P9-APA-818

PREFACE

Purpose

In the preface to the 1611 edition, the translators of the Authorized Version, known popularly as the King James Bible, state that it was not their purpose "to make a new translation . . . but to make a good one better." Indebted to the earlier work of William Tyndale and others, they saw their best contribution to consist in revising and enhancing the excellence of the English versions that had sprung from the Reformation of the sixteenth century. In harmony with the purpose of the King James scholars, the translators and editors of the present work have not pursued a goal of innovation. They have perceived the Holy Bible, New King James Version, as a continuation of the labors of the earlier translators, thus unlocking for today's readers the spiritual treasures found especially in the Authorized Version of the Holy Scriptures.

A Living Legacy

For nearly four hundred years, and throughout several revisions of its English form, the King James Bible has been deeply revered among the English-speaking peoples of the world. The precision of translation for which it is historically renowned, and its majesty of style, have enabled that monumental version of the Word of God to become the mainspring of the religion, language, and legal foundations of our civilization.

Although the Elizabethan period and our own era share in zeal for technical advance, the former period was more aggressively devoted to classical learning. Along with this awakened concern for the classics came a flourishing companion in interest in the Scriptures, an interest that was enlivened by the conviction that the manuscripts were providentially handed down and were a trustworthy record of the inspired Word of God. The King James translators were committed to producing an English Bible that would be a precise translation, and by no means a paraphrase or a broadly approximate rendering. On the one hand, the scholars were almost as familiar with the original languages of the Bible as with their native English. On the other hand, their reverence for the divine Author and His Word assured a translation of the Scriptures in which only a principle of utmost accuracy could be accepted.

In 1786 Catholic scholar Alexander Geddes said of the King James Bible, "If accuracy and strictest attention to the letter of the text be supposed to constitute an excellent version, this is of all versions the most excellent." George Bernard Shaw became a literary legend in the twentieth century because of his severe and often humorous criticisms of our most cherished values. Surprisingly, however, Shaw pays the following tribute to the scholars commissioned by King James: "The translation was extraordinarily well done because to the translators what they were translating was not merely a curious collection of ancient books written by different authors in different stages of culture, but the Word of God divinely revealed through His chosen and expressly inspired scribes. In this conviction they carried out their work with boundless reverence and care and achieved a beautifully artistic result." History agrees with these estimates. Therefore, while seeking to unveil the excellent *form* of the traditional English Bible, special care has also been taken in the present edition to preserve the work of *precision*, which is the legacy of the 1611 translators.

Complete Equivalence in Translation

Where new translation has been necessary in the New King James Version, the most complete representation of the original has been rendered by considering the history of usage and etymology of words in their contexts. This principle of complete equivalence seeks to preserve *all* of the information in the text, while presenting it in good literary form. Dynamic equivalence, a recent procedure in Bible translation, commonly results in paraphrasing where a more literal rendering is needed to reflect a specific and vital sense. For example, complete equivalence truly renders the original text in expressions such as "lifted her voice and wept" (Gen. 21:16); "I gave you cleanness of teeth" (Amos 4:6); "Jesus met them, saying, 'Rejoice!'" (Matt. 28:9); and "'Woman, what does your concern have to do with Me?'" (John 2:4). Complete equivalence translates fully, in order to provide an English text that is both accurate and readable.

In keeping with the principle of complete equivalence, it is the policy to translate interjections that are commonly omitted in modern language renderings of the Bible. As an example, the interjection *behold,* in the older King James editions, continues to have a place in English usage, especially in dramatically calling attention to a spectacular scene, or an event of profound importance such as the Immanuel prophecy of Isaiah 7:14. Consequently, *behold* is retained for these occasions in the present edition. However, the Hebrew and Greek originals for this word can be translated variously, depending on the circumstances in the passage. Therefore, in addition to *behold,* words such as *indeed, look, see,* and *surely* are also rendered to convey the appropriate sense suggested by the context in each case.

In faithfulness to God and to our readers, it was deemed appropriate that all participating scholars sign a statement affirming their belief in the verbal and plenary inspiration of Scripture, and in the inerrancy of the original autographs.

Devotional Quality

The King James scholars readily appreciated the intrinsic beauty of divine revelation. They accordingly disciplined their talents to render well-chosen English words of their time, as well as a graceful, often musical arrangement of language, which has stirred the hearts of Bible readers through the years. The translators, the committees, and the editors of the present edition, while sensitive to the late-twentieth-century English idiom, and while adhering faithfully to the Hebrew, Aramaic, and Greek texts, have sought to maintain those lyrical and devotional qualities that are so highly regarded in the Authorized Version. This devotional quality is especially apparent in the poetic and prophetic books, although even the relatively plain style of the Gospels and Epistles cannot strictly be likened, as sometimes suggested, to modern newspaper style. The Koine Greek of the New Testament is influenced by the Hebrew background of the writers, for whom even the gospel narratives were not merely flat utterance, but often song in various degrees of rhythm.

The Style

Students of the Bible applaud the timeless devotional character of our historic Bible. Yet it is also universally understood that our language, like all living languages, has undergone profound change since 1611. Subsequent revisions of the King James Bible have sought to keep abreast of changes in English speech. The present work is a further step toward this objective. Where obsolescence and other reading difficulties exist, present-day vocabulary, punctuation, and grammar have been carefully integrated. Words representing ancient objects, such as *chariot* and *phylactery,* have no modern substitutes and are therefore retained.

A special feature of the New King James Version is its conformity to the thought flow of the 1611 Bible. The reader discovers that the sequence and selection of words, phrases, and clauses of the new edition, while much clearer, are so close to the traditional that there is remarkable ease in listening to the reading of either edition while following with the other.

In the discipline of translating biblical and other ancient languages, a standard method of transliteration, that is, the English spelling of untranslated words, such as names of persons and places, has never been commonly adopted. In keeping with the design of the present work, the King James spelling of untranslated words is retained, although made uniform throughout. For example, instead of the spellings *Isaiah* and *Elijah* in the Old Testament, and *Esaias* and *Elias* in the New Testament, *Isaiah* and *Elijah* now appear in both Testaments.

King James doctrinal and theological terms, for example, *propitiation, justification,* and *sanctification,* are generally familiar to English-speaking peoples. Such terms have been retained except where the original language indicates need for a more precise translation.

Readers of the Authorized Version will immediately be struck by the absence of several pronouns: *thee, thou,* and *ye* are replaced by the simple *you,* while *your* and *yours* are substituted for *thy* and *thine* as

THE

HOLY BIBLE

CONTAINING THE OLD AND NEW TESTAMENTS

GIANT PRINT CENTER-COLUMN
REFERENCE EDITION

with Center-Column References,
Center-Column Translations,
Textual Notes, and Concordance

Words of Christ in Red

THOMAS NELSON
Since 1798

Published by Thomas Nelson in Nashville, TN. Thomas Nelson is a trademark of Thomas Nelson, Inc.

Printed in the United States of America

◆

39 40—RRD—17 16

TABLE OF CONTENTS

The Old Testament

The New Testament

BOOK ABBREVIATIONS

The Old Testament

Genesis . . . . Gen.
Exodus. . . . . Ex.
Leviticus .Lev.
Numbers . . . . Num.
Deuteronomy . . . . .Deut.
Joshua . . . . .Josh.
Judges . . . . .Judg.
Ruth. . . . . Ruth
1 Samuel . . . . 1 Sam.
2 Samuel . . . . 2 Sam.
1 Kings .1 Kin.
2 Kings .2 Kin.
1 Chronicles . . . . .1 Chr.
2 Chronicles . . . . .2 Chr.
Ezra . . . . Ezra
Nehemiah . . . . Neh.
Esther . . . . .Esth.
Job . . . . Job
Psalms. . . . . .Ps.
Proverbs .Prov.
Ecclesiastes. . . . . Eccl.
Song of Solomon . . . . .Song
Isaiah. . . . . Is.
Jeremiah . . . . Jer.
Lamentations . . . . .Lam.
Ezekiel. . . . . Ezek.
Daniel . . . . Dan.
Hosea. . . . . Hos.
Joel. . . . . .Joel
Amos . . . . .Amos
Obadiah. .Obad.
Jonah. . . . . .Jon.
Micah. . . . . Mic.
Nahum. . . . . Nah.
Habakkuk . . . . Hab.
Zephaniah. . . . . .Zeph.
Haggai. . . . . Hag.
Zechariah . . . . Zech.
Malachi . . . . Mal.

The New Testament

Matthew . . . . .Matt.
Mark . . . . .Mark
Luke. . . . . .Luke
John. . . . . .John
Acts . . . . Acts
Romans . . . . .Rom.
1 Corinthians . . . . .1 Cor.
2 Corinthians . . . . 2 Cor.
Galatians. .Gal.
Ephesians . . . . Eph.
Philippians . . . . Phil.
Colossians. Col.
1 Thessalonians . . . . 1 Thess.
2 Thessalonians . . . . 2 Thess.
1 Timothy . . . . 1 Tim.
2 Timothy . . . . 2 Tim.
Titus. . . . . Titus
Philemon. . . . . .Philem.
Hebrews . . . . Heb.
James. . . . . .James
1 Peter . . . . .1 Pet.
2 Peter . . . . .2 Pet.
1 John . . . . 1 John
2 John . . . . 2 John
3 John . . . . 3 John
Jude . . . . Jude
Revelation . . . . Rev.

applicable. *Thee, thou, thy,* and *thine* were once forms of address to express a special relationship to human as well as divine persons. These pronouns are no longer part of our language. However, reverence for God in the present work is preserved by capitalizing pronouns, including *You, Your,* and *Yours,* which refer to Him. Additionally, capitalization of these pronouns benefits the reader by clearly distinguishing divine and human persons referred to in a passage. Without such capitalization the distinction is often obscure, because the antecedent of a pronoun is not always clear in the English translation.

In addition to the pronoun usages of the seventeenth century, the *-eth* and *-est* verb endings, so familiar in the earlier King James editions, are now obsolete. Unless a speaker is schooled in these verb endings, there is common difficulty in selecting the correct form to be used with a given subject of the verb in vocal prayer. That is, should we use *love, loveth,* or *lovest*? *do, doeth, doest,* or *dost*? *have, hath,* or *hast*? Because these forms are obsolete, contemporary English usage has been substituted for the previous verb endings.

In older editions of the King James Version, the frequency of the connective *and* far exceeded the limits of present English usage. Also, biblical linguists agree that the Hebrew and Greek original words for this conjunction may commonly be translated otherwise, depending on the immediate context. Therefore, instead of *and,* alternatives such as *also, but, however, now, so, then,* and *thus* are accordingly rendered in the present edition, when the original language permits.

The real character of the Authorized Version does not reside in its archaic pronouns or verbs or other grammatical forms of the seventeenth century, but rather in the care taken by its scholars to impart the letter and spirit of the original text in a majestic and reverent style.

The Format

The format of the New King James Version is designed to enhance the vividness and devotional quality of the Holy Scriptures:

- Words or phrases in *italics* indicate expressions in the original language that require clarification by additional English words, as also done throughout the history of the King James Bible.
- Verse numbers in **bold** type indicate the beginning of a paragraph.
- *Oblique type* in the New Testament indicates a quotation from the Old Testament.
- Poetry is structured as contemporary verse to reflect the poetic form and beauty of the passage in the original language.
- The covenant name of God was usually translated from the Hebrew as "LORD" or "GOD" (using capital letters as shown) in the King James Old Testament. This tradition is maintained. In the present edition the name is so capitalized whenever the covenant name is quoted in the New Testament from a passage in the Old Testament.

The Old Testament Text

The Hebrew Bible has come down to us through the scrupulous care of ancient scribes who copied the original text in successive generations. By the sixth century A.D. the scribes were succeeded by a group known as the Masoretes, who continued to preserve the sacred Scriptures for another five hundred years in a form known as the Masoretic Text. Babylonia, Palestine, and Tiberias were the main centers of Masoretic activity; but by the tenth century A.D. the Masoretes of Tiberias, led by the family of ben Asher, gained the ascendancy. Through subsequent editions, the ben Asher text became in the twelfth century the only recognized form of the Hebrew Scriptures.

Daniel Bomberg printed the first Rabbinic Bible in 1516–17; that work was followed in 1524–25 by a second edition prepared by Jacob ben Chayyim and also published by Bomberg. The text of ben Chayyim was adopted in most subsequent Hebrew Bibles, including those used by the King James translators. The ben Chayyim text was also used for the first two editions of Rudolph Kittel's *Biblia Hebraica* of 1906 and 1912. In 1937 Paul Kahle published a third edition of *Biblia Hebraica.* This edition was based on the oldest dated manuscript of the ben Asher text, the Leningrad Manuscript B19a (A.D. 1008), which Kahle regarded as superior to that used by ben Chayyim.

For the New King James Version the text used was the 1967/1977 Stuttgart edition of the *Biblia Hebraica,* with frequent comparisons being made with the Bomberg edition of 1524–25. The Septuagint (Greek) Version of the Old Testament and the Latin Vulgate also were consulted. In addition to referring to a variety of ancient versions of the Hebrew Scriptures, the New King James Version also draws on the resources of relevant manuscripts from the Dead Sea caves. In the few places where the Hebrew was so obscure that the 1611 King James was compelled to follow one of the versions, but where information is now available to resolve the problems, the New King James Version follows the Hebrew text. Significant variations are recorded in the center reference column.

The New Testament Text

There is more manuscript support for the New Testament than for any other body of ancient literature. Over five thousand Greek, eight thousand Latin, and many more manuscripts in other languages attest the integrity of the New Testament. There is only one basic New Testament used by Protestants, Roman Catholics, and Orthodox, by conservatives and liberals. Minor variations in hand copying have appeared through the centuries, before mechanical printing began about A.D. 1450.

Some variations exist in the spelling of Greek words, in word order, and in similar details. These ordinarily do not show up in translation and do not affect the sense of the text in any way.

Other manuscript differences such as omission or inclusion of a word or a clause, and two paragraphs in the Gospels, should not overshadow the overwhelming degree of *agreement* that exists among the ancient records. Bible readers may be assured that the most important differences in English New Testaments of today are due, not to manuscript divergence, but to the way in which translators view the task of translation: How literally should the text be rendered? How does the translator view the matter of biblical inspiration? Does the translator adopt a paraphrase when a literal rendering would be quite clear and more to the point? The New King James Version follows the historic precedent of the Authorized Version in maintaining a literal approach to translation, except where the idiom of the original language cannot be translated directly into our tongue.

The King James New Testament was based on the traditional text of the Greek-speaking churches, first published in 1516, and later called the Textus Receptus or Received Text. Although based on the relatively few available manuscripts, these were representative of many more that existed at the time but only became known later. In the late nineteenth century, B. Westcott and F. Hort taught that this text had been officially edited by the fourth-century church, but a total lack of historical evidence for this event has forced a revision of the theory. It is now widely held that the Byzantine Text that largely supports the Textus Receptus has as much right as the Alexandrian or any other tradition to be weighed in determining the text of the New Testament. Those readings in the Textus Receptus that have weak support are indicated in the center reference column as being opposed by both Critical and Majority Texts (see "Center-Column Notes").

Since the 1880s most contemporary translations of the New Testament have relied upon a relatively few manuscripts discovered chiefly in the late nineteenth and early twentieth centuries. Such translations depend primarily on two manuscripts, Codex Vaticanus and Codex Sinaiticus, because of their greater age. The Greek text obtained by using these sources and the related papyri (our most ancient manuscripts) is known as the Alexandrian Text. However, some scholars have grounds for doubting the faithfulness of Vaticanus and Sinaiticus, since they often disagree with one another, and Sinaiticus exhibits excessive omission.

A third viewpoint of New Testament scholarship holds that the best text is based on the consensus of the majority of existing Greek manuscripts. This text is called the Majority Text. Most of these manuscripts are in substantial agreement. Even though many are late, and none is earlier than the fifth century, usually their readings are verified by papyri, ancient versions, quotations from the early church fathers, or a combination of these. The Majority Text is similar to the Textus Receptus, but it corrects those readings that have little or no support in the Greek manuscript tradition.

Today, scholars agree that the science of New Testament textual criticism is in a state of flux. Very few scholars still favor the Textus Receptus as such, and then often for its historical prestige as the text of Luther, Calvin, Tyndale, and the King James Version. For about a century most have followed a Critical Text (so called because it is edited according to specific principles of textual criticism), which depends heavily upon the Alexandrian type of text. More recently many have abandoned this Critical Text (which is quite similar to the one edited by Westcott and Hort) for one that is more eclectic. Finally, a small but growing number of scholars prefer the Majority Text, which is close to the traditional text except in the Revelation.

In light of these facts, and also because the New King James Version is the fifth revision of a historic document translated from specific Greek texts, the editors decided to retain the traditional text in the body of the New Testament and to indicate major Critical and Majority Text variant readings in the center reference column. Although these variations are duly indicated in the center-column notes of the present edition, it is most important to emphasize that fully 85 percent of the New Testament text is the same in the Textus Receptus, the Alexandrian Text, and the Majority Text.

Center-Column Notes

Significant explanatory notes, alternate translations, and cross-references, as well as New Testament citations of Old Testament passages, are supplied in the center reference column.

Important textual variants in the Old Testament are identified in a standard form.

The textual notes in the present edition of the New Testament make no evaluation of readings, but do clearly indicate the manuscript sources of readings. They objectively present the facts without such tendentious remarks as "the best manuscripts omit" or "the most reliable manuscripts read." Such notes are value judgments that differ according to varying viewpoints on the text. By giving a clearly defined set of variants, the New King James Version benefits readers of all textual persuasions.

Where significant variations occur in the New Testament Greek manuscripts, textual notes are classified as follows:

1. NU-Text
These variations from the traditional text generally represent the Alexandrian or Egyptian type of text described previously in "The New Testament Text." They are found in the Critical Text published in the twenty-seventh edition of the Nestle-Aland Greek New Testament (N) and in the United Bible Societies' fourth edition (U), hence the acronym, "NU-Text."

2. M-Text
This symbol indicates points of variation in the Majority Text from the traditional text, as also previously discussed in "The New Testament Text." It should be noted that M stands for whatever reading is printed in the published *Greek New Testament According to the Majority Text*, whether supported by overwhelming, strong, or only a divided majority textual tradition.

The textual notes reflect the scholarship of the past 150 years and will assist the reader to observe the variations between the different manuscript traditions of the New Testament. Such information is generally not available in English translations of the New Testament.

How to Use This Reference Bible

A LANGUAGE NOTE gives the Hebrew, Greek, or Aramaic word or phrase that underlies the English translation.

A BOLDFACED VERSE NUMERAL in the text indicates a paragraph break. When a new paragraph begins within a verse, the new paragraph is indented (see, for example, Nehemiah 13:22).

ITALIC TYPE in the text indicates words that the onginal texts do not contain but which English requires for clarity.

AN ALTERNATE TRANSLATION is *different* in meaning from the words in the text, but is justified by the original languages. That is, the translators could have understood the original word or phrase this way, although they felt their choice was more appropriate.

SQUARE BRACKETS around a cross-reference mark it as a conceptual cross-reference, which identifies a passage similar in *concept* to the referenced passage in the text.

God through the foolishness of
the message preached to save
those who believe.
22 For [a]Jews request a sign, and
Greeks seek after wisdom;
23 but we preach Christ crucified,
[a]to the Jews a [1]stumbling block
and to the [2]Greeks [b]foolishness,
24 but to those who are called,
both Jews and Greeks, Christ
[a]the power of God and [b]the wisdom of God.
25 Because the foolishness of
God is wiser than men, and the
weakness of God is stronger
than men.
26 For [1]you see your calling,
brethren, [a]that not many wise
according to the flesh, not many
mighty, not many [2]noble, *are
called.*
27 But [a]God has chosen the
foolish things of the world to put
to shame the wise, and God has
chosen the weak things of the
world to put to shame the things
which are mighty;
28 and the [1]base things of the
world and the things which are
despised God has chosen, and
the things which are not, to
bring to nothing the things that
are,
29 that no flesh should glory in
His presence.
30 But of Him you are in Christ
Jesus, who became for us wisdom
from God—and [a]righteousness
and sanctification and redemption—
31 that, as it is written, [a]*"He
who glories, let him glory in the
LORD."*

22 [a]Matt. 12:38
23 [a]Luke 2:34 [b][1 Cor. 2:14] [1]Gr. *skandalon, offense* [2]NU *Gentiles*
24 [a][Rom. 1:4] [b]Col. 2:3
26 [a]John 7:48 [1]*consider* [2]*well-born*
27 [a]Matt. 11:25
28 [1]*insignificant* or *lowly*
30 [a][2 Cor. 5:21]
31 [a]Jer. 9:23, 24

CHAPTER 2

1 [1]NU *mystery*
2 [a]Gal. 6:14
3 [a]Acts 18:1 [b][2 Cor. 4:7]
4 [a]2 Pet. 1:16 [b]Rom. 15:19 [1]NU omits *human*
5 [a]1 Thess. 1:5
7 [1]*predetermined*
8 [a]Luke 23:34 [b]Matt. 27:33–50
9 [a][Is. 64:4; 65:17]
10 [a]Matt. 11:25; 13:11; 16:17

70 [a]Rom. 1:2
[b]Acts 3:21

72 [a]Lev. 26:42

73 [a]Gen. 12:3; 22:16–18

74 [a][Heb. 9:14]

75 [a][Eph. 4:24]

76 [a]Matt. 3:3; 11:9
[b]Is. 40:3

77 [a][Mark 1:4]

78 [1]Lit. *Dawn;* the Messiah
[2]NU *shall visit*

79 [a]Is. 9:2
[b][John 10:4; 14:27; 16:33]

80 [a]Luke 2:40
[b]Matt. 3:1

CHAPTER 2

2 [a]Acts 5:37

4 [a]1 Sam. 16:1
[b]Matt. 1:16

5 [a][Matt. 1:18]
[1]NU omits *wife*

7 [a]Matt. 1:25
[1]*feed trough*

9 [a]Luke 1:12
[1]NU omits *behold*

10 [a]Luke 1:13, 30
[b]Gen. 12:3

11 [a]Is. 9:6
[b]Matt. 1:21
[c]Acts 2:36

12 [1]*feed trough*

13 [a]Dan. 7:10

2 And it came to pass in those
days *that* a decree went out
from Caesar Au·gus′tus that all
the world should be registered.
2 [a]This census first took place
while Quī·rin′i·us was governing
Syria.
3 So all went to be registered,
everyone to his own city.
4 Joseph also went up from ★
Galilee, out of the city of Nazareth, into Judea, to [a]the city of
David, which is called Bethlehem, [b]because he was of the
house and lineage of David,
5 to be registered with Mary,
[a]his betrothed [1]wife, who was
with child.
6 So it was, that while they
were there, the days were completed for her to be delivered.
7 And [a]she brought forth her
firstborn Son, and wrapped Him
in swaddling cloths, and laid Him
in a [1]manger, because there was
no room for them in the inn.
8 Now there were in the same
country shepherds living out in
the fields, keeping watch over
their flock by night.
9 And [1]behold, an angel of the
Lord stood before them, and the
glory of the Lord shone around
them, [a]and they were greatly
afraid.
10 Then the angel said to them,
[a]"Do not be afraid, for behold, I
bring you good tidings of great
joy [b]which will be to all people.
11 [a]"For there is born to you this ★
day in the city of David [b]a Savior, [c]who is Christ the Lord.
12 "And this *will be* the sign
to you: You will find a Babe
wrapped in swaddling cloths,
lying in a [1]manger."
13 [a]And suddenly there was
with the angel a multitude of

A SUPERIOR LETTER (usually preceding the referenced word or phrase in the text as space permits) indicates a cross-reference.

A SUPERIOR NUMERAL indicates an equivalent translation, alternate translation, literal translation, language note, explanatory note, or textual note.

PERSONAL PRONOUNS and certain nouns are capitalized when they refer to Deity.

AN EQUIVALENT TRANSLATION is *similar* in meaning to the translation in the text. It helps you understand the text by showing you a synonym.

A TEXTUAL NOTE points out one or more significant textual variants. The sources of the variant readings are identified by abbreviations, listed on page xiv. (See also Preface, "Center-Column Notes.")

A Boldfaced Numeral in the center column indicates the verse to which an entry applies.

An Explanatory Note explains the word or phrase in the text. Words set in roman type in translation notes are explanatory only and are not translated from the original languages.

Quotation Marks in the text follow modern English usage. For easier reading, only the marks denoting the most recently opened quotation are repeated in a new paragraph.

A Literal Translation gives the literal meaning of the word or phrase.

4 And as they went through
the cities, they delivered to them
the [a]decrees to keep, [b]which
were determined by the apostles
and elders at Jerusalem.
5 [a]So the churches were
strengthened in the faith, and
increased in number daily.
6 Now when they had gone
through Phryg′i·a and the region
of [a]Galatia, they were forbidden
by the Holy Spirit to preach the
word in [1]Asia.
7 After they had come to Mys′-
i·a, they tried to go into Bi·thyn′-
i·a, but the [1]Spirit did not permit
them.
8 So passing by Mys′i·a, they
[a]came down to Trō′as.
9 And a vision appeared to
Paul in the night. A [a]man of
Mac·e·dō′ni·a stood and pleaded
with him, saying, "Come over to
Mac·e·dō′ni·a and help us."
10 Now after he had seen the
vision, immediately we sought
to go [a]to Mac·e·dō′ni·a, concluding that the Lord had called us
to preach the gospel to them.
11 Therefore, sailing from
Trō′as, we ran a straight course
to Sam′o·thrāce, and the next
day came to Nē·ap′o·lis,
12 and from there to [a]Phi·lip′pī,
which is the [1]foremost city of
that part of Mac·e·dō′ni·a, a col-
ony. And we were staying in that
city for some days.
13 And on the Sabbath day we
went out of the city to the riverside, where prayer was custom-
arily made; and we sat down
and spoke to the women who
met *there.*
14 Now a certain woman named
Lyd′i·a heard *us.* She was a
seller of purple from the city

4 [a]Acts 15:19–21 [b]Acts 15:28, 29
5 [a]Acts 2:47; 15:41
6 [a]Gal. 1:1, 2 [1]The Roman province of Asia
7 [1]NU adds of *Jesus*
8 [a]2 Cor. 2:12
9 [a]Acts 10:30
10 [a]2 Cor. 2:13
12 [a]Phil. 1:1 [1]Lit. *first*
14 [a]Rev. 1:11; 2:18, 24 [b]Luke 24:45
15 [a]Judg. 19:21
16 [a]1 Sam. 28:3, 7 [b]Acts 19:24
18 [a]Mark 1:25, 34 [b]Mark 16:17 [1]*distressed*
19 [a]Acts 16:16; 19:25, 26 [b]Matt. 10:18
20 [a]Acts 17:8
22 [a]1 Thess. 2:2

Because He has anointed Me
To preach the gospel to the poor;
He has sent Me [1]*to heal the brokenhearted,*
To proclaim liberty to the captives
And recovery of sight to the blind,
To [b]*set at liberty those who are* [2]*oppressed;*
19 *To proclaim the acceptable year of the* LORD."

20 Then He closed the book,
and gave *it* back to the atten-
dant and sat down. And the eyes
of all who were in the synagogue were fixed on Him.
21 And He began to say to them,
"Today this Scripture is [a]fulfilled
in your hearing."
22 So all bore witness to Him,
and [a]marveled at the gracious
words which proceeded out of
His mouth. And they said, [b]"Is
this not Joseph's son?"
23 He said to them, "You will
surely say this proverb to Me,
'Physician, heal yourself! Whatever we have heard done in
[a]Ca·per′na·um,[1] do also here in
[b]Your country.' "
24 Then He said, "Assuredly, I
say to you, no [a]prophet is accepted in his own country.
25 "But I tell you truly, [a]many
widows were in Israel in the
days of E·lī′jah, when the heaven
was shut up three years and six
months, and there was a great
famine throughout all the land;
26 "but to none of them was
E·lī′jah sent except to [1]Zar′-
e·phath, *in the region* of Sī′don,
to a woman *who was* a widow.
27 [a]"And many lepers were in
Israel in the time of E·lī′sha the

POETRY is structured as contemporary verse to reflect the poetic form and beauty of the original language.

OBLIQUE TYPE in the New Testament indicates a quotation from the Old Testament. The sources of the quotations are found in cross-references.

The COVENANT NAME OF GOD in the Old Testament, represented by the Hebrew consonants YHWH, is translated "LORD" or "GOD" (using capital letters as shown), as it has been throughout the history of the King James Bible. In this edition the capitalized form is also used whenever the covenant name is quoted in the New Testament from a passage in the Old Testament.

Special Abbreviations

Arab.	Arabic
Aram.	Aramaic
Bg.	the 1524–25 edition of the Hebrew Old Testament published by Daniel Bomberg (see Preface, "The Old Testament Text")
cf.	compare
ch., chs.	chapter, chapters
DSS	Dead Sea Scrolls
e.g.	for example
et al.	and others
etc.	and so forth
fem.	feminine
f., ff.	following verse, following verses
Gr.	Greek
Heb.	Hebrew
i.e.	that is
Kt.	Kethib (literally, in Aramaic, "written")—the written words of the Hebrew Old Testament preserved by the Masoretes (see "Qr.")
Lat.	Latin
lit.	literally
LXX	Septuagint—an ancient translation of the Old Testament into Greek
M	Majority Text (see Preface, "The New Testament Text")
ms., mss.	manuscript, manuscripts
masc.	masculine
MT	Masoretic Text—the traditional Hebrew Old Testament (see Preface, "The Old Testament Text")
NU	the most prominent modern Critical Text of the Greek New Testament, published in the twenty-sixth edition of the *N*estle-Aland Greek New Testament and the third edition of the *U*nited Bible Societies' Greek New Testament (see Preface, "The New Testament Text")
pl.	plural
Qr.	Qere (literally, in Aramaic, "read")—certain words read aloud, differing from the written words, in the Masoretic tradition of the Hebrew Old Testament (see "Kt.")
Sam.	Samaritan Pentateuch—a variant Hebrew edition of the books of Moses, used by the Samaritan community
sing.	singular
Syr.	Syriac
Tg.	Targum—an Aramaic paraphrase of the Old Testament
TR	Textus Receptus or Received Text (see Preface, "The New Testament Text")
v., vv.	verse, verses
vss.	versions—ancient translations of the Bible
Vg.	Vulgate—an ancient translation of the Bible into Latin, translated and edited by Jerome

More Features of the Giant Print Center-Column Reference Bible

Messianic Stars

Throughout the Bible the use of a star has been used next to the verse to denote Messianic prophecy. An *Outline Star* "☆" indicates that the text contains a prophecy that at the time of the action had yet to be fulfilled. A *Solid Star* "★" indicates that the text contains the fulfillment of a prophecy.

Topical Running Heads

The running heads, printed in boldface italics at the top of each page, indicate important topics on that page.

The
Old Testament

The First Book of Moses Called

GENESIS

THE first part of Genesis focuses on the beginning and spread of sin in the world and culminates in the devastating flood in the days of Noah. The second part of the book focuses on God's dealings with one man, Abraham, through whom God promises to bring salvation and blessing to the world. Abraham and his descendants learn firsthand that it is always safe to trust the Lord in times of famine and feasting, blessing and bondage. From Abraham . . . to Isaac . . . to Jacob . . . to Joseph . . . God's promises begin to come to fruition in a great nation possessing a great land.

Genesis is a Greek word meaning "origin," "source," "generation," or "beginning." The original Hebrew title *Bereshith* means "In the Beginning."

The literary structure of Genesis is clear and is built around eleven separate units, each including the word *genealogy* in the phrase "This is the genealogy" or "The book of the genealogy": (1) Introduction to the Genealogies (1:1—2:3); (2) Heaven and Earth (2:4—4:26); (3) Adam (5:1—6:8); (4) Noah (6:9—9:29); (5) Sons of Noah (10:1—11:9); (6) Shem (11:10–26); (7) Terah (11:27—25:11); (8) Ishmael (25:12–18); (9) Isaac (25:19—35:29); (10) Esau (36:1—37:1); (11) Jacob (37:2—50:26).

IN the [a]beginning [b]God created
the heavens and the earth.
2 The earth was [a]without form,
and void; and darkness [1]*was* on
the face of the deep. [b]And the
Spirit of God was hovering over
the face of the waters.
3 [a]Then God said, [b]"Let there
be [c]light"; and there was light.
4 And God saw the light, that
it was good; and God divided
the light from the darkness.
5 God called the light Day, and
the [a]darkness He called Night.
[1]So the evening and the morning
were the first day.
6 Then God said, [a]"Let there
be a [1]firmament in the midst of
the waters, and let it divide the
waters from the waters."
7 Thus God made the firmament, [a]and divided the waters
which *were* under the firmament from the waters which
were [b]above the firmament; and
it was so.
8 And God called the firmament Heaven. So the evening
and the morning were the second day.
9 Then God said, [a]"Let the waters under the heavens be gathered together into one place,
and [b]let the dry *land* appear";
and it was so.
10 And God called the dry *land*
Earth, and the gathering together of the waters He called
Seas. And God saw that *it was*
good.
11 Then God said, "Let the earth
[a]bring forth grass, the herb *that*
yields seed, *and* the [b]fruit tree
that yields fruit according to its
kind, whose seed *is* in itself, on
the earth"; and it was so.
12 And the earth brought forth
grass, the herb *that* yields seed

CHAPTER 1

1 [a][John 1:1–3] [b]Acts 17:24

2 [a]Jer. 4:23 [b]Is. 40:13, 14 [1]Words in italic type have been added for clarity. They are not found in the original Hebrew or Aramaic.

3 [a]Ps. 33:6, 9 [b]2 Cor. 4:6 [c][Heb. 11:3]

5 [a]Ps. 19:2; 33:6; 74:16; 104:20; 136:5 [1]Lit. *And evening was, and morning was, a day, one.*

6 [a]Jer. 10:12 [1]*expanse*

7 [a]Prov. 8:27–29 [b]Ps. 148:4

9 [a]Job 26:10 [b]Ps. 24:1, 2; 33:7; 95:5

11 [a]Heb. 6:7 [b]2 Sam. 16:1

according to its kind, and the
tree *that* yields fruit, whose seed
is in itself according to its kind.
And God saw that *it was* good.
13 So the evening and the morning were the third day.
14 Then God said, "Let there be
[a]lights in the firmament of the
heavens to divide the day from
the night; and let them be for
signs and [b]seasons, and for days
and years;
15 "and let them be for lights in
the firmament of the heavens to
give light on the earth"; and it
was so.
16 Then God made two great
[1]lights: the [a]greater light to rule
the day, and the [b]lesser light
to rule the night. *He made* [c]the
stars also.
17 God set them in the firmament of the [a]heavens to give
light on the earth,
18 and to [a]rule over the day and
over the night, and to divide the
light from the darkness. And
God saw that *it was* good.
19 So the evening and the morning were the fourth day.
20 Then God said, "Let the waters abound with an abundance
of living [1]creatures, and let birds
fly above the earth across the
face of the [2]firmament of the
heavens."
21 So [a]God created great sea
creatures and every living thing
that moves, with which the waters abounded, according to
their kind, and every winged
bird according to its kind. And
God saw that *it was* good.
22 And God blessed them, saying, [a]"Be fruitful and multiply,
and fill the waters in the seas,
and let birds multiply on the
earth."

14 [a]Ps. 74:16; 136:5–9 [b]Ps. 104:19
16 [a]Ps. 136:8 [b]Ps. 8:3 [c]Job 38:7 [1]*luminaries*
17 [a]Gen. 15:5
18 [a]Jer. 31:35
20 [1]*souls* [2]*expanse*
21 [a]Ps. 104:25–28
22 [a]Gen. 8:17
26 [a][Eph. 4:24] [b]Gen. 9:2 [1]Syr. *all the wild animals of*
27 [a]Gen. 5:2 [b]Matt. 19:4
28 [a]Gen. 9:1, 7 [b]1 Cor. 9:27 [1]*moves about on*
29 [a]Gen. 9:3
30 [a]Ps. 145:15 [b]Job 38:41 [1]*a living soul*
31 [a][Ps. 104:24]

23 So the evening and the morning were the fifth day.
24 Then God said, "Let the
earth bring forth the living creature according to its kind: cattle
and creeping thing and beast of
the earth, *each* according to its
kind"; and it was so.
25 And God made the beast of
the earth according to its kind,
cattle according to its kind, and
everything that creeps on the
earth according to its kind. And
God saw that *it was* good.
26 Then God said, [a]"Let Us
make man in Our image, according to Our likeness; [b]let them
have dominion over the fish of
the sea, over the birds of the air,
and over the cattle, over [1]all the
earth and over every creeping
thing that creeps on the earth."
27 So God created man [a]in His
own image; in the image of God
He created him; [b]male and female He created them.
28 Then God blessed them, and
God said to them, [a]"Be fruitful
and multiply; fill the earth and
[b]subdue it; have dominion over
the fish of the sea, over the birds
of the air, and over every living
thing that [1]moves on the earth."
29 And God said, "See, I have
given you every herb *that* yields
seed which *is* on the face of all
the earth, and every tree whose
fruit yields seed; [a]to you it shall
be for food.
30 "Also, to [a]every beast of the
earth, to every [b]bird of the air,
and to everything that creeps on
the earth, in which *there is* [1]life,
I have given every green herb
for food"; and it was so.
31 Then [a]God saw everything
that He had made, and indeed *it*
was very good. So the evening

and the morning were the sixth day.

2 Thus the heavens and the earth, and [a]all the host of them, were finished.

2 [a]And on the seventh day God ended His work which He had done, and He rested on the seventh day from all His work which He had done.

3 Then God [a]blessed the seventh day and sanctified it, because in it He rested from all His work which God had created and made.

4 [a]This *is* the [1]history of the heavens and the earth when they were created, in the day that the LORD God made the earth and the heavens,

5 before any [a]plant of the field was in the earth and before any herb of the field had grown. For the LORD God had not [b]caused it to rain on the earth, and *there was* no man [c]to till the ground;

6 but a mist went up from the earth and watered the whole face of the ground.

7 And the LORD God formed man *of* the [a]dust of the ground, and [b]breathed into his [c]nostrils the breath of life; and [d]man became a living being.

8 The LORD God planted [a]a garden [b]eastward in [c]Eden, and there He put the man whom He had formed.

9 And out of the ground the LORD God made [a]every tree grow that is pleasant to the sight and good for food. [b]The tree of life *was* also in the midst of the garden, and the tree of the knowledge of good and [c]evil.

10 Now a river went out of Eden to water the garden, and from there it parted and became four riverheads.

11 The name of the first *is* Pī'shon; it *is* the one which skirts [a]the whole land of Hav'i·lah, where *there is* gold.

12 And the gold of that land *is* good. [a]Bdellium and the onyx stone *are* there.

13 The name of the second river *is* Gī'hon; it *is* the one which goes around the whole land of Cush.

14 The name of the third river *is* [a]Hid'de·kel;[1] it *is* the one which goes toward the east of [2]Assyria. The fourth river *is* the Eū·phrā'tēs.

15 Then the LORD God took [1]the man and put him in the garden of Eden to [2]tend and keep it.

16 And the LORD God commanded the man, saying, "Of every tree of the garden you may freely eat;

17 "but of the tree of the knowledge of good and evil [a]you shall not eat, for in the day that you eat of it [b]you[1] shall surely [c]die."

18 And the LORD God said, "*It is* not good that man should be alone; [a]I will make him a helper comparable to him."

19 [a]Out of the ground the LORD God formed every beast of the field and every bird of the air, and [b]brought *them* to [1]Adam to see what he would call them. And whatever Adam called each living creature, that *was* its name.

20 So Adam gave names to all cattle, to the birds of the air, and to every beast of the field. But for Adam there was not found a helper comparable to him.

21 And the LORD God caused a [a]deep sleep to fall on Adam, and

CHAPTER 2

1 [a]Ps. 33:6

2 [a]Ex. 20:9–11; 31:17

3 [a][Is. 58:13]

4 [a]Gen. 1:1 [1]Heb. *toledoth;* lit. *generations*

5 [a]Gen. 1:11, 12 [b]Gen. 7:4 [c]Gen. 3:23

7 [a]Gen. 3:19, 23 [b]Job 33:4 [c]Gen. 7:22 [d]1 Cor. 15:45

8 [a]Is. 51:3 [b]Gen. 3:23, 24 [c]Gen. 4:16

9 [a]Ezek. 31:8 [b][Gen. 3:22] [c][Deut. 1:39]

11 [a]Gen. 25:18

12 [a]Num. 11:7

14 [a]Dan. 10:4 [1]Or *Tigris* [2]Heb. *Ashshur*

15 [1]Or *Adam* [2]*cultivate*

17 [a]Gen. 3:1, 3, 11, 17 [b]Gen. 3:3, 19 [c]Rom. 5:12 [1]Lit. *dying you shall die*

18 [a]1 Cor. 11:8, 9

19 [a]Gen. 1:20, 24 [b]Ps. 8:6 [1]Or *the man*

21 [a]1 Sam. 26:12

he slept; and He took one of his
ribs, and closed up the flesh in
its place.
22 Then the rib which the LORD
God had taken from man He
[1]made into a woman, [a]and He
[b]brought her to the man.
23 And Adam said:

"This *is* now [a]bone of my
bones
And flesh of my flesh;
She shall be called [1]Woman,
Because she was [b]taken out
of [2]Man."

24 [a]Therefore a man shall leave
his father and mother and [b]be[1]
joined to his wife, and they shall
become one flesh.
25 [a]And they were both naked,
the man and his wife, and were
not [b]ashamed.

3 Now [a]the serpent was [b]more
cunning than any beast of
the field which the LORD God
had made. And he said to the
woman, "Has God indeed said,
'You shall not eat of every tree
of the garden'?"
2 And the woman said to the
serpent, "We may eat the [a]fruit
of the trees of the garden;
3 "but of the fruit of the tree
which *is* in the midst of the garden, God has said, 'You shall not
eat it, nor shall you [a]touch it, lest
you die.'"
4 [a]Then the serpent said to
the woman, "You will not surely
die.
5 "For God knows that in the
day you eat of it your eyes will
be opened, and you will be like
God, knowing good and evil."
6 So when the woman [a]saw
that the tree *was* good for food,
that it *was* [1]pleasant to the eyes,
and a tree desirable to make *one*
wise, she took of its fruit [b]and
ate. She also gave to her husband with her, and he ate.
7 Then the eyes of both of them
were opened, [a]and they knew
that they *were* naked; and they
sewed fig leaves together and
made themselves [1]coverings.
8 And they heard [a]the [1]sound
of the LORD God walking in the
garden in the [2]cool of the day,
and Adam and his wife [b]hid
themselves from the presence of
the LORD God among the trees of
the garden.
9 Then the LORD God called to
Adam and said to him, "Where
are you?"
10 So he said, "I heard Your
voice in the garden, [a]and I was
afraid because I was naked; and
I hid myself."
11 And He said, "Who told you
that you *were* naked? Have you
eaten from the tree of which I
commanded you that you should
not eat?"
12 Then the man said, [a]"The
woman whom You gave *to be*
with me, she gave me of the tree,
and I ate."
13 And the LORD God said to the
woman, "What *is* this you have
done?" The woman said, [a]"The
serpent deceived me, and I ate."
14 So the LORD God said to the
serpent:

"Because you have done this,
You *are* cursed more than
all cattle,
And more than every beast
of the field;
On your belly you shall go,
And [a]you shall eat dust
All the days of your life.
15 And I will put enmity ☆

22 [a]1 Tim. 2:13 [b]Heb. 13:4 [1]Lit. *built*
23 [a]Gen. 29:14 [b]1 Cor. 11:8, 9 [1]Heb. *Ishshah* [2]Heb. *Ish*
24 [a]Matt. 19:5 [b]Mark 10:6–8 [1]Lit. *cling*
25 [a]Gen. 3:7, 10 [b]Is. 47:3

CHAPTER 3

1 [a]1 Chr. 21:1 [b]2 Cor. 11:3
2 [a]Gen. 2:16, 17
3 [a]Ex. 19:12, 13
4 [a][2 Cor. 11:3]
6 [a]1 John 2:16 [b]1 Tim. 2:14 [1]Lit. *a desirable thing*
7 [a]Gen. 2:25 [1]*girding coverings*
8 [a]Job 38:1 [b]Job 31:33 [1]Or *voice* [2]Or *wind, breeze*
10 [a]Gen. 2:25
12 [a][Prov. 28:13]
13 [a]2 Cor. 11:3
14 [a]Deut. 28:15–20

Between you and the
woman,
And between [a]your seed and
[b]her Seed;
[c]He shall bruise your head,
And you shall bruise His
heel."

16 To the woman He said:

"I will greatly multiply
your sorrow and your
conception;
[a]In pain you shall bring forth
children;
[b]Your desire *shall be* [1]for
your husband,
And he shall [c]rule over you."

17 Then to Adam He said, [a]"Because you have heeded the voice
of your wife, and have eaten
from the tree [b]of which I commanded you, saying, 'You shall
not eat of it':

[c]"Cursed *is* the ground for
your sake;
[d]In toil you shall eat *of* it
All the days of your life.
18 Both thorns and thistles it
shall [1]bring forth for you,
And [a]you shall eat the herb
of the field.
19 [a]In the sweat of your face
you shall eat bread
Till you return to the ground,
For out of it you were taken;
[b]For dust you *are*,
And [c]to dust you shall
return."

20 And Adam called his wife's
name [a]Eve,[1] because she was the
mother of all living.
21 Also for Adam and his wife
the LORD God made tunics of
skin, and clothed them.

22 Then the LORD God said, "Behold, the man has become like
one of Us, to know good and
evil. And now, lest he put out his
hand and take also of the tree of
life, and eat, and live forever"—
23 therefore the LORD God sent
him out of the garden of Eden
[a]to till the ground from which he
was taken.
24 So [a]He drove out the man;
and He placed [b]cherubim [c]at the
east of the garden of Eden, and
a flaming sword which turned
every way, to guard the way to
the tree of [d]life.

4

Now Adam knew Eve his
wife, and she conceived and
bore [1]Cain, and said, "I have acquired a man from the LORD."
2 Then she bore again, this
time his brother [1]Abel. Now
[a]Abel was a keeper of sheep, but
Cain was a tiller of the ground.
3 And [1]in the process of time it
came to pass that Cain brought
an offering of the fruit [a]of the
ground to the LORD.
4 Abel also brought of [a]the
firstborn of his flock and of [b]their
fat. And the LORD [c]respected
Abel and his offering,
5 but He did not respect Cain
and his offering. And Cain was
very angry, and his countenance
fell.
6 So the LORD said to Cain,
"Why are you angry? And why
has your countenance fallen?
7 "If you do well, will you not
be accepted? And if you do not
do well, sin lies at the door. And
its desire *is* [1]for you, but you
should rule over it."
8 Now Cain [1]talked with Abel
his [2]brother; and it came to pass,
when they were in the field, that

---

15 [a]John 8:44 [b]Is. 7:14; Luke 1:31; Gal. 4:4 [c]Rom. 16:20
16 [a]John 16:21 [b]Gen. 4:7 [c]1 Cor. 11:3 [1]Lit. *toward*
17 [a]1 Sam. 15:23 [b]Gen. 2:17 [c]Rom. 8:20–22 [d]Eccl. 2:23
18 [a]Ps. 104:14 [1]*cause to grow*
19 [a]2 Thess. 3:10 [b]Gen. 2:7; 5:5 [c]Job 21:26
20 [a]2 Cor. 11:3 [1]Lit. *Life* or *Living*
23 [a]Gen. 4:2; 9:20
24 [a]Ezek. 31:3, 11 [b]Ps. 104:4 [c]Gen. 2:8 [d]Gen. 2:9

CHAPTER 4

1 [1]Lit. *Acquire*
2 [a]Luke 11:50, 51 [1]Lit. *Breath* or *Nothing*
3 [a]Num. 18:12 [1]Lit. *at the end of days*
4 [a]Num. 18:17 [b]Lev. 3:16 [c]Heb. 11:4
7 [1]Lit. *toward*
8 [1]Lit. *said to* [2]Sam., LXX, Syr., Vg. add *"Let us go out to the field."*

Cain rose up against Abel his
brother and [a]killed him.
9 Then the LORD said to Cain,
"Where *is* Abel your brother?"
He said, [a]"I do not know. *Am* I
[b]my brother's keeper?"
10 And He said, "What have
you done? The voice of your
brother's blood [a]cries out to Me
from the ground.
11 "So now [a]you *are* cursed from
the earth, which has opened its
mouth to receive your brother's
blood from your hand.
12 "When you till the ground, it
shall no longer yield its strength
to you. A fugitive and a vagabond you shall be on the earth."
13 And Cain said to the LORD,
"My [1]punishment *is* greater than
I can bear!
14 "Surely You have driven me
out this day from the face of the
ground; [a]I shall be [b]hidden from
Your face; I shall be a fugitive
and a vagabond on the earth,
and it will happen *that* [c]anyone
who finds me will kill me."
15 And the LORD said to him,
[1]"Therefore, whoever kills Cain,
vengeance shall be taken on
him [a]sevenfold." And the LORD
set a [b]mark on Cain, lest anyone
finding him should kill him.
16 Then Cain [a]went out from
the [b]presence of the LORD and
dwelt in the land of [1]Nod on the
east of Eden.
17 And Cain knew his wife, and
she conceived and bore Ē′noch.
And he built a city, [a]and called
the name of the city after the
name of his son—Ē′noch.
18 To Ē′noch was born Ī′rad;
and Ī′rad begot Me·hū′ja·el, and
Me·hū′ja·el begot Me·thū′sha·el,
and Me·thū′sha·el begot Lā′-
mech.
19 Then Lā′mech took for himself [a]two wives: the name of one
was Ā′dah, and the name of the
second *was* Zil′lah.
20 And Ā′dah bore Jā′bal. He
was the father of those who dwell
in tents and have livestock.
21 His brother's name *was*
Jū′bal. He was the father of all
those who play the harp and
[1]flute.
22 And as for Zil′lah, she also
bore Tū′bal-Cāin, an instructor
of every craftsman in bronze
and iron. And the sister of
Tū′bal-Cāin *was* Nā′a·mah.
23 Then Lā′mech said to his
wives:

"Ā′dah and Zil′lah, hear my
voice;
Wives of Lā′mech, listen to
my speech!
For I have [1]killed a man for
wounding me,
Even a young man [2]for
hurting me.
24 [a]If Cain shall be avenged
sevenfold,
Then Lā′mech seventy-
sevenfold."

25 And Adam knew his wife
again, and she bore a son and
[a]named him [1]Seth, "For God
has appointed another seed for
me instead of Abel, whom Cain
killed."
26 And as for Seth, [a]to him also
a son was born; and he named
him [1]Ē′nosh. Then *men* began [b]to
call on the name of the LORD.

CHAPTER 5

5 This is the book of the
[a]genealogy of Adam. In the
day that God created man, He
made him in [b]the likeness of
God.
2 He created them [a]male and

---

8 [a][1 John 3:12–15]
9 [a]John 8:44 [b]1 Cor. 8:11–13
10 [a]Heb. 12:24
11 [a]Gen. 3:14
13 [1]*iniquity*
14 [a]Ps. 51:11 [b]Is. 1:15 [c]Num. 35:19, 21, 27
15 [a]Gen. 4:24 [b]Ezek. 9:4, 6 [1]So with MT, Tg.; LXX, Syr., Vg. *Not so;*
16 [a]2 Kin. 13:23; 24:20 [b]Jon. 1:3 [1]Lit. *Wandering*
17 [a]Ps. 49:11
19 [a]Gen. 2:24; 16:3
21 [1]*pipe*
23 [1]*slain a man for my wound* [2]*for my hurt*
24 [a]Gen. 4:15
25 [a]Gen. 5:3 [1]Lit. *Appointed*
26 [a]Gen. 5:6 [b]Zeph. 3:9 [1]Gr. *Enos,* Luke 3:38

CHAPTER 5

1 [a]Gen. 2:4; 6:9 [b]Gen. 1:26; 9:6
2 [a]Mark 10:6

female, and [b]blessed them and
called them Mankind in the day
they were created.
3 And Adam lived one hun-
dred and thirty years, and begot
a son [a]in his own likeness, after his image, and [b]named him
Seth.
4 After he begot Seth, [a]the
days of Adam were eight hundred years; [b]and he had sons
and daughters.
5 So all the days that Adam
lived were nine hundred and
thirty years; [a]and he died.
6 Seth lived one hundred and
five years, and begot [a]Ē′nosh.
7 After he begot Ē′nosh,
Seth lived eight hundred and
seven years, and had sons and
daughters.
8 So all the days of Seth were
nine hundred and twelve years;
and he died.
9 Ē′nosh lived ninety years,
and begot [1]Cā·ī′nan.
10 After he begot Cā·ī′nan,
Ē′nosh lived eight hundred and
fifteen years, and had sons and
daughters.
11 So all the days of Ē′nosh
were nine hundred and five
years; and he died.
12 Cā·ī′nan lived seventy years,
and begot Ma·hal′a·lel.
13 After he begot Ma·hal′a·lel,
Cā·ī′nan lived eight hundred
and forty years, and had sons
and daughters.
14 So all the days of Cā·ī′nan
were nine hundred and ten
years; and he died.
15 Ma·hal′a·lel lived sixty-five
years, and begot Jar′ed.
16 After he begot Jar′ed, Ma·hal′-
a·lel lived eight hundred and
thirty years, and had sons and
daughters.
17 So all the days of Ma·hal′a·lel
were eight hundred and ninety-
five years; and he died.
18 Jar′ed lived one hundred
and sixty-two years, and begot
[a]Ē′noch.
19 After he begot Ē′noch, Jar′ed
lived eight hundred years, and
had sons and daughters.
20 So all the days of Jar′ed were
nine hundred and sixty-two
years; and he died.
21 Ē′noch lived sixty-five years,
and begot Me·thū′se·lah.
22 After he begot Me·thū′se·lah,
Ē′noch [a]walked with God three
hundred years, and had sons
and daughters.
23 So all the days of Ē′noch
were three hundred and sixty-
five years.
24 And [a]Ē′noch walked with
God; and he *was* not, for God
[b]took him.
25 Me·thū′se·lah lived one hundred and eighty-seven years,
and begot Lā′mech.
26 After he begot Lā′mech,
Me·thū′se·lah lived seven hundred and eighty-two years, and
had sons and daughters.
27 So all the days of Me·thū′-
se·lah were nine hundred and
sixty-nine years; and he died.
28 Lā′mech lived one hundred
and eighty-two years, and had a
son.
29 And he called his name
[a]Noah,[1] saying, "This *one* will
comfort us concerning our work
and the toil of our hands, because of the ground [b]which the
LORD has cursed."
30 After he begot Noah, Lā′-
mech lived five hundred and
ninety-five years, and had sons
and daughters.
31 So all the days of Lā′mech

2 [b]Gen. 1:28; 9:1
3 [a]1 Cor. 15:48, 49 [b]Gen. 4:25
4 [a]Luke 3:36–38 [b]Gen. 1:28; 4:25
5 [a][Heb. 9:27]
6 [a]Gen. 4:26
9 [1]Heb. *Qenan*
18 [a]Jude 14, 15
22 [a]Gen. 6:9; 17:1; 24:40; 48:15
24 [a]2 Kin. 2:11 [b]Heb. 11:5
29 [a]Luke 3:36 [b]Gen. 3:17–19; 4:11 [1]Lit. *Rest*

were seven hundred and seventy-seven years; and he died.
32 And Noah was five hundred years old, and Noah begot
[a]Shem, Ham, [b]and Jā′pheth.

6

6 Now it came to pass, [a]when
men began to multiply on
the face of the earth, and daughters were born to them,
2 that the sons of God saw the
daughters of men, that they *were*
beautiful; and they [a]took wives
for themselves of all whom they
chose.
3 And the LORD said, [a]"My
Spirit shall not [b]strive[1] with man
forever, [c]for he *is* indeed flesh;
yet his days shall be one hundred and twenty years."
4 There were [1]giants on the
earth in those [a]days, and also
afterward, when the sons of God
came in to the daughters of men
and they bore *children* to them.
Those *were* the mighty men who
were of old, men of renown.
5 Then [1]the LORD saw that the
wickedness of man *was* great in
the earth, and *that* every [a]intent[2]
of the thoughts of his heart *was*
only evil [3]continually.
6 And [a]the LORD was sorry
that He had made man on the
earth, and [b]He was grieved in
His [c]heart.
7 So the LORD said, "I will [a]de-
stroy man whom I have created
from the face of the earth, both
man and beast, creeping thing
and birds of the air, for I am
sorry that I have made them."
8 But Noah [a]found grace in the
eyes of the LORD.
9 This is the genealogy of
Noah. [a]Noah was a just man,
[1]perfect in his generations. Noah
[b]walked with God.
10 And Noah begot three sons:
[a]Shem, Ham, and Jā′pheth.
11 The earth also was corrupt
[a]before God, and the earth was
[b]filled with violence.
12 So God [a]looked upon the
earth, and indeed it was corrupt;
for [b]all flesh had corrupted their
way on the earth.
13 And God said to Noah, [a]"The
end of all flesh has come before
Me, for the earth is filled with
violence through them; [b]and behold, [c]I will destroy them with
the earth.
14 "Make yourself an ark of
gopherwood; make [1]rooms in
the ark, and cover it inside and
outside with pitch.
15 "And this is how you shall
make it: The length of the ark
shall be three hundred [1]cubits,
its width fifty cubits, and its
height thirty cubits.
16 "You shall make a window
for the ark, and you shall finish
it to a cubit from above; and set
the door of the ark in its side.
You shall make it *with* lower,
second, and third *decks*.
17 [a]"And behold, I Myself am
bringing [b]floodwaters on the
earth, to destroy from under
heaven all flesh in which *is* the
breath of life; everything that *is*
on the earth shall [c]die.
18 "But I will establish My
[a]covenant with you; and [b]you
shall go into the ark—you, your
sons, your wife, and your sons'
wives with you.
19 "And of every living thing of
all flesh you shall bring [a]two of
every *sort* into the ark, to keep
them alive with you; they shall
be male and female.
20 "Of the birds after their kind,
of animals after their kind, and

32 [a]Gen. 6:10; 7:13 [b]Gen. 10:21

CHAPTER 6

1 [a]Gen. 1:28

2 [a]Deut. 7:3, 4

3 [a][Gal. 5:16, 17] [b]2 Thess. 2:7 [c]Ps. 78:39 [1]LXX, Syr., Tg., Vg. *abide*

4 [a]Num. 13:32, 33 [1]Heb. *nephilim, fallen* or *mighty ones*

5 [a]Gen. 8:21 [1]So with MT, Tg.; Vg. *God;* LXX *LORD God* [2]*thought* [3]*all the day*

6 [a]1 Sam. 15:11, 29 [b]Is. 63:10 [c]Mark 3:5

7 [a]Gen. 7:4, 23

8 [a]Gen. 19:19

9 [a]2 Pet. 2:5 [b]Gen. 5:22, 24 [1]*blameless* or *having integrity*

10 [a]Gen. 5:32; 7:13

11 [a]Rom. 2:13 [b]Ezek. 8:17

12 [a]Ps. 14:2; 53:2, 3 [b]Ps. 14:1–3

13 [a]1 Pet. 4:7 [b]Gen. 6:17 [c]2 Pet. 2:4–10

14 [1]Lit. *compartments* or *nests*

15 [1]A cubit is about 18 inches.

17 [a]2 Pet. 2:5 [b]2 Pet. 3:6 [c]Luke 16:22

18 [a]Gen. 8:20—9:17; 17:7 [b]Gen. 7:1, 7, 13

19 [a]Gen. 7:2, 8, 9, 14–16

of every creeping thing of the earth after its kind, two of every *kind* [a]will come to you to keep *them* alive.

21 "And you shall take for yourself of all food that is eaten, and you shall gather *it* to yourself; and it shall be food for you and for them."

22 [a]Thus Noah did; [b]according to all that [c]God commanded him, so he did.

7 Then the [a]LORD said to Noah, [b]"Come into the ark, you and all your household, because I have seen *that* [c]you *are* righteous before Me in this generation.

2 "You shall take with you seven each of every [a]clean animal, a male and his female; [b]two each of animals that *are* unclean, a male and his female;

3 "also seven each of birds of the air, male and female, to keep [1]the species alive on the face of all the earth.

4 "For after [a]seven more days I will cause it to rain on the earth [b]forty days and forty nights, and I will [1]destroy from the face of the earth all living things that I have made."

5 [a]And Noah did according to all that the LORD commanded him.

6 Noah *was* [a]six hundred years old when the floodwaters were on the earth.

7 [a]So Noah, with his sons, his wife, and his sons' wives, went into the ark because of the waters of the flood.

8 Of clean animals, of animals that *are* unclean, of birds, and of everything that creeps on the earth,

9 two by two they went into the ark to Noah, male and female, as God had commanded Noah.

10 And it came to pass after seven days that the waters of the flood were on the earth.

11 In the six hundredth year of Noah's life, in the second month, the seventeenth day of the month, on [a]that day all [b]the fountains of the great deep were broken up, and the [c]windows of heaven were opened.

12 [a]And the rain was on the earth forty days and forty nights.

13 On the very same day Noah and Noah's sons, Shem, Ham, and Jā′pheth, and Noah's wife and the three wives of his sons with them, entered the ark—

14 [a]they and every beast after its kind, all cattle after their kind, every creeping thing that creeps on the earth after its kind, and every bird after its kind, every bird of every [b]sort.

15 And they [a]went into the ark to Noah, two by two, of all flesh in which *is* the breath of life.

16 So those that entered, male and female of all flesh, went in [a]as God had commanded him; and the LORD shut him in.

17 [a]Now the flood was on the earth forty days. The waters increased and lifted up the ark, and it rose high above the earth.

18 The waters prevailed and greatly increased on the earth, [a]and the ark moved about on the surface of the waters.

19 And the waters prevailed exceedingly on the earth, and all the high hills under the whole heaven were covered.

20 The waters prevailed fifteen

20 [a]Gen. 7:9, 15
22 [a]Gen. 7:5; 12:4, 5 [b]Gen. 7:5, 9, 16 [c][1 John 5:3]

CHAPTER 7

1 [a]Matt. 11:28 [b]Matt. 24:38 [c]Gen. 6:9
2 [a]Lev. 11 [b]Lev. 10:10
3 [1]Lit. *seed*
4 [a]Gen. 7:10 [b]Gen. 7:12, 17 [1]Lit. *blot out*
5 [a]Gen. 6:22
6 [a]Gen. 5:4, 32
7 [a]Matt. 24:38
11 [a]Matt. 24:39 [b]Gen. 8:2 [c]Ps. 78:23
12 [a]Gen. 7:4, 17
14 [a]Gen. 6:19 [b]Gen. 1:21
15 [a]Gen. 6:19, 20; 7:9
16 [a]Gen. 7:2, 3
17 [a]Gen. 7:4, 12; 8:6
18 [a]Ps. 104:26

cubits upward, and the mountains were covered.
21 [a]And all flesh died that moved
on [1]the earth: birds and cattle
and beasts and every creeping
thing that creeps on the earth,
and every man.
22 All in [a]whose nostrils *was*
the breath [1]of the spirit of life,
all that *was* on the dry *land,*
died.
23 So He destroyed all living
things which were on the face of
the ground: both man and cattle,
creeping thing and bird of the
air. They were destroyed from
the earth. Only [a]Noah and those
who *were* with him in the ark
remained *alive.*
24 [a]And the waters prevailed on
the earth one hundred and fifty
days.

CHAPTER 8

8 Then God [a]remembered
Noah, and every living thing,
and all the animals that *were*
with him in the ark. [b]And God
made a wind to pass over the
earth, and the waters subsided.
2 [a]The fountains of the deep
and the windows of heaven were
also [b]stopped, and [c]the rain from
heaven was restrained.
3 And the waters receded continually from the earth. At the
end [a]of the hundred and fifty
days the waters decreased.
4 Then the ark rested in the
seventh month, the seventeenth
day of the month, on the mountains of Ar′a·rat.
5 And the waters decreased
continually until the tenth month.
In the tenth *month,* on the first
day of the month, the tops of the
mountains were seen.
6 So it came to pass, at the end
of forty days, that Noah opened
[a]the window of the ark which he
had made.
7 Then he sent out a raven,
which kept going to and fro until the waters had dried up from
the earth.
8 He also sent out from himself a dove, to see if the waters
had receded from the face of the
ground.
9 But the dove found no resting place for the sole of her foot,
and she returned into the ark to
him, for the waters *were* on the
face of the whole earth. So he
put out his hand and took her,
and drew her into the ark to
himself.
10 And he waited yet another
seven days, and again he sent
the dove out from the ark.
11 Then the dove came to him
in the evening, and behold, a
freshly plucked olive leaf *was* in
her mouth; and Noah knew that
the waters had receded from the
earth.
12 So he waited yet another
seven days and sent out the
dove, which did not return again
to him anymore.
13 And it came to pass in the
six hundred and first year, in
the first *month,* the first *day* of
the month, that the waters were
dried up from the earth; and
Noah removed the covering of
the ark and looked, and indeed
the surface of the ground was
dry.
14 And in the second month, on
the twenty-seventh day of the
month, the earth was dried.
15 Then God spoke to Noah,
saying,
16 "Go out of the ark, [a]you and
your wife, and your sons and
your sons' wives with you.

21 [a]Gen. 6:7, 13, 17; 7:4 [1]*the land*
22 [a]Gen. 2:7 [1]LXX, Vg. omit *of the spirit*
23 [a]2 Pet. 2:5
24 [a]Gen. 8:3, 4

CHAPTER 8

1 [a]Gen. 19:29 [b]Ex. 14:21; 15:10
2 [a]Gen. 7:11 [b]Deut. 11:17 [c]Job 38:37
3 [a]Gen. 7:24
6 [a]Gen. 6:16
16 [a]Gen. 7:13

17 "Bring out with you every
living thing of all flesh that *is*
with you: birds and cattle and
every creeping thing that creeps
on the earth, so that they may
abound on the earth, and [a]be
fruitful and multiply on the
earth."
18 So Noah went out, and his
sons and his wife and his sons'
wives with him.
19 Every animal, every creeping
thing, every bird, *and* whatever
creeps on the earth, according
to their families, went out of the
ark.
20 Then Noah built an [a]altar
to the LORD, and took of [b]every
clean animal and of every clean
bird, and offered [c]burnt offerings on the altar.
21 And the LORD smelled [a]a
soothing aroma. Then the
LORD said in His heart, "I will
never again [b]curse the ground
for man's sake, although the
[c]imagination[1] of man's heart *is*
evil from his youth; [d]nor will I
again destroy every living thing
as I have done.

22 "While the earth [a]remains,
Seedtime and harvest,
Cold and heat,
Winter and summer,
And [b]day and night
Shall not cease."

9 So God blessed Noah and
his sons, and said to them:
[a]"Be fruitful and multiply, and
fill the earth.
2 [a]"And the fear of you and the
dread of you shall be on every
beast of the earth, on every bird
of the air, on all that move *on*
the earth, and on all the fish of
the sea. They are given into your
hand.
3 [a]"Every moving thing that
lives shall be food for you. I have
given you [b]all things, even as the
[c]green herbs.
4 [a]"But you shall not eat flesh
with its life, *that is*, its blood.
5 "Surely for your lifeblood I
will demand *a reckoning;* [a]from
the hand of every beast I will
require it, and [b]from the hand
of man. From the hand of every
[c]man's brother I will require the
life of man.

6 "Whoever [a]sheds man's
blood,
By man his blood shall be
shed;
[b]For in the image of God
He made man.
7 And as for you, [a]be fruitful
and multiply;
Bring forth abundantly in
the earth
And multiply in it."

8 Then God spoke to Noah and
to his sons with him, saying:
9 "And as for Me, [a]behold, I
establish [b]My covenant with you
and with your [1]descendants after you,
10 [a]"and with every living creature that *is* with you: the birds,
the cattle, and every beast of
the earth with you, of all that go
out of the ark, every beast of the
earth.
11 "Thus [a]I establish My covenant with you: Never again
shall all flesh be cut off by the
waters of the flood; never again
shall there be a flood to destroy
the earth."
12 And God said: [a]"This *is* the
sign of the covenant which I

---

17 [a]Gen. 1:22, 28; 9:1, 7
20 [a]Gen. 12:7 [b]Lev. 11 [c]Ex. 10:25
21 [a]Ex. 29:18, 25 [b]Gen. 3:17; 6:7, 13, 17 [c]Gen. 6:5; 11:6 [d]Gen. 9:11, 15 [1]*intent* or *thought*
22 [a]Is. 54:9 [b]Jer. 33:20, 25

CHAPTER 9

1 [a]Gen. 1:28, 29; 8:17; 9:7, 19; 10:32
2 [a]Ps. 8:6
3 [a]Deut. 12:15; 14:3, 9, 11 [b]Rom. 14:14, 20 [c]Gen. 1:29
4 [a]1 Sam. 14:33, 34
5 [a]Ex. 21:28 [b]Gen. 4:9, 10 [c]Acts 17:26
6 [a]Lev. 24:17 [b]Gen. 1:26, 27
7 [a]Gen. 9:1, 19
9 [a]Gen. 6:18 [b]Is. 54:9 [1]Lit. *seed*
10 [a]Ps. 145:9
11 [a]Is. 54:9
12 [a]Gen. 9:13, 17; 17:11

make between Me and you, and
every living creature that *is* with
you, for perpetual generations:
13 "I set [a]My rainbow in the
cloud, and it shall be for the sign
of the covenant between Me and
the earth.
14 "It shall be, when I bring a
cloud over the earth, that the
rainbow shall be seen in the
cloud;
15 "and [a]I will remember My
covenant which *is* between Me
and you and every living creature of all flesh; the waters shall
never again become a flood to
destroy all flesh.
16 "The rainbow shall be in the
cloud, and I will look on it to
remember [a]the everlasting covenant between God and every
living creature of all flesh that *is*
on the earth."
17 And God said to Noah, "This
is the sign of the covenant which
I have established between
Me and all flesh that *is* on the
earth."
18 Now the sons of Noah who
went out of the ark were Shem,
Ham, and Jā′pheth. [a]And Ham
was the father of Cā′naan.
19 [a]These three *were* the sons
of Noah, [b]and from these the
whole earth was populated.
20 And Noah began *to be*
[a]a farmer, and he planted a
vineyard.
21 Then he drank of the wine
[a]and was drunk, and became
uncovered in his tent.
22 And Ham, the father of
Cā′naan, saw the nakedness
of his father, and told his two
brothers outside.
23 [a]But Shem and Jā′pheth took
a garment, laid *it* on both their
shoulders, and went backward
and covered the nakedness of
their father. Their faces *were*
[1]turned away, and they did not
see their father's nakedness.
24 So Noah awoke from his wine,
and knew what his younger son
had done to him.
25 Then he said:

[a]"Cursed *be* Cā′naan;
A [b]servant of servants
He shall be to his brethren."

26 And he said:

[a]"Blessed *be* the LORD,
The God of Shem,
And may Cā′naan be his
servant.
27 May God [a]enlarge Jā′pheth,
[b]And may he dwell in the
tents of Shem;
And may Cā′naan be his
servant."

28 And Noah lived after the
flood three hundred and fifty
years.
29 So all the days of Noah were
nine hundred and fifty years;
and he died.

10 Now this *is* the genealogy of the sons of Noah:
Shem, Ham, and Jā′pheth. [a]And
sons were born to them after the
flood.
2 [a]The sons of Jā′pheth *were*
Gō′mer, Mā′gog, Mā′daī, Jā′van,
Tū′bal, Mē′shech, and Tī′ras.
3 The sons of Gō′mer *were* Ash′-
ke·naz, [1]Rī′phath, and Tō·gar′-
mah.
4 The sons of Jā′van *were*
E·lī′shah, Tar′shish, Kit′tim, and
[1]Dō′da·nim.
5 From these [a]the coastland
peoples of the Gentiles were separated into their lands, everyone

13 [a]Ezek. 1:28
15 [a]Lev. 26:42, 45
16 [a]Gen. 17:13, 19
18 [a]Gen. 9:25–27; 10:6
19 [a]Gen. 5:32 [b]1 Chr. 1:4
20 [a]Gen. 3:19, 23; 4:2
21 [a]Prov. 20:1
23 [a]Ex. 20:12 [1]Lit. *backwards*
25 [a]Deut. 27:16 [b]Josh. 9:23
26 [a]Gen. 14:20; 24:27
27 [a]Gen. 10:2–5; 39:3 [b]Eph. 2:13, 14; 3:6

CHAPTER 10

1 [a]Gen. 9:1, 7, 19
2 [a]1 Chr. 1:5–7
3 [1]*Diphath,* 1 Chr. 1:6
4 [1]Sam. *Rodanim* and 1 Chr. 1:7
5 [a]Ps. 72:10

according to his language, according to their families, into
their nations.
6 [a]The sons of Ham *were* Cush,
Miz′ra·im, [1]Put, and Cā′naan.
7 The sons of Cush *were* Sē′ba,
Hav′i·lah, Sab′tah, Rā′a·mah,
and Sab′te·chah; and the sons of
Rā′a·mah *were* Shē′ba and Dē′-
dan.
8 Cush begot [a]Nim′rod; he began to be a mighty one on the
earth.
9 He was a mighty [a]hunter
[b]before the LORD; therefore it is
said, "Like Nim′rod the mighty
hunter before the LORD."
10 [a]And the beginning of his
kingdom was [b]Bā′bel, Ē′rech,
Ac′cad, and Cal′neh, in the land
of Shī′nar.
11 From that land he went [a]to
Assyria and built Nin′e·veh,
Re·hō′both Ir, Cā′lah,
12 and Rē′sen between Nin′-
e·veh and Cā′lah (that *is* the
principal city).
13 Miz′ra·im begot Lū′dim, An′-
a·mim, Le·hā′bim, Naph′tū·him,
14 Path·rū′sim, and Cas·lū′him
[a](from whom came the Phi·lis′-
tines and Caph′to·rim).
15 Cā′naan begot Sī′don his
firstborn, and [a]Heth;
16 [a]the Jeb′ū·sīte, the Am′o·rīte,
and the Gir′ga·shīte;
17 the Hī′vīte, the Ar′kīte, and
the Sī′nīte;
18 the Ar′vad·īte, the Zem′a·rīte,
and the Hā′math·īte. Afterward
the families of the Cā′naan·ītes
were dispersed.
19 [a]And the border of the Cā′-
naan·ītes was from Sī′don as
you go toward Gē′rar, as far as
Gā′za; then as you go toward
Sod′om, Go·mor′rah, Ad′mah,
and Ze·boi′im, as far as Lā′sha.
20 These *were* the sons of Ham,
according to their families, according to their languages, in
their lands *and* in their nations.
21 And *children* were born also
to Shem, the father of all the
children of Ē′ber, [1]the brother of
Jā′pheth the elder.
22 The [a]sons of Shem *were*
Ē′lam, As′shur, [b]Ar·phā′xad,
Lud, and Ar′am.
23 The sons of Ar′am *were* Uz,
Hul, Gē′ther, and [1]Mash.
24 [1]Ar·phā′xad begot [a]Sā′lah,
and Sā′lah begot Ē′ber.
25 [a]To Ē′ber were born two
sons: the name of one *was* [1]Pē′-
leg, for in his days the earth was
divided; and his brother's name
was Jok′tan.
26 Jok′tan begot Al·mō′dad,
Shē′leph, Hā·zar·mā′veth, Jē′-
rah,
27 Ha·dor′am, Ū′zal, Dik′lah,
28 [1]Ō′bal, A·bim′a·el, Shē′ba,
29 Ō′phir, Hav′i·lah, and Jō′bab.
All these *were* the sons of Jok′-
tan.
30 And their dwelling place was
from Mē′sha as you go toward
Sē′phar, the mountain of the
east.
31 These *were* the sons of Shem,
according to their families, according to their languages, in
their lands, according to their
nations.
32 [a]These *were* the families of
the sons of Noah, according to
their generations, in their nations; [b]and from these the nations were divided on the earth
after the flood.

11 Now the whole earth had
one language and one
[1]speech.
2 And it came to pass, as they
journeyed from the east, that

6 [a]1 Chr. 1:8–16 [1]Or *Phut*
8 [a]Mic. 5:6
9 [a]Jer. 16:16 [b]Gen. 21:20
10 [a]Mic. 5:6 [b]Gen. 11:9
11 [a]Mic. 5:6
14 [a]1 Chr. 1:12
15 [a]Gen. 23:3
16 [a]Gen. 14:7; 15:19–21
19 [a]Num. 34:2–12
21 [1]Or *the older brother of Japheth*
22 [a]1 Chr. 1:17–28 [b]Luke 3:36
23 [1]LXX *Meshech* and 1 Chr. 1:17
24 [a]Gen. 11:12 [1]So with MT, Vg., Tg.; LXX *Arphaxad begot Cainan, and Cainan begot Salah* (cf. Luke 3:35, 36)
25 [a]1 Chr. 1:19 [1]Lit. *Division*
28 [1]*Ebal,* 1 Chr. 1:22
32 [a]Gen. 10:1 [b]Gen. 9:19; 11:8

CHAPTER 11

1 [1]Lit. *lip*

they found a plain in the land [a]of
Shi′nar, and they dwelt there.
3 Then they said to one another, "Come, let us make bricks
and [1]bake *them* thoroughly."
They had brick for stone, and
they had asphalt for mortar.
4 And they said, "Come, let
us build ourselves a city, and
a tower [a]whose top *is* in the
heavens; let us make a [b]name
for ourselves, lest we [c]be scattered abroad over the face of the
whole earth."
5 [a]But the LORD came down to
see the city and the tower which
the sons of men had built.
6 And the LORD said, "Indeed
[a]the people *are* one and they
all have [b]one language, and this
is what they begin to do; now
nothing that they [c]propose to do
will be withheld from them.
7 "Come, [a]let Us go down and
there [b]confuse their language,
that they may not understand
one another's speech."
8 So [a]the LORD scattered them
abroad from there [b]over the face
of all the earth, and they ceased
building the city.
9 Therefore its name is called
[1]Bā′bel, [a]because there the LORD
confused the language of all the
earth; and from there the LORD
scattered them abroad over the
face of all the earth.
10 [a]This *is* the genealogy of
Shem: Shem *was* one hundred
years old, and begot Ar·phā′xad
two years after the flood.
11 After he begot Ar·phā′xad,
Shem lived five hundred years,
and begot sons and daughters.
12 Ar·phā′xad lived thirty-five
years, [a]and begot Sā′lah.
13 After he begot Sā′lah, Ar·phā′-
xad lived four hundred and
three years, and begot sons and
daughters.
14 Sā′lah lived thirty years, and
begot Ē′ber.
15 After he begot Ē′ber, Sā′-
lah lived four hundred and
three years, and begot sons and
daughters.
16 [a]Ē′ber lived thirty-four years,
and begot [b]Pē′leg.
17 After he begot Pē′leg, Ē′ber
lived four hundred and thirty
years, and begot sons and
daughters.
18 Pē′leg lived thirty years, and
begot Rē′ū.
19 After he begot Rē′ū, Pē′-
leg lived two hundred and
nine years, and begot sons and
daughters.
20 Rē′ū lived thirty-two years,
and begot [a]Sē′rug.
21 After he begot Sē′rug, Rē′ū
lived two hundred and seven
years, and begot sons and
daughters.
22 Sē′rug lived thirty years, and
begot Nā′hor.
23 After he begot Nā′hor, Sē′-
rug lived two hundred years,
and begot sons and daughters.
24 Nā′hor lived twenty-nine
years, and begot [a]Tē′rah.
25 After he begot Tē′rah, Nā′-
hor lived one hundred and nineteen years, and begot sons and
daughters.
26 Now Tē′rah lived seventy
years, and [a]begot [1]Abram, Nā′-
hor, and Har′an.
27 This *is* the genealogy of Tē′-
rah: Tē′rah begot [a]Abram, Nā′-
hor, and Har′an. Har′an begot
Lot.
28 And Har′an died before his
father Tē′rah in his native land,
in Ūr of the Chal·dē′ans.
29 Then Abram and Nā′hor took

2 [a]Gen. 10:10; 14:1
3 [1]Lit. *burn*
4 [a]Deut. 1:28; 9:1 [b]Gen. 6:4 [c]Deut. 4:27
5 [a]Gen. 18:21
6 [a]Gen. 9:19 [b]Gen. 11:1 [c]Ps. 2:1
7 [a]Gen. 1:26 [b]Ex. 4:11
8 [a][Luke 1:51] [b]Gen. 10:25, 32
9 [a]1 Cor. 14:23 [1]Lit. *Confusion,* Babylon
10 [a]Gen. 10:22–25
12 [a]Luke 3:35
16 [a]1 Chr. 1:19 [b]Luke 3:35
20 [a]Luke 3:35
24 [a]Josh. 24:2
26 [a]1 Chr. 1:26 [1]*Abraham,* Gen. 17:5
27 [a]Gen. 11:31; 17:5

wives: the name of Abram's
wife *was* [a]Sar'aī,[1] and the name
of Nā'hor's wife, [b]Mil'cah, the
daughter of Har'an the father of
Mil'cah and the father of Is'cah.
30 But [a]Sar'aī was barren; she
had no child.
31 And Tē'rah [a]took his son
Abram and his grandson Lot, the
son of Har'an, and his daughter-
in-law Sar'aī, his son Abram's
wife, and they went out with
them from [b]Ūr of the Chal·dē'-
ans to go to [c]the land of Cā'-
naan; and they came to Har'an
and dwelt there.
32 So the days of Tē'rah were
two hundred and five years, and
Tē'rah died in Har'an.

12

Now the [a]LORD had said
to Abram:

"Get [b]out of your country,
From your family
And from your father's
house,
To a land that I will show
you.
2 [a]I will make you a great
nation;
[b]I will bless you
And make your name great;
[c]And you shall be a blessing.
☆ 3 [a]I will bless those who bless
you,
And I will curse him who
curses you;
And in [b]you all the families
of the earth shall be
[c]blessed."

4 So Abram departed as the
LORD had spoken to him, and
Lot went with him. And Abram
was seventy-five years old when
he departed from Har'an.
5 Then Abram took Sar'aī his
wife and Lot his brother's son,
and all their possessions that
they had gathered, and [a]the [1]peo-
ple whom they had acquired [b]in
Har'an, and they [c]departed to go
to the land of Cā'naan. So they
came to the land of Cā'naan.
6 Abram [a]passed through the
land to the place of Shē'chem,
[b]as far as [1]the terebinth tree of
Mō'reh. [c]And the Cā'naan·ītes
were then in the land.
7 [a]Then the LORD appeared to ☆
Abram and said, [b]"To your [1]de-
scendants I will give this land."
And there he built an [c]altar to the
LORD, who had appeared to him.
8 And he moved from there
to the mountain east of Beth'el,
and he pitched his tent *with*
Beth'el on the west and Aī on
the east; there he built an altar
to the LORD and [a]called on the
name of the LORD.
9 So Abram journeyed, [a]going
on still toward the [1]South.
10 Now there was [a]a famine
in the land, and Abram [b]went
down to Egypt to dwell there,
for the famine *was* [c]severe in the
land.
11 And it came to pass, when he
was close to entering Egypt, that
he said to Sar'aī his wife, "Indeed
I know that you *are* [a]a woman of
beautiful countenance.
12 "Therefore it will happen,
when the Egyptians see you,
that they will say, 'This *is* his
wife'; and they [a]will kill me, but
they will let you live.
13 [a]"Please say you *are* my
[b]sister, that it may be well with
me for your sake, and that [1]I
may live because of you."
14 So it was, when Abram came
into Egypt, that the Egyptians
saw the woman, that she *was*
very beautiful.

29 [a]Gen. 17:15; 20:12 [b]Gen. 22:20, 23; 24:15 [1]*Sarah*, Gen. 17:15
30 [a]Gen. 16:1, 2
31 [a]Gen. 12:1 [b]Acts 7:4 [c]Gen. 10:19

CHAPTER 12

1 [a]Acts 7:2, 3 [b]Gen. 13:9
2 [a]Deut. 26:5 [b]Gen. 22:17; 24:35 [c]Gen. 28:4
3 [a]Num. 24:9 [b]Acts 3:25; [Gal. 3:8] [c]Is. 41:27
5 [a]Gen. 14:14 [b]Gen. 11:31 [c]Gen. 13:18 [1]Lit. *souls*
6 [a]Heb. 11:9 [b]Deut. 11:30 [c]Gen. 10:18, 19 [1]Heb. *Alon Moreh*
7 [a]Gen. 17:1; 18:1 [b]Gen. 13:15; 15:18; 17:8; Acts 7:5; Gal. 3:16 [c]Gen. 13:4, 18; 22:9 [1]Lit. *seed*
8 [a]Gen. 4:26; 13:4; 21:33
9 [a]Gen. 13:1, 3; 20:1; 24:62 [1]Heb. *Negev*
10 [a]Gen. 26:1 [b]Ps. 105:13 [c]Gen. 43:1
11 [a]Gen. 12:14; 26:7; 29:17
12 [a]Gen. 20:11; 26:7
13 [a]Gen. 20:1–18; 26:6–11 [b]Gen. 20:12 [1]Lit. *my soul*

15 The princes of Pharaoh also saw her and commended her to Pharaoh. And the woman was taken to Pharaoh's house.

16 He [a]treated Abram well for her sake. He [b]had sheep, oxen, male donkeys, male and female servants, female donkeys, and camels.

17 But the LORD [a]plagued Pharaoh and his house with great plagues because of Sar'aī, Abram's wife.

18 And Pharaoh called Abram and said, [a]"What *is* this you have done to me? Why did you not tell me that she *was* your wife?

19 "Why did you say, 'She *is* my sister'? I might have taken her as my wife. Now therefore, here is your wife; take *her* and go your way."

20 [a]So Pharaoh commanded *his* men concerning him; and they sent him away, with his wife and all that he had.

13

Then Abram went up from Egypt, he and his wife and all that he had, and [a]Lot with him, [b]to the [1]South.

2 [a]Abram *was* very rich in livestock, in silver, and in gold.

3 And he went on his journey [a]from the South as far as Beth'el, to the place where his tent had been at the beginning, between Beth'el and Aī,

4 to the [a]place of the altar which he had made there at first. And there Abram [b]called on the name of the LORD.

5 Lot also, who went with Abram, had flocks and herds and tents.

6 Now [a]the land was not able to [1]support them, that they might dwell together, for their possessions were so great that they could not dwell together.

7 And there was [a]strife between the herdsmen of Abram's livestock and the herdsmen of Lot's livestock. [b]The Cā'naan·ītes and the Per'iz·zītes then dwelt in the land.

8 So Abram said to Lot, [a]"Please let there be no strife between you and me, and between my herdsmen and your herdsmen; for we *are* brethren.

9 [a]"*Is* not the whole land before you? Please [b]separate from me. [c]If *you take* the left, then I will go to the right; or, if *you go* to the right, then I will go to the left."

10 And Lot lifted his eyes and saw all [a]the plain of Jordan, that it *was* well watered everywhere (before the LORD [b]destroyed Sod'om and Go·mor'rah) [c]like the garden of the LORD, like the land of Egypt as you go toward [d]Zō'ar.

11 Then Lot chose for himself all the plain of Jordan, and Lot journeyed east. And they separated from each other.

12 Abram dwelt in the land of Cā'naan, and Lot [a]dwelt in the cities of the plain and [b]pitched *his* tent even as far as Sod'om.

13 But the men of Sod'om [a]*were* exceedingly wicked and [b]sinful against the LORD.

14 And the LORD said to Abram, after Lot [a]had separated from him: "Lift your eyes now and look from the place where you are—[b]northward, southward, eastward, and westward;

15 "for all the land which you see [a]I give to you and [b]your [1]descendants forever.

16 "And [a]I will make your

16 [a]Gen. 20:14 [b]Gen. 13:2
17 [a]1 Chr. 16:21
18 [a]Gen. 20:9, 10; 26:10
20 [a][Prov. 21:1]

CHAPTER 13

1 [a]Gen. 12:4; 14:12, 16 [b]Gen. 12:9 [1]Heb. *Negev*
2 [a]Gen. 24:35; 26:14
3 [a]Gen. 12:8, 9
4 [a]Gen. 12:7, 8; 21:33 [b]Ps. 116:17
6 [a]Gen. 36:7 [1]Lit. *bear*
7 [a]Gen. 26:20 [b]Gen. 12:6; 15:20, 21
8 [a]1 Cor. 6:7
9 [a]Gen. 20:15; 34:10 [b]Gen. 13:11, 14 [c][Rom. 12:18]
10 [a]Gen. 19:17–29 [b]Gen. 19:24 [c]Gen. 2:8, 10 [d]Deut. 34:3
12 [a]Gen. 19:24, 25, 29 [b]Gen. 14:12; 19:1
13 [a]Gen. 18:20, 21 [b]Gen. 6:11; 39:9
14 [a]Gen. 13:11 [b]Gen. 28:14
15 [a]Acts 7:5 [b]2 Chr. 20:7 [1]Lit. *seed*
16 [a]Gen. 22:17

descendants as the dust of the
earth; so that if a man could
number the dust of the earth,
then your descendants also
could be numbered.
17 "Arise, walk in the land
through its length and its width,
for I give it to you."
18 [a]Then Abram moved *his*
tent, and went and [b]dwelt by
[1]the terebinth trees of Mam′re,
[c]which *are* in Hē′bron, and built
an [d]altar there to the LORD.

14 And it came to pass in
the days of Am′ra·phel
king [a]of Shī′nar, Ar′i·och king of
El·lā′sar, Ched·or·la·ō′mer king
of [b]Ē′lam, and Tidal king of [1]na-
tions,
2 *that* they made war with
Bē′ra king of Sod′om, Bir′sha
king of Go·mor′rah, Shī′nab king
of [a]Ad′mah, Shem·ē′ber king of
Ze·boi′im, and the king of Bē′la
(that is, [b]Zō′ar).
3 All these joined together in
the Valley of Sid′dim [a](that is,
the Salt Sea).
4 Twelve years [a]they served
Ched·or·la·ō′mer, and in the thirteenth year they rebelled.
5 In the fourteenth year
Ched·or·la·ō′mer and the kings
that *were* with him came and
attacked [a]the Reph′a·im in Ash′-
te·roth Kar·nā′im, [b]the Zū′zim
in Ham, [c]the Ē′mim in Shā′veh
Kir·i·a·thā′im,
6 [a]and the Hor′ītes in their
mountain of Sē′ir, as far
as El Par′an, which *is* by the
wilderness.
7 Then they turned back and
came to En Mish′pat (that *is*,
Kā′desh), and attacked all the
country of the A·mal′e·kītes, and
also the Am′o·rītes who dwelt
[a]in Ha·zē′zon Tā′mar.
8 And the king of Sod′om, the
king of Go·mor′rah, the king of
Ad′mah, the king of Ze·boi′im,
and the king of Bē′la (that *is*,
Zō′ar) went out and joined together in battle in the Valley of
Sid′dim
9 against Ched·or·la·ō′mer
king of Ē′lam, Tidal king of [1]na-
tions, Am′ra·phel king of Shī′-
nar, and Ar′i·och king of El·lā′-
sar—four kings against five.
10 Now the Valley of Sid′dim
was full of [a]asphalt pits; and the
kings of Sod′om and Go·mor′rah
fled; *some* fell there, and the remainder fled [b]to the mountains.
11 Then they took [a]all the goods
of Sod′om and Go·mor′rah, and
all their provisions, and went
their way.
12 They also took Lot, Abram's
[a]brother's son [b]who dwelt in
Sod′om, and his goods, and
departed.
13 Then one who had escaped
came and told Abram the [a]He-
brew, for [b]he dwelt by [1]the terebinth trees of Mam′re the Am′-
o·rīte, brother of Esh′col and
brother of Ā′ner; [c]and they *were*
allies with Abram.
14 Now [a]when Abram heard
that [b]his brother was taken captive, he armed his three hundred and eighteen trained *servants* who were [c]born in his own
house, and went in pursuit [d]as
far as Dan.
15 He divided his forces against
them by night, and he and his
servants [a]attacked them and
pursued them as far as Hō′bah,
which *is* [1]north of Damascus.
16 So he [a]brought back all the
goods, and also brought back
his brother Lot and his goods,

18 [a]Gen. 26:17 [b]Gen. 14:13 [c]Gen. 23:2; 35:27 [d]Gen. 8:20; 22:8, 9 [1]Heb. *Alon Mamre*

CHAPTER 14

1 [a]Gen. 10:10; 11:2 [b]Is. 11:11; 21:2 [1]Heb. *goyim*

2 [a]Deut. 29:23 [b]Gen. 13:10; 19:22

3 [a]Num. 34:12

4 [a]Gen. 9:26

5 [a]Gen. 15:20 [b]Deut. 2:20 [c]Deut. 2:10

6 [a]Deut. 2:12, 22

7 [a]2 Chr. 20:2

9 [1]Heb. *goyim*

10 [a]Gen. 11:3 [b]Gen. 19:17, 30

11 [a]Gen. 14:16, 21

12 [a]Gen. 11:27; 12:5 [b]Gen. 13:12

13 [a]Gen. 39:14; 40:15 [b]Gen. 13:18 [c]Gen. 14:24; 21:27, 32 [1]Heb. *Alon Mamre*

14 [a]Gen. 19:29 [b]Gen. 13:8; 14:12 [c]Gen. 12:5; 15:3; 17:27 [d]Deut. 34:1

15 [a]Is. 41:2, 3 [1]Lit. *on the left hand of*

16 [a]Gen. 31:18

as well as the women and the
people.
17 And the king of Sod′om [a]went
out to meet him at the Valley of
Shā′veh (that *is,* the [b]King's Valley), [c]after his return from [1]the
defeat of Ched·or·la·ō′mer and
the kings who *were* with him.
18 Then [a]Mel·chiz′e·dek king of
Sā′lem brought out [b]bread and
wine; he *was* [c]the priest of [d]God
Most High.
19 And he blessed him and
said:

[a]"Blessed be Abram of God
Most High,
[b]Possessor of heaven and
earth;
20 And [a]blessed be God Most
High,
Who has delivered your
enemies into your hand."

And he [a]gave him [1]a tithe of all.
21 Now the king of Sod′om said
to Abram, "Give me the [1]per-
sons, and take the goods for
yourself."
22 But Abram [a]said to the king
of Sod′om, "I [b]have raised my
hand to the LORD, God Most
High, [c]the Possessor of heaven
and earth,
23 "that [a]I *will take* nothing,
from a thread to a sandal strap,
and that I will not take anything
that *is* yours, lest you should say,
'I have made Abram rich'—
24 "except only what the young
men have eaten, and the portion
of the men who went with me:
Ā′ner, Esh′col, and Mam′re; let
them take their portion."

15

After these things the
word of the LORD came to
Abram [a]in a vision, saying, [b]"Do
not be afraid, Abram. I *am* your

17 [a]1 Sam. 18:6 [b]2 Sam. 18:18 [c]Heb. 7:1 [1]Lit. *striking*
18 [a]Heb. 7:1–10 [b]Gen. 18:5 [c]Ps. 110:4 [d]Acts 16:17
19 [a]Ruth 3:10 [b]Gen. 14:22
20 [a]Gen. 24:27 [b]Heb. 7:4 [1]*one-tenth*
21 [1]Lit. *souls*
22 [a]Gen. 14:2, 8, 10 [b]Dan. 12:7 [c]Gen. 14:19
23 [a]2 Kin. 5:16

CHAPTER 15

1 [a]Dan. 10:1 [b]Gen. 21:17; 26:24 [c]Deut. 33:29 [d]Prov. 11:18 [1]Or *your reward shall be very great*
2 [a]Gen. 17:18 [b]Acts 7:5 [1]*am childless*
3 [a]Gen. 14:14 [1]*a servant*
4 [a]2 Sam. 7:12
5 [a]Ps. 147:4 [b]Jer. 33:22 [c]Ex. 32:13 [d]Gen. 17:19
6 [a]Rom. 4:3, 9, 22 [b]Ps. 32:2; 106:31
7 [a]Gen. 12:1 [b]Gen. 11:28, 31 [c]Ps. 105:42, 44
8 [a]Luke 1:18
10 [a]Jer. 34:18 [b]Lev. 1:17
12 [a]Gen. 2:21; 28:11

[c]shield, [1]your exceedingly [d]great
reward."
2 [a]But Abram said, "Lord GOD,
what will You give me, [b]seeing I
[1]go childless, and the heir of my
house *is* El·i·ē′zer of Damascus?"
3 Then Abram said, "Look, You
have given me no offspring; indeed [a]one[1] born in my house is
my heir!"
4 And behold, the word of the
LORD *came* to him, saying, "This
one shall not be your heir, but
one who [a]will come from your
own body shall be your heir."
5 Then He brought him outside and said, "Look now toward
heaven, and [a]count the [b]stars if
you are able to number them."
And He said to him, [c]"So shall
your [d]descendants be."
6 And he [a]believed in the LORD,
and He [b]accounted it to him for
righteousness.
7 Then He said to him, "I *am*
the LORD, who [a]brought you out
of [b]Ūr of the Chal·dē′ans, [c]to
give you this land to inherit it."
8 And he said, "Lord GOD, [a]how
shall I know that I will inherit
it?"
9 So He said to him, "Bring Me
a three-year-old heifer, a three-
year-old female goat, a three-
year-old ram, a turtledove, and a
young pigeon."
10 Then he brought all these
to Him and [a]cut them in two,
down the middle, and placed
each piece opposite the other;
but he did not cut [b]the birds in
two.
11 And when the vultures came
down on the carcasses, Abram
drove them away.
12 Now when the sun was going down, [a]a deep sleep fell upon

Abram; and behold, horror *and* great darkness fell upon him.

13 Then He said to Abram: "Know certainly [a]that your descendants will be strangers in a land *that is* not theirs, and will serve them, and [b]they will afflict them four hundred years.

14 "And also the nation whom they serve [a]I will judge; afterward [b]they shall come out with great possessions.

15 "Now as for you, [a]you shall [1]go [b]to your fathers in peace; [c]you shall be buried at a good old age.

16 "But [a]in the fourth generation they shall return here, for the iniquity [b]of the Am′o·rītes [c]*is* not yet complete."

17 And it came to pass, when the sun went down and it was dark, that behold, there appeared a smoking oven and a burning torch that [a]passed between those pieces.

18 On the same day the LORD [a]made a covenant with Abram, saying:

[b]"To your descendants I have given this land, from the river of Egypt to the great river, the River Eū·phrā′tēs—

19 "the Ken′ītes, the Kē′nez·zītes, the Kad′mon·ītes,

20 "the Hit′tītes, the Per′iz·zītes, the Reph′a·im,

21 "the Am′o·rītes, the Cā′naan·ītes, the Gir′ga·shītes, and the Jeb′ū·sītes."

16 Now Sar′aī, Abram's wife, [a]had borne him no *children.* And she had [b]an Egyptian maidservant whose name was [c]Hā′gar.

2 [a]So Sar′aī said to Abram, "See now, the LORD [b]has restrained me from bearing *children.* Please, [c]go in to my maid; perhaps I shall [1]obtain children by her." And Abram [d]heeded the voice of Sar′aī.

3 Then Sar′aī, Abram's wife, took Hā′gar her maid, the Egyptian, and gave her to her husband Abram to be his wife, after Abram [a]had dwelt ten years in the land of Cā′naan.

4 So he went in to Hā′gar, and she conceived. And when she saw that she had conceived, her mistress became [a]despised in her [1]eyes.

5 Then Sar′aī said to Abram, [1]"My wrong *be* upon you! I gave my maid into your embrace; and when she saw that she had conceived, I became despised in her eyes. [a]The LORD judge between you and me."

6 [a]So Abram said to Sar′aī, "Indeed your maid *is* in your hand; do to her as you please." And when Sar′aī dealt harshly with her, [b]she fled from her presence.

7 Now the [a]Angel of the LORD found her by a spring of water in the wilderness, [b]by the spring on the way to [c]Shūr.

8 And He said, "Hā′gar, Sar′aī's maid, where have you come from, and where are you going?" She said, "I am fleeing from the presence of my mistress Sar′aī."

9 The Angel of the LORD said to her, "Return to your mistress, and [a]submit yourself under her hand."

10 Then the Angel of the LORD said to her, [a]"I will multiply your descendants exceedingly, so that they shall not be counted for multitude."

11 And the Angel of the LORD said to her:

13 [a]Ex. 1:11 [b]Ex. 12:40
14 [a]Ex. 6:6 [b]Ex. 12:36
15 [a]Job 5:26 [b]Gen. 25:8; 47:30 [c]Gen. 25:8 [1]Die and join your ancestors
16 [a]Ex. 12:41 [b]1 Kin. 21:26 [c]Matt. 23:32
17 [a]Jer. 34:18, 19
18 [a]Gen. 24:7 [b]Gen. 12:7; 17:8

CHAPTER 16

1 [a]Gen. 11:30; 15:2, 3 [b]Gen. 12:16; 21:9 [c]Gal. 4:24
2 [a]Gen. 30:3 [b]Gen. 20:18 [c]Gen. 30:3, 9 [d]Gen. 3:17 [1]Lit. *be built up from*
3 [a]Gen. 12:4, 5
4 [a][Prov. 30:21, 23] [1]*sight*
5 [a]Gen. 31:53 [1]*The wrong done to me be*
6 [a]1 Pet. 3:7 [b]Ex. 2:15
7 [a]Gen. 21:17, 18; 22:11, 15; 31:11 [b]Gen. 20:1; 25:18 [c]Ex. 15:22
9 [a][Titus 2:9]
10 [a]Gen. 17:20

"Behold, you *are* with child,
[a]And you shall bear a son.
You shall call his name
[1]Ish′ma·el,
Because the LORD has heard
your affliction.
12 [a]He shall be a wild man;
His hand *shall be* against
every man,
And every man's hand
against him.
[b]And he shall dwell in the
presence of all his
brethren."

13 Then she called the name of
the LORD who spoke to her, You-
Are-[1]the-God-Who-Sees; for she
said, "Have I also here [2]seen
Him [a]who sees me?"
14 Therefore the well was called
[a]Bē′er La·haī′ Roi;[1] observe, *it is*
[b]between Kā′desh and Bē′red.
15 So [a]Hā′gar bore Abram a
son; and Abram named his son,
whom Hā′gar bore, Ish′ma·el.
16 Abram *was* eighty-six years
old when Hā′gar bore Ish′ma·el
to Abram.

17 When Abram was ninety-
nine years old, the LORD
[a]appeared to Abram and said to
him, [b]"I *am* [1]Almighty God; [c]walk
before Me and be [d]blameless.
2 "And I will make My [a]cove-
nant between Me and you, and
[b]will multiply you exceedingly."
3 Then Abram fell on his
face, and God talked with him,
saying:
4 "As for Me, behold, My covenant is with you, and you shall
be [a]a father of [1]many nations.
5 "No longer shall [a]your name
be called [1]Abram, but your name
shall be [2]Abraham; [b]for I have
made you a father of [3]many
nations.

11 [a]Luke 1:13, 31 [1]Lit. *God Hears*
12 [a]Gen. 21:20 [b]Gen. 25:18
13 [a]Gen. 31:42 [1]Heb. *El Roi* [2]Seen the back of
14 [a]Gen. 24:62 [b]Num. 13:26 [1]Lit. *Well of the One Who Lives and Sees Me*
15 [a]Gal. 4:22

CHAPTER 17

1 [a]Gen. 12:7; 18:1 [b]Gen. 28:3; 35:11 [c]2 Kin. 20:3 [d]Deut. 18:13 [1]Heb. *El Shaddai*
2 [a]Gen. 15:18 [b]Gen. 12:2; 13:16; 15:5; 18:18
4 [a][Rom. 4:11, 12, 16] [1]Lit. *multitude of nations*
5 [a]Neh. 9:7 [b]Rom. 4:17 [1]Lit. *Exalted Father* [2]Lit. *Father of a Multitude* [3]*a multitude of*
6 [a]Gen. 17:16; 35:11 [b]Matt. 1:6
7 [a][Gal. 3:17] [b]Gen. 26:24; 28:13 [c]Rom. 9:8; Gal. 3:16
8 [a]Acts 7:5 [b]Gen. 23:4; 28:4 [c]Lev. 26:12 [1]Lit. *of your sojournings*
9 [a]Ex. 19:5
10 [a]Acts 7:8
11 [a]Ex. 12:13, 48
12 [a]Lev. 12:3

6 "I will make you exceedingly
fruitful; and I will make [a]nations
of you, and [b]kings shall come
from you.
7 "And I will [a]establish My ☆
covenant between Me and you
and your descendants after you
in their generations, for an everlasting covenant, [b]to be God to
you and [c]your descendants after
you.
8 "Also [a]I give to you and your
descendants after you the land
[b]in[1] which you are a stranger, all
the land of Cā′naan, as an everlasting possession; and [c]I will be
their God."
9 And God said to Abraham:
"As for you, [a]you shall keep My
covenant, you and your descendants after you throughout their
generations.
10 "This *is* My covenant which
you shall keep, between Me and
you and your descendants after
you: [a]Every male child among
you shall be circumcised;
11 "and you shall be circumcised in the flesh of your foreskins, and it shall be [a]a sign of
the covenant between Me and
you.
12 "He who is eight days old
among you [a]shall be circumcised, every male child in your
generations, he who is born
in your house or bought with
money from any foreigner who
is not your descendant.
13 "He who is born in your
house and he who is bought with
your money must be circumcised, and My covenant shall be
in your flesh for an everlasting
covenant.
14 "And the uncircumcised male
child, who is not circumcised in
the flesh of his foreskin, that

person [a]shall be cut off from
his people; he has broken My
covenant."
15 Then God said to Abraham,
"As for Sar'aī your wife, you
shall not call her name Sar'aī,
but [1]Sarah *shall be* her name.
16 "And I will bless her [a]and
also give you a son by her; then
I will bless her, and she shall be
a mother [b]*of* nations; [c]kings of
peoples shall be from her."
17 Then Abraham fell on his
face [a]and laughed, and said in
his heart, "Shall *a child* be born
to a man who is one hundred
years old? And shall Sarah,
who is ninety years old, bear *a*
child?"
18 And Abraham [a]said to God,
"Oh, that Ish'ma·el might live
before You!"
☆ 19 Then God said: "No, [a]Sarah
your wife shall bear you a son,
and you shall call his name Isaac;
I will establish My [b]covenant
with him for an everlasting covenant, *and* with his descendants
after him.
20 "And as for Ish'ma·el, I have
heard you. Behold, I have blessed
him, and will make him fruitful,
and [a]will multiply him exceedingly. He shall beget [b]twelve
princes, [c]and I will make him a
great nation.
21 "But My [a]covenant I will establish with Isaac, [b]whom Sarah
shall bear to you at this [c]set time
next year."
22 Then He finished talking
with him, and God went up from
Abraham.
23 So Abraham took Ish'ma·el
his son, all who were born in his
house and all who were bought
with his money, every male
among the men of Abraham's

14 [a]Ex. 4:24–26
15 [1]Lit. *Princess*
16 [a]Gen. 18:10 [b]Gen. 35:11 [c]Gen. 17:6; 36:31
17 [a]Gen. 17:3; 18:12; 21:6
18 [a]Gen. 18:23
19 [a]Gen. 18:10; 21:2; [Gal. 4:28] [b]Gen. 22:16
20 [a]Gen. 16:10 [b]Gen. 25:12–16 [c]Gen. 21:13, 18
21 [a]Gen. 26:2–5 [b]Gen. 21:2 [c]Gen. 18:14
27 [a]Gen. 18:19

CHAPTER 18

1 [a]Gen. 13:18; 14:13 [1]Heb. *Alon Mamre*
2 [a]Heb. 13:2 [b]Gen. 19:1
4 [a]Gen. 19:2; 24:32; 43:24
5 [a]Judg. 6:18, 19; 13:15, 16 [b]Judg. 19:5 [c]Gen. 19:8; 33:10

house, and circumcised the flesh
of their foreskins that very same
day, as God had said to him.
24 Abraham *was* ninety-nine
years old when he was circumcised in the flesh of his foreskin.
25 And Ish'ma·el his son *was*
thirteen years old when he was
circumcised in the flesh of his
foreskin.
26 That very same day Abraham was circumcised, and his
son Ish'ma·el;
27 and [a]all the men of his house,
born in the house or bought
with money from a foreigner,
were circumcised with him.

18

Then the LORD appeared
to him by [1]the [a]terebinth
trees of Mam're, as he was sitting in the tent door in the heat
of the day.
2 [a]So he lifted his eyes and
looked, and behold, three men
were standing by him; [b]and
when he saw *them,* he ran from
the tent door to meet them, and
bowed himself to the ground,
3 and said, "My Lord, if I have
now found favor in Your sight,
do not pass on by Your servant.
4 "Please let [a]a little water be
brought, and wash your feet,
and rest yourselves under the
tree.
5 "And [a]I will bring a morsel
of bread, that [b]you may refresh
your hearts. After that you may
pass by, [c]inasmuch as you have
come to your servant." They
said, "Do as you have said."
6 So Abraham hurried into the
tent to Sarah and said, "Quickly,
make ready three measures of
fine meal; knead *it* and make
cakes."
7 And Abraham ran to the

herd, took a tender and good
calf, gave *it* to a young man, and
he hastened to prepare it.
8 So [a]he took butter and milk
and the calf which he had prepared, and set *it* before them;
and he stood by them under the
tree as they ate.
9 Then they said to him,
"Where *is* Sarah your wife?" So
he said, "Here, [a]in the tent."
10 And He said, "I will certainly
return to you [a]according to the
time of life, and behold, [b]Sarah
your wife shall have a son."
(Sarah was listening in the tent
door which *was* behind him.)
11 Now [a]Abraham and Sarah
were old, well advanced in age;
and [1]Sarah [b]had passed the age
of childbearing.
12 Therefore Sarah [a]laughed
within herself, saying, [b]"After
I have grown old, shall I have
pleasure, my [c]lord being old
also?"
13 And the LORD said to Abraham, "Why did Sarah laugh,
saying, 'Shall I surely bear *a*
child, since I am old?'
14 [a]"Is anything too hard for the
LORD? [b]At the appointed time I
will return to you, according to
the time of life, and Sarah shall
have a son."
15 But Sarah denied *it,* saying,
"I did not laugh," for she was
afraid. And He said, "No, but
you did laugh!"
16 Then the men rose from there
and looked toward Sod'om, and
Abraham went with them [a]to
send them on the way.
17 And the LORD said, [a]"Shall I
hide from Abraham what I am
doing,
☆18 "since Abraham shall surely
become a great and mighty
nation, and all the nations of the
earth shall be [a]blessed in him?
19 "For I have known him, in
order [a]that he may command his
children and his household after
him, that they keep the way of
the LORD, to do righteousness
and justice, that the LORD may
bring to Abraham what He has
spoken to him."
20 And the LORD said, "Because
[a]the outcry against Sod'om and
Go·mor'rah is great, and because their [b]sin is very grave,
21 [a]"I will go down now and see
whether they have done altogether according to the outcry
against it that has come to Me;
and if not, [b]I will know."
22 Then the men turned away
from there [a]and went toward
Sod'om, but Abraham still stood
before the LORD.
23 And Abraham [a]came near
and said, [b]"Would You also
[c]destroy the [d]righteous with the
wicked?
24 "Suppose there were fifty
righteous within the city; would
You also destroy the place and
not spare *it* for the fifty righteous that were in it?
25 "Far be it from You to do
such a thing as this, to slay the
righteous with the wicked, so
[a]that the righteous should be as
the wicked; far be it from You!
[b]Shall not the Judge of all the
earth do right?"
26 So the LORD said, [a]"If I find
in Sod'om fifty righteous within
the city, then I will spare all the
place for their sakes."
27 Then Abraham answered
and said, "Indeed now, I who *am*
[a]*but* dust and ashes have taken
it upon myself to speak to the
Lord:

8 [a]Gen. 19:3
9 [a]Gen. 24:67
10 [a]2 Kin. 4:16 [b]Rom. 9:9
11 [a]Gen. 17:17 [b]Gen. 31:35 [1]Lit. *the manner of women had ceased to be with Sarah*
12 [a]Gen. 17:17 [b]Luke 1:18 [c]1 Pet. 3:6
14 [a]Jer. 32:17 [b]Gen. 17:21; 18:10
16 [a]Rom. 15:24
17 [a]Ps. 25:14
18 [a][Acts 3:25, 26; Gal. 3:8]
19 [a][Deut. 4:9, 10; 6:6, 7]
20 [a]Gen. 4:10; 19:13 [b]Gen. 13:13
21 [a]Gen. 11:5 [b]Deut. 8:2; 13:3
22 [a]Gen. 18:16; 19:1
23 [a][Heb. 10:22] [b]Num. 16:22 [c]Job 9:22 [d]Gen. 20:4
25 [a]Is. 3:10, 11 [b]Deut. 1:16, 17; 32:4
26 [a]Jer. 5:1
27 [a][Gen. 3:19]

28 "Suppose there were five less
than the fifty righteous; would
You destroy all of the city for
lack of five?" So He said, "If I
find there forty-five, I will not
destroy *it*."
29 And he spoke to Him yet
again and said, "Suppose there
should be forty found there?" So
He said, "I will not do *it* for the
sake of forty."
30 Then he said, "Let not the
Lord be angry, and I will speak:
Suppose thirty should be found
there?" So He said, "I will not do
it if I find thirty there."
31 And he said, "Indeed now,
I have taken it upon myself to
speak to the Lord: Suppose
twenty should be found there?"
So He said, "I will not destroy *it*
for the sake of twenty."
32 Then he said, [a]"Let not the
Lord be angry, and I will speak
but once more: Suppose ten
should be found there?" [b]And
He said, "I will not destroy *it* for
the sake of ten."
33 So the LORD went His way as
soon as He had finished speaking with Abraham; and Abraham returned to his place.

19 Now [a]the two angels
came to Sod'om in the
evening, and [b]Lot was sitting in
the gate of Sod'om. When Lot
saw *them*, he rose to meet them,
and he bowed himself with his
face toward the ground.
2 And he said, "Here now, my
lords, please [a]turn in to your
servant's house and spend the
night, and [b]wash your feet; then
you may rise early and go on
your way." And they said, [c]"No,
but we will spend the night in
the open square."
3 But he insisted strongly; so
they turned in to him and entered
his house. [a]Then he made them
a feast, and baked [b]unleavened
bread, and they ate.
4 Now before they lay down,
the men of the city, the men of
Sod'om, both old and young, all
the people from every quarter,
surrounded the house.
5 [a]And they called to Lot and
said to him, "Where are the men
who came to you tonight? [b]Bring
them out to us that we [c]may
know them *carnally*."
6 So [a]Lot went out to them
through the doorway, shut the
door behind him,
7 and said, "Please, my brethren, do not do so wickedly!
8 [a]"See now, I have two daughters who have not known a man;
please, let me bring them out to
you, and you may do to them
as you wish; only do nothing to
these men, [b]since this is the reason they have come under the
shadow of my roof."
9 And they said, "Stand back!"
Then they said, "This one [a]came
in to [1]stay *here*, [b]and he keeps
acting as a judge; now we will
deal worse with you than with
them." So they pressed hard
against the man Lot, and came
near to break down the door.
10 But the men reached out
their hands and pulled Lot into
the house with them, and shut
the door.
11 And they [a]struck the men
who *were* at the doorway of
the house with blindness, both
small and great, so that they
became weary *trying* to find the
door.
12 Then the men said to Lot,
"Have you anyone else here?
Son-in-law, your sons, your

32 [a]Judg. 6:39 [b]James 5:16

CHAPTER 19

1 [a]Gen. 18:2, 16, 22 [b]Gen. 18:1–5

2 [a][Heb. 13:2] [b]Gen. 18:4; 24:32 [c]Luke 24:28

3 [a]Gen. 18:6–8 [b]Ex. 12:8

5 [a]Is. 3:9 [b]Judg. 19:22 [c]Gen. 4:1

6 [a]Judg. 19:23

8 [a]Judg. 19:24 [b]Gen. 18:5

9 [a]2 Pet. 2:7, 8 [b]Ex. 2:14 [1]As a resident alien

11 [a]Gen. 20:17, 18

daughters, and whomever you have in the city—[a]take *them* out of this place!

13 "For we will destroy this place, because the [a]outcry against them has grown great before the face of the LORD, and [b]the LORD has sent us to destroy it."

14 So Lot went out and spoke to his sons-in-law, [a]who had married his daughters, and said, [b]"Get up, get out of this place; for the LORD will destroy this city!" [c]But to his sons-in-law he seemed to be joking.

15 When the morning dawned, the angels urged Lot to hurry, saying, [a]"Arise, take your wife and your two daughters who are here, lest you be consumed in the punishment of the city."

16 And while he lingered, the men [a]took hold of his hand, his wife's hand, and the hands of his two daughters, the [b]LORD being merciful to him, [c]and they brought him out and set him outside the city.

17 So it came to pass, when they had brought them outside, that [1]he said, [a]"Escape for your life! [b]Do not look behind you nor stay anywhere in the plain. Escape [c]to the mountains, lest you be [2]destroyed."

18 Then Lot said to them, "Please, [a]no, my lords!

19 "Indeed now, your servant has found favor in your sight, and you have increased your mercy which you have shown me by saving my life; but I cannot escape to the mountains, lest some evil overtake me and I die.

20 "See now, this city *is* near *enough* to flee to, and it *is* a little one; please let me escape there (*is* it not a little one?) and my soul shall live."

21 And he said to him, "See, [a]I have favored you concerning this thing also, in that I will not overthrow this city for which you have spoken.

22 "Hurry, escape there. For [a]I cannot do anything until you arrive there." Therefore [b]the name of the city was called [1]Zō′ar.

23 The sun had risen upon the earth when Lot entered Zō′ar.

24 Then the LORD rained [a]brimstone and [b]fire on Sod′om and Go·mor′rah, from the LORD out of the heavens.

25 So He [1]overthrew those cities, all the plain, all the inhabitants of the cities, and [a]what grew on the ground.

26 But his wife looked back behind him, and she became [a]a pillar of salt.

27 And Abraham went early in the morning to the place where [a]he had stood before the LORD.

28 Then he looked toward Sod′om and Go·mor′rah, and toward all the land of the plain; and he saw, and behold, [a]the smoke of the land which went up like the smoke of a furnace.

29 And it came to pass, when God destroyed the cities of the plain, that God [a]remembered Abraham, and sent Lot out of the midst of the overthrow, when He overthrew the cities in which Lot had dwelt.

30 Then Lot went up out of Zō′ar and [a]dwelt in the mountains, and his two daughters were with him; for he was afraid to dwell in Zō′ar. And he and his two daughters dwelt in a cave.

31 Now the firstborn said to the

12 [a]2 Pet. 2:7, 9
13 [a]Gen. 18:20 [b]1 Chr. 21:15
14 [a]Matt. 1:18 [b]Num. 16:21, 24, 26, 45 [c]Ex. 9:21
15 [a]Rev. 18:4
16 [a]2 Pet. 2:7 [b]Luke 18:13 [c]Ps. 34:22
17 [a]Jer. 48:6 [b]Matt. 24:16–18 [c]Gen. 14:10 [1]LXX, Syr., Vg. *they* [2]Lit. *swept away*
18 [a]Acts 10:14
21 [a]Job 42:8, 9
22 [a]Ex. 32:10 [b]Gen. 13:10; 14:2 [1]Lit. *Little* or *Insignificant*
24 [a]Deut. 29:23 [b]Lev. 10:2
25 [a]Ps. 107:34 [1]*devastated*
26 [a]Luke 17:32
27 [a]Gen. 18:22
28 [a]Rev. 9:2; 18:9
29 [a]Gen. 8:1; 18:23
30 [a]Gen. 19:17, 19

younger, "Our father *is* old, and
there is no man on the earth [a]to
come in to us as is the custom of
all the earth.
32 "Come, let us make our father drink wine, and we will lie
with him, that we [a]may preserve
the [1]lineage of our father."
33 So they made their father
drink wine that night. And the
firstborn went in and lay with
her father, and he did not know
when she lay down or when she
arose.
34 It happened on the next day
that the firstborn said to the
younger, "Indeed I lay with my
father last night; let us make
him drink wine tonight also, and
you go in *and* lie with him, that
we may preserve the [1]lineage of
our father."
35 Then they made their father drink wine that night also.
And the younger arose and lay
with him, and he did not know
when she lay down or when she
arose.
36 Thus both the daughters of
Lot were with child by their
father.
37 The firstborn bore a son and
called his name Mō′ab; [a]he *is* the
father of the Mō′ab·ītes to this
day.
38 And the younger, she also
bore a son and called his name
Ben-Am′mī; [a]he *is* the father of
the people of Am′mon to this
day.

20 And Abraham journeyed
from [a]there to the South,
and dwelt between [b]Kā′desh and
Shūr, and [c]stayed in Gē′rar.
2 Now Abraham said of Sarah
his wife, [a]"She *is* my sister." And
A·bim′e·lech king of Gē′rar sent
and [b]took Sarah.
3 But [a]God came to A·bim′-
e·lech [b]in a dream by night, and
said to him, [c]"Indeed you *are* a
dead man because of the woman
whom you have taken, for she *is*
[1]a man's wife."
4 But A·bim′e·lech had not
come near her; and he said,
"Lord, [a]will You slay a righteous
nation also?
5 "Did he not say to me, 'She
is my sister'? And she, even she
herself said, 'He *is* my brother.'
[a]In the [1]integrity of my heart and
innocence of my hands I have
done this."
6 And God said to him in a
dream, "Yes, I know that you
did this in the integrity of your
heart. For [a]I also withheld you
from sinning [b]against Me; therefore I did not let you touch her.
7 "Now therefore, restore the
man's wife; [a]for he *is* a prophet,
and he will pray for you and
you shall live. But if you do not
restore *her*, [b]know that you shall
surely die, you [c]and all who *are*
yours."
8 So A·bim′e·lech rose early in
the morning, called all his servants, and told all these things
in their hearing; and the men
were very much afraid.
9 And A·bim′e·lech called
Abraham and said to him, "What
have you done to us? How have
I [1]offended you, [a]that you have
brought on me and on my kingdom a great sin? You have done
deeds to me [b]that ought not to be
done."
10 Then A·bim′e·lech said to
Abraham, "What did you have
in view, that you have done this
thing?"
11 And Abraham said, "Because
I thought, surely [a]the fear of God

31 [a]Gen. 16:2, 4; 38:8, 9
32 [a][Mark 12:19] [1]Lit. *seed*
34 [1]Lit. *seed*
37 [a]Deut. 2:9
38 [a]Deut. 2:19

CHAPTER 20

1 [a]Gen. 18:1 [b]Gen. 12:9; 16:7, 14 [c]Gen. 26:1, 6
2 [a]Gen. 12:11–13; 26:7 [b]Gen. 12:15
3 [a]Ps. 105:14 [b]Job 33:15 [c]Gen. 20:7 [1]Lit. *married to a husband*
4 [a]Gen. 18:23–25
5 [a]2 Kin. 20:3 [1]*innocence*
6 [a]1 Sam. 25:26, 34 [b]Gen. 39:9
7 [a]1 Sam. 7:5 [b]Gen. 2:17 [c]Num. 16:32, 33
9 [a]Gen. 26:10; 39:9 [b]Gen. 34:7 [1]*sinned against*
11 [a]Prov. 16:6

is not in this place; and [b]they
will kill me on account of my
wife.
12 "But indeed [a]*she is* truly my
sister. She *is* the daughter of my
father, but not the daughter of
my mother; and she became my
wife.
13 "And it came to pass, when
[a]God caused me to wander from
my father's house, that I said to
her, 'This *is* your kindness that
you should do for me: in every
place, wherever we go, [b]say of
me, "He *is* my brother." ' "
14 Then A·bim′e·lech [a]took
sheep, oxen, and male and female servants, and gave *them*
to Abraham; and he restored
Sarah his wife to him.
15 And A·bim′e·lech said, "See,
[a]my land *is* before you; dwell
where it pleases you."
16 Then to Sarah he said, "Behold, I have given your brother
a thousand *pieces* of silver;
[a]indeed this [1]vindicates you
[b]before all who *are* with you and
before everybody." Thus she was
[2]rebuked.
17 So Abraham [a]prayed to God;
and God [b]healed A·bim′e·lech,
his wife, and his female servants. Then they bore *children;*
18 for the LORD [a]had closed up
all the wombs of the house of
A·bim′e·lech because of Sarah,
Abraham's wife.

21

And the LORD [a]visited
Sarah as He had said,
and the LORD did for Sarah [b]as
He had spoken.
2 For Sarah [a]conceived and
bore Abraham a son in his old
age, [b]at the set time of which
God had spoken to him.
3 And Abraham called the
name of his son who was born
to him—whom Sarah bore to
him—[a]Isaac.[1]
4 Then Abraham [a]circumcised
his son Isaac when he was eight
days old, [b]as God had commanded him.
5 Now [a]Abraham was one
hundred years old when his son
Isaac was born to him.
6 And Sarah said, [a]"God has
[1]made me laugh, *and* all who
hear [b]will laugh with me."
7 She also said, "Who would
have said to Abraham that Sarah
would nurse children? [a]For I
have borne *him* a son in his old
age."
8 So the child grew and was
weaned. And Abraham made a
great feast on the same day that
Isaac was weaned.
9 And Sarah saw the son of
Hā′gar [a]the Egyptian, whom
she had borne to Abraham,
[b]scoffing.[1]
10 Therefore she said to Abraham, [a]"Cast out this bondwoman and her son; for the son
of this bondwoman shall not be
heir with my son, *namely* with
Isaac."
11 And the matter was very
[1]displeasing in Abraham's sight
[a]because of his son.
12 But God said to Abraham, ☆
"Do not let it be displeasing in
your sight because of the lad or
because of your bondwoman.
Whatever Sarah has said to you,
listen to her voice; for [a]in Isaac
your seed shall be called.
13 "Yet I will also make [a]a nation
of the son of the bondwoman,
because he *is* your [1]seed."
14 So Abraham rose early in
the morning, and took bread
and [1]a skin of water; and putting
it on her shoulder, he gave *it*

11 [b]Gen. 12:12; 26:7
12 [a]Gen. 11:29
13 [a]Gen. 12:1–9, 11 [b]Gen. 12:13; 20:5
14 [a]Gen. 12:16
15 [a]Gen. 13:9; 34:10; 47:6
16 [a]Gen. 26:11 [b]Mal. 2:9 [1]Lit. *is a covering of the eyes for you to all* [2]Or *justified*
17 [a]Job 42:9 [b]Gen. 21:2
18 [a]Gen. 12:17

CHAPTER 21

1 [a]1 Sam. 2:21 [b][Gal. 4:23, 28]
2 [a]Heb. 11:11, 12 [b]Gen. 17:21; 18:10, 14
3 [a]Gen. 17:19, 21 [1]Lit. *Laughter*
4 [a]Acts 7:8 [b]Gen. 17:10, 12
5 [a]Gen. 17:1, 17
6 [a]Is. 54:1 [b]Luke 1:58 [1]Lit. *made laughter for me*
7 [a]Gen. 18:11, 12
9 [a]Gen. 16:1, 4, 15 [b][Gal. 4:29] [1]Lit. *laughing*
10 [a]Gal. 3:18; 4:30
11 [a]Gen. 17:18 [1]*distressing*
12 [a]Matt. 1:2; Luke 3:34; [Rom. 9:7, 8]; Heb. 11:18
13 [a]Gen. 16:10; 17:20; 21:18; 25:12–18 [1]*descendant*
14 [1]A water bottle made of skins

and the boy to Hā′gar, and [a]sent
her away. Then she departed
and wandered in the Wilderness
of Bē·er·shē′ba.
15 And the water in the skin
was used up, and she placed the
boy under one of the shrubs.
16 Then she went and sat down
across from *him* at a distance of
about a bowshot; for she said
to herself, "Let me not see the
death of the boy." So she sat opposite *him*, and lifted her voice
and wept.
17 And [a]God heard the voice of
the lad. Then the [b]angel of God
called to Hā′gar out of heaven,
and said to her, "What ails you,
Hā′gar? Fear not, for God has
heard the voice of the lad where
he *is*.
18 "Arise, lift up the lad and
hold him with your hand, for [a]I
will make him a great nation."
19 Then [a]God opened her eyes,
and she saw a well of water. And
she went and filled the skin with
water, and gave the lad a drink.
20 So God [a]was with the lad;
and he grew and dwelt in the
wilderness, [b]and became an
archer.
21 He dwelt in the Wilderness
of Par′an; and his mother [a]took
a wife for him from the land of
Egypt.
22 And it came to pass at that
time that [a]A·bim′e·lech and
Phī′chol, the commander of his
army, spoke to Abraham, say-
ing, [b]"God *is* with you in all that
you do.
23 "Now therefore, [a]swear[1] to
me by God that you will not
deal falsely with me, with my
offspring, or with my posterity;
but that according to the kindness that I have done to you, you

14 [a]John 8:35
17 [a]Ex. 3:7 [b]Gen. 22:11
18 [a]Gen. 16:10; 21:13; 25:12–16
19 [a]Num. 22:31
20 [a]Gen. 28:15; 39:2, 3, 21 [b]Gen. 16:12
21 [a]Gen. 24:4
22 [a]Gen. 20:2, 14; 26:26 [b]Gen. 26:28
23 [a]Josh. 2:12 [1]*take an oath*
25 [a]Gen. 26:15, 18, 20–22
27 [a]Gen. 26:31; 31:44 [1]*treaty*
29 [a]Gen. 33:8
30 [a]Gen. 31:48, 52
31 [a]Gen. 21:14; 26:33 [1]Lit. *Well of the Oath* or *Well of the Seven*
33 [a]Gen. 4:26; 12:8; 13:4; 26:25 [b]Deut. 32:40; 33:27

CHAPTER 22

1 [a]Heb. 11:17

will do to me and to the land in
which you have dwelt."
24 And Abraham said, "I will
swear."
25 Then Abraham rebuked
A·bim′e·lech because of a well
of water which A·bim′e·lech's
servants [a]had seized.
26 And A·bim′e·lech said, "I do
not know who has done this
thing; you did not tell me, nor
had I heard *of it* until today."
27 So Abraham took sheep and
oxen and gave them to A·bim′-
e·lech, and the two of them
[a]made a [1]covenant.
28 And Abraham set seven
ewe lambs of the flock by
themselves.
29 Then A·bim′e·lech asked
Abraham, [a]"What *is the meaning
of* these seven ewe lambs which
you have set by themselves?"
30 And he said, "You will take
these seven ewe lambs from my
hand, that [a]they may be my witness that I have dug this well."
31 Therefore he [a]called that
place [1]Bē·er·shē′ba, because
the two of them swore an oath
there.
32 Thus they made a covenant
at Bē·er·shē′ba. So A·bim′e·lech
rose with Phī′chol, the commander of his army, and they returned to the land of the Phi·lis′-
tines.
33 Then *Abraham* planted a
tamarisk tree in Bē·er·shē′ba,
and [a]there called on the name of
the LORD, [b]the Everlasting God.
34 And Abraham stayed in the
land of the Phi·lis′tines many
days.

22 Now it came to pass after these things that [a]God
tested Abraham, and said to

him, "Abraham!" And he said,
"Here I am."
2 Then He said, "Take now
your son, [a]your only *son* Isaac,
whom you [b]love, and go [c]to the
land of Mō·rī′ah, and offer him
there as a [d]burnt offering on
one of the mountains of which I
shall tell you."
3 So Abraham rose early in
the morning and saddled his
donkey, and took two of his
young men with him, and Isaac
his son; and he split the wood
for the burnt offering, and arose
and went to the place of which
God had told him.
4 Then on the third day Abraham lifted his eyes and saw the
place afar off.
5 And Abraham said to his
young men, "Stay here with the
donkey; the [1]lad and I will go
yonder and worship, and we will
[a]come back to you."
6 So Abraham took the wood
of the burnt offering and [a]laid *it*
on Isaac his son; and he took the
fire in his hand, and a knife, and
the two of them went together.
7 But Isaac spoke to Abraham
his father and said, "My father!"
And he said, "Here I am, my
son." Then he said, "Look, the
fire and the wood, but where *is*
the [1]lamb for a burnt offering?"
8 And Abraham said, "My son,
God will provide for Himself the
[a]lamb for a [b]burnt offering." So
the two of them went together.
9 Then they came to the place
of which God had told him. And
Abraham built an altar there
and placed the wood in order;
and he bound Isaac his son and
[a]laid him on the altar, upon the
wood.
10 And Abraham stretched out
his hand and took the knife to
slay his son.
11 But the [a]Angel of the LORD
called to him from heaven and
said, "Abraham, Abraham!" So
he said, "Here I am."
12 And He said, [a]"Do not lay
your hand on the lad, or do anything to him; for [b]now I know
that you fear God, since you
have not [c]withheld your son,
your only *son*, from Me."
13 Then Abraham lifted his
eyes and looked, and there behind *him was* a ram caught in
a thicket by its horns. So Abraham went and took the ram, and
offered it up for a burnt offering
instead of his son.
14 And Abraham called the
name of the place, [1]The-LORD-
Will-Provide; as it is said *to* this
day, "In the Mount of the LORD it
shall be provided."
15 Then the Angel of the LORD
called to Abraham a second time
out of heaven,
16 and said: [a]"By Myself I have
sworn, says the LORD, because
you have done this thing, and
have not withheld your son,
your only *son*—
17 "blessing I will [a]bless you,
and multiplying I will multiply
your descendants [b]as the stars
of the heaven [c]and as the sand
which *is* on the seashore; and
[d]your descendants shall possess
the gate of their enemies.
18 [a]"In your seed all the nations ☆
of the earth shall be blessed,
[b]because you have obeyed My
voice."
19 So Abraham returned to his
young men, and they rose and
went together to [a]Bē·er·shē′ba;
and Abraham dwelt at Bē·er-
shē′ba.

2 [a]Gen. 22:12, 16 [b]John 5:20 [c]2 Chr. 3:1 [d]Gen. 8:20; 31:54
5 [a][Heb. 11:19] [1]Or *young man*
6 [a]John 19:17
7 [1]Or *goat*
8 [a]John 1:29, 36 [b]Ex. 12:3–6
9 [a][Heb. 11:17–19]
11 [a]Gen. 16:7–11; 21:17, 18; 31:11
12 [a]1 Sam. 15:22 [b]James 2:21, 22 [c]Gen. 22:2, 16
14 [1]Heb. *YHWH Yireh*
16 [a]Ps. 105:9
17 [a]Gen. 17:16; 26:3, 24 [b]Gen. 15:5; 26:4 [c]Gen. 13:16; 32:12 [d]Gen. 24:60
18 [a]Gen. 12:3; 18:18; 26:4; [Acts 3:25, 26]; Gal. 3:8, 9, 16, 18 [b]Gen. 18:19; 22:3, 10; 26:5
19 [a]Gen. 21:31

20 Now it came to pass after
these things that it was told
Abraham, saying, "Indeed [a]Mil′-
cah also has borne children to
your brother Nā′hor:
21 [a]"Huz his firstborn, Buz his
brother, Ke·mū′el the father [b]of
Ar′am,
22 "Chē′sed, Hā′zō, Pil′dash,
Jid′laph, and Be·thū′el."
23 And [a]Be·thū′el begot [1]Re-
bekah. These eight Mil′cah bore
to Nā′hor, Abraham's brother.
24 His concubine, whose name
was Re·ū′mah, also bore Tē′bah,
Gā′ham, Thā′hash, and Mā′-
a·chah.

23 Sarah lived one hundred
and twenty-seven years;
these were the years of the life
of Sarah.
2 So Sarah died in [a]Kir′jath
Ar′ba (that *is,* [b]Hē′bron) in the
land of Cā′naan, and Abraham
came to mourn for Sarah and to
weep for her.
3 Then Abraham stood up
from before his dead, and spoke
to the sons of [a]Heth, saying,
4 [a]"I *am* a foreigner and a visitor among you. [b]Give me property for a burial place among
you, that I may bury my dead
out of my sight."
5 And the sons of Heth answered Abraham, saying to
him,
6 "Hear us, my lord: You *are* [a]a
[1]mighty prince among us; bury
your dead in the choicest of our
burial places. None of us will
withhold from you his burial
place, that you may bury your
dead."
7 Then Abraham stood up and
bowed himself to the people of
the land, the sons of Heth.
8 And he spoke with them,
saying, "If it is your wish that I
bury my dead out of my sight,
hear me, and [1]meet with Ē′phron
the son of Zō′har for me,
9 "that he may give me the
cave of [a]Mach·pē′lah which he
has, which *is* at the end of his
field. Let him give it to me at
the full price, as property for a
burial place among you."
10 Now Ē′phron dwelt among
the sons of Heth; and Ē′phron
the Hit′tīte answered Abraham
in the presence of the sons of
Heth, all who [a]entered at the
gate of his city, saying,
11 [a]"No, my lord, hear me: I give
you the field and the cave that *is*
in it; I give it to you in the presence of the sons of my people. I
give it to you. Bury your dead!"
12 Then Abraham bowed himself down before the people of
the land;
13 and he spoke to Ē′phron in
the hearing of the people of the
land, saying, "If you *will give*
it, please hear me. I will give
you money for the field; take *it*
from me and I will bury my dead
there."
14 And Ē′phron answered Abraham, saying to him,
15 "My lord, listen to me; the
land *is worth* four hundred
[a]shekels of silver. What *is* that
between you and me? So bury
your dead."
16 And Abraham listened to
Ē′phron; and Abraham [a]weighed
out the silver for Ē′phron which
he had named in the hearing of
the sons of Heth, four hundred
shekels of silver, currency of the
merchants.
17 So [a]the field of Ē′phron which
was in Mach·pē′lah, which *was*
before Mam′re, the field and

20 [a]Gen. 11:29; 24:15
21 [a]Job 1:1 [b]Job 32:2
23 [a]Gen. 24:15 [1]*Rebecca,* Rom. 9:10

CHAPTER 23

2 [a]Josh. 14:15; 15:13; 21:11 [b]Gen. 13:18; 23:19
3 [a]Gen. 10:15; 15:20
4 [a][Gen. 17:8] [b]Acts 7:5, 16
6 [a]Gen. 13:2; 14:14; 24:35 [1]Lit. *prince of God*
8 [1]*entreat*
9 [a]Gen. 25:9
10 [a]Gen. 23:18; 34:20, 24
11 [a]2 Sam. 24:21–24
15 [a]Ex. 30:13
16 [a]Jer. 32:9, 10
17 [a]Gen. 25:9; 49:29–32; 50:13

the cave which *was* in it, and all
the trees that *were* in the field,
which *were* within all the surrounding borders, were deeded
18 to Abraham as a possession
in the presence of the sons of
Heth, before all who went in at
the gate of his city.
19 And after this, Abraham buried Sarah his wife in the cave of
the field of Mach·pē′lah, before
Mam′re (that *is,* Hē′bron) in the
land of Cā′naan.
20 So the field and the cave that
is in it [a]were deeded to Abraham
by the sons of Heth as property
for a burial place.

24 Now Abraham [a]was old,
well advanced in age; and
the LORD [b]had blessed Abraham
in all things.
2 So Abraham said [a]to the oldest servant of his house, who
[b]ruled over all that he had,
"Please, [c]put your hand under
my thigh,
3 "and I will make you [a]swear[1]
by the LORD, the God of heaven
and the God of the earth, that
[b]you will not take a wife for
my son from the daughters of
the Cā′naan·ītes, among whom I
dwell;
4 [a]"but you shall go [b]to my
country and to my family, and
take a wife for my son Isaac."
5 And the servant said to him,
"Perhaps the woman will not be
willing to follow me to this land.
Must I take your son back to the
land from which you came?"
6 But Abraham said to him,
"Beware that you do not take my
son back there.
7 "The LORD God of heaven,
who [a]took me from my father's
house and from the land of my
family, and who spoke to me
and swore to me, saying, [b]'To
your [1]descendants I give this
land,' [c]He will send His angel
before you, and you shall take a
wife for my son from there.
8 "And if the woman is not
willing to follow you, then [a]you
will be released from this oath;
only do not take my son back
there."
9 So the servant put his hand
under the thigh of Abraham his
master, and swore to him concerning this matter.
10 Then the servant took ten
of his master's camels and departed, [a]for all his master's
goods *were in* his hand. And he
arose and went to Mes·o·po·tā′-
mi·a, to [b]the city of Nā′hor.
11 And he made his camels
kneel down outside the city by
a well of water at evening time,
the time [a]when women go out to
draw *water.*
12 Then he [a]said, "O LORD God
of my master Abraham, please
[b]give me success this day, and
show kindness to my master
Abraham.
13 "Behold, *here* [a]I stand by the
well of water, and [b]the daughters of the men of the city are
coming out to draw water.
14 "Now let it be that the young
woman to whom I say, 'Please
let down your pitcher that I may
drink,' and she says, 'Drink, and
I will also give your camels a
drink'—*let* her *be the one* You
have appointed for Your servant
Isaac. And [a]by this I will know
that You have shown kindness to
my master."
15 And it happened, [a]before he
had finished speaking, that behold, [b]Rebekah,[1] who was born
to Be·thū′el, son of [c]Mil′cah,

20 [a]Jer. 32:10, 11

CHAPTER 24

1 [a]Gen. 18:11; 21:5 [b]Gen. 12:2; 13:2; 24:35

2 [a]Gen. 15:2 [b]Gen. 24:10; 39:4–6 [c]Gen. 47:29

3 [a]Gen. 14:19, 22 [b]Deut. 7:3 [1]*take an oath*

4 [a]Gen. 28:2 [b]Gen. 12:1

7 [a]Gen. 12:1; 24:3 [b]Gen. 12:7; 13:15; 15:18; 17:8 [c]Ex. 23:20, 23; 33:2 [1]Lit. *seed*

8 [a]Josh. 2:17–20

10 [a]Gen. 24:2, 22 [b]Gen. 11:31, 32; 22:20; 27:43; 29:5

11 [a]Ex. 2:16

12 [a]Ex. 3:6, 15 [b]Neh. 1:11

13 [a]Gen. 24:43 [b]Ex. 2:16

14 [a]Judg. 6:17, 37

15 [a]Is. 65:24 [b]Gen. 24:45; 25:20 [c]Gen. 22:20, 23 [1]*Rebecca,* Rom. 9:10

the wife of Nā'hor, Abraham's
brother, came out with her
pitcher on her shoulder.
16 Now the young woman [a]*was*
very beautiful to behold, a virgin; no man had known her. And
she went down to the well, filled
her pitcher, and came up.
17 And the servant ran to meet
her and said, "Please let me
drink a little water from your
pitcher."
18 [a]So she said, "Drink, my
lord." Then she quickly let her
pitcher down to her hand, and
gave him a drink.
19 And when she had finished
giving him a drink, she said, "I
will draw *water* for your camels
also, until they have finished
drinking."
20 Then she quickly emptied
her pitcher into the trough, ran
back to the well to draw *water,*
and drew for all his camels.
21 And the man, wondering at
her, remained silent so as to
know whether [a]the LORD had
made his journey prosperous or
not.
22 So it was, when the camels
had finished drinking, that the
man took a golden [a]nose ring
weighing half a shekel, and two
bracelets for her wrists weighing ten *shekels* of gold,
23 and said, "Whose daughter
are you? Tell me, please, is there
room *in* your father's house for
us [1]to lodge?"
24 So she said to him, [a]"I *am* the
daughter of Be·thū'el, Mil'cah's
son, whom she bore to Nā'hor."
25 Moreover she said to him,
"We have both straw and feed
enough, and room to lodge."
26 Then the man [a]bowed down
his head and worshiped the
LORD.
27 And he said, [a]"Blessed *be* the
LORD God of my master Abraham, who has not forsaken [b]His
mercy and His truth toward my
master. As for me, being on the
way, the LORD [c]led me to the
house of my master's brethren."
28 So the young woman ran
and told her mother's household
these things.
29 Now Rebekah had a brother
whose name *was* [a]Lā'ban, and
Lā'ban ran out to the man by the
well.
30 So it came to pass, when
he saw the nose ring, and the
bracelets on his sister's wrists,
and when he heard the words
of his sister Rebekah, saying,
"Thus the man spoke to me,"
that he went to the man. And
there he stood by the camels at
the well.
31 And he said, "Come in, [a]O
blessed of the LORD! Why do you
stand outside? For I have prepared the house, and a place for
the camels."
32 Then the man came to the
house. And he unloaded the
camels, and [a]provided straw and
feed for the camels, and water to
[b]wash his feet and the feet of the
men who *were* with him.
33 *Food* was set before him to
eat, but he said, [a]"I will not eat
until I have told about my er-
rand." And he said, "Speak on."
34 So he said, "I *am* Abraham's
servant.
35 "The LORD [a]has blessed my
master greatly, and he has become great; and He has given
him flocks and herds, silver and
gold, male and female servants,
and camels and donkeys.

16 [a]Gen. 12:11; 26:7; 29:17
18 [a][1 Pet. 3:8, 9]
21 [a]Gen. 24:12–14, 27, 52
22 [a]Ex. 32:2, 3
23 [1]*to spend the night*
24 [a]Gen. 22:23; 24:15
26 [a]Ex. 4:31
27 [a]Ex. 18:10 [b]Gen. 32:10 [c]Gen. 24:21, 48
29 [a]Gen. 29:5, 13
31 [a]Judg. 17:2
32 [a]Gen. 43:24 [b]Gen. 19:2
33 [a]John 4:34
35 [a]Gen. 13:2; 24:1

36 "And Sarah my master's wife
[a]bore a son to my master when
she was old; and [b]to him he has
given all that he has.
37 "Now my master [a]made me
swear, saying, 'You shall not
take a wife for my son from the
daughters of the Cā′naan·ītes, in
whose land I dwell;
38 [a]'but you shall go to my father's house and to my family,
and take a wife for my son.'
39 [a]"And I said to my master,
'Perhaps the woman will not follow me.'
40 [a]"But he said to me, 'The
LORD, [b]before whom I walk, will
send His angel with you and
[1]prosper your way; and you shall
take a wife for my son from
my family and from my father's
house.
41 [a]'You will be clear from this
oath when you arrive among my
family; for if they will not give
her to you, then you will be released from my oath.'
42 "And this day I came to the
well and said, [a]'O LORD God of
my master Abraham, if You will
now prosper the way in which I
go,
43 [a]'behold, I stand by the well
of water; and it shall come to
pass that when the virgin comes
out to draw *water,* and I say to
her, "Please give me a little water from your pitcher to drink,"
44 'and she says to me, "Drink,
and I will draw for your camels
also,"—*let* her *be* the woman
whom the LORD has appointed
for my master's son.'
45 [a]"But before I had finished
[b]speaking in my heart, there was
Rebekah, coming out with her
pitcher on her shoulder; and she
went down to the well and drew
water. And I said to her, 'Please
let me drink.'
46 "And she made haste and
let her pitcher down from her
shoulder, and said, 'Drink, and
I will give your camels a drink
also.' So I drank, and she gave
the camels a drink also.
47 "Then I asked her, and said,
'Whose daughter *are* you?'
And she said, 'The daughter of
Be·thū′el, Nā′hor's son, whom
Mil′cah bore to him.' So I put the
nose ring on her nose and the
bracelets on her wrists.
48 [a]"And I bowed my head and
worshiped the LORD, and blessed
the LORD God of my master Abraham, who had led me in the way
of truth to [b]take the daughter of
my master's brother for his son.
49 "Now if you will [a]deal kindly
and truly with my master, tell
me. And if not, tell me, that I
may turn to the right hand or to
the left."
50 Then Lā′ban and Be·thū′el
answered and said, [a]"The thing
comes from the LORD; we cannot [b]speak to you either bad or
good.
51 [a]"Here *is* Rebekah before
you; take *her* and go, and let her
be your master's son's wife, as
the LORD has spoken."
52 And it came to pass, when
Abraham's servant heard their
words, that [a]he worshiped the
LORD, *bowing himself* to the
earth.
53 Then the servant brought
out [a]jewelry of silver, jewelry
of gold, and clothing, and gave
them to Rebekah. He also gave
[b]precious things to her brother
and to her mother.
54 And he and the men who
were with him ate and drank

36 [a]Gen. 21:1–7 [b]Gen. 21:10; 25:5
37 [a]Gen. 24:2–4
38 [a]Gen. 24:4
39 [a]Gen. 24:5
40 [a]Gen. 24:7 [b]Gen. 5:22, 24; 17:1 [1]*make your way successful*
41 [a]Gen. 24:8
42 [a]Gen. 24:12
43 [a]Gen. 24:13
45 [a]Gen. 24:15 [b]1 Sam. 1:13
48 [a]Gen. 24:26, 52 [b]Gen. 22:23; 24:27
49 [a]Josh. 2:14
50 [a]Ps. 118:23 [b]Gen. 31:24, 29
51 [a]Gen. 20:15
52 [a]Gen. 24:26, 48
53 [a]Ex. 3:22; 11:2; 12:35 [b]2 Chr. 21:3

and stayed all night. Then they
arose in the morning, and he
said, [a]"Send me away to my
master."
55 But her brother and her
mother said, "Let the young
woman stay with us *a few* days,
at least ten; after that she may
go."
56 And he said to them, "Do
not [1]hinder me, since the LORD
has prospered my way; send
me away so that I may go to my
master."
57 So they said, "We will call
the young woman and ask her
personally."
58 Then they called Rebekah
and said to her, "Will you go
with this man?" And she said, "I
will go."
59 So they sent away Rebekah
their sister [a]and her nurse, and
Abraham's servant and his
men.
60 And they blessed Rebekah
and said to her:

"Our sister, *may* you *become*
[a]*The mother of* thousands of
ten thousands;
[b]And may your descendants
possess
The gates of those who hate
them."

61 Then Rebekah and her maids
arose, and they rode on the camels and followed the man. So
the servant took Rebekah and
departed.
62 Now Isaac came from the
way of [a]Bē′er La·haī′ Roi, for he
dwelt in the South.
63 And Isaac went out [a]to meditate in the field in the evening; and he lifted his eyes and
looked, and there, the camels
were coming.
64 Then Rebekah lifted her eyes,
and when she saw Isaac [a]she
dismounted from her camel;
65 for she had said to the servant, "Who *is* this man walking
in the field to meet us?" The
servant said, "It *is* my master."
So she took a veil and covered
herself.
66 And the servant told Isaac
all the things that he had done.
67 Then Isaac brought her into
his mother Sarah's tent; and he
[a]took Rebekah and she became
his wife, and he loved her. So
Isaac [b]was comforted after his
mother's *death*.

25 Abraham again took a
wife, and her name *was*
[a]Ke·tū′rah.
2 And [a]she bore him Zim′ran,
Jok′shan, Mē′dan, Mid′i·an, Ish′-
bak, and Shū′ah.
3 Jok′shan begot Shē′ba and
Dē′dan. And the sons of Dē′dan
were As·shū′rim, Le·tū′shim, and
Le·um′mim.
4 And the sons of Mid′i·an
were Ē′phah, Ē′pher, Hā′noch,
A·bī′dah, and El·dā′ah. All these
were the children of Ke·tū′rah.
5 And [a]Abraham gave all that
he had to Isaac.
6 But Abraham gave gifts
to the sons of the concubines
which Abraham had; and while
he was still living he [a]sent them
eastward, away from Isaac his
son, to [b]the country of the east.
7 This *is* the sum of the years
of Abraham's life which he
lived: one hundred and seventy-
five years.
8 Then Abraham breathed his
last and [a]died in a good old age,

54 [a]Gen. 24:56, 59; 30:25
56 [1]*delay*
59 [a]Gen. 35:8
60 [a]Gen. 17:16 [b]Gen. 22:17; 28:14
62 [a]Gen. 16:14; 25:11
63 [a]Josh. 1:8
64 [a]Josh. 15:18
67 [a]Gen. 25:20; 29:20 [b]Gen. 23:1, 2; 38:12

CHAPTER 25
1 [a]1 Chr. 1:32, 33
2 [a]1 Chr. 1:32, 33
5 [a]Gen. 24:35, 36
6 [a]Gen. 21:14 [b]Judg. 6:3
8 [a]Gen. 15:15; 47:8, 9

an old man and full *of years,* and
[b]was gathered to his people.
9 And [a]his sons Isaac and Ish′-
ma·el buried him in the cave of
[b]Mach·pē′lah, which *is* before
Mam′re, in the field of Ē′phron
the son of Zō′har the Hit′tīte,
10 [a]the field which Abraham
purchased from the sons of
Heth. [b]There Abraham was buried, and Sarah his wife.
11 And it came to pass, after
the death of Abraham, that God
blessed his son Isaac. And Isaac
dwelt at [a]Bē′er La·haī′ Roi.
12 Now this *is* the [a]genealogy of
Ish′ma·el, Abraham's son, whom
Hā′gar the Egyptian, Sarah's
maidservant, bore to Abraham.
13 And [a]these *were* the names
of the sons of Ish′ma·el, by their
names, according to their generations: The firstborn of Ish′-
ma·el, Ne·bā′joth; then Kē′dar,
Ad′bē·el, Mib′sam,
14 Mish′ma, Dū′mah, Mas′sa,
15 [1]Hā′dar, Tē′ma, Jē′tur, Nā′-
phish, and Ked′e·mah.
16 These *were* the sons of
Ish′ma·el and these *were* their
names, by their towns and their
[1]settlements, [a]twelve princes according to their nations.
17 These *were* the years of the
life of Ish′ma·el: one hundred
and thirty-seven years; and [a]he
breathed his last and died, and
was gathered to his people.
18 [a](They dwelt from Hav′i·lah
as far as Shūr, which *is* east
of Egypt as you go toward Assyria.) He [1]died [b]in the presence
of all his brethren.
19 This *is* the [a]genealogy of
Isaac, Abraham's son. [b]Abraham
begot Isaac.
20 Isaac was forty years old
when he took Rebekah as wife,

8 [b]Gen. 25:17; 35:29; 49:29, 33
9 [a]Gen. 35:29; 50:13 [b]Gen. 23:9, 17; 49:30
10 [a]Gen. 23:3–16 [b]Gen. 49:31
11 [a]Gen. 16:14
12 [a]Gen. 11:10, 27; 16:15
13 [a]1 Chr. 1:29–31
15 [1]MT *Hadad*
16 [a]Gen. 17:20 [1]*camps*
17 [a]Gen. 25:8; 49:33
18 [a]1 Sam. 15:7 [b]Gen. 16:12 [1]*fell*
19 [a]Gen. 36:1, 9 [b]Matt. 1:2
20 [a]Gen. 22:23; 24:15, 29, 67 [b]Gen. 24:29
21 [a]1 Chr. 5:20 [b]Rom. 9:10–13
22 [a]1 Sam. 1:15; 9:9; 10:22
23 [a]Gen. 17:4–6, 16; 24:60 [b]2 Sam. 8:14 [c]Rom. 9:12
25 [a]Gen. 27:11, 16, 23 [1]Lit. *Hairy*
26 [a]Hos. 12:3 [b]Gen. 27:36 [1]*Supplanter* or *Deceitful,* lit. *One Who Takes the Heel*
27 [a]Gen. 27:3, 5 [b]Job 1:1, 8 [c]Heb. 11:9 [1]Lit. *complete*
28 [a]Gen. 27:4, 19, 25, 31 [b]Gen. 27:6–10

[a]the daughter of Be·thū′el the
Syrian of Pad′an Ar′am, [b]the
sister of Lā′ban the Syrian.
21 Now Isaac pleaded with
the LORD for his wife, because
she *was* barren; [a]and the LORD
granted his plea, [b]and Rebekah
his wife conceived.
22 But the children struggled
together within her; and she
said, "If *all is* well, why *am I like*
this?" [a]So she went to inquire of
the LORD.
23 And the LORD said to her:

[a]"Two nations *are* in your
womb,
Two peoples shall be
separated from your
body;
One people shall be stronger
than [b]the other,
[c]And the older shall serve
the younger."

24 So when her days were fulfilled *for her* to give birth, indeed
there were twins in her womb.
25 And the first came out red.
He was [a]like a hairy garment
all over; so they called his name
[1]Esau.
26 Afterward his brother came
out, and [a]his hand took hold of
Esau's heel; so [b]his name was
called [1]Jacob. Isaac *was* sixty
years old when she bore them.
27 So the boys grew. And Esau
was [a]a skillful hunter, a man of
the field; but Jacob was [b]a [1]mild
man, [c]dwelling in tents.
28 And Isaac loved Esau because he [a]ate *of his* game, [b]but
Rebekah loved Jacob.
29 Now Jacob cooked a stew;
and Esau came in from the field,
and he *was* weary.
30 And Esau said to Jacob,

"Please feed me with that same
red *stew,* for I *am* weary."
Therefore his name was called
[1]Ē′dom.
31 But Jacob said, "Sell me your
birthright as of this day."
32 And Esau said, "Look, I *am*
about to die; so [a]what *is* this
birthright to me?"
33 Then Jacob said, [1]"Swear to
me as of this day." So he swore
to him, and [a]sold his birthright
to Jacob.
34 And Jacob gave Esau bread
and stew of lentils; then [a]he ate
and drank, arose, and went his
way. Thus Esau [b]despised *his*
birthright.

26 There was a famine in
the land, besides [a]the first
famine that was in the days of
Abraham. And Isaac went to
[b]A·bim′e·lech king of the Phi·lis′-
tines, in Gē′rar.
2 Then the LORD appeared to
him and said: [a]"Do not go down
to Egypt; live in [b]the land of
which I shall tell you.
3 [a]"Dwell in this land, and [b]I
will be with you and [c]bless you;
for to you and your descendants
[d]I give all these lands, and I will
perform [e]the oath which I swore
to Abraham your father.
☆4 "And [a]I will make your descendants multiply as the stars
of heaven; I will give to your descendants all these lands; [b]and
in your seed all the nations of
the earth shall be blessed;
5 [a]"because Abraham obeyed
My voice and kept My charge,
My commandments, My stat-
utes, and My laws."
6 So Isaac dwelt in Gē′rar.
7 And the men of the place
asked about his wife. And [a]he
said, "She *is* my sister"; for [b]he
was afraid to say, "*She is* my
wife," *because he thought,* "lest
the men of the place kill me
for Rebekah, because she *is*
[c]beautiful to behold."
8 Now it came to pass, when
he had been there a long time,
that A·bim′e·lech king of the
Phi·lis′tines looked through a
window, and saw, and there was
Isaac, [1]showing endearment to
Rebekah his wife.
9 Then A·bim′e·lech called
Isaac and said, "Quite obviously
she *is* your wife; so how could
you say, 'She *is* my sister'?"
Isaac said to him, "Because I
said, 'Lest I die on account of
her.' "
10 And A·bim′e·lech said, "What
is this you have done to us? One
of the people might soon have
lain with your wife, and [a]you
would have brought guilt on us."
11 So A·bim′e·lech charged
all *his* people, saying, "He who
[a]touches this man or his wife
shall surely be put to death."
12 Then Isaac sowed in that
land, and reaped in the same
year [a]a hundredfold; and the
LORD [b]blessed him.
13 The man [a]began to prosper,
and continued prospering until
he became very prosperous;
14 for he had possessions of
flocks and possessions of herds
and a great number of servants.
So the Phi·lis′tines [a]envied him.
15 Now the Phi·lis′tines had
stopped up all the wells [a]which
his father's servants had dug in
the days of Abraham his father,
and they had filled them with
earth.
16 And A·bim′e·lech said to
Isaac, "Go away from us, for [a]you
are much mightier than we."

30 [1]Lit. *Red*
32 [a]Mark 8:36, 37
33 [a]Heb. 12:16 [1]*Take an oath*
34 [a]Eccl. 8:15 [b]Heb. 12:16, 17

CHAPTER 26

1 [a]Gen. 12:10 [b]Gen. 20:1, 2
2 [a]Gen. 12:7; 17:1; 18:1; 35:9 [b]Gen. 12:1
3 [a]Heb. 11:9 [b]Gen. 28:13, 15 [c]Gen. 12:2 [d]Gen. 12:7; 13:15; 15:18 [e]Gen. 22:16
4 [a]Gen. 15:5; 22:17 [b]Gen. 12:3; 22:18; Gal. 3:8
5 [a]Gen. 22:16, 18
7 [a]Gen. 12:13; 20:2, 12, 13 [b]Prov. 29:25 [c]Gen. 12:11; 24:16; 29:17
8 [1]*caressing*
10 [a]Gen. 20:9
11 [a]Ps. 105:15
12 [a]Matt. 13:8, 23 [b]Gen. 24:1; 25:8, 11; 26:3
13 [a][Prov. 10:22]
14 [a]Gen. 37:11
15 [a]Gen. 21:25, 30
16 [a]Ex. 1:9

17 Then Isaac departed from
there and [1]pitched his tent in
the Valley of Gē′rar, and dwelt
there.
18 And Isaac dug again the
wells of water which they had
dug in the days of Abraham his
father, for the Phi·lis′tines had
stopped them up after the death
of Abraham. [a]He called them by
the names which his father had
called them.
19 Also Isaac's servants dug in
the valley, and found a well of
running water there.
20 But the herdsmen of Gē′rar
[a]quarreled with Isaac's herdsmen, saying, "The water *is* ours."
So he called the name of the
well [1]Ē′sek, because they quarreled with him.
21 Then they dug another well,
and they quarreled over that *one*
also. So he called its name [1]Sit′-
nah.
22 And he moved from there
and dug another well, and they
did not quarrel over it. So he
called its name [1]Re·hō′both, because he said, "For now the LORD
has made room for us, and we
shall [a]be fruitful in the land."
23 Then he went up from there
to Bē·er·shē′ba.
24 And the LORD [a]appeared to
him the same night and said,
[b]"I *am* the God of your father
Abraham; [c]do not fear, for [d]I *am*
with you. I will bless you and
multiply your descendants for
My servant Abraham's sake."
25 So he [a]built an altar there
and [b]called on the name of the
LORD, and he pitched his tent
there; and there Isaac's servants
dug a well.
26 Then A·bim′e·lech came to
him from Gē′rar with A·huz′-
zath, one of his friends, [a]and
Phī′chol the commander of his
army.
27 And Isaac said to them, "Why
have you come to me, [a]since you
hate me and have [b]sent me away
from you?"
28 But they said, "We have certainly seen that the LORD [a]is with
you. So we said, 'Let there now
be an oath between us, between
you and us; and let us make a
[1]covenant with you,
29 'that you will do us no harm,
since we have not touched you,
and since we have done nothing
to you but good and have sent
you away in peace. [a]You *are* now
the blessed of the LORD.' "
30 [a]So he made them a feast,
and they ate and drank.
31 Then they arose early in the
morning and [a]swore an oath
with one another; and Isaac sent
them away, and they departed
from him in peace.
32 It came to pass the same day
that Isaac's servants came and
told him about the well which
they had dug, and said to him,
"We have found water."
33 So he called it [1]Shē′bah.
[a]Therefore the name of the city
is [2]Bē·er·shē′ba to this day.
34 [a]When Esau was forty years
old, he took as wives Judith the
daughter of Be·ē′rī the Hit′tīte,
and Bas′e·math the daughter of
Ē′lon the Hit′tīte.
35 And [a]they were a grief of
mind to Isaac and Rebekah.

27

Now it came to pass,
when Isaac was [a]old and
[b]his eyes were so dim that he
could not see, that he called
Esau his older son and said to
him, "My son." And he answered
him, "Here I am."

17 [1]*camped*
18 [a]Gen. 21:31
20 [a]Gen. 21:25 [1]Lit. *Quarrel*
21 [1]Lit. *Enmity*
22 [a]Gen. 17:6; 28:3; 41:52 [1]Lit. *Spaciousness*
24 [a]Gen. 26:2 [b]Gen. 17:7, 8; 24:12 [c]Gen. 15:1 [d]Gen. 26:3, 4
25 [a]Gen. 12:7, 8; 13:4, 18; 22:9; 33:20 [b]Ps. 116:17
26 [a]Gen. 21:22
27 [a]Judg. 11:7 [b]Gen. 26:16
28 [a]Gen. 21:22, 23 [1]*treaty*
29 [a]Gen. 24:31
30 [a]Gen. 19:3
31 [a]Gen. 21:31
33 [a]Gen. 21:31; 28:10 [1]Lit. *Oath* or *Seven* [2]Lit. *Well of the Oath* or *Well of the Seven*
34 [a]Gen. 28:8; 36:2
35 [a]Gen. 27:46; 28:1, 8

CHAPTER 27

1 [a]Gen. 35:28 [b]Gen. 48:10

2 Then he said, "Behold now, I am old. I [a]do not know the day of my death.
3 [a]"Now therefore, please take your weapons, your quiver and your bow, and go out to the field and hunt game for me.
4 "And make me [1]savory food, such as I love, and bring *it* to me that I may eat, that my soul [a]may bless you before I die."
5 Now Rebekah was listening when Isaac spoke to Esau his son. And Esau went to the field to hunt game and to bring *it*.
6 So Rebekah spoke to Jacob her son, saying, "Indeed I heard your father speak to Esau your brother, saying,
7 'Bring me game and make [1]savory food for me, that I may eat it and bless you in the presence of the LORD before my death.'
8 "Now therefore, my son, [a]obey my voice according to what I command you.
9 "Go now to the flock and bring me from there two choice kids of the goats, and I will make [a]savory food from them for your father, such as he loves.
10 "Then you shall take *it* to your father, that he may eat *it*, and that he [a]may bless you before his death."
11 And Jacob said to Rebekah his mother, "Look, [a]Esau my brother *is* a hairy man, and I *am* a smooth-*skinned* man.
12 "Perhaps my father will [a]feel me, and I shall seem to be a deceiver to him; and I shall bring [b]a curse on myself and not a blessing."
13 But his mother said to him, [a]"*Let* your curse *be* on me, my son; only obey my voice, and go, get *them* for me."
14 And he went and got *them* and brought *them* to his mother, and his mother [a]made [1]savory food, such as his father loved.
15 Then Rebekah took [a]the choice clothes of her elder son Esau, which *were* with her in the house, and put them on Jacob her younger son.
16 And she put the skins of the kids of the goats on his hands and on the smooth part of his neck.
17 Then she gave the savory food and the bread, which she had prepared, into the hand of her son Jacob.
18 So he went to his father and said, "My father." And he said, "Here I am. Who *are* you, my son?"
19 Jacob said to his father, "I *am* Esau your firstborn; I have done just as you told me; please arise, sit and eat of my game, [a]that your soul may bless me."
20 But Isaac said to his son, "How *is it* that you have found *it* so quickly, my son?" And he said, "Because the LORD your God brought *it* to me."
21 Then Isaac said to Jacob, "Please come near, that I [a]may feel you, my son, whether you *are* really my son Esau or not."
22 So Jacob went near to Isaac his father, and he felt him and said, "The voice *is* Jacob's voice, but the hands *are* the hands of Esau."
23 And he did not recognize him, because [a]his hands were hairy like his brother Esau's hands; so he blessed him.
24 Then he said, "*Are* you really my son Esau?" He said, "I *am*."

2 [a][Prov. 27:1]
3 [a]Gen. 25:27, 28
4 [a]Deut. 33:1 [1]*tasty*
7 [1]*tasty*
8 [a]Gen. 27:13, 43
9 [a]Gen. 27:4
10 [a]Gen. 27:4; 48:16
11 [a]Gen. 25:25
12 [a]Gen. 27:21, 22 [b]Deut. 27:18
13 [a]Gen. 43:9
14 [a]Prov. 23:3 [1]*tasty*
15 [a]Gen. 27:27
19 [a]Gen. 27:4
21 [a]Gen. 27:12
23 [a]Gen. 27:16

25 He said, "Bring *it* near to me,
and I will eat of my son's game,
so [a]that my soul may bless you."
So he brought *it* near to him,
and he ate; and he brought him
wine, and he drank.
26 Then his father Isaac said to
him, "Come near now and kiss
me, my son."
27 And he came near and [a]kissed
him; and he smelled the smell of
his clothing, and blessed him
and said:

"Surely, [b]the smell of my son
Is like the smell of a field
Which the LORD has blessed.
28 Therefore may [a]God give
you
Of [b]the dew of heaven,
Of [c]the fatness of the earth,
And [d]plenty of grain and
wine.
29 [a]Let peoples serve you,
And nations bow down to
you.
Be master over your
brethren,
And [b]let your mother's sons
bow down to you.
[c]Cursed *be* everyone who
curses you,
And blessed *be* those who
bless you!"

30 Now it happened, as soon
as Isaac had finished blessing
Jacob, and Jacob had scarcely
gone out from the presence of
Isaac his father, that Esau his
brother came in from his hunting.
31 He also had made [1]savory
food, and brought it to his father, and said to his father, "Let
my father arise and [a]eat of his
son's game, that your soul may
bless me."
32 And his father Isaac said to
him, "Who *are* you?" So he said,
"I *am* your son, your firstborn,
Esau."
33 Then Isaac trembled exceedingly, and said, "Who? Where *is*
the one who hunted game and
brought *it* to me? I ate all *of it*
before you came, and I have
blessed him—[a]*and* indeed he
shall be blessed."
34 When Esau heard the words
of his father, [a]he cried with an
exceedingly great and bitter cry,
and said to his father, "Bless
me—me also, O my father!"
35 But he said, "Your brother
came with deceit and has taken
away your blessing."
36 And *Esau* said, [a]"Is he not
rightly named [1]Jacob? For he has
supplanted me these two times.
He took away my birthright, and
now look, he has taken away my
blessing!" And he said, "Have
you not reserved a blessing for
me?"
37 Then Isaac answered and
said to Esau, [a]"Indeed I have
made him your master, and all
his brethren I have given to
him as servants; with [b]grain
and wine I have [1]sustained him.
What shall I do now for you, my
son?"
38 And Esau said to his father,
"Have you only one blessing,
my father? Bless me—me also,
O my father!" And Esau lifted up
his voice [a]and wept.
39 Then Isaac his father answered and said to him:

"Behold, [a]your dwelling shall
be of the [1]fatness of the
earth,
And of the dew of heaven
from above.

25 [a]Gen. 27:4, 10, 19, 31
27 [a]Gen. 29:13 [b]Song 4:11
28 [a]Heb. 11:20 [b]Deut. 33:13, 28 [c]Gen. 45:18 [d]Deut. 7:13; 33:28
29 [a]Gen. 9:25; 25:23 [b]Gen. 37:7, 10; 49:8 [c]Gen. 12:2, 3
31 [a]Gen. 27:4 [1]*tasty*
33 [a]Gen. 25:23; 28:3, 4
34 [a][Heb. 12:17]
36 [a]Gen. 25:26, 32–34 [1]*Supplanter* or *Deceitful*, lit. *One Who Takes the Heel*
37 [a]2 Sam. 8:14 [b]Gen. 27:28, 29 [1]*provided support for*
38 [a]Heb. 12:17
39 [a]Heb. 11:20 [1]*fertility*

40 By your sword you shall
live,
And [a]you shall serve your
brother;
And [b]it shall come to pass,
when you become
restless,
That you shall break his
yoke from your neck."

41 So Esau [a]hated Jacob because of the blessing with which
his father blessed him, and Esau
said in his heart, [b]"The days of
mourning for my father [1]are at
hand; [c]then I will kill my brother
Jacob."
42 And the words of Esau her
older son were told to Rebekah.
So she sent and called Jacob
her younger son, and said to
him, "Surely your brother Esau
[a]comforts himself concerning
you *by intending* to kill you.
43 "Now therefore, my son,
obey my voice: arise, flee to my
brother Lā'ban [a]in Har'an.
44 "And stay with him a [a]few
days, until your brother's fury
turns away,
45 "until your brother's anger
turns away from you, and he
forgets what you have done to
him; then I will send and bring
you from there. Why should I be
bereaved also of you both in one
day?"
46 And Rebekah said to Isaac,
[a]"I am weary of my life because
of the daughters of Heth; [b]if
Jacob takes a wife of the daughters of Heth, like these *who are*
the daughters of the land, what
good will my life be to me?"

28 Then Isaac called Jacob
and [a]blessed him, and
[1]charged him, and said to him:
[b]"You shall not take a wife from
the daughters of Cā'naan.
2 [a]"Arise, go to [b]Pad'an Ar'am,
to the house of [c]Be·thū'el your
mother's father; and take yourself a wife from there of the
daughters of [d]Lā'ban your mother's brother.

3 "May [a]God Almighty bless
you,
And make you [b]fruitful and
multiply you,
That you may be an
assembly of peoples;
4 And give you [a]the blessing
of Abraham,
To you and your
descendants with you,
That you may inherit the
land
[b]In[1] which you are a stranger,
Which God gave to
Abraham."

5 So Isaac sent Jacob away,
and he went to Pad'an Ar'am, to
Lā'ban the son of Be·thū'el the
Syrian, the brother of Rebekah,
the mother of Jacob and Esau.
6 Esau saw that Isaac had
blessed Jacob and sent him
away to Pad'an Ar'am to take
himself a wife from there, *and*
that as he blessed him he gave
him a charge, saying, "You shall
not take a wife from the daughters of Cā'naan,"
7 and that Jacob had obeyed
his father and his mother and
had gone to Pad'an Ar'am.
8 Also Esau saw [a]that the
daughters of Cā'naan did not
please his father Isaac.
9 So Esau went to Ish'ma·el
and [a]took [b]Mā'ha·lath the daughter of Ish'ma·el, Abraham's son,
[c]the sister of Ne·bā'joth, to be his

40 [a]Gen. 25:23; 27:29 [b]2 Kin. 8:20–22
41 [a]Gen. 26:27; 32:3–11; 37:4, 5, 8 [b]Gen. 50:2–4, 10 [c]Obad. 10 [1]*are soon here*
42 [a]Ps. 64:5
43 [a]Gen. 11:31; 25:20; 28:2, 5
44 [a]Gen. 31:41
46 [a]Gen. 26:34, 35; 28:8 [b]Gen. 24:3

CHAPTER 28

1 [a]Gen. 27:33 [b]Gen. 24:3 [1]*commanded*
2 [a]Hos. 12:12 [b]Gen. 25:20 [c]Gen. 22:23 [d]Gen. 24:29; 27:43; 29:5
3 [a]Gen. 17:16; 35:11; 48:3 [b]Gen. 26:4, 24
4 [a]Gen. 12:2, 3; 22:17 [b]Gen. 17:8; 23:4; 36:7 [1]Lit. *Of your sojournings*
8 [a]Gen. 24:3; 26:34, 35; 27:46
9 [a]Gen. 26:34, 35 [b]Gen. 36:2, 3 [c]Gen. 25:13

wife in addition to the wives he
had.
10 Now Jacob [a]went out from
Bē·er·shē′ba and went toward
[b]Har′an.
11 So he came to a certain place
and stayed there all night, because the sun had set. And he
took one of the stones of that
place and put it at his head, and
he lay down in that place to
sleep.
12 Then he [a]dreamed, and behold, a ladder *was* set up on
the earth, and its top reached
to heaven; and there [b]the angels
of God were ascending and descending on it.
13 [a]And behold, the LORD stood
above it and said: [b]"I *am* the
LORD God of Abraham your father and the God of Isaac; [c]the
land on which you lie I will give
to you and your descendants.
☆ 14 "Also your [a]descendants
shall be as the dust of the earth;
you shall spread abroad [b]to the
west and the east, to the north
and the south; and in you and [c]in
your seed all the families of the
earth shall be blessed.
15 "Behold, [a]I *am* with you and
will [b]keep[1] you wherever you go,
and will [c]bring you back to this
land; for [d]I will not leave you
[e]until I have done what I have
spoken to you."
16 Then Jacob awoke from his
sleep and said, "Surely the LORD
is in [a]this place, and I did not
know *it*."
17 And he was afraid and said,
"How awesome *is* this place!
This *is* none other than the
house of God, and this *is* the
gate of heaven!"
18 Then Jacob rose early in the
morning, and took the stone that
he had put at his head, [a]set it up
as a pillar, [b]and poured oil on
top of it.
19 And he called the name
of [a]that place [1]Beth′el; but the
name of that city had been Luz
previously.
20 [a]Then Jacob made a vow,
saying, "If [b]God will be with me,
and keep me in this way that I
am going, and give me [c]bread to
eat and clothing to put on,
21 "so that [a]I come back to my
father's house in peace, [b]then
the LORD shall be my God.
22 "And this stone which I have
set as a pillar [a]shall be God's
house, [b]and of all that You give
me I will surely give a [1]tenth to
You."

29 So Jacob went on his
journey [a]and came to the
land of the people of the East.
2 And he looked, and saw a
[a]well in the field; and behold,
there *were* three flocks of sheep
lying by it; for out of that well
they watered the flocks. A large
stone *was* on the well's mouth.
3 Now all the flocks would be
gathered there; and they would
roll the stone from the well's
mouth, water the sheep, and put
the stone back in its place on the
well's mouth.
4 And Jacob said to them, "My
brethren, where *are* you from?"
And they said, "We *are* from
[a]Har′an."
5 Then he said to them, "Do
you know [a]Lā′ban the son of
Nā′hor?" And they said, "We
know him."
6 So he said to them, [a]"Is he
well?" And they said, "*He is* well.
And look, his daughter Rachel
[b]is coming with the sheep."
7 Then he said, "Look, *it is* still

10 [a]Hos. 12:12 [b]Gen. 12:4, 5; 27:43; 29:4
12 [a]Gen. 31:10; 41:1 [b]John 1:51
13 [a]Gen. 35:1; 48:3 [b]Gen. 26:24 [c]Gen. 13:15, 17; 26:3; 35:12
14 [a]Gen. 13:16; 22:17 [b]Gen. 13:14, 15 [c]Gen. 12:3; 18:18; 22:18; 26:4; Gal. 3:8
15 [a]Gen. 26:3, 24; 31:3 [b]Gen. 48:16 [c]Gen. 35:6; 48:21 [d]Deut. 7:9; 31:6, 8 [e]Num. 23:19 [1]*protect*
16 [a]Ex. 3:5
18 [a]Gen. 31:13, 45 [b]Lev. 8:10–12
19 [a]Judg. 1:23, 26 [1]Lit. *House of God*
20 [a]Judg. 11:30 [b]Gen. 28:15 [c]1 Tim. 6:8
21 [a]Judg. 11:31 [b]Deut. 26:17
22 [a]Gen. 35:7, 14 [b]Gen. 14:20 [1]*tithe*

CHAPTER 29

1 [a]Num. 23:7
2 [a]Gen. 24:10, 11
4 [a]Gen. 11:31; 28:10
5 [a]Gen. 24:24, 29; 28:2
6 [a]Gen. 43:27 [b]Ex. 2:16, 17

[1]high day; *it is* not time for the
cattle to be gathered together.
Water the sheep, and go and
feed *them.*"
8 But they said, "We cannot
until all the flocks are gathered
together, and they have rolled
the stone from the well's mouth;
then we water the sheep."
9 Now while he was still speaking with them, [a]Rachel came
with her father's sheep, for she
was a shepherdess.
10 And it came to pass, when
Jacob saw Rachel the daughter
of Lā'ban his mother's brother,
and the sheep of Lā'ban his
mother's brother, that Jacob
went near and [a]rolled the stone
from the well's mouth, and watered the flock of Lā'ban his
mother's brother.
11 Then Jacob [a]kissed Rachel,
and lifted up his voice and wept.
12 And Jacob told Rachel that
he *was* [a]her father's relative and
that he *was* Rebekah's son. [b]So
she ran and told her father.
13 Then it came to pass, when
Lā'ban heard the report about
Jacob his sister's son, that [a]he
ran to meet him, and embraced
him and kissed him, and brought
him to his house. So he told Lā'-
ban all these things.
14 And Lā'ban said to him,
[a]"Surely you *are* my bone and
my flesh." And he stayed with
him for a month.
15 Then Lā'ban said to Jacob,
"Because you *are* my relative,
should you therefore serve me
for nothing? Tell me, [a]what
should your wages *be?*"
16 Now Lā'ban had two daughters: the name of the elder
was Leah, and the name of the
younger *was* Rachel.
17 Leah's eyes *were* [1]delicate,
but Rachel was [a]beautiful of
form and appearance.
18 Now Jacob loved Rachel; so
he said, [a]"I will serve you seven
years for Rachel your younger
daughter."
19 And Lā'ban said, "*It is* better
that I give her to you than that I
should give her to another man.
Stay with me."
20 So Jacob [a]served seven years
for Rachel, and they seemed
only a few days to him because
of the love he had for her.
21 Then Jacob said to Lā'ban,
"Give *me* my wife, for my days
are fulfilled, that I may [a]go in to
her."
22 And Lā'ban gathered together all the men of the place
and [a]made a feast.
23 Now it came to pass in the
evening, that he took Leah his
daughter and brought her to Jacob; and he went in to her.
24 And Lā'ban gave his maid
[a]Zil'pah to his daughter Leah *as*
a maid.
25 So it came to pass in the
morning, that behold, it *was*
Leah. And he said to Lā'ban,
"What is this you have done to
me? Was it not for Rachel that I
served you? Why then have you
[a]deceived me?"
26 And Lā'ban said, "It must
not be done so in our [1]country,
to give the younger before the
firstborn.
27 [a]"Fulfill her week, and we
will give you this one also for
the service which you will serve
with me still another seven
years."
28 Then Jacob did so and fulfilled her week. So he gave him

7 [1]*early in the day*
9 [a]Ex. 2:16
10 [a]Ex. 2:17
11 [a]Gen. 33:4; 45:14, 15
12 [a]Gen. 13:8; 14:14, 16; 28:5 [b]Gen. 24:28
13 [a]Gen. 24:29–31
14 [a]Gen. 2:23; 37:27
15 [a]Gen. 30:28; 31:41
17 [a]Gen. 12:11, 14; 26:7 [1]Or *weak*
18 [a]Gen. 31:41
20 [a]Gen. 30:26
21 [a]Judg. 15:1
22 [a]John 2:1, 2
24 [a]Gen. 30:9, 10
25 [a]1 Sam. 28:12
26 [1]Lit. *place*
27 [a]Judg. 14:2

his daughter Rachel as wife
also.
29 And Lā′ban gave his maid
[a]Bil′hah to his daughter Rachel
as a maid.
30 Then *Jacob* also went in to
Rachel, and he also [a]loved Rachel more than Leah. And he
served with Lā′ban [b]still another
seven years.
31 When the LORD [a]saw that
Leah *was* [1]unloved, He [b]opened
her womb; but Rachel *was*
barren.
32 So Leah conceived and bore
a son, and she called his name
[1]Reuben; for she said, "The LORD
has surely [a]looked on my affliction. Now therefore, my husband will love me."
33 Then she conceived again
and bore a son, and said, "Because the LORD has heard that I
am [1]unloved, He has therefore
given me this *son* also." And she
called his name [2]Sim′ē·on.
34 She conceived again and
bore a son, and said, "Now this
time my husband will become
attached to me, because I have
borne him three sons." Therefore his name was called [1]Levi.
35 And she conceived again and
bore a son, and said, "Now I will
praise the LORD." Therefore she
called his name [a]Judah.[1] Then
she stopped bearing.

30 Now when Rachel saw
that [a]she bore Jacob no
children, Rachel [b]envied her sister, and said to Jacob, "Give me
children, [c]or else I die!"
2 And Jacob's anger was
aroused against Rachel, and he
said, [a]"*Am* I in the place of God,
who has withheld from you the
fruit of the womb?"
3 So she said, "Here is [a]my
maid Bil′hah; go in to her, [b]and
she will bear *a child* on my
knees, [c]that I also may [1]have
children by her."
4 Then she gave him Bil′hah
her maid [a]as wife, and Jacob
went in to her.
5 And Bil′hah conceived and
bore Jacob a son.
6 Then Rachel said, "God has
[a]judged my case; and He has
also heard my voice and given
me a son." Therefore she called
his name [1]Dan.
7 And Rachel's maid Bil′hah
conceived again and bore Jacob
a second son.
8 Then Rachel said, "With
[1]great wrestlings I have wrestled with my sister, *and* indeed
I have prevailed." So she called
his name [2]Naph′ta·lī.
9 When Leah saw that she had
stopped bearing, she took Zil′-
pah her maid and [a]gave her to
Jacob as wife.
10 And Leah's maid Zil′pah
bore Jacob a son.
11 Then Leah said, [1]"A troop
comes!" So she called his name
[2]Gad.
12 And Leah's maid Zil′pah
bore Jacob a second son.
13 Then Leah said, "I am happy,
for the daughters [a]will call me
blessed." So she called his name
[1]Ash′er.
14 Now Reuben went in the
days of wheat harvest and
found mandrakes in the field,
and brought them to his mother
Leah. Then Rachel said to Leah,
[a]"Please give me *some* of your
son's mandrakes."
15 But she said to her, [a]"*Is it* a
small matter that you have taken
away my husband? Would you
take away my son's mandrakes

29 [a]Gen. 30:3–5
30 [a]Deut. 21:15–17 [b]Gen. 30:26; 31:41
31 [a]Ps. 127:3 [b]Gen. 30:1 [1]Lit. *hated*
32 [a]Deut. 26:7 [1]Lit. *See, a Son*
33 [1]Lit. *hated* [2]Lit. *Heard*
34 [1]Lit. *Attached*
35 [a]Matt. 1:2 [1]Lit. *Praise*

CHAPTER 30

1 [a]Gen. 16:1, 2; 29:31 [b]Gen. 37:11 [c][Job 5:2]
2 [a]1 Sam. 1:5
3 [a]Gen. 16:2 [b]Gen. 50:23 [c]Gen. 16:2, 3 [1]Lit. *be built up by her*
4 [a]Gen. 16:3, 4
6 [a]Lam. 3:59 [1]Lit. *Judge*
8 [1]Lit. *wrestlings of God* [2]Lit. *My Wrestling*
9 [a]Gen. 30:4
11 [1]So with Qr., Syr., Tg.; Kt., LXX, Vg. *in fortune* [2]Lit. *Troop* or *Fortune*
13 [a]Luke 1:48 [1]Lit. *Happy*
14 [a]Gen. 25:30
15 [a][Num. 16:9, 13]

also?" And Rachel said, "Therefore he will lie with you tonight
for your son's mandrakes."
16 When Jacob came out of the
field in the evening, Leah went
out to meet him and said, "You
must come in to me, for I have
surely hired you with my son's
mandrakes." And he lay with
her that night.
17 And God listened to Leah,
and she conceived and bore Jacob a fifth son.
18 Leah said, "God has given me
my wages, because I have given
my maid to my husband." So she
called his name [1]Is′sa·char.
19 Then Leah conceived again
and bore Jacob a sixth son.
20 And Leah said, "God has
endowed me *with* a good en-
dowment; now my husband will
dwell with me, because I have
borne him six sons." So she
called his name [1]Zeb′ū·lun.
21 Afterward she bore a
[a]daughter, and called her name
[1]Dī′nah.
22 Then God [a]remembered Rachel, and God listened to her
and [b]opened her womb.
23 And she conceived and bore
a son, and said, "God has taken
away [a]my reproach."
24 So she called his name [1]Jo-
seph, and said, [a]"The LORD shall
add to me another son."
25 And it came to pass, when
Rachel had borne Joseph, that
Jacob said to Lā′ban, [a]"Send me
away, that I may go to [b]my own
place and to my country.
26 "Give *me* my wives and my
children [a]for whom I have served
you, and let me go; for you know
my service which I have done
for you."
27 And Lā′ban said to him,
"Please *stay,* if I have found
favor in your eyes, *for* [a]I have
learned by experience that the
LORD has blessed me for your
sake."
28 Then he said, [a]"Name me
your wages, and I will give *it.*"
29 So *Jacob* said to him, [a]"You
know how I have served you
and how your livestock has been
with me.
30 "For what you had before
I *came was* little, and it has
increased to a great amount;
the LORD has blessed you [1]since
my coming. And now, when
shall I also [a]provide for my own
house?"
31 So he said, "What shall I give
you?" And Jacob said, "You shall
not give me anything. If you will
do this thing for me, I will again
feed and keep your flocks:
32 "Let me pass through all
your flock today, removing from
there all the speckled and spotted sheep, and all the brown
ones among the lambs, and the
spotted and speckled among the
goats; and [a]*these* shall be my
wages.
33 "So my [a]righteousness will
answer for me in time to come,
when the subject of my wages
comes before you: every one
that *is* not speckled and spotted
among the goats, and brown
among the lambs, will be considered stolen, if *it is* with me."
34 And Lā′ban said, "Oh, that it
were according to your word!"
35 So he removed that day the
male goats that were [a]speckled
and spotted, all the female goats
that were speckled and spotted, every one that had *some*
white in it, and all the brown

18 [1]Lit. *Wages*
20 [1]Lit. *Dwelling*
21 [a]Gen. 34:1 [1]Lit. *Judgment*
22 [a]1 Sam. 1:19, 20 [b]Gen. 29:31
23 [a]Luke 1:25
24 [a]Gen. 35:16–18 [1]Lit. *He Will Add*
25 [a]Gen. 24:54, 56 [b]Gen. 18:33
26 [a]Gen. 29:18–20, 27, 30
27 [a]Gen. 26:24; 39:3
28 [a]Gen. 29:15; 31:7, 41
29 [a]Gen. 31:6, 38–40
30 [a][1 Tim. 5:8] [1]Lit. *at my foot*
32 [a]Gen. 31:8
33 [a]Ps. 37:6
35 [a]Gen. 31:9–12

ones among the lambs, and gave
them into the hand of his sons.
36 Then he put three days' journey between himself and Jacob,
and Jacob fed the rest of Lā'-
ban's flocks.
37 Now [a]Jacob took for himself rods of green poplar and of
the almond and chestnut trees,
peeled white strips in them, and
exposed the white which *was* in
the rods.
38 And the rods which he had
peeled, he set before the flocks
in the gutters, in the watering
troughs where the flocks came
to drink, so that they should
conceive when they came to
drink.
39 So the flocks conceived before the rods, and the flocks
brought forth streaked, speckled, and spotted.
40 Then Jacob separated the
lambs, and made the flocks face
toward the streaked and all the
brown in the flock of Lā'ban; but
he put his own flocks by themselves and did not put them with
Lā'ban's flock.
41 And it came to pass, whenever the stronger livestock conceived, that Jacob placed the
rods before the eyes of the livestock in the gutters, that they
might conceive among the rods.
42 But when the flocks were
feeble, he did not put *them* in;
so the feebler were Lā'ban's and
the stronger Jacob's.
43 Thus the man [a]became exceedingly prosperous, and [b]had
large flocks, female and male servants, and camels and donkeys.

31

Now *Jacob* heard the
words of Lā'ban's sons,
saying, "Jacob has taken away
all that was our father's, and
from what was our father's he
has acquired all this [a]wealth."
2 And Jacob saw the [a]coun-
tenance of Lā'ban, and indeed it
was not [b]*favorable* toward him
as before.
3 Then the LORD said to Jacob,
[a]"Return to the land of your fathers and to your family, and I
will [b]be with you."
4 So Jacob sent and called Rachel and Leah to the field, to his
flock,
5 and said to them, [a]"I see
your father's [1]countenance, that
it *is* not *favorable* toward me as
before; but the God of my father
[b]has been with me.
6 "And [a]you know that with
all my might I have served your
father.
7 "Yet your father has deceived
me and [a]changed my wages [b]ten
times, but God [c]did not allow
him to hurt me.
8 "If he said thus: [a]'The speckled shall be your wages,' then all
the flocks bore speckled. And
if he said thus: 'The streaked
shall be your wages,' then all the
flocks bore streaked.
9 "So God has [a]taken away
the livestock of your father and
given *them* to me.
10 "And it happened, at the time
when the flocks conceived, that
I lifted my eyes and saw in a
dream, and behold, the rams
which leaped upon the flocks
were streaked, speckled, and
gray-spotted.
11 "Then [a]the Angel of God
spoke to me in a dream, saying,
'Jacob.' And I said, 'Here I am.'
12 "And He said, 'Lift your eyes
now and see, all the rams which
leap on the flocks *are* streaked,

37 [a]Gen. 31:9–12
43 [a]Gen. 12:16; 30:30 [b]Gen. 13:2; 24:35; 26:13, 14

CHAPTER 31

1 [a]Ps. 49:16
2 [a]Gen. 4:5 [b]Deut. 28:54
3 [a]Gen. 28:15, 20, 21; 32:9 [b]Gen. 46:4
5 [a]Gen. 31:2, 3 [b]Is. 41:10 [1]Lit. *face*
6 [a]Gen. 30:29; 31:38–41
7 [a]Gen. 29:25; 31:41 [b]Num. 14:22 [c]Job 1:10
8 [a]Gen. 30:32
9 [a]Gen. 31:1, 16
11 [a]Gen. 16:7–11; 22:11, 15; 31:13; 48:16

speckled, and gray-spotted; for
[a]I have seen all that Lā′ban is
doing to you.
13 ‘I *am* the God of Beth′el,
[a]where you anointed the pillar
and where you made a vow to
Me. Now [b]arise, get out of this
land, and return to the land of
your family.’ ”
14 Then Rachel and Leah answered and said to him, [a]“Is
there still any portion or inheritance for us in our father’s
house?
15 “Are we not considered
strangers by him? For [a]he has
sold us, and also completely
consumed our money.
16 “For all these riches which
God has taken from our father
are *really* ours and our children’s; now then, whatever God
has said to you, do it.”
17 Then Jacob rose and set his
sons and his wives on camels.
18 And he carried away all his
livestock and all his possessions
which he had gained, his acquired livestock which he had
gained in Pad′an Ar′am, to go
to his father Isaac in the land of
[a]Cā′naan.
19 Now Lā′ban had gone to
shear his sheep, and Rachel had
stolen the [a]household[1] idols that
were her father’s.
20 And Jacob stole away, unknown to Lā′ban the Syrian, in
that he did not tell him that he
[illegible]tended to flee.
[illegible] he fled with all that he
[illegible]rose and crossed the
[illegible]ded[1] toward the
[illegible]d.
[illegible] on the
[illegible]

seven days’ journey, and he
overtook him in the mountains
of Gil′ē·ad.
24 But God [a]had come to Lā′ban
the Syrian in a dream by night,
and said to him, “Be careful
that you [b]speak to Jacob neither
good nor bad.”
25 So Lā′ban overtook Jacob.
Now Jacob had pitched his tent
in the mountains, and Lā′ban
with his brethren pitched in the
mountains of Gil′ē·ad.
26 And Lā′ban said to Jacob:
“What have you done, that you
have stolen away unknown
to me, and [a]carried away my
daughters like captives *taken*
with the sword?
27 “Why did you flee away secretly, and steal away from me,
and not tell me; for I might
have sent you away with joy and
songs, with timbrel and harp?
28 “And you did not allow me
[a]to kiss my sons and my daughters. Now [b]you have done foolishly in so doing.
29 “It is in my power to do you
harm, but the [a]God of your father spoke to me [b]last night, saying, ‘Be careful that you speak to
Jacob neither good nor bad.’
30 “And now you have surely
gone because you greatly long
for your father’s house, *but* why
did you [a]steal my gods?”
31 Then Jacob answered and
said to Lā′ban, “Because I was
[a]afraid, for I said, ‘Perhaps you
would take your daughters from
me by force.’
32 “With whomever you find
your gods, [a]do not let him live.
In the presence of our brethren,
identify what I have of yours
and take *it* with you.” For Jacob

12 [a]Ex. 3:7
13 [a]Gen. 28:16–22; 35:1, 6, 15 [b]Gen. 31:3; 32:9
14 [a]Gen. 2:24
15 [a]Gen. 29:15, 20, 23, 27
18 [a]Gen. 17:8; 33:18; 35:27
19 [a]Judg. 17:5 [1]Heb. *teraphim*
21 [a]2 Kin. 12:17 [1]Lit. *set his face toward*
23 [a]Gen. 13:8
24 [a]Gen. 20:3; 31:29; 46:2–4 [b]Gen. 24:50; 31:7, 29
26 [a]1 Sam. 30:2
28 [a]Gen. 31:55 [b]1 Sam. 13:13
29 [a]Gen. 28:13; 31:5, 24, 42, 53 [b]Gen. 31:24
30 [a]Judg. 17:5; 18:24
31 [a]Gen. 26:7; 32:7, 11
[illegible] 44:9

did not know that Rachel had
stolen them.
33 And Lā′ban went into Jacob's tent, into Leah's tent, and
into the two maids' tents, but he
did not find *them.* Then he went
out of Leah's tent and entered
Rachel's tent.
34 Now Rachel had taken the
[1]household idols, put them in the
camel's saddle, and sat on them.
And Lā′ban [2]searched all about
the tent but did not find *them.*
35 And she said to her father,
"Let it not displease my lord that
I cannot [a]rise before you, for the
manner of women *is* with me."
And he searched but did not
find the [1]household idols.
36 Then Jacob was angry and
rebuked Lā′ban, and Jacob
answered and said to Lā′ban:
"What *is* my [1]trespass? What *is*
my sin, that you have so hotly
pursued me?
37 "Although you have searched
all my things, what part of your
household things have you
found? Set *it* here before my
brethren and your brethren,
that they may judge between us
both!
38 "These twenty years I *have
been* with you; your ewes and
your female goats have not
miscarried their young, and I
have not eaten the rams of your
flock.
39 [a]"That which was torn *by
beasts* I did not bring to you; I
bore the loss of it. [b]You required
it from my hand, *whether* stolen
by day or stolen by night.
40 "*There* I was! In the day the
drought consumed me, and the
frost by night, and my sleep departed from my eyes.
41 "Thus I have been in your
house twenty years; I [a]served
you fourteen years for your two
daughters, and six years for your
flock, and [b]you have changed
my wages ten times.
42 [a]"Unless the God of my father, the God of Abraham and
[b]the Fear of Isaac, had been with
me, surely now you would have
sent me away empty-handed.
[c]God has seen my affliction
and the labor of my hands, and
[d]rebuked *you* last night."
43 And Lā′ban answered and
said to Jacob, "*These* daughters
are my daughters, and *these*
children *are* my children, and
this flock *is* my flock; all that
you see *is* mine. But what can I
do this day to these my daughters or to their children whom
they have borne?
44 "Now therefore, come, [a]let
us make a [1]covenant, [b]you and I,
and let it be a witness between
you and me."
45 So Jacob [a]took a stone and
set it up *as* a pillar.
46 Then Jacob said to his brethren, "Gather stones." And they
took stones and made a heap,
and they ate there on the heap.
47 Lā′ban called it [1]Jē′gar
Sā·ha·dū′tha, but Jacob called it
[2]Gal′e·ed.
48 And Lā′ban said, [a]"This heap
is a witness between you and
me this day." Therefore its name
was called Gal′e·ed,
49 also [a]Miz′pah,[1] because he
said, "May the LORD watch between you and me when we are
absent one from another.
50 "If you afflict my daughters,
or if you take *other* wives besides my daughters, *altho*
no man *is* with us
witness be

34 [1]Heb. *teraphim* [2]Lit. *felt*
35 [a]Lev. 19:32 [1]Heb. *teraphim*
36 [1]*transgression*
39 [a]Ex. 22:10 [b]Ex. 22:10–13
41 [a]Gen. 29:20, 27–30 [b]Gen. 31:7
42 [a]Ps. 124:1, 2 [b]Is. 8:13 [c]Ex. 3:7 [d]1 Chr. 12:17
44 [a]Gen. 21:27, 32; 26:28 [b]Josh. 24:27 [1]*treaty*
45 [a]Gen. 28:18; 35:14
47 [1]Lit., in Aram., *Heap of Witness* [2]Lit., in Heb., *Heap of Witness*
48 [a]Josh. 24:27
49 [a]Judg. 10:17; 11:29 [1]Lit. *Watch*

51 Then Lā′ban said to Jacob,
"Here is this heap and here is
this pillar, which I have placed
between you and me.
52 "This heap *is* a witness, and
this pillar *is* a witness, that I
will not pass beyond this heap
to you, and you will not pass
beyond this heap and this pillar
to me, for harm.
53 "The God of Abraham, the
God of Nā′hor, and the God of
their father [a]judge between us."
And Jacob [b]swore by [c]the [1]Fear
of his father Isaac.
54 Then Jacob offered a sacrifice on the mountain, and called
his brethren to eat bread. And
they ate bread and stayed all
night on the mountain.
55 And early in the morning
Lā′ban arose, and [a]kissed his
sons and daughters and [b]blessed
them. Then Lā′ban departed and
[c]returned to his place.

32

So Jacob went on his
way, and [a]the angels of
God met him.
2 When Jacob saw them, he
said, "This *is* God's [a]camp." And
he called the name of that place
[1]Mā·ha·na′im.
3 Then Jacob sent messengers
before him to Esau his brother
[a]in the land of Sē′ir, [b]the [1]coun-
try of Ē′dom.
4 And he commanded them,
saying, [a]"Speak thus to my lord
Esau, 'Thus your servant Jacob
says: "I have dwelt with Lā′ban
and stayed there until now.
5 [a]"I have oxen, donkeys,
flocks, and male and female servants; and I have sent to tell my
lord, that [b]I may find favor in
your sight." ' "
6 Then the messengers returned to Jacob, saying, "We
came to your brother Esau, and
[a]he also is coming to meet you,
and four hundred men *are* with
him."
7 So Jacob was greatly afraid
and [a]distressed; and he divided
the people that *were* with him,
and the flocks and herds and
camels, into two companies.
8 And he said, "If Esau comes
to the one company and [1]at-
tacks it, then the other company
which is left will escape."
9 [a]Then Jacob said, [b]"O God of
my father Abraham and God of
my father Isaac, the LORD [c]who
said to me, 'Return to your country and to your family, and I will
deal well with you':
10 "I am not worthy of the least
of all the [a]mercies and of all the
truth which You have shown Your
servant; for I crossed over this
Jordan with [b]my staff, and now I
have become two companies.
11 [a]"Deliver me, I pray, from the
hand of my brother, from the
hand of Esau; for I fear him, lest
he come and [1]attack me *and* [b]the
mother with the children.
12 "For [a]You said, 'I will surely
treat you well, and make your
descendants as the [b]sand of the
sea, which cannot be numbered
for multitude.' "
13 So he lodged there that same
night, and took what [1]came to
his hand as [a]a present for Esau
his brother:
14 two hundred female goats
and twenty male goats, two hundred ewes and twenty rams,
15 thirty milk camels with their
colts, forty cows and ten bulls,
twenty female donkeys and ten
foals.
16 Then he delivered *them* to
the hand of his servants, every

53 [a]Gen. 16:5 [b]Gen. 21:23 [c]Gen. 31:42 [1]A reference to God
55 [a]Gen. 29:11, 13; 31:28, 43 [b]Gen. 28:1 [c]Num. 24:25

CHAPTER 32

1 [a]Num. 22:31
2 [a]Josh. 5:14 [1]Lit. *Double Camp*
3 [a]Gen. 14:6; 33:14, 16 [b]Gen. 25:30; 36:6–9 [1]Lit. *field*
4 [a]Prov. 15:1
5 [a]Gen. 30:43 [b]Gen. 33:8, 15
6 [a]Gen. 33:1
7 [a]Gen. 32:11; 35:3
8 [1]Lit. *strikes*
9 [a][Ps. 50:15] [b]Gen. 28:13; 31:42 [c]Gen. 31:3, 13
10 [a]Gen. 24:27 [b]Job 8:7
11 [a]Ps. 59:1, 2 [b]Hos. 10:14 [1]Lit. *strike*
12 [a]Gen. 28:13–15 [b]Gen. 22:17
13 [a]Gen. 43:11 [1]*he had received*

drove by itself, and said to his
servants, "Pass over before me,
and put some distance between
successive droves."
17 And he commanded the first
one, saying, "When Esau my
brother meets you and asks you,
saying, 'To whom do you belong,
and where are you going? Whose
are these in front of you?'
18 "then you shall say, 'They *are*
your servant Jacob's. It *is* a present sent to my lord Esau; and
behold, he also *is* behind us.' "
19 So he commanded the second, the third, and all who followed the droves, saying, "In
this manner you shall speak to
Esau when you find him;
20 "and also say, 'Behold, your
servant Jacob *is* behind us.' "
For he said, "I will [a]appease him
with the present that goes before me, and afterward I will see
his face; perhaps he will accept
me."
21 So the present went on
over before him, but he himself
lodged that night in the camp.
22 And he arose that night and
took his two wives, his two female servants, and his eleven
sons, [a]and crossed over the ford
of Jab'bok.
23 He took them, sent them
[1]over the brook, and sent over
what he had.
24 Then Jacob was left alone;
and [a]a Man wrestled with him
until the [1]breaking of day.
25 Now when He saw that He
did not prevail against him, He
[1]touched the socket of his hip;
and [a]the socket of Jacob's hip
was out of joint as He wrestled
with him.
26 And [a]He said, "Let Me go,
for the day breaks." But he said,
[b]"I will not let You go unless You
bless me!"
27 So He said to him, "What *is*
your name?" He said, "Jacob."
28 And He said, [a]"Your name
shall no longer be called Jacob, but [1]Israel; for you have
[b]struggled with God and [c]with
men, and have prevailed."
29 Then Jacob asked, saying,
"Tell *me* Your name, I pray." And
He said, [a]"Why *is* it *that* you
ask about My name?" And He
[b]blessed him there.
30 So Jacob called the name of
the place [1]Pe·nī'el: "For [a]I have
seen God face to face, and my
life is preserved."
31 Just as he crossed over
[1]Pe·nū'el the sun rose on him,
and he limped on his hip.
32 Therefore to this day the
children of Israel do not eat the
muscle that shrank, which *is*
on the hip socket, because He
[1]touched the socket of Jacob's
hip in the muscle that shrank.

33

Now Jacob lifted his eyes
and looked, and there,
[a]Esau was coming, and with
him were four hundred men. So
he divided the children among
Leah, Rachel, and the two maidservants.
2 And he put the maidservants
and their children in front, Leah
and her children behind, and
Rachel and Joseph last.
3 Then he crossed over before them and [a]bowed himself to
the ground seven times, until he
came near to his brother.
4 [a]But Esau ran to meet him,
and embraced him, [b]and fell on
his neck and kissed him, and
they wept.
5 And he lifted his eyes and
saw the women and children,

20 [a][Prov. 21:14]
22 [a]Deut. 3:16
23 [1]*across*
24 [a]Hos. 12:2–4 [1]*dawn*
25 [a]2 Cor. 12:7 [1]*struck*
26 [a]Luke 24:28 [b]Hos. 12:4
28 [a]Gen. 35:10 [b]Hos. 12:3, 4 [c]Gen. 25:31; 27:33 [1]Lit. *Prince with God*
29 [a]Judg. 13:17, 18 [b]Gen. 35:9
30 [a]Gen. 16:13 [1]Lit. *Face of God*
31 [1]Lit. *Face of God;* same as *Peniel,* v. 30
32 [1]*struck*

CHAPTER 33

1 [a]Gen. 32:6
3 [a]Gen. 18:2; 42:6
4 [a]Gen. 32:28 [b]Gen. 45:14, 15

and said, "Who *are* these with
you?" So he said, "The children
[a]whom God has graciously given
your servant."
6 Then the maidservants came
near, they and their children,
and bowed down.
7 And Leah also came near
with her children, and they
bowed down. Afterward Joseph
and Rachel came near, and they
bowed down.
8 Then Esau said, "What *do*
you *mean by* [a]all this company
which I met?" And he said,
"*These are* [b]to find favor in the
sight of my lord."
9 But Esau said, "I have
enough, my brother; keep what
you have for yourself."
10 And Jacob said, "No, please,
if I have now found favor in your
sight, then receive my present
from my hand, inasmuch as I
[a]have seen your face as though
I had seen the face of God, and
you were pleased with me.
11 "Please, take [a]my blessing
that is brought to you, because
God has dealt [b]graciously with
me, and because I have [1]enough."
[c]So he urged him, and he took
it.
12 Then Esau said, "Let us take
our journey; let us go, and I will
go before you."
13 But Jacob said to him, "My
lord knows that the children *are*
weak, and the flocks and herds
which are nursing *are* with me.
And if the men should drive
them hard one day, all the flock
will die.
14 "Please let my lord go on
ahead before his servant. I will
lead on slowly at a pace which
the livestock that go before me,
and the children, [1]are able to
endure, until I come to my lord
[a]in Sē′ir."
15 And Esau said, "Now let me
leave with you *some* of the people who *are* with me." But he
said, "What need is there? [a]Let
me find favor in the sight of my
lord."
16 So Esau returned that day on
his way to Sē′ir.
17 And Jacob journeyed to
[a]Suc′coth, built himself a house,
and made [1]booths for his livestock. Therefore the name of the
place is called [2]Suc′coth.
18 Then Jacob came [1]safely to
[a]the city of [b]Shē′chem, which *is*
in the land of Cā′naan, when he
came from Pad′an Ar′am; and he
pitched his tent before the city.
19 And [a]he bought the parcel of
[1]land, where he had pitched his
tent, from the children of Hā′-
mor, Shē′chem's father, for one
hundred pieces of money.
20 Then he erected an altar
there and called it [a]El[1] Ē·lō′he
Israel.

34

Now [a]Dī′nah the daugh-
ter of Leah, whom she
had borne to Jacob, went out to
see the daughters of the land.
2 And when Shē′chem the son
of Hā′mor the Hī′vīte, prince of
the country, saw her, he [a]took
her and lay with her, and violated her.
3 His soul [1]was strongly at-
tracted to Dī′nah the daughter
of Jacob, and he loved the young
woman and spoke [2]kindly to the
young woman.
4 So Shē′chem [a]spoke to his
father Hā′mor, saying, "Get me
this young woman as a wife."
5 And Jacob heard that he had
defiled Dī′nah his daughter. Now
his sons were with his livestock

5 [a]Gen. 48:9
8 [a]Gen. 32:13–16 [b]Gen. 32:5
10 [a]Gen. 43:3
11 [a]1 Sam. 25:27; 30:26 [b]Ex. 33:19 [c]2 Kin. 5:23 [1]Lit. *all*
14 [a]Gen. 32:3; 36:8 [1]*can stand*
15 [a]Ruth 2:13
17 [a]Josh. 13:27 [1]*shelters* [2]Lit. *Booths*
18 [a]John 3:23 [b]Josh. 24:1 [1]Or *to Shalem, a city of*
19 [a]John 4:5 [1]Lit. *the field*
20 [a]Gen. 35:7 [1]Lit. *God, the God of Israel*

CHAPTER 34

1 [a]Gen. 30:21
2 [a]Gen. 20:2
3 [1]Lit. *clung to* [2]*tenderly*
4 [a]Judg. 14:2

in the field; so Jacob [a]held[1] his
peace until they came.
6 Then Hā′mor the father of
Shē′chem went out to Jacob to
speak with him.
7 And the sons of Jacob
came in from the field when
they heard *it;* and the men were
grieved and very angry, because
he [a]had done a disgraceful thing
in Israel by lying with Jacob's
daughter, [b]a thing which ought
not to be done.
8 But Hā′mor spoke with them,
saying, "The soul of my son
Shē′chem longs for your daughter. Please give her to him as a
wife.
9 "And make marriages with
us; give your daughters to
us, and take our daughters to
yourselves.
10 "So you shall dwell with us,
and the land shall be before you.
Dwell and trade in it, and acquire possessions for yourselves
in it."
11 Then Shē′chem said to her
father and her brothers, "Let
me find favor in your eyes, and
whatever you say to me I will
give.
12 "Ask me ever so much
[a]dowry[1] and gift, and I will give
according to what you say to me;
but give me the young woman
as a wife."
13 But the sons of Jacob answered Shē′chem and Hā′mor
his father, and spoke [a]deceitfully,
because he had defiled Dī′nah
their sister.
14 And they said to them,
"We cannot do this thing, to
give our sister to one who is
[a]uncircumcised, for [b]that *would
be* a reproach to us.
15 "But on this *condition* we

5 [a]2 Sam. 13:22 [1]*kept silent*
7 [a]Judg. 20:6 [b]2 Sam. 13:12
12 [a]Ex. 22:16, 17 [1]*bride-price*
13 [a]Gen. 31:7
14 [a]Ex. 12:48 [b]Josh. 5:2–9
19 [a]1 Chr. 4:9
20 [a]Ruth 4:1, 11
24 [a]Gen. 23:10, 18

will consent to you: If you will
become as we *are,* if every male
of you is circumcised,
16 "then we will give our daughters to you, and we will take
your daughters to us; and we
will dwell with you, and we will
become one people.
17 "But if you will not heed us
and be circumcised, then we will
take our daughter and be gone."
18 And their words pleased
Hā′mor and Shē′chem, Hā′mor's
son.
19 So the young man did not
delay to do the thing, because he
delighted in Jacob's daughter.
He *was* [a]more honorable than
all the household of his father.
20 And Hā′mor and Shē′chem
his son came to the [a]gate of their
city, and spoke with the men of
their city, saying:
21 "These men *are* at peace with
us. Therefore let them dwell in
the land and trade in it. For indeed the land *is* large enough for
them. Let us take their daughters to us as wives, and let us
give them our daughters.
22 "Only on this *condition* will
the men consent to dwell with
us, to be one people: if every
male among us is circumcised
as they *are* circumcised.
23 "*Will* not their livestock,
their property, and every animal
of theirs *be* ours? Only let us
consent to them, and they will
dwell with us."
24 And all who went out of the
gate of his city heeded Hā′mor
and Shē′chem his son; every
male was circumcised, all who
[a]went out of the gate of his city.
25 Now it came to pass on the
third day, when they were in
pain, that two of the sons of

Jacob, [a]Sim′ē·on and Levi, Dī′-
nah's brothers, each took his
sword and came boldly upon the
city and killed all the males.
26 And they [a]killed Hā′mor and
Shē′chem his son with the edge
of the sword, and took Dī′nah
from Shē′chem's house, and
went out.
27 The sons of Jacob came upon
the slain, and plundered the city,
because their sister had been
defiled.
28 They took their sheep, their
oxen, and their donkeys, what
was in the city and what *was* in
the field,
29 and all their wealth. All their
little ones and their wives they
took captive; and they plundered
even all that *was* in the houses.
30 Then Jacob said to Sim′ē·on
and Levi, [a]"You have [b]troubled
me [c]by making me obnoxious
among the inhabitants of the
land, among the Cā′naan·ītes and
the Per′iz·zītes; [d]and since I *am*
few in number, they will gather
themselves together against me
and kill me. I shall be destroyed,
my household and I."
31 But they said, "Should he
treat our sister like a harlot?"

35 Then God said to Jacob,
"Arise, go up to [a]Beth′el
and dwell there; and make an altar there to God, [b]who appeared
to you [c]when you fled from the
face of Esau your brother."
2 And Jacob said to his
[a]household and to all who *were*
with him, "Put away [b]the foreign gods that *are* among you,
[c]purify yourselves, and change
your garments.
3 "Then let us arise and go up
to Beth′el; and I will make an altar there to God, [a]who answered

25 [a]Gen. 29:33, 34; 42:24; 49:5–7

26 [a]Gen. 49:5, 6

30 [a]Gen. 49:6 [b]Josh. 7:25 [c]Ex. 5:21 [d]Deut. 4:27

CHAPTER 35

1 [a]Gen. 28:19; 31:13 [b]Gen. 28:13 [c]Gen. 27:43

2 [a]Josh. 24:15 [b]Josh. 24:2, 14, 23 [c]Ex. 19:10, 14

3 [a]Gen. 32:7, 24 [b]Gen. 28:15, 20; 31:3, 42

4 [a]Hos. 2:13 [b]Josh. 24:26 [1]*idols*

5 [a]Ex. 15:16; 23:27

6 [a]Gen. 28:19, 22; 48:3

7 [a]Eccl. 5:4 [b]Gen. 28:13 [1]Lit. *God of the House of God*

8 [a]Gen. 24:59 [1]Lit. *Terebinth of Weeping*

9 [a]Josh. 5:13 [b]Gen. 32:29

10 [a]Gen. 17:5 [b]Gen. 32:28

11 [a]Ex. 6:3 [b]Gen. 9:1, 7 [c]Gen. 17:5, 6, 16; 28:3; 48:4

12 [a]Gen. 12:7; 13:15; 26:3, 4; 28:13; 48:4

13 [a]Gen. 17:22; 18:33 [1]*departed*

me in the day of my distress
[b]and has been with me in the
way which I have gone."
4 So they gave Jacob all the
foreign [1]gods which *were* in their
hands, and the [a]earrings which
were in their ears; and Jacob hid
them under [b]the terebinth tree
which *was* by Shē′chem.
5 And they journeyed, and [a]the
terror of God was upon the cities that *were* all around them,
and they did not pursue the sons
of Jacob.
6 So Jacob came to [a]Luz (that
is, Beth′el), which *is* in the land
of Cā′naan, he and all the people
who *were* with him.
7 And he [a]built an altar there
and called the place [1]El Beth′el,
because [b]there God appeared to
him when he fled from the face
of his brother.
8 Now [a]Deb′or·ah, Rebekah's
nurse, died, and she was buried
below Beth′el under the terebinth tree. So the name of it was
called [1]Al′lon Bach′uth.
9 Then [a]God appeared to Jacob again, when he came from
Pad′an Ar′am, and [b]blessed him.
10 And God said to him, "Your
name *is* Jacob; [a]your name shall
not be called Jacob anymore,
[b]but Israel shall be your name."
So He called his name Israel.
11 Also God said to him: [a]"I *am*
God Almighty. [b]Be fruitful and
multiply; [c]a nation and a company of nations shall proceed
from you, and kings shall come
from your body.
12 "The [a]land which I gave
Abraham and Isaac I give to
you; and to your descendants
after you I give this land."
13 Then God [a]went[1] up from

him in the place where He talked
with him.
14 So Jacob [a]set up a pillar in
the place where He talked with
him, a pillar of stone; and he
poured a drink offering on it,
and he poured oil on it.
15 And Jacob called the name
of the place where God spoke
with him, [a]Beth′el.
16 Then they journeyed from
Beth′el. And when there was but
a little distance to go to Eph′-
rath, Rachel labored *in childbirth,* and she had hard labor.
17 Now it came to pass, when
she was in hard labor, that the
midwife said to her, "Do not
fear; [a]you will have this son
also."
18 And so it was, as her soul
was departing (for she died),
that she called his name [1]Ben-
Ō′ni; but his father called him
[2]Benjamin.
19 So [a]Rachel died and was buried on the way to [b]Eph′rath (that
is, Bethlehem).
20 And Jacob set a pillar on her
grave, which *is* the pillar of Rachel's grave [a]to this day.
21 Then Israel journeyed and
pitched his tent beyond [a]the
tower of Ē′der.
22 And it happened, when Israel
dwelt in that land, that Reuben
went and [a]lay with Bil′hah his
father's concubine; and Israel
heard *about it.*
Now the sons of Jacob were
twelve:
23 the sons of Leah *were*
[a]Reuben, Jacob's firstborn, and
Sim′ē·on, Levi, Judah, Is′sa·char,
and Zeb′ū·lun;
24 the sons of Rachel *were* Joseph and Benjamin;
25 the sons of Bil′hah, Rachel's
maidservant, *were* Dan and
Naph′ta·lī;
26 and the sons of Zil′pah, Leah's maidservant, *were* Gad and
Ash′er. These *were* the sons of
Jacob who were born to him in
Pad′an Ar′am.
27 Then Jacob came to his father Isaac at [a]Mam′re, or [b]Kir′-
jath Ar′ba[1] (that *is,* Hē′bron),
where Abraham and Isaac had
dwelt.
28 Now the days of Isaac were
one hundred and eighty years.
29 So Isaac breathed his last
and died, and [a]was [1]gathered to
his people, *being* old and full of
days. And [b]his sons Esau and
Jacob buried him.

36 Now this *is* the genealogy
of Esau, [a]who is Ē′dom.
2 [a]Esau took his wives from
the daughters of Cā′naan: Ā′dah
the daughter of Ē′lon the [b]Hit′-
tīte; [c]A·hol·i·bā′mah[1] the daughter of An′ah, the daughter of
Zib′ē·on the Hī′vīte;
3 and [a]Bas′e·math, Ish′ma·el's
daughter, sister of Ne·bā′joth.
4 Now [a]Ā′dah bore E·lī′phaz
to Esau, and Bas′e·math bore
Reū′el.
5 And [1]A·hol·i·bā′mah bore Jē′-
ush, Jā′a·lam, and Kō′rah. These
were the sons of Esau who were
born to him in the land of Cā′-
naan.
6 Then Esau took his wives,
his sons, his daughters, and all
the persons of his household,
his cattle and all his animals,
and all his goods which he had
gained in the land of Cā′naan,
and went to a country away
from the presence of his brother
Jacob.
7 [a]For their possessions were
too great for them to dwell

14 [a]Gen. 28:18, 19; 31:45
15 [a]Gen. 28:19
17 [a]Gen. 30:24
18 [1]Lit. *Son of My Sorrow* [2]Lit. *Son of the Right Hand*
19 [a]Gen. 48:7 [b]Mic. 5:2
20 [a]1 Sam. 10:2
21 [a]Mic. 4:8
22 [a]Gen. 49:4
23 [a]Ex. 1:1–4
27 [a]Gen. 13:18; 18:1; 23:19 [b]Josh. 14:15 [1]Lit. *Town* or *City of Arba*
29 [a]Gen. 15:15; 25:8; 49:33 [b]Gen. 25:9; 49:31 [1]Joined his ancestors

CHAPTER 36

1 [a]Gen. 25:30
2 [a]Gen. 26:34; 28:9 [b]2 Kin. 7:6 [c]Gen. 36:25 [1]Or *Oholibamah*
3 [a]Gen. 28:9
4 [a]1 Chr. 1:35
5 [1]Or *Oholibamah*
7 [a]Gen. 13:6, 11

together, and [b]the land where
they were strangers could not
support them because of their
livestock.
8 So Esau dwelt in [a]Mount
Sē′ir. [b]Esau *is* Ē′dom.
9 And this *is* the genealogy of
Esau the father of the Ē′dom·ītes
in Mount Sē′ir.
10 These *were* the names of
Esau's sons: [a]E·lī′phaz the son
of Ā′dah the wife of Esau, and
Reū′el the son of Bas′e·math the
wife of Esau.
11 And the sons of E·lī′phaz
were Tē′man, Ō′mar, [1]Zē′phō,
Gā′tam, and Kē′naz.
12 Now Tim′na was the concubine of E·lī′phaz, Esau's son,
and she bore [a]Am′a·lek to E·lī′-
phaz. These *were* the sons of
Ā′dah, Esau's wife.
13 These *were* the sons of
Reū′el: Nā′hath, Zē′rah, Sham′-
mah, and Miz′zah. These were
the sons of Bas′e·math, Esau's
wife.
14 These were the sons of
[1]A·hol·i·bā′mah, Esau's wife, the
daughter of An′ah, the daughter
of Zib′ē·on. And she bore to
Esau: Jē′ush, Jā′a·lam, and Kō′-
rah.
15 These *were* the chiefs of the
sons of Esau. The sons of E·lī′-
phaz, the firstborn *son* of Esau,
were Chief Tē′man, Chief Ō′mar,
Chief Zē′phō, Chief Kē′naz,
16 [1]Chief Kō′rah, Chief Gā′tam,
and Chief Am′a·lek. These *were*
the chiefs of E·lī′phaz in the
land of Ē′dom. They *were* the
sons of Ā′dah.
17 These *were* the sons of
Reū′el, Esau's son: Chief Nā′-
hath, Chief Zē′rah, Chief Sham′-
mah, and Chief Miz′zah. These
were the chiefs of Reū′el in the
land of Ē′dom. These *were* the
sons of Bas′e·math, Esau's wife.
18 And these *were* the sons of
[1]A·hol·i·bā′mah, Esau's wife:
Chief Jē′ush, Chief Jā′a·lam,
and Chief Kō′rah. These *were*
the chiefs *who descended* from
A·hol·i·bā′mah, Esau's wife, the
daughter of An′ah.
19 These *were* the sons of Esau,
who is Ē′dom, and these *were*
their chiefs.
20 [a]These *were* the sons of Sē′ir
[b]the Hor′īte who inhabited the
land: Lō′tan, Shō′bal, Zib′ē·on,
An′ah,
21 Dī′shon, Ē′zer, and Dī′shan.
These *were* the chiefs of the
Hor′ītes, the sons of Sē′ir, in the
land of Ē′dom.
22 And the sons of Lō′tan were
Hō′rī and [1]Hē′mam. Lō′tan's sister *was* Tim′na.
23 These *were* the sons of Shō′-
bal: [1]Al′van, Man′a·hath, Ē′bal,
[2]Shē′phō, and Ō′nam.
24 These *were* the sons of Zib′-
ē·on: both Ā′jah and An′ah. This
was the An′ah who found the
[1]water in the wilderness as he
pastured [a]the donkeys of his father Zib′ē·on.
25 These *were* the children of
An′ah: Dī′shon and [1]A·hol·i·bā′-
mah the daughter of An′ah.
26 These *were* the sons of [1]Dī′-
shon: [2]Hem′dan, Esh′ban, Ith′-
ran, and Chē′ran.
27 These *were* the sons of Ē′zer:
Bil′han, Zā′a·van, and [1]Ā′kan.
28 These *were* the sons of Dī′-
shan: [a]Uz and Ar′an.
29 These *were* the chiefs of the
Hor′ītes: Chief Lō′tan, Chief
Shō′bal, Chief Zib′ē·on, Chief
An′ah,
30 Chief Dī′shon, Chief Ē′zer,
and Chief Dī′shan. These *were*

7 [b]Gen. 17:8; 28:4
8 [a]Gen. 32:3 [b]Gen. 36:1, 19
10 [a]1 Chr. 1:35
11 [1]*Zephi*, 1 Chr. 1:36
12 [a]Num. 24:20
14 [1]Or *Oholibamah*
16 [1]Sam. omits *Chief Korah*
18 [1]Or *Oholibamah*
20 [a]1 Chr. 1:38–42 [b]Gen. 14:6
22 [1]*Homam*, 1 Chr. 1:39
23 [1]*Alian*, 1 Chr. 1:40 [2]*Shephi*, 1 Chr. 1:40
24 [a]Lev. 19:19 [1]So with MT, Vg. (*hot springs*); LXX *Jamin*; Tg. *mighty men*; Talmud *mules*
25 [1]Or *Oholibamah*
26 [1]Heb. *Dishan* [2]*Hamran*, 1 Chr. 1:41
27 [1]*Jaakan*, 1 Chr. 1:42
28 [a]Job 1:1

the chiefs of the Hor′ītes, according to their chiefs in the
land of Sē′ir.
31 [a]Now these *were* the kings
who reigned in the land of Ē′dom
before any king reigned over the
children of Israel:
32 Bē′la the son of Bē′or reigned
in Ē′dom, and the name of his
city *was* Din′ha·bah.
33 And when Bē′la died, Jō′bab
the son of Zē′rah of Boz′rah
reigned in his place.
34 When Jō′bab died, Hū′sham
of the land of the Tē′man·ītes
reigned in his place.
35 And when Hū′sham died,
Hā′dad the son of Bē′dad, who
attacked Mid′i·an in the field of
Mō′ab, reigned in his place. And
the name of his city *was* Ā′vith.
36 When Hā′dad died, Sam′-
lah of Mas·rē′kah reigned in his
place.
37 And when Sam′lah died,
Saul of [a]Re·hō′both-*by*-the-River
reigned in his place.
38 When Saul died, Bā′al-Hā′-
nan the son of Ach′bor reigned
in his place.
39 And when Bā′al-Hā′nan the
son of Ach′bor died, [1]Hā′dar
reigned in his place; and the
name of his city *was* [2]Pā′ū. His
wife's name *was* Me·het′a·bel,
the daughter of Mā′tred, the
daughter of Mez′a·hab.
40 And these *were* the names of
the chiefs of Esau, according to
their families and their places,
by their names: Chief Tim′nah,
Chief [1]Al′vah, Chief Jē′theth,
41 Chief [1]A·hol·i·bā′mah, Chief
Ē′lah, Chief Pī′non,
42 Chief Kē′naz, Chief Tē′man,
Chief Mib′zar,
43 Chief Mag′di·el, and Chief
Ī′ram. These *were* the chiefs of
Ē′dom, according to their dwelling places in the land of their
possession. Esau *was* the father
of [1]the Ē′dom·ītes.

37

37 Now Jacob dwelt in the
land [a]where his father
was a [1]stranger, in the land of
Cā′naan.
2 This *is* the history of Jacob.
Joseph, *being* seventeen years
old, was feeding the flock with
his brothers. And the lad *was*
with the sons of Bil′hah and
the sons of Zil′pah, his father's
wives; and Joseph brought [a]a
bad report of them to his father.
3 Now Israel loved Joseph
more than all his children, because he *was* [a]the son of his old
age. Also he [b]made him a tunic
of *many* colors.
4 But when his brothers saw
that their father loved him more
than all his brothers, they [a]hated
him and could not speak peaceably to him.
5 Now Joseph had a dream,
and he told *it* to his brothers;
and they hated him even more.
6 So he said to them, "Please
hear this dream which I have
dreamed:
7 [a]"There we were, binding
sheaves in the field. Then behold, my sheaf arose and also
stood upright; and indeed your
sheaves stood all around and
bowed down to my sheaf."
8 And his brothers said to him,
"Shall you indeed reign over us?
Or shall you indeed have dominion over us?" So they hated him
even more for his dreams and
for his words.
9 Then he dreamed still another
dream and told it to his brothers,
and said, "Look, I have dreamed
another dream. And this time,

31 [a]1 Chr. 1:43
37 [a]Gen. 10:11
39 [1]Sam., Syr. *Hadad* and 1 Chr. 1:50 [2]*Pai*, 1 Chr. 1:50
40 [1]*Aliah*, 1 Chr. 1:51
41 [1]Or *Oholibamah*
43 [1]Heb. *Edom*

CHAPTER 37

1 [a]Gen. 17:8; 23:4; 28:4; 36:7 [1]*sojourner*, temporary resident
2 [a]1 Sam. 2:22–24
3 [a]Gen. 44:20 [b]Gen. 37:23, 32
4 [a]Gen. 27:41; 49:23
7 [a]Gen. 42:6, 9; 43:26; 44:14

[a]the sun, the moon, and the eleven
stars bowed down to me."
10 So he told *it* to his father
and his brothers; and his father rebuked him and said to
him, "What *is* this dream that
you have dreamed? Shall your
mother and I and [a]your brothers
indeed come to bow down to the
earth before you?"
11 And [a]his brothers envied
him, but his father [b]kept the
matter *in mind.*
12 Then his brothers went to
feed their father's flock in [a]Shē′-
chem.
13 And Israel said to Joseph,
"Are not your brothers feeding
the flock in Shē′chem? Come,
I will send you to them." So he
said to him, "Here I am."
14 Then he said to him, "Please
go and see if it is well with
your brothers and well with the
flocks, and bring back word to
me." So he sent him out of the
Valley of [a]Hē′bron, and he went
to Shē′chem.
15 Now a certain man found
him, and there he was, wandering in the field. And the man
asked him, saying, "What are
you seeking?"
16 So he said, "I am seeking my
brothers. [a]Please tell me where
th... are feeding *their flocks.*"
... the man said, "They
...d from here, for I
... 'Let us go to
... went after
...hem in

other, "Look, this [1]dreamer is
coming!
20 [a]"Come therefore, let us now
kill him and cast him into some
pit; and we shall say, 'Some
wild beast has devoured him.'
We shall see what will become
of his dreams!"
21 But [a]Reuben heard *it,* and he
delivered him out of their hands,
and said, "Let us not kill him."
22 And Reuben said to them,
"Shed no blood, *but* cast him
into this pit which *is* in the
wilderness, and do not lay a
hand on him"—that he might deliver him out of their hands, and
bring him back to his father.
23 So it came to pass, when Joseph had come to his brothers,
that they [a]stripped Joseph of his
tunic, the tunic of *many* colors
that *was* on him.
24 Then they took him and cast
him into a pit. And the pit *was*
empty; *there was* no water in it.
25 [a]And they sat down to eat
a meal. Then they lifted their
eyes and looked, and there was
a company of [b]Ish′ma·el·ītes,
coming from Gil′ē·ad with their
camels, bearing spices, [c]balm,
and myrrh, on their way to carry
them down to Egypt.
26 So Judah said to his brothers, "What profit *is there* if we
kill our brother and [a]conceal his
blood?
27 "Come and let us sell him to
the Ish′ma·el·ītes, and [a]let not
our hand be upon him, for he *is*
[b]our brother *and* [c]our flesh." And
his brothers listened.
28 Then [a]Mid′i·an·īte traders
passed by; so *the brothers* pulled
Joseph up and lifted him out of
the pit, [b]and sold him to the Ish′-
ma·el·ītes for [c]twenty *shekels* of

9 [a]Gen. 46:29; 47:25
10 [a]Gen. 27:29
11 [a]Acts 7:9 [b]Dan. 7:28
12 [a]Gen. 33:18–20
14 [a]Gen. 13:18; 23:2, 19; 35:27
16 [a]Song 1:7
17 [a]2 Kin. 6:13
18 [a]Mark 14:1
19 [1]Lit. *master of dreams*
20 [a]Prov. 1:11
21 [a]Gen. 42:22
23 [a]Matt. 27:28
25 [a]Prov. 30:20 [b]Gen. 16:11, 12; 37:28, 36; 39:1 [c]Jer. 8:22
26 [a]Gen. 37:20
27 [a]1 Sam. 18:17 [b]Gen. 42:21 [c]Gen. 29:14

silver. And they took Joseph to
Egypt.
29 Then Reuben returned to
the pit, and indeed Joseph *was*
not in the pit; and he [a]tore his
clothes.
30 And he returned to his brothers and said, "The lad [a]*is* no
more; and I, where shall I go?"
31 So they took [a]Joseph's tunic,
killed a kid of the goats, and
dipped the tunic in the blood.
32 Then they sent the tunic of
many colors, and they brought
it to their father and said, "We
have found this. Do you know
whether it *is* your son's tunic or
not?"
33 And he recognized it and
said, "*It is* my son's tunic. A
[a]wild beast has devoured him.
Without doubt Joseph is torn to
pieces."
34 Then Jacob [a]tore his clothes,
put sackcloth on his waist, and
[b]mourned for his son many days.
35 And all his sons and all his
daughters [a]arose to comfort him;
but he refused to be comforted,
and he said, "For [b]I shall go
down into the grave to my son in
mourning." Thus his father wept
for him.
36 Now [a]the [1]Mid'i·an·ītes had
sold him in Egypt to Pot'i·phar,
an officer of Pharaoh *and* captain of the guard.

38 It came to pass at that
time that Judah departed
from his brothers, and [a]visited
a certain A·dul'lam·īte whose
name *was* Hī'rah.
2 And Judah [a]saw there a
daughter of a certain Cā'naan·īte
whose name *was* [b]Shū'a, and he
married her and went in to her.
3 So she conceived and bore a
son, and he called his name [a]Er.
4 She conceived again and
bore a son, and she called his
name [a]Ō'nan.
5 And she conceived yet again
and bore a son, and called his
name [a]Shē'lah. He was at Chē'-
zib when she bore him.
6 Then Judah [a]took a wife for
Er his firstborn, and her name
was [b]Tā'mar.
7 But [a]Er, Judah's firstborn,
was wicked in the sight of the
LORD, [b]and the LORD killed him.
8 And Judah said to Ō'nan,
"Go in to [a]your brother's wife
and marry her, and raise up an
heir to your brother."
9 But Ō'nan knew that the heir
would not be [a]his; and it came
to pass, when he went in to his
brother's wife, that he emitted
on the ground, lest he should
give an heir to his brother.
10 And the thing which he did
[1]displeased the LORD; therefore
He killed [a]him also.
11 Then Judah said to Tā'mar
his daughter-in-law, [a]"Remain a
widow in your father's house till
my son Shē'lah is grown." For
he said, "Lest he also die like his
brothers." And Tā'mar went and
dwelt [b]in her father's house.
12 Now in the process of time
the daughter of Shū'a, Judah's
wife, died; and Judah [a]was comforted, and went up to his sheepshearers at Tim'nah, he and his
friend Hī'rah the A·dul'lam·īte.
13 And it was told Tā'mar, saying, "Look, your father-in-law is
going up [a]to Tim'nah to shear
his sheep."
14 So she took off her widow'
garments, covered h
a veil and wr
[a]sat i

29 [a]Job 1:20
30 [a]Gen. 42:13, 36
31 [a]Gen. 37:3, 23
33 [a]Gen. 37:20
34 [a]2 Sam. 3:31 [b]Gen. 50:10
35 [a]2 Sam. 12:17 [b]Gen. 25:8; 35:29; 42:38; 44:29, 31
36 [a]Gen. 39:1 [1]MT *Medanites*

CHAPTER 38

1 [a]2 Kin. 4:8
2 [a]Gen. 34:2 [b]1 Chr. 2:3
3 [a]Gen. 46:12
4 [a]Num. 26:19
5 [a]Num. 26:20
6 [a]Gen. 21:21 [b]Ruth 4:12
7 [a]Gen. 46:12 [b]1 Chr. 2:3
8 [a]Deut. 25:5, 6
9 [a]Deut. 25:6
10 [a]Gen. 46:12 [1]Lit. *was evil in the eyes of*
11 [a]Ruth 1:12, 13 [b]Lev. 22:13
12 [a]2 Sam. 13:39
13 [a]Josh. 15:10, 57
14 [a]Prov. 7:1

saw [b]that Shē′lah was grown,
and she was not given to him as
a wife.
15 When Judah saw her, he
thought she *was* a harlot, because she had covered her face.
16 Then he turned to her by the
way, and said, "Please let me
come in to you"; for he did not
know that she *was* his daughter-
in-law. So she said, "What will
you give me, that you may come
in to me?"
17 And he said, [a]"I will send a
young goat from the flock." So
she said, [b]"Will you give *me* a
pledge till you send *it*?"
18 Then he said, "What pledge
shall I give you?" So she said,
[a]"Your signet and cord, and your
staff that *is* in your hand." Then
he gave *them* to her, and went
in to her, and she conceived by
him.
19 So she arose and went
away, and [a]laid aside her veil
and put on the garments of her
widowhood.
20 And Judah sent the young
goat by the hand of his friend
the A·dul′lam·īte, to receive *his*
pledge from the woman's hand,
but he did not find her.
21 Then he asked the men of
that place, saying, "Where is
the harlot who *was* [1]openly by
the roadside?" And they said,
"There was no harlot in this
place."
22 So he returned to Judah and
said, "I cannot find her. Also, the
men of the place said there was
no harlot in this *place*."
23 Then Judah said, "Let her
take *them* for herself, lest we
be shamed; for I sent this young
goat and you have not found
her."

24 And it came to pass, about
three months after, that Judah
was told, saying, "Tā′mar your
daughter-in-law has [a]played the
harlot; furthermore she *is* [1]with
child by harlotry." So Judah
said, "Bring her out [b]and let her
be burned!"
25 When she *was* brought out,
she sent to her father-in-law,
saying, "By the man to whom
these belong, I *am* with child."
And she said, [a]"Please determine whose these *are*—the signet and cord, and staff."
26 So Judah [a]acknowledged
them and said, [b]"She has been
more righteous than I, because
[c]I did not give her to Shē′lah my
son." And he [d]never knew her
again.
27 Now it came to pass, at the
time for giving birth, that behold, twins *were* in her womb.
28 And so it was, when she was
giving birth, that *the one* put out
his hand; and the midwife took
a scarlet *thread* and bound it on
his hand, saying, "This one came
out first."
29 Then it happened, as he drew
back his hand, that his brother
came out unexpectedly; and
she said, "How did you break
through? *This* breach *be* upon
you!" Therefore his name was
called [a]Per′ez.[1]
30 Afterward his brother came
out who had the scarlet *thread*
on his hand. And his name was
called [a]Zē′rah.

39 Now Joseph had been
taken [a]down to Egypt.
And [b]Pot′i·phar, an officer of
Pharaoh, captain of the guard,
an Egyptian, [c]bought him from
the Ish′ma·el·ītes who had taken
him down there.

14 [b]Gen. 38:11, 26
17 [a]Ezek. 16:33 [b]Gen. 38:20
18 [a]Gen. 38:25; 41:42
19 [a]Gen. 38:14
21 [1]*in full view*
24 [a]Judg. 19:2 [b]Lev. 20:14; 21:9 [1]*pregnant*
25 [a]Gen. 37:32; 38:18
26 [a]Gen. 37:33 [b]1 Sam. 24:17 [c]Gen. 38:14 [d]Job 34:31, 32
29 [a]Gen. 46:12 [1]Lit. *Breach* or *Breakthrough*
30 [a]1 Chr. 2:4

CHAPTER 39
1 [a]Gen. 12:10; 43:15 [b]Gen. 37:36 [c]Gen. 37:28; 45:4

2 [a]The LORD was with Joseph,
and he was a successful man;
and he was in the house of his
master the Egyptian.
3 And his master saw that the
LORD *was* with him and that the
LORD [a]made all he did [1]to prosper in his hand.
4 So Joseph [a]found favor in
his sight, and served him. Then
he made him [b]overseer of his
house, and all *that* he had he
put [1]under his authority.
5 So it was, from the time *that*
he had made him overseer of his
house and all that he had, that
[a]the LORD blessed the Egyptian's
house for Joseph's sake; and the
blessing of the LORD was on all
that he had in the house and in
the field.
6 Thus he left all that he had
in Joseph's [1]hand, and he did
not know what he had except
for the [2]bread which he ate. Now
Joseph [a]was handsome in form
and appearance.
7 And it came to pass after these
things that his master's wife [1]cast
longing eyes on Joseph, and she
said, [a]"Lie with me."
8 But he refused and said to
his master's wife, "Look, my
master does not know what *is*
with me in the house, and he has
committed all that he has to my
hand.
9 "*There is* no one greater in
this house than I, nor has he
kept back anything from me but
you, because you *are* his wife.
[a]How then can I do this great
wickedness, and [b]sin against
God?"
10 So it was, as she spoke to Joseph day by day, that he [a]did not
heed her, to lie with her *or* to be
with her.

2 [a]Acts 7:9
3 [a]Ps. 1:3 [1]*to be a success*
4 [a]Gen. 18:3; 19:19; 39:21 [b]Gen. 24:2, 10; 39:8, 22; 41:40 [1]Lit. *in his hand*
5 [a]Gen. 18:26; 30:27
6 [a]1 Sam. 16:12 [1]Care [2]Food
7 [a]2 Sam. 13:11 [1]Lit. *lifted up her eyes toward*
9 [a]Prov. 6:29, 32 [b]Ps. 51:4
10 [a]Prov. 1:10
12 [a]Prov. 7:13
14 [a]Gen. 14:13; 41:12 [1]*laugh at*
17 [a]Ex. 23:1
19 [a]Prov. 6:34, 35
20 [a]Ps. 105:18 [b]Gen. 40:3, 15; 41:14
21 [a]Acts 7:9, 10 [1]Caused him to be viewed with favor by

11 But it happened about this
time, when Joseph went into the
house to do his work, and none
of the men of the house *was*
inside,
12 that she [a]caught him by his
garment, saying, "Lie with me."
But he left his garment in her
hand, and fled and ran outside.
13 And so it was, when she saw
that he had left his garment in
her hand and fled outside,
14 that she called to the men of
her house and spoke to them,
saying, "See, he has brought in
to us a [a]Hebrew to [1]mock us. He
came in to me to lie with me, and
I cried out with a loud voice.
15 "And it happened, when he
heard that I lifted my voice and
cried out, that he left his garment with me, and fled and went
outside."
16 So she kept his garment with
her until his master came home.
17 Then she [a]spoke to him with
words like these, saying, "The
Hebrew servant whom you
brought to us came in to me to
mock me;
18 "so it happened, as I lifted
my voice and cried out, that he
left his garment with me and
fled outside."
19 So it was, when his master
heard the words which his wife
spoke to him, saying, "Your servant did to me after this manner,"
that his [a]anger was aroused.
20 Then Joseph's master took
him and [a]put him into the
[b]prison, a place where the king's
prisoners *were* confined. And he
was there in the prison.
21 But the LORD was with Joseph
and showed him mercy, and He
[a]gave[1] him favor in the sight of
the keeper of the prison.

22 And the keeper of the prison
[a]committed to Joseph's hand all
the prisoners who *were* in the
prison; whatever they did there,
it was his doing.
23 The keeper of the prison did
not look into anything *that was*
under [1]*Joseph's* authority, because [a]the LORD was with him;
and whatever he did, the LORD
made *it* prosper.

40 It came to pass after these
things *that* the [a]butler
and the baker of the king of
Egypt offended their lord, the
king of Egypt.
2 And Pharaoh was [a]angry
with his two officers, the chief
butler and the chief baker.
3 [a]So he put them in custody in
the house of the captain of the
guard, in the prison, the place
where Joseph *was* confined.
4 And the captain of the guard
charged Joseph with them, and
he served them; so they were in
custody for a while.
5 Then the butler and the
baker of the king of Egypt, who
were confined in the prison,
[a]had a dream, both of them,
each man's dream in one night
and each man's dream with its
own interpretation.
6 And Joseph came in to them
in the morning and looked at
them, and saw that they *were*
[1]sad.
7 So he asked Pharaoh's officers who *were* with him in the
custody of his lord's house, saying, [a]"Why do you look *so* sad
today?"
8 And they said to him, [a]"We
each have had a dream, and
there is no interpreter of it." So
Joseph said to them, [b]"Do not
interpretations belong to God?
Tell *them* to me, please."
9 Then the chief butler told
his dream to Joseph, and said
to him, "Behold, in my dream a
vine *was* before me,
10 "and in the vine *were* three
branches; it *was* as though it
budded, its blossoms shot forth,
and its clusters brought forth
ripe grapes.
11 "Then Pharaoh's cup *was* in
my hand; and I took the grapes
and pressed them into Pharaoh's
cup, and placed the cup in Pharaoh's hand."
12 And Joseph said to him,
[a]"This *is* the interpretation of it:
The three branches [b]*are* three
days.
13 "Now within three days Pharaoh will [a]lift up your head and
restore you to your [1]place, and
you will put Pharaoh's cup in
his hand according to the former manner, when you were his
butler.
14 "But [a]remember me when
it is well with you, and [b]please
show kindness to me; make
mention of me to Pharaoh, and
get me out of this house.
15 "For indeed I was [a]stolen
away from the land of the Hebrews; [b]and also I have done
nothing here that they should
put me into the dungeon."
16 When the chief baker saw
that the interpretation was good,
he said to Joseph, "I also *was* in
my dream, and there *were* three
[1]white baskets on my head.
17 "In the uppermost basket
were all kinds of baked goods
for Pharaoh, and the birds ate
them out of the basket on my
head."
18 So Joseph answered and

22 [a]Gen. 39:4; 40:3, 4
23 [a]Gen. 39:2, 3 [1]Lit. *his hand*

CHAPTER 40

1 [a]Neh. 1:11
2 [a]Prov. 16:14
3 [a]Gen. 39:1, 20, 23; 41:10
5 [a]Gen. 37:5; 41:1
6 [1]*dejected*
7 [a]Neh. 2:2
8 [a]Gen. 41:15 [b][Dan. 2:11, 20–22, 27, 28, 47]
12 [a]Dan. 2:36; 4:18, 19 [b]Gen. 40:18; 42:17
13 [a]2 Kin. 25:27 [1]*position*
14 [a]Luke 23:42 [b]Josh. 2:12
15 [a]Gen. 37:26–28 [b]Gen. 39:20
16 [1]Or *baskets of white bread*

said, [a]"This *is* the interpretation
of it: The three baskets *are* three
days.
19 [a]"Within three days Pharaoh
will lift [1]off your head from you
and [b]hang you on a tree; and the
birds will eat your flesh from
you."
20 Now it came to pass on the
third day, *which was* Pharaoh's
[a]birthday, that he [b]made a feast
for all his servants; and he [c]lifted
up the head of the chief butler
and of the chief baker among
his servants.
21 Then he [a]restored the chief
butler to his butlership again,
and [b]he placed the cup in Pharaoh's hand.
22 But he [a]hanged the chief
baker, as Joseph had interpreted
to them.
23 Yet the chief butler did not
remember Joseph, but [a]forgot
him.

41

Then it came to pass, at
the end of two full years,
that [a]Pharaoh had a dream; and
behold, he stood by the river.
2 Suddenly there came up out
of the river seven cows, fine
looking and fat; and they fed in
the meadow.
3 Then behold, seven other
cows came up after them out of
the river, ugly and gaunt, and
stood by the *other* cows on the
bank of the river.
4 And the ugly and gaunt cows
ate up the seven fine looking and
fat cows. So Pharaoh awoke.
5 He slept and dreamed a second time; and suddenly seven
heads of grain came up on one
stalk, plump and good.
6 Then behold, seven thin
heads, blighted by the [a]east
wind, sprang up after them.
7 And the seven thin heads devoured the seven plump and full
heads. So Pharaoh awoke, and
indeed, *it was* a dream.
8 Now it came to pass in the
morning [a]that his spirit was
troubled, and he sent and called
for all [b]the magicians of Egypt
and all its [c]wise men. And Pharaoh told them his dreams, but
there was no one who could
interpret them for Pharaoh.
9 Then the [a]chief butler spoke
to Pharaoh, saying: "I remember
my faults this day.
10 "When Pharaoh was [a]angry
with his servants, [b]and put me
in custody in the house of the
captain of the guard, *both* me
and the chief baker,
11 [a]"we each had a dream in
one night, he and I. Each of us
dreamed according to the interpretation of his *own* dream.
12 "Now there *was* a young
[a]Hebrew man with us there, a
[b]servant of the captain of the
guard. And we told him, and he
[c]interpreted our dreams for us;
to each man he interpreted according to his *own* dream.
13 "And it came to pass, just [a]as
he interpreted for us, so it happened. He restored me to my
office, and he hanged him."
14 [a]Then Pharaoh sent and
called Joseph, and they [b]brought
him quickly [c]out of the dungeon;
and he shaved, [d]changed his
clothing, and came to Pharaoh.
15 And Pharaoh said to Joseph,
"I have had a dream, and *there is*
no one who can interpret it. [a]But
I have heard it said of you *that*
you can understand a dream, to
interpret it."
16 So Joseph answered Pharaoh, saying, [a]"*It is* not in me;

---

18 [a]Gen. 40:12
19 [a]Gen. 40:13 [b]Deut. 21:22 [1]Lit. *up*
20 [a]Matt. 14:6–10 [b]Mark 6:21 [c]Gen. 40:13, 19
21 [a]Gen. 40:13 [b]Neh. 2:1
22 [a]Gen. 40:19
23 [a]Eccl. 9:15, 16

CHAPTER 41

1 [a]Gen. 40:5
6 [a]Ex. 10:13
8 [a]Dan. 2:1, 3; 4:5, 19 [b]Ex. 7:11, 22 [c]Matt. 2:1
9 [a]Gen. 40:1, 14, 23
10 [a]Gen. 40:2, 3 [b]Gen. 39:20
11 [a]Gen. 40:5
12 [a]Gen. 39:14; 43:32 [b]Gen. 37:36 [c]Gen. 40:12
13 [a]Gen. 40:21, 22
14 [a]Ps. 105:20 [b]Dan. 2:25 [c][1 Sam. 2:8] [d]2 Kin. 25:27–29
15 [a]Dan. 5:16
16 [a]Dan. 2:30

[b]God will give Pharaoh an answer of peace."
17 Then Pharaoh said to Joseph: "Behold, [a]in my dream I
stood on the bank of the river.
18 "Suddenly seven cows came
up out of the river, fine looking and fat; and they fed in the
meadow.
19 "Then behold, seven other
cows came up after them, poor
and very ugly and gaunt, such
ugliness as I have never seen in
all the land of Egypt.
20 "And the gaunt and ugly
cows ate up the first seven, the
fat cows.
21 "When they had eaten them
up, no one would have known
that they had eaten them, for
they *were* just as ugly as at the
beginning. So I awoke.
22 "Also I saw in my dream, and
suddenly seven [1]heads came up
on one stalk, full and good.
23 "Then behold, seven heads,
withered, thin, *and* blighted by
the east wind, sprang up after
them.
24 "And the thin heads devoured
the seven good heads. So [a]I told
this to the magicians, but *there*
was no one who could explain
it to me."
25 Then Joseph said to Pharaoh, "The dreams of Pharaoh
are one; [a]God has shown Pharaoh what He *is* about to do:
26 "The seven good cows *are*
seven years, and the seven good
[1]heads *are* seven years; the
dreams *are* one.
27 "And the seven thin and ugly
cows which came up after them
are seven years, and the seven
empty heads blighted by the
east wind are [a]seven years of
famine.

16 [b]Dan. 2:22, 28, 47
17 [a]Gen. 41:1
22 [1]Heads of grain
24 [a]Is. 8:19
25 [a]Dan. 2:28, 29, 45
26 [1]Heads of grain
27 [a]2 Kin. 8:1
28 [a][Gen. 41:25, 32]
29 [a]Gen. 41:47
30 [a]Gen. 41:54, 56 [b]Gen. 47:13
32 [a]Num. 23:19
34 [a][Prov. 6:6–8] [1]*overseers*
35 [a]Gen. 41:48 [1]Lit. *hand*
36 [a]Gen. 47:15, 19 [1]Lit. *supply* [2]*be cut off*
37 [a]Acts 7:10
38 [a]Num. 27:18

28 [a]"This *is* the thing which I
have spoken to Pharaoh. God
has shown Pharaoh what He *is*
about to do.
29 "Indeed [a]seven years of great
plenty will come throughout all
the land of Egypt;
30 "but after them seven years
of famine will [a]arise, and all the
plenty will be forgotten in the
land of Egypt; and the famine
[b]will deplete the land.
31 "So the plenty will not be
known in the land because of
the famine following, for it *will*
be very severe.
32 "And the dream was repeated
to Pharaoh twice because the
[a]thing *is* established by God,
and God will shortly bring it to
pass.
33 "Now therefore, let Pharaoh
select a discerning and wise
man, and set him over the land
of Egypt.
34 "Let Pharaoh do *this*, and let
him appoint [1]officers over the
land, [a]to collect one-fifth *of the*
produce of the land of Egypt in
the seven plentiful years.
35 "And [a]let them gather all the
food of those good years that are
coming, and store up grain under
the [1]authority of Pharaoh, and let
them keep food in the cities.
36 "Then that food shall be as
a [1]reserve for the land for the
seven years of famine which
shall be in the land of Egypt,
that the land [a]may not [2]perish
during the famine."
37 So [a]the advice was good in
the eyes of Pharaoh and in the
eyes of all his servants.
38 And Pharaoh said to his servants, "Can we find *such a one*
as this, a man [a]in whom *is* the
Spirit of God?"

39 Then Pharaoh said to Joseph,
"Inasmuch as God has shown
you all this, *there is* no one as
discerning and wise as you.
40 [a]"You shall be [1]over my
house, and all my people shall
be ruled according to your word;
only in regard to the throne will
I be greater than you."
41 And Pharaoh said to Joseph,
"See, I have [a]set you over all the
land of Egypt."
42 Then Pharaoh [a]took his
signet ring off his hand and
put it on Joseph's hand; and
he [b]clothed him in garments of
fine linen [c]and put a gold chain
around his neck.
43 And he had him ride in the
second [a]chariot which he had;
[b]and they cried out before him,
"Bow the knee!" So he set him
[c]over all the land of Egypt.
44 Pharaoh also said to Joseph,
"I *am* Pharaoh, and without
your consent no man may lift
his hand or foot in all the land
of Egypt."
45 And Pharaoh called Joseph's
name [1]Zaph'nath-Pā·a·nē'ah.
And he gave him as a wife [a]As'-
e·nath, the daughter of Pō·ti'-
Phe·rah' priest of On. So Joseph
went out over *all* the land of
Egypt.
46 Joseph was thirty years old
when he [a]stood before Pharaoh
king of Egypt. And Joseph went
out from the presence of Pharaoh, and went throughout all
the land of Egypt.
47 Now in the seven plentiful
years the ground brought forth
[1]abundantly.
48 So he gathered up all the
food of the seven years which
were in the land of Egypt, and
laid up the food in the cities; he
laid up in every city the food
of the fields which surrounded
them.
49 Joseph gathered very much
grain, [a]as the sand of the sea,
until he stopped counting, for *it*
was immeasurable.
50 [a]And to Joseph were born
two sons before the years of
famine came, whom As'e·nath,
the daughter of Pō·ti'-Phe·rah'
priest of On, bore to him.
51 Joseph called the name of
the firstborn [1]Ma·nas'seh: "For
God has made me forget all my
toil and all my [a]father's house."
52 And the name of the second
he called [1]Ē'phra·im: "For God
has caused me to be [a]fruitful in
the land of my affliction."
53 Then the seven years of
plenty which were in the land of
Egypt ended,
54 [a]and the seven years of famine began to come, [b]as Joseph
had said. The famine was in
all lands, but in all the land of
Egypt there was bread.
55 So when all the land of
Egypt was famished, the people
cried to Pharaoh for bread. Then
Pharaoh said to all the Egyptians, "Go to Joseph; [a]whatever
he says to you, do."
56 The famine was over all the
face of the earth, and Joseph
opened [1]all the storehouses and
[a]sold to the Egyptians. And the
famine became severe in the
land of Egypt.
57 [a]So all countries came to
Joseph in Egypt to [b]buy *grain*,
because the famine was severe
in all lands.

42

When [a]Jacob saw that
there was grain in Egypt,
Jacob said to his sons, "Why do
you look at one another?"

40 [a]Ps. 105:21 [1]In charge of
41 [a]Dan. 6:3
42 [a]Esth. 3:10 [b]Esth. 8:2, 15 [c]Dan. 5:7, 16, 29
43 [a]Gen. 46:29 [b]Esth. 6:9 [c]Gen. 42:6
45 [a]Gen. 46:20 [1]Probably Egyptian for *God Speaks and He Lives*
46 [a]1 Sam. 16:21
47 [1]Lit. *by handfuls*
49 [a]Gen. 22:17
50 [a]Gen. 46:20; 48:5
51 [a]Ps. 45:10 [1]Lit. *Making Forgetful*
52 [a]Gen. 17:6; 28:3; 49:22 [1]Lit. *Fruitfulness*
54 [a]Acts 7:11 [b]Gen. 41:30
55 [a]John 2:5
56 [a]Gen. 42:6 [1]Lit. *all that was in them*
57 [a]Ezek. 29:12 [b]Gen. 27:28, 37; 42:3

CHAPTER 42

1 [a]Acts 7:12

2 And he said, "Indeed I have heard that there is grain in Egypt; go down to that place and buy for us there, that we may [a]live and not die."

3 So Joseph's ten brothers went down to buy grain in Egypt.

4 But Jacob did not send Joseph's brother Benjamin with his brothers, for he said, [a]"Lest some calamity befall him."

5 And the sons of Israel went to buy *grain* among those who journeyed, for the famine was [a]in the land of Cā'naan.

6 Now Joseph *was* governor [a]over the land; and it was he who sold to all the people of the land. And Joseph's brothers came and [b]bowed down before him with *their* faces to the earth.

7 Joseph saw his brothers and recognized them, but he acted as [a]a stranger to them and spoke [1]roughly to them. Then he said to them, "Where do you come from?" And they said, "From the land of Cā'naan to buy food."

8 So Joseph recognized his brothers, but they did not recognize him.

9 Then Joseph [a]remembered the dreams which he had dreamed about them, and said to them, "You *are* spies! You have come to see the [1]nakedness of the land!"

10 And they said to him, "No, my lord, but your servants have come to buy food.

11 "We *are* all one man's sons; we *are* honest *men;* your servants are not spies."

12 But he said to them, "No, but you have come to see the nakedness of the land."

13 And they said, "Your servants *are* twelve brothers, the sons of one man in the land of Cā'naan; and in fact, the youngest *is* with our father today, and one [a]*is* no more."

14 But Joseph said to them, "It *is* as I spoke to you, saying, 'You *are* spies!'

15 "In this *manner* you shall be tested: [a]By the life of Pharaoh, you shall not leave this place unless your youngest brother comes here.

16 "Send one of you, and let him bring your brother; and you shall be [1]kept in prison, that your words may be tested to see whether *there is* any truth in you; or else, by the life of Pharaoh, surely you *are* spies!"

17 So he [1]put them all together in prison [a]three days.

18 Then Joseph said to them the third day, "Do this and live, [a]*for* I fear God:

19 "If you *are* honest *men,* let one of your brothers be confined to your prison house; but you, go and carry grain for the famine of your houses.

20 "And [a]bring your youngest brother to me; so your words will be verified, and you shall not die." And they did so.

21 Then they said to one another, [a]"We *are* truly guilty concerning our brother, for we saw the anguish of his soul when he pleaded with us, and we would not hear; [b]therefore this distress has come upon us."

22 And Reuben answered them, saying, [a]"Did I not speak to you, saying, 'Do not sin against the boy'; and you would not listen? Therefore behold, his blood is now [b]required of us."

23 But they did not know that

2 [a]Gen. 43:8
4 [a]Gen. 42:38
5 [a]Acts 7:11
6 [a]Gen. 41:41, 55 [b]Gen. 37:7–10; 41:43
7 [a]Gen. 45:1, 2 [1]*harshly*
9 [a]Gen. 37:5–9 [1]Exposed parts
13 [a]Gen. 37:30; 42:32; 44:20
15 [a]1 Sam. 1:26; 17:55
16 [1]Lit. *bound*
17 [a]Gen. 40:4, 7, 12 [1]Lit. *gathered*
18 [a]Lev. 25:43
20 [a]Gen. 42:34; 43:5; 44:23
21 [a]Hos. 5:15 [b]Prov. 21:13
22 [a]Gen. 37:21, 22, 29 [b]Gen. 9:5, 6

Joseph understood *them,* for
he spoke to them through an
interpreter.
24 And he turned himself away
from them and [a]wept. Then he
returned to them again, and
talked with them. And he took
[b]Sim′ē·on from them and bound
him before their eyes.
25 Then Joseph [a]gave a command to fill their sacks with
grain, to [b]restore every man's
money to his sack, and to give
them provisions for the journey.
[c]Thus he did for them.
26 So they loaded their donkeys
with the grain and departed
from there.
27 But as [a]one of *them* opened
his sack to give his donkey feed
at the encampment, he saw his
money; and there it was, in the
mouth of his sack.
28 So he said to his brothers,
"My money has been restored,
and there it is, in my sack!"
Then their hearts [1]failed *them*
and they were afraid, saying to
one another, "What *is* this *that*
God has done to us?"
29 Then they went to Jacob
their father in the land of Cā′-
naan and told him all that had
happened to them, saying:
30 "The man *who is* lord of the
land [a]spoke [1]roughly to us, and
took us for spies of the country.
31 "But we said to him, 'We *are*
honest *men;* we are not spies.
32 'We *are* twelve brothers,
sons of our father; one *is* no
more, and the youngest *is* with
our father this day in the land of
Cā′naan.'
33 "Then the man, the lord of
the country, said to us, [a]'By this
I will know that you *are* honest
men: Leave one of your brothers
here with me, take *food for* the
famine of your households, and
be gone.
34 'And bring your [a]youngest
brother to me; so I shall know
that you *are* not spies, but *that*
you *are* honest *men.* I will grant
your brother to you, and you
may [b]trade in the land.' "
35 Then it happened as they
emptied their sacks, that surprisingly [a]each man's bundle of
money *was* in his sack; and
when they and their father saw
the bundles of money, they were
afraid.
36 And Jacob their father said
to them, "You have [a]bereaved
me: Joseph is no *more,* Sim′ē·on
is no *more,* and you want to take
[b]Benjamin. All these things are
against me."
37 Then Reuben spoke to his
father, saying, "Kill my two sons
if I do not bring him *back* to you;
put him in my hands, and I will
bring him back to you."
38 But he said, "My son shall
not go down with you, for [a]his
brother is dead, and he is left
alone. [b]If any calamity should
befall him along the way in
which you go, then you would
[c]bring down my gray hair with
sorrow to the grave."

43 Now the famine *was*
[a]severe in the land.
2 And it came to pass, when
they had eaten up the grain
which they had brought from
Egypt, that their father said to
them, "Go [a]back, buy us a little
food."
3 But Judah spoke to him, saying, "The man solemnly warned
us, saying, 'You shall not see my
face unless your [a]brother *is* with
you.'

24 [a]Gen. 43:30; 45:14, 15 [b]Gen. 34:25, 30; 43:14, 23
25 [a]Gen. 44:1 [b]Gen. 43:12 [c][Rom. 12:17, 20, 21]
27 [a]Gen. 43:21, 22
28 [1]*sank*
30 [a]Gen. 42:7 [1]*harshly*
33 [a]Gen. 42:15, 19, 20
34 [a]Gen. 42:20; 43:3, 5 [b]Gen. 34:10
35 [a]Gen. 43:12, 15, 21
36 [a]Gen. 43:14 [b][Rom. 8:28, 31]
38 [a]Gen. 37:22; 42:13; 44:20, 28 [b]Gen. 42:4; 44:29 [c]Gen. 37:35; 44:31

CHAPTER 43

1 [a]Gen. 41:54, 57; 42:5; 45:6, 11
2 [a]Gen. 42:2; 44:25
3 [a]Gen. 42:20; 43:5; 44:23

4 "If you send our brother with us, we will go down and buy you food.

5 "But if you will not send *him*, we will not go down; for the man said to us, 'You shall not see my face unless your brother *is* with you.' "

6 And Israel said, "Why did you deal *so* [1]wrongfully with me *as* to tell the man whether you had still *another* brother?"

7 But they said, "The man asked us pointedly about ourselves and our family, saying, '*Is* your father still alive? Have you *another* brother?' And we told him according to these words. Could we possibly have known that he would say, 'Bring your brother down'?"

8 Then Judah said to Israel his father, "Send the lad with me, and we will arise and go, that we may [a]live and not die, both we and you *and* also our little ones.

9 "I myself will be surety for him; from my hand you shall require him. [a]If I do not bring him *back* to you and set him before you, then let me bear the blame forever.

10 "For if we had not lingered, surely by now we would have returned this second time."

11 And their father Israel said to them, "If *it must be* so, then do this: Take some of the best fruits of the land in your vessels and [a]carry down a present for the man—a little [b]balm and a little honey, spices and myrrh, pistachio nuts and almonds.

12 "Take double money in your hand, and take back in your hand the money [a]that was returned in the mouth of your sacks; perhaps it was an oversight.

6 [1]Lit. *wickedly*
8 [a]Gen. 42:2; 47:19
9 [a]Gen. 42:37; 44:32
11 [a]Gen. 32:20; 33:10; 43:25, 26 [b]Jer. 8:22
12 [a]Gen. 42:25, 35; 43:21, 22
14 [a]Gen. 17:1; 28:3; 35:11; 48:3 [b]Ps. 106:46 [c]Esth. 4:16
15 [a]Gen. 39:1; 46:3, 6
16 [a]Gen. 24:2; 39:4; 44:1 [1]Lit. *a slaughter*
18 [a]Gen. 42:28 [1]Lit. *roll himself upon us*
20 [a]Gen. 42:3, 10
21 [a]Gen. 42:27, 35

13 "Take your brother also, and arise, go back to the man.

14 "And may God [a]Almighty [b]give you mercy before the man, that he may release your other brother and Benjamin. [c]If I am bereaved, I am bereaved!"

15 So the men took that present and Benjamin, and they took double money in their hand, and arose and went [a]down to Egypt; and they stood before Joseph.

16 When Joseph saw Benjamin with them, he said to the [a]steward of his house, "Take *these* men to my home, and slaughter [1]an animal and make ready; for *these* men will dine with me at noon."

17 Then the man did as Joseph ordered, and the man brought the men into Joseph's house.

18 Now the men were [a]afraid because they were brought into Joseph's house; and they said, "*It is* because of the money, which was returned in our sacks the first time, that we are brought in, so that he may [1]make a case against us and seize us, to take us as slaves with our donkeys."

19 When they drew near to the steward of Joseph's house, they talked with him at the door of the house,

20 and said, "O sir, [a]we indeed came down the first time to buy food;

21 "but [a]it happened, when we came to the encampment, that we opened our sacks, and there, *each* man's money *was* in the mouth of his sack, our money in full weight; so we have brought it back in our hand.

22 "And we have brought down other money in our hands to buy food. We do not know who put our money in our sacks."

23 But he said, "Peace *be* with you, do not be afraid. Your God and the God of your father has given you treasure in your sacks; I had your money." Then he brought [a]Sim'ē·on out to them.

24 So the man brought the men into Joseph's house and [a]gave *them* water, and they washed their feet; and he gave their donkeys feed.

25 Then they made the present ready for Joseph's coming at noon, for they heard that they would eat bread there.

26 And when Joseph came home, they brought him the present which *was* in their hand into the house, and [a]bowed down before him to the earth.

27 Then he asked them about *their* well-being, and said, "*Is* your father well, the old man [a]of whom you spoke? *Is* he still alive?"

28 And they answered, "Your servant our father *is* in good health; he *is* still alive." [a]And they bowed their heads down and prostrated themselves.

29 Then he lifted his eyes and saw his brother Benjamin, [a]his mother's son, and said, "*Is* this your younger brother [b]of whom you spoke to me?" And he said, "God be gracious to you, my son."

30 Now [a]his heart yearned for his brother; so Joseph made haste and sought *somewhere* to weep. And he went into *his* chamber and [b]wept there.

31 Then he washed his face and came out; and he restrained himself, and said, "Serve the [a]bread."

32 So they set him a place by himself, and them by themselves, and the Egyptians who ate with him by themselves; because the Egyptians could not eat food with the [a]Hebrews, for that *is* [b]an abomination to the Egyptians.

33 And they sat before him, the firstborn according to his [a]birthright and the youngest according to his youth; and the men looked in astonishment at one another.

34 Then he took servings to them from before him, but Benjamin's serving was [a]five times as much as any of theirs. So they drank and were merry with him.

44 And he commanded [1]the [a]steward of his house, saying, [b]"Fill the men's sacks with food, as much as they can carry, and put each man's money in the mouth of his sack.

2 "Also put my cup, the silver cup, in the mouth of the sack of the youngest, and his grain money." So he did according to the word that Joseph had spoken.

3 As soon as the morning dawned, the men were sent away, they and their donkeys.

4 When they had gone out of the city, *and* were not *yet* far off, Joseph said to his steward, "Get up, follow the men; and when you overtake them, say to them, 'Why have you [a]repaid evil for good?

5 '*Is* not this *the one* from which my lord drinks, and with which he indeed practices divination? You have done evil in so doing.' "

6 So he overtook them, and he spoke to them these same words.

7 And they said to him, "Why

23 [a]Gen. 42:24
24 [a]Gen. 18:4; 19:2; 24:32
26 [a]Gen. 37:7, 10; 42:6; 44:14
27 [a]Gen. 29:6; 42:11, 13; 43:7; 45:3
28 [a]Gen. 37:7, 10
29 [a]Gen. 35:17, 18 [b]Gen. 42:13
30 [a]1 Kin. 3:26 [b]Gen. 42:24; 45:2, 14, 15; 46:29
31 [a]Gen. 43:25
32 [a]Gen. 41:12 [b]Gen. 46:34
33 [a]Gen. 27:36; 42:7
34 [a]Gen. 35:24; 45:22

CHAPTER 44

1 [a]Gen. 43:16 [b]Gen. 42:25 [1]Lit. *the one over*
4 [a]1 Sam. 25:21

does my lord say these words?
Far be it from us that your servants should do such a thing.
8 "Look, we brought back to
you from the land of Cā′naan
[a]the money which we found in
the mouth of our sacks. How
then could we steal silver or
gold from your lord's house?
9 "With whomever of your servants it is found, [a]let him die,
and we also will be my lord's
slaves."
10 And he said, "Now also *let*
it *be* according to your words;
he with whom it is found shall
be my slave, and you shall be
blameless."
11 Then each man speedily let
down his sack to the ground,
and each opened his sack.
12 So he searched. He began
with the oldest and [1]left off with
the youngest; and the cup was
found in Benjamin's sack.
13 Then they [a]tore their clothes,
and each man loaded his donkey and returned to the city.
14 So Judah and his brothers
came to Joseph's house, and he
was still there; and they [a]fell before him on the ground.
15 And Joseph said to them,
"What deed *is* this you have
done? Did you not know that
such a man as I can certainly
practice divination?"
16 Then Judah said, "What shall
we say to my lord? What shall
we speak? Or how shall we clear
ourselves? God has [a]found out
the iniquity of your servants;
here [b]we are, my lord's slaves,
both we and *he* also with whom
the cup was found."
17 But he said, [a]"Far be it from
me that I should do so; the man
in whose hand the cup was
found, he shall be my slave. And
as for you, go up in peace to
your father."
18 Then Judah came near to
him and said: "O my lord, please
let your servant speak a word in
my lord's hearing, and [a]do not
let your anger burn against your
servant; for you *are* even like
Pharaoh.
19 "My lord asked his servants,
saying, 'Have you a father or a
brother?'
20 "And we said to my lord, 'We
have a father, an old man, and
[a]a child of *his* old age, *who is*
young; his brother is [b]dead, and
he [c]alone is left of his mother's
children, and his [d]father loves
him.'
21 "Then you said to your servants, [a]'Bring him down to me,
that I may set my eyes on him.'
22 "And we said to my lord,
'The lad cannot leave his father,
for *if* he should leave his father,
his father would die.'
23 "But you said to your servants, [a]'Unless your youngest
brother comes down with you,
you shall see my face no more.'
24 "So it was, when we went up
to your servant my father, that
we told him the words of my
lord.
25 "And [a]our father said, 'Go
back *and* buy us a little food.'
26 "But we said, 'We cannot go
down; if our youngest brother is
with us, then we will go down;
for we may not see the man's
face unless our youngest brother
is with us.'
27 "Then your servant my father said to us, 'You know that
[a]my wife bore me two sons;
28 'and the one went out from
me, and I said, [a]"Surely he is

8 [a]Gen. 43:21
9 [a]Gen. 31:32
12 [1]*finished with*
13 [a]2 Sam. 1:11
14 [a]Gen. 37:7, 10
16 [a][Num. 32:23] [b]Gen. 44:9
17 [a]Prov. 17:15
18 [a]Ex. 32:22
20 [a]Gen. 37:3; 43:8; 44:30 [b]Gen. 42:38 [c]Gen. 46:19 [d]Gen. 42:4
21 [a]Gen. 42:15, 20
23 [a]Gen. 43:3, 5
25 [a]Gen. 43:2
27 [a]Gen. 30:22–24; 35:16–18; 46:19
28 [a]Gen. 37:31–35

torn to pieces"; and I have not seen him since.
29 'But if you [a]take this one also from me, and calamity befalls him, you shall bring down my gray hair with sorrow to the grave.'
30 "Now therefore, when I come to your servant my father, and the lad *is* not with us, since [a]his life is bound up in the lad's life,
31 "it will happen, when he sees that the lad *is* not *with us,* that he will die. So your servants will bring down the gray hair of your servant our father with sorrow to the grave.
32 "For your servant became surety for the lad to my father, saying, [a]'If I do not bring him *back* to you, then I shall bear the blame before my father forever.'
33 "Now therefore, please [a]let your servant remain instead of the lad as a slave to my lord, and let the lad go up with his brothers.
34 "For how shall I go up to my father if the lad *is* not with me, lest perhaps I see the evil that would [1]come upon my father?"

45 Then Joseph could not restrain himself before all those who stood by him, and he cried out, "Make everyone go out from me!" So no one stood with him [a]while Joseph made himself known to his brothers.
2 And he [a]wept aloud, and the Egyptians and the house of Pharaoh heard *it.*
3 Then Joseph said to his brothers, [a]"I *am* Joseph; does my father still live?" But his brothers could not answer him, for they were dismayed in his presence.
4 And Joseph said to his brothers, "Please come near to me." So they came near. Then he said: "I *am* Joseph your brother, [a]whom you sold into Egypt.
5 "But now, do not therefore be grieved or angry with yourselves because you sold me here; [a]for God sent me before you to preserve life.
6 "For these two years the [a]famine *has been* in the land, and *there are* still five years in which *there will be* neither plowing nor harvesting.
7 "And God [a]sent me before you to preserve a [1]posterity for you in the earth, and to save your lives by a great deliverance.
8 "So now *it was* not you *who* sent me here, but [a]God; and He has made me [b]a father to Pharaoh, and lord of all his house, and a [c]ruler throughout all the land of Egypt.
9 "Hurry and go up to my father, and say to him, 'Thus says your son Joseph: "God has made me lord of all Egypt; come down to me, do not [1]tarry.
10 [a]"You shall dwell in the land of Gō′shen, and you shall be near to me, you and your children, your children's children, your flocks and your herds, and all that you have.
11 "There I will [a]provide for you, lest you and your household, and all that you have, come to poverty; for *there are* still five years of famine." '
12 "And behold, your eyes and the eyes of my brother Benjamin see that *it is* [a]my mouth that speaks to you.
13 "So you shall tell my father of all my glory in Egypt, and of all that you have seen; and you

29 [a]Gen. 42:36, 38; 44:31
30 [a][1 Sam. 18:1; 25:29]
32 [a]Gen. 43:9
33 [a]Ex. 32:32
34 [1]Lit. *find*

CHAPTER 45

1 [a]Acts 7:13
2 [a]Gen. 43:30; 46:29
3 [a]Acts 7:13
4 [a]Gen. 37:28; 39:1
5 [a]Gen. 45:7, 8; 50:20
6 [a]Gen. 43:1; 47:4, 13
7 [a]Gen. 45:5; 50:20 [1]*remnant*
8 [a][Rom. 8:28] [b]Is. 22:21 [c]Gen. 41:43; 42:6
9 [1]*delay*
10 [a]Gen. 46:28, 34; 47:1, 6
11 [a]Gen. 47:12
12 [a]Gen. 42:23

shall hurry and [a]bring my father
down here."
14 Then he fell on his brother
Benjamin's neck and wept, and
Benjamin wept on his neck.
15 Moreover he [a]kissed all his
brothers and wept over them,
and after that his brothers talked
with him.
16 Now the report of it was
heard in Pharaoh's house, saying, "Joseph's brothers have
come." So it pleased Pharaoh
and his servants well.
17 And Pharaoh said to Joseph,
"Say to your brothers, 'Do this:
Load your animals and depart;
go to the land of Cā′naan.
18 'Bring your father and your
households and come to me; I
will give you the best of the land
of Egypt, and you will eat [a]the
[1]fat of the land.
19 'Now you are commanded—
do this: Take carts out of the
land of Egypt for your little ones
and your wives; bring your father and come.
20 'Also do not be concerned
about your goods, for the best of
all the land of Egypt *is* yours.' "
21 Then the sons of Israel did
so; and Joseph gave them [a]carts,[1]
according to the command of
Pharaoh, and he gave them provisions for the journey.
22 He gave to all of them, to
each man, [a]changes of garments; but to Benjamin he gave
three hundred *pieces* of silver
and [b]five changes of garments.
23 And he sent to his father
these *things:* ten donkeys loaded
with the good things of Egypt,
and ten female donkeys loaded
with grain, bread, and food for
his father for the journey.
24 So he sent his brothers away,
and they departed; and he said
to them, "See that you do not become troubled along the way."
25 Then they went up out of
Egypt, and came to the land of
Cā′naan to Jacob their father.
26 And they told him, saying,
"Joseph *is* still alive, and he
is governor over all the land
of Egypt." [a]And Jacob's heart
stood still, because he did not
believe them.
27 But when they told him all
the words which Joseph had
said to them, and when he saw
the carts which Joseph had sent
to carry him, the spirit [a]of Jacob
their father revived.
28 Then Israel said, "*It is*
enough. Joseph my son *is* still
alive. I will go and see him before I die."

46

So Israel took his journey
with all that he had, and
came to [a]Bē·er·shē′ba, and offered sacrifices [b]to the God of
his father Isaac.
2 Then God spoke to Israel
[a]in the visions of the night, and
said, "Jacob, Jacob!" And he
said, "Here I am."
3 So He said, "I *am* God, [a]the
God of your father; do not fear
to go down to Egypt, for I will
[b]make of you a great nation
there.
4 [a]"I will go down with you
to Egypt, and I will also surely
[b]bring you up *again;* and [c]Joseph
[1]will put his hand on your eyes."
5 Then [a]Jacob arose from
Bē·er·shē′ba; and the sons of
Israel carried their father Jacob,
their little ones, and their wives,
in the [1]carts [b]which Pharaoh had
sent to carry him.
6 So they took their livestock
and their goods, which they had

13 [a]Acts 7:14
15 [a]Gen. 48:10
18 [a]Gen. 27:28; 47:6 [1]The choicest produce
21 [a]Gen. 45:19; 46:5 [1]*wagons*
22 [a]2 Kin. 5:5 [b]Gen. 43:34
26 [a]Job 29:24
27 [a]Judg. 15:19

CHAPTER 46

1 [a]Gen. 21:31, 33; 26:32, 33; 28:10 [b]Gen. 26:24, 25; 28:13; 31:42; 32:9
2 [a]Gen. 15:1; 22:11; 31:11
3 [a]Gen. 17:1; 28:13 [b]Deut. 26:5
4 [a]Gen. 28:15; 31:3; 48:21 [b]Gen. 15:16; 50:12, 24, 25 [c]Gen. 50:1 [1]Will close your eyes when you die
5 [a]Acts 7:15 [b]Gen. 45:19–21 [1]*wagons*

acquired in the land of Cā′naan,
and went to Egypt, [a]Jacob and
all his descendants with him.
7 His sons and his sons′ sons,
his daughters and his sons′
daughters, and all his descendants he brought with him to
Egypt.
8 Now [a]these *were* the names
of the children of Israel, Jacob
and his sons, who went to Egypt:
[b]Reuben *was* Jacob′s firstborn.
9 The [a]sons of Reuben *were*
Hā′noch, Pal′lū, Hez′ron, and
Car′mī.
10 [a]The sons of Sim′ē·on *were*
[1]Je·mū′el, Jā′min, Ō′had, [2]Jā′-
chin, [3]Zō′har, and Shā′ūl, the
son of a Cā′naan·īte woman.
11 The sons of [a]Levi *were* Ger′-
shon, Kō′hath, and Me·rar′ī.
12 The sons of [a]Judah *were* [b]Er,
Ō′nan, Shē′lah, Per′ez, and Zē′-
rah (but Er and Ō′nan died in
the land of Cā′naan). [c]The sons
of Per′ez were Hez′ron and Hā′-
mul.
13 The sons of Is′sa·char *were*
Tō′la, [1]Pū′vah, [2]Job, and Shim′-
ron.
14 The [a]sons of Zeb′ū·lun *were*
Sē′red, Ē′lon, and Jah′lē·el.
15 These *were* the [a]sons of
Leah, whom she bore to Jacob
in Pad′an Ar′am, with his daughter Dī′nah. All the persons, his
sons and his daughters, *were*
thirty-three.
16 The sons of Gad *were* [1]Ziph′-
i·on, Hag′gī, Shū′nī, [2]Ez′bon, Ē′rī,
[3]A·rō′dī, and A·rē′lī.
17 [a]The sons of Ash′er *were*
Jim′nah, Ish′ū·ah, Is′ū·ī, Bē·rī′ah,
and Sē′rah, their sister. And the
sons of Bē·rī′ah *were* Hē′ber and
Mal′chi·el.
18 [a]These *were* the sons of Zil′-
pah, [b]whom Lā′ban gave to Leah
his daughter; and these she bore
to Jacob: sixteen persons.
19 The [a]sons of Rachel, [b]Ja-
cob′s wife, *were* Joseph and
Benjamin.
20 [a]And to Joseph in the land
of Egypt were born Ma·nas′seh
and Ē′phra·im, whom As′e·nath,
the daughter of Pō·ti′-Phe·rah′
priest of On, bore to him.
21 [a]The sons of Benjamin *were*
Bē′lah, Bē′cher, Ash′bel, Gē′ra,
Nā′a·man, [b]Ē′hī, Rosh, [c]Mup′-
pim, [1]Hup′pim, and Ard.
22 These *were* the sons of Rachel, who were born to Jacob:
fourteen persons in all.
23 The son of Dan *was* [1]Hū′-
shim.
24 [a]The sons of Naph′ta·lī *were*
[1]Jah′zē·el, Gū′nī, Jē′zer, and
[2]Shil′lem.
25 [a]These *were* the sons of Bil′-
hah, [b]whom Lā′ban gave to Rachel his daughter, and she bore
these to Jacob: seven persons
in all.
26 [a]All the persons who went
with Jacob to Egypt, who came
from his body, [b]besides Jacob′s
sons′ wives, *were* sixty-six persons in all.
27 And the sons of Joseph who
were born to him in Egypt *were*
two persons. [a]All the persons of
the house of Jacob who went to
Egypt were seventy.
28 Then he sent Judah before
him to Joseph, [a]to point out before him *the way* to Gō′shen.
And they came [b]to the land of
Gō′shen.
29 So Joseph made ready his
[a]chariot and went up to Gō′shen
to meet his father Israel; and he
presented himself to him, and
[b]fell on his neck and wept on his
neck a good while.

6 [a]Deut. 26:5
8 [a]Ex. 1:1–4 [b]Num. 26:4, 5
9 [a]Ex. 6:14
10 [a]Ex. 6:15 [1]*Nemuel,* 1 Chr. 4:24 [2]*Jarib,* 1 Chr. 4:24 [3]*Zerah,* 1 Chr. 4:24
11 [a]1 Chr. 6:1, 16
12 [a]1 Chr. 2:3; 4:21 [b]Gen. 38:3, 7, 10 [c]Gen. 38:29
13 [1]*Puah,* Num. 26:23; 1 Chr. 7:1 [2]*Jashub,* Num. 26:24; 1 Chr. 7:1
14 [a]Num. 26:26
15 [a]Gen. 35:23; 49:31
16 [1]Sam., LXX *Zephon* and Num. 26:15 [2]*Ozni,* Num. 26:16 [3]*Arod,* Num. 26:17
17 [a]1 Chr. 7:30
18 [a]Gen. 30:10; 37:2 [b]Gen. 29:24
19 [a]Gen. 35:24 [b]Gen. 44:27
20 [a]Gen. 41:45, 50–52; 48:1
21 [a]1 Chr. 7:6; 8:1 [b]Num. 26:38 [c]Num. 26:39 [1]*Hupham,* Num. 26:39
23 [1]*Shuham,* Num. 26:42
24 [a]Num. 26:48 [1]*Jahziel,* 1 Chr. 7:13 [2]*Shallum,* 1 Chr. 7:13
25 [a]Gen. 30:5, 7 [b]Gen. 29:29
26 [a]Ex. 1:5 [b]Gen. 35:11
27 [a]Deut. 10:22
28 [a]Gen. 31:21 [b]Gen. 47:1
29 [a]Gen. 41:43 [b]Gen. 45:14, 15

30 And Israel said to Joseph,
[a]"Now let me die, since I have
seen your face, because you *are*
still alive."
31 Then Joseph said to his brothers and to his father's household,
[a]"I will go up and tell Pharaoh,
and say to him, 'My brothers and
those of my father's house, who
were in the land of Cā′naan, have
come to me.
32 'And the men *are* [a]shepherds,
for their occupation has been
to feed livestock; and they have
brought their flocks, their herds,
and all that they have.'
33 "So it shall be, when Pharaoh calls you and says, [a]'What
is your occupation?'
34 "that you shall say, 'Your
servants' [a]occupation has been
with livestock [b]from our youth
even till now, both we *and* also
our fathers,' that you may dwell
in the land of Gō′shen; for every
shepherd *is* [c]an[1] abomination to
the Egyptians."

47 Then Joseph [a]went and
told Pharaoh, and said,
"My father and my brothers,
their flocks and their herds and
all that they possess, have come
from the land of Cā′naan; and
indeed they *are* in [b]the land of
Gō′shen."
2 And he took five men
from among his brothers and
[a]presented them to Pharaoh.
3 Then Pharaoh said to his
brothers, [a]"What *is* your occupation?" And they said to Pharaoh,
[b]"Your servants *are* shepherds,
both we *and* also our fathers."
4 And they said to Pharaoh,
[a]"We have come to dwell in the
land, because your servants
have no pasture for their flocks,
[b]for the famine *is* severe in the
land of Cā′naan. Now therefore,
please let your servants [c]dwell
in the land of Gō′shen."
5 Then Pharaoh spoke to Joseph, saying, "Your father and
your brothers have come to
you.
6 [a]"The land of Egypt *is* before you. Have your father and
brothers dwell in the best of the
land; let them dwell [b]in the land
of Gō′shen. And if you know *any*
competent men among them,
then make them chief herdsmen
over my livestock."
7 Then Joseph brought in his
father Jacob and set him before
Pharaoh; and Jacob [a]blessed
Pharaoh.
8 Pharaoh said to Jacob, "How
old *are* you?"
9 And Jacob said to Pharaoh,
[a]"The days of the years of my
[1]pilgrimage *are* [b]one hundred
and thirty years; [c]few and evil
have been the days of the years
of my life, and [d]they have not attained to the days of the years of
the life of my fathers in the days
of their pilgrimage."
10 So Jacob [a]blessed Pharaoh, and went out from before
Pharaoh.
11 And Joseph situated his father and his brothers, and gave
them a possession in the land of
Egypt, in the best of the land, in
the land of [a]Ram′e·sēs, [b]as Pharaoh had commanded.
12 Then Joseph provided [a]his
father, his brothers, and all his
father's household with bread,
according to the number in *their*
families.
13 Now *there was* no bread
in all the land; for the famine
was very severe, [a]so that the
land of Egypt and the land of

30 [a]Luke 2:29, 30
31 [a]Gen. 47:1
32 [a]Gen. 47:3
33 [a]Gen. 47:2, 3
34 [a]Gen. 47:3 [b]Gen. 30:35; 34:5; 37:17 [c]Gen. 43:32 [1]*loathsome*

CHAPTER 47

1 [a]Gen. 46:31 [b]Gen. 45:10; 46:28; 50:8
2 [a]Acts 7:13
3 [a]Gen. 46:33 [b]Gen. 46:32, 34
4 [a]Deut. 26:5 [b]Gen. 43:1 [c]Gen. 46:34
6 [a]Gen. 20:15; 45:10, 18; 47:11 [b]Gen. 47:4
7 [a]Gen. 47:10; 48:15, 20
9 [a][Heb. 11:9, 13] [b]Gen. 47:28 [c][Job 14:1] [d]Gen. 5:5; 11:10, 11; 25:7, 8; 35:28 [1]Lit. *sojourning*
10 [a]Gen. 47:7
11 [a]Ex. 1:11; 12:37 [b]Gen. 47:6, 27
12 [a]Gen. 45:11; 50:21
13 [a]Gen. 41:30

Cā′naan languished because of the famine.

14 [a]And Joseph gathered up all the money that was found in the land of Egypt and in the land of Cā′naan, for the grain which they bought; and Joseph brought the money into Pharaoh's house.

15 So when the money failed in the land of Egypt and in the land of Cā′naan, all the Egyptians came to Joseph and said, "Give us bread, for [a]why should we die in your presence? For the money has failed."

16 Then Joseph said, "Give your livestock, and I will give you *bread* for your livestock, if the money is gone."

17 So they brought their livestock to Joseph, and Joseph gave them bread *in exchange* for the horses, the flocks, the cattle of the herds, and for the donkeys. Thus he [1]fed them with bread *in exchange* for all their livestock that year.

18 When that year had ended, they came to him the next year and said to him, "We will not hide from my lord that our money is gone; my lord also has our herds of livestock. There is nothing left in the sight of my lord but our bodies and our lands.

19 "Why should we die before your eyes, both we and our land? Buy us and our land for bread, and we and our land will be servants of Pharaoh; give *us* seed, that we may [a]live and not die, that the land may not be desolate."

20 Then Joseph [a]bought all the land of Egypt for Pharaoh; for every man of the Egyptians sold his field, because the famine was severe upon them. So the land became Pharaoh's.

21 And as for the people, he [1]moved them into the cities, from *one* end of the borders of Egypt to the *other* end.

22 [a]Only the land of the [b]priests he did not buy; for the priests had rations *allotted to them* by Pharaoh, and they ate their rations which Pharaoh gave them; therefore they did not sell their lands.

23 Then Joseph said to the people, "Indeed I have bought you and your land this day for Pharaoh. Look, *here is* seed for you, and you shall sow the land.

24 "And it shall come to pass in the harvest that you shall give one-fifth to Pharaoh. Four-fifths shall be your own, as seed for the field and for your food, for those of your households and as food for your little ones."

25 So they said, "You have saved [a]our lives; let us find favor in the sight of my lord, and we will be Pharaoh's servants."

26 And Joseph made it a law over the land of Egypt to this day, *that* Pharaoh should have one-fifth, [a]except for the land of the priests only, *which* did not become Pharaoh's.

27 So Israel [a]dwelt in the land of Egypt, in the country of Gō′shen; and they had possessions there and [b]grew and multiplied exceedingly.

28 And Jacob lived in the land of Egypt seventeen years. So the length of Jacob's life was one hundred and forty-seven years.

29 When the time [a]drew near that Israel must die, he called his son Joseph and said to him, "Now if I have found favor in

14 [a]Gen. 41:56; 42:6
15 [a]Gen. 47:19
17 [1]*supplied*
19 [a]Gen. 43:8
20 [a]Jer. 32:43
21 [1]So with MT, Tg.; Sam., LXX, Vg. *made the people virtual slaves*
22 [a]Ezra 7:24 [b]Gen. 41:45
25 [a]Gen. 33:15
26 [a]Gen. 47:22
27 [a]Gen. 47:11 [b]Gen. 17:6; 26:4; 35:11; 46:3
29 [a]Deut. 31:14

your sight, please [b]put your hand
under my thigh, and [c]deal kindly
and truly with me. [d]Please do
not bury me in Egypt,
30 "but [a]let me lie with my fathers; you shall carry me out
of Egypt and [b]bury me in their
burial place." And he said, "I will
do as you have said."
31 Then he said, "Swear to me."
And he swore to him. So [a]Israel
bowed himself on the head of
the bed.

48 Now it came to pass after
these things that Joseph
was told, "Indeed your father
is sick"; and he took with him
his two sons, [a]Ma·nas′seh and
Ē′phra·im.
2 And Jacob was told, "Look,
your son Joseph is coming to
you"; and Israel [1]strengthened
himself and sat up on the bed.
3 Then Jacob said to Joseph:
"God [a]Almighty appeared to me
at [b]Luz in the land of Cā′naan
and blessed me,
4 "and said to me, 'Behold,
I will [a]make you fruitful and
multiply you, and I will make of
you a multitude of people, and
[b]give this land to your descendants after you [c]*as* an everlasting possession.'
5 "And now your [a]two sons,
Ē′phra·im and Ma·nas′seh, who
were born to you in the land of
Egypt before I came to you in
Egypt, *are* mine; as Reuben and
Sim′ē·on, they shall be mine.
6 "Your [1]offspring [2]whom you
beget after them shall be yours;
they will be called by the name
of their brothers in their inheritance.
7 "But as for me, when I came
from Pad′an, [a]Rachel died beside
me in the land of Cā′naan on the
way, when *there was* but a little
distance to go to Eph′rath; and I
buried her there on the way to
Eph′rath (that is, Bethlehem)."
8 Then Israel saw Joseph's
sons, and said, "Who *are* these?"
9 And Joseph said to his father, "They *are* my sons, whom
God has given me in this *place*."
And he said, "Please bring them
to me, and [a]I will bless them."
10 Now [a]the eyes of Israel were
dim with age, *so that* he could
not see. Then Joseph brought
them near him, and he [b]kissed
them and embraced them.
11 And Israel said to Joseph,
[a]"I had not thought to see your
face; but in fact, God has also
shown me your offspring!"
12 So Joseph brought them
from beside his knees, and he
bowed down with his face to the
earth.
13 And Joseph took them both,
Ē′phra·im with his right hand
toward Israel's left hand, and
Ma·nas′seh with his left hand
toward Israel's right hand, and
brought *them* near him.
14 Then Israel stretched out
his right hand and [a]laid *it* on
Ē′phra·im's head, who *was* the
younger, and his left hand on
Ma·nas′seh's head, [b]guiding his
hands knowingly, for Ma·nas′-
seh *was* the [c]firstborn.
15 And [a]he blessed Joseph, and
said:

"God, [b]before whom my
fathers Abraham and
Isaac walked,
The God who has fed me all
my life long to this day,
16 The Angel [a]who has
redeemed me from all
evil,

29 [b]Gen. 24:2–4 [c]Gen. 24:49 [d]Gen. 50:25
30 [a]2 Sam. 19:37 [b]Gen. 49:29; 50:5–13
31 [a]1 Kin. 1:47

CHAPTER 48

1 [a]Gen. 41:51, 56; 46:20; 50:23
2 [1]Collected his strength
3 [a]Gen. 43:14; 49:25 [b]Gen. 28:13, 19; 35:6, 9
4 [a]Gen. 46:3 [b]Ex. 6:8 [c]Gen. 17:8
5 [a]Josh. 13:7; 14:4
6 [1]*children* [2]Who are born to you
7 [a]Gen. 35:9, 16, 19, 20
9 [a]Gen. 27:4; 47:15
10 [a]Gen. 27:1 [b]Gen. 27:27; 45:15; 50:1
11 [a]Gen. 45:26
14 [a]Matt. 19:15 [b]Gen. 48:19 [c]Josh. 17:1
15 [a][Heb. 11:21] [b]Gen. 17:1; 24:40
16 [a]Gen. 22:11, 15–18; 28:13–15; 31:11

Bless the lads;
Let [b]my name be named
upon them,
And the name of my fathers
Abraham and Isaac;
And let them [c]grow into a
multitude in the midst of
the earth."

17 Now when Joseph saw that
his father [a]laid his right hand
on the head of Ē′phra·im, it displeased him; so he took hold
of his father's hand to remove
it from Ē′phra·im's head to
Ma·nas′seh's head.
18 And Joseph said to his father, "Not so, my father, for this
one is the firstborn; put your
right hand on his head."
19 But his father refused and
said, [a]"I know, my son, I know.
He also shall become a people,
and he also shall be great; but
truly [b]his younger brother shall
be greater than he, and his descendants shall become a multitude of nations."
20 So he blessed them that day,
saying, [a]"By you Israel will bless,
saying, 'May God make you as
Ē′phra·im and as Ma·nas′seh!' "
And thus he set Ē′phra·im before Ma·nas′seh.
21 Then Israel said to Joseph,
"Behold, I am dying, but [a]God
will be with you and bring you
back to the land of your fathers.
22 "Moreover [a]I have given to
you one [1]portion above your
brothers, which I took from the
hand [b]of the Am′o·rīte with my
sword and my bow."

49 And Jacob called his
sons and said, "Gather
together, that I may [a]tell you
what shall befall you [b]in the last
days:

2 "Gather together and hear,
you sons of Jacob,
And listen to Israel your
father.

3 "Reuben, you are [a]my
firstborn,
My might and the beginning
of my strength,
The excellency of dignity
and the excellency of
power.
4 Unstable as water, you shall
not excel,
Because you [a]went up to
your father's bed;
Then you defiled *it*—
He went up to my couch.

5 "Sim′ē·on and Levi *are*
brothers;
Instruments of [1]cruelty *are*
in their dwelling place.
6 [a]Let not my soul enter their
council;
Let not my honor be united
[b]to their assembly;
[c]For in their anger they slew
a man,
And in their self-will they
[1]hamstrung an ox.
7 Cursed *be* their anger, for *it*
is fierce;
And their wrath, for it is
cruel!
[a]I will divide them in Jacob
And scatter them in Israel.

8 "Judah,[a] you *are he* whom
your brothers shall
praise;
[b]Your hand *shall be* on the
neck of your enemies;
[c]Your father's children shall
bow down before you.
9 Judah *is* [a]a lion's whelp;
From the prey, my son, you
have gone up.

16 [b]Amos 9:12 [c]Num. 26:34, 37
17 [a]Gen. 48:14
19 [a]Gen. 48:14 [b]Num. 1:33, 35
20 [a]Ruth 4:11, 12
21 [a]Gen. 28:15; 46:4; 50:24
22 [a]Josh. 24:32 [b]Gen. 34:28 [1]Lit. *shoulder*

CHAPTER 49

1 [a]Deut. 33:1, 6–25 [b]Is. 2:2; 39:6
3 [a]Gen. 29:32
4 [a]Gen. 35:22
5 [1]*violence*
6 [a]Prov. 1:15, 16 [b]Ps. 26:9 [c]Gen. 34:26 [1]*lamed*
7 [a]Josh. 19:1, 9; 21:1–42
8 [a]Deut. 33:7 [b]Ps. 18:40 [c]1 Chr. 5:2
9 [a][Rev. 5:5]

[b]He [1]bows down, he lies
down as a lion;
And as a lion, who shall
rouse him?
☆ 10 [a]The [1]scepter shall not depart
from Judah,
Nor [b]a lawgiver from
between his feet,
[c]Until Shī'lōh comes;
[d]And to Him *shall be* the
obedience of the people.
11 Binding his donkey to the
vine,
And his donkey's colt to the
choice vine,
He washed his garments in
wine,
And his clothes in the blood
of grapes.
12 His eyes *are* darker than
wine,
And his teeth whiter than
milk.

13 "Zeb'ū·lun[a] shall dwell by the
haven of the sea;
He *shall become* a haven for
ships,
And his border shall [b]adjoin
Sī'don.

14 "Is'sa·char[a] is a strong
donkey,
Lying down between two
burdens;
15 He saw that rest *was* good,
And that the land *was*
pleasant;
He bowed [a]his shoulder to
bear *a burden*,
And became a band of slaves.

16 "Dan[a] shall judge his people
As one of the tribes of
Israel.
17 [a]Dan shall be a serpent by
the way,
A viper by the path,
That bites the horse's heels
So that its rider shall fall
backward.
18 [a]I have waited for your
salvation, O LORD!

19 "Gad,[a1] a troop shall [2]tramp
upon him,
But he shall [2]triumph at last.

20 "Bread from [a]Ash'er *shall be*
rich,
And he shall yield royal
dainties.

21 "Naph'ta·lī[a] *is* a deer let
loose;
He uses beautiful words.

22 "Joseph *is* a fruitful bough,
A fruitful bough by a well;
His branches run over the
wall.
23 The archers have [a]bitterly
grieved him,
Shot *at him* and hated him.
24 But his [a]bow remained in
strength,
And the arms of his hands
were [1]made strong
By the hands of [b]the Mighty
God of Jacob
[c](From there [d]*is* the
Shepherd, [e]the Stone of
Israel),
25 [a]By the God of your father
who will help you,
[b]And by the Almighty [c]who
will bless you
With blessings of heaven
above,
Blessings of the deep that
lies beneath,
Blessings of the breasts and
of the womb.
26 The blessings of your father
Have excelled the blessings
of my ancestors,

9 [b]Num. 23:24; 24:9 [1]*couches*
10 [a]Num. 24:17; Matt. 1:3; 2:6; Luke 3:33; Rev. 5:5 [b]Ps. 60:7 [c]Is. 11:1 [d]Ps. 2:6–9; 72:8–11 [1]A symbol of kingship
13 [a]Deut. 33:18, 19 [b]Gen. 10:19
14 [a]1 Chr. 12:32
15 [a]1 Sam. 10:9
16 [a]Deut. 33:22
17 [a]Judg. 18:27
18 [a]Is. 25:9
19 [a]Deut. 33:20 [1]Lit. *Troop* [2]Lit. *raid*
20 [a]Deut. 33:24
21 [a]Deut. 33:23
23 [a]Gen. 37:4, 24
24 [a]Job 29:20 [b]Ps. 132:2, 5 [c]Gen. 45:11; 47:12 [d][Ps. 23:1; 80:1] [e]Is. 28:16 [1]Or *supple*
25 [a]Gen. 28:13; 32:9; 35:3; 43:23; 50:17 [b]Gen. 17:1; 35:11 [c]Deut. 33:13

[a]Up to the utmost bound of
the everlasting hills.
[b]They shall be on the head of
Joseph,
And on the crown of the
head of him who was
separate from his
brothers.

27 "Benjamin is a [a]ravenous
wolf;
In the morning he shall
devour the prey,
[b]And at night he shall divide
the spoil."

28 All these *are* the twelve tribes
of Israel, and this *is* what their
father spoke to them. And he
blessed them; he blessed each
one according to his own blessing.
29 Then he charged them and
said to them: "I [a]am to be gathered to my people; [b]bury me
with my fathers [c]in the cave that
is in the field of Ē'phron the Hit'-
tīte,
30 "in the cave that *is* in the field
of Mach·pē'lah, which *is* before
Mam're in the land of Cā'naan,
[a]which Abraham bought with
the field of Ē'phron the Hit'-
tīte as a possession for a burial
place.
31 [a]"There they buried Abraham
and Sarah his wife, [b]there they
buried Isaac and Rebekah his
wife, and there I buried Leah.
32 "The field and the cave that
is there *were* purchased from
the sons of Heth."
33 And when Jacob had finished commanding his sons, he
drew his feet up into the bed
and breathed his last, and was
gathered to his people.

50
Then Joseph [a]fell on his
father's face, and [b]wept
over him, and kissed him.
2 And Joseph commanded
his servants the physicians to
[a]embalm his father. So the physicians embalmed Israel.
3 Forty days were required for
him, for such are the days required for those who are embalmed; and the Egyptians
[a]mourned[1] for him seventy days.
4 Now when the days of his
mourning were past, Joseph
spoke to [a]the household of Pharaoh, saying, "If now I have
found favor in your eyes, please
speak in the hearing of Pharaoh,
saying,
5 [a]'My father made me swear,
saying, "Behold, I am dying; in
my grave [b]which I dug for myself
in the land of Cā'naan, there you
shall bury me." Now therefore,
please let me go up and bury my
father, and I will come back.'"
6 And Pharaoh said, "Go up
and bury your father, as he made
you swear."
7 So Joseph went up to bury
his father; and with him went up
all the servants of Pharaoh, the
elders of his house, and all the
elders of the land of Egypt,
8 as well as all the house of
Joseph, his brothers, and his
father's house. Only their little ones, their flocks, and their
herds they left in the land of
Gō'shen.
9 And there went up with him
both chariots and horsemen, and
it was a very great gathering.
10 Then they came to the
threshing floor of Ā'tad, which
is beyond the Jordan, and they
[a]mourned there with a great and
very solemn lamentation. [b]He

26 [a]Deut. 33:15 [b]Deut. 33:16
27 [a]Judg. 20:21, 25 [b]Zech. 14:1
29 [a]Gen. 15:15; 25:8; 35:29 [b]Gen. 47:30 [c]Gen. 23:16–20; 50:13
30 [a]Gen. 23:3–20
31 [a]Gen. 23:19, 20; 25:9 [b]Gen. 35:29; 50:13

CHAPTER 50

1 [a]Gen. 46:4, 29 [b]2 Kin. 13:14
2 [a]Gen. 50:26
3 [a]Deut. 34:8 [1]Lit. *wept*
4 [a]Esth. 4:2
5 [a]Gen. 47:29–31 [b]Is. 22:16
10 [a]Acts 8:2 [b]1 Sam. 31:13

observed seven days of mourning for his father.

11 And when the inhabitants of the land, the Cā′naan·ītes, saw the mourning at the threshing floor of Ā′tad, they said, "This *is* a deep mourning of the Egyptians." Therefore its name was called [1]Abel Miz′ra·im, which *is* beyond the Jordan.

12 So his sons did for him just as he had commanded them.

13 For [a]his sons carried him to the land of Cā′naan, and buried him in the cave of the field of Mach·pē′lah, before Mam′re, which Abraham [b]bought with the field from Ē′phron the Hit′tīte as property for a burial place.

14 And after he had buried his father, Joseph returned to Egypt, he and his brothers and all who went up with him to bury his father.

15 When Joseph's brothers saw that their father was dead, [a]they said, "Perhaps Joseph will hate us, and may [1]actually repay us for all the evil which we did to him."

16 So they sent *messengers* to Joseph, saying, "Before your father died he commanded, saying,

17 'Thus you shall say to Joseph: "I beg you, please forgive the trespass of your brothers and their sin; [a]for they did evil to you." ' Now, please, forgive the trespass of the servants of [b]the God of your father." And Joseph wept when they spoke to him.

18 Then his brothers also went and [a]fell down before his face, and they said, "Behold, we *are* your servants."

19 Joseph said to them, [a]"Do not be afraid, [b]for *am* I in the place of God?

20 [a]"But as for you, you meant evil against me; *but* [b]God meant it for good, in order to bring it about as *it is* this day, to save many people alive.

21 "Now therefore, do not be afraid; [a]I will provide for you and your little ones." And he comforted them and spoke [1]kindly to them.

22 So Joseph dwelt in Egypt, he and his father's household. And Joseph lived one hundred and ten years.

23 Joseph saw Ē′phra·im's children [a]to the third *generation.* [b]The children of Mā′chir, the son of Ma·nas′seh, [c]were also brought up on Joseph's knees.

24 And Joseph said to his brethren, "I am dying; but [a]God will surely visit you, and bring you out of this land to the land [b]of which He swore to Abraham, to Isaac, and to Jacob."

25 Then [a]Joseph took an oath from the children of Israel, saying, "God will surely [1]visit you, and [b]you shall carry up my [c]bones from here."

26 So Joseph died, *being* one hundred and ten years old; and they embalmed him, and he was put in a coffin in Egypt.

---

11 [1]Lit. *Mourning of Egypt*
13 [a]Acts 7:16 [b]Gen. 23:16–20
15 [a][Job 15:21] [1]*fully*
17 [a][Prov. 28:13] [b]Gen. 49:25
18 [a]Gen. 37:7–10; 41:43; 44:14
19 [a]Gen. 45:5 [b]2 Kin. 5:7
20 [a]Ps. 56:5 [b][Acts 3:13–15]
21 [a][Matt. 5:44] [1]Lit. *to their hearts*
23 [a]Job 42:16 [b]Num. 26:29; 32:39 [c]Gen. 30:3
24 [a]Ex. 3:16, 17 [b]Gen. 26:3; 35:12; 46:4
25 [a]Ex. 13:19 [b]Deut. 1:8; 30:1–8 [c]Ex. 13:19 [1]*give attention to*

The Second Book of Moses Called

EXODUS

EXODUS is the record of Israel's birth as a nation. Within the protective "womb" of Egypt, the Jewish family of seventy rapidly multiplies. At the right time, accompanied with severe "birth pains," an infant nation, numbering between two and three million people, is brought into the world where it is divinely protected, fed, and nurtured.

The Hebrew title, *We'elleh Shemoth,* "Now These *Are* the Names," comes from the first phrase in 1:1. Exodus begins with "Now" to show it as a continuation of Genesis. The Greek title is *Exodus,* a word meaning "exit," "departure," or "going out." The Septuagint uses this word to describe the book by its key event (see 19:1, "gone out"). In Luke 9:31 and in Second Peter 1:15, the word *exodus* speaks of physical death (Jesus and Peter). This embodies Exodus's theme of redemption, because redemption is accomplished only through death. The Latin title is *Liber Exodus,* "Book of Departure," taken from the Greek title.

NOW [a]these *are* the names of
the children of Israel who
came to Egypt; each man and
his household came with Jacob:
2 Reuben, Sim'ē·on, Levi, and
Judah;
3 Is'sa·char, Zeb'ū·lun, and
Benjamin;
4 Dan, Naph'ta·lī, Gad, and
Ash'er.
5 All those [1]who were descendants of Jacob were [a]seventy[2]
persons (for Joseph was in Egypt
already).
6 And [a]Joseph died, all his
brothers, and all that generation.
7 [a]But the children of Israel
were fruitful and increased
abundantly, multiplied and
[1]grew exceedingly mighty; and
the land was filled with them.
8 Now there arose a new king
over Egypt, [a]who did not know
Joseph.
9 And he said to his people,
"Look, the people of the children
of Israel *are* more and [a]mightier
than we;
10 [a]"come, let us [b]deal shrewdly
with them, lest they multiply,
and it happen, in the event of
war, that they also join our enemies and fight against us, and
so go up out of the land."
11 Therefore they set taskmasters over them [a]to afflict them
with their [b]burdens. And they
built for Pharaoh [c]supply cities,
Pī'thom [d]and Rā·am'sēs.
12 But the more they afflicted
them, the more they multiplied
and grew. And they were in
dread of the children of Israel.
13 So the Egyptians made the
children of Israel [a]serve with
[1]rigor.
14 And they [a]made their lives
bitter with hard bondage—[b]in
mortar, in brick, and in all manner of service in the field. All
their service in which they made
them serve *was* with rigor.
15 Then the king of Egypt

CHAPTER 1

1 [a]Gen. 46:8–27

5 [a]Gen. 46:26, 27 [1]Lit. *who came from the loins of* [2]DSS, LXX *seventy-five;* cf. Acts 7:14

6 [a]Gen. 50:26

7 [a]Acts 7:17 [1]*became very numerous*

8 [a]Acts 7:18, 19

9 [a]Gen. 26:16

10 [a]Ps. 83:3, 4 [b]Acts 7:19

11 [a]Ex. 3:7; 5:6 [b]Ex. 1:14; 2:11; 5:4–9; 6:6 [c]1 Kin. 9:19 [d]Gen. 47:11

13 [a]Gen. 15:13 [1]*harshness*

14 [a]Num. 20:15 [b]Ps. 81:6

spoke to the [a]Hebrew midwives, of whom the name of one *was* Shiph′rah and the name of the other Pū′ah;

16 and he said, "When you do the duties of a midwife for the Hebrew women, and see *them* on the birthstools, if it *is* a [a]son, then you shall kill him; but if it *is* a daughter, then she shall live."

17 But the midwives [a]feared God, and did not do [b]as the king of Egypt commanded them, but saved the male children alive.

18 So the king of Egypt called for the midwives and said to them, "Why have you done this thing, and saved the male children alive?"

19 And [a]the midwives said to Pharaoh, "Because the Hebrew women *are* not like the Egyptian women; for they [1]*are* lively and give birth before the midwives come to them."

20 [a]Therefore God dealt well with the midwives, and the people multiplied and [1]grew very mighty.

21 And so it was, because the midwives feared God, [a]that He [1]provided households for them.

22 So Pharaoh commanded all his people, saying, [a]"Every son who is [1]born you shall cast into the river, and every daughter you shall save alive."

2 And [a]a man of the house of Levi went and took *as wife* a daughter of Levi.

2 So the woman conceived and bore a son. And [a]when she saw that he *was* a beautiful *child,* she hid him three months.

3 But when she could no longer hide him, she took an ark of [a]bulrushes for him, daubed it with [b]asphalt and [c]pitch, put the child in it, and laid *it* in the reeds [d]by the river's bank.

4 [a]And his sister stood afar off, to know what would be done to him.

5 Then the [a]daughter of Pharaoh came down to bathe at the river. And her maidens walked along the riverside; and when she saw the ark among the reeds, she sent her maid to get it.

6 And when she opened *it,* she saw the child, and behold, the baby wept. So she had compassion on him, and said, "This is one of the Hebrews' children."

7 Then his sister said to Pharaoh's daughter, "Shall I go and call a nurse for you from the Hebrew women, that she may nurse the child for you?"

8 And Pharaoh's daughter said to her, "Go." So the maiden went and called the child's mother.

9 Then Pharaoh's daughter said to her, "Take this child away and nurse him for me, and I will give *you* your wages." So the woman took the child and nursed him.

10 And the child grew, and she brought him to Pharaoh's daughter, and he became [a]her son. So she called his name [1]Moses, saying, "Because I drew him out of the water."

11 Now it came to pass in those days, [a]when Moses was grown, that he went out to his brethren and looked at their burdens. And he saw an Egyptian beating a Hebrew, one of his brethren.

12 So he looked this way and that way, and when he saw no one, he [a]killed the Egyptian and hid him in the sand.

13 And [a]when he went out the

15 [a]Ex. 2:6
16 [a]Acts 7:19
17 [a]Prov. 16:6 [b]Dan. 3:16, 18
19 [a]Josh. 2:4 [1]*have vigor of life, bear quickly, easily*
20 [a][Prov. 11:18] [1]*became very numerous*
21 [a]1 Sam. 2:35 [1]*gave them families*
22 [a]Acts 7:19 [1]Sam., LXX, Tg. add *to the Hebrews*

CHAPTER 2

1 [a]Ex. 6:16–20
2 [a]Acts 7:20
3 [a]Is. 18:2 [b]Gen. 14:10 [c]Gen. 6:14 [d]Is. 19:6
4 [a]Num. 26:59
5 [a]Acts 7:21
10 [a]Acts 7:21 [1]Heb. *Mosheh,* lit. *Drawn Out*
11 [a]Heb. 11:24–26
12 [a]Acts 7:24, 25
13 [a]Acts 7:26–28

second day, behold, two Hebrew
men [b]were fighting, and he said
to the one who did the wrong,
"Why are you striking your
companion?"
14 Then he said, [a]"Who made
you a prince and a judge over
us? Do you intend to kill me as
you killed the Egyptian?" So
Moses [b]feared and said, "Surely
this thing is known!"
15 When Pharaoh heard of this
matter, he sought to kill Moses.
But [a]Moses fled from [1]the face of
Pharaoh and dwelt in the land of
[b]Mid′i·an; and he sat down by [c]a
well.
16 [a]Now the priest of Mid′i·an
had seven daughters. [b]And they
came and drew water, and they
filled the [c]troughs to water their
father's flock.
17 Then the [a]shepherds came
and [b]drove them away; but Moses stood up and helped them,
and [c]watered their flock.
18 When they came to [a]Reū′el[1]
their father, [b]he said, "How *is*
it that you have come so soon
today?"
19 And they said, "An Egyptian
delivered us from the hand of
the shepherds, and he also drew
enough water for us and watered the flock."
20 So he said to his daughters,
"And where *is* he? Why *is* it *that*
you have left the man? Call him,
that he may [a]eat bread."
21 Then Moses was content
to live with the man, and he
gave [a]Zip·pō′rah his daughter to
Moses.
22 And she bore *him* a son. He
called his name [a]Ger′shom,[1] for
he said, "I have been [b]a [2]stranger
in a foreign land."
23 Now it happened [a]in the
process of time that the king of
Egypt died. Then the children
of Israel [b]groaned because of
the bondage, and they cried out;
and [c]their cry came up to God
because of the bondage.
24 So God [a]heard their groaning, and God [b]remembered His
[c]covenant with Abraham, with
Isaac, and with Jacob.
25 And God [a]looked upon the
children of Israel, and God
[b]acknowledged *them.*

3

Now Moses was tending the
flock of [a]Jeth′rō his father-
in-law, [b]the priest of Mid′i·an.
And he led the flock to the back
of the desert, and came to [c]Hō′-
reb, [d]the mountain of God.
2 And [a]the Angel of the LORD
appeared to him in a flame of
fire from the midst of a bush. So
he looked, and behold, the bush
was burning with fire, but the
bush *was* not consumed.
3 Then Moses said, "I will now
turn aside and see this [a]great
sight, why the bush does not
burn."
4 So when the LORD saw that
he turned aside to look, God
called [a]to him from the midst of
the bush and said, "Moses, Moses!" And he said, "Here I am."
5 Then He said, "Do not draw
near this place. [a]Take your
sandals off your feet, for the
place where you stand *is* holy
ground."
6 Moreover He said, [a]"I *am* the
God of your father—the God of
Abraham, the God of Isaac, and
the God of Jacob." And Moses
hid his face, for [b]he was afraid
to look upon God.
7 And the LORD said: [a]"I have
surely seen the oppression of
My people who *are* in Egypt, and

13 [b]Prov. 25:8
14 [a]Acts 7:27, 28 [b]Judg. 6:27
15 [a]Acts 7:29 [b]Ex. 3:1 [c]Gen. 24:11; 29:2 [1]*the presence of Pharaoh*
16 [a]Ex. 3:1; 4:18; 18:12 [b]Gen. 24:11, 13, 19; 29:6–10 [c]Gen. 30:38
17 [a]Gen. 47:3 [b]Gen. 26:19–21 [c]Gen. 29:3, 10
18 [a]Num. 10:29 [b]Ex. 3:1; 4:18 [1]*Jethro,* Ex. 3:1
20 [a]Gen. 31:54; 43:25
21 [a]Ex. 4:25; 18:2
22 [a]Ex. 4:20; 18:3, 4 [b]Acts 7:29 [1]Lit. *Stranger There* [2]*sojourner,* temporary resident
23 [a]Acts 7:34 [b]Deut. 26:7 [c]James 5:4
24 [a]Ex. 6:5 [b]Gen. 15:13; 22:16–18; 26:2–5; 28:13–15 [c]Gen. 12:1–3; 15:14; 17:1–14
25 [a]Ex. 4:31 [b]Ex. 3:7

CHAPTER 3

1 [a]Ex. 4:18 [b]Ex. 2:16 [c]Ex. 17:6 [d]Ex. 18:5
2 [a]Deut. 33:16
3 [a]Acts 7:31
4 [a]Deut. 33:16
5 [a]Josh. 5:15
6 [a][Matt. 22:32] [b]1 Kin. 19:13
7 [a]Ex. 2:23–25

have heard their cry [b]because of their taskmasters, [c]for I know their [1]sorrows.

8 "So [a]I have come down to [b]deliver them out of the hand of the Egyptians, and to bring them up from that land [c]to a good and large land, to a land [d]flowing with milk and honey, to the place of [e]the Cā′naan·ītes and the Hit′tītes and the Am′o·rītes and the Per′iz·zītes and the Hī′vītes and the Jeb′ū·sītes.

9 "Now therefore, behold, [a]the cry of the children of Israel has come to Me, and I have also seen the [b]oppression with which the Egyptians oppress them.

10 [a]"Come now, therefore, and I will send you to Pharaoh that you may bring My people, the children of Israel, out of Egypt."

11 But Moses said to God, [a]"Who *am* I that I should go to Pharaoh, and that I should bring the children of Israel out of Egypt?"

12 So He said, [a]"I will certainly be with you. And this *shall be* a [b]sign to you that I have sent you: When you have brought the people out of Egypt, you shall serve God on this mountain."

13 Then Moses said to God, "Indeed, *when* I come to the children of Israel and say to them, 'The God of your fathers has sent me to you,' and they say to me, 'What *is* His name?' what shall I say to them?"

14 And God said to Moses, "I AM WHO I AM." And He said, "Thus you shall say to the children of Israel, [a]'I AM has sent me to you.' "

15 Moreover God said to Moses, "Thus you shall say to the children of Israel: 'The LORD God of your fathers, the God of Abraham, the God of Isaac, and the God of Jacob, has sent me to you. This *is* [a]My name forever, and this *is* My memorial to all generations.'

16 "Go and [a]gather the elders of Israel together, and say to them, 'The LORD God of your fathers, the God of Abraham, of Isaac, and of Jacob, appeared to me, saying, [b]"I have surely visited you and *seen* what is done to you in Egypt;

17 "and I have said [a]I will bring you up out of the affliction of Egypt to the land of the Cā′naan·ītes and the Hit′tītes and the Am′o·rītes and the Per′iz·zītes and the Hī′vītes and the Jeb′ū·sītes, to a land flowing with milk and honey." '

18 "Then [a]they will heed your voice; and [b]you shall come, you and the elders of Israel, to the king of Egypt; and you shall say to him, 'The LORD God of the Hebrews has [c]met with us; and now, please, let us go three days' journey into the wilderness, that we may sacrifice to the LORD our God.'

19 "But I am sure that the king of Egypt [a]will not let you go, no, not even by a mighty hand.

20 "So I will [a]stretch out My hand and strike Egypt with [b]all My wonders which I will do in its midst; and [c]after that he will let you go.

21 "And [a]I will give this people favor in the sight of the Egyptians; and it shall be, when you go, that you shall not go empty-handed.

22 [a]"But every woman shall ask of her neighbor, namely, of her who dwells near her house, [b]articles of silver, articles of gold,

7 [b]Ex. 1:11 [c]Ex. 2:25 [1]*pain*
8 [a]Gen. 15:13–16; 46:4; 50:24, 25 [b]Ex. 6:6–8; 12:51 [c]Deut. 1:25; 8:7–9 [d]Jer. 11:5 [e]Gen. 15:19–21
9 [a]Ex. 2:23 [b]Ex. 1:11, 13, 14
10 [a][Mic. 6:4]
11 [a]Ex. 4:10; 6:12
12 [a]Gen. 31:3 [b]Ex. 4:8; 19:3
14 [a][John 8:24, 28, 58]
15 [a]Ps. 30:4; 97:12; 102:12; 135:13
16 [a]Ex. 4:29 [b]Ex. 2:25; 4:31
17 [a]Gen. 15:13–21; 46:4; 50:24, 25
18 [a]Ex. 4:31 [b]Ex. 5:1, 3 [c]Num. 23:3, 4, 15, 16
19 [a]Ex. 5:2
20 [a]Ex. 6:6; 9:15 [b]Deut. 6:22 [c]Ex. 11:1; 12:31–37
21 [a]Ex. 11:3; 12:36
22 [a]Ex. 11:2 [b]Ex. 33:6

and clothing; and you shall put
them on your sons and on your
daughters. So [c]you shall plunder
the Egyptians."

CHAPTER 4

4 Then Moses answered and
said, "But suppose they will
not believe me or listen to my
voice; suppose they say, 'The
LORD has not appeared to you.' "
2 So the LORD said to him,
"What *is* that in your hand?" He
said, "A rod."
3 And He said, "Cast it on the
ground." So he cast it on the
ground, and it became a serpent;
and Moses fled from it.
4 Then the LORD said to Moses,
"Reach out your hand and take
it by the tail" (and he reached
out his hand and caught it, and
it became a rod in his hand),
5 "that they may [a]believe that
the [b]LORD God of their fathers,
the God of Abraham, the God of
Isaac, and the God of Jacob, has
appeared to you."
6 Furthermore the LORD said
to him, "Now put your hand in
your bosom." And he put his
hand in his bosom, and when he
took it out, behold, his hand *was*
leprous, [a]like snow.
7 And He said, "Put your hand
in your bosom again." So he put
his hand in his bosom again,
and drew it out of his bosom,
and behold, [a]it was restored like
his *other* flesh.
8 "Then it will be, if they do
not believe you, nor heed the
message of the [a]first sign, that
they may believe the message of
the latter sign.
9 "And it shall be, if they do
not believe even these two signs,
or listen to your voice, that you
shall take water from [1]the river
and pour *it* on the dry *land.* [a]The
water which you take from the
river will become blood on the
dry *land.*"
10 Then Moses said to the LORD,
"O my Lord, I *am* not eloquent,
neither before nor since You
have spoken to Your servant; but
[a]I *am* slow of speech and [1]slow
of tongue."
11 So the LORD said to him,
[a]"Who has made man's mouth?
Or who makes the mute, the
deaf, the seeing, or the blind?
Have not I, the LORD?
12 "Now therefore, go, and I
will be [a]with your mouth and
teach you what you shall say."
13 But he said, "O my Lord,
[a]please send by the hand of
whomever *else* You may send."
14 So [a]the anger of the LORD
was kindled against Moses, and
He said: "Is not Aaron the Lē′-
vīte your [b]brother? I know that
he can speak well. And look, [c]he
is also coming out to meet you.
When he sees you, he will be
glad in his heart.
15 "Now [a]you shall speak to him
and [b]put the words in his mouth.
And I will be with your mouth
and with his mouth, and [c]I will
teach you what you shall do.
16 "So he shall be your spokesman to the people. And he himself shall be as a mouth for
you, and [a]you shall be to him as
God.
17 "And you shall take this rod
in your hand, with which you
shall do the signs."
18 So Moses went and returned
to [a]Jeth′rō his father-in-law, and
said to him, "Please let me go
and return to my brethren who
are in Egypt, and see whether
they are still alive." And Jeth′rō
said to Moses, [b]"Go in peace."

22 [c]Job 27:17
5 [a]Ex. 4:31; 19:9 [b]Ex. 3:6, 15
6 [a]Num. 12:10
7 [a]Deut. 32:39
8 [a]Ex. 7:6–13
9 [a]Ex. 7:19, 20 [1]The Nile
10 [a]Ex. 3:11; 4:1; 6:12 [1]*heavy* or *dull of tongue;* cannot talk very well
11 [a]Ps. 94:9; 146:8
12 [a]Is. 50:4
13 [a]Jon. 1:3
14 [a]Num. 11:1, 33 [b]Num. 26:59 [c]Ex. 4:27
15 [a]Ex. 4:12, 30; 7:1, 2 [b]Num. 23:5, 12 [c]Deut. 5:31
16 [a]Ex. 7:1, 2
18 [a]Ex. 2:21; 3:1; 4:18 [b]Judg. 18:6

19 Now the LORD said to Moses in [a]Mid′i·an, “Go, return to
[b]Egypt; for [c]all the men who
sought your life are dead.”
20 Then Moses [a]took his wife
and his sons and set them on a
donkey, and he returned to the
land of Egypt. And Moses took
[b]the rod of God in his hand.
21 And the LORD said to Moses,
“When you go back to Egypt, see
that you do all those [a]wonders
before Pharaoh which I have put
in your hand. But [b]I will harden
his heart, so that he will not let
the people go.
22 “Then you shall [a]say to Pharaoh, ‘Thus says the LORD: [b]“Israel
is My son, [c]My firstborn.
23 “So I say to you, let My son
go that he may serve Me. But
if you refuse to let him go, indeed [a]I will kill your son, your
firstborn.” ’ ”
24 And it came to pass on the
way, at the [a]encampment, that
the LORD [b]met him and sought to
[c]kill him.
25 Then [a]Zip·pō′rah took [b]a sharp
stone and cut off the foreskin of
her son and [1]cast *it* at [2]*Moses’*
feet, and said, “Surely you *are* a
husband of blood to me!”
26 So He let him go. Then she
said, “*You are* a [1]husband of
blood!”—because of the circumcision.
27 And the LORD said to Aaron,
“Go into the wilderness [a]to meet
Moses.” So he went and met him
on [b]the mountain of God, and
kissed him.
28 So Moses [a]told Aaron all the
words of the LORD who had sent
him, and all the [b]signs which He
had commanded him.
29 Then Moses and Aaron [a]went
and gathered together all the elders of the children of Israel.
30 [a]And Aaron spoke all the
words which the LORD had spoken to Moses. Then he did the
signs in the sight of the people.
31 So the people [a]believed; and
when they heard that the LORD
had [b]visited the children of Israel and that He [c]had looked on
their affliction, then [d]they bowed
their heads and worshiped.

5 Afterward Moses and Aaron
went in and told Pharaoh,
“Thus says the LORD God of
Israel: ‘Let My people go, that
they may [1]hold [a]a feast to Me in
the wilderness.’ ”
2 And Pharaoh said, [a]“Who *is*
the LORD, that I should obey His
voice to let Israel go? I do not
know the LORD, [b]nor will I let
Israel go.”
3 So they said, [a]“The God of
the Hebrews has [b]met with us.
Please, let us go three days’
journey into the desert and sacrifice to the LORD our God, lest
He fall upon us with [c]pestilence
or with the sword.”
4 Then the king of Egypt said
to them, “Moses and Aaron, why
do you take the people from
their work? Get *back* to your
[a]labor.”
5 And Pharaoh said, “Look,
the people of the land *are* [a]many
now, and you make them rest
from their labor!”
6 So the same day Pharaoh
commanded the [a]taskmasters of
the people and their officers,
saying,
7 “You shall no longer give the
people straw to make [a]brick as
before. Let them go and gather
straw for themselves.
8 “And you shall lay on them

19 [a]Ex. 3:1; 18:1 [b]Gen. 46:3, 6 [c]Ex. 2:15, 23
20 [a]Ex. 18:2–5 [b]Num. 20:8, 9, 11
21 [a]Ex. 3:20; 11:9, 10 [b]John 12:40
22 [a]Ex. 5:1 [b]Hos. 11:1 [c]Jer. 31:9
23 [a]Ex. 11:5; 12:29
24 [a]Gen. 42:27 [b]Num. 22:22 [c]Gen. 17:14
25 [a]Ex. 2:21; 18:2 [b]Josh. 5:2, 3 [1]Lit. *made it touch* [2]Lit. *his*
26 [1]*bridegroom*
27 [a]Ex. 4:14 [b]Ex. 3:1; 18:5; 24:13
28 [a]Ex. 4:15, 16 [b]Ex. 4:8, 9
29 [a]Ex. 3:16; 12:21
30 [a]Ex. 4:15, 16
31 [a]Ex. 3:18; 4:8, 9; 19:9 [b]Gen. 50:24 [c]Ex. 2:25; 3:7 [d]Gen. 24:26

CHAPTER 5

1 [a]Ex. 3:18; 7:16; 10:9 [1]*keep a pilgrim-feast*
2 [a]2 Kin. 18:35 [b]Ex. 3:19; 7:14
3 [a]Ex. 3:18; 7:16 [b]Num. 23:3 [c]Ex. 9:15
4 [a]Ex. 1:11; 2:11; 6:6
5 [a]Ex. 1:7, 9
6 [a]Ex. 1:11; 3:7; 5:10, 13, 14
7 [a]Ex. 1:14

the quota of bricks which they
made before. You shall not reduce it. For they are idle; therefore they cry out, saying, 'Let us
go *and* sacrifice to our God.'
9 "Let more work be laid on
the men, that they may labor in
it, and let them not regard false
words."
10 And the taskmasters of the
people and their officers went
out and spoke to the people, saying, "Thus says Pharaoh: 'I will
not give you straw.
11 'Go, get yourselves straw
where you can find it; yet none
of your work will be reduced.' "
12 So the people were scattered
abroad throughout all the land
of Egypt to gather stubble instead of straw.
13 And the taskmasters forced
them to hurry, saying, "Fulfill
your work, *your* daily quota, as
when there was straw."
14 Also the [a]officers of the children of Israel, whom Pharaoh's
taskmasters had set over them,
were [b]beaten *and* were asked,
"Why have you not fulfilled your
task in making brick both yesterday and today, as before?"
15 Then the officers of the children of Israel came and cried
out to Pharaoh, saying, "Why
are you dealing thus with your
servants?
16 "There is no straw given to
your servants, and they say to
us, 'Make brick!' And indeed
your servants *are* beaten, but
the fault *is* in your *own* people."
17 But he said, "You *are* idle!
Idle! Therefore you say, 'Let us
go *and* sacrifice to the LORD.'
18 "Therefore go now *and* work;
for no straw shall be given you,
yet you shall deliver the quota
of bricks."
19 And the officers of the children of Israel saw *that* they
were in trouble after it was said,
"You shall not reduce *any* bricks
from your daily quota."
20 Then, as they came out from
Pharaoh, they met Moses and
Aaron who stood there to meet
them.
21 [a]And they said to them, "Let
the LORD look on you and judge,
because you have made [1]us ab-
horrent in the sight of Pharaoh
and in the sight of his servants,
to put a sword in their hand to
kill us."
22 So Moses returned to the
LORD and said, "Lord, why have
You brought trouble on this people? Why *is* it You have sent me?
23 "For since I came to Pharaoh
to speak in Your name, he has
done evil to this people; neither
have You delivered Your people
at all."

6 Then the LORD said to Moses, "Now you shall see what
I will do to Pharaoh. For [a]with a
strong hand he will let them go,
and with a strong hand [b]he will
drive them out of his land."
2 And God spoke to Moses and
said to him: "I *am* [1]the LORD.
3 [a]"I appeared to Abraham, to
Isaac, and to Jacob, as [b]God Almighty, but *by* My name [c]LORD[1] I
was not known to them.
4 [a]"I have also [1]established My
covenant with them, [b]to give
them the land of Cā'naan, the
land of their [2]pilgrimage, [c]in
which they were [3]strangers.
5 "And [a]I have also heard
the groaning of the children
of Israel whom the Egyptians

14 [a]Ex. 5:6 [b]Is. 10:24

21 [a]Ex. 6:9; 14:11; 15:24; 16:2 [1]Lit. *our scent to stink before*

CHAPTER 6

1 [a]Ex. 3:19 [b]Ex. 12:31, 33, 39

2 [1]Heb. *YHWH*

3 [a]Gen. 17:1; 35:9; 48:3 [b]Gen. 28:3; 35:11 [c]Ps. 68:4; 83:18 [1]Heb. *YHWH*, traditionally *Jehovah*

4 [a]Gen. 12:7; 15:18; 17:4, 7, 8; 26:3; 28:4, 13 [b]Lev. 25:23 [c]Gen. 28:4 [1]*made* or *ratified* [2]*sojournings* [3]*sojourners*, temporary residents

5 [a]Ex. 2:24

keep in bondage, and I have remembered My covenant.
6 "Therefore say to the children of Israel: [a]'I *am* the LORD;
[b]I will bring you out from under
the burdens of the Egyptians,
I will [c]rescue you from their
bondage, and I will redeem you
with [1]an outstretched arm and
with great judgments.
7 'I will [a]take you as My people, and [b]I will be your God.
Then you shall know that I *am*
the LORD your God who brings
you out [c]from under the burdens
of the Egyptians.
8 'And I will bring you into the
land which I [a]swore[1] to give to
Abraham, Isaac, and Jacob; and
I will give it to you *as* a heritage:
I *am* the LORD.' "
9 So Moses spoke thus to the
children of Israel; [a]but they
did not heed Moses, because
of [b]anguish[1] of spirit and cruel
bondage.
10 And the LORD spoke to Moses, saying,
11 "Go in, tell Pharaoh king of
Egypt to let the children of Israel go out of his land."
12 And Moses spoke before the
LORD, saying, "The children of
Israel have not heeded me. How
then shall Pharaoh heed me, for
[a]I *am* [1]of uncircumcised lips?"
13 Then the LORD spoke to Moses and Aaron, and gave them
a [a]command[1] for the children
of Israel and for Pharaoh king
of Egypt, to bring the children of
Israel out of the land of Egypt.
14 These *are* the heads of their
fathers' houses: [a]The sons of
Reuben, the firstborn of Israel,
were Hā'noch, Pal'lū, Hez'ron,
and Car'mī. These are the families of Reuben.
15 [a]And the sons of Sim'ē·on
were [1]Je·mū'el, Jā'min, Ō'had,
Jā'chin, Zō'har, and Shā'ūl the
son of a Cā'naan·īte woman.
These *are* the families of Sim'-
ē·on.
16 These *are* the names of [a]the
sons of Levi according to their
generations: Ger'shon, Kō'hath,
and Me·rar'ī. And the years of
the life of Levi *were* one hundred and thirty-seven.
17 [a]The sons of Ger'shon *were*
Lib'nī and Shim'ī according to
their families.
18 And [a]the sons of Kō'hath
were Am'ram, Iz'har, Hē'bron,
and Uz'zi·el. And the years of
the life of Kō'hath *were* one
hundred and thirty-three.
19 [a]The sons of Me·rar'ī *were*
Mah'lī and Mū'shī. These *are*
the families of Levi according to
their generations.
20 Now [a]Am'ram took for himself [b]Joch'e·bed, his father's
sister, as wife; and she bore
him [c]Aaron and Moses. And the
years of the life of Am'ram *were*
one hundred and thirty-seven.
21 [a]The sons of Iz'har *were* Kō'-
rah, Nē'pheg, and Zich'rī.
22 And [a]the sons of Uz'zi·el
were Mish'a·el, El'za·phan, and
Zith'rī.
23 Aaron took to himself E·lish'-
e·ba, daughter of [a]Am·min'a·dab,
sister of Nah'shon, as wife; and
she bore him [b]Nā'dab, A·bī'hū,
[c]El·ē·ā'zar, and Ith'a·mar.
24 And [a]the sons of Kō'rah
were As'sir, El·kā'nah, and A·bī'-
a·saph. These are the families of
the Kō'ra·hītes.
25 El·ē·ā'zar, Aaron's son, took
for himself one of the daughters
of Pū'ti·el as wife; and [a]she bore
him Phin'e·has. These *are* the

6 [a]Deut. 6:12 [b]Deut. 26:8 [c]Deut. 7:8 [1]Mighty power
7 [a]2 Sam. 7:24 [b]Ex. 29:45, 46 [c]Ex. 5:4, 5
8 [a]Gen. 15:18; 26:3 [1]*promised,* lit. *lifted up My hand*
9 [a]Ex. 5:21 [b]Ex. 2:23 [1]Lit. *shortness*
12 [a]Jer. 1:6 [1]One who does not speak well
13 [a]Deut. 31:14 [1]*charge*
14 [a]Gen. 46:9
15 [a]Gen. 46:10 [1]*Nemuel,* Num. 26:12
16 [a]Gen. 46:11
17 [a]1 Chr. 6:17
18 [a]1 Chr. 6:2, 18
19 [a]1 Chr. 6:19; 23:21
20 [a]Ex. 2:1, 2 [b]Num. 26:59 [c]Num. 26:59
21 [a]1 Chr. 6:37, 38
22 [a]Lev. 10:4
23 [a]Ruth 4:19, 20 [b]Lev. 10:1 [c]Ex. 28:1
24 [a]Num. 26:11
25 [a]Num. 25:7, 11

heads of the fathers' houses of the Lē′vītes according to their families.

26 These *are the same* Aaron and Moses to whom the LORD said, "Bring out the children of Israel from the land of Egypt according to their [a]armies."[1]

27 These *are* the ones who spoke to Pharaoh king of Egypt, [a]to bring out the children of Israel from Egypt. These *are the same* Moses and Aaron.

28 And it came to pass, on the day the LORD spoke to Moses in the land of Egypt,

29 that the LORD spoke to Moses, saying, "I *am* the LORD. [a]Speak to Pharaoh king of Egypt all that I say to you."

30 But Moses said before the LORD, "Behold, [a]I *am* [1]of uncircumcised lips, and how shall Pharaoh heed me?"

7 So the LORD said to Moses: "See, I have made you [a]*as* God to Pharaoh, and Aaron your brother shall be [b]your prophet.

2 "You [a]shall speak all that I command you. And Aaron your brother shall tell Pharaoh to send the children of Israel out of his land.

3 "And [a]I will harden Pharaoh's heart, and [b]multiply My [c]signs and My wonders in the land of Egypt.

4 "But [a]Pharaoh will not heed you, so [b]that I may lay My hand on Egypt and bring My [1]armies *and* My people, the children of Israel, out of the land of Egypt [c]by great judgments.

5 "And the Egyptians [a]shall know that I *am* the LORD, when I [b]stretch out My hand on Egypt and [c]bring out the children of Israel from among them."

6 Then Moses and Aaron [a]did *so;* just as the LORD commanded them, so they did.

7 And Moses *was* [a]eighty years old and [b]Aaron eighty-three years old when they spoke to Pharaoh.

8 Then the LORD spoke to Moses and Aaron, saying,

9 "When Pharaoh speaks to you, saying, [a]'Show a miracle for yourselves,' then you shall say to Aaron, [b]'Take your rod and cast *it* before Pharaoh, *and* let it become a serpent.' "

10 So Moses and Aaron went in to Pharaoh, and they did so, just [a]as the LORD commanded. And Aaron cast down his rod before Pharaoh and before his servants, and it [b]became a serpent.

11 But Pharaoh also [a]called the wise men and [b]the [1]sorcerers; so the magicians of Egypt, they also [c]did in like manner with their [2]enchantments.

12 For every man threw down his rod, and they became serpents. But Aaron's rod swallowed up their rods.

13 And Pharaoh's heart grew hard, and he did not heed them, as the LORD had said.

14 So the LORD said to Moses: [a]"Pharaoh's heart *is* hard; he refuses to let the people go.

15 "Go to Pharaoh in the morning, when he goes out to the [a]water, and you shall stand by the river's bank to meet him; and [b]the rod which was turned to a serpent you shall take in your hand.

16 "And you shall say to him, [a]'The LORD God of the Hebrews has sent me to you, saying, "Let My people go, [b]that they may [1]serve Me in the wilderness"; but

---

26 [a]Ex. 7:4; 12:17, 51 [1]*hosts*
27 [a]Ps. 77:20
29 [a]Ex. 6:11; 7:2
30 [a]Ex. 4:10; 6:12 [1]One who does not speak well

CHAPTER 7

1 [a]Ex. 4:16 [b]Ex. 4:15, 16
2 [a]Ex. 4:15
3 [a]Ex. 4:21; 9:12 [b]Ex. 11:9 [c]Deut. 4:34
4 [a]Ex. 3:19, 20; 10:1; 11:9 [b]Ex. 9:14 [c]Ex. 6:6; 12:12 [1]*hosts*
5 [a]Ps. 9:16 [b]Ex. 9:15 [c]Ex. 3:20; 6:6; 12:51
6 [a]Ex. 7:2
7 [a]Deut. 29:5; 31:2; 34:7 [b]Num. 33:39
9 [a]Is. 7:11 [b]Ex. 4:2, 3, 17
10 [a]Ex. 7:9 [b]Ex. 4:3
11 [a]Gen. 41:8 [b]2 Tim. 3:8 [c]Ex. 7:22; 8:7, 18 [1]*soothsayers* [2]*secret arts*
14 [a]Ex. 8:15; 10:1, 20, 27
15 [a]Ex. 2:5; 8:20 [b]Ex. 4:2, 3; 7:10
16 [a]Ex. 3:13, 18; 4:22 [b]Ex. 3:12, 18; 4:23; 5:1, 3; 8:1 [1]*worship*

indeed, until now you would not
hear!
17 'Thus says the LORD: "By this
[a]you shall know that I *am* the
LORD. Behold, I will strike the
waters which *are* in the river
with the rod that *is* in my hand,
and [b]they shall be turned [c]to
blood.
18 "And the fish that *are* in the
river shall die, the river shall
stink, and the Egyptians will
[a]loathe[1] to drink the water of the
river." ' "
19 Then the LORD spoke to Moses, "Say to Aaron, 'Take your
rod and [a]stretch out your hand
over the waters of Egypt, over
their streams, over their rivers,
over their ponds, and over all
their pools of water, that they
may become blood. And there
shall be blood throughout all the
land of Egypt, both in *buckets of*
wood and *pitchers of* stone.' "
20 And Moses and Aaron did
so, just as the LORD commanded.
So he [a]lifted up the rod and
struck the waters that *were* in
the river, in the sight of Pharaoh
and in the sight of his servants.
And all the [b]waters that *were* in
the river were turned to blood.
21 The fish that *were* in the
river died, the river stank, and
the Egyptians [a]could not drink
the water of the river. So there
was blood throughout all the
land of Egypt.
22 [a]Then the magicians of Egypt
did [b]so with their [1]enchantments;
and Pharaoh's heart grew hard,
and he did not heed them, [c]as
the LORD had said.
23 And Pharaoh turned and
went into his house. Neither was
his heart moved by this.
24 So all the Egyptians dug all
around the river for water to
drink, because they could not
drink the water of the river.
25 And seven days passed after
the LORD had struck the river.

8

And the LORD spoke to Mo-
ses, "Go to Pharaoh and say
to him, 'Thus says the LORD: "Let
My people go, [a]that they may
serve Me.
2 "But if you [a]refuse to let *them*
go, behold, I will smite all your
territory with [b]frogs.
3 "So the river shall bring forth
frogs abundantly, which shall go
up and come into your house,
into your [a]bedroom, on your bed,
into the houses of your servants,
on your people, into your ovens,
and into your kneading bowls.
4 "And the frogs shall come up
on you, on your people, and on
all your servants." ' "
5 Then the LORD spoke to Moses, "Say to Aaron, [a]'Stretch out
your hand with your rod over
the streams, over the rivers,
and over the ponds, and cause
frogs to come up on the land of
Egypt.' "
6 So Aaron stretched out his
hand over the waters of Egypt,
and [a]the frogs came up and covered the land of Egypt.
7 [a]And the magicians did so
with their [1]enchantments, and
brought up frogs on the land of
Egypt.
8 Then Pharaoh called for
Moses and Aaron, and said,
[a]"Entreat[1] the LORD that He may
take away the frogs from me
and from my people; and I will
let the people [b]go, that they may
sacrifice to the LORD."
9 And Moses said to Pharaoh,
"Accept the honor of saying
when I shall intercede for you,

17 [a]Ex. 5:2; 7:5; 10:2 [b]Ex. 4:9; 7:20 [c]Rev. 11:6; 16:4, 6
18 [a]Ex. 7:24 [1]*be weary of drinking*
19 [a]Ex. 8:5, 6, 16; 9:22; 10:12, 21; 14:21, 26
20 [a]Ex. 17:5 [b]Ps. 78:44; 105:29, 30
21 [a]Ex. 7:18
22 [a]Ex. 7:11 [b]Ex. 8:7 [c]Ex. 3:19; 7:3 [1]*secret arts*

CHAPTER 8

1 [a]Ex. 3:12, 18; 4:23; 5:1, 3
2 [a]Ex. 7:14; 9:2 [b]Rev. 16:13
3 [a]Ps. 105:30
5 [a]Ex. 7:19
6 [a]Ps. 78:45; 105:30
7 [a]Ex. 7:11, 22 [1]*secret arts*
8 [a]Ex. 8:28; 9:28; 10:17 [b]Ex. 10:8, 24 [1]*Pray to, Make supplication to*

for your servants, and for your
people, to destroy the frogs from
you and your houses, *that* they
may remain in the river only."
10 So he said, "Tomorrow." And
he said, "*Let it be* according to
your word, that you may know
that [a]*there is* no one like the
LORD our God.
11 "And the frogs shall depart
from you, from your houses,
from your servants, and from
your people. They shall remain
in the river only."
12 Then Moses and Aaron went
out from Pharaoh. And Moses
[a]cried out to the LORD concerning
the frogs which He had brought
against Pharaoh.
13 So the LORD did according
to the word of Moses. And the
frogs died out of the houses, out
of the courtyards, and out of the
fields.
14 They gathered them together
in heaps, and the land stank.
15 But when Pharaoh saw that
there was [a]relief, [b]he hardened
his heart and did not heed them,
as the LORD had said.
16 So the LORD said to Moses,
"Say to Aaron, 'Stretch out your
rod, and strike the dust of the
land, so that it may become
[1]lice throughout all the land of
Egypt.' "
17 And they did so. For Aaron
stretched out his hand with his
rod and struck the dust of the
earth, and [a]it became lice on
man and beast. All the dust of
the land became lice throughout
all the land of Egypt.
18 Now [a]the magicians so
worked with their [1]enchant-
ments to bring forth lice, but
they [b]could not. So there were
lice on man and beast.

10 [a]Ex. 9:14; 15:11
12 [a]Ex. 8:30; 9:33; 10:18; 32:11
15 [a]Eccl. 8:11 [b]Ex. 7:14, 22; 9:34
16 [1]*gnats*
17 [a]Ps. 105:31
18 [a]Ex. 7:11, 12; 8:7 [b]Dan. 5:8 [1]*secret arts*
19 [a]Ex. 7:5; 10:7 [b]Ex. 8:15 [1]An act of God
20 [a]Ex. 7:15; 9:13 [b]Ex. 3:18; 4:23; 5:1, 3; 8:1
22 [a]Ex. 9:4, 6, 26; 10:23; 11:6, 7; 12:13 [b]Gen. 50:8 [c]Ex. 7:5, 17; 10:2; 14:4 [d]Ex. 9:29
23 [a]Ex. 4:8 [1]Lit. *set a ransom,* Ex. 9:4; 11:7
24 [a]Ps. 78:45; 105:31
26 [a]Gen. 43:32; 46:34

19 Then the magicians said to
Pharaoh, "This *is* [a]the[1] finger of
God." But Pharaoh's [b]heart grew
hard, and he did not heed them,
just as the LORD had said.
20 And the LORD said to Moses, [a]"Rise early in the morning
and stand before Pharaoh as he
comes out to the water. Then
say to him, 'Thus says the LORD:
[b]"Let My people go, that they
may serve Me.
21 "Or else, if you will not let
My people go, behold, I will send
swarms *of flies* on you and your
servants, on your people and
into your houses. The houses
of the Egyptians shall be full
of swarms *of flies,* and also the
ground on which they *stand.*
22 "And in that day [a]I will set
apart the land of [b]Gō′shen, in
which My people dwell, that no
swarms *of flies* shall be there, in
order that you may [c]know that I
am the LORD in the midst of the
[d]land.
23 "I will [1]make a difference between My people and your people. Tomorrow this [a]sign shall
be." ' "
24 And the LORD did so. [a]Thick
swarms *of flies* came into the
house of Pharaoh, *into* his servants' houses, and into all the
land of Egypt. The land was corrupted because of the swarms *of*
flies.
25 Then Pharaoh called for Moses and Aaron, and said, "Go,
sacrifice to your God in the
land."
26 And Moses said, "It is not
right to do so, for we would be
sacrificing [a]the abomination of
the Egyptians to the LORD our
God. If we sacrifice the abomination of the Egyptians before

their eyes, then will they not
[1]stone us?
27 "We will go [a]three days' journey into the wilderness and sacrifice to the LORD our God as [b]He
will command us."
28 So Pharaoh said, "I will let
you go, that you may sacrifice to
the LORD your God in the wilderness; only you shall not go very
far away. [a]Intercede for me."
29 Then Moses said, "Indeed I
am going out from you, and I
will entreat the LORD, that the
swarms *of flies* may depart tomorrow from Pharaoh, from his
servants, and from his people.
But let Pharaoh not [a]deal deceitfully anymore in not letting
the people go to sacrifice to the
LORD."
30 So Moses went out from Pharaoh and [a]entreated the LORD.
31 And the LORD did according
to the word of Moses; He removed the swarms *of flies* from
Pharaoh, from his servants,
and from his people. Not one
remained.
32 But Pharaoh [a]hardened his
heart at this time also; neither
would he let the people go.

CHAPTER 9

9 Then the LORD said to Moses,
[a]"Go in to Pharaoh and tell
him, 'Thus says the LORD God of
the Hebrews: "Let My people go,
that they may [b]serve Me.
2 "For if you [a]refuse to let *them*
go, and still hold them,
3 "behold, the [a]hand of the
LORD will be on your cattle in
the field, on the horses, on the
donkeys, on the camels, on the
oxen, and on the sheep—a very
severe pestilence.
4 "And [a]the LORD will make a
difference between the livestock
of Israel and the livestock of
Egypt. So nothing shall die of
all *that* belongs to the children
of Israel." ' "
5 Then the LORD appointed a
set time, saying, "Tomorrow the
LORD will do this thing in the
land."
6 So the LORD did this thing
on the next day, and [a]all the
livestock of Egypt died; but of
the livestock of the children of
Israel, not one died.
7 Then Pharaoh sent, and indeed, not even one of the livestock of the Israelites was dead.
But the [a]heart of Pharaoh became hard, and he did not let the
people go.
8 So the LORD said to Moses
and Aaron, "Take for yourselves
handfuls of ashes from a furnace, and let Moses scatter it
toward the heavens in the sight
of Pharaoh.
9 "And it will become fine dust
in all the land of Egypt, and it
will cause [a]boils that break out in
sores on man and beast throughout all the land of Egypt."
10 Then they took ashes from
the furnace and stood before
Pharaoh, and Moses scattered
them toward heaven. And *they*
caused [a]boils that break out in
sores on man and beast.
11 And the [a]magicians could
not stand before Moses because
of the [b]boils, for the boils were
on the magicians and on all the
Egyptians.
12 But the LORD hardened the
heart of Pharaoh; and he [a]did
not heed them, just [b]as the LORD
had spoken to Moses.
13 Then the LORD said to Moses,
[a]"Rise early in the morning and
stand before Pharaoh, and say
to him, 'Thus says the LORD God

26 [1]Put us to death by stoning
27 [a]Ex. 3:18; 5:3 [b]Ex. 3:12
28 [a]Ex. 8:8, 15, 29, 32; 9:28
29 [a]Ex. 8:8, 15
30 [a]Ex. 8:12
32 [a]Ex. 4:21; 8:8, 15

CHAPTER 9

1 [a]Ex. 4:23; 8:1 [b]Ex. 7:16
2 [a]Ex. 8:2
3 [a]Ex. 7:4
4 [a]Ex. 8:22
6 [a]Ps. 78:48, 50
7 [a]Ex. 7:14; 8:32
9 [a]Rev. 16:2
10 [a]Deut. 28:27
11 [a][Ex. 8:18, 19] [b]Job 2:7
12 [a]Ex. 7:13 [b]Ex. 4:21
13 [a]Ex. 8:20

of the Hebrews: "Let My people
go, that they may [b]serve Me,
14 "for at this time I will send
all My plagues to your very
heart, and on your servants and
on your people, [a]that you may
know that *there is* none like Me
in all the earth.
15 "Now if I had [a]stretched out
My hand and struck you and
your people with [b]pestilence,
then you would have been cut
off from the earth.
16 "But indeed for [a]this *purpose*
I have raised you up, that I may
[b]show My power *in* you, and that
My [c]name may be declared in all
the earth.
17 "As yet you exalt yourself
against My people in that you
will not let them go.
18 "Behold, tomorrow about this
time I will cause very heavy hail
to rain down, such as has not
been in Egypt since its founding
until now.
19 "Therefore send now *and*
gather your livestock and all that
you have in the field, for the hail
shall come down on every man
and every animal which is found
in the field and is not brought
home; and they shall die." ' "
20 He who [a]feared the word of
the LORD among the [b]servants of
Pharaoh made his servants and
his livestock flee to the houses.
21 But he who did not regard
the word of the LORD left his
servants and his livestock in the
field.
22 Then the LORD said to Moses,
"Stretch out your hand toward
heaven, that there may be [a]hail
in all the land of Egypt—on
man, on beast, and on every
herb of the field, throughout the
land of Egypt."
23 And Moses stretched out
his rod toward heaven; and [a]the
LORD sent thunder and hail, and
fire darted to the ground. And
the LORD rained hail on the land
of Egypt.
24 So there was hail, and fire
mingled with the hail, so very
heavy that there was none like
it in all the land of Egypt since it
became a nation.
25 And the [a]hail struck throughout the whole land of Egypt, all
that *was* in the field, both man
and beast; and the hail struck
every herb of the field and broke
every tree of the field.
26 [a]Only in the land of Gō'shen,
where the children of Israel
were, there was no hail.
27 And Pharaoh sent and [a]called
for Moses and Aaron, and said
to them, [b]"I have sinned this
time. [c]The LORD *is* righteous, and
my people and I *are* wicked.
28 [a]"Entreat[1] the LORD, that
there may be no *more* [2]mighty
thundering and hail, for *it is*
enough. I will let you [b]go, and
you shall stay no longer."
29 So Moses said to him, "As
soon as I have gone out of the
city, I will [a]spread out my hands
to the LORD; the thunder will
cease, and there will be no more
hail, that you may know that the
[b]earth *is* the LORD's.
30 "But as for you and your servants, [a]I know that you will not
yet fear the LORD God."
31 Now the flax and the barley
were struck, [a]for the barley *was*
in the head and the flax *was* in
bud.
32 But the wheat and the spelt
were not struck, for they *are*
[1]late crops.
33 So Moses went out of the

13 [b]Ex. 9:1
14 [a]Ex. 8:10
15 [a]Ex. 3:20; 7:5 [b]Ex. 5:3
16 [a][Rom. 9:17, 18] [b]Ex. 7:4, 5; 10:1; 11:9; 14:17 [c]1 Kin. 8:43
20 [a][Prov. 13:13] [b]Ex. 8:19; 10:7
22 [a]Rev. 16:21
23 [a]Josh. 10:11
25 [a]Ps. 78:47, 48; 105:32, 33
26 [a]Ex. 8:22, 23; 9:4, 6; 10:23; 11:7; 12:13
27 [a]Ex. 8:8 [b]Ex. 9:34; 10:16, 17 [c]2 Chr. 12:6
28 [a]Ex. 8:8, 28; 10:17 [b]Ex. 8:25; 10:8, 24 [1]*Pray to, Make supplication to* [2]Lit. *voices of God* or *sounds of God*
29 [a]Is. 1:15 [b]Ps. 24:1
30 [a][Is. 26:10]
31 [a]Ruth 1:22; 2:23
32 [1]Lit. *darkened*

city from Pharaoh and [a]spread
out his hands to the LORD; then
the thunder and the hail ceased,
and the rain was not poured on
the earth.
34 And when Pharaoh saw
that the rain, the hail, and the
thunder had ceased, he sinned
yet more; and he hardened his
heart, he and his servants.
35 So [a]the heart of Pharaoh was
hard; neither would he let the
children of Israel go, as the LORD
had spoken by Moses.

10 Now the LORD said to Moses, "Go in to Pharaoh;
[a]for I have hardened his heart
and the hearts of his servants,
[b]that I may show these signs of
Mine before him,
2 "and that [a]you may tell in the
hearing of your son and your
son's son the mighty things I
have done in Egypt, and My
signs which I have done among
them, that you may [b]know that I
am the LORD."
3 So Moses and Aaron came
in to Pharaoh and said to him,
"Thus says the LORD God of the
Hebrews: 'How long will you refuse to [a]humble yourself before
Me? Let My people go, that they
may [b]serve Me.
4 'Or else, if you refuse to let
My people go, behold, tomorrow
I will bring [a]locusts into your
territory.
5 'And they shall cover the
face of the earth, so that no one
will be able to see the earth;
and [a]they shall eat the residue
of what is left, which remains to
you from the hail, and they shall
eat every tree which grows up
for you out of the field.
6 'They shall [a]fill your houses,
the houses of all your servants,
and the houses of all the Egyptians—which neither your fathers nor your fathers' fathers
have seen, since the day that
they were on the earth to this
day.' " And he turned and went
out from Pharaoh.
7 Then Pharaoh's [a]servants
said to him, "How long shall this
man be [b]a snare to us? Let the
men go, that they may serve the
LORD their God. Do you not yet
know that Egypt is destroyed?"
8 So Moses and Aaron were
brought again to Pharaoh, and
he said to them, "Go, serve the
LORD your God. Who *are* the
ones that are going?"
9 And Moses said, "We will
go with our young and our old;
with our sons and our daughters, with our flocks and our
herds we will go, for [a]we must
hold a feast to the LORD."
10 Then he said to them, "The
LORD had better be with you
when I let you and your little ones go! Beware, for evil is
ahead of you.
11 "Not so! Go now, you *who
are* men, and serve the LORD, for
that is what you desired." And
they were driven [a]out from Pharaoh's presence.
12 Then the LORD said to Moses,
[a]"Stretch out your hand over the
land of Egypt for the locusts,
that they may come upon the
land of Egypt, and [b]eat every
herb of the land—all that the
hail has left."
13 So Moses stretched out his
rod over the land of Egypt, and
the LORD brought an east wind
on the land all that day and all
that night. When it was morning, the east wind brought the
locusts.

33 [a]Ex. 8:12; 9:29
35 [a]Ex. 4:21

CHAPTER 10

1 [a]John 12:40 [b]Ex. 7:4; 9:16
2 [a]Joel 1:3 [b]Ex. 7:5, 17; 8:22
3 [a][1 Kin. 21:29] [b]Ex. 4:23; 8:1; 9:1
4 [a]Rev. 9:3
5 [a]Ex. 9:32
6 [a]Ex. 8:3, 21
7 [a]Ex. 7:5; 8:19; 9:20; 12:33 [b]Ex. 23:33
9 [a]Ex. 5:1; 7:16
11 [a]Ex. 10:28
12 [a]Ex. 7:19 [b]Ex. 10:5, 15

14 And [a]the locusts went up
over all the land of Egypt and
rested on all the territory of
Egypt. *They were* very severe;
[b]previously there had been no
such locusts as they, nor shall
there be such after them.
15 For they [a]covered the face of
the whole earth, so that the land
was darkened; and they [b]ate every herb of the land and all
the fruit of the trees which the
hail had left. So there remained
nothing green on the trees or on
the plants of the field throughout all the land of Egypt.
16 Then Pharaoh called [a]for
Moses and Aaron in haste, and
said, [b]"I have sinned against the
LORD your God and against you.
17 "Now therefore, please forgive my sin only this once, and
[a]entreat[1] the LORD your God, that
He may take away from me this
death only."
18 So he [a]went out from Pharaoh and entreated the LORD.
19 And the LORD turned a very
strong west wind, which took
the locusts away and blew them
[a]into the Red Sea. There remained not one locust in all the
territory of Egypt.
20 But the LORD [a]hardened Pharaoh's heart, and he did not let
the children of Israel go.
21 Then the LORD said to Moses,
[a]"Stretch out your hand toward
heaven, that there may be darkness over the land of Egypt,
[1]darkness *which* may even be
felt."
22 So Moses stretched out his
hand toward heaven, and there
was [a]thick darkness in all the
land of Egypt [b]three days.
23 They did not see one another; nor did anyone rise from
his place for three days. [a]But all
the children of Israel had light
in their dwellings.
24 Then Pharaoh called to Moses and [a]said, "Go, serve the
LORD; only let your flocks and
your herds be kept back. Let your
[b]little ones also go with you."
25 But Moses said, "You must
also give [1]us sacrifices and burnt
offerings, that we may sacrifice
to the LORD our God.
26 "Our [a]livestock also shall go
with us; not a hoof shall be left
behind. For we must take some
of them to serve the LORD our
God, and even we do not know
with what we must serve the
LORD until we arrive there."
27 But the LORD [a]hardened Pharaoh's heart, and he would not
let them go.
28 Then Pharaoh said to him,
[a]"Get away from me! Take heed
to yourself and see my face no
more! For in the day you see my
face you shall die!"
29 So Moses said, "You have
spoken well. [a]I will never see
your face again."

11

And the LORD said to
Moses, "I will bring one
more plague on Pharaoh and on
Egypt. [a]Afterward he will let you
go from here. [b]When he lets *you*
go, he will surely drive you out
of here altogether.
2 "Speak now in the hearing
of the people, and let every man
ask from his neighbor and every woman from her neighbor,
[a]articles of silver and articles of
gold."
3 [a]And the LORD gave the people favor in the sight of the
Egyptians. Moreover the man
[b]Moses *was* very great in the
land of Egypt, in the sight of

14 [a]Ps. 78:46; 105:34 [b]Joel 1:4, 7; 2:1–11
15 [a]Ex. 10:5 [b]Ps. 105:35
16 [a]Ex. 8:8 [b]Ex. 9:27
17 [a]1 Kin. 13:6 [1]*make supplication to*
18 [a]Ex. 8:30
19 [a]Joel 2:20
20 [a]Ex. 4:21; 10:1; 11:10
21 [a]Ex. 9:22 [1]Lit. *that one may feel the darkness*
22 [a]Ps. 105:28 [b]Ex. 3:18
23 [a]Ex. 8:22, 23
24 [a]Ex. 8:8, 25; 10:8 [b]Ex. 10:10
25 [1]Lit. *into our hands*
26 [a]Ex. 10:9
27 [a]Ex. 4:21; 10:1, 20; 14:4, 8
28 [a]Ex. 10:11
29 [a]Heb. 11:27

CHAPTER 11

1 [a]Ex. 12:31, 33, 39 [b]Ex. 6:1; 12:39
2 [a]Ex. 3:22; 12:35, 36
3 [a]Ex. 3:21; 12:36 [b]Deut. 34:10–12

Pharaoh's servants and in the
sight of the people.
4 Then Moses said, "Thus says
the LORD: [a]'About midnight I will
go out into the midst of Egypt;
5 'and [a]all the firstborn in the
land of Egypt shall die, from the
firstborn of Pharaoh who sits on
his throne, even to the firstborn
of the female servant who *is*
behind the handmill, and all the
firstborn of the animals.
6 [a]'Then there shall be a great
cry throughout all the land of
Egypt, [b]such as was not like
it *before,* nor shall be like it
again.
7 [a]'But against none of the
children of Israel [b]shall a dog
[1]move its tongue, against man or
beast, that you may know that
the LORD does make a difference between the Egyptians and
Israel.'
8 "And [a]all these your servants
shall come down to me and bow
down to me, saying, 'Get out,
and all the people who follow
you!' After that I will go out."
[b]Then he went out from Pharaoh
in great anger.
9 But the LORD said to Moses,
[a]"Pharaoh will not heed you, so
that [b]My wonders may be multiplied in the land of Egypt."
10 So Moses and Aaron did all
these wonders before Pharaoh;
[a]and the LORD hardened Pharaoh's heart, and he did not let
the children of Israel go out of
his land.

12 Now the LORD spoke to
Moses and Aaron in the
land of Egypt, saying,
2 [a]"This month *shall be* your
beginning of months; it *shall be*
the first month of the year to
you.

4 [a]Ex. 12:12, 23, 29
5 [a]Ex. 4:23; 12:12, 29
6 [a]Ex. 12:30 [b]Ex. 10:14
7 [a]Ex. 8:22 [b]Josh. 10:21 [1]*sharpen*
8 [a]Ex. 12:31–33 [b]Heb. 11:27
9 [a]Ex. 3:19; 7:4; 10:1 [b]Ex. 7:3; 9:16
10 [a]Rom. 2:5

CHAPTER 12

2 [a]Deut. 16:1
3 [a]Josh. 4:19
5 [a][1 Pet. 1:19] [1]*perfect or sound* [2]*a year old*
6 [a]Lev. 23:5
8 [a]Num. 9:12 [b]Deut. 16:7 [c]1 Cor. 5:8
9 [a]Deut. 16:7
10 [a]Ex. 16:19; 23:18; 34:25
11 [a]Ex. 12:13, 21, 27, 43 [1]Made ready to travel
12 [a]Ex. 11:4, 5

3 "Speak to all the congregation of Israel, saying: 'On the
[a]tenth of this month every man
shall take for himself a lamb,
according to the house of *his*
father, a lamb for a household.
4 'And if the household is too
small for the lamb, let him and
his neighbor next to his house
take *it* according to the number of the persons; according to
each man's need you shall make
your count for the lamb.
5 'Your lamb shall be [a]without[1]
blemish, a male [2]of the first year.
You may take *it* from the sheep
or from the goats.
6 'Now you shall keep it until
the [a]fourteenth day of the same
month. Then the whole assembly of the congregation of Israel
shall kill it at twilight.
7 'And they shall take *some* of
the blood and put *it* on the two
doorposts and on the lintel of
the houses where they eat it.
8 'Then they shall eat the flesh
on that [a]night; [b]roasted in fire,
with [c]unleavened bread *and* with
bitter *herbs* they shall eat it.
9 'Do not eat it raw, nor boiled
at all with water, but [a]roasted in
fire—its head with its legs and
its entrails.
10 [a]'You shall let none of it remain until morning, and what
remains of it until morning you
shall burn with fire.
11 'And thus you shall eat it:
[1]*with* a belt on your waist, your
sandals on your feet, and your
staff in your hand. So you shall
eat it in haste. [a]It *is* the LORD's
Passover.
12 'For I [a]will pass through the
land of Egypt on that night, and
will strike all the firstborn in
the land of Egypt, both man and

beast; and [b]against all the gods
of Egypt I will execute judgment: [c]I *am* the LORD.
13 'Now the blood shall be
a sign for you on the houses
where you *are*. And when I see
the blood, I will pass over you;
and the plague shall not be on
you to destroy *you* when I strike
the land of Egypt.
14 'So this day shall be to you [a]a
memorial; and you shall keep it
as a [b]feast to the LORD throughout your generations. You shall
keep it as a feast [c]by an everlasting ordinance.
15 [a]'Seven days you shall eat
unleavened bread. On the first
day you shall remove leaven
from your houses. For whoever
eats leavened bread from the
first day until the seventh day,
[b]that [1]person shall be [2]cut off
from Israel.
16 'On the first day *there shall
be* [a]a holy convocation, and on
the seventh day there shall be
a holy convocation for you. No
manner of work shall be done
on them; but *that* which everyone must eat—that only may be
prepared by you.
17 'So you shall observe *the
Feast of* Unleavened Bread, for
[a]on this same day I will have
brought your [1]armies [b]out of the
land of Egypt. Therefore you
shall observe this day throughout your generations as an everlasting ordinance.
18 [a]'In the first *month*, on the
fourteenth day of the month at
evening, you shall eat unleavened bread, until the twenty-first
day of the month at evening.
19 'For [a]seven days no leaven
shall be found in your houses,
since whoever eats what is
leavened, that same person shall
be cut off from the congregation of Israel, whether *he is* a
stranger or a native of the land.
20 'You shall eat nothing leavened; in all your dwellings you
shall eat unleavened bread.' "
21 Then [a]Moses called for all
the [b]elders of Israel and said to
them, [c]"Pick out and take lambs
for yourselves according to your
families, and kill the Passover
lamb.
22 [a]"And you shall take a bunch
of hyssop, dip *it* in the blood
that *is* in the basin, and [b]strike
the lintel and the two doorposts
with the blood that *is* in the
basin. And none of you shall go
out of the door of his house until
morning.
23 [a]"For the LORD will pass
through to strike the Egyptians;
and when He sees the [b]blood on
the [1]lintel and on the two doorposts, the LORD will pass over
the door and [c]not allow [d]the destroyer to come into your houses
to strike *you*.
24 "And you shall [a]observe this
thing as an ordinance for you
and your sons forever.
25 "It will come to pass when
you come to the land which the
LORD will give you, [a]just as He
promised, that you shall keep
this service.
26 [a]"And it shall be, when your
children say to you, 'What do
you mean by this service?'
27 "that you shall say, [a]'It *is* the
Passover sacrifice of the LORD,
who passed over the houses of
the children of Israel in Egypt
when He struck the Egyptians
and delivered our households.' "
So the people [b]bowed their heads
and worshiped.

12 [b]Num. 33:4 [c]Ex. 6:2
14 [a]Ex. 13:9 [b]Lev. 23:4, 5 [c]Ex. 12:17, 24; 13:10
15 [a]Lev. 23:6 [b]Gen. 17:14 [1]*soul* [2]Put to death
16 [a]Lev. 23:2, 7, 8
17 [a]Ex. 12:14; 13:3, 10 [b]Num. 33:1 [1]*hosts*
18 [a]Lev. 23:5–8
19 [a]Ex. 12:15; 23:15; 34:18
21 [a][Heb. 11:28] [b]Ex. 3:16 [c]Num. 9:4
22 [a]Heb. 11:28 [b]Ex. 12:7
23 [a]Ex. 11:4; 12:12, 13 [b]Ex. 24:8 [c]Rev. 7:3; 9:4 [d]Heb. 11:28 [1]Crosspiece at top of door
24 [a]Ex. 12:14, 17; 13:5, 10
25 [a]Ex. 3:8, 17
26 [a]Ex. 10:2; 13:8, 14, 15
27 [a]Ex. 12:11 [b]Ex. 4:31

28 Then the children of Israel went away and [a]did *so;* just as the LORD had commanded Moses and Aaron, so they did.

29 [a]And it came to pass at midnight that [b]the LORD struck all the firstborn in the land of Egypt, from the firstborn of Pharaoh who sat on his throne to the firstborn of the captive who *was* [1]in the dungeon, and all the firstborn of [c]livestock.

30 So Pharaoh rose in the night, he, all his servants, and all the Egyptians; and there was a great cry in Egypt, for *there was* not a house where *there was* not one dead.

31 Then he [a]called for Moses and Aaron by night, and said, "Rise, go out from among my people, [b]both you and the children of Israel. And go, serve the LORD as you have [c]said.

32 [a]"Also take your flocks and your herds, as you have said, and be gone; and bless me also."

33 [a]And the Egyptians [b]urged the people, that they might send them out of the land in haste. For they said, "We *shall* all *be* dead."

34 So the people took their dough before it was leavened, having their kneading bowls bound up in their clothes on their shoulders.

35 Now the children of Israel had done according to the word of Moses, and they had asked from the Egyptians [a]articles of silver, articles of gold, and clothing.

36 [a]And the LORD had given the people favor in the sight of the Egyptians, so that they granted them *what they requested.* Thus [b]they plundered the Egyptians.

37 Then [a]the children of Israel journeyed from [b]Ram′e·sēs to Suc′coth, about [c]six hundred thousand men on foot, besides children.

38 A [a]mixed multitude went up with them also, and flocks and herds—a great deal of [b]livestock.

39 And they baked unleavened cakes of the dough which they had brought out of Egypt; for it was not leavened, because [a]they were driven out of Egypt and could not wait, nor had they prepared provisions for themselves.

40 Now the [1]sojourn of the children of Israel who lived in [2]Egypt *was* [a]four hundred and thirty years.

41 And it came to pass at the end of the four hundred and thirty years—on that very same day—it came to pass that [a]all the armies of the LORD went out from the land of Egypt.

42 It *is* [a]a [1]night of solemn observance to the LORD for bringing them out of the land of Egypt. This *is* that night of the LORD, a solemn observance for all the children of Israel throughout their generations.

43 And the LORD said to Moses and Aaron, "This *is* [a]the ordinance of the Passover: No foreigner shall eat it.

44 "But every man's servant who is bought for money, when you have [a]circumcised him, then he may eat it.

45 [a]"A sojourner and a hired servant shall not eat it.

46 "In one house it shall be eaten; you shall not carry any of the flesh outside the house, [a]nor shall you break one of its bones.

28 [a][Heb. 11:28]
29 [a]Ex. 11:4, 5 [b]Num. 8:17; 33:4 [c]Ex. 9:6 [1]*in prison*
31 [a]Ex. 10:28, 29 [b]Ex. 8:25; 11:1 [c]Ex. 10:9
32 [a]Ex. 10:9, 26
33 [a]Ex. 10:7 [b]Ps. 105:38
35 [a]Ex. 3:21, 22; 11:2, 3
36 [a]Ex. 3:21 [b]Gen. 15:14
37 [a]Num. 33:3, 5 [b]Gen. 47:11 [c]Ex. 38:26
38 [a]Num. 11:4 [b]Deut. 3:19
39 [a]Ex. 6:1; 11:1; 12:31–33
40 [a]Acts 7:6 [1]Length of the stay [2]Sam., LXX *Egypt and Canaan*
41 [a]Ex. 3:8, 10; 6:6; 7:4
42 [a]Deut. 16:1, 6 [1]*night of vigil*
43 [a]Num. 9:14
44 [a]Gen. 17:12, 13
45 [a]Lev. 22:10
46 [a][John 19:33, 36]

47 [a]"All the congregation of Israel shall keep it.
48 "And [a]when a stranger
[1]dwells with you *and wants* to
keep the Passover to the LORD,
let all his males be circumcised,
and then let him come near and
keep it; and he shall be as a
native of the land. For no uncircumcised person shall eat it.
49 [a]"One law shall be for the
native-born and for the stranger
who dwells among you."
50 Thus all the children of Israel
did; as the LORD commanded
Moses and Aaron, so they did.
51 [a]And it came to pass, on
that very same day, that the
LORD brought the children of
Israel out of the land of Egypt
[b]according to their armies.

13
Then the LORD spoke to
Moses, saying,
2 [a]"Consecrate[1] to Me all the
firstborn, whatever opens the
womb among the children of
Israel, *both* of man and beast; it
is Mine."
3 And Moses said to the people: [a]"Remember this day in
which you went out of Egypt,
out of the house of [1]bondage; for
[b]by strength of hand the LORD
brought you out of this *place.* [c]No
leavened bread shall be eaten.
4 [a]"On this day you are going
out, in the month Ā′bib.
5 "And it shall be, when the
LORD [a]brings you into the [b]land
of the Cā′naan·ītes and the Hit′-
tītes and the Am′o·rītes and
the Hī′vītes and the Jeb′ū·sītes,
which He [c]swore to your fathers
to give you, a land flowing with
milk and honey, [d]that you shall
keep this service in this month.
6 [a]"Seven days you shall eat
unleavened bread, and on the
seventh day *there shall be* a
feast to the LORD.
7 "Unleavened bread shall be
eaten seven days. And [a]no leavened bread shall be seen among
you, nor shall leaven be seen
among you in all your quarters.
8 "And you shall [a]tell your son
in that day, saying, '*This is done*
because of what the LORD did for
me when I came up from Egypt.'
9 "It shall be as [a]a sign to
you on your hand and as a memorial between your eyes, that
the LORD's law may be in your
mouth; for with a strong hand
the LORD has brought you out of
Egypt.
10 [a]"You shall therefore keep
this [1]ordinance in its season
from year to year.
11 "And it shall be, when the
LORD [a]brings you into the land of
the [b]Cā′naan·ītes, as He swore to
you and your fathers, and gives
it to you,
12 [a]"that you shall [1]set apart to
the LORD all that open the womb,
that is, every firstborn that comes
from an animal which you have;
the males *shall be* the LORD's.
13 "But [a]every firstborn of a
donkey you shall redeem with
a lamb; and if you will not redeem *it,* then you shall break
its neck. And all the firstborn of
man among your sons [b]you shall
redeem.
14 [a]"So it shall be, when your
son asks you in time to come,
saying, 'What *is* this?' that you
shall say to him, [b]'By strength
of hand the LORD brought us
out of Egypt, out of the house of
bondage.
15 'And it came to pass, when
Pharaoh was stubborn about letting us go, that [a]the LORD killed

47 [a]Ex. 12:6
48 [a]Num. 9:14 [1]As a resident alien
49 [a]Num. 15:15, 16
51 [a]Ex. 12:41; 20:2 [b]Ex. 6:26

CHAPTER 13

2 [a]Luke 2:23 [1]*Set apart*
3 [a]Deut. 16:3 [b]Ex. 3:20; 6:1 [c]Ex. 12:8, 19 [1]Lit. *slaves*
4 [a]Ex. 12:2; 23:15; 34:18
5 [a]Ex. 3:8, 17 [b]Gen. 17:8 [c]Ex. 6:8 [d]Ex. 12:25, 26
6 [a]Ex. 12:15–20
7 [a]Ex. 12:19
8 [a]Ex. 10:2; 12:26; 13:14
9 [a]Deut. 6:8; 11:18
10 [a]Ex. 12:14, 24 [1]*regulation*
11 [a]Ex. 13:5 [b]Num. 21:3
12 [a]Lev. 27:26 [1]Lit. *cause to pass over*
13 [a]Ex. 34:20 [b]Num. 3:46, 47; 18:15, 16
14 [a]Deut. 6:20 [b]Ex. 13:3, 9
15 [a]Ex. 12:29

all the firstborn in the land of Egypt, both the firstborn of man and the firstborn of beast. Therefore I sacrifice to the LORD all males that open the womb, but all the firstborn of my sons I redeem.'

16 "It shall be as [a]a sign on your hand and as frontlets between your eyes, for by strength of hand the LORD brought us out of Egypt."

17 Then it came to pass, when Pharaoh had let the people go, that God did not lead them *by* way of the land of the Phi·lis′-tines, although that *was* near; for God said, "Lest perhaps the people [a]change their minds when they see war, and [b]return to Egypt."

18 So God [a]led the people around *by* way of the wilderness of the Red Sea. And the children of Israel went up in orderly ranks out of the land of Egypt.

19 And Moses took the [a]bones of [b]Joseph with him, for he had placed the children of Israel under solemn oath, saying, [c]"God will surely [1]visit you, and you shall carry up my bones from here with you."

20 So [a]they took their journey from [b]Suc′coth and camped in Ē′tham at the edge of the wilderness.

21 And [a]the LORD went before them by day in a pillar of cloud to lead the way, and by night in a pillar of fire to give them light, so as to go by day and night.

22 He did not take away the pillar of cloud by day or the pillar of fire by night *from* before the people.

14

Now the LORD spoke to Moses, saying:

2 "Speak to the children of Israel, [a]that they turn and camp before [b]Pī Ha·hī′roth, between [c]Mig′dōl and the sea, opposite Bā′al Zē′phon; you shall camp before it by the sea.

3 "For Pharaoh will say of the children of Israel, [a]'They *are* bewildered by the land; the wilderness has closed them in.'

4 "Then [a]I will harden Pharaoh's heart, so that he will pursue them; and I [b]will gain honor over Pharaoh and over all his army, [c]that the Egyptians may know that I *am* the LORD." And they did so.

5 Now it was told the king of Egypt that the people had fled, and [a]the heart of Pharaoh and his servants was turned against the people; and they said, "Why have we done this, that we have let Israel go from serving us?"

6 So he [1]made ready his chariot and took his people with him.

7 Also, he took [a]six hundred choice chariots, and all the chariots of Egypt with captains over every one of them.

8 And the LORD [a]hardened the heart of Pharaoh king of Egypt, and he pursued the children of Israel; and [b]the children of Israel went out with boldness.

9 So the [a]Egyptians pursued them, all the horses *and* chariots of Pharaoh, his horsemen and his army, and overtook them camping by the sea beside Pī Ha·hī′roth, before Bā′al Zē′phon.

10 And when Pharaoh drew near, the children of Israel lifted their eyes, and behold, the Egyptians marched after them. So they were very afraid, and the children of Israel [a]cried out to the LORD.

16 [a]Ex. 13:9
17 [a]Ex. 14:11 [b]Deut. 17:16
18 [a]Num. 33:6
19 [a]Gen. 50:24, 25 [b]Ex. 1:6; Deut. 33:13–17 [c]Ex. 4:31 [1]*give attention to*
20 [a]Num. 33:6–8 [b]Ex. 12:37
21 [a]Deut. 1:33

CHAPTER 14

2 [a]Ex. 13:18 [b]Num. 33:7 [c]Jer. 44:1
3 [a]Ps. 71:11
4 [a]Ex. 4:21; 7:3; 14:17 [b]Ex. 9:16; 14:17, 18, 23 [c]Ex. 7:5; 14:25
5 [a]Ps. 105:25
6 [1]*harnessed*
7 [a]Ex. 15:4
8 [a]Ex. 14:4 [b]Num. 33:3
9 [a]Josh. 24:6
10 [a]Neh. 9:9

11 [a]Then they said to Moses,
"Because *there were* no graves
in Egypt, have you taken us
away to die in the wilderness?
Why have you so dealt with us,
to bring us up out of Egypt?
12 [a]"*Is* this not the word that we
told you in Egypt, saying, 'Let
us alone that we may serve the
Egyptians'? For *it would have
been* better for us to serve the
Egyptians than that we should
die in the wilderness."
13 And Moses said to the people,
[a]"Do not be afraid. [b]Stand still,
and see the [c]salvation[1] of the
LORD, which He will accomplish
for you today. For the Egyptians
whom you see today, you shall
[d]see again no more forever.
14 [a]"The LORD will fight for
you, and you shall [b]hold[1] your
peace."
15 And the LORD said to Moses,
"Why do you cry to Me? Tell the
children of Israel to go forward.
16 "But [a]lift up your rod, and
stretch out your hand over the
sea and divide it. And the children of Israel shall go on dry
ground through the midst of the
sea.
17 "And I indeed will [a]harden
the hearts of the Egyptians, and
they shall follow them. So I will
[b]gain honor over Pharaoh and
over all his army, his chariots,
and his horsemen.
18 "Then the Egyptians shall
know that I *am* the LORD, when
I have gained honor for Myself
over Pharaoh, his chariots, and
his horsemen."
19 And the Angel of God, [a]who
went before the camp of Israel,
moved and went behind them;
and the pillar of cloud went from
before them and stood behind
them.
20 So it came between the camp
of the Egyptians and the camp
of Israel. Thus it was a cloud and
darkness *to the one*, and it gave
light by night *to the other*, so
that the one did not come near
the other all that night.
21 Then Moses stretched out his
hand over the sea; and the LORD
caused the sea to go *back* by a
strong east wind all that night,
and [a]made the sea into dry *land*,
and the waters were [b]divided.
22 So [a]the children of Israel
went into the midst of the sea on
the dry *ground*, and the waters
were [b]a wall to them on their
right hand and on their left.
23 And the Egyptians pursued
and went after them into the
midst of the sea, all Pharaoh's
horses, his chariots, and his
horsemen.
24 Now it came to pass, in the
morning [a]watch, that [b]the LORD
looked down upon the army of
the Egyptians through the pillar
of fire and cloud, and He [1]trou-
bled the army of the Egyptians.
25 And He [1]took off their chariot wheels, so that they drove
them with difficulty; and the
Egyptians said, "Let us flee from
the face of Israel, for the LORD
[a]fights for them against the
Egyptians."
26 Then the LORD said to Moses, "Stretch out your hand over
the sea, that the waters may
come back upon the Egyptians,
on their chariots, and on their
horsemen."
27 And Moses stretched out his
hand over the sea; and when
the morning appeared, the sea
[a]returned to its full depth, while

11 [a]Ps. 106:7, 8
12 [a]Ex. 5:21; 6:9
13 [a]2 Chr. 20:15, 17 [b]Ps. 46:10, 11 [c]Ex. 14:30; 15:2 [d]Deut. 28:68 [1]*deliverance*
14 [a]Deut. 1:30; 3:22 [b][Is. 30:15] [1]Lit. *be quiet*
16 [a]Num. 20:8, 9, 11
17 [a]Ex. 14:8 [b]Ex. 14:4
19 [a][Is. 63:9]
21 [a]Ps. 66:6; 106:9; 136:13, 14 [b]Is. 63:12, 13
22 [a]Ex. 15:19 [b]Ex. 14:29; 15:8
24 [a]Judg. 7:19 [b]Ex. 13:21 [1]*confused*
25 [a]Ex. 7:5; 14:4, 14, 18 [1]Sam., LXX, Syr. *bound*
27 [a]Josh. 4:18

the Egyptians were fleeing into
it. So the LORD [b]overthrew[1] the
Egyptians in the midst of the
sea.
28 Then [a]the waters returned
and covered the chariots, the
horsemen, *and* all the army of
Pharaoh that came into the sea
after them. Not so much as one
of them remained.
29 But [a]the children of Israel
had walked on dry *land* in the
midst of the sea, and the waters
were a wall to them on their
right hand and on their left.
30 So the LORD [a]saved[1] Israel
that day out of the hand of
the Egyptians, and Israel [b]saw
the Egyptians dead on the
seashore.
31 Thus Israel saw the great
[1]work which the LORD had done
in Egypt; so the people feared
the LORD, and [a]believed the LORD
and His servant Moses.

15 Then [a]Moses and the
children of Israel sang
this song to the LORD, and spoke,
saying:

"I will [b]sing to the LORD,
For He has triumphed
gloriously!
The horse and its rider
He has thrown into the sea!
2 The LORD *is* my strength and
[a]song,
And He has become my
salvation;
He *is* my God, and [b]I will
praise Him;
My [c]father's God, and I [d]will
exalt Him.
3 The LORD *is* a man of [a]war;
The LORD *is* His [b]name.
4 [a]Pharaoh's chariots and his
army He has cast into
the sea;
[b]His chosen captains also are
drowned in the Red Sea.
5 The depths have covered
them;
[a]They sank to the bottom
like a stone.

6 "Your [a]right hand, O LORD,
has become glorious in
power;
Your right hand, O LORD,
has dashed the enemy in
pieces.
7 And in the greatness of Your
[a]excellence
You have overthrown those
who rose against You;
You sent forth [b]Your wrath;
It [c]consumed them [d]like
stubble.
8 And [a]with the blast of Your
nostrils
The waters were gathered
together;
[b]The floods stood upright
like a heap;
The depths [1]congealed in
the heart of the sea.
9 [a]The enemy said, 'I will
pursue,
I will overtake,
I will [b]divide the spoil;
My desire shall be satisfied
on them.
I will draw my sword,
My hand shall destroy
them.'
10 You blew with Your wind,
The sea covered them;
They sank like lead in the
mighty waters.

11 "Who[a] *is* like You, O LORD,
among the [1]gods?
Who *is* like You, [b]glorious in
holiness,
Fearful in [c]praises, [d]doing
wonders?

27 [b]Ex. 15:1, 7 [1]Lit. *shook off*
28 [a]Ps. 78:53; 106:11
29 [a]Ps. 66:6; 78:52, 53
30 [a]Ps. 106:8, 10 [b]Ps. 58:10; 59:10 [1]*delivered*
31 [a]John 2:11; 11:45 [1]Lit. *hand with which the LORD worked*

CHAPTER 15

1 [a]Ps. 106:12 [b]Is. 12:1–6
2 [a]Is. 12:2 [b]Gen. 28:21, 22 [c]Ex. 3:6, 15, 16 [d]Is. 25:1
3 [a]Rev. 19:11 [b]Ps. 24:8; 83:18
4 [a]Ex. 14:28 [b]Ex. 14:7
5 [a]Neh. 9:11
6 [a]Ps. 17:7; 118:15
7 [a]Deut. 33:26 [b]Ps. 78:49, 50 [c]Ps. 59:13 [d]Is. 5:24
8 [a]Ex. 14:21, 22, 29 [b]Ps. 78:13 [1]*became firm*
9 [a]Judg. 5:30 [b]Is. 53:12
11 [a]1 Kin. 8:23 [b]Is. 6:3 [c]1 Chr. 16:25 [d]Ps. 77:11, 14 [1]*mighty ones*

12 You stretched out Your right
hand;
The earth swallowed them.
13 You in Your mercy have [a]led
forth
The people whom You have
redeemed;
You have guided *them* in
Your strength
To [b]Your holy habitation.

14 "The [a]people will hear *and* be
afraid;
[b]Sorrow[1] will take hold of the
inhabitants of Phi·lis′ti·a.
15 [a]Then [b]the chiefs of Ē′dom
will be dismayed;
[c]The mighty men of Mō′ab,
Trembling will take hold of
them;
[d]All the inhabitants of
Cā′naan will [e]melt away.
16 [a]Fear and dread will fall on
them;
By the greatness of Your
arm
They will be [b]*as* still as a
stone,
Till Your people pass over,
O LORD,
Till the people pass over
[c]Whom You have purchased.
17 You will bring them in and
[a]plant them
In the [b]mountain of Your
inheritance,
In the place, O LORD, *which*
You have made
For Your own dwelling,
The [c]sanctuary, O Lord,
which Your hands have
established.

18 "The[a] LORD shall reign
forever and ever."

19 For the [a]horses of Pharaoh
went with his chariots and his
horsemen into the sea, and [b]the
LORD brought back the waters of
the sea upon them. But the children of Israel went on dry *land*
in the midst of the sea.
20 Then Miriam [a]the prophetess, [b]the sister of Aaron, [c]took
the timbrel in her hand; and all
the women went out after her
[d]with timbrels and with dances.
21 And Miriam [a]answered
them:

[b]"Sing to the LORD,
For He has triumphed
gloriously!
The horse and its rider
He has thrown into the sea!"

22 So Moses brought Israel
from the Red Sea; then they
went out into the Wilderness of
[a]Shūr. And they went three days
in the wilderness and found no
[b]water.
23 Now when they came to
[a]Mar′ah, they could not drink
the waters of Mar′ah, for they
were bitter. Therefore the name
of it was called [1]Mar′ah.
24 And the people [a]complained
against Moses, saying, "What
shall we drink?"
25 So he cried out to the LORD,
and the LORD showed him a tree.
[a]When he cast *it* into the waters,
the waters were made sweet.
There He [b]made a statute and an
[1]ordinance for them, and there
[c]He tested them,
26 and said, [a]"If you diligently
heed the voice of the LORD your
God and do what is right in His
sight, give ear to His commandments and keep all His statutes,
I will put none of the [b]diseases
on you which I have brought on

13 [a][Ps. 77:20] [b]Ps. 78:54
14 [a]Josh. 2:9 [b]Ps. 48:6 [1]*Anguish*
15 [a]Gen. 36:15, 40 [b]Deut. 2:4 [c]Num. 22:3, 4 [d]Josh. 5:1 [e]Josh. 2:9–11, 24
16 [a]Josh. 2:9 [b]1 Sam. 25:37 [c]Jer. 31:11
17 [a]Ps. 44:2; 80:8, 15 [b]Ps. 2:6; 78:54, 68 [c]Ps. 68:16; 76:2; 132:13, 14
18 [a]Is. 57:15
19 [a]Ex. 14:23 [b]Ex. 14:28
20 [a]Judg. 4:4 [b]Num. 26:59 [c]1 Sam. 18:6 [d]Judg. 11:34; 21:21
21 [a]1 Sam. 18:7 [b]Ex. 15:1
22 [a]Gen. 16:7; 20:1; 25:18 [b]Num. 20:2
23 [a]Num. 33:8 [1]Lit. *Bitter*
24 [a]Ex. 14:11; 16:2
25 [a]2 Kin. 2:21 [b]Josh. 24:25 [c]Deut. 8:2, 16 [1]*regulation*
26 [a]Deut. 7:12, 15 [b]Deut. 28:27, 58, 60

the Egyptians. For I *am* the LORD
[c]who heals you."
27 [a]Then they came to Ē'lim,
where there *were* twelve wells
of water and seventy palm trees;
so they camped there by the
waters.

16
16 And they [a]journeyed
from Ē'lim, and all the
congregation of the children of
Israel came to the Wilderness of
Sin, which is between Ē'lim and
[b]Sinai, on the fifteenth day of
the second month after they departed from the land of Egypt.
2 Then the whole congregation of the children of Israel
[a]complained against Moses and
Aaron in the wilderness.
3 And the children of Israel
said to them, [a]"Oh, that we had
died by the hand of the LORD in
the land of Egypt, [b]when we sat
by the pots of meat *and* when
we ate bread to the full! For you
have brought us out into this
wilderness to kill this whole assembly with hunger."
4 Then the LORD said to Moses,
"Behold, I will rain [a]bread from
heaven for you. And the people
shall go out and gather [1]a certain quota every day, that I may
[b]test them, whether they will
[c]walk in My law or not.
5 "And it shall be on the sixth
day that they shall prepare what
they bring in, and [a]it shall be
twice as much as they gather
daily."
6 Then Moses and Aaron said
to all the children of Israel, [a]"At
evening you shall know that the
LORD has brought you out of the
land of Egypt.
7 "And in the morning you shall
see [a]the glory of the LORD; for He
[b]hears your complaints against
the LORD. But [c]what *are* we, that
you complain against us?"
8 Also Moses said, "*This shall
be seen* when the LORD gives you
meat to eat in the evening, and
in the morning bread to the full;
for the LORD hears your complaints which you make against
Him. And what *are* we? Your
complaints *are* not against us
but [a]against the LORD."
9 Then Moses spoke to Aaron,
"Say to all the congregation of
the children of Israel, [a]'Come
near before the LORD, for He has
heard your complaints.' "
10 Now it came to pass, as
Aaron spoke to the whole congregation of the children of Israel, that they looked toward
the wilderness, and behold, the
glory of the LORD [a]appeared in
the cloud.
11 And the LORD spoke to Moses, saying,
12 [a]"I have heard the complaints
of the children of Israel. Speak
to them, saying, [b]'At twilight
you shall eat meat, and [c]in the
morning you shall be filled with
bread. And you shall know that I
am the LORD your God.' "
13 So it was that [a]quails came
up at evening and covered the
camp, and in the morning [b]the
dew lay all around the camp.
14 And when the layer of dew
lifted, there, on the surface of the
wilderness, was [a]a small round
[b]substance, *as* fine as frost on
the ground.
15 So when the children of Israel saw *it,* they said to one
another, "What is it?" For they
did not know what it *was.* And
Moses said to them, [a]"This *is* the
bread which the LORD has given
you to eat.

26 [c]Ex. 23:25
27 [a]Num. 33:9

CHAPTER 16

1 [a]Num. 33:10, 11 [b]Ex. 12:6, 51; 19:1
2 [a]1 Cor. 10:10
3 [a]Lam. 4:9 [b]Num. 11:4, 5
4 [a][John 6:31–35] [b]Deut. 8:2, 16 [c]Judg. 2:22 [1]Lit. *the portion of a day in its day*
5 [a]Lev. 25:21
6 [a]Ex. 6:7
7 [a]John 11:4, 40 [b]Num. 14:27; 17:5 [c]Num. 16:11
8 [a]1 Sam. 8:7
9 [a]Num. 16:16
10 [a]Num. 16:19
12 [a]Ex. 16:8 [b]Ex. 16:6 [c]Ex. 16:7
13 [a]Num. 11:31 [b]Num. 11:9
14 [a]Num. 11:7, 8 [b]Ps. 147:16
15 [a]1 Cor. 10:3

16 “This is the thing which the
LORD has commanded: ‘Let every man gather it [a]according to
each one’s need, one [b]omer for
each person, *according to the*
number of persons; let every
man take for *those* who *are* in
his tent.’ ”
17 Then the children of Israel
did so and gathered, some more,
some less.
18 So when they measured *it* by
omers, [a]he who gathered much
had nothing left over, and he
who gathered little had no lack.
Every man had gathered according to each one’s need.
19 And Moses said, “Let no one
[a]leave any of it till morning.”
20 Notwithstanding they did not
[1]heed Moses. But some of them
left part of it until morning, and
it bred worms and stank. And
Moses was angry with them.
21 So they gathered it every
morning, every man according
to his need. And when the sun
became hot, it melted.
22 And so it was, on the sixth
day, *that* they gathered twice
as much bread, two omers for
each one. And all the rulers of
the congregation came and told
Moses.
23 Then he said to them, “This *is*
what the LORD has said: ‘Tomorrow *is* [a]a Sabbath rest, a holy
Sabbath to the LORD. Bake what
you will bake *today,* and boil
what you will boil; and lay up
for yourselves all that remains,
to be kept until morning.’ ”
24 So they laid it up till morning, as Moses commanded; and
it did not [a]stink, nor were there
any worms in it.
25 Then Moses said, “Eat that
today, for today *is* a Sabbath to
the LORD; today you will not find
it in the field.
26 [a]“Six days you shall gather
it, but on the seventh day, the
Sabbath, there will be none.”
27 Now it happened *that some*
of the people went out on the
seventh day to gather, but they
found none.
28 And the LORD said to Moses,
“How long [a]do you refuse to
keep My commandments and
My laws?
29 “See! For the LORD has given
you the Sabbath; therefore He
gives you on the sixth day bread
for two days. Let every man remain in his place; let no man go
out of his place on the seventh
day.”
30 So the people rested on the
seventh day.
31 And the house of Israel
called its name [1]Manna. And [a]it
was like white coriander seed,
and the taste of it *was* like wafers *made* with honey.
32 Then Moses said, “This *is* the
thing which the LORD has commanded: ‘Fill an omer with it,
to be kept for your generations,
that they may see the bread with
which I fed you in the wilderness, when I brought you out of
the land of Egypt.’ ”
33 And Moses said to Aaron,
[a]“Take a pot and put an omer of
manna in it, and lay it up before
the LORD, to be kept for your
generations.”
34 As the LORD commanded Moses, so Aaron laid it up [a]before
the Testimony, to be kept.
35 And the children of Israel
[a]ate manna [b]forty years, [c]until
they came to an inhabited land;
they ate manna until they came

16 [a]Ex. 12:4 [b]Ex. 16:32, 36
18 [a]2 Cor. 8:15
19 [a]Ex. 12:10; 16:23; 23:18
20 [1]*listen to*
23 [a]Gen. 2:3
24 [a]Ex. 16:20
26 [a]Ex. 20:9, 10
28 [a]2 Kin. 17:14
31 [a]Num. 11:7–9 [1]Lit. *What?* Ex. 16:15
33 [a]Heb. 9:4
34 [a]Num. 17:10
35 [a]Deut. 8:3, 16 [b]Num. 33:38 [c]Josh. 5:12

to the border of the land of Cā′naan.

36 Now an omer *is* one-tenth of an ephah.

17 Then [a]all the congregation of the children of Israel set out on their journey from the Wilderness of [b]Sin, according to the commandment of the LORD, and camped in Reph′i·dim; but *there was* no water for the people to [c]drink.

2 [a]Therefore the people contended with Moses, and said, "Give us water, that we may drink." So Moses said to them, "Why do you contend with me? Why do you [b]tempt the LORD?"

3 And the people thirsted there for water, and the people [a]complained against Moses, and said, "Why *is* it you have brought us up out of Egypt, to kill us and our children and our [b]livestock with thirst?"

4 So Moses [a]cried out to the LORD, saying, "What shall I do with this people? They are almost ready to [b]stone[1] me!"

5 And the LORD said to Moses, [a]"Go on before the people, and take with you some of the elders of Israel. Also take in your hand your rod with which [b]you struck the river, and go.

6 [a]"Behold, I will stand before you there on the rock in Hō′reb; and you shall strike the rock, and water will come out of it, that the people may drink." And Moses did so in the sight of the elders of Israel.

7 So he called the name of the place [a]Mas′sah[1] and [2]Mer′i·bah, because of the contention of the children of Israel, and because they [3]tempted the LORD, saying, "Is the LORD among us or not?"

CHAPTER 17

1 [a]Ex. 16:1 [b]Num. 33:11–15 [c]Ex. 15:22

2 [a]Num. 20:2, 3, 13 [b][Deut. 6:16]

3 [a]Ex. 16:2, 3 [b]Ex. 12:38

4 [a]Ex. 14:15 [b]John 8:59; 10:31 [1]Put me to death by stoning

5 [a]Ezek. 2:6 [b]Num. 20:8

6 [a]Num. 20:10, 11

7 [a]Num. 20:13, 24; 27:14 [1]Lit. *Tempted* [2]Lit. *Contention* [3]*tested*

8 [a]Gen. 36:12

9 [a]Ex. 4:20

11 [a][James 5:16]

12 [1]Weary of being held up

14 [a]Ex. 24:4; 34:27 [b]1 Sam. 15:3

15 [1]Heb. *YHWH Nissi*

16 [a]Gen. 22:14–16 [1]Lit. *a hand is upon the throne of the LORD*

CHAPTER 18

1 [a]Ex. 2:16, 18; 3:1 [b][Ps. 106:2, 8]

8 [a]Now Am′a·lek came and fought with Israel in Reph′i·dim.

9 And Moses said to Joshua, "Choose us some men and go out, fight with Am′a·lek. Tomorrow I will stand on the top of the hill with [a]the rod of God in my hand."

10 So Joshua did as Moses said to him, and fought with Am′a·lek. And Moses, Aaron, and Hur went up to the top of the hill.

11 And so it was, when Moses [a]held up his hand, that Israel prevailed; and when he let down his hand, Am′a·lek prevailed.

12 But Moses' hands *became* [1]heavy; so they took a stone and put *it* under him, and he sat on it. And Aaron and Hur supported his hands, one on one side, and the other on the other side; and his hands were steady until the going down of the sun.

13 So Joshua defeated Am′a·lek and his people with the edge of the sword.

14 Then the LORD said to Moses, [a]"Write this *for* a memorial in the book and recount *it* in the hearing of Joshua, that [b]I will utterly blot out the remembrance of Am′a·lek from under heaven."

15 And Moses built an altar and called its name, [1]The-LORD-Is-My-Banner;

16 for he said, "Because [1]the LORD has [a]sworn: the LORD *will have* war with Am′a·lek from generation to generation."

18 And [a]Jeth′rō, the priest of Mid′i·an, Moses' father-in-law, heard of all that [b]God had done for Moses and for

Israel His people—that the LORD
had brought Israel out of Egypt.
2 Then Jeth′rō, Moses' father-
in-law, took [a]Zip·pō′rah, Moses' wife, after he had sent her
back,
3 with her [a]two sons, of whom
the name of one *was* [1]Ger′shom
(for he said, [b]"I have been a
[2]stranger in a foreign land")
4 and the name of the other
was [1]El·i·ē′zer (for *he said*, "The
God of my father *was* my [a]help,
and delivered me from the sword
of Pharaoh");
5 and Jeth′rō, Moses' father-in-
law, came with his sons and his
wife to Moses in the wilderness,
where he was encamped at [a]the
mountain of God.
6 Now he had said to Moses,
"I, your father-in-law Jeth′rō, am
coming to you with your wife
and her two sons with her."
7 So Moses [a]went out to meet
his father-in-law, bowed down,
and [b]kissed him. And they asked
each other about *their* well-being, and they went into the tent.
8 And Moses told his father-in-
law all that the LORD had done
to Pharaoh and to the Egyptians
for Israel's sake, all the hardship
that had come upon them on
the way, and *how* the LORD had
[a]delivered them.
9 Then Jeth′rō rejoiced for all
the [a]good which the LORD had
done for Israel, whom He had
delivered out of the hand of the
Egyptians.
10 And Jeth′rō said, [a]"Blessed
be the LORD, who has delivered
you out of the hand of the Egyptians and out of the hand of
Pharaoh, *and* who has delivered
the people from under the hand
of the Egyptians.
11 "Now I know that the LORD *is*
[a]greater than all the gods; [b]for in
the very thing in which they [1]be-
haved [c]proudly, *He was* above
them."
12 Then Jeth′rō, Moses' father-
in-law, [1]took a burnt [a]offering
and *other* sacrifices *to offer* to
God. And Aaron came with all
the elders of Israel [b]to eat bread
with Moses' father-in-law before
God.
13 And so it was, on the next
day, that Moses [a]sat to judge the
people; and the people stood before Moses from morning until
evening.
14 So when Moses' father-in-
law saw all that he did for the
people, he said, "What *is* this
thing that you are doing for
the people? Why do you alone
[1]sit, and all the people stand
before you from morning until
evening?"
15 And Moses said to his father-
in-law, "Because [a]the people
come to me to inquire of God.
16 "When they have [a]a [1]diffi-
culty, they come to me, and I
judge between one and another;
and I make known the statutes
of God and His laws."
17 So Moses' father-in-law said
to him, "The thing that you do *is*
not good.
18 "Both you and these people
who *are* with you will surely
wear yourselves out. For this
thing *is* too much for you; [a]you
are not able to perform it by
yourself.
19 "Listen now to my voice; I
will give you [1]counsel, and God
will be with you: Stand [a]before
God for the people, so that you
may [b]bring the difficulties to
God.

2 [a]Ex. 2:21; 4:20–26
3 [a]Acts 7:29 [b]Ex. 2:22 [1]Lit. *Stranger There* [2]*sojourner*, temporary resident
4 [a]Gen. 49:25 [1]Lit. *My God Is Help*
5 [a]Ex. 3:1, 12; 4:27; 24:13
7 [a]Gen. 18:2 [b]Ex. 4:27
8 [a]Ex. 15:6, 16
9 [a][Is. 63:7–14]
10 [a]Gen. 14:20
11 [a]2 Chr. 2:5 [b]Ex. 1:10, 16, 22; 5:2, 7 [c]Luke 1:51 [1]*acted presumptuously*
12 [a]Ex. 24:5 [b]Deut. 12:7 [1]So with MT, LXX; Syr., Tg., Vg. *offered*
13 [a]Matt. 23:2
14 [1]Sit as judge
15 [a]Lev. 24:12
16 [a]Ex. 24:14 [1]*dispute*
18 [a]Num. 11:14, 17
19 [a]Ex. 4:16; 20:19 [b]Num. 9:8; 27:5 [1]*advice*

20 "And you shall [a]teach them the statutes and the laws, and show them the way in which they must walk and [b]the work they must do.

21 "Moreover you shall select from all the people [a]able men, such as [b]fear God, [c]men of truth, [d]hating covetousness; and place *such* over them *to be* rulers of thousands, rulers of hundreds, rulers of fifties, and rulers of tens.

22 "And let them judge the people at all times. [a]Then it will be *that* every great matter they shall bring to you, but every small matter they themselves shall judge. So it will be easier for you, for [b]they will bear *the burden* with you.

23 "If you do this thing, and God *so* commands you, then you will be able to endure, and all this people will also go to their [a]place in peace."

24 So Moses heeded the voice of his father-in-law and did all that he had said.

25 And [a]Moses chose able men out of all Israel, and made them heads over the people: rulers of thousands, rulers of hundreds, rulers of fifties, and rulers of tens.

26 So they judged the people at all times; the [a]hard[1] cases they brought to Moses, but they judged every small case themselves.

27 Then Moses let his father-in-law depart, and [a]he went his way to his own land.

19

In the third month after the children of Israel had gone out of the land of Egypt, on the same day, [a]they came *to* the Wilderness of Sinai.

2 For they had departed from [a]Reph'i·dim, had come *to* the Wilderness of Sinai, and camped in the wilderness. So Israel camped there before [b]the mountain.

3 And [a]Moses went up to God, and the LORD [b]called to him from the mountain, saying, "Thus you shall say to the house of Jacob, and tell the children of Israel:

4 [a]'You have seen what I did to the Egyptians, and *how* [b]I [1]bore you on eagles' wings and brought you to Myself.

5 'Now [a]therefore, if you will indeed obey My voice and [b]keep My covenant, then [c]you shall be a special treasure to Me above all people; for all the earth *is* [d]Mine.

6 'And you shall be to Me a [a]kingdom of priests and a [b]holy nation.' These *are* the words which you shall speak to the children of Israel."

7 So Moses came and called for the [a]elders of the people, and [1]laid before them all these words which the LORD commanded him.

8 Then [a]all the people answered together and said, "All that the LORD has spoken we will do." So Moses brought back the words of the people to the LORD.

9 And the LORD said to Moses, "Behold, I come to you [a]in the thick cloud, [b]that the people may hear when I speak with you, and believe you forever." So Moses told the words of the people to the LORD.

10 Then the LORD said to Moses, "Go to the people and [a]consecrate them today and tomorrow, and let them wash their clothes.

20 [a]Deut. 5:1 [b]Deut. 1:18
21 [a]Acts 6:3 [b]2 Sam. 23:3 [c]Ezek. 18:8 [d]Deut. 16:19
22 [a]Deut. 1:17 [b]Num. 11:17
23 [a]Ex. 16:29
25 [a]Deut. 1:15
26 [a]Job 29:16 [1]*difficult matters*
27 [a]Num. 10:29, 30

CHAPTER 19

1 [a]Num. 33:15
2 [a]Ex. 17:1 [b]Ex. 3:1, 12; 18:5
3 [a]Acts 7:38 [b]Ex. 3:4
4 [a]Deut. 29:2 [b]Is. 63:9 [1]*sustained*
5 [a]Ex. 15:26; 23:22 [b]Deut. 5:2 [c]Ps. 135:4 [d]Ex. 9:29
6 [a][1 Pet. 2:5, 9] [b]Deut. 7:6; 14:21; 26:19
7 [a]Ex. 4:29, 30 [1]*set*
8 [a]Deut. 5:27; 26:17
9 [a]Ex. 19:16; 20:21; 24:15 [b]Deut. 4:12, 36
10 [a]Lev. 11:44, 45

11 "And let them be ready for the third day. For on the third day the LORD will come down upon Mount Sinai in the sight of all the people.

12 "You shall set bounds for the people all around, saying, 'Take heed to yourselves *that* you do *not* go up to the mountain or touch its base. [a]Whoever touches the mountain shall surely be put to death.

13 'Not a hand shall touch him, but he shall surely be stoned or shot *with an arrow;* whether man or beast, he shall not live.' When the trumpet sounds long, they shall come near the mountain."

14 So Moses went down from the mountain to the people and sanctified the people, and they washed their clothes.

15 And he said to the people, "Be ready for the third day; [a]do not come near *your* wives."

16 Then it came to pass on the third day, in the morning, that there were [a]thunderings and lightnings, and a thick cloud on the mountain; and the sound of the trumpet was very loud, so that all the people who *were* in the camp [b]trembled.

17 And [a]Moses brought the people out of the camp to meet with God, and they stood at the foot of the mountain.

18 Now [a]Mount Sinai *was* completely in smoke, because the LORD descended upon [b]it in fire. [c]Its smoke ascended like the smoke of a furnace, and [1]the [d]whole mountain quaked greatly.

19 And when the blast of the trumpet sounded long and became louder and louder, [a]Moses spoke, and [b]God answered him by voice.

20 Then the LORD came down upon Mount Sinai, on the top of the mountain. And the LORD called Moses to the top of the mountain, and Moses went up.

21 And the LORD said to Moses, "Go down and warn the people, lest they break through [a]to gaze at the LORD, and many of them perish.

22 "Also let the [a]priests who come near the LORD [b]consecrate themselves, lest the LORD [c]break out against them."

23 But Moses said to the LORD, "The people cannot come up to Mount Sinai; for You warned us, saying, [a]'Set bounds around the mountain and consecrate it.' "

24 Then the LORD said to him, "Away! Get down and then come up, you and Aaron with you. But do not let the priests and the people break through to come up to the LORD, lest He break out against them."

25 So Moses went down to the people and spoke to them.

20

And God spoke [a]all these words, saying:

2 [a]"I *am* the LORD your God, who brought you out of the land of Egypt, [b]out of the house of [1]bondage.

3 [a]"You shall have no other gods before Me.

4 [a]"You shall not make for yourself a carved image—any likeness *of anything* that *is* in heaven above, or that *is* in the earth beneath, or that *is* in the water under the earth;

5 [a]you shall not bow down to them nor [1]serve them. [b]For I, the LORD your God,

12 [a]Heb. 12:20
15 [a][1 Cor. 7:5]
16 [a]Heb. 12:18, 19 [b]Heb. 12:21
17 [a]Deut. 4:10
18 [a]Deut. 4:11 [b]Ex. 3:2; 24:17 [c]Gen. 15:17; 19:28 [d]Ps. 68:8 [1]LXX *all the people*
19 [a]Heb. 12:21 [b]Ps. 81:7
21 [a]1 Sam. 6:19
22 [a]Ex. 19:24; 24:5 [b]Lev. 10:3; 21:6–8 [c]2 Sam. 6:7, 8
23 [a]Ex. 19:12
CHAPTER 20
1 [a]Deut. 5:22
2 [a]Hos. 13:4 [b]Ex. 13:3 [1]*slaves*
3 [a]Jer. 25:6; 35:15
4 [a]Deut. 4:15–19; 27:15
5 [a]Is. 44:15, 19 [b]Deut. 4:24 [1]*worship*

am a jealous God, [c]visiting[2]
the iniquity of the fathers
upon the children to the
third and fourth *genera-
tions* of those who hate
Me,
6 but [a]showing mercy to
thousands, to those who
love Me and keep My
commandments.
7 [a]"You shall not take the name
of the LORD your God in
vain, for the LORD [b]will
not hold *him* guiltless
who takes His name in
vain.
8 [a]"Remember the Sabbath day,
to keep it holy.
9 [a]Six days you shall labor
and do all your work,
10 but the [a]seventh day *is*
the Sabbath of the LORD
your God. *In it* you shall
do no work: you, nor your
son, nor your daughter,
nor your male servant,
nor your female servant,
nor your cattle, [b]nor your
stranger who *is* within
your gates.
11 For [a]*in* six days the LORD
made the heavens and
the earth, the sea, and all
that *is* in them, and rested
the seventh day. There-
fore the LORD blessed the
Sabbath day and hal-
lowed it.
12 [a]"Honor your father and your
mother, that your days
may be [b]long upon the
land which the LORD your
God is giving you.
13 [a]"You shall not murder.
14 [a]"You shall not commit
[b]adultery.
15 [a]"You shall not steal.
16 [a]"You shall not bear false witness against your neigh-
bor.
17 [a]"You shall not covet your
neighbor's house; [b]you
shall not covet your
neighbor's wife, nor his
male servant, nor his fe-
male servant, nor his ox,
nor his donkey, nor any-
thing that *is* your neighbor's."
18 Now [a]all the people [b]wit-
nessed the thunderings, the
lightning flashes, the sound of
the trumpet, and the mountain
[c]smoking; and when the people
saw *it*, they trembled and stood
afar off.
19 Then they said to Moses,
[a]"You speak with us, and we
will hear; but [b]let not God speak
with us, lest we die."
20 And Moses said to the people, [a]"Do not fear; [b]for God has
come to test you, and [c]that His
fear may be before you, so that
you may not sin."
21 So the people stood afar off,
but Moses drew near [a]the thick
darkness where God *was*.
22 Then the LORD said to Moses,
"Thus you shall say to the children of Israel: 'You have seen
that I have talked with you [a]from
heaven.
23 'You shall not make *anything
to be* [a]with Me—gods of silver or
gods of gold you shall not make
for yourselves.
24 'An altar of [a]earth you shall
make for Me, and you shall sacrifice on it your burnt offerings
and your peace offerings, [b]your
sheep and your oxen. In every
[c]place where I [1]record My name
I will come to you, and I will
[d]bless you.
25 'And [a]if you make Me an altar

5 [c]Num. 14:18, 33 [2]*punishing*
6 [a]Deut. 7:9
7 [a]Lev. 19:12 [b]Mic. 6:11
8 [a]Lev. 26:2
9 [a]Luke 13:14
10 [a]Gen. 2:2, 3 [b]Neh. 13:16–19
11 [a]Ex. 31:17
12 [a]Lev. 19:3 [b]Deut. 5:16, 33; 6:2; 11:8, 9
13 [a]Rom. 13:9
14 [a]Matt. 5:27 [b]Deut. 5:18
15 [a]Lev. 19:11, 13
16 [a]Deut. 5:20
17 [a][Eph. 5:3, 5] [b][Matt. 5:28]
18 [a]Heb. 12:18, 19 [b]Rev. 1:10, 12 [c]Ex. 19:16, 18
19 [a]Heb. 12:19 [b]Deut. 5:5, 23–27
20 [a][Is. 41:10, 13] [b][Deut. 13:3] [c]Is. 8:13
21 [a]Ex. 19:16
22 [a]Deut. 4:36; 5:24, 26
23 [a]Ex. 32:1, 2, 4
24 [a]Ex. 20:25; 27:1–8 [b]Ex. 24:5 [c]2 Chr. 6:6 [d]Gen. 12:2 [1]*cause My name to be remembered*
25 [a]Deut. 27:5

of stone, you shall not build it of
hewn stone; for if you [b]use your
tool on it, you have profaned it.
26 ‘Nor shall you go up by steps
to My altar, that your [a]nakedness
may not be exposed on it.’

21 “Now these *are* the [1]judg-
ments which you shall
[a]set before them:
2 [a]“If you buy a Hebrew servant, he shall serve six years;
and in the seventh he shall go
out free and pay nothing.
3 “If he comes in by himself,
he shall go out by himself; if he
comes in married, then his wife
shall go out with him.
4 “If his master has given him
a wife, and she has borne him
sons or daughters, the wife and
her children shall be her master’s, and he shall go out by
himself.
5 [a]“But if the servant plainly
says, ‘I love my master, my wife,
and my children; I will not go
out free,’
6 “then his master shall bring
him to the [a]judges. He shall also
bring him to the door, or to the
doorpost, and his master shall
pierce his ear with an awl; and
he shall serve him forever.
7 “And if a man [a]sells his
daughter to be a female slave,
she shall not go out as the male
slaves do.
8 “If she [1]does not please her
master, who has betrothed her
to himself, then he shall let
her be redeemed. He shall have
no right to sell her to a foreign
people, since he has dealt deceitfully with her.
9 “And if he has betrothed her
to his son, he shall deal with
her according to the custom of
daughters.

25 [b]Josh. 8:30, 31
26 [a]Ex. 28:42, 43

CHAPTER 21

1 [a]Deut. 4:14; 6:1
[1]*ordinances*
2 [a]Jer. 34:14
5 [a]Deut. 15:16, 17
6 [a]Ex. 12:12; 22:8, 9
7 [a]Neh. 5:5
8 [1]Lit. *is evil in the eyes of*
10 [a][1 Cor. 7:3, 5]
12 [a][Matt. 26:52]
13 [a]Deut. 19:4, 5
[b]1 Sam. 24:4, 10, 18
[c]Num. 35:11
14 [a]Deut. 19:11, 12
[b]1 Kin. 2:28–34
16 [a]Deut. 24:7
[b]Gen. 37:28
[c]Ex. 22:4
17 [a]Mark 7:10
19 [a]2 Sam. 3:29
[1]*exempt from punishment*

10 “If he takes another *wife*,
he shall not diminish her food,
her clothing, [a]and her marriage
rights.
11 “And if he does not do these
three for her, then she shall go
out free, without *paying* money.
12 [a]“He who strikes a man so
that he dies shall surely be put
to death.
13 “However, [a]if he did not lie
in wait, but God [b]delivered *him*
into his hand, then [c]I will appoint for you a place where he
may flee.
14 “But if a man acts with
[a]premeditation against his
neighbor, to kill him by treachery, [b]you shall take him from My
altar, that he may die.
15 “And he who strikes his father or his mother shall surely
be put to death.
16 [a]“He who kidnaps a man and
[b]sells him, or if he is [c]found in
his hand, shall surely be put to
death.
17 “And [a]he who curses his father or his mother shall surely
be put to death.
18 “If men contend with each
other, and one strikes the other
with a stone or with *his* fist, and
he does not die but is confined
to *his* bed,
19 “if he rises again and walks
about outside [a]with his staff,
then he who struck *him* shall
be [1]acquitted. He shall only pay
for the loss of his time, and shall
provide *for him* to be thoroughly
healed.
20 “And if a man beats his male
or female servant with a rod, so
that he dies under his hand, he
shall surely be punished.
21 “Notwithstanding, if he remains alive a day or two, he

shall not be punished; for he *is*
his [a]property.
22 "If men [1]fight, and hurt a
woman with child, so that [2]she
gives birth prematurely, yet no
harm follows, he shall surely
be punished accordingly as the
woman's husband imposes on
him; and he shall [a]pay as the
judges *determine.*
23 "But if *any* harm follows,
then you shall give life for life,
24 [a]"eye for eye, tooth for tooth,
hand for hand, foot for foot,
25 "burn for burn, wound for
wound, stripe for stripe.
26 "If a man strikes the eye of
his male or female servant, and
destroys it, he shall let him go
free for the sake of his eye.
27 "And if he knocks out the
tooth of his male or female servant, he shall let him go free for
the sake of his tooth.
28 "If an ox gores a man or a
woman to death, then [a]the ox
shall surely be stoned, and its
flesh shall not be eaten; but
the owner of the ox *shall be*
[1]acquitted.
29 "But if the ox [1]tended to
thrust with its horn in times past,
and it has been made known to
his owner, and he has not kept it
confined, so that it has killed a
man or a woman, the ox shall be
stoned and its owner also shall
be put to death.
30 "If there is imposed on him a
sum of money, then he shall pay
[a]to redeem his life, whatever is
imposed on him.
31 "Whether it has gored a son
or gored a daughter, according
to this judgment it shall be done
to him.
32 "If the ox gores a male or
female servant, he shall give
to their master [a]thirty shekels
of silver, and the [b]ox shall be
stoned.
33 "And if a man opens a pit, or
if a man digs a pit and does not
cover it, and an ox or a donkey
falls in it,
34 "the owner of the pit shall
make *it* good; he shall give
money to their owner, but the
dead *animal* shall be his.
35 "If one man's ox hurts another's, so that it dies, then they
shall sell the live ox and divide
the money from it; and the dead
ox they shall also divide.
36 "Or if it was known that the
ox tended to thrust in time past,
and its owner has not kept it
confined, he shall surely pay
ox for ox, and the dead animal
shall be his own.

22

"If a man steals an ox or
a sheep, and slaughters it
or sells it, he shall [a]restore five
oxen for an ox and four sheep
for a sheep.
2 "If the thief is found [a]breaking
in, and he is struck so that he
dies, *there shall be* [b]no guilt for
his bloodshed.
3 "If the sun has risen on him,
there shall be guilt for his bloodshed. He should make full restitution; if he has nothing, then he
shall be [a]sold[1] for his theft.
4 "If the theft is certainly
[a]found alive in his hand, whether
it is an ox or donkey or sheep,
he shall [b]restore double.
5 "If a man causes a field or
vineyard to be grazed, and lets
loose his animal, and it feeds
in another man's field, he shall
make restitution from the best
of his own field and the best of
his own vineyard.
6 "If fire breaks out and catches

21 [a]Lev. 25:44–46
22 [a]Ex. 18:21, 22; 21:30 [1]*struggle* [2]Lit. *her children come out*
24 [a]Lev. 24:20
28 [a]Gen. 9:5 [1]*exempt from punishment*
29 [1]*was inclined*
30 [a]Num. 35:31
32 [a]Zech. 11:12, 13 [b]Ex. 21:28

CHAPTER 22

1 [a]2 Sam. 12:6
2 [a]Matt. 6:19; 24:43 [b]Num. 35:27
3 [a]Ex. 21:2 [1]Sold as a slave
4 [a]Ex. 21:16 [b]Prov. 6:31

in thorns, so that stacked grain,
standing grain, or the field is consumed, he who kindled the fire
shall surely make restitution.
7 "If a man [a]delivers to his
neighbor money or articles to
keep, and it is stolen out of
the man's house, [b]if the thief is
found, he shall pay double.
8 "If the thief is not found,
then the master of the house
shall be brought to the [a]judges
to see whether he has put his
hand into his neighbor's goods.
9 "For any kind of trespass,
whether it concerns an ox, a
donkey, a sheep, or clothing, *or*
for any kind of lost thing which
another claims to be his, the
[a]cause of both parties shall come
before the judges; *and* whomever the judges condemn shall
pay double to his neighbor.
10 "If a man delivers to his
neighbor a donkey, an ox, a
sheep, or any animal to keep,
and it dies, is hurt, or driven
away, no one seeing *it*,
11 "*then* an [a]oath of the LORD
shall be between them both, that
he has not put his hand into
his neighbor's goods; and the
owner of it shall accept *that*,
and he shall not make *it* good.
12 "But [a]if, in fact, it is stolen
from him, he shall make restitution to the owner of it.
13 "If it is [a]torn to pieces *by a
beast, then* he shall bring it as
evidence, *and* he shall not make
good what was torn.
14 "And if a man borrows *anything* from his neighbor, and
it becomes injured or dies, the
owner of it not *being* with it, he
shall surely make *it* good.
15 "If its owner *was* with it, he
shall not make *it* good; if it *was*
hired, it came for its hire.
16 [a]"If a man entices a virgin
who is not betrothed, and lies
with her, he shall surely pay
the bride-price for her *to be* his
wife.
17 "If her father utterly refuses
to give her to him, he shall pay
money according to the [a]bride-
price of virgins.
18 [a]"You shall not permit a sorceress to live.
19 [a]"Whoever lies with an animal shall surely be put to death.
20 [a]"He who sacrifices to *any*
god, except to the LORD only, he
shall be utterly destroyed.
21 [a]"You shall neither mistreat
a [1]stranger nor oppress him, for
you were strangers in the land
of Egypt.
22 [a]"You shall not afflict any
widow or fatherless child.
23 "If you afflict them in any
way, *and* they [a]cry at all to Me, I
will surely [b]hear their cry;
24 "and My [a]wrath will become
hot, and I will kill you with
the sword; [b]your wives shall
be widows, and your children
fatherless.
25 [a]"If you lend money to *any of*
My people *who are* poor among
you, you shall not be like a mon-
eylender to him; you shall not
charge him [b]interest.
26 [a]"If you ever take your neighbor's garment as a pledge, you
shall return it to him before the
sun goes down.
27 "For that *is* his only covering,
it *is* his garment for his skin.
What will he sleep in? And it
will be that when he cries to Me,
I will hear, for I *am* [a]gracious.
28 [a]"You shall not revile God, nor
curse a [b]ruler of your people.

7 [a]Lev. 6:1–7 [b]Ex. 22:4
8 [a]Ex. 21:6, 22; 22:28
9 [a]Deut. 25:1
11 [a]Heb. 6:16
12 [a]Gen. 31:39
13 [a]Gen. 31:39
16 [a]Deut. 22:28, 29
17 [a]Gen. 34:12
18 [a]1 Sam. 28:3–10
19 [a]Lev. 18:23; 20:15, 16
20 [a]Ex. 32:8; 34:15
21 [a]Deut. 10:19 [1]*sojourner*
22 [a][James 1:27]
23 [a][Luke 18:7] [b]Ps. 18:6
24 [a]Ps. 69:24 [b]Ps. 109:9
25 [a]Lev. 25:35–37 [b]Ps. 15:5
26 [a]Deut. 24:6, 10–13
27 [a]Ex. 34:6, 7
28 [a]Eccl. 10:20 [b]Acts 23:5

29 "You shall not delay *to offer*
[a]the first of your ripe produce
and your juices. [b]The firstborn of
your sons you shall give to Me.
30 [a]"Likewise you shall do with
your oxen *and* your sheep. It
shall be with its mother [b]seven
days; on the eighth day you
shall give it to Me.
31 "And you shall be [a]holy men
to Me: [b]you shall not eat meat
torn *by beasts* in the field; you
shall throw it to the dogs.

23

"You [a]shall not circulate
a false report. Do not put
your hand with the wicked to be
an [b]unrighteous witness.
2 [a]"You shall not follow a
crowd to do evil; [b]nor shall you
testify in a dispute so as to
turn aside after many to pervert
justice.
3 "You shall not show partiality
to a [a]poor man in his dispute.
4 [a]"If you meet your enemy's
ox or his donkey going astray,
you shall surely bring it back to
him again.
5 [a]"If you see the donkey of
one who hates you lying under
its burden, and you would refrain from helping it, you shall
surely help him with it.
6 [a]"You shall not pervert the
judgment of your poor in his
dispute.
7 [a]"Keep yourself far from a
false matter; [b]do not kill the innocent and righteous. For [c]I will
not justify the wicked.
8 "And [a]you shall take no bribe,
for a bribe blinds the discerning
and perverts the words of the
righteous.
9 "Also [a]you shall not oppress
a [1]stranger, for you know the
heart of a stranger, because you
were strangers in the land of
Egypt.
10 [a]"Six years you shall sow
your land and gather in its
produce,
11 "but the seventh *year* you
shall let it rest and lie fallow,
that the poor of your people
may eat; and what they leave,
the beasts of the field may eat.
In like manner you shall do with
your vineyard *and* your [1]olive
grove.
12 [a]"Six days you shall do your
work, and on the seventh day
you shall rest, that your ox and
your donkey may rest, and the
son of your female servant and
the stranger may be refreshed.
13 "And in all that I have said to
you, [a]be circumspect and [b]make
no mention of the name of other
gods, nor let it be heard from
your mouth.
14 [a]"Three times you shall keep
a feast to Me in the year:
15 [a]"You shall keep the Feast of
Unleavened Bread (you shall eat
unleavened bread seven days,
as I commanded you, at the time
appointed in the month of Ā′bib,
for in it you came out of Egypt;
[b]none shall appear before Me
empty);
16 [a]"and the Feast of Harvest,
the firstfruits of your labors
which you have sown in the
field; and [b]the Feast of Ingathering at the end of the year, when
you have gathered in *the fruit of*
your labors from the field.
17 [a]"Three times in the year all
your males shall appear before
the Lord [1]GOD.
18 [a]"You shall not offer the
blood of My sacrifice with leavened [b]bread; nor shall the fat

29 [a]Ex. 23:16, 19 [b]Ex. 13:2, 12, 15
30 [a]Deut. 15:19 [b]Lev. 22:27
31 [a]Lev. 11:44; 19:2 [b]Ezek. 4:14

CHAPTER 23

1 [a]Ps. 101:5 [b]Deut. 19:16–21
2 [a]Gen. 7:1 [b]Lev. 19:15
3 [a]Deut. 1:17; 16:19
4 [a][Rom. 12:20]
5 [a]Deut. 22:4
6 [a]Eccl. 5:8
7 [a]Eph. 4:25 [b]Matt. 27:4 [c]Rom. 1:18
8 [a]Prov. 15:27; 17:8, 23
9 [a]Ex. 22:21 [1]*sojourner*
10 [a]Lev.25:1–7
11 [1]*olive yards*
12 [a]Luke 13:14
13 [a]1 Tim. 4:16 [b]Josh. 23:7
14 [a]Ex. 23:17; 34:22–24
15 [a]Ex. 12:14–20 [b]Ex. 22:29; 34:20
16 [a]Ex. 34:22 [b]Deut. 16:13
17 [a]Deut. 16:16 [1]Heb. *YHWH*, usually translated LORD
18 [a]Ex. 34:25 [b]Deut. 16:4

of My [1]sacrifice remain until
morning.
19 [a]"The first of the firstfruits
of your land you shall bring into
the house of the LORD your God.
[b]You shall not boil a young goat
in its mother's milk.
20 [a]"Behold, I send an Angel before you to keep you in the way
and to bring you into the place
which I have prepared.
21 "Beware of Him and obey
His voice; [a]do not provoke Him,
for He will [b]not pardon your
transgressions; for [c]My name *is*
in Him.
22 "But if you indeed obey His
voice and do all that I speak,
then [a]I will be an enemy to your
enemies and an adversary to
your adversaries.
23 [a]"For My Angel will go before you and [b]bring you in to
the Am′o·rītes and the Hit′tītes
and the Per′iz·zītes and the Cā′-
naan·ītes and the Hī′vītes and
the Jeb′ū·sītes; and I will [1]cut
them off.
24 "You shall not [a]bow down to
their gods, nor serve them, [b]nor
do according to their works;
[c]but you shall utterly overthrow
them and completely break
down their *sacred* pillars.
25 "So you shall [a]serve the LORD
your God, and [b]He will bless
your bread and your water. And
[c]I will take sickness away from
the midst of you.
26 [a]"No one shall suffer miscarriage or be barren in your land;
I will [b]fulfill the number of your
days.
27 "I will send [a]My fear before you, I will [b]cause confusion
among all the people to whom
you come, and will make all

18 [1]*feast*
19 [a]Deut. 26:2, 10 [b]Deut. 14:21
20 [a]Ex. 3:2; 13:15; 14:19
21 [a]Ps. 78:40, 56 [b]Deut. 18:19 [c]Is. 9:6
22 [a]Deut. 30:7
23 [a]Ex. 23:20 [b]Josh. 24:8, 11 [1]*annihilate them*
24 [a]Ex. 20:5; 23:13, 33 [b]Deut. 12:30, 31 [c]Num. 33:52
25 [a]Deut. 6:13 [b]Deut. 28:5 [c]Ex. 15:26
26 [a]Deut. 7:14; 28:4 [b]1 Chr. 23:1
27 [a]Ex. 15:16 [b]Deut. 7:23
28 [a]Josh. 24:12
29 [a]Deut. 7:22
31 [a]Gen. 15:18 [b]Josh. 21:44 [1]*boundaries* [2]Heb. *Nahar*, the Euphrates
32 [a]Ex. 34:12, 15 [1]*treaty*
33 [a]Ps. 106:36

CHAPTER 24

1 [a]Lev. 10:1, 2 [b]Num. 11:16
3 [a]Ex. 19:8; 24:7 [1]*ordinances*
4 [a]Deut. 31:9

your enemies turn *their* backs
to you.
28 "And [a]I will send hornets before you, which shall drive out
the Hī′vīte, the Cā′naan·īte, and
the Hit′tīte from before you.
29 [a]"I will not drive them out
from before you in one year, lest
the land become desolate and
the beasts of the field become
too numerous for you.
30 "Little by little I will drive
them out from before you, until
you have increased, and you inherit the land.
31 "And [a]I will set your [1]bounds
from the Red Sea to the sea,
Phi·lis′ti·a, and from the desert
to the [2]River. For I will [b]deliver
the inhabitants of the land into
your hand, and you shall drive
them out before you.
32 [a]"You shall make no [1]cov-
enant with them, nor with their
gods.
33 "They shall not dwell in your
land, lest they make you sin
against Me. For *if* you serve their
gods, [a]it will surely be a snare to
you."

24 Now He said to Moses,
"Come up to the LORD,
you and Aaron, [a]Nā′dab and
A·bī′hū, [b]and seventy of the elders of Israel, and worship from
afar.
2 "And Moses alone shall come
near the LORD, but they shall not
come near; nor shall the people
go up with him."
3 So Moses came and told the
people all the words of the LORD
and all the [1]judgments. And all
the people answered with one
voice and said, [a]"All the words
which the LORD has said we
will do."
4 And Moses [a]wrote all the

words of the LORD. And he rose
early in the morning, and built an
altar at the foot of the mountain,
and twelve [b]pillars according to
the twelve tribes of Israel.
5 Then he sent young men of
the children of Israel, who offered [a]burnt offerings and sacrificed peace offerings of oxen to
the LORD.
6 And Moses [a]took half the
blood and put *it* in basins, and
half the blood he sprinkled on
the altar.
7 Then he [a]took the Book of
the Covenant and read in the
hearing of the people. And they
said, "All that the LORD has said
we will do, and be obedient."
8 And Moses took the blood,
sprinkled *it* on the people, and
said, "This is [a]the blood of the
covenant which the LORD has
made with you according to all
these words."
9 Then Moses went up, also
Aaron, Nā'dab, and A·bī'hū, and
seventy of the elders of Israel,
10 and they [a]saw the God of
Israel. And *there was* under His
feet as it were a paved work of
[b]sapphire stone, and it was like
the [c]very[1] heavens in *its* clarity.
11 But on the nobles of the children of Israel He [a]did not [1]lay
His hand. So [b]they saw God, and
they [c]ate and drank.
12 Then the LORD said to Moses,
[a]"Come up to Me on the mountain and be there; and I will give
you [b]tablets of stone, and the
law and commandments which I
have written, that you may teach
them."
13 So Moses arose with [a]his assistant Joshua, and Moses went
up to the mountain of God.
14 And he said to the elders,
"Wait here for us until we come
back to you. Indeed, Aaron and
[a]Hur *are* with you. If any man
has a difficulty, let him go to
them."
15 Then Moses went up into the
mountain, and [a]a cloud covered
the mountain.
16 Now [a]the glory of the LORD
rested on Mount Sinai, and the
cloud covered it six days. And
on the seventh day He called to
Moses out of the midst of the
cloud.
17 The sight of the glory of the
LORD *was* like [a]a consuming fire
on the top of the mountain in the
eyes of the children of Israel.
18 So Moses went into the midst
of the cloud and went up into
the mountain. And [a]Moses was
on the mountain forty days and
forty nights.

25 Then the LORD spoke to
Moses, saying:
2 "Speak to the children of
Israel, that they bring Me an
[1]offering. [a]From everyone who
gives it willingly with his heart
you shall take My offering.
3 "And this *is* the offering
which you shall take from them:
gold, silver, and bronze;
4 "blue, purple, and scarlet
thread, fine linen, and goats'
hair;
5 "ram skins dyed red, [1]badger
skins, and acacia wood;
6 [a]"oil for the light, and [b]spices
for the anointing oil and for the
sweet incense;
7 "onyx stones, and stones to
be set in the [a]ephod and in the
breastplate.
8 "And let them make Me a
[a]sanctuary,[1] that [b]I may dwell
among them.
9 "According to all that I show

4 [b]Gen. 28:18
5 [a]Ex. 18:12; 20:24
6 [a]Heb. 9:18
7 [a]Heb. 9:19
8 [a][Luke 22:20]
10 [a][John 1:18; 6:46] [b]Ezek. 1:26 [c]Matt. 17:2 [1]Lit. *substance of heaven*
11 [a]Ex. 19:21 [b]Gen. 32:30 [c]1 Cor. 10:18 [1]*stretch out His*
12 [a]Ex. 24:2, 15 [b]Ex. 31:18; 32:15
13 [a]Ex. 32:17
14 [a]Ex. 17:10, 12
15 [a]Ex. 19:9
16 [a]Ex. 16:10; 33:18
17 [a]Deut. 4:26, 36; 9:3
18 [a]Ex. 34:28

CHAPTER 25

2 [a]Ex. 35:4–9, 21 [1]*heave offering*
5 [1]Or *dolphin*
6 [a]Ex. 27:20 [b]Ex. 30:23
7 [a]Ex. 28:4, 6–14
8 [a]Heb. 9:1, 2 [b][2 Cor. 6:16] [1]*sacred place*

you, *that is,* the pattern of the
tabernacle and the pattern of all
its furnishings, just so you shall
make *it.*
10 [a]"And they shall make an ark
of acacia wood; two and a half
cubits *shall be* its length, a cubit
and a half its width, and a cubit
and a half its height.
11 "And you shall overlay it
with pure gold, inside and out
you shall overlay it, and shall
make on it a molding of [a]gold all
around.
12 "You shall cast four rings of
gold for it, and put *them* in its
four corners; two rings *shall be*
on one side, and two rings on
the other side.
13 "And you shall make poles *of*
acacia wood, and overlay them
with gold.
14 "You shall put the poles into
the rings on the sides of the ark,
that the ark may be carried by
them.
15 [a]"The poles shall be in the
rings of the ark; they shall not
be taken from it.
16 "And you shall put into the
ark [a]the Testimony which I will
give you.
17 [a]"You shall make a mercy
seat of pure gold; two and a half
cubits *shall be* its length and a
cubit and a half its width.
18 "And you shall make two
cherubim of gold; of hammered
work you shall make them at the
two ends of the mercy seat.
19 "Make one cherub at one
end, and the other cherub at the
other end; you shall make the
cherubim at the two ends of it *of*
one piece with the mercy seat.
20 "And [a]the cherubim shall
stretch out *their* wings above,
covering the mercy seat with
their wings, and they shall face
one another; the faces of the
cherubim *shall be* toward the
mercy seat.
21 [a]"You shall put the mercy
seat on top of the ark, and [b]in
the ark you shall put the Testimony that I will give you.
22 "And [a]there I will meet with
you, and I will speak with you
from above the mercy seat, from
[b]between the two cherubim
which *are* on the ark of the Testimony, about everything which
I will give you in commandment
to the children of Israel.
23 [a]"You shall also make a table of acacia wood; two cubits
shall be its length, a cubit its
width, and a cubit and a half its
height.
24 "And you shall overlay it with
pure gold, and make a molding
of gold all around.
25 "You shall make for it a frame
of a handbreadth all around,
and you shall make a gold molding for the frame all around.
26 "And you shall make for it
four rings of gold, and put the
rings on the four corners that
are at its four legs.
27 "The rings shall be close to
the frame, as holders for the
poles to bear the table.
28 "And you shall make the
poles of acacia wood, and overlay them with gold, that the
table may be carried with them.
29 "You shall make [a]its dishes,
its pans, its pitchers, and its
bowls for pouring. You shall
make them of pure gold.
30 "And you shall set the
[a]showbread on the table before
Me always.
31 [a]"You shall also make a lampstand of pure gold; the lampstand

10 [a]Ex. 37:1–9
11 [a]Ex. 37:2
15 [a]1 Kin. 8:8
16 [a]Heb. 9:4
17 [a]Ex. 37:6
20 [a]1 Kin. 8:7
21 [a]Ex. 26:34; 40:20 [b]Ex. 25:16
22 [a]Ex. 29:42, 43; 30:6, 36 [b]Num. 7:89
23 [a]Ex. 37:10–16
29 [a]Ex. 37:16
30 [a]Lev. 24:5–9
31 [a]Zech. 4:2

shall be of hammered work. Its
shaft, its branches, its bowls, its
ornamental knobs, and flowers
shall be *of one piece.*
32 “And six branches shall come
out of its sides: three branches
of the lampstand out of one side,
and three branches of the lampstand out of the other side.
33 [a]“Three bowls *shall be* made
like almond *blossoms* on one
branch, *with* an *ornamental* knob
and a flower, and three bowls
made like almond *blossoms* on
the other branch, *with* an *ornamental* knob and a flower—and
so for the six branches that come
out of the lampstand.
34 [a]“On the lampstand itself
four bowls *shall be* made like
almond *blossoms, each with* its
ornamental knob and flower.
35 “And *there shall be* a knob
under the *first* two branches of
the same, a knob under the *second* two branches of the same,
and a knob under the *third* two
branches of the same, according
to the six branches that extend
from the lampstand.
36 “Their knobs and their
branches *shall be of one piece;*
all of it *shall be* one hammered
piece of pure gold.
37 “You shall make seven lamps
for it, and [a]they shall arrange its
lamps so that they [b]give light in
front of it.
38 “And its wick-trimmers and
their trays *shall be* of pure gold.
39 “It shall be made of a talent of pure gold, with all these
utensils.
40 “And [a]see to it that you make
them according to the pattern
which was shown you on the
mountain.

26

26 “Moreover [a]you shall
make the tabernacle *with*
ten curtains *of* fine woven linen
and blue, purple, and scarlet
thread; with artistic designs
of cherubim you shall weave
them.
2 “The length of each curtain
shall be twenty-eight cubits, and
the width of each curtain four
cubits. And every one of the
curtains shall have [1]the same
measurements.
3 “Five curtains shall be coupled to one another, and *the
other* five curtains *shall be* coupled to one another.
4 “And you shall make loops of
blue *yarn* on the edge of the curtain on the selvedge of *one* set,
and likewise you shall do on the
outer edge of *the other* curtain
of the second set.
5 “Fifty loops you shall make
in the one curtain, and fifty loops
you shall make on the edge of
the curtain that *is* on the end
of the second set, that the loops
may be clasped to one another.
6 “And you shall make fifty
clasps of gold, and couple the
curtains together with the
clasps, so that it may be one
tabernacle.
7 [a]“You shall also make curtains of goats' *hair,* to be a tent
over the tabernacle. You shall
make eleven curtains.
8 “The length of each curtain
shall be thirty cubits, and the
width of each curtain four cubits;
and the eleven curtains shall all
have the same measurements.
9 “And you shall couple five
curtains by themselves and six
curtains by themselves, and you
shall double over the sixth curtain at the forefront of the tent.

33 [a]Ex. 37:19
34 [a]Ex. 37:20–22
37 [a]Lev. 24:3, 4 [b]Num. 8:2
40 [a][Heb. 8:5]

CHAPTER 26

1 [a]Ex. 36:8–19
2 [1]Lit. *one measure*
7 [a]Ex. 36:14

10 "You shall make fifty loops
on the edge of the curtain that
is outermost in *one* set, and fifty
loops on the edge of the curtain
of the second set.
11 "And you shall make fifty
bronze clasps, put the clasps
into the loops, and couple the
tent together, that it may be
one.
12 "The remnant that remains of
the curtains of the tent, the half
curtain that remains, shall hang
over the back of the tabernacle.
13 "And a cubit on one side and
a cubit on the other side, of what
remains of the length of the
curtains of the tent, shall hang
over the sides of the tabernacle,
on this side and on that side, to
cover it.
14 [a]"You shall also make a covering of ram skins dyed red for
the tent, and a covering of badger skins above that.
15 "And for the tabernacle you
shall [a]make the boards of acacia
wood, standing upright.
16 "Ten cubits *shall be* the
length of a board, and a cubit
and a half *shall be* the width of
each board.
17 "Two [1]tenons *shall be* in each
board for binding one to another. Thus you shall make for
all the boards of the tabernacle.
18 "And you shall make the
boards for the tabernacle, twenty
boards for the south side.
19 "You shall make forty sockets of silver under the twenty
boards: two sockets under each
of the boards for its two tenons.
20 "And for the second side of
the tabernacle, the north side,
there shall be twenty boards
21 "and their forty sockets of
silver: two sockets under each of
the boards.
22 "For the far side of the tabernacle, westward, you shall make
six boards.
23 "And you shall also make
two boards for the two back corners of the tabernacle.
24 "They shall be [1]coupled together at the bottom and they
shall be coupled together at the
top by one ring. Thus it shall be
for both of them. They shall be
for the two corners.
25 "So there shall be eight
boards with their sockets of silver—sixteen sockets—two sockets under each of the boards.
26 "And you shall make bars of
acacia wood: five for the boards
on one side of the tabernacle,
27 "five bars for the boards on
the other side of the tabernacle,
and five bars for the boards of
the side of the tabernacle, for
the far side westward.
28 "The [a]middle bar shall pass
through the midst of the boards
from end to end.
29 "You shall overlay the boards
with gold, make their rings of
gold *as* holders for the bars, and
overlay the bars with gold.
30 "And you shall raise up the
tabernacle [a]according to its pattern which you were shown on
the mountain.
31 [a]"You shall make a veil woven of blue, purple, and scarlet
thread, and fine woven linen. It
shall be woven with an artistic
design of cherubim.
32 "You shall hang it upon the
four pillars of acacia *wood* overlaid with gold. Their hooks *shall
be* gold, upon four sockets of
silver.
33 "And you shall hang the veil

14 [a]Ex. 35:7, 23; 36:19
15 [a]Ex. 36:20–34
17 [1]Projections for joining, lit. *hands*
24 [1]Lit. *doubled*
28 [a]Ex. 36:33
30 [a]Acts 7:44
31 [a]Matt. 27:51

from the clasps. Then you shall
bring [a]the ark of the Testimony
in there, behind the veil. The
veil shall be a divider for you
between [b]the holy *place* and the
Most Holy.
34 [a]"You shall put the mercy
seat upon the ark of the Testimony in the Most Holy.
35 [a]"You shall set the table outside the veil, and [b]the lampstand
across from the table on the
side of the tabernacle toward
the south; and you shall put the
table on the north side.
36 [a]"You shall make a screen
for the door of the tabernacle,
woven of blue, purple, and scarlet *thread,* and fine woven linen,
made by a weaver.
37 "And you shall make for the
screen [a]five pillars of acacia
wood, and overlay them with
gold; their hooks *shall be* gold,
and you shall cast five sockets
of bronze for them.

27 "You shall make [a]an altar
of acacia wood, five cu-
bits long and five cubits wide—
the altar shall be square—and
its height *shall be* three cubits.
2 "You shall make its horns on
its four corners; its horns shall
be of one piece with it. And you
shall overlay it with bronze.
3 "Also you shall make its pans
to receive its ashes, and its shovels and its basins and its forks
and its firepans; you shall make
all its utensils of bronze.
4 "You shall make a grate for
it, a network of bronze; and on
the network you shall make four
bronze rings at its four corners.
5 "You shall put it under the
rim of the altar beneath, that
the network may be midway up
the altar.
6 "And you shall make poles for
the altar, poles of acacia wood,
and overlay them with bronze.
7 "The poles shall be put in
the rings, and the poles shall be
on the two sides of the altar to
bear it.
8 "You shall make it hollow
with boards; [a]as it was shown
you on the mountain, so shall
they make *it.*
9 [a]"You shall also make the
court of the tabernacle. For the
south side *there shall be* hangings for the court *made of* fine
woven linen, one hundred cubits
long for one side.
10 "And its twenty pillars and
their twenty sockets *shall be*
bronze. The hooks of the pillars
and their bands *shall be* silver.
11 "Likewise along the length
of the north side *there shall be*
hangings one hundred *cubits*
long, with its twenty pillars and
their twenty sockets of bronze,
and the hooks of the pillars and
their bands of silver.
12 "And along the width of the
court on the west side *shall be*
hangings of fifty cubits, with
their ten pillars and their ten
sockets.
13 "The width of the court on the
east side *shall be* fifty cubits.
14 "The hangings on *one* side *of*
the gate shall be fifteen cubits,
with their three pillars and their
three sockets.
15 "And on the other side *shall*
be hangings of fifteen *cubits,*
with their three pillars and their
three sockets.
16 "For the gate of the court
there shall be a screen twenty
cubits long, *woven of* blue, purple, and scarlet *thread,* and fine
woven linen, made by a weaver.

33 [a]Ex. 25:10–16; 40:21 [b]Heb. 9:2, 3
34 [a]Ex. 25:17–22; 40:20
35 [a]Ex. 40:22 [b]Ex. 40:24
36 [a]Ex. 36:37
37 [a]Ex. 36:38

CHAPTER 27

1 [a]Ex. 38:1
8 [a]Ex. 25:40; 26:30
9 [a]Ex. 38:9–20

It *shall have* four pillars and
four sockets.
17 "All the pillars around the
court shall have bands of silver;
their [a]hooks *shall be* of silver
and their sockets of bronze.
18 "The length of the court *shall*
be one hundred cubits, the width
fifty throughout, and the height
five cubits, *made of* fine woven
linen, and its sockets of bronze.
19 "All the utensils of the tabernacle for all its service, all
its pegs, and all the pegs of the
court, *shall be* of bronze.
20 "And [a]you shall command
the children of Israel that they
bring you pure oil of pressed
olives for the light, to cause the
lamp to [1]burn continually.
21 "In the tabernacle of meeting, [a]outside the veil which *is*
before the Testimony, [b]Aaron
and his sons shall tend it from
evening until morning before
the LORD. [c]*It shall be* a statute
forever to their generations on
behalf of the children of Israel.
28 "Now take [a]Aaron your
brother, and his sons
with him, from among the children of Israel, that he may minister to Me as [b]priest, Aaron *and*
Aaron's sons: [c]Nā'dab, A·bī'hū,
[d]El·ē·ā'zar, and Ith'a·mar.
2 "And [a]you shall make [1]holy
garments for Aaron your brother,
for glory and for beauty.
3 "So [a]you shall speak to all
who are gifted artisans, [b]whom
I have filled with the spirit of
wisdom, that they may make
Aaron's garments, to consecrate
him, that he may minister to Me
as priest.
4 "And these *are* the garments which they shall make: [a]a
breastplate, [b]an [1]ephod, [c]a robe,
[d]a skillfully woven tunic, a turban, and [e]a sash. So they shall
make holy garments for Aaron
your brother and his sons, that
he may minister to Me as priest.
5 "They shall take the gold,
blue, purple, and scarlet *thread,*
and the fine linen,
6 [a]"and they shall make the
ephod of gold, blue, purple, *and*
scarlet *thread,* and fine woven
linen, artistically worked.
7 "It shall have two shoulder
straps joined at its two edges, and
so it shall be joined together.
8 "And the [1]intricately woven
band of the ephod, which *is* on
it, shall be of the same workmanship, *made of* gold, blue,
purple, and scarlet *thread,* and
fine woven linen.
9 "Then you shall take two
onyx [a]stones and engrave on
them the names of the sons of
Israel:
10 "six of their names on one
stone and six names on the other
stone, in order of their [a]birth.
11 "With the work of an
[a]engraver in stone, *like* the engravings of a signet, you shall
engrave the two stones with the
names of the sons of Israel. You
shall set them in settings of
gold.
12 "And you shall put the two
stones on the shoulders of the
ephod *as* memorial stones for
the sons of Israel. So [a]Aaron
shall bear their names before
the LORD on his two shoulders
[b]as a memorial.
13 "You shall also make settings of gold,
14 "and you shall make two
chains of pure gold like braided
cords, and fasten the braided
chains to the settings.

---

17 [a]Ex. 38:19
20 [a]Lev. 24:1–4 [1]Lit. *ascend*
21 [a]Ex. 26:31, 33 [b]Ex. 30:8 [c]Lev. 3:17; 16:34

CHAPTER 28

1 [a]Num. 3:10; 18:7 [b]Heb. 5:4 [c]Lev. 10:1 [d]Ex. 6:23
2 [a]Ex. 29:5, 29; 31:10; 39:1–31 [1]*sacred*
3 [a]Ex. 31:6; 36:1 [b]Ex. 31:3; 35:30, 31
4 [a]Ex. 28:15 [b]Ex. 28:6 [c]Ex. 28:31 [d]Ex. 28:39 [e]Lev. 8:7 [1]Ornamented vest
6 [a]Ex. 39:2–7
8 [1]*ingenious work of*
9 [a]Ex. 35:27
10 [a]Gen. 29:31—30:24; 35:16–18
11 [a]Ex. 35:35
12 [a]Ex. 28:29, 30; 39:6, 7 [b]Josh. 4:7

15 [a]"You shall make the breastplate of judgment. Artistically
woven according to the workmanship of the ephod you shall
make it: of gold, blue, purple,
and scarlet *thread*, and fine woven linen, you shall make it.
16 "It shall be doubled into a
square: a span *shall be* its length,
and a span *shall be* its width.
17 [a]"And you shall put settings
of stones in it, four rows of
stones: *The first* row *shall be* a
[1]sardius, a topaz, and an emerald; *this shall be* the first row;
18 "the second row *shall be*
a turquoise, a sapphire, and a
diamond;
19 "the third row, a [1]jacinth, an
agate, and an amethyst;
20 "and the fourth row, a [1]beryl,
an [2]onyx, and a jasper. They
shall be set in gold settings.
21 "And the stones shall have
the names of the sons of Israel,
twelve according to their names,
like the engravings of a signet,
each one with its own name;
they shall be according to the
twelve tribes.
22 "You shall make chains for
the breastplate at the end, like
braided cords of pure gold.
23 "And you shall make two
rings of gold for the breastplate,
and put the two rings on the two
ends of the breastplate.
24 "Then you shall put the two
braided *chains* of gold in the two
rings which are on the ends of
the breastplate;
25 "and the *other* two ends of
the two braided *chains* you shall
fasten to the two settings, and
put them on the shoulder straps
of the ephod in the front.
26 "You shall make two rings of
gold, and put them on the two
ends of the breastplate, on the
edge of it, which is on the inner
side of the ephod.
27 "And two *other* rings of gold
you shall make, and put them
on the two shoulder straps, underneath the ephod toward its
front, right at the seam above
the [1]intricately woven band of
the ephod.
28 "They shall bind the breastplate by means of its rings to the
rings of the ephod, using a blue
cord, so that it is above the intricately woven band of the ephod,
and so that the breastplate does
not come loose from the ephod.
29 "So Aaron shall [a]bear the
names of the sons of Israel on
the breastplate of judgment over
his heart, when he goes into the
holy *place*, as a memorial before
the LORD continually.
30 "And [a]you shall put in the
breastplate of judgment the
[1]Ū′rim and the Thum′mim, and
they shall be over Aaron's heart
when he goes in before the LORD.
So Aaron shall bear the judgment of the children of Israel
over his heart before the LORD
continually.
31 [a]"You shall make the robe of
the ephod all of blue.
32 "There shall be an opening
for his head in the middle of it;
it shall have a woven binding
all around its opening, like the
opening in a coat of mail, so that
it does not tear.
33 "And upon its hem you shall
make pomegranates of blue,
purple, and scarlet, all around
its hem, and bells of gold between them all around:
34 "a golden bell and a pomegranate, a golden bell and a

15 [a]Ex. 39:8–21
17 [a]Ex. 39:10 [1]Or *ruby*
19 [1]Or *amber*
20 [1]Or *yellow jasper* [2]Or *carnelian*
27 [1]*ingenious work of*
29 [a]Ex. 28:12
30 [a]Lev. 8:8 [1]Lit. *Lights and the Perfections*
31 [a]Ex. 39:22–26

pomegranate, upon the hem of
the robe all around.
35 “And it shall be upon Aaron
when he ministers, and its sound
will be heard when he goes into
the holy *place* before the LORD
and when he comes out, that he
may not die.
36 [a]“You shall also make a plate
of pure gold and engrave on it,
like the engraving of a signet:

HOLINESS TO THE LORD.

37 “And you shall put it on a
blue cord, that it may be on the
turban; it shall be on the front of
the turban.
38 “So it shall be on Aaron’s
forehead, that Aaron may [a]bear
the iniquity of the holy things
which the children of Israel hallow in all their [1]holy gifts; and it
shall always be on his forehead,
that they may be [b]accepted before the LORD.
39 “You shall [a]skillfully weave
the tunic of fine linen *thread,*
you shall make the turban of
fine linen, and you shall make
the sash of woven work.
40 [a]“For Aaron’s sons you shall
make tunics, and you shall make
sashes for them. And you shall
make [1]hats for them, for glory
and [b]beauty.
41 “So you shall put them on
Aaron your brother and on his
sons with him. You shall [a]anoint
them, [b]consecrate them, and
[1]sanctify them, that they may
minister to Me as priests.
42 “And you shall make [a]for
them linen trousers to cover
their [1]nakedness; they shall
[2]reach from the waist to the
thighs.
43 “They shall be on Aaron and

36 [a]Ex. 39:30, 31
38 [a][1 Pet. 2:24] [b]Lev. 1:4; 22:27; 23:11 [1]*sacred*
39 [a]Ex. 35:35; 39:27–29
40 [a]Ezek. 44:17, 18 [b]Ex. 28:2 [1]*headpieces* or *turbans*
41 [a]Lev. 10:7 [b]Lev. 8 [1]*set them apart*
42 [a]Ex. 39:28 [1]*bare flesh* [2]Lit. *be*
43 [a]Ex. 20:26 [b]Num. 9:13; 18:22 [c]Ex. 27:21 [1]*guilt*

CHAPTER 29

1 [a][Heb. 7:26–28]
2 [a]Lev. 2:4; 6:19–23
4 [a]Ex. 40:12
5 [a]Ex. 28:2 [b]Ex. 28:8
6 [a]Lev. 8:9
7 [a]Ex. 25:6; 30:25–31
8 [a]Ex. 28:39, 40
9 [a]Num. 3:10; 18:7; 25:13 [b]Ex. 28:41

on his sons when they come into
the tabernacle of meeting, or
when they come near [a]the altar
to minister in the holy *place,*
that they [b]do not incur [1]iniquity
and die. [c]*It shall be* a statute forever to him and his descendants
after him.

29

“And this is what you
shall do to them to hal-
low them for ministering to Me
as priests: [a]Take one young bull
and two rams without blemish,
2 “and [a]unleavened bread, unleavened cakes mixed with oil,
and unleavened wafers anointed
with oil (you shall make them of
wheat flour).
3 “You shall put them in one
basket and bring them in the
basket, with the bull and the two
rams.
4 “And Aaron and his sons you
shall bring to the door of the
tabernacle of meeting, [a]and you
shall wash them with water.
5 [a]“Then you shall take the garments, put the tunic on Aaron,
and the robe of the ephod, the
ephod, and the breastplate, and
gird him with [b]the intricately
woven band of the ephod.
6 [a]“You shall put the turban on
his head, and put the holy crown
on the turban.
7 “And you shall take the
anointing [a]oil, pour *it* on his
head, and anoint him.
8 “Then [a]you shall bring his
sons and put tunics on them.
9 “And you shall gird them
with sashes, Aaron and his sons,
and put the hats on them. [a]The
priesthood shall be theirs for a
perpetual statute. So you shall
[b]consecrate Aaron and his sons.
10 “You shall also have the bull
brought before the tabernacle

of meeting, and [a]Aaron and his
sons shall put their hands on the
head of the bull.
11 "Then you shall kill the bull
before the LORD, *by* the door of
the tabernacle of meeting.
12 "You shall take *some* of the
blood of the bull and put *it* on
[a]the horns of the altar with your
finger, and [b]pour all the blood
beside the base of the altar.
13 "And [a]you shall take all the
fat that covers the entrails, the
fatty lobe *attached* to the liver,
and the two kidneys and the fat
that *is* on them, and burn *them*
on the altar.
14 "But [a]the flesh of the bull,
with its skin and its offal, you
shall burn with fire outside the
camp. It *is* a sin offering.
15 [a]"You shall also take one
ram, and Aaron and his sons
shall [b]put their hands on the
head of the ram;
16 "and you shall kill the ram,
and you shall take its blood and
[a]sprinkle *it* all around on the
altar.
17 "Then you shall cut the ram
in pieces, wash its entrails and
its legs, and put *them* with its
pieces and with its head.
18 "And you shall burn the
whole ram on the altar. It *is* a
[a]burnt offering to the LORD; it *is*
a sweet aroma, an offering made
by fire to the LORD.
19 [a]"You shall also take the
other ram, and Aaron and his
sons shall put their hands on the
head of the ram.
20 "Then you shall kill the ram,
and take some of its blood and
put *it* on the tip of the right
ear of Aaron and on the tip of
the right ear of his sons, on
the thumb of their right hand
and on the big toe of their right
foot, and sprinkle the blood all
around on the altar.
21 "And you shall take some
of the blood that is on the altar,
and some of [a]the anointing oil,
and sprinkle *it* on Aaron and
on his garments, on his sons
and on the garments of his sons
with him; and [b]he and his garments shall be hallowed, and
his sons and his sons' garments
with him.
22 "Also you shall take the fat
of the ram, the fat tail, the fat
that covers the entrails, the fatty
lobe *attached to* the liver, the
two kidneys and the fat on them,
the right thigh (for it *is* a ram of
consecration),
23 [a]"one loaf of bread, one cake
made with oil, and one wafer
from the basket of the unleavened bread that *is* before the
LORD;
24 "and you shall put all these
in the hands of Aaron and in the
hands of his sons, and you shall
[a]wave them *as* a wave offering
before the LORD.
25 [a]"You shall receive them
back from their hands and burn
them on the altar as a burnt offering, as a sweet aroma before
the LORD. It *is* an offering made
by fire to the LORD.
26 "Then you shall take [a]the
breast of the ram of Aaron's
consecration and wave it *as* a
wave offering before the LORD;
and it shall be your portion.
27 "And from the ram of the
consecration you shall consecrate [a]the breast of the wave
offering which is waved, and
the thigh of the heave offering
which is raised, of *that* which *is*

10 [a]Lev. 1:4; 8:14
12 [a]Lev. 8:15 [b]Ex. 27:2; 30:2
13 [a]Lev. 1:8; 3:3, 4
14 [a]Lev. 4:11, 12, 21
15 [a]Lev. 8:18 [b]Lev. 1:4–9
16 [a]Ex. 24:6
18 [a]Ex. 20:24
19 [a]Lev. 8:22
21 [a]Ex. 30:25, 31 [b][Heb. 9:22]
23 [a]Lev. 8:26
24 [a]Lev. 7:30; 10:14
25 [a]Lev. 8:28
26 [a]Lev. 7:31, 34; 8:29
27 [a]Num. 18:11, 18

for Aaron and of *that* which is
for his sons.
28 "It shall be from the children
of Israel *for* Aaron and his sons
[a]by a statute forever. For it is
a heave offering; [b]it shall be a
heave offering from the children
of Israel from the sacrifices of
their peace offerings, *that is*,
their heave offering to the LORD.
29 "And the [a]holy garments of
Aaron [b]shall be his sons' after
him, [c]to be anointed in them and
to be consecrated in them.
30 [a]"That son who becomes
priest in his place shall put them
on for [b]seven days, when he enters the tabernacle of meeting to
minister in the [1]holy *place*.
31 "And you shall take the ram
of the consecration and [a]boil its
flesh in the holy place.
32 "Then Aaron and his sons
shall eat the flesh of the ram,
and the [a]bread that *is* in the
basket, *by* the door of the tabernacle of meeting.
33 [a]"They shall eat those things
with which the atonement was
made, to consecrate *and* to sanctify them; [b]but an outsider shall
not eat *them*, because they *are*
holy.
34 "And if any of the flesh of
the consecration offerings, or
of the bread, remains until the
morning, then [a]you shall burn
the remainder with fire. It shall
not be eaten, because it *is* holy.
35 "Thus you shall do to Aaron
and his sons, according to all
that I have commanded you.
[a]Seven days you shall consecrate them.
36 "And you [a]shall offer a bull
every day *as* a sin offering for
atonement. [b]You shall cleanse the
altar when you make atonement
for it, and you shall anoint it to
sanctify it.
37 "Seven days you shall make
atonement for the altar and
sanctify it. And the altar shall
be most holy. [a]Whatever touches
the altar must be holy.
38 "Now this *is* what you shall
offer on the altar: [a]two lambs
of the first year, [b]day by day
continually.
39 "One lamb you shall offer [a]in
the morning, and the other lamb
you shall offer [1]at twilight.
40 "With the one lamb shall be
one-tenth *of an ephah* of flour
mixed with one-fourth of a hin
of pressed oil, and one-fourth
of a hin of wine *as* a drink
offering.
41 "And the other lamb you
shall [a]offer [1]at twilight; and you
shall offer with it the grain offering and the drink offering,
as in the morning, for a sweet
aroma, an offering made by fire
to the LORD.
42 "*This shall be* [a]a continual
burnt offering throughout your
generations *at* the door of the
tabernacle of meeting before the
LORD, [b]where I will meet you to
speak with you.
43 "And there I will meet with
the children of Israel, and *the
tabernacle* [a]shall be sanctified
by My glory.
44 "So I will consecrate the tabernacle of meeting and the altar. I will also [a]consecrate both
Aaron and his sons to minister
to Me as priests.
45 [a]"I will dwell among the children of Israel and will [b]be their
God.
46 "And they shall know that
[a]I *am* the LORD their God, who
[b]brought them up out of the

28 [a]Lev. 10:15 [b]Lev. 3:1; 7:34
29 [a]Ex. 28:2 [b]Num. 20:26, 28 [c]Num. 18:8
30 [a]Num. 20:28 [b]Lev. 8:35 [1]*sanctuary*
31 [a]Lev. 8:31
32 [a]Matt. 12:4
33 [a]Lev. 10:14, 15, 17 [b]Lev. 22:10
34 [a]Lev. 7:18; 8:32
35 [a]Lev. 8:33–35
36 [a]Heb. 10:11 [b]Ex. 30:26–29; 40:10, 11
37 [a]Num. 4:15; Hag. 2:11–13; Matt. 23:19
38 [a]Num. 28:3–31; 29:6–38 [b]Dan. 12:11
39 [a]Ezek. 46:13–15 [1]Lit. *between the two evenings*
41 [a]2 Kin. 16:15 [1]Lit. *between the two evenings*
42 [a]Ex. 30:8 [b]Ex. 25:22; 33:7, 9
43 [a]1 Kin. 8:11
44 [a]Lev. 21:15
45 [a] [Rev. 21:3] [b]Gen. 17:8
46 [a]Ex. 16:12; 20:2 [b]Lev. 11:45

land of Egypt, that I may dwell
among them. I *am* the LORD their
God.

30 “You shall make [a]an altar
to burn incense on; you
shall make it of acacia wood.
2 “A cubit *shall be* its length
and a cubit its width—it shall be
square—and two cubits *shall be*
its height. Its horns *shall be* of
one piece with it.
3 “And you shall overlay its
top, its sides all around, and its
horns with pure gold; and you
shall make for it a [1]molding of
gold all around.
4 “Two gold rings you shall
make for it, under the molding
on both its sides. You shall place
them on its two sides, and they
will be holders for the poles
with which to bear it.
5 “You shall make the poles of
acacia wood, and overlay them
with gold.
6 “And you shall put it before
the [a]veil that *is* before the ark of
the Testimony, before the [b]mercy
seat that *is* over the Testimony,
where I will meet with you.
7 “Aaron shall burn on it
[a]sweet incense every morning;
when [b]he tends the lamps, he
shall burn incense on it.
8 “And when Aaron lights the
lamps [1]at twilight, he shall burn
incense on it, a perpetual incense before the LORD throughout your generations.
9 “You shall not offer [a]strange
incense on it, or a burnt offering,
or a grain offering; nor shall you
pour a drink offering on it.
10 “And [a]Aaron shall make
atonement upon its horns once a
year with the blood of the sin offering of atonement; once a year
he shall make atonement upon
it throughout your generations.
It *is* most holy to the LORD.”
11 Then the LORD spoke to Moses, saying:
12 [a]“When you take the census of the children of Israel for
their number, then every man
shall give [b]a[1] ransom for himself
to the LORD, when you num-
ber them, that there may be no
[c]plague among them when *you*
number them.
13 [a]“This is what everyone
among those who are numbered
shall give: half a shekel according to the shekel of the sanctuary [b](a shekel *is* twenty gerahs).
[c]The half-shekel *shall be* an offering to the LORD.
14 “Everyone included among
those who are numbered, from
twenty years old and above,
shall give an [1]offering to the
LORD.
15 “The [a]rich shall not give more
and the poor shall not give less
than half a shekel, when *you*
give an offering to the LORD, to
make atonement for yourselves.
16 “And you shall take the atonement money of the children of
Israel, and [a]shall [1]appoint it for
the service of the tabernacle of
meeting, that it may be [b]a memorial for the children of Israel
before the LORD, to make atonement for yourselves.”
17 Then the LORD spoke to Moses, saying:
18 [a]“You shall also make a [1]la-
ver of bronze, with its base also
of bronze, for washing. You shall
[b]put it between the tabernacle of
meeting and the altar. And you
shall put water in it,
19 “for Aaron and his sons [a]shall
wash their hands and their feet
in water from it.

CHAPTER 30
1 [a]Ex. 37:25–29
3 [1]*border*
6 [a]Ex. 26:31–35 [b]Ex. 25:21, 22
7 [a]1 Sam. 2:28 [b]Ex. 27:20, 21
8 [1]Lit. *between the two evenings*
9 [a]Lev. 10:1
10 [a]Lev. 16:3–34
12 [a]Num. 1:2; 26:2 [b][1 Pet. 1:18, 19] [c]2 Sam. 24:15 [1]*the price of a life*
13 [a]Matt. 17:24 [b]Num. 3:47 [c]Ex. 38:26
14 [1]*contribution*
15 [a][Eph. 6:9]
16 [a]Ex. 38:25–31 [b]Num. 16:40 [1]*give*
18 [a]Ex. 38:8 [b]Ex. 40:30 [1]*basin*
19 [a]Ex. 40:31, 32

20 "When they go into the tabernacle of meeting, or when they come near the altar to minister, to burn an offering made by fire to the LORD, they shall wash with water, lest they die.

21 "So they shall wash their hands and their feet, lest they die. And [a]it shall be a [1]statute forever to them—to him and his descendants throughout their generations."

22 Moreover the LORD spoke to Moses, saying:

23 "Also take for yourself [a]quality spices—five hundred *shekels* of liquid [b]myrrh, half as much sweet-smelling cinnamon (two hundred and fifty *shekels*), two hundred and fifty *shekels* of sweet-smelling [c]cane,

24 "five hundred *shekels* of [a]cassia, according to the shekel of the sanctuary, and a [b]hin of olive oil.

25 "And you shall make from these a holy anointing oil, an ointment compounded according to the art of the perfumer. It shall be [a]a holy anointing oil.

26 [a]"With it you shall anoint the tabernacle of meeting and the ark of the Testimony;

27 "the table and all its utensils, the lampstand and its utensils, and the altar of incense;

28 "the altar of burnt offering with all its utensils, and the laver and its base.

29 "You shall consecrate them, that they may be most holy; [a]whatever touches them must be holy.

30 [a]"And you shall anoint Aaron and his sons, and consecrate them, that *they* may minister to Me as priests.

31 "And you shall speak to the children of Israel, saying: 'This shall be a holy anointing oil to Me throughout your generations.

32 'It shall not be poured on man's flesh; nor shall you make *any other* like it, according to its composition. [a]It *is* holy, *and* it shall be holy to you.

33 [a]'Whoever [1]compounds *any* like it, or whoever puts *any* of it on an outsider, [b]shall be [2]cut off from his people.' "

34 And the LORD said to Moses: [a]"Take sweet spices, stacte and onycha and galbanum, and pure frankincense with *these* sweet spices; there shall be equal amounts of each.

35 "You shall make of these an incense, a compound [a]according to the art of the perfumer, salted, pure, *and* holy.

36 "And you shall beat *some* of it very fine, and put some of it before the Testimony in the tabernacle of meeting [a]where I will meet with you. [b]It shall be most holy to you.

37 "But *as for* the incense which you shall make, [a]you shall not make any for yourselves, according to its [1]composition. It shall be to you holy for the LORD.

38 [a]"Whoever makes *any* like it, to smell it, he shall be cut off from his people."

31 Then the LORD spoke to Moses, saying:

2 [a]"See, I have called by name Bez′a·lel the [b]son of Ū′rī, the son of Hur, of the tribe of Judah.

3 "And I have [a]filled him with the Spirit of God, in wisdom, in understanding, in knowledge, and in all *manner of* workmanship,

21 [a]Ex. 28:43 [1]*requirement*

23 [a]Ezek. 27:22 [b]Prov. 7:17 [c]Song 4:14

24 [a]Ps. 45:8 [b]Ex. 29:40

25 [a]Ex. 37:29; 40:9

26 [a]Lev. 8:10

29 [a]Ex. 29:37; Num. 4:15; Hag. 2:11–13

30 [a]Lev. 8:12

32 [a]Ex. 30:25, 37

33 [a]Ex. 30:38 [b]Gen. 17:14 [1]*mixes* [2]Put to death

34 [a]Ex. 25:6; 37:29

35 [a]Ex. 30:25

36 [a]Ex. 29:42 [b]Lev. 2:3

37 [a]Ex. 30:32 [1]Lit. *proportion*

38 [a]Ex. 30:33

CHAPTER 31

2 [a]Ex. 35:30—36:1 [b]1 Chr. 2:20

3 [a]1 Kin. 7:14

4 "to design artistic works, to
work in gold, in silver, in bronze,
5 "in cutting jewels for setting,
in carving wood, and to work in
all *manner of* workmanship.
6 "And I, indeed I, have appointed with him [a]A·hō′li·ab the
son of A·his′a·mach, of the tribe
of Dan; and I have put wisdom
in the hearts of all the [b]gifted
artisans, that they may make all
that I have commanded you:
7 [a]"the tabernacle of meeting, [b]the ark of the Testimony
and [c]the mercy seat that *is* on
it, and all the furniture of the
tabernacle—
8 [a]"the table and its utensils,
[b]the pure *gold* lampstand with all
its utensils, the altar of incense,
9 [a]"the altar of burnt offering
with all its utensils, and [b]the
laver and its base—
10 [a]"the [1]garments of ministry,
the holy garments for Aaron the
priest and the garments of his
sons, to minister as priests,
11 [a]"and the anointing oil and
[b]sweet incense for the holy
place. According to all that I
have commanded you they shall
do."
12 And the LORD spoke to Moses, saying,
13 "Speak also to the children
of Israel, saying: [a]'Surely My
Sabbaths you shall keep, for it
is a sign between Me and you
throughout your generations,
that *you* may know that I *am*
the LORD who [b]sanctifies[1] you.
14 [a]'You shall keep the Sabbath, therefore, for *it is* holy to
you. Everyone who [1]profanes it
shall surely be put to death; for
[b]whoever does *any* work on it,
that person shall be cut off from
among his people.
15 'Work shall be done for [a]six
days, but the [b]seventh *is* the Sabbath of rest, holy to the LORD.
Whoever does *any* work on the
Sabbath day, he shall surely be
put to death.
16 'Therefore the children of
Israel shall keep the Sabbath, to
observe the Sabbath throughout
their generations *as* a perpetual
covenant.
17 'It *is* [a]a sign between Me and
the children of Israel forever; for
[b]*in* six days the LORD made the
heavens and the earth, and on
the seventh day He rested and
was refreshed.' "
18 And when He had made an
end of speaking with him on
Mount Sinai, He gave Moses
[a]two tablets of the Testimony,
tablets of stone, written with the
finger of God.

32

Now when the people saw
that Moses [a]delayed coming down from the mountain,
the people [b]gathered together to
Aaron, and said to him, [c]"Come,
make us [1]gods that shall [d]go
before us; for *as for* this Moses,
the man who [e]brought us up out
of the land of Egypt, we do not
know what has become of him."
2 And Aaron said to them,
"Break off the [a]golden earrings which *are* in the ears
of your wives, your sons, and
your daughters, and bring *them*
to me."
3 So all the people broke off
the golden earrings which *were*
in their ears, and brought *them*
to Aaron.
4 [a]And he received *the gold*
from their hand, and he fashioned it with an engraving tool,
and made a molded calf. Then
they said, "This *is* your god,

6 [a]Ex. 35:34 [b]Ex. 28:3; 35:10, 35; 36:1
7 [a]Ex. 36:8 [b]Ex. 37:1–5 [c]Ex. 37:6–9
8 [a]Ex. 37:10–16 [b]Ex. 37:17–24
9 [a]Ex. 38:1–7 [b]Ex. 38:8
10 [a]Ex. 39:1, 41 [1]Or *woven garments*
11 [a]Ex. 30:23–33 [b]Ex. 30:34–38
13 [a]Ezek. 20:12, 20 [b]Lev. 20:8 [1]*consecrates*
14 [a]Ex. 20:8 [b]Num. 15:32–36 [1]*defiles*
15 [a]Ex. 20:9–11 [b]Gen. 2:2
17 [a]Ex. 31:13 [b]Gen. 1:31; 2:2, 3
18 [a][Ex. 24:12; 32:15, 16]

CHAPTER 32

1 [a]Ex. 24:18; Deut. 9:9–12 [b]Ex. 17:1–3 [c]Acts 7:40 [d]Ex. 13:21 [e]Ex. 32:8 [1]Or *a god*
2 [a]Ex. 11:2; 35:22
4 [a]Ex. 20:3, 4, 23

O Israel, that [b]brought you out
of the land of Egypt!"
5 So when Aaron saw *it*, he
built an altar before it. And
Aaron made a [a]proclamation
and said, "Tomorrow *is* a feast
to the LORD."
6 Then they rose early on the
next day, offered burnt offerings,
and brought peace offerings; and
the people [a]sat down to eat and
drink, and rose up to play.
7 And the LORD said to Moses,
[a]"Go, get down! For your people
whom you brought out of the
land of Egypt [b]have corrupted
themselves.
8 "They have turned aside
quickly out of the way which
[a]I commanded them. They have
made themselves a molded calf,
and worshiped it and sacrificed
to it, and said, [b]'This *is* your god,
O Israel, that brought you out of
the land of Egypt!' "
9 And the LORD said to Moses,
[a]"I have seen this people, and indeed it *is* a [1]stiff-necked people!
10 "Now therefore, [a]let Me
alone, that [b]My wrath may burn
hot against them and I may [1]con-
sume them. And [c]I will make of
you a great nation."
11 [a]Then Moses pleaded with
[1]the LORD his God, and said:
"LORD, why does Your wrath
burn hot against Your people
whom You have brought out of
the land of Egypt with great
power and with a mighty hand?
12 [a]"Why should the Egyptians
speak, and say, 'He brought them
out to harm them, to kill them in
the mountains, and to consume
them from the face of the earth'?
Turn from Your fierce wrath, and
[b]relent from this harm to Your
people.
13 "Remember Abraham, Isaac,
and Israel, Your servants, to
whom You [a]swore by Your own
self, and said to them, [b]'I will
multiply your descendants as
the stars of heaven; and all this
land that I have spoken of I give
to your descendants, and they
shall inherit *it* forever.' "
14 So the LORD [a]relented from
the harm which He said He
would do to His people.
15 And [a]Moses turned and went
down from the mountain, and
the two tablets of the Testimony
were in his hand. The tablets
were written on both sides; on
the one *side* and on the other
they were written.
16 Now the [a]tablets *were* the
work of God, and the writing
was the writing of God engraved
on the tablets.
17 And when Joshua heard
the noise of the people as they
shouted, he said to Moses,
"*There is* a noise of war in the
camp."
18 But he said:

"*It is* not the noise of the
shout of victory,
Nor the noise of the cry of
defeat,
But the sound of singing I
hear."

19 So it was, as soon as he came
near the camp, that [a]he saw the
calf *and* the dancing. So Moses'
anger became hot, and he cast
the tablets out of his hands and
broke them at the foot of the
mountain.
20 [a]Then he took the calf which
they had made, burned *it* in the
fire, and ground *it* to powder;
and he scattered *it* on the water

4 [b]Ex. 29:45, 46
5 [a]2 Kin. 10:20
6 [a]Num. 25:2
7 [a]Deut. 9:8–21 [b]Gen. 6:11, 12
8 [a]Ex. 20:3, 4, 23 [b]1 Kin. 12:28
9 [a][Acts 7:51] [1]*stubborn*
10 [a]Deut. 9:14, 19 [b]Ex. 22:24 [c]Num. 14:12 [1]*destroy*
11 [a]Deut. 9:18, 26–29 [1]Lit. *the face of the LORD*
12 [a]Num. 14:13–19 [b]Ex. 32:14
13 [a][Heb. 6:13] [b]Gen. 12:7; 13:15; 15:7, 18; 22:17; 26:4; 35:11, 12
14 [a]2 Sam. 24:16
15 [a]Deut. 9:15
16 [a]Ex. 31:18
19 [a]Deut. 9:16, 17
20 [a]Deut. 9:21

and made the children of Israel
drink *it*.
21 And Moses said to Aaron,
[a]"What did this people do to you
that you have brought *so* great a
sin upon them?"
22 So Aaron said, "Do not let
the anger of my lord become
hot. [a]You know the people, that
they *are set* on evil.
23 "For they said to me, 'Make
us gods that shall go before us;
as for this Moses, the man who
brought us out of the land of
Egypt, we do not know what has
become of him.'
24 "And I said to them, 'Whoever has any gold, let them break
it off.' So they gave *it* to me, and
I cast it into the fire, and this calf
came out."
25 Now when Moses saw that
the people *were* [a]unrestrained
(for Aaron [b]had not restrained
them, to *their* shame among
their enemies),
26 then Moses stood in the entrance of the camp, and said,
"Whoever *is* on the LORD's side—
come to me!" And all the sons
of Levi gathered themselves together to him.
27 And he said to them, "Thus
says the LORD God of Israel: 'Let
every man put his sword on his
side, and go in and out from
entrance to entrance throughout
the camp, and [a]let every man
kill his brother, every man his
companion, and every man his
neighbor.' "
28 So the sons of Levi did according to the word of Moses.
And about three thousand men
of the people fell that day.
29 [a]Then Moses said, [1]"Consecrate yourselves today to the
LORD, that He may bestow on
you a blessing this day, for every
man has opposed his son and
his brother."
30 Now it came to pass on the
next day that Moses said to the
people, [a]"You have committed a
great sin. So now I will go up to
the LORD; [b]perhaps I can [c]make
atonement for your sin."
31 Then Moses [a]returned to the
LORD and said, "Oh, these people
have committed a great sin, and
have [b]made for themselves a
god of gold!
32 "Yet now, if You will forgive
their sin—but if not, I pray, [a]blot
me [b]out of Your book which You
have written."
33 And the LORD said to Moses,
[a]"Whoever has sinned against
Me, I will [b]blot him out of My
book.
34 "Now therefore, go, lead the
people to *the place* of which I
have [a]spoken to you. [b]Behold,
My Angel shall go before you.
Nevertheless, [c]in the day when I
[d]visit for punishment, I will visit
punishment upon them for their
sin."
35 So the LORD plagued the
people because of [a]what they
did with the calf which Aaron
made.

33 Then the LORD said to
Moses, "Depart *and* go up
from here, you [a]and the people
whom you have brought out of
the land of Egypt, to the land
of which I swore to Abraham,
Isaac, and Jacob, saying, [b]'To
your descendants I will give it.'
2 [a]"And I will send *My* Angel
before you, [b]and I will drive out
the Cā′naan·īte and the Am′-
o·rīte and the Hit′tīte and the
Per′iz·zīte and the Hī′vīte and
the Jeb′ū·sīte.

21 [a]Gen. 26:10
22 [a]Deut. 9:24
25 [a]Ex. 33:4, 5 [b]2 Chr. 28:19
27 [a]Num. 25:5–13
29 [a]Ex. 28:41 [1]Lit. *Fill your hand*
30 [a]1 Sam. 12:20, 23 [b]2 Sam. 16:12 [c]Num. 25:13
31 [a]Deut. 9:18 [b]Ex. 20:23
32 [a]Ps. 69:28 [b]Dan. 12:1
33 [a][Ezek. 18:4; 33:2, 14, 15] [b]Ex. 17:14
34 [a]Ex. 3:17 [b]Ex. 23:20 [c]Deut. 32:35 [d]Ps. 89:32
35 [a]Neh. 9:18

CHAPTER 33

1 [a]Ex. 32:1, 7, 13 [b]Gen. 12:7
2 [a]Ex. 32:34 [b]Josh. 24:11

3 "*Go up* [a]to a land flowing
with milk and honey; for I will
not go up in your midst, lest [b]I
[1]consume you on the way, for
you *are* a [c]stiff-necked[2] people."
4 And when the people
heard this bad news, [a]they
mourned, [b]and no one put on his
ornaments.
5 For the LORD had said to
Moses, "Say to the children of
Israel, 'You *are* a stiff-necked
people. I could come up into
your midst in one moment and
consume you. Now therefore,
take off your [1]ornaments, that I
may [a]know what to do to you.' "
6 So the children of Israel
stripped themselves of their ornaments by Mount Hō'reb.
7 Moses took his tent and
pitched it outside the camp, far
from the camp, and [a]called it the
tabernacle of meeting. And it
came to pass *that* everyone who
[b]sought the LORD went out to
the tabernacle of meeting which
was outside the camp.
8 So it was, whenever Moses
went out to the tabernacle, *that*
all the people rose, and each
man stood [a]*at* his tent door and
watched Moses until he had
gone into the tabernacle.
9 And it came to pass, when
Moses entered the tabernacle,
that the pillar of cloud descended and stood *at* the door
of the tabernacle, and *the* LORD
[a]talked with Moses.
10 All the people saw the pillar
of cloud standing *at* the tabernacle door, and all the people
rose and [a]worshiped, each man
in his tent door.
11 So [a]the LORD spoke to Moses
face to face, as a man speaks to
his friend. And he would return
to the camp, but [b]his servant
Joshua the son of Nun, a young
man, did not depart from the
tabernacle.
12 Then Moses said to the LORD,
"See, [a]You say to me, 'Bring up
this people.' But You have not let
me know whom You will send
with me. Yet You have said, [b]'I
know you by name, and you have
also found grace in My sight.'
13 "Now therefore, I pray, [a]if I
have found grace in Your sight,
[b]show me now Your way, that I
may know You and that I may
find grace in Your sight. And
consider that this nation *is* [c]Your
people."
14 And He said, [a]"My Presence
will go *with you,* and I will give
you [b]rest."
15 Then he said to Him, [a]"If Your
Presence does not go *with us,* do
not bring us up from here.
16 "For how then will it be
known that Your people and I
have found grace in Your sight,
[a]except You go with us? So we
[b]shall be separate, Your people
and I, from all the people who
are upon the face of the earth."
17 So the LORD said to Moses,
[a]"I will also do this thing that
you have spoken; for you have
found grace in My sight, and I
know you by name."
18 And he said, "Please, show
me [a]Your glory."
19 Then He said, "I will make
all My [a]goodness pass before
you, and I will proclaim the
name of the LORD before you. [b]I
will be gracious to whom I will
be [c]gracious, and I will have
compassion on whom I will have
compassion."
20 But He said, "You cannot see

3 [a]Ex. 3:8 [b]Num. 16:21, 45 [c]Ex. 32:9; 33:5 [1]*destroy* [2]*stubborn*
4 [a]Num. 14:1, 39 [b]Ezra 9:3
5 [a][Ps. 139:23] [1]*jewelry*
7 [a]Ex. 29:42, 43 [b]Deut. 4:29
8 [a]Num. 16:27
9 [a]Ps. 99:7
10 [a]Ex. 4:31
11 [a]Num. 12:8 [b]Ex. 24:13
12 [a]Ex. 3:10; 32:34 [b]Ex. 33:17
13 [a]Ex. 34:9 [b]Ps. 25:4; 27:11; 86:11; 119:33 [c]Deut. 9:26, 29
14 [a]Is. 63:9 [b]Josh. 21:44; 22:4
15 [a]Ex. 33:3
16 [a]Num. 14:14 [b]Ex. 34:10
17 [a][James 5:16]
18 [a][1 Tim. 6:16]
19 [a]Ex. 34:6, 7 [b][Rom. 9:15, 16, 18] [c][Rom. 4:4, 16]

My face; for [a]no man shall see
Me, and live."
21 And the LORD said, "Here is a
place by Me, and you shall stand
on the rock.
22 "So it shall be, while My
glory passes by, that I will put
you [a]in the cleft of the rock, and
will [b]cover you with My hand
while I pass by.
23 "Then I will take away My
hand, and you shall see My
back; but My face shall [a]not be
seen."

34 And the LORD said to Moses, [a]"Cut two tablets of
stone like the first *ones,* and [b]I
will write on *these* tablets the
words that were on the first tablets which you broke.
2 "So be ready in the morning,
and come up in the morning to
Mount Sinai, and present yourself to Me there [a]on the top of
the mountain.
3 "And no man shall [a]come up
with you, and let no man be seen
throughout all the mountain; let
neither flocks nor herds feed
before that mountain."
4 So he cut two tablets of stone
like the first *ones.* Then Moses
rose early in the morning and
went up Mount Sinai, as the
LORD had commanded him; and
he took in his hand the two tablets of stone.
5 Now the LORD descended in
the [a]cloud and stood with him
there, and [b]proclaimed the name
of the LORD.
6 And the LORD passed before
him and proclaimed, "The LORD,
the LORD [a]God, merciful and gracious, longsuffering, and abounding in [b]goodness and [c]truth,
7 [a]"keeping mercy for thousands, [b]forgiving iniquity and
transgression and sin, [c]by no
means clearing *the guilty,* visit-
ing the iniquity of the fathers
upon the children and the children's children to the third and
the fourth generation."
8 So Moses made haste and
[a]bowed his head toward the
earth, and worshiped.
9 Then he said, "If now I
have found grace in Your sight,
O Lord, [a]let my Lord, I pray, go
among us, even though we *are*
a [b]stiff-necked[1] people; and pardon our iniquity and our sin, and
take us as [c]Your inheritance."
10 And He said: "Behold, [a]I
make a covenant. Before all
your people I will [b]do [1]marvels
such as have not been done in
all the earth, nor in any nation;
and all the people among whom
you *are* shall see the work of
the LORD. For it *is* [c]an awesome
thing that I will do with you.
11 [a]"Observe what I command
you this day. Behold, [b]I am driving out from before you the
Am'o·rīte and the Cā'naan·īte
and the Hit'tīte and the Per'-
iz·zīte and the Hī'vīte and the
Jeb'ū·sīte.
12 [a]"Take heed to yourself, lest
you make a covenant with the
inhabitants of the land where
you are going, lest it be a snare
in your midst.
13 "But you shall [a]destroy their
altars, break their *sacred* pillars,
and [b]cut down their wooden
images
14 "(for you shall worship [a]no
other god, for the LORD, whose
[b]name *is* Jealous, *is* a [c]jealous
God),
15 "lest you make a covenant
with the inhabitants of the land,
and they [a]play the harlot with

20 [a][Gen. 32:30]
22 [a]Is. 2:21 [b]Ps. 91:1, 4
23 [a][John 1:18]
CHAPTER 34
1 [a][Ex. 24:12; 31:18; 32:15, 16, 19] [b]Deut. 10:2, 4
2 [a]Ex. 19:11, 18, 20
3 [a]Ex. 19:12, 13; 24:9–11
5 [a]Ex. 19:9 [b]Ex. 33:19
6 [a]Neh. 9:17 [b]Rom. 2:4 [c]Ps. 108:4
7 [a]Ex. 20:6 [b]Ps. 103:3, 4 [c]Job 10:14
8 [a]Ex. 4:31
9 [a]Ex. 33:12–16 [b]Ex. 33:3 [c]Ps. 33:12; 94:14 [1]*stubborn*
10 [a]Deut. 5:2 [b]Ps. 77:14 [c]Ps. 145:6 [1]*wonderful acts*
11 [a]Deut. 6:25 [b]Ex. 23:20–33; 33:2
12 [a]Ex. 23:32, 33
13 [a]Deut. 12:3 [b]2 Kin. 18:4
14 [a][Ex. 20:3–5] [b][Is. 9:6; 57:15] [c][Deut. 4:24]
15 [a]Judg. 2:17

their gods and make sacrifice
to their gods, and *one of them*
[b]invites you and you [c]eat of his
sacrifice,
16 "and you take of [a]his daughters for your sons, and his
daughters [b]play the harlot with
their gods and make your sons
play the harlot with their gods.
17 [a]"You shall make no molded
gods for yourselves.
18 "The Feast of [a]Unleavened
Bread you shall keep. Seven
days you shall eat unleavened
bread, as I commanded you, in
the appointed time of the month
of Ā′bib; for in the [b]month of
Ā′bib you came out from Egypt.
19 [a]"All [1]that open the womb *are*
Mine, and every male firstborn
among your livestock, *whether*
ox or sheep.
20 "But [a]the firstborn of a donkey you shall redeem with a
lamb. And if you will not redeem *him*, then you shall break
his neck. All the firstborn of
your sons you shall redeem. And
none shall appear before Me
[b]empty-handed.
21 [a]"Six days you shall work,
but on the seventh day you shall
rest; in plowing time and in harvest you shall rest.
22 "And you shall observe the
Feast of Weeks, of the firstfruits
of wheat harvest, and the Feast
of Ingathering at the year's end.
23 [a]"Three times in the year
all your men shall appear before the Lord, the LORD God of
Israel.
24 "For I will [a]cast out the nations
before you and enlarge your borders; neither will any man covet
your land when you go up to appear before the LORD your God
three times in the year.
25 "You shall not offer the blood
of My sacrifice with leaven, [a]nor
shall the sacrifice of the Feast
of the Passover be left until
morning.
26 [a]"The first of the firstfruits of
your land you shall bring to the
house of the LORD your God. You
shall not boil a young goat in its
mother's milk."
27 Then the LORD said to Moses,
"Write [a]these words, for according to the tenor of these words I
have made a covenant with you
and with Israel."
28 [a]So he was there with the
LORD forty days and forty nights;
he neither ate bread nor drank
water. And [b]He wrote on the tablets the words of the covenant,
the [1]Ten Commandments.
29 Now it was so, when Moses
came down from Mount Sinai
(and the [a]two tablets of the Testimony *were* in Moses' hand when
he came down from the mountain), that Moses did not know
that [b]the skin of his face shone
while he talked with Him.
30 So when Aaron and all the
children of Israel saw Moses, behold, the skin of his face shone,
and they were afraid to come
near him.
31 Then Moses called to them,
and Aaron and all the rulers of
the congregation returned to him;
and Moses talked with them.
32 Afterward all the children of
Israel came near, [a]and he gave
them as commandments all that
the LORD had spoken with him
on Mount Sinai.
33 And when Moses had finished speaking with them, he
put [a]a veil on his face.
34 But [a]whenever Moses went
in before the LORD to speak with

15 [b]Num. 25:1, 2 [c]1 Cor. 8:4, 7, 10
16 [a]Gen. 28:1 [b]Num. 25:1, 2
17 [a]Ex. 20:4, 23; 32:8
18 [a]Ex. 12:15, 16 [b]Ex. 12:2; 13:4
19 [a]Ex. 13:2; 22:29 [1]*the firstborn*
20 [a]Ex. 13:13 [b]Ex. 22:29; 23:15
21 [a]Ex. 20:9; 23:12; 31:15; 35:2
23 [a]Ex. 23:14–17
24 [a][Ex. 33:2]
25 [a]Ex. 12:10
26 [a]Ex. 23:19
27 [a]Deut. 31:9
28 [a]Ex. 24:18 [b]Ex. 34:1, 4 [1]Lit. *Ten Words*
29 [a]Ex. 32:15 [b]2 Cor. 3:7
32 [a]Ex. 24:3
33 [a][2 Cor. 3:13, 14]
34 [a][2 Cor. 3:13–16]

Him, he would take the veil off until he came out; and he would come out and speak to the children of Israel whatever he had been commanded.

35 And whenever the children of Israel saw the face of Moses, that the skin of Moses' face shone, then Moses would put the veil on his face again, until he went in to speak with Him.

35 Then Moses gathered all the congregation of the children of Israel together, and said to them, [a]"These *are* the words which the LORD has commanded *you* to do:

2 "Work shall be done for [a]six days, but the seventh day shall be a holy day for you, a Sabbath of rest to the LORD. Whoever does any work on it shall be put to [b]death.

3 [a]"You shall kindle no fire throughout your dwellings on the Sabbath day."

4 And Moses spoke to all the congregation of the children of Israel, saying, [a]"This *is* the thing which the LORD commanded, saying:

5 'Take from among you an offering to the LORD. [a]Whoever *is* of a willing heart, let him bring it as an offering to the LORD: [b]gold, silver, and bronze;

6 [a]'blue, purple, and scarlet *thread,* fine linen, and [b]goats' *hair;*

7 'ram skins dyed red, badger skins, and acacia wood;

8 'oil for the light, [a]and spices for the anointing oil and for the sweet incense;

9 'onyx stones, and stones to be set in the ephod and in the breastplate.

10 [a]'All *who are* gifted artisans among you shall come and make all that the LORD has commanded:

11 [a]'the tabernacle, its tent, its covering, its clasps, its boards, its bars, its pillars, and its sockets;

12 [a]'the ark and its poles, *with* the mercy seat, and the veil of the covering;

13 'the [a]table and its poles, all its utensils, [b]and the showbread;

14 'also [a]the lampstand for the light, its utensils, its lamps, and the oil for the light;

15 [a]'the incense altar, its poles, [b]the anointing oil, [c]the sweet incense, and the screen for the door at the entrance of the tabernacle;

16 [a]'the altar of burnt offering with its bronze grating, its poles, all its utensils, *and* the laver and its base;

17 [a]'the hangings of the court, its pillars, their sockets, and the screen for the gate of the court;

18 'the pegs of the tabernacle, the pegs of the court, and their cords;

19 [a]'the [1]garments of ministry, for ministering in the holy *place*—the holy garments for Aaron the priest and the garments of his sons, to minister as priests.'"

20 And all the congregation of the children of Israel departed from the presence of Moses.

21 Then everyone came [a]whose heart [1]was stirred, and everyone whose spirit was willing, *and* they [b]brought the LORD's offering for the work of the tabernacle of meeting, for all its service, and for the holy garments.

22 They came, both men and women, as many as had a willing heart, *and* brought [a]earrings

CHAPTER 35

1 [a]Ex. 34:32

2 [a]Lev. 23:3 [b]Num. 15:32–36

3 [a]Ex. 12:16; 16:23

4 [a]Ex. 25:1, 2

5 [a]Ex. 25:2 [b]Ex. 38:24

6 [a]Ex. 36:8 [b]Ex. 36:14

8 [a]Ex. 25:6; 30:23–25

10 [a]Ex. 31:2–6; 36:1, 2

11 [a]Ex. 26:1, 2; 36:14

12 [a]Ex. 25:10–22

13 [a]Ex. 25:23 [b]Ex. 25:30

14 [a]Ex. 25:31

15 [a]Ex. 30:1 [b]Ex. 30:25 [c]Ex. 30:34–38

16 [a]Ex. 27:1–8

17 [a]Ex. 27:9–18

19 [a]Ex. 31:10; 39:1, 41 [1]Or *woven garments*

21 [a]Ex. 25:2; 35:5, 22, 26, 29; 36:2 [b]Ex. 35:24 [1]Lit. *lifted him up*

22 [a]Ex. 32:2, 3

and nose rings, rings and necklaces, all [b]jewelry of gold, that is,
every man who *made* an offering of gold to the LORD.
23 And [a]every man, with whom
was found blue, purple, and scarlet *thread,* fine linen, and goats'
hair, red skins of rams, and [1]bad-
ger skins, brought *them.*
24 Everyone who offered an
offering of silver or bronze
brought the LORD's offering. And
everyone with whom was found
acacia wood for any work of the
service, brought *it.*
25 All the women *who were*
[a]gifted artisans spun yarn with
their hands, and brought what
they had spun, of blue, purple,
and scarlet, and fine linen.
26 And all the women whose
hearts [1]stirred with wisdom
spun yarn of goats' *hair.*
27 [a]The rulers brought onyx
stones, and the stones to be set in
the ephod and in the breastplate,
28 and [a]spices and oil for the
light, for the anointing oil, and
for the sweet incense.
29 The children of Israel brought
a [a]freewill offering to the LORD,
all the men and women whose
hearts were willing to bring *material* for all kinds of work which
the LORD, by the hand of Moses,
had commanded to be done.
30 And Moses said to the children of Israel, "See, [a]the LORD
has called by name Bez'a·lel the
son of Ū'rī, the son of Hur, of the
tribe of Judah;
31 "and He has filled him with
the Spirit of God, in wisdom
and understanding, in knowledge and all manner of workmanship,
32 "to design artistic works, to
work in gold and silver and
bronze,
33 "in cutting jewels for setting, in carving wood, and to
work in all manner of artistic
workmanship.
34 "And He has put in his heart
the ability to teach, *in* him and
[a]A·hō'li·ab the son of A·his'-
a·mach, of the tribe of Dan.
35 "He has [a]filled them with skill
to do all manner of work of the
engraver and the designer and
the tapestry maker, in blue, purple, and scarlet *thread,* and fine
linen, and of the weaver—those
who do every work and those
who design artistic works.

36

"And Bez'a·lel and A·hō'-
li·ab, and every [a]gifted
artisan in whom the LORD has
put wisdom and understanding,
to know how to do all manner
of work for the service of the
[b]sanctuary,[1] shall do according
to all that the LORD has commanded."
2 Then Moses called Bez'-
a·lel and A·hō'li·ab, and every
gifted artisan in whose heart the
LORD had put wisdom, everyone
[a]whose heart [1]was stirred, to
come and do the work.
3 And they received from Moses all the [a]offering which the
children of Israel [b]had brought
for the work of the service of
making the sanctuary. So they
continued bringing to him freewill offerings every morning.
4 Then all the craftsmen who
were doing all the work of the
sanctuary came, each from the
work he was doing,
5 and they spoke to Moses,
saying, [a]"The people bring
much more than enough for the

22 [b]Ex. 11:2
23 [a]1 Chr. 29:8 [1]Or *dolphin*
25 [a]Ex. 28:3; 31:6; 36:1
26 [1]Lit. *lifted them up*
27 [a]Ezra 2:68
28 [a]Ex. 30:23
29 [a]1 Chr. 29:9
30 [a]Ex. 31:1–6
34 [a]Ex. 31:6
35 [a]1 Kin. 7:14

CHAPTER 36

1 [a]Ex. 28:3; 31:6; 35:10, 35 [b]Ex. 25:8 [1]*holy place*
2 [a]1 Chr. 29:5, 9, 17 [1]*lifted him up*
3 [a]Ex. 35:5 [b]Ex. 35:27
5 [a][2 Cor. 8:2, 3]

service of the work which the
LORD commanded *us* to do."
6 So Moses gave a commandment, and they caused it to
be proclaimed throughout the
camp, saying, "Let neither man
nor woman do any more work
for the offering of the sanctuary." And the people were restrained from bringing,
7 for the material they had
was sufficient for all the work to
be done—indeed too [a]much.
8 [a]Then all the gifted artisans
among them who worked on the
tabernacle made ten curtains
woven of fine linen, and of blue,
purple, and scarlet *thread; with*
artistic designs of cherubim they
made them.
9 The length of each curtain
was twenty-eight cubits, and the
width of each curtain four cubits; the curtains *were* all the
same size.
10 And he coupled five curtains
to one another, and *the other*
five curtains he coupled to one
another.
11 He made loops of blue *yarn*
on the edge of the curtain on
the selvedge of one set; likewise
he did on the outer edge of *the*
other curtain of the second set.
12 [a]Fifty loops he made on one
curtain, and fifty loops he made
on the edge of the curtain on the
end of the second set; the loops
held one *curtain* to another.
13 And he made fifty clasps of
gold, and coupled the curtains to
one another with the clasps, that
it might be one tabernacle.
14 [a]He made curtains of goats'
hair for the tent over the tabernacle; he made eleven curtains.
15 The length of each curtain
was thirty cubits, and the width
of each curtain four cubits; the
eleven curtains *were* the same
size.
16 He coupled five curtains by
themselves and six curtains by
themselves.
17 And he made fifty loops on
the edge of the curtain that is
outermost in one set, and fifty
loops he made on the edge of
the curtain of the second set.
18 He also made fifty bronze
clasps to couple the tent together, that it might be one.
19 [a]Then he made a covering
for the tent of ram skins dyed
red, and a covering of [1]badger
skins above *that.*
20 For the tabernacle [a]he made
boards of acacia wood, standing
upright.
21 The length of each board
was ten cubits, and the width of
each board a cubit and a half.
22 Each board had two [1]ten-
ons [a]for binding one to another.
Thus he made for all the boards
of the tabernacle.
23 And he made boards for the
tabernacle, twenty boards for
the south side.
24 Forty sockets of silver he
made to go under the twenty
boards: two sockets under each
of the boards for its two tenons.
25 And for the other side of the
tabernacle, the north side, he
made twenty boards
26 and their forty sockets of
silver: two sockets under each of
the boards.
27 For the west side of the tabernacle he made six boards.
28 He also made two boards
for the two back corners of the
tabernacle.
29 And they were coupled at the
bottom and [1]coupled together at

7 [a]1 Kin. 8:64
8 [a]Ex. 26:1–14
12 [a]Ex. 26:5
14 [a]Ex. 26:7
19 [a]Ex. 26:14 [1]Or *dolphin*
20 [a]Ex. 26:15–29
22 [a]Ex. 26:17 [1]Projections for joining, lit. *hands*
29 [1]Lit. *doubled*

the top by one ring. Thus he
made both of them for the two
corners.
30 So there were eight boards
and their sockets—sixteen sockets of silver—two sockets under
each of the boards.
31 And he made [a]bars of acacia
wood: five for the boards on one
side of the tabernacle,
32 five bars for the boards on
the other side of the tabernacle,
and five bars for the boards of
the tabernacle on the far side
westward.
33 And he made the middle bar
to pass through the boards from
one end to the other.
34 He overlaid the boards with
gold, made their rings of gold
to be holders for the bars, and
overlaid the bars with gold.
35 And he made [a]a veil of blue,
purple, and scarlet *thread,*
and fine woven linen; it was
worked *with* an artistic design
of cherubim.
36 He made for it four pillars of
acacia *wood,* and overlaid them
with gold, with their hooks of
gold; and he cast four sockets of
silver for them.
37 He also made a [a]screen for
the tabernacle door, of blue,
purple, and scarlet *thread,* and
fine woven linen, made by a
[1]weaver,
38 and its five pillars with their
hooks. And he overlaid their
capitals and their rings with
gold, but their five sockets *were*
bronze.

37 Then [a]Bez′a·lel made [b]the
ark of acacia wood; two
and a half cubits *was* its length,
a cubit and a half its width, and
a cubit and a half its height.
2 He overlaid it with pure gold

31 [a]Ex. 26:26–29

35 [a]Ex. 26:31–37

37 [a]Ex. 26:36
[1]Lit. *variegator,* a weaver in colors

CHAPTER 37

1 [a]Ex. 35:30; 36:1
[b]Ex. 25:10–20

6 [a]Ex. 25:17

9 [a]Ex. 25:20

10 [a]Ex. 25:23–29

inside and outside, and made a
molding of gold all around it.
3 And he cast for it four rings
of gold *to be set* in its four corners: two rings on one side, and
two rings on the other side of it.
4 He made poles of acacia
wood, and overlaid them with
gold.
5 And he put the poles into the
rings at the sides of the ark, to
bear the ark.
6 He also made the [a]mercy
seat of pure gold; two and a half
cubits *was* its length and a cubit
and a half its width.
7 He made two cherubim of
beaten gold; he made them of
one piece at the two ends of the
mercy seat:
8 one cherub at one end on
this side, and the other cherub
at the *other* end on that side. He
made the cherubim at the two
ends *of one piece* with the mercy
seat.
9 The cherubim spread out
their wings above, *and* covered the [a]mercy seat with their
wings. They faced one another;
the faces of the cherubim were
toward the mercy seat.
10 He made [a]the table of acacia
wood; two cubits *was* its length,
a cubit its width, and a cubit and
a half its height.
11 And he overlaid it with pure
gold, and made a molding of
gold all around it.
12 Also he made a frame of a
handbreadth all around it, and
made a molding of gold for the
frame all around it.
13 And he cast for it four rings
of gold, and put the rings on the
four corners that *were* at its four
legs.
14 The rings were close to the

frame, as holders for the poles
to bear the table.
15 And he made the poles of
acacia wood to bear the table,
and overlaid them with gold.
16 He made of pure gold the
utensils which were on the table:
its [a]dishes, its cups, its bowls,
and its pitchers for pouring.
17 He also made the [a]lampstand
of pure gold; of hammered work
he made the lampstand. Its shaft,
its branches, its bowls, its *ornamental* knobs, and its flowers
were of the same piece.
18 And six branches came out
of its sides: three branches of
the lampstand out of one side,
and three branches of the lampstand out of the other side.
19 There were three bowls
made like almond *blossoms*
on one branch, with an *ornamental* knob and a flower, and
three bowls made like almond
blossoms on the other branch,
with an *ornamental* knob and
a flower—and so for the six
branches coming out of the
lampstand.
20 And on the lampstand itself
were four bowls made like almond *blossoms, each with* its
ornamental knob and flower.
21 *There was* a knob under
the *first* two branches of the
same, a knob under the *second* two branches of the same,
and a knob under the *third* two
branches of the same, according
to the six branches extending
from it.
22 Their knobs and their
branches were of one piece; all
of it *was* one hammered piece of
pure gold.
23 And he made its seven lamps,

16 [a]Ex. 25:29
17 [a]Ex. 25:31–39
23 [a]Num. 4:9
25 [a]Ex. 30:1–5
28 [a]Ex. 30:5
29 [a]Ex. 30:23–25
CHAPTER 38
1 [a]Ex. 27:1–8

its [a]wick-trimmers, and its trays
of pure gold.
24 Of a talent of pure gold he
made it, with all its utensils.
25 [a]He made the incense altar
of acacia wood. Its length *was*
a cubit and its width a cubit—*it
was* square—and two cubits *was*
its height. Its horns were *of one
piece* with it.
26 And he overlaid it with pure
gold: its top, its sides all around,
and its horns. He also made for it
a molding of gold all around it.
27 He made two rings of gold
for it under its molding, by its
two corners on both sides, as
holders for the poles with which
to bear it.
28 And he [a]made the poles of
acacia wood, and overlaid them
with gold.
29 He also made [a]the holy
anointing oil and the pure incense of sweet spices, according
to the work of the perfumer.
38 He made [a]the altar of
burnt offering of acacia
wood; five cubits *was* its length
and five cubits its width—*it was*
square—and its height *was* three
cubits.
2 He made its horns on its four
corners; the horns were *of one
piece* with it. And he overlaid it
with bronze.
3 He made all the utensils for
the altar: the pans, the shovels,
the basins, the forks, and the
firepans; all its utensils he made
of bronze.
4 And he made a grate of
bronze network for the altar,
under its rim, midway from the
bottom.
5 He cast four rings for the
four corners of the bronze grating, *as* holders for the poles.

6 And he made the poles of acacia wood, and overlaid them with bronze.

7 Then he put the poles into the rings on the sides of the altar, with which to bear it. He made the altar hollow with boards.

8 He made [a]the laver of bronze and its base of bronze, from the bronze mirrors of the serving women who assembled at the door of the tabernacle of meeting.

9 Then he made [a]the court on the south side; the hangings of the court *were of* fine woven linen, one hundred cubits long.

10 There *were* twenty pillars for them, with twenty bronze sockets. The hooks of the pillars and their bands *were* silver.

11 On the north side *the hangings were* one hundred cubits *long,* with twenty pillars and their twenty bronze sockets. The hooks of the pillars and their bands *were* silver.

12 And on the west side *there were* hangings of fifty cubits, with ten pillars and their ten sockets. The hooks of the pillars and their bands *were* silver.

13 For the east side *the hangings were* fifty cubits.

14 The hangings of one side *of the gate were* fifteen cubits *long, with* their three pillars and their three sockets,

15 and the same for the other side of the court gate; on this side and that *were* hangings of fifteen cubits, *with* their three pillars and their three sockets.

16 All the hangings of the court all around *were of* fine woven linen.

17 The sockets for the pillars *were* bronze, the hooks of the pillars and their bands *were* silver, and the overlay of their capitals *was* silver; and all the pillars of the court had bands of silver.

18 The screen for the gate of the court *was* woven of blue, purple, and scarlet *thread,* and of fine woven linen. The length *was* twenty cubits, and the height along its width *was* five cubits, corresponding to the hangings of the court.

19 And *there were* four pillars *with* their four sockets of bronze; their hooks *were* silver, and the overlay of their capitals and their bands *was* silver.

20 All the [a]pegs of the tabernacle, and of the court all around, *were* bronze.

21 [1]This is the inventory of the tabernacle, [a]the tabernacle of the Testimony, which was counted according to the commandment of Moses, for the service of the Lē′vītes, [b]by the hand of [c]Ith′a·mar, son of Aaron the priest.

22 [a]Bez′a·lel the son of Ū′rī, the son of Hur, of the tribe of Judah, made all that the LORD had commanded Moses.

23 And with him *was* [a]A·hō′li·ab the son of A·his′a·mach, of the tribe of Dan, an engraver and [1]designer, a weaver of blue, purple, and scarlet *thread,* and of fine linen.

24 All the gold that was used in all the work of the holy *place,* that is, the gold of the [a]offering, was twenty-nine talents and seven hundred and thirty shekels, according to [b]the shekel of the sanctuary.

25 And the silver from those who were [a]numbered of the congregation *was* one hundred

8 [a]Ex. 30:18
9 [a]Ex. 27:9–19
20 [a]Ex. 27:19
21 [a]Acts 7:44 [b]Num. 4:28, 33 [c]Lev. 10:6, 16 [1]Lit. *These are the things appointed for*
22 [a]Ex. 31:2, 6
23 [a]Ex. 31:6; 36:1 [1]*skillful workman*
24 [a]Ex. 35:5, 22 [b]Ex. 30:13, 24
25 [a]Ex. 30:11–16

talents and one thousand seven
hundred and seventy-five shekels, according to the shekel of
the sanctuary:
26 [a]a bekah for [1]each man (*that
is*, half a shekel, according to
the shekel of the sanctuary), for
everyone included in the numbering from twenty years old
and above, for [b]six hundred and
three thousand, five hundred
and fifty *men*.
27 And from the hundred talents
of silver were cast [a]the sockets
of the sanctuary and the bases
of the veil: one hundred sockets
from the hundred talents, one
talent for each socket.
28 Then from the one thousand
seven hundred and seventy-five
shekels he made hooks for the
pillars, overlaid their capitals,
and [a]made bands for them.
29 The offering of bronze *was*
seventy talents and two thousand four hundred shekels.
30 And with it he made the
sockets for the door of the tabernacle of meeting, the bronze
altar, the bronze grating for it,
and all the utensils for the altar,
31 the sockets for the court all
around, the bases for the court
gate, all the pegs for the tabernacle, and all the pegs for the
court all around.

39 Of the [a]blue, purple, and
scarlet *thread* they made
[b]garments[1] of ministry, for ministering in the [2]holy *place*, and
made the holy garments for
Aaron, [c]as the LORD had commanded Moses.
2 [a]He made the [b]ephod of gold,
blue, purple, and scarlet *thread*,
and of fine woven linen.
3 And they beat the gold
into thin sheets and cut *it into*
threads, to work *it* in *with* the
blue, purple, and scarlet *thread*,
and the fine linen, *into* artistic
designs.
4 They made shoulder straps
for it to couple *it* together; it was
coupled together at its two edges.
5 And the intricately woven
band of his ephod that *was* on it
was of the same workmanship,
woven of gold, blue, purple, and
scarlet *thread*, and *of* fine woven linen, as the LORD had commanded Moses.
6 [a]And they set onyx stones,
enclosed in [1]settings of gold;
they were engraved, as signets
are engraved, with the names of
the sons of Israel.
7 He put them on the shoulders
of the ephod *as* [a]memorial stones
for the sons of Israel, as the LORD
had commanded Moses.
8 [a]And he made the breastplate, artistically woven like the
workmanship of the ephod, of
gold, blue, purple, and scarlet
thread, and of fine woven linen.
9 They made the breastplate
square by doubling it; a span
was its length and a span its
width when doubled.
10 [a]And they set in it four rows
of stones: a row with a sardius,
a topaz, and an emerald was the
first row;
11 the second row, a turquoise,
a sapphire, and a diamond;
12 the third row, a jacinth, an
agate, and an amethyst;
13 the fourth row, a beryl, an
onyx, and a jasper. *They were*
enclosed in settings of gold in
their mountings.
14 *There were* [a]twelve stones
according to the names of the
sons of Israel: according to their
names, *engraved like* a signet,

26 [a]Ex. 30:13, 15 [b]Num. 1:46; 26:51 [1]Lit. *a head*
27 [a]Ex. 26:19, 21, 25, 32
28 [a]Ex. 27:17

CHAPTER 39

1 [a]Ex. 25:4; 35:23 [b]Ex. 31:10; 35:19 [c]Ex. 28:4 [1]Or *woven garments* [2]*sanctuary*
2 [a]Ex. 28:6–14 [b]Lev. 8:7
6 [a]Ex. 28:9–11 [1]*plaited work*
7 [a]Ex. 28:12, 29
8 [a]Ex. 28:15–30
10 [a]Ex. 28:17
14 [a]Rev. 21:12

each one with its own name according to the twelve tribes.
15 And they made chains for
the breastplate at the ends, like
braided cords of pure gold.
16 They also made two settings
of gold and two gold rings, and
put the two rings on the two
ends of the breastplate.
17 And they put the two braided
chains of gold in the two rings
on the ends of the breastplate.
18 The two ends of the two
braided *chains* they fastened in
the two settings, and put them
on the shoulder straps of the
ephod in the front.
19 And they made two rings of
gold and put *them* on the two
ends of the breastplate, on the
edge of it, which *was* on the inward side of the ephod.
20 They made two *other* gold
rings and put them on the two
shoulder straps, underneath the
ephod toward its front, right at
the seam above the intricately
woven band of the ephod.
21 And they bound the breastplate by means of its rings to the
rings of the ephod with a blue
cord, so that it would be above
the intricately woven band of
the ephod, and that the breastplate would not come loose from
the ephod, as the LORD had commanded Moses.
22 [a]He made the [b]robe of the
ephod of woven work, all of blue.
23 And *there was* an opening in
the middle of the robe, like the
opening in a coat of mail, *with*
a woven binding all around the
opening, so that it would not tear.
24 They made on the hem of
the robe pomegranates of blue,
purple, and scarlet, and of fine
woven *linen*.
25 And they made [a]bells of pure
gold, and put the bells between
the pomegranates on the hem of
the robe all around between the
pomegranates:
26 a bell and a pomegranate,
a bell and a pomegranate, all
around the hem of the robe to
[1]minister in, as the LORD had
commanded Moses.
27 [a]They made tunics, artistically woven of fine linen, for
Aaron and his sons,
28 [a]a turban of fine linen, exquisite hats of fine linen, [b]short
trousers of fine woven linen,
29 [a]and a sash of fine woven
linen with blue, purple, and scarlet *thread*, made by a weaver,
as the LORD had commanded
Moses.
30 [a]Then they made the plate of
the holy crown of pure gold, and
wrote on it an inscription *like*
the engraving of a signet:

[b]HOLINESS TO THE LORD.

31 And they tied to it a blue
cord, to fasten *it* above on the
turban, as the LORD had commanded Moses.
32 Thus all the work of the tabernacle of the tent of meeting
was [a]finished. And the children
of Israel did [b]according to all
that the LORD had commanded
Moses; so they did.
33 And they brought the tabernacle to Moses, the tent and
all its furnishings: its clasps, its
boards, its bars, its pillars, and
its sockets;
34 the covering of ram skins
dyed red, the covering of badger skins, and the veil of the
covering;

22 [a]Ex. 28:31–35 [b]Ex. 29:5
25 [a]Ex. 28:33
26 [1]*serve*
27 [a]Ex. 28:39, 40
28 [a]Ex. 28:4, 39 [b]Ex. 28:42
29 [a]Ex. 28:39
30 [a]Ex. 28:36, 37 [b]Zech. 14:20
32 [a]Ex. 40:17 [b]Ex. 25:40; 39:42, 43

35 the ark of the Testimony with
its poles, and the mercy seat;
36 the table, all its utensils, and
the [a]showbread;
37 the pure *gold* lampstand
with its lamps (the lamps set in
order), all its utensils, and the oil
for light;
38 the gold altar, the anointing
oil, and the sweet incense; the
screen for the tabernacle door;
39 the bronze altar, its grate
of bronze, its poles, and all its
utensils; the laver with its base;
40 the hangings of the court, its
pillars and its sockets, the screen
for the court gate, its cords, and
its pegs; all the utensils for the
service of the tabernacle, for the
tent of meeting;
41 and the [1]garments of ministry, to [2]minister in the holy *place*:
the holy garments for Aaron the
priest, and his sons' garments,
to minister as priests.
42 According to all that the
LORD had commanded Moses,
so the children of Israel [a]did all
the work.
43 Then Moses looked over all
the work, and indeed they had
done it; as the LORD had commanded, just so they had done
it. And Moses [a]blessed them.

40

Then the LORD [a]spoke to
Moses, saying:
2 "On the first day of the [a]first
month you shall set up [b]the tabernacle of the tent of meeting.
3 [a]"You shall put in it the ark
of the Testimony, and [1]partition
off the ark with the veil.
4 [a]"You shall bring in the table
and [b]arrange the things that are
to be set in order on it; [c]and you
shall bring in the lampstand and
[1]light its lamps.
5 [a]"You shall also set the altar
of gold for the incense before
the ark of the Testimony, and
put up the screen for the door of
the tabernacle.
6 "Then you shall set the [a]altar
of the burnt offering before the
door of the tabernacle of the
tent of meeting.
7 "And [a]you shall set the laver
between the tabernacle of meeting and the altar, and put water
in it.
8 "You shall set up the court all
around, and hang up the screen
at the court gate.
9 "And you shall take the
anointing oil, and [a]anoint the
tabernacle and all that *is* in it;
and you shall hallow it and all
its utensils, and it shall be holy.
10 "You shall [a]anoint the altar
of the burnt offering and all
its utensils, and consecrate the
altar. [b]The altar shall be most
holy.
11 "And you shall anoint the laver and its base, and consecrate
it.
12 [a]"Then you shall bring Aaron
and his sons to the door of the
tabernacle of meeting and wash
them with water.
13 "You shall put the holy
[a]garments on Aaron, [b]and anoint
him and consecrate him, that he
may minister to Me as priest.
14 "And you shall bring his sons
and clothe them with tunics.
15 "You shall anoint them, as you
anointed their father, that they
may minister to Me as priests;
for their anointing shall surely
be [a]an everlasting priesthood
throughout their generations."
16 Thus Moses did; according
to all that the LORD had commanded him, so he did.
17 And it came to pass in the

36 [a]Ex. 23–30
41 [1]Or *woven garments* [2]*serve*
42 [a]Ex. 35:10
43 [a]Lev. 9:22, 23

CHAPTER 40

1 [a]Ex. 25:1—31:18
2 [a]Ex. 12:2; 13:4 [b]Ex. 26:1, 30; 40:17
3 [a]Num. 4:5 [1]*screen*
4 [a]Ex. 26:35; 40:22 [b]Ex. 25:30; 40:23 [c]Ex. 40:24, 25 [1]*set up*
5 [a]Ex. 40:26
6 [a]Ex. 39:39
7 [a]Ex. 30:18; 40:30
9 [a]Ex. 30:26
10 [a]Ex. 30:26–30 [b]Ex. 29:36, 37
12 [a]Lev. 8:1–13
13 [a]Ex. 29:5; 39:1, 41 [b][Ex. 28:41]
15 [a]Num. 25:13

first month of the second year, on
the first *day* of the month, *that*
the [a]tabernacle was [1]raised up.
18 So Moses raised up the tabernacle, fastened its sockets, set
up its boards, put in its bars, and
raised up its pillars.
19 And he spread out the tent
over the tabernacle and put the
covering of the tent on top of
it, as the LORD had commanded
Moses.
20 He took [a]the Testimony and
put *it* into the ark, inserted the
poles through the rings of the
ark, and put the mercy seat on
top of the ark.
21 And he brought the ark into
the tabernacle, [a]hung up the veil
of the covering, and partitioned
off the ark of the Testimony,
as the LORD had commanded
Moses.
22 [a]He put the table in the tabernacle of meeting, on the north
side of the tabernacle, outside
the veil;
23 [a]and he set the bread in order
upon it before the LORD, as the
LORD had commanded Moses.
24 [a]He put the lampstand in the
tabernacle of meeting, across
from the table, on the south side
of the tabernacle;
25 and [a]he lit the lamps before
the LORD, as the LORD had commanded Moses.
26 [a]He put the gold altar in the
tabernacle of meeting in front of
the veil;
27 [a]and he burned sweet incense on it, as the LORD had
commanded Moses.
28 [a]He hung up the screen *at*
the door of the tabernacle.
29 [a]And he put the altar of
burnt offering *before* the door
of the tabernacle of the tent of
meeting, and [b]offered upon it
the burnt offering and the grain
offering, as the LORD had commanded Moses.
30 [a]He set the laver between the
tabernacle of meeting and the
altar, and put water there for
washing;
31 and Moses, Aaron, and his
sons would [a]wash their hands
and their feet *with water*
from it.
32 Whenever they went into
the tabernacle of meeting, and
when they came near the altar,
they washed, [a]as the LORD had
commanded Moses.
33 [a]And he raised up the court
all around the tabernacle and
the altar, and hung up the screen
of the court gate. So Moses
[b]finished the work.
34 [a]Then the [b]cloud covered
the tabernacle of meeting, and
the [c]glory of the LORD filled the
tabernacle.
35 And Moses [a]was not able to
enter the tabernacle of meeting,
because the cloud rested above
it, and the glory of the LORD
filled the tabernacle.
36 [a]Whenever the cloud was
taken up from above the tabernacle, the children of Israel
would [1]go onward in all their
journeys.
37 But [a]if the cloud was not
taken up, then they did not
journey till the day that it was
taken up.
38 For [a]the cloud of the LORD
was above the tabernacle by
day, and fire was over it by
night, in the sight of all the
house of Israel, throughout all
their journeys.

17 [a]Ex. 40:2 [1]*erected*
20 [a]Ex. 25:16
21 [a]Ex. 26:33
22 [a]Ex. 26:35
23 [a]Ex. 40:4
24 [a]Ex. 26:35
25 [a]Ex. 25:37; 30:7, 8; 40:4
26 [a]Ex. 30:1, 6; 40:5
27 [a]Ex. 30:7
28 [a]Ex. 26:36; 40:5
29 [a]Ex. 40:6 [b]Ex. 29:38–42
30 [a]Ex. 30:18; 40:7
31 [a]Ex. 30:19, 20
32 [a]Ex. 30:19
33 [a]Ex. 27:9–18; 40:8 [b][Heb. 3:2–5]
34 [a]Num. 9:15 [b]1 Kin. 8:10, 11 [c]Lev. 9:6, 23
35 [a]1 Kin. 8:11
36 [a]Num. 9:17 [1]*journey*
37 [a]Num. 9:19–22
38 [a]Ex. 13:21

The Third Book of Moses Called

LEVITICUS

LEVITICUS is God's guidebook for His newly redeemed people, showing them how to worship, serve, and obey a holy God. Fellowship with God through sacrifice and obedience shows the awesome holiness of the God of Israel. Indeed, " 'you shall be holy, for I the LORD your God *am* holy' " (19:2).

Leviticus focuses on the worship and walk of the nation of God. In Exodus, Israel was redeemed and established as a kingdom of priests and a holy nation. Leviticus shows how God's people are to fulfill their priestly calling.

The Hebrew title is *Wayyiqra*, "And He Called." The Talmud refers to Leviticus as the "Law of the Priests," and the "Law of the Offerings." The Greek title appearing in the Septuagint is *Leuitikon*, "That Which Pertains to the Levites." From this word, the Latin Vulgate derived its name *Leviticus* which was adopted as the English title. This title is slightly misleading because the book does not deal with the Levites as a whole but more with the priests, a segment of the Levites.

NOW the LORD [a]called to Moses, and spoke to him [b]from
the tabernacle of meeting, saying,
2 "Speak to the children of
Israel, and say to them: [a]'When
any one of you brings an offering to the LORD, you shall bring
your offering of the livestock—
of the herd and of the flock.
3 'If his offering *is* a burnt sacrifice of the herd, let him offer a
male [a]without blemish; he shall
offer it of his own free will at the
door of the tabernacle of meeting before the LORD.
4 [a]'Then he shall put his hand
on the head of the burnt offering, and it will be [b]accepted on
his behalf [c]to make atonement
for him.
5 'He shall kill the [a]bull before
the LORD; [b]and the priests, Aaron's
sons, shall bring the blood [c]and
sprinkle the blood all around on
the altar that *is by* the door of the
tabernacle of meeting.
6 'And he shall [a]skin the
burnt offering and cut it into its
pieces.
7 'The sons of Aaron the priest
shall put [a]fire on the altar, and
[b]lay the wood in order on the
fire.
8 'Then the priests, Aaron's
sons, shall lay the parts, the head,
and the fat in order on the wood
that *is* on the fire upon the altar;
9 'but he shall wash its entrails
and its legs with water. And the
priest shall burn all on the altar
as a burnt sacrifice, an offering
made by fire, a [a]sweet[1] aroma to
the LORD.
10 'If his offering *is* of the
flocks—of the sheep or of the
goats—as a burnt sacrifice, he
shall bring a male [a]without
blemish.
11 [a]'He shall kill it on the north
side of the altar before the
LORD; and the priests, Aaron's
sons, shall sprinkle its blood all
around on the altar.

CHAPTER 1

1 [a]Ex. 19:3; 25:22 [b]Ex. 40:34
2 [a]Lev. 22:18, 19
3 [a]Eph. 5:27
4 [a]Lev. 3:2, 8, 13; 4:15 [b][Rom. 12:1] [c]2 Chr. 29:23, 24
5 [a]Mic. 6:6 [b]2 Chr. 35:11 [c][Heb. 12:24]
6 [a]Lev. 7:8
7 [a]Mal. 1:10 [b]Gen. 22:9
9 [a]Gen. 8:21 [1]*soothing* or *pleasing aroma*
10 [a]Lev. 1:3
11 [a]Lev. 1:5

12 'And he shall cut it into its
pieces, with its head and its fat;
and the priest shall lay them in
order on the wood that *is* on the
fire upon the altar;
13 'but he shall wash the entrails and the legs with water.
Then the priest shall bring *it*
all and burn *it* on the altar; it
is a burnt sacrifice, an [a]offering
made by fire, a sweet aroma to
the LORD.
14 'And if the burnt sacrifice
of his offering to the LORD *is* of
birds, then he shall bring his offering of [a]turtledoves or young
pigeons.
15 'The priest shall bring it to
the altar, [1]wring off its head, and
burn *it* on the altar; its blood
shall be drained out at the side
of the altar.
16 'And he shall remove its
crop with its feathers and cast it
[a]beside the altar on the east side,
into the place for ashes.
17 'Then he shall split it at its
wings, *but* [a]shall not divide *it*
completely; and the priest shall
burn it on the altar, on the wood
that *is* on the fire. [b]It *is* a burnt
sacrifice, an offering made by
fire, a [1]sweet aroma to the LORD.

2 'When anyone offers [a]a
grain offering to the LORD,
his offering shall be *of* fine flour.
And he shall pour oil on it, and
put [b]frankincense on it.
2 'He shall bring it to Aaron's
sons, the priests, one of whom
shall take from it his handful
of fine flour and oil with all
the frankincense. And the priest
shall burn [a]*it as* a memorial on
the altar, an offering made by
fire, a sweet aroma to the LORD.
3 [a]'The rest of the grain offering *shall be* Aaron's and his
[b]sons'. [c]*It is* most holy of the
offerings to the LORD made by
fire.
4 'And if you bring as an offering a grain offering baked
in the oven, *it shall be* unleavened cakes of fine flour mixed
with oil, or unleavened wafers
[a]anointed[1] with oil.
5 'But if your offering *is* a
grain offering *baked* in a [1]pan,
it shall be of fine flour, unleavened, mixed with oil.
6 'You shall break it in pieces
and pour oil on it; it *is* a grain
offering.
7 'If your offering *is* a grain offering *baked* in a [a]covered pan,
it shall be made *of* fine flour
with oil.
8 'You shall bring the grain
offering that is made of these
things to the LORD. And when
it is presented to the priest, he
shall bring it to the altar.
9 'Then the priest shall take
from the grain offering [a]a memorial portion, and burn *it* on
the altar. *It is* an [b]offering made
by fire, a sweet aroma to the
LORD.
10 'And [a]what is left of the grain
offering *shall be* Aaron's and
his sons'. *It is* most holy of the
offerings to the LORD made by
fire.
11 'No grain offering which you
bring to the LORD shall be made
with [a]leaven, for you shall burn
no leaven nor any honey in any
offering to the LORD made by
fire.
12 [a]'As for the offering of the
firstfruits, you shall offer them
to the LORD, but they shall not be
burned on the altar for a sweet
aroma.
13 'And every offering of your

13 [a]Num. 15:4–7; 28:12–14
14 [a]Lev. 5:7, 11; 12:8
15 [1]Lit. *nip* or *chop off*
16 [a]Lev. 6:10
17 [a]Gen. 15:10 [b]Lev. 1:9, 13 [1]*soothing* or *pleasing aroma*

CHAPTER 2

1 [a]Num. 15:4 [b]Lev. 5:11
2 [a]Lev. 2:9; 5:12; 6:15; 24:7
3 [a]Lev. 7:9 [b]Lev. 6:6; 10:12, 13 [c]Num. 18:9
4 [a]Ex. 29:2 [1]*spread*
5 [1]*flat plate or griddle*
7 [a]Lev. 7:9
9 [a]Lev. 2:2, 16; 5:12; 6:15 [b]Ex. 29:18
10 [a]Lev. 2:3; 6:16
11 [a]Lev. 6:16, 17
12 [a]Lev. 23:10, 11, 17, 18

grain offering [a]you shall season with salt; you shall not allow [b]the salt of the covenant of your God to be lacking from your grain offering. [c]With all your offerings you shall offer salt.

14 'If you offer a grain offering of your firstfruits to the LORD, [a]you shall offer for the grain offering of your firstfruits green heads of grain roasted on the fire, grain beaten from [b]full heads.

15 'And [a]you shall put oil on it, and lay frankincense on it. It *is* a grain offering.

16 'Then the priest shall burn [a]the memorial portion: *part* of its beaten grain and *part* of its oil, with all the frankincense, as an offering made by fire to the LORD.

3 'When his offering *is* a [a]sacrifice of a peace offering, if he offers *it* of the herd, whether male or female, he shall offer it [b]without [1]blemish before the LORD.

2 'And [a]he shall lay his hand on the head of his offering, and kill it *at* the door of the tabernacle of meeting; and Aaron's sons, the priests, shall [b]sprinkle the blood all around on the altar.

3 'Then he shall offer from the sacrifice of the peace offering an offering made by fire to the LORD. [a]The fat that covers the entrails and all the fat that *is* on the entrails,

4 'the two kidneys and the fat that *is* on them by the flanks, and the fatty lobe *attached* to the liver above the kidneys, he shall remove;

5 'and Aaron's sons [a]shall burn it on the altar upon the [b]burnt sacrifice, which *is* on the wood that *is* on the fire, *as* an [c]offering made by fire, a [d]sweet aroma to the LORD.

6 'If his offering as a sacrifice of a peace offering to the LORD *is* of the flock, *whether* male or female, [a]he shall offer it without blemish.

7 'If he offers a [a]lamb as his offering, then he shall [b]offer it [c]before the LORD.

8 'And he shall lay his hand on the head of his offering, and kill it before the tabernacle of meeting; and Aaron's sons shall sprinkle its blood all around on the altar.

9 'Then he shall offer from the sacrifice of the peace offering, as an offering made by fire to the LORD, its fat *and* the whole fat tail which he shall remove close to the backbone. And the fat that covers the entrails and all the fat that *is* on the entrails,

10 'the two kidneys and the fat that *is* on them by the flanks, and the fatty lobe *attached* to the liver above the kidneys, he shall remove;

11 'and the priest shall burn *them* on the altar *as* [a]food, an offering made by fire to the LORD.

12 'And if his [a]offering *is* a goat, then [b]he shall offer it before the LORD.

13 'He shall lay his hand on its head and kill it before the tabernacle of meeting; and the sons of Aaron shall sprinkle its blood all around on the altar.

14 'Then he shall offer from it his offering, as an offering made by fire to the LORD. The fat that covers the entrails and all the fat that *is* on the entrails,

15 'the two kidneys and the fat that *is* on them by the flanks,

13 [a][Col. 4:6] [b]Num. 18:19 [c]Ezek. 43:24
14 [a]Lev. 23:10, 14 [b]2 Kin. 4:42
15 [a]Lev. 2:1
16 [a]Lev. 2:2

CHAPTER 3

1 [a]Lev. 7:11, 29 [b]Lev. 1:3; 22:20–24 [1]*imperfection* or *defect*
2 [a]Lev. 1:4, 5; 16:21 [b]Lev. 1:5
3 [a]Lev. 1:8; 3:16; 4:8, 9
5 [a]Ex. 29:13 [b]2 Chr. 35:14 [c]Num. 28:3–10 [d]Num. 15:8–10
6 [a]Lev. 3:1; 22:20–24
7 [a]Num. 15:4, 5 [b]1 Kin. 8:62 [c]Lev. 17:8, 9
11 [a]Num. 28:2
12 [a]Num. 15:6–11 [b]Lev. 3:1, 7

and the fatty lobe *attached* to the liver above the kidneys, he shall remove;
16 'and the priest shall burn them on the altar *as* food, an offering made by fire for a sweet aroma; [a]all the fat *is* the LORD's.
17 '*This shall be* a [a]perpetual[1] statute throughout your generations in all your dwellings: you shall eat neither fat nor [b]blood.' "

CHAPTER 4

4 Now the LORD spoke to Moses, saying,
2 "Speak to the children of Israel, saying: [a]'If a person sins [1]unintentionally against any of the commandments of the LORD *in anything* which ought not to be done, and does any of them,
3 [a]'if the anointed priest sins, bringing guilt on the people, then let him offer to the LORD for his sin which he has sinned [b]a young bull without blemish as a [c]sin offering.
4 'He shall bring the bull [a]to the door of the tabernacle of meeting before the LORD, lay his hand on the bull's head, and kill the bull before the LORD.
5 'Then the anointed priest [a]shall take some of the bull's blood and bring it to the tabernacle of meeting.
6 'The priest shall dip his finger in the blood and sprinkle some of the blood seven times before the LORD, in front of the [a]veil of the sanctuary.
7 'And the priest shall [a]put some of the blood on the horns of the altar of sweet incense before the LORD, which is in the tabernacle of meeting; and he shall pour [b]the remaining blood of the bull at the base of the altar of the burnt offering, which is at the door of the tabernacle of meeting.
8 'He shall take from it all the fat of the bull as the sin offering. The fat that covers the entrails and all the fat which *is* on the entrails,
9 'the two kidneys and the fat that *is* on them by the flanks, and the fatty lobe *attached* to the liver above the kidneys, he shall remove,
10 [a]'as it was taken from the bull of the sacrifice of the peace offering; and the priest shall burn them on the altar of the burnt offering.
11 [a]'But the bull's hide and all its flesh, with its head and legs, its entrails and offal—
12 'the whole bull he shall carry outside the camp to a clean place, [a]where the ashes are poured out, and [b]burn it on wood with fire; where the ashes are poured out it shall be burned.
13 'Now [a]if the whole congregation of Israel sins unintentionally, [b]and the thing is hidden from the eyes of the assembly, and they have done *something against* any of the commandments of the LORD *in anything* which should not be done, and are guilty;
14 'when the sin which they have committed becomes known, then the assembly shall offer a young bull for the sin, and bring it before the tabernacle of meeting.
15 'And the elders of the congregation [a]shall lay their hands on the head of the bull before the LORD. Then the bull shall be killed before the LORD.
16 [a]'The anointed priest shall

16 [a]Lev. 7:23–25
17 [a]Lev. 6:18; 7:36; 17:7; 23:14 [b]Lev. 7:23, 26; 17:10, 14 [1]*everlasting* or *never-ending*
2 [a]Lev. 5:15–18 [1]*through error*
3 [a]Lev. 8:12 [b]Lev. 3:1; 9:2 [c]Lev. 9:7
4 [a]Lev. 1:3, 4; 4:15
5 [a]Lev. 16:14
6 [a]Ex. 40:21, 26
7 [a]Lev. 4:18, 25, 30, 34; 8:15; 9:9; 16:18 [b]Ex. 40:5, 6; Lev. 5:9
10 [a]Lev. 3:3–5
11 [a]Ex. 29:14
12 [a]Lev. 4:21; 6:10, 11; 16:27 [b][Heb. 13:11, 12]
13 [a]Num. 15:24–26 [b]Lev. 5:2–4, 17
15 [a]Lev. 1:3, 4
16 [a]Lev. 4:5

bring some of the bull's blood to the tabernacle of meeting.

17 'Then the priest shall dip his finger in the blood and sprinkle *it* seven times before the LORD, in front of the veil.

18 'And he shall put *some* of the blood on the horns of the altar which *is* before the LORD, which *is* in the tabernacle of meeting; and he shall pour the remaining blood at the base of the altar of burnt offering, which is at the door of the tabernacle of meeting.

19 'He shall take all the fat from it and burn *it* on the altar.

20 'And he shall do [a]with the bull as he did with the bull as a sin offering; thus he shall do with it. [b]So the priest shall make [1]atonement for them, and it shall be forgiven them.

21 'Then he shall carry the bull outside the camp, and burn it as he burned the first bull. It *is* a sin offering for the assembly.

22 'When a [1]ruler has sinned, and [a]done *something* unintentionally *against* any of the commandments of the LORD his God *in anything* which should not be done, and is guilty,

23 'or [a]if his sin which he has committed [1]comes to his knowledge, he shall bring as his offering a kid of the goats, a male without blemish.

24 'And [a]he shall lay his hand on the head of the goat, and kill it at the place where they kill the burnt offering before the LORD. It *is* a sin offering.

25 [a]'The priest shall take some of the blood of the sin offering with his finger, put *it* on the horns of the altar of burnt offering, and pour its blood at the base of the altar of burnt offering.

26 'And he shall burn all its fat on the altar, like [a]the fat of the sacrifice of the peace offering. [b]So the priest shall make [1]atonement for him concerning his sin, and it shall be forgiven him.

27 [a]'If [1]anyone of the [2]common people sins unintentionally by doing *something against* any of the commandments of the LORD *in anything* which ought not to be done, and is guilty,

28 'or [a]if his sin which he has committed comes to his knowledge, then he shall bring as his offering a kid of the goats, a female without blemish, for his sin which he has committed.

29 [a]'And he shall lay his hand on the head of the sin offering, and kill the sin offering at the place of the burnt offering.

30 'Then the priest shall take *some* of its blood with his finger, put *it* on the horns of the altar of burnt offering, and pour all *the remaining* blood at the base of the altar.

31 [a]'He shall remove all its fat, [b]as fat is removed from the sacrifice of the peace offering; and the priest shall burn it on the altar for a [c]sweet aroma to the LORD. [d]So the priest shall make atonement for him, and it shall be forgiven him.

32 'If he brings a lamb as his sin offering, [a]he shall bring a female without blemish.

33 'Then he shall [a]lay his hand on the head of the sin offering, and kill it as a sin offering at the place where they kill the burnt offering.

34 'The priest shall take *some* of the blood of the sin offering

20 [a]Lev. 4:3 [b]Num. 15:25 [1]Lit. *covering*
22 [a]Lev. 4:2, 13, 27 [1]*leader*
23 [a]Lev. 4:14; 5:4 [1]*is made known to him*
24 [a][Is. 53:6]
25 [a]Lev. 4:7, 18, 30, 34
26 [a]Lev. 3:3–5 [b]Lev. 4:20 [1]Lit. *covering*
27 [a]Num. 15:27 [1]Lit. *any soul* [2]Lit. *people of the land*
28 [a]Lev. 4:23
29 [a]Lev. 1:4; 4:4, 24
31 [a]Lev. 3:14 [b]Lev. 3:3, 4 [c]Ex. 29:18 [d]Lev. 4:26
32 [a]Lev. 4:28
33 [a]Num. 8:12

with his finger, put *it* on the
horns of the altar of burnt offering, and pour all *the remaining*
blood at the base of the altar.
35 'He shall remove all its fat,
as the fat of the lamb is removed
from the sacrifice of the peace
offering. Then the priest shall
burn it on the altar, [a]according
to the offerings made by fire
to the LORD. [b]So the priest shall
make atonement for his sin that
he has committed, and it shall
be forgiven him.

5 'If a person sins in [a]hearing
the utterance of an oath,
and *is* a witness, whether he has
seen or known *of the matter*—
if he does not tell *it*, he [b]bears
[1]guilt.
2 'Or [a]if a person touches any
unclean thing, whether *it is* the
carcass of an unclean beast, or
the carcass of unclean livestock,
or the carcass of unclean creeping things, and he is unaware of
it, he also shall be unclean and
[b]guilty.
3 'Or if he touches [a]human uncleanness—whatever uncleanness with which a man may be
defiled, and he is unaware of
it—when he realizes *it*, then he
shall be guilty.
4 'Or if a person [1]swears,
speaking thoughtlessly with *his*
lips [a]to do evil or [b]to do good,
whatever *it is* that a man may
pronounce by an oath, and he is
unaware of it—when he realizes
it, then he shall be guilty in any
of these *matters*.
5 'And it shall be, when he is
guilty in any of these *matters*,
that he shall [a]confess that he has
sinned in that *thing*;
6 'and he shall bring his trespass offering to the LORD for his
sin which he has committed, a
female from the flock, a lamb
or a kid of the goats as a sin offering. So the priest shall make
atonement for him concerning
his sin.
7 [a]'If he is not able to bring a
lamb, then he shall bring to the
LORD, for his trespass which he
has committed, two [b]turtledoves
or two young pigeons: one as a
sin offering and the other as a
burnt offering.
8 'And he shall bring them to
the priest, who shall offer *that*
which *is* for the sin offering first,
and [a]wring off its head from
its neck, but shall not divide *it*
[1]completely.
9 'Then he shall sprinkle *some*
of the blood of the sin offering on the side of the altar, and
the [a]rest of the blood shall be
drained out at the base of the
altar. It *is* a sin offering.
10 'And he shall offer the second
as a burnt offering according to
the [a]prescribed manner. So [b]the
priest shall make atonement on
his behalf for his sin which he
has committed, and it shall be
forgiven him.
11 'But if he is [a]not able to bring
two turtledoves or two young
pigeons, then he who sinned
shall bring for his offering one-
tenth of an ephah of fine flour
as a sin offering. [b]He shall put
no oil on it, nor shall he put
frankincense on it, for it *is* a sin
offering.
12 'Then he shall bring it to the
priest, and the priest shall take
his handful of it [a]as a memorial
portion, and burn *it* on the altar
[b]according to the offerings made
by fire to the LORD. It *is* a sin
offering.

35 [a]Lev. 3:5 [b]Lev. 4:26, 31

CHAPTER 5

1 [a]Prov. 29:24 [b]Num. 9:13 [1]*his iniquity*

2 [a]Num. 19:11–16 [b]Lev. 5:17

3 [a]Lev. 5:12, 13, 15

4 [a]Acts 23:12 [b][James 5:12] [1]*vows*

5 [a]Prov. 28:13

7 [a]Lev. 12:6, 8; 14:21 [b]Lev. 1:14

8 [a]Lev. 1:15–17 [1]Lit. *apart*

9 [a]Lev. 4:7, 18, 30, 34

10 [a]Lev. 1:14–17 [b]Lev. 4:20, 26; 5:13, 16

11 [a]Lev. 14:21–32 [b]Num. 5:15

12 [a]Lev. 2:2 [b]Lev. 4:35

13 [a]"The priest shall make atonement for him, [1]for his sin that he has committed in any of these matters; and it shall be forgiven him. [b]*The rest* shall be the priest's as a grain offering.' "

14 Then the LORD spoke to Moses, saying:

15 [a]"If a person commits a trespass, and sins unintentionally in regard to the holy things of the LORD, then [b]he shall bring to the LORD as his trespass offering a ram without blemish from the flocks, with your valuation in shekels of silver according to [c]the shekel of the sanctuary, as a trespass offering.

16 "And he shall make restitution for the harm that he has done in regard to the holy thing, [a]and shall add one-fifth to it and give it to the priest. [b]So the priest shall make atonement for him with the ram of the trespass offering, and it shall be forgiven him.

17 "If a person sins, and commits any of these things which are forbidden to be done by the commandments of the LORD, [a]though he does not know *it,* yet he is [b]guilty and shall bear his [1]iniquity.

18 [a]"And he shall bring to the priest a ram without blemish from the flock, with your valuation, as a trespass offering. So the priest shall make atonement for him regarding his ignorance in which he erred and did not know *it,* and it shall be forgiven him.

19 "It is a trespass offering; [a]he has certainly trespassed against the LORD."

6 And the LORD spoke to Moses, saying:

2 "If a person sins and [a]commits a trespass against the LORD by [b]lying[1] to his neighbor about [c]what was delivered to him for safekeeping, or about [2]a pledge, or about a robbery, or if he has [d]extorted from his neighbor,

3 "or if he [a]has found what was lost and lies concerning it, and [b]swears falsely—in any one of these things that a man may do in which he sins:

4 "then it shall be, because he has sinned and is guilty, that he shall [1]restore [a]what he has stolen, or the thing which he has extorted, or what was delivered to him for safekeeping, or the lost thing which he found,

5 "or all that about which he has sworn falsely. He shall [a]restore its full value, add one-fifth more to it, *and* give it to whomever it belongs, on the day of his trespass offering.

6 "And he shall bring his trespass offering to the LORD, [a]a ram without blemish from the flock, with your [1]valuation, as a trespass offering, to the priest.

7 [a]"So the priest shall make atonement for him before the LORD, and he shall be forgiven for any one of these things that he may have done in which he trespasses."

8 Then the LORD spoke to Moses, saying,

9 "Command Aaron and his sons, saying, 'This *is* the [a]law of the burnt offering: The burnt offering *shall be* on the hearth upon the altar all night until morning, and the fire of the altar shall be kept burning on it.

10 [a]'And the priest shall put on his linen garment, and his linen trousers he shall put on

13 [a]Lev. 4:26 [b]Lev. 2:3; 6:17, 26 [1]*concerning his sin*

15 [a]Lev. 4:2; 22:14 [b]Ezra 10:19 [c]Ex. 30:13

16 [a]Num. 5:7 [b]Lev. 4:26

17 [a]Lev. 4:2, 13, 22, 27 [b]Lev. 5:1, 2 [1]*punishment*

18 [a]Lev. 5:15

19 [a]Ezra 10:2

CHAPTER 6

2 [a]Num. 5:6 [b]Lev. 19:11 [c]Ex. 22:7, 10 [d]Prov. 24:28 [1]*deceiving his associate* [2]*an entrusted security*

3 [a]Deut. 22:1–4 [b]Ex. 22:11

4 [a]Lev. 24:18, 21 [1]*return*

5 [a]Lev. 5:16

6 [a]Lev. 1:3; 5:15 [1]*appraisal*

7 [a]Lev. 4:26

9 [a]Ex. 29:38–42

10 [a]Ex. 28:39–43

his body, and take up the ashes
of the burnt offering which the
fire has consumed on the altar,
and he shall put them [b]beside
the altar.
11 'Then [a]he shall take off his
garments, put on other garments, and carry the ashes outside the camp [b]to a clean place.
12 'And the fire on the altar
shall be kept burning on it; it
shall not be put out. And the
priest shall burn wood on it every morning, and lay the burnt
offering in order on it; and he
shall burn on it [a]the fat of the
peace offerings.
13 'A fire shall always be burning on the [a]altar; it shall never
go out.
14 'This *is* the law of the grain
offering: The sons of Aaron
shall offer it on the altar before
the LORD.
15 'He shall take from it his
handful of the fine flour of the
grain offering, with its oil, and
all the frankincense which *is* on
the grain offering, and shall burn
it on the altar *for* a sweet aroma,
as a memorial to the LORD.
16 'And the remainder of it
Aaron and his sons shall eat;
with unleavened bread it shall
be eaten in a holy place; in the
court of the tabernacle of meeting they shall eat it.
17 'It shall not be baked with
leaven. I have given it *as* their
[1]portion of My offerings made
by fire; it *is* most holy, like the
sin offering and the [a]trespass
offering.
18 [a]'All the males among the
children of Aaron may eat it. [b]*It*
shall be a statute forever in your
generations concerning the offerings made by fire to the LORD.
[c]Everyone who touches them
must be holy.' "
19 And the LORD spoke to Moses, saying,
20 [a]"This *is* the offering of Aaron
and his sons, which they shall
offer to the LORD, *beginning* on
the day when he is anointed:
one-tenth of an [b]ephah of fine
flour as a daily grain offering,
half of it in the morning and half
of it at night.
21 "It shall be made in a [a]pan
with oil. *When it is* mixed, you
shall bring it in. The baked
pieces of the grain offering you
shall offer *for* a [1]sweet aroma to
the LORD.
22 "The priest from among his
sons, [a]who is anointed in his
place, shall offer it. *It is* a statute
forever to the LORD. [b]It shall be
[1]wholly burned.
23 "For every grain offering
for the priest shall be wholly
burned. It shall not be eaten."
24 Also the LORD spoke to Moses, saying,
25 "Speak to Aaron and to his
sons, saying, 'This *is* the law of
the sin offering: [a]In the place
where the burnt offering is
killed, the sin offering shall be
killed before the LORD. It *is* most
holy.
26 [a]'The priest who offers it for
sin shall eat it. In a holy place it
shall be eaten, in the court of the
tabernacle of meeting.
27 [a]'Everyone who touches its
flesh [1]must be holy. And when
its blood is sprinkled on any
garment, you shall wash that on
which it was sprinkled, in a holy
place.
28 'But the earthen vessel in
which it is boiled [a]shall be broken. And if it is boiled in a bronze

10 [b]Lev. 1:16
11 [a]Ezek. 44:19 [b]Lev. 4:12
12 [a]Lev. 3:3, 5, 9, 14
13 [a]Lev. 1:7
17 [a]Lev. 7:7 [1]*share*
18 [a]Lev. 6:29; 7:6 [b]Lev. 3:17 [c]Ex. 29:37; Num. 4:15; Hag. 2:11–13
20 [a]Ex. 29:2 [b]Ex. 16:36
21 [a]Lev. 2:5; 7:9 [1]*pleasing*
22 [a]Lev. 4:3 [b]Ex. 29:25 [1]*completely*
25 [a]Lev. 1:1, 3, 5, 11
26 [a][Ezek. 44:28, 29]
27 [a]Ex. 29:37; Num. 4:15; Hag. 2:11–13 [1]Lit. *shall*
28 [a]Lev. 11:33; 15:12

pot, it shall be both scoured and
rinsed in water.
29 'All the males among the
priests may eat it. It *is* most
holy.
30 [a]'But no sin offering from
which *any* of the blood is brought
into the tabernacle of meeting,
to make atonement in [1]the holy
[b]*place,* shall be [c]eaten. It shall be
[d]burned in the fire.

7 'Likewise [a]this *is* the law of
the trespass offering (it *is*
most holy):
2 'In the place where they kill
the burnt offering they shall
kill the trespass offering. And
its blood he shall sprinkle all
around on the altar.
3 'And he shall offer from it
all its fat. The fat tail and the fat
that covers the entrails,
4 'the two kidneys and the fat
that *is* on them by the flanks,
and the fatty lobe *attached* to
the liver above the kidneys, he
shall remove;
5 'and the priest shall burn
them on the altar *as* an offering
made by fire to the LORD. It *is* a
trespass offering.
6 [a]'Every male among the
priests may eat it. It shall be
eaten in a holy place. [b]It *is* most
holy.
7 [a]'The trespass offering *is* like
the sin offering; *there is* one law
for them both: the priest who
makes atonement with it shall
have *it.*
8 'And the priest who offers
anyone's burnt offering, that
priest shall have for himself the
skin of the burnt offering which
he has offered.
9 'Also [a]every grain offering
that is baked in the oven and all
that is prepared in the covered
pan, or [1]in a pan, shall be the
priest's who offers it.
10 'Every grain offering,
whether mixed with oil or dry,
shall belong to all the sons of
Aaron, to one *as much* as the
other.
11 [a]'This *is* the law of the sacrifice of peace offerings which he
shall offer to the LORD:
12 'If he offers it for a thanksgiving, then he shall offer, with
the sacrifice of thanksgiving,
unleavened cakes mixed with
oil, unleavened wafers [a]anointed
with oil, or cakes of blended
flour mixed with oil.
13 'Besides the cakes, *as* his offering he shall offer [a]leavened
bread with the sacrifice of
thanksgiving of his peace offering.
14 'And from it he shall offer
one cake from each offering *as*
a heave offering to the LORD. [a]It
shall belong to the priest who
sprinkles the blood of the peace
offering.
15 [a]'The flesh of the sacrifice of
his peace offering for thanksgiving shall be eaten the same day
it is offered. He shall not leave
any of it until morning.
16 'But [a]if the sacrifice of his offering *is* a vow or a voluntary offering, it shall be eaten the same
day that he offers his sacrifice;
but on the next day the remainder of it also may be eaten;
17 'the remainder of the flesh
of the sacrifice on the third day
must be burned with fire.
18 'And if *any* of the flesh of the
sacrifice of his peace offering is
eaten at all on the third day, it
shall not be accepted, nor shall
it be [a]imputed to him; it shall
be an [b]abomination *to* him who

30 [a]Lev. 4:7, 11, 12, 18, 21; 10:18; 16:27 [b]Ex. 26:33 [c]Lev. 6:16, 23, 26 [d]Lev. 16:27 [1]The Most Holy Place when capitalized

CHAPTER 7

1 [a]Lev. 5:14—6:7

6 [a]Lev. 6:16–18, 29 [b]Lev. 2:3

7 [a]Lev. 6:24–30; 14:13

9 [a]Lev. 2:3, 10 [1]*on a griddle*

11 [a]Lev. 3:1; 22:18, 21

12 [a]Num. 6:15

13 [a]Amos 4:5

14 [a]Num. 18:8, 11, 19

15 [a]Lev. 22:29, 30

16 [a]Lev. 19:5–8

18 [a]Num. 18:27 [b]Lev. 11:10, 11, 41; 19:7

offers it, and the person who
eats of it shall bear [1]guilt.
19 'The flesh that touches any
unclean thing shall not be eaten.
It shall be burned with fire. And
as for the *clean* flesh, all who
are [1]clean may eat of it.
20 'But the person who eats
the flesh of the sacrifice of the
peace offering that *belongs* to
the [a]LORD, [b]while he is unclean,
that person [c]shall be cut off from
his people.
21 'Moreover the person who
touches any unclean thing,
such as [a]human uncleanness,
an [b]unclean animal, or any
[c]abominable[1] unclean thing, and
who eats the flesh of the sacrifice of the peace offering that
belongs to the LORD, that person [d]shall be cut off from his
people.' "
22 And the LORD spoke to Moses, saying,
23 "Speak to the children of
Israel, saying: [a]'You shall not eat
any fat, of ox or sheep or goat.
24 'And the fat of an animal
that dies *naturally*, and the fat of
what is torn by wild beasts, may
be used in any other way; but
you shall by no means eat it.
25 'For whoever eats the fat of
the animal of which men offer
an offering made by fire to the
LORD, the person who eats *it*
shall be cut off from his people.
26 [a]'Moreover you shall not eat
any blood in any of your dwellings, *whether* of bird or beast.
27 'Whoever eats any blood,
that person shall be cut off from
his people.' "
28 Then the LORD spoke to Moses, saying,
29 "Speak to the children of Israel, saying: [a]'He who offers the
sacrifice of his peace offering to
the LORD shall bring his offering
to the LORD from the sacrifice of
his peace offering.
30 [a]'His own hands shall bring
the offerings made by fire to the
LORD. The fat with the breast he
shall bring, that the [b]breast may
be waved *as* a wave offering before the LORD.
31 [a]'And the priest shall burn the
fat on the altar, but the [b]breast
shall be Aaron's and his sons'.
32 [a]'Also the right thigh you
shall give to the priest *as* a
heave offering from the sacrifices of your peace offerings.
33 'He among the sons of
Aaron, who offers the blood of
the peace offering and the fat,
shall have the right thigh for *his*
part.
34 'For [a]the breast of the wave
offering and the thigh of the
heave offering I have taken from
the children of Israel, from the
sacrifices of their peace offerings, and I have given them to
Aaron the priest and to his sons
from the children of Israel by a
statute forever.' "
35 This *is* the consecrated portion for Aaron and his sons,
from the offerings made by fire
to the LORD, on the day when
Moses presented them to [1]min-
ister to the LORD as priests.
36 The LORD commanded this
to be given to them by the children of Israel, [a]on the day that
He anointed them, *by* a statute forever throughout their
generations.
37 This *is* the law [a]of the burnt
offering, [b]the grain offering, [c]the
sin offering, [d]the trespass offering, [e]the consecrations, and [f]the
sacrifice of the peace offering,

18 [1]*his iniquity*
19 [1]*pure*
20 [a][Heb. 2:17] [b]Num. 19:13 [c]Gen. 17:14
21 [a]Lev. 5:2, 3, 5 [b]Lev. 11:24, 28 [c]Ezek. 4:14 [d]Lev. 7:20 [1]So with MT, LXX, Vg.; Sam., Syr., Tg. *swarming thing* (cf. 5:2)
23 [a]Lev. 3:17; 17:10–15
26 [a]Acts 15:20, 29
29 [a]Lev. 3:1; 22:21
30 [a]Lev. 3:3, 4, 9, 14 [b]Ex. 29:24, 27
31 [a]Lev. 3:5, 11, 16 [b]Deut. 18:3
32 [a]Num. 6:20
34 [a]Lev. 10:14, 15
35 [1]*serve*
36 [a]Lev. 8:12, 30
37 [a]Lev. 6:9 [b]Lev. 6:14 [c]Lev. 6:25 [d]Lev. 7:1 [e]Ex. 29:1 [f]Lev. 7:11

38 which the LORD commanded
Moses on Mount Sinai, on the
day when He commanded the
children of Israel [a]to offer their
offerings to the LORD in the Wilderness of Sinai.

8 And the LORD spoke to Moses, saying:
2 [a]"Take Aaron and his sons
with him, and [b]the garments,
[c]the anointing oil, a [d]bull as the
sin offering, two [e]rams, and a
basket of unleavened bread;
3 "and gather all the congregation together at the door of the
tabernacle of meeting."
4 So Moses did as the LORD
commanded him. And the congregation was gathered together
at the door of the tabernacle of
meeting.
5 And Moses said to the congregation, "This *is* what the LORD
commanded to be done."
6 Then Moses brought Aaron
and his sons and [a]washed them
with water.
7 And he [a]put the tunic on
him, girded him with the sash,
clothed him with the robe, and
put the ephod on him; and he
girded him with the intricately
woven band of the ephod, and
with it tied *the ephod* on him.
8 Then he put the breast-
plate on him, and he [a]put the
[1]Ū′rim and the Thum′mim in the
breastplate.
9 [a]And he put the turban on
his head. Also on the turban, on
its front, he put the golden plate,
the holy crown, as the LORD had
commanded Moses.
10 [a]Also Moses took the anointing oil, and anointed the tabernacle and all that *was* in it, and
consecrated them.
11 He sprinkled some of it on the
altar seven times, anointed the
altar and all its utensils, and the
laver and its base, to [1]consecrate
them.
12 And he [a]poured some of the
anointing oil on Aaron's head
and anointed him, to consecrate
him.
13 [a]Then Moses brought Aaron's sons and put tunics on
them, girded them with sashes,
and put [1]hats on them, as the
LORD had commanded Moses.
14 [a]And he brought the bull for
the sin offering. Then Aaron and
his sons [b]laid their hands on
the head of the bull for the sin
offering,
15 and Moses killed *it*. [a]Then he
took the blood, and put *some* on
the horns of the altar all around
with his finger, and purified the
altar. And he poured the blood
at the base of the altar, and consecrated it, to make [1]atonement
for it.
16 [a]Then he took all the fat that
was on the entrails, the fatty
lobe *attached to* the liver, and
the two kidneys with their fat,
and Moses burned *them* on the
altar.
17 But the bull, its hide, its flesh,
and its offal, he burned with fire
outside the camp, as the LORD
[a]had commanded Moses.
18 [a]Then he brought the ram as
the burnt offering. And Aaron
and his sons laid their hands on
the head of the ram,
19 and Moses killed *it*. Then he
sprinkled the blood all around
on the altar.
20 And he cut the ram into
pieces; and Moses [a]burned the
head, the pieces, and the fat.
21 Then he washed the entrails
and the legs in water. And Moses

38 [a]Lev. 1:1, 2

CHAPTER 8

2 [a]Ex. 29:1–3 [b]Ex. 28:2, 4 [c]Ex. 30:24, 25 [d]Ex. 29:10 [e]Ex. 29:15, 19

6 [a]Heb. 10:22

7 [a]Ex. 39:1–31

8 [a]Ex. 28:30 [1]Lit. *Lights and the Perfections,* Ex. 28:30

9 [a]Ex. 28:36, 37; 29:6

10 [a]Ex. 30:26–29; 40:10, 11

11 [1]*set them apart for the* LORD

12 [a]Ps. 133:2

13 [a]Ex. 29:8, 9 [1]*headpieces*

14 [a]Ezek. 43:19 [b]Lev. 4:4

15 [a]Lev. 4:7 [1]Lit. *covering*

16 [a]Ex. 29:13

17 [a]Lev. 4:11, 12

18 [a]Ex. 29:15

20 [a]Lev. 1:8

burned the whole ram on the altar. It *was* a burnt sacrifice for a
[1]sweet aroma, an offering made
by fire to the LORD, [a]as the LORD
had commanded Moses.
22 And [a]he brought the second
ram, the ram of consecration.
Then Aaron and his sons laid
their hands on the head of the
ram,
23 and Moses killed *it.* Also he
took *some* of [a]its blood and put
it on the tip of Aaron's right ear,
on the thumb of his right hand,
and on the big toe of his right
foot.
24 Then he brought Aaron's
sons. And Moses put *some* of the
[a]blood on the tips of their right
ears, on the thumbs of their
right hands, and on the big toes
of their right feet. And Moses
sprinkled the blood all around
on the altar.
25 [a]Then he took the fat and the
fat tail, all the fat that *was* on the
entrails, the fatty lobe *attached
to* the liver, the two kidneys and
their fat, and the right thigh;
26 [a]and from the basket of unleavened bread that was before
the LORD he took one unleavened
cake, a cake of bread *anointed
with* oil, and one wafer, and put
them on the fat and on the right
thigh;
27 and he put all *these* [a]in
Aaron's hands and in his sons'
hands, and waved them *as* a
wave offering before the LORD.
28 [a]Then Moses took them from
their hands and burned *them* on
the altar, on the burnt offering.
They *were* consecration offerings for a sweet aroma. That
was an offering made by fire to
the LORD.
29 And [a]Moses took the [b]breast
and waved it *as* a wave offering
before the LORD. It was Moses'
[c]part of the ram of consecration,
as the LORD had commanded
Moses.
30 Then [a]Moses took some of
the anointing oil and some of
the blood which *was* on the altar, and sprinkled *it* on Aaron,
on his garments, on his sons,
and on the garments of his sons
with him; and he consecrated
Aaron, his garments, his sons,
and the garments of his sons
with him.
31 And Moses said to Aaron
and his sons, [a]"Boil the flesh
at the door of the tabernacle of
meeting, and eat it there with
the bread that *is* in the basket of
consecration offerings, as I commanded, saying, 'Aaron and his
sons shall eat it.'
32 [a]"What remains of the flesh
and of the bread you shall burn
with fire.
33 "And you shall not go outside the door of the tabernacle
of meeting *for* seven days, until
the days of your consecration
are ended. For [a]seven days he
shall consecrate you.
34 [a]"As he has done this day, *so*
the LORD has commanded to do,
to make atonement for you.
35 "Therefore you shall stay *at*
the door of the tabernacle of
meeting day and night for seven
days, and [a]keep the [1]charge of
the LORD, so that you may not die;
for so I have been commanded."
36 So Aaron and his sons did
all the things that the LORD had
commanded by the hand of
Moses.

9 It came to pass on the [a]eighth
day that Moses called Aaron

21 [a]Ex. 29:18 [1]*pleasing*
22 [a]Ex. 29:19, 31
23 [a]Lev. 14:14
24 [a][Heb. 9:13, 14, 18–23]
25 [a]Ex. 29:22
26 [a]Ex. 29:23
27 [a]Ex. 29:24
28 [a]Ex. 29:25
29 [a]Ps. 99:6 [b]Ex. 29:27 [c]Ex. 29:26
30 [a]Ex. 29:21; 30:30
31 [a]Ex. 29:31, 32
32 [a]Ex. 29:34
33 [a]Ex. 29:30, 35
34 [a][Heb. 7:16]
35 [a]Deut. 11:1 [1]*office*

CHAPTER 9
1 [a]Ezek. 43:27

and his sons and the elders of
Israel.
2 And he said to Aaron, "Take
for yourself a young [a]bull as a
sin offering and a ram as a burnt
offering, without blemish, and
offer *them* before the LORD.
3 "And to the children of Israel
you shall speak, saying, [a]'Take a
kid of the goats as a sin offering,
and a calf and a lamb, *both* of
the first year, without blemish,
as a burnt offering,
4 'also a bull and a ram as
peace offerings, to sacrifice before the LORD, and [a]a grain offering mixed with oil; for [b]today
the LORD will appear to you.' "
5 So they brought what Moses
commanded before the tabernacle of meeting. And all the congregation drew near and stood
[1]before the LORD.
6 Then Moses said, "This *is*
the thing which the LORD commanded you to do, and the glory
of the LORD will appear to you."
7 And Moses said to Aaron,
"Go to the altar, [a]offer your sin
offering and your burnt offering, and make atonement for
yourself and for the people.
[b]Offer the offering of the people,
and make atonement for them,
as the LORD commanded."
8 Aaron therefore went to the
altar and killed the calf of the sin
offering, which *was* for himself.
9 Then the sons of Aaron
brought the blood to him. And
he dipped his finger in the blood,
put *it* on the horns of the altar,
and poured the blood at the base
of the altar.
10 [a]But the fat, the kidneys, and
the fatty lobe from the liver
of the sin offering he burned
on the altar, as the LORD had
commanded Moses.
11 [a]The flesh and the hide he
burned with fire outside the
camp.
12 And he killed the burnt offering; and Aaron's sons presented to him the blood, [a]which
he sprinkled all around on the
altar.
13 [a]Then they presented the
burnt offering to him, with its
pieces and head, and he burned
them on the altar.
14 [a]And he washed the entrails
and the legs, and burned *them*
with the burnt offering on the
altar.
15 [a]Then he brought the people's offering, and took the goat,
which *was* the sin offering for
the people, and killed it and
offered it for sin, like the first
one.
16 And he brought the burnt offering and offered it [a]according
to the [1]prescribed manner.
17 Then he brought the grain
offering, took a handful of
it, and burned *it* on the altar,
[a]besides the burnt sacrifice of
the morning.
18 He also killed the bull and
the ram *as* [a]sacrifices of peace
offerings, which *were* for the
people. And Aaron's sons presented to him the blood, which
he sprinkled all around on the
altar,
19 and the fat from the bull and
the ram—the fatty tail, what covers *the entrails* and the kidneys,
and the fatty lobe *attached to*
the liver;
20 and they put the fat on the
breasts. [a]Then he burned the fat
on the altar;
21 but the breasts and the right

2 [a]Lev. 4:1–12
3 [a]Lev. 4:23, 28
4 [a]Lev. 2:4 [b]Ex. 29:43
5 [1]*in the presence of*
7 [a][Heb. 5:3–5; 7:27] [b]Lev. 4:16, 20
10 [a]Lev. 8:16
11 [a]Lev. 4:11, 12; 8:17
12 [a]Lev. 1:5; 8:19
13 [a]Lev. 8:20
14 [a]Lev. 8:21
15 [a][Is. 53:10]
16 [a]Lev. 1:1–13 [1]*ordinance*
17 [a]Ex. 29:38, 39
18 [a]Lev. 3:1–11
20 [a]Lev. 3:5, 16

thigh Aaron waved [a]*as* a wave
offering before the LORD, as Moses had commanded.
22 Then Aaron lifted his hand
toward the people, [a]blessed
them, and came down from offering the sin offering, the burnt
offering, and peace offerings.
23 And Moses and Aaron went
into the tabernacle of meeting,
and came out and blessed the
people. Then the glory of the
LORD appeared to all the people,
24 and [a]fire came out from before the LORD and consumed the
burnt offering and the fat on the
altar. When all the people saw *it*,
they [b]shouted and fell on their
[c]faces.

10

Then [a]Nā′dab and A·bī′hū,
the sons of Aaron, [b]each
took his censer and put fire in
it, put incense on it, and offered
[c]profane fire before the LORD,
which He had not commanded
them.
2 So [a]fire went out from the
LORD and devoured them, and
they died before the LORD.
3 And Moses said to Aaron,
"This is what the LORD spoke,
saying:

'By those [a]who come
near Me
I must be regarded as holy;
And before all the people
I must be glorified.' "

So Aaron held his peace.
4 Then Moses called Mish′a·el
and El′za·phan, the sons of Uz′-
zi·el the uncle of Aaron, and said
to them, "Come near, [a]carry your
brethren from [1]before the sanctuary out of the camp."
5 So they went near and carried them by their tunics out of
the camp, as Moses had said.
6 And Moses said to Aaron,
and to El·ē·ā′zar and Ith′a·mar,
his sons, "Do not [1]uncover your
heads nor tear your clothes,
lest you die, and [a]wrath come
upon all the people. But let your
brethren, the whole house of Israel, [2]bewail the burning which
the LORD has kindled.
7 [a]"You shall not go out from
the door of the tabernacle of
meeting, lest you die, [b]for the
anointing oil of the LORD *is* upon
you." And they did according to
the word of Moses.
8 Then the LORD spoke to
Aaron, saying:
9 [a]"Do not drink wine or intoxicating drink, you, nor your sons
with you, when you go into the
tabernacle of meeting, lest you
die. *It shall be* a statute forever
throughout your generations,
10 "that you may [a]distinguish
between holy and unholy, and
between unclean and clean,
11 [a]"and that you may teach the
children of Israel all the statutes
which the LORD has spoken to
them by the hand of Moses."
12 And Moses spoke to Aaron,
and to El·ē·ā′zar and Ith′a·mar,
his sons who were left: [a]"Take
the grain offering that remains
of the offerings made by fire
to the LORD, and eat it without
leaven beside the altar; [b]for it *is*
most holy.
13 "You shall eat it in a [a]holy
place, because it *is* your [1]due
and your sons' due, of the sacrifices made by fire to the LORD;
for [b]so I have been commanded.
14 [a]"The breast of the wave offering and the thigh of the heave
offering you shall eat in a clean

21 [a]Lev. 7:30–34
22 [a]Luke 24:50
24 [a]Judg. 6:21 [b]Ezra 3:11 [c]1 Kin. 18:38, 39

CHAPTER 10

1 [a]Num. 3:2–4 [b]Lev. 16:12 [c]Ex. 30:9
2 [a]Num. 11:1; 16:35
3 [a]Ex. 19:22
4 [a]Acts 5:6, 10 [1]*in front of*
6 [a]2 Sam. 24:1 [1]An act of mourning [2]*weep bitterly*
7 [a]Lev. 8:33; 21:12 [b]Lev. 8:30
9 [a]Ezek. 44:21
10 [a]Ezek. 22:26; 44:23
11 [a]Deut. 24:8
12 [a]Num. 18:9 [b]Lev. 21:22
13 [a]Num. 18:10 [b]Lev. 2:3; 6:16 [1]*portion*
14 [a]Num. 18:11

place, you, your sons, and your
[b]daughters with you; for *they*
are your due and your sons'
[c]due, *which* are given from the
sacrifices of peace offerings of
the children of Israel.
15 [a]"The thigh of the heave
offering and the breast of the
wave offering they shall bring
with the offerings of fat made by
fire, to offer *as* a wave offering
before the LORD. And it shall be
yours and your sons' with you,
by a statute forever, as the LORD
has commanded."
16 Then Moses made careful
inquiry about [a]the goat of the
sin offering, and there it was—
burned up. And he was angry
with El·ē·ā'zar and Ith'a·mar, the
sons of Aaron *who were* left,
saying,
17 [a]"Why have you not eaten
the sin offering in a holy place,
since it *is* most holy, and *God* has
given it to you to bear [b]the guilt
of the congregation, to make
atonement for them before the
LORD?
18 "See! [a]Its blood was not
brought inside [1]the holy *place;* indeed you should have eaten it in
a holy *place,* [b]as I commanded."
19 And Aaron said to Moses,
"Look, [a]this day they have offered their sin offering and their
burnt offering before the LORD,
and such things have befallen
me! *If* I had eaten the sin offering today, [b]would it have been
accepted in the sight of the
LORD?"
20 So when Moses heard *that,*
he was content.

11 Now the LORD spoke to
Moses and Aaron, saying
to them,
2 "Speak to the children of
Israel, saying, [a]'These *are* the
animals which you may eat
among all the animals that *are*
on the earth:
3 'Among the animals, whatever divides the hoof, having
cloven hooves *and* chewing the
cud—that you may eat.
4 'Nevertheless these you shall
[a]not eat among those that chew
the cud or those that have cloven hooves: the camel, because
it chews the cud but does not
have cloven hooves, is [1]unclean
to you;
5 'the [1]rock hyrax, because it
chews the cud but does not have
cloven hooves, *is* [2]unclean to
you;
6 'the hare, because it chews
the cud but does not have cloven
hooves, *is* unclean to you;
7 'and the swine, though it divides the hoof, having cloven
hooves, yet does not chew the
cud, [a]*is* unclean to you.
8 'Their flesh you shall not eat,
and their carcasses you shall not
touch. [a]They *are* unclean to you.
9 [a]'These you may eat of all
that *are* in the water: whatever
in the water has fins and scales,
whether in the seas or in the
rivers—that you may eat.
10 'But all in the seas or in
the rivers that do not have fins
and scales, all that move in the
water or any living thing which
is in the water, they *are* [1]an
[a]abomination to you.
11 'They shall be an abomination to you; you shall not eat their
flesh, but you shall regard their
carcasses as an abomination.
12 'Whatever in the water does
not have fins or scales—that
shall be an abomination to you.
13 [a]'And these you shall regard

14 [b]Lev. 22:13 [c]Num. 18:10
15 [a]Lev. 7:29, 30, 34
16 [a]Lev. 9:3, 15
17 [a]Lev. 6:24–30 [b]Ex. 28:38
18 [a]Lev. 6:30 [b]Lev. 6:26, 30 [1]The Most Holy Place when capitalized
19 [a]Lev. 9:8, 12 [b][Is. 1:11–15]

CHAPTER 11

2 [a]Deut. 14:4
4 [a]Acts 10:14 [1]*impure*
5 [1]*rock badger* [2]*impure*
7 [a]Is. 65:4; 66:3, 17
8 [a]Is. 52:11
9 [a]Deut. 14:9
10 [a]Lev. 7:18, 21 [1]*detestable*
13 [a]Is. 66:17

as an abomination among the
birds; they shall not be eaten,
they *are* an abomination: the
eagle, the vulture, the buzzard,
14 ‘the kite, and the falcon after
its kind;
15 ‘every raven after its kind,
16 ‘the ostrich, the short-eared
owl, the sea gull, and the hawk
after its kind;
17 ‘the little owl, the fisher owl,
and the screech owl;
18 ‘the white owl, the jackdaw,
and the carrion vulture;
19 ‘the stork, the heron after its
kind, the hoopoe, and the bat.
20 ‘All flying insects that creep
on *all* fours *shall be* an abomination to you.
21 ‘Yet these you may eat of
every flying insect that creeps
on *all* fours: those which have
jointed legs above their feet with
which to leap on the earth.
22 ‘These you may eat: [a]the locust after its kind, the destroying locust after its kind, the
cricket after its kind, and the
grasshopper after its kind.
23 ‘But all *other* flying insects
which have four feet *shall be* an
abomination to you.
24 ‘By these you shall become
[1]unclean; whoever touches the
carcass of any of them shall be
unclean until evening;
25 ‘whoever carries part of the
carcass of any of them [a]shall
wash his clothes and be unclean
until evening:
26 ‘*The carcass* of any animal
which divides the foot, but is
not cloven-hoofed or does not
chew the cud, *is* unclean to you.
Everyone who touches it shall
be unclean.
27 ‘And whatever goes on
its paws, among all kinds of
animals that go on *all* fours,
those *are* unclean to you. Whoever touches any such carcass
shall be unclean until evening.
28 ‘Whoever carries *any such*
carcass shall wash his clothes
and be unclean until evening. It
is unclean to you.
29 ‘These also *shall be* unclean
to you among the creeping
things that creep on the earth:
the mole, [a]the mouse, and the
large lizard after its kind;
30 ‘the gecko, the monitor lizard, the sand reptile, the sand
lizard, and the chameleon.
31 ‘These *are* unclean to you
among all that creep. Whoever
[a]touches them when they are
dead shall be unclean until
evening.
32 ‘Anything on which *any* of
them falls, when they are dead
shall be [1]unclean, whether *it is*
any item of wood or clothing or
skin or sack, whatever item *it*
is, in which *any* work is done,
[a]it must be put in water. And it
shall be unclean until evening;
then it shall be clean.
33 ‘Any [a]earthen vessel into
which *any* of them falls [b]you
shall break; and whatever *is* in
it shall be unclean:
34 ‘in such a vessel, any edible
food upon which water falls becomes unclean, and any drink
that may be drunk from it becomes unclean.
35 ‘And everything on which *a*
part of *any such* carcass falls
shall be unclean; *whether it is*
an oven or cooking stove, it shall
be broken down; *for* they *are*
unclean, and shall be unclean to
you.
36 ‘Nevertheless a spring or a
cistern, *in which there is* plenty

22 [a]Matt. 3:4
24 [1]*impure*
25 [a]Num. 19:10, 21, 22; 31:24
29 [a]Is. 66:17
31 [a]Hag. 2:13
32 [a]Lev. 15:12 [1]*impure*
33 [a]Lev. 6:28 [b]Lev. 15:12

of water, shall be clean, but
whatever touches any such carcass becomes unclean.
37 'And if a part of *any such*
carcass falls on any planting
seed which is to be sown, it *re-*
mains clean.
38 'But if water is put on the
seed, and if *a part* of *any such*
carcass falls on it, it *becomes*
[1]unclean to you.
39 'And if any animal which you
may eat dies, he who touches its
carcass shall be [a]unclean until
evening.
40 [a]'He who eats of its carcass
shall wash his clothes and be
unclean until evening. He also
who carries its carcass shall
wash his clothes and be unclean
until evening.
41 'And every creeping thing
that creeps on the earth *shall be*
[1]an abomination. It shall not be
eaten.
42 'Whatever crawls on its
belly, whatever goes on *all*
fours, or whatever has many
feet among all creeping things
that creep on the earth—these
you shall not eat, for they *are* an
abomination.
43 [a]'You shall not make [1]your-
selves [2]abominable with any
creeping thing that creeps; nor
shall you make yourselves unclean with them, lest you be
defiled by them.
44 'For I *am* the LORD your [a]God.
You shall therefore consecrate
yourselves, and [b]you shall be
holy; for I *am* holy. Neither shall
you defile yourselves with any
creeping thing that creeps on
the earth.
45 [a]'For I *am* the LORD who
brings you up out of the land
of Egypt, to be your God. [b]You
shall therefore be holy, for I *am*
holy.
46 'This *is* the law [1]of the animals and the birds and every
living creature that moves in the
waters, and of every creature
that creeps on the earth,
47 [a]'to distinguish between the
unclean and the clean, and between the animal that may be
eaten and the animal that may
not be eaten.' "

12 Then the LORD spoke to
Moses, saying,
2 "Speak to the children of
Israel, saying: 'If a [a]woman has
conceived, and borne a male
child, then [b]she shall be [1]un-
clean seven days; [c]as in the days
of her customary impurity she
shall be unclean.
3 'And on the [a]eighth day the
flesh of his foreskin shall be
circumcised.
4 'She shall then continue in
the blood of *her* purification
thirty-three days. She shall not
touch any [1]hallowed thing, nor
come into the sanctuary until
the days of her purification are
fulfilled.
5 'But if she bears a female
child, then she shall be unclean
two weeks, as in her customary
impurity, and she shall continue
in the blood of *her* purification
sixty-six days.
6 [a]'When the days of her purification are fulfilled, whether
for a son or a daughter, she
shall bring to the priest a [b]lamb
[1]of the first year as a burnt offering, and a young pigeon or
a turtledove as a [c]sin offering,
to the door of the tabernacle of
meeting.
7 'Then he shall offer it before
the LORD, and make [1]atonement

38 [1]*impure*
39 [a]Hag. 2:11–13
40 [a]Lev. 17:15; 22:8
41 [1]*detestable*
43 [a]Lev. 20:25 [1]Lit. *your souls* [2]*impure*
44 [a]Ex. 6:7 [b]1 Pet. 1:15, 16
45 [a]Ex. 6:7; 20:2 [b]Lev. 11:44
46 [1]*concerning*
47 [a]Ezek. 44:23

CHAPTER 12
2 [a]Lev. 15:19 [b]Luke 2:22 [c]Lev. 18:19 [1]*impure*
3 [a]Gen. 17:12
4 [1]*consecrated*
6 [a]Luke 2:22 [b][John 1:29] [c]Lev. 5:7 [1]Lit. *a son of his year*
7 [1]Lit. *covering*

for her. And she shall be clean
from the flow of her blood. This
is the law for her who has borne
a male or a female.
8 [a]'And if she is not able to
bring a lamb, then she may bring
two turtledoves or two young
pigeons—one as a burnt offering and the other as a sin offering. [b]So the priest shall make
atonement for her, and she will
be [1]clean.' "

13

And the LORD spoke to
Moses and Aaron, say-
ing:
2 "When a man has on the skin
of his body a swelling, [a]a scab,
or a bright spot, and it becomes
on the skin of his body *like* a
[1]leprous sore, [b]then he shall be
brought to Aaron the priest or to
one of his sons the priests.
3 "The priest shall examine the
sore on the skin of the body; and
if the hair on the sore has turned
white, and the sore appears *to*
be deeper than the skin of his
body, it *is* a leprous sore. Then
the priest shall examine him,
and pronounce him [1]unclean.
4 "But if the bright spot *is* white
on the skin of his body, and does
not appear *to be* deeper than the
skin, and its hair has not turned
white, then the priest shall isolate *the one who has* the sore
[a]seven days.
5 "And the priest shall examine him on the seventh day; and
indeed *if* the sore appears to be
as it was, *and* the sore has not
spread on the skin, then the
priest shall isolate him another
seven days.
6 "Then the priest shall examine him again on the seventh day;
and indeed *if* the sore has faded,
and the sore has not spread on
the skin, then the priest shall
pronounce him clean; it *is only*
a scab, and he [a]shall wash his
clothes and be clean.
7 "But if the scab should at all
spread over the skin, after he
has been seen by the priest for
his cleansing, he shall be seen
by the priest again.
8 "And *if* the priest sees that
the scab has indeed spread on
the skin, then the priest shall
pronounce him [1]unclean. It *is*
leprosy.
9 "When the leprous sore is
on a person, then he shall be
brought to the priest.
10 [a]"And the priest shall examine *him;* and indeed *if* the swelling on the skin *is* white, and it
has turned the hair white, and
there is a spot of raw flesh in the
swelling,
11 "it *is* an old leprosy on the
skin of his body. The priest shall
pronounce him [1]unclean, and
shall not isolate him, for he *is*
unclean.
12 "And if leprosy breaks out
all over the skin, and the leprosy
covers all the skin of *the one*
who has the sore, from his head
to his foot, wherever the priest
looks,
13 "then the priest shall consider; and indeed *if* the leprosy
has covered all his body, he shall
pronounce *him* clean *who has*
the sore. It has all turned [a]white.
He *is* clean.
14 "But when raw flesh appears
on him, he shall be unclean.
15 "And the priest shall examine the raw flesh and pronounce
him to be unclean; *for* the raw
flesh *is* unclean. It *is* leprosy.
16 "Or if the raw flesh changes

8 [a]Lev. 5:7 [b]Lev. 4:26 [1]*pure*

CHAPTER 13

2 [a]Is. 3:17 [b]Mal. 2:7 [1]Heb. *saraath,* disfiguring skin diseases, including leprosy, and so in vv. 2–46 and 14:2–32

3 [1]*defiled*

4 [a]Lev. 14:8

6 [a]Lev. 11:25; 14:8

8 [1]*defiled*

10 [a]Num. 12:10, 12

11 [1]*defiled*

13 [a]Ex. 4:6

and turns white again, he shall come to the priest.

17 "And the priest shall examine him; and indeed *if* the sore has turned white, then the priest shall pronounce *him* clean *who has* the sore. He *is* clean.

18 "If the body develops a [a]boil in the skin, and it is healed,

19 "and in the place of the boil there comes a white swelling or a bright spot, reddish-white, then it shall be shown to the priest;

20 "and *if*, when the priest sees it, it indeed appears deeper than the skin, and its hair has turned white, the priest shall pronounce him unclean. It *is* a leprous sore which has broken out of the boil.

21 "But if the priest examines it, and indeed *there are* no white hairs in it, and it *is* not deeper than the skin, but has faded, then the priest shall isolate him seven days;

22 "and if it should at all spread over the skin, then the priest shall pronounce him unclean. It *is* a [1]leprous sore.

23 "But if the bright spot stays in one place, *and* has not spread, it *is* the scar of the boil; and the priest shall pronounce him clean.

24 "Or if the body receives a [a]burn on its skin by fire, and the raw *flesh* of the burn becomes a bright spot, reddish-white or white,

25 "then the priest shall examine it; and indeed *if* the hair of the bright spot has turned white, and it appears deeper than the skin, it *is* leprosy broken out in the burn. Therefore the priest shall pronounce him unclean. It *is* a leprous sore.

26 "But if the priest examines it, and indeed *there are* no white hairs in the bright spot, and it *is* not deeper than the skin, but has faded, then the priest shall isolate him seven days.

27 "And the priest shall examine him on the seventh day. If it has at all spread over the skin, then the priest shall pronounce him unclean. It *is* a leprous sore.

28 "But if the bright spot stays in one place, *and* has not spread on the skin, but has faded, it *is* a swelling from the burn. The priest shall pronounce him clean, for it *is* the scar from the burn.

29 "If a man or woman has a sore on the head or the beard,

30 "then the priest shall examine the sore; and indeed if it appears deeper than the skin, *and there is* in it thin yellow hair, then the priest shall pronounce him unclean. It *is* a scaly leprosy of the head or beard.

31 "But if the priest examines the scaly sore, and indeed it does not appear deeper than the skin, and *there is* no black hair in it, then the priest shall isolate *the one who has* the scale seven days.

32 "And on the seventh day the priest shall examine the sore; and indeed *if* the scale has not spread, and there is no yellow hair in it, and the scale does not appear deeper than the skin,

33 "he shall shave himself, but the scale he shall not shave. And the priest shall isolate *the one who has* the scale another seven days.

34 "On the seventh day the

18 [a]Ex. 9:9; 15:26

22 [1]*infection*

24 [a]Is. 3:24

priest shall examine the scale; and indeed *if* the scale has not spread over the skin, and does not appear deeper than the skin, then the priest shall pronounce him clean. He shall wash his clothes and be clean.

35 "But if the scale should at all spread over the skin after his cleansing,

36 "then the priest shall examine him; and indeed *if* the scale has spread over the skin, the priest need not seek for yellow hair. He *is* unclean.

37 "But if the scale appears to be at a standstill, and there is black hair grown up in it, the scale has healed. He *is* clean, and the priest shall pronounce him clean.

38 "If a man or a woman has bright spots on the skin of the body, *specifically* white bright spots,

39 "then the priest shall look; and indeed *if* the bright spots on the skin of the body *are* dull white, it *is* a white spot *that* grows on the skin. He *is* clean.

40 "As for the man whose hair has fallen from his head, he *is* bald, *but* he *is* clean.

41 "He whose hair has fallen from his forehead, he *is* bald on the forehead, *but* he *is* clean.

42 "And if there is on the bald head or bald [a]forehead a reddish-white sore, it *is* leprosy breaking out on his bald head or his bald forehead.

43 "Then the priest shall examine it; and indeed *if* the swelling of the sore *is* reddish-white on his bald head or on his bald forehead, as the appearance of leprosy on the skin of the body,

44 "he is a leprous man. He *is* unclean. The priest shall surely pronounce him [1]unclean; his sore *is* on his [a]head.

45 "Now the leper on whom the sore *is*, his clothes shall be torn and his head [a]bare; and he shall [b]cover his mustache, and cry, [c]'Unclean! Unclean!'

46 "He shall be unclean. All the days he has the sore he shall be unclean. He *is* unclean, and he shall [1]dwell alone; his dwelling *shall be* [a]outside the camp.

47 "Also, if a garment has a [1]leprous plague in it, *whether it is* a woolen garment or a linen garment,

48 "whether *it is* in the warp or woof of linen or wool, whether in leather or in anything made of leather,

49 "and if the plague is greenish or reddish in the garment or in the leather, whether in the warp or in the woof, or in anything made of leather, it *is* a leprous [1]plague and shall be shown to the priest.

50 "The priest shall examine the plague and isolate *that which has* the plague seven days.

51 "And he shall examine the plague on the seventh day. If the plague has spread in the garment, either in the warp or in the woof, in the leather *or* in anything made of leather, the plague *is* [a]an active leprosy. It *is* unclean.

52 "He shall therefore burn that garment in which is the plague, whether warp or woof, in wool or in linen, or anything of leather, for it *is* an active leprosy; *the garment* shall be burned in the fire.

53 "But if the priest examines *it*, and indeed the plague has not

42 [a]2 Chr. 26:19

44 [a]Is. 1:5 [1]*altogether defiled*

45 [a]Lev. 10:6; 21:10 [b]Ezek. 24:17, 22 [c]Lam. 4:15

46 [a]Num. 5:1–4; 12:14 [1]*live alone*

47 [1]A mold, fungus, or similar infestation, and so in vv. 47–59

49 [1]*mark*

51 [a]Lev. 14:44

spread in the garment, either in
the warp or in the woof, or in
anything made of leather,
54 "then the priest shall command that they wash *the thing*
in which *is* the plague; and he
shall isolate it another seven
days.
55 "Then the priest shall examine the plague after it has been
washed; and indeed *if* the plague
has not changed its color, though
the plague has not spread, it *is*
unclean, and you shall burn it
in the fire; it continues eating
away, *whether* the damage *is*
outside or inside.
56 "If the priest examines *it,* and
indeed the plague has faded after washing it, then he shall tear
it out of the garment, whether
out of the warp or out of the
woof, or out of the leather.
57 "But if it appears again in the
garment, either in the warp or in
the woof, or in anything made of
leather, it *is* a spreading *plague;*
you shall burn with fire that in
which is the plague.
58 "And if you wash the garment, either warp or woof, or
whatever is made of leather,
if the plague has disappeared
from it, then it shall be washed a
second time, and shall be clean.
59 "This *is* the law of the leprous plague in a garment of
wool or linen, either in the warp
or woof, or in anything made of
leather, to pronounce it clean or
to pronounce it unclean."

14

Then the LORD spoke to
Moses, saying,
2 "This shall be the law of the
[1]leper for the day of his cleansing: He [a]shall be brought to the
priest.
3 "And the priest shall go out
of the camp, and the priest shall
examine *him;* and indeed, *if* the
[1]leprosy is healed in the leper,
4 "then the priest shall command to take for him who is to
be cleansed two living *and* clean
birds, [a]cedar wood, [b]scarlet, and
[c]hyssop.
5 "And the priest shall command that one of the birds be
killed in an earthen vessel over
running water.
6 "As for the living bird, he
shall take it, the cedar wood and
the scarlet and the hyssop, and
dip them and the living bird in
the blood of the bird *that was*
killed over the running water.
7 "And he shall [a]sprinkle it
[b]seven times on him who is to be
cleansed from the leprosy, and
shall pronounce him clean, and
shall let the living bird loose in
the open field.
8 "He who is to be cleansed
[a]shall wash his clothes, shave off
all his hair, and [b]wash himself
in water, that he may be clean.
After that he shall come into the
camp, and [c]shall stay outside his
tent seven days.
9 "But on the [a]seventh day
he shall shave all the hair off
his head and his beard and his
eyebrows—all his hair he shall
shave off. He shall wash his
clothes and wash his body in
water, and he shall be clean.
10 "And on the eighth day [a]he
shall take two male lambs without blemish, one ewe lamb of
the first year without blemish,
three-tenths *of an ephah* of fine
flour mixed with oil as [b]a grain
offering, and one log of oil.
11 "Then the priest who makes
him clean shall present the man
who is to be made clean, and

CHAPTER 14

2 [a]Matt. 8:2, 4
[1]See note at 13:2

3 [1]Heb. *saraath,* disfiguring skin diseases, including leprosy, and so in vv. 2–32

4 [a]Num. 19:6
[b]Ex. 25:4
[c]Ps. 51:7

7 [a]Num. 19:18, 19
[b]Ps. 51:2

8 [a]Num. 8:7
[b][Heb. 10:22]
[c]Num. 5:2, 3; 12:14, 15

9 [a]Num. 19:19

10 [a]Matt. 8:4
[b]Lev. 2:1

those things, before the LORD, *at* the door of the tabernacle of meeting.

12 "And the priest shall take one male lamb and [a]offer it as a trespass offering, and the log of oil, and [b]wave them *as* a wave offering before the LORD.

13 "Then he shall kill the lamb [a]in the place where he kills the sin offering and the burnt offering, in a holy place; for [b]as the sin offering *is* the priest's, so *is* the trespass offering. [c]It *is* most holy.

14 "The priest shall take *some* of the blood of the trespass offering, and the priest shall put *it* [a]on the tip of the right ear of him who is to be cleansed, on the thumb of his right hand, and on the big toe of his right foot.

15 "And the priest shall take *some* of the log of oil, and pour *it* into the palm of his own left hand.

16 "Then the priest shall dip his right finger in the oil that *is* in his left hand, and shall [a]sprinkle some of the oil with his finger seven times before the LORD.

17 "And of the rest of the oil in his hand, the priest shall put *some* on the tip of the right ear of him who is to be cleansed, on the thumb of his right hand, and on the big toe of his right foot, on the blood of the trespass offering.

18 "The rest of the oil that *is* in the priest's hand he shall put on the head of him who is to be cleansed. [a]So the priest shall make [1]atonement for him before the LORD.

19 "Then the priest shall offer [a]the sin offering, and make atonement for him who is to be cleansed from his uncleanness. Afterward he shall kill the burnt offering.

20 "And the priest shall offer the burnt offering and the grain offering on the altar. So the priest shall make atonement for him, and he shall be [a]clean.

21 "But [a]if he *is* poor and cannot afford it, then he shall take one male lamb *as* a trespass offering to be waved, to make atonement for him, [1]one-tenth *of an ephah* of fine flour mixed with oil as a grain offering, a log of oil,

22 [a]"and two turtledoves or two young pigeons, such as he is able to afford: one shall be a sin offering and the other a burnt offering.

23 [a]"He shall bring them to the priest on the eighth day for his cleansing, to the door of the tabernacle of meeting, before the LORD.

24 [a]"And the priest shall take the lamb of the trespass offering and the log of oil, and the priest shall wave them *as* a wave offering before the LORD.

25 "Then he shall kill the lamb of the trespass offering, [a]and the priest shall take *some* of the blood of the trespass offering and put *it* on the tip of the right ear of him who is to be cleansed, on the thumb of his right hand, and on the big toe of his right foot.

26 "And the priest shall pour some of the oil into the palm of his own left hand.

27 "Then the priest shall sprinkle with his right finger *some* of the oil that *is* in his left hand seven times before the LORD.

28 "And the priest shall put *some* of the oil that *is* in his

12 [a]Lev. 5:6, 18; 6:6; 14:19 [b]Ex. 29:22–24, 26
13 [a]Ex. 29:11 [b]Lev. 6:24–30; 7:7 [c]Lev. 2:3; 7:6; 21:22
14 [a]Lev. 8:23, 24
16 [a]Lev. 4:6
18 [a]Lev. 4:26; 5:6 [1]Lit. *covering*
19 [a]Lev. 5:1, 6; 12:7
20 [a]Lev. 14:8, 9
21 [a]Lev. 5:7, 11; 12:8; 27:8 [1]Approximately two dry quarts
22 [a]Lev. 12:8; 15:14, 15
23 [a]Lev. 14:10, 11
24 [a]Lev. 14:12
25 [a]Lev. 14:14, 17

hand on the tip of the right ear
of him who is to be cleansed, on
the thumb of the right hand, and
on the big toe of his right foot,
on the place of the blood of the
trespass offering.
29 "The rest of the oil that *is* in
the priest's hand he shall put
on the head of him who is to be
cleansed, to make atonement for
him before the LORD.
30 "And he shall offer one of
[a]the turtledoves or young pigeons, such as he can afford—
31 "such as he is able to afford,
the one *as* a sin offering and the
other *as* a burnt offering, with
the grain offering. So the priest
shall make atonement for him
who is to be cleansed before the
LORD.
32 "This *is* the law *for one* who
had a leprous sore, who cannot
afford [a]the usual cleansing."
33 And the LORD spoke to Moses and Aaron, saying:
34 [a]"When you have come into
the land of Cā'naan, which I give
you as a possession, and [b]I put
the [1]leprous plague in a house in
the land of your possession,
35 "and he who owns the house
comes and tells the priest, saying, 'It seems to me that *there is*
[a]some plague in the house,'
36 "then the priest shall command that they empty the house,
before the priest goes *into it*
to examine the plague, that all
that *is* in the house may not be
made unclean; and afterward
the priest shall go in to examine
the house.
37 "And he shall examine the
plague; and indeed *if* the plague
is on the walls of the house
with ingrained streaks, greenish
or reddish, which appear to be
[1]deep in the wall,
38 "then the priest shall go out
of the house, to the door of the
house, and [1]shut up the house
seven days.
39 "And the priest shall come
again on the seventh day and
look; and indeed *if* the plague
has spread on the walls of the
house,
40 "then the priest shall command that they take away the
stones in which *is* the plague,
and they shall cast them into an
unclean place outside the city.
41 "And he shall cause the
house to be scraped inside, all
around, and the dust that they
scrape off they shall pour out
in an unclean place outside the
city.
42 "Then they shall take other
stones and put *them* in the place
of *those* stones, and he shall
take other mortar and plaster
the house.
43 "Now if the plague comes
back and breaks out in the house,
after he has taken away the
stones, after he has scraped the
house, and after it is plastered,
44 "then the priest shall come
and look; and indeed *if* the
plague has spread in the house,
it *is* [a]an active leprosy in the
house. It *is* unclean.
45 "And he shall break down
the house, its stones, its timber,
and all the plaster of the house,
and he shall carry *them* outside
the city to an unclean place.
46 "Moreover he who goes into
the house at all while it is shut up
shall be [1]unclean [a]until evening.
47 "And he who lies down in the
house shall [a]wash his clothes,

30 [a]Lev. 14:22; 15:14, 15
32 [a]Lev. 14:10
34 [a]Deut. 7:1; 32:49 [b][Prov. 3:33] [1]Decomposition by mildew, mold, dry rot, etc., and so in vv. 34–53
35 [a][Ps. 91:9, 10]
37 [1]Lit. *lower than the wall*
38 [1]*quarantine*
44 [a]Lev. 13:51
46 [a]Lev. 11:24; 15:5 [1]*defiled*
47 [a]Lev. 14:8

and he who eats in the house
shall wash his clothes.
48 "But if the priest comes in
and examines *it*, and indeed
the plague has not spread in
the house after the house was
plastered, then the priest shall
pronounce the house clean, because the plague is healed.
49 "And [a]he shall take, to
cleanse the house, two birds, cedar wood, scarlet, and hyssop.
50 "Then he shall kill one of the
birds in an earthen vessel over
running water;
51 "and he shall take the cedar
wood, the hyssop, the scarlet,
and the living bird, and dip them
in the blood of the slain bird
and in the running water, and
sprinkle the house seven times.
52 "And he shall [1]cleanse the
house with the blood of the bird
and the running water and the
living bird, with the cedar wood,
the hyssop, and the scarlet.
53 "Then he shall let the living
bird loose outside the city in the
open field, and [a]make atonement for the house, and it shall
be clean.
54 "This *is* the law for any
[a]leprous sore and scale,
55 "for the [a]leprosy of a garment [b]and of a house,
56 [a]"for a swelling and a scab
and a bright spot,
57 "to [a]teach when *it is* unclean
and when *it is* clean. This *is* the
law of leprosy."

15 And the LORD spoke to
Moses and Aaron, saying,
2 "Speak to the children of Israel, and say to them: [a]'When any
man has a discharge from his
body, his discharge *is* unclean.
3 'And this shall be his uncleanness in regard to his
discharge—whether his body
runs with his discharge, or his
body is stopped up by his discharge, it *is* his uncleanness.
4 'Every bed is [1]unclean on
which he who has the discharge
lies, and everything on which he
sits shall be unclean.
5 'And whoever [a]touches his
bed shall [b]wash his clothes and
[c]bathe in water, and be unclean
until evening.
6 'He who sits on anything on
which he who has the [a]discharge
sat shall wash his clothes and
bathe in water, and be unclean
until evening.
7 'And he who touches the
body of him who has the discharge shall wash his clothes
and bathe in water, and be unclean until evening.
8 'If he who has the discharge
[a]spits on him who is clean, then
he shall wash his clothes and
bathe in water, and be unclean
until evening.
9 'Any saddle on which he who
has the discharge rides shall be
unclean.
10 'Whoever touches anything
that was under him shall be
unclean until evening. He who
carries *any of* those things shall
wash his clothes and bathe in
water, and be unclean until
evening.
11 'And whomever the one who
has the discharge touches, and
has not rinsed his hands in water, he shall wash his clothes
and bathe in water, and be unclean until evening.
12 'The [a]vessel of earth that he
who has the discharge touches
shall be broken, and every vessel of wood shall be rinsed in
water.

49 [a]Lev. 14:4
52 [1]*ceremonially cleanse*
53 [a]Lev. 14:20
54 [a]Lev. 13:30; 26:21
55 [a]Lev. 13:47–52 [b]Lev. 14:34
56 [a]Lev. 13:2
57 [a]Deut. 24:8

CHAPTER 15

2 [a]Num. 5:2
4 [1]*defiled*
5 [a]Lev. 5:2; 14:46 [b]Lev. 14:8, 47 [c]Lev. 11:25; 17:15
6 [a]Deut. 23:10
8 [a]Num. 12:14
12 [a]Lev. 6:28; 11:32, 33

13 'And when he who has a
discharge is cleansed of his
discharge, then [a]he shall count
for himself seven days for his
cleansing, wash his clothes, and
bathe his body in running water;
then he shall be clean.
14 'On the eighth day he shall
take for himself [a]two turtledoves
or two young pigeons, and come
before the LORD, to the door of
the tabernacle of meeting, and
give them to the priest.
15 'Then the priest shall offer
them, [a]the one *as* a sin offering
and the other *as* a burnt offering. [b]So the priest shall make
[1]atonement for him before the
LORD because of his discharge.
16 [a]'If any man has an emission
of semen, then he shall wash all
his body in water, and be unclean until evening.
17 'And any garment and any
leather on which there is semen,
it shall be washed with water,
and be unclean until evening.
18 'Also, when a woman lies
with a man, and *there is* an
emission of semen, they shall
bathe in water, and [a]be unclean
until evening.
19 [a]'If a woman has a discharge,
and the discharge from her
body is blood, she shall be [1]set
apart seven days; and whoever
touches her shall be unclean
until evening.
20 'Everything that she lies on
during her impurity shall be unclean; also everything that she
sits on shall be unclean.
21 'Whoever touches her bed
shall wash his clothes and bathe
in water, and be unclean until
evening.
22 'And whoever touches anything that she sat on shall wash
his clothes and bathe in water,
and be unclean until evening.
23 'If *anything* is on *her* bed or
on anything on which she sits,
when he touches it, he shall be
unclean until evening.
24 'And [a]if any man lies with
her at all, so that her impurity
is on him, he shall be [1]unclean
seven days; and every bed on
which he lies shall be unclean.
25 'If [a]a woman has a discharge
of blood for many days, other
than at the time of her *customary* impurity, or if it runs
beyond her *usual time of* impurity, all the days of her unclean
discharge shall be as the days
of her *customary* impurity. She
shall be unclean.
26 'Every bed on which she lies
all the days of her discharge
shall be to her as the bed of her
impurity; and whatever she sits
on shall be unclean, as the uncleanness of her impurity.
27 'Whoever touches those
things shall be unclean; he shall
wash his clothes and bathe in
water, and be unclean until
evening.
28 'But [a]if she is cleansed of her
discharge, then she shall count
for herself seven days, and after
that she shall be clean.
29 'And on the eighth day she
shall take for herself two turtledoves or two young pigeons,
and bring them to the priest,
to the door of the tabernacle of
meeting.
30 'Then the priest shall offer
the one *as* a sin offering and the
other *as* a [a]burnt offering, and
the priest shall make atonement
for her before the LORD for the
discharge of her uncleanness.
31 'Thus you shall [a]separate the

13 [a]Lev. 14:8; 15:28
14 [a]Lev. 14:22, 23, 30, 31
15 [a]Lev. 14:30, 31 [b]Lev. 14:19, 31 [1]Lit. *covering*
16 [a]Lev. 22:4
18 [a][1 Sam. 21:4]
19 [a]Lev. 12:2 [1]Lit. *in her impurity*
24 [a]Lev. 18:19; 20:18 [1]*defiled*
25 [a]Matt. 9:20
28 [a]Lev. 15:13–15
30 [a]Lev. 5:7
31 [a]Deut. 24:8

children of Israel from their uncleanness, lest they die in their
uncleanness when they [b]defile
My tabernacle that *is* among
them.
32 [a]"This *is* the law for one who
has a discharge, [b]and *for him*
who emits semen and is unclean
thereby,
33 [a]"and for her who is indis-
posed because of her *customary* impurity, and for one who
has a discharge, either man [b]or
woman, [c]and for him who lies
with her who is unclean.' "

CHAPTER 16

16 Now the LORD spoke to
Moses after [a]the death of
the two sons of Aaron, when
they offered *profane fire* before
the LORD, and died;
2 and the LORD said to Moses:
"Tell Aaron your brother [a]not
to come at *just* any time into
the Holy *Place* inside the veil,
before the mercy seat which *is*
on the ark, lest he die; for [b]I will
appear in the cloud above the
mercy seat.
3 [1]"Thus Aaron shall [a]come
into the Holy *Place:* [b]with *the
blood of* a young bull as a sin
offering, and *of* a ram as a burnt
offering.
4 "He shall put the [a]holy linen
tunic and the linen trousers on
his body; he shall be girded with
a linen sash, and with the linen
turban he shall be attired. These
are holy garments. Therefore
[b]he shall wash his body in water,
and put them on.
5 "And he shall take from [a]the
congregation of the children of
Israel two kids of the goats as
a sin offering, and one ram as a
burnt offering.
6 "Aaron shall offer the bull
as a sin offering, which *is* for
himself, and [a]make atonement
for himself and for his house.
7 "He shall take the two goats
and present them before the
LORD *at* the door of the tabernacle of meeting.
8 "Then Aaron shall cast lots
for the two goats: one lot for the
LORD and the other lot for the
scapegoat.
9 "And Aaron shall bring the
goat on which the LORD's lot fell,
and offer it *as* a sin offering.
10 "But the goat on which the
lot fell to be the scapegoat shall
be presented alive before the
LORD, to make [a]atonement upon
it, *and* to let it go as the scapegoat into the wilderness.
11 "And Aaron shall bring the
bull of the sin offering, which
is for [a]himself, and make atonement for himself and for his
house, and shall kill the bull
as the sin offering which *is* for
himself.
12 "Then he shall take [a]a censer
full of burning coals of fire from
the altar before the LORD, with
his hands full of [b]sweet incense
beaten fine, and bring *it* inside
the veil.
13 [a]"And he shall put the incense
on the fire before the LORD, that
the cloud of incense may cover
the [b]mercy seat that *is* on the
Testimony, lest he [c]die.
14 [a]"He shall take some of the
blood of the bull and [b]sprinkle
it with his finger on the mercy
seat on the east *side;* and before
the mercy seat he shall sprinkle
some of the blood with his finger seven times.
15 [a]"Then he shall kill the goat
of the sin offering, which *is* for
the people, bring its blood [b]inside
the veil, do with that blood as he

31 [b]Num. 5:3; 19:13, 20
32 [a]Lev. 15:2 [b]Lev. 15:16
33 [a]Lev. 15:19 [b]Lev. 15:25 [c]Lev. 15:24

CHAPTER 16

1 [a]Lev. 10:1, 2
2 [a]Ex. 30:10 [b]Ex. 25:21, 22; 40:34
3 [a][Heb. 9:7, 12, 24, 25] [b]Lev. 4:3 [1]Lit. *With this*
4 [a]Ex. 28:39, 42, 43 [b]Ex. 30:20
5 [a]Lev. 4:14
6 [a][Heb. 5:3; 7:27, 28; 9:7]
10 [a][1 John 2:2]
11 [a][Heb. 7:27; 9:7]
12 [a]Lev. 10:1 [b]Ex. 30:34–38
13 [a]Ex. 30:7, 8 [b]Ex. 25:21 [c]Ex. 28:43
14 [a][Heb. 9:25; 10:4] [b]Lev. 4:6, 17
15 [a][Heb. 2:17] [b][Heb. 6:19; 7:27; 9:3, 7, 12]

did with the blood of the bull,
and sprinkle it on the mercy seat
and before the mercy seat.
16 “So he shall [a]make atonement for the Holy *Place,* because of the uncleanness of the
children of Israel, and because
of their transgressions, for all
their sins; and so he shall do
for the tabernacle of meeting
which remains among them in
the midst of their uncleanness.
17 “There shall be [a]no man in
the tabernacle of meeting when
he goes in to make atonement in
the Holy *Place,* until he comes
out, that he may make atonement for himself, for his household, and for all the assembly of
Israel.
18 “And he shall go out to the
altar that *is* before the LORD,
and make atonement for [a]it, and
shall take some of the blood of
the bull and some of the blood of
the goat, and put it on the horns
of the altar all around.
19 “Then he shall sprinkle
some of the blood on it with
his finger seven times, cleanse
it, and [a]consecrate[1] it from the
[2]uncleanness of the children of
Israel.
20 “And when he has made
an end of atoning for the Holy
Place, the tabernacle of meeting, and the altar, he shall bring
the live goat.
21 “Aaron shall lay both his
hands on the head of the live
goat, [a]confess over it all the
iniquities of the children of
Israel, and all their transgressions, concerning all their sins,
[b]putting them on the head of the
goat, and shall send *it* away into
the wilderness by the hand of a
suitable man.
22 “The goat [1]shall [a]bear on itself all their iniquities to an
[2]uninhabited land; and he
shall [b]release the goat in the
wilderness.
23 “Then Aaron shall come into
the tabernacle of meeting, [a]shall
take off the linen garments
which he put on when he went
into the Holy *Place,* and shall
leave them there.
24 “And he shall wash his body
with water in a holy place, put
on his garments, come out and
offer his burnt offering and the
burnt offering of the people, and
make [1]atonement for himself
and for the people.
25 [a]“The fat of the sin offering
he shall burn on the altar.
26 “And he who released the
goat as the scapegoat shall wash
his clothes [a]and bathe his body
in water, and afterward he may
come into the camp.
27 [a]“The bull *for* the sin offering
and the goat *for* the sin offering,
whose blood was brought in to
make atonement in the Holy
Place, shall be carried outside
the camp. And they shall burn
in the fire their skins, their flesh,
and their offal.
28 “Then he who burns them
shall wash his clothes and bathe
his body in water, and afterward
he may come into the camp.
29 “*This* shall be a statute forever for you: [a]In the seventh
month, on the tenth *day* of the
month, you shall [1]afflict your
souls, and do no work at all,
whether a native of your own
country or a stranger who
[2]dwells among you.
30 “For on that day *the priest*
shall make [1]atonement for you,
to [a]cleanse you, *that* you may be

16 [a]Ex. 29:36; 30:10
17 [a]Luke 1:10
18 [a]Ex. 29:36
19 [a]Ezek. 43:20 [1]*set it apart* [2]*impurity*
21 [a]Lev. 5:5; 26:40 [b][Is. 53:6]
22 [a][Is. 53:6, 11, 12] [b]Lev. 14:7 [1]*shall carry* [2]*solitary land*
23 [a]Ezek. 42:14; 44:19
24 [1]Lit. *covering*
25 [a]Lev. 1:8; 4:10
26 [a]Lev. 15:5
27 [a]Heb. 13:11
29 [a]Lev. 23:27–32 [1]*humble yourselves* [2]As a resident alien
30 [a]Jer. 33:8 [1]Lit. *covering*

clean from all your sins before
the LORD.
31 [a]"It *is* a sabbath of solemn
rest for you, and you shall afflict your souls. *It is* a statute
forever.
32 [a]"And the priest, who is
anointed and [b]consecrated to
minister as priest in his father's
place, shall make atonement,
and put on the linen clothes, the
holy garments;
33 "then he shall make [1]atone-
ment for [2]the Holy Sanctuary,
and he shall make atonement
for the tabernacle of meeting
and for the altar, and he shall
make atonement for the priests
and for all the people of the
assembly.
34 [a]"This shall be an everlasting
statute for you, to make atonement for the children of Israel,
for all their sins, [b]once a year."
And he did as the LORD commanded Moses.

17

17 And the LORD spoke to
Moses, saying,
2 "Speak to Aaron, to his sons,
and to all the children of Israel,
and say to them, 'This *is* the
thing which the LORD has commanded, saying:
3 "Whatever man of the house
of Israel who [a]kills an ox or
lamb or goat in the camp, or
who kills *it* outside the camp,
4 "and does not bring it to the
door of the tabernacle of meeting to offer an offering to the
LORD before the tabernacle of
the LORD, the guilt of bloodshed
shall be [a]imputed to that man.
He has shed blood; and that man
shall be [1]cut off from among his
people,
5 "to the end that the children of Israel may bring their
sacrifices [a]which they offer in
the open field, that they may
bring them to the LORD at the
door of the tabernacle of meeting, to the priest, and offer them
as peace offerings to the LORD.
6 "And the priest [a]shall sprinkle the blood on the altar of the
LORD *at* the door of the tabernacle of meeting, and [b]burn the fat
for a sweet aroma to the LORD.
7 "They shall no more offer
their sacrifices [a]to [1]demons, after whom they [b]have played the
harlot. This shall be a statute
forever for them throughout
their generations." '
8 "Also you shall say to them:
'Whatever man of the house of
Israel, or of the strangers who
dwell among you, [a]who offers a
burnt offering or sacrifice,
9 'and does not [a]bring it to
the door of the tabernacle of
meeting, to offer it to the LORD,
that man shall be [1]cut off from
among his people.
10 [a]'And whatever man of the
house of Israel, or of the strangers who dwell among you, who
eats any blood, [b]I will set My
face against that person who
eats blood, and will cut him off
from among his people.
11 'For the [a]life of the flesh *is*
in the blood, and I have given it
to you upon the altar [b]to make
atonement for your souls; for [c]it
is the blood *that* makes atonement for the soul.'
12 "Therefore I said to the children of Israel, 'No one among
you shall eat blood, nor shall
any stranger who dwells among
you eat blood.'
13 "Whatever man of the children of Israel, or of the strangers who dwell among you, who

31 [a]Lev. 23:27, 32
32 [a]Lev. 4:3, 5, 16; 21:10 [b]Ex. 29:29, 30
33 [1]Lit. *covering* [2]The Most Holy Place
34 [a]Lev. 23:31 [b][Heb. 9:7, 25, 28]

CHAPTER 17

3 [a]Deut. 12:5, 15, 21
4 [a]Rom. 5:13 [1]Put to death
5 [a]Deut. 12:1–27
6 [a]Lev. 3:2 [b]Num. 18:17
7 [a]Deut. 32:17 [b]Ezek. 23:8 [1]Having the form of a goat or satyr
8 [a]Lev. 1:2, 3; 18:26
9 [a]Lev. 14:23 [1]Put to death
10 [a]Gen. 9:4 [b]Lev. 20:3, 5, 6
11 [a]Gen. 9:4 [b][Matt. 26:28] [c][Heb. 9:22]

[a]hunts and catches any animal
or bird that may be eaten, he
shall [b]pour out its blood and
[c]cover it with dust;
14 [a]"for *it is* the life of all flesh.
Its blood sustains its life. Therefore I said to the children of Israel, 'You shall not eat the blood
of any flesh, for the life of all
flesh is its blood. Whoever eats
it shall be cut off.'
15 [a]"And every person who eats
what died *naturally* or what was
torn *by beasts, whether he is* a
native of your own country or a
stranger, [b]he shall both wash his
clothes and [c]bathe in water, and
be unclean until evening. Then
he shall be clean.
16 "But if he does not wash
them or bathe his body, then [a]he
shall bear his [1]guilt."

18 Then the LORD spoke to
Moses, saying,
2 "Speak to the children of Israel, and say to them: [a]'I am the
LORD your God.
3 [a]'According to [1]the doings
of the land of Egypt, where
you dwelt, you shall not do;
and [b]according to the doings
of the land of Cā'naan, where I
am bringing you, you shall not
do; nor shall you walk in their
[2]ordinances.
4 [a]'You shall observe My judgments and keep My ordinances,
to walk in them: I *am* the LORD
your God.
5 'You shall therefore keep
My statutes and My judgments,
which if a man does, he shall
live by them: I *am* the LORD.
6 'None of you shall approach
anyone who is near of kin to
him, to uncover his nakedness: I
am the LORD.
7 'The nakedness of your
father or the nakedness of your
mother you shall not uncover.
She *is* your mother; you shall
not uncover her nakedness.
8 'The nakedness of your [a]fa-
ther's wife you shall not uncover; it *is* your father's nakedness.
9 [a]'The nakedness of your sister, the daughter of your father,
or the daughter of your mother,
whether born at home or elsewhere, their nakedness you shall
not uncover.
10 'The nakedness of your son's
daughter or your daughter's
daughter, their nakedness you
shall not uncover; for theirs *is*
your own nakedness.
11 'The nakedness of your father's wife's daughter, begotten
by your father—she *is* your sister—you shall not uncover her
nakedness.
12 [a]'You shall not uncover the
nakedness of your father's sister; she *is* near of kin to your
father.
13 'You shall not uncover the
nakedness of your mother's sister, for she *is* near of kin to your
mother.
14 [a]'You shall not uncover the
nakedness of your father's
brother. You shall not approach
his wife; she *is* your aunt.
15 'You shall not uncover the
nakedness of your daughter-in-
law—she *is* your son's wife—
you shall not uncover her
nakedness.
16 'You shall not uncover the nakedness of your brother's wife;
it *is* your brother's nakedness.
17 'You shall not uncover the
nakedness of a woman and her
[a]daughter, nor shall you take her
son's daughter or her daughter's

13 [a]Lev. 7:26 [b]Deut. 12:16, 24 [c]Ezek. 24:7
14 [a]Gen. 9:4
15 [a]Ex. 22:31 [b]Lev. 11:25 [c]Lev. 15:5
16 [a]Lev. 5:1 [1]*iniquity*

CHAPTER 18

2 [a]Ex. 6:7
3 [a]Ezek. 20:7, 8 [b]Lev. 18:24–30; 20:23 [1]*what is done in* [2]*statutes*
4 [a]Ezek. 20:19
8 [a]Gen. 35:22
9 [a]Deut. 27:22
12 [a]Lev. 20:19
14 [a]Lev. 20:20
17 [a]Lev. 20:14

daughter, to uncover her nakedness. They *are* near of kin to her. It *is* wickedness.

18 ‘Nor shall you take a woman [a]as a rival to her sister, to uncover her nakedness while the other is alive.

19 ‘Also you shall not approach a woman to uncover her nakedness as [a]long as she is in her [b]*customary* impurity.

20 [a]‘Moreover you shall not lie carnally with your [b]neighbor’s wife, to defile yourself with her.

21 ‘And you shall not let any of your descendants [a]pass through [b]*the fire* to [c]Mō′lech, nor shall you profane the name of your God: I *am* the LORD.

22 ‘You shall not lie with [a]a male as with a woman. It *is* an abomination.

23 ‘Nor shall you mate with any [a]animal, to defile yourself with it. Nor shall any woman stand before an animal to mate with it. It *is* perversion.

24 [a]‘Do not defile yourselves with any of these things; [b]for by all these the nations are defiled, which I am casting out before you.

25 ‘For [a]the land is defiled; therefore I [b]visit[1] the punishment of its iniquity upon it, and the land [c]vomits out its inhabitants.

26 [a]‘You shall therefore [1]keep My statutes and My judgments, and shall not commit *any* of these abominations, *either* any of your own nation or any stranger who dwells among you

27 ‘(for all these abominations the men of the land have done, who *were* before you, and thus the land is defiled),

28 ‘lest [a]the land vomit you out also when you defile it, as it vomited out the nations that *were* before you.

29 ‘For whoever commits any of these abominations, the persons who commit *them* shall be [1]cut off from among their people.

30 ‘Therefore you shall keep My [1]ordinance, so [a]that *you* do not commit *any* of these abominable customs which were committed before you, and that you do not defile yourselves by them: [b]I *am* the LORD your God.’ ”

19 And the LORD spoke to Moses, saying,

2 “Speak to all the congregation of the children of Israel, and say to them: [a]‘You shall be holy, for I the LORD your God *am* holy.

3 [a]‘Every one of you shall revere his mother and his father, and [b]keep My Sabbaths: I *am* the LORD your God.

4 [a]‘Do not turn to idols, [b]nor make for yourselves [1]molded gods: I *am* the LORD your God.

5 ‘And [a]if you offer a sacrifice of a peace offering to the LORD, you shall offer it of your own free will.

6 ‘It shall be eaten the same day you offer *it*, and on the next day. And if any remains until the third day, it shall be burned in the fire.

7 ‘And if it is eaten at all on the third day, it *is* an abomination. It shall not be accepted.

8 ‘Therefore *everyone* who eats it shall bear his iniquity, because he has profaned the hallowed *offering* of the LORD; and that person shall be cut off from his people.

9 [a]‘When you reap the harvest of your land, you shall not wholly reap the corners of your

18 [a]1 Sam. 1:6, 8
19 [a]Ezek. 18:6 [b]Lev. 15:24; 20:18
20 [a][Prov. 6:25–33] [b]Lev. 20:10
21 [a]Lev. 20:2–5 [b]2 Kin. 16:3 [c]1 Kin. 11:7, 33
22 [a]Lev. 20:13
23 [a]Ex. 22:19
24 [a]Matt. 15:18–20 [b]Deut. 18:12
25 [a]Num. 35:33, 34 [b]Jer. 5:9 [c]Lev. 18:28; 20:22 [1]*bring judgment for*
26 [a]Lev. 18:5, 30 [1]*obey*
28 [a]Jer. 9:19
29 [1]Put to death
30 [a]Lev. 18:3; 22:9 [b]Lev. 18:2 [1]*charge*

CHAPTER 19

2 [a]Lev. 11:44; 20:7, 26
3 [a]Ex. 20:12 [b]Ex. 16:23; 20:8; 31:13
4 [a]Ex. 20:4 [b]Ex. 34:17 [1]*molten*
5 [a]Lev. 7:16
9 [a]Deut. 24:19–22

field, nor shall you gather the
gleanings of your harvest.
10 ‘And you shall not glean your
vineyard, nor shall you gather
every grape of your vineyard;
you shall leave them for the
poor and the stranger: I *am* the
LORD your God.
11 [a]‘You shall not steal, nor deal
falsely, [b]nor lie to one another.
12 ‘And you shall not [a]swear by
My name falsely, [b]nor shall you
profane the name of your God: I
am the LORD.
13 [a]‘You shall not cheat your
neighbor, nor rob *him.* [b]The
wages of him who is hired shall
not remain with you all night
until morning.
14 ‘You shall not curse the deaf,
[a]nor put a stumbling block before the blind, but shall fear
your God: I *am* the LORD.
15 ‘You shall do no injustice
in [a]judgment. You shall not [b]be
partial to the poor, nor honor the
person of the mighty. In righteousness you shall judge your
neighbor.
16 ‘You shall not go about *as*
a [a]talebearer among your people; nor shall you [b]take a stand
against the life of your neighbor: I *am* the LORD.
17 [a]‘You shall not hate your
brother in your heart. [b]You shall
surely [1]rebuke your neighbor,
and not bear sin because of
him.
18 [a]‘You shall not take vengeance, nor bear any grudge
against the children of your
people, [b]but you shall love your
neighbor as yourself: I *am* the
LORD.
19 ‘You shall keep My statutes.
You shall not let your livestock
breed with another kind. You
shall not sow your field with
mixed seed. Nor shall a garment
of mixed linen and wool come
upon you.
20 ‘Whoever lies carnally with
a woman who *is* [a]betrothed to
a man as a concubine, and who
has not at all been redeemed
nor given her freedom, for this
there shall be [1]scourging; *but*
they shall not be put to death,
because she was not free.
21 ‘And he shall bring his trespass offering to the LORD, to
the door of the tabernacle of
meeting, a ram as a trespass
offering.
22 ‘The priest shall make [1]atone-
ment for him with the ram of
the trespass offering before the
LORD for his sin which he has
committed. And the sin which
he has committed shall be forgiven him.
23 ‘When you come into the
land, and have planted all kinds
of trees for food, then you shall
count their fruit as [1]uncircum-
cised. Three years it shall be as
uncircumcised to you. *It* shall
not be eaten.
24 ‘But in the fourth year all its
fruit shall be holy, a praise to the
LORD.
25 ‘And in the fifth year you
may eat its fruit, that it may
yield to you its increase: I *am*
the LORD your God.
26 ‘You shall not eat *any-*
thing with the blood, nor shall
you practice divination or
soothsaying.
27 ‘You shall not shave around
the sides of your head, nor shall
you disfigure the edges of your
beard.
28 ‘You shall not [a]make any cuttings in your flesh for the dead,

11 [a]Ex. 20:15, 16 [b]Eph. 4:25
12 [a]Deut. 5:11 [b]Lev. 18:21
13 [a]Ex. 22:7–15, 21–27 [b]Deut. 24:15
14 [a]Deut. 27:18
15 [a]Deut. 16:19 [b]Ex. 23:3, 6
16 [a]Prov. 11:13; 18:8; 20:19 [b]1 Kin. 21:7–19
17 [a][1 John 2:9, 11; 3:15] [b]Matt. 18:15 [1]*reprove*
18 [a][Deut. 32:35] [b]Mark 12:31
20 [a]Deut. 22:23–27 [1]*punishment*
22 [1]Lit. *covering*
23 [1]*unclean*
28 [a]Jer. 16:6

nor tattoo any marks on you: I
am the LORD.
29 [a]'Do not prostitute your
daughter, to cause her to be a
harlot, lest the land fall into harlotry, and the land become full
of wickedness.
30 'You shall [1]keep My Sabbaths and [a]reverence My sanctuary: I *am* the LORD.
31 'Give no regard to mediums
and familiar spirits; do not seek
after [a]them, to be defiled by
them: I *am* the LORD your God.
32 [a]'You shall [1]rise before the
gray headed and honor the presence of an old man, and [b]fear
your God: I *am* the LORD.
33 'And [a]if a stranger dwells
with you in your land, you shall
not mistreat him.
34 [a]'The stranger who dwells
among you shall be to you as
[1]one born among you, and [b]you
shall love him as yourself; for
you were strangers in the land
of Egypt: I *am* the LORD your
God.
35 'You shall do no injustice in
judgment, in measurement of
length, weight, or volume.
36 'You shall have [a]honest
scales, honest weights, an honest ephah, and an honest hin:
I *am* the LORD your God, who
brought you out of the land of
Egypt.
37 [a]'Therefore you shall observe
all My statutes and all My judgments, and perform them: I *am*
the LORD.' "

CHAPTER 20

20 Then the LORD spoke to
Moses, saying,
2 [a]"Again, you shall say to the
children of Israel: [b]'Whoever of
the children of Israel, or of the
strangers who [1]dwell in Israel,
who gives *any* of his descendants
to Mō'lech, he shall surely be put
to death. The people of the land
shall [c]stone him with stones.
3 [a]'I will set My face against
that man, and will [1]cut him off
from his people, because he has
given *some* of his descendants
to Mō'lech, to defile My sanctuary and profane My holy name.
4 'And if the people of the land
should in any way [1]hide their
eyes from the man, when he
gives *some* of his descendants
to Mō'lech, and they do not kill
him,
5 'then I will set My face
against that man and against
his family; and I will cut him
off from his people, and all who
prostitute themselves with him
to commit harlotry with Mō'-
lech.
6 'And [a]the person who turns
to mediums and familiar spirits,
to prostitute himself with them,
I will set My face against that
person and cut him off from his
people.
7 [a]'Consecrate[1] yourselves
therefore, and be holy, for I *am*
the LORD your God.
8 'And you shall keep [a]My statutes, and perform them: [b]I *am*
the LORD who [1]sanctifies you.
9 'For [a]everyone who curses
his father or his mother shall
surely be put to death. He has
cursed his father or his mother.
[b]His blood *shall be* upon him.
10 [a]'The man who commits adultery with *another* man's wife, *he*
who commits adultery with his
neighbor's wife, the adulterer
and the adulteress, shall surely
be put to death.
11 'The man who lies with his
[a]father's wife has uncovered his
father's nakedness; both of them

29 [a]Deut. 22:21; 23:17, 18
30 [a]Lev. 26:2 [1]*observe*
31 [a]Lev. 20:6, 27
32 [a]1 Tim. 5:1 [b]Lev. 19:14 [1]*rise to give honor*
33 [a]Ex. 22:21
34 [a]Ex. 12:48 [b]Deut. 10:19 [1]*native among you*
36 [a]Deut. 25:13–15
37 [a]Lev. 18:4, 5

CHAPTER 20

2 [a]Lev. 18:2 [b]Lev. 18:21 [c]Deut. 17:2–5 [1]As resident aliens
3 [a]Lev. 17:10 [1]Put him to death
4 [1]*disregard*
6 [a]Lev. 19:31
7 [a]Lev. 19:2 [1]*Set yourselves apart* for the LORD
8 [a]Lev. 19:19, 37 [b]Ex. 31:13 [1]*sets you apart*
9 [a]Ex. 21:17 [b]2 Sam. 1:16
10 [a]Ex. 20:14
11 [a]Lev. 18:7, 8

shall surely be put to death.
Their blood *shall be* upon them.
12 'If a man lies with his
[a]daughter-in-law, both of them
shall surely be put to death.
They have committed perversion. Their blood *shall be* upon
them.
13 [a]'If a man lies with a male as
he lies with a woman, both of
them have committed an abomination. They shall surely be put
to death. Their blood *shall be*
upon them.
14 'If a man marries a woman
and her [a]mother, it *is* wickedness. They shall be burned with
fire, both he and they, that there
may be no wickedness among
you.
15 'If a man mates with an
[a]animal, he shall surely be put
to death, and you shall kill the
animal.
16 'If a woman approaches any
animal and mates with it, you
shall kill the woman and the
animal. They shall surely be put
to death. Their blood *is* upon
them.
17 'If a man takes his [a]sister, his
father's daughter or his mother's daughter, and sees her nakedness and she sees his nakedness, it *is* a wicked thing. And
they shall be [1]cut off in the sight
of their people. He has uncovered his sister's nakedness. He
shall bear his [2]guilt.
18 [a]'If a man lies with a woman
during her [1]sickness and uncovers her nakedness, he has
[2]exposed her flow, and she has
uncovered the flow of her blood.
Both of them shall be [3]cut off
from their people.
19 'You shall not uncover the
nakedness of your [a]mother's
sister nor of your [b]father's sister, for that would uncover his
near of kin. They shall bear their
guilt.
20 'If a man lies with his [a]uncle's
wife, he has uncovered his
uncle's nakedness. They shall
bear their sin; they shall die
childless.
21 'If a man takes his [a]brother's
wife, it *is* an [1]unclean thing.
He has uncovered his brother's nakedness. They shall be
childless.
22 'You shall therefore keep all
My [a]statutes and all My judgments, and perform them, that
the land where I am bringing
you to dwell [b]may not vomit you
out.
23 [a]'And you shall not walk in
the statutes of the nation which
I am casting out before you; for
they commit all these things,
and [b]therefore I abhor them.
24 'But [a]I have said to you, "You
shall inherit their land, and I will
give it to you to possess, a land
flowing with milk and honey." I
am the LORD your God, [b]who has
separated you from the peoples.
25 [a]'You shall therefore distinguish between clean animals
and unclean, between unclean
birds and clean, [b]and you shall
not make yourselves [1]abomina-
ble by beast or by bird, or by any
kind of living thing that creeps
on the ground, which I have
separated from you as [2]unclean.
26 'And you shall be holy to Me,
[a]for I the LORD *am* holy, and have
separated you from the peoples,
that you should be Mine.
27 [a]'A man or a woman who is
a medium, or who has familiar spirits, shall surely be put
to death; they shall stone them

12 [a]Lev. 18:15
13 [a]Lev. 18:22
14 [a]Lev. 18:17
15 [a]Lev. 18:23
17 [a]Lev. 18:9 [1]Put to death [2]*iniquity*
18 [a]Lev. 15:24; 18:19 [1]Or *customary impurity* [2]Lit. *made bare* [3]Put to death
19 [a]Lev. 18:13 [b]Lev. 18:12
20 [a]Lev. 18:14
21 [a]Lev. 18:16 [1]*indecent, impure*
22 [a]Lev. 18:26; 19:37 [b]Lev. 18:25, 28
23 [a]Lev. 18:3, 24 [b]Deut. 9:5
24 [a]Ex. 3:17; 6:8; 13:5; 33:1–3 [b]Ex. 19:5; 33:16
25 [a]Lev. 10:10; 11:1–47 [b]Lev. 11:43 [1]*detestable* or *loathsome* [2]*defiled*
26 [a]Lev. 19:2
27 [a]Lev. 19:31

with stones. Their blood *shall be* upon them.' "

21 And the LORD said to Moses, "Speak to the priests, the sons of Aaron, and say to them: [a]'None shall defile himself for the dead among his people,

2 'except for his relatives who are nearest to him: his mother, his father, his son, his daughter, and his brother;

3 'also his virgin sister who is near to him, who has had no husband, for her he may defile himself.

4 '*Otherwise* he shall not defile himself, *being* a [1]chief man among his people, to profane himself.

5 [a]'They shall not make any bald *place* on their heads, nor shall they shave the edges of their beards nor make any cuttings in their flesh.

6 'They shall be [a]holy to their God and not profane the name of their God, for they offer the offerings of the LORD made by fire, *and* the [b]bread of their God; [c]therefore they shall be holy.

7 [a]'They shall not take a wife *who is* a harlot or a defiled woman, nor shall they take a woman [b]divorced from her husband; for [1]*the priest* is holy to his God.

8 'Therefore you shall [1]consecrate him, for he offers the bread of your God. He shall be holy to you, for [a]I the LORD, who [b]sanctify you, *am* holy.

9 'The daughter of any priest, if she profanes herself by playing the harlot, she profanes her father. She shall be [a]burned with fire.

10 '*He who is* the high priest among his brethren, on whose head the anointing oil was [a]poured and who is consecrated to wear the garments, shall not [b]uncover[1] his head nor tear his clothes;

11 'nor shall he go [a]near any dead body, nor defile himself for his father or his mother;

12 [a]'nor shall he go out of the sanctuary, nor profane the sanctuary of his God; for the [b]consecration of the anointing oil of his God *is* upon him: I *am* the LORD.

13 'And he shall take a wife in her virginity.

14 'A widow or a divorced woman or a defiled woman *or* a harlot—these he shall not marry; but he shall take a virgin of his own people as wife.

15 'Nor shall he profane his posterity among his people, for I the LORD sanctify him.' "

16 And the LORD spoke to Moses, saying,

17 "Speak to Aaron, saying: 'No man of your descendants in *succeeding* generations, who has *any* defect, may approach to offer the bread of his God.

18 'For any man who has a [a]defect shall not approach: a man blind or lame, who has a marred *face* or any *limb* [b]too long,

19 'a man who has a broken foot or broken hand,

20 'or is a hunchback or a dwarf, or *a man* who has a defect in his eye, or eczema or scab, or is a eunuch.

21 'No man of the descendants of Aaron the priest, who has a defect, shall come near to offer the offerings made by fire to the LORD. He has a defect; he shall not come near to offer the bread of his God.

CHAPTER 21

1 [a]Ezek. 44:25

4 [1]Lit. *master* or *husband*

5 [a]Deut. 14:1

6 [a]Ex. 22:31 [b]Lev. 3:11 [c]Is. 52:11

7 [a]Ezek. 44:22 [b]Deut. 24:1, 2 [1]Lit. *he*

8 [a]Lev. 11:44, 45 [b]Lev. 8:12, 30 [1]*set him apart*

9 [a]Deut. 22:21

10 [a]Lev. 8:12 [b]Lev. 10:6, 7 [1]In mourning

11 [a]Num. 19:14

12 [a]Lev. 10:7 [b]Ex. 29:6, 7

18 [a]Lev. 22:19–25 [b]Lev. 22:23

22 'He may eat the bread of his
God, *both* the most holy and the
holy;
23 'only he shall not go near
the [a]veil or approach the altar,
because he has a defect, lest [b]he
profane My sanctuaries; for I
the LORD sanctify them.'"
24 And Moses told *it* to Aaron
and his sons, and to all the children of Israel.

22 Then the LORD spoke to
Moses, saying,
2 "Speak to Aaron and his
sons, that they [a]separate[1] themselves from the holy things of
the children of Israel, and that
they [b]do not profane My holy
name *by* what they [c]dedicate to
Me: I *am* the LORD.
3 "Say to them: 'Whoever of
all your descendants throughout your generations, who goes
near the holy things which the
children of Israel dedicate to the
LORD, [a]while he has [1]unclean-
ness upon him, that person shall
be cut off from My presence: I
am the LORD.
4 'Whatever man of the descendants of Aaron, who *is*
a [a]leper or has [b]a discharge,
shall not eat the holy offerings
[c]until he is clean. And [d]whoever
touches anything made unclean
by a corpse, or [e]a man who has
had an emission of semen,
5 'or [a]whoever touches any
creeping thing by which he
would be made unclean, or [b]any
person by whom he would become unclean, whatever his uncleanness may be—
6 'the person who has touched
any such thing shall be unclean
until evening, and shall not eat
the holy *offerings* unless he
[a]washes his body with water.
7 'And when the sun goes down
he shall be clean; and afterward
he may eat the holy *offerings*,
because [a]it *is* his food.
8 [a]'Whatever dies *naturally* or
is torn *by beasts* he shall not eat,
to defile himself with it: I *am* the
LORD.
9 'They shall therefore keep
[a]My [1]ordinance, [b]lest they bear
sin for it and die thereby, if they
profane it: I the LORD sanctify
them.
10 [a]'No outsider shall eat the
holy *offering;* one who [1]dwells
with the priest, or a hired servant, shall not eat the holy
thing.
11 'But if the priest [a]buys a person with his money, he may eat
it; and one who is born in his
house may eat his food.
12 'If the priest's daughter is
married to an outsider, she may
not eat of the holy offerings.
13 'But if the priest's daughter
is a widow or divorced, and has
no child, and has returned to her
father's house as in her youth,
she may eat her father's food;
but no outsider shall eat it.
14 'And if a man eats the holy
offering unintentionally, then he
shall restore a holy *offering* to
the priest, and add one-fifth to
it.
15 'They shall not profane the
[a]holy *offerings* of the children
of Israel, which they offer to the
LORD,
16 'or allow them to bear the
guilt of trespass when they eat
their holy *offerings;* for I the
LORD sanctify them.'"
17 And the LORD spoke to Moses, saying,
18 "Speak to Aaron and his sons,
and to all the children of Israel,

23 [a]Lev. 16:2 [b]Lev. 21:12

CHAPTER 22

2 [a]Num. 6:3 [b]Lev. 18:21 [c]Ex. 28:38 [1]*keep themselves apart from*
3 [a]Lev. 7:20, 21 [1]*defilement*
4 [a]Num. 5:2 [b]Lev. 15:2 [c]Lev. 14:2; 15:13 [d]Num. 19:11 [e]Lev. 15:16, 17
5 [a]Lev. 11:23–28 [b]Lev. 15:7, 19
6 [a]Lev. 15:5
7 [a]Num. 18:11, 13
8 [a]Lev. 7:24; 11:39, 40; 17:15
9 [a]Lev. 18:30 [b]Ex. 28:43 [1]*charge*
10 [a]Ex. 29:33 [1]As a visitor
11 [a]Ex. 12:44
15 [a]Num. 18:32

and say to them: [a]'Whatever
man of the house of Israel, or of
the strangers in Israel, who [1]of-
fers his sacrifice for any of his
vows or for any of his freewill
offerings, which they offer to
the LORD as a burnt offering—
19 [a]'*you shall offer* of your own
free will a male without blemish
from the cattle, from the sheep,
or from the goats.
20 [a]'Whatever has a defect, you
shall not offer, for it shall not be
acceptable on your behalf.
21 'And [a]whoever offers a sacrifice of a peace offering to the
LORD, [b]to fulfill *his* vow, or a
freewill offering from the cattle
or the sheep, it must be perfect
to be accepted; there shall be no
defect in it.
22 [a]'Those *that are* blind or
broken or maimed, or have an
[1]ulcer or eczema or scabs, you
shall not offer to the LORD, nor
make [b]an offering by fire of
them on the altar to the LORD.
23 'Either a bull or a lamb that
has any limb [a]too long or too
short you may offer *as* a freewill
offering, but for a vow it shall
not be accepted.
24 'You shall not offer to the
LORD what is bruised or crushed,
or torn or cut; nor shall you
make *any offering of them* in
your land.
25 'Nor [a]from a foreigner's hand
shall you offer any of these as
[b]the bread of your God, because
their [c]corruption *is* in them,
and defects *are* in them. They
shall not be accepted on your
behalf.' "
26 And the LORD spoke to Moses, saying:
27 [a]"When a bull or a sheep or
a goat is born, it shall be seven
days with its mother; and from
the eighth day and thereafter it
shall be accepted as an offering
made by fire to the LORD.
28 "*Whether it is* a cow or ewe,
do not kill both her [a]and her
young on the same day.
29 "And when you [a]offer a sacrifice of thanksgiving to the LORD,
offer *it* of your own free will.
30 "On the same day it shall be
eaten; you shall leave [a]none of it
until morning: I *am* the LORD.
31 [a]"Therefore you shall keep
My commandments, and per-
form them: I *am* the LORD.
32 [a]"You shall not profane
My holy name, but [b]I will be
[1]hallowed among the children
of Israel. I *am* the LORD who
[c]sanctifies you,
33 [a]"who brought you out of the
land of Egypt, to be your God: I
am the LORD."

23

And the LORD spoke to
Moses, saying,
2 "Speak to the children of Israel, and say to them: 'The feasts
of the LORD, which you shall proclaim *to be* [a]holy convocations,
these *are* My feasts.
3 [a]'Six days shall work be done,
but the seventh day *is* a Sabbath
of solemn rest, a holy convocation. You shall do no work *on it;*
it *is* the Sabbath of the LORD in
all your dwellings.
4 [a]'These *are* the feasts of the
LORD, holy convocations which
you shall proclaim at their appointed times.
5 [a]'On the fourteenth *day* of
the first month at twilight *is* the
LORD's Passover.
6 'And on the fifteenth day
of the same month *is* the Feast
of Unleavened Bread to the

18 [a]Lev. 1:2, 3, 10 [1]*brings his offering*
19 [a]Lev. 1:3
20 [a]Deut. 15:21; 17:1
21 [a]Lev. 3:1, 6 [b]Num. 15:3, 8
22 [a]Mal. 1:8 [b]Lev. 1:9, 13; 3:3, 5 [1]*running sore*
23 [a]Lev. 21:18
25 [a]Num. 15:15, 16 [b]Lev. 21:6, 17 [c]Mal. 1:14
27 [a]Ex. 22:30
28 [a]Deut. 22:6, 7
29 [a]Lev. 7:12
30 [a]Lev. 7:15
31 [a]Deut. 4:40
32 [a]Lev. 18:21 [b]Lev. 10:3 [c]Lev. 20:8 [1]*treated as holy*
33 [a]Lev. 19:36, 37

CHAPTER 23

2 [a]Ex. 12:16
3 [a]Luke 13:14
4 [a]Ex. 23:14–16
5 [a]Ex. 12:1–28

LORD; seven days you must eat
unleavened bread.
7 [a]'On the first day you shall
have a holy convocation; you
shall do no [1]customary work on
it.
8 'But you shall offer an offering made by fire to the LORD
for seven days. The seventh day
shall be a holy convocation; you
shall do no customary work *on
it.*' "
9 And the LORD spoke to Moses, saying,
10 "Speak to the children of
Israel, and say to them: [a]'When
you come into the land which I
give to you, and reap its harvest,
then you shall bring a sheaf of
[b]the firstfruits of your harvest to
the priest.
11 'He shall [a]wave the sheaf before the LORD, to be accepted on
your behalf; on the day after the
Sabbath the priest shall wave it.
12 'And you shall offer on that
day, when you wave the sheaf, a
male lamb of the first year, without blemish, as a burnt offering
to the LORD.
13 'Its grain offering *shall be*
two-tenths *of an ephah* of fine
flour mixed with oil, an offering made by fire to the LORD, for
a [1]sweet aroma; and its drink
offering *shall be* of wine, one-
fourth of a hin.
14 'You shall eat neither bread
nor parched grain nor fresh
grain until the same day that
you have brought an offering to
your God; *it shall be* a statute
forever throughout your generations in all your dwellings.
15 'And you shall count for
yourselves from the day after
the Sabbath, from the day that
you brought the sheaf of the
wave offering: seven Sabbaths
shall be completed.
16 'Count [a]fifty days to the day
after the seventh Sabbath; then
you shall offer [b]a new grain offering to the LORD.
17 'You shall bring from your
dwellings two wave *loaves* of
two-tenths *of an ephah.* They
shall be of fine flour; they shall
be baked with leaven. *They are*
[a]the firstfruits to the LORD.
18 'And you shall offer with
the bread seven lambs of the
first year, without blemish, one
young bull, and two rams. They
shall be *as* a burnt offering to
the LORD, with their grain offering and their drink offerings, an
offering made by fire for a sweet
aroma to the LORD.
19 'Then you shall sacrifice [a]one
kid of the goats as a sin offering,
and two male lambs of the first
year as a sacrifice of a [b]peace
offering.
20 'The priest shall wave them
with the bread of the firstfruits
as a wave offering before the
LORD, with the two lambs. [a]They
shall be holy to the LORD for the
priest.
21 'And you shall proclaim on
the same day *that* it is a holy
convocation to you. You shall
do no customary work *on it. It
shall be* a statute forever in all
your dwellings throughout your
generations.
22 [a]'When you reap the harvest of your land, you shall not
wholly reap the corners of your
field when you reap, nor shall
you gather any gleaning from
your harvest. You shall leave
them for the poor and for the
stranger: I *am* the LORD your
God.' "

7 [a]Ex. 12:16 [1]*occupational*
10 [a]Ex. 23:19; 34:26 [b][Rom. 11:16]
11 [a]Ex. 29:24
13 [1]*pleasing*
16 [a]Acts 2:1 [b]Num. 28:26
17 [a]Num. 15:17–21
19 [a]Num. 28:30 [b]Lev. 3:1
20 [a]Deut. 18:4
22 [a]Lev. 19:9, 10

23 Then the LORD spoke to Moses, saying,
24 "Speak to the children of
Israel, saying: 'In the [a]seventh
month, on the first *day* of the
month, you shall have a sabbath-
rest, [b]a memorial of blowing of
trumpets, a holy convocation.
25 'You shall do no customary
work *on it;* and you shall offer
an offering made by fire to the
LORD.' "
26 And the LORD spoke to Moses, saying:
27 [a]"Also the tenth *day* of this
seventh month *shall be* the Day
of Atonement. It shall be a holy
convocation for you; you shall
afflict your souls, and offer an
offering made by fire to the
LORD.
28 "And you shall do no work on
that same day, for it *is* the Day of
Atonement, [a]to make atonement
for you before the LORD your
God.
29 "For any person who is not
[a]afflicted *in soul* on that same
day [b]shall be cut off from his
people.
30 "And any person who does
any work on that same day,
[a]that person I will destroy from
among his people.
31 "You shall do no manner of
work; *it shall be* a statute forever throughout your generations in all your dwellings.
32 "It *shall be* to you a sabbath
of *solemn* rest, and you shall [1]af-
flict your souls; on the ninth *day*
of the month at evening, from
evening to evening, you shall
[2]celebrate your sabbath."
33 Then the LORD spoke to Moses, saying,
34 "Speak to the children of
Israel, saying: [a]'The fifteenth
day of this seventh month *shall
be* the Feast of Tabernacles *for*
seven days to the LORD.
35 'On the first day *there shall
be* a holy convocation. You shall
do no customary work *on it.*
36 '*For* seven days you shall offer an [a]offering made by fire to
the LORD. [b]On the eighth day you
shall have a holy convocation,
and you shall offer an offering
made by fire to the LORD. It *is* a
[c]sacred[1] assembly, *and* you shall
do no customary work *on it.*
37 [a]'These *are* the feasts of the
LORD which you shall proclaim
to be holy convocations, to offer an offering made by fire to
the LORD, a burnt offering and
a grain offering, a sacrifice and
drink offerings, everything on
its day—
38 [a]'besides the Sabbaths of the
LORD, besides your gifts, besides
all your vows, and besides all
your freewill offerings which
you give to the LORD.
39 'Also on the fifteenth day of
the seventh month, when you
have [a]gathered in the fruit of the
land, you shall keep the feast
of the LORD *for* seven days; on
the first day *there shall be* a
sabbath-*rest,* and on the eighth
day a sabbath-*rest.*
40 'And [a]you shall take for yourselves on the first day the [1]fruit
of beautiful trees, branches of
palm trees, the boughs of leafy
trees, and willows of the brook;
[b]and you shall rejoice before the
LORD your God for seven days.
41 [a]'You shall keep it as a feast
to the LORD for seven days in the
year. *It shall be* a statute forever
in your generations. You shall celebrate it in the seventh month.
42 [a]'You shall dwell in [1]booths

24 [a]Num. 29:1 [b]Lev. 25:9
27 [a]Num. 29:7
28 [a]Lev. 16:34
29 [a]Jer. 31:9 [b]Num. 5:2
30 [a]Lev. 20:3–6
32 [1]*humble yourselves* [2]*observe your sabbath*
34 [a]Num. 29:12
36 [a]Num. 29:12–34 [b]Num. 29:35–38 [c]Deut. 16:8 [1]*solemn*
37 [a]Lev. 23:2, 4
38 [a]Num. 29:39
39 [a]Ex. 23:16
40 [a]Neh. 8:15 [b]Deut. 12:7; 16:14, 15 [1]*foliage*
41 [a]Num. 29:12
42 [a][Is. 4:6] [1]*tabernacles;* shelters made of boughs

diminish its price; for he sells to
you *according* to the number *of*
the years of the crops.
17 'Therefore [a]you shall not [1]op-
press one another, [b]but you shall
fear your God; for I *am* the LORD
your God.
18 [a]'So you shall observe My
statutes and keep My judgments,
and perform them; [b]and you will
dwell in the land in safety.
19 'Then the land will yield its
fruit, and [a]you will eat your fill,
and dwell there in safety.
20 'And if you say, [a]"What shall
we eat in the seventh year, since
[b]we shall not sow nor gather in
our produce?"
21 'Then I will [a]command My
blessing on you in the [b]sixth
year, and it will bring forth produce enough for three years.
22 [a]'And you shall sow in the
eighth year, and eat [b]old produce until the ninth year; until
its produce comes in, you shall
eat of the old *harvest*.
23 'The land shall not be sold
permanently, for [a]the land *is*
Mine; for you *are* [b]strangers and
sojourners with Me.
24 'And in all the land of your
possession you shall grant redemption of the land.
25 [a]'If one of your brethren becomes poor, and has sold *some*
of his possession, and if [b]his
redeeming relative comes to redeem it, then he may redeem
what his brother sold.
26 'Or if the man has no one
to redeem it, but he himself becomes able to redeem it,
27 'then [a]let him count the years
since its sale, and restore the remainder to the man to whom he
sold it, that he may return to his
possession.
28 'But if he is not able to have
it restored to himself, then what
was sold shall remain in the hand
of him who bought it until the
Year of Jubilee; [a]and in the Jubilee it shall be released, and he
shall return to his possession.
29 'If a man sells a house in a
walled city, then he may redeem
it within a whole year after it is
sold; *within* a full year he may
redeem it.
30 'But if it is not redeemed
within the space of a full year,
then the house in the walled
city shall belong permanently to
him who bought it, throughout
his generations. It shall not be
released in the Jubilee.
31 'However the houses of villages which have no wall around
them shall be counted as the
fields of the country. They may
be redeemed, and they shall be
released in the Jubilee.
32 'Nevertheless [a]the cities of
the Lē′vītes, *and* the houses
in the cities of their possession,
the Lē′vītes may redeem at any
time.
33 'And if a man purchases a
house from the Lē′vītes, then the
house that was sold in the city of
his possession shall be released
in the Jubilee; for the houses in
the cities of the Lē′vītes *are* their
possession among the children
of Israel.
34 'But [a]the field of the common-land of their cities may not
be [b]sold, for it *is* their perpetual
possession.
35 'If one of your brethren becomes poor, and [1]falls into poverty among you, then you shall
[a]help him, like a stranger or a
sojourner, that he may live with
you.

17 [a]Lev. 25:14 [b]Lev. 19:14, 32; 25:43 [1]*mistreat*
18 [a]Lev. 19:37 [b]Deut. 12:10
19 [a]Lev. 26:5
20 [a]Matt. 6:25, 31 [b]Lev. 25:4, 5
21 [a]Deut. 28:8 [b]Ex. 16:29
22 [a]2 Kin. 19:29 [b]Josh. 5:11
23 [a]Ex. 19:5 [b]Ps. 39:12
25 [a]Ruth 2:20; 4:4, 6 [b]Ruth 3:2, 9, 12
27 [a]Lev. 25:50–52
28 [a]Lev. 25:10, 13
32 [a]Num. 35:1–8
34 [a]Num. 35:2–5 [b]Acts 4:36, 37
35 [a]Deut. 15:7–11; 24:14, 15 [1]Lit. *his hand fails*

36 [a]'Take no usury or interest
from him; but [b]fear your God,
that your brother may live with
you.
37 'You shall not lend him your
money for usury, nor lend him
your food at a profit.
38 [a]'I *am* the LORD your God,
who brought you out of the land
of Egypt, to give you the land of
Cā'naan *and* to be your God.
39 'And if *one of* your brethren *who dwells* by you becomes
poor, and sells himself to you,
you shall not compel him to
serve as a slave.
40 'As a hired servant *and* a
sojourner he shall be with you,
and shall serve you until the
Year of Jubilee.
41 'And *then* he shall depart
from you—he and his children
[a]with him—and shall return to
his own family. He shall return
to the possession of his fathers.
42 'For they *are* [a]My servants,
whom I brought out of the land
of Egypt; they shall not be sold
as slaves.
43 [a]'You shall not rule over him
[b]with [1]rigor, but you [c]shall fear
your God.
44 'And as for your male and
female slaves whom you may
have—from the nations that are
around you, from them you may
buy male and female slaves.
45 'Moreover you may buy [a]the
children of the strangers who
dwell among you, and their families who are with you, which
they beget in your land; and they
shall become your property.
46 'And [a]you may take them as
an inheritance for your children
after you, to inherit *them as* a
possession; they shall be your
permanent slaves. But regarding

36 [a]Ex. 22:25 [b]Neh. 5:9
38 [a]Lev. 11:45; 22:32, 33
41 [a]Ex. 21:3
42 [a][Rom. 6:22]
43 [a]Eph. 6:9 [b]Ex. 1:13, 14 [c]Mal. 3:5 [1]*severity*
45 [a][Is. 56:3, 6, 7]
46 [a]Is. 14:2
50 [a]Job 7:1

your brethren, the children of Israel, you shall not rule over one
another with rigor.
47 'Now if a sojourner or
stranger close to you becomes
rich, and *one of* your brethren *who dwells* by him becomes
poor, and sells himself to the
stranger *or* sojourner close
to you, or to a member of the
stranger's family,
48 'after he is sold he may be redeemed again. One of his brothers may redeem him;
49 'or his uncle or his uncle's
son may redeem him; or *anyone*
who is near of kin to him in his
family may redeem him; or if he
is able he may redeem himself.
50 'Thus he shall reckon with
him who bought him: The price
of his release shall be according
to the number of years, from the
year that he was sold to him until the Year of Jubilee; *it shall be*
[a]according to the time of a hired
servant for him.
51 'If *there are* still many years
remaining, according to them he
shall repay the price of his redemption from the money with
which he was bought.
52 'And if there remain but a
few years until the Year of Jubilee, then he shall reckon with
him, *and* according to his years
he shall repay him the price of
his redemption.
53 'He shall be with him as
a yearly hired servant, and he
shall not rule with rigor over
him in your sight.
54 'And if he is not redeemed in
these *years,* then he shall be released in the Year of Jubilee—he
and his children with him.
55 'For the children of Israel
are servants to Me; they *are* My

servants whom I brought out of
the land of Egypt: I *am* the LORD
your God.

26 'You shall [a]not make idols
for yourselves;
neither a carved image nor
a *sacred* pillar shall you
rear up for yourselves;
nor shall you set up an engraved stone in your land,
to bow down to it;
for I *am* the LORD your God.
2 [a]You shall [1]keep My Sabbaths and reverence My
sanctuary:
I *am* the LORD.

3 [a]'If you walk in My statutes and
keep My commandments,
and perform them,
4 [a]then I will give you rain in
its season, [b]the land shall
yield its produce, and the
trees of the field shall
yield their fruit.
5 [a]Your threshing shall last till
the time of vintage, and
the vintage shall last till
the time of sowing;
you shall eat your bread to
the full, and [b]dwell in
your land safely.
6 [a]I will give peace in the land,
and [b]you shall lie down,
and none will make *you*
afraid;
I will rid the land of [c]evil[1]
beasts,
and [d]the sword will not go
through your land.
7 You will chase your enemies,
and they shall fall by the
sword before you.
8 [a]Five of you shall chase a
hundred, and a hundred
of you shall put ten thousand to flight;
your enemies shall fall by
the sword before you.

9 'For I will [a]look on you favorably and [b]make you fruitful, multiply you and confirm My [c]covenant with
you.
10 You shall eat the [a]old harvest, and clear out the old
because of the new.
11 [a]I will set My [1]tabernacle
among you, and My soul
shall not abhor you.
12 [a]I will walk among you and
be your God, and you
shall be My people.
13 I *am* the LORD your God, who
brought you out of the
land of Egypt, that *you*
should not be their slaves;
I have broken the bands of
your [a]yoke and made you
walk [1]upright.

14 'But if you do not obey Me,
and do not observe all
these commandments,
15 and if you despise My statutes, or if your soul abhors My judgments, so
that you do not perform
all My commandments,
but break My covenant,
16 I also will do this to you:
I will even appoint terror
over you, [a]wasting disease and fever which
shall [b]consume the eyes
and [c]cause sorrow of
heart.
And [d]you shall sow your seed
[1]in vain, for your enemies
shall eat it.
17 I will [1]set [a]My face against
you, and [b]you shall be defeated by your enemies.

CHAPTER 26
1 [a]Ex. 20:4, 5
2 [a]Lev. 19:30 [1]*observe*
3 [a]Deut. 28:1–14
4 [a]Is. 30:23 [b]Ps. 67:6
5 [a]Amos 9:13 [b]Lev. 25:18, 19
6 [a]Is. 45:7 [b]Job 11:19 [c]2 Kin. 17:25 [d]Ezek. 14:17 [1]*wild beasts*
8 [a]Deut. 32:30
9 [a]Ex. 2:25 [b]Gen. 17:6, 7 [c]Gen. 17:1–7
10 [a]Lev. 25:22
11 [a]Ex. 25:8; 29:45, 46 [1]*dwelling place*
12 [a][2 Cor. 6:16]
13 [a]Gen. 27:40 [1]*erect*
16 [a]Deut. 28:22 [b]1 Sam. 2:33 [c]Ezek. 24:23; 33:10 [d]Judg. 6:3–6 [1]*without profit*
17 [a]Ps. 34:16 [b]Deut. 28:25 [1]*oppose you*

[c]Those who hate you shall
reign over you, and you
shall [d]flee when no one
pursues you.

18 'And after all this, if you do
not obey Me, then I will
punish you [a]seven times
more for your sins.
19 I will [a]break the pride of your
power;
I [b]will make your heavens like
iron and your earth like
bronze.
20 And your [a]strength shall be
spent in vain;
for your [b]land shall not yield
its produce, nor shall the
trees of the land yield
their fruit.

21 'Then, if you walk contrary
to Me, and are not will-
ing to obey Me, I will
bring on you seven times
more plagues, according
to your sins.
22 [a]I will also send wild beasts
among you, which shall
rob you of your children,
destroy your livestock, and
make you few in number;
and [b]your highways shall be
desolate.

23 'And if [a]by these things you
are not reformed by Me,
but walk contrary to Me,
24 [a]then I also will walk contrary
to you, and I will punish
you yet seven times for
your sins.
25 And [a]I will bring a sword
against you that will ex-
ecute the vengeance of
the covenant;
when you are gathered to-
gether within your cities
[b]I will send pestilence
among you;
and you shall be delivered into
the hand of the enemy.
26 [a]When I have cut off your supply of bread, ten women
shall bake your bread in
one oven, and they shall
bring back your bread by
weight, [b]and you shall eat
and not be satisfied.

27 'And after all this, if you do
not obey Me, but walk
contrary to Me,
28 then I also will walk contrary
to you in fury;
and I, even I, will chastise
you seven times for your
sins.
29 [a]You[1] shall eat the flesh of
your sons, and you shall
eat the flesh of your
daughters.
30 [a]I will destroy your high
places, cut down your
incense altars, and cast
your carcasses on the lifeless forms of your idols;
and My soul shall abhor
you.
31 I will lay your [a]cities waste
and [b]bring your sanctu-
aries to desolation, and
I will not [c]smell the fragrance of your [1]sweet
aromas.
32 [a]I will bring the land to desolation, and your enemies
who dwell in it shall be
astonished at it.
33 [a]I will scatter you among the
nations and draw out a
sword after you;
your land shall be desolate
and your cities waste.
34 [a]Then the land shall enjoy its
sabbaths as long as it lies

17 [c]Ps. 106:41 [d]Prov. 28:1
18 [a]1 Sam. 2:5
19 [a]Is. 25:11 [b]Deut. 28:23
20 [a]Ps. 127:1 [b]Gen. 4:12
22 [a]Deut. 32:24 [b]Judg. 5:6
23 [a]Amos 4:6–12
24 [a]Lev. 26:28, 41
25 [a]Ezek. 5:17 [b]Deut. 28:21
26 [a]Ps. 105:16 [b]Mic. 6:14
29 [a]2 Kin. 6:28, 29 [1]In time of famine
30 [a]2 Chr. 34:3
31 [a]2 Kin. 25:4, 10 [b]Ps. 74:7 [c]Is. 1:11–15 [1]*pleasing*
32 [a]Jer. 9:11; 18:16
33 [a]Deut. 4:27
34 [a]2 Chr. 36:21

desolate and you *are* in
your enemies' land;
then the land shall rest and
enjoy its sabbaths.
35 As long as *it* lies desolate it
shall rest—
for the time it did not rest on
your [a]sabbaths when you
dwelt in it.

36 'And as for those of you
who are left, I will send
[a]faintness[1] into their
hearts in the lands of
their enemies;
the sound of a shaken leaf
shall cause them to flee;
they shall flee as though
fleeing from a sword, and
they shall fall when no
one pursues.
37 [a]They shall stumble over one
another, as it were before
a sword, when no one
pursues;
and [b]you shall have no *power*
to stand before your
enemies.
38 You shall [a]perish among the
nations, and the land of
your enemies shall eat
you up.
39 And those of you who are
left [a]shall [1]waste away in
their iniquity in your enemies' lands;
also in their [b]fathers' iniquities, which are with them,
they shall waste away.

40 '*But* [a]if they confess their iniquity and the iniquity of
their fathers, with their
unfaithfulness in which
they were unfaithful to
Me, and that they also
have walked contrary
to Me,
41 and *that* I also have walked
contrary to them and have
brought them into the
land of their enemies;
if their [a]uncircumcised hearts
are [b]humbled, and they
[c]accept their guilt—
42 then I will [a]remember My
covenant with Jacob,
and My covenant with
Isaac and My covenant
with Abraham I will
remember;
I will [b]remember the land.
43 [a]The land also shall be left
empty by them, and will
enjoy its sabbaths while
it lies desolate without
them;
they will accept their guilt,
because they [b]despised
My judgments and be-
cause their soul abhorred
My statutes.
44 Yet for all that, when they
are in the land of their
enemies, [a]I will not cast
them away, nor shall I
abhor them, to utterly destroy them and break My
covenant with them;
for I *am* the LORD their God.
45 But [a]for their sake I will remember the covenant of
their ancestors, [b]whom I
brought out of the land
of Egypt [c]in the sight of
the nations, that I might
be their God:
I *am* the LORD.' "

46 [a]These *are* the statutes and
judgments and laws which the
LORD made between Himself and
the children of Israel [b]on Mount
Sinai by the hand of Moses.

27 Now the LORD spoke to
Moses, saying,

35 [a]Lev. 25:2
36 [a]Ezek. 21:7, 12, 15 [1]*fear*
37 [a]1 Sam. 14:15, 16 [b]Josh. 7:12, 13
38 [a]Deut. 4:26
39 [a]Ezek. 4:17; 33:10 [b]Ex. 34:7 [1]*rot away*
40 [a]Neh. 9:2
41 [a]Acts 7:51 [b]2 Chr. 12:6, 7, 12 [c]Dan. 9:7
42 [a]Ex. 2:24; 6:5 [b]Ps. 136:23
43 [a]Lev. 26:34, 35 [b]Lev. 26:15
44 [a]Deut. 4:31
45 [a][Rom. 11:28] [b]Lev. 22:33; 25:38 [c]Ps. 98:2
46 [a][John 1:17] [b]Lev. 25:1

2 "Speak to the children of
Israel, and say to them: [a]'When
a man [1]consecrates by a vow
certain persons to the LORD, according to your [2]valuation,
3 'if your valuation is of a male
from twenty years old up to
sixty years old, then your valuation shall be fifty shekels of
silver, [a]according to the shekel
of the sanctuary.
4 'If it *is* a female, then your valuation shall be thirty shekels;
5 'and if from five years old up
to twenty years old, then your
valuation for a male shall be
twenty shekels, and for a female
ten shekels;
6 'and if from a month old
up to five years old, then your
valuation for a male shall be
five shekels of silver, and for a
female your valuation shall be
three shekels of silver;
7 'and if from sixty years old
and above, if *it is* a male, then
your valuation shall be fifteen
shekels, and for a female ten
shekels.
8 'But if he is too poor to pay
your valuation, then he shall
present himself before the priest,
and the priest shall set a value
for [a]him; according to the ability of him who vowed, the priest
shall value him.
9 'If *it is* an animal that men
may bring as an offering to the
LORD, all that *anyone* gives to
the LORD shall be holy.
10 'He shall not substitute it
or exchange it, good for bad or
bad for good; and if he at all exchanges animal for animal, then
both it and the one exchanged
for it shall be [a]holy.
11 'If *it is* an unclean animal
which they do not offer as a
sacrifice to the LORD, then he
shall present the animal before
the priest;
12 'and the priest shall set a
value for it, whether it is good
or bad; as you, the priest, value
it, so it shall be.
13 [a]'But if he *wants* at all *to*
redeem it, then he must add one-
fifth to your valuation.
14 'And when a man [1]dedicates
his house *to be* holy to the LORD,
then the priest shall set a value
for it, whether it is good or bad;
as the priest values it, so it shall
stand.
15 'If he who dedicated it *wants*
to [1]redeem his house, then he
must add one-fifth of the money
of your valuation to it, and it
shall be his.
16 'If a man [1]dedicates to the
LORD *part* of a field of his possession, then your valuation shall
be according to the seed for it.
A homer of barley seed *shall be*
valued at fifty shekels of silver.
17 'If he dedicates his field from
the Year of Jubilee, according to
your valuation it shall stand.
18 'But if he dedicates his field
after the Jubilee, then the priest
shall [a]reckon to him the money
due according to the years that
remain till the Year of Jubilee,
and it shall be deducted from
your valuation.
19 'And if he who dedicates the
field ever wishes to redeem it,
then he must add one-fifth of
the money of your valuation to
it, and it shall belong to him.
20 'But if he does not want to
redeem the field, or if he has
sold the field to another man, it
shall not be redeemed anymore;
21 'but the field, [a]when it is
released in the Jubilee, shall be

CHAPTER 27

2 [a]Num. 6:2 [1]Or *makes a difficult or extraordinary vow* [2]*appraisal*

3 [a]Ex. 30:13

8 [a]Lev. 5:11; 14:21–24

10 [a]Lev. 27:33

13 [a]Lev. 6:5; 22:14; 27:15, 19

14 [1]*sets apart*

15 [1]*buy back*

16 [1]*sets apart*

18 [a]Lev. 25:15, 16, 28

21 [a]Lev. 25:10, 28, 31

holy to the LORD, as a [b]devoted
field; it shall be [c]the possession
of the priest.
22 'And if a man dedicates to
the LORD a field which he has
bought, which is not the field of
[a]his possession,
23 'then the priest shall reckon
to him the worth of your valuation, up to the Year of Jubilee,
and he shall give your valuation
on that day *as* a holy *offering* to
the LORD.
24 [a]'In the Year of Jubilee the
field shall return to him from
whom it was bought, to the
one who *owned* the land as a
possession.
25 'And all your valuations shall
be according to the shekel of the
sanctuary: [a]twenty gerahs to the
shekel.
26 'But the [a]firstborn of the animals, which should be the LORD's
firstborn, no man shall dedicate;
whether *it is* an ox or sheep, it *is*
the LORD's.
27 'And if *it is* an unclean animal, then he shall redeem *it*
according to your valuation,
and [a]shall add one-fifth to it;
or if it is not redeemed, then it
shall be sold according to your
valuation.
28 [a]'Nevertheless no [1]devoted
offering that a man may devote
to the LORD of all that he has,
both man and beast, or the field
of his possession, shall be sold
or redeemed; every devoted *offering is* most holy to the LORD.
29 [a]'No person under the ban,
who may become doomed to
destruction among men, shall
be redeemed, *but* shall surely be
put to death.
30 'And [a]all the tithe of the land,
whether of the seed of the land
or of the fruit of the tree, *is* the
LORD's. It *is* holy to the LORD.
31 [a]'If a man wants at all to redeem *any* of his tithes, he shall
add one-fifth to it.
32 'And concerning the tithe of
the herd or the flock, of whatever [a]passes under the rod, the
tenth one shall be holy to the
LORD.
33 'He shall not inquire whether
it is good or bad, [a]nor shall he
exchange it; and if he exchanges
it at all, then both it and the one
exchanged for it shall be holy; it
shall not be redeemed.' "
34 [a]These *are* the commandments which the LORD com-
manded Moses for the children
of Israel on Mount [b]Sinai.

21 [b]Lev. 27:28 [c]Num. 18:14
22 [a]Lev. 25:10, 25
24 [a]Lev. 25:10–13, 28
25 [a]Ex. 30:13
26 [a]Ex. 13:2, 12; 22:30
27 [a]Lev. 27:11, 12
28 [a]Josh. 6:17–19 [1]Given exclusively and irrevocably
29 [a]Num. 21:2
30 [a]Gen. 28:22
31 [a]Lev. 27:13
32 [a]Jer. 33:13
33 [a]Lev. 27:10
34 [a]Lev. 26:46 [b][Heb. 12:18–29]

The Fourth Book of Moses Called

NUMBERS

NUMBERS is the book of wanderings. It takes its name from the two numberings of the Israelites—the first at Mount Sinai and the second on the plains of Moab. Most of the book, however, describes Israel's experiences as they wander in the wilderness. The lesson of Numbers is clear. While it may be necessary to pass through wilderness experiences, one does not have to live there. For Israel, an eleven-day journey became a forty-year agony.

The title of Numbers comes from the first word in the Hebrew text, *Wayyedabber*, "And He Said." Jewish writings, however, usually refer to it by the fifth Hebrew word in 1:1, *Bemidbar*, "In the Wilderness," which more nearly indicates the content of the book. The Greek title in the Septuagint is *Arithmoi*, "Numbers." The Latin Vulgate followed this title and translated it *Liber Numeri*, "Book of Numbers." These titles are based on the two numberings: the generation of Exodus (Num. 1) and the generation that grew up in the wilderness and conquered Canaan (Num. 26). Numbers has also been called the "Book of the Journeyings," the "Book of the Murmurings," and the "Fourth Book of Moses."

CHAPTER 1

NOW the LORD spoke to Moses
[a]in the Wilderness of Sinai,
[b]in the tabernacle of meeting,
on the [c]first *day* of the second
month, in the second year after
they had come out of the land of
Egypt, saying:
2 [a]"Take a census of all the
congregation of the children of
Israel, by their families, by their
fathers' houses, according to the
number of names, every male
[b]individually,
3 "from [a]twenty years old and
above—all who *are able to* go
to war in Israel. You and Aaron
shall number them by their
armies.
4 "And with you there shall be
a man from every tribe, each one
the head of his father's house.
5 "These are the names of the
men who shall stand with you:
from Reuben, E·lī′zur the son of
Shed′ē·ur;
6 "from Sim′ē·on, She·lū′mi·el
the son of Zū·ri·shad′daī;
7 "from Judah, Nah′shon the
son of Am·min′a·dab;
8 "from Is′sa·char, Ne·than′el
the son of Zū′ar;
9 "from Zeb′ū·lun, E·lī′ab the
son of Hē′lon;
10 "from the sons of Joseph:
from Ē′phra·im, E·lish′a·ma
the son of Am·mī′hud; from
Ma·nas′seh, Ga·mā′li·el the son
of Pe·dah′zur;
11 "from Benjamin, A·bī′dan the
son of Gid·ē·ō′ni;
12 "from Dan, Ā·hī·ē′zer the son
of Am·mi·shad′daī;
13 "from Ash′er, Pā′gi·el the son
of Oc′ran;
14 "from Gad, E·lī′a·saph the
son of [a]Deū′el;[1]
15 "from Naph′ta·lī, A·hī′ra the
son of Ē′nan."
16 [a]These *were* [b]chosen[1] from
the congregation, leaders of

1 [a]Ex. 19:1 [b]Ex. 25:22 [c]Num. 9:1; 10:11
2 [a]Num. 26:2, 63, 64 [b]Ex. 30:12, 13; 38:26
3 [a]Ex. 30:14; 38:26
14 [a]Num. 7:42 [1]*Reuel*, Num. 2:14
16 [a]Num. 7:2 [b]Num. 16:2 [1]*called*

their fathers' tribes, [c]heads of
the divisions in Israel.
17 Then Moses and Aaron took
these men who had been [1]men-
tioned [a]by name,
18 and they assembled all the
congregation together on the first
day of the second month; and they
recited their [a]ancestry by families, by their fathers' houses, according to the number of names,
from twenty years old and above,
each one individually.
19 As the LORD commanded
Moses, so he numbered them in
the Wilderness of Sinai.
20 Now the [a]children of Reuben, Israel's oldest son, their
genealogies by their families, by
their fathers' house, according
to the number of names, every
male individually, from twenty
years old and above, all who
were able to go to war:
21 those who were numbered of
the tribe of Reuben *were* forty-
six thousand five hundred.
22 From the [a]children of Sim'-
ē·on, their genealogies by their
families, by their fathers' house,
of those who were numbered, according to the number of names,
every male individually, from
twenty years old and above, all
who *were able to* go to war:
23 those who were numbered of
the tribe of Sim'ē·on *were* fifty-
nine thousand three hundred.
24 From the [a]children of Gad,
their genealogies by their families, by their fathers' house, according to the number of names,
from twenty years old and above,
all who *were able to* go to war:
25 those who were numbered of
the tribe of Gad *were* forty-five
thousand six hundred and fifty.
26 From the [a]children of Judah,
their genealogies by their families, by their fathers' house, according to the number of names,
from twenty years old and above,
all who *were able to* go to war:
27 those who were numbered of
the tribe of Judah *were* [a]seventy-
four thousand six hundred.
28 From the [a]children of Is'-
sa·char, their genealogies by
their families, by their fathers'
house, according to the number
of names, from twenty years old
and above, all who *were able to*
go to war:
29 those who were numbered of
the tribe of Is'sa·char *were* fifty-
four thousand four hundred.
30 From the [a]children of Zeb'-
ū·lun, their genealogies by their
families, by their fathers' house,
according to the number of
names, from twenty years old
and above, all who *were able to*
go to war:
31 those who were numbered of
the tribe of Zeb'ū·lun *were* fifty-
seven thousand four hundred.
32 From the sons of Joseph, the
[a]children of Ē'phra·im, their genealogies by their families, by
their fathers' house, according
to the number of names, from
twenty years old and above, all
who *were able to* go to war:
33 those who were numbered of
the tribe of Ē'phra·im *were* forty
thousand five hundred.
34 From the [a]children of Ma-
nas'seh, their genealogies by
their families, by their fathers'
house, according to the number
of names, from twenty years old
and above, all who *were able to*
go to war:
35 those who were numbered
of the tribe of Ma·nas'seh *were*
thirty-two thousand two hundred.

16 [c]Ex. 18:21, 25
17 [a]Is. 43:1 [1]*designated*
18 [a]Ezra 2:59
20 [a]Num. 2:10, 11; 26:5–11; 32:6, 15, 21, 29
22 [a]Num. 2:12, 13; 26:12–14
24 [a]Num. 26:15–18
26 [a]2 Sam. 24:9
27 [a]2 Chr. 17:14
28 [a]Num. 2:5, 6
30 [a]Num. 2:7, 8; 26:26, 27
32 [a]Num. 26:28–37
34 [a]Num. 2:20, 21; 26:28–34

36 From the [a]children of Benjamin, their genealogies by their
families, by their fathers' house,
according to the number of
names, from twenty years old
and above, all who *were able to*
go to war:
37 those who were numbered of
the tribe of Benjamin *were* thirty-
five thousand four hundred.
38 From the [a]children of Dan,
their genealogies by their families, by their fathers' house, according to the number of names,
from twenty years old and above,
all who *were able to* go to war:
39 those who were numbered of
the tribe of Dan *were* sixty-two
thousand seven hundred.
40 From the [a]children of Ash′er,
their genealogies by their families, by their fathers' house, according to the number of names,
from twenty years old and above,
all who *were able to* go to war:
41 those who were numbered
of the tribe of Ash′er *were* forty-
one thousand five hundred.
42 From the children of Naph′-
ta·lī, their genealogies by their
families, by their fathers' house,
according to the number of
names, from twenty years old
and above, all who *were able to*
go to war:
43 those who were numbered of
the tribe of Naph′ta·lī *were* fifty-
three thousand four hundred.
44 [a]These are the ones who
were numbered, whom Moses
and Aaron numbered, with the
leaders of Israel, twelve men,
each one representing his father's house.
45 So all who were numbered of
the children of Israel, by their fathers' houses, from twenty years
old and above, all who *were able*
to go to war in Israel—
46 all who were numbered were
[a]six hundred and three thousand
five hundred and fifty.
47 But [a]the Lē′vītes were not
numbered among them by their
fathers' tribe;
48 for the LORD had spoken to
Moses, saying:
49 [a]"Only the tribe of Levi you
shall not number, nor take a
census of them among the children of Israel;
50 [a]"but you shall appoint the
Lē′vītes over the tabernacle of
the Testimony, over all its furnishings, and over all things that
belong to it; they shall carry the
tabernacle and all its furnishings; they shall attend to it [b]and
camp around the tabernacle.
51 [a]"And when the tabernacle
is to go forward, the Lē′vītes
shall take it down; and when
the tabernacle is to be set up,
the Lē′vītes shall set it [b]up. [c]The
outsider who comes near shall
be put to death.
52 "The children of Israel shall
pitch their tents, [a]everyone by
his own camp, everyone by his
own standard, according to their
armies;
53 [a]"but the Lē′vītes shall camp
around the tabernacle of the
Testimony, that there may be no
[b]wrath on the congregation of
the children of Israel; and the
Lē′vītes shall [c]keep[1] charge of the
tabernacle of the Testimony."
54 Thus the children of Israel
did; according to all that the
LORD commanded Moses, so
they did.

CHAPTER 2

2 And the LORD spoke to Moses and Aaron, saying:
2 [a]"Everyone of the children

36 [a]Num. 26:38–41
38 [a]Gen. 30:6; 46:23
40 [a]Num. 2:27, 28; 26:44–47
44 [a]Num. 26:64
46 [a]Ex. 12:37; 38:26
47 [a]Num. 2:33; 3:14–22; 26:57–62
49 [a]Num. 2:33; 26:62
50 [a]Ex. 38:21 [b]Num. 3:23, 29, 35, 38
51 [a]Num. 4:5–15; 10:17, 21 [b]Num. 10:21 [c]Num. 3:10, 38; 4:15, 19, 20; 18:22
52 [a]Num. 2:2, 34; 24:2
53 [a]Num. 1:50 [b]Lev. 10:6 [c]1 Chr. 23:32 [1]*have in their care*
2 [a]Num. 1:52; 24:2

of Israel shall camp by his own [1]standard, beside the emblems of his father's house; they shall camp [b]some distance from the tabernacle of meeting.
3 "On the [a]east side, toward the rising of the sun, those of the standard of the forces with Judah shall camp according to their armies; and [b]Nah'shon the son of Am·min'a·dab *shall be* the leader of the children of Judah."
4 And his army was numbered at seventy-four thousand six hundred.
5 "Those who camp next to him *shall be* the tribe of Is'sa·char, and Ne·than'el the son of Zū'ar *shall be* the leader of the children of Is'sa·char."
6 And his army was numbered at fifty-four thousand four hundred.
7 "Then *comes* the tribe of Zeb'ū·lun, and E·lī'ab the son of Hē'lon *shall be* the leader of the children of Zeb'ū·lun."
8 And his army was numbered at fifty-seven thousand four hundred.
9 "All who were numbered according to their armies of the forces with Judah, one hundred and eighty-six thousand four hundred—[a]these shall [1]break camp first.
10 "On the [a]south side *shall be* the standard of the forces with Reuben according to their armies, and the leader of the children of Reuben *shall be* E·lī'zur the son of Shed'ē·ur."
11 And his army was numbered at forty-six thousand five hundred.
12 "Those who camp next to him *shall be* the tribe of Sim'ē·on, and the leader of the children of Sim'ē·on *shall be* She·lū'mi·el the son of Zū·ri·shad'daī."
13 And his army was numbered at fifty-nine thousand three hundred.
14 "Then *comes* the tribe of Gad, and the leader of the children of Gad *shall be* E·lī'a·saph the son of [1]Reū'el."
15 And his army was numbered at forty-five thousand six hundred and fifty.
16 "All who were numbered according to their armies of the forces with Reuben, one hundred and fifty-one thousand four hundred and fifty—[a]they shall [1]be the second to break camp.
17 [a]"And the tabernacle of meeting shall move out with the [1]camp of the Lē'vītes [b]in the middle of the [2]camps; as they camp, so they shall move out, everyone in his place, by their [3]standards.
18 "On the west side *shall be* the standard of the forces with Ē'phra·im according to their armies, and the leader of the children of Ē'phra·im *shall be* E·lish'a·ma the son of Am·mī'hud."
19 And his army was numbered at forty thousand five hundred.
20 "Next to him *comes* the tribe of Ma·nas'seh, and the leader of the children of Ma·nas'seh *shall be* Ga·mā'li·el the son of Pe·dah'zur."
21 And his army was numbered at thirty-two thousand two hundred.
22 "Then *comes* the tribe of Benjamin, and the leader of the children of Benjamin *shall be* A·bī'dan the son of Gid·ē·ō'ni."
23 And his army was numbered

2 [b]Josh. 3:4 [1]*banner*
3 [a]Num. 10:5 [b]1 Chr. 2:10
9 [a]Num. 10:14 [1]Lit. *set forth*
10 [a]Num. 10:6
14 [1]*Deuel*, Num. 1:14; 7:42
16 [a]Num. 10:18 [1]Lit. *set forth second*
17 [a]Num. 10:17, 21 [b]Num. 1:53 [1]*company* [2]*whole company* [3]*banners*

at thirty-five thousand four
hundred.
24 “All who were numbered according to their armies of the
forces with Ē′phra·im, one hundred and eight thousand one
hundred—[a]they shall [1]be the
third to break camp.
25 “The [1]standard of the forces
with Dan *shall be* on the north
side according to their armies,
and the leader of the children of
Dan *shall be* Ā·hī·ē′zer the son
of Am·mi·shad′daī.”
26 And his army was numbered
at sixty-two thousand seven
hundred.
27 “Those who camp next to
him *shall be* the tribe of Ash′er,
and the leader of the children of
Ash′er *shall be* Pā′gi·el the son
of Oc′ran.”
28 And his army was num-
bered at forty-one thousand five
hundred.
29 “Then *comes* the tribe of
Naph′ta·lī, and the leader of the
children of Naph′ta·lī *shall be*
A·hī′ra the son of Ē′nan.”
30 And his army was numbered
at fifty-three thousand four
hundred.
31 “All who were numbered
of the forces with Dan, one
hundred and fifty-seven thousand six hundred—[a]they shall
[1]break camp last, with their
[2]standards.”
32 These *are* the ones who were
numbered of the children of Israel by their fathers’ houses. [a]All
who were numbered according
to their armies of the forces *were*
six hundred and three thousand
five hundred and fifty.
33 But [a]the Lē′vītes were not
numbered among the children

24 [a]Num. 10:22 [1]Lit. *set forth third*
25 [1]*banner*
31 [a]Num. 10:25 [1]Lit. *set forth last* [2]*banners*
32 [a]Ex. 38:26
33 [a]Num. 1:47; 26:57–62
34 [a]Num. 1:54 [b]Num. 24:2, 5, 6 [1]*banners*

CHAPTER 3

1 [a]Ex. 6:16–27 [1]Lit. *generations*
2 [a]Ex. 6:23 [b]Num. 26:60, 61
3 [a]Ex. 28:41 [1]Lit. *whose hands he filled*
4 [a]1 Chr. 24:2
6 [a]Num. 8:6–22; 18:1–7
7 [a]Num. 1:50; 8:11, 15, 24, 26
9 [a]Num. 8:19; 18:6, 7

of Israel, just as the LORD commanded Moses.
34 Thus the children of Israel
[a]did according to all that the
LORD commanded Moses; [b]so
they camped by their [1]standards
and so they broke camp, each
one by his family, according to
their fathers’ houses.
3 Now these *are* the [a]records[1]
of Aaron and Moses when
the LORD spoke with Moses on
Mount Sinai.
2 And these *are* the names of
the sons of Aaron: Nā′dab, the
[a]firstborn, and [b]A·bī′hū, El·ē·ā′-
zar, and Ith′a·mar.
3 These *are* the names of the
sons of Aaron, [a]the anointed
priests, [1]whom he consecrated
to minister as priests.
4 [a]Nā′dab and A·bī′hū had
died before the LORD when they
offered profane fire before the
LORD in the Wilderness of Sinai;
and they had no children. So
El·ē·ā′zar and Ith′a·mar ministered as priests in the presence
of Aaron their father.
5 And the LORD spoke to Moses, saying:
6 [a]“Bring the tribe of Levi near,
and present them before Aaron
the priest, that they may serve
him.
7 “And they shall attend to
his needs and the needs of the
whole congregation before the
tabernacle of meeting, to do
[a]the work of the tabernacle.
8 “Also they shall attend to all
the furnishings of the tabernacle
of meeting, and to the needs of
the children of Israel, to do the
work of the tabernacle.
9 “And [a]you shall give the Lē′-
vītes to Aaron and his sons; they

are given entirely to [1]him from
among the children of Israel.
10 "So you shall appoint Aaron
and his sons, [a]and they shall attend to their priesthood; [b]but the
outsider who comes near shall
be put to death."
11 Then the LORD spoke to Moses, saying:
12 "Now behold, [a]I Myself have
taken the Lē′vītes from among
the children of Israel instead of
every firstborn who opens the
womb among the children of Israel. Therefore the Lē′vītes shall
be [b]Mine,
13 "because [a]all the firstborn
are Mine. [b]On the day that I
struck all the firstborn in the
land of Egypt, I sanctified to
Myself all the firstborn in Israel,
both man and beast. They shall
be Mine: I *am* the LORD."
14 Then the LORD spoke to Moses in the Wilderness of Sinai,
saying:
15 "Number the children of
Levi by their fathers' houses, by
their families; you shall number
[a]every male from a month old
and above."
16 So Moses numbered them
according to the [1]word of the
LORD, as he was commanded.
17 [a]These were the sons of Levi
by their names: Ger′shon, Kō′-
hath, and Me·rar′ī.
18 And these *are* the names of
the sons of [a]Ger′shon by their
families: [b]Lib′nī and Shim′ē·ī.
19 And the sons of [a]Kō′hath by
their families: [b]Am′ram, Iz′e·har,
Hē′bron, and Uz′zi·el.
20 [a]And the sons of Me·rar′ī
by their families: Mah′lī and
Mū′shī. These *are* the families
of the Lē′vītes by their fathers'
houses.
21 From Ger′shon *came* the
family of the Lib′nītes and the
family of the Shim′ītes; these
were the families of the Ger′-
shon·ītes.
22 Those who were numbered,
according to the number of all
the males from a month old and
above—of those who were numbered *there were* seven thousand five hundred.
23 [a]The families of the Ger′-
shon·ītes were to camp behind
the tabernacle westward.
24 And the leader of the father's house of the Ger′shon·ītes
was E·lī′a·saph the son of Lā′el.
25 [a]The duties of the children
of Ger′shon in the tabernacle of
meeting *included* [b]the tabernacle, [c]the tent with [d]its covering,
[e]the screen for the door of the
tabernacle of meeting,
26 [a]the screen for the door of
the court, [b]the hangings of the
court which *are* around the tabernacle and the altar, and [c]their
cords, according to all the work
relating to them.
27 [a]From Kō′hath *came* the family of the Am′ram·ītes, the family
of the Iz′har·ītes, the family of
the Hē′bron·ītes, and the family
of the Uz′zi·el·ītes; these *were*
the families of the Kō′hath·ītes.
28 According to the number of
all the males, from a month
old and above, *there were* eight
thousand [1]six hundred [2]keeping
charge of the sanctuary.
29 [a]The families of the children
of Kō′hath were to camp on the
south side of the tabernacle.
30 And the leader of the fathers'
house of the families of the Kō′-
hath·ītes *was* E·li·zā′phan the
son of [a]Uz′zi·el.
31 [a]Their duty *included* [b]the ark,

9 [1]Sam., LXX *Me*
10 [a]Ex. 29:9 [b]Num. 1:51; 3:38; 16:40
12 [a]Num. 3:41; 8:16; 18:6 [b]Num. 3:45; 8:14
13 [a]Ex. 13:2 [b]Num. 8:17
15 [a]Num. 3:39; 26:62
16 [1]Lit. *mouth*
17 [a]Ex. 6:16–22
18 [a]Num. 4:38–41 [b]Ex. 6:17
19 [a]Num. 4:34–37 [b]Ex. 6:18
20 [a]Ex. 6:19
23 [a]Num. 1:53
25 [a]Num. 4:24–26 [b]Ex. 25:9 [c]Ex. 26:1 [d]Ex. 26:7, 14 [e]Ex. 26:36
26 [a]Ex. 27:9, 12, 14, 15 [b]Ex. 27:16 [c]Ex. 35:18
27 [a]1 Chr. 26:23
28 [1]Some LXX mss. *three* [2]*taking care of*
29 [a]Num. 1:53
30 [a]Lev. 10:4
31 [a]Num. 4:15 [b]Ex. 25:10

[c]the table, [d]the lampstand, [e]the
altars, the utensils of the sanctuary with which they ministered,
[f]the screen, and all the work
relating to them.
32 And El·ē·ā′zar the son of
Aaron the priest *was to be* chief
over the leaders of the Lē′vītes,
with oversight of those who kept
charge of the sanctuary.
33 From Me·rar′ī *came* the family of the Mah′lītes and the family of the Mū′shītes; these *were*
the families of Me·rar′ī.
34 And those who were numbered, according to the number
of all the males from a month
old and above, *were* six thousand two hundred.
35 The leader of the fathers’
house of the families of Me·rar′ī
was Zū′ri·el the son of Ab·i·hā′il.
[a]These *were* to camp on the
north side of the tabernacle.
36 And [a]the appointed duty of
the children of Me·rar′ī *included*
the boards of the tabernacle, its
bars, its pillars, its sockets, its
utensils, all the work relating to
them,
37 and the pillars of the court
all around, with their sockets,
their pegs, and their cords.
38 [a]Moreover those who were to
camp before the tabernacle on
the east, before the tabernacle
of meeting, *were* Moses, Aaron,
and his sons, [b]keeping charge of
the sanctuary, [c]to meet the needs
of the children of Israel; but [d]the
outsider who came near was to
be put to death.
39 [a]All who were numbered of
the Lē′vītes, whom Moses and
Aaron numbered at the commandment of the LORD, by their
families, all the males from a
month old and above, *were*
twenty-two thousand.
40 Then the LORD said to Moses: [a]“Number[1] all the firstborn
males of the children of Israel
from a month old and above,
and take the number of their
names.
41 [a]“And you shall take the Lē′-
vītes for Me—I *am* the LORD—instead of all the firstborn among
the children of Israel, and the
livestock of the Lē′vītes instead
of all the firstborn among the
livestock of the children of
Israel.”
42 So Moses numbered all the
firstborn among the children of
Israel, as the LORD commanded
him.
43 And all the firstborn males,
according to the number of
names from a month old and
above, of those who were numbered of them, were twenty-
two thousand two hundred and
seventy-three.
44 Then the LORD spoke to Moses, saying:
45 [a]“Take the Lē′vītes instead of
all the firstborn among the children of Israel, and the livestock
of the Lē′vītes instead of their
livestock. The Lē′vītes shall be
Mine: I *am* the LORD.
46 “And for [a]the redemption of
the two hundred and seventy-
three of the firstborn of the children of Israel, [b]who are more
than the number of the Lē′vītes,
47 “you shall take [a]five shekels
for each one [b]individually; you
shall take *them* in the currency
of the shekel of the sanctuary,
[c]the shekel of twenty gerahs.
48 “And you shall give the
money, with which the excess

31 [c]Ex. 25:23 [d]Ex. 25:31 [e]Ex. 27:1; 30:1 [f]Ex. 26:31–33
35 [a]Num. 1:53; 2:25
36 [a]Num. 4:31, 32
38 [a]Num. 1:53 [b]Num. 18:5 [c]Num. 3:7, 8 [d]Num. 3:10
39 [a]Num. 3:43; 4:48; 26:62
40 [a]Num. 3:15 [1]*Take a census of*
41 [a]Num. 3:12, 45
45 [a]Num. 3:12, 41
46 [a]Ex. 13:13, 15 [b]Num. 3:39, 43
47 [a]Lev. 27:6 [b]Num. 1:2, 18, 20 [c]Ex. 30:13

number of them is redeemed, to
Aaron and his sons."
49 So Moses took the redemption money from those who were
over and above those who were
redeemed by the Lē′vītes.
50 From the firstborn of the
children of Israel he took the
money, [a]one thousand three
hundred and sixty-five *shekels,*
according to the shekel of the
sanctuary.
51 And Moses [a]gave their redemption money to Aaron and
his sons, according to the word
of the LORD, as the LORD commanded Moses.

4

Then the LORD spoke to Moses and Aaron, saying:
2 "Take a census of the sons of
[a]Kō′hath from among the children of Levi, by their families,
by their fathers' house,
3 [a]"from thirty years old and
above, even to fifty years old,
all who enter the service to do
the work in the tabernacle of
meeting.
4 [a]"This *is* the service of the
sons of Kō′hath in the tabernacle of meeting, *relating to* [b]the
most holy things:
5 "When the camp prepares
to journey, Aaron and his sons
shall come, and they shall take
down [a]the covering veil and
cover the [b]ark of the Testimony
with it.
6 "Then they shall put on it a
covering of badger skins, and
spread over *that* a cloth entirely
of [a]blue; and they shall insert
[b]its poles.
7 "On the [a]table of showbread
they shall spread a blue cloth,
and put on it the dishes, the pans,
the bowls, and the [1]pitchers for

50 [a]Num. 3:46, 47

51 [a]Num. 3:48

CHAPTER 4

2 [a]Num. 3:27–32

3 [a]Num. 4:23, 30, 35; 8:24

4 [a]Num. 4:15
[b]Num. 4:19

5 [a]Ex. 26:31
[b]Ex. 25:10, 16

6 [a]Ex. 39:1
[b]Ex. 25:13

7 [a]Ex. 25:23, 29, 30
[b]Lev. 24:5–9
[1]*jars for the drink offering*
[2]Lit. *continual bread*

9 [a]Ex. 25:31
[b]Ex. 25:37, 38

11 [a]Ex. 30:1–5

12 [a]Ex. 25:9

14 [1]*bowls*

15 [a]Deut. 31:9
[b]2 Sam. 6:6, 7

pouring; and the [b]showbread[2]
shall be on it.
8 "They shall spread over them
a scarlet cloth, and cover the
same with a covering of badger
skins; and they shall insert its
poles.
9 "And they shall take a blue
cloth and cover the [a]lampstand
of the light, [b]with its lamps, its
wick-trimmers, its trays, and all
its oil vessels, with which they
service it.
10 "Then they shall put it with
all its utensils in a covering of
badger skins, and put *it* on a
carrying beam.
11 "Over [a]the golden altar they
shall spread a blue cloth, and
cover it with a covering of badger skins; and they shall insert
its poles.
12 "Then they shall take all the
[a]utensils of service with which
they minister in the sanctuary,
put *them* in a blue cloth, cover
them with a covering of badger
skins, and put *them* on a carrying beam.
13 "Also they shall take away
the ashes from the altar, and
spread a purple cloth over it.
14 "They shall put on it all its
implements with which they
minister there—the firepans, the
forks, the shovels, the [1]basins,
and all the utensils of the altar—
and they shall spread on it a
covering of badger skins, and
insert its poles.
15 "And when Aaron and his
sons have finished covering the
sanctuary and all the furnishings of the sanctuary, when the
camp is set to go, then [a]the
sons of Kō′hath shall come to
carry *them;* [b]but they shall not
touch any holy thing, lest they

die. [c]These *are* the things in the
tabernacle of meeting which the
sons of Kō′hath are to carry.
16 "The appointed duty of
El·ē·ā′zar the son of Aaron the
priest *is* [a]the oil for the light, the
[b]sweet incense, [c]the daily grain
offering, the [d]anointing oil, the
oversight of all the tabernacle,
of all that *is* in it, with the sanctuary and its furnishings."
17 Then the LORD spoke to Moses and Aaron, saying:
18 "Do not cut off the tribe of
the families of the Kō′hath·ītes
from among the Lē′vītes;
19 "but do this in regard to
them, that they may live and
not die when they approach [a]the
most holy things: Aaron and his
sons shall go in and [1]appoint
each of them to his service and
his task.
20 [a]"But they shall not go in to
watch while the holy things are
being covered, lest they die."
21 Then the LORD spoke to Moses, saying:
22 "Also take a census of the
sons of [a]Ger′shon, by their fathers' house, by their families.
23 [a]"From thirty years old and
above, even to fifty years old,
you shall number them, all who
enter to perform the service, to
do the work in the tabernacle of
meeting.
24 "This *is* the [a]service of the
families of the Ger′shon·ītes, in
serving and carrying:
25 [a]"They shall carry the
[b]curtains of the tabernacle and
the tabernacle of meeting *with*
its covering, the covering of
[c]badger skins that *is* on it, the
screen for the door of the tabernacle of meeting,
26 "the screen for the door of
the gate of the court, the hangings of the court which *are*
around the tabernacle and altar,
and their cords, all the furnishings for their service and all that
is made for these things: so shall
they serve.
27 "Aaron and his sons shall [1]as-
sign all the service of the sons of
the Ger′shon·ītes, all their tasks
and all their service. And you
shall [2]appoint to them all their
tasks as their duty.
28 "This *is* the service of the
families of the sons of Ger′shon
in the tabernacle of meeting.
And their duties *shall be* [a]under
the [1]authority of Ith′a·mar the
son of Aaron the priest.
29 "*As for* the sons of [a]Me·rar′ī,
you shall number them by their
families and by their fathers'
house.
30 [a]"From thirty years old and
above, even to fifty years old,
you shall number them, everyone who enters the service to
do the work of the tabernacle of
meeting.
31 "And [a]this *is* [b]what they must
carry as all their service for
the tabernacle of meeting: [c]the
boards of the tabernacle, its
bars, its pillars, its sockets,
32 "and the pillars around the
court with their sockets, pegs,
and cords, with all their furnishings and all their service; and
you shall [a]assign *to each man* by
name the items he must carry.
33 "This *is* the service of the
families of the sons of Me·rar′ī,
as all their service for the tabernacle of meeting, under the
[1]authority of Ith′a·mar the son
of Aaron the priest."
34 [a]And Moses, Aaron, and
the leaders of the congregation

15 [c]Num. 3:31
16 [a]Lev. 24:2 [b]Ex. 30:34 [c]Ex. 29:38 [d]Ex. 30:23–25
19 [a]Num. 4:4 [1]*assign*
20 [a]Ex. 19:21
22 [a]Num. 3:22
23 [a]Num. 4:3
24 [a]Num. 7:7
25 [a]Num. 3:25, 26 [b]Ex. 36:8 [c]Ex. 26:14
27 [1]*command* [2]*assign*
28 [a]Num. 4:33 [1]Lit. *hand*
29 [a]Num. 3:33–37
30 [a]Num. 4:3; 8:24–26
31 [a]Num. 3:36, 37 [b]Num. 7:8 [c]Ex. 26:15
32 [a]Ex. 25:9; 38:21
33 [1]Lit. *hand*
34 [a]Num. 4:2

numbered the sons of the Kō′hath·ītes by their families and by their fathers' house,

35 from thirty [a]years old and above, even to fifty years old, everyone who entered the service for work in the tabernacle of meeting;

36 and those who were numbered by their families were two thousand seven hundred and fifty.

37 These *were* the ones who were numbered of the families of the Kō′hath·ītes, all who might serve in the tabernacle of meeting, whom Moses and Aaron numbered according to the commandment of the LORD by the hand of Moses.

38 And those who were numbered of the sons of Ger′shon, by their families and by their fathers' house,

39 from thirty years old and above, even to fifty years old, everyone who entered the service for work in the tabernacle of meeting—

40 those who were numbered by their families, by their fathers' house, were two thousand six hundred and thirty.

41 [a]These *are* the ones who were numbered of the families of the sons of Ger′shon, of all who might serve in the tabernacle of meeting, whom Moses and Aaron numbered according to the commandment of the LORD.

42 Those of the families of the sons of Me·rar′ī who were numbered, by their families, by their fathers' [1]house,

43 from thirty years old and above, even to fifty years old, everyone who entered the service for work in the tabernacle of meeting—

44 those who were numbered by their families were three thousand two hundred.

45 These *are* the ones who were numbered of the families of the sons of Me·rar′ī, whom Moses and Aaron numbered [a]according to the word of the LORD by the hand of Moses.

46 All who were [a]numbered of the Lē′vītes, whom Moses, Aaron, and the leaders of Israel numbered, by their families and by their fathers' houses,

47 [a]from thirty years old and above, even to fifty years old, everyone who came to do the work of service and the work of bearing burdens in the tabernacle of meeting—

48 those who were numbered were eight thousand five hundred and eighty.

49 According to the commandment of the LORD they were numbered by the hand of Moses, [a]each according to his service and according to his task; thus were they numbered by him, [b]as the LORD commanded Moses.

5 And the LORD spoke to Moses, saying:

2 "Command the children of Israel that they put out of the camp every [a]leper, everyone who has a [b]discharge, and whoever becomes [c]defiled [1]by a corpse.

3 "You shall put out both male and female; you shall put them outside the camp, that they may not defile their camps [a]in the midst of which I dwell."

4 And the children of Israel did so, and put them outside the camp; as the LORD spoke to

35 [a]Num. 4:47
41 [a]Num. 4:22
42 [1]*household*
45 [a]Num. 4:29
46 [a]1 Chr. 23:3–23
47 [a]Num. 4:3, 23, 30
49 [a]Num. 4:15, 24, 31 [b]Num. 4:1, 21

CHAPTER 5

2 [a]Lev. 13:3, 8, 46 [b]Lev. 15:2 [c]Lev. 21:1 [1]*by contact with*
3 [a]Lev. 26:11, 12

Moses, so the children of Israel
did.
5 Then the LORD spoke to Moses, saying,
6 "Speak to the children of
Israel: [a]'When a man or woman
commits any sin that men commit in unfaithfulness against the
LORD, and that person is guilty,
7 [a]'then he shall confess the
sin which he has committed. He
shall make restitution for his
trespass [b]in full, plus one-fifth of
it, and give *it* to the one he has
wronged.
8 'But if the man has no [1]rela-
tive to whom restitution may be
made for the wrong, the restitution for the wrong *must go* to
the LORD for the priest, in addition to [a]the ram of the atonement with which atonement is
made for him.
9 'Every [a]offering[1] of all the
holy things of the children of
Israel, which they bring to the
priest, shall be [b]his.
10 'And every man's [1]holy things
shall be his; whatever any man
gives the priest shall be [a]his.' "
11 And the LORD spoke to Moses, saying,
12 "Speak to the children of
Israel, and say to them: 'If any
man's wife goes astray and be-
haves unfaithfully toward him,
13 'and a man [a]lies with her
carnally, and it is hidden from
the eyes of her husband, and it
is concealed that she has defiled
herself, and *there was* no witness against her, nor was she
[b]caught—
14 'if the spirit of jealousy
comes upon him and he be-
comes [a]jealous of his wife, who
has defiled herself; or if the
spirit of jealousy comes upon
him and he becomes jealous of
his wife, although she has not
defiled herself—
15 'then the man shall bring
his wife to the priest. He shall
[a]bring the offering required for
her, one-tenth of an ephah of
barley meal; he shall pour no oil
on it and put no frankincense
on it, because it *is* a grain offering of jealousy, an offering
for remembering, for [b]bringing
iniquity to remembrance.
16 'And the priest shall bring
her near, and set her before the
LORD.
17 'The priest shall take holy
water in an earthen vessel, and
take some of the dust that is on
the floor of the tabernacle and
put *it* into the water.
18 'Then the priest shall stand
the woman before the [a]LORD,
uncover the woman's head, and
put the offering for remembering in her hands, which *is* the
grain offering of jealousy. And
the priest shall have in his hand
the bitter water that brings a
curse.
19 'And the priest shall put
her under oath, and say to the
woman, "If no man has lain with
you, and if you have not gone
astray to uncleanness *while* under your husband's *authority*,
be free from this bitter water
that brings a curse.
20 "But if you have gone astray
while under your husband's *authority*, and if you have defiled
yourself and some man other
than your husband has lain with
you"—
21 'then the priest shall [a]put
the woman under the oath of the
curse, and he shall say to the
woman—[b]"the LORD make you a

6 [a]Lev. 5:14—6:7
7 [a]Lev. 5:5; 26:40, 41 [b]Lev. 6:4, 5
8 [a]Lev. 5:15; 6:6, 7; 7:7 [1]*redeemer*, Heb. *goel*
9 [a]Ex. 29:28 [b]Lev. 7:32–34; 10:14, 15 [1]*heave offering*
10 [a]Lev. 10:13 [1]*consecrated*
13 [a]Lev. 18:20; 20:10 [b]John 8:4
14 [a]Prov. 6:34
15 [a]Lev. 5:11 [b]1 Kin. 17:18
18 [a]Heb. 13:4
21 [a]Josh. 6:26 [b]Jer. 29:22

curse and an oath among your
people, when the LORD makes
your thigh [1]rot and your belly
swell;
22 "and may this water that
causes the curse [a]go into your
stomach, and make *your* belly
swell and *your* thigh rot." [b]Then
the woman shall say, "Amen, so
be it."
23 'Then the priest shall write
these curses in a book, and he
shall scrape *them* off into the
bitter water.
24 'And he shall make the
woman drink the bitter water
that brings a curse, and the water that brings the curse shall
enter her *to become* bitter.
25 [a]'Then the priest shall take
the grain offering of jealousy
from the woman's hand, shall
[b]wave the offering before the
LORD, and bring it to the altar;
26 'and the priest shall take a
handful of the offering, [a]as its
memorial portion, burn *it* on the
altar, and afterward make the
woman drink the water.
27 'When he has made her
drink the water, then it shall be,
if she has defiled herself and
behaved unfaithfully toward
her husband, that the water that
brings a [a]curse will enter her
and become bitter, and her belly
will swell, her thigh will rot, and
the woman [b]will become a curse
among her people.
28 'But if the woman has not
defiled herself, and is clean,
then she shall be free and may
conceive children.
29 'This *is* the law of jealousy,
when a wife, *while* under her
husband's *authority*, [a]goes
astray and defiles herself,
30 'or when the spirit of jealousy

21 [1]Lit. *fall away*

22 [a]Ps. 109:18 [b]Deut. 27:15–26

25 [a]Lev. 8:27 [b]Lev. 2:2, 9

26 [a]Lev. 2:2, 9

27 [a]Jer. 24:9; 29:18, 22; 42:18 [b]Num. 5:21

29 [a]Num. 5:19

31 [a]Lev. 20:17, 19, 20 [1]*guilt* [2]*iniquity*

CHAPTER 6

2 [a]Judg. 13:5 [1]Or *makes a difficult vow*

3 [a]Luke 1:15

4 [1]Separation as a Nazirite

5 [a]1 Sam. 1:11

6 [a]Num. 19:11–22

7 [a]Num. 9:6 [1]By touching a dead body

8 [a][2 Cor. 6:17, 18]

comes upon a man, and he becomes jealous of his wife; then
he shall stand the woman before
the LORD, and the priest shall
execute all this law upon her.
31 'Then the man shall be free
from [1]iniquity, but that woman
[a]shall bear her [2]guilt.' "
6 Then the LORD spoke to Moses, saying,
2 "Speak to the children of
Israel, and say to them: 'When
either a man or woman [1]con-
secrates an offering to take the
vow of a Naz′ir·īte, [a]to separate
himself to the LORD,
3 [a]'he shall separate himself
from wine and *similar* drink; he
shall drink neither vinegar made
from wine nor vinegar made
from *similar* drink; neither shall
he drink any grape juice, nor eat
fresh grapes or raisins.
4 'All the days of his [1]separa-
tion he shall eat nothing that is
produced by the grapevine, from
seed to skin.
5 'All the days of the vow of his
separation no [a]razor shall come
upon his head; until the days are
fulfilled for which he separated
himself to the LORD, he shall be
holy. *Then* he shall let the locks
of the hair of his head grow.
6 'All the days that he separates himself to the LORD [a]he
shall not go near a dead body.
7 [a]'He shall not [1]make himself
unclean even for his father or
his mother, for his brother or his
sister, when they die, because
his separation to God *is* on his
head.
8 [a]'All the days of his separation he shall be holy to the
LORD.
9 'And if anyone dies very suddenly beside him, and he defiles

his consecrated head, then he
shall [a]shave his head on the day
of his cleansing; on the seventh
day he shall shave it.
10 'Then [a]on the eighth day he
shall bring two turtledoves or
two young pigeons to the priest,
to the door of the tabernacle of
meeting;
11 'and the priest shall offer
one as a sin offering and *the*
other as a burnt offering, and
make atonement for him, because he sinned in regard to the
corpse; and he shall sanctify his
head that same day.
12 'He shall consecrate to the
LORD the days of his separation,
and bring a male lamb in its
first year [a]as a trespass offering; but the former days shall be
[1]lost, because his separation was
defiled.
13 'Now this *is* the law of the
Naz'ir·īte: [a]When the days of his
separation are fulfilled, he shall
be brought to the door of the
tabernacle of meeting.
14 'And he shall present his offering to the LORD: one male
lamb in its first year without
blemish as a burnt offering, one
ewe lamb in its first year without blemish [a]as a sin offering,
one ram without blemish [b]as a
peace offering,
15 'a basket of unleavened
bread, [a]cakes of fine flour
mixed with oil, unleavened wafers [b]anointed with oil, and their
grain offering with their [c]drink
offerings.
16 'Then the priest shall bring
them before the LORD and offer
his sin offering and his burnt
offering;
17 'and he shall offer the ram as
a sacrifice of a peace offering to
the LORD, with the basket of unleavened bread; the priest shall
also offer its grain offering and
its drink offering.
18 [a]'Then the Naz'ir·īte shall
shave his consecrated head *at*
the door of the tabernacle of
meeting, and shall take the hair
from his consecrated head and
put *it* on the fire which is under the sacrifice of the peace
offering.
19 'And the priest shall take the
[a]boiled shoulder of the ram, one
[b]unleavened cake from the basket, and one unleavened wafer,
and [c]put *them* upon the hands
of the Naz'ir·īte after he has
shaved his consecrated *hair*,
20 'and the priest shall wave
them as a wave offering before
the LORD; [a]they *are* holy for the
priest, together with the breast
of the wave offering and the
thigh of the heave offering. After that the Naz'ir·īte may drink
wine.'
21 "This is the law of the Naz'-
ir·īte who vows to the LORD the
offering for his separation, and
besides that, whatever else his
hand is able to provide; according to the vow which he takes,
so he must do according to the
law of his separation."
22 And the LORD spoke to Moses, saying:
23 "Speak to Aaron and his
sons, saying, 'This is the way
you shall bless the children of
Israel. Say to them:

24 "The LORD [a]bless you and
[b]keep you;
25 The LORD [a]make His face
shine upon you,
And [b]be gracious to you;

9 [a]Lev. 14:8, 9
10 [a]Lev. 5:7; 14:22; 15:14, 29
12 [a]Lev. 5:6 [1]*void*
13 [a]Acts 21:26
14 [a]Lev. 4:2, 27, 32 [b]Lev. 3:6
15 [a]Lev. 2:4 [b]Ex. 29:2 [c]Num. 15:5, 7, 10
18 [a]Acts 21:23, 24
19 [a]1 Sam. 2:15 [b]Ex. 29:23, 24 [c]Lev. 7:30
20 [a]Ex. 29:27, 28
24 [a]Deut. 28:3–6 [b]John 7:11
25 [a]Dan. 9:17 [b]Mal. 1:9

26 [a]The LORD [1]lift up His
countenance upon you,
And [b]give you peace." '

27 [a]"So they shall [1]put My name
on the children of Israel, and [b]I
will bless them."

7

7 Now it came to pass, when
Moses had finished [a]setting
up the tabernacle, that he
[b]anointed it and consecrated it
and all its furnishings, and the
altar and all its utensils; so he
anointed them and consecrated
them.
2 Then [a]the leaders of Israel,
the heads of their fathers' houses,
who *were* the leaders of the
tribes [1]and over those who were
numbered, made an offering.
3 And they brought their offering before the LORD, six covered
carts and twelve oxen, a cart
for *every* two of the leaders,
and for each one an ox; and
they presented them before the
tabernacle.
4 Then the LORD spoke to Moses, saying,
5 "Accept *these* from them,
that they may be used in doing the work of the tabernacle
of meeting; and you shall give
them to the Lē'vītes, *to* every
man according to his service."
6 So Moses took the carts and
the oxen, and gave them to the
Lē'vītes.
7 Two carts and four oxen [a]he
gave to the sons of Ger'shon, according to their service;
8 [a]and four carts and eight
oxen he gave to the sons of
Me·rar'ī, according to their service, under the [1]authority of
Ith'a·mar the son of Aaron the
priest.
9 But to the sons of Kō'hath
he gave none, because theirs
was [a]the service of the holy
things, [b]*which* they carried on
their shoulders.
10 Now the leaders offered [a]the
dedication *offering* for the altar
when it was anointed; so the
leaders offered their offering before the altar.
11 For the LORD said to Moses,
"They shall offer their offering,
one leader each day, for the
dedication of the altar."
12 And the one who offered his
offering on the first day *was*
[a]Nah'shon the son of Am·min'-
a·dab, from the tribe of Judah.
13 His offering *was* one silver
platter, the weight of which *was*
one hundred and thirty *shekels*,
and one silver bowl of seventy
shekels, according to [a]the shekel
of the sanctuary, both of them
full of fine flour mixed with oil
as a [b]grain offering;
14 one gold pan of ten *shekels*,
full of [a]incense;
15 [a]one young bull, one ram,
and one male lamb [b]in its first
year, as a burnt offering;
16 one kid of the goats as a [a]sin
offering;
17 and for [a]the sacrifice of
peace offerings: two oxen, five
rams, five male goats, and five
male lambs in their first year.
This *was* the offering of Nah'-
shon the son of Am·min'a·dab.
18 On the second day Ne·than'el
the son of Zū'ar, leader of Is'-
sa·char, presented *an offering*.
19 *For* his offering he offered
one silver platter, the weight
of which *was* one hundred and
thirty *shekels*, and one silver
bowl of seventy shekels, according to the shekel of the sanctuary, both of them full of fine

26 [a]Ps. 4:6; 89:15 [b]Lev. 26:6 [1]Look upon you with favor
27 [a]Is. 43:7 [b]Num. 23:20 [1]*invoke*

CHAPTER 7

1 [a]Ex. 40:17–33 [b]Lev. 8:10, 11
2 [a]Num. 1:4 [1]Lit. *who stood over*
7 [a]Num. 4:24–28
8 [a]Num. 4:29–33 [1]Lit. *hand*
9 [a]Num. 4:15 [b]Num. 4:6–14
10 [a]2 Chr. 7:5, 9
12 [a]Num. 2:3
13 [a]Ex. 30:13 [b]Lev. 2:1
14 [a]Ex. 30:34, 35
15 [a]Lev. 1:2 [b]Ex. 12:5
16 [a]Lev. 4:23
17 [a]Lev. 3:1

flour mixed with oil as a grain
offering;
20 one gold pan of ten *shekels,*
full of incense;
21 one young bull, one ram, and
one male lamb in its first year,
as a burnt offering;
22 one kid of the goats as a sin
offering;
23 and as the sacrifice of peace
offerings: two oxen, five rams,
five male goats, and five male
lambs in their first year. This
was the offering of Ne·than′el
the son of Zū′ar.
24 On the third day E·lī′ab the
son of Hē′lon, leader of the children of Zeb′ū·lun, *presented an
offering.*
25 His offering *was* one silver
platter, the weight of which *was*
one hundred and thirty *shekels,*
and one silver bowl of seventy
shekels, according to the shekel
of the sanctuary, both of them
full of fine flour mixed with oil
as a grain offering;
26 one gold pan of ten *shekels,*
full of incense;
27 one young bull, one ram, and
one male lamb in its first year,
as a burnt offering;
28 one kid of the goats as a sin
offering;
29 and for the sacrifice of peace
offerings: two oxen, five rams,
five male goats, and five male
lambs in their first year. This
was the offering of E·lī′ab the
son of Hē′lon.
30 On the fourth day [a]E·lī′zur
the son of Shed′ē·ur, leader of
the children of Reuben, *presented an offering.*
31 His offering *was* one silver
platter, the weight of which *was*
one hundred and thirty *shekels,*
and one silver bowl of seventy

30 [a]Num. 1:5; 2:10

36 [a]Num. 1:6; 2:12; 7:41

42 [a]Num. 1:14; 2:14; 10:20 [1]*Reuel,* Num. 2:14

shekels, according to the shekel
of the sanctuary, both of them
full of fine flour mixed with oil
as a grain offering;
32 one gold pan of ten *shekels,*
full of incense;
33 one young bull, one ram, and
one male lamb in its first year,
as a burnt offering;
34 one kid of the goats as a sin
offering;
35 and as the sacrifice of peace
offerings: two oxen, five rams,
five male goats, and five male
lambs in their first year. This
was the offering of E·lī′zur the
son of Shed′ē·ur.
36 On the fifth day [a]She·lū′mi·el
the son of Zū·ri·shad′daī, leader
of the children of Sim′ē·on, *presented an offering.*
37 His offering *was* one silver
platter, the weight of which *was*
one hundred and thirty *shekels,*
and one silver bowl of seventy
shekels, according to the shekel
of the sanctuary, both of them
full of fine flour mixed with oil
as a grain offering;
38 one gold pan of ten *shekels,*
full of incense;
39 one young bull, one ram, and
one male lamb in its first year,
as a burnt offering;
40 one kid of the goats as a sin
offering;
41 and as the sacrifice of peace
offerings: two oxen, five rams,
five male goats, and five male
lambs in their first year. This
was the offering of She·lū′mi·el
the son of Zū·ri·shad′daī.
42 On the sixth day [a]E·lī′a·saph
the son of [1]Deū′el, leader of the
children of Gad, *presented an
offering.*
43 His offering *was* one silver
platter, the weight of which *was*

one hundred and thirty *shekels*,
and one silver bowl of seventy
shekels, according to the shekel
of the sanctuary, both of them
full of fine flour mixed with oil
as a grain offering;
44 one gold pan of ten *shekels*,
full of incense;
45 one young bull, one ram, and
one male lamb in its first year,
as [a]a burnt offering;
46 one kid of the goats as a sin
offering;
47 and as the sacrifice of peace
offerings: two oxen, five rams,
five male goats, and five male
lambs in their first year. This
was the offering of E·lī′a·saph
the son of Deū′el.
48 On the seventh day [a]E·lish′-
a·ma the son of Am·mī′hud, leader of the children of Ē′phra·im,
presented an offering.
49 His offering *was* one silver
platter, the weight of which *was*
one hundred and thirty *shekels*,
and one silver bowl of seventy
shekels, according to the shekel
of the sanctuary, both of them
full of fine flour mixed with oil
as a grain offering;
50 one gold pan of ten *shekels*,
full of incense;
51 one young bull, one ram, and
one male lamb in its first year,
as a burnt offering;
52 one kid of the goats as a sin
offering;
53 and as the sacrifice of peace
offerings: two oxen, five rams,
five male goats, and five male
lambs in their first year. This
was the offering of E·lish′a·ma
the son of Am·mī′hud.
54 On the eighth day [a]Ga·mā′-
li·el the son of Pe·dah′zur, leader
of the children of Ma·nas′seh,
presented an offering.

45 [a]Ps. 40:6

48 [a]Num. 1:10; 2:18

54 [a]Num. 1:10; 2:20

60 [a]Num. 1:11; 2:22

66 [a]Num. 1:12; 2:25

55 His offering *was* one silver
platter, the weight of which *was*
one hundred and thirty *shekels*,
and one silver bowl of seventy
shekels, according to the shekel
of the sanctuary, both of them
full of fine flour mixed with oil
as a grain offering;
56 one gold pan of ten *shekels*,
full of incense;
57 one young bull, one ram, and
one male lamb in its first year,
as a burnt offering;
58 one kid of the goats as a sin
offering;
59 and as the sacrifice of peace
offerings: two oxen, five rams,
five male goats, and five male
lambs in their first year. This
was the offering of Ga·mā′li·el
the son of Pe·dah′zur.
60 On the ninth day [a]A·bī′dan
the son of Gid·ē·ō′ni, leader of
the children of Benjamin, *presented an offering.*
61 His offering *was* one silver
platter, the weight of which *was*
one hundred and thirty *shekels*,
and one silver bowl of seventy
shekels, according to the shekel
of the sanctuary, both of them
full of fine flour mixed with oil
as a grain offering;
62 one gold pan of ten *shekels*,
full of incense;
63 one young bull, one ram, and
one male lamb in its first year,
as a burnt offering;
64 one kid of the goats as a sin
offering;
65 and as the sacrifice of peace
offerings: two oxen, five rams,
five male goats, and five male
lambs in their first year. This
was the offering of A·bī′dan the
son of Gid·ē·ō′ni.
66 On the tenth day [a]Ā·hi·ē′-
zer the son of Am·mi·shad′daī,

leader of the children of Dan, *presented an offering.*
67 His offering *was* one silver platter, the weight of which *was* one hundred and thirty *shekels,* and one silver bowl of seventy shekels, according to the shekel of the sanctuary, both of them full of fine flour mixed with oil as a grain offering;
68 one gold pan of ten *shekels,* full of incense;
69 one young bull, one ram, and one male lamb in its first year, as a burnt offering;
70 one kid of the goats as a sin offering;
71 and as the sacrifice of peace offerings: two oxen, five rams, five male goats, and five male lambs in their first year. This *was* the offering of Ā·hī·ē′zer the son of Am·mi·shad′daī.
72 On the eleventh day [a]Pā′gi·el the son of Oc′ran, leader of the children of Ash′er, *presented an offering.*
73 His offering *was* one silver platter, the weight of which *was* one hundred and thirty *shekels,* and one silver bowl of seventy shekels, according to the shekel of the sanctuary, both of them full of fine flour mixed with oil as a grain offering;
74 one gold pan of ten *shekels,* full of incense;
75 one young bull, one ram, and one male lamb in its first year, as a burnt offering;
76 one kid of the goats as a sin offering;
77 and as the sacrifice of peace offerings: two oxen, five rams, five male goats, and five male lambs in their first year. This *was* the offering of Pā′gi·el the son of Oc′ran.

72 [a]Num. 1:13; 2:27
78 [a]Num. 1:15; 2:29
84 [a]Num. 7:10

78 On the twelfth day [a]A·hī′ra the son of Ē′nan, leader of the children of Naph′ta·lī, *presented an offering.*
79 His offering *was* one silver platter, the weight of which *was* one hundred and thirty *shekels,* and one silver bowl of seventy shekels, according to the shekel of the sanctuary, both of them full of fine flour mixed with oil as a grain offering;
80 one gold pan of ten *shekels,* full of incense;
81 one young bull, one ram, and one male lamb in its first year, as a burnt offering;
82 one kid of the goats as a sin offering;
83 and as the sacrifice of peace offerings: two oxen, five rams, five male goats, and five male lambs in their first year. This *was* the offering of A·hī′ra the son of Ē′nan.
84 This *was* [a]the dedication *offering* for the altar from the leaders of Israel, when it was anointed: twelve silver platters, twelve silver bowls, and twelve gold pans.
85 Each silver platter *weighed* one hundred and thirty *shekels* and each bowl seventy *shekels.* All the silver of the vessels *weighed* two thousand four hundred *shekels,* according to the shekel of the sanctuary.
86 The twelve gold pans full of incense *weighed* ten *shekels* apiece, according to the shekel of the sanctuary; all the gold of the pans *weighed* one hundred and twenty *shekels.*
87 All the oxen for the burnt offering *were* twelve young bulls, the rams twelve, the male lambs in their first year twelve, with

their grain offering, and the kids
of the goats as a sin offering
twelve.
88 And all the oxen for the sacrifice of peace offerings were
twenty-four bulls, the rams
sixty, the male goats sixty, and
the lambs in their first year
sixty. This *was* the dedication
offering for the altar after it was
[a]anointed.
89 Now when Moses went into
the tabernacle of meeting [a]to
speak with Him, he heard [b]the
voice of One speaking to him
from above the mercy seat that
was on the ark of the Testimony,
from [c]between the two cherubim; thus He spoke to him.

8

And the LORD spoke to Mo-
ses, saying:
2 "Speak to Aaron, and say
to him, 'When you [a]arrange
the lamps, the seven [b]lamps
shall give light in front of the
lampstand.' "
3 And Aaron did so; he arranged the lamps to face toward
the front of the lampstand, as
the LORD commanded Moses.
4 [a]Now this workmanship of
the lampstand *was* hammered
gold; from its shaft to its flowers it *was* [b]hammered work.
[c]According to the pattern which
the LORD had shown Moses, so
he made the lampstand.
5 Then the LORD spoke to Moses, saying:
6 "Take the Lē′vītes from
among the children of Israel and
cleanse them *ceremonially*.
7 "Thus you shall do to them
to cleanse them: Sprinkle [a]water
of purification on them, and [b]let[1]
them shave all their body, and
let them wash their clothes, and
so make themselves clean.
8 "Then let them take a young
bull with [a]its grain offering of
fine flour mixed with oil, and
you shall take another young
bull as a sin offering.
9 [a]"And you shall bring the
Lē′vītes before the tabernacle of
meeting, [b]and you shall gather
together the whole congregation
of the children of Israel.
10 "So you shall bring the Lē′-
vītes before the LORD, and the
children of Israel [a]shall lay their
hands on the Lē′vītes;
11 "and Aaron shall [1]offer the
Lē′vītes before the LORD *like* a
[a]wave offering from the children
of Israel, that they may perform
the work of the LORD.
12 [a]"Then the Lē′vītes shall lay
their hands on the heads of the
young bulls, and you shall offer
one as a sin offering and the
other as a burnt offering to the
LORD, to make atonement for
the Lē′vītes.
13 "And you shall stand the Lē′-
vītes before Aaron and his sons,
and then offer them *like* a wave
offering to the LORD.
14 "Thus you shall [a]separate the
Lē′vītes from among the children of Israel, and the Lē′vītes
shall be [b]Mine.
15 "After that the Lē′vītes shall
go in to service the tabernacle
of meeting. So you shall cleanse
them and [a]offer them, *like* a
wave offering.
16 "For they *are* [a]wholly given
to Me from among the children
of Israel; I have taken them for
Myself [b]instead of all who open
the womb, the firstborn of all
the children of Israel.
17 [a]"For all the firstborn among
the children of Israel *are* Mine,
both man and beast; on the day

88 [a]Num. 7:1, 10
89 [a][Ex. 33:9, 11] [b]Ex. 25:21, 22 [c]Ps. 80:1; 99:1

CHAPTER 8

2 [a]Lev. 24:2–4 [b]Ex. 25:37; 40:25
4 [a]Ex. 25:31 [b]Ex. 25:18 [c]Ex. 25:40
7 [a]Num. 19:9, 13, 17, 20 [b]Lev. 14:8, 9 [1]Heb. *let them cause a razor to pass over*
8 [a]Lev. 2:1
9 [a]Ex. 29:4; 40:12 [b]Lev. 8:3
10 [a]Lev. 1:4
11 [a]Num. 18:6 [1]*present*
12 [a]Ex. 29:10
14 [a]Num. 16:9 [b]Num. 3:12, 45; 16:9
15 [a]Num. 8:11, 13
16 [a]Num. 3:9 [b]Num. 3:12, 45
17 [a]Ex. 12:2, 12, 13, 15

that I struck all the firstborn in
the land of Egypt I [1]sanctified
them to Myself.
18 "I have taken the Lē′vītes
instead of all the firstborn of the
children of Israel.
19 "And [a]I have given the Lē′-
vītes as a gift to Aaron and his
sons from among the children
of Israel, to do the work for the
children of Israel in the tabernacle of meeting, and to make
atonement for the children of
Israel, [b]that there be no plague
among the children of Israel
when the children of Israel come
near the sanctuary."
20 Thus Moses and Aaron and
all the congregation of the children of Israel did to the Lē′vītes;
according to all that the LORD
commanded Moses concerning
the Lē′vītes, so the children of
Israel did to them.
21 [a]And the Lē′vītes purified
themselves and washed their
clothes; then Aaron presented
them, *like* a wave offering before the LORD, and Aaron made
atonement for them to cleanse
them.
22 [a]After that the Lē′vītes went
in to do their work in the tabernacle of meeting before Aaron
and his sons; [b]as the LORD commanded Moses concerning the
Lē′vītes, so they did to them.
23 Then the LORD spoke to Moses, saying,
24 "This *is* what *pertains* to the
Lē′vītes: [a]From twenty-five years
old and above one may enter to
perform service in the work of
the tabernacle of meeting;
25 "and at the age of fifty years
they must cease performing this
work, and shall work no more.
26 "They may minister with
their brethren in the tabernacle
of meeting, [a]to attend to needs,
but they *themselves* shall do no
work. Thus you shall do to the
Lē′vītes regarding their duties."

9 Now the LORD spoke to Moses in the Wilderness of Sinai, in the first month of the
second year after they had come
out of the land of Egypt, saying:
2 "Let the children of Israel
keep [a]the Passover at its appointed [b]time.
3 "On the fourteenth day of
this month, [1]at twilight, you shall
[2]keep it at its appointed time.
According to all its [3]rites and
ceremonies you shall keep it."
4 So Moses told the children of
Israel that they should keep the
Passover.
5 And [a]they kept the Passover
on the fourteenth day of the
first month, at twilight, in the
Wilderness of Sinai; according
to all that the LORD commanded
Moses, so the children of Israel
did.
6 Now there were *certain* men
who were [a]defiled by a human
corpse, so that they could not
keep the Passover on that day;
[b]and they came before Moses
and Aaron that day.
7 And those men said to him,
"We *became* defiled by a human corpse. Why are we kept
from presenting the offering of
the LORD at its appointed time
among the children of Israel?"
8 And Moses said to them,
"Stand still, that [a]I may hear
what the LORD will command
concerning you."
9 Then the LORD spoke to Moses, saying,
10 "Speak to the children of
Israel, saying: 'If anyone of you

17 [1]*set them apart*
19 [a]Num. 3:9 [b]Num. 1:53; 16:46; 18:5
21 [a]Num. 8:7
22 [a]Num. 8:15 [b]Num. 8:5
24 [a]Num. 4:3
26 [a]Num. 1:53

CHAPTER 9

2 [a]Lev. 23:5 [b]2 Chr. 30:1–15
3 [1]Lit. *between the evenings* [2]*observe* [3]*statutes*
5 [a]Josh. 5:10
6 [a]Num. 5:2; 19:11–22 [b]Num. 27:2
8 [a]Num. 27:5

or your [1]posterity is unclean because of a corpse, or *is* far away on a journey, he may still keep the LORD's Passover.

11 'On [a]the fourteenth day of the second month, at twilight, they may keep it. They shall [b]eat it with unleavened bread and bitter herbs.

☆ 12 [a]'They shall leave none of it until morning, [b]nor break one of its bones. [c]According to all the [1]ordinances of the Passover they shall keep it.

13 'But the man who *is* clean and is not on a journey, and ceases to keep the Passover, that same person [a]shall be cut off from among his people, because he [b]did not bring the offering of the LORD at its appointed time; that man shall [c]bear his sin.

14 'And if a stranger [1]dwells among you, and would keep the LORD's Passover, he must do so according to the rite of the Passover and according to its ceremony; [a]you shall have one [2]ordinance, both for the stranger and the native of the land.' "

15 Now [a]on the day that the tabernacle was raised up, the cloud [b]covered the tabernacle, the tent of the Testimony; [c]from evening until morning it was above the tabernacle like the appearance of fire.

16 So it was always: the cloud covered it *by day,* and the appearance of fire by night.

17 Whenever the cloud [a]was [1]taken up from above the tabernacle, after that the children of Israel would journey; and in the place where the cloud settled, there the children of Israel would pitch their tents.

18 At the [1]command of the LORD the children of Israel would journey, and at the command of the LORD they would camp; [a]as long as the cloud stayed above the tabernacle they remained encamped.

19 Even when the cloud continued long, many days above the tabernacle, the children of Israel [a]kept the charge of the LORD and did not journey.

20 So it was, when the cloud was above the tabernacle a few days: according to the command of the LORD they would remain encamped, and according to the command of the LORD they would journey.

21 So it was, when the cloud remained only from evening until morning: when the cloud was taken up in the morning, then they would journey; whether by day or by night, whenever the cloud was taken up, they would journey.

22 *Whether it was* two days, a month, or a year that the cloud remained above the tabernacle, the children of Israel [a]would remain encamped and not journey; but when it was taken up, they would journey.

23 At the command of the LORD they remained encamped, and at the command of the LORD they journeyed; they [a]kept the charge of the LORD, at the command of the LORD by the hand of Moses.

10 And the LORD spoke to Moses, saying:

2 "Make two silver trumpets for yourself; you shall make them of hammered work; you shall use them for [a]calling the congregation and for directing the movement of the camps.

3 "When [a]they blow both of

---

10 [1]*descendants*
11 [a]2 Chr. 30:2, 15 [b]Ex. 12:8
12 [a]Ex. 12:10 [b]Ex. 12:46; [John 19:33, 36] [c]Ex. 12:43 [1]*statutes*
13 [a]Ex. 12:15, 47 [b]Num. 9:7 [c]Num. 5:31
14 [a]Ex. 12:49 [1]As a resident alien [2]*statute*
15 [a]Ex. 40:33, 34 [b]Is. 4:5 [c]Ex. 13:21, 22; 40:38
17 [a]Ex. 40:36–38 [1]*lifted up*
18 [a]1 Cor. 10:1 [1]Lit. *mouth*
19 [a]Num. 1:53; 3:8
22 [a]Ex. 40:36, 37
23 [a]Num. 9:19

CHAPTER 10

2 [a]Is. 1:13
3 [a]Jer. 4:5

them, all the congregation shall
gather before you at the door of
the tabernacle of meeting.
4 "But if they blow *only* one,
then the leaders, the [a]heads
of the divisions of Israel, shall
gather to you.
5 "When you sound the
[a]advance, [b]the camps that lie on
the east side shall then begin
their journey.
6 "When you sound the ad-
vance the second time, then the
camps that lie [a]on the south side
shall begin their journey; they
shall sound the call for them to
begin their journeys.
7 "And when the assembly is
to be gathered together, [a]you
shall blow, but not [b]sound the
advance.
8 [a]"The sons of Aaron, the
priests, shall blow the trumpets;
and these shall be to you as an
[1]ordinance forever throughout
your generations.
9 [a]"When you go to war in
your land against the enemy
who [b]oppresses you, then you
shall sound an alarm with
the trumpets, and you will be
[c]remembered before the LORD
your God, and you will be saved
from your enemies.
10 "Also [a]in the day of your
gladness, in your appointed
feasts, and at the beginning of
your months, you shall blow the
trumpets over your burnt offerings and over the sacrifices of
your peace offerings; and they
shall be [b]a memorial for you
before your God: I *am* the LORD
your God."
11 Now it came to pass on
the twentieth *day* of the second month, in the second year,
that the cloud [a]was taken up
from above the tabernacle of the
Testimony.
12 And the children of Israel
set out from the [a]Wilderness of
Sinai on [b]their journeys; then
the cloud settled down in the
[c]Wilderness of Par′an.
13 So they started out for the
first time [a]according to the command of the LORD by the hand of
Moses.
14 The [1]standard of the camp
of the children of Judah [a]set out
first according to their armies;
over their army was [b]Nah′shon
the son of Am·min′a·dab.
15 Over the army of the tribe
of the children of Is′sa·char *was*
Ne·than′el the son of Zū′ar.
16 And over the army of the
tribe of the children of Zeb′ū·lun
was E·lī′ab the son of Hē′lon.
17 Then [a]the tabernacle was
taken down; and the sons of Ger′-
shon and the sons of Me·rar′ī set
out, [b]carrying the tabernacle.
18 And [a]the standard of the
camp of Reuben set out according to their armies; over their
army *was* E·lī′zur the son of
Shed′ē·ur.
19 Over the army of the tribe
of the children of Sim′ē·on
was She·lū′mi·el the son of
Zū·ri·shad′daī.
20 And over the army of the
tribe of the children of Gad *was*
E·lī′a·saph the son of Deū′el.
21 Then the Kō′hath·ītes set out,
carrying the [a]holy things. (The
tabernacle would be [1]prepared
for their arrival.)
22 And [a]the standard of the camp
of the children of Ē′phra·im set
out according to their armies;
over their army *was* E·lish′a·ma
the son of Am·mī′hud.
23 Over the army of the tribe of

4 [a]Ex. 18:21
5 [a]Joel 2:1 [b]Num. 2:3
6 [a]Num. 2:10
7 [a]Num. 10:3 [b]Joel 2:1
8 [a]Num. 31:6 [1]*statute*
9 [a]Josh. 6:5 [b]Judg. 2:18; 4:3; 6:9; 10:8, 12 [c]Gen. 8:1
10 [a]Lev. 23:24 [b]Num. 10:9
11 [a]Num. 9:17
12 [a]Ex. 19:1 [b]Ex. 40:36 [c]Gen. 21:21
13 [a]Num. 10:5, 6
14 [a]Num. 2:3–9 [b]Num. 1:7 [1]*banner*
17 [a]Num. 1:51 [b]Num. 4:21–32; 7:7–9
18 [a]Num. 2:10–16
21 [a]Num. 4:4–20; 7:9 [1]Prepared by the Gershonites and the Merarites
22 [a]Num. 2:18–24

the children of Ma·nas′seh *was*
Ga·mā′li·el the son of Pe·dah′-
zur.
24 And over the army of the
tribe of the children of Benjamin *was* A·bī′dan the son of
Gid·ē·ō′ni.
25 Then [a]the standard of the
camp of the children of Dan (the
rear guard of all the camps) set
out according to their armies;
over their army *was* Ā·hi·ē′zer
the son of Am·mi·shad′daī.
26 Over the army of the tribe of
the children of Ash′er *was* Pā′-
gi·el the son of Oc′ran.
27 And over the army of the
tribe of the children of Naph′ta·lī
was A·hī′ra the son of Ē′nan.
28 [a]Thus *was* the order of march
of the children of Israel, according to their armies, when they
began their journey.
29 Now Moses said to [a]Hō′bab
the son of [b]Reū′el[1] the Mid′-
i·an·īte, Moses' father-in-law,
"We are setting out for the place
of which the LORD said, [c]'I will
give it to you.' Come with us,
and [d]we will treat you well; for
[e]the LORD has promised good
things to Israel."
30 And he said to him, "I will
not go, but I will depart to my
own land and to my relatives."
31 So *Moses* said, "Please do
not leave, inasmuch as you
know how we are to camp in
the wilderness, and you can [1]be
our [a]eyes.
32 "And it shall be, if you go
with us—indeed it shall be—that
[a]whatever good the LORD will
do to us, the same we will do to
you."
33 So they departed from [a]the
mountain of the LORD on a journey of three days; and the ark of
the covenant of the LORD [b]went
before them for the three days'
journey, to search out a resting
place for them.
34 And [a]the cloud of the LORD
was above them by day when
they went out from the camp.
35 So it was, whenever the ark
set out, that Moses said:

[a]"Rise up, O LORD!
Let Your enemies be
scattered,
And let those who hate You
flee before You."

36 And when it rested, he said:

"Return, O LORD,
To the many thousands of
Israel."

11

Now [a]*when* the people
complained, it displeased
the LORD; [b]for the LORD heard
it, and His anger was aroused.
So the [c]fire of the LORD burned
among them, and consumed
some in the outskirts of the
camp.
2 Then the people [a]cried out
to Moses, and when Moses
[b]prayed to the LORD, the fire was
[1]quenched.
3 So he called the name of the
place [1]Tab′e·rah, because the fire
of the LORD had burned among
them.
4 Now the [a]mixed multitude
who were among them [1]yielded
to [b]intense craving; so the children of Israel also wept again
and said: [c]"Who will give us
meat to eat?
5 [a]"We remember the fish
which we ate freely in Egypt,
the cucumbers, the melons, the
leeks, the onions, and the garlic;

---

25 [a]Num. 2:25–31
28 [a]Num. 2:34
29 [a]Judg. 4:11 [b]Ex. 2:18; 3:1; 18:12 [c]Gen. 12:7 [d]Judg. 1:16 [e]Ex. 3:8 [1]*Jethro,* Ex. 3:1; LXX *Raguel*
31 [a]Job 29:15 [1]Act as our guide
32 [a]Judg. 1:16
33 [a]Ex. 3:1 [b]Deut. 1:33
34 [a]Ex. 13:21
35 [a]Ps. 68:1, 2; 132:8

CHAPTER 11

1 [a]Num. 14:2; 16:11; 17:5 [b]Ps. 78:21 [c]Lev. 10:2
2 [a]Num. 12:11, 13; 21:7 [b][James 5:16] [1]*extinguished*
3 [1]Lit. *Burning*
4 [a]Ex. 12:38 [b]1 Cor. 10:6 [c][Ps. 78:18] [1]Lit. *lusted intensely*
5 [a]Ex. 16:3

6 "but now [a]our whole being *is* dried up; *there is* nothing at all except this manna *before* our eyes!"

7 Now [a]the manna *was* like coriander seed, and its color like the color of bdellium.

8 The people went about and gathered *it*, ground *it* on millstones or beat *it* in the mortar, cooked *it* in pans, and made cakes of it; and [a]its taste was like the taste of pastry prepared with oil.

9 And [a]when the dew fell on the camp in the night, the manna fell on it.

10 Then Moses heard the people weeping throughout their families, everyone at the door of his tent; and [a]the anger of the LORD was greatly aroused; Moses also was displeased.

11 [a]So Moses said to the LORD, "Why have You afflicted Your servant? And why have I not found favor in Your sight, that You have laid the [1]burden of all these people on me?

12 "Did I conceive all these people? Did I beget them, that You should say to me, [a]'Carry them in your bosom, as a [b]guardian carries a nursing child,' to the land which You [c]swore[1] to their fathers?

13 [a]"Where am I to get meat to give to all these people? For they weep all over me, saying, 'Give us meat, that we may eat.'

14 [a]"I am not able to bear all these people alone, because the burden *is* too heavy for me.

15 "If You treat me like this, please kill me here and now—if I have found favor in Your sight—and [a]do not let me see my wretchedness!"

16 So the LORD said to Moses: "Gather to Me [a]seventy men of the elders of Israel, whom you know to be the elders of the people and [b]officers over them; bring them to the tabernacle of meeting, that they may stand there with you.

17 "Then I will come down and talk with you there. [a]I will take of the Spirit that *is* upon you and will put *the same* upon them; and they shall bear the burden of the people with you, that you may not bear *it* yourself alone.

18 "Then you shall say to the people, [1]'Consecrate yourselves for tomorrow, and you shall eat meat; for you have wept [a]in the hearing of the LORD, saying, "Who will give us meat to eat? For *it was* well with us in Egypt." Therefore the LORD will give you meat, and you shall eat.

19 'You shall eat, not one day, nor two days, nor five days, nor ten days, nor twenty days,

20 [a]'but *for* a whole month, until it comes out of your nostrils and becomes loathsome to you, because you have [b]despised the LORD who is among you, and have wept before Him, saying, [c]"Why did we ever come up out of Egypt?" ' "

21 And Moses said, [a]"The people whom I *am* among *are* six hundred thousand men on foot; yet You have said, 'I will give them meat, that they may eat *for* a whole month.'

22 [a]"Shall flocks and herds be slaughtered for them, to provide enough for them? Or shall all the fish of the sea be gathered together for them, to provide enough for them?"

6 [a]Num. 21:5
7 [a]Ex. 16:14, 31
8 [a]Ex. 16:31
9 [a]Ex. 16:13, 14
10 [a]Ps. 78:21
11 [a]Deut. 1:12 [1]*responsibility*
12 [a]Is. 40:11 [b]Is. 49:23 [c]Gen. 26:3 [1]*solemnly promised*
13 [a]Mark 8:4
14 [a]Ex. 18:18
15 [a]Rev. 3:17
16 [a]Ex. 18:25; 24:1, 9 [b]Deut. 16:18
17 [a]1 Sam. 10:6
18 [a]Ex. 16:7 [1]*Set yourselves apart*
20 [a]Ps. 78:29; 106:15 [b]1 Sam. 10:19 [c]Num. 21:5
21 [a]Gen. 12:2
22 [a]2 Kin. 7:2

13 from the tribe of Ash′er,
Seth′ur the son of Michael;
14 from the tribe of Naph′ta·lī,
Nah′bī the son of Voph′sī;
15 from the tribe of Gad, Ge·ū′el
the son of Mā′chī.
16 These *are* the names of
the men whom Moses sent to
[1]spy out the land. And Moses
called [a]Hō·shē′a[2] the son of Nun,
Joshua.
17 Then Moses sent them to
spy out the land of Cā′naan, and
said to them, "Go up this *way*
into the South, and go up to [a]the
mountains,
18 "and see what the land is
like: whether the people who
dwell in it *are* strong or weak,
few or many;
19 "whether the land they dwell
in *is* good or bad; whether the
cities they inhabit *are* like camps
or strongholds;
20 "whether the land *is* [1]rich
or poor; and whether there are
forests there or not. [a]Be of good
courage. And bring some of the
fruit of the land." Now the time
was the season of the first ripe
grapes.
21 So they went up and spied
out the land [a]from the Wilderness of Zin as far as [b]Rē′hob,
near the entrance of [c]Hā′math.
22 And they went up through
the South and came to [a]Hē′bron;
A·hī′man, Shē′shai, and Tal′maī,
the descendants of [b]Ā′nak, *were*
there. (Now Hē′bron was built
seven years before Zō′an in
Egypt.)
23 [a]Then they came to the [1]Val-
ley of Esh′col, and there cut
down a branch with one cluster
of grapes; they carried it between two of them on a pole.
They also *brought* some of the
pomegranates and figs.
24 The place was called the Valley of [1]Esh′col, because of the
cluster which the men of Israel
cut down there.
25 And they returned from
spying out the land after forty
days.
26 Now they departed and
came back to Moses and Aaron
and all the congregation of the
children of Israel in the Wilderness of Par′an, at [a]Kā′desh;
they brought back word to them
and to all the congregation, and
showed them the fruit of the
land.
27 Then they told him, and said:
"We went to the land where you
sent us. It truly [1]flows with [a]milk
and honey, [b]and this *is* its fruit.
28 "Nevertheless the [a]people
who dwell in the land *are* strong;
the cities *are* fortified *and* very
large; moreover we saw the descendants of [b]Ā′nak there.
29 [a]"The A·mal′e·kītes dwell
in the land of the South; the
Hit′tītes, the Jeb′ū·sītes, and the
Am′o·rītes dwell in the mountains; and the Cā′naan·ītes dwell
by the sea and along the banks
of the Jordan."
30 Then [a]Caleb quieted the people before Moses, and said, "Let
us go up at once and take possession, for we are well able to
overcome it."
31 [a]But the men who had gone
up with him said, "We are not
able to go up against the people,
for they *are* stronger than we."
32 And they [a]gave the children
of Israel a bad report of the land
which they had spied out, saying, "The land through which
we have gone as spies *is* a land

16 [a]Ex. 17:9 [1]*secretly search* [2]LXX, Vg. *Oshea*
17 [a]Judg. 1:9
20 [a]Deut. 31:6, 7, 23 [1]*fertile or barren*
21 [a]Num. 20:1; 27:14; 33:36 [b]Josh. 19:28 [c]Josh. 13:5
22 [a]Josh. 15:13, 14 [b]Josh. 11:21, 22
23 [a]Deut. 1:24, 25 [1]*Wadi*
24 [1]Lit. *Cluster*
26 [a]Deut. 1:19
27 [a]Ex. 3:8, 17; 13:5; 33:3 [b]Deut. 1:25 [1]Has an abundance of food
28 [a]Deut. 1:28; 9:1, 2 [b]Josh. 11:21, 22
29 [a]Judg. 6:3
30 [a]Num. 14:6, 24
31 [a]Deut. 1:28; 9:1–3
32 [a]Num. 14:36, 37

that devours its inhabitants, and
[b]all the people whom we saw in
it *are* men of *great* stature.
33 "There we saw the [1]giants
([a]the descendants of Ā′nak came
from the giants); and we were
[b]like[2] grasshoppers in our own
sight, and so we were [c]in their
sight."

14 So all the congregation
lifted up their voices and
cried, and the people [a]wept that
night.
2 [a]And all the children of Israel
complained against Moses and
Aaron, and the whole congregation said to them, "If only we
had died in the land of Egypt!
Or if only we had died in this
wilderness!
3 "Why has the LORD brought
us to this land to [1]fall by the
sword, that our wives and
[a]children should become victims? Would it not be better for
us to return to Egypt?"
4 So they said to one another,
[a]"Let us select a leader and
[b]return to Egypt."
5 Then Moses and Aaron [1]fell
on their faces before all the assembly of the congregation of
the children of Israel.
6 But Joshua the son of Nun
and Caleb the son of Je·phū′-
neh, *who were* among those who
had spied out the land, tore their
clothes;
7 and they spoke to all the
congregation of the children of
Israel, saying: [a]"The land we
passed through to spy out *is* an
exceedingly good land.
8 "If the LORD [a]delights in
us, then He will bring us into
this land and give it to us, [b]'a
land which flows with milk and
honey.'
9 "Only [a]do not rebel against
the LORD, [b]nor fear the people
of the land, for [c]they[1] *are* our
bread; their protection has departed from them, [d]and the LORD
is with us. Do not fear them."
10 [a]And all the congregation
said to stone them with stones.
Now [b]the glory of the LORD appeared in the tabernacle of
meeting before all the children
of Israel.
11 Then the LORD said to Moses: "How long will these people
[a]reject[1] Me? And how long will
they not [b]believe Me, with all the
[2]signs which I have performed
among them?
12 "I will strike them with the
pestilence and disinherit them,
and I will [a]make of you a nation
greater and mightier than they."
13 And [a]Moses said to the LORD:
[b]"Then the Egyptians will hear
it, for by Your might You brought
these people up from among
them,
14 "and they will tell *it* to the
inhabitants of this land. They
have [a]heard that You, LORD, *are*
among these people; that You,
LORD, are seen face to face and
Your cloud stands above them,
and You go before them in a pillar of cloud by day and in a pillar of fire by night.
15 "Now *if* You kill these people
as one man, then the nations
which have heard of Your fame
will speak, saying,
16 'Because the LORD was not
[a]able to bring this people to the
land which He swore to give
them, therefore He killed them
in the wilderness.'
17 "And now, I pray, let the
power of my Lord be great, just
as You have spoken, saying,

32 [b]Amos 2:9
33 [a]Deut. 1:28; 9:2 [b]Is. 40:22 [c]1 Sam. 17:42 [1]Heb. *nephilim* [2]As mere insects

CHAPTER 14

1 [a]Deut. 1:45
2 [a]Ex. 16:2; 17:3
3 [a]Deut. 1:39 [1]*be killed in battle*
4 [a]Neh. 9:17 [b]Acts 7:39
5 [1]*prostrated themselves*
7 [a]Num. 13:27
8 [a]Deut. 10:15 [b]Num. 13:27
9 [a]Deut. 1:26; 9:7, 23, 24 [b]Deut. 7:18 [c]Num. 24:8 [d]Deut. 20:1, 3, 4; 31:6–8 [1]They shall be as food for our consumption.
10 [a]Ex. 17:4 [b]Ex. 16:10
11 [a]Heb. 3:8 [b]Deut. 9:23 [1]*despise* [2]*miraculous signs*
12 [a]Ex. 32:10
13 [a]Ps. 106:23 [b]Ex. 32:12
14 [a]Deut. 2:25
16 [a]Deut. 9:28

18 [a]"The LORD is longsuffering
and abundant in mercy, forgiving iniquity and transgression;
but He by no means clears *the
guilty,* [b]visiting the iniquity of
the fathers on the children to the
third and fourth *generation.*'
19 [a]"Pardon the iniquity of this
people, I pray, [b]according to the
greatness of Your mercy, just [c]as
You have forgiven this people,
from Egypt even until now."
20 Then the LORD said: "I have
pardoned, [a]according to your
word;
21 "but truly, as I live, [a]all the
earth shall be filled with the
glory of the LORD—
22 [a]"because all these men who
have seen My glory and the
signs which I did in Egypt and in
the wilderness, and have put Me
to the test now [b]these ten times,
and have not heeded My voice,
23 "they certainly shall not [a]see
the land of which I [1]swore to
their fathers, nor shall any of
those who rejected Me see it.
24 "But My servant [a]Caleb, because he has a different spirit in
him and [b]has followed Me fully, I
will bring into the land where he
went, and his descendants shall
inherit it.
25 "Now the A·mal′e·kītes and
the Cā′naan·ītes dwell in the valley; tomorrow turn and [a]move
out into the wilderness by the
Way of the Red Sea."
26 And the LORD spoke to Moses and Aaron, saying,
27 [a]"How long *shall I bear with*
this evil congregation who complain against Me? [b]I have heard
the complaints which the children of Israel make against Me.
28 "Say to them, [a]'As I live,'
says the LORD, 'just as you have
spoken in My hearing, so I will
do to you:
29 'The carcasses of you who
have complained against Me
shall fall in this wilderness, [a]all
of you who were numbered,
according to your entire number, from twenty years old and
above.
30 [a]'Except for Caleb the son of
Je·phūn′neh and Joshua the son
of Nun, you shall by no means
enter the land which I [1]swore I
would make you dwell in.
31 [a]'But your little ones, whom
you said would be victims, I
will bring in, and they shall
[1]know the land which [b]you have
despised.
32 'But *as for* you, [a]your[1] carcasses shall fall in this wilderness.
33 'And your sons shall [a]be
[1]shepherds in the wilderness
[b]forty years, and [c]bear the brunt
of your infidelity, until your
carcasses are consumed in the
wilderness.
34 [a]'According to the number
of the days in which you spied
out the land, [b]forty days, for
each day you shall bear your
[1]guilt one year, *namely* forty
years, [c]and you shall know My
[2]rejection.
35 [a]'I the LORD have spoken this.
I will surely do so to all [b]this evil
congregation who are gathered
together against Me. In this wilderness they shall be consumed,
and there they shall die.'"
36 Now the men whom Moses
sent to spy out the land, who
returned and made all the congregation complain against him
by bringing a bad report of the
land,
37 those very men who brought

18 [a]Ex. 34:6, 7 [b]Ex. 20:5
19 [a]Ex. 32:32; 34:9 [b]Ps. 51:1; 106:45 [c]Ps. 78:38
20 [a]Mic. 7:18–20
21 [a]Ps. 72:19
22 [a]Deut. 1:35 [b]Gen. 31:7
23 [a]Num. 26:65; 32:11 [1]*solemnly promised*
24 [a]Josh. 14:6, 8, 9 [b]Num. 32:12
25 [a]Deut. 1:40
27 [a]Ex. 16:28 [b]Ex. 16:12
28 [a]Heb. 3:16–19
29 [a]Num. 1:45, 46; 26:64
30 [a]Deut. 1:36–38 [1]*solemnly promised*
31 [a]Deut. 1:39 [b]Ps. 106:24 [1]*be acquainted with*
32 [a]Num. 26:64, 65; 32:13 [1]You shall die.
33 [a]Ps. 107:40 [b]Deut. 2:14 [c]Ezek. 23:35 [1]Vg. *wanderers*
34 [a]Num. 13:25 [b]Ezek. 4:6 [c][Heb. 4:1] [1]*iniquity* [2]*opposition*
35 [a]Num. 23:19 [b]1 Cor. 10:5

the evil report about the land,
[a]died by the plague before the
LORD.
38 [a]But Joshua the son of Nun
and Caleb the son of Je·phŭn′-
neh remained alive, of the men
who went to spy out the land.
39 Then Moses told these words
to all the children of Israel, [a]and
the people mourned greatly.
40 And they rose early in the
morning and went up to the top
of the mountain, saying, [a]"Here
we are, and we will go up to the
place which the LORD has promised, for we have sinned!"
41 And Moses said, "Now why
do you [1]transgress the command
of the LORD? For this will not
succeed.
42 [a]"Do not go up, lest you be
defeated by your enemies, for
the LORD *is* not among you.
43 "For the A·mal′e·kītes and
the Cā′naan·ītes *are* there before you, and you shall fall by
the sword; [a]because you have
turned away from the LORD, the
LORD will not be with you."
44 [a]But they presumed to go
up to the mountaintop. Nevertheless, neither the ark of the
covenant of the LORD nor Moses
departed from the camp.
45 Then the A·mal′e·kītes and
the Cā′naan·ītes who dwelt in
that mountain came down and
attacked them, and drove them
back as far as [a]Hor′mah.

15

And the LORD spoke to
Moses, saying,
2 [a]"Speak to the children of
Israel, and say to them: 'When
you have come into the land you
are to inhabit, which I am giving
to you,
3 'and you [a]make an offering by
fire to the LORD, a burnt offering
or a sacrifice, [b]to fulfill a vow
or as a freewill offering or [c]in
your appointed feasts, to make a
[d]sweet[1] aroma to the LORD, from
the herd or the flock,
4 'then [a]he who presents his
offering to the LORD shall bring
[b]a grain offering of one-tenth
of an ephah of fine flour mixed
[c]with one-fourth of a hin of oil;
5 [a]'and one-fourth of a hin of
wine as a drink offering you
shall prepare with the burnt offering or the sacrifice, for each
[b]lamb.
6 [a]'Or for a ram you shall prepare as a grain offering two-
tenths *of an ephah* of fine flour
mixed with one-third of a hin of
oil;
7 'and as a drink offering you
shall offer one-third of a hin of
wine as a sweet aroma to the
LORD.
8 'And when you prepare a
young bull as a burnt offering,
or as a sacrifice to fulfill a vow,
or as a [a]peace offering to the
LORD,
9 'then shall be offered [a]with
the young bull a grain offering
of three-tenths *of an ephah* of
fine flour mixed with half a hin
of oil;
10 'and you shall bring as the
drink offering half a hin of wine
as an offering made by fire, a
sweet aroma to the LORD.
11 [a]'Thus it shall be done for
each young bull, for each ram,
or for each lamb or young goat.
12 'According to the number
that you prepare, so you shall
do with everyone according to
their number.
13 'All who are native-born shall
do these things in this manner,
in presenting an offering made

37 [a][1 Cor. 10:10]
38 [a]Josh. 14:6, 10
39 [a]Ex. 33:4
40 [a]Deut. 1:41–44
41 [1]*overstep*
42 [a]Deut. 1:42; 31:17
43 [a]2 Chr. 15:2
44 [a]Deut. 1:43
45 [a]Num. 21:3

CHAPTER 15

2 [a]Lev. 23:10
3 [a]Lev. 1:2, 3 [b]Lev. 7:16; 22:18, 21 [c]Lev. 23:2, 8, 12, 38 [d]Ex. 29:18 [1]*pleasing*
4 [a]Lev. 2:1; 6:14 [b]Ex. 29:40 [c]Num. 28:5
5 [a]Num. 28:7, 14 [b]Lev. 1:10; 3:6
6 [a]Num. 28:12, 14
8 [a]Lev. 7:11
9 [a]Num. 28:12, 14
11 [a]Num. 28

by fire, a sweet aroma to the
LORD.
14 'And if a stranger [1]dwells
with you, or whoever *is* among
you throughout your generations, and would present an offering made by fire, a sweet
aroma to the LORD, just as you
do, so shall he do.
15 [a]'One [1]ordinance *shall be* for
you of the assembly and for the
stranger who dwells *with you,*
an ordinance forever throughout your generations; as you are,
so shall the stranger be before
the LORD.
16 'One law and one custom
shall be for you and for the
stranger who dwells with you.' "
17 Again the LORD spoke to Moses, saying,
18 [a]"Speak to the children of
Israel, and say to them: 'When
you come into the land to which
I bring you,
19 'then it will be, when you eat
of [a]the bread of the land, that
you shall offer up a heave offering to the LORD.
20 [a]'You shall offer up a cake of
the first of your ground meal *as*
a heave offering; as [b]a heave offering of the threshing floor, so
shall you offer it up.
21 'Of the first of your ground
meal you shall give to the LORD a
heave offering throughout your
generations.
22 [a]'If you sin unintentionally,
and do not observe all these
commandments which the LORD
has spoken to Moses—
23 'all that the LORD has commanded you by the hand of Moses, from the day the LORD gave
commandment and onward
throughout your generations—
24 'then it will be, [a]if it is unintentionally committed, [1]without
the knowledge of the congregation, that the whole congregation shall offer one young bull
as a burnt offering, as a sweet
aroma to the LORD, [b]with its
grain offering and its drink offering, according to the ordinance, and [c]one kid of the goats
as a sin offering.
25 [a]'So the priest shall make
atonement for the whole congregation of the children of Israel,
and it shall be forgiven them,
for it was unintentional; they
shall bring their offering, an offering made by fire to the LORD,
and their sin offering before the
LORD, for their unintended sin.
26 'It shall be forgiven the
whole congregation of the children of Israel and the stranger
who dwells among them, because all the people *did it*
unintentionally.
27 'And [a]if a person sins unintentionally, then he shall bring a
female goat in its first year as a
sin offering.
28 [a]'So the priest shall make
atonement for the person who
sins unintentionally, when he
sins unintentionally before the
LORD, to make atonement for
him; and it shall be forgiven
him.
29 [a]'You shall have one law for
him who sins unintentionally, *for*
him who is native-born among
the children of Israel and for
the stranger who dwells among
them.
30 [a]'But the person who does *anything* [1]presumptuously, *whether
he is* native-born or a stranger,
that one [2]brings reproach on the
LORD, and he shall be [3]cut off
from among his people.

14 [1]As a resident alien
15 [a]Num. 9:14; 15:29 [1]*statute*
18 [a]Deut. 26:1
19 [a]Josh. 5:11, 12
20 [a]Lev. 23:10, 14, 17 [b]Lev. 2:14; 23:10, 16
22 [a]Lev. 4:2
24 [a]Lev. 4:13 [b]Num. 15:8–10 [c]Lev. 4:23 [1]Lit. *away from the eyes*
25 [a][Heb. 2:17]
27 [a]Lev. 4:27–31
28 [a]Lev. 4:35
29 [a]Num. 15:15
30 [a]Deut. 1:43; 17:12 [1]*defiantly,* lit. *with a high hand* [2]*blasphemes* [3]Put to death

31 'Because he has [a]despised the word of the LORD, and has broken His commandment, that person shall be completely cut off; his [1]guilt *shall be* upon him.' "

32 Now while the children of Israel were in the wilderness, [a]they found a man gathering sticks on the Sabbath day.

33 And those who found him gathering sticks brought him to Moses and Aaron, and to all the congregation.

34 They put him [a]under guard, because it had not been explained what should be done to him.

35 Then the LORD said to Moses, [a]"The man must surely be put to death; all the congregation shall [b]stone him with stones outside the camp."

36 So, as the LORD commanded Moses, all the congregation brought him outside the camp and stoned him with stones, and he died.

37 Again the LORD spoke to Moses, saying,

38 "Speak to the children of Israel: Tell [a]them to make tassels on the corners of their garments throughout their generations, and to put a blue thread in the tassels of the corners.

39 "And you shall have the tassel, that you may look upon it and [a]remember all the commandments of the LORD and do them, and that you [b]*may* not [c]follow the harlotry to which your own heart and your own eyes are inclined,

40 "and that you may remember and do all My commandments, and be [a]holy for your God.

41 "I *am* the LORD your God, who brought you out of the land of Egypt, to be your God: I *am* the LORD your God."

16

Now [a]Kō′rah the son of Iz′har, the son of Kō′hath, the son of Levi, with [b]Dā′than and A·bī′ram the sons of E·lī′ab, and On the son of Pē′leth, sons of Reuben, took *men;*

2 and they rose up before Moses with some of the children of Israel, two hundred and fifty leaders of the congregation, [a]representatives of the congregation, men of renown.

3 [a]They gathered together against Moses and Aaron, and said to them, "*You* [1]*take* too much upon yourselves, for [b]all the congregation *is* holy, every one of them, [c]and the LORD *is* among them. Why then do you exalt yourselves above the assembly of the LORD?"

4 So when Moses heard *it,* he [a]fell on his face;

5 and he spoke to Kō′rah and all his company, saying, "Tomorrow morning the LORD will show who *is* [a]His and *who is* [b]holy,[1] and will cause *him* to come near to Him. That one whom He chooses He will cause to [c]come near to Him.

6 "Do this: Take censers, Kō′rah and all your company;

7 "put fire in them and put incense in them before the LORD tomorrow, and it shall be *that* the man whom the LORD chooses *is* the holy one. *You take* too much upon yourselves, you sons of Levi!"

8 Then Moses said to Kō′rah, "Hear now, you sons of Levi:

9 "*Is it* [a]a small thing to you that the God of Israel has [b]separated you from the congregation of Israel, to bring you

31 [a]Prov. 13:13 [1]*iniquity*
32 [a]Ex. 31:14, 15; 35:2, 3
34 [a]Lev. 24:12
35 [a]Ex. 31:14, 15 [b]Lev. 24:14
38 [a]Matt. 23:5
39 [a]Ps. 103:18 [b]Deut. 29:19 [c]James 4:4
40 [a][Lev. 11:44, 45]

CHAPTER 16

1 [a]Ex. 6:21 [b]Num. 26:9
2 [a]Num. 1:16; 26:9
3 [a]Ps. 106:16 [b]Ex. 19:6 [c]Ex. 29:45 [1]*assume too much for*
4 [a]Num. 14:5; 20:6
5 [a][2 Tim. 2:19] [b]Lev. 21:6–8, 12 [c]Ezek. 40:46; 44:15, 16 [1]*set aside* for His use only
9 [a]Is. 7:13 [b]Deut. 10:8

near to Himself, to do the work
of the tabernacle of the LORD,
and to stand before the congregation to serve them;
10 "and that He has brought
you near *to Himself,* you and all
your brethren, the sons of Levi,
with you? And are you seeking
the priesthood also?
11 "Therefore you and all your
company *are* gathered together
against the LORD. [a]And what *is*
Aaron that you complain against
him?"
12 And Moses sent to call Dā′-
than and A·bī′ram the sons of
E·lī′ab, but they said, "We will
not come up!
13 "*Is it* a small thing that you
have brought us up out of [a]a land
flowing with milk and honey, to
kill us in the wilderness, that
you should [b]keep acting like a
prince over us?
14 "Moreover [a]you have not
brought us into [b]a land flowing with milk and honey, nor
given us inheritance of fields
and vineyards. Will you put out
the eyes of these men? We will
not come up!"
15 Then Moses was very angry, and said to the LORD, [a]"Do
not [1]respect their offering. [b]I
have not taken one donkey from
them, nor have I hurt one of
them."
16 And Moses said to Kō′rah,
"Tomorrow, you and all your
company be present [a]before the
LORD—you and they, as well as
Aaron.
17 "Let each take his censer
and put incense in it, and each
of you bring his censer before
the LORD, two hundred and fifty
censers; both you and Aaron,
each *with* his censer."
18 So every man took his censer, put fire in it, laid incense
on it, and stood at the door of
the tabernacle of meeting with
Moses and Aaron.
19 And Kō′rah gathered all
the congregation against them
at the door of the tabernacle
of meeting. Then [a]the glory of
the LORD appeared to all the
congregation.
20 And the LORD spoke to Moses and Aaron, saying,
21 [a]"Separate yourselves from
among this congregation, that
I may [b]consume them in a
moment."
22 Then they [a]fell[1] on their faces,
and said, "O God, [b]the God of
the spirits of all flesh, shall one
man sin, and You be angry with
all the [c]congregation?"
23 So the LORD spoke to Moses,
saying,
24 "Speak to the congregation,
saying, 'Get away from the tents
of Kō′rah, Dā′than, and A·bī′-
ram.' "
25 Then Moses rose and went
to Dā′than and A·bī′ram, and the
elders of Israel followed him.
26 And he spoke to the congregation, saying, [a]"Depart now
from the tents of these wicked
men! Touch nothing of theirs,
lest you be consumed in all their
sins."
27 So they got away from
around the tents of Kō′rah, Dā′-
than, and A·bī′ram; and Dā′-
than and A·bī′ram came out and
stood at the door of their tents,
with their wives, their sons, and
their little [a]children.
28 And Moses said: [a]"By this
you shall know that the LORD has
sent me to do all these works,

11 [a]Ex. 16:7, 8
13 [a]Num. 11:4–6 [b]Ex. 2:14
14 [a]Num. 14:1–4 [b]Ex. 3:8
15 [a]Gen. 4:4, 5 [b]1 Sam. 12:3 [1]*graciously regard*
16 [a]1 Sam. 12:3, 7
19 [a]Num. 14:10
21 [a]Gen. 19:17 [b]Ex. 32:10; 33:5
22 [a]Num. 14:5 [b]Num. 27:16 [c]Gen. 18:23–32; 20:4 [1]*prostrated themselves*
26 [a]Gen. 19:12, 14, 15, 17
27 [a]Num. 26:11
28 [a]John 5:36

for *I have* not *done them* [b]of my
own will.
29 "If these men die naturally
like all men, or if they are [a]visited
by the common fate of all men,
then the LORD has not sent me.
30 "But if the LORD creates [a]a
new thing, and the earth opens
its mouth and swallows them
up with all that belongs to them,
and they [b]go down alive into the
pit, then you will understand
that these men have rejected the
LORD."
31 [a]Now it came to pass, as
he finished speaking all these
words, that the ground split
apart under them,
32 and the earth opened its
mouth and swallowed them up,
with their households and [a]all
the men with Kō′rah, with all
their goods.
33 So they and all those with
them went down alive into the
pit; the earth closed over them,
and they perished from among
the assembly.
34 Then all Israel who *were*
around them fled at their cry, for
they said, "Lest the earth swallow us up *also!*"
35 And [a]a fire came out from
the LORD and consumed the two
hundred and fifty men who were
offering incense.
36 Then the LORD spoke to Moses, saying:
37 "Tell El·ē·ā′zar, the son of
Aaron the priest, to pick up the
censers out of the blaze, for
[a]they are holy, and scatter the
fire some distance away.
38 "The censers of [a]these men
who sinned [1]against their own
souls, let them be made into
hammered plates as a covering for the altar. Because they
presented them before the LORD,
therefore they are holy; [b]and
they shall be a sign to the children of Israel."
39 So El·ē·ā′zar the priest took
the bronze censers, which those
who were burned up had presented, and they were hammered
out as a covering on the altar,
40 *to be* a [1]memorial to the
children of Israel [a]that no outsider, who *is* not a descendant of
Aaron, should come near to offer incense before the LORD, that
he might not become like Kō′rah
and his companions, just as the
LORD had said to him through
Moses.
41 On the next day [a]all the congregation of the children of Israel complained against Moses
and Aaron, saying, "You have
killed the people of the LORD."
42 Now it happened, when
the congregation had gathered
against Moses and Aaron, that
they turned toward the tabernacle of meeting; and suddenly
[a]the cloud covered it, and the
glory of the LORD appeared.
43 Then Moses and Aaron
came before the tabernacle of
meeting.
44 And the LORD spoke to Moses, saying,
45 "Get away from among this
congregation, that I may consume them in a moment." And
they fell on their faces.
46 So Moses said to Aaron,
"Take a censer and put fire in it
from the altar, put incense *on it*,
and take it quickly to the congregation and make [1]atonement
for them; [a]for wrath has gone
out from the LORD. The plague
has begun."
47 Then Aaron took *it* as Moses

28 [b]John 5:30
29 [a]Ex. 20:5
30 [a]Job 31:3 [b][Ps. 55:15]
31 [a]Num. 26:10
32 [a]Num. 26:11
35 [a]Num. 11:1–3; 26:10
37 [a]Lev. 27:28
38 [a]Hab. 2:10 [b]Num. 17:10 [1]Or *at the cost of their own lives*
40 [a]Num. 3:10 [1]*reminder*
41 [a]Num. 14:2
42 [a]Ex. 40:34
46 [a]Num. 18:5 [1]Lit. *covering*

commanded, and ran into the midst of the assembly; and already the plague had begun among the people. So he put in the incense and made atonement for the people.

48 And he stood between the dead and the living; so [a]the plague was stopped.

49 Now those who died in the plague were fourteen thousand seven hundred, besides those who died in the Kō'rah incident.

50 So Aaron returned to Moses at the door of the tabernacle of meeting, for the plague had stopped.

17 And the LORD spoke to Moses, saying:

2 "Speak to the children of Israel, and get from them a rod from each father's house, all their leaders according to their fathers' houses—twelve rods. Write each man's name on his rod.

3 "And you shall write Aaron's name on the rod of Levi. For there shall be one rod for the head of *each* father's house.

4 "Then you shall place them in the tabernacle of meeting before [a]the Testimony, [b]where I meet with you.

5 "And it shall be *that* the rod of the man [a]whom I choose will blossom; thus I will rid Myself of the complaints of the children of Israel, [b]which they make against you."

6 So Moses spoke to the children of Israel, and each of their leaders gave him a rod apiece, for each leader according to their fathers' houses, twelve rods; and the rod of Aaron *was* among their rods.

7 And Moses placed the rods before the LORD in [a]the tabernacle of witness.

8 Now it came to pass on the next day that Moses went into the tabernacle of witness, and behold, the [a]rod of Aaron, of the house of Levi, had sprouted and put forth buds, had produced blossoms and yielded ripe almonds.

9 Then Moses brought out all the rods from before the LORD to all the children of Israel; and they looked, and each man took his rod.

10 And the LORD said to Moses, "Bring [a]Aaron's rod back before the Testimony, to be kept [b]as a sign against the rebels, [c]that you may put their complaints away from Me, lest they die."

11 Thus did Moses; just as the LORD had commanded him, so he did.

12 So the children of Israel spoke to Moses, saying, "Surely we die, we perish, we all perish!

13 [a]"Whoever even comes near the tabernacle of the LORD must die. Shall we all utterly die?"

18 Then the LORD said to Aaron: [a]"You and your sons and your father's house with you shall [b]bear the [1]iniquity *related to* the sanctuary, and you and your sons with you shall bear the iniquity *associated with* your priesthood.

2 "Also bring with you your brethren of the [a]tribe of Levi, the tribe of your father, that they may be [b]joined with you and serve you while you and your sons *are* with you before the tabernacle of [1]witness.

3 "They shall attend to your [1]needs and [a]all the needs of the tabernacle; [b]but they shall not

48 [a]Num. 25:8

CHAPTER 17

4 [a]Ex. 25:16 [b]Ex. 25:22; 29:42, 43; 30:36

5 [a]Num. 16:5 [b]Num. 16:11

7 [a]Ex. 38:21

8 [a][Ezek. 17:24]

10 [a]Heb. 9:4 [b]Deut. 9:7, 24 [c]Num. 17:5

13 [a]Num. 1:51, 53; 18:4, 7

CHAPTER 18

1 [a]Num. 17:13 [b]Ex. 28:38 [1]*guilt*

2 [a]Num. 1:47 [b]Num. 3:5–10 [1]*testimony*

3 [a]Num. 3:25, 31, 36 [b]Num. 16:40 [1]*service*

come near the articles of the
sanctuary and the altar, [c]lest
they die—they and you also.
4 “They shall be joined with
you and attend to the needs of
the tabernacle of meeting, for all
the work of the tabernacle; [a]but
an outsider shall not come near
you.
5 “And you shall attend to [a]the
duties of the sanctuary and the
duties of the altar, [b]that there
may be no more wrath on the
children of Israel.
6 “Behold, I Myself have [a]taken
your brethren the Lē′vītes from
among the children of Israel;
[b]*they are* a gift to you, given by
the LORD, to do the work of the
tabernacle of meeting.
7 “Therefore [a]you and your
sons with you shall attend to
your priesthood for everything
at the altar and [b]behind the
veil; and you shall serve. I give
your priesthood *to you* as a
[c]gift for service, but the outsider
who comes near shall be put to
death.”
8 And the LORD spoke to Aaron:
“Here, [a]I Myself have also given
you [1]charge of My heave offerings, all the holy gifts of the children of Israel; I have given them
[b]as a portion to you and your
sons, as an ordinance forever.
9 “This shall be yours of the
most holy things *reserved* from
the fire: every offering of theirs,
every [a]grain offering and every
[b]sin offering and every [c]trespass
offering which they render to
Me, *shall be* most holy for you
and your sons.
10 [a]“In a most holy *place* you
shall eat it; every male shall eat
it. It shall be holy to you.
11 “This also *is* yours: [a]the heave
offering of their gift, with all the
wave offerings of the children
of Israel; I have given them to
you, and your sons and daughters with you, as an ordinance
forever. [b]Everyone who is [1]clean
in your house may eat it.
12 [a]“All the [1]best of the oil, all
the best of the new wine and
the grain, [b]their firstfruits which
they offer to the LORD, I have
given them to you.
13 “Whatever first ripe fruit is
in their land, [a]which they bring
to the LORD, shall be yours. Everyone who is clean in your
house may eat it.
14 [a]“Every [1]devoted thing in Israel shall be yours.
15 “Everything that first opens
[a]the womb of all flesh, which
they bring to the LORD, whether
man or beast, shall be yours;
nevertheless [b]the firstborn of
man you shall surely redeem,
and the firstborn of unclean animals you shall redeem.
16 “And those redeemed of the
devoted things you shall redeem
when one month old, [a]according
to your valuation, for five shekels of silver, according to the
shekel of the sanctuary, which *is*
[b]twenty gerahs.
17 [a]“But the firstborn of a cow,
the firstborn of a sheep, or the
firstborn of a goat you shall not
redeem; they *are* holy. [b]You shall
sprinkle their blood on the altar,
and burn their fat *as* an offering
made by fire for a sweet aroma
to the LORD.
18 “And their flesh shall be
yours, just as the [a]wave[1] breast
and the right thigh are yours.
19 “All the heave offerings of
the holy things, which the children of Israel offer to the LORD, I

3 [c]Num. 4:15
4 [a]Num. 3:10
5 [a]Lev. 24:3 [b]Num. 8:19; 16:46
6 [a]Num. 3:12, 45 [b]Num. 3:9
7 [a]Num. 3:10; 18:5 [b]Heb. 9:3, 6 [c]1 Pet. 5:2, 3
8 [a]Lev. 6:16, 18; 7:28–34 [b]Ex. 29:29; 40:13, 15 [1]*custody*
9 [a]Lev. 2:2, 3; 10:12, 13 [b]Lev. 6:25, 26 [c]Lev. 7:7
10 [a]Lev. 6:16, 26
11 [a]Deut. 18:3–5 [b]Lev. 22:1–16 [1]*purified*
12 [a]Ex. 23:19 [b]Ex. 22:29 [1]Lit. *fat*
13 [a]Ex. 22:29; 23:19; 34:26
14 [a]Lev. 27:1–33 [1]*consecrated*
15 [a]Ex. 13:2 [b]Ex. 13:12–15
16 [a]Lev. 27:6 [b]Ex. 30:13
17 [a]Deut. 15:19 [b]Lev. 3:2, 5
18 [a]Ex. 29:26–28 [1]*breast of the wave offering*

have given to you and your sons and daughters with you as an ordinance forever; [a]it *is* a covenant of salt forever before the LORD with you and your descendants with you."

20 Then the LORD said to Aaron: "You shall have [a]no inheritance in their land, nor shall you have any portion among them; [b]I *am* your portion and your inheritance among the children of Israel.

21 "Behold, [a]I have given the children of Levi all the tithes in Israel as [1]an inheritance in return for the work which they perform, [b]the work of the tabernacle of meeting.

22 [a]"Hereafter the children of Israel shall not come near the tabernacle of meeting, [b]lest they bear sin and die.

23 "But the Lē′vītes shall perform the work of the tabernacle of meeting, and they shall bear their iniquity; *it shall be* a statute forever, throughout your generations, that among the children of Israel they shall have no inheritance.

24 "For the tithes of the children of Israel, which they offer up *as* a heave offering to the LORD, I have given to the Lē′vītes [1]as an inheritance; therefore I have said to them, 'Among the children of Israel they shall have no inheritance.' "

25 Then the LORD spoke to Moses, saying,

26 "Speak thus to the Lē′vītes, and say to them: 'When you take from the children of Israel the tithes which I have given you from them as your inheritance, then you shall offer up a heave offering of it to the LORD, [a]a tenth of the tithe.

27 'And your heave offering shall be reckoned to you as though *it were* the grain of the [a]threshing floor and as the fullness of the winepress.

28 'Thus you shall also offer a heave offering to the LORD from all your tithes which you receive from the children of Israel, and you shall give the LORD's heave offering from it to Aaron the priest.

29 'Of all your gifts you shall offer up every heave offering due to the LORD, from all the [1]best of them, the consecrated part of them.'

30 "Therefore you shall say to them: 'When you have lifted up the best of it, then *the rest* shall be accounted to the Lē′vītes as the produce of the threshing floor and as the produce of the winepress.

31 'You may eat it in any place, you and your households, for it *is* [a]your [1]reward for your work in the tabernacle of meeting.

32 'And you shall [a]bear no sin because of it, when you have lifted up the best of it. But you shall not [b]profane the holy gifts of the children of Israel, lest you die.' "

19 Now the LORD spoke to Moses and Aaron, saying,

2 "This *is* the [1]ordinance of the law which the LORD has commanded, saying: 'Speak to the children of Israel, that they bring you a red heifer without [2]blemish, in which there *is* no [a]defect [b]*and* on which a yoke has never come.

3 'You shall give it to El·ē·ā′zar

19 [a]2 Chr. 13:5
20 [a]Josh. 13:14, 33 [b]Ezek. 44:28
21 [a]Lev. 27:30–33 [b]Num. 3:7, 8 [1]*a possession*
22 [a]Num. 1:51 [b]Lev. 22:9
24 [1]*for a possession*
26 [a]Neh. 10:38
27 [a]Num. 15:20
29 [1]Lit. *fat*
31 [a][Luke 10:7] [1]*wages*
32 [a]Lev. 19:8; 22:16 [b]Lev. 22:2, 15

CHAPTER 19

2 [a]Lev. 22:20–25 [b]Deut. 21:3 [1]*statute* [2]*defect*

the priest, that he may take it [a]outside the camp, and it shall be slaughtered before him;

4 'and El·ē·ā'zar the priest shall take some of its blood with his finger, and [a]sprinkle some of its blood seven times directly in front of the tabernacle of meeting.

5 'Then the heifer shall be burned in his sight: [a]its hide, its flesh, its blood, and its offal shall be burned.

6 'And the priest shall take [a]cedar wood and [b]hyssop and scarlet, and cast *them* into the midst of the fire burning the heifer.

7 [a]'Then the priest shall wash his clothes, he shall bathe in water, and afterward he shall come into the camp; the priest shall be unclean until evening.

8 'And the one who burns it shall wash his clothes in water, bathe in water, and shall be unclean until evening.

9 'Then a man *who is* clean shall gather up [a]the ashes of the heifer, and store *them* outside the camp in a clean place; and they shall be kept for the congregation of the children of Israel [b]for the water of [1]purification; it *is* for purifying from sin.

10 'And the one who gathers the ashes of the heifer shall wash his clothes, and be unclean until evening. It shall be a statute forever to the children of Israel and to the stranger who dwells among them.

11 [a]'He who touches the dead [1]body of anyone shall be unclean seven days.

12 [a]'He shall purify himself with the water on the third day and on the seventh day; *then* he will be clean. But if he does not purify himself on the third day and on the seventh day, he will not be clean.

13 'Whoever touches the body of anyone who has died, and [a]does not purify himself, [b]defiles the tabernacle of the LORD. That person shall be cut off from Israel. He shall be unclean, because [c]the water of purification was not sprinkled on him; [d]his uncleanness *is* still on him.

14 'This *is* the law when a man dies in a tent: All who come into the tent and all who *are* in the tent shall be unclean seven days;

15 'and every [a]open vessel, which has no cover fastened on it, *is* unclean.

16 [a]'Whoever in the open field touches one who is slain by a sword or who has died, or a bone of a man, or a grave, shall be unclean seven days.

17 'And for an unclean *person* they shall take some of the [a]ashes of the heifer burnt for purification from sin, and [1]running water shall be put on them in a vessel.

18 'A clean person shall take [a]hyssop and dip *it* in the water, sprinkle *it* on the tent, on all the vessels, on the persons who were there, or on the one who touched a bone, the slain, the dead, or a grave.

19 'The clean *person* shall sprinkle the unclean on the third day and on the seventh day; [a]and on the seventh day he shall purify himself, wash his clothes, and bathe in water; and at evening he shall be clean.

20 'But the man who is unclean and does not purify himself, that person shall be cut off from

3 [a]Lev. 4:12, 21
4 [a]Lev. 4:6
5 [a]Ex. 29:14
6 [a]Lev. 14:4, 6, 49 [b]Ex. 12:22
7 [a]Lev. 11:25; 15:5; 16:26, 28
9 [a][Heb. 9:13, 14] [b]Num. 19:13, 20, 21 [1]Lit. *impurity*
11 [a]Lev. 21:1, 11 [1]Lit. *soul of man*
12 [a]Num. 19:19; 31:19
13 [a]Lev. 22:3–7 [b]Lev. 15:31 [c]Num. 8:7; 19:9 [d]Lev. 7:20; 22:3
15 [a]Num. 31:20
16 [a]Num. 19:11; 31:19
17 [a]Num. 19:9 [1]Lit. *living*
18 [a]Ps. 51:7
19 [a]Lev. 14:9

among the assembly, because he
has [a]defiled the sanctuary of the
LORD. The water of purification
has not been sprinkled on him;
he *is* unclean.
21 'It shall be a perpetual statute for them. He who sprinkles
the water of purification shall
wash his clothes; and he who
touches the water of purification
shall be unclean until evening.
22 [a]'Whatever the unclean *per-*
son touches shall be unclean; and
[b]the person who touches *it* shall
be unclean until evening.' "

20 Then[a] the children of Israel, the whole congrega-
tion, came into the Wilderness
of Zin in the first month, and
the people stayed in [b]Kā′desh;
and [c]Miriam died there and was
buried there.
2 [a]Now there was no water for
the congregation; [b]so they gathered together against Moses and
Aaron.
3 And the people [a]contended
with Moses and spoke, saying:
"If only we had died [b]when our
brethren died before the LORD!
4 [a]"Why have you brought up
the assembly of the LORD into
this wilderness, that we and our
animals should die here?
5 "And why have you made us
come up out of Egypt, to bring
us to this evil place? It *is* not a
place of grain or figs or vines or
pomegranates; nor *is* there any
water to drink."
6 So Moses and Aaron went
from the presence of the assembly to the door of the tabernacle
of meeting, and [a]they [1]fell on
their faces. And [b]the glory of the
LORD appeared to them.
7 Then the LORD spoke to Moses, saying,
8 [a]"Take the rod; you and your
brother Aaron gather the congregation together. Speak to the
rock before their eyes, and it will
yield its water; thus [b]you shall
bring water for them out of the
rock, and give drink to the congregation and their animals."
9 So Moses took the rod [a]from
before the LORD as He commanded him.
10 And Moses and Aaron gathered the assembly together before the rock; and he said to
them, [a]"Hear now, you rebels!
Must we bring water for you out
of this rock?"
11 Then Moses lifted his hand
and struck the rock twice with
his rod; [a]and water came out
abundantly, and the congregation and their animals drank.
12 Then the LORD spoke to Moses and Aaron, "Because [a]you
did not believe Me, to [b]hallow
Me in the eyes of the children
of Israel, therefore you shall not
bring this assembly into the land
which I have given them."
13 [a]This *was* the water of [1]Mer′-
i·bah, because the children of Israel contended with the LORD, and
He was hallowed among them.
14 [a]Now Moses sent messengers from Kā′desh to the king
of [b]Ē′dom. [c]"Thus says your
brother Israel: 'You know all the
hardship that has befallen us,
15 [a]how our fathers went down
to Egypt, [b]and we dwelt in Egypt
a long time, [c]and the Egyptians
[1]afflicted us and our fathers.
16 [a]'When we cried out to the
LORD, He heard our voice and
[b]sent the Angel and brought us
up out of Egypt; now here we
are in Kā′desh, a city on the
edge of your border.

20 [a]Num. 19:13
22 [a]Hag. 2:11–13 [b]Lev. 15:5

CHAPTER 20

1 [a]Num. 13:21; 33:36 [b]Num. 13:26 [c]Ex. 15:20
2 [a]Ex. 17:1 [b]Num. 16:19, 42
3 [a]Ex. 17:2 [b]Num. 11:1, 33; 14:37; 16:31–35, 49
4 [a]Ex. 17:3
6 [a]Num. 14:5; 16:4, 22, 45 [b]Num. 14:10 [1]*prostrated themselves*
8 [a]Ex. 4:17, 20; 17:5, 6 [b]Neh. 9:15
9 [a]Num. 17:10
10 [a]Ps. 106:33
11 [a][1 Cor. 10:4]
12 [a]Deut. 1:37; 3:26, 27; 34:5 [b]Lev. 10:3
13 [a]Deut. 33:8 [1]Lit. *Contention*
14 [a]Judg. 11:16, 17 [b]Gen. 36:31–39 [c]Deut. 2:4
15 [a]Gen. 46:6 [b]Ex. 12:40 [c]Deut. 26:6 [1]*did evil to*
16 [a]Ex. 2:23; 3:7 [b]Ex. 3:2; 14:19

17 'Please [a]let us pass through
your country. We will not pass
through fields or vineyards, nor
will we drink water from wells;
we will go along the King's
Highway; we will not turn aside
to the right hand or to the left
until we have passed through
your territory.' "
18 Then [a]Ē′dom said to him,
"You shall not pass through my
land, lest I come out against you
with the sword."
19 So the children of Israel said
to him, "We will go by the Highway, and if I or my livestock
drink any of your water, [a]then I
will pay for it; let me only pass
through on foot, nothing *more.*"
20 Then he said, [a]"You shall not
pass through." So Ē′dom came
out against them with many
men and with a strong hand.
21 Thus Ē′dom [a]refused to give
Israel passage through his territory; so Israel [b]turned away
from him.
22 Now the children of Israel,
the whole congregation, journeyed from [a]Kā′desh [b]and came
to Mount Hor.
23 And the LORD spoke to Moses and Aaron in Mount Hor by
the border of the land of Ē′dom,
saying:
24 "Aaron shall [1]be [a]gathered to
his people, for he shall not enter
the land which I have given to
the children of Israel, because
you rebelled against My word at
the water of Mer′i·bah.
25 [a]"Take Aaron and El·ē·ā′zar
his son, and bring them up to
Mount Hor;
26 "and strip Aaron of his garments and put them on El·ē·ā′-
zar his son; for Aaron shall be
gathered *to his people* and die
there."
27 So Moses did just as the LORD
commanded, and they went up
to Mount Hor in the sight of all
the congregation.
28 [a]Moses stripped Aaron of his
garments and put them on El·ē·ā′-
zar his son; and [b]Aaron died
there on the top of the mountain.
Then Moses and El·ē·ā′zar came
down from the mountain.
29 Now when all the congregation saw that Aaron was dead,
all the house of Israel mourned
for Aaron [a]thirty days.

21

The [a]king of Ar′ad, the
Cā′naan·īte, who dwelt in
the South, heard that Israel was
coming on the road to Ath′a·rim.
Then he fought against Israel and
took *some* of them prisoners.
2 [a]So Israel made a vow to the
LORD, and said, "If You will indeed deliver this people into my
hand, then [b]I will utterly destroy
their cities."
3 And the LORD listened to the
voice of Israel and delivered up
the Cā′naan·ītes, and they utterly destroyed them and their
cities. So the name of that place
was called [1]Hor′mah.
4 Then they journeyed from
Mount Hor by the Way of the
Red Sea, to [a]go around the land
of Ē′dom; and the soul of the
people became very [1]discour-
aged on the way.
5 And the people [a]spoke
against God and against Moses:
"Why have you brought us up
out of Egypt to die in the wilderness? For *there is* no food and
no water, and our soul [1]loathes
this worthless bread."
6 So [a]the LORD sent [b]fiery serpents among the people, and

17 [a]Num. 21:22
18 [a]Num. 24:18
19 [a]Deut. 2:6, 28
20 [a]Judg. 11:17
21 [a]Deut. 2:27, 30 [b]Judg. 11:18
22 [a]Num. 33:37 [b]Num. 21:4
24 [a]Gen. 25:8 [1]Die and join his ancestors
25 [a]Num. 33:38
28 [a]Ex. 29:29, 30 [b]Num. 33:38
29 [a]Deut. 34:8

CHAPTER 21

1 [a]Judg. 1:16
2 [a]Gen. 28:20 [b]Deut. 2:34
3 [1]Lit. *Utter Destruction*
4 [a]Judg. 11:18 [1]*impatient*
5 [a]Num. 20:4, 5 [1]*detests*
6 [a]1 Cor. 10:9 [b]Deut. 8:15

they bit the people; and many of the people of Israel died.

7 [a]Therefore the people came to Moses, and said, "We have [b]sinned, for we have spoken against the LORD and against you; [c]pray to the LORD that He take away the serpents from us." So Moses prayed for the people.

8 Then the LORD said to Moses, [a]"Make a [b]fiery *serpent*, and set it on a pole; and it shall be that everyone who is bitten, when he looks at it, shall live."

9 So [a]Moses made a bronze serpent, and put it on a pole; and so it was, if a serpent had bitten anyone, when he looked at the bronze serpent, he lived.

10 Now the children of Israel moved on and [a]camped in Ō′both.

11 And they journeyed from Ō′both and camped at [1]Ī′jē Ab′a·rim, in the wilderness which *is* east of Mō′ab, toward the sunrise.

12 [a]From there they moved and camped in the Valley of Zē′red.

13 From there they moved and camped on the other side of the Ar′non, which *is* in the wilderness that extends from the border of the Am′o·rītes; for [a]the Ar′non *is* the border of Mō′ab, between Mō′ab and the Am′o·rītes.

14 Therefore it is said in the Book of the Wars of the LORD:

[1]"Wa′heb in Sū′phah,
The brooks of the Ar′non,
15 And the slope of the brooks
That reaches to the dwelling of [a]Ar,
And lies on the border of Mō′ab."

16 From there *they went* [a]to Bē′er, which *is* the well where the LORD said to Moses, "Gather the people together, and I will give them water."

17 [a]Then Israel sang this song:

"Spring up, O well!
All of you sing to it—
18 The well the leaders sank,
Dug by the nation's nobles,
By the [a]lawgiver, with their staves."

And from the wilderness *they went* to Mat′ta·nah,

19 from Mat′ta·nah to Na·hal′i·el, from Na·hal′i·el to Bā′moth,

20 and from Bā′moth, *in* the valley that *is* in the [1]country of Mō′ab, to the top of Pis′gah which looks [a]down on the [2]wasteland.

21 Then [a]Israel sent messengers to Sī′hon king of the Am′o·rītes, saying,

22 [a]"Let me pass through your land. We will not turn aside into fields or vineyards; we will not drink water from wells. We will go by the King's Highway until we have passed through your territory."

23 [a]But Sī′hon would not allow Israel to pass through his territory. So Sī′hon gathered all his people together and [1]went out against Israel in the wilderness, [b]and he came to Jā′haz and fought against Israel.

24 Then [a]Israel defeated him with the edge of the sword, and took possession of his land from the Ar′non to the Jab′bok, as far as the people of Am′mon; for the border of the people of Am′mon *was* fortified.

25 So Israel took all these cities,

7 [a]Num. 11:2 [b]Lev. 26:40 [c]Ex. 8:8
8 [a][John 3:14, 15] [b]Is. 14:29; 30:6
9 [a]John 3:14, 15
10 [a]Num. 33:43, 44
11 [1]Lit. *The Heaps of Abarim*
12 [a]Deut. 2:13
13 [a]Num. 22:36
14 [1]Ancient unknown places; Vg. *What He did in the Red Sea*
15 [a]Deut. 2:9, 18, 29
16 [a]Judg. 9:21
17 [a]Ex. 15:1
18 [a]Is. 33:22
20 [a]Num. 23:28 [1]Lit. *field* [2]Heb. *Jeshimon*
21 [a]Deut. 2:26–37
22 [a]Num. 20:16, 17
23 [a]Deut. 29:7 [b]Judg. 11:20 [1]*attacked*
24 [a]Amos 2:9

and Israel [a]dwelt in all the cities
of the Am′o·rītes, in Hesh′bon
and in all its villages.
26 For Hesh′bon *was* the city
of Sī′hon king of the Am′o·rītes,
who had fought against the former king of Mō′ab, and had
taken all his land from his hand
as far as the Ar′non.
27 Therefore those who speak
in [1]proverbs say:

"Come to Hesh′bon, let it be
built;
Let the city of Sī′hon be
repaired.

28 "For [a]fire went out from
Hesh′bon,
A flame from the city of
Sī′hon;
It consumed [b]Ar of Mō′ab,
The lords of the [c]heights of
the Ar′non.
29 Woe to you, [a]Mō′ab!
You have perished, O people
of [b]Chē′mosh!
He has given his [c]sons as
fugitives,
And his [d]daughters into
captivity,
To Sī′hon king of the
Am′o·rītes.

30 "But we have shot at them;
Hesh′bon has perished [a]as
far as Dī′bon.
Then we laid waste as far as
Nō′phah,
Which *reaches* to
[b]Med′e·ba."

31 Thus Israel dwelt in the land
of the Am′o·rītes.
32 Then Moses sent to [1]spy out
[a]Jā′zer; and they took its villages and drove out the Am′-
o·rītes who *were* there.

25 [a]Amos 2:10

27 [1]*parables*

28 [a]Jer. 48:45, 46 [b]Is. 15:1 [c]Num. 22:41; 33:52

29 [a]Jer. 48:46 [b]Judg. 11:24 [c]Is. 15:2, 5 [d]Is. 16:2

30 [a]Num. 32:3, 34 [b]Is. 15:2

32 [a]Jer. 48:32 [1]*secretly search*

33 [a]Deut. 29:7 [b]Deut. 3:1 [c]Josh. 13:12

34 [a]Deut. 3:2 [b]Num. 21:24 [1]*given you victory over him*

35 [a]Deut. 3:3, 4; 29:7

CHAPTER 22

1 [a]Num. 33:48, 49

2 [a]Judg. 11:25

3 [a]Ex. 15:15

4 [a]Num. 25:15–18; 31:1–3 [1]*consume*

5 [a]2 Pet. 2:15 [b]Deut. 23:4 [1]The Euphrates [2]Or *the people of Amau*

6 [a]Num. 22:17; 23:7, 8 [b]Num. 22:12; 24:9

33 [a]And they turned and went
up by the way to [b]Bā′shan. So
Og king of Bā′shan went out
against them, he and all his
people, to battle [c]at Ed′rē·ī.
34 Then the LORD said to Moses,
[a]"Do not fear him, for I have [1]de-
livered him into your hand, with
all his people and his land; and
[b]you shall do to him as you did
to Sī′hon king of the Am′o·rītes,
who dwelt at Hesh′bon."
35 [a]So they defeated him, his
sons, and all his people, until
there was no survivor left him;
and they took possession of his
land.

22 Then [a]the children of Israel moved, and camped
in the plains of Mō′ab on the
side of the Jordan *across from*
Jericho.
2 Now [a]Bā′lak the son of Zip′-
por saw all that Israel had done
to the Am′o·rītes.
3 And [a]Mō′ab was exceedingly
afraid of the people because
they *were* many, and Mō′ab was
sick with dread because of the
children of Israel.
4 So Mō′ab said to [a]the elders
of Mid′i·an, "Now this company
will [1]lick up everything around
us, as an ox licks up the grass
of the field." And Bā′lak the son
of Zip′por *was* king of the Mō′-
ab·ītes at that time.
5 Then [a]he sent messengers
to Bā′laam the son of Bē′or
at [b]Pē′thor, which *is* near [1]the
River in the land of [2]the sons of
his people, to call him, saying:
"Look, a people has come from
Egypt. See, they cover the face
of the earth, and are settling
next to me!
6 [a]"Therefore please come at
once, [b]curse this people for me,

for they *are* too mighty for me.
Perhaps I shall be able to defeat
them and drive them out of the
land, for I know that he whom
you bless *is* blessed, and he
whom you curse is cursed."
7 So the elders of Mō′ab and
the elders of Mid′i·an departed
with [a]the diviner's fee in their
hand, and they came to Bā′laam
and spoke to him the words of
Bā′lak.
8 And he said to them, [a]"Lodge
here tonight, and I will bring
back word to you, as the LORD
speaks to me." So the princes of
Mō′ab stayed with Bā′laam.
9 [a]Then God came to Bā′laam
and said, "Who *are* these men
with you?"
10 So Bā′laam said to God, "Bā′-
lak the son of Zip′por, king of
Mō′ab, has sent to me, *saying*,
11 'Look, a people has come out
of Egypt, and they cover the face
of the earth. Come now, curse
them for me; perhaps I shall
be able to overpower them and
drive them out.' "
12 And God said to Bā′laam,
"You shall not go with them; you
shall not curse the people, for
[a]they *are* blessed."
13 So Bā′laam rose in the morning and said to the princes of
Bā′lak, "Go back to your land,
for the LORD has refused to give
me permission to go with you."
14 And the princes of Mō′ab
rose and went to Bā′lak, and
said, "Bā′laam refuses to come
with us."
15 Then Bā′lak again sent
princes, more numerous and
more [1]honorable than they.
16 And they came to Bā′laam
and said to him, "Thus says Bā′-
lak the son of Zip′por: 'Please let
nothing hinder you from coming
to me;
17 'for I will certainly [a]honor
you greatly, and I will do whatever you say to me. [b]Therefore
please come, curse this people
for me.' "
18 Then Bā′laam answered and
said to the servants of Bā′lak,
[a]"Though Bā′lak were to give me
his house full of silver and gold,
[b]I could not go beyond the word
of the LORD my God, to do less or
more.
19 "Now therefore, please, you
also [a]stay here tonight, that I
may know what more the LORD
will say to me."
20 [a]And God came to Bā′laam
at night and said to him, "If the
men come to call you, rise *and*
go with them; but [b]only the word
which I speak to you—that you
shall do."
21 So Bā′laam rose in the morning, saddled his donkey, and
went with the princes of Mō′ab.
22 Then God's anger was
aroused because he went, [a]and
the Angel of the LORD took His
stand in the way as an adversary
against him. And he was riding
on his donkey, and his two servants *were* with him.
23 Now [a]the donkey saw the
Angel of the LORD standing in
the way with His drawn sword
in His hand, and the donkey
turned aside out of the way and
went into the field. So Bā′laam
struck the donkey to turn her
back onto the road.
24 Then the Angel of the LORD
stood in a narrow path between
the vineyards, *with* a wall on
this side and a wall on that
side.
25 And when the donkey saw

7 [a]1 Sam. 9:7, 8
8 [a]Num. 22:19
9 [a]Gen. 20:3
12 [a][Rom. 11:28]
15 [1]*distinguished*
17 [a]Num. 24:11 [b]Num. 22:6
18 [a]Num. 22:38; 24:13 [b]1 Kin. 22:14
19 [a]Num. 22:8
20 [a]Num. 22:9 [b]Num. 22:35; 23:5, 12, 16, 26; 24:13
22 [a]Ex. 4:24
23 [a]Josh. 5:13

the Angel of the LORD, she
pushed herself against the wall
and crushed Bā′laam's foot
against the wall; so he struck
her again.
26 Then the Angel of the LORD
went further, and stood in a narrow place where there *was* no
way to turn either to the right
hand or to the left.
27 And when the donkey saw
the Angel of the LORD, she lay
down under Bā′laam; so Bā′-
laam's anger was aroused, and
he struck the donkey with his
staff.
28 Then the LORD [a]opened the
mouth of the donkey, and she
said to Bā′laam, "What have
I done to you, that you have
struck me these three times?"
29 And Bā′laam said to the donkey, "Because you have [1]abused
me. I wish there were a sword in
my hand, [a]for now I would kill
you!"
30 [a]So the donkey said to Bā′-
laam, "*Am* I not your donkey
on which you have ridden, ever
since *I became* yours, to this
day? Was I ever [1]disposed to do
this to you?" And he said, "No."
31 Then the LORD [a]opened Bā′-
laam's eyes, and he saw the
Angel of the LORD standing in
the way with His drawn sword
in His hand; and he bowed his
head and fell flat on his face.
32 And the Angel of the LORD
said to him, "Why have you
struck your donkey these three
times? Behold, I have come
out [1]to stand against you, because *your* way is [a]perverse[2]
before Me.
33 "The donkey saw Me and
turned aside from Me these three
times. If she had not turned
aside from Me, surely I would
also have killed you by now, and
let her live."
34 And Bā′laam said to the Angel of the LORD, [a]"I have sinned,
for I did not know You stood in
the way against me. Now therefore, if it [1]displeases You, I will
turn back."
35 Then the Angel of the LORD
said to Bā′laam, "Go with the
men, [a]but only the word that
I speak to you, that you shall
speak." So Bā′laam went with
the princes of Bā′lak.
36 Now when Bā′lak heard that
Bā′laam was coming, [a]he went
out to meet him at the city of
Mō′ab, [b]which *is* on the border
at the Ar′non, the boundary of
the territory.
37 Then Bā′lak said to Bā′laam,
"Did I not earnestly send to you,
calling for you? Why did you not
come to me? Am I not able [a]to
honor you?"
38 And Bā′laam said to Bā′lak,
"Look, I have come to you! Now,
have I any power at all to say
anything? [a]The word that God
puts in my mouth, that I must
speak."
39 So Bā′laam went with Bā′-
lak, and they came to Kir′jath
Hu′zoth.
40 Then Bā′lak offered oxen
and sheep, and he sent *some* to
Bā′laam and to the princes who
were with him.
41 So it was, the next day,
that Bā′lak took Bā′laam and
brought him up to the [a]high
places of Bā′al, that from there
he might observe [1]the extent of
the people.

CHAPTER 23

23 Then Bā′laam said to Bā′-
lak, [a]"Build seven altars
for me here, and prepare for

28 [a]2 Pet. 2:16
29 [a][Prov. 12:10] [1]*mocked*
30 [a]2 Pet. 2:16 [1]*accustomed*
31 [a]Gen. 21:19
32 [a][2 Pet. 2:14, 15] [1]*as an adversary* [2]*contrary*
34 [a]2 Sam. 12:13 [1]Lit. *is evil in your eyes*
35 [a]Num. 22:20
36 [a]Gen. 14:17 [b]Num. 21:13
37 [a]Num. 22:17; 24:11
38 [a]1 Kin. 22:14
41 [a]Num. 21:28 [1]*the farthest extent*
CHAPTER 23
1 [a]Num. 23:29

me here seven bulls and seven
rams."
2 And Bā′lak did just as Bā′-
laam had spoken, and Bā′lak
and Bā′laam [a]offered a bull and
a ram on *each* altar.
3 Then Bā′laam said to Bā′-
lak, [a]"Stand by your burnt offering, and I will go; perhaps the
LORD will come [b]to meet me, and
whatever He shows me I will tell
you." So he went to a desolate
height.
4 [a]And God met Bā′laam, and
he said to Him, "I have prepared
the seven altars, and I have offered on *each* altar a bull and a
ram."
5 Then the LORD [a]put a word
in Bā′laam's mouth, and said,
"Return to Bā′lak, and thus you
shall speak."
6 So he returned to him, and
there he was, standing by his
burnt offering, he and all the
princes of Mō′ab.
7 And he [a]took up his [1]oracle
and said:

"Bā′lak the king of Mō′ab
has brought me from
Ar′am,
From the mountains of the
east.
[b]'Come, curse Jacob for me,
And come, [c]denounce
Israel!'

8 "How[a] shall I curse whom
God has not cursed?
And how shall I denounce
whom the LORD has not
denounced?
9 For from the top of the
rocks I see him,
And from the hills I behold
him;
There! [a]A people dwelling
alone,
[b]Not reckoning itself among
the nations.

10 "Who[a] can count the [1]dust of
Jacob,
Or number one-fourth of
Israel?
Let me die [b]the death of the
righteous,
And let my end be like his!"

11 Then Bā′lak said to Bā′laam,
"What have you done to me? [a]I
took you to curse my enemies,
and look, you have blessed *them*
bountifully!"
12 So he answered and said,
[a]"Must I not take heed to speak
what the LORD has put in my
mouth?"
13 Then Bā′lak said to him,
"Please come with me to another place from which you may
see them; you shall see only the
outer part of them, and shall not
see them all; curse them for me
from there."
14 So he brought him to the
field of Zō′phim, to the top of
Pis′gah, [a]and built seven altars,
and offered a bull and a ram on
each altar.
15 And he said to Bā′lak, "Stand
here by your burnt offering while
I [1]meet *the LORD* over there."
16 Then the LORD met Bā′laam,
and [a]put a word in his mouth,
and said, "Go back to Bā′lak,
and thus you shall speak."
17 So he came to him, and there
he was, standing by his burnt offering, and the princes of Mō′ab
were with him. And Bā′lak said
to him, "What has the LORD
spoken?"

2 [a]Num. 23:14, 30
3 [a]Num. 23:15 [b]Num. 23:4, 16
4 [a]Num. 23:16
5 [a]Deut. 18:18
7 [a]Deut. 23:4 [b]Num. 22:6, 11, 17 [c]1 Sam. 17:10 [1]*prophetic discourse*
8 [a]Num. 22:12
9 [a]Deut. 32:8; 33:28 [b]Ex. 33:16
10 [a]Gen. 13:16; 22:17; 28:14 [b]Ps. 116:15 [1]Or *dust cloud*
11 [a]Num. 22:11
12 [a]Num. 22:38
14 [a]Num. 23:1, 2
15 [1]So with MT, Tg., Vg.; Syr. *call;* LXX *go and ask God*
16 [a]Num. 22:35; 23:5

18 Then he took up his oracle
and said:

[a]"Rise up, Bā′lak, and hear!
Listen to me, son of Zip′por!

19 "God[a] *is* not a man, that He
should lie,
Nor a son of man, that He
should repent.
Has He [b]said, and will He
not do?
Or has He spoken, and will
He not make it good?
20 Behold, I have received *a*
command to bless;
[a]He has blessed, and I cannot
reverse it.

21 "He[a] has not observed
iniquity in Jacob,
Nor has He seen
[1]wickedness in Israel.
The LORD his God *is* with
him,
[b]And the shout of a King *is*
among them.
22 [a]God brings them out of
Egypt;
He has [b]strength like a wild
ox.

23 "For *there is* no [1]sorcery
against Jacob,
Nor any [2]divination against
Israel.
It now must be said of
Jacob
And of Israel, 'Oh, [a]what
God has done!'
24 Look, a people rises [a]like a
lioness,
And lifts itself up like a lion;
[b]It shall not lie down until it
devours the prey,
And drinks the blood of the
slain."

25 Then Bā′lak said to Bā′laam,
"Neither curse them at all, nor
bless them at all!"
26 So Bā′laam answered and
said to Bā′lak, "Did I not tell
you, saying, [a]'All that the LORD
speaks, that I must do'?"
27 Then Bā′lak said to Bā′laam,
"Please come, I will take you to
another place; perhaps it will
please God that you may curse
them for me from there."
28 So Bā′lak took Bā′laam to
the top of Pē′or, that [a]overlooks
the [1]wasteland.
29 Then Bā′laam said to Bā′lak,
"Build for me here seven altars,
and prepare for me here seven
bulls and seven rams."
30 And Bā′lak did as Bā′laam
had said, and offered a bull and
a ram on *every* altar.

24

Now when Bā′laam saw
that it pleased the LORD to
bless Israel, he did not go as at
[a]other times, to seek to use [1]sor-
cery, but he set his face toward
the wilderness.
2 And Bā′laam raised his eyes,
and saw Israel [a]encamped according to their tribes; and [b]the
Spirit of God came upon him.
3 [a]Then he took up his oracle
and said:

"The utterance of Bā′laam
the son of Bē′or,
The utterance of the man
whose eyes are opened,
4 The utterance of him who
hears the words of God,
Who sees the vision of the
Almighty,
Who [a]falls down, with eyes
wide open:

5 "How lovely are your tents,
O Jacob!
Your dwellings, O Israel!

18 [a]Judg. 3:20
19 [a]Mal. 3:6 [b]1 Kin. 8:56
20 [a]Num. 22:12
21 [a][Rom. 4:7, 8] [b]Ps. 89:15–18 [1]*trouble*
22 [a]Num. 24:8 [b]Deut. 33:17
23 [a]Ps. 31:19; 44:1 [1]*enchantment* [2]*fortune-telling*
24 [a]Gen. 49:9 [b]Gen. 49:27
26 [a]Num. 22:38
28 [a]Num. 21:20 [1]Heb. *Jeshimon*

CHAPTER 24

1 [a]Num. 23:3, 15 [1]*enchantments*
2 [a]Num. 2:2, 34 [b]Num. 11:25
3 [a]Num. 23:7, 18
4 [a]Ezek. 1:28

6 Like valleys that stretch out,
Like gardens by the
riverside,
[a]Like aloes [b]planted by the
LORD,
Like cedars beside the
waters.
7 He shall pour water from
his buckets,
And his seed *shall be* [a]in
many waters.

"His king shall be higher
than [b]Ā′gag,
And his [c]kingdom shall be
exalted.

8 "God[a] brings him out of
Egypt;
He has strength like a wild
ox;
He shall [b]consume the
nations, his enemies;
He shall [c]break their bones
And [d]pierce *them* with his
arrows.
9 'He[a] bows down, he lies
down as a lion;
And as a lion, who shall
rouse him?'

[b]"Blessed *is* he who blesses
you,
And cursed *is* he who curses
you."

10 Then Bā′lak's anger was
aroused against Bā′laam, and
he [a]struck his hands together;
and Bā′lak said to Bā′laam, [b]"I
called you to curse my enemies,
and look, you have bountifully
blessed *them* these three times!
11 "Now therefore, flee to your
place. [a]I said I would greatly
honor you, but in fact, the LORD
has kept you back from honor."
12 So Bā′laam said to Bā′lak,
"Did I not also speak to your
messengers whom you sent to
me, saying,
13 'If Bā′lak were to give me
his house full of silver and gold,
I could not go beyond the word
of the LORD, to do good or bad
of my own will. What the LORD
says, that I must speak'?
14 "And now, indeed, I am going to my people. Come, [a]I will
advise you what this people will
do to your people in the [b]latter
days."
15 So he took up his oracle and
said:

"The utterance of Bā′laam
the son of Bē′or,
And the utterance of the
man whose eyes are
opened;
16 The utterance of him who
hears the words of God,
And has the knowledge of
the Most High,
Who sees the vision of the
Almighty,
Who falls down, with eyes
wide open:

17 "I[a] see Him, but not now; ☆
I behold Him, but not near;
[b]A Star shall come out of
Jacob;
[c]A Scepter shall rise out of
Israel,
And [1]batter the brow of
Mō′ab,
And destroy all the sons of
[2]tumult.

18 "And [a]Ē′dom shall be a
possession;
Sē′ir also, his enemies, shall
be a possession,
While Israel does [1]valiantly.
19 [a]Out of Jacob One [1]shall
have dominion,

6 [a]Jer. 17:8 [b]Ps. 104:16
7 [a]Jer. 51:13 [b]1 Sam. 15:8, 9 [c]2 Sam. 5:12
8 [a]Num. 23:22 [b]Num. 14:9; 23:24 [c]Ps. 2:9 [d]Ps. 45:5
9 [a]Gen. 49:9 [b]Gen. 12:3; 27:29
10 [a]Ezek. 21:14, 17 [b]Num. 23:11
11 [a]Num. 22:17, 37
14 [a][Mic. 6:5] [b]Gen. 49:1
17 [a]Matt. 1:2; Luke 3:34; Rev. 1:7 [b]Matt. 2:2 [c]Gen. 49:10 [1]*shatter the forehead* [2]Heb. *Sheth*, Jer. 48:45
18 [a]2 Sam. 8:14 [1]*mightily*
19 [a]Amos 9:11, 12 [1]*shall rule*

And destroy the remains of
the city."

20 Then he looked on Am′a·lek,
and he took up his oracle and
said:

"Am′a·lek *was* first among
the nations,
But *shall be* last until he
perishes."

21 Then he looked on the Ken′-
ītes, and he took up his oracle
and said:

"Firm is your dwelling place,
And your nest is set in the
rock;
22 Nevertheless Kāin shall be
burned.
How long until As′shur
carries you away
captive?"

23 Then he took up his oracle
and said:

"Alas! Who shall live when
God does this?
24 But ships *shall come* from
the coasts of [a]Cyprus,[1]
And they shall afflict As′shur
and afflict [b]Ē′ber,
And so shall [2]*Am′a·lek,* until
he perishes."

25 So Bā′laam rose and departed and [a]returned to his
place; Bā′lak also went his way.

25

Now Israel remained in
[a]Acacia Grove,[1] and the
[b]people began to commit harlotry with the women of Mō′ab.
2 [a]They invited the people to
[b]the sacrifices of their gods, and
the people ate and [c]bowed down
to their gods.

24 [a]Gen. 10:4 [b]Gen. 10:21, 25 [1]Heb. *Kittim* [2]Lit. *he* or *that one*

25 [a]Num. 22:5; 31:8

CHAPTER 25

1 [a]Josh. 2:1 [b]Rev. 2:14 [1]Heb. *Shittim*

2 [a]Hos. 9:10 [b]Ex. 34:15 [c]Ex. 20:5

3 [a]Ps. 106:28, 29

4 [a]Deut. 4:3 [b]Num. 25:11

5 [a]Ex. 18:21 [b]Deut. 13:6, 9

6 [a]Joel 2:17

7 [a]Ps. 106:30 [b]Ex. 6:25

8 [a]Ps. 106:30 [b]Num. 16:46–48

9 [a]Deut. 4:3

11 [a]Ps. 106:30 [b][Ex. 20:5]

3 So Israel was joined to
Bā′al of Pē′or, and [a]the anger of
the LORD was aroused against
Israel.
4 Then the LORD said to Moses, [a]"Take all the leaders of the
people and hang the offenders
before the LORD, out in the sun,
[b]that the fierce anger of the LORD
may turn away from Israel."
5 So Moses said to [a]the judges
of Israel, [b]"Every one of you
kill his men who were joined to
Bā′al of Pē′or."
6 And indeed, one of the children of Israel came and presented to his brethren a Mid′-
i·an·īte woman in the sight of
Moses and in the sight of all the
congregation of the children of
Israel, [a]who *were* weeping at
the door of the tabernacle of
meeting.
7 Now [a]when Phin′e·has [b]the
son of El·ē·ā′zar, the son of
Aaron the priest, saw *it,* he rose
from among the congregation
and took a javelin in his hand;
8 and he went after the man
of Israel into the tent and thrust
both of them through, the man of
Israel, and the woman through
her body. So [a]the plague was
[b]stopped among the children of
Israel.
9 And [a]those who died in
the plague were twenty-four
thousand.
10 Then the LORD spoke to Moses, saying:
11 [a]"Phin′e·has the son of El·ē·ā′-
zar, the son of Aaron the priest,
has turned back My wrath from
the children of Israel, because
he was zealous with My zeal
among them, so that I did not
consume the children of Israel
in [b]My zeal.

12 "Therefore say, [a]'Behold, I
give to him My [b]covenant of
peace;
13 'and it shall be to him and
[a]his descendants after him a covenant of [b]an everlasting priesthood, because he was [c]zealous
for his God, and [d]made [1]atone-
ment for the children of Israel.' "
14 Now the name of the Israelite
who was killed, who was killed
with the Mid′i·an·īte woman, *was*
Zim′rī the son of Sa′lū, a leader
of a father's house among the
Sim′ē·on·ītes.
15 And the name of the Mid′-
i·an·īte woman who was killed
was Cōz′bī the daughter of [a]Zūr;
he *was* head of the people of a
father's house in Mid′i·an.
16 Then the LORD spoke to Moses, saying:
17 [a]"Harass the Mid′i·an·ītes,
and [1]attack them;
18 "for they harassed you with
their [a]schemes[1] by which they
seduced you in the matter of
Pē′or and in the matter of Cōz′bī,
the daughter of a leader of Mid′-
i·an, their sister, who was killed
in the day of the plague because
of Pē′or."

26 And it came to pass, after
the [a]plague, that the LORD
spoke to Moses and El·ē·ā′zar
the son of Aaron the priest, saying:
2 [a]"Take a census of all the
congregation of the children of
Israel [b]from twenty years old
and above, by their fathers'
houses, all who are able to go to
war in Israel."
3 So Moses and El·ē·ā′zar the
priest spoke with them [a]in the
plains of Mō′ab by the Jordan,
across from Jericho, saying:
4 "*Take a census of the people*
from twenty years old and above,
just as the LORD [a]commanded
Moses and the children of Israel
who came out of the land of
Egypt."
5 [a]Reuben *was* the firstborn of
Israel. The children of Reuben
were: of Hā′noch, the family of
the Hā′noch·ītes; *of* Pal′lū, the
family of the Pal′lū·ītes;
6 *of* Hez′ron, the family of the
Hez′ron·ītes; *of* Car′mī, the family of the Car′mītes.
7 These *are* the families of the
Reū′ben·ītes: those who were
numbered of them were forty-
three thousand seven hundred
and thirty.
8 And the son of Pal′lū *was*
E·lī′ab.
9 The sons of E·lī′ab *were*
Nem′ū·el, Dā′than, and A·bī′-
ram. These *are* the Dā′than and
A·bī′ram, [a]representatives of the
congregation, who contended
against Moses and Aaron in the
company of Kō′rah, when they
contended against the LORD;
10 [a]and the earth opened its
mouth and swallowed them up
together with Kō′rah when that
company died, when the fire
devoured two hundred and fifty
men; [b]and they became a sign.
11 Nevertheless [a]the children of
Kō′rah did not die.
12 The sons of Sim′ē·on according to their families *were*:
of [1]Nem′ū·el, the family of the
Nem′ū·el·ītes; *of* Jā′min, the family of the Jā′min·ītes; *of* [2]Jā′chin,
the family of the Jā′chin·ītes;
13 *of* [1]Zē′rah, the family of the
Zar′hītes; *of* Shā′ūl, the family of
the Shā′u·lītes.
14 These *are* the families of the
Sim′ē·on·ītes: twenty-two thousand two hundred.

12 [a][Mal. 2:4, 5; 3:1] [b]Is. 54:10
13 [a]1 Chr. 6:4–15 [b]Ex. 40:15 [c]Acts 22:3 [d][Heb. 2:17] [1]Lit. *covering*
15 [a]Num. 31:8
17 [a]Num. 31:1–3 [1]*be hostile toward*
18 [a]Rev. 2:14 [1]*tricks*

CHAPTER 26

1 [a]Num. 25:9
2 [a]Num. 1:2; 14:29 [b]Num. 1:3
3 [a]Num. 22:1; 31:12; 33:48; 35:1
4 [a]Num. 1:1
5 [a]Ex. 6:14
9 [a]Num. 1:16; 16:1, 2
10 [a]Num. 16:32–35 [b]Num. 16:38–40
11 [a]Ex. 6:24
12 [1]*Jemuel,* Gen. 46:10; Ex. 6:15 [2]*Jarib,* 1 Chr. 4:24
13 [1]*Zohar,* Gen. 46:10

15 The sons of Gad according to
their families *were: of* [1]Zē′phon,
the family of the Zē′phon·ītes; *of*
Hag′gī, the family of the Hag′-
gītes; *of* Shū′nī, the family of the
Shū′nītes;
16 *of* [1]Oz′nī, the family of the
Oz′nītes; *of* Ē′rī, the family of
the Ē′rītes;
17 *of* [1]Ar′od, the family of the
Ar′od·ītes; *of* A·rē′lī, the family
of the A·rē′lītes.
18 These *are* the families of the
sons of Gad according to those
who were numbered of them:
forty thousand five hundred.
19 [a]The sons of Judah *were* Er
and Ō′nan; and Er and Ō′nan
died in the land of Cā′naan.
20 And [a]the sons of Judah according to their families were:
of Shē′lah, the family of the
Shē′la·nītes; *of* Per′ez, the family of the Par′zītes; *of* Zē′rah, the
family of the Zar′hītes.
21 And the sons of Per′ez were:
of Hez′ron, the family of the
Hez′ron·ītes; *of* Hā′mul, the family of the Hā′mul·ītes.
22 These *are* the families of Judah according to those who were
numbered of them: seventy-six
thousand five hundred.
23 The sons of Is′sa·char according to their families *were:*
of Tō′la, the family of the Tō′-
la·ītes; of [1]Pū′ah, the family of
the [2]Pū′nītes;
24 of [1]Jash′ub, the family of the
Jash′ub·ītes; of Shim′ron, the
family of the Shim′ron·ītes.
25 These *are* the families of Is′-
sa·char according to those who
were numbered of them: sixty-
four thousand three hundred.
26 [a]The sons of Zeb′ū·lun according to their families *were:*
of Sē′red, the family of the Sar′-
dītes; of Ē′lon, the family of the
Ē′lon·ītes; of Jah′lē·el, the family
of the Jah′lē·el·ītes.
27 These *are* the families of the
Zeb′ū·lun·ītes according to those
who were numbered of them:
sixty thousand five hundred.
28 [a]The sons of Joseph according to their families, by Ma·nas′-
seh and Ē′phra·im, *were:*
29 The sons of [a]Ma·nas′seh: of
[b]Mā′chir, the family of the Mā′-
chir·ītes; and Mā′chir begot Gil′-
ē·ad; of Gil′ē·ad, the family of
the Gil′ē·ad·ītes.
30 These *are* the sons of Gil′-
ē·ad: *of* [1]Je·ē′zer, the family of
the Je·ē′zer·ītes; of Hē′lek, the
family of the Hē′lek·ītes;
31 *of* As′ri·el, the family of the
As′ri·el·ītes; *of* Shē′chem, the
family of the Shē′chem·ītes;
32 *of* She·mī′da, the family of
the She·mī′da·ītes; *of* Hē′pher,
the family of the Hē′pher·ītes.
33 Now [a]Ze·loph′e·had the son
of Hē′pher had no sons, but
daughters; and the names of the
daughters of Ze·loph′e·had *were*
Mah′lah, Noah, Hog′lah, Mil′-
cah, and Tir′zah.
34 These *are* the families of
Ma·nas′seh; and those who were
numbered of them *were* fifty-
two thousand seven hundred.
35 These *are* the sons of
Ē′phra·im according to their
families: of Shū′the·lah, the
family of the Shū′thal·hītes; of
[1]Bē′cher, the family of the Bach′-
rītes; of Tā′han, the family of the
Tā′han·ītes.
36 And these *are* the sons of
Shū′the·lah: of Ē′ran, the family
of the Ē′ran·ītes.
37 These *are* the families of the
sons of Ē′phra·im according to
those who were numbered of

15 [1]*Ziphion,* Gen. 46:16
16 [1]*Ezbon,* Gen. 46:16
17 [1]Sam., Syr. *Arodi* and Gen. 46:16
19 [a]Gen. 38:2; 46:12
20 [a]1 Chr. 2:3
23 [1]So with Sam., LXX, Syr., Vg.; Heb. *Puvah,* Gen. 46:13; 1 Chr. 7:1 [2]Sam., LXX, Syr., Vg. *Puaites*
24 [1]*Job,* Gen. 46:13
26 [a]Gen. 46:14
28 [a]Gen. 46:20
29 [a]Josh. 17:1 [b]1 Chr. 7:14, 15
30 [1]*Abiezer,* Josh. 17:2
33 [a]Num. 27:1; 36:11
35 [1]*Bered,* 1 Chr. 7:20

them: thirty-two thousand five
hundred. These *are* the sons
of Joseph according to their
families.
38 [a]The sons of Benjamin according to their families were: of
Bē′la, the family of the Bē′la·ītes;
of Ash′bel, the family of the
Ash′bel·ītes; of [b]A·hī′ram, the
family of the A·hī′ram·ītes;
39 of [a]Shū′pham,[1] the family of
the Shū′pham·ītes; of [2]Hū′pham,
the family of the Hū′pham·ītes.
40 And the sons of Bē′la were
[1]Ard and Nā′a·man: [a]*of Ard,* the
family of the Ard′ītes; of Nā′-
a·man, the family of the Nā′-
a·mītes.
41 These *are* the sons of Benjamin according to their families;
and those who were numbered
of them *were* forty-five thousand six hundred.
42 These *are* the sons of Dan
according to their families: of
[1]Shū′ham, the family of the Shū′-
ham·ītes. These *are* the families of Dan according to their
families.
43 All the families of the Shū′-
ham·ītes, according to those
who were numbered of them,
were sixty-four thousand four
hundred.
44 [a]The sons of Ash′er according to their families *were:* of
Jim′na, the family of the Jim′-
nītes; of Jes′ū·ī, the family of the
Jes′ū·ītes; of Bē·rī′ah, the family
of the Bē·rī′ītes.
45 Of the sons of Bē·rī′ah: of
Hē′ber, the family of the Hē′-
ber·ītes; of Mal′chi·el, the family
of the Mal′chi·el·ītes.
46 And the name of the daughter of Ash′er *was* Sē′rah.
47 These *are* the families of
the sons of Ash′er according to
those who were numbered of
them: fifty-three thousand four
hundred.
48 [a]The sons of Naph′ta·lī according to their families *were:*
of [1]Jah′zē·el, the family of the
Jah′zē·el·ītes; of Gū′nī, the family of the Gū′nītes;
49 of Jē′zer, the family of the
Jē′zer·ītes; of [a]Shil′lem, the family of the Shil′lem·ītes.
50 These *are* the families of
Naph′ta·lī according to their
families; and those who were
numbered of them *were* forty-
five thousand four hundred.
51 [a]These *are* those who were
numbered of the children of Israel: six hundred and one thousand seven hundred and thirty.
52 Then the LORD spoke to Moses, saying:
53 [a]"To these the land shall
be [b]divided as an inheritance,
according to the number of
names.
54 [a]"To a large *tribe* you shall
give a larger inheritance, and
to a small *tribe* you shall give a
smaller inheritance. Each shall
be given its inheritance according to those who were numbered
of them.
55 "But the land shall be [a]divided
by lot; they shall inherit according to the names of the tribes of
their fathers.
56 "According to the lot their
inheritance shall be divided
between the larger and the
smaller."
57 [a]And these *are* those who
were numbered of the Lē′vītes
according to their families: of
Ger′shon, the family of the Ger′-
shon·ītes; of Kō′hath, the family
of the Kō′hath·ītes; of Me·rar′ī,
the family of the Me·rar′ītes.

38 [a]Gen. 46:21 [b]1 Chr. 8:1, 2
39 [a]1 Chr. 7:12 [1]MT *Shephupham; Shephuphan,* 1 Chr. 8:5 [2]*Huppim,* Gen. 46:21
40 [a]1 Chr. 8:3 [1]*Addar,* 1 Chr. 8:3
42 [1]*Hushim,* Gen. 46:23
44 [a]Gen. 46:17
48 [a]1 Chr. 7:13 [1]*Jahziel,* 1 Chr. 7:13
49 [a]1 Chr. 7:13
51 [a]Num. 1:46; 11:21
53 [a]Josh. 11:23; 14:1 [b]Num. 33:54
54 [a]Num. 33:54
55 [a]Num. 33:54; 34:13
57 [a]Gen. 46:11

58 These *are* the families of the Lē′vītes: the family of the Lib′nītes, the family of the Hē′bron·ītes, the family of the Mah′lītes, the family of the Mū′shītes, and the family of the Kō′ra·thītes. And Kō′hath begot Am′ram.

59 The name of Am′ram's wife *was* [a]Joch′e·bed the daughter of Levi, who was born to Levi in Egypt; and to Am′ram she bore Aaron and Moses and their sister Miriam.

60 [a]To Aaron were born Nā′dab and A·bī′hū, El·ē·ā′zar and Ith′a·mar.

61 And [a]Nā′dab and A·bī′hū died when they offered profane fire before the LORD.

62 [a]Now those who were numbered of them were twenty-three thousand, every male from a month old and above; [b]for they were not numbered among the other children of Israel, because there was [c]no inheritance given to them among the children of Israel.

63 These *are* those who were numbered by Moses and El·ē·ā′zar the priest, who numbered the children of Israel [a]in the plains of Mō′ab by the Jordan, *across from* Jericho.

64 [a]But among these there was not a man of those who were numbered by Moses and Aaron the priest when they numbered the children of Israel in the [b]Wilderness of Sinai.

65 For the LORD had said of them, "They [a]shall surely die in the wilderness." So there was not left a man of them, [b]except Caleb the son of Je·phūn′neh and Joshua the son of Nun.

59 [a]Ex. 2:1, 2; 6:20
60 [a]Num. 3:2
61 [a]Lev. 10:1, 2
62 [a]Num. 3:39 [b]Num. 1:49 [c]Num. 18:20, 23, 24
63 [a]Num. 26:3
64 [a]Num. 14:29–35 [b]Num. 1:1–46
65 [a]Num. 14:26–35 [b]Num. 14:30

CHAPTER 27

1 [a]Num. 26:33; 36:1, 11
3 [a]Num. 14:35; 26:64, 65 [b]Num. 16:1, 2
4 [a]Deut. 25:6 [b]Josh. 17:4 [1]*withdrawn* [2]*inheritance*
5 [a]Ex. 18:13–26
7 [a]Num. 36:2

27

Then came the daughters of [a]Ze·loph′e·had the son of Hē′pher, the son of Gil′ē·ad, the son of Mā′chir, the son of Ma·nas′seh, from the families of Ma·nas′seh the son of Joseph; and these *were* the names of his daughters: Mah′lah, Noah, Hog′lah, Mil′cah, and Tir′zah.

2 And they stood before Moses, before El·ē·ā′zar the priest, and before the leaders and all the congregation, *by* the doorway of the tabernacle of meeting, saying:

3 "Our father [a]died in the wilderness; but he was not in the company of those who gathered together against the LORD, [b]in company with Kō′rah, but he died in his own sin; and he had no sons.

4 "Why should the name of our father be [a]removed[1] from among his family because he had no son? [b]Give us a [2]possession among our father's brothers."

5 So Moses [a]brought their case before the LORD.

6 And the LORD spoke to Moses, saying:

7 "The daughters of Ze·loph′e·had speak *what is* right; [a]you shall surely give them a possession of inheritance among their father's brothers, and cause the inheritance of their father to pass to them.

8 "And you shall speak to the children of Israel, saying: 'If a man dies and has no son, then you shall cause his inheritance to pass to his daughter.

9 'If he has no daughter, then you shall give his inheritance to his brothers.

10 'If he has no brothers, then

you shall give his inheritance to
his father's brothers.
11 'And if his father has no
brothers, then you shall give his
inheritance to the relative closest to him in his family, and he
shall possess it.' " And it shall
be to the children of Israel [a]a
statute of judgment, just as the
LORD commanded Moses.
12 Now the LORD said to Moses:
[a]"Go up into this Mount Ab'-
a·rim, and see the land which
I have given to the children of
Israel.
13 "And when you have seen
it, you also [a]shall [1]be gathered
to your people, as Aaron your
brother was gathered.
14 "For in the Wilderness of Zin,
during the strife of the congregation, you [a]rebelled against My
command to hallow Me at the
waters before their eyes." (These
are the [b]waters of Mer'i·bah, at
Kā'desh in the Wilderness of
Zin.)
15 Then Moses spoke to the
LORD, saying:
16 "Let the LORD, [a]the God of
the spirits of all flesh, set a man
over the congregation,
17 [a]"who may go out before
them and go in before them, who
may lead them out and bring
them in, that the congregation of
the LORD may not be [b]like sheep
which have no shepherd."
18 And the LORD said to Moses:
"Take Joshua the son of Nun
with you, a man [a]in whom *is* the
Spirit, and [b]lay your hand on
him;
19 "set him before El·ē·ā'zar the
priest and before all the congregation, and [a]inaugurate[1] him in
their sight.
20 "And [a]you shall give *some* of
your authority to him, that all
the congregation of the children
of Israel [b]may be obedient.
21 [a]"He shall stand before
El·ē·ā'zar the priest, who shall
inquire before the LORD for
him [b]by the judgment of the
Ū'rim. [c]At his word they shall go
out, and at his word they shall
come in, he and all the children of Israel with him—all the
congregation."
22 So Moses did as the LORD
commanded him. He took Joshua
and set him before El·ē·ā'zar
the priest and before all the
congregation.
23 And he laid his hands on
him [a]and [1]inaugurated him, just
as the LORD commanded by the
hand of Moses.

28 Now the LORD spoke to
Moses, saying,
2 "Command the children of
Israel, and say to them, 'My offering, [a]My food for My offerings
made by fire as a sweet aroma to
Me, you shall be careful to offer
to Me at their appointed time.'
3 "And you shall say to them,
[a]'This *is* the offering made by
fire which you shall offer to
the LORD: two male lambs in
their first year without blemish,
day by day, as a regular burnt
offering.
4 'The one lamb you shall offer
in the morning, the other lamb
you shall offer in the evening,
5 'and [a]one-tenth of an ephah
of fine flour as a [b]grain offering
mixed with one-fourth of a hin
of pressed oil.
6 '*It is* [a]a regular burnt offering which was ordained at
Mount Sinai for a sweet aroma,
an offering made by fire to the
LORD.

11 [a]Num. 35:29
12 [a]Num. 33:47
13 [a]Deut. 10:6; 34:5, 6 [1]Die and join your ancestors
14 [a]Ps. 106:32, 33 [b]Ex. 17:7
16 [a]Num. 16:22
17 [a]Deut. 31:2 [b]Zech. 10:2
18 [a]Gen. 41:38 [b]Deut. 34:9
19 [a]Deut. 3:28; 31:3, 7, 8, 23 [1]*commission*
20 [a]Num. 11:17 [b]Josh. 1:16–18
21 [a]1 Sam. 23:9; 30:7 [b]Ex. 28:30 [c]1 Sam. 22:10
23 [a]Deut. 3:28; 31:7, 8 [1]*commissioned*

CHAPTER 28

2 [a]Lev. 3:11; 21:6, 8
3 [a]Ex. 29:38–42
5 [a]Ex. 16:36 [b]Lev. 2:1
6 [a]Ex. 29:42

7 'And its drink offering *shall*
be one-fourth of a hin for each
lamb; [a]in a holy *place* you shall
pour out the drink to the LORD as
an offering.
8 'The other lamb you shall offer in the evening; as the morning grain offering and its drink
offering, you shall offer *it* as an
offering made by fire, a [1]sweet
aroma to the LORD.
9 'And on the Sabbath day two
lambs in their first year, without
blemish, and two-tenths *of an*
ephah of fine flour as a grain
offering, mixed with oil, with its
drink offering—
10 '*this is* [a]the burnt offering for
every Sabbath, besides the regular burnt offering with its drink
offering.
11 [a]'At the beginnings of your
months you shall present a
burnt offering to the LORD: two
young bulls, one ram, and seven
lambs in their first year, without
blemish;
12 [a]'three-tenths *of an ephah*
of fine flour as a grain offering,
mixed with oil, for each bull;
two-tenths *of an ephah* of fine
flour as a grain offering, mixed
with oil, for the one ram;
13 'and one-tenth *of an ephah*
of fine flour, mixed with oil, as a
grain offering for each lamb, as
a burnt offering of sweet aroma,
an offering made by fire to the
LORD.
14 'Their drink offering shall be
half a hin of wine for a bull, one-
third of a hin for a ram, and one-
fourth of a hin for a lamb; this
is the burnt offering for each
month throughout the months
of the year.
15 'Also [a]one kid of the goats as
a sin offering to the LORD shall
be offered, besides the regular burnt offering and its drink
offering.
16 [a]'On the fourteenth day of
the first month *is* the Passover
of the LORD.
17 [a]'And on the fifteenth day of
this month *is* the feast; unleavened bread shall be eaten for
seven days.
18 'On the [a]first day *you shall*
have a holy [1]convocation. You
shall do no [2]customary work.
19 'And you shall present an
offering made by fire as a burnt
offering to the LORD: two young
bulls, one ram, and seven lambs
in their first year. [a]Be sure they
are without blemish.
20 'Their grain offering shall
be of fine flour mixed with oil:
three-tenths *of an ephah* you
shall offer for a bull, and two-
tenths for a ram;
21 'you shall offer one-tenth *of*
an ephah for each of the seven
lambs;
22 'also [a]one goat *as* a sin offering, to make [1]atonement for you.
23 'You shall offer these besides
the burnt offering of the morning, which *is* for a regular burnt
offering.
24 'In this manner you shall offer the food of the offering made
by fire daily for seven days,
as a sweet aroma to the LORD;
it shall be offered besides the
regular burnt offering and its
drink offering.
25 'And [a]on the seventh day
you shall have a holy convocation. You shall do no customary
work.
26 'Also [a]on the day of the firstfruits, when you bring a new
grain offering to the LORD at
your *Feast of* Weeks, you shall

7 [a]Ex. 29:42
8 [1]*pleasing*
10 [a]Ezek. 46:4
11 [a]Num. 10:10
12 [a]Num. 15:4–12
15 [a]Num. 15:24; 28:3, 22
16 [a]Lev. 23:5–8
17 [a]Lev. 23:6
18 [a]Lev. 23:7 [1]*assembly* or *gathering* [2]*occupational*
19 [a]Deut. 15:21
22 [a]Num. 28:15 [1]Lit. *covering*
25 [a]Lev. 23:8
26 [a]Deut. 16:9–12

have a holy convocation. You
shall do no customary work.
27 ‘You shall present a burnt
offering as a sweet aroma to the
LORD: [a]two young bulls, one ram,
and seven lambs in their first
year,
28 ‘with their grain offering of
fine flour mixed with oil: three-
tenths *of an ephah* for each bull,
two-tenths for the one ram,
29 ‘and one-tenth for each of
the seven lambs;
30 ‘*also* one kid of the goats, to
make [1]atonement for you.
31 [a]‘Be sure they are without
[1]blemish. You shall present *them*
with their drink offerings, besides the regular burnt offering
with its grain offering.

29 ‘And in the seventh
month, on the first *day* of
the month, you shall have a holy
convocation. You shall do no
customary work. For you [a]it is a
day of blowing the trumpets.
2 ‘You shall offer a burnt offering as a sweet aroma to the
LORD: one young bull, one ram,
and seven lambs in their first
year, without blemish.
3 ‘Their grain offering *shall be*
fine flour mixed with oil: three-
tenths *of an ephah* for the bull,
two-tenths for the ram,
4 ‘and one-tenth for each of
the seven lambs;
5 ‘also one kid of the goats *as*
a sin offering, to make atonement for you;
6 ‘besides [a]the burnt offering
with its grain offering for the
New Moon, [b]the regular burnt
offering with its grain offering, and their drink offerings,
[c]according to their ordinance, as
a sweet aroma, an offering made
by fire to the LORD.
7 [a]‘On the tenth *day* of this
seventh month you shall have
a holy convocation. You shall
[b]afflict your souls; you shall not
do any work.
8 ‘You shall present a burnt
offering to the LORD *as* a sweet
aroma: one young bull, one ram,
and seven lambs in their first
year. [a]Be sure they are without
blemish.
9 ‘Their grain offering *shall*
be of fine flour mixed with oil:
three-tenths *of an ephah* for
the bull, two-tenths for the one
ram,
10 ‘and one-tenth for each of
the seven lambs;
11 ‘also one kid of the goats
as a sin offering, besides [a]the
sin offering for atonement, the
regular burnt offering with its
grain offering, and their drink
offerings.
12 [a]‘On the fifteenth day of the
seventh month you shall have a
holy convocation. You shall do
no customary work, and you
shall keep a feast to the LORD
seven days.
13 [a]‘You shall present a burnt
offering, an offering made by
fire as a sweet aroma to the
LORD: thirteen young bulls, two
rams, *and* fourteen lambs in
their first year. They shall be
without blemish.
14 ‘Their grain offering *shall*
be of fine flour mixed with oil:
three-tenths *of an ephah* for
each of the thirteen bulls, two-
tenths for each of the two rams,
15 ‘and one-tenth for each of
the fourteen lambs;
16 ‘also one kid of the goats
as a sin offering, besides the
regular burnt offering, its grain
offering, and its drink offering.

27 [a]Lev. 23:18, 19
30 [1]Lit. *covering*
31 [a]Num. 28:3, 19 [1]*defect*

CHAPTER 29

1 [a]Lev. 23:23–25
6 [a]Num. 28:11–15 [b]Num. 28:3 [c]Num. 15:11, 12
7 [a]Lev. 16:29–34; 23:26–32 [b]Is. 58:5
8 [a]Num. 28:19
11 [a]Lev. 16:3, 5
12 [a]Deut. 16:13–15
13 [a]Ezra 3:4

17 'On the [a]second day *present*
twelve young bulls, two rams,
fourteen lambs in their first year
without blemish,
18 'and their grain offering and
their drink offerings for the bulls,
for the rams, and for the lambs,
by their number, [a]according to
the ordinance;
19 'also one kid of the goats
as a sin offering, besides the
regular burnt offering with its
grain offering, and their drink
offerings.
20 'On the third day *present*
eleven bulls, two rams, fourteen
lambs in their first year without
blemish,
21 'and their grain offering and
their drink offerings for the bulls,
for the rams, and for the lambs,
by their number, [a]according to
the ordinance;
22 'also one goat *as* a sin offering, besides the regular burnt
offering, its grain offering, and
its drink offering.
23 'On the fourth day *present*
ten bulls, two rams, *and* fourteen lambs in their first year,
without blemish,
24 'and their grain offering and
their drink offerings for the
bulls, for the rams, and for the
lambs, by their number, according to the ordinance;
25 'also one kid of the goats
as a sin offering, besides the
regular burnt offering, its grain
offering, and its drink offering.
26 'On the fifth day *present* nine
bulls, two rams, *and* fourteen
lambs in their first year without
blemish,
27 'and their grain offering and
their drink offerings for the bulls,
for the rams, and for the lambs,
by their number, according to
the ordinance;
28 'also one goat *as* a sin offering, besides the regular burnt
offering, its grain offering, and
its drink offering.
29 'On the sixth day *present*
eight bulls, two rams, *and* fourteen lambs in their first year
without blemish,
30 'and their grain offering and
their drink offerings for the
bulls, for the rams, and for the
lambs, by their number, according to the ordinance;
31 'also one goat *as* a sin offering, besides the regular burnt
offering, its grain offering, and
its drink offering.
32 'On the seventh day *present*
seven bulls, two rams, *and* fourteen lambs in their first year
without blemish,
33 'and their grain offering and
their drink offerings for the
bulls, for the rams, and for the
lambs, by their number, according to the ordinance;
34 'also one goat *as* a sin offering, besides the regular burnt
offering, its grain offering, and
its drink offering.
35 'On the eighth day you shall
have a [a]sacred[1] assembly. You
shall do no customary work.
36 'You shall present a burnt
offering, an offering made by
fire as a sweet aroma to the
LORD: one bull, one ram, seven
lambs in their first year without
blemish,
37 'and their grain offering and
their drink offerings for the bull,
for the ram, and for the lambs,
by their number, according to
the ordinance;
38 'also one goat *as* a sin offering, besides the regular burnt

17 [a]Lev. 23:36
18 [a]Num. 15:12; 28:7, 14; 29:3, 4, 9, 10
21 [a]Num. 29:18
35 [a]Lev. 23:36 [1]*solemn*

offering, its grain offering, and
its drink offering.
39 'These you shall present to
the LORD at your [a]appointed
feasts (besides your [b]vowed offerings and your freewill offerings) as your burnt offerings
and your grain offerings, as
your drink offerings and your
peace offerings.' "
40 So Moses told the children
of Israel everything, just as the
LORD commanded Moses.

30

Then Moses spoke to [a]the
heads of the tribes con-
cerning the children of Israel,
saying, "This *is* the thing which
the LORD has commanded:
2 [a]"If a man makes a vow to
the LORD, or [b]swears an oath
to bind himself by some agreement, he shall not break his
word; he shall [c]do according
to all that proceeds out of his
mouth.
3 "Or if a woman makes a vow
to the LORD, and binds *herself*
by some agreement while in her
father's house in her youth,
4 "and her father hears her
vow and the agreement by which
she has bound herself, and her
father [1]holds his peace, then all
her vows shall stand, and every
agreement with which she has
bound herself shall stand.
5 "But if her father overrules
her on the day that he hears,
then none of her vows nor her
agreements by which she has
bound herself shall stand; and
the LORD will release her, because her father overruled her.
6 "If indeed she takes a husband, while bound by her vows
or by a rash utterance from
her lips by which she bound
herself,

39 [a]Lev. 23:1–44 [b]Lev. 7:16; 22:18, 21, 23; 23:38

CHAPTER 30

1 [a]Num. 1:4, 16; 7:2

2 [a]Lev. 27:2 [b]Matt. 14:9 [c]Job 22:27

4 [1]*says nothing* to interfere

8 [a][Gen. 3:16]

12 [1]*annulled* or *invalidated*

7 "and her husband hears *it*,
and makes no response to her
on the day that he hears, then
her vows shall stand, and her
agreements by which she bound
herself shall stand.
8 "But if her husband [a]overrules
her on the day that he hears *it*,
he shall make void her vow
which she took and what she uttered with her lips, by which she
bound herself, and the LORD will
release her.
9 "Also any vow of a widow or
a divorced woman, by which she
has bound herself, shall stand
against her.
10 "If she vowed in her husband's house, or bound herself
by an agreement with an oath,
11 "and her husband heard *it*,
and made no response to her
and did not overrule her, then all
her vows shall stand, and every
agreement by which she bound
herself shall stand.
12 "But if her husband truly
made them void on the day he
heard *them*, then whatever proceeded from her lips concerning her vows or concerning the
agreement binding her, it shall
not stand; her husband has
made them [1]void, and the LORD
will release her.
13 "Every vow and every binding oath to afflict her soul, her
husband may confirm it, or her
husband may make it void.
14 "Now if her husband makes
no response whatever to her
from day to day, then he confirms all her vows or all the
agreements that bind her; he
confirms them, because he made
no response to her on the day
that he heard *them*.
15 "But if he does make them

void after he has heard *them*,
then he shall bear her guilt."
16 These *are* the statutes which
the LORD commanded Moses,
between a man and his wife, and
between a father and his daughter in her youth in her father's
house.

31 And the LORD spoke to
Moses, saying:
2 [a]"Take vengeance on the
Mid'i·an·ītes for the children of
Israel. Afterward you shall [b]be
gathered to your people."
3 So Moses spoke to the people, saying, "Arm some of yourselves for war, and let them
go against the Mid'i·an·ītes to
take vengeance for the LORD on
[a]Mid'i·an.
4 "A thousand from each tribe
of all the tribes of Israel you
shall send to the war."
5 So there were recruited from
the divisions of Israel one thousand from *each* tribe, twelve
thousand armed for war.
6 Then Moses sent them to
the war, one thousand from
each tribe; he sent them to the
war with Phin'e·has the son of
El·ē·ā'zar the priest, with the
holy articles and [a]the signal
trumpets in his hand.
7 And they warred against the
Mid'i·an·ītes, just as the LORD
commanded Moses, and [a]they
killed all the [b]males.
8 They killed the kings of Mid'-
i·an with *the rest of* those who
were killed—[a]Ē'vī, Rē'kem, [b]Zūr,
Hur, and Rē'ba, the five kings
of Mid'i·an. [c]Bā'laam the son of
Bē'or they also killed with the
sword.
9 And the children of Israel
took the women of Mid'i·an captive, with their little ones, and
took as spoil all their cattle, all
their flocks, and all their goods.
10 They also burned with fire
all the cities where they dwelt,
and all their forts.
11 And [a]they took all the spoil
and all the booty—of man and
beast.
12 Then they brought the captives, the booty, and the spoil to
Moses, to El·ē·ā'zar the priest,
and to the congregation of the
children of Israel, to the camp
in the plains of Mō'ab by the
Jordan, *across from* Jericho.
13 And Moses, El·ē·ā'zar the
priest, and all the leaders of
the congregation, went to meet
them outside the camp.
14 But Moses was angry with
the officers of the army, *with*
the captains over thousands and
captains over hundreds, who
had come from the battle.
15 And Moses said to them:
"Have you kept [a]all the women
alive?
16 "Look, [a]these *women* caused
the children of Israel, through
the [b]counsel of Bā'laam, to trespass against the LORD in the incident of Pē'or, and [c]there was a
plague among the congregation
of the LORD.
17 "Now therefore, [a]kill every male among the little ones,
and kill every woman who has
known a man intimately.
18 "But keep alive [a]for yourselves all the young girls
who have not known a man
intimately.
19 "And as for you, [a]remain outside the camp seven days; whoever has killed any person, and
[b]whoever has touched any slain,
purify yourselves and your cap-

CHAPTER 31
2 [a]Num. 25:17 [b]Num. 27:12, 13
3 [a]Josh. 13:21
6 [a]Num. 10:9
7 [a]Deut. 20:13 [b]Gen. 34:25
8 [a]Josh. 13:21 [b]Num. 25:15 [c]Josh. 13:22
11 [a]Deut. 20:14
15 [a]Deut. 20:14
16 [a]Num. 25:2 [b]Rev. 2:14 [c]Num. 25:9
17 [a]Deut. 7:2; 20:16–18
18 [a]Deut. 21:10–14
19 [a]Num. 5:2 [b]Num. 19:11–22

tives on the third day and on the seventh day.
20 "Purify every garment, everything made of leather, everything woven of goats' *hair,* and everything made of wood."
21 Then El·ē·ā′zar the priest said to the men of war who had gone to the battle, "This *is* the [1]ordinance of the law which the LORD commanded Moses:
22 "Only the gold, the silver, the bronze, the iron, the tin, and the lead,
23 "everything that can endure fire, you shall put through the fire, and it shall be clean; and it shall be purified [a]with the water of purification. But all that cannot endure fire you shall put through water.
24 [a]"And you shall wash your clothes on the seventh day and be clean, and afterward you may come into the camp."
25 Now the LORD spoke to Moses, saying:
26 "Count up the plunder that was [1]taken—of man and beast—you and El·ē·ā′zar the priest and the chief fathers of the congregation;
27 "and [a]divide the plunder into two parts, between those who took part in the war, who went out to battle, and all the congregation.
28 "And levy a [1]tribute for the LORD on the men of war who went out to battle: [a]one of every five hundred of the persons, the cattle, the donkeys, and the sheep;
29 "take *it* from their half, and [a]give *it* to El·ē·ā′zar the priest as a heave offering to the LORD.
30 "And from the children of Israel's half you shall take [a]one of every fifty, drawn from the persons, the cattle, the donkeys, and the sheep, from all the livestock, and give them to the Lē′vītes [b]who [1]keep charge of the tabernacle of the LORD."
31 So Moses and El·ē·ā′zar the priest did as the LORD commanded Moses.
32 The booty remaining from the plunder, which the men of war had taken, was six hundred and seventy-five thousand sheep,
33 seventy-two thousand cattle,
34 sixty-one thousand donkeys,
35 and thirty-two thousand persons in all, of women who had not known a man intimately.
36 And the half, the portion for those who had gone out to war, was in number three hundred and thirty-seven thousand five hundred sheep;
37 and the LORD's [1]tribute of the sheep was six hundred and seventy-five.
38 The cattle *were* thirty-six thousand, of which the LORD's tribute *was* seventy-two.
39 The donkeys *were* thirty thousand five hundred, of which the LORD's tribute *was* sixty-one.
40 The persons *were* sixteen thousand, of which the LORD's tribute *was* thirty-two persons.
41 So Moses gave the tribute *which was* the LORD's heave offering to El·ē·ā′zar the priest, [a]as the LORD commanded Moses.
42 And from the children of Israel's half, which Moses separated from the men who fought—
43 now the half belonging to the congregation was three hundred and thirty-seven thousand five hundred sheep,

21 [1]*statute*
23 [a]Num. 19:9, 17
24 [a]Lev. 11:25
26 [1]*captured*
27 [a]Josh. 22:8
28 [a]Num. 31:30, 47 [1]*tax*
29 [a]Deut. 18:1–5
30 [a]Num. 31:42–47 [b]Num. 3:7, 8, 25, 31, 36; 18:3, 4 [1]*perform the service*
37 [1]*tax*
41 [a]Num. 5:9, 10; 18:8, 19

44 thirty-six thousand cattle,
45 thirty thousand five hundred
donkeys,
46 and sixteen thousand
persons—
47 and [a]from the children of
Israel's half Moses took one of
every fifty, drawn from man and
beast, and gave them to the Lē′-
vītes, who kept charge of the
tabernacle of the LORD, as the
LORD commanded Moses.
48 Then the officers who *were*
over thousands of the army, the
captains of thousands and captains of hundreds, came near to
Moses;
49 and they said to Moses, "Your
servants have taken a count of
the men of war who *are* under
our command, and not a man of
us is missing.
50 "Therefore we have brought
an offering for the LORD, what every man found of ornaments of
gold: armlets and bracelets and
signet rings and earrings and
necklaces, [a]to make [1]atonement
for ourselves before the LORD."
51 So Moses and El·ē·ā′zar
the priest received the gold
from them, all the fashioned
ornaments.
52 And all the gold of the offering that they offered to the LORD,
from the captains of thousands
and captains of hundreds, was
sixteen thousand seven hundred
and fifty shekels.
53 [a](The men of war had taken
spoil, every man for himself.)
54 And Moses and El·ē·ā′zar the
priest received the gold from the
captains of thousands and of
hundreds, and brought it into
the tabernacle of meeting [a]as
a memorial for the children of
Israel before the LORD.

47 [a]Num. 31:30
50 [a]Ex. 30:12–16 [1]Lit. *covering*
53 [a]Deut. 20:14
54 [a]Ex. 30:16

CHAPTER 32
1 [a]Num. 21:32 [b]Deut. 3:13
3 [a]Num. 32:36 [b]Josh. 13:17, 26 [c]Num. 32:38 [d]Num. 32:38
4 [a]Num. 21:24, 34, 35
7 [a]Num. 13:27—14:4
8 [a]Num. 13:3, 26 [b]Deut. 1:19–25
9 [a]Deut. 1:24, 28
10 [a]Deut. 1:34–36
11 [a]Num. 14:28, 29; 26:63–65

32 Now the children of Reuben and the children of
Gad had a very great multitude
of livestock; and when they saw
the land of [a]Jā′zer and the land
of [b]Gil′ē·ad, that indeed the region *was* a place for livestock,
2 the children of Gad and the
children of Reuben came and
spoke to Moses, to El·ē·ā′zar the
priest, and to the leaders of the
congregation, saying,
3 "At′a·roth, Dī′bon, Jā′zer,
[a]Nim′rah, [b]Hesh′bon, Ē·le·ā′leh,
[c]Shē′bam, Nē′bō, and [d]Bē′on,
4 "the country [a]which the LORD
defeated before the congregation of Israel, *is* a land for livestock, and your servants have
livestock."
5 Therefore they said, "If we
have found favor in your sight,
let this land be given to your
servants as a possession. Do not
take us over the Jordan."
6 And Moses said to the children of Gad and to the children
of Reuben: "Shall your brethren
go to war while you sit here?
7 "Now why will you [a]dis-
courage the heart of the children of Israel from going over
into the land which the LORD has
given them?
8 "Thus your fathers did [a]when
I sent them away from Kā′desh
Bar·nē′a [b]to see the land.
9 "For [a]when they went up to
the Valley of Esh′col and saw
the land, they discouraged the
heart of the children of Israel, so
that they did not go into the land
which the LORD had given them.
10 [a]"So the LORD's anger was
aroused on that day, and He
swore an oath, saying,
11 'Surely none of the men
who came up from Egypt, [a]from

twenty years old and above,
shall see the land of which I
swore to Abraham, Isaac, and
Jacob, because [b]they have not
wholly followed Me,
12 'except Caleb the son of
Je·phŭn′neh, the Kē′niz·zīte, and
Joshua the son of Nun, [a]for they
have wholly followed the LORD.'
13 "So the LORD's anger was
aroused against Israel, and He
made them [a]wander in the wilderness forty years, until [b]all the
generation that had done evil in
the sight of the LORD was gone.
14 "And look! You have risen in
your fathers' place, a brood of
sinful men, to increase still more
the [a]fierce anger of the LORD
against Israel.
15 "For if you [a]turn away from
following Him, He will once
again leave them in the wilderness, and you will destroy all
these people."
16 Then they came near to him
and said: "We will build sheepfolds here for our livestock, and
cities for our little ones,
17 "but [a]we ourselves will be
armed, ready *to go* before the
children of Israel until we have
brought them to their place; and
our little ones will dwell in the
fortified cities because of the
inhabitants of the land.
18 [a]"We will not return to our
homes until every one of the
children of Israel has [1]received
his inheritance.
19 "For we will not inherit with
them on the other side of the
Jordan and beyond, [a]because
our inheritance has fallen to
us on this eastern side of the
Jordan."
20 Then [a]Moses said to them:
"If you do this thing, if you arm
yourselves before the LORD for
the war,
21 "and all your armed men
cross over the Jordan before the
LORD until He has driven out His
enemies from before Him,
22 "and [a]the land is subdued
before the LORD, then afterward
[b]you may return and be blameless before the LORD and before Israel; and [c]this land shall
be your possession before the
LORD.
23 "But if you do not do so,
then take note, you have sinned
against the LORD; and be sure
[a]your sin will find you out.
24 [a]"Build cities for your little
ones and folds for your sheep,
and do [1]what has proceeded out
of your mouth."
25 And the children of Gad and
the children of Reuben spoke to
Moses, saying: "Your servants
will do as my lord commands.
26 [a]"Our little ones, our wives,
our flocks, and all our livestock
will be there in the cities of Gil′-
ē·ad;
27 [a]"but your servants will cross
over, every man armed for war,
before the LORD to battle, just as
my lord says."
28 So Moses gave command
[a]concerning them to El·ē·ā′zar
the priest, to Joshua the son of
Nun, and to the chief fathers
of the tribes of the children of
Israel.
29 And Moses said to them: "If
the children of Gad and the
children of Reuben cross over
the Jordan with you, every man
armed for battle before the
LORD, and the land is subdued
before you, then you shall give
them the land of Gil′ē·ad as a
possession.

11 [b]Num. 14:24, 30
12 [a]Deut. 1:36
13 [a]Num. 14:33–35 [b]Num. 26:64, 65
14 [a]Deut. 1:34
15 [a]Deut. 30:17, 18
17 [a]Josh. 4:12, 13
18 [a]Josh. 22:1–4 [1]*possessed*
19 [a]Josh. 12:1; 13:8
20 [a]Deut. 3:18
22 [a]Deut. 3:20 [b]Josh. 22:4 [c]Deut. 3:12, 15, 16, 18
23 [a]Is. 59:12
24 [a]Num. 32:16 [1]*what you said you would do*
26 [a]Josh. 1:14
27 [a]Josh. 4:12
28 [a]Josh. 1:13

30 "But if they do not cross over
armed with you, they shall have
possessions among you in the
land of Cā'naan."
31 Then the children of Gad
and the children of Reuben answered, saying: "As the LORD has
said to your servants, so we will
do.
32 "We will cross over armed
before the LORD into the land
of Cā'naan, but the possession
of our inheritance *shall re-*
main with us on this side of the
Jordan."
33 So [a]Moses gave to the children of Gad, to the children of
Reuben, and to half the tribe of
Ma·nas'seh the son of Joseph,
[b]the kingdom of Sī'hon king of
the Am'o·rītes and the kingdom
of Og king of Bā'shan, the land
with its cities within the borders,
the cities of the surrounding
country.
34 And the children of Gad
built [a]Dī'bon and At'a·roth and
[b]A·rō'er,
35 At'roth and Shō'phan and
[a]Jā'zer and Jog'be·hah,
36 [a]Beth Nim'rah and Beth
Har'an, [b]fortified cities, and
folds for sheep.
37 And the children of Reuben
built [a]Hesh'bon and Ē·le·ā'leh
and Kir·jath'a·im,
38 [a]Nē'bō and [b]Bā'al Mē'on
[c](*their* names being changed)
and Shib'mah; and they gave
other names to the cities which
they built.
39 And the children of [a]Mā'chir
the son of Ma·nas'seh went to
Gil'ē·ad and took it, and [1]dispos-
sessed the Am'o·rītes who *were*
in it.
40 So Moses [a]gave Gil'ē·ad to

33 [a]Deut. 3:8–17; 29:8 [b]Num. 21:24, 33, 35
34 [a]Num. 33:45, 46 [b]Deut. 2:36
35 [a]Num. 32:1, 3
36 [a]Num. 32:3 [b]Num. 32:24
37 [a]Num. 21:27
38 [a]Is. 46:1 [b]Ezek. 25:9 [c]Ex. 23:13
39 [a]Gen. 50:23 [1]*drove out*
40 [a]Deut. 3:12, 13, 15
41 [a]Deut. 3:14 [b]Judg. 10:4 [1]Lit. *Towns of Jair*

CHAPTER 33

1 [a]Ps. 77:20
3 [a]Ex. 12:37 [b]Ex. 12:2; 13:4 [c]Ex. 14:8
4 [a]Ex. 12:29 [b]Is. 19:1
5 [a]Ex. 12:37
6 [a]Ex. 13:20
7 [a]Ex. 14:1, 2, 9
8 [a]Ex. 14:22; 15:22, 23 [1]Many Heb. mss., Sam., Syr., Tg., Vg. *from Pi Hahiroth*; cf. Num. 33:7

Mā'chir the son of Ma·nas'seh,
and he dwelt in it.
41 Also [a]Jā'ir the son of Ma·nas'-
seh went and took its small
towns, and called them [b]Hā'voth
Jā'ir.[1]
42 Then Nō'bah went and took
Kē'nath and its villages, and he
called it Nō'bah, after his own
name.

33 These *are* the journeys
of the children of Israel,
who went out of the land of
Egypt by their armies under the
[a]hand of Moses and Aaron.
2 Now Moses wrote down the
starting points of their journeys
at the command of the LORD.
And these *are* their journeys according to their starting points:
3 They [a]departed from Ram'-
e·sēs in [b]the first month, on the
fifteenth day of the first month;
on the day after the Passover the
children of Israel went out [c]with
boldness in the sight of all the
Egyptians.
4 For the Egyptians were burying all *their* firstborn, [a]whom the
LORD had killed among them.
Also [b]on their gods the LORD had
executed judgments.
5 [a]Then the children of Israel
moved from Ram'e·sēs and
camped at Suc'coth.
6 They departed from [a]Suc'-
coth and camped at Ē'tham,
which *is* on the edge of the
wilderness.
7 [a]They moved from Ē'tham
and turned back to Pī Ha·hī'-
roth, which *is* east of Bā'al Zē'-
phon; and they camped near
Mig'dōl.
8 They departed [1]from before
Ha·hī'roth and [a]passed through
the midst of the sea into the
wilderness, went three days'

journey in the Wilderness of
Ē′tham, and camped at Mar′ah.
9 They moved from Mar′ah
and [a]came to Ē′lim. At Ē′lim
were twelve springs of water
and seventy palm trees; so they
camped there.
10 They moved from Ē′lim and
camped by the Red Sea.
11 They moved from the Red Sea
and camped in the [a]Wilderness
of Sin.
12 They journeyed from the
Wilderness of Sin and camped
at Doph′kah.
13 They departed from Doph′-
kah and camped at Ā′lush.
14 They moved from Ā′lush and
camped at [a]Reph′i·dim, where
there was no water for the people to drink.
15 They departed from Reph′-
i·dim and camped in the
[a]Wilderness of Sinai.
16 They moved from the Wilderness of Sinai and camped [a]at
[1]Kib′roth Hat·tā′a·vah.
17 They departed from Kib′-
roth Hat·tā′a·vah and [a]camped
at Ha·zē′roth.
18 They departed from Ha·zē′-
roth and camped at [a]Rith′mah.
19 They departed from Rith′-
mah and camped at Rim′mon
Per′ez.
20 They departed from Rim′-
mon Per′ez and camped at Lib′-
nah.
21 They moved from Lib′nah
and camped at Ris′sah.
22 They journeyed from Ris′sah
and camped at Kē·he·lā′thah.
23 They went from Kē·he·lā′-
thah and camped at Mount Shē′-
pher.
24 They moved from Mount
Shē′pher and camped at Ha·rā′-
dah.

9 [a]Ex. 15:27
11 [a]Ex. 16:1
14 [a]Ex. 17:1; 19:2
15 [a]Ex. 16:1; 19:1, 2
16 [a]Num. 11:34 [1]Lit. *Graves of Craving*
17 [a]Num. 11:35
18 [a]Num. 12:16
30 [a]Deut. 10:6
32 [a]Deut. 10:6 [b]Deut. 10:7
35 [a]Deut. 2:8
36 [a]Num. 20:1; 27:14
37 [a]Num. 20:22, 23; 21:4
38 [a]Num. 20:25, 28
40 [a]Num. 21:1

25 They moved from Ha·rā′dah
and camped at Mak·hē′loth.
26 They moved from Mak·hē′-
loth and camped at Tā′hath.
27 They departed from Tā′hath
and camped at Tē′rah.
28 They moved from Tē′rah and
camped at Mith′kah.
29 They went from Mith′kah
and camped at Hash·mō′nah.
30 They departed from Hash-
mō′nah and [a]camped at Mō·sē′-
roth.
31 They departed from Mō·sē′-
roth and camped at Ben′ē Jā′-
a·kan.
32 They moved from [a]Ben′ē
Jā′a·kan and [b]camped at Hor
Ha·gid′gad.
33 They went from Hor Ha·gid′-
gad and camped at Jot′ba·thah.
34 They moved from Jot′ba·thah
and camped at A·brō′nah.
35 They departed from A·brō′-
nah [a]and camped at Ē′zi·on Gē′-
ber.
36 They moved from Ē′zi·on
Gē′ber and camped in the
[a]Wilderness of Zin, which *is* Kā′-
desh.
37 They moved from [a]Kā′desh
and camped at Mount Hor, on
the boundary of the land of
Ē′dom.
38 Then [a]Aaron the priest went
up to Mount Hor at the command of the LORD, and died
there in the fortieth year after
the children of Israel had come
out of the land of Egypt, on the
first *day* of the fifth month.
39 Aaron *was* one hundred and
twenty-three years old when he
died on Mount Hor.
40 Now [a]the king of Ar′ad, the
Cā′naan·īte, who dwelt in the
South in the land of Cā′naan,

heard of the coming of the children of Israel.
41 So they departed from Mount
Hor and camped at Zal·mō′nah.
42 They departed from Zal·mō′-
nah and camped at Pū′non.
43 They departed from Pū′non
and [a]camped at Ō′both.
44 [a]They departed from Ō′both
and camped at Ī′jē Ab′a·rim, at
the border of Mō′ab.
45 They departed from [1]Ī′jim
and camped [a]at Dī′bon Gad.
46 They moved from Dī′bon
Gad and camped at [a]Al′mon
Dib·la·thā′im.
47 They moved from Al′mon
Dib·la·thā′im [a]and camped in
the mountains of Ab′a·rim, before Nē′bō.
48 They departed from the mountains of Ab′a·rim and [a]camped in
the plains of Mō′ab by the Jordan, *across from* Jericho.
49 They camped by the Jordan,
from Beth Jes′i·moth as far as
the [a]Abel Acacia Grove[1] in the
plains of Mō′ab.
50 Now the LORD spoke to Moses in the plains of Mō′ab by
the Jordan, *across from* Jericho,
saying,
51 "Speak to the children of
Israel, and say to them: [a]'When
you have crossed the Jordan
into the land of Cā′naan,
52 [a]'then you shall drive out all
the inhabitants of the land from
before you, destroy all their engraved stones, destroy all their
molded images, and demolish
all their [1]high places;
53 'you shall dispossess *the inhabitants of* the land and dwell
in it, for I have given you the
land to [a]possess.
54 'And [a]you shall divide the
land by lot as an inheritance
among your families; to the
larger you shall give a larger
inheritance, and to the smaller
you shall give a smaller inheritance; there everyone's *inheritance* shall be whatever falls
to him by lot. You shall inherit
according to the tribes of your
fathers.
55 'But if you do not drive out
the inhabitants of the land from
before you, then it shall be that
those whom you let remain *shall
be* [a]irritants in your eyes and
thorns in your sides, and they
shall harass you in the land
where you dwell.
56 'Moreover it shall be *that* I
will do to you as I thought to do
to them.' "

34

Then the LORD spoke to
Moses, saying,
2 "Command the children of Israel, and say to them: 'When you
come into [a]the land of Cā′naan,
this *is* the land that shall fall to
you as an inheritance—the land
of Cā′naan to its boundaries.
3 [a]'Your southern border shall
be from the Wilderness of Zin
along the border of Ē′dom; then
your southern border shall extend eastward to the end of [b]the
Salt Sea;
4 'your border shall turn from
the southern side of [a]the Ascent
of Ak·rab′bim, continue to Zin,
and be on the south of [b]Kā′desh
Bar·nē′a; then it shall go on to
[c]Hā′zar Ad′dar, and continue to
Az′mon;
5 'the border shall turn from
Az′mon [a]to the Brook of Egypt,
and it shall end at the Sea.
6 'As for the [a]western border,
you shall have the Great Sea
for a border; this shall be your
western border.

43 [a]Num. 21:10
44 [a]Num. 21:11
45 [a]Num. 32:34
[1]Same as *Ije Abarim,* v. 44
46 [a]Jer. 48:22
47 [a]Deut. 32:49
48 [a]Num. 22:1; 31:12; 35:1
49 [a]Num. 25:1
[1]Heb. *Abel Shittim*
51 [a]Josh. 3:17
52 [a]Deut. 7:2, 5; 12:3
[1]Places for pagan worship
53 [a]Deut. 11:31
54 [a]Num. 26:53–56
55 [a]Josh. 23:13

CHAPTER 34

2 [a]Gen. 17:8
3 [a]Josh. 15:1–3
[b]Gen. 14:3
4 [a]Josh. 15:3
[b]Num. 13:26; 32:8
[c]Josh. 15:3, 4
5 [a]Josh. 15:4, 47
6 [a]Ezek. 47:20

7 'And this shall be your northern border: From the Great Sea
you shall mark out your *border*
line to [a]Mount Hor;
8 'from Mount Hor you shall
mark out *your border* [a]to the
entrance of Hā′math; then the
direction of the border shall be
toward [b]Zē′dad;
9 'the border shall proceed to
Ziph′ron, and it shall end at
[a]Hā′zar Ē′nan. This shall be your
northern border.
10 'You shall mark out your
eastern border from Hā′zar
Ē′nan to Shē′pham;
11 'the border shall go down
from Shē′pham [a]to Rib′lah on
the east side of Ā′in; the border shall go down and reach to
the eastern [1]side of the Sea [b]of
Chin′ne·reth;
12 'the border shall go down
along the Jordan, and it shall
end at [a]the Salt Sea. This shall
be your land with its surrounding boundaries.' "
13 Then Moses commanded the
children of Israel, saying: [a]"This
is the land which you shall inherit by lot, which the LORD has
commanded to give to the nine
tribes and to the half-tribe.
14 [a]"For the tribe of the children
of Reuben according to the house
of their fathers, and the tribe of
the children of Gad according to
the house of their fathers, have
received *their inheritance;* and
the half-tribe of Ma·nas′seh has
received its inheritance.
15 "The two tribes and the half-
tribe have received their inheritance on this side of the Jordan,
across from Jericho eastward,
toward the sunrise."
16 And the LORD spoke to Moses, saying,
17 "These *are* the names of the
men who shall divide the land
among you as an inheritance:
[a]El·ē·ā′zar the priest and Joshua
the son of Nun.
18 "And you shall take one
[a]leader of every tribe to divide
the land for the inheritance.
19 "These *are* the names of the
men: from the tribe of Judah,
Caleb the son of Je·phū′neh;
20 "from the tribe of the children of Sim′ē·on, She·mū′el the
son of Am·mī′hud;
21 "from the tribe of Benjamin,
Ē·lī′dad the son of Chis′lon;
22 "a leader from the tribe of
the children of Dan, Buk′kī the
son of Jog′lī;
23 "from the sons of Joseph: a
leader from the tribe of the children of Ma·nas′seh, Han′ni·el
the son of Ephod,
24 "and a leader from the tribe
of the children of Ē′phra·im,
Ke·mū′el the son of Shiph′tan;
25 "a leader from the tribe of the
children of Zeb′ū·lun, E·li·zā′-
phan the son of Par′nach;
26 "a leader from the tribe of
the children of Is′sa·char, Pal′-
ti·el the son of Az′zan;
27 "a leader from the tribe of
the children of Ash′er, A·hī′hud
the son of She·lō′mī;
28 "and a leader from the tribe
of the children of Naph′ta·lī,
Ped′a·hel the son of Am·mī′-
hud."
29 These *are* the ones the LORD
commanded to [1]divide the inheritance among the children of
Israel in the land of Cā′naan.

CHAPTER 35

35 And the LORD spoke to
Moses in [a]the plains of
Mō′ab by the Jordan *across from*
Jericho, saying:
2 [a]"Command the children of

7 [a]Num. 33:37
8 [a]Num. 13:21 [b]Ezek. 47:15
9 [a]Ezek. 47:17
11 [a]2 Kin. 23:33 [b]Deut. 3:17 [1]Lit. *shoulder*
12 [a]Num. 34:3
13 [a]Josh. 14:1–5
14 [a]Num. 32:33
17 [a]Josh. 14:1, 2; 19:51
18 [a]Num. 1:4, 16
29 [1]*apportion*
1 [a]Num. 33:50
2 [a]Josh. 14:3, 4; 21:2, 3

Israel that they give the Lē′-
vītes cities to dwell in from the
inheritance of their possession,
and you shall *also* give the Lē′-
vītes [b]common-land around the
cities.
3 “They shall have the cities to
dwell in; and their common-land
shall be for their cattle, for their
herds, and for all their animals.
4 “The common-land of the
cities which you will give the
Lē′vītes *shall extend* from
the wall of the city outward a
thousand cubits all around.
5 “And you shall measure outside the city on the east side two
thousand cubits, on the south
side two thousand cubits, on the
west side two thousand cubits,
and on the north side two thousand cubits. The city *shall be* in
the middle. This shall belong to
them as common-land for the
cities.
6 “Now among the cities which
you will give to the Lē′vītes *you
shall appoint* [a]six cities of refuge, to which a manslayer may
flee. And to these you shall add
forty-two cities.
7 “So all the cities you will give
to the Lē′vītes *shall be* [a]forty-
eight; these *you shall give* with
their common-land.
8 “And the cities which you
will give *shall be* [a]from the possession of the children of Israel;
[b]from the larger *tribe* you shall
give many, from the smaller you
shall give few. Each shall give
some of its cities to the Lē′vītes,
in proportion to the inheritance
that each receives.”
9 Then the LORD spoke to Moses, saying,
10 “Speak to the children of
Israel, and say to them: [a]‘When
you cross the Jordan into the
land of Cā′naan,
11 ‘then [a]you shall appoint cities to be cities of refuge for you,
that the manslayer who kills any
person accidentally may flee
there.
12 [a]‘They shall be cities of refuge for you from the avenger,
that the manslayer may not die
until he stands before the congregation in judgment.
13 ‘And of the cities which you
give, you shall have [a]six cities of
refuge.
14 [a]‘You shall appoint three cities on this side of the Jordan,
and three cities you shall appoint in the land of Cā′naan,
which will be cities of refuge.
15 ‘These six cities shall be for
refuge for the children of Israel, [a]for the stranger, and for
the sojourner among them, that
anyone who kills a person accidentally may flee there.
16 [a]‘But if he strikes him with an
iron implement, so that he dies,
he *is* a murderer; the murderer
shall surely be put to death.
17 ‘And if he strikes him with a
stone in the hand, by which one
could die, and he does die, he *is*
a murderer; the murderer shall
surely be put to death.
18 ‘Or *if* he strikes him with a
wooden hand weapon, by which
one could die, and he does die,
he *is* a murderer; the murderer
shall surely be put to death.
19 [a]‘The[1] avenger of blood himself shall put the murderer to
death; when he meets him, he
shall put him to death.
20 [a]‘If he pushes him out of
hatred or, [b]while lying in wait,
hurls something at him so that
he dies,

2 [b]Lev. 25:32–34
6 [a]Josh. 20:2, 7, 8; 21:3, 13
7 [a]Josh. 21:41
8 [a]Josh. 21:3 [b]Num. 26:54; 33:54
10 [a]Josh. 20:1–9
11 [a]Ex. 21:13
12 [a]Deut. 19:6
13 [a]Num. 35:6
14 [a]Deut. 4:41
15 [a]Num. 15:16
16 [a]Lev. 24:17
19 [a]Num. 35:21, 24, 27
[1]A family member who is to avenge the victim
20 [a]Gen. 4:8 [b]Ex. 21:14

21 'or in enmity he strikes him with his hand so that he dies, the one who struck *him* shall surely be put to death. He *is* a murderer. The avenger of blood shall put the murderer to death when he meets him.

22 'However, if he pushes him suddenly [a]without enmity, or throws anything at him without lying in wait,

23 'or uses a stone, by which a man could die, throwing *it* at him without seeing *him,* so that he dies, while he was not his enemy or seeking his harm,

24 'then [a]the congregation shall judge between the manslayer and the avenger of blood according to these judgments.

25 'So the congregation shall deliver the manslayer from the hand of the avenger of blood, and the congregation shall return him to the city of refuge where he had fled, and [a]he shall remain there until the death of the high priest [b]who was anointed with the holy oil.

26 'But if the manslayer at any time goes outside the limits of the city of refuge where he fled,

27 'and the avenger of blood finds him outside the limits of his city of refuge, and the avenger of blood kills the manslayer, he shall not be guilty of [1]blood,

28 'because he should have remained in his city of refuge until the death of the high priest. But after the death of the high priest the manslayer may return to the land of his possession.

29 'And these *things* shall be [a]a statute of judgment to you throughout your generations in all your dwellings.

30 'Whoever kills a person, the murderer shall be put to death on the [a]testimony of witnesses; but one witness is not *sufficient* testimony against a person for the death *penalty.*

31 'Moreover you shall take no ransom for the life of a murderer who *is* guilty of death, but he shall surely be put to death.

32 'And you shall take no ransom for him who has fled to his city of refuge, that he may return to dwell in the land before the death of the priest.

33 'So you shall not pollute the land where you *are;* for blood [a]defiles the land, and no [1]atonement can be made for the land, for the blood that is shed on it, except [b]by the blood of him who shed it.

34 'Therefore [a]do not defile the land which you inhabit, in the midst of which I dwell; for [b]I the LORD dwell among the children of Israel.' "

36

Now the chief fathers of the families of the [a]children of Gil'ē·ad the son of Mā'chir, the son of Ma·nas'seh, of the families of the sons of Joseph, came near and [b]spoke before Moses and before the leaders, the chief fathers of the children of Israel.

2 And they said: [a]"The LORD commanded my lord *Moses* to give the land as an inheritance by lot to the children of Israel, and [b]my lord was commanded by the LORD to give the inheritance of our brother Ze·loph'-e·had to his daughters.

3 "Now if they are married to any of the sons of the *other* tribes of the children of Israel, then their inheritance will be [a]taken from the inheritance of

22 [a]Ex. 21:13
24 [a]Josh. 20:6
25 [a]Josh. 20:6 [b]Ex. 29:7
27 [1]Murder
29 [a]Num. 27:11
30 [a]Deut. 17:6; 19:15
33 [a]Ps. 106:38 [b]Gen. 9:6 [1]Lit. *covering*
34 [a]Lev. 18:24, 25 [b]Ex. 29:45, 46

CHAPTER 36

1 [a]Num. 26:29 [b]Num. 27:1–11
2 [a]Josh. 17:4 [b]Num. 27:1, 5–7
3 [a]Num. 27:4

our fathers, and it will be added to the inheritance of the tribe into which they marry; so it will be taken from the lot of our inheritance.

4 "And when [a]the Jubilee of the children of Israel comes, then their inheritance will be added to the inheritance of the tribe into which they marry; so their inheritance will be taken away from the inheritance of the tribe of our fathers."

5 Then Moses commanded the children of Israel according to the word of the LORD, saying: [a]"What the tribe of the sons of Joseph speaks is right.

6 "This *is* what the LORD commands concerning the daughters of Ze·loph′e·had, saying, 'Let them [1]marry whom they think best, [a]but they may marry only within the family of their father's tribe.'

7 "So the inheritance of the children of Israel shall not change hands from tribe to tribe, for every one of the children of Israel shall [a]keep the inheritance of the tribe of his fathers.

8 "And [a]every daughter who possesses an inheritance in any tribe of the children of Israel shall be the wife of one of the family of her father's tribe, so that the children of Israel each may possess the inheritance of his fathers.

9 "Thus no inheritance shall change hands from *one* tribe to another, but every tribe of the children of Israel shall keep its own inheritance."

10 Just as the LORD commanded Moses, so did the daughters of Ze·loph′e·had;

11 [a]for Mah′lah, Tir′zah, Hog′-lah, Mil′cah, and Noah, the daughters of Ze·loph′e·had, were married to the sons of their father's brothers.

12 They were married into the families of the children of Ma·nas′seh the son of Joseph, and their inheritance remained in the tribe of their father's family.

13 These *are* the commandments and the judgments which the LORD commanded the children of Israel by the hand of Moses [a]in the plains of Mō′ab by the Jordan, *across from* Jericho.

4 [a]Lev. 25:10
5 [a]Num. 27:7
6 [a]Num. 36:11, 12 [1]Lit. *be wives to*
7 [a]1 Kin. 21:3
8 [a]1 Chr. 23:22
11 [a]Num. 26:33; 27:1
13 [a]Num. 26:3; 33:50

The Fifth Book of Moses Called

DEUTERONOMY

DEUTERONOMY, Moses' "Upper Desert Discourse," consists of a series of farewell messages by Israel's 120-year-old leader. It is addressed to the new generation destined to possess the Land of Promise—those who survived the forty years of wilderness wandering.

Like Leviticus, Deuteronomy contains a vast amount of legal detail, but its emphasis is on the laymen rather than the priests. Moses reminds the new generation of the importance of obedience if they are to learn from the sad example of their parents.

The Hebrew title of Deuteronomy is *Haddebharim*, "The Words," taken from the opening phrase in 1:1, "These are the words." The parting words of Moses to the new generation are given in oral and written form so that they will endure to all generations. Deuteronomy has been called "five-fifths of the Law" since it completes the five books of Moses. The Jewish people have also called it *Mishneh Hattorah*, "Repetition of the Law," which is translated in the Septuagint as *To Deuteronomion Touto*, "This Second Law." Deuteronomy, however, is not a second law but an adaptation and expansion of much of the original law given on Mount Sinai. The English title comes from the Greek title *Deuteronomion*, "Second Law." Deuteronomy has also been appropriately called the "Book of Remembrance."

THESE *are* the words which
Moses spoke to all Israel
[a]on this side of the Jordan in
the wilderness, in the [1]plain opposite
[2]Sūph, between Par′an,
Tō′phel, Lā′ban, Ha·zē′roth, and
Diz′a·hab.
2 *It is* eleven days' *journey*
from Hō′reb by way of Mount
Sē′ir [a]to Kā′desh Bar·nē′a.
3 Now it came to pass [a]in the
fortieth year, in the eleventh
month, on the first *day* of the
month, *that* Moses spoke to the
children of Israel according to
all that the LORD had given him
as commandments to them,
4 [a]after he had killed Sī′hon
king of the Am′o·rītes, who
dwelt in Hesh′bon, and Og king
of Bā′shan, who dwelt at Ash′ta·roth
[b]in[1] Ed′rē·ī.
5 On this side of the Jordan in
the land of Mō′ab, Moses began
to explain this law, saying,
6 "The LORD our God spoke
to us [a]in Hō′reb, saying: 'You
have dwelt long [b]enough at this
mountain.
7 'Turn and take your journey,
and go to the mountains of the
Am′o·rītes, to all the neighboring
places in the [1]plain, in the
mountains and in the lowland,
in the South and on the seacoast,
to the land of the Cā′naan·ītes
and to Lebanon, as
far as the great river, the River
Eū·phrā′tēs.
8 'See, I have set the land before
you; go in and possess the
land which the LORD [1]swore
to your fathers—to [a]Abraham,
Isaac, and Jacob—to give to

CHAPTER 1

1 [a]Deut. 4:44–46 [1]Heb. *arabah* [2]One LXX ms., Tg., Vg. *Red Sea*

2 [a]Num. 13:26; 32:8

3 [a]Num. 33:38

4 [a]Num. 21:23, 24, 33–35 [b]Josh. 13:12 [1]LXX, Syr., Vg. *and;* cf. Josh. 12:4

6 [a]Ex. 3:1, 12 [b]Ex. 19:1, 2

7 [1]Heb. *arabah*

8 [a]Gen. 12:7; 15:5; 22:17; 26:3; 28:13 [1]*promised*

them and their descendants after them.'
9 "And [a]I spoke to you at that time, saying: 'I [1]alone am not able to bear you.
10 'The LORD your God has multiplied you, [a]and here you *are* today, as the stars of heaven in multitude.
11 [a]'May the LORD God of your fathers make you a thousand times more numerous than you are, and bless you [b]as He has promised you!
12 [a]'How can I alone bear your problems and your burdens and your complaints?
13 'Choose wise, understanding, and knowledgeable men from among your tribes, and I will make them [1]heads over you.'
14 "And you answered me and said, 'The thing which you have told *us* to do *is* good.'
15 "So I took [a]the heads of your tribes, wise and knowledgeable men, and [1]made them heads over you, leaders of thousands, leaders of hundreds, leaders of fifties, leaders of tens, and officers for your tribes.
16 "Then I commanded your judges at that time, saying, 'Hear *the cases* between your brethren, and [a]judge righteously between a man and his [b]brother or the stranger who is with him.
17 [a]'You shall not show partiality in judgment; you shall hear the small as well as the great; you shall not be afraid in any man's presence, for [b]the judgment *is* God's. The case that is too hard for you, [c]bring to me, and I will hear it.'
18 "And I commanded you at that time all the things which you should do.

9 [a]Ex. 18:18, 24 [1]*am not able to bear you by myself*
10 [a]Gen. 15:5; 22:17
11 [a]2 Sam. 24:3 [b]Gen. 15:5
12 [a]1 Kin. 3:8, 9
13 [1]*rulers*
15 [a]Ex. 18:25 [1]*appointed*
16 [a]Deut. 16:18 [b]Lev. 24:22
17 [a]Prov. 24:23–26 [b]2 Chr. 19:6 [c]Ex. 18:22, 26
19 [a]Deut. 2:7; 8:15; 32:10 [b]Num. 13:26
21 [a]Josh. 1:6, 9
23 [a]Num. 13:2, 3
24 [a]Num. 13:21–25
25 [a]Num. 13:27
26 [a]Num. 14:1–4
27 [a]Ps. 106:25 [b]Deut. 9:28

19 "So we departed from Hō'reb, [a]and went through all that great and terrible wilderness which you saw on the way to the mountains of the Am'o·rītes, as the LORD our God had commanded us. Then [b]we came to Kā'desh Bar·nē'a.
20 "And I said to you, 'You have come to the mountains of the Am'o·rītes, which the LORD our God is giving us.
21 'Look, the LORD your God has set the land before you; go up *and* possess *it*, as the LORD God of your fathers has spoken to you; [a]do not fear or be discouraged.'
22 "And every one of you came near to me and said, 'Let us send men before us, and let them search out the land for us, and bring back word to us of the way by which we should go up, and of the cities into which we shall come.'
23 "The plan pleased me well; so [a]I took twelve of your men, one man from *each* tribe.
24 [a]"And they departed and went up into the mountains, and came to the Valley of Esh'col, and spied it out.
25 "They also took *some* of the fruit of the land in their hands and brought *it* down to us; and they brought back word to us, saying, '*It is* a [a]good land which the LORD our God is giving us.'
26 [a]"Nevertheless you would not go up, but rebelled against the command of the LORD your God;
27 "and you [a]complained in your tents, and said, 'Because the LORD [b]hates us, He has brought us out of the land of Egypt to deliver us into the hand of the Am'o·rītes, to destroy us.

28 'Where can we go up? Our brethren have [1]discouraged our hearts, saying, [a]"The people *are* greater and taller than we; the cities *are* great and fortified up to heaven; moreover we have seen the sons of the [b]An'a·kim there." '

29 "Then I said to you, 'Do not be terrified, [a]or afraid of them.

30 [a]'The LORD your God, who goes before you, He will fight for you, according to all He did for you in Egypt before your eyes,

31 'and in the wilderness where you saw how the LORD your God carried you, as a [a]man carries his son, in all the way that you went until you came to this place.'

32 "Yet, for all that, [a]you did not believe the LORD your God,

33 [a]"who went in the way before you [b]to search out a place for you to pitch your tents, to show you the way you should go, in the fire by night and in the cloud by day.

34 "And the LORD heard the sound of your words, and was angry, [a]and took an oath, saying,

35 [a]'Surely not one of these men of this evil generation shall see that good land of which I [1]swore to give to your fathers,

36 [a]'except Caleb the son of Je·phūn'neh; he shall see it, and to him and his children I am giving the land on which he walked, because [b]he [1]wholly followed the LORD.'

37 [a]"The LORD was also angry with me for your sakes, saying, 'Even you shall not go in there.

38 [a]'Joshua the son of Nun, [b]who stands before you, he shall go in there. [c]Encourage him, for he shall cause Israel to inherit it.

39 [a]'Moreover your little ones and your children, who [b]you say will be victims, who today [c]have no knowledge of good and evil, they shall go in there; to them I will give it, and they shall possess it.

40 [a]'But *as for* you, turn and take your journey into the wilderness by the Way of the Red Sea.'

41 "Then you answered and said to me, [a]'We have sinned against the LORD; we will go up and fight, just as the LORD our God commanded us.' And when everyone of you had girded on his weapons of war, you were ready to go up into the mountain.

42 "And the LORD said to me, 'Tell them, [a]"Do not go up nor fight, for I *am* not among you; lest you be defeated before your enemies." '

43 "So I spoke to you; yet you would not listen, but [a]rebelled against the command of the LORD, and [b]presumptuously[1] went up into the mountain.

44 "And the Am'o·rītes who dwelt in that mountain came out against you and chased you [a]as bees do, and drove you back from Sē'ir to Hor'mah.

45 "Then you returned and wept before the LORD, but the LORD would not listen to your voice nor give ear to you.

46 [a]"So you remained in Kā'desh many days, according to the days that you spent *there*.

2 "Then we turned and [a]journeyed into the wilderness of the Way of the Red Sea, [b]as the LORD spoke to me, and we [1]skirted Mount Sē'ir for many days.

28 [a]Deut. 9:1, 2 [b]Num. 13:28 [1]Lit. *melted*
29 [a]Num. 14:9
30 [a]Ex. 14:14
31 [a]Is. 46:3, 4; 63:9
32 [a]Jude 5
33 [a]Ex. 13:21 [b]Num. 10:33
34 [a]Deut. 2:14, 15
35 [a]Num. 14:22, 23 [1]*promised*
36 [a][Josh. 14:9] [b]Num. 32:11, 12 [1]*fully*
37 [a]Deut. 3:26; 4:21; 34:4
38 [a]Num. 14:30 [b]1 Sam. 16:22 [c]Deut. 31:7, 23
39 [a]Num. 14:31 [b]Num. 14:3 [c]Is. 7:15, 16
40 [a]Num. 14:25
41 [a]Num. 14:40
42 [a]Num. 14:41–43
43 [a]Num. 14:44 [b]Deut. 17:12, 13 [1]*willfully*
44 [a]Ps. 118:12
46 [a]Deut. 2:7, 14

CHAPTER 2

1 [a]Deut. 1:40 [b]Num. 14:25 [1]*circled around*

2 "And the LORD spoke to me,
saying:
3 'You have skirted this mountain [a]long enough; turn northward.
4 'And command the people,
saying, [a]"You *are about to* pass
through the territory of [b]your
brethren, the descendants of
Esau, who live in Sē'ir; and they
will be afraid of you. Therefore
watch yourselves carefully.
5 "Do not meddle with them,
for I will not give you *any* of
their land, no, not so much as
one footstep, [a]because I have
given Mount Sē'ir to Esau *as* a
possession.
6 "You shall buy food from
them with money, that you may
eat; and you shall also buy water
from them with money, that you
may drink.
7 "For the LORD your God has
blessed you in all the work
of your hand. He knows your
[1]trudging through this great wilderness. [a]These forty years the
LORD your God *has been* with
you; you have lacked nothing." '
8 "And when we passed be-
yond our brethren, the descendants of Esau who dwell in Sē'ir,
away from the road of the plain,
away from [a]Ē'lath and Ē'zi·on
Gē'ber, we [b]turned and passed
by way of the Wilderness of
Mō'ab.
9 "Then the LORD said to me,
'Do not harass Mō'ab, nor contend with them in battle, for I
will not give you *any* of their
land *as* a possession, because I
have given [a]Ar to [b]the descendants of Lot *as* a possession.' "
10 [a](The Ē'mim had dwelt there
in times past, a people as great
and numerous and tall as [b]the
An'a·kim.
11 They were also regarded as
[1]giants, like the An'a·kim, but
the Mō'ab·ītes call them Ē'mim.
12 [a]The Hor'ītes formerly dwelt
in Sē'ir, but the descendants of
Esau dispossessed them and destroyed them from before them,
and dwelt in their [1]place, just
as Israel did to the land of their
possession which the LORD gave
them.)
13 " 'Now rise and cross over
[a]the [1]Valley of the Zē'red.' So we
crossed over the Valley of the
Zē'red.
14 "And the time we took to
come [a]from Kā'desh Bar·nē'a
until we crossed over the Valley
of the Zē'red *was* thirty-eight
years, [b]until all the generation of
the men of war [1]was consumed
from the midst of the camp, [c]just
as the LORD had sworn to them.
15 "For indeed the hand of
the LORD was against them, to
destroy them from the midst
of the camp until they [1]were
consumed.
16 "So it was, when all the men
of war had finally perished from
among the people,
17 "that the LORD spoke to me,
saying:
18 'This day you are to cross
over at Ar, the boundary of
Mō'ab.
19 'And *when* you come near
the people of Am'mon, do not
harass them or meddle with
them, for I will not give you *any*
of the land of the people of Am'-
mon *as* a possession, because I
have given it to [a]the descendants
of Lot *as* a possession.' "
20 (That was also regarded as a
land of [1]giants; giants formerly

3 [a]Deut. 2:7, 14
4 [a]Num. 20:14–21 [b]Deut. 23:7
5 [a]Gen. 36:8
7 [a]Deut. 8:2–4 [1]Lit. *goings*
8 [a]Judg. 11:18 [b]Num. 21:4
9 [a]Deut. 2:18, 29 [b]Gen. 19:36–38
10 [a]Gen. 14:5 [b]Deut. 9:2
11 [1]Heb. *rephaim*
12 [a]Deut. 2:22 [1]*stead*
13 [a]Num. 21:12 [1]*Wadi* or *Brook*
14 [a]Num. 13:26 [b]Deut. 1:34, 35 [c]Num. 14:35 [1]*perished*
15 [1]*perished*
19 [a]Gen. 19:38
20 [1]Heb. *rephaim*

dwelt there. But the Am′mon·ītes
call them [a]Zam·zum′mim,
21 [a]a people as great and numerous and tall as the An′a·kim.
But the LORD destroyed them
before them, and they dispossessed them and dwelt in their
place,
22 just as He had done for the
descendants of Esau, [a]who dwelt
in Sē′ir, when He destroyed [b]the
Hor′ītes from before them. They
dispossessed them and dwelt in
their place, even to this day.
23 And [a]the Av′im, who dwelt
in villages as far as Gā′za—[b]the
Caph′to·rim, who came from
Caph′tor, destroyed them and
dwelt in their place.)
24 "'Rise, take your journey,
and [a]cross over the River Ar′-
non. Look, I have given into
your hand [b]Sī′hon the Am′o·rīte,
king of Hesh′bon, and his land.
Begin [1]to possess *it*, and engage
him in battle.
25 [a]'This day I will begin to put
the dread and fear of you upon
the nations [1]under the whole
heaven, who shall hear the report of you, and shall [b]tremble
and be in anguish because of
you.'
26 "And I [a]sent messengers from
the Wilderness of Ked′e·moth to
Sī′hon king of Hesh′bon, [b]with
words of peace, saying,
27 [a]'Let me pass through your
land; I will keep strictly to the
road, and I will turn neither to
the right nor to the left.
28 'You shall sell me food for
money, that I may eat, and give
me water for money, that I may
drink; [a]only let me pass through
on foot,
29 [a]'just as the descendants of
Esau who dwell in Sē′ir and the
Mō′ab·ītes who dwell in Ar did
for me, until I cross the Jordan
to the land which the LORD our
God is giving us.'
30 [a]"But Sī′hon king of Hesh′bon
would not let us pass through, for
[b]the LORD your God [c]hardened
his spirit and made his heart
obstinate, that He might deliver
him into your hand, as *it is* this
day.
31 "And the LORD said to me,
'See, I have begun to [a]give Sī′-
hon and his land over to you.
Begin to possess *it*, that you
may inherit his land.'
32 [a]"Then Sī′hon and all his
people came out against us to
fight at Jā′haz.
33 "And [a]the LORD our God delivered him [1]over to us; so [b]we
defeated him, his sons, and all
his people.
34 "We took all his cities at
that time, and we [a]utterly destroyed the men, women, and
little ones of every city; we left
none remaining.
35 "We took only the livestock
as plunder for ourselves, with
the spoil of the cities which we
took.
36 [a]"From A·rō′er, which *is* on
the bank of the River Ar′non,
and *from* [b]the city that *is* in the
ravine, as far as Gil′ē·ad, there
was not one city too strong for
us; [c]the LORD our God delivered
all to us.
37 "Only you did not go near
the land of the people of Am′-
mon—anywhere along the River
[a]Jab′bok, or to the cities of the
mountains, or [b]wherever the
LORD our God had forbidden us.

3 "Then we turned and went
up the road to Bā′shan; and
[a]Og king of Bā′shan came out

20 [a]Gen. 14:5
21 [a]Deut. 2:10
22 [a]Gen. 36:8 [b]Gen. 14:6; 36:20–30
23 [a]Josh. 13:3 [b]Gen. 10:14
24 [a]Judg. 11:18 [b]Deut. 1:4 [1]*to take possession*
25 [a]Ex. 23:27 [b]Ex. 15:14–16 [1]*everywhere under the heavens*
26 [a]Num. 21:21–32 [b]Deut. 20:10
27 [a]Judg. 11:19
28 [a]Num. 20:19
29 [a]Deut. 23:3, 4
30 [a]Num. 21:23 [b]Josh. 11:20 [c]Ex. 4:21
31 [a]Deut. 1:3, 8
32 [a]Num. 21:23
33 [a]Deut. 7:2 [b]Num. 21:24 [1]Lit. *before us*
34 [a]Lev. 27:28
36 [a]Deut. 3:12; 4:48 [b]Josh. 13:9, 16 [c]Ps. 44:3
37 [a]Gen. 32:22 [b]Deut. 2:5, 9, 19

CHAPTER 3

1 [a]Num. 21:33–35

against us, he and all his people,
to battle [b]at Ed′rē·ī.
2 "And the LORD said to me,
'Do not fear him, for I have delivered him and all his people
and his land into your hand; you
shall do to him as you did to [a]Sī′-
hon king of the Am′o·rītes, who
dwelt at Hesh′bon.'
3 "So the LORD our God also
delivered into our hands Og king
of Bā′shan, with all his people,
and we [1]attacked him until he
had no survivors remaining.
4 "And we took all his cities
at that time; there was not a
city which we did not take from
them: sixty cities, [a]all the region
of Ar′gob, the kingdom of Og in
Bā′shan.
5 "All these cities *were* fortified with high walls, gates, and
bars, besides a great many rural
towns.
6 "And we utterly destroyed
them, as we did to Sī′hon king
[a]of Hesh′bon, utterly destroying
the men, women, and children
of every city.
7 "But all the livestock and
the spoil of the cities we took as
booty for ourselves.
8 "And at that time we took
the [a]land from the hand of the
two kings of the Am′o·rītes who
were on this side of the Jordan,
from the River Ar′non to Mount
[b]Her′mon
9 "(the Sī·dō′ni·ans call [a]Her′-
mon Sir′i·on, and the Am′o·rītes
call it Sē′nir),
10 [a]"all the cities of the plain, all
Gil′ē·ad, and [b]all Bā′shan, as far
as Sal′cah and Ed′rē·ī, cities of
the kingdom of Og in Bā′shan.
11 [a]"For only Og king of Bā′shan
remained of the remnant of [b]the
[1]giants. Indeed his bedstead *was*
an iron bedstead. (*Is* it not in
[c]Rab′bah of the people of Am′-
mon?) Nine cubits *is* its length
and four cubits its width, according to the standard cubit.
12 "And this [a]land, *which* we
possessed at that time, [b]from
A·rō′er, which *is* by the River
Ar′non, and half the mountains
of Gil′ē·ad and [c]its cities, I gave
to the Reū′ben·ītes and the Gad′-
ītes.
13 [a]"The rest of Gil′ē·ad, and all
Bā′shan, the kingdom of Og, I
gave to half the tribe of Ma·nas′-
seh. (All the region of Ar′gob,
with all Bā′shan, was called the
land of the [1]giants.
14 [a]"Jā′ir the son of Ma·nas′seh
took all the region of Ar′gob, [b]as
far as the border of the Gesh′-
ū·rītes and the Mā′a·cha·thītes,
and [c]called Bā′shan after his
own name, [1]Hā′voth Jā′ir, to this
day.)
15 "Also I gave [a]Gil′ē·ad to Mā′-
chir.
16 "And to the Reū′ben·ītes [a]and
the Gad′ītes I gave from Gil′ē·ad
as far as the River Ar′non, the
middle of the river as *the* border,
as far as the River Jab′bok, [b]the
border of the people of Am′-
mon;
17 "the plain also, with the Jordan as *the* border, from Chin′-
ne·reth [a]as far as the east side
of the Sea of the Ar′a·bah [b](the
Salt Sea), below the slopes of
Pis′gah.
18 "Then I commanded you at
that time, saying: 'The LORD your
God has given you this land to
possess. [a]All you men of valor
shall cross over armed before
your brethren, the children of
Israel.
19 'But your wives, your little

1 [b]Deut. 1:4
2 [a]Num. 21:34
3 [1]*struck*
4 [a]Deut. 3:13, 14
6 [a]Deut. 2:24, 34, 35
8 [a]Josh. 12:6; 13:8–12 [b]1 Chr. 5:23
9 [a]1 Chr. 5:23
10 [a]Deut. 4:49 [b]Josh. 12:5; 13:11
11 [a]Amos 2:9 [b]Deut. 2:11, 20 [c]Jer. 49:2 [1]Heb. *rephaim*
12 [a]Num. 32:33 [b]Deut. 2:36 [c]Num. 34:14
13 [a]Josh. 13:29–31; 17:1 [1]Heb. *rephaim*
14 [a]1 Chr. 2:22 [b]Josh. 13:13 [c]Num. 32:41 [1]Lit. *Towns of Jair*
15 [a]Num. 32:39, 40
16 [a]2 Sam. 24:5 [b]Num. 21:24
17 [a]Num. 34:11, 12 [b]Gen. 14:3
18 [a]Num. 32:20

ones, and your livestock (I know that you have much livestock) shall stay in your cities which I have given you,

20 'until the LORD has given [a]rest to your brethren as to you, and they also possess the land which the LORD your God is giving them beyond the Jordan. Then each of you may [b]return to his possession which I have given you.'

21 "And [a]I commanded Joshua at that time, saying, 'Your eyes have seen all that the LORD your God has done to these two kings; so will the LORD do to all the kingdoms through which you pass.

22 'You must not fear them, for [a]the LORD your God Himself fights for you.'

23 "Then [a]I pleaded with the LORD at that time, saying:

24 'O Lord GOD, You have begun to show Your servant [a]Your greatness and Your [1]mighty hand, for [b]what god *is there* in heaven or on earth who can do *anything* like Your works and Your mighty *deeds?*

25 'I pray, let me cross over and see [a]the good land beyond the Jordan, those pleasant mountains, and Lebanon.'

26 "But the LORD [a]was angry with me on your account, and would not listen to me. So the LORD said to me: 'Enough of that! Speak no more to Me of this matter.

27 [a]'Go up to the top of Pis'gah, and lift your eyes toward the west, the north, the south, and the east; behold *it* with your eyes, for you shall not cross over this Jordan.

28 'But [a]command[1] Joshua, and encourage him and strengthen him; for he shall go over before this people, and he shall cause them to inherit the land which you will see.'

29 "So we stayed in [a]the valley opposite Beth Pē'or.

20 [a]Deut. 12:9, 10 [b]Josh. 22:4
21 [a][Num. 27:22, 23]
22 [a]Ex. 14:14
23 [a][2 Cor. 12:8, 9]
24 [a]Deut. 5:24; 11:2 [b]2 Sam. 7:22 [1]*strong*
25 [a]Deut. 4:22
26 [a]Num. 20:12; 27:14
27 [a]Num. 23:14; 27:12
28 [a]Num. 27:18, 23 [1]*charge*
29 [a]Deut. 4:46; 34:6

4

"Now, O Israel, listen to [a]the statutes and the judgments which I teach you to observe, that you may live, and go in and [1]possess the land which the LORD God of your fathers is giving you.

2 [a]"You shall not add to the word which I command you, nor take from it, that you may keep the commandments of the LORD your God which I command you.

3 "Your eyes have seen what the LORD did at [a]Bā'al Pē'or; for the LORD your God has destroyed from among you all the men who followed Bā'al of Pē'or.

4 "But you who held fast to the LORD your God *are* alive today, every one of you.

5 "Surely I have taught you statutes and judgments, just as the LORD my God commanded me, that you should act according *to them* in the land which you go to possess.

6 "Therefore be careful to observe *them;* for this *is* [a]your wisdom and your understanding in the sight of the peoples who will hear all these statutes, and say, 'Surely this great nation *is* a wise and understanding people.'

7 "For [a]what great nation *is there* that has [b]God[1] *so* near to it, as the LORD our God *is* to us, for whatever *reason* we may call upon Him?

8 "And what great nation *is*

CHAPTER 4

1 [a][Rom. 10:5] [1]*take possession of*
2 [a]Prov. 30:6
3 [a]Num. 25:1–9
6 [a][2 Tim. 3:15]
7 [a][2 Sam. 7:23] [b][Is. 55:6] [1]Or *a god*

there that has *such* statutes and righteous judgments as are in all this law which I set before you this day?

9 "Only take heed to yourself, and diligently [a]keep yourself, lest you [b]forget the things your eyes have seen, and lest they depart from your heart all the days of your life. And [c]teach them to your children and your grandchildren,

10 "*especially concerning* [a]the day you stood before the LORD your God in Hō′reb, when the LORD said to me, 'Gather the people to Me, and I will let them hear My words, that they may learn to fear Me all the days they live on the earth, and *that* they may teach their children.'

11 "Then you came near and stood at the foot of the mountain, and the mountain burned with fire to the midst of heaven, with darkness, cloud, and thick darkness.

12 [a]"And the LORD spoke to you out of the midst of the fire. You heard the sound of the words, but saw no [1]form; [b]*you* only *heard* a voice.

13 [a]"So He declared to you His covenant which He commanded you to perform, [b]the Ten Commandments; and [c]He wrote them on two tablets of stone.

14 "And [a]the LORD commanded me at that time to teach you statutes and judgments, that you might [1]observe them in the land which you cross over to possess.

15 [a]"Take careful heed to yourselves, for you saw no [b]form when the LORD spoke to you at Hō′reb out of the midst of the fire,

16 "lest you [a]act corruptly and [b]make for yourselves a carved image in the [1]form of any figure: [c]the likeness of male or female,

17 "the likeness of any animal that *is* on the earth or the likeness of any winged bird that flies in the air,

18 "the likeness of anything that creeps on the ground or the likeness of any fish that *is* in the water beneath the earth.

19 "And *take heed,* lest you [a]lift your eyes to heaven, and *when* you see the sun, the moon, and the stars, [b]all the host of heaven, you feel driven to [c]worship them and serve them, which the LORD your God has [1]given to all the peoples under the whole heaven as a heritage.

20 "But the LORD has taken you and [a]brought you out of the iron furnace, out of Egypt, to be [b]His people, an inheritance, as you are this day.

21 "Furthermore [a]the LORD was angry with me for your sakes, and swore that [b]I would not cross over the Jordan, and that I would not enter the good land which the LORD your God is giving you as an inheritance.

22 "But [a]I must die in this land, [b]I must not cross over the Jordan; but you shall cross over and [1]possess [c]that good land.

23 "Take heed to yourselves, lest you forget the covenant of the LORD your God which He made with you, [a]and make for yourselves a carved image in the form of anything which the LORD your God has forbidden you.

24 "For [a]the LORD your God *is* a consuming fire, [b]a jealous God.

25 "When you beget children

9 [a]Prov. 4:23 [b]Deut. 29:2–8 [c]Gen. 18:19
10 [a]Ex. 19:9, 16, 17
12 [a]Deut. 5:4, 22 [b]1 Kin. 19:11–18 [1]*similitude*
13 [a]Deut. 9:9, 11 [b]Ex. 34:28 [c]Ex. 24:12
14 [a]Ex. 21:1 [1]*do or perform*
15 [a]Josh. 23:11 [b]Is. 40:18
16 [a]Deut. 9:12; 31:29 [b]Ex. 20:4, 5 [c]Rom. 1:23 [1]*similitude*
19 [a]Deut. 17:3 [b]2 Kin. 21:3 [c][Rom. 1:25] [1]*divided*
20 [a]Jer. 11:4 [b]Deut. 7:6; 27:9
21 [a]Num. 20:12 [b]Num. 27:13, 14
22 [a]2 Pet. 1:13–15 [b]Deut. 3:27 [c]Deut. 3:25 [1]*take possession of*
23 [a]Deut. 4:16
24 [a]Deut. 9:3 [b]Ex. 20:5; 34:14

and grandchildren and have
grown old in the land, and act
corruptly and make a carved
image in the form of anything,
and [a]do evil in the sight of the
LORD your God to provoke Him
to anger,
26 [a]"I call heaven and earth to
witness against you this day,
that you will soon utterly perish
from the land which you cross
over the Jordan to possess; you
will not [1]prolong *your* days in it,
but will be utterly destroyed.
27 "And the LORD [a]will scatter
you among the peoples, and you
will be left few in number among
the nations where the LORD will
drive you.
28 "And [a]there you will serve
gods, the work of men's hands,
wood and stone, [b]which neither
see nor hear nor eat nor smell.
29 [a]"But from there you will
seek the LORD your God, and
you will find *Him* if you seek
Him with all your heart and
with all your soul.
30 "When you are in [1]distress,
and all these things come upon
you in the [a]latter days, when you
[b]turn to the LORD your God and
obey His voice
31 "(for the LORD your God *is* a
merciful God), He will not forsake you nor [a]destroy you, nor
forget the covenant of your fathers which He swore to them.
32 "For [a]ask now concerning
the days that are past, which
were before you, since the day
that God created man on the
earth, and *ask* [b]from one end of
heaven to the other, whether *any*
great *thing* like this has happened, or *anything* like it has
been heard.
33 [a]"Did *any* people *ever* hear
the voice of God speaking out of
the midst of the fire, as you have
heard, and live?
34 "Or did God *ever* try to go
and take for Himself a nation
from the midst of *another* nation, [a]by trials, [b]by signs, by
wonders, by war, [c]by a mighty
hand and [d]an outstretched arm,
[e]and by great [1]terrors, according
to all that the LORD your God
did for you in Egypt before your
eyes?
35 "To you it was shown, that
you might know that the LORD
Himself *is* God; [a]*there is* none
other besides Him.
36 [a]"Out of heaven He let you
hear His voice, that He might instruct you; on earth He showed
you His great fire, and you heard
His words out of the midst of the
fire.
37 "And because [a]He loved your
fathers, therefore He chose their
[1]descendants after them; and [b]He
brought you out of Egypt with
His Presence, with His mighty
power,
38 [a]"driving out from before you
nations greater and mightier
than you, to bring you in, to give
you their land *as* an inheritance,
as *it is* this day.
39 "Therefore know this day,
and consider *it* in your heart,
that [a]the LORD Himself *is* God in
heaven above and on the earth
beneath; *there is* no other.
40 [a]"You shall therefore keep
His statutes and His commandments which I command you
today, that [1]it may go well with
you and with your children
after you, and that you may
[2]prolong *your* days in the land
which the LORD your God is giving you for all time."

25 [a]2 Kin. 17:17
26 [a]Deut. 30:18, 19 [1]*live long on it*
27 [a]Deut. 28:62
28 [a]Jer. 16:13 [b]Ps. 115:4–7; 135:15–17
29 [a][2 Chr. 15:4]
30 [a]Hos. 3:5 [b]Joel 2:12 [1]*tribulation*
31 [a]Jer. 30:11
32 [a]Job 8:8 [b]Matt. 24:31
33 [a]Deut. 5:24–26
34 [a]Deut. 7:19 [b]Ex. 7:3 [c]Ex. 13:3 [d]Ex. 6:6 [e]Deut. 26:8 [1]*calamities*
35 [a]Mark 12:32
36 [a]Heb. 12:19, 25
37 [a]Deut. 7:7, 8; 10:15; 33:3 [b]Ex. 13:3, 9, 14 [1]Lit. *seed*
38 [a]Deut. 7:1
39 [a]Josh. 2:11
40 [a]Lev. 22:31 [1]*you may prosper* [2]*live long*

41 Then Moses [a]set apart three
cities on this side of the Jordan,
toward the rising of the sun,
42 [a]that the manslayer might
flee there, who kills his neighbor
unintentionally, without having
hated him in time past, and that
by fleeing to one of these cities
he might live:
43 [a]Bē′zer in the wilderness on
the plateau for the Reū′ben·ītes,
Rā′moth in Gil′ē·ad for the Gad′-
ītes, and Gō′lan in Bā′shan for
the Ma·nas′sītes.
44 Now this *is* the law which
Moses set before the children of
Israel.
45 These *are* the testimonies,
the statutes, and the judgments
which Moses spoke to the children of Israel after they came
out of Egypt,
46 on this side of the Jordan, [a]in
the valley opposite Beth Pē′or,
in the land of Sī′hon king of the
Am′o·rītes, who dwelt at Hesh′-
bon, whom Moses and the children of Israel [b]defeated[1] after
they came out of Egypt.
47 And they took possession
of his land and the land [a]of Og
king of Bā′shan, two kings of
the Am′o·rītes, who *were* on this
side of the Jordan, toward the
[1]rising of the sun,
48 [a]from A·rō′er, which *is* on the
bank of the River Ar′non, even to
Mount [1]Sī′on (that is, [b]Her′mon),
49 and all the plain on the east
side of the Jordan as far as the
Sea of the Ar′a·bah, below the
[a]slopes of Pis′gah.

5 And Moses called all Israel,
and said to them: "Hear, O Israel, the statutes and judgments
which I speak in your hearing
today, that you may learn them
and be careful to observe them.
2 [a]"The LORD our God made a
covenant with us in Hō′reb.
3 "The LORD [a]did not make this
covenant with our fathers, but
with us, those who *are* here today, all of us who *are* alive.
4 [a]"The LORD talked with you
face to face on the mountain
from the midst of the fire.
5 [a]"I stood between the LORD
and you at that time, to declare
to you the word of the LORD; for
[b]you were afraid because of the
fire, and you did not go up the
mountain. *He* said:

6 [a]'I *am* the LORD your God who
brought you out of the
land of Egypt, out of the
house of [1]bondage.
7 [a]'You shall have no other gods
[1]before Me.
8 [a]'You shall not make for yourself a carved image—any
likeness *of anything* that
is in heaven above, or that
is in the earth beneath, or
that *is* in the water under
the earth;
9 you shall not [a]bow[1] down
to them nor serve them.
For I, the LORD your God,
am a jealous God, [2]visit-
ing the iniquity of the
fathers upon the children
to the third and fourth
generations of those who
hate Me,
10 [a]but showing mercy to
thousands, to those who
love Me and [1]keep My
commandments.
11 [a]'You shall not take the name
of the LORD your God in
vain, for the LORD will not
hold *him* [1]guiltless who
takes His name in vain.
12 [a]'Observe the Sabbath day, to
[1]keep it holy, as the LORD

41 [a]Num. 35:6
42 [a]Deut. 19:4
43 [a]Josh. 20:8
46 [a]Deut. 3:29 [b]Num. 21:24 [1]*struck*
47 [a]Num. 21:33–35 [1]*east*
48 [a]Deut. 2:36; 3:12 [b]Deut. 3:9 [1]Syr. *Sirion*
49 [a]Deut. 3:17

CHAPTER 5

2 [a]Ex. 19:5
3 [a]Heb. 8:9
4 [a]Ex. 19:9
5 [a]Gal. 3:19 [b]Ex. 19:16
6 [a]Ex. 20:2–17 [1]*slavery*
7 [a]Hos. 13:4 [1]*besides*
8 [a]Ex. 20:4
9 [a]Ex. 34:7, 14–16 [1]*worship them* [2]*punishing*
10 [a]Dan. 9:4 [1]*observe*
11 [a]Ex. 20:7 [1]*innocent*
12 [a]Ex. 20:8 [1]*sanctify it*

your God commanded
you.
13 [a]Six days you shall labor
and do all your work,
14 but the seventh day *is*
the [a]Sabbath of the LORD
your God. *In it* you shall
do no work: you, nor your
son, nor your daughter,
nor your male servant,
nor your female servant,
nor your ox, nor your
donkey, nor any of your
cattle, nor your stranger
who *is* within your gates,
that your male servant
and your female servant
may rest as well as you.
15 [a]And remember that
you were a slave in the
land of Egypt, and the
LORD your God brought
you out from there [b]by a
mighty hand and by an
outstretched arm; there-
fore the LORD your God
commanded you to keep
the Sabbath day.
16[a]'Honor your father and your
mother, as the LORD your
God has commanded
you, [b]that your days may
be long, and that it may
be well with [c]you in the
land which the LORD your
God is giving you.
17[a]'You shall not murder.
18[a]'You shall not commit adultery.
19[a]'You shall not steal.
20[a]'You shall not bear false witness against your neigh-
bor.
21[a]'You shall not covet your
neighbor's wife; and you
shall not desire your
neighbor's house, his
field, his male servant, his
female servant, his ox, his
donkey, or anything that
is your neighbor's.'
22 "These words the LORD
spoke to all your assembly, in
the mountain from the midst of
the fire, the cloud, and the thick
darkness, with a loud voice; and
He added no more. And [a]He
wrote them on two tablets of
stone and gave them to me.
23 [a]"So it was, when you heard
the voice from the midst of the
darkness, while the mountain
was burning with fire, that you
came near to me, all the heads
of your tribes and your elders.
24 "And you said: 'Surely the
LORD our God has shown us His
glory and His greatness, and [a]we
have heard His voice from the
midst of the fire. We have seen
this day that God speaks with
man; yet he [b]*still* lives.
25 'Now therefore, why should
we die? For this great fire will
consume us; [a]if we hear the
voice of the LORD our God anymore, then we shall die.
26 [a]'For who *is there* of all flesh
who has heard the voice of the
living God speaking from the
midst of the fire, as we *have*, and
lived?
27 'You go near and hear all
that the LORD our God may say,
and [a]tell us all that the LORD our
God says to you, and we will
hear and do *it*.'
28 "Then the LORD heard the
voice of your words when you
spoke to me, and the LORD said
to me: 'I have heard the voice of
the words of this people which
they have spoken to you. [a]They
are right *in* all that they have
spoken.
29 [a]'Oh, that they had such a

13 [a]Ex. 23:12; 35:2
14 [a][Heb. 4:4]
15 [a]Deut. 15:15 [b]Deut. 4:34, 37
16 [a]Lev. 19:3 [b]Deut. 6:2 [c]Deut. 4:40
17 [a]Matt. 5:21
18 [a]Ex. 20:14
19 [a][Rom. 13:9]
20 [a]Ex. 20:16; 23:1
21 [a]Ex. 20:17
22 [a]Deut. 4:13
23 [a]Ex. 20:18, 19
24 [a]Ex. 19:19 [b]Deut. 4:33
25 [a]Deut. 18:16
26 [a]Deut. 4:33
27 [a]Ex. 20:19
28 [a]Deut. 18:17
29 [a]Ps. 81:13

heart in them that they would
fear Me and [b]always keep all My
commandments, [c]that it might
be well with them and with their
children forever!
30 'Go and say to them, "Return
to your tents."
31 'But as for you, stand here by
Me, [a]and I will speak to you all
the commandments, the statutes,
and the judgments which you
shall teach them, that they may
observe *them* in the land which
I am giving them to possess.'
32 "Therefore you shall [1]be
careful to do as the LORD your
God has commanded you; [a]you
shall not turn aside to the right
hand or to the left.
33 "You shall walk in [a]all the
ways which the LORD your God
has commanded you, that you
may live [b]and *that it may be*
well with you, and *that* you may
prolong *your* days in the land
which you shall possess.

6 "Now this *is* [a]the commandment, *and these are* the statutes and judgments which the
LORD your God has commanded
to teach you, that you may observe *them* in the land which
you are crossing over to possess,
2 [a]"that you may fear the LORD
your God, to keep all His statutes
and His commandments which I
command you, you and your son
and your grandson, all the days
of your life, [b]and that your days
may be prolonged.
3 "Therefore hear, O Israel,
and [1]be careful to observe *it*,
that it may be well with you, and
that you may [a]multiply greatly
[b]as the LORD God of your fathers
has promised you—[c]'a land flowing with milk and honey.'
4 [a]"Hear, O Israel: [1]The LORD
our God, the LORD *is* one!
5 [a]"You shall love the LORD
your God with all your heart,
[b]with all your soul, and with all
your strength.
6 "And [a]these words which I
command you today shall be in
your heart.
7 [a]"You shall teach them diligently to your children, and
shall talk of them when you sit
in your house, when you walk
by the way, when you lie down,
and when you rise up.
8 [a]"You shall bind them as a
sign on your hand, and they
shall be as frontlets between
your eyes.
9 [a]"You shall write them on the
doorposts of your house and on
your gates.
10 "So it shall be, when the
LORD your God brings you into
the land of which He [1]swore to
your fathers, to Abraham, Isaac,
and Jacob, to give you large and
beautiful cities [a]which you did
not build,
11 "houses full of all good things,
which you did not fill, hewn-out
wells which you did not dig,
vineyards and olive trees which
you did not plant—[a]when you
have eaten and are full—
12 "*then* beware, lest you forget
the [a]LORD who brought you out
of the land of Egypt, from the
house of bondage.
13 "You shall [a]fear the LORD
your God and serve Him, and
[b]shall take oaths in His name.
14 "You shall not go after other
gods, [a]the gods of the peoples
who *are* all around you
15 "(for [a]the LORD your God *is*
a jealous God [b]among you), lest
the anger of the LORD your God

29 [b]Deut. 11:1 [c]Deut. 4:40
31 [a][Gal. 3:19]
32 [a]Deut. 17:20; 28:14 [1]*observe*
33 [a]Deut. 10:12 [b]Deut. 4:40

CHAPTER 6

1 [a]Deut. 12:1
2 [a][Eccl. 12:13] [b]Deut. 4:40
3 [a]Deut. 7:13 [b]Gen. 22:17 [c]Ex. 3:8, 17 [1]Lit. *observe to do*
4 [a][1 Cor. 8:4, 6] [1]Or *The LORD is our God, the LORD alone*, i.e., the only one
5 [a]Matt. 22:37 [b]2 Kin. 23:25
6 [a]Deut. 11:18–20
7 [a]Deut. 4:9; 11:19
8 [a]Prov. 3:3; 6:21; 7:3
9 [a]Deut. 11:20
10 [a]Josh. 24:13 [1]*promised*
11 [a]Deut. 8:10; 11:15; 14:29
12 [a]Deut. 8:11–18
13 [a]Matt. 4:10 [b]Deut. 5:11
14 [a]Deut. 13:7
15 [a]Ex. 20:5 [b]Ex. 33:3

be aroused against you and destroy you from the face of the
earth.
16 [a]"You shall not [1]tempt the
LORD your God [b]as you [2]tempted
Him in Mas'sah.
17 "You shall [a]diligently keep
the commandments of the LORD
your God, His testimonies, and
His statutes which He has commanded you.
18 "And you [a]shall do *what is*
right and good in the sight of the
LORD, that it may be well with
you, and that you may go in and
possess the good land of which
the LORD swore to your fathers,
19 [a]"to cast out all your enemies
from before you, as the LORD has
spoken.
20 [a]"When your son asks you in
time to come, saying, 'What *is*
the meaning of the testimonies,
the statutes, and the judgments
which the LORD our God has
commanded you?'
21 "then you shall say to your
son: 'We were slaves of Pharaoh
in Egypt, and the LORD brought
us out of Egypt [a]with a mighty
hand;
22 'and the LORD showed signs
and wonders before our eyes,
great and severe, against Egypt,
Pharaoh, and all his household.
23 'Then He brought us out from
there, that He might bring us in,
to give us the land of which He
[1]swore to our fathers.
24 'And the LORD commanded
us to [1]observe all these [2]statutes,
[a]to fear the LORD our God, [b]for
our good always, that [c]He might
preserve us alive, as *it is* [3]this
day.
25 'Then [a]it will be righteousness for us, if we are careful to
observe all these commandments
before the LORD our God, as He
has commanded us.'

7 "When the LORD your God
brings you into the land
which you go to [a]possess, and
has cast out many [b]nations before you, [c]the Hit'tītes and the
Gir'ga·shītes and the Am'o·rītes
and the Cā'naan·ītes and the
Per'iz·zītes and the Hī'vītes and
the Jeb'ū·sītes, seven nations
greater and mightier than you,
2 "and when the LORD your
God delivers [a]them over to you,
you shall conquer them *and* utterly destroy them. [b]You shall
make no covenant with them
nor show mercy to them.
3 [a]"Nor shall you make marriages with them. You shall not
give your daughter to their son,
nor take their daughter for your
son.
4 "For they will turn your sons
away from following Me, to serve
other gods; [a]so the anger of the
LORD will be aroused against
you and destroy you suddenly.
5 "But thus you shall deal with
them: you shall [a]destroy their
altars, and break down their *sa-*
cred pillars, and cut down their
[1]wooden images, and burn their
carved images with fire.
6 "For you *are* a [1]holy people
to the LORD your God; [a]the LORD
your God has chosen you to be
a people for Himself, a special
treasure above all the peoples
on the face of the earth.
7 "The LORD did not set His
[a]love on you nor choose you because you were more in number
than any other people, for you
were [b]the least of all peoples;
8 "but [a]because the LORD loves
you, and because He would
keep [b]the oath which He swore

16 [a]Luke 4:12 [b][1 Cor. 10:9] [1]*test* [2]*tested*
17 [a]Deut. 11:22
18 [a]Ex. 15:26
19 [a]Num. 33:52, 53
20 [a]Ex. 13:8, 14
21 [a]Ex. 13:3
23 [1]*promised*
24 [a]Deut. 6:2 [b]Jer. 32:39 [c]Deut. 4:1 [1]*do* [2]*ordinances* [3]*today*
25 [a][Rom. 10:3, 5]

CHAPTER 7

1 [a]Deut. 6:10 [b]Gen. 15:19–21 [c]Ex. 33:2
2 [a]Num. 31:17 [b]Josh. 2:14
3 [a]1 Kin. 11:2
4 [a]Deut. 6:15
5 [a]Ex. 23:24; 34:13 [1]Heb. *Asherim*, Canaanite deities
6 [a]Ex. 19:5, 6 [1]*set-apart*
7 [a]Deut. 4:37 [b]Deut. 10:22
8 [a]Deut. 10:15 [b]Luke 1:55, 72, 73

to your fathers, [c]the LORD has
brought you out with a mighty
hand, and redeemed you from
the house of [1]bondage, from the
hand of Pharaoh king of Egypt.
9 "Therefore know that the
LORD your God, He *is* God, [a]the
faithful God [b]who keeps covenant and mercy for a thousand generations with those
who love Him and keep His
commandments;
10 "and He repays those who
hate Him to their face, to destroy
them. He will not [1]be [a]slack with
him who hates Him; He will repay him to his face.
11 "Therefore you shall keep
the commandment, the statutes, and the judgments which I
command you today, to observe
them.
12 "Then it shall come to pass,
because you listen to these judgments, and keep and do them,
that the LORD your God will keep
with you the covenant and the
mercy which He swore to your
fathers.
13 "And He will [a]love you and
bless you and [1]multiply you; [b]He
will also bless the fruit of your
womb and the fruit of your land,
your grain and your new wine
and your oil, the increase of
your cattle and the offspring of
your flock, in the land of which
He [2]swore to your fathers to give
you.
14 "You shall be blessed above
all peoples; there shall not be a
male or female [a]barren among
you or among your livestock.
15 "And the LORD will take away
from you all sickness, and will
afflict you with none of the
[a]terrible diseases of Egypt which

8 [c]Ex. 13:3, 14 [1]*slavery*

9 [a]1 Cor. 1:9 [b]Neh. 1:5

10 [a][2 Pet. 3:9, 10] [1]*delay*

13 [a]John 14:21 [b]Deut. 28:4 [1]*cause you to increase* [2]*promised*

14 [a]Ex. 23:26

15 [a]Ex. 9:14; 15:26

16 [a]Judg. 8:27 [1]*consume*

18 [a]Ps. 105:5

19 [a]Deut. 4:34; 29:3

20 [a]Josh. 24:12

22 [a]Ex. 23:29, 30 [1]*consume*

24 [a]Josh. 10:24, 42; 12:1–24 [b]Josh. 23:9

you have known, but will lay
them on all those who hate you.
16 "Also you shall [1]destroy all
the peoples whom the LORD your
God delivers over to you; your
eye shall have no pity on them;
nor shall you serve their gods,
for that *will* [a]*be* a snare to you.
17 "If you should say in your
heart, 'These nations are greater
than I; how can I dispossess
them?'—
18 "you shall not be afraid of
them, *but* you shall [a]remember
well what the LORD your God did
to Pharaoh and to all Egypt:
19 [a]"the great trials which your
eyes saw, the signs and the wonders, the mighty hand and the
outstretched arm, by which the
LORD your God brought you out.
So shall the LORD your God do to
all the peoples of whom you are
afraid.
20 [a]"Moreover the LORD your
God will send the hornet among
them until those who are left,
who hide themselves from you,
are destroyed.
21 "You shall not be terrified
of them; for the LORD your God,
the great and awesome God, *is*
among you.
22 "And the LORD your God will
drive out those nations before
you [a]little by little; you will be
unable to [1]destroy them at once,
lest the beasts of the field become *too* numerous for you.
23 "But the LORD your God will
deliver them over to you, and
will inflict defeat upon them until they are destroyed.
24 "And [a]He will deliver their
kings into your hand, and you
will destroy their name from
under heaven; [b]no one shall be

able to stand [1]against you until
you have destroyed them.
25 "You shall burn the carved
images of their gods with fire;
you shall not [a]covet[1] the silver
or gold *that is* on them, nor take
it for yourselves, lest you be
snared by it; for it *is* an abomination to the LORD your God.
26 "Nor shall you bring an
abomination into your house,
lest you be doomed to destruction like it. You shall utterly detest it and utterly abhor it, [a]for it
is an [1]accursed thing.

8

"Every commandment which
I command you today [a]you
must [1]be careful to observe, that
you may live and [b]multiply,[2] and
go in and possess the land of
which the LORD [3]swore to your
fathers.
2 "And you shall remember
that the LORD your God [a]led you
all the way these forty years in
the wilderness, to humble you
and [b]test you, [c]to know what
was in your heart, whether you
would keep His commandments
or not.
3 "So He humbled you, [a]al-
lowed you to hunger, and [b]fed
you with manna which you did
not know nor did your fathers
know, that He might make you
know that man shall [c]not live by
bread alone; but man lives by
every *word* that proceeds from
the mouth of the LORD.
4 [a]"Your garments did not
wear out on you, nor did your
foot swell these forty years.
5 [a]"You should [1]know in your
heart that as a man chastens his
son, *so* the LORD your God chastens you.
6 "Therefore you shall keep
the commandments of the LORD
your God, [a]to walk in His ways
and to fear Him.
7 "For the LORD your God is
bringing you into a good land,
[a]a land of brooks of water, of
fountains and springs, that flow
out of valleys and hills;
8 "a land of wheat and barley,
of vines and fig trees and pomegranates, a land of olive oil and
honey;
9 "a land in which you will eat
bread without scarcity, in which
you will lack nothing; a land
whose stones *are* iron and out of
whose hills you can dig copper.
10 [a]"When you have eaten and
are full, then you shall bless the
LORD your God for the good land
which He has given you.
11 "Beware that you do not forget the LORD your God by not
keeping His commandments,
His judgments, and His statutes
which I command you today,
12 [a]"lest—*when* you have eaten
and are [1]full, and have built
beautiful houses and dwell *in
them;*
13 "and *when* your herds and
your flocks multiply, and your
silver and your gold are [1]mul-
tiplied, and all that you have is
multiplied;
14 [a]"when your heart [1]is lifted
up, and you [b]forget the LORD
your God who brought you out
of the land of Egypt, from the
house of bondage;
15 "who [a]led you through that
great and terrible wilderness,
[b]*in which were* fiery serpents
and scorpions and thirsty land
where there was no water; [c]who
brought water for you out of the
flinty rock;
16 "who fed you in the wilderness with [a]manna, which your

24 [1]*before*
25 [a]Prov. 23:6 [1]*desire*
26 [a]Deut. 13:17 [1]*devoted or banned*

CHAPTER 8

1 [a]Deut. 4:1; 6:24 [b]Deut. 30:16 [1]*observe to do* [2]*increase in number* [3]*promised*
2 [a]Amos 2:10 [b]Ex. 16:4 [c][John 2:25]
3 [a]Ex. 16:2, 3 [b]Ex. 16:12, 14, 35 [c]Matt. 4:4
4 [a]Neh. 9:21
5 [a]2 Sam. 7:14 [1]*consider*
6 [a][Deut. 5:33]
7 [a]Deut. 11:9–12
10 [a]Deut. 6:11, 12
12 [a]Hos. 13:6 [1]*satisfied*
13 [1]*increased*
14 [a]1 Cor. 4:7 [b]Ps. 106:21 [1]*becomes proud*
15 [a]Is. 63:12–14 [b]Num. 21:6 [c]Num. 20:11
16 [a]Ex. 16:15

fathers did not know, that He
might humble you and that He
might test you, [b]to do you good
in the end—
17 "then you say in your heart,
'My power and the might of
my hand have gained me this
wealth.'
18 "And you shall remember the
LORD your God, [a]for *it is* He who
gives you power to get wealth,
[b]that He may [1]establish His covenant
which He swore to your
fathers, as *it is* this day.
19 "Then it shall be, if you by
any means forget the LORD your
God, and follow other gods, and
serve them and worship them, [a]I
testify against you this day that
you shall surely perish.
20 "As the nations which the
LORD destroys before you, [a]so
you shall perish, because you
would not be obedient to the
voice of the LORD your God.

9

"Hear, O Israel: You *are* to
cross over the Jordan today,
and go in to dispossess nations
greater and mightier than yourself,
cities great and fortified up
to heaven,
2 "a people great and tall, the
[a]descendants of the An'a·kim,
whom you know, and *of whom*
you heard *it said*, 'Who can
stand before the descendants of
Ā'nak?'
3 "Therefore understand today
that the LORD your God *is*
He who [a]goes over before you
as a [b]consuming fire. [c]He will
destroy them and bring them
down before you; [d]so you shall
drive them out and destroy them
quickly, as the LORD has said to
you.
4 [a]"Do not think in your heart,
after the LORD your God has
cast them out before you, saying,
'Because of my righteousness
the LORD has brought me
in to possess this land'; but *it
is* [b]because of the wickedness
of these nations *that* the LORD
is driving them out from before
you.
5 [a]"*It is* not because of your
righteousness or the uprightness
of your heart *that* you go
in to possess their land, but
because of the wickedness of
these nations *that* the LORD your
God drives them out from before
you, and that He may [1]fulfill the
[b]word which the LORD swore to
your fathers, to Abraham, Isaac,
and Jacob.
6 "Therefore understand that
the LORD your God is not giving
you this good land to possess because
of your righteousness, for
you *are* a [a]stiff-necked[1] people.
7 "Remember! Do not forget
how you [a]provoked the LORD
your God to wrath in the wilderness.
[b]From the day that you
departed from the land of Egypt
until you came to this place, you
have been rebellious against the
LORD.
8 "Also [a]in Hō'reb you provoked
the LORD to wrath, so that
the LORD was angry *enough* with
you to have destroyed you.
9 [a]"When I went up into the
mountain to receive the tablets
of stone, the tablets of the covenant
which the LORD made with
you, then I stayed on the mountain
forty days and [b]forty nights.
I neither ate bread nor drank
water.
10 [a]"Then the LORD delivered to
me two tablets of stone written
with the finger of God, and on
them *were* all the words which

16 [b][Heb. 12:11]
18 [a]Hos. 2:8 [b]Deut. 7:8, 12 [1]*confirm*
19 [a]Deut. 4:26; 30:18
20 [a][Dan. 9:11, 12]

CHAPTER 9

2 [a]Num. 13:22, 28, 33
3 [a]Josh. 3:11; 5:14 [b]Deut. 4:24 [c]Deut. 7:24 [d]Ex. 23:31
4 [a]Deut. 8:17 [b]Lev. 18:3, 24–30
5 [a][Titus 3:5] [b]Gen. 50:24 [1]*perform*
6 [a]Deut. 31:27 [1]*stubborn* or *rebellious*
7 [a]Num. 14:22 [b]Ex. 14:11
8 [a]Ex. 32:1–8
9 [a]Deut. 5:2–22 [b]Ex. 24:18
10 [a]Deut. 4:13

the LORD had spoken to you on
the mountain from the midst
of the fire [b]in[1] the day of the
assembly.
11 "And it came to pass, at
the end of forty days and forty
nights, *that* the LORD gave me
the two tablets of stone, the tablets of the covenant.
12 "Then the LORD said to me,
[a]'Arise, go down quickly from
here, for your people whom you
brought out of Egypt have acted
corruptly; they have [b]quickly
turned aside from the way
which I commanded them; they
have made themselves a molded
image.'
13 "Furthermore [a]the LORD
spoke to me, saying, 'I have seen
this people, and indeed [b]they are
a [1]stiff-necked people.
14 [a]'Let Me alone, that I may
destroy them and [b]blot out their
name from under heaven; [c]and
I will make of you a nation
mightier and greater than they.'
15 [a]"So I turned and came down
from the mountain, and [b]the
mountain burned with fire; and
the two tablets of the covenant
were in my two hands.
16 "And [a]I looked, and behold,
you had sinned against the LORD
your God—had made for yourselves a molded calf! You had
turned aside quickly from the
way which the LORD had commanded you.
17 "Then I took the two tablets
and threw them out of my two
hands and [a]broke them before
your eyes.
18 "And I [a]fell[1] down before
the LORD, as at the first, forty
days and forty nights; I neither
ate bread nor drank water, because of all your sin which you
committed in doing wickedly in
the sight of the LORD, to provoke
Him to anger.
19 [a]"For I was afraid of the anger and hot displeasure with
which the LORD was angry with
you, to destroy you. [b]But the
LORD listened to me at that time
also.
20 "And the LORD was very angry with Aaron *and* would have
destroyed him; so I prayed for
Aaron also at the same time.
21 "Then I took your sin, the
calf which you had made, and
burned it with fire and crushed it
and ground *it* very small, until it
was as fine as dust; and I [a]threw
its dust into the brook that descended from the mountain.
22 "Also at [a]Tab′e·rah and
[b]Mas′sah and [c]Kib′roth Hat·tā′-
a·vah you [1]provoked the LORD to
wrath.
23 "Likewise, [a]when the LORD
sent you from Kā′desh Bar·nē′a,
saying, 'Go up and possess the
land which I have given you,'
then you rebelled against the
commandment of the LORD your
God, and [b]you did not believe
Him nor obey His voice.
24 [a]"You have been rebellious
against the LORD from the day
that I knew you.
25 [a]"Thus I [1]prostrated myself
before the LORD; forty days and
forty nights I kept prostrating
myself, because the LORD had
said He would destroy you.
26 "Therefore I prayed to the
LORD, and said: 'O Lord GOD, do
not destroy Your people and [a]Your
inheritance whom You have redeemed through Your greatness,
whom You have brought out of
Egypt with a mighty hand.
27 'Remember Your servants,

10 [b]Ex. 19:17 [1]*when you were all gathered together*
12 [a]Ex. 32:7, 8 [b]Deut. 31:29
13 [a]Ex. 32:9 [b]Deut. 9:6 [1]*stubborn* or *rebellious*
14 [a]Ex. 32:10 [b]Deut. 29:20 [c]Num. 14:12
15 [a]Ex. 32:15–19 [b]Ex. 19:18
16 [a]Ex. 32:19
17 [a]Ex. 32:19
18 [a]Ex. 34:28 [1]*prostrated myself*
19 [a]Ex. 32:10, 11 [b]Ex. 32:14
21 [a]Ex. 32:20
22 [a]Num. 11:1, 3 [b]Ex. 17:7 [c]Num. 11:4, 34 [1]*caused the* LORD *to be angry*
23 [a]Num. 13:3 [b]Ps. 106:24, 25
24 [a]Deut. 9:7; 31:27
25 [a]Deut. 9:18 [1]*fell down*
26 [a]Deut. 32:9

Abraham, Isaac, and Jacob; do
not look on the stubbornness of
this people, or on their wickedness or their sin,
28 'lest the land from which
You brought us should say, "Because the LORD was not able to
bring them to the land which
He promised them, and because
He hated them, He has brought
them out to kill them in the
wilderness."
29 'Yet they *are* Your people
and Your inheritance, whom
You brought out by Your mighty
power and by Your outstretched
arm.'

10 "At that time the LORD
said to me, [1]'Hew for
yourself two tablets of stone like
the first, and come up to Me on
the mountain and make yourself
an [a]ark of wood.
2 'And I will write on the tablets the words that were on the
first tablets, which you broke;
and [a]you shall put them in the
ark.'
3 "So I made an ark of acacia wood, hewed two tablets of
stone like the first, and went up
the mountain, having the two
tablets in my hand.
4 "And He wrote on the tablets according to the first writing, the Ten [1]Commandments,
[a]which the LORD had spoken to
you in the mountain from the
midst of the fire in the day of
the assembly; and the LORD gave
them to me.
5 "Then I turned and [a]came
down from the mountain, and
[b]put the tablets in the ark
which I had made; [c]and there
they are, just as the LORD commanded me."
6 (Now the children of Israel
journeyed from the wells of
Ben'ē Jā'a·kan to Mō·sē'rah,
where Aaron [a]died, and where
he was buried; and El·ē·ā'zar his
son ministered as priest in his
[1]stead.
7 [a]From there they journeyed
to Gud'gō·dah, and from Gud'-
gō·dah to Jot'ba·thah, a land of
[1]rivers of water.
8 At that time [a]the LORD [1]sepa-
rated the tribe of Levi [b]to bear
the ark of the covenant of the
LORD, [c]to stand before the LORD
to minister to Him and [d]to bless
in His name, to this day.
9 [a]Therefore Levi has no portion nor inheritance with his
brethren; the LORD *is* his inheritance, just as the LORD your God
promised him.)
10 "As at the first time, [a]I stayed
in the mountain forty days and
forty nights; [b]the LORD also
heard me at that time, *and* the
LORD chose not to destroy you.
11 [a]"Then the LORD said to me,
'Arise, begin *your* journey before the people, that they may go
in and possess the land which I
swore to their fathers to give
them.'
12 "And now, Israel, [a]what does
the LORD your God require of
you, but to fear the LORD your
God, to walk in all His ways and
to [b]love Him, to serve the LORD
your God with all your heart
and with all your soul,
13 "*and* to keep the commandments of the LORD and His statutes which I command you today [a]for your [1]good?
14 "Indeed heaven and the highest heavens belong to the [a]LORD
your God, *also* the earth with all
that *is* in it.
15 "The LORD delighted only in

CHAPTER 10
1 [a]Ex. 25:10 [1]*Cut out*
2 [a]Ex. 25:16, 21
4 [a]Ex. 20:1; 34:28 [1]Lit. *Words*
5 [a]Ex. 34:29 [b]Ex. 40:20 [c]1 Kin. 8:9
6 [a]Num. 20:25–28; 33:38 [1]*place*
7 [a]Num. 33:32–34 [1]*brooks*
8 [a]Num. 3:6 [b]Num. 4:5, 15; 10:21 [c]Deut. 18:5 [d]Num. 6:23 [1]*set apart*
9 [a]Deut. 18:1, 2
10 [a]Deut. 9:18 [b]Ex. 32:14
11 [a]Ex. 33:1
12 [a]Mic. 6:8 [b]Deut. 6:5
13 [a]Deut. 6:24 [1]*benefit* or *welfare*
14 [a][Neh. 9:6]

your fathers, to love them; and
He chose their [1]descendants after them, you above all peoples,
as *it is* this day.
16 "Therefore circumcise the
foreskin of your [a]heart, and be
[b]stiff-necked[1] no longer.
17 "For the LORD your God *is*
[a]God of gods and [b]Lord of lords,
the great God, [c]mighty and awesome, who [d]shows no partiality
nor takes a bribe.
18 [a]"He administers justice for
the fatherless and the widow,
and loves the stranger, giving
him food and clothing.
19 "Therefore love the stranger,
for you were strangers in the
land of Egypt.
20 [a]"You shall fear the LORD
your God; you shall serve Him,
and to Him you shall hold fast,
and take oaths in His name.
21 "He *is* your praise, and He *is*
your God, who has done for you
these great and awesome things
which your eyes have seen.
22 "Your fathers went down to
Egypt with seventy persons, and
now the LORD your God has
made you as the stars of heaven
in multitude.

11

"Therefore you shall love
the LORD your God, and
keep His charge, His statutes,
His judgments, and His commandments always.
2 "Know today that *I do* not
speak with your children, who
have not known and who have
not seen the [1]chastening of the
LORD your God, His greatness
and His mighty hand and His
outstretched arm—
3 "His signs and His acts which
He did in the midst of Egypt, to
Pharaoh king of Egypt, and to
all his land;
4 "what He did to the army
of Egypt, to their horses and
their chariots: [a]how He made
the waters of the Red Sea overflow them as they pursued you,
and *how* the LORD has destroyed
them to this day;
5 "what He did for you in the
wilderness until you came to
this place;
6 "and [a]what He did to Dā′than
and A·bī′ram the sons of E·lī′ab,
the son of Reuben: how the earth
opened its mouth and swallowed
them up, their households, their
tents, and all the substance that
was [1]in their possession, in the
midst of all Israel—
7 "but your eyes have [a]seen every great [1]act of the LORD which
He did.
8 "Therefore you shall keep
every commandment which I
command you today, that you
may [a]be strong, and go in and
possess the land which you
cross over to possess,
9 "and [a]that you may prolong
your days in the land [b]which the
LORD [1]swore to give your fathers,
to them and their descendants,
[c]'a land flowing with milk and
honey.'
10 "For the land which you go
to possess *is* not like the land
of Egypt from which you have
come, where you sowed your
seed and watered *it* by foot, as a
vegetable garden;
11 [a]"but the land which you
cross over to possess *is* a land of
hills and valleys, which drinks
water from the rain of heaven,
12 "a land for which the LORD
your God cares; [a]the eyes of the
LORD your God *are* always on it,
from the beginning of the year
to the very end of the year.

15 [1]Lit. *seed*
16 [a]Jer. 4:4 [b]Deut. 9:6, 13 [1]*rebellious*
17 [a]Dan. 2:47 [b]Rev. 19:16 [c]Deut. 7:21 [d]Acts 10:34
18 [a]Ps. 68:5; 146:9
20 [a]Matt. 4:10

CHAPTER 11

2 [1]*discipline*
4 [a]Ps. 106:11
6 [a]Ps. 106:16–18 [1]*at their feet*
7 [a]Deut. 10:21; 29:2 [1]*work*
8 [a]Josh. 1:6, 7
9 [a]Deut. 4:40; 5:16, 33; 6:2 [b]Deut. 9:5 [c]Ex. 3:8 [1]*promised*
11 [a]Deut. 8:7
12 [a]1 Kin. 9:3

13 'And it shall be that if you
earnestly [1]obey My commandments which I command you
today, to love the LORD your God
and serve Him with all your
heart and with all your soul,
14 'then [a]I[1] will give *you* the
rain for your land in its season,
[b]the early rain and the latter
rain, that you may gather in
your grain, your new wine, and
your oil.
15 [a]'And I will send grass in your
fields for your livestock, that
you may [b]eat and be [1]filled.'
16 "Take heed to yourselves,
[a]lest your heart be deceived, and
you turn aside and [b]serve other
gods and worship them,
17 "lest [a]the LORD's anger be
aroused against you, and He
[b]shut up the heavens so that
there be no rain, and the land
yield no produce, and [c]you perish quickly from the good land
which the LORD is giving you.
18 "Therefore [a]you shall [1]lay up
these words of mine in your
heart and in your [b]soul, and
[c]bind them as a sign on your
hand, and they shall be as frontlets between your eyes.
19 [a]"You shall teach them to
your children, speaking of them
when you sit in your house, when
you walk by the way, when you
lie down, and when you rise up.
20 [a]"And you shall write them
on the doorposts of your house
and on your gates,
21 "that [a]your days and the days
of your children may be multiplied in the land of which the
LORD swore to your fathers to
give them, like [b]the days of the
heavens above the earth.
22 "For if [a]you carefully keep
all these commandments which
I command you to do—to love
the LORD your God, to walk in
all His ways, and [b]to hold fast to
Him—
23 "then the LORD will [a]drive
out all these nations from before
you, and you will [b]dispossess
greater and mightier nations
than yourselves.
24 [a]"Every place on which the
sole of your foot treads shall
be yours: [b]from the wilderness
and Lebanon, from the river,
the River Eū·phrā′tēs, even to
the [1]Western Sea, shall be your
territory.
25 "No man shall be able to
[a]stand [1]against you; the LORD
your God will put the [b]dread of
you and the fear of you upon all
the land where you tread, just as
He has said to you.
26 [a]"Behold, I set before you
today a blessing and a curse:
27 [a]"the blessing, if you obey
the commandments of the LORD
your God which I command you
today;
28 "and the [a]curse, if you do not
obey the commandments of the
LORD your God, but turn aside
from the way which I command
you today, to go after other gods
which you have not known.
29 "Now it shall be, when the
LORD your God has brought you
into the land which you go to
possess, that you shall put the
[a]blessing on Mount Ger′i·zim
and the [b]curse on Mount Ē′bal.
30 "*Are* they not on the other
side of the Jordan, toward
the setting sun, in the land of the
Cā′naan·ītes who dwell in the
plain opposite Gil′gal, [a]beside
the terebinth trees of Mō′reh?
31 "For you will cross over the
Jordan and go in to possess the

13 [1]Lit. *listen to*
14 [a]Deut. 28:12 [b]Joel 2:23 [1]So with MT, Tg.; Sam., LXX, Vg. *He*
15 [a]Ps. 104:14 [b]Deut. 6:11 [1]*satisfied*
16 [a]Job 31:27 [b]Deut. 8:19
17 [a]Deut. 6:15; 9:19 [b]2 Chr. 6:26; 7:13 [c]Deut. 4:26
18 [a]Deut. 6:6–9 [b]Ps. 119:2, 34 [c]Deut. 6:8 [1]Lit. *put*
19 [a]Deut. 4:9, 10; 6:7
20 [a]Deut. 6:9
21 [a]Deut. 4:40 [b]Ps. 72:5; 89:29
22 [a]Deut. 11:1 [b]Deut. 10:20
23 [a]Deut. 4:38 [b]Deut. 9:1
24 [a]Josh. 1:3; 14:9 [b]Gen. 15:18 [1]Mediterranean
25 [a]Deut. 7:24 [b]Deut. 2:25 [1]*before*
26 [a]Deut. 30:1, 15, 19
27 [a]Deut. 28:1–14
28 [a]Deut. 28:15–68
29 [a]Josh. 8:33 [b]Deut. 27:13–26
30 [a]Gen. 12:6

land which the LORD your God is giving you, and you will possess it and dwell in it.

32 “And you shall be careful to observe all the statutes and judgments which I set before you today.

12

“These [a]*are* the statutes and judgments which you shall be careful to observe in the land which the LORD God of your fathers is giving you to possess, [b]all[1] the days that you live on the earth.

2 [a]“You shall utterly destroy all the places where the nations which you shall dispossess served their gods, [b]on the high mountains and on the hills and under every green tree.

3 “And [a]you shall destroy their altars, break their *sacred* pillars, and burn their [1]wooden images with fire; you shall cut down the carved images of their gods and destroy their names from that place.

4 “You shall not [a]worship the LORD your God *with* such *things.*

5 “But you shall seek the [a]place where the LORD your God chooses, out of all your tribes, to put His name for His [b]dwelling[1] place; and there you shall go.

6 [a]“There you shall take your burnt offerings, your sacrifices, your tithes, the heave offerings of your hand, your vowed offerings, your freewill offerings, and the [b]firstborn of your herds and flocks.

7 “And [a]there you shall eat before the LORD your God, and [b]you shall rejoice in [1]all to which you have put your hand, you and your households, in which the LORD your God has blessed you.

8 “You shall not at all do as we are doing here today—[a]every man doing whatever *is* right in his own eyes—

9 “for as yet you have not come to the [a]rest[1] and the inheritance which the LORD your God is giving you.

10 “But *when* you cross over the Jordan and dwell in the land which the LORD your God is giving you to inherit, and He gives you [a]rest from all your enemies round about, so that you dwell in safety,

11 “then there will be the place where the LORD your God chooses to make His name abide. There you shall bring all that I command you: your burnt offerings, your sacrifices, your tithes, the heave offerings of your hand, and all your choice offerings which you vow to the LORD.

12 “And [a]you shall rejoice before the LORD your God, you and your sons and your daughters, your male and female servants, and the [b]Lē′vīte who *is* within your gates, since he has no portion nor inheritance with you.

13 “Take heed to yourself that you do not offer your burnt offerings in every place that you see;

14 “but in the place which the LORD chooses, in one of your tribes, there you shall offer your burnt offerings, and there you shall do all that I command you.

15 “However, [a]you may slaughter and eat meat within all your gates, whatever your heart desires, according to the blessing of the LORD your God which He has given you; [b]the unclean and the clean may eat of it, [c]of the gazelle and the deer alike.

CHAPTER 12

1 [a]Deut. 6:1 [b]Deut. 4:9, 10 [1]As long as

2 [a]Ex. 34:13 [b]2 Kin. 16:4; 17:10, 11

3 [a]Num. 33:52 [1]Heb. *Asherim*

4 [a]Deut. 12:31

5 [a]Ex. 20:24 [b]Ex. 15:13 [1]*home*

6 [a]Lev. 17:3, 4 [b]Deut. 14:23

7 [a]Deut. 14:26 [b]Deut. 12:12, 18 [1]*all that you undertake*

8 [a]Judg. 17:6; 21:25

9 [a]Deut. 3:20; 25:19 [1]Or *place of rest*

10 [a]Josh. 11:23

12 [a]Deut. 12:18; 26:11 [b]Deut. 10:9; 14:29

15 [a]Deut. 12:21 [b]Deut. 12:22 [c]Deut. 14:5

16 [a]"Only you shall not eat the blood; you shall pour it on the earth like water.

17 "You may not eat within your gates the tithe of your grain or your new wine or your oil, of the firstborn of your herd or your flock, of any of your offerings which you vow, of your freewill offerings, or of the [1]heave offering of your hand.

18 "But you must eat them before the LORD your God in the place which the LORD your God chooses, you and your son and your daughter, your male servant and your female servant, and the Lē′vīte who *is* within your gates; and you shall rejoice before the LORD your God in [1]all to which you put your hands.

19 [1]"Take heed to yourself that you do not forsake the Lē′vīte as long as you live in your land.

20 "When the LORD your God [a]enlarges your border as He has promised you, and you say, 'Let me eat meat,' because you long to eat meat, you may eat as much meat as your heart desires.

21 "If the place where the LORD your God chooses to put His name is too far from [a]you, then you may slaughter from your herd and from your flock which the LORD has given you, just as I have commanded you, and you may eat within your gates as much as your heart desires.

22 "Just as the gazelle and the deer are eaten, so you may eat them; the unclean and the clean alike may eat them.

23 "Only be sure that you do not eat the blood, [a]for the blood *is* the life; you may not eat the life with the meat.

24 "You shall not eat it; you shall pour it on the earth like water.

25 "You shall not eat it, [a]that it may go well with you and your children after you, [b]when you do *what is* right in the sight of the LORD.

26 "Only the [a]holy things which you have, and your vowed offerings, you shall take and go to the place which the LORD chooses.

27 "And [a]you shall offer your burnt offerings, the meat and the blood, on the altar of the LORD your God; and the blood of your sacrifices shall be poured out on the altar of the LORD your God, and you shall eat the meat.

28 "Observe and obey all these words which I command you, [a]that it may go well with you and your children after you forever, when you do *what is* good and right in the sight of the LORD your God.

29 "When [a]the LORD your God cuts off from before you the nations which you go to dispossess, and you displace them and dwell in their land,

30 "take heed to yourself that you are not ensnared to follow them, after they are destroyed from before you, and that you do not inquire after their gods, saying, 'How did these nations serve their gods? I also will do likewise.'

31 [a]"You shall not worship the LORD your God in that way; for every [1]abomination to the LORD which He hates they have done to their gods; for [b]they burn even their sons and daughters in the fire to their gods.

32 "Whatever I command you, be careful to observe it; [a]you

16 [a]Gen. 9:4
17 [1]*contribution*
18 [1]*all your undertakings*
19 [1]*Be careful*
20 [a]Ex. 34:24
21 [a]Deut. 14:24
23 [a]Gen. 9:4
25 [a]Deut. 4:40; 6:18 [b]Ex. 15:26
26 [a]Num. 5:9, 10; 18:19
27 [a]Lev. 1:5, 9, 13, 17
28 [a]Deut. 12:25
29 [a]Ex. 23:23
31 [a]Lev. 18:3, 26, 30; 20:1, 2 [b]Deut. 18:10 [1]*detestable action*
32 [a]Rev. 22:18, 19

shall not add to it nor take away from it.

13 "If there arises among you a prophet or a [a]dreamer of dreams, [b]and he gives you a sign or a wonder,

2 "and [a]the sign or the wonder comes to pass, of which he spoke to you, saying, 'Let us go after other gods'—which you have not known—'and let us serve them,'

3 "you shall not listen to the words of that prophet or that dreamer of dreams, for the LORD your God [a]is testing you to know whether you love the LORD your God with all your heart and with all your soul.

4 "You shall [a]walk[1] after the LORD your God and fear Him, and keep His commandments and obey His voice; you shall serve Him and [b]hold fast to Him.

5 "But [a]that prophet or that dreamer of dreams shall be put to death, because he has spoken in order to turn *you* away from the LORD your God, who brought you out of the land of Egypt and redeemed you from the house of bondage, to entice you from the way in which the LORD your God commanded you to walk. [b]So you shall [1]put away the evil from your midst.

6 [a]"If your brother, the son of your mother, your son or your daughter, [b]the wife [1]of your bosom, or your friend [c]who is as your own soul, secretly entices you, saying, 'Let us go and serve other gods,' which you have not known, neither you nor your fathers,

7 "of the gods of the people which *are* all around you, near to you or far off from you, from *one* end of the earth to the *other* end of the earth,

8 "you shall [a]not [1]consent to him or listen to him, nor shall your eye pity him, nor shall you spare him or conceal him;

9 "but you shall surely kill him; your hand shall be first against him to put him to [a]death, and afterward the hand of all the people.

10 "And you shall stone him with stones until he dies, because he sought to entice you away from the LORD your God, who brought you out of the land of Egypt, from the house of bondage.

11 "So all Israel shall hear and [a]fear, and not again do such wickedness as this among you.

12 [a]"If you hear someone in one of your cities, which the LORD your God gives you to dwell in, saying,

13 [1]'Corrupt men have gone out from among you and enticed the inhabitants of their city, saying, "Let us go and serve other gods" '—which you have not known—

14 "then you shall inquire, search out, and ask diligently. And *if it is* indeed true *and* certain *that* such an [1]abomination was committed among you,

15 "you shall surely strike the inhabitants of that city with the edge of the sword, utterly destroying it, all that is in it and its livestock—with the edge of the sword.

16 "And you shall gather all its plunder into the middle of the street, and [1]completely [a]burn with fire the city and all its plunder, for the LORD your God. It

CHAPTER 13

1 [a]Zech. 10:2 [b]Matt. 24:24

2 [a]Deut. 18:22

3 [a]Deut. 8:2, 16

4 [a]2 Kin. 23:3 [b]Deut. 30:20 [1]*follow the LORD*

5 [a]Jer. 14:15 [b]Deut. 17:5, 7 [1]*exterminate*

6 [a]Deut. 17:2 [b]Gen. 16:5 [c]1 Sam. 18:1, 3 [1]Whom you cherish

8 [a]Prov. 1:10 [1]*yield*

9 [a]Deut. 17:7

11 [a]Deut. 17:13

12 [a]Judg. 20:1–48

13 [1]Lit. *Sons of Belial*

14 [1]*detestable action*

16 [a]Josh. 6:24 [1]Or *as a whole-offering*

shall be [b]a [2]heap forever; it shall
not be built again.
17 [a]"So none of the accursed
things shall remain in your hand,
that the LORD may [b]turn from the
fierceness of His anger and show
you mercy, have compassion on
you and [1]multiply you, just as He
swore to your fathers,
18 "because you have listened
to the voice of the LORD your
God, [a]to keep all His commandments which I command you
today, to do *what is* right in the
eyes of the LORD your God.

CHAPTER 14

14 "You *are* [a]the children
of the LORD your God;
[b]you shall not cut yourselves nor
[1]shave the front of your head for
the dead.
2 [a]"For you *are* a holy people to
the LORD your God, and the LORD
has chosen you to be a people
for Himself, a special treasure
above all the peoples who *are* on
the face of the earth.
3 [a]"You shall not eat any [1]de-
testable thing.
4 [a]"These *are* the animals
which you may eat: the ox, the
sheep, the goat,
5 "the deer, the gazelle, the roe
deer, the wild goat, the [1]moun-
tain goat, the antelope, and the
mountain sheep.
6 "And you may eat every animal with cloven hooves, having
the hoof split into two parts, *and
that* chews the cud, among the
animals.
7 "Nevertheless, of those that
chew the cud or have cloven
hooves, you shall not eat, *such
as* these: the camel, the hare,
and the rock hyrax; for they
chew the cud but do not have
cloven hooves; they *are* unclean
for you.
8 "Also the swine is unclean
for you, because it has cloven
hooves, yet *does* not *chew* the
cud; you shall not eat their flesh
[a]or touch their dead carcasses.
9 [a]"These you may eat of all
that *are* in the waters: you may
eat all that have fins and scales.
10 "And whatever does not have
fins and scales you shall not eat;
it *is* unclean for you.
11 "All clean birds you may eat.
12 [a]"But these you shall not
eat: the eagle, the vulture, the
buzzard,
13 "the red kite, the falcon, and
the kite after their kinds;
14 "every raven after its kind;
15 "the ostrich, the short-eared
owl, the sea gull, and the hawk
after their kinds;
16 "the little owl, the screech
owl, the white owl,
17 "the jackdaw, the carrion
vulture, the fisher owl,
18 "the stork, the heron after
its kind, and the hoopoe and the
bat.
19 "Also [a]every [1]creeping thing
that flies is unclean for you;
[b]they shall not be eaten.
20 "You may eat all clean birds.
21 [a]"You shall not eat anything
that dies *of itself;* you may give
it to the alien who *is* within your
gates, that he may eat it, or you
may sell it to a foreigner; [b]for
you *are* a holy people to the
LORD your God. [c]You shall not
boil a young goat in its mother's
milk.
22 [a]"You shall truly tithe all the
increase of your grain that the
field produces year by year.
23 [a]"And you shall eat before
the LORD your God, in the place
where He chooses to make His
name abide, the tithe of your

16 [b]Josh. 8:28 [2]Lit. *mound* or *ruin*
17 [a]Josh. 6:18 [b]Josh. 7:26 [1]*increase*
18 [a]Deut. 12:25, 28, 32
1 [a][Rom. 8:16] [b]Lev. 19:28; 21:1–5 [1]*make any baldness between your eyes*
2 [a]Lev. 20:26
3 [a]Ezek. 4:14 [1]*abominable*
4 [a]Lev. 11:2–45
5 [1]Or *addax*
8 [a]Lev. 11:26, 27
9 [a]Lev. 11:9
12 [a]Lev. 11:13
19 [a]Lev. 11:20 [b]Lev. 11:23 [1]*swarming*
21 [a]Lev. 17:15; 22:8 [b]Deut. 14:2 [c]Ex. 23:19; 34:26
22 [a]Lev. 27:30
23 [a]Deut. 12:5–7

grain and your new wine and your oil, of [b]the firstborn of your herds and your flocks, that you may learn to fear the LORD your God always.

24 "But if the journey is too long for you, so that you are not able to carry *the tithe, or* [a]if the place where the LORD your God chooses to put His name is too far from you, when the LORD your God has blessed you,

25 "then you shall exchange *it* for money, take the money in your hand, and go to the place which the LORD your God chooses.

26 "And you shall spend that money for whatever your heart desires: for oxen or sheep, for wine or similar drink, for whatever your heart desires; you shall eat there before the LORD your God, and you shall [a]rejoice, you and your household.

27 "You shall not [1]forsake the [a]Lē′vīte who *is* within your gates, for he has no part nor inheritance with you.

28 [a]"At the end of *every* third year you shall bring out the [b]tithe of your produce of that year and store *it* up within your gates.

29 "And the Lē′vīte, because he has no portion nor inheritance with you, and the stranger and the fatherless and the widow who *are* within your gates, may come and eat and be satisfied, that the LORD your God may bless you in all the work of your hand which you do.

15 "At the end of [a]*every* seven years you shall grant a [1]release *of debts.*

2 "And this *is* the form of the release: Every creditor who has lent *anything* to his neighbor shall [1]release *it;* he shall not [2]require *it* of his neighbor or his brother, because it is called the LORD's release.

3 "Of a foreigner you may require *it;* but you shall give up your claim to what is owed by your brother,

4 "except when there may be no poor among you; for the LORD will greatly [a]bless you in the land which the LORD your God is giving you to possess *as* an inheritance—

5 "only if you carefully obey the voice of the LORD your God, to observe with care all these commandments which I command you today.

6 "For the LORD your God will bless you just as He promised you; [a]you shall lend to many nations, but you shall not borrow; you shall reign over many nations, but they shall not reign over you.

7 "If there is among you a poor man of your brethren, within any of the [1]gates in your land which the LORD your God is giving you, [a]you shall not harden your heart nor shut your hand from your poor brother,

8 "but [a]you shall [1]open your hand wide to him and willingly lend him sufficient for his need, whatever he needs.

9 "Beware lest there be a wicked thought in your heart, saying, 'The seventh year, the year of release, is at hand,' and your [a]eye be evil against your poor brother and you give him nothing, and [b]he cry out to the LORD against you, and [c]it become sin among you.

10 "You shall surely give to him,

23 [b]Deut. 15:19, 20
24 [a]Deut. 12:5, 21
26 [a]Deut. 12:7
27 [a]Deut. 12:12 [1]*neglect*
28 [a]Deut. 26:12 [b]Num. 18:21–24

CHAPTER 15

1 [a]Ex. 21:2; 23:10, 11 [1]*remission*
2 [1]*cancel the debt* [2]*exact it*
4 [a]Deut. 7:13
6 [a]Deut. 28:12, 44
7 [a]Lev. 25:35–37 [1]*towns*
8 [a]Matt. 5:42 [1]*freely open*
9 [a]Deut. 28:54, 56 [b]Deut. 24:15 [c][Matt. 25:41, 42]

and [a]your heart should not be
grieved when you give to him,
because [b]for this thing the LORD
your God will bless you in all
your works and in all to which
you put your hand.
11 "For [a]the poor will never
cease from the land; therefore
I command you, saying, 'You
shall [1]open your hand wide to
your brother, to your poor and
your needy, in your land.'
12 [a]"If your brother, a Hebrew
man, or a Hebrew woman, is
[b]sold to you and serves you six
years, then in the seventh year
you shall let him go free from
you.
13 "And when you [1]send him
away free from you, you shall not
let him go away empty-handed;
14 "you shall supply him liberally from your flock, from your
threshing floor, and from your
winepress. *From what* the LORD
your God has [a]blessed you with,
you shall give to him.
15 [a]"You shall remember that
you were a slave in the land of
Egypt, and the LORD your God
redeemed you; therefore I command you this thing today.
16 "And [a]if it happens that he
says to you, 'I will not go away
from you,' because he loves you
and your house, since he prospers with you,
17 "then you shall take an awl
and thrust *it* through his ear
to the door, and he shall be
your servant forever. Also to
your female servant you shall do
likewise.
18 "It shall not seem hard to
you when you send him away
free from you; for he has been
worth [a]a double hired servant in
serving you six years. Then the
LORD your God will bless you in
all that you do.
19 [a]"All the firstborn males that
come from your herd and your
flock you shall [1]sanctify to the
LORD your God; you shall do no
work with the firstborn of your
herd, nor shear the firstborn of
your flock.
20 [a]"You and your household
shall eat *it* before the LORD your
God year by year in the place
which the LORD chooses.
21 [a]"But if there is a defect in it,
if it is lame or blind *or has* any
serious defect, you shall not sacrifice it to the LORD your God.
22 "You may eat it within your
gates; [a]the unclean and the clean
person alike *may eat it,* as *if it
were* a gazelle or a deer.
23 "Only you shall not eat its
blood; you shall pour it on the
ground like water.

16

"Observe the [a]month of
Ā'bib, and keep the Pass-
over to the LORD your God, for
[b]in the month of Ā'bib the LORD
your God brought you out of
Egypt by night.
2 "Therefore you shall sacrifice
the Passover to the LORD your
God, from the flock and [a]the
herd, in the [b]place where the
LORD chooses to put His name.
3 "You shall eat no leavened
bread with it; [a]seven days you
shall eat unleavened bread with
it, *that is,* the bread of affliction
(for you came out of the land of
Egypt in haste), that you may
[b]remember the day in which you
came out of the land of Egypt all
the days of your life.
4 [a]"And no leaven shall be seen
among you in all your territory
for seven days, nor shall *any* of
the meat which you sacrifice the

10 [a]2 Cor. 9:5, 7 [b]Deut. 14:29
11 [a]Matt. 26:11 [1]*freely open*
12 [a]Ex. 21:2–6 [b]Lev. 25:39–46
13 [1]*set him free*
14 [a]Prov. 10:22
15 [a]Deut. 5:15
16 [a]Ex. 21:5, 6
18 [a]Is. 16:14
19 [a]Ex. 13:2, 12 [1]*set apart* or *consecrate*
20 [a]Deut. 12:5; 14:23
21 [a]Lev. 22:19–25
22 [a]Deut. 12:15, 16, 22

CHAPTER 16

1 [a]Ex. 12:2 [b]Ex. 13:4
2 [a]Num. 28:19 [b]Deut. 12:5, 26; 15:20
3 [a]Num. 29:12 [b]Ex. 13:3
4 [a]Ex. 13:7

first day at twilight remain overnight until [b]morning.
5 "You may not sacrifice the
Passover within any of your
gates which the LORD your God
gives you;
6 "but at the place where the
LORD your God chooses to make
His name abide, there you shall
sacrifice the Passover [a]at twilight, at the going down of the
sun, at the time you came out of
Egypt.
7 "And you shall roast and eat
it [a]in the place which the LORD
your God chooses, and in the
morning you shall turn and go
to your tents.
8 "Six days you shall eat unleavened bread, and [a]on the seventh day there *shall be* a [1]sacred
assembly to the LORD your God.
You shall do no work *on it.*
9 [a]"You shall count seven weeks
for yourself; begin to count the
seven weeks from *the time* you
begin *to put* the sickle to the
grain.
10 "Then you shall keep the
[a]Feast of Weeks to the LORD your
God with the tribute of a freewill
offering from your hand, which
you shall give [b]as the LORD your
God blesses you.
11 [a]"You shall rejoice before the
LORD your God, you and your son
and your daughter, your male
servant and your female servant,
the Lē′vīte who *is* within your
gates, the stranger and the fatherless and the widow who *are*
among you, at the place where
the LORD your God chooses to
make His name abide.
12 [a]"And you shall remember
that you were a slave in Egypt,
and you shall be careful to observe these statutes.

4 [b]Num. 9:12
6 [a]Ex. 12:7–10
7 [a]2 Kin. 23:23
8 [a]Lev. 23:8, 36 [1]Lit. *restraint*
10 [a]Ex. 34:22 [b]1 Cor. 16:2
11 [a]Deut. 16:14
12 [a]Deut. 15:15
13 [a]Ex. 23:16
14 [a]Neh. 8:9 [1]*towns*
15 [a]Lev. 23:39–41
16 [a]Ex. 23:14–17; 34:22–24 [b]Ex. 23:15
17 [a]Deut. 16:10
18 [a]Deut. 1:16, 17 [1]*towns*
19 [a]Ex. 23:2, 6 [b]Deut. 1:17 [c]Ex. 23:8 [1]Lit. *regard faces* [2]*perverts*
20 [a]Ezek. 18:5–9

13 [a]"You shall observe the Feast
of Tabernacles seven days, when
you have gathered from your
threshing floor and from your
winepress.
14 "And [a]you shall rejoice in
your feast, you and your son
and your daughter, your male
servant and your female servant
and the Lē′vīte, the stranger and
the fatherless and the widow,
who *are* within your [1]gates.
15 [a]"Seven days you shall keep
a sacred feast to the LORD your
God in the place which the LORD
chooses, because the LORD your
God will bless you in all your
produce and in all the work of
your hands, so that you surely
rejoice.
16 [a]"Three times a year all
your males shall appear before the LORD your God in the
place which He chooses: at the
Feast of Unleavened Bread, at
the Feast of Weeks, and at the
Feast of Tabernacles; and [b]they
shall not appear before the LORD
empty-handed.
17 "Every man *shall give* as he
is able, [a]according to the blessing of the LORD your God which
He has given you.
18 "You shall appoint [a]judges
and officers in all your [1]gates,
which the LORD your God gives
you, according to your tribes,
and they shall judge the people
with just judgment.
19 [a]"You shall not pervert justice; [b]you shall not [1]show partiality, [c]nor take a bribe, for a
bribe blinds the eyes of the wise
and [2]twists the words of the
righteous.
20 "You shall follow what is altogether just, that you may [a]live

and inherit the land which the
LORD your God is giving you.
21 [a]"You shall not plant for
yourself any tree, as a [1]wooden
image, near the altar which you
build for yourself to the LORD
your God.
22 [a]"You shall not set up a *sacred* pillar, which the LORD your
God hates.

17 "You [a]shall not sacrifice
to the LORD your God a
bull or sheep which has any
[1]blemish *or* defect, for that *is* an
[2]abomination to the LORD your
God.
2 [a]"If there is found among
you, within any of your [1]gates
which the LORD your God gives
you, a man or a woman who has
been wicked in the sight of the
LORD your God, [b]in transgressing His covenant,
3 "who has gone and served
other gods and worshiped them,
either [a]the sun or moon or any
of the host of heaven, [b]which I
have not commanded,
4 [a]"and it is told you, and you
hear *of it,* then you shall inquire
diligently. And if *it is* indeed
true *and* certain that such an
[1]abomination has been committed in Israel,
5 "then you shall bring out to
your gates that man or woman
who has committed that wicked
thing, and [a]shall stone [b]to
death that man or woman with
stones.
6 "Whoever is deserving of
death shall be put to death on
the testimony of two or three
[a]witnesses; he shall not be put
to death on the testimony of one
witness.
7 "The hands of the witnesses
shall be the first against him to
put him to death, and afterward
the hands of all the people. So
you shall put away the evil from
among [a]you.
8 [a]"If a matter arises which is
too hard for you to judge, between degrees of guilt for bloodshed, between one judgment or
another, or between one punishment or another, matters of controversy within your gates, then
you shall arise and go up to the
[b]place which the LORD your God
chooses.
9 "And [a]you shall come to the
priests, the Lē′vītes, and [b]to the
judge *there* in those days, and
inquire *of them;* [c]they shall pronounce upon you the sentence
of judgment.
10 "You shall do according to
the sentence which they pronounce upon you in that place
which the LORD chooses. And
you shall be careful to do according to all that they order
you.
11 "According to the sentence
of the law in which they instruct
you, according to the judgment
which they tell you, you shall do;
you shall not turn aside *to* the
right hand or *to* the left from the
sentence which they pronounce
upon you.
12 "Now [a]the man who acts presumptuously and will not heed
the priest who stands to minister there before the LORD your
God, or the judge, that man shall
die. So you shall put away the
evil from Israel.
13 [a]"And all the people shall
hear and fear, and no longer act
presumptuously.
14 "When you come to the land
which the LORD your God is giving you, and possess it and dwell

21 [a]Ex. 34:13 [1]Or *Asherah*
22 [a]Lev. 26:1

CHAPTER 17

1 [a]Deut. 15:21 [1]Lit. *evil thing* [2]*detestable thing*
2 [a]Deut. 13:6 [b]Josh. 7:11 [1]*towns*
3 [a]Deut. 4:19 [b]Jer. 7:22
4 [a]Deut. 13:12, 14 [1]*detestable thing*
5 [a]Lev. 24:14–16 [b]Deut. 13:6–18
6 [a]Num. 35:30
7 [a]Deut. 13:5; 19:19
8 [a]Deut. 1:17 [b]Deut. 12:5; 16:2
9 [a]Jer. 18:18 [b]Deut. 19:17–19 [c]Ezek. 44:24
12 [a]Num. 15:30
13 [a]Deut. 13:11

in it, and say, [a]'I will set a king
over me like all the nations that
are around me,'
15 "you shall surely set a king
over you [a]whom the LORD your
God chooses; *one* [b]from among
your brethren you shall set as
king over you; you may not set
a foreigner over you, who *is* not
your brother.
16 "But he shall not multiply
[a]horses for himself, nor cause
the people [b]to return to Egypt
to multiply horses, for [c]the LORD
has said to you, [d]'You shall not
return that way again.'
17 "Neither shall he multiply
wives for himself, lest his heart
turn away; nor shall he greatly
multiply silver and [a]gold for
himself.
18 "Also it shall be, when he sits
on the throne of his kingdom,
that he shall write for himself a
copy of this law in a book, from
the one [a]before the priests, the
Lē′vītes.
19 "And [a]it shall be with him,
and he shall read it all the days
of his life, that he may learn to
fear the LORD his God and be
careful to observe all the words
of this law and these statutes,
20 "that his heart may not [1]be
lifted above his brethren, that
he [a]may not turn aside from the
commandment *to* the right hand
or *to* the left, and that he may
[2]prolong *his* days in his kingdom, he and his children in the
midst of Israel.

18

"The priests, the Lē′vītes—
all the tribe of Levi—shall
have [1]no part nor [a]inheritance
with Israel; they shall eat the offerings of the LORD made by fire,
and His portion.
2 "Therefore they shall have
no inheritance among their
brethren; the LORD is their inheritance, as He said to them.
3 "And this shall be the priest's
[a]due[1] from the people, from those
who offer a sacrifice, whether *it
is* bull or sheep: they shall give
to the priest the shoulder, the
cheeks, and the stomach.
4 [a]"The firstfruits of your grain
and your new wine and your oil,
and the first of the fleece of your
sheep, you shall give him.
5 "For [a]the LORD your God has
chosen him out of all your tribes
[b]to stand to minister in the name
of the LORD, him and his sons
forever.
6 "So if a Lē′vīte comes from
any of your [1]gates, from where
he [a]dwells among all Israel, and
comes with all the desire of his
mind [b]to the place which the
LORD chooses,
7 "then he may serve in the
name of the LORD his God [a]as all
his brethren the Lē′vītes *do*, who
stand there before the LORD.
8 "They shall have equal
[a]portions to eat, besides what
comes from the sale of his
inheritance.
9 "When you come into the
land which the LORD your God is
giving you, [a]you shall not learn
to follow the [1]abominations of
those nations.
10 "There shall not be found
among you *anyone* who makes
his son or his daughter [a]pass[1]
through the fire, [b]*or one* who
practices witchcraft, *or* a sooth-
sayer, or one who interprets
omens, or a sorcerer,
11 [a]"or one who conjures spells,
or a medium, or a spiritist, or
[b]one who calls up the dead.
12 "For all who do these things

14 [a]1 Sam. 8:5, 19, 20; 10:19
15 [a]1 Sam. 9:15, 16; 10:24; 16:12, 13 [b]Jer. 30:21
16 [a]1 Kin. 4:26; 10:26–29 [b]Ezek. 17:15 [c]Ex. 13:17, 18 [d]Deut. 28:68
17 [a]1 Kin. 10:14
18 [a]Deut. 31:24–26
19 [a]Ps. 119:97, 98
20 [a]Deut. 5:32 [1]*become proud* [2]*continue long in his kingdom*

CHAPTER 18

1 [a]Deut. 10:9 [1]*no portion*
3 [a]Lev. 7:32–34; 1 Sam. 2:13–16, 29 [1]*right*
4 [a]Ex. 22:29
5 [a]Ex. 28:1 [b]Deut. 10:8
6 [a]Num. 35:2 [b]Deut. 12:5; 14:23 [1]*towns*
7 [a]2 Chr. 31:2
8 [a]2 Chr. 31:4
9 [a]Deut. 12:29, 30; 20:16–18 [1]*detestable acts*
10 [a]Deut. 12:31 [b]Is. 8:19 [1]Be burned as an offering to an idol
11 [a]Lev. 20:27 [b]1 Sam. 28:7

are [1]an abomination to the LORD,
and [a]because of these abominations the LORD your God drives
them out from before you.
13 "You shall be [1]blameless before the LORD your God.
14 "For these nations which you
will dispossess listened to soothsayers and diviners; but as for
you, the LORD your God has not
[1]appointed such for you.
☆ **15** [a]"The LORD your God will
raise up for you a Prophet like
me from your midst, from your
brethren. Him you shall hear,
16 "according to all you desired
of the LORD your God in Hō′reb
[a]in the day of the assembly, saying, [b]'Let me not hear again the
voice of the LORD my God, nor
let me see this great fire anymore, lest I die.'
17 "And the LORD said to me:
[a]'What they have spoken is good.
☆ 18 [a]'I will raise up for them a
Prophet like you from among
their brethren, and [b]will put My
words in His mouth, [c]and He
shall speak to them all that I
command Him.
☆ 19 [a]'And it shall be *that* whoever will not hear My words,
which He speaks in My name, I
will require *it* of him.
20 'But [a]the prophet who pre-
sumes to speak a word in My
name, which I have not commanded him to speak, or [b]who
speaks in the name of other
gods, that prophet shall die.'
21 "And if you say in your
heart, 'How shall we know the
word which the LORD has not
spoken?'—
22 [a]"when a prophet speaks in
the name of the LORD, [b]if the thing
does not happen or come to pass,
that *is* the thing which the LORD

12 [a]Lev. 18:24 [1]*detestable*
13 [1]Lit. *perfect*
14 [1]*allowed you to do so*
15 [a]Matt. 21:11; Luke 1:76; 2:25–34; 7:16; 24:19; John 1:45; Acts 3:22
16 [a]Deut. 5:23–27 [b]Ex. 20:18, 19
17 [a]Deut. 5:28
18 [a]John 1:45; 6:14; Acts 3:22; [b]Is. 49:2; 51:16; John 17:8 [c][John 4:25; 8:28]
19 [a]Acts 3:23; [Heb. 12:25]
20 [a]Jer. 14:14, 15 [b]Jer. 2:8
22 [a]Jer. 28:9 [b]Deut. 13:2 [c]Deut. 18:20

CHAPTER 19

1 [a]Deut. 12:29
2 [a]Num. 35:10–15
4 [a]Num. 35:9–34 [1]*ignorantly*, lit. *without knowledge*
6 [a]Num. 35:12
8 [a]Deut. 12:20 [b]Gen. 15:18–21

has not spoken; the prophet has
spoken it [c]presumptuously; you
shall not be afraid of him.

19

"When the LORD your
God [a]has cut off the nations whose land the LORD your
God is giving you, and you dispossess them and dwell in their
cities and in their houses,
2 [a]"you shall separate three
cities for yourself in the midst of
your land which the LORD your
God is giving you to possess.
3 "You shall prepare roads for
yourself, and divide into three
parts the territory of your land
which the LORD your God is
giving you to inherit, that any
manslayer may flee there.
4 "And [a]this *is* the case of the
manslayer who flees there, that
he may live: Whoever kills his
neighbor [1]unintentionally, not
having hated him in time past—
5 "as when *a man* goes to the
woods with his neighbor to cut
timber, and his hand swings a
stroke with the ax to cut down
the tree, and the head slips from
the handle and strikes his neighbor so that he dies—he shall flee
to one of these cities and live;
6 [a]"lest the avenger of blood,
while his anger is hot, pursue
the manslayer and overtake him,
because the way is long, and kill
him, though he *was* not deserving of death, since he had not
hated the victim in time past.
7 "Therefore I command you,
saying, 'You shall separate three
cities for yourself.'
8 "Now if the LORD your God
[a]enlarges your territory, as He
swore to [b]your fathers, and gives
you the land which He promised
to give to your fathers,
9 "and if you keep all these

commandments and do them,
which I command you today, to
love the LORD your God and to
walk always in His ways, [a]then
you shall add three more cities
for yourself besides these three,
10 [a]"lest innocent blood be shed
in the midst of your land which
the LORD your God is giving you
as an inheritance, and *thus* guilt
of bloodshed be upon you.
11 "But [a]if anyone hates his
neighbor, lies in wait for him,
rises against him and strikes him
mortally, so that he dies, and he
flees to one of these cities,
12 "then the elders of his city
shall send and bring him from
there, and deliver him over to
the hand of the avenger of blood,
that he may die.
13 [a]"Your eye shall not pity him,
[b]but you shall [1]put away *the
guilt of* innocent blood from Israel, that it may go well with
you.
14 [a]"You shall not remove your
neighbor's landmark, which the
men of old have set, in your inheritance which you will inherit
in the land that the LORD your
God is giving you to possess.
15 [a]"One witness shall not rise
against a man concerning any
iniquity or any sin that he commits; by the mouth of two or
three witnesses the matter shall
be established.
16 "If a false witness [a]rises
against any man to testify against
him of wrongdoing,
17 "then both men in the controversy shall stand before the
LORD, [a]before the priests and the
judges who serve in those days.
18 "And the judges shall make
careful inquiry, and indeed, *if*
the witness *is* a false witness,

9 [a]Josh. 20:7–9
10 [a]Deut. 21:1–9
11 [a]Num. 35:16, 24
13 [a]Deut. 13:8 [b]1 Kin. 2:31 [1]*purge the blood of the innocent*
14 [a]Prov. 22:28
15 [a]Num. 35:30
16 [a]Ex. 23:1
17 [a]Deut. 17:8–11; 21:5
19 [a]Prov. 19:5 [b]Deut. 13:5; 17:7; 21:21; 22:21
20 [a]Deut. 17:13; 21:21
21 [a]Deut. 19:13 [b]Ex. 21:23, 24
CHAPTER 20
1 [a]Ps. 20:7 [b]Deut. 7:18 [c]2 Chr. 13:12; 32:7, 8
4 [a]Josh. 23:10
5 [a]Neh. 12:27

who has testified falsely against
his brother,
19 [a]"then you shall do to him as
he thought to have done to his
brother; so [b]you shall put away
the evil from among you.
20 [a]"And those who remain
shall hear and fear, and hereafter they shall not again commit such evil among you.
21 [a]"Your eye shall not pity: [b]life
shall be for life, eye for eye,
tooth for tooth, hand for hand,
foot for foot.
20 "When you go out to battle against your enemies,
and see [a]horses and chariots
and people more numerous than
you, do not be [b]afraid of them;
for the LORD your God *is* [c]with
you, who brought you up from
the land of Egypt.
2 "So it shall be, when you are
on the verge of battle, that the
priest shall approach and speak
to the people.
3 "And he shall say to them,
'Hear, O Israel: Today you are
on the verge of battle with your
enemies. Do not let your heart
faint, do not be afraid, and do
not tremble or be terrified because of them;
4 'for the LORD your God *is* He
who goes with you, [a]to fight for
you against your enemies, to
save you.'
5 "Then the officers shall speak
to the people, saying: 'What man
is there who has built a new
house and has not [a]dedicated
it? Let him go and return to his
house, lest he die in the battle
and another man dedicate it.
6 'Also what man *is there* who
has planted a vineyard and has
not eaten of it? Let him go and
return to his house, lest he die in

the battle and another man eat
of it.
7 [a]'And what man *is there* who
is betrothed to a woman and has
not married her? Let him go and
return to his house, lest he die
in the battle and another man
marry her.'
8 "The officers shall speak
further to the people, and say,
[a]'What man *is there who is* fearful and fainthearted? Let him go
and return to his house, [1]lest the
heart of his brethren faint like
his heart.'
9 "And so it shall be, when the
officers have finished speaking
to the people, that they shall
make captains of the armies to
lead the people.
10 "When you go near a city to
fight against it, [a]then proclaim
an offer of peace to it.
11 "And it shall be that if they
accept your offer of peace, and
open to you, then all the people
who are found in it shall be
placed under tribute to you, and
serve you.
12 "Now if *the city* will not
make peace with you, but makes
war against you, then you shall
besiege it.
13 "And when the LORD your
God delivers it into your hands,
[a]you shall strike every male in it
with the edge of the sword.
14 "But the women, the little
ones, [a]the livestock, and all that
is in the city, all its spoil, you
shall plunder for yourself; and
[b]you shall eat the enemies' plunder which the LORD your God
gives you.
15 "Thus you shall do to all the
cities *which are* very far from
you, which *are* not of the cities
of these nations.
16 "But [a]of the cities of these
peoples which the LORD your
God gives you *as* an inheritance, you shall let nothing that
breathes remain alive,
17 "but you shall utterly destroy
them: the Hit'tīte and the Am'-
o·rīte and the Cā'naan·īte and
the Per'iz·zīte and the Hī'vīte
and the Jeb'ū·sīte, just as the
LORD your God has commanded
you,
18 "lest [a]they teach you to do
according to all their [1]abomina-
tions which they have done for
their gods, and you [b]sin against
the LORD your God.
19 "When you besiege a city for
a long time, while making war
against it to take it, you shall not
destroy its trees by wielding an
ax against them; if you can eat
of them, do not cut them down
to use in the siege, for the tree
of the field *is* man's *food.*
20 "Only the trees which you
know *are* not trees for food you
may destroy and cut down, to
build siegeworks against the
city that makes war with you,
until it is subdued.

21

"If *anyone* is found slain,
lying in the field in the
land which the LORD your God
is giving you to possess, *and* it is
not known who killed him,
2 "then your elders and your
judges shall go out and measure
the distance from the slain man
to the surrounding cities.
3 "And it shall be *that* the elders of the city nearest to the
slain man will take a heifer
which has not been worked *and*
which has not pulled with a
[a]yoke.
4 "The elders of that city shall
bring the heifer down to a valley

7 [a]Deut. 24:5
8 [a]Judg. 7:3 [1]So with MT, Tg.; Sam., LXX, Syr., Vg. *lest he make his brother's heart faint*
10 [a]2 Sam. 10:19
13 [a]Num. 31:7
14 [a]Josh. 8:2 [b]1 Sam. 14:30
16 [a]Deut. 7:1–5
18 [a]Deut. 7:4; 12:30; 18:9 [b]Ex. 23:33 [1]*detestable things*

CHAPTER 21

3 [a]Num. 19:2

with flowing water, which is neither plowed nor sown, and they
shall break the heifer's neck
there in the valley.
5 "Then the priests, the sons
of Levi, shall come near, for [a]the
LORD your God has chosen them
to minister to Him and to bless
in the name of the LORD; [b]by their
word every controversy and every [1]assault shall be *settled.*
6 "And all the elders of that
city nearest to the slain *man*
[a]shall wash their hands over the
heifer whose neck was broken
in the valley.
7 "Then they shall answer and
say, 'Our hands have not shed
this blood, nor have our eyes
seen *it.*
8 'Provide atonement, O LORD,
for Your people Israel, whom You
have redeemed, [a]and do not lay
innocent blood to the charge of
Your people Israel.' And atonement shall be provided on their
behalf for the blood.
9 "So [a]you shall put away the
guilt of innocent blood from
among you when you do *what*
is right in the sight of the LORD.
10 "When you go out to war
against your enemies, and the
LORD your God delivers them
into your hand, and you take
them captive,
11 "and you see among the captives a beautiful woman, and
desire her and would take her
for your [a]wife,
12 "then you shall bring her
home to your house, and she
shall [a]shave her head and trim
her nails.
13 "She shall put off the clothes
of her captivity, remain in your
house, and [a]mourn her father
and her mother a full month;

5 [a]1 Chr. 23:13 [b]Deut. 17:8, 9 [1]Lit. *stroke*
6 [a]Matt. 27:24
8 [a]Jon. 1:14
9 [a]Deut. 19:13
11 [a]Num. 31:18
12 [a]Lev. 14:8, 9
13 [a]Ps. 45:10
14 [a]Judg. 19:24
15 [a]Gen. 29:33
16 [a]1 Chr. 5:2; 26:10
17 [a]2 Kin. 2:9 [b]Gen. 49:3 [c]Gen. 25:31, 33
21 [a]Deut. 13:5; 19:19, 20; 22:21, 24

after that you may go in to her
and be her husband, and she
shall be your wife.
14 "And it shall be, if you have
no delight in her, then you shall
set her free, but you certainly
shall not sell her for money;
you shall not treat her brutally,
because you have [a]humbled her.
15 "If a man has two wives, one
loved [a]and the other unloved,
and they have borne him children, *both* the loved and the
unloved, and *if* the firstborn son
is of her who is unloved,
16 "then it shall be, [a]on the day
he bequeaths his possessions to
his sons, *that* he must not bestow firstborn status on the son
of the loved wife in preference
to the son of the unloved, the
true firstborn.
17 "But he shall acknowledge
the son of the unloved wife *as*
the firstborn [a]by giving him a
double portion of all that he has,
for he [b]*is* the beginning of his
strength; [c]the right of the firstborn *is* his.
18 "If a man has a stubborn and
rebellious son who will not obey
the voice of his father or the
voice of his mother, and *who,*
when they have chastened him,
will not heed them,
19 "then his father and his
mother shall take hold of him
and bring him out to the elders
of his city, to the gate of his
city.
20 "And they shall say to the
elders of his city, 'This son of
ours is stubborn and rebellious;
he will not obey our voice; he is
a glutton and a drunkard.'
21 "Then all the men of his city
shall stone him to death with
stones; [a]so you shall put away

the evil from among you, [b]and
all Israel shall hear and fear.
22 "If a man has committed a
sin [a]deserving of death, and he
is put to death, and you hang
him on a tree,
23 [a]"his body shall not remain
overnight on the tree, but you
shall surely bury him that day,
so that [b]you do not defile the
land which the LORD your God is
giving you *as* an inheritance; for
[c]he who is hanged *is* accursed of
God.

22

"You [a]shall not see your
brother's ox or his sheep
going astray, and [1]hide yourself from them; you shall certainly bring them back to your
brother.
2 "And if your brother *is* not
near you, or if you do not know
him, then you shall bring it to
your own house, and it shall remain with you until your brother
seeks it; then you shall restore it
to him.
3 "You shall do the same with
his donkey, and so shall you do
with his garment; with any lost
thing of your brother's, which
he has lost and you have found,
you shall do likewise; you [1]must
not hide yourself.
4 [a]"You shall not see your brother's donkey or his ox fall down
along the road, and hide yourself
from them; you shall surely help
him lift *them* up again.
5 "A woman shall not wear
anything that pertains to a man,
nor shall a man put on a woman's garment, for all who do so
are [1]an abomination to the LORD
your God.
6 "If a bird's nest happens to
be before you along the way, in
any tree or on the ground, with

21 [b]Deut. 13:11
22 [a]Acts 23:29
23 [a]John 19:31 [b]Lev. 18:25 [c]Gal. 3:13
CHAPTER 22
1 [a]Ex. 23:4 [1]*ignore them*
3 [1]*may not avoid responsibility*
4 [a]Ex. 23:5
5 [1]*detestable*
6 [a]Lev. 22:28
7 [a]Deut. 4:40
9 [a]Lev. 19:19
10 [a][2 Cor. 6:14–16]
11 [a]Lev. 19:19
12 [a]Num. 15:37–41
13 [a]Deut. 21:15; 24:3

young ones or eggs, with the
mother sitting on the young or
on the eggs, [a]you shall not take
the mother with the young;
7 "you shall surely let the
mother go, and take the young
for yourself, [a]that it may be well
with you and *that* you may prolong *your* days.
8 "When you build a new
house, then you shall make a
parapet for your roof, that you
may not bring guilt of bloodshed
on your household if anyone
falls from it.
9 [a]"You shall not sow your
vineyard with different kinds
of seed, lest the yield of the
seed which you have sown and
the fruit of your vineyard be
defiled.
10 [a]"You shall not plow with an
ox and a donkey together.
11 [a]"You shall not wear a garment of different sorts, *such as*
wool and linen mixed together.
12 "You shall make [a]tassels on
the four corners of the clothing
with which you cover *yourself*.
13 "If any man takes a wife, and
goes in to her, and [a]detests her,
14 "and charges her with
shameful conduct, and brings
a bad name on her, and says,
'I took this woman, and when I
came to her I found she *was* not
a virgin,'
15 "then the father and mother
of the young woman shall take
and bring out *the evidence of*
the young woman's virginity to
the elders of the city at the gate.
16 "And the young woman's father shall say to the elders, 'I
gave my daughter to this man as
wife, and he detests her.
17 'Now he has charged her
with shameful conduct, saying,

"I found your daughter *was* not a virgin," and yet these *are the evidences of* my daughter's virginity.' And they shall spread the cloth before the elders of the city.

18 "Then the elders of that city shall take that man and punish him;

19 "and they shall fine him one hundred *shekels* of silver and give *them* to the father of the young woman, because he has brought a bad name on a virgin of Israel. And she shall be his wife; he cannot divorce her all his days.

20 "But if the thing is true, *and evidences of* virginity are not found for the young woman,

21 "then they shall bring out the young woman to the door of her father's house, and the men of her city shall stone her to death with [a]stones, because she has [b]done a disgraceful thing in Israel, to play the harlot in her father's house. [c]So you shall [1]put away the evil from among you.

22 [a]"If a man is found lying with a woman married to a husband, then both of them shall die—the man that lay with the woman, and the woman; so you shall put away the evil from Israel.

23 "If a young woman *who is* a virgin is [a]betrothed to a husband, and a man finds her in the city and lies with her,

24 "then you shall bring them both out to the gate of that city, and you shall stone them to death with stones, the young woman because she did not cry out in the city, and the man because he [a]humbled his neighbor's wife; [b]so you shall put away the evil from among you.

25 "But if a man finds a betrothed young woman in the countryside, and the man forces her and lies with her, then only the man who lay with her shall die.

26 "But you shall do nothing to the young woman; *there is* in the young woman no sin *deserving* of death, for just as when a man rises against his neighbor and kills him, even so *is* this matter.

27 "For he found her in the countryside, *and* the betrothed young woman cried out, but *there was* no one to save her.

28 [a]"If a man finds a young woman *who is* a virgin, who is not betrothed, and he seizes her and lies with her, and they are found out,

29 "then the man who lay with her shall give to the young woman's father [a]fifty *shekels* of silver, and she shall be his wife [b]because he has humbled her; he shall not be permitted to divorce her all his days.

30 [a]"A man shall not take his father's wife, nor [b]uncover his father's bed.

23

"He who is emasculated by crushing or mutilation shall [a]not enter the assembly of the LORD.

2 "One of illegitimate birth shall not enter the assembly of the LORD; even to the tenth generation none of his *descendants* shall enter the assembly of the LORD.

3 [a]"An Am'mon·īte or Mō'ab·īte shall not enter the assembly of the LORD; even to the tenth generation none of his *descendants* shall enter the assembly of the LORD forever,

21 [a]Deut. 21:21 [b]Gen. 34:7 [c]Deut. 13:5 [1]*purge the evil person*
22 [a]Lev. 20:10
23 [a]Matt. 1:18, 19
24 [a]Deut. 21:14 [b]Deut. 22:21, 22
28 [a]Ex. 22:16, 17
29 [a]Ex. 22:16, 17 [b]Deut. 22:24
30 [a]Deut. 27:20 [b]Ezek. 16:8
CHAPTER 23
1 [a]Lev. 21:20; 22:24
3 [a]Neh. 13:1, 2

4 [a]"because they did not meet you with bread and water on the road when you came out of Egypt, and [b]because they hired against you Bā′laam the son of Bē′or from Pē′thor of [1]Mes·o·po·tā′mi·a, to curse you.

5 "Nevertheless the LORD your God would not listen to Bā′laam, but the LORD your God turned the curse into a blessing for you, because the LORD your God [a]loves you.

6 [a]"You shall not seek their peace nor their prosperity all your days forever.

7 "You shall not abhor an Ē′dom·īte, [a]for he *is* your brother. You shall not abhor an Egyptian, because [b]you were an alien in his land.

8 "The children of the third generation born to them may enter the assembly of the LORD.

9 "When the army goes out against your enemies, then keep yourself from every wicked thing.

10 [a]"If there is any man among you who becomes unclean by some occurrence in the night, then he shall go outside the camp; he shall not come inside the camp.

11 "But it shall be, when evening comes, that [a]he shall wash with water; and when the sun sets, he may come into the camp.

12 "Also you shall have a place outside the camp, where you may go out;

13 "and you shall have an implement among your equipment, and when you sit down outside, you shall dig with it and turn and cover your refuse.

14 "For the LORD your God [a]walks in the midst of your camp, to deliver you and give your enemies over to you; therefore your camp shall be holy, that He may see no unclean thing among you, and turn away from you.

15 [a]"You shall not give back to his master the slave who has escaped from his master to you.

16 "He may dwell with you in your midst, in the place which he chooses within one of your gates, where it [1]seems best to him; [a]you shall not oppress him.

17 "There shall be no *ritual* [1]harlot [a]of the daughters of Israel, or a [b]perverted[2] one of the sons of Israel.

18 "You shall not bring the wages of a harlot or the price of a dog to the house of the LORD your God for any vowed offering, for both of these *are* [1]an abomination to the LORD your God.

19 [a]"You shall not charge interest to your brother—interest on money *or* food *or* anything that is lent out at interest.

20 [a]"To a foreigner you may charge interest, but to your brother you shall not charge interest, [b]that the LORD your God may bless you in all to which you set your hand in the land which you are entering to possess.

21 [a]"When you make a vow to the LORD your God, you shall not delay to pay it; for the LORD your God will surely require it of you, and it would be sin to you.

22 "But if you abstain from vowing, it shall not be sin to you.

23 [a]"That which has gone from your lips you shall keep and perform, for you voluntarily vowed to the LORD your God what you have promised with your mouth.

4 [a]Deut. 2:27–30 [b]Num. 22:5, 6; 23:7 [1]Heb. *Aram Naharaim*
5 [a]Deut. 4:37
6 [a]Ezra 9:12
7 [a]Obad. 10, 12 [b]Deut. 10:19
10 [a]Lev. 15:16
11 [a]Lev. 15:5
14 [a]Lev. 26:12
15 [a]1 Sam. 30:15
16 [a]Ex. 22:21 [1]*pleases him best*
17 [a]Lev. 19:29 [b]2 Kin. 23:7 [1]Heb. *qedeshah,* fem. of *qadesh* (note 2) [2]Heb. *qadesh,* one practicing sodomy and prostitution in religious rituals
18 [1]*detestable*
19 [a]Ex. 22:25
20 [a]Deut. 15:3 [b]Deut. 15:10
21 [a]Eccl. 5:4, 5
23 [a]Ps. 66:13, 14

24 "When you come into your
neighbor's vineyard, you may
eat your fill of grapes at your
pleasure, but you shall not put
any in your container.
25 "When you come into your
neighbor's standing grain, [a]you
may pluck the heads with your
hand, but you shall not use a
sickle on your neighbor's standing grain.

24

"When a [a]man takes a
wife and marries her, and
it happens that she finds no favor in his eyes because he has
found some [1]uncleanness in her,
and he writes her a [b]certificate
of divorce, puts *it* in her hand,
and sends her out of his house,
2 "when she has departed
from his house, and goes and
becomes another man's *wife,*
3 "*if* the latter husband detests
her and writes her a certificate
of divorce, puts *it* in her hand,
and sends her out of his house,
or if the latter husband dies who
took her as his wife,
4 [a]"*then* her former husband
who divorced her must not take
her back to be his wife after
she has been defiled; for that
is [1]an abomination before the
LORD, and you shall not bring
sin on the land which the LORD
your God is giving you *as* an
inheritance.
5 [a]"When a man has taken a
new wife, he shall not go out
to war or be charged with any
business; he shall be free at
home one year, and [b]bring hap-
piness to his wife whom he has
taken.
6 "No man shall take the lower
or the upper millstone in pledge,
for he takes [1]*one's* living in
pledge.
7 "If a man is [a]found [1]kidnap-
ping any of his brethren of the
children of Israel, and mistreats
him or sells him, then that kid-
napper shall die; [b]and you shall
put away the evil from among
you.
8 "Take heed in [a]an outbreak
of leprosy, that you carefully
observe and do according to
all that the priests, the Lē′vītes,
shall teach you; just as I commanded them, *so* you shall be
careful to do.
9 [a]"Remember what the LORD
your God did [b]to Miriam on
the way when you came out of
Egypt!
10 "When you [a]lend your brother
anything, you shall not go into
his house to get his pledge.
11 "You shall stand outside, and
the man to whom you lend shall
bring the pledge out to you.
12 "And if the man *is* poor,
you shall not [1]keep his pledge
overnight.
13 [a]"You shall in any case return the pledge to him again
when the sun goes down, that he
may sleep in his own garment
and [b]bless you; and [c]it shall be
righteousness to you before the
LORD your God.
14 "You shall not [a]oppress a
hired servant *who is* poor and
needy, *whether* one of your
brethren or one of the aliens
who *is* in your land within your
gates.
15 "Each day [a]you shall give
him his wages, and not let the
sun go down on it, for he *is* poor
and has set his heart on it; [b]lest
he cry out against you to the
LORD, and it be sin to you.
16 [a]"Fathers shall not be put
to death for *their* children, nor

25 [a]Luke 6:1

CHAPTER 24

1 [a][Matt. 5:31; 19:7] [b][Jer. 3:8] [1]*indecency,* lit. *nakedness of a thing*

4 [a][Jer. 3:1] [1]*a detestable thing*

5 [a]Deut. 20:7 [b]Prov. 5:18

6 [1]*life*

7 [a]Ex. 21:16 [b]Deut. 19:19 [1]Lit. *stealing*

8 [a]Lev. 13:2; 14:2

9 [a][1 Cor. 10:6] [b]Num. 12:10

10 [a]Matt. 5:42

12 [1]Lit. *sleep with his pledge*

13 [a]Ex. 22:26 [b]2 Tim. 1:18 [c]Deut. 6:25

14 [a][Mal. 3:5]

15 [a]Lev. 19:13 [b]James 5:4

16 [a]Ezek. 18:20

shall children be put to death for *their* fathers; a person shall be put to death for his own sin.

17 [a]"You shall not pervert justice due the stranger or the fatherless, [b]nor take a widow's garment as a pledge.

18 "But [a]you shall remember that you were a slave in Egypt, and the LORD your God redeemed you from there; therefore I command you to do this thing.

19 [a]"When you reap your harvest in your field, and forget a sheaf in the field, you shall not go back to get it; it shall be for the stranger, the fatherless, and the widow, that the LORD your God may [b]bless you in all the work of your hands.

20 "When you beat your olive trees, you shall not go over the boughs again; it shall be for the stranger, the fatherless, and the widow.

21 "When you gather the grapes of your vineyard, you shall not glean *it* afterward; it shall be for the stranger, the fatherless, and the widow.

22 "And you shall remember that you were a slave in the land of Egypt; therefore I command you to do this thing.

25 "If there is a [a]dispute between men, and they come to [1]court, that *the judges* may judge them, and they [b]justify the righteous and condemn the wicked,

2 "then it shall be, if the wicked man [a]deserves to be beaten, that the judge will cause him to lie down [b]and be beaten in his presence, according to his guilt, with a certain number of blows.

3 [a]"Forty blows he may give him *and* no more, lest he should exceed this and beat him with many blows above these, and your brother [b]be humiliated in your sight.

4 [a]"You shall not muzzle an ox while it [1]treads out *the grain.*

5 [a]"If brothers dwell together, and one of them dies and has no son, the widow of the dead man shall not be *married* to a stranger outside *the family;* her husband's brother shall go in to her, take her as his wife, and perform the duty of a husband's brother to her.

6 "And it shall be *that* the firstborn son which she bears [a]will succeed to the name of his dead brother, that [b]his name may not be blotted out of Israel.

7 "But if the man does not want to take his brother's wife, then let his brother's wife go up to the [a]gate to the elders, and say, 'My husband's brother refuses to raise up a name to his brother in Israel; he will not perform the duty of my husband's brother.'

8 "Then the elders of his city shall call him and speak to him. But *if* he stands firm and says, [a]'I do not want to take her,'

9 "then his brother's wife shall come to him in the presence of the elders, [a]remove his sandal from his foot, spit in his face, and answer and say, 'So shall it be done to the man who will not [b]build up his brother's house.'

10 "And his name shall be called in Israel, 'The house of him who had his sandal removed.'

11 "If *two* men fight together, and the wife of one draws near to rescue her husband from the hand of the one attacking him, and puts out her hand and seizes him by the genitals,

17 [a]Ex. 23:6 [b]Ex. 22:26
18 [a]Deut. 24:22
19 [a]Lev. 19:9, 10 [b]Ps. 41:1

CHAPTER 25

1 [a]Deut. 17:8–13; 19:17 [b]Prov. 17:15 [1]Lit. *the judgment*
2 [a]Prov. 19:29 [b]Matt. 10:17
3 [a]2 Cor. 11:24 [b]Job 18:3
4 [a][Prov. 12:10] [1]*threshes*
5 [a]Matt. 22:24
6 [a]Gen. 38:9 [b]Ruth 4:5, 10
7 [a]Ruth 4:1, 2
8 [a]Ruth 4:6
9 [a]Ruth 4:7, 8 [b]Ruth 4:11

12 "then you shall cut off her hand; [a]your eye shall not pity *her.*

13 [a]"You shall not have in your bag differing weights, a heavy and a light.

14 "You shall not have in your house differing measures, a large and a small.

15 "You shall have a perfect and just weight, a perfect and just measure, [a]that your days may be lengthened in the land which the LORD your God is giving you.

16 "For [a]all who do such things, all who behave unrighteously, *are* [1]an abomination to the LORD your God.

17 [a]"Remember what Am′a·lek did to you on the way as you were coming out of Egypt,

18 "how he met you on the way and attacked your rear ranks, all the stragglers at your rear, when you *were* tired and weary; and he [a]did not fear God.

19 "Therefore it shall be, [a]when the LORD your God has given you rest from your enemies all around, in the land which the LORD your God is giving you to possess *as* an inheritance, *that* you will [b]blot out the remembrance of Am′a·lek from under heaven. You shall not forget.

26 "And it shall be, when you come into the land which the LORD your God is giving you *as* an inheritance, and you possess it and dwell in it,

2 [a]"that you shall take some of the first of all the produce of the ground, which you shall bring from your land that the LORD your God is giving you, and put *it* in a basket and [b]go to the place where the LORD your God chooses to make His name abide.

3 "And you shall go to the one who is priest in those days, and say to him, 'I declare today to the LORD [1]your God that I have come to the country which the LORD swore to our fathers to give us.'

4 "Then the priest shall take the basket out of your hand and set it down before the altar of the LORD your God.

5 "And you shall answer and say before the LORD your God: 'My father *was* [a]a [1]Syrian, [b]about to perish, and [c]he went down to Egypt and [2]dwelt there, [d]few in number; and there he became a nation, [e]great, mighty, and populous.

6 'But the [a]Egyptians mistreated us, afflicted us, and laid hard bondage on us.

7 [a]'Then we cried out to the LORD God of our fathers, and the LORD heard our voice and looked on our affliction and our labor and our oppression.

8 'So [a]the LORD brought us out of Egypt with a mighty hand and with an outstretched arm, [b]with great terror and with signs and wonders.

9 'He has brought us to this place and has given us this land, [a]"a land flowing with milk and honey";

10 'and now, behold, I have brought the firstfruits of the land which you, O LORD, have given me.' Then you shall set it before the LORD your God, and worship before the LORD your God.

11 "So [a]you shall rejoice in every good *thing* which the LORD your God has given to you and your

12 [a]Deut. 7:2; 19:13
13 [a]Mic. 6:11
15 [a]Ex. 20:12
16 [a]Prov. 11:1 [1]*detestable*
17 [a]Ex. 17:8–16
18 [a]Rom. 3:18
19 [a]1 Sam. 15:3 [b]Ex. 17:14

CHAPTER 26

2 [a]Ex. 22:29; 23:16, 19 [b]Deut. 12:5
3 [1]LXX *my*
5 [a]Hos. 12:12 [b]Gen. 43:1, 2; 45:7, 11 [c]Acts 7:15 [d]Deut. 10:22 [e]Deut. 1:10 [1]Or *Aramean* [2]As a resident alien
6 [a]Ex. 1:8–11, 14
7 [a]Ex. 2:23–25; 3:9; 4:31
8 [a]Deut. 5:15 [b]Deut. 4:34; 34:11, 12
9 [a]Ex. 3:8, 17
11 [a]Deut. 12:7; 16:11

house, you and the Lē′vīte and the stranger who *is* among you.

12 "When you have finished laying aside all the [a]tithe of your increase in the third year—[b]the year of tithing—and have given *it* to the Lē′vīte, the stranger, the fatherless, and the widow, so that they may eat within your gates and be filled,

13 "then you shall say before the LORD your God: 'I have removed the [1]holy *tithe* from *my* house, and also have given them to the Lē′vīte, the stranger, the fatherless, and the widow, according to all Your commandments which You have commanded me; I have not transgressed Your commandments, [a]nor have I forgotten *them.*

14 [a]'I have not eaten any of it [1]when in mourning, nor have I removed *any* of it [2]for an unclean *use,* nor given *any* of it for the dead. I have obeyed the voice of the LORD my God, and have done according to all that You have commanded me.

15 [a]'Look down from Your holy [1]habitation, from heaven, and bless Your people Israel and the land which You have given us, just as You swore to our fathers, [b]"a land flowing with milk and honey." '

16 "This day the LORD your God commands you to observe these statutes and judgments; therefore you shall be careful to observe them with all your heart and with all your soul.

17 "Today you have [a]proclaimed the LORD to be your God, and that you will walk in His ways and keep His statutes, His commandments, and His judgments, and that you will [b]obey His voice.

12 [a]Lev. 27:30 [b]Deut. 14:28, 29
13 [a]Ps. 119:141, 153, 176 [1]*hallowed things*
14 [a]Hos. 9:4 [1]Lit. *in my mourning* [2]Or *while I was unclean*
15 [a]Is. 63:15 [b]Ex. 3:8 [1]*home*
17 [a]Ex. 20:19 [b]Deut. 15:5
18 [a]Ex. 6:7; 19:5
19 [a]Deut. 4:7, 8; 28:1 [b][1 Pet. 2:9] [1]*consecrated*

CHAPTER 27

2 [a]Josh. 4:1 [b]Josh. 8:32
3 [a]Ex. 3:8
4 [a]Deut. 11:29
5 [a]Ex. 20:25
6 [1]*uncut*

18 "Also today [a]the LORD has proclaimed you to be His special people, just as He promised you, that *you* should keep all His commandments,

19 "and that He will set you [a]high above all nations which He has made, in praise, in name, and in honor, and that you may be [b]a [1]holy people to the LORD your God, just as He has spoken."

27

Now Moses, with the elders of Israel, commanded the people, saying: "Keep all the commandments which I command you today.

2 "And it shall be, on the day [a]when you cross over the Jordan to the land which the LORD your God is giving you, that [b]you shall set up for yourselves large stones, and whitewash them with lime.

3 "You shall write on them all the words of this law, when you have crossed over, that you may enter the land which the LORD your God is giving you, [a]'a land flowing with milk and honey,' just as the LORD God of your fathers promised you.

4 "Therefore it shall be, when you have crossed over the Jordan, *that* [a]on Mount Ē′bal you shall set up these stones, which I command you today, and you shall whitewash them with lime.

5 "And there you shall build an altar to the LORD your God, an altar of stones; [a]you shall not use an iron *tool* on them.

6 "You shall build with [1]whole stones the altar of the LORD your God, and offer burnt offerings on it to the LORD your God.

7 "You shall offer peace offerings, and shall eat there, and

[a]rejoice before the LORD your
God.
8 "And you shall [a]write very
plainly on the stones all the
words of this law."
9 Then Moses and the priests,
the Lē′vītes, spoke to all Israel,
saying, "Take heed and listen,
O Israel: [a]This day you have
become the people of the LORD
your God.
10 "Therefore you shall obey
the voice of the LORD your God,
and observe His commandments
and His statutes which I command you today."
11 And Moses commanded the
people on the same day, saying,
12 "These shall stand [a]on
Mount Ger′i·zim to bless the
people, when you have crossed
over the Jordan: Sim′ē·on, Levi,
Judah, Is′sa·char, Joseph, and
Benjamin;
13 "and [a]these shall stand on
Mount Ē′bal to curse: Reuben,
Gad, Ash′er, Zeb′ū·lun, Dan, and
Naph′ta·lī.
14 "And [a]the Lē′vītes shall speak
with a loud voice and say to all
the men of Israel:
15 [a]'Cursed *is* the one who
makes a carved or molded image, [1]an abomination to the
LORD, the work of the hands of
the craftsman, and sets *it* up in
secret.'
[b]"And all the people shall
answer and say, 'Amen!'
16 [a]'Cursed *is* the one who
treats his father or his mother
with contempt.'
"And all the people shall say,
'Amen!'
17 [a]'Cursed *is* the one who moves
his neighbor's landmark.'
"And all the people shall say,
'Amen!'

7 [a]Deut. 26:11
8 [a]Josh. 8:32
9 [a]Deut. 26:18
12 [a]Josh. 8:33
13 [a]Deut. 11:29
14 [a]Deut. 33:10
15 [a]Ex. 20:4, 23; 34:17 [b]Num. 5:22 [1]*a detestable thing*
16 [a]Ezek. 22:7
17 [a]Deut. 19:14
18 [a]Lev. 19:14
19 [a]Ex. 22:21, 22; 23:9
20 [a]Deut. 22:30
21 [a]Lev. 18:23; 20:15, 16
22 [a]Lev. 18:9
23 [a]Lev. 18:17; 20:14
24 [a]Ex. 20:13; 21:12
25 [a]Ex. 23:7
26 [a]Gal. 3:10
CHAPTER 28
1 [a]Ex. 15:26

18 [a]'Cursed *is* the one who
makes the blind to wander off
the road.'
"And all the people shall say,
'Amen!'
19 [a]'Cursed *is* the one who perverts the justice due the stranger,
the fatherless, and widow.'
"And all the people shall say,
'Amen!'
20 [a]'Cursed *is* the one who lies
with his father's wife, because
he has uncovered his father's
bed.'
"And all the people shall say,
'Amen!'
21 [a]'Cursed *is* the one who lies
with any kind of animal.'
"And all the people shall say,
'Amen!'
22 [a]'Cursed *is* the one who lies
with his sister, the daughter of
his father or the daughter of his
mother.'
"And all the people shall say,
'Amen!'
23 [a]'Cursed *is* the one who lies
with his mother-in-law.'
"And all the people shall say,
'Amen!'
24 [a]'Cursed *is* the one who attacks his neighbor secretly.'
"And all the people shall say,
'Amen!'
25 [a]'Cursed *is* the one who
takes a bribe to slay an innocent
person.'
"And all the people shall say,
'Amen!'
26 [a]'Cursed *is* the one who does
not confirm *all* the words of this
law by observing them.'
"And all the people shall say,
'Amen!'

28

"Now it shall come to
pass, [a]if you diligently
obey the voice of the LORD your
God, to observe carefully all His

commandments which I com-
mand you today, that the LORD
your God [b]will set you high
above all nations of the earth.
2 "And all these blessings shall
come upon you and [a]overtake
you, because you obey the voice
of the LORD your God:
3 [a]"Blessed *shall* you *be* in the
city, and blessed *shall* you *be* [b]in
the country.
4 "Blessed *shall be* [a]the [1]fruit
of your body, the produce of
your ground and the increase of
your herds, the increase of your
cattle and the offspring of your
flocks.
5 "Blessed *shall be* your basket and your kneading bowl.
6 [a]"Blessed *shall* you *be* when
you come in, and blessed *shall*
you *be* when you go out.
7 "The LORD [a]will cause your
enemies who rise against you
to be defeated before your face;
they shall come out against you
one way and flee before you
seven ways.
8 "The LORD will [a]command
the blessing on you in your
storehouses and in all to which
you [b]set your hand, and He will
bless you in the land which the
LORD your God is giving you.
9 [a]"The LORD will establish you
as a holy people to Himself, just
as He has sworn to you, if you
keep the commandments of the
LORD your God and walk in His
ways.
10 "Then all peoples of the earth
shall see that you are [a]called by
the name of the LORD, and they
shall be [b]afraid of you.
11 "And [a]the LORD will grant
you plenty of goods, in the fruit
of your body, in the increase
of your livestock, and in the
produce of your ground, in the
land of which the LORD [1]swore to
your fathers to give you.
12 "The LORD will open to you
His good [1]treasure, the heavens,
[a]to give the rain to your land in
its season, and [b]to bless all the
work of your hand. [c]You shall
lend to many nations, but you
shall not borrow.
13 "And the LORD will make
[a]you the head and not the tail;
you shall be above only, and
not be beneath, if you [1]heed
the commandments of the LORD
your God, which I command you
today, and are careful to observe
them.
14 [a]"So you shall not turn aside
from any of the words which I
command you this day, *to* the
right or the left, to go after other
gods to serve them.
15 "But it shall come to pass, [a]if
you do not obey the voice of the
LORD your God, to observe carefully all His commandments and
His statutes which I command
you today, that all these curses
will come upon you and overtake you:
16 "Cursed *shall* you *be* in the
city, and cursed *shall* you *be* in
the country.
17 "Cursed *shall be* your basket
and your kneading bowl.
18 "Cursed *shall be* the [1]fruit of
your body and the produce of
your land, the increase of your
cattle and the offspring of your
flocks.
19 "Cursed *shall* you *be* when
you come in, and cursed *shall*
you *be* when you go out.
20 "The LORD will send on you
[a]cursing, [b]confusion, and [c]rebuke
in all that you set your hand
to do, until you are destroyed

1 [b]Deut. 26:19
2 [a]Deut. 28:15
3 [a]Ps. 128:1, 4 [b]Gen. 39:5
4 [a]Gen. 22:17 [1]*offspring*
6 [a]Ps. 121:8
7 [a]Lev. 26:7, 8
8 [a]Lev. 25:21 [b]Deut. 15:10
9 [a]Ex. 19:5, 6
10 [a]Num. 6:27 [b]Deut. 11:25
11 [a]Deut. 30:9 [1]*promised*
12 [a]Lev. 26:4 [b]Deut. 14:29 [c]Deut. 15:6 [1]*storehouse*
13 [a][Is. 9:14, 15] [1]*listen to*
14 [a]Deut. 5:32
15 [a]Lev. 26:14–39
18 [1]*offspring*
20 [a]Mal. 2:2 [b]Is. 65:14 [c]Is. 30:17

and until you perish quickly,
because of the wickedness of
your doings in which you have
forsaken Me.
21 "The LORD will make the
[1]plague cling to you until He has
consumed you from the land
which you are going to possess.
22 [a]"The LORD will strike you
with consumption, with fever,
with inflammation, with severe
burning fever, with the sword,
with [b]scorching,[1] and with mildew; they shall pursue you until
you perish.
23 "And [a]your heavens which
are over your head shall be
bronze, and the earth which is
under you *shall be* iron.
24 "The LORD will change the
rain of your land to powder and
dust; from the heaven it shall
come down on you until you are
destroyed.
25 [a]"The LORD will cause you
to be defeated before your enemies; you shall go out one way
against them and flee seven
ways before them; and you shall
become [1]troublesome to all the
kingdoms of the earth.
26 [a]"Your carcasses shall be
food for all the birds of the
air and the beasts of the earth,
and no one shall frighten *them*
away.
27 "The LORD will strike you
with [a]the boils of Egypt, with
[b]tumors, with the scab, and with
the itch, from which you cannot
be healed.
28 "The LORD will strike you
with madness and blindness
and [a]confusion of heart.
29 "And you shall [a]grope at
noonday, as a blind man gropes
in darkness; you shall not prosper in your ways; you shall be
only oppressed and plundered
continually, and no one shall
save *you.*
30 [a]"You shall betroth a wife,
but another man shall lie with
her; [b]you shall build a house,
but you shall not dwell in it; [c]you
shall plant a vineyard, but shall
not gather its grapes.
31 "Your ox *shall be* slaughtered before your eyes, but you
shall not eat of it; your donkey
shall be violently taken away
from before you, and shall not
be restored to you; your sheep
shall be given to your enemies,
and you shall have no one to
rescue *them.*
32 "Your sons and your daughters *shall be* given to [a]another
people, and your eyes shall look
and [b]fail *with longing* for them
all day long; and *there shall be*
[1]no strength in your [c]hand.
33 "A nation whom you have
not known shall eat [a]the fruit
of your land and the produce
of your labor, and you shall
be only oppressed and crushed
continually.
34 "So you shall be driven mad
because of the sight which your
eyes see.
35 "The LORD will strike you in
the knees and on the legs with
severe boils which cannot be
healed, and from the sole of your
foot to the top of your head.
36 "The LORD will [a]bring you and
the king whom you set over you
to a nation which neither you
nor your fathers have known,
and [b]there you shall serve other
gods—wood and stone.
37 "And you shall become [a]an[1]
astonishment, a proverb, [b]and a
byword among all nations where
the LORD will drive you.

21 [1]*pestilence*
22 [a]Lev. 26:16 [b]Amos 4:9 [1]*blight*
23 [a]Lev. 26:19
25 [a]Deut. 32:30 [1]*a terror*
26 [a]1 Sam. 17:44
27 [a]Ex. 15:26 [b]1 Sam. 5:6
28 [a]Jer. 4:9
29 [a]Job 5:14
30 [a]Jer. 8:10 [b]Amos 5:11 [c]Deut. 20:6
32 [a]2 Chr. 29:9 [b]Ps. 119:82 [c]Neh. 5:5 [1]*nothing you can do*
33 [a]Jer. 5:15, 17
36 [a]Jer. 39:1–9 [b]Deut. 4:28
37 [a]1 Kin. 9:7, 8 [b]Ps. 44:14 [1]*a thing of horror*

38 [a]"You shall carry much seed out to the field but gather little in, for [b]the locust shall [1]consume it.

39 "You shall plant vineyards and tend *them,* but you shall neither drink *of* the [a]wine nor gather the *grapes;* for the worms shall eat them.

40 "You shall have olive trees throughout all your territory, but you shall not anoint *yourself* with the oil; for your olives shall drop off.

41 "You shall beget sons and daughters, but they shall not be yours; for [a]they shall go into captivity.

42 "Locusts shall [1]consume all your trees and the produce of your land.

43 "The alien who *is* among you shall rise higher and higher above you, and you shall come down lower and lower.

44 "He shall lend to you, but you shall not lend to him; he shall be the head, and you shall be the tail.

45 "Moreover all these curses shall come upon you and pursue and overtake you, until you are destroyed, because you [1]did not obey the voice of the LORD your God, to keep His commandments and His statutes which He commanded you.

46 "And they shall be upon [a]you for a sign and a wonder, and on your descendants forever.

47 [a]"Because you did not serve the LORD your God with joy and gladness of heart, [b]for the abundance of everything,

48 "therefore you shall serve your enemies, whom the LORD will send against you, in [a]hunger, in thirst, in nakedness, and in need of everything; and He [b]will put a yoke of iron on your neck until He has destroyed you.

49 [a]"The LORD will bring a nation against you from afar, from the end of the earth, [b]*as swift* as the eagle flies, a nation whose language you will not understand,

50 "a nation of fierce countenance, [a]which does not respect the elderly nor show favor to the young.

51 "And they shall eat the increase of your livestock and the produce of your land, until you are destroyed; they shall not leave you grain or new wine or oil, *or* the increase of your cattle or the offspring of your flocks, until they have destroyed you.

52 "They shall [a]besiege you at all your gates until your high and fortified walls, in which you trust, come down throughout all your land; and they shall besiege you at all your gates throughout all your land which the LORD your God has given you.

53 [a]"You shall eat the [1]fruit of your own body, the flesh of your sons and your daughters whom the LORD your God has given you, in the siege and desperate straits in which your enemy shall distress you.

54 "The [1]sensitive and very refined man among you [a]will[2] be hostile toward his brother, toward [b]the wife of his bosom, and toward the rest of his children whom he leaves behind,

55 "so that he will not give any of them the flesh of his children whom he will eat, because he has nothing left in the siege and desperate straits in which your enemy shall distress you at all your gates.

---

38 [a]Mic. 6:15 [b]Joel 1:4 [1]*devour*
39 [a]Zeph. 1:13
41 [a]Lam. 1:5
42 [1]*possess*
45 [1]*did not listen to*
46 [a]Is. 8:18
47 [a]Neh. 9:35–37 [b]Deut. 32:15
48 [a]Lam. 4:4–6 [b]Jer. 28:13, 14
49 [a]Jer. 5:15 [b]Jer. 48:40; 49:22
50 [a]2 Chr. 36:17
52 [a]2 Kin. 25:1, 2, 4
53 [a]Lev. 26:29 [1]*offspring*
54 [a]Deut. 15:9 [b]Deut. 13:6 [1]Lit. *tender* [2]Lit. *his eye shall be evil toward*

56 "The [1]tender and [2]delicate woman among you, who would not venture to set the sole of her foot on the ground because of her delicateness and sensitivity, [3]will refuse to the husband of her bosom, and to her son and her daughter,

57 "her [1]placenta which comes out [a]from between her feet and her children whom she bears; for she will eat them secretly for lack of everything in the siege and desperate straits in which your enemy shall distress you at all your gates.

58 "If you do not carefully observe all the words of this law that are written in this book, that you may fear [a]this glorious and awesome name, THE LORD YOUR GOD,

59 "then the LORD will bring upon you and your descendants [a]extraordinary plagues—great and prolonged plagues—and serious and prolonged sicknesses.

60 "Moreover He will bring back on you all [a]the diseases of Egypt, of which you were afraid, and they shall cling to you.

61 "Also every sickness and every plague, which *is* not written in this Book of the Law, will the LORD bring upon you until you are destroyed.

62 "You [a]shall be left few in number, whereas you were [b]as the stars of heaven in multitude, because you would not obey the voice of the LORD your God.

63 "And it shall be, *that* just as the LORD [a]rejoiced over you to do you good and multiply you, so the LORD [b]will rejoice over you to destroy you and bring you to nothing; and you shall be [c]plucked[1] from off the land which you go to possess.

64 "Then the LORD [a]will scatter you among all peoples, from one end of the earth to the other, and [b]there you shall serve other gods, which neither you nor your fathers have known—wood and stone.

65 "And [a]among those nations you shall find no rest, nor shall the sole of your foot have a resting place; [b]but there the LORD will give you a [1]trembling heart, failing eyes, and [c]anguish of soul.

66 "Your life shall hang in doubt before you; you shall fear day and night, and have no assurance of life.

67 [a]"In the morning you shall say, 'Oh, that it were evening!' And at evening you shall say, 'Oh, that it were morning!' because of the fear which terrifies your heart, and [b]because of the sight which your eyes see.

68 "And the LORD [a]will take you back to Egypt in ships, by the way of which I said to you, [b]'You shall never see it again.' And there you shall be offered for sale to your enemies as male and female slaves, but no one will buy *you*."

29

These *are* the words of the covenant which the LORD commanded Moses to make with the children of Israel in the land of Mō'ab, besides the [a]covenant which He made with them in Hō'reb.

2 Now Moses called all Israel and said to them: [a]"You have seen all that the LORD did before your eyes in the land of Egypt, to Pharaoh and to all his servants and to all his land—

56 [1]*sensitive* [2]*refined* [3]Lit. *her eye shall be evil toward*
57 [a]Gen. 49:10 [1]*afterbirth*
58 [a]Ex. 6:3
59 [a]Dan. 9:12
60 [a]Deut. 7:15
62 [a]Deut. 4:27 [b]Neh. 9:23
63 [a]Jer. 32:41 [b]Prov. 1:26 [c]Jer. 12:14; 45:4 [1]*torn*
64 [a]Jer. 16:13 [b]Deut. 28:36
65 [a]Amos 9:4 [b]Lev. 26:36 [c]Lev. 26:16 [1]*anxious*
67 [a]Job 7:4 [b]Deut. 28:34
68 [a]Hos. 8:13 [b]Deut. 17:16

CHAPTER 29

1 [a]Deut. 5:2, 3
2 [a]Ex. 19:4

3 [a]"the great trials which your
eyes have seen, the signs, and
those great wonders.
4 "Yet [a]the LORD has not given
you a heart to [1]perceive and eyes
to see and ears to hear, to this
very day.
5 [a]"And I have led you forty
years in the wilderness. [b]Your
clothes have not worn out on
you, and your sandals have not
worn out on your feet.
6 [a]"You have not eaten bread,
nor have you drunk wine or *similar* drink, that you may know
that I *am* the LORD your God.
7 "And when you came to this
place, [a]Sī′hon king of Hesh′bon
and Og king of Bā′shan came
out against us to battle, and we
conquered them.
8 "We took their land and
[a]gave it as an inheritance to the
Reū′ben·ītes, to the Gad′ītes, and
to half the tribe of Ma·nas′seh.
9 "Therefore [a]keep the words
of this covenant, and do them,
that you may [b]prosper in all that
you do.
10 "All of you stand today before the LORD your God: your
leaders and your tribes and your
elders and your officers, all the
men of Israel,
11 "your little ones and your
wives—also the stranger who *is*
in your camp, from [a]the one who
cuts your wood to the one who
draws your water—
12 "that you may enter into covenant with the LORD your God,
and [a]into His oath, which the
LORD your God makes with you
today,
13 "that He may [a]establish you
today as a people for Himself,
and *that* He may be God to you,
[b]just as He has spoken to you,
and [c]just as He has sworn to
your fathers, to Abraham, Isaac,
and Jacob.
14 "I make this covenant and
this oath, [a]not with you alone,
15 "but with *him* who stands here
with us today before the LORD our
God, [a]as well as with *him* who *is*
not here with us today
16 (for you know that we dwelt
in the land of Egypt and that we
came through the nations which
you passed by,
17 and you saw their [1]abomina-
tions and their idols which *were*
among them—wood and stone
and silver and gold);
18 "so that there may not be
among you man or woman or
family or tribe, [a]whose heart
turns away today from the LORD
our God, to go *and* serve the
gods of these nations, [b]and that
there may not be among you
a root bearing [c]bitterness or
wormwood;
19 "and so it may not happen,
when he hears the words of this
curse, that he blesses himself in
his heart, saying, 'I shall have
peace, even though I [1]follow
the [a]dictates of my heart'—[b]as
though the drunkard could be
included with the sober.
20 [a]"The LORD would not spare
him; for then [b]the anger of the
LORD and [c]His jealousy would
burn against that man, and every curse that is written in this
book would settle on him, and
the LORD [d]would blot out his
name from under heaven.
21 "And the LORD [a]would separate him from all the tribes of
Israel for adversity, according
to all the curses of the covenant
that are written in this Book of
the [b]Law,

3 [a]Deut. 4:34; 7:19
4 [a][Acts 28:26, 27] [1]*understand* or *know*
5 [a]Deut. 1:3; 8:2 [b]Deut. 8:4
6 [a]Deut. 8:3
7 [a]Num. 21:23, 24
8 [a]Deut. 3:12, 13
9 [a]Deut. 4:6 [b]Josh. 1:7
11 [a]Josh. 9:21, 23, 27
12 [a]Neh. 10:29
13 [a]Deut. 28:9 [b]Ex. 6:7 [c]Gen. 17:7, 8
14 [a][Jer. 31:31]
15 [a]Acts 2:39
17 [1]*detestable things*
18 [a]Deut. 11:16 [b]Heb. 12:15 [c]Deut. 32:32
19 [a]Jer. 3:17; 7:24 [b]Is. 30:1 [1]*walk in the stubbornness* or *imagination*
20 [a]Ezek. 14:7 [b]Ps. 74:1 [c]Ps. 79:5 [d]Deut. 9:14
21 [a][Matt. 24:51] [b]Deut. 30:10

22 "so that the coming generation of your children who rise up
after you, and the foreigner who
comes from a far land, would
say, when they [a]see the plagues
of that land and the sicknesses
which the LORD has laid on it:
23 'The whole land *is* brimstone,
[a]salt, and burning; it is not sown,
nor does it bear, nor does any
grass grow there, [b]like the overthrow of Sod′om and Go·mor′-
rah, Ad′mah, and Ze·boi′im,
which the LORD overthrew in
His anger and His wrath.'
24 "All nations would say, [a]'Why
has the LORD done so to this
land? What does the heat of this
great anger mean?'
25 "Then *people* would say: 'Because they have forsaken the
covenant of the LORD God of
their fathers, which He made
with them when He brought
them out of the land of Egypt;
26 'for they went and served
other gods and worshiped them,
gods that they did not know and
that He had not given to them.
27 'Then the anger of the LORD
was aroused against this land,
[a]to bring on it every curse that is
written in this book.
28 'And the LORD [a]uprooted
them from their land in anger, in
wrath, and in great indignation,
and cast them into another land,
as *it is* this day.'
29 "The secret *things belong* to
the LORD our God, but those
things which are revealed *be-*
long to us and to our children
forever, that *we* may do all the
words of this law.

30 "Now [a]it shall come to
pass, when [b]all these
things come upon you, the blessing and the [c]curse which I have
set before you, and [d]you [1]call
them to mind among all the nations where the LORD your God
drives you,
2 "and you [a]return to the LORD
your God and obey His voice,
according to all that I command
you today, you and your children, with all your heart and
with all your soul,
3 [a]"that the LORD your God will
bring you back from captivity,
and have compassion on you,
and [b]gather you again from all
the nations where the LORD your
God has scattered you.
4 [a]"If *any* of you are driven
out to the farthest *parts* under heaven, from there the LORD
your God will gather you, and
from there He will bring you.
5 "Then the LORD your God
will bring you to the land which
your fathers possessed, and you
shall possess it. He will prosper
you and multiply you more than
your fathers.
6 "And [a]the LORD your God
will circumcise your heart and
the heart of your descendants,
to love the LORD your God with
all your heart and with all your
soul, that you may live.
7 "Also the LORD your God will
put all these [a]curses on your
enemies and on those who hate
you, who persecuted you.
8 "And you will [a]again obey
the voice of the LORD and do
all His commandments which I
command you today.
9 [a]"The LORD your God will
make you abound in all the
work of your hand, in the [1]fruit
of your body, in the increase of
your livestock, and in the produce of your land for good. For
the LORD will again [b]rejoice over

22 [a]Jer. 19:8; 49:17; 50:13
23 [a]Zeph. 2:9 [b]Gen. 19:24, 25
24 [a]1 Kin. 9:8
27 [a]Dan. 9:11
28 [a]1 Kin. 14:15

CHAPTER 30

1 [a]Lev. 26:40 [b]Deut. 28:2 [c]Deut. 28:15–45 [d]Deut. 4:29, 30 [1]Lit. *cause them to return to your heart*
2 [a]Neh. 1:9
3 [a]Jer. 29:14 [b]Ezek. 34:13
4 [a]Neh. 1:9
6 [a]Deut. 10:16
7 [a]Jer. 30:16, 20
8 [a]Zeph. 3:20
9 [a]Deut. 28:11 [b]Jer. 32:41 [1]*offspring*

you for good as He rejoiced over
your fathers,
10 "if you obey the voice of
the LORD your God, to keep His
commandments and His statutes
which are written in this Book
of the Law, *and* if you turn to
the LORD your God with all your
heart and with all your soul.
11 "For this commandment
which I command you today [a]*is*
[1]not *too* mysterious for you, nor
is it far off.
12 [a]"It *is* not in heaven, that you
should say, 'Who will ascend
into heaven for us and bring it
to us, that we may hear it and
do it?'
13 "Nor *is* it beyond the sea,
that you should say, 'Who will
go over the sea for us and bring
it to us, that we may hear it and
do it?'
14 "But the word *is* very near
you, [a]in your mouth and in your
heart, that you may do it.
15 "See, [a]I have set before you
today life and good, death and
evil,
16 "in that I command you today to love the LORD your God,
to walk in His ways, and to keep
His commandments, His statutes, and His judgments, that
you may live and multiply; and
the LORD your God will bless
you in the land which you go to
possess.
17 "But if your heart turns away
so that you do not hear, and are
drawn away, and worship other
gods and serve them,
18 [a]"I announce to you today
that you shall surely perish; you
shall not prolong *your* days in
the land which you cross over
the Jordan to go in and possess.
19 [a]"I call heaven and earth as
witnesses today against you,
that [b]I have set before you life
and death, blessing and cursing;
therefore choose life, that both
you and your descendants may
live;
20 "that you may love the LORD
your God, that you may obey
His voice, and that you may
cling to Him, for He *is* your [a]life
and the length of your days; and
that you may dwell in the land
which the LORD swore to your
fathers, to Abraham, Isaac, and
Jacob, to give them."

31

Then Moses went and
spoke these words to all
Israel.
2 And he said to them: "I [a]*am*
one hundred and twenty years
old today. I can no longer [b]go out
and come in. Also the LORD has
said to me, [c]'You shall not cross
over this Jordan.'
3 "The LORD your God [a]Himself
crosses over before you; He
will destroy these nations from
before you, and you shall dispossess them. [b]Joshua himself
crosses over before you, just [c]as
the LORD has said.
4 [a]"And the LORD will do to
them [b]as He did to Sī′hon and
Og, the kings of the Am′o·rītes
and their land, when He destroyed them.
5 [a]"The LORD will give them
over to you, that you may do to
them according to every commandment which I have commanded you.
6 [a]"Be strong and of good courage, [b]do not fear nor be afraid of
them; for the LORD your God,
[c]He *is* the One who goes with
you. [d]He will not leave you nor
forsake you."
7 Then Moses called Joshua

11 [a]Is. 45:19 [1]*not hidden from*
12 [a]Rom. 10:6–8
14 [a]Rom. 10:8
15 [a]Deut. 30:1, 19
18 [a]Deut. 4:26; 8:19
19 [a]Deut. 4:26 [b]Deut. 30:15
20 [a][John 11:25; 14:6]

CHAPTER 31

2 [a]Deut. 34:7 [b]1 Kin. 3:7 [c]Num. 20:12
3 [a]Deut. 9:3 [b]Num. 27:18 [c]Num. 27:21
4 [a]Deut. 3:21 [b]Num. 21:24, 33
5 [a]Deut. 7:2; 20:10–20
6 [a]Josh. 10:25 [b]Deut. 1:29 [c]Deut. 20:4 [d]Heb. 13:5

and said to him in the sight of all Israel, [a]"Be strong and of good courage, for you must go with this people to the land which the LORD has sworn to their fathers to give them, and you shall cause them to inherit it.

8 "And the LORD, [a]He *is* the One who goes before you. [b]He will be with you, He will not leave you nor forsake you; do not fear nor be dismayed."

9 So Moses wrote this law [a]and delivered it to the priests, the sons of Levi, [b]who bore the ark of the covenant of the LORD, and to all the elders of Israel.

10 And Moses commanded them, saying: "At the end of *every* seven years, at the appointed time in the [a]year of release, [b]at the Feast of Tabernacles,

11 "when all Israel comes to [a]appear before the LORD your God in the [b]place which He chooses, [c]you shall read this law before all Israel in their hearing.

12 [a]"Gather the people together, men and women and little ones, and the stranger who *is* within your gates, that they may hear and that they may learn to fear the LORD your God and carefully observe all the words of this law,

13 "and *that* their children, [a]who have not known it, [b]may hear and learn to fear the LORD your God as long as you live in the land which you cross the Jordan to possess."

14 Then the LORD said to Moses, [a]"Behold, the days approach when you must die; call Joshua, and present yourselves in the tabernacle of meeting, that [b]I may [1]inaugurate him." So Moses and Joshua went and presented themselves in the tabernacle of meeting.

15 Now [a]the LORD appeared at the tabernacle in a pillar of cloud, and the pillar of cloud stood above the door of the tabernacle.

16 And the LORD said to Moses: "Behold, you will [1]rest with your fathers; and this people will [a]rise and [b]play the harlot with the gods of the foreigners of the land, where they go *to be* among them, and they will [c]forsake Me and [d]break My covenant which I have made with them.

17 "Then My anger shall be [a]aroused against them in that day, and [b]I will forsake them, and I will [c]hide My face from them, and they shall be [1]devoured. And many evils and troubles shall befall them, so that they will say in that day, [d]'Have not these evils come upon us because our God *is* [e]not among us?'

18 "And [a]I will surely hide My face in that day because of all the evil which they have done, in that they have turned to other gods.

19 "Now therefore, write down this song for yourselves, and teach it to the children of Israel; put it in their mouths, that this song may be [a]a witness for Me against the children of Israel.

20 "When I have brought them to the land flowing with milk and honey, of which I swore to their fathers, and they have eaten and filled themselves [a]and grown fat, [b]then they will turn to other gods and serve them; and they will provoke Me and break My covenant.

21 "Then it shall be, [a]when many evils and troubles have

7 [a]Deut. 31:23
8 [a]Ex. 13:21 [b]Josh. 1:5
9 [a]Deut. 17:18; 31:25, 26 [b]Josh. 3:3
10 [a]Deut. 15:1, 2 [b]Lev. 23:34
11 [a]Deut. 16:16 [b]Deut. 12:5 [c]Josh. 8:34
12 [a]Deut. 4:10
13 [a]Deut. 11:2 [b]Ps. 78:6, 7
14 [a]Num. 27:13 [b]Deut. 3:28 [1]*commission*
15 [a]Ex. 33:9
16 [a]Deut. 29:22 [b]Ex. 34:15 [c]Deut. 32:15 [d]Judg. 2:20 [1]Die and join your ancestors
17 [a]Judg. 2:14; 6:13 [b]2 Chr. 15:2 [c]Deut. 32:20 [d]Judg. 6:13 [e]Num. 14:42 [1]*consumed*
18 [a]Deut. 31:17
19 [a]Deut. 31:22, 26
20 [a]Deut. 32:15–17 [b]Deut. 31:16
21 [a]Deut. 31:17

come upon them, that this song
will testify against them as a
witness; for it will not be forgotten in the mouths of their descendants, for [b]I know the incli-
nation [c]of their behavior today,
even before I have brought them
to the land of which I swore *to*
give them."
22 Therefore Moses wrote this
song the same day, and taught it
to the children of Israel.
23 [a]Then He inaugurated Joshua
the son of Nun, and said, [b]"Be
strong and of good courage; for
you shall bring the children of
Israel into the land of which I
swore to them, and I will be with
you."
24 So it was, when Moses had
completed writing the words of
this law in a book, when they
were finished,
25 that Moses commanded the
Lē′vītes, who bore the ark of the
covenant of the LORD, saying:
26 "Take this Book of the Law,
[a]and put it beside the ark of the
covenant of the LORD your God,
that it may be there [b]as a witness against you;
27 [a]"for I know your rebellion
and your [b]stiff neck. *If* today,
while I am yet alive with you,
you have been rebellious against
the LORD, then how much more
after my death?
28 "Gather to me all the elders of
your tribes, and your officers, that
I may speak these words in their
hearing [a]and call heaven and
earth to witness against them.
29 "For I know that after my
death you will [a]become utterly
corrupt, and turn aside from the
way which I have commanded
you. And [b]evil will befall you [c]in
the latter days, because you will
do evil in the sight of the LORD,
to provoke Him to anger through
the work of your hands."
30 Then Moses spoke in the
hearing of all the assembly of Israel the words of this song until
they were ended:

32 "Give [a]ear, O heavens,
and I will speak;
And hear, O [b]earth, the
words of my mouth.
2 Let [a]my [1]teaching drop as
the rain,
My speech distill as the dew,
[b]As raindrops on the tender
herb,
And as showers on the
grass.
3 For I proclaim the [a]name of
the LORD:
[b]Ascribe greatness to our
God.
4 *He is* [a]the Rock, [b]His work *is*
perfect;
For all His ways *are* justice,
[c]A God of truth and [d]without
injustice;
Righteous and upright *is* He.
5 "They[a] have corrupted
themselves;
They are not His children,
Because of their blemish:
A [b]perverse and crooked
generation.
6 Do you thus [a]deal[1] with the
LORD,
O foolish and unwise
people?
Is He not [b]your Father, *who*
[c]bought you?
Has He not [d]made you and
established you?

7 "Remember[a] the days of old,
Consider the years of many
generations.

21 [b]Hos. 5:3 [c]Amos 5:25, 26
23 [a]Num. 27:23 [b]Deut. 31:7
26 [a]2 Kin. 22:8 [b]Deut. 31:19
27 [a]Deut. 9:7, 24 [b]Ex. 32:9
28 [a]Deut. 30:19
29 [a]Judg. 2:19 [b]Deut. 28:15 [c]Gen. 49:1

CHAPTER 32

1 [a]Deut. 4:26 [b]Jer. 6:19
2 [a]Is. 55:10, 11 [b]Ps. 72:6 [1]*doctrine*
3 [a]Deut. 28:58 [b]1 Chr. 29:11
4 [a]Ps. 18:2 [b]2 Sam. 22:31 [c]Is. 65:16 [d]Job 34:10
5 [a]Deut. 4:25; 31:29 [b]Phil. 2:15
6 [a]Ps. 116:12 [b]Is. 63:16 [c]Ps. 74:2 [d]Deut. 32:15 [1]*repay the*
7 [a]Ps. 44:1

[b]Ask your father, and he will
show you;
Your elders, and they will
tell you:
8 When the Most High
[a]divided their
inheritance to the
nations,
When He [b]separated the
sons of Adam,
He set the boundaries of the
peoples
According to the number of
the [1]children of Israel.
9 For [a]the LORD's portion *is*
His people;
Jacob *is* the place of His
inheritance.

10 "He found him [a]in a desert
land
And in the wasteland, a
howling wilderness;
He encircled him, He
instructed him,
He [b]kept him as the [1]apple
of His eye.
11 [a]As an eagle stirs up its nest,
Hovers over its young,
Spreading out its wings,
taking them up,
Carrying them on its wings,
12 *So* the LORD alone led him,
And *there was* no foreign
god with him.

13 "He[a] made him ride in the
heights of the earth,
That he might eat the
produce of the fields;
He made him draw honey
from the rock,
And oil from the flinty rock;
14 Curds from the cattle, and
milk of the flock,
[a]With fat of lambs;
And rams of the breed of
Bā'shan, and goats,
With the choicest wheat;
And you drank wine, the
[b]blood of the grapes.

15 "But Jesh'ū·run grew fat and
kicked;
[a]You grew fat, you grew
thick,
You are obese!
Then he [b]forsook God *who*
[c]made him,
And scornfully esteemed the
[d]Rock of his salvation.
16 [a]They provoked Him to
jealousy with foreign
gods;
With [1]abominations they
provoked Him to anger.
17 [a]They sacrificed to demons,
not to God,
To gods they did not know,
To new *gods,* new arrivals
That your fathers did not
fear.
18 [a]Of the Rock *who* begot you,
you are unmindful,
And have [b]forgotten the God
who fathered you.

19 "And[a] when the LORD saw *it,*
He spurned *them,*
Because of the provocation
of His sons and His
daughters.
20 And He said: 'I will hide My
face from them,
I will see what their end *will
be,*
For they *are* a perverse
generation,
[a]Children in whom *is* no
faith.
21 [a]They have provoked Me to
jealousy by *what* is not
God;
They have moved Me to
anger [b]by their [1]foolish
idols.

7 [b]Ps. 78:5–8
8 [a]Acts 17:26 [b]Gen. 11:8 [1]LXX, DSS *angels of God;* Symmachus, Lat. *sons of God*
9 [a]Ex. 19:5
10 [a]Jer. 2:6 [b]Ps. 17:8 [1]*pupil*
11 [a]Is. 31:5
13 [a]Is. 58:14
14 [a]Ps. 81:16 [b]Gen. 49:11
15 [a]Deut. 31:20 [b]Is. 1:4 [c]Is. 51:13 [d]Ps. 95:1
16 [a]1 Cor. 10:22 [1]*detestable acts*
17 [a]Rev. 9:20
18 [a]Is. 17:10 [b]Jer. 2:32
19 [a]Judg. 2:14
20 [a]Matt. 17:17
21 [a]Ps. 78:58 [b]Ps. 31:6 [1]*foolishness,* lit. *vanities*

But [c]I will provoke them to
jealousy by *those who*
are not a nation;
I will move them to anger
by a foolish nation.
22 For [a]a fire is kindled in My
anger,
And shall burn to the
[1]lowest [2]hell;
It shall consume the earth
with her increase,
And set on fire the
foundations of the
mountains.

23 'I will [a]heap disasters on
them;
[b]I will spend My arrows on
them.
24 *They shall be* wasted with
hunger,
Devoured by pestilence and
bitter destruction;
I will also send against them
the [a]teeth of beasts,
With the poison of serpents
of the dust.
25 The sword shall destroy
outside;
There shall be terror within
For the young man and
virgin,
The nursing child with the
man of gray hairs.
26 [a]I would have said, "I will
dash them in pieces,
I will make the memory
of them to cease from
among men,"
27 Had I not feared the wrath
of the enemy,
Lest their adversaries
should misunderstand,
Lest they should say, [a]"Our
hand *is* high;
And it is not the LORD who
has done all this." '

28 "For they *are* a nation void of
counsel,
Nor *is there any*
understanding in them.
29 [a]Oh, that they were wise,
that they understood
this,
That they would consider
their [b]latter end!
30 How could one chase a
thousand,
And two put ten thousand to
flight,
Unless their Rock [a]had sold
them,
And the LORD had
surrendered them?
31 For their rock *is* not like our
Rock,
[a]Even our enemies
themselves *being* judges.
32 For [a]their vine *is* of the vine
of Sod'om
And of the fields of
Go·mor'rah;
Their grapes *are* grapes of
gall,
Their clusters *are* bitter.
33 Their wine *is* [a]the poison of
serpents,
And the cruel [b]venom of
cobras.

34 '*Is* this not [a]laid up in store
with Me,
Sealed up among My
treasures?
35 [a]Vengeance is Mine, and
recompense;
Their foot shall slip in *due*
time;
[b]For the day of their calamity
is at hand,
And the things to come
hasten upon them.'

36 "For[a] the LORD will judge His
people

21 [c]Rom. 10:19
22 [a]Lam. 4:11 [1]*lowest part of* [2]Or *Sheol*
23 [a]Ex. 32:12 [b]Ps. 7:12, 13
24 [a]Lev. 26:22
26 [a]Ezek. 20:23
27 [a]Is. 10:12–15
29 [a][Luke 19:42] [b]Deut. 31:29
30 [a]Judg. 2:14
31 [a][1 Sam. 4:7, 8]
32 [a]Is. 1:8–10
33 [a]Ps. 58:4 [b]Rom. 3:13
34 [a][Jer. 2:22]
35 [a]Heb. 10:30 [b]2 Pet. 2:3
36 [a]Ps. 135:14

[b]And have compassion on
His servants,
When He sees that *their*
power is gone,
And [c]*there is* no one
remaining, bond or free.
37 He will say: [a]'Where *are*
their gods,
The rock in which they
sought refuge?
38 Who ate the fat of their
sacrifices,
And drank the wine of their
drink offering?
Let them rise and help you,
And be your refuge.

39 'Now see that [a]I, *even* I, *am*
He,
And [b]*there is* no God
besides Me;
[c]I kill and I make alive;
I wound and I heal;
Nor *is there any* who can
deliver from My hand.
40 For I raise My hand to
heaven,
And say, "*As* I live forever,
41 [a]If I [1]whet My glittering
sword,
And My hand takes hold on
judgment,
I will render vengeance to
My enemies,
And repay those who hate
Me.
42 I will make My arrows
drunk with blood,
And My sword shall devour
flesh,
With the blood of the slain
and the captives,
From the heads of the
leaders of the enemy." '

☆ 43 "Rejoice,[a]O Gentiles, *with*
His [1]people;
For He will [b]avenge the
blood of His servants,
And render vengeance to
His adversaries;
He [c]will provide atonement
for His land *and* His
people."

44 So Moses came with [1]Joshua
the son of Nun and spoke all the
words of this song in the hearing of the people.
45 Moses finished speaking all
these words to all Israel,
46 and he said to them: [a]"Set
your hearts on all the words
which I testify among you today, which you shall command
your [b]children to be careful to
observe—all the words of this
law.
47 "For it *is* not a [1]futile thing
for you, because it *is* your [a]life,
and by this word you shall prolong *your* days in the land which
you cross over the Jordan to
possess."
48 Then the LORD spoke to Moses that very same day, saying:
49 [a]"Go up this mountain of the
Ab'a·rim, Mount Nē'bō, which
is in the land of Mō'ab, across
from Jericho; view the land of
Cā'naan, which I give to the children of Israel as a possession;
50 "and die on the mountain
which you ascend, and be [1]gath-
ered to your people, just as
[a]Aaron your brother died on
Mount Hor and was gathered to
his people;
51 "because [a]you trespassed
against Me among the children
of Israel at the waters of [1]Mer'-
i·bah Kā'desh, in the Wilderness
of Zin, because you [b]did not
hallow Me in the midst of the
children of Israel.

36 [b]Jer. 31:20 [c]2 Kin. 14:26
37 [a]Judg. 10:14
39 [a]Is. 41:4; 43:10 [b]Is. 45:5 [c]1 Sam. 2:6
41 [a]Is. 1:24; 66:16 [1]*sharpen*
43 [a]Rom. 15:10 [b]Rev. 6:10; 19:2 [c]Ps. 65:3; 79:9; 85:1 [1]DSS fragment adds *And let all the gods (angels) worship Him;* cf. LXX and Heb. 1:6
44 [1]Heb. *Hoshea*, Num. 13:8, 16
46 [a]Ezek. 40:4; 44:5 [b]Deut. 11:19
47 [a]Deut. 8:3; 30:15–20 [1]*vain*
49 [a]Num. 27:12–14
50 [a]Num. 20:25, 28; 33:38 [1]Join your ancestors
51 [a]Num. 20:11–13 [b]Lev. 10:3 [1]Lit. *Contention at Kadesh*

52 [a]"Yet you shall see the land before *you*, though you shall not go there, into the land which I am giving to the children of Israel."

33

Now this *is* [a]the blessing with which Moses [b]the man of God blessed the children of Israel before his death.
2 And he said:

[a]"The LORD came from Sinai,
And dawned on them from
[b]Sē'ir;
He shone forth from [c]Mount
Par'an,
And He came with [d]ten
thousands of saints;
From His right hand
Came a fiery law for them.
3 Yes, [a]He loves the people;
[b]All His saints *are* in Your
hand;
They [c]sit down at Your feet;
Everyone [d]receives Your
words.
4 [a]Moses [1]commanded a law
for us,
[b]A heritage of the
congregation of Jacob.
5 And He was [a]King in
[b]Jesh'ū·run,
When the leaders of the
people were gathered,
All the tribes of Israel
together.

6 "Let [a]Reuben live, and not
die,
Nor let his men be few."

7 And this he said of [a]Judah:

"Hear, LORD, the voice of
Judah,
And bring him to his people;
[b]Let his hands be sufficient
for him,
And may You be [c]a help
against his enemies."

8 And of [a]Levi he said:

[b]"*Let* Your [1]Thum'mim and
Your Ū'rim *be* with Your
holy one,
[c]Whom You tested at
Mas'sah,
And with whom You
contended at the waters
of Mer'i·bah,
9 [a]Who says of his father and
mother,
'I have not [b]seen them';
[c]Nor did he acknowledge his
brothers,
Or know his own children;
For [d]they have observed
Your word
And kept Your covenant.
10 [a]They shall teach Jacob Your
judgments,
And Israel Your law.
They shall put incense
before You,
[b]And a whole burnt sacrifice
on Your altar.
11 Bless his substance, LORD,
And [a]accept the work of his
hands;
Strike the loins of those
who rise against him,
And of those who hate
him, that they rise not
again."

12 Of Benjamin he said:

"The beloved of the LORD
shall dwell in safety by
Him,
Who shelters him all the
day long;
And he shall dwell between
His shoulders."

52 [a]Deut. 34:1–5

CHAPTER 33

1 [a]Gen. 49:28 [b]Ps. 90
2 [a]Ps. 68:8, 17 [b]Deut. 2:1, 4 [c]Num. 10:12 [d]Dan. 7:10
3 [a]Hos. 11:1 [b]1 Sam. 2:9 [c][Luke 10:39] [d]Prov. 2:1
4 [a]John 1:17; 7:19 [b]Ps. 119:111 [1]*charged us with*
5 [a]Ex. 15:18 [b]Deut. 32:15
6 [a]Gen. 49:3, 4
7 [a]Gen. 49:8–12 [b]Gen. 49:8 [c]Ps. 146:5
8 [a]Gen. 49:5 [b]Ex. 28:30 [c]Ps. 81:7 [1]Lit. *Perfections and Your Lights*
9 [a][Num. 25:5–8] [b][Gen. 29:32] [c]Ex. 32:26–28 [d]Mal. 2:5, 6
10 [a]Lev. 10:11 [b]Ps. 51:19
11 [a]2 Sam. 24:23

13 And of Joseph he said:

[a]"Blessed of the LORD *is* his
land,
With the precious things of
heaven, with the [b]dew,
And the deep lying beneath,
14 With the precious fruits of
the sun,
With the precious produce
of the months,
15 With the best things of [a]the
ancient mountains,
With the precious things [b]of
the everlasting hills,
16 With the precious things of
the earth and its fullness,
And the favor of [a]Him who
dwelt in the bush.
Let *the blessing* come [b]'on
the head of Joseph,
And on the crown of the
head of him *who was*
separate from his
brothers.'
17 His glory *is like* a [a]firstborn
bull,
And his horns *like* the
[b]horns of the wild ox;
Together with them
[c]He shall push the peoples
To the ends of the earth;
[d]They *are* the ten thousands
of Ē'phra·im,
And they *are* the thousands
of Ma·nas'seh."

18 And of Zeb'ū·lun he said:

[a]"Rejoice, Zeb'ū·lun, in your
going out,
And Is'sa·char in your tents!
19 They shall [a]call the peoples
to the mountain;
There [b]they shall
offer sacrifices of
righteousness;
For they shall partake *of* the
abundance of the seas
And *of* treasures hidden in
the sand."

20 And of Gad he said:

"Blessed *is* he who [a]enlarges
Gad;
He dwells as a lion,
And tears the arm and the
crown of his head.
21 [a]He provided the first *part*
for himself,
Because a lawgiver's portion
was reserved there.
[b]He came *with* the heads of
the people;
He administered the justice
of the LORD,
And His judgments with
Israel."

22 And of Dan he said:

"Dan *is* a lion's whelp;
[a]He shall leap from Bā'shan."

23 And of Naph'ta·lī he said:

"O Naph'ta·lī, [a]satisfied with
favor,
And full of the blessing of
the LORD,
[b]Possess the west and the
south."

24 And of Ash'er he said:

[a]"Ash'er *is* most blessed of
sons;
Let him be favored by his
brothers,
And let him [b]dip his foot in
oil.
25 Your sandals *shall be* [a]iron
and bronze;

13 [a]Gen. 49:22–26 [b]Gen. 27:28
15 [a]Gen. 49:26 [b]Hab. 3:6
16 [a]Ex. 3:2–4 [b]Gen. 49:26
17 [a]1 Chr. 5:1 [b]Num. 23:22 [c]Ps. 44:5 [d]Gen. 48:19
18 [a]Gen. 49:13–15
19 [a]Is. 2:3 [b]Ps. 4:5; 51:19
20 [a]1 Chr. 12:8
21 [a]Num. 32:16, 17 [b]Josh. 4:12
22 [a]Josh. 19:47
23 [a]Gen. 49:21 [b]Josh. 19:32
24 [a]Gen. 49:20 [b]Job 29:6
25 [a]Deut. 8:9

As your days, *so shall* your
strength *be.*

26 "*There is* [a]no one like the
God of [b]Jesh'ū·run,
[c]*Who* rides the heavens to
help you,
And in His excellency on
the clouds.
27 The eternal God *is your*
[a]refuge,
And underneath *are* the
everlasting arms;
[b]He will thrust out the enemy
from before you,
And will say, 'Destroy!'
28 Then [a]Israel shall dwell in
safety,
[b]The fountain of Jacob [c]alone,
In a land of grain and new
wine;
His [d]heavens shall also drop
dew.
29 [a]Happy *are* you, O Israel!
[b]Who *is* like you, a people
saved by the LORD,
[c]The shield of your help
And the sword of your
majesty!
Your enemies [d]shall submit
to you,
And [e]you shall tread down
their [1]high places."

34 Then Moses went up
from the plains of Mō'ab
[a]to Mount Nē'bō, to the top of
Pis'gah, which is across from
Jericho. And the LORD showed
him all the land of Gil'ē·ad as
far as Dan,
2 all Naph'ta·lī and the land of
Ē'phra·im and Ma·nas'seh, all
the land of Judah as far as the
[1]Western Sea,
3 the South, and the plain of

26 [a]Ex. 15:11 [b]Deut. 32:15 [c]Ps. 68:3, 33, 34; 104:3
27 [a][Ps. 90:1; 91:2, 9] [b]Deut. 9:3–5
28 [a]Jer. 23:6; 33:16 [b]Deut. 8:7, 8 [c]Num. 23:9 [d]Gen. 27:28
29 [a]Ps. 144:15 [b]2 Sam. 7:23 [c]Ps. 115:9 [d]Ps. 18:44; 66:3 [e]Num. 33:52 [1]Places for pagan worship

CHAPTER 34

1 [a]Deut. 32:49
2 [1]Mediterranean
3 [a]2 Chr. 28:15
4 [a]Gen. 12:7 [b]Deut. 3:27
5 [a]Deut. 32:50; Josh. 1:1, 2
6 [a]Jude 9
7 [a]Deut. 31:2 [b]Gen. 27:1; 48:10 [1]*eyesight was not weakened* [2]*reduced*
8 [a]Gen. 50:3, 10
9 [a]Is. 11:2 [b]Num. 27:18, 23
10 [a]Deut. 18:15, 18 [b]Ex. 33:11
11 [a]Deut. 7:19

the Valley of Jericho, [a]the city of
palm trees, as far as Zō'ar.
4 Then the LORD said to him,
[a]"This *is* the land of which I
swore to give Abraham, Isaac,
and Jacob, saying, 'I will give
it to your descendants.' [b]I have
caused you to see *it* with your
eyes, but you shall not cross
over there."
5 [a]So Moses the servant of the
LORD died there in the land of
Mō'ab, according to the word of
the LORD.
6 And He buried him in a valley in the land of Mō'ab, opposite Beth Pē'or; but [a]no one
knows his grave to this day.
7 [a]Moses *was* one hundred and
twenty years old when he died.
[b]His [1]eyes were not dim nor his
natural vigor [2]diminished.
8 And the children of Israel
wept for Moses in the plains of
Mō'ab [a]thirty days. So the days
of weeping *and* mourning for
Moses ended.
9 Now Joshua the son of Nun
was full of the [a]spirit of wisdom,
for [b]Moses had laid his hands
on him; so the children of Israel
heeded him, and did as the LORD
had commanded Moses.
10 But since then there [a]has not
arisen in Israel a prophet like
Moses, [b]whom the LORD knew
face to face,
11 in all [a]the signs and wonders
which the LORD sent him to do
in the land of Egypt, before Pharaoh, before all his servants, and
in all his land,
12 and by all that mighty power
and all the great terror which
Moses performed in the sight of
all Israel.

The Book of
JOSHUA

JOSHUA, the first of the twelve historical books (Joshua—Esther), forges a link between the Pentateuch and the remainder of Israel's history. Through three major military campaigns involving more than thirty enemy armies, the people of Israel learn a crucial lesson under Joshua's capable leadership: victory comes through faith in God and obedience to His word, rather than through military might or numerical superiority.

The title of this book is appropriately named after its central figure, Joshua. His original name is *Hoshea*, "Salvation" (Num. 13:8); but Moses evidently changes it to *Yehoshua*, "Yahweh is Salvation" (Num. 13:16). He is also called *Yeshua*, a shortened form of *Yehoshua*. This is the Hebrew equivalent of the Greek name *Iesous* (Jesus). Thus, the Greek title given to the book in the Septuagint is *Iesous Naus*, "Joshua the Son of Nun." The Latin title is *Liber Josue*, the "Book of Joshua."

His name is symbolic of the fact that although he is the leader of the Israelite nation during the conquest, the Lord is the Conqueror.

AFTER the death of Moses the
servant of the LORD, it came
to pass that the LORD spoke to
Joshua the son of Nun, Moses'
[a]assistant, saying:
2 [a]"Moses My servant is dead.
Now therefore, arise, go over
this Jordan, you and all this
people, to the land which I am
giving to them—the children of
Israel.
3 [a]"Every place that the sole of
your foot will tread upon I have
given you, as I said to Moses.
4 [a]"From the wilderness and
this Lebanon as far as the great
river, the River Eū·phrā′tēs, all
the land of the Hit′tītes, and to
the Great Sea toward the going
down of the sun, shall be your
territory.
5 [a]"No man shall *be able to*
stand before you all the days of
your life; [b]as I was with Moses,
so [c]I will be with you. [d]I will not
leave you nor forsake you.
6 [a]"Be strong and of good
courage, for to this people you
shall [1]divide as an inheritance
the land which I swore to their
fathers to give them.
7 "Only be strong and very
courageous, that you may observe to do according to all the
law [a]which Moses My servant
commanded you; [b]do not turn
from it to the right hand or to
the left, that you may [1]prosper
wherever you go.
8 [a]"This Book of the Law shall
not depart from your mouth, but
[b]you[1] shall meditate in it day and
night, that you may observe to
do according to all that is written in it. For then you will make
your way prosperous, and then
you will have good success.
9 [a]"Have I not commanded
you? Be strong and of good courage; [b]do not be afraid, nor be
dismayed, for the LORD your God
is with you wherever you go."

CHAPTER 1

1 [a]Ex. 24:13

2 [a]Deut. 34:5

3 [a]Deut. 11:24

4 [a]Gen. 15:18

5 [a]Deut. 7:24 [b]Ex. 3:12 [c]Deut. 31:8, 23 [d]Deut. 31:6, 7

6 [a]Deut. 31:7, 23 [1]*give as a possession*

7 [a]Deut. 31:7 [b]Deut. 5:32 [1]*have success* or *act wisely*

8 [a]Josh. 8:34 [b]Ps. 1:1–3 [1]*you shall be constantly in*

9 [a]Deut. 31:7 [b]Ps. 27:1

10 Then Joshua commanded the
officers of the people, saying,
11 "Pass through the camp and
command the people, saying,
'Prepare provisions for yourselves, for [a]within three days
you will cross over this Jordan,
to go in to possess the land
which the LORD your God is giving you to possess.' "
12 And to the Reū′ben·ītes, the
Gad′ītes, and half the tribe of
Ma·nas′seh Joshua spoke, saying,
13 "Remember [a]the word which
Moses the servant of the LORD
commanded you, saying, 'The
LORD your God is giving you rest
and is giving you this land.'
14 "Your wives, your little ones,
and your livestock shall remain
in the land which Moses gave
you on this side of the Jordan.
But you shall [1]pass before your
brethren armed, all your mighty
men of valor, and help them,
15 "until the LORD has given
your brethren rest, as He *gave*
you, and they also have taken
possession of the land which
the LORD your God is giving
them. [a]Then you shall return to
the land of your possession and
enjoy it, which Moses the LORD's
servant gave you on this side of
the Jordan toward the sunrise."
16 So they answered Joshua,
saying, "All that you command
us we will do, and wherever you
send us we will go.
17 "Just as we heeded Moses in
all things, so we will heed you.
Only the LORD your God [a]be with
you, as He was with Moses.
18 "Whoever rebels against
your command and does not
heed your words, in all that you
command him, shall be put to
death. Only be strong and of
good courage."

2

Now Joshua the son of Nun
sent out two men [a]from
[1]Acacia Grove to spy secretly,
saying, "Go, view the land, especially Jericho." So they went,
and [b]came to the house of a harlot named [c]Rā′hab, and [2]lodged
there.
2 And [a]it was told the king of
Jericho, saying, "Behold, men
have come here tonight from the
children of Israel to search out
the country."
3 So the king of Jericho sent
to Rā′hab, saying, "Bring out the
men who have come to you, who
have entered your house, for
they have come to search out all
the country."
4 [a]Then the woman took the
two men and hid them. So she
said, "Yes, the men came to me,
but I did not know where they
were from.
5 "And it happened as the gate
was being shut, when it was
dark, that the men went out.
Where the men went I do not
know; pursue them quickly, for
you may overtake them."
6 (But [a]she had brought them
up to the roof and hidden them
with the stalks of flax, which she
had laid in order on the roof.)
7 Then the men pursued them
by the road to the Jordan, to the
fords. And as soon as those who
pursued them had gone out, they
shut the gate.
8 Now before they lay down,
she came up to them on the roof,
9 and said to the men: [a]"I know
that the LORD has given you
the land, that [b]the terror of you
has fallen on us, and that all

11 [a]Deut. 9:1
13 [a]Num. 32:20–28
14 [1]*cross over ahead of*
15 [a]Josh. 22:1–4
17 [a]1 Sam. 20:13

CHAPTER 2

1 [a]Num. 25:1 [b]James 2:25 [c]Matt. 1:5 [1]Heb. *Shittim* [2]Lit. *lay down*
2 [a]Josh. 2:22
4 [a]2 Sam. 17:19, 20
6 [a]Ex. 1:17
9 [a]Deut. 1:8 [b]Deut. 2:25; 11:25

the inhabitants of the land [c]are
fainthearted because of you.
10 "For we have heard how
the LORD [a]dried up the water of
the Red Sea for you when you
came out of Egypt, and [b]what
you did to the two kings of
the Am′o·rītes who *were* on the
other side of the Jordan, Sī′-
hon and Og, whom you [c]utterly
destroyed.
11 "And as soon as we [a]heard
these things, [b]our hearts melted;
neither did there remain any
more courage in anyone because of you, for [c]the LORD your
God, He *is* God in heaven above
and on earth beneath.
12 "Now therefore, I beg you,
[a]swear to me by the LORD, since
I have shown you kindness, that
you also will show kindness to
[b]my father's house, and [c]give me
[1]a true token,
13 "and [a]spare my father, my
mother, my brothers, my sisters,
and all that they have, and deliver our lives from death."
14 So the men answered her,
"Our lives for yours, if none of
you tell this business of ours. And
it shall be, when the LORD has
given us the land, that [a]we will
deal kindly and truly with you."
15 Then she [a]let them down by
a rope through the window, for
her house *was* on the city wall;
she dwelt on the wall.
16 And she said to them, "Get
to the mountain, lest the pursuers meet you. Hide there three
days, until the pursuers have
returned. Afterward you may go
your way."
17 So the men said to her: "We
will be [a]blameless[1] of this oath
of yours which you have made
us swear,
18 [a]"unless, *when* we come
into the land, you bind this line
of scarlet cord in the window
through which you let us down,
[b]and unless you [1]bring your father, your mother, your brothers,
and all your father's household
to your own home.
19 "So it shall be *that* whoever
goes outside the doors of your
house into the street, his blood
shall be on his own head, and
we *will be* [1]guiltless. And whoever is with you in the house,
[a]his [2]blood *shall be* on our head
if a hand is laid on him.
20 "And if you tell this business
of ours, then we will be [1]free
from your oath which you made
us swear."
21 Then she said, "According
to your words, so *be* it." And
she sent them away, and they
departed. And she bound the
scarlet cord in the window.
22 They departed and went to
the mountain, and stayed there
three days until the pursuers
returned. The pursuers sought
them all along the way, but did
not find *them*.
23 So the two men returned, descended from the mountain, and
crossed over; and they came to
Joshua the son of Nun, and told
him all that had befallen them.
24 And they said to Joshua,
"Truly [a]the LORD has delivered
all the land into our hands, for
indeed all the inhabitants of the
country are fainthearted because of us."

3

3 Then Joshua rose early in
the morning; and they set
out [a]from [1]Acacia Grove and
came to the Jordan, he and all
the children of Israel, and lodged
there before they crossed over.

9 [c]Josh. 5:1
10 [a]Ex. 14:21 [b]Num. 21:21–35 [c]Josh. 6:21
11 [a]Ex. 15:14, 15 [b]Josh. 5:1; 7:5 [c]Deut. 4:39
12 [a]1 Sam. 20:14, 15, 17 [b]1 Tim. 5:8 [c]Josh. 2:18 [1]*a pledge of truth*
13 [a]Josh. 6:23–25
14 [a]Judg. 1:24
15 [a]Acts 9:25
17 [a]Ex. 20:7 [1]*free from obligation to this oath*
18 [a]Josh. 2:12 [b]Josh. 6:23 [1]Lit. *gather*
19 [a]1 Kin. 2:32 [1]*free from obligation* [2]*guilt of bloodshed*
20 [1]*free from obligation to*
24 [a]Ex. 23:31
CHAPTER 3
1 [a]Josh. 2:1 [1]Heb. *Shittim*

2 So it was, [a]after three days,
that the officers went through
the camp;
3 and they commanded the
people, saying, [a]"When you see
the ark of the covenant of the
LORD your God, [b]and the priests,
the Lē′vītes, [1]bearing it, then you
shall set out from your place
and go after it.
4 [a]"Yet there shall be a space
between you and it, about two
thousand cubits by measure. Do
not come near it, that you may
know the way by which you
must go, for you have not passed
this way before."
5 And Joshua said to the people, [a]"Sanctify[1] yourselves, for
tomorrow the LORD will do wonders among you."
6 Then Joshua spoke to the
priests, saying, [a]"Take up the ark
of the covenant and cross over
before the people." So they took
up the ark of the covenant and
went before the people.
7 And the LORD said to Joshua,
"This day I will begin to [a]exalt[1]
you in the sight of all Israel, that
they may know that, [b]as I was
with Moses, *so* I will be with you.
8 "You shall command [a]the
priests who bear the ark of the
covenant, saying, 'When you
have come to the edge of the
water of the Jordan, [b]you shall
stand in the Jordan.' "
9 So Joshua said to the children of Israel, "Come here, and
hear the words of the LORD your
God."
10 And Joshua said, "By this
you shall know that [a]the living
God *is* among you, and *that* He
will without fail [b]drive out from
before you the [c]Cā′naan·ītes and
the Hit′tītes and the Hī′vītes and
the Per′iz·zītes and the Gir′-
ga·shītes and the Am′o·rītes and
the Jeb′ū·sītes:
11 "Behold, the ark of the covenant of [a]the Lord of all the earth
is crossing over before you into
the Jordan.
12 "Now therefore, [a]take for
yourselves twelve men from the
tribes of Israel, one man from
every tribe.
13 "And it shall come to pass,
[a]as soon as the soles of the feet
of the priests who bear the ark
of the LORD, [b]the Lord of all the
earth, shall rest in the waters of
the Jordan, *that* the waters of
the Jordan shall be cut off, the
waters that come down from
upstream, and they [c]shall stand
as a heap."
14 So it was, when the people
set out from their camp to cross
over the Jordan, with the priests
bearing the [a]ark of the covenant
before the people,
15 and as those who bore the
ark came to the Jordan, and
[a]the feet of the priests who bore
the ark dipped in the edge of the
water (for the [b]Jordan overflows
all its banks [c]during the whole
time of harvest),
16 that the waters which came
down from upstream stood *still,*
and rose in a heap very far away
[1]at Adam, the city that *is* beside
[a]Zar′e·tan. So the waters that
went down [b]into the Sea of the
Ar′a·bah, [c]the Salt Sea, failed,
and were cut off; and the people
crossed over opposite Jericho.
17 Then the priests who bore
the ark of the covenant of the
LORD stood firm on dry ground
in the midst of the Jordan; [a]and
all Israel crossed over on dry
ground, until all the people had

2 [a]Josh. 1:10, 11
3 [a]Num. 10:33 [b]Deut. 31:9, 25 [1]*carrying*
4 [a]Ex. 19:12
5 [a]Josh. 7:13 [1]*Consecrate*
6 [a]Num. 4:15
7 [a]Josh. 4:14 [b]Josh. 1:5, 9 [1]*make you great*
8 [a]Josh. 3:3 [b]Josh. 3:17
10 [a]1 Thess. 1:9 [b]Ex. 33:2 [c]Acts 13:19
11 [a]Zech. 4:14; 6:5
12 [a]Josh. 4:2, 4
13 [a]Josh. 3:15, 16 [b]Josh. 3:11 [c]Ps. 78:13; 114:3
14 [a]Acts 7:44, 45
15 [a]Josh. 3:13 [b]1 Chr. 12:15 [c]Josh. 4:18; 5:10, 12
16 [a]1 Kin. 4:12; 7:46 [b]Deut. 3:17 [c]Gen. 14:3 [1]Qr., many mss. and vss., *from Adam*
17 [a]Ex. 3:8; 6:1–8; 14:21, 22, 29; 33:1

crossed completely over the
Jordan.

4 And it came to pass, when
all the people had com-
pletely crossed [a]over the Jordan,
that the LORD spoke to Joshua,
saying:
2 [a]"Take for yourselves twelve
men from the people, one man
from every tribe,
3 "and command them, say-
ing, 'Take for yourselves twelve
stones from here, out of the
midst of the Jordan, from the
place where [a]the priests' feet
stood firm. You shall carry them
over with you and leave them
in [b]the lodging place where you
lodge tonight.' "
4 Then Joshua called the
twelve men whom he had appointed from the children of Israel, one man from every tribe;
5 and Joshua said to them:
"Cross over before the ark of the
LORD your God into the midst of
the Jordan, and each one of you
take up a stone on his shoulder,
according to the number of the
tribes of the children of Israel,
6 "that this may be [a]a sign
among you [b]when your children
ask in time to come, saying,
'What do these stones *mean* to
you?'
7 "Then you shall answer them
that [a]the waters of the Jordan
were cut off before the ark of
the covenant of the LORD; when
it crossed over the Jordan, the
waters of the Jordan were cut
off. And these stones shall be
for [b]a memorial to the children
of Israel forever."
8 And the children of Israel did
so, just as Joshua commanded,
and took up twelve stones from
the midst of the Jordan, as the
LORD had spoken to Joshua, according to the number of the
tribes of the children of Israel,
and carried them over with them
to the place where they lodged,
and laid them down there.
9 Then Joshua set up twelve
stones in the midst of the Jordan, in the place where the feet
of the priests who bore the ark
of the covenant stood; and they
are there to this day.
10 So the priests who bore the
ark stood in the midst of the
Jordan until everything was finished that the LORD had commanded Joshua to speak to the
people, according to all that Moses had commanded Joshua; and
the people hurried and crossed
over.
11 Then it came to pass, when
all the people had completely
crossed over, that the [a]ark of the
LORD and the priests crossed over
in the presence of the people.
12 And [a]the men of Reuben, the
men of Gad, and half the tribe of
Ma·nas'seh crossed over armed
before the children of Israel, as
Moses had spoken to them.
13 About forty thousand [1]pre-
pared for war crossed over before the LORD for battle, to the
plains of Jericho.
14 On that day the LORD [a]exalted[1]
Joshua in the sight of all Israel;
and they feared him, as they had
feared Moses, all the days of his
life.
15 Then the LORD spoke to
Joshua, saying,
16 "Command the priests who
bear [a]the ark of the Testimony to
come up from the Jordan."
17 Joshua therefore commanded
the priests, saying, "Come up
from the Jordan."

CHAPTER 4

1 [a]Deut. 27:2

2 [a]Josh. 3:12

3 [a]Josh. 3:13
[b]Josh. 4:19, 20

6 [a]Deut. 27:2
[b]Deut. 6:20

7 [a]Josh. 3:13, 16
[b]Num. 16:40

11 [a]Josh. 3:11; 6:11

12 [a]Num. 32:17, 20, 27, 28

13 [1]*equipped*

14 [a]Josh. 3:7
[1]*made Joshua great*

16 [a]Ex. 25:16, 22

18 And it came to pass, when
the priests who bore the ark of
the covenant of the LORD had
come from the midst of the Jordan, *and* the soles of the priests'
feet touched the dry land, that
the waters of the Jordan returned to their place [a]and overflowed all its banks as before.
19 Now the people came up
from the Jordan on the tenth
day of the first month, and they
camped [a]in Gil'gal on the east
border of Jericho.
20 And [a]those twelve stones
which they took out of the Jordan, Joshua set up in Gil'gal.
21 Then he spoke to the children of Israel, saying: [a]"When
your children ask their fathers
in time to come, saying, 'What
are these stones?'
22 "then you shall let your
children know, saying, [a]'Israel
crossed over this Jordan on [b]dry
land';
23 "for the LORD your God dried
up the waters of the Jordan before you until you had crossed
over, as the LORD your God did to
the Red Sea, [a]which He dried up
before us until we had crossed
over,
24 [a]"that all the peoples of the
earth may know the hand of the
LORD, that it *is* [b]mighty, that you
may [c]fear the LORD your God
[1]forever."

5

So it was, when all the kings
of the Am'o·rītes who *were*
on the west side of the Jordan,
and all the kings of the Cā'-
naan·ītes [a]who *were* by the sea,
[b]heard that the LORD had dried
up the waters of the Jordan from
before the children of Israel until [1]we had crossed over, that
[2]their heart melted; [c]and there
was no spirit in them any longer
because of the children of Israel.
2 At that time the LORD said
to Joshua, "Make [a]flint knives
for yourself, and circumcise the
sons of Israel again the second
time."
3 So Joshua made flint knives
for himself, and circumcised the
sons of Israel at [1]the hill of the
foreskins.
4 And this *is* the reason why
Joshua circumcised them: [a]All
the people who came out of
Egypt *who were* males, all the
men of war, had died in the wilderness on the way, after they
had come out of Egypt.
5 For all the people who came
out had been circumcised, but
all the people born in the wilderness, on the way as they
came out of Egypt, had not been
circumcised.
6 For the children of Israel
walked [a]forty years in the wilderness, till all the people *who
were* men of war, who came
out of Egypt, were [1]consumed,
because they did not obey the
voice of the LORD—to whom the
LORD swore that [b]He would not
show them the land which the
LORD had sworn to their fathers
that He would give us, [c]"a land
flowing with milk and honey."
7 Then Joshua circumcised
[a]their sons *whom* He raised up
in their place; for they were
uncircumcised, because they
had not been circumcised on the
way.
8 So it was, when they had finished circumcising all the people,
that they stayed in their places in
the camp [a]till they were healed.
9 Then the LORD said to Joshua,

18 [a]Josh. 3:15
19 [a]Josh. 5:9
20 [a]Josh. 4:3; 5:9, 10
21 [a]Josh. 4:6
22 [a]Deut. 26:5–9 [b]Josh. 3:17
23 [a]Ex. 14:21
24 [a]1 Kin. 8:42 [b]1 Chr. 29:12 [c]Jer. 10:7 [1]Lit. *all days*

CHAPTER 5

1 [a]Num. 13:29 [b]Ex. 15:14, 15 [c]Josh. 2:10, 11; 9:9 [1]So with Kt.; Qr., some Heb. mss. and editions, LXX, Syr., Tg., Vg. *they* [2]*their courage failed*
2 [a]Ex. 4:25
3 [1]Heb. *Gibeath Haaraloth*
4 [a]Deut. 2:14–16
6 [a]Num. 14:33 [b]Heb. 3:11 [c]Ex. 3:8 [1]*destroyed*
7 [a]Deut. 1:39
8 [a]Gen. 34:25

"This day I have rolled away [a]the
reproach of Egypt from you."
Therefore the name of the place
is called [b]Gil′gal[1] to this day.
10 Now the children of Israel
camped in Gil′gal, and kept the
Passover [a]on the fourteenth day
of the month at twilight on the
plains of Jericho.
11 And they ate of the produce
of the land on the day after the
Passover, unleavened bread and
[1]parched grain, on the very same
day.
12 Then [a]the manna ceased on
the day after they had eaten the
produce of the land; and the
children of Israel no longer had
manna, but they ate the food of
the land of Cā′naan that year.
13 And it came to pass, when
Joshua was by Jericho, that he
lifted his eyes and looked, and
behold, [a]a Man stood opposite
him [b]with His sword drawn in
His hand. And Joshua went to
Him and said to Him, "*Are* You
for us or for our adversaries?"
14 So He said, "No, but *as* Commander of the army of the LORD
I have now come." And Joshua
[a]fell on his face to the earth and
[b]worshiped, and said to Him,
"What does my Lord say to His
servant?"
15 Then the Commander of
the LORD's army said to Joshua,
[a]"Take your sandal off your foot,
for the place where you stand *is*
holy." And Joshua did so.

6

Now [a]Jericho was securely
shut up because of the children of Israel; none went out,
and none came in.
2 And the LORD said to Joshua:
"See! [a]I have given Jericho into
your hand, its [b]king, *and* the
mighty men of valor.
3 "You shall march around the
city, all *you* men of war; you
shall go all around the city once.
This you shall do six days.
4 "And seven priests shall bear
seven [a]trumpets of rams' horns
before the ark. But the seventh
day you shall march around
the city [b]seven times, and [c]the
priests shall blow the trumpets.
5 "It shall come to pass, when
they make a long *blast* with the
ram's horn, *and* when you hear
the sound of the trumpet, that
all the people shall shout with a
great shout; then the wall of the
city will fall down flat. And the
people shall go up every man
straight before him."
6 Then Joshua the son of Nun
called the priests and said to
them, "Take up the ark of the covenant, and let seven priests bear
seven trumpets of rams' horns
before the ark of the LORD."
7 And he said to the people,
"Proceed, and march around the
city, and let him who is armed
advance before the ark of the
LORD."
8 So it was, when Joshua had
spoken to the people, that the
seven priests bearing the seven
trumpets of rams' horns before
the LORD advanced and blew
the trumpets, and the ark of the
covenant of the LORD followed
them.
9 The armed men went be-
fore the priests who blew the
trumpets, [a]and the rear guard
came after the ark, while *the
priests* continued blowing the
trumpets.
10 Now Joshua had commanded
the people, saying, "You shall
not shout or make any noise
with your voice, nor shall a word

9 [a]Gen. 34:14 [b]Josh. 4:19 [1]Lit. *Rolling*
10 [a]Ex. 12:6
11 [1]*roasted*
12 [a]Ex. 16:35
13 [a]Gen. 18:1, 2; 32:24, 30 [b]Num. 22:23
14 [a]Gen. 17:3 [b]Ex. 34:8
15 [a]Ex. 3:5
CHAPTER 6
1 [a]Josh. 2:1
2 [a]Josh. 2:9, 24; 8:1 [b]Deut. 7:24
4 [a]Lev. 25:9 [b]1 Kin. 18:43 [c]Num. 10:8
9 [a]Num. 10:25

proceed out of your mouth, until the day I say to you, 'Shout!' Then you shall shout."

11 So he had [a]the ark of the LORD circle the city, going around *it* once. Then they came into the camp and [1]lodged in the camp.

12 And Joshua rose early in the morning, [a]and the priests took up the ark of the LORD.

13 Then seven priests bearing seven trumpets of rams' horns before the ark of the LORD went on continually and blew with the trumpets. And the armed men went before them. But the rear guard came after the ark of the LORD, while *the priests* continued blowing the trumpets.

14 And the second day they marched around the city once and returned to the camp. So they did six days.

15 But it came to pass on the seventh day that they rose early, about the dawning of the day, and marched around the city seven times in the same manner. On that day only they marched around the city seven times.

16 And the seventh time it happened, when the priests blew the trumpets, that Joshua said to the people: "Shout, for the LORD has given you the city!

17 "Now the city shall be [a]doomed by the LORD to destruction, it and all who *are* in it. Only [b]Rā'hab the harlot shall live, she and all who *are* with her in the house, because [c]she hid the messengers that we sent.

18 "And you, [a]by all means abstain from the accursed things, lest you become accursed when you take of the accursed things, and make the camp of Israel a curse, [b]and trouble it.

19 "But all the silver and gold, and vessels of bronze and iron, *are* [1]consecrated to the LORD; they [2]shall come into the treasury of the LORD."

20 So the people shouted when *the priests* blew the trumpets. And it happened when the people heard the sound of the trumpet, and the people shouted with a great shout, that [a]the wall fell down flat. Then the people went up into the city, every man straight before him, and they took the city.

21 And they [a]utterly destroyed all that *was* in the city, both man and woman, young and old, ox and sheep and donkey, with the edge of the sword.

22 But Joshua had said to the two men who had spied out the country, "Go into the harlot's house, and from there bring out the woman and all that she has, [a]as you swore to her."

23 And the young men who had been spies went in and brought out Rā'hab, [a]her father, her mother, her brothers, and all that she had. So they brought out all her relatives and left them outside the camp of Israel.

24 But they burned the city and all that *was* in it with fire. Only the silver and gold, and the vessels of bronze and iron, they put into the treasury of the house of the LORD.

25 And Joshua spared Rā'hab the harlot, her father's household, and all that she had. So [a]she dwells in Israel to this day, because she hid the messengers whom Joshua sent to spy out Jericho.

26 Then Joshua [1]charged *them* at that time, saying, [a]"Cursed *be*

11 [a]Josh. 4:11 [1]*spent the night*
12 [a]Deut. 31:25
17 [a]Deut. 13:17 [b]Matt. 1:5 [c]Josh. 2:4, 6
18 [a]Deut. 7:26 [b]Josh. 7:1, 12, 25
19 [1]*set apart* [2]*shall go*
20 [a]Heb. 11:30
21 [a]Deut. 7:2; 20:16, 17
22 [a]Josh. 2:12–19
23 [a]Josh. 2:13
25 [a][Matt. 1:5]
26 [a]1 Kin. 16:34 [1]*warned*

the man before the LORD who
rises up and builds this city
Jericho; he shall lay its foundation with his firstborn, and with
his youngest he shall set up its
gates."
27 So the LORD was with Joshua,
and his fame spread throughout
all the country.

7 But the children of Israel
[1]committed a [a]trespass regarding the [b]accursed[2] things,
for [c]Ā′chan the son of Car′mī,
the son of [3]Zab′dī, the son of Zē′-
rah, of the tribe of Judah, took of
the accursed things; so the anger of the LORD burned against
the children of Israel.
2 Now Joshua sent men from
Jericho to Aī, which *is* beside
Beth Ā′ven, on the east side
of Beth′el, and spoke to them,
saying, "Go up and spy out the
country." So the men went up
and spied out Aī.
3 And they returned to Joshua
and said to him, "Do not let all
the people go up, but let about
two or three thousand men go
up and attack Aī. Do not weary
all the people there, for *the people of Aī are* few."
4 So about three thousand
men went up there from the
people, [a]but they fled before the
men of Aī.
5 And the men of Aī struck
down about thirty-six men, for
they chased them *from* before
the gate as far as Sheb′a·rim,
and struck them down on the
descent; therefore [a]the[1] hearts of
the people melted and became
like water.
6 Then Joshua [a]tore his clothes,
and fell to the earth on his face
before the ark of the LORD until
evening, he and the elders of
Israel; and they [b]put dust on
their heads.
7 And Joshua said, "Alas, Lord
[1]GOD, [a]why have You brought
this people over the Jordan at
all—to deliver us into the hand
of the Am′o·rītes, to destroy us?
Oh, that we had been content,
and dwelt on the other side of
the Jordan!
8 "O Lord, what shall I say
when Israel turns its [1]back before its enemies?
9 "For the Cā′naan·ītes and all
the inhabitants of the land will
hear *it,* and surround us, and
[a]cut off our name from the earth.
Then [b]what will You do for Your
great name?"
10 So the LORD said to Joshua:
"Get up! Why do you lie thus on
your face?
11 "Israel has sinned, and they
have also transgressed My covenant which I commanded them.
[a]For they have even taken some
of the [1]accursed things, and
have both stolen and [b]deceived;
and they have also put *it* among
their own stuff.
12 [a]"Therefore the children of
Israel could not stand before
their enemies, *but* turned *their*
backs before their enemies,
because [b]they have become
doomed to destruction. Neither
will I be with you anymore, unless you destroy the accursed
from among you.
13 "Get up, [a]sanctify[1] the people,
and say, [b]'Sanctify yourselves
for tomorrow, because thus says
the LORD God of Israel: "*There is*
an accursed thing in your midst,
O Israel; you cannot stand before your enemies until you take
away the accursed thing from
among you."

CHAPTER 7

1 [a]Josh. 7:20, 21 [b]Josh. 6:17–19 [c]Josh. 22:20 [1]*acted unfaithfully* [2]*devoted* [3]*Zimri,* 1 Chr. 2:6

4 [a]Lev. 26:17

5 [a]Lev. 26:36 [1]*the people's courage failed*

6 [a]Gen. 37:29, 34 [b]1 Sam. 4:12

7 [a]Ex. 17:3 [1]Heb. *YHWH,* LORD

8 [1]Lit. *neck*

9 [a]Deut. 32:26 [b]Ex. 32:12

11 [a]Josh. 6:17–19 [b]Acts 5:1, 2 [1]*devoted*

12 [a]Judg. 2:14 [b][Hag. 2:13, 14]

13 [a]Ex. 19:10 [b]Josh. 3:5 [1]*set apart*

14 'In the morning therefore you shall be brought according to your tribes. And it shall be *that* the tribe which [a]the LORD takes shall come according to families; and the family which the LORD takes shall come by households; and the household which the LORD takes shall come man by man.

15 [a]'Then it shall be *that* he who is taken with the accursed thing shall be burned with fire, he and all that he has, because he has [b]transgressed[1] the covenant of the LORD, and because he [c]has done a disgraceful thing in Israel.' "

16 So Joshua rose early in the morning and brought Israel by their tribes, and the tribe of Judah was taken.

17 He brought the clan of Judah, and he took the family of the Zar'hītes; and he brought the family of the Zar'hītes man by man, and Zab'dī was taken.

18 Then he brought his household man by man, and Ā'chan the son of Car'mī, the son of Zab'dī, the son of Zē'rah, of the tribe of Judah, [a]was taken.

19 Now Joshua said to Ā'chan, "My son, I beg you, [a]give glory to the LORD God of Israel, [b]and make confession to Him, and [c]tell me now what you have done; do not hide *it* from me."

20 And Ā'chan answered Joshua and said, "Indeed [a]I have sinned against the LORD God of Israel, and this is what I have done:

21 "When I saw among the spoils a beautiful Babylonian garment, two hundred shekels of silver, and a wedge of gold weighing fifty shekels, I [1]coveted them and took them. And there they are, hidden in the earth in the midst of my tent, with the silver under it."

22 So Joshua sent messengers, and they ran to the tent; and there it was, hidden in his tent, with the silver under it.

23 And they took them from the midst of the tent, brought them to Joshua and to all the children of Israel, and laid them out before the LORD.

24 Then Joshua, and all Israel with him, took Ā'chan the son of Zē'rah, the silver, the garment, the wedge of gold, his sons, his daughters, his oxen, his donkeys, his sheep, his tent, and [a]all that he had, and they brought them to [b]the Valley of Ā'chor.

25 And Joshua said, [a]"Why have you troubled us? The LORD will trouble you this day." [b]So all Israel stoned him with stones; and they burned them with fire after they had stoned them with stones.

26 Then they [a]raised over him a great heap of stones, still there to this day. So [b]the LORD turned from the fierceness of His anger. Therefore the name of that place has been called [c]the Valley of [1]Ā'chor to this day.

8

Now the LORD said to Joshua: [a]"Do not be afraid, nor be dismayed; take all the people of war with you, and arise, go up to Aī. See, [b]I have given into your hand the king of Aī, his people, his city, and his land.

2 "And you shall do to Aī and its king as you did to [a]Jericho and its king. Only [b]its spoil and its cattle you shall take as booty for yourselves. Lay an ambush for the city behind it."

3 So Joshua arose, and all the

14 [a][Prov. 16:33]

15 [a]1 Sam. 14:38, 39 [b]Josh. 7:11 [c]Gen. 34:7 [1]*overstepped*

18 [a]1 Sam. 14:42

19 [a]Jer. 13:16 [b]Num. 5:6, 7 [c]1 Sam. 14:43

20 [a]Num. 22:34

21 [1]*desired*

24 [a]Num. 16:32, 33 [b]Josh. 7:26; 15:7

25 [a]Josh. 6:18 [b]Deut. 17:5

26 [a]2 Sam. 18:17 [b]Deut. 13:17 [c]Is. 65:10 [1]Lit. *Trouble*

CHAPTER 8

1 [a]Josh. 1:9; 10:8 [b]Josh. 6:2

2 [a]Josh. 6:21 [b]Deut. 20:14

people of war, to go up against
Aī; and Joshua chose thirty
thousand mighty men of valor
and sent them away by night.
4 And he commanded them,
saying: "Behold, [a]you shall lie in
ambush against the city, behind
the city. Do not go very far from
the city, but all of you be ready.
5 "Then I and all the people
who *are* with me will approach
the city; and it will come about,
when they come out against us
as at the first, that [a]we shall flee
before them.
6 "For they will come out after
us till we have drawn them from
the city, for they will say, '*They
are* fleeing before us as at the
first.' Therefore we will flee before them.
7 "Then you shall rise from the
ambush and seize the city, for
the LORD your God will deliver it
into your hand.
8 "And it will be, when you
have taken the city, *that* you
shall set the city on fire. According to the commandment of the
LORD you shall do. [a]See, I have
commanded you."
9 Joshua therefore sent them
out; and they went to lie in
ambush, and stayed between
Beth′el and Aī, on the west side
of Aī; but Joshua lodged that
night among the people.
10 Then Joshua rose up early
in the morning and mustered
the people, and went up, he and
the elders of Israel, before the
people to Aī.
11 [a]And all the people of war
who *were* with him went up and
drew near; and they came before the city and camped on the
north side of Aī. Now a valley
lay between them and Aī.

4 [a]Judg. 20:29
5 [a]Judg. 20:32
8 [a]2 Sam. 13:28
11 [a]Josh. 8:5
12 [1]Ai
14 [a]Judg. 20:34
15 [a]Judg. 20:36

12 So he took about five thousand men and set them in ambush between Beth′el and Aī, on
the west side of [1]the city.
13 And when they had set the
people, all the army that *was* on
the north of the city, and its rear
guard on the west of the city,
Joshua went that night into the
midst of the valley.
14 Now it happened, when the
king of Aī saw *it,* that the men of
the city hurried and rose early
and went out against Israel to
battle, he and all his people, at
an appointed place before the
plain. But he [a]did not know that
there was an ambush against
him behind the city.
15 And Joshua and all Israel
[a]made as if they were beaten
before them, and fled by the way
of the wilderness.
16 So all the people who *were*
in Aī were called together to
pursue them. And they pursued
Joshua and were drawn away
from the city.
17 There was not a man left in
Aī or Beth′el who did not go out
after Israel. So they left the city
open and pursued Israel.
18 Then the LORD said to Joshua,
"Stretch out the spear that *is* in
your hand toward Aī, for I will
give it into your hand." And
Joshua stretched out the spear
that *was* in his hand toward the
city.
19 So *those in* ambush arose
quickly out of their place; they
ran as soon as he had stretched
out his hand, and they entered
the city and took it, and hurried
to set the city on fire.
20 And when the men of Aī
looked behind them, they saw,
and behold, the smoke of the

city ascended to heaven. So they had no power to flee this way or that way, and the people who had fled to the wilderness turned back on the pursuers.

21 Now when Joshua and all Israel saw that the ambush had taken the city and that the smoke of the city ascended, they turned back and struck down the men of Aī.

22 Then the others came out of the city against them; so they were *caught* in the midst of Israel, some on this side and some on that side. And they struck them down, so that they [a]let none of them remain or escape.

23 But the king of Aī they took alive, and brought him to Joshua.

24 And it came to pass when Israel had made an end of slaying all the inhabitants of Aī in the field, in the wilderness where they pursued them, and when they all had fallen by the edge of the sword until they were consumed, that all the Israelites returned to Aī and struck it with the edge of the sword.

25 So it was *that* all who fell that day, both men and women, *were* twelve thousand—all the people of Aī.

26 For Joshua did not draw back his hand, with which he stretched out the spear, until he had [a]utterly destroyed all the inhabitants of Aī.

27 [a]Only the livestock and the spoil of that city Israel took as booty for themselves, according to the word of the LORD which He had [b]commanded Joshua.

28 So Joshua burned Aī and made it [a]a heap forever, a desolation to this day.

29 [a]And the king of Aī he hanged on a tree until evening. [b]And as soon as the sun was down, Joshua commanded that they should take his corpse down from the tree, cast it at the entrance of the gate of the city, and [c]raise over it a great heap of stones *that remains* to this day.

30 Now Joshua built an altar to the LORD God of Israel [a]in Mount Ē'bal,

31 as Moses the servant of the LORD had commanded the children of Israel, as it is written in the Book of the Law of Moses: [a]"an altar of whole stones over which no man has wielded an iron *tool*." And [b]they offered on it burnt offerings to the LORD, and sacrificed peace offerings.

32 And there, in the presence of the children of Israel, [a]he wrote on the stones a copy of the law of Moses, which he had written.

33 Then all Israel, with their elders and officers and judges, stood on either side of the ark before the priests, the Lē'vītes, [a]who bore the ark of the covenant of the LORD, [b]the stranger as well as he who was born among them. Half of them *were* in front of Mount Ger'i·zim and half of them in front of Mount Ē'bal, [c]as Moses the servant of the LORD had commanded before, that they should bless the people of Israel.

34 And afterward [a]he read all the words of the law, [b]the blessings and the cursings, according to all that is written in the [c]Book of the Law.

35 There was not a word of all that Moses had commanded which Joshua did not read before all the assembly of Israel,

22 [a]Deut. 7:2
26 [a]Josh. 6:21
27 [a]Num. 31:22, 26 [b]Josh. 8:2
28 [a]Deut. 13:16
29 [a]Josh. 10:26 [b]Deut. 21:22, 23 [c]Josh. 7:26; 10:27
30 [a]Deut. 27:4–8
31 [a]Ex. 20:25 [b]Ex. 20:24
32 [a]Deut. 27:2, 3, 8
33 [a]Deut. 31:9, 25 [b]Deut. 31:12 [c]Deut. 11:29; 27:12
34 [a]Neh. 8:3 [b]Deut. 28:2, 15, 45; 29:20, 21; 30:19 [c]Josh. 1:8

[a]with the women, the little ones, [b]and the strangers who were living among them.

9

And it came to pass when [a]all the kings who *were* on this side of the Jordan, in the hills and in the lowland and in all the coasts of [b]the Great Sea toward Lebanon—[c]the Hit′tīte, the Am′o·rīte, the Cā′naan·īte, the Per′iz·zīte, the Hī′vīte, and the Jeb′ū·sīte—heard *about it,*

2 that they [a]gathered together to fight with Joshua and Israel with one [1]accord.

3 But when the inhabitants of [a]Gib′ē·on [b]heard what Joshua had done to Jericho and Aī,

4 they worked craftily, and went and [1]pretended to be ambassadors. And they took old sacks on their donkeys, old wineskins torn and [2]mended,

5 old and patched sandals on their feet, and old garments on themselves; and all the bread of their provision was dry *and* moldy.

6 And they went to Joshua, [a]to the camp at Gil′gal, and said to him and to the men of Israel, "We have come from a far country; now therefore, make a [1]covenant with us."

7 Then the men of Israel said to the [a]Hī′vītes, "Perhaps you dwell among us; so [b]how can we make a covenant with you?"

8 But they said to Joshua, [a]"We *are* your servants." And Joshua said to them, "Who *are* you, and where do you come from?"

9 So they said to him: [a]"From a very far country your servants have come, because of the name of the LORD your God; for we have [b]heard of His fame, and all that He did in Egypt,

10 "and [a]all that He did to the two kings of the Am′o·rītes who *were* beyond the Jordan—to Sī′hon king of Hesh′bon, and Og king of Bā′shan, who was at Ash′ta·roth.

11 "Therefore our elders and all the inhabitants of our country spoke to us, saying, 'Take provisions with you for the journey, and go to meet them, and say to them, "We *are* your servants; now therefore, make a covenant with us." '

12 "This bread of ours we took hot *for* our provision from our houses on the day we departed to come to you. But now look, it is dry and moldy.

13 "And these wineskins which we filled *were* new, and see, they are torn; and these our garments and our sandals have become old because of the very long journey."

14 Then the men of Israel took some of their provisions; [a]but they [1]did not ask counsel of the LORD.

15 So Joshua [a]made peace with them, and made a covenant with them to let them live; and the rulers of the congregation swore to them.

16 And it happened at the end of three days, after they had made a covenant with them, that they heard that they *were* their neighbors who dwelt near them.

17 Then the children of Israel journeyed and came to their cities on the third day. Now their cities *were* [a]Gib′ē·on, Chē·phī′rah, Be·er′oth, and Kir′jath Jē′a·rim.

18 But the children of Israel did not [1]attack them, [a]because the

35 [a]Deut. 31:12 [b]Josh. 8:33

CHAPTER 9

1 [a]Josh. 3:10 [b]Num. 34:6 [c]Ex. 3:17; 23:23

2 [a]Ps. 83:3, 5 [1]Lit. *mouth*

3 [a]Josh. 9:17, 22; 10:2; 21:17 [b]Josh. 6:27

4 [1]*acted as envoys* [2]Lit. *tied up*

6 [a]Josh. 5:10 [1]*treaty*

7 [a]Josh. 9:1; 11:19 [b]Ex. 23:32

8 [a]Deut. 20:11

9 [a]Deut. 20:15 [b]Josh. 2:9, 10; 5:1

10 [a]Num. 21:24, 33

14 [a]Num. 27:21 [1]Lit. *did not inquire at the mouth of*

15 [a]2 Sam. 21:2

17 [a]Josh. 18:25

18 [a]Ps. 15:4 [1]*strike*

rulers of the congregation had
sworn to them by the LORD God
of Israel. And all the congregation complained against the
rulers.
19 Then all the rulers said to
all the congregation, "We have
sworn to them by the LORD God
of Israel; now therefore, we may
not touch them.
20 "This we will do to them: We
will let them live, lest [a]wrath
be upon us because of the oath
which we swore to them."
21 And the rulers said to them,
"Let them live, but let them be
[a]woodcutters and water carriers
for all the congregation, as the
rulers had [b]promised them."
22 Then Joshua called for them,
and he spoke to them, saying,
"Why have you deceived us, saying, [a]'We *are* very far from you,'
when [b]you dwell near us?
23 "Now therefore, you *are*
[a]cursed, and none of you shall
be freed from being slaves—
woodcutters and water carriers
for the house of my God."
24 So they answered Joshua
and said, "Because your servants were clearly told that the
LORD your God [a]commanded
His servant Moses to give you
all the land, and to destroy all
the inhabitants of the land from
before you; therefore [b]we were
very much afraid for our lives
because of you, and have done
this thing.
25 "And now, here we are, [a]in
your hands; do with us as it
seems good and right to do to
us."
26 So he did to them, and delivered them out of the hand of the
children of Israel, so that they
did not kill them.
27 And that day Joshua made
them [a]woodcutters and water
carriers for the congregation
and for the altar of the LORD,
[b]in the place which He would
choose, even to this day.

10 Now it came to pass when
A·dō′ni-Zē′dek king of
Jerusalem [a]heard how Joshua
had taken [b]Aī and had utterly
destroyed it—[c]as he had done to
Jericho and its king, so he had
done to [d]Aī and its king—and
[e]how the inhabitants of Gib′ē·on
had made peace with Israel and
were among them,
2 that they [a]feared greatly, because Gib′ē·on *was* a great city,
like one of the royal cities, and
because it *was* greater than Aī,
and all its men *were* mighty.
3 Therefore A·dō′ni-Zē′dek
king of Jerusalem sent to Hō′-
ham king of Hē′bron, Pī′ram
king of Jar′muth, Ja·phī′a king
of Lā′chish, and Dē′bir king of
Eg′lon, saying,
4 "Come up to me and help me,
that we may attack Gib′ē·on, for
[a]it has made peace with Joshua
and with the children of Israel."
5 Therefore the five kings of
the [a]Am′o·rītes, the king of Jerusalem, the king of Hē′bron,
the king of Jar′muth, the king
of Lā′chish, *and* the king of Eg′-
lon, [b]gathered together and went
up, they and all their armies,
and camped before Gib′ē·on and
made war against it.
6 And the men of Gib′ē·on sent
to Joshua at the camp [a]at Gil′gal,
saying, "Do not forsake your
servants; come up to us quickly,
save us and help us, for all the
kings of the Am′o·rītes who
dwell in the mountains have
gathered together against us."

20 [a]2 Sam. 21:1, 2, 6
21 [a]Deut. 29:11 [b]Josh. 9:15
22 [a]Josh. 9:6, 9 [b]Josh. 9:16
23 [a]Gen. 9:25
24 [a]Deut. 7:1, 2 [b]Ex. 15:14
25 [a]Gen. 16:6
27 [a]Josh. 9:21, 23 [b]Deut. 12:5

CHAPTER 10

1 [a]Josh. 9:1 [b]Josh. 8:1 [c]Josh. 6:21 [d]Josh. 8:22, 26, 28 [e]Josh. 9:15
2 [a]Ex. 15:14–16
4 [a]Josh. 9:15; 10:1
5 [a]Num. 13:29 [b]Josh. 9:2
6 [a]Josh. 5:10; 9:6

7 So Joshua ascended from
Gil′gal, he and [a]all the people of
war with him, and all the mighty
men of valor.
8 And the LORD said to Joshua,
[a]"Do not fear them, for I have
delivered them into your hand;
[b]not a man of them shall [c]stand
before you."
9 Joshua therefore came upon
them suddenly, having marched
all night from Gil′gal.
10 So the LORD [a]routed them
before Israel, killed them with
a great slaughter at Gib′ē·on,
chased them along the road that
goes [b]to Beth Hor′on, and struck
them down as far as [c]A·zē′kah
and Mak·kē′dah.
11 And it happened, as they fled
before Israel *and* were on the
descent of Beth Hor′on, [a]that the
LORD cast down large hailstones
from heaven on them as far as
A·zē′kah, and they died. *There
were* more who died from the
hailstones than the children of
Israel killed with the sword.
12 Then Joshua spoke to the
LORD in the day when the LORD
delivered up the Am′o·rītes before the children of Israel, and
he said in the sight of Israel:

[a]"Sun, stand still over
Gib′ē·on;
And Moon, in the Valley of
[b]Aī′ja·lon."
13 So the sun stood still,
And the moon stopped,
Till the people had revenge
Upon their enemies.

[a]*Is* this not written in the Book
of Jā′sher? So the sun stood still
in the midst of heaven, and did
not hasten to go *down* for about
a whole day.
14 And there has been [a]no day
like that, before it or after it, that
the LORD heeded the voice of a
man; for [b]the LORD fought for
Israel.
15 [a]Then Joshua returned, and
all Israel with him, to the camp
at Gil′gal.
16 But these five kings had fled
and hidden themselves in a cave
at Mak·kē′dah.
17 And it was told Joshua, saying, "The five kings have been
found hidden in the cave at
Mak·kē′dah."
18 So Joshua said, "Roll large
stones against the mouth of the
cave, and set men by it to guard
them.
19 "And do not stay *there* yourselves, *but* pursue your enemies,
and attack their rear *guard.* Do
not allow them to enter their cities, for the LORD your God has
delivered them into your hand."
20 Then it happened, while
Joshua and the children of Israel
made an end of slaying them
with a very great slaughter, till
they had finished, that those
who escaped entered fortified
cities.
21 And all the people returned to
the camp, to Joshua at Mak·kē′-
dah, in peace. [a]No one [1]moved
his tongue against any of the
children of Israel.
22 Then Joshua said, "Open the
mouth of the cave, and bring out
those five kings to me from the
cave."
23 And they did so, and brought
out those five kings to him from
the cave: the king of Jerusalem,
the king of Hē′bron, the king of
Jar′muth, the king of Lā′chish,
and the king of Eg′lon.
24 So it was, when they brought

7 [a]Josh. 8:1
8 [a]Josh. 11:6 [b]Josh. 1:5, 9 [c]Josh. 21:44
10 [a]Is. 28:21 [b]Josh. 16:3, 5 [c]Josh. 15:35
11 [a]Is. 30:30
12 [a]Hab. 3:11 [b]Judg. 12:12
13 [a]2 Sam. 1:18
14 [a]Is. 38:7, 8 [b]Deut. 1:30; 20:4
15 [a]Josh. 10:43
21 [a]Ex. 11:7 [1]*criticized,* lit. *sharpened his tongue*

out those kings to Joshua, that
Joshua called for all the men of
Israel, and said to the captains
of the men of war who went
with him, "Come near, put your
feet on the necks of these kings."
And they drew near and [a]put
their feet on their necks.
25 Then Joshua said to [1]them,
[a]"Do not be afraid, nor be dismayed; be strong and of good
courage, for [b]thus the LORD will
do to all your enemies against
whom you fight."
26 And afterward Joshua struck
[1]them and killed them, and
hanged them on five trees; and
they [a]were hanging on the trees
until evening.
27 So it was at the time of the
going down of the sun *that*
Joshua commanded, and they
[a]took them down from the trees,
cast them into the cave where
they had been hidden, and laid
large stones against the cave's
mouth, *which remain* until this
very day.
28 On that day Joshua took
Mak·kē′dah, and struck it and its
king with the edge of the sword.
He utterly [a]destroyed [1]them—all
the people who *were* in it. He let
none remain. He also did to the
king of Mak·kē′dah [b]as he had
done to the king of Jericho.
29 Then Joshua passed from
Mak·kē′dah, and all Israel with
him, to [a]Lib′nah; and they fought
against Lib′nah.
30 And the LORD also delivered
it and its king into the hand of
Israel; he struck it and all the
people who *were* in it with the
edge of the sword. He let none
remain in it, but did to its king
as he had done to the king of
Jericho.

31 Then Joshua passed from
Lib′nah, and all Israel with him,
to Lā′chish; and they encamped
against it and fought against it.
32 And the LORD delivered Lā′-
chish into the hand of Israel,
who took it on the second day,
and struck it and all the people
who *were* in it with the edge of
the sword, according to all that
he had done to Lib′nah.
33 Then Hō′ram king of Gē′-
zer came up to help Lā′chish;
and Joshua struck him and his
people, until he left him none
remaining.
34 From Lā′chish Joshua passed
to Eg′lon, and all Israel with
him; and they encamped against
it and fought against it.
35 They took it on that day and
struck it with the edge of the
sword; all the people who *were*
in it he utterly destroyed that
day, according to all that he had
done to Lā′chish.
36 So Joshua went up from Eg′-
lon, and all Israel with him,
to [a]Hē′bron; and they fought
against it.
37 And they took it and struck
it with the edge of the sword—
its king, all its cities, and all the
people who *were* in it; he left
none remaining, according to all
that he had done to Eg′lon, but
utterly destroyed it and all the
people who *were* in it.
38 Then Joshua returned, and
all Israel with him, to [a]Dē′bir;
and they fought against it.
39 And he took it and its king
and all its cities; they struck
them with the edge of the sword
and utterly destroyed all the
people who *were* in it. He left
none remaining; as he had done
to Hē′bron, so he did to Dē′bir

24 [a]Mal. 4:3
25 [a]Deut. 31:6–8 [b]Deut. 3:21; 7:19 [1]The captains
26 [a]Josh. 8:29 [1]The kings
27 [a]Deut. 21:22, 23
28 [a]Deut. 7:2, 16 [b]Josh. 6:21 [1]So with MT and most authorities; many Heb. mss., some LXX mss., and some Tg. mss. *it*
29 [a]Josh. 15:42; 21:13
36 [a]Josh. 14:13–15; 15:13
38 [a]Josh. 15:15

and its king, as he had done also
to Lib′nah and its king.
40 So Joshua conquered all the
land: the [a]mountain country and
the [1]South and the lowland and
the wilderness slopes, and [b]all
their kings; he left none remaining, but [c]utterly destroyed all
that breathed, as the LORD God
of Israel had commanded.
41 And Joshua conquered them
from [a]Kā′desh Bar·nē′a as far as
[b]Gā′za, [c]and all the country of
Gō′shen, even as far as Gib′ē·on.
42 All these kings and their
land Joshua took at one time,
[a]because the LORD God of Israel
fought for Israel.
43 Then Joshua returned, and
all Israel with him, to the camp
at Gil′gal.

11 And it came to pass,
when Jā′bin king of Hā′-
zor heard *these things*, that he
[a]sent to Jō′bab king of Mā′don,
to the king [b]of Shim′ron, to the
king of Ach′shaph,
2 and to the kings who *were*
from the north, in the mountains,
in the plain south of [a]Chin′-
ne·roth, in the lowland, and in
the heights [b]of Dor on the west,
3 to the Cā′naan·ītes in the
east and in the west, the [a]Am′-
o·rīte, the Hit′tīte, the Per′iz·zīte,
the Jeb′ū·sīte in the mountains,
[b]and the Hī′vīte below [c]Her′mon
[d]in the land of Miz′pah.
4 So they went out, they and all
their armies with them, *as* many
people [a]*as* the sand that *is* on the
seashore in multitude, with very
many horses and chariots.
5 And when all these kings
had [1]met together, they came
and camped together at the waters of Mē′rom to fight against
Israel.
6 But the LORD said to Joshua,
[a]"Do not be afraid because of
them, for tomorrow about this
time I will deliver all of them
slain before Israel. You shall
[b]hamstring their horses and
burn their chariots with fire."
7 So Joshua and all the people
of war with him came against
them suddenly by the waters
of Mē′rom, and they attacked
them.
8 And the LORD delivered them
into the hand of Israel, who defeated them and chased them to
[1]Greater [a]Sī′don, to the [2]Brook
[b]Mis′re·photh, and to the Valley
of Miz′pah eastward; they attacked them until they left none
of them remaining.
9 So Joshua did to them as
the LORD had told him: he ham-
strung their horses and burned
their chariots with fire.
10 Joshua turned back at that
time and took Hā′zor, and struck
its king with the sword; for Hā′-
zor was formerly the head of all
those kingdoms.
11 And they struck all the people who *were* in it with the edge
of the sword, [a]utterly destroying *them*. There was none left
[b]breathing. Then he burned Hā′-
zor with fire.
12 So all the cities of those
kings, and all their kings, Joshua
took and struck with the edge of
the sword. He utterly destroyed
them, [a]as Moses the servant of
the LORD had commanded.
13 But *as for* the cities that stood
on their [1]mounds, Israel burned
none of them, except Hā′zor
only, *which* Joshua burned.
14 And all the [a]spoil of these
cities and the livestock, the children of Israel took as booty for

40 [a]Deut. 1:7 [b]Deut. 7:24 [c]Deut. 20:16, 17 [1]Heb. *Negev*, and so throughout the book

41 [a]Deut. 9:23 [b]Gen. 10:19 [c]Josh. 11:16; 15:51

42 [a]Josh. 10:14

CHAPTER 11

1 [a]Josh. 10:3 [b]Josh. 19:15

2 [a]Num. 34:11 [b]Josh. 17:11

3 [a]Josh. 9:1 [b]Judg. 3:3, 5 [c]Josh. 11:17; 13:5, 11 [d]Gen. 31:49

4 [a]Judg. 7:12

5 [1]Lit. *assembled by appointment*

6 [a]Josh. 10:8 [b]2 Sam. 8:4

8 [a]Gen. 49:13 [b]Josh. 13:6 [1]Heb. *Sidon Rabbah* [2]Heb. *Misrephoth Maim*, lit. *Burnings of Water*

11 [a]Deut. 20:16 [b]Josh. 10:40

12 [a]Num. 33:50–56

13 [1]Heb. *tel*, a heap of successive city ruins

14 [a]Deut. 20:14–18

themselves; but they struck every
man with the edge of the sword
until they had destroyed them,
and they left none breathing.
15 [a]As the LORD had commanded Moses his servant, so
[b]Moses commanded Joshua, and
[c]so Joshua did. [1]He left nothing
undone of all that the LORD had
commanded Moses.
16 Thus Joshua took all this
land: [a]the mountain country, all
the South, [b]all the land of Gō′-
shen, the lowland, and the Jordan [1]plain—the mountains of
Israel and its lowlands,
17 [a]from [1]Mount Hā′lak and the
ascent to Sē′ir, even as far as
Bā′al Gad in the Valley of Lebanon below Mount Her′mon. He
captured [b]all their kings, and
struck them down and killed
them.
18 Joshua made war a long time
with all those kings.
19 There was not a city that
made peace with the children of
Israel, except [a]the Hī′vītes, the
inhabitants of Gib′ē·on. All *the
others* they took in battle.
20 For [a]it was of the LORD [1]to
harden their hearts, that they
should come against Israel in
battle, that He might utterly destroy them, *and* that they might
receive no mercy, but that He
might destroy them, [b]as the LORD
had commanded Moses.
21 And at that time Joshua
came and cut off [a]the An′a·kim
from the mountains: from Hē′-
bron, from Dē′bir, from Ā′nab,
from all the mountains of Judah,
and from all the mountains of
Israel; Joshua utterly destroyed
them with their cities.
22 None of the An′a·kim were
left in the land of the children
of Israel; they remained only [a]in
Gā′za, in Gath, [b]and in Ash′dod.
23 So Joshua took the whole
land, [a]according to all that the
LORD had said to Moses; and
Joshua gave it as an inheritance
to Israel [b]according to their divisions by their tribes. Then the
land [c]rested from war.

12

These *are* the kings of the
land whom the children
of Israel defeated, and whose
land they possessed on the other
side of the Jordan toward the
rising of the sun, [a]from the River
Ar′non [b]to Mount Her′mon, and
all the eastern Jordan plain:
2 *One king was* [a]Sī′hon king
of the Am′o·rītes, who dwelt in
Hesh′bon *and* ruled half of Gil′-
ē·ad, from A·rō′er, which is on
the bank of the River Ar′non,
from the middle of that river,
even as far as the River Jab′bok,
which is the border of the Am′-
mon·ītes,
3 and [a]the eastern Jordan plain
from the [1]Sea of Chin′ne·roth as
far as the [2]Sea of the Ar′a·bah
(the Salt Sea), [b]the road to Beth
Jesh′i·moth, and [3]southward below [c]the[4] slopes of Pis′gah.
4 *The other king was* [a]Og king
of Bā′shan and his territory, *who
was* of [b]the remnant of the giants, [c]who dwelt at Ash′ta·roth
and at Ed′rē·ī,
5 and reigned over [a]Mount
Her′mon, [b]over Sal′cah, over all
Bā′shan, [c]as far as the border
of the Gesh′ū·rītes and the Mā′-
a·cha·thītes, and over half of
Gil′ē·ad *to* the border of Sī′hon
king of Hesh′bon.
6 [a]These Moses the servant of
the LORD and the children of Israel had conquered; and [b]Moses
the servant of the LORD had

15 [a]Ex. 34:10–17 [b]Deut. 31:7, 8 [c]Josh. 1:7 [1]Lit. *He turned aside from nothing*
16 [a]Josh. 12:8 [b]Josh. 10:40, 41 [1]Heb. *arabah*
17 [a]Josh. 12:7 [b]Deut. 7:24 [1]Lit. *The Smooth* or *Bald Mountain*
19 [a]Josh. 9:3–7
20 [a]Deut. 2:30 [b]Deut. 20:16, 17 [1]Lit. *to make strong*
21 [a]Num. 13:22, 33
22 [a]1 Sam. 17:4 [b]Josh. 15:46
23 [a]Num. 34:2–15 [b]Num. 26:53 [c]Deut. 12:9, 10; 25:19

CHAPTER 12

1 [a]Num. 21:24 [b]Deut. 3:8
2 [a]Deut. 2:24–27
3 [a]Deut. 3:17 [b]Josh. 13:20 [c]Deut. 3:17; 4:49 [1]Sea of Galilee [2]Lit. *Sea of the Plain,* the Dead Sea [3]Or *Teman* [4]Or *Ashdoth Pisgah*
4 [a]Num. 21:33 [b]Deut. 3:11 [c]Deut. 1:4
5 [a]Deut. 3:8 [b]Deut. 3:10 [c]Deut. 3:14
6 [a]Num. 21:24, 35 [b]Num. 32:29–33

given it *as* a possession to the
Reū'ben·ītes, the Gad'ītes, and
half the tribe of Ma·nas'seh.
7 And these *are* the kings of
the country [a]which Joshua and
the children of Israel conquered
on this side of the Jordan, on the
west, from Bā'al Gad in the Valley of Lebanon as far as [1]Mount
Hā'lak and the ascent to [b]Sē'ir,
which Joshua [c]gave to the tribes
of Israel *as* a possession according to their divisions,
8 [a]in the mountain country, in
the lowlands, in the *Jordan* plain,
in the slopes, in the wilderness,
and in the South—[b]the Hit'tītes,
the Am'o·rītes, the Cā'naan·ītes,
the Per'iz·zītes, the Hī'vītes, and
the Jeb'ū·sītes:
9 [a]the king of Jericho, one;
[b]the king of Aī, which *is* beside
Beth'el, one;
10 [a]the king of Jerusalem, one;
the king of Hē'bron, one;
11 the king of Jar'muth, one;
the king of Lā'chish, one;
12 the king of Eg'lon, one; [a]the
king of Gē'zer, one;
13 [a]the king of Dē'bir, one; the
king of Gē'der, one;
14 the king of Hor'mah, one; the
king of Ar'ad, one;
15 [a]the king of Lib'nah, one; the
king of A·dul'lam, one;
16 [a]the king of Mak·kē'dah, one;
[b]the king of Beth'el, one;
17 the king of Tap'pū·ah, one;
[a]the king of Hē'pher, one;
18 the king of Ā'phek, one; the
king of [1]La·shar'on, one;
19 the king of Mā'don, one; [a]the
king of Hā'zor, one;
20 the king of [a]Shim'ron Mē'-
ron, one; the king of Ach'shaph,
one;
21 the king of Tā'a·nach, one;
the king of Me·gid'dō, one;

7 [a]Josh. 11:17 [b]Gen. 14:6; 32:3 [c]Josh. 11:23 [1]Lit. *The Bald Mountain*
8 [a]Josh. 10:40; 11:16 [b]Ex. 3:8; 23:23
9 [a]Josh. 6:2 [b]Josh. 8:29
10 [a]Josh. 10:23
12 [a]Josh. 10:33
13 [a]Josh. 10:38, 39
15 [a]Josh. 10:29, 30
16 [a]Josh. 10:28 [b]Judg. 1:22
17 [a]1 Kin. 4:10
18 [1]Or *Sharon*
19 [a]Josh. 11:10
20 [a]Josh. 11:1; 19:15
22 [a]Josh. 19:37; 20:7; 21:32
23 [a]Josh. 11:2 [b]Is. 9:1
24 [a]Deut. 7:24

CHAPTER 13

1 [a]Josh. 14:10; 23:1, 2
2 [a]Judg. 3:1–3 [b]Joel 3:4 [c]2 Sam. 3:3
3 [a]Jer. 2:18 [b]Judg. 3:3 [c]Deut. 2:23
4 [a]Josh. 12:18; 19:30 [b]Judg. 1:34
5 [a]1 Kin. 5:18; Ezek. 27:9 [b]Josh. 12:7 [1]Or *Giblites*
6 [a]Josh. 11:8 [b]Josh. 23:13 [c]Josh. 14:1, 2 [1]Heb. *Misrephoth Maim*, lit. *Burnings of Water* [2]*apportion*

22 [a]the king of Kē'desh, one; the
king of Jok'nē·am in Car'mel,
one;
23 the king of Dor in the
[a]heights of Dor, one; the king of
[b]the people of Gil'gal, one;
24 the king of Tir'zah, one—[a]all
the kings, thirty-one.

13

Now Joshua [a]was old, advanced in years. And the
LORD said to him: "You are old,
advanced in years, and there
remains very much land yet to
be possessed.
2 [a]"This is the land that yet
remains: [b]all the territory of the
Phi·lis'tines and all [c]*that of* the
Gesh'ū·rites,
3 [a]"from Sī'hor, which *is* east of
Egypt, as far as the border of Ek'-
ron northward (*which* is counted
as Cā'naan·īte); the [b]five lords of
the Phi·lis'tines—the Gā'zītes, the
Ash'dod·ītes, the Ash'ke·lon·ītes,
the Git'tītes, and the Ek'ron·ītes;
also [c]the Av'ītes;
4 "from the south, all the land
of the Cā'naan·ītes, and Me·ar'ah
that belongs to the Sī·dō'ni·ans
[a]as far as Ā'phek, to the border
of [b]the Am'o·rītes;
5 "the land of [a]the [1]Gē'bal·ītes,
and all Lebanon, toward the
sunrise, [b]from Bā'al Gad below
Mount Her'mon as far as the
entrance to Hā'math;
6 "all the inhabitants of the
mountains from Lebanon as far
as [a]the [1]Brook Mis're·photh, *and*
all the Sī·dō'ni·ans—them [b]I will
drive out from before the children of Israel; only [c]divide[2] it by
lot to Israel as an inheritance, as
I have commanded you.
7 "Now therefore, divide this
land as an inheritance to the
nine tribes and half the tribe of
Ma·nas'seh."

8 With the other half-tribe the
Reū′ben·ītes and the Gad′ītes received their inheritance, [a]which
Moses had given them, [b]beyond
the Jordan eastward, as Moses the servant of the LORD had
given them:
9 from A·rō′er which *is* on the
bank of the River Ar′non, and
the town that *is* in the midst of
the ravine, [a]and all the plain of
Med′e·ba as far as Dī′bon;
10 [a]all the cities of Sī′hon king
of the Am′o·rītes, who reigned in
Hesh′bon, as far as the border of
the children of Am′mon;
11 [a]Gil′ē·ad, and the border
of the Gesh′ū·rītes and Mā′-
a·cha·thītes, all Mount Her′mon,
and all Bā′shan as far as Sal′-
cah;
12 all the kingdom of Og in Bā′-
shan, who reigned in Ash′ta·roth
and Ed′rē·ī, who remained of
[a]the remnant of the giants; [b]for
Moses had [1]defeated and [2]cast
out these.
13 Nevertheless the children of
Israel [a]did not drive out the
Gesh′ū·rītes or the Mā′a·cha-
thītes, but the Gesh′ū·rītes and
the Mā′a·cha·thītes dwell among
the Israelites until this day.
14 [a]Only to the tribe of Levi he
had given [1]no inheritance; the
sacrifices of the LORD God of
Israel made by fire *are* their inheritance, [b]as He said to them.
15 [a]And Moses had given to
the tribe of the children of Reuben *an inheritance* according to
their families.
16 Their territory was [a]from
A·rō′er, which *is* on the bank of
the River Ar′non, [b]and the city
that *is* in the midst of the ravine,
[c]and all the plain by Med′e·ba;
17 [a]Hesh′bon and all its cities
that *are* in the plain: Dī′bon, Bā′-
moth Bā′al, Beth Bā′al Mē′on,
18 [a]Ja·hā′za, Ked′e·moth, Meph′-
a·ath,
19 [a]Kir·jath′a·im, [b]Sib′mah, Zē′-
reth Shā′har on the mountain of
the valley,
20 Beth Pē′or, [a]the slopes of
Pis′gah, and Beth Jesh′i·moth—
21 [a]all the cities of the plain and
all the kingdom of Sī′hon king
of the Am′o·rītes, who reigned
in Hesh′bon, [b]whom Moses had
struck [c]with the princes of Mid′-
i·an: Ē′vī, Rē′kem, Zūr, Hur, and
Rē′ba, who *were* princes of Sī′-
hon dwelling in the country.
22 The children of Israel also
killed with the sword [a]Bā′laam
the son of Bē′or, the [1]soothsayer,
among those who were killed by
them.
23 And the border of the children of Reuben was the bank of
the Jordan. This *was* the inheritance of the children of Reuben
according to their families, the
cities and their villages.
24 [a]Moses also had given *an inheritance* to the tribe of Gad, to
the children of Gad according to
their families.
25 [a]Their territory was Jā′zer,
and all the cities of Gil′ē·ad, [b]and
half the land of the Am′mon·ītes
as far as A·rō′er, which *is* before
[c]Rab′bah,
26 and from Hesh′bon to Rā′-
math Miz′pah and Bet′ō·nim,
and from Mā·ha·na′im to the
border of Dē′bir,
27 and in the valley [a]Beth Hā′-
ram, Beth Nim′rah, [b]Suc′coth,
and Zā′phon, the rest of the kingdom of Sī′hon king of Hesh′bon,
with the Jordan as *its* border, as
far as the edge [c]of the [1]Sea of

8 [a]Num. 32:33 [b]Josh. 12:1–6
9 [a]Num. 21:30
10 [a]Num. 21:24, 25
11 [a]Josh. 12:5
12 [a]Deut. 3:11 [b]Num. 21:24, 34, 35 [1]Lit. *struck* [2]*dispossessed*
13 [a]Josh. 13:11
14 [a]Josh. 14:3, 4 [b]Josh. 13:33 [1]*no land as a possession*
15 [a]Num. 34:14
16 [a]Josh. 12:2 [b]Num. 21:28 [c]Num. 21:30
17 [a]Num. 21:28, 30
18 [a]Num. 21:23
19 [a]Num. 32:37 [b]Num. 32:38
20 [a]Deut. 3:17
21 [a]Deut. 3:10 [b]Num. 21:24 [c]Num. 31:8
22 [a]Num. 22:5; 31:8 [1]*diviner*
24 [a]Num. 34:14
25 [a]Num. 32:1, 35 [b]Judg. 11:13, 15 [c]Deut. 3:11
27 [a]Num. 32:36 [b]Gen. 33:17 [c]Num. 34:11 [1]Sea of Galilee

Chin′ne·reth, on the other side
of the Jordan eastward.
28 This *is* the inheritance of
the children of Gad according
to their families, the cities and
their villages.
29 [a]Moses also had given *an*
inheritance to half the tribe of
Ma·nas′seh; it was for half the
tribe of the children of Ma·nas′-
seh according to their families:
30 Their territory was from
Mā·ha·na′im, all Bā′shan, all the
kingdom of Og king of Bā′shan,
and [a]all the towns of Jā′ir which
are in Bā′shan, sixty cities;
31 half of Gil′ē·ad, and [a]Ash′-
ta·roth and Ed′rē·ī, cities of the
kingdom of Og in Bā′shan, *were*
for the [b]children of Mā′chir the
son of Ma·nas′seh, for half of the
children of Mā′chir according to
their families.
32 These *are the areas* which
Moses had [1]distributed as an inheritance in the plains of Mō′ab
on the other side of the Jordan,
by Jericho eastward.
33 [a]But to the tribe of Levi Moses had given no inheritance;
the LORD God of Israel *was* their
inheritance, [b]as He had said to
them.

14 These *are the areas*
which the children of Is-
rael inherited in the land of
Cā′naan, [a]which El·ē·ā′zar the
priest, Joshua the son of Nun,
and the heads of the fathers
of the tribes of the children of
Israel distributed as an inheritance to them.
2 Their inheritance *was* [a]by
lot, as the LORD had commanded
by the hand of Moses, for the
nine tribes and the half-tribe.
3 [a]For Moses had given the
inheritance of the two tribes and
the half-tribe on the other side of
the Jordan; but to the Lē′vītes he
had given no inheritance among
them.
4 For [a]the children of Joseph
were two tribes: Ma·nas′seh and
Ē′phra·im. And they gave no
part to the Lē′vītes in the land,
except [b]cities to dwell *in,* with
their common-lands for their
livestock and their property.
5 [a]As the LORD had commanded
Moses, so the children of Israel
did; and they divided the land.
6 Then the children of Judah
came to Joshua in Gil′gal. And
Caleb the son of Je·phŭn′neh
the [a]Kē′niz·zīte said to him: "You
know [b]the word which the LORD
said to Moses the man of God
concerning [c]you and me in Kā′-
desh Bar·nē′a.
7 "I *was* forty years old when
Moses the servant of the LORD
[a]sent me from Kā′desh Bar·nē′a
to spy out the land, and I brought
back word to him as *it was* in
my heart.
8 "Nevertheless [a]my brethren
who went up with me made the
[1]heart of the people melt, but I
wholly [b]followed the LORD my
God.
9 "So Moses swore on that day,
saying, [a]'Surely the land [b]where
your foot has trodden shall be
your inheritance and your children's forever, because you have
wholly followed the LORD my
God.'
10 "And now, behold, the LORD
has kept me [a]alive, [b]as He said,
these forty-five years, ever since
the LORD spoke this word to
Moses while Israel [1]wandered
in the wilderness; and now, here
I am this day, eighty-five years
old.

29 [a]Num. 34:14
30 [a]Num. 32:41
31 [a]Josh. 9:10; 12:4; 13:12 [b]Num. 32:39, 40
32 [1]*apportioned*
33 [a]Josh. 13:14; 18:7 [b]Num. 18:20

CHAPTER 14

1 [a]Num. 34:16–29
2 [a]Num. 26:55; 33:54; 34:13
3 [a]Josh. 13:8, 32, 33
4 [a]2 Chr. 30:1 [b]Num. 35:2–8
5 [a]Josh. 21:2
6 [a]Num. 32:11, 12 [b]Num. 14:24, 30 [c]Num. 13:26
7 [a]Num. 13:6, 17; 14:6
8 [a]Num. 13:31, 32 [b]Num. 14:24 [1]*courage of the people fail*
9 [a]Num. 14:23, 24 [b]Deut. 1:36
10 [a]Num. 14:24, 30, 38 [b]Josh. 5:6 [1]Lit. *walked*

11 [a]"As yet I *am as* strong this
day as on the day that Moses
sent me; just as my strength *was*
then, so now *is* my strength for
war, both [b]for going out and for
coming in.
12 "Now therefore, give me this
mountain of which the LORD
spoke in that day; for you heard
in that day how [a]the An'a·kim
were there, and *that* the cities
were great *and* fortified. [b]It may
be that the LORD *will be* with me,
and [c]I shall be able to drive them
out as the LORD said."
13 And Joshua [a]blessed him,
[b]and gave Hē'bron to Caleb
the son of Je·phū'neh as an
inheritance.
14 [a]Hē'bron therefore became
the inheritance of Caleb the son
of Je·phū'neh the Kē'niz·zīte to
this day, because he [b]wholly followed the LORD God of Israel.
15 And [a]the name of Hē'bron
formerly was Kir'jath Ar'ba
(*Ar'ba was* the greatest man
among the An'a·kim). [b]Then the
land had rest from war.

CHAPTER 15

15 So *this* was the [1]lot of the
tribe of the children of
Judah according to their families: [a]The border of Ē'dom at
the [b]Wilderness of Zin southward *was* the extreme southern
boundary.
2 And their [a]southern border
began at the shore of the Salt
Sea, from the bay that faces
southward.
3 Then it went out to the
southern side of [a]the Ascent of
Ak·rab'bim, passed along to Zin,
ascended on the south side of
Kā'desh Bar·nē'a, passed along
to Hez'ron, went up to Ā'dar,
and went around to Kar'ka·a.
4 *From there* it passed [a]toward
Az'mon and went out to the
Brook of Egypt; and the border
ended at the sea. This shall be
your southern border.
5 The east border *was* the Salt
Sea as far as the mouth of the
Jordan. And the [a]border on
the northern quarter *began* at
the bay of the sea at the mouth
of the Jordan.
6 The border went up to [a]Beth
Hog'lah and passed north of
Beth Ar'a·bah; and the border
went up [b]to the stone of Bō'han
the son of Reuben.
7 Then the border went up toward [a]Dē'bir from [b]the Valley of
Ā'chor, and it turned northward
toward Gil'gal, which *is* before
the Ascent of A·dum'mim, which
is on the south side of the valley.
The border continued toward
the waters of En Shem'esh and
ended at [c]En Rō'gel.
8 And the border went up [a]by
the Valley of the Son of Hin'nom
to the southern slope of the [b]Jeb'-
ū·sīte *city* (which *is* Jerusalem).
The border went up to the top
of the mountain that *lies* before
the Valley of Hin'nom westward,
which *is* at the end of the Valley
[c]of [1]Reph'a·im northward.
9 Then the border went
around from the top of the hill
to [a]the fountain of the water of
Neph·tō'ah, and extended to the
cities of Mount Ē'phron. And the
border went around [b]to Bā'a·lah
(which *is* [c]Kir'jath Jē'a·rim).
10 Then the border [1]turned
westward from Bā'a·lah to
Mount Sē'ir, passed along to
the side of Mount Jē'a·rim on
the north (which *is* Ches'a·lon),
went down to Beth Shem'esh,
and passed on to [a]Tim'nah.
11 And the border went out to

11 [a]Deut. 34:7 [b]Deut. 31:2
12 [a]Num. 13:28, 33 [b]Rom. 8:31 [c]Josh. 15:14
13 [a]Josh. 22:6 [b]Josh. 10:37; 15:13
14 [a]Josh. 21:12 [b]Josh. 14:8, 9
15 [a]Gen. 23:2 [b]Josh. 11:23

CHAPTER 15

1 [a]Num. 34:3 [b]Num. 33:36 [1]*allotment*
2 [a]Num. 34:3, 4
3 [a]Num. 34:4
4 [a]Num. 34:5
5 [a]Josh. 18:15–19
6 [a]Josh. 18:19, 21 [b]Josh. 18:17
7 [a]Josh. 13:26 [b]Josh. 7:26 [c]2 Sam. 17:17
8 [a]Josh. 18:16 [b]Judg. 1:21; 19:10 [c]Josh. 18:16 [1]Lit. *Giants*
9 [a]Josh. 18:15 [b]1 Chr. 13:6 [c]Judg. 18:12
10 [a]Gen. 38:13 [1]*turned around*

the side of [a]Ek′ron northward.
Then the border went around to
Shic′ron, passed along to Mount
Bā′a·lah, and extended to Jab′-
nē·el; and the border ended at
the sea.
12 The west border *was* [a]the
coastline of the Great Sea. This
is the boundary of the children
of Judah all around according to
their families.
13 [a]Now to Caleb the son of
Je·phū′n′neh he gave a share
among the children of [b]Judah,
according to the commandment
of the LORD to Joshua, *namely,*
[c]Kir′jath Ar′ba, which *is* Hē′bron
(*Ar′ba was* the father of Ā′nak).
14 Caleb drove out [a]the three
sons of Ā′nak from there: [b]Shē′-
shai, A·hī′man, and Tal′maī, the
children of Ā′nak.
15 Then [a]he went up from there
to the inhabitants of Dē′bir (formerly the name of Dē′bir *was*
Kir′jath Sē′pher).
16 [a]And Caleb said, "He who
[1]attacks Kir′jath Sē′pher and
takes it, to him I will give Ach′-
sah my daughter as wife."
17 So [a]Oth′ni·el the [b]son of Kē′-
naz, the brother of Caleb, took
it; and he gave him [c]Ach′sah his
daughter as wife.
18 [a]Now it was so, when she
came *to him*, that she persuaded
him to ask her father for a field.
So [b]she dismounted from *her*
donkey, and Caleb said to her,
"What do you wish?"
19 She answered, "Give me a
[a]blessing; since you have given
me land in the South, give me
also springs of water." So he
gave her the upper springs and
the lower springs.
20 This *was* the inheritance of
the tribe of the children of Judah
according to their families:
21 The cities at the limits of
the tribe of the children of Judah, toward the border of Ē′dom
in the South, were Kab′zē·el,
[a]Ē′der, Jā′gur,
22 Kinah, Di·mō′nah, A·dā′dah,
23 Kē′desh, Hā′zor, Ith′nan,
24 [a]Ziph, Tē′lem, Be·ā′loth,
25 Hā′zor, Ha·dat′tah, Ker′i·oth,
Hez′ron (which *is* Hā′zor),
26 Ā′mam, Shē′ma, Mō′la·dah,
27 Hā′zar Gad′dah, Hesh′mon,
Beth Pē′let,
28 Hā′zar Shū′al, [a]Bē·er·shē′ba,
Biz·joth′jah,
29 Bā′a·lah, Ī′jim, Ē′zem,
30 El·tō′lad, Chē′sil, [a]Hor′mah,
31 [a]Zik′lag, Mad·man′nah, San-
san′nah,
32 Le·bā′oth, Shil′him, Ā′in,
and [a]Rim′mon: all the cities *are*
twenty-nine, with their villages.
33 In the lowland: [a]Esh′tā·ol,
Zō′rah, Ash′nah,
34 Za·nō′ah, En Gan′nim, Tap′-
pū·ah, Ē′nam,
35 Jar′muth, [a]A·dul′lam, Sō′cōh,
A·zē′kah,
36 Sha·rā′im, Ad·i·thā′im, Ge-
dē′rah, and Ged·e·rō·thā′im:
fourteen cities with their villages;
37 Zē′nan, Ha·dash′ah, Migdal
Gad,
38 Dil′e·an, Miz′pah, [a]Jok′the·el,
39 [a]Lā′chish, Boz′kath, [b]Eg′lon,
40 Cab′bon, [1]Lah′mas, Kith′lish,
41 Ge·dē′roth, Beth Dā′gon, Nā′-
a·mah, and Mak·kē′dah: sixteen
cities with their villages;
42 [a]Lib′nah, Ē′ther, Ā′shan,
43 Jiph′tah, Ash′nah, Nē′zib,
44 Kē·ī′lah, Ach′zib, and Ma·rē′-
shah: nine cities with their
villages;

11 [a]Josh. 19:43
12 [a]Num. 34:6, 7
13 [a]Josh. 14:13 [b]Num. 13:6 [c]Josh. 14:15
14 [a]Judg. 1:10, 20 [b]Num. 13:22
15 [a]Judg. 1:11
16 [a]Judg. 1:12 [1]Lit. *strikes*
17 [a]Judg. 1:13; 3:9 [b]Num. 32:12 [c]Judg. 1:12
18 [a]Judg. 1:14 [b]Gen. 24:64
19 [a]Gen. 33:11
21 [a]Gen. 35:21
24 [a]1 Sam. 23:14
28 [a]Gen. 21:31
30 [a]Josh. 19:4
31 [a]1 Sam. 27:6; 30:1
32 [a]Judg. 20:45, 47
33 [a]Judg. 13:25; 16:31
35 [a]1 Sam. 22:1
38 [a]2 Kin. 14:7
39 [a]2 Kin. 14:19 [b]Josh. 10:3
40 [1]Or *Lahmam*
42 [a]Josh. 21:13

45 Ek′ron, with its towns and
villages;
46 from Ek′ron to the sea, all
that *lay* near [a]Ash′dod, with
their villages;
47 Ash′dod with its towns and
villages, Gā′za with its towns
and villages—as far as [a]the
Brook of Egypt and [b]the Great
Sea with *its* coastline.
48 And in the mountain country: Shā′mir, Jat′tir, Sō′chōh,
49 Dan′nah, Kir′jath San′nah
(which *is* Dē′bir),
50 Ā′nab, Esh′te·mōh, Ā′nim,
51 [a]Gō′shen, Hō′lon, and Gī′lōh:
eleven cities with their villages;
52 Arab, Dū′mah, Esh′e·an,
53 Jā′num, Beth Tap′pū·ah,
A·phē′kah,
54 Hum′tah, [a]Kir′jath Ar′ba
(which *is* Hē′bron), and Zī′or:
nine cities with their villages;
55 [a]Mā′on, Car′mel, Ziph, Jut′-
tah,
56 Jez′rē·el, Jok′dē·am, Za·nō′ah,
57 Kāin, Gib′ē·ah, and Tim′nah:
ten cities with their villages;
58 Hal′hul, Beth Zūr, Gē′dor,
59 Mā′a·rath, Beth Ā′noth, and
El′tē·kon: six cities with their
villages;
60 [a]Kir′jath Bā′al (which *is* Kir′-
jath Jē′a·rim) and Rab′bah: two
cities with their villages.
61 In the wilderness: Beth Ar′-
a·bah, Mid′din, Se·cā′cah,
62 Nib′shan, the City of Salt,
and [a]En Ge′di: six cities with
their villages.
63 As for the Jeb′ū·sītes, the inhabitants of Jerusalem, [a]the children of Judah could not drive
them out; [b]but the Jeb′ū·sītes
dwell with the children of Judah
at Jerusalem to this day.

16 The lot [1]fell to the children of Joseph from the
Jordan, by Jericho, to the waters
of Jericho on the east, to the
[a]wilderness that goes up from
Jericho through the mountains
to [2]Beth′el,
2 then went out [1]from [a]Beth′el
to Luz, passed along to the border of the Ar′chītes at At′a·roth,
3 and went down westward to
the boundary of the Japh′let·ītes,
[a]as far as the boundary of Lower
Beth Hor′on to [b]Gē′zer; and [1]it
ended at the sea.
4 [a]So the children of Joseph,
Ma·nas′seh and Ē′phra·im, took
their [1]inheritance.
5 [a]The border of the children
of Ē′phra·im, according to their
families, was *thus:* The border
of their inheritance on the east
side was [b]At′a·roth Ad′dar [c]as
far as Upper Beth Hor′on.
6 And the border went out toward the sea on the north side of
[a]Mich·mē′thath; then the border
went around eastward to Tā′-
a·nath Shī′lōh, and passed by it
on the east of Ja·nō′hah.
7 Then it went down from
Ja·nō′hah to At′a·roth and [1]Nā′-
a·rah, reached to Jericho, and
came out at the Jordan.
8 The border went out from
[a]Tap′pū·ah westward to the
[b]Brook Kā′nah, and [1]it ended
at the sea. This *was* the inheritance of the tribe of the children
of Ē′phra·im according to their
families.
9 [a]The separate cities for the
children of Ē′phra·im *were*
among the inheritance of the
children of Ma·nas′seh, all the
cities with their villages.
10 [a]And they did not drive out
the Cā′naan·ītes who dwelt in
Gē′zer; but the Cā′naan·ītes
dwell among the Ē′phra·im·ītes

46 [a]Josh. 11:22
47 [a]Josh. 15:4 [b]Num. 34:6
51 [a]Josh. 10:41; 11:16
54 [a]Josh. 14:15
55 [a]1 Sam. 23:24, 25
60 [a]Josh. 18:14
62 [a]1 Sam. 23:29
63 [a]2 Sam. 5:6 [b]Judg. 1:21

CHAPTER 16

1 [a]Josh. 8:15; 18:12 [1]Lit. *went out* [2]LXX *Bethel Luz*
2 [a]Josh. 18:13 [1]LXX *to Bethel,*
3 [a]2 Chr. 8:5 [b]1 Kin. 9:15 [1]Lit. *the goings out of it were at the sea*
4 [a]Josh. 17:14 [1]*possession*
5 [a]Judg. 1:29 [b]Josh. 18:13 [c]2 Chr. 8:5
6 [a]Josh. 17:7
7 [1]*Naaran,* 1 Chr. 7:28
8 [a]Josh. 17:8 [b]Josh. 17:9 [1]Lit. *the goings out of it were at the sea*
9 [a]Josh. 17:9
10 [a]Judg. 1:29

to this day and have become
forced laborers.

17 There was also a lot for
the tribe of Ma·nas'seh,
for he *was* the [a]firstborn of Joseph: *namely* for [b]Mā'chir the
firstborn of Ma·nas'seh, the father of Gil'ē·ad, because he was
a man of war; therefore he was
given [c]Gil'ē·ad and Bā'shan.
2 And there was *a lot* for [a]the
rest of the children of Ma·nas'seh
according to their families: [b]for
the children of [1]Ā·bi·ē'zer, the
children of Hē'lek, [c]the children
of As'ri·el, the children of Shē'-
chem, [d]the children of Hē'pher,
and the children of She·mī'da;
these *were* the male children of
Ma·nas'seh the son of Joseph
according to their families.
3 But [a]Ze·loph'e·had the son of
Hē'pher, the son of Gil'ē·ad, the
son of Mā'chir, the son of Ma·nas'-
seh, had no sons, but only daughters. And these *are* the names
of his daughters: Mah'lah, Noah,
Hog'lah, Mil'cah, and Tir'zah.
4 And they came near be-
fore [a]El·ē·ā'zar the priest, before Joshua the son of Nun,
and before the rulers, saying,
[b]"The LORD commanded Moses to give us an [1]inheritance
among our brothers." Therefore,
according to the commandment
of the LORD, he gave them an
inheritance among their father's
brothers.
5 Ten shares fell to [a]Ma·nas'-
seh, besides the land of Gil'ē·ad
and Bā'shan, which *were* on the
other side of the Jordan,
6 because the daughters of
Ma·nas'seh received an inheritance among his sons; and the
rest of Ma·nas'seh's sons had
the land of Gil'ē·ad.

CHAPTER 17

1 [a]Gen. 41:51; 46:20; 48:18 [b]Gen. 50:23 [c]Deut. 3:15

2 [a]Num. 26:29–33 [b]1 Chr. 7:18 [c]Num. 26:31 [d]Num. 26:32 [1]*Jeezer,* Num. 26:30

3 [a]Num. 26:33; 27:1; 36:2

4 [a]Josh. 14:1 [b]Num. 27:2–11 [1]*possession*

5 [a]Josh. 22:7

7 [a]Josh. 16:6

8 [a]Josh. 16:8

9 [a]Josh. 16:9 [1]*boundary* [2]*Wadi*

11 [a]1 Chr. 7:29 [b]1 Kin. 4:12

12 [a]Judg. 1:19, 27, 28

13 [a]Josh. 16:10

14 [a]Josh. 16:4 [b]Gen. 48:22 [1]*allotment*

7 And the territory of
Ma·nas'seh was from Ash'er to
[a]Mich·mē'thath, that *lies* east of
Shē'chem; and the border went
along south to the inhabitants of
En Tap'pū·ah.
8 Ma·nas'seh had the land of
Tap'pū·ah, but [a]Tap'pū·ah on the
border of Ma·nas'seh *belonged*
to the children of Ē'phra·im.
9 And the [1]border descended
to the [2]Brook Kā'nah, southward
to the brook. [a]These cities of
Ē'phra·im *are* among the cities
of Ma·nas'seh. The border of
Ma·nas'seh *was* on the north
side of the brook; and it ended
at the sea.
10 Southward *it was* Ē'phra·im's,
northward *it was* Ma·nas'seh's,
and the sea was its border.
Ma·nas'seh's territory was adjoining Ash'er on the north and
Is'sa·char on the east.
11 And in Is'sa·char and in
Ash'er, [a]Ma·nas'seh had [b]Beth
Shē'an and its towns, Ib'lē·am
and its towns, the inhabitants of
Dor and its towns, the inhabitants of En Dor and its towns,
the inhabitants of Tā'a·nach and
its towns, and the inhabitants of
Me·gid'dō and its towns—three
hilly regions.
12 Yet [a]the children of Ma·nas'-
seh could not drive out *the inhabitants of* those cities, but the
Cā'naan·ītes were determined to
dwell in that land.
13 And it happened, when the
children of Israel grew strong,
that they put the Cā'naan·ītes to
[a]forced labor, but did not utterly
drive them out.
14 [a]Then the children of Joseph
spoke to Joshua, saying, "Why
have you given us *only* [b]one [1]lot
and one share to inherit, since

we *are* [c]a great people, inasmuch as the LORD has blessed us until now?"

15 So Joshua answered them, "If you *are* a great people, *then* go up to the forest *country* and clear a place for yourself there in the land of the Per'iz·zītes and the giants, since the mountains of Ē'phra·im are too confined for you."

16 But the children of Joseph said, "The mountain country is not enough for us; and all the Cā'naan·ītes who dwell in the land of the valley have [a]chariots of iron, *both those* who *are* of Beth Shē'an and its towns and *those* who *are* [b]of the Valley of Jez'rē·el."

17 And Joshua spoke to the house of Joseph—to Ē'phra·im and Ma·nas'seh—saying, "You *are* a great people and have great power; you shall not have *only* one [1]lot,

18 "but the mountain country shall be yours. Although it *is* wooded, you shall cut it down, and its [1]farthest extent shall be yours; for you shall drive out the Cā'naan·ītes, [a]though they have iron chariots *and* are strong."

18

Now the whole congregation of the children of Israel assembled together [a]at Shī'lōh, and [b]set up the tabernacle of meeting there. And the land was subdued before them.

2 But there remained among the children of Israel seven tribes which had not yet received their inheritance.

3 Then Joshua said to the children of Israel: [a]"How long will you neglect to go and possess the land which the LORD God of your fathers has given you?

4 "Pick out from among you three men for *each* tribe, and I will send them; they shall rise and go through the land, survey it according to their inheritance, and come *back* to me.

5 "And they shall divide it into seven parts. [a]Judah shall remain in their territory on the south, and the [b]house of Joseph shall remain in their territory on the north.

6 "You shall therefore [1]survey the land in seven parts and bring *the survey* here to me, [a]that I may cast lots for you here before the LORD our God.

7 [a]"But the Lē'vītes have no part among you, for the priesthood of the LORD *is* their inheritance. [b]And Gad, Reuben, and half the tribe of Ma·nas'seh have received their inheritance beyond the Jordan on the east, which Moses the servant of the LORD gave them."

8 Then the men arose to go away; and Joshua charged those who went to [1]survey the land, saying, "Go, walk [a]through the land, survey it, and come back to me, that I may cast lots for you here before the LORD in Shī'lōh."

9 So the men went, passed through the land, and [1]wrote the survey in a book in seven parts by cities; and they came to Joshua at the camp in Shī'lōh.

10 Then Joshua cast [a]lots for them in Shī'lōh before the LORD, and there [b]Joshua divided the land to the children of Israel according to their [1]divisions.

11 [a]Now the lot of the tribe of the children of Benjamin came up according to their families, and the territory of their lot

14 [c]Gen. 48:19
16 [a]Judg. 1:19; 4:3 [b]1 Kin. 4:12
17 [1]*allotment*
18 [a]Deut. 20:1 [1]Lit. *goings out*

CHAPTER 18

1 [a]Jer. 7:12 [b]Judg. 18:31
3 [a]Judg. 18:9
5 [a]Josh. 15:1 [b]Josh. 16:1—17:18
6 [a]Josh. 14:2; 18:10 [1]*describe in writing*
7 [a]Josh. 13:33 [b]Josh. 13:8
8 [a]Gen. 13:17 [1]*describe in writing*
9 [1]*described it in writing*
10 [a]Acts 13:19 [b]Num. 34:16–29 [1]*portions*
11 [a]Judg. 1:21

came out between the children
of Judah and the children of
Joseph.
12 [a]Their border on the north
side began at the Jordan, and
the border went up to the side of
Jericho on the north, and went
up through the mountains westward; it ended at the Wilderness
of Beth Ā′ven.
13 The border went over from
there toward Luz, to the side of
Luz [a](which *is* Beth′el) southward; and the border descended
to At′a·roth Ad′dar, near the hill
that *lies* on the south side [b]of
Lower Beth Hor′on.
14 Then the border extended
around the west side to the
south, from the hill that *lies*
before Beth Hor′on southward;
and [1]it ended at [a]Kir′jath Bā′al
(which *is* Kir′jath Jē′a·rim), a
city of the children of Judah.
This *was* the west side.
15 The south side *began* at the
end of Kir′jath Jē′a·rim, and the
border extended on the west
and went out to [a]the spring of
the waters of Neph·tō′ah.
16 Then the border came down
to the end of the mountain that
lies before [a]the Valley of the Son
of Hin′nom, which *is* in the Valley of the [1]Reph′a·im on the
north, descended to the Valley
of Hin′nom, to the side of the
Jeb′ū·sīte *city* on the south, and
descended to [b]En Rō′gel.
17 And it went around from the
north, went out to En Shem′esh,
and extended toward Ge·lī′loth,
which is before the Ascent of
A·dum′mim, and descended to
[a]the stone of Bō′han the son of
Reuben.
18 Then it passed along toward
the north side of [1]Ar′a·bah, and
went down to Ar′a·bah.
19 And the border passed along
to the north side of Beth Hog′-
lah; then [1]the border ended at
the north bay at the [a]Salt Sea, at
the south end of the Jordan. This
was the southern boundary.
20 The Jordan was its border on
the east side. This *was* the inheritance of the children of Benjamin, according to its boundaries
all around, according to their
families.
21 Now the cities of the tribe
of the children of Benjamin, according to their families, were
Jericho, Beth Hog′lah, Ē′mek
Kē′ziz,
22 Beth Ar′a·bah, Zem·a·rā′im,
Beth′el,
23 Av′im, Par′ah, Oph′rah,
24 Chē′phar Ha·am′mo·nī,
Oph′nī, and Gā′ba: twelve cities
with their villages;
25 [a]Gib′ē·on, [b]Rā′mah, Be·er′oth,
26 Miz′pah, Chē·phī′rah, Mō′zah,
27 Rē′kem, Ir′pē·el, Tar′a·lah,
28 Zē′lah, Ē′leph, [a]Jē′bus (which
is Jerusalem), Gib′ē·ath, *and* Kir′-
jath: fourteen cities with their
villages. This was the inheritance of the children of Benjamin according to their families.

19

The [a]second lot came out
for Sim′ē·on, for the tribe
of the children of Sim′ē·on according to their families. [b]And
their inheritance was within the
inheritance of the children of
Judah.
2 [a]They had in their inheritance Bē·er·shē′ba (Shē′ba), Mō′-
la·dah,
3 Hā′zar Shū′al, Bā′lah, Ē′zem,
4 El·tō′lad, Bē′thul, Hor′mah,
5 Zik′lag, Beth Mar′ca·both,
Hā′zar Sū′sah,

12 [a]Josh. 16:1
13 [a]Gen. 28:19 [b]Josh. 16:3
14 [a]Josh. 15:9 [1]Lit. *its goings out were*
15 [a]Josh. 15:9
16 [a]Josh. 15:8 [b]Josh. 15:7 [1]Lit. *Giants*
17 [a]Josh. 15:6
18 [1]*Beth Arabah,* Josh. 15:6; 18:22
19 [a]Josh. 15:2, 5 [1]Lit. *the goings out of the border were*
25 [a]1 Kin. 3:4, 5 [b]Jer. 31:15
28 [a]Josh. 15:8, 63

CHAPTER 19

1 [a]Judg. 1:3 [b]Josh. 19:9
2 [a]1 Chr. 4:28

6 Beth Le·bā′oth, and Sha·rū′-
hen: thirteen cities and their
villages;
7 Ā′in, Rim′mon, Ē′ther, and
Ā′shan: four cities and their
villages;
8 and all the villages that *were*
all around these cities as far
as Bā′a·lath Bē′er, [a]Rā′mah of
the South. This *was* the inheritance of the tribe of the children
of Sim′ē·on according to their
families.
9 The inheritance of the children of Sim′ē·on *was included*
in the share of the children of
Judah, for the share of the children of Judah was [1]too much for
them. [a]Therefore the children of
Sim′ē·on had *their* inheritance
within the inheritance of [2]that
people.
10 The third lot came out for the
children of Zeb′ū·lun according
to their families, and the border
of their inheritance was as far as
Sā′rid.
11 [a]Their border went toward
the west and to Mar′a·lah, went
to Dab′ba·sheth, and extended
along the brook that is [b]east of
Jok′nē·am.
12 Then from Sā′rid it went
eastward toward the sunrise
along the border of Chis′loth
Tā′bor, and went out toward
[a]Dab′e·rath, bypassing Ja·phī′a.
13 And from there it passed
along on the east of [a]Gath Hē′-
pher, toward Eth Kā′zin, and
extended to Rim′mon, which
borders on Nē′ah.
14 Then the border went around
it on the north side of Han·na′-
thon, and [1]it ended in the Valley
of Jiph′thah El.
15 Included were Kat′tath, Na-
hal′lal, Shim′ron, I′da·lah, and
Bethlehem: twelve cities with
their villages.
16 This *was* the inheritance of
the children of Zeb′ū·lun according to their families, these
cities with their villages.
17 The fourth lot came out to
Is′sa·char, for the children of
Is′sa·char according to their
families.
18 And their territory went to
Jez′rē·el, and *included* Che·sul′-
loth, Shū′nem,
19 Haph·rā′im, Shī′on, A·nā′-
ha·rath,
20 Rab′bith, Kish′i·on, Ā′bez,
21 Rē′meth, En Gan′nim, En
Had′dah, and Beth Paz′zez.
22 And the border reached to
Tā′bor, Shā·ha·zi′mah, and [a]Beth
Shem′esh; their border ended at
the Jordan: sixteen cities with
their villages.
23 This *was* the inheritance of
the tribe of the children of Is′-
sa·char according to their families, the cities and their villages.
24 [a]The fifth lot came out for the
tribe of the children of Ash′er
according to their families.
25 And their territory included
Hel′kath, Hā′lī, Bē′ten, Ach′-
shaph,
26 A·lam′me·lech, Ā′mad, and
Mī′shal; it reached to [a]Mount
Car′mel westward, along *the
Brook* Shī′hor Lib′nath.
27 It turned toward the sunrise
to Beth Dā′gon; and it reached
to Zeb′ū·lun and to the Valley
of Jiph′thah El, then northward
beyond Beth Ē′mek and Nē·ī′el,
bypassing [a]Cā′bul *which was* on
the left,
28 including [1]Ē′bron, Rē′hob,
Ham′mon, and Kā′nah, [a]as far as
Greater Sī′don.
29 And the border turned to

8 [a]1 Sam. 30:27
9 [a]Josh. 19:1 [1]*too large* [2]Lit. *them*
11 [a]Gen. 49:13 [b]Josh. 12:22
12 [a]1 Chr. 6:72
13 [a]2 Kin. 14:25
14 [1]Lit. *the goings out of it were*
22 [a]Josh. 15:10
24 [a]Judg. 1:31, 32
26 [a]Jer. 46:18
27 [a]1 Kin. 9:13
28 [a]Judg. 1:31 [1]So with MT, Tg., Vg.; a few Heb. mss. *Abdon* (cf. 21:30 and 1 Chr. 6:74)

Rā′mah and to the fortified city
of Tȳre; then the border turned
to Hō′sah, and ended at the sea
by the region of [a]Ach′zib.
30 Also Um′mah, Ā′phek, and
Rē′hob *were included:* twenty-
two cities with their villages.
31 This *was* the inheritance of
the tribe of the children of Ash′er
according to their families, these
cities with their villages.
32 [a]The sixth lot came out to the
children of Naph′ta·lī, for the
children of Naph′ta·lī according
to their families.
33 And their border began at
Hē′leph, enclosing the territory from the terebinth tree in
Zā·a·nan′nim, Ad′a·mī Nē′keb,
and Jab′nē·el, as far as Lak′kum;
[1]it ended at the Jordan.
34 [a]From Hē′leph the border
extended westward to Az′noth
Tā′bor, and went out from there
toward Huk′kok; it adjoined
Zeb′ū·lun on the south side and
Ash′er on the west side, and
ended at Judah by the Jordan
toward the sunrise.
35 And the fortified cities *are*
Zid′dim, Zer, Ham′math, Rak′-
kath, Chin′ne·reth,
36 Ad′a·mah, Rā′mah, Hā′zor,
37 [a]Kē′desh, Ed′rē·ī, En Hā′zor,
38 Ī′ron, Migdal El, Hō′rem,
Beth Ā′nath, and Beth Shem′-
esh: nineteen cities with their
villages.
39 This *was* the inheritance of
the tribe of the children of Naph′-
ta·lī according to their families,
the cities and their villages.
40 [a]The seventh lot came out for
the tribe of the children of Dan
according to their families.
41 And the territory of their inheritance was Zō′rah, [a]Esh′tā·ol,
Ir Shem′esh,
42 [a]Shā·a·lab′bin, [b]Aī′ja·lon,
Jeth′lah,
43 Ē′lon, Tim′nah, [a]Ek′ron,
44 El′tē·keh, Gib′be·thon, Bā′-
a·lath,
45 Jē′hud, Ben′ē Be′rak, Gath
Rim′mon,
46 Me Jar′kon, and Rak′kon,
with the region [1]near [2]Jop′pa.
47 And the [a]border of the children of Dan went beyond these,
because the children of Dan
went up to fight against Lē′shem
and took it; and they struck it
with the edge of the sword, took
possession of it, and dwelt in it.
They called Lē′shem, [b]Dan, after
the name of Dan their father.
48 This *is* the inheritance of the
tribe of the children of Dan according to their families, these
cities with their villages.
49 When they had [1]made an
end of dividing the land as an
inheritance according to their
borders, the children of Israel
gave an inheritance among them
to Joshua the son of Nun.
50 According to the word of
the LORD they gave him the city
which he asked for, [a]Tim′nath
[b]Sē′rah in the mountains of
Ē′phra·im; and he built the city
and dwelt in it.
51 [a]These *were* the inheritances
which El·ē·ā′zar the priest,
Joshua the son of Nun, and the
heads of the fathers of the tribes
of the children of Israel divided
as an inheritance by lot [b]in Shī′-
lōh before the LORD, at the door
of the tabernacle of meeting. So
they made an end of dividing
the country.

20 The LORD also spoke to
Joshua, saying,
2 "Speak to the children of
Israel, saying: [a]'Appoint[1] for

29 [a]Judg. 1:31
32 [a]Judg. 1:33
33 [1]Lit. *its goings out were*
34 [a]Deut. 33:23
37 [a]Josh. 20:7
40 [a]Judg. 1:34–36
41 [a]Josh. 15:33
42 [a]Judg. 1:35 [b]Josh. 10:12; 21:24
43 [a]Judg. 1:18
46 [1]*over against* [2]Heb. *Japho*
47 [a]Judg. 18 [b]Judg. 18:29
49 [1]*finished*
50 [a]Josh. 24:30 [b]1 Chr. 7:24
51 [a]Num. 34:17 [b]Josh. 18:1, 10

CHAPTER 20

2 [a]Num. 35:6–34 [1]*Designate*

yourselves cities of refuge, of
which I spoke to you through
Moses,
3 ‘that the slayer who kills a
person accidentally *or* unintentionally may flee there; and they
shall be your refuge from the
avenger of blood.
4 ‘And when he flees to one of
those cities, and stands at the
entrance of the gate of the city,
and [1]declares his case in the
hearing of the elders of that city,
they shall take him into the city
as one of them, and give him a
place, that he may dwell among
them.
5 [a]‘Then if the avenger of blood
pursues him, they shall not deliver the slayer into his hand,
because he struck his neighbor
unintentionally, but did not hate
him beforehand.
6 ‘And he shall dwell in that
city [a]until he stands before the
congregation for judgment, *and*
until the death of the one who is
high priest in those days. Then
the slayer may return and come
to his own city and his own
house, to the city from which he
fled.’ ”
7 So they appointed [a]Kē′-
desh in Galilee, in the mountains of Naph′ta·lī, [b]Shē′chem
in the mountains of Ē′phra·im,
and [c]Kir′jath Ar′ba (which *is*
Hē′bron) in [d]the mountains of
Judah.
8 And on the other side of
the Jordan, by Jericho eastward,
they assigned [a]Bē′zer in the wilderness on the plain, from the
tribe of Reuben, [b]Rā′moth in
Gil′ē·ad, from the tribe of Gad,
and [c]Gō′lan in Bā′shan, from the
tribe of Ma·nas′seh.
9 [a]These were the cities
appointed for all the children of
Israel and for the stranger who
[1]dwelt among them, that whoever killed a person accidentally
might flee there, and not die
by the hand of the avenger of
blood [b]until he stood before the
congregation.

21 Then the heads of the fathers’ *houses* of the [a]Lē′-
vītes came near to [b]El·ē·ā′zar the
priest, to Joshua the son of Nun,
and to the heads of the fathers’
houses of the tribes of the children of Israel.
2 And they spoke to them at
[a]Shī′lōh in the land of Cā′naan,
saying, [b]“The LORD commanded
through Moses to give us cities
to dwell in, with their common-
lands for our livestock.”
3 So the children of Israel gave
to the Lē′vītes from their inheritance, at the commandment of
the LORD, these cities and their
common-lands:
4 Now the lot came out for the
families of the Kō′hath·ītes. And
[a]the children of Aaron the priest,
who were of the Lē′vītes, [b]had
thirteen cities by lot from the
tribe of Judah, from the tribe of
Sim′ē·on, and from the tribe of
Benjamin.
5 [a]The rest of the children of
Kō′hath had ten cities by lot
from the families of the tribe
of Ē′phra·im, from the tribe of
Dan, and from the half-tribe of
Ma·nas′seh.
6 And [a]the children of Ger′-
shon had thirteen cities by lot
from the families of the tribe
of Is′sa·char, from the tribe of
Ash′er, from the tribe of Naph′-
ta·lī, and from the half-tribe of
Ma·nas′seh in Bā′shan.
7 [a]The children of Me·rar′ī

4 [1]*states*
5 [a]Num. 35:12
6 [a]Num. 35:12, 24, 25
7 [a]1 Chr. 6:76 [b]Josh. 21:21 [c]Josh. 14:15; 21:11, 13 [d]Luke 1:39
8 [a]Deut. 4:43 [b]Josh. 21:38 [c]Josh. 21:27
9 [a]Num. 35:15 [b]Josh. 20:6 [1]As a resident alien

CHAPTER 21

1 [a]Num. 35:1–8 [b]Josh. 14:1; 17:4
2 [a]Josh. 18:1 [b]Num. 35:2
4 [a]Josh. 21:8, 19 [b]Josh. 19:51
5 [a]Josh. 21:20
6 [a]Josh. 21:27
7 [a]Josh. 21:34

according to their families had
twelve cities from the tribe of
Reuben, from the tribe of Gad,
and from the tribe of Zeb′ū·lun.
8 [a]And the children of Israel
gave these cities with their common-lands by lot to the Lē′vītes,
[b]as the LORD had commanded by
the hand of Moses.
9 So they gave from the tribe
of the children of Judah and
from the tribe of the children of
Sim′ē·on these cities which are
[1]designated by name,
10 which were for the children
of Aaron, one of the families of
the Kō′hath·ītes, *who were* of
the children of Levi; for the lot
was theirs first.
11 [a]And they gave them [1]Kir′-
jath Ar′ba (*Ar′ba was* the father
of [b]Ā′nak), [c]which *is* Hē′bron, in
the mountains of Judah, with
the common-land surrounding
it.
12 But [a]the fields of the city and
its villages they gave to Caleb
the son of Je·phū′neh as his
possession.
13 Thus [a]to the children of
Aaron the priest they gave [b]Hē′-
bron with its common-land (a
city of refuge for the slayer),
[c]Lib′nah with its common-land,
14 [a]Jat′tir with its common-land,
[b]Esh·te·mō′a with its common-
land,
15 [a]Hō′lon with its common-
land, [b]Dē′bir with its common-
land,
16 [a]Ā′in with its common-land,
[b]Jut′tah with its common-land,
and [c]Beth Shem′esh with its
common-land: nine cities from
those two tribes;
17 and from the tribe of Benjamin, [a]Gib′ē·on with its common-
land, [b]Gē′ba with its common-
land,
18 An′a·thoth with its common-
land, and [a]Al′mon with its common-land: four cities.
19 All the cities of the children
of Aaron, the priests, *were* thirteen cities with their common-
lands.
20 [a]And the families of the children of Kō′hath, the Lē′vītes, the
rest of the children of Kō′hath,
even they had the cities of their
[1]lot from the tribe of Ē′phra·im.
21 For they gave them [a]Shē′-
chem with its common-land in
the mountains of Ē′phra·im (a
city of refuge for the slayer),
[b]Gē′zer with its common-land,
22 Kib′zā·im with its common-
land, and Beth Hor′on with its
common-land: four cities;
23 and from the tribe of Dan,
El′tē·keh with its common-land,
Gib′be·thon with its common-
land,
24 [a]Aī′ja·lon with its common-
land, *and* Gath Rim′mon with its
common-land: four cities;
25 and from the half-tribe of
Ma·nas′seh, Tā′nach with its
common-land and Gath Rim′-
mon with its common-land: two
cities.
26 All the ten cities with their
common-lands were for the rest
of the families of the children of
Kō′hath.
27 [a]Also to the children of Ger′-
shon, of the families of the Lē′-
vītes, from the *other* half-tribe
of Ma·nas′seh, *they gave* [b]Gō′lan
in Bā′shan with its common-
land (a city of refuge for the
slayer), and Be Esh′te·rah with
its common-land: two cities;
28 and from the tribe of
Is′sa·char, Kish′i·on with its

8 [a]Josh. 21:3 [b]Num. 35:2
9 [1]Lit. *called*
11 [a]1 Chr. 6:55 [b]Josh. 14:15; 15:13, 14 [c]Josh. 20:7 [1]Lit. *City of Arba*
12 [a]Josh. 14:14
13 [a]1 Chr. 6:57 [b]Josh. 15:54; 20:2, 7 [c]Josh. 15:42
14 [a]Josh. 15:48 [b]Josh. 15:50
15 [a]1 Chr. 6:58 [b]Josh. 15:49
16 [a]1 Chr. 6:59 [b]Josh. 15:55 [c]Josh. 15:10
17 [a]Josh. 18:25 [b]Josh. 18:24
18 [a]1 Chr. 6:60
20 [a]1 Chr. 6:66 [1]*allotment*
21 [a]Josh. 20:7 [b]Judg. 1:29
24 [a]Josh. 10:12
27 [a]1 Chr. 6:71 [b]Josh. 20:8

common-land, Dab′e·rath with its common-land,
29 Jar′muth with its common-land, *and* En Gan′nim with its common-land: four cities;
30 and from the tribe of Ash′er, Mī′shal with its common-land, Ab′don with its common-land,
31 Hel′kath with its common-land, and Rē′hob with its common-land: four cities;
32 and from the tribe of Naph′ta·lī, [a]Kē′desh in Galilee with its common-land (a city of refuge for the slayer), Ham′moth Dor with its common-land, and Kar′tan with its common-land: three cities.
33 All the cities of the Ger′shon·ītes according to their families *were* thirteen cities with their common-lands.
34 [a]And to the families of the children of Me·rar′ī, the rest of the Lē′vītes, from the tribe of Zeb′ū·lun, Jok′nē·am with its common-land, Kar′tah with its common-land,
35 Dim′nah with its common-land, *and* Na·hal′al with its common-land: four cities;
36 [1]and from the tribe of Reuben, [a]Bē′zer with its common-land, Jā′haz with its common-land,
37 Ked′e·moth with its common-land, and Meph′a·ath with its common-land: four cities;
38 and from the tribe of Gad, [a]Rā′moth in Gil′ē·ad with its common-land (a city of refuge for the slayer), Mā·ha·na′im with its common-land,
39 Hesh′bon with its common-land, *and* Jā′zer with its common-land: four cities in all.
40 So all the cities for the children of Me·rar′ī according to their families, the rest of the families of the Lē′vītes, were *by* their lot twelve cities.
41 [a]All the cities of the Lē′vītes within the possession of the children of Israel *were* forty-eight cities with their common-lands.
42 Every one of these cities had its common-land surrounding it; thus *were* all these cities.
43 So the LORD gave to Israel [a]all the land of which He had sworn to give to their fathers, and they [b]took possession of it and dwelt in it.
44 [a]The LORD gave them [b]rest all around, according to all that He had sworn to their fathers. And [c]not a man of all their enemies stood against them; the LORD delivered all their enemies into their hand.
45 [a]Not a word failed of any good thing which the LORD had spoken to the house of Israel. All came to pass.

22 Then Joshua called the Reū′ben·ītes, the Gad′ītes, and half the tribe of Ma·nas′seh,
2 and said to them: "You have kept [a]all that Moses the servant of the LORD commanded you, [b]and have obeyed my voice in all that I commanded you.
3 "You have not [1]left your brethren these many days, up to this day, but have kept the charge of the commandment of the LORD your God.
4 "And now the LORD your God has given [a]rest to your brethren, as He promised them; now therefore, return and go to your tents *and* to the land of your possession, [b]which Moses the servant of the LORD gave you on the other side of the Jordan.

32 [a]Josh. 20:7
34 [a]1 Chr. 6:77–81
36 [a]Josh. 20:8 [1]So with LXX, Vg. (cf. 1 Chr. 6:78, 79); MT, Bg., Tg. omit vv. 36, 37
38 [a]Josh. 20:8
41 [a]Num. 35:7
43 [a]Gen. 12:7; 26:3, 4; 28:4, 13, 14 [b]Num. 33:53
44 [a]Deut. 7:23, 24 [b]Josh. 1:13, 15; 11:23 [c]Deut. 7:24
45 [a]Josh. 23:14

CHAPTER 22

2 [a]Num. 32:20–22 [b]Josh. 1:12–18
3 [1]*forsaken*
4 [a]Josh. 21:44 [b]Num. 32:33

5 "But [a]take[1] careful heed to
do the commandment and the
law which Moses the servant of
the LORD commanded you, [b]to
love the LORD your God, to walk
in all His ways, to keep His commandments, to hold fast to Him,
and to serve Him with all your
heart and with all your soul."
6 So Joshua [a]blessed them and
sent them away, and they went
to their tents.
7 Now to half the tribe of
Ma·nas′seh Moses had given a
possession in Bā′shan, [a]but to
the *other* half of it Joshua gave
a possession among their brethren on this side of the Jordan,
westward. And indeed, when
Joshua sent them away to their
tents, he blessed them,
8 and spoke to them, saying,
"Return with much riches to
your tents, with very much livestock, with silver, with gold,
with bronze, with iron, and with
very much clothing. [a]Divide the
[1]spoil of your enemies with your
brethren."
9 So the children of Reuben,
the children of Gad, and half
the tribe of Ma·nas′seh returned,
and departed from the children
of Israel at Shī′lōh, which *is* in
the land of Cā′naan, to go to [a]the
country of Gil′ē·ad, to the land
of their possession, which they
had obtained according to the
word of the LORD by the hand of
Moses.
10 And when they came to the
region of the Jordan which *is* in
the land of Cā′naan, the children
of Reuben, the children of Gad,
and half the tribe of Ma·nas′seh
built an altar there by the Jordan—a great, impressive altar.
11 Now the children of Israel
[a]heard *someone* say, "Behold,
the children of Reuben, the children of Gad, and half the tribe
of Ma·nas′seh have built an altar on the [1]frontier of the land
of Cā′naan, in the region of the
Jordan—on the children of Israel's side."
12 And when the children of
Israel heard *of it*, [a]the whole
congregation of the children of
Israel gathered together at Shī′-
lōh to go to war against them.
13 Then the children of Israel
[a]sent [b]Phin′e·has the son of
El·ē·ā′zar the priest to the children of Reuben, to the children
of Gad, and to half the tribe of
Ma·nas′seh, into the land of Gil′-
ē·ad,
14 and with him ten rulers, one
ruler each from the chief house
of every tribe of Israel; and [a]each
one *was* the head of the house of
his father among the [1]divisions
of Israel.
15 Then they came to the children of Reuben, to the children
of Gad, and to half the tribe of
Ma·nas′seh, to the land of Gil′-
ē·ad, and they spoke with them,
saying,
16 "Thus says the whole congregation of the LORD: 'What
[a]treachery[1] *is* this that you have
committed against the God of
Israel, to turn away this day
from following the LORD, in that
you have built for yourselves an
altar, [b]that you might rebel this
day against the LORD?
17 '*Is* the iniquity [a]of Pē′or not
enough for us, from which we
are not cleansed till this day,
although there was a plague in
the congregation of the LORD,
18 'but that you must turn away
this day from following the

5 [a]Deut. 6:6, 17; 11:22 [b]Deut. 10:12; 11:13, 22 [1]*be very careful to do*
6 [a]2 Sam. 6:18
7 [a]Josh. 17:1–13
8 [a]1 Sam. 30:24 [1]*plunder*
9 [a]Num. 32:1, 26, 29
11 [a]Judg. 20:12, 13 [1]Lit. *front*
12 [a]Josh. 18:1
13 [a]Deut. 13:14 [b]Ex. 6:25
14 [a]Num. 1:4 [1]Lit. *thousands*
16 [a]Deut. 12:5–14 [b]Lev. 17:8, 9 [1]*unfaithful act*
17 [a]Num. 25:1–9

LORD? And it shall be, if you rebel today against the LORD, that tomorrow [a]He will be angry with the whole congregation of Israel.

19 [1]'Nevertheless, if the land of your possession *is* unclean, *then* cross over to the land of the possession of the LORD, [a]where the LORD's tabernacle stands, and take possession among us; but do not rebel against the LORD, nor rebel against us, by building yourselves an altar besides the altar of the LORD our God.

20 [a]'Did not Ā'chan the son of Zē'rah [1]commit a trespass in the [2]accursed thing, and wrath fell on all the congregation of Israel? And that man did not perish alone in his iniquity.' "

21 Then the children of Reuben, the children of Gad, and half the tribe of Ma·nas'seh answered and said to the heads of the [1]divisions of Israel:

22 "The LORD [a]God of gods, the LORD God of gods, He [b]knows, and let Israel itself know—if *it is* in rebellion, or if in treachery against the LORD, do not save us this day.

23 "If we have built ourselves an altar to turn from following the LORD, or if to offer on it burnt offerings or grain offerings, or if to offer peace offerings on it, let the LORD Himself [a]require *an account.*

24 "But in fact we have done it [1]for fear, for a reason, saying, 'In time to come your descendants may speak to our descendants, saying, "What have you to do with the LORD God of Israel?

25 "For the LORD has made the Jordan a border between you and us, *you* children of Reuben and children of Gad. You have no part in the LORD." So your descendants would make our descendants cease fearing the LORD.'

26 "Therefore we said, 'Let us now prepare to build ourselves an altar, not for burnt offering nor for sacrifice,

27 'but *that* it *may be* [a]a [1]witness between you and us and our generations after us, that we may [b]perform the service of the LORD before Him with our burnt offerings, with our sacrifices, and with our peace offerings; that your descendants may not say to our descendants in time to come, "You have no part in the LORD." '

28 "Therefore we said that it will be, when they say *this* to us or to our generations in time to come, that we may say, 'Here is the replica of the altar of the LORD which our fathers made, though not for burnt offerings nor for sacrifices; but it *is* a witness between you and us.'

29 "Far be it from us that we should rebel against the LORD, and turn from following the LORD this day, [a]to build an altar for burnt offerings, for grain offerings, or for sacrifices, besides the altar of the LORD our God which *is* before His tabernacle."

30 Now when Phin'e·has the priest and the rulers of the congregation, the heads of the [1]divisions of Israel who *were* with him, heard the words that the children of Reuben, the children of Gad, and the children of Ma·nas'seh spoke, it pleased them.

31 Then Phin'e·has the son of El·ē·ā'zar the priest said to the

18 [a]Num. 16:22
19 [a]Josh. 18:1 [1]*However*
20 [a]Josh. 7:1–26 [1]*act unfaithfully* [2]*devoted thing*
21 [1]Lit. *thousands*
22 [a]Deut. 4:35; 10:17 [b][Jer. 12:3]
23 [a]1 Sam. 20:16
24 [1]Lit. *from fear*
27 [a]Gen. 31:48 [b]Deut. 12:5, 14 [1]*testimony*
29 [a]Deut. 12:13, 14
30 [1]Lit. *thousands*

children of Reuben, the children of Gad, and the children of
Ma·nas′seh, "This day we perceive that the LORD *is* [a]among
us, because you have not committed this treachery against the
LORD. Now you have delivered
the children of Israel out of the
hand of the LORD."
32 And Phin′e·has the son of
El·ē·ā′zar the priest, and the rulers, returned from the children
of Reuben and the children of
Gad, from the land of Gil′ē·ad to
the land of Cā′naan, to the children of Israel, and brought back
word to them.
33 So the thing pleased the
children of Israel, and the children of Israel [a]blessed God; they
spoke no more of going against
them in battle, to destroy the
land where the children of Reuben and Gad dwelt.
34 The children of Reuben and
the children of [1]Gad called the
altar, *Witness*, "For *it is* a witness between us that the LORD *is*
God."

23

Now it came to pass, a
long time after the LORD
[a]had given rest to Israel from
all their enemies round about,
that Joshua [b]was old, advanced
in age.
2 And Joshua [a]called for all
Israel, for their elders, for their
heads, for their judges, and for
their officers, and said to them:
"I am old, advanced in age.
3 "You have seen all that the
[a]LORD your God has done to all
these nations because of you, for
the [b]LORD your God *is* He who
has fought for you.
4 "See, [a]I have divided to you
by lot these nations that remain,
to be an inheritance for your
tribes, from the Jordan, with all
the nations that I have cut off, as
far as the Great Sea westward.
5 "And the LORD your God [a]will
expel them from before you and
drive them out of your sight. So
you shall possess their land, [b]as
the LORD your God promised
you.
6 [a]"Therefore be very courageous to keep and to do all that
is written in the Book of the Law
of Moses, [b]lest you turn aside
from it to the right hand or to
the left,
7 "*and* lest you [a]go[1] among
these nations, these who remain among you. You shall not
[b]make mention of the name of
their gods, nor cause *anyone* to
[c]swear *by them;* you shall not
[d]serve them nor bow down to
them,
8 "but you shall [a]hold fast to
the LORD your God, as you have
done to this day.
9 [a]"For the LORD has [1]driven
out from before you great and
strong nations; but *as for* you,
no one has been able to stand
against you to this day.
10 [a]"One man of you shall chase
a thousand, for the LORD your
God *is* He who fights for you, [b]as
He promised you.
11 [a]"Therefore take careful heed
to yourselves, that you love the
LORD your God.
12 "Or else, if indeed you do [a]go
back, and cling to the remnant
of these nations—these that remain among you—and [b]make
marriages with them, and go in
to them and they to you,
13 "know for certain that [a]the
LORD your God will no longer
drive out these nations from before you. [b]But they shall be snares

31 [a]Lev. 26:11, 12
33 [a]1 Chr. 29:20
34 [1]LXX adds *and half the tribe of Manasseh.*

CHAPTER 23

1 [a]Josh. 21:44; 22:4 [b]Josh. 13:1; 24:29
2 [a]Deut. 31:28
3 [a]Ps. 44:3 [b]Deut. 1:30
4 [a]Josh. 13:2, 6; 18:10
5 [a]Ex. 23:30; 33:2 [b]Num. 33:53
6 [a]Josh. 1:7 [b]Deut. 5:32
7 [a]Deut. 7:2, 3 [b]Ex. 23:13 [c]Deut. 6:13; 10:20 [d]Ex. 20:5 [1]*associate with*
8 [a]Deut. 10:20
9 [a]Deut. 7:24; 11:23 [1]*dispossessed*
10 [a]Lev. 26:8 [b]Ex. 14:14
11 [a]Josh. 22:5
12 [a][2 Pet. 2:20, 21] [b]Deut. 7:3, 4
13 [a]Judg. 2:3 [b]Ex. 23:33; 34:12

and traps to you, and scourges on your sides and thorns in your eyes, until you perish from this good land which the LORD your God has given you.

14 "Behold, this day [a]I[1] *am* going the way of all the earth. And you know in all your hearts and in all your souls that [b]not one thing has failed of all the good things which the LORD your God spoke concerning you. All have come to pass for you; not one word of them has failed.

15 [a]"Therefore it shall come to pass, that as all the good things have come upon you which the LORD your God promised you, so the LORD will bring upon you [b]all harmful things, until He has destroyed you from this good land which the LORD your God has given you.

16 [1]"When you have transgressed the covenant of the LORD your God, which He commanded you, and have gone and served other gods, and bowed down to them, then the [a]anger of the LORD will burn against you, and you shall perish quickly from the good land which He has given you."

24

Then Joshua gathered all the tribes of Israel to [a]Shē′chem and [b]called for the elders of Israel, for their heads, for their judges, and for their officers; and they [c]presented themselves before God.

2 And Joshua said to all the people, "Thus says the LORD God of Israel: [a]'Your fathers, *including* Tē′rah, the father of Abraham and the father of Nā′hor, dwelt on the other side of [1]the River in old times; and [b]they served other gods.

3 [a]'Then I took your father Abraham from the other side of [1]the River, led him throughout all the land of Cā′naan, and multiplied his [2]descendants and [b]gave him Isaac.

4 'To Isaac I gave [a]Jacob and Esau. To [b]Esau I gave the mountains of Sē′ir to possess, [c]but Jacob and his children went down to Egypt.

5 [a]'Also I sent Moses and Aaron, and [b]I plagued Egypt, according to what I did among them. Afterward I brought you out.

6 'Then I [a]brought your fathers out of Egypt, and you came to the sea; and the Egyptians pursued your fathers with chariots and horsemen to the Red Sea.

7 'So they cried out to the LORD; and He put [a]darkness between you and the Egyptians, brought the sea upon them, and covered them. And [b]your eyes saw what I did in Egypt. Then you dwelt in the wilderness [c]a long time.

8 'And I brought you into the land of the Am′o·rītes, who dwelt on the other side of the Jordan, [a]and they fought with you. But I gave them into your hand, that you might possess their land, and I destroyed them from before you.

9 'Then [a]Bā′lak the son of Zip′por, king of Mō′ab, arose to make war against Israel, and [b]sent and called Bā′laam the son of Bē′or to curse you.

10 [a]'But I would not listen to Bā′laam; [b]therefore he continued to bless you. So I delivered you out of his hand.

11 'Then [a]you went over the Jordan and came to Jericho. And [b]the men of Jericho fought

14 [a]1 Kin. 2:2 [b]Josh. 21:45 [1]I am going to die.
15 [a]Deut. 28:63 [b]Deut. 28:15–68
16 [a]Deut. 4:24–28 [1]Or *If ever*

CHAPTER 24

1 [a]Gen. 35:4 [b]Josh. 23:2 [c]1 Sam. 10:19
2 [a]Gen. 11:7–32 [b]Josh. 24:14 [1]The Euphrates
3 [a]Gen. 12:1; Acts 7:2, 3 [b][Ps. 127:3] [1]The Euphrates [2]Lit. *seed*
4 [a]Gen. 25:24–26 [b]Deut. 2:5 [c]Gen. 46:1, 3, 6
5 [a]Ex. 3:10 [b]Ex. 7—10
6 [a]Ex. 12:37, 51; 14:2–31
7 [a]Ex. 14:20 [b]Deut. 4:34 [c]Josh. 5:6
8 [a]Num. 21:21–35
9 [a]Judg. 11:25 [b]Num. 22:2–14
10 [a]Deut. 23:5 [b]Num. 23:11, 20; 24:10
11 [a]Josh. 3:14, 17 [b]Josh. 6:1; 10:1

against you—*also* the Am′o·rītes, the Per′iz·zītes, the Cā′naan·ītes, the Hit′tītes, the Gir′ga·shītes, the Hī′vītes, and the Jeb′ū·sītes. But I delivered them into your hand.

12 [a]‘I sent the hornet before you which drove them out from before you, *also* the two kings of the Am′o·rītes, *but* [b]not with your sword or with your bow.

13 ‘I have given you a land for which you did not labor, and [a]cities which you did not build, and you dwell in them; you eat of the vineyards and olive groves which you did not plant.’

14 [a]“Now therefore, fear the LORD, serve Him in [b]sincerity and in truth, and [c]put away the gods which your fathers served on the other side of [1]the River and [d]in Egypt. Serve the LORD!

15 “And if it seems evil to you to serve the LORD, [a]choose for yourselves this day whom you will serve, whether [b]the gods which your fathers served that *were* on the other side of [1]the River, or [c]the gods of the Am′o·rītes, in whose land you dwell. [d]But as for me and my house, we will serve the LORD.”

16 So the people answered and said: “Far be it from us that we should forsake the LORD to serve other gods;

17 “for the LORD our God *is* He who brought us and our fathers up out of the land of Egypt, from the house of bondage, who did those great signs in our sight, and preserved us in all the way that we went and among all the people through whom we passed.

18 “And the LORD drove out from before us all the people, including the Am′o·rītes who dwelt in the land. [a]We also will serve the LORD, for He *is* our God.”

19 But Joshua said to the people, [a]“You cannot serve the LORD, for He *is* a [b]holy God. He *is* [c]a jealous God; [d]He will not forgive your transgressions nor your sins.

20 [a]“If you forsake the LORD and serve foreign gods, [b]then He will turn and do you harm and consume you, after He has done you good.”

21 And the people said to Joshua, “No, but we will serve the LORD!”

22 So Joshua said to the people, “You *are* witnesses against yourselves that [a]you have chosen the LORD for yourselves, to serve Him.” And they said, “*We are* witnesses!”

23 “Now therefore,” *he said,* [a]“put away the foreign gods which *are* among you, and [b]incline your heart to the LORD God of Israel.”

24 And the people [a]said to Joshua, “The LORD our God we will serve, and His voice we will obey!”

25 So Joshua [a]made[1] a covenant with the people that day, and made for them a statute and an ordinance [b]in Shē′chem.

26 Then Joshua [a]wrote these words in the Book of the Law of God. And he took [b]a large stone, and [c]set it up there [d]under the oak that *was* by the sanctuary of the LORD.

27 And Joshua said to all the people, “Behold, this stone shall be [a]a witness to us, for [b]it has heard all the words of the LORD which He spoke to us. It shall

12 [a]Ex. 23:28 [b]Ps. 44:3
13 [a]Deut. 6:10, 11
14 [a]1 Sam. 12:24 [b]2 Cor. 1:12 [c]Ezek. 20:18 [d]Ezek. 20:7, 8 [1]The Euphrates
15 [a]1 Kin. 18:21 [b]Josh. 24:2 [c]Ex. 23:24, 32 [d]Gen. 18:19 [1]The Euphrates
18 [a]Ps. 116:16
19 [a]Matt. 6:24 [b]1 Sam. 6:20 [c]Ex. 20:5 [d]Ex. 23:21
20 [a]Ezra 8:22 [b]Deut. 4:24–26
22 [a]Ps. 119:173
23 [a]Gen. 35:2 [b]1 Kin. 8:57, 58
24 [a]Deut. 5:24–27
25 [a]Ex. 15:25 [b]Josh. 24:1 [1]Lit. *cut a covenant*
26 [a]Deut. 31:24 [b]Judg. 9:6 [c]Gen. 28:18 [d]Gen. 35:4
27 [a]Gen. 31:48 [b]Deut. 32:1

therefore be a witness to you,
lest you deny your God."
28 So [a]Joshua let the people depart, each to his own
inheritance.
29 [a]Now it came to pass after
these things that Joshua the son
of Nun, the servant of the LORD,
died, *being* one hundred and ten
years old.
30 And they buried him within
the border of his inheritance at
[a]Tim′nath Sē′rah, which *is* in the
mountains of Ē′phra·im, on the
north side of Mount Gā′ash.
31 [a]Israel served the LORD all
the days of Joshua, and all the
days of the elders who outlived
Joshua, who had [b]known all the
works of the LORD which He had
done for Israel.
32 [a]The bones of Joseph, which
the children of Israel had brought
up out of Egypt, they buried at
Shē′chem, in the plot of ground
[b]which Jacob had bought from
the sons of Hā′mor the father
of Shē′chem for one hundred
[1]pieces of silver, and which had
become an inheritance of the
children of Joseph.
33 And [a]El·ē·ā′zar the son of
Aaron died. They buried him in
a hill *belonging to* [b]Phin′e·has
his son, which was given to him
in the mountains of Ē′phra·im.

28 [a]Judg. 2:6, 7
29 [a]Judg. 2:8
30 [a]Josh. 19:50
31 [a]Judg. 2:7 [b]Deut. 11:2
32 [a]Gen. 50:25 [b]Gen. 33:19 [1]Heb. *qesitah,* an unknown ancient measure of weight
33 [a]Ex. 28:1 [b]Ex. 6:25

The Book of JUDGES

THE Book of Judges stands in stark contrast to Joshua. In Joshua an obedient people conquered the land through trust in the power of God. In Judges, however, a disobedient and idolatrous people are defeated time and time again because of their rebellion against God.

In seven distinct cycles of sin to salvation, Judges shows how Israel had set aside God's law and in its place substituted "*what was* right in his own eyes" (21:25). The recurring result of abandonment from God's law is corruption from within and oppression from without. During the nearly four centuries spanned by this book, God raises up military champions to throw off the yoke of bondage and to restore the nation to pure worship. But all too soon the "sin cycle" begins again as the nation's spiritual temperature grows steadily colder.

The Hebrew title is *Shophetim*, meaning "judges," "rulers," "deliverers," or "saviors." *Shophet* not only carries the idea of maintaining justice and settling disputes, but it is also used to mean "liberating" and "delivering." First the judges deliver the people; then they rule and administer justice. The Septuagint used the Greek equivalent of this word, *Kritai* ("Judges"). The Latin Vulgate called it *Liber Judicum*, the "Book of Judges." This book could also appropriately be titled the "Book of Failure."

NOW after the [a]death of
Joshua it came to pass that
the children of Israel [b]asked
the LORD, saying, "Who shall
be first to go up for us against
the [c]Cā'naan·ītes to fight against
them?"
2 And the LORD said, [a]"Judah
shall go up. Indeed I have delivered
the land into his hand."
3 So Judah said to [a]Sim'ē·on
his brother, "Come up with me
to my allotted territory, that
we may fight against the Cā'naan·ītes;
and [b]I will likewise
go with you to your allotted territory."
And Sim'ē·on went with
him.
4 Then Judah went up, and the
LORD delivered the Cā'naan·ītes
and the Per'iz·zītes into their
hand; and they killed ten thousand
men at [a]Bē'zek.

CHAPTER 1

1 [a]Josh. 24:29 [b]Num. 27:21 [c]Josh. 17:12, 13

2 [a]Gen. 49:8, 9

3 [a]Josh. 19:1 [b]Judg. 1:17

4 [a]1 Sam. 11:8

7 [a]Lev. 24:19

8 [a]Josh. 15:63

9 [a]Josh. 10:36; 11:21; 15:13

5 And they found A·dō'ni-
Bē'zek in Bē'zek, and fought
against him; and they defeated
the Cā'naan·ītes and the Per'iz·zītes.
6 Then A·dō'ni-Bē'zek fled, and
they pursued him and caught
him and cut off his thumbs and
big toes.
7 And A·dō'ni-Bē'zek said,
"Seventy kings with their
thumbs and big toes cut off used
to gather *scraps* under my table;
[a]as I have done, so God has
repaid me." Then they brought
him to Jerusalem, and there he
died.
8 Now [a]the children of Judah
fought against Jerusalem and
took it; they struck it with the
edge of the sword and set the
city on fire.
9 [a]And afterward the children

of Judah went down to fight
against the Cā′naan·ītes who
dwelt in the mountains, in the
[1]South, and in the lowland.
10 Then Judah [1]went against
the Cā′naan·ītes who dwelt in
[a]Hē′bron. (Now the name of
Hē′bron *was* formerly [b]Kir′jath
Ar′ba.) And they killed Shē′shai,
A·hī′man, and Tal′maī.
11 [a]From there they went
against the inhabitants of Dē′-
bir. (The name of Dē′bir *was*
formerly Kir′jath Sē′pher.)
12 [a]Then Caleb said, "Whoever
attacks Kir′jath Sē′pher and
takes it, to him I will give my
daughter Ach′sah as wife."
13 And Oth′ni·el the son of Kē′-
naz, [a]Caleb's younger brother,
took it; so he gave him his
daughter Ach′sah as wife.
14 [a]Now it happened, when she
came *to him,* that [1]she urged
him to ask her father for a field.
And she dismounted from *her*
donkey, and Caleb said to her,
"What do you wish?"
15 So she said to him, [a]"Give me
a blessing; since you have given
me land in the South, give me
also springs of water." And Caleb gave her the upper springs
and the lower springs.
16 [a]Now the children of the
Ken′īte, Moses' father-in-law,
went up [b]from the City of Palms
with the children of Judah into
the Wilderness of Judah, which
lies in the South *near* [c]Ar′ad;
[d]and they went and dwelt among
the people.
17 [a]And Judah went with his
brother Sim′ē·on, and they attacked the Cā′naan·ītes who inhabited Zē′phath, and utterly
destroyed it. So the name of the
city was called [b]Hor′mah.

9 [1]Heb. *Negev,* and so throughout the book

10 [a]Josh. 15:13–19 [b]Josh. 14:15 [1]*attacked*

11 [a]Josh. 15:15

12 [a]Josh. 15:16, 17

13 [a]Judg. 3:9

14 [a]Josh. 15:18, 19 [1]LXX, Vg. *he urged her*

15 [a]Gen. 33:11

16 [a]Num. 10:29–32 [b]Deut. 34:3 [c]Josh. 12:14 [d]1 Sam. 15:6

17 [a]Judg. 1:3 [b]Num. 21:3

18 [a]Josh. 11:22

19 [a]Josh. 17:16, 18

20 [a]Josh. 14:9, 14 [b]Josh. 15:14 [1]*drove out from there*

21 [a]Josh. 15:63

22 [a]Judg. 1:19 [1]*family*

23 [a]Josh. 2:1; 7:2 [b]Gen. 28:19 [1]*family*

24 [a]Josh. 2:12, 14

27 [a]Josh. 17:11–13 [b]Josh. 21:25 [c]Josh. 17:11

18 Also Judah took [a]Gā′za with
its territory, Ash′ke·lon with its
territory, and Ek′ron with its
territory.
19 So the LORD was with Judah. And they drove out the
mountaineers, but they could
not drive out the inhabitants of
the lowland, because they had
[a]chariots of iron.
20 [a]And they gave Hē′bron to
Caleb, as Moses had said. Then
he [1]expelled from there the
[b]three sons of Ā′nak.
21 [a]But the children of Benjamin
did not drive out the Jeb′ū·sītes
who inhabited Jerusalem; so the
Jeb′ū·sītes dwell with the children of Benjamin in Jerusalem
to this day.
22 And the [1]house of Joseph
also went up against Beth′el,
[a]and the LORD *was* with them.
23 So the [1]house of Joseph [a]sent
men to spy out Beth′el. (The
name of the city *was* formerly
[b]Luz.)
24 And when the spies saw a
man coming out of the city, they
said to him, "Please show us the
entrance to the city, and [a]we will
show you mercy."
25 So he showed them the
entrance to the city, and they
struck the city with the edge of
the sword; but they let the man
and all his family go.
26 And the man went to the
land of the Hit′tītes, built a city,
and called its name Luz, which
is its name to this day.
27 [a]However, Ma·nas′seh did not
drive out *the inhabitants of* Beth
Shē′an and its villages, or [b]Tā′-
a·nach and its villages, or the inhabitants of [c]Dor and its villages,
or the inhabitants of Ib′lē·am and
its villages, or the inhabitants of

Me·gid′dō and its villages; for the
Cā′naan·ītes were determined to
dwell in that land.
28 And it came to pass, when
Israel was strong, that they put
the Cā′naan·ītes [1]under tribute,
but did not completely drive
them out.
29 [a]Nor did Ē′phra·im drive out
the Cā′naan·ītes who dwelt in
Gē′zer; so the Cā′naan·ītes dwelt
in Gē′zer among them.
30 Nor did [a]Zeb′ū·lun drive out
the inhabitants of Kit′ron or the
inhabitants of Na·hal′ol; so the
Cā′naan·ītes dwelt among them,
and [1]were put under tribute.
31 [a]Nor did Ash′er drive out
the inhabitants of Ac′cō or the
inhabitants of Sī′don, or of Ah′-
lab, Ach′zib, Hel′bah, Ā′phik, or
Rē′hob.
32 So the Ash′er·ītes [a]dwelt
among the Cā′naan·ītes, the inhabitants of the land; for they
did not drive them out.
33 [a]Nor did Naph′ta·lī drive out
the inhabitants of Beth Shem′-
esh or the inhabitants of Beth
Ā′nath; but they dwelt among
the Cā′naan·ītes, the inhabitants
of the land. Nevertheless the
inhabitants of Beth Shem′esh
and Beth Ā′nath were put under
tribute to them.
34 And the Am′o·rītes forced
the children of Dan into the
mountains, for they would not
allow them to come down to the
valley;
35 and the Am′o·rītes were determined to dwell in Mount Hē′-
res, [a]in Aī′ja·lon, and in [1]Shā·al′-
bim; yet when the strength of the
house of Joseph became greater,
they [2]were put under tribute.
36 Now the boundary of the
Am′o·rītes *was* [a]from the Ascent
of Ak·rab′bim, from Sē′la, and
upward.

2 Then the Angel of the LORD
came up from Gil′gal to Bō′-
chim, and said: [a]"I led you up
from Egypt and [b]brought you
to the land of which I swore to
your fathers; and [c]I said, 'I will
never break My covenant with
you.
2 'And [a]you shall make no [1]cov-
enant with the inhabitants of
this land; [b]you shall tear down
their altars.' [c]But you have not
obeyed My voice. Why have you
done this?
3 "Therefore I also said, 'I will
not drive them out before you;
but they shall be [a]*thorns*[1] in your
side, and [b]their gods shall [2]be a
[c]snare to you.' "
4 So it was, when the Angel of
the LORD spoke these words to
all the children of Israel, that the
people lifted up their voices and
wept.
5 Then they called the name
of that place [1]Bō′chim; and they
sacrificed there to the LORD.
6 And when [a]Joshua had dismissed the people, the children
of Israel went each to his own
inheritance to possess the land.
7 [a]So the people served the
LORD all the days of Joshua, and
all the days of the elders who
outlived Joshua, who had seen
all the great works of the LORD
which He had done for Israel.
8 Now [a]Joshua the son of Nun,
the servant of the LORD, died
when he was one hundred and
ten years old.
9 [a]And they buried him within
the border of his inheritance at
[b]Tim′nath Hē′res, in the mountains of Ē′phra·im, on the north
side of Mount Gā′ash.

28 [1]*to forced labor*
29 [a]Josh. 16:10
30 [a]Josh. 19:10–16 [1]*became forced laborers*
31 [a]Josh. 19:24–31
32 [a]Ps. 106:34, 35
33 [a]Josh. 19:32–39
35 [a]Josh. 19:42 [1]*Shaalabbin,* Josh. 19:42 [2]*became forced laborers*
36 [a]Josh. 15:3

CHAPTER 2

1 [a]Ex. 20:2 [b]Deut. 1:8 [c]Gen. 17:7, 8
2 [a]Deut. 7:2 [b]Deut. 12:3 [c]Ps. 106:34 [1]*treaty*
3 [a]Josh. 23:13 [b]Judg. 3:6 [c]Ps. 106:36 [1]LXX, Tg., Vg. *enemies to you* [2]*entrap you*
5 [1]Lit. *Weeping*
6 [a]Josh. 22:6; 24:28–31
7 [a]Josh. 24:31
8 [a]Josh. 24:29
9 [a]Josh. 24:30 [b]Josh. 19:49, 50

10 When all that generation had [1]been gathered to their fathers, another generation arose after them who [a]did not know the LORD nor the work which He had done for Israel.

11 Then the children of Israel did [a]evil in the sight of the LORD, and served the Bā′als;

12 and they [a]forsook the LORD God of their fathers, who had brought them out of the land of Egypt; and they followed [b]other gods from *among* the gods of the people who *were* all around them, and they [c]bowed down to them; and they provoked the LORD to anger.

13 They forsook the LORD [a]and served [1]Bā′al and the [2]Ash′to·reths.

14 [a]And the anger of the LORD was hot against Israel. So He [b]delivered them into the hands of plunderers who despoiled them; and [c]He sold them into the hands of their enemies all around, so that they [d]could no longer stand before their enemies.

15 Wherever they went out, the hand of the LORD was against them for calamity, as the LORD had said, and as the LORD had [a]sworn to them. And they were greatly distressed.

16 Nevertheless, [a]the LORD raised up judges who delivered them out of the hand of those who plundered them.

17 Yet they would not listen to their judges, but they [a]played the harlot with other gods, and bowed down to them. They turned quickly from the way in which their fathers walked, in obeying the commandments of the LORD; they did not do so.

18 And when the LORD raised up judges for them, [a]the LORD was with the judge and delivered them out of the hand of their enemies all the days of the judge; [b]for the LORD was moved to pity by their groaning because of those who oppressed them and harassed them.

19 And it came to pass, [a]when the judge was dead, that they reverted and behaved more corruptly than their fathers, by following other gods, to serve them and bow down to them. They did not cease from their own doings nor from their stubborn way.

20 Then the anger of the LORD was hot against Israel; and He said, "Because this nation has [a]transgressed My covenant which I commanded their fathers, and has not heeded My voice,

21 "I also will no longer drive out before them any of the nations which Joshua [a]left when he died,

22 "so [a]that through them I may [b]test Israel, whether they will keep the ways of the LORD, to walk in them as their fathers kept *them*, or not."

23 Therefore the LORD left those nations, without driving them out immediately; nor did He deliver them into the hand of Joshua.

3

Now these *are* [a]the nations which the LORD left, that He might test Israel by them, *that is,* all who had not [1]known any of the wars in Cā′naan

2 (*this was* only so that the generations of the children of Israel might be taught to know war, at least those who had not formerly known it),

3 *namely,* [a]five lords of the

10 [a]1 Sam. 2:12 [1]Died and joined their ancestors
11 [a]Judg. 3:7, 12; 4:1; 6:1
12 [a]Deut. 31:16 [b]Deut. 6:14 [c]Ex. 20:5
13 [a]Judg. 10:6 [1]A Canaanite god [2]Canaanite goddesses
14 [a]Deut. 31:17 [b]2 Kin. 17:20 [c]Is. 50:1 [d]Lev. 26:37
15 [a]Lev. 26:14–26
16 [a]Ps. 106:43–45
17 [a]Ex. 34:15
18 [a]Josh. 1:5 [b]Gen. 6:6
19 [a]Judg. 3:12
20 [a][Josh. 23:16]
21 [a]Josh. 23:4, 5, 13
22 [a]Judg. 3:1, 4 [b]Deut. 8:2, 16; 13:3

CHAPTER 3

1 [a]Judg. 1:1; 2:21, 22 [1]*experienced*
3 [a]Josh. 13:3

Phi·lis′tines, all the Cā′naan·ītes,
the Sī·dō′ni·ans, and the Hī′vītes
who dwelt in Mount Lebanon,
from Mount Bā′al Her′mon to
the entrance of Hā′math.
4 And they were *left, that He
might* test Israel by them, to
[1]know whether they would obey
the commandments of the LORD,
which He had commanded their
fathers by the hand of Moses.
5 [a]Thus the children of Israel
dwelt among the Cā′naan·ītes,
the Hit′tītes, the Am′o·rītes, the
Per′iz·zītes, the Hī′vītes, and the
Jeb′ū·sītes.
6 And [a]they took their daughters to be their wives, and gave
their daughters to their sons;
and they served their gods.
7 So the children of Israel did
[a]evil in the sight of the LORD.
They [b]forgot the LORD their
God, and served the Bā′als and
[1]A·shē′rahs.
8 Therefore the anger of the
LORD was hot against Israel, and
He [a]sold them into the hand of
[b]Cū′shan-Rish·a·thā′im king of
Mes·o·po·tā′mi·a; and the children of Israel served Cū′shan-
Rish·a·thā′im eight years.
9 When the children of Israel
[a]cried out to the LORD, the LORD
[b]raised up a deliverer for the
children of Israel, who delivered
them: [c]Oth′ni·el the son of Kē′-
naz, Caleb's younger brother.
10 [a]The Spirit of the LORD came
upon him, and he judged Israel.
He went out to war, and the LORD
delivered Cū′shan-Rish·a·thā′im
king of Mes·o·po·tā′mi·a into his
hand; and his hand prevailed
over Cū′shan-Rish·a·thā′im.
11 So the land had rest for forty
years. Then Oth′ni·el the son of
Kē′naz died.

12 [a]And the children of Israel
again did evil in the sight of the
LORD. So the LORD strengthened
[b]Eg′lon king of Mō′ab against
Israel, because they had done
evil in the sight of the LORD.
13 Then he gathered to himself
the people of Am′mon and [a]Am′-
a·lek, went and [1]defeated Israel,
and took possession of [b]the City
of Palms.
14 So the children of Israel
[a]served Eg′lon king of Mō′ab
eighteen years.
15 But when the children of
Israel [a]cried out to the LORD, the
LORD raised up a deliverer for
them: Ē′hud the son of Gē′ra, the
Ben′ja·mīte, a [b]left-handed man.
By him the children of Israel
sent tribute to Eg′lon king of
Mō′ab.
16 Now Ē′hud made himself a
dagger (it was double-edged and
a cubit in length) and fastened
it under his clothes on his right
thigh.
17 So he brought the tribute to
Eg′lon king of Mō′ab. (Now Eg′-
lon *was* a very fat man.)
18 And when he had finished
presenting the tribute, he sent
away the people who had carried the tribute.
19 But he himself turned back
[a]from the [1]stone images that
were at Gil′gal, and said, "I
have a secret message for you,
O king." He said, "Keep silence!"
And all who attended him went
out from him.
20 So Ē′hud came to him (now
he was sitting upstairs in his
cool private chamber). Then
Ē′hud said, "I have a message
from God for you." So he arose
from *his* seat.
21 Then Ē′hud reached with his

4 [1]*find out*
5 [a]Ps. 106:35
6 [a]Ex. 34:15, 16
7 [a]Judg. 2:11 [b]Deut. 32:18 [1]Name or symbol for Canaanite goddesses
8 [a]Judg. 2:14 [b]Hab. 3:7
9 [a]Judg. 3:15 [b]Judg. 2:16 [c]Judg. 1:13
10 [a]Num. 27:18
12 [a]Judg. 2:19 [b]1 Sam. 12:9
13 [a]Judg. 5:14 [b]Judg. 1:16 [1]*struck*
14 [a]Deut. 28:48
15 [a]Ps. 78:34 [b]Judg. 20:16
19 [a]Josh. 4:20 [1]Tg. *quarries*

left hand, took the dagger from
his right thigh, and thrust it into
his belly.
22 Even the [1]hilt went in after
the blade, and the fat closed
over the blade, for he did not
draw the dagger out of his belly;
and his entrails came out.
23 Then Ē′hud went out through
the porch and shut the doors of
the upper room behind him and
locked them.
24 When he had gone out,
[1]*Eg′lon's* servants came to look,
and *to their* surprise, the doors
of the upper room were locked.
So they said, "He is probably
[a]attending[2] to his needs in the
cool chamber."
25 So they waited till they were
[a]embarrassed, and still he had
not opened the doors of the upper room. Therefore they took
the key and opened *them*. And
there was their master, fallen
dead on the floor.
26 But Ē′hud had escaped while
they delayed, and passed beyond the [1]stone images and escaped to Sē·ī′rah.
27 And it happened, when he arrived, that [a]he blew the trumpet
in the [b]mountains of Ē′phra·im,
and the children of Israel went
down with him from the mountains; and [1]he led them.
28 Then he said to them, "Follow *me*, for [a]the LORD has delivered your enemies the Mō′-
ab·ītes into your hand." So they
went down after him, seized the
[b]fords of the Jordan leading to
Mō′ab, and did not allow anyone
to cross over.
29 And at that time they killed
about ten thousand men of
Mō′ab, all stout men of valor;
not a man escaped.
30 So Mō′ab was subdued that
day under the hand of Israel.
And [a]the land had rest for eighty
years.
31 After him was [a]Sham′gar the
son of Ā′nath, who killed six
hundred men of the Phi·lis′tines
[b]with an ox goad; [c]and he also
delivered [d]Israel.

4

When Ē′hud was dead, [a]the
children of Israel again did
[b]evil in the sight of the LORD.
2 So the LORD [a]sold them into
the hand of Jā′bin king of Cā′-
naan, who reigned in [b]Hā′zor.
The commander of his army *was*
[c]Sis′e·ra, who dwelt in [d]Ha·rō′-
sheth Ha·goy′im.
3 And the children of Israel
cried out to the LORD; for Jā′bin
had nine hundred [a]chariots of
iron, and for twenty years [b]he
had harshly oppressed the children of Israel.
4 Now Deb′or·ah, a prophetess, the wife of Lap′i·doth, was
judging Israel at that time.
5 [a]And she would sit under
the palm tree of Deb′or·ah between Rā′mah and Beth′el in the
mountains of Ē′phra·im. And the
children of Israel came up to her
for judgment.
6 Then she sent and called for
[a]Bar′ak the son of A·bin′ō·am
from [b]Kē′desh in Naph′ta·lī, and
said to him, "Has not the LORD
God of Israel commanded, 'Go
and [1]deploy *troops* at Mount [c]Tā′-
bor; take with you ten thousand
men of the sons of Naph′ta·lī and
of the sons of Zeb′ū·lun;
7 'and against you [a]I will de-
ploy Sis′e·ra, the commander of
Jā′bin's army, with his chariots
and his multitude at the [b]River
Kī′shon; and I will [1]deliver him
into your hand'?"

22 [1]*handle*
24 [a]1 Sam. 24:3 [1]Lit. *his* [2]Lit. *covering his feet*
25 [a]2 Kin. 2:17; 8:11
26 [1]Tg. *quarries*
27 [a]1 Sam. 13:3 [b]Josh. 17:15 [1]Lit. *he went before them*
28 [a]Judg. 7:9, 15 [b]Josh. 2:7
30 [a]Judg. 3:11
31 [a]Judg. 5:6 [b]1 Sam. 17:47 [c]Judg. 2:16 [d]1 Sam. 4:1

CHAPTER 4

1 [a]Judg. 2:19 [b]Judg. 2:11
2 [a]Judg. 2:14 [b]Josh. 11:1, 10 [c]1 Sam. 12:9 [d]Judg. 4:13, 16
3 [a]Judg. 1:19 [b]Ps. 106:42
5 [a]Gen. 35:8
6 [a]Heb. 11:32 [b]Josh. 19:37; 21:32 [c]Judg. 8:18 [1]*march*
7 [a]Ex. 14:4 [b]Ps. 83:9, 10 [1]Lit. *draw*

8 And Bar′ak said to her, "If
you will go with me, then I will
go; but if you will not go with
me, I will not go!"
9 So she said, "I will surely go
with you; nevertheless there will
be no glory for you in the journey you are taking, for the LORD
will [a]sell Sis′e·ra into the hand
of a woman." Then Deb′or·ah
arose and went with Bar′ak to
Kē′desh.
10 And Bar′ak called [a]Zeb′ū·lun
and Naph′ta·lī to Kē′desh; he
went up with ten thousand men
[b]under[1] his command, and Deb′-
or·ah went up with him.
11 Now Hē′ber [a]the Ken′īte, of
the children of [b]Hō′bab the father-in-law of Moses, had separated himself from the Ken′ītes
and pitched his tent near the
terebinth tree at Zā·a·nā′im,
[c]which *is* beside Kē′desh.
12 And they reported to Sis′e·ra
that Bar′ak the son of A·bin′-
ō·am had gone up to Mount Tā′-
bor.
13 So Sis′e·ra gathered together
all his chariots, nine hundred
chariots of iron, and all the people who *were* with him, from
Ha·rō′sheth Ha·goy′im to the
River Kī′shon.
14 Then Deb′or·ah said to
Bar′ak, [1]"Up! For this *is* the day
in which the LORD has delivered
Sis′e·ra into your hand. [a]Has not
the LORD gone out before you?"
So Bar′ak went down from
Mount Tā′bor with ten thousand
men following him.
15 And the LORD routed Sis′-
e·ra and all *his* chariots and all
his army with the edge of the
sword before Bar′ak; and Sis′-
e·ra alighted from *his* chariot
and fled away on foot.
16 But Bar′ak pursued the chariots and the army as far as
Ha·rō′sheth Ha·goy′im, and all
the army of Sis′e·ra fell by the
edge of the sword; not a man
was [a]left.
17 However, Sis′e·ra had fled
away on foot to the tent of [a]Jā′el,
the wife of Hē′ber the Ken′īte;
for *there was* peace between
Jā′bin king of Hā′zor and the
house of Hē′ber the Ken′īte.
18 And Jā′el went out to meet
Sis′e·ra, and said to him, "Turn
aside, my lord, turn aside to me;
do not fear." And when he had
turned aside with her into the
tent, she covered him with a
[1]blanket.
19 Then he said to her, "Please
give me a little water to drink,
for I am thirsty." So she opened
[a]a jug of milk, gave him a drink,
and covered him.
20 And he said to her, "Stand
at the door of the tent, and if
any man comes and inquires of
you, and says, 'Is there any man
here?' you shall say, 'No.' "
21 Then Jā′el, Hē′ber's wife,
[a]took a tent peg and took a hammer in her hand, and went softly
to him and drove the peg into
his temple, and it went down
into the ground; for he was fast
asleep and weary. So he died.
22 And then, as Bar′ak pursued
Sis′e·ra, Jā′el came out to meet
him, and said to him, "Come, I
will show you the man whom
you seek." And when he went
into her *tent*, there lay Sis′e·ra,
dead with the peg in his temple.
23 So on that day God subdued Jā′bin king of Cā′naan in
the presence of the children of
Israel.
24 And the hand of the children

9 [a]Judg. 2:14
10 [a]Judg. 5:18 [b]1 Kin. 20:10 [1]Lit. *at his feet*
11 [a]Judg. 1:16 [b]Num. 10:29 [c]Judg. 4:6
14 [a]Deut. 9:3; 31:3 [1]*Arise!*
16 [a]Ex. 14:28
17 [a]Judg. 5:6
18 [1]*rug*
19 [a]Judg. 5:24–27
21 [a]Judg. 5:24–27

of Israel grew stronger and
stronger against Jā′bin king
of Cā′naan, until they had destroyed Jā′bin king of Cā′naan.

5 Then Deb′or·ah and Bar′ak
the son of A·bin′ō·am [a]sang
on that day, saying:

2 "When[1] leaders [a]lead in
Israel,
[b]When the people [2]willingly
offer themselves,
Bless the LORD!

3 "Hear,[a] O kings! Give ear,
O princes!
I, *even* [b]I, will sing to the
LORD;
I will sing praise to the LORD
God of Israel.

4 "LORD, [a]when You went out
from Sē′ir,
When You marched from
[b]the field of Ē′dom,
The earth trembled and the
heavens poured,
The clouds also poured
water;
5 [a]The mountains [1]gushed
before the LORD,
[b]This Sinai, before the LORD
God of Israel.

6 "In the days of [a]Sham′gar,
son of Ā′nath,
In the days of [b]Jā′el,
[c]The highways were
deserted,
And the travelers walked
along the byways.
7 Village life ceased, it ceased
in Israel,
Until I, Deb′or·ah, arose,
Arose a mother in Israel.
8 They chose [a]new gods;
Then *there was* war in the
gates;
Not a shield or spear
was seen among forty
thousand in Israel.
9 My heart *is* with the rulers
of Israel
Who offered themselves
willingly with the
people.
Bless the LORD!

10 "Speak, you who ride on
white [a]donkeys,
Who sit in judges' attire,
And who walk along the
road.
11 Far from the noise of the
archers, among the
watering places,
There they shall recount
the righteous acts of the
LORD,
The righteous acts *for* His
villagers in Israel;
Then the people of the LORD
shall go down to the
gates.

12 "Awake,[a] awake, Deb′or·ah!
Awake, awake, sing a song!
Arise, Bar′ak, and lead your
captives away,
O son of A·bin′ō·am!

13 "Then the survivors came
down, the people against
the nobles;
The LORD came down for me
against the mighty.
14 From Ē′phra·im *were* those
whose roots were in
[a]Am′a·lek.
After you, Benjamin, with
your peoples,
From Mā′chir rulers came
down,
And from Zeb′ū·lun those
who bear the recruiter's
staff.

CHAPTER 5
1 [a]Judg. 4:4
2 [a]Ps. 18:47 [b]2 Chr. 17:16 [1]Or *When locks are loosed* [2]*volunteer*
3 [a]Deut. 32:1, 3 [b]Ps. 27:6
4 [a]Deut. 33:2 [b]Ps. 68:8
5 [a]Ps. 97:5 [b]Ex. 19:18 [1]*flowed*
6 [a]Judg. 3:31 [b]Judg. 4:17 [c]Is. 33:8
8 [a]Deut. 32:17
10 [a]Judg. 10:4; 12:14
12 [a]Ps. 57:8
14 [a]Judg. 3:13

15 And [1]the princes of
Is′sa·char *were* with
Deb′or·ah;
As Is′sa·char, so *was* Bar′ak
Sent into the valley [2]under
his command;
Among the divisions of
Reuben
There were great resolves of
heart.
16 Why did you sit among the
sheepfolds,
To hear the pipings for the
flocks?
The divisions of Reuben
have great searchings of
heart.
17 [a]Gil′ē·ad stayed beyond the
Jordan,
And why did Dan remain
[1]on ships?
[b]Ash′er continued at the
seashore,
And stayed by his inlets.
18 [a]Zeb′ū·lun *is* a people *who*
jeopardized their lives to
the point of death,
Naph′ta·lī also, on the
heights of the battlefield.
19 "The kings came *and* fought,
Then the kings of Cā′naan
fought
In [a]Tā′a·nach, by the waters
of Me·gid′dō;
They took no spoils of silver.
20 They fought from the
heavens;
The stars from their courses
fought against Sis′e·ra.
21 [a]The torrent of Kī′shon swept
them away,
That ancient torrent, the
torrent of Kī′shon.
O my soul, march on in
strength!
22 Then the horses' hooves
pounded,
The galloping, galloping of
his steeds.
23 'Curse Mē′roz,' said the
[1]angel of the LORD,
'Curse its inhabitants bitterly,
Because they did not come
to the help of the LORD,
To the help of the LORD
against the mighty.'
24 "Most blessed among women
is Jā′el,
The wife of Hē′ber the
Ken′īte;
[a]Blessed is she among
women in tents.
25 He asked for water, she gave
milk;
She brought out cream in a
lordly bowl.
26 She stretched her hand to
the tent peg,
Her right hand to the
workmen's hammer;
She pounded Sis′e·ra, she
pierced his head,
She split and struck through
his temple.
27 At her feet he sank, he fell,
he lay still;
At her feet he sank, he fell;
Where he sank, there he fell
[a]dead.
28 "The mother of Sis′e·ra
looked through the
window,
And cried out through the
lattice,
'Why is his chariot *so* long in
coming?
Why tarries the clatter of
his chariots?'
29 Her wisest [1]ladies answered
her,
Yes, she [2]answered herself,
30 'Are they not finding and
dividing the spoil:

15 [1]So with LXX, Syr., Tg., Vg.; MT *And my princes in Issachar* [2]Lit. *at his feet*
17 [a]Josh. 22:9 [b]Josh. 19:29, 31 [1]Or *at ease*
18 [a]Judg. 4:6, 10
19 [a]Judg. 1:27
21 [a]Judg. 4:7
23 [1]Or *Angel*
24 [a][Luke 1:28]
27 [a]Judg. 4:18–21
29 [1]*princesses* [2]Lit. *repeats her words to herself*

To every man a girl *or* two;
For Sis′e·ra, plunder of dyed
garments,
Plunder of garments
embroidered and dyed,
Two pieces of dyed
embroidery for the neck
of the looter?'

31 "Thus let all Your enemies
[a]perish, O LORD!
But *let* those who love Him
be [b]like the [c]sun
When it comes out in full
[d]strength."

So the land had rest for forty years.

6

Then the children of Israel did [a]evil in the sight of the LORD. So the LORD delivered them into the hand of [b]Mid′i·an for seven years,
2 and the hand of Mid′i·an prevailed against Israel. Because of the Mid′i·an·ītes, the children of Israel made for themselves the dens, [a]the caves, and the strongholds which *are* in the mountains.
3 So it was, whenever Israel had sown, Mid′i·an·ītes would come up; also A·mal′e·kītes and the [a]people of the East would come up against them.
4 Then they would encamp against them and [a]destroy the produce of the earth as far as Gā′za, and leave no sustenance for Israel, neither sheep nor ox nor [b]donkey.
5 For they would come up with their livestock and their tents, coming in as numerous as locusts; both they and their camels were [1]without number; and they would enter the land to destroy it.
6 So Israel was greatly impoverished because of the Mid′i·an·ītes, and the children of Israel [a]cried out to the LORD.
7 And it came to pass, when the children of Israel cried out to the LORD because of the Mid′i·an·ītes,
8 that the LORD sent a prophet to the children of Israel, who said to them, "Thus says the LORD God of Israel: 'I brought you up from Egypt and brought you out of the [a]house of [1]bondage;
9 'and I delivered you out of the hand of the Egyptians and out of the hand of all who oppressed you, and [a]drove them out before you and gave you their land.
10 'Also I said to you, "I *am* the LORD your God; [a]do not fear the gods of the Am′o·rītes, in whose land you dwell." But you have not obeyed My [b]voice.' "
11 Now the Angel of the LORD came and sat under the terebinth tree which *was* in Oph′rah, which *belonged* to Jō′ash [a]the Ā·bi·ez′rīte, while his son [b]Gideon threshed wheat in the winepress, in order to hide *it* from the Mid′i·an·ītes.
12 And the [a]Angel of the LORD appeared to him, and said to him, "The LORD *is* [b]with you, you mighty man of valor!"
13 Gideon said to Him, "O [1]my lord, if the LORD is with us, why then has all this happened to us? And [a]where *are* all His miracles [b]which our fathers told us about, saying, 'Did not the LORD bring us up from Egypt?' But now the LORD has [c]forsaken us and delivered us into the hands of the Mid′i·an·ītes."
14 Then the LORD turned to him and said, [a]"Go in this might of

31 [a]Ps. 92:9 [b]2 Sam. 23:4 [c]Ps. 37:6; 89:36, 37 [d]Ps. 19:5

CHAPTER 6

1 [a]Judg. 2:11 [b]Num. 22:4; 31:1–3
2 [a]1 Sam. 13:6
3 [a]Judg. 7:12
4 [a]Lev. 26:16 [b]Deut. 28:31
5 [1]*innumerable*
6 [a]Hos. 5:15
8 [a]Josh. 24:17 [1]*slavery*
9 [a]Ps. 44:2, 3
10 [a]2 Kin. 17:35, 37, 38 [b]Judg. 2:1, 2
11 [a]Josh. 17:2 [b]Heb. 11:32
12 [a]Judg. 13:3 [b]Josh. 1:5
13 [a][Is. 59:1] [b]Ps. 44:1 [c]Ps. 44:9–16 [1]Heb. *adoni*, used of man
14 [a]1 Sam. 12:11

yours, and you shall save Israel from the hand of the Mid′-
i·an·ītes. [b]Have I not sent you?"
15 So he said to Him, "O [1]my
Lord, how can I save Israel? Indeed [a]my clan *is* the weakest in
Ma·nas′seh, and I *am* the least in
my father's house."
16 And the LORD said to him,
[a]"Surely I will be with you, and
you shall [1]defeat the Mid′i·an·ītes
as one man."
17 Then he said to Him, "If now
I have found favor in Your sight,
then [a]show me a sign that it is
You who talk with me.
18 [a]"Do not depart from here,
I pray, until I come to You and
bring out my offering and set *it*
before You." And He said, "I will
wait until you come back."
19 [a]So Gideon went in and prepared a young goat, and unleavened bread from an ephah
of flour. The meat he put in a
basket, and he put the broth in
a pot; and he brought *them* out
to Him under the terebinth tree
and presented *them*.
20 The Angel of God said to
him, "Take the meat and the
unleavened bread and [a]lay *them*
on this rock, and [b]pour out the
broth." And he did so.
21 Then the Angel of the LORD
put out the end of the staff that
was in His hand, and touched
the meat and the unleavened
bread; and [a]fire rose out of the
rock and consumed the meat
and the unleavened bread. And
the Angel of the LORD departed
out of his sight.
22 Now Gideon [a]perceived that
He *was* the Angel of the LORD.
So Gideon said, "Alas, O Lord
GOD! [b]For I have seen the Angel
of the LORD face to face."

14 [b]Josh. 1:9
15 [a]1 Sam. 9:21 [1]Heb. *Adonai*, used of God
16 [a]Ex. 3:12 [1]Lit. *strike*
17 [a]Judg. 6:36, 37
18 [a]Gen. 18:3, 5
19 [a]Gen. 18:6–8
20 [a]Judg. 13:19 [b]1 Kin. 18:33, 34
21 [a]Lev. 9:24
22 [a]Judg. 13:21, 22 [b]Gen. 16:13
23 [a]Dan. 10:19
24 [a]Judg. 8:32 [1]Heb. *YHWH Shalom*
25 [a]Judg. 2:2 [b]Judg. 3:7 [c]Ex. 34:13 [1]Heb. *Asherah*, a Canaanite goddess
26 [1]*stronghold*

23 Then the LORD said to him,
[a]"Peace *be* with you; do not fear,
you shall not die."
24 So Gideon built an altar
there to the LORD, and called
it [1]The-LORD-*Is*-Peace. To this
day it *is* still [a]in Oph′rah of the
Ā·bi·ez′rītes.
25 Now it came to pass the
same night that the LORD said to
him, "Take your father's young
bull, the second bull of seven
years old, and [a]tear down the
altar of [b]Bā′al that your father
has, and [c]cut down the [1]wooden
image that *is* beside it;
26 "and build an altar to the
LORD your God on top of this
[1]rock in the proper arrangement, and take the second bull
and offer a burnt sacrifice with
the wood of the image which
you shall cut down."
27 So Gideon took ten men from
among his servants and did as
the LORD had said to him. But
because he feared his father's
household and the men of the
city too much to do *it* by day, he
did *it* by night.
28 And when the men of the
city arose early in the morning,
there was the altar of Bā′al, torn
down; and the wooden image
that *was* beside it was cut down,
and the second bull was being
offered on the altar *which had
been* built.
29 So they said to one another,
"Who has done this thing?"
And when they had inquired
and asked, they said, "Gideon
the son of Jō′ash has done this
thing."
30 Then the men of the city
said to Jō′ash, "Bring out your
son, that he may die, because he
has torn down the altar of Bā′al,

and because he has cut down
the wooden image that *was* beside it."
31 But Jō′ash said to all who
stood against him, "Would you
[1]plead for Bā′al? Would you save
him? Let the one who would
plead for him be put to death by
morning! If he *is* a god, let him
plead for himself, because his
altar has been torn down!"
32 Therefore on that day he
called him [a]Jer·ub·bā′al,[1] saying,
"Let Bā′al plead against him,
because he has torn down his
altar."
33 Then all [a]the Mid′i·an·ītes
and A·mal′e·kītes, the people of
the East, gathered together; and
they crossed over and encamped
in [b]the Valley of Jez′rē·el.
34 But [a]the Spirit of the LORD
came upon Gideon; then he [b]blew
the trumpet, and the Ā·bi·ez′rītes
gathered behind him.
35 And he sent messengers
throughout all Ma·nas′seh, who
also gathered behind him. He
also sent messengers to [a]Ash′er,
[b]Zeb′ū·lun, and Naph′ta·lī; and
they came up to meet them.
36 So Gideon said to God, "If
You will save Israel by my hand
as You have said—
37 [a]"look, I shall put a fleece of
wool on the threshing floor; if
there is dew on the fleece only,
and *it is* dry on all the ground,
then I shall know that You will
save Israel by my hand, as You
have said."
38 And it was so. When he rose
early the next morning and
squeezed the fleece together, he
wrung the dew out of the fleece,
a bowlful of water.
39 Then Gideon said to God,
[a]"Do not be angry with me, but
let me speak just once more: Let
me test, I pray, just once more
with the fleece; let it now be dry
only on the fleece, but on all the
ground let there be dew."
40 And God did so that night.
It was dry on the fleece only,
but there was dew on all the
ground.

7 Then [a]Jer·ub·bā′al (that *is*,
Gideon) and all the people
who *were* with him rose early
and encamped beside the well of
Har′od, so that the camp of the
Mid′i·an·ītes was on the north
side of them by the hill of Mō′-
reh in the valley.
2 And the LORD said to Gideon,
"The people who *are* with you
are too many for Me to give the
Mid′i·an·ītes into their hands,
lest Israel [a]claim glory for itself
against Me, saying, 'My own
hand has saved me.'
3 "Now therefore, proclaim in
the hearing of the people, saying, [a]'Whoever *is* fearful and
afraid, let him turn and depart
at once from Mount Gil′ē·ad.' "
And twenty-two thousand of the
people returned, and ten thousand remained.
4 But the LORD said to Gideon,
"The people *are* still *too* many;
bring them down to the water,
and I will test them for you
there. Then it will be, *that* of
whom I say to you, 'This one
shall go with you,' the same
shall go with you; and of whomever I say to you, 'This one shall
not go with you,' the same shall
not go."
5 So he brought the people
down to the water. And the LORD
said to Gideon, "Everyone who
laps from the water with his
tongue, as a dog laps, you shall

31 [1]*contend*
32 [a]1 Sam. 12:11 [1]Lit. *Let Baal Plead*
33 [a]Judg. 6:3 [b]Josh. 17:16
34 [a]Judg. 3:10 [b]Judg. 3:27
35 [a]Judg. 5:17; 7:23 [b]Judg. 4:6, 10; 5:18
37 [a][Ex. 4:3–7]
39 [a]Gen. 18:32
CHAPTER 7
1 [a]Judg. 6:32
2 [a]Deut. 8:17
3 [a]Deut. 20:8

set apart by himself; likewise
everyone who gets down on his
knees to drink."
6 And the number of those
who lapped, *putting* their hand
to their mouth, was three hundred men; but all the rest of the
people got down on their knees
to drink water.
7 Then the LORD said to Gideon,
[a]"By the three hundred men who
lapped I will save you, and deliver the Mid'i·an·ītes into your
hand. Let all the *other* people
go, every man to his [1]place."
8 So the people took provisions and their trumpets in their
hands. And he sent away all *the
rest of* Israel, every man to his
tent, and retained those three
hundred men. Now the camp of
Mid'i·an was below him in the
valley.
9 It happened on the same
[a]night that the LORD said to him,
"Arise, go down against the
camp, for I have delivered it into
your hand.
10 "But if you are afraid to go
down, go down to the camp with
Pū'rah your servant,
11 "and you shall [a]hear what
they say; and afterward [1]your
hands shall be strengthened
to go down against the camp."
Then he went down with Pū'-
rah his servant to the outpost of
the armed men who *were* in the
camp.
12 Now the Mid'i·an·ītes and
A·mal'e·kītes, [a]all the people of
the East, were lying in the valley [b]as numerous as locusts; and
their camels *were* [1]without number, as the sand by the seashore
in multitude.
13 And when Gideon had come,
there was a man telling a dream
to his companion. He said, "I
have had a dream: *To my* surprise, a loaf of barley bread
tumbled into the camp of Mid'-
i·an; it came to a tent and struck
it so that it fell and overturned,
and the tent collapsed."
14 Then his companion an-
swered and said, "This *is* nothing
else but the sword of Gideon the
son of Jō'ash, a man of Israel!
Into his hand [a]God has delivered
Mid'i·an and the whole camp."
15 And so it was, when Gideon
heard the telling of the dream
and its interpretation, that he
worshiped. He returned to the
camp of Israel, and said, "Arise,
for the LORD has delivered the
camp of Mid'i·an into your
hand."
16 Then he divided the three
hundred men *into* three companies, and he put a trumpet into
every man's hand, with empty
pitchers, and torches inside the
pitchers.
17 And he said to them, "Look
at me and do likewise; watch,
and when I come to the edge of
the camp you shall do as I do:
18 "When I blow the trumpet,
I and all who *are* with me, then
you also blow the trumpets on
every side of the whole camp,
and say, '*The sword of* the LORD
and of Gideon!' "
19 So Gideon and the hundred
men who *were* with him came
to the outpost of the camp at
the beginning of the middle
watch, just as they had posted
the watch; and they blew the
trumpets and broke the pitchers
that *were* in their hands.
20 Then the three companies
blew the trumpets and broke
the pitchers—they held the

7 [a]1 Sam. 14:6 [1]*home*
9 [a]Judg. 6:25
11 [a]1 Sam. 14:9, 10 [1]*you shall be encouraged*
12 [a]Judg. 6:3, 33; 8:10 [b]Judg. 6:5 [1]*innumerable*
14 [a]Judg. 6:14, 16

torches in their left hands and
the trumpets in their right hands
for blowing—and they cried,
"The sword of the LORD and of
Gideon!"
21 And [a]every man stood in his
place all around the camp; [b]and
the whole army ran and cried
out and fled.
22 When the three hundred
[a]blew the trumpets, [b]the LORD
set [c]every man's sword against
his companion throughout the
whole camp; and the army fled
to [1]Beth Acacia, toward Zer′-
e·rah, as far as the border of
[d]Abel Me·hō′lah, by Tab′bath.
23 And the men of Israel gathered together from [a]Naph′ta·lī,
Ash′er, and all Ma·nas′seh, and
pursued the Mid′i·an·ītes.
24 Then Gideon sent messengers
throughout all the [a]mountains of
Ē′phra·im, saying, "Come down
against the Mid′i·an·ītes, and
seize from them the watering
places as far as Beth Ba′rah and
the Jordan." Then all the men
of Ē′phra·im gathered together
and [b]seized the watering places
as far as [c]Beth Ba′rah and the
Jordan.
25 And they captured [a]two
princes of the Mid′i·an·ītes,
[b]Or′eb and Zē′eb. They killed
Or′eb at the rock of Or′eb, and
Zē′eb they killed at the winepress of Zē′eb. They pursued
Mid′i·an and brought the heads
of Or′eb and Zē′eb to Gideon on
the [c]other side of the Jordan.

8

Now [a]the men of Ē′phra·im
said to him, "Why have you
done this to us by not calling us
when you went to fight with the
Mid′i·an·ītes?" And they repri-
manded him sharply.
2 So he said to them, "What
have I done now in comparison
with you? *Is* not the [1]gleaning *of
the grapes* of Ē′phra·im better
than [2]the vintage of [a]Ā·bi·ē′zer?
3 [a]"God has delivered into
your hands the princes of Mid′-
i·an, Or′eb and Zē′eb. And what
was I able to do in comparison
with you?" Then their [b]anger toward him subsided when he said
that.
4 When Gideon came [a]to the
Jordan, he and [b]the three hundred men who *were* with him
crossed over, exhausted but still
in pursuit.
5 Then he said to the men of
[a]Suc′coth, "Please give loaves
of bread to the people who follow me, for they are exhausted,
and I am pursuing Zē′bah and
Zal·mun′na, kings of Mid′i·an."
6 And the leaders of Suc′coth
said, [a]"*Are*[1] the hands of Zē′bah
and Zal·mun′na now in your
hand, that [b]we should give bread
to your army?"
7 So Gideon said, "For this
cause, when the LORD has delivered Zē′bah and Zal·mun′na
into my hand, [a]then I will tear
your flesh with the thorns of the
wilderness and with briers!"
8 Then he went up from there
[a]to Pe·nū′el and spoke to them
in the same way. And the men
of Pe·nū′el answered him as the
men of Suc′coth had answered.
9 So he also spoke to the men
of Pe·nū′el, saying, "When I
[a]come back in peace, [b]I will tear
down this tower!"
10 Now Zē′bah and Zal·mun′na
were at Kar′kor, and their armies
with them, about fifteen thousand, all who were left of [a]all the
army of the people of the East;
for [b]one hundred and twenty

21 [a]2 Chr. 20:17 [b]2 Kin. 7:7
22 [a]Josh. 6:4, 16, 20 [b]Is. 9:4 [c]1 Sam. 14:20 [d]1 Kin. 4:12 [1]Heb. *Beth Shittah*
23 [a]Judg. 6:35
24 [a]Judg. 3:27 [b]Judg. 3:28 [c]John 1:28
25 [a]Judg. 8:3 [b]Ps. 83:11 [c]Judg. 8:4

CHAPTER 8

1 [a]Judg. 12:1
2 [a]Judg. 6:11 [1]Few grapes left after the harvest [2]The whole harvest
3 [a]Judg. 7:24, 25 [b]Prov. 15:1
4 [a]Judg. 7:25 [b]Judg. 7:6
5 [a]Gen. 33:17
6 [a]Judg. 8:15 [b]1 Sam. 25:11 [1]Lit. *Is the palm*
7 [a]Judg. 8:16
8 [a]Gen. 32:30, 31
9 [a]1 Kin. 22:27 [b]Judg. 8:17
10 [a]Judg. 7:12 [b]Judg. 6:5

thousand men who drew the sword had fallen.

11 Then Gideon went up by the road of those who dwell in tents on the east of [a]Nō′bah and Jog′be·hah; and he [1]attacked the army while the camp felt [b]secure.

12 When Zē′bah and Zal·mun′na fled, he pursued them; and he [a]took the two kings of Mid′i·an, Zē′bah and Zal·mun′na, and routed the whole army.

13 Then Gideon the son of Jō′-ash returned from battle, from the Ascent of Hē′res.

14 And he caught a young man of the men of Suc′coth and interrogated him; and he wrote down for him the leaders of Suc′coth and its elders, seventy-seven men.

15 Then he came to the men of Suc′coth and said, "Here are Zē′bah and Zal·mun′na, about whom you [a]ridiculed me, saying, '*Are* the hands of Zē′bah and Zal·mun′na now in your hand, that we should give bread to your weary men?' "

16 [a]And he took the elders of the city, and thorns of the wilderness and briers, and with them he [1]taught the men of Suc′-coth.

17 [a]Then he tore down the tower of [b]Pe·nū′el and killed the men of the city.

18 And he said to Zē′bah and Zal·mun′na, "What kind of men *were they* whom you killed at [a]Tā′bor?" So they answered, "As you *are,* so *were* they; each one resembled the son of a king."

19 Then he said, "They *were* my brothers, the sons of my mother. *As* the LORD lives, if you had let them live, I would not kill you."

20 And he said to Jē′ther his firstborn, "Rise, kill them!" But the youth would not draw his sword; for he was afraid, because he *was* still a youth.

21 So Zē′bah and Zal·mun′na said, "Rise yourself, and kill us; for as a man *is, so is* his strength." So Gideon arose and [a]killed Zē′-bah and Zal·mun′na, and took the crescent ornaments that *were* on their camels' necks.

22 Then the men of Israel said to Gideon, [a]"Rule over us, both you and your son, and your grandson also; for you have [b]delivered us from the hand of Mid′i·an."

23 But Gideon said to them, "I will not rule over you, nor shall my son rule over you; [a]the LORD shall rule over you."

24 Then Gideon said to them, "I would like to [1]make a request of you, that each of you would give me the earrings from his plunder." For they had golden earrings, [a]because they *were* Ish′ma·el·ītes.

25 So they answered, "We will gladly give *them.*" And they spread out a garment, and each man threw into it the earrings from his plunder.

26 Now the weight of the gold earrings that he requested was one thousand seven hundred *shekels* of gold, besides the crescent ornaments, pendants, and purple robes which *were* on the kings of Mid′i·an, and besides the chains that *were* around their camels' necks.

27 Then Gideon [a]made it into an ephod and set it up in his city, [b]Oph′rah. And all Israel [c]played the harlot with it there. It became [d]a snare to Gideon and to his house.

11 [a]Num. 32:35, 42 [b]Judg. 18:27 [1]Lit. *struck*
12 [a]Ps. 83:11
15 [a]Judg. 8:6
16 [a]Judg. 8:7 [1]*disciplined*
17 [a]Judg. 8:9 [b]1 Kin. 12:25
18 [a]Judg. 4:6
21 [a]Ps. 83:11
22 [a][Judg. 9:8] [b]Judg. 3:9; 9:17
23 [a]1 Sam. 8:7; 10:19; 12:12
24 [a]Gen. 37:25, 28 [1]Lit. *request a request*
27 [a]Judg. 17:5 [b]Judg. 6:11, 24 [c][Ps. 106:39] [d]Deut. 7:16

28 Thus Mid′i·an was subdued before the children of Israel, so that they lifted their heads no more. [a]And the country was quiet for forty years in the days of Gideon.

29 Then [a]Jer·ub·bā′al the son of Jō′ash went and dwelt in his own house.

30 Gideon had [a]seventy sons who were his own offspring, for he had many wives.

31 [a]And his concubine who *was* in Shē′chem also bore him a son, whose name he called A·bim′e·lech.

32 Now Gideon the son of Jō′ash died [a]at a good old age, and was buried in the tomb of Jō′ash his father, [b]in Oph′rah of the Ā·bi·ez′rītes.

33 So it was, [a]as soon as Gideon was dead, that the children of Israel again [b]played the harlot with the Bā′als, [c]and made Bā′al-Be′rith their god.

34 Thus the children of Israel [a]did not remember the LORD their God, who had delivered them from the hands of all their enemies on every side;

35 [a]nor did they show kindness to the house of Jer·ub·bā′al (Gideon) in accordance with the good he had done for Israel.

9 Then A·bim′e·lech the son of Jer·ub·bā′al went to Shē′chem, to [a]his mother's brothers, and spoke with them and with all the family of the house of his mother's father, saying,

2 "Please speak in the hearing of all the men of Shē′chem: 'Which is better for you, that all [a]seventy of the sons of Jer·ub·bā′al reign over you, or that one reign over you?' Remember that I *am* your own flesh and [b]bone."

3 And his mother's brothers spoke all these words concerning him in the hearing of all the men of Shē′chem; and their heart was inclined to follow A·bim′e·lech, for they said, "He is our [a]brother."

4 So they gave him seventy *shekels* of silver from the temple of [a]Bā′al-Be′rith, with which A·bim′e·lech hired [b]worthless and reckless men; and they followed him.

5 Then he went to his father's house [a]at Oph′rah and [b]killed his brothers, the seventy sons of Jer·ub·bā′al, on one stone. But Jō′tham the youngest son of Jer·ub·bā′al was left, because he hid himself.

6 And all the men of Shē′chem gathered together, all of Beth Mil′lō, and they went and made A·bim′e·lech king beside the terebinth tree at the pillar that *was* in Shē′chem.

7 Now when they told Jō′tham, he went and stood on top of [a]Mount Ger′i·zim, and lifted his voice and cried out. And he said to them:

"Listen to me, you men of
Shē′chem,
That God may listen to you!

8 "The[a] trees once went forth
to anoint a king over
them.
And they said to the olive
tree,
[b]'Reign over us!'

9 But the olive tree said to
them,
'Should I cease giving my oil,
[a]With which they honor God
and men,
And go to sway over trees?'

28 [a]Judg. 5:31
29 [a]Judg. 6:32; 7:1
30 [a]Judg. 9:2, 5
31 [a]Judg. 9:1
32 [a]Gen. 25:8 [b]Judg. 6:24; 8:27
33 [a]Judg. 2:19 [b]Judg. 2:17 [c]Judg. 9:4, 46
34 [a]Deut. 4:9
35 [a]Judg. 9:16–18

CHAPTER 9

1 [a]Judg. 8:31, 35
2 [a]Judg. 8:30; 9:5, 18 [b]Gen. 29:14
3 [a]Gen. 29:15
4 [a]Judg. 8:33 [b]Judg. 11:3
5 [a]Judg. 6:24 [b]2 Kin. 11:1, 2
7 [a]Deut. 11:29; 27:12
8 [a]2 Kin. 14:9 [b]Judg. 8:22, 23
9 [a][John 5:23]

10 "Then the trees said to the
fig tree,
'You come *and* reign over
us!'
11 But the fig tree said to them,
'Should I cease my sweetness
and my good fruit,
And go to sway over trees?'
12 "Then the trees said to the
vine,
'You come *and* reign over
us!'
13 But the vine said to them,
'Should I cease my new
wine,
[a]Which cheers *both* God and
men,
And go to sway over trees?'
14 "Then all the trees said to the
bramble,
'You come *and* reign over
us!'
15 And the bramble said to the
trees,
'If in truth you anoint me as
king over you,
Then come *and* take shelter
in my [a]shade;
But if not, [b]let fire come out
of the bramble
And devour the [c]cedars of
Lebanon!'

16 "Now therefore, if you have
acted in truth and sincerity in
making A·bim′e·lech king, and
if you have dealt well with
Jer·ub·bā′al and his house, and
have done to him [a]as[1] he deserves—
17 "for my [a]father fought for you,
risked his life, and [b]delivered
you out of the hand of Mid′i·an;
18 [a]"but you have risen up
against my father's house this
day, and killed his seventy sons
on one stone, and made A·bim′-
e·lech, the son of his [b]female
servant, king over the men of
Shē′chem, because he is your
brother—
19 "if then you have acted
in truth and sincerity with
Jer·ub·bā′al and with his house
this day, *then* [a]rejoice in A·bim′-
e·lech, and let him also rejoice in
you.
20 "But if not, [a]let fire come
from A·bim′e·lech and devour
the men of Shē′chem and Beth
Mil′lō; and let fire come from
the men of Shē′chem and from
Beth Mil′lō and devour A·bim′-
e·lech!"
21 And Jō′tham ran away and
fled; and he went to [a]Bē′er and
dwelt there, for fear of A·bim′-
e·lech his brother.
22 After A·bim′e·lech had
reigned over Israel three years,
23 [a]God sent a [b]spirit of ill will
between A·bim′e·lech and the
men of Shē′chem; and the men
of Shē′chem [c]dealt treacherously with A·bim′e·lech,
24 [a]that the crime *done* to the
seventy sons of Jer·ub·bā′al
might be settled and their [b]blood
be laid on A·bim′e·lech their
brother, who killed them, and
on the men of Shē′chem, who
aided him in the killing of his
brothers.
25 And the men of Shē′chem set
[1]men in ambush against him on
the tops of the mountains, and
they robbed all who passed by
them along that way; and it was
told A·bim′e·lech.
26 Now Gā′al the son of Ē′bed
came with his brothers and
went over to Shē′chem; and the
men of Shē′chem put their confidence in him.

13 [a]Ps. 104:15
15 [a]Is. 30:2 [b]Num. 21:28 [c]2 Kin. 14:9
16 [a]Judg. 8:35 [1]Lit. *according to the doing of his hands*
17 [a]Judg. 7 [b]Judg. 8:22
18 [a]Judg. 8:30, 35; 9:2, 5, 6 [b]Judg. 8:31
19 [a]Is. 8:6
20 [a]Judg. 9:15, 45, 56, 57
21 [a]Num. 21:16
23 [a]Is. 19:14 [b]1 Sam. 16:14; 18:9, 10 [c]Is. 33:1
24 [a]1 Kin. 2:32 [b]Num. 35:33
25 [1]Lit. *liers-in-wait for*

27 So they went out into the
fields, and gathered *grapes* from
their vineyards and trod *them*,
and [1]made merry. And they went
into [a]the house of their god,
and ate and drank, and cursed
A·bim′e·lech.
28 Then Gā′al the son of Ē′bed
said, [a]"Who *is* A·bim′e·lech, and
who *is* Shē′chem, that we should
serve him? *Is he* not the son of
Jer·ub·bā′al, and *is not* Zē′bul
his officer? Serve the men of
[b]Hā′mor the father of Shē′chem;
but why should we serve him?
29 [a]"If only this people were under my [1]authority! Then I would
remove A·bim′e·lech." So [2]he
said to A·bim′e·lech, "Increase
your army and come out!"
30 When Zē′bul, the ruler of the
city, heard the words of Gā′al
the son of Ē′bed, his anger was
aroused.
31 And he sent messengers to
A·bim′e·lech secretly, saying,
"Take note! Gā′al the son of Ē′bed
and his brothers have come to
Shē′chem; and here they are,
fortifying the city against you.
32 "Now therefore, get up by
night, you and the people who
are with you, and [1]lie in wait in
the field.
33 "And it shall be, as soon as
the sun is up in the morning,
that you shall rise early and
rush upon the city; and *when*
he and the people who are with
him come out against you, you
may then do to them [1]as you find
opportunity."
34 So A·bim′e·lech and all the
people who *were* with him rose
by night, and [1]lay in wait against
Shē′chem in four companies.
35 When Gā′al the son of
Ē′bed went out and stood in
the entrance to the city gate,
A·bim′e·lech and the people who
were with him rose from lying in
wait.
36 And when Gā′al saw the
people, he said to Zē′bul, "Look,
people are coming down from
the tops of the mountains!" But
Zē′bul said to him, "You see the
shadows of the mountains as *if
they were* men."
37 So Gā′al spoke again and
said, "See, people are coming
down from the center of the
land, and another company is
coming from the [1]Diviners' Terebinth Tree."
38 Then Zē′bul said to him,
"Where indeed *is* your mouth
now, with which you [a]said, 'Who
is A·bim′e·lech, that we should
serve him?' *Are* not these the
people whom you despised? Go
out, if you will, and fight with
them now."
39 So Gā′al went out, leading
the men of Shē′chem, and fought
with A·bim′e·lech.
40 And A·bim′e·lech chased
him, and he fled from him; and
many fell wounded, to the *very*
entrance of the gate.
41 Then A·bim′e·lech dwelt at
A·rū′mah, and Zē′bul [1]drove out
Gā′al and his brothers, so that
they would not dwell in Shē′-
chem.
42 And it came about on the
next day that the people went
out into the field, and they told
A·bim′e·lech.
43 So he took his people, divided them into three companies, and lay in wait in the field.
And he looked, and there were
the people, coming out of the
city; and he rose against them
and [1]attacked them.

27 [a]Judg. 9:4 [1]*rejoiced*
28 [a]1 Sam. 25:10 [b]Gen. 34:2, 6
29 [a]2 Sam. 15:4 [1]Lit. *hand* [2]So with MT, Tg.; DSS *they;* LXX *I*
32 [1]Set up an ambush
33 [1]Lit. *as your hand can find*
34 [1]Set up an ambush
37 [1]Heb. *Meonenim*
38 [a]Judg. 9:28, 29
41 [1]*exiled*
43 [1]Lit. *struck*

44 Then A·bim′e·lech and the company that *was* with him rushed forward and stood at the entrance of the gate of the city; and the *other* two companies rushed upon all who *were* in the fields and killed them.

45 So A·bim′e·lech fought against the city all that day; [a]he took the city and killed the people who *were* in it; and he [b]demolished the city and sowed it with salt.

46 Now when all the men of the tower of Shē′chem had heard *that,* they entered the [1]stronghold of the temple [a]of the god Be′rith.

47 And it was told A·bim′e·lech that all the men of the tower of Shē′chem were gathered together.

48 Then A·bim′e·lech went up to Mount [a]Zal′mon, he and all the people who *were* with him. And A·bim′e·lech took an ax in his hand and cut down a bough from the trees, and took it and laid *it* on his shoulder; then he said to the people who were with him, "What you have seen me do, make haste *and* do as I *have done.*"

49 So each of the people likewise cut down his own bough and followed A·bim′e·lech, put *them* against the [1]stronghold, and set the stronghold on fire above them, so that all the people of the tower of Shē′chem died, about a thousand men and women.

50 Then A·bim′e·lech went to Thē′bez, and he [1]encamped against Thē′bez and took it.

51 But there was a strong tower in the city, and all the men and women—all the people of the city—fled there and shut themselves in; then they went up to the top of the tower.

52 So A·bim′e·lech came as far as the tower and fought against it; and he drew near the door of the tower to burn it with fire.

53 But a certain woman [a]dropped an upper millstone on A·bim′e·lech's head and crushed his skull.

54 Then [a]he called quickly to the young man, his armorbearer, and said to him, "Draw your sword and kill me, lest men say of me, 'A woman killed him.' " So his young man thrust him through, and he died.

55 And when the men of Israel saw that A·bim′e·lech was dead, they departed, every man to his [1]place.

56 [a]Thus God repaid the wickedness of A·bim′e·lech, which he had done to his father by killing his seventy brothers.

57 And all the evil of the men of Shē′chem God returned on their own heads, and on them came [a]the curse of Jō′tham the son of Jer·ub·bā′al.

10

10 After A·bim′e·lech there [a]arose to save Israel Tō′la the son of Pū′ah, the son of Dodo, a man of Is′sa·char; and he dwelt in Shā′mir in the mountains of Ē′phra·im.

2 He judged Israel twenty-three years; and he died and was buried in Shā′mir.

3 After him arose Jā′ir, a Gil′ē·ad·īte; and he judged Israel twenty-two years.

4 Now he had thirty sons who [a]rode on thirty donkeys; they also had thirty towns, [b]which are called [1]"Hā′voth Jā′ir" to

45 [a]Judg. 9:20 [b]2 Kin. 3:25
46 [a]Judg. 8:33 [1]*fortified room*
48 [a]Ps. 68:14
49 [1]*fortified room*
50 [1]*besieged*
53 [a]2 Sam. 11:21
54 [a]1 Sam. 31:4
55 [1]*home*
56 [a]Job 31:3
57 [a]Judg. 9:20

CHAPTER 10

1 [a]Judg. 2:16
4 [a]Judg. 5:10; 12:14 [b]Deut. 3:14 [1]Lit. *Towns of Jair,* Num. 32:41; Deut. 3:14

this day, which *are* in the land of Gil′ē·ad.

5 And Jā′ir died and was buried in Cā′mon.

6 Then [a]the children of Israel again did evil in the sight of the LORD, and [b]served the Bā′als and the Ash′to·reths, [c]the gods of Syria, the gods of [d]Sī′don, the gods of Mō′ab, the gods of the people of Am′mon, and the gods of the Phi·lis′tines; and they forsook the LORD and did not serve Him.

7 So the anger of the LORD was hot against Israel; and He [a]sold them into the hands of the [b]Phi·lis′tines and into the hands of the people of [c]Am′mon.

8 From that year they [1]harassed and oppressed the children of Israel for eighteen years—all the children of Israel who *were* on the other side of the Jordan in the [a]land of the Am′o·rītes, in Gil′ē·ad.

9 Moreover the people of Am′mon crossed over the Jordan to fight against Judah also, against Benjamin, and against the house of Ē′phra·im, so that Israel was severely distressed.

10 [a]And the children of Israel cried out to the LORD, saying, "We have [b]sinned against You, because we have both forsaken our God and served the Bā′als!"

11 So the LORD said to the children of Israel, "*Did I* not *deliver you* [a]from the Egyptians and [b]from the Am′o·rītes and [c]from the people of Am′mon and [d]from the Phi·lis′tines?

12 "Also [a]the Sī·dō′ni·ans [b]and A·mal′e·kītes and [1]Mā′on·ītes [c]oppressed you; and you cried out to Me, and I delivered you from their hand.

13 [a]"Yet you have forsaken Me and served other gods. Therefore I will deliver you no more.

14 "Go and [a]cry out to the gods which you have chosen; let them deliver you in your time of distress."

15 And the children of Israel said to the LORD, "We have sinned! [a]Do to us whatever seems best to You; only deliver us this day, we pray."

16 [a]So they put away the foreign gods from among them and served the LORD. And [b]His soul could no longer endure the misery of Israel.

17 Then the people of Am′mon gathered together and encamped in Gil′ē·ad. And the children of Israel assembled together and encamped in [a]Miz′pah.

18 And the people, the leaders of Gil′ē·ad, said to one another, "Who *is* the man who will begin the fight against the people of Am′mon? He shall [a]be head over all the inhabitants of Gil′ē·ad."

11

Now [a]Jeph′thah the Gil′ē·ad·īte was [b]a mighty man of valor, but he *was* the son of a harlot; and Gil′ē·ad begot Jeph′thah.

2 Gil′ē·ad's wife bore sons; and when his wife's sons grew up, they drove Jeph′thah out, and said to him, "You shall have [a]no inheritance in our father's house, for you *are* the son of another woman."

3 Then Jeph′thah fled from his brothers and dwelt in the land of [a]Tob; and [b]worthless men banded together with Jeph′thah and went out *raiding* with him.

4 It came to pass after a time that the [a]people of Am′mon made war against Israel.

6 [a]Judg. 2:11; 3:7; 6:1; 13:1 [b]Judg. 2:13 [c]Judg. 2:12 [d]1 Kin. 11:33
7 [a]1 Sam. 12:9 [b]Judg. 13:1 [c]Judg. 3:13
8 [a]Num. 32:33 [1]Lit. *shattered*
10 [a]1 Sam. 12:10 [b]Deut. 1:41
11 [a]Ex. 14:30 [b]Num. 21:21, 24, 25 [c]Judg. 3:12, 13 [d]Judg. 3:31
12 [a]Judg. 1:31; 5:19 [b]Judg. 6:3; 7:12 [c]Ps. 106:42, 43 [1]LXX mss. *Midianites*
13 [a][Jer. 2:13]
14 [a]Deut. 32:37, 38
15 [a]1 Sam. 3:18
16 [a]Jer. 18:7, 8 [b]Is. 63:9
17 [a]Judg. 11:11, 29
18 [a]Judg. 11:8, 11

CHAPTER 11

1 [a]Heb. 11:32 [b]2 Kin. 5:1
2 [a]Gen. 21:10
3 [a]2 Sam. 10:6, 8 [b]1 Sam. 22:2
4 [a]Judg. 10:9, 17

5 And so it was, when the
people of Am′mon made war
against Israel, that the elders of
Gil′ē·ad went to get Jeph′thah
from the land of Tob.
6 Then they said to Jeph′thah,
"Come and be our commander,
that we may fight against the
people of Am′mon."
7 So Jeph′thah said to the elders of Gil′ē·ad, [a]"Did you not
hate me, and expel me from my
father's house? Why have you
come to me now when you are
in [1]distress?"
8 [a]And the elders of Gil′ē·ad
said to Jeph′thah, "That is why
we have [b]turned[1] again to you
now, that you may go with us
and fight against the people of
Am′mon, and be [c]our head over
all the inhabitants of Gil′ē·ad."
9 So Jeph′thah said to the elders of Gil′ē·ad, "If you take me
back home to fight against the
people of Am′mon, and the LORD
delivers them to me, shall I be
your head?"
10 And the elders of Gil′ē·ad
said to Jeph′thah, [a]"The LORD
will be a witness between us, if
we do not do according to your
words."
11 Then Jeph′thah went with
the elders of Gil′ē·ad, and the
people made him [a]head and
commander over them; and
Jeph′thah spoke all his words
[b]before the LORD in Miz′pah.
12 Now Jeph′thah sent messengers to the king of the people of
Am′mon, saying, [a]"What do you
have against me, that you have
come to fight against me in my
land?"
13 And the king of the people
of Am′mon answered the messengers of Jeph′thah, [a]"Because
Israel took away my land when
they came up out of Egypt, from
[b]the Ar′non as far as [c]the Jab′-
bok, and to the Jordan. Now
therefore, restore those *lands*
peaceably."
14 So Jeph′thah again sent messengers to the king of the people
of Am′mon,
15 and said to him, "Thus says
Jeph′thah: [a]'Israel did not take
away the land of Mō′ab, nor the
land of the people of Am′mon;
16 'for when Israel came up
from Egypt, they walked through
the wilderness as far as the Red
Sea and [a]came to Kā′desh.
17 'Then [a]Israel sent messengers to the king of Ē′dom, saying, "Please let me pass through
your land." [b]But the king of
Ē′dom would not heed. And in
like manner they sent to the
[c]king of Mō′ab, but he would not
consent. So Israel [d]remained in
Kā′desh.
18 'And they [a]went along
through the wilderness and
[b]bypassed the land of Ē′dom and
the land of Mō′ab, came to the
east side of the land of Mō′ab,
and encamped on the other side
of the Ar′non. But they did not
enter the border of Mō′ab, for
the Ar′non *was* the border of
Mō′ab.
19 'Then [a]Israel sent messengers to Sī′hon king of the Am′-
o·rītes, king of Hesh′bon; and
Israel said to him, "Please [b]let us
pass through your land into our
place."
20 [a]'But Sī′hon did not trust Israel to pass through his territory. So Sī′hon gathered all
his people together, encamped
in Jā′haz, and fought against
Israel.

7 [a]Gen. 26:27 [1]*trouble*
8 [a]Judg. 10:18 [b][Luke 17:4] [c]Judg. 10:18 [1]*returned*
10 [a]Jer. 29:23; 42:5
11 [a]Judg. 11:8 [b]Judg. 10:17; 20:1
12 [a]2 Sam. 16:10
13 [a]Num. 21:24–26 [b]Josh. 13:9 [c]Gen. 32:22
15 [a]Deut. 2:9, 19
16 [a]Num. 13:26; 20:1
17 [a]Num. 20:14 [b]Num. 20:14–21 [c]Josh. 24:9 [d]Num. 20:1
18 [a]Deut. 2:9, 18, 19 [b]Num. 21:4
19 [a]Num. 21:21 [b]Deut. 2:27
20 [a]Deut. 2:27

21 'And the LORD God of Israel [a]delivered Sī'hon and all his
people into the hand of Israel,
and they [b]defeated[1] them. Thus
Israel gained possession of all
the land of the Am'o·rītes, who
inhabited that country.
22 'They took possession of [a]all
the territory of the Am'o·rītes,
from the Ar'non to the Jab'bok
and from the wilderness to the
Jordan.
23 'And now the LORD God of
Israel has [1]dispossessed the
Am'o·rītes from before His people Israel; should you then possess it?
24 'Will you not possess whatever [a]Chē'mosh your god gives
you to possess? So whatever [b]the
LORD our God takes possession
of before us, we will possess.
25 'And now, *are* you any better
than [a]Bā'lak the son of Zip'-
por, king of Mō'ab? Did he ever
strive against Israel? Did he ever
fight against them?
26 'While Israel dwelt in [a]Hesh'-
bon and its villages, in [b]A·rō'er
and its villages, and in all the
cities along the banks of the
Ar'non, for three hundred years,
why did you not recover *them*
within that time?
27 'Therefore I have not sinned
against you, but you wronged
me by fighting against me. May
the LORD, [a]the Judge, [b]render
judgment this day between the
children of Israel and the people
of Am'mon.' "
28 However, the king of the
people of Am'mon did not heed
the words which Jeph'thah sent
him.
29 Then [a]the Spirit of the LORD
came upon Jeph'thah, and he
passed through Gil'ē·ad and
Ma·nas'seh, and passed through
Miz'pah of Gil'ē·ad; and from
Miz'pah of Gil'ē·ad he advanced
toward the people of Am'mon.
30 And Jeph'thah [a]made a vow
to the LORD, and said, "If You
will indeed deliver the people of
Am'mon into my hands,
31 "then it will be that whatever
comes out of the doors of my
house to meet me, when I return
in peace from the people of Am'-
mon, [a]shall surely be the LORD's,
[b]and I will offer it up as a burnt
offering."
32 So Jeph'thah advanced toward the people of Am'mon to
fight against them, and the LORD
delivered them into his hands.
33 And he [1]defeated them from
A·rō'er as far as [a]Min'nith—
twenty cities—and to [2]Abel Ker'-
a·mim, with a very great slaughter. Thus the people of Am'mon
were subdued before the children of Israel.
34 When Jeph'thah came to his
house at [a]Miz'pah, there was [b]his
daughter, coming out to meet
him with timbrels and dancing;
and she *was his* only child. Besides her he had neither son nor
daughter.
35 And it came to pass, when he
saw her, that he [a]tore his clothes,
and said, "Alas, my daughter!
You have brought me very low!
You are among those who trouble me! For I [b]have [1]given my
word to the LORD, and [c]I cannot
[2]go back on it."
36 So she said to him, "My father, *if* you have given your word
to the LORD, [a]do to me according
to what has gone out of your
mouth, because [b]the LORD has
avenged you of your enemies,
the people of Am'mon."

21 [a]Josh. 24:8 [b]Num. 21:24, 25 [1]Lit. *struck*
22 [a]Deut. 2:36, 37
23 [1]*driven out*
24 [a]Num. 21:29 [b][Deut. 9:4, 5]
25 [a]Num. 22:2
26 [a]Num. 21:25, 26 [b]Deut. 2:36
27 [a]Gen. 18:25 [b]Gen. 16:5; 31:53
29 [a]Judg. 3:10
30 [a]Gen. 28:20
31 [a]Lev. 27:2, 3, 28 [b]Ps. 66:13
33 [a]Ezek. 27:17 [1]Lit. *struck* [2]Lit. *Plain of Vineyards*
34 [a]Judg. 10:17; 11:11 [b]Ex. 15:20
35 [a]Gen. 37:29, 34 [b]Eccl. 5:2, 4, 5 [c]Num. 30:2 [1]Lit. *opened my mouth* [2]Lit. *take it back*
36 [a]Num. 30:2 [b]2 Sam. 18:19, 31

37 Then she said to her father,
"Let this thing be done for me:
let me alone for two months,
that I may go and wander on
the mountains and [1]bewail my
virginity, my [2]friends and I."
38 So he said, "Go." And he sent
her away *for* two months; and
she went with her friends, and
bewailed her virginity on the
mountains.
39 And it was so at the end of
two months that she returned to
her father, and he [a]carried out
his vow with her which he had
vowed. She [1]knew no man. And
it became a custom in Israel
40 *that* the daughters of Israel
went four days each year to [1]lament the daughter of Jeph'thah
the Gil'ē·ad·īte.

12 Then [a]the men of
Ē'phra·im [1]gathered together, crossed over toward
Zā'phon, and said to Jeph'thah,
"Why did you cross over to fight
against the people of Am'mon,
and did not call us to go with
you? We will burn your house
down on you with fire!"
2 And Jeph'thah said to them,
"My people and I were in a great
struggle with the people of Am'mon; and when I called you, you
did not deliver me out of their
hands.
3 "So when I saw that you
would not deliver *me,* I [a]took
my life in my hands and crossed
over against the people of Am'mon; and the LORD delivered
them into my hand. Why then
have you come up to me this day
to fight against me?"
4 Now Jeph'thah gathered together all the men of Gil'ē·ad
and fought against Ē'phra·im.
And the men of Gil'ē·ad defeated
Ē'phra·im, because they said,
"You Gil'ē·ad·ītes [a]*are* fugitives of Ē'phra·im among the
Ē'phra·im·ītes *and* among the
Ma·nas'sītes."
5 The Gil'ē·ad·ītes seized the
[a]fords of the Jordan before
the Ē'phra·im·ītes *arrived.* And
when *any* Ē'phra·im·īte who escaped said, "Let me cross over,"
the men of Gil'ē·ad would say to
him, "*Are* you an Ē'phra·im·īte?"
If he said, "No,"
6 then they would say to him,
"Then say, [a]'Shib'bo·leth'!"[1] And
he would say, "Sib'bo·leth," for
he could not [2]pronounce *it* right.
Then they would take him and
kill him at the fords of the Jordan. There fell at that time forty-two thousand Ē'phra·im·ītes.
7 And Jeph'thah judged Israel
six years. Then Jeph'thah the
Gil'ē·ad·īte died and was buried
among the cities of Gil'ē·ad.
8 After him, Ib'zan of Bethlehem judged Israel.
9 He had thirty sons. And he
gave away thirty daughters in
marriage, and brought in thirty
daughters from elsewhere for
his sons. He judged Israel seven
years.
10 Then Ib'zan died and was
buried at Bethlehem.
11 After him, Ē'lon the Zeb'ū·lun·īte judged Israel. He judged
Israel ten years.
12 And Ē'lon the Zeb'ū·lun·īte
died and was buried at Aī'ja·lon
in the country of Zeb'ū·lun.
13 After him, Ab'don the son of
Hil'lel the Pir'a·thon·īte judged
Israel.
14 He had forty sons and thirty
grandsons, who [a]rode on seventy young donkeys. He judged
Israel eight years.

37 [1]*lament* [2]*companions*
39 [a]Judg. 11:31 [1]Remained a virgin
40 [1]*commemorate*

CHAPTER 12

1 [a]Judg. 8:1 [1]*were summoned*
3 [a]1 Sam. 19:5; 28:21
4 [a]1 Sam. 25:10
5 [a]Josh. 22:11
6 [a]Ps. 69:2, 15 [1]Lit. *a flowing stream;* used as a test of dialect [2]Lit. *speak so*
14 [a]Judg. 5:10; 10:4

15 Then Ab′don the son of Hil′-
lel the Pir′a·thon·īte died and
was buried in Pir′a·thon in the
land of Ē′phra·im, [a]in the mountains of the A·mal′e·kītes.

13 Again the children of Israel [a]did evil in the sight
of the LORD, and the LORD delivered them [b]into the hand of the
Phi·lis′tines for forty years.
2 Now there was a certain
man from [a]Zō′rah, of the family
of the Dan′ītes, whose name *was*
Ma·nō′ah; and his wife *was* barren and had no children.
3 And the [a]Angel of the LORD
appeared to the woman and said
to her, "Indeed now, you are barren and have borne no children,
but you shall conceive and bear
a son.
4 "Now therefore, please be
careful [a]not to drink wine or
similar drink, and not to eat anything unclean.
5 "For behold, you shall conceive and bear a son. And no
[a]razor shall come upon his head,
for the child shall be [b]a Naz′ir·īte
to God from the womb; and he
shall [c]begin to deliver Israel out
of the hand of the Phi·lis′tines."
6 So the woman came and told
her husband, saying, [a]"A Man
of God came to me, and His
[b]countenance[1] *was* like the countenance of the Angel of God,
very awesome; but I [c]did not ask
Him where He *was* from, and He
did not tell me His name.
7 "And He said to me, 'Behold,
you shall conceive and bear a
son. Now drink no wine or *similar* drink, nor eat anything unclean, for the child shall be a
Naz′ir·īte to God from the womb
to the day of his death.'"
8 Then Ma·nō′ah prayed to the
LORD, and said, "O my Lord,
please let the Man of God whom
You sent come to us again and
teach us what we shall do for
the child who will be born."
9 And God listened to the voice
of Ma·nō′ah, and the Angel of
God came to the woman again
as she was sitting in the field;
but Ma·nō′ah her husband *was*
not with her.
10 Then the woman ran in haste
and told her husband, and said
to him, "Look, the Man who
came to me the *other* day has
just now appeared to me!"
11 So Ma·nō′ah arose and followed his wife. When he came
to the Man, he said to Him, "Are
You the Man who spoke to this
woman?" And He said, "I *am*."
12 Ma·nō′ah said, "Now let Your
words come *to pass!* What will
be the boy's rule of life, and his
work?"
13 So the Angel of the LORD said
to Ma·nō′ah, "Of all that I said to
the woman let her be careful.
14 "She may not eat anything
that comes from the vine, [a]nor
may she drink wine or *similar*
drink, nor eat anything unclean.
All that I commanded her let her
observe."
15 Then Ma·nō′ah said to the
Angel of the LORD, "Please [a]let
us detain You, and we will prepare a young goat for You."
16 And the Angel of the LORD
said to Ma·nō′ah, "Though you
detain Me, I will not eat your
food. But if you offer a burnt
offering, you must offer it to the
LORD." (For Ma·nō′ah did not
know He *was* the Angel of the
LORD.)
17 Then Ma·nō′ah said to the
Angel of the LORD, "What *is*

15 [a]Judg. 3:13, 27; 5:14

CHAPTER 13

1 [a]Judg. 2:11 [b]1 Sam. 12:9

2 [a]Josh. 19:41

3 [a]Judg. 6:12

4 [a]Num. 6:2, 3, 20

5 [a]Num. 6:5 [b]Num. 6:2 [c]1 Sam. 7:13

6 [a]Gen. 32:24–30 [b]Matt. 28:3 [c]Judg. 13:17, 18 [1]*appearance*

14 [a]Num. 6:3, 4

15 [a]Gen. 18:5

Your name, that when Your
words come *to pass* we may
honor You?"
18 And the Angel of the LORD
said to him, [a]"Why do you ask My
name, seeing it *is* wonderful?"
19 So Ma·nō′ah took the young
goat with the grain offering,
[a]and offered it upon the rock
to the LORD. And He did a wondrous thing while Ma·nō′ah and
his wife looked on—
20 it happened as the flame
went up toward heaven from
the altar—the Angel of the LORD
ascended in the flame of the altar! When Ma·nō′ah and his wife
saw *this,* they [a]fell on their faces
to the ground.
21 When the Angel of the LORD
appeared no more to Ma·nō′ah
and his wife, [a]then Ma·nō′ah
knew that He *was* the Angel of
the LORD.
22 And Ma·nō′ah said to his
wife, [a]"We shall surely die, because we have seen God!"
23 But his wife said to him,
"If the LORD had desired to kill
us, He would not have accepted
a burnt offering and a grain
offering from our hands, nor
would He have shown us all
these *things,* nor would He have
told us *such things* as these at
this time."
24 So the woman bore a son
and called his name [a]Samson;
and [b]the child grew, and the
LORD blessed him.
25 [a]And the Spirit of the LORD
began to move upon him at
[1]Mā′ha·neh Dan [b]between Zō′-
rah and [c]Esh′tā·ol.

14

Now Samson went down
[a]to Tim′nah, and [b]saw a
woman in Tim′nah of the daughters of the Phi·lis′tines.

18 [a]Gen. 32:29
19 [a]Judg. 6:19–21
20 [a]Ezek. 1:28
21 [a]Judg. 6:22
22 [a]Deut. 5:26
24 [a]Heb. 11:32 [b]1 Sam. 3:19
25 [a]Judg. 3:10 [b]Judg. 18:11 [c]Judg. 16:31 [1]Lit. *Camp of Dan,* Judg. 18:12

CHAPTER 14

1 [a]Josh. 15:10, 57 [b]Gen. 34:2
2 [a]Gen. 21:21
3 [a]Gen. 24:3, 4 [b]Gen. 34:14 [1]Lit. *she is right in my eyes*
4 [a]Josh. 11:20 [b]Deut. 28:48
6 [a]Judg. 3:10

2 So he went up and told his
father and mother, saying, "I
have seen a woman in Tim′nah
of the daughters of the Phi·lis′-
tines; now therefore, [a]get her for
me as a wife."
3 Then his father and mother
said to him, "*Is there* no woman
among the daughters of [a]your
brethren, or among all my people, that you must go and get a
wife from the [b]uncircumcised
Phi·lis′tines?" And Samson said
to his father, "Get her for me, for
[1]she pleases me well."
4 But his father and mother
did not know that it was [a]of the
LORD—that He was seeking an
occasion to move against the
Phi·lis′tines. For at that time [b]the
Phi·lis′tines had dominion over
Israel.
5 So Samson went down to
Tim′nah with his father and
mother, and came to the vineyards of Tim′nah.
Now *to his* surprise, a young
lion *came* roaring against him.
6 And [a]the Spirit of the LORD
came mightily upon him, and he
tore the lion apart as one would
have torn apart a young goat,
though *he had* nothing in his
hand. But he did not tell his father or his mother what he had
done.
7 Then he went down and
talked with the woman; and she
pleased Samson well.
8 After some time, when he
returned to get her, he turned
aside to see the carcass of the
lion. And behold, a swarm of
bees and honey *were* in the carcass of the lion.
9 He took some of it in his
hands and went along, eating.
When he came to his father and

mother, he gave *some* to them,
and they also ate. But he did not
tell them that he had taken the
honey out of the [a]carcass of the
lion.
10 So his father went down to
the woman. And Samson gave a
feast there, for young men used
to do so.
11 And it happened, when they
saw him, that they brought thirty
companions to be with him.
12 Then Samson said to them,
"Let me [a]pose a riddle to you. If
you can correctly solve and explain it to me [b]within the seven
days of the feast, then I will give
you thirty linen garments and
thirty [c]changes of clothing.
13 "But if you cannot explain
it to me, then you shall give me
thirty linen garments and thirty
changes of clothing." And they
said to him, [a]"Pose your riddle,
that we may hear it."
14 So he said to them:

"Out of the eater came
something to eat,
And out of the strong came
something sweet."

Now for three days they could
not explain the riddle.
15 But it came to pass on the
[1]seventh day that they said to
Samson's wife, [a]"Entice your
husband, that he may explain
the riddle to us, [b]or else we
will burn you and your father's
house with fire. Have you invited us in order to take what is
ours? *Is that* not *so*?"
16 Then Samson's wife wept
on him, and said, [a]"You only
hate me! You do not love me!
You have posed a riddle to the
sons of my people, but you have
not explained *it* to me." And he
said to her, "Look, I have not
explained *it* to my father or my
mother; so should I explain *it* to
you?"
17 Now she had wept on him
the seven days while their feast
lasted. And it happened on the
seventh day that he told her, because she pressed him so much.
Then she explained the riddle to
the sons of her people.
18 So the men of the city said to
him on the seventh day before
the sun went down:

"What *is* sweeter than
honey?
And what *is* stronger than a
lion?"

And he said to them:

"If you had not plowed with
my heifer,
You would not have solved
my riddle!"

19 Then [a]the Spirit of the LORD
came upon him mightily, and
he went down to Ash'ke·lon
and killed thirty of their men,
took their apparel, and gave the
changes *of clothing* to those who
had explained the riddle. So his
anger was aroused, and he went
back up to his father's house.
20 And Samson's wife [a]was
given to his companion, who
had been [b]his best man.

15 After a while, in the time
of wheat harvest, it hap-
pened that Samson visited his
wife with a [a]young goat. And he
said, "Let me go in to my wife,
into *her* room." But her father
would not permit him to go in.
2 Her father said, "I really

9 [a]Lev. 11:27
12 [a]Ezek. 17:2 [b]Gen. 29:27 [c]2 Kin. 5:22
13 [a]Ezek. 17:2
15 [a]Judg. 16:5 [b]Judg. 15:6 [1]So with MT, Tg., Vg.; LXX, Syr. *fourth*
16 [a]Judg. 16:15
19 [a]Judg. 3:10; 13:25
20 [a]Judg. 15:2 [b]John 3:29
CHAPTER 15
1 [a]Gen. 38:17

thought that you thoroughly
[a]hated her; therefore I gave her
to your companion. *Is* not her
younger sister better than she?
Please, take her instead."
3 And Samson said to them,
"This time I shall be blameless
regarding the Phi·lis′tines if I
harm them!"
4 Then Samson went and
caught three hundred foxes;
and he took torches, turned *the*
foxes tail to tail, and put a torch
between each pair of tails.
5 When he had set the torches
on fire, he let *the foxes* go into
the standing grain of the Phi·lis′-
tines, and burned up both the
shocks and the standing grain,
as well as the vineyards *and* olive groves.
6 Then the Phi·lis′tines said,
"Who has done this?" And they
answered, "Samson, the son-in-
law of the Tim′nīte, because he
has taken his wife and given
her to his companion." [a]So the
Phi·lis′tines came up and burned
her and her father with fire.
7 Samson said to them, "Since
you would do a thing like this, I
will surely take revenge on you,
and after that I will cease."
8 So he attacked them hip and
thigh with a great slaughter;
then he went down and dwelt in
the cleft of the rock of [a]Ē′tam.
9 Now the Phi·lis′tines went
up, encamped in Judah, and
deployed themselves [a]against
Lē′hi.
10 And the men of Judah said,
"Why have you come up against
us?" So they answered, "We have
come up to [1]arrest Samson, to
do to him as he has done to us."
11 Then three thousand men
of Judah went down to the cleft
of the rock of Ē′tam, and said
to Samson, "Do you not know
that the Phi·lis′tines [a]rule over
us? What *is* this you have done
to us?" And he said to them, "As
they did to me, so I have done to
them."
12 But they said to him, "We
have come down to arrest you,
that we may deliver you into the
hand of the Phi·lis′tines." Then
Samson said to them, "Swear
to me that you will not kill me
yourselves."
13 So they spoke to him, saying,
"No, but we will tie you securely
and deliver you into their hand;
but we will surely not kill you."
And they bound him with two
[a]new ropes and brought him up
from the rock.
14 When he came to Lē′hi,
the Phi·lis′tines came shouting
against him. Then [a]the Spirit of
the LORD came mightily upon
him; and the ropes that *were* on
his arms became like flax that is
burned with fire, and his bonds
[1]broke loose from his hands.
15 He found a fresh jawbone of
a donkey, reached out his hand
and took it, and [a]killed a thousand men with it.
16 Then Samson said:

"With the jawbone of a
donkey,
Heaps upon heaps,
With the jawbone of a
donkey
I have slain a thousand
men!"

17 And so it was, when he had
finished speaking, that he threw
the jawbone from his hand, and
called that place [1]Rā′math Lē′hi.
18 Then he became very thirsty;

2 [a]Judg. 14:20
6 [a]Judg. 14:15
8 [a]2 Chr. 11:6
9 [a]Judg. 15:19
10 [1]Lit. *bind*
11 [a]Judg. 13:1; 14:4
13 [a]Judg. 16:11, 12
14 [a]Judg. 3:10; 14:6 [1]Lit. *were melted*
15 [a]Lev. 26:8
17 [1]Lit. *Jawbone Height*

so he cried out to the LORD and
said, [a]"You have given this great
deliverance by the hand of Your
servant; and now shall I die of
thirst and fall into the hand of
the uncircumcised?"
19 So God split the hollow place
that *is* in [1]Lē'hi, and water came
out, and he drank; and [a]his spirit
returned, and he revived. Therefore he called its name [2]En Hak'-
ko·rē, which is in Lē'hi to this
day.
20 And [a]he judged Israel [b]twenty
years [c]in the days of the Phi·lis'-
tines.

16 Now Samson went to
[a]Gā'za and saw a harlot
there, and went in to her.
2 *When* the Gā'zītes *were told,*
"Samson has come here!" they
[a]surrounded *the place* and lay in
wait for him all night at the gate
of the city. They were quiet all
night, saying, "In the morning,
when it is daylight, we will kill
him."
3 And Samson lay *low* till midnight; then he arose at midnight,
took hold of the doors of the
gate of the city and the two gateposts, pulled them up, bar and
all, put *them* on his shoulders,
and carried them to the top of
the hill that faces Hē'bron.
4 Afterward it happened that
he loved a woman in the Valley of Sō'rek, whose name *was*
Dē·lī'lah.
5 And the [a]lords of the Phi·lis'-
tines came up to her and said to
her, [b]"Entice him, and find out
where his great strength *lies,*
and by what *means* we may
overpower him, that we may
bind him to afflict him; and every one of us will give you eleven
hundred *pieces* of silver."

18 [a]Ps. 3:7

19 [a]Is. 40:29
[1]Lit. *Jawbone,* Judg. 15:14
[2]Lit. *Spring of the Caller*

20 [a]Judg. 10:2; 12:7–14
[b]Judg. 16:31
[c]Judg. 13:1

CHAPTER 16

1 [a]Josh. 15:47

2 [a]1 Sam. 23:26

5 [a]Josh. 13:3
[b]Judg. 14:15

11 [a]Judg. 15:13
[1]Lit. *with which work has never been done*

6 So Dē·lī'lah said to Samson,
"Please tell me where your great
strength *lies,* and with what you
may be bound to afflict you."
7 And Samson said to her, "If
they bind me with seven fresh
bowstrings, not yet dried, then I
shall become weak, and be like
any *other* man."
8 So the lords of the Phi·lis'-
tines brought up to her seven
fresh bowstrings, not yet dried,
and she bound him with them.
9 Now *men were* lying in wait,
staying with her in the room. And
she said to him, "The Phi·lis'-
tines *are* upon you, Samson!"
But he broke the bowstrings as
a strand of yarn breaks when it
touches fire. So the secret of his
strength was not known.
10 Then Dē·lī'lah said to Samson, "Look, you have mocked
me and told me lies. Now, please
tell me what you may be bound
with."
11 So he said to her, "If they bind
me securely with [a]new ropes
[1]that have never been used, then
I shall become weak, and be like
any *other* man."
12 Therefore Dē·lī'lah took new
ropes and bound him with them,
and said to him, "The Phi·lis'-
tines *are* upon you, Samson!"
And *men were* lying in wait,
staying in the room. But he
broke them off his arms like a
thread.
13 Dē·lī'lah said to Samson,
"Until now you have mocked me
and told me lies. Tell me what
you may be bound with." And
he said to her, "If you weave the
seven locks of my head into the
web of the loom"—
14 So she wove *it* tightly with
the batten of the loom, and

to me, since I have a Lē′vīte as
[a]priest!"

18 In [a]those days *there was*
no king in Israel. And
in those days [b]the tribe of the
Dan′ītes was seeking an inheritance for itself to dwell in; for
until that day *their* inheritance
among the tribes of Israel had
not fallen to them.
2 So the children of Dan sent
five men of their family from
their territory, men of valor from
[a]Zō′rah and Esh′tā·ol, [b]to spy out
the land and search it. They said
to them, "Go, search the land."
So they went to the mountains
of Ē′phra·im, to the [c]house of
Mī′cah, and lodged there.
3 While they *were* at the house
of Mī′cah, they recognized the
voice of the young Lē′vīte. They
turned aside and said to him,
"Who brought you here? What
are you doing in this *place*?
What do you have here?"
4 He said to them, "Thus and
so Mī′cah did for me. He has
[a]hired me, and I have become
his priest."
5 So they said to him, "Please
[a]inquire [b]of God, that we may
know whether the journey on
which we go will be prosperous."
6 And the priest said to them,
[a]"Go in peace. [1]The presence of
the LORD *be* with you on your
way."
7 So the five men departed
and went to [a]Lā′ish. They saw
the people who *were* there, [b]how
they dwelt safely, in the manner
of the Sī·dō′ni·ans, quiet and
secure. *There were* no rulers in
the land who might put *them* to
shame for anything. They *were*
far from the [c]Sī·dō′ni·ans, and
they had no ties [1]with anyone.
8 Then *the spies* came back
to their brethren at [a]Zō′rah and
Esh′tā·ol, and their brethren said
to them, "What *is* your *report?*"
9 So they said, [a]"Arise, let us
go up against them. For we have
seen the land, and indeed it *is*
very good. *Would* you [b]*do* nothing? Do not hesitate to go, *and*
enter to possess the land.
10 "When you go, you will come
to a [a]secure people and a large
land. For God has given it into
your hands, [b]a place where *there*
is no lack of anything that *is* on
the earth."
11 And six hundred men of the
family of the Dan′ītes went from
there, from Zō′rah and Esh′tā·ol,
armed with weapons of war.
12 Then they went up and encamped in [a]Kir′jath Jē′a·rim in
Judah. (Therefore they call that
place [b]Mā′ha·neh Dan[1] to this
day. There *it is,* west of Kir′jath
Jē′a·rim.)
13 And they passed from there
to the mountains of Ē′phra·im,
and came to [a]the house of Mī′-
cah.
14 [a]Then the five men who had
gone to spy out the country of
Lā′ish answered and said to
their brethren, "Do you know
that [b]there are in these houses
an ephod, household idols, a
carved image, and a molded image? Now therefore, consider
what you should do."
15 So they turned aside there,
and came to the house of the
young Lē′vīte man—to the house
of Mī′cah—and greeted him.
16 The [a]six hundred men armed
with their weapons of war, who
were of the children of Dan,
stood by the entrance of the
gate.

13 [a]Judg. 18:4

CHAPTER 18

1 [a]Judg. 17:6; 19:1; 21:25 [b]Josh. 19:40–48

2 [a]Judg. 13:25 [b]Num. 13:17 [c]Judg. 17:1

4 [a]Judg. 17:10, 12

5 [a]Hos. 4:12 [b]Judg. 1:1; 17:5; 18:14

6 [a]1 Kin. 22:6 [1]Lit. *The LORD is before the way in which you go*

7 [a]Josh. 19:47 [b]Judg. 18:27–29 [c]Judg. 10:12 [1]So with MT, Tg., Vg.; LXX *with Syria*

8 [a]Judg. 18:2

9 [a]Num. 13:30 [b]1 Kin. 22:3

10 [a]Judg. 18:7, 27 [b]Deut. 8:9

12 [a]Josh. 15:60 [b]Judg. 13:25 [1]Lit. *Camp of Dan*

13 [a]Judg. 18:2

14 [a]1 Sam. 14:28 [b]Judg. 17:5

16 [a]Judg. 18:11

17 Then [a]the five men who had gone to spy out the land went up. Entering there, they took [b]the carved image, the ephod, the household idols, and the molded image. The priest stood at the entrance of the gate with the six hundred men *who were* armed with weapons of war.

18 When these went into Mī′cah's house and took the carved image, the ephod, the household idols, and the molded image, the priest said to them, "What are you doing?"

19 And they said to him, "Be quiet, [a]put your hand over your mouth, and come with us; [b]be a father and a priest to us. *Is it* better for you to be a priest to the household of one man, or that you be a priest to a tribe and a family in Israel?"

20 So the priest's heart was glad; and he took the ephod, the household idols, and the carved image, and took his place among the people.

21 Then they turned and departed, and put the little ones, the livestock, and the goods in front of them.

22 When they were a good way from the house of Mī′cah, the men who *were* in the houses near Mī′cah's house gathered together and overtook the children of Dan.

23 And they called out to the children of Dan. So they turned around and said to Mī′cah, [a]"What ails you, that you have gathered such a company?"

24 So he said, "You have [a]taken away my [1]gods which I made, and the priest, and you have gone away. Now what more do I have? How can you say to me, 'What ails you?' "

25 And the children of Dan said to him, "Do not let your voice be heard among us, lest [1]angry men fall upon you, and you lose your life, with the lives of your household!"

26 Then the children of Dan went their way. And when Mī′cah saw that they *were* too strong for him, he turned and went back to his house.

27 So they took *the things* Mī′cah had made, and the priest who had belonged to him, and went to Lā′ish, to a people quiet and secure; [a]and they struck them with the edge of the sword and burned the city with fire.

28 *There was* no deliverer, because it *was* [a]far from Sī′don, and they had no ties with anyone. It was in the valley that belongs [b]to Beth Rē′hob. So they rebuilt the city and dwelt there.

29 And [a]they called the name of the city [b]Dan, after the name of Dan their father, who was born to Israel. However, the name of the city formerly *was* Lā′ish.

30 Then the children of Dan set up for themselves the carved image; and Jonathan the son of Ger′shom, the son of [1]Ma·nas′seh, and his sons were priests to the tribe of Dan [a]until the day of the captivity of the land.

31 So they set up for themselves Mī′cah's carved image which he made, [a]all the time that the house of God was in Shī′lōh.

CHAPTER 19

19 And it came to pass in those days, [a]when *there was* no king in Israel, that there was a certain Lē′vīte staying in the remote mountains of Ē′phra·im. He took for himself

17 [a]Judg. 18:2, 14 [b]Judg. 17:4, 5
19 [a]Job 21:5; 29:9; 40:4 [b]Judg. 17:10
23 [a]2 Kin. 6:28
24 [a]Gen. 31:30 [1]*idols*
25 [1]Lit. *bitter of soul*
27 [a]Josh. 19:47
28 [a]Judg. 18:7 [b]2 Sam. 10:6
29 [a]Josh. 19:47 [b]Judg. 20:1
30 [a]2 Kin. 15:29 [1]LXX, Vg. *Moses*
31 [a]Josh. 18:1, 8

CHAPTER 19

1 [a]Judg. 17:6; 18:1; 21:25

a concubine from [b]Bethlehem in Judah.

2 But his concubine played the harlot against him, and went away from him to her father's house at Bethlehem in Judah, and was there four whole months.

3 Then her husband arose and went after her, to [a]speak [1]kindly to her *and* bring her back, having his servant and a couple of donkeys with him. So she brought him into her father's house; and when the father of the young woman saw him, he was glad to meet him.

4 Now his father-in-law, the young woman's father, detained him; and he stayed with him three days. So they ate and drank and lodged there.

5 Then it came to pass on the fourth day that they arose early in the morning, and he stood to depart; but the young woman's father said to his son-in-law, [a]"Refresh your heart with a morsel of bread, and afterward go your way."

6 So they sat down, and the two of them ate and drank together. Then the young woman's father said to the man, "Please be content to stay all night, and let your heart be merry."

7 And when the man stood to depart, his father-in-law urged him; so he lodged there again.

8 Then he arose early in the morning on the fifth day to depart, but the young woman's father said, "Please refresh your heart." So they delayed until afternoon; and both of them ate.

9 And when the man stood to depart—he and his concubine and his servant—his father-in-law, the young woman's father, said to him, "Look, the day is now drawing toward evening; please spend the night. See, the day is coming to an end; lodge here, that your heart may be merry. Tomorrow go your way early, so that you may get [1]home."

10 However, the man was not willing to spend that night; so he rose and departed, and came to opposite [a]Jē′bus (that *is*, Jerusalem). With him were the two saddled donkeys; his concubine *was* also with him.

11 They *were* near Jē′bus, and the day was far spent; and the servant said to his master, "Come, please, and let us turn aside into this city [a]of the Jeb′ū·sītes and lodge in it."

12 But his master said to him, "We will not turn aside here into a city of foreigners, who *are* not of the children of Israel; we will go on [a]to Gib′ē·ah."

13 So he said to his servant, "Come, let us draw near to one of these places, and spend the night in Gib′ē·ah or in [a]Rā′mah."

14 And they passed by and went their way; and the sun went down on them near Gib′ē·ah, which belongs to Benjamin.

15 They turned aside there to go in to lodge in Gib′ē·ah. And when he went in, he sat down in the open square of the city, for no one would [a]take them into *his* house to spend the night.

16 Just then an old man came in from [a]his work in the field at evening, who also *was* from the mountains of Ē′phra·im; he was staying in Gib′ē·ah, whereas the men of the place *were* Ben′ja·mītes.

1 [b]Judg. 17:7
3 [a]Gen. 34:3; 50:21 [1]Lit. *to her heart*
5 [a]Gen. 18:5
9 [1]Lit. *to your tent*
10 [a]1 Chr. 11:4, 5
11 [a]Josh. 15:8, 63
12 [a]Josh. 18:28
13 [a]Josh. 18:25
15 [a]Matt. 25:43
16 [a]Ps. 104:23

17 And when he raised his eyes, he saw the traveler in the open square of the city; and the old man said, "Where are you going, and where do you come from?"

18 So he said to him, "We *are* passing from Bethlehem in Judah toward the remote mountains of Ē′phra·im; I *am* from there. I went to Bethlehem in Judah; *now* I am going to [a]the house of the LORD. But there *is* no one who will take me into his house,

19 "although we have both straw and fodder for our donkeys, and bread and wine for myself, for your female servant, and for the young man *who is* with your servant; *there is* no lack of anything."

20 And the old man said, [a]"Peace *be* with you! However, *let* all your needs *be* my responsibility; [b]only do not spend the night in the open square."

21 [a]So he brought him into his house, and gave fodder to the donkeys. [b]And they washed their feet, and ate and drank.

22 As they were [a]enjoying themselves, suddenly [b]certain men of the city, [c]perverted[1] men, surrounded the house *and* beat on the door. They spoke to the master of the house, the old man, saying, [d]"Bring out the man who came to your house, that we may know him *carnally!*"

23 But [a]the man, the master of the house, went out to them and said to them, "No, my brethren! I beg you, do not act *so* wickedly! Seeing this man has come into my house, [b]do not commit this outrage.

24 [a]"Look, *here is* my virgin daughter and [1]*the man's* concubine; let me bring them out now. [b]Humble them, and do with them as you please; but to this man do not do such a vile thing!"

25 But the men would not heed him. So the man took his concubine and brought *her* out to them. And they [a]knew her and abused her all night until morning; and when the day began to break, they let her go.

26 Then the woman came as the day was dawning, and fell down at the door of the man's house where her master *was,* till it was light.

27 When her master arose in the morning, and opened the doors of the house and went out to go his way, there was his concubine, fallen *at* the door of the house with her hands on the threshold.

28 And he said to her, "Get up and let us be going." But [a]there was no answer. So the man lifted her onto the donkey; and the man got up and went to his place.

29 When he entered his house he took a knife, laid hold of his concubine, and [a]divided her into twelve pieces, [1]limb by limb, and sent her throughout all the territory of Israel.

30 And so it was that all who saw it said, "No such deed has been done or seen from the day that the children of Israel came up from the land of Egypt until this day. Consider it, [a]confer, and speak up!"

20

So [a]all the children of Israel came out, from [b]Dan to [c]Bē·er·shē′ba, as well as from the land of Gil′ē·ad, and the congregation gathered together

18 [a]Josh. 18:1
20 [a]Gen. 43:23 [b]Gen. 19:2
21 [a]Gen. 24:32; 43:24 [b]John 13:5
22 [a]Judg. 16:25; 19:6, 9 [b]Hos. 9:9; 10:9 [c]Deut. 13:13 [d][Rom. 1:26, 27] [1]Lit. *sons of Belial*
23 [a]Gen. 19:6, 7 [b]2 Sam. 13:12
24 [a]Gen. 19:8 [b]Gen. 34:2 [1]Lit. *his*
25 [a]Gen. 4:1
28 [a]Judg. 20:5
29 [a]1 Sam. 11:7 [1]Lit. *with her bones*
30 [a]Judg. 20:7

CHAPTER 20
1 [a]Josh. 22:12 [b]2 Sam. 3:10; 24:2 [c]Josh. 19:2

as one man before the LORD [d]at Miz'pah.

2 And the leaders of all the people, all the tribes of Israel, presented themselves in the assembly of the people of God, four hundred thousand foot soldiers [a]who drew the sword.

3 (Now the children of Benjamin heard that the children of Israel had gone up to Miz'pah.) Then the children of Israel said, "Tell *us*, how did this wicked deed happen?"

4 So the Lē'vīte, the husband of the woman who was murdered, answered and said, "My concubine and [a]I went into Gib'ē·ah, which belongs to Benjamin, to spend the night.

5 [a]"And the men of Gib'ē·ah rose against me, and surrounded the house at night because of me. They intended to kill me, [b]but instead they ravished my concubine so that she died.

6 "So [a]I took hold of my concubine, cut her in pieces, and sent her throughout all the territory of the inheritance of Israel, because they [b]committed lewdness and outrage in Israel.

7 "Look! All of you *are* children of Israel; [a]give your advice and counsel here and now!"

8 So all the people arose as one man, saying, "None *of us* will go to his tent, nor will any turn back to his house;

9 "but now this *is* the thing which we will do to Gib'ē·ah: *We will go up* [a]against it by lot.

10 "We will take ten men out of *every* hundred throughout all the tribes of Israel, a hundred out of *every* thousand, and a thousand out of *every* ten thousand, to make provisions for the people, that when they come to Gib'ē·ah in Benjamin, they may repay all the vileness that they have done in Israel."

11 So all the men of Israel were gathered against the city, united together as one man.

12 [a]Then the tribes of Israel sent men through all the tribe of Benjamin, saying, "What *is* this wickedness that has occurred among you?

13 "Now therefore, deliver up the men, [a]the [1]perverted men who *are* in Gib'ē·ah, that we may put them to death and [b]remove the evil from Israel!" But the children of Benjamin would not listen to the voice of their brethren, the children of Israel.

14 Instead, the children of Benjamin gathered together from their cities to Gib'ē·ah, to go to battle against the children of Israel.

15 And from their cities at that time [a]the children of Benjamin numbered twenty-six thousand men who drew the sword, besides the inhabitants of Gib'ē·ah, who numbered seven hundred select men.

16 Among all this people *were* seven hundred select men *who were* [a]left-handed; every one could sling a stone at a hair's *breadth* and not miss.

17 Now besides Benjamin, the men of Israel numbered four hundred thousand men who drew the sword; all of these *were* men of war.

18 Then the children of Israel arose and [a]went up to [1]the house of God to [b]inquire of God. They said, "Which of us shall go up first to battle against the

1 [d]1 Sam. 7:5
2 [a]Judg. 8:10
4 [a]Judg. 19:15
5 [a]Judg. 19:22 [b]Judg. 19:25, 26
6 [a]Judg. 19:29 [b]Josh. 7:15
7 [a]Judg. 19:30
9 [a]Judg. 1:3
12 [a]Deut. 13:14
13 [a]Deut. 13:13 [b]Deut. 17:12 [1]Lit. *sons of Belial*
15 [a]Num. 1:36, 37; 2:23; 26:41
16 [a]1 Chr. 12:2
18 [a]Judg. 20:23, 26 [b]Num. 27:21 [1]Or *Bethel*

children of Benjamin?" The LORD
said, [c]"Judah first!"
19 So the children of Israel rose
in the morning and encamped
against Gib′ē·ah.
20 And the men of Israel went
out to battle against Benjamin,
and the men of Israel put themselves in battle array to fight
against them at Gib′ē·ah.
21 Then [a]the children of Benjamin came out of Gib′ē·ah, and on
that day cut down to the ground
twenty-two thousand men of the
Israelites.
22 And the people, that is, the
men of Israel, encouraged themselves and again formed the battle line at the place where they
had put themselves in array on
the first day.
23 [a]Then the children of Israel
went up and wept before the
LORD until evening, and asked
counsel of the LORD, saying,
"Shall I again draw near for
battle against the children of
my brother Benjamin?" And the
LORD said, "Go up against him."
24 So the children of Israel approached the children of Benjamin on the second day.
25 And [a]Benjamin went out
against them from Gib′ē·ah on
the second day, and cut down to
the ground eighteen thousand
more of the children of Israel;
all these drew the sword.
26 Then all the children of Israel, that is, all the people, [a]went
up and came to [1]the house of
God and wept. They sat there
before the LORD and fasted that
day until evening; and they offered burnt offerings and peace
offerings before the LORD.
27 So the children of Israel inquired of the LORD ([a]the ark of

18 [c]Judg. 1:1, 2
21 [a][Gen. 49:27]
23 [a]Judg. 20:26, 27
25 [a]Judg. 20:21
26 [a]Judg. 20:18, 23; 21:2 [1]Or *Bethel*
27 [a]Josh. 18:1
28 [a]Josh. 24:33 [b]Deut. 10:8; 18:5
29 [a]Josh. 8:4
31 [a]Judg. 21:19
34 [a]Josh. 8:14 [1]Lit. *they*
35 [1]Lit. *struck*

the covenant of God *was* there
in those days,
28 [a]and Phin′e·has the son of
El·ē·ā′zar, the son of Aaron,
[b]stood before it in those days),
saying, "Shall I yet again go out
to battle against the children of
my brother Benjamin, or shall I
cease?" And the LORD said, "Go
up, for tomorrow I will deliver
them into your hand."
29 Then Israel [a]set men in ambush all around Gib′ē·ah.
30 And the children of Israel
went up against the children of
Benjamin on the third day, and
put themselves in battle array
against Gib′ē·ah as at the other
times.
31 So the children of Benjamin
went out against the people, *and*
were drawn away from the city.
They began to strike down *and*
kill some of the people, as at
the other times, in the highways
[a](one of which goes up to Beth′el
and the other to Gib′ē·ah) and
in the field, about thirty men of
Israel.
32 And the children of Benjamin said, "They *are* defeated
before us, as at first." But the
children of Israel said, "Let us
flee and draw them away from
the city to the highways."
33 So all the men of Israel rose
from their place and put themselves in battle array at Bā′al
Tā′mar. Then Israel's men in
ambush burst forth from their
position in the plain of Gē′ba.
34 And ten thousand select men
from all Israel came against
Gib′ē·ah, and the battle was
fierce. [a]But [1]*the Ben′ja·mītes* did
not know that disaster *was* upon
them.
35 The LORD [1]defeated Benjamin

before Israel. And the children
of Israel destroyed that day
twenty-five thousand one hundred Ben′ja·mītes; all these drew
the sword.
36 So the children of Benjamin
saw that they were defeated.
[a]The men of Israel had given
ground to the Ben′ja·mītes, because they relied on the men
in ambush whom they had set
against Gib′ē·ah.
37 [a]And the men in ambush
quickly rushed upon Gib′ē·ah;
the men in ambush spread out
and struck the whole city with
the edge of the sword.
38 Now the appointed signal
between the men of Israel and
the men in ambush was that
they would make a great cloud
of [a]smoke rise up from the city,
39 whereupon the men of Israel
would turn in battle. Now Benjamin had begun [1]to strike *and* kill
about thirty of the men of Israel.
For they said, "Surely they are
defeated before us, as *in* the first
battle."
40 But when the cloud began to
rise from the city in a column of
smoke, the Ben′ja·mītes [a]looked
behind them, and there was the
whole city going up *in smoke* to
heaven.
41 And when the men of Israel
turned back, the men of Benjamin panicked, for they saw that
disaster had come upon them.
42 Therefore they [1]turned *their*
backs before the men of Israel
in the direction of the wilderness; but the battle overtook
them, and whoever *came* out of
the cities they destroyed in their
midst.
43 They surrounded the Ben′-
ja·mītes, chased them, *and* easily
trampled them down as far as
the front of Gib′ē·ah toward the
east.
44 And eighteen thousand men
of Benjamin fell; all these *were*
men of valor.
45 Then [1]they turned and fled
toward the wilderness to the
rock of [a]Rim′mon; and they cut
down five thousand of them on
the highways. Then they pursued them relentlessly up to Gī′-
dom, and killed two thousand of
them.
46 So all who fell of Benjamin
that day were twenty-five thousand men who drew the sword;
all these *were* [1]men of valor.
47 [a]But six hundred men turned
and fled toward the wilderness
to the rock of Rim′mon, and
they stayed at the rock of Rim′-
mon for four months.
48 And the men of Israel turned
back against the children of Benjamin, and struck them down
with the edge of the sword—
from *every* city, men and beasts,
all who were found. They also
set fire to all the cities they came
to.

21

Now [a]the men of Israel
had sworn an oath at
Miz′pah, saying, "None of us
shall give his daughter to Benjamin as a wife."
2 Then the people came [a]to
[1]the house of God, and remained
there before God till evening.
They lifted up their voices and
wept bitterly,
3 and said, "O LORD God of Israel, why has this come to pass
in Israel, that today there should
be one tribe *missing* in Israel?"
4 So it was, on the next morning, that the people rose early
and [a]built an altar there, and

36 [a]Josh. 8:15
37 [a]Josh. 8:19
38 [a]Josh. 8:20
39 [1]Lit. *to strike the slain ones*
40 [a]Josh. 8:20
42 [1]*fled*
45 [a]Josh. 15:32 [1]LXX *the rest*
46 [1]*valiant warriors*
47 [a]Judg. 21:13

CHAPTER 21

1 [a]Judg. 20:1
2 [a]Judg. 20:18, 26 [1]Or *Bethel*
4 [a]2 Sam. 24:25

offered burnt offerings and peace offerings.

5 The children of Israel said, "Who *is there* among all the tribes of Israel who did not come up with the assembly to the LORD?" [a]For they had made a great oath concerning anyone who had not come up to the LORD at Miz′pah, saying, "He shall surely be put to death."

6 And the children of Israel grieved for Benjamin their brother, and said, "One tribe is cut off from Israel today.

7 "What shall we do for wives for those who remain, seeing we have sworn by the LORD that we will not give them our daughters as wives?"

8 And they said, "What one *is there* from the tribes of Israel who did not come up to Miz′pah to the LORD?" And, in fact, no one had come to the camp from [a]Jā′besh Gil′ē·ad to the assembly.

9 For when the people were counted, indeed, not one of the inhabitants of Jā′besh Gil′ē·ad *was* there.

10 So the congregation sent out there twelve thousand of their most valiant men, and commanded them, saying, [a]"Go and strike the inhabitants of Jā′besh Gil′ē·ad with the edge of the sword, including the women and children.

11 "And this *is* the thing that you shall do: [a]You shall utterly destroy every male, and every woman who has known a man intimately."

12 So they found among the inhabitants of Jā′besh Gil′ē·ad four hundred young virgins who had not known a man intimately; and they brought them to the camp at [a]Shī′lōh, which is in the land of Cā′naan.

13 Then the whole congregation sent *word* to the children of Benjamin [a]who *were* at the rock of Rim′mon, and announced peace to them.

14 So Benjamin came back at that time, and they gave them the women whom they had saved alive of the women of Jā′besh Gil′ē·ad; and yet they had not found enough for them.

15 And the people [a]grieved for Benjamin, because the LORD had made a void in the tribes of Israel.

16 Then the elders of the congregation said, "What shall we do for wives for those who remain, since the women of Benjamin have been destroyed?"

17 And they said, "*There must be* an inheritance for the survivors of Benjamin, that a tribe may not be destroyed from Israel.

18 "However, we cannot give them wives from our daughters, [a]for the children of Israel have sworn an oath, saying, 'Cursed *be* the one who gives a wife to Benjamin.' "

19 Then they said, "In fact, *there is* a yearly [a]feast of the LORD in [b]Shī′lōh, which *is* north of Beth′el, on the east side of the [c]highway that goes up from Beth′el to Shē′chem, and south of Le·bō′nah."

20 Therefore they instructed the children of Benjamin, saying, "Go, lie in wait in the vineyards,

21 "and watch; and just when the daughters of Shī′lōh come out [a]to perform their dances, then come out from the vineyards, and every man catch a

5 [a]Judg. 20:1–3
8 [a]1 Sam. 11:1; 31:11
10 [a]Num. 31:17
11 [a]Num. 31:17
12 [a]Josh. 18:1
13 [a]Judg. 20:47
15 [a]Judg. 21:6
18 [a]Judg. 11:35; 21:1
19 [a]Lev. 23:2 [b]1 Sam. 1:3 [c]Judg. 20:31
21 [a]Judg. 11:34

wife for himself from the daughters of Shī'lōh; then go to the
land of Benjamin.
22 "Then it shall be, when their
fathers or their brothers come to
us to complain, that we will say
to them, 'Be kind to them for our
sakes, because we did not take a
wife for any of them in the war;
for *it is* not *as though* you have
given the *women* to them at this
time, making yourselves guilty
of your oath.' "
23 And the children of Benjamin
did so; they took enough wives
for their number from those who
danced, whom they caught. Then
they went and returned to their
inheritance, and they [a]rebuilt the
cities and dwelt in them.
24 So the children of Israel departed from there at that time,
every man to his tribe and family; they went out from there,
every man to his inheritance.
25 [a]In those days *there was* no
king in Israel; [b]everyone did
what was right in his own eyes.

23 [a]Judg. 20:48

25 [a]Judg. 17:6; 18:1; 19:1 [b]Judg. 17:6

The Book of RUTH

RUTH is a cameo story of love, devotion, and redemption set in the black context of the days of the judges. It is the story of a Moabite woman who forsakes her pagan heritage in order to cling to the people of Israel and to the God of Israel. Because of the *faithfulness* in a time of national *faithlessness*, God rewards her by giving her a new husband (Boaz), a son (Obed), and a privileged position in the lineage of David and Christ (she is the great-grandmother of David).

Ruth is the Hebrew title of this book. This name may be a Moabite modification of the Hebrew word *reuit*, meaning "friendship" or "association." The Septuagint entitles the book *Routh*, the Greek equivalent of the Hebrew name. The Latin title of *Ruth* is a transliteration of *Routh*.

CHAPTER 1

NOW it came to pass, in the
days when [a]the judges [1]ruled,
that there was [b]a famine in the
land. And a certain man of [c]Beth-
lehem, Judah, went to [2]dwell in
the country of [d]Mō′ab, he and his
wife and his two sons.
2 The name of the man *was*
Ē·lim′e·lech, the name of his wife
was Nā′o·mī, and the names of
his two sons *were* Mah′lon and
Chil′i·on—[a]Eph′ra·thītes of Bethlehem, Judah. And they went [b]to
the country of Mō′ab and remained there.
3 Then Ē·lim′e·lech, Nā′o·mī's
husband, died; and she was left,
and her two sons.
4 Now they took wives of the
women of Mō′ab: the name of
the one *was* Or′pah, and the
name of the other Ruth. And they
[1]dwelt there about ten years.
5 Then both Mah′lon and Chil′-
i·on also died; so the woman
survived her two sons and her
husband.
6 Then she arose with her
daughters-in-law that she might
return from the country of Mō′ab,
for she had heard in the country of Mō′ab that the LORD had
[a]visited[1] His people by [b]giving
them bread.
7 Therefore she went out from
the place where she was, and
her two daughters-in-law with
her; and they went on the way
to return to the land of Judah.
8 And Nā′o·mī said to her two
daughters-in-law, [a]"Go, return
each to her mother's house. [b]The
LORD deal kindly with you, as
you have dealt [c]with the dead
and with me.
9 "The LORD grant that you
may find [a]rest, each in the house
of her husband." So she kissed
them, and they lifted up their
voices and wept.
10 And they said to her, "Surely
we will return with you to your
people."
11 But Nā′o·mī said, "Turn back,
my daughters; why will you go
with me? *Are* there still sons
in my womb, [a]that they may be
your husbands?
12 "Turn back, my daughters,
go—for I am too old to have a

1 [a]Judg. 2:16–18 [b]Gen. 12:10; 26:1 [c]Judg. 17:8 [d]Gen. 19:37 [1]Lit. *judged* [2]As a resident alien

2 [a]Gen. 35:19 [b]Judg. 3:30

4 [1]*lived*

6 [a]Ex. 3:16; 4:31 [b]Matt. 6:11 [1]*attended to*

8 [a]Josh. 24:15 [b]2 Tim. 1:16–18 [c]Ruth 2:20

9 [a]Ruth 3:1

11 [a]Deut. 25:5

husband. If I should say I have
hope, *if* I should have a husband
tonight and should also bear
sons,
13 "would you wait for them till
they were grown? Would you
restrain yourselves from having
husbands? No, my daughters;
for it grieves me very much for
your sakes that [a]the hand of the
LORD has gone out against me!"
14 Then they lifted up their
voices and wept again; and Or′-
pah kissed her mother-in-law,
but Ruth [a]clung to her.
15 And she said, "Look, your
sister-in-law has gone back to
[a]her people and to her gods;
[b]return after your sister-in-law."
16 But Ruth said:

[a]"Entreat[1] me not to leave you,
Or to turn back from
following after you;
For wherever you go, I will
go;
And wherever you lodge, I
will lodge;
[b]Your people *shall be* my
people,
And your God, my God.
17 Where you die, I will die,
And there will I be buried.
[a]The LORD do so to me, and
more also,
If *anything but* death parts
you and me."

18 [a]When she saw that she [1]was
determined to go with her, she
stopped speaking to her.
19 Now the two of them went
until they came to Bethlehem.
And it happened, when they
had come to Bethlehem, that [a]all
the city was excited because of
them; and the women said, [b]"*Is*
this Nā′o·mī?"
20 But she said to them, "Do not
call me [1]Nā′o·mī; call me [2]Mar′a,
for the Almighty has dealt very
bitterly with me.
21 "I went out full, [a]and the
LORD has brought me home
again empty. Why do you call
me Nā′o·mī, since the LORD has
testified against me, and [1]the
Almighty has afflicted me?"
22 So Nā′o·mī returned, and
Ruth the Mō′ab·ī·tess her daughter-in-law with her, who returned
from the country of Mō′ab. Now
they came to Bethlehem [a]at the
beginning of barley harvest.

2 There was a [a]relative of
Nā′o·mī's husband, a man
of great wealth, of the family
of [b]Ē·lim′e·lech. His name *was*
[c]Bō′az.
2 So Ruth the Mō′ab·ī·tess said
to Nā′o·mī, "Please let me go to
the [a]field, and glean heads of
grain after *him* in whose sight I
may find favor." And she said to
her, "Go, my daughter."
3 Then she left, and went and
gleaned in the field after the
reapers. And she happened to
come to the part of the field *be-*
longing to Bō′az, who *was* of the
family of Ē·lim′e·lech.
4 Now behold, Bō′az came
from [a]Bethlehem, and said to
the reapers, [b]"The LORD *be* with
you!" And they answered him,
"The LORD bless you!"
5 Then Bō′az said to his servant who was in charge of the
reapers, "Whose young woman
is this?"
6 So the servant who was in
charge of the reapers answered
and said, "It *is* the young Mō′-
ab·īte woman [a]who came back
with Nā′o·mī from the country
of Mō′ab.

13 [a]Judg. 2:15
14 [a][Prov. 17:17]
15 [a]Judg. 11:24 [b]Josh. 1:15
16 [a]2 Kin. 2:2, 4, 6 [b]Ruth 2:11, 12 [1]*Urge me not*
17 [a]1 Sam. 3:17
18 [a]Acts 21:14 [1]Lit. *made herself strong to go*
19 [a]Matt. 21:10 [b]Lam. 2:15
20 [1]Lit. *Pleasant* [2]Lit. *Bitter*
21 [a]Job 1:21 [1]Heb. *Shaddai*
22 [a]2 Sam. 21:9

CHAPTER 2

1 [a]Ruth 3:2, 12 [b]Ruth 1:2 [c]Ruth 4:21
2 [a]Lev. 19:9, 10; 23:22
4 [a]Ruth 1:1 [b]Ps. 129:7, 8
6 [a]Ruth 1:22

7 "And she said, 'Please let me
glean and gather after the reapers among the sheaves.' So she
came and has continued from
morning until now, though she
rested a little in the house."
8 Then Bō'az said to Ruth,
"You will listen, my daughter,
will you not? Do not go to glean
in another field, nor go from
here, but stay close by my young
women.
9 "*Let* your eyes *be* on the field
which they reap, and go after
them. Have I not commanded
the young men not to touch you?
And when you are thirsty, go to
the vessels and drink from what
the young men have drawn."
10 So she [a]fell on her face,
bowed down to the ground, and
said to him, "Why have I found
[b]favor in your eyes, that you
should take notice of me, since I
am a foreigner?"
11 And Bō'az answered and
said to her, "It has been fully
reported to me, [a]all that you
have done for your mother-in-
law since the death of your husband, and *how* you have left
your father and your mother
and the land of your birth, and
have come to a people whom
you did not know before.
12 [a]"The LORD repay your work,
and a full reward be given you
by the LORD God of Israel, [b]under
whose wings you have come for
refuge."
13 Then she said, [a]"Let me find
favor in your sight, my lord; for
you have comforted me, and
have spoken [1]kindly to your
maidservant, [b]though I am not
like one of your maidservants."
14 Now Bō'az said to her at
mealtime, "Come here, and eat
of the bread, and dip your piece
of bread in the vinegar." So she
sat beside the reapers, and he
passed parched *grain* to her; and
she ate and [a]was satisfied, and
kept some back.
15 And when she rose up to
[1]glean, Bō'az commanded his
young men, saying, "Let her
glean even among the sheaves,
and do not [2]reproach her.
16 "Also let *grain* from the bundles fall purposely for her; leave
it that she may glean, and do not
rebuke her."
17 So she gleaned in the field
until evening, and beat out what
she had gleaned, and it was
about an ephah of [a]barley.
18 Then she took *it* up and went
into the city, and her mother-in-
law saw what she had gleaned.
So she brought out and gave
to her [a]what she had kept back
after she had been satisfied.
19 And her mother-in-law
said to her, "Where have you
gleaned today? And where did
you work? Blessed be the one
who [a]took notice of you." So
she told her mother-in-law with
whom she had worked, and said,
"The man's name with whom I
worked today *is* Bō'az."
20 Then Nā'o·mī said to her
daughter-in-law, [a]"Blessed *be* he
of the LORD, who [b]has not forsaken His kindness to the living and the dead!" And Nā'o·mī
said to her, "This man *is* a rela-
tion of ours, [c]one of [1]our close
relatives."
21 Ruth the Mō'ab·ī·tess said,
"He also said to me, 'You shall
stay close by my young men
until they have finished all my
harvest.' "
22 And Nā'o·mī said to Ruth her

10 [a]1 Sam. 25:23 [b]1 Sam. 1:18
11 [a]Ruth 1:14–18
12 [a]1 Sam. 24:19 [b]Ruth 1:16
13 [a]Gen. 33:15 [b]1 Sam. 25:41 [1]Lit. *to the heart of*
14 [a]Ruth 2:18
15 [1]Gather after the reapers [2]*rebuke*
17 [a]Ruth 1:22
18 [a]Ruth 2:14
19 [a][Ps. 41:1]
20 [a]2 Sam. 2:5 [b]Prov. 17:17 [c]Ruth 3:9; 4:4, 6 [1]*our redeemers*, Heb. *goalenu*

daughter-in-law, "*It is* good, my
daughter, that you go out with
his young women, and that people do not [1]meet you in any other
field."
23 So she stayed close by the
young women of Bō′az, to glean
until the end of barley harvest
and wheat harvest; and she
dwelt with her mother-in-law.
3 Then Nā′o·mī her mother-in-
law said to her, "My daugh-
ter, [a]shall I not seek [b]security[1]
for you, that it may be well with
you?
2 "Now Bō′az, [a]whose young
women you were with, *is he* not
our relative? In fact, he is winnowing barley tonight at the
threshing floor.
3 "Therefore wash yourself
and [a]anoint yourself, put on
your *best* garment and go down
to the threshing floor; *but* do
not make yourself known to the
man until he has finished eating
and drinking.
4 "Then it shall be, when he
lies down, that you shall notice
the place where he lies; and you
shall go in, uncover his feet, and
lie down; and he will tell you
what you should do."
5 And she said to her, "All that
you say to me I will do."
6 So she went down to the
threshing floor and did according to all that her mother-in-law
instructed her.
7 And after Bō′az had eaten
and drunk, and [a]his heart was
cheerful, he went to lie down at
the end of the heap of grain; and
she came softly, uncovered his
feet, and lay down.
8 Now it happened at mid-
night that the man was startled,
and turned himself; and there, a
woman was lying at his feet.
9 And he said, "Who *are* you?"
So she answered, "I *am* Ruth,
your maidservant. [a]Take[1] your
maidservant under your wing,
for you are [b]a [2]close relative."
10 Then he said, [a]"Blessed *are*
you of the LORD, my daughter!
For you have shown more kindness at the end than [b]at the beginning, in that you did not go
after young men, whether poor
or rich.
11 "And now, my daughter, do
not fear. I will do for you all that
you request, for all the people of
my town know that you *are* [a]a
virtuous woman.
12 "Now it is true that I *am* a
[a]close relative; however, [b]there
is a relative closer than I.
13 "Stay this night, and in the
morning it shall be *that* if he
will [a]perform the duty of a close
relative for you—good; let him
do it. But if he does not want to
perform the duty for you, then
I will perform the duty for you,
[b]*as* the LORD lives! Lie down until morning."
14 So she lay at his feet until
morning, and she arose before
one could recognize another.
Then he said, [a]"Do not let it be
known that the woman came to
the threshing floor."
15 Also he said, "Bring the
[1]shawl that *is* on you and hold
it." And when she held it, he
measured six *ephahs* of barley,
and laid *it* on her. Then [2]she
went into the city.
16 When she came to her
mother-in-law, she said, [1]"*Is* that
you, my daughter?" Then she
told her all that the man had
done for her.

22 [1]*encounter*

CHAPTER 3

1 [a]1 Tim. 5:8 [b]Ruth 1:9 [1]Lit. *rest*

2 [a]Ruth 2:3, 8

3 [a]2 Sam. 14:2

7 [a]Judg. 19:6, 9, 22

9 [a]Ezek. 16:8 [b]Ruth 2:20; 3:12 [1]Or *Spread the corner of your garment over your maidservant* [2]*redeemer*, Heb. *goel*

10 [a]Ruth 2:20 [b]Ruth 1:8

11 [a]Prov. 12:4; 31:10–31

12 [a]Ruth 3:9 [b]Ruth 4:1

13 [a]Deut. 25:5–10 [b]Jer. 4:2; 12:16

14 [a][1 Cor. 10:32]

15 [1]*cloak* [2]Many Heb. mss., Syr., Vg. *she*; MT, LXX, Tg. *he*

16 [1]Or *How are you,*

17 And she said, "These six *ephahs* of barley he gave me; for he said to me, 'Do not go empty-handed to your mother-in-law.' "

18 Then she said, [a]"Sit still, my daughter, until you know how the matter will turn out; for the man will not rest until he has concluded the matter this day."

CHAPTER 4

4 Now Bō′az went up to the gate and sat down there; and behold, [a]the close relative of whom Bō′az had spoken came by. So Bō′az said, "Come aside, [1]friend, sit down here." So he came aside and sat down.

2 And he took ten men of [a]the elders of the city, and said, "Sit down here." So they sat down.

3 Then he said to the close relative, "Nā′o·mī, who has come back from the country of Mō′ab, sold the piece of land [a]which *belonged* to our brother Ē·lim′e·lech.

4 "And I thought to [1]inform you, saying, [a]'Buy *it* back [b]in the presence of the inhabitants and the elders of my people. If you will redeem *it*, redeem *it;* but if [2]you will not redeem *it, then* tell me, that I may know; [c]for *there is* no one but you to redeem *it*, and I *am* next after you.' " And he said, "I will redeem *it*."

5 Then Bō′az said, "On the day you buy the field from the hand of Nā′o·mī, you must also buy *it* from Ruth the Mō′ab·ī·tess, the wife of the dead, [a]to [1]perpetuate the name of the dead through his inheritance."

6 [a]And the close relative said, "I cannot redeem *it* for myself, lest I ruin my own inheritance. You redeem my right of redemption for yourself, for I cannot redeem *it*."

7 [a]Now this *was the custom* in former times in Israel concerning redeeming and exchanging, to confirm anything: one man took off his sandal and gave *it* to the other, and this *was* a confirmation in Israel.

8 Therefore the close relative said to Bō′az, "Buy *it* for yourself." So he took off his sandal.

9 And Bō′az said to the elders and all the people, "You *are* witnesses this day that I have bought all that was Ē·lim′e·lech's, and all that *was* Chil′i·on's and Mah′lon's, from the hand of Nā′o·mī.

10 "Moreover, Ruth the Mō′ab·ī·tess, the widow of Mah′lon, I have acquired as my wife, to perpetuate the name of the dead through his inheritance, [a]that the name of the dead may not be cut off from among his brethren and from [1]his position at the gate. You *are* witnesses this day."

11 And all the people who *were* at the gate, and the elders, said, "*We are* witnesses. [a]The LORD make the woman who is coming to your house like Rachel and Leah, the two who [b]built the house of Israel; and may you prosper in [c]Eph′ra·thah and be famous in [d]Bethlehem.

12 "May your house be like the house of [a]Per′ez, [b]whom Tā′mar bore to Judah, because of [c]the offspring which the LORD will give you from this young woman."

13 So Bō′az [a]took Ruth and she became his wife; and when he went in to her, [b]the LORD gave her conception, and she bore a son.

14 Then [a]the women said to

---

18 [a][Ps. 37:3, 5]

CHAPTER 4

1 [a]Ruth 3:12 [1]Heb. *peloni almoni*, lit. *so and so*

2 [a]1 Kin. 21:8

3 [a]Lev. 25:25

4 [a]Jer. 32:7, 8 [b]Gen. 23:18 [c]Lev. 25:25 [1]Lit. *uncover your ear* [2]So with many Heb. mss., LXX, Syr., Tg., Vg.; MT *he*

5 [a]Matt. 22:24 [1]Lit. *raise up*

6 [a]Ruth 3:12, 13

7 [a]Deut. 25:7–10

10 [a]Deut. 25:6 [1]Probably his civic office

11 [a]Ps. 127:3; 128:3 [b]Gen. 29:25–30 [c]Gen. 35:16–18 [d]Mic. 5:2

12 [a]Matt. 1:3 [b]Gen. 38:6–29 [c]1 Sam. 2:20

13 [a]Ruth 3:11 [b]Gen. 29:31; 33:5

14 [a]Luke 1:58

Nā′o·mī, "Blessed *be* the LORD,
who has not left you this day
without a [1]close relative; and may
his name be famous in Israel!
15 "And may he be to you a restorer of life and a [1]nourisher of
your old age; for your daughter-
in-law, who loves you, who is
[a]better to you than seven sons,
has borne him."
16 Then Nā′o·mī took the child
and laid him on her bosom, and
became a nurse to him.
17 [a]Also the neighbor women
gave him a name, saying, "There
is a son born to Nā′o·mī." And
they called his name Ō′bed. He
is the father of Jesse, the father
of David.
18 [a]Now this *is* the genealogy of
Per′ez: [b]Per′ez begot Hez′ron;
19 Hez′ron begot Ram, and Ram
begot Am·min′a·dab;
20 Am·min′a·dab begot [a]Nah′-
shon, and Nah′shon begot [b]Sal′-
mon;[1]
21 Sal′mon begot Bō′az, and
Bō′az begot Ō′bed;
22 Ō′bed begot Jesse, and Jesse
begot [a]David.

14 [1]*redeemer*, Heb. *goel*
15 [a]1 Sam. 1:8 [1]*sustainer*
17 [a]Luke 1:58
18 [a]1 Chr. 2:4, 5 [b]Num. 26:20, 21
20 [a]Num. 1:7 [b]Matt. 1:4 [1]Heb. *Salmah*
22 [a]Matt. 1:6

The First Book of SAMUEL

THE Book of First Samuel describes the transition of leadership in Israel from judges to kings. Three characters are prominent in the book: Samuel, the last judge and first prophet; Saul, the first king of Israel; and David, the king-elect, anointed but not yet recognized as Saul's successor.

The books of First and Second Samuel were originally one book in the Hebrew Bible, known as the "Book of Samuel" or simply "Samuel." This name has been variously translated "The Name of God," "His Name Is God," "Heard of God," and "Asked of God." The Septuagint divides Samuel into two books even though it is one continuous account. This division artificially breaks up the history of David. The Greek (Septuagint) title is *Bibloi Basileion,* "Books of Kingdoms," referring to the later kingdoms of Israel and Judah. First Samuel is called *Basileion Alpha,* "First Kingdoms." Second Samuel and First and Second Kings are called "Second, Third, and Fourth Kingdoms." The Latin Vulgate originally called the books of Samuel and Kings *Libri Regum,* "Books of the Kings." Later the Latin Bible combined the Hebrew and Greek titles for the first of these books, calling it *Liber I Samuelis,* the "First Book of Samuel," or simply "First Samuel."

NOW there was a certain man
of Rā·ma·thā'im Zō'phim, of
the [a]mountains of Ē'phra·im, and
his name *was* [b]El·kā'nah the son
of Je·rō'ham, the son of [1]E·lī'hū,
the son of [2]Tō'hū, the son of
Zuph, [c]an Ē'phra·im·īte.
2 And he had [a]two wives: the
name of one *was* Hannah, and
the name of the other Pe·nin'-
nah. Pe·nin'nah had children,
but Hannah had no children.
3 This man went up from his
city [a]yearly [b]to worship and sacrifice to the LORD of hosts in
[c]Shī'lōh. Also the two sons of
Ē'lī, Hoph'nī and Phin'e·has, the
priests of the LORD, *were* there.
4 And whenever the time
came for El·kā'nah to make an
[a]offering, he would give portions
to Pe·nin'nah his wife and to all
her sons and daughters.
5 But to Hannah he would give
a double portion, for he loved
Hannah, [a]although the LORD had
closed her womb.
6 And her rival also [a]provoked
her severely, to make her miserable, because the LORD had
closed her womb.
7 So it was, year by year, when
she went up to the house of the
LORD, that she provoked her;
therefore she wept and did not
eat.
8 Then El·kā'nah her husband
said to her, "Hannah, why do
you weep? Why do you not eat?
And why is your heart grieved?
Am I not [a]better to you than ten
sons?"
9 So Hannah arose after they
had finished eating and drinking in Shī'lōh. Now Ē'lī the
priest was sitting on the seat by
the doorpost of [a]the [1]tabernacle
of the LORD.

CHAPTER 1

1 [a]Josh. 17:17, 18; 24:33 [b]1 Chr. 6:27, 33–38 [c]Ruth 1:2 [1]*Eliel,* 1 Chr. 6:34 [2]*Toah,* 1 Chr. 6:34

2 [a]Deut. 21:15–17

3 [a]Luke 2:41 [b]Deut. 12:5–7; 16:16 [c]Josh. 18:1

4 [a]Deut. 12:17, 18

5 [a]Gen. 16:1; 30:1, 2

6 [a]Job 24:21

8 [a]Ruth 4:15

9 [a]1 Sam. 3:3 [1]*palace* or *temple,* Heb. *heykal*

10 [a]And she *was* in bitterness of
soul, and prayed to the LORD and
[1]wept in anguish.
11 Then she [a]made a vow and
said, "O LORD of hosts, if You
will indeed [b]look on the affliction of Your maidservant and
[c]remember me, and not forget
Your maidservant, but will give
Your maidservant a male child,
then I will give him to the LORD
all the days of his life, and [d]no razor shall come upon his head."
12 And it happened, as she continued praying before the LORD,
that Ē′lī watched her mouth.
13 Now Hannah spoke in her
heart; only her lips moved, but
her voice was not heard. Therefore Ē′lī thought she was drunk.
14 So Ē′lī said to her, "How long
will you be drunk? Put your
wine away from you!"
15 But Hannah answered and
said, "No, my lord, I *am* a woman
of sorrowful spirit. I have drunk
neither wine nor intoxicating
drink, but have [a]poured out my
soul before the LORD.
16 "Do not consider your maidservant a [a]wicked[1] woman, for
out of the abundance of my
complaint and grief I have spoken until now."
17 Then Ē′lī answered and said,
[a]"Go in peace, and [b]the God of
Israel grant your petition which
you have asked of Him."
18 And she said, [a]"Let your
maidservant find favor in your
sight." So the woman [b]went her
way and ate, and her face was
no longer *sad*.
19 Then they rose early in the
morning and worshiped before
the LORD, and returned and came
to their house at Rā′mah. And
El·kā′nah [a]knew Hannah his
wife, and the LORD [b]remembered
her.
20 So it came to pass in the
process of time that Hannah
conceived and bore a son, and
called his name [1]Samuel, *saying*,
"Because I have asked for him
from the LORD."
21 Now the man El·kā′nah and
all his house [a]went up to offer to
the LORD the yearly sacrifice and
his vow.
22 But Hannah did not go up,
for she said to her husband,
"*Not* until the child is weaned;
then I will [a]take him, that he
may appear before the LORD and
[b]remain there [c]forever."
23 So [a]El·kā′nah her husband
said to her, "Do what seems
best to you; wait until you have
weaned him. Only let the LORD
[1]establish [2]His word." Then the
woman stayed and nursed her
son until she had weaned him.
24 Now when she had weaned
him, she [a]took him up with her,
with [1]three bulls, one ephah of
flour, and a skin of wine, and
brought him to [b]the house of the
LORD in Shī′lōh. And the child
was young.
25 Then they slaughtered a bull,
and [a]brought the child to Ē′lī.
26 And she said, "O my lord!
[a]As your soul lives, my lord, I *am*
the woman who stood by you
here, praying to the LORD.
27 [a]"For this child I prayed, and
the LORD has granted me my petition which I asked of Him.
28 "Therefore I also have lent
him to the LORD; as long as he
lives he shall be [1]lent to the
LORD." So they [a]worshiped the
LORD there.

2 And Hannah [a]prayed and
said:

10 [a]Job 7:11 [1]Lit. *wept greatly*
11 [a]Num. 30:6–11 [b]Ps. 25:18 [c]Gen. 8:1 [d]Num. 6:5
15 [a]Ps. 42:4; 62:8
16 [a]Deut. 13:13 [1]Lit. *daughter of Belial*
17 [a]Mark 5:34 [b]Ps. 20:3–5
18 [a]Ruth 2:13 [b]Rom. 15:13
19 [a]Gen. 4:1 [b]Gen. 21:1; 30:22
20 [1]Lit. *Heard by God*
21 [a]1 Sam. 1:3
22 [a]Luke 2:22 [b]1 Sam. 1:11, 28 [c]Ex. 21:6
23 [a]Num. 30:7, 10, 11 [1]*confirm* [2]So with MT, Tg., Vg.; DSS, LXX, Syr. *your*
24 [a]Num. 15:9, 10 [b]Josh. 18:1 [1]DSS, LXX, Syr. *a three-year-old bull*
25 [a]Luke 2:22
26 [a]2 Kin. 2:2, 4, 6; 4:30
27 [a][Matt. 7:7]
28 [a]Gen. 24:26, 52 [1]*granted*

CHAPTER 2

1 [a]Phil. 4:6

[b]"My heart rejoices in the
LORD;
[c]My [1]horn is exalted in the
LORD.
[2]I smile at my enemies,
Because I [d]rejoice in Your
salvation.

2 "No[a] one is holy like the
LORD,
For *there is* [b]none besides
You,
Nor *is there* any [c]rock like
our God.

3 "Talk no more so very
proudly;
[a]Let no arrogance come from
your mouth,
For the LORD *is* the God of
[b]knowledge;
And by Him actions are
weighed.

4 "The[a] bows of the mighty
men *are* broken,
And those who stumbled
are girded with strength.
5 *Those who were* full have
hired themselves out for
bread,
And the hungry have ceased
to hunger.
Even [a]the barren has borne
seven,
And [b]she who has many
children has become
feeble.

6 "The[a] LORD kills and makes
alive;
He brings down to the grave
and brings up.
7 The LORD [a]makes poor and
makes rich;
[b]He brings low and lifts up.
8 [a]He raises the poor from the
dust

1 [b]Luke 1:46–55 [c]Ps. 75:10; 89:17, 24; 92:10; 112:9 [d]Ps. 9:14; 13:5; 35:9 [1]Strength [2]Lit. *My mouth is enlarged*
2 [a]Ex. 15:11 [b]Deut. 4:35 [c]Deut. 32:4, 30, 31
3 [a]Ps. 94:4 [b]1 Sam. 16:7
4 [a]Ps. 37:15; 46:9
5 [a]Ps. 113:9 [b]Is. 54:1
6 [a]Deut. 32:39
7 [a]Deut. 8:17, 18 [b]Ps. 75:7
8 [a]Luke 1:52 [b]Job 36:7 [c]Job 38:4–6
9 [a][1 Pet. 1:5] [b][Rom. 3:19]
10 [a]Ps. 2:9 [b]Ps. 18:13, 14 [c]Ps. 96:13; 98:9 [d][Matt. 28:18] [e]Ps. 21:1, 7 [f]Ps. 89:24 [1]Strength
11 [1]*served*
12 [a]Deut. 13:13 [b]Judg. 2:10 [1]Lit. *sons of Belial*

And lifts the beggar from
the ash heap,
[b]To set *them* among princes
And make them inherit the
throne of glory.

[c]"For the pillars of the earth
are the LORD's,
And He has set the world
upon them.
9 [a]He will guard the feet of His
saints,
But the [b]wicked shall be
silent in darkness.

"For by strength no man
shall prevail.
10 The adversaries of the
LORD shall be [a]broken in
pieces;
[b]From heaven He will
thunder against them.
[c]The LORD will judge the
ends of the earth.

[d]"He will give [e]strength to His
king,
And [f]exalt the [1]horn of His
anointed."

11 Then El·kā′nah went to his
house at Rā′mah. But the child
[1]ministered to the LORD before
Ē′lī the priest.
12 Now the sons of Ē′lī *were*
[a]corrupt;[1] [b]they did not know the
LORD.
13 And the priests' custom with
the people *was that* when any
man offered a sacrifice, the
priest's servant would come
with a three-pronged fleshhook
in his hand while the meat was
boiling.
14 Then he would thrust *it* into
the pan, or kettle, or caldron, or
pot; and the priest would take
for himself all that the fleshhook

brought up. So they did in [a]Shī'-
lōh to all the Israelites who came
there.
15 Also, before they [a]burned the
fat, the priest's servant would
come and say to the man who
sacrificed, "Give meat for roast-
ing to the priest, for he will not
take boiled meat from you, but
raw."
16 And *if* the man said to him,
"They should really burn the fat
first; *then* you may take *as much*
as your heart desires," he would
then answer him, "*No*, but you
must give *it* now; and if not, I
will take *it* by force."
17 Therefore the sin of the
young men was very great [a]be-
fore the LORD, for men [b]abhorred[1]
the offering of the LORD.
18 [a]But Samuel ministered before the LORD, *even as* a child,
[b]wearing a linen ephod.
19 Moreover his mother used to
make him a little robe, and bring
it to him year by year when she
[a]came up with her husband to
offer the yearly sacrifice.
20 And Ē'lī [a]would bless El·kā'-
nah and his wife, and say, "The
LORD give you descendants from
this woman for the [1]loan that
was [b]given to the LORD." Then
they would go to their own
home.
21 And the LORD [a]visited[1] Hannah, so that she conceived and
bore three sons and two daughters. Meanwhile the child Samuel [b]grew before the LORD.
22 Now Ē'lī was very old; and
he heard everything his sons did
to all Israel, [1]and how they lay
with [a]the women who assembled
at the door of the tabernacle of
meeting.
23 So he said to them, "Why do

14 [a]1 Sam. 1:3
15 [a]Lev. 3:3–5, 16
17 [a]Gen. 6:11 [b][Mal. 2:7–9] [1]*despised*
18 [a]1 Sam. 2:11; 3:1 [b]Ex. 28:4
19 [a]1 Sam. 1:3, 21
20 [a]Gen. 14:19 [b]1 Sam. 1:11, 27, 28 [1]*gift*
21 [a]Gen. 21:1 [b]1 Sam. 2:26; 3:19–21 [1]*attended to*
22 [a]Ex. 38:8 [1]So with MT, Tg., Vg.; DSS, LXX omit rest of verse
25 [a]Deut. 1:17; 25:1, 2 [b]Num. 15:30 [c]Josh. 11:20 [1]Tg. *the Judge*
26 [a]1 Sam. 2:21 [b]Prov. 3:4
27 [a]1 Kin. 13:1 [b]Ex. 4:14–16; 12:1
28 [a]Ex. 28:1, 4 [b]Num. 5:9
29 [a]Deut. 32:15 [b]Deut. 12:5 [c]Matt. 10:37
30 [a]Ex. 29:9 [b]Jer. 18:9, 10 [c]Mal. 2:9–12
31 [a]1 Kin. 2:27, 35

you do such things? For I hear
of your evil dealings from all the
people.
24 "No, my sons! For *it is* not a
good report that I hear. You make
the LORD's people transgress.
25 "If one man sins against another, [a]God[1] will judge him. But
if a man [b]sins against the LORD,
who will intercede for him?"
Nevertheless they did not heed
the voice of their father, [c]because
the LORD desired to kill them.
26 And the child Samuel [a]grew
in stature, and [b]in favor both
with the LORD and men.
27 Then a [a]man of God came to
Ē'lī and said to him, "Thus says
the LORD: [b]'Did I not clearly reveal Myself to the house of your
father when they were in Egypt
in Pharaoh's house?
28 'Did I not [a]choose him out of
all the tribes of Israel *to be* My
priest, to offer upon My altar,
to burn incense, and to wear an
ephod before Me? And [b]did I not
give to the house of your father
all the offerings of the children
of Israel made by fire?
29 'Why do you [a]kick at My
sacrifice and My offering which
I have commanded *in My*
[b]dwelling place, and honor your
sons more than [c]Me, to make
yourselves fat with the best of
all the offerings of Israel My
people?'
30 "Therefore the LORD God
of Israel says: [a]'I said indeed
that your house and the house
of your father would walk before Me forever.' But now the
LORD says: [b]'Far be it from Me;
for those who honor Me I will
honor, and [c]those who despise
Me shall be lightly esteemed.
31 'Behold, [a]the days are coming

that I will cut off your [1]arm and
the arm of your father's house,
so that there will not be an old
man in your house.
32 'And you will see an enemy
in My dwelling place, *despite*
all the good which God does for
Israel. And there shall not be [a]an
old man in your house forever.
33 'But any of your men *whom*
I do not cut off from My altar
shall consume your eyes and
grieve your heart. And all the
descendants of your house shall
die in the flower of their age.
34 'Now this *shall be* [a]a sign to
you that will come upon your
two sons, on Hoph'nī and Phin'-
e·has: [b]in one day they shall die,
both of them.
35 'Then [a]I will raise up for Myself a faithful priest *who* shall
do according to what *is* in My
heart and in My mind. [b]I will
build him a sure house, and he
shall walk before [c]My anointed
forever.
36 [a]'And it shall come to pass
that everyone who is left in
your house will come *and* bow
down to him for a piece of silver
and a morsel of bread, and say,
"Please, [1]put me in one of the
priestly positions, that I may eat
a piece of bread." ' "

3

Now [a]the boy Samuel ministered to the LORD before Ē'lī.
And [b]the word of the LORD was
rare in those days; *there was* no
widespread revelation.
2 And it came to pass at that
time, while Ē'lī *was* lying down
in his place, and when his eyes
had begun to grow [a]so dim that
he could not see,
3 and before [a]the lamp of God
went out in the [1]tabernacle of
the LORD where the ark of God
was, and while Samuel was lying down,
4 that the LORD called Samuel.
And he answered, "Here I am!"
5 So he ran to Ē'lī and said,
"Here I am, for you called me."
And he said, "I did not call; lie
down again." And he went and
lay down.
6 Then the LORD called yet
again, "Samuel!" So Samuel
arose and went to Ē'lī, and said,
"Here I am, for you called me."
He answered, "I did not call, my
son; lie down again."
7 (Now Samuel [a]did not yet
know the LORD, nor was the
word of the LORD yet revealed to
him.)
8 And the LORD called Samuel
again the third time. So he arose
and went to Ē'lī, and said, "Here
I am, for you did call me." Then
Ē'lī perceived that the LORD had
called the boy.
9 Therefore Ē'lī said to Samuel, "Go, lie down; and it shall
be, if He calls you, that you must
say, [a]'Speak, LORD, for Your servant hears.' " So Samuel went
and lay down in his place.
10 Now the LORD came and
stood and called as at other
times, "Samuel! Samuel!" And
Samuel answered, "Speak, for
Your servant hears."
11 Then the LORD said to Samuel: "Behold, I will do something
in Israel [a]at which both ears
of everyone who hears it will
tingle.
12 "In that day I will perform
against Ē'lī [a]all that I have spoken concerning his house, from
beginning to end.
13 [a]"For I have told him that I
will [b]judge his house forever for
the iniquity which he knows,

31 [1]*strength*
32 [a]Zech. 8:4
34 [a]1 Kin. 13:3 [b]1 Sam. 4:11, 17
35 [a]1 Kin. 2:35 [b]1 Kin. 11:38 [c]Ps. 18:50
36 [a]1 Kin. 2:27 [1]*assign*
CHAPTER 3
1 [a]1 Sam. 2:11, 18 [b]Ps. 74:9
2 [a]1 Sam. 4:15
3 [a]Ex. 27:20, 21 [1]*palace or temple*
7 [a]1 Sam. 2:12
9 [a]1 Kin. 2:17
11 [a]2 Kin. 21:12
12 [a]1 Sam. 2:27–36
13 [a]1 Sam. 2:29–31 [b]1 Sam. 2:22

because [c]his sons made themselves vile, and he [d]did not [1]re-
strain them.
14 "And therefore I have sworn
to the house of Ē′lī that the iniquity of Ē′lī's house [a]shall not be
atoned for by sacrifice or offering forever."
15 So Samuel lay down until
[1]morning, and opened the doors
of the house of the LORD. And
Samuel was afraid to tell Ē′lī the
vision.
16 Then Ē′lī called Samuel and
said, "Samuel, my son!" He answered, "Here I am."
17 And he said, "What *is* the
word that *the* LORD spoke to
you? Please do not hide *it* from
me. [a]God do so to you, and more
also, if you hide anything from
me of all the things that He said
to you."
18 Then Samuel told him everything, and hid nothing from him.
And he said, [a]"It *is* the LORD.
Let Him do what seems good to
Him."
19 So Samuel [a]grew, and [b]the
LORD was with him [c]and let none
of his words [1]fall to the ground.
20 And all Israel [a]from Dan to
Bē·er·shē′ba knew that Samuel *had been* [1]established as a
prophet of the LORD.
21 Then the LORD appeared
again in Shī′lōh. For the LORD
revealed Himself to Samuel in
Shī′lōh by [a]the word of the LORD.

4

And the word of Samuel
came to all [1]Israel.
Now Israel went out to battle against the Phi·lis′tines, and
encamped beside [a]Eb·e·nē′zer;
and the Phi·lis′tines encamped
in Ā′phek.
2 Then the [a]Phi·lis′tines put
themselves in battle array
against Israel. And when they
joined battle, Israel was [1]de-
feated by the Phi·lis′tines, who
killed about four thousand men
of the army in the field.
3 And when the people had
come into the camp, the elders
of Israel said, "Why has the
LORD defeated us today before
the Phi·lis′tines? [a]Let us bring
the ark of the covenant of the
LORD from Shī′lōh to us, that
when it comes among us it may
save us from the hand of our
enemies."
4 So the people sent to Shī′-
lōh, that they might bring from
there the ark of the covenant of
the LORD of hosts, [a]who dwells
between [b]the cherubim. And the
[c]two sons of Ē′lī, Hoph′nī and
Phin′e·has, *were* there with the
ark of the covenant of God.
5 And when the ark of the
covenant of the LORD came into
the camp, all Israel shouted so
loudly that the earth shook.
6 Now when the Phi·lis′tines
heard the noise of the shout,
they said, "What *does* the sound
of this great shout in the camp
of the Hebrews *mean?*" Then
they understood that the ark
of the LORD had come into the
camp.
7 So the Phi·lis′tines were
afraid, for they said, "God has
come into the camp!" And they
said, [a]"Woe to us! For such a thing
has never happened before.
8 "Woe to us! Who will deliver
us from the hand of these mighty
gods? These *are* the gods who
struck the Egyptians with all the
plagues in the wilderness.
9 [a]"Be strong and conduct
yourselves like men, you Phi·lis′-
tines, that you do not become

---

13 [c]1 Sam. 2:12, 17, 22 [d]1 Sam. 2:23, 25 [1]Lit. *rebuke*
14 [a]Num. 15:30, 31
15 [1]So with MT, Tg., Vg.; LXX adds *and he arose in the morning*
17 [a]Ruth 1:17
18 [a]Is. 39:8
19 [a]1 Sam. 2:21 [b]Gen. 21:22; 28:15; 39:2, 21, 23 [c]1 Sam. 9:6 [1]*fail*
20 [a]Judg. 20:1 [1]*confirmed*
21 [a]1 Sam.3:1, 4

CHAPTER 4

1 [a]1 Sam. 7:12 [1]So with MT, Tg.; LXX, Vg. add *And it came to pass in those days that the Philistines gathered themselves together to fight;* LXX adds further *against Israel*
2 [a]1 Sam. 12:9 [1]Lit. *struck*
3 [a]Josh. 6:6–21
4 [a]1 Sam. 6:2 [b]Num. 7:89 [c]1 Sam. 2:12
7 [a]Ex. 15:14
9 [a]1 Cor. 16:13

servants of the Hebrews, [b]as they have been to you. [1]Conduct yourselves like men, and fight!”

10 So the Phi·lis′tines fought, and [a]Israel was [1]defeated, and every man fled to his tent. There was a very great slaughter, and there fell of Israel thirty thousand foot soldiers.

11 Also [a]the ark of God was captured; and [b]the two sons of Ē′lī, Hoph′nī and Phin′e·has, died.

12 Then a man of Benjamin ran from the battle line the same day, and [a]came to Shī′lōh with his clothes torn and [b]dirt on his head.

13 Now when he came, there was Ē′lī, sitting on [a]a seat [1]by the wayside watching, for his heart [2]trembled for the ark of God. And when the man came into the city and told *it*, all the city cried out.

14 When Ē′lī heard the noise of the outcry, he said, “What *does* the sound of this tumult *mean?*” And the man came quickly and told Ē′lī.

15 Ē′lī was ninety-eight years old, and [a]his eyes were so [1]dim that he could not see.

16 Then the man said to Ē′lī, “I *am* he who came from the battle. And I fled today from the battle line.” And he said, [a]“What happened, my son?”

17 So the messenger answered and said, “Israel has fled before the Phi·lis′tines, and there has been a great slaughter among the people. Also your two sons, Hoph′nī and Phin′e·has, are dead; and the ark of God has been captured.”

18 Then it happened, when he made mention of the ark of God, that Ē′lī fell off the seat backward by the side of the gate; and his neck was broken and he died, for the man was old and heavy. And he had judged Israel forty years.

19 Now his daughter-in-law, Phin′e·has′ wife, was with child, *due* to be delivered; and when she heard the news that the ark of God was captured, and that her father-in-law and her husband were dead, she bowed herself and gave birth, for her labor pains came upon her.

20 And about the time of her death [a]the women who stood by her said to her, “Do not fear, for you have borne a son.” But she did not answer, nor did she [1]regard *it*.

21 Then she named the child [a]Ich′a·bod,[1] saying, [b]“The glory has departed from Israel!” because the ark of God had been captured and because of her father-in-law and her husband.

22 And she said, “The glory has departed from Israel, for the ark of God has been captured.”

5

Then the Phi·lis′tines took the ark of God and brought it [a]from Eb·e·nē′zer to Ash′dod.

2 When the Phi·lis′tines took the ark of God, they brought it into the house of [a]Dā′gon[1] and set it by Dā′gon.

3 And when the people of Ash′dod arose early in the morning, there was Dā′gon, [a]fallen on its face to the earth before the ark of the LORD. So they took Dā′gon and [b]set it in its place again.

4 And when they arose early the next morning, there was Dā′gon, fallen on its face to the ground before the ark of the LORD. [a]The head of Dā′gon and both the palms of its hands *were*

9 [b]Judg. 13:1 [1]Lit. *Be men*

10 [a]Deut. 28:15, 25 [1]Lit. *struck down*

11 [a]Ps. 78:60, 61 [b]1 Sam. 2:34

12 [a]2 Sam. 1:2 [b]Josh. 7:6

13 [a]1 Sam. 1:9; 4:18 [1]So with MT, Vg.; LXX *beside the gate watching the road* [2]*trembled with anxiety*

15 [a]1 Sam. 3:2 [1]*fixed*

16 [a]2 Sam. 1:4

20 [a]Gen. 35:16–19 [1]*pay any attention to*

21 [a]1 Sam. 14:3 [b]Ps. 26:8; 78:61 [1]Lit. *Inglorious*

CHAPTER 5

1 [a]1 Sam. 4:1; 7:12

2 [a]1 Chr. 10:8–10 [1]A Philistine idol

3 [a]Is. 19:1; 46:1, 2 [b]Is. 46:7

4 [a]Mic. 1:7

broken off on the threshold; only
[1]Dā′gon's *torso* was left of it.
5 Therefore neither the priests
of Dā′gon nor any who come
into Dā′gon's house [a]tread on
the threshold of Dā′gon in Ash′-
dod to this day.
6 But the [a]hand of the LORD
was heavy on the people of Ash′-
dod, and He [b]ravaged them and
struck them with [c]tumors,[1] *both*
Ash′dod and its [d]territory.
7 And when the men of Ash′-
dod saw how *it was*, they said,
"The ark of the [a]God of Israel
must not remain with us, for
His hand is harsh toward us and
Dā′gon our god."
8 Therefore they sent and
gathered to themselves all the
[a]lords of the Phi·lis′tines, and
said, "What shall we do with
the ark of the God of Israel?"
And they answered, "Let the ark
of the God of Israel be carried
away to [b]Gath." So they carried the ark of the God of Israel
away.
9 So it was, after they had carried it away, that [a]the hand of
the LORD was against the city
with a very great destruction;
and He struck the men of the
city, both small and great, [1]and
tumors broke out on them.
10 Therefore they sent the ark
of God to Ek′ron. So it was, as
the ark of God came to Ek′ron,
that the Ek′ron·ites cried out,
saying, "They have brought the
ark of the God of Israel to us, to
kill us and our people!"
11 So they sent and gathered
together all the lords of the
Phi·lis′tines, and said, "Send
away the ark of the God of Israel, and let it go back to its own
place, so that it does not kill us
and our people." For there was
a deadly destruction throughout
all the city; the hand of God was
very heavy there.
12 And the men who did not die
were stricken with the tumors,
and the [a]cry of the city went up
to heaven.

6 Now the ark of the LORD was
in the country of the Phi·lis′-
tines seven months.
2 And the Phi·lis′tines [a]called
for the priests and the diviners,
saying, "What shall we do with
the ark of the LORD? Tell us how
we should send it to its place."
3 So they said, "If you send
away the ark of the God of Israel, do not send it [a]empty; but
by all means return *it* to Him
with [b]a trespass offering. Then
you will be healed, and it will be
known to you why His hand is
not removed from you."
4 Then they said, "What *is*
the trespass offering which we
shall return to Him?" They answered, [a]"Five golden tumors
and five golden rats, *according
to* the number of the lords of
the Phi·lis′tines. For the same
plague *was* on all of [1]you and on
your lords.
5 "Therefore you shall make
images of your tumors and images of your rats that [a]ravage
the land, and you shall [b]give
glory to the God of Israel; perhaps He will [c]lighten[1] His hand
from you, from [d]your gods, and
from your land.
6 "Why then do you harden
your hearts [a]as the Egyptians
and Pharaoh hardened their
hearts? When He did mighty
things among them, [b]did they
not let the people go, that they
might depart?

4 [1]So with LXX, Syr., Tg., Vg.; MT *Dagon*
5 [a]Zeph. 1:9
6 [a]Ex. 9:3 [b]1 Sam. 6:5 [c]Deut. 28:27; Ps. 78:66 [d]Josh. 15:46, 47 [1]Probably bubonic plague. LXX, Vg. add *And in the midst of their land rats sprang up, and there was a great death panic in the city.*
7 [a]1 Sam. 6:5
8 [a]1 Sam. 6:4 [b]Josh. 11:22
9 [a]Deut. 2:15 [1]Vg. *and they had tumors in their secret parts*
12 [a]Jer. 14:2
CHAPTER 6
2 [a]Gen. 41:8
3 [a]Deut. 16:16 [b]Lev. 5:15, 16
4 [a]1 Sam. 5:6, 9, 12; 6:17 [1]Lit. *them*
5 [a]1 Sam. 5:6 [b]Josh. 7:19 [c]1 Sam. 5:6, 11 [d]1 Sam. 5:3, 4, 7 [1]*ease*
6 [a]Ex. 7:13; 8:15; 9:34; 14:17 [b]Ex. 12:31

7 "Now therefore, make [a]a new
cart, take two milk cows [b]which
have never been yoked, and
hitch the cows to the cart; and
take their calves home, away
from them.
8 "Then take the ark of the
LORD and set it on the cart; and
put [a]the articles of gold which
you are returning to Him *as* a
trespass offering in a chest by
its side. Then send it away, and
let it go.
9 "And watch: if it goes up the
road to its own territory, to [a]Beth
Shem'esh, *then* He has done [1]us
this great evil. But if not, then
[b]we shall know that *it is* not His
hand *that* struck us—it happened to us by chance."
10 Then the men did so; they
took two milk cows and hitched
them to the cart, and shut up
their calves at home.
11 And they set the ark of the
LORD on the cart, and the chest
with the gold rats and the images of their tumors.
12 Then the cows headed
straight for the road to Beth
Shem'esh, *and* went along the
[a]highway, lowing as they went,
and did not turn aside to the
right hand or the left. And the
lords of the Phi·lis'tines went
after them to the border of Beth
Shem'esh.
13 Now *the people of* Beth
Shem'esh *were* reaping their
[a]wheat harvest in the valley; and
they lifted their eyes and saw
the ark, and rejoiced to see *it*.
14 Then the cart came into the
field of Joshua of Beth Shem'esh,
and stood there; a large stone
was there. So they split the wood
of the cart and offered the cows
as a burnt offering to the LORD.
15 The Lē'vītes took down the
ark of the LORD and the chest
that *was* with it, in which *were*
the articles of gold, and put *them*
on the large stone. Then the men
of Beth Shem'esh offered burnt
offerings and made sacrifices
the same day to the LORD.
16 So when [a]the five lords of the
Phi·lis'tines had seen *it*, they returned to Ek'ron the same day.
17 [a]These *are* the golden tumors which the Phi·lis'tines returned *as* a trespass offering to
the LORD: one for Ash'dod, one
for Gā'za, one for Ash'ke·lon,
one for [b]Gath, one for Ek'ron;
18 and the golden rats, *according to* the number of all the cities of the Phi·lis'tines *belonging*
to the five lords, *both* fortified
cities and country villages, even
as far as the large *stone of* Abel
on which they set the ark of the
LORD, *which stone remains* to
this day in the field of Joshua of
Beth Shem'esh.
19 Then [a]He struck the men
of Beth Shem'esh, because they
had looked into the ark of the
LORD. [1]He [b]struck fifty thousand
and seventy men of the people,
and the people lamented because the LORD had struck the
people with a great slaughter.
20 And the men of Beth Shem'-
esh said, [a]"Who is able to stand
before this holy LORD God? And
to whom shall it go up from us?"
21 So they sent messengers to
the inhabitants of [a]Kir'jath Jē'-
a·rim, saying, "The Phi·lis'tines
have brought back the ark of the
LORD; come down *and* take it up
with you."

7

Then the men of [a]Kir'jath
Jē'a·rim came and took the
ark of the LORD, and brought it

7 [a]2 Sam. 6:3 [b]Num. 19:2
8 [a]1 Sam. 6:4, 5
9 [a]Josh. 15:10; 21:16 [b]1 Sam. 6:3 [1]*this calamity to us*
12 [a]Num. 20:19
13 [a]1 Sam. 12:17
16 [a]Josh. 13:3
17 [a]1 Sam. 6:4 [b]1 Sam. 5:8
19 [a]Ex. 19:21 [b]2 Sam. 6:7 [1]Or *He struck seventy men of the people and fifty oxen of a man*
20 [a]Mal. 3:2
21 [a]1 Chr. 13:5, 6

CHAPTER 7

1 [a]1 Sam. 6:21

into the house of [b]A·bin′a·dab
on the hill, and [c]consecrated
El·ē·ā′zar his son to keep the ark
of the LORD.
2 So it was that the ark remained in Kir′jath Jē′a·rim a
long time; it was there twenty
years. And all the house of Israel
lamented after the LORD.
3 Then Samuel spoke to all the
house of Israel, saying, "If you
[a]return to the LORD with all your
hearts, *then* [b]put away the foreign gods and the [c]Ash′to·reths[1]
from among you, and [d]prepare
your hearts for the LORD, and
[e]serve Him only; and He will
deliver you from the hand of the
Phi·lis′tines."
4 So the children of Israel put
away the [a]Bā′als and the [1]Ash′-
to·reths, and served the LORD
only.
5 And Samuel said, [a]"Gather
all Israel to Miz′pah, and [b]I will
pray to the LORD for you."
6 So they gathered together
at Miz′pah, [a]drew water, and
poured *it* out before the LORD.
And they [b]fasted that day, and
said there, [c]"We have sinned
against the LORD." And Samuel
judged the children of Israel at
Miz′pah.
7 Now when the Phi·lis′tines
heard that the children of Israel
had gathered together at Miz′-
pah, the lords of the Phi·lis′-
tines went up against Israel.
And when the children of Israel
heard *of it*, they were afraid of
the Phi·lis′tines.
8 So the children of Israel said
to Samuel, [a]"Do not cease to cry
out to the LORD our God for us,
that He may save us from the
hand of the Phi·lis′tines."
9 And Samuel took a [a]suckling
lamb and offered *it as* a whole
burnt offering to the LORD. Then
[b]Samuel cried out to the LORD for
Israel, and the LORD answered
him.
10 Now as Samuel was offering up the burnt offering, the
Phi·lis′tines drew near to battle
against Israel. [a]But the LORD
thundered with a loud thunder
upon the Phi·lis′tines that day,
and so confused them that they
were overcome before Israel.
11 And the men of Israel went
out of Miz′pah and pursued the
Phi·lis′tines, and [1]drove them
back as far as below Beth Car.
12 Then Samuel [a]took a stone
and set *it* up between Miz′pah
and Shen, and called its name
[1]Eb·e·nē′zer, saying, "Thus far
the LORD has helped us."
13 [a]So the Phi·lis′tines were
subdued, and they [b]did not come
anymore into the territory of
Israel. And the hand of the LORD
was against the Phi·lis′tines all
the days of Samuel.
14 Then the cities which the
Phi·lis′tines had taken from
Israel were restored to Israel,
from Ek′ron to Gath; and Israel
recovered its territory from the
hands of the Phi·lis′tines. Also
there was peace between Israel
and the Am′o·rītes.
15 And Samuel [a]judged Israel
all the days of his life.
16 He went from year to year on
a circuit to Beth′el, Gil′gal, and
Miz′pah, and judged Israel in all
those places.
17 But [a]he always returned to
Rā′mah, for his home *was* there.
There he judged Israel, and there
he [b]built an altar to the LORD.

CHAPTER 8

8 Now it came to pass when
Samuel was [a]old that he

---

1 [b]2 Sam. 6:3, 4 [c]Lev. 21:8
3 [a]Deut. 30:2–10 [b]Gen. 35:2 [c]Judg. 2:13 [d]Job 11:13 [e]Luke 4:8 [1]Images of Canaanite goddesses
4 [a]Judg. 2:11; 10:16 [1]Images of Canaanite goddesses
5 [a]Judg. 10:17; 20:1 [b]1 Sam. 12:17–19
6 [a]2 Sam. 14:14 [b]Neh. 9:1, 2 [c]1 Sam. 12:10
8 [a]Is. 37:4
9 [a]Lev. 22:27 [b]1 Sam. 12:18
10 [a]2 Sam. 22:14, 15
11 [1]*struck them down*
12 [a]Josh. 4:9; 24:26 [1]Lit. *Stone of Help*
13 [a]Judg. 13:1 [b]1 Sam. 13:5
15 [a]1 Sam. 12:11
17 [a]1 Sam. 8:4 [b]Judg. 21:4

CHAPTER 8

1 [a]1 Sam. 12:2

[b]made his [c]sons judges over Israel.
2 The name of his firstborn was
Jō′el, and the name of his second, A·bī′jah; *they were* judges
in Bē·er·shē′ba.
3 But his sons [a]did not walk in
his ways; they turned aside [b]after
dishonest gain, [c]took bribes, and
perverted justice.
4 Then all the elders of Israel
gathered together and came to
Samuel at Rā′mah,
5 and said to him, "Look, you
are old, and your sons do not
walk in your ways. Now [a]make
us a king to judge us like all the
nations."
6 But the thing [a]displeased
Samuel when they said, "Give us
a king to judge us." So Samuel
[b]prayed to the LORD.
7 And the LORD said to Samuel,
"Heed the voice of the people in
all that they say to you; for [a]they
have not rejected you, but [b]they
have rejected Me, that I should
not reign over them.
8 "According to all the works
which they have done since the
day that I brought them up out
of Egypt, even to this day—with
which they have forsaken Me
and served other gods—so they
are doing to you also.
9 "Now therefore, heed their
voice. However, you shall solemnly forewarn them, and
[a]show them the behavior of the
king who will reign over them."
10 So Samuel told all the words
of the LORD to the people who
asked him for a king.
11 And he said, [a]"This will be
the behavior of the king who
will reign over you: He will take
your [b]sons and appoint *them* for
his own [c]chariots and *to be* his
horsemen, and *some* will run
before his chariots.
12 "He will [a]appoint captains
over his thousands and captains
over his fifties, *will set some* to
plow his ground and reap his
harvest, and *some* to make his
weapons of war and equipment
for his chariots.
13 "He will take your daughters *to be* perfumers, cooks, and
bakers.
14 "And [a]he will take the best of
your fields, your vineyards, and
your olive groves, and give *them*
to his servants.
15 "He will take a tenth of your
grain and your vintage, and give
it to his officers and servants.
16 "And he will take your male
servants, your female servants,
your finest [1]young men, and
your donkeys, and put *them* to
his work.
17 "He will take a tenth of
your sheep. And you will be his
servants.
18 "And you will cry out in that
day because of your king whom
you have chosen for yourselves,
and the LORD [a]will not hear you
in that day."
19 Nevertheless the people
[a]refused to obey the voice of
Samuel; and they said, "No, but
we will have a king over us,
20 "that we also may be [a]like all
the nations, and that our king
may judge us and go out before
us and fight our battles."
21 And Samuel heard all the
words of the people, and he
repeated them in the hearing of
the LORD.
22 So the LORD said to Samuel,
[a]"Heed their voice, and make
them a king." And Samuel said

1 [b]Deut. 16:18, 19 [c]Judg. 10:4
3 [a]Jer. 22:15–17 [b]Ex. 18:21 [c]Ex. 23:6–8
5 [a]Deut. 17:14, 15
6 [a]1 Sam. 12:17 [b]1 Sam. 7:9
7 [a]Ex. 16:8 [b]1 Sam. 10:19
9 [a]1 Sam. 8:11–18
11 [a]Deut. 17:14–20 [b]1 Sam. 14:52 [c]2 Sam. 15:1
12 [a]1 Sam. 22:7
14 [a]1 Kin. 21:7
16 [1]LXX *cattle*
18 [a]Is. 1:15
19 [a]Jer. 44:16
20 [a]1 Sam. 8:5
22 [a]Hos. 13:11

to the men of Israel, "Every man
go to his city."

9 There was a man of Benjamin whose name *was* [a]Kish
the son of A·bī′el, the son of Zē′-
ror, the son of Be·chō′rath, the
son of A·phī′ah, a Ben′ja·mīte, a
mighty man of [1]power.
2 And he had a choice and
handsome son whose name *was*
Saul. *There was* not a more
handsome person than he among
the children of Israel. [a]From his
shoulders upward *he was* taller
than any of the people.
3 Now the donkeys of Kish,
Saul's father, were lost. And Kish
said to his son Saul, "Please take
one of the servants with you,
and arise, go and look for the
donkeys."
4 So he passed through the
mountains of Ē′phra·im and
through the land of [a]Shal′i·sha,
but they did not find *them*. Then
they passed through the land
of Shā′a·lim, and *they were* not
there. Then he passed through
the land of the Ben′ja·mītes, but
they did not find *them*.
5 When they had come to
the land of [a]Zuph, Saul said to
his servant who *was* with him,
"Come, let [b]us return, lest my
father cease *caring* about the
donkeys and become worried
about us."
6 And he said to him, "Look
now, *there is* in this city [a]a man
of God, and *he is* an honorable
man; [b]all that he says surely
comes to pass. So let us go
there; perhaps he can show us
the way that we should go."
7 Then Saul said to his servant, "But look, *if* we go, [a]what
shall we bring the man? For the
bread in our vessels is all gone,
and *there is* no present to bring
to the man of God. What do we
have?"
8 And the servant answered
Saul again and said, "Look, I
have here at hand one-fourth of
a shekel of silver. I will give *that*
to the man of God, to tell us our
way."
9 (Formerly in Israel, when a
man [a]went [1]to inquire of God,
he spoke thus: "Come, let us go
to the seer"; for *he who is* now
called a prophet was formerly
called [b]a seer.)
10 Then Saul said to his servant,
[1]"Well said; come, let us go." So
they went to the city where the
man of God *was*.
11 As they went up the hill to
the city, [a]they met some young
women going out to draw water,
and said to them, "Is the seer
here?"
12 And they answered them and
said, "Yes, there he is, just ahead
of you. Hurry now; for today he
came to this city, because [a]there
is a sacrifice of the people today
[b]on the high place.
13 "As soon as you come into
the city, you will surely find him
before he goes up to the high
place to eat. For the people will
not eat until he comes, because
he must bless the sacrifice; afterward those who are invited
will eat. Now therefore, go up,
for about this time you will find
him."
14 So they went up to the city.
As they were coming into the
city, there was Samuel, coming
out toward them on his way up
to the high place.
15 [a]Now the LORD had told
Samuel in his ear the day before
Saul came, saying,

CHAPTER 9

1 [a]1 Chr. 8:33; 9:36–39 [1]*wealth*

2 [a]1 Sam. 10:23

4 [a]2 Kin. 4:42

5 [a]1 Sam. 1:1 [b]1 Sam. 10:2

6 [a]Deut. 33:1 [b]1 Sam. 3:19

7 [a]Judg. 6:18; 13:17

9 [a]Gen. 25:22 [b]2 Kin. 17:13 [1]Lit. *to seek God*

10 [1]Lit. *Your word is good*

11 [a]Ex. 2:16

12 [a]Gen. 31:54 [b]1 Kin. 3:2

15 [a]1 Sam. 15:1

16 "Tomorrow about this time
[a]I will send you a man from the
land of Benjamin, [b]and you shall
anoint him [1]commander over My
people Israel, that he may save
My people from the hand of the
Phi·lis′tines; for I have [c]looked
upon My people, because their
cry has come to Me."
17 So when Samuel saw Saul,
the LORD said to him, [a]"There he
is, the man of whom I spoke to
you. This one shall reign over My
people."
18 Then Saul drew near to Samuel in the gate, and said, "Please
tell me, where *is* the seer's
house?"
19 Samuel answered Saul and
said, "I *am* the seer. Go up before
me to the high place, for you
shall eat with me today; and tomorrow I will let you go and will
tell you all that *is* in your heart.
20 "But as for [a]your donkeys
that were lost three days ago, do
not be anxious about them, for
they have been found. And [1]on
whom [b]*is* all the desire of Israel?
Is it not on you and on all your
father's house?"
21 And Saul answered and said,
[a]"*Am* I not a Ben′ja·mīte, of the
[b]smallest of the tribes of Israel,
and [c]my family the least of all
the families of the [1]tribe of Benjamin? Why then do you speak
like this to me?"
22 Now Samuel took Saul and
his servant and brought them
into the hall, and had them sit in
the place of honor among those
who were invited; there *were*
about thirty persons.
23 And Samuel said to the cook,
"Bring the portion which I gave
you, of which I said to you, 'Set
it apart.' "
24 So the cook took up [a]the
thigh with its upper part and set
it before Saul. And *Samuel* said,
"Here it is, what was kept back.
It was set apart for you. Eat; for
until this time it has been kept
for you, since I said I invited
the people." So Saul ate with
Samuel that day.
25 When they had come down
from the high place into the city,
[1]*Samuel* spoke with Saul on [a]the
top of the house.
26 They arose early; and it was
about the dawning of the day
that Samuel called to Saul on
the top of the house, saying,
"Get up, that I may send you on
your way." And Saul arose, and
both of them went outside, he
and Samuel.
27 As they were going down to
the outskirts of the city, Samuel
said to Saul, "Tell the servant to
go on ahead of us." And he went
on. "But you stand here [1]awhile,
that I may announce to you the
word of God."

10

Then [a]Samuel took a flask
of oil and poured *it* on his
head, [b]and kissed him and said:
"*Is it* not because [c]the LORD has
anointed you commander over
[d]His [1]inheritance?
2 "When you have departed
from me today, you will find two
men by [a]Rachel's tomb in the
territory of Benjamin [b]at Zel′zah;
and they will say to you, 'The
donkeys which you went to look
for have been found. And now
your father has ceased caring
about the donkeys and is wor-
rying about [c]you, saying, "What
shall I do about my son?" '
3 "Then you shall go on forward from there and come to the
terebinth tree of Tā′bor. There

---

16 [a]Deut. 17:15 [b]1 Sam. 10:1 [c]Ex. 2:23–25; 3:7, 9 [1]*prince or ruler*

17 [a]1 Sam. 16:12

20 [a]1 Sam. 9:3 [b]1 Sam. 8:5, 19; 12:13 [1]*for whom*

21 [a]1 Sam. 15:17 [b]Judg. 20:46–48 [c]Judg. 6:15 [1]Lit. *tribes*

24 [a]Lev. 7:32, 33

25 [a]Deut. 22:8 [1]So with MT, Tg.; LXX omits *He spoke with Saul on the top of the house;* LXX, Vg. afterward add *And he prepared a bed for Saul on the top of the house, and he slept.*

27 [1]*now*

CHAPTER 10

1 [a]2 Kin. 9:3, 6 [b]Ps. 2:12 [c]Acts 13:21 [d]Deut. 32:9 [1]So with MT, Tg., Vg.; LXX *people Israel; and you shall rule the people of the Lord;* LXX, Vg. add *And you shall deliver His people from the hands of their enemies all around them. And this shall be a sign to you, that God has anointed you to be a prince.*

2 [a]Gen. 35:16–20; 48:7 [b]Josh. 18:28 [c]1 Sam. 9:3–5

three men going up [a]to God at
Beth'el will meet you, one carrying three young goats, another
carrying three loaves of bread,
and another carrying a skin of
wine.
4 "And they will [1]greet you and
give you two *loaves* of bread,
which you shall receive from
their hands.
5 "After that you shall come
to the hill of God [a]where the
Phi·lis'tine garrison *is.* And it
will happen, when you have
come there to the city, that you
will meet a group of prophets
coming down [b]from the high
place with a stringed instrument, a tambourine, a flute, and
a harp before them; [c]and they
will be prophesying.
6 "Then [a]the Spirit of the LORD
will come upon you, and [b]you
will prophesy with them and be
turned into another man.
7 "And let it be, when these
[a]signs come to you, *that* you do
as the occasion demands; for
[b]God *is* with you.
8 "You shall go down before
me [a]to Gil'gal; and surely I will
come down to you to offer burnt
offerings *and* make sacrifices of
peace offerings. [b]Seven days you
shall wait, till I come to you and
show you what you should do."
9 So it was, when he had turned
his back to go from Samuel, that
God [1]gave him another heart;
and all those signs came to pass
that day.
10 [a]When they came there to
the hill, there was [b]a group of
prophets to meet him; then the
Spirit of God came upon him,
and he prophesied among them.
11 And it happened, when all
who knew him formerly saw that
he indeed prophesied among the
prophets, that the people said
to one another, "What *is* this
that has come upon the son of
Kish? [a]*Is* Saul also among the
prophets?"
12 Then a man from there answered and said, "But [a]who *is*
their father?" Therefore it became a proverb: "*Is* Saul also
among the prophets?"
13 And when he had finished
prophesying, he went to the high
place.
14 Then Saul's [a]uncle said to
him and his servant, "Where did
you go?" So he said, "To look for
the donkeys. When we saw that
they were nowhere *to be found,*
we went to Samuel."
15 And Saul's uncle said, "Tell
me, please, what Samuel said to
you."
16 So Saul said to his uncle, "He
told us plainly that the donkeys
had been [a]found." But about the
matter of the kingdom, he did
not tell him what Samuel had
said.
17 Then Samuel called the people together [a]to the LORD [b]at
Miz'pah,
18 and said to the children of
Israel, [a]"Thus says the LORD God
of Israel: 'I brought up Israel
out of Egypt, and delivered you
from the hand of the Egyptians
and from the hand of all kingdoms and from those who oppressed you.'
19 [a]"But you have today rejected
your God, who Himself saved
you from all your adversities
and your tribulations; and you
have said to Him, 'No, set a king
over us!' Now therefore, present
yourselves before the LORD by
your tribes and by your [1]clans."

3 [a]Gen. 28:22; 35:1, 3, 7
4 [1]*ask you about your welfare*
5 [a]1 Sam. 13:2, 3 [b]1 Sam. 19:12, 20 [c]2 Kin. 3:15
6 [a]Num. 11:25, 29 [b]1 Sam. 10:10; 19:23, 24
7 [a]Ex. 4:8 [b]Judg. 6:12
8 [a]1 Sam. 11:14, 15; 13:8 [b]1 Sam. 13:8–10
9 [1]*changed his heart*
10 [a]1 Sam. 10:5 [b]1 Sam. 19:20
11 [a]Matt. 13:54–57
12 [a]John 5:30, 36
14 [a]1 Sam. 14:50
16 [a]1 Sam. 9:20
17 [a]Judg. 20:1 [b]1 Sam. 7:5, 6
18 [a]Judg. 6:8, 9
19 [a]1 Sam. 8:7, 19; 12:12 [1]Lit. *thousands*

20 And when Samuel had
[a]caused all the tribes of Israel to
come near, the tribe of Benjamin
was chosen.
21 When he had caused the
tribe of Benjamin to come near
by their families, the family of
Mā′trī was chosen. And Saul
the son of Kish was chosen. But
when they sought him, he could
not be found.
22 Therefore they [a]inquired of
the LORD further, "Has the man
come here yet?" And the LORD
answered, "There he is, hidden
among the equipment."
23 So they ran and brought him
from there; and when he stood
among the people, [a]he was taller
than any of the people from his
shoulders upward.
24 And Samuel said to all the
people, "Do you see him [a]whom
the LORD has chosen, that *there*
is no one like him among all
the people?" So all the people
shouted and said, [b]"Long[1] live
the king!"
25 Then Samuel explained to
the people [a]the behavior of royalty, and wrote *it* in a book and
laid *it* up before the LORD. And
Samuel sent all the people away,
every man to his house.
26 And Saul also went home [a]to
Gib′ē·ah; and valiant *men* went
with him, whose hearts God had
touched.
27 [a]But some [b]rebels said, "How
can this man save us?" So they
despised him, [c]and brought him
no presents. But he [1]held his
peace.

CHAPTER 11

11 Then [a]Nā′hash the Am′-
mon·īte came up and
[1]encamped against [b]Jā′besh
Gil′ē·ad; and all the men of Jā′-
besh said to Nā′hash, [c]"Make a
covenant with us, and we will
serve you."
2 And Nā′hash the Am′mon·īte
answered them, "On this *condi-*
tion I will make *a covenant* with
you, that I may put out all your
right eyes, and bring [a]reproach
on all Israel."
3 Then the elders of Jā′besh
said to him, "Hold off for seven
days, that we may send messengers to all the territory of Israel.
And then, if *there is* no one to
[1]save us, we will come out to
you."
4 So the messengers came [a]to
Gib′ē·ah of Saul and told the
news in the hearing of the people. And [b]all the people lifted up
their voices and wept.
5 Now there was Saul, coming
behind the herd from the field;
and Saul said, "What *troubles*
the people, that they weep?"
And they told him the words of
the men of Jā′besh.
6 [a]Then the Spirit of God came
upon Saul when he heard this
news, and his anger was greatly
aroused.
7 So he took a yoke of oxen
and [a]cut them in pieces, and sent
them throughout all the territory of Israel by the hands of
messengers, saying, [b]"Whoever
does not go out with Saul and
Samuel to battle, so it shall be
done to his oxen." And the fear
of the LORD fell on the people,
and they came out [1]with one
consent.
8 When he numbered them in
[a]Bē′zek, the children [b]of Israel
were three hundred thousand,
and the men of Judah thirty
thousand.
9 And they said to the messengers who came, "Thus you shall

20 [a]Acts 1:24, 26
22 [a]1 Sam. 23:2, 4, 10, 11
23 [a]1 Sam. 9:2
24 [a]2 Sam. 21:6 [b]1 Kin. 1:25, 39 [1]Lit. *May the king live*
25 [a]1 Sam. 8:11–18
26 [a]Judg. 20:14
27 [a]1 Sam. 11:12 [b]Deut. 13:13 [c]1 Kin. 4:21; 10:25 [1]*kept silent*

CHAPTER 11

1 [a]1 Sam. 12:12 [b]Judg. 21:8 [c]Gen. 26:28 [1]*besieged*
2 [a]Gen. 34:14
3 [1]*deliver*
4 [a]1 Sam. 10:26; 15:34 [b]Judg. 2:4; 20:23, 26; 21:2
6 [a]Judg. 3:10; 6:34; 11:29; 13:25; 14:6
7 [a]Judg. 19:29 [b]Judg. 21:5, 8, 10 [1]Lit. *as one man*
8 [a]Judg. 1:5 [b]2 Sam. 24:9

say to the men of Jā′besh Gil′-
ē·ad: ‘Tomorrow, by *the time* the
sun is hot, you shall have help.’ ”
Then the messengers came and
reported *it* to the men of Jā′-
besh, and they were glad.
10 Therefore the men of Jā′besh
said, “Tomorrow we will come
out to you, and you may do
with us whatever seems good to
you.”
11 So it was, on the next day,
that [a]Saul put the people [b]in
three companies; and they came
into the midst of the camp in the
morning watch, and killed Am′-
mon·ītes until the heat of the
day. And it happened that those
who survived were scattered, so
that no two of them were left
together.
12 Then the people said to Samuel, [a]“Who *is* he who said, ‘Shall
Saul reign over us?’ [b]Bring the
men, that we may put them to
death.”
13 But Saul said, [a]“Not a man
shall be put to death this day,
for today [b]the LORD has accomplished salvation in Israel.”
14 Then Samuel said to the people, “Come, let us go [a]to Gil′gal
and renew the kingdom there.”
15 So all the people went to Gil′-
gal, and there they made Saul
king [a]before the LORD in Gil′gal.
[b]There they made sacrifices of
peace offerings before the LORD,
and there Saul and all the men
of Israel rejoiced greatly.

12 Now Samuel said to all
Israel: “Indeed I have
[1]heeded [a]your voice in all that
you said to me, and [b]have made
a king over you.
2 “And now here is the king,
[a]walking before you; [b]and I am
old and grayheaded, and look,

11 [a]1 Sam. 31:11 [b]Judg. 7:16, 20
12 [a]1 Sam. 10:27 [b]Luke 19:27
13 [a]2 Sam. 19:22 [b]Ex. 14:13, 30
14 [a]1 Sam. 7:16; 10:8
15 [a]1 Sam. 10:17 [b]1 Sam. 10:8

CHAPTER 12

1 [a]1 Sam. 8:5, 7, 9, 20, 22 [b]1 Sam. 10:24; 11:14, 15 [1]*listened to*
2 [a]Num. 27:17 [b]1 Sam. 8:1, 5
3 [a]1 Sam. 10:1; 24:6 [b]Num. 16:15 [c]Ex. 23:8 [d]Deut. 16:19
4 [a]Lev. 19:13
5 [a]Acts 23:9; 24:20 [b]Ex. 22:4
6 [a]Mic. 6:4
7 [a]Is. 1:18 [b]Judg. 5:11
8 [a]Gen. 46:5, 6 [b]Ex. 2:23–25 [c]Ex. 3:10; 4:14–16 [1]So with MT, Tg., Vg.; LXX adds *and the Egyptians afflicted them*
9 [a]Judg. 3:7 [b]Judg. 4:2 [c]Judg. 3:31; 10:7; 13:1 [d]Judg. 3:12–30

my sons *are* with you. I have
walked before you from my
childhood to this day.
3 “Here I am. Witness against
me before the LORD and before
[a]His anointed: [b]Whose ox have
I taken, or whose donkey have I
taken, or whom have I cheated?
Whom have I oppressed, or from
whose hand have I received *any*
[c]bribe with which to [d]blind my
eyes? I will restore *it* to you.”
4 And they said, [a]“You have
not cheated us or oppressed us,
nor have you taken anything
from any man’s hand.”
5 Then he said to them, “The
LORD *is* witness against you, and
His anointed *is* witness this day,
[a]that you have not found anything [b]in my hand.” And they
answered, “*He is* witness.”
6 Then Samuel said to the people, [a]“*It is* the LORD who raised
up Moses and Aaron, and who
brought your fathers up from
the land of Egypt.
7 “Now therefore, stand still,
that I may [a]reason with you
before the LORD concerning all
the [b]righteous acts of the LORD
which He did to you and your
fathers:
8 [a]“When Jacob had gone
into [1]Egypt, and your fathers
[b]cried out to the LORD, then the
LORD [c]sent Moses and Aaron,
who brought your fathers out of
Egypt and made them dwell in
this place.
9 “And when they [a]forgot the
LORD their God, He sold them
into the hand of [b]Sis′e·ra, commander of the army of Hā′zor,
into the hand of the [c]Phi·lis′-
tines, and into the hand of the
king of [d]Mō′ab; and they fought
against them.

10 "Then they cried out to the
LORD, and said, [a]'We have sinned,
because we have forsaken the
LORD [b]and served the Bā'als and
[1]Ash'to·reths; but now deliver us
from the hand of our enemies,
and we will serve You.'
11 "And the LORD sent [1]Jer·ub-
bā'al, [2]Bē'dan, [a]Jeph'thah, and
[b]Samuel,[3] and delivered you out
of the hand of your enemies on
every side; and you dwelt in
safety.
12 "And when you saw that
[a]Nā'hash king of the Am'mon-
ītes came against you, [b]you said
to me, 'No, but a king shall reign
over us,' when [c]the LORD your
God *was* your king.
13 "Now therefore, [a]here is the
king [b]whom you have chosen
and whom you have desired.
And take note, [c]the LORD has set
a king over you.
14 "If you [a]fear the LORD and
serve Him and obey His voice,
and do not rebel against the
commandment of the LORD,
then both you and the king who
reigns over you will continue
following the LORD your God.
15 "However, if you do [a]not obey
the voice of the LORD, but [b]rebel
against the commandment of
the LORD, then the hand of the
LORD will be against you, as *it*
was against your fathers.
16 "Now therefore, [a]stand and
see this great thing which the
LORD will do before your eyes:
17 "*Is* today not the [a]wheat harvest? [b]I will call to the LORD, and
He will send thunder and [c]rain,
that you may perceive and see
that [d]your wickedness *is* great,
which you have done in the
sight of the LORD, in asking a
king for yourselves."
18 So Samuel called to the
LORD, and the LORD sent thunder
and rain that day; and [a]all the
people greatly feared the LORD
and Samuel.
19 And all the people said to
Samuel, [a]"Pray for your servants
to the LORD your God, that we
may not die; for we have added
to all our sins the evil of asking
a king for ourselves."
20 Then Samuel said to the people, "Do not fear. You have done
all this wickedness; [a]yet do not
turn aside from following the
LORD, but serve the LORD with all
your heart.
21 "And [a]do not turn aside; [b]for
then you would go after empty
things which cannot profit or
deliver, for they *are* nothing.
22 "For [a]the LORD will not forsake [b]His people, [c]for His great
name's sake, because [d]it has
pleased the LORD to make you
His people.
23 "Moreover, as for me, far
be it from me that I should sin
against the LORD [a]in ceasing to
pray for you; but [b]I will teach you
the [c]good and the right way.
24 [a]"Only fear the LORD, and
serve Him in truth with all your
heart; for [b]consider what [c]great
things He has done for you.
25 "But if you still do wickedly,
[a]you shall be swept away, [b]both
you and your king."

13

13 Saul [1]reigned one year;
and when he had reigned
two years over Israel,
2 Saul chose for himself three
thousand *men* of Israel. Two
thousand were with Saul in
[a]Mich'mash and in the mountains of Beth'el, and a thousand
were with [b]Jonathan in [c]Gib'ē·ah
of Benjamin. The rest of the

10 [a]Judg. 10:10 [b]Judg. 2:13; 3:7 [1]Images of Canaanite goddesses

11 [a]Judg. 11:1 [b]1 Sam. 7:13 [1]Gideon, cf. Judg. 6:25–32; Syr. *Deborah;* Tg. *Gideon* [2]LXX, Syr. *Barak;* Tg. *Simson* [3]Syr. *Simson*

12 [a]1 Sam. 11:1, 2 [b]1 Sam. 8:5, 19, 20 [c]Judg. 8:23

13 [a]1 Sam. 10:24 [b]1 Sam. 8:5; 12:17, 19 [c]Hos. 13:11

14 [a]Josh. 24:14

15 [a]Deut. 28:15 [b]Is. 1:20

16 [a]Ex. 14:13, 31

17 [a]Gen. 30:14 [b][James 5:16–18] [c]Ezra 10:9 [d]1 Sam. 8:7

18 [a]Ex. 14:31

19 [a]Ex. 9:28

20 [a]Deut. 11:16

21 [a]2 Chr. 25:15 [b]Is. 41:29

22 [a]Deut. 31:6 [b]Is. 43:21 [c]Jer. 14:21 [d]Deut. 7:6–11

23 [a]Rom. 1:9 [b]Ps. 34:11 [c]1 Kin. 8:36

24 [a]Eccl. 12:13 [b]Is. 5:12 [c]Deut. 10:21

25 [a]Josh. 24:20 [b]Deut. 28:36

CHAPTER 13

1 [1]Heb. is difficult; cf. 2 Sam. 5:4; 2 Kin. 14:2; see also 2 Sam. 2:10; Acts 13:21

2 [a]1 Sam. 14:5, 31 [b]1 Sam. 14:1 [c]1 Sam. 10:26

people he sent away, every man
to his tent.
3 And Jonathan attacked [a]the
garrison of the Phi·lis′tines that
was in [b]Gē′ba, and the Phi·lis′-
tines heard *of it*. Then Saul blew
the trumpet throughout all the
land, saying, "Let the Hebrews
hear!"
4 Now all Israel heard it said
that Saul had attacked a garrison of the Phi·lis′tines, and
that Israel had also become [1]an
abomination to the Phi·lis′tines.
And the people were called together to Saul at Gil′gal.
5 Then the Phi·lis′tines gathered together to fight with Israel, [1]thirty thousand chariots
and six thousand horsemen, and
people [a]as the sand which *is* on
the seashore in multitude. And
they came up and encamped in
Mich′mash, to the east of [b]Beth
Ā′ven.
6 When the men of Israel saw
that they were in danger (for the
people were distressed), then the
people [a]hid in caves, in thickets,
in rocks, in holes, and in pits.
7 And *some of* the Hebrews
crossed over the Jordan to the
[a]land of Gad and Gil′ē·ad. As
for Saul, he *was* still in Gil′gal,
and all the people followed him
trembling.
8 [a]Then he waited seven days,
according to the time set by
Samuel. But Samuel did not
come to Gil′gal; and the people
were scattered from him.
9 So Saul said, "Bring a burnt
offering and peace offerings
here to me." And he offered the
burnt offering.
10 Now it happened, as soon
as he had finished presenting
the burnt offering, that Samuel
came; and Saul went out to meet
him, that he might [1]greet him.
11 And Samuel said, "What
have you done?" Saul said,
"When I saw that the people
were scattered from me, and
that you did not come within
the days appointed, and *that* the
Phi·lis′tines gathered together at
Mich′mash,
12 "then I said, 'The Phi·lis′tines
will now come down on me at
Gil′gal, and I have not made
supplication to the LORD.' Therefore I felt compelled, and offered
a burnt offering."
13 And Samuel said to Saul,
[a]"You have done foolishly. [b]You
have not kept the commandment of the LORD your God,
which He commanded you. For
now the LORD would have established your kingdom over Israel
forever.
14 [a]"But now your kingdom
shall not continue. [b]The LORD
has sought for Himself a man
[c]after His own heart, and the
LORD has commanded him *to
be* commander over His people,
because you have [d]not kept what
the LORD commanded you."
15 Then Samuel arose and went
up from Gil′gal to Gib′ē·ah of
[1]Benjamin. And Saul numbered
the people present with him,
[a]about six hundred men.
16 Saul, Jonathan his son, and
the people present with them
remained in [1]Gib′ē·ah of Benjamin. But the Phi·lis′tines encamped in Mich′mash.
17 Then raiders came out of
the camp of the Phi·lis′tines in
three companies. One company
turned onto the road to [a]Oph′-
rah, to the land of Shū′al,
18 another company turned to

3 [a]1 Sam. 10:5 [b]2 Sam. 5:25
4 [1]*odious*
5 [a]Judg. 7:12 [b]Josh. 7:2 [1]So with MT, LXX, Tg., Vg.; Syr. and some mss. of LXX *three thousand*
6 [a]Judg. 6:2
7 [a]Num.32:1–42
8 [a]1 Sam. 10:8
10 [1]Lit. *bless him*
13 [a]2 Chr. 16:9 [b]1 Sam. 15:11, 22, 28
14 [a]1 Sam. 15:28; 31:6 [b]1 Sam. 16:1 [c]Acts 7:46; 13:22 [d]1 Sam. 15:11, 19
15 [a]1 Sam. 13:2, 6, 7; 14:2 [1]So with MT, Tg.; LXX, Vg. add *And the rest of the people went up after Saul to meet the people who fought against them, going from Gilgal to Gibeah in the hill of Benjamin.*
16 [1]Heb. *Geba*
17 [a]Josh. 18:23

the road *to* [a]Beth Hor′on, and
another company turned *to* the
road of the border that over-
looks the Valley of [b]Ze·bō′im toward the wilderness.
19 Now [a]there was no blacksmith to be found throughout all
the land of Israel, for the Phi·lis′-
tines said, "Lest the Hebrews
make swords or spears."
20 But all the Israelites would
go down to the Phi·lis′tines to
sharpen each man's plowshare,
his mattock, his ax, and his
sickle;
21 and the charge for a sharp-
ening was a [1]pim for the plowshares, the mattocks, the forks,
and the axes, and to set the
points of the goads.
22 So it came about, on the day
of battle, that [a]there was neither
sword nor spear found in the
hand of any of the people who
were with Saul and Jonathan.
But they were found with Saul
and Jonathan his son.
23 [a]And the garrison of the
Phi·lis′tines went out to the pass
of Mich′mash.

14

Now it happened one day
that Jonathan the son of
Saul said to the young man who
[1]bore his armor, "Come, let us go
over to the Phi·lis′tines' garrison
that *is* on the other side." But he
did not tell his father.
2 And Saul was sitting in the
outskirts of [a]Gib′ē·ah under a
pomegranate tree which *is* in
Mig′ron. The people who *were*
with him *were* about six hundred men.
3 [a]A·hī′jah the son of A·hī′-
tub, [b]Ich′a·bod's brother, the
son of Phin′e·has, the son of
Ē′lī, the LORD's priest in Shī′lōh,
was [c]wearing an ephod. But the
people did not know that Jonathan had gone.
4 Between the passes, by
which Jonathan sought to go
over [a]to the Phi·lis′tines' garrison, *there was* a sharp rock on
one side and a sharp rock on the
other side. And the name of one
was Bō′zez, and the name of the
other Sē′neh.
5 The front of one faced northward opposite Mich′mash, and
the other southward opposite
Gib′ē·ah.
6 Then Jonathan said to the
young man who bore his armor,
"Come, let us go over to the garrison of these [a]uncircumcised; it
may be that the LORD will work
for us. For nothing restrains the
LORD [b]from saving by many or
by few."
7 So his armorbearer said to
him, "Do all that is in your heart.
Go then; here I am with you, according to your heart."
8 Then Jonathan said, "Very
well, let us cross over to *these*
men, and we will show ourselves to them.
9 "If they say thus to us, 'Wait
until we come to you,' then we
will stand still in our place and
not go up to them.
10 "But if they say thus, 'Come
up to us,' then we will go up.
For the LORD has delivered them
into our hand, and [a]this *will be* a
sign to us."
11 So both of them showed
themselves to the garrison of the
Phi·lis′tines. And the Phi·lis′tines
said, "Look, the Hebrews are
coming out of the holes where
they have [a]hidden."
12 Then the men of the garrison called to Jonathan and his
armorbearer, and said, "Come

18 [a]Josh. 16:3; 18:13, 14 [b]Neh. 11:34
19 [a]Judg. 5:8
21 [1]About two-thirds shekel weight
22 [a]Judg. 5:8
23 [a]1 Sam. 14:1, 4
CHAPTER 14
1 [1]*carried*
2 [a]1 Sam. 13:15, 16
3 [a]1 Sam. 22:9, 11, 20 [b]1 Sam. 4:21 [c]1 Sam. 2:28
4 [a]1 Sam. 13:23
6 [a]1 Sam. 17:26, 36 [b]Judg. 7:4, 7
10 [a]Gen. 24:14
11 [a]1 Sam. 13:6; 14:22

up to us, and we will [1]show you
something." Jonathan said to
his armorbearer, "Come up after
me, for the LORD has delivered
them into the hand of Israel."
13 And Jonathan climbed up
on his hands and knees with his
armorbearer after him; and they
[a]fell before Jonathan. And as he
came after him, his armorbearer
killed them.
14 That first slaughter which
Jonathan and his armorbearer
made was about twenty men
within about [1]half an acre of
land.
15 And [a]there was [1]trembling in
the camp, in the field, and among
all the people. The garrison and
[b]the raiders also trembled; and
the earth quaked, so that it was
[c]a very great trembling.
16 Now the watchmen of Saul
in Gib'ē·ah of Benjamin looked,
and *there* was the multitude,
melting away; and they [a]went
here and there.
17 Then Saul said to the people
who *were* with him, "Now call
the roll and see who has gone
from us." And when they had
called the roll, surprisingly, Jonathan and his armorbearer *were*
not *there.*
18 And Saul said to A·hī'jah,
"Bring the [1]ark of God here" (for
at that time the [1]ark of God was
with the children of Israel).
19 Now it happened, while Saul
[a]talked to the priest, that the
noise which *was* in the camp of
the Phi·lis'tines continued to increase; so Saul said to the priest,
"Withdraw your hand."
20 Then Saul and all the people
who *were* with him assembled,
and they went to the battle; and
indeed [a]every man's sword was
against his neighbor, *and there
was* very great confusion.
21 Moreover the Hebrews *who*
were with the Phi·lis'tines before that time, who went up with
them into the camp *from the*
surrounding *country,* they also
joined the Israelites who *were*
with Saul and Jonathan.
22 Likewise all the men of Israel who [a]had hidden in the
mountains of Ē'phra·im, *when*
they heard that the Phi·lis'tines
fled, they also followed hard after them in the battle.
23 [a]So the LORD saved Israel
that day, and the battle shifted
[b]to Beth Ā'ven.
24 And the men of Israel were
distressed that day, for Saul had
[a]placed the people under oath,
saying, "Cursed *is* the man who
eats *any* food until evening, before I have taken vengeance on
my enemies." So none of the
people tasted food.
25 [a]Now all *the people* of the
land came to a forest; and there
was [b]honey on the ground.
26 And when the people had
come into the woods, there was
the honey, dripping; but no one
put his hand to his mouth, for
the people feared the oath.
27 But Jonathan had not heard
his father charge the people with
the oath; therefore he stretched
out the end of the rod that *was*
in his hand and dipped it in a
honeycomb, and put his hand to
his mouth; and his [1]countenance
brightened.
28 Then one of the people said,
"Your father strictly charged
the people with an oath, saying,
'Cursed *is* the man who eats
food this day.'" And the people
were faint.

12 [1]*teach*
13 [a]Lev. 26:8
14 [1]Lit. *half the area plowed by a yoke* of oxen in a day
15 [a]Job 18:11 [b]1 Sam. 13:17 [c]Gen. 35:5 [1]*terror*
16 [a]1 Sam. 14:20
18 [1]So with MT, Tg., Vg.; LXX *ephod*
19 [a]Num. 27:21
20 [a]Judg. 7:22
22 [a]1 Sam. 13:6
23 [a]Ex. 14:30 [b]1 Sam. 13:5
24 [a]Josh. 6:26
25 [a]Deut. 9:28 [b]Ex. 3:8
27 [1]Lit. *eyes*

29 But Jonathan said, "My father has troubled the land. Look
now, how my countenance has
brightened because I tasted a
little of this honey.
30 "How much better if the people had eaten freely today of
the spoil of their enemies which
they found! For now would there
not have been a much greater
slaughter among the Phi·lis′-
tines?"
31 Now they had [1]driven back
the Phi·lis′tines that day from
Mich′mash to Ai′ja·lon. So the
people were very faint.
32 And the people rushed on the
[1]spoil, and took sheep, oxen, and
calves, and slaughtered *them* on
the ground; and the people ate
them [a]with the blood.
33 Then they told Saul, saying,
"Look, the people are sinning
against the LORD by eating with
the blood!" So he said, "You
have dealt treacherously; roll a
large stone to me this day."
34 Then Saul said, "Disperse
yourselves among the people,
and say to them, 'Bring me here
every man's ox and every man's
sheep, slaughter *them* here, and
eat; and do not sin against the
LORD by eating with the blood.' "
So every one of the people
brought his ox with him that
night, and slaughtered *it* there.
35 Then Saul [a]built an altar to
the LORD. This was the first altar
that he built to the LORD.
36 Now Saul said, "Let us go
down after the Phi·lis′tines by
night, and plunder them until
the morning light; and let us not
leave a man of them." And they
said, "Do whatever seems good
to you." Then the priest said,
"Let us draw near to God here."
37 So Saul [a]asked counsel of
God, "Shall I go down after the
Phi·lis′tines? Will You deliver
them into the hand of Israel?"
But [b]He did not answer him that
day.
38 And Saul said, [a]"Come over
here, all you chiefs of the people, and know and see what this
sin was today.
39 "For [a]*as* the LORD lives, who
saves Israel, though it be in Jonathan my son, he shall surely
die." But not a man among all
the people answered him.
40 Then he said to all Israel,
"You be on one side, and my son
Jonathan and I will be on the
other side." And the people said
to Saul, "Do what seems good to
you."
41 Therefore Saul said to the
LORD God of Israel, [a]"Give[1] a
perfect *lot.*" [b]So Saul and Jonathan were taken, but the people
escaped.
42 And Saul said, "Cast *lots*
between my son Jonathan and
me." So Jonathan was taken.
43 Then Saul said to Jonathan,
[a]"Tell me what you have done."
And Jonathan told him, and said,
[b]"I only tasted a little honey with
the end of the rod that *was* in
my hand. So now I must die!"
44 Saul answered, [a]"God do so
and more also; [b]for you shall
surely die, Jonathan."
45 But the people said to Saul,
"Shall Jonathan die, who has
accomplished this great deliverance in Israel? Certainly not!
[a]*As* the LORD lives, not one hair
of his head shall fall to the
ground, for he has worked [b]with
God this day." So the people rescued Jonathan, and he did not
die.

31 [1]Lit. *struck*
32 [a]Deut. 12:16, 23, 24 [1]*plunder*
35 [a]1 Sam. 7:12, 17
37 [a]Judg. 20:18 [b]1 Sam. 28:6
38 [a]Josh. 7:14
39 [a]2 Sam. 12:5
41 [a]Acts 1:24–26 [b]1 Sam. 10:20, 21 [1]So with MT, Tg.; LXX, Vg. *Why do You not answer Your servant today? If the injustice is with me or Jonathan my son, O LORD God of Israel, give proof; and if You say it is with Your people Israel, give holiness.*
43 [a]Josh. 7:19 [b]1 Sam. 14:27
44 [a]Ruth 1:17 [b]1 Sam. 14:39
45 [a]1 Kin. 1:52 [b][2 Cor. 6:1]

46 Then Saul returned from
pursuing the Phi·lis′tines, and
the Phi·lis′tines went to their
own place.
47 So Saul established his sovereignty over Israel, and fought
against all his enemies on every side, against Mō′ab, against
the people of [a]Am′mon, against
Ē′dom, against the kings of [b]Zō′-
bah, and against the Phi·lis′-
tines. Wherever he turned, he
[1]harassed *them.*
48 And he gathered an army
and [a]attacked[1] the A·mal′e·kītes,
and delivered Israel from the
hands of those who plundered
them.
49 [a]The sons of Saul were Jonathan, [1]Jish′ū·ī, and Mal·chī·shū′a.
And the names of his two daughters *were these:* the name of the
firstborn Mē′rab, and the name
of the younger [b]Mī′chal.
50 The name of Saul's wife
was A·hin′ō·am the daughter of
A·him′a·az. And the name of the
commander of his army *was* Abner the son of Ner, Saul's [a]uncle.
51 [a]Kish *was* the father of Saul,
and Ner the father of Abner *was*
the son of A·bī′el.
52 Now there was fierce war
with the Phi·lis′tines all the days
of Saul. And when Saul saw any
strong man or any valiant man,
[a]he took him for himself.

15

Samuel also said to Saul,
[a]"The LORD sent me to
anoint you king over His people,
over Israel. Now therefore, heed
the voice of the words of the
LORD.
2 "Thus says the LORD of hosts:
'I will punish Am′a·lek *for* what
he did to Israel, [a]how he am-
bushed him on the way when he
came up from Egypt.
3 'Now go and [a]attack[1] Am′-
a·lek, and [b]utterly destroy all that
they have, and do not spare them.
But kill both man and woman,
infant and nursing child, ox and
sheep, camel and donkey.' "
4 So Saul gathered the people
together and numbered them in
Te·lā′im, two hundred thousand
foot soldiers and ten thousand
men of Judah.
5 And Saul came to a city of
Am′a·lek, and lay in wait in the
valley.
6 Then Saul said to [a]the Ken′-
ītes, [b]"Go, depart, get down from
among the A·mal′e·kītes, lest I
destroy you with them. For [c]you
showed kindness to all the children of Israel when they came
up out of Egypt." So the Ken′-
ītes departed from among the
A·mal′e·kītes.
7 [a]And Saul attacked the
A·mal′e·kītes, from [b]Hav′i·lah all
the way to [c]Shūr, which is east of
Egypt.
8 [a]He also took Ā′gag king
of the A·mal′e·kītes alive, and
[b]utterly destroyed all the people
with the edge of the sword.
9 But Saul and the people
[a]spared Ā′gag and the best of
the sheep, the oxen, the fatlings,
the lambs, and all *that was* good,
and were unwilling to utterly
destroy them. But everything despised and worthless, that they
utterly destroyed.
10 Now the word of the LORD
came to Samuel, saying,
11 [a]"I greatly regret that I have
set up Saul *as* king, for he has
[b]turned back from following
Me, [c]and has not performed My
commandments." And it [d]grieved
Samuel, and he cried out to the
LORD all night.

47 [a]1 Sam. 11:1–13 [b]2 Sam. 10:6 [1]LXX, Vg. *prospered*
48 [a]1 Sam. 15:3–7 [1]Lit. *struck*
49 [a]1 Sam. 31:2 [b]1 Sam. 18:17–20, 27; 19:12 [1]*Abinadab,* 1 Chr. 8:33; 9:39
50 [a]1 Sam. 10:14
51 [a]1 Sam. 9:1, 21
52 [a]1 Sam. 8:11

CHAPTER 15

1 [a]1 Sam. 9:16; 10:1
2 [a]Deut. 25:17–19
3 [a]Deut. 25:19 [b]Num. 24:20 [1]Lit. *strike*
6 [a]Num. 24:21 [b]Gen. 18:25; 19:12, 14 [c]Ex. 18:10, 19
7 [a]1 Sam. 14:48 [b]Gen. 2:11; 25:17, 18 [c]Gen. 16:7
8 [a]1 Sam. 15:32, 33 [b]1 Sam. 27:8, 9
9 [a]1 Sam. 15:3, 15, 19
11 [a]Gen. 6:6, 7 [b]1 Kin. 9:6 [c]1 Sam. 13:13; 15:3, 9 [d]1 Sam. 15:35; 16:1

12 So when Samuel rose early
in the morning to meet Saul, it
was told Samuel, saying, "Saul
went to [a]Car′mel, and indeed, he
set up a monument for himself;
and he has gone on around,
passed by, and gone down to
Gil′gal."
13 Then Samuel went to Saul,
and Saul said to him, [a]"Blessed
are you of the LORD! I have performed the commandment of
the LORD."
14 But Samuel said, "What then
is this bleating of the sheep in
my ears, and the lowing of the
oxen which I hear?"
15 And Saul said, "They have
brought them from the A·mal′-
e·kītes; [a]for the people spared
the best of the sheep and the
oxen, to sacrifice to the LORD
your God; and the rest we have
utterly destroyed."
16 Then Samuel said to Saul,
"Be quiet! And I will tell you
what the LORD said to me last
night." And he said to him,
"Speak on."
17 So Samuel said, [a]"When you
were little in your own eyes,
were you not head of the tribes
of Israel? And did not the LORD
anoint you king over Israel?
18 "Now the LORD sent you on
a mission, and said, 'Go, and
utterly destroy the sinners, the
A·mal′e·kītes, and fight against
them until they are [1]consumed.'
19 "Why then did you not obey
the voice of the LORD? Why did
you swoop down on the [1]spoil,
and do evil in the sight of the
LORD?"
20 And Saul said to Samuel,
[a]"But I have obeyed the voice of
the LORD, and gone on the mission on which the LORD sent me,
and brought back Ā′gag king
of Am′a·lek; I have utterly destroyed the A·mal′e·kītes.
21 [a]"But the people took of the
plunder, sheep and oxen, the
best of the things which should
have been utterly destroyed, to
sacrifice to the LORD your God in
Gil′gal."
22 So Samuel said:

[a]"Has the LORD *as great*
delight in burnt offerings
and sacrifices,
As in obeying the voice of
the LORD?
Behold, [b]to obey is better
than sacrifice,
And to heed than the fat of
rams.
23 For rebellion *is as* the sin of
[1]witchcraft,
And stubbornness *is* as
iniquity and idolatry.
Because you have rejected
the word of the LORD,
[a]He also has rejected you
from *being* king."

24 [a]Then Saul said to Samuel,
"I have sinned, for I have transgressed the commandment of
the LORD and your words, because I [b]feared the people and
obeyed their voice.
25 "Now therefore, please pardon my sin, and return with me,
that I may worship the LORD."
26 But Samuel said to Saul, "I
will not return with you, [a]for
you have rejected the word of
the LORD, and the LORD has rejected you from being king over
Israel."
27 And as Samuel turned
around to go away, [a]*Saul* seized
the edge of his robe, and it tore.
28 So Samuel said to him, [a]"The

12 [a]Josh. 15:55
13 [a]Judg. 17:2
15 [a][Gen. 3:12, 13]; 1 Sam. 15:9, 21
17 [a]1 Sam. 9:21; 10:22
18 [1]*exterminated*
19 [1]*plunder*
20 [a]1 Sam. 15:13
21 [a]1 Sam. 15:15
22 [a][Is. 1:11–17] [b][Hos. 6:6]
23 [a]1 Sam. 13:14; 16:1 [1]*divination*
24 [a]Josh. 7:20 [b][Is. 51:12, 13]
26 [a]1 Sam. 2:30
27 [a]1 Kin. 11:30, 31
28 [a]1 Kin. 11:31

LORD has torn the kingdom of
Israel from you today, and has
given it to a neighbor of yours,
who is better than you.
29 "And also the Strength of
Israel [a]will not lie nor relent. For
He *is* not a man, that He should
relent."
30 Then he said, "I have sinned;
yet [a]honor me now, please, before the elders of my people and
before Israel, and return with
me, that I may worship the LORD
your God."
31 So Samuel turned back after
Saul, and Saul worshiped the
LORD.
32 Then Samuel said, "Bring
Ā′gag king of the A·mal′e·kītes
here to me." So Ā′gag came to
him cautiously. And Ā′gag said,
"Surely the bitterness of death is
past."
33 But Samuel said, [a]"As your
sword has made women childless, so shall your mother be
childless among women." And
Samuel hacked Ā′gag in pieces
before the LORD in Gil′gal.
34 Then Samuel went to [a]Rā′-
mah, and Saul went up to his
house at [b]Gib′ē·ah of Saul.
35 And [a]Samuel went no more
to see Saul until the day of
his death. Nevertheless Samuel
mourned for Saul, and the LORD
regretted that He had made Saul
king over Israel.

16

Now the LORD said to
Samuel, [a]"How long will
you mourn for Saul, seeing I
have rejected him from reigning
over Israel? [b]Fill your horn with
oil, and go; I am sending you to
[c]Jesse the Beth′le·hem·īte. For
[d]I have [1]provided Myself a king
among his sons."
2 And Samuel said, "How can
I go? If Saul hears *it*, he will kill
me." But the LORD said, "Take a
heifer with you, and say, [a]'I have
come to sacrifice to the LORD.'
3 "Then invite Jesse to the sacrifice, and I will show you what
you shall do; you shall anoint
for Me the one I name to you."
4 So Samuel did what the LORD
said, and went to Bethlehem. And
the elders of the town [a]trembled
at his coming, and said, [b]"Do
you come peaceably?"
5 And he said, "Peaceably; I
have come to sacrifice to the
LORD. [a]Sanctify[1] yourselves, and
come with me to the sacrifice."
Then he consecrated Jesse and
his sons, and invited them to the
sacrifice.
6 So it was, when they came,
that he looked at [a]E·lī′ab
and [b]said, "Surely the LORD's
anointed *is* before Him!"
7 But the LORD said to Samuel,
[a]"Do not look at his appearance
or at his physical stature, because I have [1]refused him. [b]For[2]
the LORD *does* not *see* as man
sees; for man [c]looks at the outward appearance, but the LORD
looks at the [d]heart."
8 So Jesse called A·bin′a·dab,
and made him pass before Samuel. And he said, "Neither has
the LORD chosen this one."
9 Then Jesse made Sham′mah
pass by. And he said, "Neither
has the LORD chosen this one."
10 Thus Jesse made seven of his
sons pass before Samuel. And
Samuel said to Jesse, "The LORD
has not chosen these."
11 And Samuel said to Jesse,
"Are all the young men here?"
Then he said, "There remains
yet the youngest, and there he
is, keeping the [a]sheep." And

29 [a]Num. 23:19
30 [a][John 5:44; 12:43]
33 [a][Gen. 9:6]
34 [a]1 Sam. 7:17 [b]1 Sam. 11:4
35 [a]1 Sam. 19:24

CHAPTER 16

1 [a]1 Sam. 15:23, 35 [b]1 Sam. 9:16; 10:1 [c]Ruth 4:18–22 [d]Acts 13:22 [1]Lit. *seen*
2 [a]1 Sam. 9:12
4 [a]1 Sam. 21:1 [b]1 Kin. 2:13
5 [a]Ex. 19:10 [1]*Consecrate*
6 [a]1 Sam. 17:13, 28 [b]1 Kin. 12:26
7 [a]Ps. 147:10 [b]Is. 55:8, 9 [c]2 Cor. 10:7 [d]1 Kin. 8:39 [1]*rejected* [2]LXX *For God does not see as man sees;* Tg. *It is not by the appearance of a man;* Vg. *Nor do I judge according to the looks of a man*
11 [a]2 Sam. 7:8

Samuel said to Jesse, "Send and
bring him. For we will not [1]sit
down till he comes here."
12 So he sent and brought him
in. Now he *was* [a]ruddy, [b]with
[1]bright eyes, and good-looking.
[c]And the LORD said, "Arise,
anoint him; for this *is* the one!"
13 Then Samuel took the horn
of oil and anointed him in the
midst of his brothers; and [a]the
Spirit of the LORD came upon
David from that day forward. So
Samuel arose and went to Rā′-
mah.
14 [a]But the Spirit of the LORD
departed from Saul, and [b]a distressing spirit from the LORD
troubled him.
15 And Saul's servants said to
him, "Surely, a distressing spirit
from God is troubling you.
16 "Let our master now command your servants, *who are* before you, to seek out a man *who*
is a skillful player on the harp.
And it shall be that he will [a]play
it with his hand when the [1]dis-
tressing spirit from God is upon
you, and you shall be well."
17 So Saul said to his servants,
[1]"Provide me now a man who
can play well, and bring *him* to
me."
18 Then one of the servants answered and said, "Look, I have
seen a son of Jesse the Beth′-
le·hem·īte, *who is* skillful in
playing, a mighty man of valor,
a man of war, prudent in speech,
and a handsome person; and
[a]the LORD *is* with him."
19 Therefore Saul sent messengers to Jesse, and said, "Send
me your son David, who *is* with
the sheep."
20 And Jesse [a]took a donkey
loaded with bread, a skin of

11 [1]So with LXX, Vg.; MT *turn around;* Tg., Syr. *turn away*

12 [a]1 Sam. 17:42 [b]Gen. 39:6 [c]1 Sam. 9:17 [1]Lit. *beautiful*

13 [a]Num. 27:18

14 [a]Judg. 16:20 [b]Judg. 9:23

16 [a]1 Sam. 18:10; 19:9 [1]Lit. *evil*

17 [1]Lit. *Look now for a man for me*

18 [a]1 Sam. 3:19; 18:12, 14

20 [a]1 Sam. 10:4, 27

21 [a]Gen. 41:46

CHAPTER 17

1 [a]Josh. 15:35

4 [a]2 Sam. 21:19 [b]Josh. 11:21, 22

5 [1]*clothed with scaled body armor*

wine, and a young goat, and sent
them by his son David to Saul.
21 So David came to Saul and
[a]stood before him. And he loved
him greatly, and he became his
armorbearer.
22 Then Saul sent to Jesse, saying, "Please let David stand before me, for he has found favor
in my sight."
23 And so it was, whenever the
spirit from God was upon Saul,
that David would take a harp
and play *it* with his hand. Then
Saul would become refreshed
and well, and the distressing
spirit would depart from him.

17 Now the Phi·lis′tines
gathered their armies to-
gether to battle, and were gathered at [a]Sō′chōh, which *belongs*
to Judah; they encamped between Sō′chōh and A·zē′kah, in
Ē′phes Dam′mim.
2 And Saul and the men of
Israel were gathered together,
and they encamped in the Valley
of Ē′lah, and drew up in battle
array against the Phi·lis′tines.
3 The Phi·lis′tines stood on a
mountain on one side, and Israel stood on a mountain on the
other side, with a valley between
them.
4 And a champion went out
from the camp of the Phi·lis′-
tines, named [a]Goliath, from
[b]Gath, whose height *was* six cubits and a span.
5 *He had* a bronze helmet on
his head, and he *was* [1]armed
with a coat of mail, and the
weight of the coat *was* five thousand shekels of bronze.
6 And *he had* bronze armor
on his legs and a bronze javelin
between his shoulders.
7 Now the staff of his spear

was like a weaver's beam, and
his iron spearhead *weighed* six
hundred shekels; and a shield-
bearer went before him.
8 Then he stood and cried out
to the armies of Israel, and said
to them, "Why have you come
out to line up for battle? *Am* I
not a Phi·lis′tine, and you the
[a]servants of Saul? Choose a man
for yourselves, and let him come
down to me.
9 "If he is able to fight with me
and kill me, then we will be your
servants. But if I prevail against
him and kill him, then you shall
be our servants and [a]serve us."
10 And the Phi·lis′tine said, "I
[a]defy the armies of Israel this
day; give me a man, that we may
fight together."
11 When Saul and all Israel
heard these words of the Phi·lis′-
tine, they were dismayed and
greatly afraid.
12 Now David *was* [a]the son of
that [b]Eph′ra·thīte of Bethlehem
Judah, whose name *was* Jesse,
and who had [c]eight sons. And
the man was old, advanced *in*
years, in the days of Saul.
13 The three oldest sons of Jesse
had gone to follow Saul to the
battle. The [a]names of his three
sons who went to the battle
were E·lī′ab the firstborn, next
to him A·bin′a·dab, and the third
Sham′mah.
14 David *was* the youngest. And
the three oldest followed Saul.
15 But David occasionally went
and returned from Saul [a]to feed
his father's sheep at Bethlehem.
16 And the Phi·lis′tine drew
near and presented himself forty
days, morning and evening.
17 Then Jesse said to his son David, "Take now for your brothers

8 [a]1 Sam. 8:17
9 [a]1 Sam. 11:1
10 [a]1 Sam. 17:26, 36, 45
12 [a]Ruth 4:22 [b]Gen. 35:19 [c]1 Sam. 16:10, 11
13 [a]1 Sam. 16:6, 8, 9
15 [a]1 Sam. 16:11, 19
18 [a]Gen. 37:13, 14
23 [a]1 Sam. 17:8–10
25 [a]Josh. 15:16

an ephah of this dried *grain* and
these ten loaves, and run to your
brothers at the camp.
18 "And carry these ten cheeses
to the captain of *their* thousand,
and [a]see how your brothers fare,
and bring back news of them."
19 Now Saul and they and all
the men of Israel *were* in the
Valley of Ē′lah, fighting with the
Phi·lis′tines.
20 So David rose early in the
morning, left the sheep with a
keeper, and took *the things* and
went as Jesse had commanded
him. And he came to the camp
as the army was going out to
the fight and shouting for the
battle.
21 For Israel and the Phi·lis′-
tines had drawn up in battle array, army against army.
22 And David left his supplies
in the hand of the supply keeper,
ran to the army, and came and
greeted his brothers.
23 Then as he talked with them,
there was the champion, the
Phi·lis′tine of Gath, Goliath
by name, coming up from the
armies of the Phi·lis′tines; and
he spoke [a]according to the same
words. So David heard *them.*
24 And all the men of Israel,
when they saw the man, fled
from him and were dreadfully
afraid.
25 So the men of Israel said,
"Have you seen this man who
has come up? Surely he has
come up to defy Israel; and it
shall be *that* the man who kills
him the king will enrich with
great riches, [a]will give him his
daughter, and give his father's
house exemption *from taxes* in
Israel."
26 Then David spoke to the men

who stood by him, saying, "What
shall be done for the man who
kills this Phi·lis′tine and takes
away [a]the reproach from Israel?
For who *is* this [b]uncircumcised
Phi·lis′tine, that he should [c]defy
the armies of [d]the living God?"
27 And the people answered
him in this manner, saying, [a]"So
shall it be done for the man who
kills him."
28 Now E·lī′ab his oldest brother
heard when he spoke to the
men; and E·lī′ab's [a]anger was
aroused against David, and he
said, "Why did you come down
here? And with whom have you
left those few sheep in the wilderness? I know your pride and
the insolence of your heart, for
you have come down to see the
battle."
29 And David said, "What have
I done now? [a]*Is*[1] *there* not a
cause?"
30 Then he turned from him toward another and [a]said the same
thing; and these people answered
him as the first ones *did*.
31 Now when the words which
David spoke were heard, they
reported *them* to Saul; and he
sent for him.
32 Then David said to Saul,
[a]"Let no man's heart fail because
of him; [b]your servant will go and
fight with this Phi·lis′tine."
33 And Saul said to David, [a]"You
are not able to go against this
Phi·lis′tine to fight with him; for
you *are* a youth, and he a man of
war from his youth."
34 But David said to Saul, "Your
servant used to keep his father's
sheep, and when a [a]lion or a
bear came and took a lamb out
of the flock,
35 "I went out after it and struck
it, and delivered *the lamb* from
its mouth; and when it arose
against me, I caught *it* by its
beard, and struck and killed it.
36 "Your servant has killed both
lion and bear; and this uncircumcised Phi·lis′tine will be like
one of them, seeing he has defied the armies of the living
God."
37 Moreover David said, [a]"The
LORD, who delivered me from
the paw of the lion and from
the paw of the bear, He will deliver me from the hand of this
Phi·lis′tine." And Saul said to
David, [b]"Go, and the LORD be
with you!"
38 So Saul clothed David with
his [1]armor, and he put a bronze
helmet on his head; he also
clothed him with a coat of mail.
39 David fastened his sword to
his armor and tried to walk, for
he had not tested *them*. And David said to Saul, "I cannot walk
with these, for I have not tested
them." So David took them off.
40 Then he took his staff in his
hand; and he chose for himself five smooth stones from the
brook, and put them in a shepherd's bag, in a pouch which
he had, and his sling was in his
hand. And he drew near to the
Phi·lis′tine.
41 So the Phi·lis′tine came, and
began drawing near to David,
and the man who bore the shield
went before him.
42 And when the Phi·lis′tine
looked about and saw David,
he [a]disdained[1] him; for he was
only a youth, [b]ruddy and good-
looking.
43 So the Phi·lis′tine [a]said to
David, "*Am* I a dog, that you
come to me with sticks?" And

26 [a]1 Sam. 11:2 [b]1 Sam. 14:6; 17:36 [c]1 Sam. 17:10 [d]Deut. 5:26
27 [a]1 Sam. 17:25
28 [a][Matt. 10:36]
29 [a]1 Sam. 17:17 [1]Lit. *Is it not a word?* or *matter?*
30 [a]1 Sam. 17:26, 27
32 [a]Deut. 20:1–4 [b]1 Sam. 16:18
33 [a]Num. 13:31
34 [a]Judg. 14:5
37 [a][2 Cor. 1:10] [b]1 Chr. 22:11, 16
38 [1]Lit. *clothes*
42 [a][Ps. 123:4] [b]1 Sam. 16:12 [1]*belittled*
43 [a]2 Kin. 8:13

the Phi·lis′tine cursed David by
his gods.
44 And the Phi·lis′tine [a]said to
David, "Come to me, and I will
give your flesh to the birds of
the air and the beasts of the
field!"
45 Then David said to the
Phi·lis′tine, "You come to me
with a sword, with a spear, and
with a javelin. [a]But I come to you
in the name of the LORD of hosts,
the God of the armies of Israel,
whom you have [b]defied.
46 "This day the LORD will deliver you into my hand, and I
will strike you and take your
head from you. And this day I
will give [a]the carcasses of the
camp of the Phi·lis′tines to the
birds of the air and the wild
beasts of the earth, [b]that all the
earth may know that there is a
God in Israel.
47 "Then all this assembly shall
know that the LORD [a]does not
save with sword and spear; for
[b]the battle *is* the LORD's, and He
will give you into our hands."
48 So it was, when the Phi·lis′-
tine arose and came and drew
near to meet David, that David hurried and [a]ran toward the
army to meet the Phi·lis′tine.
49 Then David put his hand in
his bag and took out a stone;
and he slung *it* and struck the
Phi·lis′tine in his forehead, so
that the stone sank into his forehead, and he fell on his face to
the earth.
50 So David prevailed over the
Phi·lis′tine with a [a]sling and a
stone, and struck the Phi·lis′tine
and killed him. But *there was* no
sword in the hand of David.
51 Therefore David ran and
stood over the Phi·lis′tine, took
his [a]sword and drew it out of its
sheath and killed him, and cut
off his head with it. And when
the Phi·lis′tines saw that their
champion was dead, [b]they fled.
52 Now the men of Israel and
Judah arose and shouted, and
pursued the Phi·lis′tines as far
as the entrance of [1]the valley and
to the gates of Ek′ron. And the
wounded of the Phi·lis′tines fell
along the road to [a]Shā·a·rā′im,
even as far as Gath and Ek′ron.
53 Then the children of Israel returned from chasing the
Phi·lis′tines, and they plundered
their tents.
54 And David took the head of
the Phi·lis′tine and brought it to
Jerusalem, but he put his armor
in his tent.
55 When Saul saw David going
out against the Phi·lis′tine, he
said to [a]Abner, the commander
of the army, "Abner, [b]whose son
is this youth?" And Abner said,
"As your soul lives, O king, I do
not know."
56 So the king said, "Inquire
whose son this young man *is*."
57 Then, as David returned from
the slaughter of the Phi·lis′tine,
Abner took him and brought
him before Saul [a]with the head
of the Phi·lis′tine in his hand.
58 And Saul said to him, "Whose
son *are* you, young man?" So
David answered, [a]"*I am* the son
of your servant Jesse the Beth′-
le·hem·īte."

18 Now when he had fin-
ished speaking to Saul,
[a]the [1]soul of Jonathan was knit
to the soul of David, [b]and Jonathan loved him as his own soul.
2 Saul took him that day, [a]and
would not let him go home to his
father's house anymore.

44 [a]1 Kin. 20:10, 11
45 [a]Heb. 11:33, 34 [b]1 Sam. 17:10
46 [a]Deut. 28:26 [b]Josh. 4:24
47 [a]Hos. 1:7 [b]2 Chr. 20:15
48 [a]Ps. 27:3
50 [a]Judg. 3:31; 15:15; 20:16
51 [a]1 Sam. 21:9 [b]Heb. 11:34
52 [a]Josh. 15:36 [1]So with MT, Syr., Tg., Vg.; LXX *Gath*
55 [a]1 Sam. 14:50 [b]1 Sam. 16:21, 22
57 [a]1 Sam. 17:54
58 [a]1 Sam. 17:12

CHAPTER 18

1 [a]Gen. 44:30 [b]1 Sam. 20:17 [1]*life of Jonathan was bound up with the life of*
2 [a]1 Sam. 17:15

3 Then Jonathan and David
made a [a]covenant, because he
loved him as his own soul.
4 And Jonathan took off the
robe that *was* on him and gave
it to David, with his armor, even
to his sword and his bow and his
belt.
5 So David went out wherever Saul sent him, *and* [1]be-
haved wisely. And Saul set him
over the men of war, and he was
accepted in the sight of all the
people and also in the sight of
Saul's servants.
6 Now it had happened as
they were coming *home,* when
David was returning from the
slaughter of the [1]Phi·lis′tine, that
[a]the women had come out of all
the cities of Israel, singing and
dancing, to meet King Saul, with
tambourines, with joy, and with
musical instruments.
7 So the women [a]sang as they
danced, and said:

[b]"Saul has slain his
thousands,
And David his ten
thousands."

8 Then Saul was very angry,
and the saying [a]displeased him;
and he said, "They have ascribed to David ten thousands,
and to me they have ascribed
only thousands. Now *what* more
can he have but [b]the kingdom?"
9 So Saul [1]eyed David from
that day forward.
10 And it happened on the next
day that [a]the distressing spirit
from God came upon Saul, [b]and
he prophesied inside the house.
So David [c]played *music* with his
hand, as at other times; [d]but *there*
was a spear in Saul's hand.
11 And Saul [a]cast the spear, for
he said, "I will pin David to the
wall!" But David escaped his
presence twice.
12 Now Saul was [a]afraid of David, because [b]the LORD was with
him, but had [c]departed from
Saul.
13 Therefore Saul removed him
from [1]his presence, and made
him his captain over a thousand;
and [a]he went out and came in
before the people.
14 And David behaved wisely
in all his ways, and [a]the LORD
was with him.
15 Therefore, when Saul saw
that he behaved very wisely, he
was afraid of him.
16 But [a]all Israel and Judah
loved David, because he went
out and came in before them.
17 Then Saul said to David,
"Here is my older daughter Mē′-
rab; [a]I will give her to you as a
wife. Only be valiant for me, and
fight [b]the LORD's battles." For Saul
thought, [c]"Let my hand not be
against him, but let the hand of
the Phi·lis′tines be against him."
18 So David said to Saul, [a]"Who
am I, and what *is* my life *or* my
father's family in Israel, that
I should be son-in-law to the
king?"
19 But it happened at the time
when Mē′rab, Saul's daughter,
should have been given to David,
that she was given to [a]Ā′dri·el the
[b]Me·hō′la·thīte as a wife.
20 [a]Now Mī′chal, Saul's daughter, loved David. And they told
Saul, and the thing pleased him.
21 So Saul said, "I will give her
to him, that she may [1]be a snare
to him, and that [a]the hand of the
Phi·lis′tines may be against him."
Therefore Saul said to David a

3 [a]1 Sam. 20:8–17
5 [1]Or *prospered*
6 [a]Ex. 15:20, 21 [1]*Philistines*
7 [a]Ex. 15:21 [b]1 Sam. 21:11; 29:5
8 [a]Eccl. 4:4 [b]1 Sam. 15:28
9 [1]Viewed with suspicion
10 [a]1 Sam. 16:14 [b]1 Sam. 19:24 [c]1 Sam. 16:23 [d]1 Sam. 19:9, 10
11 [a]1 Sam. 19:10; 20:33
12 [a]1 Sam. 18:15, 29 [b]1 Sam. 16:13, 18 [c]1 Sam. 16:14; 28:15
13 [a]Num. 27:17 [1]Lit. *himself*
14 [a]Josh. 6:27
16 [a]1 Sam. 18:5
17 [a]1 Sam. 14:49; 17:25 [b]Num. 32:20, 27, 29 [c]1 Sam. 18:21, 25
18 [a]2 Sam. 7:18
19 [a]2 Sam. 21:8 [b]Judg. 7:22
20 [a]1 Sam. 18:28
21 [a]1 Sam. 18:17 [1]*be bait for*

second time, [b]"You shall be my
son-in-law today."
22 And Saul commanded his
servants, "Communicate with
David secretly, and say, 'Look,
the king has delight in you, and
all his servants love you. Now
therefore, become the king's
son-in-law.' "
23 So Saul's servants spoke
those words in the hearing of
David. And David said, "Does
it seem to you *a* light *thing* to
be a king's son-in-law, seeing I
am a poor and lightly esteemed
man?"
24 And the servants of Saul told
him, saying, [1]"In this manner
David spoke."
25 Then Saul said, "Thus you
shall say to David: 'The king
does not desire any [a]dowry but
one hundred foreskins of the
Phi·lis′tines, to take [b]vengeance
on the king's enemies.' " But
Saul [c]thought to make David fall
by the hand of the Phi·lis′tines.
26 So when his servants told
David these words, it pleased
David well to become the king's
son-in-law. Now [a]the days had
not expired;
27 therefore David arose and
went, he and [a]his men, and killed
two hundred men of the Phi·lis′-
tines. And [b]David brought their
foreskins, and they gave them
in full count to the king, that he
might become the king's son-in-
law. Then Saul gave him Mī′chal
his daughter as a wife.
28 Thus Saul saw and knew
that the LORD *was* with David,
and *that* Mī′chal, Saul's daughter, loved him;
29 and Saul was still more
afraid of David. So Saul became
David's enemy [1]continually.

21 [b]1 Sam. 18:26
24 [1]Lit. *According to these words*
25 [a]Ex. 22:17 [b]1 Sam. 14:24 [c]1 Sam. 18:17
26 [a]1 Sam. 18:21
27 [a]1 Sam. 18:13 [b]2 Sam. 3:14
29 [1]*all the days*
30 [a]2 Sam. 11:1 [b]1 Sam. 18:5

CHAPTER 19

1 [a]1 Sam. 8:8, 9 [b]1 Sam. 18:1
3 [a]1 Sam. 20:8–13
4 [a][Prov. 31:8, 9] [b][Prov. 17:13]
5 [a]Judg. 9:17; 12:3 [b]1 Sam. 17:49, 50 [c]1 Sam. 11:13 [d]1 Sam. 20:32 [e][Deut. 19:10–13]
7 [a]1 Sam. 16:21; 18:2, 10, 13

30 Then the princes of the
Phi·lis′tines [a]went out *to war.*
And so it was, whenever they
went out, *that* David [b]behaved
more wisely than all the servants of Saul, so that his name
became highly esteemed.

19 Now Saul spoke to Jonathan his son and to all
his servants, that they should
kill [a]David; but Jonathan, Saul's
son, [b]delighted greatly in David.
2 So Jonathan told David, saying, "My father Saul seeks to
kill you. Therefore please be on
your guard until morning, and
stay in a secret *place* and hide.
3 "And I will go out and stand
beside my father in the field
where you *are,* and I will speak
with my father about you. Then
what I observe, I will tell [a]you."
4 Thus Jonathan [a]spoke well
of David to Saul his father, and
said to him, "Let not the king [b]sin
against his servant, against David, because he has not sinned
against you, and because his
works *have been* very good toward you.
5 "For he took his [a]life in his
hands and [b]killed the Phi·lis′tine,
and [c]the LORD brought about a
great deliverance for all Israel.
You saw *it* and rejoiced. [d]Why
then will you [e]sin against innocent blood, to kill David without
a cause?"
6 So Saul heeded the voice of
Jonathan, and Saul swore, "*As*
the LORD lives, he shall not be
killed."
7 Then Jonathan called David,
and Jonathan told him all these
things. So Jonathan brought David to Saul, and he was in his
presence [a]as in times past.
8 And there was war again; and

David went out and fought with the Phi·lis′tines, [a]and struck them with a mighty blow, and they fled from him.

9 Now [a]the distressing spirit from the LORD came upon Saul as he sat in his house with his spear in his hand. And David was playing *music* with *his* hand.

10 Then Saul sought to pin David to the wall with the spear, but he slipped away from Saul's presence; and he drove the spear into the wall. So David fled and escaped that night.

11 [a]Saul also sent messengers to David's house to watch him and to kill him in the morning. And Mī′chal, David's wife, told him, saying, "If you do not save your life tonight, tomorrow you will be killed."

12 So Mī′chal [a]let David down through a window. And he went and fled and escaped.

13 And Mī′chal took [1]an image and laid *it* in the bed, put a cover of goats' *hair* for his head, and covered *it* with clothes.

14 So when Saul sent messengers to take David, she said, "He *is* sick."

15 Then Saul sent the messengers *back* to see David, saying, "Bring him up to me in the bed, that I may kill him."

16 And when the messengers had come in, there was the image in the bed, with a cover of goats' *hair* for his head.

17 Then Saul said to Mī′chal, "Why have you deceived me like this, and sent my enemy away, so that he has escaped?" And Mī′chal answered Saul, "He said to me, 'Let me go! [a]Why should I kill you?' "

18 So David fled and escaped, and went to [a]Samuel at [b]Rā′mah, and told him all that Saul had done to him. And he and Samuel went and stayed in Naī′oth.

19 Now it was told Saul, saying, "Take note, David *is* at Naī′oth in Rā′mah!"

20 Then [a]Saul sent messengers to take David. [b]And when they saw the group of prophets prophesying, and Samuel standing *as* leader over them, the Spirit of God came upon the messengers of Saul, and they also [c]prophesied.

21 And when Saul was told, he sent other messengers, and they prophesied likewise. Then Saul sent messengers again the third time, and they prophesied also.

22 Then he also went to Rā′mah, and came to the great well that *is* at Sē′chu. So he asked, and said, "Where *are* Samuel and David?" And *someone* said, "Indeed *they are* at Naī′oth in Rā′mah."

23 So he went there to Naī′oth in Rā′mah. Then [a]the Spirit of God was upon him also, and he went on and prophesied until he came to Naī′oth in Rā′mah.

24 [a]And he also stripped off his clothes and prophesied before Samuel in like manner, and lay down [b]naked all that day and all that night. Therefore they say, [c]"*Is* Saul also among the prophets?"

20

Then David fled from Naī′oth in Rā′mah, and went and said to Jonathan, "What have I done? What *is* my iniquity, and what *is* my sin before your father, that he seeks my life?"

2 So Jonathan said to him, "By

8 [a]1 Sam. 18:27; 23:5
9 [a]1 Sam. 16:14; 18:10, 11
11 [a]Ps. 59:title
12 [a]Josh. 2:15
13 [1]*household idols*, Heb. *teraphim*
17 [a]2 Sam. 2:22
18 [a]1 Sam. 16:13 [b]1 Sam. 7:17
20 [a]John 7:32 [b]1 Sam. 10:5, 6, 10 [c]Joel 2:28
23 [a]1 Sam. 10:10
24 [a]Is. 20:2 [b]Mic. 1:8 [c]1 Sam. 10:10–12

no means! You shall not die! Indeed, my father will do nothing either great or small without first telling me. And why should my father hide this thing from me? It *is* not *so!*"

3 Then David took an oath again, and said, "Your father certainly knows that I have found favor in your eyes, and he has said, 'Do not let Jonathan know this, lest he be grieved.' But [a]truly, *as* the LORD lives and *as* your soul lives, *there is* but a step between me and death."

4 So Jonathan said to David, "Whatever you yourself desire, I will do *it* for you."

5 And David said to Jonathan, "Indeed tomorrow *is* the [a]New Moon, and I should not fail to sit with the king to eat. But let me go, that I may [b]hide in the field until the third *day* at evening.

6 "If your father misses me at all, then say, 'David earnestly asked *permission* of me that he might run over [a]to Bethlehem, his city, for *there is* a yearly sacrifice there for all the family.'

7 [a]"If he says thus: '*It is* well,' your servant will be safe. But if he is very angry, be sure that [b]evil is determined by him.

8 "Therefore you shall [a]deal kindly with your servant, for [b]you have brought your servant into a covenant of the LORD with you. Nevertheless, [c]if there is iniquity in me, kill me yourself, for why should you bring me to your father?"

9 But Jonathan said, "Far be it from you! For if I knew certainly that evil was determined by my father to come upon you, then would I not tell you?"

10 Then David said to Jonathan, "Who will tell me, or what *if* your father answers you roughly?"

11 And Jonathan said to David, "Come, let us go out into the field." So both of them went out into the field.

12 Then Jonathan said to David: "The LORD God of Israel *is witness!* When I have [1]sounded out my father sometime tomorrow, *or* the third *day,* and indeed *there is* good toward David, and I do not send to you and tell you,

13 "may [a]the LORD do so and much more to Jonathan. But if it pleases my father *to do* you evil, then I will report it to you and send you away, that you may go in safety. And [b]the LORD be with you as He has [c]been with my father.

14 "And you shall not only show me the kindness of the LORD while I still live, that I may not die;

15 "but [a]you shall not [1]cut off your kindness from my [2]house forever, no, not when the LORD has cut off every one of the enemies of David from the face of the earth."

16 So Jonathan made *a covenant* with the [1]house of David, *saying,* [a]"Let the LORD require *it* at the hand of David's enemies."

17 Now Jonathan again caused David to vow, because he loved him; [a]for he loved him as he loved his own soul.

18 Then Jonathan said to David, [a]"Tomorrow *is* the New Moon; and you will be missed, because your seat will be empty.

19 "And *when* you have stayed three days, go down quickly and come to [a]the place where you

CHAPTER 20

3 [a]1 Sam. 27:1

5 [a]Num. 10:10; 28:11–15 [b]1 Sam. 19:2, 3

6 [a]1 Sam. 16:4; 17:12

7 [a]2 Sam. 17:4 [b]1 Sam. 25:17

8 [a]Josh. 2:14 [b]1 Sam. 18:3; 20:16; 23:18 [c]2 Sam. 14:32

12 [1]*searched out*

13 [a]Ruth 1:17 [b]Josh. 1:5 [c]1 Sam. 10:7

15 [a]2 Sam. 9:1, 3, 7; 21:7 [1]*stop being kind* [2]*family*

16 [a]1 Sam. 25:22; 31:2 [1]*family*

17 [a]1 Sam. 18:1

18 [a]1 Sam. 20:5, 24

19 [a]1 Sam. 19:2

hid on the day of the deed; and
remain by the stone Ē'zel.
20 "Then I will shoot three arrows to the side, as though I shot
at a target;
21 "and there I will send a lad,
saying, 'Go, find the arrows.' If I
expressly say to the lad, 'Look,
the arrows *are* on this side of
you; get them and come'—then,
[a]as the LORD lives, *there is* safety
for you and no harm.
22 "But if I say thus to the young
man, 'Look, the arrows *are* beyond you'—go your way, for the
LORD has sent you away.
23 "And as for [a]the matter which
you and I have spoken of, indeed
the LORD *be* between you and me
forever."
24 Then David hid in the field.
And when the New Moon had
come, the king sat down to eat
the feast.
25 Now the king sat on his seat,
as at other times, on a seat by
the wall. And [1]Jonathan arose,
and Abner sat by Saul's side, but
David's place was empty.
26 Nevertheless Saul did not
say anything that day, for he
thought, "Something has happened to him; he *is* unclean,
surely he *is* [a]unclean."
27 And it happened the next
day, the second *day* of the month,
that David's place was empty.
And Saul said to Jonathan his
son, "Why has the son of Jesse
not come to eat, either yesterday
or today?"
28 So Jonathan [a]answered Saul,
"David earnestly asked *permission* of me *to go* to Bethlehem.
29 "And he said, 'Please let me
go, for our family has a sacrifice in the city, and my brother
has commanded me *to be there.*
And now, if I have found favor in your eyes, please let me
get away and see my brothers.'
Therefore he has not come to
the king's table."
30 Then Saul's anger was
aroused against Jonathan, and
he said to him, "You son of a
perverse, rebellious *woman!* Do
I not know that you have chosen
the son of Jesse to your own
shame and to the shame of your
mother's nakedness?
31 "For as long as the son of
Jesse lives on the earth, you
shall not be established, nor
your kingdom. Now therefore,
send and bring him to me, for he
[1]shall surely die."
32 And Jonathan answered
Saul his father, and said to him,
[a]"Why should he be killed? What
has he done?"
33 Then Saul [a]cast a spear at him
to [1]kill him, [b]by which Jonathan
knew that it was determined by
his father to kill David.
34 So Jonathan arose from the
table in fierce anger, and ate
no food the second day of the
month, for he was grieved for
David, because his father had
treated him shamefully.
35 And so it was, in the morning, that Jonathan went out into
the field at the time appointed
with David, and a little lad *was*
with him.
36 Then he said to his lad, "Now
run, find the arrows which I
shoot." As the lad ran, he shot an
arrow beyond him.
37 When the lad had come to
the place where the arrow was
which Jonathan had shot, Jonathan cried out after the lad and
said, "*Is* not the arrow beyond
you?"

21 [a]Jer. 4:2
23 [a]1 Sam. 20:14, 15
25 [1]So with MT, Syr., Tg., Vg.; LXX *he sat across from Jonathan*
26 [a]Lev. 7:20, 21; 15:5
28 [a]1 Sam. 20:6
31 [1]Lit. *is a son of death*
32 [a]Gen. 31:36
33 [a]1 Sam. 18:11; 19:10 [b]1 Sam. 20:7 [1]*strike him down*

38 And Jonathan cried out after the lad, "Make haste, hurry,
do not delay!" So Jonathan's
lad gathered up the arrows and
came back to his master.
39 But the lad did not know
anything. Only Jonathan and
David knew of the matter.
40 Then Jonathan gave his [1]wea-
pons to his lad, and said to him,
"Go, carry *them* to the city."
41 As soon as the lad had gone,
David arose from *a place* toward
the south, fell on his face to the
ground, and bowed down three
times. And they kissed one another; and they wept together,
but David more so.
42 Then Jonathan said to David, [a]"Go in peace, since we have
both sworn in the name of the
LORD, saying, 'May the LORD be
between you and me, and between your descendants and my
descendants, forever.' " So he
arose and departed, and Jonathan went into the city.

21 Now David came to Nob,
to A·him′e·lech the priest.
And [a]A·him′e·lech was [b]afraid
when he met David, and said to
him, "Why *are* you alone, and no
one is with you?"
2 So David said to A·him′e·lech
the priest, "The king has ordered
me on some business, and said
to me, 'Do not let anyone know
anything about the business on
which I send you, or what I have
commanded you.' And I have
directed *my* young men to such
and such a place.
3 "Now therefore, what have
you on hand? Give *me* five
loaves of bread in my hand, or
whatever can be found."
4 And the priest answered
David and said, "*There is* no
[1]common bread on hand; but
there is [a]holy[2] bread, [b]if the
young men have at least kept
themselves from women."
5 Then David answered the
priest, and said to him, "Truly,
women *have been* kept from us
about three days since I came
out. And [1]the [a]vessels of the
young men are holy, and *the
bread is* in effect common, even
though it was consecrated [b]in
the vessel this day."
6 So the priest [a]gave him holy
bread; for there was no bread
there but the showbread [b]which
had been taken from before the
LORD, in order to put hot bread
in its place on the day when it
was taken away.
7 Now a certain man of the
servants of Saul *was* there that
day, detained before the LORD.
And his name *was* [a]Dō′eg, an
Ē′dom·īte, the chief of the herdsmen who *belonged* to Saul.
8 And David said to A·him′-
e·lech, "Is there not here on
hand a spear or a sword? For I
have brought neither my sword
nor my weapons with me, because the king's business required haste."
9 So the priest said, "The sword
of Goliath the Phi·lis′tine, whom
you killed in [a]the Valley of Ē′lah,
[b]there it is, wrapped in a cloth
behind the ephod. If you will
take that, take *it*. For *there is* no
other except that one here." And
David said, "*There is* none like
it; give it to me."
10 Then David arose and fled
that day from before Saul, and
went to Ā′chish the king of
Gath.
11 And [a]the servants of Ā′chish
said to him, "*Is* this not David

40 [1]*equipment*
42 [a]1 Sam. 1:17

CHAPTER 21

1 [a]1 Sam. 14:3 [b]1 Sam. 16:4
4 [a]Lev. 24:5–9 [b]Ex. 19:15 [1]*ordinary* [2]*consecrated*
5 [a]1 Thess. 4:4 [b]Lev. 8:26 [1]The young men are ceremonially undefiled
6 [a]Luke 6:3, 4 [b]Lev. 24:8, 9
7 [a]1 Sam. 14:47; 22:9
9 [a]1 Sam. 17:2, 50 [b]1 Sam. 31:10
11 [a]Ps. 56:title

the king of the land? Did they
not sing of him to one another
in dances, saying:

[b]'Saul has slain his
thousands,
And David his ten
thousands'?"

12 Now David [a]took these
words [1]to heart, and was very
much afraid of Ā'chish the king
of Gath.
13 So [a]he changed his behavior
before them, pretended [1]mad-
ness in their hands, [2]scratched
on the doors of the gate, and
let his saliva fall down on his
beard.
14 Then Ā'chish said to his servants, "Look, you see the man is
insane. Why have you brought
him to me?
15 "Have I need of madmen,
that you have brought this *fel-*
low to play the madman in my
presence? Shall this *fellow* come
into my house?"

22

22 David therefore departed
from there and [a]escaped
[b]to the cave of A·dul'lam. So
when his brothers and all his father's house heard *it*, they went
down there to him.
2 [a]And everyone *who was* in
distress, everyone who *was* in
debt, and everyone *who was*
[1]discontented gathered to him.
So he became captain over them.
And there were about [b]four hundred men with him.
3 Then David went from there
to Miz'pah of [a]Mō'ab; and he
said to the king of Mō'ab, "Please
let my father and mother come
here with you, till I know what
God will do for me."
4 So he brought them before
the king of Mō'ab, and they
dwelt with him all the time that
David was in the stronghold.
5 Now the prophet [a]Gad said
to David, "Do not stay in the
stronghold; depart, and go to
the land of Judah." So David departed and went into the forest
of Hē'reth.
6 When Saul heard that David
and the men who *were* with him
had been discovered—now Saul
was staying in [a]Gib'ē·ah under
a tamarisk tree in Rā'mah, with
his spear in his hand, and all his
servants standing about him—
7 then Saul said to his servants
who stood about him, "Hear now,
you Ben'ja·mītes! Will the son of
Jesse [a]give every one of you
fields and vineyards, *and* make
you all captains of thousands
and captains of hundreds?
8 "All of you have conspired
against me, and *there is* no one
who reveals to me that [a]my son
has made a covenant with the
son of Jesse; and *there is* not
one of you who is sorry for me
or reveals to me that my son has
stirred up my servant against me,
to lie in wait, as *it is* this day."
9 Then answered [a]Dō'eg the
Ē'dom·īte, who was set over the
servants of Saul, and said, "I
saw the son of Jesse going to
Nob, to [b]A·him'e·lech the son of
[c]A·hī'tub.
10 [a]"And he inquired of the
LORD for him, [b]gave him provisions, and gave him the sword of
Goliath the Phi·lis'tine."
11 So the king sent to call
A·him'e·lech the priest, the son
of A·hī'tub, and all his father's
house, the priests who *were* in
Nob. And they all came to the
king.

11 [b]1 Sam. 18:6–8; 29:5
12 [a]Luke 2:19 [1]Lit. *in his heart*
13 [a]Ps. 34:title [1]*insanity* [2]*scribbled*

CHAPTER 22

1 [a]Ps. 57:title; 142:title [b]2 Sam. 23:13
2 [a]Judg. 11:3 [b]1 Sam. 25:13 [1]Lit. *bitter of soul*
3 [a]2 Sam. 8:2
5 [a]2 Sam. 24:11
6 [a]1 Sam. 15:34
7 [a]1 Sam. 8:14
8 [a]1 Sam. 18:3; 20:16, 30
9 [a]1 Sam. 21:7; 22:22 [b]1 Sam. 21:1 [c]1 Sam. 14:3
10 [a]Num. 27:21 [b]1 Sam. 21:6, 9

12 And Saul said, "Hear now,
son of A·hī′tub!" He answered,
"Here I am, my lord."
13 Then Saul said to him, "Why
have you conspired against me,
you and the son of Jesse, in that
you have given him bread and
a sword, and have inquired of
God for him, that he should rise
against me, to lie in wait, as it is
this day?"
14 So A·him′e·lech answered
the king and said, "And who
among all your servants *is as*
[a]faithful as David, who is the
king's son-in-law, who goes at
your bidding, and is honorable
in your house?
15 "Did I then begin to inquire
of God for him? Far be it from
me! Let not the king impute anything to his servant, *or* to any in
the house of my father. For your
servant knew nothing of all this,
little or much."
16 And the king said, "You shall
surely die, A·him′e·lech, you and
all [a]your father's house!"
17 Then the king said to the
guards who stood about him,
"Turn and kill the priests of the
LORD, because their hand also
is with David, and because they
knew when he fled and did not
tell it to me." But the servants
of the king [a]would not lift their
hands to strike the priests of the
LORD.
18 And the king said to Dō′eg,
"You turn and kill the priests!"
So Dō′eg the Ē′dom·īte turned
and [1]struck the priests, and
[a]killed on that day eighty-five
men who wore a linen ephod.
19 [a]Also Nob, the city of the
priests, he struck with the edge
of the sword, both men and
women, children and nursing
infants, oxen and donkeys and
sheep—with the edge of the
sword.
20 [a]Now one of the sons of
A·him′e·lech the son of A·hī′tub,
named A·bī′a·thar, [b]escaped and
fled after David.
21 And A·bī′a·thar told David
that Saul had killed the LORD's
priests.
22 So David said to A·bī′a·thar,
"I knew that day, when Dō′eg
the Ē′dom·īte *was* there, that he
would surely tell Saul. I have
caused *the death* of all the persons of your father's [1]house.
23 "Stay with me; do not fear.
[a]For he who seeks my life seeks
your life, but with me you *shall*
be safe."

23

Then they told David,
saying, "Look, the Phi·lis′-
tines are fighting against [a]Kē·ī′-
lah, and they are robbing the
threshing floors."
2 Therefore David [a]inquired of
the LORD, saying, "Shall I go and
[1]attack these Phi·lis′tines?" And
the LORD said to David, "Go and
attack the Phi·lis′tines, and save
Kē·ī′lah."
3 But David's men said to him,
"Look, we are afraid here in Judah. How much more then if we
go to Kē·ī′lah against the armies
of the Phi·lis′tines?"
4 Then David inquired of the
LORD once again. And the LORD
answered him and said, "Arise,
go down to Kē·ī′lah. For I will
deliver the Phi·lis′tines into your
hand."
5 And David and his men went
to Kē·ī′lah and [a]fought with the
Phi·lis′tines, struck them with
a mighty blow, and took away
their livestock. So David saved
the inhabitants of Kē·ī′lah.

14 [a]1 Sam. 19:4, 5; 20:32; 24:11
16 [a]Deut. 24:16
17 [a]Ex. 1:17
18 [a]1 Sam. 2:31 [1]*attacked*
19 [a]1 Sam. 22:9, 11
20 [a]1 Sam. 23:6, 9; 30:7 [b]1 Sam. 2:33
22 [1]*family*
23 [a]1 Kin. 2:26

CHAPTER 23

1 [a]Josh. 15:44
2 [a]2 Sam. 5:19, 23 [1]Lit. *strike*
5 [a]1 Sam. 19:8

6 Now it happened, when A·bī′-
a·thar the son of A·him′e·lech
[a]fled to David at Kē·ī′lah, *that* he
went down *with* an ephod in his
hand.
7 And Saul was told that David had gone to Kē·ī′lah. So Saul
said, "God has delivered him
into my hand, for he has shut
himself in by entering a town
that has gates and bars."
8 Then Saul called all the people together for war, to go down
to Kē·ī′lah to besiege David and
his men.
9 When David knew that Saul
plotted evil against him, [a]he said
to A·bī′a·thar the priest, "Bring
the ephod here."
10 Then David said, "O LORD
God of Israel, Your servant has
certainly heard that Saul seeks
to come to Kē·ī′lah [a]to destroy
the city for my sake.
11 "Will the men of Kē·ī′lah deliver me into his hand? Will Saul
come down, as Your servant has
heard? O LORD God of Israel,
I pray, tell Your servant." And
the LORD said, "He will come
down."
12 Then David said, "Will the
men of Kē·ī′lah [1]deliver me and
my men into the hand of Saul?"
And the LORD said, "They will
deliver *you*."
13 So David and his men, [a]about
six hundred, arose and departed
from Kē·ī′lah and went wherever
they could go. Then it was told
Saul that David had escaped
from Kē·ī′lah; so he halted the
expedition.
14 And David stayed in strongholds in the wilderness, and remained in [a]the mountains in
the Wilderness of [b]Ziph. Saul
[c]sought him every day, but God
did not deliver him into his
hand.
15 So David saw that Saul had
come out to seek his life. And
David *was* in the Wilderness of
Ziph [1]in a forest.
16 Then Jonathan, Saul's son,
arose and went to David in the
woods and [1]strengthened his
hand in God.
17 And he said to him, [a]"Do not
fear, for the hand of Saul my father shall not find you. You shall
be king over Israel, and I shall
be next to you. [b]Even my father
Saul knows that."
18 So the two of them [a]made a
covenant before the LORD. And
David stayed in the woods, and
Jonathan went to his own house.
19 Then the Ziph′ītes [a]came
up to Saul at Gib′ē·ah, saying,
"Is David not hiding with us in
strongholds in the woods, in the
hill of Ha·chī′lah, which *is* on
the south of Jē·shī′mon?
20 "Now therefore, O king, come
down according to all the desire
of your soul to come down; and
[a]our part *shall be* to deliver him
into the king's hand."
21 And Saul said, "Blessed *are*
you of the LORD, for you have
compassion on me.
22 "Please go and find out for
sure, and see the place where
his hideout is, *and* who has seen
him there. For I am told he is
very crafty.
23 "See therefore, and take
knowledge of all the lurking
places where he hides; and come
back to me with certainty, and I
will go with you. And it shall be,
if he is in the land, that I will
search for him throughout all
the [1]clans of Judah."
24 So they arose and went to

6 [a]1 Sam. 22:20
9 [a]1 Sam. 23:6; 30:7
10 [a]1 Sam. 22:19
12 [1]Lit. *shut up*
13 [a]1 Sam. 22:2; 25:13
14 [a]Ps. 11:1 [b]Josh. 15:55 [c]Ps. 32:7; 54:3, 4
15 [1]Or *in Horesh*
16 [1]*encouraged him*
17 [a][Heb. 13:6] [b]1 Sam. 20:31; 24:20
18 [a]2 Sam. 9:1; 21:7
19 [a]1 Sam. 26:1
20 [a]Ps. 54:3
23 [1]Lit. *thousands*

Ziph before Saul. But David and
his men *were* in the Wilderness
[a]of Mā'on, in the plain on the
south of Jē·shī'mon.
25 When Saul and his men went
to seek *him*, they told David.
Therefore he went down [1]to the
rock, and stayed in the Wilderness of Mā'on. And when Saul
heard *that*, he pursued David in
the Wilderness of Mā'on.
26 Then Saul went on one side
of the mountain, and David and
his men on the other side of
the mountain. [a]So David made
haste to get away from Saul, for
Saul and his men [b]were encircling David and his men to take
them.
27 [a]But a messenger came to
Saul, saying, "Hurry and come,
for the Phi·lis'tines have invaded
the land!"
28 Therefore Saul returned
from pursuing David, and went
against the Phi·lis'tines; so they
called that place [1]the Rock of
Escape.
29 Then David went up from
there and dwelt in strongholds
at [a]En Ge'di.

24

Now it happened, [a]when
Saul had returned from
following the Phi·lis'tines, that
it was told him, saying, "Take
note! David *is* in the Wilderness
of En Ge'di."
2 Then Saul took three thousand chosen men from all Israel,
and [a]went to seek David and his
men on the Rocks of the Wild
Goats.
3 So he came to the sheepfolds by the road, where there
was a cave; and [a]Saul went in
to [b]attend to his needs. ([c]David
and his men were staying in the
recesses of the cave.)
4 [a]Then the men of David said
to him, "This is the day of which
the LORD said to you, 'Behold,
I will deliver your enemy into
your hand, that you may do to
him as it seems good to you.' "
And David arose and secretly
cut off a corner of Saul's robe.
5 Now it happened afterward
that [a]David's heart troubled him
because he had cut Saul's robe.
6 And he said to his men, [a]"The
LORD forbid that I should do this
thing to my master, the LORD's
anointed, to stretch out my hand
against him, seeing he *is* the
anointed of the LORD."
7 So David [a]restrained his servants with *these* words, and did
not allow them to rise against
Saul. And Saul got up from the
cave and went on *his* way.
8 David also arose afterward,
went out of the cave, and called
out to Saul, saying, "My lord the
king!" And when Saul looked
behind him, David stooped with
his face to the earth, and bowed
down.
9 And David said to Saul:
[a]"Why do you listen to the words
of men who say, 'Indeed David
seeks your harm'?
10 "Look, this day your eyes
have seen that the LORD delivered you today into my hand in
the cave, and *someone* urged *me*
to kill you. But *my eye* spared
you, and I said, 'I will not stretch
out my hand against my lord, for
he *is* the LORD's anointed.'
11 "Moreover, my father, see!
Yes, see the corner of your robe
in my hand! For in that I cut off
the corner of your robe, and
did not kill you, know and see
that *there is* [a]neither evil nor
rebellion in my hand, and I have

24 [a]1 Sam. 25:2
25 [1]Or *from the rock*
26 [a]Ps. 31:22 [b]Ps. 17:9
27 [a]2 Kin. 19:9
28 [1]Heb. *Sela Hammahlekoth*
29 [a]2 Chr. 20:2

CHAPTER 24

1 [a]1 Sam. 23:19, 28, 29
2 [a]1 Sam. 26:2
3 [a]1 Sam. 24:10 [b]Judg. 3:24 [c]Ps. 57:title; 142:title
4 [a]1 Sam. 26:8–11
5 [a]2 Sam. 24:10
6 [a]1 Sam. 26:11
7 [a][Matt. 5:44]
9 [a]Ps. 141:6
11 [a]Ps. 7:3; 35:7

not sinned against you. Yet you
[b]hunt my life to take it.
12 [a]"Let the LORD judge between
you and me, and let the LORD
avenge me on you. But my hand
shall not be against you.
13 "As the proverb of the an-
cients says, [a]'Wickedness proceeds from the wicked.' But my
hand shall not be against you.
14 "After whom has the king of
Israel come out? Whom do you
pursue? [a]A dead dog? [b]A flea?
15 [a]"Therefore let the LORD be
judge, and judge between you
and me, and [b]see and [c]plead my
case, and deliver me out of your
hand."
16 So it was, when David had
finished speaking these words
to Saul, that Saul said, [a]"*Is* this
your voice, my son David?"
And Saul lifted up his voice and
wept.
17 [a]Then he said to David: "You
are [b]more righteous than I; for
[c]you have rewarded me with
good, whereas I have rewarded
you with evil.
18 "And you have shown this
day how you have dealt well
with me; for when [a]the LORD delivered me into your hand, you
did not kill me.
19 "For if a man finds his enemy, will he let him get away
safely? Therefore may the LORD
reward you with good for what
you have done to me this day.
20 "And now [a]I know indeed
that you shall surely be king, and
that the kingdom of Israel shall
be established in your hand.
21 [a]"Therefore swear now to me
by the LORD [b]that you will not
cut off my descendants after me,
and that you will not destroy my
name from my father's house."
22 So David swore to Saul.
And Saul went home, but David
and his men went up to [a]the
stronghold.

25 Then [a]Samuel died; and
the Israelites gathered together and [b]lamented for him,
and buried him at his home in
Rā′mah. And David arose and
went down [c]to the Wilderness of
[1]Par′an.
2 Now *there was* a man [a]in
Mā′on whose business *was* in
[b]Car′mel, and the man *was* very
rich. He had three thousand
sheep and a thousand goats.
And he was shearing his sheep
in Car′mel.
3 The name of the man *was*
Nā′bal, and the name of his
wife Ab′i·gāil. And *she was* a
woman of good understanding
and beautiful appearance; but
the man *was* harsh and evil in
his doings. He *was of the house*
of [a]Caleb.
4 When David heard in the
wilderness that Nā′bal was
[a]shearing his sheep,
5 David sent ten young men;
and David said to the young
men, "Go up to Car′mel, go to
Nā′bal, and greet him in my
name.
6 "And thus you shall say to
him who lives *in prosperity*:
[a]'Peace *be* to you, peace to your
house, and peace to all that you
have!
7 'Now I have heard that you
have shearers. Your shepherds
were with us, and we did not
hurt them, [a]nor was there anything missing from them all the
while they were in Car′mel.
8 'Ask your young men, and
they will tell you. Therefore [1]let
my young men find favor in

11 [b]1 Sam. 26:20
12 [a]1 Sam. 26:10–23
13 [a][Matt. 7:16–20]
14 [a]2 Sam. 9:8 [b]1 Sam. 26:20
15 [a]1 Sam. 24:12 [b]2 Chr. 24:22 [c]Ps. 35:1; 43:1; 119:154
16 [a]1 Sam. 26:17
17 [a]1 Sam. 26:21 [b]Gen. 38:26 [c][Matt. 5:44]
18 [a]1 Sam. 26:23
20 [a]1 Sam. 23:17
21 [a]Gen. 21:23 [b]2 Sam. 21:6–8
22 [a]1 Sam. 23:29

CHAPTER 25

1 [a]1 Sam. 28:3 [b]Deut. 34:8 [c]Gen. 21:21 [1]So with MT, Syr., Tg., Vg.; LXX *Maon*
2 [a]1 Sam. 23:24 [b]Josh. 15:55
3 [a]Josh. 15:13
4 [a]Gen. 38:13
6 [a]1 Chr. 12:18
7 [a]1 Sam. 25:15, 21
8 [1]*be gracious to the young men*

your eyes, for we come on [a]a
feast day. Please give whatever
comes to your hand to your servants and to your son David.' "
9 So when David's young men
came, they spoke to Nā'bal according to all these words in the
name of David, and waited.
10 Then Nā'bal answered David's servants, and said, [a]"Who
is David, and who *is* the son of
Jesse? There are many servants
nowadays who break away each
one from his master.
11 [a]"Shall I then take my bread
and my water and my [1]meat that
I have killed for my shearers,
and give *it* to men when I do not
know where they *are* from?"
12 So David's young men turned
on their heels and went back;
and they came and told him all
these words.
13 Then David said to his men,
"Every man gird on his sword."
So every man girded on his
sword, and David also girded
on his sword. And about four
hundred men went with David,
and two hundred [a]stayed with
the supplies.
14 Now one of the young men
told Ab'i·gāil, Nā'bal's wife,
saying, "Look, David sent messengers from the wilderness to
greet our master; and he [1]reviled
them.
15 "But the men *were* very good
to us, and [a]we were not hurt, nor
did we miss anything as long as
we accompanied them, when we
were in the fields.
16 "They were [a]a wall to us both
by night and day, all the time
we were with them keeping the
sheep.
17 "Now therefore, know and
consider what you will do, for
[a]harm is determined against our
master and against all his household. For he *is such* a [b]scoundrel[1]
that *one* cannot speak to him."
18 Then Ab'i·gāil made haste
and [a]took two hundred *loaves*
of bread, two skins of wine,
five sheep already dressed, five
seahs of roasted *grain*, one hundred clusters of raisins, and
two hundred cakes of figs, and
loaded *them* on donkeys.
19 And she said to her servants,
[a]"Go on before me; see, I am
coming after you." But she did
not tell her husband Nā'bal.
20 So it was, *as* she rode on the
donkey, that she went down under cover of the hill; and there
were David and his men, coming down toward her, and she
met them.
21 Now David had said, "Surely
in vain I have protected all that
this *fellow* has in the wilderness,
so that nothing was missed of all
that *belongs* to him. And he has
[a]repaid me evil for good.
22 [a]"May God do so, and more
also, to the enemies of David, if
I [b]leave [c]one male of all who *belong* to him by morning light."
23 Now when Ab'i·gāil saw David, she [a]dismounted quickly
from the donkey, fell on her face
before David, and bowed down
to the ground.
24 So she fell at his feet and
said: "On me, my lord, *on* me *let*
this iniquity *be!* And please let
your maidservant [1]speak in your
ears, and hear the words of your
maidservant.
25 "Please, let not my lord [1]re-
gard this scoundrel Nā'bal. For
as his name *is,* so *is* he: [2]Nā'bal
is his name, and folly *is* with
him! But I, your maidservant,

8 [a]Esth. 8:17; 9:19, 22
10 [a]Judg. 9:28
11 [a]Judg. 8:6, 15 [1]Lit. *slaughter*
13 [a]1 Sam. 30:24
14 [1]*scolded or scorned at*
15 [a]1 Sam. 25:7, 21
16 [a]Ex. 14:22
17 [a]1 Sam. 20:7 [b]Deut. 13:13 [1]Lit. *son of Belial*
18 [a]Gen. 32:13
19 [a]Gen. 32:16, 20
21 [a]Ps. 109:5
22 [a]1 Sam. 3:17; 20:13, 16 [b]1 Sam. 25:34 [c]1 Kin. 14:10; 21:21
23 [a]Judg. 1:14
24 [1]*speak to you*
25 [1]*pay attention to* [2]Lit. *Fool*

did not see the young men of my
lord whom you sent.
26 "Now therefore, my lord,
[a]*as* the LORD lives and *as* your
soul lives, since the LORD has
[b]held you back from coming to
bloodshed and from [c]avenging[1]
yourself with your own hand,
now then, [d]let your enemies and
those who seek harm for my
lord be as Nā′bal.
27 "And now [a]this present which
your maidservant has brought
to my lord, let it be given to the
young men who follow my lord.
28 "Please forgive the trespass
of your maidservant. For [a]the
LORD will certainly make for my
lord an enduring house, because
my lord [b]fights the battles of the
LORD, [c]and evil is not found in
you throughout your days.
29 "Yet a man has risen to
pursue you and seek your life,
but the life of my lord shall be
[a]bound in the bundle of the living with the LORD your God;
and the lives of your enemies
He shall [b]sling out, *as from* the
pocket of a sling.
30 "And it shall come to pass,
when the LORD has done for my
lord according to all the good
that He has spoken concerning you, and has appointed you
[a]ruler over Israel,
31 "that this will be no grief to
you, nor offense of heart to my
lord, either that you have shed
blood without cause, or that my
lord has avenged himself. But
when the LORD has dealt well
with my lord, then remember
your maidservant."
32 Then David said to Ab′i·gāil:
[a]"Blessed *is* the LORD God of
Israel, who sent you this day to
meet me!

26 [a]2 Kin. 2:2 [b]Gen. 20:6 [c][Rom. 12:19] [d]2 Sam. 18:32 [1]Lit. *saving yourself*
27 [a]Gen. 33:11
28 [a]2 Sam. 7:11–16, 27 [b]1 Sam. 18:17 [c]1 Sam. 24:11
29 [a][Col. 3:3] [b]Jer. 10:18
30 [a]1 Sam. 13:14; 15:28
32 [a]Luke 1:68
33 [a]1 Sam. 25:26
34 [a]1 Sam. 25:26 [b]1 Sam. 25:22
35 [a]2 Kin. 5:19 [b]Gen. 19:21
36 [a]2 Sam. 13:28
38 [a]1 Sam. 26:10
39 [a]1 Sam. 25:32 [b]Prov. 22:23 [c]1 Sam. 25:26, 34 [d]1 Kin. 2:44

33 "And blessed *is* your advice
and blessed *are* you, because
you have [a]kept me this day from
coming to bloodshed and from
avenging myself with my own
hand.
34 "For indeed, *as* the LORD God
of Israel lives, who has [a]kept
me back from hurting you, unless you had hurried and come
to meet me, surely [b]by morning
light no males would have been
left to Nā′bal!"
35 So David received from her
hand what she had brought him,
and said to her, [a]"Go up in peace
to your house. See, I have heeded
your voice and [b]respected your
person."
36 Now Ab′i·gāil went to Nā′-
bal, and there he was, [a]holding a
feast in his house, like the feast
of a king. And Nā′bal's heart
was merry within him, for he
was very drunk; therefore she
told him nothing, little or much,
until morning light.
37 So it was, in the morning,
when the wine had gone from
Nā′bal, and his wife had told
him these things, that his heart
died within him, and he became
like a stone.
38 Then it happened, *after*
about ten days, that the LORD
[a]struck Nā′bal, and he died.
39 So when David heard that
Nā′bal was dead, he said,
[a]"Blessed *be* the LORD, who has
[b]pleaded the cause of my reproach from the hand of Nā′bal,
and has [c]kept His servant from
evil! For the LORD has [d]returned
the wickedness of Nā′bal on his
own head." And David sent and
proposed to Ab′i·gāil, to take her
as his wife.
40 When the servants of David

had come to Ab′i·gāil at Car′mel, they spoke to her saying, "David sent us to you, to ask you to become his wife."

41 Then she arose, bowed her face to the earth, and said, "Here is your maidservant, a servant to [a]wash the feet of the servants of my lord."

42 So Ab′i·gāil rose in haste and rode on a donkey, [1]attended by five of her maidens; and she followed the messengers of David, and became his wife.

43 David also took A·hin′ō·am [a]of Jez′rē·el, [b]and so both of them were his wives.

44 But Saul had given [a]Mī′chal his daughter, David's wife, to [1]Pal′tī the son of Lā′ish, who *was* from [b]Gal′lim.

26 Now the Ziph′ītes came to Saul at Gib′ē·ah, saying, [a]"Is David not hiding in the hill of Ha·chī′lah, opposite Jē·shī′mon?"

2 Then Saul arose and went down to the Wilderness of Ziph, having [a]three thousand chosen men of Israel with him, to seek David in the Wilderness of Ziph.

3 And Saul encamped in the hill of Ha·chī′lah, which *is* opposite Jē·shī′mon, by the road. But David stayed in the wilderness, and he saw that Saul came after him into the wilderness.

4 David therefore sent out spies, and understood that Saul had indeed come.

5 So David arose and came to the place where Saul had encamped. And David saw the place where Saul lay, and [a]Abner the son of Ner, the commander of his army. Now Saul lay within the camp, with the people encamped all around him.

6 Then David answered, and said to A·him′e·lech the Hit′tīte and to A·bi′shaī [a]the son of Ze·rū′i·ah, brother of [b]Jō′ab, saying, "Who will [c]go down with me to Saul in the camp?" And [d]A·bi′shaī said, "I will go down with you."

7 So David and A·bi′shaī came to the people by night; and there Saul lay sleeping within the camp, with his spear stuck in the ground by his head. And Abner and the people lay all around him.

8 Then A·bi′shaī said to David, [a]"God has delivered your enemy into your hand this day. Now therefore, please, let me strike him [1]at once with the spear, right to the earth; and I will not *have to strike* him a second time!"

9 But David said to A·bi′shaī, "Do not destroy him; [a]for who can stretch out his hand against the LORD's anointed, and be guiltless?"

10 David said furthermore, "*As* the LORD lives, [a]the LORD shall strike him, or [b]his day shall come to die, or he shall [c]go out to battle and perish.

11 [a]"The LORD forbid that I should stretch out my hand against the LORD's anointed. But please, take now the spear and the jug of water that *are* by his head, and let us go."

12 So David took the spear and the jug of water *by* Saul's head, and they got away; and no man saw or knew *it* or awoke. For they *were* all asleep, because [a]a deep sleep from the LORD had fallen on them.

41 [a]Luke 7:38, 44
42 [1]Lit. *with five of her maidens at her feet*
43 [a]Josh. 15:56 [b]1 Sam. 27:3; 30:5
44 [a]2 Sam. 3:14 [b]Is. 10:30 [1]*Paltiel,* 2 Sam. 3:15

CHAPTER 26

1 [a]1 Sam. 23:19
2 [a]1 Sam. 13:2; 24:2
5 [a]1 Sam. 14:50, 51; 17:55
6 [a]1 Chr. 2:16 [b]2 Sam. 2:13 [c]Judg. 7:10, 11 [d]2 Sam. 2:18, 24
8 [a]1 Sam. 24:4 [1]Or *one time*
9 [a]1 Sam. 24:6, 7
10 [a]1 Sam. 25:26, 38 [b][Job 7:1; 14:5] [c]1 Sam. 31:6
11 [a]1 Sam. 24:6–12
12 [a]Gen. 2:21; 15:12

13 Now David went over to the
other side, and stood on the top
of a hill afar off, a great distance
being between them.
14 And David called out to the
people and to Abner the son of
Ner, saying, "Do you not answer,
Abner?" Then Abner answered
and said, "Who *are* you, calling
out to the king?"
15 So David said to Abner, "*Are*
you not a man? And who *is*
like you in Israel? Why then
have you not guarded your lord
the king? For one of the people
came in to destroy your lord the
king.
16 "This thing that you have
done *is* not good. *As* the LORD
lives, you deserve to die, because
you have not guarded your master, the LORD's anointed. And
now see where the king's spear
is, and the jug of water that *was*
by his head."
17 Then Saul knew David's
voice, and said, [a]"*Is* that your
voice, my son David?" David
said, "*It is* my voice, my lord,
O king."
18 And he said, [a]"Why does my
lord thus pursue his servant?
For what have I done, or what
evil *is* in my hand?
19 "Now therefore, please, let
my lord the king hear the words
of his servant: If the LORD has
[a]stirred you up against me, let
Him accept an offering. But if *it
is* the children of men, *may* they
be cursed before the LORD, [b]for
they have driven me out this day
from sharing in the [c]inheritance
of the LORD, saying, 'Go, serve
other gods.'
20 "So now, do not let my blood
fall to the earth before the face
of the LORD. For the king of
Israel has come out to seek [a]a
flea, as when one hunts a partridge in the mountains."
21 Then Saul said, [a]"I have
sinned. Return, my son David.
For I will harm you no more,
because my life was precious
in your eyes this day. Indeed I
have played the fool and erred
exceedingly."
22 And David answered and
said, "Here is the king's spear.
Let one of the young men come
over and get it.
23 [a]"May the LORD [b]repay every
man *for* his righteousness and
his faithfulness; for the LORD
delivered you into *my* hand
today, but I would not stretch
out my hand against the LORD's
anointed.
24 "And indeed, as your life was
valued much this day in my
eyes, so let my life be valued
much in the eyes of the LORD,
and let Him deliver me out of all
tribulation."
25 Then Saul said to David,
"*May* you *be* blessed, my son
David! You shall both do great
things and also still [a]prevail." So
David went on his way, and Saul
returned to his place.

27 And David said in his
heart, "Now I shall per-
ish someday by the hand of
Saul. *There is* nothing better for
me than that I should speedily
escape to the land of the Phi·lis′-
tines; and Saul will [1]despair of
me, to seek me anymore in any
part of Israel. So I shall escape
out of his hand."
2 Then David arose [a]and went
over with the six hundred men
who *were* with him [b]to Ā′chish
the son of Mā′och, king of Gath.
3 So David dwelt with Ā′chish

17 [a]1 Sam. 24:16
18 [a]1 Sam. 24:9, 11–14
19 [a]2 Sam. 16:11; 24:1 [b]Deut. 4:27, 28 [c]2 Sam. 14:16; 20:19
20 [a]1 Sam. 24:14
21 [a]1 Sam. 15:24, 30; 24:17
23 [a]Ps. 7:8; 18:20; 62:12 [b]2 Sam. 22:21
25 [a]Gen. 32:28

CHAPTER 27

1 [1]*despair of searching for*
2 [a]1 Sam. 25:13 [b]1 Sam. 21:10

at Gath, he and his men, each
man with his household, *and*
David [a]with his two wives,
A·hin′ō·am the Jez′rē·el·ī·tess,
and Ab′i·gāil the Car′mel·ī·tess,
Nā′bal's widow.
4 And it was told Saul that
David had fled to Gath; so he
sought him no more.
5 Then David said to Ā′chish,
"If I have now found favor in
your eyes, let them give me a
place in some town in the country, that I may dwell there. For
why should your servant dwell
in the royal city with you?"
6 So Ā′chish gave him Zik′lag
that day. Therefore [a]Zik′lag has
belonged to the kings of Judah
to this day.
7 Now [1]the time that David
[a]dwelt in the country of the
Phi·lis′tines was one full year
and four months.
8 And David and his men went
up and raided [a]the Gesh′ū·rītes,
[b]the [1]Gir′zītes, and the [c]A·mal′-
e·kītes. For those *nations* were
the inhabitants of the land from
[2]of old, [d]as you go to Shūr, even
as far as the land of Egypt.
9 Whenever David [1]attacked
the land, he left neither man nor
woman alive, but took away the
sheep, the oxen, the donkeys,
the camels, and the apparel, and
returned and came to Ā′chish.
10 Then Ā′chish would say,
"Where have you made a raid
today?" And David would say,
"Against the southern *area* of
Judah, or against the southern
area of [a]the Je·rah′mē·el·ītes, or
against the southern *area* of [b]the
Ken′ītes."
11 David would save neither
man nor woman alive, to bring
news to Gath, saying, "Lest they

3 [a]1 Sam. 25:42, 43
6 [a]Josh. 15:31; 19:5
7 [a]1 Sam. 29:3
[1]Lit. *the number of days*
8 [a]Josh. 13:2, 13
[b]Judg. 1:29
[c]Ex. 17:8, 16
[d]Gen. 25:18
[1]Or *Gezrites*
[2]*ancient times*
9 [1]Lit. *struck*
10 [a]1 Chr. 2:9, 25
[b]Judg. 1:16

CHAPTER 28

1 [a]1 Sam. 29:1, 2
3 [a]1 Sam. 25:1
[b]1 Sam. 1:19
[c]Deut. 18:10, 11
4 [a]Josh. 19:18
[b]1 Sam. 31:1
5 [a]Job 18:11
6 [a]1 Sam. 14:37
[b]Num. 12:6
[c]Ex. 28:30
7 [a]1 Chr. 10:13

should inform on us, saying,
'Thus David did.' " And thus
was his behavior all the time
he dwelt in the country of the
Phi·lis′tines.
12 So Ā′chish believed David,
saying, "He has made his people Israel utterly abhor him;
therefore he will be my servant
forever."

28 Now [a]it happened in those
days that the Phi·lis′tines
gathered their armies together
for war, to fight with Israel. And
Ā′chish said to David, "You assuredly know that you will go
out with me to battle, you and
your men."
2 So David said to Ā′chish,
"Surely you know what your
servant can do." And Ā′chish
said to David, "Therefore I will
make you one of my chief guardians forever."
3 Now [a]Samuel had died, and
all Israel had lamented for him
and buried him in [b]Rā′mah, in
his own city. And Saul had put
[c]the mediums and the spiritists
out of the land.
4 Then the Phi·lis′tines gathered together, and came and
encamped at [a]Shū′nem. So Saul
gathered all Israel together, and
they encamped at [b]Gil·bō′a.
5 When Saul saw the army of
the Phi·lis′tines, he was [a]afraid,
and his heart trembled greatly.
6 And when Saul inquired of
the LORD, [a]the LORD did not answer him, either by [b]dreams or
[c]by Ū′rim or by the prophets.
7 Then Saul said to his servants, "Find me a woman who is
a medium, [a]that I may go to her
and inquire of her." And his servants said to him, "In fact, *there*

is a woman who is a medium at
En Dor."
8 So Saul disguised himself
and put on other clothes, and
he went, and two men with him;
and they came to the woman by
night. And [a]he said, "Please conduct a séance for me, and bring
up for me the one I shall name
to you."
9 Then the woman said to him,
"Look, you know what Saul has
done, how he has [a]cut off the
mediums and the spiritists from
the land. Why then do you lay a
snare for my life, to cause me to
die?"
10 And Saul swore to her by the
LORD, saying, "*As* the LORD lives,
no punishment shall come upon
you for this thing."
11 Then the woman said, "Whom
shall I bring up for you?" And he
said, "Bring up Samuel for me."
12 When the woman saw Samuel, she cried out with a loud
voice. And the woman spoke to
Saul, saying, "Why have you deceived me? For you *are* Saul!"
13 And the king said to her,
"Do not be afraid. What did you
see?" And the woman said to
Saul, "I saw [a]a[1] spirit ascending
out of the earth."
14 So he said to her, "What *is*
his form?" And she said, "An old
man is coming up, and he *is* covered with [a]a mantle." And Saul
perceived that it *was* Samuel,
and he stooped with *his* face to
the ground and bowed down.
15 Now Samuel said to Saul,
"Why have you [a]disturbed me by
bringing me up?" And Saul answered, "I am deeply distressed;
for the Phi·lis′tines make war
against me, and [b]God has departed from me and [c]does not

8 [a]Deut. 18:10, 11
9 [a]1 Sam. 28:3
13 [a]Ex. 22:28 [1]Heb. *elohim*
14 [a]1 Sam. 15:27
15 [a]Is. 14:9 [b]1 Sam. 16:14; 18:12 [c]1 Sam. 28:6
17 [a]1 Sam. 15:28 [1]Or *him*, i.e., David
18 [a]1 Chr. 10:13 [b]1 Sam. 15:3–9
19 [a]Job 3:17–19
21 [a]Job 13:14

answer me anymore, neither
by prophets nor by dreams.
Therefore I have called you, that
you may reveal to me what I
should do."
16 Then Samuel said: "So why
do you ask me, seeing the LORD
has departed from you and has
become your enemy?
17 "And the LORD has done for
[1]Himself [a]as He spoke by me.
For the LORD has torn the kingdom out of your hand and given
it to your neighbor, David.
18 [a]"Because you did not obey
the voice of the LORD nor execute
His fierce wrath upon [b]Am′a·lek,
therefore the LORD has done this
thing to you this day.
19 "Moreover the LORD will also
deliver Israel with you into the
hand of the Phi·lis′tines. And tomorrow you and your sons *will*
be with [a]me. The LORD will also
deliver the army of Israel into
the hand of the Phi·lis′tines."
20 Immediately Saul fell full
length on the ground, and was
dreadfully afraid because of the
words of Samuel. And there was
no strength in him, for he had
eaten no food all day or all
night.
21 And the woman came to Saul
and saw that he was severely
troubled, and said to him, "Look,
your maidservant has obeyed
your voice, and I have [a]put my
life in my hands and heeded the
words which you spoke to me.
22 "Now therefore, please, heed
also the voice of your maidservant, and let me set a piece of
bread before you; and eat, that
you may have strength when
you go on *your* way."
23 But he refused and said, "I
will not eat." So his servants,

together with the woman, urged
him; and he heeded their voice.
Then he arose from the ground
and sat on the bed.
24 Now the woman had a fatted calf in the house, and she
hastened to kill it. And she took
flour and kneaded *it*, and baked
unleavened bread from it.
25 So she brought *it* before Saul
and his servants, and they ate.
Then they rose and went away
that night.

CHAPTER 29

29 Then [a]the Phi·lis′tines
gathered together all
their armies [b]at Ā′phek, and the
Israelites encamped by a fountain which *is* in Jez′rē·el.
2 And the [a]lords of the Phi·lis′-
tines [1]passed in review by hundreds and by thousands, but
[b]David and his men passed in
review at the rear with Ā′chish.
3 Then the princes of the
Phi·lis′tines said, "What *are*
these Hebrews *doing here*?" And
Ā′chish said to the princes of
the Phi·lis′tines, "*Is* this not David, the servant of Saul king of
Israel, who has been with me
[a]these days, or these years? And
to this day I have [b]found no fault
in him since he defected *to me*."
4 But the princes of the Phi·lis′-
tines were angry with him; so
the princes of the Phi·lis′tines
said to him, [a]"Make this fellow
return, that he may go back to
the place which you have appointed for him, and do not let
him go down with us to [b]battle,
lest [c]in the battle he become our
adversary. For with what could
he reconcile himself to his master, if not with the heads of these
[d]men?
5 "*Is* this not David, [a]of whom
they sang to one another in
dances, saying:

[b]'Saul has slain his
thousands,
And David his ten
thousands'?"

6 Then Ā′chish called David
and said to him, "Surely, *as* the
LORD lives, you have been upright, and [a]your going out and
your coming in with me in the
army *is* good in my sight. For to
this day [b]I have not found evil in
you since the day of your coming to me. Nevertheless the lords
do not favor you.
7 "Therefore return now, and
go in peace, that you may not
displease the lords of the Phi·lis′-
tines."
8 So David said to Ā′chish,
"But what have I done? And to
this day what have you found in
your servant as long as I have
been with you, that I may not go
and fight against the enemies of
my lord the king?"
9 Then Ā′chish answered and
said to David, "I know that you
are as good in my sight [a]as an
angel of God; nevertheless [b]the
princes of the Phi·lis′tines have
said, 'He shall not go up with us
to the battle.'
10 "Now therefore, rise early in
the morning with your master's
servants [a]who have come with
[1]you. And as soon as you are up
early in the morning and have
light, depart."
11 So David and his men rose
early to depart in the morning, to return to the land of the
Phi·lis′tines. [a]And the Phi·lis′-
tines went up to Jez′rē·el.

CHAPTER 29

1 [a]1 Sam. 28:1 [b]1 Sam. 4:1
2 [a]1 Sam. 6:4; 7:7 [b]1 Sam. 28:1, 2 [1]*passed on in the rear*
3 [a]1 Sam. 27:7 [b]Dan. 6:5
4 [a]1 Sam. 27:6 [b]1 Sam. 14:21 [c]1 Sam. 29:9 [d]1 Chr. 12:19, 20
5 [a]1 Sam. 21:11 [b]1 Sam. 18:7
6 [a]2 Sam. 3:25 [b]1 Sam. 29:3
9 [a]2 Sam. 14:17, 20; 19:27 [b]1 Sam. 29:4
10 [a]1 Chr. 12:19, 22 [1]So with MT, Tg., Vg.; LXX adds *and go to the place which I have selected for you there; and set no bothersome word in your heart, for you are good before me. And rise on your way*
11 [a]2 Sam. 4:4

30 Now it happened, when David and his men came to [a]Zik'lag, on the third day, that the [b]A·mal'e·kītes had invaded the South and Zik'lag, attacked Zik'lag and burned it with fire,

2 and had taken captive the [a]women and those who *were* there, from small to great; they did not kill anyone, but carried *them* away and went their way.

3 So David and his men came to the city, and there it was, burned with fire; and their wives, their sons, and their daughters had been taken captive.

4 Then David and the people who *were* with him lifted up their voices and wept, until they had no more power to weep.

5 And David's two [a]wives, A·hin'ō·am the Jez'rē·el·ī·tess, and Ab'i·gāil the widow of Nā'bal the Car'mel·īte, had been taken captive.

6 Now David was greatly distressed, for [a]the people spoke of stoning him, because the soul of all the people was [1]grieved, every man for his sons and his daughters. [b]But David strengthened himself in the LORD his God.

7 [a]Then David said to A·bī'a·thar the priest, A·him'e·lech's son, "Please bring the ephod here to me." And [b]A·bī'a·thar brought the ephod to David.

8 [a]So David inquired of the LORD, saying, "Shall I pursue this troop? Shall I overtake them?" And He answered him, "Pursue, for you shall surely overtake *them* and without fail recover *all.*"

9 So David went, he and the six hundred men who *were* with him, and came to the Brook Bē'sor, where those stayed who were left behind.

10 But David pursued, he and four hundred men; [a]for two hundred stayed *behind,* who were so weary that they could not cross the Brook Bē'sor.

11 Then they found an Egyptian in the field, and brought him to David; and they gave him bread and he ate, and they let him drink water.

12 And they gave him a piece of [a]a cake of figs and two clusters of raisins. So [b]when he had eaten, his strength came back to him; for he had eaten no bread nor drunk water for three days and three nights.

13 Then David said to him, "To whom do you *belong,* and where *are* you from?" And he said, "I *am* a young man from Egypt, servant of an A·mal'e·kīte; and my master left me behind, because three days ago I fell sick.

14 "We made an invasion of the southern *area* of [a]the Cher'e·thītes, in the *territory* which *belongs* to Judah, and of the southern *area* [b]of Caleb; and we burned Zik'lag with fire."

15 And David said to him, "Can you take me down to this troop?" So he said, "Swear to me by God that you will neither kill me nor deliver me into the hands of my [a]master, and I will take you down to this troop."

16 And when he had brought him down, there they were, spread out over all the land, [a]eating and drinking and dancing, because of all the great spoil which they had taken from the land of the Phi·lis'tines and from the land of Judah.

17 Then David attacked them

CHAPTER 30

1 [a]1 Sam. 27:6 [b]1 Sam. 15:7; 27:8

2 [a]1 Sam. 27:2, 3

5 [a]1 Sam. 25:42, 43

6 [a]Ex. 17:4 [b]Hab. 3:17–19 [1]Lit. *bitter*

7 [a]1 Sam. 23:2–9 [b]1 Sam. 23:6

8 [a]1 Sam. 23:2, 4

10 [a]1 Sam. 30:9, 21

12 [a]1 Sam. 25:18 [b]Judg. 15:19

14 [a]2 Sam. 8:18 [b]Josh. 14:13; 15:13

15 [a]Deut. 23:15

16 [a]1 Thess. 5:3

from twilight until the evening
of the next day. Not a man of
them escaped, except four hundred young men who rode on
camels and fled.
18 So David recovered all that
the A·mal′e·kītes had carried
away, and David rescued his two
wives.
19 And nothing of theirs was
lacking, either small or great,
sons or daughters, spoil or anything which they had taken from
them; [a]David recovered all.
20 Then David took all the
flocks and herds they had driven
before those *other* livestock, and
said, "This *is* David's spoil."
21 Now David came to the [a]two
hundred men who had been so
weary that they could not follow David, whom they also had
made to stay at the Brook Bē′-
sor. So they went out to meet
David and to meet the people
who *were* with him. And when
David came near the people, he
[1]greeted them.
22 Then all the wicked and
[a]worthless[1] men of those who
went with David answered and
said, "Because they did not go
with us, we will not give them
any of the spoil that we have recovered, except for every man's
wife and children, that they may
lead *them* away and depart."
23 But David said, "My brethren, you shall not do so with
what the LORD has given us, who
has preserved us and delivered
into our hand the troop that
came against us.
24 "For who will heed you in
this matter? But [a]as his part *is*
who goes down to the battle, so
shall his part *be* who stays by

19 [a]1 Sam. 30:8
21 [a]1 Sam. 30:10 [1]*asked them concerning their welfare*
22 [a]Deut. 13:13 [1]Lit. *men of Belial*
24 [a]Josh. 22:8
26 [1]*booty*
27 [a]Josh. 19:8 [b]Josh. 15:48; 21:14
28 [a]Josh. 13:16 [b]1 Chr. 27:27 [c]Josh. 15:50
29 [a]1 Sam. 27:10 [b]Judg. 1:16
30 [a]Judg. 1:17 [1]Or *Borashan*
31 [a]2 Sam. 2:1 [b]1 Sam. 23:22

CHAPTER 31

1 [a]1 Chr. 10:1–12 [b]1 Sam. 28:4
2 [a]1 Sam. 14:49
3 [a]2 Sam. 1:6 [1]Lit. *found him*
4 [a]Judg. 9:54

the supplies; they shall share
alike."
25 So it was, from that day forward; he made it a statute and
an ordinance for Israel to this
day.
26 Now when David came to
Zik′lag, he sent *some* of the
[1]spoil to the elders of Judah, to
his friends, saying, "Here is a
present for you from the spoil of
the enemies of the LORD"—
27 to *those* who *were* in Beth′el,
those who *were* in [a]Rā′moth of
the South, *those* who *were* in
[b]Jat′tir,
28 *those* who *were* in [a]A·rō′er,
those who *were* in [b]Siph′moth,
those who *were* in [c]Esh·te·mō′a,
29 *those* who *were* in Rā′chal,
those who *were* in the cities of
[a]the Je·rah′mē·el·ītes, *those* who
were in the cities of the [b]Ken′-
ītes,
30 *those* who *were* in [a]Hor′mah,
those who *were* in [1]Chor·ash′an,
those who *were* in Ā′thach,
31 *those* who *were* in [a]Hē′bron,
and to all the places where David himself and his men were
accustomed to [b]rove.

31

Now [a]the Phi·lis′tines
fought against Israel; and
the men of Israel fled from before the Phi·lis′tines, and fell
slain on Mount [b]Gil·bō′a.
2 Then the Phi·lis′tines followed hard after Saul and his
sons. And the Phi·lis′tines killed
[a]Jonathan, A·bin′a·dab, and
Mal·chī·shū′a, Saul's sons.
3 [a]The battle became fierce
against Saul. The archers
[1]hit him, and he was severely
wounded by the archers.
4 [a]Then Saul said to his armorbearer, "Draw your sword,

and thrust me through with it,
lest [b]these uncircumcised men
come and thrust me through
and [1]abuse me." But his armorbearer would not, [c]for he was
greatly afraid. Therefore Saul
took a sword and [d]fell on it.
5 And when his armorbearer
saw that Saul was dead, he also
fell on his sword, and died with
him.
6 So Saul, his three sons, his
armorbearer, and all his men
died together that same day.
7 And when the men of Israel
who *were* on the other side of
the valley, and *those* who *were*
on the other side of the Jordan,
saw that the men of Israel had
fled and that Saul and his sons
were dead, they forsook the cities and fled; and the Phi·lis′tines
came and dwelt in them.
8 So it happened the next day,
when the Phi·lis′tines came to
strip the slain, that they found
Saul and his three sons fallen on
Mount Gil·bō′a.
9 And they cut off his head
and stripped off his armor, and
sent *word* throughout the land
of the Phi·lis′tines, to [a]proclaim
it in the temple of their idols and
among the people.
10 [a]Then they put his armor in
the temple of the [b]Ash′to·reths,
and [c]they fastened his body to
the wall of [d]Beth[1] Shan.
11 [a]Now when the inhabitants
of Jā′besh Gil′ē·ad heard what
the Phi·lis′tines had done to
Saul,
12 [a]all the valiant men arose
and traveled all night, and took
the body of Saul and the bodies
of his sons from the wall of Beth
Shan; and they came to Jā′besh
and [b]burned them there.
13 Then they took their bones
and [a]buried *them* under the tamarisk tree at Jā′besh, [b]and fasted
seven days.

4 [b]1 Sam. 14:6; 17:26, 36 [c]2 Sam. 1:14 [d]2 Sam. 1:6, 10 [1]*torture*
9 [a]2 Sam. 1:20
10 [a]1 Sam. 21:9 [b]Judg. 2:13 [c]2 Sam. 21:12 [d]Judg. 1:27 [1]*Beth Shean,* Josh. 17:11
11 [a]1 Sam. 11:1–13
12 [a]2 Sam. 2:4–7 [b]2 Chr. 16:14
13 [a]2 Sam. 2:4, 5; 21:12–14 [b]Gen. 50:10

The Second Book of
SAMUEL

THE Book of Second Samuel records the highlights of David's reign, first over the territory of Judah, and finally over the entire nation of Israel. It traces the ascension of David to the throne, his climactic sins of adultery and murder, and the shattering consequences of those sins upon his family and the nation.

See First Samuel for details on the titles of the books of Samuel. The Hebrew title for both books (originally one) is "Samuel." The Greek title for Second Samuel is *Basileion Beta,* "Second Kingdoms." The Latin title is *Liber II Samuelis,* the "Second Book of Samuel," or simply "Second Samuel."

CHAPTER 1

NOW it came to pass after
the [a]death of Saul, when
David had returned from [b]the
slaughter of the A·mal′e·kītes,
and David had stayed two days
in Zik′lag,
2 on the third day, behold, it
happened that [a]a man came from
Saul's camp [b]with his clothes
[1]torn and dust on his head. So
it was, when he came to David,
that he [c]fell to the ground and
prostrated himself.
3 And David said to him,
"Where have you come from?"
So he said to him, "I have escaped from the camp of Israel."
4 Then David said to him,
[a]"How did the matter go? Please
tell me." And he answered, "The
people have fled from the battle,
many of the people are fallen and
dead, and Saul and [b]Jonathan
his son are dead also."
5 So David said to the young
man who told him, "How do you
know that Saul and Jonathan
his son are dead?"
6 Then the young man who
told him said, "As I happened by
chance *to be* on [a]Mount Gil·bō′a,
there was [b]Saul, leaning on his
spear; and indeed the chariots
and horsemen followed hard after him.
7 "Now when he looked behind
him, he saw me and called to me.
And I answered, 'Here I am.'
8 "And he said to me, 'Who *are*
you?' So I answered him, 'I *am*
an A·mal′e·kīte.'
9 "He said to me again, 'Please
stand over me and kill me, for
[1]anguish has come upon me, but
my life still *remains* in me.'
10 "So I stood over him and
[a]killed him, because I was sure
that he could not live after he
had fallen. And I took the crown
that *was* on his head and the
bracelet that *was* on his arm,
and have brought them here to
my lord."
11 Therefore David took hold of
his own clothes and [a]tore them,
and *so did* all the men who *were*
with him.
12 And they [a]mourned and wept
and [b]fasted until evening for
Saul and for Jonathan his son,
for the [c]people of the LORD and
for the house of Israel, because
they had fallen by the sword.
13 Then David said to the young

1 [a]1 Sam. 31:6 [b]1 Sam. 30:1, 17, 26
2 [a]2 Sam. 4:10 [b]1 Sam. 4:12 [c]1 Sam. 25:23 [1]To show grief
4 [a]1 Sam. 4:16; 31:3 [b]1 Sam. 31:2
6 [a]1 Sam. 31:1 [b]1 Sam. 31:2–4
9 [1]*agony*
10 [a]Judg. 9:54
11 [a]2 Sam. 3:31; 13:31
12 [a]2 Sam. 3:31 [b]1 Sam. 31:13 [c]2 Sam. 6:21

man who told him, "Where *are*
you from?" And he answered,
"I *am* the son of an alien, an
A·mal′e·kīte."
14 So David said to him, "How
[a]was it you were not [b]afraid to
[c]put forth your hand to destroy
the LORD's anointed?"
15 Then [a]David called one of
the young men and said, "Go
near, *and* execute him!" And he
struck him so that he died.
16 So David said to him, [a]"Your
blood *is* on your own head, for
[b]your own mouth has testified
against you, saying, 'I have
killed the LORD's anointed.' "
17 Then David lamented with
this lamentation over Saul and
over Jonathan his son,
18 [a]and he told *them* to teach
the children of Judah *the Song
of* the Bow; indeed *it is* written
[b]in the Book [1]of Jā′sher:

19 "The beauty of Israel is slain
on your high places!
[a]How the mighty have fallen!
20 [a]Tell *it* not in Gath,
Proclaim *it* not in the streets
of [b]Ash′ke·lon—
Lest [c]the daughters of the
Phi·lis′tines rejoice,
Lest the daughters of [d]the
uncircumcised triumph.

21 "O [a]mountains of Gil·bō′a,
[b]*Let there be* no dew nor
rain upon you,
Nor fields of offerings.
For the shield of the mighty
is [1]cast away there!
The shield of Saul, not
[c]anointed with oil.
22 From the blood of the slain,
From the fat of the mighty,
[a]The bow of Jonathan did
not turn back,
And the sword of Saul did
not return empty.

23 "Saul and Jonathan *were*
beloved and pleasant in
their lives,
And in their [a]death they
were not divided;
They were swifter than
eagles,
They were [b]stronger than
lions.

24 "O daughters of Israel, weep
over Saul,
Who clothed you in scarlet,
with luxury;
Who put ornaments of gold
on your apparel.

25 "How the mighty have fallen
in the midst of the battle!
Jonathan *was* slain in your
high places.
26 I am distressed for you, my
brother Jonathan;
You have been very pleasant
to me;
[a]Your love to me was
wonderful,
Surpassing the love of
women.

27 "How[a] the mighty have
fallen,
And the weapons of war
perished!"

2 It happened after this that
David [a]inquired of the LORD,
saying, "Shall I go up to any of
the cities of Judah?" And the
LORD said to him, "Go up." David
said, "Where shall I go up?" And
He said, "To [b]Hē′bron."
2 So David went up there, and
his [a]two wives also, A·hin′ō·am
the Jez′rē·el·ī·tess, and Ab′i·gāil

14 [a]Num. 12:8 [b]1 Sam. 31:4 [c]1 Sam. 24:6; 26:9
15 [a]2 Sam. 4:10, 12
16 [a]1 Kin. 2:32–37 [b]Luke 19:22
18 [a]1 Sam. 31:3 [b]Josh. 10:13 [1]Lit. *of the Upright*
19 [a]2 Sam. 1:27
20 [a]Mic. 1:10 [b]Jer. 25:20 [c]Ex. 15:20 [d]1 Sam. 31:4
21 [a]1 Sam. 31:1 [b]Ezek. 31:15 [c]1 Sam. 10:1 [1]Lit. *defiled*
22 [a]1 Sam. 18:4
23 [a]1 Sam. 31:2–4 [b]Judg. 14:18
26 [a]1 Sam. 18:1–4; 19:2; 20:17
27 [a]2 Sam. 1:19, 25

CHAPTER 2

1 [a]Judg. 1:1 [b]1 Sam. 30:31
2 [a]1 Sam. 25:42, 43; 30:5

the widow of Nā′bal the Car′-
mel·īte.
3 And David brought up [a]the
men who *were* with him, every
man with his household. So they
dwelt in the cities of Hē′bron.
4 [a]Then the men of Judah
came, and there they [b]anointed
David king over the house of Judah. And they told David, saying,
[c]"The men of Jā′besh Gil′ē·ad
were the ones who buried Saul."
5 So David sent messengers to
the men of Jā′besh Gil′ē·ad, and
said to them, [a]"You *are* blessed
of the LORD, for you have shown
this kindness to your lord, to
Saul, and have buried him.
6 "And now may [a]the LORD
show kindness and truth to you.
I also will repay you this kindness, because you have done
this thing.
7 "Now therefore, let your
hands be strengthened, and be
valiant; for your master Saul is
dead, and also the house of Judah has anointed me king over
them."
8 But [a]Abner the son of Ner,
commander of Saul's army, took
[1]Ish·bō′sheth the son of Saul
and brought him over to [b]Mā·ha-
na′im;
9 and he made him king over
[a]Gil′ē·ad, over the [b]Ash′ur·ītes,
over [c]Jez′rē·el, over Ē′phra·im,
over Benjamin, and over all
Israel.
10 Ish·bō′sheth, Saul's son, *was*
forty years old when he began to
reign over Israel, and he reigned
two years. Only the house of Judah followed David.
11 And [a]the [1]time that David
was king in Hē′bron over the
house of Judah was seven years
and six months.

3 [a]1 Chr. 12:1
4 [a]1 Sam. 30:26 [b]1 Sam. 16:13 [c]1 Sam. 31:11–13
5 [a]Ruth 2:20; 3:10
6 [a]2 Tim. 1:16, 18
8 [a]1 Sam. 14:50 [b]2 Sam. 17:24 [1]*Esh-Baal*, 1 Chr. 8:33; 9:39
9 [a]Josh. 22:9 [b]Judg. 1:32 [c]1 Sam. 29:1
11 [a]2 Sam. 5:5 [1]Lit. *number of days*
12 [a]Josh. 10:2–12; 18:25
13 [a]1 Chr. 2:16; 11:6 [b]Jer. 41:12
16 [1]Heb. *Helkath Hazzurim*
18 [a]1 Chr. 2:16 [b]1 Chr. 12:8 [c]Ps. 18:33

12 Now Abner the son of Ner,
and the servants of Ish·bō′sheth
the son of Saul, went out from
Mā·ha·na′im to [a]Gib′ē·on.
13 And [a]Jō′ab the son of Ze·rū′-
i·ah, and the servants of David,
went out and met them by [b]the
pool of Gib′ē·on. So they sat
down, one on one side of the
pool and the other on the other
side of the pool.
14 Then Abner said to Jō′ab,
"Let the young men now arise
and compete before us." And
Jō′ab said, "Let them arise."
15 So they arose and went over
by number, twelve from Benjamin, *followers* of Ish·bō′sheth
the son of Saul, and twelve from
the servants of David.
16 And each one grasped his
opponent by the head and
thrust his sword in his opponent's side; so they fell down
together. Therefore that place
was called [1]the Field of Sharp
Swords, which *is* in Gib′ē·on.
17 So there was a very fierce
battle that day, and Abner and
the men of Israel were beaten
before the servants of David.
18 Now the [a]three sons of
Ze·rū′i·ah were there: Jō′ab and
A·bi′shaī and As′a·hel. And As′-
a·hel *was* [b]*as* fleet of foot [c]as a
wild gazelle.
19 So As′a·hel pursued Abner,
and in going he did not turn to
the right hand or to the left from
following Abner.
20 Then Abner looked behind
him and said, "*Are* you As′-
a·hel?" He answered, "I *am*."
21 And Abner said to him, "Turn
aside to your right hand or to
your left, and lay hold on one
of the young men and take his
armor for yourself." But As′a·hel

would not turn aside from following him.

22 So Abner said again to As′a·hel, "Turn aside from following me. Why should I strike you to the ground? How then could I face your brother Jō′ab?"

23 However, he refused to turn aside. Therefore Abner struck him [a]in the stomach with the blunt end of the spear, so that the spear came out of his back; and he fell down there and died on the spot. So it was *that* as many as came to the place where As′a·hel fell down and died, stood [b]still.

24 Jō′ab and A·bi′shaī also pursued Abner. And the sun was going down when they came to the hill of Am′mah, which *is* before Gī′ah by the road to the Wilderness of Gib′ē·on.

25 Now the children of Benjamin gathered together behind Abner and became [1]a unit, and took their stand on top of a hill.

26 Then Abner called to Jō′ab and said, "Shall the sword devour forever? Do you not know that it will be bitter in the latter end? How long will it be then until you tell the people to return from pursuing their brethren?"

27 And Jō′ab said, "*As* God lives, [1]unless [a]you had spoken, surely then by morning all the people would have given up pursuing their brethren."

28 So Jō′ab blew a trumpet; and all the people stood still and did not pursue Israel anymore, nor did they fight anymore.

29 Then Abner and his men went on all that night through the plain, crossed over the Jordan, and went through all Bith′ron; and they came to Mā·ha·na′im.

30 So Jō′ab returned from pursuing Abner. And when he had gathered all the people together, there were missing of David's servants nineteen men and As′a·hel.

31 But the servants of David had struck down, of Benjamin and Abner's men, three hundred and sixty men who died.

32 Then they took up As′a·hel and buried him in his father's tomb, which *was in* [a]Bethlehem. And Jō′ab and his men went all night, and they came to Hē′bron at daybreak.

CHAPTER 3

3 Now there was a long [a]war between the house of Saul and the house of David. But David grew stronger and stronger, and the house of Saul grew weaker and weaker.

2 Sons were born [a]to David in Hē′bron: His firstborn was Am′non [b]by A·hin′ō·am the Jez′rē·el·ī·tess;

3 his second, [1]Chil′ē·ab, by Ab′i·gāil the widow of Nā′bal the Car′mel·īte; the third, [a]Ab′sa·lom the son of Mā′a·cah, the daughter of Tal′maī, king [b]of Gē′shur;

4 the fourth, [a]Ad·o·nī′jah the son of Hag′gith; the fifth, Sheph·a·tī′ah the son of A·bī′tal;

5 and the sixth, Ith′rē·am, by David's wife Eg′lah. These were born to David in Hē′bron.

6 Now it was so, while there was war between the house of Saul and the house of David, that Abner was strengthening *his hold* on the house of Saul.

7 And Saul had a concubine, whose name *was* [a]Riz′pah, the daughter of Ā′i·ah. So *Ish·bō′sheth* said to Abner, "Why have you [b]gone in to my father's concubine?"

23 [a]2 Sam. 3:27; 4:6; 20:10 [b]2 Sam. 20:12
25 [1]*one band*
27 [a]2 Sam. 2:14 [1]*if you had not spoken*
32 [a]1 Sam. 20:6
CHAPTER 3
1 [a]1 Kin. 14:30
2 [a]1 Chr. 3:1–4 [b]1 Sam. 25:42, 43
3 [a]2 Sam. 15:1–10 [b]Josh. 13:13 [1]*Daniel*, 1 Chr. 3:1
4 [a]1 Kin. 1:5
7 [a]2 Sam. 21:8–11 [b]2 Sam. 16:21

8 Then Abner became very angry at the words of Ish·bō′sheth, and said, "*Am* I [a]a dog's head that belongs to Judah? Today I show loyalty to the house of Saul your father, to his brothers, and to his friends, and have not delivered you into the hand of David; and you charge me today with a fault concerning this woman?

9 [a]"May God do so to Abner, and more also, if I do not do for David [b]as the LORD has sworn to him—

10 "to transfer the kingdom from the [1]house of Saul, and set up the throne of David over Israel and over Judah, [a]from Dan to Bē·er·shē′ba."

11 And he could not answer Abner another word, because he feared him.

12 Then Abner sent messengers on his behalf to David, saying, "Whose *is* the land?" saying *also*, "Make your covenant with me, and indeed my hand *shall be* with you to bring all Israel to you."

13 And *David* said, "Good, I will make a covenant with you. But one thing I require of you: [a]you shall not see my face unless you first bring [b]Mī′chal, Saul's daughter, when you come to see my face."

14 So David sent messengers to [a]Ish·bō′sheth, Saul's son, saying, "Give *me* my wife Mī′chal, whom I betrothed to myself [b]for a hundred foreskins of the Phi·lis′tines."

15 And Ish·bō′sheth sent and took her from *her* husband, from [1]Pal′ti·el the son of Lā′ish.

16 Then her husband went along with her to [a]Ba·hū′rim, [1]weeping behind her. So Abner said to him, "Go, return!" And he returned.

17 Now Abner had communicated with the elders of Israel, saying, "In time past you were seeking for David *to be* king over you.

18 "Now then, do *it!* [a]For the LORD has spoken of David, saying, 'By the hand of My servant David, [1]I will save My people Israel from the hand of the Phi·lis′tines and the hand of all their enemies.' "

19 And Abner also spoke in the hearing of [a]Benjamin. Then Abner also went to speak in the hearing of David in Hē′bron all that seemed good to Israel and the whole house of Benjamin.

20 So Abner and twenty men with him came to David at Hē′bron. And David made a feast for Abner and the men who *were* with him.

21 Then Abner said to David, "I will arise and go, and [a]gather all Israel to my lord the king, that they may make a covenant with you, and that you may [b]reign over all that your heart desires." So David sent Abner away, and he went in peace.

22 At that moment the servants of David and Jō′ab came from a raid and brought much [1]spoil with them. But Abner *was* not with David in Hē′bron, for he had sent him away, and he had gone in peace.

23 When Jō′ab and all the troops that *were* with him had come, they told Jō′ab, saying, "Abner the son of Ner came to the king, and he sent him away, and he has gone in peace."

24 Then Jō′ab came to the king and said, "What have you done?

8 [a]1 Sam. 24:14
9 [a]1 Kin. 19:2 [b]1 Chr. 12:23
10 [a]1 Sam. 3:20 [1]*family*
13 [a]Gen. 43:3 [b]1 Sam. 18:20; 19:11; 25:44
14 [a]2 Sam. 2:10 [b]1 Sam. 18:25–27
15 [1]*Palti,* 1 Sam. 25:44
16 [a]2 Sam. 16:5; 19:16 [1]Lit. *going and weeping*
18 [a]2 Sam. 3:9 [1]So with many Heb. mss., LXX, Syr., Tg.; MT *he*
19 [a]1 Chr. 12:29
21 [a]2 Sam. 3:10, 12 [b]1 Kin. 11:37
22 [1]*booty*

Look, Abner came to you; why
is it *that* you sent him away, and
he has already gone?
25 "Surely you realize that Abner the son of Ner came to deceive you, to know [a]your going
out and your coming in, and to
know all that you are doing."
26 And when Jō′ab had gone
from David's presence, he sent
messengers after Abner, who
brought him back from the well
of Sī′rah. But David did not
know *it*.
27 Now when Abner had re-
turned to Hē′bron, Jō′ab [a]took
him aside in the gate to speak
with him privately, and there
[1]stabbed him [b]in the stomach,
so that he died for the blood of
[c]As′a·hel his brother.
28 Afterward, when David
heard *it*, he said, "My kingdom
and I *are* [1]guiltless before the
LORD forever of the blood of Abner the son of Ner.
29 [a]"Let it rest on the head of
Jō′ab and on all his father's
house; and let there never fail
to be in the [1]house of Jō′ab one
[b]who has a discharge or is a
leper, who leans on a staff or
falls by the sword, or who lacks
bread."
30 So Jō′ab and A·bi′shaī his
brother killed Abner, because
he had killed their brother [a]As′-
a·hel at Gib′ē·on in the battle.
31 Then David said to Jō′ab and
to all the people who were with
him, [a]"Tear your clothes, [b]gird
yourselves with sackcloth, and
mourn for Abner." And King David followed the coffin.
32 So they buried Abner in Hē′-
bron; and the king lifted up his
voice and wept at the grave of
Abner, and all the people wept.
33 And the king sang *a lament*
over Abner and said:

"Should Abner die as a [a]fool
dies?
34 Your hands were not bound
Nor your feet put into
fetters;
As a man falls before
wicked men, *so* you fell."

Then all the people wept over
him again.
35 And when all the people
came [a]to persuade David to eat
food while it was still day, David
took an oath, saying, [b]"God do
so to me, and more also, if I taste
bread or anything else [c]till the
sun goes down!"
36 Now all the people took note
of it, and it pleased them, since
whatever the king did pleased
all the people.
37 For all the people and all
Israel understood that day that
it had not been the king's *intent*
to kill Abner the son of Ner.
38 Then the king said to his
servants, "Do you not know that
a prince and a great man has
fallen this day in Israel?
39 "And I *am* weak today,
though anointed king; and these
men, the sons of Ze·rū′i·ah, [a]*are*
too harsh for me. [b]The LORD
shall repay the evildoer according to his wickedness."

4 When Saul's [1]son heard that
Abner had died in Hē′bron,
[a]he[2] lost heart, and all Israel was
[b]troubled.
2 Now Saul's son *had* two men
who were captains of troops.
The name of one *was* Bā′a·nah
and the name of the other Rē′-
chab, the sons of Rim′mon the
Be·er′oth·īte, of the children of

25 [a]1 Sam. 29:6
27 [a]1 Kin. 2:5 [b]2 Sam. 4:6 [c]2 Sam. 2:23 [1]Lit. *struck*
28 [1]*innocent*
29 [a]1 Kin. 2:32, 33 [b]Lev. 15:2 [1]*family*
30 [a]2 Sam. 2:23
31 [a]Josh. 7:6 [b]Gen. 37:34
33 [a]2 Sam. 13:12, 13
35 [a]2 Sam. 12:17 [b]Ruth 1:17 [c]2 Sam. 1:12
39 [a]2 Sam. 19:5–7 [b]1 Kin. 2:5, 6, 32–34

CHAPTER 4

1 [a]Ezra 4:4 [b]Matt. 2:3 [1]Ishbosheth [2]Lit. *his hands dropped*

Benjamin. (For [a]Be·er′oth also
was [1]*part* of Benjamin,
3 because the Be·er′oth·ītes
fled to [a]Git′ta·im and have been
sojourners there until this day.)
4 [a]Jonathan, Saul's son, had
a son *who was* lame in *his* feet.
He was five years old when the
news about Saul and Jonathan
came [b]from Jez′rē·el; and his
nurse took him up and fled. And
it happened, as she made haste
to flee, that he fell and became
lame. His name *was* [c]Me·phib′-
o·sheth.[1]
5 Then the sons of Rim′mon
the Be·er′oth·īte, Rē′chab and
Bā′a·nah, set out and came at
about the heat of the day to the
[a]house of Ish·bō′sheth, who was
lying on his bed at noon.
6 And they came there, all the
way into the house, *as though*
to get wheat, and they [1]stabbed
him [a]in the stomach. Then Rē′-
chab and Bā′a·nah his brother
escaped.
7 For when they came into the
house, he was lying on his bed
in his bedroom; then they struck
him and killed him, beheaded
him and took his head, and were
all night escaping through the
plain.
8 And they brought the head
of Ish·bō′sheth to David at Hē′-
bron, and said to the king, "Here
is the head of Ish·bō′sheth,
the son of Saul your enemy,
[a]who sought your life; and the
LORD has avenged my lord the
king this day of Saul and his
descendants."
9 But David answered Rē′-
chab and Bā′a·nah his brother,
the sons of Rim′mon the Be·er′-
oth·īte, and said to them, "*As* the
LORD lives, [a]who has redeemed
my life from all adversity,
10 "when [a]someone told me,
saying, 'Look, Saul is dead,'
thinking to have brought good
news, I arrested him and had
him executed in Zik′lag—the
one who *thought* I would give
him a reward for *his* news.
11 "How much more, when
wicked men have killed a righteous person in his own house
on his bed? Therefore, shall I not
now [a]require his [1]blood at your
hand and [2]remove you from the
earth?"
12 So David [a]commanded his
young men, and they executed
them, cut off their hands and
feet, and hanged *them* by the
pool in Hē′bron. But they took
the head of Ish·bō′sheth and
buried *it* in the [b]tomb of Abner
in Hē′bron.

5

Then all the tribes of Israel
[a]came to David at Hē′bron
and spoke, saying, "Indeed [b]we
are your bone and your flesh.
2 "Also, in time past, when
Saul was king over us, [a]you were
the one who led Israel out and
brought them in; and the LORD
said to you, [b]'You shall shepherd
My people Israel, and be ruler
over Israel.' "
3 [a]Therefore all the elders of
Israel came to the king at Hē′-
bron, [b]and King David made
a covenant with them at Hē′-
bron [c]before the LORD. And they
anointed David king over Israel.
4 David *was* [a]thirty years old
when he began to reign, *and* [b]he
reigned forty years.
5 In Hē′bron he reigned over
Judah [a]seven years and six
months, and in Jerusalem he

2 [a]Josh. 18:25 [1]*considered part of*
3 [a]Neh. 11:33
4 [a]2 Sam. 9:3 [b]1 Sam. 29:1, 11 [c]2 Sam. 9:6 [1]*Merib-Baal*, 1 Chr. 8:34; 9:40
5 [a]2 Sam. 2:8, 9
6 [a]2 Sam. 2:23; 20:10 [1]Lit. *struck*
8 [a]1 Sam. 19:2, 10, 11; 23:15; 25:29
9 [a]Gen. 48:16
10 [a]2 Sam. 1:2–16
11 [a][Gen. 9:5, 6] [1]Or *bloodshed* [2]Lit. *consume you*
12 [a]2 Sam. 1:15 [b]2 Sam. 3:32

CHAPTER 5

1 [a]1 Chr. 11:1–3 [b]2 Sam. 19:12, 13
2 [a]1 Sam. 18:5, 13, 16 [b]1 Sam. 16:1
3 [a]2 Sam. 3:17 [b]2 Kin. 11:17 [c]1 Sam. 23:18
4 [a]Gen. 41:46 [b]1 Chr. 26:31; 29:27
5 [a]2 Sam. 2:11

reigned thirty-three years over
all Israel and Judah.
6 [a]And the king and his men
went to Jerusalem against [b]the
Jeb′ū·sītes, the inhabitants of
the land, who spoke to David,
saying, "You shall not come in
here; but the blind and the lame
will repel you," thinking, "David
cannot come in here."
7 Nevertheless David took the
stronghold of Zion [a](that *is*, the
City of David).
8 Now David said on that day,
"Whoever climbs up by way of
the water shaft and defeats the
Jeb′ū·sītes (the lame and the
blind, *who are* hated by David's
soul), [a]*he shall be chief and captain.*" Therefore they say, "The
blind and the lame shall not
come into the house."
9 Then David dwelt in the
stronghold, and called it [a]the
City of David. And David built
all around from [1]the Mil′lō and
inward.
10 So David went on and became great, and [a]the LORD God
of hosts *was* with [b]him.
11 Then [a]Hī′ram [b]king of Tȳre
sent messengers to David, and
cedar trees, and carpenters and
masons. And they built David a
house.
12 So David knew that the LORD
had established him as king over
Israel, and that He had [a]exalted
His kingdom [b]for the sake of His
people Israel.
13 And [a]David took more concubines and wives from Jerusalem, after he had come from
Hē′bron. Also more sons and
daughters were born to David.
14 Now [a]these *are* the names
of those who were born to him
in Jerusalem: [1]Sham′mū·a, Shō′-
bab, Nathan, [b]Solomon,
15 Ib′har, [1]E·lish′ū·a, Nē′pheg,
Ja·phī′a,
16 E·lish′a·ma, E·lī′a·da, and
E·liph′e·let.
17 [a]Now when the Phi·lis′tines
heard that they had anointed
David king over Israel, all the
Phi·lis′tines went up to search
for David. And David heard *of*
it [b]and went down to the stronghold.
18 The Phi·lis′tines also went
and deployed themselves in [a]the
Valley of Reph′a·im.
19 So David [a]inquired of the
LORD, saying, "Shall I go up
against the Phi·lis′tines? Will
You deliver them into my hand?"
And the LORD said to David, "Go
up, for I will doubtless deliver
the Phi·lis′tines into your hand."
20 So David went to [a]Bā′al
Pe·rā′zim, and David defeated
them there; and he said, "The
LORD has broken through my
enemies before me, like a breakthrough of water." Therefore he
called the name of that place
[1]Bā′al Pe·rā′zim.
21 And they left their [1]images
there, and David and his men
[a]carried them away.
22 [a]Then the Phi·lis′tines went
up once again and deployed
themselves in the Valley of
Reph′a·im.
23 Therefore [a]David inquired of
the LORD, and He said, "You shall
not go up; circle around behind
them, and come upon them in
front of the mulberry trees.
24 "And it shall be, when you
[a]hear the sound of marching in
the tops of the mulberry trees,
then you shall advance quickly.
For then [b]the LORD will go out

6 [a]Judg. 1:21 [b]Josh. 15:63
7 [a]1 Kin. 2:10; 8:1; 9:24
8 [a]1 Chr. 11:6–9
9 [a]2 Sam. 5:7 [1]Lit. *The Landfill*
10 [a]1 Sam. 17:45 [b]1 Sam. 18:12, 28
11 [a]1 Kin. 5:1–18 [b]1 Chr. 14:1
12 [a]Num. 24:7 [b]Is. 45:4
13 [a][Deut. 17:17]
14 [a]1 Chr. 3:5–8 [b]2 Sam. 12:24 [1]*Shimea,* 1 Chr. 3:5
15 [1]*Elishama,* 1 Chr. 3:6
17 [a]1 Chr. 11:16 [b]2 Sam. 23:14
18 [a]1 Chr. 11:15
19 [a]1 Sam. 23:2
20 [a]Is. 28:21 [1]Lit. *Master of Breakthroughs*
21 [a]Deut. 7:5, 25 [1]*idols*
22 [a]1 Chr. 14:13
23 [a]2 Sam. 5:19
24 [a]1 Chr. 14:15 [b]Judg. 4:14

before you to strike the camp of the Phi·lis′tines."

25 And David did so, as the LORD commanded him; and he drove back the Phi·lis′tines from [a]Gē′ba[1] as far as [b]Gē′zer.

6

Again David gathered all *the* choice *men* of Israel, thirty thousand.

2 And [a]David arose and went with all the people who *were* with him from [1]Bā′a·lē Judah to bring up from there the ark of God, whose name is called [2]by the Name, the LORD of Hosts, [b]who dwells *between* the cherubim.

3 So they set the ark of God on a new cart, and brought it out of the house of A·bin′a·dab, which *was* on [a]the hill; and Uz′zah and A·hī′ō, the sons of A·bin′a·dab, drove the new [1]cart.

4 And they brought it out of [a]the house of A·bin′a·dab, which *was* on the hill, accompanying the ark of God; and A·hī′ō went before the ark.

5 Then David and all the house of Israel [a]played *music* before the LORD on all kinds of *instruments of* fir wood, on harps, on stringed instruments, on tambourines, on sistrums, and on cymbals.

6 And when they came to [a]Nā′chon's threshing floor, Uz′zah put out *his* [b]*hand* to the ark of God and [1]took hold of it, for the oxen stumbled.

7 Then the anger of the LORD was aroused against Uz′zah, and God struck him there for *his* [1]error; and he died there by the ark of God.

8 And David became angry because of the LORD's outbreak against Uz′zah; and he called the name of the place [1]Per′ez Uz′zah to this day.

9 [a]David was afraid of the LORD that day; and he said, "How can the ark of the LORD come to me?"

10 So David would not move the ark of the LORD with him into the [a]City of David; but David took it aside into the house of Ō′bed-Ē′dom the [b]Git′tīte.

11 [a]The ark of the LORD remained in the house of Ō′bed-Ē′dom the Git′tīte three months. And the LORD [b]blessed Ō′bed-Ē′dom and all his household.

12 Now it was told King David, saying, "The LORD has blessed the house of Ō′bed-Ē′dom and all that *belongs* to him, because of the ark of God." [a]So David went and brought up the ark of God from the house of Ō′bed-Ē′dom to the City of David with gladness.

13 And so it was, when [a]those bearing the ark of the LORD had gone six paces, that he sacrificed [b]oxen and fatted sheep.

14 Then David [a]danced[1] before the LORD with all *his* might; and David *was* wearing [b]a linen ephod.

15 [a]So David and all the house of Israel brought up the ark of the LORD with shouting and with the sound of the trumpet.

16 Now as the ark of the LORD came into the City of David, [a]Mī′chal, Saul's daughter, looked through a window and saw King David leaping and whirling before the LORD; and she despised him in her heart.

17 So [a]they brought the ark of the LORD, and set it in [b]its place in the midst of the tabernacle that David had erected for it.

25 [a]1 Chr. 14:16 [b]Josh. 16:10 [1]So with MT, Tg., Vg.; LXX *Gibeon*

CHAPTER 6

2 [a]1 Chr. 13:5, 6 [b]Ps. 80:1 [1]*Baalah, Kirjath Jearim,* Josh. 15:9; 1 Chr. 13:6 [2]LXX, Tg., Vg. omit *by the Name;* many Heb. mss., Syr. *there*

3 [a]1 Sam. 26:1 [1]LXX adds *with the ark*

4 [a]1 Sam. 7:1

5 [a]1 Sam. 18:6, 7

6 [a]1 Chr. 13:9 [b]Num. 4:15, 19, 20 [1]*held it*

7 [1]Or *irreverence*

8 [1]Lit. *Outburst Against Uzzah*

9 [a]Ps. 119:120

10 [a]2 Sam. 5:7 [b]1 Chr. 13:13; 26:4–8

11 [a]1 Chr. 13:14 [b]Gen. 30:27; 39:5

12 [a]1 Chr. 15:25—16:3

13 [a]Josh. 3:3 [b]1 Kin. 8:5

14 [a]Ps. 30:11; 149:3 [b]1 Sam. 2:18, 28 [1]*whirled about*

15 [a]1 Chr. 15:28

16 [a]2 Sam. 3:14

17 [a]1 Chr. 16:1 [b]1 Chr. 15:1

Then David [c]offered burnt offerings and peace offerings before the LORD.

18 And when David had finished offering burnt offerings and peace offerings, [a]he blessed the people in the name of the LORD of hosts.

19 [a]Then he distributed among all the people, among the whole multitude of Israel, both the women and the men, to everyone a loaf of bread, a piece *of meat,* and a cake of raisins. So all the people departed, everyone to his house.

20 [a]Then David returned to bless his household. And Mī'chal the daughter of Saul came out to meet David, and said, "How glorious was the king of Israel today, [b]uncovering himself today in the eyes of the maids of his servants, as one of the [c]base fellows [1]shamelessly uncovers himself!"

21 So David said to Mī'chal, "*It was* before the LORD, [a]who chose me instead of your father and all his house, to appoint me ruler over the [b]people of the LORD, over Israel. Therefore I will play *music* before the LORD.

22 "And I will be even more undignified than this, and will be humble in my own sight. But as for the maidservants of whom you have spoken, by them I will be held in honor."

23 Therefore Mī'chal the daughter of Saul had no children [a]to the day of her death.

7 Now it came to pass [a]when the king was dwelling in his house, and the LORD had given him rest from all his enemies all around,

2 that the king said to Nathan the prophet, "See now, I dwell in [a]a house of cedar, [b]but the ark of God dwells inside tent [c]curtains."

3 Then Nathan said to the king, "Go, do all that *is* in your [a]heart, for the LORD *is* with you."

4 But it happened that night that the word of the LORD came to Nathan, saying,

5 "Go and tell My servant David, 'Thus says the LORD: [a]"Would you build a house for Me to dwell in?

6 "For I have not dwelt in a house [a]since the time that I brought the children of Israel up from Egypt, even to this day, but have moved about in [b]a tent and in a tabernacle.

7 "Wherever I have [a]moved about with all the children of Israel, have I ever spoken a word to anyone from the tribes of Israel, whom I commanded [b]to shepherd My people Israel, saying, 'Why have you not built Me a house of cedar?' " '

8 "Now therefore, thus shall you say to My servant David, 'Thus says the LORD of hosts: [a]"I took you from the sheepfold, from following the sheep, to be ruler over My people, over Israel.

9 "And [a]I have been with you wherever you have gone, [b]and have [1]cut off all your enemies from before you, and have made you a great name, like the name of the great men who *are* on the earth.

10 "Moreover I will appoint a place for My people Israel, and will [a]plant them, that they may dwell in a place of their own and move no more; [b]nor shall

17 [c]1 Kin. 8:5, 62, 63
18 [a]1 Kin. 8:14, 15, 55
19 [a]1 Chr. 16:3
20 [a]Ps. 30:title [b]2 Sam. 6:14, 16 [c]Judg. 9:4 [1]*openly*
21 [a]1 Sam. 13:14; 15:28 [b]2 Kin. 11:17
23 [a]Is. 22:14

CHAPTER 7

1 [a]1 Chr. 17:1–27
2 [a]2 Sam. 5:11 [b]Acts 7:46 [c]Ex. 26:1
3 [a]1 Kin. 8:17, 18
5 [a]1 Kin. 5:3, 4; 8:19
6 [a]1 Kin. 8:16 [b]Ex. 40:18, 34
7 [a]Lev. 26:11, 12 [b]2 Sam. 5:2
8 [a]1 Sam. 16:11, 12
9 [a]2 Sam. 5:10 [b]1 Sam. 31:6 [1]*destroyed*
10 [a]Ps. 44:2; 80:8 [b]Ps. 89:22, 23

the sons of wickedness oppress
them anymore, as previously,
11 [a]"since the time that I commanded judges *to be* over My
people Israel, and have caused
you to rest from all your enemies.
Also the LORD [1]tells you [b]that He
will make you a [2]house.
☆ **12** [a]"When your days are fulfilled and you [b]rest with your
fathers, [c]I will set up your seed
after you, who will come from
your body, and I will establish
his kingdom.
☆ 13 [a]"He shall build a house for
My name, and I will [b]establish
the throne of his kingdom
forever.
14 [a]"I will be his Father, and he
shall be [b]My son. If he commits
iniquity, I will chasten him with
the rod of men and with the
[1]blows of the sons of men.
15 "But My mercy shall not depart from him, [a]as I took *it* from
Saul, whom I removed from before you.
16 "And [a]your house and your
kingdom shall be established
forever before [1]you. Your throne
shall be established forever." ' "
17 According to all these words
and according to all this vision,
so Nathan spoke to David.
18 Then King David went in
and sat before the LORD; and he
said: [a]"Who *am* I, O Lord GOD?
And what is my house, that You
have brought me this far?
19 "And yet this was a small
thing in Your sight, O Lord GOD;
and You have also spoken of
Your servant's house for a great
while to come. [a]*Is* this the manner of man, O Lord GOD?
20 "Now what more can David
say to You? For You, Lord GOD,
[a]know Your servant.
21 "For Your word's sake, and
according to Your own heart,
You have done all these great
things, to make Your servant
know *them.*
22 "Therefore [a]You are great,
[1]O Lord GOD. For [b]*there is* none
like You, nor *is there any* God
besides You, according to all that
we have heard with our [c]ears.
23 "And who *is* like Your people,
like Israel, [a]the one nation on
the earth whom God went to redeem for Himself as a people, to
make for Himself a name—and
to do for Yourself great and awesome deeds for Your land—before [b]Your people whom You redeemed for Yourself from Egypt,
the nations, and their gods?
24 "For [a]You have made Your
people Israel Your very own people forever; [b]and You, LORD, have
become their God.
25 "Now, O LORD God, the word
which You have spoken concerning Your servant and concerning
his house, establish *it* forever
and do as You have said.
26 "So let Your name be magnified forever, saying, 'The LORD of
hosts *is* the God over Israel.' And
let the house of Your servant David be established before You.
27 "For You, O LORD of hosts,
God of Israel, have revealed *this*
to Your servant, saying, 'I will
build you a house.' Therefore
Your servant has found it in his
heart to pray this prayer to You.
28 "And now, O Lord GOD, You
are God, and [a]Your words are
true, and You have promised this
goodness to Your servant.
29 "Now therefore, let it please
You to bless the house of Your
servant, that it may continue
before You forever; for You,

11 [a]Judg. 2:14–16 [b]2 Sam. 7:27 [1]*declares to you* [2]Royal dynasty
12 [a]1 Kin. 2:1 [b]Deut. 31:16 [c]Ps. 132:11; Matt. 1:6; 19:28; 25:31; Luke 3:31
13 [a]1 Kin. 5:5; 8:19 [b][Is. 9:7; 49:8]; Matt. 19:28; 25:31
14 [a][Heb. 1:5] [b][Ps. 2:7; 89:26, 27, 30] [1]*strokes*
15 [a]1 Sam. 15:23, 28; 16:14
16 [a]2 Sam. 7:13 [1]LXX *Me*
18 [a]Ex. 3:11
19 [a][Is. 55:8, 9]
20 [a]John 21:17
22 [a]Deut. 10:17 [b]Ex. 15:11 [c]Ex. 10:2 [1]Tg., Syr. *O LORD God*
23 [a]Ps. 147:20 [b]Deut. 9:26; 33:29
24 [a][Deut. 26:18] [b]Ps. 48:14
28 [a]John 17:17

O Lord GOD, have spoken *it*,
and with Your blessing let the
house of Your servant be blessed
[a]forever."

8 After this it came to pass that
David [1]attacked the Phi·lis'-
tines and subdued them. And
David took [2]Meth'eg Am'mah
from the hand of the Phi·lis'-
tines.
2 Then [a]he defeated Mō'ab.
Forcing them down to the
ground, he measured them
off with a line. With two lines
he measured off those to be
put to death, and with one full
line those to be kept alive. So
the Mō'ab·ītes became David's
[b]servants, *and* [c]brought tribute.
3 David also defeated
Had·a·dē'zer the son of Rē'hob,
king of [a]Zō'bah, as he went to
recover [b]his territory at the River
Eū·phrā'tēs.
4 David took from him one
thousand *chariots,* [1]seven hundred horsemen, and twenty
thousand foot soldiers. Also David [a]hamstrung all the chariot
horses, except that he spared
enough of them for one hundred
chariots.
5 [a]When the Syrians of Damascus came to help Had·a·dē'-
zer king of Zō'bah, David killed
twenty-two thousand of the
Syrians.
6 Then David put garrisons in
Syria of Damascus; and the Syrians became David's servants,
and brought tribute. So [a]the
LORD preserved David wherever
he went.
7 And David took [a]the shields
of gold that had belonged to
the servants of Had·a·dē'zer, and
brought them to Jerusalem.
8 Also from [1]Bē'tah and from
[a]Berothai,[2] cities of Had·a·dē'zer,
King David took a large amount
of bronze.
9 When [1]Tō'ī king of [a]Hā'math
heard that David had defeated
all the army of Had·a·dē'zer,
10 then Tō'ī sent [1]Jō'ram his
son to King David, to [2]greet him
and bless him, because he had
fought against Had·a·dē'zer and
defeated him (for Had·a·dē'zer
had been at war with Tō'ī); and
Jō'ram [b]brought with him articles of silver, articles of gold,
and articles of bronze.
11 King David also [a]dedicated
these to the LORD, along with
the silver and gold that he had
dedicated from all the nations
which he had subdued—
12 from [1]Syria, from Mō'ab,
from the people of Am'mon,
from the [a]Phi·lis'tines, from
Am'a·lek, and from the spoil of
Had·a·dē'zer the son of Rē'hob,
king of Zō'bah.
13 And David made *himself* a
[a]name when he returned from
killing [b]eighteen thousand [1]Syr-
ians in [c]the Valley of Salt.
14 He also put garrisons in
Ē'dom; throughout all Ē'dom
he put garrisons, and [a]all the
Ē'dom·ītes became David's servants. And the LORD preserved
David wherever he went.
15 So David reigned over all
Israel; and David administered
judgment and justice to all his
people.
16 [a]Jō'ab the son of Ze·rū'i·ah
was over the army; [b]Je·hosh'-
a·phat the son of A·hī'lud *was*
recorder;
17 [a]Zā'dok the son of A·hī'-
tub and A·him'e·lech the son
of A·bī'a·thar *were* the priests;
[1]Se·rāi'ah *was* the [2]scribe;

29 [a]2 Sam. 22:51

CHAPTER 8

1 [1]Lit. *struck* [2]Lit. *The Bridle of the Mother City*
2 [a]Num. 24:17 [b]2 Sam. 12:31 [c]1 Kin. 4:21
3 [a]1 Sam. 14:47 [b]2 Sam. 10:15–19
4 [a]Josh. 11:6, 9 [1]*seven thousand,* 1 Chr. 18:4
5 [a]1 Kin. 11:23–25
6 [a]2 Sam. 7:9; 8:14
7 [a]1 Kin. 10:16
8 [a]Ezek. 47:16 [1]*Tibhath,* 1 Chr. 18:8 [2]*Chun,* 1 Chr. 18:8
9 [a]1 Kin. 8:65 [1]*Tou,* 1 Chr. 18:9
10 [1]*Hadoram,* 1 Chr. 18:10 [2]Lit. *ask him of his welfare*
11 [a]1 Kin. 7:51
12 [a]2 Sam. 5:17–25 [1]LXX, Syr., Heb. mss. *Edom*
13 [a]2 Sam. 7:9 [b]2 Kin. 14:7 [c]1 Chr. 18:12 [1]LXX, Syr., Heb. mss. *Edomites* and 1 Chr. 18:12
14 [a]Gen. 27:29, 37–40
16 [a]2 Sam. 19:13; 20:23 [b]1 Kin. 4:3
17 [a]1 Chr. 6:4–8; 24:3 [1]*Shavsha,* 1 Chr. 18:16 [2]*secretary*

18 [a]Be·nā′i·ah the son of Je·hoi′-
a·da *was over* both the [b]Cher′-
e·thītes and the Pel′eth·ītes;
and David's sons were [1]chief
ministers.

CHAPTER 9

9 Now David said, "Is there
still anyone who is left of
the house of Saul, that I may
[a]show him [1]kindness for Jonathan's sake?"
2 And *there was* a servant of
the house of Saul whose name
was [a]Zī′ba. So when they had
called him to David, the king
said to him, "*Are* you Zī′ba?" He
said, "At your service!"
3 Then the king said, "*Is* there
not still someone of the house of
Saul, to whom I may show [a]the
kindness of God?" And Zī′ba
said to the king, "There is still a
son of Jonathan *who is* [b]lame in
his feet."
4 So the king said to him,
"Where *is* he?" And Zī′ba said
to the king, "Indeed he *is* in the
house of [a]Mā′chir the son of
Am′mi·el, in Lo Dē′bar."
5 Then King David sent and
brought him out of the house
of Mā′chir the son of Am′mi·el,
from Lo Dē′bar.
6 Now when [a]Me·phib′o·sheth[1]
the son of Jonathan, the son of
Saul, had come to David, he fell
on his face and prostrated himself. Then David said, "Me·phib′-
o·sheth?" And he answered,
"Here is your servant!"
7 So David said to him, "Do
not fear, for I will surely show
you kindness for Jonathan your
father's sake, and will restore
to you all the land of Saul your
grandfather; and you shall eat
bread at my table continually."
8 Then he bowed himself, and
said, "What *is* your servant, that
you should look upon such [a]a
dead dog as I?"
9 And the king called to Zī′ba,
Saul's servant, and said to him,
[a]"I have given to your master's
son all that belonged to Saul
and to all his house.
10 "You therefore, and your sons
and your servants, shall work
the land for him, and you shall
bring in *the harvest*, that your
master's son may have food to
eat. But Me·phib′o·sheth your
master's son [a]shall eat bread
at my table always." Now Zī′ba
had [b]fifteen sons and twenty
servants.
11 Then Zī′ba said to the king,
"According to all that my lord
the king has commanded his
servant, so will your servant
do." "As for Me·phib′o·sheth,"
said the king, "he shall eat at
[1]my table like one of the king's
sons."
12 Me·phib′o·sheth had a young
son [a]whose name *was* Mī′-
cha. And all who dwelt in the
house of Zī′ba *were* servants of
Me·phib′o·sheth.
13 So Me·phib′o·sheth dwelt in
Jerusalem, [a]for he ate continually at the king's table. And he
[b]was lame in both his feet.

CHAPTER 10

10 It happened after this that
the [a]king of the people of
Am′mon died, and Hā′nun his
son reigned in his place.
2 Then David said, "I will show
[a]kindness to Hā′nun the son of
[b]Nā′hash, as his father showed
kindness to me." So David sent
by the hand of his servants to
comfort him concerning his father. And David's servants came
into the land of the people of
Am′mon.
3 And the princes of the people

18 [a]1 Chr. 18:17 [b]1 Sam. 30:14 [1]Lit. *priests*
1 [a]1 Sam. 18:3; 20:14–16 [1]*covenant faithfulness*
2 [a]2 Sam. 16:1–4; 19:17, 29
3 [a]1 Sam. 20:14 [b]2 Sam. 4:4
4 [a]2 Sam. 17:27–29
6 [a]2 Sam. 16:4; 19:24–30 [1]Or *Merib-Baal*
8 [a]2 Sam. 16:9
9 [a]2 Sam. 16:4; 19:29
10 [a]2 Sam. 9:7, 11, 13; 19:28 [b]2 Sam. 19:17
11 [1]LXX *David's table*
12 [a]1 Chr. 8:34
13 [a]2 Sam. 9:7, 10, 11 [b]2 Sam. 9:3
1 [a]1 Chr. 19:1
2 [a]2 Sam. 9:1 [b]1 Sam. 11:1

of Am′mon said to Hā′nun their
lord, "Do you think that David
really honors your father because he has sent comforters to
you? Has David not *rather* sent
his servants to you to search the
city, to spy it out, and to overthrow it?"
4 Therefore Hā′nun took David's servants, shaved off half
of their beards, cut off their
garments in the middle, [a]at their
buttocks, and sent them away.
5 When they told David, he
sent to meet them, because the
men were greatly [1]ashamed. And
the king said, "Wait at Jericho
until your beards have grown,
and *then* return."
6 When the people of Am′-
mon saw that they [a]had made
themselves repulsive to David,
the people of Am′mon sent and
hired [b]the Syrians of [c]Beth Rē′-
hob and the Syrians of Zō′ba,
twenty thousand foot soldiers;
and from the king of [d]Mā′a·cah
one thousand men, and from
[e]Ish-Tob twelve thousand men.
7 Now when David heard *of it,*
he sent Jō′ab and all the army of
[a]the mighty men.
8 Then the people of Am′mon
came out and put themselves
in battle array at the entrance
of the gate. And [a]the Syrians of
Zō′ba, Beth Rē′hob, Ish-Tob, and
Mā′a·cah *were* by themselves in
the field.
9 When Jō′ab saw that the battle line was against him before
and behind, he chose some of
Israel's best and put *them* in
battle array against the Syrians.
10 And the rest of the people
he put under the command of
[a]A·bi′shaī his brother, that he
might set *them* in battle array
against the people of Am′mon.
11 Then he said, "If the Syrians
are too strong for me, then you
shall help me; but if the people
of Am′mon are too strong for
you, then I will come and help
you.
12 [a]"Be of good courage, and let
us [b]be strong for our people and
for the cities of our God. And
may [c]the LORD do *what is* good
in His sight."
13 So Jō′ab and the people who
were with him drew near for the
battle against the Syrians, and
they fled before him.
14 When the people of Am′-
mon saw that the Syrians were
fleeing, they also fled before
A·bi′shaī, and entered the city.
So Jō′ab returned from the
people of Am′mon and went to
[a]Jerusalem.
15 When the Syrians saw that
they had been defeated by Israel, they gathered together.
16 Then [1]Had·a·dē′zer sent and
brought out the Syrians who
were beyond [2]the River, and they
came to Hē′lam. And [3]Shō′bach
the commander of Had·a·dē′-
zer's army *went* before them.
17 When it was told David, he
gathered all Israel, crossed over
the Jordan, and came to Hē′lam.
And the Syrians set themselves
in battle array against David
and fought with him.
18 Then the Syrians fled before
Israel; and David killed seven
hundred charioteers and forty
thousand [a]horsemen of the Syrians, and struck Shō′bach the
commander of their army, who
died there.
19 And when all the kings *who*
were servants to [1]Had·a·dē′zer

4 [a]Is. 20:4; 47:2
5 [1]*humiliated*
6 [a]Gen. 34:30 [b]2 Sam. 8:3, 5 [c]Judg. 18:28 [d]Deut. 3:14 [e]Judg. 11:3, 5
7 [a]2 Sam. 23:8
8 [a]2 Sam. 10:6
10 [a]2 Sam. 3:30
12 [a]Deut. 31:6 [b]1 Cor. 16:13 [c]1 Sam. 3:18
14 [a]2 Sam. 11:1
16 [1]Heb. *Hadarezer* [2]The Euphrates [3]*Shophach,* 1 Chr. 19:16
18 [a]1 Chr. 19:18
19 [1]Heb. *Hadarezer*

saw that they were defeated by
Israel, they made peace with
Israel and [a]served them. So the
Syrians were afraid to help the
people of Am′mon anymore.

11 It happened in the spring
of the year, at the [a]time
when kings go out *to battle,*
that [b]David sent Jō′ab and his
servants with him, and all Israel;
and they destroyed the people
of Am′mon and besieged [c]Rab′-
bah. But David remained at
Jerusalem.
2 Then it happened one evening that David arose from his
bed [a]and walked on the roof of
the king's house. And from the
roof he [b]saw a woman bathing,
and the woman *was* very beautiful to behold.
3 So David sent and inquired
about the woman. And *someone*
said, "*Is* this not [1]Bath·shē′ba,
the daughter of [2]E·lī′am, the wife
[a]of Ū·rī′ah the [b]Hit′tīte?"
4 Then David sent messengers,
and took her; and she came to
him, and [a]he lay with her, for
she was [b]cleansed from her impurity; and she returned to her
house.
5 And the woman conceived;
so she sent and told David, and
said, "I *am* with child."
6 Then David sent to Jō′ab,
saying, "Send me Ū·rī′ah the
Hit′tīte." And Jō′ab sent Ū·rī′ah
to David.
7 When Ū·rī′ah had come to
him, David asked how Jō′ab
was doing, and how the people
were doing, and how the war
prospered.
8 And David said to Ū·rī′ah,
"Go down to your house and
[a]wash your feet." So Ū·rī′ah departed from the king's house,
and a gift *of food* from the king
followed him.
9 But Ū·rī′ah slept at the [a]door
of the king's house with all the
servants of his lord, and did not
go down to his house.
10 So when they told David,
saying, "Ū·rī′ah did not go down
to his house," David said to
Ū·rī′ah, "Did you not come from
a journey? Why did you not go
down to your house?"
11 And Ū·rī′ah said to David,
[a]"The ark and Israel and Judah
are dwelling in tents, and [b]my
lord Jō′ab and the servants of
my lord are encamped in the
open fields. Shall I then go to
my house to eat and drink, and
to lie with my wife? *As* you live,
and *as* your soul lives, I will not
do this thing."
12 Then David said to Ū·rī′ah,
"Wait here today also, and tomorrow I will let you depart." So
Ū·rī′ah remained in Jerusalem
that day and the next.
13 Now when David called him,
he ate and drank before him;
and he made him [a]drunk. And
at evening he went out to lie on
his bed [b]with the servants of his
lord, but he did not go down to
his house.
14 In the morning it happened
that David [a]wrote a letter to
Jō′ab and sent *it* by the hand of
Ū·rī′ah.
15 And he wrote in the letter,
saying, "Set Ū·rī′ah in the forefront of the [1]hottest battle, and
retreat from him, that he may
[a]be struck down and die."
16 So it was, while Jō′ab besieged the city, that he assigned
Ū·rī′ah to a place where he knew
there *were* valiant men.
17 Then the men of the city

19 [a]2 Sam. 8:6

CHAPTER 11

1 [a]1 Kin. 20:22–26 [b]1 Chr. 20:1 [c]2 Sam. 12:26

2 [a]Deut. 22:8 [b]Gen. 34:2

3 [a]2 Sam. 23:39 [b]1 Sam. 26:6 [1]*Bathshua,* 1 Chr. 3:5 [2]*Ammiel,* 1 Chr. 3:5

4 [a][James 1:14, 15] [b]Lev. 15:19, 28

8 [a]Gen. 18:4; 19:2

9 [a]1 Kin. 14:27, 28

11 [a]2 Sam. 7:2, 6 [b]2 Sam. 20:6–22

13 [a]Gen. 19:33, 35 [b]2 Sam. 11:9

14 [a]1 Kin. 21:8, 9

15 [a]2 Sam. 12:9 [1]*fiercest*

came out and fought with Jō′ab. And *some* of the people of the servants of David fell; and Ū·rī′ah the Hit′tīte died also.

18 Then Jō′ab sent and told David all the things concerning the war,

19 and charged the messenger, saying, "When you have finished telling the matters of the war to the king,

20 "if it happens that the king's wrath rises, and he says to you: 'Why did you approach so near to the city when you fought? Did you not know that they would shoot from the wall?

21 'Who struck [a]A·bim′e·lech the son of [1]Je·rub′be·sheth? Was it not a woman who cast a piece of a millstone on him from the wall, so that he died in Thē′bez? Why did you go near the wall?'—then you shall say, 'Your servant Ū·rī′ah the Hit′tīte is dead also.' "

22 So the messenger went, and came and told David all that Jō′ab had sent by him.

23 And the messenger said to David, "Surely the men prevailed against us and came out to us in the field; then we drove them back as far as the entrance of the gate.

24 "The archers shot from the wall at your servants; and *some* of the king's servants are dead, and your servant Ū·rī′ah the Hit′tīte is dead also."

25 Then David said to the messenger, "Thus you shall say to Jō′ab: 'Do not let this thing [1]displease you, for the sword devours one as well as another. Strengthen your attack against the city, and overthrow it.' So encourage him."

26 When the wife of Ū·rī′ah heard that Ū·rī′ah her husband was dead, she mourned for her husband.

27 And when her mourning was over, David sent and brought her to his house, and she [a]became his wife and bore him a son. But the thing that David had done [b]displeased[1] the LORD.

12

Then the LORD sent Nathan to David. And [a]he came to him, and [b]said to him: "There were two men in one city, one rich and the other poor.

2 "The rich *man* had exceedingly many flocks and herds.

3 "But the poor *man* had nothing, except one little ewe lamb which he had bought and nourished; and it grew up together with him and with his children. It ate of his own food and drank from his own cup and lay in his bosom; and it was like a daughter to him.

4 "And a traveler came to the rich man, who refused to take from his own flock and from his own herd to prepare one for the wayfaring man who had come to him; but he took the poor man's lamb and prepared it for the man who had come to him."

5 So David's anger was greatly aroused against the man, and he said to Nathan, "*As* the LORD lives, the man who has done this [1]shall surely die!

6 "And he shall restore [a]fourfold for the lamb, because he did this thing and because he had no pity."

7 Then Nathan said to David, "You *are* the man! Thus says the LORD God of Israel: 'I [a]anointed you king over Israel, and I delivered you from the hand of Saul.

21 [a]Judg. 9:50–54 [1]*Jerubbaal* (Gideon), Judg. 6:32ff.

25 [1]Lit. *be evil in your sight*

27 [a]2 Sam. 12:9 [b]1 Chr. 21:7 [1]Lit. *was evil in the eyes of*

CHAPTER 12

1 [a]Ps. 51:title [b]1 Kin. 20:35–41

5 [1]*deserves to die,* lit. *is a son of death*

6 [a][Ex. 22:1]

7 [a]1 Sam. 16:13

8 'I gave you your master's house and your master's wives into your keeping, and gave you the house of Israel and Judah. And if *that had been* too little, I also would have given you much more!

9 [a]'Why have you [b]despised the commandment of the LORD, to do evil in His sight? [c]You have killed Ū·rīʹah the Hitʹtīte with the sword; you have taken his wife *to be* your wife, and have killed him with the sword of the people of Amʹmon.

10 'Now therefore, [a]the sword shall never depart from your house, because you have despised Me, and have taken the wife of Ū·rīʹah the Hitʹtīte to be your wife.'

11 "Thus says the LORD: 'Behold, I will raise up adversity against you from your own house; and I will [a]take your wives before your eyes and give *them* to your neighbor, and he shall lie with your wives in the sight of this sun.

12 'For you did *it* secretly, [a]but I will do this thing before all Israel, before the sun.' "

13 [a]So David said to Nathan, [b]"I have sinned against the LORD." And Nathan said to David, "The LORD also has [c]put away your sin; you shall not die.

14 "However, because by this deed you have given great occasion to the enemies of the LORD [a]to blaspheme, the child also *who is* born to you shall surely die."

15 Then Nathan departed to his house.

And the [a]LORD struck the child that Ū·rīʹah's wife bore to David, and it became ill.

16 David therefore pleaded with God for the child, and David fasted and went in and [a]lay all night on the ground.

17 So the elders of his house arose *and went* to him, to raise him up from the ground. But he would not, nor did he eat food with them.

18 Then on the seventh day it came to pass that the child died. And the servants of David were afraid to tell him that the child was dead. For they said, "Indeed, while the child was alive, we spoke to him, and he would not heed our voice. How can we tell him that the child is dead? He may do some harm!"

19 When David saw that his servants were whispering, David perceived that the child was dead. Therefore David said to his servants, "Is the child dead?" And they said, "He is dead."

20 So David arose from the ground, washed and [a]anointed himself, and changed his clothes; and he went into the house of the LORD and [b]worshiped. Then he went to his own house; and when he requested, they set food before him, and he ate.

21 Then his servants said to him, "What *is* this that you have done? You fasted and wept for the child *while he was* alive, but when the child died, you arose and ate food."

22 And he said, "While the child was alive, I fasted and wept; [a]for I said, 'Who can tell *whether* [1]the LORD will be gracious to me, that the child may live?'

23 "But now he is dead; why should I fast? Can I bring him back again? I shall go [a]to him, but [b]he shall not return to me."

---

9 [a]1 Sam. 15:19 [b]Num. 15:31 [c]2 Sam. 11:14–17, 27
10 [a][Amos 7:9]
11 [a]2 Sam. 16:21, 22
12 [a]2 Sam. 16:22
13 [a]1 Sam. 15:24 [b]2 Sam. 24:10 [c][Mic. 7:18]
14 [a]Is. 52:5
15 [a]1 Sam. 25:38
16 [a]2 Sam. 13:31
20 [a]Ruth 3:3 [b]Job 1:20
22 [a]Jon. 3:9 [1]Heb. mss., Syr. *God*
23 [a]Gen. 37:35 [b]Job 7:8–10

24 Then David comforted Bath·shē′ba his wife, and went in to her and lay with her. So [a]she bore a son, and [b]he[1] called his name Solomon. Now the LORD loved him,

25 and He sent *word* by the hand of Nathan the prophet: So [1]he called his name [2]Jed·i·dī′ah, because of the LORD.

26 Now [a]Jō′ab fought against [b]Rab′bah of the people of Am′mon, and took the royal city.

27 And Jō′ab sent messengers to David, and said, "I have fought against Rab′bah, and I have taken the city's water *supply.*

28 "Now therefore, gather the rest of the people together and encamp against the city and take it, lest I take the city and it be called after my name."

29 So David gathered all the people together and went to Rab′bah, fought against it, and took it.

30 [a]Then he took their king's crown from his head. Its weight *was* a talent of gold, with precious stones. And it was *set* on David's head. Also he brought out the [1]spoil of the city in great abundance.

31 And he brought out the people who *were* in it, and put *them to work* with saws and iron picks and iron axes, and made them cross over to the brick works. So he did to all the cities of the people of Am′mon. Then David and all the people returned to Jerusalem.

13 After this [a]Ab′sa·lom the son of David had a lovely sister, whose name *was* [b]Tā′mar; and [c]Am′non the son of David loved her.

2 Am′non was so distressed over his sister Tā′mar that he became sick; for she *was* a virgin. And it was improper for Am′non to do anything to her.

3 But Am′non had a friend whose name *was* Jon′a·dab [a]the son of Shim′ē·ah, David's brother. Now Jon′a·dab *was* a very crafty man.

4 And he said to him, "Why *are* you, the king's son, becoming thinner day after day? Will you not tell me?" Am′non said to him, "I love Tā′mar, my brother Ab′sa·lom's sister."

5 So Jon′a·dab said to him, "Lie down on your bed and pretend to be ill. And when your father comes to see you, say to him, 'Please let my sister Tā′mar come and give me food, and prepare the food in my sight, that I may see *it* and eat it from her hand.' "

6 Then Am′non lay down and pretended to be ill; and when the king came to see him, Am′non said to the king, "Please let Tā′mar my sister come and [a]make a couple of cakes for me in my sight, that I may eat from her hand."

7 And David sent home to Tā′mar, saying, "Now go to your brother Am′non's house, and prepare food for him."

8 So Tā′mar went to her brother Am′non's house; and he was lying down. Then she took flour and kneaded *it,* made cakes in his sight, and baked the cakes.

9 And she took the pan and placed *them* out before him, but he refused to eat. Then Am′non said, [a]"Have everyone go out from me." And they all went out from him.

24 [a]Matt. 1:6 [b]1 Chr. 22:9 [1]So with Kt., LXX, Vg.; Qr., a few Heb. mss., Syr., Tg. *she*

25 [1]Qr., some Heb. mss., Syr., Tg. *she* [2]Lit. *Beloved of the LORD*

26 [a]1 Chr. 20:1 [b]Deut. 3:11

30 [a]1 Chr. 20:2 [1]*plunder*

CHAPTER 13

1 [a]2 Sam. 3:2, 3 [b]1 Chr. 3:9 [c]2 Sam. 3:2

3 [a]1 Sam. 16:9

6 [a]Gen. 18:6

9 [a]Gen. 45:1

10 Then Am′non said to Tā′-
mar, "Bring the food into the
bedroom, that I may eat from
your hand." And Tā′mar took
the cakes which she had made,
and brought *them* to Am′non
her brother in the bedroom.
11 Now when she had brought
them to him to eat, [a]he took hold
of her and said to her, "Come, lie
with me, my sister."
12 But she answered him, "No,
my brother, do not [1]force me,
for [a]no such thing should be
done in Israel. Do not do this
[b]disgraceful thing!
13 "And I, where could I take
my shame? And as for you, you
would be like one of the fools
in Israel. Now therefore, please
speak to the king; [a]for he will
not withhold me from you."
14 However, he would not heed
her voice; and being stronger
than she, he [a]forced her and lay
with her.
15 Then Am′non hated her [1]ex-
ceedingly, so that the hatred
with which he hated her *was*
greater than the love with which
he had loved her. And Am′non
said to her, "Arise, be gone!"
16 So she said to him, "No, indeed! This evil of sending me
away *is* worse than the other
that you did to me." But he
would not listen to her.
17 Then he called his servant
who attended him, and said,
"Here! Put this *woman* out, away
from me, and bolt the door behind her."
18 Now she had on [a]a robe of
many colors, for the king's virgin daughters wore such apparel. And his servant put her
out and bolted the door behind
her.
19 Then Tā′mar put [a]ashes on
her head, and tore her robe of
many colors that *was* on her,
and [b]laid her hand on her head
and went away crying bitterly.
20 And Ab′sa·lom her brother
said to her, "Has Am′non your
brother been with you? But now
hold your peace, my sister. He
is your brother; do not take this
thing to heart." So Tā′mar remained desolate in her brother
Ab′sa·lom's house.
21 But when King David heard
of all these things, he was very
angry.
22 And Ab′sa·lom spoke to his
brother Am′non [a]neither good
nor bad. For Ab′sa·lom [b]hated
Am′non, because he had forced
his sister Tā′mar.
23 And it came to pass, after
two full years, that Ab′sa·lom
[a]had sheepshearers in Bā′al Hā′-
zor, which *is* near Ē′phra·im; so
Ab′sa·lom invited all the king's
sons.
24 Then Ab′sa·lom came to the
king and said, "Kindly note,
your servant has sheepshearers;
please, let the king and his servants go with your servant."
25 But the king said to Ab′-
sa·lom, "No, my son, let us not
all go now, lest we be a burden
to you." Then he urged him, but
he would not go; and he blessed
him.
26 Then Ab′sa·lom said, "If not,
please let my brother Am′non
go with us." And the king said
to him, "Why should he go with
you?"
27 But Ab′sa·lom urged him; so
he let Am′non and all the king's
sons go with him.
28 Now Ab′sa·lom had commanded his servants, saying,

11 [a]Gen. 39:12
12 [a][Lev. 18:9–11; 20:17] [b]Judg. 19:23; 20:6 [1]Lit. *humble me*
13 [a]Gen. 20:12
14 [a]2 Sam. 12:11
15 [1]*with a very great hatred*
18 [a]Gen. 37:3
19 [a]Josh. 7:6 [b]Jer. 2:37
22 [a]Gen. 24:50; 31:24 [b][Lev. 19:17, 18]
23 [a]1 Sam. 25:4

“Watch now, when Am′non’s
[a]heart is merry with wine,
and when I say to you, ‘Strike
Am′non!’ then kill him. Do
not be afraid. Have I not commanded you? Be courageous
and [1]valiant.”
29 So the servants of Ab′sa·lom
[a]did to Am′non as Ab′sa·lom had
commanded. Then all the king’s
sons arose, and each one got on
[b]his mule and fled.
30 And it came to pass, while
they were on the way, that news
came to David, saying, “Ab′-
sa·lom has killed all the king’s
sons, and not one of them is
left!”
31 So the king arose and [a]tore
his garments and [b]lay on the
ground, and all his servants
stood by with their clothes torn.
32 Then [a]Jon′a·dab the son of
Shim′ē·ah, David’s brother, answered and said, “Let not my
lord suppose they have killed all
the young men, the king’s sons,
for only Am′non is dead. For by
the command of Ab′sa·lom this
has been determined from the
day that he forced his sister Tā′-
mar.
33 “Now therefore, [a]let not my
lord the king take the thing to
his heart, to think that all the
king’s sons are dead. For only
Am′non is dead.”
34 [a]Then Ab′sa·lom fled. And
the young man who was keeping watch lifted his eyes and
looked, and there, many people
were coming from the road on
the hillside behind [1]him.
35 And Jon′a·dab said to the
king, “Look, the king’s sons are
coming; as your servant said, so
it is.”
36 So it was, as soon as he had
finished speaking, that the king’s
sons indeed came, and they lifted
up their voice and wept. Also the
king and all his servants wept
very bitterly.
37 But Ab′sa·lom fled and went
to [a]Tal′maī the son of Am·mī′-
hud, king of Gē′shur. And *David*
mourned for his son every day.
38 So Ab′sa·lom fled and went
to [a]Gē′shur, and was there three
years.
39 And [1]King David [2]longed to
go to Ab′sa·lom. For he had been
[a]comforted concerning Am′non,
because he was dead.

14

So Jō′ab the son of
Ze·rū′i·ah perceived that
the king’s heart *was* concerned
[a]about Ab′sa·lom.
2 And Jō′ab sent to [a]Te·kō′a
and brought from there a wise
woman, and said to her, “Please
pretend to be a mourner, [b]and
put on mourning apparel; do
not anoint yourself with oil, but
act like a woman who has been
mourning a long time for the
dead.
3 “Go to the king and speak
to him in this manner.” So Jō′ab
[a]put the words in her mouth.
4 And when the woman of
Te·kō′a [1]spoke to the king, she
[a]fell on her face to the ground
and prostrated herself, and said,
[b]“Help, O king!”
5 Then the king said to her,
“What troubles you?” And she
answered, [a]“Indeed I *am* a
widow, my husband is dead.
6 “Now your maidservant had
two sons; and the two fought
with each other in the field, and
there was no one to part them,
but the one struck the other and
killed him.
7 “And now the whole family

28 [a]1 Sam. 25:36 [1]Lit. *sons of valor*
29 [a]2 Sam. 12:10 [b]2 Sam. 18:9
31 [a]2 Sam. 1:11 [b]2 Sam. 12:16
32 [a]2 Sam. 13:3–5
33 [a]2 Sam. 19:19
34 [a]2 Sam. 13:37, 38 [1]LXX adds *And the watchman went and told the king, and said, “I see men from the way of Horonaim, from the regions of the mountains.”*
37 [a]2 Sam. 3:3
38 [a]2 Sam. 14:23, 32; 15:8
39 [a]2 Sam. 12:19, 23 [1]So with MT, Syr., Vg.; LXX *the spirit of the king;* Tg. *the soul of King David* [2]So with MT, Tg.; LXX, Vg. *ceased to pursue after*

CHAPTER 14

1 [a]2 Sam. 13:39
2 [a]2 Chr. 11:6 [b]Ruth 3:3
3 [a]2 Sam. 14:19
4 [a]1 Sam. 20:41; 25:23 [b]2 Kin. 6:26, 28 [1]Many Heb. mss., LXX, Syr., Vg. *came*
5 [a][Zech. 7:10]

has risen up against your maidservant, and they said, 'Deliver him who struck his brother, that we may execute him [a]for the life of his brother whom he killed; and we will destroy the heir also.' So they would extinguish my ember that is left, and leave to my husband *neither* name nor remnant on the earth."

8 Then the king said to the woman, "Go to your house, and I will give orders concerning you."

9 And the woman of Te·kō'a said to the king, "My lord, O king, *let* [a]the [1]iniquity *be* on me and on my father's house, [b]and the king and his throne *be* guiltless."

10 So the king said, "Whoever says *anything* to you, bring him to me, and he shall not touch you anymore."

11 Then she said, "Please let the king remember the LORD your God, and do not permit [a]the avenger of blood to destroy anymore, lest they destroy my son." And he said, [b]"*As* the LORD lives, not one hair of your son shall fall to the ground."

12 Therefore the woman said, "Please, let your maidservant speak *another* word to my lord the king." And he said, "Say on."

13 So the woman said: "Why then have you schemed such a thing against [a]the people of God? For the king speaks this thing as one who is guilty, *in that* the king does not bring [b]his banished one home again.

14 "For we [a]will surely die and *become* like water spilled on the ground, which cannot be gathered up again. Yet God does not [b]take away a life; but He [c]devises means, so that His banished ones are not [1]expelled from Him.

15 "Now therefore, I have come to speak of this thing to my lord the king because the people have made me afraid. And your maidservant said, 'I will now speak to the king; it may be that the king will perform the request of his maidservant.

16 'For the king will hear and deliver his maidservant from the hand of the man *who would* destroy me and my son together from the [a]inheritance of God.'

17 "Your maidservant said, 'The word of my lord the king will now be comforting; for [a]as the angel of God, so *is* my lord the king in [b]discerning good and evil. And may the LORD your God be with you.' "

18 Then the king answered and said to the woman, "Please do not hide from me anything that I ask you." And the woman said, "Please, let my lord the king speak."

19 So the king said, "*Is* the hand of Jō'ab with you in all this?" And the woman answered and said, "*As* you live, my lord the king, no one can turn to the right hand or to the left from anything that my lord the king has spoken. For your servant Jō'ab commanded me, and [a]he put all these words in the mouth of your maidservant.

20 "To bring about this change of affairs your servant Jō'ab has done this thing; but my lord *is* wise, [a]according to the wisdom of the angel of God, to know everything that *is* in the earth."

21 And the king said to Jō'ab, "All right, I have granted this

7 [a]Deut. 19:12, 13
9 [a]1 Sam. 25:24 [b]1 Kin. 2:33 [1]*guilt*
11 [a]Num. 35:19, 21 [b]1 Sam. 14:45
13 [a]Judg. 20:2 [b]2 Sam. 13:37, 38
14 [a][Heb. 9:27] [b]Job 34:19 [c]Num. 35:15 [1]*cast out*
16 [a]Deut. 32:9
17 [a]2 Sam. 19:27 [b]1 Kin. 3:9
19 [a]2 Sam. 14:3
20 [a]2 Sam. 14:17; 19:27

thing. Go therefore, bring back
the young man Ab′sa·lom."
22 Then Jō′ab fell to the ground
on his face and bowed himself, and [1]thanked the king. And
Jō′ab said, "Today your servant
knows that I have found favor
in your sight, my lord, O king,
in that the king has fulfilled the
request of his servant."
23 So Jō′ab arose [a]and went to
Gē′shur, and brought Ab′sa·lom
to Jerusalem.
24 And the king said, "Let him
return to his own house, but
[a]do not let him see my face." So
Ab′sa·lom returned to his own
house, but did not see the king's
face.
25 Now in all Israel there was
no one who was praised as much
as Ab′sa·lom for his good looks.
[a]From the sole of his foot to the
crown of his head there was no
blemish in him.
26 And when he cut the hair of
his head—at the end of every
year he cut *it* because it was
heavy on him—when he cut it,
he weighed the hair of his head
at two hundred shekels according to the king's standard.
27 [a]To Ab′sa·lom were born
three sons, and one daughter whose name *was* Tā′mar.
She was a woman of beautiful
appearance.
28 And Ab′sa·lom dwelt two full
years in Jerusalem, [a]but did not
see the king's face.
29 Therefore Ab′sa·lom sent for
Jō′ab, to send him to the king,
but he would not come to him.
And when he sent again the second time, he would not come.
30 So he said to his servants,
"See, Jō′ab's field is near mine,
and he has barley there; go and
set it on fire." And Ab′sa·lom's
servants set the field on fire.
31 Then Jō′ab arose and came
to Ab′sa·lom's house, and said
to him, "Why have your servants
set my field on fire?"
32 And Ab′sa·lom answered
Jō′ab, "Look, I sent to you, saying, 'Come here, so that I may
send you to the king, to say,
"Why have I come from Gē′-
shur? *It would be* better for me
to be there still."' Now therefore, let me see the king's face;
but [a]if there is iniquity in me, let
him execute me."
33 So Jō′ab went to the king
and told him. And when he had
called for Ab′sa·lom, he came to
the king and bowed himself on
his face to the ground before the
king. Then the king [a]kissed Ab′-
sa·lom.

15

After this [a]it happened
that Ab′sa·lom [b]provided
himself with chariots and
horses, and fifty men to run
before him.
2 Now Ab′sa·lom would rise
early and stand beside the way
to the gate. *So* it was, whenever anyone who had a [a]lawsuit[1]
came to the king for a decision, that Ab′sa·lom would call
to him and say, "What city *are*
you from?" And he would say,
"Your servant *is* from such and
such a tribe of Israel."
3 Then Ab′sa·lom would say to
him, "Look, your [1]case *is* good
and right; but *there is* no [2]dep-
uty of the king to hear you."
4 Moreover Ab′sa·lom would
say, [a]"Oh, that I were made
judge in the land, and everyone
who has any suit or cause would
come to me; then I would give
him justice."

22 [1]Lit. *blessed*
23 [a]2 Sam. 13:37, 38
24 [a]2 Sam. 3:13
25 [a]Is. 1:6
27 [a]2 Sam. 13:1; 18:18
28 [a]2 Sam. 14:24
32 [a]1 Sam. 20:8
33 [a]Luke 15:20

CHAPTER 15

1 [a]2 Sam. 12:11 [b]1 Kin. 1:5
2 [a]Deut. 19:17 [1]Lit. *controversy*
3 [1]Lit. *words* [2]Lit. *listener*
4 [a]Judg. 9:29

5 And *so* it was, whenever
anyone came near to bow down
to him, that he would put out
his hand and take him and [a]kiss
him.
6 In this manner Ab′sa·lom
acted toward all Israel who
came to the king for judgment.
[a]So Ab′sa·lom stole the hearts of
the men of Israel.
7 Now it came to pass [a]after
[1]forty years that Ab′sa·lom said
to the king, "Please, let me go to
[b]Hē′bron and pay the vow which
I made to the LORD.
8 [a]"For your servant [b]took a
vow [c]while I dwelt at Gē′shur in
Syria, saying, 'If the LORD indeed
brings me back to Jerusalem,
then I will serve the LORD.' "
9 And the king said to him,
"Go in peace." So he arose and
went to Hē′bron.
10 Then Ab′sa·lom sent spies
throughout all the tribes of Israel, saying, "As soon as you
hear the sound of the trumpet,
then you shall say, 'Ab′sa·lom
[a]reigns in Hē′bron!' "
11 And with Ab′sa·lom went
two hundred men [a]invited from
Jerusalem, and they [b]went along
innocently and did not know
anything.
12 Then Ab′sa·lom sent for
A·hith′o·phel the Gī′lo·nīte, [a]Da-
vid's counselor, from his city—
from [b]Gī′lōh—while he offered
sacrifices. And the conspiracy
grew strong, for the people with
Ab′sa·lom [c]continually increased
in number.
13 Now a messenger came to
David, saying, [a]"The hearts of
the men of Israel are [1]with Ab′-
sa·lom."
14 So David said to all his servants who *were* with him at
Jerusalem, "Arise, and let us
[a]flee, or we shall not escape
from Ab′sa·lom. Make haste to
depart, lest he overtake us suddenly and bring disaster upon
us, and strike the city with the
edge of the sword."
15 And the king's servants said
to the king, "We *are* your servants, *ready to do* whatever my
lord the king commands."
16 Then [a]the king went out with
all his household after him. But
the king left [b]ten women, concubines, to keep the house.
17 And the king went out with
all the people after him, and
stopped at the outskirts.
18 Then all his servants passed
[1]before him; [a]and all the Cher′-
e·thītes, all the Pel′eth·ītes, and
all the Git′tītes, [b]six hundred
men who had followed him from
Gath, passed before the king.
19 Then the king said to [a]It′taī
the Git′tīte, "Why are you also
going with us? Return and remain with the king. For you *are*
a foreigner and also an exile
from your own place.
20 "In fact, you came *only* yesterday. Should I make you wander up and down with us today,
since I go [a]I know not where?
Return, and take your brethren
back. Mercy and truth *be* with
you."
21 But It′taī answered the king
and said, [a]"*As* the LORD lives,
and *as* my lord the king lives,
surely in whatever place my lord
the king shall be, whether in
death or life, even there also
your servant will be."
22 So David said to It′taī, "Go,
and cross over." Then It′taī the
Git′tīte and all his men and all

5 [a]2 Sam. 14:33; 20:9
6 [a][Rom. 16:18]
7 [a][Deut. 23:21] [b]2 Sam. 3:2, 3 [1]LXX mss., Syr., Josephus *four*
8 [a]1 Sam. 16:2 [b]Gen. 28:20, 21 [c]2 Sam. 13:38
10 [a]1 Kin. 1:34
11 [a]1 Sam. 16:3, 5 [b]Gen. 20:5
12 [a]1 Chr. 27:33 [b]Josh. 15:51 [c]Ps. 3:1
13 [a]Judg. 9:3 [1]Lit. *after*
14 [a]Ps. 3:title
16 [a]Ps. 3:title [b]2 Sam. 12:11; 16:21, 22
18 [a]2 Sam. 8:18 [b]1 Sam. 23:13; 25:13; 30:1, 9 [1]Lit. *by his hand*
19 [a]2 Sam. 18:2
20 [a]1 Sam. 23:13
21 [a]Ruth 1:16, 17

the little ones who *were* with
him crossed over.
23 And all the country wept
with a loud voice, and all the
people crossed over. The king
himself also crossed over the
Brook Kid′ron, and all the people crossed over toward the way
of the [a]wilderness.
24 There was [a]Zā′dok also, and
all the Lē′vītes with him, bearing the [b]ark of the covenant of
God. And they set down the ark
of God, and [c]A·bī′a·thar went up
until all the people had finished
crossing over from the city.
25 Then the king said to Zā′dok,
"Carry the ark of God back into
the city. If I find favor in the eyes
of the LORD, He [a]will bring me
back and show me *both* it and
[b]His dwelling place.
26 "But if He says thus: 'I have
no [a]delight in you,' here I am,
[b]let Him do to me as seems good
to Him."
27 The king also said to Zā′dok
the priest, "*Are* you *not* a [a]seer?[1]
Return to the city in peace, and
[b]your two sons with you, A·him′-
a·az your son, and Jonathan the
son of A·bī′a·thar.
28 "See, [a]I will wait in the plains
of the wilderness until word
comes from you to inform me."
29 Therefore Zā′dok and A·bī′-
a·thar carried the ark of God
back to Jerusalem. And they
remained there.
30 So David went up by the
Ascent of the *Mount of* Olives,
and wept as he went up; and he
[a]had his head covered and went
[b]barefoot. And all the people who
were with him [c]covered their
heads and went up, [d]weeping as
they went up.
31 Then *someone* told David,

23 [a]2 Sam. 15:28; 16:2
24 [a]2 Sam. 8:17 [b]Num. 4:15 [c]1 Sam. 22:20
25 [a][Ps. 43:3] [b]Ex. 15:13
26 [a]Num. 14:8 [b]1 Sam. 3:18
27 [a]1 Sam. 9:6–9 [b]2 Sam. 17:17–20 [1]*prophet*
28 [a]2 Sam. 17:16
30 [a]Esth. 6:12 [b]Is. 20:2–4 [c]Jer. 14:3, 4 [d][Ps. 126:6]
31 [a]Ps. 3:1, 2; 55:12 [b]2 Sam. 16:23; 17:14, 23
32 [a]Josh. 16:2 [b]2 Sam. 1:2
33 [a]2 Sam. 19:35
34 [a]2 Sam. 16:19
35 [a]2 Sam. 17:15, 16
36 [a]2 Sam. 15:27
37 [a]1 Chr. 27:33 [b]2 Sam. 16:15

CHAPTER 16

1 [a]2 Sam. 15:30, 32 [b]2 Sam. 9:2; 19:17, 29

saying, [a]"A·hith′o·phel *is* among
the conspirators with Ab′sa·lom."
And David said, "O LORD, I pray,
[b]turn the counsel of A·hith′o·phel
into foolishness!"
32 Now it happened when David had come to the top *of the
mountain,* where he worshiped
God—there was Hū′shai the
[a]Ar′chīte coming to meet him
[b]with his robe torn and dust on
his head.
33 David said to him, "If you go
on with me, then you will become [a]a burden to me.
34 "But if you return to the city,
and say to Ab′sa·lom, [a]'I will be
your servant, O king; *as* I *was*
your father's servant previously,
so I *will* now also *be* your servant,' then you may defeat the
counsel of A·hith′o·phel for me.
35 "And *do* you not *have* Zā′dok
and A·bī′a·thar the priests with
you there? Therefore it will be
that whatever you hear from
the king's house, you shall tell
to [a]Zā′dok and A·bī′a·thar the
priests.
36 "Indeed *they have* there [a]with
them their two sons, A·him′a·az,
Zā′dok's *son,* and Jonathan,
A·bī′a·thar's *son;* and by them
you shall send me everything
you hear."
37 So Hū′shai, [a]David's friend,
went into the city. [b]And Ab′-
sa·lom came into Jerusalem.

16

When[a] David was a lit-
tle past the top *of the
mountain,* there was [b]Zī′ba the
servant of Me·phib′o·sheth,
who met him with a couple of
saddled donkeys, and on them
two hundred *loaves* of bread,
one hundred clusters of raisins,
one hundred summer fruits, and
a skin of wine.

2 And the king said to Zī′ba,
"What do you mean to do with
these?" So Zī′ba said, "The donkeys *are* for the king's household to ride on, the bread and
summer fruit for the young men
to eat, and the wine for [a]those
who are faint in the wilderness
to drink."
3 Then the king said, "And
where *is* your [a]master's son?"
[b]And Zī′ba said to the king, "Indeed he is staying in Jerusalem,
for he said, 'Today the house of
Israel will restore the kingdom
of my father to me.' "
4 So the king said to Zī′ba,
"Here, all that *belongs* to
Me·phib′o·sheth *is* yours." And
Zī′ba said, "I humbly bow before
you, *that* I may find favor in
your sight, my lord, O king!"
5 Now when King David came
to [a]Ba·hū′rim, there was a man
from the family of the house of
Saul, whose name *was* [b]Shim′ē·ī
the son of Gē′ra, coming from
there. He came out, cursing continuously as he came.
6 And he threw stones at David and at all the servants of
King David. And all the people
and all the mighty men *were* on
his right hand and on his left.
7 Also Shim′ē·ī said thus when
he cursed: "Come out! Come
out! You [1]bloodthirsty man, [a]you
[2]rogue!
8 "The LORD has [a]brought upon
you all [b]the blood of the house of
Saul, in whose place you have
reigned; and the LORD has delivered the kingdom into the hand
of Ab′sa·lom your son. So now
you *are caught* in your own evil,
because you are a [1]bloodthirsty
man!"
9 Then A·bi′shaī the son of
Ze·rū′i·ah said to the king, "Why
should this [a]dead dog [b]curse my
lord the king? Please, let me go
over and take off his head!"
10 But the king said, [a]"What
have I to do with you, you sons
of Ze·rū′i·ah? So let him curse,
because [b]the LORD has said to
him, 'Curse David.' [c]Who then
shall say, 'Why have you done
so?' "
11 And David said to A·bi′shaī
and all his servants, "See how
[a]my son who [b]came from my
own body seeks my life. How
much more now *may this* Ben′-
ja·mīte? Let him alone, and let
him curse; for so the LORD has
ordered him.
12 "It may be that the LORD will
look on [1]my affliction, and that
the LORD will [a]repay me with
[b]good for his cursing this day."
13 And as David and his men
went along the road, Shim′ē·ī
went along the hillside opposite him and cursed as he went,
threw stones at him and [1]kicked
up dust.
14 Now the king and all the
people who *were* with him became weary; so they refreshed
themselves there.
15 Meanwhile [a]Ab′sa·lom and
all the people, the men of Israel,
came to Jerusalem; and A·hith′-
o·phel *was* with him.
16 And so it was, when Hū′shai
the Ar′chīte, [a]David's friend,
came to Ab′sa·lom, that [b]Hū′shai
said to Ab′sa·lom, "*Long* live the
king! *Long* live the king!"
17 So Ab′sa·lom said to Hū′-
shai, "*Is* this your loyalty to your
friend? [a]Why did you not go
with your friend?"
18 And Hū′shai said to Ab′-
sa·lom, "No, but whom the LORD

2 [a]2 Sam. 15:23; 17:29
3 [a]2 Sam. 9:9, 10 [b]2 Sam. 19:27
5 [a]2 Sam. 3:16 [b]2 Sam. 19:21
7 [a]Deut. 13:13 [1]Lit. *man of bloodshed* [2]*worthless man*
8 [a]Judg. 9:24, 56, 57 [b]2 Sam. 1:16; 3:28, 29; 4:11, 12 [1]Lit. *man of bloodshed*
9 [a]2 Sam. 9:8 [b]Ex. 22:28
10 [a]2 Sam. 3:39; 19:22 [b][Lam. 3:38] [c][Rom. 9:20]
11 [a]2 Sam. 12:11 [b]Gen. 15:4
12 [a]Prov. 20:22 [b][Rom. 8:28] [1]So with Kt., LXX, Syr., Vg.; Qr. *my eyes;* Tg. *tears of my eyes*
13 [1]Lit. *dusted him with dust*
15 [a]2 Sam. 15:12, 37
16 [a]2 Sam. 15:37 [b]2 Sam. 15:34
17 [a]2 Sam. 19:25

and this people and all the men
of Israel choose, his I will be,
and with him I will remain.
19 "Furthermore, [a]whom should
I serve? *Should I* not *serve* in the
presence of his son? As I have
served in your father's presence,
so will I be in your presence."
20 Then Ab′sa·lom said to
[a]A·hith′o·phel, "Give advice as
to what we should do."
21 And A·hith′o·phel said to
Ab′sa·lom, "Go in to your father's [a]concubines, whom he has
left to keep the house; and all
Israel will hear that you [b]are abhorred by your father. Then [c]the
hands of all who are with you
will be strong."
22 So they pitched a tent for
Ab′sa·lom on the top of the
house, and Ab′sa·lom went in to
his father's concubines [a]in the
sight of all Israel.
23 Now the advice of A·hith′-
o·phel, which he gave in those
days, *was* as if one had inquired
at the oracle of God. So *was* all
the advice of A·hith′o·phel [a]both
with David and with Ab′sa·lom.

17 Moreover A·hith′o·phel
said to Ab′sa·lom, "Now
let me choose twelve thousand
men, and I will arise and pursue
David tonight.
2 "I will come upon him while
he *is* [a]weary and weak, and make
him [1]afraid. And all the people
who *are* with him will flee, and I
will [b]strike only the king.
3 "Then I will bring back all
the people to you. When all return except the man whom you
seek, all the people will be at
peace."
4 And the saying pleased Ab′-
sa·lom and all the [a]elders of
Israel.

19 [a]2 Sam. 15:34
20 [a]2 Sam. 15:12
21 [a]2 Sam. 15:16; 20:3 [b]Gen. 34:30 [c]2 Sam. 2:7
22 [a]2 Sam. 12:11, 12
23 [a]2 Sam. 15:12

CHAPTER 17

2 [a]2 Sam. 16:14 [b]Zech. 13:7 [1]*tremble with fear*
4 [a]2 Sam. 5:3; 19:11
5 [a]2 Sam. 15:32–34
8 [a]Hos. 13:8
10 [a]Josh. 2:11
11 [a]2 Sam. 3:10 [b]Gen. 22:17

5 Then Ab′sa·lom said, "Now
call Hū′shai the Ar′chīte also,
and let us hear what he [a]says
too."
6 And when Hū′shai came to
Ab′sa·lom, Ab′sa·lom spoke to
him, saying, "A·hith′o·phel has
spoken in this manner. Shall we
do as he says? If not, speak up."
7 So Hū′shai said to Ab′sa·lom:
"The advice that A·hith′o·phel
has given *is* not good at this
time.
8 "For," said Hū′shai, "you
know your father and his men,
that they *are* mighty men, and
they *are* enraged in their minds,
like [a]a bear robbed of her cubs
in the field; and your father *is* a
man of war, and will not camp
with the people.
9 "Surely by now he is hidden in some pit, or in some
other place. And it will be, when
some of them are overthrown
at the first, that whoever hears
it will say, 'There is a slaughter
among the people who follow
Ab′sa·lom.'
10 "And even he *who is* valiant,
whose heart *is* like the heart of
a lion, will [a]melt completely. For
all Israel knows that your father
is a mighty man, and *those* who
are with him *are* valiant men.
11 "Therefore I advise that all
Israel be fully gathered to you,
[a]from Dan to Bē·er·shē′ba, [b]like
the sand that *is* by the sea for
multitude, and that you go to
battle in person.
12 "So we will come upon him
in some place where he may be
found, and we will fall on him as
the dew falls on the ground. And
of him and all the men who *are*
with him there shall not be left
so much as one.

13 "Moreover, if he has withdrawn into a city, then all Israel
shall bring ropes to that city;
and we will [a]pull it into the river,
until there is not one small stone
found there."
14 So Ab′sa·lom and all the men
of Israel said, "The advice of Hū′-
shai the Ar′chīte *is* better than
the advice of A·hith′o·phel." For
[a]the LORD had purposed to defeat
the good advice of A·hith′o·phel,
to the intent that the LORD might
bring disaster on Ab′sa·lom.
15 [a]Then Hū′shai said to Zā′-
dok and A·bī′a·thar the priests,
"Thus and so A·hith′o·phel advised Ab′sa·lom and the elders
of Israel, and thus and so I have
advised.
16 "Now therefore, send quickly
and tell David, saying, 'Do not
spend this night [a]in the plains
of the wilderness, but speedily
cross over, lest the king and all
the people who *are* with him be
swallowed up.' "
17 [a]Now Jonathan and A·him′-
a·az [b]stayed at [c]En Rō′gel, for
they dared not be seen coming
into the city; so a female servant
would come and tell them, and
they would go and tell King
David.
18 Nevertheless a lad saw them,
and told Ab′sa·lom. But both
of them went away quickly
and came to a man's house [a]in
Ba·hū′rim, who had a well in his
court; and they went down into
it.
19 [a]Then the woman took and
spread a covering over the well's
mouth, and spread ground grain
on it; and the thing was not
known.
20 And when Ab′sa·lom's servants came to the woman at the
house, they said, "Where *are*
A·him′a·az and Jonathan?" So
[a]the woman said to them, "They
have gone over the water brook."
And when they had searched
and could not find *them*, they
returned to Jerusalem.
21 Now it came to pass, after they had departed, that they
came up out of the well and went
and told King David, and said to
David, [a]"Arise and cross over
the water quickly. For thus has
A·hith′o·phel advised against
you."
22 So David and all the people who *were* with him arose
and crossed over the Jordan. By
morning light not one of them
was left who had not gone over
the Jordan.
23 Now when A·hith′o·phel
saw that his advice was not
followed, he saddled a donkey,
and arose and went home to
[a]his house, to his city. Then he
[1]put his [b]household in order, and
[c]hanged himself, and died; and
he was buried in his father's
tomb.
24 Then David went to
[a]Mā·ha·na′im. And Ab′sa·lom
crossed over the Jordan, he and
all the men of Israel with him.
25 And Ab′sa·lom made
[a]A·mā′sa captain of the army
instead of Jō′ab. This A·mā′sa
was the son of a man whose
name *was* [1]Jith′ra, an [2]Israelite,
who had gone in to [b]Ab′i·gāil
the daughter of Nā′hash, sister
of Ze·rū′i·ah, Jō′ab's mother.
26 So Israel and Ab′sa·lom encamped in the land of Gil′ē·ad.
27 Now it happened, when David had come to Mā·ha·na′im,
that [a]Shō′bī the son of Nā′hash
from Rab′bah of the people of

13 [a]Mic. 1:6
14 [a]2 Sam. 15:31, 34
15 [a]2 Sam. 15:35, 36
16 [a]2 Sam. 15:28
17 [a]2 Sam. 15:27, 36 [b]Josh. 2:4–6 [c]Josh. 15:7; 18:16
18 [a]2 Sam. 3:16; 16:5
19 [a]Josh. 2:4–6
20 [a]Josh. 2:3–5
21 [a]2 Sam. 17:15, 16
23 [a]2 Sam. 15:12 [b]2 Kin. 20:1 [c]Matt. 27:5 [1]Lit. *gave charge concerning his house*
24 [a]2 Sam. 2:8; 19:32
25 [a]1 Kin. 2:5, 32 [b]1 Chr. 2:16 [1]*Jether*, 1 Chr. 2:17 [2]So with MT, some LXX mss., Tg.; some LXX mss. *Ishmaelite* (cf. 1 Chr. 2:17); Vg. *of Jezrael*
27 [a]2 Sam. 10:1; 12:29

Am′mon, [b]Mā′chir the son of
Am′mi·el from Lo Dē′bar, and
[c]Bar·zil′laī the Gil′ē·ad·īte from
Rō′ge·lim,
28 brought beds and basins,
earthen vessels and wheat, barley and flour, parched *grain*
and beans, lentils and parched
seeds,
29 honey and curds, sheep and
cheese of the herd, for David
and the people who *were* with
him to eat. For they said, "The
people are hungry and weary
and thirsty [a]in the wilderness."

CHAPTER 18

18 And David [1]numbered
the people who *were* with
him, and [a]set captains of thousands and captains of hundreds
over them.
2 Then David sent out one
third of the people under the
hand of Jō′ab, [a]one third under
the hand of A·bi′shaī the son of
Ze·rū′i·ah, Jō′ab's brother, and
one third under the hand of [b]It′-
taī the Git′tīte. And the king said
to the people, "I also will surely
go out with you myself."
3 [a]But the people answered,
"You shall not go out! For if we
flee away, they will not care
about us; nor if half of us die,
will they care about us. But *you*
are worth ten thousand of us
now. For you are now more help
to us in the city."
4 Then the king said to them,
"Whatever seems best to you I
will do." So the king stood beside the gate, and all the people
went out by hundreds and by
thousands.
5 Now the king had com-
manded Jō′ab, A·bi′shaī, and
It′taī, saying, "*Deal* gently for
my sake with the young man
Ab′sa·lom." [a]And all the people
heard when the king gave all
the captains orders concerning
Ab′sa·lom.
6 So the people went out into
the field of battle against Israel.
And the battle was in the [a]woods
of Ē′phra·im.
7 The people of Israel were
overthrown there before the
servants of David, and a great
slaughter of twenty thousand
took place there that day.
8 For the battle there was scattered over the face of the whole
countryside, and the woods devoured more people that day
than the sword devoured.
9 Then Ab′sa·lom met the servants of David. Ab′sa·lom rode
on a mule. The mule went under
the thick boughs of a great terebinth tree, and [a]his head caught
in the terebinth; so he was left
hanging between heaven and
earth. And the mule which *was*
under him went on.
10 Now a certain man saw *it*
and told Jō′ab, and said, "I just
saw Ab′sa·lom hanging in a
terebinth tree!"
11 So Jō′ab said to the man who
told him, "You just saw *him!* And
why did you not strike him there
to the ground? I would have
given you ten *shekels* of silver
and a belt."
12 But the man said to Jō′ab,
"Though I were to receive a
thousand *shekels* of silver in
my hand, I would not raise my
hand against the king's son. [a]For
in our hearing the king commanded you and A·bi′shaī and
It′taī, saying, [1]'Beware lest anyone *touch* the young man Ab′-
sa·lom!'
13 "Otherwise I would have
dealt falsely against my own life.

27 [b]2 Sam. 9:4 [c]2 Sam. 19:31, 32
29 [a]2 Sam. 16:2, 14
1 [a]Ex. 18:25 [1]Lit. *attended to*
2 [a]Judg. 7:16 [b]2 Sam. 15:19–22
3 [a]2 Sam. 21:17
5 [a]2 Sam. 18:12
6 [a]Josh. 17:15, 18
9 [a]2 Sam. 14:26
12 [a]2 Sam. 18:5 [1]Vss. *'Protect the young man Absalom for me!'*

For there is nothing hidden from
the king, and you yourself would
have set yourself against *me*."
14 Then Jō′ab said, "I cannot
linger with you." And he took
three spears in his hand and
thrust them through Ab′sa·lom's
heart, while he was *still* alive in
the midst of the terebinth tree.
15 And ten young men who
bore Jō′ab's armor surrounded
Ab′sa·lom, and struck and killed
him.
16 So Jō′ab blew the trumpet,
and the people returned from
pursuing Israel. For Jō′ab held
back the people.
17 And they took Ab′sa·lom and
cast him into a large pit in the
woods, and [a]laid a very large
heap of stones over him. Then
all Israel [b]fled, everyone to his
tent.
18 Now Ab′sa·lom in his lifetime had taken and set up a
[1]pillar for himself, which *is* in
[a]the King's Valley. For he said,
[b]"I have no son to keep my name
in remembrance." He called the
pillar after his own name. And to
this day it is called Ab′sa·lom's
Monument.
19 Then [a]A·him′a·az the son of
Zā′dok said, "Let me run now
and take the news to the king,
how the LORD has [1]avenged him
of his enemies."
20 And Jō′ab said to him, "You
shall not take the news this day,
for you shall take the news another day. But today you shall
take no news, because the king's
son is dead."
21 Then Jō′ab said to the Cū′-
shīte, "Go, tell the king what
you have seen." So the Cū′shīte
bowed himself to Jō′ab and ran.
22 And A·him′a·az the son of
Zā′dok said again to Jō′ab, "But
[1]whatever happens, please let
me also run after the Cū′shīte."
So Jō′ab said, "Why will you
run, my son, since you have no
news ready?"
23 "But whatever happens," *he
said*, "let me run." So he said to
him, "Run." Then A·him′a·az ran
by way of the plain, and outran
the Cū′shīte.
24 Now David was sitting between the [a]two gates. And the
watchman went up to the roof
over the gate, to the wall, lifted
his eyes and looked, and there
was a man, running alone.
25 Then the watchman cried
out and told the king. And the
king said, "If he *is* alone, *there
is* news in his mouth." And he
came rapidly and drew near.
26 Then the watchman saw
another man running, and the
watchman called to the gatekeeper and said, "There is *another* man, running alone!" And
the king said, "He also brings
news."
27 So the watchman said, [1]"I
think the running of the first is
like the running of A·him′a·az
the son of Zā′dok." And the king
said, "He *is* a good man, and
comes with [a]good news."
28 So A·him′a·az called out and
said to the king, [1]"All is well!"
Then he bowed down with his
face to the earth before the king,
and said, [a]"Blessed *be* the LORD
your God, who has delivered up
the men who raised their hand
against my lord the king!"
29 The king said, "Is the young
man Ab′sa·lom safe?" A·him′a·az
answered, "When Jō′ab sent the
king's servant and *me* your servant, I saw a great tumult, but

17 [a]Josh. 7:26; 8:29 [b]2 Sam. 19:8; 20:1, 22
18 [a]Gen. 14:17 [b]2 Sam. 14:27 [1]*monument*
19 [a]2 Sam. 15:36; 17:17 [1]*vindicated*
22 [1]Lit. *be what may*
24 [a]2 Kin. 9:17
27 [a]1 Kin. 1:42 [1]Lit. *I see the running*
28 [a]2 Sam. 16:12 [1]*Peace be to you*

I did not know what *it was*
about."
30 And the king said, "Turn
aside *and* stand here." So he
turned aside and stood still.
31 Just then the Cū′shīte came,
and the Cū′shīte said, "There is
good news, my lord the king!
For the LORD has avenged you
this day of all those who rose
against you."
32 And the king said to the
Cū′shīte, "Is the young man Ab′-
sa·lom safe?" So the Cū′shīte
answered, "May the enemies of
my lord the king, and all who
rise against you to do harm, be
like *that* young man!"
33 Then the king was deeply
moved, and went up to the chamber over the gate, and wept. And
as he went, he said thus: [a]"O my
son Ab′sa·lom—my son, my son
Ab′sa·lom—if only I had died in
your place! O Ab′sa·lom my son,
[b]my son!"

19

And Jō′ab was told, "Be-
hold, the king is weeping
and [a]mourning for Ab′sa·lom."
2 So the victory that day was
turned into [a]mourning for all
the people. For the people heard
it said that day, "The king is
grieved for his son."
3 And the people [1]stole back
[a]into the city that day, as people
who are ashamed steal away
when they flee in battle.
4 But the king [a]covered his
face, and the king cried out with
a loud voice, [b]"O my son Ab′-
sa·lom! O Ab′sa·lom, my son, my
son!"
5 Then [a]Jō′ab came into the
house to the king, and said,
"Today you have disgraced all
your servants who today have
saved your life, the lives of your
sons and daughters, the lives of
your wives and the lives of your
concubines,
6 "in that you love your enemies and hate your friends. For
you have declared today that
you [1]regard neither princes nor
servants; for today I perceive
that if Ab′sa·lom had lived and
all of us had died today, then it
would have pleased you well.
7 "Now therefore, arise, go out
and speak [1]comfort to your servants. For I swear by the LORD, if
you do not go out, not one will
stay with you this night. And
that will be worse for you than
all the evil that has befallen you
from your youth until now."
8 Then the king arose and sat
in the [a]gate. And they told all
the people, saying, "There is the
king, sitting in the gate." So all
the people came before the king.
For everyone of Israel had [b]fled
to his tent.
9 Now all the people were in a
dispute throughout all the tribes
of Israel, saying, "The king
saved us from the hand of our
[a]enemies, he delivered us from
the hand of the [b]Phi·lis′tines,
and now he has [c]fled from the
land because of Ab′sa·lom.
10 "But Ab′sa·lom, whom we
anointed over us, has died in
battle. Now therefore, why do
you say nothing about bringing
back the king?"
11 So King David sent to [a]Zā′-
dok and A·bī′a·thar the priests,
saying, "Speak to the elders of
Judah, saying, 'Why are you the
last to bring the king back to
his house, since the words of all
Israel have come to the king, to
his *very* house?
12 'You *are* my brethren, you

33 [a]2 Sam. 12:10 [b]2 Sam. 19:4

CHAPTER 19

1 [a]Jer. 14:2

2 [a]Esth. 4:3

3 [a]2 Sam. 17:24, 27; 19:32 [1]*went by stealth*

4 [a]2 Sam. 15:30 [b]2 Sam. 18:33

5 [a]2 Sam. 18:14

6 [1]*have no respect for*

7 [1]Lit. *to the heart of*

8 [a]2 Sam. 15:2; 18:24 [b]2 Sam. 18:17

9 [a]2 Sam. 8:1–14 [b]2 Sam. 3:18 [c]2 Sam. 15:14

11 [a]2 Sam. 15:24

are [a]my bone and my flesh. Why
then are you the last to bring
back the king?'
13 [a]"And say to A·mā′sa, '*Are*
you not my bone and my flesh?
[b]God do so to me, and more also,
if you are not commander of the
army before me [1]continually in
place of Jō′ab.' "
14 So he swayed the hearts
of all the men of Judah, [a]just
as *the heart of* one man, so
that they sent *this word* to the
king: "Return, you and all your
servants!"
15 Then the king returned and
came to the Jordan. And Judah came to [a]Gil′gal, to go to
meet the king, to escort the king
[b]across the Jordan.
16 And [a]Shim′ē·ī the son of
Gē′ra, a Ben′ja·mīte, who *was*
from Ba·hū′rim, hurried and
came down with the men of Judah to meet King David.
17 *There were* a thousand men
of [a]Benjamin with him, and
[b]Zī′ba the servant of the house
of Saul, and his fifteen sons and
his twenty servants with him;
and they went over the Jordan
before the king.
18 Then a ferryboat went across
to carry over the king's household, and to do what he thought
good.
Now Shim′ē·ī the son of Gē′ra
fell down before the king when
he had crossed the Jordan.
19 Then he said to the king,
[a]"Do not let my lord [1]impute iniquity to me, or remember what
[b]wrong your servant did on the
day that my lord the king left
Jerusalem, that the king should
[c]take *it* to heart.
20 "For I, your servant, know
that I have sinned. Therefore
here I am, the first to come today of all [a]the house of Joseph
to go down to meet my lord the
king."
21 But A·bi′shaī the son of
Ze·rū′i·ah answered and said,
"Shall not Shim′ē·ī be put to
death for this, [a]because he
[b]cursed the LORD's anointed?"
22 And David said, [a]"What have
I to do with you, you sons of
Ze·rū′i·ah, that you should be
adversaries to me today? [b]Shall
any man be put to death today
in Israel? For do I not know that
today I *am* king over Israel?"
23 Therefore [a]the king said to
Shim′ē·ī, "You shall not die."
And the king swore to him.
24 Now [a]Me·phib′o·sheth the
son of Saul came down to meet
the king. And he had not cared
for his feet, nor trimmed his mustache, nor washed his clothes,
from the day the king departed
until the day he returned in
peace.
25 So it was, when he had
come to Jerusalem to meet the
king, that the king said to him,
[a]"Why did you not go with me,
Me·phib′o·sheth?"
26 And he answered, "My lord,
O king, my servant deceived
me. For your servant said, 'I will
saddle a donkey for myself, that
I may ride on it and go to the
king,' because your servant *is*
lame.
27 "And [a]he has slandered your
servant to my lord the king, [b]but
my lord the king *is* like the angel
of God. Therefore do *what is*
good in your eyes.
28 "For all my father's house
were but dead men before my
lord the king. [a]Yet you set your
servant among those who eat at

12 [a]2 Sam. 5:1
13 [a]2 Sam. 17:25 [b]Ruth 1:17 [1]*permanently*
14 [a]Judg. 20:1
15 [a]Josh. 5:9 [b]2 Sam. 17:22
16 [a]2 Sam. 16:5
17 [a]1 Kin. 12:21 [b]2 Sam. 9:2, 10; 16:1, 2
19 [a]1 Sam. 22:15 [b]2 Sam. 16:5, 6 [c]2 Sam. 13:33 [1]*charge me with iniquity*
20 [a]Judg. 1:22
21 [a][Ex. 22:28] [b][1 Sam. 26:9]
22 [a]2 Sam. 3:39; 16:10 [b]1 Sam. 11:13
23 [a]1 Kin. 2:8, 9, 37, 46
24 [a]2 Sam. 9:6; 21:7
25 [a]2 Sam. 16:17
27 [a]2 Sam. 16:3, 4 [b]2 Sam. 14:17, 20
28 [a]2 Sam. 9:7–13

your own table. Therefore what
right have I still to [1]cry out anymore to the king?"
29 So the king said to him,
"Why do you speak anymore of
your matters? I have said, 'You
and Zī'ba divide the land.' "
30 Then Me·phib'o·sheth said to
the king, "Rather, let him take
it all, inasmuch as my lord the
king has come back in peace to
his own house."
31 And [a]Bar·zil'laī the Gil'-
ē·ad·īte came down from Rō'-
ge·lim and went across the Jordan with the king, to escort him
across the Jordan.
32 Now Bar·zil'laī was a very
aged man, eighty years old.
And [a]he had provided the king
with supplies while he stayed at
Mā·ha·na'im, for he *was* a very
rich man.
33 And the king said to Bar·zil'-
laī, "Come across with me, and
I will provide for you while you
are with me in Jerusalem."
34 But Bar·zil'laī said to the
king, "How long have I to live,
that I should go up with the king
to Jerusalem?
35 "I *am* today [a]eighty years
old. Can I discern between the
good and bad? Can your servant taste what I eat or what I
drink? Can I hear any longer the
voice of singing men and singing women? Why then should
your servant be a further burden
to my lord the king?
36 "Your servant will go a little
way across the Jordan with the
king. And why should the king
repay me *with* such a reward?
37 "Please let your servant turn
back again, that I may die in my
own city, near the grave of my
father and mother. But here is
your servant [a]Chim'ham; let him
cross over with my lord the king,
and do for him what seems good
to you."
38 And the king answered,
"Chim'ham shall cross over with
me, and I will do for him what
seems good to you. Now whatever you request of me, I will do
for you."
39 Then all the people went
over the Jordan. And when the
king had crossed over, the king
[a]kissed Bar·zil'laī and blessed
him, and he returned to his own
place.
40 Now the king went on to
Gil'gal, and [1]Chim'ham went on
with him. And all the people of
Judah escorted the king, and
also half the people of Israel.
41 Just then all the men of Israel
came to the king, and said to the
king, "Why have our brethren,
the men of Judah, stolen you
away and [a]brought the king, his
household, and all David's men
with him across the Jordan?"
42 So all the men of Judah answered the men of Israel, "Because the king *is* [a]a close relative
of ours. Why then are you angry
over this matter? Have we ever
eaten at the king's *expense*? Or
has he given us any gift?"
43 And the men of Israel answered the men of Judah, and
said, "We have [a]ten shares in
the king; therefore we also have
more *right* to David than you.
Why then do you despise us—
were we not the first to advise
bringing back our king?" Yet
[b]the words of the men of Judah
were [1]fiercer than the words of
the men of Israel.

20

And there happened to
be there a [1]rebel, whose

28 [1]*complain*
31 [a]1 Kin. 2:7
32 [a]2 Sam. 17:27–29
35 [a]Ps. 90:10
37 [a]Jer. 41:17
39 [a]Gen. 31:55
40 [1]MT *Chimhan*
41 [a]2 Sam. 19:15
42 [a]2 Sam. 19:12
43 [a]1 Kin. 11:30, 31 [b]Judg. 8:1; 12:1 [1]*harsher*

CHAPTER 20
1 [1]Lit. *man of Belial*

name *was* Shē′ba the son of
Bich′rī, a Ben′ja·mīte. And he
blew a trumpet, and said:

[a]"We have no share in David,
Nor do we have inheritance
in the son of Jesse;
[b]Every man to his tents,
O Israel!"

2 So every man of Israel deserted David, *and* followed
Shē′ba the son of Bich′rī. But the
[a]men of Judah, from the Jordan
as far as Jerusalem, remained
loyal to their king.
3 Now David came to his house
at Jerusalem. And the king took
the ten women, [a]his concubines
whom he had left to keep the
house, and put them in seclusion
and supported them, but did not
go in to them. So they were shut
up to the day of their death, living in widowhood.
4 And the king said to A·mā′sa,
[a]"Assemble the men of Judah for
me within three days, and be
present here yourself."
5 So A·mā′sa went to assemble
the men of Judah. But he delayed
longer than the set time which
David had appointed him.
6 And David said to [a]A·bi′shaī,
"Now Shē′ba the son of Bich′rī
will do us more harm than Ab′-
sa·lom. Take [b]your lord's servants and pursue him, lest he
find for himself fortified cities,
and escape us."
7 So Jō′ab's men, with the
[a]Cher′e·thītes, the Pel′eth·ītes,
and [b]all the mighty men, went
out after him. And they went out
of Jerusalem to pursue Shē′ba
the son of Bich′rī.
8 When they *were* at the large
stone which *is* in Gib′ē·on,
A·mā′sa came before them. Now
Jō′ab was dressed in battle armor; on it was a belt *with* a
sword fastened in its sheath at
his hips; and as he was going
forward, it fell out.
9 Then Jō′ab said to A·mā′sa,
"*Are* you in health, my brother?"
[a]And Jō′ab took A·mā′sa by the
beard with his right hand to kiss
him.
10 But A·mā′sa did not notice
the sword that *was* in Jō′ab's
hand. And [a]he struck him with
it [b]in the stomach, and his entrails poured out on the ground;
and he did not *strike* him again.
Thus he died. Then Jō′ab and
A·bi′shaī his brother pursued
Shē′ba the son of Bich′rī.
11 Meanwhile one of Jō′ab's
men stood near A·mā′sa, and
said, "Whoever favors Jō′ab and
whoever *is* for David—follow
Jō′ab!"
12 But A·mā′sa wallowed in *his*
blood in the middle of the highway. And when the man saw
that all the people stood still, he
moved A·mā′sa from the highway to the field and threw a
garment over him, when he saw
that everyone who came upon
him halted.
13 When he was removed from
the highway, all the people went
on after Jō′ab to pursue Shē′ba
the son of Bich′rī.
14 And he went through all the
tribes of Israel to [a]Abel and Beth
Mā′a·chah and all the Be′rītes.
So they were gathered together
and also went after [1]*Shē′ba.*
15 Then they came and besieged
him in Abel of Beth Mā′a·chah;
and they [a]cast up a siege mound
against the city, and it stood by
the rampart. And all the people

1 [a]1 Kin. 12:16 [b]2 Sam. 18:17
2 [a]2 Sam. 19:14
3 [a]2 Sam. 15:16; 16:21, 22
4 [a]2 Sam. 17:25; 19:13
6 [a]2 Sam. 21:17 [b]2 Sam. 11:11
7 [a]1 Kin. 1:38, 44 [b]2 Sam. 15:18
9 [a]Matt. 26:49
10 [a]1 Kin. 2:5 [b]2 Sam. 2:23
14 [a]2 Kin. 15:29 [1]Lit. *him*
15 [a]2 Kin. 19:32

who *were* with Jō′ab battered
the wall to throw it down.
16 Then a wise woman cried out
from the city, "Hear, hear! Please
say to Jō′ab, 'Come nearby, that
I may speak with you.' "
17 When he had come near to
her, the woman said, "*Are* you
Jō′ab?" He answered, "I *am*."
Then she said to him, "Hear the
words of your maidservant." And
he answered, "I am listening."
18 So she spoke, saying, "They
used to talk in former times,
saying, 'They shall surely seek
guidance at Abel,' and so they
would end *disputes*.
19 "I *am among the* peaceable
and faithful in Israel. You seek
to destroy a city and a mother
in Israel. Why would you swallow up [a]the inheritance of the
LORD?"
20 And Jō′ab answered and
said, "Far be it, far be it from
me, that I should swallow up or
destroy!
21 "That *is* not so. But a
man from the mountains of
Ē′phra·im, Shē′ba the son of
Bich′rī by name, has raised his
hand against the king, against
David. Deliver him only, and I
will depart from the city." So the
woman said to Jō′ab, "Watch,
his head will be thrown to you
over the wall."
22 Then the woman [a]in her wisdom went to all the people. And
they cut off the head of Shē′ba
the son of Bich′rī, and threw
it out to Jō′ab. Then he blew
a trumpet, and they withdrew
from the city, every man to his
tent. So Jō′ab returned to the
king at Jerusalem.
23 And [a]Jō′ab *was* over all
the army of Israel; Be·nā′i·ah
the son of Je·hoi′a·da *was* over
the Cher′e·thītes and the Pel′-
eth·ītes;
24 A·dor′am *was* [a]in charge of
revenue; [b]Je·hosh′a·phat the son
of A·hī′lud *was* recorder;
25 Shē′va *was* scribe; [a]Zā′dok
and A·bī′a·thar *were* the priests;
26 [a]and Ī′ra the Jā′i·rīte was [1]a
chief minister under David.

21

Now there was a fam-
ine in the days of David
for three years, year after year;
and David [a]inquired of the LORD.
And the LORD answered, "*It is*
because of Saul and *his* [1]blood-
thirsty house, because he killed
the Gib′ē·on·ītes."
2 So the king called the Gib′-
ē·on·ītes and spoke to them.
Now the Gib′ē·on·ītes *were* not
of the children of Israel, but [a]of
the remnant of the Am′o·rītes;
the children of Israel had sworn
protection to them, but Saul had
sought to kill them [b]in his zeal
for the children of Israel and
Judah.
3 Therefore David said to the
Gib′ē·on·ītes, "What shall I do for
you? And with what shall I make
atonement, that you may bless
[a]the inheritance of the LORD?"
4 And the Gib′ē·on·ītes said
to him, "We will have no silver
or gold from Saul or from his
house, nor shall you kill any
man in Israel for us." So he said,
"Whatever you say, I will do for
you."
5 Then they answered the king,
"As for the man who consumed
us and plotted against us, *that*
we should be destroyed from remaining in any of the territories
of Israel,
6 "let seven men of his descendants be delivered [a]to us, and we

19 [a]1 Sam. 26:19
22 [a][Eccl. 9:13–16]
23 [a]2 Sam. 8:16–18
24 [a]1 Kin. 4:6 [b]2 Sam. 8:16
25 [a]1 Kin. 4:4
26 [a]2 Sam. 8:18 [1]Or *David's priest*

CHAPTER 21

1 [a]Num. 27:21 [1]Lit. *house of bloodshed*
2 [a]Josh. 9:3, 15–20 [b][Ex. 34:11–16]
3 [a]2 Sam. 20:19
6 [a]Num. 25:4

will hang them before the LORD
[b]in Gib′ē·ah of Saul, [c]*whom* the
LORD chose." And the king said,
"I will give *them.*"
7 But the king spared [a]Me-
phib′o·sheth the son of Jonathan, the son of Saul, because
of [b]the LORD's oath that *was* between them, between David and
Jonathan the son of Saul.
8 So the king took Ar·mō′nī
and Me·phib′o·sheth, the two
sons of [a]Riz′pah the daughter of
Ā′i·ah, whom she bore to Saul,
and the five sons of [1]Mī′chal
the daughter of Saul, whom she
[2]brought up for Ā′dri·el the son
of Bar·zil′laī the Me·hō′la·thīte;
9 and he delivered them into
the hands of the Gib′ē·on·ītes,
and they hanged them on the
hill [a]before the LORD. So they
fell, *all* seven together, and were
put to death in the days of harvest, in the first *days,* in the beginning of barley harvest.
10 Now [a]Riz′pah the daughter
of Ā′i·ah took sackcloth and
spread it for herself on the rock,
[b]from the beginning of harvest
until the late rains poured on
them from heaven. And she did
not allow the birds of the air
to rest on them by day nor the
beasts of the field by night.
11 And David was told what
Riz′pah the daughter of Ā′i·ah,
the concubine of Saul, had done.
12 Then David went and took
the bones of Saul, and the bones
of Jonathan his son, from the
men of [a]Jā′besh Gil′ē·ad who had
stolen them from the street of
[1]Beth Shan, where the [b]Phi·lis′-
tines had hung them up, after
the Phi·lis′tines had struck down
Saul in Gil·bō′a.
13 So he brought up the bones
of Saul and the bones of Jonathan his son from there; and
they gathered the bones of those
who had been hanged.
14 They buried the bones of
Saul and Jonathan his son in the
country of Benjamin in [a]Zē′lah,
in the tomb of Kish his father.
So they performed all that the
king commanded. And after that
[b]God heeded the prayer for the
land.
15 When the Phi·lis′tines were
at war again with Israel, David and his servants with him
went down and fought against
the Phi·lis′tines; and David grew
faint.
16 Then Ish′bi-Bē′nob, who *was*
one of the sons of [1]the [a]giant, the
weight of whose bronze spear
was three hundred *shekels,*
who was bearing a new *sword,*
thought he could kill David.
17 But [a]A·bi′shaī the son of
Ze·rū′i·ah came to his aid, and
struck the Phi·lis′tine and killed
him. Then the men of David
swore to him, saying, [b]"You shall
go out no more with us to battle,
lest you quench the [c]lamp of
Israel."
18 [a]Now it happened afterward that there was again a
battle with the Phi·lis′tines at
Gob. Then [b]Sib′be·chaī the Hū′-
sha·thīte killed [1]Saph, who *was*
one of the sons of [2]the giant.
19 Again there was war at Gob
with the Phi·lis′tines, where
[a]El·hā′nan the son of [1]Jā′a·rē-
Or′e·gim the Beth′le·hem·īte
killed [b]*the brother of* Goliath the
Git′tīte, the shaft of whose spear
was like a weaver's beam.
20 Yet again [a]there was war at
Gath, where there was a man
of *great* stature, who had six

6 [b]1 Sam. 10:26 [c]1 Sam. 10:24
7 [a]2 Sam. 4:4; 9:10 [b]2 Sam. 9:1–7
8 [a]2 Sam. 3:7 [1]*Merab,* 1 Sam. 18:19; 25:44; 2 Sam. 3:14; 6:23 [2]Lit. *bore to Adriel*
9 [a]2 Sam. 6:17
10 [a]2 Sam. 3:7; 21:8 [b]Deut. 21:23
12 [a]1 Sam. 31:11–13 [b]1 Sam. 31:8 [1]*Beth Shean,* Josh. 17:11
14 [a]Josh. 18:28 [b]2 Sam. 24:25
16 [a]2 Sam. 21:18–22 [1]Or *Rapha*
17 [a]2 Sam. 20:6–10 [b]2 Sam. 18:3 [c]1 Kin. 11:36
18 [a]1 Chr. 20:4–8 [b]1 Chr. 11:29; 27:11 [1]*Sippai,* 1 Chr. 20:4 [2]Or *Rapha*
19 [a]2 Sam. 23:24 [b]1 Chr. 20:5 [1]*Jair,* 1 Chr. 20:5
20 [a]1 Chr. 20:6

fingers on each hand and six
toes on each foot, twenty-four in
number; and he also was born to
[1]the giant.
21 So when he [a]defied Israel,
Jonathan the son of [1]Shim'ē·a,
David's brother, killed him.
22 [a]These four were born to [1]the
giant in Gath, and fell by the
hand of David and by the hand
of his servants.

22

Then David [a]spoke to
the LORD the words of
this song, on the day when the
LORD had [b]delivered him from
the hand of all his enemies, and
from the hand of Saul.
2 And he [a]said:

[b]"The LORD *is* my rock and
my [c]fortress and my
deliverer;
3 The God of my strength, [a]in
whom I will trust;
My [b]shield and the [c]horn[1] of
my salvation,
My [d]stronghold and my
[e]refuge;
My Savior, You save me
from violence.
4 I will call upon the LORD,
who is worthy to be
praised;
So shall I be saved from my
enemies.

5 "When the waves of death
surrounded me,
The floods of ungodliness
[1]made me afraid.
6 The [a]sorrows of Shē'ōl
surrounded me;
The snares of death
confronted me.
7 In my distress [a]I called upon
the LORD,
And cried out to my God;
He [b]heard my voice from
His temple,
And my cry *entered* His
ears.

8 "Then [a]the earth shook and
trembled;
[b]The foundations of [1]heaven
quaked and were
shaken,
Because He was angry.
9 Smoke went up from His
nostrils,
And devouring [a]fire from
His mouth;
Coals were kindled by it.
10 He [a]bowed the heavens also,
and came down
With [b]darkness under His
feet.
11 He rode upon a cherub, and
flew;
And He [1]was seen [a]upon the
wings of the wind.
12 He made [a]darkness canopies
around Him,
Dark waters *and* thick
clouds of the skies.
13 From the brightness before
Him
Coals of fire were kindled.

14 "The LORD [a]thundered from
heaven,
And the Most High uttered
His voice.
15 He sent out [a]arrows and
scattered them;
Lightning bolts, and He
vanquished them.
16 Then the channels of the sea
[a]were seen,
The foundations of the
world were uncovered,
At the [b]rebuke of the LORD,
At the blast of the breath of
His nostrils.

20 [1]Or *Rapha*

21 [a]1 Sam. 17:10 [1]*Shammah*, 1 Sam. 16:9 and elsewhere

22 [a]1 Chr. 20:8 [1]Or *Rapha*

CHAPTER 22

1 [a]Ex. 15:1 [b]Ps. 18:title; 34:19

2 [a]Ps. 18 [b]Deut. 32:4 [c]Ps. 91:2

3 [a]Heb. 2:13 [b]Gen. 15:1 [c]Luke 1:69 [d]Prov. 18:10 [e]Ps. 9:9; 46:1, 7, 11 [1]Strength

5 [1]Or *overwhelmed*

6 [a]Ps. 116:3

7 [a]Ps. 116:4; 120:1 [b]Ex. 3:7

8 [a]Judg. 5:4 [b]Job 26:11 [1]So with MT, LXX, Tg.; Syr., Vg. *hills* (cf. Ps. 18:7)

9 [a]Heb. 12:29

10 [a]Is. 64:1 [b]Ex. 20:21

11 [a]Ps. 104:3 [1]So with MT, LXX; many Heb. mss., Syr., Vg. *flew* (cf. Ps. 18:10); Tg. *spoke with power*

12 [a]Job 36:29

14 [a]Job 37:2–5

15 [a]Deut. 32:23

16 [a]Nah. 1:4 [b]Ex. 15:8

17 "He[a] sent from above, He took me,
He drew me out of many waters.
18 He delivered me from my strong enemy,
From those who hated me;
For they were too strong for me.
19 They confronted me in the day of my calamity,
But the LORD was my [a]support.
20 [a]He also brought me out into a broad place;
He delivered me because He [b]delighted in me.

21 "The[a] LORD rewarded me according to my righteousness;
According to the [b]cleanness of my hands
He has recompensed me.
22 For I have [a]kept the ways of the LORD,
And have not wickedly departed from my God.
23 For all His [a]judgments *were* before me;
And *as for* His statutes, I did not depart from them.
24 I was also [a]blameless before Him,
And I kept myself from my iniquity.
25 Therefore [a]the LORD has [1]recompensed me according to my righteousness,
According to [2]my cleanness in His eyes.

26 "With [a]the merciful You will show Yourself merciful;
With a blameless man You will show Yourself blameless;
27 With the pure You will show Yourself pure;
And [a]with the devious You will show Yourself shrewd.
28 You will save the [a]humble[1] people;
But Your eyes *are* on [b]the haughty, *that* You may bring *them* down.

29 "For You *are* my [a]lamp, O LORD;
The LORD shall enlighten my darkness.
30 For by You I can run against a troop;
By my God I can leap over a [a]wall.
31 *As for* God, [a]His way *is* perfect;
[b]The word of the LORD *is* proven;
He *is* a shield to all who trust in Him.

32 "For [a]who *is* God, except the LORD?
And who *is* a rock, except our God?
33 [1]God *is* my [a]strength *and* power,
And He [b]makes [2]my way [c]perfect.
34 He makes [1]my feet [a]like the *feet* of deer,
And [b]sets me on my high places.
35 He teaches my hands [1]to make war,
So that my arms can bend a bow of bronze.

36 "You have also given me the shield of Your salvation;
Your gentleness has made me great.

17 [a]Ps. 144:7
19 [a]Is. 10:20
20 [a]Ps. 31:8; 118:5 [b]2 Sam. 15:26
21 [a]1 Sam. 26:23 [b]Ps. 24:4
22 [a]Ps. 119:3
23 [a][Deut. 6:6–9; 7:12]
24 [a][Eph. 1:4]
25 [a]2 Sam. 22:21 [1]*rewarded* [2]LXX, Syr., Vg. *the cleanness of my hands in His sight* (cf. Ps. 18:24); Tg. *my cleanness before His word*
26 [a][Matt. 5:7]
27 [a][Lev. 26:23, 24]
28 [a]Ps. 72:12 [b]Job 40:11 [1]*afflicted*
29 [a]Ps. 119:105; 132:17
30 [a]2 Sam. 5:6–8
31 [a][Matt. 5:48] [b]Ps. 12:6
32 [a]Is. 45:5, 6
33 [a]Ps. 27:1 [b][Heb. 13:21] [c]Ps. 101:2, 6 [1]DSS, LXX, Syr., Vg. *It is God who arms me with strength* (cf. Ps. 18:32); Tg. *It is God who sustains me with strength* [2]So with Qr., LXX, Syr., Tg., Vg. (cf. Ps. 18:32); Kt. *His*
34 [a]2 Sam. 2:18 [b]Is. 33:16 [1]So with Qr., LXX, Syr., Tg., Vg. (cf. Ps. 18:33); Kt. *His*
35 [1]Lit. *for the war*

37 You [a]enlarged my path
under me;
So my feet did not slip.

38 "I have pursued my enemies
and destroyed them;
Neither did I turn back
again till they were
destroyed.
39 And I have destroyed them
and wounded them,
So that they could not rise;
They have fallen [a]under my
feet.
40 For You have [a]armed me
with strength for the
battle;
You have [1]subdued under
me [b]those who rose
against me.
41 You have also [1]given me the
[a]necks of my enemies,
So that I destroyed those
who hated me.
42 They looked, but *there was*
none to save;
Even [a]to the LORD, but He
did not answer them.
43 Then I beat them as fine [a]as
the dust of the earth;
I trod them [b]like dirt in the
streets,
And I [1]spread them out.

44 "You[a] have also delivered me
from the [1]strivings of my
people;
You have kept me as the
[b]head of the nations.
[c]A people I have not known
shall serve me.
45 The foreigners submit
to me;
As soon as they hear, they
obey me.
46 The foreigners fade away,
And [1]come frightened [a]from
their hideouts.

47 "The LORD lives!
Blessed *be* my Rock!
Let God be exalted,
The [a]Rock of my salvation!
48 *It is* God who avenges me,
And [a]subdues the peoples
under me;
49 He delivers me from my
enemies.
You also lift me up
above those who rise
against me;
You have delivered me from
the [a]violent man.
50 Therefore I will give thanks
to You, O LORD, among
[a]the Gentiles,
And sing praises to Your
[b]name.

51 "*He*[a] *is* the tower of salvation
to His king,
And shows mercy to His
[b]anointed,
To David and [c]his
descendants
forevermore."

23

Now these *are* the last words of David.

Thus says David the son of
Jesse;
Thus says [a]the man raised
up on high,
[b]The anointed of the God of
Jacob,
And the sweet psalmist of
Israel:

2 "The[a] Spirit of the LORD
spoke by me,
And His word *was* on my
tongue.
3 The God of Israel said,
[a]The Rock of Israel spoke
to me:

37 [a]Prov. 4:12
39 [a]Mal. 4:3
40 [a][Ps. 18:32] [b][Ps. 44:5] [1]Lit. *caused to bow down*
41 [a]Gen. 49:8 [1]*given me victory over*
42 [a]1 Sam. 28:6
43 [a]Ps. 18:42 [b]Is. 10:6 [1]*scattered*
44 [a]2 Sam. 3:1 [b]Deut. 28:13 [c][Is. 55:5] [1]*contentions*
46 [a][Mic. 7:17] [1]So with LXX, Tg., Vg. (cf. Ps. 18:45); MT *gird themselves*
47 [a]Ps. 89:26
48 [a]Ps. 144:2
49 [a]Ps. 140:1, 4, 11
50 [a]2 Sam. 8:1–14 [b]Rom. 15:9
51 [a]Ps. 144:10 [b]Ps. 89:20 [c]2 Sam. 7:12–16

CHAPTER 23

1 [a]2 Sam. 7:8, 9 [b]1 Sam. 16:12, 13
2 [a][2 Pet. 1:21]
3 [a][Deut. 32:4]

'He who rules over men
must be just,
Ruling [b]in the fear of God.
4 And [a]*he shall be* like the
light of the morning
when the sun rises,
A morning without clouds,
Like the tender grass
springing out of the
earth,
By clear shining after rain.'

5 "Although my house *is* not so
with God,
[a]Yet He has made with me an
everlasting covenant,
Ordered in all *things* and
secure.
For *this is* all my salvation
and all *my* desire;
Will He not make *it*
increase?
6 But *the sons* of rebellion
shall all *be* as thorns
thrust away,
Because they cannot be
taken with hands.
7 But the man *who* touches
them
Must be [1]armed with iron
and the shaft of a spear,
And they shall be utterly
burned with fire in *their*
place."

8 These *are* the names of the
mighty men whom David had:
[1]Jō'sheb-Bas·shē'beth the Tach'-
mo·nīte, chief among [2]the captains. He was called Ad'i·nō the
Ez'nīte, because he had killed
eight hundred men at one time.
9 And after him *was* [a]El·ē·ā'zar
the son of [1]Dodo, the A·hō'hīte,
one of the three mighty men
with David when they defied the
Phi·lis'tines *who* were gathered
there for battle, and the men of
Israel had retreated.
10 He arose and attacked the
Phi·lis'tines until his hand was
[a]weary, and his hand stuck to
the sword. The LORD brought
about a great victory that day;
and the people returned after
him only to [b]plunder.
11 And after him *was* [a]Sham'-
mah the son of Ā'gee the Har'-
a·rīte. [b]The Phi·lis'tines had gathered together into a troop where
there was a piece of ground full
of lentils. So the people fled
from the Phi·lis'tines.
12 But he stationed himself in
the middle of the field, defended
it, and killed the Phi·lis'tines. So
the LORD brought about a great
victory.
13 Then [a]three of the thirty
chief men went down at harvest
time and came to David at [b]the
cave of A·dul'lam. And the troop
of Phi·lis'tines encamped in [c]the
Valley of Reph'a·im.
14 David *was* then in [a]the
stronghold, and the garrison
of the Phi·lis'tines *was* then *in*
Bethlehem.
15 And David said with longing,
"Oh, that someone would give
me a drink of the water from the
well of Bethlehem, which *is* by
the gate!"
16 So the three mighty men
broke through the camp of the
Phi·lis'tines, drew water from
the well of Bethlehem that *was*
by the gate, and took it and
brought *it* to David. Nevertheless he would not drink it, but
poured it out to the LORD.
17 And he said, "Far be it from
me, O LORD, that I should do
this! Is *this not* [a]the blood of the
men who went in *jeopardy of*

3 [b]Ex. 18:21
4 [a]Ps. 89:36
5 [a]Ps. 89:29
7 [1]Lit. *filled*
8 [1]Lit. *One Who Sits in the Seat* (1 Chr. 11:11) [2]So with MT, Tg.; LXX, Vg. *the three*
9 [a]1 Chr. 11:12; 27:4 [1]*Dodai*, 1 Chr. 27:4
10 [a]Judg. 8:4 [b]1 Sam. 30:24, 25
11 [a]1 Chr. 11:27 [b]1 Chr. 11:13, 14
13 [a]1 Chr. 11:15 [b]1 Sam. 22:1 [c]2 Sam. 5:18
14 [a]1 Sam. 22:4, 5
17 [a][Lev. 17:10]

their lives?" Therefore he would
not drink it. These things were
done by the three mighty men.
18 Now [a]A·bi'shaī the brother
of Jō'ab, the son of Ze·rū'i·ah,
was chief of [1]*another* three. He
lifted his spear against three
hundred *men,* killed *them,* and
won a name among *these* three.
19 Was he not the most honored
of three? Therefore he became
their captain. However, he did
not attain to the *first* three.
20 Be·nā'i·ah *was* the son of
Je·hoi'a·da, the son of a valiant
man from [a]Kab'zē·el, [1]who had
done many deeds. [b]He had killed
two lion-like heroes of Mō'ab.
He also had gone down and
killed a lion in the midst of a pit
on a snowy day.
21 And he killed an Egyptian, [1]a
spectacular man. The Egyptian
had a spear in his hand; so he
went down to him with a staff,
wrested the spear out of the
Egyptian's hand, and killed him
with his own spear.
22 These *things* Be·nā'i·ah the
son of Je·hoi'a·da did, and won a
name among three mighty men.
23 He was more honored than
the thirty, but he did not attain
to the *first* three. And David appointed him [a]over his guard.
24 [a]As'a·hel the brother of Jō'ab
was one of the thirty; El·hā'nan
the son of Dodo of Bethlehem,
25 [a]Sham'mah the Har'od·īte,
E·lī'ka the Har'od·īte,
26 Hē'lez the Pal'tīte, Ī'ra the
son of Ik'kesh the Te·kō'īte,
27 Ā·bi·ē'zer the An'a·thoth·īte,
Me·bun'nai the Hū'sha·thīte,
28 Zal'mon the A·hō'hīte, Mā'-
ha·raī the Ne·toph'a·thīte,
29 Hē'leb the son of Bā'a·nah
(the Ne·toph'a·thīte), It'taī the

18 [a]1 Chr. 11:20 [1]So with MT, LXX, Vg.; some Heb. mss., Syr. *thirty;* Tg. *the mighty men*
20 [a]Josh. 15:21 [b]Ex. 15:15 [1]Lit. *great of acts*
21 [1]Lit. *a man of appearance*
23 [a]2 Sam. 8:18; 20:23
24 [a]2 Sam. 2:18
25 [a]1 Chr. 11:27
30 [a]Judg. 2:9
33 [a]2 Sam. 23:11 [1]Or *Ararite*
34 [a]2 Sam. 15:12
35 [1]*Hezro,* 1 Chr. 11:37
36 [a]2 Sam. 8:3
38 [a]1 Chr. 2:53
39 [a]2 Sam. 11:3, 6

CHAPTER 24

1 [a]2 Sam. 21:1, 2 [b]1 Chr. 27:23, 24 [1]*take a census of*
2 [a]Judg. 20:1 [b][Jer. 17:5]
3 [a]Deut. 1:11

son of Rī'baī from Gib'ē·ah of
the children of Benjamin,
30 Be·nā'i·ah a Pir'a·thon·īte,
Hid'daī from the brooks of [a]Gā'-
ash,
31 Ā'bi-Al'bon the Ar'ba·thīte,
Az'ma·veth the Bar·hū'mīte,
32 Ē·lī'ah·ba the Shā·al'-
bon·īte (of the sons of Jā'shen),
Jonathan,
33 [a]Sham'mah the [1]Har'a·rīte,
A·hī'am the son of Shar'ar the
Har'a·rīte,
34 E·liph'e·let the son of A·has'-
baī, the son of the Mā'a·cha·thīte,
E·lī'am the son of [a]A·hith'o·phel
the Gī'lo·nīte,
35 [1]Hez'raī the Car'mel·īte, Pā'-
a·raī the Ar'bīte,
36 Ī'gal the son of Nathan of
[a]Zō'bah, Bā'nī the Gad'īte,
37 Zē'lek the Am'mon·īte, Nā'-
ha·raī the Be·er'oth·īte (armorbearer of Jō'ab the son of Ze·rū'-
i·ah),
38 [a]Ī'ra the Ith'rīte, Gā'reb the
Ith'rīte,
39 *and* [a]Ū·rī'ah the Hit'tīte:
thirty-seven in all.

24 Again [a]the anger of the
LORD was aroused against
Israel, and He moved David
against them to say, [b]"Go, [1]num-
ber Israel and Judah."
2 So the king said to Jō'ab the
commander of the army who
was with him, "Now go throughout all the tribes of Israel, [a]from
Dan to Bē·er·shē'ba, and count
the people, that [b]I may know the
number of the people."
3 And Jō'ab said to the king,
"Now may the LORD your God
[a]add to the people a hundred
times more than there are, and
may the eyes of my lord the king
see *it.* But why does my lord the
king desire this thing?"

4 Nevertheless the king's word
[1]prevailed against Jō′ab and
against the captains of the army.
Therefore Jō′ab and the captains
of the army went out from the
presence of the king to count the
people of Israel.
5 And they crossed over the
Jordan and camped in [a]A·rō′er,
on the right side of the town
which *is* in the midst of the ravine of Gad, and toward [b]Jā′zer.
6 Then they came to Gil′ē·ad
and to the land of Tah′tim Hod′-
shī; they came to [a]Dan Jā′an and
around to [b]Sī′don;
7 and they came to the stronghold of [a]Tȳre and to all the cities of the [b]Hī′vītes and the Cā′-
naan·ītes. Then they went out
to South Judah *as far as* Bē·er-
shē′ba.
8 So when they had gone
through all the land, they came
to Jerusalem at the end of nine
months and twenty days.
9 Then Jō′ab gave the sum of
the number of the people to the
king. [a]And there were in Israel
eight hundred thousand valiant
men who drew the sword, and
the men of Judah were five hundred thousand men.
10 And [a]David's heart condemned him after he had numbered the people. So [b]David
said to the LORD, [c]"I have sinned
greatly in what I have done; but
now, I pray, O LORD, take away
the iniquity of Your servant, for I
have [d]done very foolishly."
11 Now when David arose in
the morning, the word of the
LORD came to the prophet [a]Gad,
David's [b]seer, saying,
12 "Go and tell David, 'Thus
says the LORD: "I offer you three
things; choose one of them for
yourself, that I may do *it* to
you." ' "
13 So Gad came to David and
told him; and he said to him,
"Shall [a]seven[1] years of famine
come to you in your land? Or
shall you flee three months before your enemies, while they
pursue you? Or shall there be
three days' plague in your land?
Now consider and see what answer I should take back to Him
who sent me."
14 And David said to Gad, "I
am in great distress. Please let
us fall into the hand of the LORD,
[a]for His mercies *are* great; but
[b]do not let me fall into the hand
of man."
15 So [a]the LORD sent a plague
upon Israel from the morning till
the appointed time. From Dan to
Bē·er·shē′ba seventy thousand
men of the people died.
16 [a]And when the [1]angel
stretched out His hand over Jerusalem to destroy it, [b]the LORD
relented from the destruction,
and said to the [1]angel who
was destroying the people, "It
is enough; now restrain your
hand." And the [1]angel of the
LORD was by the threshing floor
of [2]A·rau′nah the Jeb′ū·sīte.
17 Then David spoke to the LORD
when he saw the angel who was
striking the people, and said,
"Surely [a]I have sinned, and I
have done wickedly; but these
sheep, what have they done? Let
Your hand, I pray, be against me
and against my father's house."
18 And Gad came that day to
David and said to him, [a]"Go up,
erect an altar to the LORD on the
threshing floor of A·rau′nah the
Jeb′ū·sīte."
19 So David, according to the

4 [1]*overruled*
5 [a]Deut. 2:36 [b]Num. 32:1, 3
6 [a]Judg. 18:29 [b]Josh. 19:28
7 [a]Josh. 19:29 [b]Josh. 11:3
9 [a]1 Chr. 21:5
10 [a]1 Sam. 24:5 [b]2 Sam. 23:1 [c]2 Sam. 12:13 [d]1 Sam. 13:13
11 [a]1 Sam. 22:5 [b]1 Sam. 9:9
13 [a]Ezek. 14:21 [1]So with MT, Syr., Tg., Vg.; LXX *three* (cf. 1 Chr. 21:12)
14 [a][Ps. 51:1; 103:8, 13, 14; 119:156; 130:4, 7] [b][Is. 47:6]
15 [a]1 Chr. 21:14
16 [a]Ex. 12:23 [b]Gen. 6:6 [1]Or *Angel* [2]*Ornan,* 1 Chr. 21:15
17 [a]Ps. 74:1
18 [a]1 Chr. 21:18

word of Gad, went up as the
LORD commanded.
20 Now A·rau′nah looked, and
saw the king and his servants
coming toward him. So A·rau′-
nah went out and bowed before
the king with his face to the
ground.
21 Then A·rau′nah said, "Why
has my lord the king come to
his servant?" [a]And David said,
"To buy the threshing floor from
you, to build an altar to the
LORD, that [b]the plague may be
withdrawn from the people."
22 Now A·rau′nah said to David, "Let my lord the king take
and offer up whatever *seems*
good to him. [a]Look, *here are*
oxen for burnt sacrifice, and
threshing implements and the
yokes of the oxen for wood.
23 "All these, O king, A·rau′-
nah has given to the king." And
A·rau′nah said to the king, "May
the LORD your God [a]accept you."
24 Then the king said to A·rau′-
nah, "No, but I will surely buy *it*
from you for a price; nor will I
offer burnt offerings to the LORD
my God with that which costs
me nothing." So [a]David bought
the threshing floor and the oxen
for fifty shekels of silver.
25 And David built there an altar to the LORD, and offered burnt
offerings and peace offerings.
[a]So the LORD heeded the prayers
for the land, and [b]the plague was
withdrawn from Israel.

21 [a]Gen. 23:8–16 [b]Num. 16:48, 50
22 [a]1 Kin. 19:21
23 [a][Ezek. 20:40, 41]
24 [a]1 Chr. 21:24, 25
25 [a]2 Sam. 21:14 [b]2 Sam. 24:21

The First Book of the

KINGS

THE first half of First Kings traces the life of Solomon. Under his leadership Israel rises to the peak of her size and glory. Solomon's great accomplishments, including the unsurpassed splendor of the temple he constructs in Jerusalem, bring him worldwide fame and respect. However, Solomon's zeal for God diminishes in his later years, as pagan wives turn his heart away from worship in the temple of God. As a result, the king with the divided heart leaves behind a divided kingdom. The Book of First Kings goes on to present the twin histories of two sets of kings and two nations of disobedient people who are growing indifferent to God's prophets and precepts in the century following Solomon's death.

Like the two books of Samuel, the two books of Kings were originally one in the Hebrew Bible. The original title was *Melechim,* "Kings," taken from the first word in 1:1, *Vehamelech,* "Now King." The Septuagint artificially divided the book of Kings in the middle of the story of Ahaziah into two books. It called the books of Samuel "First and Second Kingdoms" and the books of Kings "Third and Fourth Kingdoms." The Septuagint may have divided Samuel, Kings, and Chronicles into two books each because the Greek required a greater amount of scroll space than did the Hebrew. The Latin title for these books is *Liber Regum Tertius et Quartus,* "Third and Fourth Books of Kings."

NOW King David was [a]old,
[1]advanced in years; and they
put covers on him, but he could
not get warm.
2 Therefore his servants said
to him, "Let a young woman, a
virgin, be sought for our lord the
king, and let her [1]stand before
the king, and let her care for
him; and let her lie in your bosom,
that our lord the king may
be warm."
3 So they sought for a lovely
young woman throughout all
the territory of Israel, and found
[a]Ab'i·shag the [b]Shū'nam·mīte,
and brought her to the king.
4 The young woman *was* very
lovely; and she cared for the
king, and served him; but the
king did not know her.
5 Then [a]Ad·o·nī'jah the [1]son of
Hag'gith exalted himself, saying,
"I will [2]be king"; and [b]he prepared
for himself chariots and
horsemen, and fifty men to run
before him.
6 (And his father had not [1]rebuked
him at any time by saying,
"Why have you done so?"
He *was* also very good-looking.
[a]*His mother* had borne him after
Ab'sa·lom.)
7 Then he conferred with
[a]Jō'ab the son of Ze·rū'i·ah and
with [b]A·bī'a·thar the priest,
and [c]they followed and helped
Ad·o·nī'jah.
8 But [a]Zā'dok the priest,
[b]Be·nā'i·ah the son of Je·hoi'a·da,
[c]Nathan the prophet, [d]Shim'ē·ī,
Rē'ī, and [e]the mighty men who
belonged to David were not with
Ad·o·nī'jah.
9 And Ad·o·nī'jah sacrificed
sheep and oxen and fattened

CHAPTER 1

1 [a]1 Chr. 23:1 [1]Seventy years

2 [1]Or *serve*

3 [a]1 Kin. 2:17 [b]Josh. 19:18

5 [a]2 Sam. 3:4 [b]2 Sam. 15:1 [1]The fourth son [2]Lit. *reign*

6 [a]2 Sam. 3:3, 4 [1]Lit. *pained*

7 [a]1 Chr. 11:6 [b]2 Sam. 20:25 [c]1 Kin. 2:22, 28

8 [a]1 Kin. 2:35 [b]1 Kin. 2:25 [c]2 Sam. 12:1 [d]1 Kin. 4:18 [e]2 Sam. 23:8

cattle by the stone of [1]Zō′he·leth, which *is* by [a]En Rō′gel;[2] he also invited all his brothers, the king's sons, and all the men of Judah, the king's servants.

10 But he did not invite Na·than the prophet, Be·nā′i·ah, the mighty men, or [a]Solomon his brother.

11 So Nathan spoke to Bath·shē′ba the mother of Sol·omon, saying, "Have you not heard that Ad·o·nī′jah the son of [a]Hag′gith has become king, and David our lord does not know *it?*

12 "Come, please, let me now give you advice, that you may save your own life and the life of your son Solomon.

13 "Go immediately to King David and say to him, 'Did you not, my lord, O king, swear to your maidservant, saying, [a]"Assuredly your son Solomon shall reign after me, and he shall sit on my throne"? Why then has Ad·o·nī′jah become king?'

14 "Then, while you are still talking there with the king, I also will come in after you and confirm your words."

15 So Bath·shē′ba went into the chamber to the king. (Now the king was very old, and Ab′i·shag the Shū′nam·mīte was serving the king.)

16 And Bath·shē′ba bowed and did homage to the king. Then the king said, "What is your wish?"

17 Then she said to him, "My lord, [a]you swore by the LORD your God to your maidservant, *saying,* 'Assuredly Solomon your son shall reign after me, and he shall sit on my throne.'

18 "So now, look! Ad·o·nī′jah has become king; and now, my lord the king, you do not know about *it.*

19 [a]"He has sacrificed oxen and fattened cattle and sheep in abundance, and has invited all the sons of the king, A·bī′a·thar the priest, and Jō′ab the commander of the army; but Solomon your servant he has not invited.

20 "And as for you, my lord, O king, the eyes of all Israel *are* on you, that you should tell them who will sit on the throne of my lord the king after him.

21 "Otherwise it will happen, when my lord the king [a]rests with his fathers, that I and my son Solomon will be counted as offenders."

22 And just then, while she was still talking with the king, Nathan the prophet also came in.

23 So they told the king, saying, "Here is Nathan the prophet." And when he came in before the king, he bowed down before the king with his face to the ground.

24 And Nathan said, "My lord, O king, have you said, 'Ad·o·nī′jah shall reign after me, and he shall sit on my throne'?

25 [a]"For he has gone down today, and has sacrificed oxen and fattened cattle and sheep in abundance, and has invited all the king's sons, and the commanders of the army, and A·bī′a·thar the priest; and look! They are eating and drinking before him; and they say, [b]'*Long*[1] live King Ad·o·nī′jah!'

26 "But he has not invited me—me your servant—nor Zā′dok the priest, nor Be·nā′i·ah the son of Je·hoi′a·da, nor your servant Solomon.

9 [a]Josh. 15:7; 18:16 [1]Lit. *Serpent* [2]A spring south of Jerusalem in the Kidron Valley

10 [a]2 Sam. 12:24

11 [a]2 Sam. 3:4

13 [a]1 Chr. 22:9–13

17 [a]1 Kin. 1:13, 30

19 [a]1 Kin. 1:7–9, 25

21 [a]Deut. 31:16

25 [a]1 Kin. 1:9, 19 [b]1 Sam. 10:24 [1]Lit. *Let King Adonijah live*

27 "Has this thing been done by my lord the king, and you have not told your servant who should sit on the throne of my lord the king after him?"

28 Then King David answered and said, "Call Bath·shē′ba to me." So she came into the king's presence and stood before the king.

29 And the king took an oath and said, [a]"*As* the LORD lives, who has redeemed my life from every distress,

30 [a]"just as I swore to you by the LORD God of Israel, saying, 'Assuredly Solomon your son shall be king after me, and he shall sit on my throne in my place,' so I certainly will do this day."

31 Then Bath·shē′ba bowed with *her* face to the earth, and paid homage to the king, and said, [a]"Let my lord King David live forever!"

32 And King David said, "Call to me Zā′dok the priest, Nathan the prophet, and Be·nā′i·ah the son of Je·hoi′a·da." So they came before the king.

33 The king also said to them, [a]"Take with you the servants of your lord, and have Solomon my son ride on my own [b]mule, and take him down to [c]Gī′hon.[1]

34 "There let Zā′dok the priest and Nathan the prophet [a]anoint him king over Israel; and [b]blow the horn, and say, [1]'*Long* live King Solomon!'

35 "Then you shall come up after him, and he shall come and sit on my throne, and he shall be king in my place. For I have appointed him to be ruler over Israel and Judah."

36 Be·nā′i·ah the son of Je·hoi′a·da answered the king and said, [a]"Amen! May the LORD God of my lord the king say so *too*.

37 [a]"As the LORD has been with my lord the king, even so may He be with Solomon, and [b]make his throne greater than the throne of my lord King David."

38 So Zā′dok the priest, Nathan the prophet, [a]Be·nā′i·ah the son of Je·hoi′a·da, the [b]Cher′e·thītes, and the Pel′eth·ītes went down and had Solomon ride on King David's mule, and took him to Gī′hon.

39 Then Zā′dok the priest took a horn of [a]oil from the tabernacle and [b]anointed Solomon. And they blew the horn, [c]and all the people said, [1]"*Long* live King Solomon!"

40 And all the people went up after him; and the people played the flutes and rejoiced with great joy, so that the earth *seemed to* split with their sound.

41 Now Ad·o·nī′jah and all the guests who *were* with him heard *it* as they finished eating. And when Jō′ab heard the sound of the horn, he said, "Why *is* the city in such a noisy uproar?"

42 While he was still speaking, there came [a]Jonathan, the son of A·bī′a·thar the priest. And Ad·o·nī′jah said to him, "Come in, for [b]you *are* a prominent man, and bring good news."

43 Then Jonathan answered and said to Ad·o·nī′jah, "No! Our lord King David has made Solomon king.

44 "The king has sent with him Zā′dok the priest, Nathan the prophet, Be·nā′i·ah the son of Je·hoi′a·da, the Cher′e·thītes, and the Pel′eth·ītes; and they have made him ride on the king's mule.

29 [a]2 Sam. 4:9; 12:5
30 [a]1 Kin. 1:13, 17
31 [a]Dan. 2:4; 3:9
33 [a]2 Sam. 20:6 [b]Esth. 6:8 [c]2 Chr. 32:30; 33:14 [1]A spring east of Jerusalem in the Kidron Valley
34 [a]1 Sam. 10:1; 16:3, 12 [b]2 Sam. 15:10 [1]Lit. *Let King Solomon live*
36 [a]Jer. 28:6
37 [a]1 Sam. 20:13 [b]1 Kin. 1:47
38 [a]2 Sam. 8:18; 23:20–23 [b]2 Sam. 20:7
39 [a]Ps. 89:20 [b]1 Chr. 29:22 [c]1 Sam. 10:24 [1]Lit. *Let King Solomon live*
42 [a]2 Sam. 17:17, 20 [b]2 Sam. 18:27

45 "So Zā′dok the priest and Nathan the prophet have anointed him king at Gī′hon; and they have gone up from there rejoicing, so that the city is in an uproar. This *is* the noise that you have heard.

46 "Also Solomon [a]sits on the throne of the kingdom.

47 "And moreover the king's servants have gone to bless our lord King David, saying, [a]'May God make the name of Solomon better than your name, and may He make his throne greater than your throne.' [b]Then the king bowed himself on the bed.

48 "Also the king said thus, 'Blessed *be* the LORD God of Israel, who has [a]given *one* to sit on my throne this day, while my eyes see [b]*it!*' "

49 So all the guests who were with Ad·o·nī′jah were afraid, and arose, and each one went his way.

50 Now Ad·o·nī′jah was afraid of Solomon; so he arose, and went and [a]took hold of the horns of the altar.

51 And it was told Solomon, saying, "Indeed Ad·o·nī′jah is afraid of King Solomon; for look, he has taken hold of the horns of the altar, saying, 'Let King Solomon swear to me today that he will not put his servant to death with the sword.' "

52 Then Solomon said, "If he proves himself a worthy man, [a]not one hair of him shall fall to the earth; but if wickedness is found in him, he shall die."

53 So King Solomon sent them to bring him down from the altar. And he came and fell down before King Solomon; and Solomon said to him, "Go to your house."

46 [a]1 Chr. 29:23
47 [a]1 Kin. 1:37 [b]Gen. 47:31
48 [a]1 Kin. 3:6 [b]2 Sam. 7:12
50 [a]1 Kin. 2:28
52 [a]1 Sam. 14:45

CHAPTER 2

1 [a]Gen. 47:29 [1]*commanded*
2 [a]Josh. 23:14 [b]Deut. 31:7, 23
3 [a][Deut. 29:9]
4 [a]2 Sam. 7:25 [b][Ps. 132:12] [c]2 Kin. 20:3 [d]2 Sam. 7:12, 13
5 [a]2 Sam. 3:39; 18:5, 12, 14 [b]2 Sam. 3:27 [c]2 Sam. 20:10
6 [a]1 Kin. 2:9
7 [a]2 Sam. 19:31–39 [b]2 Sam. 9:7, 10; 19:28 [c]2 Sam. 17:17–29

2

Now [a]the days of David drew near that he should die, and he [1]charged Solomon his son, saying:

2 [a]"I go the way of all the earth; [b]be strong, therefore, and prove yourself a man.

3 "And keep the charge of the LORD your God: to walk in His ways, to keep His statutes, His commandments, His judgments, and His testimonies, as it is written in the Law of Moses, that you may [a]prosper in all that you do and wherever you turn;

4 "that the LORD may [a]fulfill His word which He spoke concerning me, saying, [b]'If your sons take heed to their way, to [c]walk before Me in truth with all their heart and with all their soul,' He said, [d]'you shall not lack a man on the throne of Israel.'

5 "Moreover you know also what Jō′ab the son of Ze·rū′i·ah [a]did to me, *and* what he did to the two commanders of the armies of Israel, to [b]Abner the son of Ner and [c]A·mā′sa the son of Jē′ther, whom he killed. And he shed the blood of war in peacetime, and put the blood of war on his belt that *was* around his waist, and on his sandals that *were* on his feet.

6 "Therefore do [a]according to your wisdom, and do not let his gray hair go down to the grave in peace.

7 "But show kindness to the sons of [a]Bar·zil′laī the Gil′ē·ad·īte, and let them be among those who [b]eat at your table, for so [c]they came to me when I fled from Ab′sa·lom your brother.

8 "And see, *you have* with

you [a]Shim′ē·ī the son of Gē′ra,
a Ben′ja·mīte from Ba·hū′rim,
who cursed me with a malicious
curse in the day when I went
to Mā·ha·na′im. But [b]he came
down to meet me at the Jordan,
and [c]I swore to him by the LORD,
saying, 'I will not put you to
death with the sword.'
9 "Now therefore, [a]do not hold
him guiltless, for you *are* a wise
man and know what you ought
to do to him; but [b]bring his gray
hair down to the grave with
blood."
10 So [a]David [1]rested with his
fathers, and was buried in [b]the
City of David.
11 The period that David
[a]reigned over Israel *was* forty
years; seven years he reigned
in Hē′bron, and in Jerusalem he
reigned thirty-three years.
12 [a]Then Solomon sat on the
throne of his father David; and
his kingdom was [b]firmly established.
13 Now Ad·o·nī′jah the son of
Hag′gith came to Bath·shē′ba
the mother of Solomon. So she
said, [a]"Do you come peaceably?"
And he said, "Peaceably."
14 Moreover he said, "I have
something *to say* to you." And
she said, "Say it."
15 Then he said, "You know that
the kingdom was [a]mine, and
all Israel had set their expecta-
tions on me, that I should reign.
However, the kingdom has been
turned over, and has become my
brother's; for [b]it was his from
the LORD.
16 "Now I ask one petition of
you; do not [1]deny me." And she
said to him, "Say it."
17 Then he said, "Please speak
to King Solomon, for he will not
refuse you, that he may give me
[a]Ab′i·shag the Shū′nam·mīte as
wife."
18 So Bath·shē′ba said, "Very
well, I will speak for you to the
king."
19 Bath·shē′ba therefore went
to King Solomon, to speak to
him for Ad·o·nī′jah. And the king
rose up to meet her and [a]bowed
down to her, and sat down on
his throne and had a throne set
for the king's mother; [b]so she sat
at his right hand.
20 Then she said, "I desire one
small petition of you; do not [1]re-
fuse me." And the king said to
her, "Ask it, my mother, for I will
not refuse you."
21 So she said, "Let Ab′i·shag
the Shū′nam·mīte be given to
Ad·o·nī′jah your brother as
wife."
22 And King Solomon answered
and said to his mother, "Now
why do you ask Ab′i·shag the
Shū′nam·mīte for Ad·o·nī′jah?
Ask for him the kingdom also—
for he *is* my [a]older brother—
for him, and for [b]A·bī′a·thar the
priest, and for Jō′ab the son of
Ze·rū′i·ah."
23 Then King Solomon swore
by the LORD, saying, [a]"May God
do so to me, and more also, if
Ad·o·nī′jah has not spoken this
word against his own life!
24 "Now therefore, *as* the LORD
lives, who has confirmed me
and set me on the throne of
David my father, and who has
established a [1]house for me, as
He [a]promised, Ad·o·nī′jah shall
be put to death today!"
25 So King Solomon sent by the
hand of [a]Be·nā′i·ah the son of
Je·hoi′a·da; and he struck him
down, and he died.

8 [a]2 Sam. 16:5–13 [b]2 Sam. 19:18 [c]2 Sam. 19:23
9 [a]Ex. 20:7 [b]Gen. 42:38; 44:31
10 [a]Acts 2:29; 13:36 [b]2 Sam. 5:7 [1]Died and joined his ancestors
11 [a]2 Sam. 5:4, 5
12 [a]1 Chr. 29:23 [b]2 Chr. 1:1
13 [a]1 Sam. 16:4, 5
15 [a]1 Kin. 1:11, 18 [b][Dan. 2:21]
16 [1]Lit. *turn away the face*
17 [a]1 Kin. 1:3, 4
19 [a][Ex. 20:12] [b]Ps. 45:9
20 [1]Lit. *turn away the face*
22 [a]1 Chr. 3:2, 5 [b]1 Kin. 1:7
23 [a]Ruth 1:17
24 [a]2 Sam. 7:11, 13 [1]Royal dynasty
25 [a]2 Sam. 8:18

26 And to A·bī′a·thar the priest
the king said, “Go to [a]An′a·thoth,
to your own fields, for [1]you *are*
deserving of death; but I will
not put you to death at this time,
[b]because you carried the ark of
the Lord GOD before my father
David, and because you were afflicted every time my father was
afflicted.”
27 So Solomon removed A·bī′-
a·thar from being priest to the
LORD, that he might [a]fulfill the
word of the LORD which He
spoke concerning the house of
Ē′lī at Shī′lōh.
28 Then news came to Jō′ab, for
Jō′ab [a]had defected to Ad·o·nī′-
jah, though he had not defected
to Ab′sa·lom. So Jō′ab fled to
the tabernacle of the LORD, and
[b]took hold of the horns of the
altar.
29 And King Solomon was told,
“Jō′ab has fled to the tabernacle of the LORD; there *he is,* by
the altar.” Then Solomon sent
Be·nā′i·ah the son of Je·hoi′a·da,
saying, “Go, [a]strike him down.”
30 So Be·nā′i·ah went to the
tabernacle of the LORD, and said
to him, “Thus says the king,
[a]‘Come out!’ ” And he said, “No,
but I will die here.” And Be·nā′-
i·ah brought back word to the
king, saying, “Thus said Jō′ab,
and thus he answered me.”
31 Then the king said to him,
[a]“Do as he has said, and strike
him down and bury him, [b]that
you may take away from me
and from the house of my father
the innocent blood which Jō′ab
shed.
32 “So the LORD [a]will return his
[1]blood on his head, because he
struck down two men more righteous [b]and better than he, and
killed them with the sword—
[c]Abner the son of Ner, the commander of the army of Israel,
and [d]A·mā′sa the son of Jē′ther,
the commander of the army of
Judah—though my father David
did not know *it.*
33 “Their blood shall therefore
return upon the head of Jō′ab
and [a]upon the head of his descendants forever. [b]But upon David and his descendants, upon
his house and his throne, there
shall be peace forever from the
LORD.”
34 So Be·nā′i·ah the son of
Je·hoi′a·da went up and struck
and killed him; and he was buried in his own house in the
wilderness.
35 The king put Be·nā′i·ah the
son of Je·hoi′a·da in his place
over the army, and the king put
[a]Zā′dok the priest in the place of
[b]A·bī′a·thar.
36 Then the king sent and
called for [a]Shim′ē·ī, and said
to him, “Build yourself a house
in Jerusalem and dwell there,
and do not go out from there
anywhere.
37 “For it shall be, on the day
you go out and cross [a]the Brook
Kid′ron, know for certain you
shall surely die; [b]your [1]blood
shall be on your own head.”
38 And Shim′ē·ī said to the king,
“The saying *is* good. As my lord
the king has said, so your servant will do.” So Shim′ē·ī dwelt
in Jerusalem many days.
39 Now it happened at the end
of three years, that two slaves
of Shim′ē·ī ran away to [a]Ā′chish
the son of Mā′a·chah, king of
Gath. And they told Shim′ē·ī,
saying, “Look, your slaves *are* in
Gath!”

26 [a]Josh. 21:18 [b]2 Sam. 15:14, 29 [1]Lit. *you are a man of death*
27 [a]1 Sam. 2:31–35
28 [a]1 Kin. 1:7 [b]1 Kin. 1:50
29 [a]1 Kin. 2:5, 6
30 [a][Ex. 21:14]
31 [a][Ex. 21:14] [b][Num. 35:33]
32 [a]Judg. 9:24, 57 [b]2 Chr. 21:13, 14 [c]2 Sam. 3:27 [d]2 Sam. 20:9, 10 [1]Or *bloodshed*
33 [a]2 Sam. 3:29 [b][Prov. 25:5]
35 [a]1 Sam. 2:35 [b]1 Kin. 2:27
36 [a]1 Kin. 2:8
37 [a]2 Sam. 15:23 [b]Josh. 2:19 [1]Or *bloodshed*
39 [a]1 Sam. 27:2

40 So Shim′ē·ī arose, saddled
his donkey, and went to Ā′chish
at Gath to seek his slaves. And
Shim′ē·ī went and brought his
slaves from Gath.
41 And Solomon was told that
Shim′ē·ī had gone from Jerusalem to Gath and had come
back.
42 Then the king sent and
called for Shim′ē·ī, and said to
him, "Did I not make you swear
by the LORD, and warn you, saying, 'Know for certain that on
the day you go out and travel
anywhere, you shall surely die'?
And you said to me, 'The word I
have heard *is* good.'
43 "Why then have you not
kept the oath of the LORD and
the commandment that I gave
you?"
44 The king said moreover to
Shim′ē·ī, "You know, as your
heart acknowledges, [a]all the
wickedness that you did to my
father David; therefore the LORD
will [b]return your wickedness on
your own head.
45 "But King Solomon *shall be*
blessed, and [a]the throne of David shall be established before
the LORD forever."
46 So the king commanded
Be·nā′i·ah the son of Je·hoi′a·da;
and he went out and struck him
down, and he died. Thus the
[a]kingdom was established in the
hand of Solomon.

3 Now [a]Solomon made [1]a
treaty with Pharaoh king of
Egypt, and married Pharaoh's
daughter; then he brought her
[b]to the City of David until he
had finished building his [c]own
house, and [d]the house of the
LORD, and [e]the wall all around
Jerusalem.

44 [a]2 Sam. 16:5–13 [b]1 Sam. 25:39
45 [a][Prov. 25:5]
46 [a]2 Chr. 1:1

CHAPTER 3

1 [a]1 Kin. 7:8; 9:24 [b]2 Sam. 5:7 [c]1 Kin. 7:1 [d]1 Kin. 6 [e]1 Kin. 9:15, 19 [1]*an alliance*
2 [a][Deut. 12:2–5, 13, 14]
3 [a][Rom. 8:28] [b][1 Kin. 3:6, 14]
4 [a]2 Chr. 1:3 [b]1 Chr. 16:39; 21:29
5 [a]1 Kin. 9:2; 11:9 [b]Num. 12:6
6 [a]2 Chr. 1:8 [b]1 Kin. 2:4; 9:4 [c]1 Kin. 1:48
7 [a]Jer. 1:6, 7 [b]Num. 27:17
8 [a][Deut. 7:6] [b]Gen. 13:6; 15:5; 22:17
9 [a]2 Chr. 1:10 [b]Ps. 72:1, 2 [c][Heb. 5:14] [1]Lit. *hearing*

2 [a]Meanwhile the people sacrificed at the high places, because
there was no house built for the
name of the LORD until those
days.
3 And Solomon [a]loved the
LORD, [b]walking in the statutes of
his father David, except that he
sacrificed and burned incense at
the high places.
4 Now [a]the king went to Gib′-
ē·on to sacrifice there, [b]for that
was the great high place: Solomon offered a thousand burnt
offerings on that altar.
5 [a]At Gib′ē·on the LORD appeared to Solomon [b]in a dream
by night; and God said, "Ask!
What shall I give you?"
6 [a]And Solomon said: "You
have shown great mercy to Your
servant David my father, because he [b]walked before You in
truth, in righteousness, and in
uprightness of heart with You;
You have continued this great
kindness for him, and You [c]have
given him a son to sit on his
throne, as *it is* this day.
7 "Now, O LORD my God, You
have made Your servant king
instead of my father David, but I
am a [a]little child; I do not know
how [b]to go out or come in.
8 "And Your servant *is* in the
midst of Your people whom You
[a]have chosen, a great people,
[b]too numerous to be numbered
or counted.
9 [a]"Therefore give to Your servant an [1]understanding heart [b]to
judge Your people, that I may
[c]discern between good and evil.
For who is able to judge this
great people of Yours?"
10 The speech pleased the Lord,
that Solomon had asked this
thing.

11 Then God said to him: "Because you have asked this thing, and have [a]not asked long life for yourself, nor have asked riches for yourself, nor have asked the life of your enemies, but have asked for yourself understanding to discern justice,

12 [a]"behold, I have done according to your words; [b]see, I have given you a wise and understanding heart, so that there has not been anyone like you before you, nor shall any like you arise after you.

13 "And I have also [a]given you what you have not asked: both [b]riches and honor, so that there shall not be anyone like you among the kings all your days.

14 "So [a]if you walk in My ways, to keep My statutes and My commandments, [b]as your father David walked, then I will [c]lengthen[1] your days."

15 Then Solomon [a]awoke; and indeed it had been a dream. And he came to Jerusalem and stood before the ark of the covenant of the LORD, offered up burnt offerings, offered peace offerings, and [b]made a feast for all his servants.

16 Now two women *who were* harlots came to the king, and [a]stood before him.

17 And one woman said, "O my lord, this woman and I dwell in the same house; and I gave birth while she *was* in the house.

18 "Then it happened, the third day after I had given birth, that this woman also gave birth. And we *were* together; [1]no one *was* with us in the house, except the two of us in the house.

19 "And this woman's son died in the night, because she lay on him.

20 "So she arose in the middle of the night and took my son from my side, while your maidservant slept, and laid him in her bosom, and laid her dead child in my bosom.

21 "And when I rose in the morning to nurse my son, there he was, dead. But when I had examined him in the morning, indeed, he was not my son whom I had borne."

22 Then the other woman said, "No! But the living one *is* my son, and the dead one *is* your son." And the first woman said, "No! But the dead one *is* your son, and the living one *is* my son." Thus they spoke before the king.

23 And the king said, "The one says, 'This *is* my son, who lives, and your son *is* the dead one'; and the other says, 'No! But your son *is* the dead one, and my son *is* the living one.' "

24 Then the king said, "Bring me a sword." So they brought a sword before the king.

25 And the king said, "Divide the living child in two, and give half to one, and half to the other."

26 Then the woman whose son *was* living spoke to the king, for [a]she yearned with compassion for her son; and she said, "O my lord, give her the living child, and by no means kill him!" But the other said, "Let him be neither mine nor yours, *but* divide *him*."

27 So the king answered and said, "Give the first woman the living child, and by no means kill him; she *is* his mother."

11 [a][James 4:3]
12 [a][1 John 5:14, 15] [b]Eccl. 1:16
13 [a][Matt. 6:33] [b]1 Kin. 4:21, 24; 10:23
14 [a][1 Kin. 6:12] [b]1 Kin. 15:5 [c]Ps. 91:16 [1]*prolong*
15 [a]Gen. 41:7 [b]1 Kin. 8:65
16 [a]Num. 27:2
18 [1]Lit. *no stranger*
26 [a]Jer. 31:20

Blessed *be* the LORD this
day, for He has given David
a wise son over this great
people!

8 Then Hī'ram sent to Solomon,
saying:

I have considered *the*
message which you sent me,
and I will do all you desire
concerning the cedar and
cypress logs.
9 My servants shall bring
them down [a]from Lebanon
to the sea; I will float them
in rafts by sea to the place
you indicate to me, and will
have them broken apart
there; then you can take
them away. And you shall
fulfill my desire [b]by giving
food for my household.

10 Then Hī'ram gave Solomon
cedar and cypress logs *accord-*
ing to all his desire.
11 [a]And Solomon gave Hī'ram
twenty thousand [1]kors of wheat
as food for his household, and
[2]twenty kors of pressed oil. Thus
Solomon gave to Hī'ram year by
year.
12 So the LORD gave Solomon
wisdom, [a]as He had promised
him; and there was peace between Hī'ram and Solomon, and
the two of them made a treaty
together.
13 Then King Solomon raised
up a labor force out of all Israel;
and the labor force was thirty
thousand men.
14 And he sent them to Lebanon,
ten thousand a month in shifts:
they were one month in Lebanon *and* two months at home;
[a]Ad·o·nī'ram *was* in charge of
the labor force.
15 [a]Solomon had seventy thousand who carried burdens, and
eighty thousand who quarried
stone in the mountains,
16 besides three thousand [1]three
hundred from the [a]chiefs of Solomon's deputies, who super-
vised the people who labored in
the work.
17 And the king commanded
them to quarry large stones,
costly stones, *and* [a]hewn stones,
to lay the foundation of the
[1]temple.
18 So Solomon's builders, Hī'-
ram's builders, and the Gē'-
bal·ītes quarried *them;* and they
prepared timber and stones to
build the [1]temple.

6 And [a]it came to pass in the
four hundred and [1]eighti-
eth year after the children of
Israel had come out of the land
of Egypt, in the fourth year of
Solomon's reign over Israel, in
the month of [2]Ziv, which *is* the
second month, [b]that he began to
build the house of the LORD.
2 Now [a]the house which King
Solomon built for the LORD, its
length *was* sixty cubits, its width
twenty, and its height thirty
cubits.
3 The vestibule in front of the
[1]sanctuary of the house *was*
[2]twenty cubits long across the
width of the house, *and* the
width of [3]*the vestibule extended*
[4]ten cubits from the front of the
house.
4 And he made for the house
[a]windows with beveled frames.
5 Against the wall of the [1]tem-
ple he built [a]chambers all around,
against the walls of the temple,
all around the sanctuary [b]and the

---

9 [a]Ezra 3:7 [b]Ezek. 27:17

11 [a]2 Chr. 2:10 [1]Each about 5 bushels [2]So with MT, Tg., Vg.; LXX, Syr. *twenty thousand kors*

12 [a]1 Kin. 3:12

14 [a]1 Kin. 12:18

15 [a]2 Chr. 2:17, 18

16 [a]1 Kin. 9:23 [1]So with MT, Tg., Vg.; LXX *six hundred*

17 [a]1 Kin. 6:7 [1]Lit. *house*

18 [1]Lit. *house*

CHAPTER 6

1 [a]2 Chr. 3:1, 2 [b]Acts 7:47 [1]So with MT, Tg., Vg.; LXX *fortieth* [2]Or *Ayyar*, April or May

2 [a]Ezek. 41:1

3 [1]Heb. *heykal;* here the main room of the temple; elsewhere called the holy place, Ex. 26:33; Ezek. 41:1 [2]About 30 feet [3]Lit. *it* [4]About 15 feet

4 [a]Ezek. 40:16; 41:16

5 [a]Ezek. 41:6 [b]1 Kin. 6:16, 19–21, 31 [1]Lit. *house*

[2]inner sanctuary. Thus he made
side chambers all around it.
6 The lowest chamber *was* five
cubits wide, the middle *was* six
cubits wide, and the third *was*
seven cubits wide; for he made
narrow ledges around the outside
of the temple, so that *the support
beams* would not be fastened
into the walls of the [1]temple.
7 And [a]the temple, when it was
being built, was built with stone
finished at the quarry, so that
no hammer or chisel *or* any iron
tool was heard in the temple
while it was being built.
8 The doorway for the [1]middle
story *was* on the right side of the
temple. They went up by stairs
to the middle *story,* and from
the middle to the third.
9 [a]So he built the [1]temple and
finished it, and he paneled the
temple with beams and boards
of cedar.
10 And he built side chambers
against the entire temple, each
five cubits high; they were attached to the temple with cedar
beams.
11 Then the word of the LORD
came to Solomon, saying:
12 "*Concerning* this [1]temple
which you are building, [a]if you
walk in My statutes, execute My
judgments, keep all My commandments, and walk in them,
then I will perform My [2]word
with you, [b]which I spoke to your
father David.
13 "And [a]I will dwell among the
children of Israel, and will not
[b]forsake My people Israel."
14 So Solomon built the temple
and finished it.
15 And he built the inside walls
of the temple with cedar boards;
from the floor of the temple to
the ceiling he paneled the inside
with wood; and he covered the
floor of the temple with planks
of cypress.
16 Then he built the twenty-
cubit room at the rear of the
temple, from floor to ceiling,
with cedar boards; he built *it*
inside as the inner sanctuary, as
the [a]Most Holy *Place.*
17 And in front of it the temple
sanctuary was forty cubits *long.*
18 The inside of the temple was
cedar, carved with ornamental
buds and open flowers. All *was*
cedar; there was no stone *to be*
seen.
19 And he prepared the [1]inner
sanctuary inside the temple, to
set the ark of the covenant of the
LORD there.
20 The inner sanctuary *was*
twenty cubits long, twenty cubits
wide, and twenty cubits high. He
overlaid it with pure gold, and
overlaid the altar of cedar.
21 So Solomon overlaid the inside of the temple with pure
gold. He stretched gold chains
across the front of the inner
sanctuary, and overlaid it with
gold.
22 The whole temple he overlaid
with gold, until he had finished
all the temple; also he overlaid
with gold [a]the entire altar that
was by the inner sanctuary.
23 Inside the inner sanctuary
[a]he made two cherubim *of* olive
wood, *each* ten cubits high.
24 One wing of the cherub *was*
five cubits, and the other wing
of the cherub five cubits: ten
cubits from the tip of one wing
to the tip of the other.
25 And the other cherub *was*
ten cubits; both cherubim *were*
of the same size and shape.

5 [2]Heb. *debir;* here the inner room of the temple; elsewhere called the Most Holy Place, v. 16
6 [1]Lit. *house*
7 [a]Deut. 27:5, 6
8 [1]So with MT, Vg.; LXX *upper story;* Tg. *ground story*
9 [a]1 Kin. 6:14, 38 [1]Lit. *house*
12 [a]1 Kin. 2:4; 9:4 [b][2 Sam. 7:13] [1]Lit. *house* [2]*promise*
13 [a]Ex. 25:8 [b][Deut. 31:6]
16 [a]Ex. 26:33
19 [1]The Most Holy Place
22 [a]Ex. 30:1, 3, 6
23 [a]2 Chr. 3:10–12

26 The height of one cherub *was* ten cubits, and so *was* the other cherub.

27 Then he set the cherubim inside the inner [1]room; and [a]they stretched out the wings of the cherubim so that the wing of the one touched *one* wall, and the wing of the other cherub touched the other wall. And their wings touched each other in the middle of the room.

28 Also he overlaid the cherubim with gold.

29 Then he carved all the walls of the temple all around, both the inner and outer *sanctuaries,* with carved [a]figures of cherubim, palm trees, and open flowers.

30 And the floor of the temple he overlaid with gold, both the inner and outer *sanctuaries.*

31 For the entrance of the inner sanctuary he made doors *of* olive wood; the lintel *and* doorposts *were* [1]one-fifth *of the wall.*

32 The two doors *were of* olive wood; and he carved on them figures of cherubim, palm trees, and open flowers, and overlaid *them* with gold; and he spread gold on the cherubim and on the palm trees.

33 So for the door of the [1]sanctuary he also made doorposts *of* olive wood, [2]one-fourth *of the wall.*

34 And the two doors *were of* cypress wood; [a]two panels *comprised* one folding door, and two panels *comprised* the other folding door.

35 Then he carved cherubim, palm trees, and open flowers *on them,* and overlaid *them* with gold applied evenly on the carved work.

36 And he built the [a]inner court with three rows of hewn stone and a row of cedar beams.

37 [a]In the fourth year the foundation of the house of the LORD was laid, in the month of [1]Ziv.

38 And in the eleventh year, in the month of [1]Bul, which is the eighth month, the house was finished in all its details and according to all its plans. So he was [a]seven years in building it.

7 But Solomon took [a]thirteen years to build his own house; so he finished all his house.

2 He also built the [a]House of the Forest of Lebanon; its length *was* [1]one hundred cubits, its width [2]fifty cubits, and its height thirty cubits, with four rows of cedar pillars, and cedar beams on the pillars.

3 And *it was* paneled with cedar above the beams that *were* on forty-five pillars, fifteen *to* a row.

4 *There were* windows *with beveled frames in* three rows, and window *was* opposite window *in* three tiers.

5 And all the doorways and doorposts *had* rectangular frames; and window *was* opposite window *in* three tiers.

6 He also made the Hall of Pillars: its length *was* fifty cubits, and its width thirty cubits; and in front of them *was* a portico with pillars, and a canopy *was* in front of them.

7 Then he made a hall for the throne, the Hall of Judgment, where he might judge; and *it was* paneled with cedar from floor to [1]ceiling.

8 And the house where he dwelt *had* another court inside the hall, of like workmanship.

27 [a]2 Chr. 5:8 [1]Lit. *house*
29 [a]Ex. 36:8, 35
31 [1]Or *five-sided*
33 [1]*temple* [2]Or *four-sided*
34 [a]Ezek. 41:23–25
36 [a]1 Kin. 7:12
37 [a]1 Kin. 6:1 [1]Or *Ayyar,* April or May
38 [a]1 Kin. 5:5; 6:1; 8:19 [1]Or *Heshvan,* October or November

CHAPTER 7

1 [a]2 Chr. 8:1
2 [a]2 Chr. 9:16 [1]About 150 feet [2]About 75 feet
7 [1]Lit. *floor* of the upper level

Solomon also made a house like
this hall for Pharaoh's daughter,
[a]whom he had taken *as wife.*
9 All these *were of* costly
stones cut to size, trimmed with
saws, inside and out, from the
foundation to the eaves, and
also on the outside to the great
court.
10 The foundation *was of* costly
stones, large stones, some ten
cubits and some eight cubits.
11 And above *were* costly
stones, hewn to size, and cedar
wood.
12 The great court *was* enclosed
with three rows of hewn stones
and a row of cedar beams. So
were the [a]inner court of the
house of the LORD [b]and the vestibule of the temple.
13 Now King Solomon sent and
brought [1]Hū′ram from Tȳre.
14 [a]He *was* the son of a widow
from the tribe of Naph′ta·lī, and
[b]his father *was* a man of Tȳre,
a bronze worker; [c]he was filled
with wisdom and understanding and skill in working with
all kinds of bronze work. So he
came to King Solomon and did
all his work.
15 And he [1]cast [a]two pillars of
bronze, each one eighteen cubits
high, and a line of twelve cubits
measured the circumference of
each.
16 Then he made two capitals
of cast bronze, to set on the tops
of the pillars. The height of one
capital *was* five cubits, and the
height of the other capital *was*
five cubits.
17 *He made* a lattice network,
with wreaths of chainwork, for
the capitals which *were* on top
of the pillars: seven chains for
one capital and seven for the
other capital.
18 So he made the pillars, and
two rows of pomegranates above
the network all around to cover
the capitals that *were* on top;
and thus he did for the other
capital.
19 The capitals which *were* on
top of the pillars in the hall
were in the shape of lilies, four
cubits.
20 The capitals on the two pillars also *had pomegranates*
above, by the convex surface
which *was* next to the network;
and there *were* [a]two hundred
such pomegranates in rows on
each of the capitals all around.
21 [a]Then he set up the pillars by
the vestibule of the temple; he
set up the pillar on the right and
called its name [1]Jā′chin, and he
set up the pillar on the left and
called its name [2]Bō′az.
22 The tops of the pillars were
in the shape of lilies. So the
work of the pillars was finished.
23 And he made [a]the Sea of cast
bronze, ten cubits from one brim
to the other; *it was* completely
round. Its height *was* five cubits,
and a line of thirty cubits measured its circumference.
24 Below its brim *were* ornamental buds encircling it all
around, ten to a cubit, [a]all the
way around the Sea. The ornamental buds *were* cast in two
rows when it was cast.
25 It stood on [a]twelve oxen:
three looking toward the
north, three looking toward the
west, three looking toward
the south, and three looking
toward the east; the Sea *was set*
upon them, and all their back
parts *pointed* inward.

8 [a]2 Chr. 8:11
12 [a]1 Kin. 6:36 [b]John 10:23
13 [1]Heb. *Hiram;* cf. 2 Chr. 2:13, 14
14 [a]2 Chr. 2:14 [b]2 Chr. 4:16 [c]Ex. 31:3; 36:1
15 [a]Jer. 52:21 [1]*fashioned*
20 [a]Jer. 52:23
21 [a]2 Chr. 3:17 [1]Lit. *He Shall Establish* [2]Lit. *In It Is Strength*
23 [a]2 Chr. 4:2
24 [a]2 Chr. 4:3
25 [a]Jer. 52:20

26 It *was* a handbreadth thick;
and its brim was shaped like the
brim of a cup, *like* a lily blossom. It contained [1]two thousand
baths.
27 He also made ten [1]carts of
bronze; four cubits *was* the
length of each cart, four cubits
its width, and three cubits its
height.
28 And this *was* the design
of the carts: They had panels,
and the panels *were* between
frames;
29 on the panels that *were* between the frames *were* lions,
oxen, and cherubim. And on the
frames *was* a pedestal on top.
Below the lions and oxen *were*
wreaths of plaited work.
30 Every cart had four bronze
wheels and axles of bronze, and
its four feet had supports. Under
the laver *were* supports of cast
bronze beside each wreath.
31 Its opening inside the crown
at the top *was* one cubit in diameter; and the opening *was*
round, shaped *like* a pedestal,
one and a half cubits in outside
diameter; and also on the opening *were* engravings, but the
panels were square, not round.
32 Under the panels *were* the
four wheels, and the axles of the
wheels *were joined* to the cart.
The height of a wheel *was* one
and a half cubits.
33 The workmanship of the
wheels *was* like the workmanship of a chariot wheel; their
axle pins, their rims, their
spokes, and their hubs *were* all
of cast *bronze*.
34 And *there were* four supports at the four corners of each
cart; its supports *were* part of
the cart itself.
35 On the top of the cart, at the
height of half a cubit, *it was* perfectly round. And on the top of
the cart, its flanges and its panels *were* of the same casting.
36 On the plates of its flanges
and on its panels he engraved
cherubim, lions, and palm trees,
wherever there was a clear
space on each, with wreaths all
around.
37 Thus he made the ten carts.
All of them were of [1]the same
mold, one measure, *and* one
shape.
38 Then [a]he made ten lavers
of bronze; each laver contained
[1]forty baths, *and* each laver *was*
four cubits. On each of the ten
carts *was* a laver.
39 And he put five carts on the
right side of the house, and five
on the left side of the house. He
set the Sea on the right side of
the house, toward the southeast.
40 [a]Hū′ram[1] made the lavers
and the shovels and the bowls.
So Hū′ram finished doing all the
work that he was to do for King
Solomon *for* the house of the
LORD:
41 the two pillars, the *two*
bowl-shaped capitals that *were*
on top of the two pillars; the
two [a]networks covering the two
bowl-shaped capitals which
were on top of the pillars;
42 [a]four hundred pomegranates for the two networks (two
rows of pomegranates for each
network, to cover the two bowl-
shaped capitals that *were* on top
of the pillars);
43 the ten carts, and ten lavers
on the carts;
44 one Sea, and twelve oxen
under the Sea;
45 [a]the pots, the shovels, and

26 [1]About 12,000 gallons; *three thousand,* 2 Chr. 4:5
27 [1]Or *stands*
37 [1]*one*
38 [a]2 Chr. 4:6 [1]About 240 gallons
40 [a]2 Chr. 4:11—5:1 [1]Heb. *Hiram;* cf. 2 Chr. 2:13, 14
41 [a]1 Kin. 7:17, 18
42 [a]1 Kin. 7:20
45 [a]Ex. 27:3

the bowls. All these articles which [1]Hū′ram made for King Solomon *for* the house of the LORD *were of* burnished bronze.

46 [a]In the plain of Jordan the king had them cast in clay molds, between [b]Suc′coth and [c]Zar′e·tan.

47 And Solomon did not weigh all the articles, because *there were* so many; the weight of the bronze was not [a]determined.

48 Thus Solomon had all the furnishings made for the house of the LORD: [a]the altar of gold, and [b]the table of gold on which *was* [c]the showbread;

49 the lampstands of pure gold, five on the right *side* and five on the left in front of the inner sanctuary, with the flowers and the lamps and the wick-trimmers of gold;

50 the basins, the trimmers, the bowls, the ladles, and the [1]censers of pure gold; and the hinges of gold, *both* for the doors of the inner room (the Most Holy *Place*) *and* for the doors of the main hall of the temple.

51 So all the work that King Solomon had done for the house of the LORD was finished; and Solomon brought in the things [a]which his father David had dedicated: the silver and the gold and the furnishings. He put them in the treasuries of the house of the LORD.

CHAPTER 8

8 Now [a]Solomon assembled the elders of Israel and all the heads of the tribes, the chief fathers of the children of Israel, to King Solomon in Jerusalem, [b]that they might bring [c]up the ark of the covenant of the LORD from the City of David, which *is* Zion.

2 Therefore all the men of Israel assembled with King Solomon at the [a]feast in the month of [1]Eth′a·nim, which *is* the seventh month.

3 So all the elders of Israel came, [a]and the priests took up the ark.

4 Then they brought up the ark of the LORD, [a]the [1]tabernacle of meeting, and all the holy furnishings that *were* in the tabernacle. The priests and the Lē′vītes brought them up.

5 Also King Solomon, and all the congregation of Israel who were assembled with him, *were* with him before the ark, [a]sacrificing sheep and oxen that could not be counted or numbered for multitude.

6 Then the priests [a]brought in the ark of the covenant of the LORD to [b]its place, into the inner sanctuary of the temple, to the Most Holy *Place*, [c]under the wings of the cherubim.

7 For the cherubim spread *their* two wings over the place of the ark, and the cherubim overshadowed the ark and its poles.

8 The poles [a]extended so that the [1]ends of the poles could be seen from the holy *place*, in front of the inner sanctuary; but they could not be seen from outside. And they are there to this day.

9 [a]Nothing *was* in the ark [b]except the two tablets of stone which Moses [c]put there at Hō′reb, [d]when the LORD made *a covenant* with the children of Israel, when they came out of the land of Egypt.

10 And it came to pass, when the priests came out of the holy *place*, that the cloud [a]filled the house of the LORD,

45 [1]Heb. *Hiram;* cf. 2 Chr. 2:13, 14
46 [a]2 Chr. 4:17 [b]Gen. 33:17 [c]Josh. 3:16
47 [a]1 Chr. 22:3, 14
48 [a]Ex. 37:25, 26; 2 Chr. 4:8 [b]Ex. 37:10, 11 [c]Lev. 24:5–8
50 [1]*firepans*
51 [a]2 Sam. 8:11

CHAPTER 8

1 [a]2 Chr. 5:2–14 [b]2 Sam. 6:12–17 [c]2 Sam. 5:7; 6:12, 16
2 [a]Lev. 23:34 [1]Or *Tishri,* September or October
3 [a]Num. 4:15; 7:9
4 [a]2 Chr. 1:3 [1]*tent*
5 [a]2 Sam. 6:13
6 [a]2 Sam. 6:17 [b]1 Kin. 6:19 [c]1 Kin. 6:27
8 [a]Ex. 25:13–15; 37:4, 5 [1]*heads*
9 [a]Ex. 25:21 [b]Deut. 10:5 [c]Ex. 24:7, 8; 40:20 [d]Ex. 34:27, 28
10 [a]Ex. 40:34, 35

11 so that the priests could not
continue ministering because
of the cloud; for the [a]glory of
the LORD filled the house of the
LORD.
12 [a]Then Solomon spoke:

“The LORD said He would
dwell [b]in the dark cloud.
13 [a]I have surely built You an
exalted house,
[b]And a place for You to dwell
in forever.”

14 Then the king turned around
and [a]blessed the whole assembly
of Israel, while all the assembly
of Israel was standing.
15 And he said: [a]“Blessed *be* the
LORD God of Israel, who [b]spoke
with His mouth to my father
David, and with His hand has
fulfilled *it,* saying,
16 ‘Since the day that I brought
My people Israel out of Egypt,
I have chosen no city from any
tribe of Israel *in which* to build
a house, that [a]My name might
be there; but I chose [b]David to
be over My people Israel.’
17 “Now [a]it was in the heart
of my father David to build a
[1]temple for the name of the LORD
God of Israel.
18 [a]“But the LORD said to my
father David, ‘Whereas it was in
your heart to build a temple for
My name, you did well that it
was in your heart.
19 ‘Nevertheless [a]you shall not
build the temple, but your son
who will come from your body,
he shall build the temple for My
name.’
20 “So the LORD has fulfilled
His word which He spoke; and
I have [1]filled the position of
my father David, and sit on the
throne of Israel, [a]as the LORD
promised; and I have built a
temple for the name of the LORD
God of Israel.
21 “And there I have made a
place for the ark, in which *is* [a]the
covenant of the LORD which He
made with our fathers, when He
brought them out of the land of
Egypt.”
22 Then Solomon stood before
[a]the altar of the LORD in the
presence of all the assembly of
Israel, and [b]spread out his hands
toward heaven;
23 and he said: “LORD God of Israel, [a]*there is* no God in heaven
above or on earth below like
You, [b]who keep *Your* covenant
and mercy with Your servants
who [c]walk before You with all
their hearts.
24 “You have kept what You
promised Your servant David my
father; You have both spoken
with Your mouth and fulfilled *it*
with Your hand, as *it is* this day.
25 “Therefore, LORD God of Israel, now keep what You promised Your servant David my father, saying, [a]‘You shall not fail
to have a man sit before Me on
the throne of Israel, only if your
sons take heed to their way, that
they walk before Me as you
have walked before Me.’
26 [a]“And now I pray, O God of
Israel, let Your word come true,
which You have spoken to Your
servant David my father.
27 “But [a]will God indeed dwell
on the earth? Behold, heaven
and the [b]heaven of heavens cannot contain You. How much less
this temple which I have built!
28 “Yet regard the prayer of
Your servant and his supplication, O LORD my God, and listen

11 [a]2 Chr. 7:1, 2
12 [a]2 Chr. 6:1 [b]Ps. 18:11; 97:2
13 [a]2 Sam. 7:13 [b]Ps. 132:14
14 [a]2 Sam. 6:18
15 [a]Luke 1:68 [b]2 Sam. 7:2, 12, 13, 25
16 [a]1 Kin. 8:29 [b]2 Sam. 7:8
17 [a]2 Sam. 7:2, 3 [1]Lit. *house,* and so in vv. 18–20
18 [a]2 Chr. 6:8, 9
19 [a]2 Sam. 7:5, 12, 13
20 [a]1 Chr. 28:5, 6 [1]*risen in the place of*
21 [a]Deut. 31:26
22 [a]2 Chr. 6:12 [b]Ezra 9:5
23 [a]Ex. 15:11 [b][Neh. 1:5] [c][Gen. 17:1]
25 [a]1 Kin. 2:4; 9:5
26 [a]2 Sam. 7:25
27 [a][Acts 7:49; 17:24] [b]2 Cor. 12:2

to the cry and the prayer which
Your servant is praying before
You today:
29 “that Your eyes may be open
toward this [1]temple night and
day, toward the place of which
You said, [a]‘My name shall be
[b]there,’ that You may hear the
prayer which Your servant
makes [c]toward this place.
30 [a]“And may You hear the supplication of Your servant and of
Your people Israel, when they
pray toward this place. Hear in
heaven Your dwelling place; and
when You hear, forgive.
31 “When anyone sins against
his neighbor, and is forced to
take [a]an oath, and comes *and*
takes an oath before Your altar
in this temple,
32 “then hear in heaven, and
act, and judge Your servants,
[a]condemning the wicked, bringing his way on his head, and
justifying the righteous by
giving him according to his
righteousness.
33 [a]“When Your people Israel
are defeated before an enemy
because they have sinned against
You, and [b]when they turn back
to You and confess Your name,
and pray and make supplication
to You in this temple,
34 “then hear in heaven, and
forgive the sin of Your people
Israel, and bring them back to
the land which You gave to their
[a]fathers.
35 [a]“When the heavens are shut
up and there is no rain because
they have sinned against You,
when they pray toward this
place and confess Your name,
and turn from their sin because
You afflict them,
36 “then hear in heaven, and
forgive the sin of Your servants,
Your people Israel, that You may
[a]teach them [b]the good way in
which they should walk; and
send rain on Your land which
You have given to Your people as
an inheritance.
37 [a]“When there is famine in
the land, pestilence *or* blight
or mildew, locusts *or* grasshoppers; when their enemy besieges
them in the land of their [1]cities;
whatever plague or whatever
sickness *there is;*
38 “whatever prayer, whatever
supplication is made by anyone,
or by all Your people Israel, when
each one knows the plague of
his own heart, and spreads out
his hands toward this temple:
39 “then hear in heaven Your
dwelling place, and forgive, and
act, and give to everyone according to all his ways, whose
heart You know (for You alone
[a]know the hearts of all the sons
of men),
40 [a]“that they may fear You all
the days that they live in the land
which You gave to our fathers.
41 “Moreover, concerning a foreigner, who *is* not of Your people
Israel, but has come from a far
country for Your name’s sake
42 “(for they will hear of Your
great name and Your [a]strong
hand and Your outstretched
arm), when he comes and prays
toward this temple,
43 “hear in heaven Your dwelling place, and do according to
all for which the foreigner calls
to You, [a]that all peoples of the
earth may know Your name and
[b]fear You, as *do* Your people Israel, and that they may know

29 [a]Deut. 12:11 [b]1 Kin. 9:3 [c]Dan. 6:10 [1]Lit. *house*
30 [a]Neh. 1:6
31 [a]Ex. 22:8–11
32 [a]Deut. 25:1
33 [a]Deut. 28:25 [b]Lev. 26:39, 40
34 [a][Lev. 26:40–42]
35 [a]Deut. 28:23
36 [a]Ps. 25:4; 27:11; 94:12 [b]1 Sam. 12:23
37 [a]Lev. 26:16, 25, 26 [1]Lit. *gates*
39 [a][1 Sam. 16:7]
40 [a][Ps. 130:4]
42 [a]Deut. 3:24
43 [a][1 Sam. 17:46] [b]Ps. 102:15

that this temple which I have built is called by Your name.

44 "When Your people go out to battle against their enemy, wherever You send them, and when they pray to the LORD toward the city which You have chosen and the temple which I have built for Your name,

45 "then hear in heaven their prayer and their supplication, and maintain their [1]cause.

46 "When they sin against You [a](for *there is* no one who does not sin), and You become angry with them and deliver them to the enemy, and they take them captive [b]to the land of the enemy, far or near;

47 [a]"*yet* when they [1]come to themselves in the land where they were carried captive, and repent, and make supplication to You in the land of those who took them captive, [b]saying, 'We have sinned and done wrong, we have committed wickedness';

48 "and *when* they [a]return to You with all their heart and with all their soul in the land of their enemies who led them away captive, and [b]pray to You toward their land which You gave to their fathers, the city which You have chosen and the temple which I have built for Your name:

49 "then hear in heaven Your dwelling place their prayer and their supplication, and maintain their [1]cause,

50 "and forgive Your people who have sinned against You, and all their transgressions which they have transgressed against You; and [a]grant them compassion before those who took them captive, that they may have compassion on them

51 "(for [a]they *are* Your people and Your inheritance, whom You brought out of Egypt, [b]out of the iron furnace),

52 [a]"that Your eyes may be open to the supplication of Your servant and the supplication of Your people Israel, to listen to them whenever they call to You.

53 "For You separated them from among all the peoples of the earth *to be* Your inheritance, [a]as You spoke by Your servant Moses, when You brought our fathers out of Egypt, O Lord GOD."

54 [a]And so it was, when Solomon had finished praying all this prayer and supplication to the LORD, that he arose from before the altar of the LORD, from kneeling on his knees with his hands spread up to heaven.

55 Then he stood [a]and blessed all the assembly of Israel with a loud voice, saying:

56 "Blessed *be* the LORD, who has given [a]rest[1] to His people Israel, according to all that He promised. [b]There has not failed one word of all His good promise, which He promised through His servant Moses.

57 "May the LORD our God be with us, as He was with our fathers. [a]May He not leave us nor forsake us,

58 "that He may [a]incline our hearts to Himself, to walk in all His ways, and to keep His commandments and His statutes and His judgments, which He commanded our fathers.

59 "And may these words of mine, with which I have made supplication before the LORD,

45 [1]*justice*
46 [a]Ps. 130:3 [b]Lev. 26:34, 44
47 [a][Lev. 26:40–42] [b]Dan. 9:5 [1]Lit. *bring back to their heart*
48 [a]Jer. 29:12–14 [b]Dan. 6:10
49 [1]*justice*
50 [a]Ps. 106:46
51 [a]Deut. 9:26–29 [b]Jer. 11:4
52 [a]1 Kin. 8:29
53 [a]Ex. 19:5, 6
54 [a]2 Chr. 7:1
55 [a]2 Sam. 6:18
56 [a]1 Chr. 22:18 [b]Deut. 12:10 [1]*peace*
57 [a]Deut. 31:6
58 [a]Ps. 119:36

be near the LORD our God day
and night, that He may maintain
the cause of His servant and the
cause of His people Israel, as
each day may require,
60 [a]"that all the peoples of the
earth may know that [b]the LORD
is God; *there is* no other.
61 "Let your [a]heart therefore
be [1]loyal to the LORD our God,
to walk in His statutes and keep
His commandments, as at this
day."
62 Then [a]the king and all Israel
with him offered sacrifices before the LORD.
63 And Solomon offered a sacrifice of peace offerings, which he
offered to the LORD, twenty-two
thousand bulls and one hundred
and twenty thousand sheep. So
the king and all the children of
Israel dedicated the house of the
LORD.
64 On [a]the same day the king
consecrated the middle of the
court that *was* in front of the
house of the LORD; for there he
offered burnt offerings, grain offerings, and the fat of the peace
offerings, because the [b]bronze
altar that *was* before the LORD
was too small to receive the
burnt offerings, the grain offerings, and the fat of the peace
offerings.
65 At that time Solomon held
[a]a feast, and all Israel with him,
a great assembly from [b]the entrance of Hā′math to [c]the Brook
of Egypt, before the LORD our
God, [d]seven days and seven
more days—fourteen days.
66 [a]On the eighth day he sent the
people away; and they [1]blessed
the king, and went to their tents
joyful and glad of heart for all
the good that the LORD had done

60 [a]1 Sam. 17:46 [b]Deut. 4:35, 39
61 [a]Deut. 18:13 [1]Lit. *at peace with*
62 [a]2 Chr. 7:4–10
64 [a]2 Chr. 7:7 [b]2 Chr. 4:1
65 [a]Lev. 23:34 [b]Num. 34:8 [c]Gen. 15:18 [d]2 Chr. 7:8
66 [a]2 Chr. 7:9 [1]*thanked*

CHAPTER 9

1 [a]2 Chr. 7:11 [b]1 Kin. 7:1 [c]2 Chr. 8:6
2 [a]1 Kin. 3:5; 11:9
3 [a]Ps. 10:17 [b]1 Kin. 8:29 [c]Deut. 11:12
4 [a]Gen. 17:1 [b]1 Kin. 11:4, 6; 15:5 [c]1 Kin. 8:61
5 [a]2 Sam. 7:12, 16
6 [a]2 Sam. 7:14–16 [1]*turn back*
7 [a][Lev. 18:24–29] [b][Jer. 7:4–14] [c]Ps. 44:14 [1]*destroy*
8 [a]2 Chr. 7:21

for His servant David, and for
Israel His people.
9 And [a]it came to pass, when
Solomon had finished building the house of the LORD [b]and
the king's house, and [c]all Solomon's desire which he wanted
to do,
2 that the LORD appeared to
Solomon the second time, [a]as
He had appeared to him at Gib′-
ē·on.
3 And the LORD said to him: [a]"I
have heard your prayer and your
supplication that you have made
before Me; I have consecrated
this house which you have built
[b]to put My name there forever,
[c]and My eyes and My heart will
be there perpetually.
4 "Now if you [a]walk before Me
[b]as your father David walked, in
integrity of heart and in uprightness, to do according to all that
I have commanded you, *and* if
you [c]keep My statutes and My
judgments,
5 "then I will establish the
throne of your kingdom over
Israel forever, [a]as I promised
David your father, saying, 'You
shall not fail to have a man on
the throne of Israel.'
6 [a]"*But* if you or your sons at
all [1]turn from following Me, and
do not keep My commandments
and My statutes which I have
set before you, but go and serve
other gods and worship them,
7 [a]"then I will [1]cut off Israel
from the land which I have given
them; and this house which I
have consecrated [b]for My name
I will cast out of My sight. [c]Israel
will be a proverb and a byword
among all peoples.
8 "And *as for* [a]this house,
which is exalted, everyone who

passes by it will be astonished
and will hiss, and say, [b]'Why has
the LORD done thus to this land
and to this house?'
9 "Then they will answer, 'Because they forsook the LORD
their God, who brought their
fathers out of the land of Egypt,
and have embraced other gods,
and worshiped them and served
them; therefore the LORD has
brought all this [a]calamity on
them.' "
10 Now [a]it happened at the end
of twenty years, when Solomon
had built the two houses, the
house of the LORD and the king's
house
11 [a](Hī′ram the king of Tȳre had
supplied Solomon with cedar
and cypress and gold, as much
as he desired), *that* King Solomon then gave Hī′ram twenty
cities in the land of Galilee.
12 Then Hī′ram went from Tȳre
to see the cities which Solomon
had given him, but they did not
please him.
13 So he said, "What *kind of*
cities *are* these which you have
given me, my brother?" [a]And he
called them the land of [1]Cā′bul,
as they are to this day.
14 Then Hī′ram sent the king
one hundred and twenty talents
of gold.
15 And this *is* the reason for
[a]the labor force which King Solomon raised: to build the house
of the LORD, his own house, [1]the
[b]Mil′lō, the wall of Jerusalem,
[c]Hā′zor, [d]Me·gid′dō, and [e]Gē′zer.
16 (Pharaoh king of Egypt had
gone up and taken Gē′zer and
burned it with fire, [a]had killed
the Cā′naan·ītes who dwelt in the
city, and had given it *as* a dowry
to his daughter, Solomon's wife.)
17 And Solomon built Gē′zer,
Lower [a]Beth Hor′on,
18 [a]Bā′a·lath, and Tad′mor in
the wilderness, in the land *of
Judah*,
19 all the storage cities that Solomon had, cities for [a]his chariots and cities for his [b]cavalry,
and whatever Solomon [c]desired
to build in Jerusalem, in Lebanon, and in all the land of his
dominion.
20 [a]All the people *who were* left
of the Am′o·rītes, Hit′tītes, Per′-
iz·zītes, Hī′vītes, and Jeb′ū·sītes,
who *were* not of the children of
Israel—
21 that is, their descendants
[a]who were left in the land after
them, [b]whom the children of
Israel had not been able to destroy completely—[c]from these
Solomon raised [d]forced labor, as
it is to this day.
22 But of the children of Israel
Solomon [a]made no forced laborers, because they *were* men of
war and his servants: his officers, his captains, commanders
of his chariots, and his cavalry.
23 Others *were* chiefs of the officials who *were* over Solomon's
work: [a]five hundred and fifty,
who ruled over the people who
did the work.
24 But [a]Pharaoh's daughter
came up from the City of David
to [b]her house which [1]*Solomon*
had built for her. [c]Then he built
the Mil′lō.
25 [a]Now three times a year Solomon offered burnt offerings
and peace offerings on the altar which he had built for the
LORD, and he burned incense
with them *on the altar* that *was*
before the LORD. So he finished
the temple.

8 [b][Deut. 29:24–26]
9 [a][Deut. 29:25–28]
10 [a]2 Chr. 8:1
11 [a]1 Kin. 5:1
13 [a]Josh. 19:27 [1]Lit. *Good for Nothing*
15 [a]1 Kin. 5:13 [b]2 Sam. 5:9 [c]Josh. 11:1; 19:36 [d]Josh. 17:11 [e]Josh. 16:10 [1]Lit. *The Landfill*
16 [a]Josh. 16:10
17 [a]2 Chr. 8:5
18 [a]Josh. 19:44
19 [a]1 Kin. 10:26 [b]1 Kin. 4:26 [c]1 Kin. 9:1
20 [a]2 Chr. 8:7
21 [a]Judg. 1:21–36; 3:1 [b]Josh. 15:63; 17:12, 13 [c]Judg. 1:28, 35 [d]Ezra 2:55, 58
22 [a][Lev. 25:39]
23 [a]2 Chr. 8:10
24 [a]1 Kin. 3:1 [b]1 Kin. 7:8 [c]2 Sam. 5:9 [1]Lit. *he;* cf. 2 Chr. 8:11
25 [a]Ex. 23:14–17

26 [a]King Solomon also built a
fleet of ships at [b]Ē′zi·on Gē′ber,
which *is* near [1]Ē′lath on the
shore of the Red Sea, in the land
of Ē′dom.
27 [a]Then Hī′ram sent his servants with the fleet, seamen who
knew the sea, to work with the
servants of Solomon.
28 And they went to [a]Ō′phir,
and acquired four hundred and
twenty talents of gold from
there, and brought *it* to King
Solomon.

10 Now when the [a]queen of
Shē′ba heard of the fame
of Solomon concerning the
name of the LORD, she came [b]to
test him with hard questions.
2 She came to Jerusalem with
a very great [1]retinue, with camels that bore spices, very much
gold, and precious stones; and
when she came to Solomon, she
spoke with him about all that
was in her heart.
3 So Solomon answered all
her questions; there was nothing [1]so difficult for the king that
he could not explain *it* to her.
4 And when the queen of
Shē′ba had seen all the wisdom
of Solomon, the house that he
had built,
5 the food on his table, the
seating of his servants, the service of his waiters and their apparel, his cupbearers, [a]and his
entryway by which he went up
to the house of the LORD, there
was no more spirit in her.
6 Then she said to the king:
"It was a true report which I
heard in my own land about
your words and your wisdom.
7 "However I did not believe
the words until I came and saw
with my own eyes; and indeed
the half was not told me. Your
wisdom and prosperity exceed
the fame of which I heard.
8 [a]"Happy *are* your men and
happy *are* these your servants,
who stand continually before
you *and* hear your wisdom!
9 [a]"Blessed be the LORD your
God, who [b]delighted in you, setting you on the throne of Israel!
Because the LORD has loved Israel forever, therefore He made
you king, [c]to do justice and
righteousness."
10 Then she [a]gave the king one
hundred and twenty talents of
gold, spices in great quantity,
and precious stones. There never
again came such abundance of
spices as the queen of Shē′ba
gave to King Solomon.
11 [a]Also, the ships of Hī′ram,
which brought gold from Ō′phir,
brought great quantities of [1]al-
mug wood and precious stones
from Ō′phir.
12 [a]And the king made [1]steps of
the almug wood for the house
of the LORD and for the king's
house, also harps and stringed
instruments for singers. There
never again came such [b]almug
wood, nor has the like been seen
to this day.
13 Now King Solomon gave the
queen of Shē′ba all she desired,
whatever she asked, besides
what Solomon had given her
according to the royal generosity. So she turned and went to
her own country, she and her
servants.
14 The weight of gold that came
to Solomon yearly was six hundred and sixty-six talents of
gold,
15 besides *that* from the [a]travel-
ing merchants, from the income

26 [a]2 Chr. 8:17, 18 [b]Num. 33:35 [1]Heb. *Eloth*
27 [a]1 Kin. 5:6, 9; 10:11
28 [a]Job 22:24

CHAPTER 10

1 [a]Matt. 12:42 [b]Judg. 14:12
2 [1]*company*
3 [1]*too*
5 [a]1 Chr. 26:16
8 [a]Prov. 8:34
9 [a]1 Kin. 5:7 [b]2 Sam. 22:20 [c]Ps. 72:2
10 [a]Ps. 72:10, 15
11 [a]1 Kin. 9:27, 28 [1]*algum*, 2 Chr. 9:10, 11
12 [a]2 Chr. 9:11 [b]2 Chr. 9:10 [1]Or *supports*
15 [a]2 Chr. 1:16

of traders, [b]from all the kings of
Arabia, and from the governors
of the country.
16 And King Solomon made
two hundred large shields *of*
hammered gold; six hundred
shekels of gold went into each
shield.
17 He also *made* [a]three hundred
shields *of* hammered gold; three
minas of gold went into each
shield. The king put them in the
[b]House of the Forest of Lebanon.
18 [a]Moreover the king made a
great throne of ivory, and overlaid it with pure gold.
19 The throne had six steps, and
the top of the throne *was* round
at the back; *there were* armrests
on either side of the place of the
seat, and two lions stood beside
the armrests.
20 Twelve lions stood there, one
on each side of the six steps;
nothing like *this* had been made
for any *other* kingdom.
21 [a]All King Solomon's drinking vessels *were* gold, and all
the vessels of the House of the
Forest of Lebanon *were* pure
gold. Not *one was* silver, for this
was accounted as nothing in the
days of Solomon.
22 For the king had [a]merchant[1]
ships at sea with the fleet of
Hī′ram. Once every three years
the merchant [b]ships came bringing gold, silver, ivory, apes, and
[2]monkeys.
23 So [a]King Solomon surpassed
all the kings of the earth in
riches and wisdom.
24 Now all the earth sought the
presence of Solomon to hear his
wisdom, which God had put in
his heart.
25 Each man brought his present: articles of silver and gold,

15 [b]Ps. 72:10

17 [a]1 Kin. 14:26 [b]1 Kin. 7:2

18 [a]2 Chr. 9:17

21 [a]2 Chr. 9:20

22 [a]Gen. 10:4 [b]1 Kin. 9:26–28; 22:48 [1]Lit. *ships of Tarshish*, deep-sea vessels [2]Or *peacocks*

23 [a]1 Kin. 3:12, 13; 4:30

26 [a]1 Kin. 4:26 [b]1 Kin. 9:19 [1]So with LXX, Syr., Tg., Vg. (cf. 2 Chr. 9:25); MT *led*

27 [a]2 Chr. 1:15–17

28 [a][Deut. 17:16]

29 [a]2 Kin. 7:6, 7 [1]Lit. *by their hands*

CHAPTER 11

1 [a][Neh. 13:26] [b][Deut. 17:17]

2 [a][Deut. 7:3, 4]

4 [a][Deut. 17:17]

garments, armor, spices, horses,
and mules, at a set rate year by
year.
26 [a]And Solomon [b]gathered
chariots and horsemen; he had
one thousand four hundred
chariots and twelve thousand
horsemen, whom he [1]stationed
in the chariot cities and with the
king at Jerusalem.
27 [a]The king made silver *as
common* in Jerusalem as stones,
and he made cedar trees as
abundant as the sycamores
which *are* in the lowland.
28 [a]Also Solomon had horses
imported from Egypt and
Ke·veh′; the king's merchants
bought them in Ke·veh′ at the
current price.
29 Now a chariot that was imported from Egypt cost six hundred *shekels* of silver, and a
horse one hundred and fifty;
[a]and [1]thus, through their agents,
they exported *them* to all the
kings of the Hit′tītes and the
kings of Syria.

11 But [a]King Solomon loved
[b]many foreign women, as
well as the daughter of Pharaoh: women of the Mō′ab·ītes,
Am′mon·ītes, Ē′dom·ītes, Sī·dō′-
ni·ans, *and* Hit′tītes—
2 from the nations of whom
the LORD had said to the children of Israel, [a]"You shall not
intermarry with them, nor they
with you. Surely they will turn
away your hearts after their
gods." Solomon clung to these
in love.
3 And he had seven hundred
wives, princesses, and three
hundred concubines; and his
wives turned away his heart.
4 For it was so, when Solomon
was old, [a]that his wives turned

his heart after other gods; and
his [b]heart was not [1]loyal to the
LORD his God, [c]as *was* the heart
of his father David.
5 For Solomon went after
[a]Ash′to·reth the goddess of the
Sī·dō′ni·ans, and after [b]Mil′com[1]
the abomination of the [c]Am′-
mon·ītes.
6 Solomon did evil in the sight
of the LORD, and did not fully
follow the LORD, as *did* his father
David.
7 [a]Then Solomon built a [1]high
place for [b]Chē′mosh the abomination of Mō′ab, on [c]the hill that
is east of Jerusalem, and for
Mō′lech the abomination of the
people of Am′mon.
8 And he did likewise for all
his foreign wives, who burned
incense and sacrificed to their
gods.
9 So the LORD became angry
with Solomon, because his heart
had turned from the LORD God
of Israel, [a]who had appeared to
him twice,
10 and [a]had commanded him
concerning this thing, that he
should not go after other gods;
but he did not keep what the
LORD had commanded.
11 Therefore the LORD said to
Solomon, "Because you have
done this, and have not kept
My covenant and My statutes,
which I have commanded you,
[a]I will surely tear the kingdom
away from you and give it to
your [b]servant.
12 "Nevertheless I will not do
it in your days, for the sake of
your father David; I will tear it
out of the hand of your son.
13 [a]"However I will not tear
away the whole kingdom; I will
give [b]one tribe to your son [c]for

4 [b]1 Kin. 8:61 [c]1 Kin. 9:4 [1]Lit. *at peace with*
5 [a]Judg. 2:13 [b][Lev. 20:2–5] [c]2 Kin. 23:13 [1]Or *Molech*
7 [a]Num. 33:52 [b]Judg. 11:24 [c]2 Kin. 23:13 [1]A place for pagan worship
9 [a]1 Kin. 3:5; 9:2
10 [a]1 Kin. 6:12; 9:6, 7
11 [a]1 Kin. 11:31; 12:15, 16 [b]1 Kin. 11:31, 37
13 [a]2 Sam. 7:15 [b]1 Kin. 12:20 [c]2 Sam. 7:15, 16 [d]Deut. 12:11
14 [a]1 Chr. 5:26
15 [a]2 Sam. 8:14 [b]Num. 24:18, 19
21 [a]1 Kin. 2:10, 34 [1]Died and joined his ancestors [2]Lit. *Send me away*

the sake of My servant David,
and for the sake of Jerusalem
[d]which I have chosen."
14 Now the LORD [a]raised up an
adversary against Solomon, Hā′-
dad the Ē′dom·īte; he *was* a descendant of the king in Ē′dom.
15 [a]For it happened, when David was in Ē′dom, and Jō′ab
the commander of the army
had gone up to bury the slain,
[b]after he had killed every male
in Ē′dom
16 (because for six months
Jō′ab remained there with all Israel, until he had cut down every
male in Ē′dom),
17 that Hā′dad fled to go to
Egypt, he and certain Ē′dom·ītes
of his father's servants with him.
Hā′dad *was* still a little child.
18 Then they arose from Mid′-
i·an and came to Par′an; and they
took men with them from Par′an
and came to Egypt, to Pharaoh
king of Egypt, who gave him
a house, apportioned food for
him, and gave him land.
19 And Hā′dad found great favor in the sight of Pharaoh, so
that he gave him as wife the
sister of his own wife, that is, the
sister of Queen Tah′pe·nēs.
20 Then the sister of Tah′pe·nēs
bore him Ge·nū′bath his son,
whom Tah′pe·nēs weaned in
Pharaoh's house. And Ge·nū′-
bath was in Pharaoh's household
among the sons of Pharaoh.
21 [a]So when Hā′dad heard in
Egypt that David [1]rested with
his fathers, and that Jō′ab the
commander of the army was
dead, Hā′dad said to Pharaoh,
[2]"Let me depart, that I may go to
my own country."
22 Then Pharaoh said to him,
"But what have you lacked with

me, that suddenly you seek to
go to your own country?" So he
answered, "Nothing, but do let
me go anyway."
23 And God raised up *another*
adversary against him, Rē'zon
the son of E·lī'a·dah, who had
fled from his lord, [a]Had·a·dē'zer
king of Zō'bah.
24 So he gathered men to him
and became captain over a band
of raiders, [a]when David killed
those *of Zō'bah.* And they went
to Damascus and dwelt there,
and reigned in Damascus.
25 He was an adversary of Israel all the days of Solomon
(besides the trouble that Hā'dad
caused); and he abhorred Israel,
and reigned over Syria.
26 Then Solomon's servant,
[a]Jer·o·bō'am the son of Nē'bat,
an Ē'phra·im·īte from Zer'e·da,
whose mother's name *was*
Ze·rū'ah, a widow, [b]also [c]rebelled
against the king.
27 And this *is* what caused him
to rebel against the king: [a]Sol-
omon had built the Mil'lō *and*
[1]repaired the damages to the
City of David his father.
28 The man Jer·o·bō'am *was* a
mighty man of valor; and Solomon, seeing that the young
man was [a]industrious, made him
the officer over all the labor
force of the house of Joseph.
29 Now it happened at that
time, when Jer·o·bō'am went out
of Jerusalem, that the prophet
[a]A·hī'jah the Shī'lo·nīte met him
on the way; and he had clothed
himself with a new garment,
and the two *were* alone in the
field.
30 Then A·hī'jah took hold of the
new garment that *was* on him,
and [a]tore it *into* twelve pieces.
31 And he said to Jer·o·bō'am,
"Take for yourself ten pieces,
for [a]thus says the LORD, the God
of Israel: 'Behold, I will tear the
kingdom out of the hand of Solomon and will give ten tribes to
you
32 '(but he shall have one tribe
for the sake of My servant David,
and for the sake of Jerusalem,
the city which I have chosen out
of all the tribes of Israel),
33 [a]'because [1]they have forsaken Me, and worshiped Ash'-
to·reth the goddess of the Sī·dō'-
ni·ans, Chē'mosh the god of the
Mō'ab·ītes, and Mil'com the god
of the people of Am'mon, and
have not walked in My ways to
do *what is* right in My eyes and
keep My statutes and My judgments, as *did* his father David.
34 'However I will not take the
whole kingdom out of his hand,
because I have made him ruler
all the days of his life for the
sake of My servant David, whom
I chose because he kept My commandments and My statutes.
35 'But [a]I will take the kingdom
out of his son's hand and give it
to you—ten tribes.
36 'And to his son I will give one
tribe, that [a]My servant David
may always have a lamp before
Me in Jerusalem, the city which
I have chosen for Myself, to put
My name there.
37 'So I will take you, and you
shall reign over all your heart
desires, and you shall be king
over Israel.
38 'Then it shall be, if you heed
all that I command you, walk in
My ways, and do *what is* right
in My sight, to keep My statutes
and My commandments, as My
servant David did, then [a]I will

23 [a]2 Sam. 8:3; 10:16
24 [a]2 Sam. 8:3; 10:8, 18
26 [a]1 Kin. 12:2 [b]2 Chr. 13:6 [c]2 Sam. 20:21
27 [a]1 Kin. 9:15, 24 [1]Lit. *closed up the breaches*
28 [a][Prov. 22:29]
29 [a]2 Chr. 9:29
30 [a]1 Sam. 15:27, 28; 24:5
31 [a]1 Kin. 11:11, 13
33 [a]1 Kin. 11:5–8 [1]So with MT, Tg.; LXX, Syr., Vg. *he has*
35 [a]1 Kin. 12:16, 17
36 [a][1 Kin. 15:4]
38 [a]Josh. 1:5

be with you and [b]build for you
an enduring house, as I built for
David, and will give Israel to
you.
39 'And I will afflict the descendants of David because of this,
but not forever.' "
40 Solomon therefore sought to
kill Jer·o·bō′am. But Jer·o·bō′am
arose and fled to Egypt, to [a]Shī′-
shak king of Egypt, and was
in Egypt until the death of Solomon.
41 Now [a]the rest of the acts of
Solomon, all that he did, and
his wisdom, *are* they not written
in the book of the acts of Solomon?
42 [a]And the period that Solomon reigned in Jerusalem over
all Israel *was* forty years.
43 [a]Then Solomon [1]rested with
his fathers, and was buried in
the City of David his father. And
Rē·ho·bō′am his son reigned in
his [b]place.
12 And [a]Rē·ho·bō′am went
to [b]Shē′chem, for all Israel had gone to Shē′chem to
make him king.
2 So it happened, when
[a]Jer·o·bō′am the son of Nē′bat
heard *it* (he was still in [b]Egypt,
for he had fled from the presence of King Solomon and had
been dwelling in Egypt),
3 that they sent and called him.
Then Jer·o·bō′am and the whole
assembly of Israel came and
spoke to Rē·ho·bō′am, saying,
4 "Your father made our [a]yoke
[1]heavy; now therefore, lighten
the burdensome service of your
father, and his heavy yoke which
he put on us, and we will serve
you."
5 So he said to them, "Depart

38 [b]2 Sam. 7:11, 27
40 [a]2 Chr. 12:2–9
41 [a]2 Chr. 9:29
42 [a]2 Chr. 9:30
43 [a]2 Chr. 9:31 [b]2 Chr. 10:1 [1]Died and joined his ancestors

CHAPTER 12

1 [a]2 Chr. 10:1 [b]Judg. 9:6
2 [a]1 Kin. 11:26 [b]1 Kin. 11:40
4 [a]1 Sam. 8:11–18 [1]*hard*
7 [a]2 Chr. 10:7
11 [1]Scourges with points or barbs, lit. *scorpions*

for three days, then come back to
me." And the people departed.
6 Then King Rē·ho·bō′am consulted the elders who stood before his father Solomon while
he still lived, and he said, "How
do you advise *me* to answer
these people?"
7 And they spoke to him, saying, [a]"If you will be a servant to
these people today, and serve
them, and answer them, and
speak good words to them,
then they will be your servants
forever."
8 But he rejected the advice
which the elders had given him,
and consulted the young men
who had grown up with him,
who stood before him.
9 And he said to them, "What
advice do you give? How should
we answer this people who have
spoken to me, saying, 'Lighten
the yoke which your father put
on us'?"
10 Then the young men who
had grown up with him spoke to
him, saying, "Thus you should
speak to this people who have
spoken to you, saying, 'Your father made our yoke heavy, but
you make *it* lighter on us'—thus
you shall say to them: 'My little
finger shall be thicker than my
father's waist!
11 'And now, whereas my father put a heavy yoke on you,
I will add to your yoke; my father chastised you with whips,
but I will chastise you with
[1]scourges!' "
12 So Jer·o·bō′am and all the
people came to Rē·ho·bō′am the
third day, as the king had directed, saying, "Come back to
me the third day."
13 Then the king answered the

people [1]roughly, and rejected
the advice which the elders had
given him;
14 and he spoke to them according to the advice of the young
men, saying, "My father made
your yoke heavy, but I will add
to your yoke; my father chastised you with whips, but I will
chastise you with [1]scourges!"
15 So the king did not listen
to the people; for [a]the turn *of
events* was from the LORD, that
He might fulfill His word, which
the LORD had [b]spoken by A·hī'-
jah the Shī'lo·nīte to Jer·o·bō'am
the son of Nē'bat.
16 Now when all Israel saw that
the king did not listen to them,
the people answered the king,
saying:

[a]"What share have we in
David?
We have no inheritance in
the son of Jesse.
To your tents, O Israel!
Now, see to your own house,
O David!"

So Israel departed to their tents.
17 But Rē·ho·bō'am reigned
over [a]the children of Israel who
dwelt in the cities of Judah.
18 Then King Rē·ho·bō'am [a]sent
A·dor'am, who *was* in charge of
the revenue; but all Israel stoned
him with stones, and he died.
Therefore King Rē·ho·bō'am
mounted his chariot in haste to
flee to Jerusalem.
19 So [a]Israel has been in rebellion against the house of David
to this day.
20 Now it came to pass when all
Israel heard that Jer·o·bō'am had
come back, they sent for him and
called him to the congregation,
and made him king over all
[a]Israel. There was none who followed the house of David, but
the tribe of Judah [b]only.
21 And when [a]Rē·ho·bō'am came
to Jerusalem, he assembled all
the house of Judah with the tribe
of [b]Benjamin, one hundred and
eighty thousand chosen *men*
who were warriors, to fight
against the house of Israel, that
he might restore the kingdom to
Rē·ho·bō'am the son of Solomon.
22 But [a]the word of God came
to She·māi'ah the man of God,
saying,
23 "Speak to Rē·ho·bō'am the
son of Solomon, king of Judah,
to all the house of Judah and
Benjamin, and to the rest of the
people, saying,
24 'Thus says the LORD: "You
shall not go up nor fight against
your brethren the children of
Israel. Let every man return to
his house, [a]for this thing is from
Me." ' " Therefore they obeyed
the word of the LORD, and turned
back, according to the word of
the LORD.
25 Then Jer·o·bō'am [a]built[1]
Shē'chem in the mountains of
Ē'phra·im, and dwelt there. Also
he went out from there and built
[b]Pe·nū'el.
26 And Jer·o·bō'am said in his
heart, "Now the kingdom may
return to the house of David:
27 "If these people [a]go up to
offer sacrifices in the house of
the LORD at Jerusalem, then the
heart of this people will turn
back to their lord, Rē·ho·bō'am
king of Judah, and they will kill
me and go back to Rē·ho·bō'am
king of Judah."
28 Therefore the king asked

13 [1]*harshly*
14 [1]Lit. *scorpions*
15 [a]Judg. 14:4 [b]1 Kin. 11:11, 29, 31
16 [a]2 Sam. 20:1
17 [a]1 Kin. 11:13, 36
18 [a]1 Kin. 4:6; 5:14
19 [a]2 Kin. 17:21
20 [a]2 Kin. 17:21 [b]1 Kin. 11:13, 32, 36
21 [a]2 Chr. 11:1–4 [b]2 Sam. 19:17
22 [a]2 Chr. 11:2; 12:5–7
24 [a]1 Kin. 12:15
25 [a]Judg. 9:45–49 [b]Judg. 8:8, 17 [1]*fortified*
27 [a][Deut. 12:5–7, 14]

advice, [a]made two calves of
gold, and said to the people, "It
is too much for you to go up to
Jerusalem. [b]Here are your gods,
O Israel, which brought you up
from the land of Egypt!"
29 And he set up one in [a]Beth'el,
and the other he put in [b]Dan.
30 Now this thing became [a]a sin,
for the people went *to worship*
before the one as far as Dan.
31 He made [1]shrines on the high
places, [a]and made priests from
every class of people, who were
not of the sons of Levi.
32 Jer·o·bō'am [1]ordained a feast
on the fifteenth day of the eighth
month, like [a]the feast that *was*
in Judah, and offered sacrifices
on the altar. So he did at Beth'el,
sacrificing to the calves that he
had made. [b]And at Beth'el he
installed the priests of the high
places which he had made.
33 So he made offerings on
the altar which he had made at
Beth'el on the fifteenth day of
the eighth month, in the month
which he had [a]devised in his
own heart. And he [1]ordained a
feast for the children of Israel,
and offered sacrifices on the
altar and [b]burned incense.

13 And behold, [a]a man of
God went from Judah to
Beth'el [1]by the word of the LORD,
[b]and Jer·o·bō'am stood by the
altar to burn incense.
2 Then he cried out against the
altar [1]by the word of the LORD,
and said, "O altar, altar! Thus
says the LORD: 'Behold, a child,
[a]Jō·sī'ah by name, shall be born
to the house of David; and on
you he shall sacrifice the priests
of the high places who burn incense on you, and men's bones
shall be [b]burned on you.' "

28 [a]2 Kin. 10:29; 17:16 [b]Ex. 32:4, 8
29 [a]Gen. 28:19 [b]Judg. 18:26–31
30 [a]1 Kin. 13:34
31 [a]2 Kin. 17:32 [1]Lit. *a house;* cf. 1 Kin. 13:32, lit. *houses*
32 [a]Lev. 23:33, 34 [b]Amos 7:10–13 [1]*instituted*
33 [a]Num. 15:39 [b]1 Kin. 13:1 [1]*instituted*

CHAPTER 13

1 [a]2 Kin. 23:17 [b]1 Kin. 12:32, 33 [1]*at the LORD's command*
2 [a]2 Kin. 23:15, 16 [b][Lev. 26:30] [1]*at the LORD's command*
3 [a]Is. 7:14; 38:7
6 [a][James 5:16]
7 [a]1 Sam. 9:7
8 [a]Num. 22:18; 24:13
9 [a][1 Cor. 5:11]

3 And he gave [a]a sign the same
day, saying, "This *is* the sign
which the LORD has spoken:
Surely the altar shall split apart,
and the ashes on it shall be
poured out."
4 So it came to pass when
King Jer·o·bō'am heard the saying of the man of God, who cried
out against the altar in Beth'el,
that he stretched out his hand
from the altar, saying, "Arrest
him!" Then his hand, which he
stretched out toward him, withered, so that he could not pull it
back to himself.
5 The altar also was split apart,
and the ashes poured out from
the altar, according to the sign
which the man of God had given
by the word of the LORD.
6 Then the king answered and
said to the man of God, "Please
[a]entreat the favor of the LORD
your God, and pray for me, that
my hand may be restored to me."
So the man of God entreated the
LORD, and the king's hand was
restored to him, and became as
before.
7 Then the king said to the
man of God, "Come home with
me and refresh yourself, and [a]I
will give you a reward."
8 But the man of God said to
the king, [a]"If you were to give
me half your house, I would not
go in with you; nor would I eat
bread nor drink water in this
place.
9 "For so it was commanded
me by the word of the LORD, saying, [a]'You shall not eat bread,
nor drink water, nor return by
the same way you came.' "
10 So he went another way and
did not return by the way he
came to Beth'el.

11 Now an [a]old prophet dwelt in
Beth'el, and his [1]sons came and
told him all the works that the
man of God had done that day
in Beth'el; they also told their
father the words which he had
spoken to the king.
12 And their father said to them,
"Which way did he go?" For his
sons [1]had seen which way the
man of God went who came
from Judah.
13 Then he said to his sons,
"Saddle the donkey for me." So
they saddled the donkey for him;
and he rode on it,
14 and went after the man of
God, and found him sitting under an oak. Then he said to him,
"*Are* you the man of God who
came from Judah?" And he said,
"I *am*."
15 Then he said to him, "Come
home with me and eat bread."
16 And he said, [a]"I cannot return with you nor go in with
you; neither can I eat bread nor
drink water with you in this
place.
17 "For [1]I have been told [a]by the
word of the LORD, 'You shall not
eat bread nor drink water there,
nor return by going the way you
came.' "
18 He said to him, "I too *am*
a prophet as you *are,* and an
angel spoke to me by the word
of the LORD, saying, 'Bring him
back with you to your house,
that he may eat bread and drink
water.' " (He was lying to him.)
19 So he went back with him,
and ate bread in his house, and
drank water.
20 Now it happened, as they sat
at the table, that the word of the
LORD came to the prophet who
had brought him back;

11 [a]1 Kin. 13:25 [1]Lit. *son*
12 [1]LXX, Syr., Tg., Vg. *showed him*
16 [a]1 Kin. 13:8, 9
17 [a]1 Kin. 20:35 [1]Lit. *a command came to me by*
22 [a]1 Kin. 13:9
24 [a]1 Kin. 20:36

21 and he cried out to the man
of God who came from Judah,
saying, "Thus says the LORD:
'Because you have disobeyed the
word of the LORD, and have not
kept the commandment which
the LORD your God commanded
you,
22 'but you came back, ate
bread, and drank water in the
[a]place of which *the* LORD said
to you, "Eat no bread and drink
no water," your corpse shall
not come to the tomb of your
fathers.' "
23 So it was, after he had eaten
bread and after he had drunk,
that he saddled the donkey for
him, the prophet whom he had
brought back.
24 When he was gone, [a]a lion
met him on the road and killed
him. And his corpse was thrown
on the road, and the donkey
stood by it. The lion also stood
by the corpse.
25 And there, men passed by
and saw the corpse thrown on
the road, and the lion standing
by the corpse. Then they went
and told *it* in the city where the
old prophet dwelt.
26 Now when the prophet who
had brought him back from the
way heard *it,* he said, "It *is* the
man of God who was disobedient to the word of the LORD.
Therefore the LORD has delivered him to the lion, which has
torn him and killed him, according to the word of the LORD
which He spoke to him."
27 And he spoke to his sons,
saying, "Saddle the donkey for
me." So they saddled *it.*
28 Then he went and found his
corpse thrown on the road, and
the donkey and the lion standing

by the corpse. The lion had not
eaten the corpse nor torn the
donkey.
29 And the prophet took up the
corpse of the man of God, laid
it on the donkey, and brought it
back. So the old prophet came
to the city to mourn, and to bury
him.
30 Then he laid the corpse in his
own tomb; and they mourned
over him, *saying,* [a]"Alas, my
brother!"
31 So it was, after he had buried
him, that he spoke to his sons,
saying, "When I am dead, then
bury me in the tomb where the
man of God *is* buried; [a]lay my
bones beside his bones.
32 [a]"For the [1]saying which he
cried out by the word of the
LORD against the altar in Beth′el,
and against all the [2]shrines on
the high places which *are* in the
cities of [b]Samaria, will surely
come to pass."
33 [a]After this event Jer·o·bō′am
did not turn from his evil way,
but again he made priests from
every class of people for the
high places; whoever wished, he
consecrated him, and he became
one of the priests of the high
places.
34 [a]And this thing was the sin
of the house of Jer·o·bō′am, so
as [b]to exterminate and destroy
it from the face of the earth.

14 At that time A·bī′jah the
son of Jer·o·bō′am be-
came sick.
2 And Jer·o·bō′am said to his
wife, "Please arise, and disguise yourself, that they may
not recognize you as the wife of
Jer·o·bō′am, and go to Shī′lōh.
Indeed, A·hī′jah the prophet *is*
there, who told me that [a]*I would
be* king over this people.
3 [a]"Also take [1]with you ten
loaves, *some* cakes, and a jar
of honey, and go to him; he will
tell you what will become of the
child."
4 And Jer·o·bō′am's wife did
so; she arose [a]and went to Shī′-
lōh, and came to the house of
A·hī′jah. But A·hī′jah could not
see, for his eyes were [1]glazed by
reason of his age.
5 Now the LORD had said to
A·hī′jah, "Here is the wife of
Jer·o·bō′am, coming to ask you
something about her son, for he
is sick. Thus and thus you shall
say to her; for it will be, when
she comes in, that she will pretend *to be* another *woman.*"
6 And so it was, when A·hī′jah
heard the sound of her footsteps as she came through the
door, he said, "Come in, wife of
Jer·o·bō′am. Why do you pretend
to be another *person?* For I *have
been* sent to you *with* bad *news.*
7 "Go, tell Jer·o·bō′am, 'Thus
says the LORD God of Israel:
[a]"Because I exalted you from
among the people, and made
you ruler over My people Israel,
8 "and [a]tore the kingdom away
from the house of David, and
gave it to you; and *yet* you have
not been as My servant David,
[b]who kept My commandments
and who followed Me with all
his heart, to do only *what was*
right in My eyes;
9 "but you have done more evil
than all who were before you,
[a]for you have gone and made for
yourself other gods and molded
images to provoke Me to anger,
and [b]have cast Me behind your
back—

30 [a]Jer. 22:18
31 [a]2 Kin. 23:17, 18
32 [a]2 Kin. 23:16, 19 [b]1 Kin. 16:24 [1]Lit. *word* [2]Lit. *houses*
33 [a]1 Kin. 12:31, 32
34 [a]1 Kin. 12:30 [b][1 Kin. 14:10; 15:29, 30]

CHAPTER 14

2 [a]1 Kin. 11:29–31
3 [a]1 Sam. 9:7, 8 [1]Lit. *in your hand*
4 [a]1 Kin. 11:29 [1]Lit. *set*
7 [a]1 Kin. 16:2
8 [a]1 Kin. 11:31 [b]1 Kin. 11:33, 38; 15:5
9 [a]1 Kin. 12:28 [b]Ps. 50:17

10 "therefore behold! [a]I will bring disaster on the house of Jer·o·bō′am, and [b]will cut off from Jer·o·bō′am every male in Israel, [c]bond and free; I will take away the remnant of the house of Jer·o·bō′am, as one takes away refuse until it is all gone.

11 "The dogs shall eat [a]whoever belongs to Jer·o·bō′am and dies in the city, and the birds of the air shall eat whoever dies in the field; for the LORD has spoken!"'

12 "Arise therefore, go to your own house. [a]When your feet enter the city, the child shall die.

13 "And all Israel shall mourn for him and bury him, for he is the only one of Jer·o·bō′am who shall [1]come to the grave, because in him [a]there is found something good toward the LORD God of Israel in the house of Jer·o·bō′am.

14 [a]"Moreover the LORD will raise up for Himself a king over Israel who shall cut off the house of Jer·o·bō′am; [1]this is the day. What? Even now!

15 "For the LORD will strike Israel, as a reed is shaken in the water. He will [a]uproot Israel from this [b]good land which He gave to their fathers, and will scatter them [c]beyond [1]the River, [d]because they have made their [2]wooden images, provoking the LORD to anger.

16 "And He will give Israel up because of the sins of Jer·o·bō′am, [a]who sinned and who made Israel sin."

17 Then Jer·o·bō′am's wife arose and departed, and came to [a]Tir′zah. [b]When she came to the threshold of the house, the child died.

18 And they buried him; and all Israel mourned for him, [a]according to the word of the LORD which He spoke through His servant A·hī′jah the prophet.

19 Now the rest of the acts of Jer·o·bō′am, how he [a]made war and how he reigned, indeed they *are* written in the book of the chronicles of the kings of Israel.

20 The period that Jer·o·bō′am reigned *was* twenty-two years. So he rested with his fathers. Then [a]Nā′dab his son reigned in his place.

21 And Rē·ho·bō′am the son of Solomon reigned in Judah. [a]Rē·ho·bō′am *was* forty-one years old when he became king. He reigned seventeen years in Jerusalem, the city [b]which the LORD had chosen out of all the tribes of Israel, to put His name there. [c]His mother's name *was* Nā′a·mah, an Am′mon·ī·tess.

22 [a]Now Judah did evil in the sight of the LORD, and they [b]provoked Him to jealousy with their sins which they committed, more than all that their fathers had done.

23 For they also built for themselves [a]high[1] places, [b]*sacred* pillars, and [c]wooden images on every high hill and [d]under every green tree.

24 [a]And there were also [1]perverted persons in the land. They did according to all the [b]abominations of the nations which the LORD had cast out before the children of [c]Israel.

25 [a]It happened in the fifth year of King Rē·ho·bō′am *that* Shī′shak king of Egypt came up against Jerusalem.

26 [a]And he took away the treasures of the house of the LORD and the treasures of the king's

10 [a]1 Kin. 15:29 [b]1 Kin. 21:21 [c]Deut. 32:36
11 [a]1 Kin. 16:4; 21:24
12 [a]1 Kin. 14:17
13 [a]2 Chr. 12:12; 19:3 [1]Be buried
14 [a]1 Kin. 15:27–29 [1]Or *this day and from now on*
15 [a]2 Kin. 17:6 [b][Josh. 23:15, 16] [c]2 Kin. 15:29 [d][Ex. 34:13, 14] [1]The Euphrates [2]Heb. *Asherim,* Canaanite deities
16 [a]1 Kin. 12:30; 13:34; 15:30, 34; 16:2
17 [a]Song 6:4 [b]1 Kin. 14:12
18 [a]1 Kin. 14:13
19 [a]2 Chr. 13:2–20
20 [a]1 Kin. 15:25
21 [a]2 Chr. 12:13 [b]1 Kin. 11:32, 36 [c]1 Kin. 14:31
22 [a]2 Chr. 12:1, 14 [b]Deut. 32:21
23 [a]Deut. 12:2 [b][Deut. 16:22] [c][2 Kin. 17:9, 10] [d]Is. 57:5 [1]Places for pagan worship
24 [a]Deut. 23:17 [b]Deut. 20:18 [c][Deut. 9:4, 5] [1]Heb. *qadesh,* one practicing sodomy and prostitution in religious rituals
25 [a]1 Kin. 11:40
26 [a]2 Chr. 12:9–11

house; he took away everything.
He also took away all the gold
shields [b]which Solomon had
made.
27 Then King Rē·ho·bō′am
made bronze shields in their
place, and [1]committed *them* to
the hands of the captains of the
[2]guard, who guarded the doorway of the king's house.
28 And whenever the king entered the house of the LORD,
the guards carried them, then
brought them back into the
guardroom.
29 [a]Now the rest of the acts of
Rē·ho·bō′am, and all that he did,
are they not written in the book
of the chronicles of the kings of
Judah?
30 And there was [a]war between
Rē·ho·bō′am and Jer·o·bō′am all
their days.
31 [a]So Rē·ho·bō′am [1]rested with
his fathers, and was buried with
his fathers in the City of David.
[b]His mother's name *was* Nā′-
a·mah, an Am′mon·ī·tess. Then
[c]A·bī′jam[2] his son reigned in his
place.

15 [a]In the eighteenth year of
King Jer·o·bō′am the son
of Nē′bat, A·bī′jam became king
over Judah.
2 He reigned three years in
Jerusalem. [a]His mother's name
was [b]Mā′a·chah the granddaughter of [c]A·bish′a·lom.
3 And he walked in all the sins
of his father, which he had done
before him; [a]his heart was not
[1]loyal to the LORD his God, as was
the heart of his father David.
4 Nevertheless [a]for David's
sake the LORD his God gave him
a lamp in Jerusalem, by setting
up his son after him and by es-
tablishing Jerusalem;
5 because David [a]did *what was*
right in the eyes of the LORD, and
had not turned aside from anything that He commanded him
all the days of his life, [b]except in
the matter of Ū·rī′ah the Hit′tīte.
6 [a]And there was war between
[1]Rē·ho·bō′am and Jer·o·bō′am
all the days of his life.
7 [a]Now the rest of the acts of
A·bī′jam, and all that he did, *are*
they not written in the book of
the chronicles of the kings of
Judah? And there was war between A·bī′jam and Jer·o·bō′am.
8 [a]So A·bī′jam [1]rested with his
fathers, and they buried him in
the City of David. Then Ā′sa his
son reigned in his place.
9 In the twentieth year of
Jer·o·bō′am king of Israel, Ā′sa
became king over Judah.
10 And he reigned forty-one
years in Jerusalem. His grandmother's name *was* Mā′a·chah
the granddaughter of A·bish′-
a·lom.
11 [a]Ā′sa did *what was* right in
the eyes of the LORD, as *did* his
father David.
12 [a]And he banished the [1]per-
verted persons from the land,
and removed all the idols that
his fathers had made.
13 Also he removed [a]Mā′a·chah
his grandmother from *being*
queen mother, because she
had made an obscene image of
[1]A·shē′rah. And Ā′sa cut down
her obscene image and [b]burned
it by the Brook Kid′ron.
14 [a]But the [1]high places were
not removed. Nevertheless
Ā′sa's [b]heart was loyal to the
LORD all his days.
15 He also brought into the
house of the LORD the things
which his father [a]had dedicated,

---

26 [b]1 Kin. 10:17
27 [1]*entrusted* [2]Lit. *runners*
29 [a]2 Chr. 12:15, 16
30 [a]1 Kin. 12:21–24; 15:6
31 [a]2 Chr. 12:16 [b]1 Kin. 14:21 [c]2 Chr. 12:16 [1]Died and joined his ancestors [2]*Abijah,* 2 Chr. 12:16

CHAPTER 15

1 [a]2 Chr. 13:1
2 [a]2 Chr. 11:20–22 [b]2 Chr. 13:2 [c]2 Chr. 11:21
3 [a]Ps. 119:80 [1]Lit. *at peace with*
4 [a]2 Sam. 21:17
5 [a]1 Kin. 9:4; 14:8 [b]2 Sam. 11:3, 15–17; 12:9, 10
6 [a]1 Kin. 14:30 [1]So with MT, LXX, Tg., Vg.; some Heb. mss., Syr. *Abijam*
7 [a]2 Chr. 13:2–22
8 [a]2 Chr. 14:1 [1]Died and joined his ancestors
11 [a]2 Chr. 14:2
12 [a]1 Kin. 14:24; 22:46 [1]Heb. *qedeshim,* those practicing sodomy and prostitution in religious rituals
13 [a]2 Chr. 15:16–18 [b]Ex. 32:20 [1]A Canaanite goddess
14 [a]1 Kin. 3:2; 22:43 [b]1 Kin. 8:61; 15:3 [1]Places for pagan worship
15 [a]1 Kin. 7:51

and the things which he himself
had dedicated: silver and gold
and utensils.
16 Now there was war between
Ā′sa and Bā′a·sha king of Israel
all their days.
17 And [a]Bā′a·sha king of Israel came up against Judah, and
built [b]Rā′mah, [c]that he might let
none go out or come in to Ā′sa
king of Judah.
18 Then Ā′sa took all the silver
and gold *that was* left in the
treasuries of the house of the
LORD and the treasuries of
the king's house, and delivered
them into the hand of his servants. And King Ā′sa sent them
to [a]Ben-Hā′dad the son of Tab-
rim′mon, the son of Hē′zi·on,
king of Syria, who dwelt in
[b]Damascus, saying,
19 "*Let there be* a treaty between you and me, as there was
between my father and your father. See, I have sent you a present of silver and gold. Come and
break your treaty with Bā′a·sha
king of Israel, so that he will
withdraw from me."
20 So Ben-Hā′dad heeded King
Ā′sa, and [a]sent the captains of
his armies against the cities of
Israel. He attacked [b]Ī′jon, [c]Dan,
[d]Abel Beth Mā′a·chah, and all
Chin′ne·roth, with all the land of
Naph′ta·lī.
21 Now it happened, when Bā′-
a·sha heard *it*, that he stopped
building Rā′mah, and remained
in [a]Tir′zah.
22 [a]Then King Ā′sa made a
proclamation throughout all Judah; none *was* exempted. And
they took away the stones and
timber of Rā′mah, which Bā′-
a·sha had used for building; and
with them King Ā′sa built [b]Gē′ba
of Benjamin, and [c]Miz′pah.
23 The rest of all the acts of
Ā′sa, all his might, all that he
did, and the cities which he built,
are they not written in the book
of the chronicles of the kings of
Judah? But [a]in the time of his old
age he was diseased in his feet.
24 So Ā′sa [1]rested with his fathers, and was buried with his
fathers in the City of David
his father. [a]Then [b]Je·hosh′a·phat
his son reigned in his place.
25 Now [a]Nā′dab the son of
Jer·o·bō′am became king over
Israel in the second year of Ā′sa
king of Judah, and he reigned
over Israel two years.
26 And he did evil in the sight
of the LORD, and walked in the
way of his father, and in [a]his sin
by which he had made Israel
sin.
27 [a]Then Bā′a·sha the son of
A·hī′jah, of the house of Is′-
sa·char, conspired against him.
And Bā′a·sha killed him at
[b]Gib′be·thon, which *belonged* to
the Phi·lis′tines, while Nā′dab
and all Israel laid siege to Gib′-
be·thon.
28 Bā′a·sha killed him in the
third year of Ā′sa king of Judah,
and reigned in his place.
29 And it was so, when he became king, *that* he killed all the
house of Jer·o·bō′am. He did not
leave to Jer·o·bō′am anyone that
breathed, until he had destroyed
him, according to [a]the word of
the LORD which He had spoken
by His servant A·hī′jah the Shī′-
lo·nīte,
30 [a]because of the sins of Jer·o-
bō′am, which he had sinned and
by which he had made Israel sin,
because of his provocation with

17 [a]2 Chr. 16:1–6 [b]Josh. 18:25 [c]1 Kin. 12:26–29
18 [a]2 Chr. 16:2 [b]1 Kin. 11:23, 24
20 [a]1 Kin. 20:1 [b]2 Kin. 15:29 [c]Judg. 18:29 [d]2 Sam. 20:14, 15
21 [a]1 Kin. 14:17; 16:15–18
22 [a]2 Chr. 16:6 [b]Josh. 21:17 [c]Josh. 18:26
23 [a]2 Chr. 16:11–14
24 [a]2 Chr. 17:1 [b]Matt. 1:8 [1]Died and joined his ancestors
25 [a]1 Kin. 14:20
26 [a]1 Kin. 12:28–33; 14:16
27 [a]1 Kin. 14:14 [b]Josh. 19:44; 21:23
29 [a]1 Kin. 14:10–14
30 [a]1 Kin. 14:9, 16

which he had provoked the LORD God of Israel to anger.

31 Now the rest of the acts of Nā′dab, and all that he did, *are* they not written in the book of the chronicles of the kings of Israel?

32 [a]And there was war between Ā′sa and Bā′a·sha king of Israel all their days.

33 In the third year of Ā′sa king of Judah, Bā′a·sha the son of A·hī′jah became king over all Israel in Tir′zah, and *reigned* twenty-four years.

34 He did evil in the sight of the LORD, and walked in [a]the way of Jer·o·bō′am, and in his sin by which he had made Israel sin.

16 Then the word of the LORD came to [a]Jē′hū the son of [b]Ha·nā′nī, against [c]Bā′a·sha, saying:

2 [a]"Inasmuch as I lifted you out of the dust and made you ruler over My people Israel, and [b]you have walked in the way of Jer·o·bō′am, and have made My people Israel sin, to provoke Me to anger with their sins,

3 "surely I will [a]take[1] away the posterity of Bā′a·sha and the posterity of his house, and I will make your house like [b]the house of Jer·o·bō′am the son of Nē′bat.

4 "The dogs shall eat [a]whoever belongs to Bā′a·sha and dies in the city, and the birds of the air shall eat whoever dies in the fields."

5 Now the rest of the acts of Bā′a·sha, what he did, and his might, [a]*are* they not written in the book of the chronicles of the kings of Israel?

6 So Bā′a·sha [1]rested with his fathers and was buried in [a]Tir′zah. Then Ē′lah his son reigned in his place.

7 And also the word of the LORD came by the prophet [a]Jē′hū the son of Ha·nā′nī against Bā′a·sha and his house, because of all the evil that he did in the sight of the LORD in provoking Him to anger with the work of his hands, in being like the house of Jer·o·bō′am, and because [b]he killed them.

8 In the twenty-sixth year of Ā′sa king of Judah, Ē′lah the son of Bā′a·sha became king over Israel, *and reigned* two years in Tir′zah.

9 [a]Now his servant Zim′rī, commander of half *his* chariots, conspired against him as he was in Tir′zah drinking himself drunk in the house of Ar′za, [b]steward[1] of *his* house in Tir′zah.

10 And Zim′rī went in and struck him and killed him in the twenty-seventh year of Ā′sa king of Judah, and reigned in his place.

11 Then it came to pass, when he began to reign, as soon as he was seated on his throne, *that* he killed all the household of Bā′a·sha; he [a]did not leave him one male, neither of his relatives nor of his friends.

12 Thus Zim′rī destroyed all the household of Bā′a·sha, [a]according to the word of the LORD, which He spoke against Bā′a·sha by Jē′hū the prophet,

13 for all the sins of Bā′a·sha and the sins of Ē′lah his son, by which they had sinned and by which they had made Israel sin, in provoking the LORD God of Israel to anger [a]with their [1]idols.

14 Now the rest of the acts of Ē′lah, and all that he did, *are*

32 [a]1 Kin. 15:16

34 [a]1 Kin. 13:33; 14:16

CHAPTER 16

1 [a]2 Chr. 19:2; 20:34 [b]2 Chr. 16:7–10 [c]1 Kin. 15:27

2 [a]1 Kin. 14:7 [b]1 Kin. 12:25–33; 15:34

3 [a]1 Kin. 16:11; 21:21 [b]1 Kin. 14:10; 15:29 [1]*consume*

4 [a]1 Kin. 14:11; 21:24

5 [a]2 Chr. 16:11

6 [a]1 Kin. 14:17; 15:21 [1]Died and joined his ancestors

7 [a]1 Kin. 16:1 [b]1 Kin. 15:27, 29

9 [a]2 Kin. 9:30–33 [b]1 Kin. 18:3 [1]Lit. *who was over the house*

11 [a]1 Sam. 25:22

12 [a]1 Kin. 16:3

13 [a]Deut. 32:21 [1]Lit. *vanities*

they not written in the book of
the chronicles of the kings of
Israel?
15 In the twenty-seventh year of
Ā'sa king of Judah, Zim'rī had
reigned in Tir'zah seven days.
And the people *were* encamped
[a]against Gib'be·thon, which *be-*
longed to the Phi·lis'tines.
16 Now the people *who were*
encamped heard it said, "Zim'rī
has conspired and also has
killed the king." So all Israel
made Om'rī, the commander of
the army, king over Israel that
day in the camp.
17 Then Om'rī and all Israel
with him went up from Gib'-
be·thon, and they besieged Tir'-
zah.
18 And it happened, when Zim'rī
saw that the city was [1]taken, that
he went into the citadel of the
king's house and burned the
king's house [2]down upon himself with fire, and died,
19 because of the sins which he
had committed in doing evil in
the sight of the LORD, [a]in walking in the [b]way of Jer·o·bō'am,
and in his sin which he had
committed to make Israel sin.
20 Now the rest of the acts of
Zim'rī, and the treason he committed, *are* they not written in
the book of the chronicles of the
kings of Israel?
21 Then the people of Israel
were divided into two parts: half
of the people followed Tib'nī
the son of Gī'nath, to make him
king, and half followed Om'rī.
22 But the people who followed
Om'rī prevailed over the people
who followed Tib'nī the son of
Gī'nath. So Tib'nī died and Om'rī
reigned.
23 In the thirty-first year of
Ā'sa king of Judah, Om'rī became king over Israel, *and*
reigned twelve years. Six years
he reigned in [a]Tir'zah.
24 And he bought the hill of
Samaria from Shē'mer for
two talents of silver; then he
built on the hill, and called the
name of the city which he built,
[a]Samaria,[1] after the name of
Shē'mer, owner of the hill.
25 [a]Om'rī did evil in the eyes of
the LORD, and did worse than all
who *were* before him.
26 For he [a]walked in all the
ways of Jer·o·bō'am the son of
Nē'bat, and in his sin by which
he had made Israel sin, provoking the LORD God of Israel to
anger with their [b]idols.[1]
27 Now the rest of the acts of
Om'rī which he did, and the
might that he showed, *are*
they not written in the book of
the chronicles of the kings of
Israel?
28 So Om'rī rested with his fathers and was buried in Samaria.
Then Ā'hab his son reigned in
his place.
29 In the thirty-eighth year of
Ā'sa king of Judah, Ā'hab the
son of Om'rī became king over
Israel; and Ā'hab the son of
Om'rī reigned over Israel in Samaria twenty-two years.
30 Now Ā'hab the son of Om'rī
did evil in the sight of the LORD,
more than all who *were* before
him.
31 And it came to pass, as
though it had been a trivial
thing for him to walk in the sins
of Jer·o·bō'am the son of Nē'bat,
[a]that he took as wife Jez'e·bel
the daughter of Eth·bā'al, king
of the [b]Sī·dō'ni·ans; [c]and he went

15 [a]1 Kin. 15:27
18 [1]*captured* [2]Lit. *over him*
19 [a]1 Kin. 15:26, 34 [b]1 Kin. 12:25–33
23 [a]1 Kin. 15:21
24 [a]1 Kin. 13:32 [1]Heb. *Shomeron*
25 [a]Mic. 6:16
26 [a]1 Kin. 16:19 [b]1 Kin. 16:13 [1]Lit. *vanities*
31 [a]Deut. 7:3 [b]Judg. 18:7 [c]1 Kin. 21:25, 26

and served Bā′al and worshiped
him.
32 Then he set up an altar for
Bā′al in [a]the temple of Bā′al,
which he had built in Samaria.
33 [a]And Ā′hab made a [1]wooden
image. Ā′hab [b]did more to provoke the LORD God of Israel to
anger than all the kings of Israel
who were before him.
34 In his days Hī′el of Beth′el
built Jericho. He laid its foundation [1]with A·bī′ram his firstborn,
and with his youngest *son* Sē′gub
he set up its gates, [a]according to
the word of the LORD, which He
had spoken through Joshua the
son of Nun.

17 And E·lī′jah the Tish′bīte,
of the [a]inhabitants of Gil′-
ē·ad, said to Ā′hab, [b]"*As* the
LORD God of Israel lives, [c]before
whom I stand, [d]there shall not
be dew nor rain [e]these years,
except at my word."
2 Then the word of the LORD
came to him, saying,
3 "Get away from here and
turn eastward, and hide by the
Brook Chē′rith, which flows into
the Jordan.
4 "And it will be *that* you shall
drink from the brook, and I have
commanded the [a]ravens to feed
you there."
5 So he went and did according to the word of the LORD, for
he went and stayed by the Brook
Chē′rith, which flows into the
Jordan.
6 The ravens brought him
bread and meat in the morning, and bread and meat in the
evening; and he drank from the
brook.
7 And it happened after a
while that the brook dried up,
because there had been no rain
in the land.
8 Then the word of the LORD
came to him, saying,
9 "Arise, go to [a]Zar′e·phath,
which *belongs* to [b]Sī′don, and
dwell there. See, I have commanded a widow there to provide for you."
10 So he arose and went to
Zar′e·phath. And when he came
to the gate of the city, indeed
a widow *was* there gathering
sticks. And he called to her and
said, "Please bring me a little water in a cup, that I may drink."
11 And as she was going to
get *it*, he called to her and said,
"Please bring me a morsel of
bread in your hand."
12 So she said, "As the LORD
your God lives, I do not have
bread, only a handful of flour
in a bin, and a little oil in a
[1]jar; and see, I *am* gathering a
couple of sticks that I may go
in and prepare it for myself and
my son, that we may eat it, and
[a]die."
13 And E·lī′jah said to her, "Do
not fear; go *and* do as you have
said, but make me a small cake
from it first, and bring *it* to me;
and afterward make *some* for
yourself and your son.
14 "For thus says the LORD God
of Israel: 'The bin of flour shall
not be used up, nor shall the jar
of oil run dry, until the day the
LORD sends rain on the earth.' "
15 So she went away and did
according to the word of E·lī′jah;
and she and he and her household ate for *many* days.
16 The bin of flour was not used
up, nor did the jar of oil run dry,
according to the word of the

32 [a]2 Kin. 10:21, 26, 27
33 [a]2 Kin. 13:6 [b]1 Kin. 14:9; 16:29, 30; 21:25 [1]Heb. *Asherah*, a Canaanite goddess
34 [a]Josh. 6:26 [1]At the cost of the life of

CHAPTER 17

1 [a]Judg. 12:4 [b]2 Kin. 3:14; 5:20 [c]Deut. 10:8 [d]James 5:17 [e]Luke 4:25
4 [a]Job 38:41
9 [a]Obad. 20 [b]2 Sam. 24:6
12 [a]Deut. 28:23, 24 [1]Lit. *pitcher* or *water jar*

LORD which He spoke by E·lī′-
jah.
17 Now it happened after
these things *that* the son of the
woman who owned the house
became sick. And his sickness
was so [1]serious that [2]there was
no breath left in him.
18 So she said to E·lī′jah, [a]"What
have I to do with you, O man of
God? Have you come to me to
bring my sin to remembrance,
and to kill my son?"
19 And he said to her, "Give me
your son." So he took him out
of her arms and carried him to
the upper room where he was
staying, and laid him on his own
bed.
20 Then he cried out to the LORD
and said, "O LORD my God, have
You also brought tragedy on the
widow with whom I lodge, by
killing her son?"
21 [a]And he stretched himself
out on the child three times, and
cried out to the LORD and said,
"O LORD my God, I pray, let this
child's soul come back to him."
22 Then the LORD heard the
voice of E·lī′jah; and the soul of
the child came back to him, and
he [a]revived.
23 And E·lī′jah took the child
and brought him down from
the upper room into the house,
and gave him to his mother.
And E·lī′jah said, "See, your son
lives!"
24 Then the woman said to E·lī′-
jah, "Now by this [a]I know that
you *are* a man of God, *and* that
the word of the LORD in your
mouth *is* the truth."

18 And it came to pass *after*
[a]many days that the word
of the LORD came to E·lī′jah,
in the third year, saying, "Go,
present yourself to Ā′hab, and [b]I
will send rain on the earth."
2 So E·lī′jah went to present
himself to Ā′hab; and *there was*
a severe famine in Samaria.
3 And Ā′hab had called
Ō·ba·dī′ah, who *was* [1]in charge
of *his* house. (Now Ō·ba·dī′ah
feared the LORD greatly.
4 For so it was, while Jez′e·bel
[1]massacred the prophets of the
LORD, that Ō·ba·dī′ah had taken
one hundred prophets and hidden them, fifty to a cave, and
had fed them with bread and
water.)
5 And Ā′hab had said to
Ō·ba·dī′ah, "Go into the land to
all the springs of water and to all
the brooks; perhaps we may
find grass to keep the horses
and mules alive, so that we will
not have to kill any livestock."
6 So they divided the land between them to explore it; Ā′hab
went one way by himself, and
Ō·ba·dī′ah went another way by
himself.
7 Now as Ō·ba·dī′ah was on
his way, suddenly E·lī′jah met
him; and he [a]recognized him,
and fell on his face, and said, "*Is*
that you, my lord E·lī′jah?"
8 And he answered him, "*It is*
I. Go, tell your master, 'E·lī′jah *is*
here.' "
9 So he said, "How have I
sinned, that you are delivering
your servant into the hand of
Ā′hab, to kill me?
10 "*As* the LORD your God lives,
there is no nation or kingdom
where my master has not sent
someone to hunt for you; and
when they said, '*He is* not *here,*'
he took an oath from the kingdom or nation that they could
not find you.

17 [1]*severe* [2]He died.
18 [a]Luke 5:8
21 [a]2 Kin. 4:34, 35
22 [a]Heb. 11:35
24 [a]John 2:11; 3:2; 16:30

CHAPTER 18

1 [a]Luke 4:25 [b]Deut. 28:12
3 [1]Lit. *over the house*
4 [1]Lit. *cut off*
7 [a]2 Kin. 1:6–8

11 "And now you say, 'Go, tell your master, "E·lī'jah *is here*" '!

12 "And it shall come to pass, *as soon as* I am gone from you, that [a]the Spirit of the LORD will carry you to a place I do not know; so when I go and tell Ā'hab, and he cannot find you, he will kill me. But I your servant have feared the LORD from my youth.

13 "Was it not reported to my lord what I did when Jez'e·bel killed the prophets of the LORD, how I hid one hundred men of the LORD's prophets, fifty to a cave, and fed them with bread and water?

14 "And now you say, 'Go, tell your master, "E·lī'jah *is here.*" ' He will kill me!"

15 Then E·lī'jah said, "*As* the LORD of hosts lives, before whom I stand, I will surely present myself to him today."

16 So Ō·ba·dī'ah went to meet Ā'hab, and told him; and Ā'hab went to meet E·lī'jah.

17 Then it happened, when Ā'hab saw E·lī'jah, that Ā'hab said to him, [a]"*Is that* you, O [b]troubler of Israel?"

18 And he answered, "I have not troubled Israel, but you and your father's house *have,* [a]in that you have forsaken the commandments of the LORD and have followed the Bā'als.

19 "Now therefore, send *and* gather all Israel to me on [a]Mount Car'mel, the four hundred and fifty prophets of Bā'al, [b]and the four hundred prophets of [1]A·shē'rah, who [2]eat at Jez'e·bel's table."

20 So Ā'hab sent for all the children of Israel, and [a]gathered the prophets together on Mount Car'mel.

21 And E·lī'jah came to all the people, and said, [a]"How long will you falter between two opinions? If the LORD *is* God, follow Him; but if Bā'al, [b]follow him." But the people answered him not a word.

22 Then E·lī'jah said to the people, [a]"I alone am left a prophet of the LORD; [b]but Bā'al's prophets *are* four hundred and fifty men.

23 "Therefore let them give us two bulls; and let them choose one bull for themselves, cut it in pieces, and lay *it* on the wood, but put no fire *under it;* and I will prepare the other bull, and lay *it* on the wood, but put no fire *under it.*

24 "Then you call on the name of your gods, and I will call on the name of the LORD; and the God who [a]answers by fire, He is God." So all the people answered and said, [1]"It is well spoken."

25 Now E·lī'jah said to the prophets of Bā'al, "Choose one bull for yourselves and prepare *it* first, for you *are* many; and call on the name of your god, but put no fire *under it.*"

26 So they took the bull which was given them, and they prepared *it,* and called on the name of Bā'al from morning even till noon, saying, "O Bā'al, [1]hear us!" But *there was* [a]no voice; no one answered. Then they [2]leaped about the altar which they had made.

27 And so it was, at noon, that E·lī'jah mocked them and said, "Cry [1]aloud, for he *is* a god; either he is meditating, or he is busy, or he is on a journey, *or* perhaps he is sleeping and must be awakened."

28 So they cried aloud, and [a]cut

12 [a]Acts 8:39
17 [a]1 Kin. 21:20 [b]Josh. 7:25
18 [a][2 Chr. 15:2]
19 [a]Josh. 19:26 [b]1 Kin. 16:33 [1]A Canaanite goddess [2]Are provided for by Jezebel
20 [a]1 Kin. 22:6
21 [a][Matt. 6:24] [b]Josh. 24:15
22 [a]1 Kin. 19:10, 14 [b]1 Kin. 18:19
24 [a]1 Chr. 21:26 [1]Lit. *The word is good*
26 [a]Jer. 10:5 [1]*answer* [2]Lit. *limped about, leaped in dancing around*
27 [1]*with a loud voice*
28 [a][Deut. 14:1]

themselves, as was their custom,
with [1]knives and lances, until
the blood gushed out on them.
29 And when midday was past,
[a]they prophesied until the *time*
of the offering of the *evening*
sacrifice. But *there was* [b]no
voice; no one answered, no one
paid attention.
30 Then E·lī′jah said to all the
people, "Come near to me." So
all the people came near to him.
[a]And he repaired the altar of the
LORD *that was* broken down.
31 And E·lī′jah took twelve
stones, according to the number
of the tribes of the sons of Jacob,
to whom the word of the LORD
had come, saying, [a]"Israel shall
be your name."
32 Then with the stones he built
an altar [a]in the name of the
LORD; and he made a trench
around the altar large enough to
hold two seahs of seed.
33 And he [a]put the wood in order,
cut the bull in pieces, and
laid *it* on the wood, and said,
"Fill four waterpots with water,
and [b]pour *it* on the burnt sacrifice
and on the wood."
34 Then he said, "Do *it* a second
time," and they did *it* a
second time; and he said, "Do *it*
a third time," and they did *it* a
third time.
35 So the water ran all around
the altar; and he also filled [a]the
trench with water.
36 And it came to pass, at *the
time of* the offering of the *evening*
sacrifice, that E·lī′jah the
prophet came near and said,
"LORD [a]God of Abraham, Isaac,
and Israel, [b]let it be known this
day that You *are* God in Israel
and I *am* Your servant, and *that*

28 [1]*swords*
29 [a]Ex. 29:39, 41 [b]1 Kin. 18:26
30 [a]2 Chr. 33:16
31 [a]Gen. 32:28; 35:10
32 [a][Col. 3:17]
33 [a]Lev. 1:6–8 [b]Judg. 6:20
35 [a]1 Kin. 18:32, 38
36 [a]Ex. 3:6; 4:5 [b]1 Kin. 8:43 [c]Num. 16:28
38 [a]1 Chr. 21:26
39 [a]1 Kin. 18:21, 24
40 [a]2 Kin. 10:25 [b]Judg. 4:7; 5:21 [c][Deut. 13:5; 18:20]
42 [a]James 5:17, 18
44 [1]Lit. *Bind* or *Harness*

[c]I have done all these things at
Your word.
37 "Hear me, O LORD, hear me,
that this people may know that
You *are* the LORD God, and *that*
You have turned their hearts
back *to You* again."
38 Then [a]the fire of the LORD
fell and consumed the burnt sacrifice,
and the wood and the
stones and the dust, and it licked
up the water that *was* in the
trench.
39 Now when all the people
saw *it*, they fell on their faces;
and they said, [a]"The LORD, He *is*
God! The LORD, He *is* God!"
40 And E·lī′jah said to them,
[a]"Seize the prophets of Bā′al!
Do not let one of them escape!"
So they seized them; and E·lī′jah
brought them down to the
Brook [b]Kī′shon and [c]executed
them there.
41 Then E·lī′jah said to Ā′hab,
"Go up, eat and drink; for *there
is* the sound of abundance of
rain."
42 So Ā′hab went up to eat
and drink. And E·lī′jah went up
to the top of Car′mel; [a]then he
bowed down on the ground, and
put his face between his knees,
43 and said to his servant, "Go
up now, look toward the sea." So
he went up and looked, and said,
"*There is* nothing." And seven
times he said, "Go again."
44 Then it came to pass the seventh
time, that he said, "There
is a cloud, as small as a man's
hand, rising out of the sea!" So
he said, "Go up, say to Ā′hab,
[1]'Prepare *your chariot*, and
go down before the rain stops
you.' "
45 Now it happened in the
meantime that the sky became

black with clouds and wind, and
there was a heavy rain. So Ā′hab
rode away and went to Jez′rē·el.
46 Then the [a]hand of the LORD
came upon E·lī′jah; and he
[b]girded[1] up his loins and ran
ahead of Ā′hab to the entrance
of Jez′rē·el.

19 And Ā′hab told Jez′e·bel
all that E·lī′jah had done,
also how he had [a]executed all
the prophets with the sword.
2 Then Jez′e·bel sent a messenger to E·lī′jah, saying, [a]"So
let the gods do *to me,* and more
also, if I do not make your life as
the life of one of them by tomorrow about this time."
3 And when he saw *that,* he
arose and ran for his life, and
went to Bē·er·shē′ba, which *belongs* to Judah, and left his servant there.
4 But he himself went a day's
journey into the wilderness,
and came and sat down under
a [1]broom tree. And he [a]prayed
that he might die, and said, "It
is enough! Now, LORD, take my
life, for I *am* no better than my
fathers!"
5 Then as he lay and slept under a broom tree, suddenly an
[1]angel touched him, and said to
him, "Arise *and* eat."
6 Then he looked, and there
by his head *was* a cake baked
on [1]coals, and a jar of water. So
he ate and drank, and lay down
again.
7 And the [1]angel of the LORD
came back the second time, and
touched him, and said, "Arise
and eat, because the journey *is*
too great for you."
8 So he arose, and ate and
drank; and he went in the
strength of that food forty days
and [a]forty nights as far as [b]Hō′-
reb, the mountain of God.
9 And there he went into a
cave, and spent the night in that
place; and behold, the word of
the LORD *came* to him, and He
said to him, "What are you doing here, E·lī′jah?"
10 So he said, [a]"I have been
very [b]zealous for the LORD God
of hosts; for the children of Israel have forsaken Your covenant, torn down Your altars, and
[c]killed Your prophets with the
sword. [d]I alone am left; and they
seek to take my life."
11 Then He said, "Go out, and
stand [a]on the mountain before
the LORD." And behold, the LORD
[b]passed by, and [c]a great and
strong wind tore into the mountains and broke the rocks in
pieces before the LORD, *but* the
LORD *was* not in the wind; and
after the wind an earthquake,
but the LORD *was* not in the
earthquake;
12 and after the earthquake a
fire, *but* the LORD *was* not in
the fire; and after the fire [1]a still
small voice.
13 So it was, when E·lī′jah
heard *it,* that [a]he wrapped his
face in his mantle and went out
and stood in the entrance of the
cave. [b]Suddenly a voice *came* to
him, and said, "What are you doing here, E·lī′jah?"
14 [a]And he said, "I have been
very zealous for the LORD God
of hosts; because the children of
Israel have forsaken Your covenant, torn down Your altars,
and killed Your prophets with
the sword. I alone am left; and
they seek to take my life."
15 Then the LORD said to him:
"Go, return on your way to the

46 [a]2 Kin. 3:15 [b]2 Kin. 4:29; 9:1 [1]Tucked the skirts of his robe in his belt in preparation for quick travel

CHAPTER 19

1 [a]1 Kin. 18:40
2 [a]Ruth 1:17
4 [a]Num. 11:15 [1]*juniper*
5 [1]Or *Angel*
6 [1]*hot stones*
7 [1]Or *Angel*
8 [a]Matt. 4:2 [b]Ex. 3:1; 4:27
10 [a]Rom. 11:3 [b]Ps. 69:9 [c]1 Kin. 18:4 [d]1 Kin. 18:22
11 [a]Ex. 19:20; 24:12, 18 [b]Ex. 33:21, 22 [c]Ezek. 1:4; 37:7
12 [1]*a delicate whispering voice*
13 [a]Ex. 3:6 [b]1 Kin. 19:9
14 [a]1 Kin. 19:10

Wilderness of Damascus; [a]and
when you arrive, anoint Haz′a·el
as king over Syria.
16 "Also you shall anoint [a]Jē′hū
the son of Nim′shī *as* king over
Israel. And [b]E·lī′sha the son of
Shā′phat of Abel Me·hō′lah you
shall anoint *as* prophet in your
place.
17 [a]"It shall be *that* whoever
escapes the sword of Haz′a·el,
Jē′hū will [b]kill; and whoever escapes the sword of Jē′hū, [c]E·lī′-
sha will kill.
18 [a]"Yet I have reserved seven
thousand in Israel, all whose
knees have not bowed to Bā′al,
[b]and every mouth that has not
kissed him."
19 So he departed from there,
and found E·lī′sha the son of
Shā′phat, who *was* plowing *with*
twelve yoke *of oxen* before him,
and he was with the twelfth.
Then E·lī′jah passed by him and
threw his [a]mantle on him.
20 And he left the oxen and ran
after E·lī′jah, and said, [a]"Please
let me kiss my father and my
mother, and *then* I will follow
you." And he said to him, "Go
back again, for what have I done
to you?"
21 So *E·lī′sha* turned back
from him, and took a yoke of
oxen and slaughtered them and
[a]boiled their flesh, using the ox-
en's equipment, and gave it to
the people, and they ate. Then
he arose and followed E·lī′jah,
and became his servant.

20

Now [a]Ben-Hā′dad the
king of Syria gathered
all his forces together; thirty-
two kings *were* with him, with
horses and chariots. And he
went up and besieged [b]Samaria,
and made war against it.
2 Then he sent messengers
into the city to Ā′hab king of Israel, and said to him, "Thus says
Ben-Hā′dad:
3 'Your silver and your gold
are mine; your loveliest wives
and children are mine.' "
4 And the king of Israel answered and said, "My lord,
O king, just as you say, I and all
that I have *are* yours."
5 Then the messengers came
back and said, "Thus speaks
Ben-Hā′dad, saying, 'Indeed I
have sent to you, saying, "You
shall deliver to me your silver
and your gold, your wives and
your children";
6 'but I will send my servants
to you tomorrow about this time,
and they shall search your house
and the houses of your servants.
And it shall be, *that* whatever
is [1]pleasant in your eyes, they
will put *it* in their hands and
take *it*.' "
7 So the king of Israel called
all the elders of the land, and
said, "Notice, please, and see
how this *man* seeks trouble, for
he sent to me for my wives, my
children, my silver, and my gold;
and I did not deny him."
8 And all the elders and all
the people said to him, "Do not
listen or consent."
9 Therefore he said to the messengers of Ben-Hā′dad, "Tell my
lord the king, 'All that you sent
for to your servant the first time
I will do, but this thing I cannot
do.' " And the messengers departed and brought back word
to him.
10 Then Ben-Hā′dad sent to him
and said, [a]"The gods do so to me,
and more also, if enough dust
is left of Samaria for a handful

15 [a]2 Kin. 8:8–15
16 [a]2 Kin. 9:1–10 [b]2 Kin. 2:9–15
17 [a]2 Kin. 8:12; 13:3, 22 [b]2 Kin. 9:14—10:28 [c][Hos. 6:5]
18 [a]Rom. 11:4 [b]Hos. 13:2
19 [a]2 Kin. 2:8, 13, 14
20 [a][Matt. 8:21, 22]
21 [a]2 Sam. 24:22

CHAPTER 20

1 [a]2 Kin. 6:24 [b]1 Kin. 16:24
6 [1]*pleasing*
10 [a]1 Kin. 19:2

for each of the people [1]who follow me."
11 So the king of Israel answered and said, "Tell *him*, 'Let
not the one who puts on *his*
armor [a]boast like the one who
takes *it off.*' "
12 And it happened when *Ben-*
Hā´dad heard this message, as
he and the kings *were* [a]drinking
at the [1]command post, that he
said to his servants, "Get ready."
And they got ready to attack the
city.
13 Suddenly a prophet approached Ā´hab king of Israel,
saying, "Thus says the LORD:
'Have you seen all this great
multitude? Behold, [a]I will deliver
it into your hand today, and
you shall know that I *am* the
LORD.' "
14 So Ā´hab said, "By whom?"
And he said, "Thus says the
LORD: 'By the young leaders of
the provinces.' " Then he said,
"Who will set the battle in order?" And he answered, "You."
15 Then he mustered the young
leaders of the provinces, and
there were two hundred and
thirty-two; and after them he
mustered all the people, all
the children of Israel—seven
thousand.
16 So they went out at noon.
Meanwhile Ben-Hā´dad and the
thirty-two kings helping him
were [a]getting drunk at the command post.
17 The young leaders of the
provinces went out first. And
Ben-Hā´dad sent out *a patrol*,
and they told him, saying, "Men
are coming out of Samaria!"
18 So he said, "If they have
come out for peace, take them
alive; and if they have come out
for war, take them alive."
19 Then these young leaders of
the provinces went out of the
city with the army which followed them.
20 And each one killed his man;
so the Syrians fled, and Israel
pursued them; and Ben-Hā´dad
the king of Syria escaped on a
horse with the cavalry.
21 Then the king of Israel went
out and attacked the horses and
chariots, and killed the Syrians
with a great slaughter.
22 And the prophet came to the
king of Israel and said to him,
"Go, strengthen yourself; take
note, and see what you should
do, [a]for [1]in the spring of the year
the king of Syria will come up
against you."
23 Then the servants of the king
of Syria said to him, "Their gods
are gods of the hills. Therefore
they were stronger than we; but
if we fight against them in the
plain, surely we will be stronger
than they.
24 "So do this thing: Dismiss
the kings, each from his position, and put captains in their
[1]places;
25 "and you shall muster an
army like the army [1]that you
have lost, horse for horse and
chariot for chariot. Then we will
fight against them in the plain;
surely we will be stronger than
they." And he listened to their
voice and did so.
26 So it was, in the spring of
the year, that Ben-Hā´dad mustered the Syrians and went up to
[a]Ā´phek to fight against Israel.
27 And the children of Israel
were mustered and given provisions, and they went against

10 [1]Lit. *at my feet*
11 [a]Prov. 27:1
12 [a]1 Kin. 20:16 [1]Lit. *booths or shelters*
13 [a]1 Kin. 20:28
16 [a]1 Kin. 16:9; 20:12
22 [a]2 Sam. 11:1 [1]Lit. *at the return*
24 [1]*positions*
25 [1]Lit. *that fell from you*
26 [a]Josh. 13:4

them. Now the children of Israel
encamped before them like two
little flocks of goats, while the
Syrians filled the [a]countryside.
28 Then a [a]man of God came
and spoke to the king of Israel,
and said, "Thus says the LORD:
'Because the Syrians have said,
"The LORD *is* God of the hills, but
He *is* not God of the valleys,"
therefore [b]I will deliver all this
great multitude into your hand,
and you shall know that I *am* the
LORD.' "
29 And they encamped opposite each other for seven days.
So it was that on the seventh
day the battle was joined; and
the children of Israel killed one
hundred thousand foot soldiers
of the Syrians in one day.
30 But the rest fled to Ā'phek,
into the city; then a wall fell on
twenty-seven thousand of the
men *who were* left. And Ben-
Hā'dad fled and went into the
city, into an inner chamber.
31 Then his servants said to
him, "Look now, we have heard
that the kings of the house of
Israel *are* merciful kings. Please,
let us [a]put sackcloth around our
waists and ropes around our
heads, and go out to the king
of Israel; perhaps he will spare
your life."
32 So they wore sackcloth
around their waists and *put*
ropes around their heads, and
came to the king of Israel and
said, "Your servant Ben-Hā'dad
says, 'Please let me live.' " And
he said, "*Is* he still alive? He *is*
my brother."
33 Now the men were watching
closely to see whether *any sign*
of mercy would come from him;
and they quickly grasped *at this*
word and said, "Your brother
Ben-Hā'dad." So he said, "Go,
bring him." Then Ben-Hā'dad
came out to him; and he had him
come up into the chariot.
34 So *Ben-Hā'dad* said to him,
[a]"The cities which my father
took from your father I will
restore; and you may set up
marketplaces for yourself in Damascus, as my father did in Samaria." Then *Ā'hab said,* "I will
send you away with this treaty."
So he made a treaty with him
and sent him away.
35 Now a certain man of [a]the
sons of the prophets said to his
neighbor [b]by the word of the
LORD, "Strike me, please." And
the man refused to strike him.
36 Then he said to him, "Because you have not obeyed the
voice of the LORD, surely, as
soon as you depart from me, a
lion shall kill you." And as soon
as he left him, [a]a lion found him
and killed him.
37 And he found another man,
and said, "Strike me, please." So
the man struck him, inflicting a
wound.
38 Then the prophet departed
and waited for the king by the
road, and disguised himself with
a bandage over his eyes.
39 Now [a]as the king passed by,
he cried out to the king and said,
"Your servant went out into the
midst of the battle; and there,
a man came over and brought
a man to me, and said, 'Guard
this man; if by any means he is
missing, [b]your life shall be for
his life, or else you shall [1]pay a
talent of silver.'
40 "While your servant was
busy here and there, he was
gone." Then the king of Israel

27 [a]Judg. 6:3–5
28 [a]1 Kin. 17:18 [b]1 Kin. 20:13
31 [a]Gen. 37:34
34 [a]1 Kin. 15:20
35 [a]2 Kin. 2:3, 5, 7, 15 [b]1 Kin. 13:17, 18
36 [a]1 Kin. 13:24
39 [a]2 Sam. 12:1 [b]2 Kin. 10:24 [1]Lit. *weigh*

said to him, "So *shall* your judgment *be;* you yourself have decided *it*."
41 And he hastened to take the
bandage away from his eyes;
and the king of Israel recognized
him as one of the prophets.
42 Then he said to him, "Thus
says the LORD: [a]'Because you
have let slip out of *your* hand a
man whom I appointed to utter
destruction, therefore your life
shall go for his life, and your
people for his people.' "
43 So the king of Israel [a]went to
his house sullen and displeased,
and came to Samaria.

21 And it came to pass after
these things *that* Nā'both
the Jez'rē·el·īte had a vineyard
which *was* in [a]Jez'rē·el, next
to the palace of Ā'hab king of
Samaria.
2 So Ā'hab spoke to Nā'both,
saying, "Give me your [a]vineyard,
that I may have it for a vegetable
garden, because it *is* near, next
to my house; and for it I will give
you a vineyard better than it. *Or,*
if it seems good to you, I will
give you its worth in money."
3 But Nā'both said to Ā'hab,
"The LORD forbid [a]that I should
give the inheritance of my fathers to you!"
4 So Ā'hab went into his house
sullen and displeased because
of the word which Nā'both the
Jez'rē·el·īte had spoken to him;
for he had said, "I will not give
you the inheritance of my fathers." And he lay down on his
bed, and turned away his face,
and would eat no food.
5 But [a]Jez'e·bel his wife came
to him, and said to him, "Why is
your spirit so sullen that you eat
no food?"
6 He said to her, "Because I
spoke to Nā'both the Jez'rē·el·īte,
and said to him, 'Give me your
vineyard for money; or else, if
it pleases you, I will give you
another vineyard for it.' And he
answered, 'I will not give you
my vineyard.' "
7 Then Jez'e·bel his wife said to
him, "You now exercise authority over Israel! Arise, eat food,
and let your heart be cheerful;
I will give you the vineyard of
Nā'both the Jez'rē·el·īte."
8 And she wrote letters in
Ā'hab's name, sealed *them* with
his seal, and sent the letters to
the elders and the nobles who
were dwelling in the city with
Nā'both.
9 She wrote in the letters,
saying,

Proclaim a fast, and seat
Nā'both [1]with high honor
among the people;
10 and seat two men,
scoundrels, before him
to bear witness against
him, saying, "You have
[a]blasphemed God and the
king." *Then* take him out,
and [b]stone him, that he may
die.

11 So the men of his city, the
elders and nobles who were inhabitants of his city, did as Jez'-
e·bel had sent to them, as it *was*
written in the letters which she
had sent to them.
12 [a]They proclaimed a fast, and
seated Nā'both with high honor
among the people.
13 And two men, scoundrels,
came in and sat before him;
and the scoundrels [a]witnessed
against him, against Nā'both, in

42 [a]1 Kin. 22:31–37
43 [a]1 Kin. 21:4

CHAPTER 21

1 [a]1 Kin. 18:45, 46
2 [a]1 Sam. 8:14
3 [a][Num. 36:7]
5 [a]1 Kin. 19:1, 2
9 [1]Lit. *at the head*
10 [a][Ex. 22:28] [b][Lev. 24:14]
12 [a]Is. 58:4
13 [a][Ex. 20:16; 23:1, 7]

the presence of the people, saying, "Nā′both has blasphemed
God and the king!" [b]Then they
took him outside the city and
stoned him with stones, so that
he died.
14 Then they sent to Jez′e·bel,
saying, "Nā′both has been stoned
and is dead."
15 And it came to pass, when
Jez′e·bel heard that Nā′both had
been stoned and was dead, that
Jez′e·bel said to Ā′hab, "Arise,
take possession of the vineyard of Nā′both the Jez′rē·el·īte,
which he refused to give you for
money; for Nā′both is not alive,
but dead."
16 So it was, when Ā′hab heard
that Nā′both was dead, that
Ā′hab got up and went down to
take possession of the vineyard
of Nā′both the Jez′rē·el·īte.
17 [a]Then the word of the LORD
came to [b]E·lī′jah the Tish′bīte,
saying,
18 "Arise, go down to meet
Ā′hab king of Israel, [a]who *lives*
in Samaria. There *he is,* in the
vineyard of Nā′both, where he
has gone down to take possession of it.
19 "You shall speak to him, saying, 'Thus says the LORD: "Have
you murdered and also taken
possession?" ' And you shall
speak to him, saying, 'Thus says
the LORD: [a]"In the place where
dogs licked the blood of Nā′-
both, dogs shall lick your blood,
even yours." ' "
20 So Ā′hab said to E·lī′jah,
[a]"Have you found me, O my enemy?" And he answered, "I have
found *you,* because [b]you have
sold yourself to do evil in the
sight of the LORD:
21 'Behold, [a]I will bring calamity

13 [b]2 Kin. 9:26
17 [a][Ps. 9:12] [b]1 Kin. 19:1
18 [a]2 Chr. 22:9
19 [a]1 Kin. 22:38
20 [a]1 Kin. 18:17 [b][Rom. 7:14]
21 [a]1 Kin. 14:10 [b]2 Kin. 10:10 [c]1 Sam. 25:22 [d]1 Kin. 14:10
22 [a]1 Kin. 15:29 [b]1 Kin. 16:3, 11
23 [a]2 Kin. 9:10, 30–37 [1]So with MT, LXX; some Heb. mss., Syr., Tg., Vg. *plot of ground* instead of *wall* (cf. 2 Kin. 9:36)
24 [a]1 Kin. 14:11; 16:4
25 [a]1 Kin. 16:30–33; 21:20 [b]1 Kin. 16:31 [1]*incited him*
26 [a]2 Kin. 21:11
27 [a]Gen. 37:34
29 [a][2 Kin. 22:19] [b]2 Kin. 9:25; 10:11, 17

on you. I will take away your
[b]posterity, and will cut off from
Ā′hab [c]every male in Israel, both
[d]bond and free.
22 'I will make your house like
the house of [a]Jer·o·bō′am the
son of Nē′bat, and like the house
of [b]Bā′a·sha the son of A·hī′jah,
because of the provocation with
which you have provoked *Me* to
anger, and made Israel sin.'
23 "And [a]concerning Jez′e·bel
the LORD also spoke, saying,
'The dogs shall eat Jez′e·bel by
the [1]wall of Jez′rē·el.'
24 "The dogs shall eat [a]whoever
belongs to Ā′hab and dies in the
city, and the birds of the air shall
eat whoever dies in the field."
25 But [a]there was no one like
Ā′hab who sold himself to do
wickedness in the sight of the
LORD, [b]because Jez′e·bel his wife
[1]stirred him up.
26 And he behaved very abomi-
nably in following idols, according to all [a]*that* the Am′o·rītes had
done, whom the LORD had cast
out before the children of Israel.
27 So it was, when Ā′hab heard
those words, that he tore his
clothes and [a]put sackcloth on
his body, and fasted and lay
in sackcloth, and went about
mourning.
28 And the word of the LORD
came to E·lī′jah the Tish′bīte,
saying,
29 "See how Ā′hab has humbled
himself before Me? Because he
[a]has humbled himself before
Me, I will not bring the calamity
in his days. [b]In the days of his
son I will bring the calamity on
his house."

22
Now three years passed
without war between
Syria and Israel.

2 Then it came to pass, in the third year, that [a]Je·hosh′a·phat the king of Judah went down to *visit* the king of Israel.

3 And the king of Israel said to his servants, "Do you know that [a]Rā′moth in Gil′ē·ad *is* ours, but we hesitate to take it out of the hand of the king of Syria?"

4 So he said to Je·hosh′a·phat, "Will you go with me to fight at Rā′moth Gil′ē·ad?" Je·hosh′a·phat said to the king of Israel, [a]"I *am* as you *are,* my people as your people, my horses as your horses."

5 Also Je·hosh′a·phat said to the king of Israel, [a]"Please inquire for the word of the LORD today."

6 Then the king of Israel [a]gathered [1]the prophets together, about four hundred men, and said to them, "Shall I go against Rā′moth Gil′ē·ad to fight, or shall I refrain?" So they said, "Go up, for the Lord will deliver *it* into the hand of the king."

7 And [a]Je·hosh′a·phat said, "*Is there* not still a prophet of the LORD here, that we may inquire of [1]Him?"

8 So the king of Israel said to Je·hosh′a·phat, "*There is* still one man, Mī·cāi′ah the son of Im′lah, by whom we may inquire of the LORD; but I hate him, because he does not prophesy good concerning me, but evil." And Je·hosh′a·phat said, "Let not the king say such things!"

9 Then the king of Israel called an officer and said, "Bring Mī·cāi′ah the son of Im′lah quickly!"

10 The king of Israel and Je·hosh′a·phat the king of Judah, having put on *their* robes, sat each on his throne, at a threshing floor at the entrance of the gate of Samaria; and all the prophets prophesied before them.

11 Now Zed·e·kī′ah the son of Che·nā′a·nah had made [a]horns of iron for himself; and he said, "Thus says the LORD: 'With these you shall [b]gore the Syrians until they are destroyed.' "

12 And all the prophets prophesied so, saying, "Go up to Rā′moth Gil′ē·ad and prosper, for the LORD will deliver *it* into the king's hand."

13 Then the messenger who had gone to call Mī·cāi′ah spoke to him, saying, "Now listen, the words of the prophets with one accord encourage the king. Please, let your word be like the word of one of them, and speak encouragement."

14 And Mī·cāi′ah said, "*As* the LORD lives, [a]whatever the LORD says to me, that I will speak."

15 Then he came to the king; and the king said to him, "Mī·cāi′ah, shall we go to war against Rā′moth Gil′ē·ad, or shall we refrain?" And he answered him, "Go and prosper, for the LORD will deliver *it* into the hand of the king!"

16 So the king said to him, "How many times shall I make you swear that you tell me nothing but the truth in the name of the LORD?"

17 Then he said, "I saw all Israel [a]scattered on the mountains, as sheep that have no shepherd. And the LORD said, 'These have no master. Let each return to his house in peace.' "

18 And the king of Israel said to Je·hosh′a·phat, "Did I not tell

CHAPTER 22

2 [a]2 Chr. 18:2

3 [a]Deut. 4:43

4 [a]2 Kin. 3:7

5 [a]2 Kin. 3:11

6 [a]1 Kin. 18:19 [1]The false prophets

7 [a]2 Kin. 3:11 [1]Or *him*

11 [a]Zech. 1:18–21 [b]Deut. 33:17

14 [a]Num. 22:38; 24:13

17 [a]Matt. 9:36

you he would not prophesy good concerning me, but evil?”

19 Then *Mī·cāi′ah* said, “Therefore hear the word of the LORD: [a]I saw the LORD sitting on His throne, [b]and all the host of heaven standing by, on His right hand and on His left.

20 “And the LORD said, ‘Who will persuade Ā′hab to go up, that he may fall at Rā′moth Gil′ē·ad?’ So one spoke in this manner, and another spoke in that manner.

21 “Then a spirit came forward and stood before the LORD, and said, ‘I will persuade him.’

22 “The LORD said to him, ‘In what way?’ So he said, ‘I will go out and be a lying spirit in the mouth of all his prophets.’ And the LORD said, [a]‘You shall persuade *him,* and also prevail. Go out and do so.’

23 [a]“Therefore look! The LORD has put a lying spirit in the mouth of all these prophets of yours, and the LORD has declared disaster against you.”

24 Now Zed·e·kī′ah the son of Che·nā′a·nah went near and [a]struck Mī·cāi′ah on the cheek, and said, [b]“Which way did the spirit from the LORD go from me to speak to you?”

25 And Mī·cāi′ah said, “Indeed, you shall see on that day when you go into an [a]inner chamber to hide!”

26 So the king of Israel said, “Take Mī·cāi′ah, and return him to Ā′mon the governor of the city and to Jō′ash the king’s son;

27 “and say, ‘Thus says the king: “Put this *fellow* in [a]prison, and feed him with bread of affliction and water of affliction, until I come in peace.” ’ ”

28 But Mī·cāi′ah said, “If you ever return in peace, [a]the LORD has not spoken by me.” And he said, “Take heed, all you people!”

29 So the king of Israel and Je·hosh′a·phat the king of Judah went up to Rā′moth Gil′ē·ad.

30 And the king of Israel said to Je·hosh′a·phat, “I will disguise myself and go into battle; but you put on your robes.” So the king of Israel [a]disguised himself and went into battle.

31 Now the [a]king of Syria had commanded the thirty-two [b]captains of his chariots, saying, “Fight with no one small or great, but only with the king of Israel.”

32 So it was, when the captains of the chariots saw Je·hosh′a·phat, that they said, “Surely it *is* the king of Israel!” Therefore they turned aside to fight against him, and Je·hosh′a·phat [a]cried out.

33 And it happened, when the captains of the chariots saw that it *was* not the king of Israel, that they turned back from pursuing him.

34 Now a *certain* man drew a bow at random, and struck the king of Israel between the joints of his armor. So he said to the driver of his chariot, “Turn around and take me out of the battle, for I am wounded.”

35 The battle increased that day; and the king was propped up in his chariot, facing the Syrians, and died at evening. The blood ran out from the wound onto the floor of the chariot.

36 Then, as the sun was going down, a shout went throughout

19 [a]Is. 6:1 [b]Dan. 7:10
22 [a]Judg. 9:23
23 [a][Ezek. 14:9]
24 [a]Jer. 20:2 [b]2 Chr. 18:23
25 [a]1 Kin. 20:30
27 [a]2 Chr. 16:10; 18:25–27
28 [a]Num. 16:29
30 [a]2 Chr. 35:22
31 [a]1 Kin. 20:1 [b]1 Kin. 20:24
32 [a]2 Chr. 18:31

the army, saying, "Every man
to his city, and every man to his
own country!"
37 So the king died, and was
brought to Samaria. And they
buried the king in Samaria.
38 Then *someone* washed the
chariot at a pool in Samaria,
and the dogs licked up his blood
while [1]the harlots bathed, according [a]to the word of the LORD
which He had spoken.
39 Now the rest of the acts of
Ā'hab, and all that he did, [a]the
ivory house which he built and
all the cities that he built, *are*
they not written in the book of
the chronicles of the kings of
Israel?
40 So Ā'hab [1]rested with his
fathers. Then [a]Ā·ha·zī'ah his son
reigned in his place.
41 [a]Je·hosh'a·phat the son of
Ā'sa had become king over Judah in the fourth year of Ā'hab
king of Israel.
42 Je·hosh'a·phat *was* thirty-
five years old when he became
king, and he reigned twenty-five
years in Jerusalem. His mother's
name *was* A·zū'bah the daughter of Shil'hī.
43 And [a]he walked in all the
ways of his father Ā'sa. He did
not turn aside from them, doing
what was right in the eyes of
the LORD. Nevertheless [b]the high
places were not taken away, *for*
the people offered sacrifices
and burned incense on the high
places.
44 Also [a]Je·hosh'a·phat made
[b]peace with the king of Israel.
45 Now the rest of the acts of
Je·hosh'a·phat, the might that he
showed, and how he made war,
are they not written [a]in the book
of the chronicles of the kings of
Judah?
46 [a]And the rest of the [1]per-
verted persons, who remained
in the days of his father Ā'sa, he
banished from the land.
47 [a]*There was* then no king in
Ē'dom, only a deputy of the
king.
48 [a]Je·hosh'a·phat [b]made [1]mer-
chant ships to go to [c]Ō'phir for
gold; [d]but they never sailed,
for the ships were wrecked at
[e]Ē'zi·on Gē'ber.
49 Then Ā·ha·zī'ah the son of
Ā'hab said to Je·hosh'a·phat,
"Let my servants go with your
servants in the ships." But
Je·hosh'a·phat would not.
50 And [a]Je·hosh'a·phat [1]rested
with his fathers, and was buried
with his fathers in the City of
David his father. Then Je·hō'ram
his son reigned in his place.
51 [a]Ā·ha·zī'ah the son of Ā'hab
became king over Israel in Samaria in the seventeenth year
of Je·hosh'a·phat king of Judah, and reigned two years over
Israel.
52 He did evil in the sight of the
LORD, and [a]walked in the way
of his father and in the way of
his mother and in the way of
Jer·o·bō'am the son of Nē'bat,
who had made Israel sin;
53 for [a]he served Bā'al and worshiped him, and provoked the
LORD God of Israel to anger,
[b]according[1] to all that his father
had done.

38 [a]1 Kin. 21:19 [1]Tg., Syr. *they washed his armor*
39 [a]Amos 3:15
40 [a]2 Kin. 1:2, 18 [1]Died and joined his ancestors
41 [a]2 Chr. 20:31
43 [a]2 Chr. 17:3; 20:32, 33 [b]2 Kin. 12:3
44 [a]2 Chr. 19:2 [b]2 Chr. 18:1
45 [a]2 Chr. 20:34
46 [a]1 Kin. 14:24; 15:12 [1]Heb. *qadesh,* one practicing sodomy and prostitution in religious rituals
47 [a]2 Sam. 8:14
48 [a]2 Chr. 20:35–37 [b]1 Kin. 10:22 [c]1 Kin. 9:28 [d]2 Chr. 20:37 [e]1 Kin. 9:26 [1]Or *ships of Tarshish*
50 [a]2 Chr. 21:1 [1]Died and joined his ancestors
51 [a]1 Kin. 22:40
52 [a]1 Kin. 15:26; 21:25
53 [a]Judg. 2:11 [b]1 Kin. 16:30–32 [1]In the same way that

The Second Book of the
KINGS

THE Book of Second Kings continues the drama begun in First Kings—the tragic history of two nations on a collision course with captivity. The author systematically traces the reigning monarchs of Israel and Judah, first by carrying one nation's history forward, then retracing the same period for the other nation.

Nineteen consecutive evil kings rule in Israel, leading to the captivity by Assyria. The picture is somewhat brighter in Judah, where godly kings occasionally emerge to reform the evils of their predecessors. In the end, however, sin outweighs righteousness and Judah is marched off to Babylon.

CHAPTER 1

MOAB [a]rebelled against Israel [b]after the death of
Ā'hab.
2 Now [a]Ā·ha·zī'ah fell through
the lattice of his upper room in
Samaria, and was injured; so
he sent messengers and said
to them, "Go, inquire of [b]Bā'al-
Zebub,[1] the god of [c]Ek'ron,
whether I shall recover from this
injury."
3 But the [1]angel of the LORD
said to E·lī'jah the Tish'bīte,
"Arise, go up to meet the messengers of the king of Samaria, and
say to them, '*Is it* because *there*
is no God in Israel *that* you are
going to inquire of Bā'al-Zebub,
the god of Ek'ron?'
4 "Now therefore, thus says the
LORD: 'You shall not come down
from the bed to which you have
gone up, but you shall surely
die.' " So E·lī'jah departed.
5 And when the messengers
returned to [1]him, he said to them,
"Why have you come back?"
6 So they said to him, "A man
came up to meet us, and said to
us, 'Go, return to the king who
sent you, and say to him, "Thus
says the LORD: '*Is it* because
there is no God in Israel *that*
you are sending to inquire of
Bā'al-Zebub, the god of Ek'ron?
Therefore you shall not come
down from the bed to which
you have gone up, but you shall
surely die.' " ' "
7 Then he said to them, "What
kind of man *was it* who came up
to meet you and told you these
words?"
8 So they answered him, [a]"A
hairy man wearing a leather belt
around his waist." And he said,
[b]"It *is* E·lī'jah the Tish'bīte."
9 Then the king sent to him
a captain of fifty with his fifty
men. So he went up to him; and
there he was, sitting on the top
of a hill. And he spoke to him:
"Man of God, the king has said,
'Come down!' "
10 So E·lī'jah answered and said
to the captain of fifty, "If I *am* a
man of God, then [a]let fire come
down from heaven and consume
you and your fifty men." And
fire came down from heaven
and consumed him and his fifty.
11 Then he sent to him another
captain of fifty with his fifty men.
And he answered and said to him:

1 [a]2 Sam. 8:2 [b]2 Kin. 3:5
2 [a]1 Kin. 22:40 [b]Matt. 10:25 [c]1 Sam. 5:10 [1]Lit. *Lord of Flies*
3 [1]Or *Angel*
5 [1]Ahaziah
8 [a]Zech. 13:4 [b]1 Kin. 18:7
10 [a]Luke 9:54

"Man of God, thus has the king
said, 'Come down quickly!' "
12 So E·lī'jah answered and
said to them, "If I *am* a man of
God, let fire come down from
heaven and consume you and
your fifty men." And the fire of
God came down from heaven
and consumed him and his fifty.
13 Again, he sent a third captain of fifty with his fifty men.
And the third captain of fifty
went up, and came and [1]fell on
his knees before E·lī'jah, and
pleaded with him, and said to
him: "Man of God, please let
my life and the life of these fifty
servants of yours [a]be precious in
your sight.
14 "Look, fire has come down
from heaven and burned up the
first two captains of fifties with
their fifties. But let my life now
be precious in your sight."
15 And the [1]angel of the LORD
said to E·lī'jah, "Go down with
him; do not be afraid of him." So
he arose and went down with
him to the king.
16 Then he said to him, "Thus
says the LORD: 'Because you
have sent messengers to inquire
of Bā'al-Zebub, the god of Ek'-
ron, *is it* because *there is* no God
in Israel to inquire of His word?
Therefore you shall not come
down from the bed to which
you have gone up, but you shall
surely die.' "
17 So *Ā·ha·zī'ah* died according
to the word of the LORD which
E·lī'jah had spoken. Because he
had no son, [a]Je·hō'ram[1] became
king in his place, in the second
year of Je·hō'ram the son of
Je·hosh'a·phat, king of Judah.
18 Now the rest of the acts of
Ā·ha·zī'ah which he did, *are*
they not written in the book of
the chronicles of the kings of
Israel?

2

And it came to pass, when
the LORD was about to
[a]take up E·lī'jah into heaven by
a whirlwind, that E·lī'jah went
with [b]E·lī'sha from Gil'gal.
2 Then E·lī'jah said to E·lī'sha,
[a]"Stay here, please, for the LORD
has sent me on to Beth'el." But
E·lī'sha said, "*As* the LORD lives,
and [b]*as* your soul lives, I will not
leave you!" So they went down
to Beth'el.
3 Now [a]the sons of the prophets who *were* at Beth'el came
out to E·lī'sha, and said to him,
"Do you know that the LORD will
take away your master [1]from
over you today?" And he said,
"Yes, I know; keep silent!"
4 Then E·lī'jah said to him,
"E·lī'sha, stay here, please, for
the LORD has sent me on to Jericho." But he said, "*As* the LORD
lives, and *as* your soul lives,
I will not leave you!" So they
came to Jericho.
5 Now the sons of the prophets who *were* at Jericho came
to E·lī'sha and said to him, "Do
you know that the LORD will take
away your master from over you
today?" So he answered, "Yes, I
know; keep silent!"
6 Then E·lī'jah said to him,
"Stay here, please, for the LORD
has sent me on to the Jordan."
But he said, "*As* the LORD lives,
and *as* your soul lives, I will not
leave you!" So the two of them
went on.
7 And fifty men of the sons
of the prophets went and stood
facing *them* at a distance, while
the two of them stood by the
Jordan.

13 [a]1 Sam. 26:21 [1]Lit. *bowed down*

15 [1]Or *Angel*

17 [a]1 Kin. 22:50 [1]The son of Ahab king of Israel, 2 Kin. 3:1

CHAPTER 2

1 [a]Gen. 5:24 [b]1 Kin. 19:16–21

2 [a]Ruth 1:15, 16 [b]1 Sam. 1:26

3 [a]1 Kin. 20:35 [1]Lit. *from your head*

8 Now E·lī′jah took his mantle,
rolled *it* up, and struck the water; and [a]it was divided this way
and that, so that the two of them
crossed over on dry [b]ground.
9 And so it was, when they
had crossed over, that E·lī′jah
said to E·lī′sha, "Ask! What may
I do for you, before I am taken
away from you?" E·lī′sha said,
"Please let a double portion of
your spirit be upon me."
10 So he said, "You have asked
a hard thing. *Nevertheless,* if
you see me *when I am* taken
from you, it shall be so for you;
but if not, it shall not be *so.*"
11 Then it happened, as they
continued on and talked, that
suddenly [a]a chariot of fire *ap-*
peared with horses of fire, and
separated the two of them; and
E·lī′jah [b]went up by a whirlwind
into heaven.
12 And E·lī′sha saw *it,* and he
cried out, [a]"My father, my father, the chariot of Israel and its
horsemen!" So he saw him no
more. And he took hold of his
own clothes and tore them into
two pieces.
13 He also took up the mantle
of E·lī′jah that had fallen from
him, and went back and stood
by the bank of the Jordan.
14 Then he took the mantle of
E·lī′jah that had fallen from him,
and struck the water, and said,
"Where *is* the LORD God of E·lī′-
jah?" And when he also had
struck the water, [a]it was divided
this way and that; and E·lī′sha
crossed over.
15 Now when the sons of the
prophets who *were* [a]from[1] Jericho saw him, they said, "The
spirit of E·lī′jah rests on E·lī′-
sha." And they came to meet
him, and bowed to the ground
before him.
16 Then they said to him, "Look
now, there are fifty strong men
with your servants. Please let
them go and search for your
master, [a]lest perhaps the Spirit
of the LORD has taken him up
and cast him upon some mountain or into some valley." And
he said, "You shall not send
anyone."
17 But when they urged him till
he was [a]ashamed, he said, "Send
them!" Therefore they sent fifty
men, and they searched for three
days but did not find him.
18 And when they came back
to him, for he had stayed in Jericho, he said to them, "Did I not
say to you, 'Do not go'?"
19 Then the men of the city said
to E·lī′sha, "Please notice, the
situation of this city *is* pleasant,
as my lord sees; but the water *is*
bad, and the ground barren."
20 And he said, "Bring me a
new bowl, and put salt in it." So
they brought *it* to him.
21 Then he went out to the
source of the water, and [a]cast in
the salt there, and said, "Thus
says the LORD: 'I have [1]healed
this water; from it there shall be
no more death or barrenness.' "
22 So the water remains [a]healed
to this day, according to the word
of E·lī′sha which he spoke.
23 Then he went up from there
to Beth′el; and as he was going
up the road, some youths came
from the city and mocked him,
and said to him, "Go up, you baldhead! Go up, you baldhead!"
24 So he turned around and
looked at them, and [a]pronounced
a curse on them in the name of
the LORD. And two female bears

8 [a]Ex. 14:21, 22 [b]Josh. 3:17
11 [a]2 Kin. 6:17 [b]Heb. 11:5
12 [a]2 Kin. 13:14
14 [a]2 Kin. 2:8
15 [a]2 Kin. 2:7 [1]Or *at Jericho opposite him saw*
16 [a]1 Kin. 18:12
17 [a]2 Kin. 8:11
21 [a]Ex. 15:25, 26 [1]*purified*
22 [a]Ezek. 47:8, 9
24 [a]Deut. 27:13–26

came out of the woods and
mauled forty-two of the youths.
25 Then he went from there to
[a]Mount Car′mel, and from there
he returned to Samaria.

3 Now [a]Je·hō′ram the son of
Ā′hab became king over Israel at Samaria in the eighteenth
year of Je·hosh′a·phat king of Judah, and reigned twelve years.
2 And he did evil in the sight
of the LORD, but not like his
father and mother; for he put
away the *sacred* pillar of Bā′al
[a]that his father had made.
3 Nevertheless he persisted in
[a]the sins of Jer·o·bō′am the son
of Nē′bat, who had made Israel sin; he did not depart from
them.
4 Now Mē′sha king of Mō′ab
was a sheepbreeder, and he
[a]regularly paid the king of Israel
one hundred thousand [b]lambs
and the wool of one hundred
thousand rams.
5 But it happened, when [a]Ā′hab
died, that the king of Mō′ab rebelled against the king of Israel.
6 So King Je·hō′ram went out
of Samaria at that time and
mustered all Israel.
7 Then he went and sent to
Je·hosh′a·phat king of Judah,
saying, "The king of Mō′ab has
rebelled against me. Will you go
with me to fight against Mō′ab?"
And he said, "I will go up; [a]I
am as you *are*, my people as
your people, my horses as your
horses."
8 Then he said, "Which way
shall we go up?" And he answered, "By way of the Wilderness of Ē′dom."
9 So the king of Israel went
with the king of Judah and the
king of Ē′dom, and they marched
on that roundabout route seven
days; and there was no water
for the army, nor for the animals
that followed them.
10 And the king of Israel said,
"Alas! For the LORD has called
these three kings together to
deliver them into the hand of
Mō′ab."
11 But [a]Je·hosh′a·phat said, "*Is
there* no prophet of the LORD
here, that we may inquire of
the LORD by him?" So one of the
servants of the king of Israel
answered and said, "E·lī′sha the
son of Shā′phat *is* here, who
[b]poured[1] water on the hands of
E·lī′jah."
12 And Je·hosh′a·phat said,
"The word of the LORD is with
him." So the king of Israel and
Je·hosh′a·phat and the king of
Ē′dom [a]went down to him.
13 Then E·lī′sha said to the king
of Israel, [a]"What have I to do
with you? [b]Go to [c]the prophets
of your father and the [d]prophets
of your mother." But the king
of Israel said to him, "No, for
the LORD has called these three
kings *together* to deliver them
into the hand of Mō′ab."
14 And E·lī′sha said, [a]"*As* the
LORD of hosts lives, before whom
I stand, surely were it not that I
regard the presence of Je·hosh′-
a·phat king of Judah, I would
not look at you, nor see you.
15 "But now bring me [a]a musician." Then it happened, when
the musician [b]played, that [c]the
hand of the LORD came upon
him.
16 And he said, "Thus says the
LORD: [a]'Make this valley full of
[1]ditches.'
17 "For thus says the LORD: 'You
shall not see wind, nor shall you

25 [a]2 Kin. 4:25

CHAPTER 3

1 [a]2 Kin. 1:17

2 [a]1 Kin. 16:31, 32

3 [a]1 Kin. 12:28–32

4 [a]2 Sam. 8:2 [b]Is. 16:1, 2

5 [a]2 Kin. 1:1

7 [a]1 Kin. 22:4

11 [a]1 Kin. 22:7 [b]1 Kin. 19:21 [1]Was the personal servant of

12 [a]2 Kin. 2:25

13 [a][Ezek. 14:3] [b]Judg. 10:14 [c]1 Kin. 22:6–11 [d]1 Kin. 18:19

14 [a]1 Kin. 17:1

15 [a]1 Sam. 10:5 [b]1 Sam. 16:16, 23 [c]Ezek. 1:3; 3:14, 22; 8:1

16 [a]Jer. 14:3 [1]*water canals*

see rain; yet that valley shall be filled with water, so that you, your cattle, and your animals may drink.'

18 "And this is a simple matter in the sight of the LORD; He will also deliver the Mō'ab·ītes into your hand.

19 "Also you shall attack every fortified city and every choice city, and shall cut down every good tree, and stop up every spring of water, and ruin every good piece of land with stones."

20 Now it happened in the morning, when [a]the grain offering was offered, that suddenly water came by way of Ē'dom, and the land was filled with water.

21 And when all the Mō'ab·ītes heard that the kings had come up to fight against them, all who were able to bear arms and older were [1]gathered; and they stood at the border.

22 Then they rose up early in the morning, and the sun was shining on the water; and the Mō'ab·ītes saw the water on the other side *as* red as blood.

23 And they said, "This is blood; the kings have surely struck swords and have killed one another; now therefore, Mō'ab, to the spoil!"

24 So when they came to the camp of Israel, Israel rose up and attacked the Mō'ab·ītes, so that they fled before them; and they entered *their* land, killing the Mō'ab·ītes.

25 Then they destroyed the cities, and each man threw a stone on every good piece of land and filled it; and they stopped up all the springs of water and cut down all the good trees. But they left the stones of [a]Kir Har'-a·seth *intact*. However the slingers surrounded and attacked it.

26 And when the king of Mō'ab saw that the battle was too fierce for him, he took with him seven hundred men who drew swords, to break through to the king of Ē'dom, but they could not.

27 Then [a]he took his eldest son who would have reigned in his place, and offered him *as* a burnt offering upon the wall; and there was great [1]indignation against Israel. [b]So they departed from him and returned to *their own* land.

4

1 A certain woman of the wives of [a]the sons of the prophets cried out to E·lī'sha, saying, "Your servant my husband is dead, and you know that your servant feared the LORD. And the creditor is coming [b]to take my two sons to be his slaves."

2 So E·lī'sha said to her, "What shall I do for you? Tell me, what do you have in the house?" And she said, "Your maidservant has nothing in the house but a jar of oil."

3 Then he said, "Go, borrow vessels from everywhere, from all your neighbors—empty vessels; [a]do not gather just a few.

4 "And when you have come in, you shall shut the door behind you and your sons; then pour it into all those vessels, and set aside the full ones."

5 So she went from him and shut the door behind her and her sons, who brought *the vessels* to her; and she poured *it* out.

6 Now it came to pass, when the vessels were full, that she

20 [a]Ex. 29:39, 40

21 [1]*summoned*

25 [a]Is. 16:7, 11

27 [a][Amos 2:1] [b]2 Kin. 8:20 [1]*wrath*

CHAPTER 4

1 [a]1 Kin. 20:35 [b][Lev. 25:39–41, 48]

3 [a]2 Kin. 3:16

said to her son, "Bring me another vessel." And he said to her,
"*There is* not another vessel." So
the oil ceased.
7 Then she came and told the
man of God. And he said, "Go,
sell the oil and pay your debt;
and you *and* your sons live on
the rest."
8 Now it happened one day
that E·lī′sha went to [a]Shū′nem,
where there *was* a [1]notable
woman, and she [2]persuaded him
to eat some food. So it was, as
often as he passed by, he would
turn in there to eat some food.
9 And she said to her husband,
"Look now, I know that this *is* a
holy man of God, who passes by
us regularly.
10 "Please, let us make [1]a small
upper room on the wall; and let
us put a bed for him there, and
a table and a chair and a lampstand; so it will be, whenever
he comes to us, he can turn in
there."
11 And it happened one day that
he came there, and he turned in
to the upper room and lay down
there.
12 Then he said to [a]Ge·hā′zī his
servant, "Call this Shū′nam·mīte
woman." When he had called
her, she stood before him.
13 And he said to him, "Say
now to her, 'Look, you have
been concerned for us with all
this care. What *can I* do for you?
Do you want me to speak on
your behalf to the king or to the
commander of the army?' " She
answered, "I dwell among my
own people."
14 So he said, "What then *is* to
be done for her?" And Ge·hā′zī
answered, "Actually, she has no
son, and her husband is old."
15 So he said, "Call her." When
he had called her, she stood in
the doorway.
16 Then he said, [1]"About this
time next year you shall embrace a son." And she said, "No,
my lord. Man of God, [a]do not lie
to your maidservant!"
17 But the woman conceived,
and bore a son when the appointed time had come, of which
E·lī′sha had told her.
18 And the child grew. Now it
happened one day that he went
out to his father, to the reapers.
19 And he said to his father,
"My head, my head!" So he said
to a servant, "Carry him to his
mother."
20 When he had taken him and
brought him to his mother, he
sat on her knees till noon, and
then died.
21 And she went up and laid
him on the bed of the man of
God, shut *the door* upon him,
and went out.
22 Then she called to her husband, and said, "Please send me
one of the young men and one
of the donkeys, that I may run
to the man of God and come
back."
23 So he said, "Why are you
going to him today? *It is* neither
the [a]New Moon nor the Sab-
bath." And she said, [1]"*It is* well."
24 Then she saddled a donkey,
and said to her servant, "Drive,
and go forward; do not slacken
the pace for me unless I tell
you."
25 And so she departed, and
went to the man of God [a]at
Mount Car′mel.
So it was, when the man of
God saw her afar off, that he said

8 [a]Josh. 19:18 [1]Lit. *great* [2]Lit. *laid hold on him*

10 [1]Or *a small walled upper chamber*

12 [a]2 Kin. 4:29–31; 5:20–27; 8:4, 5

16 [a]2 Kin. 4:28 [1]Lit. *About this season, as the time of life*

23 [a]1 Chr. 23:31 [1]Or *It will be well*

25 [a]2 Kin. 2:25

to his servant Ge·hā′zī, “Look,
the Shū′nam·mīte woman!
26 “Please run now to meet her,
and say to her, ‘*Is it* well with
you? *Is it* well with your husband? *Is it* well with the child?’ ”
And she answered, “*It is* well.”
27 Now when she came to
the man of God at the hill, she
caught him by the feet, but
Ge·hā′zī came near to push her
away. But the man of God said,
“Let her alone; for her soul *is* in
deep distress, and the LORD has
hidden *it* from me, and has not
told me.”
28 So she said, “Did I ask a son
of my lord? [a]Did I not say, ‘Do
not deceive me’?”
29 Then he said to Ge·hā′zī,
[a]“Get[1] yourself ready, and take
my staff in your hand, and be on
your way. If you meet anyone,
[b]do not greet him; and if anyone
greets you, do not answer him;
but [c]lay my staff on the face of
the child.”
30 And the mother of the child
said, [a]“*As* the LORD lives, and *as*
your soul lives, I will not [b]leave
you.” So he arose and followed
her.
31 Now Ge·hā′zī went on ahead
of them, and laid the staff on
the face of the child; but *there*
was neither voice nor hearing.
Therefore he went back to meet
him, and told him, saying, “The
child has [a]not awakened.”
32 When E·lī′sha came into the
house, there was the child, lying
dead on his bed.
33 He [a]went in therefore, shut
the door behind the two of them,
[b]and prayed to the LORD.
34 And he went up and lay on
the child, and put his mouth on
his mouth, his eyes on his eyes,
and his hands on his hands; and
[a]he stretched himself out on the
child, and the flesh of the child
became warm.
35 He returned and walked
back and forth in the house, and
again went up [a]and stretched
himself out on him; then [b]the
child sneezed seven times, and
the child opened his eyes.
36 And he called Ge·hā′zī and
said, “Call this Shū′nam·mīte
woman.” So he called her. And
when she came in to him, he
said, “Pick up your son.”
37 So she went in, fell at his
feet, and bowed to the ground;
then she [a]picked up her son and
went out.
38 And E·lī′sha returned to
[a]Gil′gal, and *there was* a [b]famine
in the land. Now the sons of
the prophets *were* [c]sitting before him; and he said to his
servant, “Put on the large pot,
and boil stew for the sons of the
prophets.”
39 So one went out into the
field to gather herbs, and found
a wild vine, and gathered from
it a lapful of wild gourds, and
came and sliced *them* into the
pot of stew, though they did not
know *what they were.*
40 Then they served it to the
men to eat. Now it happened, as
they were eating the stew, that
they cried out and said, “Man of
God, *there is* [a]death in the pot!”
And they could not eat *it.*
41 So he said, “Then bring some
flour.” And [a]he put *it* into the
pot, and said, “Serve *it* to the
people, that they may eat.” And
there was nothing harmful in
the pot.
42 Then a man came from [a]Bā′al
Shal′i·sha, [b]and brought the man

28 [a]2 Kin. 4:16
29 [a]1 Kin. 18:46 [b]Luke 10:4 [c]Ex. 7:19; 14:16 [1]Lit. *Gird up your loins.* The skirt of the robe was wrapped around the legs and tucked in the belt to gain freedom of movement.
30 [a]2 Kin. 2:2 [b]2 Kin. 2:4
31 [a]John 11:11
33 [a][Matt. 6:6] [b]1 Kin. 17:20
34 [a]1 Kin. 17:21–23
35 [a]1 Kin. 17:21 [b]2 Kin. 8:1, 5
37 [a][Heb. 11:35]
38 [a]2 Kin. 2:1 [b]2 Kin. 8:1 [c]Acts 22:3
40 [a]Ex. 10:17
41 [a]Ex. 15:25
42 [a]1 Sam. 9:4 [b][1 Cor. 9:11]

of God bread of the firstfruits,
twenty loaves of barley bread,
and newly ripened grain in his
knapsack. And he said, "Give
it to the people, that they may
eat."
43 But his servant said, [a]"What?
Shall I set this before one hundred men?" He said again, "Give
it to the people, that they may
eat; for thus says the LORD:
[b]'They shall eat and have *some*
left over.' "
44 So he set *it* before them; and
they ate [a]and had *some* left over,
according to the word of the
LORD.

5 Now [a]Nā′a·man, commander
of the army of the king of
Syria, was [b]a great and honorable man in the eyes of his master, because by him the LORD had
given victory to Syria. He was
also a mighty man of valor, *but*
a leper.
2 And the Syrians had gone
out [a]on[1] raids, and had brought
back captive a young girl from
the land of Israel. She [2]waited
on Nā′a·man's wife.
3 Then she said to her mistress, "If only my master *were*
with the prophet who *is* in Samaria! For he would heal him of
his leprosy."
4 And *Nā′a·man* went in and
told his master, saying, "Thus
and thus said the girl who *is*
from the land of Israel."
5 Then the king of Syria said,
"Go now, and I will send a letter to the king of Israel." So he
departed and [a]took with him ten
talents of silver, six thousand
shekels of gold, and ten changes
of clothing.
6 Then he brought the letter to
the king of Israel, which said,

43 [a]John 6:9
[b]Luke 9:17
44 [a]John 6:13

CHAPTER 5

1 [a]Luke 4:27
[b]Ex. 11:3
2 [a]2 Kin. 6:23; 13:20
[1]Or *in bands*
[2]Served, lit. *was before*
5 [a]1 Sam. 9:8
7 [a][Gen. 30:2]
10 [a]John 9:7
12 [1]So with Kt., LXX, Vg.; Qr., Syr., Tg. *Amanah*
13 [a]1 Sam. 28:23

Now be advised, when this
letter comes to you, that
I have sent Nā′a·man my
servant to you, that you may
heal him of his leprosy.

7 And it happened, when the
king of Israel read the letter,
that he tore his clothes and said,
"*Am* I [a]God, to kill and make
alive, that this man sends a man
to me to heal him of his leprosy?
Therefore please consider, and
see how he seeks a quarrel with
me."
8 So it was, when E·lī′sha the
man of God heard that the king
of Israel had torn his clothes,
that he sent to the king, saying, "Why have you torn your
clothes? Please let him come to
me, and he shall know that there
is a prophet in Israel."
9 Then Nā′a·man went with
his horses and chariot, and he
stood at the door of E·lī′sha's
house.
10 And E·lī′sha sent a messenger to him, saying, "Go and
[a]wash in the Jordan seven times,
and your flesh shall be restored
to you, and *you shall* be clean."
11 But Nā′a·man became furious, and went away and said,
"Indeed, I said to myself, 'He
will surely come out *to me,* and
stand and call on the name of
the LORD his God, and wave his
hand over the place, and heal
the leprosy.'
12 "*Are* not the [1]A·bā′nah and
the Phar′par, the rivers of Damascus, better than all the
waters of Israel? Could I not
wash in them and be clean?" So
he turned and went away in a
rage.
13 And his [a]servants came near

and spoke to him, and said,
"My father, *if* the prophet had
told you *to do* something great,
would you not have done *it*?
How much more then, when
he says to you, 'Wash, and be
clean'?"
14 So he went down and dipped
seven times in the Jordan, according to the saying of the
man of God; and his [a]flesh was
restored like the flesh of a little
child, and [b]he was clean.
15 And he returned to the man
of God, he and all his aides, and
came and stood before him; and
he said, "Indeed, now I know that
there is [a]no God in all the earth,
except in Israel; now therefore,
please take [b]a gift from your
servant."
16 But he said, [a]"*As* the LORD
lives, before whom I stand, [b]I
will receive nothing." And he
urged him to take *it*, but he
refused.
17 So Nā′a·man said, "Then, if
not, please let your servant be
given two mule-loads of earth;
for your servant will no longer
offer either burnt offering or
sacrifice to other gods, but to the
LORD.
18 "Yet in this thing may the
LORD pardon your servant: when
my master goes into the temple
of Rim′mon to worship there,
and [a]he leans on my hand, and
I bow down in the temple of
Rim′mon—when I bow down in
the temple of Rim′mon, may the
LORD please pardon your servant in this thing."
19 Then he said to him, "Go in
peace." So he departed from him
a short distance.
20 But [a]Ge·hā′zī, the servant of
E·lī′sha the man of God, said,
"Look, my master has spared
Nā′a·man this Syrian, while not
receiving from his hands what
he brought; but *as* the LORD
lives, I will run after him and
take something from him."
21 So Ge·hā′zī pursued Nā′-
a·man. When Nā′a·man saw *him*
running after him, he got down
from the chariot to meet him,
and said, "*Is* all well?"
22 And he said, "All *is* [a]well. My
master has sent me, saying, 'Indeed, just now two young men
of the sons of the prophets have
come to me from the mountains
of Ē′phra·im. Please give them a
talent of silver and two changes
of garments.' "
23 So Nā′a·man said, "Please,
take two talents." And he urged
him, and bound two talents of
silver in two bags, with two
changes of garments, and
handed *them* to two of his servants; and they carried *them* on
ahead of him.
24 When he came to [1]the citadel, he took *them* from their
hand, and stored *them* away in
the house; then he let the men
go, and they departed.
25 Now he went in and stood
before his master. E·lī′sha said
to him, "Where *did you go*,
Ge·hā′zī?" And he said, "Your
servant did not go anywhere."
26 Then he said to him, "Did
not my heart go *with you* when
the man turned back from his
chariot to meet you? *Is it* [a]time
to receive money and to receive
clothing, olive groves and vineyards, sheep and oxen, male and
female servants?
27 "Therefore the leprosy of
Nā′a·man [a]shall cling to you and
your descendants forever." And

14 [a]Job 33:25 [b]Luke 4:27; 5:13
15 [a]Dan. 2:47; 3:29; 6:26, 27 [b]Gen. 33:11
16 [a]2 Kin. 3:14 [b]Gen. 14:22, 23
18 [a]2 Kin. 7:2, 17
20 [a]2 Kin. 4:12; 8:4, 5
22 [a]2 Kin. 4:26
24 [1]Lit. *the hill*
26 [a][Eccl. 3:1, 6]
27 [a][1 Tim. 6:10]

he went out from his presence
[b]leprous, *as white* as snow.

6 And [a]the sons of the prophets said to E·lī′sha, "See now,
the place where we dwell with
you is too small for us.
2 "Please, let us go to the Jordan, and let every man take
a beam from there, and let us
make there a place where we
may dwell." So he answered,
"Go."
3 Then one said, [a]"Please consent to go with your servants."
And he answered, "I will go."
4 So he went with them. And
when they came to the Jordan,
they cut down trees.
5 But as one was cutting down
a tree, the iron *ax head* fell into
the water; and he cried out and
said, "Alas, master! For it was
[a]borrowed."
6 So the man of God said,
"Where did it fall?" And he
showed him the place. So [a]he cut
off a stick, and threw *it* in there;
and he made the iron float.
7 Therefore he said, "Pick *it* up
for yourself." So he reached out
his hand and took it.
8 Now the [a]king of Syria was
making war against Israel; and
he consulted with his servants,
saying, "My camp *will be* in such
and such a place."
9 And the man of God sent to
the king of Israel, saying, "Beware that you do not pass this
place, for the Syrians are coming down there."
10 Then the king of Israel sent
someone to the place of which
the man of God had told him.
Thus he warned him, and he was
watchful there, not just once or
twice.
11 Therefore the heart of the

27 [b]Ex. 4:6

CHAPTER 6

1 [a]2 Kin. 4:38

3 [a]2 Kin. 5:23

5 [a][Ex. 22:14]

6 [a]2 Kin. 2:21; 4:41

8 [a]2 Kin. 8:28, 29

13 [a]Gen. 37:17

16 [a]Ex. 14:13
[b][Rom. 8:31]

17 [a]Num. 22:31
[b]2 Kin. 2:11

18 [a]Gen. 19:11

king of Syria was greatly troubled by this thing; and he called
his servants and said to them,
"Will you not show me which of
us *is* for the king of Israel?"
12 And one of his servants said,
"None, my lord, O king; but
E·lī′sha, the prophet who *is* in
Israel, tells the king of Israel the
words that you speak in your
bedroom."
13 So he said, "Go and see
where he *is*, that I may send and
get him." And it was told him,
saying, "Surely *he is* in [a]Dō′-
than."
14 Therefore he sent horses and
chariots and a great army there,
and they came by night and surrounded the city.
15 And when the servant of the
man of God arose early and
went out, there was an army,
surrounding the city with horses
and chariots. And his servant
said to him, "Alas, my master!
What shall we do?"
16 So he answered, [a]"Do not
fear, for [b]those who *are* with us
are more than those who *are*
with them."
17 And E·lī′sha prayed, and
said, "LORD, I pray, open his eyes
that he may see." Then the LORD
[a]opened the eyes of the young
man, and he saw. And behold,
the mountain *was* full of [b]horses
and chariots of fire all around
E·lī′sha.
18 So when *the Syrians* came
down to him, E·lī′sha prayed to
the LORD, and said, "Strike this
people, I pray, with blindness."
And [a]He struck them with blindness according to the word of
E·lī′sha.
19 Now E·lī′sha said to them,
"This *is* not the way, nor *is* this

the city. Follow me, and I will
bring you to the man whom
you seek." But he led them to
Samaria.
20 So it was, when they had
come to Samaria, that E·lī′sha
said, "LORD, open the eyes of
these *men*, that they may see."
And the LORD opened their eyes,
and they saw; and there *they*
were, inside Samaria!
21 Now when the king of Israel
saw them, he said to E·lī′sha,
"My [a]father, shall I kill *them?*
Shall I kill *them?*"
22 But he answered, "You shall
not kill *them.* Would you kill
those whom you have taken captive with your sword and your
bow? [a]Set food and water before
them, that they may eat and
drink and go to their master."
23 Then he prepared a great
feast for them; and after they ate
and drank, he sent them away
and they went to their master.
So [a]the bands of Syrian *raiders*
came no more into the land of
Israel.
24 And it happened after this
that [a]Ben-Hā′dad king of Syria
gathered all his army, and went
up and besieged Samaria.
25 And there was a great
[a]famine in Samaria; and indeed
they besieged it until a donkey's
head was *sold* for eighty *shekels*
of silver, and one-fourth of a
[1]kab of dove droppings for five
shekels of silver.
26 Then, as the king of Israel
was passing by on the wall, a
woman cried out to him, saying,
"Help, my lord, O king!"
27 And he said, "If the LORD
does not help you, where can
I find help for you? From the

21 [a]2 Kin. 2:12; 5:13; 8:9
22 [a][Rom. 12:20]
23 [a]2 Kin. 5:2; 6:8, 9
24 [a]1 Kin. 20:1
25 [a]2 Kin. 4:38; 8:1 [1]Approximately 1 pint
29 [a]Lev. 26:27–29
30 [a]1 Kin. 21:27
31 [a]Ruth 1:17
32 [a]Ezek. 8:1; 14:1; 20:1 [b]Luke 13:32 [c]1 Kin. 18:4, 13, 14; 21:10, 13
33 [a]Job 2:9

CHAPTER 7

1 [a]2 Kin. 7:18, 19 [1]A third of an ephah, or about 8 gallons

threshing floor or from the
winepress?"
28 Then the king said to her,
"What is troubling you?" And
she answered, "This woman said
to me, 'Give your son, that we
may eat him today, and we will
eat my son tomorrow.'
29 "So [a]we boiled my son, and
ate him. And I said to her on the
next day, 'Give your son, that we
may eat him'; but she has hidden her son."
30 Now it happened, when the
king heard the words of the
woman, that he [a]tore his clothes;
and as he passed by on the wall,
the people looked, and there
underneath *he had* sackcloth on
his body.
31 Then he said, [a]"God do so to
me and more also, if the head
of E·lī′sha the son of Shā′phat
remains on him today!"
32 But E·lī′sha was sitting in his
house, and [a]the elders were sitting with him. And *the king* sent
a man ahead of him, but before
the messenger came to him, he
said to the elders, [b]"Do you see
how this son of [c]a murderer has
sent someone to take away my
head? Look, when the messenger comes, shut the door, and
hold him fast at the door. *Is* not
the sound of his master's feet
behind him?"
33 And while he was still talking with them, there was the
messenger, coming down to him;
and then *the king* said, "Surely
this calamity *is* from the LORD;
[a]why should I wait for the LORD
any longer?"
7 Then E·lī′sha said, "Hear the
word of the LORD. Thus says
the LORD: [a]"Tomorrow about this
time a [1]seah of fine flour *shall be*

sold for a shekel, and two seahs
of barley for a shekel, at the gate
of Samaria.' "
2 [a]So an officer on whose hand
the king leaned answered the
man of God and said, "Look, [b]*if*
the LORD would make windows
in heaven, could this thing be?"
And he said, "In fact, you shall
see *it* with your eyes, but you
shall not eat of it."
3 Now there were four leprous
men [a]at the entrance of the gate;
and they said to one another,
"Why are we sitting here until
we die?
4 "If we say, 'We will enter the
city,' the famine *is* in the city,
and we shall die there. And if
we sit here, we die also. Now
therefore, come, let us surrender
to the [a]army of the Syrians. If
they keep us alive, we shall live;
and if they kill us, we shall only
die."
5 And they rose at twilight to
go to the camp of the Syrians;
and when they had come to the
outskirts of the Syrian camp, to
their surprise no one *was* there.
6 For the Lord had caused the
army of the Syrians [a]to hear the
noise of chariots and the noise
of horses—the noise of a great
army; so they said to one another,
"Look, the king of Israel
has hired against us [b]the kings
of the Hit'tītes and the kings of
the Egyptians to attack us!"
7 Therefore they [a]arose and
fled at twilight, and left the
camp intact—their tents, their
horses, and their donkeys—and
they fled for their lives.
8 And when these lepers came
to the outskirts of the camp, they
went into one tent and ate and
drank, and carried from it silver

2 [a]2 Kin. 5:18; 7:17, 19, 20 [b]Mal. 3:10
3 [a][Num. 5:2–4;12:10–14]
4 [a]2 Kin. 6:24
6 [a]2 Sam. 5:24 [b]1 Kin. 10:29
7 [a]Ps. 48:4–6
9 [1]Calamity
12 [a]2 Kin. 6:24–29 [1]Hide themselves in ambush

and gold and clothing, and went
and hid *them;* then they came
back and entered another tent,
and carried *some* from there
also, and went and hid *it.*
9 Then they said to one another,
"We are not doing right.
This day *is* a day of good news,
and we remain silent. If we wait
until morning light, some [1]punishment
will come upon us. Now
therefore, come, let us go and
tell the king's household."
10 So they went and called to
the gatekeepers of the city, and
told them, saying, "We went to
the Syrian camp, and surprisingly
no one *was* there, not a
human sound—only horses
and donkeys tied, and the tents
intact."
11 And the gatekeepers called
out, and they told *it* to the king's
household inside.
12 So the king arose in the night
and said to his servants, "Let me
now tell you what the Syrians
have done to us. They know
that we *are* [a]hungry; therefore
they have gone out of the camp
to [1]hide themselves in the field,
saying, 'When they come out
of the city, we shall catch them
alive, and get into the city.' "
13 And one of his servants answered
and said, "Please, let
several *men* take five of the remaining
horses which are left in
the city. Look, they *may either
become* like all the multitude
of Israel that are left in it; or
indeed, *I say,* they *may become*
like all the multitude of Israel
left from those who are consumed;
so let us send them and
see."
14 Therefore they took two
chariots with horses; and the

king sent them in the direction of the Syrian army, saying, "Go and see."

15 And they went after them to the Jordan; and indeed all the road *was* full of garments and weapons which the Syrians had thrown away in their haste. So the messengers returned and told the king.

16 Then the people went out and plundered the tents of the Syrians. So a seah of fine flour was *sold* for a shekel, and two seahs of barley for a shekel, [a]according to the word of the LORD.

17 Now the king had appointed the officer on whose hand he leaned to have charge of the gate. But the people trampled him in the gate, and he died, just [a]as the man of God had said, who spoke when the king came down to him.

18 So it happened just as the man of God had spoken to the king, saying, [a]"Two seahs of barley for a shekel, and a seah of fine flour for a shekel, shall be *sold* tomorrow about this time in the gate of Samaria."

19 Then that officer had answered the man of God, and said, "Now look, *if* the LORD would make windows in heaven, could such a thing be?" And he had said, "In fact, you shall see *it* with your eyes, but you shall not eat of it."

20 And so it happened to him, for the people trampled him in the gate, and he died.

8 Then E·lī′sha spoke to the woman [a]whose son he had restored to life, saying, "Arise and go, you and your household, and stay wherever you can; for the LORD [b]has called for a [c]famine, and furthermore, it will come upon the land for seven years."

2 So the woman arose and did according to the saying of the man of God, and she went with her household and dwelt in the land of the Phi·lis′tines seven years.

3 It came to pass, at the end of seven years, that the woman returned from the land of the Phi·lis′tines; and she went to make an appeal to the king for her house and for her land.

4 Then the king talked with [a]Ge·hā′zī, the servant of the man of God, saying, "Tell me, please, all the great things E·lī′sha has done."

5 Now it happened, as he was telling the king how he had restored the dead to life, that there was the woman whose son he had [a]restored to life, appealing to the king for her house and for her land. And Ge·hā′zī said, "My lord, O king, this *is* the woman, and this *is* her son whom E·lī′sha restored to life."

6 And when the king asked the woman, she told him. So the king appointed a certain officer for her, saying, "Restore all that *was* hers, and all the proceeds of the field from the day that she left the land until now."

7 Then E·lī′sha went to Damascus, and [a]Ben-Hā′dad king of Syria was sick; and it was told him, saying, "The man of God has come here."

8 And the king said to [a]Haz′a·el, [b]"Take a present in your hand, and go to meet the man of God, and [c]inquire of the LORD

16 [a]2 Kin. 7:1
17 [a]2 Kin. 6:32; 7:2
18 [a]2 Kin. 7:1

CHAPTER 8

1 [a]2 Kin. 4:18, 31–35 [b]Hag. 1:11 [c]2 Sam. 21:1
4 [a]2 Kin. 4:12; 5:20–27
5 [a]2 Kin. 4:35
7 [a]2 Kin. 6:24
8 [a]1 Kin. 19:15 [b]1 Sam. 9:7 [c]2 Kin. 1:2

by him, saying, 'Shall I recover
from this disease?' "
9 So [a]Haz′a·el went to meet
him and took a present with
him, of every good thing of Damascus, forty camel-loads; and
he came and stood before him,
and said, "Your son Ben-Hā′dad
king of Syria has sent me to you,
saying, 'Shall I recover from this
disease?' "
10 And E·lī′sha said to him, "Go,
say to him, 'You shall certainly
recover.' However the LORD has
shown me that [a]he will really
die."
11 Then he [1]set his countenance
in a stare until he was ashamed;
and the man of God [a]wept.
12 And Haz′a·el said, "Why is
my lord weeping?" He answered,
"Because I know [a]the evil that
you will do to the children of Israel: Their strongholds you will
set on fire, and their young men
you will kill with the sword; and
you [b]will dash their children,
and rip open their women with
child."
13 So Haz′a·el said, "But what
[a]*is* your servant—a dog, that he
should do this gross thing?" And
E·lī′sha answered, [b]"The LORD
has shown me that you *will be-*
come king over Syria."
14 Then he departed from E·lī′-
sha, and came to his master, who
said to him, "What did E·lī′sha
say to you?" And he answered,
"He told me you would surely
recover."
15 But it happened on the next
day that he took a thick cloth and
dipped *it* in water, and spread *it*
over his face so that he died; and
Haz′a·el reigned in his place.
16 Now [a]in the fifth year of
Jō′ram the son of Ā′hab, king
of Israel, Je·hosh′a·phat *having*
been king of Judah, [b]Je·hō′ram
the son of Je·hosh′a·phat began
to reign as [1]king of Judah.
17 He was [a]thirty-two years
old when he became king,
and he reigned eight years in
Jerusalem.
18 And he walked in the way
of the kings of Israel, just as the
house of Ā′hab had done, for
[a]the daughter of Ā′hab was his
wife; and he did evil in the sight
of the LORD.
19 Yet the LORD would not destroy Judah, for the sake of His
servant David, [a]as He promised
him to give a lamp to him *and*
his sons forever.
20 In his days [a]Ē′dom revolted
against Judah's authority, [b]and
made a king over themselves.
21 So [1]Jō′ram went to Zā′ir, and
all his chariots with him. Then
he rose by night and attacked
the Ē′dom·ītes who had surrounded him and the captains
of the chariots; and the troops
fled to their tents.
22 Thus Ē′dom has been in revolt against Judah's authority to
this day. [a]And Lib′nah revolted
at that time.
23 Now the rest of the acts of
Jō′ram, and all that he did, *are*
they not written in the book of
the chronicles of the kings of
Judah?
24 So Jō′ram [1]rested with his
fathers, and was buried with
his fathers in the City of David. Then [a]Ā·ha·zī′ah[2] his son
reigned in his place.
25 In the twelfth year of Jō′ram
the son of Ā′hab, king of Israel,
Ā·ha·zī′ah the son of Je·hō′ram,
king of Judah, began to reign.
26 Ā·ha·zī′ah *was* [a]twenty-two

9 [a]1 Kin. 19:15
10 [a]2 Kin. 8:15
11 [a]Luke 19:41 [1]*fixed his gaze*
12 [a]Amos 1:3, 4 [b]Hos. 13:16
13 [a]1 Sam. 17:43 [b]1 Kin. 19:15
16 [a]2 Kin. 1:17; 3:1 [b]2 Chr. 21:3 [1]Co-regent with his father
17 [a]2 Chr. 21:5–10
18 [a]2 Kin. 8:26, 27
19 [a]2 Sam. 7:13
20 [a]Gen. 27:40 [b]1 Kin. 22:47
21 [1]*Jehoram,* v. 16
22 [a]Josh. 21:13
24 [a]2 Chr. 22:1, 7 [1]Died and joined his ancestors [2]Or *Azariah* or *Jehoahaz*
26 [a]2 Chr. 22:2

years old when he became king,
and he reigned one year in Jerusalem. His mother's name *was*
Ath·a·lī'ah the granddaughter of
Om'rī, king of Israel.
27 [a]And he walked in the way
of the house of Ā'hab, and did
evil in the sight of the LORD, like
the house of Ā'hab, for he *was*
the son-in-law of the house of
Ā'hab.
28 Now he went [a]with Jō'ram
the son of Ā'hab to war against
Haz'a·el king of Syria at [b]Rā'-
moth Gil'ē·ad; and the Syrians
wounded Jō'ram.
29 Then [a]King Jō'ram went
back to Jez'rē·el to recover from
the wounds which the Syrians
had inflicted on him at [1]Rā'mah,
when he fought against Haz'a·el
king of Syria. [b]And Ā·ha·zī'ah
the son of Je·hō'ram, king of
Judah, went down to see Jō'ram
the son of Ā'hab in Jez'rē·el, because he was sick.

9

And E·lī'sha the prophet
called one of [a]the sons of
the prophets, and said to him,
[b]"Get[1] yourself ready, take this
flask of oil in your hand, [c]and go
to Rā'moth Gil'ē·ad.
2 "Now when you arrive at
that place, look there for Jē'hū
the son of Je·hosh'a·phat, the
son of Nim'shī, and go in and
make him rise up from among
[a]his associates, and take him to
an inner room.
3 "Then [a]take the flask of oil,
and pour *it* on his head, and
say, 'Thus says the LORD: "I have
anointed you king over Israel." '
Then open the door and flee,
and do not delay."
4 So the young man, the servant of the prophet, went to Rā'-
moth Gil'ē·ad.
5 And when he arrived, there
were the captains of the army
sitting; and he said, "I have a
message for you, Commander."
Jē'hū said, "For which *one* of
us?" And he said, "For you,
Commander."
6 Then he arose and went into
the house. And he poured the
oil on his head, and said to him,
[a]"Thus says the LORD God of
Israel: 'I have anointed you king
over the people of the LORD, over
Israel.
7 'You shall strike down the
house of Ā'hab your master, that
I may [a]avenge the blood of My
servants the prophets, and the
blood of all the servants of the
LORD, [b]at the hand of Jez'e·bel.
8 'For the whole house of
Ā'hab shall perish; and [a]I will
cut off from Ā'hab all [b]the males
in Israel, both [c]bond and free.
9 'So I will make the house
of Ā'hab like the house of
[a]Jer·o·bō'am the son of Nē'bat,
and like the house of [b]Bā'a·sha
the son of A·hī'jah.
10 [a]'The dogs shall eat Jez'e·bel
on the plot *of ground* at Jez'rē·el,
and *there shall be* none to bury
her.' " And he opened the door
and fled.
11 Then Jē'hū came out to the
servants of his master, and *one*
said to him, "*Is* all well? Why
did [a]this madman come to you?"
And he said to them, "You know
the man and his babble."
12 And they said, "A lie! Tell us
now." So he said, "Thus and thus
he spoke to me, saying, 'Thus
says the LORD: "I have anointed
you king over Israel." ' "
13 Then each man hastened [a]to
take his garment and put *it* [1]un-
der him on the top of the steps;

27 [a]2 Chr. 22:3, 4
28 [a]2 Chr. 22:5 [b]1 Kin. 22:3, 29
29 [a]2 Kin. 9:15 [b]2 Chr. 22:6, 7 [1]*Ramoth*, v. 28

CHAPTER 9

1 [a]1 Kin. 20:35 [b]2 Kin. 4:29 [c]2 Kin. 8:28, 29 [1]Lit. *Gird up your loins*
2 [a]2 Kin. 9:5, 11
3 [a]1 Kin. 19:16
6 [a]2 Chr. 22:7
7 [a][Deut. 32:35, 41] [b]1 Kin. 18:4; 21:15
8 [a]2 Kin. 10:17 [b]1 Sam. 25:22 [c]Deut. 32:36
9 [a]1 Kin. 14:10; 15:29; 21:22 [b]1 Kin. 16:3, 11
10 [a]1 Kin. 21:23
11 [a]Jer. 29:26
13 [a]Matt. 21:7, 8 [1]Lit. *under his feet*

and they blew trumpets, saying,
"Jē′hū is king!"
14 So Jē′hū the son of Je·hosh′-
a·phat, the son of Nim′shī, conspired against [a]Jō′ram. (Now
Jō′ram had been defending Rā′-
moth Gil′ē·ad, he and all Israel,
against Haz′a·el king of Syria.
15 But [a]King [1]Jō′ram had returned to Jez′rē·el to recover
from the wounds which the Syrians had inflicted on him when
he fought with Haz′a·el king of
Syria.) And Jē′hū said, "If you
are so minded, let no one leave
or escape from the city to go and
tell *it* in Jez′rē·el."
16 So Jē′hū rode in a chariot
and went to Jez′rē·el, for Jō′-
ram was laid up there; [a]and
Ā·ha·zī′ah king of Judah had
come down to see Jō′ram.
17 Now a watchman stood on
the tower in Jez′rē·el, and he
saw the company of Jē′hū as he
came, and said, "I see a company of men." And Jō′ram said,
"Get a horseman and send him
to meet them, and let him say,
'[1]*Is it* peace?' "
18 So the horseman went to
meet him, and said, "Thus says
the king: '*Is it* peace?' " And
Jē′hū said, "What have you to do
with peace? [1]Turn around and
follow me." So the watchman reported, saying, "The messenger
went to them, but is not coming
back."
19 Then he sent out a second
horseman who came to them,
and said, "Thus says the king:
'*Is it* peace?' " And Jē′hū answered, "What have you to do
with peace? Turn around and
follow me."
20 So the watchman reported,
saying, "He went up to them
and is not coming back; and
the driving *is* like the driving of
Jē′hū the son of Nim′shī, for he
drives furiously!"
21 Then Jō′ram said, [1]"Make
ready." And his chariot was
made ready. Then [a]Jō′ram king
of Israel and Ā·ha·zī′ah king
of Judah went out, each in his
chariot; and they went out to
meet Jē′hū, and [2]met him [b]on
the property of Nā′both the Jez′-
rē·el·īte.
22 Now it happened, when Jō′-
ram saw Jē′hū, that he said,
"*Is it* peace, Jē′hū?" So he answered, "What peace, as long
as the harlotries of your mother
Jez′e·bel and her witchcraft *are*
so many?"
23 Then Jō′ram turned around
and fled, and said to Ā·ha·zī′ah,
"Treachery, Ā·ha·zī′ah!"
24 Now Jē′hū [1]drew his bow with
full strength and shot Je·hō′ram
between his arms; and the arrow
came out at his heart, and he
sank down in his chariot.
25 Then *Jē′hū* said to Bid′kar
his captain, "Pick *him* up, *and*
throw him into the tract of the
field of Nā′both the Jez′rē·el·īte;
for remember, when you and
I were riding together behind
Ā′hab his father, that [a]the LORD
laid this [b]burden upon him:
26 'Surely I saw yesterday the
blood of Nā′both and the blood
of his sons,' says the LORD, [a]'and
I will repay you [1]in this plot,'
says the LORD. Now therefore,
take *and* throw him on the plot
of ground, according to the word
of the LORD."
27 But when Ā·ha·zī′ah king of
Judah saw *this,* he fled by the
road to [1]Beth Hag′gan. So Jē′hū
pursued him, and said, [2]"Shoot

14 [a]2 Kin. 8:28
15 [a]2 Kin. 8:29 [1]*Jehoram,* v. 24
16 [a]2 Kin. 8:29
17 [1]Are you peaceful?
18 [1]Lit. *Turn behind me*
21 [a]1 Kin. 19:17 [b]1 Kin. 21:1–14 [1]*Harness up* [2]Lit. *found*
24 [1]Lit. *filled his hand*
25 [a]1 Kin. 21:19, 24–29 [b]Is. 13:1
26 [a]1 Kin. 21:13, 19 [1]*on this property*
27 [1]Lit. *The Garden House* [2]Lit. *Strike*

him also in the chariot." *And*
they shot him at the Ascent of
Gur, which is by Ib′lē·am. Then
he fled to [a]Me·gid′dō, and died
there.
28 And his servants carried him
in the chariot to Jerusalem, and
buried him in his tomb with his
fathers in the City of David.
29 In the eleventh year of Jō′-
ram the son of Ā′hab, Ā·ha·zī′ah
had become king over Judah.
30 Now when Jē′hū had come
to Jez′rē·el, Jez′e·bel heard *of*
it; [a]and she put paint on her
eyes and adorned her head, and
looked through a window.
31 Then, as Jē′hū entered at
the gate, she said, [a]"*Is it* peace,
Zim′rī, murderer of your master?"
32 And he looked up at the
window, and said, "Who *is* on
my side? Who?" So two *or* three
eunuchs looked out at him.
33 Then he said, "Throw her
down." So they threw her down,
and *some* of her blood spattered
on the wall and on the horses;
and he trampled her underfoot.
34 And when he had gone in,
he ate and drank. Then he said,
"Go now, see to this accursed
woman, and bury her, for [a]she
was a king's daughter."
35 So they went to bury her, but
they found no more of her than
the skull and the feet and the
palms of *her* hands.
36 Therefore they came back
and told him. And he said, "This
is the word of the LORD, which
He spoke by His servant E·lī′jah
the Tish′bīte, saying, [a]'On the
plot *of ground* at Jez′rē·el dogs
shall eat the flesh of Jez′e·bel;
37 'and the corpse of Jez′e·bel
shall be [a]as refuse on the surface

27 [a]2 Chr. 22:7, 9
30 [a]Ezek. 23:40
31 [a]1 Kin. 16:9–20
34 [a]1 Kin. 16:31
36 [a]1 Kin. 21:23
37 [a]Ps. 83:10

CHAPTER 10

1 [1]So with MT, Syr., Tg.; LXX *Samaria;* Vg. *city* [2]*the guardians of*
3 [1]*most upright*
4 [a]2 Kin. 9:24, 27 [1]Lit. *stand before*

of the field, in the plot at Jez′-
rē·el, so that they shall not say,
"Here *lies* Jez′e·bel." ' "

10 Now Ā′hab had sev-
enty sons in Samaria.
And Jē′hū wrote and sent letters to Samaria, to the rulers of
[1]Jez′rē·el, to the elders, and to
[2]those who reared Ā′hab's *sons,*
saying:

2 Now as soon as this letter
comes to you, since your
master's sons *are* with you,
and you have chariots and
horses, a fortified city also,
and weapons,
3 choose the [1]best qualified
of your master's sons, set
him on his father's throne,
and fight for your master's
house.

4 But they were exceedingly
afraid, and said, "Look, [a]two
kings could not [1]stand up to
him; how then can we stand?"
5 And he who *was* in charge
of the house, and he who *was*
in charge of the city, the elders
also, and those who reared *the*
sons, sent to Jē′hū, saying, "We
are your servants, we will do all
you tell us; but we will not make
anyone king. Do *what is* good in
your sight."
6 Then he wrote a second letter to them, saying:

If you *are* for me and will
obey my voice, take the
heads of the men, your
master's sons, and come to
me at Jez′rē·el by this time
tomorrow.

Now the king's sons, seventy
persons, *were* with the great

men of the city, *who* were rear-
ing them.
7 So it was, when the letter
came to them, that they took
the king's sons and [a]slaughtered
seventy persons, put their heads
in baskets and sent *them* to him
at Jez'rē·el.
8 Then a messenger came and
told him, saying, "They have
brought the heads of the king's
sons." And he said, "Lay them in
two heaps at the entrance of the
gate until morning."
9 So it was, in the morning,
that he went out and stood, and
said to all the people, "You *are*
righteous. Indeed [a]I conspired
against my master and killed
him; but who killed all these?
10 "Know now that nothing
shall [a]fall to the earth of the
word of the LORD which the LORD
spoke concerning the house of
Ā'hab; for the LORD has done
what He spoke [b]by His servant
E·lī'jah."
11 So Jē'hū killed all who remained of the house of Ā'hab in
Jez'rē·el, and all his great men
and his close acquaintances and
his priests, until he left him none
remaining.
12 And he arose and departed
and went to Samaria. On the way,
at [1]Beth Ē'ked of the Shepherds,
13 [a]Jē'hū met with the brothers
of Ā·ha·zī'ah king of Judah, and
said, "Who *are* you?" So they answered, "We *are* the brothers of
Ā·ha·zī'ah; we have come down
to greet the sons of the king and
the sons of the queen mother."
14 And he said, "Take them
alive!" So they took them alive,
and [a]killed them at the well of
[1]Beth Ē'ked, forty-two men; and
he left none of them.
15 Now when he departed from
there, he [1]met [a]Je·hon'a·dab the
son of [b]Rē'chab, *coming* to meet
him; and he greeted him and said
to him, "Is your heart right, as
my heart *is* toward your heart?"
And Je·hon'a·dab answered, "It
is." *Jē'hū said,* "If it is, [c]give *me*
your hand." So he gave *him* his
hand, and he took him up to him
into the chariot.
16 Then he said, "Come with
me, and see my [a]zeal for the
LORD." So they had him ride in
his chariot.
17 And when he came to Samaria, [a]he killed all who remained to Ā'hab in Samaria,
till he had destroyed them, according to the word of the LORD
[b]which He spoke to E·lī'jah.
18 Then Jē'hū gathered all the
people together, and said to
them, [a]"Ā'hab served Bā'al a little, Jē'hū will serve him much.
19 "Now therefore, call to me
all the [a]prophets of Bā'al, all his
servants, and all his priests. Let
no one be missing, for I have a
great sacrifice for Bā'al. Whoever is missing shall not live."
But Jē'hū acted deceptively, with
the intent of destroying the worshipers of Bā'al.
20 And Jē'hū said, [1]"Proclaim a
solemn assembly for Bā'al." So
they proclaimed *it.*
21 Then Jē'hū sent throughout
all Israel; and all the worshipers
of Bā'al came, so that there was
not a man left who did not come.
So they came into the [1]temple of
Bā'al, and the [a]temple of Bā'al
was full from one end to the
other.
22 And he said to the one
in charge of the wardrobe,
"Bring out vestments for all the

7 [a]1 Kin. 21:21
9 [a]2 Kin. 9:14–24
10 [a]1 Sam. 3:19 [b]1 Kin. 21:17–24, 29
12 [1]Or *The Shearing House*
13 [a]2 Chr. 22:8
14 [a]2 Chr. 22:8 [1]Or *The Shearing House*
15 [a]Jer. 35:6 [b]1 Chr. 2:55 [c]Ezra 10:19 [1]Lit. *found*
16 [a]1 Kin. 19:10
17 [a]2 Kin. 9:8 [b]1 Kin. 21:21, 29
18 [a]1 Kin. 16:31, 32
19 [a]1 Kin. 18:19; 22:6
20 [1]Consecrate
21 [a]1 Kin. 16:32 [1]Lit. *house*

worshipers of Bā′al." So he brought out vestments for them.

23 Then Jē′hū and Je·hon′a·dab the son of Rē′chab went into the temple of Bā′al, and said to the worshipers of Bā′al, "Search and see that no servants of the LORD are here with you, but only the worshipers of Bā′al."

24 So they went in to offer sacrifices and burnt offerings. Now Jē′hū had appointed for himself eighty men on the outside, and had said, "*If* any of the men whom I have brought into your hands escapes, *whoever lets him escape, it shall be* [a]his life for the life of the other."

25 Now it happened, as soon as he had made an end of offering the burnt offering, that Jē′hū said to the guard and to the captains, "Go in *and* kill them; let no one come out!" And they killed them with the edge of the sword; then the guards and the officers threw *them* out, and went into the [1]inner room of the temple of Bā′al.

26 And they brought the [a]*sacred* pillars out of the temple of Bā′al and burned them.

27 Then they broke down the *sacred* pillar of Bā′al, and tore down the [1]temple of Bā′al and [a]made it a refuse dump to this day.

28 Thus Jē′hū destroyed Bā′al from Israel.

29 However Jē′hū did not turn away from the sins of Jer·o·bō′am the son of Nē′bat, who had made Israel sin, *that is*, from [a]the golden calves that *were* at Beth′el and Dan.

30 And the LORD [a]said to Jē′hū, "Because you have done well in doing *what is* right in My sight, *and* have done to the house of Ā′hab all that *was* in My heart, [b]your sons shall sit on the throne of Israel to the fourth *generation*."

31 But Jē′hū [1]took no heed to walk in the law of the LORD God of Israel with all his heart; for he did not depart from [a]the sins of Jer·o·bō′am, who had made Israel sin.

32 In those days the LORD began to cut off *parts* of Israel; and [a]Haz′a·el conquered them in all the territory of Israel

33 from the Jordan eastward: all the land of Gil′ē·ad—Gad, Reuben, and Ma·nas′seh—from [a]A·rō′er, which *is* by the River Ar′non, including [b]Gil′ē·ad and Bā′shan.

34 Now the rest of the acts of Jē′hū, all that he did, and all his might, *are* they not written in the book of the chronicles of the kings of Israel?

35 So Jē′hū [1]rested with his fathers, and they buried him in Samaria. Then [a]Je·hō′a·haz his son reigned in his place.

36 And the period that Jē′hū reigned over Israel in Samaria *was* twenty-eight years.

11 When [a]Ath·a·lī′ah [b]the mother of Ā·ha·zī′ah saw that her son was [c]dead, she arose and destroyed all the royal heirs.

2 But [1]Je·hosh′e·ba, the daughter of King Jō′ram, sister of [a]Ā·ha·zī′ah, took [2]Jō′ash the son of Ā·ha·zī′ah, and stole him away from among the king's sons *who were* being murdered; and they hid him and his nurse in the bedroom, from Ath·a·lī′ah, so that he was not killed.

3 So he was hidden with her

24 [a]1 Kin. 20:39
25 [1]Lit. *city*
26 [a][Deut. 7:5, 25]
27 [a]Ezra 6:11 [1]Lit. *house*
29 [a]1 Kin. 12:28–30; 13:33, 34
30 [a]2 Kin. 9:6, 7 [b]2 Kin. 13:1, 10; 14:23; 15:8, 12
31 [a]1 Kin. 14:16 [1]*was not careful*
32 [a]2 Kin. 8:12; 13:22
33 [a]Deut. 2:36 [b]Amos 1:3–5
35 [a]2 Kin. 13:1 [1]Died and joined his ancestors

CHAPTER 11

1 [a]2 Chr. 22:10 [b]2 Kin. 8:26 [c]2 Kin. 9:27
2 [a]2 Kin. 8:25 [1]*Jehoshabeath*, 2 Chr. 22:11 [2]Or *Jehoash*

in the house of the LORD for six years, while Ath·a·lī′ah reigned over the land.

4 In [a]the seventh year Je·hoi′a·da sent and brought the captains of hundreds—of the bodyguards and the [1]escorts—and brought them into the house of the LORD to him. And he made a covenant with them and took an oath from them in the house of the LORD, and showed them the king's son.

5 Then he commanded them, saying, "This *is* what you shall do: One-third of you who [1]come on duty [a]on the Sabbath shall be keeping watch over the king's house,

6 "one-third *shall be* at the gate of Sūr, and one-third at the gate behind the escorts. You shall keep the watch of the house, lest it be broken down.

7 "The two [1]contingents of you who go off duty on the Sabbath shall keep the watch of the house of the LORD for the king.

8 "But you shall surround the king on all sides, every man with his weapons in his hand; and whoever comes within range, let him be put to death. You are to be with the king as he goes out and as he comes in."

9 [a]So the captains of the hundreds did according to all that Je·hoi′a·da the priest commanded. Each of them took his men who were to be on duty on the Sabbath, with those who were going off duty on the Sabbath, and came to Je·hoi′a·da the priest.

10 And the priest gave the captains of hundreds the spears and shields which *had belonged* to King David, [a]that were in the temple of the LORD.

11 Then the escorts stood, every man with his weapons in his hand, all around the king, from the right [1]side of the temple to the left side of the temple, by the altar and the house.

12 And he brought out the king's son, put the crown on him, and *gave him* the [a]Testimony;[1] they made him king and anointed him, and they clapped their hands and said, [b]"Long live the king!"

13 [a]Now when Ath·a·lī′ah heard the noise of the escorts *and* the people, she came to the people *in* the temple of the LORD.

14 When she looked, there was the king standing by [a]a pillar according to custom; and the leaders and the trumpeters were by the king. All the people of the land were rejoicing and blowing trumpets. So Ath·a·lī′ah tore her clothes and cried out, "Treason! Treason!"

15 And Je·hoi′a·da the priest commanded the captains of the hundreds, the officers of the army, and said to them, "Take her outside [1]under guard, and slay with the sword whoever follows her." For the priest had said, "Do not let her be killed in the house of the LORD."

16 So they seized her; and she went by way of the horses' entrance *into* the king's house, and there she was killed.

17 [a]Then Je·hoi′a·da [b]made a covenant between the LORD, the king, and the people, that they should be the LORD's people, and *also* [c]between the king and the people.

18 And all the people of the land

4 [a]2 Chr. 23:1 [1]*guards*
5 [a]1 Chr. 9:25 [1]Lit. *enter in*
7 [1]*companies*
9 [a]2 Chr. 23:8
10 [a]2 Sam. 8:7
11 [1]Lit. *shoulder*
12 [a]Ex. 25:16; 31:18 [b]1 Sam. 10:24 [1]Law, Ex. 25:16, 21; Deut. 31:9
13 [a]2 Chr. 23:12
14 [a]2 Chr. 34:31
15 [1]Lit. *between ranks*
17 [a]2 Chr. 23:16 [b]Josh. 24:24, 25 [c]2 Sam. 5:3

went to the [a]temple of Bā'al, and
tore it down. They thoroughly
[b]broke in pieces its altars and
[1]images, and [c]killed Mat'tan the
priest of Bā'al before the altars.
And [d]the priest appointed [2]offi-
cers over the house of the LORD.
19 Then he took the captains
of hundreds, the bodyguards,
the escorts, and all the people
of the land; and they brought
the king down from the house
of the LORD, and went by way
of the gate of the escorts to the
king's house. Then he sat on the
throne of the kings.
20 So all the people of the land
rejoiced; and the city was quiet,
for they had slain Ath·a·lī'ah
with the sword *in* the king's
house.
21 Je·hō'ash *was* [a]seven years
old when he became king.

12 In the seventh year of
Jē'hū, [a]Je·hō'ash[1] became
king, and he reigned forty years
in Jerusalem. His mother's name
was Zib'i·ah of Bē·er·shē'ba.
2 Je·hō'ash did *what was* right
in the sight of the LORD all the
days in which [a]Je·hoi'a·da the
priest instructed him.
3 But [a]the [1]high places were
not taken away; the people still
sacrificed and burned incense
on the high places.
4 And Je·hō'ash said to the
priests, [a]"All the money of the
dedicated gifts that are brought
into the house of the LORD—each
man's [b]census[1] money, each
man's [c]assessment money—
and all the money that [2]a man
[d]purposes in his heart to bring
into the house of the LORD,
5 "let the priests take *it* themselves, each from his constituency; and let them repair the
[1]damages of the temple, wherever any dilapidation is found."
6 Now it was so, by the twenty-
third year of King Je·hō'ash,
[a]*that* the priests had not repaired
the damages of the temple.
7 [a]So King Je·hō'ash called
Je·hoi'a·da the priest and the
other priests, and said to them,
"Why have you not repaired the
damages of the temple? Now
therefore, do not take *more*
money from your constituency,
but deliver it for repairing the
damages of the temple."
8 And the priests agreed that
they would neither receive *more*
money from the people, nor repair the damages of the temple.
9 Then Je·hoi'a·da the priest
took [a]a chest, bored a hole in its
lid, and set it beside the altar, on
the right side as one comes into
the house of the LORD; and the
priests who [1]kept the door put
[b]there all the money brought
into the house of the LORD.
10 So it was, whenever they saw
that *there was* much money in
the chest, that the king's [a]scribe[1]
and the high priest came up and
[2]put it in bags, and counted the
money that was found in the
house of the LORD.
11 Then they gave the money,
which had been apportioned,
into the hands of those who did
the work, who had the oversight
of the house of the LORD; and
they [1]paid it out to the carpenters and builders who worked
on the house of the LORD,
12 and to masons and stonecutters, and for buying timber and
hewn stone, to [a]repair the damage of the house of the LORD,
and for all that was paid out to
repair the temple.

18 [a]2 Kin. 10:26, 27 [b][Deut. 12:3] [c]1 Kin. 18:40 [d]2 Chr. 23:18 [1]Idols [2]Lit. *offices*
21 [a]2 Chr. 24:1–14

CHAPTER 12

1 [a]2 Chr. 24:1 [1]*Joash,* 2 Kin. 11:2ff.
2 [a]2 Kin. 11:4
3 [a]2 Kin. 14:4; 15:35 [1]Places for pagan worship
4 [a]2 Kin. 22:4 [b]Ex. 30:13–16 [c]Lev. 27:2–28 [d]Ex. 35:5 [1]Lit. *the money coming over* [2]*any man's heart prompts him to bring*
5 [1]Lit. *breaches*
6 [a]2 Chr. 24:5
7 [a]2 Chr. 24:6
9 [a]2 Chr. 23:1; 24:8 [b]Mark 12:41 [1]*guarded at the door*
10 [a]2 Sam. 8:17 [1]*secretary* [2]*tied it up*
11 [1]Lit. *weighed*
12 [a]2 Kin. 22:5, 6

13 However [a]there were not
made for the house of the
LORD basins of silver, trimmers,
sprinkling-bowls, trumpets, any
articles of gold or articles of
silver, from the money brought
into the house of the LORD.
14 But they gave that to the
workmen, and they repaired the
house of the LORD with it.
15 Moreover [a]they did not require an account from the men
into whose hand they delivered
the money to be paid to workmen, for they dealt faithfully.
16 [a]The money from the trespass offerings and the money
from the sin offerings was not
brought into the house of the
LORD. [b]It belonged to the priests.
17 [a]Haz′a·el king of Syria went
up and fought against Gath, and
took it; then [b]Haz′a·el set his
face to [1]go up to Jerusalem.
18 And Je·hō′ash king of Judah
[a]took all the sacred things that
his fathers, Je·hosh′a·phat and
Je·hō′ram and Ā·ha·zī′ah, kings
of Judah, had dedicated, and his
own sacred things, and all the
gold found in the treasuries of
the house of the LORD and in the
king's house, and sent *them* to
Haz′a·el king of Syria. Then he
went away from Jerusalem.
19 Now the rest of the acts of
[1]Jō′ash, and all that he did, *are*
they not written in the book of
the chronicles of the kings of
Judah?
20 And [a]his servants arose and
formed a conspiracy, and killed
Jō′ash in the house of [1]the Mil′lō,
which goes down to Sil′la.
21 For [1]Joz′a·char the son of
Shim′ē·ath and Je·hō′za·bad the
son of [2]Shō′mer, his servants,
struck him. So he died, and they
buried him with his fathers in the
City of David. Then [a]Am·a·zī′ah
his son reigned in his place.

13

In the twenty-third year
of [a]Jō′ash[1] the son of
Ā·ha·zī′ah, king of Judah, [b]Je·hō′-
a·haz the son of Jē′hū became
king over Israel in Samaria, *and
reigned* seventeen years.
2 And he did evil in the sight
of the LORD, and followed the
[a]sins of Jer·o·bō′am the son of
Nē′bat, who had made Israel sin.
He did not [1]depart from them.
3 Then [a]the anger of the LORD
was aroused against Israel, and
He delivered them into the hand
of [b]Haz′a·el king of Syria, and
into the hand of [c]Ben-Hā′dad the
son of Haz′a·el, all *their* days.
4 So Je·hō′a·haz [a]pleaded with
the LORD, and the LORD listened
to him; for [b]He saw the oppression of Israel, because the king
of Syria oppressed them.
5 [a]Then the LORD gave Israel a
deliverer, so that they escaped
from under the hand of the Syrians; and the children of Israel
dwelt in their tents as before.
6 Nevertheless they did not depart from the sins of the house
of Jer·o·bō′am, who had made
Israel sin, *but* walked in them;
[a]and the [1]wooden image also
remained in Samaria.
7 For He left of the army of
Je·hō′a·haz only fifty horsemen,
ten chariots, and ten thousand
foot soldiers; for the king of
Syria had destroyed them [a]and
made them [b]like the dust at
threshing.
8 Now the rest of the acts of
Je·hō′a·haz, all that he did, and
his might, *are* they not written in
the book of the chronicles of the
kings of Israel?

13 [a]2 Chr. 24:14
15 [a]2 Kin. 22:7
16 [a][Lev. 5:15, 18] [b][Num. 18:9]
17 [a]2 Kin. 8:12 [b]2 Chr. 24:23 [1]Advance upon
18 [a]1 Kin. 15:18
19 [1]*Jehoash,* vv. 1–18
20 [a]2 Kin. 14:5 [1]Lit. *The Landfill*
21 [a]2 Chr. 24:27 [1]*Zabad,* 2 Chr. 24:26 [2]*Shimrith,* 2 Chr. 24:26

CHAPTER 13

1 [a]2 Kin. 12:1 [b]2 Kin. 10:35 [1]*Jehoash,* 2 Kin. 12:1–18
2 [a]1 Kin. 12:26–33 [1]Lit. *turn*
3 [a]Judg. 2:14 [b]2 Kin. 8:12 [c]Amos 1:4
4 [a][Ps. 78:34] [b][Ex. 3:7, 9]
5 [a]2 Kin. 13:25; 14:25, 27
6 [a]1 Kin. 16:33 [1]Heb. *Asherah,* a Canaanite goddess
7 [a]2 Kin. 10:32 [b][Amos 1:3]

9 So Je·hō′a·haz [1]rested with his fathers, and they buried him in Samaria. Then [2]Jō′ash his son reigned in his place.

10 In the thirty-seventh year of Jō′ash king of Judah, [1]Je·hō′ash the son of Je·hō′a·haz became king over Israel in Samaria, *and reigned* sixteen years.

11 And he did evil in the sight of the LORD. He did not depart from all the sins of Jer·o·bō′am the son of Nē′bat, who made Israel sin, *but* walked in them.

12 [a]Now the rest of the acts of Jō′ash, [b]all that he did, and [c]his might with which he fought against Am·a·zī′ah king of Judah, *are* they not written in the book of the chronicles of the kings of Israel?

13 So Jō′ash [a]rested[1] with his fathers. Then Jer·o·bō′am sat on his throne. And Jō′ash was buried in Samaria with the kings of Israel.

14 E·lī′sha had become sick with the illness of which he would die. Then Jō′ash the king of Israel came down to him, and wept over his face, and said, "O my father, my father, [a]the chariots of Israel and their horsemen!"

15 And E·lī′sha said to him, "Take a bow and some arrows." So he took himself a bow and some arrows.

16 Then he said to the king of Israel, "Put your hand on the bow." So he put his hand *on it*, and E·lī′sha put his hands on the king's hands.

17 And he said, "Open the east window"; and he opened *it*. Then E·lī′sha said, "Shoot"; and he shot. And he said, "The arrow of the LORD's deliverance and the arrow of deliverance from Syria; for you must strike the Syrians at [a]Ā′phek till you have destroyed *them*."

18 Then he said, "Take the arrows"; so he took *them*. And he said to the king of Israel, "Strike the ground"; so he struck three times, and stopped.

19 And the man of God was angry with him, and said, "You should have struck five or six times; then you would have struck Syria till you had destroyed *it!* [a]But now you will strike Syria *only* three times."

20 Then E·lī′sha [1]died, and they buried him. And the [a]*raiding* bands from Mō′ab invaded the land in the spring of the year.

21 So it was, as they were burying a man, that suddenly they spied a band *of raiders;* and they put the man in the tomb of E·lī′sha; and when the man was let down and touched the bones of E·lī′sha, he revived and stood on his feet.

22 And [a]Haz′a·el king of Syria oppressed Israel all the days of Je·hō′a·haz.

23 But the LORD was [a]gracious to them, had compassion on them, and [b]regarded them, [c]because of His covenant with Abraham, Isaac, and Jacob, and would not yet destroy them or cast them from His presence.

24 Now Haz′a·el king of Syria died. Then Ben-Hā′dad his son reigned in his place.

25 And [1]Je·hō′ash the son of Je·hō′a·haz recaptured from the hand of Ben-Hā′dad, the son of Haz′a·el, the cities which he had taken out of the hand of Je·hō′a·haz his father by war. [a]Three

9 [1]Died and joined his ancestors [2]Or *Jehoash*
10 [1]*Joash*, v. 9
12 [a]2 Kin. 14:8–15 [b]2 Kin. 13:14–19, 25 [c]2 Kin. 14:9
13 [a]2 Kin. 14:16 [1]Died and joined his ancestors
14 [a]2 Kin. 2:12
17 [a]1 Kin. 20:26
19 [a]2 Kin. 13:25
20 [a]2 Kin. 3:5; 24:2 [1]Having prophesied at least 55 years
22 [a]2 Kin. 8:12, 13
23 [a]2 Kin. 14:27 [b][Ex. 2:24, 25] [c]Ex. 32:13
25 [a]2 Kin. 13:18, 19 [1]*Joash*, vv. 12–14, 25

times Jō′ash defeated him and
recaptured the cities of Israel.

14 In [a]the second year of
Jō′ash the son of Je·hō′-
a·haz, king of Israel, [b]Am·a·zī′ah
the son of Jō′ash, king of Judah,
became king.
2 He was twenty-five years old
when he became king, and he
reigned twenty-nine years in Jerusalem. His mother's name was
Jē·hō·ad′dan of Jerusalem.
3 And he did *what was* right in
the sight of the LORD, yet not like
his father David; he did everything [a]as his father Jō′ash had
done.
4 [a]However the [1]high places
were not taken away, and the
people still sacrificed and burned
incense on the high places.
5 Now it happened, as soon as
the kingdom was established in
his hand, that he executed his
servants [a]who had murdered his
father the king.
6 But the children of the murderers he did not execute, according to what is written in
the Book of the Law of Moses,
in which the LORD commanded,
saying, [a]"Fathers shall not be put
to death for their children, nor
shall children be put to death for
their fathers; but a person shall
be put to death for his own sin."
7 [a]He killed ten thousand
Ē′dom·ītes in [b]the Valley of Salt,
and took [1]Sē′la by war, [c]and
called its name Jok′the·el to this
day.
8 [a]Then Am·a·zī′ah sent messengers to [1]Je·hō′ash the son
of Je·hō′a·haz, the son of Jē′hū,
king of Israel, saying, "Come, let
us face one another *in battle*."
9 And Je·hō′ash king of Israel
sent to Am·a·zī′ah king of Judah,
saying, [a]"The thistle that *was*
in Lebanon sent to the [b]cedar
that *was* in Lebanon, saying,
'Give your daughter to my son
as wife'; and a wild beast that
was in Lebanon passed by and
trampled the thistle.
10 "You have indeed defeated
Ē′dom, and [a]your heart has
[1]lifted you up. Glory *in that*, and
stay at home; for why should
you meddle with trouble so that
you fall—you and Judah with
you?"
11 But Am·a·zī′ah would not
heed. Therefore Je·hō′ash king
of Israel went out; so he and
Am·a·zī′ah king of Judah faced
one another at [a]Beth Shem′esh,
which *belongs* to Judah.
12 And Judah was defeated by
Israel, and every man fled to his
tent.
13 Then Je·hō′ash king of Israel captured Am·a·zī′ah king
of Judah, the son of Je·hō′ash,
the son of Ā·ha·zī′ah, at Beth
Shem′esh; and he went to Jerusalem, and broke down the wall
of Jerusalem from [a]the Gate of
Ē′phra·im to [b]the Corner Gate—
[1]four hundred cubits.
14 And he took all [a]the gold
and silver, all the articles that
were found in the house of the
LORD and in the treasuries of the
king's house, and hostages, and
returned to Samaria.
15 [a]Now the rest of the acts
of Je·hō′ash which he did—his
might, and how he fought with
Am·a·zī′ah king of Judah—*are*
they not written in the book of
the chronicles of the kings of
Israel?
16 So Je·hō′ash [1]rested with his
fathers, and was buried in Samaria with the kings of Israel.

CHAPTER 14

1 [a]2 Kin. 13:10 [b]2 Chr. 25:1, 2

3 [a]2 Kin. 12:2

4 [a]2 Kin. 12:3 [1]Places for pagan worship

5 [a]2 Kin. 12:20

6 [a][Ezek. 18:4, 20]

7 [a]2 Chr. 25:5–16 [b]2 Sam. 8:13 [c]Josh. 15:38 [1]Lit. *The Rock;* the city of Petra

8 [a]2 Chr. 25:17, 18 [1]*Joash*, 2 Kin. 13:9, 12–14, 25; 2 Chr. 25:17ff.

9 [a]Judg. 9:8–15 [b]1 Kin. 4:33

10 [a]Deut. 8:14 [1]Made you proud

11 [a]Josh. 19:38; 21:16

13 [a]Neh. 8:16; 12:39 [b]Jer. 31:38 [1]About 600 feet

14 [a]1 Kin. 7:51

15 [a]2 Kin. 13:12, 13

16 [1]Died and joined his ancestors

Then Jer·o·bō′am his son reigned in his place.

17 [a]Am·a·zī′ah the son of Jō′ash, king of Judah, lived fifteen years after the death of Je·hō′ash the son of Je·hō′a·haz, king of Israel.

18 Now the rest of the acts of Am·a·zī′ah, *are* they not written in the book of the chronicles of the kings of Judah?

19 And [a]they formed a conspiracy against him in Jerusalem, and he fled to [b]Lā′chish; but they sent after him to Lā′chish and killed him there.

20 Then they brought him on horses, and he was buried at Jerusalem with his fathers in the City of David.

21 And all the people of Judah took [a]Az·a·rī′ah,[1] who *was* sixteen years old, and made him king instead of his father Am·a·zī′ah.

22 He built [a]Ē′lath[1] and restored it to Judah, after [2]the king rested with his fathers.

23 In the fifteenth year of Am·a·zī′ah the son of Jō′ash, king of Judah, Jer·o·bō′am the son of Jō′ash, king of Israel, became king in Samaria, *and reigned* forty-one years.

24 And he did evil in the sight of the LORD; he did not depart from all the [a]sins of Jer·o·bō′am the son of Nē′bat, who had made Israel sin.

25 He [a]restored the [1]territory of Israel [b]from the entrance of Hā′math to [c]the[2] Sea of the Ar′a·bah, according to the word of the LORD God of Israel, which He had spoken through His servant [d]Jonah the son of A·mit′taī, the prophet who *was* from [e]Gath Hē′pher.

26 For the LORD [a]saw *that* the affliction of Israel *was* very bitter; and whether bond or free, [b]there was no helper for Israel.

27 [a]And the LORD did not say that He would blot out the name of Israel from under heaven; but He saved them by the hand of Jer·o·bō′am the son of Jō′ash.

28 Now the rest of the acts of Jer·o·bō′am, and all that he did—his might, how he made war, and how he recaptured for Israel, from [a]Damascus and Hā′math, [b]*what had belonged* to Judah—*are* they not written in the book of the chronicles of the kings of Israel?

29 So Jer·o·bō′am [1]rested with his fathers, the kings of Israel. Then [a]Zech·a·rī′ah his son reigned in his place.

15 In the twenty-seventh year of Jer·o·bō′am king of Israel, [a]Az·a·rī′ah the son of Am·a·zī′ah, king of Judah, [b]became king.

2 He was sixteen years old when he became king, and he reigned fifty-two years in Jerusalem. His mother's name *was* Jech·o·lī′ah of Jerusalem.

3 And he did *what was* right in the sight of the LORD, according to all that his father Am·a·zī′ah had done,

4 [a]except that the [1]high places were not removed; the people still sacrificed and burned incense on the high places.

5 Then the LORD [a]struck the king, so that he was a leper until the day of his [b]death; so he [c]dwelt in an isolated house. And Jō′tham the king's son *was* over the *royal* house, judging the people of the land.

6 Now the rest of the acts of

17 [a]2 Chr. 25:25–28
19 [a]2 Chr. 25:27 [b]Josh. 10:31
21 [a]2 Kin. 15:13 [1]*Uzziah,* 2 Chr. 26:1ff.; Is. 6:1; etc.
22 [a]2 Kin. 16:6 [1]Heb. *Eloth* [2]Amaziah died and joined his ancestors.
24 [a]1 Kin. 12:26–33
25 [a]2 Kin. 10:32; 13:5, 25 [b]1 Kin. 8:65 [c]Deut. 3:17 [d]Jon. 1:1 [e]Josh. 19:13 [1]*border* [2]The Dead Sea
26 [a]2 Kin. 13:4 [b]Deut. 32:36
27 [a][2 Kin. 13:5, 23]
28 [a]1 Kin. 11:24 [b]2 Chr. 8:3
29 [a]2 Kin. 15:8 [1]Died and joined his ancestors

CHAPTER 15

1 [a]2 Kin. 15:13, 30 [b]2 Kin. 14:21
4 [a]2 Kin. 12:3; 14:4; 15:35 [1]Places for pagan worship
5 [a]2 Chr. 26:19–23 [b]Is. 6:1 [c][Lev. 13:46]

Az·a·rī'ah, and all that he did,
are they not written in the book
of the chronicles of the kings of
Judah?
7 So Az·a·rī'ah [1]rested with his
fathers, and [a]they buried him
with his fathers in the City of
David. Then Jō'tham his son
reigned in his place.
8 In the thirty-eighth year of
Az·a·rī'ah king of Judah, [a]Zech-
a·rī'ah the son of Jer·o·bō'am
reigned over Israel in Samaria
six months.
9 And he did evil in the sight
of the LORD, [a]as his fathers had
done; he did not depart from
the sins of Jer·o·bō'am the son
of Nē'bat, who had made Israel
sin.
10 Then Shal'lum the son of Jā'-
besh conspired against him, and
[a]struck and killed him in front of
the people; and he reigned in his
place.
11 Now the rest of the acts of
Zech·a·rī'ah, indeed they *are*
written in the book of the chronicles of the kings of Israel.
12 This *was* the word of the
LORD which He spoke to Jē'hū,
saying, [a]"Your sons shall sit on
the throne of Israel to the fourth
generation." And so it was.
13 Shal'lum the son of Jā'besh
became king in the thirty-ninth
year of [1]Uz·zī'ah king of Judah;
and he reigned a full month in
Samaria.
14 For Men'a·hem the son of
Gā'dī went up from [a]Tir'zah,
came to Samaria, and struck
Shal'lum the son of Jā'besh in
Samaria and killed him; and he
reigned in his place.
15 Now the rest of the acts of
Shal'lum, and the conspiracy
which he [1]led, indeed they *are*
written in the book of the chronicles of the kings of Israel.
16 Then from Tir'zah, Men'-
a·hem attacked [a]Tiph'sah, all
who *were* there, and its territory.
Because they did not surrender,
therefore he attacked *it.* All [b]the
women there who were with
child he ripped open.
17 In the thirty-ninth year of
Az·a·rī'ah king of Judah, Men'-
a·hem the son of Gā'dī became
king over Israel, *and reigned* ten
years in Samaria.
18 And he did evil in the sight
of the LORD; he did not depart
all his days from the sins of
Jer·o·bō'am the son of Nē'bat,
who had made Israel sin.
19 [a]Pūl[1] king of Assyria came
against the land; and Men'a·hem
gave Pūl a thousand talents of
silver, that his [2]hand might be
with him to [b]strengthen the
kingdom under his control.
20 And Men'a·hem [a]exacted[1]
the money from Israel, from all
the very wealthy, from each man
fifty shekels of silver, to give to
the king of Assyria. So the king
of Assyria turned back, and did
not stay there in the land.
21 Now the rest of the acts of
Men'a·hem, and all that he did,
are they not written in the book
of the chronicles of the kings of
Israel?
22 So Men'a·hem [1]rested with
his fathers. Then Pek·a·hī'ah his
son reigned in his place.
23 In the fiftieth year of Az·a-
rī'ah king of Judah, Pek·a·hī'ah
the son of Men'a·hem became
king over Israel in Samaria, *and
reigned* two years.
24 And he did evil in the sight
of the LORD; he did not depart
from the sins of Jer·o·bō'am the

7 [a]2 Chr. 26:23 [1]Died and joined his ancestors
8 [a]2 Kin. 14:29
9 [a]2 Kin. 14:24
10 [a]Amos 7:9
12 [a]2 Kin. 10:30
13 [1]*Azariah,* 2 Kin. 14:21ff.; 15:1ff.
14 [a]1 Kin. 14:17
15 [1]Lit. *conspired*
16 [a]1 Kin. 4:24 [b]2 Kin. 8:12
19 [a]Hos. 8:9 [b]2 Kin. 14:5 [1]Tiglath-Pileser III, v. 29 [2]Support
20 [a]2 Kin. 23:35 [1]*took*
22 [1]Died and joined his ancestors

son of Nē′bat, who had made
Israel sin.
25 Then Pē′kah the son of
Rem·a·lī′ah, an officer of his,
conspired against him and [1]killed
him in Samaria, in the [a]citadel
of the king's house, along with
Ar′gob and A·ri′eh; and with
him were fifty men of Gil′ē·ad.
He killed him and reigned in his
place.
26 Now the rest of the acts of
Pek·a·hī′ah, and all that he did,
indeed they *are* written in the
book of the chronicles of the
kings of Israel.
27 In the fifty-second year of
Az·a·rī′ah king of Judah, [a]Pē′kah
the son of Rem·a·lī′ah became
king over Israel in Samaria, *and
reigned* twenty years.
28 And he did evil in the sight
of the LORD; he did not depart
from the sins of Jer·o·bō′am the
son of Nē′bat, who had made
Israel sin.
29 In the days of Pē′kah king of
Israel, [1]Tig′lath-Pī·lē′ser king of
Assyria [a]came and took [b]Ī′jon,
Abel Beth Mā′a·chah, Ja·nō′ah,
Kē′desh, Hā′zor, Gil′ē·ad, and
Galilee, all the land of Naph′-
ta·lī; and he [c]carried them captive to Assyria.
30 Then Hō·shē′a the son of
Ē′lah led a conspiracy against
Pē′kah the son of Rem·a·lī′ah,
and struck and killed him; so he
[a]reigned in his place in the twentieth year of Jō′tham the son of
Uz·zī′ah.
31 Now the rest of the acts of
Pē′kah, and all that he did, indeed they *are* written in the
book of the chronicles of the
kings of Israel.
32 In the second year of Pē′-
kah the son of Rem·a·lī′ah, king
of Israel, [a]Jō′tham the son of
Uz·zī′ah, king of Judah, began
to reign.
33 He was twenty-five years old
when he became king, and he
reigned sixteen years in Jerusalem. His mother's name *was*
[1]Je·rū′sha the daughter of Zā′-
dok.
34 And he did *what was* right
in the sight of the LORD; he did
[a]according to all that his father
Uz·zī′ah had done.
35 [a]However the [1]high places
were not removed; the people
still sacrificed and burned incense on the high places. [b]He
built the Upper Gate of the house
of the LORD.
36 Now the rest of the acts of
Jō′tham, and all that he did, *are*
they not written in the book of
the chronicles of the kings of
Judah?
37 In those days the LORD began
to send [a]Rē′zin king of Syria and
[b]Pē′kah the son of Rem·a·lī′ah
against Judah.
38 So Jō′tham [1]rested with his
fathers, and was buried with
his fathers in the City of David
his father. Then Ā′haz his son
reigned in his place.

16

In the seventeenth year
of Pē′kah the son of
Rem·a·lī′ah, Ā′haz the son of
Jō′tham, king of Judah, began
to reign.
2 Ā′haz *was* twenty years old
when he became king, and he
reigned sixteen years in Jerusalem; and he did not do *what was*
right in the sight of the LORD his
God, as his father David *had
done*.
3 But he walked in the way of
the kings of Israel; indeed [a]he
made his son pass through the

25 [a]1 Kin. 16:18 [1]Lit. *struck*
27 [a]Is. 7:1
29 [a]1 Chr. 5:26 [b]1 Kin. 15:20 [c]2 Kin. 17:6 [1]A later name of *Pul*, v. 19
30 [a][Hos. 10:3, 7, 15]
32 [a]2 Chr. 27:1
33 [1]*Jerushah*, 2 Chr. 27:1
34 [a]2 Kin. 15:3, 4
35 [a]2 Kin. 15:4 [b]2 Chr. 23:20; 27:3 [1]Places for pagan worship
37 [a]2 Kin. 16:5–9 [b]2 Kin. 15:26, 27
38 [1]Died and joined his ancestors

CHAPTER 16

3 [a][Lev. 18:21]

fire, according to the [b]abomina-
tions of the nations whom the
LORD had cast out from before
the children of Israel.
4 And he sacrificed and burned
incense on the [a]high places, [b]on
the hills, and under every green
tree.
5 [a]Then Rē′zin king of Syria
and Pē′kah the son of Rem·a-
lī′ah, king of Israel, came up
to Jerusalem to *make* war; and
they besieged Ā′haz but could
not overcome *him*.
6 At that time Rē′zin king of
Syria [a]captured [1]Ē′lath for Syria,
and drove the men of Judah from
Ē′lath. Then the [2]Ē′dom·ītes went
to Ē′lath, and dwell there to this
day.
7 So Ā′haz sent messengers
to [a]Tig′lath-Pī·lē′ser[1] king of Assyria, saying, "I *am* your servant
and your son. Come up and save
me from the hand of the king
of Syria and from the hand of
the king of Israel, who rise up
against me."
8 And Ā′haz [a]took the silver
and gold that was found in the
house of the LORD, and in the
treasuries of the king's house,
and sent *it as* a present to the
king of Assyria.
9 So the king of Assyria heeded
him; for the king of Assyria went
up against [a]Damascus and [b]took
it, carried *its people* captive to
[c]Kir, and killed Rē′zin.
10 Now King Ā′haz went to Damascus to meet Tig′lath-Pī·lē′ser
king of Assyria, and saw an
altar that *was* at Damascus; and
King Ā′haz sent to Ū·rī′jah the
priest the design of the altar and
its pattern, according to all its
workmanship.
11 Then [a]Ū·rī′jah the priest built
an altar according to all that
King Ā′haz had sent from Damascus. So Ū·rī′jah the priest
made *it* before King Ā′haz came
back from Damascus.
12 And when the king came
back from Damascus, the king
saw the altar; and [a]the king approached the altar and made
offerings on it.
13 So he burned his burnt offering and his grain offering; and
he poured his drink offering and
sprinkled the blood of his peace
offerings on the altar.
14 He also brought [a]the bronze
altar which *was* before the LORD,
from the front of the [1]temple—
from between the *new* altar and
the house of the LORD—and put
it on the north side of the *new*
altar.
15 Then King Ā′haz commanded
Ū·rī′jah the priest, saying, "On
the great *new* altar burn [a]the
morning burnt offering, the evening grain offering, the king's
burnt sacrifice, and his grain offering, with the burnt offering of
all the people of the land, their
grain offering, and their drink
offerings; and sprinkle on it all
the blood of the burnt offering
and all the blood of the sacrifice.
And the bronze altar shall be for
me to inquire *by*."
16 Thus did Ū·rī′jah the priest,
according to all that King Ā′haz
commanded.
17 [a]And King Ā′haz cut off [b]the
panels of the carts, and removed
the lavers from them; and he
took down [c]the Sea from the
bronze oxen that *were* under
it, and put it on a pavement of
stones.
18 Also he removed the Sabbath
pavilion which they had built in

3 [b][Deut. 12:31]
4 [a]2 Kin. 15:34, 35 [b][Deut. 12:2]
5 [a]Is. 7:1, 4
6 [a]2 Kin. 14:22 [1]Lit. *Large Tree*; sing. of *Eloth* [2]A few ancient mss. *Syrians*
7 [a]1 Chr. 5:26 [1]A later name of *Pul*, 2 Kin. 15:19
8 [a]2 Kin. 12:17, 18
9 [a]2 Kin. 14:28 [b]Amos 1:5 [c]Amos 9:7
11 [a]Is. 8:2
12 [a]2 Chr. 26:16, 19
14 [a]2 Chr. 4:1 [1]Lit. *house*
15 [a]Ex. 29:39–41
17 [a]2 Chr. 28:24 [b]1 Kin. 7:27–29 [c]1 Kin. 7:23–25

the temple, and he removed the
king's outer entrance from the
house of the LORD, on account of
the king of Assyria.
19 Now the rest of the acts of
Ā'haz which he did, *are* they not
written in the book of the chronicles of the kings of Judah?
20 So Ā'haz rested with his fathers, and [a]was buried with his
fathers in the City of David.
Then Hez·e·kī'ah his son reigned
in his place.

17 In the twelfth year of
Ā'haz king of Judah,
[a]Hō·shē'a the son of Ē'lah became king of Israel in Samaria,
and he reigned nine years.
2 And he did evil in the sight
of the LORD, but not as the kings
of Israel who were before him.
3 [a]Shal·man·ē'ser king of Assyria came up against him; and
Hō·shē'a [b]became his vassal,
and paid him tribute money.
4 And the king of Assyria
uncovered a conspiracy by
Hō·shē'a; for he had sent messengers to So, king of Egypt,
and brought no tribute to the
king of Assyria, as *he had done*
year by year. Therefore the king
of Assyria shut him up, and
bound him in prison.
5 Now [a]the king of Assyria
went throughout all the land,
and went up to Samaria and besieged it for three years.
6 [a]In the ninth year of Hō·shē'a,
the king of Assyria took Samaria and [b]carried Israel away
to Assyria, [c]and placed them in
Hā'lah and by the Hā'bor, the
River of Gō'zan, and in the cities
of the Mēdes.
7 For [a]so it was that the children of Israel had sinned against
the LORD their God, who had
brought them up out of the land
of Egypt, from under the hand of
Pharaoh king of Egypt; and they
had [b]feared other gods,
8 and [a]had walked in the statutes of the nations whom the
LORD had cast out from before
the children of Israel, and of the
kings of Israel, which they had
made.
9 Also the children of Israel
secretly did against the LORD
their God things that *were* not
right, and they built for themselves [1]high places in all their
cities, [a]from watchtower to fortified city.
10 [a]They set up for themselves
sacred pillars and [b]wooden images[1] [c]on every high hill and
under every green tree.
11 There they burned incense
on all the high places, like the
nations whom the LORD had carried away before them; and they
did wicked things to provoke the
LORD to anger,
12 for they served idols, [a]of
which the LORD had said to them,
[b]"You shall not do this thing."
13 Yet the LORD testified against
Israel and against Judah, by all
of His [a]prophets, [b]every seer,
saying, [c]"Turn from your evil
ways, and keep My commandments *and* My statutes, according to all the law which I commanded your fathers, and which
I sent to you by My servants the
prophets."
14 Nevertheless they would not
hear, but [a]stiffened their necks,
like the necks of their fathers,
who [b]did not believe in the LORD
their God.
15 And they [a]rejected His statutes [b]and His covenant that He
had made with their fathers, and

20 [a]2 Chr. 28:27

CHAPTER 17

1 [a]2 Kin. 15:30

3 [a]2 Kin. 18:9–12 [b]2 Kin. 24:1

5 [a]Hos. 13:16

6 [a]Hos. 1:4; 13:16 [b][Deut. 28:36, 64; 29:27, 28] [c]1 Chr. 5:26

7 [a][Josh. 23:16] [b]Judg. 6:10

8 [a][Lev. 18:3]

9 [a]2 Kin. 18:8 [1]Places for pagan worship

10 [a]Is. 57:5 [b][Ex. 34:12–14] [c][Deut. 12:2] [1]Heb. *Asherim*, Canaanite deities

12 [a][Ex. 20:3–5] [b][Deut. 4:19]

13 [a]Neh. 9:29, 30 [b]1 Sam. 9:9 [c][Jer. 18:11; 25:5; 35:15]

14 [a][Acts 7:51] [b]Deut. 9:23

15 [a]Jer. 44:3 [b]Deut. 29:25

His testimonies which He had testified against them; they followed [c]idols, [d]became idolaters, and *went* after the nations who *were* all around them, *concerning* whom the LORD had charged them that they should [e]not do like them.

16 So they left all the commandments of the LORD their God, [a]made for themselves a molded image *and* two calves, [b]made a wooden image and worshiped all the [c]host of heaven, [d]and served Bā′al.

17 [a]And they caused their sons and daughters to pass through the fire, [b]practiced witchcraft and soothsaying, and [c]sold themselves to do evil in the sight of the LORD, to provoke Him to anger.

18 Therefore the LORD was very angry with Israel, and removed them from His sight; there was none left [a]but the tribe of Judah alone.

19 Also [a]Judah did not keep the commandments of the LORD their God, but walked in the statutes of Israel which they made.

20 And the LORD rejected all the descendants of Israel, afflicted them, and [a]delivered them into the hand of plunderers, until He had cast them from His [b]sight.

21 For [a]He tore Israel from the house of David, and [b]they made Jer·o·bō′am the son of Nē′bat king. Then Jer·o·bō′am drove Israel from following the LORD, and made them commit a great sin.

22 For the children of Israel walked in all the sins of Jer·o·bō′am which he did; they did not depart from them,

23 until the LORD removed Israel out of His sight, [a]as He had said by all His servants the prophets. [b]So Israel was carried away from their own land to Assyria, *as it is* to this day.

24 [a]Then the king of Assyria brought *people* from Babylon, Cū′thah, [b]Ā′va, Hā′math, and from Seph·ar·vā′im, and placed *them* in the cities of Samaria instead of the children of Israel; and they took possession of Samaria and dwelt in its cities.

25 And it was so, at the beginning of their dwelling there, *that* they did not fear the LORD; therefore the LORD sent lions among them, which killed *some* of them.

26 So they spoke to the king of Assyria, saying, "The nations whom you have removed and placed in the cities of Samaria do not know the rituals of the God of the land; therefore He has sent lions among them, and indeed, they are killing them because they do not know the rituals of the God of the land."

27 Then the king of Assyria commanded, saying, "Send there one of the priests whom you brought from there; let him go and dwell there, and let him teach them the rituals of the God of the land."

28 Then one of the priests whom they had carried away from Samaria came and dwelt in Beth′el, and taught them how they should fear the LORD.

29 However every nation continued to make gods of its own, and put *them* [a]in the shrines on the high places which the Samaritans had made, *every* nation in the cities where they dwelt.

30 The men of [a]Babylon made

15 [c]Deut. 32:21 [d][Rom. 1:21–23] [e][Deut. 12:30, 31]
16 [a]1 Kin. 12:28 [b][1 Kin. 14:15] [c][Deut. 4:19] [d]1 Kin. 16:31; 22:53
17 [a]2 Kin. 16:3 [b][Deut. 18:10–12] [c]1 Kin. 21:20
18 [a]1 Kin. 11:13, 32
19 [a]Jer. 3:8
20 [a]2 Kin. 13:3; 15:29 [b]2 Kin. 24:20
21 [a]1 Kin. 11:11, 31 [b]1 Kin. 12:20, 28
23 [a]1 Kin. 14:16 [b]2 Kin. 17:6
24 [a]Ezra 4:2, 10 [b]2 Kin. 18:34
29 [a]1 Kin. 12:31; 13:32
30 [a]2 Kin. 17:24

Suc′coth Be·noth′, the men of
Cūth made Ner′gal, the men of
Hā′math made A·shī′ma,
31 [a]and the Av′ītes made Nib′-
haz and Tar′tak; and the Se-
phar′vītes [b]burned their children in fire to A·dram′me·lech
and A·nam′me·lech, the gods of
Seph·ar·vā′im.
32 So they feared the LORD, [a]and
from every class they appointed
for themselves priests of the
[1]high places, who sacrificed for
them in the shrines of the high
places.
33 [a]They feared the LORD, yet
served their own gods—according to the rituals of the nations
from among whom they were
carried away.
34 To this day they continue
practicing the former rituals;
they do not fear the LORD, nor
do they follow their statutes or
their ordinances, or the law and
commandment which the LORD
had commanded the children of
Jacob, [a]whom He named Israel,
35 with whom the LORD had
made a covenant and charged
them, saying: [a]"You shall not
fear other gods, nor [b]bow down
to them nor serve them nor sacrifice to them;
36 "but the LORD, who [a]brought
you up from the land of Egypt
with great power and [b]an outstretched arm, [c]Him you shall
fear, Him you shall worship, and
to Him you shall offer sacrifice.
37 "And the statutes, the ordinances, the law, and the commandment which He wrote for
you, [a]you shall be careful to observe forever; you shall not fear
other gods.
38 "And the covenant that I have
made with you, [a]you shall not
forget, nor shall you fear other
gods.
39 "But the LORD your God you
shall fear; and He will deliver
you from the hand of all your
enemies."
40 However they did not obey,
but they followed their former
rituals.
41 [a]So these nations feared the
LORD, yet served their carved
images; also their children and
their children's children have
continued doing as their fathers
did, even to this day.

18 Now it came to pass in the
third year of [a]Hō·shē′a the
son of Ē′lah, king of Israel, *that*
[b]Hez·e·kī′ah the son of Ā′haz,
king of Judah, began to reign.
2 He was twenty-five years
old when he became king, and
he reigned twenty-nine years in
Jerusalem. His mother's name
was [a]Ā′bī[1] the daughter of Zech-
a·rī′ah.
3 And he did *what was* right in
the sight of the LORD, according
to all that his father David had
done.
4 [a]He removed the [1]high places
and broke the *sacred* pillars, cut
down the [2]wooden image and
broke in pieces the [b]bronze serpent that Moses had made; for
until those days the children of
Israel burned incense to it, and
called it [3]Ne·hush′tan.
5 He [a]trusted in the LORD God
of Israel, [b]so that after him was
none like him among all the
kings of Judah, nor who were
before him.
6 For he [a]held fast to the LORD;
he did not depart from following
Him, but kept His commandments, which the LORD had commanded Moses.

31 [a]Ezra 4:9 [b][Deut. 12:31]
32 [a]1 Kin. 12:31; 13:33 [1]Places for pagan worship
33 [a]Zeph. 1:5
34 [a]Gen. 32:28; 35:10
35 [a]Judg. 6:10 [b][Ex. 20:5]
36 [a]Ex. 14:15–30 [b]Ex. 6:6; 9:15 [c][Deut. 10:20]
37 [a]Deut. 5:32
38 [a]Deut. 4:23; 6:12
41 [a]2 Kin. 17:32, 33

CHAPTER 18

1 [a]2 Kin. 17:1 [b]2 Chr. 28:27; 29:1
2 [a]Is. 38:5 [1]*Abijah,* 2 Chr. 29:1ff.
4 [a]2 Chr. 31:1 [b]Num. 21:5–9 [1]Places for pagan worship [2]Heb. *Asherah,* a Canaanite goddess [3]Lit. *Bronze Thing,* also similar to Heb. *nahash, serpent*
5 [a]2 Kin. 19:10 [b]2 Kin. 23:25
6 [a]Deut. 10:20

7 The LORD [a]was with him; he [b]prospered wherever he went. And he [c]rebelled against the king of Assyria and did not serve him.
8 [a]He [1]subdued the Phi·lis′-tines, as far as Gā′za and its territory, [b]from watchtower to fortified city.
9 Now [a]it came to pass in the fourth year of King Hez·e·kī′ah, which *was* the seventh year of Hō·shē′a the son of Ē′lah, king of Israel, *that* Shal·man·ē′ser king of Assyria came up against Samaria and besieged it.
10 And at the end of three years they took it. In the sixth year of Hez·e·kī′ah, that *is,* [a]the ninth year of Hō·shē′a king of Israel, Samaria was taken.
11 [a]Then the king of Assyria carried Israel away captive to Assyria, and put them [b]in Hā′lah and by the Hā′bor, the River of Gō′zan, and in the cities of the Mēdes,
12 because they [a]did not obey the voice of the LORD their God, but transgressed His covenant *and* all that Moses the servant of the LORD had commanded; and they would neither hear nor do *them.*
13 And [a]in the fourteenth year of King Hez·e·kī′ah, Sen·nach′-e·rib king of Assyria came up against all the fortified cities of Judah and took them.
14 Then Hez·e·kī′ah king of Judah sent to the king of Assyria at Lā′chish, saying, "I have done wrong; turn away from me; whatever you impose on me I will pay." And the king of Assyria assessed Hez·e·kī′ah king of Judah three hundred talents of silver and thirty talents of gold.
15 So Hez·e·kī′ah [a]gave *him* all the silver that was found in the house of the LORD and in the treasuries of the king's house.
16 At that time Hez·e·kī′ah stripped *the gold from* the doors of the temple of the LORD, and *from* the pillars which Hez·e·kī′ah king of Judah had overlaid, and gave [1]it to the king of Assyria.
17 Then the king of Assyria sent *the* [1]Tartan, *the* [2]Rab·sar′is, *and the* [3]Rab′sha·keh from Lā′-chish, with a great army against Jerusalem, to King Hez·e·kī′ah. And they went up and came to Jerusalem. When they had come up, they went and stood by the [a]aqueduct from the upper pool, [b]which *was* on the highway to the Fuller's Field.
18 And when they had called to the king, [a]E·lī′a·kim the son of Hil·kī′ah, who *was* over the household, Sheb′na the [1]scribe, and Jō′ah the son of Ā′saph, the recorder, came out to them.
19 Then *the* Rab′sha·keh said to them, "Say now to Hez·e·kī′ah, 'Thus says the great king, the king of Assyria: [a]"What confidence *is* this in which you trust?
20 "You speak of *having* plans and power for war; but *they are* [1]mere words. And in whom do you trust, that you rebel against me?
21 [a]"Now look! You are trusting in the staff of this broken reed, Egypt, on which if a man leans, it will go into his hand and pierce it. So *is* Pharaoh king of Egypt to all who trust in him.
22 "But if you say to me, 'We trust in the LORD our God,' *is*

7 [a][2 Chr. 15:2] [b]1 Sam. 18:5, 14 [c]2 Kin. 16:7
8 [a]Is. 14:29 [b]2 Kin. 17:9 [1]Lit. *struck*
9 [a]2 Kin. 17:3
10 [a]2 Kin. 17:6
11 [a]2 Kin. 17:6 [b]1 Chr. 5:26
12 [a]2 Kin. 17:7–18
13 [a]2 Chr. 32:1
15 [a]2 Kin. 12:18; 16:8
16 [1]Lit. *them*
17 [a]2 Kin. 20:20 [b]Is. 7:3 [1]A title, probably *Commander in Chief* [2]A title, probably *Chief Officer* [3]A title, probably *Chief of Staff* or *Governor*
18 [a]Is. 22:20 [1]*secretary*
19 [a]2 Chr. 32:10
20 [1]Lit. *a word of the lips*
21 [a]Ezek. 29:6, 7

it not He [a]whose [1]high places
and whose altars Hez·e·kī′ah
has taken away, and said to Judah and Jerusalem, 'You shall
worship before this altar in
Jerusalem'?" '
23 "Now therefore, I urge you,
give a pledge to my master the
king of Assyria, and I will give
you two thousand horses—if
you are able on your part to put
riders on them!
24 "How then will you repel
one captain of the least of my
master's servants, and put your
trust in Egypt for chariots and
horsemen?
25 "Have I now come up without the LORD against this place
to destroy it? The LORD said to
me, 'Go up against this land, and
destroy it.' "
26 [a]Then E·lī′a·kim the son of
Hil·kī′ah, Sheb′na, and Jō′ah
said to *the* Rab′sha·keh, "Please
speak to your servants in
[b]Ar·a·mā′ic, for we understand
it; and do not speak to us in
[1]Hebrew in the hearing of the
people who *are* on the wall."
27 But *the* Rab′sha·keh said to
them, "Has my master sent me
to your master and to you to
speak these words, and not to
the men who sit on the wall,
who will eat and drink their own
waste with you?"
28 Then *the* Rab′sha·keh stood
and called out with a loud voice
in [1]Hebrew, and spoke, saying,
"Hear the word of the great
king, the king of Assyria!
29 "Thus says the king: [a]'Do not
let Hez·e·kī′ah deceive you, for
he shall not be able to deliver
you from his hand;
30 'nor let Hez·e·kī′ah make you
trust in the LORD, saying, "The

22 [a]2 Kin. 18:4 [1]Places for pagan worship
26 [a]Is. 36:11—39:8 [b]Ezra 4:7 [1]Lit. *Judean*
28 [1]Lit. *Judean*
29 [a]2 Chr. 32:15
31 [a]1 Kin. 4:20, 25 [1]By paying tribute
32 [a]Deut. 8:7–9; 11:12
33 [a]2 Kin. 19:12
34 [a]2 Kin. 19:13 [b]2 Kin. 17:24
35 [a]Dan. 3:15
37 [a]Is. 33:7

LORD will surely deliver us; this
city shall not be given into the
hand of the king of Assyria." '
31 "Do not listen to Hez·e·kī′ah;
for thus says the king of Assyria: 'Make *peace* with me [1]by
a present and come out to me;
and every one of you eat from
his own [a]vine and every one
from his own fig tree, and every
one of you drink the waters of
his own cistern;
32 'until I come and take you
away to a land like your own
land, [a]a land of grain and new
wine, a land of bread and vineyards, a land of olive groves
and honey, that you may live
and not die. But do not listen
to Hez·e·kī′ah, lest he persuade
you, saying, "The LORD will deliver us."
33 [a]'Has any of the gods of the
nations at all delivered its land
from the hand of the king of
Assyria?
34 'Where *are* the gods of [a]Hā′-
math and Ar′pad? Where *are*
the gods of Seph·ar·vā′im and
Hē′na and [b]Ī′vah? Indeed, have
they delivered Samaria from my
hand?
35 'Who among all the gods of
the lands have delivered their
countries from my hand, [a]that
the LORD should deliver Jerusalem from my hand?' "
36 But the people held their
peace and answered him not a
word; for the king's commandment was, "Do not answer him."
37 Then E·lī′a·kim the son of
Hil·kī′ah, who *was* over the
household, Sheb′na the scribe,
and Jō′ah the son of Ā′saph, the
recorder, came to Hez·e·kī′ah
[a]with *their* clothes torn, and

told him the words of *the* Rab′-
sha·keh.

19 And [a]so it was, when King
Hez·e·kī′ah heard *it,* that
he tore his clothes, covered himself with [b]sackcloth, and went
into the house of the LORD.
2 Then he sent E·lī′a·kim, who
was over the household, Sheb′na
the scribe, and the elders of the
priests, covered with sackcloth,
to Ī·sāi′ah the prophet, the son
of Ā′moz.
3 And they said to him, "Thus
says Hez·e·kī′ah: 'This day *is*
a day of trouble, and rebuke,
and blasphemy; for the children
have come to birth, but *there*
is no strength to [1]bring them
forth.
4 [a]'It may be that the LORD your
God will hear all the words of
the Rab′sha·keh, whom his master the king of Assyria has sent
to [b]reproach the living God, and
will [c]rebuke the words which
the LORD your God has heard.
Therefore lift up *your* prayer for
the remnant that is left.' "
5 So the servants of King
Hez·e·kī′ah came to Ī·sāi′ah.
6 [a]And Ī·sāi′ah said to them,
"Thus you shall say to your master, 'Thus says the LORD: "Do not
be [b]afraid of the words which
you have heard, with which the
[c]servants of the king of Assyria
have blasphemed Me.
7 "Surely I will send [a]a spirit
upon him, and he shall hear a
rumor and return to his own
land; and I will cause him to
fall by the sword in his own
land." ' "
8 Then *the* Rab′sha·keh returned and found the king of
Assyria warring against Lib′-
nah, for he heard that he had
departed [a]from Lā′chish.
9 And [a]the king heard concerning Tir·hā′kah king of Ethiopia, "Look, he has come out to
make war with you." So he again
sent messengers to Hez·e·kī′ah,
saying,
10 "Thus you shall speak to
Hez·e·kī′ah king of Judah, saying: 'Do not let your God [a]in
whom you trust deceive you,
saying, "Jerusalem shall not be
given into the hand of the king
of Assyria."
11 'Look! You have heard what
the kings of Assyria have done
to all lands by utterly destroying them; and shall you be
delivered?
12 [a]'Have the gods of the nations delivered those whom my
fathers have destroyed, Gō′zan
and Har′an and Rē′zeph, and
the people of [b]Eden who *were* in
Te·las′sar?
13 [a]'Where *is* the king of Hā′-
math, the king of Ar′pad, and the
king of the city of Seph·ar·vā′im,
Hē′na, and Ī′vah?' "
14 [a]And Hez·e·kī′ah received
the letter from the hand of the
messengers, and read it; and
Hez·e·kī′ah went up to the house
of the LORD, and spread it before
the LORD.
15 Then Hez·e·kī′ah prayed before the LORD, and said: "O LORD
God of Israel, *the One* [a]who
dwells *between* the cherubim,
[b]You are God, You alone, of all
the kingdoms of the earth. You
have made heaven and earth.
16 [a]"Incline Your ear, O LORD,
and hear; [b]open Your eyes,
O LORD, and see; and hear the
words of Sen·nach′e·rib, [c]which

CHAPTER 19
1 [a]Is. 37:1 [b]Ps. 69:11
3 [1]*give birth*
4 [a]2 Sam. 16:12 [b]2 Kin. 18:35 [c]Ps. 50:21
6 [a]Is. 37:6 [b][Ps. 112:7] [c]2 Kin. 18:17
7 [a]2 Kin. 19:35–37
8 [a]2 Kin. 18:14, 17
9 [a]1 Sam. 23:27
10 [a]2 Kin. 18:5
12 [a]2 Kin. 18:33, 34 [b]Ezek. 27:23
13 [a]2 Kin. 18:34
14 [a]Is. 37:14
15 [a]Ex. 25:22 [b][Is. 44:6]
16 [a]Ps. 31:2 [b]2 Chr. 6:40 [c]2 Kin. 19:4

he has sent to reproach the living God.
17 "Truly, LORD, the kings of Assyria have laid waste the nations and their lands,
18 "and have cast their gods into the fire; for they *were* [a]not gods, but [b]the work of men's hands—wood and stone. Therefore they destroyed them.
19 "Now therefore, O LORD our God, I pray, save us from his hand, [a]that all the kingdoms of the earth may [b]know that You *are* the LORD God, You alone."
20 Then Ī·sāi′ah the son of Ā′moz sent to Hez·e·kī′ah, saying, "Thus says the LORD God of Israel: [a]'Because you have prayed to Me against Sen·nach′e·rib king of Assyria, [b]I have heard.'
21 "This *is* the word which the LORD has spoken concerning him:

'The virgin, [a]the daughter of Zion,
Has despised you, laughed you to scorn;
The daughter of Jerusalem
[b]Has shaken *her* head behind your back!

22 'Whom have you reproached and blasphemed?
Against whom have you raised *your* voice,
And lifted up your eyes on high?
Against [a]the Holy *One* of Israel.
23 [a]By your messengers you have reproached the Lord,
And said: [b]"By the multitude of my chariots
I have come up to the height of the mountains,
To the limits of Lebanon;
I will cut down its tall cedars
And its choice cypress trees;
I will enter the extremity of its borders,
To its fruitful forest.
24 I have dug and drunk strange water,
And with the soles of my feet I have [a]dried up
All the brooks of defense."

25 'Did you not hear long ago
How [a]I made it,
From ancient times that I formed it?
Now I have brought it to pass,
That [b]you should be
For crushing fortified cities *into* heaps of ruins.
26 Therefore their inhabitants had little power;
They were dismayed and confounded;
They were *as* the grass of the field
And the green herb,
As [a]the grass on the housetops
And *grain* blighted before it is grown.

27 'But [a]I know your dwelling place,
Your going out and your coming in,
And your rage against Me.
28 Because your rage against Me and your tumult
Have come up to My ears,
Therefore [a]I will put My hook in your nose
And My bridle in your lips,
And I will turn you back
[b]By the way which you came.

18 [a][Jer. 10:3–5] [b][Acts 17:29]
19 [a]Ps. 83:18 [b]1 Kin. 8:42, 43
20 [a]Is. 37:21 [b]2 Kin. 20:5
21 [a]Lam. 2:13 [b]Ps. 22:7, 8
22 [a]Jer. 51:5
23 [a]2 Kin. 18:17 [b]Ps. 20:7
24 [a]Is. 19:6
25 [a][Is. 45:7] [b]Is. 10:5, 6
26 [a]Ps. 129:6
27 [a]Ps. 139:1–3
28 [a]Ezek. 29:4; 38:4 [b]2 Kin. 19:33, 36

29 'This *shall be* a [a]sign to you:

You shall eat this year such
as grows [1]of itself,
And in the second year
what springs from the
same;
Also in the third year sow
and reap,
Plant vineyards and eat the
fruit of them.
30 [a]And the remnant who have
escaped of the house of
Judah
Shall again take root
downward,
And bear fruit upward.
31 For out of Jerusalem shall
go a remnant,
And those who escape from
Mount Zion.
[a]The zeal of the LORD [1]of
hosts will do this.'

32 "Therefore thus says the LORD concerning the king of Assyria:

'He shall [a]not come into this
city,
Nor shoot an arrow there,
Nor come before it with
shield,
Nor build a siege mound
against it.
33 By the way that he came,
By the same shall he return;
And he shall not come into
this city,'
Says the LORD.
34 'For [a]I will [b]defend this city,
to save it
For My own sake and [c]for
My servant David's
sake.' "

35 And [a]it came to pass on a certain night that the [1]angel of the LORD went out, and killed in the camp of the Assyrians one hundred and eighty-five thousand; and when *people* arose early in the morning, there were the corpses—all dead.

36 So Sen·nach′e·rib king of Assyria departed and went away, returned *home,* and remained at [a]Nin′e·veh.

37 Now it came to pass, as he was worshiping in the temple of Nis′roch his god, that his sons [a]A·dram′me·lech and Sha·rē′zer [b]struck him down with the sword; and they escaped into the land of Ar′a·rat. Then [c]Ē·sar·had′don his son reigned in his place.

20

In [a]those days Hez·e·kī′ah was sick and near death. And Ī·sāi′ah the prophet, the son of Ā′moz, went to him and said to him, "Thus says the LORD: 'Set your house in order, for you shall die, and not live.' "

2 Then he turned his face toward the wall, and prayed to the LORD, saying,

3 [a]"Remember now, O LORD, I pray, how I have walked before You in truth and with a loyal heart, and have done *what was* good in Your sight." And Hez·e·kī′ah wept bitterly.

4 And it happened, before Ī·sāi′ah had gone out into the middle court, that the word of the LORD came to him, saying,

5 "Return and tell Hez·e·kī′ah [a]the leader of My people, 'Thus says the LORD, the God of David your father: [b]"I have heard your prayer, I have seen [c]your tears; surely I will heal you. On the third day you shall go up to the house of the LORD.

6 "And I will add to your days

29 [a]2 Kin. 20:8, 9 [1]Without cultivation
30 [a]2 Chr. 32:22, 23
31 [a]Is. 9:7 [1]So with many Heb. mss. and ancient vss. (cf. Is. 37:32); MT omits *of hosts*
32 [a]Is. 8:7–10
34 [a]2 Kin. 20:6 [b]Is. 31:5 [c]1 Kin. 11:12, 13
35 [a]Is. 10:12–19; 37:36 [1]Or *Angel*
36 [a]Gen. 10:11
37 [a]2 Kin. 17:31 [b]2 Kin. 19:7 [c]Ezra 4:2

CHAPTER 20

1 [a]Is. 38:1–22
3 [a]Neh. 13:22
5 [a]1 Sam. 9:16; 10:1 [b]Ps. 65:2 [c]Ps. 39:12; 56:8

fifteen years. I will deliver you
and this city from the hand of
the king of Assyria; and [a]I will
defend this city for My own
sake, and for the sake of My
servant David." ' "
7 Then [a]Ī·sāi'ah said, "Take
a lump of figs." So they took
and laid *it* on the boil, and he
recovered.
8 And Hez·e·kī'ah said to
Ī·sāi'ah, [a]"What *is* the sign that
the LORD will heal me, and that
I shall go up to the house of the
LORD the third day?"
9 Then Ī·sāi'ah said, [a]"This is
the sign to you from the LORD,
that the LORD will do the thing
which He has spoken: *shall* the
shadow go forward ten degrees
or go backward ten degrees?"
10 And Hez·e·kī'ah answered, "It
is an easy thing for the shadow
to go down ten [1]degrees; no, but
let the shadow go backward ten
degrees."
11 So Ī·sāi'ah the prophet cried
out to the LORD, and [a]He brought
the shadow ten [1]degrees backward, by which it had gone down
on the sundial of Ā'haz.
12 [a]At that time [1]Be·rō'dach-
Bal'a·dan the son of Bal'a·dan,
king of Babylon, sent letters and
a present to Hez·e·kī'ah, for he
heard that Hez·e·kī'ah had been
sick.
13 And [a]Hez·e·kī'ah was attentive to them, and showed them
all the house of his treasures—
the silver and gold, the spices
and precious ointment, and [1]all
[2]his armory—all that was found
among his treasures. There was
nothing in his house or in all his
dominion that Hez·e·kī'ah did
not show them.
14 Then Ī·sāi'ah the prophet
went to King Hez·e·kī'ah, and
said to him, "What did these men
say, and from where did they
come to you?" So Hez·e·kī'ah
said, "They came from a far
country, from Babylon."
15 And he said, "What have
they seen in your house?" So
Hez·e·kī'ah answered, [a]"They
have seen all that *is* in my house;
there is nothing among my treasures that I have not shown
them."
16 Then Ī·sāi'ah said to Hez·e-
kī'ah, "Hear the word of the
LORD:
17 'Behold, the days are coming
when all that *is* in your house,
and what your fathers have ac-
cumulated until this day, [a]shall
be carried to Babylon; nothing
shall be left,' says the LORD.
18 'And [a]they shall take away
some of your sons who will
[1]descend from you, whom you
will beget; [b]and they shall be
[c]eunuchs in the palace of the
king of Babylon.' "
19 So Hez·e·kī'ah said to Ī·sāi'ah,
[a]"The word of the LORD which
you have spoken *is* good!" For
he said, "Will there not be peace
and truth at least in my days?"
20 [a]Now the rest of the acts of
Hez·e·kī'ah—all his might, and
how he [b]made a [c]pool and a
[1]tunnel and [d]brought water into
the city—*are* they not written in
the book of the chronicles of the
kings of Judah?
21 So [a]Hez·e·kī'ah [1]rested with
his fathers. Then Ma·nas'seh his
son reigned in his place.

21

Ma·nas'seh [a]*was* twelve
years old when he became
king, and he reigned fifty-five
years in Jerusalem. His mother's
name *was* Heph'zi·bah.

6 [a]2 Kin. 19:34
7 [a]Is. 38:21
8 [a]Judg. 6:17, 37, 39
9 [a]Is. 38:7, 8
10 [1]Lit. *steps*
11 [a]Is. 38:8 [1]Lit. *steps*
12 [a]Is. 39:1–8 [1]*Merodach-Baladan*, Is. 39:1
13 [a]2 Chr. 32:27, 31 [1]So with many Heb. mss., Syr., Tg.; MT omits *all* [2]Lit. *the house of his armor*
15 [a]2 Kin. 20:13
17 [a]Jer. 27:21, 22; 52:17
18 [a]2 Kin. 24:12 [b]Dan. 1:3–7 [c]Dan. 1:11, 18 [1]*be born from*
19 [a]1 Sam. 3:18
20 [a]2 Chr. 32:32 [b]Neh. 3:16 [c]Is. 7:3 [d]2 Chr. 32:3, 30 [1]*aqueduct*
21 [a]2 Chr. 32:33 [1]Died and joined his ancestors

CHAPTER 21

1 [a]2 Chr. 33:1–9

2 And he did evil in the sight
of the LORD, [a]according to the
abominations of the nations
whom the LORD had cast out before the children of Israel.
3 For he rebuilt the [1]high places
[a]which Hez·e·kī'ah his father had
destroyed; he raised up altars
for Bā'al, and made a [2]wooden
image, [b]as Ā'hab king of Israel
had done; and he [c]worshiped all
[3]the host of heaven and served
them.
4 [a]He also built altars in the
house of the LORD, of which the
LORD had said, [b]"In Jerusalem I
will put My name."
5 And he built altars for all the
host of heaven in the [a]two courts
of the house of the LORD.
6 [a]Also he made his son pass
through the fire, practiced
[b]soothsaying, used witchcraft,
and consulted spiritists and mediums. He did much evil in the
sight of the LORD, to provoke
Him to anger.
7 He even set a carved image
of [1]A·shē'rah that he had made,
in the [2]house of which the LORD
had said to David and to Solomon his son, [a]"In this house
and in Jerusalem, which I have
chosen out of all the tribes of
Israel, I will put My name forever;
8 [a]"and I will not make the
feet of Israel wander anymore
from the land which I gave their
fathers—only if they are careful
to do according to all that I have
commanded them, and according to all the law that My servant Moses commanded them."
9 But they paid no attention,
and Ma·nas'seh [a]seduced them
to do more evil than the nations
whom the LORD had destroyed
before the children of Israel.
10 And the LORD spoke [a]by His
servants the prophets, saying,
11 [a]"Because Ma·nas'seh king
of Judah has done these abominations ([b]he has acted more
wickedly than all the [c]Am'o·rītes
who *were* before him, and [d]has
also made Judah sin with his
idols),
12 "therefore thus says the
LORD God of Israel: 'Behold, *I*
am bringing *such* calamity upon
Jerusalem and Judah, that whoever hears of it, both [a]his ears
will tingle.
13 'And I will stretch over Jerusalem [a]the measuring line of
Samaria and the plummet of
the house of Ā'hab; [b]I will wipe
Jerusalem as *one* wipes a dish,
wiping *it* and turning *it* upside
down.
14 'So I will forsake the
[a]remnant of My inheritance and
deliver them into the hand of
their enemies; and they shall
become victims of plunder to all
their enemies,
15 'because they have done evil
in My sight, and have provoked
Me to anger since the day their
fathers came out of Egypt, even
to this day.' "
16 [a]Moreover Ma·nas'seh shed
very much innocent blood, till
he had filled Jerusalem from
one end to another, besides his
sin by which he made Judah sin,
in doing evil in the sight of the
LORD.
17 Now [a]the rest of the acts
of [b]Ma·nas'seh—all that he did,
and the sin that he committed—
are they not written in the book
of the chronicles of the kings of
Judah?

2 [a]2 Kin. 16:3
3 [a]2 Kin. 18:4, 22 [b]1 Kin. 16:31–33 [c][Deut. 4:19; 17:2–5] [1]Places for pagan worship [2]Heb. *Asherah*, a Canaanite goddess [3]The gods of the Assyrians
4 [a]Jer. 7:30; 32:34 [b]1 Kin. 11:13
5 [a]1 Kin. 6:36; 7:12
6 [a][Lev. 18:21; 20:2] [b][Deut. 18:10–14]
7 [a]1 Kin. 8:29; 9:3 [1]A Canaanite goddess [2]Temple
8 [a]2 Sam. 7:10
9 [a][Prov. 29:12]
10 [a]2 Kin. 17:13
11 [a]2 Kin. 23:26, 27; 24:3, 4 [b]1 Kin. 21:26 [c]Gen. 15:16 [d]2 Kin. 21:9
12 [a]Jer. 19:3
13 [a]Amos 7:7, 8 [b]2 Kin. 22:16–19; 25:4–11
14 [a]Jer. 6:9
16 [a]2 Kin. 24:4
17 [a]2 Chr. 33:11–19 [b]2 Kin. 20:21

18 So [a]Ma·nas′seh [1]rested with his fathers, and was buried in the garden of his own house, in the garden of Uz′za. Then his son Ā′mon reigned in his place.

19 [a]Ā′mon *was* twenty-two years old when he became king, and he reigned two years in Jerusalem. His mother's name *was* Me·shul′le·meth the daughter of Ha′ruz of Jot′bah.

20 And he did evil in the sight of the LORD, [a]as his father Ma·nas′seh had done.

21 So he walked in all the ways that his father had walked; and he served the idols that his father had served, and worshiped them.

22 He [a]forsook the LORD God of his fathers, and did not walk in the way of the LORD.

23 [a]Then the servants of Ā′mon [b]conspired against him, and killed the king in his own house.

24 But the people of the land [a]executed all those who had conspired against King Ā′mon. Then the people of the land made his son Jō·sī′ah king in his place.

25 Now the rest of the acts of Ā′mon which he did, *are* they not written in the book of the chronicles of the kings of Judah?

26 And he was buried in his tomb in the garden of Uz′za. Then Jō·sī′ah his son reigned in his place.

22 Jō·sī′ah [a]*was* eight years old when he became king, and he reigned thirty-one years in Jerusalem. His mother's name *was* Je·dī′dah the daughter of A·dāi′ah of [b]Boz′kath.

2 And he did *what was* right in the sight of the LORD, and walked in all the ways of his father David; he [a]did not turn aside to the right hand or to the left.

3 [a]Now it came to pass, in the eighteenth year of King Jō·sī′ah, *that* the king sent Shā′phan the scribe, the son of Az·a·lī′ah, the son of Me·shul′lam, to the house of the LORD, saying:

4 "Go up to Hil·kī′ah the high priest, that he may count the money which has been [a]brought into the house of the LORD, which [b]the doorkeepers have gathered from the people.

5 "And let them [a]deliver it into the hand of those doing the work, who are the overseers in the house of the LORD; let them give it to those who *are* in the house of the LORD doing the work, to repair the damages of the house—

6 "to carpenters and builders and masons—and to buy timber and hewn stone to repair the house.

7 "However [a]there need be no accounting made with them of the money delivered into their hand, because they deal faithfully."

8 Then Hil·kī′ah the high priest said to Shā′phan the scribe, [a]"I have found the Book of the Law in the house of the LORD." And Hil·kī′ah gave the book to Shā′phan, and he read it.

9 So Shā′phan the scribe went to the king, bringing the king word, saying, "Your servants have [1]gathered the money that was found in the house, and have delivered it into the hand of those who do the work, who oversee the house of the LORD."

10 Then Shā′phan the scribe

18 [a]2 Chr. 33:20 [1]Died and joined his ancestors
19 [a]2 Chr. 33:21–23
20 [a]2 Kin. 21:2–6, 11, 16
22 [a]1 Kin. 11:33
23 [a]2 Chr. 33:24, 25 [b]2 Kin. 12:20; 14:19
24 [a]2 Kin. 14:5

CHAPTER 22

1 [a]2 Chr. 34:1 [b]Josh. 15:39
2 [a]Deut. 5:32
3 [a]2 Chr. 34:8
4 [a]2 Kin. 12:4 [b]2 Kin. 12:9, 10
5 [a]2 Kin. 12:11–14
7 [a]2 Kin. 12:15
8 [a]Deut. 31:24–26
9 [1]Lit. *poured out*

showed the king, saying, "Hil·kī′ah the priest has given me a book." And Shā′phan read it before the king.

11 Now it happened, when the king heard the words of the Book of the Law, that he tore his clothes.

12 Then the king commanded Hil·kī′ah the priest, [a]A·hī′kam the son of Shā′phan, [1]Ach′bor the son of Mī·chaī′ah, Shā′phan the scribe, and A·sāi′ah a servant of the king, saying,

13 "Go, inquire of the LORD for me, for the people and for all Judah, concerning the words of this book that has been found; for great *is* [a]the wrath of the LORD that is aroused against us, because our fathers have not obeyed the words of this book, to do according to all that is written concerning us."

14 So Hil·kī′ah the priest, A·hī′kam, Ach′bor, Shā′phan, and A·sāi′ah went to Hul′dah the prophetess, the wife of Shal′lum the son of [a]Tik′vah, the son of Har′has, keeper of the wardrobe. (She dwelt in Jerusalem in the Second Quarter.) And they spoke with her.

15 Then she said to them, "Thus says the LORD God of Israel, 'Tell the man who sent you to Me,

16 "Thus says the LORD: 'Behold, [a]I will bring calamity on this place and on its inhabitants—all the words of the book which the king of Judah has read—

17 [a]'because they have forsaken Me and burned incense to other gods, that they might provoke Me to anger with all the works of their hands. Therefore My wrath shall be aroused against this place and shall not be quenched.' " '

18 "But as for [a]the king of Judah, who sent you to inquire of the LORD, in this manner you shall speak to him, 'Thus says the LORD God of Israel: "*Concerning* the words which you have heard—

19 "because your [a]heart was tender, and you [b]humbled yourself before the LORD when you heard what I spoke against this place and against its inhabitants, that they would become [c]a desolation and [d]a curse, and you tore your clothes and wept before Me, I also have heard *you*," says the LORD.

20 "Surely, therefore, I will [1]gather you to your fathers, and you [a]shall [2]be gathered to your grave in peace; and your eyes shall not see all the calamity which I will bring on this place." ' " So they brought back word to the king.

23

Now [a]the king sent them to gather all the elders of Judah and Jerusalem to him.

2 The king went up to the house of the LORD with all the men of Judah, and with him all the inhabitants of Jerusalem—the priests and the prophets and all the people, both small and great. And he [a]read in their hearing all the words of the Book of the Covenant [b]which had been found in the house of the LORD.

3 Then the king [a]stood by a pillar and made a [b]covenant before the LORD, to follow the LORD and to keep His commandments and His testimonies and His statutes, with all *his* heart and all *his* soul, to perform the words of this covenant that were written

12 [a]Jer. 26:24 [1]*Abdon the son of Micah,* 2 Chr. 34:20
13 [a][Deut. 29:23–28; 31:17, 18]
14 [a]2 Chr. 34:22
16 [a]Deut. 29:27
17 [a]Deut. 29:25–27
18 [a]2 Chr. 34:26
19 [a][Ps. 51:17] [b]1 Kin. 21:29 [c]Lev. 26:31, 32 [d]Jer. 26:6; 44:22
20 [a][Is. 57:1, 2] [1]Cause you to join your ancestors in death [2]Die a natural death

CHAPTER 23

1 [a]2 Chr. 34:29, 30
2 [a]Deut. 31:10–13 [b]2 Kin. 22:8
3 [a]2 Kin. 11:14 [b]2 Kin. 11:17

in this book. And all the people took a stand for the covenant.

4 And the king commanded Hil·kī′ah the high priest, the [a]priests of the second order, and the doorkeepers, to bring [b]out of the temple of the LORD all the articles that were made for Bā′al, for [1]A·shē′rah, and for all [2]the host of heaven; and he burned them outside Jerusalem in the fields of Kid′ron, and carried their ashes to Beth′el.

5 Then he removed the idolatrous priests whom the kings of Judah had ordained to burn incense on the high places in the cities of Judah and in the places all around Jerusalem, and those who burned incense to Bā′al, to the sun, to the moon, to the [1]constellations, and to [a]all the host of heaven.

6 And he brought out the [a]wooden[1] image from the house of the LORD, to the Brook Kid′ron outside Jerusalem, burned it at the Brook Kid′ron and ground *it* to [b]ashes, and threw its ashes on [c]the graves of the common people.

7 Then he tore down the *ritual* [1]booths [a]of the [2]perverted persons that *were* in the house of the LORD, [b]where the [c]women wove hangings for the wooden image.

8 And he brought all the priests from the cities of Judah, and defiled the high places where the priests had burned incense, from [a]Gē′ba to Bē·er·shē′ba; also he broke down the high places at the gates which *were* at the entrance of the Gate of Joshua the governor of the city, which *were* to the left of the city gate.

9 [a]Nevertheless the priests of the high places did not come up to the altar of the LORD in Jerusalem, [b]but they ate unleavened bread among their brethren.

10 And he defiled [a]Tō′pheth, which *is* in [b]the Valley of the [1]Son of Hin′nom, [c]that no man might make his son or his daughter [d]pass through the fire to Mō′lech.

11 Then he removed the horses that the kings of Judah had [1]dedicated to the sun, at the entrance to the house of the LORD, by the chamber of Nā′than-Mē′lech, the officer who *was* in the court; and he burned the chariots of the sun with fire.

12 The altars that *were* [a]on the roof, the upper chamber of Ā′haz, which the kings of Judah had made, and the altars which [b]Ma·nas′seh had made in the two courts of the house of the LORD, the king broke down and pulverized there, and threw their dust into the Brook Kid′ron.

13 Then the king defiled the [1]high places that *were* east of Jerusalem, which *were* on the [2]south of [3]the Mount of Corruption, which [a]Solomon king of Israel had built for Ash′to·reth the abomination of the Sī·dō′ni·ans, for Chē′mosh the abomination of the Mō′ab·ītes, and for Mil′com the abomination of the people of Am′mon.

14 And he [a]broke in pieces the *sacred* pillars and cut down the wooden images, and filled their places with the bones of men.

15 Moreover the altar that *was* at Beth′el, *and* the [1]high place [a]which Jer·o·bō′am the son of Nē′bat, who made Israel sin, had made, both that altar and

4 [a]2 Kin. 25:18 [b]2 Kin. 21:3–7 [1]A Canaanite goddess [2]The gods of the Assyrians

5 [a]2 Kin. 21:3 [1]Of the Zodiac

6 [a]2 Kin. 21:7 [b]Ex. 32:20 [c]2 Chr. 34:4 [1]Heb. *Asherah*, a Canaanite goddess

7 [a]1 Kin. 14:24; 15:12 [b]Ezek. 16:16 [c]Ex. 38:8 [1]Lit. *houses* [2]Heb. *qedeshim*, those practicing sodomy and prostitution in religious rituals

8 [a]Josh. 21:17

9 [a][Ezek. 44:10–14] [b]1 Sam. 2:36

10 [a]Is. 30:33 [b]Josh. 15:8 [c][Lev. 18:21] [d]2 Kin. 21:6 [1]Kt. *Sons*

11 [1]*given*

12 [a]Jer. 19:13 [b]2 Kin. 21:5

13 [a]1 Kin. 11:5–7 [1]Places for pagan worship [2]Lit. *right of* [3]The Mount of Olives

14 [a][Ex. 23:24]

15 [a]1 Kin. 12:28–33 [1]A place for pagan worship

the high place he broke down;
and he burned the high place
and crushed *it* to powder, and
burned the wooden image.
16 As Jō·sī′ah turned, he saw
the tombs that *were* there on
the mountain. And he sent and
took the bones out of the tombs
and burned *them* on the altar,
and defiled it according to the
[a]word of the LORD which the
man of God proclaimed, who
proclaimed these words.
17 Then he said, "What grave-
stone *is* this that I see?" So the
men of the city told him, "*It is*
[a]the tomb of the man of God
who came from Judah and proclaimed these things which you
have done against the altar of
Beth′el."
18 And he said, "Let him alone;
let no one move his bones." So
they let his bones alone, with the
bones of [a]the prophet who came
from Samaria.
19 Now Jō·sī′ah also took away
all the [1]shrines of the [2]high
places that *were* [a]in the cities
of Samaria, which the kings of
Israel had made to provoke [3]the
LORD to anger; and he did to
them according to all the deeds
he had done in Beth′el.
20 [a]He [b]executed all the priests
of the [1]high places who *were*
there, on the altars, and [c]burned
men's bones on them; and he
returned to Jerusalem.
21 Then the king commanded
all the people, saying, [a]"Keep the
Passover to the LORD your God,
[b]as *it is* written in this Book of
the Covenant."
22 [a]Such a Passover surely had
never been held since the days
of the judges who judged Israel,
nor in all the days of the kings of
Israel and the kings of Judah.
23 But in the eighteenth year
of King Jō·sī′ah this Passover
was held before the LORD in
Jerusalem.
24 Moreover Jō·sī′ah put away
those who consulted mediums
and spiritists, the household
gods and idols, all the abominations that were seen in the
land of Judah and in Jerusalem,
that he might perform the words
of [a]the law which were written
in the book [b]that Hil·kī′ah the
priest found in the house of the
LORD.
25 [a]Now before him there was
no king like him, who turned
to the LORD with all his heart,
with all his soul, and with all his
might, according to all the Law
of Moses; nor after him did *any*
arise like him.
26 Nevertheless the LORD did
not turn from the fierceness of
His great wrath, with which His
anger was aroused against Judah, [a]because of all the provocations with which Ma·nas′seh
had provoked Him.
27 And the LORD said, "I will
also remove Judah from My
sight, as [a]I have removed Israel,
and will cast off this city Jerusalem which I have chosen, and
the house of which I said, [b]'My
name shall be there.' "
28 Now the rest of the acts of
Jō·sī′ah, and all that he did, *are*
they not written in the book of
the chronicles of the kings of
Judah?
29 [a]In his days Pharaoh Nē′cho
king of Egypt went [1]to the aid of
the king of Assyria, to the River
Eū·phrā′tēs; and King Jō·sī′ah
went against him. And *Pharaoh*

16 [a]1 Kin. 13:2
17 [a]1 Kin. 13:1, 30, 31
18 [a]1 Kin. 13:11, 31
19 [a]2 Chr. 34:6, 7 [1]Lit. *houses* [2]Places for pagan worship [3]So with LXX, Syr., Vg.; MT, Tg. omit *the LORD*
20 [a]1 Kin. 13:2 [b]2 Kin. 10:25; 11:18 [c]2 Chr. 34:5 [1]Places for pagan worship
21 [a]2 Chr. 35:1 [b]Deut. 16:2–8
22 [a]2 Chr. 35:18, 19
24 [a][Lev. 19:31; 20:27] [b]2 Kin. 22:8
25 [a]2 Kin. 18:5
26 [a]Jer. 15:4
27 [a]2 Kin. 17:18, 20; 18:11; 21:13 [b]1 Kin. 8:29; 9:3
29 [a]Jer. 2:16; 46:2 [1]Or *to attack*, Heb. *al* can mean *together with* or *against*

Nē´cho killed him at [b]Me·gid´dō
when he [c]confronted him.
30 [a]Then his servants moved his
body in a chariot from Me·gid´dō,
brought him to Jerusalem, and
buried him in his own tomb.
And [b]the people of the land took
Je·hō´a·haz the son of Jō·sī´ah,
anointed him, and made him
king in his father's place.
31 [a]Je·hō´a·haz *was* twenty-
three years old when he became king, and he reigned three
months in Jerusalem. His mother's name *was* [b]Ha·mū´tal the
daughter of Jer·e·mī´ah of Lib´-
nah.
32 And he did evil in the sight
of the LORD, according to all that
his fathers had done.
33 Now Pharaoh Nē´cho put
him in prison [a]at Rib´lah in the
land of Hā´math, that he might
not reign in Jerusalem; and he
imposed on the land a tribute
of one hundred talents of silver
and a talent of gold.
34 Then [a]Pharaoh Nē´cho made
E·lī´a·kim the son of Jō·sī´ah
king in place of his father
Jō·sī´ah, and [b]changed his name
to [c]Je·hoi´a·kim. And *Pharaoh*
took Je·hō´a·haz [d]and went to
Egypt, and [1]he died there.
35 So Je·hoi´a·kim gave [a]the silver and gold to Pharaoh; but he
taxed the land to give money
according to the command of
Pharaoh; he exacted the silver
and gold from the people of the
land, from every one according
to his assessment, to give *it* to
Pharaoh Nē´cho.
36 [a]Je·hoi´a·kim *was* twenty-five
years old when he became king,
and he reigned eleven years in
Jerusalem. His mother's name

29 [b]Zech. 12:11 [c]2 Kin. 14:8
30 [a]2 Chr. 35:24 [b]2 Chr. 36:1–4
31 [a]Jer. 22:11 [b]2 Kin. 24:18
33 [a]2 Kin. 25:6
34 [a]2 Chr. 36:4 [b]Dan. 1:7 [c]Matt. 1:11 [d]Ezek. 19:3, 4 [1]Jehoahaz
35 [a]2 Kin. 23:33
36 [a]2 Chr. 36:5

CHAPTER 24

1 [a]Dan. 1:1 [b]2 Kin. 20:14
2 [a]Jer. 25:9; 32:28; 35:11 [b]2 Kin. 20:17; 21:12–14; 23:27 [1]*troops*
3 [a]2 Kin. 21:2, 11; 23:26
4 [a]2 Kin. 21:16
6 [a]Jer. 22:18, 19
7 [a]Jer. 37:5–7 [b]Jer. 46:2
8 [a]2 Chr. 36:9 [1]*Jeconiah,* 1 Chr. 3:16; Jer. 24:1; or *Coniah,* Jer. 22:24, 28

was Ze·bū´dah the daughter of
Pe·dāi´ah of Rū´mah.
37 And he did evil in the sight
of the LORD, according to all that
his fathers had done.

24 In [a]his days Ne·bū·chad-
nez´zar king of [b]Babylon
came up, and Je·hoi´a·kim became his vassal *for* three years.
Then he turned and rebelled
against him.
2 [a]And the LORD sent against
him *raiding* [1]bands of Chal·dē´-
ans, bands of Syrians, bands
of Mō´ab·ītes, and bands of the
people of Am´mon; He sent
them against Judah to destroy
it, [b]according to the word of the
LORD which He had spoken by
His servants the prophets.
3 Surely at the commandment
of the LORD *this* came upon Judah, to remove *them* from His
sight [a]because of the sins of
Ma·nas´seh, according to all that
he had done,
4 [a]and also because of the innocent blood that he had shed;
for he had filled Jerusalem with
innocent blood, which the LORD
would not pardon.
5 Now the rest of the acts of
Je·hoi´a·kim, and all that he did,
are they not written in the book
of the chronicles of the kings of
Judah?
6 [a]So Je·hoi´a·kim rested with
his fathers. Then Je·hoi´a·chin
his son reigned in his place.
7 And [a]the king of Egypt did
not come out of his land anymore, for [b]the king of Babylon
had taken all that belonged
to the king of Egypt from the
Brook of Egypt to the River
Eū·phrā´tēs.
8 [a]Je·hoi´a·chin[1] *was* eighteen
years old when he became king,

and he reigned in Jerusalem
three months. His mother's name
was Ne·hush'ta the daughter of
El·nā'than of Jerusalem.
9 And he did evil in the sight
of the LORD, according to all that
his father had done.
10 [a]At that time the servants of
Ne·bū·chad·nez'zar king of Babylon came up against Jerusalem,
and the city [1]was besieged.
11 And Ne·bū·chad·nez'zar king
of Babylon came against the
city, as his servants were besieging it.
12 [a]Then Je·hoi'a·chin king of
Judah, his mother, his servants,
his princes, and his officers
went out to the king of Babylon;
and the king of Babylon, [b]in the
eighth year of his reign, took
him prisoner.
13 [a]And he carried out from
there all the treasures of the
house of the LORD and the treasures of the king's house, and
he [b]cut in pieces all the articles
of gold which Solomon king of
Israel had made in the temple of
the LORD, [c]as the LORD had said.
14 Also [a]he carried into captivity all Jerusalem: all the captains
and all the mighty men of valor,
[b]ten thousand captives, and [c]all
the craftsmen and smiths. None
remained except [d]the poorest
people of the land.
15 And [a]he carried Je·hoi'a·chin
captive to Babylon. The king's
mother, the king's wives, his
officers, and the mighty of the
land he carried into captivity
from Jerusalem to Babylon.
16 [a]All the valiant men, seven
thousand, and craftsmen and
smiths, one thousand, all *who*
were strong *and* fit for war, these

10 [a]Dan. 1:1 [1]Lit. *came into siege*
12 [a]Jer. 22:24–30; 24:1; 29:1, 2 [b]2 Chr. 36:10
13 [a]Is. 39:6 [b]Dan. 5:2, 3 [c]Jer. 20:5
14 [a]Jer. 24:1 [b]2 Kin. 24:16 [c]1 Sam. 13:19 [d]2 Kin. 25:12
15 [a]Jer. 22:24–28
16 [a]Jer. 52:28
17 [a]Jer. 37:1 [b]2 Chr. 36:10 [c]2 Chr. 36:4 [1]Lit. *his*
18 [a]Jer. 52:1 [b]2 Kin. 23:31
19 [a]2 Chr. 36:12
20 [a]Ezek. 17:15

CHAPTER 25

1 [a]Jer. 6:6; 34:2
3 [a]Lam. 4:9, 10
4 [a]Jer. 39:2 [b]Ezek. 12:12 [1]Lit. *he* [2]Or *Arabah*, the Jordan Valley

the king of Babylon brought
captive to Babylon.
17 Then [a]the king of Babylon made Mat·ta·nī'ah, [b]*Je-
hoi'a·chin's*[1] uncle, king in his
place, and [c]changed his name to
Zed·e·kī'ah.
18 [a]Zed·e·kī'ah *was* twenty-one
years old when he became king,
and he reigned eleven years in
Jerusalem. His mother's name
was [b]Ha·mū'tal the daughter of
Jer·e·mī'ah of Lib'nah.
19 [a]He also did evil in the sight
of the LORD, according to all that
Je·hoi'a·kim had done.
20 For because of the anger of
the LORD *this* happened in Jerusalem and Judah, that He finally
cast them out from His presence. [a]Then Zed·e·kī'ah rebelled
against the king of Babylon.

25 Now it came to pass [a]in
the ninth year of his
reign, in the tenth month, on the
tenth *day* of the month, *that* Ne-
bū·chad·nez'zar king of Babylon
and all his army came against Jerusalem and encamped against
it; and they built a siege wall
against it all around.
2 So the city was besieged until the eleventh year of King
Zed·e·kī'ah.
3 By the ninth *day* of the
[a]*fourth* month the famine had
become so severe in the city that
there was no food for the people
of the land.
4 Then [a]the city wall was broken through, and all the men of
war *fled* at night by way of the
gate between two walls, which
was by the king's garden, even
though the Chal·dē'ans *were* still
encamped all around against the
city. And [b]*the king*[1] went by way
of the [2]plain.

5 But the army of the Chal·dē′-
ans pursued the king, and they
overtook him in the plains of
Jericho. All his army was scattered from him.
6 So they took the king and
brought him up to the king of
Babylon [a]at Rib′lah, and they
pronounced judgment on him.
7 Then they killed the sons
of Zed·e·kī′ah before his eyes,
[a]put[1] out the eyes of Zed·e·kī′ah,
bound him with bronze fetters,
and took him to Babylon.
8 And in the fifth month, [a]on
the seventh *day* of the month
(which *was* [b]the nineteenth year
of King Ne·bū·chad·nez′zar king
of Babylon), [c]Ne·bū·za·rad′an
the captain of the guard, a servant of the king of Babylon,
came to Jerusalem.
9 [a]He burned the house of the
LORD [b]and the king's house; all
the houses of Jerusalem, that is,
all the houses of the great, [c]he
burned with fire.
10 And all the army of the
Chal·dē′ans who *were with* the
captain of the guard [a]broke
down the walls of Jerusalem all
around.
11 Then Ne·bū·za·rad′an the
captain of the guard carried
away captive [a]the rest of the
people *who* remained in the city
and the defectors who had deserted to the king of Babylon,
with the rest of the multitude.
12 But the captain of the guard
[a]left *some* of the poor of the land
as vinedressers and farmers.
13 [a]The bronze [b]pillars that
were in the house of the LORD,
and [c]the carts and [d]the bronze
Sea that *were* in the house of the
LORD, the Chal·dē′ans broke in
pieces, and [e]carried their bronze
to Babylon.
14 They also took away [a]the
pots, the shovels, the trimmers,
the spoons, and all the bronze
utensils with which the priests
ministered.
15 The firepans and the basins,
the things of solid gold and solid
silver, the captain of the guard
took away.
16 The two pillars, one Sea, and
the carts, which Solomon had
made for the house of the LORD,
[a]the bronze of all these articles
was beyond measure.
17 [a]The height of one pillar *was*
[1]eighteen cubits, and the capital
on it *was* of bronze. The height
of the capital was three cubits,
and the network and pomegranates all around the capital were
all of bronze. The second pillar
was the same, with a network.
18 [a]And the captain of the guard
took [b]Se·rāi′ah the chief priest,
[c]Zeph·a·nī′ah the second priest,
and the three doorkeepers.
19 He also took out of the city
an officer who had charge of
the men of war, [a]five men of
[1]the king's close associates who
were found in the city, the chief
recruiting officer of the army,
who mustered the people of the
land, and sixty men of the people of the land *who were* found
in the city.
20 So Ne·bū·za·rad′an, captain
of the guard, took these and
brought them to the king of Babylon at Rib′lah.
21 Then the king of Babylon
struck them and put them to
death at Rib′lah in the land of
Hā′math. [a]Thus Judah was carried away captive from its own
land.

6 [a]Jer. 52:9
7 [a]Jer. 39:7 [1]*blinded*
8 [a]Jer. 52:12 [b]2 Kin. 24:12 [c]Jer. 39:9
9 [a]2 Chr. 36:19 [b]Jer. 39:8 [c]Jer. 17:27
10 [a]Neh. 1:3
11 [a]Jer. 5:19; 39:9
12 [a]Jer. 39:10; 40:7; 52:16
13 [a]Jer. 52:17 [b]1 Kin. 7:15 [c]1 Kin. 7:27 [d]1 Kin. 7:23 [e]Jer. 27:19–22
14 [a]Ex. 27:3
16 [a]1 Kin. 7:47
17 [a]1 Kin. 7:15–22 [1]About 27 feet
18 [a]Jer. 39:9–13; 52:12–16, 24 [b]Ezra 7:1 [c]Jer. 21:1; 29:25, 29
19 [a]Jer. 52:25 [1]Lit. *those seeing the king's face*
21 [a]Deut. 28:36, 64

22 Then he made Ged·a·lī′ah the son of [a]A·hī′kam, the son of Shā′phan, governor over [b]the people who remained in the land of Judah, whom Ne·bū·chad·nez′zar king of Babylon had left.

23 Now when all the [a]captains of the armies, they and *their* men, heard that the king of Babylon had made Ged·a·lī′ah governor, they came to Ged·a·lī′ah at Miz′pah—Ish′ma·el the son of Neth·a·nī′ah, Jō·hā′nan the son of Ca·rē′ah, Se·rāi′ah the son of Tan′hu·meth the Ne·toph′a·thīte, and [1]Jā·az·a·nī′ah the son of a Mā′a·cha·thīte, they and their men.

24 And Ged·a·lī′ah took an oath before them and their men, and said to them, "Do not be afraid of the servants of the Chal·dē′ans. Dwell in the land and serve the king of Babylon, and it shall be well with you."

25 But [a]it happened in the seventh month that Ish′ma·el the son of Neth·a·nī′ah, the son of E·lish′a·ma, of the royal family, came with ten men and struck and killed Ged·a·lī′ah, the Jews, as well as the Chal·dē′ans who were with him at Miz′pah.

26 And all the people, small and great, and the captains of the armies, arose [a]and went to Egypt; for they were afraid of the Chal·dē′ans.

27 [a]Now it came to pass in the thirty-seventh year of the captivity of Je·hoi′a·chin king of Judah, in the twelfth month, on the twenty-seventh *day* of the month, *that* [1]Ē′vil-Me·rō′dach king of Babylon, in the year that he began to reign, [b]released Je·hoi′a·chin king of Judah from prison.

28 He spoke kindly to him, and gave him a more prominent seat than those of the kings who *were* with him in Babylon.

29 So Je·hoi′a·chin changed from his prison garments, and he [a]ate [1]bread regularly before the king all the days of his life.

30 And as for his [1]provisions, *there was* a [2]regular ration given him by the king, a portion for each day, all the days of his life.

22 [a]2 Kin. 22:12 [b]Is. 1:9; Jer. 40:5
23 [a]Jer. 40:7–9 [1]*Jezaniah*, Jer. 40:8
25 [a]Jer. 41:1–3
26 [a]Jer. 43:4–7
27 [a]Jer. 52:31–34 [b]Gen. 40:13, 20 [1]Lit. *Man of Marduk*
29 [a]2 Sam. 9:7 [1]Food
30 [1]Lit. *allowance* [2]Lit. *allowance*

The First Book of the

CHRONICLES

THE books of First and Second Chronicles cover the same period of Jewish history described in Second Samuel through Second Kings, but the perspective is different. These books are no mere repetition of the same material, but rather form a divine editorial on the history of God's people. While Second Samuel and First and Second Kings give a political history of Israel and Judah, First and Second Chronicles present a religious history of the Davidic dynasty of Judah. The former are written from a prophetic and moral viewpoint and the latter from a priestly and spiritual perspective. The Book of First Chronicles begins with the royal line of David and then traces the spiritual significance of David's righteous reign.

The books of First and Second Chronicles were originally one continuous work in the Hebrew. The title was *Dibere Hayyamim,* meaning "The Words [accounts, events] of the Days." The equivalent meaning today would be "The Events of the Times." Chronicles was divided into two parts in the third-century B.C. Greek translation of the Hebrew Bible (the Septuagint). At that time it was given the name *Paraleipomenon.* "Of Things Omitted," referring to the things omitted from Samuel and Kings. Some copies add the phrase, *Basileon Iouda,* "Concerning the Kings of Judah." The first book of Chronicles was called *Paraleipomenon Primus,* "The First Book of Things Omitted." The name "Chronicles" comes from Jerome in his Latin Vulgate Bible (A.D. 385–405): *Chronicorum Liber.* He meant his title in the sense of the "Chronicles of the Whole of Sacred History."

ADAM,[a] [b]Seth, Ē′nosh,
2 Cā·ī′nan, Ma·hal′a·lel,
Jar′ed,
3 Ē′noch, Me·thū′se·lah, Lā′-
mech,
4 [a]Noah,[1] Shem, Ham, and Jā′-
pheth.
5 [a]The sons of Jā′pheth *were*
Gō′mer, Mā′gog, Mā′daī, Jā′van,
Tū′bal, Mē′shech, and Tī′ras.
6 The sons of Gō′mer *were*
Ash′ke·naz, [1]Dī′phath, and Tō-
gar′mah.
7 The sons of Jā′van *were* E·li′-
shah, [1]Tar·shish′ah, Kit′tim, and
[2]Rod′a·nim.
8 [a]The sons of Ham *were* Cush,
Miz′ra·im, Put, and Cā′naan.
9 The sons of Cush *were* Sē′ba,
Hav′i·lah, [1]Sab′ta, [2]Rā′a·ma, and
Sab′te·cha. The sons of Rā′a·ma
were Shē′ba and Dē′dan.
10 Cush [a]begot Nim′rod; he began to be a mighty one on the
earth.
11 Miz′ra·im begot Lū′dim, An′-
a·mim, Le·hā′bim, Naph′tū·him,
12 Path·rū′sim, Cas·lū′him (from
whom came the Phi·lis′tines and
the [a]Caph′to·rim).
13 [a]Cā′naan begot Sī′don, his
firstborn, and Heth;
14 the Jeb′ū·sīte, the Am′o·rīte,
and the Gir′ga·shīte;
15 the Hī′vīte, the Ar′kīte, and
the Sī′nīte;
16 the Ar′vad·īte, the Zem′a·rīte,
and the Hā′math·īte.

CHAPTER 1

1 [a]Gen. 1:27; 2:7; 5:1, 2, 5 [b]Gen. 4:25, 26; 5:3–9
4 [a]Gen. 5:28—10:1 [1]So with MT, Vg.; LXX adds *the sons of Noah*
5 [a]Gen. 10:2–4
6 [1]*Riphath,* Gen. 10:3
7 [1]*Tarshish,* Gen. 10:4 [2]*Dodanim,* Gen. 10:4
8 [a]Gen. 10:6
9 [1]*Sabtah,* Gen. 10:7 [2]*Raamah,* Gen. 10:7
10 [a]Gen. 10:8–10, 13
12 [a]Deut. 2:23
13 [a]Gen. 9:18, 25–27; 10:15

17 The sons of [a]Shem *were*
Ē′lam, As′shur, [b]Ar·phā′xad,
Lud, Ar′am, Uz, Hul, Gē′ther,
and [1]Mē′shech.
18 Ar·phā′xad begot Shē′lah,
and Shē′lah begot Ē′ber.
19 To Ē′ber were born two sons:
the name of one *was* [1]Pē′leg,
for in his days the [2]earth was
divided; and his brother's name
was Jok′tan.
20 [a]Jok′tan begot Al·mō′dad,
Shē′leph, Hā·zar·mā′veth, Jē′-
rah,
21 Ha·dor′am, Ū′zal, Dik′lah,
22 [1]Ē′bal, A·bim′a·el, Shē′ba,
23 Ō′phir, Hav′i·lah, and Jō′bab.
All these *were* the sons of Jok′-
tan.
24 [a]Shem, Ar·phā′xad, Shē′lah,
25 [a]Ē′ber, Pē′leg, Rē′ū,
26 Sē′rug, Nā′hor, Tē′rah,
27 and [a]Abram, who *is* Abraham.
28 [a]The sons of Abraham *were*
[b]Isaac and [c]Ish′ma·el.
29 These *are* their genealogies:
The [a]firstborn of Ish′ma·el *was*
Ne·bā′joth; then Kē′dar, Ad′-
bē·el, Mib′sam,
30 Mish′ma, Dū′mah, Mas′sa,
[1]Hā′dad, Tē′ma,
31 Jē′tur, Nā′phish, and Ked′-
e·mah. These *were* the sons of
Ish′ma·el.
32 Now [a]the sons born to Ke·tū′-
rah, Abraham's concubine, *were*
Zim′ran, Jok′shan, Mē′dan, Mid′-
i·an, Ish′bak, and Shū′ah. The
sons of Jok′shan *were* Shē′ba
and Dē′dan.
33 The sons of Mid′i·an *were*
Ē′phah, Ē′pher, Hā′noch, A·bī′da,
and El·dā′ah. All these were the
children of Ke·tū′rah.
34 And [a]Abraham begot Isaac.
[b]The sons of Isaac *were* Esau
and Israel.

35 The sons of [a]Esau *were* E·lī′-
phaz, Reū′el, Jē′ush, Jā′a·lam,
and Kō′rah.
36 And the sons of E·lī′phaz
were Tē′man, Ō′mar, [1]Zē′phī,
Gā′tam, *and* Kē′naz; and *by*
[a]Tim′na, Am′a·lek.
37 The sons of Reū′el *were* Nā′-
hath, Zē′rah, Sham′mah, and
Miz′zah.
38 [a]The sons of Sē′ir *were* Lō′-
tan, Shō′bal, Zib′ē·on, An′ah,
Dī′shon, Ē′zer, and Dī′shan.
39 And the sons of Lō′tan *were*
Hō′rī and [1]Hō′mam; Lō′tan's sister *was* Tim′na.
40 The sons of Shō′bal *were* [1]Al′-
i·an, Man′a·hath, Ē′bal, [2]Shē′phī,
and Ō′nam. The sons of Zib′ē·on
were Ā′jah and An′ah.
41 The son of An′ah *was* [a]Dī′-
shon. The sons of Dī′shon *were*
[1]Ham′ran, Esh′ban, Ith′ran, and
Chē′ran.
42 The sons of Ē′zer *were* Bil′-
han, Zā′a·van, *and* [1]Jā′a·kan.
The sons of Dī′shan *were* Uz
and Ar′an.
43 Now these *were* the [a]kings
who reigned in the land of
Ē′dom before a king reigned
over the children of Israel: Bē′la
the son of Bē′or, and the name of
his city was Din′ha·bah.
44 And when Bē′la died, Jō′bab
the son of Zē′rah of Boz′rah
reigned in his place.
45 When Jō′bab died, Hū′sham
of the land of the Tē′man·ītes
reigned in his place.
46 And when Hū′sham died,
Hā′dad the son of Bē′dad, who
[1]attacked Mid′i·an in the field of
Mō′ab, reigned in his place. The
name of his city *was* Ā′vith.
47 When Hā′dad died, Sam′-
lah of Mas·rē′kah reigned in his
place.

17 [a]Gen. 10:22–29; 11:10 [b]Luke 3:36 [1]*Mash*, Gen. 10:23
19 [1]Lit. *Division*, Gen. 10:25 [2]Or *land*
20 [a]Gen. 10:26
22 [1]*Obal*, Gen. 10:28
24 [a]Luke 3:34–36
25 [a]Gen. 11:15
27 [a]Gen. 17:5
28 [a]Gen. 21:2, 3 [b]Gen. 21:2 [c]Gen. 16:11, 15
29 [a]Gen. 25:13–16
30 [1]*Hadar*, Gen. 25:15
32 [a]Gen. 25:1–4
34 [a]Gen. 21:2 [b]Gen. 25:9, 25, 26, 29; 32:28
35 [a]Gen. 36:10–19
36 [a]Gen. 36:12 [1]*Zepho*, Gen. 36:11
38 [a]Gen. 36:20–28
39 [1]*Hemam* or *Heman*, Gen. 36:22
40 [1]*Alvan*, Gen. 36:23 [2]*Shepho*, Gen. 36:23
41 [a]Gen. 36:25 [1]*Hemdan*, Gen. 36:26
42 [1]*Akan*, Gen. 36:27
43 [a]Gen. 36:31–43
46 [1]Lit. *struck*

48 [a]And when Sam′lah died,
Saul of Re·hō′both-by-the-River
reigned in his place.
49 When Saul died, Bā′al-Hā′-
nan the son of Ach′bor reigned
in his place.
50 And when Bā′al-Hā′nan died,
[1]Hā′dad reigned in his place; and
the name of his city was [2]Pā′ī.
His wife's name was Me·het′-
a·bel the daughter of Mā′tred,
the daughter of Mez′a·hab.
51 Hā′dad died also. And the
chiefs of Ē′dom were Chief Tim′-
nah, Chief [1]Al′i·ah, Chief Jē′-
theth,
52 Chief A·hol·i·bā′mah, Chief
Ē′lah, Chief Pī′non,
53 Chief Kē′naz, Chief Tē′man,
Chief Mib′zar,
54 Chief Mag′di·el, and Chief
Ī′ram. These *were* the chiefs of
Ē′dom.

2 These *were* the [a]sons of [1]Is-
rael: [b]Reuben, Sim′ē·on, Levi,
Judah, Is′sa·char, Zeb′ū·lun,
2 Dan, Joseph, Benjamin,
Naph′ta·lī, Gad, and Ash′er.
3 The sons of [a]Judah *were* Er,
Ō′nan, and Shē′lah. *These* three
were born to him by the daughter of [b]Shū′a, the Cā′naan·ī·tess.
[c]Er, the firstborn of Judah, was
wicked in the sight of the LORD;
so He killed him.
4 And [a]Tā′mar, his daughter-
in-law, [b]bore him Per′ez and Zē′-
rah. All the sons of Judah *were*
five.
5 The sons of [a]Per′ez *were*
Hez′ron and Hā′mul.
6 The sons of Zē′rah *were*
[1]Zim′rī, [a]Ē′than, Hē′man, Cal′col,
and [2]Dar′a—five of them in all.
7 The son of [a]Car′mī *was*
[1]Ā′char, the troubler of Israel,
who transgressed in the [b]ac-
cursed[2] thing.
8 The son of Ē′than *was* Az·a-
rī′ah.
9 Also the sons of Hez′ron who
were born to him *were* Je·rah′-
mē·el, [1]Ram, and [2]Che·lū′baī.
10 Ram [a]begot Am·min′a·dab,
and Am·min′a·dab begot Nah′-
shon, [b]leader of the children of
Judah;
11 Nah′shon begot [1]Sal′ma, and
Sal′ma begot Bō′az;
12 Bō′az begot Ō′bed, and Ō′bed
begot Jesse;
13 [a]Jesse begot E·lī′ab his firstborn, A·bin′a·dab the second,
[1]Shim′ē·a the third,
14 Ne·than′el the fourth, Rad′-
daī the fifth,
15 Ō′zem the sixth, *and* David
the [a]seventh.
16 Now their sisters *were*
Ze·rū′i·ah and Ab′i·gāil. [a]And
the sons of Ze·rū′i·ah *were* A·bi′-
shaī, Jō′ab, and As′a·hel—three.
17 Ab′i·gāil bore A·mā′sa; and
the father of A·mā′sa *was* [1]Jē′-
ther the Ish′ma·el·īte.
18 Caleb the son of Hez′ron had
children by A·zū′bah, *his* wife,
and by Jer′i·oth. Now these were
her sons: Jē′sher, Shō′bab, and
Ar′don.
19 When A·zū′bah died, Caleb
[1]took [a]Eph′rath[2] as his wife, who
bore him Hur.
20 And Hur begot Ū′rī, and Ū′rī
begot [a]Bez′a·lel.
21 Now afterward Hez′ron went
in to the daughter of [a]Mā′chir the
father of Gil′ē·ad, whom he married when he *was* sixty years
old; and she bore him Sē′gub.
22 Sē′gub begot [a]Jā′ir,[1] who had
twenty-three cities in the land of
Gil′ē·ad.
23 [a](Gē′shur and Syria took
from them the towns of Jā′ir,
with Kē′nath and its towns—

48 [a]Gen. 36:37
50 [1]*Hadar*, Gen. 36:39 [2]*Pau*, Gen. 36:39
51 [1]*Alvah*, Gen. 36:40

CHAPTER 2

1 [a]Gen. 29:32–35; 35:23, 26; 46:8–27 [b]Gen. 29:32; 35:22 [1]*Jacob*, Gen. 32:28
3 [a]Num. 26:19 [b]Gen. 38:2 [c]Gen. 38:7
4 [a]Gen. 38:6 [b]Matt. 1:3
5 [a]Ruth 4:18
6 [a]1 Kin. 4:31 [1]*Zabdi*, Josh. 7:1 [2]*Darda*, 1 Kin. 4:31
7 [a]1 Chr. 4:1 [b]Josh. 6:18 [1]*Achan*, Josh. 7:1 [2]*banned* or *devoted*
9 [1]*Aram*, Matt. 1:3, 4 [2]*Caleb*, vv. 18, 42
10 [a]Matt. 1:4 [b]Num. 1:7; 2:3
11 [1]*Salmon*, Ruth 4:21; Luke 3:32
13 [a]1 Sam. 16:6 [1]*Shammah*, 1 Sam. 16:9
15 [a]1 Sam. 16:10, 11; 17:12
16 [a]2 Sam. 2:18
17 [1]*Jithra the Israelite*, 2 Sam. 17:25
19 [a]1 Chr. 2:50 [1]Lit. *took to himself* [2]Or *Ephrathah*
20 [a]Ex. 31:2; 38:22
21 [a]Num. 27:1
22 [a]Judg. 10:3 [1]Reckoned to Manasseh through the daughter of Machir, Num. 32:41; Deut. 3:14; 25:5, 6; 1 Kin. 4:13; 1 Chr. 7:14
23 [a]Deut. 3:14

sixty towns.) All these *belonged*
to the sons of Mā′chir the father
of Gil′ē·ad.
24 After Hez′ron died in Caleb Eph′ra·thah, Hez′ron's wife
A·bī′jah bore him [a]Ash′hur the
father of Te·kō′a.
25 The sons of Je·rah′mē·el, the
firstborn of Hez′ron, *were* Ram,
the firstborn, and Bū′nah, Ō′ren,
Ō′zem, *and* A·hī′jah.
26 Je·rah′mē·el had another
wife, whose name was At′a·rah;
she was the mother of Ō′nam.
27 The sons of Ram, the firstborn of Je·rah′mē·el, were Mā′az,
Jā′min, and Ē′ker.
28 The sons of Ō′nam were
Sham′maī and Jā′da. The sons
of Sham′maī *were* Nā′dab and
A·bī′shur.
29 And the name of the wife of
A·bī′shur *was* Ab·i·hā′il, and she
bore him Ah′ban and Mō′lid.
30 The sons of Nā′dab *were*
Sē′led and Ap′pa·im; Sē′led died
without children.
31 The son of Ap′pa·im *was*
Ish′ī, the son of Ish′ī *was* Shē′-
shan, and [a]Shē′shan's son *was*
Ah′laī.
32 The sons of Jā′da, the brother
of Sham′maī, *were* Jē′ther and
Jonathan; Jē′ther died without
children.
33 The sons of Jonathan *were*
Pē′leth and Zā′za. These were
the sons of Je·rah′mē·el.
34 Now Shē′shan had no sons,
only daughters. And Shē′shan
had an Egyptian servant whose
name *was* Jar′ha.
35 Shē′shan gave his daughter
to Jar′ha his servant as wife, and
she bore him At′taī.
36 At′taī begot Nathan, and Nathan begot [a]Zā′bad;

24 [a]1 Chr. 4:5
31 [a]1 Chr. 2:34, 35
36 [a]1 Chr. 11:41
37 [a]2 Chr. 23:1
49 [a]Josh. 15:17 [1]Or *Achsa*
50 [a]1 Chr. 4:4 [b]Josh. 9:17; 18:14 [1]*Ephrath*, v. 19

37 Zā′bad begot Eph′lal, and
Eph′lal begot [a]Ō′bed;
38 Ō′bed begot Jē′hū, and Jē′hū
begot Az·a·rī′ah;
39 Az·a·rī′ah begot Hē′lez, and
Hē′lez begot El·e·ā′sah;
40 El·e·ā′sah begot Sis′maī, and
Sis′maī begot Shal′lum;
41 Shal′lum begot Jek·a·mī′ah,
and Jek·a·mī′ah begot E·lish′-
a·ma.
42 The descendants of Caleb
the brother of Je·rah′mē·el *were*
Mē′sha, his firstborn, who was
the father of Ziph, and the sons
of Ma·rē′shah the father of Hē′-
bron.
43 The sons of Hē′bron *were*
Kō′rah, Tap′pū·ah, Rē′kem, and
Shē′ma.
44 Shē′ma begot Rā′ham the
father of Jor·kō′am, and Rē′kem
begot Sham′maī.
45 And the son of Sham′maī
was Mā′on, and Mā′on *was* the
father of Beth Zūr.
46 Ē′phah, Caleb's concubine,
bore Har′an, Mō′za, and Gā′zez;
and Har′an begot Gā′zez.
47 And the sons of Jah′daī *were*
Rē′gem, Jō′tham, Gē′shan, Pē′-
let, Ē′phah, and Shā′aph.
48 Mā′a·chah, Caleb's concubine, bore Shē′ber and Tir′-
hā·nah.
49 She also bore Shā′aph the father of Mad·man′nah, Shē′va the
father of Mach·bē′nah and the father of Gib′ē·a. And the daughter
of Caleb *was* [a]Ach′sah.[1]
50 These were the descendants
of Caleb: The sons of [a]Hur, the
firstborn of [1]Eph′ra·thah, *were*
Shō′bal the father of [b]Kir′jath
Jē′a·rim,
51 Sal′ma the father of Bethlehem, *and* Har′eph the father of
Beth Gā′der.

52 And Shō′bal the father of
Kir′jath Jē′a·rim had descendants: [1]Ha·rō′eh, *and* half of the
[2]*families of* Ma·nū′hoth.
53 The families of Kir′jath Jē′-
a·rim *were* the Ith′rītes, the Pū′-
thītes, the Shū′ma·thītes, and the
Mish′ra·ītes. From these came
the Zō′ra·thītes and the Esh′-
ta·o·lītes.
54 The sons of Sal′ma *were*
Bethlehem, the Ne·toph′a·thītes,
[1]At′roth Beth Jō′ab, half of the
Ma·nā′heth·ītes, and the Zō′-
rītes.
55 And the families of the
scribes who dwelt at Jā′bez
were the Tī′ra·thītes, the Shim′-
ē·a·thītes, *and* the Sū′cha·thītes.
These *were* the [a]Ken′ītes who
came from Ham′math, the father
of the house of [b]Rē′chab.

3 Now these were the sons
of David who were born to
him in Hē′bron: The firstborn
was [a]Am′non, by [b]A·hin′ō·am
the [c]Jez′rē·el·ī·tess; the second,
[1]Daniel, by [d]Ab′i·gāil the Car′-
mel·ī·tess;
2 the third, [a]Ab′sa·lom the son
of Mā′a·cah, the daughter of Tal′-
maī, king of Gē′shur; the fourth,
[b]Ad·o·nī′jah the son of Hag′gith;
3 the fifth, Sheph·a·tī′ah, by
A·bī′tal; the sixth, Ith′rē·am, by
his wife [a]Eg′lah.
4 *These* six were born to him
in Hē′bron. [a]There he reigned
seven years and six months, and
[b]in Jerusalem he reigned thirty-
three years.
5 [a]And these were born to him
in Jerusalem: [1]Shim′ē·a, Shō′-
bab, Nathan, and [b]Solomon—
four by [2]Bath·shū′a the daughter
of [3]Am′mi·el.
6 Also *there* were Ib′har,
[1]E·lish′a·ma, [2]E·liph′e·let,
7 Nō′gah, Nē′pheg, Ja·phī′a,
8 E·lish′a·ma, [1]E·lī′a·da, and
E·liph′e·let—[a]nine *in all.*
9 *These were* all the sons of
David, besides the sons of the
concubines, and [a]Tā′mar their
sister.
10 Solomon's son *was* [a]Rē·ho-
bō′am; [1]A·bī′jah *was* his son,
Ā′sa his son, Je·hosh′a·phat his
son,
11 [1]Jō′ram his son, [2]Ā·ha·zī′ah
his son, [3]Jō′ash his son,
12 Am·a·zī′ah his son, [1]Az·a·rī′ah
his son, Jō′tham his son,
13 Ā′haz his son, Hez·e·kī′ah
his son, Ma·nas′seh his son,
14 Ā′mon his son, *and* Jō·sī′ah
his son.
15 The sons of Jō·sī′ah *were*
Jō·hā′nan the firstborn, the
second [1]Je·hoi′a·kim, the third
Zed·e·kī′ah, and the fourth
[2]Shal′lum.
16 The sons of [a]Je·hoi′a·kim
were [1]Jec·o·nī′ah his son *and*
[2]Zed·e·kī′ah his son.
17 And the sons of [1]Jec·o·nī′ah
[2]*were* As′sir, She·al′ti·el [a]his son,
18 *and* Mal·chī′ram, Pe·dāi′ah,
Shen·az′zar, Jec·a·mī′ah, Hosh′-
a·ma, and Ned·a·bī′ah.
19 The sons of Pe·dāi′ah *were*
Ze·rub′ba·bel and Shim′ē·ī. The
sons of Ze·rub′ba·bel *were* Me-
shul′lam, Han·a·nī′ah, She·lō′-
mith their sister,
20 and Ha·shū′bah, Ō′hel, Ber-
e·chī′ah, Has·a·dī′ah, and Jū′-
shab-Hē′sed—five *in all.*
21 The sons of Han·a·nī′ah *were*
Pel·a·tī′ah and Je·shā′i·ah, the
sons of Reph·āi′ah, the sons of
Ar′nan, the sons of Ō·ba·dī′ah,
and the sons of Shech·a·nī′ah.
22 The son of Shech·a·nī′ah
was She·māi′ah. The sons of
She·māi′ah *were* [a]Hat′tush, Ī′gal,

52 [1]*Reaiah,* 1 Chr. 4:2 [2]Or *Manuhothites,* same as *Manahethites,* v. 54
54 [1]Or *Ataroth of the house of Joab*
55 [a]Judg. 1:16 [b]Jer. 35:2

CHAPTER 3

1 [a]2 Sam. 3:2–5 [b]1 Sam. 25:43 [c]Josh. 15:56 [d]1 Sam. 25:39–42 [1]*Chileab,* 2 Sam. 3:3
2 [a]2 Sam. 13:37; 15:1 [b]1 Kin. 1:5
3 [a]2 Sam. 3:5
4 [a]2 Sam. 2:11 [b]2 Sam. 5:5
5 [a]1 Chr. 14:4–7 [b]2 Sam. 12:24, 25 [1]*Shammua,* 1 Chr. 14:4; 2 Sam. 5:14 [2]*Bathsheba,* 2 Sam. 11:3 [3]*Eliam,* 2 Sam. 11:3
6 [1]*Elishua,* 1 Chr. 14:5; 2 Sam. 5:15 [2]*Elpelet,* 1 Chr. 14:5
8 [a]2 Sam. 5:14–16 [1]*Beeliada,* 1 Chr. 14:7
9 [a]2 Sam. 13:1
10 [a]1 Kin. 11:43 [1]*Abijam,* 1 Kin. 15:1
11 [1]*Jehoram,* 2 Kin. 1:17; 8:16 [2]Or *Azariah* or *Jehoahaz* [3]*Jehoash,* 2 Kin. 12:1
12 [1]*Uzziah,* Is. 6:1
15 [1]*Eliakim,* 2 Kin. 23:34 [2]*Jehoahaz,* 2 Kin. 23:31
16 [a]Matt. 1:11 [1]*Jehoiachin,* 2 Kin. 24:8, or *Coniah,* Jer. 22:24 [2]*Mattaniah,* 2 Kin. 24:17
17 [a]Matt. 1:12 [1]*Jehoiachin,* 2 Kin. 24:8, or *Coniah,* Jer. 22:24 [2]Or *the captive were Shealtiel*
22 [a]Ezra 8:2

Ba·rī′ah, Nē·a·rī′ah, and Shā′-
phat—six *in all.*
23 The sons of Nē·a·rī′ah *were*
El·i·ō·ē′naī, Hez·e·kī′ah, and Az-
rī′kam—three *in all.*
24 The sons of El·i·ō·ē′naī *were*
Hod·a·vī′ah, E·lī′a·shib, Pe·lāi′ah,
Ak′kub, Jō·hā′nan, De·laī′ah,
and A·nā′nī—seven *in all.*

4 The sons of Judah *were*
[a]Per′ez, Hez′ron, [1]Car′mī,
Hur, and Shō′bal.
2 And [1]Rē·āi′ah the son of
Shō′bal begot Jā′hath, and Jā′-
hath begot A·hū′māi and Lā′had.
These *were* the families of the
Zō′ra·thītes.
3 These *were the sons of* the
father of Ē′tam: Jez′rē·el, Ish′ma,
and Id′bash; and the name of
their sister *was* Haz·e·lel·pō′ni;
4 and Pe·nū′el *was* the father of
Gē′dor, and Ē′zer *was the* father
of Hū′shah. These *were* the sons
of [a]Hur, the firstborn of Eph′-
ra·thah the father of Bethlehem.
5 And [a]Ash′hur the father of
Te·kō′a had two wives, Hē′lah
and Nā′a·rah.
6 Nā′a·rah bore him A·huz′-
zam, Hē′pher, Tē′me·nī, and Hā-
a·hash′ta·rī. These *were* the sons
of Nā′a·rah.
7 The sons of Hē′lah *were* Zē′-
reth, Zō′har, and Eth′nan;
8 and Koz begot Ā′nub, Zō·bē′-
bah, and the families of A·har′-
hel the son of Har′um.
9 Now Jā′bez was [a]more honorable than his brothers, and his
mother called his name [1]Jā′bez,
saying, "Because I bore *him* in
pain."
10 And Jā′bez called on the
God of Israel saying, "Oh, that
You would bless me indeed, and
enlarge my [1]territory, that Your
hand would be with me, and
that You would keep *me* from
evil, that I may not cause pain!"
So God granted him what he
requested.
11 Chē′lub the brother of [a]Shū′-
hah begot Mē′hir, who *was* the
father of Esh′ton.
12 And Esh′ton begot Beth-Rā′-
pha, Pa·sē′ah, and Te·hin′nah the
father of [1]Ir-Nā′hash. These *were*
the men of Rē′chah.
13 The sons of Kē′naz *were*
[a]Oth′ni·el and Se·rāi′ah. The sons
of Oth′ni·el *were* [1]Hā′thath,
14 and Me·on′o·thaī *who* begot
Oph′rah. Se·rāi′ah begot Jō′ab
the father of [a]Ge Ha·ra′shim,[1]
for they were craftsmen.
15 The sons of [a]Caleb the son
of Je·phūn′neh *were* Ī′rū, Ē′lah,
and Nā′am. The son of Ē′lah *was*
[1]Kē′naz.
16 The sons of Je·hal′le·lel *were*
Ziph, Zī′phah, Tir′i·a, and As′-
a·rel.
17 The sons of Ez′rah *were* Jē′-
ther, Mē′red, Ē′pher, and Jā′lon.
And [1]*Mē′red's wife* bore Miriam,
Sham′maī, and Ish′bah the father of Esh·te·mō′a.
18 ([1]His wife Jē·hu·dī′jah bore
Jē′red the father of Gē′dor,
Hē′ber the father of Sō′chōh,
and Je·kū′thi·el the father of
Za·nō′ah.) And these were the
sons of Bith′i·ah the daughter of
Pharaoh, whom Mē′red took.
19 The sons of Hō·dī′ah's wife,
the sister of Nā′ham, *were* the
fathers of Kē·ī′lah the Gar′mīte
and of Esh·te·mō′a the [a]Mā′-
a·cha·thīte.
20 And the sons of Shī′mon
were Am′non, Rin′nah, Ben-Hā′-
nan, and Tī′lon. And the sons of
Ish′ī *were* Zō′heth and Ben-Zō′-
heth.
21 The sons of [a]Shē′lah [b]the son

CHAPTER 4

1 [a]Gen. 38:29; 46:12 [1]*Chelubai,* 1 Chr. 2:9 or *Caleb,* 1 Chr. 2:18

2 [1]*Haroeh,* 1 Chr. 2:52

4 [a]1 Chr. 2:50

5 [a]1 Chr. 2:24

9 [a]Gen. 34:19 [1]Lit. *He Will Cause Pain*

10 [1]*border*

11 [a]Job 8:1

12 [1]Lit. *City of Nahash*

13 [a]Josh. 15:17 [1]LXX, Vg. add *and Meonothai*

14 [a]Neh. 11:35 [1]Lit. *Valley of Craftsmen*

15 [a]1 Chr. 6:56 [1]Or *Uknaz*

17 [1]Lit. *she*

18 [1]Or *His Judean wife*

19 [a]2 Kin. 25:23

21 [a]Gen. 38:11, 14 [b]Gen. 38:1–5; 46:12

of Judah *were* Er the father of
Lē′cah, Lā′a·dah the father of
Ma·rē′shah, and the families
of the house of the linen workers of the house of Ash′bē·a;
22 also Jō′kim, the men of
Cho·zē′ba, and Jō′ash; Sar′aph,
who ruled in Mō′ab, and Ja·shū′-
bī-Lē′hem. Now the [1]records are
ancient.
23 These *were* the potters and
those who dwell at [1]Ne·tā′im
and [2]Ge·dē′rah; there they dwelt
with the king for his work.
24 The [a]sons of Sim′ē·on *were*
[1]Nem′ū·el, Jā′min, [2]Jā′rib, [3]Zē′-
rah, *and* Shā′ūl,
25 Shal′lum his son, Mib′sam
his son, and Mish′ma his son.
26 And the sons of Mish′ma
were Ham′ū·el his son, Zac′chur
his son, and Shim′ē·ī his son.
27 Shim′ē·ī had sixteen sons
and six daughters; but his brothers did not have many children,
[a]nor did any of their families
multiply as much as the children
of Judah.
28 They dwelt at Bē·er·shē′ba,
Mō′la·dah, Hā′zar Shū′al,
29 [1]Bil′hah, Ē′zem, [2]Tō′lad,
30 Be·thū′el, Hor′mah, Zik′lag,
31 Beth Mar′ca·both, [1]Hā′-zar
Sū′sim, Beth Bi′ri, and at Shā·a-
rā′im. These *were* their cities
until the reign of David.
32 And their villages *were*
[1]Ē′tam, Ā′in, Rim′mon, Tō′chen,
and Ā′shan—five cities—
33 and all the villages that *were*
around these cities as far as
[1]Bā′al. These *were* their dwelling places, and they maintained
their genealogy:
34 Me·shō′bab, Jam′lech, and
Jō′shah the son of Am·a·zī′ah;
35 Jō′el, and Jē′hū the son of
Josh·i·bī′ah, the son of Se·rāi′ah,
the son of As′i·el;
36 El·i·ō·ē′naī, Jā·a·kō′bah, Jesh-
ō·hāi′ah, A·sāi′ah, Ad′i·el, Je·sim′-
i·el, and Be·nā′i·ah;
37 Zī′za the son of Shī′phī,
the son of Al′lon, the son of
Je·daī′ah, the son of Shim′rī, the
son of She·māi′ah—
38 these mentioned by name
were leaders in their families,
and their father's house increased greatly.
39 So they went to the entrance
of Gē′dor, as far as the east side
of the valley, to seek pasture for
their flocks.
40 And they found rich, good
pasture, and the land *was* broad,
quiet, and peaceful; for some
Ham′ītes formerly lived there.
41 These recorded by name
came in the days of Hez·e·kī′ah
king of Judah; and they [a]at-
tacked[1] their tents and the Me·ū′-
nītes who were found there, and
[b]utterly destroyed them, as it is
to this day. So they dwelt in their
place, because *there was* pasture
for their flocks there.
42 Now *some* of them, five hundred men of the sons of Sim′-
ē·on, went to Mount Sē′ir, having as their captains Pel·a·tī′ah,
Nē·a·rī′ah, Reph·āi′ah, and Uz′-
zi·el, the sons of Ish′ī.
43 And they [1]defeated [a]the rest
of the A·mal′e·kītes who had
escaped. They have dwelt there
to this day.

5 Now the sons of Reuben the
firstborn of Israel—[a]he *was*
indeed the firstborn, but because
he [b]defiled his father's bed, [c]his
birthright was given to the sons
of Joseph, the son of Israel, so
that the genealogy is not listed
according to the birthright;

22 [1]Lit. *words*
23 [1]Lit. *Plants* [2]Lit. *Hedges*
24 [a]Num. 26:12–14 [1]*Jemuel,* Gen. 46:10; Ex. 6:15; Num. 26:12 [2]*Jachin,* Gen. 46:10; Num. 26:12 [3]*Zohar,* Gen. 46:10; Ex. 6:15
27 [a]Num. 2:9
29 [1]*Balah,* Josh. 19:3 [2]*Eltolad,* Josh. 19:4
31 [1]*Hazar Susah,* Josh. 19:5
32 [1]*Ether,* Josh. 19:7
33 [1]*Baalath Beer,* Josh. 19:8
41 [a]2 Kin. 18:8 [b]2 Kin. 19:11 [1]Lit. *struck*
43 [a]1 Sam. 15:8; 30:17 [1]Lit. *struck*

CHAPTER 5
1 [a]Gen. 29:32; 49:3 [b]Gen. 35:22; 49:4 [c]Gen. 48:15, 22

2 yet [a]Judah prevailed over his
brothers, and from him *came* a
[b]ruler, although [1]the birthright
was Joseph's—
3 the sons of [a]Reuben the firstborn of Israel were Hā′noch,
Pal′lū, Hez′ron, and Car′mī.
4 The sons of Jō′el *were*
She·māi′ah his son, Gog his son,
Shim′ē·ī his son,
5 Mī′cah his son, Rē·āi′ah his
son, Bā′al his son,
6 and Be·er′ah his son, whom
[1]Tig′lath-Pī·lē′ser king of Assyria [a]carried into captivity. He
was leader of the Reū′ben·ītes.
7 And his brethren by their
families, [a]when the genealogy
of their generations was registered: the chief, Je·ī′el, and
Zech·a·rī′ah,
8 and Bē′la the son of Ā′zaz,
the son of Shē′ma, the son of
Jō′el, who dwelt in [a]A·rō′er, as
far as Nē′bō and Bā′al Mē′on.
9 Eastward they settled as
far as the [1]entrance of the wilderness this side of the River
Eū·phrā′tēs, because their cattle
had [2]multiplied [a]in the land of
Gil′ē·ad.
10 Now in the days of Saul they
made war [a]with the Hag′rītes,
who fell by their hand; and they
dwelt in their tents throughout
the entire *area* east of Gil′ē·ad.
11 And the [a]children of Gad
dwelt next to them in the land of
[b]Bā′shan as far as [c]Sal′cah:
12 Jō′el *was* the chief, Shā′pham
the next, then Jā′a·naī and Shā′-
phat in Bā′shan,
13 and their brethren of their father's house: Michael, Me·shul′-
lam, Shē′ba, Jō′raī, Jā′chan, Zī′a,
and Ē′ber—seven *in all.*
14 These *were* the children of
Ab·i·hā′il the son of Hū′rī, the
son of Ja·rō′ah, the son of Gil′-
ē·ad, the son of Michael, the son
of Je·shish′aī, the son of Jah′dō,
the son of Buz;
15 Ā′hī the son of Ab′di·el, the
son of Gū′nī, *was* chief of their
father's house.
16 And *the Gad′ītes* dwelt in
Gil′ē·ad, in Bā′shan and in its
villages, and in all the [1]common-
lands of [a]Sharon within their
borders.
17 All these were registered
by genealogies in the days of
[a]Jō′tham king of Judah, and in
the days of [b]Jer·o·bō′am king of
Israel.
18 The sons of Reuben, the
Gad′ītes, and half the tribe of
Ma·nas′seh *had* forty-four thousand seven hundred and sixty
valiant men, men able to bear
shield and sword, to shoot with
the bow, and skillful in war, who
went to war.
19 They made war with the
Hag′rītes, [a]Jē′tur, Nā′phish, and
Nō′dab.
20 And [a]they were helped
against them, and the Hag′rītes
were delivered into their hand,
and all who *were* with them,
for they [b]cried out to God in the
battle. He [1]heeded their prayer,
because they [c]put their trust in
Him.
21 Then they took away their
livestock—fifty thousand of their
camels, two hundred and fifty
thousand of their sheep, and two
thousand of their donkeys—also
one hundred thousand of their
men;
22 for many fell dead, because
the war [a]*was* God's. And they
dwelt in their place until [b]the
captivity.
23 So the children of the half-

2 [a]Gen. 49:8, 10 [b]Mic. 5:2 [1]*the right of the firstborn*
3 [a]Ex. 6:14
6 [a]2 Kin. 18:11 [1]Heb. *Tilgath-Pilneser*
7 [a]1 Chr. 5:17
8 [a]Josh. 12:2; 13:15, 16
9 [a]Josh. 22:8, 9 [1]*beginning* [2]*increased*
10 [a]Gen. 25:12
11 [a]Num. 26:15–18 [b]Josh. 13:11, 24–28 [c]Deut. 3:10
16 [a]1 Chr. 27:29 [1]*open lands*
17 [a]2 Kin. 15:5, 32 [b]2 Kin. 14:16, 28
19 [a]Gen. 25:15
20 [a][1 Chr. 5:22] [b]2 Chr. 14:11–13 [c]Ps. 9:10; 20:7, 8; 22:4, 5 [1]Lit. *was entreated for them*
22 [a][Josh. 23:10] [b]2 Kin. 15:29; 17:6

tribe of Ma·nas′seh dwelt in the
land. Their *numbers* increased
from Bā′shan to Bā′al Her′-
mon, that is, to [a]Sē′nir, or Mount
Her′mon.
24 These *were* the heads of
their fathers' houses: Ē′pher,
Ish′ī, E·lī′el, Az′ri·el, Jer·e·mī′ah,
Hod·a·vī′ah, and Jah′di·el. They
were mighty men of valor, famous men, *and* heads of their
fathers' houses.
25 And they were unfaithful to
the God of their fathers, and
[a]played the harlot after the gods
of the peoples of the land, whom
God had destroyed before them.
26 So the God of Israel stirred
up the spirit of [a]Pūl king of Assyria, that is, [b]Tig′lath-Pī·lē′ser[1]
king of Assyria. He carried the
Reū′ben·ītes, the Gad′ītes, and
the half-tribe of Ma·nas′seh into
captivity. He took them to [c]Hā′-
lah, Hā′bor, Hā′ra, and the river
of Gō′zan to this day.

6

6 The sons of Levi *were* [a]Ger′-
shon,[1] Kō′hath, and Me-
rar′ī.
2 The sons of Kō′hath *were*
Am′ram, [a]Iz′har, Hē′bron, and
Uz′zi·el.
3 The children of Am′ram *were*
Aaron, Moses, and Miriam. And
the sons of Aaron *were* [a]Nā′-
dab, A·bī′hū, El·ē·ā′zar, and Ith′-
a·mar.
4 El·ē·ā′zar begot Phin′e·has,
and Phin′e·has begot Ab·i·shū′a;
5 Ab·i·shū′a begot Buk′kī, and
Buk′kī begot Uz′zī;
6 Uz′zī begot Zer·a·hī′ah, and
Zer·a·hī′ah begot Me·rā′i·oth;
7 Me·rā′i·oth begot Am·a·rī′ah,
and Am·a·rī′ah begot A·hī′tub;
8 [a]A·hī′tub begot [b]Zā′dok, and
Zā′dok begot A·him′a·az;
9 A·him′a·az begot Az·a·rī′ah,
and Az·a·rī′ah begot Jō·hā′nan;
10 Jō·hā′nan begot Az·a·rī′ah
(it was he [a]who ministered as
priest in the [b]temple[1] that Solomon built in Jerusalem);
11 [a]Az·a·rī′ah begot [b]Am·a·rī′ah,
and Am·a·rī′ah begot A·hī′tub;
12 A·hī′tub begot Zā′dok, and
Zā′dok begot [1]Shal′lum;
13 Shal′lum begot Hil·kī′ah, and
Hil·kī′ah begot Az·a·rī′ah;
14 Az·a·rī′ah begot [a]Se·rāi′ah,
and Se·rāi′ah begot Je·hoz′-
a·dak.
15 Je·hoz′a·dak went *into captivity* [a]when the LORD carried Judah and Jerusalem into captivity
by the hand of Ne·bū·chad·nez′-
zar.
16 The sons of Levi *were* [a]Ger′-
shon,[1] Kō′hath, and Me·rar′ī.
17 These are the names of the
sons of Ger′shon: Lib′nī and
Shim′ē·ī.
18 The sons of Kō′hath *were*
Am′ram, Iz′har, Hē′bron, and
Uz′zi·el.
19 The sons of Me·rar′ī *were*
Mah′lī and Mū′shī. Now these
are the families of the Lē′vītes
according to their fathers:
20 Of Ger′shon *were* Lib′nī his
son, Jā′hath his son, [a]Zim′mah
his son,
21 [1]Jō′ah his son, [2]Id′dō his son,
Zē′rah his son, *and* [3]Jē·ath′e·raī
his son.
22 The sons of Kō′hath *were*
[1]Am·min′a·dab his son, [a]Kō′rah
his son, As′sir his son,
23 El·kā′nah his son, E·bī′a·saph
his son, As′sir his son,
24 Tā′hath his son, Ū·rī′el his
son, Uz·zī′ah his son, and Shā′ūl
his son.
25 The sons of El·kā′nah *were*
[a]A·mā′saī and A·hī′moth.

23 [a]Deut. 3:9
25 [a]2 Kin. 17:7
26 [a]2 Kin. 15:19 [b]2 Kin. 15:29 [c]2 Kin. 17:6; 18:11 [1]Heb. *Tilgath-Pilneser*

CHAPTER 6

1 [a]Ex. 6:16 [1]Or *Gershom*, v. 16
2 [a]1 Chr. 6:18, 22
3 [a]Lev. 10:1, 2
8 [a]2 Sam. 8:17 [b]2 Sam. 15:27
10 [a]2 Chr. 26:17, 18 [b]1 Kin. 6:1 [1]Lit. *house*
11 [a]Ezra 7:3 [b]2 Chr. 19:11
12 [1]*Meshullam*, 1 Chr. 9:11
14 [a]Neh. 11:11
15 [a]2 Kin. 25:21
16 [a]Ex. 6:16 [1]Heb. *Gershom*, an alternate spelling for *Gershon*, vv. 1, 17, 20, 43, 62, 71
20 [a]1 Chr. 6:42
21 [1]*Ethan*, v. 42 [2]*Adaiah*, v. 41 [3]*Ethni*, v. 41
22 [a]Num. 16:1 [1]*Izhar*, vv. 2, 18
25 [a]1 Chr. 6:35, 36

26 *As for* El·kā′nah, the sons of El·kā′nah *were* [1]Zō′phai his son, [2]Nā′hath his son,

27 [1]E·lī′ab his son, Je·rō′ham his son, *and* El·kā′nah his son.

28 The sons of Samuel *were* [1]*Jō′el* the firstborn, and A·bī′jah [2]the second.

29 The sons of Me·rar′ī *were* Mah′lī, Lib′nī his son, Shim′ē·ī his son, Uz′zah his son,

30 Shim′ē·a his son, Hag·gī′ah his son, *and* A·sāi′ah his son.

31 Now these are [a]the men whom David appointed over the service of song in the house of the LORD, after the [b]ark came to rest.

32 They were ministering with music before the dwelling place of the tabernacle of meeting, until Solomon had built the house of the LORD in Jerusalem, and they served in their office according to their order.

33 And these *are* the ones who [1]ministered with their sons: Of the sons of the [a]Kō′hath·ites *were* Hē′man the singer, the son of Jō′el, the son of Samuel,

34 the son of El·kā′nah, the son of Je·rō′ham, the son of [1]E·lī′el, the son of [2]Tō′ah,

35 the son of Zuph, the son of El·kā′nah, the son of Mā′hath, the son of A·mā′sai,

36 the son of El·kā′nah, the son of Jō′el, the son of Az·a·rī′ah, the son of Zeph·a·nī′ah,

37 the son of Tā′hath, the son of As′sir, the son of [a]E·bī′a·saph, the son of Kō′rah,

38 the son of Iz′har, the son of Kō′hath, the son of Levi, the son of Israel.

39 And his brother [a]Ā′saph, who stood at his right hand, *was* Ā′saph the son of Ber·a·chī′ah, the son of Shim′ē·a,

40 the son of Michael, the son of Bā·a·sē′i·ah, the son of Mal·chī′jah,

41 the son of [a]Eth′nī, the son of Zē′rah, the son of A·dāi′ah,

42 the son of Ē′than, the son of Zim′mah, the son of Shim′ē·ī,

43 the son of Jā′hath, the son of Ger′shon, the son of Levi.

44 Their brethren, the sons of Me·rar′ī, on the left hand, *were* [1]Ē′than the son of [2]Kish′ī, the son of Ab′dī, the son of Mal′luch,

45 the son of Hash·a·bī′ah, the son of Am·a·zī′ah, the son of Hil·kī′ah,

46 the son of Am′zī, the son of Bā′nī, the son of Shamer,

47 the son of Mah′lī, the son of Mū′shī, the son of Me·rar′ī, the son of Levi.

48 And their brethren, the Lē′vites, *were* appointed to every [a]kind of service of the tabernacle of the house of God.

49 [a]But Aaron and his sons offered sacrifices [b]on the altar of burnt offering and [c]on the altar of incense, for all the work of the Most Holy *Place*, and to make atonement for Israel, according to all that Moses the servant of God had commanded.

50 Now these *are* the [a]sons of Aaron: El·ē·ā′zar his son, Phin′e·has his son, Ab·i·shū′a his son,

51 Buk′kī his son, Uz′zī his son, Zer·a·hī′ah his son,

52 Me·rā′i·oth his son, Am·a·rī′ah his son, A·hī′tub his son,

53 Zā′dok his son, *and* A·him′a·az his son.

54 [a]Now these *are* their dwelling places throughout their settlements in their territory, for

26 [1]*Zuph*, v. 35; 1 Sam. 1:1 [2]*Toah*, v. 34
27 [1]*Eliel*, v. 34
28 [1]So with LXX, Syr., Arab.; cf. v. 33 and 1 Sam. 8:2 [2]Heb. *Vasheni*
31 [a]1 Chr. 15:16–22, 27; 16:4–6 [b]1 Chr. 15:25—16:1
33 [a]Num. 26:57 [1]Lit. *stood with*
34 [1]*Elihu*, 1 Sam. 1:1 [2]*Tohu*, 1 Sam. 1:1
37 [a]Ex. 6:24
39 [a]2 Chr. 5:12
41 [a]1 Chr. 6:21
44 [1]*Jeduthun*, 1 Chr. 9:16; 25:1, 3, 6; 2 Chr. 35:15; Ps. 62:title [2]Or *Kushaiah*
48 [a]1 Chr. 9:14–34
49 [a][Num. 18:1–8] [b]Lev. 1:8, 9 [c]Ex. 30:7
50 [a]1 Chr. 6:4–8
54 [a]Josh. 21

they were *given* by lot to the
sons of Aaron, of the family of
the Kō′hath·ītes:
55 [a]They gave them Hē′bron in
the land of Judah, with its surrounding [1]common-lands.
56 [a]But the fields of the city and
its villages they gave to Caleb
the son of Je·phŭn′neh.
57 And [a]to the sons of Aaron
they gave *one of* the cities of
refuge, Hē′bron; also Lib′nah
with its common-lands, Jat′tir,
Esh·te·mō′a with its common-
lands,
58 [1]Hī′len with its common-
lands, Dē′bir with its common-
lands,
59 [1]Ā′shan with its common-
lands, and Beth Shem′esh with
its common-lands.
60 And from the tribe of Benjamin: Gē′ba with its common-
lands, [1]Al′e·meth with its common-lands, and An′a·thoth with
its common-lands. All their cities among their families *were*
thirteen.
61 [a]To the rest of the family of
the tribe of the Kō′hath·ītes *they*
gave [b]by lot ten cities from half
the tribe of Ma·nas′seh.
62 And to the sons of Ger′-
shon, throughout their families,
they gave thirteen cities from
the tribe of Is′sa·char, from the
tribe of Ash′er, from the tribe of
Naph′ta·lī, and from the tribe of
Ma·nas′seh in Bā′shan.
63 To the sons of Me·rar′ī,
throughout their families, *they*
gave [a]twelve cities from the tribe
of Reuben, from the tribe of Gad,
and from the tribe of Zeb′ū·lun.
64 So the children of Israel gave
these cities with their [1]common-
lands to the Lē′vītes.
65 And they gave by lot from
the tribe of the children of Judah, from the tribe of the children of Sim′ē·on, and from the
tribe of the children of Benjamin
these cities which are called by
their names.
66 Now [a]some of the families of
the sons of Kō′hath *were given*
cities as their territory from the
tribe of Ē′phra·im.
67 [a]And they gave them *one of*
the cities of refuge, Shē′chem
with its common-lands, in the
mountains of Ē′phra·im, also
Gē′zer with its common-lands,
68 [a]Jok′mē·am with its common-lands, Beth Hor′on with its
common-lands,
69 Aī′ja·lon with its common-
lands, and Gath Rim′mon with
its common-lands.
70 And from the half-tribe of
Ma·nas′seh: Ā′ner with its common-lands and Bil′ē·am with its
common-lands, for the rest of
the family of the sons of Kō′-
hath.
71 From the family of the half-
tribe of Ma·nas′seh the sons
of Ger′shon *were given* Gō′lan
in Bā′shan with its common-
lands and [1]Ash′ta·roth with its
common-lands.
72 And from the tribe of Is′-
sa·char: [1]Kē′desh with its common-lands, Dab′e·rath with its
common-lands,
73 Rā′moth with its common-
lands, and Ā′nem with its
common-lands.
74 And from the tribe of Ash′er:
Mā′shal with its common-lands,
Ab′don with its common-lands,
75 Hū′kok with its common-
lands, and Rē′hob with its
common-lands.
76 And from the tribe of Naph′-
ta·lī: Kē′desh in Galilee with its

55 [a]Josh. 14:13; 21:11, 12 [1]*open lands*
56 [a]Josh. 14:13; 15:13
57 [a]Josh. 21:13, 19
58 [1]*Holon*, Josh. 21:15
59 [1]*Ain*, Josh. 21:16
60 [1]*Almon*, Josh. 21:18
61 [a]1 Chr. 6:66–70 [b]Josh. 21:5
63 [a]Josh. 21:7, 34–40
64 [1]*open lands*
66 [a]1 Chr. 6:61
67 [a]Josh. 21:21
68 [a]Josh. 21:22
71 [1]*Beeshterah*, Josh. 21:27
72 [1]*Kishon*, Josh. 21:28

common-lands, Ham′mon with
its common-lands, and Kir·jath′-
a·im with its common-lands.
77 From the tribe of Zeb′ū-
lun the rest of the children of
Me·rar′ī *were given* [1]Rim′mon
with its common-lands and Tā′-
bor with its common-lands.
78 And on the other side of
the Jordan, across from Jericho,
on the east side of the Jordan,
they were given from the tribe
of Reuben: Bē′zer in the wilderness with its common-lands,
Jah′zah with its common-lands,
79 Ked′e·moth with its common-
lands, and Meph′a·ath with its
common-lands.
80 And from the tribe of Gad:
Rā′moth in Gil′ē·ad with its common-lands, Mā·ha·na′im with its
common-lands,
81 Hesh′bon with its common-
lands, and Jā′zer with its
common-lands.

7

The sons of Is′sa·char *were*
[a]Tō′la, [1]Pū′ah, [2]Jash′ub, and
Shim′ron—four *in all.*
2 The sons of Tō′la *were* Uz′zī,
Reph·āi′ah, Jē′ri·el, Jah′maī,
Jib′sam, and She·mū′el, heads
of their father's house. *The sons*
of Tō′la *were* mighty men of
valor in their generations; [a]their
number in the days of David
was twenty-two thousand six
hundred.
3 The son of Uz′zī *was* Iz·ra-
hī′ah, and the sons of Iz·ra·hī′ah
were Michael, Ō·ba·dī′ah, Jō′el,
and Ish·ī′ah. All five of them
were chief men.
4 And with them, by their
generations, according to their
fathers' houses, *were* thirty-six
thousand troops ready for war;
for they had many wives and
sons.
5 Now their brethren among
all the families of Is′sa·char *were*
mighty men of valor, listed by
their genealogies, eighty-seven
thousand in all.
6 *The sons* of [a]Benjamin *were*
Bē′la, Bē′cher, and Je·dī′a·el—
three *in all.*
7 The sons of Bē′la were Ez′-
bon, Uz′zī, Uz′zi·el, Jer′i·moth,
and Iri—five *in all.* They *were*
heads of *their* fathers' houses,
and they were listed by their genealogies, twenty-two thousand
and thirty-four mighty men of
valor.
8 The sons of Bē′cher *were*
Ze·mī′rah, Jō′ash, El·i·ē′zer, El·i-
ō·ē′naī, Om′rī, Jer′i·moth, A·bī′-
jah, An′a·thoth, and Al′e·meth.
All these *are* the sons of Bē′-
cher.
9 And they were recorded by
genealogy according to their
generations, heads of their fathers' houses, twenty thousand
two hundred mighty men of
valor.
10 The son of Je·dī′a·el *was* Bil′-
han, and the sons of Bil′han
were Jē′ush, Benjamin, Ē′hud,
Che·nā′a·nah, Zē′than, Thar′-
shish, and A·hish′a·har.
11 All these sons of Je·dī′a·el
were heads of their fathers'
houses; *there were* seventeen
thousand two hundred mighty
men of valor fit to go out for war
and battle.
12 [1]Shup′pim and [2]Hup′pim
were the sons of [3]Ir, *and* Hū′-
shim *was* the son of [4]Ā′her.
13 The [a]sons of Naph′ta·lī *were*
[1]Jah′zi·el, Gū′nī, Jē′zer, and
[2]Shal′lum, the sons of Bil′hah.
14 The [a]descendants of Ma·nas′-
seh: his Syrian concubine bore

77 [1]Heb. *Rimmono,* an alternate spelling of *Rimmon,* 1 Chr. 4:32

CHAPTER 7

1 [a]Num. 26:23–25 [1]*Puvah,* Gen. 46:13 [2]*Job,* Gen. 46:13

2 [a]2 Sam. 24:1–9

6 [a]Gen. 46:21

12 [1]*Shupham,* Num. 26:39 [2]*Hupham,* Num. 26:39 [3]*Iri,* v. 7 [4]*Ahiram,* Num. 26:38

13 [a]Num. 26:48–50 [1]*Jahzeel,* Gen. 46:24 [2]*Shillem,* Gen. 46:24

14 [a]Num. 26:29–34

him [b]Mā′chir the father of Gil′-
ē·ad, the father of As′ri·el.
15 Mā′chir took as his wife *the*
sister of [1]Hup′pim and [2]Shup′-
pim, whose name *was* Mā′-
a·chah. The name of *Gil′ē·ad's*
[3]grandson *was* [a]Ze·loph′e·had,
but Ze·loph′e·had begot only
daughters.
16 (Mā′a·chah the wife of Mā′-
chir bore a son, and she called
his name Pē′resh. The name
of his brother *was* Shē′resh,
and his sons *were* Ū′lam and
Rā′kem.
17 The son of Ū′lam *was* [a]Bē′-
dan.) These *were* the descendants of Gil′ē·ad the son of Mā′-
chir, the son of Ma·nas′seh.
18 His sister Ham·mo′le·keth
bore Ish′hod, [1]Ā·bi·ē′zer, and
Mah′lah.
19 And the sons of She·mī′da
were A·hī′an, Shē′chem, Lik′hī,
and A·nī′am.
20 [a]The sons of Ē′phra·im *were*
Shū′the·lah, Bē′red his son, Tā′-
hath his son, El′a·dah his son,
Tā′hath his son,
21 Zā′bad his son, Shū′the·lah
his son, and Ē′zer and Ē′lē·ad.
The men of Gath who were born
in *that* land killed *them* because
they came down to take away
their cattle.
22 Then Ē′phra·im their father
mourned many days, and his
brethren came to comfort him.
23 And when he went in to his
wife, she conceived and bore
a son; and he called his name
[1]Bē·rī′ah, because tragedy had
come upon his house.
24 Now his daughter *was* Shē′-
e·rah, who built Lower and Upper [a]Beth Hor′on and Uz′zen
Shē′e·rah;
25 and Rē′phah *was* his son, *as*
well as Rē′sheph, and Tē′lah his
son, Tā′han his son,
26 Lā′a·dan his son, Am·mī′hud
his son, [a]E·lish′a·ma his son,
27 [1]Nun his son, and [a]Joshua
his son.
28 Now their [a]possessions and
dwelling places *were* Beth′el
and its towns: to the east [1]Nā′-
a·ran, to the west Gē′zer and
its towns, and Shē′chem and its
towns, as far as [2]Āy′yah and its
towns;
29 and by the borders of the
children of [a]Ma·nas′seh *were*
Beth Shē′an and its towns, Tā′-
a·nach and its towns, [b]Me·gid′dō
and its towns, Dor and its towns.
In these dwelt the children of
Joseph, the son of Israel.
30 [a]The sons of Ash′er *were* Im′-
nah, Ish′vah, Ish′vī, Bē·rī′ah, and
their sister Sē′rah.
31 The sons of Bē·rī′ah *were*
Hē′ber and Mal′chi·el, who was
the father of [1]Bir′zā·ith.
32 And Hē′ber begot Japh′let,
[1]Shō′mer, [2]Hō′tham, and their
sister Shū′a.
33 The sons of Japh′let *were*
Pā′sach, Bim′hal, and Ash′vath.
These *were* the children of
Japh′let.
34 The sons of [a]Shē′mer *were*
Ā′hī, Rōh′gah, Je·hub′bah, and
Ar′am.
35 And the sons of his brother
Hē′lem *were* Zō′phah, Im′na,
Shē′lesh, and Ā′mal.
36 The sons of Zō′phah *were*
Sū′ah, Har′ne·pher, Shū′al, Bē′rī,
Im′rah,
37 Bē′zer, Hod, Sham′ma, Shil′-
shah, [1]Jith′ran, and Be·ē′ra.
38 The sons of Jē′ther *were*
Je·phun′neh, Pis′pah, and Ar′a.
39 The sons of Ul′la *were* Ā′rah,
Han′i·el, and Rī·zī′a.

14 [b]1 Chr. 2:21
15 [a]Num. 26:30–33; 27:1 [1]*Hupham*, v. 12; Num. 26:39 [2]*Shupham*, v. 12; Num. 26:39 [3]Lit. *the second*
17 [a]1 Sam. 12:11
18 [1]*Jeezer*, Num. 26:30
20 [a]Num. 26:35–37
23 [1]Lit. *In Tragedy*
24 [a]Josh. 16:3, 5
26 [a]Num. 10:22
27 [a]Ex. 17:9, 14; 24:13; 33:11 [1]Heb. *Non*
28 [a]Josh. 16:1–10 [1]*Naarath*, Josh. 16:7 [2]Many Heb. mss., Bg., LXX, Tg., Vg. *Gazza*
29 [a]Josh. 17:7 [b]Josh. 17:11
30 [a]Num. 26:44–47
31 [1]Or *Birzavith* or *Birzoth*
32 [1]*Shemer*, 1 Chr. 7:34 [2]*Helem*, 1 Chr. 7:35
34 [a]1 Chr. 7:32
37 [1]*Jether*, v. 38

40 All these *were* the children
of Ash′er, heads of *their* fathers′
houses, choice men, mighty men
of valor, chief leaders. And they
were recorded by genealogies
among the army fit for battle;
their number *was* twenty-six
thousand.

8

Now Benjamin begot [a]Bē′la
his firstborn, Ash′bel the
second, [1]A′har·ah the third,
2 Nō′hah the fourth, and Rā′-
pha the fifth.
3 The sons of Bē′la *were* [1]Ad′-
dar, Gē′ra, A·bī′hud,
4 Ab·i·shū′a, Nā′a·man, A·hō′ah,
5 Gē′ra, [1]She·phū′phan, and
Hū′ram.
6 These *are* the sons of Ē′hud,
who were the heads of the fa-
thers′ *houses* of the inhabitants
of [a]Gē′ba, and who forced them
to move to [b]Man′a·hath:
7 Nā′a·man, A·hī′jah, and Gē′ra
who forced them to move. He
begot Uz′za and A·hī′hud.
8 Also Shā·ha·rā′im had children in the country of Mō′ab,
after he had sent away Hū′shim
and Bā′a·ra his wives.
9 By Hō′desh his wife he begot Jō′bab, Zib′i·a, Mē′sha, Mal′-
cam,
10 Jē′uz, Sa·chī′ah, and Mir′-
mah. These *were* his sons, heads
of their fathers′ *houses*.
11 And by Hū′shim he begot
A·bī′tub and El·pā′al.
12 The sons of El·pā′al *were*
Ē′ber, Mī′sham, and Shē′med,
who built Ō′nō and Lod with its
towns;
13 and Bē·rī′ah and [a]Shē′ma,
who *were* heads of their fathers′
houses of the inhabitants of Aī′-
ja·lon, who drove out the inhabitants of Gath.
14 A·hī′ō, Shā′shak, Jer′e·moth,
15 Zeb·a·dī′ah, Ar′ad, Ē′der,
16 Michael, Is′pah, and Jō′ha
were the sons of Bē·rī′ah.
17 Zeb·a·dī′ah, Me·shul′lam,
Hiz′kī, Hē′ber,
18 Ish′me·raī, Jiz·lī′ah, and Jō′-
bab *were* the sons of El·pā′al.
19 Jā′kim, Zich′rī, Zab′dī,
20 E·li·ē′naī, Zil′le·thaī, E·lī′el,
21 A·dāi′ah, Be·rā′i·ah, and
Shim′rath *were* the sons of
[1]Shim′ē·ī.
22 Ish′pan, Ē′ber, E·lī′el,
23 Ab′don, Zich′rī, Hā′nan,
24 Han·a·nī′ah, Ē′lam, An·to-
thī′jah,
25 Iph·dē′i·ah, and Pe·nū′el *were*
the sons of Shā′shak.
26 Sham′she·raī, Shē·ha·rī′ah,
Ath·a·lī′ah,
27 Jā·ar·e·shī′ah, E·lī′jah, and
Zich′rī *were* the sons of Je·rō′-
ham.
28 These *were* heads of the fa-
thers′ *houses* by their generations, chief men. These dwelt in
Jerusalem.
29 Now [1]the father of Gib′ē·on,
whose [a]wife′s name *was* Mā′a-
cah, dwelt at Gib′ē·on.
30 And his firstborn son *was*
Ab′don, then Zūr, Kish, Bā′al,
Nā′dab,
31 Gē′dor, A·hī′ō, [1]Zē′cher,
32 and Mik′loth, *who* begot
[1]Shim′ē·ah. They also dwelt
[2]alongside their [3]relatives in Jerusalem, with their brethren.
33 [a]Ner[1] begot Kish, Kish begot
Saul, and Saul begot Jonathan,
Mal·chī·shū′a, [2]A·bin′a·dab, and
[3]Esh-Bā′al.
34 The son of Jonathan *was*
[1]Mer′ib-Bā′al, and Mer′ib-Bā′al
begot [a]Mī′cah.
35 The sons of Mī′cah *were*
Pī′thon, Mē′lech, [1]Ta·rē′a, and
Ā′haz.

CHAPTER 8

1 [a]Gen. 46:21 [1]*Ahiram*, Num. 26:38
3 [1]*Ard*, Num. 26:40
5 [1]*Shupham*, Num. 26:39, or *Shuppim*, 1 Chr. 7:12
6 [a]1 Chr. 6:60 [b]1 Chr. 2:52
13 [a]1 Chr. 8:21
21 [1]*Shema*, 1 Chr. 7:13
29 [a]1 Chr. 9:35–38 [1]*Jeiel*, 1 Chr. 9:35
31 [1]*Zechariah*, 1 Chr. 9:37
32 [1]*Shimeam*, 1 Chr. 9:38 [2]Lit. *opposite* [3]*brethren*
33 [a]1 Sam. 14:51 [1]Also the son of Gibeon, 1 Chr. 9:36, 39 [2]*Jishui*, 1 Sam. 14:49 [3]*Ishbosheth*, 2 Sam. 2:8
34 [a]2 Sam. 9:12 [1]*Mephibosheth*, 2 Sam. 4:4
35 [1]*Tahrea*, 1 Chr. 9:41

36 And Ā′haz begot [1]Je·hō′ad·dah; Je·hō′ad·dah begot Al′e·meth, Az′ma·veth, and Zim′rī; and Zim′rī begot Mō′za.

37 Mō′za begot Bin′ē·a, [1]Rā′phah his son, El·e·ā′sah his son, *and* Ā′zel his son.

38 Ā′zel had six sons whose names *were* these: Az·rī′kam, Bō′che·rū, Ish′ma·el, Shē·a·rī′ah, Ō·ba·dī′ah, and Hā′nan. All these *were* the sons of Ā′zel.

39 And the sons of Ē′shek his brother *were* Ū′lam his firstborn, Jē′ush the second, and E·liph′e·let the third.

40 The sons of Ū′lam were mighty men of valor—archers. *They* had many sons and grandsons, one hundred and fifty *in all*. These *were* all sons of Benjamin.

CHAPTER 9

9 So [a]all Israel was [1]recorded by genealogies, and indeed, they *were* inscribed in the book of the kings of Israel. But Judah was carried away captive to Babylon because of their unfaithfulness.

2 [a]And the first inhabitants who *dwelt* in their possessions in their cities *were* Israelites, priests, Lē′vītes, and [b]the Neth′i·nim.

3 Now in [a]Jerusalem the children of Judah dwelt, and some of the children of Benjamin, and of the children of Ē′phra·im and Ma·nas′seh:

4 Ū′thaī the son of Am·mī′hud, the son of Om′rī, the son of Im′rī, the son of Bā′nī, of the descendants of Per′ez, the son of Judah.

5 Of the Shī′lo·nītes: A·sāi′ah the firstborn and his sons.

6 Of the sons of Zē′rah: Je·ū′el, and their brethren—six hundred and ninety.

7 Of the sons of Benjamin: Sal′lū the son of Me·shul′lam, the son of Hod·a·vī′ah, the son of Has·se·nū′ah;

8 Ib·nē′i·ah the son of Je·rō′ham; Ē′lah the son of Uz′zī, the son of Mich′rī; Me·shul′lam the son of Sheph·a·tī′ah, the son of Reū′el, the son of Ib·nī′jah;

9 and their brethren, according to their generations—nine hundred and fifty-six. All these men *were* heads of a father's *house* in their fathers' houses.

10 [a]Of the priests: Je·daī′ah, Je·hoi′a·rib, and Jā′chin;

11 [1]Az·a·rī′ah the son of Hil·kī′ah, the son of Me·shul′lam, the son of Zā′dok, the son of Me·rā′i·oth, the son of A·hī′tub, the [a]officer over the house of God;

12 A·dāi′ah the son of Je·rō′ham, the son of Pash′ur, the son of Mal·chī′jah; Mā′a·saī the son of Ad′i·el, the son of Jah′ze·rah, the son of Me·shul′lam, the son of Me·shil′le·mith, the son of Im′mer;

13 and their brethren, heads of their fathers' houses—one thousand seven hundred and sixty. *They were* [1]very able men for the work of the service of the house of God.

14 Of the Lē′vītes: She·māi′ah the son of Has′shub, the son of Az·rī′kam, the son of Hash·a·bī′ah, of the sons of Me·rar′ī;

15 Bak·bak′kar, Hē′resh, Gā′lal, and Mat·ta·nī′ah the son of Mī′cah, the son of [a]Zich′rī, the son of Ā′saph;

16 [a]Ō·ba·dī′ah the son of [b]She·māi′ah, the son of Gā′lal, the son of Je·dū′thun; and Ber·e·chī′ah

36 [1]*Jarah*, 1 Chr. 9:42
37 [1]*Raphaiah*, 1 Chr. 9:43
1 [a]Ezra 2:59 [1]*enrolled*
2 [a]Neh. 7:73 [b]Ezra 2:43; 8:20
3 [a]Neh. 11:1, 2
10 [a]Neh. 11:10–14
11 [a]Jer. 20:1 [1]*Seraiah*, Neh. 11:11
13 [1]Lit. *mighty men of strength*
15 [a]Neh. 11:17
16 [a]Neh. 11:17 [b]Neh. 11:17

the son of Ā′sa, the son of El·kā′-
nah, who lived in the villages of
the Ne·toph′a·thītes.
17 And the gatekeepers *were*
Shal′lum, Ak′kub, Tal′mon, A·hī′-
man, and their brethren. Shal′lum
was the chief.
18 Until then *they had been*
gatekeepers for the camps of
the children of Levi at the King's
Gate on the east.
19 Shal′lum the son of Kō′re,
the son of E·bī′a·saph, the son
of Kō′rah, and his brethren,
from his father's house, the Kō′-
ra·hītes, *were* in charge of the
work of the service, [1]gatekeep-
ers of the tabernacle. Their fathers had been keepers of the
entrance to the camp of the
LORD.
20 And [a]Phin′e·has the son of
El·ē·ā′zar had been the officer
over them in time past; the LORD
was with him.
21 [a]Zech·a·rī′ah the son of Me-
shel·e·mī′ah *was* [1]keeper of
the door of the tabernacle of
meeting.
22 All those chosen as gatekeepers *were* two hundred and
twelve. [a]They were recorded by
their genealogy, in their villages.
David and Samuel [b]the seer had
appointed them to their trusted
office.
23 So they and their children
were in charge of the gates of the
house of the LORD, the house of
the tabernacle, by assignment.
24 The gatekeepers were assigned to the four directions:
the east, west, north, and south.
25 And their brethren in their
villages *had* to come with them
from time to time [a]for seven
days.
26 For in this trusted office

19 [1]Lit. *thresholds*
20 [a]Num. 25:6–13; 31:6
21 [a]1 Chr. 26:2, 14 [1]*gatekeeper*
22 [a]1 Chr. 26:1, 2 [b]1 Sam. 9:9
25 [a]2 Kin. 11:4–7
27 [a]1 Chr. 23:30–32 [1]*the watch was committed to them*
29 [a]1 Chr. 23:29
30 [a]Ex. 30:22–25
31 [a]Lev. 2:5; 6:21
32 [a]Lev. 24:5–8
33 [a]1 Chr. 6:31; 25:1
35 [a]1 Chr. 8:29–32

were four chief gatekeepers;
they were Lē′vītes. And they
had charge over the chambers
and treasuries of the house of
God.
27 And they lodged *all* around
the house of God because [1]they
had the [a]responsibility, and they
were in charge of opening *it* every morning.
28 Now *some* of them were in
charge of the serving vessels,
for they brought them in and
took them out by count.
29 *Some* of them *were* appointed
over the furnishings and over all
the implements of the sanctuary,
and over the [a]fine flour and the
wine and the oil and the incense
and the spices.
30 And *some* of the sons of the
priests made [a]the ointment of
the spices.
31 Mat·ti·thī′ah of the Lē′vītes,
the firstborn of Shal′lum the
Kō′ra·hīte, had the trusted office
[a]over the things that were baked
in the pans.
32 And some of their brethren
of the sons of the Kō′hath·ītes
[a]*were* in charge of preparing the
showbread for every Sabbath.
33 These are [a]the singers, heads
of the fathers' *houses* of the Lē′-
vītes, *who lodged* in the chambers, *and were* free *from other
duties;* for they were employed
in *that* work day and night.
34 These heads of the fathers'
houses of the Lē′vītes *were*
heads throughout their generations. They dwelt at Jerusalem.
35 Je·ī′el the father of Gib′ē·on,
whose wife's name *was* [a]Mā′-
a·cah, dwelt at Gib′ē·on.
36 His firstborn son *was* Ab′-
don, then Zūr, Kish, Bā′al, Ner,
Nā′dab,

37 Gē′dor, A·hī′ō, [1]Zech·a·rī′ah,
and Mik′loth.
38 And Mik′loth begot [1]Shim′-
ē·am. They also dwelt alongside
their relatives in Jerusalem, with
their brethren.
39 [a]Ner begot Kish, Kish begot
Saul, and Saul begot Jonathan,
Mal·chī·shū′a, A·bin′a·dab, and
Esh-Bā′al.
40 The son of Jonathan *was*
Mer′ib-Bā′al, and Mer′ib-Bā′al
begot Mī′cah.
41 The sons of Mī′cah *were* Pī′-
thon, Mē′lech, [1]Tah′rē·a, [a]and[2]
Ā′haz.
42 And Ā′haz begot [1]Jar′ah;
Jar′ah begot Al′e·meth, Az′ma-
veth, and Zim′rī; and Zim′rī begot Mō′za;
43 Mō′za begot Bin′ē·a, [1]Reph-
āi′ah his son, El·e·ā′sah his son,
and Ā′zel his son.
44 And Ā′zel had six sons whose
names *were* these: Az·rī′kam,
Bō′che·rū, Ish′ma·el, Shē·a·rī′ah,
Ō·ba·dī′ah, and Hā′nan; these
were the sons of Ā′zel.

CHAPTER 10

10 Now [a]the Phi·lis′tines
fought against Israel; and
the men of Israel fled from before the Phi·lis′tines, and fell
slain on Mount Gil·bō′a.
2 Then the Phi·lis′tines followed hard after Saul and his
sons. And the Phi·lis′tines killed
Jonathan, [1]A·bin′a·dab, and Mal-
chī·shū′a, Saul's sons.
3 The battle became fierce
against Saul. The archers hit
him, and he was wounded by the
archers.
4 Then Saul said to his armorbearer, "Draw your sword, and
thrust me through with it, lest
these uncircumcised men come
and abuse me." But his armorbearer would not, for he was
greatly afraid. Therefore Saul
took a sword and fell on it.
5 And when his armorbearer
saw that Saul was dead, he also
fell on his sword and died.
6 So Saul and his three sons
died, and all his house died
together.
7 And when all the men of Israel who *were* in the valley saw
that they had fled and that Saul
and his sons were dead, they
forsook their cities and fled;
then the Phi·lis′tines came and
dwelt in them.
8 So it happened the next day,
when the Phi·lis′tines came to
[1]strip the slain, that they found
Saul and his sons fallen on
Mount Gil·bō′a.
9 And they stripped him and
took his head and his armor, and
sent word throughout the land
of the Phi·lis′tines to proclaim
the news *in the temple* of their
idols and among the people.
10 [a]Then they put his armor in
the [1]temple of their gods, and
fastened his head in the temple
of Dā′gon.
11 And when all Jā′besh Gil′-
ē·ad heard all that the Phi·lis′-
tines had done to Saul,
12 all the [a]valiant men arose
and took the body of Saul and
the bodies of his sons; and they
brought them to [b]Jā′besh, and
buried their bones under the
tamarisk tree at Jā′besh, and
fasted seven days.
13 So Saul died for his unfaithfulness which he had [1]commit-
ted against the LORD, [a]because
he did not keep the word of the
LORD, and also because [b]he consulted a medium for guidance.
14 But *he* did not inquire of the
LORD; therefore He killed him,

37 [1]*Zecher,* 1 Chr. 8:31
38 [1]*Shimeah,* 1 Chr. 8:32
39 [a]1 Chr. 8:33–38
41 [a]1 Chr. 8:35 [1]*Tarea,* 1 Chr. 8:35 [2]So with Arab., Syr., Tg., Vg. (cf. 8:35); MT, LXX omit *and Ahaz*
42 [1]*Jehoaddah,* 1 Chr. 8:36
43 [1]*Raphah,* 1 Chr. 8:37
1 [a]1 Sam. 31:1, 2
2 [1]*Jishui,* 1 Sam. 14:49
8 [1]*plunder*
10 [a]1 Sam. 31:10 [1]Lit. *house*
12 [a]1 Sam. 14:52 [b]2 Sam. 21:12
13 [a]1 Sam. 13:13, 14; 15:22–26 [b]1 Sam. 28:7 [1]Lit. *transgressed*

and [a]turned the kingdom over to
David the son of Jesse.

11

Then [a]all Israel came together to David at Hē′-
bron, saying, "Indeed we *are*
your bone and your flesh.
2 "Also, in time past, even when
Saul was king, you *were* the one
who led Israel out and brought
them in; and the LORD your [a]God
said to you, 'You shall [b]shepherd
My people Israel, and be ruler
over My people Israel.' "
3 Therefore all the elders of Israel came to the king at Hē′bron,
and David made a covenant with
them at Hē′bron before the LORD.
And [a]they anointed David king
over Israel, according to the
word of the LORD [1]by [b]Samuel.
4 And David and all Israel
[a]went to Jerusalem, which is Jē′-
bus, [b]where the Jeb′ū·sītes *were,*
the inhabitants of the land.
5 But the inhabitants of Jē′bus
said to David, "You shall not
come in here!" Nevertheless David took the stronghold of Zion
(that is, the City of David).
6 Now David said, "Whoever
attacks the Jeb′ū·sītes first shall
be [1]chief and captain." And Jō′ab
the son of Ze·rū′i·ah went up
first, and became chief.
7 Then David dwelt in the
stronghold; therefore they called
it [1]the City of David.
8 And he built the city around
it, from [1]the Mil′lō to the surrounding area. Jō′ab [2]repaired
the rest of the city.
9 So David [a]went on and became great, and the LORD of
hosts *was* with [b]him.
10 Now [a]these *were* the heads
of the mighty men whom David
had, who strengthened themselves with him in his kingdom,
with all Israel, to make him
king, according to [b]the word of
the LORD concerning Israel.
11 And this *is* the number of
the mighty men whom David
had: [a]Ja·shō′bē·am the son of a
Hach′mo·nīte, [b]chief of [1]the captains; he had lifted up his spear
against three hundred, killed *by*
him at one time.
12 After him *was* El·ē·ā′zar the
son of [a]Dodo, the A·hō′hīte, who
was one of the three mighty
men.
13 He was with David at [1]Pas-
dam′mim. Now there the Phi·lis′-
tines were gathered for battle,
and there was a piece of ground
full of barley. So the people fled
from the Phi·lis′tines.
14 But they [1]stationed themselves in the middle of *that*
field, defended it, and killed the
Phi·lis′tines. So the LORD brought
about a great victory.
15 Now three of the thirty chief
men [a]went down to the rock to
David, into the cave of A·dul′-
lam; and the army of the Phi·lis′-
tines encamped [b]in the Valley of
[1]Reph′a·im.
16 David *was* then in the
stronghold, and the garrison
of the Phi·lis′tines *was* then in
Bethlehem.
17 And David said with longing, "Oh, that someone would
give me a drink of water from
the well of Bethlehem, which is
by the gate!"
18 So the three broke through
the camp of the Phi·lis′tines,
drew water from the well of
Bethlehem that *was* by the gate,
and took *it* and brought *it* to David. Nevertheless David would
not drink it, but poured it out to
the LORD.

14 [a]1 Sam. 15:28
CHAPTER 11
1 [a]2 Sam. 5:1
2 [a]Ps. 78:70–72 [b]2 Sam. 7:7
3 [a]2 Sam. 5:3 [b]1 Sam. 16:1, 4, 12, 13 [1]Lit. *by the hand of Samuel*
4 [a]2 Sam. 5:6 [b]Judg. 1:21; 19:10, 11
6 [1]Lit. *head*
7 [1]*Zion,* 2 Sam. 5:7
8 [1]Lit. *The Landfill* [2]Lit. *revived*
9 [a]2 Sam. 3:1 [b]1 Sam. 16:18
10 [a]2 Sam. 23:8 [b]1 Sam. 16:1, 12
11 [a]1 Chr. 27:2 [b]1 Chr. 12:18 [1]So with Qr.; Kt., LXX, Vg. *the thirty* (cf. 2 Sam. 23:8)
12 [a]1 Chr. 27:4
13 [1]*Ephes Dammim,* 1 Sam. 17:1
14 [1]Lit. *took their stand*
15 [a]2 Sam. 23:13 [b]2 Sam. 5:18 [1]Lit. *Giants*

19 And he said, "Far be it from
me, O my God, that I should do
this! Shall I drink the blood of
these men *who have put* their
lives *in jeopardy*? For at the risk
of their lives they brought it."
Therefore he would not drink it.
These things were done by the
three mighty men.
20 [a]A·bi′shaī the brother of Jō′ab
was chief of *another* [1]three. He
had lifted up his spear against
three hundred *men*, killed *them*,
and won a name among *these*
three.
21 [a]Of the three he was more
honored than the other two men.
Therefore he became their captain. However he did not attain
to the *first* three.
22 Be·nā′i·ah was the son of
Je·hoi′a·da, the son of a valiant
man from Kab′zē·el, who [1]had
done many deeds. [a]He had killed
two lion-like heroes of Mō′ab.
He also had gone down and
killed a lion in the midst of a pit
on a snowy day.
23 And he killed an Egyptian,
a man of *great* height, [1]five cubits tall. In the Egyptian's hand
there was a spear like a weaver's
beam; and he went down to him
with a staff, wrested the spear
out of the Egyptian's hand, and
killed him with his own spear.
24 These *things* Be·nā′i·ah the
son of Je·hoi′a·da did, and won a
name among three mighty men.
25 Indeed he was more honored
than the thirty, but he did not attain to the *first* three. And David
appointed him over his guard.
26 Also the mighty warriors
were [a]As′a·hel the brother of
Jō′ab, El·hā′nan the son of Dodo
of Bethlehem,
27 [1]Sham′moth the Ha′rō·rīte,
[a]Hē′lez the [2]Pel′o·nīte,
28 [a]Ī′ra the son of Ik′kesh the
Te·kō′īte, [b]Ā·bi·ē′zer the An′a-
thoth·īte,
29 [1]Sib′be·chaī the Hū′sha·thīte,
[2]Ī′lāi the A·hō′hīte,
30 [a]Mā′ha·raī the Ne·toph′-
a·thīte, [1]Hē′led the son of Bā′-
a·nah the Ne·toph′a·thīte,
31 [1]Ith′aī the son of Rī′baī of
Gib′ē·ah, of the sons of Benjamin,
[a]Be·nā′i·ah the Pir′a·thon·īte,
32 [1]Hū′raī of the brooks of Gā′-
ash, [2]A·bī′el the Ar′ba·thīte,
33 Az′ma·veth the [1]Ba·har′um-
īte, Ē·lī′ah·ba the Shā·al′bon-
īte,
34 the sons of [1]Hā′shem the
Gī′zō·nīte, Jonathan the son of
Shā′geh the Har′a·rīte,
35 A·hī′am the son of [1]Sā′car
the Har′a·rīte, [2]E·lī′phal the son
of [3]Ūr,
36 Hē′pher the Me·chē′ra·thīte,
A·hī′jah the Pel′o·nīte,
37 [1]Hez′rō the Car′mel·īte, [2]Nā′-
a·raī the son of Ez′baī,
38 Jō′el the brother of Nathan,
Mib′har the son of Hag′rī,
39 Zē′lek the Am′mon·īte, Nā′-
ha·raī the [1]Be·rō′thīte (the armorbearer of Jō′ab the son of
Ze·rū′i·ah),
40 Ī′ra the Ith′rīte, Gā′reb the
Ith′rīte,
41 [a]Ū·rī′ah the Hit′tīte, [1]Zā′bad
the son of Ah′laī,
42 Ad′i·na the son of Shī′za the
Reū′ben·īte (a chief of the Reū′-
ben·ītes) and thirty with him,
43 Hā′nan the son of Mā′a·chah,
Josh′a·phat the Mith′nīte,
44 Uz·zī′a the Ash′te·ra·thīte,
Shā′ma and Je·ī′el the sons of
Hō′tham the A·rō′er·īte,
45 Je·dī′a·el the son of Shim′rī,

20 [a]2 Sam. 23:18 [1]So with MT, LXX, Vg.; Syr. *thirty*
21 [a]2 Sam. 23:19
22 [a]2 Sam. 23:20 [1]*was great in deeds*
23 [1]About 7½ feet
26 [a]2 Sam. 23:24
27 [a]1 Chr. 27:10 [1]*Shammah the Harodite*, 2 Sam. 23:25 [2]*Paltite*, 2 Sam. 23:26
28 [a]1 Chr. 27:9 [b]1 Chr. 27:12
29 [1]*Mebunnai*, 2 Sam. 23:27 [2]*Zalmon*, 2 Sam. 23:28
30 [a]1 Chr. 27:13 [1]*Heleb*, 2 Sam. 23:29, or *Heldai*, 1 Chr. 27:15
31 [a]1 Chr. 27:14 [1]*Ittai*, 2 Sam. 23:29
32 [1]*Hiddai*, 2 Sam. 23:30 [2]*Abi-Albon*, 2 Sam. 23:31
33 [1]*Barhumite*, 2 Sam. 23:31
34 [1]*Jashen*, 2 Sam. 23:32
35 [1]*Sharar*, 2 Sam. 23:33 [2]*Eliphelet*, 2 Sam. 23:34 [3]*Ahasbai*, 2 Sam. 23:34
37 [1]*Hezrai*, 2 Sam. 23:38 [2]*Paarai the Arbite*, 2 Sam. 23:35
39 [1]*Beerothite*, 2 Sam. 23:37
41 [a]2 Sam. 11 [1]The last sixteen are not added in 2 Sam. 23.

and Jō'ha his brother, the Tī'-
zīte,
46 E·lī'el the Mā'ha·vīte, Jer'-
i·baī and Josh·a·vī'ah the sons of
El'nā·am, Ith'mah the Mō'ab·īte,
47 E·lī'el, Ō'bed, and Jā·a·sī'el
the Me·zō'ba·īte.

12 Now [a]these *were* the men
who came to David at
[b]Zik'lag while he was still a
fugitive from Saul the son of
Kish; and they *were* among the
mighty men, helpers in the war,
2 armed with bows, using both
the right hand and [a]the left in
hurling stones and *shooting* arrows with the bow. *They were* of
Benjamin, Saul's brethren.
3 The chief *was* Ā·hī·ē'zer, then
Jō'ash, the sons of [1]She·mā'ah
the Gib'ē·a·thīte; Jē'zi·el and
Pē'let the sons of Az'ma·veth;
Ber'a·chah, and Jē'hū the An'-
a·thoth·īte;
4 Ish·mā'i·ah the Gib'ē·on·īte,
a mighty man among the thirty,
and over the thirty; Jer·e·mī'ah,
Ja·hā'zi·el, Jō·hā'nan, and Joz'-
a·bad the Ge·dē'ra·thīte;
5 E·lū'zaī, Jer'i·moth, Bē·a·lī'ah,
Shem·a·rī'ah, and Sheph·a·tī'ah
the Ha·rū'phīte;
6 El·kā'nah, Jis·shī'ah, Az'-
a·rel, Jō·ē'zer, and Ja·shō'bē·am,
the Kō'ra·hītes;
7 and Jō·ē'lah and Zeb·a·dī'ah
the sons of Je·rō'ham of Gē'dor.
8 *Some* Gad'ītes [1]joined David
at the stronghold in the wilderness, mighty men of valor, men
trained for battle, who could
handle shield and spear, whose
faces *were like* the faces of lions,
and *were* [a]as swift as gazelles on
the mountains:
9 Ē'zer the first, Ō·ba·dī'ah the
second, E·lī'ab the third,
10 Mish·man'nah the fourth,
Jer·e·mī'ah the fifth,
11 At'taī the sixth, E·lī'el the
seventh,
12 Jō·hā'nan the eighth, El·zā'-
bad the ninth,
13 Jer·e·mī'ah the tenth, and
Mach'ba·naī the eleventh.
14 These *were* from the sons
of Gad, captains of the army;
the least was over a hundred,
and the greatest was over a
[a]thousand.
15 These *are* the ones who
crossed the Jordan in the first
month, when it had overflowed
all its [a]banks; and they put to
flight all *those* in the valleys, to
the east and to the west.
16 Then some of the sons of
Benjamin and Judah came to
David at the stronghold.
17 And David went out [1]to meet
them, and answered and said to
them, "If you have come peaceably to me to help me, my heart
will be united with you; but if to
betray me to my enemies, since
there is no [2]wrong in my hands,
may the God of our fathers look
and bring judgment."
18 Then the Spirit [1]came upon
[a]A·mā'saī, chief of the captains,
and he said:

"*We are* yours, O David;
We *are* on your side, O son
of Jesse!
Peace, peace to you,
And peace to your helpers!
For your God helps you."

So David received them, and
made them captains of the troop.
19 And *some* from Ma·nas'seh
defected to David [a]when he was
going with the Phi·lis'tines to
battle against Saul; but they did

CHAPTER 12
1 [a]1 Sam. 27:2 [b]1 Sam. 27:6
2 [a]Judg. 3:15; 20:16
3 [1]Or *Hasmaah*
8 [a]2 Sam. 2:18 [1]Lit. *separated themselves to*
14 [a]1 Sam. 18:13
15 [a]Josh. 3:15; 4:18, 19
17 [1]Lit. *before them* [2]Lit. *violence*
18 [a]2 Sam. 17:25 [1]Lit. *clothed*
19 [a]1 Sam. 29:2

not help them, for the lords of the Phi·lis'tines sent him away by agreement, saying, [b]"He may defect to his master Saul *and endanger* our heads."

20 When he went to Zik'lag, those of Ma·nas'seh who defected to him were Ad'nah, Joz'a·bad, Je·dī'a·el, Michael, Joz'a·bad, E·lī'hū, and Zil'le·thaī, captains of the thousands who *were* from Ma·nas'seh.

21 And they helped David against [a]the bands *of raiders,* for they *were* all mighty men of valor, and they were captains in the army.

22 For at *that* time they came to David day by day to help him, until *it was* a great army, [a]like the army of God.

23 Now these *were* the numbers of the [1]divisions *that were* equipped for war, *and* [a]came to David at [b]Hē'bron to [c]turn *over* the kingdom of Saul to him, [d]according to the word of the LORD:

24 of the sons of Judah bearing shield and spear, six thousand eight hundred [1]armed for war;

25 of the sons of Sim'ē·on, mighty men of valor fit for war, seven thousand one hundred;

26 of the sons of Levi four thousand six hundred;

27 Je·hoi'a·da, the leader of the Aaronites, and with him three thousand seven hundred;

28 [a]Zā'dok, a young man, a valiant warrior, and from his father's house twenty-two captains;

29 of the sons of Benjamin, relatives of Saul, three thousand (until then [a]the greatest part of them had remained loyal to the house of Saul);

30 of the sons of Ē'phra·im twenty thousand eight hundred, mighty men of valor, [1]famous men throughout their father's house;

31 of the half-tribe of Ma·nas'seh eighteen thousand, who were designated by name to come and make David king;

32 of the sons of Is'sa·char [a]who had understanding of the times, to know what Israel ought to do, their chiefs were two hundred; and all their brethren were at their command;

33 of Zeb'ū·lun there were fifty thousand who went out to battle, expert in war with all weapons of war, [a]stouthearted men who could keep ranks;

34 of Naph'ta·lī one thousand captains, and with them thirty-seven thousand with shield and spear;

35 of the Dan'ītes who could keep battle formation, twenty-eight thousand six hundred;

36 of Ash'er, those who could go out to war, able to keep battle formation, forty thousand;

37 of the Reū'ben·ītes and the Gad'ītes and the half-tribe of Ma·nas'seh, from the other side of the Jordan, one hundred and twenty thousand armed for battle with every *kind* of weapon of war.

38 All these men of war, who could keep ranks, came to Hē'bron with a loyal heart, to make David king over all Israel; and all the rest of Israel *were* of [a]one mind to make David king.

39 And they were there with David three days, eating and drinking, for their brethren had prepared for them.

40 Moreover those who were

19 [b]1 Sam. 29:4
21 [a]1 Sam. 30:1, 9, 10
22 [a]Josh. 5:13–15
23 [a]2 Sam. 2:1–4 [b]1 Chr. 11:1 [c]1 Chr. 10:14 [d]1 Sam. 16:1–4 [1]Lit. *heads of those*
24 [1]*equipped*
28 [a]2 Sam. 8:17
29 [a]2 Sam. 2:8, 9
30 [1]Lit. *men of names*
32 [a]Esth. 1:13
33 [a]Ps. 12:2
38 [a]2 Chr. 30:12

near to them, from as far away
as Is′sa·char and Zeb′ū·lun and
Naph′ta·lī, were bringing food
on donkeys and camels, on
mules and oxen—provisions of
flour and cakes of figs and cakes
of raisins, wine and oil and oxen
and sheep abundantly, for *there*
was joy in Israel.

13 Then David consulted with
the [a]captains of thousands
and hundreds, *and* with every
leader.
2 And David said to all the
assembly of Israel, "If *it seems*
good to you, and if it is of the
LORD our God, let us send out to
our brethren everywhere *who*
are [a]left in all the land of Israel,
and with them to the priests and
Lē′vītes *who are* in their cities
and their common-lands, that
they may gather together to us;
3 "and let us bring the ark of
our God back to us, [a]for we have
not inquired at it since the days
of Saul."
4 Then all the assembly said
that they would do so, for the
thing was right in the eyes of all
the people.
5 So [a]David gathered all Israel
together, from [b]Shī′hor in Egypt
to as far as the entrance of Hā′-
math, to bring the ark of God
[c]from Kir′jath Jē′a·rim.
6 And David and all Israel
went up to [a]Bā′a·lah,[1] to Kir′-
jath Jē′a·rim, which belonged
to Judah, to bring up from there
the ark of God the LORD, [b]who
dwells *between* the cherubim,
where *His* name is proclaimed.
7 So they [1]carried the ark of
God [a]on a new cart [b]from the
house of A·bin′a·dab, and Uz′za
and A·hī′ō drove the cart.
8 Then [a]David and all Israel
played *music* before God with
all *their* might, with [1]singing, on
harps, on stringed instruments,
on tambourines, on cymbals,
and with trumpets.
9 And when they came to
[1]Chī′don's threshing floor, Uz′za
put out his hand to hold the ark,
for the oxen [2]stumbled.
10 Then the anger of the LORD
was aroused against Uz′za, and
He struck him [a]because he put
his hand to the ark; and he [b]died
there before God.
11 And David became angry
because of the LORD's outbreak
against Uz′za; therefore that
place is called [1]Per′ez Uz′za to
this day.
12 David was afraid of God that
day, saying, "How can I bring
the ark of God to me?"
13 So David would not move
the ark with him into the City of
David, but took it aside into the
house of Ō′bed-Ē′dom the Git′-
tīte.
14 [a]The ark of God remained
with the family of Ō′bed-Ē′dom
in his house three months. And
the LORD blessed [b]the house of
Ō′bed-Ē′dom and all that he
had.

14 Now [a]Hī′ram king of Tȳre
sent messengers to Da-
vid, and cedar trees, with masons and carpenters, to build
him a house.
2 So David knew that the LORD
had established him as king
over Israel, for his kingdom was
[a]highly exalted for the sake of
His people Israel.
3 Then David took more wives
in Jerusalem, and David begot
more sons and daughters.
4 And [a]these are the names
of his children whom he had in

CHAPTER 13

1 [a]1 Chr. 11:15; 12:34
2 [a]Is. 37:4
3 [a]1 Sam. 7:1, 2
5 [a]1 Sam. 7:5 [b]Josh. 13:3 [c]1 Sam. 6:21; 7:1, 2
6 [a]Josh. 15:9, 60 [b]Ex. 25:22 [1]*Baale Judah*, 2 Sam. 6:2
7 [a]1 Sam. 6:7 [b]1 Sam. 7:1 [1]Lit. *caused the ark of God to ride*
8 [a]2 Sam. 6:5 [1]*songs*
9 [1]*Nachon*, 2 Sam. 6:6 [2]Or *let it go off*
10 [a][Num. 4:15] [b]Lev. 10:2
11 [1]Lit. *Outburst Against Uzza*
14 [a]2 Sam. 6:11 [b]1 Chr. 26:4–8

CHAPTER 14

1 [a]2 Sam. 5:11
2 [a]Num. 24:7
4 [a]1 Chr. 3:5–8

Jerusalem: [1]Sham′mū·a, Shō′bab,
Nathan, Solomon,
5 Ib′har, [1]E·lish′ū·a, [2]El′pe·let,
6 Nō′gah, Nē′pheg, Ja·phī′a,
7 E·lish′a·ma, [1]Bē·e·lī′a·da, and
E·liph′e·let.
8 Now when the Phi·lis′tines
heard that [a]David had been
anointed king over all Israel,
all the Phi·lis′tines went up to
search for David. And David
heard *of it* and went out against
them.
9 Then the Phi·lis′tines went
and made a raid [a]on the Valley
of [1]Reph′a·im.
10 And David [a]inquired of God,
saying, "Shall I go up against
the Phi·lis′tines? Will You deliver
them into my hand?" The LORD
said to him, "Go up, for I will
deliver them into your hand."
11 So they went up to Bā′al
Pe·rā′zim, and David defeated
them there. Then David said,
"God has broken through my
enemies by my hand like a
breakthrough of water." Therefore they called the name of that
place [1]Bā′al Pe·rā′zim.
12 And when they left their gods
there, David gave a commandment, and they were burned
with fire.
13 [a]Then the Phi·lis′tines once
again made a raid on the valley.
14 Therefore David inquired
again of God, and God said to
him, "You shall not go up after
them; circle around them, [a]and
come upon them in front of the
mulberry trees.
15 "And it shall be, when you
hear a sound of marching in the
tops of the mulberry trees, then
you shall go out to battle, for God
has gone out before you to strike
the camp of the Phi·lis′tines."
16 So David did as God commanded him, and they drove
back the army of the Phi·lis′tines
from [1]Gib′ē·on as far as Gē′zer.
17 Then [a]the fame of David
went out into all lands, and the
LORD [b]brought the fear of him
upon all nations.

15 David built houses for
himself in the City of David; and he prepared a place for
the ark of God, [a]and pitched a
tent for it.
2 Then David said, "No one
may carry the [a]ark of God but
the Lē′vītes, for [b]the LORD has
chosen them to carry the ark of
God and to minister before Him
forever."
3 And David [a]gathered all Israel together at Jerusalem, to
bring up the ark of the LORD to
its place, which he had prepared
for it.
4 Then David assembled the
children of Aaron and the Lē′-
vītes:
5 of the sons of Kō′hath, Ū·rī′el
the chief, and one hundred and
twenty of his [1]brethren;
6 of the sons of Me·rar′ī,
A·sāi′ah the chief, and two hundred and twenty of his brethren;
7 of the sons of Ger′shom, Jō′el
the chief, and one hundred and
thirty of his brethren;
8 of the sons of [a]E·li·zā′phan,
She·māi′ah the chief, and two
hundred of his brethren;
9 of the sons of [a]Hē′bron,
E·lī′el the chief, and eighty of his
brethren;
10 of the sons of Uz′zi·el, Am-
min′a·dab the chief, and one hundred and twelve of his brethren.
11 And David called for [a]Zā′-
dok and [b]A·bī′a·thar the priests,
and for the Lē′vītes: for Ū·rī′el,

4 [1]*Shimea,* 1 Chr. 3:5
5 [1]*Elishama,* 1 Chr. 3:6 [2]*Eliphelet,* 1 Chr. 3:6
7 [1]*Eliada,* 2 Sam. 5:6; 1 Chr. 3:8
8 [a]2 Sam. 5:17–21
9 [a]1 Chr. 11:15; 14:13 [1]Lit. *Giants*
10 [a]1 Sam. 23:2, 4; 30:8
11 [1]Lit. *Master of Breakthroughs*
13 [a]2 Sam. 5:22–25
14 [a]2 Sam. 5:23
16 [1]*Geba,* 2 Sam. 5:25
17 [a]Josh. 6:27 [b][Deut. 2:25; 11:25]

CHAPTER 15

1 [a]1 Chr. 16:1
2 [a][Num. 4:15] [b]Deut. 10:8; 31:9
3 [a]1 Kin. 8:1
5 [1]*kinsmen*
8 [a]Ex. 6:22
9 [a]Ex. 6:18
11 [a]1 Chr. 12:28 [b]1 Kin. 2:22, 26, 27

A·sāi′ah, Jō′el, She·māi′ah, E·lī′el,
and Am·min′a·dab.
12 He said to them, "You *are*
the heads of the fathers' *houses*
of the Lē′vītes; [1]sanctify yourselves, you and your brethren,
that you may bring up the ark
of the LORD God of Israel to *the*
place I have prepared for it.
13 "For [a]because you *did* not
do it the first *time*, [b]the LORD
our God broke out against us,
because we did not consult Him
[1]about the proper order."
14 So the priests and the Lē′-
vītes [1]sanctified themselves to
bring up the ark of the LORD God
of Israel.
15 And the children of the Lē′-
vītes bore the ark of God on
their shoulders, by its poles, as
[a]Moses had commanded according to the word of the LORD.
16 Then David spoke to the
leaders of the Lē′vītes to appoint
their brethren *to be* the singers accompanied by instruments
of music, stringed instruments,
harps, and cymbals, by raising
the voice with resounding joy.
17 So the Lē′vītes appointed
[a]Hē′man the son of Jō′el; and of
his brethren, [b]Ā′saph the son of
Ber·e·chī′ah; and of their brethren, the sons of Me·rar′ī, [c]Ē′than
the son of Kū·shā′i·ah;
18 and with them their brethren
of the second *rank*: Zech·a·rī′ah,
[1]Ben, Ja·ā′zi·el, She·mir′a·moth,
Je·hī′el, Un′nī, E·lī′ab, Be·nā′i·ah,
Mā·a·sēi′ah, Mat·ti·thī′ah, E·liph′-
e·leh, Mik·nē′i·ah, Ō′bed-Ē′dom,
and Je·ī′el, the gatekeepers;
19 the singers, Hē′man, Ā′saph,
and Ē′than, *were* to sound the
cymbals of bronze;
20 Zech·a·rī′ah, [1]Ā′zi·el, She-
mir′a·moth, Je·hī′el, Un′nī, E·lī′ab,

12 [1]*consecrate*
13 [a]2 Sam. 6:3 [b]1 Chr. 13:7–11 [1]*regarding the ordinance*
14 [1]*consecrated*
15 [a]Ex. 25:14
17 [a]1 Chr. 6:33; 25:1 [b]1 Chr. 6:39 [c]1 Chr. 6:44
18 [1]So with MT, Vg.; LXX omits *Ben*
20 [a]Ps. 46:title [1]*Jaaziel*, v. 18
21 [a]Ps. 6:title
24 [a][Num. 10:8] [b]1 Chr. 13:13, 14
25 [a]1 Kin. 8:1
27 [a]1 Sam. 2:18, 28
28 [a]1 Chr. 13:8
29 [a]2 Sam. 3:13, 14; 6:16, 20–23

Mā·a·sēi′ah, and Be·nā′i·ah, with
strings according to [a]Al′a·moth;
21 Mat·ti·thī′ah, E·liph′e·leh,
Mik·nē′i·ah, Ō′bed-Ē′dom, Je·ī′el,
and Az·a·zī′ah, to direct with
harps on the [a]Shem′i·nith;
22 Chen·a·nī′ah, leader of the
Lē′vītes, was instructor *in charge*
of the music, because he *was*
skillful;
23 Ber·e·chī′ah and El·kā′nah
were doorkeepers for the ark;
24 Sheb·a·nī′ah, Josh′a·phat, Ne-
than′el, A·mā′saī, Zech·a·rī′ah,
Be·nā′i·ah, and El·i·ē′zer, the
priests, [a]were to blow the trumpets before the ark of God; and
[b]Ō′bed-Ē′dom and Je·hī′ah, doorkeepers for the ark.
25 So [a]David, the elders of Israel, and the captains over thousands went to bring up the ark
of the covenant of the LORD from
the house of Ō′bed-Ē′dom with
joy.
26 And so it was, when God
helped the Lē′vītes who bore the
ark of the covenant of the LORD,
that they offered seven bulls and
seven rams.
27 David was clothed with a
robe of fine [a]linen, as were all
the Lē′vītes who bore the ark,
the singers, and Chen·a·nī′ah the
music master *with* the singers.
David also wore a linen ephod.
28 [a]Thus all Israel brought up
the ark of the covenant of the
LORD with shouting and with the
sound of the horn, with trumpets and with cymbals, making
music with stringed instruments
and harps.
29 And it happened, [a]*as* the
ark of the covenant of the LORD
came to the City of David, that
Mī′chal, Saul's daughter, looked
through a window and saw King

David whirling and playing music; and she despised him in her
heart.

16 So [a]they brought the ark
of God, and set it in the
midst of the tabernacle that
David had erected for it. Then
they offered burnt offerings and
peace offerings before God.
2 And when David had fin-
ished offering the burnt offerings and the peace offerings, [a]he
blessed the people in the name
of the LORD.
3 Then he distributed to everyone of Israel, both man and
woman, to everyone a loaf of
bread, a piece *of meat,* and a
cake of raisins.
4 And he appointed some
of the Lē′vītes to minister before the ark of the LORD, to
[a]commemorate, to thank, and to
praise the LORD God of Israel:
5 Ā′saph the chief, and next
to him Zech·a·rī′ah, *then* [a]Je-
ī′el, She·mir′a·moth, Je·hī′el,
Mat·ti·thī′ah, E·lī′ab, Be·nā′i·ah,
and Ō′bed-Ē′dom: Je·ī′el with
stringed instruments and harps,
but Ā′saph made music with
cymbals;
6 Be·nā′i·ah and Ja·hā′zi·el the
priests regularly *blew* the trumpets before the ark of the covenant of God.
7 On that day [a]David [b]first delivered *this psalm* into the hand
of Ā′saph and his brethren, to
thank the LORD:

8 [a]Oh, give thanks to the LORD!
Call upon His name;
Make known His deeds
among the peoples!
9 Sing to Him, sing psalms to
Him;
Talk of all His wondrous
works!
10 Glory in His holy name;
Let the hearts of those
rejoice who seek the
LORD!
11 Seek the LORD and His
strength;
Seek His face evermore!
12 Remember His marvelous
works which He has
done,
His wonders, and the
judgments of His mouth,
13 O seed of Israel His servant,
You children of Jacob, His
chosen ones!

14 He *is* the LORD our God;
His [a]judgments *are* in all the
earth.
15 Remember His covenant
forever,
The word which He
commanded, for a
thousand generations,
16 *The* [a]*covenant which* He
made with Abraham,
And His oath to Isaac,
17 And [a]confirmed it to [b]Jacob
for a statute,
To Israel *for* an everlasting
covenant,
18 Saying, "To you I will give
the land of Cā′naan
As the allotment of your
inheritance,"
19 When you were [a]few in
number,
Indeed very few, and
strangers in it.
20 When they went from one
nation to another,
And from *one* kingdom to
another people,
21 He permitted no man to do
them wrong;

CHAPTER 16

1 [a]2 Sam. 6:17
2 [a]1 Kin. 8:14
4 [a]Ps. 38:title; 70:title
5 [a]1 Chr. 15:18
7 [a]2 Sam. 22:1; 23:1 [b]Ps. 105:1–15
8 [a]Ps. 105:1–15
14 [a][Is. 26:9]
16 [a]Gen. 17:2; 26:3; 28:13; 35:11
17 [a]Gen. 35:11, 12 [b]Gen. 28:10–15
19 [a]Gen. 34:30

Yes, He [a]rebuked kings for
their sakes,
22 *Saying,* [a]"Do not touch My
anointed ones,
And do My prophets no
harm."

23 [a]Sing to the LORD, all the
earth;
Proclaim the good news of
His salvation from day
to day.
24 Declare His glory among
the nations,
His wonders among all
peoples.

25 For the LORD *is* great and
greatly to be praised;
He *is* also to be feared
above all gods.
26 For all the gods [a]of the
peoples *are* [1]idols,
But the LORD made the
heavens.
27 Honor and majesty *are*
before Him;
Strength and gladness are
in His place.
28 Give to the LORD, O families
of the peoples,
Give to the LORD glory and
strength.
29 Give to the LORD the glory
due His name;
Bring an offering, and come
before Him.
Oh, worship the LORD in the
beauty of holiness!
30 Tremble before Him, all the
earth.
The world also is firmly
established,
It shall not be moved.
31 Let the heavens rejoice, and
let the earth be glad;
And let them say among
the nations, "The LORD
reigns."
32 Let the sea roar, and all its
fullness;
Let the field rejoice, and all
that *is* in it.
33 Then the [a]trees of the woods
shall rejoice before the
LORD,
For He is [b]coming to judge
the earth.

34 [a]Oh, give thanks to the LORD,
for *He is* good!
For His mercy *endures*
forever.
35 [a]And say, "Save us, O God of
our salvation;
Gather us together, and
deliver us from the
Gentiles,
To give thanks to Your holy
name,
To triumph in Your praise."

36 [a]Blessed *be* the LORD God of
Israel
From everlasting to
everlasting!

And all [a]the people said, "Amen!"
and praised the LORD.
37 So he left [a]Ā′saph and his
brothers there before the ark of
the covenant of the LORD to minister before the ark regularly, as
every day's work [b]required;
38 and [a]Ō′bed-Ē′dom with his
sixty-eight brethren, including Ō′bed-Ē′dom the son of
Je·dū′thun, and Hō′sah, *to be*
gatekeepers;
39 and Zā′dok the priest and his
brethren the priests, [a]before the
tabernacle of the LORD [b]at the
[1]high place that *was* at Gib′ē·on,
40 to offer burnt offerings to

21 [a]Gen. 12:17; 20:3
22 [a]Gen. 20:7
23 [a]Ps. 96:1–13
26 [a]Lev. 19:4 [1]*worthless things*
33 [a]Is. 55:12, 13 [b][Matt. 25:31–46]
34 [a]Ps. 106:1; 107:1; 118:1; 136:1
35 [a]Ps. 106:47, 48
36 [a]1 Kin. 8:15, 56 [b]Deut. 27:15
37 [a]1 Chr. 16:4, 5 [b]Ezra 3:4
38 [a]1 Chr. 13:14
39 [a]2 Chr. 1:3 [b]1 Kin. 3:4 [1]Place for pagan worship

the LORD on the altar of burnt offering regularly [a]morning and evening, and *to do* according to all that is written in the Law of the LORD which He commanded Israel;

41 and with them Hē'man and Je·dū'thun and the rest who were chosen, who were designated by name, to give thanks to the LORD, [a]because His mercy *endures* forever;

42 and with them Hē'man and Je·dū'thun, to sound aloud with trumpets and cymbals and the musical instruments of God. Now the sons of Je·dū'thun *were* gatekeepers.

43 [a]Then all the people departed, every man to his house; and David returned to bless his house.

17 Now [a]it came to pass, when David was dwelling in his house, that David said to Nathan the prophet, "See now, I dwell in a house of cedar, but the ark of the covenant of the LORD *is* under tent curtains."

2 Then Nathan said to David, "Do all that *is* in your heart, for God *is* with you."

3 But it happened that night that the word of God came to Nathan, saying,

4 "Go and tell My servant David, 'Thus says the LORD: "You shall [a]not build Me a house to dwell in.

5 "For I have not dwelt in a house since the time that I brought up Israel, even to this day, but have gone from tent to tent, and from *one* tabernacle *to another.*

6 "Wherever I have moved about with all Israel, have I ever spoken a word to any of the judges of Israel, whom I commanded to shepherd My people, saying, 'Why have you not built Me a house of cedar?' " '

7 "Now therefore, thus shall you say to My servant David, 'Thus says the LORD of hosts: "I took you [a]from the sheepfold, from following the sheep, to be [1]ruler over My people Israel.

8 "And I have been with you wherever you have gone, and have cut off all your enemies from before you, and have [1]made you a name like the name of the great men who *are* on the earth.

9 "Moreover I will appoint a place for My people Israel, and will [a]plant them, that they may dwell in a place of their own and move no more; nor shall the sons of wickedness oppress them anymore, as previously,

10 "since the time that I commanded judges *to be* over My people Israel. Also I will subdue all your enemies. Furthermore I tell you that the LORD will build you a [1]house.

11 "And it shall be, when your days are [a]fulfilled, when you must [1]go *to be* with your fathers, that I will set up your [b]seed after you, who will be of your sons; and I will establish his kingdom. ☆

12 [a]"He shall build Me a house, and I will establish his throne forever. ☆

13 [a]"I will be his Father, and he shall be My son; and I will not take My mercy away from him, [b]as I took *it* from *him* who was before you. ☆

14 "And [a]I will establish him in My house and in My kingdom forever; and his throne shall be established forever." ' " ☆

40 [a][Ex. 29:38–42]
41 [a]2 Chr. 5:13; 7:3
43 [a]2 Sam. 6:18–20

CHAPTER 17

1 [a]2 Sam. 7:1
4 [a][1 Chr. 28:2, 3]
7 [a]1 Sam. 16:11–13 [1]*leader*
8 [1]*given you prestige*
9 [a]Amos 9:14
10 [1]Royal dynasty
11 [a]1 Kin. 2:10 [b][1 Chr. 22:9–13; 28:20]; Matt. 1:6; Luke 3:31 [1]Die and join your ancestors
12 [a][Ps. 89:20–37; Luke 1:33]
13 [a]Heb. 1:5 [b][1 Sam. 15:23–28]
14 [a]Matt. 19:28; 25:31; [Luke 1:31–33]; Acts 2:30

15 According to all these words and according to all this vision, so Nathan spoke to David.

16 [a]Then King David went in and sat before the LORD; and he said: "Who *am* I, O LORD God? And what is my house, that You have brought me this far?

17 "And *yet* this was a small thing in Your sight, O God; and You have *also* spoken of Your servant's house for a great while to come, and have regarded me according to the rank of a man of high degree, O LORD God.

18 "What more can David *say* to You for the honor of Your servant? For You know Your servant.

19 "O LORD, for Your servant's sake, and according to Your own heart, You have done all this greatness, in making known all these great things.

20 "O LORD, *there is* none like You, nor *is there any* God besides You, according to all that we have heard with our ears.

21 [a]"And who *is* like Your people Israel, the one nation on the earth whom God went to redeem for Himself *as* a people—to make for Yourself a name by great and awesome deeds, by driving out nations from before Your people whom You redeemed from Egypt?

22 "For You have made Your people Israel Your very own people forever; and You, LORD, have become their God.

23 "And now, O LORD, the word which You have spoken concerning Your servant and concerning his house, *let it* be established forever, and do as You have said.

24 "So let it be established, that Your name may be magnified forever, saying, 'The LORD of hosts, the God of Israel, *is* Israel's God.' And let the house of Your servant David be established before You.

25 "For You, O my God, [1]have revealed to Your servant that You will build him a house. Therefore Your servant has found it *in his heart* to pray before You.

26 "And now, LORD, [1]You are God, and have promised this goodness to Your servant.

27 "Now You have been pleased to bless the house of Your servant, that it may continue before You forever; for You have blessed it, O LORD, and *it shall be* blessed forever."

18 After this [a]it came to pass that David [1]attacked the Phi·lis′tines, subdued them, and took Gath and its towns from the hand of the Phi·lis′tines.

2 Then he [1]defeated [a]Mō′ab, and the Mō′ab·ītes became David's [b]servants, *and* brought tribute.

3 And [a]David [1]defeated [2]Had·a·dē′zer king of Zō′bah *as far as* Hā′math, as he went to establish his power by the River Eū·phrā′tēs.

4 David took from him one thousand chariots, [1]seven thousand horsemen, and twenty thousand foot soldiers. Also David [2]hamstrung all the chariot *horses*, except that he spared enough of them for one hundred chariots.

5 When the [a]Syrians of Damascus came to help Had·a·dē′zer king of Zō′bah, David killed twenty-two thousand of the Syrians.

6 Then David put *garrisons* in

16 [a]2 Sam. 7:18
21 [a]Ps. 147:20
25 [1]Lit. *have uncovered the ear of*
26 [1]Or *You alone are*

CHAPTER 18

1 [a]2 Sam. 8:1–18 [1]Lit. *struck*
2 [a]2 Sam. 8:2 [b]Ps. 60:8 [1]Lit. *struck*
3 [a]2 Sam. 8:3 [1]Lit. *struck* [2]Heb. *Hadarezer*
4 [1]*seven hundred*, 2 Sam. 8:4 [2]*crippled*
5 [a]2 Sam. 8:5, 6

Syria of Damascus; and the Syrians became David's servants,
and brought tribute. So the LORD
preserved David wherever he
went.
7 And David took the shields
of gold that were on the servants
of Had·a·dē′zer, and brought
them to Jerusalem.
8 Also from [1]Tib′hath and from
[2]Chun, cities of [3]Had·a·dē′zer,
David brought a large amount
of [a]bronze, with which [b]Solomon
made the bronze [4]Sea, the pillars, and the articles of bronze.
9 Now when [1]Tō′ū king of Hā′-
math heard that David had [2]de-
feated all the army of Had·a·dē′-
zer king of Zō′bah,
10 he sent [1]Ha·dor′am his son
to King David, to greet him
and bless him, because he had
fought against Had·a·dē′zer and
[2]defeated him (for Had·a·dē′zer
had been at war with Tō′ū); and
Ha·dor′am brought with him all
kinds of [a]articles of gold, silver,
and bronze.
11 King David also dedicated
these to the LORD, along with
the silver and gold that he had
brought from all *these* nations—
from Ē′dom, from Mō′ab, from
the [a]people of Am′mon, from
the [b]Phi·lis′tines, and from [c]Am′-
a·lek.
12 Moreover [a]A·bi′shaī the son
of Ze·rū′i·ah killed [b]eighteen
thousand [1]Ē′dom·ītes in the Valley of Salt.
13 [a]He also put garrisons in
Ē′dom, and all the Ē′dom·ītes
became David's servants. And
the LORD preserved David wherever he went.
14 So David reigned over all Israel, and administered judgment
and justice to all his people.
15 Jō′ab the son of Ze·rū′i·ah
was over the army; Je·hosh′-
a·phat the son of A·hī′lud *was*
recorder;
16 Zā′dok the son of A·hī′-
tub and [1]A·bim′e·lech the son
of A·bī′a·thar *were* the priests;
[2]Shav′sha *was* the scribe;
17 [a]Be·nā′i·ah the son of Je·hoi′-
a·da *was* over the Cher′e·thītes
and the Pel′eth·ītes; and David's
sons *were* [1]chief ministers at the
king's side.

19 It[a] happened after this
that Nā′hash the king of
the people of Am′mon died, and
his son reigned in his place.
2 Then David said, "I will
show kindness to Hā′nun the
son of Nā′hash, because his father showed kindness to me." So
David sent messengers to comfort him concerning his father.
And David's servants came to
Hā′nun in the land of the people
of Am′mon to comfort him.
3 And the princes of the people of Am′mon said to Hā′nun,
[1]"Do you think that David really
honors your father because he
has sent comforters to you? Did
his servants not come to you to
search and to overthrow and to
spy out the land?"
4 Therefore Hā′nun took David's servants, shaved them, and
cut off their garments [1]in the
middle, at their [a]buttocks, and
sent them away.
5 Then *some* went and told
David about the men; and he
sent to meet them, because the
men were greatly ashamed. And
the king said, "Wait at Jericho
until your beards have grown,
and *then* return."
6 When the people of Am′-
mon saw that they had made

8 [a]2 Sam. 8:8 [b]1 Kin. 7:15, 23 [1]*Betah,* 2 Sam. 8:8 [2]*Berothai,* 2 Sam. 8:8 [3]Heb. *Hadarezer* [4]Great laver or basin

9 [1]*Toi,* 2 Sam. 8:9, 10 [2]Lit. *struck*

10 [a]2 Sam. 8:10–12 [1]*Joram,* 2 Sam. 8:10 [2]Lit. *struck*

11 [a]2 Sam. 10:14 [b]2 Sam. 5:17–25 [c]2 Sam. 1:1

12 [a]2 Sam. 23:18 [b]2 Sam. 8:13 [1]*Syrians,* 2 Sam. 8:13

13 [a]2 Sam. 8:14

16 [1]*Ahimelech,* 2 Sam. 8:17 [2]*Seraiah,* 2 Sam. 8:17, or *Shisha,* 1 Kin. 4:3

17 [a]2 Sam. 8:18 [1]Lit. *at the hand of the king*

CHAPTER 19

1 [a]2 Sam. 10:1–19

3 [1]Lit. *In your eyes is David honoring your father because*

4 [a]Is. 20:4 [1]*in half*

themselves repulsive to David, Hā′nun and the people of Am′mon sent a thousand talents of silver to hire for themselves chariots and horsemen from [1]Mes·o·po·tā′mi·a, from Syrian Mā′a·cah, [a]and from [2]Zō′bah.
7 So they hired for themselves thirty-two thousand chariots, with the king of Mā′a·cah and his people, who came and encamped before Med′e·ba. Also the people of Am′mon gathered together from their cities, and came to battle.
8 Now when David heard *of it,* he sent Jō′ab and all the army of the mighty men.
9 Then the people of Am′mon came out and put themselves in battle array before the gate of the city, and the kings who had come *were* by themselves in the field.
10 When Jō′ab saw that the battle line was against him before and behind, he chose some of Israel's best and put *them* in battle array against the Syrians.
11 And the rest of the people he put under the command of A·bi′shaī his brother, and they set *themselves* in battle array against the people of Am′mon.
12 Then he said, "If the Syrians are too strong for me, then you shall help me; but if the people of Am′mon are too strong for you, then I will help you.
13 "Be of good courage, and let us be strong for our people and for the cities of our God. And may the LORD do *what is* good in His sight."
14 So Jō′ab and the people who *were* with him drew near for the battle against the Syrians, and they fled before him.
15 When the people of Am′mon saw that the Syrians were fleeing, they also fled before A·bi′shaī his brother, and entered the city. So Jō′ab went to Jerusalem.
16 Now when the Syrians saw that they had been defeated by Israel, they sent messengers and brought the Syrians who were beyond [1]the River, and [2]Shō′phach the commander of Had·a·dē′zer's army *went* before them.
17 When it was told David, he gathered all Israel, crossed over the Jordan and came upon them, and set up in *battle* array against them. So when David had set up in battle array against the Syrians, they fought with him.
18 Then the Syrians fled before Israel; and David killed [1]seven thousand charioteers and forty thousand [2]foot soldiers of the Syrians, and killed Shō′phach the commander of the army.
19 And when the servants of Had·a·dē′zer saw that they were defeated by Israel, they made peace with David and became his servants. So the Syrians were not willing to help the people of Am′mon anymore.

20

It[a] happened [1]in the spring of the year, at the time kings go out *to battle,* that Jō′ab led out the armed forces and ravaged the country of the people of Am′mon, and came and besieged Rab′bah. But [b]David stayed at Jerusalem. And [c]Jō′ab defeated Rab′bah and overthrew it.
2 Then David [a]took their king's crown from his head, and found it to weigh a talent of gold, and *there were* precious stones in it. And it was set on David's head.

6 [a]1 Chr. 18:5, 9 [1]Heb. *Aram Naharaim* [2]*Zoba,* 2 Sam. 10:6
16 [1]The Euphrates [2]*Zoba,* 2 Sam. 10:6, or *Shobach,* 2 Sam. 10:16
18 [1]*seven hundred,* 2 Sam. 10:18 [2]*horsemen,* 2 Sam. 10:18

CHAPTER 20

1 [a]2 Sam. 11:1 [b]2 Sam. 11:2—12:25 [c]2 Sam. 12:26 [1]Lit. *at the return of the year*
2 [a]2 Sam. 12:30, 31

Also he brought out the [1]spoil of
the city in great abundance.
3 And he brought out the people who *were* in it, and [1]put
them to work with saws, with
iron picks, and with axes. So
David did to all the cities of the
people of Am′mon. Then David
and all the people returned *to*
Jerusalem.
4 Now it happened afterward
[a]that war broke out at [1]Gē′zer
with the Phi·lis′tines, at which
time [b]Sib′be·chaī the Hū′sha-
thīte killed [2]Sip′paī, *who was
one* of the sons of [3]the giant.
And they were subdued.
5 Again there was war with
the Phi·lis′tines, and El·hā′nan
the son of [1]Jā′ir killed Lah′mī the
brother of Goliath the Git′tīte,
the shaft of whose spear *was*
like a weaver's [a]beam.
6 Yet again [a]there was war at
Gath, where there was a man of
great stature, with twenty-four
fingers and toes, six *on each
hand* and six *on each foot;* and
he also was born to [1]the giant.
7 So when he defied Israel,
Jonathan the son of [1]Shim′ē·a,
David's brother, killed him.
8 These were born to the giant in Gath, and they fell by the
hand of David and by the hand
of his servants.

21 Now [a]Satan stood up
against Israel, and moved
David to [1]number Israel.
2 So David said to Jō′ab and
to the leaders of the people, "Go,
number Israel from Bē·er·shē′ba
to Dan, [a]and bring the number of
them to me that I may know *it.*"
3 And Jō′ab answered, "May
the LORD make His people a
hundred times more than they
are. But, my lord the king, *are*
they not all my lord's servants?
Why then does my lord require
this thing? Why should he be a
cause of guilt in Israel?"
4 Nevertheless the king's word
prevailed against Jō′ab. Therefore Jō′ab departed and went
throughout all Israel and came
to Jerusalem.
5 Then Jō′ab gave the sum of
the number of the people to
David. All Israel *had* one million
one hundred thousand men who
drew the sword, and Judah *had*
four hundred and seventy thousand men who drew the sword.
6 [a]But he did not count Levi
and Benjamin among them, for
the king's [1]word was abominable to Jō′ab.
7 And [1]God was displeased
with this thing; therefore He
struck Israel.
8 So David said to God, [a]"I
have sinned greatly, because I
have done this thing; [b]but now,
I pray, take away the iniquity
of Your servant, for I have done
very foolishly."
9 Then the LORD spoke to Gad,
David's [a]seer, saying,
10 "Go and tell David, [a]saying,
'Thus says the LORD: "I offer you
three *things;* choose one of them
for yourself, that I may do *it* to
you." ' "
11 So Gad came to David and
said to him, "Thus says the LORD:
'Choose for yourself,
12 [a]'either [1]three years of famine, or three months to be defeated by your foes with the
sword of your enemies overtak-
ing *you,* or else for three days the
sword of the LORD—the plague
in the land, with the [2]angel of
the LORD destroying throughout
all the territory of Israel.' Now

2 [1]*plunder*
3 [1]LXX *cut them with*
4 [a]2 Sam. 21:18 [b]1 Chr. 11:29 [1]*Gob,* 2 Sam. 21:18 [2]*Saph,* 2 Sam. 21:18 [3]Or *Raphah*
5 [a]1 Sam. 17:7 [1]*Jaare-Oregim,* 2 Sam. 21:19
6 [a]2 Sam. 21:20 [1]Or *Raphah*
7 [1]*Shammah,* 1 Sam. 16:9 or *Shimeah,* 2 Sam. 21:21

CHAPTER 21

1 [a]2 Sam. 24:1–25 [1]*take a census of*
2 [a]1 Chr. 27:23, 24
6 [a]1 Chr. 27:24 [1]*command*
7 [1]Lit. *it was evil in the eyes of God*
8 [a]2 Sam. 24:10 [b]2 Sam. 12:13
9 [a]1 Sam. 9:9
10 [a]2 Sam. 24:12–14
12 [a]2 Sam. 24:13 [1]*seven,* 2 Sam. 24:13 [2]Or *Angel,* and so throughout the chapter

consider what answer I should
take back to Him who sent me."
13 And David said to Gad, "I am
in great distress. Please let me
fall into the hand of the LORD,
for His [a]mercies *are* very great;
but do not let me fall into the
hand of man."
14 So the LORD sent a [a]plague
upon Israel, and seventy thousand men of Israel fell.
15 And God sent [1]an [a]angel to
Jerusalem to destroy it. As [2]he
was destroying, the LORD looked
and [b]relented of the disaster,
and said to the angel who was
destroying, "It is enough; now
restrain [3]your hand." And the
angel of the LORD stood by
the [c]threshing floor of [4]Or'nan
the Jeb'ū·sīte.
16 Then David lifted his eyes
and [a]saw the angel of the LORD
standing between earth and
heaven, having in his hand a
drawn sword stretched out over
Jerusalem. So David and the
elders, clothed in sackcloth, fell
on their faces.
17 And David said to God, "Was
it not I who commanded the people to be numbered? I am the one
who has sinned and done evil
indeed; but these [a]sheep, what
have they done? Let Your hand, I
pray, O LORD my God, be against
me and my father's house, but
not against Your people that they
should be plagued."
18 Therefore, the [a]angel of the
LORD commanded Gad to say to
David that David should go and
erect an altar to the LORD on the
threshing floor of Or'nan the
Jeb'ū·sīte.
19 So David went up at the
word of Gad, which he had spoken in the name of the LORD.

13 [a]Ps. 51:1; 130:4, 7
14 [a]1 Chr. 27:24
15 [a]2 Sam. 24:16 [b]Gen. 6:6 [c]2 Chr. 3:1 [1]Or *the Angel* [2]Or *He* [3]Or *Your* [4]*Araunah*, 2 Sam. 24:16, 18–24
16 [a]2 Chr. 3:1
17 [a]2 Sam. 7:8
18 [a]2 Chr. 3:1
22 [1]Lit. *Give*
25 [a]2 Sam. 24:24
26 [a]Lev. 9:24

20 Now Or'nan turned and saw
the angel; and his four sons *who*
were with him hid themselves,
but Or'nan continued threshing
wheat.
21 So David came to Or'nan,
and Or'nan looked and saw David. And he went out from the
threshing floor, and bowed before David with *his* face to the
ground.
22 Then David said to Or'nan,
[1]"Grant me the place of *this*
threshing floor, that I may build
an altar on it to the LORD. You
shall grant it to me at the full
price, that the plague may be
withdrawn from the people."
23 But Or'nan said to David,
"Take *it* to yourself, and let my
lord the king do *what is* good in
his eyes. Look, I *also* give *you*
the oxen for burnt offerings, the
threshing implements for wood,
and the wheat for the grain offering; I give *it* all."
24 Then King David said to Or'-
nan, "No, but I will surely buy *it*
for the full price, for I will not
take what is yours for the LORD,
nor offer burnt offerings with
that which costs *me* nothing."
25 So [a]David gave Or'nan six
hundred shekels of gold by
weight for the place.
26 And David built there an
altar to the LORD, and offered
burnt offerings and peace offerings, and called on the LORD; and
[a]He answered him from heaven
by fire on the altar of burnt
offering.
27 So the LORD commanded the
angel, and he returned his sword
to its sheath.
28 At that time, when David
saw that the LORD had answered
him on the threshing floor of

Or′nan the Jeb′ū·sīte, he sacrificed there.

29 [a]For the tabernacle of the LORD and the altar of the burnt offering, which Moses had made in the wilderness, *were* at that time at the high place in [b]Gib′ē·on.

30 But David could not go before it to inquire of God, for he was afraid of the sword of the angel of the LORD.

22 Then David said, [a]"This *is* the house of the LORD God, and this *is* the altar of burnt offering for Israel."

2 So David commanded to gather the [a]aliens who *were* in the land of Israel; and he appointed masons to [b]cut hewn stones to build the house of God.

3 And David prepared iron in abundance for the nails of the doors of the gates and for the joints, and bronze in abundance [a]beyond measure,

4 and cedar trees in abundance; for the [a]Sī·dō′ni·ans and those from Tȳre brought much cedar wood to David.

5 Now David said, [a]"Solomon my son *is* young and inexperienced, and the house to be built for the LORD *must be* exceedingly magnificent, famous and glorious throughout all countries. I will now make preparation for it." So David made abundant preparations before his death.

6 Then he called for his son Solomon, and [1]charged him to build a house for the LORD God of Israel.

7 And David said to Solomon: "My son, as for me, [a]it was in my mind to build a house [b]to the name of the LORD my God;

8 "but the word of the LORD came to me, saying, [a]'You have shed much blood and have made great wars; you shall not build a house for My name, because you have shed much blood on the earth in My sight.

9 [a]'Behold, a son shall be born to you, who shall be a man of rest; and I will give him [b]rest from all his enemies all around. His name shall be [1]Solomon, for I will give peace and quietness to Israel in his days.

10 [a]'He shall build a house for My name, and [b]he shall be My son, and I *will be* his Father; and I will establish the throne of his kingdom over Israel forever.' ☆

11 "Now, my son, may [a]the LORD be with you; and may you prosper, and build the house of the LORD your God, as He has said to you.

12 "Only may the LORD [a]give you wisdom and understanding, and give you charge concerning Israel, that you may keep the law of the LORD your God.

13 [a]"Then you will prosper, if you take care to fulfill the statutes and judgments with which the LORD [1]charged Moses concerning Israel. [b]Be strong and of good courage; do not fear nor be dismayed.

14 "Indeed I have taken much trouble to prepare for the house of the LORD one hundred thousand talents of gold and one million talents of silver, and bronze and iron [a]beyond measure, for it is so abundant. I have prepared timber and stone also, and you may add to them.

15 "Moreover *there are* workmen with you in abundance: woodsmen and stonecutters,

29 [a]1 Kin. 3:4 [b]1 Chr. 16:39

CHAPTER 22

1 [a]Deut. 12:5

2 [a]1 Kin. 9:20, 21 [b]1 Kin. 5:17, 18

3 [a]1 Kin. 7:47

4 [a]1 Kin. 5:6–10

5 [a]1 Chr. 29:1, 2

6 [1]*commanded*

7 [a]2 Sam. 7:1, 2 [b]Deut. 12:5, 11

8 [a]1 Chr. 28:3

9 [a]1 Chr. 28:5 [b]1 Kin. 4:20, 25; 5:4 [1]Lit. *Peaceful*

10 [a]1 Chr. 17:12, 13; 28:6 [b]Matt. 1:6; Heb. 1:5

11 [a]1 Chr. 22:16

12 [a]1 Kin. 3:9–12

13 [a]1 Chr. 28:7 [b][Josh. 1:6, 7, 9] [1]*commanded*

14 [a]1 Chr. 22:3

and all types of skillful men for
every kind of work.
16 "Of gold and silver and
bronze and iron *there is* no limit.
Arise and begin working, and
[a]the LORD be with you."
17 David also commanded all
the [a]leaders of Israel to help Solomon his son, *saying,*
18 "*Is* not the LORD your God
with you? [a]And has He *not* given
you rest on every side? For He
has given the inhabitants of the
land into my hand, and the land
is subdued before the LORD and
before His people.
19 "Now set your heart and your
soul to seek the LORD your God.
Therefore arise and build the
sanctuary of the LORD God, to
[a]bring the ark of the covenant of
the LORD and the holy articles of
God into the house that is to be
built [b]for the name of the LORD."

23 So when David was old
and full of days, he made
his son [a]Solomon king over
Israel.
2 And he gathered together all
the leaders of Israel, with the
priests and the Lē′vītes.
3 Now the Lē′vītes were numbered from the age of [a]thirty
years and above; and the number of individual males was
thirty-eight thousand.
4 Of these, twenty-four thousand *were* to [a]look after the
work of the house of the LORD,
six thousand *were* [b]officers and
judges,
5 four thousand *were* gatekeepers, and four thousand
[a]praised the LORD with *musical*
instruments, [b]"which I made,"
said David, "for giving praise."
6 Also [a]David separated them
into [1]divisions among the sons
of Levi: Ger′shon, Kō′hath, and
Me·rar′ī.
7 Of the [a]Ger′shon·ītes: [1]Lā′-
a·dan and Shim′ē·ī.
8 The sons of Lā′a·dan: the
first Je·hī′el, then Zē′tham and
Jō′el—three *in all.*
9 The sons of Shim′ē·ī: She·lō′-
mith, Hā′zi·el, and Har′an—three
in all. These were the heads of
the fathers' *houses* of Lā′a·dan.
10 And the sons of Shim′ē·ī: Jā′-
hath, [1]Zī′na, Jē′ush, and Bē·rī′ah.
These *were* the four sons of
Shim′ē·ī.
11 Jā′hath was the first and Zī′-
zah the second. But Jē′ush and
Bē·rī′ah did not have many sons;
therefore they were assigned as
one father's house.
12 [a]The sons of Kō′hath: Am′-
ram, Iz′har, Hē′bron, and Uz′-
zi·el—four *in all.*
13 The sons of [a]Am′ram: Aaron
and Moses; and [b]Aaron was set
apart, he and his sons forever,
that he should [1]sanctify the most
holy things, [c]to burn incense
before the LORD, [d]to minister to
Him, and [e]to give the blessing in
His name forever.
14 Now [a]the sons of Moses the
man of God were reckoned to
the tribe of Levi.
15 [a]The sons of Moses *were*
[1]Ger′shon and El·i·ē′zer.
16 Of the sons of Ger′shon,
[a]She·bū′el[1] *was* the first.
17 Of the descendants of El·i·ē′-
zer, [a]Rē·ha·bī′ah was the first.
And El·i·ē′zer had no other sons,
but the sons of Rē·ha·bī′ah were
very many.
18 Of the sons of Iz′har, [a]She·lō′-
mith *was* the first.
19 [a]Of the sons of Hē′bron,
Je·rī′ah *was* the first, Am·a·rī′ah

16 [a]1 Chr. 22:11
17 [a]1 Chr. 28:1–6
18 [a]Josh. 22:4
19 [a]2 Chr. 5:2–14 [b]1 Kin. 5:3

CHAPTER 23

1 [a]1 Kin. 1:33–40
3 [a]Num. 4:1–3
4 [a]Ezra 3:8, 9 [b]Deut. 16:18–20
5 [a]1 Chr. 15:16 [b]2 Chr. 29:25–27
6 [a]Ex. 6:16 [1]*groups*
7 [a]1 Chr. 26:21 [1]*Libni,* Ex. 6:17
10 [1]LXX, Vg. *Zizah* and v. 11
12 [a]Ex. 6:18
13 [a]Ex. 6:20 [b]Heb. 5:4 [c]1 Sam. 2:28 [d][Deut. 21:5] [e]Num. 6:23 [1]*consecrate*
14 [a]1 Chr. 26:20–24
15 [a]Ex. 18:3, 4 [1]Heb. *Gershom,* 1 Chr. 6:16
16 [a]1 Chr. 26:24 [1]*Shubael,* 1 Chr. 24:20
17 [a]1 Chr. 26:25
18 [a]1 Chr. 24:22
19 [a]1 Chr. 24:23

the second, Ja·hā′zi·el the third,
and Jek·a·mē′am the fourth.
20 Of the sons of Uz′zi·el, Mī′-
chah *was* the first and Jes·shī′ah
the second.
21 [a]The sons of Me·rar′ī *were*
Mah′lī and Mū′shī. The sons
of Mah′lī *were* El·ē·ā′zar and
[b]Kish.
22 And El·ē·ā′zar died, and [a]had
no sons, but only daughters; and
their [1]brethren, the sons of Kish,
[b]took them *as wives.*
23 [a]The sons of Mū′shī *were*
Mah′lī, Ē′der, and Jer′e·moth—
three *in all.*
24 These *were* the sons of [a]Levi
by their fathers' houses—the
heads of the fathers' *houses* as
they were counted individually
by the number of their names,
who did the work for the service
of the house of the LORD, from
the age of [b]twenty years and
above.
25 For David said, "The LORD
God of Israel [a]has given rest to
His people, that they may dwell
in Jerusalem forever";
26 and also to the Lē′vītes,
"They shall no longer [a]carry the
tabernacle, or any of the articles
for its service."
27 For by the [a]last words of
David the Lē′vītes *were* numbered from twenty years old and
above;
28 because their duty *was* to
help the sons of Aaron in the
service of the house of the LORD,
in the courts and in the chambers, in the purifying of all holy
things and the work of the service of the house of God,
29 both with [a]the showbread
and [b]the fine flour for the grain
offering, with [c]the unleavened
cakes and [d]*what is baked in* the
pan, with what is mixed and
with all kinds of [e]measures and
sizes;
30 to stand every morning to
thank and praise the LORD, and
likewise at evening;
31 and at every presentation of
a burnt offering to the LORD [a]on
the Sabbaths and on the New
Moons and on the [b]set[1] feasts,
by number according to the ordinance governing them, regularly before the LORD;
32 and that they should [a]attend
to the [b]needs of the tabernacle
of meeting, the needs of the holy
place, and the [c]needs of the sons
of Aaron their brethren in the
work of the house of the LORD.

24 Now *these are* the divisions of the sons of
Aaron. [a]The sons of Aaron *were*
Nā′dab, A·bī′hū, El·ē·ā′zar, and
Ith′a·mar.
2 And [a]Nā′dab and A·bī′hū
died before their father, and had
no children; therefore El·ē·ā′-
zar and Ith′a·mar ministered as
priests.
3 Then David with Zā′dok
of the sons of El·ē·ā′zar, and
[a]A·him′e·lech of the sons of Ith′-
a·mar, divided them according
to the schedule of their service.
4 There were more leaders
found of the sons of El·ē·ā′zar
than of the sons of Ith′a·mar,
and *thus* they were divided.
Among the sons of El·ē·ā′zar
were sixteen heads of *their* fathers' houses, and eight heads of
their fathers' houses among the
sons of Ith′a·mar.
5 Thus they were divided
by lot, one group as another,
for there were officials of the
sanctuary and officials *of the
house* of God, from the sons of

21 [a]1 Chr. 24:26 [b]1 Chr. 24:29
22 [a]1 Chr. 24:28 [b]Num. 36:6 [1]*kinsmen*
23 [a]1 Chr. 24:30
24 [a]Num. 10:17, 21 [b]Ezra 3:8
25 [a]1 Chr. 22:18
26 [a]Num. 4:5, 15; 7:9
27 [a]2 Sam. 23:1
29 [a]Ex. 25:30 [b]Lev. 6:20 [c]Lev. 2:1, 4 [d]Lev. 2:5, 7 [e]Lev. 19:35
31 [a]Num. 10:10 [b]Lev. 23:2–4 [1]*appointed feasts*
32 [a]2 Chr. 13:10, 11 [b][Num. 1:53] [c]Num. 3:6–9, 38

CHAPTER 24

1 [a]Lev. 10:1–6
2 [a]Num. 3:1–4; 26:61
3 [a]1 Chr. 18:16

El·ē·ā′zar and from the sons of
Ith′a·mar.
6 And the scribe, She·māi′ah
the son of Ne·than′el, *one* of
the Lē′vītes, wrote them down
before the king, the leaders, Zā′-
dok the priest, A·him′e·lech the
son of A·bī′a·thar, and the heads
of the fathers′ *houses* of the
priests and Lē′vītes, one father′s
house taken for El·ē·ā′zar and
one for Ith′a·mar.
7 Now the first lot fell to Je·hoi′-
a·rib, the second to Je·daī′ah,
8 the third to Hā′rim, the fourth
to Sē·ō′rim,
9 the fifth to Mal·chī′jah, the
sixth to Mij′a·min,
10 the seventh to Hak′koz, the
eighth to [a]A·bī′jah,
11 the ninth to Jesh′ū·a, the
tenth to Shec·a·nī′ah,
12 the eleventh to E·lī′a·shib,
the twelfth to Jā′kim,
13 the thirteenth to Hup′pah,
the fourteenth to Je·sheb′e·ab,
14 the fifteenth to Bil′gah, the
sixteenth to Im′mer,
15 the seventeenth to Hē′zir, the
eighteenth to [1]Hap′piz·zez,
16 the nineteenth to Peth·a·hī′ah,
the twentieth to [1]Je·hez′e·kel,
17 the twenty-first to Jā′chin,
the twenty-second to Gā′mūl,
18 the twenty-third to De·laī′ah,
the twenty-fourth to Mā·a·zī′ah.
19 This *was* the schedule of
their service [a]for coming into
the house of the LORD according to their ordinance by the
hand of Aaron their father, as
the LORD God of Israel had commanded him.
20 And the rest of the sons of
Levi: of the sons of Am′ram,
[1]Shū′ba·el; of the sons of Shū′-
ba·el, Jeh·dē′i·ah.
21 Concerning [a]Rē·ha·bī′ah, of
the sons of Rē·ha·bī′ah, the first
was Is·shī′ah.
22 Of the Iz′har·ītes, [1]She·lō′-
moth; of the sons of She·lō′-
moth, Jā′hath.
23 Of the sons [1]*of* [a]*Hē′bron,*
Je·rī′ah [1]*was the first,* Am·a·rī′ah
the second, Ja·hā′zi·el the third,
and Jek·a·mē′am the fourth.
24 *Of* the sons of Uz′zi·el, Mī′-
chah; of the sons of Mī′chah,
Shā′mir.
25 The brother of Mī′chah,
Is·shī′ah; of the sons of Is·shī′ah,
Zech·a·rī′ah.
26 [a]The sons of Me·rar′ī *were*
Mah′lī and Mū′shī; the son of
Jā·a·zī′ah, Bē′no.
27 The sons of Me·rar′ī by
Jā·a·zī′ah *were* Bē′no, Shō′ham,
Zac′cur, and Ib′rī.
28 Of Mah′lī: El·ē·ā′zar, [a]who
had no sons.
29 Of Kish: the son of Kish,
Je·rah′mē·el.
30 Also [a]the sons of Mū′shī *were*
Mah′lī, Ē′der, and Jer′i·moth.
These *were* the sons of the Lē′-
vītes according to their fathers′
houses.
31 These also cast lots just as
their brothers the sons of Aaron
did, in the presence of King David, Zā′dok, A·him′e·lech, and
the heads of the fathers′ *houses*
of the priests and Lē′vītes. The
chief fathers *did* just as their
younger brethren.

25 Moreover David and the
captains of the army
separated for the service *some*
of the sons of [a]Ā′saph, of Hē′-
man, and of Je·dū′thun, who
should prophesy with harps,
stringed instruments, and cymbals. And the number of the
skilled men performing their
service was:

10 [a]Luke 1:5
15 [1]LXX, Vg. *Aphses*
16 [1]MT *Jehezkel*
19 [a]1 Chr. 9:25
20 [1]*Shebuel,* 1 Chr. 23:16
21 [a]1 Chr. 23:17
22 [1]*Shelomith,* 1 Chr. 23:18
23 [a]1 Chr. 23:19; 26:31 [1]Supplied from 23:19 (following some Heb. mss. and LXX mss.)
26 [a]Ex. 6:19
28 [a]1 Chr. 23:22
30 [a]1 Chr. 23:23

CHAPTER 25

1 [a]1 Chr. 6:30, 33, 39, 44

2 Of the sons of Ā′saph: Zac′cur, Joseph, Neth·a·nī′ah, and [1]Ash·a·rē′lah; the sons of Ā′saph *were* [2]under the direction of Ā′saph, who prophesied according to the order of the king.

3 Of [a]Je·dū′thun, the sons of Je·dū′thun: Ged·a·lī′ah, [1]Zē′rī, Je·shā′i·ah, [2]*Shim′ē·ī*, Hash·a·bī′ah, and Mat·ti·thī′ah, [3]six, under the direction of their father Je·dū′thun, who prophesied with a harp to give thanks and to praise the LORD.

4 Of Hē′man, the sons of Hē′man: Buk·kī′ah, Mat·ta·nī′ah, [1]Uz′zi·el, [2]She·bū′el, [3]Jer′i·moth, Han·a·nī′ah, Ha·nā′nī, E·lī′a·thah, Gid·dal′tī, Rō·mam′ti-Ē′zer, Josh·be·kash′ah, Mal·lō′thī, Hō′thir, *and* Ma·hā′zi·oth.

5 All these *were* the sons of Hē′man the king's seer in the words of God, to [1]exalt his [a]horn. For God gave Hē′man fourteen sons and three daughters.

6 All these *were* under the direction of their father for the music *in* the house of the LORD, with cymbals, stringed instruments, and [a]harps, for the service of the house of God. Ā′saph, Je·dū′thun, and Hē′man *were* [b]under the authority of the king.

7 So the [a]number of them, with their brethren who were instructed in the songs of the LORD, all who were skillful, *was* two hundred and eighty-eight.

8 And they cast lots for their duty, the small as well as the great, [a]the teacher with the student.

9 Now the first lot for Ā′saph came out for Joseph; the second for Ged·a·lī′ah, him with his brethren and sons, twelve;

10 the third for Zac′cur, his sons and his brethren, twelve;

11 the fourth for [1]Jiz′rī, his sons and his brethren, twelve;

12 the fifth for Neth·a·nī′ah, his sons and his brethren, twelve;

13 the sixth for Buk·kī′ah, his sons and his brethren, twelve;

14 the seventh for [1]Jesh·a·rē′lah, his sons and his brethren, twelve;

15 the eighth for Je·shā′i·ah, his sons and his brethren, twelve;

16 the ninth for Mat·ta·nī′ah, his sons and his brethren, twelve;

17 the tenth for Shim′ē·ī, his sons and his brethren, twelve;

18 the eleventh for [1]Az′a·rel, his sons and his brethren, twelve;

19 the twelfth for Hash·a·bī′ah, his sons and his brethren, twelve;

20 the thirteenth for [1]Shū′ba·el, his sons and his brethren, twelve;

21 the fourteenth for Mat·ti·thī′ah, his sons and his brethren, twelve;

22 the fifteenth for [1]Jer′e·moth, his sons and his brethren, twelve;

23 the sixteenth for Han·a·nī′ah, his sons and his brethren, twelve;

24 the seventeenth for Josh·be·kash′ah, his sons and his brethren, twelve;

25 the eighteenth for Ha·nā′nī, his sons and his brethren, twelve;

26 the nineteenth for Mal·lō′thī, his sons and his brethren, twelve;

27 the twentieth for E·lī′a·thah, his sons and his brethren, twelve;

28 the twenty-first for Hō′thir, his sons and his brethren, twelve;

29 the twenty-second for Gid·dal′tī, his sons and his brethren, twelve;

2 [1]*Jesharelah*, v. 14 [2]Lit. *at the hands of*

3 [a]1 Chr. 16:41, 42 [1]*Jizri*, v. 11 [2]So with one Heb. ms., LXX mss. [3]Shimei is the sixth, v. 17

4 [1]*Azarel*, v. 18 [2]*Shubael*, v. 20 [3]*Jeremoth*, v. 22

5 [a]1 Chr. 16:42 [1]Increase his power or influence

6 [a]1 Chr. 15:16 [b]1 Chr. 15:19; 25:2

7 [a]1 Chr. 23:5

8 [a]2 Chr. 23:13

11 [1]*Zeri*, v. 3

14 [1]*Asharelah*, v. 2

18 [1]*Uzziel*, v. 4

20 [1]*Shebuel*, v. 4

22 [1]*Jerimoth*, v. 4

30 the twenty-third for Ma·hā′-
zi·oth, his sons and his brethren,
twelve;
31 the twenty-fourth for Rō·mam′-
ti-Ē′zer, his sons and his brethren, twelve.

26

Concerning the divisions
of the gatekeepers: of the
Kō′ra·hītes, [1]Me·shel·e·mī′ah the
son of [a]Kō′re, of the sons of
[2]Ā′saph.
2 And the sons of Me·shel·e-
mī′ah *were* [a]Zech·a·rī′ah the
firstborn, Je·dī′a·el the second,
Zeb·a·dī′ah the third, Jath′ni·el
the fourth,
3 Ē′lam the fifth, Jē·hō·hā′-
nan the sixth, El·i·ē·hō·ē′naī the
seventh.
4 Moreover the sons of [a]Ō′bed-
Ē′dom *were* She·māi′ah the
firstborn, Je·hō′za·bad the second, Jō′ah the third, Sā′car the
fourth, Ne·than′el the fifth,
5 Am′mi·el the sixth, Is′sa-
char the seventh, Pē·ul′thaī the
eighth; for God blessed him.
6 Also to She·māi′ah his son
were sons born who governed
their fathers' houses, because
they *were* men of great ability.
7 The sons of She·māi′ah
were Oth′nī, Reph′a·el, Ō′bed,
and El·zā′bad, whose brothers
E·lī′hū and Sem·a·chī′ah *were*
able men.
8 All these *were* of the sons
of Ō′bed-Ē′dom, they and their
sons and their brethren, [a]able
men with strength for the work:
sixty-two of Ō′bed-Ē′dom.
9 And Me·shel·e·mī′ah had
sons and brethren, eighteen able
men.
10 Also [a]Hō′sah, of the children
of Me·rar′ī, had sons: Shim′rī the
first (for *though* he was not the
firstborn, his father made him
the first),
11 Hil·kī′ah the second, Teb·a-
lī′ah the third, Zech·a·rī′ah the
fourth; all the sons and brethren
of Hō′sah *were* thirteen.
12 Among these *were* the divisions of the gatekeepers, among
the chief men, *having* duties just
like their brethren, to serve in
the house of the LORD.
13 And they [a]cast lots for each
gate, the small as well as the
great, according to their father's
house.
14 The lot for the East *Gate* fell
to [1]Shel·e·mī′ah. Then they cast
lots *for* his son Zech·a·rī′ah, a
wise counselor, and his lot came
out for the North Gate;
15 to Ō′bed-Ē′dom the South
Gate, and to his sons the [1]store-
house.
16 To Shup′pim and Hō′sah *the
lot came out* for the West Gate,
with the Shal′le·cheth Gate on
the [a]ascending highway—watchman opposite watchman.
17 On the east *were* six Lē′vītes,
on the north four each day, on
the south four each day, and for
the [1]storehouse two by two.
18 As for the [1]Par′bar on the
west, *there were* four on the
highway *and* two at the Par′bar.
19 These were the divisions of
the gatekeepers among the sons
of Kō′rah and among the sons of
Me·rar′ī.
20 Of the Lē′vītes, A·hī′jah *was*
[a]over the treasuries of the house
of God and over the treasuries
of the [b]dedicated[1] things.
21 The sons of [1]Lā′a·dan, the
descendants of the Ger′shon·ītes
of Lā′a·dan, heads of their fathers' *houses*, of Lā′a·dan the
Ger′shon·īte: [2]Je·hī′e·lī.

CHAPTER 26

1 [a]Ps. 42:title [1]*Shelemiah*, v. 14 [2]*Ebiasaph*, 1 Chr. 6:37; 9:19

2 [a]1 Chr. 9:21

4 [a]1 Chr. 15:18, 21

8 [a]1 Chr. 9:13

10 [a]1 Chr. 16:38

13 [a]1 Chr. 24:5, 31; 25:8

14 [1]*Meshelemiah*, v. 1

15 [1]Heb. *asuppim*

16 [a]1 Kin. 10:5

17 [1]Heb. *asuppim*

18 [1]Probably a court or colonnade extending west of the temple

20 [a]1 Chr. 9:26 [b]1 Chr. 26:22, 24, 26; 28:12 [1]*holy things*

21 [1]*Libni*, 1 Chr. 6:17 [2]*Jehiel*, 1 Chr. 23:8; 29:8

22 The sons of Je·hī′e·lī, Zē′tham and Jō′el his brother, *were* over the treasuries of the house of the LORD.

23 Of the [a]Am′ram·ītes, the Iz′har·ītes, the Hē′bron·ītes, and the Uz′zi·el·ītes:

24 [a]She·bū′el the son of Ger′shom, the son of Moses, *was* overseer of the treasuries.

25 And his brethren by El·i·ē′zer *were* Rē·ha·bī′ah his son, Je·shā′i·ah his son, Jō′ram his son, Zich′rī his son, and [a]She·lō′mith his son.

26 This She·lō′mith and his brethren *were* over all the treasuries of the dedicated things [a]which King David and the heads of fathers' *houses*, the captains over thousands and hundreds, and the captains of the army, had dedicated.

27 Some of the [1]spoils won in battles they dedicated to maintain the house of the LORD.

28 And all that Samuel [a]the seer, Saul the son of Kish, Abner the son of Ner, and Jō′ab the son of Ze·rū′i·ah had dedicated, every dedicated *thing*, was under the hand of She·lō′mith and his brethren.

29 Of the Iz′har·ītes, Chen·a·nī′ah and his sons [a]*performed* duties as [b]officials and judges over Israel outside Jerusalem.

30 Of the Hē′bron·ītes, [a]Hash·a·bī′ah and his brethren, one thousand seven hundred able men, had the oversight of Israel on the west side of the Jordan for all the business of the LORD, and in the service of the king.

31 Among the Hē′bron·ītes, [a]Je·rī′jah *was* head of the Hē′bron·ītes according to his genealogy of the fathers. In the fortieth year of the reign of David they were sought, and there were found among them capable men [b]at Jā′zer of Gil′ē·ad.

32 And his brethren *were* two thousand seven hundred able men, heads of fathers' *houses*, whom King David made officials over the Reū′ben·ītes, the Gad′ītes, and the half-tribe of Ma·nas′seh, for every matter pertaining to God and the [a]affairs of the king.

27

And the children of Israel, according to their number, the heads of fathers' *houses*, the captains of thousands and hundreds and their officers, served the king in every matter of the *military* divisions. *These divisions* came in and went out month by month throughout all the months of the year, each division *having* twenty-four thousand.

2 Over the first division for the first month *was* [a]Ja·shō′bē·am the son of Zab′di·el, and in his division *were* twenty-four thousand;

3 *he was* of the children of Per′ez, and the chief of all the captains of the army for the first month.

4 Over the division of the second month *was* [1]Dō′daī an A·hō′hīte, and of his division Mik′loth also *was* the leader; in his division *were* twenty-four thousand.

5 The third captain of the army for the third month *was* [a]Be·nā′i·ah, the son of Je·hoi′a·da the priest, who was chief; in his division *were* twenty-four thousand.

6 This was the Be·nā′i·ah *who was* [a]mighty *among* the thirty,

23 [a]Ex. 6:18
24 [a]1 Chr. 23:16
25 [a]1 Chr. 23:18
26 [a]2 Sam. 8:11
27 [1]*plunder*
28 [a]1 Sam. 9:9
29 [a]Neh. 11:16 [b]1 Chr. 23:4
30 [a]1 Chr. 27:17
31 [a]1 Chr. 23:19 [b]Josh. 21:39
32 [a]2 Chr. 19:11

CHAPTER 27

2 [a]1 Chr. 11:11
4 [1]Heb. *Dodai*, usually spelled *Dodo*, 2 Sam. 23:9
5 [a]1 Chr. 18:17
6 [a]2 Sam. 23:20–23

and was over the thirty; in his
division *was* Am·miz′a·bad his
son.
7 The fourth *captain* for the
fourth month *was* [a]As′a·hel the
brother of Jō′ab, and Zeb·a·dī′ah
his son after him; in his division
were twenty-four thousand.
8 The fifth captain for the
fifth month *was* [1]Sham′huth the
Iz′ra·hīte; in his division were
twenty-four thousand.
9 The sixth *captain* for the
sixth month *was* [a]Ī′ra the son of
Ik′kesh the Te·kō′īte; in his division *were* twenty-four thousand.
10 The seventh *captain* for the
seventh month *was* [a]Hē′lez the
Pel′o·nīte, of the children of
Ē′phra·im; in his division *were*
twenty-four thousand.
11 The eighth *captain* for the
eighth month *was* [a]Sib′be·chaī
the Hū′sha·thīte, of the Zar′hītes;
in his division *were* twenty-four
thousand.
12 The ninth *captain* for the
ninth month *was* [a]Ā·bi·ē′zer
the An′a·thoth·īte, of the Ben′-
ja·mītes; in his division *were*
twenty-four thousand.
13 The tenth *captain* for the
tenth month *was* [a]Mā′ha·raī the
Ne·toph′a·thīte, of the Zar′hītes;
in his division *were* twenty-four
thousand.
14 The eleventh *captain* for the
eleventh month *was* [a]Be·nā′i·ah
the Pir′a·thon·īte, of the children
of Ē′phra·im; in his division *were*
twenty-four thousand.
15 The twelfth *captain* for the
twelfth month *was* [1]Hel′daī the
Ne·toph′a·thīte, of Oth′ni·el; in
his division *were* twenty-four
thousand.
16 Furthermore, over the tribes
of Israel: the officer over the
Reū′ben·ītes *was* El·i·ē′zer the
son of Zich′rī; over the Sim′-
ē·on·ītes, Sheph·a·tī′ah the son
of Mā′a·chah;
17 *over* the Lē′vītes, [a]Hash·a-
bī′ah the son of Ke·mū′el; over
the Aaronites, Zā′dok;
18 *over* Judah, [a]E·lī′hū, *one* of
David's brothers; *over* Is′sa·char,
Om′rī the son of Michael;
19 *over* Zeb′ū·lun, Ish·mā′i·ah
the son of Ō·ba·dī′ah; *over*
Naph′ta·lī, Jer′i·moth the son of
Az′ri·el;
20 *over* the children of Ē′phra-
im, Hō·shē′a the son of Az·a-
zī′ah; *over* the half-tribe of
Ma·nas′seh, Jō′el the son of Pe-
dāi′ah;
21 *over* the half-*tribe* of Ma-
nas′seh in Gil′ē·ad, Id′dō the son
of Zech·a·rī′ah; *over* Benjamin,
Jā·a·sī′el the son of Abner;
22 *over* Dan, Az′a·rel the son of
Je·rō′ham. These *were* the leaders of the tribes of Israel.
23 But David did not take the
number of those twenty years
old and under, because [a]the
LORD had said He would multiply Israel like the [b]stars of the
heavens.
24 Jō′ab the son of Ze·rū′i·ah
began a census, but he did not
finish, for [a]wrath came upon
Israel because of this census;
nor was the number recorded in
the account of the chronicles of
King David.
25 And Az′ma·veth the son of
Ad′i·el *was* over the king's treasuries; and Je·hon′a·than the
son of Uz·zī′ah was over the
storehouses in the field, in
the cities, in the villages, and in
the fortresses.
26 Ez′rī the son of Chē′lub was

7 [a]1 Chr. 11:26
8 [1]*Shammah*, 2 Sam. 23:11, or *Shammoth*, 1 Chr. 11:27
9 [a]1 Chr. 11:28
10 [a]1 Chr. 11:27
11 [a]2 Sam. 21:18
12 [a]1 Chr. 11:28
13 [a]1 Chr. 11:30
14 [a]1 Chr. 11:31
15 [1]*Heleb*, 2 Sam. 23:29, or *Heled*, 1 Chr. 11:30
17 [a]1 Chr. 26:30
18 [a]1 Sam. 16:6
23 [a][Deut. 6:3] [b]Gen. 15:5; 22:17; 26:4
24 [a]1 Chr. 21:1–7

over those who did the work of
the field for tilling the ground.
27 And Shim'ē·ī the Rā'ma·thīte
was over the vineyards, and
Zab'dī the Shiph'mīte was over
the produce of the vineyards for
the supply of wine.
28 Bā'al-Hā'nan the Ge·dē'rīte
was over the olive trees and the
sycamore trees that *were* in the
lowlands, and Jō'ash *was* over
the store of oil.
29 And Shit'raī the Shar'on·īte
was over the herds that fed in
Sharon, and Shā'phat the son of
Ad'lā·ī was over the herds *that*
were in the valleys.
30 Ō'bil the Ish'ma·el·īte *was*
over the camels, Jeh·dē'i·ah
the Me·ron'o·thīte *was* over the
donkeys,
31 and Jā'ziz the [a]Hag'rīte *was*
over the flocks. All these *were*
the officials over King David's
property.
32 Also Je·hon'a·than, David's
uncle, *was* a counselor, a wise
man, and a [1]scribe; and Je·hī'el
the [2]son of Hach'mo·nī *was* with
the king's sons.
33 [a]A·hith'o·phel *was* the king's
counselor, and [b]Hū'shai the Ar'-
chīte *was* the king's companion.
34 After A·hith'o·phel *was*
Je·hoi'a·da the son of Be·nā'-
i·ah, then [a]A·bī'a·thar. And the
general of the king's army *was*
[b]Jō'ab.

28

Now David assembled at
Jerusalem all [a]the leaders of Israel: the officers of the
tribes and [b]the captains of the
divisions who served the king,
the captains over thousands and
captains over hundreds, and
[c]the stewards over all the substance and [1]possessions of the
king and of his sons, with the
officials, the valiant men, and
all [d]the mighty men of valor.
2 Then King David rose to his
feet and said, "Hear me, my
brethren and my people: [a]I *had*
it in my heart to build a house of
rest for the ark of the covenant
of the LORD, and for [b]the footstool of our God, and had made
preparations to build it.
3 "But God said to me, [a]'You
shall not build a house for My
name, because you *have been*
a man of war and have shed
[b]blood.'
4 "However the LORD God of
Israel [a]chose me above all the
house of my father to be king
over Israel forever, for He has
chosen [b]Judah *to be* the ruler.
And of the house of Judah, [c]the
house of my father, and [d]among
the sons of my father, He was
pleased with me to make *me*
king over all Israel.
5 [a]"And of all my sons (for the
LORD has given me many sons)
[b]He has chosen my son Solomon
to sit on the throne of the kingdom of the LORD over Israel.
6 "Now He said to me, 'It is
[a]your son Solomon *who* shall
build My house and My courts;
for I have chosen him *to be* My
son, and I will be his Father.
7 'Moreover I will establish his
kingdom forever, [a]if he is steadfast to observe My commandments and My judgments, as it
is this day.'
8 "Now therefore, in the sight
of all Israel, the assembly of the
LORD, and in the hearing of our
God, be careful to seek out all
the commandments of the LORD
your God, that you may possess
this good land, and leave *it* as

31 [a]1 Chr. 5:10
32 [1]*secretary* [2]Or *Hachmonite*
33 [a]2 Sam. 15:12 [b]2 Sam. 15:32–37
34 [a]1 Kin. 1:7 [b]1 Chr. 11:6
CHAPTER 28
1 [a]1 Chr. 27:16 [b]1 Chr. 27:1, 2 [c]1 Chr. 27:25 [d]1 Chr. 11:10–47 [1]Or *livestock*
2 [a]2 Sam. 7:2 [b]Ps. 99:5; 132:7
3 [a]2 Sam. 7:5, 13 [b][1 Chr. 17:4; 22:8]
4 [a]1 Sam. 16:6–13 [b]Gen. 49:8–10 [c]1 Sam. 16:1 [d]1 Sam. 13:14; 16:12, 13
5 [a]1 Chr. 3:1–9; 14:3–7; 23:1 [b]1 Chr. 22:9; 29:1
6 [a]2 Sam. 7:13, 14
7 [a]1 Chr. 22:13

an inheritance for your children after you forever.

9 "As for you, my son Solomon, [a]know the God of your father, and serve Him [b]with a loyal heart and with a willing mind; for [c]the LORD searches all hearts and understands all the intent of the thoughts. [d]If you seek Him, He will be found by you; but if you forsake Him, He will [e]cast you off forever.

10 "Consider now, [a]for the LORD has chosen you to build a house for the sanctuary; be strong, and do it."

11 Then David gave his son Solomon [a]the plans for the vestibule, its houses, its treasuries, its upper chambers, its inner chambers, and the place of the mercy seat;

12 and the [a]plans for all that he had by the Spirit, of the courts of the house of the LORD, of all the chambers all around, [b]of the treasuries of the house of God, and of the treasuries for the dedicated things;

13 also for the division of the priests and the [a]Lē′vītes, for all the work of the service of the house of the LORD, and for all the articles of service in the house of the LORD.

14 *He gave* gold by weight for *things* of gold, for all articles used in every kind of service; also *silver* for all articles of silver by weight, for all articles used in every kind of service;

15 the weight for the [a]lampstands of gold, and their lamps of gold, by weight for each lampstand and its lamps; for the lampstands of silver by weight, for the lampstand and its lamps, according to the use of each lampstand.

16 And by weight *he gave* gold for the tables of the showbread, for each [a]table, and silver for the tables of silver;

17 also pure gold for the forks, the basins, the pitchers of pure gold, and the golden bowls—*he gave gold* by weight for every bowl; and for the silver bowls, *silver* by weight for every bowl;

18 and refined gold by weight for the [a]altar of incense, and for the construction of the chariot, that is, the gold [b]cherubim that spread *their wings* and overshadowed the ark of the covenant of the LORD.

19 "All *this,*" *said David,* [a]"the LORD made me understand in writing, by *His* hand upon me, all the [1]works of these plans."

20 And David said to his son Solomon, [a]"Be strong and of good courage, and do *it;* do not fear nor be dismayed, for the LORD God—my God—*will be* with you. [b]He will not leave you nor forsake you, until you have finished all the work for the service of the house of the LORD.

21 "*Here are* [a]the divisions of the priests and the Lē′vītes for all the service of the house of God; and [b]every willing craftsman *will be* with you for all manner of workmanship, for every kind of service; also the leaders and all the people *will be* completely at your command."

29

Furthermore King David said to all the assembly: "My son Solomon, whom alone God has [a]chosen, *is* [b]young and inexperienced; and the work *is* great, because the [1]temple *is* not for man but for the LORD God.

9 [a][John 17:3] [b]2 Kin. 20:3 [c][1 Sam. 16:7] [d]2 Chr. 15:2 [e]Deut. 31:17
10 [a]1 Chr. 22:13; 28:6
11 [a]1 Chr. 28:19
12 [a]Heb. 8:5 [b]1 Chr. 26:20, 28
13 [a]1 Chr. 23:6
15 [a]Ex. 25:31–39
16 [a]1 Kin. 7:48
18 [a]Ex. 30:1–10 [b]Ex. 25:18–22
19 [a]Ex. 25:40 [1]*details*
20 [a]1 Chr. 22:13 [b]Josh. 1:5
21 [a]1 Chr. 24—26 [b]Ex. 35:25–35; 36:1, 2

CHAPTER 29

1 [a]1 Chr. 28:5 [b]1 Kin. 3:7 [1]Lit. *palace*

2 "Now for the house of my God I have prepared with all my might: gold for *things to be made of* gold, silver for *things of* silver, bronze for *things of* bronze, iron for *things of* iron, wood for *things of* wood, [a]onyx stones, *stones* to be set, glistening stones of various colors, all kinds of precious stones, and marble slabs in abundance.
3 "Moreover, because I have set my affection on the house of my God, I have given to the house of my God, over and above all that I have prepared for the holy house, my own special treasure of gold and silver:
4 "three thousand talents of gold, of the gold of [a]Ō′phir, and seven thousand talents of refined silver, to overlay the walls of the houses;
5 "the gold for *things of* gold and the silver for *things of* silver, and for all kinds of work *to be done* by the hands of craftsmen. Who *then* is [a]willing to [1]consecrate himself this day to the LORD?"
6 Then [a]the leaders of the fathers' *houses*, leaders of the tribes of Israel, the captains of thousands and of hundreds, with [b]the officers over the king's work, [c]offered willingly.
7 They gave for the work of the house of God five thousand talents and ten thousand darics of gold, ten thousand talents of silver, eighteen thousand talents of bronze, and one hundred thousand talents of iron.
8 And whoever had *precious* stones gave *them* to the treasury of the house of the LORD, into the hand of [a]Je·hī′el[1] the Ger′shon·īte.

2 [a]Is. 54:11, 12
4 [a]1 Kin. 9:28
5 [a][2 Cor. 8:5, 12] [1]Lit. *fill his hand*
6 [a]1 Chr. 27:1; 28:1 [b]1 Chr. 27:25–31 [c]Ex. 35:21–35
8 [a]1 Chr. 23:8 [1]Possibly the same as *Jehieli*, 1 Chr. 26:21, 22
9 [a]2 Cor. 9:7
11 [a]1 Tim. 1:17
12 [a]Rom. 11:36
14 [1]Lit. *of Your hand*
15 [a]Heb. 11:13, 14 [1]*sojourners*, temporary residents [2]*transients*, temporary residents in an even more temporary sense

9 Then the people rejoiced, for they had offered willingly, because with a loyal heart they had [a]offered willingly to the LORD; and King David also rejoiced greatly.
10 Therefore David blessed the LORD before all the assembly; and David said:

"Blessed are You, LORD God
of Israel, our Father,
forever and ever.
11 [a]Yours, O LORD, *is* the
greatness,
The power and the glory,
The victory and the
majesty;
For all *that is* in heaven and
in earth *is Yours;*
Yours *is* the kingdom,
O LORD,
And You are exalted as head
over all.
12 [a]Both riches and honor *come*
from You,
And You reign over all.
In Your hand *is* power and
might;
In Your hand *it is* to make
great
And to give strength to all.

13 "Now therefore, our God,
We thank You
And praise Your glorious
name.
14 But who *am* I, and who *are*
my people,
That we should be able to
offer so willingly as this?
For all things *come* from
You,
And [1]of Your own we have
given You.
15 For [a]we *are* [1]aliens and
[2]pilgrims before You,
As *were* all our fathers;

[b]Our days on earth *are* as a
shadow,
And without hope.

16 "O LORD our God, all this abundance that we have prepared to build You a house for Your holy name is from Your hand, and *is* all Your own.

17 "I know also, my God, that You [a]test the heart and [b]have pleasure in uprightness. As for me, in the uprightness of my heart I have willingly offered all these *things;* and now with joy I have seen Your people, who are present here to offer willingly to You.

18 "O LORD God of Abraham, Isaac, and Israel, our fathers, keep this forever in the intent of the thoughts of the heart of Your people, and fix their heart toward You.

19 "And [a]give my son Solomon a loyal heart to keep Your commandments and Your testimonies and Your statutes, to do all *these things,* and to build the [1]temple for which [b]I have made provision."

20 Then David said to all the assembly, "Now bless the LORD your God." So all the assembly blessed the LORD God of their fathers, and bowed their heads and prostrated themselves before the LORD and the king.

21 And they made sacrifices to the LORD and offered burnt offerings to the LORD on the next day: a thousand bulls, a thousand rams, a thousand lambs, with their drink offerings, and [a]sacrifices in abundance for all Israel.

22 So they ate and drank before the LORD with great gladness on that day. And they made Solomon the son of David king the second time, and [a]anointed *him* before the LORD *to be* the leader, and Zā′dok *to be* priest.

23 Then Solomon sat on the throne of the LORD as king instead of David his father, and prospered; and all Israel obeyed him.

24 All the leaders and the mighty men, and also all the sons of King David, [a]submitted[1] themselves to King Solomon.

25 So the LORD exalted Solomon exceedingly in the sight of all Israel, and [a]bestowed on him *such* royal majesty as had not been on any king before him in Israel.

26 Thus David the son of Jesse reigned over all Israel.

27 [a]And the period that he reigned over Israel *was* forty years; [b]seven years he reigned in Hē′bron, and thirty-three *years* he reigned in Jerusalem.

28 So he [a]died in a good old age, [b]full of days and riches and honor; and Solomon his son reigned in his place.

29 Now the acts of King David, first and last, indeed they *are* written in the [1]book of Samuel the seer, in the book of Nathan the prophet, and in the book of Gad the seer,

30 with all his reign and his might, [a]and the events that happened to him, to Israel, and to all the kingdoms of the lands.

15 [b]Job 14:2
17 [a][1 Chr. 28:9] [b]Prov. 11:20
19 [a][1 Chr. 28:9] [b]1 Chr. 29:1, 2 [1]Lit. *palace*
21 [a]1 Kin. 8:62, 63
22 [a]1 Kin. 1:32–35, 39
24 [a]Eccl. 8:2 [1]Lit. *gave the hand*
25 [a]1 Kin. 3:13
27 [a]1 Kin. 2:11 [b]2 Sam. 5:5
28 [a]Gen. 25:8 [b]1 Chr. 23:1
29 [1]Lit. *words*
30 [a]Dan. 2:21; 4:23, 25

The Second Book of the
CHRONICLES

THE Book of Second Chronicles parallels First and Second Kings but virtually ignores the northern kingdom of Israel because of its false worship and refusal to acknowledge the temple in Jerusalem. Chronicles focuses on those kings who pattern their lives and reigns after the life and reign of godly King David. It gives extended treatment to such zealous reformers as Asa, Jehoshaphat, Joash, Hezekiah, and Josiah.

The temple and temple worship, central throughout the book, befit a nation whose worship of God is central to its very survival. The book begins with Solomon's glorious temple and concludes with Cyrus's edict to rebuild the temple more than four hundred years later.

NOW [a]Solomon the son of
David was strengthened in
his kingdom, and [b]the LORD his
God *was* with him and [c]exalted
him exceedingly.
2 And Solomon spoke to all
Israel, to [a]the captains of thousands
and of hundreds, to the
judges, and to every leader in all
Israel, the heads of the fathers'
houses.
3 Then Solomon, and all the
assembly with him, went to [1]the
high place that *was* at [a]Gib'ē·on;
for the tabernacle of meeting
with God was there, which Moses
the servant of the LORD had
[b]made in the wilderness.
4 [a]But David had brought up
the ark of God from Kir'jath Jē'a·rim
to *the place* David had prepared
for it, for he had pitched a
tent for it at Jerusalem.
5 Now [a]the bronze altar that
[b]Bez'a·lel the son of Ū'rī, the son
of Hur, had made, [1]he put before
the tabernacle of the LORD; Solomon
and the assembly sought
Him *there.*
6 And Solomon went up there
to the bronze altar before the
LORD, which *was* at the tabernacle
of meeting, and [a]offered a
thousand burnt offerings on it.
7 [a]On that night God appeared
to Solomon, and said to him,
"Ask! What shall I give you?"
8 And Solomon said to God:
"You have shown great [a]mercy
to David my father, and have
made me [b]king in his place.
9 "Now, O LORD God, let Your
promise to David my father be
established, [a]for You have made
me king over a people like the
[b]dust of the earth in multitude.
10 [a]"Now give me wisdom and
knowledge, that I may [b]go out
and come in before this people;
for who can judge this great
people of Yours?"
11 [a]Then God said to Solomon:
"Because this was in your heart,
and you have not asked riches
or wealth or honor or the life
of your enemies, nor have you
asked long life—but have asked
wisdom and knowledge for
yourself, that you may judge My
people over whom I have made
you king—
12 "wisdom and knowledge *are*

CHAPTER 1

1 [a]1 Kin. 2:46 [b]Gen. 39:2 [c]1 Chr. 29:25
2 [a]1 Chr. 27:1–34
3 [a]1 Kin. 3:4 [b]Ex. 25—27; 35:4—36:38 [1]Place for worship
4 [a]2 Sam. 6:2–17
5 [a]Ex. 27:1, 2; 38:1, 2 [b]Ex. 31:2 [1]Some authorities *it was there*
6 [a]1 Kin. 3:4
7 [a]1 Kin. 3:5–14; 9:2
8 [a]Ps. 18:50 [b]1 Chr. 28:5
9 [a]2 Sam. 7:8–16 [b]Gen. 13:16
10 [a]1 Kin. 3:9 [b]Deut. 31:2
11 [a]1 Kin. 3:11–13

granted to you; and I will give
you riches and wealth and honor,
such as [a]none of the kings have
had who *were* before you, nor
shall any after you have the like."
13 So Solomon came to Jerusalem from [1]the high place that
was at Gib′ē·on, from before
the tabernacle of meeting, and
reigned over Israel.
14 [a]And Solomon gathered
chariots and horsemen; he had
one thousand four hundred
chariots and twelve thousand
horsemen, whom he stationed
in the chariot cities and with the
king in Jerusalem.
15 [a]Also the king made silver
and gold as common in Jerusalem as stones, and he made
cedars as abundant as the sycamores which *are* in the lowland.
16 [a]And Solomon had horses imported from Egypt and Ke·veh′;
the king's merchants bought
them in Ke·veh′ at the *current*
price.
17 They also acquired and imported from Egypt a chariot for
six hundred *shekels* of silver,
and a horse for one hundred and
fifty; thus, [1]through their agents,
they exported them to all the
kings of the Hit′tītes and the
kings of Syria.

2 Then Solomon [a]determined
to build a temple for the
name of the LORD, and a royal
house for himself.
2 [a]Solomon selected seventy
thousand men to bear burdens,
eighty thousand to quarry *stone*
in the mountains, and three
thousand six hundred to oversee
them.
3 Then Solomon sent to [1]Hī′-
ram king of Tȳre, saying:
[a]As you have dealt with
David my father, and sent
him cedars to build himself
a house to dwell in, *so deal
with me.*
4 Behold, [a]I am building a
temple for the name of the
LORD my God, to dedicate
it to Him, [b]to burn before
Him [1]sweet incense, for
[c]the continual showbread,
for [d]the burnt offerings
morning and evening, on
the [e]Sabbaths, on the New
Moons, and on the [2]set
feasts of the LORD our God.
This *is an ordinance* forever
to Israel.
5 And the temple which I
build *will be* great, for [a]our
God is greater than all gods.
6 [a]But who is able to build
Him a temple, since heaven
and the heaven of heavens
cannot contain Him? Who
am I then, that I should build
Him a temple, except to burn
sacrifice before Him?
7 Therefore send me at once
a man skillful to work in
gold and silver, in bronze
and iron, in purple and
crimson and blue, who has
skill to engrave with the
skillful men who are with
me in Judah and Jerusalem,
[a]whom David my father
provided.
8 [a]Also send me cedar and
cypress and algum logs
from Lebanon, for I know
that your servants have skill
to cut timber in Lebanon;
and indeed my servants *will
be* with your servants,
9 to prepare timber for me
in abundance, for the
[1]temple which I am about

12 [a]2 Chr. 9:22
13 [1]Place for worship
14 [a]1 Kin. 10:26
15 [a]2 Chr. 9:27
16 [a]1 Kin. 10:28; 22:36
17 [1]Lit. *by their hands*

CHAPTER 2

1 [a]1 Kin. 5:5
2 [a]2 Chr. 2:18
3 [a]1 Chr. 14:1 [1]Heb. *Huram;* cf. 1 Kin. 5:1
4 [a]2 Chr. 2:1 [b]Ex. 30:7 [c]Ex. 25:30 [d]Ex. 29:38–42 [e]Num. 28:3, 9–11 [1]Lit. *incense of spices* [2]*appointed*
5 [a]Ps. 135:5
6 [a]1 Kin. 8:27
7 [a]1 Chr. 22:15
8 [a]1 Kin. 5:6
9 [1]Lit. *house*

to build *shall be* great and
wonderful.
10 [a]And indeed I will give
to your servants, the
woodsmen who cut timber,
twenty thousand kors of
ground wheat, twenty
thousand kors of barley,
twenty thousand baths of
wine, and twenty thousand
baths of oil.

11 Then Hī′ram king of Tȳre
answered in writing, which he
sent to Solomon:

[a]Because the LORD loves His
people, He has made you
king over them.

12 [1]Hī′ram also said:

[a]Blessed *be* the LORD God of
Israel, [b]who made heaven
and earth, for He has given
King David a wise son,
endowed with prudence
and understanding, who
will build a temple for the
LORD and a royal house for
himself!
13 And now I have sent a
skillful man, endowed with
understanding, [1]Hū′ram my
[2]master *craftsman*
14 [a](the son of a woman of the
daughters of Dan, and his
father was a man of Tȳre),
skilled to work in gold and
silver, bronze and iron,
stone and wood, purple and
blue, fine linen and crimson,
and to make any engraving
and to accomplish any plan
which may be given to him,
with your skillful men and
with the skillful men of my
lord David your father.

15 Now therefore, the wheat,
the barley, the oil, and the
wine which [a]my lord has
spoken of, let him send to
his servants.
16 [a]And we will cut wood from
Lebanon, as much as you
need; we will bring it to you
in rafts by sea to [1]Jop′pa,
and you will carry it up to
Jerusalem.

17 [a]Then Solomon numbered
all the aliens who *were* in the
land of Israel, after the census in which [b]David his father
had numbered them; and there
were found to be one hundred
and fifty-three thousand six
hundred.
18 And he made [a]seventy thousand of them bearers of burdens, eighty thousand stonecutters in the mountain, and three
thousand six hundred overseers
to make the people work.

CHAPTER 3

3 Now [a]Solomon began to
build the house of the LORD
at [b]Jerusalem on Mount Mō·rī′ah,
where [1]*the* LORD had appeared
to his father David, at the place
that David had prepared on the
threshing floor of [c]Or′nan[2] the
Jeb′ū·sīte.
2 And he began to build on the
second *day* of the second month
in the fourth year of his reign.
3 This is the foundation [a]which
Solomon laid for building the
house of God: The length *was*
sixty cubits (by cubits according
to the former measure) and the
width twenty cubits.
4 And the [a]vestibule that *was*
in front *of* [1]*the sanctuary* was
twenty cubits long across the
width of the house, and the
height *was* [2]one hundred and

10 [a]1 Kin. 5:11
11 [a]2 Chr. 9:8
12 [a]1 Kin. 5:7 [b]Rev. 10:6 [1]Heb. *Huram;* cf. 1 Kin. 5:1
13 [1]*Hiram,* 1 Kin. 7:13 [2]Lit. *father,* 1 Kin. 7:13, 14
14 [a]1 Kin. 7:13, 14
15 [a]2 Chr. 2:10
16 [a]1 Kin. 5:8, 9 [1]Heb. *Japho*
17 [a]1 Kin. 5:13; 2 Chr. 8:7, 8 [b]1 Chr. 22:2
18 [a]2 Chr. 2:2
CHAPTER 3
1 [a]1 Kin. 6:1 [b]Gen. 22:2–14 [c]1 Chr. 21:18; 22:1 [1]Lit. *He,* following MT, Vg.; LXX *the* LORD; Tg. *the Angel of the* LORD [2]*Araunah,* 2 Sam. 24:16
3 [a]1 Kin. 6:2
4 [a]1 Kin. 6:3 [1]The holy place, the main room of the temple, 1 Kin. 6:3 [2]So with MT, LXX, Vg.; Arab., some LXX mss., Syr. *twenty*

twenty. He overlaid the inside
with pure gold.
5 [a]The larger [1]room he [b]paneled
with cypress which he overlaid
with fine gold, and he carved
palm trees and chainwork on it.
6 And he decorated the house
with precious stones for beauty,
and the gold *was* gold from
Par·vā′im.
7 He also overlaid the house—
the beams and doorposts, its
walls and doors—with gold;
and he carved cherubim on the
walls.
8 And he made the [a]Most Holy
Place. Its length was according
to the width of the house, twenty
cubits, and its width twenty cubits. He overlaid it with six hundred talents of fine gold.
9 The weight of the nails *was*
fifty shekels of gold; and he overlaid the upper [a]area with gold.
10 [a]In the Most Holy Place he
made two cherubim, fashioned
by carving, and overlaid them
with gold.
11 The wings of the cherubim
were twenty cubits in *overall*
length: one wing *of the one
cherub was* five cubits, touching the wall of the room, and
the other wing *was* five cubits,
touching the wing of the other
cherub;
12 *one* wing of the other cherub
was five cubits, touching the wall
of the room, and the other wing
also was five cubits, touching
the wing of the other cherub.
13 The wings of these cherubim
spanned twenty cubits overall.
They stood on their feet, and
they faced inward.
14 And he made the [a]veil of blue,
purple, crimson, and fine linen,
and wove cherubim into it.

15 Also he made in front of the
[1]temple [a]two pillars [2]thirty-five
cubits [3]high, and the capital that
was on the top of each of *them*
was five cubits.
16 He made wreaths of chainwork, as in the inner sanctuary,
and put *them* on top of the pillars; and he made [a]one hundred
pomegranates, and put *them* on
the wreaths of chainwork.
17 Then he [a]set up the pillars
before the temple, one on the
right hand and the other on
the left; he called the name of
the one on the right hand [1]Jā′-
chin, and the name of the one
on the left [2]Bō′az.

4

Moreover he made [a]a bronze
altar: twenty cubits was its
length, twenty cubits its width,
and ten cubits its height.
2 [a]Then he made the [1]Sea of
cast *bronze,* ten cubits from one
brim to the other; *it was* completely round. Its height *was* five
cubits, and a line of thirty cubits
measured its circumference.
3 [a]And under it *was* the likeness of oxen encircling it all
around, ten to a cubit, all the
way around the Sea. The oxen
were cast in two rows, when it
was cast.
4 It stood on twelve [a]oxen:
three looking toward the
north, three looking toward
the west, three looking toward
the south, and three looking
toward the east; the Sea *was set*
upon them, and all their back
parts *pointed* inward.
5 It *was* a handbreadth thick;
and its brim was shaped like the
brim of a cup, *like* a lily blossom. It contained [1]three thousand baths.
6 He also made [a]ten lavers, and

5 [a]1 Kin. 6:17 [b]1 Kin. 6:15 [1]Lit. *house*
8 [a]Ex. 26:33
9 [a]1 Chr. 28:11
10 [a]1 Kin. 6:23–28
14 [a]Ex. 26:31
15 [a]1 Kin. 7:15–20 [1]Lit. *house* [2]*eighteen,* 1 Kin. 7:15; 2 Kin. 25:17; Jer. 52:21 [3]Lit. *long*
16 [a]1 Kin. 7:20
17 [a]1 Kin. 7:21 [1]Lit. *He Shall Establish* [2]Lit. *In It Is Strength*

CHAPTER 4

1 [a]Ex. 27:1, 2
2 [a]1 Kin. 7:23–26 [1]Great laver or basin
3 [a]1 Kin. 7:24–26
4 [a]1 Kin. 7:25
5 [1]About 8,000 gallons; *two thousand,* 1 Kin. 7:26
6 [a]1 Kin. 7:38, 40

put five on the right side and five
on the left, to wash in them; such
things as they offered for the
burnt offering they would wash
in them, but the [1]Sea *was* for the
[b]priests to wash in.
7 [a]And he made ten lampstands of gold [b]according to
their design, and set *them* in the
temple, five on the right side and
five on the left.
8 [a]He also made ten tables,
and placed *them* in the temple,
five on the right side and five on
the left. And he made one hundred [b]bowls of gold.
9 Furthermore [a]he made the
court of the priests, and the
[b]great court and doors for
the court; and he overlaid these
doors with bronze.
10 [a]He set the Sea on the right
side, toward the southeast.
11 Then [a]Hū′ram made the pots
and the shovels and the bowls.
So Hū′ram finished doing the
work that he was to do for King
Solomon for the house of God:
12 the two pillars and [a]the bowl-
shaped capitals *that were* on
top of the two pillars; the two
networks covering the two bowl-
shaped capitals which *were* on
top of the pillars;
13 [a]four hundred pomegranates for the two networks (two
rows of pomegranates for each
network, to cover the two bowl-
shaped capitals that *were* on the
pillars);
14 he also made [a]carts and the
lavers on the carts;
15 one Sea and twelve oxen under it;
16 also the pots, the shovels,
the forks—and all their articles
[a]Hū′ram his [1]master *craftsman*
made of burnished bronze for
King Solomon for the house of
the LORD.
17 In the plain of Jordan the
king had them cast in clay
molds, between Suc′coth and
[1]Zer′e·dah.
18 [a]And Solomon had all these
articles made in such great
abundance that the weight of
the bronze was not determined.
19 Thus [a]Solomon had all the
furnishings made for the house
of God: the altar of gold and
the tables on which *was* [b]the
showbread;
20 the lampstands with their
lamps of pure gold, to burn [a]in
the prescribed manner in front
of the inner sanctuary,
21 with [a]the flowers and the
lamps and the wick-trimmers of
gold, of purest gold;
22 the trimmers, the bowls, the
ladles, and the censers of pure
gold. As for the entry of the
[1]sanctuary, its inner doors to the
Most Holy *Place,* and the doors
of the main hall of the temple,
were gold.

5 So [a]all the work that Solomon had done for the
house of the LORD was finished;
and Solomon brought in the
things which his father David
had dedicated: the silver and
the gold and all the furnishings.
And he put *them* in the treasuries of the house of God.
2 [a]Now Solomon assembled
the elders of Israel and all the
heads of the tribes, the chief fathers of the children of Israel, in
Jerusalem, that they might bring
the ark of the covenant of the
LORD up [b]from the City of David,
which *is* Zion.
3 [a]Therefore all the men of
Israel assembled with the king

6 [b]Ex. 30:19–21 [1]Great basin
7 [a]1 Kin. 7:49 [b]Ex. 25:31
8 [a]1 Kin. 7:48 [b]1 Chr. 28:17
9 [a]1 Kin. 6:36 [b]2 Kin. 21:5
10 [a]1 Kin. 7:39
11 [a]1 Kin. 7:40–51
12 [a]1 Kin. 7:41
13 [a]1 Kin. 7:20
14 [a]1 Kin. 7:27, 43
16 [a]1 Kin. 7:45 [1]Lit. *father*
17 [1]*Zaretan,* 1 Kin. 7:46
18 [a]1 Kin. 7:47
19 [a]1 Kin. 7:48–50 [b]Ex. 25:30
20 [a]Ex. 27:20, 21
21 [a]Ex. 25:31
22 [1]Lit. *house*

CHAPTER 5
1 [a]1 Kin. 7:51
2 [a]1 Kin. 8:1–9 [b]2 Sam. 6:12
3 [a]1 Kin. 8:2

[b]at the feast, which *was* in the
seventh month.
4 So all the elders of Israel
came, and the [a]Lē′vītes took up
the ark.
5 Then they brought up the
ark, the tabernacle of meeting,
and all the holy furnishings
that *were* in the tabernacle. The
priests and the Lē′vītes brought
them up.
6 Also King Solomon, and all
the congregation of Israel who
were assembled with him before the ark, were sacrificing
sheep and oxen that could not
be counted or numbered for
multitude.
7 Then the priests brought in
the ark of the covenant of the
LORD to its place, into the [a]inner
sanctuary of the [1]temple, to the
Most Holy *Place,* under the
wings of the cherubim.
8 For the cherubim spread
their wings over the place of the
ark, and the cherubim overshadowed the ark and its poles.
9 The poles extended so that
the ends of the [a]poles of the
ark could be seen from *the holy
place,* in front of the inner sanctuary; but they could not be
seen from outside. And [1]they are
there to this day.
10 Nothing was in the ark except the two tablets which Moses [a]put *there* at Hō′reb, [1]when
the LORD made *a covenant* with
the children of Israel, when they
had come out of Egypt.
11 And it came to pass when
the priests came out of the *Most
Holy Place* (for all the priests
who *were* present had [1]sancti-
fied themselves, without keeping to their [a]divisions),
12 [a]and the Lē′vītes *who were*
the singers, all those of Ā′saph
and Hē′man and Je·dū′thun,
with their sons and their brethren, stood at the east end of
the altar, clothed in white linen,
having cymbals, stringed instruments and harps, [b]and with them
one hundred and twenty priests
sounding with trumpets—
13 indeed it came to pass, when
the trumpeters and singers *were*
as one, to make one sound to be
heard in praising and thanking
the LORD, and when they lifted
up their voice with the trumpets
and cymbals and instruments
of music, and praised the LORD,
saying:

[a]"*For He is* good,
For His mercy *endures*
forever,"

that the house, the house of the
LORD, was filled with a cloud,
14 so that the priests could not
[1]continue ministering because
of the cloud; [a]for the glory of the
LORD filled the house of God.

6 Then [a]Solomon spoke:

"The LORD said He would
dwell in the [b]dark cloud.
2 I have surely built You an
exalted house,
And [a]a place for You to
dwell in forever."

3 Then the king turned around
and [a]blessed the whole assembly
of Israel, while all the assembly
of Israel was standing.
4 And he said: "Blessed *be* the
LORD God of Israel, who has
fulfilled with His hands *what*
He spoke with His mouth to my
father David, [a]saying,
5 'Since the day that I brought

3 [b]2 Chr. 7:8–10
4 [a]1 Chr. 15:2; 15
7 [a]2 Chr. 4:20 [1]Lit. *house*
9 [a]Ex. 25:13–15 [1]Lit. *it is*
10 [a]Deut. 10:2, 5 [1]Or *where*
11 [a]1 Chr. 24:1–5 [1]*consecrated*
12 [a]1 Chr. 25:1–7 [b]1 Chr. 13:8; 15:16, 24
13 [a]1 Chr. 16:34, 41; Ps. 100:5; 106:1; 136
14 [a]Ex. 40:35 [1]Lit. *stand to minister*

CHAPTER 6

1 [a]1 Kin. 8:12–21 [b][Lev. 16:2]
2 [a]2 Chr. 7:12
3 [a]2 Sam. 6:18
4 [a]1 Chr. 17:5

My people out of the land of
Egypt, I have chosen no city
from any tribe of Israel *in which*
to build a house, that My name
might be there, nor did I choose
any man to be a ruler over My
people Israel.
6 [a]'Yet I have chosen Jerusalem, that My name may be there,
and I [b]have chosen David to be
over My people Israel.'
7 "Now [a]it was in the heart
of my father David to build a
[1]temple for the name of the LORD
God of Israel.
8 "But the LORD said to my
father David, 'Whereas it was in
your heart to build a temple for
My name, you did well in that it
was in your heart.
9 'Nevertheless you shall not
build the temple, but your son
who will come from your body,
he shall build the temple for My
[a]name.'
10 "So the LORD has fulfilled
His word which He spoke, and
I have filled the position of my
father David, and [a]sit on the
throne of Israel, as the LORD
promised; and I have built the
temple for the name of the LORD
God of Israel.
11 "And there I have put the
ark, [a]in which *is* the covenant of
the LORD which He made with
the children of Israel."
12 [a]Then [1]*Solomon* stood before the altar of the LORD in the
presence of all the assembly of
Israel, and spread out his hands
13 (for Solomon had made a
bronze platform five cubits long,
five cubits wide, and three cubits high, and had set it in the
midst of the court; and he stood
on it, knelt down on his knees
before all the assembly of Israel,
and spread out his hands toward
heaven);
14 and he said: "LORD God of Israel, [a]*there is* no God in heaven
or on earth like You, who keep
Your [b]covenant and mercy with
Your servants who walk before
You with all their hearts.
15 [a]"You have kept what You
promised Your servant David my
father; You have both spoken
with Your mouth and fulfilled *it*
with Your hand, as *it is* this day.
16 "Therefore, LORD God of Israel, now keep what You promised Your servant David my father, saying, [a]'You shall not fail
to have a man sit before Me on
the throne of Israel, [b]only if your
sons take heed to their way, that
they walk in My law as you have
walked before Me.'
17 "And now, O LORD God of
Israel, let Your word come true,
which You have spoken to Your
servant David.
18 "But will God indeed dwell
with men on the earth? [a]Behold,
heaven and the heaven of heavens cannot contain You. How
much less this [1]temple which I
have built!
19 "Yet regard the prayer of
Your servant and his supplication, O LORD my God, and listen
to the cry and the prayer which
Your servant is praying before
You:
20 "that Your eyes may be [a]open
toward this temple day and night,
toward the place where You said
You would put Your name, that
You may hear the prayer which
Your servant makes [b]toward this
place.
21 "And may You hear the supplications of Your servant and
of Your people Israel, when they

6 [a]Deut. 12:5–7 [b]1 Chr. 28:4
7 [a]2 Sam. 7:2 [1]Lit. *house*, and so in vv. 8–10
9 [a]1 Chr. 28:3–6
10 [a]1 Kin. 2:12; 10:9
11 [a]2 Chr. 5:7–10
12 [a]1 Kin. 8:22 [1]Lit. *he*
14 [a][Ex. 15:11] [b][Deut. 7:9]
15 [a]1 Chr. 22:9, 10
16 [a]2 Chr. 7:18 [b]Ps. 132:12
18 [a][2 Chr. 2:6] [1]Lit. *house*
20 [a]2 Chr. 7:15 [b]Dan. 6:10

pray toward this place. Hear
from heaven Your dwelling place,
and when You hear, [a]forgive.
22 "If anyone sins against his
neighbor, and is forced to take
an [a]oath, and comes *and* takes
an oath before Your altar in this
temple,
23 "then hear from heaven, and
act, and judge Your servants,
bringing retribution on the
wicked by bringing his way on
his own head, and justifying the
righteous by giving him according to his [a]righteousness.
24 "Or if Your people Israel are
defeated before an [a]enemy because they have sinned against
You, and return and confess
Your name, and pray and make
supplication before You in this
temple,
25 "then hear from heaven and
forgive the sin of Your people
Israel, and bring them back to
the land which You gave to them
and their fathers.
26 "When the [a]heavens are shut
up and there is no rain because
they have sinned against You,
when they pray toward this
place and confess Your name,
and turn from their sin because
You afflict them,
27 "then hear *in* heaven, and
forgive the sin of Your servants,
Your people Israel, that You may
teach them the good way in
which they should walk; and
send rain on Your land which
You have given to Your people as
an inheritance.
28 "When there [a]is famine in
the land, pestilence or blight or
mildew, locusts or grasshoppers;
when their enemies besiege
them in the land of their cities;
whatever plague or whatever
[b]sickness *there is;*
29 "whatever prayer, whatever
supplication is *made* by anyone, or by all Your people Israel,
when each one knows his own
burden and his own grief, and
spreads out his hands to this
temple:
30 "then hear from heaven Your
dwelling place, and forgive, and
give to everyone according to all
his ways, whose heart You know
(for You alone [a]know the [b]hearts
of the sons of men),
31 "that they may fear You, to
walk in Your ways as long as
they live in the land which You
gave to our fathers.
32 "Moreover, concerning a
foreigner, [a]who is not of Your
people Israel, but has come
from a far country for the sake
of Your great name and Your
mighty hand and Your out-
stretched arm, when they come
and pray in this temple;
33 "then hear from heaven Your
dwelling place, and do according to all for which the foreigner
calls to You, that all peoples of
the earth may know Your name
and fear You, as *do* Your people
Israel, and that they may know
that [1]this temple which I have
built is called by Your name.
34 "When Your people go out
to battle against their enemies,
wherever You send them, and
when they pray to You toward
this city which You have chosen
and the temple which I have
built for Your name,
35 "then hear from heaven their
prayer and their supplication,
and maintain their cause.
36 "When they sin against You
(for *there is* [a]no one who does

21 [a][Mic. 7:18]
22 [a]Ex. 22:8–11
23 [a][Job 34:11]
24 [a]2 Kin. 21:14, 15
26 [a]1 Kin. 17:1
28 [a]2 Chr. 20:9 [b][Mic. 6:13]
30 [a][1 Chr. 28:9] [b][1 Sam. 16:7]
32 [a]John 12:20
33 [1]Lit. *Your name is called upon this house*
36 [a][Rom. 3:9, 19; 5:12]

not sin), and You become angry with them and deliver them to the enemy, and they take them [b]captive to a land far or near;
37 "*yet* when they [1]come to themselves in the land where they were carried captive, and repent, and make supplication to You in the land of their captivity, saying, 'We have sinned, we have done wrong, and have committed wickedness';
38 "and *when* they return to You with all their heart and with all their soul in the land of their captivity, where they have been carried captive, and pray toward their land which You gave to their fathers, the [a]city which You have chosen, and toward the temple which I have built for Your name:
39 "then hear from heaven Your dwelling place their prayer and their supplications, and maintain their cause, and forgive Your people who have sinned against You.
40 "Now, my God, I pray, let Your eyes be [a]open and *let* Your ears *be* attentive to the prayer *made* in this place.

41 "Now[a] therefore,
Arise, O LORD God, to Your
[b]resting place,
You and the ark of Your
strength.
Let Your priests, O LORD God,
be clothed with salvation,
And let Your saints [c]rejoice
in goodness.

42 "O LORD God, do not turn
away the face of Your
Anointed;
[a]Remember the mercies of
Your servant David."

7 When [a]Solomon had finished praying, [b]fire came down from heaven and consumed the burnt offering and the sacrifices; and [c]the glory of the LORD filled the [1]temple.
2 [a]And the priests could not enter the house of the LORD, because the glory of the LORD had filled the LORD's house.
3 When all the children of Israel saw how the fire came down, and the glory of the LORD on the temple, they bowed their faces to the ground on the pavement, and worshiped and praised the LORD, *saying:*

[a]"For *He is* good,
[b]For His mercy *endures*
forever."

4 [a]Then the king and all the people offered sacrifices before the LORD.
5 King Solomon offered a sacrifice of twenty-two thousand bulls and one hundred and twenty thousand sheep. So the king and all the people dedicated the house of God.
6 [a]And the priests attended to their services; the Lē′vītes also with instruments of the music of the LORD, which King David had made to praise the LORD, saying, "For His mercy *endures* forever," whenever David offered praise by their [1]ministry. [b]The priests sounded trumpets opposite them, while all Israel stood.
7 Furthermore [a]Solomon consecrated the middle of the court that *was* in front of the house of the LORD; for there he offered burnt offerings and the fat of the peace offerings, because the bronze altar which Solomon had

36 [b]Deut. 28:63–68
37 [1]Lit. *bring back to their hearts*
38 [a]Dan. 6:10
40 [a]2 Chr. 6:20
41 [a]Ps. 132:8–10, 16 [b]1 Chr. 28:2 [c]Neh. 9:25
42 [a]Ps. 89:49; 132:1, 8–10

CHAPTER 7

1 [a]1 Kin. 8:54 [b]Lev. 9:24 [c]1 Kin. 8:10, 11 [1]Lit. *house*
2 [a]2 Chr. 5:14
3 [a]Ps. 106:1; 136:1 [b]2 Chr. 20:21
4 [a]1 Kin. 8:62, 63
6 [a]1 Chr. 15:16 [b]2 Chr. 5:12 [1]Lit. *hand*
7 [a]1 Kin. 8:64–66; 9:3

made was not able to receive the
burnt offerings, the grain offerings, and the fat.
8 [a]At that time Solomon kept
the feast seven days, and all Israel with him, a very great assembly [b]from the entrance of
Hā′math to [c]the[1] Brook of Egypt.
9 And on the eighth day they
held a [a]sacred assembly, for they
observed the dedication of the
altar seven days, and the feast
seven days.
10 [a]On the twenty-third day of
the seventh month he sent the
people away to their tents, joyful and glad of heart for the
good that the LORD had done for
David, for Solomon, and for His
people Israel.
11 Thus [a]Solomon finished the
house of the LORD and the king's
house; and Solomon successfully accomplished all that came
into his heart to make in the
house of the LORD and in his
own house.
12 Then the LORD [a]appeared to
Solomon by night, and said to
him: "I have heard your prayer,
[b]and have chosen this [c]place for
Myself as a house of sacrifice.
13 [a]"When I shut up heaven and
there is no rain, or command
the locusts to devour the land,
or send pestilence among My
people,
14 "if My people who are [a]called
by My name will [b]humble themselves, and pray and seek My
face, and turn from their wicked
ways, [c]then I will hear from
heaven, and will forgive their
sin and heal their land.
15 "Now [a]My eyes will be open
and My ears attentive to prayer
made in this place.
16 "For now [a]I have chosen and
[1]sanctified this house, that My
name may be there forever; and
[2]My eyes and [3]My heart will be
there perpetually.
17 [a]"As for you, if you walk
before Me as your father David
walked, and do according to all
that I have commanded you, and
if you keep My statutes and My
judgments,
18 "then I will establish the
throne of your kingdom, as I
covenanted with David your
father, saying, [a]'You shall not
fail *to have* a man as ruler in
Israel.'
19 [a]"But if you turn away and
forsake My statutes and My
commandments which I have
set before you, and go and serve
other gods, and worship them,
20 [a]"then I will uproot them
from My land which I have given
them; and this house which I
have [1]sanctified for My name
I will cast out of My sight, and
will make it a proverb and a
[b]byword among all peoples.
21 "And *as for* [a]this [1]house,
which [2]is exalted, everyone who
passes by it will be [b]astonished
and say, [c]'Why has the LORD
done thus to this land and this
house?'
22 "Then they will answer, 'Because they forsook the LORD God
of their fathers, who brought
them out of the land of Egypt,
and embraced other gods, and
worshiped them and served
them; therefore He has brought
all this calamity on them.' "

8 It [a]came to pass at the end
of [b]twenty years, when Solomon had built the house of the
LORD and his own house,
2 that the cities which [1]Hī′ram

8 [a]1 Kin. 8:65 [b]1 Kin. 4:21, 24 [c]Josh. 13:3 [1]The Shihor, 1 Chr. 13:5
9 [a]Lev. 23:36
10 [a]1 Kin. 8:66
11 [a]1 Kin. 9:1
12 [a]1 Kin. 3:5; 11:9 [b]Deut. 12:5, 11 [c]2 Chr. 6:20
13 [a]2 Chr. 6:26–28
14 [a][Is. 43:7] [b][James 4:10] [c]2 Chr. 6:27, 30
15 [a]2 Chr. 6:20, 40
16 [a]2 Chr. 6:6 [1]*set apart* [2]My attention [3]My concern
17 [a]1 Kin. 9:4
18 [a]2 Chr. 6:16
19 [a]Lev. 26:14, 33
20 [a]Deut. 28:63–68 [b]Ps. 44:14 [1]*set apart*
21 [a]2 Kin. 25:9 [b]2 Chr. 29:8 [c][Deut. 29:24, 25] [1]Temple [2]Or *was*

CHAPTER 8

1 [a]1 Kin. 9:10–14 [b]1 Kin. 6:38—7:1
2 [1]Heb. *Huram,* 2 Chr. 2:3

had given to Solomon, Solomon built them; and he settled the children of Israel there.

3 And Solomon went to Hā′math Zō′bah and seized it.

4 [a]He also built Tad′mor in the wilderness, and all the storage cities which he built in [b]Hā′math.

5 He built Upper Beth Hor′on and [a]Lower Beth Hor′on, fortified cities *with* walls, gates, and bars,

6 also Bā′a·lath and all the storage cities that Solomon had, and all the chariot cities and the cities of the cavalry, and all that Solomon [a]desired to build in Jerusalem, in Lebanon, and in all the land of his dominion.

7 [a]All the people *who were* left of the Hit′tītes, Am′o·rītes, Per′iz·zītes, Hī′vītes, and Jeb′ū·sītes, who *were* not of Israel—

8 that is, their descendants who were left in the land after them, whom the children of Israel did not destroy—from these Solomon raised forced labor, as it is to this day.

9 But Solomon did not make the children of Israel [1]servants for his work. Some *were* men of war, captains of his officers, captains of his chariots, and his cavalry.

10 And others *were* chiefs of the officials of King Solomon: [a]two hundred and fifty, who ruled over the people.

11 Now Solomon [a]brought the daughter of Pharaoh up from the City of David to the house he had built for her, for he said, "My wife shall not dwell in the house of David king of Israel, because *the places* to which the ark of the LORD has come are holy."

12 Then Solomon offered burnt offerings to the LORD on the altar of the LORD which he had built before the vestibule,

13 according to the [a]daily rate, offering according to the commandment of Moses, for the Sabbaths, the New Moons, and the [b]three appointed yearly [c]feasts—the Feast of Unleavened Bread, the Feast of Weeks, and the Feast of Tabernacles.

14 And, according to the [1]order of David his father, he appointed the [a]divisions of the priests for their service, [b]the Lē′vītes for their duties (to praise and serve before the priests) as the duty of each day required, and the [c]gatekeepers by their divisions at each gate; for so David the man of God had commanded.

15 They did not depart from the command of the king to the priests and Lē′vītes concerning any matter or concerning the [a]treasuries.

16 Now all the work of Solomon was well-ordered [1]from the day of the foundation of the house of the LORD until it was finished. So the house of the LORD was completed.

17 Then Solomon went to [a]Ē′zi·on Gē′ber and [1]Ē′lath on the seacoast, in the land of Ē′dom.

18 [a]And Hī′ram sent him ships by the hand of his servants, and servants who knew the sea. They went with the servants of Solomon to [b]Ō′phir, and acquired four hundred and fifty talents of gold from there, and brought it to King Solomon.

9 Now [a]when the queen of Shē′ba heard of the fame of

4 [a]1 Kin. 9:17, 18 [b]1 Chr. 18:3, 9
5 [a]1 Chr. 7:24
6 [a]2 Chr. 7:11
7 [a]1 Kin. 9:20
9 [1]*slaves*
10 [a]1 Kin. 9:23
11 [a]1 Kin. 3:1; 7:8; 9:24; 11:1
13 [a]Num. 28:3, 9, 11, 26; 29:1 [b]Ex. 23:14–17; 34:22, 23 [c]Lev. 23:1–44
14 [a]1 Chr. 24:3 [b]1 Chr. 25:1 [c]1 Chr. 9:17; 26:1 [1]*ordinance*
15 [a]1 Chr. 26:20–28
16 [1]So with LXX, Syr., Vg.; MT *as far as*
17 [a]1 Kin. 9:26 [1]Heb. *Eloth*, 2 Kin. 14:22
18 [a]2 Chr. 9:10, 13 [b]1 Chr. 29:4

CHAPTER 9

1 [a][Matt. 12:42]

Solomon, she came to Jerusalem to test Solomon with hard
questions, *having* a very great
retinue, camels that bore spices,
gold in abundance, and precious
stones; and when she came to
Solomon, she spoke with him
about all that was in her heart.
2 So Solomon answered all
her questions; there was nothing so difficult for Solomon that
he could not explain it to her.
3 And when the queen of
Shē′ba had seen the wisdom of
Solomon, the house that he had
built,
4 the food on his table, the
seating of his servants, the service of his waiters and their apparel, his [a]cupbearers and their
apparel, and his entryway by
which he went up to the house
of the LORD, there was no more
spirit in her.
5 Then she said to the king:
"*It was* a true report which I
heard in my own land about
your words and your wisdom.
6 "However I did not believe
their words until I came and saw
with my own eyes; and indeed
the half of the greatness of your
wisdom was not told me. You exceed the fame of which I heard.
7 "Happy *are* your men and
happy *are* these your servants,
who stand continually before
you and hear your wisdom!
8 "Blessed be the LORD your
God, who delighted in you, setting you on His throne *to be* king
for the LORD your God! Because
your God has [a]loved Israel, to
establish them forever, therefore
He made you king over them, to
do justice and righteousness."
9 And she gave the king one
hundred and twenty talents of
gold, spices in great abundance,
and precious stones; there never
were any spices such as those
the queen of Shē′ba gave to
King Solomon.
10 Also, the servants of Hī′ram
and the servants of Solomon,
[a]who brought gold from Ō′phir,
brought [1]algum wood and precious stones.
11 And the king made walk-
ways *of* the [1]algum wood for
the house of the LORD and for
the king's house, also harps and
stringed instruments for singers; and there were none such *as*
these seen before in the land of
Judah.
12 Now King Solomon gave to
the queen of Shē′ba all she desired, whatever she asked, *much*
more than she had brought to
the king. So she turned and
went to her own country, she
and her servants.
13 [a]The weight of gold that
came to Solomon yearly was six
hundred and sixty-six talents of
gold,
14 besides *what* the traveling
merchants and traders brought.
And all the kings of Arabia and
governors of the country brought
gold and silver to Solomon.
15 And King Solomon made
two hundred large shields of
hammered gold; six hundred
shekels of hammered gold went
into each shield.
16 *He* also *made* three hundred
shields of hammered gold; [1]three
hundred *shekels* of gold went
into each shield. The king put
them in the [a]House of the Forest
of Lebanon.
17 Moreover the king made a
great throne of ivory, and overlaid it with pure gold.

4 [a]Neh. 1:11
8 [a]Deut. 7:8
10 [a]2 Chr. 8:18 [1]*almug*, 1 Kin. 10:11, 12
11 [1]*almug*, 1 Kin. 10:11, 12
13 [a]1 Kin. 10:14–29
16 [a]1 Kin. 7:2 [1]*three minas*, 1 Kin. 10:17

18 The throne *had* six steps,
with a footstool of gold, *which*
were fastened to the throne;
there were [1]armrests on either
side of the place of the seat,
and two lions stood beside the
armrests.
19 Twelve lions stood there, one
on each side of the six steps;
nothing like *this* had been made
for any *other* kingdom.
20 All King Solomon's drinking vessels *were* gold, and all
the vessels of the House of the
Forest of Lebanon *were* pure
gold. Not *one was* silver, for this
was accounted as nothing in the
days of Solomon.
21 For the king's ships went
to [a]Tar'shish with the servants
of [1]Hī'ram. Once every three
years the [2]merchant ships came,
bringing gold, silver, ivory, apes,
and [3]monkeys.
22 So King Solomon surpassed
all the kings of the earth in
riches and wisdom.
23 And all the kings of the earth
sought the presence of Solomon
to hear his wisdom, which God
had put in his heart.
24 Each man brought his present: articles of silver and gold,
garments, [a]armor, spices, horses,
and mules, at a set rate year by
year.
25 Solomon [a]had four thousand
stalls for horses and chariots,
and twelve thousand horsemen
whom he stationed in the chariot cities and with the king at
Jerusalem.
26 [a]So he reigned over all the
kings [b]from [1]the River to the
land of the Phi·lis'tines, as far as
the border of Egypt.
27 [a]The king made silver *as*
common in Jerusalem as stones,

18 [1]Lit. *hands*

21 [a]2 Chr. 20:36, 37 [1]Heb. *Huram;* cf. 1 Kin. 10:22 [2]Lit. *ships of Tarshish,* deep-sea vessels [3]Or *peacocks*

24 [a]1 Kin. 20:11

25 [a]1 Kin. 4:26; 10:26

26 [a]1 Kin. 4:21 [b]Gen. 15:18 [1]The Euphrates

27 [a]1 Kin. 10:27 [b]2 Chr. 1:15–17

28 [a]2 Chr. 1:16

29 [a]1 Kin. 11:41 [b]1 Kin. 11:29 [c]2 Chr. 12:15; 13:22

30 [a]1 Kin. 4:21; 11:42, 43

31 [1]Died and joined his ancestors

CHAPTER 10

1 [a]1 Kin. 12:1–20

2 [a]1 Kin. 11:40

and he made cedar trees [b]as
abundant as the sycamores
which *are* in the lowland.
28 [a]And they brought horses to
Solomon from Egypt and from
all lands.
29 [a]Now the rest of the acts of
Solomon, first and last, *are* they
not written in the book of Nathan the prophet, in the prophecy of [b]A·hī'jah the Shī'lo·nīte,
and in the visions of [c]Id'dō the
seer concerning Jer·o·bō'am the
son of Nē'bat?
30 [a]Solomon reigned in Jerusalem over all Israel forty years.
31 Then Solomon [1]rested with
his fathers, and was buried in
the City of David his father. And
Rē·ho·bō'am his son reigned in
his place.

10 And [a]Rē·ho·bō'am went
to Shē'chem, for all Israel
had gone to Shē'chem to make
him king.
2 So it happened, when Jer·o-
bō'am the son of Nē'bat heard
it (he was in Egypt, [a]where he
had fled from the presence of
King Solomon), that Jer·o·bō'am
returned from Egypt.
3 Then they sent for him and
called him. And Jer·o·bō'am and
all Israel came and spoke to
Rē·ho·bō'am, saying,
4 "Your father made our yoke
heavy; now therefore, lighten
the burdensome service of your
father and his heavy yoke which
he put on us, and we will serve
you."
5 So he said to them, "Come
back to me after three days."
And the people departed.
6 Then King Rē·ho·bō'am consulted the elders who stood before his father Solomon while
he still lived, saying, "How do

you advise *me* to answer these people?"

7 And they spoke to him, saying, "If you are kind to these people, and please them, and speak good words to them, they will be your servants forever."

8 [a]But he rejected the advice which the elders had given him, and consulted the young men who had grown up with him, who stood before him.

9 And he said to them, "What advice do you give? How should we answer this people who have spoken to me, saying, 'Lighten the yoke which your father put on us'?"

10 Then the young men who had grown up with him spoke to him, saying, "Thus you should speak to the people who have spoken to you, saying, 'Your father made our yoke heavy, but you make *it* lighter on us'—thus you shall say to them: 'My little *finger* shall be thicker than my father's waist!

11 'And now, whereas my father put a heavy yoke on you, I will add to your yoke; my father chastised you with whips, but I *will chastise you* with [1]scourges!' "

12 So [a]Jer·o·bō′am and all the people came to Rē·ho·bō′am on the third day, as the king had directed, saying, "Come back to me the third day."

13 Then the king answered them roughly. King Rē·ho·bō′am rejected the advice of the elders,

14 and he spoke to them according to the advice of the young men, saying, [1]"My father made your yoke heavy, but I will add to it; my father chastised you with whips, but I *will chastise you* with [2]scourges!"

15 So the king did not listen to the people; [a]for the turn *of events* was from God, that the LORD might fulfill His [b]word, which He had spoken by the hand of A·hī′jah the Shī′lo·nīte to Jer·o·bō′am the son of Nē′bat.

16 Now when all Israel *saw* that the king did not listen to them, the people answered the king, saying:

"What share have we in
 David?
We have no inheritance in
 the son of Jesse.
Every man to your tents,
 O Israel!
Now see to your own house,
 O David!"

So all Israel departed to their tents.

17 But Rē·ho·bō′am reigned over the children of Israel who dwelt in the cities of Judah.

18 Then King Rē·ho·bō′am sent Ha·dor′am, who *was* in charge of revenue; but the children of Israel stoned him with stones, and he died. Therefore King Rē·ho·bō′am mounted *his* chariot in haste to flee to Jerusalem.

19 [a]So Israel has been in rebellion against the house of David to this day.

11 Now [a]when Rē·ho·bō′am came to Jerusalem, he assembled from the house of Judah and Benjamin one hundred and eighty thousand chosen *men* who were warriors, to fight against Israel, that he might restore the kingdom to Rē·ho·bō′am.

2 But the word of the LORD

8 [a]1 Kin. 12:8–11

11 [1]Scourges with points or barbs, lit. *scorpions*

12 [a]1 Kin. 12:12–14

14 [1]So with many Heb. mss., LXX, Syr., Vg. (cf. v. 10; 1 Kin. 12:14); MT I [2]Lit. *scorpions*

15 [a]1 Chr. 5:22 [b]1 Kin. 11:29–39

19 [a]1 Kin. 12:19

CHAPTER 11

1 [a]1 Kin. 12:21–24

came [a]to She·māi'ah the man of God, saying,

3 "Speak to Rē·ho·bō'am the son of Solomon, king of Judah, and to all Israel in Judah and Benjamin, saying,

4 'Thus says the LORD: "You shall not go up or fight against your brethren! Let every man return to his house, for this thing is from Me." ' " Therefore they obeyed the words of the LORD, and turned back from attacking Jer·o·bō'am.

5 So Rē·ho·bō'am dwelt in Jerusalem, and built cities for defense in Judah.

6 And he built Bethlehem, Ē'tam, Te·kō'a,

7 Beth Zūr, Sō'chōh, A·dul'lam,

8 Gath, Ma·rē'shah, Ziph,

9 Ad·o·rā'im, Lā'chish, A·zē'kah,

10 Zō'rah, Aī'ja·lon, and Hē'bron, which are in Judah and Benjamin, fortified cities.

11 And he fortified the strongholds, and put captains in them, and stores of food, oil, and wine.

12 Also in every city *he put* shields and spears, and made them very strong, having Judah and Benjamin on his side.

13 And from all their territories the priests and the Lē'vītes who *were* in all Israel took their stand with him.

14 For the Lē'vītes left [a]their common-lands and their possessions and came to Judah and Jerusalem, for [b]Jer·o·bō'am and his sons had rejected them from serving as priests to the LORD.

15 [a]Then he appointed for himself priests for the [1]high places, for [b]the demons, and [c]the calf idols which he had made.

16 [a]And [1]after *the Lē'vītes left,* those from all the tribes of Israel, such as set their heart to seek the LORD God of Israel, [b]came to Jerusalem to sacrifice to the LORD God of their fathers.

17 So they [a]strengthened the kingdom of Judah, and made Rē·ho·bō'am the son of Solomon strong for three years, because they walked in the way of David and Solomon for three years.

18 Then Rē·ho·bō'am took for himself as wife Mā'ha·lath the daughter of Jer'i·moth the son of David, *and of* Ab·i·hā'il the daughter of [a]E·lī'ah the son of Jesse.

19 And she bore him children: Jē'ush, Sham·a·rī'ah, and Zā'ham.

20 After her he took [a]Mā'a·chah the [1]granddaughter of [b]Ab'sa·lom; and she bore him [c]A·bī'jah, At'taī, Zī'za, and She·lō'mith.

21 Now Rē·ho·bō'am loved Mā'a·chah the granddaughter of Ab'sa·lom more than all his [a]wives and his concubines; for he took eighteen wives and sixty concubines, and begot twenty-eight sons and sixty daughters.

22 And Rē·ho·bō'am [a]appointed [b]A·bī'jah the son of Mā'a·chah as chief, *to be* leader among his brothers; for he *intended* to make him king.

23 He dealt wisely, and [1]dispersed some of his sons throughout all the territories of Judah and Benjamin, to every [a]fortified city; and he gave them provisions in abundance. He also sought many wives *for them.*

CHAPTER 12

12 Now [a]it came to pass, when Rē·ho·bō'am had

2 [a]1 Chr. 12:5

14 [a]Num. 35:2–5 [b]2 Chr. 13:9

15 [a]1 Kin. 12:31; 13:33; 14:9 [b][Lev. 17:7] [c]1 Kin. 12:28 [1]Places for pagan worship

16 [a]2 Chr. 14:7 [b]2 Chr. 15:9, 10; 30:11, 18 [1]Lit. *after them*

17 [a]2 Chr. 12:1, 13

18 [a]1 Sam. 16:6

20 [a]2 Chr. 13:2 [b]1 Kin. 15:2 [c]1 Kin. 14:31 [1]Lit. *daughter,* but in the broader sense of granddaughter

21 [a]Deut. 17:17

22 [a]Deut. 21:15–17 [b]2 Chr. 13:1

23 [a]2 Chr. 11:5 [1]*distributed*

1 [a]2 Chr. 11:17

established the kingdom and had strengthened himself, that [b]he forsook the law of the LORD, and all Israel along with him.

2 [a]And it happened in the fifth year of King Rē·ho·bō′am *that* Shī′shak king of Egypt came up against Jerusalem, because they had transgressed against the LORD,

3 with twelve hundred chariots, sixty thousand horsemen, and people without number who came with him out of Egypt—[a]the Lū′bim and the Suk′ki·im and the Ethiopians.

4 And he took the fortified cities of Judah and came to Jerusalem.

5 Then [a]She·māi′ah the prophet came to Rē·ho·bō′am and the leaders of Judah, who were gathered together in Jerusalem because of Shī′shak, and said to them, "Thus says the LORD: 'You have forsaken Me, and therefore I also have left you in the hand of Shī′shak.' "

6 So the leaders of Israel and the king [a]humbled themselves; and they said, [b]"The LORD *is* righteous."

7 Now when the LORD saw that they humbled themselves, [a]the word of the LORD came to She·māi′ah, saying, "They have humbled themselves; *therefore* I will not destroy them, but I will grant them some deliverance. My wrath shall not be poured out on Jerusalem by the hand of Shī′shak.

8 "Nevertheless [a]they will be his servants, that they may distinguish [b]My service from the service of the kingdoms of the nations."

9 [a]So Shī′shak king of Egypt came up against Jerusalem, and took away the treasures of the house of the LORD and the treasures of the king's house; he took everything. He also carried away the gold shields which Solomon had [b]made.

10 Then King Rē·ho·bō′am made bronze shields in their place, and committed *them* [a]to the hands of the captains of the guard, who guarded the doorway of the king's house.

11 And whenever the king entered the house of the LORD, the guard would go and bring them out; then they would take them back into the guardroom.

12 When he humbled himself, the wrath of the LORD turned from him, so as not to destroy *him* completely; and things also went well in Judah.

13 Thus King Rē·ho·bō′am strengthened himself in Jerusalem and reigned. Now [a]Rē·ho·bō′am *was* forty-one years old when he became king; and he reigned seventeen years in Jerusalem, [b]the city which the LORD had chosen out of all the tribes of Israel, to put His name there. His mother's name *was* Nā′a·mah, an [c]Am′mon·i·tess.

14 And he did evil, because he did not prepare his heart to seek the LORD.

15 The acts of Rē·ho·bō′am, first and last, *are* they not written in the book of She·māi′ah the prophet, [a]and of Id′dō the seer concerning genealogies? [b]And *there were* wars between Rē·ho·bō′am and Jer·o·bō′am all their days.

16 So Rē·ho·bō′am [1]rested with his fathers, and was buried in

1 [b]1 Kin. 14:22–24
2 [a]1 Kin. 11:40; 14:25
3 [a]2 Chr. 16:8
5 [a]2 Chr. 11:2
6 [a][James 4:10] [b]Ex. 9:27
7 [a]1 Kin. 21:28, 29
8 [a]Is. 26:13 [b][Deut. 28:47, 48]
9 [a]1 Kin. 14:25, 26 [b]2 Chr. 9:15, 16
10 [a]1 Kin. 14:27
13 [a]1 Kin. 14:21 [b]2 Chr. 6:6 [c]1 Kin. 11:1, 5
15 [a]2 Chr. 9:29; 13:22 [b]1 Kin. 14:30
16 [1]Died and joined his ancestors

the City of David. Then [a]A·bī′jah[2]
his son reigned in his place.

13 In [a]the eighteenth year of
King Jer·o·bō′am, A·bī′-
jah became king over [b]Judah.
2 He reigned three years in
Jerusalem. His mother's name
was [1]Mī·chaī′ah the daughter
of Ū·rī′el of Gib′ē·ah. And there
was war between A·bī′jah and
Jer·o·bō′am.
3 A·bī′jah set the battle in
order with an army of valiant
warriors, four hundred thousand choice men. Jer·o·bō′am
also drew up in battle formation
against him with eight hundred
thousand choice men, mighty
men of valor.
4 Then A·bī′jah stood on
Mount [a]Zem·a·rā′im, which *is* in
the mountains of Ē′phra·im, and
said, "Hear me, Jer·o·bō′am and
all Israel:
5 "Should you not know that
the LORD God of Israel [a]gave the
dominion over Israel to David
forever, to him and his sons, [b]by
a covenant of salt?
6 "Yet Jer·o·bō′am the son of
Nē′bat, the servant of Solomon
the son of David, rose up and
[a]rebelled against his lord.
7 "Then [a]worthless rogues
gathered to him, and strengthened themselves against Rē·ho-
bō′am the son of Solomon, when
Rē·ho·bō′am was [b]young and inexperienced and could not withstand them.
8 "And now you think to withstand the kingdom of the LORD,
which is in the hand of the sons
of David; and you *are* a great
multitude, and with you are the
gold calves which Jer·o·bō′am
[a]made for you as gods.
9 [a]"Have you not cast out the
priests of the LORD, the sons
of Aaron, and the Lē′vītes, and
made for yourselves priests, like
the peoples of *other* lands, [b]so
that whoever comes to consecrate himself with a young bull
and seven rams may be a priest
of [c]*things that are* not gods?
10 "But as for us, the LORD *is*
our [a]God, and we have not forsaken Him; and the priests who
minister to the LORD *are* the sons
of Aaron, and the Lē′vītes *attend* to *their* duties.
11 [a]"And they burn to the
LORD every morning and every
evening burnt sacrifices and
sweet incense; *they* also *set* the
[b]showbread *in order on* the pure
gold table, and the lampstand
of gold with its lamps [c]to burn
every evening; for we keep the
command of the LORD our God,
but you have forsaken Him.
12 "Now look, God Himself is
with us as *our* [a]head, [b]and His
priests with sounding trumpets to sound the alarm against
you. O children of Israel, do not
fight against the LORD God of
your fathers, for you shall not
prosper!"
13 But Jer·o·bō′am caused an
ambush to go around behind
them; so they were in front of
Judah, and the ambush *was* behind them.
14 And when Judah looked
around, to their surprise the
battle line *was* at both front and
rear; and they [a]cried out to the
LORD, and the priests sounded
the trumpets.
15 Then the men of Judah gave
a shout; and as the men of Judah
shouted, it happened that God
[a]struck Jer·o·bō′am and all Israel before A·bī′jah and Judah.

16 [a]2 Chr. 11:20–22 [2]*Abijam*, 1 Kin. 14:31

CHAPTER 13

1 [a]1 Kin. 15:1 [b]1 Kin. 12:17
2 [1]*Maachah*, 1 Kin. 15:2; 2 Chr. 11:20, 21
4 [a]Josh. 18:22
5 [a]2 Sam. 7:8–16 [b]Num. 18:19
6 [a]1 Kin. 11:28; 12:20
7 [a]Judg. 9:4 [b]2 Chr. 12:13
8 [a]1 Kin. 12:28; 14:9
9 [a]2 Chr. 11:13–15 [b]Ex. 29:29–33 [c]Jer. 2:11; 5:7
10 [a]Josh. 24:15
11 [a]2 Chr. 2:4 [b]Lev. 24:5–9 [c]Ex. 27:20, 21
12 [a][Heb. 2:10] [b][Num. 10:8–10]
14 [a]2 Chr. 6:34, 35; 14:11
15 [a]2 Chr. 14:12

16 And the children of Israel
fled before Judah, and God delivered them into their hand.
17 Then A·bī′jah and his people
struck them with a great slaughter; so five hundred thousand
choice men of Israel fell slain.
18 Thus the children of Israel
were subdued at that time; and
the children of Judah prevailed,
[a]because they relied on the LORD
God of their fathers.
19 And A·bī′jah pursued Jer·o-
bō′am and took cities from
him: Beth′el with its villages,
Je·shā′nah with its villages, and
[a]Ē′phra·in[1] with its villages.
20 So Jer·o·bō′am did not recover strength again in the days
of A·bī′jah; and the LORD [a]struck
him, and [b]he died.
21 But A·bī′jah grew mighty,
married fourteen wives, and begot twenty-two sons and sixteen
daughters.
22 Now the rest of the acts of
A·bī′jah, his ways, and his sayings *are* written in [a]the [1]annals
of the prophet Id′dō.

14

So A·bī′jah rested with
his fathers, and they buried him in the City of David.
Then [a]Ā′sa his son reigned in his
place. In his days the land was
quiet for ten years.
2 Ā′sa did *what was* good and
right in the eyes of the LORD his
God,
3 for he removed the altars of
the foreign *gods* and [a]the [1]high
places, and [b]broke down the *sacred* pillars [c]and cut down the
wooden images.
4 He commanded Judah to
[a]seek the LORD God of their fathers, and to observe the law
and the commandment.
5 He also removed the [1]high
places and the incense altars
from all the cities of Judah, and
the kingdom was quiet under
him.
6 And he built fortified cities
in Judah, for the land had rest;
he had no war in those years,
because the LORD had given him
[a]rest.
7 Therefore he said to Judah,
"Let us build these cities and
make walls around *them,* and
towers, gates, and bars, *while* the
land *is* yet before us, because we
have sought the LORD our God;
we have sought *Him,* and He has
given us rest on every side." So
they built and prospered.
8 And Ā′sa had an army of
three hundred thousand from
Judah who carried [1]shields and
spears, and from Benjamin
two hundred and eighty thousand men who carried shields
and drew [a]bows; all these *were*
mighty men of [b]valor.
9 [a]Then Zē′rah the Ethiopian
came out against them with an
army of a million men and three
hundred chariots, and he came
to [b]Ma·rē′shah.
10 So Ā′sa went out against
him, and they set the troops
in battle array in the Valley of
Zeph′a·thah at Ma·rē′shah.
11 And Ā′sa [a]cried out to the
LORD his God, and said, "LORD,
it is [b]nothing for You to help,
whether with many or with
those who have no power; help
us, O LORD our God, for we rest
on You, and [c]in Your name we go
against this multitude. O LORD,
You *are* our God; do not let man
prevail against You!"
12 So the LORD [a]struck the Ethiopians before Ā′sa and Judah,
and the Ethiopians fled.

18 [a]2 Chr. 14:11
19 [a]Josh. 15:9 [1]Or *Ephron*
20 [a]1 Sam. 2:6; 25:38 [b]1 Kin. 14:20
22 [a]2 Chr. 9:29 [1]Or *commentary,* Heb. *midrash*

CHAPTER 14

1 [a]1 Kin. 15:8
3 [a]1 Kin. 15:14 [b][Ex. 34:13] [c]1 Kin. 11:7 [1]Places for pagan worship
4 [a][2 Chr. 7:14]
5 [1]Places for pagan worship
6 [a]2 Chr. 15:15
8 [a]1 Chr. 12:2 [b]2 Chr. 13:3 [1]*large shields*
9 [a]2 Chr. 12:2, 3; 16:8 [b]Josh. 15:44
11 [a]Ex. 14:10 [b][1 Sam. 14:6] [c]1 Sam. 17:45
12 [a]2 Chr. 13:15

13 And Ā′sa and the people who
were with him pursued them to
[a]Gē′rar. So the Ethiopians were
overthrown, and they could not
recover, for they were broken
before the LORD and His army.
And they carried away very
much [1]spoil.
14 Then they defeated all the
cities around Gē′rar, for [a]the
fear of the LORD came upon
them; and they plundered all the
cities, for there was exceedingly
much [1]spoil in them.
15 They also [1]attacked the livestock enclosures, and carried off
sheep and camels in abundance,
and returned to Jerusalem.

15 Now [a]the Spirit of God
came upon Az·a·rī′ah the
son of Ō′ded.
2 And he went out [1]to meet
Ā′sa, and said to him: "Hear me,
Ā′sa, and all Judah and Benjamin. [a]The LORD *is* with you while
you are with Him. [b]If you seek
Him, He will be found by you;
but [c]if you forsake Him, He will
forsake you.
3 [a]"For a long time Israel *has
been* without the true God, without a [b]teaching priest, and without [c]law;
4 "but [a]when in their trouble
they turned to the LORD God of
Israel, and sought Him, He was
found by them.
5 "And in those times *there
was* no peace to the one who
went out, nor to the one who
came in, but great turmoil *was*
on all the inhabitants of the
lands.
6 [a]"So nation was [1]destroyed
by nation, and city by city, for
God troubled them with every
adversity.
7 "But you, be strong and do
not let your hands be weak, for
your work shall be rewarded!"
8 And when Ā′sa heard these
words and the prophecy of
[1]Ō′ded the prophet, he took courage, and removed the abominable idols from all the land of
Judah and Benjamin and from
the cities [a]which he had taken in
the mountains of Ē′phra·im; and
he restored the altar of the LORD
that *was* before the vestibule of
the LORD.
9 Then he gathered all Judah
and Benjamin, and [a]those who
dwelt with them from Ē′phra·im,
Ma·nas′seh, and Sim′ē·on, for
they came over to him in great
numbers from Israel when they
saw that the LORD his God was
with him.
10 So they gathered together at
Jerusalem in the third month, in
the fifteenth year of the reign of
Ā′sa.
11 [a]And they offered to the LORD
[1]at that time seven hundred bulls
and seven thousand sheep from
the [2]spoil they had brought.
12 Then they [a]entered into a
covenant to seek the LORD God
of their fathers with all their
heart and with all their soul;
13 [a]and whoever would not seek
the LORD God of Israel [b]was to be
put to death, whether small or
great, whether man or woman.
14 Then they took an oath before the LORD with a loud voice,
with shouting and trumpets and
rams' horns.
15 And all Judah rejoiced at the
oath, for they had sworn with
all their heart and [a]sought Him
with all their soul; and He was
found by them, and the LORD
gave them [b]rest all around.
16 Also he removed [a]Mā′a·chah,

13 [a]Gen. 10:19; 20:1 [1]*plunder*
14 [a]2 Chr. 17:10 [1]*plunder*
15 [1]Lit. *struck*

CHAPTER 15

1 [a]2 Chr. 20:14; 24:20
2 [a][James 4:8] [b][1 Chr. 28:9] [c]2 Chr. 24:20 [1]Lit. *before*
3 [a]Hos. 3:4 [b]2 Kin. 12:2 [c]Lev. 10:11
4 [a][Deut. 4:29]
6 [a]Matt. 24:7 [1]Lit. *beaten in pieces*
8 [a]2 Chr. 13:19 [1]So with MT, LXX; Syr., Vg. *Azariah the son of Oded* (cf. v. 1)
9 [a]2 Chr. 11:16
11 [a]2 Chr. 14:13–15 [1]Lit. *in that day* [2]*plunder*
12 [a]2 Kin. 23:3
13 [a]Ex. 22:20 [b]Deut. 13:5–15
15 [a]2 Chr. 15:2 [b]2 Chr. 14:7
16 [a]1 Kin. 15:2, 10, 13

the [1]mother of Ā′sa the king,
from *being* queen mother, because she had made an obscene
image of [2]A·shē′rah; and Ā′sa
cut down her obscene image,
then crushed and burned *it* by
the Brook Kid′ron.
17 But [a]the [1]high places were
not removed from Israel. Nevertheless the heart of Ā′sa was
loyal all his days.
18 He also brought into the
house of God the things that his
father had dedicated and that
he himself had dedicated: silver
and gold and utensils.
19 And there was no war until
the thirty-fifth year of the reign
of Ā′sa.

16 In the thirty-sixth year
of the reign of Ā′sa, [a]Bā′-
a·sha king of Israel came up
against Judah and built Rā′mah,
[b]that he might let none go out or
come in to Ā′sa king of Judah.
2 Then Ā′sa brought silver and
gold from the treasuries of the
house of the LORD and of the
king's house, and sent to Ben-
Hā′dad king of Syria, who dwelt
in Damascus, saying,
3 "*Let there be* a treaty between you and me, as there was
between my father and your
father. See, I have sent you silver and gold; come, break your
treaty with Bā′a·sha king of Israel, so that he will withdraw
from me."
4 So Ben-Hā′dad heeded King
Ā′sa, and sent the captains of
his armies against the cities of
Israel. They attacked Ī′jon, Dan,
Abel Mā′im, and all the storage
cities of Naph′ta·lī.
5 Now it happened, when Bā′-
a·sha heard *it*, that he stopped
building Rā′mah and ceased his
work.
6 Then King Ā′sa took all Judah, and they carried away the
stones and timber of Rā′mah,
which Bā′a·sha had used for
building; and with them he built
Gē′ba and Miz′pah.
7 And at that time [a]Ha·nā′nī
the seer came to Ā′sa king of Judah, and said to him: [b]"Because
you have relied on the king of
Syria, and have not relied on
the LORD your God, therefore the
army of the king of Syria has
escaped from your hand.
8 "Were [a]the Ethiopians and
[b]the Lū′bim not a huge army
with very many chariots and
horsemen? Yet, because you relied on the LORD, He delivered
them into your [c]hand.
9 [a]"For the eyes of the LORD run
to and fro throughout the whole
earth, to show Himself strong
on behalf of *those* whose heart
is loyal to Him. In this [b]you have
done foolishly; therefore from
now on [c]you shall have wars."
10 Then Ā′sa was angry with
the seer, and [a]put him in prison,
for *he was* enraged at him
because of this. And Ā′sa oppressed *some* of the people at
that time.
11 [a]Note that the acts of Ā′sa,
first and last, are indeed written
in the book of the kings of Judah
and Israel.
12 And in the thirty-ninth year
of his reign, Ā′sa became diseased in his feet, and his malady
was severe; yet in his disease he
[a]did not seek the LORD, but the
physicians.
13 [a]So Ā′sa [1]rested with his fathers; he died in the forty-first
year of his reign.

16 [1]Or *grandmother* [2]A Canaanite deity
17 [a]1 Kin. 15:14 [1]Places for pagan worship

CHAPTER 16

1 [a]1 Kin. 15:17–22 [b]2 Chr. 15:9
7 [a]2 Chr. 19:2 [b][Jer. 17:5]
8 [a]2 Chr. 14:9 [b]2 Chr. 12:3 [c]2 Chr. 13:16, 18
9 [a]Zech. 4:10 [b]1 Sam. 13:13 [c]1 Kin. 15:32
10 [a]Jer. 20:2
11 [a]1 Kin. 15:23, 24
12 [a][Jer. 17:5]
13 [a]1 Kin. 15:24 [1]Died and joined his ancestors

14 They buried him in his own
tomb, which he had [1]made for
himself in the City of David; and
they laid him in the bed which
was filled [a]with spices and various ingredients prepared in
a mixture of ointments. They
made [b]a very great burning for
him.

17 Then [a]Je·hosh'a·phat his
son reigned in his place,
and strengthened himself against
Israel.
2 And he placed troops in all
the fortified cities of Judah,
and set garrisons in the land
of [a]Judah and in the cities of
Ē'phra·im [b]which Ā'sa his father
had taken.
3 Now the LORD was with Je-
hosh'a·phat, because he walked
in the former ways of his father David; he did not seek the
Bā'als,
4 but sought [1]the God of his
father, and walked in His commandments and not according
to [a]the acts of Israel.
5 Therefore the LORD established the kingdom in his hand;
and all Judah [a]gave presents
to Je·hosh'a·phat, [b]and he had
riches and honor in abundance.
6 And his heart took delight in
the ways of the LORD; moreover
[a]he removed the [1]high places and
wooden images from Judah.
7 Also in the third year of his
reign he sent his leaders, Ben-
Hā'il, Ō·ba·dī'ah, Zech·a·rī'ah,
Ne·than'el, and Mī·chaī'ah, [a]to
teach in the cities of Judah.
8 And with them *he sent* Lē'-
vītes: She·māi'ah, Neth·a·nī'ah,
Zeb·a·dī'ah, As'a·hel, She·mir'-
a·moth, Je·hon'a·than, Ad·o·nī'-
jah, Tō·bī'jah, and Tob·ad·o·nī'-
jah—the Lē'vītes; and with them
E·lish'a·ma and Je·hō'ram, the
priests.
9 [a]So they taught in Judah,
and *had* the Book of the Law of
the LORD with them; they went
throughout all the cities of Judah and taught the people.
10 And [a]the fear of the LORD fell
on all the kingdoms of the lands
that *were* around Judah, so that
they did not make war against
Je·hosh'a·phat.
11 Also *some* of the Phi·lis'tines
[a]brought Je·hosh'a·phat presents
and silver as tribute; and the
Arabians brought him flocks,
seven thousand seven hundred
rams and seven thousand seven
hundred male goats.
12 So Je·hosh'a·phat became
increasingly powerful, and he
built fortresses and storage cities in Judah.
13 He had much property in the
cities of Judah; and the men of
war, mighty men of valor, *were*
in Jerusalem.
14 These *are* their numbers, according to their fathers' houses.
Of Judah, the captains of thousands: Ad'nah the captain, and
with him three hundred thousand mighty men of valor;
15 and next to him *was* Jē·hō-
hā'nan the captain, and with
him two hundred and eighty
thousand;
16 and next to him *was* Am·a-
sī'ah the son of Zich'rī, [a]who
willingly offered himself to the
LORD, and with him two hundred
thousand mighty men of valor.
17 Of Benjamin: E·lī'a·da a
mighty man of valor, and with
him two hundred thousand men
armed with bow and shield;
18 and next to him *was* Je·hō'-
za·bad, and with him one hundred

14 [a]John 19:39, 40 [b]2 Chr. 21:19 [1]Lit. *dug*

CHAPTER 17

1 [a]1 Kin. 15:24

2 [a]2 Chr. 11:5 [b]2 Chr. 15:8

4 [a]1 Kin. 12:28 [1]LXX *the LORD God*

5 [a]1 Kin. 10:25 [b]2 Chr. 18:1

6 [a]1 Kin. 22:43 [1]Places for pagan worship

7 [a]2 Chr. 15:3; 35:3

9 [a]Neh. 8:3, 7

10 [a]2 Chr. 14:14

11 [a]2 Chr. 9:14; 26:8

16 [a]Judg. 5:2, 9

and eighty thousand prepared for
war.
19 These served the king, besides [a]those the king put in the
fortified cities throughout all
Judah.

18 Je·hosh′a·phat [a]had riches
and honor in abundance;
and by marriage he [b]allied himself with [c]Ā′hab.
2 [a]After some years he went
down to *visit* Ā′hab in Samaria; and Ā′hab killed sheep and
oxen in abundance for him and
the people who were with him,
and persuaded him to go up
with him to Rā′moth Gil′ē·ad.
3 So Ā′hab king of Israel said
to Je·hosh′a·phat king of Judah,
"Will you go with me *against*
Rā′moth Gil′ē·ad?" And he answered him, "I *am* as you *are*,
and my people as your people;
we will be with you in the war."
4 Also Je·hosh′a·phat said to
the king of Israel, [a]"Please inquire for the word of the LORD
today."
5 Then the king of Israel gathered the prophets together, four
hundred men, and said to them,
"Shall we go to war against
Rā′moth Gil′ē·ad, or shall I refrain?" So they said, "Go up, for
God will deliver it into the king's
hand."
6 But Je·hosh′a·phat said, "*Is
there* not still a prophet of the
LORD here, that we may inquire
of [a]Him?"[1]
7 So the king of Israel said to
Je·hosh′a·phat, "*There is* still one
man by whom we may inquire
of the LORD; but I hate him, because he never prophesies good
concerning me, but always evil.
He *is* Mī·cāi′ah the son of Im′la."

19 [a]2 Chr. 17:2

CHAPTER 18

1 [a]2 Chr. 17:5 [b]2 Kin. 8:18 [c]1 Kin. 22:40

2 [a]1 Kin. 22:2

4 [a]2 Sam. 2:1

6 [a]2 Kin. 3:11 [1]Or *him*

10 [a]Zech. 1:18–21

13 [a]Num. 22:18–20, 35; 23:12, 26

And Je·hosh′a·phat said, "Let
not the king say such things!"
8 Then the king of Israel called
one *of his* officers and said,
"Bring Mī·cāi′ah the son of Im′la
quickly!"
9 The king of Israel and
Je·hosh′a·phat king of Judah,
clothed in *their* robes, sat each
on his throne; and they sat at a
threshing floor at the entrance
of the gate of Samaria; and all
the prophets prophesied before
them.
10 Now Zed·e·kī′ah the son of
Che·nā′a·nah had made [a]horns
of iron for himself; and he said,
"Thus says the LORD: 'With these
you shall gore the Syrians until
they are destroyed.' "
11 And all the prophets prophesied so, saying, "Go up to Rā′moth Gil′ē·ad and prosper, for
the LORD will deliver *it* into the
king's hand."
12 Then the messenger who
had gone to call Mī·cāi′ah spoke
to him, saying, "Now listen,
the words of the prophets with
one accord encourage the king.
Therefore please let your word
be like *the word of* one of them,
and speak encouragement."
13 And Mī·cāi′ah said, "*As* the
LORD lives, [a]whatever my God
says, that I will speak."
14 Then he came to the king; and
the king said to him, "Mī·cāi′ah,
shall we go to war against Rā′moth Gil′ē·ad, or shall I refrain?"
And he said, "Go and prosper,
and they shall be delivered into
your hand!"
15 So the king said to him,
"How many times shall I make
you swear that you tell me nothing but the truth in the name of
the LORD?"

16 Then he said, "I saw all Israel
[a]scattered on the mountains, as
sheep that have no [b]shepherd.
And the LORD said, 'These have
no master. Let each return to his
house in peace.' "
17 And the king of Israel said
to Je·hosh′a·phat, "Did I not tell
you he would not prophesy good
concerning me, but evil?"
18 Then *Mī·cāi′ah* said, "Therefore hear the word of the LORD:
I saw the LORD sitting on His
[a]throne, and all the host of
heaven standing on His right
hand and His left.
19 "And the LORD said, 'Who will
persuade Ā′hab king of Israel to
go up, that he may fall at Rā′-
moth Gil′ē·ad?' So one spoke in
this manner, and another spoke
in that manner.
20 "Then a [a]spirit came forward and stood before the LORD,
and said, 'I will persuade him.'
The LORD said to him, 'In what
way?'
21 "So he said, 'I will go out and
be a lying spirit in the mouth of
all his prophets.' And *the LORD*
said, 'You shall persuade *him*
and also prevail; go out and
do so.'
22 "Therefore look! [a]The LORD
has put a lying spirit in the mouth
of these prophets of yours, and
the LORD has declared disaster
against you."
23 Then Zed·e·kī′ah the son
of Che·nā′a·nah went near and
[a]struck Mī·cāi′ah on the cheek,
and said, "Which way did the
spirit from the LORD go from me
to speak to you?"
24 And Mī·cāi′ah said, "Indeed
you shall see on that day when
you go into an inner chamber to
hide!"

16 [a][Jer. 23:1–8; 31:10] [b]Matt. 9:36
18 [a]Is. 6:1–5
20 [a]Job 1:6
22 [a]Ezek. 14:9
23 [a]Jer. 20:2
26 [a]2 Chr. 16:10
27 [a]Deut. 18:22
29 [a]2 Chr. 35:22
31 [a]2 Chr. 13:14, 15
33 [1]Or *scale armor and the breastplate*

25 Then the king of Israel said,
"Take Mī·cāi′ah, and return him
to Ā′mon the governor of the city
and to Jō′ash the king's son;
26 "and say, 'Thus says the king:
[a]"Put this *fellow* in prison, and
feed him with bread of affliction
and water of affliction, until I
return in peace." ' "
27 But Mī·cāi′ah said, "If you
ever return in peace, the LORD
has not spoken by [a]me." And
he said, "Take heed, all you
people!"
28 So the king of Israel and
Je·hosh′a·phat the king of Judah
went up to Rā′moth Gil′ē·ad.
29 And the king of Israel said to
Je·hosh′a·phat, "I will [a]disguise
myself and go into battle; but
you put on your robes." So the
king of Israel disguised himself,
and they went into battle.
30 Now the king of Syria had
commanded the captains of the
chariots who *were* with him,
saying, "Fight with no one small
or great, but only with the king
of Israel."
31 So it was, when the captains
of the chariots saw Je·hosh′-
a·phat, that they said, "It *is* the
king of Israel!" Therefore they
surrounded him to attack; but
Je·hosh′a·phat [a]cried out, and
the LORD helped him, and God
diverted them from him.
32 For so it was, when the captains of the chariots saw that it
was not the king of Israel, that
they turned back from pursuing
him.
33 Now a certain man drew
a bow at random, and struck
the king of Israel between the
[1]joints of his armor. So he said
to the driver of his chariot, "Turn

around and take me out of the
battle, for I am wounded."
34 The battle increased that day,
and the king of Israel propped
himself up in *his* chariot facing the Syrians until evening;
and about the time of sunset he
died.

19 Then Je·hosh'a·phat the
king of Judah returned
safely to his house in Jerusalem.
2 And Jē'hū the son of Ha·nā'nī
[a]the seer went out to meet him,
and said to King Je·hosh'a·phat,
"Should you help the wicked
and [b]love those who hate the
LORD? Therefore the [c]wrath of
the LORD *is* upon you.
3 "Nevertheless [a]good things
are found in you, in that you
have removed the [1]wooden images from the land, and have
[b]prepared your heart to seek
God."
4 So Je·hosh'a·phat dwelt at
Jerusalem; and he went out
again among the people from
Bē·er·shē'ba to the mountains
of Ē'phra·im, and brought them
back to the LORD God of their
[a]fathers.
5 Then he set [a]judges in the
land throughout all the fortified
cities of Judah, city by city,
6 and said to the judges, "Take
heed to what you are doing, for
[a]you do not judge for man but
for the LORD, [b]who *is* with you
[1]in the judgment.
7 "Now therefore, let the fear
of the LORD be upon you; take
care and do *it*, for [a]*there is*
no iniquity with the LORD our
God, no [b]partiality, nor taking of
bribes."
8 Moreover in Jerusalem, for
the judgment of the LORD and
for controversies, Je·hosh'a·phat
[a]appointed some of the Lē'vītes
and priests, and some of the
chief fathers of Israel, [1]when
they returned to Jerusalem.
9 And he commanded them,
saying, "Thus you shall act [a]in
the fear of the LORD, faithfully
and with a loyal heart:
10 [a]"Whatever case comes to
you from your brethren who
dwell in their cities, whether of
bloodshed or offenses against
law or commandment, against
statutes or ordinances, you shall
warn them, lest they trespass
against the LORD and [b]wrath
come upon [c]you and your brethren. Do this, and you will not be
guilty.
11 "And take notice: [a]Am·a·rī'ah
the chief priest *is* over you [b]in
all matters of the LORD; and
Zeb·a·dī'ah the son of Ish'ma·el,
the ruler of the house of Judah,
for all the king's matters; also
the Lē'vītes *will be* officials before you. Behave courageously,
and the LORD will be [c]with the
good."

20 It happened after this
that the people of [a]Mō'ab
with the people of [b]Am'mon,
and *others* with them besides
the [c]Am'mon·ītes,[1] came to battle against Je·hosh'a·phat.
2 Then some came and told
Je·hosh'a·phat, saying, "A great
multitude is coming against
you from beyond the sea, from
[1]Syria; and they are [a]in Haz'-
a·zon Tā'mar" (which *is* [b]En
Ge'di).
3 And Je·hosh'a·phat feared,
and set [1]himself to [a]seek the
LORD, and [b]proclaimed a fast
throughout all Judah.
4 So Judah gathered together
to ask [a]*help* from the LORD; and

CHAPTER 19

2 [a]1 Kin. 16:1 [b]Ps. 139:21 [c]2 Chr. 32:25

3 [a]2 Chr. 17:4, 6 [b]2 Chr. 30:19 [1]Or *Asherim*, Heb. *Asheroth*

4 [a]2 Chr. 15:8–13

5 [a][Deut. 16:18–20]

6 [a][Deut. 1:17] [b]Ps. 82:1 [1]Lit. *in the matter of the judgment*

7 [a][Deut. 32:4] [b][Deut. 10:17, 18]

8 [a]2 Chr. 17:8 [1]LXX, Vg. *for the inhabitants of Jerusalem*

9 [a][2 Sam. 23:3]

10 [a]Deut. 17:8 [b]Num. 16:46 [c][Ezek. 3:18]

11 [a]Ezra 7:3 [b]1 Chr. 26:30 [c][2 Chr. 15:2; 20:17]

CHAPTER 20

1 [a]1 Chr. 18:2 [b]1 Chr. 19:15 [c]2 Chr. 26:7 [1]So with MT, Vg.; LXX *Meunites* (cf. 2 Chr. 26:7)

2 [a]Gen. 14:7 [b]Josh. 15:62 [1]So with MT, LXX, Vg.; Heb. mss., Old Lat. *Edom*

3 [a]2 Chr. 19:3 [b]Ezra 8:21 [1]Lit. *his face*

4 [a]2 Chr. 14:11

from all the cities of Judah they
came to seek the LORD.
5 Then Je·hosh′a·phat stood in
the assembly of Judah and Jerusalem, in the house of the LORD,
before the new court,
6 and said: "O LORD God of
our fathers, *are* You not [a]God
in heaven, and [b]do You *not* rule
over all the kingdoms of the nations, and [c]in Your hand *is there*
not power and might, so that no
one is able to withstand You?
7 "*Are* You not [a]our God, *who*
[b]drove out the inhabitants of this
land before Your people Israel,
and gave it to the descendants of
Abraham [c]Your friend forever?
8 "And they dwell in it, and
have built You a sanctuary in it
for Your name, saying,
9 [a]'If disaster comes upon us—
sword, judgment, pestilence, or
famine—we will stand before
this temple and in Your presence
(for Your [b]name *is* in this temple),
and cry out to You in our affliction, and You will hear and save.'
10 "And now, here are the
people of Am′mon, Mō′ab, and
Mount Sē′ir—whom You [a]would
not let Israel invade when they
came out of the land of Egypt,
but [b]they turned from them and
did not destroy them—
11 "here they are, rewarding us
[a]by coming to throw us out of
Your possession which You have
given us to inherit.
12 "O our God, will You not
[a]judge them? For we have no
power against this great multitude that is coming against us;
nor do we know what to do, but
[b]our eyes *are* upon You."
13 Now all Judah, with their
little ones, their wives, and their
children, stood before the LORD.

6 [a]Deut. 4:39 [b]Dan. 4:17, 25, 32 [c]1 Chr. 29:12
7 [a]Ex. 6:7 [b]Ps. 44:2 [c]Is. 41:8
9 [a]2 Chr. 6:28–30 [b]2 Chr. 6:20
10 [a]Deut. 2:4, 9, 19 [b]Num. 20:21
11 [a]Ps. 83:1–18
12 [a]Judg. 11:27 [b]Ps. 25:15; 121:1, 2; 123:1, 2; 141:8
14 [a]2 Chr. 15:1; 24:20
15 [a][Deut. 1:29, 30; 31:6, 8] [b]1 Sam. 17:47
16 [1]*streambed* or *wadi*
17 [a]Ex. 14:13, 14 [b]Num. 14:9
18 [a]Ex. 4:31
20 [a]Is. 7:9

14 Then [a]the Spirit of the LORD
came upon Ja·hā′zi·el the son of
Zech·a·rī′ah, the son of Be·nā′-
i·ah, the son of Je·ī′el, the son
of Mat·ta·nī′ah, a Lē′vīte of the
sons of Ā′saph, in the midst of
the assembly.
15 And he said, "Listen, all you
of Judah and you inhabitants
of Jerusalem, and you, King
Je·hosh′a·phat! Thus says the
LORD to you: [a]'Do not be afraid
nor dismayed because of this
great multitude, [b]for the battle *is*
not yours, but God's.
16 'Tomorrow go down against
them. They will surely come up
by the Ascent of Ziz, and you
will find them at the end of the
[1]brook before the Wilderness of
Je·rū′el.
17 [a]'You will not *need* to fight in
this *battle*. Position yourselves,
stand still and see the salvation
of the LORD, who is with you,
O Judah and Jerusalem!' Do not
fear or be dismayed; tomorrow
go out against them, [b]for the
LORD *is* with you."
18 And Je·hosh′a·phat [a]bowed
his head with *his* face to the
ground, and all Judah and the
inhabitants of Jerusalem bowed
before the LORD, worshiping the
LORD.
19 Then the Lē′vītes of the children of the Kō′hath·ītes and of
the children of the Kō′ra·hītes
stood up to praise the LORD God
of Israel with voices loud and
high.
20 So they rose early in the morning and went out into the Wilderness of Te·kō′a; and as they went
out, Je·hosh′a·phat stood and
said, "Hear me, O Judah and you
inhabitants of Jerusalem: [a]Be-
lieve in the LORD your God, and

you shall be established; believe His prophets, and you shall
prosper."
21 And when he had consulted
with the people, he appointed
those who should sing to the
LORD, [a]and who should praise
the beauty of holiness, as they
went out before the army and
were saying:

[b]"Praise the LORD,
[c]For His mercy *endures*
forever."

22 Now when they began to
sing and to praise, [a]the LORD
set ambushes against the people
of Am'mon, Mō'ab, and Mount
Sē'ir, who had come against Judah; and they were defeated.
23 For the people of Am'mon
and Mō'ab stood up against the
inhabitants of Mount Sē'ir to utterly kill and destroy *them*. And
when they [1]had made an end of
the inhabitants of Sē'ir, [a]they
helped to destroy one another.
24 So when Judah came to a
place overlooking the wilderness, they looked toward the
multitude; and there *were* their
dead bodies, fallen on the earth.
No one had escaped.
25 When Je·hosh'a·phat and his
people came to take away their
spoil, they found among them
an abundance of valuables on
the [1]dead bodies, and precious
jewelry, which they stripped off
for themselves, more than they
could carry away; and they were
three days gathering the spoil
because there was so much.
26 And on the fourth day they
assembled in the Valley of [1]Ber'-
a·chah, for there they blessed
the LORD; therefore the name of

21 [a]1 Chr. 16:29 [b]Ps. 106:1; 136:1 [c]2 Chr. 5:13
22 [a]Judg. 7:22
23 [a]1 Sam. 14:20 [1]*had finished*
25 [1]A few Heb. mss., Old Lat., Vg. *garments;* LXX *armor*
26 [1]Lit. *Blessing*
27 [a]Neh. 12:43
29 [a]2 Chr. 14:14; 17:10
30 [a]Job 34:29
31 [a][1 Kin. 22:41–43]
32 [a]2 Chr. 14:2
33 [a]2 Chr. 15:17; 17:6 [b]2 Chr. 12:14; 19:3 [1]Places for pagan worship
34 [a]1 Kin. 16:1, 7
35 [a]2 Chr. 18:1 [b]1 Kin. 22:48–53 [c][2 Chr. 19:2]
36 [a]1 Kin. 9:26; 10:22

that place was called The Valley
of Ber'a·chah until this day.
27 Then they returned, every
man of Judah and Jerusalem,
with Je·hosh'a·phat in front of
them, to go back to Jerusalem
with joy, for the LORD had [a]made
them rejoice over their enemies.
28 So they came to Jerusalem,
with stringed instruments and
harps and trumpets, to the house
of the LORD.
29 And [a]the fear of God was
on all the kingdoms of *those*
countries when they heard that
the LORD had fought against the
enemies of Israel.
30 Then the realm of Je·hosh'-
a·phat was quiet, for his [a]God
gave him rest all around.
31 [a]So Je·hosh'a·phat was king
over Judah. *He was* thirty-five
years old when he became king,
and he reigned twenty-five years
in Jerusalem. His mother's name
was A·zū'bah the daughter of
Shil'hī.
32 And he walked in the way of
his father [a]Ā'sa, and did not turn
aside from it, doing *what was*
right in the sight of the LORD.
33 Nevertheless [a]the [1]high
places were not taken away, for
as yet the people had not [b]di-
rected their hearts to the God of
their fathers.
34 Now the rest of the acts of
Je·hosh'a·phat, first and last, indeed they *are* written in the book
of Jē'hū the son of Ha·nā'nī,
[a]which *is* mentioned in the book
of the kings of Israel.
35 After this [a]Je·hosh'a·phat
king of Judah allied himself
with Ā·ha·zī'ah king of Israel,
[b]who acted very [c]wickedly.
36 And he allied himself with
him [a]to make ships to go to

Tar′shish, and they made the
ships in Ē′zi·on Gē′ber.
37 But El·i·ē′zer the son of Dō′-
da·vah of Ma·rē′shah prophesied against Je·hosh′a·phat, saying, "Because you have allied
yourself with Ā·ha·zī′ah, the
LORD has destroyed your works."
[a]Then the ships were wrecked,
so that they were not able to go
[b]to Tar′shish.

21

And [a]Je·hosh′a·phat
[1]rested with his fathers,
and was buried with his fathers in the City of David. Then
Je·hō′ram his son reigned in his
place.
2 He had brothers, the sons
of Je·hosh′a·phat: Az·a·rī′ah, Je-
hī′el, Zech·a·rī′ah, Az′ar·ya·hu,
Michael, and Sheph·a·tī′ah; all
these *were* the sons of Je·hosh′-
a·phat king of Israel.
3 Their father gave them great
gifts of silver and gold and precious things, with fortified cities
in Judah; but he gave the kingdom to Je·hō′ram, because he
was the firstborn.
4 Now when Je·hō′ram [1]was
established over the kingdom of
his father, he strengthened himself and killed all his brothers
with the sword, and also *others*
of the princes of Israel.
5 [a]Je·hō′ram *was* thirty-two
years old when he became king,
and he reigned eight years in
Jerusalem.
6 And he walked in the way
of the kings of Israel, just as the
house of Ā′hab had done, for he
had the daughter of [a]Ā′hab as a
wife; and he did evil in the sight
of the LORD.
7 Yet the LORD would not destroy the house of David, because of the [a]covenant that He
had made with David, and since
He had promised to give a lamp
to him and to his [b]sons forever.
8 [a]In his days Ē′dom revolted
against Judah's authority, and
made a king over themselves.
9 So Je·hō′ram went out with
his officers, and all his chariots
with him. And he rose by night
and attacked the Ē′dom·ītes who
had surrounded him and the
captains of the chariots.
10 Thus Ē′dom has been in revolt against Judah's authority to
this day. At that time Lib′nah revolted against his rule, because
he had forsaken the LORD God of
his fathers.
11 Moreover he made [1]high
places in the mountains of Judah, and caused the inhabitants
of Jerusalem to [a]commit harlotry, and led Judah astray.
12 And a letter came to him from
E·lī′jah the prophet, saying,

Thus says the LORD God of
your father David:
Because you have not walked
in the ways of Je·hosh′a·phat
your father, or in the ways of
Ā′sa king of Judah,
13 but have walked in the way
of the kings of Israel, and
have [a]made Judah and the
inhabitants of Jerusalem
to [b]play the harlot like the
[c]harlotry of the house of
Ā′hab, and also have [d]killed
your brothers, those of your
father's household, *who*
were better than yourself,
14 behold, the LORD will strike
your people with a serious
affliction—your children,
your wives, and all your
possessions;
15 and you *will become* very

37 [a]1 Kin. 22:48 [b]2 Chr. 9:21

CHAPTER 21

1 [a]1 Kin. 22:50 [1]Died and joined his ancestors

4 [1]Lit. *arose*

5 [a]2 Kin. 8:17–22

6 [a]2 Chr. 18:1

7 [a]2 Sam. 7:8–17 [b]1 Kin. 11:36

8 [a]2 Kin. 8:20; 14:7, 10

11 [a][Lev. 20:5] [1]Places for pagan worship

13 [a]2 Chr. 21:11 [b]Deut. 31:16 [c]2 Kin. 9:22 [d]2 Chr. 21:4

sick with a [a]disease of
your intestines, until your
intestines come out by
reason of the sickness, day
by day.

16 Moreover the [a]LORD [b]stirred
up against Je·hō'ram the spirit
of the Phi·lis'tines and the [c]Ara-
bians who *were* near the Ethiopians.
17 And they came up into Judah and invaded it, and carried
away all the possessions that
were found in the king's house,
and also [a]his sons and his wives,
so that there was not a son left
to him except [1]Je·hō'a·haz, the
youngest of his sons.
18 After all this the LORD struck
him [a]in his intestines with an
incurable disease.
19 Then it happened in the
course of time, after the end of
two years, that his intestines
came out because of his sickness; so he died in severe pain.
And his people made no [1]burn-
ing for him, like [a]the burning for
his fathers.
20 He was thirty-two years
old when he became king. He
reigned in Jerusalem eight years
and, to no one's sorrow, departed. However they buried
him in the City of David, but not
in the tombs of the kings.

22

22 Then the inhabitants of
Jerusalem made [a]Ā·ha-
zī'ah his youngest son king in
his place, for the raiders who
came with the [b]Arabians into
the camp had killed all the
[c]older *sons*. So Ā·ha·zī'ah the
son of Je·hō'ram, king of Judah,
reigned.
2 Ā·ha·zī'ah *was* [1]forty-two
years old when he became king,
and he reigned one year in Jerusalem. His mother's name *was*
[a]Ath·a·lī'ah the [2]granddaughter
of Om'rī.
3 He also walked in the ways
of the house of Ā'hab, for his
mother advised him to do wickedly.
4 Therefore he did evil in the
sight of the LORD, like the house
of Ā'hab; for they were his counselors after the death of his father, to his destruction.
5 He also followed their advice, and went with [1]Je·hō'ram
the son of Ā'hab king of Israel
to war against Haz'a·el king of
Syria at Rā'moth Gil'ē·ad; and
the Syrians wounded Jō'ram.
6 [a]Then he returned to Jez'-
rē·el to recover from the wounds
which he had received at Rā'-
mah, when he fought against
Haz'a·el king of Syria. And
[1]Az·a·rī'ah the son of Je·hō'ram,
king of Judah, went down to see
Je·hō'ram the son of Ā'hab in
Jez'rē·el, because he was sick.
7 His going to Jō'ram [a]was
God's occasion for Ā·ha·zī'ah's
[1]downfall; for when he arrived,
[b]he went out with [2]Je·hō'ram
against Jē'hū the son of Nim'shī,
[c]whom the LORD had anointed to
[3]cut off the house of Ā'hab.
8 And it happened, when Jē'hū
was [a]executing judgment on the
house of Ā'hab, and [b]found the
princes of Judah and the sons of
Ā·ha·zī'ah's brothers who served
Ā·ha·zī'ah, that he killed them.
9 [a]Then he searched for Ā·ha-
zī'ah; and they caught him (he
was hiding in Samaria), and
brought him to Jē'hū. When
they had killed him, they buried
him, "because," they said, "he is
the son of [b]Je·hosh'a·phat, who

15 [a]2 Chr. 21:18, 19

16 [a]2 Chr. 33:11 [b]1 Kin. 11:14, 23 [c]2 Chr. 17:11

17 [a]2 Chr. 24:7 [1]*Ahaziah* or *Azariah*, 2 Chr. 22:1

18 [a]2 Chr. 13:20; 21:15

19 [a]2 Chr. 16:14 [1]Burning of spices

CHAPTER 22

1 [a]2 Chr. 21:17; 22:6 [b]2 Chr. 21:16 [c]2 Chr. 21:17

2 [a]2 Chr. 21:6 [1]*twenty-two*, 2 Kin. 8:26 [2]Lit. *daughter*

5 [1]*Joram*, v. 7; 2 Kin. 8:28

6 [a]2 Kin. 9:15 [1]Heb. mss., LXX, Syr., Vg. *Ahaziah* and 2 Kin. 8:29

7 [a]2 Chr. 10:15 [b]2 Kin. 9:21–24 [c]2 Kin. 9:6, 7 [1]Lit. *crushing* [2]*Joram*, vv. 5, 7; 2 Kin. 8:28 [3]*destroy*

8 [a]2 Kin. 9:22–24 [b]2 Kin. 10:10–14

9 [a][2 Kin. 9:27] [b]1 Kin. 15:24

[c]sought the LORD with all his
heart." So the house of Ā·ha·zī′ah
had no one to assume power
over the kingdom.
10 [a]Now when Ath·a·lī′ah the
mother of Ā·ha·zī′ah saw that
her son was dead, she arose and
destroyed all the royal heirs of
the house of Judah.
11 But [1]Jē·hō·shab′e·ath, the
daughter of the king, took [a]Jō′-
ash the son of Ā·ha·zī′ah, and
stole him away from among
the king's sons who were being
murdered, and put him and his
nurse in a bedroom. So Jē·hō-
shab′e·ath, the daughter of King
Je·hō′ram, the wife of Je·hoi′-
a·da the priest (for she was the
sister of Ā·ha·zī′ah), hid him
from Ath·a·lī′ah so that she did
not kill him.
12 And he was hidden with
them in the house of God for six
years, while Ath·a·lī′ah reigned
over the land.

23

In [a]the seventh year
[b]Je·hoi′a·da strengthened
himself, *and made a* covenant
with the captains of hundreds:
Az·a·rī′ah the son of Je·rō′ham,
Ish′ma·el the son of Jē·hō·hā′-
nan, Az·a·rī′ah the son of [c]Ō′bed,
Mā·a·sēi′ah the son of A·dāi′ah,
and El·i·shā′phat the son of
Zich′rī.
2 And they went throughout
Judah and gathered the Lē′vītes
from all the cities of Judah, and
the [a]chief fathers of Israel, and
they came to Jerusalem.
3 Then all the assembly made
a covenant with the king in the
house of God. And he said to
them, "Behold, the king's son
shall reign, as the LORD has [a]said
of the sons of David.
4 "This *is* what you shall do:
One-third of you [a]entering on
the Sabbath, of the priests and
the Lē′vītes, *shall be* keeping
watch over the doors;
5 "one-third *shall be* at the
king's house; and one-third at
the Gate of the Foundation. All
the people *shall be* in the courts
of the house of the LORD.
6 "But let no one come into
the house of the LORD except
the priests and [a]those of the Lē′-
vītes who serve. They may go
in, for they *are* holy; but all the
people shall keep the watch of
the LORD.
7 "And the Lē′vītes shall surround the king on all sides, every man with his weapons in
his hand; and whoever comes
into the house, let him be put
to death. You are to be with the
king when he comes in and
when he goes out."
8 So the Lē′vītes and all Judah
did according to all that Je·hoi′-
a·da the priest commanded. And
each man took his men who
were to be on duty on the Sabbath, with those who were going *off duty* on the Sabbath; for
Je·hoi′a·da the priest had not
dismissed [a]the divisions.
9 And Je·hoi′a·da the priest
gave to the captains of hundreds the spears and the large
and small [a]shields which *had belonged* to King David, that *were*
in the temple of God.
10 Then he set all the people,
every man with his weapon in
his hand, from the right side of
the temple to the left side of the
temple, along by the altar and
by the temple, all around the
king.
11 And they brought out the
king's son, put the crown on him,

9 [c]2 Chr. 17:4; 20:3, 4
10 [a]2 Kin. 11:1–3
11 [a]2 Kin. 12:18 [1]*Jehosheba,* 2 Kin. 11:2

CHAPTER 23
1 [a]2 Kin. 11:4 [b]2 Kin. 12:2 [c]1 Chr. 2:37, 38
2 [a]Ezra 1:5
3 [a]2 Sam. 7:12
4 [a]1 Chr. 9:25
6 [a]1 Chr. 23:28–32
8 [a]1 Chr. 24:1–31
9 [a]2 Sam. 8:7

[a]*gave him* the [1]Testimony, and
made him king. Then Je·hoi′a·da
and his sons anointed him, and
said, "*Long* live the king!"
12 Now when [a]Ath·a·lī′ah heard
the noise of the people running
and praising the king, she came
to the people *in* the temple of the
LORD.
13 *When* she looked, there was
the king standing by his pillar
at the entrance; and the leaders and the trumpeters *were* by
the king. All the people of the
land were rejoicing and blowing trumpets, also the singers
with musical instruments, and
[a]those who led in praise. So
Ath·a·lī′ah tore her clothes and
said, [b]"Treason! Treason!"
14 And Je·hoi′a·da the priest
brought out the captains of hundreds who were set over the
army, and said to them, "Take
her outside under guard, and
slay with the sword whoever
follows her." For the priest had
said, "Do not kill her in the
house of the LORD."
15 So they seized her; and she
went by way of the entrance [a]of
the Horse Gate *into* the king's
house, and they killed her there.
16 Then Je·hoi′a·da made a
[a]covenant between himself, the
people, and the king, that they
should be the LORD's people.
17 And all the people went to
the [1]temple of Bā′al, and tore it
down. They broke in pieces its
altars and images, and [a]killed
Mat′tan the priest of Bā′al before the altars.
18 Also Je·hoi′a·da appointed
the oversight of the house of the
LORD to the hand of the priests,
the Lē′vītes, whom David had
[a]assigned in the house of the
LORD, to offer the burnt offerings
of the LORD, as *it is* written in
the [b]Law of Moses, with rejoicing and with singing, *as it was
established* by David.
19 And he set the [a]gatekeepers
at the gates of the house of the
LORD, so that no one *who was* in
any way unclean should enter.
20 [a]Then he took the captains of
hundreds, the nobles, the governors of the people, and all the
people of the land, and brought
the king down from the house of
the LORD; and they went through
the Upper Gate to the king's
house, and set the king on the
throne of the kingdom.
21 So all the people of the land
rejoiced; and the city was quiet,
for they had slain Ath·a·lī′ah
with the sword.

24 Jō′ash [a]*was* seven years
old when he became king,
and he reigned forty years in Jerusalem. His mother's name *was*
Zib′i·ah of Bē·er·shē′ba.
2 Jō′ash [a]did *what was* right in
the sight of the LORD all the days
of Je·hoi′a·da the priest.
3 And Je·hoi′a·da took two
wives for him, and he had sons
and daughters.
4 Now it happened after this
that Jō′ash set his heart on repairing the house of the LORD.
5 Then he gathered the priests
and the Lē′vītes, and said to
them, "Go out to the cities of
Judah, and [a]gather from all Israel money to repair the house
of your God from year to year,
and see that you do it quickly."
However the Lē′vītes did not do
it quickly.
6 [a]So the king called Je·hoi′-
a·da the chief *priest,* and said
to him, "Why have you not

11 [a]Deut. 17:18 [1]Law, Ex. 25:16, 21; 31:18
12 [a]2 Chr. 22:10
13 [a]1 Chr. 25:6–8 [b]2 Kin. 9:23
15 [a]Neh. 3:28
16 [a]Josh. 24:24, 25
17 [a]Deut. 13:6–9 [1]Lit. *house*
18 [a]1 Chr. 23:6, 30, 31; 24:1 [b]Num. 28:2
19 [a]1 Chr. 26:1–19
20 [a]2 Kin. 11:19

CHAPTER 24

1 [a]2 Kin. 11:21; 12:1–15
2 [a]2 Chr. 26:4, 5
5 [a]2 Kin. 12:4
6 [a]2 Kin. 12:7

required the Lē′vītes to bring in from Judah and from Jerusalem the collection, *according to the commandment* of [b]Moses the servant of the LORD and of the assembly of Israel, for the [c]tabernacle of witness?"

7 For [a]the sons of Ath·a·lī′ah, that wicked woman, had broken into the house of God, and had also presented all the [b]dedicated things of the house of the LORD to the Bā′als.

8 Then at the king's command [a]they made a chest, and set it outside at the gate of the house of the LORD.

9 And they made a proclamation throughout Judah and Jerusalem to bring to the LORD [a]the collection *that* Moses the servant of God *had imposed* on Israel in the wilderness.

10 Then all the leaders and all the people rejoiced, brought their contributions, and put *them* into the chest until all had given.

11 So it was, at that time, when the chest was brought to the king's official by the hand of the Lē′vītes, and [a]when they saw that *there was* much money, that the king's scribe and the high priest's officer came and emptied the chest, and took it and returned it to its place. Thus they did day by day, and gathered money in abundance.

12 The king and Je·hoi′a·da gave it to those who did the work of the service of the house of the LORD; and they hired masons and carpenters to [a]repair the house of the LORD, and also those who worked in iron and bronze to restore the house of the LORD.

13 So the workmen labored, and the work was completed by them; they restored the house of God to its original condition and reinforced it.

14 When they had finished, they brought the rest of the money before the king and Je·hoi′a·da; [a]they made from it articles for the house of the LORD, articles for serving and offering, spoons and vessels of gold and silver. And they offered burnt offerings in the house of the LORD continually all the days of Je·hoi′a·da.

15 But Je·hoi′a·da grew old and was full of days, and he died; *he was* one hundred and thirty years old when he died.

16 And they buried him in the City of David among the kings, because he had done good in Israel, both toward God and His house.

17 Now after the death of Je·hoi′a·da the leaders of Judah came and bowed down to the king. And the king listened to them.

18 Therefore they left the house of the LORD God of their fathers, and served [a]wooden images and idols; and [b]wrath came upon Judah and Jerusalem because of their trespass.

19 Yet He [a]sent prophets to them, to bring them back to the LORD; and they testified against them, but they would not listen.

20 Then the Spirit of God [1]came upon [a]Zech·a·rī′ah the son of Je·hoi′a·da the priest, who stood above the people, and said to them, "Thus says God: [b]'Why do you transgress the commandments of the LORD, so that you cannot prosper? [c]Because you

6 [b]Ex. 30:12–16 [c]Num. 1:50
7 [a]2 Chr. 21:17 [b]2 Kin. 12:4
8 [a]2 Kin. 12:9
9 [a]2 Chr. 24:6
11 [a]2 Kin. 12:10
12 [a]2 Chr. 30:12
14 [a]2 Kin. 12:13
18 [a]1 Kin. 14:23 [b][Ex. 34:12–14]
19 [a]2 Chr. 36:15, 16
20 [a]Matt. 23:35 [b]Num. 14:41 [c][2 Chr. 15:2] [1]Lit. *clothed*

have forsaken the LORD, He also
has forsaken you.' "
21 So they conspired against
him, and at the command of
the king they [a]stoned him with
stones in the court of the house
of the LORD.
22 Thus Jō'ash the king did not
remember the kindness which
Je·hoi'a·da his [1]father had done
to him, but killed his son; and as
he died, he said, "The LORD look
on *it*, and [a]repay!"
23 So it happened in the spring
of the year *that* [a]the army of
Syria came up against him; and
they came to Judah and Jerusalem, and destroyed all the leaders of the people from among
the people, and sent all their
[1]spoil to the king of Damascus.
24 For the army of the Syrians
[a]came with a small company of
men; but the LORD [b]delivered a
very great army into their hand,
because they had forsaken the
LORD God of their fathers. So
they [c]executed judgment against
Jō'ash.
25 And when they had withdrawn from him (for they left
him severely wounded), [a]his
own servants conspired against
him because of the blood of the
[1]sons of Je·hoi'a·da the priest,
and killed him on his bed. So
he died. And they buried him in
the City of David, but they did
not bury him in the tombs of the
kings.
26 These are the ones who
conspired against him: [1]Zā'bad
the son of Shim'ē·ath the Am'-
mon·ī·tess, and Je·hō'za·bad the
son of [2]Shim'rith the Mō'ab·ī-
tess.
27 Now *concerning* his sons,
and [a]the many oracles about him,
and the repairing of the house of
God, indeed they *are* written in
the [1]annals of the book of the
kings. [b]Then Am·a·zī'ah his son
reigned in his place.

25

Am·a·zī'ah [a]*was* twenty-
five years old *when* he
became king, and he reigned
twenty-nine years in Jerusalem. His mother's name *was*
Jē·hō·ad'dan of Jerusalem.
2 And he did *what was* right
in the sight of the LORD, [a]but not
with a loyal heart.
3 [a]Now it happened, as soon
as the kingdom was established
for him, that he executed his
servants who had murdered his
father the king.
4 However he did not execute
their children, but *did* as *it is*
written in the Law in the Book
of Moses, where the LORD commanded, saying, [a]"The fathers
shall not be put to death for
their children, nor shall the children be put to death for their
fathers; but a person shall die
for his own sin."
5 Moreover Am·a·zī'ah gathered Judah together and set over
them captains of thousands and
captains of hundreds, according
to *their* fathers' houses, throughout all Judah and Benjamin; and
he numbered them [a]from twenty
years old and above, and found
them to be three hundred thousand choice *men*, *able* to go to
war, who could handle spear
and shield.
6 He also hired one hundred
thousand mighty men of valor
from Israel for one hundred talents of silver.
7 But a [a]man of God came to
him, saying, "O king, do not let
the army of Israel go with you,

21 [a][Neh. 9:26]
22 [a][Gen. 9:5] [1]Foster father
23 [a]2 Kin. 12:17 [1]*plunder*
24 [a]Lev. 26:8; Is. 30:17 [b]Lev. 26:25 [c]2 Chr. 22:8
25 [a]2 Kin. 12:20, 21 [1]LXX, Vg. *son* and vv. 20–22
26 [1]*Jozachar*, 2 Kin. 12:21 [2]*Shomer*, 2 Kin. 12:21
27 [a]2 Kin. 12:18 [b]2 Kin. 12:21 [1]Or *commentary*, Heb. *midrash*

CHAPTER 25

1 [a]2 Kin. 14:1–6
2 [a]2 Chr. 25:14
3 [a]2 Kin. 14:5
4 [a]Deut. 24:16
5 [a]Num. 1:3
7 [a]2 Chr. 11:2

for the LORD *is* not with Israel—*not with* any of the children of Ē′phra·im.

8 "But if you go, be gone! Be strong in battle! *Even so,* God shall make you fall before the enemy; for God has [a]power to help and to overthrow."

9 Then Am·a·zī′ah said to the man of God, "But what *shall we* do about the hundred talents which I have given to the troops of Israel?" And the man of God answered, [a]"The LORD is able to give you much more than this."

10 So Am·a·zī′ah discharged the troops that had come to him from Ē′phra·im, to go back home. Therefore their anger was greatly aroused against Judah, and they returned home in great anger.

11 Then Am·a·zī′ah strengthened himself, and leading his people, he went to [a]the Valley of Salt and killed ten thousand of the people of Sē′ir.

12 Also the children of Judah took captive ten thousand alive, brought them to the top of the rock, and cast them down from the top of the rock, so that they all were dashed in pieces.

13 But as for the soldiers of the army which Am·a·zī′ah had discharged, so that they would not go with him to battle, they raided the cities of Judah from Samaria to Beth Hor′on, killed three thousand in them, and took much [1]spoil.

14 Now it was so, after Am·a·zī′ah came from the slaughter of the Ē′dom·ītes, that [a]he brought the gods of the people of Sē′ir, set them up *to be* [b]his gods, and bowed down before them and burned incense to them.

8 [a]2 Chr. 14:11; 20:6
9 [a][Deut. 8:18]
11 [a]2 Kin. 14:7
13 [1]*plunder*
14 [a]2 Chr. 28:23 [b][Ex. 20:3, 5]
15 [a][Ps. 96:5] [b]2 Chr. 25:11
16 [a][1 Sam. 2:25]
17 [a]2 Kin. 14:8–14 [1]*Jehoash,* 2 Kin. 14:8ff.
19 [a]2 Chr. 26:16; 32:25
20 [a]1 Kin. 12:15 [b]2 Chr. 25:14

15 Therefore the anger of the LORD was aroused against Am·a·zī′ah, and He sent him a prophet who said to him, "Why have you sought [a]the gods of the people, which [b]could not rescue their own people from your hand?"

16 So it was, as he talked with him, that *the king* said to him, "Have we made you the king's counselor? Cease! Why should you be killed?" Then the prophet ceased, and said, "I know that God has [a]determined to destroy you, because you have done this and have not heeded my advice."

17 Now [a]Am·a·zī′ah king of Judah asked advice and sent to [1]Jō′ash the son of Je·hō′a·haz, the son of Jē′hū, king of Israel, saying, "Come, let us face one another *in battle.*"

18 And Jō′ash king of Israel sent to Am·a·zī′ah king of Judah, saying, "The thistle that *was* in Lebanon sent to the cedar that was in Lebanon, saying, 'Give your daughter to my son as wife'; and a wild beast that *was* in Lebanon passed by and trampled the thistle.

19 "Indeed you say that you have defeated the Ē′dom·ītes, and your heart is lifted up to [a]boast. Stay at home now; why should you meddle with trouble, that you should fall—you and Judah with you?"

20 But Am·a·zī′ah would not heed, for [a]it *came* from God, that He might give them into the hand *of their enemies,* because they [b]sought the gods of Ē′dom.

21 So Jō′ash king of Israel went out; and he and Am·a·zī′ah king of Judah faced one another at

[a]Beth Shem′esh, which *belongs*
to Judah.
22 And Judah was defeated by
Israel, and every man fled to his
tent.
23 Then Jō′ash the king of Israel captured Am·a·zī′ah king of
Judah, the son of Jō′ash, the son
of [a]Je·hō′a·haz, at Beth Shem′-
esh; and he brought him to Jerusalem, and broke down the wall
of Jerusalem from the Gate of
Ē′phra·im to the Corner Gate—
four hundred cubits.
24 And *he took* all the gold and
silver, all the articles that were
found in the house of God with
[a]Ō′bed-Ē′dom, the treasures of
the king's house, and hostages,
and returned to Samaria.
25 [a]Am·a·zī′ah the son of Jō′ash,
king of Judah, lived fifteen years
after the death of Jō′ash the son
of Je·hō′a·haz, king of Israel.
26 Now the rest of the acts of
Am·a·zī′ah, from first to last, indeed *are* they not written in the
book of the kings of Judah and
Israel?
27 After the time that Am·a·zī′ah
turned away from following the
LORD, they made a conspiracy
against him in Jerusalem, and
he fled to Lā′chish; but they sent
after him to Lā′chish and killed
him there.
28 Then they brought him on
horses and buried him with his
fathers in [1]the City of Judah.

26 Now all the people of Judah took [1]Uz·zī′ah, who
was sixteen years old, and made
him king instead of his father
Am·a·zī′ah.
2 He built [1]Ē′lath and restored
it to Judah, after the king rested
with his fathers.
3 Uz·zī′ah *was* sixteen years
old when he became king, and
he reigned fifty-two years in Jerusalem. His mother's name was
Jech·o·lī′ah of Jerusalem.
4 And he did *what was* [a]right
in the sight of the LORD, according to all that his father
Am·a·zī′ah had done.
5 [a]He sought God in the days
of Zech·a·rī′ah, who [b]had understanding in the [1]visions of God;
and as long as he sought the
LORD, God made him [c]prosper.
6 Now he went out and [a]made
war against the Phi·lis′tines, and
broke down the wall of Gath,
the wall of Jab′neh, and the wall
of Ash′dod; and he built cities
around Ash′dod and among the
Phi·lis′tines.
7 God helped him against [a]the
Phi·lis′tines, against the Arabians who lived in Gur Bā′al, and
against the Me·ū′nītes.
8 Also the Am′mon·ītes [a]brought
tribute to Uz·zī′ah. His fame
spread as far as the entrance of
Egypt, for he became exceedingly
strong.
9 And Uz·zī′ah built towers in
Jerusalem at the [a]Corner Gate,
at the Valley Gate, and at the
corner buttress of the wall; then
he fortified them.
10 Also he built towers in the
desert. He dug many wells, for
he had much livestock, both in
the lowlands and in the plains;
he also had farmers and vinedressers in the mountains and in
[1]Car′mel, for he loved the soil.
11 Moreover Uz·zī′ah had an
army of fighting men who went
out to war by companies, according to the number on their roll
as prepared by Je·ī′el the scribe
and Mā·a·sēi′ah the officer, un-

21 [a]Josh. 19:38
23 [a]2 Chr. 21:17; 22:1, 6
24 [a]1 Chr. 26:15
25 [a]2 Kin. 14:17–22
28 [1]The City of David

CHAPTER 26

1 [1]*Azariah,* 2 Kin. 14:21ff.
2 [1]Heb. *Eloth*
4 [a]2 Chr. 24:2
5 [a]2 Chr. 24:2 [b]Dan. 1:17; 10:1 [c][2 Chr. 15:2; 20:20; 31:21] [1]Heb. mss., LXX, Syr., Tg., Arab. *fear*
6 [a]Is. 14:29
7 [a]2 Chr. 21:16
8 [a]2 Chr. 17:11
9 [a]Neh. 3:13, 19, 32
10 [1]Or *the fertile fields*

der the hand of Han·a·nī′ah, *one*
of the king's captains.
12 The total number of [1]chief officers of the mighty men of valor
was two thousand six hundred.
13 And under their authority
was an army of three hundred
and seven thousand five hundred, that made war with mighty
power, to help the king against
the enemy.
14 Then Uz·zī′ah prepared
for them, for the entire army,
shields, spears, helmets, body
armor, bows, and slings *to cast*
stones.
15 And he made devices in Jerusalem, invented by [a]skillful
men, to be on the towers and
the corners, to shoot arrows and
large stones. So his fame spread
far and wide, for he was marvelously helped till he became
strong.
16 But [a]when he was strong
his heart was [b]lifted up, to *his*
destruction, for he transgressed
against the LORD his God [c]by
entering the temple of the LORD
to burn incense on the altar of
incense.
17 So [a]Az·a·rī′ah the priest went
in after him, and with him were
eighty priests of the LORD—valiant men.
18 And they withstood King
Uz·zī′ah, and said to him, "*It*
[a]*is* not for you, Uz·zī′ah, to burn
incense to the LORD, but for the
[b]priests, the sons of Aaron, who
are consecrated to burn incense.
Get out of the sanctuary, for you
have trespassed! You *shall have*
no honor from the LORD God."
19 Then Uz·zī′ah became furious; and he *had* a censer in his
hand to burn incense. And while
he was angry with the priests,
[a]leprosy broke out on his forehead, before the priests in the
house of the LORD, beside the
incense altar.
20 And Az·a·rī′ah the chief
priest and all the priests looked
at him, and there, on his forehead, he *was* leprous; so they
thrust him out of that place. Indeed he also [a]hurried to get out,
because the LORD had struck
him.
21 [a]King Uz·zī′ah was a leper
until the day of his death. He
dwelt in an [b]isolated house, because he was a leper; for he was
cut off from the house of the
LORD. Then Jō′tham his son *was*
over the king's house, judging
the people of the land.
22 Now the rest of the acts
of Uz·zī′ah, from first to last,
the prophet [a]Ī·sāi′ah the son of
Ā′moz wrote.
23 [a]So Uz·zī′ah [1]rested with his
fathers, and they buried him with
his fathers in the field of burial
which *belonged* to the kings, for
they said, "He is a leper." Then
Jō′tham his son reigned in his
place.

27

Jō′tham [a]*was* twenty-
five years old when he
became king, and he reigned
sixteen years in Jerusalem. His
mother's name *was* [1]Je·rū′shah
the daughter of Zā′dok.
2 And he did *what was* right in
the sight of the LORD, according
to all that his father Uz·zī′ah had
done (although he did not enter
the temple of the LORD). But still
[a]the people acted corruptly.
3 He built the Upper Gate of
the house of the LORD, and he
built extensively on the wall of
[a]Ō′phel.
4 Moreover he built cities in

12 [1]Lit. *chief fathers*
15 [a]Ex. 39:3, 8
16 [a][Deut. 32:15] [b]2 Chr. 25:19 [c]2 Kin. 16:12, 13
17 [a]1 Chr. 6:10
18 [a][Num. 3:10; 16:39, 40; 18:7] [b]Ex. 30:7, 8
19 [a]2 Kin. 5:25–27
20 [a]Esth. 6:12
21 [a]2 Kin. 15:5 [b][Lev. 13:46]
22 [a]Is. 1:1
23 [a]Is. 6:1 [1]Died and joined his ancestors

CHAPTER 27

1 [a]2 Kin. 15:32–35 [1]*Jerusha,* 2 Kin. 15:33
2 [a]2 Kin. 15:35
3 [a]2 Chr. 33:14

the mountains of Judah, and in the forests he built fortresses and towers.

5 He also fought with the king of the [a]Am′mon·ītes and defeated them. And the people of Am′mon gave him in that year one hundred talents of silver, ten thousand kors of wheat, and ten thousand of barley. The people of Am′mon paid this to him in the second and third years also.

6 So Jō′tham became mighty, [a]because he prepared his ways before the LORD his God.

7 Now the rest of the acts of Jō′tham, and all his wars and his ways, indeed they *are* written in the book of the kings of Israel and Judah.

8 He was twenty-five years old when he became king, and he reigned sixteen years in Jerusalem.

9 [a]So Jō′tham [1]rested with his fathers, and they buried him in the City of David. Then [b]Ā′haz his son reigned in his place.

28 Ā′haz [a]*was* twenty years old when he became king, and he reigned sixteen years in Jerusalem; and he did not do *what was* right in the sight of the LORD, as his father David *had done.*

2 For he walked in the ways of the kings of Israel, and made [a]molded images for [b]the Bā′als.

3 He burned incense in [a]the Valley of the Son of Hin′nom, and burned [b]his children in the [c]fire, according to the abominations of the nations whom the LORD had [d]cast out before the children of Israel.

4 And he sacrificed and burned incense on the [1]high places, on the hills, and under every green tree.

5 Therefore [a]the LORD his God delivered him into the hand of the king of Syria. They [b]defeated him, and carried away a great multitude of them as captives, and brought *them* to Damascus. Then he was also delivered into the hand of the king of Israel, who defeated him with a great slaughter.

6 For [a]Pē′kah the son of Rem·a·lī′ah killed one hundred and twenty thousand in Judah in one day, all valiant men, [b]because they had forsaken the LORD God of their fathers.

7 Zich′rī, a mighty man of Ē′phra·im, killed Mā·a·sē′ah the king's son, Az·rī′kam the officer over the house, and El·kā′nah *who was* second to the king.

8 And the children of Israel carried away captive of their [a]brethren two hundred thousand women, sons, and daughters; and they also took away much [1]spoil from them, and brought the spoil to Samaria.

9 But a [a]prophet of the LORD was there, whose name *was* Ō′ded; and he went out before the army that came to Samaria, and said to them: "Look, [b]because the LORD God of your fathers was angry with Judah, He has delivered them into your hand; but you have killed them in a rage *that* [c]reaches up to heaven.

10 "And now you propose to force the children of Judah and Jerusalem to be your [a]male and female slaves; *but are* you not also guilty before the LORD your God?

11 "Now hear me, therefore, and

5 [a]2 Chr. 26:8
6 [a]2 Chr. 26:5
9 [a]2 Kin. 15:38 [b]Is. 1:1 [1]Died and joined his ancestors

CHAPTER 28

1 [a]2 Kin. 16:2–4
2 [a]Ex. 34:17 [b]Judg. 2:11
3 [a]Josh. 15:8 [b]2 Kin. 23:10 [c][Lev. 18:21] [d][Lev. 18:24–30]
4 [1]Places for pagan worship
5 [a][Is. 10:5] [b]Is. 7:1, 17
6 [a]2 Kin. 15:27 [b][2 Chr. 29:8]
8 [a]Deut. 28:25, 41 [1]*plunder*
9 [a]2 Chr. 25:15 [b][Is. 10:5; 47:6] [c]Rev. 18:5
10 [a][Lev. 25:39, 42, 43, 46]

return the captives, whom you
have taken captive from your
brethren, [a]for the fierce wrath of
the LORD *is* upon you."
12 Then some of the heads of
the children of Ē′phra·im, Az-
a·rī′ah the son of Jō·hā′nan,
Ber·e·chī′ah the son of Me·shil′-
le·moth, Jē·hiz·kī′ah the son
of Shal′lum, and A·mā′sa the
son of Had′laī, stood up against
those who came from the war,
13 and said to them, "You shall
not bring the captives here, for
we *already* have offended the
LORD. You intend to add to our
sins and to our guilt; for our
guilt is great, and *there is* fierce
wrath against Israel."
14 So the armed men left the
captives and the [1]spoil before the
leaders and all the assembly.
15 Then the men [a]who were
designated by name rose up and
took the captives, and from the
[1]spoil they clothed all who were
naked among them, dressed
them and gave them sandals,
[b]gave them food and drink, and
anointed them; and they let all
the feeble ones ride on donkeys.
So they brought them to their
brethren at Jericho, [c]the city of
palm trees. Then they returned
to Samaria.
16 [a]At the same time King Ā′haz
sent to the [1]kings of Assyria to
help him.
17 For again the [a]Ē′dom·ītes
had come, attacked Judah, and
carried away captives.
18 [a]The Phi·lis′tines also had
invaded the cities of the lowland and of the South of Judah,
and had taken Beth Shem′esh,
Aī′ja·lon, Ge·dē′roth, Sō′chōh
with its villages, Tim′nah with
its villages, and Gim′zō with its
villages; and they dwelt there.
19 For the LORD [1]brought Judah
low because of Ā′haz king of
[a]Israel, for he had [b]encouraged
moral decline in Judah and had
been continually unfaithful to
the LORD.
20 Also [a]Tig′lath-Pī·lē′ser[1] king
of Assyria came to him and distressed him, and did not assist
him.
21 For Ā′haz took part *of the*
treasures from the house of
the LORD, from the house of the
king, and from the leaders, and
he gave *it* to the king of Assyria;
but he did not help him.
22 Now in the time of his distress
King Ā′haz became increasingly
unfaithful to the LORD. This *is*
that King Ā′haz.
23 For [a]he sacrificed to the gods
of Damascus which had defeated
him, saying, "Because the gods
of the kings of Syria help them,
I will sacrifice to them [b]that they
may help me." But they were the
ruin of him and of all Israel.
24 So Ā′haz gathered the articles of the house of God, cut in
pieces the articles of the house
of God, [a]shut up the doors of the
house of the LORD, and made for
himself altars in every corner of
Jerusalem.
25 And in every single city of
Judah he made [1]high places to
burn incense to other gods, and
provoked to anger the LORD God
of his fathers.
26 [a]Now the rest of his acts and
all his ways, from first to last,
indeed they *are* written in the
book of the kings of Judah and
Israel.
27 So Ā′haz [1]rested with his fathers, and they buried him in the

11 [a]James 2:13
14 [1]*plunder*
15 [a]2 Chr. 28:12 [b][Prov. 25:21, 22] [c]Deut. 34:3 [1]*plunder*
16 [a]2 Kin. 16:7 [1]LXX, Syr., Vg. *king* (cf. v. 20)
17 [a]Obad. 10–14
18 [a]Ezek. 16:27, 57
19 [a]2 Chr. 21:2 [b]Ex. 32:25 [1]*humbled Judah*
20 [a]1 Chr. 5:26 [1]Heb. *Tilgath-Pilneser*
23 [a]2 Chr. 25:14 [b]Jer. 44:17, 18
24 [a]2 Chr. 29:3, 7
25 [1]Places for pagan worship
26 [a]2 Kin. 16:19, 20
27 [1]Died and joined his ancestors

city, in Jerusalem; but they [a]did
not bring him into the tombs
of the kings of Israel. Then
Hez·e·kī′ah his son reigned in
his place.

29 Hez·e·kī′ah [a]became king
when he was twenty-
five years old, and he reigned
twenty-nine years in Jerusalem.
His mother's name *was* [1]A·bī′jah
the daughter of Zech·a·rī′ah.
2 And he did *what was* right in
the sight of the LORD, according
to all that his father David had
done.
3 In the first year of his reign,
in the first month, he [a]opened
the doors of the house of the
LORD and repaired them.
4 Then he brought in the priests
and the Lē′vītes, and gathered
them in the East Square,
5 and said to them: "Hear me,
Lē′vītes! Now [1]sanctify yourselves, [a]sanctify the house of the
LORD God of your fathers, and
carry out the rubbish from the
holy *place*.
6 "For our fathers have trespassed and done evil in the eyes
of the LORD our God; they have
forsaken Him, have [a]turned their
faces away from the [1]dwelling
place of the LORD, and turned
their backs *on Him*.
7 [a]"They have also shut up the
doors of the vestibule, put out
the lamps, and have not burned
incense or offered burnt offerings in the holy *place* to the God
of Israel.
8 "Therefore the [a]wrath of the
LORD fell upon Judah and Jerusalem, and He has [b]given them
up to trouble, to desolation, and
to [c]jeering, as you see with your
[d]eyes.
9 "For indeed, because of this
[a]our fathers have fallen by the
sword; and our sons, our daughters, and our wives *are* in captivity.
10 "Now *it is* in my heart to
make [a]a covenant with the LORD
God of Israel, that His fierce
wrath may turn away from us.
11 "My sons, do not be negligent now, for the LORD has
[a]chosen you to stand before
Him, to serve Him, and that you
should minister to Him and burn
incense."
12 Then these Lē′vītes arose:
[a]Mā′hath the son of A·mā′saī
and Jō′el the son of Az·a·rī′ah,
of the sons of the [b]Kō′hath·ītes;
of the sons of Me·rar′ī, Kish the
son of Ab′dī and Az·a·rī′ah the
son of Je·hal′le·lel; of the Ger′-
shon·ītes, Jō′ah the son of Zim′-
mah and Eden the son of Jō′ah;
13 of the sons of E·li·zā′phan,
Shim′rī and Je·ī′el; of the sons
of Ā′saph, Zech·a·rī′ah and Mat-
ta·nī′ah;
14 of the sons of Hē′man, Je·hī′el
and Shim′ē·ī; and of the sons of
Je·dū′thun, She·māi′ah and Uz′-
zi·el.
15 And they gathered their brethren, [a]sanctified[1] themselves, and
went according to the commandment of the king, at the words of
the LORD, [b]to cleanse the house of
the LORD.
16 Then the priests went into
the inner part of the house of the
LORD to cleanse *it*, and brought
out all the debris that they found
in the temple of the LORD to the
court of the house of the LORD.
And the Lē′vītes took *it* out and
carried *it* to the Brook [a]Kid′ron.
17 Now they began to [1]sanc-
tify on the first *day* of the first
month, and on the eighth day

27 [a]2 Chr. 21:20; 24:25

CHAPTER 29

1 [a]2 Kin. 18:1 [1]*Abi,* 2 Kin. 18:2
3 [a]2 Chr. 28:24; 29:7
5 [a]2 Chr. 29:15, 34; 35:6 [1]*consecrate*
6 [a]Ezek. 8:16 [1]Temple
7 [a]2 Chr. 28:24
8 [a]2 Chr. 24:18 [b]2 Chr. 28:5 [c]1 Kin. 9:8 [d]Deut. 28:32
9 [a]2 Chr. 28:5–8, 17
10 [a]2 Chr. 15:12; 23:16
11 [a]Num. 3:6; 8:14; 18:2, 6
12 [a]2 Chr. 31:13 [b]Num. 3:19, 20
15 [a]2 Chr. 29:5 [b]1 Chr. 23:28 [1]*consecrated*
16 [a]2 Chr. 15:16; 30:14
17 [1]*consecrate*

of the month they came to the vestibule of the LORD. So they sanctified the house of the LORD in eight days, and on the sixteenth day of the first month they finished.

18 Then they went in to King Hez·e·kī′ah and said, "We have cleansed all the house of the LORD, the altar of burnt offerings with all its articles, and the table of the showbread with all its articles.

19 "Moreover all the articles which King Ā′haz in his reign had [a]cast aside in his transgression we have prepared and [1]sanctified; and there they *are*, before the altar of the LORD."

20 Then King Hez·e·kī′ah rose early, gathered the rulers of the city, and went up to the house of the LORD.

21 And they brought seven bulls, seven rams, seven lambs, and seven male goats for a [a]sin offering for the kingdom, for the sanctuary, and for Judah. Then he commanded the priests, the sons of Aaron, to offer *them* on the altar of the LORD.

22 So they killed the bulls, and the priests received the blood and [a]sprinkled *it* on the altar. Likewise they killed the rams and sprinkled the blood on the altar. They also killed the lambs and sprinkled the blood on the altar.

23 Then they brought out the male goats *for* the sin offering before the king and the assembly, and they laid their [a]hands on them.

24 And the priests killed them; and they presented their blood on the altar as a sin offering [a]to make an atonement for all Israel, for the king commanded *that* the burnt offering and the sin offering *be made* for all Israel.

25 [a]And he stationed the Lē′vītes in the house of the LORD with cymbals, with stringed instruments, and with harps, [b]according to the commandment of David, of [c]Gad the king's seer, and of Nathan the prophet; [d]for thus *was* the commandment of the LORD by His prophets.

26 The Lē′vītes stood with the instruments [a]of David, and the priests with [b]the trumpets.

27 Then Hez·e·kī′ah commanded *them* to offer the burnt offering on the altar. And when the burnt offering began, [a]the song of the LORD *also* began, with the trumpets and with the instruments of David king of Israel.

28 So all the assembly worshiped, the singers sang, and the trumpeters sounded; all *this continued* until the burnt offering was finished.

29 And when they had finished offering, [a]the king and all who were present with him bowed and worshiped.

30 Moreover King Hez·e·kī′ah and the leaders commanded the Lē′vītes to sing praise to the LORD with the words of David and of Ā′saph the seer. So they sang praises with gladness, and they bowed their heads and worshiped.

31 Then Hez·e·kī′ah answered and said, "Now *that* you have consecrated yourselves to the LORD, come near, and bring sacrifices and [a]thank offerings into the house of the LORD." So the assembly brought in sacrifices and thank offerings, and as many as

19 [a]2 Chr. 28:24 [1]*consecrated*
21 [a]Lev. 4:3–14
22 [a]Lev. 8:14, 15, 19, 24
23 [a]Lev. 4:15, 24; 8:14
24 [a]Lev. 14:20
25 [a]1 Chr. 16:4; 25:6 [b]2 Chr. 8:14 [c]2 Sam. 24:11 [d]2 Chr. 30:12
26 [a]1 Chr. 23:5 [b]2 Chr. 5:12
27 [a]2 Chr. 23:18
29 [a]2 Chr. 20:18
31 [a]Lev. 7:12

were of a [b]willing heart *brought*
burnt offerings.
32 And the number of the burnt
offerings which the assembly
brought was seventy bulls, one
hundred rams, *and* two hundred
lambs; all these *were* for a burnt
offering to the LORD.
33 The consecrated things *were*
six hundred bulls and three
thousand sheep.
34 But the priests were too few,
so that they could not skin all
the burnt offerings; therefore
[a]their brethren the Lē′vītes
helped them until the work was
ended and until the *other* priests
had [1]sanctified themselves, [b]for
the Lē′vītes were [c]more diligent
in [d]sanctifying themselves than
the priests.
35 Also the burnt offerings
were in abundance, with [a]the fat
of the peace offerings and *with*
[b]the drink offerings for *every*
burnt offering. So the service of
the house of the LORD was set in
order.
36 Then Hez·e·kī′ah and all the
people rejoiced that God had
prepared the people, since the
events took place so suddenly.

30

And Hez·e·kī′ah sent to
all Israel and Judah, and
also wrote letters to Ē′phra·im
and Ma·nas′seh, that they should
come to the house of the LORD at
Jerusalem, to keep the Passover
to the LORD God of Israel.
2 For the king and his leaders
and all the assembly in Jerusalem had agreed to keep the
Passover in the second [a]month.
3 For they could not keep it [a]at
[1]the regular time, [b]because a sufficient number of priests had not
consecrated themselves, nor had

31 [b]Ex. 35:5, 22

34 [a]2 Chr. 35:11 [b]2 Chr. 30:3 [c]Ps. 7:10 [d]2 Chr. 29:5 [1]*consecrated*

35 [a]Lev. 3:15, 16 [b]Num. 15:5–10

CHAPTER 30

2 [a]Num. 9:10, 11

3 [a]Ex. 12:6, 18 [b]2 Chr. 29:17, 34 [1]The first month, Lev. 23:5; lit. *that time*

5 [1]*established a decree to*

6 [a]Esth. 8:14 [b][Jer. 4:1] [c]2 Kin. 15:19, 29 [d]2 Chr. 28:20

7 [a]Ezek. 20:18 [b]Is. 1:9 [c]2 Chr. 29:8

8 [a]Ex. 32:9 [b]2 Chr. 29:10 [1]Rebellious

9 [a]Ps. 106:46 [b][Ex. 34:6] [c][Is. 55:7]

the people gathered together at
Jerusalem.
4 And the matter pleased the
king and all the assembly.
5 So they [1]resolved to make
a proclamation throughout all
Israel, from Bē·er·shē′ba to Dan,
that they should come to keep
the Passover to the LORD God of
Israel at Jerusalem, since they
had not done *it* for a long *time*
in the *prescribed* manner.
6 Then the [a]runners went
throughout all Israel and Judah with the letters from the
king and his leaders, and spoke
according to the command of
the king: "Children of Israel,
[b]return to the LORD God of Abraham, Isaac, and Israel; then He
will return to the remnant of
you who have escaped from the
hand of [c]the kings of [d]Assyria.
7 "And do not be [a]like your
fathers and your brethren, who
trespassed against the LORD God
of their fathers, so that He [b]gave
them up to [c]desolation, as you
see.
8 "Now do not be [a]stiff-necked,[1]
as your fathers *were, but* yield
yourselves to the LORD; and enter His sanctuary, which He has
sanctified forever, and serve the
LORD your God, [b]that the fierceness of His wrath may turn away
from you.
9 "For if you return to the LORD,
your brethren and your children
will be treated with [a]compassion
by those who lead them captive,
so that they may come back to
this land; for the LORD your God
is [b]gracious and merciful, and
will not turn *His* face from you
if you [c]return to Him."
10 So the runners passed from
city to city through the country

of Ē′phra·im and Ma·nas′seh, as far as Zeb′ū·lun; but [a]they laughed at them and mocked them.

11 Nevertheless [a]some from Ash′er, Ma·nas′seh, and Zeb′ū·lun humbled themselves and came to Jerusalem.

12 Also [a]the hand of God was on Judah to give them singleness of heart to obey the command of the king and the leaders, [b]at the word of the LORD.

13 Now many people, a very great assembly, gathered at Jerusalem to keep the Feast of [a]Unleavened Bread in the second month.

14 They arose and took away the [a]altars that *were* in Jerusalem, and they took away all the incense altars and cast *them* into the Brook [b]Kid′ron.

15 Then they slaughtered the Passover *lambs* on the fourteenth *day* of the second month. The priests and the Lē′vītes [1]were [a]ashamed, and [2]sanctified themselves, and brought the burnt offerings to the house of the LORD.

16 They stood in their [a]place [1]according to their custom, according to the Law of Moses the man of God; the priests sprinkled the blood *received* from the hand of the Lē′vītes.

17 For *there were* many in the assembly who had not [1]sanctified themselves; [a]therefore the Lē′vītes had charge of the slaughter of the Passover *lambs* for everyone *who was* not clean, to sanctify *them* to the LORD.

18 For a multitude of the people, [a]many from Ē′phra·im, Ma·nas′seh, Is′sa·char, and Zeb′ū·lun, had not cleansed themselves, [b]yet they ate the Passover contrary to what was written. But Hez·e·kī′ah prayed for them, saying, "May the good LORD provide atonement for everyone

19 "*who* [a]prepares his heart to seek God, the LORD God of his fathers, though *he is* not *cleansed* according to the purification of the sanctuary."

20 And the LORD listened to Hez·e·kī′ah and healed the people.

21 So the children of Israel who were present at Jerusalem kept [a]the Feast of Unleavened Bread seven days with great gladness; and the Lē′vītes and the priests praised the LORD day by day, *singing* to the LORD, accompanied by loud instruments.

22 And Hez·e·kī′ah gave encouragement to all the Lē′vītes [a]who taught the good knowledge of the LORD; and they ate throughout the feast seven days, offering peace offerings and [b]making confession to the LORD God of their fathers.

23 Then the whole assembly agreed to keep *the feast* [a]another seven days, and they kept it *another* seven days with gladness.

24 For Hez·e·kī′ah king of Judah [a]gave to the assembly a thousand bulls and seven thousand sheep, and the leaders gave to the assembly a thousand bulls and ten thousand sheep; and a great number of priests [b]sanctified[1] themselves.

25 The whole assembly of Judah rejoiced, also the priests and Lē′vītes, all the assembly that came from Israel, the sojourners [a]who came from the land of Israel, and those who dwelt in Judah.

10 [a]2 Chr. 36:16
11 [a]2 Chr. 11:16; 30:18, 21
12 [a][Phil. 2:13] [b]2 Chr. 29:25
13 [a]Lev. 23:6
14 [a]2 Chr. 28:24 [b]2 Chr. 29:16
15 [a]2 Chr. 29:34 [1]*humbled themselves* [2]*set themselves apart*
16 [a]2 Chr. 35:10, 15 [1]Or *in their proper order*
17 [a]2 Chr. 29:34 [1]*consecrated*
18 [a]2 Chr. 30:1, 11, 25 [b][Num. 9:10]
19 [a]2 Chr. 19:3
21 [a]Ex. 12:15; 13:6
22 [a]2 Chr. 17:9; 35:3 [b]Ezra 10:11
23 [a]1 Kin. 8:65
24 [a]2 Chr. 35:7, 8 [b]2 Chr. 29:34 [1]*consecrated*
25 [a]2 Chr. 30:11, 18

26 So there was great joy in Jerusalem, for since the time of [a]Solomon the son of David, king of Israel, *there had* been nothing like this in Jerusalem.

27 Then the priests, the Lē′vītes, arose and [a]blessed the people, and their voice was heard; and their prayer came *up* to [b]His holy dwelling place, to heaven.

CHAPTER 31

31 Now when all this was finished, all Israel who were present went out to the cities of Judah and [a]broke the *sacred* pillars in pieces, cut down the wooden images, and threw down the [1]high places and the altars—from all Judah, Benjamin, Ē′phra·im, and Ma·nas′seh—until they had utterly destroyed them all. Then all the children of Israel returned to their own cities, every man to his possession.

2 And Hez·e·kī′ah appointed [a]the divisions of the priests and the Lē′vītes according to their divisions, each man according to his service, the priests and Lē′vītes [b]for burnt offerings and peace offerings, to serve, to give thanks, and to praise in the gates of the [1]camp of the LORD.

3 The king also *appointed* a [1]portion of his [a]possessions[2] for the burnt offerings: for the morning and evening burnt offerings, the burnt offerings for the Sabbaths and the New Moons and the set feasts, as *it is* written in the [b]Law of the LORD.

4 Moreover he commanded the people who dwelt in Jerusalem to contribute [a]support[1] for the priests and the Lē′vītes, that they might devote themselves to [b]the Law of the LORD.

5 As soon as the commandment was circulated, the children of Israel brought in abundance [a]the firstfruits of grain and wine, oil and honey, and of all the produce of the field; and they brought in abundantly the [b]tithe of everything.

6 And the children of Israel and Judah, who dwelt in the cities of Judah, brought the tithe of oxen and sheep; also the [a]tithe of holy things which were consecrated to the LORD their God they laid in heaps.

7 In the third month they began laying them in heaps, and they finished in the seventh month.

8 And when Hez·e·kī′ah and the leaders came and saw the heaps, they blessed the LORD and His people Israel.

9 Then Hez·e·kī′ah questioned the priests and the Lē′vītes concerning the heaps.

10 And Az·a·rī′ah the chief priest, from the [a]house of Zā′dok, answered him and said, [b]"Since *the people* began to bring the offerings into the house of the LORD, we have had enough to eat and have plenty left, for the LORD has blessed His people; and what is left *is* this great [c]abundance."

11 Now Hez·e·kī′ah commanded *them* to prepare [a]rooms[1] in the house of the LORD, and they prepared them.

12 Then they faithfully brought in the offerings, the tithes, and the dedicated things; [a]Con·o·nī′ah the Lē′vīte had charge of them, and Shim′ē·ī his brother *was* the next.

13 Je·hī′el, Az·a·zī′ah, Nā′hath, As′a·hel, Jer′i·moth, Joz′a·bad, E·lī′el, Is·ma·chī′ah, Mā′hath,

26 [a]2 Chr. 7:8–10
27 [a]Num. 6:23 [b]Deut. 26:15
1 [a]2 Kin. 18:4 [1]Places for pagan worship
2 [a]1 Chr. 23:6; 24:1 [b]1 Chr. 23:30, 31 [1]Temple
3 [a]2 Chr. 35:7 [b]Num. 28:1—29:40 [1]*share* [2]*property*
4 [a]Num. 18:8 [b]Mal. 2:7 [1]*the portion due*
5 [a]Ex. 22:29 [b][Lev. 27:30]
6 [a]Deut. 14:28
10 [a]1 Chr. 6:8, 9 [b][Mal. 3:10] [c]Ex. 36:5
11 [a]1 Kin. 6:5–8 [1]*storerooms*
12 [a]2 Chr. 35:9

and Be·nā'i·ah *were* overseers
under the hand of Con·o·nī'ah
and Shim'ē·ī his brother, at the
commandment of Hez·e·kī'ah
the king and Az·a·rī'ah the [a]ruler
of the house of God.
14 Kō're the son of Im'nah the
Lē'vīte, the keeper of the East
Gate, *was* over the [a]freewill offerings to God, to distribute the
offerings of the LORD and the
most holy things.
15 And under him *were* [a]Eden,
Min'ia·min, Jesh'ū·a, She·māi'ah,
Am·a·rī'ah, and Shec·a·nī'ah, *his*
faithful assistants in [b]the cities of the priests, to distribute
[c]allotments to their brethren by
divisions, to the great as well as
the small.
16 Besides those males from
three years old and up who were
written in the genealogy, they
distributed to everyone who entered the house of the LORD his
daily portion for the work of his
service, by his division,
17 and to the priests who were
written in the genealogy according to their father's house,
and to the Lē'vītes [a]from twenty
years old and up according to
their work, by their divisions,
18 and to all who were written in the genealogy—their little
ones and their wives, their sons
and daughters, the whole company of them—for in their faithfulness they [1]sanctified themselves in holiness.
19 Also for the sons of Aaron the
priests, *who were* in [a]the fields
of the common-lands of their
cities, in every single city, *there
were* men who were [b]designated
by name to distribute portions to
all the males among the priests
and to all who were listed by genealogies among the Lē'vītes.
20 Thus Hez·e·kī'ah did throughout all Judah, and he [a]did what
was good and right and true
before the LORD his God.
21 And in every work that he
began in the service of the house
of God, in the law and in the
commandment, to seek his God,
he did *it* with all his heart. So he
[a]prospered.

32 After [a]these deeds of
faithfulness, Sen·nach'-
e·rib king of Assyria came and
entered Judah; he encamped
against the fortified cities, thinking to win them over to himself.
2 And when Hez·e·kī'ah saw
that Sen·nach'e·rib had come,
and that his purpose was to
make war against Jerusalem,
3 he consulted with his leaders
and [1]commanders to stop the
water from the springs which
were outside the city; and they
helped him.
4 Thus many people gathered
together who stopped all the
[a]springs and the brook that ran
through the land, saying, "Why
should the [1]kings of Assyria
come and find much water?"
5 And [a]he strengthened himself, [b]built up all the wall that
was broken, raised *it* up to the
towers, and *built* another wall
outside; also he repaired [1]the
[c]Mil'lō *in* the City of David, and
made [2]weapons and shields in
abundance.
6 Then he set military captains over the people, gathered
them together to him in the open
square of the city gate, and [a]gave
them encouragement, saying,
7 [a]"Be strong and courageous;
[b]do not be afraid nor dismayed

13 [a]Jer. 20:1
14 [a]Deut. 23:23
15 [a]2 Chr. 29:12 [b]Josh. 21:1–3, 9 [c]1 Chr. 9:26
17 [a]1 Chr. 23:24, 27
18 [1]*consecrated*
19 [a]Lev. 25:34 [b]2 Chr. 31:12–15
20 [a]2 Kin. 20:3; 22:2
21 [a]Ps. 1:3

CHAPTER 32

1 [a]2 Kin. 18:13—19:37
3 [1]Lit. *mighty men*
4 [a]2 Kin. 20:20 [1]So with MT, Vg.; Arab., LXX, Syr. *king*
5 [a]Is. 22:9, 10 [b]2 Chr. 25:23 [c]2 Sam. 5:9 [1]Lit. *The Landfill* [2]*javelins*
6 [a]2 Chr. 30:22
7 [a][Deut. 31:6] [b]2 Chr. 20:15

before the king of Assyria, nor
before all the multitude that *is*
with him; for [c]*there are* more
with us than with him.
8 "With him *is* an [a]arm of flesh;
but [b]with us *is* the LORD our
God, to help us and to fight our
battles." And the people were
strengthened by the words of
Hez·e·kī′ah king of Judah.
9 [a]After this Sen·nach′e·rib
king of Assyria sent his servants to Jerusalem (but he and
all the forces with him *laid siege*
against Lā′chish), to Hez·e·kī′ah
king of Judah, and to all Judah
who *were* in Jerusalem, saying,
10 [a]"Thus says Sen·nach′e·rib
king of Assyria: 'In what do
you trust, that you remain under
siege in Jerusalem?
11 'Does not Hez·e·kī′ah persuade you to give yourselves
over to die by famine and by
thirst, saying, [a]"The LORD our
God will deliver us from the
hand of the king of Assyria"?
12 [a]'Has not the same Hez·e-
kī′ah taken away His high places
and His altars, and commanded
Judah and Jerusalem, saying,
"You shall worship before one
altar and burn incense on [b]it"?
13 'Do you not know what I and
my fathers have done to all the
peoples of *other* lands? [a]Were
the gods of the nations of those
lands in any way able to deliver
their lands out of my hand?
14 'Who *was there* among all
the gods of those nations that
my fathers utterly destroyed that
could deliver his people from
my hand, that your God should
be able to deliver you from my
[a]hand?
15 'Now therefore, [a]do not
let Hez·e·kī′ah deceive you or
persuade you like this, and do
not believe him; for no god of
any nation or kingdom was able
to deliver his people from my
hand or the hand of my fathers.
How much less will your God
deliver you from my hand?' "
16 Furthermore, his servants
spoke against the LORD God and
against His servant Hez·e·kī′ah.
17 He also wrote letters to revile the LORD God of Israel, and
to speak against Him, saying,
[a]"As the gods of the nations
of *other* lands have not delivered their people from my hand,
so the God of Hez·e·kī′ah will
not deliver His people from my
[b]hand."
18 [a]Then they called out with
a loud voice in [1]Hebrew to the
people of Jerusalem who *were*
on the wall, to frighten them and
trouble them, that they might
take the city.
19 And they spoke against the
God of Jerusalem, as against the
gods of the people of the earth—
[a]the work of men's hands.
20 [a]Now because of this King
Hez·e·kī′ah and [b]the prophet
Ī·sāi′ah, the son of Ā′moz, prayed
and cried out to heaven.
21 [a]Then the LORD sent an angel
who cut down every mighty man
of valor, leader, and captain in
the camp of the king of Assyria.
So he returned [b]shamefaced to
his own land. And when he had
gone into the temple of his god,
some of his own offspring struck
him down with the sword there.
22 Thus the LORD saved Hez·e-
kī′ah and the inhabitants of
Jerusalem from the hand of
Sen·nach′e·rib the king of Assyria, and from the hand of all

7 [c]2 Kin. 6:16
8 [a][Jer. 17:5] [b][Rom. 8:31]
9 [a]2 Kin. 18:17
10 [a]2 Kin. 18:19
11 [a]2 Kin. 18:30
12 [a]2 Kin. 18:22 [b]2 Chr. 31:1, 2
13 [a]2 Kin. 18:33–35
14 [a][Is. 10:5–12]
15 [a]2 Kin. 18:29
17 [a]2 Kin. 19:9 [b]2 Kin. 19:12
18 [a]2 Kin. 18:28 [1]Lit. *Judean*
19 [a][Ps. 96:5; 115:4–8]
20 [a]2 Kin. 19:15 [b]2 Kin. 19:2
21 [a]Zech. 14:3 [b]Ps. 44:7

others, and [1]guided them on
every side.
23 And many brought gifts to the
LORD at Jerusalem, and [a]presents[1]
to Hez·e·kī′ah king of Judah, so
that he was [b]exalted in the sight
of all nations thereafter.
24 [a]In those days Hez·e·kī′ah
was sick and near death, and
he prayed to the LORD; and He
spoke to him and gave him a
sign.
25 But Hez·e·kī′ah [a]did not
repay according to the favor
shown him, for [b]his heart was
lifted up; [c]therefore wrath was
looming over him and over Judah and Jerusalem.
26 [a]Then Hez·e·kī′ah humbled
himself for the pride of his heart,
he and the inhabitants of Jerusalem, so that the wrath of the
LORD did not come upon them
[b]in the days of Hez·e·kī′ah.
27 Hez·e·kī′ah had very great
riches and honor. And he made
himself treasuries for silver, for
gold, for precious stones, for
spices, for shields, and for all
kinds of desirable items;
28 storehouses for the harvest
of grain, wine, and oil; and stalls
for all kinds of livestock, and
[1]folds for flocks.
29 Moreover he provided cities
for himself, and possessions of
flocks and herds in abundance;
for [a]God had given him very
much property.
30 [a]This same Hez·e·kī′ah also
stopped the water outlet of Upper Gī′hon, and [1]brought the
water by tunnel to the west side
of the City of David. Hez·e·kī′ah
[b]prospered in all his works.
31 However, *regarding* the ambassadors of the princes of
Babylon, whom they [a]sent to him

22 [1]LXX *gave them rest;* Vg. *gave them treasures*

23 [a]2 Sam. 8:10 [b]2 Chr. 1:1 [1]Lit. *precious things*

24 [a]Is. 38:1–8

25 [a]Ps. 116:12 [b][Hab. 2:4] [c]2 Chr. 24:18

26 [a]Jer. 26:18, 19 [b]2 Kin. 20:19

28 [1]So with LXX, Vg.; Arab., Syr. omit *folds for flocks;* MT *flocks for sheepfolds*

29 [a]1 Chr. 29:12

30 [a]Is. 22:9–11 [b]2 Chr. 31:21 [1]Lit. *brought it straight to* (cf. 2 Kin. 20:20)

31 [a]Is. 39:1 [b][Deut. 8:2, 16]

32 [a]Is. 36—39 [b]2 Kin. 18—20

33 [a]2 Kin. 20:21 [b]Prov. 10:7 [1]Died and joined his ancestors

CHAPTER 33

1 [a]2 Kin. 21:1–9

2 [a]2 Chr. 28:3

3 [a]2 Kin. 18:4 [b]Deut. 16:21 [c]Deut. 17:3 [1]Places for pagan worship [2]The gods of the Assyrians

4 [a]2 Chr. 6:6; 7:16

5 [a]2 Chr. 4:9

6 [a][Lev. 18:21] [b]Deut. 18:11 [c]2 Kin. 21:6

to inquire about the wonder that
was *done* in the land, God withdrew from him, in order to [b]test
him, that He might know all *that*
was in his heart.
32 Now the rest of the acts of
Hez·e·kī′ah, and his goodness,
indeed they *are* written in [a]the
vision of Ī·sāi′ah the prophet,
the son of Ā′moz, *and* in the
[b]book of the kings of Judah and
Israel.
33 [a]So Hez·e·kī′ah [1]rested with
his fathers, and they buried him
in the upper tombs of the sons of
David; and all Judah and the inhabitants of Jerusalem [b]honored
him at his death. Then Ma·nas′-
seh his son reigned in his place.

33

Ma·nas′seh [a]*was* twelve
years old when he be-
came king, and he reigned fifty-
five years in Jerusalem.
2 But he did evil in the sight of
the LORD, according to the [a]abom-
inations of the nations whom the
LORD had cast out before the children of Israel.
3 For he rebuilt the [1]high places
which Hez·e·kī′ah his father had
[a]broken down; he raised up altars for the Bā′als, and [b]made
wooden images; and he worshiped [c]all [2]the host of heaven
and served them.
4 He also built altars in the
house of the LORD, of which the
LORD had said, [a]"In Jerusalem
shall My name be forever."
5 And he built altars for all the
host of heaven [a]in the two courts
of the house of the LORD.
6 [a]Also he caused his sons to
pass through the fire in the Valley
of the Son of Hin′nom; he practiced [b]soothsaying, used witchcraft and sorcery, and [c]consulted
mediums and spiritists. He did

much evil in the sight of the
LORD, to provoke Him to anger.
7 [a]He even set a carved image,
the idol which he had made, in
the [1]house of God, of which God
had said to David and to Solomon his son, [b]"In this house and
in Jerusalem, which I have chosen out of all the tribes of Israel,
I will put My name forever;
8 [a]"and I will not again remove
the foot of Israel from the land
which I have appointed for your
fathers—only if they are careful to do all that I have commanded them, according to the
whole law and the statutes and
the ordinances by the hand of
Moses."
9 So Ma·nas'seh seduced Judah and the inhabitants of Jerusalem to do more evil than
the nations whom the LORD had
destroyed before the children of
Israel.
10 And the LORD spoke to
Ma·nas'seh and his people, but
they would not [1]listen.
11 [a]Therefore the LORD brought
upon them the captains of the
army of the king of Assyria, who
took Ma·nas'seh with [1]hooks,
[b]bound him with [2]bronze *fetters*,
and carried him off to Babylon.
12 Now when he was in af-
fliction, he implored the LORD
his God, and [a]humbled himself
greatly before the God of his
fathers,
13 and prayed to Him; and He
[a]received his entreaty, heard his
supplication, and brought him
back to Jerusalem into his kingdom. Then Ma·nas'seh [b]knew
that the LORD *was* God.
14 After this he built a wall
outside the City of David on
the west side of [a]Gī'hon, in the
valley, as far as the entrance of
the Fish Gate; and *it* [b]enclosed
Ō'phel, and he raised it to a very
great height. Then he put military captains in all the fortified
cities of Judah.
15 He took away [a]the foreign
gods and the idol from the house
of the LORD, and all the altars
that he had built in the mount
of the house of the LORD and in
Jerusalem; and he cast *them* out
of the city.
16 He also repaired the altar of
the LORD, sacrificed peace offerings and [a]thank offerings on it,
and commanded Judah to serve
the LORD God of Israel.
17 [a]Nevertheless the people still
sacrificed on the [1]high places,
but only to the LORD their God.
18 Now the rest of the acts of
Ma·nas'seh, his prayer to his
God, and the words of [a]the seers
who spoke to him in the name
of the LORD God of Israel, indeed
they *are written* in the [1]book of
the kings of Israel.
19 Also his prayer and *how
God* received his entreaty, and
all his sin and trespass, and the
sites where he built [1]high places
and set up wooden images and
carved images, before he was
humbled, indeed they *are* written
among the sayings of [2]Hō'zā·ī.
20 [a]So Ma·nas'seh rested with
his fathers, and they buried him
in his own house. Then his son
Ā'mon reigned in his place.
21 [a]Ā'mon *was* twenty-two
years old when he became king,
and he reigned two years in
Jerusalem.
22 But he did evil in the sight of
the LORD, as his father Ma·nas'-
seh had done; for Ā'mon sacrificed to all the carved images

7 [a]2 Chr. 25:14 [b]Ps. 132:14 [1]Temple
8 [a]2 Sam. 7:10
10 [1]*obey*
11 [a]Deut. 28:36 [b]2 Chr. 36:6 [1]Nose hooks, 2 Kin. 19:28 [2]*chains*
12 [a]2 Chr. 7:14; 32:26
13 [a]Ezra 8:23 [b]Dan. 4:25
14 [a]1 Kin. 1:33 [b]2 Chr. 27:3
15 [a]2 Chr. 33:3, 5, 7
16 [a]Lev. 7:12
17 [a]2 Chr. 32:12 [1]Places for pagan worship
18 [a]1 Sam. 9:9 [1]Lit. *words*
19 [1]Places for pagan worship [2]LXX *the seers*
20 [a]2 Kin. 21:18
21 [a]2 Kin. 21:19–24

which his father Ma·nas′seh had
made, and served them.
23 And he did not humble himself before the LORD, [a]as his father Ma·nas′seh had humbled
himself; but Ā′mon trespassed
more and more.
24 [a]Then his servants conspired
against him, and [b]killed him in
his own house.
25 But the people of the land
executed all those who had conspired against King Ā′mon. Then
the people of the land made his
son Jō·sī′ah king in his place.
34 Jō·sī′ah [a]*was* eight years
old when he became king,
and he reigned thirty-one years
in Jerusalem.
2 And he did *what was* right
in the sight of the LORD, and
walked in the ways of his father
David; *he* did *not* turn aside to
the right hand or to the left.
3 For in the eighth year of his
reign, while he was still [a]young,
he began to [b]seek the God of his
father David; and in the twelfth
year he began [c]to purge Judah
and Jerusalem [d]of the [1]high
places, the wooden images, the
carved images, and the molded
images.
4 [a]They broke down the altars
of the Bā′als in his presence, and
the incense altars which *were*
above them he cut down; and
the wooden images, the carved
images, and the molded images
he broke in pieces, and made
dust of them [b]and scattered *it*
on the graves of those who had
sacrificed to them.
5 He also [a]burned the bones of
the priests on their [b]altars, and
cleansed Judah and Jerusalem.
6 And *so he did* in the cities
of Ma·nas′seh, Ē′phra·im, and
Sim′ē·on, as far as Naph′ta·lī
and all around, with [1]axes.
7 When he had broken down
the altars and the wooden images, had [a]beaten the carved images into powder, and cut down
all the incense altars throughout
all the land of Israel, he returned
to Jerusalem.
8 [a]In the eighteenth year of his
reign, when he had purged the
land and the [1]temple, he sent
[b]Shā′phan the son of Az·a·lī′ah,
Mā·a·sēi′ah the [c]governor of the
city, and Jō′ah the son of Jō′-
a·haz the recorder, to repair the
house of the LORD his God.
9 When they came to Hil·kī′ah
the high priest, they delivered
[a]the money that was brought
into the house of God, which
the Lē′vītes who kept the doors
had gathered from the hand of
Ma·nas′seh and Ē′phra·im, from
all the [b]remnant of Israel, from
all Judah and Benjamin, and
which they had brought back to
Jerusalem.
10 Then they put *it* in the hand
of the foremen who had the oversight of the house of the LORD;
and they gave it to the workmen
who worked in the house of the
LORD, to repair and restore the
house.
11 They gave *it* to the craftsmen
and builders to buy hewn stone
and timber for beams, and to
floor the houses which the kings
of Judah had destroyed.
12 And the men did the work
faithfully. Their overseers *were*
Jā′hath and Ō·ba·dī′ah the Lē′-
vītes, of the sons of Me·rar′ī, and
Zech·a·rī′ah and Me·shul′lam, of
the sons of the Kō′hath·ītes, to
supervise. *Others of* the Lē′vītes,

23 [a]2 Chr. 33:12, 19
24 [a]2 Chr. 24:25 [b]2 Chr. 25:27

CHAPTER 34

1 [a]2 Kin. 22:1, 2
3 [a]Eccl. 12:1 [b]2 Chr. 15:2 [c]1 Kin. 13:2 [d]2 Chr. 33:17–19, 22 [1]Places for pagan worship
4 [a]Lev. 26:30 [b]2 Kin. 23:6
5 [a]1 Kin. 13:2 [b]2 Kin. 23:20
6 [1]Lit. *swords*
7 [a]Deut. 9:21
8 [a]2 Kin. 22:3–20 [b]2 Kin. 25:22 [c]2 Chr. 18:25 [1]Lit. *house*
9 [a]2 Kin. 12:4 [b]2 Chr. 30:6

all of whom were skillful with
instruments of music,
13 *were* [a]over the burden bearers and *were* overseers of all
who did work in any kind of
service. [b]And *some* of the Lē′-
vītes *were* scribes, officers, and
gatekeepers.
14 Now when they brought out
the money that was brought
into the house of the LORD,
Hil·kī′ah the priest [a]found the
Book of the Law of the LORD
given by Moses.
15 Then Hil·kī′ah answered and
said to Shā′phan the scribe, "I
have found the Book of the Law
in the house of the LORD." And
Hil·kī′ah gave the [a]book to Shā′-
phan.
16 So Shā′phan carried the
book to the king, bringing the
king word, saying, "All that was
committed to your servants they
are doing.
17 "And they have [1]gathered the
money that was found in the
house of the LORD, and have
delivered it into the hand of the
overseers and the workmen."
18 Then Shā′phan the scribe
told the king, saying, "Hil·kī′ah
the priest has given me a book."
And Shā′phan read it before the
king.
19 Thus it happened, when the
king heard the words of the Law,
that he tore his clothes.
20 Then the king commanded
Hil·kī′ah, [a]A·hī′kam the son of
Shā′phan, [1]Ab′don the son of
Mī′cah, Shā′phan the scribe, and
A·sāi′ah a servant of the king,
saying,
21 "Go, inquire of the LORD for
me, and for those who are left in
Israel and Judah, concerning the
words of the book that is found;
for great *is* the wrath of the LORD
that is poured out on us, because
our fathers have not [a]kept the
word of the LORD, to do according to all that is written in this
book."
22 So Hil·kī′ah and those the
king *had appointed* went to
Hul′dah the prophetess, the wife
of Shal′lum the son of [1]Tok′hath,
the son of [2]Has′rah, keeper of
the wardrobe. (She dwelt in Jerusalem in the Second Quarter.)
And they spoke to her to that
effect.
23 Then she answered them,
"Thus says the LORD God of Israel, 'Tell the man who sent you
to Me,
24 "Thus says the LORD: 'Behold, I will [a]bring calamity on
this place and on its inhabitants,
all the curses that are written in
the [b]book which they have read
before the king of Judah,
25 'because they have forsaken
Me and burned incense to other
gods, that they might provoke
Me to anger with all the works
of their hands. Therefore My
wrath will be poured out on this
place, and not be quenched.' " '
26 "But as for the king of Judah,
who sent you to inquire of the
LORD, in this manner you shall
speak to him, 'Thus says the
LORD God of Israel: "*Concerning* the words which you have
heard—
27 "because your heart was tender, and you humbled yourself
before God when you heard His
words against this place and
against its inhabitants, and you
humbled yourself before Me,
and you tore your clothes and
wept before Me, I also have
heard *you*," says the [a]LORD.

13 [a]2 Chr. 8:10 [b]1 Chr. 23:4, 5
14 [a]2 Kin. 22:8
15 [a]Deut. 31:24, 26
17 [1]Lit. *poured out*
20 [a]Jer. 26:24 [1]*Achbor the son of Michaiah*, 2 Kin. 22:12
21 [a]2 Kin. 17:15–19
22 [1]*Tikvah*, 2 Kin. 22:14 [2]*Harhas*, 2 Kin. 22:14
24 [a]2 Chr. 36:14–20 [b]Deut. 28:15–68
27 [a]2 Chr. 12:7; 30:6; 33:12, 13

28 "Surely I will gather you to
your fathers, and you shall be
gathered to your grave in peace;
and your eyes shall not see all
the calamity which I will bring
on this place and its inhabitants." ' " So they brought back
word to the king.
29 [a]Then the king sent and gathered all the elders of Judah and
Jerusalem.
30 The king went up to the
house of the LORD, with all the
men of Judah and the inhabitants of Jerusalem—the priests
and the Lē′vītes, and all the
people, great and small. And
he [a]read in their hearing all the
words of the Book of the Covenant which had been found in
the house of the LORD.
31 Then the king [a]stood in [b]his
place and made a [c]covenant before the LORD, to follow the LORD,
and to keep His commandments
and His testimonies and His
statutes with all his heart and all
his soul, to perform the words of
the covenant that were written
in this book.
32 And he made all who were
present in Jerusalem and Benjamin take a stand. So the inhabitants of Jerusalem did according
to the covenant of God, the God
of their fathers.
33 Thus Jō·sī′ah removed all
the [a]abominations from all the
country that *belonged* to the
children of Israel, and made all
who were present in Israel [1]dili-
gently serve the LORD their God.
[b]All his days they did not depart
from following the LORD God of
their fathers.

35

Now [a]Jō·sī′ah kept a
Passover to the LORD in
Jerusalem, and they slaughtered
the Passover *lambs* on the [b]four-
teenth *day* of the first month.
2 And he set the priests in
their [a]duties and [b]encouraged
them for the service of the house
of the LORD.
3 Then he said to the Lē′vītes
[a]who taught all Israel, who were
holy to the LORD: [b]"Put the holy
ark [c]in the house which Solomon the son of David, king of
Israel, built. [d]*It shall* no longer
be a burden on *your* shoulders.
Now serve the LORD your God
and His people Israel.
4 "Prepare *yourselves* [a]accord-
ing to your fathers' [1]houses, according to your divisions, following the [b]written instruction
of David king of Israel and the
[c]written instruction of Solomon
his son.
5 "And [a]stand in the holy *place*
according to the divisions of the
fathers' houses of your brethren
the *lay* people, and *according to*
the division of the father's house
of the Lē′vītes.
6 "So slaughter the Passover
offerings, [a]consecrate yourselves,
and prepare *them* for your brethren, that *they* may do according to
the word of the LORD by the hand
of Moses."
7 Then Jō·sī′ah [a]gave the *lay*
people lambs and young goats
from the flock, all for Passover
offerings for all who were present, to the number of thirty
thousand, as well as three thousand cattle; these *were* from the
king's [b]possessions.
8 And his [a]leaders gave willingly to the people, to the priests,
and to the Lē′vītes. Hil·kī′ah,
Zech·a·rī′ah, and Je·hī′el, rulers
of the house of God, gave to the
priests for the Passover *offerings*

29 [a]2 Kin. 23:1–3
30 [a]Neh. 8:1–3
31 [a]2 Chr. 6:13 [b]2 Kin. 11:14; 23:3 [c]2 Chr. 23:16; 29:10
33 [a]1 Kin. 11:5 [b]Jer. 3:10 [1]Lit. *serve to serve*

CHAPTER 35

1 [a]2 Kin. 23:21, 22 [b]Ex. 12:6
2 [a]2 Chr. 23:18 [b]2 Chr. 29:5–15
3 [a]Deut. 33:10 [b]2 Chr. 34:14 [c]2 Chr. 5:7 [d]1 Chr. 23:26
4 [a]1 Chr. 9:10–13 [b]1 Chr. 23—26 [c]2 Chr. 8:14 [1]*households*
5 [a]Ps. 134:1
6 [a]2 Chr. 29:5, 15
7 [a]2 Chr. 30:24 [b]2 Chr. 31:3
8 [a]Num. 7:2

two thousand six hundred *from the flock,* and three hundred cattle.

9 Also [a]Con·a·nī′ah, his brothers She·māi′ah and Ne·than′el, and Hash·a·bī′ah and Je·ī′el and Joz′a·bad, chief of the Lē′vītes, gave to the Lē′vītes for Passover *offerings* five thousand *from the flock* and five hundred cattle.

10 So the service was prepared, and the priests [a]stood in their places, and the [b]Lē′vītes in their divisions, according to the king's command.

11 And they slaughtered the Passover *offerings;* and the priests [a]sprinkled *the blood* with their hands, while the Lē′vītes [b]skinned *the animals.*

12 Then they removed the burnt offerings that *they* might give them to the divisions of the fathers' houses of the *lay* people, to offer to the LORD, as *it is* written [a]in the Book of Moses. And so *they did* with the cattle.

13 Also they [a]roasted the Passover *offerings* with fire according to the ordinance; but the *other* holy *offerings* they [b]boiled in pots, in caldrons, and in pans, and divided *them* quickly among all the *lay* people.

14 Then afterward they prepared portions for themselves and for the priests, because the priests, the sons of Aaron, *were busy* in offering burnt offerings and fat until night; therefore the Lē′vītes prepared portions for themselves and for the priests, the sons of Aaron.

15 And the singers, the sons of Ā′saph, *were* in their places, according to the [a]command of David, Ā′saph, Hē′man, and Je·dū′thun the king's seer. Also the gatekeepers [b]were at each gate; they did not have to leave their position, because their brethren the Lē′vītes prepared portions for them.

16 So all the service of the LORD was prepared the same day, to keep the Passover and to offer burnt offerings on the altar of the LORD, according to the command of King Jō·sī′ah.

17 And the children of Israel who were present kept the Passover at that time, and the Feast of [a]Unleavened Bread for seven days.

18 [a]There had been no Passover kept in Israel like that since the days of Samuel the prophet; and none of the kings of Israel had kept such a Passover as Jō·sī′ah kept, with the priests and the Lē′vītes, all Judah and Israel who were present, and the inhabitants of Jerusalem.

19 In the eighteenth year of the reign of Jō·sī′ah this Passover was kept.

20 [a]After all this, when Jō·sī′ah had prepared the temple, Nē′cho king of Egypt came up to fight against [b]Car′chem·ish by the Eū·phrā′tēs; and Jō·sī′ah went out against him.

21 But he sent messengers to him, saying, "What have I to do with you, king of Judah? *I have* not *come* against you this day, but against the house with which I have war; for God commanded me to make haste. Refrain *from meddling with* God, who *is* with me, lest He destroy you."

22 Nevertheless Jō·sī′ah would not turn his face from him, but [a]disguised himself so that he might fight with him, and did

9 [a]2 Chr. 31:12
10 [a]Ezra 6:18 [b]2 Chr. 5:12; 7:6; 8:14, 15; 13:10; 29:25–34
11 [a]2 Chr. 29:22 [b]2 Chr. 29:34
12 [a]Ezra 6:18
13 [a]Ex. 12:8, 9 [b]1 Sam. 2:13–15
15 [a]1 Chr. 25:1–6 [b]1 Chr. 9:17, 18
17 [a]Ex. 12:15; 13:6
18 [a]2 Kin. 23:22, 23
20 [a]2 Kin. 23:29 [b]Jer. 46:2
22 [a]2 Chr. 18:29

not heed the words of Nē′cho
from the mouth of God. So he
came to fight in the Valley of
Me·gid′dō.
23 And the archers shot King
Jō·sī′ah; and the king said to his
servants, “Take me away, for I
am severely wounded.”
24 [a]His servants therefore took
him out of that chariot and put
him in the second chariot that
he had, and they brought him to
Jerusalem. So he died, and was
buried in *one of* the tombs of
his fathers. And [b]all Judah and
Jerusalem mourned for Jō·sī′ah.
25 Jer·e·mī′ah also [a]lamented
for [b]Jō·sī′ah. And to this day [c]all
the singing men and the sing-
ing women speak of Jō·sī′ah in
their lamentations. [d]They made
it a custom in Israel; and indeed
they *are* written in the Laments.
26 Now the rest of the acts of
Jō·sī′ah and his goodness, according to *what was* written in
the Law of the LORD,
27 and his deeds from first to
last, indeed they *are* written in
the book of the kings of Israel
and Judah.

36 Then [a]the people of the
land took Je·hō′a·haz
the son of Jō·sī′ah, and made
him king in his father’s place in
Jerusalem.
2 [1]Je·hō′a·haz *was* twenty-
three years old when he became king, and he reigned three
months in Jerusalem.
3 Now the king of Egypt deposed him at Jerusalem; and he
imposed on the land a tribute
of one hundred talents of silver
and a talent of gold.
4 Then the king of Egypt made
[1]*Je·hō′a·haz’s* brother E·lī′a·kim
king over Judah and Jerusalem,
and changed his name to Je·hoi′-
a·kim. And Nē′cho took [2]Je·hō′-
a·haz his brother and carried
him off to Egypt.
5 [a]Je·hoi′a·kim *was* twenty-five
years old when he became king,
and he reigned eleven years in
Jerusalem. And he did [b]evil in
the sight of the LORD his God.
6 [a]Ne·bū·chad·nez′zar king of
Babylon came up against him,
and bound him in [1]bronze *fetters* to [b]carry him off to Babylon.
7 [a]Ne·bū·chad·nez′zar also carried off *some* of the articles from
the house of the LORD to Babylon, and put them in his temple
at Babylon.
8 Now the rest of the acts of
Je·hoi′a·kim, the abominations
which he did, and what was
found against him, indeed they
are written in the book of the
kings of Israel and Judah. Then
[1]Je·hoi′a·chin his son reigned in
his place.
9 [a]Je·hoi′a·chin *was* [1]eight
years old when he became king,
and he reigned in Jerusalem
three months and ten days. And
he did evil in the sight of the
LORD.
10 At the turn of the year
[a]King Ne·bū·chad·nez′zar summoned *him* and took him to
Babylon, [b]with the costly articles from the house of the
LORD, and made [c]Zed·e·kī′ah,[1]
[2]*Je·hoi′a·kim’s* brother, king
over Judah and Jerusalem.
11 [a]Zed·e·kī′ah *was* twenty-one
years old when he became king,
and he reigned eleven years in
Jerusalem.
12 He did evil in the sight of the
LORD his God, *and* [a]did not humble himself before Jer·e·mī′ah

---

24 [a]2 Kin. 23:30 [b]Zech. 12:11
25 [a]Lam. 4:20 [b]Jer. 22:10, 11 [c]Matt. 9:23 [d]Jer. 22:20

CHAPTER 36

1 [a]2 Kin. 23:30–34
2 [1]MT *Joahaz*
4 [1]Lit. *his* [2]MT *Joahaz*
5 [a]2 Kin. 23:36, 37 [b][Jer. 22:13–19]
6 [a]2 Kin. 24:1 [b]Jer. 36:30 [1]*chains*
7 [a]Dan. 1:1, 2
8 [1]Or *Jeconiah*
9 [a]2 Kin. 24:8–17 [1]Heb. mss., LXX, Syr. *eighteen* and 2 Kin. 24:8
10 [a]2 Kin. 24:10–17 [b]Dan. 1:1, 2 [c]Jer. 37:1 [1]Or *Mattaniah* [2]Lit. *his brother,* 2 Kin. 24:17
11 [a]Jer. 52:1
12 [a]Jer. 21:3–7; 44:10

the prophet, *who spoke* from the mouth of the LORD.

13 And he also [a]rebelled against King Ne·bū·chad·nez′zar, who had made him swear *an oath* by God; but he [b]stiffened his neck and hardened his heart against turning to the LORD God of Israel.

14 Moreover all the leaders of the priests and the people transgressed more and more, *according* to all the abominations of the nations, and defiled the house of the LORD which He had consecrated in Jerusalem.

15 [a]And the LORD God of their fathers sent *warnings* to them by His messengers, rising up early and sending *them,* because He had compassion on His people and on His dwelling place.

16 But [a]they mocked the messengers of God, [b]despised His words, and [c]scoffed at His prophets, until the [d]wrath of the LORD arose against His people, till *there was* no remedy.

17 [a]Therefore He brought against them the king of the Chal·dē′ans, who [b]killed their young men with the sword in the house of their sanctuary, and had no compassion on young man or virgin, on the aged or the weak; He gave *them* all into his hand.

18 [a]And all the articles from the house of God, great and small, the treasures of the house of the LORD, and the treasures of the king and of his leaders, all *these* he took to Babylon.

19 [a]Then they burned the house of God, broke down the wall of Jerusalem, burned all its palaces with fire, and destroyed all its precious possessions.

20 And [a]those who escaped from the sword he carried away to Babylon, [b]where they became servants to him and his sons until the rule of the kingdom of Persia,

21 to fulfill the word of the LORD by the mouth of [a]Jer·e·mī′ah, until the land [b]had enjoyed her Sabbaths. As long as she lay desolate [c]she kept Sabbath, to fulfill seventy years.

22 [a]Now in the first year of Cyrus king of Persia, that the word of the LORD by the mouth of [b]Jer·e·mī′ah might be fulfilled, the LORD stirred up the spirit of [c]Cyrus king of Persia, so that he made a proclamation throughout all his kingdom, and also *put it* in writing, saying,

23 [a]Thus says Cyrus king of
Persia: All the kingdoms
of the earth the LORD God
of heaven has given me.
And He has commanded
me to build Him a [1]house
at Jerusalem which is in
Judah. Who *is* among you
of all His people? May the
LORD his God *be* with him,
and let him go up!

13 [a]Ezek. 17:15 [b]2 Kin. 17:14
15 [a]Jer. 7:13; 25:3, 4
16 [a]Jer. 5:12, 13 [b][Prov. 1:24–32] [c]Jer. 38:6 [d]Ps. 79:5
17 [a]2 Kin. 25:1 [b]Ps. 74:20
18 [a]2 Kin. 25:13–15
19 [a]2 Kin. 25:9
20 [a]2 Kin. 25:11 [b]Jer. 17:4; 27:7
21 [a]Jer. 25:9–12; 27:6–8; 29:10 [b]Lev. 26:34–43 [c]Lev. 25:4, 5
22 [a]Ezra 1:1–3 [b]Jer. 29:10 [c]Is. 44:28; 45:1
23 [a]Ezra 1:2, 3 [1]Temple

The Book of
EZRA

EZRA continues the Old Testament narrative of Second Chronicles by showing how God fulfills His promise to return His people to the Land of Promise after seventy years of exile. Israel's "second exodus," this one from Babylon, is less impressive than the return from Egypt because only a remnant chooses to leave Babylon.

Ezra relates the story of two returns from Babylon—the first led by Zerubbabel to rebuild the temple (1—6), and the second under the leadership of Ezra to rebuild the spiritual condition of the people (7—10). Sandwiched between these two accounts is a gap of nearly six decades, during which Esther lives and rules as queen in Persia.

Ezra is the Aramaic form of the Hebrew word *ezer*, "help," and perhaps means "Yahweh helps." Ezra and Nehemiah were originally bound together as one book because Chronicles, Ezra, and Nehemiah were viewed as one continuous history. The Septuagint, a Greek-language version of the Old Testament translated in the third century B.C., refers to Ezra–Nehemiah as *Esdras Deuteron*, or "Second Esdras." First Esdras is the name of the apocryphal book of Esdras. The Latin title is *Liber Primus Esdrae*, "First Book of Ezra." In the Latin Bible, Ezra is called First Ezra and Nehemiah is called Second Ezra.

CHAPTER 1

NOW in the first year of Cyrus
king of Persia, that the word
of the LORD [a]by the mouth of
Jer·e·mi′ah might be fulfilled,
the LORD stirred up the spirit of
Cyrus king of Persia, [b]so that he
made a proclamation throughout all his kingdom, and also
put it in writing, saying,

2 Thus says Cyrus king of
Persia: All the kingdoms
of the earth the LORD God
of heaven has given me.
And He has [a]commanded
me to build Him a [1]house
at Jerusalem which *is* in
Judah.
3 Who *is* among you of all
His people? May his God
be with him, and let him go
up to Jerusalem which *is* in
Judah, and build the house
of the LORD God of Israel
[a](He *is* God), which *is* in
Jerusalem.
4 And whoever is left in any
place where he dwells, let
the men of his place help
him with silver and gold,
with goods and livestock,
besides the freewill
offerings for the house of
God which *is* in Jerusalem.

5 Then the heads of the fathers' *houses* of Judah and Benjamin, and the priests and the
Lē′vītes, with all whose spirits
[a]God [1]had moved, arose to go up
and build the house of the LORD
which *is* in Jerusalem.
6 And all those who *were*
around them [1]encouraged them
with articles of silver and gold,
with goods and livestock, and

1 [a]2 Chr. 36:22, 23 [b]Ezra 5:13, 14
2 [a]Is. 44:28; 45:1, 13 [1]Temple
3 [a]Dan. 6:26
5 [a][Phil. 2:13] [1]*stirred up*
6 [1]Lit. *strengthened their hands*

with precious things, besides all
that was [a]willingly offered.
7 [a]King Cyrus also brought out
the articles of the house of the
LORD, [b]which Ne·bū·chad·nez′-
zar had taken from Jerusalem
and put in the [1]temple of his
gods;
8 and Cyrus king of Persia
brought them out by the hand of
Mith′re·dath the treasurer, and
counted them out to [a]Shesh·baz′-
zar the prince of Judah.
9 This *is* the number of them:
thirty gold platters, one thousand silver platters, twenty-nine
knives,
10 thirty gold basins, four hundred and ten silver basins of a
similar *kind, and* one thousand
other articles.
11 All the articles of gold and
silver *were* five thousand four
hundred. All *these* Shesh·baz′-
zar took with the captives who
were brought from Babylon to
Jerusalem.

2 Now [a]these *are* the people of
the province who came back
from the captivity, of those who
had been carried away, [b]whom
Ne·bū·chad·nez′zar the king of
Babylon had carried away to
Babylon, and who returned to
Jerusalem and Judah, everyone
to his *own* city.
2 *Those* who came with
Ze·rub′ba·bel *were* Jesh′ū·a, Nē-
he·mī′ah, [1]Se·rāi′ah, [2]Rē·el·āi′ah,
Mor′de·caī, Bil′shan, [3]Mis′par,
Big′vaī, [4]Rē′hum, *and* Bā′a·nah.
The number of the men of the
people of Israel:
3 the people of Pā′rosh, two
thousand one hundred and
seventy-two;
4 the people of Sheph·a·tī′ah,
three hundred and seventy-two;

6 [a]Ezra 2:68
7 [a]Ezra 5:14; 6:5 [b]2 Kin. 24:13 [1]Lit. *house*
8 [a]Ezra 5:14, 16

CHAPTER 2

1 [a]Neh. 7:6–73 [b]2 Kin. 24:14–16; 25:11
2 [1]*Azariah,* Neh. 7:7 [2]*Raamiah,* Neh. 7:7 [3]*Mispereth,* Neh. 7:7 [4]*Nehum,* Neh. 7:7
5 [a]Neh. 7:10
6 [a]Neh. 7:11
10 [1]*Binnui,* Neh. 7:15
18 [1]*Hariph,* Neh. 7:24
20 [1]*Gibeon,* Neh. 7:25
24 [1]*Beth Azmaveth,* Neh. 7:28
25 [1]*Kirjath Jearim,* Neh. 7:29

5 the people of Ā′rah, [a]seven
hundred and seventy-five;
6 the people of [a]Pā′hath-Mō′ab,
of the people of Jesh′ū·a *and*
Jō′ab, two thousand eight hundred and twelve;
7 the people of Ē′lam, one
thousand two hundred and fifty-
four;
8 the people of Zat′tū, nine
hundred and forty-five;
9 the people of Zac′caī, seven
hundred and sixty;
10 the people of [1]Bā′nī, six hundred and forty-two;
11 the people of Bē′baī, six hundred and twenty-three;
12 the people of Az′gad, one
thousand two hundred and
twenty-two;
13 the people of Ad·o·nī′kam,
six hundred and sixty-six;
14 the people of Big′vaī, two
thousand and fifty-six;
15 the people of Ā′din, four
hundred and fifty-four;
16 the people of Ā′ter of
Hez·e·kī′ah, ninety-eight;
17 the people of Bē′zaī, three
hundred and twenty-three;
18 the people of [1]Jō′rah, one
hundred and twelve;
19 the people of Hā′shum, two
hundred and twenty-three;
20 the people of [1]Gib′bar, ninety-
five;
21 the people of Bethlehem, one
hundred and twenty-three;
22 the men of Ne·toph′ah, fifty-
six;
23 the men of An′a·thoth, one
hundred and twenty-eight;
24 the people of [1]Az′ma·veth,
forty-two;
25 the people of [1]Kir′jath Ar′im,
Chē·phī′rah, and Be·er′oth, seven
hundred and forty-three;
26 the people of Rā′mah and

Gē′ba, six hundred and twenty-
one;
27 the men of Mich′mas, one
hundred and twenty-two;
28 the men of Beth′el and Aī,
two hundred and twenty-three;
29 the people of Nē′bō, fifty-
two;
30 the people of Mag′bish, one
hundred and fifty-six;
31 the people of the other
[a]Ē′lam, one thousand two hundred and fifty-four;
32 the people of Hā′rim, three
hundred and twenty;
33 the people of Lod, Hā′did,
and Ō′nō, seven hundred and
twenty-five;
34 the people of Jericho, three
hundred and forty-five;
35 the people of Se·nā′ah, three
thousand six hundred and
thirty.
36 The priests: the sons of [a]Je-
daī′ah, of the house of Jesh′-
ū·a, nine hundred and seventy-
three;
37 the sons of [a]Im′mer, one
thousand and fifty-two;
38 the sons of [a]Pash′hur, one
thousand two hundred and
forty-seven;
39 the sons of [a]Hā′rim, one
thousand and seventeen.
40 The Lē′vītes: the sons of
Jesh′ū·a and Kad′mi·el, of the
sons of [1]Hod·a·vī′ah, seventy-
four.
41 The singers: the sons of
Ā′saph, one hundred and twenty-
eight.
42 The sons of the gatekeepers:
the sons of Shal′lum, the sons
of Ā′ter, the sons of Tal′mon,
the sons of Ak′kub, the sons of
Ha·tī′ta, and the sons of Shō′-
baī, one hundred and thirty-nine
in all.

43 [a]The Neth′i·nim: the sons of
Zī′ha, the sons of Ha·sū′pha, the
sons of Tab·bā′oth,
44 the sons of Kē′ros, the sons
of [1]Sī′a·ha, the sons of Pā′don,
45 the sons of Le·bā′nah, the
sons of Hag′a·bah, the sons of
Ak′kub,
46 the sons of Hā′gab, the sons
of Shal′maī, the sons of Hā′nan,
47 the sons of Gid′del, the sons
of Gā′har, the sons of Rē·āi′ah,
48 the sons of Rē′zin, the sons
of Ne·kō′da, the sons of Gaz′-
zam,
49 the sons of Uz′za, the sons of
Pa·sē′ah, the sons of Bē′saī,
50 the sons of As′nah, the
sons of Me·ū′nim, the sons of
[1]Ne·phū′sim,
51 the sons of Bak′buk, the sons
of Ha·kū′pha, the sons of Har′-
hur,
52 the sons of [1]Baz′luth, the
sons of Me·hī′da, the sons of
Har′sha,
53 the sons of Bar′kos, the sons
of Sis′e·ra, the sons of Tam′ah,
54 the sons of Ne·zī′ah, and the
sons of Ha·tī′pha.
55 The sons of [a]Solomon's servants: the sons of Sō′taī, the
sons of [b]Sō′phe·reth, the sons of
[1]Pe·rū′da,
56 the sons of Jā′a·la, the sons
of Dar′kon, the sons of Gid′del,
57 the sons of Sheph·a·tī′ah, the
sons of Hat′til, the sons of Poch′-
e·reth of Ze·bā′im, and the sons
of [1]Ā′mī.
58 All the [a]Neth′i·nim and the
children of [b]Solomon's servants
were three hundred and ninety-
two.
59 And these *were* the ones
who came up from Tel Mē′lah,
Tel Har′sha, Chē′rub, [1]Ad′dan,
and Im′mer; but they could not

31 [a]Ezra 2:7
36 [a]1 Chr. 24:7–18
37 [a]1 Chr. 24:14
38 [a]1 Chr. 9:12
39 [a]1 Chr. 24:8
40 [1]*Judah*, Ezra 3:9, or *Hodevah*, Neh. 7:43
43 [a]1 Chr. 9:2
44 [1]*Sia*, Neh. 7:47
50 [1]*Nephishesim*, Neh. 7:52
52 [1]*Bazlith*, Neh. 7:54
55 [a]1 Kin. 9:21 [b]Neh. 7:57–60 [1]*Perida*, Neh. 7:57
57 [1]*Amon*, Neh. 7:59
58 [a]1 Chr. 9:2 [b]1 Kin. 9:21
59 [1]Or *Addon*, Neh. 7:61

[2]identify their father's house or
their [3]genealogy, whether they
were of Israel:
60 the sons of De·laī'ah, the
sons of Tō·bī'ah, and the sons of
Ne·kō'da, six hundred and fifty-
two;
61 and of the sons of the priests:
the sons of [a]Ha·baī'ah, the sons
of [1]Koz, and the sons of [b]Bar·zil'-
laī, who took a wife of the daughters of Bar·zil'laī the Gil'ē·ad·īte,
and was called by their name.
62 These sought their listing
among those who were registered by genealogy, but they
were not found; [a]therefore they
were excluded from the priesthood as defiled.
63 And the [1]governor said to
them that they [a]should not eat of
the most holy things till a priest
could consult with the [b]Ū'rim
and Thum'mim.
64 [a]The whole assembly together *was* forty-two thousand
three hundred *and* sixty,
65 besides their male and female servants, of whom *there
were* seven thousand three
hundred and thirty-seven; and
they had two hundred men and
women singers.
66 Their horses *were* seven hundred and thirty-six, their mules
two hundred and forty-five,
67 their camels four hundred
and thirty-five, and *their* donkeys six thousand seven hundred and twenty.
68 [a]*Some* of the heads of the
fathers' *houses*, when they came
to the house of the LORD which *is*
in Jerusalem, offered freely for
the house of God, to erect it in
its place:
69 According to their ability,
they gave to the [a]treasury for
the work sixty-one thousand
gold drachmas, five thousand
minas of silver, and one hundred
priestly garments.
70 [a]So the priests and the Lē'-
vītes, *some* of the people, the
singers, the gatekeepers, and
the Neth'i·nim, dwelt in their cities, and all Israel in their cities.

3

3 And when the [a]seventh
month had come, and the
children of Israel *were* in the cities, the people gathered together
as one man to Jerusalem.
2 Then [1]Jesh'ū·a the son of
[a]Jō'za·dak[2] and his brethren the
priests, [b]and Ze·rub'ba·bel the
son of [c]She·al'ti·el and his brethren, arose and built the altar of
the God of Israel, to offer burnt
offerings on it, as *it is* [d]written
in the Law of Moses the man of
God.
3 Though fear *had come* upon
them because of the people of
those countries, they set the altar on its [1]bases; and they offered [a]burnt offerings on it to
the LORD, *both* the morning and
evening burnt offerings.
4 [a]They also kept the Feast of
Tabernacles, [b]as *it is* written,
and [c]*offered* the daily burnt offerings in the number required
by ordinance for each day.
5 Afterwards *they offered* the
[a]regular burnt offering, and
those for New Moons and for
all the appointed feasts of the
LORD that were consecrated, and
those of everyone who willingly
offered a freewill offering to the
LORD.
6 From the first day of the
seventh month they began to offer burnt offerings to the LORD,
although the foundation of the

59 [2]Lit. *tell* [3]Lit. *seed*
61 [a]Neh. 7:63 [b]2 Sam. 17:27 [1]Or *Hakkoz*
62 [a]Num. 3:10
63 [a]Lev. 22:2, 10, 15, 16 [b]Ex. 28:30 [1]Heb. *Tirshatha*
64 [a]Neh. 7:66
68 [a]Neh. 7:70
69 [a]Ezra 8:25–35
70 [a]Neh. 7:73

CHAPTER 3

1 [a]Neh. 7:73; 8:1, 2
2 [a]Neh. 12:1, 8 [b]Ezra 2:2; 4:2, 3; 5:2 [c]1 Chr. 3:17 [d]Deut. 12:5, 6 [1]Or *Joshua* [2]*Jehozadak*, 1 Chr. 6:14
3 [a]Num. 28:3 [1]*foundations*
4 [a]Neh. 8:14–18 [b]Ex. 23:16 [c]Num. 29:12, 13
5 [a]Ex. 29:38

temple of the LORD had not been
laid.
7 They also gave money to the
masons and the carpenters, and
[a]food, drink, and oil to the people of Sī′don and Tȳre to bring
cedar logs from Lebanon to the
sea, to [b]Jop′pa, [c]according to the
permission which they had from
Cyrus king of Persia.
8 Now in the second month of
the second year of their coming to the house of God at Jerusalem, [a]Ze·rub′ba·bel the son
of She·al′ti·el, Jesh′ū·a the son
of [1]Jō′za·dak, and the rest of
their brethren the priests and
the Lē′vītes, and all those who
had come out of the captivity to
Jerusalem, began *work* [b]and appointed the Lē′vītes from twenty
years old and above to oversee
the work of the house of the
LORD.
9 Then Jesh′ū·a *with* his sons
and brothers, Kad′mi·el *with* his
sons, and the sons of [1]Judah,
arose as one to oversee those
working on the house of God:
the sons of Hen′a·dad *with* their
sons and their brethren the Lē′-
vītes.
10 When the builders laid the
foundation of the temple of the
LORD, [a]the[1] priests stood in their
apparel with trumpets, and the
Lē′vītes, the sons of Ā′saph, with
cymbals, to praise the LORD, according to the [b]ordinance[2] of
David king of Israel.
11 [a]And they sang responsively,
praising and giving thanks to
the LORD:

[b]"For *He is* good,
[c]For His mercy *endures*
forever toward Israel."

Then all the people shouted with
a great shout, when they praised
the LORD, because the foundation of the house of the LORD
was laid.
12 But many of the priests and
Lē′vītes and [a]heads of the fathers' *houses,* old men who had
seen the first temple, wept with a
loud voice when the foundation
of this temple was laid before
their eyes. Yet many shouted
aloud for joy,
13 so that the people could not
discern the noise of the shout of
joy from the noise of the weeping of the people, for the people
shouted with a loud shout, and
the sound was heard afar off.

4

Now when [a]the [1]adversar-
ies of Judah and Benjamin
heard that the descendants of
the captivity were building the
temple of the LORD God of Israel,
2 they came to Ze·rub′ba·bel
and the heads of the fathers'
houses, and said to them, "Let us
build with you, for we seek your
God as you *do;* and we have sacrificed to Him [a]since the days of
Ē·sar·had′don king of Assyria,
who brought us here."
3 But Ze·rub′ba·bel and Jesh′-
ū·a and the rest of the heads of
the fathers' *houses* of Israel said
to them, [a]"You may do nothing
with us to build a [1]house for our
God; but we alone will build to
the LORD God of Israel, as [b]King
Cyrus the king of Persia has
commanded us."
4 Then [a]the people of the land
tried to discourage the people
of Judah. They troubled them in
building,
5 and hired counselors against
them to frustrate their purpose

7 [a]Acts 12:20 [b]2 Chr. 2:16 [c]Ezra 1:2; 6:3
8 [a]Ezra 3:2; 4:3 [b]1 Chr. 23:4, 24 [1]*Jehozadak,* 1 Chr. 6:14
9 [1]*Hodaviah,* Ezra 2:40
10 [a]1 Chr. 16:5, 6 [b]1 Chr. 6:31; 16:4; 25:1 [1]So with LXX, Syr., Vg.; MT *they stationed the priests* [2]Lit. *hands*
11 [a]Neh. 12:24 [b]Ps. 136:1 [c]Jer. 33:11
12 [a]Ezra 2:68

CHAPTER 4

1 [a]Ezra 4:7–9 [1]*enemies*
2 [a]2 Kin. 17:24; 19:37
3 [a]Neh. 2:20 [b]Ezra 1:1–4 [1]Temple
4 [a]Ezra 3:3

all the days of Cyrus king of
Persia, even until the reign of
[a]Da·rī′us king of Persia.
6 In the reign of A·has·ū·ē′rus,
in the beginning of his reign,
they wrote an accusation against
the inhabitants of Judah and
Jerusalem.
7 In the days of [a]Ar·ta·xerx′ēs
also, [1]Bish′lam, Mith′re·dath,
Tā′bel, and the rest of their companions
wrote to Ar·ta·xerx′ēs
king of Persia; and the letter *was*
written in [b]Ar·a·mā′ic script, and
translated into the Ar·a·mā′ic
language.
8 [1]Rē′hum the commander and
Shim′shaī the scribe wrote a letter
against Jerusalem to King
Ar·ta·xerx′ēs in this fashion:

9 [1]From Rē′hum the
commander, Shim′shaī
the scribe, and the rest
of their companions—
representatives of
[a]the Dī′na·ītes, the
A·phar′sath·chites, the
Tar′pel·ītes, the people
of Persia and Ē′rech and
Babylon and [2]Shū′shan, the
De·hā′vītes, the Ē′lam·ītes,
10 [a]and the rest of the nations
whom the great and noble
Os·nap′per took captive
and settled in the cities of
Samaria and the remainder
beyond [1]the River—[b]and[2] so
forth.

11 (This *is* a copy of the letter
that they sent him)

To King Ar·ta·xerx′ēs from
your servants, the men *of
the region* beyond the River,
[1]and so forth:

5 [a]Ezra 5:5; 6:1

7 [a]Ezra 7:1, 7, 21 [b]2 Kin. 18:26 [1]Or *in peace*

8 [1]The original language of Ezra 4:8 through 6:18 is Aramaic.

9 [a]2 Kin. 17:30, 31 [1]Lit. *Then* [2]Or *Susa*

10 [a]2 Kin. 17:24 [b]Ezra 4:11, 17; 7:12 [1]The Euphrates [2]Lit. *and now*

11 [1]Lit. *and now*

12 [a]2 Chr. 36:13 [b]Ezra 5:3, 9

13 [a]Ezra 4:20; 7:24

12 Let it be known to the king
that the Jews who came
up from you have come to
us at Jerusalem, and are
building the [a]rebellious and
evil city, and are finishing
its [b]walls and repairing the
foundations.
13 Let it now be known to the
king that, if this city is built
and the walls completed,
they will not pay [a]tax,
tribute, or custom, and
the king's treasury will be
diminished.
14 Now because we receive
support from the palace,
it was not proper for us to
see the king's dishonor;
therefore we have sent and
informed the king,
15 that search may be made
in the book of the records
of your fathers. And you
will find in the book of
the records and know that
this city *is* a rebellious
city, harmful to kings and
provinces, and that they
have incited sedition within
the city in former times, for
which cause this city was
destroyed.
16 We inform the king that if
this city is rebuilt and its
walls are completed, the
result will be that you will
have no dominion beyond
the River.

17 The king sent an answer:

To Rē′hum the commander,
to Shim′shaī the scribe, *to*
the rest of their companions
who dwell in Samaria, and
to the remainder beyond the
River:

Peace, [1]and so forth.
18 The letter which you sent
to us has been clearly read
before me.
19 And [1]I gave the command,
and a search has been
made, and it was found that
this city in former times has
revolted against kings, and
rebellion and sedition have
been fostered in it.
20 There have also been
mighty kings over
Jerusalem, who have [a]ruled
over all *the region* [b]beyond
the River; and tax, tribute,
and custom were paid to
them.
21 Now [1]give the command to
make these men cease, that
this city may not be built
until the command is given
by me.
22 Take heed now that you
do not fail to do this. Why
should damage increase to
the hurt of the kings?

23 Now when the copy of King
Ar·ta·xerx′ēs′ letter *was* read
before Rē′hum, Shim′shaī the
scribe, and their companions,
they went up in haste to Jerusalem against the Jews, and by
force of arms made them cease.
24 Thus the work of the house
of God which *is* at Jerusalem
ceased, and it was discontin-
ued until the second year of the
reign of Da·rī′us king of Persia.

5

Then the prophet [a]Hag′gaī
and [b]Zech·a·rī′ah the son of
Id′dō, prophets, prophesied to
the Jews who *were* in Judah
and Jerusalem, in the name of
the God of Israel, *who was* over
them.
2 So [a]Ze·rub′ba·bel the son of
She·al′ti·el and Jesh′ū·a the son
of [1]Jō′za·dak rose up and began
to build the house of God which
is in Jerusalem; and [b]the prophets of God *were* with them, helping them.
3 At the same time [a]Tat′te·naī
the governor of *the region* beyond [1]the River and Shē′thar-
Boz′nai and their companions
came to them and spoke thus to
them: [b]"Who has commanded
you to build this [2]temple and finish this wall?"
4 [a]Then, accordingly, we told
them the names of the men who
were constructing this building.
5 But [a]the eye of their God was
upon the elders of the Jews, so
that they could not make them
cease till a report could go to
Da·rī′us. Then a [b]written answer
was returned concerning this
matter.
6 This is a copy of the letter
that Tat′te·naī sent:

The governor of *the region*
beyond the River, and
Shē′thar-Boz′nai, [a]and his
companions, the Persians
who *were in the region*
beyond the River, to Da·rī′us
the king.

7 (They sent a letter to him, in
which was written thus)

To Da·rī′us the king:

All peace.

8 Let it be known to the
king that we went into the
province of Judea, to the
[1]temple of the great God,
which is being built with

17 [1]Lit. *and now*
19 [1]Lit. *by me a decree has been put forth*
20 [a]Ps. 72:8 [b]Gen. 15:18
21 [1]*put forth a decree*

CHAPTER 5

1 [a]Hag. 1:1 [b]Zech. 1:1
2 [a]Ezra 3:2 [b]Hag. 2:4 [1]*Jehozadak*, 1 Chr. 6:14
3 [a]Ezra 5:6; 6:6 [b]Ezra 1:3; 5:9 [1]The Euphrates [2]Lit. *house*
4 [a]Ezra 5:10
5 [a]Ps. 33:18 [b]Ezra 6:6
6 [a]Ezra 4:7–10
8 [1]Lit. *house*

[2]heavy stones, and timber is
being laid in the walls; and
this work goes on diligently
and prospers in their hands.
9 Then we asked those elders,
and spoke thus to them:
[a]"Who commanded you to
build this temple and to
finish these walls?"
10 We also asked them their
names to inform you, that
we might write the names
of the men who *were* chief
among them.
11 And thus they returned us
an answer, saying: "We are
the servants of the God of
heaven and earth, and we
are rebuilding the [1]temple
that was built many years
ago, which a great king of
Israel built [a]and completed.
12 "But [a]because our fathers
provoked the God of
heaven to wrath, He gave
them into the hand of
[b]Ne·bū·chad·nez′zar king
of Babylon, the Chal·dē′an,
who destroyed this temple
and [c]carried the people
away to Babylon.
13 "However, in the first year
of [a]Cyrus king of Babylon,
King Cyrus issued a decree
to build this [1]house of God.
14 "Also, [a]the gold and silver
articles of the house of God,
which Ne·bū·chad·nez′zar
had taken from the temple
that *was* in Jerusalem and
carried into the temple of
Babylon—those King Cyrus
took from the temple of
Babylon, and they were
given to [b]one named
Shesh·baz′zar, whom he had
made governor.
15 "And he said to him, 'Take
these articles; go, carry
them to the temple *site* that
is in Jerusalem, and let the
house of God be rebuilt on
its former site.'
16 "Then the same
Shesh·baz′zar came *and*
[a]laid the foundation of the
house of God which *is* in
Jerusalem; but from that
time even until now it has
been under construction,
and [b]it is not finished."
17 Now therefore, if *it seems*
good to the king, [a]let a
search be made in the king's
treasure house, which *is*
there in Babylon, whether
it is *so* that a decree was
issued by King Cyrus to
build this house of God
at Jerusalem, and let the
king send us his pleasure
concerning this *matter*.

6 Then King Da·rī′us issued
a decree, [a]and a search was
made in the [1]archives, where the
treasures were stored in Babylon.
2 And at [1]Ach′me·tha, in the
palace that *is* in the province of
[a]Media, a scroll was found, and
in it a record *was* written thus:

3 In the first year of King
Cyrus, King Cyrus issued
a [a]decree *concerning* the
house of God at Jerusalem:
"Let the house be rebuilt,
the place where they offered
sacrifices; and let the
foundations of it be firmly
laid, its height sixty cubits
and its width sixty cubits,
4 [a]*with* three rows of heavy
stones and one row of new
timber. Let the [b]expenses

8 [2]Lit. *stones of rolling*, stones too heavy to be carried
9 [a]Ezra 5:3, 4
11 [a]1 Kin. 6:1, 38 [1]Lit. *house*
12 [a]2 Chr. 34:25; 36:16, 17 [b]2 Kin. 24:2; 25:8–11 [c]Jer. 13:19
13 [a]Ezra 1:1 [1]Temple
14 [a]Ezra 1:7, 8; 6:5 [b]Hag. 1:14; 2:2, 21
16 [a]Ezra 3:8–10 [b]Ezra 6:15
17 [a]Ezra 6:1, 2

CHAPTER 6

1 [a]Ezra 5:17 [1]Lit. *house of the scrolls*
2 [a]2 Kin. 17:6 [1]Probably *Ecbatana*, the ancient capital of Media
3 [a]Ezra 1:1; 5:13
4 [a]1 Kin. 6:36 [b]Ezra 3:7

be paid from the king's
treasury.
5 Also let [a]the gold and silver
articles of the house of God,
which Ne·bū·chad·nez′zar
took from the temple which
is in Jerusalem and brought
to Babylon, be restored and
taken back to the temple
which *is* in Jerusalem, *each*
to its place; and deposit
them in the house of God"—
6 [a]Now *therefore,* Tat′te·naī,
governor of *the region*
beyond the River, and
Shē′thar-Boz′nai, and your
companions the Persians
who *are* beyond the River,
keep yourselves far from
there.
7 Let the work of this house
of God alone; let the
governor of the Jews and
the elders of the Jews build
this house of God on its site.
8 Moreover I issue a decree
as to what you shall do for
the elders of these Jews, for
the building of this [1]house
of God: Let the cost be paid
at the king's expense from
taxes *on the region* beyond
the River; this is to be
given immediately to these
men, so that they are not
hindered.
9 And whatever they
need—young bulls, rams,
and lambs for the burnt
offerings of the God of
heaven, wheat, salt, wine,
and oil, according to the
request of the priests who
are in Jerusalem—let it
be given them day by day
without fail,
10 [a]that they may offer
sacrifices of sweet aroma to
the God of heaven, and pray
for the life of the king and
his sons.
11 Also I issue a decree that
whoever alters this edict, let
a timber be pulled from his
house and erected, and let
him be hanged on it; [a]and
let his house be made a
refuse heap because of this.
12 And may the God who
causes His [a]name to dwell
there destroy any king or
people who put their hand
to alter it, or to destroy this
[1]house of God which is in
Jerusalem. I Da·rī′us issue
a decree; let it be done
diligently.

13 Then Tat′te·naī, governor of
the region beyond the River,
Shē′thar-Boz′nai, and their companions diligently did according
to what King Da·rī′us had sent.
14 [a]So the elders of the Jews
built, and they prospered through
the prophesying of Hag′gaī the
prophet and Zech·a·rī′ah the son
of Id′dō. And they built and finished *it,* according to the commandment of the God of Israel,
and according to the [1]com-
mand of [b]Cyrus, [c]Da·rī′us, and
[d]Ar·ta·xerx′ēs king of Persia.
15 Now the temple was finished on the third day of the
month of Ā′dar, which was in
the sixth year of the reign of
King Da·rī′us.
16 Then the children of Israel,
the priests and the Lē′vītes and
the rest of the descendants of
the captivity, celebrated [a]the
dedication of this [1]house of God
with joy.
17 And they [a]offered sacrifices
at the dedication of this house

5 [a]Ezra 1:7, 8; 5:14
6 [a]Ezra 5:3, 6
8 [1]Temple
10 [a]Ezra 7:23
11 [a]Dan. 2:5; 3:29
12 [a]1 Kin. 9:3 [1]Temple
14 [a]Ezra 5:1, 2 [b]Ezra 1:1; 5:13; 6:3 [c]Ezra 4:24; 6:12 [d]Ezra 7:1, 11 [1]*decree*
16 [a]1 Kin. 8:63 [1]Temple
17 [a]Ezra 8:35

of God, one hundred bulls, two
hundred rams, four hundred
lambs, and as a sin offering for
all Israel twelve male goats, according to the number of the
tribes of Israel.
18 They assigned the priests to
their [a]divisions and the Lē′vītes
to their [b]divisions, over the service of God in Jerusalem, [c]as it is
written in the Book of Moses.
19 [1]And the descendants of the
captivity kept the Passover [a]on
the fourteenth *day* of the first
month.
20 For the priests and the Lē′-
vītes had [a]purified themselves;
all of them *were ritually* clean.
And they [b]slaughtered the Passover *lambs* for all the descendants of the captivity, for their
brethren the priests, and for
themselves.
21 Then the children of Israel
who had returned from the captivity ate together with all who
had separated themselves from
the [a]filth[1] of the nations of the
land in order to seek the LORD
God of Israel.
22 And they kept the [a]Feast of
Unleavened Bread seven days
with joy; for the LORD made
them joyful, and [b]turned the
heart [c]of the king of Assyria
toward them, to strengthen their
hands in the work of the house
of God, the God of Israel.

7 Now after these things, in
the reign of [a]Ar·ta·xerx′ēs
king of Persia, Ezra the [b]son of
Se·rāi′ah, [c]the son of Az·a·rī′ah,
the son of [d]Hil·kī′ah,
2 the son of Shal′lum, the son
of Zā′dok, the son of A·hī′tub,
3 the son of Am·a·rī′ah, the son
of Az·a·rī′ah, the son of Me·rā′-
i·oth,
4 the son of Zer·a·hī′ah, the
son of Uz′zī, the son of Buk′kī,
5 the son of Ab·i·shū′a, the son
of Phin′e·has, the son of El·ē·ā′-
zar, the son of Aaron the chief
priest—
6 this Ezra came up from Babylon; and he *was* [a]a skilled scribe
in the Law of Moses, which the
LORD God of Israel had given.
The king granted him all his request, [b]according to the hand of
the LORD his God upon him.
7 [a]*Some* of the children of Israel, the priests, [b]the Lē′vītes,
the singers, the gatekeepers,
and [c]the Neth′i·nim came up to
Jerusalem in the seventh year of
King Ar·ta·xerx′ēs.
8 And Ezra came to Jerusalem
in the fifth month, which *was* in
the seventh year of the king.
9 On the first *day* of the first
month he began *his* journey from
Babylon, and on the first *day* of
the fifth month he came to Jerusalem, [a]according to the good
hand of his God upon him.
10 For Ezra had prepared his
heart to [a]seek[1] the Law of the
LORD, and to do *it*, and to [b]teach
statutes and ordinances in
Israel.
11 This *is* a copy of the letter that King Ar·ta·xerx′ēs gave
Ezra the priest, the scribe, expert in the words of the commandments of the LORD, and of
His statutes to Israel:

12 [1]Ar·ta·xerx′ēs, [a]king of kings,

To Ezra the priest, a scribe
of the Law of the God of
heaven:

Perfect *peace*, [b]and[2] so forth.

18 [a]1 Chr. 24:1 [b]1 Chr. 23:6 [c]Num. 3:6; 8:9
19 [a]Ex. 12:6 [1]The Hebrew language resumes in Ezra 6:19 and continues through 7:11.
20 [a]2 Chr. 29:34; 30:15 [b]2 Chr. 35:11
21 [a]Ezra 9:11 [1]*uncleanness*
22 [a]Ex. 12:15; 13:6, 7 [b][Prov. 21:1] [c]Ezra 1:1; 6:1

CHAPTER 7

1 [a]Neh. 2:1 [b]1 Chr. 6:14 [c]Jer. 52:24 [d]2 Chr. 35:8
6 [a]Ezra 7:11, 12, 21 [b]Ezra 7:9, 28; 8:22
7 [a]Ezra 8:1–14 [b]Ezra 8:15 [c]Ezra 2:43; 8:20
9 [a]Neh. 2:8, 18
10 [a]Ps. 119:45 [b]Deut. 33:10 [1]Study
12 [a]Dan. 2:37 [b]Ezra 4:10 [1]The original language of Ezra 7:12–26 is Aramaic. [2]Lit. *and now*

13 I issue a decree that all
those of the people of Israel
and the priests and Lē′vītes
in my realm, who volunteer
to go up to Jerusalem, may
go with you.
14 And whereas you are being
sent [1]by the king and his
[a]seven counselors to inquire
concerning Judah and
Jerusalem, with regard to
the Law of your God which
is in your hand;
15 and *whereas you are* to
carry the silver and gold
which the king and his
counselors have freely
offered to the God of Israel,
[a]whose dwelling *is* in
Jerusalem;
16 [a]and *whereas* all the silver
and gold that you may
find in all the province of
Babylon, along with the
freewill offering of the
people and the priests, *are
to be* [b]freely offered for
the [1]house of their God in
Jerusalem—
17 now therefore, be careful
to buy with this money
bulls, rams, and lambs, with
their [a]grain offerings and
their drink offerings, and
[b]offer them on the altar of
the house of your God in
Jerusalem.
18 And whatever seems good
to you and your brethren to
do with the rest of the silver
and the gold, do it according
to the will of your God.
19 Also the articles that are
given to you for the service
of the house of your God,
deliver in full before the
God of Jerusalem.
20 And whatever more may
be needed for the house of
your God, which you may
have occasion to provide,
pay *for it* from the king's
treasury.
21 And I, *even* I, Ar·ta·xerx′ēs
the king, issue a decree to
all the treasurers who *are in
the region* beyond the River,
that whatever Ezra the
priest, the scribe of the Law
of the God of heaven, may
require of you, let it be done
diligently,
22 up to one hundred talents of
silver, one hundred kors of
wheat, one hundred baths
of wine, one hundred baths
of oil, and salt without
prescribed limit.
23 Whatever [1]is commanded
by the God of heaven, let it
diligently be done for the
[2]house of the God of heaven.
For why should there be
wrath against the realm of
the king and his sons?
24 Also we inform you that
it shall not be lawful to
impose tax, tribute, or
custom on any of the
priests, Lē′vītes, singers,
gatekeepers, Neth′i·nim, or
servants of this house of
God.
25 And you, Ezra, according to
your God-given wisdom, [a]set
magistrates and judges who
may judge all the people
who *are in the region*
beyond the River, all such as
know the laws of your God;
and [b]teach those who do not
know *them.*
26 Whoever will not observe
the law of your God and the
law of the king, let judgment
be executed speedily on

14 [a]Esth. 1:14 [1]*from before*
15 [a]Ezra 6:12
16 [a]Ezra 8:25 [b]1 Chr. 29:6, 9 [1]Temple
17 [a]Num. 15:4–13 [b]Deut. 12:5–11
23 [1]Lit. *is from the decree* [2]Temple
25 [a]Ex. 18:21, 22 [b][Mal. 2:7]

him, whether *it be* death, or
[1]banishment, or confiscation
of goods, or imprisonment.

27 [a]Blessed[1] *be* the LORD God of
our fathers, [b]who has put *such a*
thing as this in the king's heart,
to beautify the house of the LORD
which *is* in Jerusalem,
28 and [a]has extended mercy
to me before the king and his
counselors, and before all the
king's mighty princes.
So I was encouraged, as [b]the
hand of the LORD my God *was*
upon me; and I gathered leading
men of Israel to go up with me.

8 These *are* the heads of their
fathers' *houses,* and *this is*
the genealogy of those who went
up with me from Babylon, in the
reign of King Ar·ta·xerx′ēs:
2 of the sons of Phin′e·has,
Ger′shom; of the sons of Ith′-
a·mar, Daniel; of the sons of
David, [a]Hat′tush;
3 of the sons of Shec·a·nī′ah, of
the sons of [a]Pā′rosh, Zech·a·rī′ah;
and registered with him *were*
one hundred and fifty males;
4 of the sons of [a]Pā′hath-
Mō′ab, El·i·ē·hō·ē′naī the son of
Zer·a·hī′ah, and with him two
hundred males;
5 of [1]the sons of Shech·a·nī′ah,
Ben-Ja·hā′zi·el, and with him
three hundred males;
6 of the sons of Ā′din, Ē′bed
the son of Jonathan, and with
him fifty males;
7 of the sons of Ē′lam, Je·shā′-
i·ah the son of Ath·a·lī′ah, and
with him seventy males;
8 of the sons of Sheph·a·tī′ah,
Zeb·a·dī′ah the son of Michael,
and with him eighty males;
9 of the sons of Jō′ab, Ō·ba-
dī′ah the son of Je·hī′el, and with
him two hundred and eighteen
males;
10 of [1]the sons of She·lō′mith,
Ben-Jō·si·phī′ah, and with him
one hundred and sixty males;
11 of the sons of [a]Bē′baī, Zech-
a·rī′ah the son of Bē′baī, and
with him twenty-eight males;
12 of the sons of Az′gad, Jō·hā′-
nan [1]the son of Hak′ka·tan, and
with him one hundred and ten
males;
13 of the last sons of Ad·o·nī′-
kam, whose names *are* these—
E·liph′e·let, Je·ī′el, and She-
māī′ah—and with them sixty
males;
14 also of the sons of Big′vaī,
Ū′thaī and [1]Zab′bud, and with
them seventy males.
15 Now I gathered them by the
river that flows to A·hā′va, and
we camped there three days.
And I looked among the people
and the priests, and found none
of the [a]sons of Levi there.
16 Then I sent for El·i·ē′zer, Ar′-
i·el, She·māī′ah, El·nā′than, Jā′rib,
El·nā′than, Nathan, Zech·a·rī′ah,
and [a]Me·shul′lam, leaders; also
for Joi′ā·rib and El·nā′than, men
of understanding.
17 And I gave them a command
for Id′dō the chief man at the
place Cas·i·phī′a, and [1]I told them
what they should say to [2]Id′dō
and his brethren the Neth′i·nim
at the place Cas·i·phī′a—that
they should bring us servants
for the house of our God.
18 Then, by the good hand of
our God upon us, they [a]brought
us a man of understanding, of
the sons of Mah′lī the son of
Levi, the son of Israel, namely
Sher·e·bī′ah, with his sons and
brothers, eighteen men;
19 and [a]Hash·a·bī′ah, and with

26 [1]Lit. *rooting out*

27 [a]1 Chr. 29:10 [b]Ezra 6:22 [1]The Hebrew language resumes in Ezra 7:27.

28 [a]Ezra 9:9 [b]Ezra 5:5; 7:6, 9; 8:18

CHAPTER 8

2 [a]1 Chr. 3:22

3 [a]Ezra 2:3

4 [a]Ezra 10:30

5 [1]So with MT, Vg.; LXX *the sons of Zatho, Shechaniah*

10 [1]So with MT, Vg.; LXX *the sons of Banni, Shelomith*

11 [a]Ezra 10:28

12 [1]Or *the youngest son,*

14 [1]Or *Zakkur*

15 [a]Ezra 7:7; 8:2

16 [a]Ezra 10:15

17 [1]Lit. *I put words in their mouths to say* [2]So with Vg.; MT *to Iddo his brother;* LXX *to their brethren*

18 [a]Neh. 8:7

19 [a]Neh. 12:24

him Je·shā′i·ah of the sons of
Me·rar′ī, his brothers and their
sons, twenty men;
20 [a]also of the Neth′i·nim,
whom David and the leaders
had appointed for the service of
the Lē′vītes, two hundred and
twenty Neth′i·nim. All of them
were designated by name.
21 Then I [a]proclaimed a fast
there at the river of A·hā′va, that
we might [b]humble ourselves before our God, to seek from Him
the [c]right way for us and our little ones and all our possessions.
22 For [a]I was ashamed to request of the king an escort of
soldiers and horsemen to help
us against the enemy on the
road, because we had spoken
to the king, saying, [b]"The hand
of our God *is* upon all those
for [c]good who seek Him, but
His power and His wrath *are*
[d]against all those who [e]forsake
Him."
23 So we fasted and entreated
our God for this, and He
[a]answered our prayer.
24 And I separated twelve of
the leaders of the priests—Sher-
e·bī′ah, Hash·a·bī′ah, and ten of
their brethren with them—
25 and weighed out to them [a]the
silver, the gold, and the articles,
the offering for the house of
our God which the king and his
counselors and his princes, and
all Israel *who were* present, had
offered.
26 I weighed into their hand six
hundred and fifty talents of silver, silver articles *weighing* one
hundred talents, one hundred
talents of gold,
27 twenty gold basins *worth*
a thousand drachmas, and two
vessels of fine polished bronze,
precious as gold.
28 And I said to them, "You *are*
[a]holy[1] to the LORD; the articles
are [b]holy also; and the silver and
the gold *are* a freewill offering
to the LORD God of your fathers.
29 "Watch and keep *them* until
you weigh *them* before the leaders of the priests and the Lē′-
vītes and [a]heads of the fathers'
houses of Israel in Jerusalem, *in*
the chambers of the house of the
LORD."
30 So the priests and the Lē′-
vītes received the silver and the
gold and the articles by weight,
to bring *them* to Jerusalem to
the house of our God.
31 Then we departed from the
river of A·hā′va on the twelfth
day of the first month, to go to
Jerusalem. And [a]the hand of our
God was upon us, and He delivered us from the hand of the
enemy and from ambush along
the road.
32 So we [a]came to Jerusalem,
and stayed there three days.
33 Now on the fourth day the
silver and the gold and the articles were [a]weighed in the house
of our God by the hand of Mer′-
e·moth the son of Ū·rī′ah the
priest, and with him *was* El·ē·ā′-
zar the son of Phin′e·has; with
them *were* the Lē′vītes, [b]Joz′-
a·bad the son of Jesh′ū·a and
Nō·a·dī′ah the son of Bin′nū·ī,
34 with the number *and* weight
of everything. All the weight
was written down at that time.
35 The children of those who
had been [a]carried away captive,
who had come from the captivity, [b]offered burnt offerings to
the God of Israel: twelve bulls
for all Israel, ninety-six rams,

20 [a]Ezra 2:43; 7:7
21 [a]1 Sam. 7:6 [b]Is. 58:3, 5 [c]Ps. 5:8
22 [a]1 Cor. 9:15 [b]Ezra 7:6, 9, 28 [c][Rom. 8:28] [d][Ps. 34:16] [e][2 Chr. 15:2]
23 [a]2 Chr. 33:13
25 [a]Ezra 7:15, 16
28 [a]Lev. 21:6–9 [b]Lev. 22:2, 3 [1]*consecrated*
29 [a]Ezra 4:3
31 [a]Ezra 7:6, 9, 28
32 [a]Neh. 2:11
33 [a]Ezra 8:26, 30 [b]Neh. 11:16
35 [a]Ezra 2:1 [b]Ezra 6:17

seventy-seven lambs, and twelve
male goats *as* a sin offering. All
this was a burnt offering to the
LORD.
36 And they delivered the king's
[a]orders to the king's satraps and
the governors *in the region* beyond [1]the River. So they gave
support to the people and the
[2]house of God.

9 When these things were
done, the leaders came to
me, saying, "The people of Israel
and the priests and the Lē′vītes
have not [a]separated themselves
from the peoples of the lands,
[b]with respect to the abominations of the Cā′naan·ītes, the
Hit′tītes, the Per′iz·zītes, the
Jeb′ū·sītes, the Am′mon·ītes,
the Mō′ab·ītes, the Egyptians,
and the Am′o·rītes.
2 "For they have [a]taken some
of their daughters *as wives* for
themselves and their sons, so
that the [b]holy seed is [c]mixed
with the peoples of *those* lands.
Indeed, the hand of the leaders
and rulers has been foremost in
this [1]trespass."
3 So when I heard this thing,
[a]I tore my garment and my robe,
and plucked out some of the
hair of my head and beard, and
sat down [b]astonished.
4 Then everyone who [a]trembled
at the words of the God of Israel
assembled to me, because of the
transgression of those who had
been carried away captive, and I
sat astonished until the [b]evening
sacrifice.
5 At the evening sacrifice I
arose from my fasting; and having torn my garment and my
robe, I fell on my knees and
[a]spread out my hands to the
LORD my God.

36 [a]Ezra 7:21–24 [1]The Euphrates [2]Temple

CHAPTER 9

1 [a]Neh. 9:2 [b]Deut. 12:30, 31

2 [a][Deut. 7:3] [b]Ex. 22:31 [c][2 Cor. 6:14] [1]*unfaithfulness*

3 [a]Job 1:20 [b]Ps. 143:4

4 [a]Ezra 10:3 [b]Ex. 29:39

5 [a]Ex. 9:29

6 [a]Dan. 9:7, 8 [b]Ps. 38:4 [c]Rev. 18:5

7 [a]Dan. 9:5, 6 [b]Deut. 28:36 [c]Deut. 32:25 [d]Dan. 9:7, 8 [1]Lit. *shame of faces*

8 [a]Ps. 34:5

9 [a]Neh. 9:36 [b]Ps. 136:23 [c]Ezra 7:28 [d]Is. 5:2

11 [a]Ezra 6:21

12 [a][Deut. 7:3, 4]

6 And I said: "O my God, I
am too [a]ashamed and humiliated to lift up my face to You,
my God; for [b]our iniquities have
risen higher than *our* heads, and
our guilt has [c]grown up to the
heavens.
7 "Since the days of our fathers
to this day [a]we *have been* very
guilty, and for our iniquities [b]we,
our kings, *and* our priests have
been delivered into the hand
of the kings of the lands, to the
[c]sword, to captivity, to plunder,
and to [d]humiliation,[1] as *it is* this
day.
8 "And now for a little while
grace has been *shown* from the
LORD our God, to leave us a remnant to escape, and to give us a
peg in His holy place, that our
God may [a]enlighten our eyes
and give us a measure of revival
in our bondage.
9 [a]"For we *were* slaves. [b]Yet
our God did not forsake us in
our bondage; but [c]He extended
mercy to us in the sight of the
kings of Persia, to revive us, to
repair the house of our God, to
rebuild its ruins, and to give us
[d]a wall in Judah and Jerusalem.
10 "And now, O our God, what
shall we say after this? For we
have forsaken Your commandments,
11 "which You commanded by
Your servants the prophets, saying, 'The land which you are entering to possess is an unclean
land, with the [a]uncleanness of
the peoples of the lands, with
their abominations which have
filled it from one end to another
with their impurity.
12 'Now therefore, [a]do not give
your daughters as wives for their
sons, nor take their daughters

to your sons; and [b]never seek
their peace or prosperity, that
you may be strong and eat the
good of the land, and [c]leave *it* as
an inheritance to your children
forever.'
13 "And after all that has come
upon us for our evil deeds and
for our great guilt, since You our
God [a]have punished us less than
our iniquities *deserve*, and have
given us *such* deliverance as
this,
14 "should we [a]again break Your
commandments, and [b]join in
marriage with the people *committing*
these abominations?
Would You not be [c]angry with us
until You had [1]consumed *us*, so
that *there would be* no remnant
or survivor?
15 "O LORD God of Israel, [a]You
are righteous, for we are left as
a remnant, as *it is* this day. [b]Here
we *are* before You, [c]in our guilt,
though no one can stand before
You because of this!"

CHAPTER 10

10 Now [a]while Ezra was
praying, and while he
was confessing, weeping, and
bowing down [b]before the house
of God, a very large assembly of
men, women, and children gathered
to him from Israel; for the
people wept very [c]bitterly.
2 And Shech·a·nī′ah the son of
Je·hī′el, *one* of the sons of Ē′lam,
spoke up and said to Ezra, "We
have [a]trespassed[1] against our
God, and have taken pagan
wives from the peoples of the
land; yet now there is hope in
Israel in spite of this.
3 "Now therefore, let us make
[a]a covenant with our God to
put away all these wives and
those who have been born to
them, according to the advice
of my master and of those who
[b]tremble at [c]the commandment
of our God; and let it be done
according to the [d]law.
4 "Arise, for *this* matter *is* your
responsibility. We also *are* with
you. [a]Be of good courage, and do
it."
5 Then Ezra arose, and made
the leaders of the priests, the
Lē′vītes, and all Israel [a]swear an
oath that they would do according
to this word. So they swore
an oath.
6 Then Ezra rose up from before
the house of God, and went
into the chamber of Jē·hō·hā′-
nan the son of E·lī′a·shib; and
when he came there, he [a]ate no
bread and drank no water, for
he mourned because of the guilt
of those from the captivity.
7 And they issued a proclamation
throughout Judah and
Jerusalem to all the descendants
of the captivity, that they must
gather at Jerusalem,
8 and that whoever would not
come within three days, according
to the instructions of the
leaders and elders, all his property
would be confiscated, and
he himself would be separated
from the assembly of those from
the captivity.
9 So all the men of Judah and
Benjamin gathered at Jerusalem
within three days. It *was*
the ninth month, on the twentieth
of the month; and [a]all the
people sat in the open square
of the house of God, trembling
because of *this* matter and because
of heavy rain.
10 Then Ezra the priest stood
up and said to them, "You have
[1]transgressed and [2]have taken

12 [b]Deut. 23:6 [c][Prov. 13:22; 20:7]
13 [a][Ps. 103:10]
14 [a][John 5:14] [b]Neh. 13:23 [c]Deut. 9:8 [1]*destroyed*
15 [a]Dan. 9:14 [b][Rom. 3:19] [c]1 Cor. 15:17

CHAPTER 10

1 [a]Dan. 9:4, 20 [b]2 Chr. 20:9 [c]Neh. 8:1–9
2 [a]Neh. 13:23–27 [1]*been unfaithful to*
3 [a]2 Chr. 34:31 [b]Ezra 9:4 [c]Deut. 7:2, 3 [d]Deut. 24:1, 2
4 [a]1 Chr. 28:10
5 [a]Neh. 5:12; 13:25
6 [a]Deut. 9:18
9 [a]1 Sam. 12:18
10 [1]*acted unfaithfully* [2]Heb. *have caused to dwell* or *have brought back*

pagan wives, adding to the guilt of Israel.

11 "Now therefore, [a]make confession to the LORD God of your fathers, and do His will; [b]separate yourselves from the peoples of the land, and from the pagan wives."

12 Then all the assembly answered and said with a loud voice, "Yes! As you have said, so we must do.

13 "But *there are* many people; *it is* the season for heavy rain, and we are not able to stand outside. Nor *is this* the work of one or two days, for *there are* many of us who have transgressed in this matter.

14 "Please, let the leaders of our entire assembly stand; and let all those in our cities who have taken pagan wives come at appointed times, together with the elders and judges of their cities, until [a]the fierce wrath of our God is turned away from us in this matter."

15 Only Jonathan the son of As′a·hel and Jā·ha·zī′ah the son of Tik′vah opposed this, and [a]Me·shul′lam and Shab′be·thaī the Lē′vīte gave them support.

16 Then the descendants of the captivity did so. And Ezra the priest, *with* certain [a]heads of the fathers' *households,* were set apart by the fathers' households, each of them by name; and they sat down on the first day of the tenth month to examine the matter.

17 By the first day of the first month they finished *questioning* all the men who had taken pagan wives.

18 And among the sons of the priests who had taken pagan wives *the following* were found of the sons of [a]Jesh′ū·a the son of [1]Jō′za·dak, and his brothers: Mā·a·sēi′ah, El·i·ē′zer, Jā′rib, and Ged·a·lī′ah.

19 And they [a]gave their promise that they would put away their wives; and *being* [b]guilty, *they presented* a ram of the flock as their [c]trespass offering.

20 Also of the sons of Im′mer: Ha·nā′nī and Zeb·a·dī′ah;

21 of the sons of Hā′rim: Mā·a·sēi′ah, E·lī′jah, She·māi′ah, Je·hī′el, and Uz·zī′ah;

22 of the sons of Pash′hur: El·i·ō·ē′naī, Mā·a·sēi′ah, Ish′ma·el, Ne·than′el, Joz′a·bad, and El·ā′sah.

23 Also of the Lē′vītes: Joz′a·bad, Shim′ē·ī, Ke·lāi′ah (the same *is* Ke·lī′ta), Peth·a·hī′ah, Judah, and El·i·ē′zer.

24 Also of the singers: E·lī′a·shib; and of the gatekeepers: Shal′lum, Tē′lem, and Ū′rī.

25 And others of Israel: of the [a]sons of Pā′rosh: Ra·mī′ah, Je·zī′ah, Mal·chī′ah, Mij′a·min, El·ē·ā′zar, Mal·chī′jah, and Be·nā′i·ah;

26 of the sons of Ē′lam: Mat·ta·nī′ah, Zech·a·rī′ah, Je·hī′el, Ab′dī, Jer′e·moth, and E·lī′ah;

27 of the sons of Zat′tū: El·i·ō·ē′naī, E·lī′a·shib, Mat·ta·nī′ah, Jer′e·moth, Zā′bad, and A·zī′za;

28 of the [a]sons of Bē′baī: Jē·hō·hā′nan, Han·a·nī′ah, Zab′baī, *and* Ath′laī;

29 of the sons of Bā′nī: Me·shul′lam, Mal′luch, A·dāi′ah, Jash′ub, Shē′al, *and* [1]Rā′moth;

30 of the [a]sons of Pā′hath-Mō′ab: Ad′na, Chē′lal, Be·nā′i·ah, Mā·a·sēi′ah, Mat·ta·nī′ah, Bez′a·lel, Bin′nū·ī, and Ma·nas′seh;

11 [a][Prov. 28:13] [b]Ezra 10:3
14 [a]2 Chr. 28:11–13; 29:10; 30:8
15 [a]Neh. 3:4
16 [a]Ezra 4:3
18 [a]Ezra 5:2 [1]*Jehozadak,* 1 Chr. 6:14
19 [a]2 Kin. 10:15 [b]Lev. 6:4, 6 [c]Lev. 5:6, 15
25 [a]Ezra 2:3; 8:3
28 [a]Ezra 8:11
29 [1]Or *Jeremoth*
30 [a]Ezra 8:4

31 *of* the sons of Hā′rim: El·i·ē′-
zer, Ish·ī′jah, Mal·chī′jah, She-
māi′ah, Shim′ē·on,
32 Benjamin, Mal′luch, *and*
Shem·a·rī′ah;
33 of the sons of Hā′shum:
Mat·tē′naī, Mat·tat′tah, Zā′bad,
E·liph′e·let, Jer′e·maī, Ma·nas′-
seh, *and* Shim′ē·ī;
34 of the sons of Bā′nī: Mā·a·dā′ī,
Am′ram, Ū′el,
35 Be·nā′i·ah, Bē·dēi′ah, [1]Chel′ūh,
36 Va·nī′ah, Mer′e·moth, E·lī′-
a·shib,
37 Mat·ta·nī′ah, Mat·tē′naī, [1]Jā′-
a·sai,
38 Bā′nī, Bin′nū·ī, Shim′ē·ī,
39 Shel·e·mī′ah, Nathan, A·dāi′-
ah,
40 Mach·nad′e·baī, Shā′shaī, Shā′-
raī,
41 Az′a·rel, Shel·e·mī′ah, Shem-
a·rī′ah,
42 Shal′lum, Am·a·rī′ah, *and*
Joseph;
43 of the sons of Nē′bō: Je·ī′el,
Mat·ti·thī′ah, Zā′bad, Ze·bī′na,
[1]Jad′daī, Jō′el, *and* Be·nā′i·ah.
44 All these had taken pa-
gan wives, and *some* of them
had wives *by whom* they had
children.

35 [1]Or *Cheluhi* or *Cheluhu*
37 [1]Or *Jaasu*
43 [1]Or *Jaddu*

The Book of

NEHEMIAH

NEHEMIAH, contemporary of Ezra and cupbearer to the king in the Persian palace, leads the third and last return to Jerusalem after the Babylonian exile. His concern for the welfare of Jerusalem and its inhabitants prompts him to take bold action. Granted permission to return to his homeland, Nehemiah challenges his countrymen to arise and rebuild the shattered wall of Jerusalem. In spite of opposition from without and abuse from within, the task is completed in only fifty-two days, a feat even the enemies of Israel must attribute to God's enabling. By contrast, the task of reviving and reforming the people of God within the rebuilt wall demands years of Nehemiah's godly life and leadership.

The Hebrew for Nehemiah is *Nehemyah,* "Comfort of Yahweh." The book is named after its chief character, whose name appears in the opening verse. The combined Ezra–Nehemiah is given the Greek title *Esdras Deuteron,* or "Second Esdras," in the Septuagint, a third-century B.C. Greek-language translation of the Hebrew Old Testament. The Latin title of Nehemiah is *Liber Secundus Esdrae,* "Second Book of Ezra" (Ezra was the first). At this point, it is considered a separate book from Ezra, and is later called *Liber Nehemiae,* "Book of Nehemiah."

THE words of [a]Nē·he·mī′ah
the son of Ha·cha·lī′ah.
It came to pass in the month
of Chis′lev, *in* the [b]twentieth
year, as I was in [c]Shū′shan[1] the
[2]citadel,
2 that [a]Ha·nā′nī one of my
brethren came with men from Judah; and I asked them concerning the Jews who had escaped,
who had survived the captivity,
and concerning Jerusalem.
3 And they said to me, "The
survivors who are left from
the captivity in the [a]province
are there in great distress and
[b]reproach. [c]The wall of Jerusalem [d]*is* also broken down, and
its gates are burned with fire."
4 So it was, when I heard these
words, that I sat down and wept,
and mourned *for many* days; I

CHAPTER 1

1 [a]Neh. 10:1 [b]Neh. 2:1 [c]Esth. 1:1, 2, 5 [1]Or *Susa* [2]Or *fortified palace,* and so elsewhere in the book

2 [a]Neh. 7:2

3 [a]Neh. 7:6 [b]Neh. 2:17 [c]Neh. 2:17 [d]2 Kin. 25:10

5 [a]Dan. 9:4 [b]Neh. 4:14 [c][Ex. 20:6; 34:6, 7] [1]Lit. *Him* [2]Lit. *His*

6 [a]2 Chr. 6:40 [b]Dan. 9:20

7 [a]Dan. 9:5 [b]Deut. 28:15

was fasting and praying before
the God of heaven.
5 And I said: "I pray, [a]LORD
God of heaven, O great and
[b]awesome God, [c]*You* who keep
Your covenant and mercy with
those who love [1]You and observe [2]Your commandments,
6 "please let Your ear be attentive and [a]Your eyes open, that
You may hear the prayer of Your
servant which I pray before You
now, day and night, for the children of Israel Your servants, and
[b]confess the sins of the children
of Israel which we have sinned
against You. Both my father's
house and I have sinned.
7 [a]"We have acted very corruptly against You, and have
[b]not kept the commandments,
the statutes, nor the ordinances

which You commanded Your servant Moses.
8 "Remember, I pray, the word
that You commanded Your ser-
vant Moses, saying, [a]'*If* you [1]are
unfaithful, I will scatter you
among the nations;
9 [a]'but *if* you return to Me, and
keep My commandments and
do them, [b]though some of you
were cast out to the farthest part
of the heavens, *yet* I will gather
them from there, and bring them
to the place which I have chosen
as a dwelling for My name.'
10 [a]"Now these *are* Your servants and Your people, whom
You have redeemed by Your
great power, and by Your strong
hand.
11 "O Lord, I pray, please [a]let
Your ear be attentive to the
prayer of Your servant, and to
the prayer of Your servants who
[b]desire to fear Your name; and
let Your servant prosper this day,
I pray, and grant him mercy in
the sight of this man." For I was
the king's [c]cupbearer.

CHAPTER 2

2 And it came to pass in the
month of Nī′san, in the twentieth year of [a]King [1]Ar·ta·xerx′ēs,
when wine *was* before him, that
[b]I took the wine and gave it to
the king. Now I had never been
sad in his presence before.
2 Therefore the king said to
me, "Why *is* your face sad, since
you *are* not sick? This *is* nothing but [a]sorrow of heart." So I
became [1]dreadfully afraid,
3 and said to the king, [a]"May
the king live forever! Why
should my face not be sad, when
[b]the city, the place of my fathers'
tombs, *lies* waste, and its gates
are burned with [c]fire?"
4 Then the king said to me,
"What do you request?" So I
[a]prayed to the God of heaven.
5 And I said to the king, "If
it pleases the king, and if your
servant has found favor in your
sight, I ask that you send me to
Judah, to the city of my fathers'
tombs, that I may rebuild it."
6 Then the king said to me (the
queen also sitting beside him),
"How long will your journey be?
And when will you return?" So it
pleased the king to send me; and
I set him [a]a time.
7 Furthermore I said to the
king, "If it pleases the king, let
letters be given to me for the
[a]governors *of the region* beyond
[1]the River, that they must permit
me to pass through till I come to
Judah,
8 "and a letter to Ā′saph the
keeper of the king's forest, that
he must give me timber to make
beams for the gates of the [1]cita-
del which *pertains* [a]to the [2]tem-
ple, for the city wall, and for the
house that I will occupy." And
the king granted *them* to me
[b]according to the good hand of
my God upon me.
9 Then I went to the governors
in the region beyond the River,
and gave them the king's letters.
Now the king had sent captains of the army and horsemen
with me.
10 When [a]San·bal′lat the Hor′-
o·nīte and Tō·bī′ah the Am′-
mon·īte [1]official heard *of it*, they
were deeply disturbed that a
man had come to seek the well-
being of the children of Israel.
11 So I [a]came to Jerusalem and
was there three days.
12 Then I arose in the night, I
and a few men with me; I told
no one what my God had put in

8 [a]Lev. 26:33 [1]*act treacherously*
9 [a][Deut. 4:29–31; 30:2–5] [b]Deut. 30:4
10 [a]Deut. 9:29
11 [a]Neh. 1:6 [b]Is. 26:8 [c]Neh. 2:1

CHAPTER 2

1 [a]Ezra 7:1 [b]Neh. 1:11 [1]Artaxerxes Longimanus
2 [a]Prov. 15:13 [1]Lit. *very much*
3 [a]Dan. 2:4; 5:10; 6:6, 21 [b]2 Chr. 36:19 [c]Neh. 1:3
4 [a]Neh. 1:4
6 [a]Neh. 5:14; 13:6
7 [a]Ezra 7:21; 8:36 [1]The Euphrates
8 [a]Neh. 3:7 [b]Ezra 5:5; 7:6, 9, 28 [1]*palace* [2]Lit. *house*
10 [a]Neh. 2:19; 4:1 [1]Lit. *servant*
11 [a]Ezra 8:32

my heart to do at Jerusalem; nor
was there any animal with me,
except the one on which I rode.
13 And I went out by night
[a]through the Valley Gate to the
Serpent Well and the [1]Refuse
Gate, and [2]viewed the walls of
Jerusalem which were [b]broken
down and its gates which were
burned with fire.
14 Then I went on to the
[a]Fountain Gate and to the [b]King's
Pool, but *there was* no room for
the animal under me to pass.
15 So I went up in the night
by the [a]valley,[1] and [2]viewed the
wall; then I turned back and entered by the Valley Gate, and so
returned.
16 And the officials did not
know where I had gone or what
I had done; I had not yet told the
Jews, the priests, the nobles, the
officials, or the others who did
the work.
17 Then I said to them, "You
see the distress that we *are* in,
how Jerusalem *lies* [1]waste, and
its gates are burned with fire.
Come and let us build the wall
of Jerusalem, that we may no
longer be [a]a reproach."
18 And I told them of [a]the hand
of my God which had been good
upon me, and also of the king's
words that he had spoken to
me. So they said, "Let us rise up
and build." Then they [b]set[1] their
hands to *this* good *work*.
19 But when San·bal'lat the
Hor'o·nīte, Tō·bī'ah the Am'-
mon·īte official, and Gē'shem the
Arab heard *of it*, they laughed at
us and despised us, and said,
"What *is* this thing that you are
doing? [a]Will you rebel against
the king?"
20 So I answered them, and said

13 [a]Neh. 3:13 [b]Neh. 1:3; 2:17 [1]*Dung* [2]*examined*
14 [a]Neh. 3:15 [b]2 Kin. 20:20
15 [a]2 Sam. 15:23 [1]*torrent valley, wadi* [2]*examined*
17 [a]Neh. 1:3 [1]*desolate*
18 [a]Neh. 2:8 [b]2 Sam. 2:7 [1]Lit. *strengthened*
19 [a]Neh. 6:6
20 [a]Ezra 4:3

CHAPTER 3

1 [a]Neh. 3:20; 12:10; 13:4, 7, 28 [b]John 5:2 [c]Neh. 12:39 [d]Jer. 31:38 [1]Heb. *Hammeah*
2 [a]Neh. 7:36 [1]Lit. *On his hand*
3 [a]Zeph. 1:10 [b]Neh. 6:1; 7:1
4 [a]Ezra 8:33 [b]Ezra 10:15 [1]Or *Hakkoz*
5 [a][Judg. 5:23] [1]Lit. *necks*
6 [a]Neh. 12:39
7 [a]Neh. 7:25 [b]Neh. 2:7–9 [1]Lit. *throne* [2]West of the Euphrates

to them, "The God of heaven
Himself will prosper us; therefore we His servants will arise
and build, [a]but you have no heritage or right or memorial in
Jerusalem."

3 Then [a]E·lī'a·shib the high
priest rose up with his brethren the priests [b]and built the
Sheep Gate; they consecrated it
and hung its doors. They built
[c]as far as the Tower of [1]the Hundred, *and* consecrated it, then as
far as the Tower of [d]Ha·nan'el.
2 [1]Next to *E·lī'a·shib* [a]the men
of Jericho built. And next to
them Zac'cur the son of Im'rī
built.
3 Also the sons of Has·se·nā'ah
built [a]the Fish Gate; they laid its
beams and [b]hung its doors with
its bolts and bars.
4 And next to them [a]Mer'-
e·moth the son of Ū·rī'jah, the
son of [1]Koz, made repairs. Next
to them [b]Me·shul'lam the son of
Ber·e·chī'ah, the son of Me·shez'-
a·bel, made repairs. Next to them
Zā'dok the son of Bā'a·na made
repairs.
5 Next to them the Te·kō'ītes
made repairs; but their nobles
did not put their [1]shoulders to
[a]the work of their Lord.
6 Moreover Je·hoi'a·da the son
of Pa·sē'ah and Me·shul'lam the
son of Bes·o·dēi'ah repaired [a]the
Old Gate; they laid its beams
and hung its doors, with its bolts
and bars.
7 And next to them Me·la·tī'ah
the Gib'ē·on·īte, Jā'don the Me-
ron'o·thīte, the [a]men of Gib'-
ē·on and Miz'pah, repaired the
[b]residence[1] of the governor *of
the region* [2]beyond the River.
8 Next to him Uz'zi·el the
son of Har·hai'ah, one of the

goldsmiths, made repairs. Also
next to him Han·a·nī′ah, [1]one
of the perfumers, made repairs;
and they [2]fortified Jerusalem as
far as the [a]Broad Wall.
9 And next to them Reph·āi′ah
the son of Hur, leader of half
the district of Jerusalem, made
repairs.
10 Next to them Je·daī′ah the
son of Har·ū′maph made repairs in front of his house. And
next to him Hat′tush the son of
Ha·shab·nī′ah made repairs.
11 Mal·chī′jah the son of Hā′rim
and Hash′ub the son of Pā′hath-
Mō′ab repaired another section,
[a]as well as the Tower of the
Ovens.
12 And next to him was Shal′-
lum the son of Hal·lō′hesh,
leader of half the district of Jerusalem; he and his daughters
made repairs.
13 Hā′nun and the inhabitants
of Za·nō′ah repaired [a]the Valley Gate. They built it, hung its
doors with its bolts and bars,
and *repaired* a thousand cubits
of the wall as far as [b]the Refuse
Gate.
14 Mal·chī′jah the son of Rē′-
chab, leader of the district of
[a]Beth Hac′ce·rem, repaired the
Refuse Gate; he built it and hung
its doors with its bolts and bars.
15 Shal′lun the son of Col-Hō′-
zeh, leader of the district of
Miz′pah, repaired [a]the Fountain
Gate; he built it, covered it, hung
its doors with its bolts and bars,
and repaired the wall of the Pool
of [b]Shē′lah[1] by the [c]King's Garden, as far as the stairs that go
down from the City of David.
16 After him Nē·he·mī′ah the
son of Az′buk, leader of half
the district of Beth Zūr, made
repairs as far as *the place* in
front of the [1]tombs of David, to
the [a]man-made pool, and as far
as the House of the Mighty.
17 After him the Lē′vītes, *un-*
der Rē′hum the son of Bā′nī,
made repairs. Next to him Hash-
a·bī′ah, leader of half the district
of Kē·ī′lah, made repairs for his
district.
18 After him their brethren,
under [1]Bav′a·ī the son of Hen′-
a·dad, leader of the *other* half
of the district of Kē·ī′lah, made
repairs.
19 And next to him Ē′zer the
son of Jesh′ū·a, the leader of
Miz′pah, repaired another section in front of the Ascent to the
Armory at the [a]buttress.[1]
20 After him Bar′uch the son of
[1]Zab′baī carefully repaired the
other section, from the [2]buttress
to the door of the house of E·lī′-
a·shib the high priest.
21 After him Mer′e·moth the
son of Ū·rī′jah, the son of [1]Koz,
repaired another section, from
the door of the house of E·lī′-
a·shib to the end of the house of
E·lī′a·shib.
22 And after him the priests, the
men of the plain, made repairs.
23 After him Benjamin and
Has′shub made repairs opposite
their house. After them Az·a·rī′ah
the son of Mā·a·sēi′ah, the son of
An·a·nī′ah, made repairs by his
house.
24 After him [a]Bin′nū·ī the son of
Hen′a·dad repaired another section, from the house of Az·a·rī′ah
to [b]the [1]buttress, even as far as
the corner.
25 Pā′lal the son of Ū′zaī *made*
repairs opposite the [1]buttress,
and on the tower which projects
from the king's upper house that

8 [a]Neh. 12:38 [1]Lit. *the son* [2]*restored*
11 [a]Neh. 12:38
13 [a]Neh. 2:13, 15 [b]Neh. 2:13
14 [a]Jer. 6:1
15 [a]Neh. 2:14 [b]Is. 8:6 [c]2 Kin. 25:4 [1]Or *Shiloah*
16 [a]2 Kin. 20:20 [1]LXX, Syr., Vg. *tomb*
18 [1]So with MT, Vg.; some Heb. mss., LXX, Syr. *Binnui* (cf. v. 24)
19 [a]2 Chr. 26:9 [1]Lit. *turning*
20 [1]A few Heb. mss., Syr., Vg. *Zaccai* [2]Lit. *turning*
21 [1]Or *Hakkoz*
24 [a]Ezra 8:33 [b]Neh. 3:19 [1]Lit. *turning*
25 [1]Lit. *turning*

was by the [a]court of the prison.
After him Pe·dāi′ah the son of
Pā′rosh *made repairs.*
26 Moreover [a]the Neth′i·nim
who dwelt in [b]Ō′phel *made*
repairs as far as *the place* in
front of [c]the Water Gate toward
the east, and on the projecting
tower.
27 After them the Te·kō′ītes repaired another section, next to
the great projecting tower, and
as far as the wall of Ō′phel.
28 Beyond the [a]Horse Gate the
priests made repairs, each in
front of his *own* house.
29 After them Zā′dok the son
of Im′mer made repairs in front
of his *own* house. After him
She·māi′ah the son of Shech·a-
nī′ah, the keeper of the East
Gate, made repairs.
30 After him Han·a·nī′ah the
son of Shel·e·mī′ah, and Hā′-
nun, the sixth son of Zā′laph,
repaired another section. After
him Me·shul′lam the son of Ber-
e·chī′ah made repairs in front of
his [1]dwelling.
31 After him Mal·chī′jah, [1]one
of the goldsmiths, made repairs
as far as the house of the Neth′-
i·nim and of the merchants, in
front of the [2]Miph′kad Gate, and
as far as the upper room at the
corner.
32 And between the upper
room at the corner, as far as the
[a]Sheep Gate, the goldsmiths and
the merchants made repairs.

4 But it so happened, [a]when
San·bal′lat heard that we
were rebuilding the wall, that he
was furious and very indignant,
and mocked the Jews.
2 And he spoke before his
brethren and the army of Samaria, and said, "What are these
feeble Jews doing? Will they fortify themselves? Will they offer
sacrifices? Will they complete
it in a day? Will they revive the
stones from the heaps of rubbish—*stones* that are burned?"
3 Now [a]Tō·bī′ah the Am′-
mon·īte *was* beside him, and he
said, "Whatever they build, if
even a fox goes up *on it,* he will
break down their stone wall."
4 [a]Hear, O our God, for we are
despised; [b]turn their reproach
on their own heads, and give
them as plunder to a land of
captivity!
5 [a]Do not cover their iniquity,
and do not let their sin be blotted out from before You; for they
have provoked *You* to anger before the builders.
6 So we built the wall, and the
entire wall was joined together
up to half its *height,* for the
people had a mind to work.
7 Now it happened, [a]when
San·bal′lat, Tō·bī′ah, [b]the Arabs,
the Am′mon·ītes, and the Ash′-
dod·ītes heard that the walls of
Jerusalem were being restored
and the [1]gaps were beginning to
be closed, that they became very
angry,
8 and all of them [a]conspired
together to come *and* attack Jerusalem and create confusion.
9 Nevertheless [a]we made our
prayer to our God, and because
of them we set a watch against
them day and night.
10 Then Judah said, "The
strength of the laborers is failing, and *there is* so much rubbish that we are not able to build
the wall."
11 And our adversaries said,
"They will neither know nor see
anything, till we come into their

25 [a]Jer. 32:2; 33:1; 37:21
26 [a]Neh. 11:21 [b]2 Chr. 27:3 [c]Neh. 8:1, 3; 12:37
28 [a]2 Chr. 23:15
30 [1]Lit. *room*
31 [1]Lit. *a son of the goldsmiths* [2]Lit. *Inspection* or *Recruiting*
32 [a]Neh. 3:1; 12:39

CHAPTER 4

1 [a]Neh. 2:10, 19
3 [a]Neh. 2:10, 19
4 [a]Ps. 123:3, 4 [b]Ps. 79:12
5 [a]Jer. 18:23
7 [a]Neh. 4:1 [b]Neh. 2:19 [1]Lit. *breaks*
8 [a]Ps. 83:3–5
9 [a][Ps. 50:15]

midst and kill them and cause
the work to cease."
12 So it was, when the Jews
who dwelt near them came, that
they told us ten times, "From
whatever place you turn, *they*
will be upon us."
13 Therefore I positioned *men*
behind the lower parts of the
wall, at the openings; and I set
the people according to their
families, with their swords, their
spears, and their bows.
14 And I looked, and arose and
said to the nobles, to the leaders,
and to the rest of the people, [a]"Do
not be afraid of them. Remember the Lord, [b]great and awesome, and [c]fight for your brethren, your sons, your daughters,
your wives, and your houses."
15 And it happened, when our
enemies heard that it was known
to us, and [a]*that* God had brought
their plot to nothing, that all of
us returned to the wall, everyone
to his work.
16 So it was, from that time on,
that half of my servants worked
at construction, while the other
half held the spears, the shields,
the bows, and *wore* armor; and
the leaders [1]*were* behind all the
house of Judah.
17 Those who built on the wall,
and those who carried burdens,
loaded themselves so that with
one hand they worked at construction, and with the other
held a weapon.
18 Every one of the builders
had his sword girded at his side
as he built. And the one who
sounded the trumpet *was* beside me.
19 Then I said to the nobles,
the rulers, and the rest of the
people, "The work *is* great and
extensive, and we are separated
far from one another on the
wall.
20 "Wherever you hear the
sound of the trumpet, rally to
us there. [a]Our God will fight for
us."
21 So we labored in the work,
and half of [1]*the men* held the
spears from daybreak until the
stars appeared.
22 At the same time I also said
to the people, "Let each man
and his servant stay at night in
Jerusalem, that they may be our
guard by night and a working
party by day."
23 So neither I, my brethren,
my servants, nor the men of the
guard who followed me took off
our clothes, *except* that everyone took them off for washing.

CHAPTER 5

5 And there was a great [a]out-
cry of the people and their
wives against their [b]Jewish
brethren.
2 For there were those who
said, "We, our sons, and our
daughters *are* many; therefore
let us get grain, that we may eat
and live."
3 There were also *some* who
said, "We have mortgaged our
lands and vineyards and houses,
that we might buy grain because
of the famine."
4 There were also those who
said, "We have borrowed money
for the king's tax *on* our lands
and vineyards.
5 "Yet now [a]our flesh *is* as
the flesh of our brethren, our
children as their children; and
indeed we [b]are forcing our sons
and our daughters to be slaves,
and *some* of our daughters have
been brought into slavery. *It is*
not in our power *to redeem*

14 [a]Deut. 1:29 [b][Deut. 10:17] [c]2 Sam. 10:12
15 [a]Job 5:12
16 [1]Supported
20 [a]Ex. 14:14, 25
21 [1]Lit. *them*
CHAPTER 5
1 [a]Neh. 5:7, 8 [b]Deut. 15:7
5 [a]Is. 58:7 [b]Ex. 21:7

them, for other men have our lands and vineyards."

6 And I became very angry when I heard their outcry and these words.

7 After serious thought, I rebuked the nobles and rulers, and said to them, [a]"Each of you is [1]exacting usury from his brother." So I [2]called a great assembly against them.

8 And I said to them, "According to our ability we have [a]redeemed our Jewish brethren who were sold to the nations. Now indeed, will you even sell your brethren? Or should they be sold to us?" Then they were silenced and found nothing *to say.*

9 Then I said, "What you are doing *is* not good. Should you not walk [a]in the fear of our God [b]because of the reproach of the nations, our enemies?

10 "I also, *with* my brethren and my servants, am lending them money and grain. Please, let us stop this [1]usury!

11 "Restore now to them, even this day, their lands, their vineyards, their olive groves, and their houses, also a hundredth of the money and the grain, the new wine and the oil, that you have charged them."

12 So they said, "We will restore *it,* and will require nothing from them; we will do as you say." Then I called the priests, [a]and required an oath from them that they would do according to this promise.

13 Then [a]I shook out [1]the fold of my garment and said, "So may God shake out each man from his house, and from his property, who does not perform this promise. Even thus may he be shaken out and emptied." And all the assembly said, "Amen!" and praised the LORD. [b]Then the people did according to this promise.

14 Moreover, from the time that I was appointed to be their governor in the land of Judah, from the twentieth year [a]until the thirty-second year of King Ar·ta·xerx′ēs, twelve years, neither I nor my brothers [b]ate the governor's provisions.

15 But the former governors who *were* before me laid burdens on the people, and took from them bread and wine, besides forty shekels of silver. Yes, even their servants bore rule over the people, but [a]I did not do so, because of the [b]fear of God.

16 Indeed, I also continued the [a]work on this wall, and [1]we did not buy any land. All my servants *were* gathered there for the work.

17 And [a]at my table *were* one hundred and fifty Jews and rulers, besides those who came to us from the nations around us.

18 Now *that* [a]which was prepared daily *was* one ox *and* six choice sheep. Also fowl were prepared for me, and once every ten days an abundance of all kinds of wine. Yet in spite of this [b]I did not demand the governor's provisions, because the bondage was heavy on this people.

19 [a]Remember me, my God, for good, *according to* all that I have done for this people.

6

Now it happened [a]when San·bal′lat, Tō·bī′ah, [1]Gē′shem the Arab, and the rest of our enemies heard that I had rebuilt the wall, and *that* there

7 [a][Ex. 22:25] [1]*charging interest* [2]Lit. *held*
8 [a]Lev. 25:48
9 [a]Lev. 25:36 [b]2 Sam. 12:14
10 [1]*interest*
12 [a]Ezra 10:5
13 [a]Acts 13:51; 18:6 [b]2 Kin. 23:3 [1]Lit. *my lap*
14 [a]Neh. 2:1; 13:6 [b][1 Cor. 9:4–15]
15 [a]2 Cor. 11:9; 12:13 [b]Neh. 5:9
16 [a]Neh. 4:1; 6:1 [1]So with MT; LXX, Syr., Vg. *I*
17 [a]1 Kin. 18:19
18 [a]1 Kin. 4:22 [b]Neh. 5:14, 15
19 [a]Neh. 13:14, 22, 31

CHAPTER 6

1 [a]Neh. 2:10, 19; 4:1, 7; 13:28 [1]Or *Gashmu*

were no breaks left in it [b](though
at that time I had not hung the
doors in the gates),
2 that San·bal′lat and [1]Gē′shem
[a]sent to me, saying, "Come, let
us meet together [2]among the villages in the plain of [b]Ō′nō." But
they [c]thought to do me harm.
3 So I sent messengers to them,
saying, "I *am* doing a great work,
so that I cannot come down. Why
should the work cease while I
leave it and go down to you?"
4 But they sent me this message four times, and I answered
them in the same manner.
5 Then San·bal′lat sent his servant to me as before, the fifth
time, with an open letter in his
hand.
6 In it *was* written:

It is reported among the
nations, and [1]Gē′shem says,
that you and the Jews
plan to rebel; therefore,
according to these rumors,
you are rebuilding the wall,
[a]that you may be their king.
7 And you have also
appointed prophets to
proclaim concerning you at
Jerusalem, saying, "*There is*
a king in Judah!" Now these
matters will be reported to
the king. So come, therefore,
and let us consult together.

8 Then I sent to him, saying,
"No such things as you say are
being done, but you invent them
in your own heart."
9 For they all *were trying* to
make us afraid, saying, "Their
hands will be weakened in the
work, and it will not be done."
Now therefore, O God,
strengthen my hands.

1 [b]Neh. 3:1, 3

2 [a]Prov. 26:24, 25
[b]1 Chr. 8:12
[c]Ps. 37:12, 32
[1]Or *Gashmu*
[2]Or *in Kephirim*, exact location unknown

6 [a]Neh. 2:19
[1]Heb. *Gashmu*

10 [1]Lit. *house*

12 [a]Ezek. 13:22

14 [a]Neh. 13:29
[b]Ezek. 13:17

16 [a]Neh. 2:10, 20; 4:1, 7; 6:1
[b]Ps. 126:2

10 Afterward I came to the
house of She·māi′ah the son of
De·lai′ah, the son of Me·het′a·bel,
who *was* a secret informer; and
he said, "Let us meet together
in the house of God, within the
[1]temple, and let us close the
doors of the temple, for they are
coming to kill you; indeed, at
night they will come to kill you."
11 And I said, "Should such a
man as I flee? And who *is there*
such as I who would go into the
temple to save his life? I will not
go in!"
12 Then I perceived that God
had not sent him at all, but that
[a]he pronounced *this* prophecy
against me because Tō·bī′ah and
San·bal′lat had hired him.
13 For this reason he *was* hired,
that I should be afraid and
act that way and sin, so *that*
they might have *cause* for an
evil report, that they might reproach me.
14 [a]My God, remember Tō·bī′ah
and San·bal′lat, according
to these their works, and the
[b]prophetess Nō·a·dī′ah and the
rest of the prophets who would
have made me afraid.
15 So the wall was finished on
the twenty-fifth *day* of Ē′lul, in
fifty-two days.
16 And it happened, [a]when all
our enemies heard *of it*, and all
the nations around us saw *these
things*, that they were very dis-
heartened in their own eyes; for
[b]they perceived that this work
was done by our God.
17 Also in those days the nobles of Judah sent many letters
to Tō·bī′ah, and *the letters of*
Tō·bī′ah came to them.
18 For many in Judah were
pledged to him, because he was

the [a]son-in-law of Shech·a·nī′ah
the son of Ā′rah, and his son
Jē·hō·hā′nan had married the
daughter of [b]Me·shul′lam the
son of Ber·e·chī′ah.
19 Also they reported his good
deeds before me, and reported
my [1]words to him. Tō·bī′ah sent
letters to frighten me.

7 Then it was, when the wall
was built and I had [a]hung
the doors, when the gatekeepers,
the singers, and the Lē′vītes
had been appointed,
2 that I gave the charge of Jerusalem
to my brother [a]Ha·nā′nī,
and Han·a·nī′ah the leader [b]of
the [1]citadel, for he *was* a faithful
man and [c]feared God more than
many.
3 And I said to them, "Do not
let the gates of Jerusalem be
opened until the sun is hot; and
while they stand *guard,* let them
shut and bar the doors; and appoint
guards from among the
inhabitants of Jerusalem, one at
his watch station and another in
front of his own house."
4 Now the city *was* large and
spacious, but the people in it
were [a]few, and the houses *were*
not rebuilt.
5 Then my God put it into my
heart to gather the nobles, the
rulers, and the people, that they
might be registered by genealogy.
And I found a register of
the genealogy of those who had
come up in the first *return,* and
found written in it:

6 [a]These *are* the people of the
province who came back
from the captivity, of those
who had been carried away,
whom Ne·bū·chad·nez′zar
the king of Babylon had
carried away, and who
returned to Jerusalem and
Judah, everyone to his city.
7 Those who came with
[a]Ze·rub′ba·bel *were* Jesh′ū·a,
Nē·he·mī′ah, [1]Az·a·rī′ah,
Rā·a·mī′ah, Nā·ham′a·nī,
Mor′de·caī, Bil′shan,
[2]Mis′pe·reth, Big′vaī,
Nē′hum, and Bā′a·nah.
The number of the men
of the people of Israel:
8 the sons of Pā′rosh, two
thousand one hundred and
seventy-two;
9 the sons of Sheph·a·tī′ah,
three hundred and seventy-two;
10 the sons of Ā′rah, six
hundred and fifty-two;
11 the sons of Pā′hath-Mō′ab,
of the sons of Jesh′ū·a and
Jō′ab, two thousand eight
hundred and eighteen;
12 the sons of Ē′lam, one
thousand two hundred and
fifty-four;
13 the sons of Zat′tū, eight
hundred and forty-five;
14 the sons of Zac′caī, seven
hundred and sixty;
15 the sons of [1]Bin′nū·ī, six
hundred and forty-eight;
16 the sons of Bē′baī, six
hundred and twenty-eight;
17 the sons of Az′gad, two
thousand three hundred and
twenty-two;
18 the sons of Ad·o·nī′kam, six
hundred and sixty-seven;
19 the sons of Big′vaī, two
thousand and sixty-seven;
20 the sons of Ā′din, six
hundred and fifty-five;
21 the sons of Ā′ter of
Hez·e·kī′ah, ninety-eight;
22 the sons of Hā′shum, three
hundred and twenty-eight;

18 [a]Neh. 13:4, 28 [b]Ezra 10:15
19 [1]Or *affairs*

CHAPTER 7

1 [a]Neh. 6:1, 15
2 [a]Neh. 1:2 [b]Neh. 2:8; 10:23 [c]Ex. 18:21 [1]*palace*
4 [a]Deut. 4:27
6 [a]Ezra 2:1–70
7 [a]Ezra 5:2 [1]*Seraiah,* Ezra 2:2 [2]*Mispar,* Ezra 2:2
15 [1]*Bani,* Ezra 2:10

23 the sons of Bē′zaī, three hundred and twenty-four;
24 the sons of [1]Hā′riph, one hundred and twelve;
25 the sons of [1]Gib′ē·on, ninety-five;
26 the men of Bethlehem and Ne·toph′ah, one hundred and eighty-eight;
27 the men of An′a·thoth, one hundred and twenty-eight;
28 the men of [1]Beth Az′ma·veth, forty-two;
29 the men of [1]Kir′jath Jē′a·rim, Chē·phī′rah, and Be·er′oth, seven hundred and forty-three;
30 the men of Rā′mah and Gē′ba, six hundred and twenty-one;
31 the men of Mich′mas, one hundred and twenty-two;
32 the men of Beth′el and Aī, one hundred and twenty-three;
33 the men of the other Nē′bō, fifty-two;
34 the sons of the other [a]Ē′lam, one thousand two hundred and fifty-four;
35 the sons of Hā′rim, three hundred and twenty;
36 the sons of Jericho, three hundred and forty-five;
37 the sons of Lod, Hā′did, and Ō′nō, seven hundred and twenty-one;
38 the sons of Se·nā′ah, three thousand nine hundred and thirty.

39 The priests: the sons of [a]Je·daī′ah, of the house of Jesh′ū·a, nine hundred and seventy-three;
40 the sons of [a]Im′mer, one thousand and fifty-two;
41 the sons of [a]Pash′hur, one thousand two hundred and forty-seven;
42 the sons of [a]Hā′rim, one thousand and seventeen.

43 The Lē′vītes: the sons of Jesh′ū·a, of Kad′mi·el, *and* of the sons of [1]Hō′de·vah, seventy-four.
44 The singers: the sons of Ā′saph, one hundred and forty-eight.
45 The gatekeepers: the sons of Shal′lum, the sons of Ā′ter, the sons of Tal′mon, the sons of Ak′kub, the sons of Ha·tī′ta, the sons of Shō′baī, one hundred and thirty-eight.

46 The Neth′i·nim: the sons of Zī′ha, the sons of Ha·sū′pha, the sons of Tab·bā′oth,
47 the sons of Kē′ros, the sons of [1]Sī′a, the sons of Pā′don,
48 the sons of [1]Le·bā′na, the sons of [2]Hag′a·ba, the sons of [3]Sal′maī,
49 the sons of Hā′nan, the sons of Gid′del, the sons of Gā′har,
50 the sons of Rē·āi′ah, the sons of Rē′zin, the sons of Ne·kō′da,
51 the sons of Gaz′zam, the sons of Uz′za, the sons of Pa·sē′ah,
52 the sons of Bē′saī, the sons of Me·ū′nim, the sons of [1]Ne·phish′e·sim,
53 the sons of Bak′buk, the sons of Ha·kū′pha, the sons of Har′hur,
54 the sons of [1]Baz′lith, the sons of Me·hī′da, the sons of Har′sha,
55 the sons of Bar′kos, the sons of Sis′e·ra, the sons of Tam′ah,

---

24 [1]*Jorah,* Ezra 2:18
25 [1]*Gibbar,* Ezra 2:20
28 [1]*Azmaveth,* Ezra 2:24
29 [1]*Kirjath Arim,* Ezra 2:25
34 [a]Neh. 7:12
39 [a]1 Chr. 24:7
40 [a]1 Chr. 9:12
41 [a]Ezra 2:38; 10:22
42 [a]1 Chr. 24:8
43 [1]*Hodaviah,* Ezra 2:40; or *Judah,* Ezra 3:9
47 [1]*Siaha,* Ezra 2:44
48 [1]MT *Lebanah* [2]MT *Hogabah* [3]*Shalmai,* Ezra 2:46; or *Shamlai*
52 [1]*Nephusim,* Ezra 2:50
54 [1]*Bazluth,* Ezra 2:52

56 the sons of Ne·zī'ah, and the sons of Ha·tī'pha.
57 The sons of Solomon's servants: the sons of Sō'taī, the sons of Sō'phe·reth, the sons of [1]Pe·rī'da,
58 the sons of Jā'a·la, the sons of Dar'kon, the sons of Gid'del,
59 the sons of Sheph·a·tī'ah, the sons of Hat'til, the sons of Poch'e·reth of Ze·bā'im, and the sons of [1]Ā'mon.
60 All the Neth'i·nim, and the sons of Solomon's servants, *were* three hundred and ninety-two.
61 And these *were* the ones who came up from Tel Mē'lah, Tel Har'sha, Chē'rub, [1]Ad'don, and Im'mer, but they could not identify their father's house nor their lineage, whether they *were* of Israel:
62 the sons of De·laī'ah, the sons of Tō·bī'ah, the sons of Ne·kō'da, six hundred and forty-two;
63 and of the priests: the sons of Ha·baī'ah, the sons of [1]Koz, the sons of Bar·zil'laī, who took a wife of the daughters of Bar·zil'laī the Gil'ē·ad·īte, and was called by their name.
64 These sought their listing *among* those who were registered by genealogy, but it was not found; therefore they were excluded from the priesthood as defiled.
65 And the [1]governor said to them that they should not eat of the most holy things till a priest could consult with the Ū'rim and Thum'mim.

57 [1]*Peruda,* Ezra 2:55
59 [1]*Ami,* Ezra 2:57
61 [1]*Addan,* Ezra 2:59
63 [1]Or *Hakkoz*
65 [1]Heb. *Tirshatha*
70 [a]Neh. 8:9 [1]Heb. *Tirshatha*
71 [a]Ezra 2:69
73 [a]Ezra 3:1

66 Altogether the whole assembly *was* forty-two thousand three hundred and sixty,
67 besides their male and female servants, of whom *there were* seven thousand three hundred and thirty-seven; and they had two hundred and forty-five men and women singers.
68 Their horses were seven hundred and thirty-six, their mules two hundred and forty-five,
69 *their* camels four hundred and thirty-five, *and* donkeys six thousand seven hundred and twenty.
70 And some of the heads of the fathers' *houses* gave to the work. [a]The [1]governor gave to the treasury one thousand gold drachmas, fifty basins, and five hundred and thirty priestly garments.
71 Some of the heads of the fathers' *houses* gave to the treasury of the work [a]twenty thousand gold drachmas, and two thousand two hundred silver minas.
72 And that which the rest of the people gave *was* twenty thousand gold drachmas, two thousand silver minas, and sixty-seven priestly garments.

73 So the priests, the Lē'vītes, the gatekeepers, the singers, *some* of the people, the Neth'i-nim, and all Israel dwelt in their cities.

[a]When the seventh month came, the children of Israel *were* in their cities.

8 Now all [a]the people gathered together as one man
in the open square that *was* [b]in
front of the Water Gate; and they
told Ezra the [c]scribe to bring
the Book of the Law of Moses,
which the LORD had commanded
Israel.
2 So Ezra the priest brought
[a]the Law before the assembly
of men and women and all who
could hear with understanding
[b]on the first day of the seventh
month.
3 Then he [a]read from it in the
open square that *was* in front
of the Water Gate [1]from morning until midday, before the
men and women and those who
could understand; and the ears
of all the people *were attentive*
to the Book of the Law.
4 So Ezra the scribe stood on
a platform of wood which they
had made for the purpose; and
beside him, at his right hand,
stood Mat·ti·thī′ah, Shē′ma,
A·naī′ah, Ū·rī′jah, Hil·kī′ah, and
Mā·a·sēi′ah; and at his left hand
Pe·dāi′ah, Mish′a·el, Mal·chī′-
jah, Hā′shum, Hash·ba·da′na,
Zech·a·rī′ah, *and* Me·shul′lam.
5 And Ezra opened the book
in the sight of all the people, for
he was *standing* above all the
people; and when he opened it,
all the people [a]stood up.
6 And Ezra blessed the LORD,
the great God. Then all the people [a]answered, "Amen, Amen!"
while [b]lifting up their hands.
And they [c]bowed their heads
and worshiped the LORD with
their faces to the ground.
7 Also Jesh′ū·a, Bā′nī, Sher·e-
bī′ah, Jā′min, Ak′kub, Shab′-
be·thaī, Hō·dī′jah, Mā·a·sēi′ah,
Ke·lī′ta, Az·a·rī′ah, Joz′a·bad,
Hā′nan, Pe·lāi′ah, and the Lē′-
vītes, [a]helped the people to
understand the Law; and the
people [b]*stood* in their place.
8 So they read distinctly from
the book, in the Law of God;
and they gave the sense, and
helped *them* to understand the
reading.
9 [a]And Nē·he·mī′ah, who *was*
the [1]governor, Ezra the priest
and scribe, and the Lē′vītes who
taught the people said to all
the people, [b]"This day *is* holy
to the LORD your God; [c]do not
mourn nor weep." For all the
people wept, when they heard
the words of the Law.
10 Then he said to them, "Go
your way, eat the fat, drink the
sweet, [a]and send portions to
those for whom nothing is prepared; for *this* day *is* holy to our
Lord. Do not sorrow, for the joy
of the LORD is your strength."
11 So the Lē′vītes quieted all the
people, saying, "Be still, for the
day *is* holy; do not be grieved."
12 And all the people went their
way to eat and drink, to [a]send
portions and rejoice greatly,
because they [b]understood the
words that were declared to
them.
13 Now on the second day the
heads of the fathers' *houses* of
all the people, with the priests
and Lē′vītes, were gathered to
Ezra the scribe, in order to understand the words of the Law.
14 And they found written in
the Law, which the LORD had
commanded by Moses, that the
children of Israel should dwell
in [a]booths[1] during the feast of
the seventh month,
15 and [a]that they should announce and proclaim in all their

CHAPTER 8
1 [a]Ezra 3:1 [b]Neh. 3:26 [c]Ezra 7:6
2 [a][Deut. 31:11, 12] [b]Lev. 23:24
3 [a]2 Kin. 23:2 [1]Lit. *from the light*
5 [a]Judg. 3:20
6 [a]Neh. 5:13 [b]Ps. 28:2 [c]2 Chr. 20:18
7 [a][Mal. 2:7] [b]Neh. 9:3
9 [a]Neh. 7:65, 70; 10:1 [b]Num. 29:1 [c]Deut. 16:14 [1]Heb. *Tirshatha*
10 [a]Rev. 11:10
12 [a]Neh. 8:10 [b]Neh. 8:7, 8
14 [a]Lev. 23:34, 40, 42 [1]Temporary shelters
15 [a]Lev. 23:4

cities and [b]in Jerusalem, saying,
"Go out to the mountain, and
[c]bring olive branches, branches
of oil trees, myrtle branches,
palm branches, and branches of
leafy trees, to make booths, as *it*
is written."
16 Then the people went out
and brought *them* and made
themselves booths, each one on
the [a]roof of his house, or in their
courtyards or the courts of the
house of God, and in the open
square of the [b]Water Gate [c]and
in the open square of the Gate of
Ē′phra·im.
17 So the whole assembly of
those who had returned from
the captivity made [1]booths and
sat under the booths; for since
the days of Joshua the son of
Nun until that day the children
of Israel had not done so. And
there was very [a]great gladness.
18 Also [a]day by day, from the
first day until the last day, he
read from the Book of the Law
of God. And they kept the feast
[b]seven days; and on the [c]eighth
day *there was* a sacred assembly, according to the *prescribed*
manner.

9 Now on the twenty-fourth
day of [a]this month the children of Israel were assembled
with fasting, in sackcloth, [b]and
with [1]dust on their heads.
2 Then [a]those of Israelite lineage separated themselves from
all foreigners; and they stood
and [b]confessed their sins and
the iniquities of their fathers.
3 And they stood up in their
place and [a]read from the Book
of the Law of the LORD their God
for one-fourth of the day; and *for*
another fourth they confessed
and worshiped the LORD their
God.
4 Then Jesh′ū·a, Bā′nī, Kad′-
mi·el, Sheb·a·nī′ah, Bun′nī, Sher-
e·bī′ah, Bā′nī, *and* Che·nā′nī
stood on the [1]stairs of the Lē′-
vītes and cried out with a loud
voice to the LORD their God.
5 And the Lē′vītes, Jesh′ū·a,
Kad′mi·el, Bā′nī, Ha·shab·nī′ah,
Sher·e·bī′ah, Hō·dī′jah, Sheb·a-
nī′ah, *and* Peth·a·hī′ah, said:

"Stand up *and* bless the LORD
your God
Forever and ever!

"Blessed be [a]Your glorious
name,
Which is exalted above all
blessing and praise!
6 [a]You alone *are* the LORD;
[b]You have made heaven,
[c]The heaven of heavens, with
[d]all their host,
The earth and everything
on it,
The seas and all that is in
them,
And You [e]preserve them all.
The host of heaven worships
You.

7 "You *are* the LORD God,
Who chose [a]Abram,
And brought him out of Ūr
of the Chal·dē′ans,
And gave him the name
[b]Abraham;
8 You found his heart [a]faithful
before You,
And made a [b]covenant with
him
To give the land of the
Cā′naan·ītes,
The Hit′tītes, the Am′o·rītes,
The Per′iz·zītes, the
Jeb′ū·sītes,

15 [b]Deut. 16:16 [c]Lev. 23:40
16 [a]Deut. 22:8 [b]Neh. 12:37 [c]2 Kin. 14:13
17 [a]2 Chr. 30:21 [1]Temporary shelters
18 [a]Deut. 31:11 [b]Lev. 23:36 [c]Num. 29:35

CHAPTER 9

1 [a]Neh. 8:2 [b]1 Sam. 4:12 [1]Lit. *earth on them*
2 [a]Neh. 13:3, 30 [b]Neh. 1:6
3 [a]Neh. 8:7, 8
4 [1]Lit. *ascent*
5 [a]1 Chr. 29:13
6 [a]2 Kin. 19:15, 19 [b]Rev. 14:7 [c][Deut. 10:14] [d]Gen. 2:1 [e][Ps. 36:6]
7 [a]Gen. 11:31 [b]Gen. 17:5
8 [a]Gen. 15:6; 22:1–3 [b]Gen. 15:18

And the Gir'ga·shites—
To give *it* to his
descendants.
You [c]have performed Your
words,
For You *are* righteous.

9 "You[a] saw the affliction of
our fathers in Egypt,
And [b]heard their cry by the
Red Sea.
10 You [a]showed signs and
wonders against
Pharaoh,
Against all his servants,
And against all the people
of his land.
For You knew that they
[b]acted [1]proudly against
them.
So You [c]made a name for
Yourself, as *it is* this day.
11 [a]And You divided the sea
before them,
So that they went through
the midst of the sea on
the dry land;
And their persecutors You
threw into the deep,
[b]As a stone into the mighty
waters.
12 Moreover You [a]led them by
day with a cloudy pillar,
And by night with a pillar
of fire,
To give them light on the
road
Which they should travel.

13 "You[a] came down also on
Mount Sinai,
And spoke with them from
heaven,
And gave them [b]just
ordinances and true
laws,
Good statutes and
commandments.
14 You made known to them
Your [a]holy Sabbath,
And commanded them
precepts, statutes and
laws,
By the hand of Moses Your
servant.
15 You [a]gave them bread from
heaven for their hunger,
And [b]brought them water
out of the rock for their
thirst,
And told them to [c]go in to
possess the land
Which You had [1]sworn to
give them.

16 "But[a] they and our fathers
acted [1]proudly,
[b]Hardened[2] their necks,
And did not heed Your
commandments.
17 They refused to obey,
And [a]they were not mindful
of Your wonders
That You did among them.
But they hardened their
necks,
And [1]in their rebellion
They appointed [b]a leader
To return to their bondage.
But You *are* God,
Ready to pardon,
[c]Gracious and merciful,
Slow to anger,
Abundant in kindness,
And did not forsake them.

18 "Even [a]when they made
a molded calf for
themselves,
And said, 'This *is* your god
That brought you up out of
Egypt,'
And worked great
provocations,
19 Yet in Your [a]manifold
mercies

---

8 [c]Josh. 23:14
9 [a]Ex. 2:25; 3:7 [b]Ex. 14:10
10 [a]Ex. 7—14 [b]Ex. 18:11 [c]Jer. 32:20 [1]*presumptuously* or *insolently*
11 [a]Ex. 14:20–28 [b]Ex. 15:1, 5
12 [a]Ex. 13:21, 22
13 [a]Ex. 20:1–18 [b][Rom. 7:12]
14 [a]Gen. 2:3
15 [a]Ex. 16:14–17 [b]Ex. 17:6 [c]Deut. 1:8 [1]Lit. *raised Your hand to*
16 [a]Ps. 106:6 [b]Deut. 1:26–33; 31:27 [1]*presumptuously* [2]*Stiffened their necks*, became stubborn
17 [a]Ps. 78:11, 42–45 [b]Num. 14:4 [c]Joel 2:13 [1]So with MT, Vg.; LXX *in Egypt*
18 [a]Ex. 32:4–8, 31
19 [a]Ps. 106:45

You did not forsake them in
the wilderness.
The [b]pillar of the cloud did
not depart from them by
day,
To lead them on the road;
Nor the pillar of fire by
night,
To show them light,
And the way they should go.
20 You also gave Your [a]good
Spirit to instruct them,
And did not withhold Your
[b]manna from their
mouth,
And gave them [c]water for
their thirst.
21 [a]Forty years You sustained
them in the wilderness;
They lacked nothing;
Their [b]clothes did not wear
out
And their feet did not swell.

22 "Moreover You gave them
kingdoms and nations,
And divided them into
[1]districts.
So they took possession of
the land of [a]Sī'hon,
[2]The land of the king of
Hesh'bon,
And the land of Og king of
Bā'shan.
23 You also multiplied [a]their
children as the stars of
heaven,
And brought them into the
land
Which You had told their
fathers
To go in and possess.
24 So [a]the [1]people went in
And possessed the land;
[b]You subdued before them
the inhabitants of the
land,
The Cā'naan·ītes,
And gave them into their
hands,
With their kings
And the people of the land,
That they might do with
them as they wished.
25 And they took strong cities
and a [a]rich land,
And possessed [b]houses full
of all goods,
Cisterns *already* dug,
vineyards, olive groves,
And [1]fruit trees in
abundance.
So they ate and were filled
and [c]grew fat,
And delighted themselves in
Your great [d]goodness.

26 "Nevertheless they [a]were
disobedient
And rebelled against You,
[b]Cast Your law behind their
backs
And killed Your [c]prophets,
who [1]testified against
them
To turn them to Yourself;
And they worked great
provocations.
27 [a]Therefore You delivered
them into the hand of
their enemies,
Who oppressed them;
And in the time of their
trouble,
When they cried to You,
You [b]heard from heaven;
And according to Your
abundant mercies
[c]You gave them deliverers
who saved them
From the hand of their
enemies.

28 "But after they had rest,
[a]They again did evil before
You.

19 [b]1 Cor. 10:1
20 [a]Num. 11:17 [b]Ex. 16:14–16 [c]Ex. 17:6
21 [a]Deut. 2:7 [b]Deut. 8:4; 29:5
22 [a]Num. 21:21–35 [1]Lit. *corners* [2]So with MT, Vg.; LXX omits *The land of*
23 [a]Gen. 15:5; 22:17
24 [a]Josh. 1:2–4 [b][Ps. 44:2, 3] [1]Lit. *sons*
25 [a]Num. 13:27 [b]Deut. 6:11 [c][Deut. 32:15] [d]Hos. 3:5 [1]Lit. *trees for eating*
26 [a]Judg. 2:11 [b]1 Kin. 14:9 [c]1 Kin. 18:4; 19:10 [1]*admonished* or *warned them*
27 [a]Judg. 2:14 [b]Ps. 106:44 [c]Judg. 2:18
28 [a]Judg. 3:12

Therefore You left them
in the hand of their
enemies,
So that they had dominion
over them;
Yet when they returned and
cried out to You,
You heard from heaven;
And [b]many times You
delivered them
according to Your
mercies,
29 And [1]testified against them,
That You might bring them
back to Your law.
Yet they acted [2]proudly,
And did not heed Your
commandments,
But sinned against Your
judgments,
[a]'Which if a man does, he
shall live by them.'
And they shrugged their
shoulders,
[3]Stiffened their necks,
And would not hear.
30 Yet for many years You had
patience with them,
And [1]testified [a]against them
by Your Spirit [b]in Your
prophets.
Yet they would not listen;
[c]Therefore You gave them
into the hand of the
peoples of the lands.
31 Nevertheless in Your great
mercy
[a]You did not utterly consume
them nor forsake them;
For You *are* God, gracious
and merciful.

32 "Now therefore, our God,
The great, the [a]mighty, and
awesome God,
Who keeps covenant and
mercy:
Do not let all the [1]trouble
seem small before You
That has come upon us,
Our kings and our princes,
Our priests and our prophets,
Our fathers and on all Your
people,
[b]From the days of the kings
of Assyria until this day.
33 However, [a]You *are* just in all
that has befallen us;
For You have dealt faithfully,
But [b]we have done wickedly.
34 Neither our kings nor our
princes,
Our priests nor our fathers,
Have kept Your law,
Nor heeded Your
commandments and Your
testimonies,
With which You testified
against them.
35 For they have [a]not served
You in their kingdom,
Or in the many good *things*
that You gave them,
Or in the large and rich land
which You set before
them;
Nor did they turn from their
wicked works.

36 "Here [a]we *are*, servants
today!
And the land that You gave
to our fathers,
To eat its fruit and its
bounty,
Here we *are*, servants in it!
37 And [a]it yields much increase
to the kings
You have set over us,
Because of our sins;
Also they have [b]dominion
over our bodies and our
cattle
At their pleasure;
And we *are* in great distress.

28 [b]Ps. 106:43
29 [a]Lev. 18:5 [1]*admonished them* [2]*presumptuously* [3]Became stubborn
30 [a]Jer. 7:25 [b][Acts 7:51] [c]Is. 5:5 [1]*admonished* or *warned them*
31 [a]Jer. 4:27
32 [a][Ex. 34:6, 7] [b]2 Kin. 15:19; 17:3–6 [1]*hardship*
33 [a][Dan. 9:14] [b][Dan. 9:5, 6, 8]
35 [a]Deut. 28:47
36 [a]Deut. 28:48
37 [a]Deut. 28:33, 51 [b]Deut. 28:48

38 "And because of all this,
We [a]make a sure *covenant*
and write *it;*
Our leaders, our Lē′vītes,
and our priests [b]seal *it.*"

10

Now those who placed *their* seal on *the document were:*

Nē·he·mī′ah the [1]governor,
[a]the son of Hac·a·lī′ah, and Zed-
e·kī′ah,
2 [a]Se·rāi′ah, Az·a·rī′ah, Jer·e-
mī′ah,
3 Pash′hur, Am·a·rī′ah, Mal-
chī′jah,
4 Hat′tush, Sheb·a·nī′ah, Mal′-
luch,
5 Hā′rim, Mer′e·moth, Ō·ba-
dī′ah,
6 Daniel, Gin′ñe·thon, Bar′-
uch,
7 Me·shul′lam, A·bī′jah, Mij′a-
min,
8 Mā·a·zī′ah, Bil′gaī, *and* She-
māi′ah. These *were* the priests.
9 The Lē′vītes: Jesh′ū·a the son
of Az·a·nī′ah, Bin′nū·ī of the sons
of Hen′a·dad, *and* Kad′mi·el.
10 Their brethren: Sheb·a·nī′ah,
Hō·dī′jah, Ke·lī′ta, Pe·lāi′ah, Hā′-
nan,
11 Mī′cha, Rē′hob, Hash·a-
bī′ah,
12 Zac′cur, Sher·e·bī′ah, Sheb-
a·nī′ah,
13 Hō·dī′jah, Bā′nī, *and* Be-
nī′nū.
14 The leaders of the people:
[a]Pā′rosh, Pā′hath-Mō′ab, Ē′lam,
Zat′tū, Bā′nī,
15 Bun′nī, Az′gad, Bē′baī,
16 Ad·o·nī′jah, Big′vaī, Ā′din,
17 Ā′ter, Hez·e·kī′ah, Az′zur,
18 Hō·dī′jah, Hā′shum, Bē′zaī,
19 Hā′riph, An′a·thoth, Nē′baī,
20 Mag′pi·ash, Me·shul′lam, Hē′-
zir,
21 Me·shez′a·bel, Zā′dok, Jad′-
dū·a,
22 Pel·a·tī′ah, Hā′nan, A·naī′ah,
23 Hō·shē′a, Han·a·nī′ah, Has′-
shub,
24 Hal·lō′hesh, Pil′ha, Shō′bek,
25 Rē′hum, Ha·shab′nah, Mā·a-
sēi′ah,
26 A·hī′jah, Hā′nan, Ā′nan,
27 Mal′luch, Hā′rim, *and* Bā′a-
nah.
28 [a]Now the rest of the people—the priests, the Lē′vītes,
the gatekeepers, the singers, the
Neth′i·nim, [b]and all those who
had separated themselves from
the peoples of the lands to the
Law of God, their wives, their
sons, and their daughters, everyone who had knowledge and
understanding—
29 these joined with their brethren, their nobles, [a]and entered
into a curse and an oath [b]to walk
in God's Law, which was given
by Moses the servant of God,
and to observe and do all the
commandments of the LORD our
Lord, and His ordinances and
His statutes:
30 We would not give [a]our
daughters as wives to the peoples of the land, nor take their
daughters for our sons;
31 [a]*if* the peoples of the land
brought [1]wares or any grain
to sell on the Sabbath day, we
would not buy it from them
on the Sabbath, or on a holy
day; and we would forego the
[b]seventh year's *produce* and the
[c]exacting[2] of every debt.
32 Also we made ordinances
for ourselves, to exact from
ourselves yearly [a]one-third of
a shekel for the service of the
house of our God:
33 for [a]the showbread, for the

38 [a]2 Kin. 23:3 [b]Neh. 10:1

CHAPTER 10

1 [a]Neh. 1:1 [1]Heb. *Tirshatha*

2 [a]Neh. 12:1–21

14 [a]Ezra 2:3

28 [a]Ezra 2:36–43 [b]Neh. 13:3

29 [a]Deut. 29:12 [b]2 Kin. 23:3

30 [a]Ex. 34:16

31 [a]Ex. 20:10 [b]Lev. 25:4 [c][Deut. 15:1, 2] [1]*merchandise* [2]*collection*

32 [a]Matt. 17:24

33 [a]Lev. 24:5

regular grain offering, for the
[b]regular burnt offering of the
Sabbaths, the New Moons, and
the set feasts; for the holy things,
for the sin offerings to make
atonement for Israel, and all the
work of the house of our God.
34 We cast lots among the
priests, the Lē′vītes, and the
people, [a]for bringing the wood
offering into the house of our
God, according to our fathers'
houses, at the appointed times
year by year, to burn on the altar of the LORD our God [b]as *it is*
written in the Law.
35 And *we made ordinances*
[a]to bring the firstfruits of our
ground and the firstfruits of all
fruit of all trees, year by year, to
the house of the LORD;
36 to bring the [a]firstborn of our
sons and our cattle, as *it is* written in the Law, and the firstborn
of our herds and our flocks,
to the house of our God, to
the priests who minister in the
house of our God;
37 [a]to bring the firstfruits of our
dough, our offerings, the fruit
from all kinds of trees, *the* new
wine and oil, to the priests, to the
storerooms of the [1]house of our
God; and to bring [b]the tithes of
our land to the Lē′vītes, for the
Lē′vītes should receive the tithes
in all our farming communities.
38 And the priest, the descendant of Aaron, shall be with
the Lē′vītes [a]when the Lē′vītes
receive tithes; and the Lē′vītes
shall bring up a tenth of the
tithes to the house of our God,
to [b]the rooms of the storehouse.
39 For the children of Israel and
the children of Levi [a]shall bring
the offering of the grain, of the
new wine and the oil, to the

33 [b]Num. 28; 29
34 [a]Neh. 13:31 [b]Lev. 6:12
35 [a]Ex. 23:19; 34:26
36 [a]Ex. 13:2, 12, 13
37 [a]Lev. 23:17 [b]Lev. 27:30 [1]Temple
38 [a]Num. 18:26 [b]1 Chr. 9:26
39 [a]Deut. 12:6, 11 [b]Neh. 13:10, 11 [c][Heb. 10:25]

CHAPTER 11

1 [a]Matt. 4:5; 5:35; 27:53
2 [a]Judg. 5:9
3 [a]1 Chr. 9:2, 3 [b]Ezra 2:43 [c]Ezra 2:55
4 [a]1 Chr. 9:3 [b]Gen. 38:29

storerooms where the articles
of the sanctuary *are, where* the
priests who minister and the
gatekeepers [b]and the singers
are; and we will not [c]neglect the
house of our God.

11 Now the leaders of the
people dwelt at Jerusa-
lem; the rest of the people cast
lots to bring one out of ten to
dwell in Jerusalem, [a]the holy
city, and nine-tenths *were to*
dwell in *other* cities.
2 And the people blessed all
the men who [a]willingly offered
themselves to dwell at Jerusalem.
3 [a]These *are* the heads of the
province who dwelt in Jerusalem. (But in the cities of Judah
everyone dwelt in his own possession in their cities—Israelites,
priests, Lē′vītes, [b]Neth′i·nim,
and [c]descendants of Solomon's
servants.)
4 Also [a]in Jerusalem dwelt
some of the children of Judah and
of the children of Benjamin.
The children of Judah:
A·thaī′ah the son of Uz·zī′ah,
the son of Zech·a·rī′ah, the son
of Am·a·rī′ah, the son of Sheph-
a·tī′ah, the son of Ma·hal′a·lel, of
the children of [b]Per′ez;
5 and Mā·a·sēi′ah the son of
Bar′uch, the son of Col-Hō′zeh,
the son of Ha·zaī′ah, the son of
A·dāi′ah, the son of Joi′ā·rib, the
son of Zech·a·rī′ah, the son of
Shi·lō′nī.
6 All the sons of Per′ez who
dwelt at Jerusalem *were* four
hundred and sixty-eight valiant
men.
7 And these are the sons of
Benjamin: Sal′lū the son of
Me·shul′lam, the son of Jō′ed,
the son of Pe·dāi′ah, the son of

Kō·laī′ah, the son of Mā·a·sēī′ah,
the son of Ith′i·el, the son of
Je·shā′i·ah;
8 and after him Gab·bā′ī
and Sal′laī, nine hundred and
twenty-eight.
9 Jō′el the son of Zich′rī *was*
their overseer, and Judah the
son of [1]Se·nū′ah *was* second
over the city.
10 [a]Of the priests: Je·daī′ah the
son of Joi′ā·rib, and Jā′chin;
11 Se·rāī′ah the son of Hil·kī′ah,
the son of Me·shul′lam, the son
of Zā′dok, the son of Me·rā′-
i·oth, the son of A·hī′tub, *was* the
leader of the house of God.
12 Their brethren who did the
work of the house *were* eight
hundred and twenty-two; and
A·dāī′ah the son of Je·rō′ham,
the son of Pel·a·lī′ah, the son of
Am′zī, the son of Zech·a·rī′ah,
the son of Pash′hur, the son of
Mal·chī′jah,
13 and his brethren, heads of
the fathers′ *houses*, *were* two
hundred and forty-two; and
A·mash′aī the son of Az′a·rel,
the son of Ah′zaī, the son of
Me·shil′le·moth, the son of Im′-
mer,
14 and their brethren, mighty
men of valor, *were* one hundred
and twenty-eight. Their overseer
was Zab′di·el [1]the son of *one of*
the great men.
15 Also of the Lē′vītes:
She·māī′ah the son of Has′shub,
the son of Az·rī′kam, the son of
Hash·a·bī′ah, the son of Bun′nī;
16 [a]Shab′be·thaī and [b]Joz′a·bad,
of the heads of the Lē′vītes, *had*
the oversight of [c]the business
outside of the [1]house of God;
17 Mat·ta·nī′ah the son of [1]Mī′-
cha, the son of Zab′dī, the son
of Ā′saph, the leader *who* began
the thanksgiving with prayer;
Bak·bū·kī′ah, the second among
his brethren; and Ab′da the son
of Sham′mū·a, the son of Gā′lal,
the son of Je·dū′thun.
18 All the Lē′vītes in [a]the holy
city *were* two hundred and
eighty-four.
19 Moreover the gatekeepers,
Ak′kub, Tal′mon, and their
brethren who kept the gates,
were one hundred and seventy-
two.
20 And the rest of Israel, of the
priests *and* Lē′vītes, *were* in all
the cities of Judah, everyone in
his inheritance.
21 [a]But the Neth′i·nim dwelt in
Ō′phel. And Zī′ha and Gish′pa
were over the Neth′i·nim.
22 Also the overseer of the Lē′-
vītes at Jerusalem *was* Uz′zī the
son of Bā′nī, the son of Hash-
a·bī′ah, the son of Mat·ta·nī′ah,
the son of Mī′cha, of the sons
of Ā′saph, the singers in charge
of the [1]service of the [2]house of
God.
23 For [a]*it was* the king′s command concerning them that a
[1]certain portion should be for
the singers, a quota day by day.
24 Peth·a·hī′ah the son of Me-
shez′a·bel, of the children of
[a]Zē′rah the son of Judah, *was*
[b]the[1] king′s deputy in all matters
concerning the people.
25 And as for the villages with
their fields, *some* of the children of Judah dwelt in [a]Kir′jath
Ar′ba and its villages, Dī′bon
and its villages, Je·kab′zē·el and
its villages;
26 in Jesh′ū·a, Mō′la·dah, Beth
Pē′let,
27 Hā′zar Shū′al, and Bē·er-
shē′ba and its villages;

9 [1]Or *Hassenuah*
10 [a]1 Chr. 9:10
14 [1]Or *the son of Haggedolim*
16 [a]Ezra 10:15 [b]Ezra 8:33 [c]1 Chr. 26:29 [1]Temple
17 [1]Or *Michah*
18 [a]Neh. 11:1
21 [a]Neh. 3:26
22 [1]*work* [2]Temple
23 [a]Ezra 6:8, 9; 7:20 [1]*fixed share*
24 [a]Gen. 38:30 [b]1 Chr. 18:17 [1]Lit. *at the king's hand*
25 [a]Josh. 14:15

28 in Zik′lag and Mē·cō′nah and
its villages;
29 in En Rim′mon, Zō′rah, Jar′-
muth,
30 Za·nō′ah, A·dul′lam, and
their villages; in Lā′chish and
its fields; in A·zē′kah and its
villages. They dwelt from Bē·er-
shē′ba to the Valley of Hin′nom.
31 Also the children of Benjamin from Gē′ba *dwelt* in Mich′-
mash, Āi′ja, and Beth′el, and
their villages;
32 in An′a·thoth, Nob, An·a-
nī′ah;
33 in Hā′zor, Rā′mah, Git′ta·im;
34 in Hā′did, Ze·bō′im, Ne·bal′-
lat;
35 in Lod, Ō′nō, *and* [a]the Valley
of Craftsmen.
36 Some of the Judean divisions
of Lē′vītes *were* in Benjamin.

12 Now these *are* the [a]priests
and the Lē′vītes who
came up with [b]Ze·rub′ba·bel the
son of She·al′ti·el, and Jesh′ū·a:
[c]Se·rāi′ah, Jer·e·mī′ah, Ezra,
2 Am·a·rī′ah, [1]Mal′luch, Hat′-
tush,
3 [1]Shech·a·nī′ah, [2]Rē′hum, [3]Mer′-
e·moth,
4 Id′dō, [1]Gin′ne·thoi, [a]A·bī′jah,
5 [1]Mij′a·min, [2]Mā·a·dī′ah, Bil′-
gah,
6 She·māi′ah, Joi′ā·rib, Je-
daī′ah,
7 [1]Sal′lū, Ā′mok, Hil·kī′ah, *and*
Je·daī′ah.
These *were* the heads of the
priests and their brethren in the
days of [a]Jesh′ū·a.
8 Moreover the Lē′vītes *were*
Jesh′ū·a, Bin′nū·ī, Kad′mi·el,
Sher·e·bī′ah, Judah, *and* Mat·ta-
nī′ah [a]*who led* the thanksgiving
psalms, he and his brethren.
9 Also Bak·bū·kī′ah and Un′nī,
their brethren, *stood* across
from them in *their* duties.
10 Jesh′ū·a begot Joi′a·kim,
Joi′a·kim begot E·lī′a·shib, E·lī′-
a·shib begot Joi′a·da,
11 Joi′a·da begot Jonathan, and
Jonathan begot Jad′dū·a.
12 Now in the days of Joi′a·kim,
the priests, the [a]heads of the fa-
thers′ *houses were:* of Se·rāi′ah,
Me·raī′ah; of Jer·e·mī′ah, Han·a-
nī′ah;
13 of Ezra, Me·shul′lam; of Am-
a·rī′ah, Jē·hō·hā′nan;
14 of [1]Mel′i·chū, Jonathan; of
[2]Sheb·a·nī′ah, Joseph;
15 of [1]Hā′rim, Ad′na; of [2]Me·rā′-
i·oth, Hel′kaī;
16 of Id′dō, Zech·a·rī′ah; of Gin′-
ne·thon, Me·shul′lam;
17 of A·bī′jah, Zich′rī; *the son*
of [1]Min′ja·min; of [2]Mō·a·dī′ah,
Pil′taī;
18 of Bil′gah, Sham′mū·a; of
She·māi′ah, Je·hon′a·than;
19 of Joi′ā·rib, Mat·tē′naī; of
Je·daī′ah, Uz′zī;
20 of [1]Sal′laī, Kal′laī; of Ā′mok,
Ē′ber;
21 of Hil·kī′ah, Hash·a·bī′ah;
and of Je·daī′ah, Ne·than′el.
22 During the reign of Da·rī′us
the Persian, a record *was also*
kept of the Lē′vītes and priests
who had been [a]heads of their
fathers′ *houses* in the days of
E·lī′a·shib, Joi′a·da, Jō·hā′nan,
and Jad′dū·a.
23 The sons of Levi, the heads
of the fathers′ *houses* until the
days of Jō·hā′nan the son of
E·lī′a·shib, *were* written in the
book of the [a]chronicles.
24 And the heads of the Lē′vītes
were Hash·a·bī′ah, Sher·e·bī′ah,
and Jesh′ū·a the son of Kad′-
mi·el, with their brothers across
from them, to [a]praise *and* give

35 [a]1 Chr. 4:14

CHAPTER 12

1 [a]Ezra 2:1, 2; 7:7 [b]Neh. 7:7 [c]Neh. 10:2–8

2 [1]*Melichu*, v. 14

3 [1]*Shebaniah*, v. 14 [2]*Harim*, v. 15 [3]*Meraioth*, v. 15

4 [a]Luke 1:5 [1]*Ginnethon*, v. 16

5 [1]*Minjamin*, v. 17 [2]*Moadiah*, v. 17

7 [a]Zech. 3:1 [1]*Sallai*, v. 20

8 [a]Neh. 11:17

12 [a]Neh. 7:70, 71; 8:13; 11:13

14 [1]*Malluch*, v. 2 [2]*Shechaniah*, v. 3

15 [1]*Rehum*, v. 3 [2]*Meremoth*, v. 3

17 [1]*Mijamin*, v. 5 [2]*Maadiah*, v. 5

20 [1]*Sallu*, v. 7

22 [a]1 Chr. 24:6

23 [a]1 Chr. 9:14–22

24 [a]Neh. 11:17

thanks, [b]group[1] alternating with
group, [c]according to the command of David the man of God.
25 Mat·ta·nī′ah, Bak·bū·kī′ah,
Ō·ba·dī′ah, Me·shul′lam, Tal′-
mon, and Ak′kub *were* gatekeepers keeping the watch at
the storerooms of the gates.
26 These *lived* in the days of
Joi′a·kim the son of Jesh′ū·a,
the son of [1]Jō′za·dak, and in the
days of Nē·he·mī′ah [a]the governor, and of Ezra the priest, [b]the
scribe.
27 Now at [a]the dedication of the
wall of Jerusalem they sought out
the Lē′vītes in all their places, to
bring them to Jerusalem to celebrate the dedication with gladness, [b]both with thanksgivings
and singing, *with* cymbals and
stringed instruments and harps.
28 And the sons of the singers gathered together from the
countryside around Jerusalem,
from the [a]villages of the Ne-
toph′a·thītes,
29 from the house of Gil′gal,
and from the fields of Gē′ba
and Az′ma·veth; for the singers
had built themselves villages all
around Jerusalem.
30 Then the priests and Lē′vītes
[a]purified themselves, and purified the people, the gates, and
the wall.
31 So I brought the leaders of
Judah up on the wall, and appointed two large thanksgiving
choirs. [a]*One* went to the right
hand on the wall [b]toward the
Refuse Gate.
32 After them went Hō·shaī′ah
and half of the leaders of
Judah,
33 and Az·a·rī′ah, Ezra, Me-
shul′lam,
34 Judah, Benjamin, She·māi′-
ah, Jer·e·mī′ah,
35 and some of the priests' sons
[a]with trumpets—Zech·a·rī′ah
the son of Jonathan, the son of
She·māi′ah, the son of Mat·ta-
nī′ah, the son of Mī·chaī′ah,
the son of Zac′cur, the son of
Ā′saph,
36 and his brethren, She·māi′ah,
Az′a·rel, Mil′a·laī, Gil′a·laī, Mā′aī,
Ne·than′el, Judah, *and* Ha·nā′nī,
with [a]the musical [b]instruments
of David the man of God. Ezra
the scribe *went* before them.
37 [a]By the Fountain Gate, in
front of them, they went up [b]the
stairs of the [c]City of David, on
the stairway of the wall, beyond
the house of David, as far as [d]the
Water Gate eastward.
38 [a]The other thanksgiving
choir went the opposite *way*,
and I *was* behind them with half
of the people on the wall, going
past the [b]Tower of the Ovens as
far as [c]the Broad Wall,
39 [a]and above the Gate of
Ē′phra·im, above [b]the Old Gate,
above [c]the Fish Gate, [d]the Tower
of Ha·nan′el, the Tower of [1]the
Hundred, as far as [e]the Sheep
Gate; and they stopped by [f]the
Gate of the Prison.
40 So the two thanksgiving
choirs stood in the house of
God, likewise I and the half of
the rulers with me;
41 and the priests, E·lī′a·kim,
Mā·a·sēi′ah, [1]Min′ja·min, Mī-
chaī′ah, El·i·ō·ē′naī, Zech·a·rī′ah,
and Han·a·nī′ah, with trumpets;
42 also Mā·a·sēi′ah, She·māi′ah,
El·ē·ā′zar, Uz′zī, Jē·hō·hā′nan,
Mal·chī′jah, Ē′lam, and Ē′zer.
The singers [1]sang loudly with
Jez·ra·hī′ah the director.
43 Also that day they offered

24 [b]Ezra 3:11 [c]1 Chr. 23—26 [1]Lit. *watch by watch*
26 [a]Neh. 8:9 [b]Ezra 7:6, 11 [1]*Jehozadak*, 1 Chr. 6:14
27 [a]Deut. 20:5 [b]1 Chr. 25:6
28 [a]1 Chr. 9:16
30 [a]Neh. 13:22, 30
31 [a]Neh. 12:38 [b]Neh. 2:13; 3:13
35 [a]Num. 10:2, 8
36 [a]1 Chr. 23:5 [b]2 Chr. 29:26, 27
37 [a]Neh. 2:14; 3:15 [b]Neh. 3:15 [c]2 Sam. 5:7–9 [d]Neh. 3:26; 8:1, 3, 16
38 [a]Neh. 12:31 [b]Neh. 3:11 [c]Neh. 3:8
39 [a]2 Kin. 14:13 [b]Neh. 3:6 [c]Neh. 3:3 [d]Neh. 3:1 [e]Neh. 3:32 [f]Jer. 32:2 [1]Heb. *Hammeah*
41 [1]Or *Mijamin*, v. 5
42 [1]Lit. *made their voice to be heard*

great sacrifices, and rejoiced,
for God had made them rejoice
with great joy; the women and
the children also rejoiced, so
that the joy of Jerusalem was
heard [a]afar off.
44 [a]And at the same time some
were appointed over the rooms
of the storehouse for the offerings,
the firstfruits, and the
[b]tithes, to gather into them from
the fields of the cities the portions
specified by the Law for
the priests and Lē′vītes; for Judah
rejoiced over the priests and
Lē′vītes who [1]ministered.
45 Both the singers and the
gatekeepers kept the charge of
their God and the charge of
the purification, [a]according to
the command of David *and* Solomon
his son.
46 For in the days of David
[a]and Ā′saph of old *there were*
chiefs of the singers, and songs
of praise and thanksgiving to
God.
47 In the days of Ze·rub′ba·bel
and in the days of Nē·he·mī′ah
all Israel gave the portions for
the singers and the gatekeepers,
a portion for [a]each day. [b]They
also [1]consecrated *holy things*
for the Lē′vītes, [c]and the Lē′vītes
consecrated *them* for the children
of Aaron.

13 On that day [a]they read
from the Book of Moses
in the hearing of the people, and
in it was found written [b]that no
Am′mon·īte or Mō′ab·īte should
ever come into the assembly of
God,
2 because they had not met
the children of Israel with bread
and water, but [a]hired Bā′laam
against them to curse them.
[b]However, our God turned the
curse into a blessing.
3 So it was, when they had
heard the Law, [a]that they separated
all the mixed multitude
from Israel.
4 Now before this, [a]E·lī′a·shib
the priest, having authority over
the storerooms of the house
of our God, *was* allied with
[b]Tō·bī′ah.
5 And he had prepared for
him a large room, [a]where previously
they had stored the grain
offerings, the frankincense, the
articles, the tithes of grain, the
new wine and oil, [b]which were
commanded *to be given* to the
Lē′vītes and singers and gatekeepers,
and the offerings for
the priests.
6 But during all this I was not
in Jerusalem, [a]for in the thirty-second
year of Ar·ta·xerx′ēs
king of Babylon I had returned
to the king. Then after certain
days I obtained leave from the
king,
7 and I came to Jerusalem and
discovered the evil that E·lī′a·shib
had done for Tō·bī′ah, in
[a]preparing a room for him in the
courts of the [1]house of God.
8 And it grieved me bitterly;
therefore I threw all the household
goods of Tō·bī′ah out of the
room.
9 Then I commanded them
to [a]cleanse the rooms; and I
brought back into them the
articles of the house of God,
with the grain offering and the
frankincense.
10 I also realized that the portions
for the Lē′vītes had [a]not
been given *them;* for each of the
Lē′vītes and the singers who did

43 [a]Ezra 3:13
44 [a]Neh. 13:5, 12, 13 [b]Neh. 10:37–39 [1]Lit. *stood*
45 [a]1 Chr. 25, 26
46 [a]2 Chr. 29:30
47 [a]Neh. 11:23 [b]Num. 18:21, 24 [c]Num. 18:26 [1]*set apart*

CHAPTER 13

1 [a]Neh. 8:3, 8; 9:3 [b]Deut. 23:3, 4
2 [a]Num. 22:5 [b]Num. 23:1; 24:10
3 [a]Neh. 9:2; 10:28
4 [a]Neh. 12:10 [b]Neh. 2:10; 4:3; 6:1
5 [a]Neh. 12:44 [b]Num. 18:21, 24
6 [a]Neh. 5:14–16
7 [a]Neh. 13:1, 5 [1]Temple
9 [a]2 Chr. 29:5, 15, 16
10 [a]Neh. 10:37

the work had gone back to [b]his
field.
11 So [a]I contended with the rulers, and said, [b]"Why is the house
of God forsaken?" And I gathered them together and set them
in their place.
12 [a]Then all Judah brought the
tithe of the grain and the new
wine and the oil to the storehouse.
13 [a]And I appointed as treasurers over the storehouse Shel-
e·mī'ah the priest and Zā'dok
the scribe, and of the Lē'vītes,
Pe·dāi'ah; and next to them *was*
Hā'nan the son of Zac'cur, the
son of Mat·ta·nī'ah; for they
were considered [b]faithful, and
their task *was* to distribute to
their brethren.
14 [a]Remember me, O my God,
concerning this, and do not wipe
out my good deeds that I have
done for the house of my God,
and for its services!
15 In those days I saw *people*
in Judah treading wine presses
[a]on the Sabbath, and bringing
in sheaves, and loading donkeys with wine, grapes, figs,
and all *kinds of* burdens, [b]which
they brought into Jerusalem on
the Sabbath day. And I warned
them about the day on which
they were selling provisions.
16 Men of Tȳre dwelt there
also, who brought in fish and all
kinds of goods, and sold *them*
on the Sabbath to the children
of Judah, and in Jerusalem.
17 Then I contended with the
nobles of Judah, and said to
them, "What evil thing *is* this
that you do, by which you profane the Sabbath day?
18 [a]"Did not your fathers do
thus, and did not our God bring

10 [b]Num. 35:2
11 [a]Neh. 13:17, 25 [b]Neh. 10:39
12 [a]Neh. 10:38; 12:44
13 [a]2 Chr. 31:12 [b]1 Cor. 4:2
14 [a]Neh. 5:19; 13:22, 31
15 [a][Ex. 20:10] [b][Jer. 17:21]
18 [a][Jer. 17:21]
19 [a]Lev. 23:32 [b]Jer. 17:21, 22
20 [1]*merchandise* [2]*spent the night*
21 [1]Lit. *before*
22 [a]Neh. 12:30
23 [a]Ezra 9:2 [b]Neh. 4:7
25 [a]Prov. 28:4 [b]Neh. 10:29, 30 [1]*pronounced them cursed*

all this disaster on us and on
this city? Yet you bring added
wrath on Israel by profaning the
Sabbath."
19 So it was, at the gates of Jerusalem, as it [a]began to be dark
before the Sabbath, that I commanded the gates to be shut,
and charged that they must not
be opened till after the Sabbath.
[b]Then I posted *some* of my servants at the gates, *so that* no
burdens would be brought in on
the Sabbath day.
20 Now the merchants and
sellers of all kinds of [1]wares
[2]lodged outside Jerusalem once
or twice.
21 Then I warned them, and
said to them, "Why do you spend
the night [1]around the wall? If
you do *so* again, I will lay hands
on you!" From that time on they
came no *more* on the Sabbath.
22 And I commanded the Lē'-
vītes that [a]they should cleanse
themselves, and that they should
go and guard the gates, to sanctify the Sabbath day.

Remember me, O my God,
concerning this also, and spare
me according to the greatness of
Your mercy!
23 In those days I also saw Jews
who [a]had married women of
[b]Ash'dod, Am'mon, *and* Mō'ab.
24 And half of their children
spoke the language of Ash'dod,
and could not speak the language of Judah, but spoke according to the language of one
or the other people.
25 So I [a]contended with them
and [1]cursed them, struck some
of them and pulled out their
hair, and made them [b]swear by
God, *saying*, "You shall not give
your daughters as wives to their

sons, nor take their daughters
for your sons or yourselves.
26 [a]"Did not Solomon king
of Israel sin by these things?
Yet among many nations there
was no king like him, [b]who was
beloved of his God; and God
made him king over all Israel.
[c]Nevertheless pagan women
caused even him to sin.
27 "Should we then hear of
your doing all this great evil,
[a]transgressing against our God
by marrying pagan women?"
28 And *one* of the sons [a]of Joi′-
a·da, the son of E·lī′a·shib the
high priest, *was* a son-in-law
of [b]San·bal′lat the Hor′o·nīte;
therefore I drove him from me.
29 [a]Remember them, O my God,
because they have defiled the
priesthood and [b]the covenant of
the priesthood and the Lē′vītes.
30 [a]Thus I cleansed them of everything pagan. I also [b]assigned
duties to the priests and the Lē′-
vītes, each to his service,
31 and *to bringing* [a]the wood
offering and the firstfruits at appointed times.

[b]Remember me, O my God,
for good!

26 [a]1 Kin. 11:1, 2 [b]2 Sam. 12:24, 25 [c]1 Kin. 11:4–8

27 [a][Ezra 10:2]

28 [a]Neh. 12:10, 12 [b]Neh. 4:1, 7; 6:1, 2

29 [a]Neh. 6:14 [b]Mal. 2:4, 11, 12

30 [a]Neh. 10:30 [b]Neh. 12:1

31 [a]Neh. 10:34 [b]Neh. 13:14, 22

The Book of
ESTHER

GOD'S hand of providence and protection on behalf of His people is evident throughout the Book of Esther, though His name does not appear once. Haman's plot brings grave danger to the Jews and is countered by the courage of beautiful Esther and the counsel of her wise cousin Mordecai, resulting in a great deliverance. The Feast of Purim becomes an annual reminder of God's faithfulness on behalf of His people.

Esther's Hebrew name was *Hadassah,* "Myrtle" (2:7), but her Persian name *Ester* was derived from the Persian word for "Star" (*Stara*). The Greek title for this book is *Esther,* and the Latin title is *Hester.*

CHAPTER 1

NOW it came to pass in the
days of [a]A·has·ū·ē′rus[1] (this
was the A·has·ū·ē′rus who
reigned [b]over one hundred and
twenty-seven provinces, [c]from
India to Ethiopia),
2 in those days when King
A·has·ū·ē′rus [a]sat on the throne
of his kingdom, which *was* in
[b]Shū′shan[1] the [2]citadel,
3 *that* in the third year of his
reign he [a]made a feast for all
his officials and servants—the
powers of Persia and Media,
the nobles, and the princes of the
provinces *being* before him—
4 when he showed the riches
of his glorious kingdom and the
splendor of his excellent majesty for many days, one hundred
and eighty days *in all.*
5 And when these days were
completed, the king made a
feast lasting seven days for all
the people who were present
in [1]Shū′shan the [2]citadel, from
great to small, in the court of the
garden of the king's palace.
6 *There were* white and blue
linen *curtains* fastened with
cords of fine linen and purple on
silver rods and marble pillars;
and the [a]couches *were* of gold
and silver on a *mosaic* pavement of alabaster, turquoise,
and white and black marble.
7 And they served drinks in
golden vessels, each vessel being different from the other,
with royal wine in abundance,
[a]according to the [1]generosity of
the king.
8 In accordance with the law,
the drinking was not compul-
sory; for so the king had ordered
all the officers of his household,
that they should do according to
each man's pleasure.
9 Queen Vash′tī also made a
feast for the women *in* the royal
palace which *belonged* to King
A·has·ū·ē′rus.
10 On the seventh day, when
the heart of the king was merry
with wine, he commanded
Me·hū′man, Biz′tha, [a]Har·bō′na,
Big′tha, A·bag′tha, Zē′thar, and
Car′cas, seven eunuchs who
served in the presence of King
A·has·ū·ē′rus,
11 to bring Queen Vash′tī before the king, *wearing* her royal
crown, in order to show her
beauty to the people and the

1 [a]Ezra 4:6 [b]Esth. 8:9 [c]Dan. 6:1 [1]Generally identified with Xerxes I (485–464 B.C.)

2 [a]1 Kin. 1:46 [b]Neh. 1:1 [1]Or *Susa* [2]Or *fortified palace,* and so elsewhere in the book

3 [a]Gen. 40:20

5 [1]Or *Susa* [2]*palace*

6 [a]Amos 2:8; 6:4

7 [a]Esth. 2:18 [1]Lit. *hand*

10 [a]Esth. 7:9

officials, for she *was* beautiful to
behold.
12 But Queen Vash′tī refused to
come at the king's command
brought by *his* eunuchs; therefore the king was furious, and
his anger burned within him.
13 Then the king said to the
[a]wise men [b]who understood the
times (for this *was* the king's
manner toward all who knew
law and justice,
14 those closest to him *being*
Car·shē′na, Shē′thar, Ad·mā′tha,
Tar′shish, Mē′rēs, Mar·sē′na, and
Mē·mū′can, the [a]seven princes
of Persia and Media, [b]who had
access to the king's presence,
and who [1]ranked highest in the
kingdom):
15 "What *shall we* do to Queen
Vash′tī, according to law, because
she did not obey the command
of King A·has·ū·ē′rus *brought to
her* by the eunuchs?"
16 And Mē·mū′can answered
before the king and the princes:
"Queen Vash′tī has not only
wronged the king, but also all
the princes, and all the people
who *are* in all the provinces of
King A·has·ū·ē′rus.
17 "For the queen's behavior
will become known to all women,
so that they will [a]despise their
husbands in their eyes, when
they report, 'King A·has·ū·ē′rus
commanded Queen Vash′tī to be
brought in before him, but she
did not come.'
18 "This very day the *noble* la-
dies of Persia and Media will
say to all the king's officials that
they have heard of the behavior
of the queen. Thus *there will be*
excessive contempt and wrath.
19 "If it pleases the king, let a
royal [1]decree go out from him,
and let it be recorded in the laws
of the Persians and the Mēdes,
so that it will [a]not [2]be altered,
that Vash′tī shall come no more
before King A·has·ū·ē′rus; and
let the king give her royal position to another who is better
than she.
20 "When the king's decree
which he will make is proclaimed throughout all his em-
pire (for it is great), all wives
will [a]honor their husbands, both
great and small."
21 And the reply pleased the
king and the princes, and the
king did according to the word
of Mē·mū′can.
22 Then he sent letters to all
the king's provinces, [a]to each
province in its own script, and
to every people in their own
language, that each man should
[b]be master in his own house,
and speak in the language of his
own people.

2
After these things, when the
wrath of King A·has·ū·ē′-
rus subsided, he remembered
Vash′tī, [a]what she had done, and
what had been decreed against
her.
2 Then the king's servants who
attended him said: "Let beautiful young virgins be sought for
the king;
3 "and let the king appoint officers in all the provinces of his
kingdom, that they may gather
all the beautiful young virgins
to [1]Shū′shan the [2]citadel, into
the women's quarters, under the
custody of [3]Heg′aī the king's eunuch, custodian of the women.
And let beauty preparations be
given *them*.
4 "Then let the young woman
who pleases the king be queen

13 [a]Dan. 2:12 [b]1 Chr. 12:32
14 [a]Ezra 7:14 [b]2 Kin. 25:19 [1]Lit. *sat in first place*
17 [a][Eph. 5:33]
19 [a]Esth. 8:8 [1]Lit. *word* [2]*pass away*
20 [a][Col. 3:18]
22 [a]Esth. 3:12; 8:9 [b][Eph. 5:22–24]

CHAPTER 2

1 [a]Esth. 1:19, 20
3 [1]Or *Susa* [2]*palace* [3]Heb. *Hege*

instead of Vash′tī.” This thing
pleased the king, and he did so.
5 In [1]Shū′shan the [2]citadel
there was a certain Jew whose
name *was* Mor′de·caī the son of
Jā′ir, the son of Shim′ē·ī, the son
of [a]Kish, a Ben′ja·mīte.
6 [a]*Kish*[1] had been carried away
from Jerusalem with the captives who had been captured
with [2]Jec·o·nī′ah king of Judah,
whom Ne·bū·chad·nez′zar the
king of Babylon had carried
away.
7 And *Mor′de·caī* had brought
up Ha·das′sah, that *is,* Esther,
[a]his uncle’s daughter, for she
had neither father nor mother.
The young woman *was* lovely
and beautiful. When her father
and mother died, Mor′de·caī
took her as his own daughter.
8 So it was, when the king’s
command and decree were
heard, and when many young
women were [a]gathered at [1]Shū′-
shan the [2]citadel, *under* the custody of Heg′aī, that Esther also
was taken to the king’s palace,
into the care of Heg′aī the custodian of the women.
9 Now the young woman
pleased him, and she obtained
his favor; so he readily gave
[a]beauty preparations to her,
besides [1]her allowance. Then
seven choice maidservants
were provided for her from the
king’s palace, and he moved
her and her maidservants to the
best *place* in the house of the
women.
10 [a]Esther had not [1]revealed
her people or family, for Mor′-
de·caī had charged her not to
reveal *it.*
11 And every day Mor′de·caī
paced in front of the court of the
women’s quarters, to learn of
Esther’s welfare and what was
happening to her.
12 Each young woman’s turn
came to go in to King A·has·ū·ē′-
rus after she had completed
twelve months’ preparation, according to the regulations for
the women, for thus were the
days of their preparation apportioned: six months with oil
of myrrh, and six months with
perfumes and preparations for
beautifying women.
13 Thus *prepared, each* young
woman went to the king, and
she was given whatever she desired to take with her from the
women’s quarters to the king’s
palace.
14 In the evening she went, and
in the morning she returned to
the second house of the women,
to the custody of Sha·ash′gaz,
the king’s eunuch who kept the
concubines. She would not go in
to the king again unless the king
delighted in her and called for
her by name.
15 Now when the turn came for
Esther [a]the daughter of Ab·i·hā′il
the uncle of Mor′de·caī, who had
taken her as his daughter, to go
in to the king, she requested
nothing but what Heg′aī the
king’s eunuch, the custodian of
the women, advised. And Esther
[b]obtained favor in the sight of all
who saw her.
16 So Esther was taken to King
A·has·ū·ē′rus, into his royal palace, in the tenth month, which
is the month of Tē′beth, in the
seventh year of his reign.
17 The king loved Esther more
than all the *other* women, and
she obtained grace and favor
in his sight more than all the

5 [a]1 Sam. 9:1 [1]Or *Susa* [2]*palace*
6 [a]2 Kin. 24:14, 15 [1]Lit. *Who* [2]*Jehoiachin,* 2 Kin. 24:6
7 [a]Esth. 2:15
8 [a]Esth. 2:3 [1]Or *Susa* [2]*palace*
9 [a]Esth. 2:3, 12 [1]Lit. *her portions*
10 [a]Esth. 2:20 [1]Revealed the identity of
15 [a]Esth. 2:7; 9:29 [b]Esth. 5:2, 8

virgins; so he set the royal
[a]crown upon her head and made
her queen instead of Vash′tī.
18 Then the king [a]made a great
feast, the Feast of Esther, for all
his officials and servants; and
he proclaimed a holiday in the
provinces and gave gifts according to the [1]generosity of a king.
19 When virgins were gathered
together a second time, Mor′-
de·caī sat within the king's gate.
20 [a]*Now* Esther had not revealed
her family and her people, just
as Mor′de·caī had charged her,
for Esther obeyed the command
of Mor′de·caī as when she was
brought up by him.
21 In those days, while Mor′-
de·caī sat within the king's gate,
two of the king's eunuchs, [1]Big′-
than and Tē′resh, doorkeepers,
became furious and sought to
lay hands on King A·has·ū·ē′-
rus.
22 So the matter became known
to Mor′de·caī, [a]who told Queen
Esther, and Esther informed the
king in Mor′de·caī's name.
23 And when an inquiry was
made into the matter, it was confirmed, and both were hanged
on a gallows; and it was written
in [a]the book of the chronicles in
the presence of the king.

3

After these things King
A·has·ū·ē′rus promoted Hā′-
man, the son of Ham·me·dā′tha
the [a]Ag′ag·īte, and [b]advanced
him and set his seat above all
the princes who *were* with him.
2 And all the king's servants
who *were* [a]within the king's gate
bowed and paid homage to Hā′-
man, for so the king had commanded concerning him. But
Mor′de·caī [b]would not bow or
pay homage.
3 Then the king's servants
who *were* within the king's gate
said to Mor′de·caī, "Why do
you transgress the [a]king's command?"
4 Now it happened, when they
spoke to him daily and he would
not listen to them, that they told
it to Hā′man, to see whether
Mor′de·caī's words would stand;
for *Mor′de·caī* had told them
that he *was* a Jew.
5 When Hā′man saw that Mor′-
de·caī [a]did not bow or pay him
homage, Hā′man was [b]filled with
wrath.
6 But he disdained to lay
hands on Mor′de·caī alone, for
they had told him of the people
of Mor′de·caī. Instead, Hā′man
[a]sought to destroy all the Jews
who *were* throughout the whole
kingdom of A·has·ū·ē′rus—the
people of Mor′de·caī.
7 In the first month, which
is the month of Nī′san, in the
twelfth year of King A·has·ū·ē′-
rus, [a]they cast Pūr (that *is*, the
lot), before Hā′man [1]to determine
the day and the [2]month, [3]until *it*
fell on the twelfth *month,* which
is the month of Ā′dar.
8 Then Hā′man said to King
A·has·ū·ē′rus, "There is a certain people scattered and dispersed among the people in all
the provinces of your kingdom;
[a]their laws *are* different from all
other people's, and they do not
keep the king's laws. Therefore
it *is* not fitting for the king to let
them remain.
9 "If it pleases the king, let *a*
decree be written that they be
destroyed, and I will pay ten
thousand talents of silver into
the hands of those who do the

17 [a]Esth. 1:11
18 [a]Esth. 1:3 [1]Lit. *hand*
20 [a]Esth. 2:10
21 [1]*Bigthana,* Esth. 6:2
22 [a]Esth. 6:1, 2
23 [a]Esth. 6:1

CHAPTER 3

1 [a]Num. 24:7 [b]Esth. 5:11
2 [a]Esth. 2:19, 21; 5:9 [b]Ps. 15:4
3 [a]Esth. 3:2
5 [a]Esth. 3:2; 5:9 [b]Dan. 3:19
6 [a]Ps. 83:4
7 [a]Esth. 9:24–26 [1]Lit. *from day to day and month to month* [2]LXX adds *to destroy the people of Mordecai in one day;* Vg. adds *the nation of the Jews should be destroyed* [3]So with MT, Vg.; LXX *and the lot fell on the fourteenth of the month*
8 [a]Acts 16:20, 21

work, to bring *it* into the king's
treasuries."
10 So the king [a]took [b]his signet
ring from his hand and gave it to
Hā′man, the son of Ham·me·dā′-
tha the Ag′ag·īte, the [c]enemy of
the Jews.
11 And the king said to Hā′man,
"The money and the people *are*
given to you, to do with them as
seems good to you."
12 [a]Then the king's scribes were
called on the thirteenth day of
the first month, and *a decree*
was written according to all that
Hā′man commanded—to the
king's satraps, to the governors
who *were* over each province,
to the officials of all people, to
every province [b]according to its
script, and to every people in
their language. [c]In the name of
King A·has·ū·ē′rus it was written, and sealed with the king's
signet ring.
13 And the letters were [a]sent
by couriers into all the king's
provinces, to destroy, to kill, and
to annihilate all the Jews, both
young and old, little children and
women, [b]in one day, on the thirteenth *day* of the twelfth month,
which *is* the month of Ā′dar, and
[c]to plunder their [1]possessions.
14 [a]A copy of the document was
to be issued as law in every
province, being published for
all people, that they should be
ready for that day.
15 The couriers went out, hastened by the king's command;
and the decree was proclaimed
in [1]Shū′shan the [2]citadel. So the
king and Hā′man sat down to
drink, but [a]the city of Shū′shan
was [3]perplexed.

4 When Mor′de·caī learned all
that had happened, [1]he [a]tore
his clothes and put on sackcloth
[b]and ashes, and went out into
the midst of the city. He [c]cried
out with a loud and bitter cry.
2 He went as far as the front of
the king's gate, for no one *might*
enter the king's gate clothed
with sackcloth.
3 And in every province where
the king's command and decree arrived, *there was* great
mourning among the Jews, with
fasting, weeping, and wailing;
and many lay in sackcloth and
ashes.
4 So Esther's maids and eunuchs came and told her, and
the queen was deeply distressed.
Then she sent garments to clothe
Mor′de·caī and take his sackcloth
away from him, but he would not
accept *them.*
5 Then Esther called Hā′thach,
one of the king's eunuchs whom
he had appointed to attend her,
and she gave him a command
concerning Mor′de·caī, to learn
what and why this *was.*
6 So Hā′thach went out to
Mor′de·caī in the city square
that *was* in front of the king's
gate.
7 And Mor′de·caī told him all
that had happened to him, and
[a]the sum of money that Hā′man
had promised to pay into the
king's treasuries to destroy the
Jews.
8 He also gave him [a]a copy
of the written decree for their
destruction, which was given at
[1]Shū′shan, that he might show it
to Esther and explain it to her,
and that he might command
her to go in to the king to make
supplication to him and plead
before him for her people.
9 So Hā′thach returned and

10 [a]Gen. 41:42 [b]Esth. 8:2, 8 [c]Esth. 7:6
12 [a]Esth. 8:9 [b]Esth. 1:22 [c]Esth. 8:8–10
13 [a]Esth. 8:10, 14 [b]Esth. 8:12 [c]Esth. 8:11; 9:10 [1]LXX adds the text of the letter here
14 [a]Esth. 8:13, 14
15 [a]Esth. 8:15 [1]Or *Susa* [2]*palace* [3]*in confusion*

CHAPTER 4

1 [a]2 Sam. 1:11 [b]Josh. 7:6 [c]Gen. 27:34 [1]Lit. *Mordecai*
7 [a]Esth. 3:9
8 [a]Esth. 3:14, 15 [1]Or *Susa*

told Esther the words of Mor′-
de·caī.
10 Then Esther spoke to Hā′-
thach, and gave him a command
for Mor′de·caī:
11 "All the king's servants and
the people of the king's provinces know that any man or
woman who goes into [a]the inner court to the king, who has
not been called, [b]*he has* but one
law: put *all* to death, except the
one [c]to whom the king holds out
the golden scepter, that he may
live. Yet I myself have not been
[d]called to go in to the king these
thirty days."
12 So they told Mor′de·caī Esther's words.
13 And Mor′de·caī told *them* to
answer Esther: "Do not think in
your heart that you will escape
in the king's palace any more
than all the other Jews.
14 "For if you remain completely silent at this time, relief
and deliverance will arise for
the Jews from another place, but
you and your father's house will
perish. Yet who knows whether
you have come to the kingdom
for *such* a time as this?"
15 Then Esther told *them* to
reply to Mor′de·caī:
16 "Go, gather all the Jews who
are present in [1]Shū′shan, and
fast for me; neither eat nor drink
for [a]three days, night or day. My
maids and I will fast likewise.
And so I will go to the king,
which *is* against the law; [b]and if
I perish, I perish!"
17 So Mor′de·caī went his way
and did according to all that Esther commanded [1]him.

5 Now it happened [a]on the
third day that Esther put on
her royal *robes* and stood in [b]the
inner court of the king's palace,
across from the king's house,
while the king sat on his royal
throne in the royal house, facing
the entrance of the [1]house.
2 So it was, when the king saw
Queen Esther standing in the
court, *that* [a]she found favor in
his sight, and [b]the king held out
to Esther the golden scepter that
was in his hand. Then Esther
went near and touched the top
of the scepter.
3 And the king said to her,
"What do you wish, Queen Esther? What *is* your request? [a]It
shall be given to you—up to half
the kingdom!"
4 So Esther answered, "If it
pleases the king, let the king
and Hā′man come today to the
banquet that I have prepared for
him."
5 Then the king said, "Bring
Hā′man quickly, that he may do
as Esther has said." So the king
and Hā′man went to the banquet
that Esther had prepared.
6 At the banquet of wine [a]the
king said to Esther, [b]"What *is*
your petition? It shall be granted
you. What *is* your request, up
to half the kingdom? It shall be
done!"
7 Then Esther answered and
said, "My petition and request *is*
this:
8 "If I have found favor in the
sight of the king, and if it pleases
the king to grant my petition
and [1]fulfill my request, then let
the king and Hā′man come to
the [a]banquet which I will prepare for them, and tomorrow I
will do as the king has said."
9 So Hā′man went out that day
[a]joyful and with a glad heart; but
when Hā′man saw Mor′de·caī in

11 [a]Esth. 5:1; 6:4 [b]Dan. 2:9 [c]Esth. 5:2; 8:4 [d]Esth. 2:14
16 [a]Esth. 5:1 [b]Gen. 43:14 [1]Or *Susa*
17 [1]LXX adds a prayer of Mordecai here

CHAPTER 5

1 [a]Esth. 4:16 [b]Esth. 4:11; 6:4 [1]LXX adds many extra details in vv. 1, 2
2 [a][Prov. 21:1] [b]Esth. 4:11; 8:4
3 [a]Mark 6:23
6 [a]Esth. 7:2 [b]Esth. 9:12
8 [a]Esth. 6:14 [1]Lit. *to do*
9 [a][Job 20:5]

the king's gate, and [b]that he did not stand or tremble before him, he was filled with indignation against Mor′de·caī.

10 Nevertheless Hā′man [a]restrained himself and went home, and he sent and called for his friends and his wife Zē′resh.

11 Then Hā′man told them of his great riches, [a]the multitude of his children, everything in which the king had promoted him, and how he had [b]advanced him above the officials and servants of the king.

12 Moreover Hā′man said, "Besides, Queen Esther invited no one but me to come in with the king to the banquet that she prepared; and tomorrow I am again invited by her, along with the king.

13 "Yet all this avails me nothing, so long as I see Mor′de·caī the Jew sitting at the king's gate."

14 Then his wife Zē′resh and all his friends said to him, "Let a [a]gallows[1] be made, [2]fifty cubits high, and in the morning [b]suggest to the king that Mor′de·caī be hanged on it; then go merrily with the king to the banquet." And the thing pleased Hā′man; so he had [c]the gallows made.

6

That night [1]the king could not sleep. So one was commanded to bring [a]the book of the records of the chronicles; and they were read before the king.

2 And it was found written that Mor′de·caī had told of [1]Big·thā′na and Tē′resh, two of the king's eunuchs, the doorkeepers who had sought to lay hands on King A·has·ū·ē′rus.

3 Then the king said, "What honor or dignity has been bestowed on Mor′de·caī for this?" And the king's servants who attended him said, "Nothing has been done for him."

4 So the king said, "Who *is* in the court?" Now Hā′man had *just* entered [a]the outer court of the king's palace [b]to suggest that the king hang Mor′de·caī on the gallows that he had prepared for him.

5 The king's servants said to him, "Hā′man is there, standing in the court." And the king said, "Let him come in."

6 So Hā′man came in, and the king asked him, "What shall be done for the man whom the king delights to honor?" Now Hā′man thought in his heart, "Whom would the king delight to honor more than [a]me?"

7 And Hā′man answered the king, "*For* the man whom the king delights to honor,

8 "let a royal robe be brought which the king has worn, and [a]a horse on which the king has ridden, which has a royal [1]crest placed on its head.

9 "Then let this robe and horse be delivered to the hand of one of the king's most noble princes, that he may array the man whom the king delights to honor. Then [1]parade him on horseback through the city square, [a]and proclaim before him: 'Thus shall it be done to the man whom the king delights to honor!' "

10 Then the king said to Hā′man, "Hurry, take the robe and the horse, as you have suggested, and do so for Mor′de·caī the Jew who sits within the king's gate!

9 [b]Esth. 3:5

10 [a]2 Sam. 13:22

11 [a]Esth. 9:7–10 [b]Esth. 3:1

14 [a]Esth. 7:9 [b]Esth. 6:4 [c]Esth. 7:10 [1]Lit. *tree or wood* [2]About 75 feet

CHAPTER 6

1 [a]Esth. 2:23; 10:2 [1]Lit. *the king's sleep fled away*

2 [1]*Bigthan*, Esth. 2:21

4 [a]Esth. 5:1 [b]Esth. 5:14

6 [a][Prov. 16:18; 18:12]

8 [a]1 Kin. 1:33 [1]*crown*

9 [a]Gen. 41:43 [1]Lit. *cause him to ride*

Leave nothing undone of all that
you have spoken."
11 So Hā′man took the robe
and the horse, arrayed Mor′-
de·caī and led him on horseback
through the city square, and proclaimed before him, "Thus shall
it be done to the man whom the
king delights to honor!"
12 Afterward Mor′de·caī went
back to the king's gate. But
Hā′man [a]hurried to his house,
mourning [b]and with his head
covered.
13 When Hā′man told his wife
Zē′resh and all his friends everything that had happened to him,
his wise men and his wife Zē′-
resh said to him, "If Mor′de·caī,
before whom you have begun
to fall, is of Jewish descent, you
will not prevail against [a]him but
will surely fall before him."
14 While they *were* still talking
with him, the king's eunuchs
came, and hastened to bring
Hā′man to [a]the banquet which
Esther had prepared.

7

So the king and Hā′man
went to dine with Queen
Esther.
2 And on the second day, [a]at
the banquet of wine, the king
again said to Esther, "What *is*
your petition, Queen Esther? It
shall be granted you. And what
is your request, up to half the
kingdom? It shall be done!"
3 Then Queen Esther answered
and said, "If I have found favor
in your sight, O king, and if it
pleases the king, let my life be
given me at my petition, and my
people at my request.
4 "For we have been [a]sold, my
people and I, to be destroyed, to
be killed, and to be annihilated.
Had we been sold as [b]male and
female slaves, I would have held
my tongue, although the enemy
could never compensate for the
king's loss."
5 So King A·has·ū·ē′rus answered and said to Queen Esther, "Who is he, and where is
he, who would dare presume in
his heart to do such a thing?"
6 And Esther said, "The adversary and [a]enemy *is* this wicked
Hā′man!" So Hā′man was terrified before the king and queen.
7 Then the king arose in his
wrath from the banquet of wine
and went into the palace garden;
but Hā′man stood before Queen
Esther, pleading for his life, for
he saw that evil was determined
against him by the king.
8 When the king returned
from the palace garden to the
place of the banquet of wine,
Hā′man had fallen across [a]the
couch where Esther *was*. Then
the king said, "Will he also assault the queen while I *am* in
the house?" As the word left the
king's mouth, they [b]covered Hā′-
man's face.
9 Now [a]Har·bō′nah, one of
the eunuchs, said to the king,
"Look! [b]The [1]gallows, fifty cubits high, which Hā′man made
for Mor′de·caī, who spoke [c]good
on the king's behalf, is standing
at the house of Hā′man." Then
the king said, "Hang him on it!"
10 So [a]they [b]hanged Hā′man on
the gallows that he had prepared for Mor′de·caī. Then the
king's wrath subsided.

8

On that day King A·has·ū·ē′-
rus gave Queen Esther the
house of Hā′man, the [a]enemy of
the Jews. And Mor′de·caī came
before the king, for Esther had
told [b]how he *was related* to her.

12 [a]2 Chr. 26:20 [b]2 Sam. 15:30
13 [a]Zech. 2:8
14 [a]Esth. 5:8

CHAPTER 7

2 [a]Esth. 5:6
4 [a]Esth. 3:9; 4:7 [b]Deut. 28:68
6 [a]Esth. 3:10
8 [a]Esth. 1:6 [b]Job 9:24
9 [a]Esth. 1:10 [b]Esth. 5:14 [c]Esth. 6:2 [1]Lit. *tree* or *wood*
10 [a][Ps. 7:16; 94:23] [b]Dan. 6:24

CHAPTER 8

1 [a]Esth. 7:6 [b]Esth. 2:7, 15

2 So the king took off [a]his
signet ring, which he had
taken from Hā′man, and gave
it to Mor′de·caī; and Esther appointed Mor′de·caī over the
house of Hā′man.
3 Now Esther spoke again to
the king, fell down at his feet,
and implored him with tears to
counteract the evil of Hā′man
the Ag′ag·īte, and the scheme
which he had devised against
the Jews.
4 And [a]the king held out the
golden scepter toward Esther.
So Esther arose and stood before the king,
5 and said, "If it pleases the
king, and if I have found favor
in his sight and the thing *seems*
right to the king and I am pleasing in his eyes, let it be written
to revoke the [a]letters devised by
Hā′man, the son of Ham·me·dā′-
tha the Ag′ag·īte, which he wrote
to annihilate the Jews who *are*
in all the king's provinces.
6 "For how can I endure to see
[a]the evil that will come to my
people? Or how can I endure
to see the destruction of my
countrymen?"
7 Then King A·has·ū·ē′rus said
to Queen Esther and Mor′de·caī
the Jew, "Indeed, [a]I have given
Esther the house of Hā′man, and
they have hanged him on the
gallows because he *tried to* lay
his hand on the Jews.
8 "You yourselves write *a decree* concerning the Jews, [1]as
you please, in the king's name,
and seal *it* with the king's signet
ring; for whatever is written in
the king's name and sealed with
the king's signet ring [a]no one
can revoke."
9 [a]So the king's scribes were
called at that time, in the third
month, which *is* the month of
Sī′van, on the twenty-third *day;*
and it was written, according to
all that Mor′de·caī commanded,
to the Jews, the satraps, the governors, and the princes of the
provinces [b]from India to Ethiopia, one hundred and twenty-
seven provinces *in all,* to every
province [c]in its own script, to
every people in their own language, and to the Jews in their
own script and language.
10 [a]And he wrote in the name
of King A·has·ū·ē′rus, sealed *it*
with the king's signet ring, and
sent letters by couriers on horseback, riding on royal horses
[1]bred from swift steeds.
11 By these letters the king permitted the Jews who *were* in every city to [a]gather together and
protect their lives—to [b]destroy,
kill, and annihilate all the forces
of any people or province that
would assault them, *both* little children and women, and to
plunder their possessions,
12 [a]on one day in all the provinces of King A·has·ū·ē′rus, on
the thirteenth *day* of the twelfth
month, which *is* the month of
[1]Ā′dar.
13 [a]A copy of the document was
to be issued as a decree in every
province and published for all
people, so that the Jews would
be ready on that day to avenge
themselves on their enemies.
14 The couriers who rode on
royal horses went out, hastened
and pressed on by the king's
command. And the decree was
issued in [1]Shū′shan the [2]citadel.
15 So Mor′de·caī went out from
the presence of the king in royal
apparel of [1]blue and white, with

2 [a]Esth. 3:10
4 [a]Esth. 4:11; 5:2
5 [a]Esth. 3:13
6 [a]Neh. 2:3
7 [a]Prov. 13:22
8 [a]Dan. 6:8, 12, 15 [1]Lit. *as is good in your eyes*
9 [a]Esth. 3:12 [b]Esth. 1:1 [c]Esth. 1:22; 3:12
10 [a]1 Kin. 21:8 [1]Lit. *sons of the swift horses*
11 [a]Esth. 9:2 [b]Esth. 9:10, 15, 16
12 [a]Esth. 3:13; 9:1 [1]LXX adds the text of the letter here
13 [a]Esth. 3:14, 15
14 [1]Or *Susa* [2]*palace*
15 [1]*violet*

a great crown of gold and a garment of fine linen and purple;
and [a]the city of [2]Shū′shan rejoiced and was glad.
16 The Jews had [a]light and gladness, joy and honor.
17 And in every province and
city, wherever the king's command and decree came, the Jews
had joy and gladness, a feast
[a]and a holiday. Then many of
the people of the land [b]became
Jews, because [c]fear of the Jews
fell upon them.

9 Now [a]in the twelfth month,
that *is*, the month of Ā′dar,
on the thirteenth day, [b]*the time*
came for the king's command
and his decree to be executed.
On the day that the enemies
of the Jews had hoped to overpower them, the opposite occurred, in that the Jews themselves [c]overpowered those who
hated them.
2 The Jews [a]gathered together
in their cities throughout all
the provinces of King A·has-
ū·ē′rus to lay hands on those
who [b]sought their harm. And
no one could withstand them,
[c]because fear of them fell upon
all people.
3 And all the officials of the
provinces, the satraps, the governors, and all those doing the
king's work, helped the Jews,
because the fear of Mor′de·caī
fell upon them.
4 For Mor′de·caī *was* great
in the king's palace, and his
fame spread throughout all the
provinces; for this man Mor′-
de·caī [a]became increasingly
prominent.
5 Thus the Jews defeated all
their enemies with the stroke of
the sword, with slaughter and
destruction, and did what they
pleased with those who hated
them.
6 And in [a]Shū′shan[1] the [2]cit-
adel the Jews killed and destroyed five hundred men.
7 Also Par·shan·dā′tha, Dal′-
phon, As·pā′tha,
8 Pō·rā′tha, A·dā′li·a, Ar·i·dā′-
tha,
9 Par·mash′ta, Ar′i·saī, Ar′i·daī,
and Va·jez′a·tha—
10 [a]the ten sons of Hā′man the
son of Ham·me·dā′tha, the enemy of the Jews—they killed;
[b]but they did not lay a hand on
the [1]plunder.
11 On that day the number of
those who were killed in [1]Shū′-
shan the [2]citadel [3]was brought to
the king.
12 And the king said to Queen
Esther, "The Jews have killed
and destroyed five hundred men
in Shū′shan the citadel, and the
ten sons of Hā′man. What have
they done in the rest of the
king's provinces? Now [a]what *is*
your petition? It shall be granted
to you. Or what *is* your further
request? It shall be done."
13 Then Esther said, "If it pleases
the king, let it be granted to the
Jews who *are* in Shū′shan to
do again tomorrow [a]according
to today's decree, and let Hā′-
man's ten sons [b]be hanged on
the gallows."
14 So the king commanded
this to be done; the decree was
issued in Shū′shan, and they
hanged Hā′man's ten sons.
15 And the Jews who *were* in
[1]Shū′shan [a]gathered together
again on the fourteenth day of
the month of Ā′dar and killed
three hundred men at Shū′shan;

15 [a]Prov. 29:2 [2]Or *Susa*
16 [a]Ps. 97:11; 112:4
17 [a]Esth. 9:19 [b]Ps. 18:43 [c]Gen. 35:5

CHAPTER 9

1 [a]Esth. 8:12 [b]Esth. 3:13 [c]2 Sam. 22:41
2 [a]Esth. 8:11; 9:15–18 [b]Ps. 71:13, 14 [c]Esth. 8:17
4 [a]2 Sam. 3:1
6 [a]Esth. 1:2; 3:15; 4:16 [1]Or *Susa* [2]*palace*
10 [a]Esth. 5:11; 9:7–10 [b]Esth. 8:11 [1]*spoil*
11 [1]Or *Susa* [2]*palace* [3]Lit. *came*
12 [a]Esth. 5:6; 7:2
13 [a]Esth. 8:11; 9:15 [b]2 Sam. 21:6, 9
15 [a]Esth. 8:11; 9:2 [1]Or *Susa*

[b]but they did not lay a hand on
the plunder.
16 The remainder of the Jews in
the king's provinces [a]gathered
together and protected their
lives, had rest from their enemies, and killed seventy-five
thousand of their enemies; [b]but
they did not lay a hand on the
plunder.
17 *This was* on the thirteenth
day of the month of Ā'dar. And
on the fourteenth of [1]*the month*
they rested and made it a day of
feasting and gladness.
18 But the Jews who *were* at
[1]Shū'shan assembled together
[a]on the thirteenth *day*, as well
as on the fourteenth; and on
the fifteenth of [2]*the month* they
rested, and made it a day of
feasting and gladness.
19 Therefore the Jews of the villages who dwelt in the unwalled
towns celebrated the fourteenth
day of the month of Ā'dar [a]*with*
gladness and feasting, [b]as a holiday, and for [c]sending presents to
one another.
20 And Mor'de·caī wrote these
things and sent letters to all the
Jews, near and far, who *were* in
all the provinces of King A·has-
ū·ē'rus,
21 to establish among them that
they should celebrate yearly the
fourteenth and fifteenth days of
the month of Ā'dar,
22 as the days on which the
Jews had rest from their enemies, as the month which was
turned from sorrow to joy for
them, and from mourning to a
holiday; that they should make
them days of feasting and joy,
of [a]sending presents to one another and gifts to the [b]poor.
23 So the Jews accepted the
custom which they had begun, as
Mor'de·caī had written to them,
24 because Hā'man, the son of
Ham·me·dā'tha the Ag'ag·īte,
the enemy of all the Jews, [a]had
plotted against the Jews to annihilate them, and had cast Pūr
(that *is*, the lot), to consume
them and destroy them;
25 but [a]when [1]*Esther* came before the king, he commanded
by letter that [2]this wicked plot
which *Hā'man* had devised
against the Jews should [b]return
on his own head, and that he
and his sons should be hanged
on the gallows.
26 So they called these days
Pūr'im, after the name [1]Pūr.
Therefore, because of all the
words of [a]this letter, what they
had seen concerning this matter, and what had happened to
them,
27 the Jews established and imposed it upon themselves and
their descendants and all who
would [a]join them, that without
fail they should celebrate these
two days every year, according to
the written *instructions* and according to the *prescribed* time,
28 *that* these days *should be*
remembered and kept throughout every generation, every family, every province, and every
city, that these days of Pūr'im
should not fail *to be observed*
among the Jews, and *that* the
memory of them should not perish among their descendants.
29 Then Queen Esther, [a]the
daughter of Ab·i·hā'il, with Mor'-
de·caī the Jew, wrote with full
authority to confirm this [b]second
letter about Pūr'im.
30 And *Mor'de·caī* sent letters to
all the Jews, to [a]the one hundred

15 [b]Esth. 9:10
16 [a]Esth. 9:2 [b]Esth. 8:11
17 [1]Lit. *it*
18 [a]Esth. 9:11, 15 [1]Or *Susa* [2]Lit. *it*
19 [a]Deut. 16:11, 14 [b]Esth. 8:16, 17 [c]Neh. 8:10, 12
22 [a]Neh. 8:10 [b][Deut. 15:7–11]
24 [a]Esth. 3:6, 7; 9:26
25 [a]Esth. 7:4–10; 8:3; 9:13, 14 [b]Esth. 7:10 [1]Lit. *she* or *it* [2]Lit. *his*
26 [a]Esth. 9:20 [1]Lit. *Lot*
27 [a]Esth. 8:17
29 [a]Esth. 2:15 [b]Esth. 8:10; 9:20, 21
30 [a]Esth. 1:1

and twenty-seven provinces of
the kingdom of A·has·ū·ē′rus,
with words of peace and truth,
31 to confirm these days of
Pūr′im at their *appointed* time,
as Mor′de·caī the Jew and
Queen Esther had prescribed
for them, and as they had decreed for themselves and their
descendants concerning matters
of their [a]fasting and lamenting.
32 So the decree of Esther confirmed these matters of Pūr′im,
and it was written in the book.

10 And King A·has·ū·ē′rus
imposed tribute on the
land and *on* [a]the islands of the
sea.
2 Now all the acts of his power
and his might, and the account
of the greatness of Mor′de·caī,
[a]to which the king [1]advanced
him, *are* they not written in the
book of the [b]chronicles of the
kings of Media and Persia?
3 For Mor′de·caī the Jew *was*
[a]second to King A·has·ū·ē′rus,
and was great among the Jews
and well received by the multitude of his brethren, [b]seeking the
good of his people and speaking
peace to all his [1]countrymen.

31 [a]Esth. 4:3, 16

CHAPTER 10

1 [a]Is. 11:11; 24:15

2 [a]Esth. 8:15; 9:4 [b]Esth. 6:1 [1]Lit. *made him great*

3 [a]Gen. 41:40, 43, 44 [b]Neh. 2:10 [1]Lit. *seed.* LXX, Vg. add a dream of Mordecai here; Vg. adds six more chapters

The Book of
JOB

JOB is perhaps the earliest book of the Bible. Set in the period of the patriarchs (Abraham, Isaac, Jacob, and Joseph), it tells the story of a man who loses everything—his wealth, his family, his health—and wrestles with the question, Why?

The book begins with a heavenly debate between God and Satan, moves through three cycles of earthly debates between Job and his friends, and concludes with a dramatic "divine diagnosis" of Job's problem. In the end, Job acknowledges the sovereignty of God in his life and receives back more than he had before his trials.

Iyyōb is the Hebrew title for this book, and the name has two possible meanings. If derived from the Hebrew word for "Persecution," it means "Persecuted One." It is more likely that it comes from the Arabic word meaning "To Come Back" or "Repent." If so, it may be defined "Repentant One." Both meanings apply to the book. The Greek title is *Iob*, and the Latin title is *Iob*.

CHAPTER 1

THERE was a man [a]in the land of Uz, whose name *was* [b]Job; and that man was [c]blameless and upright, and one who [d]feared God and [1]shunned evil.

2 And seven sons and three daughters were born to him.

3 Also, his possessions were seven thousand sheep, three thousand camels, five hundred yoke of oxen, five hundred female donkeys, and a very large household, so that this man was the greatest of all the [1]people of the East.

4 And his sons would go and feast *in their* houses, each on his *appointed* day, and would send and invite their three sisters to eat and drink with them.

5 So it was, when the days of feasting had run their course, that Job would send and [1]sanctify them, and he would rise early in the morning [a]and offer burnt offerings *according to* the number of them all. For Job said, "It may be that my sons have sinned and [b]cursed[2] God in their hearts." Thus Job did regularly.

6 Now [a]there was a day when the sons of God came to present themselves before the LORD, and [1]Satan also came among them.

7 And the LORD said to [1]Satan, "From where do you come?" So Satan answered the LORD and said, "From [a]going to and fro on the earth, and from walking back and forth on it."

8 Then the LORD said to Satan, "Have you [1]considered My servant Job, that *there is* none like him on the earth, a blameless and upright man, one who fears God and [2]shuns evil?"

9 So Satan answered the LORD and said, "Does Job fear God for nothing?

10 [a]"Have You not [1]made a hedge around him, around his household, and around all that he has on every side? [b]You have blessed the work of his hands,

1 [a]1 Chr. 1:17 [b]Ezek. 14:14, 20 [c]Gen. 6:9; 17:1 [d][Prov. 16:6] [1]Lit. *turned away from*

3 [1]Lit. *sons*

5 [a][Job 42:8] [b]1 Kin. 21:10, 13 [1]*consecrate* [2]Lit. *blessed*, but in an evil sense; cf. Job 1:11; 2:5, 9

6 [a]Job 2:1 [1]Lit. *the Adversary*

7 [a][1 Pet. 5:8] [1]Lit. *the Adversary*

8 [1]Lit. *set your heart on* [2]Lit. *turns away from*

10 [a]Ps. 34:7 [b][Prov. 10:22] [1]Protected him

and his possessions have increased in the land.
11 [a]"But now, stretch out Your
hand and touch all that he has,
and he will surely [b]curse[1] You to
Your face!"
12 And the LORD said to Satan,
"Behold, all that he has *is* in
your [1]power; only do not lay a
hand on his *person*." So Satan
went out from the presence of
the LORD.
13 Now there was a day [a]when
his sons and daughters *were* eating and drinking wine in their
oldest brother's house;
14 and a messenger came to
Job and said, "The oxen were
plowing and the donkeys feeding beside them,
15 "when the [1]Sa·bē′ans [2]raided
them and took them away—
indeed they have killed the servants with the edge of the sword;
and I alone have escaped to tell
you!"
16 While he *was* still speaking, another also came and said,
"The fire of God fell from heaven
and burned up the sheep and the
servants, and [1]consumed them;
and I alone have escaped to tell
you!"
17 While he *was* still speaking, another also came and said,
"The Chal·dē′ans formed three
bands, raided the camels and
took them away, yes, and killed
the servants with the edge of the
sword; and I alone have escaped
to tell you!"
18 While he *was* still speaking, another also came and said,
[a]"Your sons and daughters *were*
eating and drinking wine in their
oldest brother's house,
19 "and suddenly a great wind
came from [1]across the wilderness
and struck the four corners of the
house, and it fell on the young
people, and they are dead; and I
alone have escaped to tell you!"
20 Then Job arose, [a]tore his robe,
and shaved his head; and he [b]fell
to the ground and worshiped.
21 And he said:

[a]"Naked I came from my
mother's womb,
And naked shall I return
there.
The LORD [b]gave, and the
LORD has [c]taken away;
[d]Blessed be the name of the
LORD."

22 [a]In all this Job did not sin nor
charge God with wrong.

2 Again [a]there was a day
when the sons of God came
to present themselves before
the LORD, and Satan came also
among them to present himself
before the LORD.
2 And the LORD said to Satan,
"From where do you come?"
[a]Satan answered the LORD and
said, "From going to and fro
on the earth, and from walking
back and forth on it."
3 Then the LORD said to Satan,
"Have you considered My servant Job, that *there is* none like
him on the earth, [a]a blameless
and upright man, one who fears
God and shuns evil? And still
he [b]holds fast to his integrity,
although you incited Me against
him, [c]to [1]destroy him without
cause."
4 So Satan answered the LORD
and said, "Skin for skin! Yes, all
that a man has he will give for
his life.
5 [a]"But stretch out Your hand
now, and touch his [b]bone and his

11 [a]Job 2:5; 19:21 [b]Is. 8:21 [1]Lit. *bless*, but in an evil sense; cf. Job 1:5
12 [1]Lit. *hand*
13 [a][Eccl. 9:12]
15 [1]Lit. *Sheba;* cf. Job 6:19 [2]Lit. *fell upon*
16 [1]*destroyed*
18 [a]Job 1:4, 13
19 [1]LXX omits *across*
20 [a]Gen. 37:29, 34 [b][1 Pet. 5:6]
21 [a][Eccl. 5:15] [b][James 1:17] [c]Gen. 31:16 [d]Eph. 5:20
22 [a]Job 2:10

CHAPTER 2

1 [a]Job 1:6–8
2 [a]Job 1:7
3 [a]Job 1:1, 8 [b]Job 27:5, 6 [c]Job 9:17 [1]Lit. *consume*
5 [a]Job 1:11 [b]Job 19:20

flesh, and he will surely [1]curse You to Your face!"

6 [a]And the LORD said to Satan, "Behold, he *is* in your hand, but spare his life."

7 So Satan went out from the presence of the LORD, and struck Job with painful boils [a]from the sole of his foot to the crown of his head.

8 And he took for himself a potsherd with which to scrape himself [a]while he sat in the midst of the ashes.

9 Then his wife said to him, "Do you still hold fast to your integrity? [1]Curse God and die!"

10 But he said to her, "You speak as one of the foolish women speaks. [a]Shall we indeed accept good from God, and shall we not accept adversity?" [b]In all this Job did not [c]sin with his lips.

11 Now when Job's three friends heard of all this adversity that had come upon him, each one came from his own place—E·lī′phaz the [a]Tē′man·īte, Bil′dad the [b]Shū′hīte, and Zō′phar the Nā′a·ma·thīte. For they had made an appointment together to come [c]and mourn with him, and to comfort him.

12 And when they raised their eyes from afar, and did not recognize him, they lifted their voices and wept; and each one tore his robe and [a]sprinkled dust on his head toward heaven.

13 So they sat down with him on the ground [a]seven days and seven nights, and no one spoke a word to him, for they saw that *his* grief was very great.

3 After this Job opened his mouth and cursed the day of his *birth.*

2 And Job [1]spoke, and said:

3 "May[a] the day perish on
which I was born,
And the night *in which* it
was said,
'A male child is conceived.'
4 May that day be darkness;
May God above not seek it,
Nor the light shine upon it.
5 May darkness and [a]the
shadow of death claim it;
May a cloud settle on it;
May the blackness of the
day terrify it.
6 *As for* that night, may
darkness seize it;
May it not [1]rejoice among
the days of the year,
May it not come into the
number of the months.
7 Oh, may that night be
barren!
May no joyful shout come
into it!
8 May those curse it who
curse the day,
Those [a]who are ready to
arouse Le·vī′a·than.
9 May the stars of its morning
be dark;
May it look for light, but
have none,
And not see the [1]dawning of
the day;
10 Because it did not shut up
the doors of my *mother's*
womb,
Nor hide sorrow from my
eyes.

11 "Why[a] did I not die at birth?
Why did I *not* [1]perish when
I came from the womb?
12 [a]Why did the knees receive
me?
Or why the breasts, that I
should nurse?
13 For now I would have lain
still and been quiet,

5 [1]Lit. *bless,* but in an evil sense; cf. Job 1:5
6 [a]Job 1:12
7 [a]Is. 1:6
8 [a]Ezek. 27:30
9 [1]Lit. *Bless,* but in an evil sense; cf. Job 1:5
10 [a]Job 1:21, 22 [b]Job 1:22 [c]Ps. 39:1
11 [a]Gen. 36:11 [b]Gen. 25:2 [c]Rom. 12:15
12 [a]Neh. 9:1
13 [a]Gen. 50:10

CHAPTER 3

2 [1]Lit. *answered*
3 [a]Jer. 20:14–18
5 [a]Jer. 13:16
6 [1]LXX, Syr., Tg., Vg. *be joined*
8 [a]Jer. 9:17
9 [1]*eyelids of the dawn*
11 [a]Job 10:18, 19 [1]*expire*
12 [a]Gen. 30:3

I would have been asleep;
Then I would have been at rest
14 With kings and counselors of the earth,
Who [a]built ruins for themselves,
15 Or with princes who had gold,
Who filled their houses *with* silver;
16 Or *why* was I not hidden
[a]like a stillborn child,
Like infants who never saw light?
17 There the wicked cease *from* troubling,
And there the [1]weary are at [a]rest.
18 *There* the prisoners [1]rest together;
[a]They do not hear the voice of the oppressor.
19 The small and great are there,
And the servant *is* free from his master.

20 "Why[a] is light given to him who is in misery,
And life to the [b]bitter of soul,
21 Who [a]long[1] for death, but it does not *come,*
And search for it more than [b]hidden treasures;
22 Who rejoice exceedingly,
And are glad when they can find the [a]grave?
23 *Why is light given* to a man whose way is hidden,
[a]And whom God has hedged in?
24 For my sighing comes before [1]I eat,
And my groanings pour out like water.
25 For the thing I greatly [a]feared has come upon me,
And what I dreaded has happened to me.
26 I am not at ease, nor am I quiet;
I have no rest, for trouble comes."

4 Then E·lī′phaz the Tē′man·īte answered and said:

2 "*If* one attempts a word with you, will you become weary?
But who can withhold himself from speaking?
3 Surely you have instructed many,
And you [a]have strengthened weak hands.
4 Your words have upheld him who was stumbling,
And you [a]have strengthened the [1]feeble knees;
5 But now it comes upon you, and you are weary;
It touches you, and you are troubled.
6 *Is* not [a]your reverence [b]your confidence?
And the integrity of your ways your hope?

7 "Remember now, [a]who *ever* perished being innocent?
Or where were the upright *ever* cut off?
8 Even as I have seen,
[a]Those who plow iniquity
And sow trouble reap the same.
9 By the blast of God they perish,
And by the breath of His anger they are consumed.
10 The roaring of the lion,

14 [a]Job 15:28
16 [a]Ps. 58:8
17 [a]Job 17:16 [1]Lit. *weary of strength*
18 [a]Job 39:7 [1]*are at ease*
20 [a]Jer. 20:18 [b]2 Kin. 4:27
21 [a]Rev. 9:6 [b]Prov. 2:4 [1]Lit. *wait*
22 [a]Job 7:15, 16
23 [a]Job 19:8
24 [1]Lit. *my bread*
25 [a][Job 9:28; 30:15]

CHAPTER 4

3 [a]Is. 35:3
4 [a]Is. 35:3 [1]Lit. *bending*
6 [a]Job 1:1 [b]Prov. 3:26
7 [a][Ps. 37:25]
8 [a][Prov. 22:8]

The voice of the fierce lion,
And [a]the teeth of the young lions are broken.
11 [a]The old lion perishes for lack of prey,
And the cubs of the lioness are scattered.

12 "Now a word was secretly brought to me,
And my ear received a whisper of it.
13 [a]In disquieting thoughts from the visions of the night,
When deep sleep falls on men,
14 Fear came upon me, and [a]trembling,
Which made all my bones shake.
15 Then a spirit passed before my face;
The hair on my body stood up.
16 It stood still,
But I could not discern its appearance.
A form *was* before my eyes;
There was silence;
Then I heard a voice *saying*:
17 'Can a mortal be more righteous than God?
Can a man be more pure than his Maker?
18 If He [a]puts no trust in His servants,
If He charges His angels with error,
19 How much more those who dwell in houses of clay,
Whose foundation is in the dust,
Who are crushed before a moth?
20 [a]They are broken in pieces from morning till evening;
They perish forever, with no one regarding.
21 Does not their own excellence go away?
They die, even without wisdom.'

5 "Call out now;
Is there anyone who will answer you?
And to which of the holy ones will you turn?
2 For wrath kills a foolish man,
And envy slays a simple one.
3 [a]I have seen the foolish taking root,
But suddenly I cursed his dwelling place.
4 His sons are [a]far from safety,
They are crushed in the gate,
And [b]*there is* no deliverer.
5 Because the hungry eat up his harvest,
[1]Taking it even from the thorns,
[2]And a snare snatches their [3]substance.
6 For affliction does not come from the dust,
Nor does trouble spring from the ground;
7 Yet man is [a]born to [1]trouble,
As the sparks fly upward.

8 "But as for me, I would seek God,
And to God I would commit my cause—
9 Who does great things, and unsearchable,
Marvelous things without number.
10 [a]He gives rain on the earth,

10 [a]Ps. 58:6
11 [a]Ps. 34:10
13 [a]Job 33:15
14 [a]Hab. 3:16
18 [a]Job 15:15
20 [a]Ps. 90:5, 6

CHAPTER 5

3 [a]Jer. 12:1–3
4 [a]Ps. 119:155 [b]Ps. 109:12
5 [1]LXX *They shall not be taken from evil men;* Vg. *And the armed man shall take him by violence* [2]LXX *The might shall draw them off;* Vg. *And the thirsty shall drink up their riches* [3]*wealth*
7 [a]Job 14:1 [1]*labor*
10 [a][Job 36:27–29; 37:6–11; 38:26]

And sends waters on the
fields.
11 [a]He sets on high those who
are lowly,
And those who mourn are
lifted to safety.
12 [a]He frustrates the devices of
the crafty,
So that their hands cannot
carry out their plans.
13 He catches the [a]wise in their
own craftiness,
And the counsel of the
cunning comes quickly
upon them.
14 They meet with darkness in
the daytime,
And grope at noontime as in
the night.
15 But [a]He saves the needy
from the sword,
From the mouth of the
mighty,
And from their hand.
16 [a]So the poor have hope,
And injustice shuts her
mouth.

17 "Behold,[a] happy *is* the man
whom God corrects;
Therefore do not despise
the chastening of the
Almighty.
18 [a]For He bruises, but He
binds up;
He wounds, but His hands
make whole.
19 [a]He shall deliver you in six
troubles,
Yes, in seven [b]no evil shall
touch you.
20 [a]In famine He shall redeem
you from death,
And in war from the [1]power
of the sword.
21 [a]You shall be hidden from
the scourge of the
tongue,
And you shall not be afraid
of destruction when it
comes.
22 You shall laugh at
destruction and famine,
And [a]you shall not be afraid
of the [b]beasts of the
earth.
23 [a]For you shall have a
covenant with the stones
of the field,
And the beasts of the field
shall be at peace with
you.
24 You shall know that your
tent *is* in peace;
You shall visit your dwelling
and find nothing amiss.
25 You shall also know that
[a]your descendants *shall*
be many,
And your offspring [b]like the
grass of the earth.
26 [a]You shall come to the grave
at a full age,
As a sheaf of grain ripens in
its season.
27 Behold, this we have
[a]searched out;
It *is* true.
Hear it, and know for
yourself."

6

Then Job answered and said:

2 "Oh, that my grief were fully
weighed,
And my calamity laid with it
on the scales!
3 For then it would be heavier
than the sand of the
sea—
Therefore my words have
been rash.
4 [a]For the arrows of the
Almighty *are* within me;

11 [a]Ps. 113:7
12 [a]Neh. 4:15
13 [a][1 Cor. 3:19]
15 [a]Ps. 35:10
16 [a]1 Sam. 2:8
17 [a]Ps. 94:12
18 [a][1 Sam. 2:6, 7]
19 [a]Ps. 34:19; 91:3 [b]Ps. 91:10
20 [a]Ps. 33:19, 20; 37:19 [1]Lit. *hand*
21 [a]Ps. 31:20
22 [a]Ezek. 34:25 [b]Hos. 2:18
23 [a]Ps. 91:12
25 [a]Ps. 112:2 [b]Ps. 72:16
26 [a][Prov. 9:11; 10:27]
27 [a]Ps. 111:2

CHAPTER 6

4 [a]Ps. 38:2

My spirit drinks in their
poison;
[b]The terrors of God are
arrayed [c]against me.
5 Does the [a]wild donkey bray
when it has grass,
Or does the ox low over its
fodder?
6 Can flavorless food be eaten
without salt?
Or is there *any* taste in the
white of an egg?
7 My soul refuses to touch
them;
They *are* as loathsome food
to me.

8 "Oh, that I might have my
request,
That God would grant *me*
the thing that I long for!
9 That it would please God to
crush me,
That He would loose His
hand and [a]cut me off!
10 Then I would still have
comfort;
Though in anguish I would
exult,
He will not spare;
For [a]I have not concealed
the words of [b]the Holy
One.

11 "What strength do I have,
that I should hope?
And what *is* my end, that I
should prolong my life?
12 *Is* my strength the strength
of stones?
Or is my flesh bronze?
13 *Is* my help not within me?
And is success driven from
me?

14 "To[a] him who is [1]afflicted,
kindness *should be
shown* by his friend,
Even though he forsakes the
fear of the Almighty.
15 [a]My brothers have dealt
deceitfully like a brook,
[b]Like the streams of the
brooks that pass away,
16 Which are dark because of
the ice,
And into which the snow
vanishes.
17 When it is warm, they cease
to flow;
When it is hot, they vanish
from their place.
18 The paths of their way turn
aside,
They go nowhere and perish.
19 The caravans of [a]Tē′ma
look,
The travelers of [b]Shē′ba
hope for them.
20 They are [a]disappointed[1]
because they were
confident;
They come there and are
confused.
21 For now [a]you are nothing,
You see terror and [b]are
afraid.
22 Did I ever say, 'Bring
something to me'?
Or, 'Offer a bribe for me
from your wealth'?
23 Or, 'Deliver me from the
enemy's hand'?
Or, 'Redeem me from the
hand of oppressors'?

24 "Teach me, and I will hold
my tongue;
Cause me to understand
wherein I have erred.
25 How forceful are right
words!
But what does your arguing
prove?
26 Do you intend to rebuke *my*
words,

4 [b]Ps. 88:15, 16 [c]Job 30:15
5 [a]Job 39:5–8
9 [a]Job 7:16; 9:21; 10:1
10 [a]Acts 20:20 [b][Is. 57:15]
14 [a][Prov. 17:17] [1]Or *despairing*
15 [a]Ps. 38:11 [b]Jer. 15:18
19 [a]Gen. 25:15 [b]1 Kin. 10:1
20 [a]Jer. 14:3 [1]Lit. *ashamed*
21 [a]Job 13:4 [b]Ps. 38:11

And the speeches of a
desperate one, *which are*
as wind?
27 Yes, you overwhelm the
fatherless,
And you [a]undermine your
friend.
28 Now therefore, be pleased
to look at me;
For I would never lie to your
face.
29 [a]Yield now, let there be no
injustice!
Yes, concede, my
[b]righteousness [1]still
stands!
30 Is there injustice on my
tongue?
Cannot my [1]taste discern
the unsavory?

7

"*Is there* not [a]a time of hard
service for man on earth?
Are not his days also like
the days of a hired man?
2 Like a servant who
[1]earnestly desires the
shade,
And like a hired man who
eagerly looks for his
wages,
3 So I have been allotted
[a]months of futility,
And wearisome nights have
been appointed to me.
4 [a]When I lie down, I say,
'When shall I arise,
And the night be ended?'
For I have had my fill of
tossing till dawn.
5 My flesh is [a]caked with
worms and dust,
My skin is cracked and
breaks out afresh.

6 "My[a] days are swifter than a
weaver's shuttle,
And are spent without hope.
7 Oh, remember that [a]my life
is a breath!
My eye will never again see
good.
8 [a]The eye of him who sees me
will see me no *more;*
While your eyes *are* upon
me, I shall no longer *be.*
9 *As* the cloud disappears and
vanishes away,
So [a]he who goes down
to the grave does not
come up.
10 He shall never return to his
house,
[a]Nor shall his place know
him anymore.

11 "Therefore I will [a]not restrain
my mouth;
I will speak in the anguish
of my spirit;
I will [b]complain in the
bitterness of my soul.
12 *Am* I a sea, or a sea serpent,
That You set a guard over
me?
13 [a]When I say, 'My bed will
comfort me,
My couch will ease my
complaint,'
14 Then You scare me with
dreams
And terrify me with visions,
15 So that my soul chooses
strangling
And death rather than [1]my
body.
16 [a]I loathe *my life;*
I would not live forever.
[b]Let me alone,
For [c]my days *are but* [1]a
breath.

17 "What[a] *is* man, that You
should exalt him,
That You should set Your
heart on him,

27 [a]Ps. 57:6
29 [a]Job 17:10 [b]Job 27:5, 6; 34:5 [1]Lit. *is in it*
30 [1]*palate*

CHAPTER 7

1 [a][Job 14:5, 13, 14]
2 [1]Lit. *pants for*
3 [a][Job 15:31]
4 [a]Deut. 28:67
5 [a]Is. 14:11
6 [a]Job 9:25; 16:22; 17:11
7 [a]Ps. 78:39; 89:47
8 [a]Job 8:18; 20:9
9 [a]2 Sam. 12:23
10 [a]Ps. 103:16
11 [a]Ps. 39:1, 9 [b]1 Sam. 1:10
13 [a]Job 9:27
15 [1]Lit. *my bones*
16 [a]Job 10:1 [b]Job 14:6 [c]Ps. 62:9 [1]Without substance, futile
17 [a]Ps. 8:4; 144:3

18 That You should [1]visit him
every morning,
And test him every moment?
19 How long?
Will You not look away
from me,
And let me alone till I
swallow my saliva?
20 Have I sinned?
What have I done to You,
[a]O watcher of men?
Why [b]have You set me as
Your target,
So that I am a burden [1]to
myself?
21 Why then do You not pardon
my transgression,
And take away my iniquity?
For now I will lie down in
the dust,
And You will seek me
diligently,
But I *will* no longer *be*."

8 Then Bil'dad the Shū'hīte
answered and said:

2 "How long will you speak
these *things*,
And the words of your
mouth *be like* a strong
wind?
3 [a]Does God subvert
judgment?
Or does the Almighty
pervert justice?
4 If [a]your sons have sinned
against Him,
He has cast them away [1]for
their transgression.
5 [a]If you would earnestly seek
God
And make your supplication
to the Almighty,
6 If you *were* pure and
upright,
Surely now He would
[1]awake for you,
And prosper your rightful
dwelling place.
7 Though your beginning was
small,
Yet your latter end would
[a]increase abundantly.

8 "For[a] inquire, please, of the
former age,
And consider the things
discovered by their
fathers;
9 For [a]we *were born* yesterday,
and know [1]nothing,
Because our days on earth
are a shadow.
10 Will they not teach you and
tell you,
And utter words from their
heart?

11 "Can the papyrus grow up
without a marsh?
Can the reeds flourish
without water?
12 [a]While it *is* yet green *and* not
cut down,
It withers before any *other*
plant.
13 So *are* the paths of all who
[a]forget God;
And the hope of the
[b]hypocrite shall perish,
14 Whose confidence shall be
cut off,
And whose trust *is* [1]a
spider's web.
15 [a]He leans on his house, but it
does not stand.
He holds it fast, but it does
not endure.
16 He grows green in the sun,
And his branches spread
out in his garden.
17 His roots wrap around the
rock heap,
And look for a place in the
stones.

18 [1]*attend to*
20 [a]Ps. 36:6 [b]Ps. 21:12 [1]So with MT, Tg., Vg.; LXX, Jewish tradition *to You*

CHAPTER 8

3 [a][Deut. 32:4]
4 [a]Job 1:5, 18, 19 [1]Lit. *into the hand of their transgression*
5 [a][Job 5:17–27; 11:13]
6 [1]*arise*
7 [a]Job 42:12
8 [a]Deut. 4:32; 32:7
9 [a]Gen. 47:9 [1]Lit. *not*
12 [a]Ps. 129:6
13 [a]Ps. 9:17 [b]Job 11:20; 18:14; 27:8
14 [1]Lit. *a spider's house*
15 [a]Job 8:22; 27:18

18 [a]If he is destroyed from his place,
Then *it* will deny him,
saying, 'I have not seen you.'

19 "Behold, this is the joy of His way,
And [a]out of the earth others will grow.
20 Behold, [a]God will not [1]cast away the blameless,
Nor will He uphold the evildoers.
21 He will yet fill your mouth with laughing,
And your lips with [1]rejoicing.
22 Those who hate you will be [a]clothed with shame,
And the dwelling place of the wicked [1]will come to nothing."

9

Then Job answered and said:

2 "Truly I know *it is* so,
But how can a [a]man be [b]righteous before God?
3 If one wished to [1]contend with Him,
He could not answer Him one time out of a thousand.
4 [a]*God is* wise in heart and mighty in strength.
Who has hardened *himself* against Him and prospered?
5 He removes the mountains, and they do not know
When He overturns them in His anger;
6 He [a]shakes the earth out of its place,
And its [b]pillars tremble;
7 He commands the sun, and it does not rise;
He seals off the stars;
8 [a]He alone spreads out the heavens,
And [1]treads on the [2]waves of the sea;
9 [a]He made [1]the Bear, Ō·rī′on, and the Plē′a·dēs,
And the chambers of the south;
10 [a]He does great things past finding out,
Yes, wonders without number.
11 [a]If He goes by me, I do not see *Him;*
If He moves past, I do not perceive Him;
12 [a]If He takes away, [1]who can hinder Him?
Who can say to Him, 'What are You doing?'
13 God will not withdraw His anger,
[a]The allies of [1]the proud lie prostrate beneath Him.

14 "How then can I answer Him,
And choose my words *to reason* with Him?
15 [a]For though I were righteous, I could not answer Him;
I would beg mercy of my Judge.
16 If I called and He answered me,
I would not believe that He was listening to my voice.
17 For He crushes me with a tempest,
And multiplies my wounds [a]without cause.
18 He will not allow me to catch my breath,
But fills me with bitterness.

18 [a]Job 7:10
19 [a]Ps. 113:7
20 [a]Job 4:7 [1]*reject*
21 [1]Lit. *shouts of joy*
22 [a]Ps. 35:26; 109:29 [1]Lit. *will not be*

CHAPTER 9

2 [a][Job 4:17; 15:14–16] [b][Hab. 2:4]
3 [1]*argue*
4 [a]Job 36:5
6 [a]Heb. 12:26 [b]Job 26:11
8 [a]Ps. 104:2, 3 [1]*walks* [2]Lit. *heights*
9 [a]Amos 5:8 [1]Heb. *Ash, Kesil,* and *Kimah*
10 [a]Job 5:9
11 [a][Job 23:8, 9; 35:14]
12 [a][Is. 45:9] [1]Lit. *who can turn Him back?*
13 [a]Job 26:12 [1]Heb. *rahab*
15 [a]Job 10:15; 23:1–7
17 [a]Job 2:3

19 If *it is a matter* of strength,
indeed *He is* strong;
And if of justice, who will
appoint my day *in court?*
20 Though I were righteous,
my own mouth would
condemn me;
Though I *were* blameless,
it would prove me
perverse.

21 "I am blameless, yet I do not
know myself;
I despise my life.
22 It *is* all one *thing;*
Therefore I say, [a]'He
destroys the blameless
and the wicked.'
23 If the scourge slays
suddenly,
He laughs at the plight of
the innocent.
24 The earth is given into the
hand of the wicked.
He covers the faces of its
judges.
If it is not *He,* who else
could it be?

25 "Now [a]my days are swifter
than a runner;
They flee away, they see no
good.
26 They pass by like [1]swift
ships,
[a]Like an eagle swooping on
its prey.
27 [a]If I say, 'I will forget my
complaint,
I will put off my sad face
and wear a smile,'
28 [a]I am afraid of all my
sufferings;
I know that You [b]will not
hold me innocent.
29 *If* I am condemned,
Why then do I labor in vain?

22 [a]Ezek. 21:3
25 [a]Job 7:6, 7
26 [a]Hab. 1:8 [1]Lit. *ships of reeds*
27 [a]Job 7:13
28 [a]Ps. 119:120 [b]Ex. 20:7
30 [a][Jer. 2:22] [1]*lye*
31 [1]*loathe*
32 [a][Is. 45:9]
33 [a][1 Sam. 2:25]
34 [a]Job 13:20, 21

CHAPTER 10

1 [a]Job 7:16 [b]Job 7:11 [1]Lit. *leave on myself*
4 [a][1 Sam. 16:7]

30 [a]If I wash myself with snow
water,
And cleanse my hands with
[1]soap,
31 Yet You will plunge me into
the pit,
And my own clothes will
[1]abhor me.

32 "For [a]*He is* not a man, as I
am,
That I may answer Him,
And that we should go to
court together.
33 [a]Nor is there any mediator
between us,
Who may lay his hand on us
both.
34 [a]Let Him take His rod away
from me,
And do not let dread of Him
terrify me.
35 *Then* I would speak and not
fear Him,
But it is not so with me.

10

"My [a]soul loathes my life;
I will [1]give free course
to my complaint,
[b]I will speak in the bitterness
of my soul.
2 I will say to God, 'Do not
condemn me;
Show me why You contend
with me.
3 *Does it* seem good to You
that You should oppress,
That You should despise the
work of Your hands,
And smile on the counsel of
the wicked?
4 Do You have eyes of flesh?
Or [a]do You see as man sees?
5 *Are* Your days like the days
of a mortal man?
Are Your years like the days
of a mighty man,

6 That You should seek for my iniquity
And search out my sin,
7 Although You know that I am not wicked,
And *there is* no one who can deliver from Your hand?

8 'Your[a] hands have made me and fashioned me,
An intricate unity;
Yet You would [b]destroy me.
9 Remember, I pray, [a]that You have made me like clay.
And will You turn me into dust again?
10 [a]Did You not pour me out like milk,
And curdle me like cheese,
11 Clothe me with skin and flesh,
And knit me together with bones and sinews?
12 You have granted me life and favor,
And Your care has preserved my spirit.

13 'And these *things* You have hidden in Your heart;
I know that this *was* with You:
14 If I sin, then [a]You mark me,
And will not acquit me of my iniquity.
15 If I am wicked, [a]woe to me;
[b]Even *if* I am righteous, I [1]cannot lift up my head.
I am full of disgrace;
[c]See my misery!
16 If *my head* is exalted,
[a]You hunt me like a fierce lion,
And again You show Yourself awesome against me.
17 You renew Your witnesses against me,
And increase Your indignation toward me;
Changes and war are *ever* with me.

18 'Why[a] then have You brought me out of the womb?
Oh, that I had perished and no eye had seen me!
19 I would have been as though I had not been.
I would have been carried from the womb to the grave.
20 [a]Are not my days few?
Cease! [b]Leave me alone, that I may take a little comfort,
21 Before I go *to the place from which* I shall not return,
[a]To the land of darkness [b]and the shadow of death,
22 A land as dark as darkness *itself*,
As the shadow of death, without any order,
Where even the light *is* like darkness.' "

11

Then Zō′phar the Nā′a·ma·thīte answered and said:

2 "Should not the multitude of words be answered?
And should [1]a man full of talk be vindicated?
3 Should your empty talk make men [1]hold their peace?
And when you mock, should no one rebuke you?
4 For you have said,
[a]'My doctrine *is* pure,

8 [a]Ps. 119:73 [b][Job 9:22]
9 [a]Gen. 2:7
10 [a][Ps. 139:14–16]
14 [a]Ps. 139:1
15 [a]Is. 3:11 [b][Job 9:12, 15] [c]Ps. 25:18 [1]Lit. *will not*
16 [a]Is. 38:13
18 [a]Job 3:11–13
20 [a]Ps. 39:5 [b]Job 7:16, 19
21 [a]Ps. 88:12 [b]Ps. 23:4

CHAPTER 11
2 [1]Lit. *a man of lips*
3 [1]*be silent*
4 [a]Job 6:30

And I am clean in your eyes.'
5 But oh, that God would speak,
And open His lips against you,
6 That He would show you the secrets of wisdom!
For *they would* double *your* prudence.
Know therefore that [a]God [1]exacts from you
Less than your iniquity *deserves*.

7 "Can[a] you search out the deep things of God?
Can you find out the limits of the Almighty?
8 *They are* higher than heaven— what can you do?
Deeper than [1]Shē'ōl— what can you know?
9 Their measure *is* longer than the earth
And broader than the sea.

10 "If[a] He passes by, imprisons, and gathers *to judgment*,
Then who can [1]hinder Him?
11 For [a]He knows deceitful men;
He sees wickedness also.
Will He not then consider *it*?
12 For an [a]empty-headed man will be wise,
When a wild donkey's colt is born a man.

13 "If you would [a]prepare your heart,
And [b]stretch out your hands toward Him;
14 If iniquity *were* in your hand, *and you* put it far away,
And [a]would not let wickedness dwell in your tents;
15 [a]Then surely you could lift up your face without spot;
Yes, you could be steadfast, and not fear;
16 Because you would [a]forget *your* misery,
And remember *it* as waters *that have* passed away,
17 And *your* life [a]would be brighter than noonday.
Though you were dark, you would be like the morning.
18 And you would be secure, because there is hope;
Yes, you would dig *around you, and* [a]take your rest in safety.
19 You would also lie down, and no one would make *you* afraid;
Yes, many would court your favor.
20 But [a]the eyes of the wicked will fail,
And they shall not escape,
And [b]their hope—[1]loss of life!"

12

Then Job answered and said:

2 "No doubt you *are* the people,
And wisdom will die with you!
3 But I have [1]understanding as well as you;
I *am* not [a]inferior to you.
Indeed, who does not *know* such things as these?

4 "I[a] am one mocked by his friends,

6 [a][Ezra 9:13] [1]Lit. *forgets some of your iniquity for you*
7 [a][Eccl. 3:11]
8 [1]The abode of the dead
10 [a][Rev. 3:7] [1]*restrain*
11 [a][Ps. 10:14]
12 [a]Rom. 1:22
13 [a][1 Sam. 7:3] [b]Ps. 88:9
14 [a]Ps. 101:3
15 [a]Ps. 119:6
16 [a]Is. 65:16
17 [a]Is. 58:8, 10
18 [a]Lev. 26:5, 6
20 [a]Deut. 28:65 [b][Prov. 11:7] [1]Lit. *the breathing out of life*

CHAPTER 12

3 [a]Job 13:2 [1]Lit. *a heart*
4 [a]Job 21:3

Who [b]called on God, and He
answered him,
The just and blameless *who*
is ridiculed.
5 A [1]lamp is despised in the
thought of one who is at
ease;
It is made ready for [a]those
whose feet slip.
6 [a]The tents of robbers prosper,
And those who provoke God
are secure—
In what God provides by His
hand.

7 "But now ask the beasts, and
they will teach you;
And the birds of the air, and
they will tell you;
8 Or speak to the earth, and it
will teach you;
And the fish of the sea will
explain to you.
9 Who among all these does
not know
That the hand of the LORD
has done this,
10 [a]In whose hand *is* the [1]life of
every living thing,
And the [b]breath of [2]all
mankind?
11 Does not the ear test words
And the [1]mouth taste its
food?
12 Wisdom *is* with aged men,
And with [1]length of days,
understanding.

13 "With Him *are* [a]wisdom and
strength,
He has counsel and
understanding.
14 If [a]He breaks *a thing* down,
it cannot be rebuilt;
If He imprisons a man, there
can be no release.
15 If He [a]withholds the waters,
they dry up;
If He [b]sends them out, they
overwhelm the earth.
16 With Him *are* strength and
prudence.
The deceived and the
deceiver *are* His.
17 He leads counselors away
plundered,
And makes fools of the
judges.
18 He loosens the bonds of
kings,
And binds their waist with
a belt.
19 He leads [1]princes away
plundered,
And overthrows the mighty.
20 [a]He deprives the trusted ones
of speech,
And takes away the
discernment of the
elders.
21 [a]He pours contempt on
princes,
And [1]disarms the mighty.
22 He [a]uncovers deep things
out of darkness,
And brings the shadow of
death to light.
23 [a]He makes nations great, and
destroys them;
He [1]enlarges nations, and
guides them.
24 He takes away the
[1]understanding of the
chiefs of the people of
the earth,
And [a]makes them wander in
a pathless wilderness.
25 [a]They grope in the dark
without light,
And He makes them [b]stagger
like a drunken *man.*

13 "Behold, my eye has seen
all *this,*
My ear has heard and
understood it.

4 [b]Ps. 91:15
5 [a]Prov. 14:2 [1]Or *disaster*
6 [a][Job 9:24; 21:6–16]
10 [a][Acts 17:28] [b]Job 27:3; 33:4 [1]Or *soul* [2]Lit. *all flesh of men*
11 [1]*palate*
12 [1]Long life
13 [a]Job 9:4; 36:5
14 [a]Job 11:10
15 [a][1 Kin. 8:35, 36] [b]Gen. 7:11–24
19 [1]Lit. *priests,* but not in a technical sense
20 [a]Job 32:9
21 [a]Ps. 107:40 [1]*loosens the belt of*
22 [a][1 Cor. 4:5]
23 [a]Is. 9:3; 26:15 [1]Lit. *spreads out*
24 [a]Ps. 107:4 [1]Lit. *heart*
25 [a]Job 5:14; 15:30; 18:18 [b]Ps. 107:27

2 [a]What you know, I also
know;
I *am* not inferior to you.
3 [a]But I would speak to the
Almighty,
And I desire to reason with
God.
4 But you forgers of lies,
[a]You *are* all worthless
physicians.
5 Oh, that you would be silent,
And [a]it would be your
wisdom!
6 Now hear my reasoning,
And heed the pleadings of
my lips.
7 [a]Will you speak [1]wickedly for
God,
And talk deceitfully for
Him?
8 Will you show partiality for
Him?
Will you contend for God?
9 Will it be well when He
searches you out?
Or can you mock Him as
one mocks a man?
10 He will surely rebuke you
If you secretly show
partiality.
11 Will not His [1]excellence
make you afraid,
And the dread of Him fall
upon you?
12 Your platitudes *are* proverbs
of ashes,
Your defenses are defenses
of clay.

13 "Hold[1] your peace with me,
and let me speak,
Then let come on me what
may!
14 Why [a]do I take my flesh in
my teeth,
And put my life in my
hands?
15 [a]Though He slay me, yet will
I trust Him.
[b]Even so, I will defend my
own ways before Him.
16 He also *shall* be my
salvation,
For a [a]hypocrite could not
come before Him.
17 Listen carefully to my
speech,
And to my declaration with
your ears.
18 See now, I have prepared
my case,
I know that I shall be
[a]vindicated.
19 [a]Who *is* he *who* will contend
with me?
If now I hold my tongue, I
perish.

20 "Only[a] two *things* do not do
to me,
Then I will not hide myself
from You:
21 [a]Withdraw Your hand far
from me,
And let not the dread of You
make me afraid.
22 Then call, and I will
[a]answer;
Or let me speak, then You
respond to me.
23 How many *are* my iniquities
and sins?
Make me know my
transgression and my
sin.
24 [a]Why do You hide Your
face,
And [b]regard me as Your
enemy?
25 [a]Will You frighten a leaf
driven to and fro?
And will You pursue dry
stubble?
26 For You write bitter things
against me,

CHAPTER 13
2 [a]Job 12:3
3 [a]Job 23:3; 31:35
4 [a]Job 6:21
5 [a]Prov. 17:28
7 [a]Job 27:4; 36:4 [1]*unrighteously*
11 [1]Lit. *exaltation*
13 [1]*Be silent*
14 [a]Job 18:4
15 [a]Ps. 23:4 [b]Job 27:5
16 [a]Job 8:13
18 [a][Rom. 8:34]
19 [a]Is. 50:8
20 [a]Job 9:34
21 [a]Ps. 39:10
22 [a]Job 9:16; 14:15
24 [a][Deut. 32:20] [b]Lam. 2:5
25 [a]Is. 42:3

And [a]make me inherit the
iniquities of my youth.
27 [a]You put my feet in the
stocks,
And watch closely all my
paths.
You [1]set a limit for the [2]soles
of my feet.

28 "*Man*[1] decays like a rotten
thing,
Like a garment that is moth-
eaten.

CHAPTER 14

14 "Man *who is* born of
woman
Is of few days and [a]full of
[1]trouble.
2 [a]He comes forth like a flower
and fades away;
He flees like a shadow and
does not continue.
3 And [a]do You open Your eyes
on such a one,
And [b]bring [1]me to judgment
with Yourself?
4 Who [a]can bring a clean
thing out of an unclean?
No one!
5 [a]Since his days *are*
determined,
The number of his months
is with You;
You have appointed his
limits, so that he cannot
pass.
6 [a]Look away from him that he
may [1]rest,
Till [b]like a hired man he
finishes his day.

7 "For there is hope for a tree,
If it is cut down, that it will
sprout again,
And that its tender shoots
will not cease.
8 Though its root may grow
old in the earth,
And its stump may die in
the ground,
9 *Yet* at the scent of water it
will bud
And bring forth branches
like a plant.
10 But man dies and [1]is laid
away;
Indeed he [2]breathes his last
And where *is* [a]he?
11 *As* water disappears from
the sea,
And a river becomes
parched and dries up,
12 So man lies down and does
not rise.
[a]Till the heavens *are* no
more,
They will not awake
Nor be roused from their
sleep.

13 "Oh, that You would hide me
in the grave,
That You would conceal me
until Your wrath is past,
That You would appoint
me a set time, and
remember me!
14 If a man dies, shall he live
again?
All the days of my hard
service [a]I will wait,
Till my change comes.
15 [a]You shall call, and I will
answer You;
You shall desire the work of
Your hands.
16 For now [a]You number my
steps,
But do not watch over my
sin.
17 [a]My transgression *is* sealed
up in a bag,
And You [1]cover my iniquity.

18 "But *as* a mountain falls *and*
crumbles away,

---

26 [a]Job 20:11
27 [a]Job 33:11 [1]Lit. *inscribe a print* [2]Lit. *roots*
28 [1]Lit. *He*
1 [a]Eccl. 2:23 [1]*turmoil*
2 [a]Job 8:9
3 [a]Ps. 8:4; 144:3 [b][Ps. 143:2] [1]LXX, Syr., Vg. *him*
4 [a][Ps. 51:2, 5, 10]
5 [a]Job 7:1; 21:21
6 [a]Ps. 39:13 [b]Job 7:1 [1]Lit. *cease*
10 [a]Job 10:21, 22 [1]*lies prostrate* [2]*expires*
12 [a][Is. 51:6; 65:17; 66:22]
14 [a]Job 13:15
15 [a]Job 13:22
16 [a]Prov. 5:21
17 [a]Deut. 32:32–34 [1]Lit. *plaster over*

And *as* a rock is moved
from its place;
19 *As* water wears away
stones,
And as torrents wash away
the soil of the earth;
So You destroy the hope of
man.
20 You prevail forever against
him, and he passes on;
You change his countenance
and send him away.
21 His sons come to honor, and
[a]he does not know *it;*
They are brought low, and
he does not perceive *it.*
22 But his flesh will be in pain
over it,
And his soul will mourn
over it."

15

Then [a]E·lī'phaz the Tē'man·īte answered and said:

2 "Should a wise man answer
with empty knowledge,
And fill [1]himself with the
east wind?
3 Should he reason with
unprofitable talk,
Or by speeches with which
he can do no good?
4 Yes, you cast off fear,
And restrain [1]prayer before
God.
5 For your iniquity teaches
your mouth,
And you choose the tongue
of the crafty.
6 [a]Your own mouth condemns
you, and not I;
Yes, your own lips testify
against you.

7 "*Are* you the first man *who*
was born?
[a]Or were you made before
the hills?
8 [a]Have you heard the counsel
of God?
Do you limit wisdom to
yourself?
9 [a]What do you know that we
do not know?
What do you understand
that *is* not in us?
10 [a]Both the gray-haired and
the aged *are* among us,
Much older than your
father.
11 *Are* the consolations of God
too small for you,
And the word *spoken*
[1]gently with you?
12 Why does your heart carry
you away,
And [1]what do your eyes
wink at,
13 That you turn your spirit
against God,
And let *such* words go out
of your mouth?

14 "What[a] *is* man, that he could
be pure?
And *he who is* born of a
woman, that he could be
righteous?
15 [a]If *God* puts no trust in His
saints,
And the heavens are not
pure in His sight,
16 [a]How much less man, *who is*
abominable and filthy,
[b]Who drinks iniquity like
water!

17 "I will tell you, hear me;
What I have seen I will
declare,
18 What wise men have told,
Not hiding *anything*
received [a]from their
fathers,

21 [a]Eccl. 9:5

CHAPTER 15

1 [a]Job 4:1

2 [1]Lit. *his belly*

4 [1]*meditation* or *complaint*

6 [a][Luke 19:22]

7 [a]Prov. 8:25

8 [a]Rom. 11:34

9 [a]Job 12:3; 13:2

10 [a]Job 8:8–10; 12:12; 32:6, 7

11 [1]Or *a secret thing*

12 [1]Or *why do your eyes flash*

14 [a]Prov. 20:9

15 [a]Job 4:18; 25:5

16 [a]Ps. 14:3; 53:3 [b]Prov. 19:28

18 [a]Job 8:8; 20:4

19 To whom alone the [1]land
was given,
And [a]no alien passed among
them:
20 The wicked man writhes
with pain all *his* days,
[a]And the number of years
is hidden from the
oppressor.
21 [1]Dreadful sounds *are* in his
ears;
[a]In prosperity the destroyer
comes upon him.
22 He does not believe that
he will [a]return from
darkness,
For a sword is waiting for
him.
23 He [a]wanders about for
bread, *saying*, 'Where *is*
it?'
He knows [b]that a day of
darkness is ready at his
hand.
24 Trouble and anguish make
him afraid;
They overpower him, like a
king ready for [1]battle.
25 For he stretches out his
hand against God,
And acts defiantly against
the Almighty,
26 Running stubbornly against
Him
With his strong, embossed
shield.

27 "Though[a] he has covered his
face with his fatness,
And made *his* waist heavy
with fat,
28 He dwells in desolate cities,
In houses which no one
inhabits,
Which are destined to
become ruins.
29 He will not be rich,
Nor will his wealth
[a]continue,
Nor will his possessions
overspread the earth.
30 He will not depart from
darkness;
The flame will dry out his
branches,
And [a]by the breath of His
mouth he will go away.
31 Let him not [a]trust in futile
things, deceiving
himself,
For futility will be his
reward.
32 It will be accomplished
[a]before his time,
And his branch will not be
green.
33 He will shake off his unripe
grape like a vine,
And cast off his blossom
like an olive tree.
34 For the company of
hypocrites *will be*
barren,
And fire will consume the
tents of bribery.
35 [a]They conceive trouble and
bring forth futility;
Their womb prepares
deceit."

16

Then Job answered and
said:

2 "I have heard many such
things;
[a]Miserable[1] comforters *are*
you all!
3 Shall [1]words of wind have
an end?
Or what provokes you that
you answer?
4 I also could speak as you
do,
If your soul were in my
soul's place.

19 [a]Joel 3:17
[1]Or *earth*
20 [a]Ps. 90:12
21 [a]1 Thess. 5:3
[1]*Terrifying*
22 [a]Job 14:10–12
23 [a]Ps. 59:15; 109:10
[b]Job 18:12
24 [1]*attack*
27 [a]Ps. 17:10; 73:7; 119:70
29 [a]Job 20:28; 27:16, 17
30 [a]Job 4:9
31 [a]Is. 59:4
32 [a]Job 22:16
35 [a]Is. 59:4

CHAPTER 16
2 [a]Job 13:4; 21:34
[1]*Troublesome*
3 [1]Empty words

I could heap up words
against you,
And [a]shake my head at
you;
5 *But* I would strengthen you
with my mouth,
And the comfort of my lips
would relieve *your grief.*

6 "Though I speak, my grief is
not relieved;
And *if* I remain silent, how
am I eased?
7 But now He has [a]worn me
out;
You [b]have made desolate all
my company.
8 You have shriveled me up,
And it is a [a]witness *against
me;*
My leanness rises up
against me
And bears witness to my
face.
9 [a]He tears *me* in His wrath,
and hates me;
He gnashes at me with His
teeth;
[b]My adversary sharpens His
gaze on me.
10 They [a]gape at me with their
mouth,
They [b]strike me
reproachfully on the
cheek,
They gather together
against me.
11 God [a]has delivered me to
the ungodly,
And turned me over to the
hands of the wicked.
12 I was at ease, but He has
[a]shattered me;
He also has taken *me* by my
neck, and shaken me to
pieces;
He has [b]set me up for His
target,

4 [a]Ps. 22:7; 109:25
7 [a]Job 7:3 [b]Job 16:20; 19:13–15
8 [a]Job 10:17
9 [a]Hos. 6:1 [b]Job 13:24; 33:10
10 [a]Ps. 22:13; 35:21 [b]Lam. 3:30
11 [a]Job 1:15, 17
12 [a]Job 9:17 [b]Job 7:20
13 [1]Lit. *kidneys*
14 [1]Vg. *giant*
15 [a]Ps. 7:5 [1]Lit. *horn*
16 [1]Lit. *red*
18 [a][Ps. 66:18]
19 [a]Rom. 1:9
21 [a]Job 31:35 [1]*friend*
22 [a]Eccl. 12:5
CHAPTER 17
1 [a]Ps. 88:3, 4

13 His archers surround me.
He pierces my [1]heart and
does not pity;
He pours out my gall on the
ground.
14 He breaks me with wound
upon wound;
He runs at me like a
[1]warrior.

15 "I have sewn sackcloth over
my skin,
And [a]laid my [1]head in the
dust.
16 My face is [1]flushed from
weeping,
And on my eyelids *is* the
shadow of death;
17 Although no violence *is* in
my hands,
And my prayer *is* pure.

18 "O earth, do not cover my
blood,
And [a]let my cry have no
resting place!
19 Surely even now [a]my
witness *is* in heaven,
And my evidence *is* on
high.
20 My friends scorn me;
My eyes pour out *tears* to
God.
21 [a]Oh, that one might plead for
a man with God,
As a man *pleads* for his
[1]neighbor!
22 For when a few years are
finished,
I shall [a]go the way of no
return.

17 "My spirit is broken,
My days are
extinguished,
[a]The grave *is ready* for me.
2 *Are* not mockers with me?

And does not my eye [1]dwell
on their [a]provocation?

3 "Now put down a pledge for
me with Yourself.
Who *is* he *who* [a]will shake
hands with me?
4 For You have hidden
their heart from
[a]understanding;
Therefore You will not exalt
them.
5 He who speaks flattery to
his friends,
Even the eyes of his
children will [a]fail.

6 "But He has made me [a]a
byword of the people,
And I have become one in
whose face men spit.
7 [a]My eye has also grown dim
because of sorrow,
And all my members *are*
like shadows.
8 Upright *men* are astonished
at this,
And the innocent stirs
himself up against the
hypocrite.
9 Yet the righteous will hold
to his [a]way,
And he who has [b]clean
hands will be stronger
and stronger.

10 "But please, [a]come back
again, [1]all of you,
For I shall not find *one* wise
man among you.
11 [a]My days are past,
My purposes are broken off,
Even the [1]thoughts of my
heart.
12 They change the night into
day;
'The light *is* near,' *they say,*
in the face of darkness.

2 [a]Job 12:4; 17:6; 30:1, 9; 34:7 [1]Lit. *lodge*
3 [a]Prov. 6:1; 17:18; 22:26
4 [a]Job 12:20; 32:9
5 [a]Job 11:20
6 [a]Job 30:9
7 [a]Ps. 6:7; 31:9
9 [a]Prov. 4:18 [b]Ps. 24:4
10 [a]Job 6:29 [1]So with some Heb. mss., LXX, Syr., Vg.; MT, Tg. *all of them*
11 [a]Job 7:6 [1]*desires*
15 [a]Job 7:6; 13:15; 14:19; 19:10
16 [a]Jon. 2:6 [b]Job 3:17–19; 21:33 [1]The abode of the dead

CHAPTER 18

1 [a]Job 8:1
3 [a]Ps. 73:22
4 [a]Job 13:14 [1]Lit. *one who tears his soul*
5 [a]Prov. 13:9; 20:20; 24:20
6 [a]Job 21:17
7 [a]Job 5:12, 13; 15:6

13 If I wait *for* the grave *as* my
house,
If I make my bed in the
darkness,
14 If I say to corruption, 'You
are my father,'
And to the worm, 'You
are my mother and my
sister,'
15 Where then *is* my [a]hope?
As for my hope, who can
see it?
16 *Will* they go down [a]to the
gates of [1]Shē′ōl?
Shall *we have* [b]rest together
in the dust?"

18

Then [a]Bil′dad the Shū′hīte answered and said:

2 "How long *till* you put an
end to words?
Gain understanding, and
afterward we will
speak.
3 Why are we counted [a]as
beasts,
And regarded as stupid in
your sight?
4 [a]You[1] who tear yourself in
anger,
Shall the earth be forsaken
for you?
Or shall the rock be
removed from its place?

5 "The[a] light of the wicked
indeed goes out,
And the flame of his fire
does not shine.
6 The light is dark in his tent,
[a]And his lamp beside him is
put out.
7 The steps of his strength are
shortened,
And [a]his own counsel casts
him down.

8 For [a]he is cast into a net by
his own feet,
And he walks into a snare.
9 The net takes *him* by the
heel,
And [a]a snare lays hold of
him.
10 A noose *is* hidden for him
on the ground,
And a trap for him in the
road.
11 [a]Terrors frighten him on
every side,
And drive him to his feet.
12 His strength is starved,
And [a]destruction *is* ready at
his side.
13 It devours patches of his
skin;
The firstborn of death
devours his [1]limbs.
14 He is uprooted from [a]the
shelter of his tent,
And they parade him before
the king of terrors.
15 They dwell in his tent *who
are* none of his;
Brimstone is scattered on
his dwelling.
16 [a]His roots are dried out
below,
And his branch withers
above.
17 [a]The memory of him perishes
from the earth,
And he has no name
[1]among the renowned.
18 [1]He is driven from light into
darkness,
And chased out of the
world.
19 [a]He has neither son nor
posterity among his
people,
Nor any remaining in his
dwellings.
20 Those [1]in the west are
astonished [a]at his day,
As those [2]in the east are
frightened.
21 Surely such *are* the
dwellings of the wicked,
And this *is* the place *of him
who* [a]does not know
God."

19 Then Job answered and
said:

2 "How long will you torment
my soul,
And break me in pieces
with words?
3 These ten times you have
[1]reproached me;
You are not ashamed *that*
you [2]have wronged me.
4 And if indeed I have erred,
My error remains with me.
5 If indeed you [a]exalt
yourselves against me,
And plead my disgrace
against me,
6 Know then that [a]God has
wronged me,
And has surrounded me
with His net.

7 "If I cry out concerning
[1]wrong, I am not heard.
If I cry aloud, *there is* no
justice.
8 [a]He has [1]fenced up my way,
so that I cannot pass;
And He has set darkness in
my paths.
9 [a]He has stripped me of my
glory,
And taken the crown *from*
my head.
10 He breaks me down on
every side,
And I am gone;
My [a]hope He has uprooted
like a tree.

8 [a]Job 22:10
9 [a]Job 5:5
11 [a]Jer. 6:25
12 [a]Job 15:23
13 [1]*parts*
14 [a]Job 11:20
16 [a]Job 29:19
17 [a][Ps. 34:16] [1]Lit. *before the outside,* i.e., the distinguished or famous
18 [1]Or *They drive him*
19 [a]Is. 14:22
20 [a]Ps. 37:13 [1]Lit. *who came after* [2]Lit. *who have gone before*
21 [a]Jer. 9:3

CHAPTER 19

3 [1]*shamed* or *disgraced* [2]A Jewish tradition *make yourselves strange to me*
5 [a]Ps. 35:26; 38:16; 55:12, 13
6 [a]Job 16:11
7 [1]*violence*
8 [a]Job 3:23 [1]*walled off my way*
9 [a]Ps. 89:44
10 [a]Job 17:14–16

11 He has also kindled His
wrath against me,
And [a]He counts me as *one*
of His enemies.
12 His troops come together
And build up their road
against me;
They encamp all around my
tent.

13 "He[a] has removed my
brothers far from me,
And my acquaintances are
completely estranged
from me.
14 My relatives have failed,
And my close friends have
forgotten me.
15 Those who dwell in
my house, and my
maidservants,
Count me as a stranger;
I am an alien in their sight.
16 I call my servant, but he
gives no answer;
I beg him with my mouth.
17 My breath is offensive to my
wife,
And I am [1]repulsive to the
children of my own
body.
18 Even [a]young children
despise me;
I arise, and they speak
against me.
19 [a]All my close friends abhor
me,
And those whom I love have
turned against me.
20 [a]My bone clings to my skin
and to my flesh,
And I have escaped by the
skin of my teeth.

21 "Have pity on me, have pity
on me, O you my friends,
For the hand of God has
struck me!

22 Why do you [a]persecute me
as God *does*,
And are not satisfied with
my flesh?

23 "Oh, that my words were
written!
Oh, that they were inscribed
in a book!
24 That they were engraved on
a rock
With an iron pen and lead,
forever!
25 For I know *that* my ☆
[a]Redeemer lives,
And He shall stand at last
on the earth;
26 And after my skin is
[1]destroyed, this *I know*,
That [a]in my flesh I shall see
God,
27 Whom I shall see for myself,
And my eyes shall behold,
and not another.
How my [1]heart yearns
within me!
28 If you should say, 'How shall
we persecute him?'—
Since the root of the matter
is found in me,
29 Be afraid of the sword for
yourselves;
For wrath *brings* the
punishment of the
sword,
That you may know *there is*
a judgment."

20 Then [a]Zō′phar the Nā′-
a·ma·thīte answered and
said:

2 "Therefore my anxious
thoughts make me
answer,
Because of the turmoil
within me.

11 [a]Job 13:24; 33:10
13 [a]Ps. 31:11; 38:11; 69:8; 88:8, 18
17 [1]Lit. *strange*
18 [a]2 Kin. 2:23
19 [a]Ps. 38:11; 55:12, 13
20 [a]Ps. 102:5
22 [a]Ps. 69:26
25 [a]1 Cor. 1:30; Gal. 3:13; Heb. 9:12
26 [a][Ps. 17:15] [1]Lit. *struck off*
27 [1]Lit. *kidneys*

CHAPTER 20

1 [a]Job 11:1

3 I have heard the rebuke
[1]that reproaches me,
And the spirit of my
understanding causes
me to answer.

4 "Do you *not* know this of
[a]old,
Since man was placed on
earth,
5 [a]That the triumphing of the
wicked is short,
And the joy of the hypocrite
is *but* for a [b]moment?
6 [a]Though his haughtiness
mounts up to the
heavens,
And his head reaches to the
clouds,
7 *Yet* he will perish forever
like his own refuse;
Those who have seen him
will say, 'Where is he?'
8 He will fly away [a]like a
dream, and not be found;
Yes, he [b]will be chased away
like a vision of the night.
9 The eye *that* saw him will
see him no more,
Nor will his place behold
him anymore.
10 His children will seek the
favor of the poor,
And his hands will restore
his wealth.
11 His bones are full of [a]his
youthful vigor,
[b]But it will lie down with him
in the dust.

12 "Though evil is sweet in his
mouth,
And he hides it under his
tongue,
13 *Though* he spares it and
does not forsake it,
But still keeps it in his
[1]mouth,
14 *Yet* his food in his stomach
turns sour;
It becomes cobra venom
within him.
15 He swallows down riches
And vomits them up again;
God casts them out of his
belly.
16 He will suck the poison of
cobras;
The viper's tongue will slay
him.
17 He will not see [a]the streams,
The rivers flowing with
honey and cream.
18 He will restore that for
which he labored,
And will not swallow *it*
down;
From the proceeds of
business
He will get no enjoyment.
19 For he has [1]oppressed *and*
forsaken the poor,
He has violently seized a
house which he did not
build.

20 "Because[a] he knows no
quietness in his [1]heart,
He will not save anything he
desires.
21 Nothing is left for him to
eat;
Therefore his well-being
will not last.
22 In his self-sufficiency he will
be in distress;
Every hand of [1]misery will
come against him.
23 *When* he is about to fill his
stomach,
God will cast on him the
fury of His wrath,
And will rain *it* on him
while he is eating.
24 [a]He will flee from the iron
weapon;

3 [1]Lit. *of my insulting correction*
4 [a]Job 8:8; 15:10
5 [a]Ps. 37:35, 36 [b][Job 8:13; 13:16; 15:34; 27:8]
6 [a]Is. 14:13, 14
8 [a]Ps. 73:20; 90:5 [b]Job 18:18; 27:21–23
11 [a]Job 13:26 [b]Job 21:26
13 [1]Lit. *palate*
17 [a]Jer. 17:8
19 [1]*crushed*
20 [a]Eccl. 5:13–15 [1]Lit. *belly*
22 [1]Or *the wretched* or *sufferer*
24 [a]Amos 5:19

A bronze bow will pierce him through.
25 It is drawn, and comes out of the body;
Yes, [a]the glittering *point comes* out of his [1]gall.
[b]Terrors *come* upon him;
26 Total darkness *is* reserved for his treasures.
[a]An unfanned fire will consume him;
It shall go ill with him who is left in his tent.
27 The heavens will reveal his iniquity,
And the earth will rise up against him.
28 The increase of his house will depart,
And his goods will flow away in the day of His [a]wrath.
29 [a]This *is* the portion from God for a wicked man,
The heritage appointed to him by God."

21

Then Job answered and said:

2 "Listen carefully to my speech,
And let this be your [1]consolation.
3 Bear with me that I may speak,
And after I have spoken, keep [a]mocking.

4 "As for me, *is* my complaint against man?
And if *it were*, why should I not be impatient?
5 Look at me and be astonished;
[a]Put *your* hand over *your* mouth.
6 Even when I remember I am terrified,
And trembling takes hold of my flesh.
7 [a]Why do the wicked live *and* become old,
Yes, become mighty in power?
8 Their descendants are established with them in their sight,
And their offspring before their eyes.
9 Their houses *are* safe from fear,
[a]Neither *is* [1]the rod of God upon them.
10 Their bull breeds without failure;
Their cow calves [a]without miscarriage.
11 They send forth their little ones like a flock,
And their children dance.
12 They sing to the tambourine and harp,
And rejoice to the sound of the flute.
13 They [a]spend their days in wealth,
And [1]in a moment go down to the [2]grave.
14 [a]Yet they say to God, 'Depart from us,
For we do not desire the knowledge of Your ways.
15 [a]Who *is* the Almighty, that we should serve Him?
And [b]what profit do we have if we pray to Him?'
16 Indeed [1]their prosperity *is* not in their hand;
[a]The counsel of the wicked is far from me.

17 "How often is the lamp of the wicked put out?

25 [a]Job 16:13 [b]Job 18:11, 14 [1]Gallbladder
26 [a]Ps. 21:9
28 [a]Job 20:15; 21:30
29 [a]Job 27:13; 31:2, 3

CHAPTER 21

2 [1]*comfort*
3 [a]Job 16:10
5 [a]Judg. 18:19
7 [a][Jer. 12:1]
9 [a]Ps. 73:5 [1]The rod of God's chastisement
10 [a]Ex. 23:26
13 [a]Job 21:23; 36:11 [1]Without lingering [2]Or *Sheol*
14 [a]Job 22:17
15 [a]Ex. 5:2 [b]Mal. 3:14
16 [a]Prov. 1:10 [1]Lit. *their goal*

How often does their
destruction come upon
them,
The sorrows *God*
[a]distributes in His anger?
18 [a]They are like straw before
the wind,
And like chaff that a storm
[1]carries away.
19 *They say*, 'God [1]lays up
[2]one's iniquity [a]for his
children';
Let Him recompense him,
that he may know *it*.
20 Let his eyes see his
destruction,
And [a]let him drink of the
wrath of the Almighty.
21 For what does he care about
his household after him,
When the number of his
months is cut in half?

22 "Can[a] *anyone* teach God
knowledge,
Since He judges those on
high?
23 One dies in his full strength,
Being wholly at ease and
secure;
24 His [1]pails are full of milk,
And the marrow of his
bones is moist.
25 Another man dies in the
bitterness of his soul,
Never having eaten with
pleasure.
26 They [a]lie down alike in the
dust,
And worms cover them.

27 "Look, I know your thoughts,
And the schemes *with which*
you would wrong me.
28 For you say,
'Where *is* the house of the
prince?
And where *is* [1]the tent,
The dwelling place of the
wicked?'
29 Have you not asked those
who travel the road?
And do you not know their
signs?
30 [a]For the wicked are reserved
for the day of doom;
They shall be brought out
on the day of wrath.
31 Who condemns his way to
his face?
And who repays him *for
what* he has done?
32 Yet he shall be brought to
the grave,
And a vigil kept over the
tomb.
33 The clods of the valley shall
be sweet to him;
[a]Everyone shall follow him,
As countless *have gone*
before him.
34 How then can you comfort
me with empty words,
Since [1]falsehood remains in
your answers?"

22 Then [a]E·lī'phaz the Tē'man·īte answered and
said:

2 "Can[a] a man be profitable to
God,
Though he who is wise may
be profitable to himself?
3 *Is it* any pleasure to the
Almighty that you are
righteous?
Or *is it* gain *to Him* that
you make your ways
blameless?

4 "Is it because of your fear
of Him that He corrects
you,
And enters into judgment
with you?

17 [a][Luke 12:46]
18 [a]Ps. 1:4; 35:5 [1]*steals away*
19 [a][Ex. 20:5] [1]*stores up* [2]Lit. *his*
20 [a]Is. 51:17
22 [a][Is. 40:13; 45:9]
24 [1]LXX, Vg. *bowels;* Syr. *sides;* Tg. *breasts*
26 [a]Eccl. 9:2
28 [1]Vg. omits *the tent*
30 [a][Prov. 16:4]
33 [a]Heb. 9:27
34 [1]*faithlessness*

CHAPTER 22

1 [a]Job 4:1; 15:1; 42:9
2 [a][Luke 17:10]

5 *Is* not your wickedness
great,
And your iniquity without
end?
6 For you have [a]taken pledges
from your brother for no
reason,
And stripped the naked of
their clothing.
7 You have not given the
weary water to drink,
And you [a]have withheld
bread from the hungry.
8 But the [1]mighty man
possessed the land,
And the honorable man
dwelt in it.
9 You have sent widows away
empty,
And the [1]strength of the
fatherless was crushed.
10 Therefore snares *are* all
around you,
And sudden fear troubles
you,
11 Or darkness *so that* you
cannot see;
And an abundance of [a]water
covers you.

12 "Is not God in the height of
heaven?
And see the highest stars,
how lofty they are!
13 And you say, [a]'What does
God know?
Can He judge through the
deep darkness?
14 [a]Thick clouds cover Him, so
that He cannot see,
And He walks above the
circle of heaven.'
15 Will you keep to the old way
Which wicked men have
trod,
16 Who [a]were cut down before
their time,
Whose foundations were
swept away by a flood?
17 [a]They said to God, 'Depart
from us!
What can the Almighty do
to [1]them?'
18 Yet He filled their houses
with good *things;*
But the counsel of the
wicked is far from me.

19 "The[a] righteous see *it* and
are glad,
And the innocent laugh at
them:
20 'Surely our [1]adversaries are
cut down,
And the fire consumes their
remnant.'

21 "Now acquaint yourself with
Him, and [a]be at peace;
Thereby good will come to
you.
22 Receive, please, [a]instruction
from His mouth,
And [b]lay up His words in
your heart.
23 If you return to the
Almighty, you will be
built up;
You will remove iniquity far
from your tents.
24 Then you will [a]lay your gold
in the dust,
And the *gold* of Ōphir
among the stones of the
brooks.
25 Yes, the Almighty will be
your [1]gold
And your precious silver;
26 For then you will have your
[a]delight in the Almighty,
And lift up your face to God.
27 [a]You will make your prayer
to Him,
He will hear you,
And you will pay your vows.

6 [a][Ex. 22:26, 27]
7 [a]Deut. 15:7
8 [1]Lit. *man of arm*
9 [1]Lit. *arms*
11 [a]Ps. 69:1, 2; 124:5
13 [a]Ps. 73:11
14 [a]Ps. 139:11, 12
16 [a]Job 14:19; 15:32
17 [a]Job 21:14, 15 [1]LXX, Syr. *us*
19 [a]Ps. 52:6; 58:10; 107:42
20 [1]LXX *substance is*
21 [a]Is. 27:5
22 [a]Prov. 2:6 [b][Ps. 119:11]
24 [a]2 Chr. 1:15
25 [1]Ancient vss. suggest *defense;* MT *gold,* as in v. 24
26 [a]Job 27:10; Ps. 37:4; Is. 58:14
27 [a][Is. 58:9–11]

28 You will also declare a thing,
And it will be established for you;
So light will shine on your ways.
29 When they cast *you* down, and you say, 'Exaltation *will come!*'
Then [a]He will save the humble *person.*
30 He will *even* deliver one who is not innocent;
Yes, he will be delivered by the purity of your hands."

23

Then Job answered and said:

2 "Even today my [a]complaint is bitter;
[1]My hand is listless because of my groaning.
3 [a]Oh, that I knew where I might find Him,
That I might come to His seat!
4 I would present *my* case before Him,
And fill my mouth with arguments.
5 I would know the words *which* He would answer me,
And understand what He would say to me.
6 [a]Would He contend with me in His great power?
No! But He would take *note* of me.
7 There the upright could reason with Him,
And I would be delivered forever from my Judge.

8 "Look,[a] I go forward, but He is not *there,*
And backward, but I cannot perceive Him;
9 When He works on the left hand, I cannot behold *Him;*
When He turns to the right hand, I cannot see *Him.*
10 But [a]He knows the way that I take;
When [b]He has tested me, I shall come forth as gold.
11 [a]My foot has held fast to His steps;
I have kept His way and not turned aside.
12 I have not departed from the [a]commandment of His lips;
[b]I have treasured the words of His mouth
More than my [1]necessary *food.*

13 "But He *is* unique, and who can make Him change?
And *whatever* [a]His soul desires, *that* He does.
14 For He performs *what is* [a]appointed for me,
And many such *things are* with Him.
15 Therefore I am terrified at His presence;
When I consider *this,* I am afraid of Him.
16 For God [a]made my heart weak,
And the Almighty terrifies me;
17 Because I was not [a]cut off [1]from the presence of darkness,
And He did *not* hide deep darkness from my face.

24

"*Since* [a]times are not hidden from the Almighty,

---

29 [a][1 Pet. 5:5]

CHAPTER 23

2 [a]Job 7:11 [1]So with MT, Tg., Vg.; LXX, Syr. *His*

3 [a]Job 13:3, 18; 16:21; 31:35

6 [a]Is. 57:16

8 [a]Job 9:11; 35:14

10 [a][Ps. 1:6; 139:1–3] [b][James 1:12]

11 [a]Ps. 17:5

12 [a]Job 6:10; 22:22 [b]Ps. 44:18 [1]Lit. *appointed portion*

13 [a][Ps. 115:3]

14 [a][1 Thess. 3:2–4]

16 [a]Ps. 22:14

17 [a]Job 10:18, 19 [1]Or *by* or *before*

CHAPTER 24

1 [a][Acts 1:7]

Why do those who know
Him see not His [b]days?

2 "*Some* remove [a]landmarks;
They seize flocks violently
and feed *on them;*
3 They drive away the donkey
of the fatherless;
They [a]take the widow's ox
as a pledge.
4 They push the needy off the
road;
All the [a]poor of the land are
forced to hide.
5 Indeed, *like* wild donkeys in
the desert,
They go out to their work,
searching for food.
The wilderness *yields* food
for them *and* for *their*
children.
6 They gather their fodder in
the field
And glean in the vineyard of
the wicked.
7 They [a]spend the night
naked, without clothing,
And have no covering in the
cold.
8 They are wet with
the showers of the
mountains,
And [a]huddle around the
rock for want of shelter.

9 "*Some* snatch the fatherless
from the breast,
And take a pledge from the
poor.
10 They cause *the poor* to go
naked, without [a]clothing;
And they take away the
sheaves from the hungry.
11 They press out oil within
their walls,
And tread winepresses, yet
suffer thirst.
12 The dying groan in the city,
And the souls of the
wounded cry out;
Yet God does not charge
them with wrong.

13 "There are those who rebel
against the light;
They do not know its ways
Nor abide in its paths.
14 [a]The murderer rises with the
light;
He kills the poor and needy;
And in the night he is like a
thief.
15 [a]The eye of the adulterer
waits for the twilight,
[b]Saying, 'No eye will see me';
And he [1]disguises *his* face.
16 In the dark they break into
houses
Which they marked for
themselves in the
daytime;
[a]They do not know the light.
17 For the morning is the same
to them as the shadow of
death;
If *someone* recognizes *them,*
They are in the terrors of
the shadow of death.

18 "They *should be* swift on the
face of the waters,
Their portion *should be*
cursed in the earth,
So that no *one would* turn
into the way of their
vineyards.
19 As drought and heat
[1]consume the snow
waters,
So [2]the grave *consumes*
those who have sinned.
20 The womb *should* forget
him,
The worm *should* feed
sweetly on him;

1 [b][Is. 2:12]
2 [a][Deut. 19:14; 27:17]
3 [a][Deut. 24:6, 10, 12, 17]
4 [a]Prov. 28:28
7 [a]Ex. 22:26, 27
8 [a]Lam. 4:5
10 [a]Job 31:19
14 [a]Ps. 10:8
15 [a]Prov. 7:7–10 [b]Ps. 10:11 [1]Lit. *puts a covering on his face*
16 [a][John 3:20]
19 [1]Lit. *seize* [2]Or *Sheol*

[a]He *should* be remembered
no more,
And wickedness *should* be
broken like a tree.
21 For he [1]preys on the barren
who do not bear,
And does no good for the
widow.

22 "But *God* draws the mighty
away with His power;
He rises up, but no *man* is
sure of life.
23 He gives them security, and
they rely *on it;*
Yet [a]His eyes *are* on their
ways.
24 They are exalted for a little
while,
Then they are gone.
They are brought low;
They are [1]taken out of the
way like all *others;*
They dry out like the heads
of grain.

25 "Now if *it is* not *so,* who will
prove me a liar,
And make my speech worth
nothing?"

25

Then [a]Bil′dad the Shū′-
hite answered and said:

2 "Dominion and fear *belong*
to Him;
He makes peace in His high
places.
3 [1]Is there any number to His
armies?
Upon whom does [a]His light
not rise?
4 [a]How then can man be
righteous before God?
Or how can he be [b]pure *who*
is born of a woman?
5 If even the moon does not
shine,
And the stars are not pure
in His [a]sight,
6 How much less man, *who is*
[a]a maggot,
And a son of man, *who is* a
worm?"

26

But Job answered and
said:

2 "How have you helped *him*
who is without power?
How have you saved
the arm *that has* no
strength?
3 How have you counseled
one who has no wisdom?
And *how* have you declared
sound advice to many?
4 To whom have you uttered
words?
And whose spirit came from
you?

5 "The dead tremble,
Those under the waters and
those inhabiting them.
6 [a]Shē′ōl *is* naked before Him,
And Destruction has no
covering.
7 [a]He stretches out the north
over empty space;
He hangs the earth on
nothing.
8 [a]He binds up the water in His
thick clouds,
Yet the clouds [1]are not
broken under it.
9 He covers the face of *His*
throne,
And spreads His cloud over
it.
10 [a]He drew a circular horizon
on the face of the waters,
At the boundary of light and
darkness.
11 The pillars of heaven
tremble,

20 [a]Prov. 10:7
21 [1]Lit. *feeds on*
23 [a][Prov. 15:3]
24 [1]Lit. *gathered up*

CHAPTER 25

1 [a]Job 8:1; 18:1
3 [a]James 1:17 [1]Can His armies be counted?
4 [a]Job 4:17; 15:14 [b][Job 14:4]
5 [a]Job 15:15
6 [a]Ps. 22:6

CHAPTER 26

6 [a]Prov. 15:11
7 [a]Job 9:8
8 [a]Prov. 30:4 [1]*do not break*
10 [a]Prov. 8:29

And are [1]astonished at His
rebuke.
12 [a]He stirs up the sea with His
power,
And by His understanding
He breaks up [1]the storm.
13 [a]By His Spirit He adorned
the heavens;
His hand pierced [b]the
fleeing serpent.
14 Indeed these *are* the mere
edges of His ways,
And how small a whisper
we hear of Him!
But the thunder of His
power who can
understand?"

27

Moreover Job continued his discourse, and said:

2 "*As* God lives, [a]*who* has
taken away my justice,
And the Almighty, *who* has
made my soul bitter,
3 As long as my breath *is* in
me,
And the breath of God in
my nostrils,
4 My lips will not speak
wickedness,
Nor my tongue utter deceit.
5 Far be it from me
That I should say you are
right;
Till I die [a]I will not put away
my integrity from me.
6 My righteousness I [a]hold
fast, and will not let it
go;
[b]My heart shall not [1]reproach
me as long as I live.

7 "May my enemy be like the
wicked,
And he who rises up against
me like the unrighteous.
8 [a]For what is the hope of the
hypocrite,
Though he may gain *much,*
If God takes away his life?
9 [a]Will God hear his cry
When trouble comes upon
him?
10 [a]Will he delight himself in
the Almighty?
Will he always call on God?

11 "I will teach you [1]about the
hand of God;
What *is* with the Almighty I
will not conceal.
12 Surely all of you have seen
it;
Why then do you behave
with complete nonsense?

13 "This[a] is the portion of a
wicked man with God,
And the heritage of
oppressors, received
from the Almighty:
14 [a]If his children are
multiplied, *it is* for the
sword;
And his offspring shall not
be satisfied with bread.
15 Those who survive him shall
be buried in death,
And [a]their[1] widows shall not
weep,
16 Though he heaps up silver
like dust,
And piles up clothing like
clay—
17 He may pile *it* up, but [a]the
just will wear *it,*
And the innocent will divide
the silver.
18 He builds his house like a
[1]moth,
[a]Like a [2]booth *which* a
watchman makes.
19 The rich man will lie down,
[1]But not be gathered *up;*

11 [1]*amazed*
12 [a]Is. 51:15 [1]Heb. *rahab*
13 [a]Ps. 33:6 [b]Is. 27:1

CHAPTER 27

2 [a]Job 34:5
5 [a]Job 2:9; 13:15
6 [a]Job 2:3; 33:9 [b]Acts 24:16 [1]*reprove*
8 [a]Matt. 16:26
9 [a]Jer. 14:12
10 [a]Job 22:26, 27
11 [1]Or *by*
13 [a]Job 20:29
14 [a]Deut. 28:41
15 [a]Ps. 78:64 [1]Lit. *his*
17 [a]Prov. 28:8
18 [a]Is. 1:8 [1]So with MT, Vg.; LXX, Syr. *spider* (cf. 8:14); Tg. *decay* [2]Temporary shelter
19 [1]So with MT, Tg.; LXX, Syr. *But shall not add* (i.e., do it again); Vg. *But take away nothing*

He opens his eyes,
And he *is* [a]no more.
20 [a]Terrors overtake him like a flood;
A tempest steals him away in the night.
21 The east wind carries him away, and he is gone;
It sweeps him out of his place.
22 It hurls against him and does not [a]spare;
He flees desperately from its [1]power.
23 *Men* shall clap their hands at him,
And shall hiss him out of his place.

28 "Surely there is a mine for silver,
And a place *where* gold is refined.
2 Iron is taken from the [1]earth,
And copper *is* smelted *from* ore.
3 *Man* puts an end to darkness,
And searches every recess
For ore in the darkness and the shadow of death.
4 He breaks open a shaft away from people;
In places forgotten by feet
They hang far away from men;
They swing to and fro.
5 *As for* the earth, from it comes bread,
But underneath it is turned up as by fire;
6 Its stones *are* the source of sapphires,
And it contains gold dust.
7 *That* path no bird knows,
Nor has the falcon's eye seen it.
8 The [1]proud lions have not trodden it,
Nor has the fierce lion passed over it.
9 He puts his hand on the flint;
He overturns the mountains [1]at the roots.
10 He cuts out channels in the rocks,
And his eye sees every precious thing.
11 He dams up the streams from trickling;
What is hidden he brings forth to light.

12 "But[a] where can wisdom be found?
And where *is* the place of understanding?
13 Man does not know its [a]value,
Nor is it found in the land of the living.
14 [a]The deep says, '*It is* not in me';
And the sea says, '*It is* not with me.'
15 It [a]cannot be purchased for gold,
Nor can silver be weighed *for* its price.
16 It cannot be valued in the gold of Ō'phir,
In precious onyx or sapphire.
17 Neither [a]gold nor crystal can equal it,
Nor can it be exchanged for [1]jewelry of fine gold.
18 No mention shall be made of [1]coral or quartz,
For the price of wisdom *is* above [a]rubies.
19 The topaz of Ethiopia cannot equal it,

---

19 [a]Job 7:8, 21; 20:7
20 [a]Job 18:11
22 [a]Jer. 13:14 [1]Lit. *hand*

CHAPTER 28

2 [1]Lit. *dust*
8 [1]Lit. *sons of pride*, figurative of the great lions
9 [1]At the base
12 [a]Eccl. 7:24
13 [a]Prov. 3:15
14 [a]Job 28:22
15 [a]Prov. 3:13–15; 8:10, 11, 19
17 [a]Prov. 8:10; 16:16 [1]*vessels*
18 [a]Prov. 3:15; 8:11 [1]Heb. *ramoth*

Nor can it be valued in pure
[a]gold.
20 "From[a] where then does
wisdom come?
And where *is* the place of
understanding?
21 It is hidden from the eyes of
all living,
And concealed from the
birds of the [1]air.
22 [a]Destruction[1] and Death say,
'We have heard a report
about it with our ears.'
23 God understands its way,
And He knows its place.
24 For He looks to the ends of
the earth,
And [a]sees under the whole
heavens,
25 [a]To establish a weight for the
wind,
And apportion the waters by
measure.
26 When He [a]made a law for
the rain,
And a path for the
thunderbolt,
27 Then He saw [1]*wisdom* and
declared it;
He prepared it, indeed, He
searched it out.
28 And to man He said,
'Behold, [a]the fear of the
Lord, that *is* wisdom,
And to depart from evil *is*
understanding.' "

29

Job further continued his discourse, and said:

2 "Oh, that I were as *in* months
[a]past,
As *in* the days *when* God
[b]watched over me;
3 [a]When His lamp shone upon
my head,
And when by His light
I walked *through*
darkness;
4 Just as I was in the days of
my prime,
When [a]the friendly counsel
of God *was* over my
tent;
5 When the Almighty *was* yet
with me,
When my children *were*
around me;
6 When [a]my steps were
bathed with [1]cream,
And [b]the rock poured out
rivers of oil for me!

7 "When I went out to the gate
by the city,
When I took my seat in the
open square,
8 The young men saw me and
hid,
And the aged arose *and*
stood;
9 The princes refrained from
talking,
And [a]put *their* hand on their
mouth;
10 The voice of nobles was
hushed,
And their [a]tongue stuck to
the roof of their mouth.
11 When the ear heard, then it
blessed me,
And when the eye saw, then
it approved me;
12 Because [a]I delivered the
poor who cried out,
The fatherless and *the one*
who had no helper.
13 The blessing of a perishing
man came upon me,
And I caused the widow's
heart to sing for joy.
14 [a]I put on righteousness, and
it clothed me;

19 [a]Prov. 8:19
20 [a]Job 28:12
21 [1]*heaven*
22 [a]Job 28:14 [1]Heb. *Abaddon*
24 [a][Prov. 15:3]
25 [a]Ps. 135:7
26 [a]Job 37:3; 38:25
27 [1]Lit. *it*
28 [a][Prov. 1:7; 9:10]

CHAPTER 29

2 [a]Job 1:1–5 [b]Job 1:10
3 [a]Job 18:6
4 [a][Ps. 25:14]
6 [a]Deut. 32:14; Job 20:17 [b]Ps. 81:16 [1]So with ancient vss. and a few Heb. mss. (cf. Job 20:17); MT *wrath*
9 [a]Job 21:5
10 [a]Ps. 137:6
12 [a][Ps. 72:12]
14 [a][Is. 59:17; 61:10]

My justice *was* like a robe
and a turban.
15 I *was* [a]eyes to the blind,
And I *was* feet to the lame.
16 I *was* a father to the poor,
And [a]I searched out the case
that I did not know.
17 I broke [a]the fangs of the
wicked,
And plucked the victim
from his teeth.

18 "Then I said, [a]'I shall die in
my nest,
And multiply *my* days as
the sand.
19 [a]My root *is* spread out [b]to the
waters,
And the dew lies all night
on my branch.
20 My glory *is* fresh within me,
And my [a]bow is renewed in
my hand.'

21 "*Men* listened to me and
waited,
And kept silence for my
counsel.
22 After my words they did not
speak again,
And my speech settled on
them *as dew.*
23 They waited for me *as* for
the rain,
And they opened their
mouth wide *as* for [a]the
spring rain.
24 *If* I mocked at them, they
did not believe *it*,
And the light of my
countenance they did
not cast down.
25 I chose the way for them,
and sat as chief;
So I dwelt as a king in the
army,
As one *who* comforts
mourners.

15 [a]Num. 10:31
16 [a]Prov. 29:7
17 [a]Prov. 30:14
18 [a]Ps. 30:6
19 [a]Job 18:16 [b]Ps. 1:3
20 [a]Gen. 49:24
23 [a][Zech. 10:1]

CHAPTER 30

1 [1]Lit. *of fewer days*
4 [1]A plant of the salty marshes
6 [1]*wadis* [2]Lit. *holes*
9 [a]Job 17:6
10 [a]Is. 50:6
11 [a]Job 12:18 [1]So with MT, Syr., Tg.; LXX, Vg. *His*

30

"But now they mock at
me, *men* [1]younger
than I,
Whose fathers I disdained
to put with the dogs of
my flock.
2 Indeed, what *profit* is the
strength of their hands
to me?
Their vigor has perished.
3 *They are* gaunt from want
and famine,
Fleeing late to the
wilderness, desolate and
waste,
4 Who pluck [1]mallow by the
bushes,
And broom tree roots *for*
their food.
5 They were driven out from
among *men*,
They shouted at them as *at*
a thief.
6 *They had* to live in the clefts
of the [1]valleys,
In [2]caves of the earth and
the rocks.
7 Among the bushes they
brayed,
Under the nettles they
nestled.
8 *They were* sons of fools,
Yes, sons of vile men;
They were scourged from
the land.

9 "And[a] now I am their
taunting song;
Yes, I am their byword.
10 They abhor me, they keep
far from me;
They do not hesitate [a]to spit
in my face.
11 Because [a]He has loosed
[1]my bowstring and
afflicted me,
They have cast off restraint
before me.

12 At *my* right *hand* the rabble
arises;
They push away my feet,
And [a]they raise against me
their ways of destruction.
13 They break up my path,
They promote my calamity;
They have no helper.
14 They come as broad
breakers;
Under the ruinous storm
they roll along.
15 Terrors are turned upon me;
They pursue my honor as
the wind,
And my prosperity has
passed like a cloud.

16 "And[a] now my soul is
[b]poured out because of
my *plight;*
The days of affliction take
hold of me.
17 My bones are pierced in me
at night,
And my gnawing pains take
no rest.
18 By great force my garment
is disfigured;
It binds me about as the
collar of my coat.
19 He has cast me into the
mire,
And I have become like dust
and ashes.

20 "I [a]cry out to You, but You do
not answer me;
I stand up, and You regard
me.
21 *But* You have become cruel
to me;
With the strength of Your
hand You [a]oppose me.
22 You lift me up to the wind
and cause me to ride
on it;
You spoil my success.

12 [a]Job 19:12
16 [a]Ps. 42:4 [b]Ps. 22:14
20 [a]Job 19:7
21 [a]Job 10:3; 16:9, 14; 19:6, 22
23 [a][Heb. 9:27]
25 [a]Ps. 35:13, 14
26 [a]Jer. 8:15
27 [1]*I seethe inside*
28 [a]Ps. 38:6; 42:9; 43:2
29 [a]Mic. 1:8
30 [a]Ps. 119:83 [b]Ps. 102:3

CHAPTER 31

1 [a][Matt. 5:28] [1]*look intently* or *gaze*
2 [a]Job 20:29

23 For I know *that* You will
bring me *to* death,
And *to* the house [a]appointed
for all living.

24 "Surely He would not stretch
out *His* hand against a
heap of ruins,
If they cry out when He
destroys *it.*
25 [a]Have I not wept for him who
was in trouble?
Has *not* my soul grieved for
the poor?
26 [a]But when I looked for good,
evil came *to me;*
And when I waited for light,
then came darkness.
27 [1]My heart is in turmoil and
cannot rest;
Days of affliction confront
me.
28 [a]I go about mourning, but
not in the sun;
I stand up in the assembly
and cry out for help.
29 [a]I am a brother of jackals,
And a companion of
ostriches.
30 [a]My skin grows black and
falls from me;
[b]My bones burn with fever.
31 My harp is *turned* to
mourning,
And my flute to the voice of
those who weep.

31

"I have made a covenant
with my eyes;
Why then should I [1]look
upon a [a]young woman?
2 For what *is* the [a]allotment of
God from above,
And the inheritance of the
Almighty from on high?
3 *Is* it not destruction for the
wicked,

And disaster for the
workers of iniquity?
4 [a]Does He not see my ways,
And count all my steps?

5 "If I have walked with
falsehood,
Or if my foot has hastened
to deceit,
6 [1]Let me be weighed on
honest scales,
That God may know my
[a]integrity.
7 If my step has turned from
the way,
Or [a]my heart walked after
my eyes,
Or if any spot adheres to my
hands,
8 *Then* [a]let me sow, and
another eat;
Yes, let my harvest be
[1]rooted out.

9 "If my heart has been enticed
by a woman,
Or *if* I have lurked at my
neighbor's door,
10 *Then* let my wife grind for
[a]another,
And let others bow down
over her.
11 For that *would be*
wickedness;
Yes, [a]it *would be* iniquity
deserving of judgment.
12 For that *would be* a fire *that*
consumes to destruction,
And would root out all my
increase.

13 "If I have [a]despised the cause
of my male or female
servant
When they complained
against me,
14 What then shall I do when
[a]God rises up?
When He punishes, how
shall I answer Him?
15 [a]Did not He who made me in
the womb make them?
Did not the same One
fashion us in the womb?

16 "If I have kept the poor from
their desire,
Or caused the eyes of the
widow to [a]fail,
17 Or eaten my morsel by
myself,
So that the fatherless could
not eat of it
18 (But from my youth I reared
him as a father,
And from my mother's
womb I guided [1]*the
widow*);
19 If I have seen anyone perish
for lack of clothing,
Or any poor *man* without
covering;
20 If his [1]heart has not [a]blessed
me,
And *if* he was *not* warmed
with the fleece of my
sheep;
21 If I have raised my hand
[a]against the fatherless,
When I saw I had help in
the gate;
22 *Then* let my arm fall from
my shoulder,
Let my arm be torn from the
socket.
23 For [a]destruction *from* God *is*
a terror to me,
And because of His
magnificence I cannot
endure.

24 "If[a] I have made gold my
hope,
Or said to fine gold, '*You are*
my confidence';

4 [a][2 Chr. 16:9]
6 [a]Job 23:10; 27:5, 6 [1]Lit. *Let Him weigh me*
7 [a]Ezek. 6:9
8 [a]Lev. 26:16 [1]*uprooted*
10 [a]Jer. 8:10
11 [a]Gen. 38:24
13 [a][Deut. 24:14, 15]
14 [a][Ps. 44:21]
15 [a]Job 34:19
16 [a]Job 29:12
18 [1]Lit. *her*
20 [a][Deut. 24:13] [1]Lit. *loins*
21 [a]Job 22:9
23 [a]Is. 13:6
24 [a][Mark 10:23–25]

25 [a]If I have rejoiced because
my wealth *was* great,
And because my hand had
gained much;
26 [a]If I have observed the [1]sun
when it shines,
Or the moon moving *in*
brightness,
27 So that my heart has been
secretly enticed,
And my mouth has kissed
my hand;
28 This also *would be* an
iniquity *deserving of*
judgment,
For I would have denied
God *who is* above.

29 "If[a] I have rejoiced at the
destruction of him who
hated me,
Or lifted myself up when
evil found him
30 [a](Indeed I have not allowed
my mouth to sin
By asking for a curse on his
[1]soul);
31 If the men of my tent have
not said,
'Who is there that has not
been satisfied with his
meat?'
32 [a](*But* no sojourner had to
lodge in the street,
For I have opened my doors
to the [1]traveler);
33 If I have covered my
transgressions [a]as[1]
Adam,
By hiding my iniquity in my
bosom,
34 Because I feared the great
[a]multitude,
And dreaded the contempt
of families,
So that I kept silence
And did not go out of the
door—

35 [a]Oh, that I had one to
hear me!
Here is my mark.
Oh, [b]*that* the Almighty
would answer me,
That my [1]Prosecutor had
written a book!
36 Surely I would carry it on
my shoulder,
And bind it on me *like* a
crown;
37 I would declare to Him the
number of my steps;
Like a prince I would
approach Him.

38 "If my land cries out
against me,
And its furrows weep
together;
39 If [a]I have eaten its [1]fruit
without money,
Or [b]caused its owners to
lose their lives;
40 *Then* let [a]thistles grow
instead of wheat,
And weeds instead of
barley."

The words of Job are ended.

32

So these three men
ceased answering Job,
because he *was* [a]righteous in his
own eyes.
2 Then the wrath of E·lī′hū, the
son of Bar′a·chel the [a]Būz′īte, of
the family of Ram, was aroused
against Job; his wrath was
aroused because he [b]justified
himself rather than God.
3 Also against his three friends
his wrath was aroused, because
they had found no answer, and
yet had condemned Job.
4 Now because they *were* years
older than he, E·lī′hū had waited
[1]to speak to Job.

25 [a]Ps. 62:10
26 [a]Ezek. 8:16 [1]Lit. *light*
29 [a][Prov. 17:5; 24:17]
30 [a][Matt. 5:44] [1]Or *life*
32 [a]Gen. 19:2, 3 [1]So with LXX, Syr., Tg., Vg.; MT *road*
33 [a][Prov. 28:13] [1]Or *as men do*
34 [a]Ex. 23:2
35 [a]Job 19:7; 30:20, 24, 28 [b]Job 13:22, 24; 33:10 [1]Lit. *Accuser*
39 [a]Job 24:6, 10–12 [b]1 Kin. 21:19 [1]Lit. *strength*
40 [a]Gen. 3:18

CHAPTER 32

1 [a]Job 6:29; 31:6; 33:9
2 [a]Gen. 22:21 [b]Job 27:5, 6
4 [1]Vg. *till Job had spoken*

5 When E·lī′hū saw that *there*
was no answer in the mouth of
these three men, his wrath was
aroused.
6 So E·lī′hū, the son of Bar′-
a·chel the Būz′ite, answered and
said:

"I *am* [a]young in years, and
you *are* very old;
Therefore I was afraid,
And dared not declare my
opinion to you.
7 I said, [1]'Age should speak,
And multitude of years
should teach wisdom.'
8 But *there is* a spirit in man,
And [a]the breath of the
Almighty gives him
understanding.
9 [a]Great[1] men are not *always*
wise,
Nor do the aged *always*
understand justice.

10 "Therefore I say, 'Listen
to me,
I also will declare my
opinion.'
11 Indeed I waited for your
words,
I listened to your reasonings,
while you searched out
what to say.
12 I paid close attention to you;
And surely not one of you
convinced Job,
Or answered his words—
13 [a]Lest you say,
'We have found wisdom';
God will vanquish him, not
man.
14 Now he has not [1]directed *his*
words against me;
So I will not answer him
with your words.

6 [a]Lev. 19:32

7 [1]Lit. *Days*, i.e., years

8 [a][Prov. 2:6]

9 [a][1 Cor. 1:26] [1]Or *Men of many years*

13 [a][Jer. 9:23]

14 [1]*ordered*

19 [1]*bosom* [2]*opening*

22 [a]Job 27:8

CHAPTER 33

4 [a][Gen. 2:7]

15 "They are dismayed and
answer no more;
Words escape them.
16 And I have waited, because
they did not speak,
Because they stood still *and*
answered no more.
17 I also will answer my part,
I too will declare my
opinion.
18 For I am full of words;
The spirit within me
compels me.
19 Indeed my [1]belly *is* like wine
that has no [2]vent;
It is ready to burst like new
wineskins.
20 I will speak, that I may find
relief;
I must open my lips and
answer.
21 Let me not, I pray, show
partiality to anyone;
Nor let me flatter any man.
22 For I do not know how to
flatter,
Else my Maker would soon
take me [a]away.

33 "But please, Job, hear my
speech,
And listen to all my words.
2 Now, I open my mouth;
My tongue speaks in my
mouth.
3 My words *come* from my
upright heart;
My lips utter pure
knowledge.
4 [a]The Spirit of God has
made me,
And the breath of the
Almighty gives me life.
5 If you can answer me,
Set *your words* in order
before me;
Take your stand.

6 [a]Truly I *am* [1]as your
spokesman before God;
I also have been formed out
of clay.
7 [a]Surely no fear of me will
terrify you,
Nor will my hand be heavy
on you.

8 "Surely you have spoken [1]in
my hearing,
And I have heard the sound
of *your* words, *saying*,
9 'I[a] *am* pure, without
transgression;
I *am* innocent, and *there is*
no iniquity in me.
10 Yet He finds occasions
against me,
[a]He counts me as His enemy;
11 [a]He puts my feet in the
stocks,
He watches all my paths.'

12 "Look, *in* this you are not
righteous.
I will answer you,
For God is greater than
man.
13 Why do you [a]contend with
Him?
For He does not give an
accounting of any of His
words.
14 [a]For God may speak in one
way, or in another,
Yet man does not perceive
it.
15 [a]In a dream, in a vision of
the night,
When deep sleep falls upon
men,
While slumbering on their
beds,
16 [a]Then He opens the ears of
men,
And seals their instruction.

6 [a]Job 4:19 [1]Lit. *as your mouth*
7 [a]Job 9:34
8 [1]Lit. *in my ears*
9 [a]Job 10:7
10 [a]Job 13:24; 16:9
11 [a]Job 13:27; 19:8
13 [a][Is. 45:9]
14 [a]Ps. 62:11
15 [a][Num. 12:6]
16 [a][Job 36:10, 15]
18 [1]Lit. *passing*
19 [a]Job 30:17
20 [a]Ps. 107:18 [b]Job 3:24; 6:7 [1]*desirable*
24 [1]*an atonement*

17 In order to turn man *from*
his deed,
And conceal pride from
man,
18 He keeps back his soul from
the Pit,
And his life from [1]perishing
by the sword.

19 "*Man* is also chastened with
pain on his [a]bed,
And with strong *pain* in
many of his bones,
20 [a]So that his life abhors
[b]bread,
And his soul [1]succulent
food.
21 His flesh wastes away from
sight,
And his bones stick out
which once were not
seen.
22 Yes, his soul draws near the
Pit,
And his life to the
executioners.

23 "If there is a messenger for
him,
A mediator, one among a
thousand,
To show man His
uprightness,
24 Then He is gracious to him,
and says,
'Deliver him from going
down to the Pit;
I have found [1]a ransom';
25 His flesh shall be young like
a child's,
He shall return to the days
of his youth.
26 He shall pray to God, and
He will delight in him,
He shall see His face with
joy,
For He restores to man His
righteousness.

27 Then he looks at men and [a]says,
'I have sinned, and perverted *what was* right,
And it [b]did not profit me.'
28 He will [a]redeem [1]his soul from going down to the Pit,
And [1]his life shall see the light.

29 "Behold, God works all these *things*,
Twice, *in fact*, three *times* with a man,
30 [a]To bring back his soul from the Pit,
That he may be enlightened with the light of life.

31 "Give ear, Job, listen to me;
Hold your peace, and I will speak.
32 If you have anything to say, answer me;
Speak, for I desire to justify you.
33 If not, [a]listen to me;
[1]Hold your peace, and I will teach you wisdom."

34

E·lī'hū further answered and said:

2 "Hear my words, you wise *men*;
Give ear to me, you who have knowledge.
3 [a]For the ear tests words
As the palate tastes food.
4 Let us choose justice for ourselves;
Let us know among ourselves what *is* good.

5 "For Job has said, [a]'I am righteous,
But [b]God has taken away my justice;
6 [a]Should I lie concerning my right?
My [1]wound *is* incurable, *though I am* without transgression.'
7 What man *is* like Job,
[a]*Who* drinks [1]scorn like water,
8 Who goes in company with the workers of iniquity,
And walks with wicked men?
9 For [a]he has said, 'It profits a man nothing
That he should delight in God.'

10 "Therefore listen to me, you [1]men of understanding:
[a]Far be it from God *to do* wickedness,
And *from* the Almighty to *commit* iniquity.
11 [a]For He repays man *according to* his work,
And makes man to find a reward according to *his* way.
12 Surely God will never do wickedly,
Nor will the Almighty [a]pervert justice.
13 Who gave Him charge over the earth?
Or who appointed *Him over* the whole world?
14 If He should set His heart on it,
If He should [a]gather to Himself His Spirit and His breath,
15 [a]All flesh would perish together,
And man would return to dust.

27 [a][Luke 15:21] [b][Rom. 6:21]
28 [a]Is. 38:17 [1]Kt. *my*
30 [a]Ps. 56:13
33 [a]Ps. 34:11 [1]*Keep silent*

CHAPTER 34

3 [a]Job 6:30; 12:11
5 [a]Job 13:18; 33:9 [b]Job 27:2
6 [a]Job 6:4; 9:17 [1]Lit. *arrow*
7 [a]Job 15:16 [1]*derision*
9 [a]Mal. 3:14
10 [a]Job 8:3; 36:23 [1]*men of heart*
11 [a]Ps. 62:12
12 [a]Job 8:3
14 [a]Ps. 104:29
15 [a][Gen. 3:19]

16 "If *you have* understanding,
hear this;
Listen to the sound of my
words:
17 [a]Should one who hates
justice govern?
Will you [b]condemn *Him who*
is most just?
18 [a]*Is it fitting* to say to a king,
'*You are* worthless,'
And to nobles, '*You are*
wicked'?
19 Yet He [a]is not partial to
princes,
Nor does He regard the
rich more than the
poor;
For [b]they *are* all the work
of His hands.
20 In a moment they die, [a]in
the middle of the night;
The people are shaken and
pass away;
The mighty are taken away
without a hand.

21 "For[a] His eyes *are* on the
ways of man,
And He sees all his steps.
22 [a]There is no darkness nor
shadow of death
Where the workers of
iniquity may hide
themselves.
23 For He need not further
consider a man,
That he should go before
God in judgment.
24 [a]He breaks in pieces mighty
men without inquiry,
And sets others in their
place.
25 Therefore He knows their
works;
He overthrows *them* in the
night,
And they are crushed.
26 He strikes them as wicked
men
In the open sight of others,
27 Because they [a]turned back
from Him,
And [b]would not consider
any of His ways,
28 So that they [a]caused the cry
of the poor to come to
Him;
For He [b]hears the cry of the
afflicted.
29 When He gives quietness,
who then can make
trouble?
And when He hides *His*
face, who then can see
Him,
Whether *it is* against a
nation or a man alone?—
30 That the hypocrite should
not reign,
Lest the people be ensnared.

31 "For has *anyone* said to God,
'I have borne *chastening*;
I will offend no more;
32 Teach me *what* I do not see;
If I have done iniquity, I will
do no more'?
33 Should He repay *it*
according to your *terms*,
Just because you disavow
it?
You must choose, and not I;
Therefore speak what you
know.

34 "Men of understanding say
to me,
Wise men who listen to me:
35 'Job[a] speaks without
knowledge,
His words *are* without
wisdom.'
36 Oh, that Job were tried to
the utmost,

17 [a]2 Sam. 23:3 [b]Job 40:8
18 [a]Ex. 22:28
19 [a][Deut. 10:17] [b]Job 31:15
20 [a]Ex. 12:29
21 [a]Job 31:4
22 [a][Amos 9:2, 3]
24 [a][Dan. 2:21]
27 [a]1 Sam. 15:11 [b]Is. 5:12
28 [a]Job 35:9 [b][Ex. 22:23]
35 [a]Job 35:16; 38:2

Because *his* answers *are like*
those of wicked men!
37 For he adds [a]rebellion to his
sin;
He claps *his hands* among us,
And multiplies his words
against God."

35 Moreover E·lī′hū answered and said:

2 "Do you think this is right?
Do you say,
'My righteousness is more
than God's'?
3 For [a]you say,
'What advantage will it be to
You?
What profit shall I have,
more than *if* I had
sinned?'

4 "I will answer you,
And [a]your companions with
you.
5 [a]Look to the heavens and see;
And behold the clouds—
They are higher than you.
6 If you sin, what do you
accomplish [a]against
Him?
Or, *if* your transgressions
are multiplied, what do
you do to Him?
7 [a]If you are righteous, what
do you give Him?
Or what does He receive
from your hand?
8 Your wickedness affects a
man such as you,
And your righteousness a
son of man.

9 "Because[a] of the multitude of
oppressions they cry out;
They cry out for help
because of the arm of
the mighty.
10 But no one says, [a]'Where *is*
God my Maker,
[b]Who gives songs in the
night,
11 Who [a]teaches us more than
the beasts of the earth,
And makes us wiser than
the birds of heaven?'
12 [a]There they cry out, but He
does not answer,
Because of the pride of evil
men.
13 [a]Surely God will not listen to
empty *talk*,
Nor will the Almighty
regard it.
14 [a]Although you say you do
not see Him,
Yet justice *is* before Him, and
[b]you must wait for Him.
15 And now, because He has
not [a]punished in His
anger,
Nor taken much notice of
folly,
16 [a]Therefore Job opens his
mouth in vain;
He multiplies words without
knowledge."

36 E·lī′hū also proceeded and said:

2 "Bear with me a little, and I
will show you
That *there are* yet words to
speak on God's behalf.
3 I will fetch my knowledge
from afar;
I will ascribe righteousness
to my Maker.
4 For truly my words *are* not
false;
One who is perfect in
knowledge *is* with you.

5 "Behold, God *is* mighty, but
despises *no one;*

37 [a]Job 7:11; 10:1

CHAPTER 35

3 [a]Job 21:15; 34:9

4 [a]Job 34:8

5 [a][Job 22:12]

6 [a][Jer. 7:19]

7 [a]Prov. 9:12

9 [a]Job 34:28

10 [a]Is. 51:13 [b]Acts 16:25

11 [a]Ps. 94:12

12 [a]Prov. 1:28

13 [a][Is. 1:15]

14 [a]Job 9:11 [b][Ps. 37:5, 6]

15 [a]Ps. 89:32

16 [a]Job 34:35; 38:2

[a]*He is* mighty in strength [1]of
understanding.
6 He does not preserve the life
of the wicked,
But gives justice to the
[a]oppressed.
7 [a]He does not withdraw His
eyes from the righteous;
But [b]*they are* on the throne
with kings,
For He has seated them
forever,
And they are exalted.
8 And [a]if *they are* bound in
[1]fetters,
Held in the cords of
affliction,
9 Then He tells them
their work and their
transgressions—
That they have acted
[1]defiantly.
10 [a]He also opens their ear to
[1]instruction,
And commands that they
turn from iniquity.
11 If they obey and serve *Him,*
They shall [a]spend their days
in prosperity,
And their years in
pleasures.
12 But if they do not obey,
They shall perish by the
sword,
And they shall die [1]without
[a]knowledge.

13 "But the hypocrites in heart
[a]store up wrath;
They do not cry for help
when He binds them.
14 [a]They[1] die in youth,
And their life *ends* among
the [2]perverted persons.
15 He delivers the poor in their
affliction,
And opens their ears in
oppression.

16 "Indeed He would have
brought you out of dire
distress,
[a]*Into* a broad place where
there is no restraint;
And [b]what is set on your table
would be full of [c]richness.
17 But you are filled with
the judgment due the
[a]wicked;
Judgment and justice take
hold *of you.*
18 Because *there is* wrath,
beware lest He take you
away with *one* blow;
For [a]a large ransom would
not help you avoid *it.*
19 [a]Will your riches,
Or all the mighty forces,
Keep you from distress?
20 Do not desire the night,
When people are cut off in
their place.
21 Take heed, [a]do not turn to
iniquity,
For [b]you have chosen this
rather than affliction.

22 "Behold, God is exalted by
His power;
Who teaches like Him?
23 [a]Who has assigned Him His
way,
Or who has said, 'You have
done [b]wrong'?

24 "Remember to [a]magnify His
work,
Of which men have sung.
25 Everyone has seen it;
Man looks on *it* from afar.

26 "Behold, God *is* great, and
we [a]do not know *Him;*
[b]Nor can the number of His
years *be* discovered.
27 For He [a]draws up drops of
water,

CHAPTER 36

5 [a]Job 12:13, 16; 37:23 [1]*of heart*

6 [a]Job 5:15

7 [a][Ps. 33:18; 34:15] [b]Ps. 113:8

8 [a]Ps. 107:10 [1]*chains*

9 [1]*proudly*

10 [a]Job 33:16; 36:15 [1]*discipline*

11 [a][Is. 1:19, 20]

12 [a]Job 4:21 [1]MT *as one without knowledge*

13 [a][Rom. 2:5]

14 [a]Ps. 55:23 [1]Lit. *Their soul dies* [2]Heb. *qedeshim,* those practicing sodomy or prostitution in religious rituals

16 [a]Ps. 18:19; 31:8; 118:5 [b]Ps. 23:5 [c]Ps. 36:8

17 [a]Job 22:5, 10, 11

18 [a]Ps. 49:7

19 [a][Prov. 11:4]

21 [a][Ps. 31:6; 66:18] [b][Heb. 11:25]

23 [a]Job 34:13; [Is. 40:13, 14] [b]Job 8:3

24 [a][Rev. 15:3]

26 [a][1 Cor. 13:12] [b]Heb. 1:12

27 [a]Ps. 147:8

Which distill as rain from
the mist,
28 [a]Which the clouds drop
down
And pour abundantly on
man.
29 Indeed, can *anyone*
understand the
spreading of clouds,
The thunder from His
canopy?
30 Look, He [a]scatters His light
upon it,
And covers the depths of
the sea.
31 For [a]by these He judges the
peoples;
He [b]gives food in
abundance.
32 [a]He covers *His* hands with
lightning,
And commands it to [1]strike.
33 [a]His thunder declares it,
The cattle also, concerning
[1]the rising *storm*.

37 "At this also my heart
trembles,
And leaps from its place.
2 Hear attentively the thunder
of His voice,
And the rumbling *that*
comes from His mouth.
3 He sends it forth under the
whole heaven,
His [1]lightning to the ends of
the earth.
4 After it [a]a voice roars;
He thunders with His
majestic voice,
And He does not restrain
them when His voice is
heard.
5 God thunders marvelously
with His voice;
[a]He does great things which
we cannot comprehend.
6 For [a]He says to the snow,
'Fall *on* the earth';
Likewise to the [1]gentle rain
and the heavy rain of
His strength.
7 He seals the hand of every
man,
[a]That [b]all men may know His
work.
8 The beasts [a]go into dens,
And remain in their lairs.
9 From the chamber *of*
the south comes the
whirlwind,
And cold from the scattering
winds *of the north.*
10 [a]By the breath of God ice is
given,
And the broad waters are
frozen.
11 Also with moisture He
saturates the thick
clouds;
He scatters His [1]bright
clouds.
12 And they swirl about, being
turned by His guidance,
That they may [a]do whatever
He commands them
On the face of [1]the whole
earth.
13 [a]He causes it to come,
Whether for [1]correction,
Or [b]for His land,
Or [c]for mercy.

14 "Listen to this, O Job;
Stand still and [a]consider the
wondrous works of God.
15 Do you know when God
[1]dispatches them,
And causes the light of His
cloud to shine?
16 [a]Do you know how the
clouds are balanced,
Those wondrous works of
[b]Him who is perfect in
knowledge?

28 [a][Prov. 3:20]
30 [a]Job 37:3
31 [a][Acts 14:17] [b]Ps. 104:14, 15
32 [a]Ps. 147:8 [1]*strike the mark*
33 [a]1 Kin. 18:41 [1]Lit. *what is rising*

CHAPTER 37

3 [1]Or *light*
4 [a]Ps. 29:3
5 [a]Job 5:9; 9:10; 36:26
6 [a]Ps. 147:16, 17 [1]Lit. *shower of rain*
7 [a]Ps. 109:27 [b]Ps. 19:3, 4
8 [a]Ps. 104:21, 22
10 [a]Ps. 147:17, 18
11 [1]*clouds of light*
12 [a]Job 36:32 [1]Lit. *the world of the earth*
13 [a]Ex. 9:18, 23 [b]Job 38:26, 27 [c]1 Kin. 18:41–46 [1]Lit. *a rod*
14 [a]Ps. 111:2
15 [1]*places them*
16 [a]Job 36:29 [b]Job 36:4

17 Why *are* your garments hot,
When He quiets the earth
by the south *wind*?
18 With Him, have you [a]spread
out the [b]skies,
Strong as a cast metal
mirror?

19 "Teach us what we should
say to Him,
For we can prepare nothing
because of the darkness.
20 Should He be told that I
wish to speak?
If a man were to speak,
surely he would be
swallowed up.
21 Even now *men* cannot look
at the light *when it is*
bright in the skies,
When the wind has passed
and cleared them.
22 He comes from the north *as*
golden *splendor;*
With God *is* awesome
majesty.
23 *As for* the Almighty, [a]we
cannot find Him;
[b]*He is* excellent in power,
In judgment and abundant
justice;
He does not oppress.
24 Therefore men [a]fear Him;
He shows no partiality to
any *who are* [b]wise of
heart."

38 Then the LORD answered
Job [a]out of the whirlwind,
and said:

2 "Who[a] *is* this who darkens
counsel
By [b]words without
knowledge?
3 [a]Now [1]prepare yourself like a
man;
I will question you, and you
shall answer Me.

4 "Where[a] were you when I
laid the foundations of
the earth?
Tell *Me*, if you have
understanding.
5 Who determined its
measurements?
Surely you know!
Or who stretched the [1]line
upon it?
6 To what were its
foundations fastened?
Or who laid its cornerstone,
7 When the morning stars
sang together,
And all [a]the sons of God
shouted for joy?

8 "Or[a] *who* shut in the sea with
doors,
When it burst forth *and*
issued from the womb;
9 When I made the clouds its
garment,
And thick darkness its
swaddling band;
10 When [a]I fixed My limit for it,
And set bars and doors;
11 When I said,
'This far you may come, but
no farther,
And here your proud waves
[a]must stop!'

12 "Have you [a]commanded the
morning since your days
began,
And caused the dawn to
know its place,
13 That it might take hold of
the ends of the earth,
And [a]the wicked be shaken
out of it?
14 It takes on form like clay
under a seal,

18 [a][Is. 44:24] [b]Ps. 104:2
23 [a][1 Tim. 6:16] [b][Job 9:4; 36:5]
24 [a][Matt. 10:28] [b][Matt. 11:25]

CHAPTER 38

1 [a]Ex. 19:16
2 [a]Job 34:35; 42:3 [b]1 Tim. 1:7
3 [a]Job 40:7 [1]Lit. *gird up your loins like*
4 [a]Ps. 104:5
5 [1]*measuring line*
7 [a]Job 1:6
8 [a]Gen. 1:9
10 [a]Job 26:10
11 [a][Ps. 89:9; 93:4]
12 [a][Ps. 74:16; 148:5]
13 [a]Ps. 104:35

And stands out like a garment.
15 From the wicked their [a]light is withheld,
And [b]the [1]upraised arm is broken.

16 "Have you [a]entered the springs of the sea?
Or have you walked in search of the depths?
17 Have [a]the gates of death been [1]revealed to you?
Or have you seen the doors of the shadow of death?
18 Have you comprehended the breadth of the earth?
Tell *Me,* if you know all this.

19 "Where *is* the way *to* the dwelling of light?
And darkness, where *is* its place,
20 That you may take it to its territory,
That you may know the paths *to* its home?
21 Do you know *it,* because you were born then,
Or *because* the number of your days *is* great?

22 "Have you entered [a]the treasury of snow,
Or have you seen the treasury of hail,
23 [a]Which I have reserved for the time of trouble,
For the day of battle and war?
24 By what way is light [1]diffused,
Or the east wind scattered over the earth?

25 "Who [a]has divided a channel for the overflowing *water,*
Or a path for the thunderbolt,
26 To cause it to rain on a land *where there is* no one,
A wilderness in which *there is* no man;
27 [a]To satisfy the desolate waste,
And cause to spring forth the growth of tender grass?
28 [a]Has the rain a father?
Or who has begotten the drops of dew?
29 From whose womb comes the ice?
And the [a]frost of heaven, who gives it birth?
30 The waters harden like stone,
And the surface of the deep is [a]frozen.[1]

31 "Can you bind the cluster of the [a]Plē′a·dēs,[1]
Or loose the belt of Ō·rī′on?
32 Can you bring out [1]Maz′za·roth in its season?
Or can you guide [2]the Great Bear with its cubs?
33 Do you know [a]the ordinances of the heavens?
Can you set their dominion over the earth?

34 "Can you lift up your voice to the clouds,
That an abundance of water may cover you?
35 Can you send out lightnings, that they may go,
And say to you, 'Here we *are!*'?
36 [a]Who has put wisdom in [1]the mind?
Or who has given understanding to the heart?

15 [a]Job 18:5 [b]Ps. 10:15; 37:17 [1]Lit. *high*
16 [a][Ps. 77:19]
17 [a]Ps. 9:13 [1]Lit. *opened*
22 [a]Ps. 135:7
23 [a]Is. 30:30
24 [1]Lit. *divided*
25 [a]Job 28:26
27 [a]Ps. 104:13, 14; 107:35
28 [a]Job 36:27, 28
29 [a]Ps. 147:16, 17
30 [a][Job 37:10] [1]Lit. *imprisoned*
31 [a]Amos 5:8 [1]Or *the Seven Stars*
32 [1]Lit. *Constellations* [2]Or *Arcturus*
33 [a]Jer. 31:35, 36
36 [a][Ps. 51:6] [1]Lit. *the inward parts*

37 Who can number the clouds
by wisdom?
Or who can pour out the
bottles of heaven,
38 When the dust hardens in
clumps,
And the clods cling together?

39 "Can[a] you hunt the prey for
the lion,
Or satisfy the appetite of the
young lions,
40 When they crouch in *their*
dens,
Or lurk in their lairs to lie in
wait?
41 [a]Who provides food for the
raven,
When its young ones cry to
God,
And wander about for lack
of food?

39

"Do you know the
time when the wild
[a]mountain goats bear
young?
Or can you mark when [b]the
deer gives birth?
2 Can you number the months
that they fulfill?
Or do you know the time
when they bear young?
3 They bow down,
They bring forth their
young,
They deliver their [1]offspring.
4 Their young ones are
healthy,
They grow strong with
grain;
They depart and do not
return to them.

5 "Who set the wild donkey
free?
Who loosed the bonds of the
[1]onager,
6 [a]Whose home I have made
the wilderness,
And the [1]barren land his
dwelling?
7 He scorns the tumult of the
city;
He does not heed the shouts
of the driver.
8 The range of the mountains
is his pasture,
And he searches after [a]every
green thing.

9 "Will the [a]wild ox be willing
to serve you?
Will he bed by your
manger?
10 Can you bind the wild ox in
the furrow with ropes?
Or will he plow the valleys
behind you?
11 Will you trust him because
his strength *is* great?
Or will you leave your labor
to him?
12 Will you trust him to bring
home your [1]grain,
And gather it to your
threshing floor?

13 "The wings of the ostrich
wave proudly,
But are her wings and
pinions *like the* kindly
stork's?
14 For she leaves her eggs on
the ground,
And warms them in the
dust;
15 She forgets that a foot may
crush them,
Or that a wild beast may
break them.
16 She [a]treats her young
harshly, as though *they*
were not hers;
Her labor is in vain, without
[1]concern,

39 [a]Ps. 104:21
41 [a][Matt. 6:26]

CHAPTER 39

1 [a]Ps. 104:18
[b]Ps. 29:9
3 [1]Lit. *pangs*
5 [1]A species of wild donkey
6 [a]Jer. 2:24
[1]Lit. *salt land*
8 [a]Gen. 1:29
9 [a]Num. 23:22
12 [1]Lit. *seed*
16 [a]Lam. 4:3
[1]Lit. *fear*

17 Because God deprived her of wisdom,
And did not [a]endow her with understanding.
18 When she lifts herself on high,
She scorns the horse and its rider.

19 "Have you given the horse strength?
Have you clothed his neck with [1]thunder?
20 Can you [1]frighten him like a locust?
His majestic snorting strikes terror.
21 He paws in the valley, and rejoices in *his* strength;
[a]He gallops into the clash of arms.
22 He mocks at fear, and is not frightened;
Nor does he turn back from the sword.
23 The quiver rattles against him,
The glittering spear and javelin.
24 He devours the distance with fierceness and rage;
Nor does he come to a halt because the trumpet *has* sounded.
25 At *the blast of* the trumpet he says, 'Aha!'
He smells the battle from afar,
The thunder of captains and shouting.

26 "Does the hawk fly by your wisdom,
And spread its wings toward the south?
27 Does the [a]eagle mount up at your command,
And [b]make its nest on high?
28 On the rock it dwells and resides,
On the crag of the rock and the stronghold.
29 From there it spies out the prey;
Its eyes observe from afar.
30 Its young ones suck up blood;
And [a]where the slain *are*, there it *is*."

40

Moreover the LORD [a]answered Job, and said:

2 "Shall [a]the one who contends with the Almighty correct *Him*?
He who [b]rebukes God, let him answer it."

3 Then Job answered the LORD and said:

4 "Behold,[a] I am vile;
What shall I answer You?
[b]I lay my hand over my mouth.
5 Once I have spoken, but I will not answer;
Yes, twice, but I will proceed no further."

6 [a]Then the LORD answered Job out of the whirlwind, and said:

7 "Now[a] [1]prepare yourself like a man;
[b]I will question you, and you shall answer Me:

8 "Would[a] you indeed [1]annul My judgment?
Would you condemn Me that you may be justified?
9 Have you an arm like God?

17 [a]Job 35:11
19 [1]Or *a mane*
20 [1]*make him spring*
21 [a]Jer. 8:6
27 [a]Prov. 30:18, 19 [b]Jer. 49:16
30 [a]Matt. 24:28

CHAPTER 40

1 [a]Job 38:1
2 [a]Job 9:3; 10:2; 33:13 [b]Job 13:3; 23:4
4 [a]Ezra 9:6 [b]Job 29:9
6 [a]Job 38:1
7 [a]Job 38:3 [b]Job 42:4 [1]Lit. *gird up your loins*
8 [a][Rom. 3:4] [1]*nullify*

Or can you thunder with [a]a
voice like His?
10 [a]Then adorn yourself *with*
majesty and splendor,
And array yourself with
glory and beauty.
11 Disperse the rage of your
wrath;
Look on everyone *who is*
proud, and humble him.
12 Look on everyone *who is*
[a]proud, *and* bring him
low;
Tread down the wicked in
their place.
13 Hide them in the dust
together,
Bind their faces in hidden
darkness.
14 Then I will also confess to
you
That your own right hand
can save you.

15 "Look now at the [1]behemoth,
which I made *along* with
you;
He eats grass like an ox.
16 See now, his strength *is* in
his hips,
And his power *is* in his
stomach muscles.
17 He moves his tail like a
cedar;
The sinews of his thighs are
tightly knit.
18 His bones *are like* beams of
bronze,
His ribs like bars of iron.
19 He *is* the first of the [a]ways
of God;
Only He who made him can
bring near His sword.
20 Surely the mountains [a]yield
food for him,
And all the beasts of the
field play there.
21 He lies under the lotus trees,
In a covert of reeds and
marsh.
22 The lotus trees cover him
with their shade;
The willows by the brook
surround him.
23 Indeed the river may rage,
Yet he is not disturbed;
He is confident, though the
Jordan gushes into his
mouth,
24 *Though* he takes it in his
eyes,
Or one pierces *his* nose with
a snare.

41

"Can you draw out
[a]Le·vi′a·than[1] with a
hook,
Or *snare* his tongue with a
line *which* you lower?
2 Can you [a]put a reed through
his nose,
Or pierce his jaw with a
[1]hook?
3 Will he make many
supplications to you?
Will he speak softly to you?
4 Will he make a covenant
with you?
Will you take him as a
servant forever?
5 Will you play with him as
with a bird,
Or will you leash him for
your maidens?
6 Will *your* companions
[1]make a banquet of him?
Will they apportion him
among the merchants?
7 Can you fill his skin with
harpoons,
Or his head with fishing
spears?
8 Lay your hand on him;
Remember the battle—
Never do it again!

9 [a][Ps. 29:3, 4]
10 [a]Ps. 93:1; 104:1
12 [a]Dan. 4:37
15 [1]A large animal, exact identity unknown
19 [a]Job 26:14
20 [a]Ps. 104:14

CHAPTER 41

1 [a]Is. 27:1
[1]A large sea creature, exact identity unknown
2 [a]Is. 37:29
[1]*thorn*
6 [1]Or *bargain over him*

9 Indeed, *any* hope of
overcoming him is false;
Shall *one not* be
overwhelmed at the sight
of him?
10 No one *is so* fierce that he
would dare stir him up.
Who then is able to stand
against Me?
11 [a]Who has preceded Me, that
I should pay *him*?
[b]Everything under heaven is
Mine.

12 "I will not [1]conceal his limbs,
His mighty power, or his
graceful proportions.
13 Who can [1]remove his outer
coat?
Who can approach *him* with
a double bridle?
14 Who can open the doors of
his face,
With his terrible teeth all
around?
15 *His* rows of [1]scales are *his*
pride,
Shut up tightly *as with* a
seal;
16 One is so near another
That no air can come
between them;
17 They are joined one to
another,
They stick together and
cannot be parted.
18 His sneezings flash forth
light,
And his eyes *are* like the
eyelids of the morning.
19 Out of his mouth go burning
lights;
Sparks of fire shoot out.
20 Smoke goes out of his
nostrils,
As *from* a boiling pot and
burning rushes.
21 His breath kindles coals,
And a flame goes out of his
mouth.
22 Strength dwells in his neck,
And [1]sorrow dances before
him.
23 The folds of his flesh are
joined together;
They are firm on him and
cannot be moved.
24 His heart is as hard as stone,
Even as hard as the lower
millstone.
25 When he raises himself up,
the mighty are afraid;
Because of his crashings
they [1]are beside
themselves.
26 *Though* the sword reaches
him, it cannot avail;
Nor does spear, dart, or
javelin.
27 He regards iron as straw,
And bronze as rotten wood.
28 The arrow cannot make him
flee;
Slingstones become like
stubble to him.
29 Darts are regarded as straw;
He laughs at the threat of
javelins.
30 His undersides *are* like
sharp potsherds;
He spreads pointed *marks*
in the mire.
31 He makes the deep boil like
a pot;
He makes the sea like a pot
of ointment.
32 He leaves a shining wake
behind him;
One would think the deep
had white hair.
33 On earth there is nothing
like him,
Which is made without fear.
34 He beholds every high *thing*;
He *is* king over all the
children of pride."

11 [a][Rom. 11:35] [b]Ps. 24:1; 50:12

12 [1]Lit. *keep silent about*

13 [1]Lit. *take off the face of his garment*

15 [1]Lit. *shields*

22 [1]*despair*

25 [1]Or *purify themselves*

CHAPTER 42

42 Then Job answered the LORD and said:

2 "I know that You [a]can do
everything,
And that no purpose *of*
Yours can be withheld
from You.
3 *You asked,* [a]'Who *is* this
who hides counsel
without knowledge?'
Therefore I have uttered
what I did not
understand,
[b]Things too wonderful for me,
which I did not know.
4 Listen, please, and let me
speak;
You said, [a]'I will question
you, and you shall
answer Me.'

5 "I have [a]heard of You by the
hearing of the ear,
But now my eye sees You.
6 Therefore I [a]abhor[1] *myself,*
And repent in dust and
ashes."

7 And so it was, after the LORD
had spoken these words to Job,
that the LORD said to E·lī′phaz
the Tē′man·īte, "My wrath is
aroused against you and your
two friends, for you have not
spoken of Me *what is* right, as
My servant Job *has.*
8 "Now therefore, take for
yourselves [a]seven bulls and
seven rams, [b]go to My servant
Job, and offer up for yourselves
a burnt offering; and My servant
Job shall [c]pray for you. For I will
accept [1]him, lest I deal with you
according to your folly; because
you have not spoken of Me *what*
is right, as My servant Job *has.*"

9 So E·lī′phaz the Tē′man·īte
and Bil′dad the Shū′hīte *and*
Zō′phar the Nā′a·ma·thīte went
and did as the LORD commanded
them; for the LORD had [1]accepted
Job.
10 [a]And the LORD [1]restored Job's
losses when he prayed for his
friends. Indeed the LORD gave
Job [b]twice as much as he had
before.
11 Then [a]all his brothers, all his
sisters, and all those who had
been his acquaintances before,
came to him and ate food with
him in his house; and they con-
soled him and comforted him
for all the adversity that the
LORD had brought upon him.
Each one gave him a piece of
silver and each a ring of gold.
12 Now the LORD blessed [a]the
latter *days* of Job more than his
beginning; for he had [b]fourteen
thousand sheep, six thousand
camels, one thousand yoke of
oxen, and one thousand female
donkeys.
13 [a]He also had seven sons and
three daughters.
14 And he called the name of
the first [1]Je·mī′mah, the name
of the second [2]Ke·zī′ah, and the
name of the third [3]Ker′en-Hap′-
puch.
15 In all the land were found
no women *so* beautiful as the
daughters of Job; and their father gave them an inheritance
among their brothers.
16 After this Job [a]lived one hundred and forty years, and saw
his children and grandchildren
for four generations.
17 So Job died, old and [a]full of
days.

2 [a][Matt. 19:26]
3 [a]Job 38:2 [b]Ps. 40:5; 131:1; 139:6
4 [a]Job 38:3; 40:7
5 [a]Job 26:14
6 [a]Ezra 9:6 [1]*despise*
8 [a]Num. 23:1 [b][Matt. 5:24] [c]Gen. 20:17 [1]Lit. *his face*
9 [1]Lit. *lifted up the face of Job*
10 [a]Deut. 30:3 [b]Is. 40:2 [1]Lit. *turned the captivity of Job,* what was captured from Job
11 [a]Job 19:13
12 [a]James 5:11 [b]Job 1:3
13 [a]Job 1:2
14 [1]Lit. *Handsome as the Day* [2]*Cassia,* a fragrance [3]Lit. *The Horn of Color* or *The Colorful Ray*
16 [a]Job 5:26; Prov. 3:16
17 [a]Gen. 15:15; 25:8

The Book of PSALMS

THE Book of Psalms is the largest and perhaps most widely used book in the Bible. It explores the full range of human experience in a very personal and practical way. Its 150 "songs" run from the Creation through the patriarchal, theocratic, monarchical, exilic, and postexilic periods. The tremendous breadth of subject matter in the Psalms includes diverse topics, such as jubilation, war, peace, worship, judgment, messianic prophecy, praise, and lament. The Psalms were set to the accompaniment of stringed instruments and served as the temple hymnbook and devotional guide for the Jewish people.

The Book of Psalms was gradually collected and originally unnamed, perhaps due to the great variety of material. It came to be known as *Sepher Tehillim*—"Book of Praises"—because almost every psalm contains some note of praise to God. The Septuagint uses the Greek word *Psalmoi* as its title for this book, meaning "Poems Sung to the Accompaniment of Musical Instruments." It also calls it the *Psalterium* ("A Collection of Songs"), and this word is the basis for the term *Psalter*. The Latin title is *Liber Psalmorum*, "Book of Psalms."

BOOK ONE
Psalms 1—41

PSALM 1

BLESSED [a]*is* the man
Who walks not in the counsel of the [1]ungodly,
Nor stands in the path of sinners,
[b]Nor sits in the seat of the scornful;
2 But [a]his delight *is* in the law of the LORD,
[b]And in His law he [1]meditates day and night.
3 He shall be like a tree
[a]Planted by the [1]rivers of water,
That brings forth its fruit in its season,
Whose leaf also shall not wither;
And whatever he does shall [b]prosper.
4 The ungodly *are* not so,
But *are* [a]like the chaff which the wind drives away.
5 Therefore the ungodly shall not stand in the judgment,
Nor sinners in the congregation of the righteous.
6 For [a]the LORD knows the way of the righteous,
But the way of the ungodly shall perish.

PSALM 1

1 [a]Prov. 4:14 [b]Jer. 15:17 [1]*wicked*

2 [a]Ps. 119:14, 16, 35 [b][Josh. 1:8] [1]*ponders* by talking to himself

3 [a]Jer. 17:8 [b]Gen. 39:2, 3, 23 [1]*channels*

4 [a]Job 21:18

6 [a]Ps. 37:18

PSALM 2

1 [a]Acts 4:25, 26 [1]*Gentiles* [2]*throng tumultuously* [3]*worthless* or *empty*

2 [a][Matt. 12:14; 26:3, 4, 59–66; 27:1, 2; Mark 3:6; 11:18]; Acts 4:25, 26

PSALM 2

WHY [a]do the [1]nations [2]rage, ☆
And the people plot a [3]vain thing?
2 The kings of the earth set themselves, ☆
And the [a]rulers take counsel together,

Against the LORD and
against His [b]Anointed,[1]
saying,

3 "Let [a]us break Their bonds in
pieces
And cast away Their cords
from us."

4 He who sits in the heavens
[a]shall laugh;
The Lord shall hold them in
derision.

5 Then He shall speak to them
in His wrath,
And distress them in His
deep displeasure:

6 "Yet I have [1]set My King
[2]On My holy hill of Zion."

☆7 "I will declare the [1]decree:
The LORD has said to Me,
[a]'You *are* My Son,
Today I have begotten You.

8 Ask of Me, and I will give
You
The nations *for* Your
inheritance,
And the ends of the earth
for Your possession.

☆9 [a]You shall [1]break them with
a rod of iron;
You shall dash them to
pieces like a potter's
vessel.' "

10 Now therefore, be wise,
O kings;
Be instructed, you judges of
the earth.

11 Serve the LORD with fear,
And rejoice with trembling.

12 [1]Kiss the Son, lest [2]He be
angry,
And you perish *in* the
way,
When [a]His wrath is kindled
but a little.

2 [b][John 1:41] [1]Christ, Commissioned One, Heb. *Messiah*

3 [a]Luke 19:14

4 [a]Ps. 37:13

6 [1]Lit. *installed* [2]Lit. *Upon Zion, the hill of My holiness*

7 [a]Matt. 3:17; Mark 1:1, 11; Luke 3:22; John 1:18; Acts 13:33 [Heb. 1:5; 5:5] [1]Or *decree of the* LORD*: He said to Me*

9 [a]Ps. 89:23; 110:5, 6; [Rev. 2:26, 27; 12:5; 19:15] [1]So with MT, Tg.; LXX, Syr., Vg. *rule* (cf. Rev. 2:27)

12 [a][Rev. 6:16, 17] [b][Ps. 5:11; 34:22] [1]LXX, Vg. *Embrace discipline;* Tg. *Receive instruction* [2]*LXX the* LORD

PSALM 3

title [a]2 Sam. 15:13–17

3 [a]Ps. 5:12; 28:7 [b]Ps. 9:13; 27:6 [1]Lit. *around*

4 [a]Ps. 4:3; 34:4 [b]Ps. 2:6; 15:1; 43:3

5 [a]Lev. 26:6

6 [a]Ps. 23:4; 27:3

7 [a]Job 16:10

8 [a][Is. 43:11]

[b]Blessed *are* all those who
put their trust in Him.

PSALM 3

A Psalm of David [a]when he fled
from Ab′sa·lom his son.

LORD, how they have
increased who
trouble me!
Many *are* they who rise up
against me.

2 Many *are* they who say
of me,
"*There is* no help for him in
God." Sē′lah

3 But You, O LORD, *are* [a]a
shield [1]for me,
My glory and [b]the One who
lifts up my head.

4 I cried to the LORD with my
voice,
And [a]He heard me from His
[b]holy hill. Sē′lah

5 [a]I lay down and slept;
I awoke, for the LORD
sustained me.

6 [a]I will not be afraid of ten
thousands of people
Who have set *themselves*
against me all around.

7 Arise, O LORD;
Save me, O my God!
[a]For You have struck all
my enemies on the
cheekbone;
You have broken the teeth
of the ungodly.

8 [a]Salvation *belongs* to the
LORD.
Your blessing *is* upon Your
people. Sē′lah

PSALM 4

To the [1]Chief Musician. With stringed instruments. A Psalm of David.

HEAR me when I call, O God of my righteousness!
You have relieved me in *my* distress;
[1]Have mercy on me, and hear my prayer.

2 How long, O you sons of men,
Will you turn my glory to shame?
How long will you love worthlessness
And seek falsehood? Sē′lah
3 But know that [a]the LORD has [1]set apart for Himself him who is godly;
The LORD will hear when I call to Him.

4 [a]Be[1] angry, and do not sin.
[b]Meditate within your heart on your bed, and be still. Sē′lah
5 Offer [a]the sacrifices of righteousness,
And [b]put your trust in the LORD.

6 *There are* many who say,
"Who will show us *any* good?"
[a]LORD, lift up the light of Your countenance upon us.
7 You have put [a]gladness in my heart,
More than in the season that their grain and wine increased.
8 [a]I will both lie down in peace, and sleep;
[b]For You alone, O LORD, make me dwell in safety.

PSALM 4

title [1]*Choir Director*

1 [1]*Be gracious to me*

3 [a][2 Tim. 2:19] [1]Many Heb. mss., LXX, Tg., Vg. *made wonderful*

4 [a][Eph. 4:26] [b]Ps. 77:6 [1]Lit. *Tremble* or *Be agitated*

5 [a]Deut. 33:19 [b]Ps. 37:3, 5; 62:8

6 [a]Num. 6:26

7 [a]Is. 9:3

8 [a]Ps. 3:5 [b][Lev. 25:18]

PSALM 5

title [1]Heb. *nehiloth*

1 [a]Ps. 4:1 [1]Lit. *groaning*

3 [a]Ps. 55:17; 88:13

4 [1]Lit. *sojourn*

5 [a][Hab. 1:13] [b]Ps. 1:5

6 [a]Ps. 55:23

7 [1]Lit. *the temple of Your holiness*

8 [a]Ps. 25:4, 5; 27:11; 31:3

9 [1]*uprightness*

PSALM 5

To the Chief Musician. With [1]flutes. A Psalm of David.

GIVE [a]ear to my words, O LORD,
Consider my [1]meditation.
2 Give heed to the voice of my cry,
My King and my God,
For to You I will pray.
3 My voice You shall hear in the morning, O LORD;
[a]In the morning I will direct *it* to You,
And I will look up.

4 For You *are* not a God who takes pleasure in wickedness,
Nor shall evil [1]dwell with You.
5 The [a]boastful shall not [b]stand in Your sight;
You hate all workers of iniquity.
6 You shall destroy those who speak falsehood;
The LORD abhors the [a]bloodthirsty and deceitful man.

7 But as for me, I will come into Your house in the multitude of Your mercy;
In fear of You I will worship toward [1]Your holy temple.
8 [a]Lead me, O LORD, in Your righteousness because of my enemies;
Make Your way straight before my face.

9 For *there is* no [1]faithfulness in their mouth;
Their inward part *is* destruction;

[a]Their throat *is* an open tomb;
They flatter with their tongue.
10 Pronounce them guilty, O God!
Let them fall by their own counsels;
Cast them out in the multitude of their transgressions,
For they have rebelled against You.

11 But let all those rejoice who put their trust in You;
Let them ever shout for joy, because You [1]defend them;
Let those also who love Your name
Be joyful in You.
12 For You, O LORD, will bless the righteous;
With favor You will surround him as *with* a shield.

PSALM 6

To the Chief Musician. With stringed instruments. [a]On [1]an eight-stringed harp. A Psalm of David.

O LORD, [a]do not rebuke me in Your anger,
Nor chasten me in Your hot displeasure.
2 Have mercy on me, O LORD, for I *am* weak;
O LORD, [a]heal me, for my bones are troubled.
3 My soul also is greatly [a]troubled;
But You, O LORD—how long?

4 Return, O LORD, deliver me!
Oh, save me for Your mercies' sake!
5 [a]For in death *there is* no remembrance of You;
In the grave who will give You thanks?

6 I am weary with my groaning;
[1]All night I make my bed swim;
I drench my couch with my tears.
7 [a]My eye wastes away because of grief;
It grows old because of all my enemies.

8 [a]Depart from me, all you workers of iniquity;
For the LORD has [b]heard the voice of my weeping.
9 The LORD has heard my supplication;
The LORD will receive my prayer.
10 Let all my enemies be ashamed and greatly troubled;
Let them turn back *and* be ashamed suddenly.

PSALM 7

A [a]Meditation[1] of David, which he sang to the LORD [b]concerning the words of Cush, a Ben'ja·mīte.

O LORD my God, in You I put my trust;
[a]Save me from all those who persecute me;
And deliver me,
2 [a]Lest they tear me like a lion,
[b]Rending *me* in pieces, while *there is* none to deliver.

3 O LORD my God, [a]if I have done this:

---

9 [a]Rom. 3:13
11 [1]*protect*, lit. *cover*

PSALM 6

title [a]Ps. 12:title [1]Heb. *sheminith*
1 [a]Ps. 38:1; 118:18
2 [a][Hos. 6:1]
3 [a]Ps. 88:3
5 [a][Eccl. 9:10]
6 [1]Or *Every night*
7 [a]Job 17:7
8 [a][Matt. 25:41] [b]Ps. 3:4; 28:6

PSALM 7

title [a]Hab. 3:1 [b]2 Sam. 16 [1]Heb. *Shiggaion*
1 [a]Ps. 31:15
2 [a]Is. 38:13 [b]Ps. 50:22
3 [a]2 Sam. 16:7

If there is [b]iniquity in my hands,
4 If I have repaid evil to him who was at peace with me,
Or [a]have plundered my enemy without cause,
5 Let the enemy pursue me and overtake *me;*
Yes, let him trample my life to the earth,
And lay my honor in the dust. Sē′lah

6 Arise, O LORD, in Your anger;
[a]Lift Yourself up because of the rage of my enemies;
[b]Rise up [1]for me *to* the judgment You have commanded!
7 So the congregation of the peoples shall surround You;
For their sakes, therefore, return on high.
8 The LORD shall judge the peoples;
[a]Judge me, O LORD, [b]according to my righteousness,
And according to my integrity within me.

9 Oh, let the wickedness of the wicked come to an end,
But establish the just;
[a]For the righteous God tests the hearts and [1]minds.
10 [1]My defense *is* of God,
Who saves the [a]upright in heart.

11 God *is* a just judge,
And God is angry *with the wicked* every day.
12 If he does not turn back,
He will [a]sharpen His sword;
He bends His bow and makes it ready.
13 He also prepares for Himself instruments of death;
He makes His arrows into fiery shafts.

14 [a]Behold, *the wicked* brings forth iniquity;
Yes, he conceives trouble and brings forth falsehood.
15 He made a pit and dug it out,
[a]And has fallen into the ditch *which* he made.
16 [a]His trouble shall return upon his own head,
And his violent dealing shall come down on [1]his own crown.

17 I will praise the LORD according to His righteousness,
And will sing praise to the name of the LORD Most High.

PSALM 8

To the Chief Musician. [1]On the instrument of Gath. A Psalm of David.

O LORD, our Lord,
How [a]excellent *is* Your name in all the earth,
Who have [b]set Your glory above the heavens!

2 [a]Out of the mouth of babes and nursing infants
You have [1]ordained strength,
Because of Your enemies,
That You may silence [b]the enemy and the avenger.

3 [b]1 Sam. 24:11
4 [a]1 Sam. 24:7; 26:9
6 [a]Ps. 94:2 [b]Ps. 35:23; 44:23 [1]So with MT, Tg., Vg.; LXX *O LORD my God*
8 [a]Ps. 26:1; 35:24; 43:1 [b]Ps. 18:20; 35:24
9 [a][1 Sam. 16:7] [1]Lit. *kidneys*, the most secret part of man
10 [a]Ps. 97:10, 11; 125:4 [1]Lit. *My shield is upon God*
12 [a]Deut. 32:41
14 [a]Is. 59:4
15 [a][Job 4:8]
16 [a]Esth. 9:25 [1]The crown of his own head

PSALM 8

title [1]Heb. *Al Gittith*
1 [a]Ps. 148:13 [b]Ps. 113:4
2 [a][1 Cor. 1:27] [b]Ps. 44:16 [1]*established*

3 When I [a]consider Your
heavens, the work of
Your fingers,
The moon and the stars,
which You have ordained,
4 [a]What is man that You are
mindful of him,
And the son of man that You
[b]visit[1] him?
5 For You have made him a
little lower than [1]the
angels,
And You have crowned him
with glory and honor.

☆6 [a]You have made him to have
dominion over the works
of Your hands;
[b]You have put all *things*
under his feet,
7 All sheep and oxen—
Even the beasts of the field,
8 The birds of the air,
And the fish of the sea
That pass through the paths
of the seas.

9 [a]O LORD, our Lord,
How excellent *is* Your name
in all the earth!

PSALM 9

To the Chief Musician. To *the tune of* [1]"Death of the Son." A Psalm of David.

I WILL praise *You,* O LORD,
with my whole heart;
I will tell of all Your
marvelous works.
2 I will be glad and [a]rejoice in
You;
I will sing praise to Your
name, [b]O Most High.

3 When my enemies turn
back,
They shall fall and perish at
Your presence.
4 For You have maintained my
right and my cause;
You sat on the throne
judging in righteousness.
5 You have rebuked the
[1]nations,
You have destroyed the
wicked;
You have [a]blotted out their
name forever and ever.

6 O enemy, destructions are
finished forever!
And you have destroyed
cities;
Even their memory has
[a]perished.
7 [a]But the LORD shall endure
forever;
He has prepared His throne
for judgment.
8 [a]He shall judge the world in
righteousness,
And He shall administer
judgment for the peoples
in uprightness.

9 The LORD also will be
a [a]refuge[1] for the
oppressed,
A refuge in times of trouble.
10 And those who [a]know Your
name will put their trust
in You;
For You, LORD, have not
forsaken those who seek
You.

11 Sing praises to the LORD,
who dwells in Zion!
[a]Declare His deeds among
the people.
12 [a]When He avenges blood, He
remembers them;
He does not forget the cry
of the [1]humble.

3 [a]Ps. 111:2
4 [a]Job 7:17, 18 [b][Job 10:12] [1]*give attention to* or *care for*
5 [1]Heb. *Elohim, God;* LXX, Syr., Tg., Jewish tradition *angels*
6 [a][Gen. 1:26, 28] [b][1 Cor. 15:27; Eph. 1:22; Heb. 2:8]
9 [a]Ps. 8:1

PSALM 9

title [1]Heb. *Muth Labben*
2 [a]Ps. 5:11; 104:34 [b][Ps. 83:18; 92:1]
5 [a]Prov. 10:7 [1]*Gentiles*
6 [a][Ps. 34:16]
7 [a]Heb. 1:11
8 [a][Ps. 96:13; 98:9]
9 [a]Ps. 32:7; 46:1; 91:2 [1]Lit. *secure height*
10 [a]Ps. 91:14
11 [a]Ps. 66:16; 107:22
12 [a][Ps. 72:14] [1]*afflicted*

13 Have mercy on me, O LORD!
Consider my trouble from
those who hate me,
You who lift me up from the
gates of death,
14 That I may tell of all Your
praise
In the gates of [1]the daughter
of Zion.
I will [a]rejoice in Your
salvation.

15 [a]The [1]nations have sunk
down in the pit *which*
they made;
In the net which they hid,
their own foot is caught.
16 The LORD is [a]known *by* the
judgment He executes;
The wicked is snared in the
work of his own hands.
[b]Meditation.[1] Sēʹlah

17 The wicked shall be turned
into hell,
And all the [1]nations [a]that
forget God.
18 [a]For the needy shall not
always be forgotten;
[b]The expectation of the poor
shall *not* perish forever.

19 Arise, O LORD,
Do not let man prevail;
Let the [1]nations be judged in
Your sight.
20 Put them in fear, O LORD,
That the [1]nations may know
themselves *to be but*
men. Sēʹlah

PSALM 10

WHY do You stand afar off,
O LORD?
Why do You hide in times of
trouble?

2 The wicked in *his* pride
[1]persecutes the poor;
[a]Let them be caught in the
plots which they have
devised.

3 For the wicked [a]boasts of
his heart's desire;
[1]He [b]blesses the greedy *and*
renounces the LORD.
4 The wicked in his proud
countenance does not
seek *God;*
[1]God *is* in none of his
[a]thoughts.

5 His ways [1]are always
prospering;
Your judgments *are* far
above, out of his sight;
As for all his enemies, he
sneers at them.
6 [a]He has said in his heart, "I
shall not be moved;
[b]I shall never be in adversity."
7 [a]His mouth is full of
cursing and [b]deceit and
oppression;
Under his tongue *is* trouble
and iniquity.

8 He sits in the lurking places
of the villages;
In the secret places he
murders the innocent;
His eyes are secretly fixed
on the helpless.
9 He lies in wait secretly, as a
lion in his den;
He lies in wait to catch the
poor;
He catches the poor when he
draws him into his net.
10 So [1]he crouches, he lies low,
That the helpless may fall
by his [2]strength.
11 He has said in his heart,
"God has forgotten;

---

14 [a]Ps. 13:5; 20:5; 35:9 [1]Jerusalem
15 [a]Ps. 7:15, 16 [1]*Gentiles*
16 [a]Ex. 7:5 [b]Ps. 92:3 [1]Heb. *Higgaion*
17 [a]Job 8:13 [1]*Gentiles*
18 [a]Ps. 9:12; 12:5 [b]Prov. 23:18
19 [1]*Gentiles*
20 [1]*Gentiles*

PSALM 10

2 [a]Ps. 7:16; 9:16 [1]*hotly pursues*
3 [a]Ps. 49:6; 94:3, 4 [b]Prov. 28:4 [1]Or *The greedy man curses and spurns the* LORD
4 [a]Ps. 14:1; 36:1 [1]Or *All his thoughts are, "There is no God"*
5 [1]Lit. *are strong*
6 [a][Eccl. 8:11] [b]Rev. 18:7
7 [a][Rom. 3:14] [b]Ps. 55:10, 11
10 [1]Or *he is crushed, is bowed* [2]Or *mighty ones*

He hides His face;
He will never see."

12 Arise, O LORD!
O God, [a]lift up Your hand!
Do not forget the [b]humble.
13 Why do the wicked renounce God?
He has said in his heart,
"You will not require *an account*."

14 But You have [a]seen, for You observe trouble and grief,
To repay *it* by Your hand.
The helpless [b]commits[1] himself to You;
[c]You are the helper of the fatherless.
15 Break the arm of the wicked and the evil *man;*
Seek out his wickedness *until* You find none.

16 [a]The LORD *is* King forever and ever;
The nations have perished out of His land.
17 LORD, You have heard the desire of the humble;
You will prepare their heart;
You will cause Your ear to hear,
18 To [1]do justice to the fatherless and the oppressed,
That the man of the earth may [2]oppress no more.

PSALM 11

To the Chief Musician. *A Psalm* of David.

IN [a]the LORD I put my trust;
How can you say to my soul,
"Flee *as* a bird to your mountain"?
2 For look! [a]The wicked bend *their* bow,
They make ready their arrow on the string,
That they may shoot [1]secretly at the upright in heart.
3 [a]If the foundations are destroyed,
What can the righteous do?

4 The LORD *is* in His holy temple,
The LORD's [a]throne *is* in heaven;
[b]His eyes behold,
His eyelids test the sons of men.
5 The LORD [a]tests the righteous,
But the wicked and the one who loves violence His soul hates.
6 Upon the wicked He will rain coals;
Fire and brimstone and a burning wind
[a]*Shall be* [1]the portion of their cup.

7 For the LORD *is* righteous,
He [a]loves righteousness;
[1]His countenance beholds the upright.

PSALM 12

To the Chief Musician. [a]On [1]an eight-stringed harp. A Psalm of David.

HELP,[1] LORD, for the godly man [a]ceases!
For the faithful disappear from among the sons of men.

---

12 [a]Mic. 5:9 [b]Ps. 9:12
14 [a][Ps. 11:4] [b][2 Tim. 1:12] [c]Ps. 68:5 [1]Lit. *leaves, entrusts*
16 [a]Ps. 29:10
18 [1]*vindicate* [2]*terrify*

PSALM 11

1 [a]Ps. 56:11
2 [a]Ps. 64:3, 4 [1]Lit. *in darkness*
3 [a]Ps. 82:5; 87:1; 119:152
4 [a][Is. 66:1] [b][Ps. 33:18; 34:15, 16]
5 [a]Gen. 22:1
6 [a]Ps. 75:8 [1]Their allotted portion or serving
7 [a]Ps. 33:5; 45:7 [1]Or *The upright beholds His countenance*

PSALM 12

title [a]Ps. 6:title [1]Heb. *sheminith*
1 [a][Is. 57:1] [1]*Save*

2 [a]They speak idly everyone
with his neighbor;
With flattering lips *and* [1]a
double heart they speak.

3 May the LORD [1]cut off all
flattering lips,
And the tongue that speaks
[2]proud things,
4 Who have said,
"With our tongue we will
prevail;
Our lips *are* our own;
Who *is* lord over us?"

5 "For the oppression of the
poor, for the sighing of
the needy,
Now I will arise," says the
LORD;
"I will set *him* in the safety
for which he yearns."

6 The words of the LORD *are*
[a]pure words,
Like silver tried in a furnace
of earth,
Purified seven times.
7 You shall keep them,
O LORD,
You shall preserve them
from this generation
forever.

8 The wicked prowl on every
side,
When vileness is exalted
among the sons of men.

PSALM 13

To the Chief Musician. A Psalm
of David.

HOW long, O LORD? Will You
forget me forever?
[a]How long will You hide Your
face from me?
2 How long shall I take
counsel in my soul,
Having sorrow in my heart
daily?
How long will my enemy be
exalted over me?

3 Consider *and* hear me,
O LORD my God;
[a]Enlighten my eyes,
[b]Lest I sleep the *sleep of*
death;
4 Lest my enemy say,
"I have prevailed against
him";
Lest those who trouble
me rejoice when I am
moved.

5 But I have trusted in Your
mercy;
My heart shall rejoice in
Your salvation.
6 I will sing to the LORD,
Because He has dealt
bountifully with me.

PSALM 14

To the Chief Musician. *A Psalm*
of David.

THE [a]fool has said in his
heart,
"*There is* no God."
They are corrupt,
They have done abominable
works,
There is none who does
good.

2 [a]The LORD looks down
from heaven upon the
children of men,
To see if there are any who
understand, who seek
God.
3 [a]They have all turned aside,

Psalm 12: 2 [a]Ps. 10:7; 41:6 [1]An inconsistent mind
3 [1]*destroy* [2]*great*
6 [a]2 Sam. 22:31; Ps. 18:30; 119:140

PSALM 13
1 [a]Job 13:24
3 [a]Ezra 9:8 [b]Jer. 51:39

PSALM 14
1 [a]Ps. 10:4; 53:1
2 [a]Ps. 33:13, 14; 102:19
3 [a]Rom. 3:12

They have together become
corrupt;
There is none who does
good,
No, not one.

4 Have all the workers of
iniquity no knowledge,
Who eat up my people *as*
they eat bread,
And [a]do not call on the
LORD?
5 There they are in great fear,
For God *is* with the
generation of the
righteous.
6 You shame the counsel of
the poor,
But the LORD *is* his [a]refuge.

7 [a]Oh,[1] that the salvation of
Israel *would come* out of
Zion!
[b]When the LORD brings back
[2]the captivity of His
people,
Let Jacob rejoice *and* Israel
be glad.

PSALM 15

A Psalm of David.

LORD, [a]who may [1]abide in
Your tabernacle?
Who may dwell in Your holy
hill?

2 He who walks uprightly,
And works righteousness,
And speaks the [a]truth in
his heart;
3 He *who* [a]does not backbite
with his tongue,
Nor does evil to his
neighbor,
[b]Nor does he [1]take up a
reproach against his
friend;
4 [a]In whose eyes a vile person
is despised,
But he honors those who
fear the LORD;
He *who* [b]swears to his
own hurt and does not
change;
5 He *who* does not put out his
money at usury,
Nor does he take a bribe
against the innocent.

He who does these *things*
[a]shall never be moved.

PSALM 16

A [a]Mich'tam of David.

PRESERVE[1] me, O God, for
in You I put my trust.

2 *O my soul,* you have said to
the LORD,
"You *are* my Lord,
[a]My goodness is nothing
apart from You."
3 As for the saints who *are* on
the earth,
"They are the excellent
ones, in [a]whom is all my
delight."

4 Their sorrows shall be
multiplied who hasten
after another *god;*
Their drink offerings of
[a]blood I will not offer,
[b]Nor take up their names on
my lips.

5 O LORD, *You are* the portion
of my inheritance and
my cup;
You [1]maintain my lot.

4 [a]Is. 64:7
6 [a]Ps. 9:9; 40:17; 46:1; 142:5
7 [a]Ps. 53:6 [b]Job 42:10 [1]Lit. *Who will give out of Zion the salvation of Israel?* [2]Or *His captive people*

PSALM 15
1 [a]Ps. 24:3–5 [1]*sojourn*
2 [a][Eph. 4:25]
3 [a][Lev. 19:16–18] [b]Ex. 23:1 [1]*receive*
4 [a]Esth. 3:2 [b]Lev. 5:4
5 [a]2 Pet. 1:10

PSALM 16
title [a]Ps. 56—60
1 [1]*Watch over*
2 [a]Job 35:7
3 [a]Ps. 119:63
4 [a]Ps. 106:37, 38 [b][Ex. 23:13]
5 [1]Lit. *uphold*

6 The lines have fallen to me in pleasant *places;*
Yes, I have a good inheritance.

7 I will bless the LORD who has given me counsel;
My [1]heart also instructs me in the night seasons.
8 [a]I have set the LORD always before me;
Because *He is* at my right hand I shall not be moved.

9 Therefore my heart is glad, and my glory rejoices;
My flesh also will [1]rest in hope.
☆ 10 [a]For You will not leave my soul in [1]Shē'ōl,
Nor will You allow Your Holy One to [2]see corruption.
11 You will show me the [a]path of life;
In Your presence *is* fullness of joy;
At Your right hand *are* pleasures forevermore.

PSALM 17

A Prayer of David.

HEAR a just cause, O LORD,
Attend to my cry;
Give ear to my prayer *which is* not from deceitful lips.
2 Let my vindication come from Your presence;
Let Your eyes look on the things that are upright.

3 You have tested my heart;
You have visited *me* in the night;
[a]You have [1]tried me and have found [2]nothing;
I have purposed that my mouth shall not [b]transgress.
4 Concerning the works of men,
By the word of Your lips,
I have kept away from the paths of the destroyer.
5 [a]Uphold my steps in Your paths,
That my footsteps may not slip.

6 [a]I have called upon You, for You will hear me, O God;
Incline Your ear to me, *and* hear my speech.
7 Show Your marvelous lovingkindness by Your right hand,
O You who [1]save those who trust *in You*
From those who rise up *against them.*
8 Keep me as the [1]apple of Your eye;
Hide me under the shadow of Your wings,
9 From the wicked who oppress me,
From my deadly enemies who surround me.

10 They have closed up their [a]fat *hearts;*
With their mouths they [b]speak proudly.
11 They have now surrounded us in our steps;
They have set their eyes, crouching down to the earth,
12 As a lion is eager to tear his prey,
And like a young lion lurking in secret places.

7 [1]Mind, lit. *kidneys*
8 [a][Acts 2:25–28]
9 [1]Or *dwell securely*
10 [a]Ps. 49:15; 86:13; Acts 2:31, 32; Heb. 13:20 [1]The abode of the dead [2]*undergo*
11 [a][Matt. 7:14]

PSALM 17

3 [a]Job 23:10 [b]Ps. 39:1 [1]*examined* [2]Nothing evil
5 [a]Ps. 44:18; 119:133
6 [a]Ps. 86:7; 116:2
7 [1]*deliver*
8 [1]*pupil*
10 [a]Ezek. 16:49 [b][1 Sam. 2:3]

13 Arise, O LORD,
Confront him, cast him down;
Deliver my life from the wicked with Your sword,
14 With Your hand from men, O LORD,
From men of the world *who have* their portion in *this* life,
And whose belly You fill with Your hidden treasure.
They are satisfied with children,
And leave the rest of their *possession* for their babes.

15 As for me, [a]I will see Your face in righteousness;
[b]I shall be satisfied when I [c]awake in Your likeness.

PSALM 18

To the Chief Musician. *A Psalm* of David [a]the servant of the LORD, who spoke to the LORD the words of [b]this song on the day that the LORD delivered him from the hand of all his enemies and from the hand of Saul. And he said:

I [a]WILL love You, O LORD, my strength.
2 The LORD is my rock and my fortress and my deliverer;
My God, my [1]strength, [a]in whom I will trust;
My shield and the [2]horn of my salvation, my stronghold.
3 I will call upon the LORD, [a]*who is worthy* to be praised;
So shall I be saved from my enemies.

4 [a]The pangs of death surrounded me,
And the floods of [1]ungodliness made me afraid.
5 The sorrows of She'ōl surrounded me;
The snares of death confronted me.
6 In my distress I called upon the LORD,
And cried out to my God;
He heard my voice from His temple,
And my cry came before Him, *even* to His ears.

7 [a]Then the earth shook and trembled;
The foundations of the hills also quaked and were shaken,
Because He was angry.
8 Smoke went up from His nostrils,
And devouring fire from His mouth;
Coals were kindled by it.
9 [a]He bowed the heavens also, and came down
With darkness under His feet.
10 [a]And He rode upon a cherub, and flew;
[b]He flew upon the wings of the wind.
11 He made darkness His secret place;
[a]His canopy around Him *was* dark waters
And thick clouds of the skies.
12 [a]From the brightness before Him,

15 [a][1 John 3:2] [b]Ps. 4:6, 7; 16:11 [c][Is. 26:19]

PSALM 18

title [a]Ps. 36:title [b]2 Sam. 22

1 [a]Ps. 144:1

2 [a]Heb. 2:13 [1]Lit. *rock* [2]Strength

3 [a]Rev. 5:12

4 [a]Ps. 116:3 [1]Lit. *Belial*

7 [a]Acts 4:31

9 [a]Ps. 144:5

10 [a]Ps. 80:1; 99:1 [b][Ps. 104:3]

11 [a]Ps. 97:2

12 [a]Ps. 97:3; 140:10

His thick clouds passed with
hailstones and coals of
fire.
13 The LORD thundered from
heaven,
And the Most High uttered
[a]His voice,
[1]Hailstones and coals of fire.
14 [a]He sent out His arrows and
scattered [1]the foe,
Lightnings in abundance,
and He vanquished
them.
15 Then the channels of the sea
were seen,
The foundations of the
world were uncovered
At Your rebuke, O LORD,
At the blast of the breath of
Your nostrils.
16 [a]He sent from above, He took
me;
He drew me out of many
waters.
17 He delivered me from my
strong enemy,
From those who hated me,
For they were too strong
for me.
18 They confronted me in the
day of my calamity,
But the LORD was my
support.
19 [a]He also brought me out into
a broad place;
He delivered me because He
delighted in me.
20 [a]The LORD rewarded me
according to my
righteousness;
According to the cleanness
of my hands
He has recompensed me.
21 For I have kept the ways of
the LORD,
And have not wickedly
departed from my God.
22 For all His judgments *were*
before me,
And I did not put away His
statutes from me.
23 I was also blameless [1]before
Him,
And I kept myself from my
iniquity.
24 [a]Therefore the LORD has
recompensed me
according to my
righteousness,
According to the cleanness
of my hands in His sight.
25 [a]With the merciful You will
show Yourself merciful;
With a blameless man
You will show Yourself
blameless;
26 With the pure You will show
Yourself pure;
And [a]with the devious
You will show Yourself
shrewd.
27 For You will save the humble
people,
But will bring down
[a]haughty looks.
28 [a]For You will light my lamp;
The LORD my God will
enlighten my darkness.
29 For by You I can [1]run against
a troop,
By my God I can leap over
a wall.
30 *As for* God, [a]His way *is*
perfect;
[b]The word of the LORD is
[1]proven;
He *is* a shield [c]to all who
trust in Him.
31 [a]For who *is* God, except the
LORD?

13 [a][Ps. 29:3–9; 104:7] [1]So with MT, Tg., Vg.; a few Heb. mss., LXX omit *Hailstones and coals of fire*
14 [a]Ps. 144:6 [1]Lit. *them*
16 [a]Ps. 144:7
19 [a]Ps. 4:1; 31:8; 118:5
20 [a]1 Sam. 24:19
23 [1]*with*
24 [a]1 Sam. 26:23
25 [a][1 Kin. 8:32]
26 [a][Lev. 26:23–28]
27 [a][Ps. 101:5]
28 [a]Job 18:6
29 [1]Or *run through*
30 [a]Rev. 15:3 [b]Ps. 12:6; 119:140 [c][Ps. 17:7] [1]Lit. *refined*
31 [a][1 Sam. 2:2]

And who *is* a rock, except our God?
32 *It is* God who [a]arms me with strength,
And makes my way perfect.
33 [a]He makes my feet like the *feet of* deer,
And [b]sets me on my high places.
34 [a]He teaches my hands to make war,
So that my arms can bend a bow of bronze.
35 You have also given me the shield of Your salvation;
Your right hand has held me up,
Your gentleness has made me great.
36 You enlarged my path under me,
[a]So my feet did not slip.
37 I have pursued my enemies and overtaken them;
Neither did I turn back again till they were destroyed.
38 I have wounded them,
So that they could not rise;
They have fallen under my feet.
39 For You have armed me with strength for the battle;
You have [1]subdued under me those who rose up against me.
40 You have also given me the necks of my enemies,
So that I destroyed those who hated me.
41 They cried out, but *there was* none to save;
[a]*Even* to the LORD, but He did not answer them.
42 Then I beat them as fine as the dust before the wind;
I [a]cast them out like dirt in the streets.
43 You have delivered me from the strivings of the people;
[a]You have made me the head of the [1]nations;
[b]A people I have not known shall serve me.
44 As soon as they hear of me they obey me;
The foreigners [1]submit to me.
45 [a]The foreigners fade away,
And come frightened from their hideouts.

46 The LORD lives!
Blessed *be* my Rock!
Let the God of my salvation be exalted.
47 *It is* God who avenges me,
[a]And subdues the peoples under me;
48 He delivers me from my enemies.
[a]You also lift me up above those who rise against me;
You have delivered me from the violent man.
49 [a]Therefore I will give thanks to You, O LORD, among the [1]Gentiles,
And sing praises to Your name.

50 [a]Great deliverance He gives to His king,
And shows mercy to His anointed,
To David and his [1]descendants forevermore.

32 [a][Ps. 91:2]
33 [a]Hab. 3:19 [b]Deut. 32:13; 33:29
34 [a]Ps. 144:1
36 [a]Prov. 4:12
39 [1]Lit. *caused to bow*
41 [a]Job 27:9
42 [a]Zech. 10:5
43 [a]2 Sam. 8 [b]Is. 52:15 [1]*Gentiles*
44 [1]*feign submission*
45 [a]Mic. 7:17
47 [a]Ps. 47:3
48 [a]Ps. 27:6; 59:1
49 [a]Rom. 15:9 [1]*nations*
50 [a]Ps. 21:1; 144:10 [1]Lit. *seed*

PSALM 19

To the Chief Musician. A Psalm of David.

THE [a]heavens declare the glory of God;
And the [b]firmament[1] shows [2]His handiwork.
2 Day unto day utters speech,
And night unto night reveals knowledge.
3 *There is* no speech nor language
Where their voice is not heard.
4 [a]Their [1]line has gone out through all the earth,
And their words to the end of the world.

In them He has set a [2]tabernacle for the sun,
5 Which *is* like a bridegroom coming out of his chamber,
[a]*And* rejoices like a strong man to run its race.
6 Its rising *is* from one end of heaven,
And its circuit to the other end;
And there is nothing hidden from its heat.

7 [a]The law of the LORD *is* perfect, [1]converting the soul;
The testimony of the LORD *is* sure, making [b]wise the simple;
8 The statutes of the LORD *are* right, rejoicing the heart;
The commandment of the LORD *is* pure, enlightening the eyes;
9 The fear of the LORD *is* clean, enduring forever;
The judgments of the LORD *are* true *and* righteous altogether.
10 More to be desired *are they* than [a]gold,
Yea, than much fine gold;
Sweeter also than honey and the [1]honeycomb.
11 Moreover by them Your servant is warned,
And in keeping them *there is* great reward.

12 Who can understand *his* errors?
[a]Cleanse me from secret *faults*.
13 Keep back Your servant also from [a]presumptuous *sins*;
Let them not have [b]dominion over me.
Then I shall be blameless,
And I shall be innocent of [1]great transgression.

14 [a]Let the words of my mouth and the meditation of my heart
Be acceptable in Your sight,
O LORD, my [1]strength and my [b]Redeemer.

PSALM 20

To the Chief Musician. A Psalm of David.

MAY the LORD answer you in the day of trouble;
May the name of the God of Jacob [1]defend you;
2 May He send you help from the sanctuary,
And strengthen you out of Zion;
3 May He remember all your offerings,

PSALM 19

1 [a]Is. 40:22 [b]Gen. 1:6, 7 [1]*expanse* of heaven [2]*the work of His hands*

4 [a]Rom. 10:18 [1]LXX, Syr., Vg. *sound*; Tg. *business* [2]*tent*

5 [a]Eccl. 1:5

7 [a]Ps. 111:7 [b]Ps. 119:130 [1]*restoring*

10 [a]Ps. 119:72, 127 [1]*honey in the combs*

12 [a][Ps. 51:1, 2]

13 [a]Num. 15:30 [b]Ps. 119:133 [1]Or *much*

14 [a]Ps. 51:15 [b]Is. 47:4 [1]Lit. *rock*

PSALM 20

1 [1]Lit. *set you on high*

And accept your burnt
sacrifice. Sē'lah

4 May He grant you
according to your
heart's *desire*,
And [a]fulfill all your
[1]purpose.
5 We will rejoice in your
salvation,
And in the name of our
God we will set up *our*
banners!
May the LORD fulfill all your
petitions.

6 Now I know that the LORD
saves His [1]anointed;
He will answer him from
His holy heaven
With the saving strength of
His right hand.

7 Some *trust* in chariots, and
some in [a]horses;
But we will remember the
name of the LORD our
God.
8 They have bowed down and
fallen;
But we have risen and stand
upright.

9 Save, LORD!
May the King answer us
when we call.

PSALM 21

To the Chief Musician. A Psalm
of David.

THE king shall have joy in
Your strength, O LORD;
And in Your salvation how
greatly shall he rejoice!
2 You have given him his
heart's desire,
And have not withheld the
[a]request of his lips.
Sē'lah

3 For You meet him with the
blessings of goodness;
You set a crown of pure
gold upon his head.
4 [a]He asked life from You, *and*
You gave *it* to him—
Length of days forever and
ever.
5 His glory *is* great in Your
salvation;
Honor and majesty You have
placed upon him.
6 For You have made him
most blessed forever;
[a]You have made him
[1]exceedingly glad with
Your presence.
7 For the king trusts in the
LORD,
And through the mercy of
the Most High he shall
not be [1]moved.

8 Your hand will find all Your
enemies;
Your right hand will find
those who hate You.
9 You shall make them as a
fiery oven in the time of
Your anger;
The LORD shall swallow
them up in His wrath,
And the fire shall devour
them.
10 Their offspring You shall
destroy from the earth,
And their [1]descendants from
among the sons of men.
11 For they intended evil
against You;
They devised a plot *which*
they are not able to
[a]*perform*.

4 [a]Ps. 21:2 [1]*counsel*

6 [1]Commissioned one, Heb. *messiah*

7 [a]Ps. 33:16, 17

PSALM 21

2 [a]2 Sam. 7:26–29

4 [a]Ps. 61:5, 6; 133:3

6 [a]Ps. 16:11; 45:7 [1]Lit. *joyful with gladness*

7 [1]*shaken*

10 [1]Lit. *seed*

11 [a]Ps. 2:1–4

12 Therefore You will make
them turn their back;
You will make ready *Your*
arrows on Your string
toward their faces.

13 Be exalted, O LORD, in Your
own strength!
We will sing and praise Your
power.

PSALM 22

To the Chief Musician. Set to
[1]"The Deer of the Dawn." A
Psalm of David.

☆ MY [a]God, My God, why have
You forsaken Me?
Why are You so far from
helping Me,
And from the words of My
groaning?
2 O My God, I cry in the
daytime, but You do not
hear;
And in the night season,
and am not silent.

3 But You *are* holy,
Enthroned in the [a]praises of
Israel.
4 Our fathers trusted in You;
They trusted, and You
delivered them.
5 They cried to You, and were
delivered;
[a]They trusted in You, and
were not ashamed.

6 But I *am* [a]a worm, and no
man;
[b]A reproach of men, and
despised by the people.
☆ 7 [a]All those who see Me
ridicule Me;
They [1]shoot out the lip, they
shake the head, *saying*,

PSALM 22

title [1]Heb. *Aijeleth Hashahar*

1 [a][Matt. 27:46; Mark 15:34]

3 [a]Deut. 10:21

5 [a]Is. 49:23

6 [a]Is. 41:14 [b][Is. 53:3]

7 [a]Matt. 27:39; Mark 15:29; Luke 23:35 [1]Show contempt with their mouth

8 [a]Matt. 27:43; Luke 23:35 [b]Ps. 91:14 [1]LXX, Syr., Vg. *hoped;* Tg. *praised*

9 [a][Ps. 71:5, 6]

10 [a][Is. 46:3; 49:1]

12 [a]Ps. 22:21; 68:30 [b]Deut. 32:14

13 [a]Job 16:10 [1]Lit. *have opened their mouths at Me*

14 [a]Dan. 5:6 [1]Lit. *in the midst of My bowels*

15 [a]Prov. 17:22 [b]John 19:28

16 [a]Matt. 27:35; John 20:25, 27 [1]So with some Heb. mss., LXX, Syr., Vg.; MT *Like a lion* instead of *They pierced*

17 [a]Matt. 27:36, 39; Luke 23:27, 35; John 19:37

18 [a]Matt. 27:35; Mark 15:24; Luke 23:34; John 19:24

8 "He[a] [1]trusted in the LORD, let ☆
Him rescue Him;
[b]Let Him deliver Him, since
He delights in Him!"

9 [a]But You *are* He who took Me
out of the womb;
You made Me trust *while* on
My mother's breasts.
10 I was cast upon You from
birth.
From My mother's womb
[a]You *have been* My God.
11 Be not far from Me,
For trouble *is* near;
For *there is* none to help.

12 [a]Many bulls have surrounded
Me;
Strong *bulls* of [b]Bā'shan
have encircled Me.
13 [a]They [1]gape at Me *with* their
mouths,
Like a raging and roaring
lion.

14 I am poured out like water,
[a]And all My bones are out of
joint;
My heart is like wax;
It has melted [1]within Me.
15 [a]My strength is dried up like
a potsherd,
And [b]My tongue clings to
My jaws;
You have brought Me to the
dust of death.

16 For dogs have surrounded ☆
Me;
The congregation of the
wicked has enclosed Me.
[a]They[1] pierced My hands and
My feet;
17 I can count all My bones. ☆
[a]They look *and* stare at Me.
18 [a]They divide My garments ☆
among them,

And for My clothing they
cast lots.

19 But You, O LORD, do not be
far from Me;
O My Strength, hasten to
help Me!
20 Deliver Me from the sword,
[a]My[1] precious *life* from the
power of the dog.
21 [a]Save Me from the lion's
mouth
And from the horns of the
wild oxen!

[b]You have answered Me.

☆ 22 [a]I will declare Your name to
[b]My brethren;
In the midst of the assembly
I will praise You.
23 [a]You who fear the LORD,
praise Him!
All you [1]descendants of
Jacob, glorify Him,
And fear Him, all you
offspring of Israel!
24 For He has not despised nor
abhorred the affliction of
the afflicted;
Nor has He hidden His face
from Him;
But [a]when He cried to Him,
He heard.

25 [a]My praise *shall be* of You in
the great assembly;
[b]I will pay My vows before
those who fear Him.
26 The poor shall eat and be
satisfied;
Those who seek Him will
praise the LORD.
Let your heart live forever!

27 All the ends of the world
Shall remember and turn to
the LORD,
And all the families of the
[1]nations
Shall worship before [2]You.
28 [a]For the kingdom *is* the
LORD's,
And He rules over the
nations.

29 [a]All the prosperous of the
earth
Shall eat and worship;
[b]All those who go down to
[1]the dust
Shall bow before Him,
Even he who cannot keep
himself alive.

30 A posterity shall serve Him.
It will be recounted of
the Lord to the *next*
generation,
31 They will come and declare
His righteousness to a
people who will be born,
That He has done *this*.

PSALM 23

A Psalm of David.

THE LORD *is* [a]my shepherd;
[b]I shall not [1]want.
2 [a]He makes me to lie down in
[1]green pastures;
[b]He leads me beside the [2]still
waters.
3 He restores my soul;
[a]He leads me in the paths of
righteousness
For His name's sake.

4 Yea, though I walk through
the valley of [a]the shadow
of death,
[b]I will fear no evil;
[c]For You *are* with me;
Your rod and Your staff, they
comfort me.

---

20 [a]Ps. 35:17 [1]Lit. *My only one*

21 [a]2 Tim. 4:17 [b]Is. 34:7

22 [a]Heb. 2:12 [b][Rom. 8:29]

23 [a]Ps. 135:19, 20 [1]Lit. *seed*

24 [a]Heb. 5:7

25 [a]Ps. 35:18; 40:9, 10 [b]Eccl. 5:4

27 [1]*Gentiles* [2]So with MT, LXX, Tg.; Arab., Syr., Vg. *Him*

28 [a]Matt. 6:13

29 [a]Ps. 17:10; 45:12 [b][Is. 26:19] [1]Death

PSALM 23

1 [a][Is. 40:11] [b][Phil. 4:19] [1]*lack*

2 [a]Ezek. 34:14 [b][Rev. 7:17] [1]Lit. *pastures of tender grass* [2]Lit. *waters of rest*

3 [a]Ps. 5:8; 31:3

4 [a]Job 3:5; 10:21, 22; 24:17 [b][Ps. 3:6; 27:1] [c][Is. 43:2]

5 You [a]prepare a table before
me in the presence of my
enemies;
You [b]anoint my head with
oil;
My cup runs over.
6 Surely goodness and mercy
shall follow me
All the days of my life;
And I will [1]dwell in the
house of the LORD
[2]Forever.

PSALM 24

A Psalm of David.

THE [a]earth *is* the LORD's, and
all its fullness,
The world and those who
dwell therein.
2 For He has [a]founded it upon
the seas,
And established it upon the
[1]waters.

3 [a]Who may ascend into the
hill of the LORD?
Or who may stand in His
holy place?
4 He who has [a]clean hands
and [b]a pure heart,
Who has not lifted up his
soul to an idol,
Nor [c]sworn deceitfully.
5 He shall receive blessing
from the LORD,
And righteousness from the
God of his salvation.
6 This *is* Jacob, the generation
of those who [a]seek Him,
Who seek Your face. Sē′lah

7 [a]Lift up your heads, O you
gates!
And be lifted up, you
everlasting doors!
[b]And the King of glory shall
come in.
8 Who *is* this King of glory?
The LORD strong and mighty,
The LORD mighty in [a]battle.
9 Lift up your heads, O you
gates!
Lift up, you everlasting
doors!
And the King of glory shall
come in.
10 Who is this King of glory?
The LORD of hosts,
He *is* the King of glory.
Sē′lah

PSALM 25

A Psalm of David.

TO [a]You, O LORD, I lift up my
soul.
2 O my God, I [a]trust in You;
Let me not be ashamed;
[b]Let not my enemies triumph
over me.
3 Indeed, let no one who
[1]waits on You be
ashamed;
Let those be ashamed who
deal treacherously
without cause.

4 [a]Show me Your ways, O LORD;
Teach me Your paths.
5 Lead me in Your truth and
teach me,
For You *are* the God of my
salvation;
On You I wait all the day.

6 Remember, O LORD, [a]Your
tender mercies and Your
lovingkindnesses,
For they *are* from of old.
7 Do not remember [a]the sins
of my youth, nor my
transgressions;

5 [a]Ps. 104:15 [b]Ps. 92:10
6 [1]So with LXX, Syr., Tg., Vg.; MT *return* [2]Or *To the end of my days*, lit. *For length of days*

PSALM 24
1 [a]1 Cor. 10:26, 28
2 [a]Ps. 89:11 [1]Lit. *rivers*
3 [a]Ps. 15:1–5
4 [a][Job 17:9] [b][Matt. 5:8] [c]Ps. 15:4
6 [a]Ps. 27:4, 8
7 [a]Is. 26:2 [b]Ps. 29:2, 9; 97:6
8 [a]Rev. 19:13–16

PSALM 25
1 [a]Ps. 86:4; 143:8
2 [a]Ps. 34:8 [b]Ps. 13:4; 41:11
3 [1]Waits for You in faith
4 [a]Ex. 33:13
6 [a]Ps. 103:17; 106:1
7 [a][Jer. 3:25]

[b]According to Your mercy remember me,
For Your goodness' sake, O LORD.

8 Good and upright *is* the LORD;
Therefore He teaches sinners in the way.
9 The humble He guides in justice,
And the humble He teaches His way.
10 All the paths of the LORD *are* mercy and truth,
To such as keep His covenant and His testimonies.
11 [a]For Your name's sake, O LORD,
Pardon my iniquity, for it *is* great.

12 Who *is* the man that fears the LORD?
[a]Him shall [1]He teach in the way [1]He chooses.
13 [a]He himself shall dwell in [1]prosperity,
And [b]his descendants shall inherit the earth.
14 [a]The secret of the LORD *is* with those who fear Him,
And He will show them His covenant.
15 [a]My eyes *are* ever toward the LORD,
For He shall [1]pluck my feet out of the net.

16 [a]Turn Yourself to me, and have mercy on me,
For I *am* [1]desolate and afflicted.
17 The troubles of my heart have enlarged;
Bring me out of my distresses!
18 [a]Look on my affliction and my pain,
And forgive all my sins.
19 Consider my enemies, for they are many;
And they hate me with [1]cruel hatred.
20 Keep my soul, and deliver me;
Let me not be ashamed, for I put my trust in You.
21 Let integrity and uprightness preserve me,
For I wait for You.

22 [a]Redeem Israel, O God,
Out of all their troubles!

PSALM 26

A Psalm of David.

VINDICATE [a]me, O LORD,
For I have [b]walked in my integrity.
[c]I have also trusted in the LORD;
I shall not slip.
2 [a]Examine me, O LORD, and [1]prove me;
Try my mind and my heart.
3 For Your lovingkindness *is* before my eyes,
And [a]I have walked in Your truth.
4 I have not [a]sat with idolatrous mortals,
Nor will I go in with hypocrites.
5 I have [a]hated the assembly of evildoers,
And will not sit with the wicked.

6 I will wash my hands in innocence;

---

7 [b]Ps. 51:1
11 [a]Ps. 31:3; 79:9; 109:21; 143:11
12 [a][Ps. 25:8; 37:23] [1]Or *he*
13 [a][Prov. 19:23] [b]Matt. 5:5 [1]Lit. *goodness*
14 [a][John 7:17]
15 [a][Ps. 123:2; 141:8] [1]Lit. *bring out*
16 [a]Ps. 69:16 [1]*lonely*
18 [a]2 Sam. 16:12
19 [1]*violent hatred*
22 [a][Ps. 130:8]

PSALM 26

1 [a]Ps. 7:8 [b]2 Kin. 20:3 [c][Ps. 13:5; 28:7]
2 [a]Ps. 17:3; 139:23 [1]*test me*
3 [a]2 Kin. 20:3
4 [a]Ps. 1:1
5 [a]Ps. 31:6; 139:21

So I will go about Your altar,
O LORD,
7 That I may proclaim
with the voice of
thanksgiving,
And tell of all Your
wondrous works.
8 LORD, [a]I have loved the
habitation of Your house,
And the place [1]where Your
glory dwells.

9 [a]Do[1] not gather my soul with
sinners,
Nor my life with
bloodthirsty men,
10 In whose hands *is* a sinister
scheme,
And whose right hand is full
of [a]bribes.

11 But as for me, I will walk in
my integrity;
Redeem me and be merciful
to me.
12 [a]My foot stands in an even
place;
In the congregations I will
bless the LORD.

PSALM 27

A Psalm of David.

THE LORD *is* my [a]light and my
salvation;
Whom shall I fear?
The [b]LORD *is* the strength of
my life;
Of whom shall I be afraid?
☆2 When the wicked came
against me
To [a]eat[1] up my flesh,
My enemies and foes,
They stumbled and fell.
3 [a]Though an army may
encamp against me,
My heart shall not fear;
Though war may rise
against me,
In this I *will be* confident.

4 [a]One *thing* I have desired of
the LORD,
That will I seek:
That I may [b]dwell in the
house of the LORD
All the days of my life,
To behold the [1]beauty of the
LORD,
And to inquire in His
temple.
5 For [a]in the time of trouble
He shall hide me in His
pavilion;
In the secret place of His
tabernacle
He shall hide me;
He shall [b]set me high upon
a rock.

6 And now [a]my head shall
be [1]lifted up above my
enemies all around me;
Therefore I will offer
sacrifices of [2]joy in His
tabernacle;
I will sing, yes, I will sing
praises to the LORD.

7 Hear, O LORD, *when* I cry
with my voice!
Have mercy also upon me,
and answer me.
8 *When You said,* "Seek My
face,"
My heart said to You, "Your
face, LORD, I will seek."
9 [a]Do not hide Your face from
me;
Do not turn Your servant
away in anger;
You have been my help;
Do not leave me nor
forsake me,
O God of my salvation.

---

8 [a]Ps. 27:4; 84:1–4, 10 [1]Lit. *of the tabernacle of Your glory*
9 [a]Ps. 28:3 [1]*Do not take away*
10 [a]1 Sam. 8:3
12 [a]Ps. 40:2

PSALM 27

1 [a][Mic. 7:8] [b]Ps. 62:7; 118:14
2 [a]Ps. 14:4; John 18:6 [1]*devour*
3 [a]Ps. 3:6
4 [a]Ps. 26:8; 65:4 [b]Luke 2:37 [1]*delightfulness*
5 [a]Ps. 31:20; 91:1 [b]Ps. 40:2
6 [a]Ps. 3:3 [1]Lifted up in honor [2]*joyous shouts*
9 [a]Ps. 69:17; 143:7

10 [a]When my father and my
mother forsake me,
Then the LORD will take care
of me.

11 [a]Teach me Your way, O LORD,
And lead me in a smooth
path, because of my
enemies.
☆ 12 Do not deliver me to the will
of my adversaries;
For [a]false witnesses have
risen against me,
And such as breathe out
violence.
13 *I would have lost heart,*
unless I had believed
That I would see the
goodness of the LORD
[a]In the land of the living.

14 [a]Wait[1] on the LORD;
Be of good courage,
And He shall strengthen
your heart;
Wait, I say, on the LORD!

PSALM 28

A Psalm of David.

TO You I will cry, O LORD my
Rock:
[a]Do not be silent to me,
[b]Lest, if You *are* silent to me,
I become like those who go
down to the pit.
2 Hear the voice of my
supplications
When I cry to You,
[a]When I lift up my hands
[b]toward Your holy
sanctuary.

3 Do not [1]take me away with
the wicked
And with the workers of
iniquity,
[a]Who speak peace to their
neighbors,
But evil *is* in their hearts.
4 [a]Give them according to their
deeds,
And according to the
wickedness of their
endeavors;
Give them according to the
work of their hands;
Render to them what they
deserve.
5 Because [a]they do not regard
the works of the LORD,
Nor the operation of His
hands,
He shall destroy them
And not build them up.

6 Blessed *be* the LORD,
Because He has heard
the voice of my
supplications!
7 The LORD *is* [a]my strength
and my shield;
My heart [b]trusted in Him,
and I am helped;
Therefore my heart greatly
rejoices,
And with my song I will
praise Him.

8 The LORD *is* [1]their strength,
And He *is* the [a]saving refuge
of His [2]anointed.
9 Save Your people,
And bless [a]Your inheritance;
Shepherd them also,
[b]And bear them up forever.

PSALM 29

A Psalm of David.

GIVE[1] [a]unto the LORD, O you
mighty ones,
Give unto the LORD glory
and strength.

---

10 [a]Is. 49:15
11 [a]Ps. 25:4; 86:11; 119:33
12 [a]Ps. 35:11; Matt. 26:60, 61; Mark 14:56
13 [a]Ezek. 26:20
14 [a]Is. 25:9
[1]Wait in faith

PSALM 28

1 [a]Ps. 35:22; 39:12; 83:1
[b]Ps. 88:4; 143:7
2 [a]Ps. 5:7
[b]Ps. 138:2
3 [a]Ps. 12:2; 55:21; 62:4
[1]*drag*
4 [a][Rev. 18:6; 22:12]
5 [a]Is. 5:12
7 [a]Ps. 18:2; 59:17
[b]Ps. 13:5; 112:7
8 [a]Ps. 20:6
[1]So with MT, Tg.; LXX, Syr., Vg. *the strength of His people*
[2]Commissioned one, Heb. *messiah*
9 [a][Deut. 9:29; 32:9]
[b]Deut. 1:31

PSALM 29

1 [a]1 Chr. 16:28, 29
[1]*Ascribe*

2 [1]Give unto the LORD the
glory [2]due to His name;
Worship the LORD in [a]the
[3]beauty of holiness.

3 The voice of the LORD *is*
over the waters;
[a]The God of glory
thunders;
The LORD *is* over many
waters.
4 The voice of the LORD *is*
powerful;
The voice of the LORD *is* full
of majesty.

5 The voice of the LORD
breaks [a]the cedars,
Yes, the LORD splinters the
cedars of Lebanon.
6 [a]He makes them also skip
like a calf,
Lebanon and [b]Sir'i·on like a
young wild ox.
7 The voice of the LORD
[1]divides the flames of
fire.

8 The voice of the LORD
shakes the wilderness;
The LORD shakes the
Wilderness of [a]Kā'desh.
9 The voice of the LORD makes
the [a]deer give birth,
And strips the forests
bare;
And in His temple everyone
says, "Glory!"

10 The [a]LORD sat *enthroned* at
the Flood,
And [b]the LORD sits as King
forever.
11 [a]The LORD will give strength
to His people;
The LORD will bless His
people with peace.

2 [a]2 Chr. 20:21 [1]*Ascribe* [2]Lit. *of His name* [3]*majesty*
3 [a][Job 37:4, 5]
5 [a]Is. 2:13; 14:8
6 [a]Ps. 114:4 [b]Deut. 3:9
7 [1]*stirs up*, lit. *hews out*
8 [a]Num. 13:26
9 [a]Job 39:1
10 [a]Gen. 6:17 [b]Ps. 10:16
11 [a]Ps. 28:8; 68:35

PSALM 30

title [a]Deut. 20:5
1 [a]Ps. 28:9 [b]Ps. 25:2
2 [a]Ps. 6:2; 103:3
3 [a]Ps. 86:13 [1]So with Qr., Tg.; Kt., LXX, Syr., Vg. *from those who descend to the pit*
4 [a]Ps. 97:12 [1]Or *His holiness*
5 [a]Ps. 103:9 [b]Ps. 63:3 [1]*a shout of joy*
6 [1]*shaken*
7 [a][Ps. 104:29; 143:7]
9 [a][Ps. 6:5]

PSALM 30

A Psalm. A Song [a]at the
dedication of the house of
David.

I WILL extol You, O LORD, for
You have [a]lifted me up,
And have not let my foes
[b]rejoice over me.
2 O LORD my God, I cried out
to You,
And You [a]healed me.
3 O LORD, [a]You brought my
soul up from the grave;
You have kept me alive,
[1]that I should not go
down to the pit.

4 [a]Sing praise to the LORD, you
saints of His,
And give thanks at the
remembrance of [1]His
holy name.
5 For [a]His anger *is but for* a
moment,
[b]His favor *is for* life;
Weeping may endure for a
night,
But [1]joy *comes* in the
morning.

6 Now in my prosperity I said,
"I shall never be [1]moved."
7 LORD, by Your favor You
have made my mountain
stand strong;
[a]You hid Your face, *and* I was
troubled.

8 I cried out to You, O LORD;
And to the LORD I made
supplication:
9 "What profit *is there* in my
blood,
When I go down to the pit?
[a]Will the dust praise You?
Will it declare Your truth?

10 Hear, O LORD, and have
mercy on me;
LORD, be my helper!"

11 [a]You have turned for me my
mourning into dancing;
You have put off [1]my
sackcloth and clothed
me with gladness,
12 To the end that *my* [1]glory
may sing praise to You
and not be silent.
O LORD my God, I will give
thanks to You forever.

PSALM 31

To the Chief Musician. A Psalm of David.

IN [a]You, O LORD, I [1]put my
trust;
Let me never be ashamed;
Deliver me in Your
righteousness.
2 [a]Bow down Your ear to me,
Deliver me speedily;
Be my rock of [1]refuge,
A [2]fortress of defense to
save me.

3 [a]For You *are* my rock and my
fortress;
Therefore, [b]for Your name's
sake,
Lead me and guide me.
4 Pull me out of the net which
they have secretly laid
for me,
For You *are* my strength.
5 [a]Into Your hand I commit my
spirit;
You have redeemed me,
O LORD God of [b]truth.

6 I have hated those [a]who
regard useless idols;
But I trust in the LORD.
7 I will be glad and rejoice in
Your mercy,
For You have considered my
trouble;
You have [a]known my soul in
[1]adversities,
8 And have not [a]shut[1] me
up into the hand of the
enemy;
[b]You have set my feet in a
wide place.

9 Have mercy on me, O LORD,
for I am in trouble;
[a]My eye wastes away with
grief,
Yes, my soul and my [1]body!
10 For my life is spent with
grief,
And my years with sighing;
My strength fails because of
my iniquity,
And my bones waste away.
11 [a]I am a [1]reproach among all
my enemies,
But [b]especially among my
neighbors,
And *am* repulsive to my
acquaintances;
[c]Those who see me outside
flee from me.
12 [a]I am forgotten like a dead
man, out of mind;
I am like a [1]broken vessel.
13 [a]For I hear the slander of
many;
[b]Fear *is* on every side;
While they [c]take counsel
together against me,
They scheme to take away
my life.

14 But as for me, I trust in You,
O LORD;
I say, "You *are* my God."
15 My times *are* in Your [a]hand;
Deliver me from the hand of
my enemies,

11 [a]Jer. 31:4 [1]The sackcloth of my mourning
12 [1]*soul*

PSALM 31

1 [a]Ps. 22:5 [1]*have taken refuge*
2 [a]Ps. 17:6; 71:2; 86:1; 102:2 [1]*strength* [2]Lit. *house of fortresses*
3 [a][Ps. 18:2] [b]Ps. 23:3; 25:11
5 [a]Luke 23:46 [b][Deut. 32:4]
6 [a]Jon. 2:8
7 [a][John 10:27] [1]*troubles*
8 [a][Deut. 32:30] [b][Ps. 4:1; 18:19] [1]*given me over*
9 [a]Ps. 6:7 [1]Lit. *belly*
11 [a][Is. 53:4] [b]Job 19:13 [c]Ps. 64:8 [1]*despised thing*
12 [a]Ps. 88:4, 5 [1]Lit. *perishing*
13 [a]Jer. 20:10 [b]Lam. 2:22 [c]Matt. 27:1
15 [a][Job 14:5; 24:1]

And from those who
persecute me.
16 [a]Make Your face shine upon
Your servant;
Save me for Your mercies'
sake.
17 [a]Do not let me be ashamed,
O LORD, for I have called
upon You;
Let the wicked be ashamed;
[b]Let them be silent in the
grave.
18 [a]Let the lying lips be put to
silence,
Which [b]speak insolent
things proudly and
contemptuously against
the righteous.

19 [a]Oh, how great *is* Your
goodness,
Which You have laid up for
those who fear You,
Which You have prepared
for those who trust in
You
In the presence of the sons
of men!
20 [a]You shall hide them in the
secret place of Your
presence
From the plots of man;
[b]You shall keep them secretly
in a [1]pavilion
From the strife of tongues.

21 Blessed *be* the LORD,
For [a]He has shown me His
marvelous kindness in a
[1]strong city!
22 For I said in my haste,
"I am cut off from before
Your eyes";
Nevertheless You heard
the voice of my
supplications
When I cried out to You.

16 [a]Ps. 4:6; 80:3
17 [a]Ps. 25:2, 20 [b]Ps. 94:17; 115:17
18 [a]Ps. 109:2; 120:2 [b]Ps. 94:4
19 [a][Rom. 2:4; 11:22]
20 [a][Ps. 27:5; 32:7] [b]Job 5:21 [1]*shelter*
21 [a][Ps. 17:7] [1]*fortified*
24 [a][Ps. 27:14]

PSALM 32
title [1]Heb. *Maschil*
1 [a][Ps. 85:2; 103:3]
2 [a][2 Cor. 5:19] [b]John 1:47 [1]*charge his account with*
4 [a]1 Sam. 5:6
5 [a][Prov. 28:13]
6 [a][1 Tim. 1:16] [b]Is. 55:6

23 Oh, love the LORD, all you
His saints!
For the LORD preserves the
faithful,
And fully repays the proud
person.
24 [a]Be of good courage,
And He shall strengthen
your heart,
All you who hope in the
LORD.

PSALM 32

A Psalm of David. A
[1]Contemplation.

BLESSED *is he whose*
[a]transgression *is* forgiven,
Whose sin *is* covered.
2 Blessed *is* the man to whom
the LORD [a]does not
[1]impute iniquity,
And [b]in whose spirit *there is*
no deceit.

3 When I kept silent, my
bones grew old
Through my groaning all
the day long.
4 For day and night Your
[a]hand was heavy
upon me;
My vitality was turned into
the drought of summer.
Sēlah
5 I acknowledged my sin to
You,
And my iniquity I have not
hidden.
[a]I said, "I will confess my
transgressions to the
LORD,"
And You forgave the iniquity
of my sin. Sēlah

6 [a]For this cause everyone who
is godly shall [b]pray to You

In a time when You may be found;
Surely in a flood of great waters
They shall not come near him.
7 [a]You *are* my hiding place;
You shall preserve me from trouble;
You shall surround me with [b]songs of deliverance.
Sē′lah

8 I will instruct you and teach you in the way you should go;
I will guide you with My eye.
9 Do not be like the [a]horse *or* like the mule,
Which have no understanding,
Which must be harnessed with bit and bridle,
Else they will not come near you.

10 [a]Many sorrows *shall be* to the wicked;
But [b]he who trusts in the LORD, mercy shall surround him.
11 [a]Be glad in the LORD and rejoice, you righteous;
And shout for joy, all *you* upright in heart!

PSALM 33

REJOICE [a]in the LORD, O you righteous!
For praise from the upright is beautiful.
2 Praise the LORD with the harp;
[1]Make melody to Him with an instrument of ten strings.
3 Sing to Him a new song;
Play skillfully with a shout of joy.

4 For the word of the LORD *is* right,
And all His work *is done* in truth.
5 He loves righteousness and justice;
The earth is full of the goodness of the LORD.

6 [a]By the word of the LORD the heavens were made,
And all the [b]host of them [c]by the breath of His mouth.
7 [a]He gathers the waters of the sea together [1]as a heap;
He lays up the deep in storehouses.

8 Let all the earth fear the LORD;
Let all the inhabitants of the world stand in awe of Him.
9 For [a]He spoke, and it was *done;*
He commanded, and it stood fast.

10 [a]The LORD brings the counsel of the nations to nothing;
He makes the plans of the peoples of no effect.
11 [a]The counsel of the LORD stands forever,
The plans of His heart to all generations.
12 Blessed *is* the nation whose God *is* the LORD,

---

7 [a]Ps. 9:9 [b]Ex. 15:1
9 [a]Prov. 26:3
10 [a][Rom. 2:9] [b]Prov. 16:20
11 [a]Ps. 64:10; 68:3; 97:12

PSALM 33

1 [a]Ps. 32:11; 97:12
2 [1]Lit. *Sing to Him*
6 [a][Heb. 11:3] [b]Gen. 2:1 [c][Job 26:13]
7 [a]Job 26:10; 38:8 [1]LXX, Tg., Vg. *in a vessel*
9 [a]Gen. 1:3
10 [a]Is. 8:10; 19:3
11 [a][Job 23:13]

The people He has [a]chosen
as His own inheritance.

13 [a]The LORD looks from
heaven;
He sees all the sons of
men.
14 From the place of His
dwelling He looks
On all the inhabitants of
the earth;
15 He fashions their hearts
individually;
[a]He [1]considers all their
works.

16 [a]No king *is* saved by the
multitude of an army;
A mighty man is not
delivered by great
strength.
17 [a]A horse *is* a [1]vain hope for
safety;
Neither shall it deliver *any*
by its great strength.

18 [a]Behold, the eye of the LORD
is on those who fear
Him,
On those who hope in His
mercy,
19 To deliver their soul from
death,
And [a]to keep them alive in
famine.

20 Our soul waits for the
LORD;
He *is* our help and our
shield.
21 For our heart shall rejoice in
Him,
Because we have trusted in
His holy name.
22 Let Your mercy, O LORD, be
upon us,
Just as we hope in You.

12 [a][Ex. 19:5]
13 [a]Job 28:24
15 [a][Jer. 32:19] [1]*understands*
16 [a]Ps. 44:6; 60:11
17 [a][Prov. 21:31] [1]*false*
18 [a][Job 36:7]
19 [a]Job 5:20

PSALM 34

title [a]1 Sam. 21:10–15
1 [a][Eph. 5:20]
4 [a][Matt. 7:7]
7 [a]Dan. 6:22 [b]2 Kin. 6:17 [1]Or *Angel*
8 [a]1 Pet. 2:3 [b]Ps. 2:12
9 [1]*lack*

PSALM 34

A *Psalm* of David [a]when he
pretended madness before
A·bim′e·lech, who drove him
away, and he departed.

I WILL [a]bless the LORD at all
times;
His praise *shall* continually
be in my mouth.
2 My soul shall make its boast
in the LORD;
The humble shall hear *of it*
and be glad.
3 Oh, magnify the LORD with
me,
And let us exalt His name
together.

4 I [a]sought the LORD, and He
heard me,
And delivered me from all
my fears.
5 They looked to Him and
were radiant,
And their faces were not
ashamed.
6 This poor man cried out,
and the LORD heard
him,
And saved him out of all his
troubles.
7 [a]The [1]angel of the LORD
[b]encamps all around
those who fear Him,
And delivers them.

8 Oh, [a]taste and see that the
LORD *is* good;
[b]Blessed *is* the man *who*
trusts in Him!
9 Oh, fear the LORD, you His
saints!
There is no [1]want to those
who fear Him.
10 The young lions lack and
suffer hunger;

[a]But those who seek the
LORD shall not lack any
good *thing*.

11 Come, you children, listen to
me;
[a]I will teach you the fear of
the LORD.
12 [a]Who *is* the man *who* desires
life,
And loves *many* days, that
he may see good?
13 Keep your tongue from
evil,
And your lips from speaking
[a]deceit.
14 [a]Depart from evil and do
good;
[b]Seek peace and pursue it.
15 [a]The eyes of the LORD *are* on
the righteous,
And His ears *are open* to
their cry.
16 [a]The face of the LORD *is*
against those who do
evil,
[b]To [1]cut off the remembrance
of them from the earth.

17 *The righteous* cry out, and
[a]the LORD hears,
And delivers them out of all
their troubles.
18 [a]The LORD *is* near [b]to those
who have a broken
heart,
And saves such as [1]have a
contrite spirit.

19 [a]Many *are* the afflictions of
the righteous,
[b]But the LORD delivers him
out of them all.
☆ 20 He guards all his bones;
[a]Not one of them is broken.
21 [a]Evil shall slay the wicked,
And those who hate the
righteous shall be
[1]condemned.
22 The LORD [a]redeems the soul
of His servants,
And none of those who
trust in Him shall be
condemned.

PSALM 35

A Psalm of David.

PLEAD[1] *my cause,* O LORD,
with those who strive
with me;
Fight against those who
fight against me.
2 Take hold of shield and
[1]buckler,
And stand up for my help.
3 Also draw out the spear,
And stop those who
pursue me.
Say to my soul,
"I *am* your salvation."

4 [a]Let those be put to shame
and brought to dishonor
Who seek after my life;
Let those be [b]turned back
and brought to confusion
Who plot my hurt.
5 [a]Let them be like chaff
before the wind,
And let the [1]angel of the
LORD chase *them.*
6 Let their way be [a]dark and
slippery,
And let the angel of the
LORD pursue them.
7 For without cause they have
[a]hidden their net for me
in a pit,
Which they have dug
without cause for my
life.

10 [a][Ps. 84:11]
11 [a]Ps. 32:8
12 [a][1 Pet. 3:10–12]
13 [a][Eph. 4:25]
14 [a]Ps. 37:27 [b][Rom. 14:19]
15 [a]Job 36:7
16 [a]Lev. 17:10 [b][Prov. 10:7] [1]*destroy*
17 [a]Ps. 34:6; 145:19
18 [a][Ps. 145:18] [b][Is. 57:15] [1]*are crushed in spirit*
19 [a]Prov. 24:16 [b]Ps. 34:4, 6, 17
20 [a]John 19:33, 36
21 [a]Ps. 94:23; 140:11 [1]*held guilty*
22 [a]1 Kin. 1:29

PSALM 35
1 [1]*Contend for me*
2 [1]A small shield
4 [a]Ps. 40:14, 15; 70:2, 3 [b]Ps. 129:5
5 [a]Job 21:18 [1]Or *Angel*
6 [a]Ps. 73:18
7 [a]Ps. 9:15

8 [1]Let [a]destruction come upon
him unexpectedly,
And let his net that he has
hidden catch himself;
Into that very destruction let
him fall.

9 And my soul shall be joyful
in the LORD;
It shall rejoice in His
salvation.
10 [a]All my bones shall say,
"LORD, [b]who *is* like You,
Delivering the poor from
him who is too strong
for him,
Yes, the poor and the needy
from him who plunders
him?"

☆ 11 Fierce [a]witnesses rise up;
They ask me *things* that I do
not know.
12 [a]They reward me evil for
good,
To the sorrow of my soul.
13 But as for me, [a]when they
were sick,
My clothing *was* sackcloth;
I humbled myself with
fasting;
And my prayer would return
to my own [1]heart.
14 I paced about as though
he were my friend *or*
brother;
I bowed down [1]heavily, as
one who mourns *for his*
mother.

15 But in my [1]adversity they
rejoiced
And gathered together;
Attackers gathered against
me,
And I did not know *it;*
They tore *at me* and did not
cease;

8 [a][1 Thess. 5:3] [1]Lit. *Let destruction he does not know come upon him,*

10 [a]Ps. 51:8 [b][Ex. 15:11]

11 [a]Matt. 26:3, 4, 59–66; 27:1, 2

12 [a]John 10:32

13 [a]Job 30:25 [1]Lit. *bosom*

14 [1]*in mourning*

15 [1]*limping, stumbling*

17 [a][Hab. 1:13]

18 [1]*a mighty*

19 [a]Ps. 69:4; 109:3; [John 15:24, 25]

16 With ungodly mockers at
feasts
They gnashed at me with
their teeth.

17 Lord, how long will You
[a]look on?
Rescue me from their
destructions,
My precious *life* from the
lions.
18 I will give You thanks in the
great assembly;
I will praise You among
[1]many people.

19 [a]Let them not rejoice over ☆
me who are wrongfully
my enemies;
Nor let them wink with the
eye who hate me without
a cause.
20 For they do not speak peace,
But they devise deceitful
matters
Against *the* quiet ones in
the land.
21 They also opened their
mouth wide against me,
And said, "Aha, aha!
Our eyes have seen *it.*"

22 *This* You have seen, O LORD;
Do not keep silence.
O Lord, do not be far
from me.
23 Stir up Yourself, and awake
to my vindication,
To my cause, my God and
my Lord.
24 Vindicate me, O LORD my
God, according to Your
righteousness;
And let them not rejoice
over me.
25 Let them not say in their
hearts, "Ah, so we would
have it!"

Let them not say, "We have
swallowed him up."
26 Let them be ashamed and
brought to mutual
confusion
Who rejoice at my hurt;
Let them be [a]clothed with
shame and dishonor
Who exalt themselves
against me.

27 [a]Let them shout for joy and
be glad,
Who favor my righteous
cause;
And let them say
continually,
"Let the LORD be magnified,
Who has pleasure in
the prosperity of His
servant."
28 And my tongue shall speak
of Your righteousness
And of Your praise all the
day long.

PSALM 36

To the Chief Musician. *A Psalm* of David the servant of the LORD.

AN oracle within my heart
concerning the
transgression of the
wicked:
[a]*There is* no fear of God
before his eyes.
2 For he flatters himself in his
own eyes,
When he finds out his
iniquity *and* when he
hates.
3 The words of his mouth *are*
wickedness and deceit;
[a]He has ceased to be wise
and to do good.
4 [a]He devises wickedness on
his bed;
He sets himself [b]in a way
that is not good;
He does not [1]abhor [c]evil.

5 Your mercy, O LORD, *is* in
the heavens;
Your faithfulness *reaches* to
the clouds.
6 Your righteousness *is* like
the [1]great mountains;
[a]Your judgments *are* a great
deep;
O LORD, You preserve man
and beast.

7 How precious *is* Your
lovingkindness, O God!
Therefore the children of
men [a]put their trust
under the shadow of
Your wings.
8 [a]They are abundantly
satisfied with the
fullness of Your house,
And You give them drink
from [b]the river of Your
pleasures.
9 [a]For with You *is* the fountain
of life;
[b]In Your light we see light.

10 Oh, continue Your
lovingkindness to those
who know You,
And Your righteousness to
the upright in heart.
11 Let not the foot of pride
come against me,
And let not the hand of the
wicked drive me away.
12 There the workers of
iniquity have fallen;
They have been cast down
and are not able to rise.

---

26 [a]Ps. 109:29
27 [a]Rom. 12:15

PSALM 36

1 [a]Rom. 3:18
3 [a]Jer. 4:22
4 [a]Prov. 4:16 [b]Is. 65:2 [c][Rom. 12:9] [1]*reject, loathe*
6 [a][Rom. 11:33] [1]Lit. *mountains of God*
7 [a]Ps. 17:8; 57:1; 91:4
8 [a]Ps. 63:5; 65:4 [b]Rev. 22:1
9 [a][Jer. 2:13] [b][1 Pet. 2:9]

PSALM 37

A Psalm of David.

DO[a] not fret because of
evildoers,
Nor be envious of the
workers of iniquity.
2 For they shall soon be cut
down [a]like the grass,
And wither as the green
herb.

3 Trust in the LORD, and do
good;
Dwell in the land, and feed
on His faithfulness.
4 [a]Delight yourself also in the
LORD,
And He shall give you the
desires of your [b]heart.

5 [a]Commit[1] your way to the
LORD,
Trust also in Him,
And He shall bring *it* to
pass.
6 [a]He shall bring forth your
righteousness as the
light,
And your justice as the
noonday.

7 Rest in the LORD, [a]and wait
patiently for Him;
Do not fret because of him
who [b]prospers in his
way,
Because of the man who
brings wicked schemes
to pass.
8 [a]Cease from anger, and
forsake wrath;
[b]Do not fret—*it* only *causes*
harm.

9 For evildoers shall be [1]cut
off;
But those who wait on the
LORD,
They shall [a]inherit the earth.
10 For [a]yet a little while and
the wicked *shall be* no
more;
Indeed, [b]you will look
carefully for his place,
But it *shall be* no *more.*
11 [a]But the meek shall inherit
the earth,
And shall delight
themselves in the
abundance of peace.

12 The wicked plots against the
just,
[a]And gnashes at him with his
teeth.
13 [a]The Lord laughs at him,
For He sees that [b]his day is
coming.
14 The wicked have drawn the
sword
And have bent their bow,
To cast down the poor and
needy,
To slay those who are of
upright conduct.
15 Their sword shall enter their
own heart,
And their bows shall be
broken.

16 [a]A little that a righteous man
has
Is better than the riches of
many wicked.
17 For the arms of the wicked
shall be broken,
But the LORD upholds the
righteous.

18 The LORD knows the days of
the upright,
And their inheritance shall
be forever.

PSALM 37

1 [a]Ps. 73:3
2 [a]Ps. 90:5, 6; 92:7
4 [a]Is. 58:14 [b]Ps. 21:2; 145:19
5 [a][Ps. 55:22] [1]Lit. *Roll off onto*
6 [a]Job 11:17
7 [a][Lam. 3:26] [b][Ps. 73:3–12]
8 [a][Eph. 4:26] [b]Ps. 73:3
9 [a][Is. 57:13; 60:21] [1]*destroyed*
10 [a][Heb. 10:37] [b]Job 7:10
11 [a][Matt. 5:5]
12 [a]Ps. 35:16
13 [a]Ps. 2:4; 59:8 [b]1 Sam. 26:10
16 [a]Prov. 15:16; 16:8

19 They shall not be ashamed
in the evil time,
And in the days of famine
they shall be satisfied.
20 But the wicked shall perish;
And the enemies of the
LORD,
Like the splendor of the
meadows, shall vanish.
Into smoke they shall vanish
away.

21 The wicked borrows and
does not repay,
But [a]the righteous shows
mercy and gives.
22 [a]For *those* blessed by Him
shall inherit the earth,
But *those* cursed by Him
shall be [1]cut off.

23 [a]The steps of a *good* man are
[1]ordered by the LORD,
And He delights in his way.
24 [a]Though he fall, he shall not
be utterly cast down;
For the LORD upholds *him*
with His hand.

25 I have been young, and *now*
am old;
Yet I have not seen the
righteous forsaken,
Nor his descendants
begging bread.
26 [a]*He is* [1]ever merciful, and
lends;
And his descendants *are*
blessed.

27 Depart from evil, and do
good;
And dwell forevermore.
28 For the LORD loves justice,
And does not forsake His
saints;
They are preserved forever,
But the descendants of the
wicked shall be cut off.
29 [a]The righteous shall inherit
the land,
And dwell in it forever.

30 [a]The mouth of the righteous
speaks wisdom,
And his tongue talks of
justice.
31 The law of his God *is* in his
heart;
None of his steps shall
[1]slide.

32 The wicked [a]watches the
righteous,
And seeks to slay him.
33 The LORD [a]will not leave him
in his hand,
Nor condemn him when he
is judged.

34 [a]Wait on the LORD,
And keep His way,
And He shall exalt you to
inherit the land;
When the wicked are cut
off, you shall see *it*.
35 I have seen the wicked in
great power,
And spreading himself like
a native green tree.
36 Yet [1]he passed away, and
behold, he *was* no
more;
Indeed I sought him, but he
could not be found.

37 Mark the blameless *man*,
and observe the upright;
For the future of *that* man *is*
peace.
38 [a]But the transgressors shall
be destroyed together;
The future of the wicked
shall be cut off.

21 [a]Ps. 112:5, 9
22 [a][Prov. 3:33] [1]*destroyed*
23 [a][1 Sam. 2:9] [1]*established*
24 [a]Prov. 24:16
26 [a][Deut. 15:8] [1]Lit. *all the day*
29 [a]Prov. 2:21
30 [a][Matt. 12:35]
31 [1]*slip*
32 [a]Ps. 10:8; 17:11
33 [a][2 Pet. 2:9]
34 [a]Ps. 27:14; 37:9
36 [1]So with MT, LXX, Tg.; Syr., Vg. *I passed by*
38 [a][Ps. 1:4–6; 37:20, 28]

39 But the salvation of the righteous *is* from the LORD;
He *is* their strength [a]in the time of trouble.
40 And [a]the LORD shall help them and deliver them;
He shall deliver them from the wicked,
And save them,
[b]Because they trust in Him.

PSALM 38

A Psalm of David. [a]To bring to remembrance.

O LORD, do not [a]rebuke me in Your wrath,
Nor chasten me in Your hot displeasure!
2 For Your arrows pierce me deeply,
And Your hand presses me down.

3 *There is* no soundness in my flesh
Because of Your anger,
Nor *any* health in my bones
Because of my sin.
4 For my iniquities have gone over my head;
Like a heavy burden they are too heavy for me.
5 My wounds are foul *and* festering
Because of my foolishness.

6 I am [1]troubled, I am bowed down greatly;
I go mourning all the day long.
7 For my loins are full of inflammation,
And *there is* no soundness in my flesh.
8 I am feeble and severely broken;
I groan because of the turmoil of my heart.

9 Lord, all my desire *is* before You;
And my sighing is not hidden from You.
10 My heart pants, my strength fails me;
As for the light of my eyes, it also has gone from me.

11 My loved ones and my friends [a]stand aloof from my plague,
And my relatives stand afar off.
12 Those also who seek my life lay snares *for me;*
Those who seek my hurt speak of destruction,
And plan deception all the day long.

13 But I, like a deaf *man*, do not hear; ☆
And *I am* like a [a]mute *who* does not open his mouth.
14 Thus I am like a man who does not hear,
And in whose mouth *is* no response.

15 For [1]in You, O LORD, [a]I hope;
You will [2]hear, O Lord my God.
16 For I said, "*Hear me,* lest they rejoice over me,
Lest, when my foot slips, they exalt *themselves* against me."

17 [a]For I *am* ready to fall,
And my sorrow *is* continually before me.

39 [a]Ps. 9:9; 37:19
40 [a]Is. 31:5 [b]1 Chr. 5:20
PSALM 38
title [a]Ps. 70:title
1 [a]Ps. 6:1
6 [1]Lit. *bent down*
11 [a]Ps. 31:11; 88:18
13 [a]Matt. 26:62, 63; 27:12–14
15 [a][Ps. 39:7] [1]*I wait for You, O LORD* [2]*answer*
17 [a]Ps. 51:3

18 For I will [a]declare my
iniquity;
I will be [b]in [1]anguish over
my sin.
19 But my enemies *are*
vigorous, *and* they are
strong;
And those who hate
me wrongfully have
multiplied.
20 Those also [a]who render evil
for good,
They are my adversaries,
because I follow *what is*
good.

21 Do not forsake me, O LORD;
O my God, [a]be not far from
me!
22 Make haste to help me,
O Lord, my salvation!

PSALM 39

To the Chief Musician. To
Je·dū'thun. A Psalm of David.

I SAID, "I will guard my ways,
Lest I sin with my [a]tongue;
I will restrain my mouth
with a muzzle,
While the wicked are before
me."
2 [a]I was mute with silence,
I held my peace *even* from
good;
And my sorrow was stirred
up.
3 My heart was hot within
me;
While I was [1]musing, the
fire burned.
Then I spoke with my
tongue:

4 "LORD, [a]make me to know my
end,
And what *is* the measure of
my days,
That I may know how frail
I *am*.
5 Indeed, You have made my
days *as* handbreadths,
And my age *is* as nothing
before You;
Certainly every man at his
best state *is* but [a]vapor.
Sē'lah
6 Surely every man walks
about like a shadow;
Surely they [1]busy
themselves in vain;
He heaps up *riches*,
And does not know who
will gather them.

7 "And now, Lord, what do I
wait for?
My [a]hope *is* in You.
8 Deliver me from all my
transgressions;
Do not make me [a]the
reproach of the foolish.
9 [a]I was mute, I did not open
my mouth,
Because it was [b]You who
did *it*.
10 [a]Remove Your plague from
me;
I am consumed by the blow
of Your hand.
11 When with rebukes You
correct man for iniquity,
You make his beauty [a]melt
away like a moth;
Surely every man *is* vapor.
Sē'lah

12 "Hear my prayer, O LORD,
And give ear to my cry;
Do not be silent at my tears;
For I *am* a stranger with
You,
A sojourner, [a]as all my
fathers *were*.

18 [a]Ps. 32:5 [b][2 Cor. 7:9, 10] [1]*anxiety*
20 [a]Ps. 35:12
21 [a]Ps. 22:19; 35:22

PSALM 39

1 [a][James 3:5–12]
2 [a]Ps. 38:13
3 [1]*meditating*
4 [a]Ps. 90:12; 119:84
5 [a]Ps. 62:9
6 [1]*make an uproar for nothing*
7 [a]Ps. 38:15
8 [a]Ps. 44:13; 79:4; 119:22
9 [a]Ps. 39:2 [b]Job 2:10
10 [a]Job 9:34; 13:21
11 [a]Job 13:28
12 [a]Gen. 47:9

13 [a]Remove Your gaze from
me, that I may regain
strength,
Before I go away and [b]am
no more."

PSALM 40

To the Chief Musician. A Psalm
of David.

I [a]WAITED patiently for the
LORD;
And He inclined to me,
And heard my cry.
2 He also brought me up out
of a horrible pit,
Out of [a]the miry clay,
And [b]set my feet upon a
rock,
And established my steps.
3 [a]He has put a new song in
my mouth—
Praise to our God;
Many will see *it* and fear,
And will trust in the LORD.

4 [a]Blessed *is* that man who
makes the LORD his trust,
And does not respect the
proud, nor such as turn
aside to lies.
5 [a]Many, O LORD my God, *are*
Your wonderful works
Which You have done;
[b]And Your thoughts
toward us
Cannot be recounted to You
in order;
If I would declare and speak
of them,
They are more than can be
numbered.

☆ 6 [a]Sacrifice and offering You
did not desire;
My ears You have opened.
Burnt offering and sin
offering You did not
require.
7 [a]Then I said, "Behold, I come; ☆
In the scroll of the book *it is*
written of me.
8 [a]I delight to do Your will,
O my God,
And Your law *is* [b]within my
heart."

9 [a]I have proclaimed the good
news of righteousness
In the great assembly;
Indeed, [b]I do not restrain my
lips,
O LORD, You Yourself know.
10 [a]I have not hidden Your
righteousness within my
heart;
I have declared Your
faithfulness and Your
salvation;
I have not concealed Your
lovingkindness and Your
truth
From the great assembly.

11 Do not withhold Your
tender mercies from me,
O LORD;
[a]Let Your lovingkindness and
Your truth continually
preserve me.
12 For innumerable evils have
surrounded me;
[a]My iniquities have
overtaken me, so that I
am not able to look up;
They are more than the
hairs of my head;
Therefore my heart fails me.

13 [a]Be pleased, O LORD, to
deliver me;
O LORD, make haste to
help me!

---

13 [a]Job 7:19; 10:20, 21; 14:6 [b][Job 14:10]

PSALM 40

1 [a]Ps. 25:5; 27:14; 37:7

2 [a]Ps. 69:2, 14 [b]Ps. 27:5

3 [a]Ps. 32:7; 33:3

4 [a]Ps. 34:8; 84:12

5 [a]Job 9:10 [b][Is. 55:8]

6 [a][Heb. 10:5–9]

7 [a][Heb. 10:5–9]

8 [a][John 4:34; 6:38] [b][Jer. 31:33]

9 [a]Ps. 22:22, 25 [b]Ps. 119:13

10 [a]Acts 20:20, 27

11 [a]Ps. 61:7

12 [a]Ps. 38:4; 65:3

13 [a]Ps. 70:1

14 [a]Let them be ashamed and brought to mutual confusion
Who seek to destroy my [1]life;
Let them be driven backward and brought to dishonor
Who wish me evil.
15 Let them be [a]confounded because of their shame,
Who say to me, "Aha, aha!"

16 [a]Let all those who seek You rejoice and be glad in You;
Let such as love Your salvation [b]say continually,
"The LORD be magnified!"
17 [a]But I *am* poor and needy;
[b]*Yet* the LORD thinks upon me.
You *are* my help and my deliverer;
Do not delay, O my God.

PSALM 41

To the Chief Musician. A Psalm of David.

BLESSED *is* he who considers the [1]poor;
The LORD will deliver him in time of trouble.
2 The LORD will preserve him and keep him alive,
And he will be blessed on the earth;
[a]You will not deliver him to the will of his enemies.
3 The LORD will strengthen him on his bed of illness;
You will [1]sustain him on his sickbed.

4 I said, "LORD, be merciful to me;
[a]Heal my soul, for I have sinned against You."
5 My enemies speak evil of me:
"When will he die, and his name perish?"
6 And if he comes to see *me*, he speaks [1]lies;
His heart gathers iniquity to itself;
When he goes out, he tells *it*.

7 All who hate me whisper together against me;
Against me they [1]devise my hurt.
8 "An[1] evil disease," *they say*, "clings to him.
And *now* that he lies down, he will rise up no more."
9 [a]Even my own familiar friend in whom I trusted, ☆
[b]Who ate my bread,
Has [1]lifted up *his* heel against me.

10 But You, O LORD, be merciful to me, and raise me up,
That I may repay them.
11 By this I know that You are well pleased with me,
Because my enemy does not triumph over me.
12 As for me, You uphold me in my integrity,
And [a]set me before Your face forever.

13 [a]Blessed *be* the LORD God of Israel
From everlasting to everlasting!
Amen and Amen.

---

14 [a]Ps. 35:4, 26; 70:2; 71:13 [1]Lit. *soul*
15 [a]Ps. 73:19
16 [a]Ps. 70:4 [b]Ps. 35:27
17 [a]Ps. 70:5; 86:1; 109:22 [b]1 Pet. 5:7

PSALM 41
1 [1]*helpless* or *powerless*
2 [a]Ps. 27:12
3 [1]*restore*
4 [a]Ps. 6:2; 103:3; 147:3
6 [1]*empty words*
7 [1]*plot*
8 [1]Lit. *A thing of Belial*
9 [a]2 Sam. 15:12 [b]Matt. 26:14–16, 21–25, 47–50; John 13:18, 21–30; Acts 1:16, 17 [1]Acted as a traitor
12 [a][Job 36:7]
13 [a]Ps. 72:18, 19; 89:52; 106:48; 150:6

BOOK TWO
Psalms 42—72

PSALM 42

To the Chief Musician. A [1]Contemplation of the sons of Kō'rah.

AS the deer [1]pants for the water brooks,
So pants my soul for You, O God.
2 [a]My soul thirsts for God, for the [b]living God.
When shall I come and [1]appear before God?
3 [a]My tears have been my food day and night,
While they continually say to me,
[b]"Where *is* your God?"
4 When I remember these *things*,
[a]I pour out my soul within me.
For I used to go with the multitude;
[b]I went with them to the house of God,
With the voice of joy and praise,
With a multitude that kept a pilgrim feast.
5 [a]Why are you [1]cast down, O my soul?
And *why* are you disquieted within me?
[b]Hope in God, for I shall yet praise Him
[2]*For* the help of His countenance.
6 [1]O my God, my soul is cast down within me;
Therefore I will remember You from the land of the Jordan,
And from the heights of Her'mon,
From [2]the Hill Mī'zar.
7 Deep calls unto deep at the noise of Your waterfalls;
[a]All Your waves and billows have gone over me.
8 The LORD will [a]command His lovingkindness in the daytime,
And [b]in the night His song *shall be* with me—
A prayer to the God of my life.

9 I will say to God my Rock,
[a]"Why have You forgotten me?
Why do I go mourning because of the oppression of the enemy?"
10 *As* with a [1]breaking of my bones,
My enemies [2]reproach me,
[a]While they say to me all day long,
"Where *is* your God?"
11 [a]Why are you cast down, O my soul?
And why are you disquieted within me?
Hope in God;
For I shall yet praise Him,
The [1]help of my countenance and my God.

PSALM 43

VINDICATE [a]me, O God,
And [b]plead my cause against an ungodly nation;

PSALM 42

title [1]Heb. *Maschil*

1 [1]Lit. *longs for*

2 [a]Ps. 63:1; 84:2; 143:6 [b]1 Thess. 1:9 [1]So with MT, Vg.; some Heb. mss., LXX, Syr., Tg. *I see the face of God*

3 [a]Ps. 80:5; 102:9 [b]Ps. 79:10; 115:2

4 [a]Job 30:16 [b]Is. 30:29

5 [a]Ps. 42:11; 43:5 [b]Lam. 3:24 [1]Lit. *bowed down* [2]So with MT, Tg.; a few Heb. mss., LXX, Syr., Vg. *The help of my countenance, my God*

6 [1]So with MT, Tg.; a few Heb. mss., LXX, Syr., Vg. put *my God* at the end of v. 5 [2]Or *Mount*

7 [a]Ps. 69:1, 2; 88:7

8 [a]Deut. 28:8 [b]Job 35:10

9 [a]Ps. 38:6

10 [a]Joel 2:17 [1]Lit. *shattering* [2]*revile*

11 [a]Ps. 43:5 [1]Lit. *salvation*

PSALM 43

1 [a][Ps. 26:1; 35:24] [b]Ps. 35:1

Oh, deliver me from the
deceitful and unjust
man!
2 For You *are* the God of my
strength;
Why do You cast me off?
[a]Why do I go mourning
because of the
oppression of the
enemy?

3 [a]Oh, send out Your light and
Your truth!
Let them lead me;
Let them bring me to [b]Your
holy hill
And to Your [1]tabernacle.
4 Then I will go to the altar of
God,
To God my exceeding joy;
And on the harp I will
praise You,
O God, my God.

5 [a]Why are you cast down,
O my soul?
And why are you disquieted
within me?
Hope in God;
For I shall yet praise Him,
The [1]help of my
countenance and my
God.

PSALM 44

To the Chief Musician.
A [a]Contemplation[1] of the sons
of Kō′rah.

WE have heard with our
ears, O God,
[a]Our fathers have told us,
The deeds You did in their
days,
In days of old:
2 [a]You drove out the [1]nations
with Your hand,
But them You planted;
You afflicted the peoples,
and cast them out.
3 For [a]they did not gain
possession of the land by
their own sword,
Nor did their own arm save
them;
But it was Your right hand,
Your arm, and the light
of Your countenance,
[b]Because You favored them.

4 [a]You are my King, [1]O God;
[2]Command victories for
Jacob.
5 Through You [a]we will push
down our enemies;
Through Your name we will
trample those who rise
up against us.
6 For [a]I will not trust in my
bow,
Nor shall my sword save me.
7 But You have saved us from
our enemies,
And have put to shame
those who hated us.
8 [a]In God we boast all day
long,
And praise Your name
forever. Sē′lah

9 But [a]You have cast *us* off
and put us to shame,
And You do not go out with
our armies.
10 You make us [a]turn back
from the enemy,
And those who hate us
have taken [1]spoil for
themselves.
11 [a]You have given us up like
sheep *intended* for food,
And have [b]scattered us
among the nations.
12 [a]You sell Your people for
next to nothing,

---

2 [a]Ps. 42:9
3 [a][Ps. 40:11] [b]Ps. 3:4 [1]*dwelling places*
5 [a]Ps. 42:5, 11 [1]Lit. *salvation*

PSALM 44

title [a]Ps. 42:title [1]Heb. *Maschil*
1 [a][Ex. 12:26, 27]
2 [a]Ex. 15:17 [1]*Gentiles, heathen*
3 [a][Deut. 8:17, 18] [b][Deut. 4:37; 7:7, 8]
4 [a][Ps. 74:12] [1]So with MT, Tg.; LXX, Vg. *and my God* [2]So with MT, Tg.; LXX, Syr., Vg. *Who commands*
5 [a][Dan. 8:4]
6 [a]Ps. 33:16
8 [a]Ps. 34:2
9 [a]Ps. 60:1
10 [a]Lev. 26:17 [1]*plunder*
11 [a]Rom. 8:36 [b]Deut. 4:27; 28:64
12 [a]Is. 52:3, 4

And are not enriched by
selling them.

13 [a]You make us a reproach to
our neighbors,
A scorn and a derision to
those all around us.
14 [a]You make us a byword
among the nations,
[b]A shaking of the head
among the peoples.
15 My dishonor *is* continually
before me,
And the shame of my face
has covered me,
16 Because of the voice of him
who reproaches and
reviles,
[a]Because of the enemy and
the avenger.

17 [a]All this has come upon us;
But we have not forgotten
You,
Nor have we dealt falsely
with Your covenant.
18 Our heart has not turned
back,
[a]Nor have our steps departed
from Your way;
19 But You have severely
broken us in [a]the place
of jackals,
And covered us [b]with the
shadow of death.

20 If we had forgotten the
name of our God,
Or [a]stretched[1] out our hands
to a foreign god,
21 [a]Would not God search this
out?
For He knows the secrets of
the heart.
22 [a]Yet for Your sake we are
killed all day long;
We are accounted as sheep
for the slaughter.

23 [a]Awake! Why do You sleep,
O Lord?
Arise! Do not cast *us* off
forever.
24 [a]Why do You hide Your face,
And forget our affliction
and our oppression?
25 For [a]our soul is bowed down
to the [1]dust;
Our body clings to the
ground.
26 Arise for our help,
And redeem us for Your
mercies' sake.

PSALM 45

To the Chief Musician. [a]Set to [1]"The Lilies." A [2]Contemplation of the sons of Kō′rah. A Song of Love.

MY heart is overflowing
with a good theme;
I recite my composition
concerning the King;
My tongue *is* the pen of a
[1]ready writer.

2 You are fairer than the sons
of men;
[a]Grace is poured upon Your
lips;
Therefore God has blessed
You forever.
3 [1]Gird Your [a]sword upon
Your thigh, [b]O Mighty
One,
With Your [c]glory and Your
majesty.
4 [a]And in Your majesty ride
prosperously because
of truth, humility, *and*
righteousness;
And Your right hand shall
teach You awesome
things.

---

13 [a]Jer. 24:9
14 [a]Deut. 28:37 [b]Job 16:4
16 [a]Ps. 8:2
17 [a]Dan. 9:13
18 [a]Job 23:11
19 [a]Is. 34:13 [b][Ps. 23:4]
20 [a][Deut. 6:14] [1]Worshiped
21 [a][Ps. 139:1, 2]
22 [a]Rom. 8:36
23 [a]Ps. 7:6
24 [a]Job 13:24
25 [a]Ps. 119:25 [1]Ground, in humiliation

PSALM 45

title [a]Ps. 69:title [1]Heb. *Shoshannim* [2]Heb. *Maschil*
1 [1]*skillful*
2 [a]Luke 4:22
3 [a][Heb. 4:12] [b][Is. 9:6] [c]Jude 25 [1]*Belt on*
4 [a]Rev. 6:2

5 Your arrows *are* sharp in
the heart of the King's
enemies;
The peoples fall under You.

☆6 [a]Your throne, O God, *is*
forever and ever;
A [b]scepter of righteousness
is the scepter of Your
kingdom.
7 You love righteousness and
hate wickedness;
Therefore God, Your God,
has [a]anointed You
With the oil of [b]gladness
more than Your
companions.
8 All Your garments *are*
[a]*scented* with myrrh and
aloes *and* cassia,
Out of the ivory palaces, by
which they have made
You glad.
9 [a]Kings' daughters *are* among
Your honorable women;
[b]At Your right hand stands
the queen in gold from
Ō'phir.

10 Listen, O daughter,
Consider and incline your
ear;
[a]Forget your own people also,
and your father's house;
11 So the King will greatly
desire your beauty;
[a]Because He *is* your Lord,
worship Him.
12 And the daughter of Tȳre
will come with a gift;
[a]The rich among the people
will seek your favor.

13 The royal daughter *is* all
glorious within *the*
palace;
Her clothing *is* woven with
gold.
14 [a]She shall be brought to the
King in robes of many
colors;
The virgins, her companions
who follow her, shall be
brought to You.
15 With gladness and rejoicing
they shall be brought;
They shall enter the King's
palace.

16 Instead of Your fathers shall
be Your sons,
[a]Whom You shall make
princes in all the earth.
17 [a]I will make Your name to
be remembered in all
generations;
Therefore the people shall
praise You forever and
ever.

PSALM 46

To the Chief Musician. *A Psalm*
of the sons of Kō'rah. A Song
[a]for Al'a·moth.

GOD *is* our [a]refuge and
strength,
[b]A[1] very present help in
trouble.
2 Therefore we will not fear,
Even though the earth be
removed,
And though the mountains
be carried into the [1]midst
of the sea;
3 [a]*Though* its waters roar *and*
be troubled,
Though the mountains
shake with its swelling.
Sē'lah

4 *There is* a [a]river whose
streams shall make glad
the [b]city of God,

6 [a][Ps. 93:2]; Heb. 1:8, 9 [b][Num. 24:17]
7 [a]Ps. 2:2 [b]Ps. 21:6
8 [a]Song 1:12, 13
9 [a]Song 6:8 [b]1 Kin. 2:19
10 [a]Deut. 21:13
11 [a][Is. 54:5]
12 [a]Is. 49:23
14 [a]Song 1:4
16 [a][1 Pet. 2:9]
17 [a]Mal. 1:11
PSALM 46
title [a]1 Chr. 15:20
1 [a]Ps. 62:7, 8 [b][Deut. 4:7] [1]*An abundantly available help*
2 [1]Lit. *heart*
3 [a][Ps. 93:3, 4]
4 [a][Ezek. 47:1–12] [b]Is. 60:14

The holy *place* of the
[1]tabernacle of the Most
High.
5 God *is* [a]in the midst of her,
she shall not be [1]moved;
God shall help her, just [2]at
the break of dawn.
6 [a]The nations raged, the
kingdoms were moved;
He uttered His voice, the
earth melted.

7 The [a]LORD of hosts *is*
with us;
The God of Jacob *is* our
refuge. Sē′lah

8 Come, behold the works of
the LORD,
Who has made desolations
in the earth.
9 [a]He makes wars cease to the
end of the earth;
[b]He breaks the bow and cuts
the spear in two;
[c]He burns the chariot in the
fire.

10 Be still, and know that I *am*
God;
[a]I will be exalted among the
nations,
I will be exalted in the
earth!

11 The LORD of hosts *is* with us;
The God of Jacob *is* our
refuge. Sē′lah

PSALM 47

To the Chief Musician. A Psalm
of the sons of Kō′rah.

OH, clap your hands, all you
peoples!
Shout to God with the voice
of triumph!
2 For the LORD Most High *is*
awesome;
He is a great [a]King over all
the earth.
3 [a]He will subdue the peoples
under us,
And the nations under our
feet.
4 He will choose our
[a]inheritance for us,
The excellence of Jacob
whom He loves. Sē′lah

5 [a]God has gone up with a
shout,
The LORD with the sound of
a trumpet.
6 Sing praises to God, sing
praises!
Sing praises to our King,
sing praises!
7 [a]For God *is* the King of all
the earth;
[b]Sing praises with
understanding.

8 [a]God reigns over the nations;
God [b]sits on His [c]holy
throne.
9 The princes of the people
have gathered together,
[a]The people of the God of
Abraham.
[b]For the shields of the earth
belong to God;
He is greatly exalted.

PSALM 48

A Song. A Psalm of the sons of
Kō′rah.

GREAT *is* the LORD, and
greatly to be praised
In the [a]city of our God,
In His holy mountain.
2 [a]Beautiful in [1]elevation,
The joy of the whole earth,

4 [1]*dwelling places*
5 [a][Zeph. 3:15] [1]*shaken* [2]Lit. *at the turning of the morning*
6 [a]Ps. 2:1, 2
7 [a]Num. 14:9
9 [a]Is. 2:4 [b]Ps. 76:3 [c]Ezek. 39:9
10 [a][Is. 2:11, 17]

PSALM 47
2 [a]Neh. 1:5
3 [a]Ps. 18:47
4 [a][1 Pet. 1:4]
5 [a]Ps. 68:24, 25
7 [a]Zech. 14:9 [b]1 Cor. 14:15
8 [a]1 Chr. 16:31 [b]Ps. 97:2 [c]Ps. 48:1
9 [a][Rom. 4:11, 12] [b][Ps. 89:18]

PSALM 48
1 [a]Ps. 46:4; 87:3
2 [a]Ps. 50:2 [1]*height*

Is Mount Zion *on* the sides
of the north,
The city of the great King.
3 God *is* in her palaces;
He is known as her refuge.

4 For behold, [a]the kings
assembled,
They passed by together.
5 They saw *it, and* so they
marveled;
They were troubled, they
hastened away.
6 Fear [a]took hold of them
there,
And pain, as of a woman in
birth pangs,
7 *As when* You break the
[a]ships of Tar′shish
With an east wind.

8 As we have heard,
So we have seen
In the city of the LORD of
hosts,
In the city of our God:
God will [a]establish it
forever. Sē′lah

9 We have thought, O God, on
[a]Your lovingkindness,
In the midst of Your temple.
10 According to [a]Your name,
O God,
So *is* Your praise to the ends
of the earth;
Your right hand is full of
righteousness.
11 Let Mount Zion rejoice,
Let the daughters of Judah
be glad,
Because of Your judgments.

12 Walk about Zion,
And go all around her.
Count her towers;
13 Mark well her bulwarks;
Consider her palaces;
That you may [a]tell *it* to the
generation following.
14 For this *is* God,
Our God forever and ever;
[a]He will be our guide
[1]*Even* to death.

PSALM 49

To the Chief Musician. A Psalm
of the sons of Kō′rah.

HEAR this, all peoples;
Give ear, all inhabitants of
the world,
2 Both low and high,
Rich and poor together.
3 My mouth shall speak
wisdom,
And the meditation of
my heart *shall give*
understanding.
4 I will incline my ear to a
proverb;
I will disclose my [1]dark
saying on the harp.

5 Why should I fear in the
days of evil,
When the iniquity at my
heels surrounds me?
6 Those who [a]trust in their
wealth
And boast in the multitude
of their riches,
7 None *of them* can by any
means redeem *his*
brother,
Nor [a]give to God a ransom
for him—
8 For [a]the redemption of their
souls *is* costly,
And it shall cease
forever—
9 That he should continue to
live eternally,
And [a]not [1]see the Pit.

4 [a]2 Sam. 10:6, 14
6 [a]Ex. 15:15
7 [a]Ezek. 27:25
8 [a][Ps. 87:5]
9 [a]Ps. 26:3
10 [a]Mal. 1:11
13 [a][Ps. 78:5–7]
14 [a]Is. 58:11 [1]So with MT, Syr.; LXX, Vg. *Forever*

PSALM 49

4 [1]*riddle*
6 [a][Mark 10:23, 24]
7 [a]Job 36:18, 19
8 [a][Matt. 16:26]
9 [a]Ps. 89:48 [1]*experience corruption*

10 For he sees wise men die;
Likewise the fool and the senseless person perish,
And leave their wealth to others.
11 [1]Their inner thought *is that* their houses *will last* forever,
Their dwelling places to all generations;
They [a]call *their* lands after their own names.
12 Nevertheless man, *though* in honor, does not [1]remain;
He is like the beasts *that* perish.

13 This is the way of those who *are* [a]foolish,
And of their posterity who approve their sayings. Sē′lah
14 Like sheep they are laid in the grave;
Death shall feed on them;
[a]The upright shall have dominion over them in the morning;
[b]And their beauty shall be consumed in [1]the grave, far from their dwelling.
☆ 15 But God [a]will redeem my soul from the power of [1]the grave,
For He shall [b]receive me. Sē′lah

16 Do not be afraid when one becomes rich,
When the glory of his house is increased;
17 For when he dies he shall carry nothing away;
His glory shall not descend after him.
18 Though while he lives [a]he blesses himself
(For *men* will praise you when you do well for yourself),
19 He shall go to the generation of his fathers;
They shall never see [a]light.[1]
20 A man *who is* in honor, yet does not understand,
[a]Is like the beasts *that* perish.

PSALM 50

A Psalm of Ā′saph.

THE [a]Mighty One, God the LORD,
Has spoken and called the earth
From the rising of the sun to its going down.
2 Out of Zion, the perfection of beauty,
[a]God will shine forth.
3 Our God shall come, and shall not keep silent;
[a]A fire shall devour before Him,
And it shall be very tempestuous all around Him.

4 [a]He shall call to the heavens from above,
And to the earth, that He may judge His people:
5 "Gather [a]My saints together to Me,
[b]Those who have [1]made a covenant with Me by sacrifice."
6 Let the [a]heavens declare His righteousness,
For [b]God Himself *is* Judge. Sē′lah

---

11 [a]Gen. 4:17 [1]LXX, Syr., Tg., Vg. *Their graves shall be their houses forever*
12 [1]So with MT, Tg.; LXX, Syr., Vg. *understand* (cf. v. 20)
13 [a][Luke 12:20]
14 [a][Dan. 7:18] [b]Job 4:21 [1]Or *Sheol*
15 [a][Hos. 13:4]; Mark 16:6, 7; Acts 2:31, 32 [b]Ps. 73:24 [1]Or *Sheol*
18 [a]Deut. 29:19
19 [a]Job 33:30 [1]The light of life
20 [a]Eccl. 3:19

PSALM 50

1 [a]Is. 9:6
2 [a]Ps. 80:1
3 [a][Ps. 97:3]
4 [a]Is. 1:2
5 [a]Deut. 33:3 [b]Ex. 24:7 [1]Lit. *cut*
6 [a][Ps. 97:6] [b]Ps. 75:7

7 "Hear, O My people, and I
will speak,
O Israel, and I will testify
against you;
[a]I *am* God, your God!
8 [a]I will not [1]rebuke you [b]for
your sacrifices
Or your burnt offerings,
Which are continually
before Me.
9 [a]I will not take a bull from
your house,
Nor goats out of your folds.
10 For every beast of the forest
is Mine,
And the cattle on a
thousand hills.
11 I know all the birds of the
mountains,
And the wild beasts of the
field *are* Mine.

12 "If I were hungry, I would not
tell you;
[a]For the world *is* Mine, and
all its fullness.
13 [a]Will I eat the flesh of bulls,
Or drink the blood of goats?
14 [a]Offer to God thanksgiving,
And [b]pay your vows to the
Most High.
15 [a]Call upon Me in the day of
trouble;
I will deliver you, and you
shall glorify Me."

16 But to the wicked God says:
"What *right* have you to
declare My statutes,
Or take My covenant in
your mouth,
17 [a]Seeing you hate instruction
And cast My words behind
you?
18 When you saw a thief, you
[a]consented[1] with him,
And have been a [b]partaker
with adulterers.
19 You give your mouth to evil,
And [a]your tongue frames
deceit.
20 You sit *and* speak against
your brother;
You slander your own
mother's son.
21 These *things* you have done,
and I kept silent;
[a]You thought that I was
altogether like you;
But I will rebuke you,
And [b]set *them* in order
before your eyes.

22 "Now consider this, you who
[a]forget God,
Lest I tear *you* in pieces,
And *there be* none to
deliver:
23 Whoever offers praise
glorifies Me;
And [a]to him who orders *his*
conduct *aright*
I will show the salvation of
God."

PSALM 51

To the Chief Musician. A Psalm of David [a]when Nathan the prophet went to him, after he had gone in to Bath-shē′ba.

HAVE mercy upon me,
O God,
According to Your
lovingkindness;
According to the multitude
of Your tender mercies,
[a]Blot out my transgressions.
2 [a]Wash me thoroughly from
my iniquity,
And cleanse me from my
sin.

3 For I acknowledge my
transgressions,

---

7 [a]Ex. 20:2
8 [a]Jer. 7:22 [b][Hos. 6:6] [1]*reprove*
9 [a]Ps. 69:31
12 [a]Ex. 19:5
13 [a][Ps. 51:15–17]
14 [a]Heb. 13:15 [b]Deut. 23:21
15 [a][Zech. 13:9]
17 [a]Rom. 2:21
18 [a][Rom. 1:32] [b]1 Tim. 5:22 [1]LXX, Syr., Tg., Vg. *ran*
19 [a]Ps. 52:2
21 [a][Rom. 2:4] [b][Ps. 90:8]
22 [a][Job 8:13]
23 [a]Gal. 6:16

PSALM 51
title [a]2 Sam. 12:1
1 [a][Is. 43:25; 44:22]
2 [a][Heb. 9:14]

And my sin *is* always
before me.
4 [a]Against You, You only, have I
sinned,
And done *this* evil [b]in Your
sight—
[c]That You may be found just
[1]when You speak,
And blameless when You
judge.
5 [a]Behold, I was brought forth
in iniquity,
And in sin my mother
conceived me.
6 Behold, You desire truth in
the inward parts,
And in the hidden *part* You
will make me to know
wisdom.

7 [a]Purge me with hyssop, and I
shall be clean;
Wash me, and I shall be
[b]whiter than snow.
8 Make me hear joy and
gladness,
That the bones You have
broken [a]may rejoice.
9 Hide Your face from my sins,
And blot out all my
iniquities.

10 [a]Create in me a clean heart,
O God,
And renew a steadfast spirit
within me.
11 Do not cast me away from
Your presence,
And do not take Your [a]Holy
Spirit from me.

12 Restore to me the joy of
Your salvation,
And uphold me *by Your*
[a]generous Spirit.
13 *Then* I will teach
transgressors Your ways,
And sinners shall be
converted to You.

14 Deliver me from the guilt of
bloodshed, O God,
The God of my salvation,
And my tongue shall
sing aloud of Your
righteousness.
15 O Lord, open my lips,
And my mouth shall show
forth Your praise.
16 For [a]You do not desire
sacrifice, or else I would
give *it;*
You do not delight in burnt
offering.
17 [a]The sacrifices of God *are* a
broken spirit,
A broken and a contrite
heart—
These, O God, You will not
despise.

18 Do good in Your good
pleasure to Zion;
Build the walls of Jerusalem.
19 Then You shall be pleased
with [a]the sacrifices of
righteousness,
With burnt offering and
whole burnt offering;
Then they shall offer bulls
on Your altar.

PSALM 52

To the Chief Musician. A
[1]Contemplation of David [a]when
Dō′eg the Ē′dom·ite went and
[b]told Saul, and said to him,
"David has gone to the house
of A·him′e·lech."

WHY do you boast in evil,
O mighty man?
The goodness of God
endures continually.

---

4 [a]2 Sam. 12:13 [b][Luke 5:21] [c]Rom. 3:4 [1]LXX, Tg., Vg. *in Your words*
5 [a][Job 14:4]
7 [a]Heb. 9:19 [b][Is. 1:18]
8 [a][Matt. 5:4]
10 [a][Ezek. 18:31]
11 [a][Luke 11:13]
12 [a][2 Cor. 3:17]
16 [a][1 Sam. 15:22]
17 [a]Ps. 34:18
19 [a]Ps. 4:5

PSALM 52

title [a]1 Sam. 22:9 [b]Ezek. 22:9 [1]Heb. *Maschil*

2 Your tongue devises destruction,
Like a sharp razor, working deceitfully.
3 You love evil more than good,
Lying rather than speaking righteousness. Sē′lah
4 You love all devouring words,
You deceitful tongue.

5 God shall likewise destroy you forever;
He shall take you away, and pluck you out of *your* dwelling place,
And uproot you from the land of the living. Sē′lah
6 The righteous also shall see and fear,
And shall laugh at him, *saying,*
7 "Here is the man *who* did not make God his strength,
But trusted in the abundance of his riches,
And strengthened himself in his [1]wickedness."

8 But I *am* [a]like a green olive tree in the house of God;
I trust in the mercy of God forever and ever.
9 I will praise You forever,
Because You have done *it;*
And in the presence of Your saints
I will wait on Your name, for *it* [1]*is* good.

PSALM 53

To the Chief Musician. Set to "Mā′ha·lath." A [1]Contemplation of David.

THE [a]fool has said in his heart,
"*There is* no God."
They are corrupt, and have done abominable iniquity;
[b]*There is* none who does good.

2 God looks down from heaven upon the children of men,
To see if there are *any* who understand, who [a]seek God.
3 Every one of them has turned aside;
They have together become corrupt;
There is none who does good,
No, not one.

4 Have the workers of iniquity [a]no knowledge,
Who eat up my people *as* they eat bread,
And do not call upon God?
5 [a]There they are in great fear
Where no fear was,
For God has scattered the bones of him who encamps against you;
You have put *them* to shame,
Because God has despised them.

6 [a]Oh, that the salvation of Israel would come out of Zion!
When God brings back [1]the captivity of His people,
Let Jacob rejoice *and* Israel be glad.

---

7 [1]Lit. *desire,* in evil sense

8 [a]Jer. 11:16

9 [1]Or *has a good reputation*

PSALM 53

title [1]Heb. *Maschil*

1 [a]Ps. 10:4 [b]Rom. 3:10–12

2 [a][2 Chr. 15:2]

4 [a]Jer. 4:22

5 [a]Prov. 28:1

6 [a]Ps. 14:7 [1]Or *His captive people*

PSALM 54

To the Chief Musician. With [1]stringed instruments. A [2]Contemplation of David [a]when the Ziph′ītes went and said to Saul, "Is David not hiding with us?"

SAVE me, O God, by Your name,
And vindicate me by Your strength.
2 Hear my prayer, O God;
Give ear to the words of my mouth.
3 For strangers have risen up against me,
And oppressors have sought after my life;
They have not set God before them. Sē′lah

4 Behold, God *is* my helper;
The Lord *is* with those who [1]uphold my life.
5 He will repay my enemies for their evil.
[1]Cut them off in Your [2]truth.

6 I will freely sacrifice to You;
I will praise Your name,
O LORD, for *it is* good.
7 For He has delivered me out of all trouble;
[a]And my eye has seen *its desire* upon my enemies.

PSALM 55

To the Chief Musician. With [1]stringed instruments. A [2]Contemplation of David.

GIVE ear to my prayer, O God,
And do not hide Yourself from my supplication.
2 Attend to me, and hear me;
I [a]am[1] restless in my complaint, and moan noisily,
3 Because of the voice of the enemy,
Because of the oppression of the wicked;
[a]For they bring down trouble upon me,
And in wrath they hate me.

4 [a]My heart is severely pained within me,
And the terrors of death have fallen upon me.
5 Fearfulness and trembling have come upon me,
And horror has overwhelmed me.
6 So I said, "Oh, that I had wings like a dove!
I would fly away and be at rest.
7 Indeed, I would wander far off,
And remain in the wilderness. Sē′lah
8 I would hasten my escape
From the windy storm *and* tempest."

9 Destroy, O Lord, *and* divide their [1]tongues,
For I have seen [a]violence and strife in the city.
10 Day and night they go around it on its walls;
[a]Iniquity and trouble *are* also in the midst of it.
11 Destruction *is* in its midst;
[a]Oppression and deceit do not depart from its streets.

12 [a]For *it is* not an enemy *who* reproaches me;
Then I could bear *it*.

PSALM 54

title [a]1 Sam. 23:19 [1]Heb. *neginoth* [2]Heb. *Maschil*

4 [1]*sustain my soul*

5 [1]*Destroy them* [2]Or *faithfulness*

7 [a]Ps. 59:10

PSALM 55

title [1]Heb. *neginoth* [2]Heb. *Maschil*

2 [a]Is. 38:14; 59:11 [1]*wander*

3 [a]2 Sam. 16:7, 8

4 [a]Ps. 116:3

9 [a]Jer. 6:7 [1]*speech*, their counsel

10 [a]Ps. 10:7

11 [a]Ps. 10:7

12 [a]Ps. 41:9

Nor *is it* one *who* hates me
who has [b]exalted *himself*
against me;
Then I could hide from him.
13 But *it was* you, a man my
equal,
[a]My companion and my
acquaintance.
14 We took sweet counsel
together,
And [a]walked to the house of
God in the throng.

15 Let death seize them;
Let them [a]go down alive
into [1]hell,
For wickedness *is* in their
dwellings *and* among
them.

16 As for me, I will call upon
God,
And the LORD shall save me.
17 [a]Evening and morning and at
noon
I will pray, and cry aloud,
And He shall hear my voice.
18 He has redeemed my soul
in peace from the battle
that was against me,
For [a]there were many
against me.
19 God will hear, and afflict
them,
[a]Even He who abides from of
old. Sē′lah
Because they do not change,
Therefore they do not fear
God.

20 He has [a]put forth his hands
against those who [b]were
at peace with him;
He has broken his
[1]covenant.
21 [a]*The words* of his mouth were
smoother than butter,
But war *was* in his heart;
His words were softer than
oil,
Yet they *were* drawn swords.

22 [a]Cast your burden on the
LORD,
And [b]He shall sustain you;
He shall never permit the
righteous to be [1]moved.

23 But You, O God, shall bring
them down to the pit of
destruction;
[a]Bloodthirsty and deceitful
men [b]shall not live out
half their days;
But I will trust in You.

PSALM 56

To the Chief Musician. Set to [1]"The Silent Dove in Distant Lands." A Mich′tam of David when the [a]Phi·lis′tines captured him in Gath.

BE [a]merciful to me, O God,
for man would swallow
me up;
Fighting all day he
oppresses me.
2 My enemies would [a]hound
me all day,
For *there are* many who
fight against me, O Most
High.

3 Whenever I am afraid,
I will trust in You.
4 In God (I will praise His
word),
In God I have put my trust;
[a]I will not fear.
What can flesh do to me?

5 All day they twist my words;
All their thoughts *are*
against me for evil.

12 [b]Ps. 35:26; 38:16
13 [a]2 Sam. 15:12
14 [a]Ps. 42:4
15 [a]Num. 16:30, 33 [1]Or *Sheol*
17 [a]Dan. 6:10
18 [a]2 Chr. 32:7, 8
19 [a][Deut. 33:27]
20 [a]Acts 12:1 [b]Ps. 7:4 [1]*treaty*
21 [a]Ps. 28:3; 57:4
22 [a][Ps. 37:5] [b]Ps. 37:24 [1]*shaken*
23 [a]Ps. 5:6 [b]Prov. 10:27

PSALM 56

title [a]1 Sam. 21:11 [1]Heb. *Jonath Elem Rechokim*
1 [a]Ps. 57:1
2 [a]Ps. 57:3
4 [a]Ps. 118:6

6 They gather together,
They hide, they mark my steps,
When they lie in wait for my life.
7 Shall they escape by iniquity?
In anger cast down the peoples, O God!

8 You number my wanderings;
Put my tears into Your bottle;
[a]*Are they* not in Your book?
9 When I cry out *to You*,
Then my enemies will turn back;
This I know, because [a]God *is* for me.
10 In God (I will praise *His* word),
In the LORD (I will praise *His* word),
11 In God I have put my trust;
I will not be afraid.
What can man do to me?

12 Vows *made* to You *are binding* upon me, O God;
I will render praises to You,
13 [a]For You have delivered my soul from death.
Have You not *kept* my feet from falling,
That I may walk before God
In the [b]light of the living?

PSALM 57

To the Chief Musician. Set to [1]"Do Not Destroy." A Mich'tam of David [a]when he fled from Saul into the cave.

BE merciful to me, O God, be merciful to me!
For my soul trusts in You;
[a]And in the shadow of Your wings I will make my refuge,
[b]Until *these* calamities have passed by.

2 I will cry out to God Most High,
To God [a]who performs *all things* for me.
3 [a]He shall send from heaven and save me;
He reproaches the one who [1]would swallow me up. Se̅'lah
God [b]shall send forth His mercy and His truth.

4 My soul *is* among lions;
I lie *among* the sons of men
Who are set on fire,
[a]Whose teeth *are* spears and arrows,
And their tongue a sharp sword.
5 [a]Be exalted, O God, above the heavens;
Let Your glory *be* above all the earth.

6 [a]They have prepared a net for my steps;
My soul is bowed down;
They have dug a pit before me;
Into the midst of it they *themselves* have fallen. Se̅'lah

7 [a]My heart is steadfast, O God, my heart is steadfast;
I will sing and give praise.
8 Awake, [a]my glory!
Awake, lute and harp!
I will awaken the dawn.

9 [a]I will praise You, O Lord, among the peoples;

8 [a][Mal. 3:16]
9 [a][Rom. 8:31]
13 [a]Ps. 116:8, 9 [b]Job 33:30

PSALM 57

title [a]1 Sam. 22:1 [1]Heb. *Al Tashcheth*
1 [a]Ps. 17:8; 63:7 [b]Is. 26:20
2 [a][Ps. 138:8]
3 [a]Ps. 144:5, 7 [b]Ps. 43:3 [1]*snaps at* or *hounds me*, or *crushes me*
4 [a]Prov. 30:14
5 [a]Ps. 108:5
6 [a]Ps. 9:15
7 [a]Ps. 108:1–5
8 [a]Ps. 16:9
9 [a]Ps. 108:3

I will sing to You among the [1]nations.
10 [a]For Your mercy reaches unto the heavens,
And Your truth unto the clouds.

11 [a]Be exalted, O God, above the heavens;
Let Your glory *be* above all the earth.

PSALM 58

To the Chief Musician. Set to [1]"Do Not Destroy." A Mich'tam of David.

DO you indeed speak righteousness, you silent ones?
Do you judge uprightly, you sons of men?
2 No, in heart you work wickedness;
You weigh out the violence of your hands in the earth.

3 [a]The wicked are estranged from the womb;
They go astray as soon as they are born, speaking lies.
4 [a]Their poison *is* like the poison of a serpent;
They are like the deaf cobra *that* stops its ear,
5 Which will not [a]heed the voice of charmers,
Charming ever so skillfully.

6 [a]Break[1] their teeth in their mouth, O God!
Break out the fangs of the young lions, O LORD!
7 [a]Let them flow away as waters *which* run continually;
When he bends *his bow,*
Let his arrows be as if cut in pieces.
8 *Let them be* like a snail which melts away as it goes,
[a]*Like* a stillborn child of a woman, that they may not see the sun.

9 Before your [a]pots can feel *the burning* thorns,
He shall take them away [b]as with a whirlwind,
As in His living and burning wrath.
10 The righteous shall rejoice when he sees the [a]vengeance;
[b]He shall wash his feet in the blood of the wicked,
11 [a]So that men will say,
"Surely *there is* a reward for the righteous;
Surely He is God who [b]judges in the earth."

PSALM 59

To the Chief Musician. Set to [1]"Do Not Destroy." A Mich'tam of David [a]when Saul sent men, and they watched the house in order to kill him.

DELIVER me from my enemies, O my God;
[1]Defend me from those who rise up against me.
2 Deliver me from the workers of iniquity,
And save me from bloodthirsty men.

3 For look, they lie in wait for my life;
[a]The mighty gather against me,

---

9 [1]*Gentiles*
10 [a]Ps. 103:11
11 [a]Ps. 57:5

PSALM 58

title [1]Heb. *Al Tashcheth*
3 [a][Is. 48:8]
4 [a]Eccl. 10:11
5 [a]Jer. 8:17
6 [a]Job 4:10 [1]*Break away*
7 [a]Josh. 2:11; 7:5
8 [a]Job 3:16
9 [a]Eccl. 7:6 [b]Prov. 10:25
10 [a]Jer. 11:20 [b]Ps. 68:23
11 [a]Ps. 92:15 [b]Ps. 50:6; 75:7

PSALM 59

title [a]1 Sam. 19:11 [1]Heb. *Al Tashcheth*
1 [1]Lit. *Set me on high*
3 [a]Ps. 56:6

Not *for* my transgression
nor *for* my sin, O LORD.
4 They run and prepare
themselves through no
fault *of mine.*

[a]Awake to help me, and
behold!
5 You therefore, O LORD God
of hosts, the God of
Israel,
Awake to punish all the
[1]nations;
Do not be merciful to any
wicked transgressors.
Sē'lah

6 [a]At evening they return,
They growl like a dog,
And go all around the city.
7 Indeed, they belch with their
mouth;
[a]Swords *are* in their lips;
For *they say,* [b]"Who hears?"

8 But [a]You, O LORD, shall
laugh at them;
You shall have all the
[1]nations in derision.
9 I will wait for You, O You [1]his
Strength;
[a]For God *is* my [2]defense.
10 [1]My God of mercy shall
[a]come to meet me;
God shall let [b]me see *my*
desire on my enemies.

11 Do not slay them, lest my
people forget;
Scatter them by Your power,
And bring them down,
O Lord our shield.
12 [a]*For* the sin of their mouth
and the words of their
lips,
Let them even be taken in
their pride,

4 [a]Ps. 35:23
5 [1]*Gentiles*
6 [a]Ps. 59:14
7 [a]Prov. 12:18 [b]Ps. 10:11
8 [a]Prov. 1:26 [1]*Gentiles*
9 [a][Ps. 62:2] [1]So with MT, Syr.; some Heb. mss., LXX, Tg., Vg. *my Strength* [2]Lit. *fortress*
10 [a]Ps. 21:3 [b]Ps. 54:7 [1]So with Qr.; some Heb. mss., LXX, Vg. *My God, His mercy;* Kt., some Heb. mss., Tg. *O God, my mercy;* Syr. *O God, Your mercy*
12 [a]Prov. 12:13
13 [a]Ps. 104:35 [b]Ps. 83:18
14 [a]Ps. 59:6
15 [a]Job 15:23 [1]So with LXX, Vg.; MT, Syr., Tg. *spend the night*
17 [a]Ps. 18:1

PSALM 60
title [a]Ps. 80 [b]2 Sam. 8:3, 13 [1]Heb. *Shushan Eduth*
1 [a]Ps. 44:9

And for the cursing and
lying *which* they speak.
13 [a]Consume *them* in wrath,
consume *them,*
That they *may* not *be;*
And [b]let them know that
God rules in Jacob
To the ends of the earth.
Sē'lah

14 And [a]at evening they return,
They growl like a dog,
And go all around the city.
15 They [a]wander up and down
for food,
And [1]howl if they are not
satisfied.

16 But I will sing of Your
power;
Yes, I will sing aloud of Your
mercy in the morning;
For You have been my
defense
And refuge in the day of my
trouble.
17 To You, [a]O my Strength,
I will sing praises;
For God *is* my defense,
My God of mercy.

PSALM 60

To the Chief Musician. [a]Set to [1]"Lily of the Testimony." A Mich'tam of David. For teaching. [b]When he fought against Mes·o·po·tā'mi·a and Syria of Zō'bah, and Jō'ab returned and killed twelve thousand Ē'dom·ītes in the Valley of Salt.

O GOD, [a]You have cast us off;
You have broken us down;
You have been displeased;
Oh, restore us again!

2 You have made the earth
tremble;
You have broken it;
[a]Heal its breaches, for it is
shaking.
3 [a]You have shown Your people
hard things;
[b]You have made us drink the
wine of [1]confusion.

4 [a]You have given a banner to
those who fear You,
That it may be displayed
because of the truth.
Sē′lah
5 [a]That Your beloved may be
delivered,
Save *with* Your right hand,
and hear me.

6 God has [a]spoken in His
holiness:
"I will rejoice;
I will [b]divide [c]Shē′chem
And measure out [d]the Valley
of Suc′coth.
7 Gil′ē·ad *is* Mine, and
Ma·nas′seh *is* Mine;
[a]Ē′phra·im also *is* the [1]helmet
for My head;
[b]Judah *is* My lawgiver.
8 [a]Mō′ab *is* My washpot;
[b]Over Ē′dom I will cast My
shoe;
[c]Phi·lis′ti·a, shout in triumph
because of Me."

9 Who will bring me *to* the
strong city?
Who will lead me to Ē′dom?
10 *Is it* not You, O God, [a]*who*
cast us off?
And You, O God, *who* did
[b]not go out with our
armies?
11 Give us help from trouble,
[a]For the help of man *is*
useless.
12 Through God [a]we will do
valiantly,
For *it is* He *who* shall tread
down our enemies.

PSALM 61

To the Chief Musician. On [1]a
stringed instrument. *A Psalm*
of David.

HEAR my cry, O God;
Attend to my prayer.
2 From the end of the earth I
will cry to You,
When my heart is
overwhelmed;
Lead me to the rock that is
higher than I.

3 For You have been a shelter
for me,
[a]A strong tower from the
enemy.
4 I will abide in Your
[1]tabernacle forever;
[a]I will trust in the shelter of
Your wings. Sē′lah

5 For You, O God, have heard
my vows;
You have given *me* the
heritage of those who
fear Your name.
6 You will prolong the king's
life,
His years as many
generations.
7 He shall abide before God
forever.
Oh, prepare mercy [a]and
truth, *which* may
[1]preserve him!

8 So I will sing praise to Your
name forever,
That I may daily perform
my vows.

2 [a][2 Chr. 7:14]
3 [a]Ps. 71:20 [b]Jer. 25:15 [1]*staggering*
4 [a]Ps. 20:5
5 [a]Ps. 108:6–13
6 [a]Ps. 89:35 [b]Josh. 1:6 [c]Gen. 12:6 [d]Josh. 13:27
7 [a]Deut. 33:17 [b][Gen. 49:10] [1]Lit. *protection*
8 [a]2 Sam. 8:2 [b]2 Sam. 8:14 [c]2 Sam. 8:1
10 [a]Ps. 108:11 [b]Josh. 7:12
11 [a]Ps. 118:8; 146:3
12 [a]Num. 24:18

PSALM 61

title [1]Heb. *neginah*
3 [a]Prov. 18:10
4 [a]Ps. 91:4 [1]*tent*
7 [a]Ps. 40:11 [1]Lit. *guard* or *keep*

PSALM 62

To the Chief Musician. To [a]Je·dū'thun. A Psalm of David.

TRULY [a]my soul silently *waits* for God;
From Him *comes* my salvation.
2 He only *is* my rock and my salvation;
He is my [1]defense;
I shall not be greatly [a]moved.[2]
3 How long will you attack a man?
You shall be slain, all of you,
[a]Like a leaning wall and a tottering fence.
4 They only consult to cast *him* down from his high position;
They [a]delight in lies;
They bless with their mouth,
But they curse inwardly. Sē'lah
5 My soul, wait silently for God alone,
For my [1]expectation *is* from Him.
6 He only *is* my rock and my salvation;
He is my defense;
I shall not be [1]moved.
7 [a]In God *is* my salvation and my glory;
The rock of my strength,
And my refuge, *is* in God.
8 Trust in Him at all times, you people;
[a]Pour out your heart before Him;
God *is* a refuge for us. Sē'lah
9 [a]Surely men of low degree *are* [1]a vapor,
Men of high degree *are* a lie;
If they are weighed on the scales,
They *are* altogether *lighter* than vapor.
10 Do not trust in oppression,
Nor vainly hope in robbery;
[a]If riches increase,
Do not set *your* heart *on them.*
11 God has spoken once,
Twice I have heard this:
That power *belongs* to God.
12 Also to You, O Lord, *belongs* mercy;
For [a]You [1]render to each one according to his work.

PSALM 63

A Psalm of David [a]when he was in the wilderness of Judah.

O GOD, You *are* my God;
Early will I seek You;
[a]My soul thirsts for You;
My flesh longs for You
In a dry and thirsty land
Where there is no water.
2 So I have looked for You in the sanctuary,
To see [a]Your power and Your glory.
3 [a]Because Your lovingkindness *is* better than life,
My lips shall praise You.
4 Thus I will bless You while I live;
I will [a]lift up my hands in Your name.
5 My soul shall be satisfied as with [1]marrow and [2]fatness,
And my mouth shall praise *You* with joyful lips.

PSALM 62
title [a]1 Chr. 25:1
1 [a]Ps. 33:20
2 [a]Ps. 55:22 [1]*strong tower* [2]*shaken*
3 [a]Is. 30:13
4 [a]Ps. 28:3
5 [1]*hope*
6 [1]*shaken*
7 [a][Jer. 3:23]
8 [a]1 Sam. 1:15
9 [a]Is. 40:17 [1]*vanity*
10 [a][Luke 12:15]
12 [a][Matt. 16:27] [1]*reward*

PSALM 63
title [a]1 Sam. 22:5
1 [a]Ps. 42:2
2 [a]Ps. 27:4
3 [a]Ps. 138:2
4 [a]Ps. 28:2; 143:6
5 [1]Lit. *fat* [2]Abundance

6 When [a]I remember You on
my bed,
I meditate on You in the
night watches.
7 Because You have been my
help,
Therefore in the shadow of
Your wings I will
rejoice.
8 My soul follows close
behind You;
Your right hand upholds me.

9 But those *who* seek my life,
to destroy *it*,
Shall go into the lower parts
of the earth.
10 They shall [1]fall by the
sword;
They shall be [2]a portion for
jackals.

11 But the king shall rejoice in
God;
[a]Everyone who swears by
Him shall glory;
But the mouth of those
who speak lies shall be
stopped.

PSALM 64

To the Chief Musician. A Psalm of David.

HEAR my voice, O God, in
my [1]meditation;
Preserve my life from fear
of the enemy.
2 Hide me from the secret
plots of the wicked,
From the rebellion of the
workers of iniquity,
3 Who sharpen their tongue
like a sword,
[a]And bend *their bows to*
shoot their arrows—
bitter words,
4 That they may shoot in
secret at the blameless;
Suddenly they shoot at him
and do not fear.

5 They encourage themselves
in an evil matter;
They talk of laying snares
secretly;
[a]They say, "Who will see
them?"
6 They devise iniquities:
"We have perfected a shrewd
scheme."
Both the inward thought
and the heart of man are
deep.

7 But God shall shoot at them
with an arrow;
Suddenly they shall be
wounded.
8 So He will make them
stumble over their own
tongue;
[a]All who see them shall flee
away.
9 All men shall fear,
And shall [a]declare the work
of God;
For they shall wisely
consider His doing.

10 [a]The righteous shall be glad
in the LORD, and trust in
Him.
And all the upright in heart
shall glory.

PSALM 65

To the Chief Musician. A Psalm of David. A Song.

PRAISE is awaiting You,
O God, in Zion;
And to You the [1]vow shall be
performed.

6 [a]Ps. 42:8
10 [1]Lit. *pour him out by the hand of the sword* [2]Prey
11 [a]Deut. 6:13

PSALM 64
1 [1]*complaint*
3 [a]Ps. 58:7
5 [a]Ps. 10:11; 59:7
8 [a]Ps. 31:11
9 [a]Jer. 50:28; 51:10
10 [a]Ps. 32:11

PSALM 65
1 [1]A promised deed

2 O You who hear prayer,
[a]To You all flesh will come.
3 Iniquities prevail against me;
As for our transgressions,
You will [a]provide atonement for them.

4 [a]Blessed *is the man* You [b]choose,
And cause to approach *You*,
That he may dwell in Your courts.
[c]We shall be satisfied with the goodness of Your house,
Of Your holy temple.

5 *By* awesome deeds in righteousness You will answer us,
O God of our salvation,
You who are the confidence of all the ends of the earth,
And of the far-off seas;
6 Who established the mountains by His strength,
[a]*Being* clothed with power;
7 [a]You who still the noise of the seas,
The noise of their waves,
[b]And the tumult of the peoples.
8 They also who dwell in the farthest parts are afraid of Your signs;
You make the outgoings of the morning and evening [1]rejoice.

9 You [1]visit the earth and [a]water it,
You greatly enrich it;
[b]The river of God is full of water;
You provide their grain,
For so You have prepared it.
10 You water its ridges abundantly,
You settle its furrows;
You make it soft with showers,
You bless its growth.
11 You crown the year with Your goodness,
And Your paths drip *with* abundance.
12 They drop *on* the pastures of the wilderness,
And the little hills rejoice on every side.
13 The pastures are clothed with flocks;
[a]The valleys also are covered with grain;
They shout for joy, they also sing.

PSALM 66

To the Chief Musician. A Song. A Psalm.

MAKE [a]a joyful shout to God, all the earth!
2 Sing out the honor of His name;
Make His praise glorious.
3 Say to God,
"How [a]awesome are Your works!
[b]Through the greatness of Your power
Your enemies shall submit themselves to You.
4 [a]All the earth shall worship You
And sing praises to You;
They shall sing praises *to* Your name." Sē′lah

5 Come and see the works of God;

2 [a][Is. 66:23]
3 [a][Heb. 9:14]
4 [a]Ps. 33:12 [b]Ps. 4:3 [c]Ps. 36:8
6 [a]Ps. 93:1
7 [a]Matt. 8:26 [b]Is. 17:12, 13
8 [1]*shout for joy*
9 [a]Jer. 5:24 [b]Ps. 46:4; 104:13; 147:8 [1]*give attention to*
13 [a]Is. 44:23; 55:12

PSALM 66

1 [a]Ps. 100:1
3 [a]Ps. 65:5 [b]Ps. 18:44
4 [a]Ps. 117:1

He is awesome *in His* doing
toward the sons of men.
6 [a]He turned the sea into dry
land;
[b]They went through the river
on foot.
There we will rejoice in
Him.
7 He rules by His power
forever;
His eyes observe the
nations;
Do not let the rebellious
exalt themselves. Sē′lah

8 Oh, bless our God, you
peoples!
And make the voice of His
praise to be heard,
9 Who keeps our soul among
the living,
And does not allow our feet
to [1]be moved.
10 For [a]You, O God, have tested
us;
[b]You have refined us as silver
is refined.
11 [a]You brought us into the net;
You laid affliction on our
backs.
12 [a]You have caused men to ride
over our heads;
[b]We went through fire and
through water;
But You brought us out to
[1]rich *fulfillment.*

13 [a]I will go into Your house
with burnt offerings;
[b]I will pay You my [1]vows,
14 Which my lips have uttered
And my mouth has spoken
when I was in trouble.
15 I will offer You burnt
sacrifices of fat animals,
With the sweet aroma of
rams;
I will offer bulls with goats.
Sē′lah

16 Come *and* hear, all you who
fear God,
And I will declare what He
has done for my soul.
17 I cried to Him with my
mouth,
And He was [1]extolled with
my tongue.
18 [a]If I regard iniquity in my
heart,
The Lord will not hear.
19 *But* certainly God [a]has
heard *me;*
He has attended to the voice
of my prayer.

20 Blessed *be* God,
Who has not turned away
my prayer,
Nor His mercy from me!

PSALM 67

To the Chief Musician. On
[1]stringed instruments. A Psalm.
A Song.

GOD be merciful to us and
bless us,
And [a]cause His face to shine
upon us, Sē′lah
2 That [a]Your way may be
known on earth,
[b]Your salvation among all
nations.
3 Let the peoples praise You,
O God;
Let all the peoples praise
You.
4 Oh, let the nations be glad
and sing for joy!
For [a]You shall judge the
people righteously,

---

6 [a]Ex. 14:21 [b]Josh. 3:14–16
9 [1]*slip*
10 [a]Ps. 17:3 [b][1 Pet. 1:7]
11 [a]Lam. 1:13
12 [a]Is. 51:23 [b]Is. 43:2 [1]*abundance*
13 [a]Ps. 100:4; 116:14, 17–19 [b][Eccl. 5:4] [1]Promised deeds
17 [1]*praised*
18 [a]Is. 1:15
19 [a]Ps. 116:1, 2

PSALM 67
title [1]Heb. *neginoth*
1 [a]Num. 6:25
2 [a]Acts 18:25 [b]Titus 2:11
4 [a][Ps. 96:10, 13; 98:9]

And govern the nations on
earth. Sē′lah

5 Let the peoples praise You,
O God;
Let all the peoples praise
You.
6 [a]*Then* the earth shall [1]yield
her increase;
God, our own God, shall
bless us.
7 God shall bless us,
And all the ends of the earth
shall fear Him.

PSALM 68

To the Chief Musician. A Psalm
of David. A Song.

LET [a]God arise,
Let His enemies be
scattered;
Let those also who hate Him
flee before Him.
2 [a]As smoke is driven away,
So drive *them* away;
[b]As wax melts before the
fire,
So let the wicked perish at
the presence of God.
3 But [a]let the righteous be
glad;
Let them rejoice before God;
Yes, let them rejoice
exceedingly.

4 Sing to God, sing praises to
His name;
[a]Extol[1] Him who rides on the
[2]clouds,
[b]By His name [3]YAH,
And rejoice before Him.

5 [a]A father of the fatherless, a
defender of widows,
Is God in His holy
habitation.

6 [a]God sets the solitary in
families;
[b]He brings out those who are
bound into prosperity;
But [c]the rebellious dwell in
a dry *land.*

7 O God, [a]when You went out
before Your people,
When You marched through
the wilderness, Sē′lah
8 The earth shook;
The heavens also dropped
rain at the presence of
God;
Sinai itself *was moved* at
the presence of God, the
God of Israel.
9 [a]You, O God, sent a plentiful
rain,
Whereby You confirmed
Your inheritance,
When it was weary.
10 Your congregation dwelt in
it;
[a]You, O God, provided from
Your goodness for the
poor.

11 The Lord gave the word;
Great *was* the [1]company of
those who proclaimed *it:*
12 "Kings[a] of armies flee, they
flee,
And she who remains at
home divides the [1]spoil.
13 [a]Though you lie down among
the [1]sheepfolds,
[b]*You will be* like the wings
of a dove covered with
silver,
And her feathers with
yellow gold."
14 [a]When the Almighty
scattered kings in it,
It was *white* as snow in
Zal′mon.

---

6 [a]Lev. 26:4 [1]*give her produce*

PSALM 68

1 [a]Num. 10:35
2 [a][Is. 9:18] [b]Mic. 1:4
3 [a]Ps. 32:11
4 [a]Deut. 33:26 [b][Ex. 6:3] [1]*Praise* [2]MT *deserts;* Tg. *heavens* (cf. v. 34 and Is. 19:1) [3]Lit. *LORD,* a shortened Heb. form
5 [a][Ps. 10:14, 18; 146:9]
6 [a]Ps. 107:4–7 [b]Acts 12:6–11 [c]Ps. 107:34
7 [a]Ex. 13:21
9 [a]Deut. 11:11
10 [a]Deut. 26:5
11 [1]*host*
12 [a]Josh. 10:16 [1]*plunder*
13 [a]Ps. 81:6 [b]Ps. 105:37 [1]Or *saddlebags*
14 [a]Josh. 10:10

15 A mountain of God *is* the
mountain of Bā′shan;
A mountain *of many* peaks
is the mountain of
Bā′shan.
16 Why do you [1]fume with
envy, you mountains of
many peaks?
[a]*This is* the mountain *which*
God desires to dwell in;
Yes, the LORD will dwell *in it*
forever.

17 [a]The chariots of God *are*
twenty thousand,
Even thousands of
thousands;
The Lord is among them
as in Sinai, in the Holy
Place.
☆ 18 [a]You have ascended on high,
[b]You have led captivity
captive;
[c]You have received gifts
among men,
Even *from* [d]the rebellious,
[e]That the LORD God might
dwell *there.*

19 Blessed *be* the Lord,
Who daily loads us *with*
benefits,
The God of our salvation!
Sē′lah
20 Our God *is* the God of
salvation;
And [a]to GOD the Lord *belong*
escapes from death.

21 But [a]God will wound the
head of His enemies,
[b]The hairy scalp of the one
who still goes on in his
trespasses.
22 The Lord said, "I will bring
[a]back from Bā′shan,
I will bring *them* back [b]from
the depths of the sea,
23 [a]That [1]your foot may crush
them in blood,
[b]And the tongues of your
dogs *may have* their
portion from *your*
enemies."

24 They have seen Your
[1]procession, O God,
The procession of my
God, my King, into the
sanctuary.
25 [a]The singers went before, the
players on instruments
followed after;
Among *them were* the
maidens playing
timbrels.
26 Bless God in the
congregations,
The Lord, from [a]the fountain
of Israel.
27 [a]There *is* little Benjamin,
their leader,
The princes of Judah *and*
their [1]company,
The princes of Zeb′ū·lun *and*
the princes of Naph′ta·lī.

28 [1]Your God has [a]commanded
your strength;
Strengthen, O God, what
You have done for us.
29 Because of Your temple at
Jerusalem,
[a]Kings will bring presents to
You.
30 Rebuke the beasts of the
reeds,
[a]The herd of bulls with the
calves of the peoples,
Till everyone [b]submits
himself with pieces of
silver.
Scatter the peoples *who*
delight in war.
31 [a]Envoys will come out of
Egypt;

---

16 [a][Deut. 12:5] [1]Lit. *stare*
17 [a]Deut. 33:2
18 [a]Mark 16:19; Acts 1:9; Eph. 4:8; Phil. 2:9; Col. 3:1; Heb. 1:3 [b]Judg. 5:12 [c]Acts 2:4, 33; 10:44–46 [d][1 Tim. 1:13] [e]Ps. 78:60
20 [a][Deut. 32:39]
21 [a]Hab. 3:13 [b]Ps. 55:23
22 [a]Num. 21:33 [b]Ex. 14:22
23 [a]Ps. 58:10 [b]1 Kin. 21:19 [1]LXX, Syr., Tg., Vg. *you may dip your foot*
24 [1]Lit. *goings*
25 [a]1 Chr. 13:8
26 [a]Deut. 33:28
27 [a]1 Sam. 9:21 [1]*throng*
28 [a]Is. 26:12 [1]LXX, Syr., Tg., Vg. *Command, O God*
29 [a]Ps. 45:12; 72:10
30 [a]Ps. 22:12 [b]2 Sam. 8:2
31 [a]Is. 19:19–23

[b]Ethiopia will quickly
[c]stretch out her hands to
God.

32 Sing to God, you [a]kingdoms
of the earth;
Oh, sing praises to the Lord,
Sē′lah
33 To Him [a]who rides on the
heaven of heavens,
which were of old!
Indeed, He sends out His
voice, a [b]mighty voice.
34 [a]Ascribe strength to God;
His excellence *is* over
Israel,
And His strength *is* in the
clouds.
35 O God, [a]*You are* more
awesome than Your holy
places.
The God of Israel *is* He who
gives strength and power
to *His* people.

Blessed *be* God!

PSALM 69

To the Chief Musician. Set to [1]"The Lilies." *A Psalm* of David.

SAVE me, O God!
For [a]the waters have come
up to *my* [1]neck.
2 [a]I sink in deep mire,
Where *there is* no standing;
I have come into deep
waters,
Where the floods
overflow me.
3 [a]I am weary with my crying;
My throat is dry;
[b]My eyes fail while I wait for
my God.

☆ 4 Those who [a]hate me without
a cause
Are more than the hairs of
my head;
They are mighty who would
destroy me,
Being my enemies
wrongfully;
Though I have stolen
nothing,
I *still* must restore *it*.

5 O God, You know my
foolishness;
And my sins are not hidden
from You.
6 Let not those who [1]wait
for You, O Lord GOD
of hosts, be ashamed
because of me;
Let not those who seek You
be [2]confounded because
of me, O God of Israel.
7 Because for Your sake I have ☆
borne [a]reproach;
Shame has covered my face.
8 [a]I have become a stranger to ☆
my brothers,
And an alien to my mother's
children;
9 [a]Because zeal for Your house ☆
has eaten me up,
[b]And the reproaches of those
who reproach You have
fallen on me.
10 When I wept *and chastened*
my soul with fasting,
That became my reproach.
11 I also [1]made sackcloth my
garment;
I became a byword to them.
12 Those who [1]sit in the gate
speak against me,
And I *am* the song of the
[a]drunkards.

13 But as for me, my prayer *is*
to You,
O LORD, *in* the acceptable
time;

31 [b]Is. 45:14 [c]Ps. 44:20
32 [a][Ps. 67:3, 4]
33 [a]Ps. 18:10 [b]Ps. 46:6
34 [a]Ps. 29:1
35 [a]Ps. 76:12

PSALM 69

title [1]Heb. *Shoshannim*
1 [a]Jon. 2:5 [1]Lit. *soul*
2 [a]Ps. 40:2
3 [a]Ps. 6:6 [b]Ps. 119:82, 123
4 [a]John 15:25
6 [1]Wait in faith [2]*dishonored*
7 [a]Rom. 15:3
8 [a]Is. 53:3; Mark 3:21; Luke 8:19; John 7:3–5
9 [a]John 2:17 [b]Rom. 15:3
11 [1]Symbolic of sorrow
12 [a]Job 30:9 [1]Sit as judges

O God, in the multitude of
Your mercy,
Hear me in the truth of Your
salvation.
14 Deliver me out of the mire,
And let me not sink;
Let me be delivered from
those who hate me,
And out of the deep waters.
15 Let not the floodwater
overflow me,
Nor let the deep swallow
me up;
And let not the pit shut its
mouth on me.

16 Hear me, O LORD, for Your
lovingkindness *is* good;
Turn to me according to the
multitude of Your tender
mercies.
17 And do not hide Your face
from Your servant,
For I am in trouble;
Hear me speedily.
18 Draw near to my soul, *and*
redeem it;
Deliver me because of my
enemies.

19 You know [a]my reproach, my
shame, and my dishonor;
My adversaries *are* all
before You.
☆ 20 Reproach has broken my
heart,
And I am full of [1]heaviness;
[a]I looked *for someone* to take
pity, but *there was* none;
And for [b]comforters, but I
found none.
☆ 21 They also gave me gall for
my food,
[a]And for my thirst they gave
me vinegar to drink.

☆ 22 [a]Let their table become a
snare before them,
And their well-being a
trap.
23 [a]Let their eyes be darkened,
so that they do not see;
And make their loins shake
continually.
24 [a]Pour out Your indignation
upon them,
And let Your wrathful anger
take hold of them.
25 [a]Let their dwelling place be ☆
desolate;
Let no one live in their
tents.
26 For they persecute the *ones*
[a]You have struck,
And talk of the grief of
those You have wounded.
27 [a]Add iniquity to their
iniquity,
[b]And let them not come into
Your righteousness.
28 Let them [a]be blotted out of
the book of the living,
[b]And not be written with the
righteous.

29 But I *am* poor and
sorrowful;
Let Your salvation, O God,
set me up on high.
30 [a]I will praise the name of
God with a song,
And will magnify Him with
thanksgiving.
31 [a]*This* also shall please the
LORD better than an ox
or bull,
Which has horns and
hooves.
32 [a]The humble shall see *this*
and be glad;
And you who seek God,
[b]your hearts shall live.
33 For the LORD hears the poor,
And does not despise [a]His
prisoners.

19 [a]Ps. 22:6, 7
20 [a]Is. 63:5; Rom. 15:3 [b]Job 16:2 [1]Lit. *sickness*
21 [a]Matt. 27:34, 48; Mark 15:23, 36; Luke 23:36; John 19:28–30
22 [a]Rom. 11:9, 10
23 [a]Is. 6:9, 10
24 [a][1 Thess. 2:16]
25 [a]Matt. 23:38; Luke 13:35; Acts 1:20
26 [a][Is. 53:4]
27 [a][Rom. 1:28] [b][Is. 26:10]
28 [a][Ex. 32:32] [b]Ezek. 13:9
30 [a][Ps. 28:7]
31 [a]Ps. 50:13, 14, 23; 51:16
32 [a]Ps. 34:2 [b]Ps. 22:26
33 [a]Eph. 3:1

34 [a]Let heaven and earth praise
Him,
The seas [b]and everything
that moves in them.
35 [a]For God will save Zion
And build the cities of
Judah,
That they may dwell there
and possess it.
36 Also, [a]the [1]descendants of
His servants shall
inherit it,
And those who love His
name shall dwell in it.

PSALM 70

To the Chief Musician. *A Psalm* of David. [a]To bring to remembrance.

MAKE *haste,* [a]O God, to
deliver me!
Make haste to help me,
O LORD!

2 [a]Let them be ashamed and
confounded
Who seek my life;
Let them be [1]turned back
and confused
Who desire my hurt.
3 [a]Let them be turned back
because of their shame,
Who say, [1]"Aha, aha!"

4 Let all those who seek You
rejoice and be glad in
You;
And let those who love Your
salvation say continually,
"Let God be magnified!"

5 [a]But I *am* poor and needy;
[b]Make haste to me, O God!
You *are* my help and my
deliverer;
O LORD, do not delay.

34 [a]Ps. 96:11 [b]Is. 55:12
35 [a]Is. 44:26
36 [a]Ps. 102:28 [1]Lit. *seed*

PSALM 70
title [a]Ps. 38:title
1 [a]Ps. 40:13–17
2 [a]Ps. 35:4, 26 [1]So with MT, LXX, Tg., Vg.; some Heb. mss., Syr. *appalled* (cf. 40:15)
3 [a]Ps. 40:15 [1]An expression of scorn
5 [a]Ps. 72:12, 13 [b]Ps. 141:1

PSALM 71
1 [a]Ps. 25:2, 3
2 [a]Ps. 31:1 [b]Ps. 17:6
3 [a]Ps. 31:2, 3 [b]Ps. 44:4 [1]Lit. *rock of refuge* or *rock of habitation*
4 [a]Ps. 140:1, 3
5 [a]Jer. 14:8; 17:7, 13, 17; 50:7
6 [a]Ps. 22:9, 10 [1]*sustained from the womb*
7 [a]Is. 8:18
8 [a]Ps. 35:28

PSALM 71

IN [a]You, O LORD, I put my
trust;
Let me never be put to
shame.
2 [a]Deliver me in Your
righteousness, and cause
me to escape;
[b]Incline Your ear to me, and
save me.
3 [a]Be my [1]strong refuge,
To which I may resort
continually;
You have given the
[b]commandment to save
me,
For You *are* my rock and my
fortress.

4 [a]Deliver me, O my God,
out of the hand of the
wicked,
Out of the hand of the
unrighteous and cruel
man.
5 For You are [a]my hope,
O Lord GOD;
You are my trust from my
youth.
6 [a]By You I have been [1]upheld
from birth;
You are He who took me out
of my mother's womb.
My praise *shall be*
continually of You.

7 [a]I have become as a wonder
to many,
But You *are* my strong
refuge.
8 Let [a]my mouth be filled *with*
Your praise
And with Your glory all the
day.

9 Do not cast me off in the
time of old age;

Do not forsake me when my
strength fails.
10 For my enemies speak
against me;
And those who lie in wait
for my life [a]take counsel
together,
11 Saying, "God has forsaken
him;
Pursue and take him, for
there is none to deliver
him."

12 [a]O God, do not be far from
me;
O my God, [b]make haste to
help me!
13 Let them be [1]confounded
and consumed
Who are adversaries of my
life;
Let them be covered *with*
reproach and dishonor
Who seek my hurt.

14 But I will hope continually,
And will praise You yet
more and more.
15 My mouth shall tell of Your
righteousness
And Your salvation all the
day,
For I do not know *their*
limits.
16 I will go in the strength of
the Lord GOD;
I will make mention of Your
righteousness, of Yours
only.

17 O God, You have taught me
from my [a]youth;
And to this *day* I declare
Your wondrous works.
18 Now also [a]when *I am* old
and grayheaded,
O God, do not forsake me,
Until I declare Your strength
to *this* generation,
Your power to everyone *who*
is to come.

19 Also [a]Your righteousness,
O God, *is* [1]very high,
You who have done great
things;
[b]O God, who *is* like You?
20 [a]*You,* who have shown
me great and severe
troubles,
[b]Shall revive me again,
And bring me up again from
the depths of the earth.
21 You shall increase my
greatness,
And comfort me on every
side.

22 Also [a]with the lute I will
praise You—
And Your faithfulness, O my
God!
To You I will sing with the
harp,
O [b]Holy One of Israel.
23 My lips shall greatly rejoice
when I sing to You,
And [a]my soul, which You
have redeemed.
24 My tongue also shall talk of
Your righteousness all
the day long;
For they are confounded,
For they are brought to
shame
Who seek my hurt.

PSALM 72

A Psalm [a]of Solomon.

GIVE the king Your
judgments, O God,
And Your righteousness to
the king's Son.

10 [a]2 Sam. 17:1
12 [a]Ps. 35:22 [b]Ps. 70:1
13 [1]*ashamed*
17 [a]Deut. 4:5; 6:7
18 [a][Is. 46:4]
19 [a]Ps. 57:10 [b]Ps. 35:10 [1]*great,* lit. *to the height* of heaven
20 [a]Ps. 60:3 [b]Hos. 6:1, 2
22 [a]Ps. 92:1–3 [b]2 Kin. 19:22
23 [a]Ps. 103:4
PSALM 72
title [a]Ps. 127:title

2 [a]He will judge Your people
with righteousness,
And Your poor with justice.
3 [a]The mountains will bring
peace to the people,
And the little hills, by
righteousness.
4 [a]He will bring justice to the
poor of the people;
He will save the children of
the needy,
And will [1]break in pieces
the oppressor.

5 [1]They shall fear You
[a]As long as the sun and
moon endure,
Throughout all generations.
6 [a]He shall come down like
rain upon the grass
before mowing,
Like showers *that* water the
earth.
7 In His days the righteous
shall flourish,
[a]And abundance of peace,
Until the moon is no more.

8 [a]He shall have dominion also
from sea to sea,
And from the River to the
ends of the earth.
9 [a]Those who dwell in the
wilderness will bow
before Him,
[b]And His enemies will lick
the dust.
10 [a]The kings of Tar′shish and
of the isles
Will bring presents;
The kings of Shē′ba and
Sē′ba
Will offer gifts.
11 [a]Yes, all kings shall fall down
before Him;
All nations shall serve Him.

12 For He [a]will deliver the
needy when he cries,
The poor also, and *him* who
has no helper.
13 He will spare the poor and
needy,
And will save the souls of
the needy.
14 He will redeem their life from
oppression and violence;
And [a]precious shall be their
blood in His sight.

15 And He shall live;
And the gold of [a]Shē′ba will
be given to Him;
Prayer also will be made for
Him continually,
And daily He shall be
praised.

16 There will be an abundance
of grain in the earth,
On the top of the mountains;
Its fruit shall wave like
Lebanon;
[a]And *those* of the city shall
flourish like grass of the
earth.

17 [a]His name shall endure
forever;
His name shall continue as
long as the sun.
And [b]*men* shall be blessed
in Him;
[c]All nations shall call Him
blessed.

18 [a]Blessed *be* the LORD God,
the God of Israel,
[b]Who only does wondrous
things!
19 And [a]blessed *be* His glorious
name forever!
[b]And let the whole earth be
filled *with* His glory.
Amen and Amen.

2 [a][Is. 9:7; 11:2–5; 32:1]
3 [a]Ps. 85:10
4 [a]Is. 11:4 [1]*crush*
5 [a]Ps. 72:7, 17; 89:36 [1]So with MT, Tg.; LXX, Vg. *They shall continue*
6 [a]Hos. 6:3
7 [a]Is. 2:4
8 [a]Ex. 23:31
9 [a]Is. 23:13 [b]Is. 49:23
10 [a]2 Chr. 9:21
11 [a]Is. 49:23
12 [a]Job 29:12
14 [a][Ps. 116:15]
15 [a]Is. 60:6
16 [a]1 Kin. 4:20
17 [a][Ps. 89:36] [b][Gen. 12:3] [c]Luke 1:48
18 [a]1 Chr. 29:10 [b]Ex. 15:11
19 [a][Neh. 9:5] [b]Num. 14:21

20 The prayers of David the
son of Jesse are ended.

BOOK THREE
Psalms 73—89

PSALM 73

A Psalm of [a]Ā'saph.

TRULY God *is* good to Israel,
To such as are pure in heart.
2 But as for me, my feet had
almost stumbled;
My steps had nearly
[a]slipped.
3 [a]For I *was* envious of the
boastful,
When I saw the prosperity
of the [b]wicked.

4 For *there are* no [1]pangs in
their death,
But their strength *is* firm.
5 [a]They *are* not in trouble *as*
other men,
Nor are they plagued like
other men.
6 Therefore pride serves as
their necklace;
Violence covers them [a]*like* a
garment.
7 [a]Their [1]eyes bulge with
abundance;
They have more than heart
could wish.
8 [a]They scoff and speak
wickedly *concerning*
oppression;
They [b]speak [1]loftily.
9 They set their mouth
[a]against the heavens,
And their tongue walks
through the earth.

10 Therefore his people return
here,
[a]And waters of a full *cup* are
drained by them.
11 And they say, [a]"How does
God know?
And is there knowledge in
the Most High?"
12 Behold, these *are* the
ungodly,
Who are always at ease;
They increase *in* riches.
13 Surely I have [1]cleansed my
heart *in* [a]vain,
And washed my hands in
innocence.
14 For all day long I have been
plagued,
And chastened every
morning.

15 If I had said, "I will speak
thus,"
Behold, I would have been
untrue to the generation
of Your children.
16 When I thought *how* to
understand this,
It *was* [1]too painful for
me—
17 Until I went into the
sanctuary of God;
Then I understood their
[a]end.

18 Surely [a]You set them in
slippery places;
You cast them down to
destruction.
19 Oh, how they are *brought*
to desolation, as in a
moment!
They are utterly consumed
with terrors.
20 As a dream when *one*
awakes,
So, Lord, when You awake,
You shall despise their
image.

PSALM 73

title [a]Ps. 50:title

2 [a]Job 12:5

3 [a]Ps. 37:1, 7 [b]Job 21:5–16

4 [1]*pains*

5 [a]Job 21:9

6 [a]Ps. 109:18

7 [a]Jer. 5:28 [1]Tg. *face bulges;* LXX, Syr., Vg. *iniquity bulges*

8 [a]Ps. 53:1 [b]2 Pet. 2:18 [1]Proudly

9 [a]Rev. 13:6

10 [a][Ps. 75:8]

11 [a]Job 22:13

13 [a]Job 21:15; 35:3 [1]*kept my heart pure in vain*

16 [1]*troublesome in my eyes*

17 [a][Ps. 37:38; 55:23]

18 [a]Ps. 35:6

21 Thus my heart was grieved,
And I was [1]vexed in my mind.
22 [a]I *was* so foolish and ignorant;
I was *like* a beast before You.
23 Nevertheless I *am* continually with You;
You hold *me* by my right hand.
24 [a]You will guide me with Your counsel,
And afterward receive me *to* glory.

25 [a]Whom have I in heaven *but You?*
And *there is* none upon earth *that* I desire besides You.
26 [a]My flesh and my heart fail;
But God *is* the [1]strength of my heart and my [b]portion forever.

27 For indeed, [a]those who are far from You shall perish;
You have destroyed all those who [1]desert You for harlotry.
28 But *it is* good for me to [a]draw near to God;
I have put my trust in the Lord God,
That I may [b]declare all Your works.

PSALM 74

A [1]Contemplation of Ā′saph.

O GOD, why have You cast *us* off forever?
Why does Your anger smoke against the sheep of Your pasture?
2 Remember Your congregation, *which* You have purchased of old,
The tribe of Your inheritance, *which* You have redeemed—
This Mount Zion where You have dwelt.
3 Lift up Your feet to the perpetual desolations.
The enemy has damaged everything in the sanctuary.
4 [a]Your enemies roar in the midst of Your meeting place;
[b]They set up their banners *for* signs.
5 They seem like men who lift up
Axes among the thick trees.
6 And now they break down its carved work, all at once,
With axes and hammers.
7 They have set fire to Your sanctuary;
They have defiled the dwelling place of Your name to the ground.
8 [a]They said in their hearts,
"Let us [1]destroy them altogether."
They have burned up all the meeting places of God in the land.

9 We do not see our signs;
[a]*There is* no longer any prophet;
Nor *is there* any among us who knows how long.
10 O God, how long will the adversary [1]reproach?
Will the enemy blaspheme Your name forever?

21 [1]Lit. *pierced in my kidneys*
22 [a]Ps. 92:6
24 [a]Ps. 32:8; 48:14
25 [a][Phil. 3:8]
26 [a]Ps. 84:2 [b]Ps. 16:5 [1]Lit. *rock*
27 [a][Ps. 119:155] [1]Are unfaithful to You
28 [a][Heb. 10:22] [b]2 Cor. 4:13

PSALM 74

title [1]Heb. *Maschil*
4 [a]Lam. 2:7 [b]Num. 2:2
8 [a]Ps. 83:4 [1]*oppress*
9 [a]Amos 8:11
10 [1]*revile*

11 [a]Why do You withdraw Your
hand, even Your right
hand?
Take it out of Your bosom
and destroy *them.*
12 For [a]God *is* my King from of
old,
Working salvation in the
midst of the earth.
13 [a]You divided the sea by Your
strength;
You broke the heads of
the [1]sea serpents in the
waters.
14 You broke the heads of
[1]Le·vi'a·than in pieces,
And gave him *as* food to the
people inhabiting the
wilderness.
15 [a]You broke open the fountain
and the flood;
[b]You dried up mighty rivers.
16 The day *is* Yours, the night
also *is* [a]Yours;
[b]You have prepared the light
and the sun.
17 You have [a]set all the borders
of the earth;
[b]You have made summer and
winter.

18 Remember this, *that* the
enemy has reproached,
O LORD,
And *that* a foolish people
has blasphemed Your
name.
19 Oh, do not deliver the life
of Your turtledove to the
wild beast!
Do not forget the life of Your
poor forever.
20 [a]Have respect to the
covenant;
For the [1]dark places of the
earth are full of the
[2]haunts of [3]cruelty.

11 [a]Lam. 2:3

12 [a]Ps. 44:4

13 [a]Ex. 14:21
[1]*sea monsters*

14 [1]A large sea creature of unknown identity

15 [a]Ex. 17:5, 6
[b]Josh. 2:10; 3:13

16 [a]Job 38:12
[b]Gen. 1:14–18

17 [a]Acts 17:26
[b]Gen. 8:22

20 [a]Lev. 26:44, 45
[1]*hiding places*
[2]*homes*
[3]*violence*

22 [1]*reviles* or *taunts*

PSALM 75

title [a]Ps. 57:title
[1]Heb. *Al Tashcheth*

2 [1]*appointed*

4 [a][1 Sam. 2:3]
[1]Raise the head proudly like a horned animal

5 [1]Insolent pride

21 Oh, do not let the oppressed
return ashamed!
Let the poor and needy
praise Your name.

22 Arise, O God, plead Your
own cause;
Remember how the foolish
man [1]reproaches You
daily.
23 Do not forget the voice of
Your enemies;
The tumult of those who
rise up against You
increases continually.

PSALM 75

To the Chief Musician. Set to [a]"Do[1] Not Destroy." A Psalm of Ā'saph. A Song.

WE give thanks to You,
O God, we give thanks!
For Your wondrous works
declare *that* Your name
is near.

2 "When I choose the [1]proper
time,
I will judge uprightly.
3 The earth and all its
inhabitants are
dissolved;
I set up its pillars firmly.
Sē'lah

4 "I said to the boastful, 'Do
not deal boastfully,'
And to the wicked, [a]'Do not
[1]lift up the horn.
5 Do not lift up your horn on
high;
Do *not* speak with [1]a stiff
neck.' "

6 For exaltation *comes* neither
from the east

Nor from the west nor from
the south.
7 But [a]God *is* the Judge:
[b]He puts down one,
And exalts another.
8 For [a]in the hand of the LORD
there is a cup,
And the wine is red;
It is fully mixed, and He
pours it out;
Surely its dregs shall all the
wicked of the earth
Drain *and* drink down.

9 But I will declare forever,
I will sing praises to the
God of Jacob.

10 "All[a] the [1]horns of the wicked
I will also cut off,
But [b]the horns of the
righteous shall be
[c]exalted."

PSALM 76

To the Chief Musician. On [1]stringed instruments. A Psalm of Ā′saph. A Song.

IN [a]Judah God *is* known;
His name *is* great in Israel.
2 In [1]Sā′lem also is His
tabernacle,
And His dwelling place in
Zion.
3 There He broke the arrows
of the bow,
The shield and sword of
battle. Sē′lah

4 You *are* more glorious and
excellent
[a]*Than* the mountains of prey.
5 [a]The stouthearted were
plundered;
[b]They [1]have sunk into their
sleep;
And none of the mighty
men have found the use
of their hands.
6 [a]At Your rebuke, O God of
Jacob,
Both the chariot and horse
were cast into a dead
sleep.

7 You, Yourself, *are* to be
feared;
And [a]who may stand in Your
presence
When once You are angry?
8 [a]You caused judgment to be
heard from heaven;
[b]The earth feared and was
still,
9 When God [a]arose to
judgment,
To deliver all the oppressed
of the earth. Sē′lah

10 [a]Surely the wrath of man
shall praise You;
With the remainder of wrath
You shall gird Yourself.

11 [a]Make vows to the LORD your
God, and pay *them;*
[b]Let all who are around Him
bring presents to Him
who ought to be feared.
12 He shall cut off the spirit of
princes;
[a]*He is* awesome to the kings
of the earth.

PSALM 77

To the Chief Musician. [a]To Je·dū′thun. A Psalm of Ā′saph.

I CRIED out to God with my
voice—
To God with my voice;
And He gave ear to me.

7 [a]Ps. 50:6 [b]1 Sam. 2:7
8 [a]Jer. 25:15
10 [a]Jer. 48:25 [b]Ps. 89:17; 148:14 [c]1 Sam. 2:1 [1]Strength

PSALM 76
title [1]Heb. *neginoth*
1 [a]Ps. 48:1, 3
2 [1]Jerusalem
4 [a]Ezek. 38:12
5 [a]Is. 10:12; 46:12 [b]Ps. 13:3 [1]Lit. *have slumbered their sleep*
6 [a]Ex. 15:1–21
7 [a][Nah. 1:6]
8 [a]Ex. 19:9 [b]2 Chr. 20:29
9 [a][Ps. 9:7–9]
10 [a]Rom. 9:17
11 [a][Eccl. 5:4–6] [b]2 Chr. 32:22, 23
12 [a]Ps. 68:35

PSALM 77
title [a]Ps. 39:title

2 In the day of my trouble I sought the Lord;
My hand was stretched out in the night without ceasing;
My soul refused to be comforted.
3 I remembered God, and was troubled;
I complained, and my spirit was overwhelmed. Sē′lah

4 You hold my eyelids *open;*
I am so troubled that I cannot speak.
5 I have considered the days of old,
The years of ancient times.
6 I call to remembrance my song in the night;
I meditate within my heart,
And my spirit [1]makes diligent search.

7 Will the Lord cast off forever?
And will He be favorable no more?
8 Has His mercy ceased forever?
Has *His* [a]promise failed [1]forevermore?
9 Has God forgotten to be gracious?
Has He in anger shut up His tender mercies? Sē′lah

10 And I said, "This *is* my [1]anguish;
But I will remember the years of the right hand of the Most High."
11 I will remember the works of the LORD;
Surely I will remember Your wonders of old.
12 I will also meditate on all Your work,
And talk of Your deeds.
13 Your way, O God, *is* in [1]the [a]sanctuary;
Who *is* so great a God as *our* God?
14 You *are* the God who does wonders;
You have declared Your strength among the peoples.
15 You have with *Your* arm redeemed Your people,
The sons of Jacob and Joseph. Sē′lah

16 The waters saw You, O God;
The waters saw You, they were [a]afraid;
The depths also trembled.
17 The clouds poured out water;
The skies sent out a sound;
Your arrows also flashed about.
18 The voice of Your thunder *was* in the whirlwind;
The lightnings lit up the world;
The earth trembled and shook.
19 Your way *was* in the sea,
Your path in the great waters,
And Your footsteps were not known.
20 You led Your people like a flock
By the hand of Moses and Aaron.

PSALM 78

A [a]Contemplation[1] of Ā′saph.

GIVE ear, O my people, *to* my law;
Incline your ears to the words of my mouth.

---

6 [1]*ponders diligently*

8 [a][2 Pet. 3:8, 9] [1]Lit. *unto generation and generation*

10 [1]Lit. *infirmity*

13 [a]Ps. 73:17 [1]Or *holiness*

16 [a]Ex. 14:21

PSALM 78

title [a]Ps. 74:title [1]Heb. *Maschil*

☆2 I will open my mouth in a [a]parable;
I will utter [1]dark sayings of old,
3 Which we have heard and known,
And our fathers have told us.
4 [a]We will not hide *them* from their children,
[b]Telling to the generation to come the praises of the LORD,
And His strength and His wonderful works that He has done.

5 For [a]He established a testimony in Jacob,
And appointed a law in Israel,
Which He commanded our fathers,
That [b]they should make them known to their children;
6 [a]That the generation to come might know *them,*
The children *who* would be born,
That they may arise and declare *them* to their children,
7 That they may set their hope in God,
And not forget the works of God,
But keep His commandments;
8 And [a]may not be like their fathers,
[b]A stubborn and rebellious generation,
A generation [c]*that* did not [1]set its heart aright,
And whose spirit was not faithful to God.

9 The children of Ē′phra·im, *being* armed *and* [1]carrying bows,
Turned back in the day of battle.
10 [a]They did not keep the covenant of God;
They refused to walk in His law,
11 And [a]forgot His works
And His wonders that He had shown them.

12 [a]Marvelous things He did in the sight of their fathers,
In the land of Egypt, [b]*in* the field of Zō′an.
13 [a]He divided the sea and caused them to pass through;
And [b]He made the waters stand up like a heap.
14 [a]In the daytime also He led them with the cloud,
And all the night with a light of fire.
15 [a]He split the rocks in the wilderness,
And gave *them* drink in abundance like the depths.
16 He also brought [a]streams out of the rock,
And caused waters to run down like rivers.

17 But they sinned even more against Him
By [a]rebelling against the Most High in the wilderness.
18 And [a]they tested God in their heart
By asking for the food of their fancy.
19 [a]Yes, they spoke against God:

2 [a]Matt. 13:34, 35 [1]*obscure sayings* or *riddles*
4 [a]Deut. 4:9; 6:7 [b]Ex. 13:8, 14
5 [a]Ps. 147:19 [b]Deut. 4:9; 11:19
6 [a]Ps. 102:18
8 [a]2 Kin. 17:14 [b]Ex. 32:9 [c]Ps. 78:37 [1]Lit. *prepare its heart*
9 [1]Lit. *bow shooters*
10 [a]2 Kin. 17:15
11 [a]Ps. 106:13
12 [a]Ex. 7—12 [b]Num. 13:22
13 [a]Ex. 14:21 [b]Ex. 15:8
14 [a]Ex. 13:21
15 [a]Num. 20:11
16 [a]Num. 20:8, 10, 11
17 [a]Heb. 3:16
18 [a]Ex. 16:2
19 [a]Num. 11:4; 20:3; 21:5

They said, "Can God
prepare a table in the
wilderness?
20 [a]Behold, He struck the rock,
So that the waters gushed
out,
And the streams overflowed.
Can He give bread also?
Can He provide meat for
His people?"

21 Therefore the LORD heard
this and [a]was furious;
So a fire was kindled
against Jacob,
And anger also came up
against Israel,
22 Because they [a]did not
believe in God,
And did not trust in His
salvation.
23 Yet He had commanded the
clouds above,
[a]And opened the doors of
heaven,
24 [a]Had rained down manna on
them to eat,
And given them of the
[1]bread of [b]heaven.
25 Men ate angels' food;
He sent them food to [1]the
full.

26 [a]He caused an east wind to
blow in the heavens;
And by His power He
brought in the south
wind.
27 He also rained meat on
them like the dust,
Feathered fowl like the sand
of the seas;
28 And He let *them* fall in the
midst of their camp,
All around their dwellings.
29 [a]So they ate and were well
filled,
For He gave them their own
desire.
30 They were not [1]deprived of
their craving;
But [a]while their food *was*
still in their mouths,
31 The wrath of God came
against them,
And slew the stoutest of
them,
And struck down the choice
men of Israel.

32 In spite of this [a]they still
sinned,
And [b]did not believe in His
wondrous works.
33 [a]Therefore their days He
consumed in futility,
And their years in fear.

34 [a]When He slew them, then
they sought Him;
And they returned and
sought earnestly for
God.
35 Then they remembered that
[a]God *was* their rock,
And the Most High God
[b]their Redeemer.
36 Nevertheless they [a]flattered
Him with their mouth,
And they lied to Him with
their tongue;
37 For their heart was not
steadfast with Him,
Nor were they faithful in
His covenant.
38 [a]But He, *being* full of
[b]compassion, forgave
their iniquity,
And did not destroy *them.*
Yes, many a time [c]He turned
His anger away,
And [d]did not stir up all His
wrath;
39 For [a]He remembered [b]that
they *were but* flesh,

20 [a]Num. 20:11
21 [a]Num. 11:1
22 [a][Heb. 3:18]
23 [a][Mal. 3:10]
24 [a]Ex. 16:4 [b]John 6:31 [1]Lit. *grain*
25 [1]*satiation*
26 [a]Num. 11:31
29 [a]Num. 11:19, 20
30 [a]Num. 11:33 [1]Lit. *separated*
32 [a]Num. 14:16, 17 [b]Num. 14:11
33 [a]Num. 14:29, 35
34 [a][Hos. 5:15]
35 [a][Deut. 32:4, 15] [b]Is. 41:14; 44:6; 63:9
36 [a]Ezek. 33:31
38 [a][Num. 14:18–20] [b]Ex. 34:6 [c][Is. 48:9] [d]1 Kin. 21:29
39 [a]Job 10:9 [b]John 3:6

[c]A breath that passes away
and does not come
again.

40 How often they [a]provoked[1]
Him in the wilderness,
And grieved Him in the
desert!
41 Yes, [a]again and again they
tempted God,
And limited the Holy One of
Israel.
42 They did not remember His
[1]power:
The day when He redeemed
them from the enemy,
43 When He worked His signs
in Egypt,
And His wonders in the
field of Zō′an;
44 [a]Turned their rivers into
blood,
And their streams, that they
could not drink.
45 [a]He sent swarms of flies
among them, which
devoured them,
And [b]frogs, which destroyed
them.
46 He also gave their crops to
the caterpillar,
And their labor to the
[a]locust.
47 [a]He destroyed their vines
with hail,
And their sycamore trees
with frost.
48 He also gave up their [a]cattle
to the hail,
And their flocks to fiery
[1]lightning.
49 He cast on them the
fierceness of His anger,
Wrath, indignation, and
trouble,
By sending angels of
destruction *among them.*

39 [c][Job 7:7, 16]
40 [a]Heb. 3:16 [1]*rebelled against Him*
41 [a]Num. 14:22
42 [1]Lit. *hand*
44 [a]Ex. 7:20
45 [a]Ex. 8:24 [b]Ex. 8:6
46 [a]Ex. 10:14
47 [a]Ex. 9:23–25
48 [a]Ex. 9:19 [1]*lightning bolts*
50 [1]Or *their beasts*
51 [a]Ex. 12:29, 30
52 [a]Ps. 77:20
53 [a]Ex. 14:19, 20 [b]Ex. 14:27, 28
54 [a]Ex. 15:17 [b]Ps. 44:3
55 [a]Ps. 44:2 [b]Josh. 13:7; 19:51; 23:4 [1]*surveyed measurement*, lit. *measuring cord*
56 [a]Judg. 2:11–13
57 [a]Ezek. 20:27, 28 [b]Hos. 7:16
58 [a]Judg. 2:12 [b]Deut. 12:2

50 He made a path for His
anger;
He did not spare their soul
from death,
But gave [1]their life over to
the plague,
51 And destroyed all the
[a]firstborn in Egypt,
The first of *their* strength in
the tents of Ham.
52 But He [a]made His own
people go forth like
sheep,
And guided them in the
wilderness like a flock;
53 And He [a]led them on safely,
so that they did not fear;
But the sea [b]overwhelmed
their enemies.
54 And He brought them to His
[a]holy border,
This mountain [b]*which* His
right hand had acquired.
55 [a]He also drove out the
nations before them,
[b]Allotted them an inheritance
by [1]survey,
And made the tribes of
Israel dwell in their tents.

56 [a]Yet they tested and
provoked the Most High
God,
And did not keep His
testimonies,
57 But [a]turned back and acted
unfaithfully like their
fathers;
They were turned aside [b]like
a deceitful bow.
58 [a]For they provoked Him to
anger with their [b]high
places,
And moved Him to jealousy
with their carved images.
59 When God heard *this,* He
was furious,
And greatly abhorred Israel,

60 [a]So that He forsook the
tabernacle of Shī′lōh,
The tent He had placed
among men,
61 [a]And delivered His strength
into captivity,
And His glory into the
enemy's hand.
62 [a]He also gave His people
over to the sword,
And was furious with His
inheritance.
63 The fire consumed their
young men,
And [a]their maidens were not
given in marriage.
64 [a]Their priests fell by the
sword,
And [b]their widows made no
lamentation.

65 Then the Lord awoke as
from sleep,
[a]Like a mighty man who
shouts because of wine.
66 And [a]He beat back His
enemies;
He put them to a perpetual
reproach.

67 Moreover He rejected the
tent of Joseph,
And did not choose the tribe
of Ē′phra·im,
68 But chose the tribe of Judah,
Mount Zion [a]which He
loved.
69 And He built His [a]sanctuary
like the heights,
Like the earth which He has
established forever.
70 [a]He also chose David His
servant,
And took him from the
sheepfolds;
71 From following [a]the ewes
that had young He
brought him,
[b]To shepherd Jacob His
people,
And Israel His inheritance.
72 So he shepherded them
according to the
[a]integrity of his heart,
And guided them by the
skillfulness of his hands.

PSALM 79

A Psalm of Ā′saph.

O GOD, the [1]nations have
come into [a]Your
inheritance;
Your holy temple they have
defiled;
[b]They have laid Jerusalem [2]in
heaps.
2 [a]The dead bodies of Your
servants
They have given *as* food for
the birds of the heavens,
The flesh of Your saints to
the beasts of the earth.
3 Their blood they have shed
like water all around
Jerusalem,
And *there was* no one to
bury *them*.
4 We have become a reproach
to our [a]neighbors,
A scorn and derision to
those who are around us.

5 [a]How long, LORD?
Will You be angry forever?
Will Your [b]jealousy burn like
fire?
6 [a]Pour out Your wrath on the
[1]nations that [b]do not
know You,
And on the kingdoms that
[c]do not call on Your
name.
7 For they have devoured
Jacob,

60 [a]1 Sam. 4:11
61 [a]Judg. 18:30
62 [a]1 Sam. 4:10
63 [a]Jer. 7:34; 16:9; 25:10
64 [a]1 Sam. 4:17; 22:18 [b]Job 27:15; Ezek. 24:23
65 [a]Is. 42:13
66 [a]1 Sam. 5:6
68 [a][Ps. 87:2]
69 [a]1 Kin. 6:1–38
70 [a]1 Sam. 16:11, 12
71 [a][Is. 40:11] [b]2 Sam. 5:2
72 [a]1 Kin. 9:4

PSALM 79

1 [a]Ps. 74:2 [b]Mic. 3:12 [1]*Gentiles* [2]*in ruins*
2 [a]Jer. 7:33; 19:7; 34:20
4 [a]Ps. 44:13
5 [a]Ps. 74:1, 9 [b][Zeph. 3:8]
6 [a]Jer. 10:25 [b]Is. 45:4, 5 [c]Ps. 53:4 [1]*Gentiles*

And laid waste his dwelling
place.

8 [a]Oh, do not remember
[1]former iniquities
against us!
Let Your tender mercies
come speedily to
meet us,
For we have been brought
very low.
9 Help us, O God of our
salvation,
For the glory of Your
name;
And deliver us, and
provide atonement for
our sins,
[a]For Your name's sake!
10 [a]Why should the [1]nations
say,
"Where *is* their God?"
Let there be known among
the nations in our sight
The avenging of the blood
of Your servants *which*
has been shed.

11 Let [a]the groaning of the
prisoner come before
You;
According to the greatness
of Your [1]power
Preserve those who are
appointed to die;
12 And return to our neighbors
[a]sevenfold into their
bosom
[b]Their reproach with which
they have reproached
You, O Lord.

13 So [a]we, Your people and
sheep of Your pasture,
Will give You thanks forever;
[b]We will show forth Your
praise to all generations.

8 [a]Is. 64:9 [1]Or *against us the iniquities of those who were before us*
9 [a]Jer. 14:7, 21
10 [a]Ps. 42:10 [1]*Gentiles*
11 [a]Ps. 102:20 [1]Lit. *arm*
12 [a]Gen. 4:15 [b]Ps. 74:10, 18, 22
13 [a]Ps. 74:1; 95:7 [b]Is. 43:21

PSALM 80

title [a]Ps. 45:title [1]Heb. *Shoshannim* [2]Heb. *Eduth*
1 [a][Ex. 25:20–22] [b]Ps. 77:20 [c]Deut. 33:2
2 [a]Ps. 78:9, 67
3 [a]Lam. 5:21 [b]Num. 6:25
4 [a]Ps. 79:5
5 [a]Is. 30:20
8 [a][Is. 5:1, 7] [b]Ps. 44:2 [1]*Gentiles*

PSALM 80

To the Chief Musician. [a]Set to
[1]"The Lilies." A [2]Testimony of
Ā'saph. A Psalm.

GIVE ear, O Shepherd of
Israel,
[a]You who lead Joseph [b]like a
flock;
You who dwell *between* the
cherubim, [c]shine forth!
2 Before [a]Ē'phra·im,
Benjamin, and
Ma·nas'seh,
Stir up Your strength,
And come *and* save us!

3 [a]Restore us, O God;
[b]Cause Your face to shine,
And we shall be saved!

4 O LORD God of hosts,
[a]How long will You be
angry
Against the prayer of Your
people?
5 [a]You have fed them with the
bread of tears,
And given them tears to
drink in great measure.
6 You have made us a strife to
our neighbors,
And our enemies laugh
among themselves.

7 Restore us, O God of hosts;
Cause Your face to shine,
And we shall be saved!

8 You have brought [a]a vine
out of Egypt;
[b]You have cast out the
[1]nations, and planted it.
9 You prepared *room* for it,
And caused it to take deep
root,
And it filled the land.

10 The hills were covered with
its shadow,
And the [1]mighty cedars with
its [a]boughs.
11 She sent out her boughs to
[1]the Sea,
And her branches to [2]the
River.

12 Why have You [a]broken down
her [1]hedges,
So that all who pass by the
way pluck her *fruit?*
13 The boar out of the woods
uproots it,
And the wild beast of the
field devours it.

14 Return, we beseech You,
O God of hosts;
[a]Look down from heaven
and see,
And visit this vine
15 And the vineyard which
Your right hand has
planted,
And the branch *that*
You made strong [a]for
Yourself.
16 *It is* burned with fire, *it is*
cut down;
[a]They perish at the rebuke of
Your countenance.
17 [a]Let Your hand be upon the
man of Your right hand,
Upon the son of man *whom*
You made strong for
Yourself.
18 Then we will not turn back
from You;
Revive us, and we will call
upon Your name.

19 Restore us, O LORD God of
hosts;
Cause Your face to shine,
And we shall be saved!

10 [a]Lev. 23:40 [1]Lit. *cedars of God*
11 [1]The Mediterranean [2]The Euphrates
12 [a]Is. 5:5 [1]*walls or fences*
14 [a]Is. 63:15
15 [a][Is. 49:5]
16 [a][Ps. 39:11]
17 [a]Ps. 89:21

PSALM 81

title [a]Ps. 8:title [1]Heb. *Al Gittith*
4 [a]Num. 10:10
5 [a]Ps. 114:1
7 [a]Ex. 2:23; 14:10 [b]Ex. 19:19; 20:18 [c]Ex. 17:6, 7 [1]Lit. *Strife* or *Contention*
8 [a][Ps. 50:7]
9 [a][Is. 43:12]
10 [a]Ex. 20:2

PSALM 81

To the Chief Musician. [a]On[1] an instrument of Gath. *A Psalm* of Ā′saph.

SING aloud to God our
strength;
Make a joyful shout to the
God of Jacob.
2 Raise a song and strike the
timbrel,
The pleasant harp with the
lute.

3 Blow the trumpet at the
time of the New Moon,
At the full moon, on our
solemn feast day.
4 For [a]this *is* a statute for
Israel,
A law of the God of Jacob.
5 This He established in
Joseph *as* a testimony,
When He went throughout
the land of Egypt,
[a]*Where* I heard a language I
did not understand.

6 "I removed his shoulder from
the burden;
His hands were freed from
the baskets.
7 [a]You called in trouble, and I
delivered you;
[b]I answered you in the secret
place of thunder;
I [c]tested you at the waters of
[1]Mer′i·bah. Sē′lah

8 "Hear,[a] O My people, and I
will admonish you!
O Israel, if you will listen to
Me!
9 There shall be no [a]foreign
god among you;
Nor shall you worship any
foreign god.
10 [a]I *am* the LORD your God,

Who brought you out of the
land of Egypt;
[b]Open your mouth wide, and
I will fill it.

11 "But My people would not
heed My voice,
And Israel would *have*
[a]none of Me.
12 [a]So I gave them over to [1]their
own stubborn heart,
To walk in their own
counsels.

13 "Oh,[a] that My people would
listen to Me,
That Israel would walk in
My ways!
14 I would soon subdue their
enemies,
And turn My hand against
their adversaries.
15 [a]The haters of the LORD
would pretend
submission to Him,
But their [1]fate would endure
forever.
16 He would [a]have fed them
also with [1]the finest of
wheat;
And with honey [b]from
the rock I would have
satisfied you."

PSALM 82

A Psalm of Ā'saph.

GOD [a]stands in the
congregation of [1]the
mighty;
He judges among [b]the [2]gods.
2 How long will you judge
unjustly,
And [a]show partiality to the
wicked? Sē'lah
3 [1]Defend the poor and
fatherless;
Do justice to the afflicted
and [a]needy.
4 Deliver the poor and needy;
Free *them* from the hand of
the wicked.

5 They do not know, nor do
they understand;
They walk about in
darkness;
All the [a]foundations of the
earth are [1]unstable.

6 I said, [a]"You *are* [1]gods,
And all of you *are* children
of the Most High.
7 But you shall die like men,
And fall like one of the
princes."

8 Arise, O God, judge the
earth;
[a]For You shall inherit all
nations.

PSALM 83

A Song. A Psalm of Ā'saph.

DO[a] not keep silent, O God!
Do not hold Your peace,
And do not be still, O God!
2 For behold, [a]Your enemies
make a [1]tumult;
And those who hate You
have [2]lifted up their head.
3 They have taken crafty
counsel against Your
people,
And consulted together
[a]against Your sheltered
ones.
4 They have said, "Come, and
[a]let us cut them off from
being a nation,
That the name of Israel
may be remembered no
more."

---

10 [b]Ps. 103:5
11 [a]Deut. 32:15
12 [a][Acts 7:42] [1]*the dictates of their heart*
13 [a][Is. 48:18]
15 [a]Rom. 1:30 [1]Lit. *time*
16 [a]Deut. 32:14 [b]Job 29:6 [1]Lit. *fat of wheat*

PSALM 82

1 [a][2 Chr. 19:6] [b]Ps. 82:6 [1]Heb. *El*, lit. *God* [2]Judges; Heb. *elohim*, lit. *mighty ones* or *gods*
2 [a][Deut. 1:17]
3 [a][Deut. 24:17] [1]*Vindicate*
5 [a]Ps. 11:3 [1]*moved*
6 [a]John 10:34 [1]Judges; Heb. *elohim*, lit. *mighty ones* or *gods*
8 [a][Rev. 11:15]

PSALM 83

1 [a]Ps. 28:1
2 [a]Ps. 81:15 [1]*uproar* [2]Exalted themselves
3 [a][Ps. 27:5]
4 [a]Jer. 11:19; 31:36

5 For they have consulted
together with one
[1]consent;
They [2]form a confederacy
against You:
6 [a]The tents of Ē′dom and the
Ish′ma·el·ītes;
Mō′ab and the Hag′rītes;
7 Gē′bal, Am′mon, and
Am′a·lek;
Phi·lis′ti·a with the
inhabitants of Tȳre;
8 Assyria also has joined with
them;
They have helped the
children of Lot. Sē′lah

9 Deal with them as *with*
[a]Mid′i·an,
As *with* [b]Sis′e·ra,
As *with* Jā′bin at the Brook
Kī′shon,
10 Who perished at En Dor,
[a]*Who* became *as* refuse on
the earth.
11 Make their nobles like
[a]Or′eb and like Zē′eb,
Yes, all their princes like
[b]Zē′bah and Zal·mun′na,
12 Who said, "Let us take for
ourselves
The pastures of God for a
possession."

13 [a]O my God, make them like
the whirling dust,
[b]Like the chaff before the
wind!
14 As the fire burns the woods,
And as the flame [a]sets the
mountains on fire,
15 So pursue them with Your
tempest,
And frighten them with Your
storm.
16 Fill their faces with shame,
That they may seek Your
name, O LORD.
17 Let them be [1]confounded
and dismayed forever;
Yes, let them be put to
shame and perish,
18 [a]That they may know that
You, whose [b]name alone
is the LORD,
Are [c]the Most High over all
the earth.

PSALM 84

To the Chief Musician. [a]On[1] an instrument of Gath. A Psalm of the sons of Kō′rah.

HOW [a]lovely [1]*is* Your
tabernacle,
O LORD of hosts!
2 [a]My soul longs, yes, even
faints
For the courts of the LORD;
My heart and my flesh cry
out for the living God.

3 Even the sparrow has found
a home,
And the swallow a nest for
herself,
Where she may lay her
young—
Even Your altars, O LORD of
hosts,
My King and my God.
4 Blessed *are* those who dwell
in Your [a]house;
They will still be praising
You. Sē′lah

5 Blessed *is* the man whose
strength *is* in You,
Whose heart *is* set on
pilgrimage.
6 *As they* pass through the
Valley [a]of [1]Bā′ca,
They make it a spring;
The rain also covers it with
[2]pools.

5 [1]Lit. *heart* [2]Lit. *cut a covenant*
6 [a]2 Chr. 20:1, 10, 11
9 [a]Judg. 7:22 [b]Judg. 4:15–24; 5:20, 21
10 [a]Zeph. 1:17
11 [a]Judg. 7:25 [b]Judg. 8:12–21
13 [a]Is. 17:13 [b]Ps. 35:5
14 [a]Deut. 32:22
17 [1]*ashamed*
18 [a]Ps. 59:13 [b]Ex. 6:3 [c][Ps. 92:8]
PSALM 84
title [a]Ps. 8:title [1]Heb. *Al Gittith*
1 [a]Ps. 27:4; 46:4, 5 [1]*are Your dwellings*
2 [a]Ps. 42:1, 2
4 [a][Ps. 65:4]
6 [a]2 Sam. 5:22–25 [1]Lit. *Weeping* [2]Or *blessings*

7 They go [a]from strength to strength;
[1]*Each one* [b]appears before God in Zion.

8 O LORD God of hosts, hear my prayer;
Give ear, O God of Jacob! Sē′lah
9 [a]O God, behold our shield,
And look upon the face of Your [1]anointed.

10 For a day in Your courts *is* better than a thousand.
I would rather [1]be a doorkeeper in the house of my God
Than dwell in the tents of wickedness.
11 For the LORD God *is* [a]a sun and [b]shield;
The LORD will give grace and glory;
[c]No good *thing* will He withhold
From those who walk uprightly.

12 O LORD of hosts,
[a]Blessed *is* the man who trusts in You!

PSALM 85

To the Chief Musician. A Psalm [a]of the sons of Kō′rah.

LORD, You have been favorable to Your land;
You have [a]brought back the captivity of Jacob.
2 You have forgiven the iniquity of Your people;
You have covered all their sin. Sē′lah
3 You have taken away all Your wrath;
You have turned from the fierceness of Your anger.

4 [a]Restore us, O God of our salvation,
And cause Your anger toward us to cease.
5 [a]Will You be angry with us forever?
Will You prolong Your anger to all generations?
6 Will You not [a]revive us again,
That Your people may rejoice in You?
7 Show us Your mercy, LORD,
And grant us Your salvation.

8 I will hear what God the LORD will speak,
For He will speak peace
To His people and to His saints;
But let them not turn back to [1]folly.
9 Surely [a]His salvation *is* near to those who fear Him,
[b]That glory may dwell in our land.

10 Mercy and truth have met together;
[a]Righteousness and peace have kissed.
11 Truth shall spring out of the earth,
And righteousness shall look down from heaven.
12 [a]Yes, the LORD will give *what is* good;
And our land will yield its increase.
13 Righteousness will go before Him,
And shall make His footsteps *our* pathway.

---

7 [a]Prov. 4:18 [b]Deut. 16:16 [1]LXX, Syr., Vg. *The God of gods shall be seen*
9 [a]Gen. 15:1 [1]Commissioned one, Heb. *messiah*
10 [1]*stand at the threshold*
11 [a]Is. 60:19, 20 [b]Gen. 15:1 [c]Ps. 34:9, 10
12 [a][Ps. 2:12; 40:4]

PSALM 85

title [a]Ps. 42:title
1 [a]Joel 3:1
4 [a]Ps. 80:3, 7
5 [a]Ps. 79:5
6 [a]Hab. 3:2
8 [1]*foolishness*
9 [a]Is. 46:13 [b]Zech. 2:5
10 [a]Ps. 72:3
12 [a][Ps. 84:11]

PSALM 86

A Prayer of David.

BOW down Your ear, O LORD, hear me;
For I *am* poor and needy.
2 Preserve my [1]life, for I *am* holy;
You are my God;
Save Your servant who trusts in You!
3 Be merciful to me, O Lord,
For I cry to You all day long.
4 [1]Rejoice the soul of Your servant,
[a]For to You, O Lord, I lift up my soul.
5 For [a]You, Lord, *are* good, and ready to forgive,
And abundant in mercy to all those who call upon You.

6 Give ear, O LORD, to my prayer;
And attend to the voice of my supplications.
7 In the day of my trouble I will call upon You,
For You will answer me.

8 [a]Among the gods *there is* none like You, O Lord;
Nor *are there any works* like Your works.
9 All nations whom You have made
Shall come and worship before You, O Lord,
And shall glorify Your name.
10 For You *are* great, and [a]do wondrous things;
[b]You alone *are* God.

11 [a]Teach me Your way, O LORD;
I will walk in Your truth;
[1]Unite my heart to fear Your name.

PSALM 86
2 [1]Lit. *soul*
4 [a]Ps. 25:1; 143:8 [1]*Make glad*
5 [a][Joel 2:13]
8 [a][Ex. 15:11]
10 [a][Ex. 15:11] [b]Deut. 6:4
11 [a]Ps. 27:11; 143:8 [1]Give me singleness of heart
13 [1]The abode of the dead
15 [a]Ex. 34:6

PSALM 87
2 [a]Ps. 78:67, 68

12 I will praise You, O Lord my God, with all my heart,
And I will glorify Your name forevermore.
13 For great *is* Your mercy toward me,
And You have delivered my soul from the depths of [1]Shē′ōl.

14 O God, the proud have risen against me,
And a mob of violent *men* have sought my life,
And have not set You before them.
15 But [a]You, O Lord, *are* a God full of compassion, and gracious,
Longsuffering and abundant in mercy and truth.

16 Oh, turn to me, and have mercy on me!
Give Your strength to Your servant,
And save the son of Your maidservant.
17 Show me a sign for good,
That those who hate me may see *it* and be ashamed,
Because You, LORD, have helped me and comforted me.

PSALM 87

A Psalm of the sons of Kō′rah. A Song.

HIS foundation *is* in the holy mountains.
2 [a]The LORD loves the gates of Zion
More than all the dwellings of Jacob.

3 [a]Glorious things are spoken
of you,
O city of God! Sē′lah

4 "I will make mention of
[1]Rā′hab and Babylon to
those who know Me;
Behold, O Phi·lis′ti·a and
Tȳre, with Ethiopia:
'This *one* was born there.' "

5 And of Zion it will be said,
"This *one* and that *one* were
born in her;
And the Most High Himself
shall establish her."

6 The LORD will record,
When He [a]registers the
peoples:
"This *one* was born there."
Sē′lah

7 Both the singers and the
players on instruments
say,
"All my springs *are* in you."

PSALM 88

A Song. A Psalm of the sons of Kō′rah. To the Chief Musician. Set to "Mā′ha·lath Le·an′noth." A [1]Contemplation of [a]Hē′man the Ez′ra·hīte.

O LORD, [a]God of my
salvation,
I have cried out day and
night before You.

2 Let my prayer come before
You;
[1]Incline Your ear to my cry.

3 For my soul is full of
troubles,
And my life [a]draws near to
the grave.

4 I am counted with those
who [a]go[1] down to the pit;
[b]I am like a man *who has* no
strength,

5 [1]Adrift among the dead,
Like the slain who lie in the
grave,
Whom You remember no
more,
And who are cut off from
Your hand.

6 You have laid me in the
lowest pit,
In darkness, in the depths.

7 Your wrath lies heavy upon
me,
And You have afflicted *me*
with all [a]Your waves.
Sē′lah

8 [a]You have [1]put away my
acquaintances far from
me;
You have made me an
abomination to them;
[b]*I am* shut up, and I cannot
get out;

9 My eye wastes away
because of affliction.

[a]LORD, I have called daily
upon You;
I have stretched out my
hands to You.

10 Will You work wonders for
the dead?
Shall [1]the dead arise *and*
praise You? Sē′lah

11 Shall Your lovingkindness
be declared in the grave?
Or Your faithfulness in the
place of destruction?

12 Shall Your wonders be
known in the dark?
And Your righteousness
in the land of
forgetfulness?

---

3 [a]Is. 60:1
4 [1]Egypt
6 [a]Is. 4:3

PSALM 88

title [a]1 Kin. 4:31 [1]Heb. *Maschil*
1 [a]Ps. 27:9
2 [1]Listen to
3 [a]Ps. 107:18
4 [a][Ps. 28:1] [b]Ps. 31:12 [1]Die
5 [1]Lit. *Free*
7 [a]Ps. 42:7
8 [a]Job 19:13, 19 [b]Lam. 3:7 [1]*taken away my friends*
9 [a]Ps. 86:3
10 [1]*shades, ghosts*

13 But to You I have cried out,
O LORD,
And in the morning my
prayer comes before You.
14 LORD, why do You cast off
my soul?
Why do You hide Your face
from me?
15 I *have been* afflicted and
ready to die from *my*
youth;
I suffer Your terrors;
I am distraught.
16 Your fierce wrath has gone
over me;
Your terrors have [1]cut me
off.
17 They came around me all
day long like water;
They engulfed me
altogether.
18 [a]Loved one and friend You
have put far from me,
And my acquaintances into
darkness.

PSALM 89

A [1]Contemplation of [a]Ē'than the
Ez'ra·hite.

I WILL sing of the mercies of
the LORD forever;
With my mouth will I make
known Your faithfulness
to all generations.
2 For I have said, "Mercy shall
be built up forever;
[a]Your faithfulness You shall
establish in the very
heavens."
3 "I[a] have made a covenant
with My chosen,
I have [b]sworn to My servant
David:
4 'Your seed I will establish
forever,
And build up your throne
[a]to all generations.' "
Sē'lah
5 And [a]the heavens will praise
Your wonders, O LORD;
Your faithfulness also in the
assembly of the saints.
6 [a]For who in the heavens
can be compared to the
LORD?
Who among the sons of the
mighty can be likened to
the LORD?
7 [a]God is greatly to be feared
in the assembly of the
saints,
And to be held in reverence
by all *those* around Him.
8 O LORD God of hosts,
Who *is* mighty like You,
O LORD?
Your faithfulness also
surrounds You.
9 [a]You rule the raging of the
sea;
When its waves rise, You
still them.
10 [a]You have broken [1]Rā'hab
in pieces, as one who is
slain;
You have scattered Your
enemies with Your
mighty arm.
11 [a]The heavens *are* Yours, the
earth also *is* Yours;
The world and all its
fullness, You have
founded them.
12 The north and the south,
You have created them;
[a]Tā'bor and [b]Her'mon rejoice
in Your name.
13 You have a mighty arm;
Strong is Your hand, *and*
high is Your right hand.

16 [1]*destroyed me*
18 [a]Ps. 31:11; 38:11

PSALM 89

title [a]1 Kin. 4:31
[1]Heb. *Maschil*
2 [a][Ps. 119:89, 90]
3 [a]1 Kin. 8:16
[b]2 Sam. 7:11
4 [a][Luke 1:33]
5 [a][Ps. 19:1]
6 [a]Ps. 86:8; 113:5
7 [a]Ps. 76:7, 11
9 [a]Ps. 65:7; 93:3, 4; 107:29
10 [a]Ps. 87:4
[1]Egypt
11 [a][Gen. 1:1]
12 [a]Josh. 19:22
[b]Josh. 11:17; 12:1

14 Righteousness and justice
are the foundation of
Your throne;
Mercy and truth go before
Your face.
15 Blessed *are* the people who
know the [a]joyful sound!
They walk, O LORD, in
the light of Your
countenance.
16 In Your name they rejoice all
day long,
And in Your righteousness
they are exalted.
17 For You *are* the glory of
their strength,
And in Your favor our [1]horn
is [a]exalted.
18 For our shield *belongs* to the
LORD,
And our king to the Holy
One of Israel.

19 Then You spoke in a vision
to Your [1]holy one,
And said: "I have given help
to *one who is* mighty;
I have exalted one [a]chosen
from the people.
20 [a]I have found My servant
David;
With My holy oil I have
anointed him,
21 [a]With whom My hand shall
be established;
Also My arm shall
strengthen him.
22 The enemy shall not [1]outwit
him,
Nor the son of wickedness
afflict him.
23 I will beat down his foes
before his face,
And plague those who hate
him.

24 "But My faithfulness and My
mercy *shall be* with him,
And in My name his horn
shall be exalted.
25 Also I will [a]set his hand over
the sea,
And his right hand over the
rivers.
26 He shall cry to Me, 'You *are*
[a]my Father,
My God, and [b]the rock of
my salvation.'
27 Also I will make him [a]*My*
firstborn,
[b]The highest of the kings of
the earth.
28 [a]My mercy I will keep for
him forever,
And My covenant shall
stand firm with him.
29 His seed also I will make *to*
endure forever,
[a]And his throne [b]as the days
of heaven.

30 "If[a] his sons [b]forsake My law
And do not walk in My
judgments,
31 If they [1]break My statutes
And do not keep My
commandments,
32 Then I will punish their
transgression with the
rod,
And their iniquity with
stripes.
33 [a]Nevertheless My
lovingkindness I will not
[1]utterly take from him,
Nor [2]allow My faithfulness
to fail.
34 My covenant I will not
break,
Nor [a]alter the word that has
gone out of My lips.
35 Once I have sworn [a]by My
holiness;
I will not lie to David:
36 [a]His seed shall endure
forever,

15 [a]Ps. 98:6
17 [a]Ps. 75:10; 92:10; 132:17 [1]Strength
19 [a]1 Kin. 11:34 [1]So with many Heb. mss.; MT, LXX, Tg., Vg. *holy ones*
20 [a]1 Sam. 13:14; 16:1–12
21 [a]Ps. 80:17
22 [1]Or *exact usury from him*
25 [a]Ps. 72:8
26 [a][1 Chr. 22:10] [b]2 Sam. 22:47
27 [a][Col. 1:15, 18] [b]Rev. 19:16
28 [a]Is. 55:3
29 [a]Jer. 33:17 [b]Deut. 11:21
30 [a][2 Sam. 7:14] [b]Ps. 119:53
31 [1]*profane*
33 [a]2 Sam. 7:14, 15 [1]Lit. *break off* [2]Lit. *deal falsely with My faithfulness*
34 [a]Jer. 33:20–22
35 [a]Amos 4:2
36 [a][Luke 1:33]

And his throne [b]as the sun
before Me;
37 It shall be established
forever like the moon,
Even *like* the faithful
witness in the sky."
Sē'lah

38 But You have [a]cast off and
[b]abhorred,[1]
You have been furious with
Your [2]anointed.
39 You have renounced the
covenant of Your servant;
[a]You have [1]profaned his
crown *by casting it* to
the ground.
40 You have broken down all
his hedges;
You have brought his
[1]strongholds to ruin.
41 All who pass by the way
[a]plunder him;
He is a reproach to his
neighbors.
42 You have exalted the right
hand of his adversaries;
You have made all his
enemies rejoice.
43 You have also turned back
the edge of his sword,
And have not sustained him
in the battle.
44 You have made his [1]glory
cease,
And cast his throne down to
the ground.
45 The days of his youth You
have shortened;
You have covered him with
shame. Sē'lah

46 How long, LORD?
Will You hide Yourself
forever?
Will Your wrath burn like
fire?

36 [b]Ps. 72:17

38 [a][1 Chr. 28:9] [b]Deut. 32:19 [1]*rejected* [2]Commissioned one, Heb. *messiah*

39 [a]Lam. 5:16 [1]*defiled*

40 [1]*fortresses*

41 [a]Ps. 80:12

44 [1]*splendor* or *brightness*

47 [a]Ps. 90:9 [b]Ps. 62:9

48 [a][Eccl. 3:19] [1]*experience death* [2]Or *Sheol*

49 [a][2 Sam. 7:15] [b]Ps. 54:5

50 [a]Ps. 69:9, 19

51 [a]Ps. 74:10, 18, 22 [1]Commissioned one, Heb. *messiah*

52 [a]Ps. 41:13

PSALM 90

title [a]Deut. 33:1

1 [a][Ezek. 11:16] [1]LXX, Tg., Vg. *refuge*

2 [a][Prov. 8:25, 26] [1]Lit. *gave birth to*

47 Remember how short my
time [a]is;
For what [b]futility have You
created all the children
of men?
48 What man can live and not
[1]see [a]death?
Can he deliver his life from
the power of [2]the grave?
Sē'lah

49 Lord, where *are* Your former
lovingkindnesses,
Which You [a]swore to David
[b]in Your truth?
50 Remember, Lord, the
reproach of Your
servants—
[a]*How* I bear in my bosom *the
reproach of* all the many
peoples,
51 [a]With which Your enemies
have reproached,
O LORD,
With which they have
reproached the footsteps
of Your [1]anointed.

52 [a]Blessed *be* the LORD
forevermore!
Amen and Amen.

BOOK FOUR
Psalms 90—106

PSALM 90

A Prayer [a]of Moses the man
of God.

LORD, [a]You have been our
[1]dwelling place in all
generations.
2 [a]Before the mountains were
brought forth,
Or ever You [1]had formed the
earth and the world,

Even from everlasting to
everlasting, You *are* God.

3 You turn man to destruction,
And say, [a]"Return,
O children of men."
4 [a]For a thousand years in Your
sight
Are like yesterday when it
is past,
And *like* a watch in the
night.
5 You carry them away *like* a
flood;
[a]*They are* like a sleep.
In the morning [b]they are
like grass *which* grows
up:
6 In the morning it flourishes
and grows up;
In the evening it is cut down
and withers.

7 For we have been consumed
by Your anger,
And by Your wrath we are
terrified.
8 [a]You have set our iniquities
before You,
Our [b]secret *sins* in the light
of Your countenance.
9 For all our days have passed
away in Your wrath;
We finish our years like a
sigh.
10 The days of our lives *are*
seventy years;
And if by reason of strength
they are eighty years,
Yet their boast *is* only labor
and sorrow;
For it is soon cut off, and we
fly away.
11 Who knows the power of
Your anger?
For as the fear of You, *so is*
Your wrath.

3 [a]Gen. 3:19
4 [a]2 Pet. 3:8
5 [a]Ps. 73:20 [b]Is. 40:6
8 [a]Ps. 50:21 [b]Ps. 19:12
12 [a]Ps. 39:4
13 [a]Deut. 32:36
14 [a]Ps. 85:6
16 [a]Hab. 3:2
17 [a]Ps. 27:4 [b]Is. 26:12

12 [a]So teach *us* to number our
days,
That we may gain a heart of
wisdom.

13 Return, O LORD!
How long?
And [a]have compassion on
Your servants.
14 Oh, satisfy us early with
Your mercy,
[a]That we may rejoice and be
glad all our days!
15 Make us glad according to
the days *in which* You
have afflicted us,
The years *in which* we have
seen evil.
16 Let [a]Your work appear to
Your servants,
And Your glory to their
children.
17 [a]And let the beauty of the
LORD our God be upon
us,
And [b]establish the work of
our hands for us;
Yes, establish the work of
our hands.

PSALM 91

1 [a]Ps. 27:5; 31:20; 32:7 [b]Ps. 17:8
2 [a]Ps. 142:5
3 [a]Ps. 124:7 [1]One who catches birds in a trap or snare
4 [a]Ps. 17:8

PSALM 91

HE [a]who dwells in the secret
place of the Most High
Shall abide [b]under the
shadow of the Almighty.
2 [a]I will say of the LORD, "*He*
is my refuge and my
fortress;
My God, in Him I will trust."

3 Surely [a]He shall deliver you
from the snare of the
[1]fowler
And from the perilous
pestilence.
4 [a]He shall cover you with His
feathers,

And under His wings you
shall take refuge;
His truth *shall be your*
shield and [1]buckler.
5 [a]You shall not be afraid of
the terror by night,
Nor of the arrow *that* flies
by day,
6 *Nor* of the pestilence *that*
walks in darkness,
Nor of the destruction *that*
lays waste at noonday.

7 A thousand may fall at your
side,
And ten thousand at your
right hand;
But it shall not come near
you.
8 Only [a]with your eyes shall
you look,
And see the reward of the
wicked.

9 Because you have made the
LORD, *who is* [a]my refuge,
Even the Most High, [b]your
dwelling place,
10 [a]No evil shall befall you,
Nor shall any plague come
near your dwelling;
11 [a]For He shall give His angels
charge over you,
To keep you in all your
ways.
12 In *their* hands they shall
[1]bear you up,
[a]Lest you [2]dash your foot
against a stone.
13 You shall tread upon the
lion and the cobra,
The young lion and the
serpent you shall
trample underfoot.

14 "Because he has set his love
upon Me, therefore I will
deliver him;
I will [1]set him on high,
because he has [a]known
My name.
15 He shall [a]call upon Me, and
I will answer him;
I *will be* [b]with him in
trouble;
I will deliver him and honor
him.
16 With [1]long life I will satisfy
him,
And show him My
salvation."

4 [1]A small shield
5 [a][Job 5:19]
8 [a]Mal. 1:5
9 [a]Ps. 91:2 [b]Ps. 90:1
10 [a][Prov. 12:21]
11 [a][Heb. 1:14]
12 [a]Matt. 4:6 [1]*lift* [2]*strike*
14 [a][Ps. 9:10] [1]*exalt him*
15 [a]Ps. 50:15 [b]Is. 43:2
16 [1]Lit. *length of days*

PSALM 92

A Psalm. A Song for the
Sabbath day.

IT *is* [a]good to give thanks to
the LORD,
And to sing praises to Your
name, O Most High;
2 To [a]declare Your
lovingkindness in the
morning,
And Your faithfulness every
night,
3 [a]On an instrument of ten
strings,
On the lute,
And on the harp,
With harmonious sound.
4 For You, LORD, have made
me glad through Your
work;
I will triumph in the works
of Your hands.

5 [a]O LORD, how great are Your
works!
[b]Your thoughts are very deep.
6 [a]A senseless man does not
know,
Nor does a fool understand
this.
7 When [a]the wicked [1]spring
up like grass,

PSALM 92
1 [a]Ps. 147:1
2 [a]Ps. 89:1
3 [a]1 Chr. 23:5
5 [a]Ps. 40:5 [b][Is. 28:29]
6 [a]Ps. 73:22
7 [a]Job 12:6 [1]*sprout*

And when all the workers of iniquity flourish,
It is that they may be destroyed forever.

8 [a]But You, LORD, *are* on high forevermore.
9 For behold, Your enemies, O LORD,
For behold, Your enemies shall perish;
All the workers of iniquity shall [a]be scattered.

10 But [a]my [1]horn You have exalted like a wild ox;
I have been [b]anointed with fresh oil.
11 [a]My eye also has seen *my desire* on my enemies;
My ears hear *my desire* on the wicked
Who rise up against me.

12 [a]The righteous shall flourish like a palm tree,
He shall grow like a cedar in Lebanon.
13 Those who are planted in the house of the LORD
Shall flourish in the courts of our God.
14 They shall still bear fruit in old age;
They shall be [1]fresh and [2]flourishing,
15 To declare that the LORD is upright;
[a]*He is* my rock, and [b]*there is* no unrighteousness in Him.

PSALM 93

THE [a]LORD reigns, He is clothed with majesty;
The LORD is clothed,
[b]He has girded Himself with strength.
Surely the world is established, so that it cannot be [1]moved.
2 [a]Your throne *is* established from of old;
You *are* from everlasting.

3 The floods have [1]lifted up, O LORD,
The floods have lifted up their voice;
The floods lift up their waves.
4 [a]The LORD on high *is* mightier
Than the noise of many waters,
Than the mighty waves of the sea.

5 Your testimonies are very sure;
Holiness adorns Your house, O LORD, [1]forever.

PSALM 94

O LORD God, [a]to whom vengeance belongs—
O God, to whom vengeance belongs, shine forth!
2 Rise up, O [a]Judge of the earth;
[1]Render punishment to the proud.
3 LORD, [a]how long will the wicked,
How long will the wicked triumph?

4 They [a]utter speech, *and* speak insolent things;
All the workers of iniquity boast in themselves.
5 They break in pieces Your people, O LORD,
And afflict Your heritage.

---

8 [a][Ps. 83:18]
9 [a]Ps. 68:1
10 [a]Ps. 89:17 [b]Ps. 23:5 [1]Strength
11 [a]Ps. 54:7
12 [a]Ps. 52:8
14 [1]Full of oil or sap, lit. *fat* [2]*green*
15 [a][Deut. 32:4] [b][Rom. 9:14]

PSALM 93
1 [a]Ps. 96:10 [b]Ps. 65:6 [1]*shaken*
2 [a]Ps. 45:6
3 [1]*raised up*
4 [a]Ps. 65:7
5 [1]Lit. *for length of days*

PSALM 94
1 [a][Nah. 1:2]
2 [a][Gen. 18:25] [1]*Repay with*
3 [a][Job 20:5]
4 [a]Ps. 31:18

6 They slay the widow and
the stranger,
And murder the fatherless.
7 [a]Yet they say, "The LORD does
not see,
Nor does the God of Jacob
[1]understand."

8 Understand, you senseless
among the people;
And *you* fools, when will
you be wise?
9 [a]He who planted the ear,
shall He not hear?
He who formed the eye,
shall He not see?
10 He who [1]instructs the
[2]nations, shall He not
correct,
He who teaches man
knowledge?
11 The LORD [a]knows the
thoughts of man,
That they *are* futile.

12 Blessed *is* the man whom
You [a]instruct, O LORD,
And teach out of Your law,
13 That You may give him
[1]rest from the days of
adversity,
Until the pit is dug for the
wicked.
14 For the LORD will not [1]cast
off His people,
Nor will He forsake His
inheritance.
15 But judgment will return to
righteousness,
And all the upright in heart
will follow it.

16 Who will rise up for me
against the evildoers?
Who will stand up for me
against the workers of
iniquity?
17 Unless the LORD *had been*
my help,
My soul would soon have
settled in silence.
18 If I say, "My foot slips,"
Your mercy, O LORD, will
hold me up.
19 In the multitude of my
anxieties within me,
Your comforts delight my
soul.

20 Shall [a]the throne of iniquity,
which devises evil by
law,
Have fellowship with You?
21 They gather together
against the life of the
righteous,
And condemn [a]innocent
blood.
22 But the LORD has been my
defense,
And my God the rock of my
refuge.
23 He has brought on them
their own iniquity,
And shall [1]cut them off in
their own wickedness;
The LORD our God shall cut
them off.

PSALM 95

Oh come, let us sing to the
LORD!
Let us shout joyfully to the
Rock of our salvation.
2 Let us come before
His presence with
thanksgiving;
Let us shout joyfully to Him
with [a]psalms.
3 For [a]the LORD *is* the great
God,
And the great King above
all gods.

7 [a]Ps. 10:11 [1]*pay attention*
9 [a][Ex. 4:11]
10 [1]*disciplines* [2]*Gentiles*
11 [a]1 Cor. 3:20
12 [a][Heb. 12:5, 6]
13 [1]*relief*
14 [1]*abandon*
20 [a]Amos 6:3
21 [a][Ex. 23:7]
23 [1]*destroy them*
PSALM 95
2 [a]James 5:13
3 [a][Ps. 96:4]

4 [1]In His hand *are* the deep
places of the earth;
The heights of the hills *are*
His also.
5 [a]The sea *is* His, for He made
it;
And His hands formed the
dry *land.*

6 Oh come, let us worship and
bow down;
Let [a]us kneel before the
LORD our Maker.
7 For He *is* our God,
And [a]we *are* the people of
His pasture,
And the sheep [1]of His hand.

[b]Today, if you will hear His
voice:
8 "Do not harden your hearts,
as in the [1]rebellion,
[a]As *in* the day of [2]trial in the
wilderness,
9 When [a]your fathers tested
Me;
They tried Me, though they
[b]saw My work.
10 For [a]forty years I was
[1]grieved with *that*
generation,
And said, 'It *is* a people who
go astray in their hearts,
And they do not know My
ways.'
11 So [a]I swore in My wrath,
'They shall not enter My
rest.' "

PSALM 96

OH, [a]sing to the LORD a new
song!
Sing to the LORD, all the
earth.
2 Sing to the LORD, bless His
name;
Proclaim the good news of
His salvation from day
to day.
3 Declare His glory among
the [1]nations,
His wonders among all
peoples.

4 For [a]the LORD *is* great and
[b]greatly to be praised;
[c]He *is* to be feared above all
gods.
5 For [a]all the gods of the
peoples *are* idols,
[b]But the LORD made the
heavens.
6 Honor and majesty *are*
before Him;
Strength and [a]beauty *are* in
His sanctuary.

7 [a]Give[1] to the LORD, O families
of the peoples,
Give to the LORD glory and
strength.
8 [1]Give to the LORD the glory
due His name;
Bring an offering, and come
into His courts.
9 Oh, worship the LORD [a]in the
beauty of holiness!
Tremble before Him, all the
earth.

10 Say among the [1]nations,
[a]"The LORD reigns;
The world also is firmly
established,
It shall not be [2]moved;
[b]He shall judge the peoples
righteously."

11 [a]Let the heavens rejoice, and
let the earth be glad;
[b]Let the sea roar, and [1]all its
fullness;
12 Let the field be joyful, and
all that *is* in it.

---

4 [1]In His possession
5 [a]Gen. 1:9, 10
6 [a][Phil. 2:10]
7 [a]Ps. 79:13 [b]Heb. 3:7–11, 15; 4:7 [1]Under His care
8 [a]Ex. 17:2–7 [1]Or *Meribah,* lit. *Strife, Contention* [2]Or *Massah,* lit. *Trial, Testing*
9 [a]Ps. 78:18 [b]Num. 14:22
10 [a]Heb. 3:10, 17 [1]*disgusted*
11 [a]Heb. 4:3, 5

PSALM 96

1 [a]1 Chr. 16:23–33
3 [1]*Gentiles*
4 [a]Ps. 145:3 [b]Ps. 18:3 [c]Ps. 95:3
5 [a][Jer. 10:11] [b]Is. 42:5
6 [a]Ps. 29:2
7 [a]Ps. 29:1, 2 [1]*Ascribe*
8 [1]*Ascribe*
9 [a]Ps. 29:2
10 [a]Ps. 93:1; 97:1 [b]Ps. 67:4 [1]*Gentiles* [2]*shaken*
11 [a]Ps. 69:34 [b]Ps. 98:7 [1]*all that is in it*

Then all the trees of the woods will rejoice
13 before the LORD.
For He is coming, for He is coming to judge the earth.
[a]He shall judge the world with righteousness,
And the peoples with His truth.

PSALM 97

THE LORD [a]reigns;
Let the earth rejoice;
Let the multitude of [1]isles be glad!

2 [a]Clouds and darkness surround Him;
[b]Righteousness and justice *are* the foundation of His throne.
3 [a]A fire goes before Him,
And burns up His enemies round about.
4 [a]His lightnings light the world;
The earth sees and trembles.
5 [a]The mountains melt like wax at the presence of the LORD,
At the presence of the Lord of the whole earth.
6 [a]The heavens declare His righteousness,
And all the peoples see His glory.

7 [a]Let all be put to shame who serve carved images,
Who boast of idols.
[b]Worship Him, all *you* gods.
8 Zion hears and is glad,
And the daughters of Judah rejoice
Because of Your judgments, O LORD.
9 For You, LORD, *are* [a]most high above all the earth;
[b]You are exalted far above all gods.

10 You who love the LORD, [a]hate evil!
[b]He preserves the souls of His saints;
[c]He delivers them out of the hand of the wicked.
11 [a]Light is sown for the righteous,
And gladness for the upright in heart.
12 [a]Rejoice in the LORD, you righteous,
[b]And give thanks [1]at the remembrance of [2]His holy name.

PSALM 98

A Psalm.

OH, [a]sing to the LORD a new song!
For He has [b]done marvelous things;
His right hand and His holy arm have gained Him the victory.
2 [a]The LORD has made known His salvation;
[b]His righteousness He has revealed in the sight of the [1]nations.
3 He has remembered His mercy and His faithfulness to the house of Israel;
[a]All the ends of the earth have seen the salvation of our God.

4 Shout joyfully to the LORD, all the earth;

---

13 [a][Rev. 19:11]

PSALM 97

1 [a][Ps. 96:10]
[1]Or *coastlands*

2 [a]Ps. 18:11
[b][Ps. 89:14]

3 [a]Ps. 18:8

4 [a]Ex. 19:18

5 [a]Mic. 1:4

6 [a]Ps. 19:1

7 [a][Ex. 20:4]
[b][Heb. 1:6]

9 [a]Ps. 83:18
[b]Ex. 18:11

10 [a][Ps. 34:14]
[b]Prov. 2:8
[c]Ps. 37:40

11 [a]Job 22:28

12 [a]Ps. 33:1
[b]Ps. 30:4
[1]Or *for the memory*
[2]Or *His holiness*

PSALM 98

1 [a]Is. 42:10
[b]Ex. 15:11

2 [a]Is. 52:10
[b]Is. 62:2
[1]*Gentiles*

3 [a]Luke 3:6

Break forth in song, rejoice,
and sing praises.
5 Sing to the LORD with the
harp,
With the harp and the sound
of a psalm,
6 With trumpets and the
sound of a horn;
Shout joyfully before the
LORD, the King.

7 Let the sea roar, and all its
fullness,
The world and those who
dwell in it;
8 Let the rivers clap *their*
hands;
Let the hills be joyful
together
9 before the LORD,
[a]For He is coming to judge
the earth.
With righteousness He shall
judge the world,
And the peoples with
[1]equity.

PSALM 99

THE LORD reigns;
Let the peoples tremble!
[a]He dwells *between* the
cherubim;
Let the earth be [1]moved!
2 The LORD *is* great in Zion,
And He *is* high above all the
peoples.
3 Let them praise Your great
and awesome name—
[1]He *is* holy.

4 The King's strength also
loves justice;
You have established equity;
You have executed justice
and righteousness in
Jacob.
5 Exalt the LORD our God,
And worship at His
footstool—
He *is* holy.

6 Moses and Aaron were
among His priests,
And Samuel was among
those who [a]called upon
His name;
They called upon the LORD,
and He answered them.
7 He spoke to them in the
cloudy pillar;
They kept His testimonies
and the [1]ordinance He
gave them.

8 You answered them, O LORD
our God;
You were to them God-Who-
Forgives,
Though You took vengeance
on their deeds.
9 Exalt the LORD our God,
And worship at His holy
hill;
For the LORD our God *is*
holy.

PSALM 100

[a]A Psalm of Thanksgiving.

MAKE [a]a joyful shout to the
LORD, [1]all you lands!
2 Serve the LORD with
gladness;
Come before His presence
with singing.
3 Know that the LORD, He *is*
God;
[a]*It is* He *who* has made us,
and [1]not we ourselves;
[b]*We are* His people and the
sheep of His pasture.

4 [a]Enter into His gates with
thanksgiving,

---

9 [a][Ps. 96:10, 13] [1]*uprightness*

PSALM 99

1 [a]Ex. 25:22 [1]*shaken*

3 [1]Or *It*

6 [a]1 Sam. 7:9; 12:18

7 [1]*statute*

PSALM 100

title [a]Ps. 145:title

1 [a]Ps. 95:1 [1]Lit. *all the earth*

3 [a][Eph. 2:10] [b]Ezek. 34:30, 31 [1]So with Kt., LXX, Vg.; Qr., many Heb. mss., Tg. *we are His*

4 [a]Ps. 66:13; 116:17–19

And into His courts with praise.
Be thankful to Him, *and* bless His name.
5 For the LORD *is* good;
[a]His mercy *is* everlasting,
And His truth *endures* to all generations.

PSALM 101

A Psalm of David.

I WILL sing of mercy and justice;
To You, O LORD, I will sing praises.
2 I will behave wisely in a [1]perfect way.
Oh, when will You come to me?
I will [a]walk within my house with a perfect heart.
3 I will set nothing [1]wicked before my eyes;
[a]I hate the work of those [b]who fall away;
It shall not cling to me.
4 A perverse heart shall depart from me;
I will not [a]know wickedness.
5 Whoever secretly slanders his neighbor,
Him I will destroy;
[a]The one who has a haughty look and a proud heart,
Him I will not endure.
6 My eyes *shall be* on the faithful of the land,
That they may dwell with me;
He who walks in a [1]perfect way,
He shall serve me.
7 He who works deceit shall not dwell within my house;
He who tells lies shall not [1]continue in my presence.
8 [a]Early I will destroy all the wicked of the land,
That I may cut off all the evildoers [b]from the city of the LORD.

PSALM 102

A Prayer of the afflicted, [a]when he is overwhelmed and pours out his complaint before the LORD.

HEAR my prayer, O LORD,
And let my cry come to You.
2 [a]Do not hide Your face from me in the day of my trouble;
Incline Your ear to me;
In the day that I call, answer me speedily.
3 For my days [1]are [a]consumed like smoke,
And my bones are burned like a hearth.
4 My heart is stricken and withered like grass,
So that I forget to eat my bread.
5 Because of the sound of my groaning
My bones cling to my [1]skin.
6 I am like a pelican of the wilderness;
I am like an owl of the desert.
7 I lie awake,
And am like a sparrow alone on the housetop.

---

5 [a]Ps. 136:1

PSALM 101

2 [a]1 Kin. 11:4 [1]*blameless*
3 [a]Ps. 97:10 [b]Josh. 23:6 [1]*worthless*
4 [a][Ps. 119:115]
5 [a]Prov. 6:17
6 [1]*blameless*
7 [1]Lit. *be established*
8 [a]Jer. 21:12 [b]Ps. 48:2, 8

PSALM 102

title [a]Ps. 61:2
2 [a]Ps. 27:9; 69:17
3 [a]James 4:14 [1]Lit. *end in*
5 [1]*flesh*

8 My enemies reproach me all day long;
Those who deride me swear an oath against me.
9 For I have eaten ashes like bread,
And mingled my drink with weeping,
10 Because of Your indignation and Your wrath;
For You have lifted me up and cast me away.
11 My days *are* like a shadow that lengthens,
And I wither away like grass.

12 But You, O Lord, shall endure forever,
And the remembrance of Your name to all generations.
13 You will arise *and* have mercy on Zion;
For the time to favor her,
Yes, the set time, has come.
14 For Your servants take pleasure in her stones,
And show favor to her dust.
15 So the [1]nations shall [a]fear the name of the Lord,
And all the kings of the earth Your glory.
16 For the Lord shall build up Zion;
[a]He shall appear in His glory.
17 [a]He shall regard the prayer of the destitute,
And shall not despise their prayer.

18 This will be [a]written for the generation to come,
That [b]a people yet to be created may praise the Lord.
19 For He [a]looked down from the height of His sanctuary;
From heaven the Lord viewed the earth,
20 [a]To hear the groaning of the prisoner,
To release those appointed to death,
21 To [a]declare the name of the Lord in Zion,
And His praise in Jerusalem,
22 [a]When the peoples are gathered together,
And the kingdoms, to serve the Lord.

23 He weakened my strength in the way;
He [a]shortened my days.
24 [a]I said, "O my God,
Do not take me away in the midst of my days;
[b]Your years *are* throughout all generations.
25 [a]Of old You laid the foundation of the earth,
And the heavens *are* the work of Your hands.
26 [a]They will perish, but You will [1]endure;
Yes, they will all grow old like a garment;
Like a cloak You will change them,
And they will be changed.
27 But [a]You *are* the same,
And Your years will have no end.
28 [a]The children of Your servants will continue,
And their descendants will be established before You."

15 [a]1 Kin. 8:43 [1]*Gentiles*
16 [a][Is. 60:1, 2]
17 [a]Neh. 1:6
18 [a][Rom. 15:4] [b]Ps. 22:31
19 [a]Deut. 26:15
20 [a]Ps. 79:11
21 [a]Ps. 22:22
22 [a][Is. 2:2, 3; 49:22, 23; 60:3]
23 [a]Job 21:21
24 [a]Is. 38:10 [b][Ps. 90:2]
25 [a][Heb. 1:10–12]
26 [a]Is. 34:4; 51:6 [1]*continue*
27 [a][Mal. 3:6]
28 [a]Ps. 69:36

PSALM 103

A Psalm of David.

BLESS [a]the LORD, O my soul;
And all that is within me,
bless His holy name!
2 Bless the LORD, O my soul,
And forget not all His benefits:
3 [a]Who forgives all your iniquities,
Who [b]heals all your diseases,
4 Who redeems your life from destruction,
[a]Who crowns you with lovingkindness and tender mercies,
5 Who satisfies your mouth with good *things*,
So that [a]your youth is renewed like the eagle's.

6 The LORD executes righteousness
And justice for all who are oppressed.
7 [a]He made known His ways to Moses,
His acts to the children of Israel.
8 [a]The LORD *is* merciful and gracious,
Slow to anger, and abounding in mercy.
9 [a]He will not always strive *with us*,
Nor will He keep *His anger* forever.
10 [a]He has not dealt with us according to our sins,
Nor punished us according to our iniquities.

11 For as the heavens are high above the earth,
So great is His mercy toward those who fear Him;
12 As far as the east is from the west,
So far has He [a]removed our transgressions from us.
13 [a]As a father pities *his* children,
So the LORD pities those who fear Him.
14 For He [1]knows our frame;
He remembers that we *are* dust.

15 *As for* man, [a]his days *are* like grass;
As a flower of the field, so he flourishes.
16 [a]For the wind passes over it, and it is [1]gone,
And [b]its place remembers it no more.
17 But the mercy of the LORD *is* from everlasting to everlasting
On those who fear Him,
And His righteousness to children's children,
18 [a]To such as keep His covenant,
And to those who remember His commandments to do them.

19 The LORD has established His throne in heaven,
And [a]His kingdom rules over all.

20 [a]Bless the LORD, you His angels,
Who excel in strength, who [b]do His word,
Heeding the voice of His word.
21 Bless the LORD, all *you* His hosts,

PSALM 103
1 [a]Ps. 104:1, 35
3 [a]Ps. 130:8 [b][Ex. 15:26]
4 [a][Ps. 5:12]
5 [a][Is. 40:31]
7 [a]Ps. 147:19
8 [a][Ex. 34:6, 7]
9 [a][Ps. 30:5]
10 [a][Ezra 9:13]
12 [a][Is. 38:17; 43:25]
13 [a]Mal. 3:17
14 [1]Understands our constitution
15 [a]1 Pet. 1:24
16 [a][Is. 40:7] [b]Job 7:10 [1]*not*
18 [a][Deut. 7:9]
19 [a][Dan. 4:17, 25]
20 [a]Ps. 148:2 [b][Matt. 6:10]

[a]*You* [1]ministers of His, who
do His pleasure.
22 Bless the LORD, all His
works,
In all places of His
dominion.
Bless the LORD, O my soul!

PSALM 104

BLESS [a]the LORD, O my soul!
O LORD my God, You are
very great:
You are clothed with honor
and majesty,
2 Who cover *Yourself* with
light as *with* a garment,
Who stretch out the heavens
like a curtain.

3 [a]He lays the beams of His
upper chambers in the
waters,
Who makes the clouds His
chariot,
Who walks on the wings of
the wind,
4 Who makes His angels
spirits,
His [1]ministers a flame of
fire.

5 *You who* [1]laid the
foundations of the earth,
So *that* it should not be
moved forever,
6 You [a]covered it with the
deep as *with* a garment;
The waters stood above the
mountains.
7 At Your rebuke they fled;
At the voice of Your thunder
they hastened away.
8 [1]They went up over the
mountains;
They went down into the
valleys,
To the place which You
founded for them.
9 You have [a]set a boundary
that they may not pass
over,
[b]That they may not return to
cover the earth.

10 He sends the springs into
the valleys;
They flow among the hills.
11 They give drink to every
beast of the field;
The wild donkeys quench
their thirst.
12 By them the birds of the
heavens have their
home;
They sing among the
branches.
13 [a]He waters the hills from His
upper chambers;
The earth is satisfied with
[b]the fruit of Your works.

14 [a]He causes the grass to grow
for the cattle,
And vegetation for the
service of man,
That he may bring forth
[b]food from the earth,
15 And [a]wine *that* makes glad
the heart of man,
Oil to make *his* face shine,
And bread *which*
strengthens man's heart.
16 The trees of the LORD are
full *of sap*,
The cedars of Lebanon
which He planted,
17 Where the birds make their
nests;
The stork has her home in
the fir trees.
18 The high hills *are* for the
wild goats;

21 [a][Heb. 1:14] [1]*servants*

PSALM 104

1 [a]Ps. 103:1

3 [a][Amos 9:6]

4 [1]*servants*

5 [1]Lit. *founded the earth upon her bases*

6 [a]Gen. 1:6

8 [1]Or *The mountains rose up; The valleys sank down*

9 [a][Jer. 5:22] [b]Gen. 9:11–15

13 [a]Ps. 147:8 [b]Jer. 10:13

14 [a]Gen. 1:29 [b]Job 28:5

15 [a]Judg. 9:13

The cliffs are a refuge for
the [a]rock[1] badgers.

19 [a]He appointed the moon for
seasons;
The [b]sun knows its going
down.
20 [a]You make darkness, and it
is night,
In which all the beasts of
the forest creep about.
21 [a]The young lions roar after
their prey,
And seek their food from
God.
22 *When* the sun rises, they
gather together
And lie down in their dens.
23 Man goes out to [a]his work
And to his labor until the
evening.

24 [a]O LORD, how manifold are
Your works!
In wisdom You have made
them all.
The earth is full of Your
[b]possessions—
25 This great and wide sea,
In which *are* innumerable
teeming things,
Living things both small
and great.
26 There the ships sail about;
There is that [a]Le·vi′a·than[1]
Which You have [2]made to
play there.

27 [a]These all wait for You,
That You may give *them*
their food in due season.
28 *What* You give them they
gather in;
You open Your hand, they
are filled with good.
29 You hide Your face, they are
troubled;
[a]You take away their breath,
they die and return to
their dust.
30 [a]You send forth Your Spirit,
they are created;
And You renew the face of
the earth.

31 May the glory of the LORD
endure forever;
May the LORD [a]rejoice in His
works.
32 He looks on the earth, and it
[a]trembles;
[b]He touches the hills, and
they smoke.

33 [a]I will sing to the LORD as
long as I live;
I will sing praise to my God
while I have my being.
34 May my [a]meditation be
sweet to Him;
I will be glad in the LORD.
35 May [a]sinners be consumed
from the earth,
And the wicked be no more.

Bless the LORD, O my soul!
[1]Praise the LORD!

PSALM 105

OH, [a]give thanks to the LORD!
Call upon His name;
[b]Make known His deeds
among the peoples!
2 Sing to Him, sing psalms to
Him;
[a]Talk of all His wondrous
works!
3 Glory in His holy name;
Let the hearts of those
rejoice who seek the
LORD!
4 Seek the LORD and His
strength;
[a]Seek His face evermore!

18 [a]Lev. 11:5 [1]*rock hyraxes*
19 [a]Gen. 1:14 [b]Ps. 19:6
20 [a][Is. 45:7]
21 [a]Job 38:39
23 [a]Gen. 3:19
24 [a]Prov. 3:19 [b]Ps. 65:9
26 [a]Job 41:1 [1]A large sea creature of unknown identity [2]Lit. *formed*
27 [a]Ps. 136:25
29 [a]Job 34:15
30 [a]Is. 32:15
31 [a]Gen. 1:31
32 [a]Hab. 3:10 [b]Ps. 144:5
33 [a]Ps. 63:4
34 [a]Ps. 19:14
35 [a]Ps. 37:38 [1]Heb. *Hallelujah*

PSALM 105
1 [a]Is. 12:4 [b]Ps. 145:12
2 [a]Ps. 119:27
4 [a]Ps. 27:8

5 [a]Remember His marvelous works which He has done,
His wonders, and the judgments of His mouth,
6 O seed of Abraham His servant,
You children of Jacob, His chosen ones!

7 He *is* the LORD our God;
[a]His judgments *are* in all the earth.
8 He [a]remembers His covenant forever,
The word *which* He commanded, for a thousand generations,
9 [a]*The covenant* which He made with Abraham,
And His oath to Isaac,
10 And confirmed it to Jacob for a statute,
To Israel *as* an everlasting covenant,
11 Saying, [a]"To you I will give the land of Cā′naan
As the allotment of your inheritance,"
12 [a]When they were few in number,
Indeed very few, [b]and strangers in it.

13 When they went from one nation to another,
From *one* kingdom to another people,
14 [a]He permitted no one to do them wrong;
Yes, [b]He rebuked kings for their sakes,
15 *Saying*, "Do not touch My anointed ones,
And do My prophets no harm."

16 Moreover [a]He called for a famine in the land;
He destroyed all the [b]provision of bread.
17 [a]He sent a man before them—
Joseph—*who* [b]was sold as a slave.
18 [a]They hurt his feet with fetters,
[1]He was laid in irons.
19 Until the time that his word came to pass,
[a]The word of the LORD tested him.
20 [a]The king sent and released him,
The ruler of the people let him go free.
21 [a]He made him lord of his house,
And ruler of all his possessions,
22 To [1]bind his princes at his pleasure,
And teach his elders wisdom.

23 [a]Israel also came into Egypt,
And Jacob dwelt [b]in the land of Ham.
24 [a]He increased His people greatly,
And made them stronger than their enemies.
25 [a]He turned their heart to hate His people,
To deal craftily with His servants.

26 [a]He sent Moses His servant,
And Aaron whom He had chosen.
27 They [a]performed His signs among them,
And wonders in the land of Ham.

5 [a]Ps. 77:11
7 [a][Is. 26:9]
8 [a]Luke 1:72
9 [a]Gen. 17:2
11 [a]Gen. 13:15; 15:18
12 [a][Deut. 7:7] [b]Heb. 11:9
14 [a]Gen. 35:5 [b]Gen. 12:17
16 [a]Gen. 41:54 [b]Lev. 26:26
17 [a][Gen. 45:5] [b]Gen. 37:28, 36
18 [a]Gen. 40:15 [1]*His soul came into iron*
19 [a]Gen. 39:11–21; 41:25, 42, 43
20 [a]Gen. 41:14
21 [a]Gen. 41:40–44
22 [1]Bind as prisoners
23 [a]Gen. 46:6 [b]Ps. 78:51
24 [a]Ex. 1:7, 9
25 [a]Ex. 1:8–10; 4:21
26 [a]Ex. 3:10; 4:12–15
27 [a]Ps. 78:43

28 He sent darkness, and made *it* dark;
And they did not rebel against His word.
29 [a]He turned their waters into blood,
And killed their fish.
30 [a]Their land abounded with frogs,
Even in the chambers of their kings.
31 [a]He spoke, and there came swarms of flies,
And lice in all their territory.
32 [a]He gave them hail for rain,
And flaming fire in their land.
33 [a]He struck their vines also, and their fig trees,
And splintered the trees of their territory.
34 [a]He spoke, and locusts came,
Young locusts without number,
35 And ate up all the vegetation in their land,
And devoured the fruit of their ground.
36 [a]He also [1]destroyed all the firstborn in their land,
[b]The first of all their strength.

37 [a]He also brought them out with silver and gold,
And *there was* none feeble among His tribes.
38 [a]Egypt was glad when they departed,
For the fear of them had fallen upon them.
39 [a]He spread a cloud for a covering,
And fire to give light in the night.
40 [a]*The people* asked, and He brought quail,
And [b]satisfied them with the bread of heaven.
41 [a]He opened the rock, and water gushed out;
It ran in the dry places *like* a river.

42 For He remembered [a]His holy promise,
And Abraham His servant.
43 He brought out His people with joy,
His chosen ones with [1]gladness.
44 [a]He gave them the lands of the [1]Gentiles,
And they inherited the labor of the nations,
45 [a]That they might observe His statutes
And keep His laws.

[1]Praise the LORD!

PSALM 106

PRAISE[1] the LORD!

[a]Oh, give thanks to the LORD, for *He is* good!
For His mercy *endures* forever.

2 Who can [1]utter the mighty acts of the LORD?
Who can declare all His praise?
3 Blessed *are* those who keep justice,
And [1]he who [a]does righteousness at [b]all times!

4 [a]Remember me, O LORD, with the favor *You have toward* Your people.
Oh, visit me with Your salvation,

29 [a]Ex. 7:20, 21
30 [a]Ex. 8:6
31 [a]Ex. 8:16, 17
32 [a]Ex. 9:23–25
33 [a]Ps. 78:47
34 [a]Ex. 10:4
36 [a]Ex. 12:29; 13:15 [b]Gen. 49:3 [1]Lit. *struck down*
37 [a]Ex. 12:35, 36
38 [a]Ex. 12:33
39 [a]Ex. 13:21
40 [a]Ex. 16:12 [b]Ps. 78:24
41 [a]Ex. 17:6
42 [a]Gen. 15:13, 14
43 [1]*a joyful shout*
44 [a]Josh. 11:16–23; 13:7 [1]*nations*
45 [a][Deut. 4:1, 40] [1]Heb. *Hallelujah*

PSALM 106
1 [a]1 Chr. 16:34, 41 [1]Heb. *Hallelujah*
2 [1]*express*
3 [a]Ps. 15:2 [b][Gal. 6:9] [1]LXX, Syr., Tg., Vg. *those who do*
4 [a]Ps. 119:132

5 That I may see the benefit of
Your chosen ones,
That I may rejoice in the
gladness of Your nation,
That I may glory with [1]Your
inheritance.

6 [a]We have sinned with our
fathers,
We have committed iniquity,
We have done wickedly.
7 Our fathers in Egypt did
not understand Your
wonders;
They did not remember
the multitude of Your
mercies,
[a]But rebelled by the sea—the
Red Sea.

8 Nevertheless He saved them
for His name's sake,
[a]That He might make His
mighty power known.
9 [a]He rebuked the Red Sea
also, and it dried up;
So [b]He led them through the
depths,
As through the wilderness.
10 He [a]saved them from the
hand of him who hated
them,
And redeemed them from
the hand of the enemy.
11 [a]The waters covered their
enemies;
There was not one of them
left.
12 [a]Then they believed His
words;
They sang His praise.

13 [a]They soon forgot His works;
They did not wait for His
counsel,
14 [a]But lusted exceedingly in
the wilderness,
And tested God in the
desert.
15 [a]And He gave them their
request,
But [b]sent leanness into their
soul.

16 When [a]they envied Moses in
the camp,
And Aaron the saint of the
LORD,
17 [a]The earth opened up and
swallowed Dā'than,
And covered the faction of
A·bī'ram.
18 [a]A fire was kindled in their
company;
The flame burned up the
wicked.

19 [a]They made a calf in Hō'reb,
And worshiped the molded
image.
20 Thus [a]they changed their
glory
Into the image of an ox that
eats grass.
21 They forgot God their
Savior,
Who had done great things
in Egypt,
22 Wondrous works in the land
of Ham,
Awesome things by the Red
Sea.
23 [a]Therefore He said that He
would destroy them,
Had not Moses His chosen
one [b]stood before Him in
the breach,
To turn away His wrath, lest
He destroy *them*.

24 Then they despised [a]the
pleasant land;
They [b]did not believe His
word,

5 [1]The people of Your inheritance
6 [a][Dan. 9:5]
7 [a]Ex. 14:11, 12
8 [a]Ex. 9:16
9 [a]Ex. 14:21 [b]Is. 63:11–13
10 [a]Ex. 14:30
11 [a]Ex. 14:27, 28; 15:5
12 [a]Ex. 15:1–21
13 [a]Ex. 15:24; 16:2; 17:2
14 [a]1 Cor. 10:6
15 [a]Num. 11:31 [b]Is. 10:16
16 [a]Num. 16:1–3
17 [a]Deut. 11:6
18 [a]Num. 16:35, 46
19 [a]Ex. 32:1–4
20 [a]Rom. 1:23
23 [a]Ex. 32:10 [b]Ezek. 22:30
24 [a]Deut. 8:7 [b][Heb. 3:18, 19]

25 [a]But complained in their
tents,
And did not heed the voice
of the LORD.
26 [a]Therefore He raised His
hand *in an oath* against
them,
[b]To [1]overthrow them in the
wilderness,
27 [a]To [1]overthrow their
descendants among the
[2]nations,
And to scatter them in the
lands.

28 [a]They joined themselves also
to Bā'al of Pē'or,
And ate sacrifices [1]made to
the dead.
29 Thus they provoked *Him* to
anger with their deeds,
And the plague broke out
among them.
30 [a]Then Phin'e·has stood up
and intervened,
And the plague was stopped.
31 And that was accounted to
him [a]for righteousness
To all generations
forevermore.

32 [a]They angered *Him* also at
the waters of [1]strife,
[b]So that it went ill with
Moses on account of
them;
33 [a]Because they rebelled
against His Spirit,
So that he spoke rashly with
his lips.

34 [a]They did not destroy the
peoples,
[b]Concerning whom the LORD
had commanded them,
35 [a]But they mingled with the
Gentiles
And learned their works;
36 [a]They served their idols,
[b]Which became a snare to
them.
37 [a]They even sacrificed their
sons
And their daughters to
[b]demons,
38 And shed innocent blood,
The blood of their sons and
daughters,
Whom they sacrificed to the
idols of Cā'naan;
And [a]the land was polluted
with blood.
39 Thus they [1]were [a]defiled by
their own works,
And [b]played[2] the harlot by
their own deeds.

40 Therefore [a]the wrath of
the LORD was kindled
against His people,
So that He abhorred [b]His
own inheritance.
41 And [a]He gave them into
the hand of the
Gentiles,
And those who hated them
ruled over them.
42 Their enemies also
oppressed them,
And they were brought into
subjection under their
hand.
43 [a]Many times He delivered
them;
But they rebelled in their
counsel,
And were brought low for
their iniquity.

44 Nevertheless He regarded
their affliction,
When [a]He heard their cry;
45 [a]And for their sake He
remembered His
covenant,

25 [a]Num. 14:2, 27
26 [a]Ezek. 20:15, 16 [b]Num. 14:28–30 [1]*make them fall*
27 [a]Lev. 26:33 [1]*make their descendants fall also* [2]*Gentiles*
28 [a]Hos. 9:10 [1]*offered*
30 [a]Num. 25:7, 8
31 [a]Num. 25:11–13
32 [a]Num. 20:3–13 [b]Deut. 1:37; 3:26 [1]Or *Meribah*
33 [a]Num. 20:3, 10
34 [a]Judg. 1:21 [b][Deut. 7:2, 16]
35 [a]Judg. 3:5, 6
36 [a]Judg. 2:12 [b]Deut. 7:16
37 [a]2 Kin. 16:3; 17:17 [b][Lev. 17:7]
38 [a][Num. 35:33]
39 [a]Ezek. 20:18 [b][Lev. 17:7] [1]*became unclean* [2]Were unfaithful
40 [a]Judg. 2:14 [b][Deut. 9:29; 32:9]
41 [a]Judg. 2:14
43 [a]Judg. 2:16
44 [a]Judg. 3:9; 6:7; 10:10
45 [a][Lev. 26:41, 42]

And [b]relented [c]according
to the multitude of His
mercies.
46 [a]He also made them to be
pitied
By all those who carried
them away captive.

47 [a]Save us, O LORD our God,
And gather us from among
the Gentiles,
To give thanks to Your holy
name,
To triumph in Your praise.

48 [a]Blessed *be* the LORD God of
Israel
From everlasting to
everlasting!
And let all the people say,
"Amen!"

[1]Praise the LORD!

BOOK FIVE
Psalms 107—150

PSALM 107

OH, [a]give thanks to the LORD,
for *He is* good!
For His [1]mercy *endures*
forever.
2 Let the redeemed of the
LORD say *so,*
Whom He has redeemed
from the hand of the
enemy,
3 And [a]gathered out of the
lands,
From the east and from the
west,
From the north and from the
south.

4 They wandered in [a]the
wilderness in a desolate
way;
They found no city to
dwell in.
5 Hungry and thirsty,
Their soul fainted in them.
6 [a]Then they cried out to the
LORD in their trouble,
And He delivered them out
of their distresses.
7 And He led them forth by
the [a]right way,
That they might go to a city
for a dwelling place.
8 [a]Oh, that *men* would give
thanks to the LORD *for*
His goodness,
And *for* His wonderful works
to the children of men!
9 For [a]He satisfies the longing
soul,
And fills the hungry soul
with goodness.

10 Those who [a]sat in darkness
and in the shadow of
death,
[b]Bound[1] in affliction and
irons—
11 Because they [a]rebelled
against the words of
God,
And [1]despised [b]the counsel
of the Most High,
12 Therefore He brought down
their heart with labor;
They fell down, and *there*
was [a]none to help.
13 Then they cried out to the
LORD in their trouble,
And He saved them out of
their distresses.
14 [a]He brought them out
of darkness and the
shadow of death,
And broke their chains in
pieces.

45 [b]Judg. 2:18 [c]Ps. 69:16
46 [a]Ezra 9:9
47 [a]1 Chr. 16:35, 36
48 [a]Ps. 41:13 [1]Heb. *Hallelujah*

PSALM 107
1 [a]Ps. 106:1 [1]Heb. same as *goodness*, vv. 8, 15, 21, 31, and *loving-kindness*, v. 43
3 [a]Is. 43:5, 6
4 [a][Deut. 2:7; 32:10]
6 [a]Ps. 50:15
7 [a]Ezra 8:21
8 [a]Ps. 107:15, 21
9 [a][Ps. 34:10]
10 [a][Luke 1:79] [b]Job 36:8 [1]*Prisoners*
11 [a]Lam. 3:42 [b][Ps. 73:24] [1]*scorned*
12 [a]Ps. 22:11
14 [a]Ps. 68:6

15 Oh, that *men* would give
thanks to the LORD *for*
His goodness,
And *for* His wonderful
works to the children of
men!
16 For He has [a]broken the
gates of bronze,
And cut the bars of iron in
two.

17 Fools, [a]because of their
transgression,
And because of their
iniquities, were afflicted.
18 [a]Their soul abhorred all
manner of food,
And they [b]drew near to the
gates of death.
19 Then they cried out to the
LORD in their trouble,
And He saved them out of
their distresses.
20 [a]He sent His word and
[b]healed them,
And [c]delivered *them* from
their destructions.
21 Oh, that *men* would give
thanks to the LORD *for*
His goodness,
And *for* His wonderful
works to the children of
men!
22 [a]Let them sacrifice
the sacrifices of
thanksgiving,
And [b]declare His works
with [1]rejoicing.

23 Those who go down to the
sea in ships,
Who do business on great
waters,
24 They see the works of the
LORD,
And His wonders in the
deep.
25 For He commands and
[a]raises the stormy wind,
Which lifts up the waves of
the sea.
26 They mount up to the
heavens,
They go down again to the
depths;
[a]Their soul melts because of
trouble.
27 They reel to and fro, and
stagger like a drunken
man,
And [1]are at their wits' end.
28 Then they cry out to the
LORD in their trouble,
And He brings them out of
their distresses.
29 [a]He calms the storm,
So that its waves are still.
30 Then they are glad because
they are quiet;
So He guides them to their
desired haven.
31 [a]Oh, that *men* would give
thanks to the LORD *for*
His goodness,
And *for* His wonderful
works to the children of
men!
32 Let them exalt Him also
[a]in the assembly of the
people,
And praise Him in the
company of the elders.

33 He [a]turns rivers into a
wilderness,
And the watersprings into
dry ground;
34 A [a]fruitful land into
[1]barrenness,
For the wickedness of those
who dwell in it.
35 [a]He turns a wilderness into
pools of water,
And dry land into
watersprings.

16 [a]Is. 45:1, 2
17 [a]Lam. 3:39
18 [a]Job 33:20 [b]Job 33:22
20 [a]Matt. 8:8 [b]Ps. 30:2 [c]Job 33:28, 30
22 [a]Lev. 7:12 [b]Ps. 9:11 [1]*joyful singing*
25 [a]Jon. 1:4
26 [a]Ps. 22:14
27 [1]Lit. *all their wisdom is swallowed up*
29 [a]Ps. 89:9
31 [a]Ps. 107:8, 15, 21
32 [a]Ps. 22:22, 25
33 [a]1 Kin. 17:1, 7
34 [a]Gen. 13:10 [1]Lit. *a salty waste*
35 [a]Ps. 114:8

36 There He makes the hungry dwell,
That they may establish a city for a dwelling place,
37 And sow fields and plant vineyards,
That they may yield a fruitful harvest.
38 [a]He also blesses them, and they multiply greatly;
And He does not let their cattle [b]decrease.

39 When they are [a]diminished and brought low
Through oppression, affliction, and sorrow,
40 [a]He pours contempt on princes,
And causes them to wander in the wilderness *where there is* no way;
41 [a]Yet He sets the poor on high, far from affliction,
And [b]makes *their* families like a flock.
42 [a]The righteous see *it* and rejoice,
And all [b]iniquity stops its mouth.

43 [a]Whoever *is* wise will observe these *things*,
And they will understand the lovingkindness of the LORD.

PSALM 108

A Song. A Psalm of David.

O [a]GOD, my heart is steadfast;
I will sing and give praise, even with my glory.
2 [a]Awake, lute and harp!
I will awaken the dawn.
3 I will praise You, O LORD, among the peoples,
And I will sing praises to You among the nations.
4 For Your mercy *is* great above the [1]heavens,
And Your truth *reaches* to the clouds.

5 [a]Be exalted, O God, above the heavens,
And Your glory above all the earth;
6 [a]That Your beloved may be delivered,
Save *with* Your right hand, and [1]hear me.

7 God has spoken in His holiness:
"I will rejoice;
I will divide Shē'chem
And measure out the Valley of Suc'coth.
8 Gil'ē·ad *is* Mine; Ma·nas'seh *is* Mine;
Ē'phra·im also *is* the [1]helmet for My head;
[a]Judah *is* My lawgiver.
9 Mō'ab *is* My washpot;
Over Ē'dom I will cast My shoe;
Over Phi·lis'ti·a I will triumph."

10 [a]Who will bring me *into* the strong city?
Who will lead me to Ē'dom?
11 *Is it* not *You*, O God, *who* cast us off?
And *You*, O God, *who* did not go out with our armies?
12 Give us help from trouble,
For the help of man is useless.
13 [a]Through God we will do valiantly,

38 [a]Gen. 12:2; 17:16, 20 [b][Deut. 7:14]
39 [a]2 Kin. 10:32
40 [a]Job 12:21, 24
41 [a]1 Sam. 2:8 [b]Ps. 78:52
42 [a]Job 5:15, 16 [b][Rom. 3:19]
43 [a]Jer. 9:12

PSALM 108

1 [a]Ps. 57:7–11
2 [a]Ps. 57:8–11
4 [1]*skies*
5 [a]Ps. 57:5, 11
6 [a]Ps. 60:5–12 [1]Lit. *answer*
8 [a][Gen. 49:10] [1]Lit. *protection*
10 [a]Ps. 60:9
13 [a]Ps. 60:12

For *it is* He *who* shall tread
down our enemies.

PSALM 109

To the Chief Musician. A Psalm of David.

Do[a] not keep silent,
O God of my praise!
2 For the mouth of the wicked
and the mouth of the deceitful
Have opened against me;
They have spoken against
me with a [a]lying tongue.
☆3 They have also surrounded
me with words of hatred,
And fought against me
[a]without a cause.
4 In return for my love they
are my accusers,
But I *give myself to* prayer.
5 Thus [a]they have rewarded
me evil for good,
And hatred for my love.

6 Set a wicked man over him,
And let [a]an [1]accuser stand
at his right hand.
7 When he is judged, let him
be found guilty,
And [a]let his prayer become
sin.
8 Let his days be [a]few,
And [b]let another take his
office.
9 [a]Let his children be
fatherless,
And his wife a widow.
10 Let his children [1]continually
be vagabonds, and beg;
Let them [2]seek *their bread*
also from their desolate
places.
11 [a]Let the creditor seize all
that he has,
And let strangers plunder
his labor.
12 Let there be none to extend
mercy to him,
Nor let there be any to favor
his fatherless children.
13 [a]Let his [1]posterity be cut off,
And in the generation
following let their [b]name
be blotted out.

14 [a]Let the iniquity of his
fathers be remembered
before the LORD,
And let not the sin of his
mother [b]be blotted out.
15 Let them be continually
before the LORD,
That He may [a]cut off the
memory of them from
the earth;
16 Because he did not
remember to show
mercy,
But persecuted the poor and
needy man,
That he might even slay the
[a]broken in heart.
17 [a]As he loved cursing, so let it
come to him;
As he did not delight in
blessing, so let it be far
from him.
18 As he clothed himself with
cursing as with his
garment,
So let it [a]enter his body like
water,
And like oil into his bones.
19 Let it be to him like the
garment which covers
him,
And for a belt with which
he girds himself
continually.
20 *Let* this *be* the LORD's
reward to my accusers,

PSALM 109

1 [a]Ps. 83:1
2 [a]Ps. 27:12
3 [a]John 15:23–25
5 [a]Ps. 35:7, 12; 38:20
6 [a]Zech. 3:1 [1]Heb. *satan*
7 [a][Prov. 28:9]
8 [a][Ps. 55:23] [b]Acts 1:20
9 [a]Ex. 22:24
10 [1]*wander continuously* [2]So with MT, Tg.; LXX, Vg. *be cast out*
11 [a]Job 5:5; 18:9
13 [a]Job 18:19 [b]Prov. 10:7 [1]*descendants be destroyed*
14 [a][Ex. 20:5] [b]Neh. 4:5
15 [a]Job 18:17
16 [a][Ps. 34:18]
17 [a]Prov. 14:14
18 [a]Num. 5:22

And to those who speak evil
against my person.
21 But You, O GOD the Lord,
Deal with me for Your
name's sake;
Because Your mercy *is* good,
deliver me.
22 For I *am* poor and needy,
And my heart is wounded
within me.
23 I am gone [a]like a shadow
when it lengthens;
I am shaken off like a
locust.
24 My [a]knees are weak through
fasting,
And my flesh is feeble from
lack of fatness.
25 I also have become [a]a
reproach to them;
When they look at me, [b]they
shake their heads.

26 Help me, O LORD my God!
Oh, save me according to
Your mercy,
27 [a]That they may know that
this *is* Your hand—
That You, LORD, have done
it!
28 [a]Let them curse, but You
bless;
When they arise, let them be
ashamed,
But let [b]Your servant rejoice.
29 [a]Let my accusers be clothed
with shame,
And let them cover
themselves with their
own disgrace as with a
mantle.

30 I will greatly praise the
LORD with my mouth;
Yes, [a]I will praise Him
among the multitude.

23 [a]Ps. 102:11
24 [a]Heb. 12:12
25 [a]Ps. 22:7 [b]Matt. 27:39
27 [a]Job 37:7
28 [a]2 Sam. 6:11, 12 [b]Is. 65:14
29 [a]Ps. 35:26
30 [a]Ps. 35:18; 111:1
31 [a][Ps. 16:8] [1]Lit. *judging his soul*

PSALM 110

1 [a]Matt. 22:44; Mark 12:36; 16:19; Luke 20:42, 43; Acts 2:34, 35, Col. 3:1; Heb. 1:13 [b][1 Cor. 15:25; Eph. 1:22]
2 [a][Rom. 11:26, 27] [b][Dan. 7:13, 14]
3 [a]Judg. 5:2 [b]Ps. 96:9
4 [a][Num. 23:19] [b][Zech. 6:13] [c][Heb. 5:6, 10; 6:20]
5 [a][Ps. 16:8] [b]Ps. 2:5, 12 [1]Lit. *break kings in pieces*
6 [a]Ps. 68:21 [1]Lit. *break in pieces*
7 [a][Is. 53:12]

31 For [a]He shall stand at the
right hand of the poor,
To save *him* from those
[1]who condemn him.

PSALM 110

A Psalm of David.

THE [a]LORD said to my Lord, ☆
"Sit at My right hand,
Till I make Your enemies
Your [b]footstool."
2 The LORD shall send the rod
of Your strength [a]out of
Zion.
[b]Rule in the midst of Your
enemies!

3 [a]Your people *shall be*
volunteers
In the day of Your power;
[b]In the beauties of holiness,
from the womb of the
morning,
You have the dew of Your
youth.
4 The LORD has sworn ☆
And [a]will not relent,
"You *are* a [b]priest forever
According to the order of
[c]Mel·chiz′e·dek."

5 The Lord *is* [a]at Your right
hand;
He shall [1]execute kings [b]in
the day of His wrath.
6 He shall judge among the
nations,
He shall fill *the places* with
dead bodies,
[a]He shall [1]execute the heads
of many countries.
7 He shall drink of the brook
by the wayside;
[a]Therefore He shall lift up
the head.

PSALM 111

PRAISE[1] the LORD!

[a]I will praise the LORD with
my whole heart,
In the assembly of the
upright and *in* the
congregation.

2 [a]The works of the LORD *are*
great,
[b]Studied by all who have
pleasure in them.
3 His work *is* [a]honorable and
glorious,
And His righteousness
endures forever.
4 He has made His
wonderful works to be
remembered;
[a]The LORD *is* gracious and
full of compassion.
5 He has given food to those
who fear Him;
He will ever be mindful of
His covenant.
6 He has declared to His
people the power of His
works,
In giving them the [1]heritage
of the nations.

7 The works of His hands *are*
[a]verity[1] and justice;
All His precepts *are* sure.
8 [a]They stand fast forever and
ever,
And are [b]done in truth and
uprightness.
9 [a]He has sent redemption to
His people;
He has commanded His
covenant forever:
[b]Holy and awesome *is* His
name.
10 [a]The fear of the LORD *is* the
beginning of wisdom;
A good understanding have
all those who do *His
commandments.*
His praise endures forever.

PSALM 111

1 [a]Ps. 35:18
[1]Heb. *Hallelujah*

2 [a]Ps. 92:5
[b]Ps. 143:5

3 [a]Ps. 145:4, 5

4 [a][Ps. 86:5]

6 [1]*inheritance*

7 [a][Rev. 15:3]
[1]*truth*

8 [a]Is. 40:8
[b][Rev. 15:3]

9 [a]Luke 1:68
[b]Luke 1:49

10 [a]Eccl. 12:13

PSALM 112

PRAISE[1] the LORD!

Blessed *is* the man *who*
fears the LORD,
Who [a]delights greatly in His
commandments.

2 [a]His descendants will be
mighty on earth;
The generation of the
upright will be blessed.
3 [a]Wealth and riches *will be* in
his house,
And his righteousness
[1]endures forever.
4 [a]Unto the upright there
arises light in the
darkness;
He is gracious, and full
of compassion, and
righteous.
5 [a]A good man deals
graciously and lends;
He will guide his affairs
[b]with discretion.
6 Surely he will never be
shaken;
[a]The righteous will
be in everlasting
remembrance.
7 [a]He will not be afraid of evil
tidings;
His heart is steadfast,
trusting in the LORD.
8 His [a]heart *is* established;
[b]He will not be afraid,
Until he [c]sees *his desire*
upon his enemies.

PSALM 112

1 [a]Ps. 128:1
[1]Heb. *Hallelujah*

2 [a][Ps. 102:28]

3 [a][Matt. 6:33]
[1]*stands*

4 [a]Job 11:17

5 [a][Luke 6:35]
[b][Eph. 5:15]

6 [a]Prov. 10:7

7 [a][Prov. 1:33]

8 [a]Heb. 13:9
[b]Prov. 1:33; 3:24
[c]Ps. 59:10

9 He has dispersed abroad,
He has given to the poor;
His righteousness endures forever;
His [1]horn will be exalted with honor.
10 The wicked will see *it* and be grieved;
He will gnash his teeth and melt away;
The desire of the wicked shall perish.

PSALM 113

PRAISE[1] the LORD!

[a]Praise, O servants of the LORD,
Praise the name of the LORD!
2 [a]Blessed be the name of the LORD
From this time forth and forevermore!
3 [a]From the rising of the sun to its going down
The LORD's name *is* to be praised.

4 The LORD *is* [a]high above all nations,
[b]His glory above the heavens.
5 [a]Who *is* like the LORD our God,
Who dwells on high,
6 [a]Who humbles Himself to behold
The things that are in the heavens and in the earth?

7 [a]He raises the poor out of the dust,
And lifts the [b]needy out of the ash heap,
8 That He may [a]seat *him* with princes—
With the princes of His people.
9 [a]He grants the [1]barren woman a home,
Like a joyful mother of children.

Praise the LORD!

PSALM 114

WHEN [a]Israel went out of Egypt,
The house of Jacob [b]from a people [1]of strange language,
2 [a]Judah became His sanctuary,
And Israel His dominion.

3 [a]The sea saw *it* and fled;
[b]Jordan turned back.
4 [a]The mountains skipped like rams,
The little hills like lambs.
5 [a]What ails you, O sea, that you fled?
O Jordan, *that* you turned back?
6 O mountains, *that* you skipped like rams?
O little hills, like lambs?

7 Tremble, O earth, at the presence of the Lord,
At the presence of the God of Jacob,
8 [a]Who turned the rock *into* a pool of water,
The flint into a fountain of waters.

PSALM 115

NOT [a]unto us, O LORD, not unto us,
But to Your name give glory,
Because of Your mercy,
Because of Your truth.

---

9 [1]Strength

PSALM 113

1 [a]Ps. 135:1 [1]Heb. *Hallelujah*

2 [a][Dan. 2:20]

3 [a]Is. 59:19

4 [a]Ps. 97:9; 99:2 [b][Ps. 8:1]

5 [a][Is. 57:15]

6 [a][Ps. 11:4]

7 [a]1 Sam. 2:8 [b]Ps. 72:12

8 [a][Job 36:7]

9 [a]1 Sam. 2:5 [1]*childless*

PSALM 114

1 [a]Ex. 12:51; 13:3 [b]Ps. 81:5 [1]*who spoke unintelligibly*

2 [a]Ex. 6:7; 19:6; 25:8; 29:45, 46

3 [a]Ex. 14:21 [b]Josh. 3:13–16

4 [a]Ps. 29:6

5 [a]Hab. 3:8

8 [a]Ex. 17:6

PSALM 115

1 [a][Is. 48:11]

2 Why should the [1]Gentiles say,
[a]"So where *is* their God?"

3 [a]But our God *is* in heaven;
He does whatever He pleases.
4 [a]Their idols *are* silver and gold,
The work of men's hands.
5 They have mouths, but they do not speak;
Eyes they have, but they do not see;
6 They have ears, but they do not hear;
Noses they have, but they do not smell;
7 They have hands, but they do not handle;
Feet they have, but they do not walk;
Nor do they mutter through their throat.
8 [a]Those who make them are like them;
So is everyone who trusts in them.

9 [a]O Israel, trust in the LORD;
[b]He *is* their help and their shield.
10 O house of Aaron, trust in the LORD;
He *is* their help and their shield.
11 You who fear the LORD, trust in the LORD;
He *is* their help and their shield.

12 The LORD [1]has been mindful of *us;*
He will bless us;
He will bless the house of Israel;
He will bless the house of Aaron.
13 [a]He will bless those who fear the LORD,
Both small and great.

14 May the LORD give you increase more and more,
You and your children.
15 *May* you *be* [a]blessed by the LORD,
[b]Who made heaven and earth.

16 The heaven, *even* the heavens, *are* the LORD'S;
But the earth He has given to the children of men.
17 [a]The dead do not praise the LORD,
Nor any who go down into silence.
18 [a]But we will bless the LORD
From this time forth and forevermore.

Praise the LORD!

PSALM 116

I [a]LOVE the LORD, because He has heard
My voice *and* my supplications.
2 Because He has inclined His ear to me,
Therefore I will call *upon Him* as long as I live.

3 [a]The [1]pains of death surrounded me,
And the [2]pangs of Shē′ōl [3]laid hold of me;
I found trouble and sorrow.
4 Then I called upon the name of the LORD:
"O LORD, I implore You, deliver my soul!"

2 [a]Ps. 42:3, 10 [1]*nations*
3 [a][1 Chr. 16:26]
4 [a]Jer. 10:3
8 [a]Is. 44:9–11
9 [a]Ps. 118:2, 3 [b]Ps. 33:20
12 [1]*has remembered us*
13 [a]Ps. 128:1, 4
15 [a][Gen. 14:19] [b]Gen. 1:1
17 [a][Is. 38:18]
18 [a]Dan. 2:20

PSALM 116
1 [a]Ps. 18:1
3 [a]Ps. 18:4–6 [1]Lit. *cords* [2]*distresses* [3]Lit. *found me*

5 [a]Gracious *is* the LORD, and
[b]righteous;
Yes, our God *is* merciful.
6 The LORD preserves the
simple;
I was brought low, and He
saved me.
7 Return to your [a]rest, O my
soul,
For [b]the LORD has dealt
bountifully with you.

8 [a]For You have delivered my
soul from death,
My eyes from tears,
And my feet from falling.
9 I will walk before the LORD
[a]In the land of the living.
10 [a]I believed, therefore I spoke,
"I am greatly afflicted."
11 [a]I said in my haste,
[b]"All men *are* liars."

12 What shall I render to the
LORD
For all His benefits
toward me?
13 I will take up the cup of
salvation,
And call upon the name of
the LORD.
14 [a]I will pay my vows to the
LORD
Now in the presence of all
His people.
15 [a]Precious in the sight of the
LORD
Is the death of His saints.

16 O LORD, truly [a]I *am* Your
servant;
I *am* Your servant, [b]the son
of Your maidservant;
You have loosed my bonds.
17 I will offer to You [a]the
sacrifice of thanksgiving,
And will call upon the name
of the LORD.
18 I will pay my vows to the
LORD
Now in the presence of all
His people,
19 In the [a]courts of the LORD's
house,
In the midst of you,
O Jerusalem.

[1]Praise the LORD!

PSALM 117

PRAISE [a]the LORD, all you
Gentiles!
[1]Laud Him, all you peoples!
2 For His merciful kindness is
great toward us,
And [a]the truth of the LORD
endures forever.

Praise the LORD!

PSALM 118

OH, [a]give thanks to the LORD,
for *He is* good!
[b]For His mercy *endures*
forever.

2 [a]Let Israel now say,
"His mercy *endures* forever."
3 Let the house of Aaron now
say,
"His mercy *endures* forever."
4 Let those who fear the LORD
now say,
"His mercy *endures* forever."

5 [a]I called on the LORD in
distress;
The LORD answered me *and*
[b]*set me* in a broad place.

---

5 [a][Ps. 103:8] [b][Ezra 9:15]
7 [a][Jer. 6:16] [b]Ps. 13:6
8 [a]Ps. 56:13
9 [a]Ps. 27:13
10 [a]2 Cor. 4:13
11 [a]Ps. 31:22 [b]Rom. 3:4
14 [a]Ps. 116:18
15 [a]Ps. 72:14
16 [a]Ps. 119:125; 143:12 [b]Ps. 86:16
17 [a]Lev. 7:12
19 [a]Ps. 96:8 [1]Heb. *Hallelujah*

PSALM 117
1 [a]Rom. 15:11 [1]*Praise*
2 [a][Ps. 100:5]

PSALM 118
1 [a]1 Chr. 16:8, 34 [b][Ps. 136:1–26]
2 [a][Ps. 115:9]
5 [a]Ps. 120:1 [b]Ps. 18:19

6 [a]The LORD *is* on my side;
I will not fear.
What can man do to me?
7 [a]The LORD is for me among
those who help me;
Therefore [b]I shall see *my desire* on those who
hate me.
8 [a]*It is* better to trust in the
LORD
Than to put confidence in
man.
9 [a]*It is* better to trust in the
LORD
Than to put confidence in
princes.

10 All nations surrounded me,
But in the name of the LORD
I will destroy them.
11 They [a]surrounded me,
Yes, they surrounded me;
But in the name of the LORD
I will destroy them.
12 They surrounded me [a]like
bees;
They were quenched [b]like a
fire of thorns;
For in the name of the LORD
I will [1]destroy them.
13 You pushed me violently,
that I might fall,
But the LORD helped me.
14 [a]The LORD *is* my strength and
song,
And He has become my
salvation.

15 The voice of rejoicing and
salvation
Is in the tents of the
righteous;
The right hand of the LORD
does valiantly.
16 [a]The right hand of the LORD
is exalted;
The right hand of the LORD
does valiantly.

6 [a]Ps. 27:1; 56:9
7 [a]Ps. 54:4 [b]Ps. 59:10
8 [a]Ps. 40:4
9 [a]Ps. 146:3
11 [a]Ps. 88:17
12 [a]Deut. 1:44 [b]Nah. 1:10 [1]*cut them off*
14 [a]Is. 12:2
16 [a]Ex. 15:6
17 [a]Hab. 1:12 [b]Ps. 73:28
18 [a]2 Cor. 6:9 [1]*disciplined*
19 [a]Is. 26:2
20 [a]Ps. 24:7 [b]Is. 35:8
21 [a]Ps. 116:1
22 [a]Matt. 21:42; Mark 12:10, 11; Luke 20:17; Acts 4:11; [Eph. 2:20; 1 Pet. 2:7, 8]
23 [1]Lit. *This is from the LORD*
26 [a]Matt. 21:9 Mark 11:9; Luke 13:35; 19:38
27 [a][1 Pet. 2:9]
28 [a]Is. 25:1

17 [a]I shall not die, but live,
And [b]declare the works of
the LORD.
18 The LORD has [a]chastened[1]
me severely,
But He has not given me
over to death.

19 [a]Open to me the gates of
righteousness;
I will go through them,
And I will praise the LORD.
20 [a]This is the gate of the LORD,
[b]Through which the
righteous shall enter.

21 I will praise You,
For You have [a]answered me,
And have become my
salvation.

22 [a]The stone *which* the
builders rejected
Has become the chief
cornerstone. ☆
23 [1]This was the LORD's doing;
It *is* marvelous in our eyes.
24 This *is* the day the LORD has
made;
We will rejoice and be glad
in it.

25 Save now, I pray, O LORD;
O LORD, I pray, send now
prosperity.
26 [a]Blessed *is* he who comes in
the name of the LORD! ☆
We have blessed you from
the house of the LORD.
27 God *is* the LORD,
And He has given us [a]light;
Bind the sacrifice with cords
to the horns of the altar.
28 You *are* my God, and I will
praise You;
[a]*You are* my God, I will exalt
You.

29 Oh, give thanks to the LORD,
for *He is* good!
For His mercy *endures*
forever.

PSALM 119

א ALEPH

BLESSED *are* the [1]undefiled
in the way,
[a]Who walk in the law of the
LORD!
2 Blessed *are* those who keep
His testimonies,
Who seek Him with the
[a]whole heart!
3 [a]They also do no iniquity;
They walk in His ways.
4 You have commanded *us*
To keep Your precepts
diligently.
5 Oh, that my ways were
directed
To keep Your statutes!
6 [a]Then I would not be
ashamed,
When I look into all Your
commandments.
7 I will praise You with
uprightness of heart,
When I learn Your righteous
judgments.
8 I will keep Your statutes;
Oh, do not forsake me
utterly!

ב BETH

9 How can a young man
cleanse his way?
By taking heed according to
Your word.
10 With my whole heart I have
[a]sought You;
Oh, let me not wander from
Your commandments!
11 [a]Your word I have hidden in
my heart,
That I might not sin against
You.
12 Blessed *are* You, O LORD!
Teach me Your statutes.
13 With my lips I have
[a]declared
All the judgments of Your
mouth.
14 I have rejoiced in the way of
Your testimonies,
As *much as* in all riches.
15 I will meditate on Your
precepts,
And [1]contemplate Your
ways.
16 I will [a]delight myself in Your
statutes;
I will not forget Your word.

ג GIMEL

17 [a]Deal bountifully with Your
servant,
That I may live and keep
Your word.
18 Open my eyes, that I may
see
Wondrous things from Your
law.
19 [a]I *am* a stranger in the earth;
Do not hide Your
commandments
from me.
20 [a]My soul [1]breaks with
longing
For Your judgments at all
times.
21 You rebuke the proud—
the cursed,
Who stray from Your
commandments.
22 [a]Remove from me reproach
and contempt,
For I have kept Your
testimonies.
23 Princes also sit *and* speak
against me,
But Your servant meditates
on Your statutes.

PSALM 119

1 [a]Ps. 128:1 [1]*blameless*
2 [a]Deut. 6:5; 10:12; 11:13; 13:3
3 [a][1 John 3:9; 5:18]
6 [a]Job 22:26
10 [a]2 Chr. 15:15
11 [a]Luke 2:19
13 [a]Ps. 34:11
15 [1]*look into*
16 [a]Ps. 1:2
17 [a]Ps. 116:7
19 [a]Heb. 11:13
20 [a]Ps. 42:1, 2; 63:1; 84:2 [1]*is crushed*
22 [a]Ps. 39:8

24 Your testimonies also *are* my delight
And my counselors.

ד DALETH

25 [a]My soul clings to the dust;
[b]Revive me according to Your word.
26 I have declared my ways, and You answered me;
[a]Teach me Your statutes.
27 Make me understand the way of Your precepts;
So [a]shall I meditate on Your wonderful works.
28 [a]My soul [1]melts from [2]heaviness;
Strengthen me according to Your word.
29 Remove from me the way of lying,
And grant me Your law graciously.
30 I have chosen the way of truth;
Your judgments I have laid *before me.*
31 I cling to Your testimonies;
O LORD, do not put me to shame!
32 I will run the course of Your commandments,
For You shall [a]enlarge my heart.

ה HE

33 [a]Teach me, O LORD, the way of Your statutes,
And I shall keep it *to* the end.
34 [a]Give me understanding, and I shall keep Your law;
Indeed, I shall observe it with *my* whole heart.
35 Make me walk in the path of Your commandments,
For I delight in it.
36 [1]Incline my heart to Your testimonies,
And not to [a]covetousness.
37 [a]Turn[1] away my eyes from [b]looking at worthless things,
And revive me in [2]Your way.
38 [a]Establish Your word to Your servant,
Who *is devoted* to fearing You.
39 Turn away my reproach which I dread,
For Your judgments *are* good.
40 Behold, I long for Your precepts;
Revive me in Your righteousness.

ו WAW

41 Let Your mercies come also to me, O LORD—
Your salvation according to Your word.
42 So shall I have an answer for him who [1]reproaches me,
For I trust in Your word.
43 And take not the word of truth utterly out of my mouth,
For I have hoped in Your ordinances.
44 So shall I keep Your law continually,
Forever and ever.
45 And I will walk [1]at [a]liberty,
For I seek Your precepts.
46 [a]I will speak of Your testimonies also before kings,
And will not be ashamed.
47 And I will delight myself in Your commandments,
Which I love.
48 My hands also I will lift up to Your commandments,

25 [a]Ps. 44:25 [b]Ps. 143:11
26 [a]Ps. 25:4; 27:11; 86:11
27 [a]Ps. 145:5, 6
28 [a]Ps. 107:26 [1]Lit. *drops* [2]*grief*
32 [a]Is. 60:5
33 [a][Rev. 2:26]
34 [a][Prov. 2:6]
36 [a]Ezek. 33:31 [1]Cause me to long for
37 [a]Is. 33:15 [b]Prov. 23:5 [1]Lit. *Cause my eyes to pass away from* [2]So with MT, LXX, Vg.; Tg. *Your words*
38 [a]2 Sam. 7:25
42 [1]*taunts*
45 [a]Prov. 4:12 [1]Lit. *in a wide place*
46 [a]Matt. 10:18

Which I love,
And I will meditate on Your statutes.

ז ZAYIN

49 Remember the word to Your servant,
Upon which You have caused me to hope.
50 This *is* my [a]comfort in my affliction,
For Your word has given me life.
51 The proud have me in great derision,
Yet I do not turn aside from Your law.
52 I remembered Your judgments of old,
O LORD,
And have comforted myself.
53 [a]Indignation has taken hold of me
Because of the wicked, who forsake Your law.
54 Your statutes have been my songs
In the house of my pilgrimage.
55 [a]I remember Your name in the night, O LORD,
And I keep Your law.
56 This has become mine,
Because I kept Your precepts.

ח HETH

57 [a]*You are* my portion, O LORD;
I have said that I would keep Your words.
58 I entreated Your favor with *my* whole heart;
Be merciful to me according to Your word.
59 I [a]thought about my ways,
And turned my feet to Your testimonies.
60 I made haste, and did not delay
To keep Your commandments.
61 The cords of the wicked have bound me,
But I have not forgotten Your law.
62 [a]At midnight I will rise to give thanks to You,
Because of Your righteous judgments.
63 I *am* a companion of all who fear You,
And of those who keep Your precepts.
64 [a]The earth, O LORD, is full of Your mercy;
Teach me Your statutes.

ט TETH

65 You have dealt well with Your servant,
O LORD, according to Your word.
66 Teach me good judgment and [a]knowledge,
For I believe Your commandments.
67 Before I was [a]afflicted I went astray,
But now I keep Your word.
68 You *are* [a]good, and do good;
Teach me Your statutes.
69 The proud have [a]forged[1] a lie against me,
But I will keep Your precepts with *my* whole heart.
70 [a]Their heart is [1]as fat as grease,
But I delight in Your law.
71 *It is* good for me that I have been afflicted,
That I may learn Your statutes.
72 [a]The law of Your mouth *is* better to me

50 [a][Rom. 15:4]
53 [a]Ezra 9:3
55 [a]Ps. 63:6
57 [a]Jer. 10:16
59 [a]Luke 15:17
62 [a]Acts 16:25
64 [a]Ps. 33:5
66 [a]Phil. 1:9
67 [a][Heb. 12:5–11]
68 [a][Matt. 19:17]
69 [a]Job 13:4 [1]Lit. *smeared me with a lie*
70 [a]Acts 28:27 [1]Insensible
72 [a]Ps. 19:10

Than thousands of *coins* of
gold and silver.

י YOD

73 [a]Your hands have made me
and fashioned me;
Give me understanding,
that I may learn Your
commandments.
74 [a]Those who fear You will be
glad when they see me,
Because I have hoped in
Your word.
75 I know, O LORD, [a]that Your
judgments *are* [1]right,
And *that* in faithfulness You
have afflicted me.
76 Let, I pray, Your merciful
kindness be for my
comfort,
According to Your word to
Your servant.
77 Let Your tender mercies
come to me, that I may
live;
For Your law *is* my delight.
78 Let the proud [a]be ashamed,
For they treated me
wrongfully with
falsehood;
But I will meditate on Your
precepts.
79 Let those who fear You turn
to me,
Those who know Your
testimonies.
80 Let my heart be blameless
regarding Your statutes,
That I may not be ashamed.

כ KAPH

81 [a]My soul faints for Your
salvation,
But I hope in Your word.
82 My eyes fail *from searching*
Your word,
Saying, "When will You
comfort me?"
83 For [a]I have become like a
wineskin in smoke,
Yet I do not forget Your
statutes.
84 [a]How many *are* the days of
Your servant?
[b]When will You execute
judgment on those who
persecute me?
85 [a]The proud have dug pits for
me,
Which *is* not according to
Your law.
86 All Your commandments *are*
faithful;
They persecute me
[a]wrongfully;
Help me!
87 They almost made an end of
me on earth,
But I did not forsake Your
precepts.
88 Revive me according to Your
lovingkindness,
So that I may keep the
testimony of Your mouth.

ל LAMED

89 [a]Forever, O LORD,
Your word [1]is settled in
heaven.
90 Your faithfulness *endures* to
all generations;
You established the earth,
and it [1]abides.
91 They continue this day
according to [a]Your
ordinances,
For all *are* Your servants.
92 Unless Your law *had been*
my delight,
I would then have perished
in my affliction.
93 I will never forget Your
precepts,
For by them You have given
me life.
94 I *am* Yours, save me;

73 [a]Job 10:8; 31:15
74 [a]Ps. 34:2
75 [a][Heb. 12:10] [1]Lit. *righteous*
78 [a]Ps. 25:3
81 [a]Ps. 73:26; 84:2
83 [a]Job 30:30
84 [a]Ps. 39:4 [b]Rev. 6:10
85 [a]Ps. 35:7
86 [a]Ps. 35:19
89 [a]Matt. 24:35 [1]Lit. *stands firm*
90 [1]Lit. *stands*
91 [a]Jer. 33:25

For I have sought Your
precepts.
95 The wicked wait for me to
destroy me,
But I will [1]consider Your
testimonies.
96 [a]I have seen the
consummation of all
perfection,
But Your commandment *is*
exceedingly broad.

מ MEM

97 Oh, how I love Your law!
[a]It *is* my meditation all the
day.
98 You, through Your
commandments, make
me [a]wiser than my
enemies;
For they *are* ever with me.
99 I have more understanding
than all my teachers,
[a]For Your testimonies *are*
my meditation.
100 [a]I understand more than the
[1]ancients,
Because I keep Your
precepts.
101 I have restrained my feet
from every evil way,
That I may keep Your word.
102 I have not departed from
Your judgments,
For You Yourself have
taught me.
103 [a]How sweet are Your words
to my taste,
Sweeter than honey to my
mouth!
104 Through Your precepts I
get understanding;
Therefore I hate every
false way.

נ NUN

105 [a]Your word *is* a lamp to my
feet
And a light to my path.
106 [a]I have sworn and
confirmed
That I will keep Your
righteous judgments.
107 I am afflicted very much;
Revive me, O LORD,
according to Your word.
108 Accept, I pray, [a]the freewill
offerings of my mouth,
O LORD,
And teach me Your
judgments.
109 [a]My life *is* continually [1]in
my hand,
Yet I do not forget Your
law.
110 [a]The wicked have laid a
snare for me,
Yet I have not strayed from
Your precepts.
111 [a]Your testimonies I have
taken as a [1]heritage
forever,
For they *are* the rejoicing
of my heart.
112 I have inclined my heart to
perform Your statutes
Forever, to the very end.

ס SAMEK

113 I hate the [1]double-minded,
But I love Your law.
114 [a]You *are* my hiding place
and my shield;
I hope in Your word.
115 [a]Depart from me, you
evildoers,
For I will keep the
commandments of my
God!
116 Uphold me according to
Your word, that I may
live;
And do not let me [a]be
ashamed of my hope.
117 [1]Hold me up, and I shall be
safe,

95 [1]*give attention to*
96 [a]Matt. 5:18
97 [a]Ps. 1:2
98 [a]Deut. 4:6
99 [a][2 Tim. 3:15]
100 [a][Job 32:7–9] [1]*aged*
103 [a]Prov. 8:11
105 [a]Prov. 6:23
106 [a]Neh. 10:29
108 [a]Hos. 14:2
109 [a]Job 13:14 [1]In danger
110 [a]Ps. 140:5
111 [a]Deut. 33:4 [1]*inheritance*
113 [1]Lit. *divided* in heart or mind
114 [a][Ps. 32:7]
115 [a]Matt. 7:23
116 [a][Rom. 5:5; 9:33; 10:11]
117 [1]*Uphold me*

And I shall observe Your
statutes continually.
118 You reject all those
who stray from Your
statutes,
For their deceit *is*
falsehood.
119 You [1]put away all the
wicked of the earth
[a]*like* [2]dross;
Therefore I love Your
testimonies.
120 [a]My flesh trembles for fear
of You,
And I am afraid of Your
judgments.

ע AYIN

121 I have done justice and
righteousness;
Do not leave me to my
oppressors.
122 Be [a]surety[1] for Your servant
for good;
Do not let the proud
oppress me.
123 My eyes fail *from seeking*
Your salvation
And Your righteous word.
124 Deal with Your servant
according to Your
mercy,
And teach me Your
statutes.
125 [a]I *am* Your servant;
Give me understanding,
That I may know Your
testimonies.
126 *It is* time for *You* to act,
O LORD,
For they have [1]regarded
Your law as void.
127 [a]Therefore I love Your
commandments
More than gold, yes, than
fine gold!
128 Therefore all *Your* precepts
concerning all *things*
I consider *to be* right;
I hate every false way.

פ PE

129 Your testimonies are
wonderful;
Therefore my soul keeps
them.
130 The entrance of Your words
gives light;
[a]It gives understanding to
the [b]simple.
131 I opened my mouth and
[a]panted,
For I longed for Your
commandments.
132 [a]Look upon me and be
merciful to me,
As Your custom *is* toward
those who love Your
name.
133 [a]Direct my steps by Your
word,
And [b]let no iniquity have
dominion over me.
134 [a]Redeem me from the
oppression of man,
That I may keep Your
precepts.
135 [a]Make Your face shine upon
Your servant,
And teach me Your
statutes.
136 [a]Rivers of water run down
from my eyes,
Because *men* do not keep
Your law.

צ TSADDE

137 [a]Righteous *are* You, O LORD,
And upright *are* Your
judgments.
138 [a]Your testimonies, *which*
You have commanded,
Are righteous and very
faithful.
139 [a]My zeal has [1]consumed me,

119 [a]Ezek. 22:18, 19 [1]*destroy,* lit. *cause to cease* [2]*slag* or *refuse*
120 [a]Hab. 3:16
122 [a]Heb. 7:22 [1]*guaranty*
125 [a]Ps. 116:16
126 [1]*broken Your law*
127 [a]Ps. 19:10
130 [a]Prov. 6:23 [b][Ps. 19:7]
131 [a]Ps. 42:1
132 [a]Ps. 106:4 [b][2 Thess. 1:6]
133 [a]Ps. 17:5 [b][Rom. 6:12]
134 [a]Luke 1:74
135 [a]Ps. 4:6
136 [a]Jer. 9:1, 18; 14:17
137 [a]Neh. 9:33
138 [a][Ps. 19:7–9]
139 [a]John 2:17 [1]*put an end to*

Because my enemies have
forgotten Your words.
140 [a]Your word *is* very [1]pure;
Therefore Your servant
loves it.
141 I *am* small and despised,
Yet I do not forget Your
precepts.
142 Your righteousness
is an everlasting
righteousness,
And Your law *is* [a]truth.
143 Trouble and anguish have
[1]overtaken me,
Yet Your commandments
are my delights.
144 The righteousness of
Your testimonies *is*
everlasting;
Give me understanding,
and I shall live.

ק QOPH

145 I cry out with *my* whole
heart;
Hear me, O LORD!
I will keep Your statutes.
146 I cry out to You;
Save me, and I will keep
Your testimonies.
147 [a]I rise before the dawning
of the morning,
And cry for help;
I hope in Your word.
148 [a]My eyes are awake
through the *night*
watches,
That I may meditate on
Your word.
149 Hear my voice according
to Your lovingkindness;
O LORD, revive me
according to Your
justice.
150 They draw near who follow
after wickedness;
They are far from Your law.
151 You *are* [a]near, O LORD,
And all Your
commandments *are*
truth.
152 Concerning Your
testimonies,
I have known of old that
You have founded them
[a]forever.

ר RESH

153 [a]Consider my affliction and
deliver me,
For I do not forget Your
law.
154 [a]Plead my cause and
redeem me;
Revive me according to
Your word.
155 Salvation *is* far from the
wicked,
For they do not seek Your
statutes.
156 [1]Great *are* Your tender
mercies, O LORD;
Revive me according to
Your judgments.
157 Many *are* my persecutors
and my enemies,
Yet I do not [a]turn from
Your testimonies.
158 I see the treacherous, and
[a]am disgusted,
Because they do not keep
Your word.
159 Consider how I love Your
precepts;
Revive me, O LORD,
according to Your
lovingkindness.
160 The entirety of Your word
is truth,
And every one of Your
righteous judgments
endures forever.

ש SHIN

161 [a]Princes persecute me
without a cause,

140 [a]Ps. 12:6 [1]Lit. *refined* or *tried*
142 [a][John 17:17]
143 [1]Lit. *found*
147 [a]Ps. 5:3
148 [a]Ps. 63:1, 6
151 [a][Ps. 145:18]
152 [a]Luke 21:33
153 [a]Lam. 5:1
154 [a]1 Sam. 24:15
156 [1]Or *Many*
157 [a]Ps. 44:18
158 [a]Ezek. 9:4
161 [a]1 Sam. 24:11; 26:18

But my heart stands in awe
of Your word.
162 I rejoice at Your word
As one who finds great
treasure.
163 I hate and abhor lying,
But I love Your law.
164 Seven times a day I praise
You,
Because of Your righteous
judgments.
165 [a]Great peace have those
who love Your law,
And [1]nothing causes them
to stumble.
166 [a]LORD, I hope for Your
salvation,
And I do Your
commandments.
167 My soul keeps Your
testimonies,
And I love them
exceedingly.
168 I keep Your precepts and
Your testimonies,
[a]For all my ways *are* before
You.

ת TAU

169 Let my cry come before
You, O LORD;
[a]Give me understanding
according to Your word.
170 Let my [1]supplication come
before You;
Deliver me according to
Your word.
171 [a]My lips shall utter praise,
For You teach me Your
statutes.
172 My tongue shall speak of
Your word,
For all Your commandments
are righteousness.
173 Let Your hand become my
help,
For [a]I have chosen Your
precepts.
174 [a]I long for Your salvation,
O LORD,
And [b]Your law *is* my
delight.
175 Let my soul live, and it
shall praise You;
And let Your judgments
help me.
176 [a]I have gone astray like a
lost sheep;
Seek Your servant,
For I do not forget Your
commandments.

PSALM 120

A Song of Ascents.

IN [a]my distress I cried to the
LORD,
And He heard me.
2 Deliver my soul, O LORD,
from lying lips
And from a deceitful tongue.

3 What shall be given to you,
Or what shall be done to
you,
You false tongue?
4 Sharp arrows of the [1]warrior,
With coals of the broom tree!

5 Woe is me, that I dwell in
[a]Mēʹshech,
[b]*That* I dwell among the
tents of Kēʹdar!
6 My soul has dwelt too long
With one who hates peace.
7 I *am for* peace;
But when I speak, they *are*
for war.

PSALM 121

A Song of Ascents.

I [a]WILL lift up my eyes to the
hills—

---

165 [a]Prov. 3:2 [1]Lit. *they have no stumbling block*
166 [a]Gen. 49:18
168 [a]Prov. 5:21
169 [a]Ps. 119:27, 144
170 [1]Prayer of supplication
171 [a]Ps. 119:7
173 [a]Josh. 24:22
174 [a]Ps. 119:166 [b]Ps. 119:16, 24
176 [a][Is. 53:6]

PSALM 120
1 [a]Jon. 2:2
4 [1]*mighty one*
5 [a]Gen. 10:2 [b]Gen. 25:13

PSALM 121
1 [a][Jer. 3:23]

From whence comes my help?
2 [a]My help *comes* from the LORD,
Who made heaven and earth.

3 [a]He will not allow your foot to [1]be moved;
[b]He who keeps you will not slumber.
4 Behold, He who keeps Israel
Shall neither slumber nor sleep.

5 The LORD *is* your [1]keeper;
The LORD *is* [a]your shade [b]at your right hand.
6 [a]The sun shall not strike you by day,
Nor the moon by night.

7 The LORD shall [1]preserve you from all evil;
He shall [a]preserve your soul.
8 The LORD shall [a]preserve[1] your going out and your coming in
From this time forth, and even forevermore.

PSALM 122

A Song of Ascents. Of David.

I WAS glad when they said to me,
[a]"Let us go into the house of the LORD."
2 Our feet have been standing
Within your gates, O Jerusalem!

3 Jerusalem is built
As a city that is [a]compact together,
4 [a]Where the tribes go up,
The tribes of the LORD,
[1]To [b]the Testimony of Israel,
To give thanks to the name of the LORD.
5 [a]For thrones are set there for judgment,
The thrones of the house of David.

6 [a]Pray for the peace of Jerusalem:
"May they prosper who love you.
7 Peace be within your walls,
Prosperity within your palaces."
8 For the sake of my brethren and companions,
I will now say, "Peace *be* within you."
9 Because of the house of the LORD our God
I will [a]seek your good.

PSALM 123

A Song of Ascents.

UNTO You [a]I lift up my eyes,
O You [b]who dwell in the heavens.
2 Behold, as the eyes of servants *look* to the hand of their masters,
As the eyes of a maid to the hand of her mistress,
[a]So our eyes *look* to the LORD our God,
Until He has mercy on us.

3 Have mercy on us, O LORD, have mercy on us!
For we are exceedingly filled with contempt.
4 Our soul is exceedingly filled
With the scorn of those who are at ease,

2 [a][Ps. 124:8]
3 [a]1 Sam. 2:9 [b]Is. 27:3 [1]*slip*
5 [a]Is. 25:4 [b]Ps. 16:8 [1]*protector*
6 [a]Is. 49:10
7 [a]Ps. 41:2 [1]*keep*
8 [a]Deut. 28:6 [1]*keep*

PSALM 122
1 [a][Is. 2:3]
3 [a]2 Sam. 5:9
4 [a]Deut. 16:16 [b]Ex. 16:34 [1]Or *As a testimony to*
5 [a]Deut. 17:8
6 [a]Ps. 51:18
9 [a]Neh. 2:10

PSALM 123
1 [a]Ps. 121:1; 141:8 [b]Ps. 2:4; 11:4; 115:3
2 [a]Ps. 25:15

With the contempt of the
proud.

PSALM 124

A Song of Ascents. Of David.

"IF it had not been the LORD
who was on our [a]side,"
[b]Let Israel now say—
2 "If it had not been the LORD
who was on our side,
When men rose up against
us,
3 Then they would have
[a]swallowed us alive,
When their wrath was
kindled against us;
4 Then the waters would have
overwhelmed us,
The stream would have
[1]gone over our soul;
5 Then the swollen waters
Would have [1]gone over our
soul."

6 Blessed *be* the LORD,
Who has not given us *as*
prey to their teeth.
7 [a]Our soul has escaped [b]as a
bird from the snare of
the [1]fowlers;
The snare is broken, and we
have escaped.
8 [a]Our help *is* in the name of
the LORD,
[b]Who made heaven and
earth.

PSALM 125

A Song of Ascents.

THOSE who trust in the LORD
Are like Mount Zion,
Which cannot be moved,
but abides forever.
2 As the mountains surround
Jerusalem,
So the LORD surrounds His
people
From this time forth and
forever.

3 For [a]the scepter of
wickedness shall not
rest
On the land allotted to the
righteous,
Lest the righteous reach out
their hands to iniquity.

4 Do good, O LORD, to *those
who are* good,
And to *those who are*
upright in their hearts.

5 As for such as turn aside to
their [a]crooked ways,
The LORD shall lead them
away
With the workers of
iniquity.

[b]Peace *be* upon Israel!

PSALM 126

A Song of Ascents.

WHEN [a]the LORD brought
back [1]the captivity of
Zion,
[b]We were like those who
dream.
2 Then [a]our mouth was filled
with laughter,
And our tongue with
singing.
Then they said among the
[1]nations,
"The LORD has done great
things for them."
3 The LORD has done great
things for us,
And we are glad.

PSALM 124

1 [a][Rom. 8:31] [b]Ps. 129:1

3 [a]Prov. 1:12

4 [1]*swept over*

5 [1]*swept over*

7 [a]Ps. 91:3 [b]Prov. 6:5 [1]Persons who catch birds in a trap or snare

8 [a][Ps. 121:2] [b]Gen. 1:1

PSALM 125

3 [a]Prov. 22:8

5 [a]Prov. 2:15 [b][Gal. 6:16]

PSALM 126

1 [a]Hos. 6:11 [b]Acts 12:9 [1]Those of the captivity

2 [a]Job 8:21 [1]*Gentiles*

4 Bring back our captivity,
O LORD,
As the streams in the South.
5 [a]Those who sow in tears
Shall reap in joy.
6 He who continually goes [1]forth weeping,
Bearing [2]seed for sowing,
Shall doubtless come again [3]with [a]rejoicing,
Bringing his sheaves *with* him.

PSALM 127

A Song of Ascents. Of Solomon.

UNLESS the LORD builds the house,
They labor in vain who build it;
Unless [a]the LORD guards the city,
The watchman stays awake in vain.
2 *It is* vain for you to rise up early,
To sit up late,
To [a]eat the bread of sorrows;
For so He gives His beloved sleep.
3 Behold, [a]children *are* a heritage from the LORD,
[b]The fruit of the womb *is* a [c]reward.
4 Like arrows in the hand of a warrior,
So *are* the children of one's youth.
5 [a]Happy *is* the man who has his quiver full of them;
[b]They shall not be ashamed,
But shall speak with their enemies in the gate.

5 [a]Jer. 31:9
6 [a]Is. 61:3 [1]*to and fro* [2]Lit. *a bag of seed for sowing* [3]*with shouts of joy*

PSALM 127
1 [a][Ps. 121:3–5]
2 [a][Gen. 3:17, 19]
3 [a][Josh. 24:3, 4] [b]Deut. 7:13; 28:4 [c][Ps. 113:9]
5 [a]Ps. 128:2, 3 [b]Prov. 27:11

PSALM 128
1 [a]Ps. 119:1
2 [a]Is. 3:10 [b]Deut. 4:40 [1]Fruit of the labor
3 [a]Ezek. 19:10 [b]Ps. 127:3–5 [c]Ps. 52:8; 144:12
5 [a]Ps. 134:3
6 [a]Job 42:16 [b]Ps. 125:5

PSALM 129
1 [a][Jer. 1:19; 15:20] [b]Ezek. 23:3 [c]Ps. 124:1 [1]*persecuted*

PSALM 128

A Song of Ascents.

BLESSED [a]*is* every one who fears the LORD,
Who walks in His ways.
2 [a]When you eat the [1]labor of your hands,
You *shall be* happy, and *it shall be* [b]well with you.
3 Your wife *shall be* [a]like a fruitful vine
In the very heart of your house,
Your [b]children [c]like olive plants
All around your table.
4 Behold, thus shall the man be blessed
Who fears the LORD.
5 [a]The LORD bless you out of Zion,
And may you see the good of Jerusalem
All the days of your life.
6 Yes, may you [a]see your children's children.

[b]Peace *be* upon Israel!

PSALM 129

A Song of Ascents.

"MANY a time they have [a]afflicted[1] me from [b]my youth,"
[c]Let Israel now say—
2 "Many a time they have afflicted me from my youth;
Yet they have not prevailed against me.
3 The plowers plowed on my back;

They made their furrows long."
4 The LORD *is* righteous;
He has cut in pieces the cords of the wicked.

5 Let all those who hate Zion
Be put to shame and turned back.
6 Let them be as the [a]grass *on* the housetops,
Which withers before it grows up,
7 With which the reaper does not fill his hand,
Nor he who binds sheaves, his [1]arms.
8 Neither let those who pass by them say,
[a]"The blessing of the LORD *be* upon you;
We bless you in the name of the LORD!"

PSALM 130

A Song of Ascents.

OUT [a]of the depths I have cried to You, O LORD;
2 Lord, hear my voice!
Let Your ears be attentive
To the voice of my supplications.

3 [a]If You, LORD, should [1]mark iniquities,
O Lord, who could [b]stand?
4 But *there is* [a]forgiveness with You,
That [b]You may be feared.

5 [a]I wait for the LORD, my soul waits,
And [b]in His word I do hope.
6 [a]My soul *waits* for the Lord
More than those who watch for the morning—
Yes, more than those who watch for the morning.

7 [a]O Israel, hope in the LORD;
For [b]with the LORD *there is* mercy,
And with Him *is* abundant redemption.
8 And [a]He shall redeem Israel
From all his iniquities.

PSALM 131

A Song of Ascents. Of David.

LORD, my heart is not [1]haughty,
Nor my eyes [2]lofty.
[a]Neither do I [3]concern myself with great matters,
Nor with things too [4]profound for me.

2 Surely I have calmed and quieted my soul,
[a]Like a weaned child with his mother;
Like a weaned child *is* my soul within me.

3 [a]O Israel, hope in the LORD
From this time forth and forever.

PSALM 132

A Song of Ascents.

LORD, remember David
And all his afflictions;
2 How he swore to the LORD,
[a]*And* vowed to [b]the Mighty One of Jacob:
3 "Surely I will not go into the chamber of my house,

6 [a]Ps. 37:2
7 [1]*armsful,* lit. *bosom*
8 [a]Ruth 2:4

PSALM 130
1 [a]Lam. 3:55
3 [a][Ps. 143:2] [b][Nah. 1:6] [1]*take note of*
4 [a][Ex. 34:7] [b][1 Kin. 8:39, 40]
5 [a][Ps. 27:14] [b]Ps. 119:81
6 [a]Ps. 119:147
7 [a]Ps. 131:3 [b][Is. 55:7]
8 [a][Ps. 103:3, 4]

PSALM 131
1 [a][Rom. 12:16] [1]Proud [2]Arrogant [3]Lit. *walk in* [4]*difficult*
2 [a][Matt. 18:3]
3 [a][Ps. 130:7]

PSALM 132
2 [a]Ps. 65:1 [b]Gen. 49:24

Or go up to the comfort of
my bed;
4 I will [a]not give sleep to my
eyes
Or slumber to my eyelids,
5 Until I [a]find a place for the
LORD,
A dwelling place for the
Mighty One of Jacob."

6 Behold, we heard of it [a]in
Eph'ra·thah;
[b]We found it [c]in the fields of
[1]the woods.
7 Let us go into His
tabernacle;
[a]Let us worship at His
footstool.
8 [a]Arise, O LORD, to Your
resting place,
You and [b]the ark of Your
strength.
9 Let Your priests [a]be clothed
with righteousness,
And let Your saints shout for
joy.

10 For Your servant David's
sake,
Do not turn away the face of
Your [1]Anointed.

11 [a]The LORD has sworn *in* truth
to David;
He will not turn from it:
"I will set upon your throne
[b]the [1]fruit of your body.
12 If your sons will keep My
covenant
And My testimony which I
shall teach them,
Their sons also shall sit
upon your throne
forevermore."

13 [a]For the LORD has chosen
Zion;
He has desired *it* for His
[1]dwelling place:
14 "This[a] *is* My resting place
forever;
Here I will dwell, for I have
desired it.
15 [a]I will abundantly bless her
[1]provision;
I will satisfy her poor with
bread.
16 [a]I will also clothe her priests
with salvation,
[b]And her saints shall shout
aloud for joy.
17 [a]There I will make the [1]horn
of David grow;
[b]I will prepare a lamp for My
[2]Anointed.
18 His enemies I will [a]clothe
with shame,
But upon Himself His crown
shall flourish."

PSALM 133

A Song of Ascents. Of David.

BEHOLD, how good and how
pleasant *it is*
For [a]brethren to dwell
together in unity!

2 *It is* like the precious oil
upon the head,
Running down on the
beard,
The beard of Aaron,
Running down on the edge
of his garments.
3 *It is* like the dew of
[a]Her'mon,
Descending upon the
mountains of Zion;
For [b]there the LORD
commanded the
blessing—
Life forevermore.

---

4 [a]Prov. 6:4
5 [a]Acts 7:46
6 [a]1 Sam. 17:12 [b]1 Sam. 7:1 [c]1 Chr. 13:5 [1]Heb. *Jaar*, lit. *Woods*
7 [a]Ps. 5:7; 99:5
8 [a]Num. 10:35 [b]Ps. 78:61
9 [a]Job 29:14
10 [1]Commissioned One, Heb. *Messiah*
11 [a][Ps. 89:3, 4, 35; 110:4] [b]2 Sam. 7:12 [1]*offspring*
13 [a][Ps. 48:1, 2] [1]*home*
14 [a]Ps. 68:16
15 [a]Ps. 147:14 [1]*supply of food*
16 [a]2 Chr. 6:41 [b]1 Sam. 4:5
17 [a]Ezek. 29:21 [b]1 Kin. 11:36; 15:4 [1]Government [2]Heb. *Messiah*
18 [a]Ps. 35:26

PSALM 133
1 [a]Gen. 13:8
3 [a]Deut. 4:48 [b]Lev. 25:21

PSALM 134

A Song of Ascents.

BEHOLD, bless the LORD,
All *you* servants of the LORD,
Who by night stand in the house of the LORD!
2 [a]Lift up your hands *in* the sanctuary,
And bless the LORD.

3 The LORD who made heaven and earth
Bless you from Zion!

PSALM 135

PRAISE the LORD!

Praise the name of the LORD;
[a]Praise *Him,* O you servants of the LORD!
2 [a]You who stand in the house of the LORD,
In [b]the courts of the house of our God,
3 Praise the LORD, for [a]the LORD *is* good;
Sing praises to His name, [b]for *it is* pleasant.
4 For [a]the LORD has chosen Jacob for Himself,
Israel for His [1]special treasure.

5 For I know that [a]the LORD *is* great,
And our Lord *is* above all gods.
6 [a]Whatever the LORD pleases He does,
In heaven and in earth,
In the seas and in all deep places.
7 [a]He causes the [1]vapors to ascend from the ends of the earth;
[b]He makes lightning for the rain;
He brings the wind out of His [c]treasuries.

8 [a]He [1]destroyed the firstborn of Egypt,
[2]Both of man and beast.
9 [a]He sent signs and wonders into the midst of you, O Egypt,
[b]Upon Pharaoh and all his servants.
10 [a]He defeated many nations
And slew mighty kings—
11 Sī'hon king of the Am'o·rītes,
Og king of Bā'shan,
And [a]all the kingdoms of Cā'naan—
12 [a]And gave their land *as* a [1]heritage,
A heritage to Israel His people.

13 [a]Your name, O LORD, *endures* forever,
Your fame, O LORD, throughout all generations.
14 [a]For the LORD will judge His people,
And He will have compassion on His servants.

15 [a]The idols of the nations *are* silver and gold,
The work of men's hands.
16 They have mouths, but they do not speak;
Eyes they have, but they do not see;
17 They have ears, but they do not hear;
Nor is there *any* breath in their mouths.

PSALM 134
2 [a][1 Tim. 2:8]

PSALM 135
1 [a]Ps. 113:1
2 [a]Luke 2:37 [b]Ps. 116:19
3 [a][Ps. 119:68] [b]Ps. 147:1
4 [a][Ex. 19:5] [1]*precious possession*
5 [a]Ps. 95:3; 97:9
6 [a]Ps. 115:3
7 [a]Jer. 10:13 [b]Job 28:25, 26; 38:24–28 [c]Jer. 51:16 [1]Water vapor
8 [a]Ex. 12:12 [1]Lit. *struck down* [2]Lit. *From man to beast*
9 [a]Ex. 7:10 [b]Ps. 136:15
10 [a]Num. 21:24
11 [a]Josh. 12:7–24
12 [a]Ps. 78:55; 136:21, 22 [1]*inheritance*
13 [a][Ex. 3:15]
14 [a]Deut. 32:36
15 [a][Ps. 115:4–8]

18 Those who make them are
like them;
So is everyone who trusts in
them.

19 [a]Bless the LORD, O house of
Israel!
Bless the LORD, O house of
Aaron!
20 Bless the LORD, O house of
Levi!
You who fear the LORD,
bless the LORD!
21 Blessed be the LORD [a]out of
Zion,
Who dwells in Jerusalem!

Praise the LORD!

PSALM 136

OH, [a]give thanks to the LORD,
for *He is* good!
[b]For His mercy *endures*
forever.
2 Oh, give thanks to [a]the God
of gods!
For His mercy *endures*
forever.
3 Oh, give thanks to the Lord
of lords!
For His mercy *endures*
forever:

4 To Him [a]who alone does
great wonders,
For His mercy *endures*
forever;
5 [a]To Him who by wisdom
made the heavens,
For His mercy *endures*
forever;
6 [a]To Him who laid out the
earth above the waters,
For His mercy *endures*
forever;
7 [a]To Him who made great
lights,
For His mercy *endures*
forever—
8 [a]The sun to rule by day,
For His mercy *endures*
forever;
9 The moon and stars to rule
by night,
For His mercy *endures*
forever.

10 [a]To Him who struck Egypt in
their firstborn,
For His mercy *endures*
forever;
11 [a]And brought out Israel from
among them,
For His mercy *endures*
forever;
12 [a]With a strong hand, and
with [1]an outstretched
arm,
For His mercy *endures*
forever;
13 [a]To Him who divided the Red
Sea in two,
For His mercy *endures*
forever;
14 And made Israel pass
through the midst of it,
For His mercy *endures*
forever;
15 [a]But overthrew Pharaoh and
his army in the Red Sea,
For His mercy *endures*
forever;
16 [a]To Him who led His people
through the wilderness,
For His mercy *endures*
forever;
17 [a]To Him who struck down
great kings,
For His mercy *endures*
forever;
18 [a]And slew famous kings,
For His mercy *endures*
forever—
19 [a]Sī′hon king of the
Am′o·rītes,

19 [a][Ps. 115:9]
21 [a]Ps. 134:3

PSALM 136

1 [a]Ps. 106:1 [b]1 Chr. 16:34
2 [a][Deut. 10:17]
4 [a]Ps. 72:18
5 [a]Jer. 51:15
6 [a]Jer. 10:12
7 [a]Gen. 1:14–18
8 [a]Gen. 1:16
10 [a]Ex. 12:29
11 [a]Ex. 12:51; 13:3, 16
12 [a]Ex. 6:6 [1]Mighty power
13 [a]Ex. 14:21
15 [a]Ex. 14:27
16 [a]Ex. 13:18; 15:22
17 [a]Ps. 135:10–12
18 [a]Deut. 29:7
19 [a]Num. 21:21

For His mercy *endures*
forever;
20 [a]And Og king of Bā′shan,
For His mercy *endures*
forever—
21 [a]And gave their land as a
[1]heritage,
For His mercy *endures*
forever;
22 A heritage to Israel His
servant,
For His mercy *endures*
forever.

23 Who [a]remembered us in our
lowly state,
For His mercy *endures*
forever;
24 And [a]rescued us from our
enemies,
For His mercy *endures*
forever;
25 [a]Who gives food to all flesh,
For His mercy *endures*
forever.

26 Oh, give thanks to the God
of heaven!
For His mercy *endures*
forever.

PSALM 137

BY the rivers of Babylon,
There we sat down, yea, we
wept
When we remembered Zion.
2 We hung our harps
Upon the willows in the
midst of it.
3 For there those who carried
us away captive asked of
us a song,
And those who [a]plundered
us *requested* mirth,
Saying, "Sing us *one* of the
songs of Zion!"

4 How shall we sing the
LORD's song
In a foreign land?
5 If I forget you, O Jerusalem,
Let my right hand forget *its*
skill!
6 If I do not remember you,
Let my [a]tongue cling to the
roof of my mouth—
If I do not exalt Jerusalem
Above my chief joy.

7 Remember, O LORD, against
[a]the sons of Ē′dom
The day of Jerusalem,
Who said, [1]"Raze *it,* raze *it,*
To its very foundation!"

8 O daughter of Babylon,
[a]who are to be destroyed,
Happy the one [b]who repays
you as you have served
us!
9 Happy the one who takes
and [a]dashes
Your little ones against the
rock!

PSALM 138

A Psalm of David.

I WILL praise You with my
whole heart;
[a]Before the gods I will sing
praises to You.
2 [a]I will worship [b]toward Your
holy temple,
And praise Your name
For Your lovingkindness and
Your truth;
For You have [c]magnified
Your word above all Your
name.
3 In the day when I cried out,
You answered me,
And made me bold *with*
strength in my soul.

136:20 [a]Num. 21:33
136:21 [a]Josh. 12:1 [1]*inheritance*
136:23 [a]Gen. 8:1
136:24 [a]Ps. 44:7
136:25 [a]Ps. 104:27; 145:15

PSALM 137
3 [a]Ps. 79:1
6 [a]Ezek. 3:26
7 [a]Jer. 49:7–22 [1]Lit. *Make bare*
8 [a]Is. 13:1–6; 47:1 [b]Jer. 50:15
9 [a]Is. 13:16

PSALM 138
1 [a]Ps. 119:46
2 [a]Ps. 28:2 [b]1 Kin. 8:29 [c]Is. 42:21

4 [a]All the kings of the earth
shall praise You, O LORD,
When they hear the words
of Your mouth.
5 Yes, they shall sing of the
ways of the LORD,
For great *is* the glory of the
LORD.
6 [a]Though the LORD *is* on high,
Yet [b]He regards the lowly;
But the proud He knows
from afar.

7 [a]Though I walk in the midst
of trouble, You will
revive me;
You will stretch out Your
hand
Against the wrath of my
enemies,
And Your right hand will
save me.
8 [a]The LORD will [1]perfect *that
which* concerns me;
Your mercy, O LORD, *endures*
forever;
[b]Do not forsake the works of
Your hands.

PSALM 139

For the Chief Musician. A
Psalm of David.

O LORD, [a]You have searched
me and known *me*.
2 [a]You know my sitting down
and my rising up;
You [b]understand my thought
afar off.
3 [a]You [1]comprehend my path
and my lying down,
And are acquainted with all
my ways.
4 For *there is* not a word on
my tongue,
But behold, O LORD, [a]You
know it altogether.

4 [a]Ps. 102:15
6 [a][Ps. 113:4–7] [b][James 4:6]
7 [a][Ps. 23:3, 4]
8 [a]Ps. 57:2 [b]Job 10:3, 8 [1]*complete*

PSALM 139

1 [a]Ps. 17:3
2 [a]2 Kin. 19:27 [b]Matt. 9:4
3 [a]Job 14:16; 31:4 [1]Lit. *winnow*
4 [a][Heb. 4:13]
5 [1]*enclosed*
6 [a]Job 42:3
7 [a][Jer. 23:24]
8 [a][Amos 9:2–4] [b][Job 26:6] [1]Or *Sheol*
11 [1]Vg., Symmachus *cover*
12 [a]Job 26:6; 34:22 [1]Lit. *is not dark*
13 [1]*wove*
14 [1]So with MT, Tg.; LXX, Syr., Vg. *You are fearfully wonderful*
15 [a]Job 10:8, 9 [1]Lit. *bones were*

5 You have [1]hedged me
behind and before,
And laid Your hand
upon me.
6 [a]*Such* knowledge *is* too
wonderful for me;
It is high, I cannot *attain* it.

7 [a]Where can I go from Your
Spirit?
Or where can I flee from
Your presence?
8 [a]If I ascend into heaven, You
are there;
[b]If I make my bed in [1]hell,
behold, You *are there.*
9 *If* I take the wings of the
morning,
And dwell in the uttermost
parts of the sea,
10 Even there Your hand shall
lead me,
And Your right hand shall
hold me.
11 If I say, "Surely the darkness
shall [1]fall on me,"
Even the night shall be light
about me;
12 Indeed, [a]the darkness [1]shall
not hide from You,
But the night shines as the
day;
The darkness and the light
are both alike *to You.*

13 For You formed my inward
parts;
You [1]covered me in my
mother's womb.
14 I will praise You, for [1]I
am fearfully *and*
wonderfully made;
Marvelous are Your works,
And *that* my soul knows
very well.
15 [a]My [1]frame was not hidden
from You,
When I was made in secret,

And skillfully wrought in
the lowest parts of the
earth.
16 Your eyes saw my
substance, being yet
unformed.
And in Your book they all
were written,
The days fashioned for me,
When *as yet there were*
none of them.

17 [a]How precious also are Your
thoughts to me, O God!
How great is the sum of
them!
18 *If* I should count them,
they would be more in
number than the sand;
When I awake, I am still
with You.

19 Oh, that You would [a]slay the
wicked, O God!
[b]Depart from me, therefore,
you [1]bloodthirsty men.
20 For they [a]speak against You
wickedly;
[1]Your enemies take *Your*
name in vain.
21 [a]Do I not hate them, O LORD,
who hate You?
And do I not loathe those
who rise up against
You?
22 I hate them with [1]perfect
hatred;
I count them my enemies.

23 [a]Search me, O God, and
know my heart;
Try me, and know my
anxieties;
24 And see if *there is any*
wicked way in me,
And [a]lead me in the way
everlasting.

17 [a][Ps. 40:5]
19 [a][Is. 11:4] [b]Ps. 119:115 [1]Lit. *men of bloodshed*
20 [a]Jude 15 [1]LXX, Vg. *They take Your cities in vain*
21 [a]2 Chr. 19:2
22 [1]*complete*
23 [a]Job 31:6
24 [a]Ps. 5:8; 143:10

PSALM 140
2 [a]Ps. 56:6
3 [a]Ps. 58:4
4 [a]Ps. 71:4
5 [a]Jer. 18:22
7 [1]*sheltered*
8 [a]Deut. 32:27

PSALM 140

To the Chief Musician. A Psalm
of David.

DELIVER me, O LORD, from
evil men;
Preserve me from violent
men,
2 Who plan evil things in
their hearts;
[a]They continually gather
together *for* war.
3 They sharpen their tongues
like a serpent;
The [a]poison of asps *is* under
their lips. Sē'lah

4 [a]Keep me, O LORD, from the
hands of the wicked;
Preserve me from violent
men,
Who have purposed to make
my steps stumble.
5 The proud have hidden a
[a]snare for me, and cords;
They have spread a net by
the wayside;
They have set traps for me.
Sē'lah

6 I said to the LORD: "You *are*
my God;
Hear the voice of my
supplications, O LORD.
7 O GOD the Lord, the strength
of my salvation,
You have [1]covered my head
in the day of battle.
8 Do not grant, O LORD, the
desires of the wicked;
Do not further his *wicked*
scheme,
[a]*Lest* they be exalted. Sē'lah

9 "*As for* the head of those
who surround me,
Let the evil of their lips
cover them;

10 [a]Let burning coals fall upon
them;
Let them be cast into the
fire,
Into deep pits, that they rise
not up again.
11 Let not a slanderer be
established in the earth;
Let evil hunt the violent
man to overthrow *him*."

12 I know that the LORD will
[a]maintain
The cause of the afflicted,
And justice for the poor.
13 Surely the righteous shall
give thanks to Your
name;
The upright shall dwell in
Your presence.

PSALM 141

A Psalm of David.

LORD, I cry out to You;
Make haste to me!
Give ear to my voice when I
cry out to You.
2 Let my prayer be set before
You [a]*as* incense,
[b]The lifting up of my hands
as [c]the evening sacrifice.

3 Set a guard, O LORD, over
my [a]mouth;
Keep watch over the door of
my lips.
4 Do not incline my heart to
any evil thing,
To practice wicked works
With men who work
iniquity;
[a]And do not let me eat of
their delicacies.

5 [a]Let the righteous strike me;
It shall be a kindness.
And let him rebuke me;
It shall be as excellent oil;
Let my head not refuse it.

For still my prayer *is* against
the deeds of the wicked.
6 Their judges are overthrown
by the sides of the [1]cliff,
And they hear my words,
for they are sweet.
7 Our bones are scattered at
the mouth of the grave,
As when one plows and
breaks up the earth.

8 But [a]my eyes *are* upon You,
O GOD the Lord;
In You I take refuge;
[1]Do not leave my soul
destitute.
9 Keep me from [a]the snares
they have laid for me,
And from the traps of the
workers of iniquity.
10 [a]Let the wicked fall into their
own nets,
While I escape safely.

PSALM 142

A [a]Contemplation[1] of David.
A Prayer [b]when he was in the
cave.

I CRY out to the LORD with my
voice;
With my voice to the LORD I
make my supplication.
2 I pour out my complaint
before Him;
I declare before Him my
trouble.

3 When my spirit [1]was
[a]overwhelmed within me,
Then You knew my path.
In the way in which I walk

10 [a]Ps. 11:6
12 [a]1 Kin. 8:45

PSALM 141

2 [a][Rev. 5:8; 8:3, 4] [b][1 Tim. 2:8] [c]Ex. 29:39, 41
3 [a][Prov. 13:3; 21:23]
4 [a]Prov. 23:6
5 [a][Prov. 9:8]
6 [1]*rock*
8 [a]Ps. 25:15 [1]Lit. *Do not make my soul bare*
9 [a]Ps. 119:110
10 [a]Ps. 35:8

PSALM 142

title [a]Ps. 32:title [b]1 Sam. 22:1 [1]Heb. *Maschil*
3 [a]Ps. 77:3 [1]Lit. *fainted*

They have secretly [b]set a snare for me.
4 Look on *my* right hand and see,
For *there is* no one who acknowledges me;
Refuge has failed me;
No one cares for my soul.

5 I cried out to You, O LORD:
I said, "You *are* my refuge,
My portion in the land of the living.
6 [1]Attend to my cry,
For I am brought very low;
Deliver me from my persecutors,
For they are stronger than I.
7 Bring my soul out of prison,
That I may [a]praise Your name;
The righteous shall surround me,
For You shall deal bountifully with me."

PSALM 143

A Psalm of David.

HEAR my prayer, O LORD,
Give ear to my supplications!
In Your faithfulness answer me,
And in Your righteousness.
2 Do not enter into judgment with Your servant,
[a]For in Your sight no one living is righteous.

3 For the enemy has persecuted my soul;
He has crushed my life to the ground;
He has made me dwell in [1]darkness,
Like those who have long been dead.
4 [a]Therefore my spirit is overwhelmed within me;
My heart within me is distressed.

5 [a]I remember the days of old;
I meditate on all Your works;
I [1]muse on the work of Your hands.
6 I spread out my hands to You;
[a]My soul *longs* for You like a thirsty land. Sēlah

7 Answer me speedily, O LORD;
My spirit fails!
Do not hide Your face from me,
[a]Lest I [1]be like those who [2]go down into the pit.
8 Cause me to hear Your lovingkindness [a]in the morning,
For in You do I trust;
[b]Cause me to know the way in which I should walk,
For [c]I lift up my soul to You.

9 Deliver me, O LORD, from my enemies;
[1]In You I take shelter.
10 [a]Teach me to do Your will,
For You *are* my God;
[b]Your Spirit *is* good.
Lead me in [c]the land of uprightness.

11 [a]Revive me, O LORD, for Your name's sake!
For Your righteousness' sake bring my soul out of trouble.
12 In Your mercy [a]cut[1] off my enemies,

3 [b]Ps. 141:9
6 [1]*Give heed*
7 [a]Ps. 34:1, 2

PSALM 143

2 [a][Gal. 2:16]
3 [1]*dark places*
4 [a]Ps. 77:3
5 [a]Ps. 77:5, 10, 11 [1]*ponder*
6 [a]Ps. 63:1
7 [a]Ps. 28:1 [1]*become* [2]*Die*
8 [a]Ps. 46:5 [b]Ps. 5:8 [c]Ps. 25:1
9 [1]LXX, Vg. *To You I flee*
10 [a]Ps. 25:4, 5 [b]Neh. 9:20 [c]Is. 26:10
11 [a]Ps. 119:25
12 [a]Ps. 54:5 [1]*put an end to*

And destroy all those who
afflict my soul;
For I *am* Your servant.

PSALM 144

A Psalm of David.

BLESSED *be* the LORD my
Rock,
[a]Who trains my hands for
war,
And my fingers for battle—
2 My lovingkindness and my
fortress,
My high tower and my
deliverer,
My shield and *the One* in
whom I take refuge,
Who subdues [1]my people
under me.

3 [a]LORD, what *is* man, that You
take knowledge of him?
Or the son of man, that You
are mindful of him?
4 [a]Man is like a breath;
[b]His days *are* like a passing
shadow.

5 [a]Bow down Your heavens,
O LORD, and come down;
[b]Touch the mountains, and
they shall smoke.
6 [a]Flash forth lightning and
scatter them;
Shoot out Your arrows and
destroy them.
7 Stretch out Your hand from
above;
Rescue me and deliver me
out of great waters,
From the hand of foreigners,
8 Whose mouth [a]speaks [1]lying
words,
And whose right hand *is* a
right hand of falsehood.

9 I will [a]sing a new song to
You, O God;
On a harp of ten strings I
will sing praises to You,
10 *The One* who gives
[1]salvation to kings,
[a]Who delivers David His
servant
From the deadly sword.

11 Rescue me and deliver
me from the hand of
foreigners,
Whose mouth speaks lying
words,
And whose right hand
is a right hand of
falsehood—
12 That our sons *may be* [a]as
plants grown up in their
youth;
That our daughters *may be*
as [1]pillars,
Sculptured in palace style;
13 *That* our barns *may be* full,
Supplying all kinds of
produce;
That our sheep may bring
forth thousands
And ten thousands in our
fields;
14 *That* our oxen *may be* well
laden;
That there be no [1]breaking
in or going out;
That there be no outcry in
our streets.
15 [a]Happy *are* the people who
are in such a state;
Happy *are* the people whose
God *is* the LORD!

PSALM 145

[a]A Praise of David.

I WILL [1]extol You, my God,
O King;

PSALM 144

1 [a]2 Sam. 22:35

2 [1]So with MT, LXX, Vg.; Syr., Tg. *the peoples* (cf. 18:47)

3 [a]Heb. 2:6

4 [a]Ps. 39:11
[b]Job 8:9; 14:2

5 [a]Ps. 18:9
[b]Ps. 104:32

6 [a]Ps. 18:13, 14

8 [a]Ps. 12:2
[1]*empty* or *worthless*

9 [a]Ps. 33:2, 3; 40:3

10 [a]Ps. 18:50
[1]*deliverance*

12 [a]Ps. 128:3
[1]*corner pillars*

14 [1]Lit. *breach*

15 [a][Ps. 33:12]

PSALM 145

title [a]Ps. 100:title

1 [1]*praise*

And I will bless Your name
forever and ever.
2 Every day I will bless You,
And I will praise Your name
forever and ever.
3 [a]Great *is* the LORD, and
greatly to be praised;
And [b]His greatness *is*
[1]unsearchable.
4 [a]One generation shall praise
Your works to another,
And shall declare Your
mighty acts.
5 [1]I will meditate on the
glorious splendor of Your
majesty,
And [2]on Your wondrous
works.
6 *Men* shall speak of the
might of Your awesome
acts,
And I will declare Your
greatness.
7 They shall [1]utter the
memory of Your great
goodness,
And shall sing of Your
righteousness.
8 [a]The LORD *is* gracious and
full of compassion,
Slow to anger and great in
mercy.
9 [a]The LORD *is* good to all,
And His tender mercies *are*
over all His works.
10 [a]All Your works shall praise
You, O LORD,
And Your saints shall bless
You.
11 They shall speak of the
glory of Your kingdom,
And talk of Your power,
12 To make known to the sons
of men His mighty acts,
And the glorious majesty of
His kingdom.
13 [a]Your kingdom *is* an
everlasting kingdom,
And Your dominion
endures throughout all
[1]generations.
14 The LORD upholds all who
fall,
And [a]raises up all *who are*
bowed down.
15 [a]The eyes of all look
expectantly to You,
And [b]You give them their
food in due season.
16 You open Your hand
[a]And satisfy the desire of
every living thing.
17 The LORD *is* righteous in all
His ways,
Gracious in all His works.
18 [a]The LORD *is* near to all who
call upon Him,
To all who call upon Him [b]in
truth.
19 He will fulfill the desire of
those who fear Him;
He also will hear their cry
and save them.
20 [a]The LORD preserves all who
love Him,
But all the wicked He will
destroy.
21 My mouth shall speak the
praise of the LORD,
And all flesh shall bless His
holy name
Forever and ever.

PSALM 146

PRAISE[1] the LORD!
[a]Praise the LORD, O my soul!
2 [a]While I live I will praise the
LORD;

3 [a][Ps. 147:5] [b][Rom. 11:33] [1]Beyond our understanding
4 [a]Is. 38:19
5 [1]So with MT, Tg.; DSS, LXX, Syr., Vg. *They* [2]Lit. *on the words of Your wondrous works*
7 [1]*eagerly utter,* lit. *bubble forth*
8 [a][Num. 14:18]
9 [a]Nah. 1:7
10 [a]Ps. 19:1
13 [a][1 Tim. 1:17] [1]So with MT, Tg.; DSS, LXX, Syr., Vg. add *The LORD is faithful in all His words, And holy in all His works*
14 [a]Ps. 146:8
15 [a]Ps. 104:27 [b]Ps. 136:25
16 [a]Ps. 104:21, 28
18 [a][Deut. 4:7] [b][John 4:24]
20 [a][Ps. 31:23]
PSALM 146
1 [a]Ps. 103:1 [1]Heb. *Hallelujah*
2 [a]Ps. 104:33

I will sing praises to my God
while I have my being.

3 [a]Do not put your trust in
princes,
Nor in [1]a son of man, in
whom *there is* no [2]help.
4 [a]His spirit departs, he returns
to his earth;
In that very day [b]his plans
perish.

5 [a]Happy *is he* who *has* the
God of Jacob for his
help,
Whose hope *is* in the LORD
his God,
6 [a]Who made heaven and
earth,
The sea, and all that *is* in
them;
Who keeps truth forever,
7 [a]Who executes justice for the
oppressed,
[b]Who gives food to the
hungry.
[c]The LORD gives freedom to
the prisoners.

8 [a]The LORD opens *the eyes of*
the blind;
[b]The LORD raises those who
are bowed down;
The LORD loves the
righteous.
9 [a]The LORD watches over the
strangers;
He relieves the fatherless
and widow;
[b]But the way of the wicked
He [1]turns upside down.

10 [a]The LORD shall reign
forever—
Your God, O Zion, to all
generations.

Praise the LORD!

3 [a][Is. 2:22] [1]A human being [2]*salvation*
4 [a][Eccl. 12:7] [b][1 Cor. 2:6]
5 [a]Jer. 17:7
6 [a]Rev. 14:7
7 [a]Ps. 103:6 [b]Ps. 107:9 [c]Ps. 107:10
8 [a]Matt. 9:30 [b]Luke 13:13
9 [a]Deut. 10:18 [b]Ps. 147:6 [1]Lit. *makes crooked*
10 [a]Ex. 15:18

PSALM 147
1 [a]Ps. 92:1 [b]Ps. 135:3 [c]Ps. 33:1 [1]Heb. *Hallelujah*
2 [a]Ps. 102:16 [b]Deut. 30:3
3 [a][Ps. 51:17] [1]Lit. *sorrows*
4 [a]Is. 40:26
5 [a]Ps. 48:1 [b]Nah. 1:3 [c]Is. 40:28
6 [a]Ps. 146:8, 9
8 [a]Job 38:26
9 [a]Job 38:41 [b][Matt. 6:26]
10 [a]Ps. 33:16, 17

PSALM 147

PRAISE[1] the LORD!
For [a]*it is* good to sing
praises to our God;
[b]For *it is* pleasant, *and*
[c]praise is beautiful.

2 The LORD [a]builds up
Jerusalem;
[b]He gathers together the
outcasts of Israel.
3 [a]He heals the brokenhearted
And binds up their [1]wounds.
4 [a]He counts the number of the
stars;
He calls them all by name.
5 [a]Great *is* our Lord, and
[b]mighty in power;
[c]His understanding *is* infinite.
6 [a]The LORD lifts up the
humble;
He casts the wicked down to
the ground.

7 Sing to the LORD with
thanksgiving;
Sing praises on the harp to
our God,
8 [a]Who covers the heavens
with clouds,
Who prepares rain for the
earth,
Who makes grass to grow
on the mountains.
9 [a]He gives to the beast its
food,
And [b]to the young ravens
that cry.

10 [a]He does not delight in the
strength of the horse;
He takes no pleasure in the
legs of a man.
11 The LORD takes pleasure in
those who fear Him,
In those who hope in His
mercy.

12 Praise the LORD,
O Jerusalem!
Praise your God, O Zion!
13 For He has strengthened the
bars of your gates;
He has blessed your
children within you.
14 [a]He makes peace *in* your
borders,
And [b]fills you with [1]the
finest wheat.

15 [a]He sends out His command
to the earth;
His word runs very swiftly.
16 [a]He gives snow like wool;
He scatters the frost like
ashes;
17 He casts out His hail like
[1]morsels;
Who can stand before His
cold?
18 [a]He sends out His word and
melts them;
He causes His wind to blow,
and the waters flow.

19 [a]He declares His word to
Jacob,
[b]His statutes and His
judgments to Israel.
20 [a]He has not dealt thus with
any nation;
And *as for His* judgments,
they have not known
them.

[1]Praise the LORD!

PSALM 148

PRAISE[1] the LORD!

Praise the LORD from the
heavens;
Praise Him in the heights!
2 Praise Him, all His angels;
Praise Him, all His hosts!

14 [a]Is. 54:13; 60:17, 18 [b]Ps. 132:15 [1]Lit. *fat of wheat*
15 [a][Ps. 107:20]
16 [a]Job 37:6
17 [1]*fragments* of food
18 [a]Job 37:10
19 [a]Deut. 33:4 [b]Mal. 4:4
20 [a][Rom. 3:1, 2] [1]Heb. *Hallelujah*

PSALM 148
1 [1]Heb. *Hallelujah*
4 [a]1 Kin. 8:27 [b]Gen. 1:7
5 [a]Gen. 1:1, 6
6 [a]Ps. 89:37
7 [a]Is. 43:20
9 [a]Is. 44:23; 49:13
13 [a]Ps. 8:1
14 [a]Ps. 75:10 [b]Ps. 149:9 [1]Strength or dominion

3 Praise Him, sun and moon;
Praise Him, all you stars of
light!
4 Praise Him, [a]you heavens of
heavens,
And [b]you waters above the
heavens!

5 Let them praise the name of
the LORD,
For [a]He commanded and
they were created.
6 [a]He also established them
forever and ever;
He made a decree which
shall not pass away.

7 Praise the LORD from the
earth,
[a]You great sea creatures and
all the depths;
8 Fire and hail, snow and
clouds;
Stormy wind, fulfilling His
word;
9 [a]Mountains and all hills;
Fruitful trees and all cedars;
10 Beasts and all cattle;
Creeping things and flying
fowl;
11 Kings of the earth and all
peoples;
Princes and all judges of the
earth;
12 Both young men and
maidens;
Old men and children.

13 Let them praise the name of
the LORD,
For His [a]name alone is
exalted;
His glory *is* above the earth
and heaven.
14 And He [a]has exalted the
[1]horn of His people,
The praise of [b]all His
saints—

Of the children of Israel,
[c]A people near to Him.

[2]Praise the LORD!

PSALM 149

PRAISE[1] the LORD!

[a]Sing to the LORD a new song,
And His praise in the assembly of saints.

2 Let Israel rejoice in their Maker;
Let the children of Zion be joyful in their [a]King.
3 [a]Let them praise His name with the dance;
Let them sing praises to Him with the timbrel and harp.
4 For [a]the LORD takes pleasure in His people;
[b]He will beautify the [1]humble with salvation.

5 Let the saints be joyful in glory;
Let them [a]sing aloud on their beds.
6 *Let* the high praises of God *be* in their mouth,
And [a]a two-edged sword in their hand,
7 To execute vengeance on the nations,
And punishments on the peoples;
8 To bind their kings with chains,
And their nobles with fetters of iron;
9 [a]To execute on them the written judgment—
[b]This honor have all His saints.

[1]Praise the LORD!

PSALM 150

PRAISE[a1] the LORD!

Praise God in His sanctuary;
Praise Him in His mighty [2]firmament!

2 Praise Him for His mighty acts;
Praise Him according to His excellent [a]greatness!

3 Praise Him with the sound of the [1]trumpet;
Praise Him with the lute and harp!
4 Praise Him with the timbrel and dance;
Praise Him with stringed instruments and flutes!
5 Praise Him with loud cymbals;
Praise Him with clashing cymbals!

6 Let everything that has breath praise the LORD.

[1]Praise the LORD!

---

14 [c]Eph. 2:17 [2]Heb. *Hallelujah*

PSALM 149

1 [a]Ps. 33:3 [1]Heb. *Hallelujah*
2 [a]Zech. 9:9
3 [a]Ps. 81:2
4 [a]Ps. 35:27 [b]Ps. 132:16 [1]*meek*
5 [a]Job 35:10
6 [a]Heb. 4:12
9 [a]Deut. 7:1, 2 [b]1 Cor. 6:2 [1]Heb. *Hallelujah*

PSALM 150

1 [a]Ps. 145:5, 6 [1]Heb. *Hallelujah* [2]*expanse* of heaven
2 [a]Deut. 3:24
3 [1]*cornet*
6 [1]Heb. *Hallelujah*

The Book of
PROVERBS

THE key word in Proverbs is *wisdom*, "the ability to live life skillfully." A godly life in an ungodly world, however, is no simple assignment. Proverbs provides God's detailed instructions for His people to deal successfully with the practical affairs of everyday life: how to relate to God, parents, children, neighbors, and government. Solomon, the principal author, uses a combination of poetry, parables, pithy questions, short stories, and wise maxims to give in strikingly memorable form the common sense and divine perspective necessary to handle life's issues.

Because Solomon, the pinnacle of Israel's wise men, was the principal contributor, the Hebrew title of this book is *Mishle Shelomoh*, "Proverbs of Solomon" (1:1). The Greek title is *Paroimiai Salomontos*, "Proverbs of Solomon." The Latin title *Liber Proverbiorum*, "Book of Proverbs," combines the words *pro* "for" and *verba* "words" to describe the way the proverbs concentrate many words into a few. The rabbinical writings called Proverbs *Sepher Hokhmah*, "Book of Wisdom."

THE [a]proverbs of Solomon the
son of David, king of Israel:

2 To know wisdom and
instruction,
To [1]perceive the words of
understanding,
3 To receive the instruction of
wisdom,
Justice, judgment, and
equity;
4 To give prudence to the
[a]simple,
To the young man knowledge
and discretion—
5 [a]A wise *man* will hear and
increase learning,
And a man of understanding
will [1]attain wise counsel,
6 To understand a proverb
and an enigma,
The words of the wise and
their [a]riddles.

7 [a]The fear of the LORD *is* the
beginning of knowledge,
But fools despise wisdom
and instruction.

8 [a]My son, hear the instruction
of your father,
And do not forsake the law
of your mother;
9 For they *will be* a [a]graceful
ornament on your head,
And chains about your
neck.

10 My son, if sinners entice
you,
[a]Do not consent.
11 If they say, "Come with us,
Let us [a]lie in wait to *shed*
blood;
Let us lurk secretly for the
innocent without cause;
12 Let us swallow them alive
like [1]Shē′ōl,
And whole, [a]like those who
go down to the Pit;
13 We shall find all *kinds* of
precious [1]possessions,

CHAPTER 1

1 [a]1 Kin. 4:32
2 [1]*understand* or *discern*
4 [a]Prov. 9:4
5 [a]Prov. 9:9 [1]*acquire*
6 [a]Ps. 78:2
7 [a]Job 28:28
8 [a]Prov. 4:1
9 [a]Prov. 3:22
10 [a]Gen. 39:7–10
11 [a]Jer. 5:26
12 [a]Ps. 28:1 [1]Or *the grave*
13 [1]Lit. *wealth*

We shall fill our houses with
[2]spoil;
14 Cast in your lot among us,
Let us all have one purse"—
15 My son, [a]do not walk in the
way with them,
[b]Keep your foot from their
path;
16 [a]For their feet run to evil,
And they make haste to
shed blood.
17 Surely, in [1]vain the net is
spread
In the sight of any [2]bird;
18 But they lie in wait for their
own blood,
They lurk secretly for their
own lives.
19 [a]So *are* the ways of everyone
who is greedy for gain;
It takes away the life of its
owners.

20 [a]Wisdom calls aloud [1]outside;
She raises her voice in the
open squares.
21 She cries out in the [1]chief
concourses,
At the openings of the gates
in the city
She speaks her words:
22 "How long, you [1]simple ones,
will you love [2]simplicity?
For scorners delight in their
scorning,
And fools hate knowledge.
23 Turn at my rebuke;
Surely [a]I will pour out my
spirit on you;
I will make my words
known to you.
24 [a]Because I have called and
you refused,
I have stretched out my
hand and no one
regarded,
25 Because you [a]disdained all
my counsel,
And would have none of my
rebuke,
26 [a]I also will laugh at your
calamity;
I will mock when your
terror comes,
27 When [a]your terror comes
like a storm,
And your destruction comes
like a whirlwind,
When distress and anguish
come upon you.
28 "Then[a] they will call on me,
but I will not answer;
They will seek me diligently,
but they will not find me.
29 Because they [a]hated
knowledge
And did not [b]choose the fear
of the LORD,
30 [a]They would have none of
my counsel
And despised my every
rebuke.
31 Therefore [a]they shall eat the
fruit of their own way,
And be filled to the full with
their own fancies.
32 For the [1]turning away of the
simple will slay them,
And the complacency of
fools will destroy them;
33 But whoever listens to me
will dwell [a]safely,
And [b]will be [1]secure,
without fear of evil."

2 My son, if you receive my
words,
And [a]treasure my
commands within you,
2 So that you incline your ear
to wisdom,
And apply your heart to
understanding;
3 Yes, if you cry out for
discernment,

13 [2]*plunder*
15 [a]Ps. 1:1 [b]Ps. 119:101
16 [a][Is. 59:7]
17 [1]*futility* [2]Lit. *lord of the wing*
19 [a][1 Tim. 6:10]
20 [a][John 7:37] [1]*in the street*
21 [1]LXX, Syr., Tg. *top of the walls;* Vg. *the head of multitudes*
22 [1]*naive* [2]*naivete*
23 [a]Joel 2:28
24 [a]Jer. 7:13
25 [a]Luke 7:30
26 [a]Ps. 2:4
27 [a][Prov. 10:24, 25]
28 [a]Is. 1:15
29 [a]Job 21:14 [b]Ps. 119:173
30 [a]Ps. 81:11
31 [a]Job 4:8
32 [1]*waywardness*
33 [a]Prov. 3:24–26 [b]Ps. 112:7 [1]*at ease*

CHAPTER 2

1 [a][Prov. 4:21]

And lift up your voice for
understanding,
4 [a]If you seek her as silver,
And search for her as *for*
hidden treasures;
5 [a]Then you will understand
the fear of the LORD,
And find the knowledge of
God.
6 [a]For the LORD gives wisdom;
From His mouth *come*
knowledge and
understanding;
7 He stores up sound wisdom
for the upright;
[a]*He is* a shield to those who
walk uprightly;
8 He guards the paths of
justice,
And [a]preserves the way of
His saints.
9 Then you will understand
righteousness and
justice,
Equity *and* every good path.

10 When wisdom enters your
heart,
And knowledge is pleasant
to your soul,
11 Discretion will preserve
you;
[a]Understanding will keep
you,
12 To deliver you from the way
of evil,
From the man who speaks
perverse things,
13 From those who leave the
paths of uprightness
To [a]walk in the ways of
darkness;
14 [a]Who rejoice in doing evil,
And delight in the perversity
of the wicked;
15 [a]Whose ways *are* crooked,
And *who are* devious in
their paths;
16 To deliver you from [a]the
immoral woman,
[b]From the seductress *who*
flatters with her words,
17 Who forsakes the
companion of her youth,
And forgets the covenant of
her God.
18 For [a]her house [1]leads down
to death,
And her paths to the dead;
19 None who go to her return,
Nor do they [1]regain the
paths of life—
20 So you may walk in the way
of goodness,
And keep *to* the paths of
righteousness.
21 For the upright will dwell in
the [a]land,
And the blameless will
remain in it;
22 But the wicked will be [1]cut
off from the [2]earth,
And the unfaithful will be
uprooted from it.

3 My son, do not forget my
law,
[a]But let your heart keep my
commands;
2 For length of days and long
life
And [a]peace they will add to
you.

3 Let not mercy and truth
forsake you;
[a]Bind them around your
neck,
[b]Write them on the tablet of
your heart,
4 [a]*And* so find favor and [1]high
esteem
In the sight of God and man.

5 [a]Trust in the LORD with all
your heart,

4 [a][Prov. 3:14]
5 [a][James 1:5, 6]
6 [a]1 Kin. 3:9, 12
7 [a][Ps. 84:11]
8 [a][1 Sam. 2:9]
11 [a]Prov. 4:6; 6:22
13 [a][John 3:19, 20]
14 [a][Rom. 1:32]
15 [a]Ps. 125:5
16 [a]Prov. 5:20; 6:24; 7:5 [b]Prov. 5:3
18 [a]Prov. 7:27 [1]*sinks*
19 [1]Lit. *reach*
21 [a]Ps. 37:3
22 [1]*destroyed* [2]*land*

CHAPTER 3

1 [a]Deut. 8:1
2 [a]Ps. 119:165
3 [a]Prov. 6:21 [b][2 Cor. 3:3]
4 [a]Rom. 14:18 [1]Lit. *good understanding*
5 [a][Ps. 37:3, 5]

[b]And lean not on your own
understanding;
6 [a]In all your ways
acknowledge Him,
And He shall [1]direct your
paths.

7 Do not be wise in your own
[a]eyes;
Fear the LORD and depart
from evil.
8 It will be health to your
[1]flesh,
And [a]strength[2] to your
bones.

9 [a]Honor the LORD with your
possessions,
And with the firstfruits of
all your increase;
10 [a]So your barns will be filled
with plenty,
And your vats will overflow
with new wine.

11 [a]My son, do not despise the
chastening of the LORD,
Nor detest His correction;
12 For whom the LORD loves He
corrects,
[a]Just as a father the son *in
whom* he delights.

13 [a]Happy *is* the man *who* finds
wisdom,
And the man *who* gains
understanding;
14 [a]For her proceeds *are* better
than the profits of silver,
And her gain than fine gold.
15 She *is* more precious than
rubies,
And [a]all the things you may
desire cannot compare
with her.
16 [a]Length of days *is* in her
right hand,
In her left hand riches and
honor.
17 [a]Her ways *are* ways of
pleasantness,
And all her paths *are* peace.
18 She *is* [a]a tree of life to those
who take hold of her,
And happy *are all* who
[1]retain her.

19 [a]The LORD by wisdom
founded the earth;
By understanding He
established the heavens;
20 By His knowledge the
depths were [a]broken up,
And clouds drop down the
dew.

21 My son, let them not depart
from your eyes—
Keep sound wisdom and
discretion;
22 So they will be life to your
soul
And grace to your neck.
23 [a]Then you will walk safely in
your way,
And your foot will not
stumble.
24 When you lie down, you will
not be afraid;
Yes, you will lie down and
your sleep will be sweet.
25 [a]Do not be afraid of sudden
terror,
Nor of trouble from the
wicked when it comes;
26 For the LORD will be your
confidence,
And will keep your foot
from being caught.

27 [a]Do not withhold good from
[1]those to whom it is due,
When it is in the power of
your hand to do so.

5 [b][Jer. 9:23, 24]
6 [a][1 Chr. 28:9] [1]Or *make smooth* or *straight*
7 [a]Rom. 12:16
8 [a]Job 21:24 [1]Body, lit. *navel* [2]Lit. *drink*
9 [a]Ex. 22:29
10 [a]Deut. 28:8
11 [a]Job 5:17
12 [a]Deut. 8:5
13 [a]Prov. 8:32, 34, 35
14 [a]Job 28:13
15 [a]Matt. 13:44
16 [a][1 Tim. 4:8]
17 [a][Matt. 11:29]
18 [a]Gen. 2:9 [1]*hold her fast*
19 [a]Ps. 104:24
20 [a]Gen. 7:11
23 [a]Prov. 10:9
25 [a]Ps. 91:5
27 [a]Rom. 13:7 [1]Lit. *its owners*

28 [a]Do not say to your neighbor,
"Go, and come back,
And tomorrow I will
give *it*,"
When you have it with you.
29 Do not devise evil against
your neighbor,
For he dwells by you for
safety's sake.
30 [a]Do not strive with a man
without cause,
If he has done you no harm.

31 [a]Do not envy the oppressor,
And choose none of his
ways;
32 For the perverse *person is*
an abomination to the
LORD,
[a]But His secret counsel *is*
with the upright.
33 [a]The curse of the LORD *is* on
the house of the wicked,
But [b]He blesses the home of
the just.
34 [a]Surely He scorns the
scornful,
But gives grace to the
humble.
35 The wise shall inherit glory,
But shame shall be the
legacy of fools.

4

Hear, [a]*my* children, the
instruction of a father,
And give attention to know
understanding;
2 For I give you good doctrine:
Do not forsake my law.
3 When I was my father's son,
[a]Tender and the only one in
the sight of my mother,
4 [a]He also taught me, and said
to me:
"Let your heart retain my
words;
[b]Keep my commands, and
live.
5 [a]Get wisdom! Get
understanding!
Do not forget, nor turn away
from the words of my
mouth.
6 Do not forsake her, and she
will preserve you;
[a]Love her, and she will keep
you.
7 [a]Wisdom *is* the principal
thing;
Therefore get wisdom.
And in all your getting, get
understanding.
8 [a]Exalt her, and she will
promote you;
She will bring you honor,
when you embrace her.
9 She will place on your head
[a]an ornament of grace;
A crown of glory she will
deliver to you."

10 Hear, my son, and receive
my sayings,
[a]And the years of your life
will be many.
11 I have [a]taught you in the
way of wisdom;
I have led you in right paths.
12 When you walk, [a]your steps
will not be hindered,
[b]And when you run, you will
not stumble.
13 Take firm hold of
instruction, do not let go;
Keep her, for she *is* your life.

14 [a]Do not enter the path of the
wicked,
And do not walk in the way
of evil.
15 Avoid it, do not travel on it;
Turn away from it and
pass on.
16 [a]For they do not sleep unless
they have done evil;

28 [a]Lev. 19:13
30 [a][Rom. 12:18]
31 [a]Ps. 37:1
32 [a]Ps. 25:14
33 [a]Zech. 5:3, 4 [b]Ps. 1:3
34 [a]James 4:6

CHAPTER 4

1 [a]Ps. 34:11
3 [a]1 Chr. 29:1
4 [a]1 Chr. 28:9 [b]Prov. 7:2
5 [a]Prov. 2:2, 3
6 [a]2 Thess. 2:10
7 [a]Matt. 13:44
8 [a]1 Sam. 2:30
9 [a]Prov. 3:22
10 [a]Prov. 3:2
11 [a]1 Sam. 12:23
12 [a]Ps. 18:36 [b][Ps. 91:11]
14 [a]Ps. 1:1
16 [a]Ps. 36:4

And their sleep is [1]taken
away unless they make
someone fall.
17 For they eat the bread of
wickedness,
And drink the wine of
violence.
18 [a]But the path of the just [b]*is*
like the shining [1]sun,
That shines ever brighter
unto the perfect day.
19 [a]The way of the wicked *is*
like darkness;
They do not know what
makes them stumble.

20 My son, give attention to my
words;
Incline your ear to my
sayings.
21 Do not let them depart from
your eyes;
Keep them in the midst of
your heart;
22 For they *are* life to those
who find them,
And health to all their flesh.
23 Keep your heart with all
diligence,
For out of it *spring* the
issues of [a]life.
24 Put away from you a
[1]deceitful mouth,
And put perverse lips far
from you.
25 Let your eyes look straight
ahead,
And your eyelids look right
before you.
26 Ponder the path of your
[a]feet,
And let all your ways be
established.
27 Do not turn to the right or
the left;
Remove your foot from evil.

5 My son, pay attention to my
wisdom;
[1]Lend your ear to my
understanding,
2 That you may [1]preserve
discretion,
And your lips [a]may keep
knowledge.
3 [a]For the lips of [1]an immoral
woman drip honey,
And her mouth *is* [b]smoother
than oil;
4 But in the end she is bitter
as wormwood,
Sharp as a two-edged
sword.
5 Her feet go down to death,
[a]Her steps lay hold of [1]hell.
6 Lest you ponder *her* path of
life—
Her ways are unstable;
You do not know *them.*

7 Therefore hear me now, *my*
children,
And do not depart from the
words of my mouth.
8 Remove your way far from
her,
And do not go near the door
of her house,
9 Lest you give your [1]honor to
others,
And your years to the cruel
one;
10 Lest aliens be filled with
your [1]wealth,
And your labors *go* to the
house of a foreigner;
11 And you mourn at last,
When your flesh and your
body are consumed,
12 And say:
"How I have hated
instruction,
And my heart despised
correction!

16 [1]Lit. *robbed*
18 [a]Matt. 5:14, 45 [b]2 Sam. 23:4 [1]Lit. *light*
19 [a][Is. 59:9, 10]
23 [a][Matt. 12:34; 15:18, 19]
24 [1]*devious*
26 [a]Heb. 12:13

CHAPTER 5

1 [1]Lit. *Bow*
2 [a]Mal. 2:7 [1]*appreciate good judgment*
3 [a]Prov. 2:16 [b]Ps. 55:21 [1]Lit. *a strange*
5 [a]Prov. 7:27 [1]Or *Sheol*
9 [1]*vigor*
10 [1]Lit. *strength*

13 I have not obeyed the voice
of my teachers,
Nor inclined my ear to those
who instructed me!
14 I was on the verge of total
ruin,
In the midst of the assembly
and congregation."

15 Drink water from your own
cistern,
And running water from
your own well.
16 Should your fountains be
dispersed abroad,
[1]Streams of water in the
streets?
17 Let them be only your own,
And not for strangers with
you.
18 Let your fountain be
blessed,
And rejoice with [a]the wife of
your youth.
19 [a]*As a* loving deer and a
graceful doe,
Let her breasts satisfy you
at all times;
And always be [1]enraptured
with her love.
20 For why should you, my son,
be enraptured by [a]an
immoral woman,
And be embraced in the
arms of a seductress?

21 [a]For the ways of man *are*
before the eyes of the
LORD,
And He [1]ponders all his
paths.
22 [a]His own iniquities entrap
the wicked *man,*
And he is caught in the
cords of his sin.
23 [a]He shall die for lack of
instruction,
And in the greatness of his
folly he shall go astray.

6 My son, [a]if you become
[1]surety for your friend,
If you have [2]shaken hands
in pledge for a stranger,
2 You are snared by the words
of your mouth;
You are taken by the words
of your mouth.
3 So do this, my son, and
deliver yourself;
For you have come into the
hand of your friend:
Go and humble yourself;
Plead with your friend.
4 [a]Give no sleep to your eyes,
Nor slumber to your
eyelids.
5 Deliver yourself like a
gazelle from the hand *of
the hunter,*
And like a bird from the
hand of the [1]fowler.

6 [a]Go to the ant, you sluggard!
Consider her ways and be
wise,
7 Which, having no [1]captain,
Overseer or ruler,
8 Provides her [1]supplies in the
summer,
And gathers her food in the
harvest.
9 [a]How long will you [1]slumber,
O sluggard?
When will you rise from
your sleep?
10 A little sleep, a little
slumber,
A little folding of the hands
to sleep—
11 [a]So shall your poverty come
on you like a prowler,
And your need like an
armed man.

---

16 [1]*Channels*
18 [a]Mal. 2:14
19 [a]Song 2:9 [1]Lit. *intoxicated*
20 [a]Prov. 2:16
21 [a]Hos. 7:2 [1]*observes*, lit. *weighs*
22 [a]Num. 32:23
23 [a]Job 4:21

CHAPTER 6

1 [a]Prov. 11:15 [1]*guaranty* or *collateral* [2]Lit. *struck*
4 [a]Ps. 132:4
5 [1]One who catches birds in a trap or snare
6 [a]Job 12:7
7 [1]Lit. *leader*
8 [1]Lit. *bread*
9 [a]Prov. 24:33, 34 [1]Lit. *lie down*
11 [a]Prov. 10:4

12 A worthless person, a
wicked man,
Walks with a perverse
mouth;
13 [a]He winks with his eyes,
He [1]shuffles his feet,
He points with his fingers;
14 Perversity *is* in his heart,
[a]He devises evil continually,
[b]He sows discord.
15 Therefore his calamity shall
come [a]suddenly;
Suddenly he shall [b]be
broken [c]without remedy.

16 These six *things* the LORD
hates,
Yes, seven *are* an
abomination to [1]Him:
17 [a]A[1] proud look,
[b]A lying tongue,
[c]Hands that shed innocent
blood,
18 [a]A heart that devises wicked
plans,
[b]Feet that are swift in
running to evil,
19 [a]A false witness *who* speaks
lies,
And one who [b]sows discord
among brethren.

20 [a]My son, keep your father's
command,
And do not forsake the law
of your mother.
21 [a]Bind them continually upon
your heart;
Tie them around your neck.
22 [a]When you roam, [1]they will
lead you;
When you sleep, [b]they will
keep you;
And *when* you awake, they
will speak with you.
23 [a]For the commandment *is* a
lamp,
And the law a light;
Reproofs of instruction *are*
the way of life,
24 [a]To keep you from the evil
woman,
From the flattering tongue
of a seductress.
25 [a]Do not lust after her beauty
in your heart,
Nor let her allure you with
her eyelids.
26 For [a]by means of a harlot
A man is reduced to a crust
of bread;
[b]And [1]an adulteress will
[c]prey upon his precious
life.
27 Can a man take fire to his
bosom,
And his clothes not be
burned?
28 Can one walk on hot coals,
And his feet not be seared?
29 So *is* he who goes in to his
neighbor's wife;
Whoever touches her shall
not be innocent.

30 *People* do not despise a thief
If he steals to satisfy himself
when he is starving.
31 Yet *when* he is found, [a]he
must restore sevenfold;
He may have to give up
all the substance of his
house.
32 Whoever commits adultery
with a woman [a]lacks
understanding;
He *who* does so destroys his
own soul.
33 Wounds and dishonor he
will get,
And his reproach will not be
wiped away.
34 For [a]jealousy *is* a husband's
fury;
Therefore he will not spare
in the day of vengeance.

13 [a]Job 15:12 [1]*gives signals,* lit. *scrapes*
14 [a]Mic. 2:1 [b]Prov. 6:19
15 [a]Is. 30:13 [b]Jer. 19:11 [c]2 Chr. 36:16
16 [1]Lit. *His soul*
17 [a]Ps. 101:5 [b]Ps. 120:2 [c]Is. 1:15 [1]Lit. *Haughty eyes*
18 [a]Gen. 6:5 [b]Is. 59:7
19 [a]Ps. 27:12 [b]Prov. 6:14
20 [a]Eph. 6:1
21 [a]Prov. 3:3
22 [a][Prov. 3:23] [b]Prov. 2:11 [1]Lit. *it*
23 [a]Ps. 19:8
24 [a]Prov. 2:16
25 [a]Matt. 5:28
26 [a]Prov. 29:3 [b]Gen. 39:14 [c]Ezek. 13:18 [1]Wife of another, lit. *a man's wife*
31 [a]Ex. 22:1–4
32 [a]Prov. 7:7
34 [a]Song 8:6

35 He will [1]accept no
recompense,
Nor will he be appeased
though you give many
gifts.

35 [1]Lit. *lift up the face of any*

CHAPTER 7

7 My son, keep my words,
And [a]treasure my
commands within you.
2 [a]Keep my commands and
live,
[b]And my law as the apple of
your eye.
3 [a]Bind them on your fingers;
Write them on the tablet of
your heart.
4 Say to wisdom, "You *are* my
sister,"
And call understanding *your*
nearest kin,
5 [a]That they may keep you
from the immoral
woman,
From the seductress *who*
flatters with her words.

6 For at the window of my
house
I looked through my lattice,
7 And saw among the simple,
I perceived among the
[1]youths,
A young man [a]devoid[2] of
understanding,
8 Passing along the street
near her corner;
And he took the path to her
house
9 [a]In the twilight, in the
evening,
In the black and dark night.

10 And there a woman met him,
With the attire of a harlot,
and a crafty heart.
11 [a]She *was* loud and rebellious,
[b]Her feet would not stay at
home.
12 At times *she was* outside, at
times in the open square,
Lurking at every corner.
13 So she caught him and
kissed him;
With an [1]impudent face she
said to him:
14 "*I have* peace offerings with
me;
Today I have paid my vows.
15 So I came out to meet you,
Diligently to seek your face,
And I have found you.
16 I have spread my bed with
tapestry,
Colored coverings of
[a]Egyptian linen.
17 I have perfumed my bed
With myrrh, aloes, and
cinnamon.
18 Come, let us take our fill of
love until morning;
Let us delight ourselves
with love.
19 For [1]my husband *is* not at
home;
He has gone on a long
journey;
20 He has taken a bag of
money [1]with him,
And will come home [2]on the
appointed day."

21 [1]With [a]her enticing speech
she caused him to yield,
[b]With her flattering lips she
[2]seduced him.
22 Immediately he went after
her, as an ox goes to the
slaughter,
Or [1]as a fool to the
correction of the [2]stocks,
23 Till an arrow struck his
liver.
[a]As a bird hastens to the
snare,
He did not know it [1]*would
cost* his life.

1 [a]Prov. 2:1
2 [a]Lev. 18:5 [b]Deut. 32:10
3 [a]Deut. 6:8
5 [a]Prov. 2:16; 5:3
7 [a][Prov. 6:32; 9:4, 16] [1]Lit. *sons* [2]*lacking*
9 [a]Job 24:15
11 [a]Prov. 9:13 [b]Titus 2:5
13 [1]*shameless*
16 [a]Is. 19:9
19 [1]Lit. *the man*
20 [1]Lit. *in his hand* [2]*at the full moon*
21 [a]Prov. 5:3 [b]Ps. 12:2 [1]*By the greatness of her words* [2]*compelled*
22 [1]LXX, Syr., Tg. *as a dog to bonds;* Vg. *as a lamb . . . to bonds* [2]*shackles*
23 [a]Eccl. 9:12 [1]Lit. *is for*

24 Now therefore, listen to me, *my* children;
Pay attention to the words of my mouth:
25 Do not let your heart turn aside to her ways,
Do not stray into her paths;
26 For she has cast down many wounded,
And [a]all who were slain by her were strong *men.*
27 [a]Her house *is* the way to [1]hell,
Descending to the chambers of death.

8 Does not [a]wisdom cry out,
And understanding lift up her voice?
2 She takes her stand on the top of the [1]high hill,
Beside the way, where the paths meet.
3 She cries out by the gates, at the entry of the city,
At the entrance of the doors:
4 "To you, O men, I call,
And my voice *is* to the sons of men.
5 O you [1]simple ones, understand prudence,
And you fools, be of an understanding heart.
6 Listen, for I will speak of [a]excellent things,
And from the opening of my lips *will come* right things;
7 For my mouth will speak truth;
Wickedness *is* an abomination to my lips.
8 All the words of my mouth *are* with righteousness;
Nothing crooked or perverse *is* in them.
9 They *are* all plain to him who understands,
And right to those who find knowledge.
10 Receive my instruction, and not silver,
And knowledge rather than choice gold;
11 [a]For wisdom *is* better than rubies,
And all the things one may desire cannot be compared with her.

12 "I, wisdom, dwell with prudence,
And find out knowledge *and* discretion.
13 [a]The fear of the LORD *is* to hate evil;
[b]Pride and arrogance and the evil way
And [c]the perverse mouth I hate.
14 Counsel *is* mine, and sound wisdom;
I *am* understanding, [a]I have strength.
15 [a]By me kings reign,
And rulers decree justice.
16 By me princes rule, and nobles,
All the judges of [1]the earth.
17 [a]I love those who love me,
And [b]those who seek me diligently will find me.
18 [a]Riches and honor *are* with me,
Enduring riches and righteousness.
19 My fruit *is* better than gold, yes, than fine gold,
And my revenue than choice silver.
20 I [1]traverse the way of righteousness,
In the midst of the paths of justice,
21 That I may cause those who love me to inherit wealth,

26 [a]Neh. 13:26
27 [a]Prov. 2:18; 5:5; 9:18
[1]Or *Sheol*

CHAPTER 8

1 [a]Prov. 1:20, 21; 9:3
2 [1]Lit. *heights*
5 [1]*naive*
6 [a]Prov. 22:20
11 [a]Job 28:15
13 [a]Prov. 3:7; 16:6 [b][Prov. 16:17, 18] [c]Prov. 4:24
14 [a]Eccl. 7:19; 9:16
15 [a]Rom. 13:1
16 [1]MT, Syr., Tg., Vg. *righteousness;* LXX, Bg., some mss. and editions *earth*
17 [a][John 14:21] [b]James 1:5
18 [a]Prov. 3:16
20 [1]*walk about on*

That I may fill their
treasuries.

22 "The[a] LORD possessed me
at the beginning of His
way,
Before His works of old.
23 [a]I have been established
from everlasting,
From the beginning, before
there was ever an earth.
24 When *there were* no depths
I was brought forth,
When *there were* no
fountains abounding
with water.
25 [a]Before the mountains were
settled,
Before the hills, I was
brought forth;
26 While as yet He had not
made the earth or the
[1]fields,
Or the [2]primal dust of the
world.
27 When He prepared the
heavens, I *was* there,
When He drew a circle on
the face of the deep,
28 When He established the
clouds above,
When He strengthened the
fountains of the deep,
29 [a]When He assigned to the
sea its limit,
So that the waters would
not transgress His
command,
When [b]He marked out the
foundations of the earth,
30 [a]Then I was beside Him *as* [1]a
master craftsman;
[b]And I was daily *His* delight,
Rejoicing always before
Him,
31 Rejoicing in His inhabited
world,
And [a]my delight *was* with
the sons of men.

32 "Now therefore, listen to me,
my children,
For [a]blessed *are those who*
keep my ways.
33 Hear instruction and be
wise,
And do not disdain *it*.
34 [a]Blessed is the man who
listens to me,
Watching daily at my gates,
Waiting at the posts of my
doors.
35 For whoever finds me finds
life,
And [a]obtains favor from the
LORD;
36 But he who sins against me
[a]wrongs his own soul;
All those who hate me love
death."

9

Wisdom has [a]built her
house,
She has hewn out her seven
pillars;
2 [a]She has slaughtered her
meat,
[b]She has mixed her wine,
She has also [1]furnished her
table.
3 She has sent out her
maidens,
She cries out from the
highest places of the city,
4 "Whoever[a] *is* simple, let him
turn in here!"
As for him who lacks
understanding, she says
to him,
5 "Come,[a] eat of my bread
And drink of the wine I
have mixed.
6 Forsake foolishness and
live,

22 [a]Prov. 3:19
23 [a][Ps. 2:6]
25 [a]Job 15:7, 8
26 [1]*outer places* [2]Lit. *beginning of the dust*
29 [a]Gen. 1:9, 10 [b]Job 28:4, 6
30 [a][John 1:1–3, 18] [b][Matt. 3:17] [1]A Jewish tradition *one brought up*
31 [a]Ps. 16:3
32 [a]Luke 11:28
34 [a]Prov. 3:13, 18
35 [a][John 17:3]
36 [a]Prov. 20:2

CHAPTER 9

1 [a][Matt. 16:18]
2 [a]Matt. 22:4 [b]Prov. 23:30 [1]*arranged*
4 [a]Ps. 19:7
5 [a]Is. 55:1

And go in the way of
understanding.

7 "He who corrects a scoffer
gets shame for himself,
And he who rebukes a
wicked *man only* harms
himself.
8 [a]Do not correct a scoffer, lest
he hate you;
[b]Rebuke a wise *man*, and he
will love you.
9 Give *instruction* to a wise
man, and he will be still
wiser;
Teach a just *man*, [a]and he
will increase in learning.

10 "The[a] fear of the LORD *is* the
beginning of wisdom,
And the knowledge
of the Holy One *is*
understanding.
11 [a]For by me your days will be
multiplied,
And years of life will be
added to you.
12 [a]If you are wise, you are wise
for yourself,
And *if* you scoff, you will
bear *it* alone."

13 [a]A foolish woman is
[1]clamorous;
She is simple, and knows
nothing.
14 For she sits at the door of
her house,
On a seat [a]*by* the highest
places of the city,
15 To call to those who pass by,
Who go straight on their
way:
16 "Whoever[a] *is* [1]simple, let him
turn in here";
And *as for* him who lacks
understanding, she says
to him,

8 [a]Matt. 7:6 [b]Ps. 141:5
9 [a][Matt. 13:12]
10 [a]Job 28:28
11 [a]Prov. 3:2, 16
12 [a]Job 35:6, 7
13 [a]Prov. 7:11 [1]*boisterous*
14 [a]Prov. 9:3
16 [a]Prov. 7:7, 8 [1]*naive*
17 [a]Prov. 20:17
18 [a]Prov. 2:18; 7:27 [1]Or *Sheol*

CHAPTER 10

1 [a]Prov. 1:1; 25:1 [b]Prov. 15:20; 17:21, 25; 19:13; 29:3, 15
2 [a][Luke 12:19, 20] [b]Dan. 4:27
3 [a]Ps. 34:9, 10; 37:25
4 [a]Prov. 19:15 [b]Prov. 12:24; 13:4; 21:5
5 [a]Prov. 6:8 [b]Prov. 19:26
7 [a]Eccl. 8:10
8 [a]Prov. 10:10 [1]Lit. *the foolish of lips* [2]*be thrust down* or *ruined*

17 "Stolen[a] water is sweet,
And bread *eaten* in secret is
pleasant."
18 But he does not know that
[a]the dead *are* there,
That her guests *are* in the
depths of [1]hell.

10

The proverbs of [a]Solomon:

[b]A wise son makes a glad
father,
But a foolish son *is* the grief
of his mother.

2 [a]Treasures of wickedness
profit nothing,
[b]But righteousness delivers
from death.
3 [a]The LORD will not allow the
righteous soul to famish,
But He casts away the
desire of the wicked.

4 [a]He who has a slack hand
becomes poor,
But [b]the hand of the diligent
makes rich.
5 He who gathers in [a]summer
is a wise son;
He who sleeps in harvest
is [b]a son who causes
shame.

6 Blessings *are* on the head of
the righteous,
But violence covers the
mouth of the wicked.
7 [a]The memory of the
righteous *is* blessed,
But the name of the wicked
will rot.

8 The wise in heart will
receive commands,
[a]But [1]a prating fool will [2]fall.

9 [a]He who walks with integrity
walks securely,
But he who perverts his
ways will become
known.

10 He who winks with the eye
causes trouble,
But a prating fool will fall.

11 The mouth of the righteous
is a well of life,
But violence covers the
mouth of the wicked.

12 Hatred stirs up strife,
But [a]love covers all sins.

13 Wisdom is found on the
lips of him who has
understanding,
But [a]a rod *is* for the back
of him who [1]is devoid of
understanding.

14 Wise *people* store up
knowledge,
But [a]the mouth of
the foolish *is* near
destruction.

15 The [a]rich man's wealth *is*
his strong city;
The destruction of the poor
is their poverty.

16 The labor of the righteous
leads to [a]life,
The wages of the wicked to
sin.

17 He who keeps instruction *is*
in the way of life,
But he who refuses
correction [1]goes astray.

18 Whoever [a]hides hatred *has*
lying lips,
And [b]whoever spreads
slander *is* a fool.

19 [a]In the multitude of words
sin is not lacking,
But [b]he who restrains his
lips *is* wise.

20 The tongue of the righteous
is choice silver;
The heart of the wicked *is*
worth little.

21 The lips of the righteous
feed many,
But fools die for lack of
[1]wisdom.

22 [a]The blessing of the LORD
makes *one* rich,
And He adds no sorrow
with it.

23 [a]To do evil *is* like sport to a
fool,
But a man of understanding
has wisdom.

24 [a]The fear of the wicked will
come upon him,
And [b]the desire of the
righteous will be granted.

25 When the whirlwind passes
by, [a]the wicked *is* no
more,
But [b]the righteous *has* an
everlasting foundation.

26 As vinegar to the teeth and
smoke to the eyes,
So *is* the lazy *man* to those
who send him.

27 [a]The fear of the LORD
prolongs days,
But [b]the years of the wicked
will be shortened.

28 The hope of the righteous
will be gladness,
But the [a]expectation of the
wicked will perish.

9 [a][Ps. 23:4]
12 [a][1 Cor. 13:4–7]
13 [a]Prov. 26:3 [1]Lit. *lacks heart*
14 [a]Prov. 18:7
15 [a]Job 31:24
16 [a]Prov. 6:23
17 [1]*leads*
18 [a]Prov. 26:24 [b]Ps. 15:3; 101:5
19 [a]Eccl. 5:3 [b][James 1:19; 3:2]
21 [1]Lit. *heart*
22 [a]Gen. 24:35; 26:12
23 [a]Prov. 2:14; 15:21
24 [a]Job 15:21 [b]Ps. 145:19
25 [a]Ps. 37:9, 10 [b]Ps. 15:5
27 [a]Prov. 9:11 [b]Job 15:32
28 [a]Job 8:13

29 The way of the LORD *is*
strength for the upright,
But [a]destruction *will come*
to the workers of
iniquity.
30 [a]The righteous will never be
removed,
But the wicked will not
inhabit the [1]earth.
31 [a]The mouth of the righteous
brings forth wisdom,
But the perverse tongue will
be cut out.
32 The lips of the righteous
know what is acceptable,
But the mouth of the wicked
what is perverse.

CHAPTER 11

11 [a]Dishonest[1] scales *are*
an abomination to the
LORD,
But a [2]just weight *is* His
delight.

2 When pride comes, then
comes [a]shame;
But with the humble *is*
wisdom.
3 The integrity of the upright
will guide [a]them,
But the perversity of the
unfaithful will destroy
them.
4 [a]Riches do not profit in the
day of wrath,
But [b]righteousness delivers
from death.
5 The righteousness of the
blameless will [1]direct his
way aright,
But the wicked will fall by
his own [a]wickedness.
6 The righteousness of the
upright will deliver
them,
But the unfaithful will be
caught by *their* lust.

7 When a wicked man dies,
his expectation will
[a]perish,
And the hope of the unjust
perishes.
8 [a]The righteous is delivered
from trouble,
And it comes to the wicked
instead.
9 The hypocrite with *his*
mouth destroys his
neighbor,
But through knowledge
the righteous will be
delivered.
10 [a]When it goes well with
the righteous, the city
rejoices;
And when the wicked
perish, *there is*
jubilation.
11 By the blessing of the
upright the city is
[a]exalted,
But it is overthrown by the
mouth of the wicked.

12 He who [1]is devoid of
wisdom despises his
neighbor,
But a man of understanding
holds his peace.

13 [a]A talebearer reveals
secrets,
But he who is of a faithful
spirit [b]conceals a
matter.

14 [a]Where *there is* no counsel,
the people fall;
But in the multitude of
counselors *there is*
safety.

29 [a]Ps. 1:6
30 [a]Ps. 37:22 [1]*land*
31 [a]Ps. 37:30

CHAPTER 11

1 [a]Lev. 19:35, 36 [1]*deceptive* [2]Lit. *perfect stone*
2 [a]Prov. 16:18; 18:12; 29:23
3 [a]Prov. 13:6
4 [a]Ezek. 7:19 [b]Gen. 7:1
5 [a]Prov. 5:22 [1]Or *make smooth* or *straight*
7 [a]Prov. 10:28
8 [a]Prov. 21:18
10 [a]Prov. 28:12
11 [a]Prov. 14:34
12 [1]Lit. *lacks heart*
13 [a]Lev. 19:16 [b]Prov. 19:11
14 [a]1 Kin. 12:1

15 He who is [a]surety[1] for a
stranger will suffer,
But one who hates [2]being
surety is secure.

16 A gracious woman retains
honor,
But ruthless *men* retain
riches.
17 [a]The merciful man does good
for his own soul,
But *he who is* cruel troubles
his own flesh.
18 The wicked *man* does
deceptive work,
But [a]he who sows
righteousness *will have*
a sure reward.
19 As righteousness *leads* to
[a]life,
So he who pursues evil
pursues it to his own
[b]death.
20 Those who are of a
perverse heart *are* an
abomination to the LORD,
But *the* blameless in their
ways *are* His delight.
21 [a]*Though they join* [1]forces,
the wicked will not go
unpunished;
But [b]the posterity of the
righteous will be
delivered.

22 *As* a ring of gold in a
swine's snout,
So is a lovely woman who
lacks [1]discretion.

23 The desire of the righteous
is only good,
But the expectation of the
wicked [a]*is* wrath.

24 There is *one* who [a]scatters,
yet increases more;
And there is *one* who
withholds more than is
right,
But it *leads* to poverty.
25 [a]The generous soul will be
made rich,
[b]And he who waters will also
be watered himself.
26 The people will curse [a]him
who withholds grain,
But [b]blessing *will be* on the
head of him who sells *it*.

27 He who earnestly seeks
good [1]finds favor,
[a]But trouble will come to him
who seeks *evil*.

28 [a]He who trusts in his riches
will fall,
But [b]the righteous will
flourish like foliage.

29 He who troubles his own
house [a]will inherit the
wind,
And the fool *will be* [b]servant
to the wise of heart.

30 The fruit of the righteous *is*
a tree of life,
And [a]he who [1]wins souls *is*
wise.

31 [a]If the righteous will be
[1]recompensed on the
earth,
How much more the
ungodly and the sinner.

12 Whoever loves
instruction loves
knowledge,
But he who hates correction
is stupid.

2 A good *man* obtains favor
from the LORD,

---

15 [a]Prov. 6:1, 2 [1]*guaranty* [2]*those pledging guaranty,* lit. *those who strike hands*
17 [a][Matt. 5:7; 25:34–36]
18 [a]Hos. 10:12
19 [a]Prov. 10:16; 12:28 [b][Rom. 6:23]
21 [a]Prov. 16:5 [b]Ps. 112:2 [1]Lit. *hand to hand*
22 [1]*taste*
23 [a]Rom. 2:8, 9
24 [a]Ps. 112:9
25 [a][2 Cor. 9:6, 7] [b][Matt. 5:7]
26 [a]Amos 8:5, 6 [b]Job 29:13
27 [a]Esth. 7:10 [1]Lit. *seeks*
28 [a]Job 31:24 [b]Ps. 1:3
29 [a]Eccl. 5:16 [b]Prov. 14:19
30 [a][Dan. 12:3] [1]Lit. *takes,* in the sense of *brings,* cf. 1 Sam. 16:11
31 [a]Jer. 25:29 [1]*rewarded*

But a man of wicked
intentions He will
condemn.

3 A man is not established by
wickedness,
But the [a]root of the righteous
cannot be moved.

4 [a]An[1] excellent wife *is* the
crown of her husband,
But she who causes shame
is [b]like rottenness in his
bones.

5 The thoughts of the
righteous *are* right,
But the counsels of the
wicked *are* deceitful.
6 [a]The words of the wicked
are, "Lie in wait for
blood,"
[b]But the mouth of the upright
will deliver them.

7 [a]The wicked are overthrown
and *are* no more,
But the house of the
righteous will stand.

8 A man will be commended
according to his wisdom,
[a]But he who is of a perverse
heart will be despised.

9 [a]Better *is the one* who is
[1]slighted but has a
servant,
Than he who honors himself
but lacks bread.

10 [a]A righteous *man* regards the
life of his animal,
But the tender mercies of
the wicked *are* cruel.

11 [a]He who [1]tills his land will be
satisfied with [b]bread,
But he who follows
[2]frivolity [c]*is* devoid of
[3]understanding.

12 The wicked covet the catch
of evil *men*,
But the root of the righteous
yields *fruit*.
13 [a]The wicked is ensnared by
the transgression of *his*
lips,
[b]But the righteous will come
through trouble.
14 [a]A man will be satisfied with
good by the fruit of *his*
mouth,
[b]And the recompense of a
man's hands will be
rendered to him.

15 [a]The way of a fool *is* right in
his own eyes,
But he who heeds counsel *is*
wise.
16 [a]A fool's wrath is known at
once,
But a prudent *man* covers
shame.

17 [a]He *who* speaks truth
declares righteousness,
But a false witness, deceit.
18 [a]There is one who speaks
like the piercings of a
sword,
But the tongue of the wise
promotes health.
19 The truthful lip shall be
established forever,
[a]But a lying tongue *is* but for
a moment.
20 Deceit is in the heart of
those who devise evil,
But counselors of peace
have joy.
21 [a]No grave [1]trouble will
overtake the righteous,

CHAPTER 12

3 [a][Prov. 10:25]

4 [a]1 Cor. 11:7 [b]Prov. 14:30 [1]Lit. *A wife of valor*

6 [a]Prov. 1:11, 18 [b]Prov. 14:3

7 [a]Matt. 7:24–27

8 [a]1 Sam. 25:17

9 [a]Prov. 13:7 [1]*lightly esteemed*

10 [a]Deut. 25:4

11 [a]Gen. 3:19 [b]Prov. 28:19 [c]Prov. 6:32 [1]*works* or *cultivates* [2]Lit. *vain things* [3]Lit. *heart*

13 [a]Prov. 18:7 [b][2 Pet. 2:9]

14 [a]Prov. 13:2; 15:23; 18:20 [b][Is. 3:10, 11]

15 [a]Luke 18:11

16 [a]Prov. 11:13; 29:11

17 [a]Prov. 14:5

18 [a]Ps. 57:4

19 [a]Prov. 19:9

21 [a]1 Pet. 3:13 [1]*harm*

But the wicked shall be
filled with evil.
22 [a]Lying lips *are* an
abomination to the LORD,
But those who deal
truthfully *are* His
delight.

23 [a]A prudent man conceals
knowledge,
But the heart of fools
proclaims foolishness.

24 [a]The hand of the diligent will
rule,
But the lazy *man* will be put
to forced labor.

25 [a]Anxiety in the heart of man
causes depression,
But [b]a good word makes it
glad.

26 The righteous should choose
his friends carefully,
For the way of the wicked
leads them astray.

27 The lazy *man* does not roast
what he took in hunting,
But diligence *is* man's
precious possession.

28 In the way of righteousness
is life,
And in *its* pathway *there is*
no death.

13 A wise son *heeds* his
father's instruction,
[a]But a scoffer does not listen
to rebuke.

2 [a]A man shall eat well by the
fruit of *his* mouth,
But the soul of the
unfaithful feeds on
violence.

22 [a]Rev. 22:15
23 [a]Prov. 13:16
24 [a]Prov. 10:4
25 [a]Prov. 15:13 [b]Is. 50:4

CHAPTER 13

1 [a]Is. 28:14, 15
2 [a]Prov. 12:14
3 [a]Prov. 21:23
4 [a]Prov. 10:4
6 [a]Prov. 11:3, 5, 6
7 [a][Prov. 11:24; 12:9]
9 [a]Prov. 24:20
10 [a]Prov. 10:12
11 [a]Prov. 10:2; 20:21

3 [a]He who guards his mouth
preserves his life,
But he who opens wide
his lips shall have
destruction.

4 [a]The soul of a lazy *man*
desires, and *has* nothing;
But the soul of the diligent
shall be made rich.

5 A righteous *man* hates
lying,
But a wicked *man* is
loathsome and comes to
shame.
6 [a]Righteousness guards *him*
whose way is blameless,
But wickedness overthrows
the sinner.

7 [a]There is one who makes
himself rich, yet *has*
nothing;
And one who makes himself
poor, yet *has* great
riches.

8 The ransom of a man's life
is his riches,
But the poor does not hear
rebuke.

9 The light of the righteous
rejoices,
[a]But the lamp of the wicked
will be put out.

10 By pride comes nothing but
[a]strife,
But with the well-advised *is*
wisdom.

11 [a]Wealth *gained by* dishonesty
will be diminished,
But he who gathers by labor
will increase.

12 Hope deferred makes the
heart sick,
But [a]*when* the desire comes,
it is a tree of life.

13 He who [a]despises the word
will be destroyed,
But he who fears the
commandment will be
rewarded.

14 [a]The law of the wise *is* a
fountain of life,
To turn *one* away from [b]the
snares of death.

15 Good understanding [1]gains
[a]favor,
But the way of the
unfaithful *is* hard.

16 [a]Every prudent *man* acts
with knowledge,
But a fool lays open *his*
folly.

17 A wicked messenger falls
into trouble,
But [a]a faithful ambassador
brings health.

18 Poverty and shame *will*
come to him who
[1]disdains correction,
But [a]he who regards a
rebuke will be honored.

19 A desire accomplished is
sweet to the soul,
But *it is* an abomination to
fools to depart from evil.

20 He who walks with wise
men will be wise,
But the companion of fools
will be destroyed.

21 [a]Evil pursues sinners,
But to the righteous, good
shall be repaid.

12 [a]Prov. 13:19

13 [a]Num. 15:31

14 [a]Prov. 6:22; 10:11; 14:27
[b]2 Sam. 22:6

15 [a]Prov. 3:4
[1]*gives*

16 [a]Prov. 12:23

17 [a]Prov. 25:13

18 [a]Prov. 15:5, 31, 32
[1]Lit. *ignores*

21 [a]Ps. 32:10

22 [a][Eccl. 2:26]

23 [a]Prov. 12:11
[1]*uncultivated*
[2]Lit. *what is swept away*

24 [a]Prov. 19:18
[1]*early*

25 [a]Ps. 34:10

CHAPTER 14

2 [a][Rom. 2:4]

3 [a]Prov. 12:6

4 [1]*manger or feed trough*

5 [a]Rev. 1:5; 3:14
[b]Prov. 6:19; 12:17

22 A good *man* leaves an
inheritance to his
children's children,
But [a]the wealth of the sinner
is stored up for the
righteous.

23 [a]Much food *is in* the [1]fallow
ground of the poor,
And for lack of justice there
is [2]waste.

24 [a]He who spares his rod hates
his son,
But he who loves him
disciplines him
[1]promptly.

25 [a]The righteous eats to the
satisfying of his soul,
But the stomach of the
wicked shall be in want.

14 The wise woman builds
her house,
But the foolish pulls it down
with her hands.

2 He who walks in his
uprightness fears the
LORD,
[a]But *he who is* perverse in
his ways despises Him.

3 In the mouth of a fool *is* a
rod of pride,
[a]But the lips of the wise will
preserve them.

4 Where no oxen *are,* the
[1]trough *is* clean;
But much increase *comes* by
the strength of an ox.

5 A [a]faithful witness does not
lie,
But a false witness will utter
[b]lies.

6 A scoffer seeks wisdom and
does not *find it,*
But [a]knowledge *is* easy to
him who understands.
7 Go from the presence of a
foolish man,
When you do not perceive
in him the lips of
[a]knowledge.
8 The wisdom of the prudent
is to understand his way,
But the folly of fools *is*
deceit.

9 [a]Fools mock at [1]sin,
But among the upright *there*
is favor.

10 The heart knows its own
bitterness,
And a stranger does not
share its joy.

11 [a]The house of the wicked
will be overthrown,
But the tent of the upright
will flourish.

12 [a]There is a way *that seems*
right to a man,
But [b]its end *is* the way of
[c]death.

13 Even in laughter the heart
may sorrow,
And [a]the end of mirth *may*
be grief.

14 The backslider in heart will
be [a]filled with his own
ways,
But a good man *will be*
satisfied [1]from [b]above.

15 The simple believes every
word,
But the prudent considers
well his steps.

16 [a]A wise *man* fears and
departs from evil,
But a fool rages and is self-
confident.
17 A quick-tempered *man* acts
foolishly,
And a man of wicked
intentions is hated.
18 The simple inherit folly,
But the prudent are crowned
with knowledge.
19 The evil will bow before the
good,
And the wicked at the gates
of the righteous.

20 [a]The poor *man* is hated even
by his own neighbor,
But [1]the rich *has* many
[b]friends.
21 He who despises his
neighbor sins;
[a]But he who has mercy on
the poor, happy *is* he.

22 Do they not go astray who
devise evil?
But mercy and truth *belong*
to those who devise
good.

23 In all labor there is profit,
But [1]idle chatter *leads* only
to poverty.

24 The crown of the wise is
their riches,
But the foolishness of fools
is folly.

25 A true witness [1]delivers
[a]souls,
But a deceitful *witness*
speaks lies.

26 In the fear of the LORD *there*
is strong confidence,

6 [a]Prov. 8:9; 17:24
7 [a]Prov. 23:9
9 [a]Prov. 10:23 [1]Lit. *guilt*
11 [a]Job 8:15
12 [a]Prov. 16:25 [b]Rom. 6:21 [c]Prov. 12:15
13 [a]Eccl. 2:1, 2
14 [a]Prov. 1:31; 12:15 [b]Prov. 13:2; 18:20 [1]Lit. *from above himself*
16 [a]Prov. 22:3
20 [a]Prov. 19:7 [b]Prov. 19:4 [1]Lit. *many are the lovers of the rich*
21 [a]Ps. 112:9
23 [1]Lit. *talk of the lips*
25 [a][Ezek. 3:18–21] [1]*saves lives*

And His children will have a
place of refuge.
27 [a]The fear of the LORD *is* a
fountain of life,
To turn *one* away from the
snares of death.

28 In a multitude of people *is* a
king's honor,
But in the lack of people *is*
the downfall of a prince.

29 [a]*He who is* slow to wrath has
great understanding,
But *he who is* [1]impulsive
exalts folly.

30 A sound heart *is* life to the
body,
But [a]envy *is* [b]rottenness to
the bones.

31 [a]He who oppresses the poor
reproaches [b]his Maker,
But he who honors Him has
mercy on the needy.

32 The wicked is banished in
his wickedness,
But [a]the righteous has a
refuge in his death.

33 Wisdom rests in the
heart of him who has
understanding,
But [a]*what is* in the heart of
fools is made known.

34 Righteousness exalts a
[a]nation,
But sin *is* a [1]reproach to *any*
people.

35 [a]The king's favor *is* toward a
wise servant,
But his wrath *is against* him
who causes shame.

27 [a]Prov. 13:14
29 [a]James 1:19 [1]Lit. *short of spirit*
30 [a]Ps. 112:10 [b]Prov. 12:4
31 [a]Matt. 25:40 [b][Prov. 22:2]
32 [a]Job 13:15
33 [a]Prov. 12:16
34 [a]Prov. 11:11 [1]*shame* or *disgrace*
35 [a]Matt. 24:45–47

CHAPTER 15
1 [a]Prov. 25:15 [b]1 Sam. 25:10
2 [a]Prov. 12:23
3 [a]Job 34:21
4 [1]Lit. *healing*
5 [a]Prov. 10:1 [b]Prov. 13:18 [1]Lit. *keeps*
7 [1]*spread*
8 [a]Is. 1:11
9 [a]Prov. 21:21
10 [a]1 Kin. 22:8 [b]Prov. 5:12

15 A [a]soft answer turns
away wrath,
But [b]a harsh word stirs up
anger.
2 The tongue of the wise uses
knowledge rightly,
[a]But the mouth of fools pours
forth foolishness.

3 [a]The eyes of the LORD *are* in
every place,
Keeping watch on the evil
and the good.

4 A [1]wholesome tongue *is* a
tree of life,
But perverseness in it
breaks the spirit.

5 [a]A fool despises his father's
instruction,
[b]But he who [1]receives
correction is prudent.

6 *In* the house of the righteous
there is much treasure,
But in the revenue of the
wicked is trouble.

7 The lips of the wise
[1]disperse knowledge,
But the heart of the fool
does not *do* so.

8 [a]The sacrifice of the wicked
is an abomination to the
LORD,
But the prayer of the upright
is His delight.
9 The way of the wicked *is* an
abomination to the LORD,
But He loves him who
[a]follows righteousness.

10 [a]Harsh discipline *is* for him
who forsakes the way,
And [b]he who hates
correction will die.

11 [a]Hell[1] and [2]Destruction *are*
before the LORD;
So how much more [b]the
hearts of the sons of
men.

12 [a]A scoffer does not love one
who corrects him,
Nor will he go to the wise.

13 [a]A merry heart makes a
cheerful [1]countenance,
But [b]by sorrow of the heart
the spirit is broken.

14 The heart of him who has
understanding seeks
knowledge,
But the mouth of fools feeds
on foolishness.

15 All the days of the afflicted
are evil,
[a]But he who is of a merry
heart *has* a continual
feast.

16 [a]Better *is* a little with the fear
of the LORD,
Than great treasure with
trouble.

17 [a]Better *is* a dinner of [1]herbs
where love is,
Than a fatted calf with
hatred.

18 [a]A wrathful man stirs up
strife,
But *he who is* slow to anger
allays contention.

19 [a]The way of the lazy *man* is
like a hedge of thorns,
But the way of the upright *is*
a highway.

20 [a]A wise son makes a father
glad,
But a foolish man despises
his mother.

21 [a]Folly *is* joy *to him who is*
destitute of [1]discernment,
[b]But a man of understanding
walks uprightly.

22 [a]Without counsel, plans go
awry,
But in the multitude of
counselors they are
established.

23 A man has joy by the
answer of his mouth,
And [a]a word *spoken* [1]in due
season, how good *it is!*

24 [a]The way of life *winds*
upward for the wise,
That he may [b]turn away
from [1]hell below.

25 [a]The LORD will destroy the
house of the proud,
But [b]He will establish the
boundary of the widow.

26 [a]The thoughts of the wicked
are an abomination to
the LORD,
[b]But the words of the pure
are pleasant.

27 [a]He who is greedy for gain
troubles his own house,
But he who hates bribes will
live.

28 The heart of the righteous
[a]studies how to answer,
But the mouth of the wicked
pours forth evil.

29 [a]The LORD *is* far from the
wicked,

11 [a]Job 26:6 [b]2 Chr. 6:30 [1]Or *Sheol* [2]Heb. *Abaddon*
12 [a]Amos 5:10
13 [a]Prov. 12:25 [b]Prov. 17:22 [1]*face*
15 [a]Prov. 17:22
16 [a]Ps. 37:16
17 [a]Prov. 17:1 [1]Or *vegetables*
18 [a]Prov. 26:21
19 [a]Prov. 22:5
20 [a]Prov. 10:1
21 [a]Prov. 10:23 [b]Eph. 5:15 [1]Lit. *heart*
22 [a]Prov. 11:14
23 [a]Prov. 25:11 [1]Lit. *in its time*
24 [a]Phil. 3:20 [b]Prov. 14:16 [1]Or *Sheol*
25 [a]Prov. 12:7 [b]Ps. 68:5, 6
26 [a]Prov. 6:16, 18 [b]Ps. 37:30
27 [a]Is. 5:8
28 [a]1 Pet. 3:15
29 [a]Ps. 10:1; 34:16

But [b]He hears the prayer of
the righteous.

30 The light of the eyes rejoices
the heart,
And a good report makes
the bones [1]healthy.

31 The ear that hears the
rebukes of life
Will abide among the wise.
32 He who disdains instruction
despises his own soul,
But he who heeds rebuke
gets understanding.
33 [a]The fear of the LORD *is* the
instruction of wisdom,
And [b]before honor *is*
humility.

16

1 The [a]preparations[1] of the
heart *belong* to man,
[b]But the answer of the
tongue *is* from the LORD.

2 All the ways of a man *are*
pure in his own [a]eyes,
But the LORD weighs the
spirits.

3 [a]Commit[1] your works to the
LORD,
And your thoughts will be
established.

4 The [a]LORD has made all for
Himself,
[b]Yes, even the wicked for the
day of [1]doom.

5 [a]Everyone proud in heart *is* an
abomination to the LORD;
Though they join [1]forces,
none will go unpunished.

6 [a]In mercy and truth
Atonement is provided for
iniquity;
And [b]by the fear of the LORD
one departs from evil.

7 When a man's ways please
the LORD,
He makes even his enemies
to be at peace with him.

8 [a]Better *is* a little with
righteousness,
Than vast revenues without
justice.

9 [a]A man's heart plans his way,
[b]But the LORD directs his
steps.

10 Divination *is* on the lips of
the king;
His mouth must not
transgress in judgment.
11 [a]Honest weights and scales
are the LORD's;
All the weights in the bag
are His [1]work.
12 *It is* an abomination
for kings to commit
wickedness,
For [a]a throne is established
by righteousness.
13 [a]Righteous lips *are* the
delight of kings,
And they love him who
speaks *what is* right.
14 As messengers of death *is*
the king's wrath,
But a wise man will
[a]appease it.
15 In the light of the king's
face *is* life,
And his favor *is* like a
[a]cloud of the latter rain.

16 [a]How much better to get
wisdom than gold!
And to get understanding is
to be chosen rather than
silver.

29 [b]Ps. 145:18
30 [1]Lit. *fat*
33 [a]Prov. 1:7 [b]Prov. 18:12

CHAPTER 16

1 [a]Jer. 10:23 [b]Matt. 10:19 [1]*plans*
2 [a]Prov. 21:2
3 [a]Ps. 37:5 [1]Lit. *Roll*
4 [a]Is. 43:7 [b][Rom. 9:22] [1]Lit. *evil*
5 [a]Prov. 6:17; 8:13 [1]Lit. *hand to hand*
6 [a]Dan. 4:27 [b]Prov. 8:13; 14:16
8 [a]Ps. 37:16
9 [a]Prov. 19:21 [b]Jer. 10:23
11 [a]Lev. 19:36 [1]*concern*
12 [a]Prov. 25:5
13 [a]Prov. 14:35
14 [a]Prov. 25:15
15 [a]Zech. 10:1
16 [a]Prov. 8:10, 11, 19

17 The highway of the upright
is to depart from evil;
He who keeps his way
preserves his soul.

18 Pride *goes* before
destruction,
And a haughty spirit before
[1]a fall.
19 Better *to be* of a humble
spirit with the lowly,
Than to divide the [1]spoil
with the proud.

20 He who heeds the word
wisely will find good,
And whoever [a]trusts in the
LORD, happy *is* he.

21 The wise in heart will be
called prudent,
And sweetness of the lips
increases learning.

22 Understanding *is* a
wellspring of life to him
who has it.
But the correction of fools
is folly.

23 The heart of the wise
teaches his mouth,
And adds learning to his lips.
24 Pleasant words *are like* a
honeycomb,
Sweetness to the soul and
health to the bones.

25 There is a way *that seems*
right to a man,
But its end *is* the way of
[a]death.

26 The person who labors,
labors for himself,
For his *hungry* mouth drives
[a]him *on*.

18 [1]*stumbling*
19 [1]*plunder*
20 [a]Ps. 34:8
25 [a]Prov. 14:12
26 [a][Eccl. 6:7]
27 [a][James 3:6] [1]Lit. *A man of Belial*
28 [a]Prov. 17:9
30 [1]Lit. *compresses*
31 [a]Prov. 20:29
32 [a]Prov. 14:29; 19:11
CHAPTER 17
1 [a]Prov. 15:17 [1]Or *sacrificial meals*
2 [a]Prov. 10:5
3 [a]Jer. 17:10

27 [1]An ungodly man digs up
evil,
And *it is* on his lips like a
burning [a]fire.
28 A perverse man sows strife,
And [a]a whisperer separates
the best of friends.
29 A violent man entices his
neighbor,
And leads him in a way *that*
is not good.
30 He winks his eye to devise
perverse things;
He [1]purses his lips *and*
brings about evil.

31 [a]The silver-haired head *is* a
crown of glory,
If it is found in the way of
righteousness.

32 [a]*He who is* slow to anger *is*
better than the mighty,
And he who rules his spirit
than he who takes a city.

33 The lot is cast into the lap,
But its every decision *is*
from the LORD.

17

Better *is* [a]a dry morsel
with quietness,
Than a house full of
[1]feasting *with* strife.

2 A wise servant will rule
over [a]a son who causes
shame,
And will share an
inheritance among the
brothers.

3 The refining pot *is* for silver
and the furnace for gold,
[a]But the LORD tests the hearts.

4 An evildoer gives heed to
false lips;

A liar listens eagerly to a
[1]spiteful tongue.

5 [a]He who mocks the poor
reproaches his Maker;
[b]He who is glad at calamity
will not go unpunished.

6 [a]Children's children *are* the
crown of old men,
And the glory of children *is*
their father.

7 Excellent speech is not
becoming to a fool,
Much less lying lips to a
prince.

8 A present *is* a precious
stone in the eyes of its
possessor;
Wherever he turns, he
prospers.

9 [a]He who covers a
transgression seeks love,
But [b]he who repeats a
matter separates friends.

10 [a]Rebuke is more effective for
a wise *man*
Than a hundred blows on a
fool.

11 An evil *man* seeks only
rebellion;
Therefore a cruel messenger
will be sent against him.

12 Let a man meet [a]a bear
robbed of her cubs,
Rather than a fool in his
folly.

13 Whoever [a]rewards evil for
good,
Evil will not depart from his
house.

14 The beginning of strife *is*
like releasing water;
Therefore [a]stop contention
before a quarrel starts.

15 [a]He who justifies the wicked,
and he who condemns
the just,
Both of them alike *are* an
abomination to the LORD.

16 Why *is there* in the hand of
a fool the purchase price
of wisdom,
Since *he has* no heart *for it*?

17 [a]A friend loves at all times,
And a brother is born for
adversity.

18 [a]A man devoid of
[1]understanding [2]shakes
hands in a pledge,
And becomes [3]surety for his
friend.

19 He who loves transgression
loves strife,
And [a]he who exalts his gate
seeks destruction.

20 He who has a [1]deceitful
heart finds no good,
And he who has [a]a perverse
tongue falls into evil.

21 He who begets a scoffer
does so to his sorrow,
And the father of a fool has
no joy.

22 A [a]merry heart [1]does good,
like medicine,
But a broken spirit dries the
bones.

23 A wicked *man* accepts a
bribe [1]behind the back

---

4 [1]Lit. *destructive*
5 [a]Prov. 14:31 [b]Job 31:29
6 [a][Ps. 127:3; 128:3]
9 [a][Prov. 10:12] [b]Prov. 16:28
10 [a][Mic. 7:9]
12 [a]Hos. 13:8
13 [a]Ps. 109:4, 5
14 [a][Prov. 20:3]
15 [a]Ex. 23:7
17 [a]Ruth 1:16
18 [a]Prov. 6:1 [1]Lit. *heart* [2]Lit. *strikes the hands* [3]*guaranty* or *collateral*
19 [a]Prov. 16:18
20 [a]James 3:8 [1]*crooked*
22 [a]Prov. 12:25; 15:13, 15 [1]Or *makes medicine even better*
23 [1]Under cover, lit. *from the bosom*

To pervert the ways of
justice.

24 [a]Wisdom *is* in the sight
of him who has
understanding,
But the eyes of a fool *are* on
the ends of the earth.

25 A [a]foolish son *is* a grief to
his father,
And bitterness to her who
bore him.

26 Also, to punish the
righteous *is* not good,
Nor to strike princes for
their uprightness.

27 [a]He who has knowledge
spares his words,
And a man of understanding
is of a calm spirit.

28 [a]Even a fool is counted wise
when he holds his peace;
When he shuts his lips, *he is*
considered perceptive.

18

A man who isolates
himself seeks his own
desire;
He rages against all [1]wise
judgment.

2 A fool has no delight in
understanding,
But in expressing his [a]own
heart.

3 When the wicked comes,
contempt comes also;
And with dishonor *comes*
reproach.

4 [a]The words of a man's mouth
are deep waters;
[b]The wellspring of wisdom *is*
a flowing brook.

5 *It is* not good to show
partiality to the wicked,
Or to overthrow the
righteous in [a]judgment.

6 A fool's lips enter into
contention,
And his mouth calls for
blows.

7 [a]A fool's mouth *is* his
destruction,
And his lips *are* the snare of
his [b]soul.

8 [a]The words of a [1]talebearer
are like [2]tasty trifles,
And they go down into the
[3]inmost body.

9 He who is slothful in his
work
Is a brother to him who is a
great destroyer.

10 The name of the LORD *is* a
strong [a]tower;
The righteous run to it and
are [1]safe.

11 The rich man's wealth *is* his
strong city,
And like a high wall in his
own esteem.

12 [a]Before destruction the heart
of a man is haughty,
And before honor *is*
humility.

13 He who answers a matter
before he hears *it*,
It *is* folly and shame to him.

14 The spirit of a man will
sustain him in sickness,
But who can bear a broken
spirit?

15 The heart of the prudent
acquires knowledge,

---

24 [a]Eccl. 2:14
25 [a]Prov. 10:1; 15:20; 19:13
27 [a]James 1:19
28 [a]Job 13:5

CHAPTER 18

1 [1]*sound wisdom*
2 [a]Eccl. 10:3
4 [a]Prov. 10:11 [b][James 3:17]
5 [a]Prov. 17:15
7 [a]Prov. 10:14 [b]Eccl. 10:12
8 [a]Prov. 12:18 [1]*gossip* or *slanderer* [2]A Jewish tradition *wounds* [3]Lit. *rooms of the belly*
10 [a]2 Sam. 22:2, 3, 33 [1]*secure*, lit. *set on high*
12 [a]Prov. 15:33; 16:18

And the ear of the wise
seeks knowledge.

16 [a]A man's gift makes room
for him,
And brings him before great
men.

17 The first *one* to plead his
cause *seems* right,
Until his neighbor comes
and examines him.

18 Casting [a]lots causes
contentions to cease,
And keeps the mighty apart.

19 A brother offended *is harder
to win* than a strong city,
And contentions *are* like the
bars of a castle.

20 [a]A man's stomach shall be
satisfied from the fruit of
his mouth;
From the produce of his lips
he shall be filled.

21 [a]Death and life *are* in the
power of the tongue,
And those who love it will
eat its fruit.

22 [a]*He who* finds a wife finds a
good *thing*,
And obtains favor from the
LORD.

23 The poor *man* uses
entreaties,
But the rich answers
[a]roughly.

24 A man *who has* friends
[1]must himself be friendly,
[a]But there is a friend *who*
sticks closer than a
brother.

16 [a]Gen. 32:20, 21
18 [a][Prov. 16:33]
20 [a]Prov. 12:14; 14:14
21 [a]Matt. 12:37
22 [a][Prov. 12:4; 19:14]
23 [a]James 2:3, 6
24 [a]Prov. 17:17 [1]So with Gr. mss., Syr., Tg., Vg.; MT *may come to ruin*

CHAPTER 19

1 [a]Prov. 28:6
4 [a]Prov. 14:20
5 [a]Ex. 23:1
7 [a]Prov. 14:20 [b]Ps. 38:11 [1]Lit. *are not*
8 [a]Prov. 16:20 [1]Lit. *heart*

19 Better [a]*is* the poor who
walks in his integrity
Than *one who is* perverse in
his lips, and is a fool.

2 Also it is not good *for*
a soul *to be* without
knowledge,
And he sins who hastens
with *his* feet.

3 The foolishness of a man
twists his way,
And his heart frets against
the LORD.

4 [a]Wealth makes many friends,
But the poor is separated
from his friend.

5 A [a]false witness will not go
unpunished,
And *he who* speaks lies will
not escape.

6 Many entreat the favor of
the nobility,
And every man *is* a friend to
one who gives gifts.

7 [a]All the brothers of the poor
hate him;
How much more do his
friends go [b]far from him!
He may pursue *them with*
words, *yet* they [1]abandon
him.

8 He who gets [1]wisdom loves
his own soul;
He who keeps
understanding [a]will find
good.

9 A false witness will not go
unpunished,
And *he who* speaks lies
shall perish.

10 Luxury is not fitting for a fool,
Much less [a]for a servant to rule over princes.

11 [a]The discretion of a man makes him slow to anger,
[b]And his glory *is* to overlook a transgression.

12 [a]The king's wrath *is* like the roaring of a lion,
But his favor *is* [b]like dew on the grass.

13 [a]A foolish son *is* the ruin of his father,
[b]And the contentions of a wife *are* a continual [1]dripping.

14 [a]Houses and riches *are* an inheritance from fathers,
But [b]a prudent wife *is* from the Lord.

15 [a]Laziness casts *one* into a deep sleep,
And an idle person will [b]suffer hunger.

16 [a]He who keeps the commandment keeps his soul,
But he who [1]is careless of his ways will die.

17 [a]He who has pity on the poor lends to the Lord,
And He will pay back what he has given.

18 [a]Chasten your son while there is hope,
And do not set your heart [1]on his destruction.

19 *A man of* great wrath will suffer punishment;
For if you rescue *him,* you will have to do it again.

20 Listen to counsel and receive instruction,
That you may be wise [a]in your latter days.

21 There are many plans in a man's heart,
[a]Nevertheless the Lord's counsel—that will stand.

22 What is desired in a man is [1]kindness,
And a poor man is better than a liar.

23 [a]The fear of the Lord *leads* to life,
And *he who has it* will abide in satisfaction;
He will not be visited with evil.

24 [a]A lazy *man* buries his hand in the [1]bowl,
And will not so much as bring it to his mouth again.

25 Strike a scoffer, and the simple [a]will become wary;
[b]Rebuke one who has understanding, *and* he will discern knowledge.

26 He who mistreats *his* father *and* chases away *his* mother
Is [a]a son who causes shame and brings reproach.

27 Cease listening to instruction, my son,

---

10 [a]Prov. 30:21, 22
11 [a]James 1:19 [b]Eph. 4:32
12 [a]Prov. 16:14 [b]Hos. 14:5
13 [a]Prov. 10:1 [b]Prov. 21:9, 19 [1]Irritation
14 [a]2 Cor. 12:14 [b]Prov. 18:22
15 [a]Prov. 6:9 [b]Prov. 10:4
16 [a]Luke 10:28; 11:28 [1]Is reckless, lit. *despises*
17 [a][2 Cor. 9:6–8]
18 [a]Prov. 13:24 [1]Lit. *to put him to death;* a Jewish tradition *on his crying*
20 [a]Ps. 37:37
21 [a]Heb. 6:17
22 [1]Lit. *lovingkindness*
23 [a][1 Tim. 4:8]
24 [a]Prov. 15:19 [1]LXX, Syr. *bosom;* Tg., Vg. *armpit*
25 [a]Deut. 13:11 [b]Prov. 9:8
26 [a]Prov. 17:2

And you will stray from the
words of knowledge.

28 A [1]disreputable witness
scorns justice,
And [a]the mouth of the
wicked devours iniquity.

29 Judgments are prepared for
scoffers,
[a]And beatings for the backs
of fools.

20

Wine [a]*is* a mocker,
Strong drink *is* a brawler,
And whoever is led astray
by it is not wise.

2 The [1]wrath of a king *is* like
the roaring of a lion;
Whoever provokes him to
anger sins *against* his
own life.

3 [a]*It is* honorable for a man to
stop striving,
Since any fool can start a
quarrel.

4 [a]The lazy *man* will not plow
because of winter;
[b]He will beg during harvest
and *have* nothing.

5 Counsel in the heart of man
is like deep water,
But a man of understanding
will draw it out.

6 Most men will proclaim
each his own [1]goodness,
But who can find a faithful
man?

7 [a]The righteous *man* walks in
his integrity;
[b]His children *are* blessed
after him.

8 A king who sits on the
throne of judgment
Scatters all evil with his
eyes.

9 [a]Who can say, "I have made
my heart clean,
I am pure from my sin"?

10 [a]Diverse weights *and* diverse
measures,
They *are* both alike, an
abomination to the LORD.

11 Even a child is [a]known by
his deeds,
Whether what he does *is*
pure and right.

12 [a]The hearing ear and the
seeing eye,
The LORD has made them
both.

13 [a]Do not love sleep, lest you
come to poverty;
Open your eyes, *and* you will
be satisfied with bread.

14 "*It is* [1]good for nothing,"
cries the buyer;
But when he has gone his
way, then he boasts.

15 There is gold and a
multitude of rubies,
But [a]the lips of knowledge
are a precious jewel.

16 [a]Take the garment of one
who is surety *for* a
stranger,
And hold it as a pledge
when it is for a
seductress.

17 [a]Bread gained by deceit *is*
sweet to a man,

---

28 [a]Job 15:16 [1]Lit. *witness of Belial, worthless witness*
29 [a]Prov. 26:3

CHAPTER 20

1 [a]Gen. 9:21
2 [1]Lit. *fear* or *terror,* produced by the king's wrath
3 [a]Prov. 17:14
4 [a]Prov. 10:4 [b]Prov. 19:15
6 [1]Lit. *mercy*
7 [a]2 Cor. 1:12 [b]Ps. 37:26
9 [a][1 Kin. 8:46]
10 [a]Deut. 25:13
11 [a]Matt. 7:16
12 [a]Ex. 4:11
13 [a]Rom. 12:11
14 [1]Lit. *evil, evil*
15 [a][Prov. 3:13–15]
16 [a]Prov. 22:26
17 [a]Prov. 9:17

But afterward his mouth
will be filled with gravel.

18 [a]Plans are established by
counsel;
[b]By wise counsel wage war.

19 [a]He who goes about *as*
a talebearer reveals
secrets;
Therefore do not associate
with one [b]who flatters
with his lips.

20 [a]Whoever curses his father
or his mother,
[b]His lamp will be put out in
deep darkness.

21 [a]An inheritance gained
hastily at the beginning
[b]Will not be blessed at the
end.

22 [a]Do not say, "I will
[1]recompense evil";
[b]Wait for the LORD, and He
will save you.

23 Diverse weights *are* an
abomination to the LORD,
And dishonest scales *are*
not good.

24 A man's steps *are* of the
LORD;
How then can a man
understand his own
way?

25 *It is* a snare for a man to
devote rashly *something*
as holy,
And afterward to reconsider
his vows.

26 [a]A wise king sifts out the
wicked,
And brings the threshing
wheel over them.

27 [a]The spirit of a man *is* the
lamp of the LORD,
Searching all the [1]inner
depths of his heart.

28 [a]Mercy and truth preserve
the king,
And by [1]lovingkindness he
upholds his throne.

29 The glory of young men *is*
their strength,
And [a]the splendor of old
men *is* their gray head.

30 Blows that hurt cleanse
away evil,
As *do* stripes the [1]inner
depths of the heart.

21

The king's heart *is* in the
hand of the LORD,
Like the [1]rivers of water;
He turns it wherever He
wishes.

2 [a]Every way of a man *is* right
in his own eyes,
[b]But the LORD weighs the
hearts.

3 [a]To do righteousness and
justice
Is more acceptable to the
LORD than sacrifice.

4 [a]A haughty look, a proud
heart,
And the [1]plowing of the
wicked *are* sin.

5 [a]The plans of the diligent
lead surely to plenty,
But *those of* everyone *who is*
hasty, surely to poverty.

18 [a]Prov. 24:6 [b]Luke 14:31
19 [a]Prov. 11:13 [b]Rom. 16:18
20 [a]Matt. 15:4 [b]Job 18:5, 6
21 [a]Prov. 28:20 [b]Hab. 2:6
22 [a][Rom. 12:17–19] [b]2 Sam. 16:12 [1]*repay*
26 [a]Ps. 101:8
27 [a]1 Cor. 2:11 [1]Lit. *rooms of the belly*
28 [a]Prov. 21:21 [1]*mercy*
29 [a]Prov. 16:31
30 [1]Lit. *rooms of the belly*

CHAPTER 21

1 [1]*channels*
2 [a]Prov. 16:2 [b]Prov. 24:12
3 [a]1 Sam. 15:22
4 [a]Prov. 6:17 [1]Or *lamp*
5 [a]Prov. 10:4

6 [a]Getting treasures by a lying
tongue
[1]*Is* the fleeting fantasy of
those who seek death.

7 The violence of the wicked
will [1]destroy them,
Because they refuse to do
justice.

8 The way of [1]a guilty man *is*
perverse;
But *as for* the pure, his work
is right.

9 Better to dwell in a corner
of a housetop,
Than in a house shared with
[a]a contentious woman.

10 [a]The soul of the wicked
desires evil;
His neighbor finds no favor
in his eyes.

11 When the scoffer is
punished, the simple is
made wise;
But when the [a]wise is
instructed, he receives
knowledge.

12 The righteous *God* wisely
considers the house of
the wicked,
Overthrowing the wicked
for *their* wickedness.

13 [a]Whoever shuts his ears to
the cry of the poor
Will also cry himself and
not be heard.

14 A gift in secret pacifies
anger,
And a bribe [1]behind the
back, strong wrath.

15 *It is* a joy for the just to do
justice,
But destruction *will come* to
the workers of iniquity.

16 A man who wanders
from the way of
understanding
Will rest in the assembly of
the [a]dead.

17 He who loves pleasure *will
be* a poor man;
He who loves wine and oil
will not be rich.

18 The wicked *shall be*
a ransom for the
righteous,
And the unfaithful for the
upright.

19 Better to dwell [1]in the
wilderness,
Than with a contentious and
angry woman.

20 [a]*There is* desirable treasure,
And oil in the dwelling of
the wise,
But a foolish man squanders
it.

21 [a]He who follows
righteousness and mercy
Finds life, righteousness,
and honor.

22 A [a]wise *man* [1]scales the city
of the mighty,
And brings down the
trusted stronghold.

23 [a]Whoever guards his mouth
and tongue
Keeps his soul from
troubles.

6 [a]2 Pet. 2:3 [1]LXX *Pursue vanity on the snares of death;* Vg. *Is vain and foolish, and shall stumble on the snares of death;* Tg. *They shall be destroyed, and they shall fall who seek death*

7 [1]Lit. *drag them away*

8 [1]Or *The way of a man is perverse and strange;*

9 [a]Prov. 19:13

10 [a]James 4:5

11 [a]Prov. 19:25

13 [a][Matt. 7:2; 18:30–34]

14 [1]Under cover, lit. *in the bosom*

16 [a]Ps. 49:14

19 [1]Lit. *in the land of the desert*

20 [a]Ps. 112:3

21 [a]Matt. 5:6

22 [a]Prov. 24:5 [1]Climbs over the walls of

23 [a][James 3:2]

24 A proud *and* haughty *man*—
"Scoffer" *is* his name;
He acts with arrogant pride.

25 The [a]desire of the lazy *man* kills him,
For his hands refuse to labor.
26 He covets greedily all day long,
But the righteous [a]gives and does not spare.

27 [a]The sacrifice of the wicked *is* an abomination;
How much more *when* he brings it with wicked intent!

28 A false witness shall perish,
But the man who hears *him* will speak endlessly.

29 A wicked man hardens his face,
But *as for* the upright, he [1]establishes his way.

30 [a]*There is* no wisdom or understanding
Or counsel against the LORD.

31 The horse *is* prepared for the day of battle,
But [a]deliverance *is* of the LORD.

22

1 A [a]*good* name is to be chosen rather than great riches,
Loving favor rather than silver and gold.

2 The [a]rich and the poor have this in common,
The [b]LORD *is* the maker of them all.

3 A prudent *man* foresees evil and hides himself,
But the simple pass on and are [a]punished.

4 By humility *and* the fear of the LORD
Are riches and honor and life.

5 Thorns *and* snares *are* in the way of the perverse;
He who guards his soul will be far from them.

6 [a]Train up a child in the way he should go,
[1]And when he is old he will not depart from it.

7 The [a]rich rules over the poor,
And the borrower *is* servant to the lender.

8 He who sows iniquity will reap [a]sorrow,[1]
And the rod of his anger will fail.

9 [a]He who has a [1]generous eye will be [b]blessed,
For he gives of his bread to the poor.

10 [a]Cast out the scoffer, and contention will leave;
Yes, strife and reproach will cease.

11 [a]He who loves purity of heart
And has grace on his lips,
The king *will be* his friend.

12 The eyes of the LORD preserve knowledge,
But He overthrows the words of the faithless.

21:25 [a]Prov. 13:4
21:26 [a][Prov. 22:9]
21:27 [a]Jer. 6:20
21:29 [1]Qr., LXX *understands*
21:30 [a][Jer. 9:23, 24]
21:31 [a]Ps. 3:8

CHAPTER 22

22:1 [a]Eccl. 7:1
22:2 [a]Prov. 29:13 [b]Job 31:15
22:3 [a]Prov. 27:12
22:6 [a]Eph. 6:4 [1]*Even*
22:7 [a]James 2:6
22:8 [a]Job 4:8 [1]*trouble*
22:9 [a]2 Cor. 9:6 [b][Prov. 19:17] [1]Lit. *good*
22:10 [a]Ps. 101:5
22:11 [a]Ps. 101:6

13 [a]The lazy *man* says, "*There is*
a lion outside!
I shall be slain in the
streets!"

14 [a]The mouth of an immoral
woman *is* a deep pit;
[b]He who is abhorred by the
LORD will fall there.

15 Foolishness *is* bound up in
the heart of a child;
[a]The rod of correction will
drive it far from him.

16 He who oppresses the poor
to increase his *riches*,
And he who gives to the
rich, *will* surely *come* to
poverty.

17 Incline your ear and hear
the words of the wise,
And apply your heart to my
knowledge;
18 For *it is* a pleasant thing if
you keep them within
you;
Let them all be fixed upon
your lips,
19 So that your trust may be in
the LORD;
I have instructed you today,
even you.
20 Have I not written to you
excellent things
Of counsels and knowledge,
21 [a]That I may make you know
the certainty of the
words of truth,
[b]That you may answer words
of truth
To those who [1]send to you?

22 Do not rob the [a]poor
because he *is* poor,
Nor oppress the afflicted at
the gate;
23 [a]For the LORD will plead their
cause,
And plunder the soul of
those who plunder them.

24 Make no friendship with an
angry man,
And with a [a]furious man do
not go,
25 Lest you learn his ways
And set a snare for your
soul.

26 [a]Do not be one of those
who [1]shakes hands in a
pledge,
One of those who is [2]surety
for debts;
27 If you have nothing *with
which* to pay,
Why should he take away
your bed from under
you?

28 [a]Do not remove the ancient
[1]landmark
Which your fathers have set.

29 Do you see a man *who*
[1]excels in his work?
He will stand before kings;
He will not stand before
[2]unknown *men*.

23

When you sit down to eat
with a ruler,
Consider carefully what *is*
before you;
2 And put a knife to your
throat
If you *are* a man given to
appetite.
3 Do not desire his delicacies,
For they *are* deceptive food.

4 [a]Do not overwork to be rich;
[b]Because of your own
understanding, cease!

13 [a]Prov. 26:13
14 [a]Prov. 2:16; 5:3; 7:5 [b]Eccl. 7:26
15 [a]Prov. 13:24; 23:13, 14
21 [a]Luke 1:3, 4 [b]1 Pet. 3:15 [1]Or *send you*
22 [a]Ex. 23:6
23 [a]1 Sam. 24:12
24 [a]Prov. 29:22
26 [a]Prov. 11:15 [1]Lit. *strikes* [2]*guaranty*
28 [a]Deut. 19:14; 27:17 [1]*boundary*
29 [1]*is prompt in his business* [2]*obscure*

CHAPTER 23

4 [a][1 Tim. 6:9, 10] [b]Rom. 12:16

5 [1]Will you set your eyes on
that which is not?
For *riches* certainly make
themselves wings;
They fly away like an eagle
toward heaven.

6 Do not eat the bread of [a]a[1]
miser,
Nor desire his delicacies;
7 For as he thinks in his heart,
so *is* he.
"Eat and drink!" [a]he says to
you,
But his heart is not with
you.
8 The morsel you have eaten,
you will vomit up,
And waste your pleasant
words.

9 [a]Do not speak in the hearing
of a fool,
For he will despise the
wisdom of your words.

10 Do not remove the ancient
[1]landmark,
Nor enter the fields of the
fatherless;
11 [a]For their Redeemer *is*
mighty;
He will plead their cause
against you.

12 Apply your heart to
instruction,
And your ears to words of
knowledge.

13 [a]Do not withhold correction
from a child,
For *if* you beat him with a
rod, he will not die.
14 You shall beat him with a
rod,
And deliver his soul from
[1]hell.

15 My son, if your heart is
wise,
My heart will rejoice—
indeed, I myself;
16 Yes, my [1]inmost being will
rejoice
When your lips speak right
things.

17 [a]Do not let your heart envy
sinners,
But [b]*be zealous* for the fear
of the LORD all the day;
18 [a]For surely there is a
[1]hereafter,
And your hope will not be
cut off.

19 Hear, my son, and be wise;
And guide your heart in the
way.
20 [a]Do not mix with winebibbers,
Or with gluttonous eaters of
meat;
21 For the drunkard and the
glutton will come to
poverty,
And drowsiness will clothe
a man with rags.

22 [a]Listen to your father who
begot you,
And do not despise your
mother when she is old.

23 [a]Buy the truth, and do not
sell *it*,
Also wisdom and instruction
and understanding.

24 [a]The father of the righteous
will greatly rejoice,
And he who begets a wise
child will delight in him.
25 Let your father and your
mother be glad,
And let her who bore you
rejoice.

---

5 [1]Lit. *Will you cause your eyes to fly upon it and it is not?*
6 [a]Deut. 15:9 [1]Lit. *one who has an evil eye*
7 [a]Prov. 12:2
9 [a]Matt. 7:6
10 [1]*boundary*
11 [a]Prov. 22:23
13 [a]Prov. 13:24
14 [1]Or *Sheol*
16 [1]Lit. *kidneys*
17 [a]Ps. 37:1 [b]Prov. 28:14
18 [a][Ps. 37:37] [1]Future, lit. *latter end*
20 [a]Is. 5:22
22 [a]Prov. 1:8
23 [a][Matt. 13:44]
24 [a]Prov. 10:1

26 My son, give me your heart,
And let your eyes observe
my ways.
27 [a]For a harlot *is* a deep pit,
And a seductress *is* a
narrow well.
28 [a]She also lies in wait as *for* a
victim,
And increases the unfaithful
among men.

29 [a]Who has woe?
Who has sorrow?
Who has contentions?
Who has complaints?
Who has wounds without
cause?
Who [b]has redness of eyes?
30 [a]Those who linger long at the
wine,
Those who go in search of
[b]mixed wine.
31 Do not look on the wine
when it is red,
When it sparkles in the
cup,
When it [1]swirls around
smoothly;
32 At the last it bites like a
serpent,
And stings like a viper.
33 Your eyes will see strange
things,
And your heart will utter
perverse things.
34 Yes, you will be like one
who lies down in the
[1]midst of the sea,
Or like one who lies at the
top of the mast, *saying*:
35 "They[a] have struck me, *but* I
was not hurt;
They have beaten me, but I
did not feel *it*.
When shall [b]I awake, that
I may seek another
drink?"

27 [a]Prov. 22:14
28 [a]Prov. 7:12
29 [a]Is. 5:11, 22 [b]Gen. 49:12
30 [a][Eph. 5:18] [b]Ps. 75:8
31 [1]*goes around*
34 [1]Lit. *heart*
35 [a]Jer. 5:3 [b]Eph. 4:19

CHAPTER 24

1 [a]Ps. 1:1; 37:1
5 [a]Prov. 21:22
6 [a]Luke 14:31
7 [a]Ps. 10:5
8 [a]Rom. 1:30 [1]Lit. *master of evil plots*
10 [a]Heb. 12:3
11 [a]Ps. 82:4

24

Do not be [a]envious of
evil men,
Nor desire to be with them;
2 For their heart devises
violence,
And their lips talk of
troublemaking.

3 Through wisdom a house is
built,
And by understanding it is
established;
4 By knowledge the rooms
are filled
With all precious and
pleasant riches.

5 [a]A wise man *is* strong,
Yes, a man of knowledge
increases strength;
6 [a]For by wise counsel you will
wage your own war,
And in a multitude of
counselors *there is*
safety.

7 [a]Wisdom *is* too lofty for a
fool;
He does not open his mouth
in the gate.

8 He who [a]plots to do evil
Will be called a [1]schemer.
9 The devising of foolishness
is sin,
And the scoffer *is* an
abomination to men.

10 *If* you [a]faint in the day of
adversity,
Your strength *is* small.

11 [a]Deliver *those who* are
drawn toward death,
And hold back *those*
stumbling to the
slaughter.

And a gentle tongue breaks
a bone.

16 Have you found honey?
Eat only as much as you
need,
Lest you be filled with it
and vomit.

17 Seldom set foot in your
neighbor's house,
Lest he become weary of
you and hate you.

18 [a]A man who bears false
witness against his
neighbor
Is like a club, a sword, and a
sharp arrow.

19 Confidence in an unfaithful
man in time of trouble
Is like a bad tooth and a
foot out of joint.

20 *Like* one who takes away a
garment in cold weather,
And like vinegar on soda,
Is one who [a]sings songs to a
heavy heart.

21 [a]If your enemy is hungry,
give him bread to eat;
And if he is thirsty, give him
water to drink;
22 For *so* you will heap coals of
fire on his head,
[a]And the LORD will reward
you.

23 The north wind brings forth
rain,
And [a]a backbiting tongue an
angry countenance.

24 [a]*It is* better to dwell in a
corner of a housetop,
Than in a house shared with
a contentious woman.

25 *As* cold water to a weary
soul,
So *is* [a]good news from a far
country.

26 A righteous *man* who falters
before the wicked
Is like a murky spring and a
[1]polluted well.

27 *It is* not good to eat much
honey;
So [a]to seek one's own glory
is not glory.

28 [a]Whoever *has* no rule over
his own spirit
Is like a city broken down,
without walls.

26

As snow in summer [a]and
rain in harvest,
So honor is not fitting for a
fool.

2 Like a flitting sparrow, like
a flying swallow,
So [a]a curse without cause
shall not alight.

3 [a]A whip for the horse,
A bridle for the donkey,
And a rod for the fool's
back.
4 Do not answer a fool
according to his folly,
Lest you also be like him.
5 [a]Answer a fool according to
his folly,
Lest he be wise in his own
eyes.
6 He who sends a message by
the hand of a fool
Cuts off *his own* feet *and*
drinks violence.

18 [a]Ps. 57:4
20 [a]Dan. 6:18
21 [a]Rom. 12:20
22 [a]2 Sam. 16:12
23 [a]Ps. 101:5
24 [a]Prov. 19:13
25 [a]Prov. 15:30
26 [1]*ruined*
27 [a]Prov. 27:2
28 [a]Prov. 16:32

CHAPTER 26

1 [a]1 Sam. 12:17
2 [a]Deut. 23:5
3 [a]Ps. 32:9
5 [a]Matt. 16:1–4

7 *Like* the legs of the lame
that hang limp
Is a proverb in the mouth of
fools.
8 Like one who binds a stone
in a sling
Is he who gives honor to a
fool.
9 *Like* a thorn *that* goes into
the hand of a drunkard
Is a proverb in the mouth of
fools.
10 [1]The great *God* who formed
everything
Gives the fool *his* hire and
the transgressor *his*
wages.
11 [a]As a dog returns to his own
vomit,
[b]So a fool repeats his folly.
12 [a]Do you see a man wise in
his own eyes?
There is more hope for a
fool than for him.

13 The lazy *man* says, "*There is*
a lion in the road!
A fierce lion *is* in the
[1]streets!"
14 *As* a door turns on its
hinges,
So *does* the lazy *man* on his
bed.
15 The [a]lazy *man* buries his
hand in the [1]bowl;
It wearies him to bring it
back to his mouth.
16 The lazy *man is* wiser in his
own eyes
Than seven men who can
answer sensibly.

17 He who passes by *and*
meddles in a quarrel not
his own
Is like one who takes a dog
by the ears.
18 Like a madman who throws
firebrands, arrows, and
death,
19 *Is* the man *who* deceives his
neighbor,
And says, [a]"I was only
joking!"
20 Where *there is* no wood, the
fire goes out;
And where *there is* no
[1]talebearer, strife ceases.
21 [a]*As* charcoal *is* to burning
coals, and wood to fire,
So *is* a contentious man to
kindle strife.
22 The words of a [1]talebearer
are like [2]tasty trifles,
And they go down into the
[3]inmost body.
23 Fervent lips with a wicked
heart
Are like earthenware
covered with silver
dross.
24 He who hates, disguises *it*
with his lips,
And lays up deceit within
himself;
25 [a]When [1]he speaks kindly, do
not believe him,
For *there are* seven
abominations in his
heart;
26 *Though his* hatred is
covered by deceit,
His wickedness will be
revealed before the
assembly.
27 [a]Whoever digs a pit will fall
into it,
And he who rolls a stone
will have it roll back on
him.

10 [1]Heb. difficult in v. 10; ancient and modern translators differ greatly
11 [a]2 Pet. 2:22 [b]Ex. 8:15
12 [a][Rev. 3:17]
13 [1]Or *plazas, squares*
15 [a]Prov. 19:24 [1]LXX, Syr. *bosom;* Tg., Vg. *armpit*
19 [a]Eph. 5:4
20 [1]gossip or *slanderer,* lit. *whisperer*
21 [a]Prov. 15:18
22 [1]gossip or *slanderer* [2]A Jewish tradition *wounds* [3]Lit. *rooms of the belly*
25 [a]Ps. 28:3 [1]Lit. *his voice is gracious*
27 [a]Ps. 7:15

28 A lying tongue hates *those who are* crushed by it,
And a flattering mouth works [a]ruin.

CHAPTER 27

27 Do[a] not boast about tomorrow,
For you do not know what a day may bring forth.

2 [a]Let another man praise you, and not your own mouth;
A stranger, and not your own lips.

3 A stone *is* heavy and sand *is* weighty,
But a fool's wrath *is* heavier than both of them.

4 Wrath *is* cruel and anger a torrent,
But [a]who *is* able to stand before jealousy?

5 [a]Open rebuke *is* better
Than love carefully concealed.

6 Faithful *are* the wounds of a friend,
But the kisses of an enemy *are* [a]deceitful.

7 A satisfied soul [1]loathes the honeycomb,
But to a hungry soul every bitter thing *is* sweet.

8 Like a bird that wanders from its nest
Is a man who wanders from his place.

9 Ointment and perfume delight the heart,
And the sweetness of a man's friend *gives delight* by [1]hearty counsel.

10 Do not forsake your own friend or your father's friend,
Nor go to your brother's house in the day of your calamity;
[a]Better *is* a neighbor nearby than a brother far away.

11 My son, be wise, and make my heart glad,
[a]That I may answer him who reproaches me.

12 A prudent *man* foresees evil *and* hides himself;
The simple pass on *and* are [a]punished.

13 Take the garment of him who is surety for a stranger,
And hold it in pledge *when* he is surety for a seductress.

14 He who blesses his friend with a loud voice, rising early in the morning,
It will be counted a curse to him.

15 A [a]continual dripping on a very rainy day
And a contentious woman are alike;
16 Whoever [1]restrains her restrains the wind,
And grasps oil with his right hand.

17 *As* iron sharpens iron,
So a man sharpens the countenance of his friend.

28 [a]Prov. 29:5
1 [a]James 4:13–16
2 [a]Prov. 25:27
4 [a]1 John 3:12
5 [a][Prov. 28:23]
6 [a]Matt. 26:49
7 [1]*tramples on*
9 [1]Lit. *counsel of the soul*
10 [a]Prov. 17:17; 18:24
11 [a]Prov. 10:1; 23:15–26
12 [a]Prov. 22:3
15 [a]Prov. 19:13
16 [1]Lit. *hides*

18 [a]Whoever [1]keeps the fig tree
will eat its fruit;
So he who waits on his
master will be honored.

19 As in water face *reflects*
face,
So a man's heart *reveals* the
man.

20 [a]Hell[1] and [2]Destruction are
never full;
So [b]the eyes of man are
never satisfied.

21 [a]The refining pot *is* for silver
and the furnace for gold,
And a man *is valued* by
what others say of him.

22 [a]Though you grind a fool in
a mortar with a pestle
along with crushed
grain,
Yet his foolishness will not
depart from him.

23 Be diligent to know the state
of your [a]flocks,
And attend to your herds;
24 For riches *are* not forever,
Nor does a crown *endure* to
all generations.
25 [a]*When* the hay is removed,
and the tender grass
shows itself,
And the herbs of the
mountains are gathered
in,
26 The lambs *will provide* your
clothing,
And the goats the price of a
field;
27 *You shall have* enough
goats' milk for your
food,
For the food of your
household,
And the nourishment of
your maidservants.

28

The [a]wicked flee when
no one pursues,
But the righteous are bold
as a lion.

2 Because of the transgression
of a land, many *are* its
princes;
But by a man of
understanding *and*
knowledge
Right will be prolonged.

3 [a]A poor man who oppresses
the poor
Is like a driving rain [1]which
leaves no food.

4 [a]Those who forsake the law
praise the wicked,
[b]But such as keep the law
contend with them.

5 [a]Evil men do not understand
justice,
But [b]those who seek the
LORD understand all.

6 Better *is* the poor who walks
in his integrity
Than one perverse *in his*
ways, though he *be*
rich.

7 Whoever keeps the law *is* a
discerning son,
But a companion of gluttons
shames his father.

8 One who increases his
possessions by usury
and extortion
Gathers it for him who will
pity the poor.

18 [a][1 Cor. 3:8; 9:7–13] [1]*protects* or *tends*
20 [a]Hab. 2:5 [b]Eccl. 1:8; 4:8 [1]Or *Sheol* [2]Heb. *Abaddon*
21 [a]Prov. 17:3
22 [a]Jer. 5:3
23 [a]Prov. 24:27
25 [a]Ps. 104:14

CHAPTER 28

1 [a]Ps. 53:5
3 [a]Matt. 18:28 [1]Lit. *and there is no bread*
4 [a]Ps. 49:18 [b]1 Kin. 18:18
5 [a]Ps. 92:6 [b]John 17:17

9 One who turns away his ear
from hearing the law,
[a]Even his prayer *is* an
abomination.

10 [a]Whoever causes the upright
to go astray in an evil
way,
He himself will fall into his
own pit;
[b]But the blameless will
inherit good.

11 The rich man *is* wise in his
own eyes,
But the poor who has
understanding searches
him out.

12 When the righteous rejoice,
there is great [a]glory;
But when the wicked arise,
men [1]hide themselves.

13 [a]He who covers his sins will
not prosper,
But whoever confesses and
forsakes *them* will have
mercy.

14 Happy *is* the man who is
always reverent,
But he who hardens his
heart will fall into
calamity.

15 [a]*Like* a roaring lion and a
charging bear
[b]*Is* a wicked ruler over poor
people.

16 A ruler who lacks
understanding *is* a great
[a]oppressor,
But he who hates
covetousness will
prolong *his* days.

17 [a]A man burdened with
bloodshed will flee into a
pit;
Let no one help him.

18 Whoever walks blamelessly
will be [1]saved,
But *he who is* perverse *in
his* ways will suddenly
fall.

19 [a]He who tills his land will
have plenty of bread,
But he who follows frivolity
will have poverty
enough!

20 A faithful man will abound
with blessings,
[a]But he who hastens to
be rich will not go
unpunished.

21 [a]To [1]show partiality *is* not
good,
[b]Because for a piece of
bread a man will
transgress.

22 A man with an evil eye
hastens after riches,
And does not consider that
[a]poverty will come upon
him.

23 [a]He who rebukes a man
will find more favor
afterward
Than he who flatters with
the tongue.

24 Whoever robs his father or
his mother,
And says, "*It is* no
transgression,"
The same [a]*is* companion to
a destroyer.

9 [a]Prov. 15:8
10 [a]Prov. 26:27 [b][Matt. 6:33]
12 [a]Prov. 11:10; 29:2 [1]Lit. *will be searched for*
13 [a]Ps. 32:3–5
15 [a]1 Pet. 5:8 [b]Matt. 2:16
16 [a]Eccl. 10:16
17 [a]Gen. 9:6
18 [1]*delivered*
19 [a]Prov. 12:11; 20:13
20 [a]1 Tim. 6:9
21 [a]Prov. 18:5 [b]Ezek. 13:19 [1]Lit. *recognize faces*
22 [a]Prov. 21:5
23 [a]Prov. 27:5, 6
24 [a]Prov. 18:9

25 [a]He who is of a proud heart
stirs up strife,
[b]But he who trusts in the
LORD will be prospered.

26 He who [a]trusts in his own
heart is a fool,
But whoever walks wisely
will be delivered.

27 [a]He who gives to the poor
will not lack,
But he who hides his eyes
will have many curses.

28 When the wicked arise,
[a]men hide themselves;
But when they perish, the
righteous increase.

29

1 He[a] who is often
rebuked, *and* hardens
his neck,
Will suddenly be destroyed,
and that without remedy.

2 When the righteous [1]are in
authority, the [a]people
rejoice;
But when a wicked *man*
rules, [b]the people groan.

3 Whoever loves wisdom
makes his father rejoice,
But a companion of harlots
wastes *his* wealth.

4 The king establishes the
land by justice,
But he who receives bribes
overthrows it.

5 A man who [a]flatters his
neighbor
Spreads a net for his feet.

6 By transgression an evil
man is snared,
But the righteous sings and
rejoices.

7 The righteous [a]considers the
cause of the poor,
But the wicked does
not understand *such*
knowledge.

8 Scoffers [a]set a city aflame,
But wise *men* turn away
wrath.

9 *If* a wise man contends with
a foolish man,
[a]Whether *the fool* rages or
laughs, *there is* no peace.

10 [a]The bloodthirsty hate the
blameless,
But the upright seek his
[1]well-being.

11 A fool vents all his [a]feelings,[1]
But a wise *man* holds them
back.

12 If a ruler pays attention to
lies,
All his servants *become*
wicked.

13 The poor *man* and the
oppressor have this in
common:
[a]The LORD gives light to the
eyes of both.

14 The king who judges the
[a]poor with truth,
His throne will be
established forever.

15 The rod and rebuke give
[a]wisdom,
But a child left *to himself*
brings shame to his
mother.

28:25 [a]Prov. 13:10 [b]1 Tim. 6:6
26 [a]Prov. 3:5
27 [a]Deut. 15:7
28 [a]Job 24:4

CHAPTER 29

1 [a]2 Chr. 36:16
2 [a]Prov. 28:12 [b]Esth. 4:3 [1]*become great*
5 [a]Prov. 26:28
7 [a]Job 29:16
8 [a]Prov. 11:11
9 [a]Matt. 11:17
10 [a]1 John 3:12 [1]Lit. *soul* or *life*
11 [a]Prov. 14:33 [1]Lit. *spirit*
13 [a][Matt. 5:45]
14 [a]Is. 11:4
15 [a]Prov. 22:15

16 When the wicked are
multiplied, transgression
increases;
But the righteous will see
their [a]fall.

17 Correct your son, and he
will give you rest;
Yes, he will give delight to
your soul.

18 [a]Where *there is* no
[1]revelation, the people
cast off restraint;
But [b]happy *is* he who keeps
the law.

19 A servant will not be
corrected by mere
words;
For though he understands,
he will not respond.

20 Do you see a man hasty in
his words?
[a]*There is* more hope for a
fool than for him.

21 He who pampers his servant
from childhood
Will have him as a son in
the end.

22 [a]An angry man stirs up
strife,
And a furious man abounds
in transgression.

23 [a]A man's pride will bring
him low,
But the humble in spirit will
retain honor.

24 Whoever is a partner with a
thief hates his own life;
[a]He [1]swears to tell the truth,
but reveals nothing.

16 [a]Ps. 37:34

18 [a]1 Sam. 3:1
[b]John 13:17
[1]*prophetic vision*

20 [a]Prov. 26:12

22 [a]Prov. 26:21

23 [a]Is. 66:2

24 [a]Lev. 5:1
[1]Lit. *hears the adjuration* or *oath*

25 [a]Gen. 12:12; 20:2
[1]*secure*, lit. *set on high*

26 [a]Ps. 20:9
[1]Lit. *face*

CHAPTER 30

2 [a]Ps. 73:22

3 [a][Prov. 9:10]

4 [a][John 3:13]
[b]Job 38:4

5 [a]Ps. 12:6; 19:8; 119:140
[b]Ps. 18:30; 84:11; 115:9–11
[1]*tested, refined, found pure*

6 [a]Deut. 4:2; 12:32

25 [a]The fear of man brings a
snare,
But whoever trusts in the
LORD shall be [1]safe.

26 [a]Many seek the ruler's [1]favor,
But justice for man *comes*
from the LORD.

27 An unjust man *is* an
abomination to the
righteous,
And *he who is* upright in the
way *is* an abomination to
the wicked.

30

The words of Ā′gur the
son of Jā′keh, *his* utterance. This man declared to Ith′-
i·el—to Ith′i·el and Ū′cal:

2 [a]Surely I *am* more stupid
than *any* man,
And do not have the
understanding of a
man.
3 I neither learned wisdom
Nor have [a]knowledge of the
Holy One.

4 [a]Who has ascended into
heaven, or descended?
[b]Who has gathered the wind
in His fists?
Who has bound the waters
in a garment?
Who has established all the
ends of the earth?
What *is* His name, and what
is His Son's name,
If you know?

5 [a]Every word of God *is* [1]pure;
[b]He *is* a shield to those who
put their trust in Him.
6 [a]Do not add to His words,
Lest He rebuke you, and
you be found a liar.

7 Two *things* I request of You
(Deprive me not before I die):
8 Remove falsehood and lies far from me;
Give me neither poverty nor riches—
[a]Feed me with the food allotted to me;
9 [a]Lest I be full and deny *You*,
And say, "Who *is* the LORD?"
Or lest I be poor and steal,
And profane the name of my God.

10 Do not malign a servant to his master,
Lest he curse you, and you be found guilty.

11 *There is* a generation *that* curses its [a]father,
And does not bless its mother.
12 *There is* a generation [a]*that is* pure in its own eyes,
Yet is not washed from its filthiness.
13 *There is* a generation—oh, how [a]lofty are their eyes!
And their eyelids are [1]lifted up.
14 [a]*There is* a generation whose teeth *are like* swords,
And whose fangs *are like* knives,
[b]To devour the poor from off the earth,
And the needy from *among* men.

15 The leech has two daughters—
Give *and* Give!

There are three *things that* are never satisfied,
Four never say, "Enough!":
16 [a]The[1] grave,
The barren womb,
The earth *that* is not satisfied with water—
And the fire never says, "Enough!"

17 [a]The eye *that* mocks *his* father,
And scorns obedience to *his* mother,
The ravens of the valley will pick it out,
And the young eagles will eat it.

18 There are three *things which* are too wonderful for me,
Yes, four *which* I do not understand:
19 The way of an eagle in the air,
The way of a serpent on a rock,
The way of a ship in the [1]midst of the sea,
And the way of a man with a virgin.

20 This *is* the way of an adulterous woman:
She eats and wipes her mouth,
And says, "I have done no wickedness."

21 For three *things* the earth is perturbed,
Yes, for four it cannot bear up:
22 [a]For a servant when he reigns,
A fool when he is filled with food,
23 A [1]hateful *woman* when she is married,

8 [a]Matt. 6:11
9 [a]Deut. 8:12–14
11 [a]Ex. 21:17
12 [a]Luke 18:11
13 [a]Prov. 6:17 [1]In arrogance
14 [a]Job 29:17 [b]Amos 8:4
16 [a]Prov. 27:20 [1]Or *Sheol*
17 [a]Gen. 9:22
19 [1]Lit. *heart*
22 [a]Prov. 19:10
23 [1]Or *hated*

And a maidservant who
succeeds her mistress.

24 There are four *things which*
are little on the earth,
But they *are* exceedingly
wise:
25 [a]The ants *are* a people not
strong,
Yet they prepare their food
in the summer;
26 [a]The [1]rock badgers are a
feeble folk,
Yet they make their homes
in the crags;
27 The locusts have no king,
Yet they all advance in
ranks;
28 The [1]spider skillfully grasps
with its hands,
And it is in kings' palaces.

29 There are three *things
which* are majestic in
pace,
Yes, four *which* are stately
in walk:
30 A lion, *which is* mighty
among beasts
And does not turn away
from any;
31 A [1]greyhound,
A male goat also,
And [2]a king *whose* troops
are with him.

32 If you have been foolish in
exalting yourself,
Or if you have devised evil,
[a]*put your* hand on *your*
mouth.
33 For *as* the churning of milk
produces butter,
And wringing the nose
produces blood,
So the forcing of wrath
produces strife.

31 The words of King Lem'ū·el, the utterance which
his mother taught him:

2 What, my son?
And what, son of my womb?
And what, [a]son of my vows?
3 [a]Do not give your strength to
women,
Nor your ways [b]to that
which destroys kings.

4 [a]*It is* not for kings,
O Lem'ū·el,
It is not for kings to drink
wine,
Nor for princes intoxicating
drink;
5 [a]Lest they drink and forget
the law,
And pervert the justice of all
[1]the afflicted.
6 [a]Give strong drink to him
who is perishing,
And wine to those who are
bitter of heart.
7 Let him drink and forget his
poverty,
And remember his misery
no more.

8 [a]Open your mouth for the
speechless,
In the cause of all *who are*
[1]appointed to die.
9 Open your mouth, [a]judge
righteously,
And [b]plead the cause of the
poor and needy.

10 [a]Who[1] can find a [2]virtuous
wife?
For her worth *is* far above
rubies.
11 The heart of her husband
safely trusts her;
So he will have no lack of
gain.

25 [a]Prov. 6:6
26 [a]Ps. 104:18 [1]*rock hyraxes*
28 [1]Or *lizard*
31 [1]Or perhaps *strutting rooster,* lit. *girded of waist* [2]A Jewish tradition *a king against whom there is no uprising*
32 [a]Mic. 7:16

CHAPTER 31

2 [a]Is. 49:15
3 [a]Prov. 5:9 [b]Deut. 17:17
4 [a]Eccl. 10:17
5 [a]Hos. 4:11 [1]Lit. *sons of affliction*
6 [a]Ps. 104:15
8 [a]Job 29:15, 16 [1]Lit. *sons of passing away*
9 [a]Lev. 19:15 [b]Jer. 22:16
10 [a]Prov. 12:4; 19:14 [1]Vv. 10–31 are an alphabetic acrostic in Hebrew; cf. Ps. 119 [2]Lit. *a wife of valor,* in the sense of all forms of excellence

12 She does him good and not
evil
All the days of her life.
13 She seeks wool and flax,
And willingly works with
her hands.
14 She is like the merchant
ships,
She brings her food from
afar.
15 [a]She also rises while it is yet
night,
And [b]provides food for her
household,
And a portion for her
maidservants.
16 She considers a field and
buys it;
From [1]her profits she plants
a vineyard.
17 She girds herself with
strength,
And strengthens her
arms.
18 She perceives that her
merchandise *is* good,
And her lamp does not go
out by night.
19 She stretches out her hands
to the distaff,
And her hand holds the
spindle.
20 [a]She extends her hand to the
poor,
Yes, she reaches out her
hands to the needy.
21 She is not afraid of snow for
her household,
For all her household *is*
clothed with scarlet.

15 [a]Rom. 12:11 [b]Luke 12:42

16 [1]Lit. *the fruit of her hands*

20 [a]Eph. 4:28

23 [a]Prov. 12:4

22 She makes tapestry for
herself;
Her clothing *is* fine linen
and purple.
23 [a]Her husband is known in
the gates,
When he sits among the
elders of the land.
24 She makes linen garments
and sells *them,*
And supplies sashes for the
merchants.
25 Strength and honor *are* her
clothing;
She shall rejoice in time to
come.
26 She opens her mouth with
wisdom,
And on her tongue *is* the
law of kindness.
27 She watches over the ways
of her household,
And does not eat the bread
of idleness.
28 Her children rise up and call
her blessed;
Her husband *also,* and he
praises her:
29 "Many daughters have done
well,
But you excel them all."
30 Charm *is* deceitful and
beauty *is* passing,
But a woman *who* fears
the LORD, she shall be
praised.
31 Give her of the fruit of her
hands,
And let her own works
praise her in the gates.

The Book of ECCLESIASTES

THE key word in Ecclesiastes is *vanity*, "the futile emptiness of trying to be happy apart from God." The Preacher (traditionally taken to be Solomon—1:1, 12—the wisest, richest, most influential king in Israel's history) looks at life "under the sun" (1:9) and, from the human perspective, declares it all to be empty. Power, popularity, prestige, pleasure—nothing can fill the God-shaped void in man's life but God Himself! But once seen from God's perspective, life takes on meaning and purpose, causing Solomon to exclaim, "Eat . . . drink . . . rejoice . . . do good . . . live joyfully . . . fear God . . . keep His commandments!" Skepticism and despair melt away when life is viewed as a daily gift from God.

The Hebrew title *Qoheleth* is a rare term, found only in Ecclesiastes (1:1, 2, 12; 7:27; 12:8–10). It comes from the word *qahal*, "to convoke an assembly, to assemble." Thus, it means "One Who Addresses an Assembly," "A Preacher." The Septuagint used the Greek word *Ekklesiastes* as its title for this book. Derived from the word *ekklesia*, "assembly," "congregation," "church," it simply means "Preacher." The Latin *Ecclesiastes* means "Speaker Before an Assembly."

THE words of the Preacher, the son of David, [a]king in Jerusalem.

2 "Vanity[a1] of vanities," says
the Preacher;
"Vanity[1] of vanities, [b]all *is*
vanity."

3 [a]What profit has a man from
all his labor
In which he [1]toils under the
sun?

4 *One* generation passes away,
and *another* generation
comes;
[a]But the earth abides forever.

5 [a]The sun also rises, and the
sun goes down,
And [1]hastens to the place
where it arose.

6 [a]The wind goes toward the
south,
And turns around to the
north;
The wind whirls about
continually,
And comes again on its
circuit.

7 [a]All the rivers run into the
sea,
Yet the sea *is* not full;
To the place from which the
rivers come,
There they return again.

8 All things *are* [1]full of labor;
Man cannot express *it*.
[a]The eye is not satisfied with
seeing,
Nor the ear filled with
hearing.

9 [a]That which has been *is* what
will be,
That which *is* done is what
will be done,

CHAPTER 1

1 [a]Prov. 1:1

2 [a]Ps. 39:5, 6; 62:9; 144:4
[b][Rom. 8:20, 21]
[1]Or *Absurdity, Frustration, Futility, Nonsense;* and so throughout the book

3 [a]Eccl. 2:22; 3:9
[1]*labors*

4 [a]Ps. 104:5; 119:90

5 [a]Ps. 19:4–6
[1]Is eager for, lit. *panting*

6 [a]John 3:8

7 [a][Jer. 5:22]

8 [a]Prov. 27:20
[1]*wearisome*

9 [a]Eccl. 3:15

And *there is* nothing new
under the sun.
10 Is there anything of which it
may be said,
"See, this *is* new"?
It has already been in
ancient times before us.
11 *There is* [a]no remembrance
of former *things*,
Nor will there be any
remembrance of *things*
that are to come
By *those* who will come
after.

12 I, the Preacher, was king over
Israel in Jerusalem.
13 And I set my heart to seek
and [a]search out by wisdom concerning all that is done under
heaven; [b]this burdensome task
God has given to the sons of
man, by which they may be
[1]exercised.
14 I have seen all the works that
are done under the sun; and indeed, all *is* vanity and grasping
for the wind.

15 [a]*What is* crooked cannot be
made straight,
And what is lacking cannot
be numbered.

16 I communed with my heart,
saying, "Look, I have attained
greatness, and have gained
[a]more wisdom than all who
were before me in Jerusalem.
My heart has [1]understood great
wisdom and knowledge."
17 [a]And I set my heart to know
wisdom and to know madness
and folly. I perceived that this
also is grasping for the wind.

18 For [a]in much wisdom *is*
much grief,
And he who increases
knowledge increases
sorrow.

2 I said [a]in my heart, "Come
now, I will test you with
[b]mirth;[1] therefore enjoy pleasure"; but surely, [c]this also *was*
vanity.
2 I said of laughter—"Madness!"; and of mirth, "What does
it accomplish?"
3 [a]I searched in my heart *how*
[1]to gratify my flesh with wine,
while guiding my heart with wisdom, and how to lay hold on folly,
till I might see what *was* [b]good
for the sons of men to do under
heaven all the days of their lives.
4 I made my works great, I
built myself [a]houses, and planted
myself vineyards.
5 I made myself gardens and
orchards, and I planted all *kinds*
of fruit trees in them.
6 I made myself water pools
from which to [1]water the growing trees of the grove.
7 I acquired male and female
servants, and had [1]servants born
in my house. Yes, I had greater
possessions of herds and flocks
than all who were in Jerusalem
before me.
8 [a]I also gathered for myself
silver and gold and the special
treasures of kings and of the
provinces. I acquired male and
female singers, the delights of
the sons of men, *and* [1]musical
instruments of all kinds.
9 [a]So I became great and [1]ex-
celled [b]more than all who were
before me in Jerusalem. Also my
wisdom remained with me.

10 Whatever my eyes desired I
did not keep from them.

---

11 [a]Eccl. 2:16
13 [a][Eccl. 7:25; 8:16, 17] [b]Eccl. 3:10 [1]Or *afflicted*
15 [a]Eccl. 7:13
16 [a]1 Kin. 3:12, 13 [1]Lit. *seen*
17 [a]Eccl. 2:3, 12; 7:23, 25
18 [a]Eccl. 12:12

CHAPTER 2

1 [a]Luke 12:19 [b][Eccl. 7:4; 8:15] [c]Eccl. 1:2 [1]*gladness*
3 [a]Eccl. 1:17 [b][Eccl. 3:12, 13; 5:18; 6:12] [1]Lit. *to draw my flesh*
4 [a]1 Kin. 7:1–12
6 [1]*irrigate*
7 [1]Lit. *sons of my house*
8 [a]1 Kin. 9:28; 10:10, 14, 21 [1]Exact meaning unknown
9 [a]Eccl. 1:16 [b]2 Chr. 9:22 [1]Lit. *increased*

I did not withhold my heart
from any pleasure,
For my heart rejoiced in all
my labor;
And [a]this was my [1]reward
from all my labor.
11 Then I looked on all the
works that my hands
had done
And on the labor in which I
had toiled;
And indeed all *was* [a]vanity
and grasping for the
wind.
There was no profit under
the sun.

12 Then I turned myself to
consider wisdom [a]and
madness and folly;
For what *can* the man *do*
who succeeds the king?—
Only what he has already
[b]done.
13 Then I saw that wisdom
[a]excels folly
As light excels darkness.
14 [a]The wise man's eyes *are* in
his head,
But the fool walks in
darkness.
Yet I myself perceived
That [b]the same event
happens to them all.

15 So I said in my heart,
"As it happens to the fool,
It also happens to me,
And why was I then more
wise?"
Then I said in my heart,
"This also *is* vanity."
16 For *there is* [a]no more
remembrance of the wise
than of the fool forever,
Since all that now *is* will be
forgotten in the days to
come.

And how does a wise *man*
die?
As the fool!

17 Therefore I hated life because the work that was done
under the sun *was* distressing to
me, for all *is* vanity and grasping for the wind.
18 Then I hated all my labor in
which I had toiled under the sun,
because [a]I must leave it to the
man who will come after me.
19 And who knows whether he
will be wise or a fool? Yet he will
rule over all my labor in which
I toiled and in which I have
shown myself wise under the
sun. This also *is* vanity.
20 Therefore I turned my heart
and despaired of all the labor
in which I had toiled under the
sun.
21 For there is a man whose labor *is* with wisdom, knowledge,
and skill; yet he must leave his
[1]heritage to a man who has not
labored for it. This also *is* vanity
and a great evil.
22 [a]For what has man for all his
labor, and for the striving of his
heart with which he has toiled
under the sun?
23 For all his days *are* [a]sorrowful,
and his work burdensome; even
in the night his heart takes no
rest. This also is vanity.
24 [a]Nothing *is* better for a man
than that he should eat and drink,
and *that* his soul should enjoy
good in his labor. This also, I saw,
was from the hand of God.
25 For who can eat, or who can
have enjoyment, [1]more than I?
26 For *God* gives [a]wisdom and
knowledge and joy to a man
who *is* good in His sight; but to
the sinner He gives the work of

10 [a]Eccl. 3:22; 5:18; 9:9 [1]Lit. *portion*
11 [a]Eccl. 1:3, 14
12 [a]Eccl. 1:17; 7:25 [b]Eccl. 1:9
13 [a]Eccl. 7:11, 12, 19; 9:18; 10:10
14 [a]Prov. 17:24 [b]Ps. 49:10
16 [a]Eccl. 1:11; 4:16
18 [a]Ps. 49:10
21 [1]Lit. *portion*
22 [a]Eccl. 1:3; 3:9
23 [a]Job 5:7; 14:1
24 [a]Eccl. 3:12, 13, 22
25 [1]So with MT, Tg., Vg.; some Heb. mss., LXX, Syr. *without Him*
26 [a]Prov. 2:6

gathering and collecting, that [b]he may give to *him who is* good before God. This also *is* vanity and grasping for the wind.

CHAPTER 3

3 To everything *there is* a season,
A [a]time for every purpose under heaven:

2 A time [1]to be born,
And [a]a time to die;
A time to plant,
And a time to pluck *what is* planted;
3 A time to kill,
And a time to heal;
A time to break down,
And a time to build up;
4 A time to [a]weep,
And a time to laugh;
A time to mourn,
And a time to dance;
5 A time to cast away stones,
And a time to gather stones;
[a]A time to embrace,
And a time to refrain from embracing;
6 A time to gain,
And a time to lose;
A time to keep,
And a time to throw away;
7 A time to tear,
And a time to sew;
[a]A time to keep silence,
And a time to [b]speak;
8 A time to love,
And a time to [a]hate;
A time of war,
And a time of peace.

9 [a]What profit has the worker
from that in which he labors?
10 [a]I have seen the God-given
task with which the sons of men
are to be occupied.
11 He has made everything
beautiful in its time. Also He has
put eternity in their hearts, except that [a]no one can find out the
work that God does from beginning to end.
12 I know that nothing *is* [a]better
for them than to rejoice, and to
do good in their lives,
13 and also that [a]every man
should eat and drink and enjoy
the good of all his labor—it *is*
the gift of God.

14 I know that whatever God does,
It shall be forever.
[a]Nothing can be added to it,
And nothing taken from it.
God does *it,* that men should fear before Him.
15 [a]That which is has already been,
And what is to be has already been;
And God [1]requires an account of [2]what is past.

16 Moreover [a]I saw under the
sun:

In the place of [1]judgment,
Wickedness *was* there;
And *in* the place of righteousness,
[2]Iniquity *was* there.

17 I said in my heart,

[a]"God shall judge the righteous and the wicked,
For *there is* a time there for every [1]purpose and for every work."

18 I said in my heart, "Concerning the condition of the sons of
men, God tests them, that they

---

26 [b]Prov. 28:8

1 [a]Eccl. 3:17; 8:6

2 [a]Heb. 9:27 [1]Lit. *to bear*

4 [a]Rom. 12:15

5 [a]Joel 2:16

7 [a]Amos 5:13 [b]Prov. 25:11

8 [a]Luke 14:26

9 [a]Eccl. 1:3

10 [a]Eccl. 1:13

11 [a]Rom. 11:33

12 [a]Eccl. 2:3, 24

13 [a]Eccl. 2:24

14 [a]James 1:17

15 [a]Eccl. 1:9 [1]Lit. *seeks* [2]*what is pursued*

16 [a]Eccl. 5:8 [1]*justice* [2]*Wickedness*

17 [a][Rom. 2:6–10] [1]*desire*

may see that they themselves
are *like* animals."
19 [a]For what happens to the
sons of men also happens to
animals; one thing befalls them:
as one dies, so dies the other.
Surely, they all have one breath;
man has no advantage over animals, for all *is* vanity.
20 All go to one place: [a]all are
from the dust, and all return to
dust.
21 [a]Who[1] knows the spirit of
the sons of men, which goes upward, and the spirit of the animal,
which goes down to the earth?
22 [a]So I perceived that nothing
is better than that a man should
rejoice in his own works, for
[b]that *is* his [1]heritage. [c]For who
can bring him to see what will
happen after him?

4 Then I returned and considered all the [a]oppression that
is done under the sun:

And look! The tears of the
oppressed,
But they have no
comforter—
[1]On the side of their
oppressors *there is*
power,
But they have no comforter.
2 [a]Therefore I praised the dead
who were already dead,
More than the living who
are still alive.
3 [a]Yet, better than both *is he*
who has never existed,
Who has not seen the evil
work that is done under
the sun.

4 Again, I saw that for all toil
and every skillful work a man is
envied by his neighbor. This also
is vanity and grasping for the
wind.

5 [a]The fool folds his hands
And consumes his own
flesh.
6 [a]Better a handful *with*
quietness
Than both hands full,
together with toil and
grasping for the wind.

7 Then I returned, and I saw
vanity under the sun:

8 There is one alone, without
[1]companion:
He has neither son nor
brother.
Yet *there is* no end to all his
labors,
Nor is his [a]eye satisfied with
riches.
But [b]*he never asks,*
"For whom do I toil and
deprive myself of
[c]good?"
This also *is* vanity and a
[2]grave misfortune.

9 Two *are* better than one,
Because they have a good
reward for their labor.
10 For if they fall, one will lift
up his companion.
But woe to him *who is* alone
when he falls,
For *he has* no one to help
him up.
11 Again, if two lie down
together, they will keep
warm;
But how can one be warm
alone?
12 Though one may be
overpowered by another,
two can withstand him.

19 [a][Eccl. 2:16]
20 [a]Gen. 3:19
21 [a]Eccl. 12:7 [1]LXX, Syr., Tg., Vg. *Who knows whether the spirit . . . goes upward, and whether . . . goes downward to the earth?*
22 [a]Eccl. 2:24; 5:18 [b]Eccl. 2:10 [c]Eccl. 6:12; 8:7 [1]*portion or lot*

CHAPTER 4

1 [a]Eccl. 3:16; 5:8 [1]Lit. *At the hand*
2 [a]Job 3:17, 18
3 [a]Job 3:11–22
5 [a]Prov. 6:10; 24:33
6 [a]Prov. 15:16, 17; 16:8
8 [a][1 John 2:16] [b]Ps. 39:6 [c]Eccl. 2:18–21 [1]Lit. *a second* [2]Lit. *evil task*

And a threefold cord is not
quickly broken.

13 Better a poor and wise
youth
Than an old and foolish
king who will be
admonished no more.
14 For he comes out of prison
to be king,
Although [1]he was born poor
in his kingdom.
15 I saw all the living who
walk under the sun;
They were with the second
youth who stands in his
place.
16 *There was* no end of all the
people [1]over whom he
was made king;
Yet those who come
afterward will not
rejoice in him.
Surely this also *is* vanity
and grasping for the
wind.

5

Walk [a]prudently when you
go to the house of God; and
draw near to hear rather [b]than
to give the sacrifice of fools, for
they do not know that they do
evil.

2 Do not be [a]rash with your
mouth,
And let not your heart utter
anything hastily before
God.
For God *is* in heaven, and
you on earth;
Therefore let your words [b]be
few.
3 For a dream comes through
much activity,
And [a]a fool's voice *is known*
by *his* many words.

14 [1]The youth

16 [1]Lit. *to all before whom he was to be*

CHAPTER 5

1 [a]Ex. 3:5 [b][1 Sam. 15:22]

2 [a]Prov. 20:25 [b]Matt. 6:7

3 [a]Prov. 10:19

4 [a]Num. 30:2 [b]Ps. 66:13, 14

5 [a]Acts 5:4

6 [a]Prov. 6:2 [b]1 Cor. 11:10 [1]Lit. *voice*

7 [a][Eccl. 12:13]

8 [a]Eccl. 3:16 [b][Ps. 12:5; 58:11; 82:1] [1]*wresting*

4 [a]When you make a vow to
God, do not delay to [b]pay
it;
For *He has* no pleasure in
fools.
Pay what you have vowed—
5 [a]Better not to vow than to
vow and not pay.

6 Do not let your [a]mouth cause
your flesh to sin, [b]nor say before
the messenger *of God* that it *was*
an error. Why should God be angry at your [1]excuse and destroy
the work of your hands?
7 For in the multitude of
dreams and many words *there*
is also vanity. But [a]fear God.
8 If you [a]see the oppression of
the poor, and the violent [1]per-
version of justice and righteousness in a province, do not marvel
at the matter; for [b]high official
watches over high official, and
higher officials are over them.
9 Moreover the profit of the
land is for all; *even* the king is
served from the field.

10 He who loves silver will not
be satisfied with silver;
Nor he who loves
abundance, with
increase.
This also *is* vanity.

11 When goods increase,
They increase who eat them;
So what profit have the
owners
Except to see *them* with
their eyes?

12 The sleep of a laboring man
is sweet,
Whether he eats little or
much;

But the abundance of the
rich will not permit him
to sleep.

13 [a]There is a severe evil *which*
I have seen under the
sun:
Riches kept for their owner
to his hurt.
14 But those riches perish
through [1]misfortune;
When he begets a son, *there*
is nothing in his hand.
15 [a]As he came from his
mother's womb, naked
shall he return,
To go as he came;
And he shall take nothing
from his labor
Which he may carry away
in his hand.

16 And this also *is* a severe
evil—
Just exactly as he came, so
shall he go.
And [a]what profit has he
[b]who has labored for the
wind?
17 All his days [a]he also eats in
darkness,
And *he has* much sorrow
and sickness and anger.

18 Here is what I have seen: [a]*It*
is good and fitting *for one* to eat
and drink, and to enjoy the good
of all his labor in which he toils
under the sun all the days of his
life which God gives him; [b]for it
is his [1]heritage.
19 As for [a]every man to whom
God has given riches and wealth,
and given him power to eat of
it, to receive his [1]heritage and
rejoice in his labor—this *is* the
[b]gift of God.
20 For he will not dwell unduly
on the days of his life, because
God keeps *him* busy with the joy
of his heart.

6

There[a] is an evil which I
have seen under the sun,
and it *is* common among men:
2 A man to whom God has
given riches and wealth and
honor, [a]so that he lacks nothing
for himself of all he desires; [b]yet
God does not give him power
to eat of it, but a foreigner consumes it. This *is* vanity, and it *is*
an evil [1]affliction.
3 If a man begets a hundred
children and lives many years,
so that the days of his years are
many, but his soul is not satisfied with goodness, or [a]indeed
he has no burial, I say *that* [b]a
[1]stillborn child *is* better than
he—
4 for it comes in vanity and departs in darkness, and its name
is covered with darkness.
5 Though it has not seen the
sun or known *anything*, this has
more rest than that man,
6 even if he lives a thousand
years twice—but has not seen
goodness. Do not all go to one
[a]place?

7 [a]All the labor of man *is* for
his mouth,
And yet the soul is not
satisfied.
8 For what more has the wise
man than the fool?
What does the poor man
have,
Who knows *how* to walk
before the living?
9 Better *is* [1]the [a]sight of the
eyes than the wandering
of [2]desire.
This also *is* vanity and
grasping for the wind.

13 [a]Eccl. 6:1, 2
14 [1]Lit. *bad business*
15 [a]1 Tim. 6:7
16 [a]Eccl. 1:3 [b]Prov. 11:29
17 [a]Ps. 127:2
18 [a][1 Tim. 6:17] [b]Eccl. 2:10; 3:22 [1]Lit. *portion*
19 [a][Eccl. 6:2] [b]Eccl. 2:24; 3:13 [1]Lit. *portion*

CHAPTER 6

1 [a]Eccl. 5:13
2 [a]Job 21:10 [b]Luke 12:20 [1]*disease*
3 [a]Is. 14:19, 20 [b]Job 3:16 [1]Or *miscarriage*
6 [a]Eccl. 2:14, 15
7 [a]Prov. 16:26
9 [a]Eccl. 11:9 [1]What the eyes see [2]Lit. *soul*

10 Whatever one is, he has
been named [a]already,
For it is known that he *is*
man;
[b]And he cannot contend with
Him who is mightier
than he.
11 Since there are many things
that increase vanity,
How *is* man the better?

12 For who knows what *is* good
for man in life, [1]all the days of
his [2]vain life which he passes
like [a]a shadow? [b]Who can tell a
man what will happen after him
under the sun?

7 A [a]good name *is* better than
precious ointment,
And the day of death than
the day of one's [b]birth;
2 Better to go to the house of
mourning
Than to go to the house of
feasting,
For that *is* the end of all
men;
And the living will take *it* to
[a]heart.
3 [1]Sorrow *is* better than
laughter,
[a]For by a sad countenance
the heart is made [2]better.
4 The heart of the wise *is* in
the house of mourning,
But the heart of fools *is* in
the house of mirth.

5 [a]*It is* better to [1]hear the
rebuke of the wise
Than for a man to hear the
song of fools.
6 [a]For like the [1]crackling of
thorns under a pot,
So *is* the laughter of the
fool.
This also is vanity.

7 Surely oppression destroys
a wise *man's* reason,
[a]And a bribe [1]debases the
heart.

8 The end of a thing *is* better
than its beginning;
[a]The patient in spirit *is* better
than the proud in spirit.
9 [a]Do not hasten in your spirit
to be angry,
For anger rests in the bosom
of fools.
10 Do not say,
"Why were the former days
better than these?"
For you do not inquire
wisely concerning this.

11 Wisdom *is* good with an
inheritance,
And profitable [a]to those
who see the sun.
12 For wisdom *is* [1]a [a]defense *as*
money *is* a defense,
But the [2]excellence of
knowledge *is that*
wisdom gives [b]life to
those who have it.

13 Consider the work of God;
For [a]who can make straight
what He has made
crooked?
14 [a]In the day of prosperity be
joyful,
But in the day of adversity
consider:
Surely God has appointed
the one [1]as well as the
other,
So that man can find out
nothing *that will come*
after him.

15 I have seen everything in my
days of vanity:

---

10 [a]Eccl. 1:9; 3:15 [b]Job 9:32

12 [a]James 4:14 [b]Eccl. 3:22 [1]Lit. *the number of the days* [2]*futile*

CHAPTER 7

1 [a]Prov. 22:1 [b]Eccl. 4:2

2 [a][Ps. 90:12]

3 [a][2 Cor. 7:10] [1]*Vexation* or *Grief* [2]*well* or *pleasing*

5 [a]Ps. 141:5 [1]*listen to*

6 [a]Eccl. 2:2 [1]Lit. *sound*

7 [a]Ex. 23:8 [1]*destroys*

8 [a]Prov. 14:29

9 [a]James 1:19

11 [a]Eccl. 11:7

12 [a]Eccl. 9:18 [b]Prov. 3:18 [1]A protective shade, lit. *shadow* [2]*advantage* or *profit*

13 [a]Job 12:14

14 [a]Deut. 28:47 [1]*alongside*

[a]There is a just *man*
who perishes in his
righteousness,
And there is a wicked *man*
who prolongs *life* in his
wickedness.

16 [a]Do not be overly righteous,
[b]Nor be overly wise:
Why should you destroy
yourself?
17 Do not be overly wicked,
Nor be foolish:
[a]Why should you die before
your time?
18 *It is* good that you grasp
this,
And also not remove your
hand from the other;
For he who [a]fears God will
[1]escape them all.

19 [a]Wisdom strengthens the
wise
More than ten rulers of the
city.

20 [a]For *there is* not a just man
on earth who does good
And does not sin.

21 Also do not take to heart
everything people say,
Lest you hear your servant
cursing you.
22 For many times, also, your
own heart has known
That even you have cursed
others.

23 All this I have [1]proved by
wisdom.
[a]I said, "I will be wise";
But it *was* far from me.
24 [a]As for that which is far off
and [b]exceedingly deep,
Who can find it out?
25 [a]I applied my heart to know,
To search and seek out
wisdom and the reason
of things,
To know the wickedness of
folly,
Even of foolishness *and*
madness.
26 [a]And I find more bitter than
death
The woman whose heart *is*
snares and nets,
Whose hands *are* fetters.
[1]He who pleases God shall
escape from her,
But the sinner shall be
trapped by her.

27 "Here is what I have found,"
says [a]the Preacher,
"*Adding* one thing to the
other to find out the
reason,
28 Which my soul still seeks
but I cannot find:
[a]One man among a thousand
I have found,
But a woman among all
these I have not found.
29 Truly, this only I have found:
[a]That God made man
upright,
But [b]they have sought out
many schemes."

8

Who *is* like a wise *man*?
And who knows the
interpretation of a thing?
[a]A man's wisdom makes his
face shine,
And [b]the [1]sternness of his
face is changed.

2 I *say*, "Keep the king's commandment [a]for the sake of your
oath to God.
3 [a]"Do not be hasty to go from
his presence. Do not take your

15 [a]Eccl. 8:12–14
16 [a]Prov. 25:16 [b]Rom. 12:3
17 [a]Job 15:32
18 [a]Eccl. 3:14; 5:7; 8:12, 13 [1]Lit. *come forth from all of them*
19 [a]Prov. 21:22
20 [a]1 John 1:8
23 [a]Rom. 1:22 [1]*tested*
24 [a]1 Tim. 6:16 [b]Rom. 11:33
25 [a]Eccl. 1:17
26 [a]Prov. 5:3, 4 [1]Lit. *He who is good before God*
27 [a]Eccl. 1:1, 2
28 [a]Job 33:23
29 [a]Gen. 1:27 [b]Gen. 3:6, 7

CHAPTER 8

1 [a]Acts 6:15 [b]Deut. 28:50 [1]Lit. *strength*
2 [a]1 Chr. 29:24
3 [a]Eccl. 10:4

stand for an evil thing, for he
does whatever pleases him."

4 Where the word of a king *is,*
there is power;
And [a]who may say to him,
"What are you doing?"
5 He who keeps his command
will experience nothing
harmful;
And a wise man's heart
[1]discerns both time and
judgment,
6 Because [a]for every matter
there is a time and
judgment,
Though the misery of man
[1]increases greatly.
7 [a]For he does not know what
will happen;
So who can tell him when it
will occur?
8 [a]No one has power over the
spirit to retain the spirit,
And no one has power in
the day of death.
There is [b]no release from
that war,
And wickedness will not
deliver those who are
given to it.

9 All this I have seen, and applied my heart to every work
that is done under the sun: *There*
is a time in which one man rules
over another to his own hurt.
10 Then I saw the wicked buried, who had come and gone
from the place of holiness, and
they were [a]forgotten[1] in the city
where they had so done. This
also *is* vanity.
11 [a]Because the sentence
against an evil work is not executed speedily, therefore the
heart of the sons of men is fully
set in them to do evil.

4 [a]Job 34:18
5 [1]Lit. *knows*
6 [a]Eccl. 3:1, 17 [1]*is great upon him*
7 [a]Eccl. 6:12
8 [a]Ps. 49:6, 7 [b]Deut. 20:5–8
10 [a]Eccl. 2:16; 9:5 [1]Some Heb. mss., LXX, Vg. *praised*
11 [a]Is. 26:10
12 [a]Is. 65:20 [b][Is. 3:10]
14 [a]Ps. 73:14 [b]Eccl. 2:14; 7:15; 9:1–3
15 [a]Eccl. 2:24
17 [a]Rom. 11:33
CHAPTER 9
1 [a]Eccl. 8:14 [1]Lit. *put*
2 [a]Mal. 3:15

12 [a]Though a sinner does evil
a hundred *times,* and his *days*
are prolonged, yet I surely know
that [b]it will be well with those
who fear God, who fear before
Him.
13 But it will not be well with
the wicked; nor will he prolong
his days, *which are* as a shadow,
because he does not fear before
God.
14 There is a vanity which occurs on earth, that there are
just *men* to whom it [a]happens
according to the work of the
wicked; again, there are wicked
men to whom it happens according to the work of the [b]righteous.
I said that this also *is* vanity.
15 [a]So I commended enjoyment,
because a man has nothing better under the sun than to eat,
drink, and be merry; for this will
remain with him in his labor *all*
the days of his life which God
gives him under the sun.
16 When I applied my heart to
know wisdom and to see the
business that is done on earth,
even though one sees no sleep
day or night,
17 then I saw all the work of
God, that [a]a man cannot find out
the work that is done under the
sun. For though a man labors to
discover *it,* yet he will not find
it; moreover, though a wise *man*
attempts to know *it,* he will not
be able to find *it.*

9 For I [1]considered all this in
my heart, so that I could
declare it all: [a]that the righteous
and the wise and their works
are in the hand of God. People
know neither love nor hatred *by*
anything *they see* before them.
2 [a]All things *come* alike to all:

One event *happens* to the
righteous and the
wicked;
To the [1]good, the clean, and
the unclean;
To him who sacrifices
and him who does not
sacrifice.
As is the good, so *is* the
sinner;
He who takes an oath as *he*
who fears an oath.

3 This *is* an evil in all that is
done under the sun: that one
thing *happens* to all. Truly the
hearts of the sons of men are
full of evil; madness *is* in their
hearts while they live, and after
that *they go* to the dead.
4 But for him who is joined to
all the living there is hope, for a
living dog is better than a dead
lion.

5 For the living know that
they will die;
But [a]the dead know nothing,
And they have no more
reward,
For [b]the memory of them is
forgotten.
6 Also their love, their hatred,
and their envy have now
perished;
Nevermore will they have a
share
In anything done under the
sun.

7 Go, [a]eat your bread with joy,
And drink your wine with a
merry heart;
For God has already
accepted your works.
8 Let your garments always
be white,
And let your head lack no
oil.

9 [1]Live joyfully with the wife
whom you love all the days of
your vain life which He has
given you under the sun, all
your days of vanity; [a]for that *is*
your portion in life, and in the
labor which you perform under
the sun.
10 [a]Whatever your hand finds
to do, do *it* with your [b]might;
for *there is* no work or device
or knowledge or wisdom in the
grave where you are going.
11 I returned [a]and saw under
the sun that—

The race *is* not to the swift,
Nor the battle to the strong,
Nor bread to the wise,
Nor riches to men of
understanding,
Nor favor to men of skill;
But time and [b]chance
happen to them all.
12 For [a]man also does not
know his time:
Like fish taken in a cruel
net,
Like birds caught in a snare,
So the sons of men *are*
[b]snared in an evil time,
When it falls suddenly upon
them.

13 This wisdom I have also seen
under the sun, and it *seemed*
great to me:
14 [a]*There was* a little city with
few men in it; and a great king
came against it, besieged it, and
built great [1]snares around it.
15 Now there was found in it
a poor wise man, and he by his
wisdom delivered the city. Yet no

2 [1]LXX, Syr., Vg. *good and bad,*
5 [a]Is. 63:16 [b]Is. 26:14
7 [a]Eccl. 8:15
9 [a]Eccl. 2:10 [1]Lit. *See life*
10 [a][Col. 3:17] [b]Rom. 12:11
11 [a]Amos 2:14, 15 [b]1 Sam. 6:9
12 [a]Eccl. 8:7 [b]Prov. 29:6
14 [a]2 Sam. 20:16–22 [1]LXX, Syr., Vg. *bulwarks*

one remembered that same poor man.
16 Then I said:
"Wisdom *is* better than [a]strength.
Nevertheless [b]the poor man's wisdom *is* despised,
And his words are not heard.
17 Words of the wise, *spoken* quietly, *should be* heard
Rather than the shout of a ruler of fools.
18 Wisdom *is* better than weapons of war;
But [a]one sinner destroys much good."

10 Dead[1] flies [2]putrefy the perfumer's ointment,
And cause it to give off a foul odor;
So does a little folly to one respected for wisdom *and* honor.
2 A wise man's heart *is* at his right hand,
But a fool's heart at his left.
3 Even when a fool walks along the way,
He lacks wisdom,
[a]And he shows everyone *that* he *is* a fool.
4 If the spirit of the ruler rises against you,
[a]Do not leave your post;
For [b]conciliation[1] pacifies great offenses.

5 There is an evil I have seen under the sun,
As an error proceeding from the ruler:
6 [a]Folly is set in [1]great dignity,
While the rich sit in a lowly place.
7 I have seen servants [a]on horses,
While princes walk on the ground like servants.
8 [a]He who digs a pit will fall into it,
And whoever breaks through a wall will be bitten by a serpent.
9 He who quarries stones may be hurt by them,
And he who splits wood may be endangered by it.
10 If the ax is dull,
And one does not sharpen the edge,
Then he must use more strength;
But wisdom [1]brings success.

11 A serpent may bite [a]when *it is* not charmed;
The [1]babbler is no different.
12 [a]The words of a wise man's mouth *are* gracious,
But [b]the lips of a fool shall swallow him up;
13 The words of his mouth begin with foolishness,
And the end of his talk *is* raving madness.
14 [a]A fool also multiplies words.
No man knows what is to be;
Who can tell him [b]what will be after him?
15 The labor of fools wearies them,
For they do not even know how to go to the city!

16 [a]Woe to you, O land, when your king *is* a child,
And your princes feast in the morning!
17 Blessed *are* you, O land, when your king *is* the son of nobles,

16 [a]Eccl. 7:12, 19 [b]Mark 6:2, 3
18 [a]Josh. 7:1–26

CHAPTER 10

1 [1]Lit. *Flies of death* [2]Tg., Vg. omit *putrefy*
3 [a]Prov. 13:16; 18:2
4 [a]Eccl. 8:3 [b]1 Sam. 25:24–33 [1]Lit. *healing, health*
6 [a]Esth. 3:1 [1]*exalted positions*
7 [a]Prov. 19:10; 30:22
8 [a]Prov. 26:27
10 [1]Lit. *is a successful advantage*
11 [a]Jer. 8:17 [1]Lit. *master of the tongue*
12 [a]Prov. 10:32 [b]Prov. 10:14
14 [a][Prov. 15:2] [b]Eccl. 3:22; 8:7
16 [a]Is. 3:4, 5; 5:11

And your [a]princes feast at
the proper time—
For strength and not for
drunkenness!
18 Because of laziness the
[1]building decays,
And [a]through idleness of
hands the house leaks.
19 A feast is made for laughter,
And [a]wine makes merry;
But money answers
everything.

20 [a]Do not curse the king, even
in your thought;
Do not curse the rich, even
in your bedroom;
For a bird of the air may
carry your voice,
And a bird in flight may tell
the matter.

11 Cast your bread [a]upon
the waters,
[b]For you will find it after
many days.
2 [a]Give a serving [b]to seven,
and also to eight,
[c]For you do not know what
evil will be on the earth.
3 If the clouds are full of rain,
They empty *themselves*
upon the earth;
And if a tree falls to the
south or the north,
In the place where the tree
falls, there it shall lie.
4 He who observes the wind
will not sow,
And he who regards the
clouds will not reap.

5 As [a]you do not know what *is*
the way of the [1]wind,
[b]*Or* how the bones *grow* in
the womb of her who is
with child,
So you do not know the
works of God who
makes everything.
6 In the morning sow your
seed,
And in the evening do not
withhold your hand;
For you do not know which
will prosper,
Either this or that,
Or whether both alike *will
be* good.

7 Truly the light is sweet,
And *it is* pleasant for the
eyes [a]to behold the sun;
8 But if a man lives many
years
And [a]rejoices in them all,
Yet let him [b]remember the
days of darkness,
For they will be many.
All that is coming *is* vanity.

9 Rejoice, O young man, in
your youth,
And let your heart cheer
you in the days of your
youth;
[a]Walk in the [1]ways of your
heart,
And [2]in the sight of your
eyes;
But know that for all these
[b]God will bring you into
judgment.
10 Therefore remove [1]sorrow
from your heart,
And [a]put away evil from
your flesh,
[b]For childhood and [2]youth
are vanity.

12 Remember[a] now your
Creator in the days of
your youth,
Before the [1]difficult days
come,

17 [a]Prov. 31:4
18 [a]Prov. 24:30–34 [1]Lit. *rafters sink*
19 [a]Ps. 104:15
20 [a]Acts 23:5

CHAPTER 11

1 [a]Is. 32:20 [b][Deut. 15:10]
2 [a][1 Tim. 6:18, 19] [b]Mic. 5:5 [c]Eph. 5:16
5 [a]John 3:8 [b]Ps. 139:14 [1]Or *spirit*
7 [a]Eccl. 7:11
8 [a]Eccl. 9:7 [b]Eccl. 12:1
9 [a]Num. 15:39 [b]Eccl. 3:17; 12:14 [1]Impulses [2]As you see to be best
10 [a]2 Cor. 7:1 [b]Ps. 39:5 [1]*vexation* [2]Prime of life

CHAPTER 12

1 [a]Lam. 3:27 [1]Lit. *evil*

And the years draw near
[b]when you say,
"I have no pleasure in them":
2 While the sun and the light,
The moon and the stars,
Are not darkened,
And the clouds do not
return after the rain;
3 In the day when the keepers
of the house tremble,
And the strong men bow
down;
When the grinders cease
because they are few,
And those that look through
the windows grow dim;
4 When the doors are shut in
the streets,
And the sound of grinding
is low;
When one rises up at the
sound of a bird,
And all [a]the daughters of
music are brought low.
5 Also they are afraid of
height,
And of terrors in the way;
When the almond tree
blossoms,
The grasshopper is a
burden,
And desire fails.
For man goes to [a]his eternal
home,
And [b]the mourners go about
the streets.

6 *Remember your Creator*
before the silver cord is
[1]loosed,
Or the golden bowl is
broken,
Or the pitcher shattered at
the fountain,
Or the wheel broken at the
well.
7 [a]Then the dust will return to
the earth as it was,
[b]And the spirit will return to
God [c]who gave it.

8 "Vanity[a] of vanities," says the
Preacher,
"All *is* vanity."

9 And moreover, because
the Preacher was wise, he still
taught the people knowledge;
yes, he pondered and sought out
and [a]set[1] in order many proverbs.
10 The Preacher sought to find
[1]acceptable words; and *what*
was written *was* upright—words
of truth.
11 The words of the wise are
like goads, and the words of
[1]scholars are like well-driven
nails, given by one Shepherd.
12 And further, my son, be admonished by these. Of making
many books *there is* no end, and
[a]much study *is* wearisome to the
flesh.
13 Let us hear the conclusion of
the whole matter:

[a]Fear God and keep His
commandments,
For this is man's all.
14 For [a]God will bring every
work into judgment,
Including every secret thing,
Whether good or evil.

1 [b]2 Sam. 19:35
4 [a]2 Sam. 19:35
5 [a]Job 17:13 [b]Jer. 9:17
6 [1]So with Qr., Tg.; Kt. *removed;* LXX, Vg. *broken*
7 [a]Gen. 3:19 [b]Eccl. 3:21 [c]Job 34:14
8 [a]Ps. 62:9
9 [a]1 Kin. 4:32 [1]*arranged*
10 [1]Lit. *delightful*
11 [1]Lit. *masters of assemblies*
12 [a]Eccl. 1:18
13 [a][Deut. 6:2; 10:12]
14 [a]Matt. 12:36

The SONG OF SOLOMON

THE Song of Solomon is a love song written by Solomon and abounding in metaphors and oriental imagery. Historically, it depicts the wooing and wedding of a shepherdess by King Solomon, and the joys and heartaches of wedded love.

Allegorically, it pictures Israel as God's betrothed bride (Hos. 2:19, 20), and the church as the bride of Christ. As human life finds its highest fulfillment in the love of man and woman, so spiritual life finds its highest fulfillment in the love of God for His people and Christ for His church.

The book is arranged like scenes in a drama with three main speakers: the bride (Shulamite), the king (Solomon), and a chorus (daughters of Jerusalem).

The Hebrew title *Shir Hashirim* comes from 1:1, "The song of songs." This is in the superlative and speaks of Solomon's most exquisite song. The Greek title *Asma Asmaton* and the Latin *Canticum Canticorum* also mean "Song of Songs" or "The Best Song." The name *Canticles* ("Songs") is derived from the Latin title. Because Solomon is mentioned in 1:1, the book is also known as the Song of Solomon.

CHAPTER 1

THE [a]song of songs, which *is*
Solomon's.

THE [1]SHULAMITE

2 Let him kiss me with the
kisses of his mouth—
[a]For [1]your love *is* better than
wine.
3 Because of the fragrance of
your good ointments,
Your name *is* ointment
poured forth;
Therefore the virgins love
you.
4 [a]Draw me away!

THE DAUGHTERS OF JERUSALEM

[b]We will run after [1]you.

THE SHULAMITE

The king [c]has brought me
into his chambers.

THE DAUGHTERS OF JERUSALEM

We will be glad and rejoice
in [2]you.
We will remember [1]your
love more than wine.

THE SHULAMITE

Rightly do they love [1]you.

5 I *am* dark, but lovely,
O daughters of Jerusalem,
Like the tents of Kē'dar,
Like the curtains of
Solomon.
6 Do not look upon me,
because I *am* dark,
Because the sun has
[1]tanned me.
My mother's sons were
angry with me;
They made me the keeper of
the vineyards,
But my own [a]vineyard I
have not kept.

(TO HER BELOVED)

7 Tell me, O you whom I love,
Where you feed *your flock*,

1 [a]1 Kin. 4:32 [1]A young woman from the town of Shulam or Shunem, Song 6:13. The speaker and audience are identified according to the number, gender, and person of the Hebrew words. Occasionally the identity is not certain.

2 [a]Song 4:10 [1]Masc. sing.: the Beloved

4 [a]Hos. 11:4 [b]Phil. 3:12–14 [c]Ps. 45:14, 15 [1]Masc. sing.: the Beloved [2]Fem. sing.: the Shulamite

6 [a]Song 8:11, 12 [1]Lit. *looked upon me*

Where you make *it* rest at noon.
For why should I be as one who [1]veils herself
By the flocks of your companions?

THE BELOVED

8 If you do not know,
[a]O fairest among women,
[1]Follow in the footsteps of the flock,
And feed your little goats
Beside the shepherds' tents.

9 I have compared you, [a]my love,
[b]To my filly among Pharaoh's chariots.

10 [a]Your cheeks are lovely with ornaments,
Your neck with chains *of gold.*

THE DAUGHTERS OF JERUSALEM

11 We will make [1]you ornaments of gold
With studs of silver.

THE SHULAMITE

12 While the king *is* at his table,
My [1]spikenard sends forth its fragrance.

13 A bundle of myrrh *is* my beloved to me,
That lies all night between my breasts.

14 My beloved *is* to me a cluster of henna *blooms*
In the vineyards of En Ge′di.

THE BELOVED

15 [a]Behold, you *are* fair, [1]my love!
Behold, you *are* fair!
You *have* dove's eyes.

THE SHULAMITE

16 Behold, you *are* [a]handsome, my beloved!
Yes, pleasant!
Also our [1]bed *is* green.

17 The beams of our houses *are* cedar,
And our rafters of fir.

2 I *am* the rose of Sharon,
And the lily of the valleys.

THE BELOVED

2 Like a lily among thorns,
So is my love among the daughters.

THE SHULAMITE

3 Like an apple tree among the trees of the woods,
So *is* my beloved among the sons.
I sat down in his shade with great delight,
And [a]his fruit *was* sweet to my taste.

THE SHULAMITE TO THE DAUGHTERS OF JERUSALEM

4 He brought me to the [1]banqueting house,
And his banner over me *was* love.

5 Sustain me with cakes of raisins,
Refresh me with apples,
For I *am* lovesick.

6 [a]His left hand *is* under my head,
And his right hand embraces me.

7 [a]I [1]charge you, O daughters of Jerusalem,
By the gazelles or by the does of the field,

---

7 [1]LXX, Syr., Vg. *wanders*
8 [a]Song 5:9 [1]Lit. *Go out*
9 [a]Song 2:2, 10, 13; 4:1, 7 [b]2 Chr. 1:16
10 [a]Ezek. 16:11
11 [1]Fem. sing.: the Shulamite
12 [1]*perfume*
15 [a]Song 4:1; 5:12 [1]*my companion, friend*
16 [a]Song 5:10–16 [1]*couch*

CHAPTER 2

3 [a]Rev. 22:1, 2
4 [1]Lit. *house of wine*
6 [a]Song 8:3
7 [a]Song 3:5; 8:4 [1]*adjure*

Do not stir up nor awaken love
Until it pleases.

THE SHULAMITE

8 The voice of my beloved!
Behold, he comes
Leaping upon the mountains,
Skipping upon the hills.
9 [a]My beloved is like a gazelle or a young stag.
Behold, he stands behind our wall;
He is looking through the windows,
Gazing through the lattice.

10 My beloved spoke, and said to me:
"Rise up, my love, my fair one,
And come away.
11 For lo, the winter is past,
The rain is over *and* gone.
12 The flowers appear on the earth;
The time of singing has come,
And the voice of the turtledove
Is heard in our land.
13 The fig tree puts forth her green figs,
And the vines *with* the tender grapes
Give a *good* smell.
Rise up, my love, my fair one,
And come away!

14 "O my [a]dove, in the clefts of the rock,
In the secret *places* of the cliff,
Let me see your [1]face,
[b]Let me hear your voice;
For your voice *is* sweet,
And your face *is* lovely."

HER BROTHERS

15 Catch us [a]the foxes,
The little foxes that spoil the vines,
For our vines *have* tender grapes.

THE SHULAMITE

16 [a]My beloved *is* mine, and I *am* his.
He feeds *his flock* among the lilies.

(TO HER BELOVED)

17 [a]Until the day breaks
And the shadows flee away,
Turn, my beloved,
And be [b]like a gazelle
Or a young stag
Upon the mountains of [1]Bē′ther.

THE SHULAMITE

3 By [a]night on my bed I sought the one I love;
I sought him, but I did not find him.
2 "I will rise now," *I said,*
"And go about the city;
In the streets and in the squares
I will seek the one I love."
I sought him, but I did not find him.
3 [a]The watchmen who go about the city found me;
I said,
"Have you seen the one I love?"

4 Scarcely had I passed by them,
When I found the one I love.
I held him and would not let him go,
Until I had brought him to the [a]house of my mother,

9 [a]Song 2:17
14 [a]Song 5:2 [b]Song 8:13 [1]Lit. *appearance*
15 [a]Ezek. 13:4
16 [a]Song 6:3
17 [a]Song 4:6 [b]Song 8:14 [1]Lit. *Separation*

CHAPTER 3

1 [a]Is. 26:9
3 [a]Song 5:7
4 [a]Song 8:2

And into the [1]chamber of
her who conceived me.

5 [a]I [1]charge you, O daughters
of Jerusalem,
By the gazelles or by the
does of the field,
Do not stir up nor awaken
love
Until it pleases.

THE SHULAMITE

6 [a]Who *is* this coming out of
the wilderness
Like pillars of smoke,
Perfumed with myrrh and
frankincense,
With all the merchant's
fragrant powders?
7 Behold, it *is* Solomon's
couch,
With sixty valiant men
around it,
Of the valiant of Israel.
8 They all hold swords,
Being expert in war.
Every man *has* his sword on
his thigh
Because of fear in the night.

9 Of the wood of Lebanon
Solomon the King
Made himself a [1]palanquin:
10 He made its pillars *of* silver,
Its support *of* gold,
Its seat *of* purple,
Its interior paved *with* love
By the daughters of
Jerusalem.
11 Go forth, O daughters of
Zion,
And see King Solomon with
the crown
With which his mother
crowned him
On the day of his wedding,
The day of the gladness of
his heart.

4 [1]*room*

5 [a]Song 2:7; 8:4
[1]*adjure*

6 [a]Song 8:5

9 [1]A portable enclosed chair

CHAPTER 4

1 [a]Song 1:15; 5:12
[b]Song 6:5

2 [a]Song 6:6
[1]*bereaved*

3 [a]Song 6:7

4 [a]Song 7:4
[b]Neh. 3:19
[1]Small shields

5 [a]Song 7:3

6 [a]Song 2:17

7 [a]Eph. 5:27

THE BELOVED

4 Behold, [a]you *are* fair, my
love!
Behold, you *are* fair!
You *have* dove's eyes behind
your veil.
Your hair *is* like a [b]flock of
goats,
Going down from Mount
Gil′ē·ad.
2 [a]Your teeth *are* like a flock of
shorn *sheep*
Which have come up from
the washing,
Every one of which bears
twins,
And none *is* [1]barren among
them.
3 Your lips *are* like a strand of
scarlet,
And your mouth is lovely.
[a]Your temples behind your
veil
Are like a piece of
pomegranate.
4 [a]Your neck *is* like the tower
of David,
Built [b]for an armory,
On which hang a thousand
[1]bucklers,
All shields of mighty men.
5 [a]Your two breasts *are* like
two fawns,
Twins of a gazelle,
Which feed among the lilies.

6 [a]Until the day breaks
And the shadows flee away,
I will go my way to the
mountain of myrrh
And to the hill of
frankincense.

7 [a]You *are* all fair, my love,
And *there is* no spot in you.
8 Come with me from
Lebanon, *my* spouse,

With me from Lebanon.
Look from the top of A·ma′na,
From the top of Sē′nir [a]and Her′mon,
From the lions' dens,
From the mountains of the leopards.

9 You have ravished my heart,
My sister, *my* spouse;
You have ravished my heart
With one *look* of your eyes,
With one link of your necklace.
10 How fair is your love,
My sister, *my* spouse!
[a]How much better than wine is your love,
And the [1]scent of your perfumes
Than all spices!
11 Your lips, O *my* spouse,
Drip as the honeycomb;
[a]Honey and milk *are* under your tongue;
And the fragrance of your garments
Is [b]like the fragrance of Lebanon.

12 A garden [1]enclosed
Is my sister, *my* spouse,
A spring shut up,
A fountain sealed.
13 Your plants *are* an orchard of pomegranates
With pleasant fruits,
Fragrant henna with spikenard,
14 Spikenard and saffron,
Calamus and cinnamon,
With all trees of frankincense,
Myrrh and aloes,
With all the chief spices—

8 [a]Deut. 3:9

10 [a]Song 1:2, 4 [1]*fragrance*

11 [a]Prov. 24:13, 14 [b]Hos. 14:6, 7

12 [1]*locked* or *barred*

15 [a]Zech. 14:8

16 [a]Song 5:1 [b]Song 7:13

CHAPTER 5

1 [a]Song 4:16 [b]Song 4:9 [c]Song 4:11 [d]Luke 15:7, 10

2 [a]Rev. 3:20 [1]*my companion, friend* [2]*curls* or *hair*

3 [1]*dirty*

15 A fountain of gardens,
A well of [a]living waters,
And streams from Lebanon.

THE SHULAMITE

16 Awake, O north *wind*,
And come, O south!
Blow upon my garden,
That its spices may flow out.
[a]Let my beloved come to his garden
And eat its pleasant [b]fruits.

THE BELOVED

5 I [a]have come to my garden, my [b]sister, *my* spouse;
I have gathered my myrrh with my spice;
[c]I have eaten my honeycomb with my honey;
I have drunk my wine with my milk.

(TO HIS FRIENDS)

Eat, O [d]friends!
Drink, yes, drink deeply,
O beloved ones!

THE SHULAMITE

2 I sleep, but my heart is awake;
It is the voice of my beloved!
[a]He knocks, *saying*,
"Open for me, my sister, [1]my love,
My dove, my perfect one;
For my head is covered with dew,
My [2]locks with the drops of the night."

3 I have taken off my robe;
How can I put it on *again*?
I have washed my feet;
How can I [1]defile them?
4 My beloved put his hand

By the [1]latch *of the door,*
And my heart yearned for him.
5 I arose to open for my beloved,
And my hands dripped *with* myrrh,
My fingers with liquid myrrh,
On the handles of the lock.

6 I opened for my beloved,
But my beloved had turned away *and* was gone.
My [1]heart leaped up when he spoke.
[a]I sought him, but I could not find him;
I called him, but he gave me no answer.
7 [a]The watchmen who went about the city found me.
They struck me, they wounded me;
The keepers of the walls
Took my veil away from me.
8 I charge you, O daughters of Jerusalem,
If you find my beloved,
That you tell him I *am* lovesick!

THE DAUGHTERS OF JERUSALEM

9 What *is* your beloved
More than *another* beloved,
[a]O fairest among women?
What *is* your beloved
More than *another* beloved,
That you so [1]charge us?

THE SHULAMITE

10 My beloved *is* white and ruddy,
[1]Chief among ten thousand.
11 His head *is like* the finest gold;
His locks *are* wavy,
And black as a raven.

4 [1]*opening*

6 [a]Song 3:1 [1]Lit. *soul*

7 [a]Song 3:3

9 [a]Song 1:8; 6:1 [1]*adjure*

10 [1]*Distinguished*

12 [a]Song 1:15; 4:1 [1]*sitting in a setting*

CHAPTER 6

1 [a]Song 1:8; 5:9

2 [a]Song 4:16; 5:1

3 [a]Song 2:16; 7:10

12 [a]His eyes *are* like doves
By the rivers of waters,
Washed with milk,
And [1]fitly set.
13 His cheeks *are* like a bed of spices,
Banks of scented herbs.
His lips *are* lilies,
Dripping liquid myrrh.

14 His hands *are* rods of gold
Set with beryl.
His body *is* carved ivory
Inlaid *with* sapphires.
15 His legs *are* pillars of marble
Set on bases of fine gold.
His countenance *is* like Lebanon,
Excellent as the cedars.
16 His mouth *is* most sweet,
Yes, he *is* altogether lovely.
This *is* my beloved,
And this *is* my friend,
O daughters of Jerusalem!

THE DAUGHTERS OF JERUSALEM

6 Where has your beloved gone,
[a]O fairest among women?
Where has your beloved turned aside,
That we may seek him with you?

THE SHULAMITE

2 My beloved has gone to his [a]garden,
To the beds of spices,
To feed *his flock* in the gardens,
And to gather lilies.
3 [a]I *am* my beloved's,
And my beloved *is* mine.
He feeds *his flock* among the lilies.

THE BELOVED

4 O my love, you *are as*
beautiful as Tir′zah,
Lovely as Jerusalem,
Awesome as *an army* with
banners!
5 Turn your eyes away
from me,
For they have [1]overcome me.
Your hair *is* [a]like a flock of
goats
Going down from Gil′ē·ad.
6 [a]Your teeth *are* like a flock of
sheep
Which have come up from
the washing;
Every one bears twins,
And none *is* [1]barren among
them.
7 [a]Like a piece of pomegranate
Are your temples behind
your veil.

8 There are sixty queens
And eighty concubines,
And [a]virgins without number.
9 My dove, my [a]perfect one,
Is the only one,
The only one of her mother,
The favorite of the one who
bore her.
The daughters saw her
And called her blessed,
The queens and the
concubines,
And they praised her.

10 Who is she who looks forth
as the morning,
Fair as the moon,
Clear as the sun,
[a]Awesome as *an army* with
banners?

THE SHULAMITE

11 I went down to the garden
of nuts
To see the verdure of the
valley,
[a]To see whether the vine had
budded
And the pomegranates had
bloomed.
12 Before I was even aware,
My soul had made me
As the chariots of [1]my noble
people.

THE BELOVED AND HIS FRIENDS

13 Return, return,
O Shū′lam·īte;
Return, return, that we may
look upon you!

THE SHULAMITE

What would you see in the
Shū′lam·īte—
As it were, the dance of [1]the
two camps?

THE BELOVED

7 How beautiful are your feet
in sandals,
[a]O prince's daughter!
The curves of your thighs
are like jewels,
The work of the hands of a
skillful workman.
2 Your navel *is* a rounded
goblet;
It lacks no [1]blended
beverage.
Your waist *is* a heap of
wheat
Set about with lilies.
3 [a]Your two breasts *are* like
two fawns,
Twins of a gazelle.
4 [a]Your neck *is* like an ivory
tower,
Your eyes *like* the pools in
Hesh′bon
By the gate of Bath Rab′bim.
Your nose *is* like the tower
of Lebanon

5 [a]Song 4:1 [1]*overwhelmed*
6 [a]Song 4:2 [1]*bereaved*
7 [a]Song 4:3
8 [a]Song 1:3
9 [a]Song 2:14; 5:2
10 [a]Song 6:4
11 [a]Song 7:12
12 [1]Heb. *Ammi Nadib*
13 [1]Heb. *Mahanaim*

CHAPTER 7

1 [a]Ps. 45:13
2 [1]Lit. *mixed* or *spiced drink*
3 [a]Song 4:5
4 [a]Song 4:4

Which looks toward
Damascus.
5 Your head *crowns* you like
Mount Car′mel,
And the hair of your head *is*
like purple;
A king *is* held captive by
your tresses.

6 How fair and how pleasant
you are,
O love, with your delights!
7 This stature of yours is like
a palm tree,
And your breasts *like* its
clusters.
8 I said, "I will go up to the
palm tree,
I will take hold of its
branches."
Let now your breasts be like
clusters of the vine,
The fragrance of your
[1]breath like apples,
9 And the roof of your mouth
like the best wine.

THE SHULAMITE

The wine goes *down*
smoothly for my
beloved,
[1]Moving gently the [2]lips of
sleepers.
10 [a]I *am* my beloved's,
And [b]his desire *is* toward
me.

11 Come, my beloved,
Let us go forth to the field;
Let us lodge in the villages.
12 Let us get up early to the
vineyards;
Let us [a]see if the vine has
budded,
Whether the grape blossoms
are open,
And the pomegranates are
in bloom.
There I will give you my
love.
13 The [a]mandrakes give off a
fragrance,
And at our gates [b]*are*
pleasant *fruits*,
All manner, new and old,
Which I have laid up for
you, my beloved.

8 Oh, that you were like my
brother,
Who nursed at my mother's
breasts!
If I should find you outside,
I would kiss you;
I would not be despised.
2 I would lead you *and* bring
you
Into the [a]house of my
mother,
She *who* used to instruct
me.
I would cause you to drink
of [b]spiced wine,
Of the juice of my
pomegranate.

(TO THE DAUGHTERS OF JERUSALEM)

3 [a]His left hand *is* under my
head,
And his right hand
embraces me.
4 [a]I charge you, O daughters of
Jerusalem,
Do not stir up nor awaken
love
Until it pleases.

A RELATIVE

5 [a]Who *is* this coming up from
the wilderness,
Leaning upon her beloved?

I awakened you under the
apple tree.
There your mother brought
you forth;

8 [1]Lit. *nose*
9 [1]*Gliding over* [2]LXX, Syr., Vg. *lips and teeth.*
10 [a]Song 2:16; 6:3 [b]Ps. 45:11
12 [a]Song 6:11
13 [a]Gen. 30:14 [b]Matt. 13:52

CHAPTER 8

2 [a]Song 3:4 [b]Prov. 9:2
3 [a]Song 2:6
4 [a]Song 2:7; 3:5
5 [a]Song 3:6

There she *who* bore you
brought *you* forth.

THE SHULAMITE TO HER BELOVED

6 [a]Set me as a seal upon your
heart,
As a seal upon your arm;
For love *is as* strong as
death,
[b]Jealousy *as* [1]cruel as [2]the
grave;
Its flames *are* flames of fire,
[3]A most vehement flame.[b]

7 Many waters cannot quench
love,
Nor can the floods drown it.
[a]If a man would give for love
All the wealth of his house,
It would be utterly despised.

THE SHULAMITE'S BROTHERS

8 [a]We have a little sister,
And she has no breasts.
What shall we do for our
sister
In the day when she is
spoken for?
9 If she *is* a wall,
We will build upon her
A battlement of silver;
And if she *is* a door,
We will enclose her
With boards of cedar.

THE SHULAMITE

10 I *am* a wall,
And my breasts like towers;
Then I became in his eyes
As one who found peace.
11 Solomon had a vineyard at
Bā'al Hā'mon;
[a]He leased the vineyard to
keepers;
Everyone was to bring for
its fruit
A thousand silver *coins*.

(TO SOLOMON)

12 My own vineyard *is* before
me.
You, O Solomon, *may have*
a thousand,
And those who tend its fruit
two hundred.

THE BELOVED

13 You who dwell in the
gardens,
The companions listen for
your voice—
[a]Let me hear it!

THE SHULAMITE

14 [a]Make[1] haste, my beloved,
And [b]be like a gazelle
Or a young stag
On the mountains of spices.

6 [a]Jer. 22:24 [b]Prov. 6:34, 35 [1]*severe*, lit. *hard* [2]Or *Sheol* [3]Lit. *A flame of* YAH, poetic form of *YHWH, the* LORD

7 [a]Prov. 6:35

8 [a]Ezek. 23:33

11 [a]Matt. 21:33

13 [a]Song 2:14

14 [a]Rev. 22:17, 20 [b]Song 2:7, 9, 17 [1]*Hurry*, lit. *Flee*

The Book of

ISAIAH

ISAIAH is like a miniature Bible. The first thirty-nine chapters (like the thirty-nine books of the Old Testament) are filled with judgment upon immoral and idolatrous men. Judah has sinned; the surrounding nations have sinned; the whole earth has sinned. Judgment must come, for God cannot allow such blatant sin to go unpunished forever. But the final twenty-seven chapters (like the twenty-seven books of the New Testament) declare a message of hope. The Messiah is coming as a Savior and Sovereign to bear a cross and to wear a crown.

Isaiah's prophetic ministry, spanning the reigns of four kings of Judah, covers at least forty years.

Yesha'yahu and its shortened form *Yeshaiah* mean "Yahweh Is Salvation." This name is an excellent summary of the contents of the book. The Greek form in the Septuagint is *Hesaias*, and the Latin form is *Esaias* or *Isaias*.

CHAPTER 1

THE [a]vision of Ī·sāi'ah the son of Ā'moz, which he saw concerning Judah and Jerusalem in the [b]days of Uz·zī'ah, Jō'tham, Ā'haz, *and* Hez·e·kī'ah, kings of Judah.

2 [a]Hear, O heavens, and give ear, O earth!
For the LORD has spoken:
"I have nourished and brought up children,
And they have rebelled against Me;
3 [a]The ox knows its owner
And the donkey its master's [1]crib;
But Israel [b]does not know,
My people do not [2]consider."

4 Alas, sinful nation,
A people [1]laden with iniquity,
[a]A [2]brood of evildoers,
Children who are corrupters!
They have forsaken the LORD,
They have provoked to anger
The Holy One of Israel,
They have turned away backward.

5 [a]Why should you be stricken again?
You will revolt more and more.
The whole head is sick,
And the whole heart faints.
6 From the sole of the foot even to the head,
There is no soundness in it,
But wounds and bruises and putrefying sores;
They have not been closed or bound up,
Or soothed with ointment.

7 [a]Your country *is* desolate,
Your cities *are* burned with fire;
Strangers devour your land in your presence;
And *it is* desolate, as overthrown by strangers.

1 [a]Num. 12:6 [b]2 Chr. 26—32
2 [a]Jer. 2:12
3 [a]Jer. 8:7 [b]Jer. 9:3, 6 [1]*manger or feed trough* [2]*understand*
4 [a]Matt. 3:7 [1]Lit. *heavy, weighed down* [2]*offspring, seed*
5 [a]Jer. 5:3
7 [a]Deut. 28:51, 52

8 So the daughter of Zion
is left [a]as a [1]booth in a
vineyard,
As a hut in a garden of
cucumbers,
[b]As a besieged city.
9 [a]Unless the LORD of hosts
Had left to us a very small
remnant,
We would have become like
[b]Sod′om,
We would have been made
like Go·mor′rah.

10 Hear the word of the LORD,
You rulers [a]of Sod′om;
Give ear to the law of our
God,
You people of Go·mor′rah:
11 "To what purpose *is* the
multitude of your
[a]sacrifices to Me?"
Says the LORD.
"I have had enough of burnt
offerings of rams
And the fat of fed cattle.
I do not delight in the blood
of bulls,
Or of lambs or goats.

12 "When you come [a]to appear
before Me,
Who has required this from
your hand,
To trample My courts?
13 Bring no more [a]futile[1]
sacrifices;
Incense is an abomination
to Me.
The New Moons, the
Sabbaths, and [b]the
calling of assemblies—
I cannot endure iniquity and
the sacred meeting.
14 Your [a]New Moons and your
[b]appointed feasts
My soul hates;
They are a trouble to Me,
I am weary of bearing *them.*
15 [a]When you [1]spread out your
hands,
I will hide My eyes from
you;
[b]Even though you make
many prayers,
I will not hear.
Your hands are full of
[2]blood.

16 "Wash[a] yourselves, make
yourselves clean;
Put away the evil of your
doings from before My
eyes.
[b]Cease to do evil,
17 Learn to do good;
Seek justice,
Rebuke [1]the oppressor;
[2]Defend the fatherless,
Plead for the widow.

18 "Come now, and let us
[a]reason together,"
Says the LORD,
"Though your sins are like
scarlet,
[b]They shall be as white as
snow;
Though they are red like
crimson,
They shall be as wool.
19 If you are willing and
obedient,
You shall eat the good of the
land;
20 But if you refuse and rebel,
You shall be devoured by
the sword";
[a]For the mouth of the LORD
has spoken.

21 [a]How the faithful city has
become a [1]harlot!
It was full of justice;

8 [a]Job 27:18 [b]Jer. 4:17 [1]*shelter*
9 [a]Lam. 3:22 [b]Gen. 19:24
10 [a]Deut. 32:32
11 [a][1 Sam. 15:22]
12 [a]Ex. 23:17
13 [a]Matt. 15:9 [b]Joel 1:14 [1]*worthless*
14 [a]Num. 28:11 [b]Lam. 2:6
15 [a]Prov. 1:28 [b]Mic. 3:4 [1]Pray [2]*bloodshed*
16 [a]Jer. 4:14 [b]Rom. 12:9
17 [1]Some ancient vss. *the oppressed* [2]*Vindicate*
18 [a]Is. 43:26 [b]Ps. 51:7
20 [a][Titus 1:2]
21 [a]Jer. 2:20 [1]Unfaithful

Righteousness lodged in it,
But now [b]murderers.
22 [a]Your silver has become dross,
Your wine mixed with water.
23 [a]Your princes *are* rebellious,
And [b]companions of thieves;
[c]Everyone loves bribes,
And follows after rewards.
They [d]do not defend the fatherless,
Nor does the cause of the widow come before them.

24 Therefore the Lord says,
The LORD of hosts, the Mighty One of Israel,
"Ah, [a]I will [1]rid Myself of My adversaries,
And [2]take vengeance on My enemies.
25 I will turn My hand against you,
And [a]thoroughly[1] purge away your dross,
And take away all your alloy.
26 I will restore your judges [a]as at the first,
And your counselors as at the beginning.
Afterward [b]you shall be called the city of righteousness, the faithful city."

27 Zion shall be redeemed with justice,
And her [1]penitents with righteousness.
28 The [a]destruction of transgressors and of sinners *shall be* together,
And those who forsake the LORD shall be consumed.
29 For [1]they shall be ashamed of the [2]terebinth trees
Which you have desired;
And you shall be embarrassed because of the gardens
Which you have chosen.
30 For you shall be as a terebinth whose leaf fades,
And as a garden that has no water.
31 [a]The strong shall be as tinder,
And the work of it as a spark;
Both will burn together,
And no one shall [b]quench *them.*

2 The word that Ī·sāi′ah the son of Ā′moz saw concerning Judah and Jerusalem.

2 Now [a]it shall come to pass [b]in the latter days
[c]*That* the mountain of the LORD's house
Shall be established on the top of the mountains,
And shall be exalted above the hills;
And all nations shall flow to it.
3 Many people shall come and say,
[a]"Come, and let us go up to the mountain of the LORD,
To the house of the God of Jacob;
He will teach us His ways,
And we shall walk in His paths."
[b]For out of Zion shall go forth the law,
And the word of the LORD from Jerusalem.
4 He shall judge between the nations,

21 [b]Mic. 3:1–3
22 [a]Jer. 6:28
23 [a]Hos. 9:15 [b]Prov. 29:24 [c]Jer. 22:17 [d]Jer. 5:28
24 [a]Deut. 28:63 [1]*be relieved of* [2]*avenge Myself*
25 [a]Mal. 3:3 [1]*refine with lye*
26 [a]Jer. 33:7–11 [b]Zech. 8:3
27 [1]Lit. *returners*
28 [a][2 Thess. 1:8, 9]
29 [1]So with MT, LXX, Vg.; some Heb. mss., Tg. *you* [2]Sites of pagan worship
31 [a]Ezek. 32:21 [b]Mark 9:43

CHAPTER 2

2 [a]Mic. 4:1 [b]Gen. 49:1 [c]Ps. 68:15
3 [a]Jer. 50:5 [b]Luke 24:47

And rebuke many people;
They shall beat their swords
into plowshares,
And their spears into
pruning [1]hooks;
Nation shall not lift up
sword against nation,
Neither shall they learn war
anymore.

5 O house of Jacob, come and
let us [a]walk
In the light of the LORD.

6 For You have forsaken Your
people, the house of
Jacob,
Because they are filled [a]with
eastern ways;
They *are* [b]soothsayers like
the Phi·lis′tines,
[c]And they [1]are pleased
with the children of
foreigners.
7 [a]Their land is also full of
silver and gold,
And there is no end to their
treasures;
Their land is also full of
horses,
And there is no end to their
chariots.
8 [a]Their land is also full of
idols;
They worship the work of
their own hands,
That which their own
fingers have made.
9 People bow down,
And each man humbles
himself;
Therefore do not forgive
them.

10 [a]Enter into the rock, and hide
in the dust,
From the terror of the LORD
And the glory of His
majesty.
11 The [1]lofty looks of man
shall be [a]humbled,
The haughtiness of men
shall be bowed down,
And the LORD alone shall be
exalted [b]in that day.

12 For the day of the LORD of
hosts
Shall come upon everything
proud and lofty,
Upon everything lifted up—
And it shall be brought
low—
13 Upon all [a]the cedars of
Lebanon *that are* high
and lifted up,
And upon all the oaks of
Bā′shan;
14 [a]Upon all the high
mountains,
And upon all the hills *that
are* lifted up;
15 Upon every high tower,
And upon every fortified
wall;
16 [a]Upon all the ships of
Tar′shish,
And upon all the beautiful
sloops.
17 The [1]loftiness of man shall
be bowed down,
And the haughtiness of men
shall be brought low;
The LORD alone will be
exalted in that day,
18 But the idols [1]He shall
utterly abolish.

19 They shall go into the [a]holes
of the rocks,
And into the caves of the
[1]earth,
[b]From the terror of the LORD
And the glory of His
majesty,

4 [1]*knives*
5 [a]Eph. 5:8
6 [a]Num. 23:7 [b]Deut. 18:14 [c]Ps. 106:35 [1]Or *clap, shake hands to make bargains with the children*
7 [a]Deut. 17:16
8 [a]Jer. 2:28
10 [a]Rev. 6:15, 16
11 [a]Prov. 16:5 [b]Hos. 2:16 [1]*proud*
13 [a]Zech. 11:1, 2
14 [a]Is. 30:25
16 [a]1 Kin. 10:22
17 [1]*pride*
18 [1]Or *shall utterly vanish*
19 [a]Hos. 10:8 [b][2 Thess. 1:9] [1]Lit. *dust*

When He arises [c]to shake
the earth mightily.

20 In that day a man will cast
away his idols of silver
And his idols of gold,
Which they made, *each* for
himself to worship,
To the moles and bats,
21 To go into the clefts of the
rocks,
And into the crags of the
rugged rocks,
From the terror of the LORD
And the glory of His
majesty,
When He arises to shake
the earth mightily.

22 [a]Sever[1] yourselves from such
a man,
Whose [b]breath *is* in his
nostrils;
For [2]of what account is he?

3

For behold, the Lord, the
LORD of hosts,
[a]Takes away from Jerusalem
and from Judah
[b]The[1] stock and the store,
The whole supply of bread
and the whole supply of
water;
2 [a]The mighty man and the
man of war,
The judge and the prophet,
And the diviner and the
elder;
3 The captain of fifty and the
[1]honorable man,
The counselor and the
skillful artisan,
And the expert enchanter.

4 "I will give [a]children[1] *to be*
their princes,
And [2]babes shall rule over
them.

5 The people will be
oppressed,
Every one by another
and every one by his
neighbor;
The child will be insolent
toward the [1]elder,
And the [2]base toward the
honorable."

6 When a man takes hold of
his brother
In the house of his father,
saying,
"You have clothing;
You be our ruler,
And *let* these ruins *be* under
your [1]power,"
7 In that day he will protest,
saying,
"I cannot cure *your* ills,
For in my house *is* neither
food nor clothing;
Do not make me a ruler of
the people."

8 For [a]Jerusalem stumbled,
And Judah is fallen,
Because their tongue and
their doings
Are against the LORD,
To provoke the eyes of His
glory.
9 The look on their
countenance witnesses
against them,
And they declare their sin
as [a]Sod'om;
They do not hide *it*.
Woe to their soul!
For they have brought evil
upon themselves.

10 "Say to the righteous [a]that *it*
shall be well *with them,*
[b]For they shall eat the fruit of
their doings.

---

19 [c]Hag. 2:6, 7

22 [a]Jer. 17:5 [b]Job 27:3 [1]Lit. *Cease yourselves from the man* [2]Lit. *in what is he to be esteemed*

CHAPTER 3

1 [a]Jer. 37:21 [b]Lev. 26:26 [1]Every support

2 [a]2 Kin. 24:14

3 [1]Eminent looking men

4 [a]Eccl. 10:16 [1]*boys* [2]Or *capricious ones*

5 [1]*aged* [2]*despised, lightly esteemed*

6 [1]Lit. *hand*

8 [a]Mic. 3:12

9 [a]Gen. 13:13

10 [a][Eccl. 8:12] [b]Ps. 128:2

11 Woe to the wicked! [a]*It shall be* ill *with him,*
For the reward of his hands shall be [1]given him.
12 *As for* My people, children *are* their oppressors,
And women rule over them.
O My people! [a]Those who lead you [1]cause *you* to err,
And destroy the way of your paths."

13 The LORD stands up [a]to [1]plead,
And stands to judge the people.
14 The LORD will enter into judgment
With the elders of His people
And His princes:
"For you have [1]eaten up [a]the vineyard;
The plunder of the poor *is* in your houses.
15 What do you mean by [a]crushing My people
And grinding the faces of the poor?"
Says the Lord GOD of hosts.

16 Moreover the LORD says:

"Because the daughters of Zion are haughty,
And walk with [1]outstretched necks
And [2]wanton eyes,
Walking and [3]mincing *as* they go,
Making a jingling with their feet,
17 Therefore the Lord will strike with [a]a scab
The crown of the head of the daughters of Zion,
And the LORD will [b]uncover their secret parts."

18 In that day the Lord will take away the finery:
The jingling anklets, the [1]scarves, and the [a]crescents;
19 The pendants, the bracelets, and the veils;
20 The headdresses, the leg ornaments, and the headbands;
The perfume boxes, the charms,
21 and the rings;
The nose jewels,
22 the festal apparel, and the mantles;
The outer garments, the purses,
23 and the mirrors;
The fine linen, the turbans, and the robes.

24 And so it shall be:

Instead of a sweet smell there will be a stench;
Instead of a sash, a rope;
Instead of well-set hair, [a]baldness;
Instead of a rich robe, a girding of sackcloth;
And [1]branding instead of beauty.
25 Your men shall fall by the sword,
And your [1]mighty in the war.

26 [a]Her gates shall lament and mourn,
And she *being* desolate [b]shall sit on the ground.

4

And [a]in that day seven women shall take hold of one man, saying,

11 [a][Ps. 11:6] [1]*done to him*
12 [a]Is. 9:16 [1]*lead you astray*
13 [a]Mic. 6:2 [1]*contend, plead His case*
14 [a]Matt. 21:33 [1]*burned*
15 [a]Mic. 3:2, 3
16 [1]Head held high [2]*seductive, ogling* [3]*tripping* or *skipping*
17 [a]Deut. 28:27 [b]Jer. 13:22
18 [a]Judg. 8:21, 26 [1]*headbands*
24 [a]Is. 22:12 [1]*burning scar*
25 [1]Lit. *strength*
26 [a]Jer. 14:2 [b]Lam. 2:10

CHAPTER 4

1 [a]Is. 2:11, 17

"We will [b]eat our own food
and wear our own
apparel;
Only let us be called by your
name,
To take away [c]our reproach."

2 In that day [a]the Branch
of the LORD shall be
beautiful and glorious;
And the fruit of the earth
shall be excellent and
appealing
For those of Israel who have
escaped.

3 And it shall come to pass
that *he who is* left in Zion and
remains in Jerusalem [a]will be
called holy—everyone who is
[b]recorded among the living in
Jerusalem.
4 When [a]the Lord has washed
away the filth of the daughters
of Zion, and purged the [1]blood
of Jerusalem from her midst, by
the spirit of judgment and by the
spirit of burning,
5 then the LORD will create
above every dwelling place of
Mount Zion, and above her assemblies, [a]a cloud and smoke by
day and [b]the shining of a flaming fire by night. For over all the
glory there *will be* a [1]covering.
6 And there will be a tabernacle for shade in the daytime
from the heat, [a]for a place of
refuge, and for a shelter from
storm and rain.

5 Now let me sing to my Well-
beloved
A song of my Beloved
[a]regarding His vineyard:

My Well-beloved has a
vineyard
[1]On a very fruitful hill.
2 He dug it up and cleared out
its stones,
And planted it with the
choicest vine.
He built a tower in its midst,
And also [1]made a winepress
in it;
[a]So He expected *it* to bring
forth *good* grapes,
But it brought forth wild
grapes.

3 "And now, O inhabitants of
Jerusalem and men of
Judah,
[a]Judge, please, between Me
and My vineyard.
4 What more could have been
done to My vineyard
That I have not done in [a]it?
Why then, when I expected
it to bring forth *good*
grapes,
Did it bring forth wild
grapes?
5 And now, please let Me tell
you what I will do to My
vineyard:
[a]I will take away its hedge,
and it shall be burned;
And break down its wall,
and it shall be trampled
down.
6 I will lay it [a]waste;
It shall not be pruned or
[1]dug,
But there shall come up
briers and [b]thorns.
I will also command the
clouds
That they rain no rain on it."

7 For the vineyard of the LORD
of hosts *is* the house of
Israel,
And the men of Judah are
His pleasant plant.

1 [b]2 Thess. 3:12 [c]Luke 1:25
2 [a][Jer. 23:5]
3 [a]Is. 60:21 [b]Phil. 4:3
4 [a]Mal. 3:2, 3 [1]*bloodshed*
5 [a]Ex. 13:21, 22 [b]Zech. 2:5 [1]*canopy*
6 [a]Is. 25:4

CHAPTER 5

1 [a]Matt. 21:33 [1]Lit. *In a horn, the son of fatness*
2 [a]Deut. 32:6 [1]Lit. *hewed out*
3 [a][Rom. 3:4]
4 [a]2 Chr. 36:15, 16
5 [a]Ps. 80:12; 89:40, 41
6 [a]2 Chr. 36:19–21 [b]Is. 7:19–25 [1]*hoed*

He looked for justice, but
behold, oppression;
For righteousness, but
behold, [1]a cry *for help*.

8 Woe to those who [1]join
[a]house to house;
They add field to field,
Till *there is* no place
Where they may dwell alone
in the midst of the land!
9 [a]In my hearing the LORD of
hosts *said*,
"Truly, many houses shall be
desolate,
Great and beautiful ones,
without inhabitant.
10 For ten acres of vineyard
shall yield one [a]bath,[1]
And a [2]homer of seed shall
yield one ephah."

11 [a]Woe to those who rise early
in the morning,
That they may [1]follow
intoxicating drink;
Who continue until night,
till wine inflames them!
12 [a]The harp and the strings,
The tambourine and flute,
And wine are in their feasts;
But [b]they do not regard the
work of the LORD,
Nor consider the operation
of His hands.

13 [a]Therefore my people have
gone into captivity,
Because *they have* no
[b]knowledge;
Their honorable men *are*
famished,
And their multitude dried
up with thirst.
14 Therefore Shē'ōl has
enlarged itself
And opened its mouth
beyond measure;
Their glory and their
multitude and their pomp,
And he who is jubilant, shall
descend into it.
15 People shall be brought
down,
[a]Each man shall be humbled,
And the eyes of the lofty
shall be humbled.
16 But the LORD of hosts shall
be [a]exalted in judgment,
And God who is holy
shall be hallowed in
righteousness.
17 Then the lambs shall feed in
their pasture,
And in the waste places of
[a]the [1]fat ones strangers
shall eat.

18 Woe to those who [1]draw
iniquity with cords of
[2]vanity,
And sin as if with a cart
rope;
19 [a]That say, "Let Him make
speed *and* hasten His
work,
That we may see *it*;
And let the counsel of the
Holy One of Israel draw
near and come,
That we may know *it*."

20 Woe to those who call evil
good, and good evil;
Who put darkness for light,
and light for darkness;
Who put bitter for sweet,
and sweet for bitter!

21 Woe to *those who are* [a]wise
in their own eyes,
And prudent in their own
sight!

22 Woe to men mighty at
drinking wine,

7 [1]*wailing*
8 [a]Mic. 2:2 [1]Accumulate houses
9 [a]Is. 22:14
10 [a]Ezek. 45:11 [1]1 bath = 1/10 homer [2]1 homer = 1/10 ephah
11 [a]Prov. 23:29, 30 [1]*pursue*
12 [a]Amos 6:5 [b]Job 34:27
13 [a]2 Kin. 24:14–16 [b]Hos. 4:6
15 [a]Is. 2:9, 11
16 [a]Is. 2:11
17 [a]Is. 10:16 [1]Lit. *fatlings*, rich ones
18 [1]*drag* [2]*emptiness* or *falsehood*
19 [a]Jer. 17:15
21 [a]Rom. 1:22; 12:16

Woe to men valiant for
mixing intoxicating
drink,
23 Who [a]justify the wicked for
a bribe,
And take away justice from
the righteous man!

24 Therefore, [a]as the [1]fire
devours the stubble,
And the flame consumes the
chaff,
So [b]their root will be as
rottenness,
And their blossom will
ascend like dust;
Because they have rejected
the law of the LORD of
hosts,
And despised the word of
the Holy One of Israel.
25 [a]Therefore the anger of the
LORD is aroused against
His people;
He has stretched out His
hand against them
And stricken them,
And [b]the hills trembled.
Their carcasses *were* as
refuse in the midst of the
streets.

[c]For all this His anger is not
turned away,
But His hand *is* stretched
out still.

26 [a]He will lift up a banner to
the nations from afar,
And will [b]whistle to them
from [c]the end of the
earth;
Surely [d]they shall come with
speed, swiftly.
27 No one will be weary or
stumble among them,
No one will slumber or
sleep;
Nor [a]will the belt on their
loins be loosed,
Nor the strap of their
sandals be broken;
28 [a]Whose arrows *are* sharp,
And all their bows bent;
Their horses' hooves will
[1]seem like flint,
And their wheels like a
whirlwind.
29 Their roaring *will be* like a
lion,
They will roar like young
lions;
Yes, they will roar
And lay hold of the prey;
They will carry *it* away
safely,
And no one will deliver.
30 In that day they will roar
against them
Like the roaring of the sea.
And if *one* [a]looks to the land,
Behold, darkness *and*
[1]sorrow;
And the light is darkened by
the clouds.

6 In the year that [a]King
Uz·zī'ah died, I [b]saw the
Lord sitting on a throne, high
and lifted up, and the train of
His *robe* filled the temple.
2 Above it stood seraphim;
each one had six wings: with
two he covered his face, [a]with
two he covered his feet, and
with two he flew.
3 And one cried to another
and said:

[a]"Holy, holy, holy *is* the LORD
of hosts;
[b]The whole earth *is* full of
His glory!"

4 And the posts of the door
were shaken by the voice of him

23 [a]Prov. 17:15
24 [a]Ex. 15:7 [b]Job 18:16 [1]Lit. *tongue of fire*
25 [a]2 Kin. 22:13, 17 [b]Jer. 4:24 [c]Is. 9:12, 17
26 [a]Is. 11:10, 12 [b]Is. 7:18 [c]Mal. 1:11 [d]Joel 2:7
27 [a]Dan. 5:6
28 [a]Jer. 5:16 [1]Lit. *be regarded as*
30 [a]Is. 8:22 [1]*distress*

CHAPTER 6

1 [a]2 Kin. 15:7 [b]John 12:41
2 [a]Ezek. 1:11
3 [a]Rev. 4:8 [b]Num. 14:21

who cried out, and the house was filled with smoke.
5 So I said:

"Woe *is* me, for I am
[1]undone!
Because I *am* a man of
[a]unclean lips,
And I dwell in the midst of a
people of unclean lips;
For my eyes have seen the
King,
The LORD of hosts."

6 Then one of the seraphim
flew to me, having in his hand
a live coal *which* he had taken
with the tongs from [a]the altar.
7 And he [a]touched my mouth
with it, and said:

"Behold, this has touched
your lips;
Your iniquity is taken away,
And your sin [1]purged."

8 Also I heard the voice of the
Lord, saying:

"Whom shall I send,
And who will go for [a]Us?"

Then I said, "Here *am* I! Send
me."
☆9 And He said, "Go, and [a]tell
this people:

'Keep on hearing, but do not
understand;
Keep on seeing, but do not
perceive.'

☆10 "Make [a]the heart of this
people dull,
And their ears heavy,
And shut their eyes;
[b]Lest they see with their
eyes,
And hear with their ears,
And understand with their
heart,
And return and be healed."

11 Then I said, "Lord, how
long?" And He answered:

[a]"Until the cities are laid
waste and without
inhabitant,
The houses are without a
man,
The land is utterly desolate,
12 [a]The LORD has removed men
far away,
And the forsaken places *are*
many in the midst of the
land.
13 But yet a tenth *will be* in it,
And will return and be for
consuming,
As a terebinth tree or as an
oak,
Whose stump *remains* when
it is cut down.
So [a]the holy seed *shall be* its
stump."

7 Now it came to pass in the
days of [a]Ā'haz the son of
Jō'tham, the son of Uz·zī'ah,
king of Judah, *that* Rē'zin king
of Syria and Pē'kah the son of
Rem·a·lī'ah, king of Israel, went
up to Jerusalem to *make* war
against [b]it, but could not [1]prevail
against it.
2 And it was told to the house
of David, saying, "Syria's forces
are [1]deployed in Ē'phra·im." So
his heart and the heart of his
people were moved as the trees
of the woods are moved with the
wind.
3 Then the LORD said to Ī·sāi'ah,
"Go out now to meet Ā'haz, you
and [1]Shē'ar-Jā'shub your son, at

5 [a]Ex. 6:12, 30 [1]*destroyed, cut off*
6 [a]Rev. 8:3
7 [a]Jer. 1:9 [1]*atoned for*
8 [a]Gen. 1:26
9 [a]Matt. 13:14, 15; Mark 4:12; Luke 8:10; John 12:40; Acts 28:26, 27; Rom. 11:8
10 [a]Ps. 119:70; Matt. 13:14, 15; Mark 6:1–6; Acts 7:51 [b]Jer. 5:21; Mark 4:12; John 12:40; Rom. 10:1–4; 11:8
11 [a]Mic. 3:12
12 [a]2 Kin. 25:21
13 [a]Ezra 9:2

CHAPTER 7

1 [a]2 Chr. 28 [b]2 Kin. 16:5, 9 [1]*conquer it*
2 [1]Lit. *settled upon*
3 [1]Lit. *A Remnant Shall Return*

the end of the aqueduct from the
upper pool, on the highway to
the Fuller's Field,
4 "and say to him: [1]'Take heed,
and [2]be [a]quiet; do not fear or be
fainthearted for these two stubs
of smoking firebrands, for the
fierce anger of Rē′zin and Syria,
and the son of Rem·a·lī′ah.
5 'Because Syria, Ē′phra·im,
and the son of Rem·a·lī′ah have
plotted evil against you, saying,
6 "Let us go up against Judah
and [1]trouble it, and let us make a
gap in its wall for ourselves, and
set a king over them, the son of
Tā′bel"—
7 'thus says the Lord GOD:

[a]"It shall not stand,
Nor shall it come to pass.
8 [a]For the head of Syria *is*
Damascus,
And the head of Damascus
is Rē′zin.
Within sixty-five years
Ē′phra·im will be
[1]broken,
So that it will not *be* a
people.
9 The head of Ē′phra·im *is*
Samaria,
And the head of Samaria *is*
Rem·a·lī′ah's son.
[a]If you will not believe,
Surely you shall not be
established." ' "

10 Moreover the LORD spoke
again to Ā′haz, saying,
11 [a]"Ask a sign for yourself
from the LORD your God; [1]ask
it either in the depth or in the
height above."
12 But Ā′haz said, "I will not
ask, nor will I test the LORD!"
13 Then he said, "Hear now,
O house of David! *Is it* a small
thing for you to weary men, but
will you weary my God also?
14 "Therefore the Lord Himself
will give you a sign: [a]Behold, the
virgin shall conceive and bear
[b]a Son, and shall call His name
[c]Im·man′ū·el.[1]
15 "Curds and honey He shall
eat, that He may know to refuse
the evil and choose the good.
16 [a]"For before the Child shall
know to refuse the evil and
choose the good, the land that
you dread will be forsaken by
[b]both her kings.
17 [a]"The LORD will bring the
king of Assyria upon you and
your people and your father's
house—days that have not come
since the day that [b]Ē′phra·im
departed from Judah."

18 And it shall come to pass in
that day
That the LORD [a]will whistle
for the fly
That *is* in the farthest part
of the rivers of Egypt,
And for the bee that *is* in
the land of Assyria.
19 They will come, and all of
them will rest
In the desolate valleys
and in [a]the clefts of the
rocks,
And on all thorns and in all
pastures.

20 In the same day the Lord
will shave with a [a]hired
[b]razor,
With those from beyond [1]the
River, with the king of
Assyria,
The head and the hair of the
legs,
And will also remove the
beard.

4 [a]Is. 30:15 [1]*Be careful* [2]*be calm*
6 [1]*cause a sickening dread*
7 [a]Is. 8:10
8 [a]2 Sam. 8:6 [1]Lit. *shattered*
9 [a]2 Chr. 20:20
11 [a]Matt. 12:38 [1]Lit. *make the request deep or make it high above*
14 [a]Matt. 1:23; Luke 1:31, 34, 35; John 1:45; Rev. 12:5 [b][Is. 9:6] [c]Is. 8:8, 10 [1]Lit. *God-With-Us*
16 [a]Is. 8:4 [b]2 Kin. 15:30
17 [a]2 Chr. 28:19, 20 [b]1 Kin. 12:16
18 [a]Is. 5:26
19 [a]Jer. 16:16
20 [a]Is. 10:5, 15 [b]2 Kin. 16:7 [1]The Euphrates

21 It shall be in that day
That a man will keep alive
a young cow and two
sheep;
22 So it shall be, from the
abundance of milk they
give,
That he will eat curds;
For curds and honey
everyone will eat who is
left in the land.

23 It shall happen in that day,
That wherever there could
be a thousand vines
Worth a thousand *shekels* of
silver,
[a]It will be for briers and
thorns.
24 With arrows and bows *men*
will come there,
Because all the land will
become briers and
thorns.

25 And to any hill which could
be dug with the hoe,
You will not go there for
fear of briers and thorns;
But it will become a range
for oxen
And a place for sheep to
roam.

8 Moreover the LORD said to
me, "Take a large scroll,
and [a]write on it with a man's
pen concerning [1]Mā'her-Shal'al-
Hash-Baz.
2 "And I will take for Myself faithful witnesses to record, [a]Ū·rī'ah the priest and
Zech·a·rī'ah the son of Je·ber·e-
chī'ah."
3 Then I went to the prophetess, and she conceived and bore
a son. Then the LORD said to me,

23 [a]Is. 5:6

CHAPTER 8

1 [a]Hab. 2:2
[1]Lit. *Speed the Spoil, Hasten the Booty*

2 [a]2 Kin. 16:10

4 [a]2 Kin. 17:6; Is. 7:16
[b]2 Kin. 15:29
[1]*knows how*
[2]*plunder*

6 [a]John 9:7
[b]Is. 7:1, 2

7 [1]The Euphrates
[2]Overflow

8 [a]Is. 30:28
[b]Is. 7:14
[1]Lit. *be the fullness of*
[2]Lit. *God-With-Us*

9 [a]Joel 3:9

10 [a]Is. 7:7

"Call his name Mā'her-Shal'al-
Hash-Baz;
4 [a]"for before the child [1]shall
have knowledge to cry 'My father' and 'My mother,' [b]the riches
of Damascus and the [2]spoil of
Samaria will be taken away before the king of Assyria."
5 The LORD also spoke to me
again, saying:

6 "Inasmuch as these people
refused
The waters of [a]Shī·lō'ah that
flow softly,
And rejoice [b]in Rē'zin and
in Rem·a·lī'ah's son;
7 Now therefore, behold, the
Lord brings up over
them
The waters of [1]the River,
strong and mighty—
The king of Assyria and all
his glory;
He will [2]go up over all his
channels
And go over all his banks.
8 He will pass through Judah,
He will overflow and pass
over,
[a]He will reach up to the
neck;
And the stretching out of his
wings
Will [1]fill the breadth of Your
land, O [b]Im·man'ū·el.[2]

9 "Be[a] shattered, O you
peoples, and be broken
in pieces!
Give ear, all you from far
countries.
Gird yourselves, but be
broken in pieces;
Gird yourselves, but be
broken in pieces.
10 [a]Take counsel together, but it
will come to nothing;

Speak the word, [b]but it will
not stand,
[c]For [1]God *is* with us."
11 For the LORD spoke thus to
me with [1]a strong hand, and
instructed me that I should not
walk in the way of this people,
saying:
12 "Do not say, 'A conspiracy,'
Concerning all that this
people call a conspiracy,
Nor be afraid of their
[1]threats, nor be [2]troubled.
13 The LORD of hosts, Him you
shall hallow;
Let Him *be* your fear,
And *let* Him *be* your dread.
☆ 14 [a]He will be as a [1]sanctuary,
But [b]a stone of stumbling
and a rock of [2]offense
To both the houses of Israel,
As a trap and a snare to the
inhabitants of Jerusalem.
15 And many among them
shall [a]stumble;
They shall fall and be
broken,
Be snared and [1]taken."

16 Bind up the testimony,
Seal the law among my
disciples.
17 And I will wait on the LORD,
Who [a]hides His face from
the house of Jacob;
And I [b]will hope in Him.
☆ 18 [a]Here am I and the children
whom the LORD has
given me!
We [b]are for signs and
wonders in Israel
From the LORD of hosts,
Who dwells in Mount Zion.

19 And when they say to you,
[a]"Seek those who are mediums
and wizards, [b]who whisper and
mutter," should not a people seek
their God? *Should they* [c]*seek* the
dead on behalf of the living?
20 [a]To the law and to the testimony! If they do not speak
according to this word, *it is*
because [b]*there*[1] *is* no light in
them.
21 They will pass through it
hard-pressed and hungry; and
it shall happen, when they are
hungry, that they will be enraged and [a]curse [1]their king and
their God, and look upward.
22 Then they will look to the
earth, and see trouble and darkness, gloom of anguish; and *they*
will be driven into darkness.

9 Nevertheless [a]the gloom *will* ☆
not *be* upon her who *is*
distressed,
As when at [b]first He lightly
esteemed
The land of Zeb′ū·lun and
the land of Naph′ta·lī,
And [c]afterward more
heavily oppressed *her*,
By the way of the sea,
beyond the Jordan,
In Galilee of the Gentiles.
2 [a]The people who walked in ☆
darkness
Have seen a great light;
Those who dwelt in the land
of the shadow of death,
Upon them a light has
shined.

3 You have multiplied the
nation
And [1]increased its joy;
They rejoice before You
According to the joy of
harvest,
As *men* rejoice [a]when they
divide the spoil.

10 [b]Is. 7:14 [c]Rom. 8:31 [1]Heb. *Immanuel*

11 [1]Mighty power

12 [1]Lit. *fear* or *terror* [2]Lit. *in dread*

14 [a]Ezek. 11:16 [b]Luke 2:34; 20:17; Rom. 9:33; 1 Pet. 2:8 [1]*holy abode* [2]*stumbling over*

15 [a]Matt. 21:44 [1]*captured*

17 [a]Is. 54:8 [b]Hab. 2:3

18 [a]Heb. 2:13 [b]Ps. 71:7

19 [a]1 Sam. 28:8 [b]Is. 29:4 [c]Ps. 106:28

20 [a]Luke 16:29 [b]Mic. 3:6 [1]Or *they have no dawn*

21 [a]Rev. 16:11 [1]Or *by their king and by their God*

CHAPTER 9

1 [a]Is. 8:22 [b]2 Kin. 15:29 [c]Matt. 4:13–16

2 [a]Matt. 4:16; Luke 1:79; 2 Cor. 4:6; Eph. 5:8

3 [a]Judg. 5:30 [1]So with Qr., Tg.; Kt., Vg. *not increased joy;* LXX *Most of the people You brought down in Your joy*

4 For You have broken the
yoke of his burden
And the staff of his
shoulder,
The rod of his oppressor,
As in the day of [a]Mid'i·an.
5 For every warrior's [1]sandal
from the noisy battle,
And garments rolled in
blood,
[a]Will be used for burning
and fuel [2]of fire.

☆6 [a]For unto us a Child is born,
Unto us a [b]Son is given;
And [c]the government will be
upon His shoulder.
And His name will be called
[d]Wonderful, Counselor,
[e]Mighty God,
Everlasting Father, [f]Prince
of Peace.
☆7 Of the increase of *His*
government and peace
[a]*There will be* no end,
Upon the throne of David
and over His kingdom,
To order it and establish
it with judgment and
justice
From that time forward,
even forever.
The [b]zeal of the LORD of
hosts will perform this.

8 The Lord sent a word
against [a]Jacob,
And it has fallen on Israel.
9 All the people will know—
Ē'phra·im and the
inhabitant of Samaria—
Who say in pride and
arrogance of heart:
10 "The bricks have fallen
down,
But we will rebuild with
hewn stones;
The sycamores are cut
down,
But we will replace *them*
with cedars."
11 Therefore the LORD shall
set up
The adversaries of Rē'zin
against him,
And spur his enemies on,
12 The Syrians before and the
Phi·lis'tines behind;
And they shall devour Israel
with an open mouth.

For all this His anger is not
turned away,
But His hand *is* [1]stretched
out still.

13 For the people do not turn
to Him who strikes them,
Nor do they seek the LORD
of hosts.
14 Therefore the LORD will cut
off head and tail from
Israel,
Palm branch and bulrush [a]in
one day.
15 The elder and honorable, he
is the head;
The prophet who teaches
lies, he *is* the tail.
16 For [a]the leaders of this
people cause *them* to err,
And *those who are* led by
them are destroyed.
17 Therefore the Lord [a]will
have no joy in their
young men,
Nor have mercy on their
fatherless and widows;
For everyone *is* a hypocrite
and an evildoer,
And every mouth speaks
[1]folly.

[b]For all this His anger is not
turned away,

---

4 [a]Judg. 7:22
5 [a]Is. 66:15 [1]*boot* [2]*for the fire*
6 [a][Luke 2:11]; John 1:45 [b]Luke 2:7; [John 3:16; 1 John 4:9] [c][Matt. 28:18; 1 Cor. 15:25]; Rev. 12:5 [d]Judg. 13:18 [e]Titus 2:13 [f]Eph. 2:14
7 [a]Dan. 2:44; Matt. 1:16; Luke 1:32, 33; John 7:42 [b]Is. 37:32
8 [a]Gen. 32:28
12 [1]In judgment
14 [a]Rev. 18:8
16 [a]Is. 3:12
17 [a]Ps. 147:10 [b]Is. 5:25 [1]*foolishness*

But His hand *is* stretched
out still.

18 For wickedness [a]burns as
the fire;
It shall devour the briers
and thorns,
And kindle in the thickets of
the forest;
They shall mount up *like*
rising smoke.
19 Through the wrath of the
LORD of hosts
[a]The land is burned up,
And the people shall be as
fuel for the fire;
[b]No man shall spare his
brother.
20 And he shall [1]snatch on the
right hand
And be hungry;
He shall devour on the left
hand
[a]And not be satisfied;
[b]Every man shall eat the
flesh of his own arm.
21 Ma·nas′seh *shall devour*
Ē′phra·im, and Ē′phra·im
Ma·nas′seh;
Together they *shall be*
[a]against Judah.

[b]For all this His anger is not
turned away,
But His hand *is* stretched
out still.

10

"Woe to those who
[a]decree unrighteous
decrees,
Who write misfortune,
Which they have prescribed
2 To rob the needy of justice,
And to take what is right
from the poor of My
people,
That widows may be their
prey,
And *that* they may rob the
fatherless.
3 [a]What will you do in [b]the day
of punishment,
And in the desolation *which*
will come from [c]afar?
To whom will you flee for
help?
And where will you leave
your glory?
4 Without Me they shall
bow down among the
[a]prisoners,
And they shall fall [1]among
the slain."

[b]For all this His anger is not
turned away,
But His hand *is* stretched
out still.

5 "Woe to Assyria, [a]the rod of
My anger
And the staff in whose hand
is My indignation.
6 I will send him against [a]an
ungodly nation,
And against the people of
My wrath
I will [b]give him charge,
To seize the spoil, to take
the prey,
And to tread them down
like the mire of the
streets.
7 [a]Yet he does not mean so,
Nor does his heart think so;
But *it is* in his heart to
destroy,
And cut off not a few
nations.
8 [a]For he says,
'*Are* not my princes
altogether kings?
9 *Is* not [a]Cal′nō [b]like
Car′chem·ish?
Is not Hā′math like Ar′pad?

---

18 [a]Mal. 4:1
19 [a]Is. 8:22 [b]Mic. 7:2, 6
20 [a]Lev. 26:26 [b]Jer. 19:9 [1]*slice off* or *tear*
21 [a]2 Chr. 28:6, 8 [b]Is. 9:12, 17

CHAPTER 10

1 [a]Ps. 58:2
3 [a]Job 31:14 [b]Hos. 9:7 [c]Is. 5:26
4 [a]Is. 24:22 [b]Is. 5:25 [1]Lit. *under*
5 [a]Jer. 51:20
6 [a]Is. 9:17 [b]Jer. 34:22
7 [a]Gen. 50:20
8 [a]2 Kin. 19:10
9 [a]Amos 6:2 [b]2 Chr. 35:20

Is not Samaria [c]like
Damascus?
10 As my hand has found the
kingdoms of the idols,
Whose carved images
excelled those of
Jerusalem and Samaria,
11 As I have done to Samaria
and her idols,
Shall I not do also to
Jerusalem and her
idols?' "

12 Therefore it shall come to
pass, when the Lord has [1]per-
formed all His work [a]on Mount
Zion and on Jerusalem, *that He
will say,* [b]"I will punish the fruit
of the arrogant heart of the king
of Assyria, and the glory of his
haughty looks."
13 [a]For he says:

"By the strength of my hand
I have done *it,*
And by my wisdom, for I am
prudent;
Also I have removed the
boundaries of the people,
And have robbed their
treasuries;
So I have put down the
inhabitants like a
[1]valiant *man.*
14 [a]My hand has found like a
nest the riches of the
people,
And as one gathers eggs
that are left,
I have gathered all the earth;
And there was no one who
moved *his* wing,
Nor opened *his* mouth with
even a peep."

15 Shall [a]the ax boast itself
against him who chops
with it?
Or shall the saw exalt itself
against him who saws
with it?
As if a rod could wield *itself*
against those who lift it
up,
Or as if a staff could lift up,
as if it were not wood!
16 Therefore the Lord, the
[1]Lord of hosts,
Will send leanness among
his fat ones;
And under his glory
He will kindle a burning
Like the burning of a fire.
17 So the Light of Israel will be
for a fire,
And his Holy One for a
flame;
[a]It will burn and devour
His thorns and his briers in
one day.
18 And it will consume the
glory of his forest and of
[a]his fruitful field,
Both soul and body;
And they will be as when a
sick man wastes away.
19 Then the rest of the trees of
his forest
Will be so few in number
That a child may write
them.

20 And it shall come to pass in
that day
That the remnant of Israel,
And such as have escaped
of the house of Jacob,
[a]Will never again depend on
him who [1]defeated them,
But will depend on the LORD,
the Holy One of Israel, in
truth.
21 The remnant will return, the
remnant of Jacob,
To the [a]Mighty God.

---

9 [c]2 Kin. 16:9
12 [a]2 Kin. 19:31 [b]Jer. 50:18 [1]*completed*
13 [a]Is. 37:24–27 [1]*mighty*
14 [a]Job 31:25
15 [a]Jer. 51:20
16 [1]So with Bg.; MT, DSS *YHWH (the* LORD*)*
17 [a]Is. 9:18
18 [a]2 Kin. 19:23
20 [a]2 Kin. 16:7 [1]Lit. *struck*
21 [a][Is. 9:6]

22 [a]For though your people,
O Israel, be as the sand
of the sea,
[b]A remnant of them will
return;
The destruction decreed
shall overflow with
righteousness.
23 [a]For the Lord GOD of hosts
Will make a determined end
In the midst of all the land.

24 Therefore thus says the Lord
GOD of hosts: "O My people, who
dwell in Zion, [a]do not be afraid
of the Assyrian. He shall strike
you with a rod and lift up his
staff against you, in the manner
of [b]Egypt.
25 "For yet a very little while
[a]and the indignation will cease,
as will My anger in their
destruction."
26 And the LORD of hosts will
[1]stir up [a]a scourge for him like
the slaughter of [b]Mid′i·an at the
rock of Or′eb; [c]*as* His rod was on
the sea, so will He lift it up in the
manner of Egypt.

27 It shall come to pass in that
day
That his burden will be
taken away from your
shoulder,
And his yoke from your
neck,
And the yoke will be
destroyed because of
[a]the anointing oil.

28 He has come to Aī′ath,
He has passed Mig′ron;
At Mich′mash he has
attended to his
equipment.
29 They have gone [1]along [a]the
ridge,
They have taken up lodging
at Gē′ba.
Rā′mah is afraid,
[b]Gib′ē·ah of Saul has fled.
30 [1]Lift up your voice,
O daughter [a]of Gal′lim!
Cause it to be heard as far
as [b]Lā′ish—
[2]O poor An′a·thoth!
31 [a]Mad·mē′nah has fled,
The inhabitants of Gē′bim
seek refuge.
32 As yet he will remain [a]at
Nob that day;
He will [b]shake his fist at the
mount of [c]the daughter
of Zion,
The hill of Jerusalem.

33 Behold, the Lord,
The LORD of hosts,
Will lop off the bough with
terror;
[a]Those of high stature *will be*
hewn down,
And the haughty will be
humbled.
34 He will cut down the thickets
of the forest with iron,
And Lebanon will fall by
the Mighty One.

11

There [a]shall come forth a ☆
[1]Rod from the [2]stem of
[b]Jesse,
And [c]a Branch shall [3]grow
out of his roots.
2 [a]The Spirit of the LORD shall ☆
rest upon Him,
The Spirit of wisdom and
understanding,
The Spirit of counsel and
might,
The Spirit of knowledge and
of the fear of the LORD.

3 His delight *is* in the fear of ☆
the LORD,

22 [a]Rom. 9:27, 28 [b]Is. 6:13
23 [a]Dan. 9:27
24 [a]Is. 7:4; 12:2 [b]Ex. 14
25 [a]Dan. 11:36
26 [a]2 Kin. 19:35 [b]Is. 9:4 [c]Ex. 14:26, 27 [1]*arouse*
27 [a]Ps. 105:15
29 [a]1 Sam. 13:23 [b]1 Sam. 11:4 [1]Or *over the pass*
30 [a]1 Sam. 25:44 [b]Judg. 18:7 [1]Or *Cry shrilly* [2]So with MT, Tg., Vg.; LXX, Syr. *Listen to her, O Anathoth*
31 [a]Josh. 15:31
32 [a]1 Sam. 21:1 [b]Is. 13:2 [c]Is. 37:22
33 [a]Amos 2:9

CHAPTER 11

1 [a][Zech. 6:12]; Rev. 5:5 [b]Matt. 1:5; [Acts 13:23] [c]Is. 4:2 [1]*Shoot* [2]*stock* or *trunk* [3]*be fruitful*
2 [a][Matt. 3:16]; Mark 1:10; Luke 3:22; [John 1:32]

[a]And He shall not judge by the sight of His eyes,
Nor decide by the hearing of His ears;
☆4 But [a]with righteousness He shall judge the poor,
And decide with equity for the meek of the earth;
He shall [b]strike the earth with the rod of His mouth,
And with the breath of His lips He shall slay the wicked.
5 Righteousness shall be the belt of His loins,
And faithfulness the belt of His waist.

6 "The[a] wolf also shall dwell with the lamb,
The leopard shall lie down with the young goat,
The calf and the young lion and the fatling together;
And a little child shall lead them.
7 The cow and the bear shall graze;
Their young ones shall lie down together;
And the lion shall eat straw like the ox.
8 The nursing child shall play by the cobra's hole,
And the weaned child shall put his hand in the viper's den.
9 [a]They shall not hurt nor destroy in all My holy mountain,
For [b]the earth shall be full of the knowledge of the LORD
As the waters cover the sea.

☆ **10** "And[a] in that day [b]there shall be a Root of Jesse,
Who shall stand as a [c]banner to the people;
For the [d]Gentiles shall seek Him,
And His resting place shall be glorious."

11 It shall come to pass in that day
That the Lord shall set His hand again the second time
To recover the remnant of His people who are left,
[a]From Assyria and Egypt,
From Path'ros and Cush,
From Ē'lam and Shī'nar,
From Hā'math and the [1]islands of the sea.

12 He will set up a banner for the nations,
And will [1]assemble the outcasts of Israel,
And gather together [a]the dispersed of Judah
From the four [2]corners of the earth.
13 Also [a]the envy of Ē'phra·im shall depart,
And the adversaries of Judah shall be cut off;
Ē'phra·im shall not envy Judah,
And Judah shall not harass Ē'phra·im.
14 But they shall fly down upon the shoulder of the Phi·lis'tines toward the west;
Together they shall plunder the [1]people of the East;
[a]They shall lay their hand on Ē'dom and Mō'ab;
And the people of Am'mon shall obey them.

3 [a]John 2:25
4 [a]Rev. 19:11 [b]Job 4:9; 2 Thess. 2:8
6 [a]Hos. 2:18
9 [a]Job 5:23 [b]Hab. 2:14
10 [a]Is. 2:11 [b]Rom. 15:12 [c]Is. 27:12, 13 [d]Rom. 15:10
11 [a]Zech. 10:10 [1]Or *coastlands*
12 [a]John 7:35 [1]*gather* [2]Lit. *wings*
13 [a]Jer. 3:18
14 [a]Dan. 11:41 [1]Lit. *sons*

15 The LORD [a]will utterly
[1]destroy the tongue of
the Sea of Egypt;
With His mighty wind He
will shake His fist over
[2]the River,
And strike it in the seven
streams,
And make *men* cross over
[3]dry-shod.
16 [a]There will be a highway
for the remnant of His
people
Who will be left from
Assyria,
[b]As it was for Israel
In the day that he came up
from the land of Egypt.

12

And [a]in that day you will say:

"O LORD, I will praise You;
Though You were angry
with me,
Your anger is turned away,
and You comfort me.
2 Behold, God *is* my salvation,
I will trust and not be
afraid;
[a]'For [b]YAH, the LORD, *is* my
strength and song;
He also has become my
salvation.' "
3 Therefore with joy you will
draw [a]water
From the wells of salvation.

4 And in that day you will say:

[a]"Praise the LORD, call upon
His name;
[b]Declare His deeds among
the peoples,
Make mention that His
[c]name is exalted.
5 [a]Sing to the LORD,
For He has done excellent
things;
This *is* known in all the
earth.
6 [a]Cry out and shout,
O inhabitant of Zion,
For great *is* [b]the Holy One of
Israel in your midst!"

13

The [a]burden[1] against Babylon which Ī·sāi′ah the son of Ā′moz saw.

2 "Lift[a] up a banner [b]on the
high mountain,
Raise your voice to them;
[c]Wave your hand, that they
may enter the gates of
the nobles.
3 I have commanded My
[1]sanctified ones;
I have also called [a]My
mighty ones for My
anger—
Those who [b]rejoice in My
exaltation."

4 The [a]noise of a multitude in
the mountains,
Like that of many people!
A tumultuous noise of the
kingdoms of nations
gathered together!
The LORD of hosts musters
The army for battle.
5 They come from a far
country,
From the end of heaven—
The [a]LORD and His [1]weapons
of indignation,
To destroy the whole [b]land.

6 Wail, [a]for the day of the
LORD *is* at hand!
[b]It will come as destruction
from the Almighty.

---

15 [a]Zech. 10:10, 11 [1]So with MT, Vg.; LXX, Syr., Tg. *dry up* [2]The Euphrates [3]Lit. *in sandals*
16 [a]Is. 19:23 [b]Ex. 14:29

CHAPTER 12

1 [a]Is. 2:11
2 [a]Ps. 83:18 [b]Ex. 15:2
3 [a][John 4:10, 14; 7:37, 38]
4 [a]1 Chr. 16:8 [b]Ps. 145:4–6 [c]Ps. 34:3
5 [a]Ex. 15:1
6 [a]Zeph. 3:14, 15 [b]Ps. 89:18

CHAPTER 13

1 [a]Jer. 50; 51 [1]*oracle, prophecy*
2 [a]Is. 18:3 [b]Jer. 51:25 [c]Is. 10:32
3 [a]Joel 3:11 [b]Ps. 149:2 [1]*consecrated* or *set apart*
4 [a]Is. 17:12
5 [a]Is. 42:13 [b]Is. 24:1; 34:2 [1]Or *instruments*
6 [a]Zeph. 1:7 [b]Joel 1:15

7 Therefore all hands will be limp,
Every man's heart will melt,
8 And they will be afraid.
[a]Pangs[1] and sorrows will take hold of *them;*
They will be in pain as a woman in childbirth;
They will be amazed at one another;
Their faces *will be like* flames.

9 Behold, [a]the day of the LORD comes,
Cruel, with both wrath and fierce anger,
To lay the land desolate;
And He will destroy [b]its sinners from it.
10 For the stars of heaven and their constellations
Will not give their light;
The sun will be [a]darkened in its going forth,
And the moon will not cause its light to shine.

11 "I will [a]punish the world for *its* evil,
And the wicked for their iniquity;
[b]I will halt the arrogance of the proud,
And will lay low the haughtiness of the [1]terrible.
12 I will make a mortal more rare than fine gold,
A man more than the golden wedge of Ō′phir.
13 [a]Therefore I will shake the heavens,
And the earth will move out of her place,
In the wrath of the LORD of hosts

8 [a]Ps. 48:6
[1]*Sharp pains*
9 [a]Mal. 4:1
[b]Prov. 2:22
10 [a]Joel 2:31
11 [a]Is. 26:21
[b][Is. 2:17]
[1]Or *tyrants*
13 [a]Hag. 2:6
[b]Lam. 1:12
14 [a]Jer. 50:16; 51:9
[1]*gathers*
16 [a]Nah. 3:10
[b]Zech. 14:2
17 [a]Dan. 5:28, 31
[1]*esteem*
19 [a]Is. 14:4
[b]Gen. 19:24
20 [a]Jer. 50:3

And in [b]the day of His fierce anger.
14 It shall be as the hunted gazelle,
And as a sheep that no man [1]takes up;
[a]Every man will turn to his own people,
And everyone will flee to his own land.
15 Everyone who is found will be thrust through,
And everyone who is captured will fall by the sword.
16 Their children also will be [a]dashed to pieces before their eyes;
Their houses will be plundered
And their wives [b]ravished.

17 "Behold,[a] I will stir up the Mēdes against them,
Who will not [1]regard silver;
And *as for* gold, they will not delight in it.
18 Also *their* bows will dash the young men to pieces,
And they will have no pity on the fruit of the womb;
Their eye will not spare children.
19 [a]And Babylon, the glory of kingdoms,
The beauty of the Chal·dē′ans' pride,
Will be as when God overthrew [b]Sod′om and Go·mor′rah.
20 [a]It will never be inhabited,
Nor will it be settled from generation to generation;
Nor will the Arabian pitch tents there,
Nor will the shepherds make their sheepfolds there.

21 [a]But wild beasts of the desert
will lie there,
And their houses will be full
of [1]owls;
Ostriches will dwell there,
And wild goats will caper
there.
22 The hyenas will howl in
their citadels,
And jackals in their
pleasant palaces.
[a]Her time *is* near to come,
And her days will not be
prolonged."

14 For the LORD [a]will have
mercy on Jacob, and [b]will
still choose Israel, and settle
them in their own land. [c]The
strangers will be joined with
them, and they will cling to the
house of Jacob.
2 Then people will take them
[a]and bring them to their place,
and the house of Israel will possess them for servants and maids
in the land of the LORD; they will
take them captive whose captives they were, [b]and rule over
their oppressors.
3 It shall come to pass in the
day the LORD gives you rest from
your sorrow, and from your fear
and the hard bondage in which
you were made to serve,
4 that you [a]will take up this
proverb against the king of Babylon, and say:

"How the oppressor has
ceased,
The [b]golden[1] city ceased!
5 The LORD has broken [a]the
staff of the wicked,
The scepter of the rulers;
6 He who struck the people in
wrath with a continual
stroke,
He who ruled the nations in
anger,
Is persecuted *and* no one
hinders.
7 The whole earth is at rest
and quiet;
They break forth into
singing.
8 [a]Indeed the cypress trees
rejoice over you,
And the cedars of Lebanon,
Saying, 'Since you [1]were cut
down,
No woodsman has come up
against us.'

9 "Hell[a1] from beneath is
excited about you,
To meet *you* at your coming;
It stirs up the dead for you,
All the chief ones of the
earth;
It has raised up from their
thrones
All the kings of the nations.
10 They all shall [a]speak and
say to you:
'Have you also become as
weak as we?
Have you become like us?
11 Your pomp is brought down
to Shē′ōl,
And the sound of your
stringed instruments;
The maggot is spread under
you,
And worms cover you.'

12 "How[a] you are fallen from
heaven,
O [1]Lū′ci·fer, son of the
morning!
How you are cut down to
the ground,
You who weakened the
nations!
13 For you have said in your
heart:

21 [a]Is. 34:11–15 [1]Or *howling creatures*
22 [a]Jer. 51:33

CHAPTER 14

1 [a]Ps. 102:13 [b]Zech. 1:17; 2:12 [c]Is. 60:4, 5, 10
2 [a]Is. 49:22; 60:9; 66:20 [b]Is. 60:14
4 [a]Hab. 2:6 [b]Rev. 18:16 [1]Or *insolent*
5 [a]Ps. 125:3
8 [a]Ezek. 31:16 [1]*have lain down*
9 [a]Ezek. 32:21 [1]Or *Sheol*
10 [a]Ezek. 32:21
12 [a]Is. 34:4 [1]Lit. *Day Star*

[a]"I will ascend into heaven,
[b]I will exalt my throne above
the stars of God;
I will also sit on the [c]mount
of the congregation
[d]On the farthest sides of the
north;
14 I will ascend above the
heights of the clouds,
[a]I will be like the Most High.'
15 Yet you [a]shall be brought
down to Shē′ōl,
To the [1]lowest depths of the
Pit.

16 "Those who see you will gaze
at you,
And consider you, *saying:*
'*Is* this the man who made
the earth tremble,
Who shook kingdoms,
17 Who made the world as a
wilderness
And destroyed its cities,
Who [1]did not open the
house of his prisoners?'

18 "All the kings of the nations,
All of them, sleep in glory,
Everyone in his own house;
19 But you are cast out of your
grave
Like an [1]abominable branch,
Like the garment of those
who are slain,
[2]Thrust through with a
sword,
Who go down to the stones
of the pit,
Like a corpse trodden
underfoot.
20 You will not be joined with
them in burial,
Because you have destroyed
your land
And slain your people.
[a]The brood of evildoers shall
never be named.

13 [a]Ezek. 28:2 [b]Dan. 8:10 [c]Ezek. 28:14 [d]Ps. 48:2
14 [a]2 Thess. 2:4
15 [a]Matt. 11:23 [1]Lit. *recesses*
17 [1]Would not release
19 [1]*despised* [2]*Pierced*
20 [a]Ps. 21:10; 109:13
21 [a]Ex. 20:5
22 [a]Prov. 10:7 [b]1 Kin. 14:10 [c]Job 18:19
23 [a]Zeph. 2:14
24 [a]Is. 43:13
25 [a]Mic. 5:5, 6 [b]Is. 10:27
26 [a]Is. 23:9
27 [a]Dan. 4:31, 35

21 Prepare slaughter for his
children
[a]Because of the iniquity of
their fathers,
Lest they rise up and
possess the land,
And fill the face of the
world with cities."

22 "For I will rise up against
them," says the LORD of
hosts,
"And cut off from Babylon
[a]the name and [b]remnant,
[c]And offspring and
posterity," says the LORD.
23 "I will also make it a
possession for the
[a]porcupine,
And marshes of muddy
water;
I will sweep it with the
broom of destruction,"
says the LORD of hosts.

24 The LORD of hosts has
sworn, saying,
"Surely, as I have thought, so
it shall come to pass,
And as I have purposed, *so*
it shall [a]stand:
25 That I will break the
[a]Assyrian in My land,
And on My mountains tread
him underfoot.
Then [b]his yoke shall be
removed from them,
And his burden removed
from their shoulders.
26 This *is* the [a]purpose that is
purposed against the
whole earth,
And this *is* the hand that is
stretched out over all the
nations.
27 For the LORD of hosts has
[a]purposed,
And who will annul *it*?

His hand *is* stretched out,
And who will turn it back?"

28 This is the [1]burden which came in the year that [a]King Ā'haz died.

29 "Do not rejoice, all you of Phi·lis'ti·a,
[a]Because the rod that struck you is broken;
For out of the serpent's roots will come forth a viper,
[b]And its offspring *will be* a fiery flying serpent.
30 The firstborn of the poor will feed,
And the needy will lie down in safety;
I will kill your roots with famine,
And it will slay your remnant.
31 Wail, O gate! Cry, O city!
All you of Phi·lis'ti·a *are* dissolved;
For smoke will come from the north,
And no one *will be* alone in his [1]appointed times."

32 What will they answer the messengers of the nation?
That [a]the LORD has founded Zion,
And [b]the poor of His people shall take refuge in it.

15

The [a]burden[1] against Mō'ab.

Because in the night [b]Ar of [c]Mō'ab is laid waste
And destroyed,
Because in the night Kir of Mō'ab is laid waste
And destroyed,

28 [a]2 Kin. 16:20 [1]*oracle, prophecy*
29 [a]2 Chr. 26:6 [b]2 Kin. 18:8
31 [1]Or *ranks*
32 [a]Ps. 87:1, 5 [b]Zech. 11:11

CHAPTER 15

1 [a]2 Kin. 3:4 [b]Deut. 2:9 [c]Amos 2:1–3 [1]*oracle, prophecy*
2 [a]Lev. 21:5 [1]Heb. *bayith*, lit. *house*
3 [a]Jer. 48:38
4 [a]Jer. 48:34 [1]So with MT, Tg., Vg.; LXX, Syr. *loins*
5 [a]Jer. 48:31 [b]Jer. 48:5 [1]Or *The Third Eglath*, an unknown city, Jer. 48:34
6 [a]Num. 32:36

2 He has gone up to the [1]temple and Dī'bon,
To the high places to weep.
Mō'ab will wail over Nē'bō and over Med'e·ba;
[a]On all their heads *will be* baldness,
And every beard cut off.
3 In their streets they will clothe themselves with sackcloth;
On the tops of their houses
And in their streets
Everyone will wail, [a]weeping bitterly.
4 Hesh'bon and Ē·le·ā'leh will cry out,
Their voice shall be heard as far as [a]Jā'haz;
Therefore the [1]armed soldiers of Mō'ab will cry out;
His life will be burdensome to him.

5 "My[a] heart will cry out for Mō'ab;
His fugitives *shall flee* to Zō'ar,
Like [1]a three-year-old heifer.
For [b]by the Ascent of Lū'hith
They will go up with weeping;
For in the way of Hor·ō·nā'īm
They will raise up a cry of destruction,
6 For the waters [a]of Nim'rim will be desolate,
For the green grass has withered away;
The grass fails, there is nothing green.
7 Therefore the abundance they have gained,
And what they have laid up,
They will carry away to the Brook of the Willows.

8 For the cry has gone all
around the borders of
Mō′ab,
Its wailing to Eg·lā′im
And its wailing to Bē′er
Ē′lim.
9 For the waters of [1]Dī′mon
will be full of blood;
Because I will bring more
upon [1]Dī′mon,
[a]Lions upon him who
escapes from Mō′ab,
And on the remnant of the
land."

16

Send [a]the lamb to the
ruler of the land,
[b]From [1]Sē′la to the
wilderness,
To the mount of the
daughter of Zion.
2 For it shall be as a
[a]wandering bird thrown
out of the nest;
So shall be the daughters of
Mō′ab at the fords of the
[b]Ar′non.

3 "Take counsel, execute
judgment;
Make your shadow like the
night in the middle of
the day;
Hide the outcasts,
Do not betray him who
escapes.
4 Let My outcasts dwell with
you, O Mō′ab;
Be a shelter to them from
the face of the [1]spoiler.
For the extortioner is at an
end,
Devastation ceases,
The oppressors are
consumed out of the
land.
5 In mercy [a]the throne will be
established;
And One will sit on it in
truth, in the tabernacle
of David,
[b]Judging and seeking
justice and hastening
[c]righteousness."

6 We have heard of the [a]pride
of Mō′ab—
He is very proud—
Of his haughtiness and his
pride and his wrath;
[b]*But* his [1]lies *shall* not *be* so.
7 Therefore Mō′ab shall [a]wail
for Mō′ab;
Everyone shall wail.
For the foundations [b]of Kir
Har′e·seth you shall
mourn;
Surely *they are* stricken.

8 For [a]the fields of Hesh′bon
languish,
And [b]the vine of Sib′mah;
The lords of the nations
have broken down its
choice plants,
Which have reached to
Jā′zer
And wandered through the
wilderness.
Her branches are stretched
out,
They are gone over the [c]sea.
9 Therefore I will bewail the
vine of Sib′mah,
With the weeping of Jā′zer;
I will drench you with my
tears,
[a]O Hesh′bon and Ē·le·ā′leh;
For [1]battle cries have fallen
Over your summer fruits
and your harvest.

10 [a]Gladness is taken away,
And joy from the plentiful
field;

---

9 [a]2 Kin. 17:25 [1]So with MT, Tg.; DSS, Vg. *Dibon;* LXX *Rimon*

CHAPTER 16

1 [a]2 Kin. 3:4 [b]2 Kin. 14:7 [1]Lit. *Rock*

2 [a]Prov. 27:8 [b]Num. 21:13

4 [1]*devastator*

5 [a][Dan. 7:14] [b]Ps. 72:2 [c]Is. 9:7

6 [a]Jer. 48:29 [b]Is. 28:15 [1]Lit. *vain talk*

7 [a]Jer. 48:20 [b]2 Kin. 3:25

8 [a]Is. 24:7 [b]Is. 16:9 [c]Jer. 48:32

9 [a]Is. 15:4 [1]Or *shouting has*

10 [a]Is. 24:8

In the vineyards there will
be no singing,
Nor will there be shouting;
No treaders will tread out
wine in the presses;
I have made their shouting
cease.
11 Therefore [a]my [1]heart shall
resound like a harp for
Mō′ab,
And my inner being for [2]Kir
Hē′res.

12 And it shall come to pass,
When it is seen that Mō′ab
is weary on [a]the high
place,
That he will come to his
sanctuary to pray;
But he will not prevail.

13 This *is* the word which the
LORD has spoken concerning
Mō′ab since that time.
14 But now the LORD has spoken, saying, "Within three years,
[a]as the years of a hired man, the
glory of Mō′ab will be despised
with all that great multitude,
and the remnant *will be* very
small *and* feeble."

17

The [a]burden[1] against Damascus.

"Behold, Damascus will
cease from *being* a city,
And it will be a ruinous
heap.
2 [1]The cities of [a]A·rō′er *are*
forsaken;
They will be for flocks
Which lie down, and [b]no
one will make *them*
afraid.
3 [a]The fortress also will cease
from Ē′phra·im,
The kingdom from
Damascus,
And the remnant of Syria;
They will be as the glory of
the children of Israel,"
Says the LORD of hosts.

4 "In that day it shall come to
pass
That the glory of Jacob will
[1]wane,
And [a]the fatness of his flesh
grow lean.
5 [a]It shall be as when the
harvester gathers the
grain,
And reaps the heads with
his arm;
It shall be as he who gathers
heads of grain
In the Valley of Reph′a·im.
6 [a]Yet gleaning grapes will be
left in it,
Like the shaking of an olive
tree,
Two *or* three olives at the
top of the uppermost
bough,
Four *or* five in its most
fruitful branches,"
Says the LORD God of Israel.

7 In that day a man will [a]look
to his Maker,
And his eyes will have
respect for the Holy One
of Israel.
8 He will not look to the
altars,
The work of his hands;
He will not respect what his
[a]fingers have made,
Nor the [1]wooden images nor
the incense altars.

9 In that day his strong cities
will be as a forsaken
[1]bough
And [2]an uppermost branch,

11 [a]Jer. 48:36 [1]Lit. *belly* [2]*Kir Hareseth*, v. 7
12 [a]Is. 15:2
14 [a]Is. 21:16

CHAPTER 17

1 [a]Zech. 9:1 [1]*oracle, prophecy*
2 [a]Num. 32:34 [b]Jer. 7:33 [1]So with MT, Vg.; LXX *It shall be forsaken forever;* Tg. *Its cities shall be forsaken and desolate*
3 [a]Is. 7:16; 8:4
4 [a]Is. 10:16 [1]*fade*
5 [a]Jer. 51:33
6 [a]Is. 24:13
7 [a]Mic. 7:7
8 [a]Is. 2:8; 31:7 [1]Heb. *Asherim*, Canaanite deities
9 [1]LXX *Hivites;* Tg. *laid waste;* Vg. *as the plows* [2]LXX *Amorites;* Tg. *in ruins;* Vg. *corn*

Which they left because of
the children of Israel;
And there will be
desolation.

10 Because you have forgotten
[a]the God of your
salvation,
And have not been mindful
of the Rock of your
[1]stronghold,
Therefore you will plant
pleasant plants
And set out foreign
seedlings;
11 In the day you will make
your plant to grow,
And in the morning you
will make your seed to
flourish;
But the harvest *will be* a
heap of ruins
In the day of grief and
desperate sorrow.

12 Woe to the multitude of
many people
Who make a noise [a]like the
roar of the seas,
And to the rushing of
nations
That make a rushing like
the rushing of mighty
waters!
13 The nations will rush like
the rushing of many
waters;
But *God* will [a]rebuke them
and they will flee far
away,
And [b]be chased like the
chaff of the mountains
before the wind,
Like a rolling thing before
the whirlwind.
14 Then behold, at eventide,
trouble!
And before the morning, he
is no more.
This *is* the portion of those
who plunder us,
And the lot of those who
rob us.

18

Woe [a]to the land
shadowed with
buzzing wings,
Which *is* beyond the rivers
of [1]Ethiopia,
2 Which sends ambassadors
by sea,
Even in vessels of reed on
the waters, *saying,*
"Go, swift messengers, to a
nation tall and smooth
of *skin,*
To a people terrible from
their beginning onward,
A nation powerful and
treading down,
Whose land the rivers
divide."

3 All inhabitants of the world
and dwellers on the
earth:
[a]When he lifts up a banner
on the mountains, you
see *it;*
And when he blows a
trumpet, you hear *it.*
4 For so the LORD said to me,
"I will take My rest,
And I will [1]look from My
dwelling place
Like clear heat in sunshine,
Like a cloud of dew in the
heat of harvest."
5 For before the harvest, when
the bud is perfect
And the sour grape is
ripening in the flower,
He will both cut off the
sprigs with pruning
hooks

10 [a]Ps. 68:19 [1]*refuge*
12 [a]Jer. 6:23
13 [a]Ps. 9:5 [b]Hos. 13:3

CHAPTER 18

1 [a]Zeph. 2:12; 3:10 [1]Heb. *Cush*
3 [a]Is. 5:26
4 [1]*watch*

And take away *and* cut
down the branches.
6 They will be left together
for the mountain birds of
prey
And for the beasts of the
earth;
The birds of prey will
summer on them,
And all the beasts of the
earth will winter on
them.

7 In that time [a]a present will
be brought to the LORD
of hosts
[1]From a people tall and
smooth *of skin,*
And from a people terrible
from their beginning
onward,
A nation powerful and
treading down,
Whose land the rivers
divide—
To the place of the name of
the LORD of hosts,
To Mount Zion.

19

The [a]burden[1] against Egypt.

Behold, the LORD [b]rides on a
swift cloud,
And will come into Egypt;
[c]The idols of Egypt will
[2]totter at His presence,
And the heart of Egypt will
melt in its midst.

2 "I will [a]set Egyptians against
Egyptians;
Everyone will fight against
his brother,
And everyone against his
neighbor,
City against city, kingdom
against kingdom.
3 The spirit of Egypt will fail
in its midst;
I will destroy their counsel,
And they will [a]consult the
idols and the charmers,
The mediums and the
sorcerers.
4 And the Egyptians I will
give
[a]Into the hand of a cruel
master,
And a fierce king will rule
over them,"
Says the Lord, the LORD of
hosts.

5 [a]The waters will fail from the
sea,
And the river will be wasted
and dried up.
6 The rivers will turn foul;
The brooks [a]of defense will
be emptied and dried up;
The reeds and rushes will
wither.
7 The papyrus reeds by [1]the
River, by the mouth of
the River,
And everything sown by the
River,
Will wither, be driven away,
and be no more.
8 The fishermen also will
mourn;
All those will lament who
cast hooks into the
River,
And they will languish
who spread nets on the
waters.
9 Moreover those who work
in [a]fine flax
And those who weave fine
fabric will be ashamed;
10 And its foundations will be
broken.
All who make wages *will be*
troubled of soul.

7 [a]Zeph. 3:10 [1]So with DSS, LXX, Vg.; MT omits *From;* Tg. *To*

CHAPTER 19

1 [a]Joel 3:19 [b]Ps. 18:10; 104:3 [c]Jer. 43:12 [1]*oracle, prophecy* [2]Lit. *shake*

2 [a]Judg. 7:22

3 [a]Is. 8:19; 47:12

4 [a]Ezek. 29:19

5 [a]Jer. 51:36

6 [a]2 Kin. 19:24

7 [1]The Nile

9 [a]Prov. 7:16

11 Surely the princes of [a]Zō′an
are fools;
Pharaoh's wise counselors
give foolish counsel.
[b]How do you say to Pharaoh,
"I *am* the son of the
wise,
The son of ancient kings?"
12 [a]Where *are* they?
Where are your wise men?
Let them tell you now,
And let them know what
the LORD of hosts has
[b]purposed against Egypt.
13 The princes of Zō′an have
become fools;
[a]The princes of [1]Noph are
deceived;
They have also [2]deluded
Egypt,
Those who are the
[3]mainstay of its tribes.
14 The LORD has mingled [a]a
perverse spirit in her
midst;
And they have caused Egypt
to err in all her work,
As a drunken man staggers
in his vomit.
15 Neither will there be *any*
work for Egypt,
Which [a]the head or tail,
Palm branch or bulrush,
may do.

16 In that day Egypt will [a]be
like women, and will be afraid
and fear because of the waving
of the hand of the LORD of hosts,
[b]which He waves over it.
17 And the land of Judah will
be a terror to Egypt; everyone
who makes mention of it will
be afraid in himself, because
of the counsel of the LORD of
hosts which He has [a]determined
against it.
18 In that day five cities in the
land of Egypt will [a]speak the
language of Cā′naan and [b]swear
by the LORD of hosts; one will be
called the City of [1]Destruction.
19 In that day [a]there will be an
altar to the LORD in the midst of
the land of Egypt, and a pillar to
the [b]LORD at its border.
20 And [a]it will be for a sign
and for a witness to the LORD
of hosts in the land of Egypt;
for they will cry to the LORD because of the oppressors, and He
will send them a [b]Savior and a
Mighty One, and He will deliver
them.
21 Then the LORD will be known
to Egypt, and the Egyptians will
[a]know the LORD in that day, and
[b]will make sacrifice and offering; yes, they will make a vow to
the LORD and perform *it.*
22 And the LORD will strike
Egypt, He will strike and [a]heal
it; they will return to the LORD,
and He will be entreated by
them and heal them.
23 In that day [a]there will be a
highway from Egypt to Assyria,
and the Assyrian will come into
Egypt and the Egyptian into Assyria, and the Egyptians will
[b]serve with the Assyrians.
24 In that day Israel will be
one of three with Egypt and
Assyria—a blessing in the midst
of the land,
25 whom the LORD of hosts shall
bless, saying, "Blessed *is* Egypt
My people, and Assyria [a]the
work of My hands, and Israel
My inheritance."

20

In the year that [a]Tartan[1]
came to Ash′dod, when
Sar′gon the king of Assyria sent
him, and he fought against Ash′-
dod and took it,
2 at the same time the LORD

11 [a]Num. 13:22 [b]1 Kin. 4:29, 30
12 [a]1 Cor. 1:20 [b]Ps. 33:11
13 [a]Jer. 2:16 [1]Ancient Memphis [2]Lit. *caused to stagger* [3]*cornerstone*
14 [a]Is. 29:10
15 [a]Is. 9:14–16
16 [a]Nah. 3:13 [b]Is. 11:15
17 [a]Dan. 4:35
18 [a]Zeph. 3:9 [b]Is. 45:23 [1]Some Heb. mss., Arab., DSS, Tg., Vg. *Sun;* LXX *Asedek,* lit. *Righteousness*
19 [a]Ex. 24:4 [b]Ps. 68:31
20 [a]Josh. 4:20; 22:27 [b]Is. 43:11
21 [a][Is. 2:3, 4; 11:9] [b]Mal. 1:11
22 [a]Deut. 32:39
23 [a]Is. 11:16; 35:8; 49:11; 62:10 [b]Is. 27:13
25 [a]Is. 29:23

CHAPTER 20

1 [a]2 Kin. 18:17 [1]Or *the Commander in Chief*

spoke by Ī·sāi′ah the son of
Ā′moz, saying, "Go, and remove
[a]the sackcloth from your [1]body,
and take your sandals off your
feet." And he did so, [b]walking
naked and barefoot.
3 Then the LORD said, "Just as
My servant Ī·sāi′ah has walked
naked and barefoot three years
[a]*for* a sign and a wonder against
Egypt and Ethiopia,
4 "so shall the [a]king of Assyria
lead away the Egyptians as prisoners and the Ethiopians as
captives, young and old, naked
and barefoot, [b]with their buttocks uncovered, to the shame
of Egypt.
5 [a]"Then they shall be afraid
and ashamed of Ethiopia their
expectation and Egypt their
glory.
6 "And the inhabitant of this
territory will say in that day,
'Surely such *is* our expectation, wherever we flee for [a]help
to be delivered from the king
of Assyria; and how shall we
escape?' "

21 The [1]burden against the Wilderness of the Sea.

As [a]whirlwinds in the South
pass through,
So it comes from the desert,
from a terrible land.
2 A distressing vision is
declared to me;
[a]The treacherous dealer
deals treacherously,
And the plunderer plunders.
[b]Go up, O Ē′lam!
Besiege, O Media!
All its sighing I have made
to cease.

3 Therefore [a]my loins are
filled with pain;
[b]Pangs have taken hold of
me, like the pangs of a
woman in labor.
I was [1]distressed when *I*
heard *it;*
I was dismayed when *I* saw
it.
4 My heart wavered,
fearfulness frightened
me;
[a]The night for which I longed
He turned into fear for
me.
5 [a]Prepare the table,
Set a watchman in the
tower,
Eat and drink.
Arise, you princes,
Anoint the shield!

6 For thus has the Lord said
to me:
"Go, set a watchman,
Let him declare what he
sees."
7 And he saw a chariot *with* a
pair of horsemen,
A chariot of donkeys, *and* a
chariot of camels,
And he listened earnestly
with great care.
8 [1]Then he cried, "A lion, my
Lord!
I stand continually on the
[a]watchtower in the
daytime;
I have sat at my post every
night.
9 And look, here comes a
chariot of men *with* a
pair of horsemen!"
Then he answered and said,
[a]"Babylon is fallen, is fallen!
And [b]all the carved images
of her gods
He has broken to the
ground."

2 [a]Zech. 13:4 [b]1 Sam. 19:24 [1]Lit. *loins*
3 [a]Is. 8:18
4 [a]Is. 19:4 [b]Jer. 13:22
5 [a]2 Kin. 18:21
6 [a]Is. 30:5, 7

CHAPTER 21
1 [a]Zech. 9:14 [1]*oracle, prophecy*
2 [a]Is. 33:1 [b]Jer. 49:34
3 [a]Is. 15:5; 16:11 [b]Is. 13:8 [1]Lit. *bowed*
4 [a]Deut. 28:67
5 [a]Dan. 5:5
8 [a]Hab. 2:1 [1]DSS *Then the observer cried, "My Lord!*
9 [a]Jer. 51:8 [b]Is. 46:1

10 [a]Oh, my threshing and the
grain of my floor!
That which I have heard
from the LORD of hosts,
The God of Israel,
I have declared to you.

11 [a]The [1]burden against Dū′-
mah.

He calls to me out of [b]Sē′ir,
"Watchman, what of the
night?
Watchman, what of the
night?"
12 The watchman said,
"The morning comes, and
also the night.
If you will inquire, inquire;
Return! Come back!"

13 [a]The [1]burden against Arabia.

In the forest in Arabia you
will lodge,
O you traveling companies
[b]of Ded′an·ītes.
14 O inhabitants of the land of
Tē′ma,
Bring water to him who is
thirsty;
With their bread they met
him who fled.
15 For they fled from the
swords, from the drawn
sword,
From the bent bow, and
from the distress of war.

16 For thus the LORD has said to
me: "Within a year, [a]according
to the year of a hired man, all
the glory of [b]Kē′dar will fail;
17 "and the remainder of the
number of archers, the mighty
men of the people of Kē′dar, will
be diminished; for the LORD God
of Israel has spoken *it*."

22

The [1]burden against the Valley of Vision.

What ails you now, that you
have all gone up to the
housetops,
2 You who are full of noise,
A [1]tumultuous city, [a]a joyous
city?
Your slain *men are* not slain
with the sword,
Nor dead in battle.
3 All your rulers have fled
together;
They are captured by the
archers.
All who are found in you
are bound together;
They have fled from afar.
4 Therefore I said, "Look
away from me,
[a]I will weep bitterly;
Do not labor to comfort
me
Because of the plundering
of the daughter of my
people."

5 [a]For *it is* a day of trouble
and treading down and
perplexity
[b]By the Lord GOD of hosts
In the Valley of Vision—
Breaking down the walls
And of crying to the
mountain.
6 [a]Ē′lam bore the quiver
With chariots of men *and*
horsemen,
And [b]Kir uncovered the
shield.
7 It shall come to pass *that*
your choicest valleys
Shall be full of chariots,
And the horsemen shall set
themselves in array at
the gate.

10 [a]Jer. 51:33
11 [a]Gen. 25:14 [b]Gen. 32:3 [1]*oracle, prophecy*
13 [a]Jer. 25:24; 49:28 [b]1 Chr. 1:9, 32 [1]*oracle, prophecy*
16 [a]Is. 16:14 [b]Ps. 120:5

CHAPTER 22

1 [1]*oracle, prophecy*
2 [a]Is. 32:13 [1]*boisterous*
4 [a]Jer. 4:19
5 [a]Is. 37:3 [b]Lam. 1:5; 2:2
6 [a]Jer. 49:35 [b]Is. 15:1

8 [a]He removed the [1]protection
of Judah.
You looked in that day to
the armor [b]of the House
of the Forest;
9 [a]You also saw the [1]damage to
the city of David,
That it was great;
And you gathered together
the waters of the lower
pool.
10 You numbered the houses of
Jerusalem,
And the houses you broke
down
To fortify the wall.
11 [a]You also made a reservoir
between the two walls
For the water of the old
[b]pool.
But you did not look to its
Maker,
Nor did you have respect
for Him who fashioned it
long ago.

12 And in that day the Lord
GOD of hosts
[a]Called for weeping and for
mourning,
[b]For baldness and for girding
with sackcloth.
13 But instead, joy and
gladness,
Slaying oxen and killing
sheep,
Eating meat and [a]drinking
wine:
[b]"Let us eat and drink, for
tomorrow we die!"

14 [a]Then it was revealed in my
hearing by the LORD of
hosts,
"Surely for this iniquity there
[b]will be no atonement
for you,

8 [a]2 Kin. 18:15, 16 [b]1 Kin. 7:2; 10:17 [1]Lit. *covering*
9 [a]2 Kin. 20:20 [1]Lit. *breaches* in the city walls
11 [a]Neh. 3:16 [b]2 Chr. 32:3, 4
12 [a]Joel 1:13; 2:17 [b]Mic. 1:16
13 [a]Luke 17:26–29 [b]1 Cor. 15:32
14 [a]Is. 5:9 [b]Ezek. 24:13
15 [a]Is. 36:3
16 [a]Matt. 27:60
17 [a]Esth. 7:8
18 [a]Is. 2:7
19 [1]LXX omits *he will pull you down;* Syr., Tg., Vg. *I will pull you down*
20 [a]2 Kin. 18:18

Even to your death," says
the Lord GOD of hosts.

15 Thus says the Lord GOD of
hosts:

"Go, proceed to this steward,
To [a]Sheb′na, who *is* over the
house, *and say:*
16 'What have you here, and
whom have you here,
That you have hewn a
sepulcher here,
As he [a]who hews himself a
sepulcher on high,
Who carves a tomb for
himself in a rock?
17 Indeed, the LORD will throw
you away violently,
O mighty man,
[a]And will surely seize you.
18 He will surely turn violently
and toss you like a ball
Into a large country;
There you shall die, and
there [a]your glorious
chariots
Shall be the shame of your
master's house.
19 So I will drive you out of
your office,
And from your position [1]he
will pull you down.

20 'Then it shall be in that day,
That I will call My servant
[a]E·lī′a·kim the son of
Hil·kī′ah;
21 I will clothe him with your
robe
And strengthen him with
your belt;
I will commit your
responsibility into his
hand.
He shall be a father to the
inhabitants of Jerusalem
And to the house of Judah.

☆ 22 The key of the house of
David
I will lay on his [a]shoulder;
So he shall [b]open, and no
one shall shut;
And he shall shut, and no
one shall open.
23 I will fasten him *as* [a]a peg in
a secure place,
And he will become a
glorious throne to his
father's house.

24 'They will hang on him all
the glory of his father's house,
the offspring and the posterity, all vessels of small quantity,
from the cups to all the pitchers.
25 'In that day,' says the LORD of
hosts, 'the peg that is fastened in
the secure place will be removed
and be cut down and fall, and the
burden that *was* on it will be cut
off; for the LORD has spoken.' "

23

The [a]burden[1] against Tȳre.

Wail, you ships of Tar'shish!
For it is laid waste,
So that there is no house, no
harbor;
From the land of [2]Cyprus it
is revealed to them.

2 Be still, you inhabitants of
the coastland,
You merchants of Sī'don,
[1]Whom those who cross the
sea have filled.
3 And on great waters the
grain of Shī'hor,
The harvest of [1]the River, *is*
her revenue;
And [a]she is a marketplace
for the nations.

4 Be ashamed, O Sī'don;
For the sea has spoken,
The strength of the sea,
saying,
"I do not labor, nor bring
forth children;
Neither do I rear young
men,
Nor bring up virgins."
5 [a]When the report *reaches*
Egypt,
They also will be in agony
at the report of Tȳre.

6 Cross over to Tar'shish;
Wail, you inhabitants of the
coastland!
7 *Is* this your [a]joyous *city,*
Whose antiquity *is* from
ancient days,
Whose feet carried her far
off to dwell?
8 Who has taken this counsel
against Tȳre, [a]the
crowning *city,*
Whose merchants *are*
princes,
Whose traders *are* the
honorable of the earth?
9 The LORD of hosts has
[a]purposed it,
To [1]bring to dishonor the
[b]pride of all glory,
To bring into contempt all
the honorable of the
earth.

10 Overflow through your land
like [1]the River,
O daughter of Tar'shish;
There is no more [2]strength.
11 He stretched out His hand
over the sea,
He shook the kingdoms;
The LORD has given a
commandment [a]against
Cā'naan
To destroy its strongholds.
12 And He said, "You will
rejoice no more,

22 [a]Is. 9:6 [b]Job 12:14; Rev. 3:7
23 [a]Ezra 9:8

CHAPTER 23

1 [a]Zech. 9:2, 4 [1]*oracle, prophecy* [2]Heb. *Kittim,* western lands, especially Cyprus
2 [1]So with MT, Vg.; LXX, Tg. *Passing over the water;* DSS *Your messengers passing over the sea*
3 [a]Ezek. 27:3–23 [1]The Nile
5 [a]Is. 19:16
7 [a]Is. 22:2; 32:13
8 [a]Ezek. 28:2, 12
9 [a]Is. 14:26 [b]Dan. 4:37 [1]*pollute*
10 [1]The Nile [2]*restraint,* lit. *belt*
11 [a]Zech. 9:2–4

O you oppressed virgin
daughter of Sī′don.
Arise, [a]cross over to Cyprus;
There also you will have no
rest."

13 Behold, the land of the
[a]Chal·dē′ans,
This people *which* was not;
Assyria founded it for [b]wild
beasts of the desert.
They set up its towers,
They raised up its palaces,
And brought it to ruin.

14 [a]Wail, you ships of Tar′shish!
For your strength is laid
waste.

15 Now it shall come to pass in
that day that Tȳre will be forgotten seventy years, according
to the days of one king. At the
end of seventy years it will happen to Tȳre as *in* the song of the
harlot:

16 "Take a harp, go about the
city,
You forgotten harlot;
Make sweet melody, sing
many songs,
That you may be
remembered."

17 And it shall be, at the end of
seventy years, that the LORD will
deal with Tȳre. She will return
to her hire, and [a]commit fornication with all the kingdoms of the
world on the face of the earth.
18 Her gain and her pay [a]will
be set apart for the LORD; it will
not be treasured nor laid up, for
her gain will be for those who
dwell before the LORD, to eat sufficiently, and for [1]fine clothing.

12 [a]Rev. 18:22
13 [a]Is. 47:1 [b]Ps. 72:9
14 [a]Ezek. 27:25–30
17 [a]Rev. 17:2
18 [a]Zech. 14:20, 21 [1]*choice*

CHAPTER 24

2 [a]Hos. 4:9 [b]Ezek. 7:12, 13
4 [a]Is. 25:11 [1]*proud*
5 [a]Num. 35:33 [b]Is. 59:12 [c]1 Chr. 16:14–19
6 [a]Mal. 4:6 [b]Is. 9:19 [1]Or *held guilty*
7 [a]Joel 1:10, 12

24

Behold, the LORD makes
the earth empty and
makes it waste,
Distorts its surface
And scatters abroad its
inhabitants.
2 And it shall be:
As with the people, so with
the [a]priest;
As with the servant, so with
his master;
As with the maid, so with
her mistress;
[b]As with the buyer, so with
the seller;
As with the lender, so with
the borrower;
As with the creditor, so with
the debtor.
3 The land shall be entirely
emptied and utterly
plundered,
For the LORD has spoken
this word.

4 The earth mourns *and* fades
away,
The world languishes *and*
fades away;
The [a]haughty[1] people of the
earth languish.
5 [a]The earth is also defiled
under its inhabitants,
Because they have
[b]transgressed the laws,
Changed the ordinance,
Broken the [c]everlasting
covenant.
6 Therefore [a]the curse has
devoured the earth,
And those who dwell in it
are [1]desolate.
Therefore the inhabitants of
the earth are [b]burned,
And few men *are* left.

7 [a]The new wine fails, the vine
languishes,

All the merry-hearted
sigh.
8 The mirth [a]of the
tambourine ceases,
The noise of the jubilant
ends,
The joy of the harp ceases.
9 They shall not drink wine
with a song;
Strong drink is bitter to
those who drink it.
10 The city of confusion is
broken down;
Every house is shut up, so
that none may go in.
11 *There is* a cry for wine in
the streets,
All joy is darkened,
The mirth of the land is
gone.
12 In the city desolation is left,
And the gate is stricken
with destruction.
13 When it shall be thus in the
midst of the land among
the people,
[a]*It shall be* like the shaking
of an olive tree,
Like the gleaning of grapes
when the vintage is
done.

14 They shall lift up their voice,
they shall sing;
For the majesty of the LORD
They shall cry aloud from
the sea.
15 Therefore [a]glorify the LORD
in the dawning light,
[b]The name of the LORD
God of Israel in the
coastlands of the sea.
16 From the ends of the earth
we have heard songs:
"Glory to the righteous!"
But I said, [1]"I am ruined,
ruined!
Woe to me!
[a]The treacherous dealers
have dealt treacherously,
Indeed, the treacherous
dealers have dealt very
treacherously."

17 [a]Fear and the pit and the
snare
Are upon you, O inhabitant
of the earth.
18 And it shall be
That he who flees from the
noise of the fear
Shall fall into the pit,
And he who comes up from
the midst of the pit
Shall be [1]caught in the
snare;
For [a]the windows from on
high are open,
And [b]the foundations of the
earth are shaken.

19 [a]The earth is violently
broken,
The earth is split open,
The earth is shaken
exceedingly.
20 The earth shall [a]reel[1] to and
fro like a drunkard,
And shall totter like a hut;
Its transgression shall be
heavy upon it,
And it will fall, and not rise
again.

21 It shall come to pass in that
day
That the LORD will punish
on high the host of
exalted ones,
And on the earth [a]the kings
of the earth.
22 They will be gathered
together,
As prisoners are gathered in
the [1]pit,

8 [a]Ezek. 26:13
13 [a][Is. 17:5, 6; 27:12]
15 [a]Is. 25:3 [b]Mal. 1:11
16 [a]Jer. 3:20; 5:11 [1]Lit. *Leanness to me, leanness to me*
17 [a]Jer. 48:43
18 [a]Gen. 7:11 [b]Ps. 18:7; 46:2 [1]Lit. *taken*
19 [a]Jer. 4:23
20 [a]Is. 19:14; 24:1; 28:7 [1]*stagger*
21 [a]Ps. 76:12
22 [1]*dungeon*

And will be shut up in the
prison;
After many days they will
be punished.
23 Then the [a]moon will be
disgraced
And the sun ashamed;
For the LORD of hosts will
[b]reign
On [c]Mount Zion and in
Jerusalem
And before His elders,
gloriously.

25 O LORD, You *are* my God.
[a]I will exalt You,
I will praise Your name,
[b]For You have done
wonderful *things;*
[c]*Your* counsels of old *are*
faithfulness *and* truth.
2 For You have made [a]a city a
ruin,
A fortified city a ruin,
A palace of foreigners to be
a city no more;
It will never be rebuilt.
3 Therefore the strong people
will [a]glorify You;
The city of the [1]terrible
nations will fear You.
4 For You have been a
strength to the poor,
A strength to the needy in
his distress,
[a]A refuge from the storm,
A shade from the heat;
For the blast of the terrible
ones *is* as a storm
against the wall.
5 You will reduce the noise of
aliens,
As heat in a dry place;
As heat in the shadow of a
cloud,
The song of the terrible
ones will be [1]diminished.

23 [a]Is. 13:10; 60:19 [b]Rev. 19:4, 6 [c][Heb. 12:22]

CHAPTER 25

1 [a]Ex. 15:2 [b]Ps. 98:1 [c]Num. 23:19

2 [a]Jer. 51:37

3 [a]Is. 24:15 [1]*terrifying*

4 [a]Is. 4:6

5 [1]*humbled*

6 [a][Is. 2:2–4; 56:7] [b]Prov. 9:2 [c][Dan. 7:14] [1]Lit. *fat things* [2]*wines matured on the sediment*

7 [a][Eph. 4:18]

8 [a][Hos. 13:14] [b]Rev. 7:17; 21:4

9 [a]Gen. 49:18 [b]Ps. 20:5

10 [a]Amos 2:1–3

11 [a]Is. 24:4; 26:5

6 And in [a]this mountain
[b]The LORD of hosts will make
for [c]all people
A feast of [1]choice pieces,
A feast of [2]wines on the lees,
Of fat things full of marrow,
Of well-refined wines on the
lees.
7 And He will destroy on this
mountain
The surface of the covering
cast over all people,
And [a]the veil that is spread
over all nations.
8 He will [a]swallow up death
forever,
And the Lord GOD will [b]wipe
away tears from all
faces;
The rebuke of His people
He will take away from all
the earth;
For the LORD has spoken.

9 And it will be said in that
day:
"Behold, this *is* our God;
[a]We have waited for Him,
and He will save us.
This *is* the LORD;
We have waited for Him;
[b]We will be glad and rejoice
in His salvation."

10 For on this mountain the
hand of the LORD will
rest,
And [a]Mō'ab shall be
trampled down under
Him,
As straw is trampled down
for the refuse heap.
11 And He will spread out His
hands in their midst
As a swimmer reaches out
to swim,
And He will bring down
their [a]pride

Together with the trickery of
their hands.
12 The [a]fortress of the high fort
of your walls
He will bring down, lay low,
And bring to the ground,
down to the dust.

26

In [a]that day this song will
be sung in the land of Judah:

"We have a strong city;
[b]*God* will appoint salvation
for walls and bulwarks.
2 [a]Open the gates,
That the righteous nation
which [1]keeps the truth
may enter in.
3 You will keep *him* in perfect
[a]peace,
Whose mind *is* stayed *on*
You,
Because he trusts in You.
4 Trust in the LORD forever,
[a]For in YAH, the LORD, *is*
[1]everlasting strength.
5 For He brings [1]down those
who dwell on high,
[a]The lofty city;
He lays it low,
He lays it low to the ground,
He brings it down to the
dust.
6 The foot shall [1]tread it
down—
The feet of the poor
And the steps of the needy."

7 The way of the just *is*
uprightness;
[a]O Most Upright,
You [1]weigh the path of the
just.
8 Yes, [a]in the way of Your
judgments,
O LORD, we have [b]waited for
You;
The desire of *our* soul *is* for
Your name
And for the remembrance
of You.
9 [a]With my soul I have desired
You in the night,
Yes, by my spirit within me I
will seek You early;
For when Your judgments
are in the earth,
The inhabitants of the world
will learn righteousness.

10 [a]Let grace be shown to the
wicked,
Yet he will not learn
righteousness;
In [b]the land of uprightness
he will deal unjustly,
And will not behold the
majesty of the LORD.
11 LORD, *when* Your hand is
lifted up, [a]they will not
see.
But they will see and be
ashamed
For [1]*their* envy of people;
Yes, the fire of Your enemies
shall devour them.

12 LORD, You will establish
peace for us,
For You have also done all
our works [1]in us.
13 O LORD our God, [a]masters
besides You
Have had dominion over us;
But by You only we make
mention of Your name.
14 *They are* dead, they will not
live;
They are deceased, they will
not rise.
Therefore You have
punished and destroyed
them,
And made all their memory
to [a]perish.

12 [a]Is. 26:5

CHAPTER 26

1 [a]Is. 2:11; 12:1 [b]Is. 60:18

2 [a]Ps. 118:19, 20 [1]Or *remains faithful*

3 [a]Is. 57:19

4 [a]Is. 12:2; 45:17 [1]Or *Rock of Ages*

5 [a]Is. 25:11, 12 [1]*low*

6 [1]*trample*

7 [a]Ps. 37:23 [1]Or *make level*

8 [a]Is. 64:5 [b]Is. 25:9; 33:2

9 [a]Ps. 63:6

10 [a][Rom. 2:4] [b]Ps. 143:10

11 [a]Is. 5:12 [1]Or *Your zeal for the people*

12 [1]Or *for us*

13 [a]2 Chr. 12:8

14 [a]Eccl. 9:5

15 You have increased the
nation, O LORD,
You have [a]increased the
nation;
You are glorified;
You have expanded all the
[1]borders of the land.

16 LORD, [a]in trouble they have
visited You,
They poured out a prayer
when Your chastening
was upon them.
17 As [a]a woman with child
Is in pain and cries out in
her [1]pangs,
When she draws near the
time of her delivery,
So have we been in Your
sight, O LORD.
18 We have been with child, we
have been in pain;
We have, as it were,
[1]brought forth wind;
We have not accomplished
any deliverance in the
earth,
Nor have [a]the inhabitants of
the world fallen.

19 [a]Your dead shall live;
Together with [1]my dead
body they shall arise.
[b]Awake and sing, you who
dwell in dust;
For your dew *is like* the dew
of herbs,
And the earth shall cast out
the dead.

20 Come, my people, [a]enter
your chambers,
And shut your doors behind
you;
Hide yourself, as it were,
[b]for a little moment,
Until the indignation is past.

21 For behold, the LORD [a]comes
out of His place
To punish the inhabitants
of the earth for their
iniquity;
The earth will also disclose
her [1]blood,
And will no more cover her
slain.

27

In that day the LORD with
His severe sword,
great and strong,
Will punish Le·vi'a·than the
fleeing serpent,
[a]Le·vi'a·than that twisted
serpent;
And He will slay [b]the reptile
that *is* in the sea.

2 In that day [a]sing to her,
[b]"A vineyard of [1]red wine!
3 [a]I, the LORD, keep it,
I water it every moment;
Lest any hurt it,
I keep it night and day.
4 Fury *is* not in Me.
Who would set [a]briers *and*
thorns
Against Me in battle?
I would go through them,
I would burn them
together.
5 Or let him take hold [a]of My
strength,
That he may [b]make peace
with Me;
And he shall make peace
with Me."

6 Those who come He shall
cause [a]to take root in
Jacob;
Israel shall blossom and
bud,
And fill the face of the
world with fruit.

15 [a]Is. 9:3
[1]Or *ends*

16 [a]Hos. 5:15

17 [a][John 16:21]
[1]*sharp pains*

18 [a]Ps. 17:14
[1]*given birth to*

19 [a][Ezek. 37:1–14]
[b][Dan. 12:2]
[1]So with MT, Vg.; Syr., Tg. *their dead bodies;* LXX *those in the tombs*

20 [a]Ex. 12:22, 23
[b][Ps. 30:5]

21 [a]Mic. 1:3
[1]Or *bloodshed*

CHAPTER 27

1 [a]Ps. 74:13, 14
[b]Is. 51:9

2 [a]Is. 5:1
[b]Is. 5:7
[1]So with MT (Kittel's *Biblia Hebraica*), Bg., Vg.; MT (*Biblia Hebraica Stuttgartensia*), some Heb. mss., LXX *delight;* Tg. *choice vineyard*

3 [a]Is. 31:5

4 [a]2 Sam. 23:6

5 [a]Is. 25:4
[b]Job 22:21

6 [a]Is. 37:31

7 [a]Has He struck [1]Israel as He
struck those who struck
him?
Or has He been slain
according to the
slaughter of those who
were slain by Him?
8 [a]In measure, by sending it
away,
You contended with it.
[b]He removes *it* by His rough
wind
In the day of the east wind.
9 Therefore by this the
iniquity of Jacob will be
covered;
And this *is* all the fruit of
taking away his sin:
When he makes all the
stones of the altar
Like chalkstones that are
beaten to dust,
[1]Wooden images and incense
altars shall not stand.

10 Yet the fortified city *will be*
[a]desolate,
The habitation forsaken and
left like a wilderness;
There the calf will feed, and
there it will lie down
And consume its branches.
11 When its boughs are
withered, they will be
broken off;
The women come *and* set
them on fire.
For [a]it *is* a people of no
understanding;
Therefore He who made
them will [b]not have
mercy on them,
And [c]He who formed them
will show them no favor.

12 And it shall come to pass in
that day
That the LORD will thresh,
From the channel of [1]the
River to the Brook of
Egypt;
And you will be [a]gathered
one by one,
O you children of Israel.

13 [a]So it shall be in that day:
[b]The great trumpet will be
blown;
They will come, who are
about to perish in the
land of Assyria,
And they who are outcasts
in the land of [c]Egypt,
And shall [d]worship the LORD
in the holy mount at
Jerusalem.

28

Woe to the crown of
pride, to the drunkards
of E͞′phra·im,
Whose glorious beauty *is* a
fading flower
Which *is* at the head of the
[1]verdant valleys,
To those who are overcome
with wine!
2 Behold, the Lord has a
mighty and strong one,
[a]Like a tempest of hail and a
destroying storm,
Like a flood of mighty
waters overflowing,
Who will bring *them* down
to the earth with *His*
hand.
3 The crown of pride, the
drunkards of E͞′phra·im,
Will be trampled underfoot;
4 And the glorious beauty is a
fading flower
Which *is* at the head of the
[1]verdant valley,
Like the first fruit before the
summer,
Which an observer sees;

7 [a]Is. 10:12, 17; 30:30–33 [1]Lit. *him*
8 [a]Job 23:6 [b][Ps. 78:38]
9 [1]Heb. *Asherim,* Canaanite deities
10 [a]Is. 5:6, 17; 32:14
11 [a]Deut. 32:28 [b]Is. 9:17 [c]Deut. 32:18
12 [a][Is. 11:11; 56:8] [1]The Euphrates
13 [a]Is. 2:11 [b]Rev. 11:15 [c]Is. 19:21, 22 [d]Zech. 14:16

CHAPTER 28

1 [1]Lit. *valleys of fatness*
2 [a]Ezek. 13:11
4 [1]Lit. *valley of fatness*

He eats it up while it is still
in his hand.

5 In that day the LORD of hosts
will be
For a crown of glory and a
diadem of beauty
To the remnant of His
people,
6 For a spirit of justice to him
who sits in judgment,
And for strength to those
who turn back the battle
at the gate.

7 But they also [a]have erred
through wine,
And through intoxicating
drink are out of the way;
[b]The priest and the prophet
have erred through
intoxicating drink,
They are swallowed up by
wine,
They are out of the way
through intoxicating
drink;
They err in vision, they
stumble *in* judgment.
8 For all tables are full of
vomit *and* filth;
No place *is clean.*

9 "Whom[a] will he teach
knowledge?
And whom will he make to
understand the message?
Those *just* weaned from
milk?
Those *just* drawn from the
breasts?
10 [a]For precept *must be* upon
precept, precept upon
precept,
Line upon line, line upon
line,
Here a little, there a little."

11 For with [a]stammering lips
and another tongue
He will speak to this people,
12 To whom He said, "This *is*
the [a]rest *with which*
You may cause the weary to
rest,"
And, "This *is* the refreshing";
Yet they would not hear.
13 But the word of the LORD
was to them,
"Precept upon precept,
precept upon precept,
Line upon line, line upon
line,
Here a little, there a little,"
That they might go and
fall backward, and be
broken
And snared and caught.

14 Therefore hear the word of
the LORD, you scornful
men,
Who rule this people who
are in Jerusalem,
15 Because you have said, "We
have made a covenant
with death,
And with Shē'ōl we are in
agreement.
When the overflowing
scourge passes through,
It will not come to us,
[a]For we have made lies our
refuge,
And under falsehood we
have hidden ourselves."

16 Therefore thus says the Lord ☆
GOD:

"Behold, I lay in Zion [a]a
stone for a foundation,
A tried stone, a precious
cornerstone, a sure
foundation;

7 [a]Hos. 4:11 [b]Is. 56:10, 12
9 [a]Jer. 6:10
10 [a][2 Chr. 36:15]
11 [a]1 Cor. 14:21
12 [a]Is. 30:15
15 [a]Is. 9:15
16 [a]Matt. 21:42; Mark 12:10; Luke 20:17; Acts 4:11; Rom. 9:33; 10:11; Eph. 2:20; 1 Pet. 2:6–8

Whoever believes will not
act hastily.
17 Also I will make justice the
measuring line,
And righteousness the
plummet;
The hail will sweep away
the refuge of lies,
And the waters will overflow
the hiding place.
18 Your covenant with death
will be annulled,
And your agreement with
Shē'ōl will not stand;
When the overflowing
scourge passes through,
Then you will be trampled
down by it.
19 As often as it goes out it will
take you;
For morning by morning it
will pass over,
And by day and by night;
It will be a terror just to
understand the report."

20 For the bed is too short to
stretch out *on*,
And the covering so narrow
that one cannot wrap
himself *in it*.
21 For the LORD will rise up as
at Mount [a]Pe·rā'zim,
He will be angry as in the
Valley of [b]Gib'ē·on—
That He may do His work,
[c]His awesome work,
And bring to pass His act,
His [1]unusual act.
22 Now therefore, do not be
mockers,
Lest your bonds be made
strong;
For I have heard from the
Lord GOD of hosts,
[a]A [1]destruction determined
even upon the whole
earth.

23 Give ear and hear my voice,
Listen and hear my speech.
24 Does the plowman keep
plowing all day to sow?
Does he keep turning his
soil and breaking the
clods?
25 When he has leveled its
surface,
Does he not sow the black
cummin
And scatter the cummin,
Plant the wheat in rows,
The barley in the appointed
place,
And the [1]spelt in its place?
26 For He instructs him in right
judgment,
His God teaches him.

27 For the black cummin is
not threshed with a
threshing sledge,
Nor is a cartwheel rolled
over the cummin;
But the black cummin is
beaten out with a stick,
And the cummin with a rod.
28 Bread *flour* must be ground;
Therefore he does not
thresh it forever,
Break *it with* his cartwheel,
Or crush it *with* his
horsemen.
29 This also comes from the
LORD of hosts,
[a]*Who* is wonderful in
counsel *and* excellent in
[1]guidance.

29

"Woe [a]to [1]Ar'i·el, to
Ar'i·el, the city [b]*where*
David dwelt!
Add year to year;
Let feasts come around.
2 Yet I will distress Ar'i·el;
There shall be heaviness
and sorrow,

21 [a]2 Sam. 5:20 [b]Josh. 10:10, 12 [c][Lam. 3:33] [1]Lit. *foreign*

22 [a]Is. 10:22 [1]Lit. *complete end*

25 [1]*rye*

29 [a]Ps. 92:5 [1]*sound wisdom*

CHAPTER 29

1 [a]Ezek. 24:6, 9 [b]2 Sam. 5:9 [1]Jerusalem, lit. *Lion of God*

And it shall be to Me as
Ar′i·el.
3 I will encamp against you
all around,
I will lay siege against you
with a mound,
And I will raise siegeworks
against you.
4 You shall be brought down,
You shall speak out of the
ground;
Your speech shall be low,
out of the dust;
Your voice shall be like a
medium's, [a]out of the
ground;
And your speech shall
whisper out of the dust.

5 "Moreover the multitude of
your [a]foes
Shall be like fine dust,
And the multitude of the
terrible ones
Like [b]chaff that passes
away;
Yes, it shall be [c]in an
instant, suddenly.
6 [a]You will be punished by the
LORD of hosts
With thunder and
[b]earthquake and great
noise,
With storm and tempest
And the flame of devouring
fire.
7 [a]The multitude of all the
nations who fight
against [1]Ar′i·el,
Even all who fight against
her and her fortress,
And distress her,
Shall be [b]as a dream of a
night vision.
8 [a]It shall even be as when a
hungry man dreams,
And look—he eats;
But he awakes, and his soul
is still empty;
Or as when a thirsty man
dreams,
And look—he drinks;
But he awakes, and indeed
he is faint,
And his soul still craves:
So the multitude of all the
nations shall be,
Who fight against Mount
Zion."

9 Pause and wonder!
Blind yourselves and be
blind!
[a]They are drunk, [b]but not
with wine;
They stagger, but not with
intoxicating drink.
10 For [a]the LORD has poured
out on you
The spirit of deep sleep,
And has [b]closed your eyes,
namely, the prophets;
And He has covered your
heads, *namely,* [c]the
seers.

11 The whole vision has become to you like the words of
a [1]book [a]that is sealed, which
men deliver to one who is literate, saying, "Read this, please."
[b]And he says, "I cannot, for it *is*
sealed."
12 Then the book is delivered
to one who [1]is illiterate, saying,
"Read this, please." And he says,
"I am not literate."
13 Therefore the Lord said: ☆

[a]"Inasmuch as these people
draw near with their
mouths
And honor Me [b]with their
lips,

4 [a]Is. 8:19
5 [a]Is. 25:5 [b]Job 21:18 [c]Is. 30:13; 47:11
6 [a]Is. 28:2; 30:30 [b]Rev. 16:18, 19
7 [a]Mic. 4:11, 12 [b]Job 20:8 [1]Jerusalem
8 [a]Ps. 73:20
9 [a]Is. 28:7, 8 [b]Is. 51:21
10 [a]Rom. 11:8 [b]Ps. 69:23 [c]Is. 44:18
11 [a]Is. 8:16 [b]Dan. 12:4, 9 [1]*scroll*
12 [1]Lit. *does not know books*
13 [a]Ezek. 33:31; Matt. 15:8, 9; Mark 7:6, 7 [b]Col. 2:22

But have removed their hearts far from Me,
And their fear toward Me is taught by the commandment of men,
14 [a]Therefore, behold, I will again do a marvelous work
Among this people,
A marvelous work and a wonder;
[b]For the wisdom of their wise *men* shall perish,
And the understanding of their prudent *men* shall be hidden."

15 [a]Woe to those who seek deep to hide their counsel far from the LORD,
And their works are in the dark;
[b]They say, "Who sees us?" and, "Who knows us?"
16 Surely you have things turned around!
Shall the potter be esteemed as the clay;
For shall the [a]thing made say of him who made it,
"He did not make me"?
Or shall the thing formed say of him who formed it,
"He has no understanding"?

17 *Is* it not yet a very little while
Till [a]Lebanon shall be turned into a fruitful field,
And the fruitful field be esteemed as a forest?
18 [a]In that day the deaf shall hear the words of the book,
And the eyes of the blind shall see out of obscurity and out of darkness.

14 [a]Hab. 1:5 [b]Jer. 49:7
15 [a]Is. 30:1 [b]Ps. 10:11; 94:7
16 [a]Is. 45:9
17 [a]Is. 32:15
18 [a]Is. 35:5
19 [a][Is. 11:4; 61:1] [b][James 2:5]
20 [a]Is. 28:14 [b]Mic. 2:1 [1]*terrifying*
21 [a]Amos 5:10, 12 [b]Prov. 28:21
22 [a]Josh. 24:3 [b]Is. 45:17
23 [a][Is. 45:11; 49:20–26]
24 [a]Is. 28:7
CHAPTER 30
1 [a]Is. 29:15 [1]Lit. *weave a web*

19 [a]The humble also shall increase *their* joy in the LORD,
And [b]the poor among men shall rejoice
In the Holy One of Israel.
20 For the [1]terrible one is brought to nothing,
[a]The scornful one is consumed,
And all who [b]watch for iniquity are cut off—
21 Who make a man an offender by a word,
And [a]lay a snare for him who reproves in the gate,
And turn aside the just [b]by empty words.

22 Therefore thus says the LORD, [a]who redeemed Abraham, concerning the house of Jacob:

"Jacob shall not now be [b]ashamed,
Nor shall his face now grow pale;
23 But when he sees his children,
[a]The work of My hands, in his midst,
They will hallow My name,
And hallow the Holy One of Jacob,
And fear the God of Israel.
24 These also [a]who erred in spirit will come to understanding,
And those who complained will learn doctrine."

30

"Woe to the rebellious children," says the LORD,
[a]"Who take counsel, but not of Me,
And who [1]devise plans, but not of My Spirit,

[b]That they may add sin to
sin;
2 [a]Who walk to go down to
Egypt,
And [b]have not asked My
advice,
To strengthen themselves in
the strength of Pharaoh,
And to trust in the shadow
of Egypt!
3 [a]Therefore the strength of
Pharaoh
Shall be your shame,
And trust in the shadow of
Egypt
Shall be *your* humiliation.
4 For his princes were at
[a]Zō′an,
And his ambassadors came
to Hā′nēs.
5 [a]They were all ashamed of
a people *who* could not
benefit them,
Or be help or benefit,
But a shame and also a
reproach."

6 [a]The [1]burden against the
beasts of the South.

Through a land of trouble
and anguish,
From which *came* the
lioness and lion,
[b]The viper and fiery flying
serpent,
They will carry their riches
on the backs of young
donkeys,
And their treasures on the
humps of camels,
To a people *who* shall not
profit;
7 [a]For the Egyptians shall
help in vain and to no
purpose.
Therefore I have called her
[1]Rā′hab-Hem-Shē′beth.

1 [b]Deut. 29:19
2 [a]Is. 31:1 [b]Josh. 9:14
3 [a]Is. 20:5
4 [a]Is. 19:11
5 [a]Jer. 2:36
6 [a]Is. 57:9 [b]Deut. 8:15 [1]*oracle, prophecy*
7 [a]Jer. 37:7 [1]Lit. *Rahab Sits Idle*
8 [a]Hab. 2:2
9 [a]Is. 1:2, 4; 65:2
10 [a]Jer. 11:21 [b]1 Kin. 22:8, 13
12 [a]Is. 5:24
13 [a]Ps. 62:3, 4 [b]Is. 29:5
14 [a]Jer. 19:11 [1]A piece of broken pottery

8 Now go, [a]write it before
them on a tablet,
And note it on a scroll,
That it may be for time to
come,
Forever and ever:
9 That [a]this *is* a rebellious
people,
Lying children,
Children *who* will not hear
the law of the LORD;
10 [a]Who say to the seers, "Do
not see,"
And to the prophets, "Do
not prophesy to us right
things;
[b]Speak to us smooth things,
prophesy deceits.
11 Get out of the way,
Turn aside from the path,
Cause the Holy One of
Israel
To cease from before us."

12 Therefore thus says the Holy
One of Israel:

"Because you [a]despise this
word,
And trust in oppression and
perversity,
And rely on them,
13 Therefore this iniquity shall
be to you
[a]Like a breach ready to fall,
A bulge in a high wall,
Whose breaking [b]comes
suddenly, in an instant.
14 And [a]He shall break it like
the breaking of the
potter's vessel,
Which is broken in pieces;
He shall not spare.
So there shall not be found
among its fragments
[1]A shard to take fire from the
hearth,

Or to take water from the
cistern."

15 For thus says the Lord GOD,
the Holy One of Israel:

[a]"In returning and rest you
shall be saved;
In quietness and confidence
shall be your strength."
[b]But you would not,
16 And you said, "No, for we
will flee on horses"—
Therefore you shall flee!
And, "We will ride on swift
horses"—
Therefore those who pursue
you shall be swift!

17 [a]One thousand *shall flee* at
the threat of one,
At the threat of five you
shall flee,
Till you are left as a [1]pole on
top of a mountain
And as a banner on a hill.

18 Therefore the LORD will
wait, that He may be
[a]gracious to you;
And therefore He will be
exalted, that He may
have mercy on you.
For the LORD *is* a God of
justice;
[b]Blessed *are* all those who
[c]wait for Him.

19 For the people [a]shall dwell
in Zion at Jerusalem;
You shall [b]weep no more.
He will be very gracious to
you at the sound of your
cry;
When He hears it, He will
[c]answer you.
20 And *though* the Lord gives
you
[a]The bread of adversity and
the water of [1]affliction,
Yet [b]your teachers will not
be moved into a corner
anymore,
But your eyes shall see your
teachers.
21 Your ears shall hear a word
behind you, saying,
"This *is* the way, walk in it,"
Whenever you [a]turn to the
right hand
Or whenever you turn to the
left.
22 [a]You will also defile the
covering of your images
of silver,
And the ornament of your
molded images of gold.
You will throw them away
as an unclean thing;
[b]You will say to them, "Get
away!"

23 [a]Then He will give the rain
for your seed
With which you sow the
ground,
And bread of the increase of
the earth;
It will be [1]fat and plentiful.
In that day your cattle will
feed
In large pastures.
24 Likewise the oxen and the
young donkeys that
work the ground
Will eat cured fodder,
Which has been winnowed
with the shovel and fan.
25 There will be [a]on every high
mountain
And on every high hill
Rivers *and* streams of
waters,
In the day of the [b]great
slaughter,
When the towers fall.

15 [a]Is. 7:4; 28:12 [b]Matt. 23:37
17 [a]Josh. 23:10 [1]A tree stripped of branches
18 [a]Is. 33:2 [b]Jer. 17:7 [c]Is. 26:8
19 [a]Is. 65:9 [b]Is. 25:8 [c]Is. 65:24
20 [a]1 Kin. 22:27 [b]Amos 8:11 [1]*oppression*
21 [a]Josh. 1:7
22 [a]Is. 2:20; 31:7 [b]Hos. 14:8
23 [a][Matt. 6:33] [1]*rich*
25 [a]Is. 2:14, 15 [b]Is. 2:10–21; 34:2

26 Moreover [a]the light of the moon will be as the light of the sun,
And the light of the sun will be sevenfold,
As the light of seven days,
In the day that the LORD binds up the bruise of His people
And heals the stroke of their wound.

27 Behold, the name of the LORD comes from afar,
Burning *with* His anger,
And *His* burden *is* heavy;
His lips are full of indignation,
And His tongue like a devouring fire.
28 [a]His breath is like an overflowing stream,
[b]Which reaches up to the neck,
To sift the nations with the sieve of futility;
And *there shall be* [c]a bridle in the jaws of the people,
Causing *them* to err.

29 You shall have a song
As in the night *when* a holy festival is kept,
And gladness of heart as when one goes with a flute,
To come into [a]the mountain of the LORD,
To [1]the Mighty One of Israel.
30 [a]The LORD will cause His glorious voice to be heard,
And show the descent of His arm,
With the indignation of *His* anger
And the flame of a devouring fire,
With scattering, tempest, [b]and hailstones.
31 For [a]through the voice of the LORD
Assyria will be [1]beaten down,
As He strikes with the [b]rod.
32 And *in* every place where the staff of punishment passes,
Which the LORD lays on him,
It will be with tambourines and harps;
And in battles of [a]brandishing He will fight with it.
33 [a]For Tō'phet *was* established of old,
Yes, for the king it is prepared.
He has made *it* deep and large;
Its pyre *is* fire with much wood;
The breath of the LORD, like a stream of brimstone,
Kindles it.

31

Woe to those [a]who go down to Egypt for help,
And [b]rely on horses,
Who trust in chariots because *they are* many,
And in horsemen because they are very strong,
But who do not look to the Holy One of Israel,
[c]Nor seek the LORD!
2 Yet He also *is* wise and will bring disaster,
And [a]will not [1]call back His words,
But will arise against the house of evildoers,
And against the help of those who work iniquity.

---

26 [a][Is. 60:19, 20]
28 [a]Is. 11:4 [b]Is. 8:8 [c]Is. 37:29
29 [a][Is. 2:3] [1]Lit. *the Rock*
30 [a]Is. 29:6 [b]Is. 28:2
31 [a]Is. 14:25; 37:36 [b]Is. 10:5, 24 [1]Lit. *shattered*
32 [a]Is. 11:15
33 [a]Jer. 7:31

CHAPTER 31

1 [a]Is. 30:1, 2 [b]Ps. 20:7 [c]Dan. 9:13
2 [a]Num. 23:19 [1]*retract*

3 Now the Egyptians *are* men,
and not God;
And their horses are flesh,
and not spirit.
When the LORD stretches out
His hand,
Both he who helps will fall,
And he who is helped will
fall down;
They all will perish
[a]together.

4 For thus the LORD has spoken to me:

[a]"As a lion roars,
And a young lion over his
prey
(When a multitude of
shepherds is summoned
against him,
He will not be afraid of their
voice
Nor be disturbed by their
noise),
So the LORD of hosts will
come down
To fight for Mount Zion and
for its hill.
5 [a]Like birds flying about,
So will the LORD of hosts
defend Jerusalem.
Defending, He will also
deliver *it;*
Passing over, He will
preserve *it.*"

6 Return *to Him* against whom
the children of Israel have
[a]deeply revolted.
7 For in that day every man
shall [a]throw away his idols of
silver and his idols of gold—[b]sin,
which your own hands have
made for yourselves.

8 "Then Assyria shall [a]fall by a
sword not of man,
And a sword not of mankind
shall [b]devour him.
But he shall flee from the
sword,
And his young men shall
become forced labor.
9 [a]He shall cross over to his
stronghold for fear,
And his princes shall be
afraid of the banner,"
Says the LORD,
Whose fire *is* in Zion
And whose furnace *is* in
Jerusalem.

32

Behold, [a]a king will reign
in righteousness,
And princes will rule with
justice.
2 A man will be as a hiding
place from the wind,
And [a]a [1]cover from the
tempest,
As rivers of water in a dry
place,
As the shadow of a great
rock in a weary land.
3 [a]The eyes of those who see
will not be dim,
And the ears of those who
hear will listen.
4 Also the heart of the
[1]rash will [a]understand
knowledge,
And the tongue of the
stammerers will be
ready to speak plainly.

5 The foolish person will
no longer be called
[1]generous,
Nor the miser said *to be*
bountiful;
6 For the foolish person will
speak foolishness,
And his heart will work
[a]iniquity:
To practice ungodliness,

3 [a]Is. 20:6
4 [a]Hos. 11:10
5 [a]Deut. 32:11
6 [a]Hos. 9:9
7 [a]Is. 2:20; 30:22 [b]1 Kin. 12:30
8 [a]2 Kin. 19:35, 36 [b]Is. 37:36
9 [a]Is. 37:37

CHAPTER 32

1 [a]Ps. 45:1
2 [a]Is. 4:6 [1]*shelter*
3 [a]Is. 29:18; 35:5
4 [a]Is. 29:24 [1]*hasty*
5 [1]*noble*
6 [a]Prov. 24:7–9

To utter error against the
LORD,
To keep the hungry
unsatisfied,
And he will cause the drink
of the thirsty to fail.
7 Also the schemes of the
schemer *are* evil;
He devises wicked plans
To destroy the poor with
[a]lying words,
Even when the needy
speaks justice.
8 But a [1]generous man devises
generous things,
And by generosity he shall
stand.

9 Rise up, you women [a]who
are at ease,
Hear my voice;
You complacent daughters,
Give ear to my speech.
10 In a year and *some* days
You will be troubled, you
complacent women;
For the vintage will fail,
The gathering will not come.
11 Tremble, you *women* who
are at ease;
Be troubled, you complacent
ones;
Strip yourselves, make
yourselves bare,
And gird *sackcloth* on *your*
waists.

12 People shall mourn upon
their breasts
For the pleasant fields, for
the fruitful vine.
13 [a]On the land of my people
will come up thorns *and*
briers,
Yes, on all the happy homes
in [b]the joyous city;
14 [a]Because the palaces will be
forsaken,
The bustling city will be
deserted.
The forts and towers will
become lairs forever,
A joy of wild donkeys, a
pasture of flocks—
15 Until [a]the Spirit is poured
upon us from on high,
And [b]the wilderness
becomes a fruitful field,
And the fruitful field is
counted as a forest.

16 Then justice will dwell in
the wilderness,
And righteousness remain
in the fruitful field.
17 [a]The work of righteousness
will be peace,
And the effect of
righteousness, quietness
and assurance forever.
18 My people will dwell in a
peaceful habitation,
In secure dwellings, and in
quiet [a]resting places,
19 [a]Though hail comes down
[b]on the forest,
And the city is brought low
in humiliation.

20 Blessed *are* you who sow
beside all waters,
Who send out freely the
feet of [a]the ox and the
donkey.

33 Woe to you [a]who plunder,
though you *have* not
been plundered;
And you who deal
treacherously, though
they have not dealt
treacherously with you!
[b]When you cease plundering,
You will be [c]plundered;
When you make an end of
dealing treacherously,

7 [a]Jer. 5:26–28
8 [1]*noble*
9 [a]Amos 6:1
13 [a]Hos. 9:6 [b]Is. 22:2
14 [a]Is. 27:10
15 [a][Joel 2:28] [b]Is. 29:17
17 [a]James 3:18
18 [a][Zech. 2:5; 3:10]
19 [a]Is. 30:30 [b]Zech. 11:2
20 [a]Is. 30:23, 24
CHAPTER 33
1 [a]Hab. 2:8 [b]Rev. 13:10 [c]Is. 10:12; 14:25; 31:8

They will deal treacherously
with you.

2 O LORD, be gracious to us;
[a]We have waited for You.
Be [1]their arm every
morning,
Our salvation also in the
time of trouble.
3 At the noise of the tumult
the people [a]shall flee;
When You lift Yourself up,
the nations shall be
scattered;
4 And Your plunder shall be
gathered
Like the gathering of the
caterpillar;
As the running to and fro of
locusts,
He shall run upon them.

5 [a]The LORD is exalted, for He
dwells on high;
He has filled Zion
with justice and
righteousness.
6 Wisdom and knowledge will
be the stability of your
times,
And the strength of
salvation;
The fear of the LORD *is* His
treasure.

7 Surely their valiant ones
shall cry outside,
[a]The ambassadors of peace
shall weep bitterly.
8 [a]The highways lie waste,
The traveling man ceases.
[b]He has broken the covenant,
[1]He has despised the [2]cities,
He regards no man.
9 [a]The earth mourns *and*
languishes,
Lebanon is shamed *and*
shriveled;
Sharon is like a wilderness,
And Bā′shan and Car′mel
shake off *their fruits.*

10 "Now[a] I will rise," says the
LORD;
"Now I will be exalted,
Now I will lift Myself up.
11 [a]You shall conceive chaff,
You shall bring forth stubble;
Your breath, *as* fire, shall
devour you.
12 And the people shall be *like*
the burnings of lime;
[a]*Like* thorns cut up they shall
be burned in the fire.
13 Hear, [a]you *who are* afar off,
what I have done;
And you *who are* near,
acknowledge My might."

14 The sinners in Zion are
afraid;
Fearfulness has seized the
hypocrites:
"Who among us shall dwell
with the devouring [a]fire?
Who among us shall
dwell with everlasting
burnings?"
15 He who [a]walks righteously
and speaks uprightly,
He who despises the gain of
oppressions,
Who gestures with his
hands, refusing bribes,
Who stops his ears from
hearing of bloodshed,
And [b]shuts his eyes from
seeing evil:
16 He will dwell on [1]high;
His place of defense *will be*
the fortress of rocks;
Bread will be given him,
His water *will be* sure.

17 Your eyes will see the King
in His [a]beauty;

---

2 [a]Is. 25:9; 26:8 [1]LXX omits *their;* Syr., Tg., Vg. *our*
3 [a]Is. 17:13
5 [a]Ps. 97:9
7 [a]2 Kin. 18:18, 37
8 [a]Judg. 5:6 [b]2 Kin. 18:13–17 [1]Tg. *They have been removed from their cities* [2]So with MT, Vg.; DSS *witnesses;* LXX omits *cities*
9 [a]Is. 24:4
10 [a]Ps. 12:5
11 [a][Ps. 7:14]
12 [a]Is. 9:18
13 [a]Is. 49:1
14 [a]Heb. 12:29
15 [a]Ps. 15:2; 24:3, 4 [b]Ps. 119:37
16 [1]Lit. *heights*
17 [a]Ps. 27:4

They will see the land that
is very far off.
18 Your heart will meditate on
terror:
[a]"Where *is* the scribe?
Where *is* he who weighs?
Where *is* he who counts the
towers?"
19 [a]You will not see a fierce
people,
[b]A people of obscure speech,
beyond perception,
Of a [1]stammering tongue
that you cannot
understand.

20 [a]Look upon Zion, the city of
our appointed feasts;
Your eyes will see
[b]Jerusalem, a quiet home,
A tabernacle *that* will not
be taken down;
[c]Not one of [d]its stakes will
ever be removed,
Nor will any of its cords be
broken.
21 But there the majestic LORD
will be for us
A place of broad rivers *and*
streams,
In which no [1]galley with
oars will sail,
Nor majestic ships pass by
22 (For the LORD *is* our [a]Judge,
The LORD *is* our [b]Lawgiver,
[c]The LORD *is* our King;
He will save us);
23 Your tackle is loosed,
They could not strengthen
their mast,
They could not spread the
sail.

Then the prey of great
plunder is divided;
The lame take the prey.
24 And the inhabitant will not
say, "I am sick";
[a]The people who dwell in
it *will be* forgiven *their*
iniquity.

34 Come [a]near, you nations,
to hear;
And heed, you people!
[b]Let the earth hear, and all
that is in it,
The world and all things
that come forth from it.
2 For the indignation of
the LORD *is* against all
nations,
And *His* fury against all
their armies;
He has utterly destroyed
them,
He has given them over to
the [a]slaughter.
3 Also their slain shall be
thrown out;
[a]Their stench shall rise from
their corpses,
And the mountains shall be
melted with their blood.
4 [a]All the host of heaven shall
be dissolved,
And the heavens shall be
rolled up like a scroll;
[b]All their host shall fall down
As the leaf falls from the
vine,
And as [c]*fruit* falling from a
fig tree.

5 "For [a]My sword shall be
bathed in heaven;
Indeed it [b]shall come down
on Ē′dom,
And on the people of My
curse, for judgment.
6 The [a]sword of the LORD is
filled with blood,
It is made [1]overflowing with
fatness,
With the blood of lambs and
goats,

18 [a]1 Cor. 1:20
19 [a]2 Kin. 19:32 [b]Jer. 5:15 [1]Unintelligible speech
20 [a]Ps. 48:12 [b]Ps. 46:5; 125:1 [c]Is. 37:33 [d]Is. 54:2
21 [1]*ship*
22 [a][Acts 10:42] [b]James 4:12 [c]Ps. 89:18
24 [a]Is. 40:2

CHAPTER 34

1 [a]Ps. 49:1 [b]Deut. 32:1
2 [a]Is. 13:5
3 [a]Joel 2:20
4 [a]Is. 13:13 [b]Is. 14:12 [c]Rev. 6:12–14
5 [a]Jer. 46:10 [b]Mal. 1:4
6 [a]Is. 66:16 [1]Lit. *fat*

With the fat of the kidneys
of rams.
For [b]the LORD has a sacrifice
in Boz′rah,
And a great slaughter in the
land of Ē′dom.
7 The wild oxen shall come
down with them,
And the young bulls with
the mighty bulls;
Their land shall be soaked
with blood,
And their dust [1]saturated
with fatness."

8 For *it is* the day of the
LORD's [a]vengeance,
The year of recompense for
the cause of Zion.
9 [a]Its streams shall be turned
into pitch,
And its dust into brimstone;
Its land shall become
burning pitch.
10 It shall not be quenched
night or day;
[a]Its smoke shall ascend
forever.
[b]From generation to
generation it shall lie
waste;
No one shall pass through it
forever and ever.
11 [a]But the [1]pelican and the
[2]porcupine shall possess
it,
Also the owl and the raven
shall dwell in it.
And [b]He shall stretch out
over it
The line of confusion and
the stones of emptiness.
12 They shall call its nobles to
the kingdom,
But none *shall be* there, and
all its princes shall be
nothing.
13 And [a]thorns shall come up
in its palaces,
Nettles and brambles in its
fortresses;
[b]It shall be a habitation of
jackals,
A courtyard for ostriches.
14 The wild beasts of the
desert shall also meet
with the [1]jackals,
And the wild goat shall
bleat to its companion;
Also [2]the night creature
shall rest there,
And find for herself a place
of rest.
15 There the arrow snake shall
make her nest and lay
eggs
And hatch, and gather *them*
under her shadow;
There also shall the hawks
be gathered,
Every one with her mate.

16 "Search from [a]the book of
the LORD, and read:
Not one of these shall fail;
Not one shall lack her
mate.
For My mouth has
commanded it, and His
Spirit has gathered
them.
17 He has cast the lot for them,
And His hand has divided
it among them with a
measuring line.
They shall possess it
forever;
From generation to
generation they shall
dwell in it."

35 The [a]wilderness and the
[1]wasteland shall be
glad for them,

6 [b]Zeph. 1:7
7 [1]Lit. *made fat*
8 [a]Is. 63:4
9 [a]Deut. 29:23
10 [a]Rev. 14:11; 18:18; 19:3 [b]Mal. 1:3, 4
11 [a]Zeph. 2:14 [b]Lam. 2:8 [1]Or *owl* [2]Or *hedgehog*
13 [a]Is. 32:13 [b]Is. 13:21
14 [1]Lit. *howling creatures* [2]Heb. *lilith*
16 [a][Mal. 3:16]

CHAPTER 35

1 [a]Is. 32:15; 55:12 [1]*desert*

And the [b]desert[2] shall rejoice
and blossom as the rose;
2 [a]It shall blossom abundantly
and rejoice,
Even with joy and singing.
The glory of Lebanon shall
be given to it,
The excellence of Car′mel
and Sharon.
They shall see the [b]glory of
the LORD,
The excellency of our God.

3 [a]Strengthen the [1]weak hands,
And make firm the [2]feeble
knees.
4 Say to those *who are*
fearful-hearted,
"Be strong, do not fear!
Behold, your God will come
with [a]vengeance,
With the recompense of
God;
He will come and [b]save
you."

☆5 Then the [a]eyes of the blind
shall be opened,
And [b]the ears of the deaf
shall be unstopped.
☆6 Then the [a]lame shall leap
like a deer,
And the [b]tongue of the
dumb sing.
For [c]waters shall burst forth
in the wilderness,
And streams in the desert.
7 The parched ground shall
become a pool,
And the thirsty land springs
of water;
In [a]the habitation of jackals,
where each lay,
There shall be grass with
reeds and rushes.

8 A [a]highway shall be there,
and a road,
And it shall be called the
Highway of Holiness.
[b]The unclean shall not pass
over it,
But it *shall be* for others.
Whoever walks the road,
although a fool,
Shall not go astray.
9 [a]No lion shall be there,
Nor shall *any* ravenous
beast go up on it;
It shall not be found there.
But the redeemed shall walk
there,
10 And the [a]ransomed of the
LORD shall return,
And come to Zion with
singing,
With everlasting joy on their
heads.
They shall obtain joy and
gladness,
And [b]sorrow and sighing
shall flee away.

36

Now [a]it came to pass in
the fourteenth year of
King Hez·e·kī′ah *that* Sen·nach′-
e·rib king of Assyria came up
against all the fortified cities of
Judah and took them.
2 Then the king of Assyria sent
the [1]Rab′sha·keh with a great
army from Lā′chish to King
Hez·e·kī′ah at Jerusalem. And
he stood by the aqueduct from
the upper pool, on the highway
to the Fuller's Field.
3 And [a]E·lī′a·kim the son of
Hil·kī′ah, who was over the
household, [b]Sheb′na the scribe,
and Jō′ah the son of Ā′saph, the
recorder, came out to him.
4 [a]Then *the* Rab′sha·keh said
to them, "Say now to Hez·e·kī′ah,
'Thus says the great king, the
king of Assyria: "What confidence is this in which you trust?

1 [b]Is. 41:19; 51:3 [2]Heb. *arabah*
2 [a]Is. 32:15 [b]Is. 40:5
3 [a]Heb. 12:12 [1]Lit. *sinking* [2]*tottering* or *stumbling*
4 [a]Is. 34:8 [b]Is. 33:22
5 [a]Is. 29:18; Matt. 9:27–30; John 9:6, 7 [b][Matt. 11:5]
6 [a]Matt. 11:5; 15:30; John 5:8, 9; Acts 8:7 [b]Is. 32:4; Matt. 9:32, 33; 12:22 [c][John 7:38]
7 [a]Is. 34:13
8 [a]Is. 19:23 [b]Joel 3:17
9 [a]Lev. 26:6
10 [a]Is. 51:11 [b][Rev. 7:17; 21:4]

CHAPTER 36
1 [a]2 Chr. 32:1
2 [1]A title, probably *Chief of Staff* or *Governor*
3 [a]Is. 22:20 [b]Is. 22:15
4 [a]2 Kin. 18:19

5 "I say you speak of having plans and power for war; but *they are* [1]mere words. Now in whom do you trust, that you rebel against me?

6 "Look! You are trusting in the [a]staff of this broken reed, Egypt, on which if a man leans, it will go into his hand and pierce it. So *is* Pharaoh king of Egypt to all who [b]trust in him.

7 "But if you say to me, 'We trust in the LORD our God,' *is it* not He whose high places and whose altars Hez·e·kī′ah has taken away, and said to Judah and Jerusalem, 'You shall worship before this altar'?" '

8 "Now therefore, I urge you, give a pledge to my master the king of Assyria, and I will give you two thousand horses—if you are able on your part to put riders on them!

9 "How then will you repel one captain of the least of my master's servants, and put your trust in Egypt for chariots and horsemen?

10 "Have I now come up without the LORD against this land to destroy it? The LORD said to me, 'Go up against this land, and destroy it.' "

11 Then E·lī′a·kim, Sheb′na, and Jō′ah said to *the* Rab′sha·keh, "Please speak to your servants in Ar·a·mā′ic, for we understand *it;* and do not speak to us in [1]Hebrew in the hearing of the people who *are* on the wall."

12 But *the* Rab′sha·keh said, "Has my master sent me to your master and to you to speak these words, and not to the men who sit on the wall, who will eat and drink their own waste with you?"

13 Then *the* Rab′sha·keh stood and called out with a loud voice in Hebrew, and said, "Hear the words of the great king, the king of Assyria!

14 "Thus says the king: 'Do not let Hez·e·kī′ah deceive you, for he will not be able to deliver you;

15 'nor let Hez·e·kī′ah make you trust in the LORD, saying, "The LORD will surely deliver us; this city will not be given into the hand of the king of Assyria." '

16 "Do not listen to Hez·e·kī′ah; for thus says the king of Assyria: 'Make *peace* with me *by a* present and come out to me; [a]and every one of you eat from his own vine and every one from his own fig tree, and every one of you drink the waters of his own cistern;

17 'until I come and take you away to a land like your own land, a land of grain and new wine, a land of bread and vineyards.

18 '*Beware* lest Hez·e·kī′ah persuade you, saying, "The LORD will deliver us." Has any one of the [a]gods of the nations delivered its land from the hand of the king of Assyria?

19 'Where *are* the gods of Hā′math and Ar′pad? Where *are* the gods of Seph·ar·vā′im? Indeed, have they delivered [a]Samaria from my hand?

20 'Who among all the gods of these lands have delivered their countries from my hand, that the LORD should deliver Jerusalem from my hand?' "

21 But they [1]held their peace and answered him not a word; for the king's commandment was, "Do not answer him."

5 [1]Lit. *a word of the lips*

6 [a]Ezek. 29:6 [b]Ps. 146:3

11 [1]Lit. *Judean*

16 [a]Zech. 3:10

18 [a]Is. 37:12

19 [a]2 Kin. 17:6

21 [1]*were silent*

22 Then E·lī′a·kim the son of Hil·kī′ah, who *was* over the household, Sheb′na the scribe, and Jō′ah the son of Ā′saph, the recorder, came to Hez·e·kī′ah with *their* clothes torn, and told him the words of *the* Rab′sha·keh.

37

And [a]so it was, when King Hez·e·kī′ah heard *it*, that he tore his clothes, covered himself with sackcloth, and went into the house of the LORD.

2 Then he sent E·lī′a·kim, who *was* over the household, Sheb′na the scribe, and the elders of the priests, covered with sackcloth, to Ī·sāi′ah the prophet, the son of Ā′moz.

3 And they said to him, "Thus says Hez·e·kī′ah: 'This day *is* a day of [a]trouble and rebuke and [1]blasphemy; for the children have come to birth, but *there is* no strength to bring them forth.

4 'It may be that the LORD your God will hear the words of *the* Rab′sha·keh, whom his master the king of Assyria has sent to [a]reproach the living God, and will rebuke the words which the LORD your God has heard. Therefore lift up *your* prayer for the remnant that is left.' "

5 So the servants of King Hez·e·kī′ah came to Ī·sāi′ah.

6 And Ī·sāi′ah said to them, "Thus you shall say to your master, 'Thus says the LORD: "Do not be afraid of the words which you have heard, with which the servants of the king of Assyria have blasphemed Me.

7 "Surely I will send a spirit upon him, and he shall hear a rumor and return to his own land; and I will cause him to fall by the sword in his own land." ' "

8 Then *the* Rab′sha·keh returned, and found the king of Assyria warring against Lib′nah, for he heard that he had departed from Lā′chish.

9 And the king heard concerning Tir·hā′kah king of Ethiopia, "He has come out to make war with you." So when he heard *it*, he sent messengers to Hez·e·kī′ah, saying,

10 "Thus you shall speak to Hez·e·kī′ah king of Judah, saying: 'Do not let your God in whom you trust deceive you, saying, "Jerusalem shall not be given into the hand of the king of Assyria."

11 'Look! You have heard what the kings of Assyria have done to all lands by utterly destroying them; and shall you be delivered?

12 'Have the [a]gods of the nations delivered those whom my fathers have destroyed, Gō′zan and Har′an and Rē′zeph, and the people of Eden who *were* in Te·las′sar?

13 'Where *is* the king of [a]Hā′math, the king of Ar′pad, and the king of the city of Seph·ar·vā′im, Hē′na, and Ī′vah?' "

14 And Hez·e·kī′ah received the letter from the hand of the messengers, and read it; and Hez·e·kī′ah went up to the house of the LORD, and spread it before the LORD.

15 Then Hez·e·kī′ah prayed to the LORD, saying:

16 "O LORD of hosts, God of Israel, *the One* who dwells *between* the cherubim, You *are* God, You [a]alone, of all the kingdoms of the

CHAPTER 37

1 [a]2 Kin. 19:1–37

3 [a]Is. 22:5; 26:16; 33:2 [1]*contempt*

4 [a]Is. 36:15, 18, 20

12 [a]Is. 36:18, 19

13 [a]Is. 49:23

16 [a]Is. 43:10, 11

earth. You have made heaven and
earth.
17 [a]"Incline Your ear, O LORD, and
hear; open Your eyes, O LORD,
and see; and [b]hear all the words
of Sen·nach′e·rib, which he has
sent to reproach the living God.
18 "Truly, LORD, the kings of
Assyria have laid waste all the
nations and their [a]lands,
19 "and have cast their gods
into the fire; for they *were* [a]not
gods, but the work of men's
hands—wood and stone. Therefore they destroyed them.
20 "Now therefore, O LORD our
God, [a]save us from his hand,
that all the kingdoms of the
earth may [b]know that You *are*
the LORD, You alone."
21 Then Ī·sāi′ah the son of
Ā′moz sent to Hez·e·kī′ah, saying, "Thus says the LORD God of
Israel, 'Because you have prayed
to Me against Sen·nach′e·rib
king of Assyria,
22 'this *is* the word which the
LORD has spoken concerning
him:

"The virgin, the daughter of
Zion,
Has despised you, laughed
you to scorn;
The daughter of Jerusalem
Has shaken *her* head behind
your back!

23 "Whom have you reproached
and blasphemed?
Against whom have you
raised *your* voice,
And lifted up your eyes on
high?
Against the Holy One of
Israel.
24 By your servants you have
reproached the Lord,
And said, 'By the multitude
of my chariots
I have come up to the height
of the mountains,
To the limits of Lebanon;
I will cut down its tall
cedars
And its choice cypress trees;
I will enter its farthest
height,
To its fruitful forest.
25 I have dug and drunk water,
And with the soles of my
feet I have dried up
All the brooks of [1]defense.'

26 "Did you not hear [a]long ago
How I made it,
From ancient times that I
formed it?
Now I have brought it to
pass,
That you should be
For crushing fortified cities
into heaps of ruins.
27 Therefore their inhabitants
had little power;
They were dismayed and
confounded;
They were *as* the grass of
the field
And the green herb,
As the grass on the
housetops
And *grain* blighted before it
is grown.

28 "But I know your dwelling
place,
Your going out and your
coming in,
And your rage against Me.
29 Because your rage against
Me and your tumult
Have come up to My ears,
Therefore [a]I will put My
hook in your nose
And My bridle in your lips,

17 [a]Dan. 9:18 [b]Ps. 74:22
18 [a]2 Kin. 15:29; 16:9; 17:6, 24
19 [a]Is. 40:19, 20
20 [a]Is. 33:22 [b]Ps. 83:18
25 [1]Or perhaps *Egypt*
26 [a]Is. 25:1; 40:21; 45:21
29 [a]Is. 30:28

And I will [b]turn you back
By the way which you
came." '

30 "This *shall be* a sign to you:

You shall eat this year such
as grows of itself,
And the second year what
springs from the same;
Also in the third year sow
and reap,
Plant vineyards and eat the
fruit of them.
31 And the remnant who have
escaped of the house of
Judah
Shall again take root
downward,
And bear fruit upward.
32 For out of Jerusalem shall
go a remnant,
And those who escape from
Mount Zion.
The [a]zeal of the LORD of
hosts will do this.

33 "Therefore thus says the
LORD concerning the king of Assyria:

'He shall not come into this
city,
Nor shoot an arrow there,
Nor come before it with
shield,
Nor build a siege mound
against it.
34 By the way that he came,
By the same shall he return;
And he shall not come into
this city,'
Says the LORD.
35 'For I will [a]defend this city, to
save it
For My own sake and for
My servant [b]David's
sake.' "

36 Then the [a]angel[1] of the LORD
went out, and [2]killed in the
camp of the Assyrians one hundred and eighty-five thousand;
and when *people* arose early
in the morning, there were the
corpses—all dead.
37 So Sen·nach′e·rib king of Assyria departed and went away,
returned *home,* and remained at
Nin′e·veh.
38 Now it came to pass, as he
was worshiping in the house of
Nis′roch his god, that his sons
A·dram′me·lech and Sha·rē′zer
struck him down with the sword;
and they escaped into the land
of Ar′a·rat. Then [a]Ē·sar·had′don
his son reigned in his place.

38 In [a]those days Hez·e·kī′ah
was sick and near death.
And Ī·sāi′ah the prophet, the son
of Ā′moz, went to him and said
to him, "Thus says the LORD:
[b]'Set your house in order, for
you shall die and not live.' "
2 Then Hez·e·kī′ah turned his
face toward the wall, and prayed
to the LORD,
3 and said, [a]"Remember now,
O LORD, I pray, how I have walked
before You in truth and with
a [1]loyal heart, and have done
what is good in Your [b]sight."
And Hez·e·kī′ah wept bitterly.
4 And the word of the LORD
came to Ī·sāi′ah, saying,
5 "Go and tell Hez·e·kī′ah,
'Thus says the LORD, the God of
David your father: "I have heard
your prayer, I have seen your
tears; surely I will add to your
days fifteen years.
6 "I will deliver you and this
city from the hand of the king of
Assyria, and [a]I will defend this
city." '
7 "And this *is* [a]the sign to you

29 [b]Ezek. 38:4; 39:2
32 [a]2 Kin. 19:31
35 [a]Is. 31:5; 38:6 [b]1 Kin. 11:13
36 [a]2 Kin. 19:35 [1]Or *Angel* [2]Lit. *struck*
38 [a]Ezra 4:2

CHAPTER 38

1 [a]2 Chr. 32:24 [b]2 Sam. 17:23
3 [a]Neh. 13:14 [b]2 Kin. 18:5, 6 [1]*whole* or *peaceful*
6 [a]Is. 31:5; 37:35
7 [a]Is. 7:11

from the LORD, that the LORD
will do this thing which He has
spoken:
8 "Behold, I will bring the
shadow on the sundial, which
has gone down with the sun on
the sundial of Ā′haz, ten degrees
backward." So the sun returned
ten degrees on the dial by which
it had gone down.
9 This is the writing of Hez·e-
kī′ah king of Judah, when he
had been sick and had recovered from his sickness:

10 I said,
"In the prime of my life
I shall go to the gates of
Shē′ōl;
I am deprived of the
remainder of my years."
11 I said,
"I shall not see [1]YAH,
The LORD [a]in the land of the
living;
I shall observe man no more
[2]among the inhabitants
of [3]the world.
12 [a]My life span is gone,
Taken from me like a
shepherd's tent;
I have cut off my life like a
weaver.
He cuts me off from the
loom;
From day until night You
make an end of me.
13 I have considered until
morning—
Like a lion,
So He breaks all my bones;
From day until night You
make an end of me.
14 Like a crane *or* a swallow,
so I chattered;
[a]I mourned like a dove;
My eyes fail *from looking*
upward.
O [1]LORD, I am oppressed;
[2]Undertake for me!
15 "What shall I say?
[1]He has both spoken to me,
And He Himself has done *it*.
I shall walk carefully all my
years
[a]In the bitterness of my soul.
16 O Lord, by these *things men*
live;
And in all these *things is*
the life of my spirit;
So You will restore me and
make me live.
17 Indeed *it was* for *my own*
peace
That I had great bitterness;
But You have lovingly
delivered my soul from
the pit of corruption,
For You have cast all my sins
behind Your back.
18 For [a]Shē′ōl cannot thank
You,
Death cannot praise You;
Those who go down to the
pit cannot hope for Your
truth.
19 The living, the living man,
he shall praise You,
As I *do* this day;
[a]The father shall make
known Your truth to the
children.

20 "The LORD *was ready* to save
me;
Therefore we will sing my
songs with stringed
instruments
All the days of our life, in
the house of the LORD."

21 Now [a]Ī·sāi′ah had said, "Let
them take a lump of figs, and
apply *it* as a poultice on the boil,
and he shall recover."

11 [a]Ps. 27:13; 116:9 [1]Heb. *YAH, YAH* [2]LXX omits *among the inhabitants of the world* [3]So with some Heb. mss.; MT, Vg. *rest;* Tg. *land*

12 [a]Job 7:6

14 [a]Is. 59:11 [1]So with Bg.; MT, DSS *Lord* [2]*Be my surety*

15 [a]Job 7:11; 10:1 [1]So with MT, Vg.; DSS, Tg. *And shall I say to Him;* LXX omits first half of this verse

18 [a]Ps. 6:5; 30:9; 88:11; 115:17

19 [a]Deut. 4:9; 6:7

21 [a]2 Kin. 20:7

22 And [a]Hez·e·kī′ah had said,
"What *is* the sign that I shall go
up to the house of the LORD?"

39 At [a]that time [1]Mer′o·dach-
Bal′a·dan the son of Bal′-
a·dan, king of Babylon, sent letters and a present to Hez·e·kī′ah,
for he heard that he had been
sick and had recovered.
2 [a]And Hez·e·kī′ah was pleased
with them, and showed them
the house of his treasures—
the silver and gold, the spices
and precious ointment, and all
his armory—all that was found
among his treasures. There was
nothing in his house or in all his
dominion that Hez·e·kī′ah did
not show them.
3 Then Ī·sāi′ah the prophet
went to King Hez·e·kī′ah, and
said to him, "What did these men
say, and from where did they
come to you?" So Hez·e·kī′ah
said, "They came to me from a
[a]far country, from Babylon."
4 And he said, "What have
they seen in your house?" So
Hez·e·kī′ah answered, "They
have seen all that *is* in my house;
there is nothing among my treasures that I have not shown
them."
5 Then Ī·sāi′ah said to Hez·e-
kī′ah, "Hear the word of the
LORD of hosts:
6 'Behold, the days are coming
[a]when all that *is* in your house,
and what your fathers have ac-
cumulated until this day, shall
be carried to Babylon; nothing
shall be left,' says the LORD.
7 'And they shall take away
some of your [a]sons who will descend from you, whom you will
beget; and they shall be eunuchs
in the palace of the king of Babylon.'"

22 [a]2 Kin. 20:8

CHAPTER 39

1 [a]2 Kin. 20:12–19
[1]*Berodach-Baladan*, 2 Kin. 20:12

2 [a]2 Chr. 32:25, 31

3 [a]Deut. 28:49

6 [a]Jer. 20:5

7 [a]Dan. 1:1–7

8 [a]1 Sam. 3:18

CHAPTER 40

2 [a]Is. 61:7
[1]Lit. *to the heart of*

3 [a]Matt. 3:3; Mark 1:3; Luke 3:4–6; John 1:23
[b][Mal. 3:1; 4:5, 6]
[c]Ps. 68:4
[1]So with MT, Tg., Vg.; LXX omits *in the desert*

4 [a]Is. 45:2
[1]Or *a plain*

5 [a]Is. 35:2

6 [a]Job 14:2
[1]So with MT, Tg.; DSS, LXX, Vg. *I*

8 So Hez·e·kī′ah said to Ī·sāi′ah,
[a]"The word of the LORD which
you have spoken *is* good!" For
he said, "At least there will be
peace and truth in my days."

40 "Comfort, yes, comfort
My people!"
Says your God.
2 "Speak [1]comfort to
Jerusalem, and cry out
to her,
That her warfare is ended,
That her iniquity is
pardoned;
[a]For she has received from
the LORD's hand
Double for all her sins."

3 [a]The voice of one crying in ☆
the wilderness:
[b]"Prepare the way of the
LORD;
[c]Make straight [1]in the desert
A highway for our God.
4 Every valley shall be exalted
And every mountain and
hill brought low;
[a]The crooked places shall be
made [1]straight
And the rough places
smooth;
5 The [a]glory of the LORD shall
be revealed,
And all flesh shall see *it*
together;
For the mouth of the LORD
has spoken."

6 The voice said, "Cry out!"
And [1]he said, "What shall I
cry?"

[a]"All flesh *is* grass,
And all its loveliness *is* like
the flower of the field.
7 The grass withers, the
flower fades,

Because the breath of the
LORD blows upon it;
Surely the people *are* grass.
8 The grass withers, the
flower fades,
But [a]the word of our God
stands forever."

9 O Zion,
You who bring good tidings,
Get up into the high
mountain;
O Jerusalem,
You who bring good tidings,
Lift up your voice with
strength,
Lift *it* up, be not afraid;
Say to the cities of Judah,
"Behold your God!"

10 Behold, the Lord GOD shall
come [1]with a strong
hand,
And [a]His arm shall rule for
Him;
Behold, [b]His reward *is* with
Him,
And His [2]work before Him.
☆ 11 He will [a]feed His flock like a
shepherd;
He will gather the lambs
with His arm,
And carry *them* in His
bosom,
And gently lead those who
are with young.

12 [a]Who has measured the
[1]waters in the hollow of
His hand,
Measured heaven with a
[2]span
And calculated the dust of
the earth in a measure?
Weighed the mountains in
scales
And the hills in a balance?

13 [a]Who has directed the Spirit
of the LORD,
Or *as* His counselor has
taught Him?
14 With whom did He take
counsel, and *who*
instructed Him,
And [a]taught Him in the path
of justice?
Who taught Him knowledge,
And showed Him the way of
understanding?

15 Behold, the nations *are* as a
drop in a bucket,
And are counted as the
small dust on the scales;
Look, He lifts up the isles as
a very little thing.
16 And Lebanon *is* not
sufficient to burn,
Nor its beasts sufficient for
a burnt offering.
17 All nations before Him *are*
as [a]nothing,
And [b]they are counted by
Him less than nothing
and worthless.

18 To whom then will you
[a]liken God?
Or what likeness will you
compare to Him?
19 [a]The workman molds an
image,
The goldsmith overspreads
it with gold,
And the silversmith casts
silver chains.
20 Whoever *is* too
impoverished for *such* [1]a
contribution
Chooses a tree *that* will not
rot;
He seeks for himself a
skillful workman
[a]To prepare a carved image
that will not totter.

8 [a][John 12:34]

10 [a]Is. 59:16, 18 [b]Is. 62:11 [1]*in strength* [2]*recompense*

11 [a][John 10:11, 14–16; Heb. 13:20; 1 Pet. 2:25]

12 [a]Prov. 30:4 [1]So with MT, LXX, Vg.; DSS adds *of the sea*; Tg. adds *of the world* [2]A span = 1/2 cubit, 9 inches; or the width of His hand

13 [a][1 Cor. 2:16]

14 [a]Job 36:22, 23

17 [a]Dan. 4:35 [b]Ps. 62:9

18 [a]Is. 46:5

19 [a]Is. 41:7; 44:10

20 [a]Is. 41:7; 46:7 [1]*an offering*

21 [a]Have you not known?
Have you not heard?
Has it not been told you
from the beginning?
Have you not understood
from the foundations of
the earth?
22 *It is* He who sits above the
circle of the earth,
And its inhabitants *are* like
grasshoppers,
Who [a]stretches out the
heavens like a curtain,
And spreads them out like a
[b]tent to dwell in.
23 He [1]brings the [a]princes to
nothing;
He makes the judges of the
earth useless.

24 Scarcely shall they be
planted,
Scarcely shall they be sown,
Scarcely shall their stock
take root in the earth,
When He will also blow on
them,
And they will wither,
And the whirlwind will take
them away like stubble.

25 "To[a] whom then will you
liken Me,
Or *to whom* shall I be
equal?" says the Holy
One.
26 Lift up your eyes on high,
And see who has created
these *things*,
Who brings out their host
by number;
[a]He calls them all by name,
By the greatness of His
might
And the strength of *His*
power;
Not one is missing.

27 [a]Why do you say, O Jacob,
And speak, O Israel:
"My way is hidden from the
LORD,
And my just claim is passed
over by my God"?
28 Have you not known?
Have you not heard?
The everlasting God, the
LORD,
The Creator of the ends of
the earth,
Neither faints nor is weary.
[a]His understanding is
unsearchable.
29 He gives power to the weak,
And to *those who have*
no might He increases
strength.
30 Even the youths shall faint
and be weary,
And the young men shall
utterly fall,
31 But those who [a]wait on the
LORD
[b]Shall renew *their* strength;
They shall mount up with
wings like eagles,
They shall run and not be
weary,
They shall walk and not
faint.

41

"Keep [a]silence before Me,
O coastlands,
And let the people renew
their strength!
Let them come near, then let
them speak;
Let us [b]come near together
for judgment.

2 "Who raised up one [a]from
the east?
Who in righteousness called
him to His feet?
Who [b]gave the nations
before him,

21 [a]Rom. 1:19
22 [a]Jer. 10:12 [b]Ps. 19:4
23 [a]Ps. 107:40 [1]*reduces*
25 [a]Is. 40:18
26 [a]Ps. 147:4
27 [a]Is. 54:7, 8
28 [a]Rom. 11:33
31 [a]Is. 30:15; 49:23 [b]Ps. 103:5

CHAPTER 41

1 [a]Zech. 2:13 [b]Is. 1:18
2 [a]Is. 46:11 [b]Is. 45:1, 13

And made *him* rule over
kings?
Who gave *them* as the dust
to his sword,
As driven stubble to his
bow?
3 Who pursued them, *and*
passed [1]safely
By the way *that* he had not
gone with his feet?
4 [a]Who has performed and
done *it*,
Calling the generations
from the beginning?
'I, the LORD, am [b]the first;
And with the last I *am*
[c]He.' "

5 The coastlands saw *it* and
feared,
The ends of the earth were
afraid;
They drew near and came.
6 [a]Everyone helped his
neighbor,
And said to his brother,
[1]"Be of good courage!"
7 [a]So the craftsman
encouraged the
[b]goldsmith;[1]
He who smooths *with* the
hammer *inspired* him
who strikes the anvil,
Saying, [2]"It *is* ready for the
soldering";
Then he fastened it with
pegs,
[c]*That* it might not totter.

8 "But you, Israel, *are* My
servant,
Jacob whom I have [a]chosen,
The descendants of
Abraham My [b]friend.
9 *You* whom I have taken
from the ends of the
earth,
And called from its farthest
regions,
And said to you,
'You *are* My servant,
I have chosen you and have
not cast you away:
10 [a]Fear not, [b]for I *am* with you;
Be not dismayed, for I *am*
your God.
I will strengthen you,
Yes, I will help you,
I will uphold you with My
righteous right hand.'

11 "Behold, all those who were
incensed against you
Shall be [a]ashamed and
disgraced;
They shall be as nothing,
And those who strive with
you shall perish.
12 You shall seek them and not
find them—
[1]Those who contended with
you.
Those who war against you
Shall be as nothing,
As a nonexistent thing.
13 For I, the LORD your God,
will hold your right
hand,
Saying to you, 'Fear not, I
will help you.'

14 "Fear not, you [a]worm Jacob,
You men of Israel!
I will help you," says the
LORD
And your Redeemer, the
Holy One of Israel.
15 "Behold, [a]I will make you
into a new threshing
sledge with sharp teeth;
You shall thresh the
mountains and beat
them small,
And make the hills like
chaff.

3 [1]Lit. *in peace*
4 [a]Is. 41:26 [b]Rev. 1:8, 17; 22:13 [c]Is. 43:10; 44:6
6 [a]Is. 40:19 [1]Lit. *Be strong*
7 [a]Is. 44:13 [b]Is. 40:19 [c]Is. 40:20 [1]*refiner* [2]Or *The soldering is good*
8 [a]Deut. 7:6; 10:15 [b]James 2:23
10 [a]Is. 41:13, 14; 43:5 [b][Deut. 31:6]
11 [a]Zech. 12:3
12 [1]Lit. *Men of your strife*
14 [a]Job 25:6
15 [a]Mic. 4:13

16 You shall [a]winnow them, the wind shall carry them away,
And the whirlwind shall scatter them;
You shall rejoice in the LORD,
And [b]glory in the Holy One of Israel.

17 "The poor and needy seek water, but *there is* none,
Their tongues fail for thirst.
I, the LORD, will hear them;
I, the God of Israel, will not [a]forsake them.
18 I will open [a]rivers in desolate heights,
And fountains in the midst of the valleys;
I will make the [b]wilderness a pool of water,
And the dry land springs of water.
19 I will plant in the wilderness the cedar and the acacia tree,
The myrtle and the oil tree;
I will set in the [a]desert the cypress tree *and* the pine
And the box tree together,
20 [a]That they may see and know,
And consider and understand together,
That the hand of the LORD has done this,
And the Holy One of Israel has created it.

21 "Present your case," says the LORD.
"Bring forth your strong *reasons*," says the [a]King of Jacob.
22 "Let[a] them bring forth and show us what will happen;
Let them show the [b]former things, what they *were*,
That we may [1]consider them,
And know the latter end of them;
Or declare to us things to come.
23 [a]Show the things that are to come hereafter,
That we may know that you *are* gods;
Yes, [b]do good or do evil,
That we may be dismayed and see *it* together.
24 Indeed [a]you *are* nothing,
And your work *is* nothing;
He who chooses you *is* an abomination.

25 "I have raised up one from the north,
And he shall come;
From the [1]rising of the sun [a]he shall call on My name;
[b]And he shall come against princes as *though* mortar,
As the potter treads clay.
26 [a]Who has declared from the beginning, that we may know?
And former times, that we may say, '*He is* righteous'?
Surely *there is* no one who shows,
Surely *there is* no one who declares,
Surely *there is* no one who hears your words.
27 [a]The first time [b]*I said* to Zion,
'Look, there they are!'
And I will give to Jerusalem one who brings good tidings.

16 [a]Jer. 51:2 [b]Is. 45:25
17 [a]Rom. 11:2
18 [a]Is. 35:6, 7; 43:19; 44:3 [b]Ps. 107:35
19 [a]Is. 35:1
20 [a]Job 12:9
21 [a]Is. 43:15
22 [a]Is. 45:21 [b]Is. 43:9 [1]Lit. *set our heart on them*
23 [a][John 13:19] [b]Jer. 10:5
24 [a][1 Cor. 8:4]
25 [a]Ezra 1:2 [b]Is. 41:2 [1]East
26 [a]Is. 43:9
27 [a]Is. 41:4 [b]Is. 40:9

28 [a]For I looked, and *there was* no man;
I looked among them, but *there was* no counselor,
Who, when I asked of them, could answer a word.
29 [a]Indeed they *are* all [1]worthless;
Their works *are* nothing;
Their molded images *are* wind and confusion.

☆ **42** "Behold! [a]My Servant whom I uphold,
My [1]Elect One *in whom* My soul [b]delights!
[c]I have put My Spirit upon Him;
He will bring forth justice to the Gentiles.
☆ 2 [a]He will not cry out, nor raise *His voice*,
Nor cause His voice to be heard in the street.
3 A bruised reed He will not break,
And [1]smoking flax He will not [2]quench;
He will bring forth justice for truth.
4 He will not fail nor be discouraged,
Till He has established justice in the earth;
[a]And the coastlands shall wait for His law."

5 Thus says God the LORD,
[a]Who created the heavens and stretched them out,
Who spread forth the earth and that which comes from it,
[b]Who gives breath to the people on it,
And spirit to those who walk on it:
6 "I,[a] the LORD, have called You in righteousness, ☆
And will hold Your hand;
I will keep You [b]and give You as a covenant to the people,
As [c]a light to the Gentiles,
7 [a]To open blind eyes, ☆
To [b]bring out prisoners from the prison,
Those who sit in [c]darkness from the prison house.
8 I *am* the LORD, that *is* My name;
And My [a]glory I will not give to another,
Nor My praise to carved images.
9 Behold, the former things have come to pass,
And new things I declare;
Before they spring forth I tell you of them."

10 [a]Sing to the LORD a new song,
And His praise from the ends of the earth,
[b]You who go down to the sea, and [1]all that is in it,
You coastlands and you inhabitants of them!
11 Let the wilderness and its cities lift up *their voice*,
The villages *that* Kē'dar inhabits.
Let the inhabitants of Sē'la sing,
Let them shout from the top of the mountains.
12 Let them give glory to the LORD,
And declare His praise in the coastlands.
13 The LORD shall go forth like a mighty man;
He shall stir up *His* zeal like a man of war.

28 [a]Is. 63:5

29 [a]Is. 41:24 [1]So with MT, Vg.; DSS, Syr., Tg. *nothing;* LXX omits first line

CHAPTER 42

1 [a]Matt 12:18; [Phil. 2:7] [b]Matt. 3:17; 17:5; Mark 1:11; Luke 3:22; Eph. 1:6 [c][Is. 11:2]; Matt. 3:16; [Luke 4:18, 19, 21]; John 3:34 [1]*Chosen*

2 [a]Matt. 12:19

3 [1]*dimly burning* [2]*extinguish*

4 [a][Gen. 49:10]

5 [a]Zech. 12:1 [b]Acts 17:25

6 [a]Is. 43:1 [b]Is. 49:8 [c]Luke 2:32; [Acts 10:45; 13:47; Gal. 3:14]

7 [a]Is. 35:5 [b]Luke 4:18; [Heb. 2:14] [c]Is. 9:2

8 [a]Is. 48:11

10 [a]Ps. 33:3; 40:3; 98:1 [b]Ps. 107:23 [1]Lit. *its fullness*

He shall cry out, [a]yes, shout
aloud;
He shall prevail against His
enemies.

14 "I have held My peace a long
time,
I have been still and
restrained Myself.
Now I will cry like a woman
in [1]labor,
I will pant and gasp at once.
15 I will lay waste the
mountains and hills,
And dry up all their
vegetation;
I will make the rivers
coastlands,
And I will dry up the pools.
16 I will bring the blind by a
way they did not know;
I will lead them in paths
they have not known.
I will make darkness light
before them,
And crooked places straight.
These things I will do for
them,
And not forsake them.
17 They shall be [a]turned back,
They shall be greatly
ashamed,
Who trust in carved images,
Who say to the molded
images,
'You *are* our gods.'

18 "Hear, you deaf;
And look, you blind, that
you may see.
19 [a]Who *is* blind but My
servant,
Or deaf as My messenger
whom I send?
Who *is* blind as *he who is*
perfect,
And blind as the LORD's
servant?

13 [a]Is. 31:4
14 [1]*childbirth*
17 [a]Ps. 97:7
19 [a][John 9:39, 41]
20 [a]Rom. 2:21
22 [1]Or *trapped in caves*
24 [a]Is. 65:2
25 [a]2 Kin. 25:9
[b]Hos. 7:9
[c]Is. 29:13

20 Seeing many things, [a]but
you do not observe;
Opening the ears, but he
does not hear."

21 The LORD is well pleased for
His righteousness' sake;
He will exalt the law and
make *it* honorable.
22 But this *is* a people robbed
and plundered;
All of them are [1]snared in
holes,
And they are hidden in
prison houses;
They are for prey, and no
one delivers;
For plunder, and no one
says, "Restore!"

23 Who among you will give
ear to this?
Who will listen and hear for
the time to come?
24 Who gave Jacob for
plunder, and Israel to the
robbers?
Was it not the LORD,
He against whom we have
sinned?
[a]For they would not walk in
His ways,
Nor were they obedient to
His law.
25 Therefore He has poured
on him the fury of His
anger
And the strength of battle;
[a]It has set him on fire all
around,
[b]Yet he did not know;
And it burned him,
Yet he did not take *it* to
[c]heart.

43 But now, thus says the
LORD, who created
you, O Jacob,

And He who formed you,
O Israel:
"Fear not, [a]for I have
redeemed you;
[b]I have called *you* by your
name;
You *are* Mine.
2 [a]When you pass through the
waters, [b]I *will be* with
you;
And through the rivers, they
shall not overflow you.
When you [c]walk through
the fire, you shall not be
burned,
Nor shall the flame scorch
you.
3 For I *am* the LORD your God,
The Holy One of Israel, your
Savior;
[a]I gave Egypt for your
ransom,
Ethiopia and Sē′ba in your
place.
4 Since you were precious in
My sight,
You have been honored,
And I have [a]loved you;
Therefore I will give men
for you,
And people for your life.
5 [a]Fear not, for I *am* with you;
I will bring your
descendants from the
east,
And [b]gather you from the
west;
6 I will say to the [a]north, 'Give
them up!'
And to the south, 'Do not
keep them back!'
Bring My sons from afar,
And My daughters from the
ends of the earth—
7 Everyone who is [a]called by
My name,
Whom [b]I have created for
My glory;

CHAPTER 43

1 [a]Is. 43:5; 44:6 [b]Is. 42:6; 45:4
2 [a][Ps. 66:12; 91:3] [b][Deut. 31:6] [c]Dan. 3:25
3 [a][Prov. 11:8; 21:18]
4 [a]Is. 63:9
5 [a]Is. 41:10; 44:2 [b]Is. 54:7
6 [a]Is. 49:12
7 [a]James 2:7 [b][2 Cor. 5:17]
8 [a]Ezek. 12:2 [b]Is. 29:18
9 [a]Is. 41:21, 22, 26
10 [a]Is. 44:8 [b]Is. 55:4 [c]Is. 41:4; 44:6
11 [a]Hos. 13:4
12 [a]Deut. 32:16 [b]Is. 44:8
13 [a]Ps. 90:2 [b]Job 9:12

I have formed him, yes, I
have made him."
8 [a]Bring out the blind people
who have eyes,
And the [b]deaf who have
ears.
9 Let all the nations be
gathered together,
And let the people be
assembled.
[a]Who among them can
declare this,
And show us former things?
Let them bring out their
witnesses, that they may
be justified;
Or let them hear and say, "*It*
is truth."
10 "You[a] *are* My witnesses,"
says the LORD,
[b]"And My servant whom I
have chosen,
That you may know and
[c]believe Me,
And understand that I *am*
He.
Before Me there was no God
formed,
Nor shall there be after Me.
11 I, *even* I, [a]*am* the LORD,
And besides Me *there is* no
savior.
12 I have declared and saved,
I have proclaimed,
And *there was* no [a]foreign
god among you;
[b]Therefore you *are* My
witnesses,"
Says the LORD, "that I *am*
God.
13 [a]Indeed before the day *was*, I
am He;
And *there is* no one who
can deliver out of My
hand;
I work, and who will
[b]reverse it?"

14 Thus says the LORD, your
Redeemer,
The Holy One of Israel:
"For your sake I will send to
Babylon,
And bring them all down as
fugitives—
The Chal·dē′ans, who
rejoice in their ships.
15 I *am* the LORD, your Holy
One,
The Creator of Israel, your
[a]King."

16 Thus says the LORD, who
[a]makes a way in the sea
And a [b]path through the
mighty waters,
17 Who [a]brings forth the
chariot and horse,
The army and the power
(They shall lie down
together, they shall not
rise;
They are extinguished, they
are quenched like a
wick):
18 "Do[a] not remember the
former things,
Nor consider the things of
old.
19 Behold, I will do a [a]new
thing,
Now it shall spring forth;
Shall you not know it?
[b]I will even make a road in
the wilderness
And rivers in the desert.
20 The beast of the field will
honor Me,
The jackals and the
ostriches,
Because [a]I give waters in the
wilderness
And rivers in the desert,
To give drink to My people,
My chosen.

15 [a]Is. 41:20, 21
16 [a]Ex. 14:16, 21, 22 [b]Josh. 3:13
17 [a]Ex. 14:4–9, 25
18 [a]Jer. 16:14
19 [a][2 Cor. 5:17] [b]Ex. 17:6
20 [a]Is. 48:21
21 [a]Ps. 102:18 [b]Jer. 13:11
22 [a]Mal. 1:13; 3:14
23 [a]Amos 5:25
24 [a]Is. 1:14; 7:13
25 [a]Jer. 50:20 [b]Ezek. 36:22 [c]Is. 1:18
26 [1]*justified*
27 [1]*interpreters*
28 [a]Dan. 9:11

21 [a]This people I have formed
for Myself;
They shall declare My
[b]praise.

22 "But you have not called
upon Me, O Jacob;
And you [a]have been weary
of Me, O Israel.
23 [a]You have not brought Me
the sheep for your burnt
offerings,
Nor have you honored Me
with your sacrifices.
I have not caused you
to serve with grain
offerings,
Nor wearied you with
incense.
24 You have bought Me no
sweet cane with money,
Nor have you satisfied Me
with the fat of your
sacrifices;
But you have burdened Me
with your sins,
You have [a]wearied Me with
your iniquities.

25 "I, *even* I, *am* He who [a]blots
out your transgressions
[b]for My own sake;
[c]And I will not remember
your sins.
26 Put Me in remembrance;
Let us contend together;
State your *case,* that you
may be [1]acquitted.
27 Your first father sinned,
And your [1]mediators have
transgressed against Me.
28 Therefore I will profane
the princes of the
sanctuary;
[a]I will give Jacob to the
curse,
And Israel to reproaches.

44 "Yet hear now, O Jacob
My servant,
And Israel whom I have
chosen.
2 Thus says the LORD who
made you
And formed you from the
womb, *who* will help
you:
'Fear not, O Jacob My
servant;
And you, Jesh'ū·run, whom I
have chosen.
3 For I will pour water on him
who is thirsty,
And floods on the dry
ground;
I will pour My Spirit on
your descendants,
And My blessing on your
offspring;
4 They will spring up among
the grass
Like willows by the
watercourses.'
5 One will say, 'I *am* the
LORD's';
Another will call *himself* by
the name of Jacob;
Another will write *with* his
hand, 'The LORD's,'
And name *himself* by the
name of Israel.

6 "Thus says the LORD, the
King of Israel,
And his Redeemer, the LORD
of hosts:
[a]'I *am* the First and I *am* the
Last;
Besides Me *there is* no God.
7 And [a]who can proclaim as I
do?
Then let him declare it and
set it in order for Me,
Since I appointed the
ancient people.
And the things that are
coming and shall come,
Let them show these to
them.
8 Do not fear, nor be afraid;
[a]Have I not told you
from that time, and
declared *it*?
[b]You *are* My witnesses.
Is there a God besides Me?
Indeed [c]*there is* no other
Rock;
I know not *one*.' "

9 [a]Those who make an image,
all of them *are* useless,
And their precious things
shall not profit;
They *are* their own
witnesses;
[b]They neither see nor
know, that they may be
ashamed.
10 Who would form a god or
mold an image
[a]*That* profits him nothing?
11 Surely all his companions
would be [a]ashamed;
And the workmen, they *are*
mere men.
Let them all be gathered
together,
Let them stand up;
Yet they shall fear,
They shall be ashamed
together.

12 [a]The blacksmith with the
tongs works one in the
coals,
Fashions it with hammers,
And works it with the
strength of his arms.
Even so, he is hungry, and
his strength fails;
He drinks no water and is
faint.

CHAPTER 44
6 [a]Is. 41:4
7 [a]Is. 41:4, 22, 26
8 [a]Is. 41:22 [b]Is. 43:10, 12 [c]1 Sam. 2:2
9 [a]Is. 41:24 [b]Ps. 115:4
10 [a]Hab. 2:18
11 [a]Ps. 97:7
12 [a]Jer. 10:3–5

13 The craftsman stretches out *his* rule,
He marks one out with chalk;
He fashions it with a plane,
He marks it out with the compass,
And makes it like the figure of a man,
According to the beauty of a man, that it may remain in the house.
14 He cuts down cedars for himself,
And takes the cypress and the oak;
He [1]secures *it* for himself among the trees of the forest.
He plants a pine, and the rain nourishes *it*.

15 Then it shall be for a man to burn,
For he will take some of it and warm himself;
Yes, he kindles *it* and bakes bread;
Indeed he makes a god and worships *it;*
He makes it a carved image, and falls down to it.
16 He burns half of it in the fire;
With this half he eats meat;
He roasts a roast, and is satisfied.
He even warms *himself* and says,
"Ah! I am warm,
I have seen the fire."
17 And the rest of it he makes into a god,
His carved image.
He falls down before it and worships *it,*
Prays to it and says,
"Deliver me, for you *are* my god!"

14 [1]Lit. *appropriates*

18 [a]Is. 45:20 [b]Is. 6:9, 10; 29:10 [c]Jer. 10:14 [1]Lit. *smeared over*

19 [a]Is. 46:8

20 [a]2 Thess. 2:11 [b]Rom. 1:25

21 [a]Is. 49:15

22 [a]Is. 43:25 [b]1 Cor. 6:20

23 [a]Ps. 69:34

18 [a]They do not know nor understand;
For [b]He has [1]shut their eyes, so that they cannot see,
And their hearts, so that they cannot [c]understand.
19 And no one [a]considers in his heart,
Nor *is there* knowledge nor understanding to say,
"I have burned half of it in the fire,
Yes, I have also baked bread on its coals;
I have roasted meat and eaten *it;*
And shall I make the rest of it an abomination?
Shall I fall down before a block of wood?"
20 He feeds on ashes;
[a]A deceived heart has turned him aside;
And he cannot deliver his soul,
Nor say, "*Is there* not a [b]lie in my right hand?"

21 "Remember these, O Jacob,
And Israel, for you *are* My servant;
I have formed you, you *are* My servant;
O Israel, you will not be [a]forgotten by Me!
22 [a]I have blotted out, like a thick cloud, your transgressions,
And like a cloud, your sins.
Return to Me, for [b]I have redeemed you."

23 [a]Sing, O heavens, for the LORD has done *it!*
Shout, you lower parts of the earth;
Break forth into singing, you mountains,

O forest, and every tree
in it!
For the LORD has redeemed
Jacob,
And [b]glorified Himself in
Israel.

24 Thus says the LORD, [a]your
Redeemer,
And [b]He who formed you
from the womb:
"I *am* the LORD, who makes
all *things*,
[c]Who stretches out the
heavens [1]all alone,
Who spreads abroad the
earth by Myself;
25 Who [a]frustrates the signs [b]of
the babblers,
And drives diviners mad;
Who turns wise men
backward,
[c]And makes their knowledge
foolishness;
26 [a]Who confirms the word of
His servant,
And performs the counsel of
His messengers;
Who says to Jerusalem, 'You
shall be inhabited,'
To the cities of Judah, 'You
shall be built,'
And I will raise up her
waste places;
27 [a]Who says to the deep, 'Be
dry!
And I will dry up your
rivers';
28 Who says of [a]Cyrus, '*He is*
My shepherd,
And he shall perform all My
pleasure,
Saying to Jerusalem, [b]"You
shall be built,"
And to the temple, "Your
foundation shall be
laid." '

45

"Thus says the LORD to
His anointed,
To [a]Cyrus, whose [b]right
hand I have [1]held—
[c]To subdue nations before
him
And [d]loose the armor of
kings,
To open before him the
double doors,
So that the gates will not be
shut:
2 'I will go before you
[a]And[1] make the [2]crooked
places straight;
[b]I will break in pieces the
gates of bronze
And cut the bars of iron.
3 I will give you the treasures
of darkness
And hidden riches of secret
places,
[a]That you may know that I,
the LORD,
Who [b]call *you* by your
name,
Am the God of Israel.
4 For [a]Jacob My servant's
sake,
And Israel My elect,
I have even called you by
your name;
I have named you, though
you have not known Me.
5 I [a]*am* the LORD, and [b]*there is*
no other;
There is no God besides Me.
[c]I will gird you, though you
have not known Me,
6 [a]That they may [b]know from
the rising of the sun to
its setting
That *there is* none besides
Me.
I *am* the LORD, and *there is*
no other;
7 I form the light and create
darkness,

23 [b]Is. 49:3; 60:21
24 [a]Is. 43:14 [b]Is. 43:1 [c]Job 9:8 [1]By Himself
25 [a]Is. 47:13 [b]Jer. 50:36 [c]1 Cor. 1:20, 27
26 [a]Zech. 1:6
27 [a]Jer. 50:38; 51:36
28 [a]Ezra 1:1 [b]Ezra 6:7

CHAPTER 45

1 [a]Is. 44:28 [b]Is. 41:13 [c]Dan. 5:30 [d]Job 12:21 [1]*strengthened* or *sustained*
2 [a]Is. 40:4 [b]Ps. 107:16 [1]Tg. *I will trample down the walls;* Vg. *I will humble the great ones of the earth* [2]DSS, LXX *mountains*
3 [a]Is. 41:23 [b]Ex. 33:12
4 [a]Is. 44:1
5 [a]Deut. 4:35; 32:39 [b]Is. 45:14, 18 [c]Ps. 18:32
6 [a]Mal. 1:11 [b][Is. 11:9; 52:10]

I make peace and [a]create
calamity;
I, the LORD, do all these
things.'

8 "Rain[a] down, you heavens,
from above,
And let the skies pour down
righteousness;
Let the earth open, let them
bring forth salvation,
And let righteousness
spring up together.
I, the LORD, have created it.

9 "Woe to him who strives with
[a]his Maker!
Let the potsherd *strive* with
the potsherds of the
earth!
[b]Shall the clay say to him
who forms it, 'What are
you making?'
Or shall your handiwork
say, 'He has no hands'?
10 Woe to him who says to *his*
father, 'What are you
begetting?'
Or to the woman, 'What
have you brought
forth?' "

11 Thus says the LORD,
The Holy One of Israel, and
his Maker:
[a]"Ask Me of things to come
concerning [b]My sons;
And concerning [c]the work
of My hands, you
command Me.
12 [a]I have made the earth,
And [b]created man on it.
I—My hands—stretched out
the heavens,
And [c]all their host I have
commanded.
13 [a]I have raised him up in
righteousness,
And I will [1]direct all his
ways;
He shall [b]build My city
And let My exiles go free,
[c]Not for price nor reward,"
Says the LORD of hosts.

14 Thus says the LORD:

[a]"The labor of Egypt and
merchandise of Cush
And of the Sa·bē′ans, men
of stature,
Shall come over to you, and
they shall be yours;
They shall walk behind you,
They shall come over [b]in
chains;
And they shall bow down to
you.
They will make supplication
to you, *saying,* [c]'Surely
God *is* in you,
And *there is* no other;
[d]*There is* no other God.' "

15 Truly You *are* God, [a]who
hide Yourself,
O God of Israel, the Savior!
16 They shall be [a]ashamed
And also disgraced, all of
them;
They shall go in confusion
together,
Who are makers of idols.
17 [a]*But* Israel shall be saved by
the LORD
With an [b]everlasting
salvation;
You shall not be ashamed or
[c]disgraced
Forever and ever.

18 For thus says the LORD,
[a]Who created the heavens,
Who is God,
Who formed the earth and
made it,

7 [a]Amos 3:6
8 [a]Ps. 85:11
9 [a]Is. 64:8 [b]Jer. 18:6
11 [a]Is. 8:19 [b]Jer. 31:9 [c]Is. 29:23; 60:21; 64:8
12 [a]Is. 42:5 [b]Gen. 1:26 [c]Gen. 2:1
13 [a]Is. 41:2 [b]2 Chr. 36:22 [c][Rom. 3:24] [1]Or *make all his ways straight*
14 [a]Zech. 8:22, 23 [b]Ps. 149:8 [c]1 Cor. 14:25 [d]Is. 45:5
15 [a]Ps. 44:24
16 [a]Is. 44:11
17 [a]Is. 26:4 [b]Is. 51:6 [c]Is. 29:22
18 [a]Is. 42:5

Who has established it,
Who did not create it [1]in
vain,
Who formed it to be
[b]inhabited:
[c]"I *am* the LORD, and *there is*
no other.
19 I have not spoken in [a]secret,
In a dark place of the earth;
I did not say to the seed of
Jacob,
'Seek Me [1]in vain';
[b]I, the LORD, speak
righteousness,
I declare things that are
right.

20 "Assemble yourselves and
come;
Draw near together,
You *who have* escaped from
the nations.
[a]They have no knowledge,
Who carry the wood of their
carved image,
And pray to a god *that*
cannot save.
21 Tell and bring forth *your*
case;
Yes, let them take counsel
together.
[a]Who has declared this from
ancient time?
Who has told it from that
time?
Have not I, the LORD?
[b]And *there is* no other God
besides Me,
A just God and a Savior;
There is none besides Me.

22 "Look to Me, and be saved,
[a]All you ends of the earth!
For I *am* God, and *there is*
no other.
☆ 23 [a]I have sworn by Myself;
The word has gone out of My
mouth *in* righteousness,
And shall not return,
That to Me every [b]knee shall
bow,
[c]Every tongue shall take an
oath.
24 He shall say,
[1]'Surely in the LORD I have
[a]righteousness and
strength.
To Him *men* shall come,
And [b]all shall be ashamed
Who are incensed against
Him.
25 [a]In the LORD all the
descendants of Israel
Shall be justified, and [b]shall
glory.' "

46

Bel [a]bows down, Nē′bō
stoops;
Their idols were on the
beasts and on the cattle.
Your carriages *were* heavily
loaded,
[b]A burden to the weary
beast.
2 They stoop, they bow down
together;
They could not deliver the
burden,
[a]But have themselves gone
into captivity.

3 "Listen to Me, O house of
Jacob,
And all the remnant of the
house of Israel,
[a]Who have been upheld *by*
Me from [1]birth,
Who have been carried from
the womb:
4 Even to *your* old age, [a]I *am*
He,
And *even* to gray hairs [b]I
will carry *you!*
I have made, and I will bear;
Even I will carry, and will
deliver *you.*

18 [b]Ps. 115:16 [c]Is. 45:5 [1]Or *empty, a waste*
19 [a]Deut. 30:11 [b]Ps. 19:8 [1]Or *in a waste place*
20 [a]Is. 44:9; 46:7
21 [a]Is. 41:22; 43:9 [b]Is. 44:8
22 [a]Ps. 22:27; 65:5
23 [a][Heb. 6:13] [b]Rom. 14:11; [Phil. 2:10] [c]Deut. 6:13
24 [a][1 Cor. 1:30] [b]Is. 41:11 [1]Or *Only in the LORD are all righteousness and strength*
25 [a]Is. 45:17 [b]1 Cor. 1:31

CHAPTER 46
1 [a]Jer. 50:2 [b]Jer. 10:5
2 [a]Jer. 48:7
3 [a]Ps. 71:6 [1]Lit. *the belly*
4 [a]Mal. 3:6 [b]Ps. 48:14

5 "To[a] whom will you liken Me,
and make *Me* equal
And compare Me, that we
should be alike?
6 [a]They lavish gold out of the
bag,
And weigh silver on the
scales;
They hire a [b]goldsmith, and
he makes it a god;
They prostrate themselves,
yes, they worship.
7 [a]They bear it on the shoulder,
they carry it
And set it in its place, and it
stands;
From its place it shall not
move.
Though [b]*one* cries out to it,
yet it cannot answer
Nor save him out of his
trouble.

8 "Remember this, and [1]show
yourselves men;
[a]Recall to mind, O you
transgressors.
9 [a]Remember the former
things of old,
For I *am* God, and [b]*there is*
no other;
I am God, and *there is* none
like Me,
10 [a]Declaring the end from the
beginning,
And from ancient times
things that are not *yet*
done,
Saying, [b]'My counsel shall
stand,
And I will do all My
pleasure,'
11 Calling a bird of prey [a]from
the east,
The man [b]who executes
My counsel, from a far
country.
Indeed [c]I have spoken *it;*
I will also bring it to pass.
I have purposed *it;*
I will also do it.

12 "Listen to Me, you [a]stubborn-
hearted,
[b]Who *are* far from
righteousness:
13 [a]I bring My righteousness
near, it shall not be far
off;
My salvation [b]shall not
[1]linger.
And I will place [c]salvation
in Zion,
For Israel My glory.

47 "Come [a]down and [b]sit in
the dust,
O virgin daughter of
[c]Babylon;
Sit on the ground without a
throne,
O daughter of the
Chal·dē´ans!
For you shall no more be
called
Tender and [1]delicate.
2 [a]Take the millstones and
grind meal.
Remove your veil,
Take off the skirt,
Uncover the thigh,
Pass through the rivers.
3 [a]Your nakedness shall be
uncovered,
Yes, your shame will be seen;
[b]I will take vengeance,
And I will not arbitrate with
a man."

4 *As for* [a]our Redeemer, the
LORD of hosts *is* His
name,
The Holy One of Israel.

5 "Sit in [a]silence, and go into
darkness,

5 [a]Is. 40:18, 25
6 [a]Is. 40:19; 41:6 [b]Is. 44:12
7 [a]Jer. 10:5 [b]Is. 45:20
8 [a]Is. 44:19 [1]*be men*, take courage
9 [a]Deut. 32:7 [b]Is. 45:5, 21
10 [a]Is. 45:21; 48:3 [b]Ps. 33:11
11 [a]Is. 41:2, 25 [b]Is. 44:28 [c]Num. 23:19
12 [a]Ps. 76:5 [b][Rom. 10:3]
13 [a][Rom. 1:17] [b]Hab. 2:3 [c]Is. 62:11 [1]*delay*

CHAPTER 47

1 [a]Jer. 48:18 [b]Is. 3:26 [c]Jer. 25:12; 50:1—51:64 [1]*dainty*
2 [a]Ex. 11:5
3 [a]Is. 3:17; 20:4 [b][Rom. 12:19]
4 [a]Jer. 50:34
5 [a]1 Sam. 2:9

O daughter of the
Chal·dē′ans;
[b]For you shall no longer be
called
The Lady of Kingdoms.
6 [a]I was angry with My people;
[b]I have profaned My
inheritance,
And given them into your
hand.
You showed them no
mercy;
[c]On the elderly you laid your
yoke very heavily.
7 And you said, 'I shall be [a]a
lady forever,'
So that you did not [b]take
these *things* to heart,
[c]Nor remember the latter end
of them.

8 "Therefore hear this now,
you who are given to
pleasures,
Who dwell securely,
Who say in your heart,
'I *am,* and *there is* no one
else besides me;
I shall not sit *as* a widow,
Nor shall I know the loss of
children';
9 But these two *things* shall
come to you
[a]In a moment, in one day:
The loss of children, and
widowhood.
They shall come upon you
in their fullness
Because of the multitude of
your sorceries,
For the great abundance of
your enchantments.

10 "For you have trusted in your
wickedness;
You have said, 'No one
[a]sees me';

5 [b][Dan. 2:37]

6 [a]2 Sam. 24:14
[b]Is. 43:28
[c]Deut. 28:49, 50

7 [a]Rev. 18:7
[b]Is. 42:25; 46:8
[c]Deut. 32:29

9 [a]1 Thess. 5:3

10 [a]Is. 29:15
[1]*led you astray*

11 [a]1 Thess. 5:3
[b]Is. 29:5
[1]Lit. *to cover it* or *atone for it*

13 [a]Is. 57:10
[b]Dan. 2:2, 10
[1]Lit. *viewers of the heavens*
[2]Lit. *those giving knowledge for new moons*

14 [a]Nah. 1:10
[b]Jer. 51:58

Your wisdom and your
knowledge have [1]warped
you;
And you have said in your
heart,
'I *am,* and *there is* no one
else besides me.'
11 Therefore evil shall come
upon you;
You shall not know from
where it arises.
And trouble shall fall upon
you;
You will not be able [1]to put
it off.
And [a]desolation shall come
upon you [b]suddenly,
Which you shall not know.

12 "Stand now with your
enchantments
And the multitude of your
sorceries,
In which you have labored
from your youth—
Perhaps you will be able to
profit,
Perhaps you will prevail.
13 [a]You are wearied in the
multitude of your
counsels;
Let now [b]the[1] astrologers,
the stargazers,
And [2]the monthly
prognosticators
Stand up and save you
From what shall come upon
you.
14 Behold, they shall be [a]as
stubble,
The fire shall [b]burn them;
They shall not deliver
themselves
From the power of the
flame;
It shall not *be* a coal to be
warmed by,
Nor a fire to sit before!

15 Thus shall they be to you
With whom you have
labored,
[a]Your merchants from your
youth;
They shall wander each one
to his [1]quarter.
No one shall save you.

48 "Hear this, O house of
Jacob,
Who are called by the name
of Israel,
And have come forth from
the wellsprings of Judah;
Who swear by the name of
the LORD,
And make mention of the
God of Israel,
But [a]not in truth or in
righteousness;
2 For they call themselves
[a]after the holy city,
And [b]lean on the God of
Israel;
The LORD of hosts *is* His
name:

3 "I have [a]declared the
former things from the
beginning;
They went forth from My
mouth, and I caused
them to hear it.
Suddenly I did *them*, [b]and
they came to pass.
4 Because I knew that you
were [1]obstinate,
And [a]your neck *was* an iron
sinew,
And your brow bronze,
5 Even from the beginning I
have declared *it* to you;
Before it came to pass I
proclaimed *it* to you,
Lest you should say, 'My
idol has done them,
And my carved image and
my molded image
Have commanded them.'
6 "You have heard;
See all this.
And will you not declare *it*?
I have made you hear new
things from this time,
Even hidden things, and you
did not know them.
7 They are created now and
not from the beginning;
And before this day you
have not heard them,
Lest you should say, 'Of
course I knew them.'
8 Surely you did not hear,
Surely you did not know;
Surely from long ago your
ear was not opened.
For I knew that you would
deal very treacherously,
And were called [a]a
transgressor from the
womb.

9 "For[a] My name's sake [b]I will
[1]defer My anger,
And *for* My praise I will
restrain it from you,
So that I do not cut you off.
10 Behold, [a]I have refined you,
but not as silver;
I have tested you in the
[b]furnace of affliction.
11 For My own sake, for My
own sake, I will do *it;*
For [a]how should *My name*
be profaned?
And [b]I will not give My
glory to another.

12 "Listen to Me, O Jacob,
And Israel, My called:
I *am* He, [a]I *am* the [b]First,
I *am* also the Last.

---

15 [a]Rev. 18:11 [1]*own side* or *way*

CHAPTER 48

1 [a]Jer. 4:2; 5:2

2 [a]Is. 52:1; 64:10 [b]Mic. 3:11

3 [a]Is. 44:7, 8; 46:10 [b]Josh. 21:45

4 [a]Deut. 31:27 [1]Heb. *hard*

8 [a]Ps. 58:3

9 [a]Ezek. 20:9, 14, 22, 44 [b]Ps. 78:38 [1]*delay*

10 [a]Ps. 66:10 [b]Deut. 4:20

11 [a]Ezek. 20:9 [b]Is. 42:8

12 [a]Deut. 32:39 [b][Rev. 22:13]

13 Indeed [a]My hand has laid
the foundation of the
earth,
And My right hand has
stretched out the
heavens;
When [b]I call to them,
They stand up together.

14 "All of you, assemble
yourselves, and hear!
Who among them has
declared these *things*?
[a]The LORD loves him;
[b]He shall do His pleasure on
Babylon,
And His arm *shall be
against* the Chal·dē′ans.
15 I, *even* I, have spoken;
Yes, [a]I have called him,
I have brought him, and his
way will prosper.

16 "Come near to Me, hear this:
[a]I have not spoken in secret
from the beginning;
From the time that it was, I
was there.
And now [b]the Lord GOD and
His Spirit
[1]Have sent Me."

17 Thus says [a]the LORD, your
Redeemer,
The Holy One of Israel:
"I *am* the LORD your God,
Who teaches you to profit,
[b]Who leads you by the way
you should go.
18 [a]Oh, that you had heeded My
commandments!
[b]Then your peace would have
been like a river,
And your righteousness like
the waves of the sea.
19 [a]Your descendants also
would have been like the
sand,
And the offspring of your
body like the grains of
sand;
His name would not have
been cut off
Nor destroyed from before
Me."

20 [a]Go forth from Babylon!
Flee from the Chal·dē′ans!
With a voice of singing,
Declare, proclaim this,
Utter it to the end of the
earth;
Say, "The LORD has
[b]redeemed
His servant Jacob!"
21 And they [a]did not thirst
When He led them through
the deserts;
He [b]caused the waters to
flow from the rock for
them;
He also split the rock, and
the waters gushed out.

22 "*There*[a] *is* no peace," says the
LORD, "for the wicked."

49 "Listen, [a]O coastlands, to
Me,
And take heed, you peoples
from afar!
[b]The LORD has called Me
from the womb;
From the [1]matrix of My
mother He has made
mention of My name.
2 And He has made [a]My
mouth like a sharp
sword;
[b]In the shadow of His hand
He has hidden Me,
And made Me [c]a polished
shaft;
In His quiver He has
hidden Me."

13 [a]Ps. 102:25 [b]Is. 40:26
14 [a]Is. 45:1 [b]Is. 44:28; 47:1–15
15 [a]Is. 45:1, 2
16 [a]Is. 45:19 [b]Zech. 2:8, 9, 11 [1]Heb. verb is sing.; or *Has sent Me and His Spirit*
17 [a]Is. 43:14 [b]Ps. 32:8
18 [a]Ps. 81:13 [b]Ps. 119:165
19 [a]Gen. 22:17
20 [a]Zech. 2:6, 7 [b][Ex. 19:4–6]
21 [a][Is. 41:17, 18] [b]Ex. 17:6
22 [a][Is. 57:21]

CHAPTER 49

1 [a]Is. 41:1 [b]Jer. 1:5 [1]Lit. *inward parts*
2 [a]Rev. 1:16; 2:12 [b]Is. 51:16 [c]Ps. 45:5

3 "And He said to me,
[a]'You *are* My servant,
O Israel,
[b]In whom I will be glorified.'
4 [a]Then I said, 'I have labored
in vain,
I have spent my strength for
nothing and in vain;
Yet surely my [1]just reward *is*
with the LORD,
And my [2]work with my
God.' "

☆ 5 "And now the LORD says,
Who formed Me from the
womb *to be* His Servant,
To bring Jacob back to Him,
So that Israel [a]is [1]gathered
to Him
(For I shall be glorious in
the eyes of the LORD,
And My God shall be My
strength),
☆ 6 Indeed He says,
'It is too small a thing that
You should be My
Servant
To raise up the tribes of
Jacob,
And to restore the preserved
ones of Israel;
I will also give You as a
[a]light to the Gentiles,
That You should be My
salvation to the ends of
the earth.' "

☆ 7 Thus says the LORD,
The Redeemer of Israel,
[1]their Holy One,
[a]To Him [2]whom man
despises,
To Him whom the nation
abhors,
To the Servant of rulers:
[b]"Kings shall see and arise,
Princes also shall worship,
Because of the LORD who is
faithful,
The Holy One of Israel;
And He has chosen You."

8 Thus says the LORD: ☆

"In an [a]acceptable[1] time I
have heard You,
And in the day of salvation I
have helped You;
I will [2]preserve You [b]and
give You
As a covenant to the people,
To restore the earth,
To cause them to inherit the
desolate [3]heritages;
9 That You may say [a]to the ☆
prisoners, 'Go forth,'
To those who *are* in
darkness, 'Show
yourselves.'

"They shall feed along the
roads,
And their pastures *shall be*
on all desolate heights.
10 They shall neither [a]hunger ☆
nor thirst,
[b]Neither heat nor sun shall
strike them;
For He who has mercy on
them [c]will lead them,
Even by the springs of water
He will guide them.
11 [a]I will make each of My
mountains a road,
And My highways shall be
elevated.
12 Surely [a]these shall come
from afar;
Look! Those from the north
and the west,
And these from the land of
Sin'im."

13 [a]Sing, O heavens!
Be joyful, O earth!

---

3 [a][Zech. 3:8] [b]Is. 44:23
4 [a][Ezek. 3:19] [1]*justice* [2]*recompense*
5 [a]Matt. 23:37; [Rom. 11:25–29] [1]Qr., DSS, LXX *gathered to Him;* Kt. *not gathered*
6 [a][Luke 2:32]; Acts 13:47; [Gal. 3:14]
7 [a][Is. 53:3; Matt. 26:67; 27:41]; Mark 15:29; Luke 23:35 [b][Is. 52:15] [1]Lit. *his or its* [2]Lit. *who is despised of soul*
8 [a]2 Cor. 6:2 [b]Is. 42:6 [1]*favorable* [2]*keep* [3]*inheritances*
9 [a]Is. 61:1; Luke 4:18
10 [a]Rev. 7:16, 17 [b]Ps. 121:6 [c]Ps. 23:2
11 [a]Is. 40:4
12 [a]Is. 43:5, 6
13 [a]Is. 44:23

And break out in singing,
O mountains!
For the LORD has comforted
His people,
And will have mercy on His
afflicted.

14 [a]But Zion said, "The LORD
has forsaken me,
And my Lord has
forgotten me."

15 "Can[a] a woman forget her
nursing child,
[1]And not have compassion
on the son of her womb?
Surely they may forget,
[b]Yet I will not forget you.
16 See, [a]I have inscribed you on
the palms *of My hands;*
Your walls *are* continually
before Me.
17 Your [1]sons shall make haste;
Your destroyers and those
who laid you waste
Shall go away from you.
18 [a]Lift up your eyes, look
around and see;
All these gather together
and come to you.
As I live," says the LORD,
"You shall surely clothe
yourselves with them all
[b]as an ornament,
And bind them *on you* as a
bride *does.*

19 "For your waste and desolate
places,
And the land of your
destruction,
[a]Will even now be too small
for the inhabitants;
And those who swallowed
you up will be far away.
20 [a]The children you will have,
[b]After you have lost the
others,

Will say again in your ears,
'The place *is* too small
for me;
Give me a place where I
may dwell.'
21 Then you will say in your
heart,
'Who has begotten these
for me,
Since I have lost my
children and am
desolate,
A captive, and wandering to
and fro?
And who has brought
these up?
There I was, left alone;
But these, where *were*
they?' "

22 [a]Thus says the Lord GOD:

"Behold, I will lift My hand
in an oath to the nations,
And set up My [1]standard for
the peoples;
They shall bring your sons
in *their* [2]arms,
And your daughters shall
be carried on *their*
shoulders;
23 [a]Kings shall be your foster
fathers,
And their queens your
nursing mothers;
They shall bow down to you
with *their* faces to the
earth,
And [b]lick up the dust of
your feet.
Then you will know that I
am the LORD,
[c]For they shall not be
ashamed who wait
for Me."

24 [a]Shall the prey be taken from
the mighty,

14 [a]Is. 40:27
15 [a]Ps. 103:13 [b]Rom. 11:29 [1]Lit. *From having compassion*
16 [a]Song 8:6
17 [1]DSS, LXX, Tg., Vg. *builders*
18 [a]Is. 60:4 [b]Prov. 17:6
19 [a]Zech. 10:10
20 [a]Is. 60:4 [b][Rom. 11:11]
22 [a]Is. 60:4 [1]*banner* [2]Lit. *bosom*
23 [a]Is. 52:15 [b]Ps. 72:9 [c][Rom. 5:5]
24 [a]Luke 11:21, 22

Or the captives [1]of the
righteous be delivered?

25 But thus says the LORD:

"Even the captives of the
mighty shall be taken
away,
And the prey of the terrible
be delivered;
For I will contend with him
who contends with you,
And I will save your
children.
26 I will [a]feed those who
oppress you with their
own flesh,
And they shall be drunk
with their own [b]blood as
with sweet wine.
All flesh [c]shall know
That I, the LORD, *am* your
Savior,
And your Redeemer, the
Mighty One of Jacob."

50

Thus says the LORD:

"Where *is* [a]the certificate of
your mother's divorce,
Whom I have put away?
Or which of My [b]creditors
is it to whom I have sold
you?
For your iniquities [c]you have
sold yourselves,
And for your transgressions
your mother has been
put away.
2 Why, when I came, *was
there* no man?
Why, when I called, *was
there* none to answer?
Is My hand shortened at all
that it cannot redeem?
Or have I no power to
deliver?
Indeed with My [a]rebuke I
dry up the sea,
I make the rivers a
wilderness;
Their fish stink because
there is no water,
And die of thirst.
3 [a]I clothe the heavens with
blackness,
[b]And I make sackcloth their
covering."

4 "The[a] Lord GOD has given Me
The tongue of the learned,
That I should know how to
speak
A word in season to *him
who is* [b]weary.
He awakens Me morning by
morning,
He awakens My ear
To hear as the learned.
5 The Lord GOD [a]has opened ☆
My ear;
And I was not [b]rebellious,
Nor did I turn away.
6 [a]I gave My back to those ☆
who struck *Me,*
And [b]My cheeks to those
who plucked out the
beard;
I did not hide My face from
shame and [c]spitting.

7 "For the Lord GOD will help ☆
Me;
Therefore I will not be
disgraced;
Therefore [a]I have set My
face like a flint,
And I know that I will not
be ashamed.
8 [a]*He is* near who justifies Me;
Who will contend with Me?
Let us stand together.
Who *is* [1]My adversary?
Let him come near Me.

---

24 [1]So with MT, Tg.; DSS, Syr., Vg. *of the mighty;* LXX *unjustly*

26 [a]Is. 9:20 [b]Rev. 14:20 [c]Ps. 9:16

CHAPTER 50

1 [a]Deut. 24:1 [b]Deut. 32:30; 2 Kin. 4:1 [c]Is. 52:3

2 [a]Nah. 1:4

3 [a]Ex. 10:21 [b]Rev. 6:12

4 [a]Ex. 4:11 [b]Matt. 11:28

5 [a]Ps. 40:6 [b]Matt. 26:39; Mark 14:36; Luke 22:42; John 8:29; 14:31; 15:10; [Phil. 2:8; Heb. 5:8; 10:7]

6 [a]Matt. 27:26; John 18:22 [b]Matt. 26:67; 27:30; Mark 14:65; 15:19 [c]Lam. 3:30

7 [a]Ezek. 3:8, 9; Luke 9:51

8 [a][Rom. 8:32–34] [1]Lit. *master of My judgment*

☆9 Surely the Lord God will
help Me;
Who *is* he *who* will
condemn Me?
[a]Indeed they will all grow old
like a garment;
[b]The moth will eat them up.

10 "Who among you fears the
Lord?
Who obeys the voice of His
Servant?
Who [a]walks in darkness
And has no light?
[b]Let him trust in the name of
the Lord
And rely upon his God.
11 Look, all you who kindle a
fire,
Who encircle *yourselves*
with sparks:
Walk in the light of your fire
and in the sparks you
have kindled—
[a]This you shall have from My
hand:
You shall lie down [b]in
torment.

51

"Listen to Me, [a]you
who [1]follow after
righteousness,
You who seek the Lord:
Look to the rock *from which*
you were hewn,
And to the hole of the pit
from which you were
dug.
2 [a]Look to Abraham your
father,
And to Sarah *who* bore you;
[b]For I called him alone,
And [c]blessed him and
increased him."

3 For the Lord will [a]comfort
Zion,
He will comfort all her
waste places;
He will make her wilderness
like Eden,
And her desert [b]like the
garden of the Lord;
Joy and gladness will be
found in it,
Thanksgiving and the voice
of melody.

4 "Listen to Me, My people;
And give ear to Me, O My
nation:
[a]For law will proceed from
Me,
And I will make My justice
rest
[b]As a light of the peoples.
5 [a]My righteousness *is* near,
My salvation has gone forth,
[b]And My arms will judge the
peoples;
[c]The coastlands will wait
upon Me,
And [d]on My arm they will
trust.
6 [a]Lift up your eyes to the
heavens,
And look on the earth
beneath.
For [b]the heavens will vanish
away like smoke,
[c]The earth will grow old like
a garment,
And those who dwell in it
will die in like manner;
But My salvation will be
[d]forever,
And My righteousness will
not be [1]abolished.

7 "Listen to Me, you who know
righteousness,
You people [a]in whose heart
is My law:
[b]Do not fear the reproach of
men,

9 [a]Job 13:28; Acts 2:24; Heb. 1:11 [b]Is. 51:6, 8
10 [a]Ps. 23:4 [b]2 Chr. 20:20
11 [a][John 9:39] [b]Ps. 16:4
CHAPTER 51
1 [a][Rom. 9:30–32] [1]*pursue*
2 [a]Heb. 11:11 [b]Gen. 12:1 [c]Gen. 24:35
3 [a]Is. 40:1; 52:9 [b]Gen. 13:10
4 [a]Is. 2:3 [b]Is. 42:6
5 [a]Is. 46:13 [b]Ps. 67:4 [c]Is. 60:9 [d][Rom. 1:16]
6 [a]Is. 40:26 [b]Matt. 24:35 [c]Is. 24:19, 20; 50:9 [d]Is. 45:17 [1]*broken*
7 [a]Ps. 37:31 [b][Matt. 5:11, 12; 10:28]

Nor be afraid of their
insults.
8 For [a]the moth will eat them
up like a garment,
And the worm will eat them
like wool;
But My righteousness will
be forever,
And My salvation
from generation to
generation."

9 [a]Awake, awake, [b]put on
strength,
O arm of the LORD!
Awake [c]as in the ancient
days,
In the generations of old.
[d]*Are* You not *the arm* that cut
[e]Rā'hab apart,
And wounded the [f]serpent?
10 *Are* You not *the One* who
[a]dried up the sea,
The waters of the great
deep;
That made the depths of the
sea a road
For the redeemed to cross
over?
11 So [a]the ransomed of the
LORD shall return,
And come to Zion with
singing,
With everlasting joy on their
heads.
They shall obtain joy and
gladness;
Sorrow and sighing shall
flee away.

12 "I, *even* I, *am* He [a]who
comforts you.
Who *are* you that you
should be afraid
[b]Of a man *who* will die,
And of the son of a man *who*
will be made [c]like grass?

8 [a]Is. 50:9
9 [a]Ps. 44:23 [b]Ps. 93:1 [c]Ps. 44:1 [d]Job 26:12 [e]Ps. 87:4 [f]Ps. 74:13
10 [a]Ex. 14:21
11 [a]Is. 35:10
12 [a]2 Cor. 1:3 [b]Ps. 118:6 [c]Is. 40:6, 7
13 [a]Is. 17:10 [b]Ps. 104:2 [c]Job 20:7
14 [a]Zech. 9:11
15 [a]Job 26:12
16 [a]Deut. 18:18 [b]Is. 49:2 [c]Is. 65:17 [1]*establish*
17 [a]Is. 52:1 [b]Job 21:20

13 And [a]you forget the LORD
your Maker,
[b]Who stretched out the
heavens
And laid the foundations of
the earth;
You have feared continually
every day
Because of the fury of the
oppressor,
When *he has* prepared to
destroy.
[c]And where *is* the fury of the
oppressor?
14 The captive exile hastens,
that he may be loosed,
[a]That he should not die in
the pit,
And that his bread should
not fail.
15 But I *am* the LORD your God,
Who [a]divided the sea whose
waves roared—
The LORD of hosts *is* His
name.
16 And [a]I have put My words
in your mouth;
[b]I have covered you with the
shadow of My hand,
[c]That I may [1]plant the
heavens,
Lay the foundations of the
earth,
And say to Zion, 'You *are*
My people.' "

17 [a]Awake, awake!
Stand up, O Jerusalem,
You who [b]have drunk at the
hand of the LORD
The cup of His fury;
You have drunk the dregs of
the cup of trembling,
And drained *it* out.
18 *There is* no one to guide her
Among all the sons she has
brought forth;

Nor *is there any* who takes
her by the hand
Among all the sons she has
brought up.
19 [a]These two *things* have come
to you;
Who will be sorry for
you?—
Desolation and destruction,
famine and sword—
[b]By whom will I comfort
you?
20 [a]Your sons have fainted,
They lie at the head of all
the streets,
Like an antelope in a net;
They are full of the fury of
the LORD,
The rebuke of your God.

21 Therefore please hear this,
you afflicted,
And drunk [a]but not with
wine.
22 Thus says your Lord,
The LORD and your God,
Who [a]pleads the cause of
His people:
"See, I have taken out of
your hand
The cup of trembling,
The dregs of the cup of My
fury;
You shall no longer drink it.
23 [a]But I will put it into the
hand of those who afflict
you,
Who have said to [1]you,
'Lie down, that we may walk
over you.'
And you have laid your
body like the ground,
And as the street, for those
who walk over."

52

Awake, awake!
Put on your strength,
O Zion;
Put on your beautiful
garments,
O Jerusalem, the holy city!
For the uncircumcised [a]and
the unclean
Shall no longer come to you.
2 [a]Shake yourself from the
dust, arise;
Sit down, O Jerusalem!
[b]Loose yourself from the
bonds of your neck,
O captive daughter of Zion!

3 For thus says the LORD:

[a]"You have sold yourselves for
nothing,
And you shall be redeemed
[b]without money."

4 For thus says the Lord GOD:

"My people went down at
first
Into [a]Egypt to [1]dwell there;
Then the Assyrian
oppressed them without
cause.
5 Now therefore, what have I
here," says the LORD,
"That My people are taken
away for nothing?
Those who rule over them
[1]Make them wail," says the
LORD,
"And My name *is*
[a]blasphemed continually
every day.
6 Therefore My people shall
know My name;
Therefore *they shall know*
in that day
That I *am* He who speaks:
'Behold, *it is* I.' "

7 [a]How beautiful upon the
mountains

19 [a]Is. 47:9 [b]Amos 7:2
20 [a]Lam. 2:11
21 [a]Lam. 3:15
22 [a]Jer. 50:34
23 [a]Zech. 12:2 [1]Lit. *your soul*

CHAPTER 52

1 [a][Rev. 21:2–27]
2 [a]Is. 3:26 [b]Zech. 2:7
3 [a]Ps. 44:12 [b]Is. 45:13
4 [a]Gen. 46:6 [1]As resident aliens
5 [a]Ezek. 36:20, 23 [1]DSS *Mock;* LXX *Marvel and wail;* Tg. *Boast themselves;* Vg. *Treat them unjustly*
7 [a]Rom. 10:15

Are the feet of him who
brings good news,
Who proclaims peace,
Who brings glad tidings of
good *things*,
Who proclaims salvation,
Who says to Zion,
[b]"Your God reigns!"
8 Your watchmen shall lift up
their voices,
With their voices they shall
sing together;
For they shall see eye to eye
When the LORD brings back
Zion.
9 Break forth into joy, sing
together,
You waste places of
Jerusalem!
For the LORD has comforted
His people,
He has redeemed Jerusalem.
10 [a]The LORD has [1]made bare
His holy arm
In the eyes of [b]all the
nations;
And all the ends of the earth
shall see
The salvation of our God.

11 [a]Depart! Depart! Go out from
there,
Touch no unclean *thing*;
Go out from the midst of
her,
[b]Be clean,
You who bear the vessels of
the LORD.
12 For [a]you shall not go out
with haste,
Nor go by flight;
[b]For the LORD will go before
you,
[c]And the God of Israel *will*
be your rear guard.

☆ **13** Behold, [a]My Servant shall
[1]deal prudently;

7 [b]Ps. 93:1

10 [a]Ps. 98:1–3 [b]Luke 3:6 [1]Revealed His power

11 [a]Is. 48:20 [b]Lev. 22:2

12 [a]Ex. 12:11, 33 [b]Mic. 2:13 [c]Ex. 14:19, 20

13 [a]Is. 42:1 [b]Phil. 2:9 [1]*prosper* [2]Lit. *be lifted up*

14 [a]Ps. 22:6, 7; Matt. 26:67; 27:30; John 19:3 [1]*appearance*

15 [a]Ezek. 36:25 [b]Rom. 15:21; [Eph. 3:5, 9]; 1 Pet. 1:2 [1]Or *startle*

CHAPTER 53

1 [a]John 12:38; Rom. 10:16

2 [1]Stately form [2]*splendor* [3]Lit. *appearance*

3 [a]Ps. 22:6; [Matt. 27:30, 31; Luke 18:31–33; 23:18] [b][Heb. 4:15] [c][John 1:10, 11] [1]Or *forsaken* [2]Lit. *pains* [3]Lit. *sickness*

4 [a][Matt. 8:17; Heb. 9:28; 1 Pet. 2:24] [1]Lit. *sicknesses* [2]Lit. *pains* [3]*reckoned* [4]*Struck down*

[b]He shall be exalted and
[2]extolled and be very
high.
14 Just as many were ☆
astonished at you,
So His [a]visage[1] was marred
more than any man,
And His form more than the
sons of men;
15 [a]So shall He [1]sprinkle many ☆
nations.
Kings shall shut their
mouths at Him;
For [b]what had not been told
them they shall see,
And what they had not
heard they shall
consider.

53

Who [a]has believed our ☆
report?
And to whom has the arm of
the LORD been revealed?
2 For He shall grow up before
Him as a tender plant,
And as a root out of dry
ground.
He has no [1]form or
[2]comeliness;
And when we see Him,
There is no [3]beauty that we
should desire Him.
3 [a]He is despised and [1]rejected ☆
by men,
A Man of [2]sorrows and
[b]acquainted with [3]grief.
And we hid, as it were, *our*
faces from Him;
He was despised, and [c]we
did not esteem Him.

4 Surely [a]He has borne our ☆
[1]griefs
And carried our [2]sorrows;
Yet we [3]esteemed Him
stricken,
[4]Smitten by God, and
afflicted.

☆ 5 But He *was* [a]wounded[1] for our transgressions,
He was [2]bruised for our iniquities;
The chastisement for our peace *was* upon Him,
And by His [b]stripes[3] we are healed.
6 [a]All we like sheep have gone astray;
We have turned, every one, to his own way;
And the LORD [1]has laid on Him the iniquity of us all.

☆ 7 He was oppressed and He was afflicted,
Yet [a]He opened not His mouth;
[b]He was led as a lamb to the slaughter,
And as a sheep before its shearers is silent,
So He opened not His mouth.
☆ 8 He was [a]taken from [1]prison and from judgment,
And who will declare His generation?
For [b]He was cut off from the land of the living;
For the transgressions of My people He was stricken.
☆ 9 [a]And [1]they made His grave with the wicked—
But with the rich at His death,
Because He had done no violence,
Nor *was any* [b]deceit in His mouth.

☆ 10 Yet it pleased the LORD to [1]bruise Him;
He has put *Him* to grief.
When You make His soul [a]an offering for sin,
He shall see *His* seed, He shall prolong *His* days,
And the pleasure of the LORD shall prosper in His hand.
11 [1]He shall see the labor of His soul, *and* be satisfied. ☆
By His knowledge [a]My righteous [b]Servant shall [c]justify many,
For He shall bear their iniquities.
12 [a]Therefore I will divide Him a portion with the great, ☆
[b]And He shall divide the [1]spoil with the strong,
Because He [c]poured out His soul unto death,
And He was [d]numbered with the transgressors,
And He bore the sin of many,
And [e]made intercession for the transgressors.

54

"Sing, O [a]barren,
You *who* have not borne!
Break forth into singing, and cry aloud,
You *who* have not labored with child!
For more *are* the children of the desolate
Than the children of the married woman," says the LORD.
2 "Enlarge[a] the place of your tent,
And let them stretch out the curtains of your dwellings;
Do not spare;
Lengthen your cords,
And strengthen your stakes.
3 For you shall expand to the right and to the left,

---

5 [a][Rom. 4:25; 1 Cor. 15:3, 4] [b][1 Pet. 2:24, 25] [1]*Or pierced through* [2]*crushed* [3]*Blows that cut in*

6 [a]Heb. 9:28; 1 Pet. 2:24, 25 [1]Lit. *has caused to land on Him*

7 [a]Matt. 26:63; 27:12–14; Mark 14:61; 15:4, 5; Luke 23:9; John 19:9 [b]Acts 8:32, 33; Rev. 5:6

8 [a]Matt. 27:11–26; Luke 23:1–25; 1 Cor. 15:3 [b][Dan. 9:26] [1]*confinement*

9 [a]Matt. 27:57–60; Luke 23:33 [b]1 Pet. 2:22; 1 John 3:5 [1]Lit. *he* or *He*

10 [a]John 1:29; Acts 2:24; [2 Cor. 5:21] [1]*crush*

11 [a][1 John 2:1] [b]Is. 42:1 [c][Acts 13:38, 39; Rom. 5:15–19] [1]So with MT, Tg., Vg.; DSS, LXX *From the labor of His soul He shall see light*

12 [a]Ps. 2:8 [b]Col. 2:15 [c]Is. 50:6; [Rom. 3:25] [d]Matt. 27:38; Mark 15:28; Luke 22:37; 23:34; 2 Cor. 5:21 [e]Luke 23:34 [1]*plunder*

CHAPTER 54

1 [a]Gal. 4:27

2 [a]Is. 49:19, 20

And your descendants will
[a]inherit the nations,
And make the desolate
cities inhabited.

4 "Do[a] not fear, for you will not
be ashamed;
Neither be disgraced, for
you will not be put to
shame;
For you will forget the
shame of your youth,
And will not remember
the reproach of your
widowhood anymore.
5 [a]For your Maker *is* your
husband,
The LORD of hosts *is* His
name;
And your Redeemer *is* the
Holy One of Israel;
He is called [b]the God of the
whole earth.
6 For the LORD [a]has called you
Like a woman forsaken and
grieved in spirit,
Like a youthful wife when
you were refused,"
Says your God.
7 "For[a] a mere moment I have
forsaken you,
But with great mercies [b]I
will gather you.
8 With a little wrath I hid
My face from you for a
moment;
[a]But with everlasting
kindness I will have
mercy on you,"
Says the LORD, your
Redeemer.

9 "For this *is* like the waters of
[a]Noah to Me;
For as I have sworn
That the waters of Noah
would no longer cover
the earth,
So have I sworn
That I would not be angry
with [b]you, nor rebuke
you.
10 For [a]the mountains shall
depart
And the hills be removed,
[b]But My kindness shall not
depart from you,
Nor shall My covenant of
peace be removed,"
Says the LORD, who has
mercy on you.

11 "O you afflicted one,
Tossed with tempest, *and*
not comforted,
Behold, I will lay your
stones with [a]colorful
gems,
And lay your foundations
with sapphires.
12 I will make your pinnacles
of rubies,
Your gates of crystal,
And all your walls of
precious stones.
13 All your children *shall be* ☆
[a]taught by the LORD,
And [b]great *shall be* the
peace of your children.
14 In righteousness you shall
be established;
You shall be far from
oppression, for you shall
not fear;
And from terror, for it shall
not come near you.
15 Indeed they shall surely
assemble, *but* not
because of Me.
Whoever assembles against
you shall [a]fall for your
sake.

16 "Behold, I have created the
blacksmith

3 [a]Is. 14:2; 49:22, 23; 60:9
4 [a]Is. 41:10
5 [a]Jer. 3:14 [b]Zech. 14:9
6 [a]Is. 62:4
7 [a]Is. 26:20; 60:10 [b][Is. 43:5; 56:8]
8 [a]Jer. 31:3
9 [a]Gen. 8:21; 9:11 [b]Ezek. 39:29
10 [a]Is. 51:6 [b]Ps. 89:33, 34
11 [a]Rev. 21:18, 19
13 [a][John 6:45] [b]Ps. 119:165
15 [a]Is. 41:11–16

Who blows the coals in the fire,
Who brings forth an [1]instrument for his work;
And I have created the [2]spoiler to destroy.
17 No weapon formed against you shall [a]prosper,
And every tongue *which* rises against you in judgment
You shall condemn.
This *is* the heritage of the servants of the LORD,
[b]And their righteousness *is* from Me,"
Says the LORD.

55 "Ho! [a]Everyone who thirsts,
Come to the waters;
And you who have no money,
[b]Come, buy and eat.
Yes, come, buy wine and milk
Without money and without price.
2 Why do you [1]spend money for *what is* not bread,
And your wages for *what* does not satisfy?
Listen carefully to Me, and eat *what is* good,
And let your soul delight itself in abundance.
3 Incline your ear, and [a]come to Me.
Hear, and your soul shall live;
[b]And I will make an everlasting covenant with you—
The [c]sure mercies of David.
4 Indeed I have given him *as* [a]a witness to the people,
[b]A leader and commander for the people.

16 [1]Or *weapon* [2]*destroyer*
17 [a]Is. 17:12–14; 29:8 [b]Is. 45:24, 25; 54:14

CHAPTER 55

1 [a][John 4:14; 7:37] [b][Rev. 3:18]
2 [1]Lit. *weigh out silver*
3 [a]Matt. 11:28 [b]Jer. 32:40 [c]2 Sam. 7:8
4 [a][Rev. 1:5] [b][Dan. 9:25]
5 [a]Eph. 2:11–13 [b]Is. 60:5 [c]Is. 60:9
6 [a][Heb. 3:13] [b]Ps. 32:6
7 [a]Is. 1:16 [b]Zech. 8:17 [c]Jer. 3:12 [1]Lit. *man of iniquity*
8 [a]2 Sam. 7:19
9 [a]Ps. 103:11
10 [a]Deut. 32:2

5 [a]Surely you shall call a nation you do not know, ☆
[b]And nations *who* do not know you shall run to you,
Because of the LORD your God,
And the Holy One of Israel;
[c]For He has glorified you."

6 [a]Seek the LORD while He may be [b]found,
Call upon Him while He is near.
7 [a]Let the [1]wicked forsake his way,
And the unrighteous man [b]his thoughts;
Let him return to the LORD,
[c]And He will have mercy on him;
And to our God,
For He will abundantly pardon.

8 "For[a] My thoughts *are* not your thoughts,
Nor *are* your ways My ways," says the LORD.
9 "For[a] *as* the heavens are higher than the earth,
So are My ways higher than your ways,
And My thoughts than your thoughts.

10 "For [a]as the rain comes down, and the snow from heaven,
And do not return there,
But water the earth,
And make it bring forth and bud,
That it may give seed to the sower
And bread to the eater,

11 [a]So shall My word be that
goes forth from My
mouth;
It shall not return to Me
[1]void,
But it shall accomplish what
I please,
And it shall [b]prosper *in the
thing* for which I sent it.

12 "For[a] you shall go out with
joy,
And be led out with peace;
The mountains and the hills
Shall [b]break forth into
singing before you,
And [c]all the trees of the field
shall clap *their* hands.
13 [a]Instead of [b]the thorn shall
come up the cypress tree,
And instead of the brier
shall come up the myrtle
tree;
And it shall be to the LORD
[c]for a name,
For an everlasting sign *that*
shall not be cut off."

56

Thus says the LORD:
"Keep justice, and do
righteousness,
[a]For My salvation *is* about to
come,
And My righteousness to be
revealed.
2 Blessed *is* the man *who*
does this,
And the son of man *who*
lays hold on it;
[a]Who keeps from defiling the
Sabbath,
And keeps his hand from
doing any evil."

3 Do not let [a]the son of the
foreigner
Who has joined himself to
the LORD
Speak, saying,
"The LORD has utterly
separated me from His
people";
Nor let the [b]eunuch say,
"Here I am, a dry tree."
4 For thus says the LORD:
"To the eunuchs who keep
My Sabbaths,
And choose what pleases
Me,
And hold fast My covenant,
5 Even to them I will give in
[a]My house
And within My walls a place
[b]and a name
Better than that of sons and
daughters;
I will give [1]them an
everlasting name
That shall not be cut off.

6 "Also the sons of the foreigner
Who join themselves to the
LORD, to serve Him,
And to love the name of
the LORD, to be His
servants—
Everyone who keeps from
defiling the Sabbath,
And holds fast My
covenant—
7 Even them I will [a]bring to
My holy mountain,
And make them joyful in
My [b]house of prayer.
[c]Their burnt offerings and
their sacrifices
Will be [d]accepted on My
altar;
For [e]My house shall be
called a house of prayer
[f]for all nations."
8 The Lord GOD, [a]who gathers
the outcasts of Israel,
says,

---

11 [a]Is. 45:23 [b]Is. 46:9–11 [1]*empty*, without fruit
12 [a]Is. 35:10 [b]Ps. 98:8 [c]1 Chr. 16:33
13 [a]Is. 41:19 [b]Mic. 7:4 [c]Jer. 13:11

CHAPTER 56

1 [a]Matt. 3:2; 4:17
2 [a]Is. 58:13
3 [a][Eph. 2:12–19] [b]Acts 8:27
5 [a]1 Tim. 3:15 [b][1 John 3:1, 2] [1]Lit. *him*
7 [a][Is. 2:2, 3; 60:11] [b]Mark 11:17 [c][Rom. 12:1] [d]Is. 60:7 [e]Matt. 21:13 [f][Mal. 1:11]
8 [a]Is. 11:12; 27:12; 54:7

[b]"Yet I will gather to him
Others besides those who
are gathered to him."

9 [a]All you beasts of the field,
come to devour,
All you beasts in the forest.
10 His watchmen *are* [a]blind,
They are all ignorant;
[b]They *are* all dumb dogs,
They cannot bark;
[1]Sleeping, lying down, loving
to slumber.
11 Yes, *they are* [a]greedy[1] dogs
Which [b]never[2] have enough.
And they *are* shepherds
Who cannot understand;
They all look to their own
way,
Every one for his own gain,
From his *own* territory.
12 "Come," *one says,* "I will
bring wine,
And we will fill ourselves
with intoxicating [a]drink;
[b]Tomorrow will be [c]as today,
And much more abundant."

57

The righteous perishes,
And no man takes *it* to
heart;
[a]Merciful men *are* taken
away,
[b]While no one considers
That the righteous is taken
away from [1]evil.
2 He shall enter into peace;
They shall rest in [a]their
beds,
Each one walking *in* his
uprightness.

3 "But come here,
[a]You sons of the sorceress,
You offspring of the
adulterer and the harlot!
4 Whom do you ridicule?
Against whom do you make
a wide mouth
And stick out the tongue?
Are you not children of
transgression,
Offspring of falsehood,
5 Inflaming yourselves with
gods [a]under every green
tree,
[b]Slaying the children in the
valleys,
Under the clefts of the
rocks?
6 Among the smooth [a]*stones*
of the stream
Is your portion;
They, they, *are* your lot!
Even to them you have
poured a drink offering,
You have offered a grain
offering.
Should I receive comfort in
[b]these?

7 "On[a] a lofty and high
mountain
You have set [b]your bed;
Even there you went up
To offer sacrifice.
8 Also behind the doors and
their posts
You have set up your
remembrance;
For you have uncovered
yourself *to those other*
than Me,
And have gone up to them;
You have enlarged your bed
And [1]made *a covenant* with
them;
[a]You have loved their bed,
Where you saw *their*
[2]nudity.
9 [a]You went to the king with
ointment,
And increased your
perfumes;

8 [b][John 10:16]
9 [a]Jer. 12:9
10 [a]Matt. 15:14 [b]Phil. 3:2 [1]Or *Dreaming*
11 [a][Mic. 3:5, 11] [b]Ezek. 34:2–10 [1]Lit. *strong of soul* [2]Lit. *do not know satisfaction*
12 [a]Is. 28:7 [b]Luke 12:19 [c]2 Pet. 3:4

CHAPTER 57

1 [a]Ps. 12:1 [b]1 Kin. 14:13 [1]Lit. *the face of evil*
2 [a]2 Chr. 16:14
3 [a]Matt. 16:4
5 [a]2 Kin. 16:4 [b]Jer. 7:31
6 [a]Jer. 3:9 [b]Jer. 5:9, 29; 9:9
7 [a]Ezek. 16:16 [b]Ezek. 23:41
8 [a]Ezek. 16:26 [1]Lit. *cut* [2]Lit. *hand,* a euphemism
9 [a]Hos. 7:11

You sent your [b]messengers
far off,
And *even* descended to
Shē′ōl.
10 You are wearied in the
length of your way;
[a]*Yet* you did not say, 'There
is no hope.'
You have found the life of
your hand;
Therefore you were not
grieved.

11 "And [a]of whom have you
been afraid, or feared,
That you have lied
And not remembered Me,
Nor taken *it* to your heart?
Is it not because [b]I have
[1]held My peace from of
old
That you do not fear Me?
12 I will declare your
righteousness
And your works,
For they will not profit you.
13 When you cry out,
Let your collection *of idols*
deliver you.
But the wind will carry
them all away,
A breath will take *them.*
But he who puts his trust
in Me shall possess the
land,
And shall inherit My holy
mountain."

14 And one shall say,
[a]"Heap it up! Heap it up!
Prepare the way,
Take the stumbling block
out of the way of My
people."

15 For thus says the High and
Lofty One
Who inhabits eternity,
[a]whose name *is* Holy:
[b]"I dwell in the high and holy
place,
[c]With him *who* has a contrite
and humble spirit,
[d]To revive the spirit of the
humble,
And to revive the heart of
the contrite ones.
16 [a]For I will not contend
forever,
Nor will I always be angry;
For the spirit would fail
before Me,
And the souls [b]*which* I have
made.
17 For the iniquity of [a]his
covetousness
I was angry and struck him;
[b]I hid and was angry,
[c]And he went on [1]backsliding
in the way of his heart.
18 I have seen his ways, and
[a]will heal him;
I will also lead him,
And restore comforts to him
And to [b]his mourners.

19 "I create [a]the fruit of the lips:
Peace, peace [b]to *him who is*
far off and to *him who is*
near,"
Says the LORD,
"And I will heal him."
20 [a]But the wicked *are* like the
troubled sea,
When it cannot rest,
Whose waters cast up mire
and dirt.

21 "*There*[a] *is* no peace,"
Says my God, "for the
wicked."

58 "Cry aloud, [1]spare not;
Lift up your voice like a
trumpet;

9 [b]Ezek. 23:16, 40
10 [a]Jer. 2:25; 18:12
11 [a]Is. 51:12, 13 [b]Ps. 50:21 [1]*remained silent*
14 [a]Is. 40:3; 62:10
15 [a]Job 6:10 [b]Zech. 2:13 [c]Ps. 34:18; 51:17 [d]Is. 61:1–3
16 [a][Mic. 7:18] [b]Num. 16:22
17 [a]Jer. 6:13 [b]Is. 8:17; 45:15; 59:2 [c]Is. 9:13 [1]Or *turning back*
18 [a]Jer. 3:22 [b]Is. 61:2
19 [a]Heb. 13:15 [b]Eph. 2:17
20 [a]Job 15:20
21 [a]Is. 48:22

CHAPTER 58
1 [1]*do not hold back*

[a]Tell My people their
transgression,
And the house of Jacob
their sins.
2 Yet they seek Me daily,
And delight to know My
ways,
As a nation that did
righteousness,
And did not forsake the
ordinance of their God.
They ask of Me the
ordinances of justice;
They take delight in
approaching God.
3 'Why[a] have we fasted,' *they
say,* 'and You have not
seen?
Why have we [b]afflicted our
souls, and You take no
notice?'

"In fact, in the day of your
fast you find pleasure,
And [1]exploit all your
laborers.
4 [a]Indeed you fast for strife
and debate,
And to strike with the fist of
wickedness.
You will not fast as *you do*
this day,
To make your voice heard
on high.
5 Is [a]it a fast that I have
chosen,
[b]A day for a man to afflict
his soul?
Is it to bow down his head
like a bulrush,
And [c]to spread out
sackcloth and ashes?
Would you call this a fast,
And an acceptable day to
the LORD?

6 "*Is* this not the fast that I
have chosen:
To [a]loose the bonds of
wickedness,
[b]To undo the [1]heavy burdens,
[c]To let the oppressed go free,
And that you break every
yoke?
7 *Is it* not [a]to share your
bread with the hungry,
And that you bring to your
house the poor who are
[1]cast out;
[b]When you see the naked,
that you cover him,
And not hide yourself from
[c]your own flesh?
8 [a]Then your light shall break
forth like the morning,
Your healing shall spring
forth speedily,
And your righteousness
shall go before you;
[b]The glory of the LORD shall
be your rear guard.
9 Then you shall call, and the
LORD will answer;
You shall cry, and He will
say, 'Here I *am.*'

"If you take away the yoke
from your midst,
The [1]pointing of the
finger, and [a]speaking
wickedness,
10 *If* you extend your soul to
the hungry
And satisfy the afflicted
soul,
Then your light shall dawn
in the darkness,
And your [1]darkness shall *be*
as the noonday.
11 The LORD will guide you
continually,
And satisfy your soul in
drought,
And strengthen your bones;
You shall be like a watered
garden,

1 [a]Mic. 3:8
3 [a]Mal. 3:13–18 [b]Lev. 16:29; 23:27 [1]Lit. *drive hard*
4 [a]1 Kin. 21:9
5 [a]Zech. 7:5 [b]Lev. 16:29 [c]Esth. 4:3
6 [a]Luke 4:18, 19 [b]Neh. 5:10–12 [c]Jer. 34:9 [1]Lit. *bonds of the yoke*
7 [a]Ezek. 18:7 [b]Job 31:19–22 [c]Neh. 5:5 [1]*wandering*
8 [a]Job 11:17 [b]Ex. 14:19
9 [a]Ps. 12:2 [1]Lit. *sending out of*
10 [1]Or *gloom*

And like a spring of water,
whose waters do not
fail.
12 Those from among you
[a]Shall build the old waste
places;
You shall raise up the
foundations of many
generations;
And you shall be called the
Repairer of the Breach,
The Restorer of [1]Streets to
Dwell In.

13 "If [a]you turn away your foot
from the Sabbath,
From doing your pleasure
on My holy day,
And call the Sabbath a
delight,
The holy *day* of the LORD
honorable,
And shall honor Him, not
doing your own ways,
Nor finding your own
pleasure,
Nor speaking *your own*
words,
14 [a]Then you shall delight
yourself in the LORD;
And I will cause you to [b]ride
on the high hills of the
earth,
And feed you with the
heritage of Jacob your
father.
[c]The mouth of the LORD has
spoken."

59 Behold, the LORD's hand
is not [a]shortened,
That it cannot save;
Nor His ear heavy,
That it cannot hear.
2 But your iniquities have
separated you from your
God;
And your sins have hidden
His face from you,
So that He will [a]not hear.
3 For [a]your hands are defiled
with [1]blood,
And your fingers with
iniquity;
Your lips have spoken lies,
Your tongue has muttered
perversity.

4 No one calls for justice,
Nor does *any* plead for
truth.
They trust in [a]empty words
and speak lies;
[b]They conceive [1]evil and
bring forth iniquity.
5 They hatch vipers' eggs and
weave the spider's web;
He who eats of their eggs
dies,
And *from* that which is
crushed a viper breaks
out.

6 [a]Their webs will not become
garments,
Nor will they cover
themselves with their
works;
Their works *are* works of
iniquity,
And the act of violence *is* in
their hands.
7 [a]Their feet run to evil,
And they make haste to
shed [b]innocent blood;
[c]Their thoughts *are* thoughts
of iniquity;
Wasting and [d]destruction
are in their paths.
8 The way of [a]peace they have
not known,
And *there is* no justice in
their ways;
[b]They have made themselves
crooked paths;

12 [a]Is. 61:4 [1]Lit. *Paths*
13 [a]Is. 56:2, 4, 6
14 [a]Job 22:26 [b]Deut. 32:13; 33:29 [c]Is. 1:20; 40:5

CHAPTER 59

1 [a]Num. 11:23
2 [a]Is. 1:15
3 [a]Ezek. 7:23 [1]*bloodshed*
4 [a]Jer. 7:4 [b]Job 15:35 [1]*trouble*
6 [a]Job 8:14
7 [a]Rom. 3:15 [b]Prov. 6:17 [c]Is. 55:7 [d]Rom. 3:16, 17
8 [a]Is. 57:20, 21 [b]Prov. 2:15

Whoever takes that way
shall not know peace.

9 Therefore justice is far
from us,
Nor does righteousness
overtake us;
[a]We look for light, but there
is darkness!
For brightness, *but* we walk
in blackness!
10 [a]We grope for the wall like
the blind,
And we grope as if *we had*
no eyes;
We stumble at noonday as
at twilight;
We are as dead *men* in
desolate places.
11 We all growl like bears,
And [a]moan sadly like doves;
We look for justice, but
there is none;
For salvation, *but* it is far
from us.
12 For our [a]transgressions are
multiplied before You,
And our sins testify
against us;
For our transgressions *are*
with us,
And *as for* our iniquities, we
know them:
13 In transgressing and lying
against the LORD,
And departing from our
God,
Speaking oppression and
revolt,
Conceiving and uttering
[a]from the heart words of
falsehood.
14 Justice is turned back,
And righteousness stands
afar off;
For truth is fallen in the
street,
And equity cannot enter.
15 So truth fails,
And he *who* departs from
evil makes himself a
[a]prey.

Then the LORD saw *it,* and [1]it
displeased Him
That *there was* no justice.
16 [a]He saw that *there was* no
man,
And [b]wondered that *there
was* no intercessor;
[c]Therefore His own arm
brought salvation for
Him;
And His own righteousness,
it sustained Him.
17 [a]For He put on righteousness
as a breastplate,
And a helmet of salvation
on His head;
He put on the garments of
vengeance for clothing,
And was clad with zeal as a
cloak.
18 [a]According to *their* deeds,
accordingly He will
repay,
Fury to His adversaries,
Recompense to His enemies;
The coastlands He will fully
repay.
19 [a]So shall they fear
The name of the LORD from
the west,
And His glory from the
rising of the sun;
When the enemy comes in
[b]like a flood,
The Spirit of the LORD will
lift up a standard against
him.

20 "The[a] Redeemer will come to ☆
Zion,
And to those who turn from
transgression in Jacob,"
Says the LORD.

9 [a]Jer. 8:15
10 [a]Job 5:14
11 [a]Ezek. 7:16
12 [a]Is. 24:5; 58:1
13 [a]Matt. 12:34
15 [a]Is. 5:23; 10:2; 29:21; 32:7 [1]Lit. *it was evil in His eyes*
16 [a]Ezek. 22:30 [b]Mark 6:6 [c]Ps. 98:1
17 [a]Eph. 6:14, 17
18 [a]Is. 63:6
19 [a]Mal. 1:11 [b]Rev. 12:15
20 [a]Rom. 11:26

21 "As[a] for Me," says the LORD, "this *is* My covenant with them: My Spirit who *is* upon you, and My words which I have put in your mouth, shall not depart from your mouth, nor from the mouth of your descendants, nor from the mouth of your descendants' descendants," says the LORD, "from this time and forevermore."

60

Arise, [a]shine;
For your light has come!
And [b]the glory of the LORD
is risen upon you.
2 For behold, the darkness
shall cover the earth,
And deep darkness the
people;
But the LORD will arise over
you,
And His glory will be seen
upon you.
☆ 3 The [a]Gentiles shall come to
your light,
And kings to the brightness
of your rising.

4 "Lift[a] up your eyes all
around, and see:
They all gather together,
[b]they come to you;
Your sons shall come from
afar,
And your daughters shall be
nursed at *your* side.
5 Then you shall see and
become radiant,
And your heart shall swell
with joy;
Because [a]the abundance of
the sea shall be turned
to you,
The wealth of the Gentiles
shall come to you.
6 The multitude of camels
shall cover your *land*,
The dromedaries of Mid′i·an
and [a]Ē′phah;
All those from [b]Shē′ba shall
come;
They shall bring [c]gold and
incense,
And they shall proclaim the
praises of the LORD.
7 All the flocks of [a]Kē′dar
shall be gathered
together to you,
The rams of Ne·bā′i·oth
shall minister to you;
They shall ascend with
[b]acceptance on My altar,
And [c]I will glorify the house
of My glory.

8 "Who *are* these *who* fly like
a cloud,
And like doves to their
roosts?
9 [a]Surely the coastlands shall
wait for Me;
And the ships of Tar′shish
will come first,
[b]To bring your sons from
afar,
[c]Their silver and their gold
with them,
To the name of the LORD
your God,
And to the Holy One of
Israel,
[d]Because He has glorified
you.

10 "The[a] sons of foreigners shall
build up your walls,
[b]And their kings shall
minister to you;
For [c]in My wrath I struck
you,
[d]But in My favor I have had
mercy on you.
11 Therefore your gates [a]shall
be open continually;

21 [a][Heb. 8:10; 10:16]

CHAPTER 60

1 [a]Eph. 5:14 [b]Mal. 4:2

3 [a]Is. 49:6, 23; John 8:12; 12:46; Acts 13:47, 48; 26:17, 18; Rev. 21:24

4 [a]Is. 49:18 [b]Is. 49:20–22

5 [a][Rom. 11:25–27]

6 [a]Gen. 25:4 [b]Ps. 72:10 [c]Matt. 2:11

7 [a]Gen. 25:13 [b]Is. 56:7 [c]Hag. 2:7, 9

9 [a]Ps. 72:10 [b][Gal. 4:26] [c]Jer. 3:17 [d]Is. 55:5

10 [a]Zech. 6:15 [b]Rev. 21:24 [c]Is. 57:17 [d]Is. 54:7, 8

11 [a]Rev. 21:25, 26

They shall not be shut day
or night,
That *men* may bring to
you the wealth of the
Gentiles,
And their kings in
procession.
12 [a]For the nation and kingdom
which will not serve you
shall perish,
And *those* nations shall be
utterly ruined.

13 "The[a] glory of Lebanon shall
come to you,
The cypress, the pine, and
the box tree together,
To beautify the place of My
sanctuary;
And I will make [b]the place
of My feet glorious.
14 Also the sons of those who
afflicted you
Shall come [a]bowing to you,
And all those who despised
you shall [b]fall prostrate
at the soles of your feet;
And they shall call you The
City of the LORD,
[c]Zion of the Holy One of
Israel.

15 "Whereas you have been
forsaken and hated,
So that no one went through
you,
I will make you an eternal
excellence,
A joy of many generations.
16 You shall drink the milk of
the Gentiles,
[a]And milk the breast of
kings;
You shall know that [b]I, the
LORD, *am* your Savior
And your Redeemer, the
Mighty One of Jacob.

12 [a]Zech. 14:17
13 [a]Is. 35:2 [b]1 Chr. 28:2
14 [a]Is. 45:14 [b]Rev. 3:9 [c][Heb. 12:22]
16 [a]Is. 49:23 [b]Is. 43:3
18 [a]Is. 26:1 [1]*devastation*
19 [a]Rev. 21:23; 22:5 [b]Zech. 2:5
20 [a]Amos 8:9
21 [a]Rev. 21:27 [b]Ps. 37:11 [c]Is. 61:3 [d][Eph. 2:10]
22 [a]Matt. 13:31, 32

17 "Instead of bronze I will
bring gold,
Instead of iron I will bring
silver,
Instead of wood, bronze,
And instead of stones, iron.
I will also make your
officers peace,
And your magistrates
righteousness.
18 Violence shall no longer be
heard in your land,
Neither [1]wasting nor
destruction within your
borders;
But you shall call [a]your
walls Salvation,
And your gates Praise.

19 "The [a]sun shall no longer be
your light by day,
Nor for brightness shall the
moon give light to you;
But the LORD will be to you
an everlasting light,
And [b]your God your glory.
20 [a]Your sun shall no longer go
down,
Nor shall your moon
withdraw itself;
For the LORD will be your
everlasting light,
And the days of your
mourning shall be
ended.
21 [a]Also your people *shall* all *be*
righteous;
[b]They shall inherit the land
forever,
[c]The branch of My planting,
[d]The work of My hands,
That I may be glorified.
22 [a]A little one shall become a
thousand,
And a small one a strong
nation.
I, the LORD, will hasten it in
its time."

CHAPTER 61

☆ 61 "The [a]Spirit of the Lord GOD *is* upon Me,
Because the LORD [b]has anointed Me
To preach good tidings to the poor;
He has sent Me [c]to [1]heal the brokenhearted,
To proclaim [d]liberty to the captives,
And the opening of the prison to *those who are* bound;
2 [a]To proclaim the acceptable year of the LORD,
And [b]the day of vengeance of our God;
[c]To comfort all who mourn,
3 To [1]console those who mourn in Zion,
[a]To give them beauty for ashes,
The oil of joy for mourning,
The garment of praise for the spirit of heaviness;
That they may be called trees of righteousness,
[b]The planting of the LORD, [c]that He may be glorified."

4 And they shall [a]rebuild the old ruins,
They shall raise up the former desolations,
And they shall repair the ruined cities,
The desolations of many generations.
5 [a]Strangers shall stand and feed your flocks,
And the sons of the foreigner
Shall be your plowmen and your vinedressers.
6 [a]But you shall be named the priests of the LORD,
They shall call you the servants of our God.
[b]You shall eat the riches of the Gentiles,
And in their glory you shall boast.
7 [a]Instead of your shame *you shall have* double *honor*,
And *instead of* confusion they shall rejoice in their portion.
Therefore in their land they shall possess double;
Everlasting joy shall be theirs.

8 "For [a]I, the LORD, love justice;
[b]I hate robbery [1]for burnt offering;
I will direct their work in truth,
[c]And will make with them an everlasting covenant.
9 Their descendants shall be known among the Gentiles,
And their offspring among the people.
All who see them shall acknowledge them,
[a]That they *are* the posterity *whom* the LORD has blessed."

10 [a]I will greatly rejoice in the LORD,
My soul shall be joyful in my God;
For [b]He has clothed me with the garments of salvation,
He has covered me with the robe of righteousness,
[c]As a bridegroom decks *himself* with ornaments,
And as a bride adorns *herself* with her jewels.

---

1 [a]Matt. 3:16, 17; Luke 4:18, 19; John 1:32; 3:34 [b]Matt. 11:5; Luke 7:22 [c]Ps. 147:3 [d]Is. 42:7 [1]Lit. *bind up*
2 [a]Lev. 25:9 [b]Is. 34:8 [c]Matt. 5:4
3 [a]Ps. 30:11 [b]Is. 60:21 [c][John 15:8] [1]Lit. *appoint*
4 [a]Ezek. 36:33
5 [a][Eph. 2:12]
6 [a]Ex. 19:6 [b]Is. 60:5, 11
7 [a]Zech. 9:12
8 [a]Ps. 11:7 [b]Is. 1:11, 13 [c]Is. 55:3 [1]Or *in*
9 [a]Is. 65:23
10 [a]Hab. 3:18 [b]Ps. 132:9, 16 [c]Is. 49:18

11 For as the earth brings forth
its bud,
As the garden causes the
things that are sown in it
to spring forth,
So the Lord GOD will cause
[a]righteousness and
[b]praise to spring forth
before all the nations.

62

For Zion's sake I will not
[1]hold My peace,
And for Jerusalem's sake I
will not rest,
Until her righteousness goes
forth as brightness,
And her salvation as a lamp
that burns.
2 [a]The Gentiles shall see your
righteousness,
And all [b]kings your glory.
[c]You shall be called by a new
name,
Which the mouth of the
LORD will name.
3 You shall also be [a]a crown
of glory
In the hand of the LORD,
And a royal diadem
In the hand of your God.
4 [a]You shall no longer be
termed [b]Forsaken,[1]
Nor shall your land any more
be termed [c]Desolate;[2]
But you shall be called
[3]Heph'zi·bah, and your
land [4]Beū'lah;
For the LORD delights in you,
And your land shall be
married.
5 For *as* a young man marries
a virgin,
So shall your sons marry
you;
And *as* the bridegroom
rejoices over the bride,
[a]So shall your God rejoice
over you.

6 [a]I have set watchmen on
your walls, O Jerusalem;
They shall [1]never hold their
peace day or night.
You who [2]make mention of
the LORD, do not keep
silent,
7 And give Him no rest till He
establishes
And till He makes
Jerusalem [a]a praise in
the earth.

8 The LORD has sworn by His
right hand
And by the arm of His
strength:
"Surely I will no longer [a]give
your grain
As food for your enemies;
And the sons of the
foreigner shall not drink
your new wine,
For which you have labored.
9 But those who have
gathered it shall eat it,
And praise the LORD;
Those who have brought it
together shall drink it [a]in
My holy courts."

10 Go through,
Go through the gates!
[a]Prepare the way for the
people;
Build up,
Build up the highway!
Take out the stones,
[b]Lift up a banner for the
peoples!

11 Indeed the LORD has ☆
proclaimed
To the end of the world:
[a]"Say to the daughter of Zion,
'Surely your salvation is
coming;

11 [a]Ps. 72:3; 85:11 [b]Is. 60:18; 62:7

CHAPTER 62

1 [1]*keep silent*

2 [a]Is. 60:3 [b]Ps. 102:15, 16; 138:4, 5; 148:11, 13 [c]Is. 62:4, 12; 65:15

3 [a]Zech. 9:16

4 [a]Hos. 1:10 [b]Is. 49:14; 54:6, 7 [c]Is. 54:1 [1]Heb. *Azubah* [2]Heb. *Shemamah* [3]Lit. *My Delight Is in Her* [4]Lit. *Married*

5 [a]Is. 65:19

6 [a]Ezek. 3:17; 33:7 [1]*not be silent* [2]*remember*

7 [a]Zeph. 3:19, 20

8 [a]Deut. 28:31, 33

9 [a]Deut. 12:12; 14:23, 26

10 [a]Is. 40:3; 57:14 [b]Is. 11:12

11 [a]Zech. 9:9; Matt. 21:5; John 12:15

Behold, His [b]reward *is* with
Him,
And His [1]work before
Him.' "
12 And they shall call them
The Holy People,
The Redeemed of the LORD;
And you shall be called
Sought Out,
A City Not Forsaken.

63 Who *is* this who comes
from Ē'dom,
With dyed garments from
Boz'rah,
This *One who is* [1]glorious in
His apparel,
Traveling in the greatness of
His strength?—

"I who speak in
righteousness, mighty to
save."

☆ 2 Why [a]*is* Your apparel red,
And Your garments like
one who treads in the
winepress?

☆ 3 "I have [a]trodden the
winepress alone,
And from the peoples no
one *was* with Me.
For I have trodden them in
My anger,
And trampled them in My
fury;
Their blood is sprinkled
upon My garments,
And I have stained all My
robes.
4 For the [a]day of vengeance *is*
in My heart,
And the year of My
redeemed has come.
5 [a]I looked, but [b]*there was* no
one to help,
And I wondered
That *there was* no one to
uphold;
Therefore My own [c]arm
brought salvation for
Me;
And My own fury, it
sustained Me.
6 I have trodden down the
peoples in My anger,
Made them drunk in My
fury,
And brought down their
strength to the earth."

7 I will mention the
lovingkindnesses of the
LORD
And the praises of the LORD,
According to all that the
LORD has bestowed on
us,
And the great goodness
toward the house of
Israel,
Which He has bestowed on
them according to His
mercies,
According to the multitude
of His lovingkindnesses.
8 For He said, "Surely they
are My people,
Children *who* will not lie."
So He became their Savior.
9 [a]In all their affliction He was
[1]afflicted,
[b]And the Angel of His
Presence saved them;
[c]In His love and in His pity
He redeemed them;
And [d]He bore them and
carried them
All the days of old.
10 But they [a]rebelled and
[b]grieved His Holy Spirit;
[c]So He turned Himself
against them as an
enemy,

11 [b][Rev. 22:12]
[1]*recompense*

CHAPTER 63

1 [1]Or *adorned*

2 [a][Rev. 19:13, 15]

3 [a]Rev. 14:19, 20; 19:15

4 [a]Is. 34:8; 35:4; 61:2

5 [a]Is. 41:28; 59:16 [b][John 16:32] [c]Ps. 98:1

9 [a]Judg. 10:16 [b]Ex. 14:19 [c]Deut. 7:7 [d]Ex. 19:4 [1]Kt., LXX, Syr. *not afflicted*

10 [a]Ex. 15:24 [b]Ps. 78:40 [c]Ex. 23:21

And He fought against
them.

11 Then he [a]remembered the
days of old,
Moses *and* his people,
saying:
"Where *is* He who [b]brought
them up out of the sea
With the [1]shepherd of His
flock?
[c]Where *is* He who put His
Holy Spirit within them,
12 Who led *them* by the right
hand of Moses,
[a]With His glorious arm,
[b]Dividing the water before
them
To make for Himself an
everlasting name,
13 [a]Who led them through the
deep,
As a horse in the
wilderness,
That they might not
stumble?"

14 As a beast goes down into
the valley,
And the Spirit of the LORD
causes him to rest,
So You lead Your people,
[a]To make Yourself a glorious
name.

15 [a]Look down from heaven,
And see [b]from Your
habitation, holy and
glorious.
Where *are* Your zeal and
Your strength,
The yearning [c]of Your heart
and Your mercies toward
me?
Are they restrained?
16 [a]Doubtless You *are* our
Father,
Though Abraham [b]was
ignorant of us,
And Israel does not
acknowledge us.
You, O LORD, *are* our Father;
Our Redeemer from
Everlasting *is* Your name.
17 O LORD, why have You [a]made
us stray from Your ways,
And hardened our heart
from Your fear?
Return for Your servants'
sake,
The tribes of Your
inheritance.
18 [a]Your holy people have
possessed *it* but a little
while;
[b]Our adversaries have
trodden down Your
sanctuary.
19 We have become *like* those
of old, over whom You
never ruled,
Those who were never
called by Your name.

64 Oh, that You would [1]rend
the heavens!
That You would come down!
That the mountains might
shake at Your [a]presence—
2 As fire burns brushwood,
As fire causes water to
boil—
To make Your name known
to Your adversaries,
That the nations may
tremble at Your
presence!
3 When [a]You did awesome
things *for which* we did
not look,
You came down,
The mountains shook at
Your presence.
4 For since the beginning of
the world

11 [a]Ps. 106:44, 45 [b]Ex. 14:30 [c]Num. 11:17, 25, 29 [1]MT, Vg. *shepherds*
12 [a]Ex. 15:6 [b]Ex. 14:21, 22
13 [a]Ps. 106:9
14 [a]2 Sam. 7:23
15 [a]Deut. 26:15 [b]Ps. 33:14 [c]Jer. 31:20
16 [a]Deut. 32:6 [b]Job 14:21
17 [a]John 12:40
18 [a]Deut. 7:6 [b]Ps. 74:3–7

CHAPTER 64

1 [a]Mic. 1:3, 4 [1]*tear open*
3 [a]Ex. 34:10

[a]*Men* have not heard nor
perceived by the ear,
Nor has the eye seen any
God besides You,
Who acts for the one who
waits for Him.
5 You meet him who rejoices
and does righteousness,
Who remembers You in Your
ways.
You are indeed angry, for
we have sinned—
[a]In these ways we continue;
And we need to be saved.

6 But we are all like an
unclean *thing,*
And all [a]our righteousnesses
are like [1]filthy rags;
We all [b]fade as a leaf,
And our iniquities, like the
wind,
Have taken us away.
7 And *there is* no one who
calls on Your name,
Who stirs himself up to take
hold of You;
For You have hidden Your
face from us,
And have [1]consumed us
because of our iniquities.

8 But now, O LORD,
You *are* our Father;
We *are* the clay, and You our
[a]potter;
And all we *are* the work of
Your hand.
9 Do not be furious, O LORD,
Nor remember iniquity
forever;
Indeed, please look—we all
are Your people!
10 Your holy cities are a
wilderness,
Zion is a wilderness,
Jerusalem a desolation.

4 [a]Ps. 31:19

5 [a]Mal. 3:6

6 [a][Phil. 3:9] [b]Ps. 90:5, 6 [1]Lit. *a filthy garment*

7 [1]Lit. *caused us to melt*

8 [a]Is. 29:16; 45:9

11 [a]Ezek. 24:21 [1]Lit. *house* [2]*have become a ruin*

12 [a]Is. 42:14 [b]Ps. 83:1 [1]*keep silent*

CHAPTER 65

1 [a]Rom. 9:24; 10:20 [b]Is. 63:19

2 [a]Rom. 10:21 [b]Is. 1:2, 23 [c]Is. 42:24

3 [a]Deut. 32:21 [b]Is. 1:29

4 [a]Deut. 18:11 [b]Is. 66:17 [1]Unclean meats, Lev. 7:18; 19:7

5 [a]Matt. 9:11 [1]Cause My wrath to smoke

11 Our holy and beautiful
[1]temple,
Where our fathers praised
You,
Is burned up with fire;
And all [a]our pleasant things
[2]are laid waste.
12 [a]Will You restrain Yourself
because of these *things,*
O LORD?
[b]Will You [1]hold Your peace,
and afflict us very
severely?

65

"I was [a]sought by *those*
who did not ask
for Me;
I was found by *those who*
did not seek Me.
I said, 'Here I am, here I am,'
To a nation *that* [b]was not
called by My name.
2 [a]I have stretched out My
hands all day long to a
[b]rebellious people,
Who [c]walk in a way *that is*
not good,
According to their own
thoughts;
3 A people [a]who provoke Me
to anger continually to
My face;
[b]Who sacrifice in gardens,
And burn incense on altars
of brick;
4 [a]Who sit among the graves,
And spend the night in the
tombs;
[b]Who eat swine's flesh,
And the broth of
[1]abominable things is *in*
their vessels;
5 [a]Who say, 'Keep to yourself,
Do not come near me,
For I am holier than you!'
These [1]*are* smoke in My
nostrils,
A fire that burns all the day.

6 "Behold, [a]*it is* written before
Me:
[b]I will not keep silence, [c]but
will repay—
Even repay into their
bosom—
7 Your iniquities and [a]the
iniquities of your fathers
together,"
Says the LORD,
[b]"Who have burned incense
on the mountains
[c]And blasphemed Me on the
hills;
Therefore I will measure
their former work into
their bosom."

8 Thus says the LORD:

"As the new wine is found in
the cluster,
And *one* says, 'Do not
destroy it,
For [a]a blessing *is* in it,'
So will I do for My servants'
sake,
That I may not destroy them
[b]all.
9 I will bring forth
descendants from Jacob,
And from Judah an heir of
My mountains;
My [a]elect shall inherit it,
And My servants shall dwell
there.
10 [a]Sharon shall be a fold of
flocks,
And [b]the Valley of Ā′chor
a place for herds to lie
down,
For My people who have
[c]sought Me.

11 "But you *are* those who
forsake the LORD,
Who forget [a]My holy
mountain,
Who prepare [b]a table for
[1]Gad,
And who furnish a drink
offering for [2]Men′ī.
12 Therefore I will number you
for the sword,
And you shall all bow down
to the slaughter;
[a]Because, when I called, you
did not answer;
When I spoke, you did not
hear,
But did evil before My eyes,
And chose *that* in which I
do not delight."

13 Therefore thus says the Lord
GOD:

"Behold, My servants shall
eat,
But you shall be hungry;
Behold, My servants shall
drink,
But you shall be thirsty;
Behold, My servants shall
rejoice,
But you shall be ashamed;
14 Behold, My servants shall
sing for joy of heart,
But you shall cry for sorrow
of heart,
And [a]wail for [1]grief of spirit.
15 You shall leave your name
[a]as a curse to [b]My
chosen;
For the Lord GOD will slay
you,
And [c]call His servants by
another name;
16 [a]So that he who blesses
himself in the earth
Shall bless himself in the
God of truth;
And [b]he who swears in the
earth
Shall swear by the God of
truth;

---

6 [a]Deut. 32:34 [b]Ps. 50:3 [c]Ps. 79:12
7 [a]Ex. 20:5 [b]Ezek. 18:6 [c]Ezek. 20:27, 28
8 [a]Joel 2:14 [b]Is. 1:9
9 [a]Matt. 24:22
10 [a]Is. 33:9 [b]Josh. 7:24 [c]Is. 55:6
11 [a]Is. 56:7 [b]Ezek. 23:41 [1]Lit. *Troop* or *Fortune;* a pagan deity [2]Lit. *Number* or *Destiny;* a pagan deity
12 [a]Prov. 1:24
14 [a]Matt. 8:12 [1]Or *a broken spirit*
15 [a]Jer. 29:22 [b]Is. 65:9, 22 [c][Acts 11:26]
16 [a]Jer. 4:2 [b]Zeph. 1:5

Because the former troubles
are forgotten,
And because they are
hidden from My eyes.

17 "For behold, I create [a]new
heavens and a new
earth;
And the former shall not be
remembered or [1]come to
mind.
18 But be glad and rejoice
forever in what I create;
For behold, I create
Jerusalem *as* a rejoicing,
And her people a joy.
19 [a]I will rejoice in Jerusalem,
And joy in My people;
The [b]voice of weeping shall
no longer be heard in
her,
Nor the voice of crying.

20 "No more shall an infant
from there *live but a few*
days,
Nor an old man who has not
fulfilled his days;
For the child shall die one
hundred years old,
[a]But the sinner *being* one
hundred years old shall
be accursed.
21 [a]They shall build houses and
inhabit *them;*
They shall plant vineyards
and eat their fruit.
22 They shall not build and
another inhabit;
They shall not plant and
[a]another eat;
For [b]as the days of a tree, *so
shall be* the days of My
people,
And [c]My elect shall long
enjoy the work of their
hands.
23 They shall not labor in vain,
[a]Nor bring forth children for
trouble;
For [b]they *shall be* the
descendants of the
blessed of the LORD,
And their offspring with
them.

24 "It shall come to pass
That [a]before they call, I will
answer;
And while they are still
speaking, I will [b]hear.
25 The [a]wolf and the lamb shall
feed together,
The lion shall eat straw like
the ox,
[b]And dust *shall be* the
serpent's food.
They shall not hurt nor
destroy in all My holy
mountain,"
Says the LORD.

66 Thus says the LORD:

[a]"Heaven *is* My throne,
And earth *is* My footstool.
Where *is* the house that you
will build Me?
And where *is* the place of
My rest?
2 For all those *things* My
hand has made,
And all those *things* exist,"
Says the LORD.
[a]"But on this *one* will I look:
[b]On *him who is* poor and of a
contrite spirit,
And who trembles at My
word.

3 "He[a] who kills a bull *is as if*
he slays a man;
He who sacrifices a lamb,
as if he [b]breaks a dog's
neck;

17 [a]Rev. 21:1 [1]Lit. *come upon the heart*
19 [a]Is. 62:4, 5 [b]Rev. 7:17; 21:4
20 [a]Eccl. 8:12, 13
21 [a]Amos 9:14
22 [a]Is. 62:8, 9 [b]Ps. 92:12 [c]Is. 65:9, 15
23 [a]Hos. 9:12 [b]Is. 61:9
24 [a]Is. 58:9 [b]Dan. 9:20–23
25 [a]Is. 11:6–9 [b]Gen. 3:14

CHAPTER 66

1 [a]1 Kin. 8:27
2 [a][Is. 57:15; 61:1] [b]Ps. 34:18; 51:17
3 [a][Is. 1:10–17; 58:1–7] [b]Deut. 23:18

He who offers a grain
offering, *as if he offers*
swine's blood;
He who burns incense, *as if*
he blesses an idol.
Just as they have chosen
their own ways,
And their soul delights in
their abominations,
4 So will I choose their
delusions,
And bring their fears on
them;
[a]Because, when I called, no
one answered,
When I spoke they did not
hear;
But they did evil before My
eyes,
And chose *that* in which I
do not delight."

5 Hear the word of the LORD,
You who tremble at His
word:
"Your brethren who [a]hated
you,
Who cast you out for My
name's sake, said,
[b]'Let the LORD be glorified,
That [c]we may see your joy.'
But they shall be ashamed."

6 The sound of noise from the
city!
A voice from the temple!
The voice of the LORD,
Who fully repays His
enemies!

7 "Before she was in labor, she
gave birth;
Before her pain came,
She delivered a male child.
8 Who has heard such a
thing?
Who has seen such things?
Shall the earth be made to
give birth in one day?
Or shall a nation be born at
once?
For as soon as Zion was in
labor,
She gave birth to her
children.
9 Shall I bring to the time
of birth, and not cause
delivery?" says the LORD.
"Shall I who cause delivery
shut up *the womb?*" says
your God.
10 "Rejoice with Jerusalem,
And be glad with her, all
you who love her;
Rejoice for joy with her, all
you who mourn for her;
11 That you may feed and be
satisfied
With the consolation of her
bosom,
That you may drink deeply
and be delighted
With the abundance of her
glory."

12 For thus says the LORD:

"Behold, [a]I will extend peace
to her like a river,
And the glory of the
Gentiles like a flowing
stream.
Then you shall [b]feed;
On *her* sides shall you be
[c]carried,
And be dandled on *her*
knees.
13 As one whom his mother
comforts,
So I will [a]comfort you;
And you shall be comforted
in Jerusalem."

14 When you see *this*, your
heart shall rejoice,
And [a]your bones shall
flourish like grass;

4 [a]Is. 65:12
5 [a]Is. 60:15 [b]Is. 5:19 [c][Titus 2:13]
12 [a]Is. 48:18; 60:5 [b]Is. 60:16 [c]Is. 49:22; 60:4
13 [a]Is. 51:3
14 [a]Ezek. 37:1

The hand of the LORD
shall be known to His
servants,
And *His* indignation to His
enemies.
15 [a]For behold, the LORD will
come with fire
And with His chariots, like a
whirlwind,
To render His anger with
fury,
And His rebuke with flames
of fire.
16 For by fire and by [a]His
sword
The LORD will judge all
flesh;
And the slain of the LORD
shall be [b]many.

17 "Those[a] who sanctify
themselves and purify
themselves,
To go to the gardens
[1]After an *idol* in the midst,
Eating swine's flesh and
the abomination and the
mouse,
Shall [2]be consumed
together," says the LORD.

18 "For I *know* their works and
their [a]thoughts. It shall be that
I will [b]gather all nations and
tongues; and they shall come
and see My glory.
19 [a]"I will set a sign among
them; and those among them
who escape I will send to the
nations: *to* Tar'shish and [1]Pūl
and Lud, who draw the bow,
and Tū'bal and Jā'van, *to* the
coastlands afar off who have
not heard My fame nor seen My
glory. [b]And they shall declare
My glory among the Gentiles.
20 "Then they shall [a]bring all
your brethren [b]for an offering
to the LORD out of all nations, on
horses and in chariots and in lit-
ters, on mules and on camels, to
My holy mountain Jerusalem,"
says the LORD, "as the children
of Israel bring an offering in a
clean vessel into the house of
the LORD.
21 "And I will also take some of
them for [a]priests *and* Lē'vītes,"
says the LORD.

22 "For as [a]the new heavens and
the new earth
Which I will make shall
remain before Me," says
the LORD,
"So shall your descendants
and your name remain.
23 And [a]it shall come to pass
That from one New Moon to
another,
And from one Sabbath to
another,
[b]All flesh shall come to
worship before Me," says
the LORD.

24 "And they shall go forth and
look
Upon the corpses of the
men
Who have transgressed
against Me.
For their [a]worm does not
die,
And their fire is not
quenched.
They shall be an abhorrence
to all flesh."

15 [a]Is. 9:5
16 [a]Is. 27:1 [b]Is. 34:6
17 [a]Is. 65:3–8 [1]Lit. *After one* [2]*come to an end*
18 [a]Is. 59:7 [b]Jer. 3:17
19 [a]Luke 2:34 [b]Mal. 1:11 [1]So with MT, Tg.; LXX *Put* (cf. Jer. 46:9)
20 [a]Is. 49:22 [b][Rom. 15:16]
21 [a]Ex. 19:6
22 [a]Rev. 21:1
23 [a]Zech. 14:16 [b]Zech. 14:17–21
24 [a]Mark 9:44, 46, 48

The Book of JEREMIAH

THE Book of Jeremiah is the prophecy of a man divinely called in his youth from the priest-city of Anathoth. A heartbroken prophet with a heartbreaking message, Jeremiah labors for more that forty years proclaiming a message of doom to the stiff-necked people of Judah. Despised and persecuted by his countrymen, Jeremiah bathes his harsh prophecies in tears of compassion. His broken heart causes him to write a broken book, which is difficult to arrange chronologically or topically. But through his sermons and signs he faithfully declares that surrender to God's will is the only way to escape calamity.

Yirmeyahu or *Yirmeyah* literally means "Yahweh Throws," perhaps in the sense of laying a foundation. It may effectively mean "Yahweh Establishes, Appoints, or Sends." The Greek form of the Hebrew name in the Septuagint is *Hieremias*, and the Latin form is *Jeremias*.

THE words of Jer·e·mi'ah the
son of Hil·ki'ah, of the priests
who *were* [a]in An'a·thoth in the
land of Benjamin,
2 to whom the word of the LORD
came in the days of [a]Jō·sī'ah the
son of Ā'mon, king of Judah, [b]in
the thirteenth year of his reign.
3 It came also in the days of
[a]Je·hoi'a·kim the son of Jō·sī'ah,
king of Judah, [b]until the end of
the eleventh year of Zed·e·kī'ah
the son of Jō·sī'ah, king of Judah, [c]until the carrying away of
Jerusalem captive [d]in the fifth
month.
4 Then the word of the LORD
came to me, saying:

5 "Before I [a]formed you in the
womb [b]I knew you;
Before you were born I
[c]sanctified[1] you;
I [2]ordained you a prophet to
the nations."

6 Then said I:

[a]"Ah, Lord GOD!
Behold, I cannot speak, for I
am a youth."

7 But the LORD said to me:

"Do not say, 'I *am* a youth,'
For you shall go to all to
whom I send you,
And [a]whatever I command
you, you shall speak.
8 [a]Do not be afraid of their
faces,
For [b]I *am* with you to deliver
you," says the LORD.

9 Then the LORD put forth His
hand and [a]touched my mouth,
and the LORD said to me:

"Behold, I have [b]put My
words in your mouth.
10 [a]See, I have this day set you
over the nations and
over the kingdoms,
To [b]root out and to pull
down,
To destroy and to throw
down,
To build and to plant."

11 Moreover the word of the
LORD came to me, saying,

CHAPTER 1

1 [a]Josh. 21:18

2 [a]2 Kin. 21:24 [b]Jer. 25:3

3 [a]2 Kin. 23:34 [b]Jer. 39:2 [c]Jer. 52:12 [d]2 Kin. 25:8

5 [a]Is. 49:1, 5 [b]Ex. 33:12 [c][Luke 1:15] [1]*set you apart* [2]*appointed*

6 [a]Ex. 4:10; 6:12, 30

7 [a]Num. 22:20, 38

8 [a]Ezek. 2:6; 3:9 [b]Ex. 3:12

9 [a]Is. 6:7 [b]Is. 51:16

10 [a]1 Kin. 19:17 [b][2 Cor. 10:4, 5]

"Jer·e·mi′ah, what do you see?"
And I said, "I see a [1]branch of an
almond tree."
12 Then the LORD said to me,
"You have seen well, for I am
[1]ready to perform My word."
13 And the word of the LORD
came to me the second time,
saying, "What do you see?" And
I said, "I see [a]a boiling pot, and it
is facing away from the north."
14 Then the LORD said to me:

"Out of the [a]north calamity
shall break forth
On all the inhabitants of the
land.
15 For behold, I am [a]calling
All the families of the
kingdoms of the north,"
says the LORD;
"They shall come and [b]each
one set his throne
At the entrance of the gates
of Jerusalem,
Against all its walls all
around,
And against all the cities of
Judah.
16 I will utter My judgments
Against them concerning all
their wickedness,
Because [a]they have forsaken
Me,
Burned [b]incense to other
gods,
And worshiped the works of
their own [c]hands.

17 "Therefore [a]prepare yourself
and arise,
And speak to them all that I
command you.
[b]Do not be dismayed before
their faces,
Lest I dismay you before
them.
18 For behold, I have made you
this day
[a]A fortified city and an iron
pillar,
And bronze walls against
the whole land—
Against the kings of Judah,
Against its princes,
Against its priests,
And against the people of
the land.
19 They will fight against you,
But they shall not prevail
against you.
For I *am* with you," says the
LORD, "to deliver you."

2 Moreover the word of the
LORD came to me, saying,
2 "Go and cry in the hearing
of Jerusalem, saying, 'Thus says
the LORD:

"I remember you,
The kindness of your [a]youth,
The love of your betrothal,
[b]When you [1]went after Me in
the wilderness,
In a land not sown.
3 [a]Israel *was* holiness to the
LORD,
[b]The firstfruits of His
increase.
[c]All that devour him will
offend;
Disaster will [d]come upon
them," says the LORD.' "

4 Hear the word of the LORD,
O house of Jacob and all the
families of the house of Israel.
5 Thus says the LORD:

[a]"What injustice have your
fathers found in Me,
That they have gone far
from Me,
[b]Have followed [1]idols,
And have become idolaters?

11 [1]Lit. *rod*
12 [1]Lit. *watching*
13 [a]Ezek. 11:3; 24:3
14 [a]Jer. 6:1
15 [a]Jer. 6:22; 25:9 [b]Jer. 39:3
16 [a]Deut. 28:20 [b]Jer. 7:9 [c]Is. 37:19
17 [a]Job 38:3 [b]Ezek. 2:6
18 [a]Is. 50:7

CHAPTER 2

2 [a]Ezek. 16:8 [b]Deut. 2:7 [1]*followed*
3 [a][Ex. 19:5, 6] [b]Rev. 14:4 [c]Jer. 12:14 [d]Is. 41:11
5 [a]Is. 5:4 [b]2 Kin. 17:15 [1]*vanities* or *futilities*

6 Neither did they say, 'Where *is* the LORD,
Who [a]brought us up out of the land of Egypt,
Who led us through [b]the wilderness,
Through a land of deserts and pits,
Through a land of drought and the shadow of death,
Through a land that no one crossed
And where no one dwelt?'
7 I brought you into [a]a bountiful country,
To eat its fruit and its goodness.
But when you entered, you [b]defiled My land
And made My heritage an abomination.
8 The priests did not say, 'Where *is* the LORD?'
And those who handle the [a]law did not know Me;
The rulers also transgressed against Me;
[b]The prophets prophesied by Bā′al,
And walked after *things that* do not profit.

9 "Therefore [a]I will yet [1]bring charges against you,"
says the LORD,
"And against your children's children I will bring charges.
10 For pass beyond the coasts of [1]Cyprus and see,
Send to [2]Kē′dar and consider diligently,
And see if there has been such *a* [a]*thing*.
11 [a]Has a nation changed *its* gods,
Which *are* [b]not gods?
[c]But My people have changed their Glory
For *what* does not profit.
12 Be astonished, O heavens, at this,
And be horribly afraid;
Be very desolate," says the LORD.
13 "For My people have committed two evils:
They have forsaken Me, the [a]fountain of living waters,
And hewn themselves cisterns—broken cisterns that can hold no water.

14 "*Is* Israel [a]a servant?
Is he a homeborn *slave*?
Why is he plundered?
15 [a]The young lions roared at him, *and* growled;
They made his land waste;
His cities are burned, without inhabitant.
16 Also the people of [1]Noph and [a]Tah′pan·hēs
Have [2]broken the crown of your head.
17 [a]Have you not brought this on yourself,
In that you have forsaken the LORD your God
When [b]He led you in the way?
18 And now why take [a]the road to Egypt,
To drink the waters of [b]Sī′hor?
Or why take the road to [c]Assyria,
To drink the waters of [1]the River?
19 Your own wickedness will [a]correct you,
And your backslidings will rebuke you.

6 [a]Is. 63:11 [b]Deut. 8:15; 32:10
7 [a]Num. 13:27 [b]Num. 35:33
8 [a]Rom. 2:20 [b]Jer. 23:13
9 [a]Mic. 6:2 [1]*contend with*
10 [a]Jer. 18:13 [1]Heb. *Kittim*, representative of western cultures [2]In northern Arabian desert, representative of eastern cultures
11 [a]Mic. 4:5 [b]Is. 37:19 [c]Rom. 1:23
13 [a]Ps. 36:9
14 [a][Ex. 4:22]
15 [a]Is. 1:7
16 [a]Jer. 43:7–9 [1]Memphis in ancient Egypt [2]Or *grazed*
17 [a]Jer. 4:18 [b]Deut. 32:10
18 [a]Is. 30:1–3 [b]Josh. 13:3 [c]Hos. 5:13 [1]The Euphrates
19 [a]Jer. 4:18

Know therefore and see that *it is* an evil and bitter *thing*
That you have forsaken the LORD your God,
And the [1]fear of Me *is* not in you,"
Says the Lord GOD of hosts.

20 "For of old I have [a]broken your yoke *and* burst your bonds;
And [b]you said, 'I will not [1]transgress,'
When [c]on every high hill and under every green tree
You lay down, [d]playing the harlot.
21 Yet I had [a]planted you a noble vine, a seed of highest quality.
How then have you turned before Me
Into [b]the degenerate plant of an alien vine?
22 For though you wash yourself with lye, and use much soap,
Yet your iniquity is [a]marked[1] before Me,"
says the Lord GOD.

23 "How[a] can you say, 'I am not [1]polluted,
I have not gone after the Bā'als'?
See your way in the valley;
Know what you have done:
You are a swift dromedary breaking loose in her ways,
24 A wild donkey used to the wilderness,
That sniffs at the wind in her desire;
In her time of mating, who can turn her away?
All those who seek her will not weary themselves;
In her month they will find her.
25 Withhold your foot from being unshod, and your throat from thirst.
But you said, [a]'There is no hope.
No! For I have loved [b]aliens, and after them I will go.'

26 "As the thief is ashamed when he is found out,
So is the house of Israel ashamed;
They and their kings and their princes, and their priests and their [a]prophets,
27 Saying to a tree, 'You *are* my father,'
And to a [a]stone, 'You gave birth to me.'
For they have turned *their* back to Me, and not *their* face.
But in the time of their [b]trouble
They will say, 'Arise and save us.'
28 But [a]where *are* your gods that you have made for yourselves?
Let them arise,
If they [b]can save you in the time of your [1]trouble;
For [c]*according to* the number of your cities
Are your gods, O Judah.

29 "Why will you plead with Me?
You all have transgressed against Me," says the LORD.
30 "In vain I have [a]chastened your children;

19 [1]*dread*
20 [a]Lev. 26:13 [b]Judg. 10:16 [c]Deut. 12:2 [d]Ex. 34:15 [1]Kt. *serve*
21 [a]Ex. 15:17 [b]Is. 5:4
22 [a]Job 14:16, 17 [1]*stained*
23 [a]Prov. 30:12 [1]*defiled*
25 [a]Jer. 18:12 [b]Jer. 3:13
26 [a]Is. 28:7
27 [a]Jer. 3:9 [b]Is. 26:16
28 [a]Judg. 10:14 [b]Is. 45:20 [c]Jer. 11:13 [1]Or *evil*
30 [a]Is. 9:13

They [b]received no correction.
Your sword has [c]devoured
your prophets
Like a destroying lion.

31 "O generation, see the word
of the LORD!
Have I been a wilderness to
Israel,
Or a land of darkness?
Why do My people say, 'We
[1]are lords;
[a]We will come no more to
You'?
32 Can a virgin forget her
ornaments,
Or a bride her attire?
Yet My people [a]have
forgotten Me days
without number.

33 "Why do you beautify your
way to seek love?
Therefore you have also
taught
The wicked women your
ways.
34 Also on your skirts is found
[a]The blood of the lives of the
poor innocents.
I have not found it by [1]secret
search,
But plainly on all these
things.
35 [a]Yet you say, 'Because I am
innocent,
Surely His anger shall turn
from me.'
Behold, [b]I will plead My
case against you,
[c]Because you say, 'I have not
sinned.'
36 [a]Why do you gad about so
much to change your
way?
Also [b]you shall be ashamed
of Egypt [c]as you were
ashamed of Assyria.
37 Indeed you will go forth
from him
With your hands on [a]your
head;
For the LORD has rejected
your trusted allies,
And you will [b]not prosper
by them.

3 "They say, 'If a man
divorces his wife,
And she goes from him
And becomes another
man's,
[a]May he return to her again?'
Would not that [b]land be
greatly polluted?
But you have [c]played the
harlot with many lovers;
[d]Yet return to Me," says the
LORD.

2 "Lift up your eyes to [a]the
desolate heights and see:
Where have you not [1]lain
with men?
[b]By the road you have sat for
them
Like an Arabian in the
wilderness;
[c]And you have polluted the
land
With your harlotries and
your wickedness.
3 Therefore the [a]showers have
been withheld,
And there has been no latter
rain.
You have had a [b]harlot's
forehead;
You refuse to be ashamed.
4 Will you not from this time
cry to Me,
'My Father, You *are* [a]the
guide of [b]my youth?
5 [a]Will He remain angry
forever?
Will He keep it to the end?'

30 [b]Jer. 5:3; 7:28 [c]Neh. 9:26
31 [a]Deut. 32:15 [1]*have dominion*
32 [a]Ps. 106:21
34 [a]Ps. 106:38 [1]*digging*
35 [a]Jer. 2:23, 29 [b]Jer. 2:9 [c][Prov. 28:13]
36 [a]Hos. 5:13; 12:1 [b]Is. 30:3 [c]2 Chr. 28:16
37 [a]2 Sam. 13:19 [b]Jer. 37:7–10

CHAPTER 3

1 [a]Deut. 24:1–4 [b]Jer. 2:7 [c]Ezek. 16:26 [d][Zech. 1:3]
2 [a]Deut. 12:2 [b]Prov. 23:28 [c]Jer. 2:7 [1]Kt. *been violated*
3 [a]Lev. 26:19 [b]Zeph. 3:5
4 [a]Prov. 2:17 [b]Jer. 2:2
5 [a][Is. 57:16]

Behold, you have spoken
and done evil things,
As you were able."

6 The LORD said also to me in
the days of Jō·sī′ah the king:
"Have you seen what [a]backslid-
ing Israel has done? She has
[b]gone up on every high mountain and under every green tree,
and there played the harlot.
7 [a]"And I said, after she had
done all these *things*, 'Return to
Me.' But she did not return. And
her treacherous [b]sister Judah
saw it.
8 "Then I saw that [a]for all the
causes for which backsliding Israel had committed adultery, I
had [b]put her away and given her
a certificate of divorce; [c]yet her
treacherous sister Judah did not
fear, but went and played the
harlot also.
9 "So it came to pass, through
her casual harlotry, that she
[a]defiled the land and committed
adultery with [b]stones and trees.
10 "And yet for all this her
treacherous sister Judah has not
turned to Me [a]with her whole
heart, but in pretense," says the
LORD.
11 Then the LORD said to me,
[a]"Backsliding Israel has shown
herself more righteous than
treacherous Judah.
12 "Go and proclaim these
words toward [a]the north, and say:

'Return, backsliding Israel,'
says the LORD;
'I will not cause My anger to
fall on you.
For I *am* [b]merciful,' says the
LORD;
'I will not remain angry
forever.

6 [a]Jer. 7:24 [b]Jer. 2:20
7 [a]2 Kin. 17:13 [b]Ezek. 16:47, 48
8 [a]Ezek. 23:9 [b]2 Kin. 17:6 [c]Ezek. 23:11
9 [a]Jer. 2:7 [b]Jer. 2:27
10 [a]Jer. 12:2
11 [a]Ezek. 16:51, 52
12 [a]2 Kin. 17:6 [b]Ps. 86:15
13 [a]Deut. 30:1, 2 [b]Ezek. 16:15 [c]Jer. 2:25 [d]Deut. 12:2 [1]Lit. *ways*
14 [a]Hos. 2:19, 20 [b]Jer. 31:6 [c][Rom. 11:5]
15 [a]Eph. 4:11 [b]Acts 20:28
16 [a]Is. 49:19 [b]Is. 65:17
17 [a]Is. 60:9 [b]Deut. 29:19; Jer. 7:24 [1]*walk after the stubbornness* or *imagination*
18 [a]Is. 11:13 [b]Jer. 31:8 [c]Amos 9:15

13 [a]Only acknowledge your
iniquity,
That you have transgressed
against the LORD your
God,
And have [b]scattered your
[1]charms
To [c]alien deities [d]under
every green tree,
And you have not obeyed
My voice,' says the LORD.

14 "Return, O backsliding children," says the LORD; [a]"for I am
married to you. I will take you,
[b]one from a city and two from
a family, and I will bring you to
[c]Zion.
15 "And I will give you
[a]shepherds according to My
heart, who will [b]feed you with
knowledge and understanding.
16 "Then it shall come to pass,
when you are multiplied and
[a]increased in the land in those
days," says the LORD, "that they
will say no more, 'The ark of
the covenant of the LORD.' [b]It
shall not come to mind, nor
shall they remember it, nor shall
they visit *it*, nor shall it be made
anymore.
17 "At that time Jerusalem shall
be called The Throne of the
LORD, and all the nations shall
be gathered to it, [a]to the name of
the LORD, to Jerusalem. No more
shall they [b]follow[1] the dictates of
their evil hearts.
18 "In those days [a]the house of
Judah shall walk with the house
of Israel, and they shall come
together out of the land of [b]the
north to [c]the land that I have
given as an inheritance to your
fathers.
19 "But I said:

'How can I put you among
the children
And give you [a]a pleasant
land,
A beautiful heritage of the
hosts of nations?'

"And I said:

'You shall call Me, [b]"My
Father,"
And not turn away
from Me.'
20 Surely, *as* a wife
treacherously departs
from her [1]husband,
So [a]have you dealt
treacherously with Me,
O house of Israel," says the
LORD.

21 A voice was heard on [a]the
desolate heights,
Weeping *and* supplications
of the children of Israel.
For they have perverted
their way;
They have forgotten the
LORD their God.

22 "Return, you backsliding
children,
And I will [a]heal your
backslidings."

"Indeed we do come to You,
For You are the LORD our
God.
23 [a]Truly, in vain *is salvation*
hoped for from the hills,
And from the multitude of
mountains;
[b]Truly, in the LORD our God
Is the salvation of Israel.
24 [a]For shame has devoured
The labor of our fathers
from our youth—
Their flocks and their herds,
Their sons and their
daughters.
25 We lie down in our shame,
And our [1]reproach
covers us.
[a]For we have sinned against
the LORD our God,
We and our fathers,
From our youth even to this
day,
And [b]have not obeyed the
voice of the LORD our
God."

4 "If you will return,
O Israel," says the LORD,
[a]"Return to Me;
And if you will put away
your abominations out
of My sight,
Then you shall not be
moved.
2 [a]And you shall swear, 'The
LORD lives,'
[b]In truth, in [1]judgment, and
in righteousness;
[c]The nations shall bless
themselves in Him,
And in Him they shall
[d]glory."

3 For thus says the LORD to the
men of Judah and Jerusalem:

[a]"Break up your [1]fallow
ground,
And [b]do not sow among
thorns.
4 [a]Circumcise yourselves to the
LORD,
And take away the foreskins
of your hearts,
You men of Judah and
inhabitants of Jerusalem,
Lest My fury come forth
like fire,
And burn so that no one can
quench *it*,

19 [a]Ps. 106:24 [b]Is. 63:16
20 [a]Is. 48:8 [1]Lit. *companion*
21 [a]Is. 15:2
22 [a]Hos. 6:1; 14:4
23 [a]Ps. 121:1, 2 [b]Ps. 3:8
24 [a]Hos. 9:10
25 [a]Ezra 9:6, 7 [b]Jer. 22:21 [1]*disgrace*

CHAPTER 4

1 [a]Joel 2:12
2 [a]Deut. 10:20 [b]Zech. 8:8 [c][Gen. 22:18] [d]1 Cor. 1:31 [1]*justice*
3 [a]Hos. 10:12 [b]Matt. 13:7 [1]*untilled*
4 [a]Deut. 10:16; 30:6

Because of the evil of your
doings."

5 Declare in Judah and proclaim in Jerusalem, and say:
[a]"Blow the trumpet in the
land;
Cry, 'Gather together,'
And say, [b]'Assemble
yourselves,
And let us go into the
fortified cities.'
6 Set up the [1]standard toward
Zion.
Take refuge! Do not delay!
For I will bring disaster
from the [a]north,
And great destruction."

7 [a]The lion has come up from
his thicket,
And [b]the destroyer of
nations is on his way.
He has gone forth from his
place
[c]To make your land desolate.
Your cities will be laid
waste,
Without inhabitant.
8 For this, [a]clothe yourself
with sackcloth,
Lament and wail.
For the fierce anger of the
LORD
Has not turned back from
us.

9 "And it shall come to pass in
that day," says the LORD,
"*That* the heart of the king
shall perish,
And the heart of the
princes;
The priests shall be
astonished,
And the prophets shall
wonder."

5 [a]Hos. 8:1 [b]Jer. 8:14
6 [a]Jer. 1:13–15; 6:1, 22; 50:17 [1]banner
7 [a]Dan. 7:4 [b]Jer. 25:9 [c]Is. 1:7; 6:11
8 [a]Is. 22:12
10 [a]Ezek. 14:9 [b]Jer. 5:12; 14:13 [1]Lit. *soul*
11 [a]Hos. 13:15
12 [a]Jer. 1:16
13 [a]Is. 5:28 [b]Deut. 28:49
14 [a]James 4:8
15 [a]Jer. 8:16; 50:17 [1]Or *wickedness*
16 [a]Is. 39:3

10 Then I said, "Ah, Lord GOD!
[a]Surely You have greatly
deceived this people and
Jerusalem,
[b]Saying, 'You shall have
peace,'
Whereas the sword reaches
to the [1]heart."

11 At that time it will be said
To this people and to
Jerusalem,
[a]"A dry wind of the desolate
heights *blows* in the
wilderness
Toward the daughter of My
people—
Not to fan or to cleanse—
12 A wind too strong for these
will come for Me;
Now [a]I will also speak
judgment against them."

13 "Behold, he shall come up
like clouds,
And [a]his chariots like a
whirlwind.
[b]His horses are swifter than
eagles.
Woe to us, for we are
plundered!"

14 O Jerusalem, [a]wash your
heart from wickedness,
That you may be saved.
How long shall your evil
thoughts lodge within
you?
15 For a voice declares [a]from
Dan
And proclaims [1]affliction
from Mount Ē′phra·im:
16 "Make mention to the
nations,
Yes, proclaim against
Jerusalem,
That watchers come from a
[a]far country

And raise their voice against
the cities of Judah.
17 [a]Like keepers of a field
they are against her all
around,
Because she has been
rebellious against Me,"
says the LORD.
18 "Your[a] ways and your doings
Have procured these *things*
for you.
This *is* your wickedness,
Because it is bitter,
Because it reaches to your
heart."

19 O my [a]soul, my soul!
I am pained in my very
heart!
My heart makes a noise in
me;
I cannot hold my peace,
Because you have heard,
O my soul,
The sound of the trumpet,
The alarm of war.
20 [a]Destruction upon
destruction is cried,
For the whole land is
plundered.
Suddenly [b]my tents are
plundered,
And my curtains in a
moment.
21 How long will I see the
[1]standard,
And hear the sound of the
trumpet?

22 "For My people *are* foolish,
They have not known Me.
They *are* [1]silly children,
And they have no
understanding.
[a]They *are* wise to do evil,
But to do good they have no
knowledge."

23 [a]I beheld the earth, and
indeed *it was* [b]without
form, and void;
And the heavens, they *had*
no light.
24 [a]I beheld the mountains, and
indeed they trembled,
And all the hills moved back
and forth.
25 I beheld, and indeed *there
was* no man,
And [a]all the birds of the
heavens had fled.
26 I beheld, and indeed the
fruitful land *was* a
[a]wilderness,
And all its cities were
broken down
At the presence of the LORD,
By His fierce anger.

27 For thus says the LORD:

"The whole land shall be
desolate;
[a]Yet I will not make a full
end.
28 For this [a]shall the earth
mourn,
And [b]the heavens above be
black,
Because I have spoken.
I have [c]purposed and [d]will
not relent,
Nor will I turn back from it.
29 The whole city shall flee
from the noise of the
horsemen and bowmen.
They shall go into thickets
and climb up on the
rocks.
Every city *shall be* forsaken,
And not a man shall dwell
in it.

30 "And *when* you *are*
plundered,
What will you do?

17 [a]2 Kin. 25:1, 4
18 [a]Is. 50:1
19 [a]Is. 15:5; 16:11; 21:3; 22:4
20 [a]Ezek. 7:26 [b]Jer. 10:20
21 [1]*banner*
22 [a]Rom. 16:19 [1]*foolish*
23 [a]Is. 24:19 [b]Gen. 1:2
24 [a]Ezek. 38:20
25 [a]Zeph. 1:3
26 [a]Jer. 9:10
27 [a]Jer. 5:10, 18; 30:11; 46:28
28 [a]Hos. 4:3 [b]Is. 5:30; 50:3 [c][Dan. 4:35] [d][Num. 23:19]

Though you clothe yourself
with crimson,
Though you adorn *yourself*
with ornaments of gold,
[a]Though you enlarge your
eyes with paint,
In vain you will make
yourself fair;
[b]*Your* lovers will despise you;
They will seek your life.

31 "For I have heard a voice as
of a woman in [1]labor,
The anguish as of her who
brings forth her first
child,
The voice of the daughter of
Zion bewailing herself;
She [a]spreads her hands,
saying,
'Woe *is* me now, for my soul
is [2]weary
Because of murderers!'

5 "Run to and fro through the
streets of Jerusalem;
See now and know;
And seek in her open places
[a]If you can find a man,
[b]If there is *anyone* who
executes [1]judgment,
Who seeks the truth,
[c]And I will pardon her.
2 [a]Though they say, '*As* [b]the
LORD lives,'
Surely they [c]swear falsely."

3 O LORD, *are* not [a]Your eyes
on the truth?
You have [b]stricken them,
But they have not grieved;
You have consumed them,
But [c]they have refused to
receive correction.
They have made their faces
harder than rock;
They have refused to return.

30 [a]2 Kin. 9:30 [b]Jer. 22:20, 22
31 [a]Lam. 1:17 [1]*childbirth* [2]*faint*

CHAPTER 5

1 [a]Ezek. 22:30 [b]Gen. 18:23–32 [c]Gen. 18:26 [1]*justice*
2 [a]Titus 1:16 [b]Jer. 4:2 [c]Jer. 7:9
3 [a][2 Chr. 16:9] [b]Is. 1:5; 9:13 [c]Zeph. 3:2
4 [a]Jer. 8:7
5 [a]Mic. 3:1 [b]Ps. 2:3
6 [a]Jer. 4:7 [b]Zeph. 3:3 [c]Hos. 13:7
7 [a]Zeph. 1:5 [b]Deut. 32:21 [c]Deut. 32:15
8 [a]Ezek. 22:11

4 Therefore I said, "Surely
these *are* poor.
They are foolish;
For [a]they do not know the
way of the LORD,
The judgment of their
God.
5 I will go to the great men
and speak to them,
For [a]they have known the
way of the LORD,
The judgment of their
God."

But these have altogether
[b]broken the yoke
And burst the bonds.
6 Therefore [a]a lion from the
forest shall slay them,
[b]A wolf of the deserts shall
destroy them;
[c]A leopard will watch over
their cities.
Everyone who goes out
from there shall be torn
in pieces,
Because their transgressions
are many;
Their backslidings have
increased.

7 "How shall I pardon you for
this?
Your children have forsaken
Me
And [a]sworn by *those* [b]*that*
are not gods.
[c]When I had fed them to the
full,
Then they committed
adultery
And assembled themselves
by troops in the harlots'
houses.
8 [a]They were *like* well-fed
lusty stallions;
Every one neighed after his
neighbor's wife.

9 Shall I not punish *them* for
these *things?*" says the
LORD.
"And shall I not [a]avenge
Myself on such a nation
as this?

10 "Go up on her walls and
destroy,
But do not [1]make a
[a]complete end.
Take away her branches,
For they *are* not the LORD's.
11 For [a]the house of Israel and
the house of Judah
Have dealt very
treacherously with Me,"
says the LORD.

12 [a]They have lied about the
LORD,
And said, [b]"*It is* not He.
[c]Neither will [1]evil come upon
us,
Nor shall we see sword or
famine.
13 And the prophets become
wind,
For the word *is* not in them.
Thus shall it be done to
them."

14 Therefore thus says the LORD
God of hosts:

"Because you speak this
word,
[a]Behold, I will make My
words in your mouth
fire,
And this people wood,
And it shall devour them.
15 Behold, I will bring a
[a]nation against you
[b]from afar,
O house of Israel," says the
LORD.
"It *is* a mighty nation,

9 [a]Jer. 9:9

10 [a]Jer. 4:27
[1]*completely destroy*

11 [a]Jer. 3:6, 7, 20

12 [a]2 Chr. 36:16
[b]Jer. 23:17
[c]Jer. 14:13
[1]*disaster*

14 [a]Jer. 1:9; 23:29

15 [a]Deut. 28:49
[b]Jer. 4:16

17 [a]Lev. 26:16

18 [a]Jer. 30:11
[1]*completely destroy*

19 [a]Deut. 29:24–29
[b]Jer. 1:16; 2:13
[c]Deut. 28:48

21 [a]Matt. 13:14
[1]Lit. *heart*

22 [a][Rev. 15:4]

It *is* an ancient nation,
A nation whose language
you do not know,
Nor can you understand
what they say.
16 Their quiver *is* like an open
tomb;
They *are* all mighty men.
17 And they shall eat up your
[a]harvest and your bread,
Which your sons and
daughters should eat.
They shall eat up your
flocks and your herds;
They shall eat up your vines
and your fig trees;
They shall destroy your
fortified cities,
In which you trust, with the
sword.

18 "Nevertheless in those days,"
says the LORD, "I [a]will not [1]make
a complete end of you.
19 "And it will be when you say,
[a]'Why does the LORD our God do
all these *things* to us?' then you
shall answer them, 'Just as you
have [b]forsaken Me and served
foreign gods in your land, so
[c]you shall serve aliens in a land
that is not yours.'

20 "Declare this in the house of
Jacob
And proclaim it in Judah,
saying,
21 'Hear this now, O [a]foolish
people,
Without [1]understanding,
Who have eyes and see not,
And who have ears and
hear not:
22 [a]'Do you not fear Me?' says
the LORD.
'Will you not tremble at My
presence,

Who have placed the sand
as the [b]bound of the sea,
By a perpetual decree, that
it cannot pass beyond it?
And though its waves toss
to and fro,
Yet they cannot prevail;
Though they roar, yet they
cannot pass over it.
23 But this people has a defiant
and rebellious heart;
They have revolted and
departed.
24 They do not say in their
heart,
"Let us now fear the LORD
our God,
[a]Who gives rain, both the
[b]former and the latter, in
its season.
[c]He reserves for us the
appointed weeks of the
harvest."
25 [a]Your iniquities have turned
these *things* away,
And your sins have withheld
good from you.

26 'For among My people are
found wicked *men;*
They [a]lie in wait as one who
sets snares;
They set a trap;
They catch men.
27 As a cage is full of birds,
So their houses *are* full of
deceit.
Therefore they have become
great and grown rich.
28 They have grown [a]fat, they
are sleek;
Yes, they [1]surpass the deeds
of the wicked;
They do not plead [b]the
cause,
The cause of the fatherless;
[c]Yet they prosper,

22 [b]Job 26:10
24 [a]Acts 14:17 [b]Joel 2:23 [c][Gen. 8:22]
25 [a]Jer. 3:3
26 [a]Hab. 1:15
28 [a]Deut. 32:15 [b]Zech. 7:10 [c]Job 12:6 [1]Or *pass over* or *overlook*
29 [a]Mal. 3:5
30 [a]Hos. 6:10
31 [a]Ezek. 13:6 [b]Mic. 2:11

CHAPTER 6

1 [a]Neh. 3:14 [b]Jer. 4:6
3 [a]2 Kin. 25:1–4
4 [a]Joel 3:9 [b]Jer. 15:8

And the right of the needy
they do not defend.
29 [a]Shall I not punish *them* for
these *things?*' says the
LORD.
'Shall I not avenge Myself on
such a nation as this?'

30 "An astonishing and [a]horrible
thing
Has been committed in the
land:
31 The prophets prophesy
[a]falsely,
And the priests rule by their
own power;
And My people [b]love *to*
have it so.
But what will you do in the
end?

6 "O you children of Benjamin,
Gather yourselves to flee
from the midst of
Jerusalem!
Blow the trumpet in Te·kō′a,
And set up a signal-fire in
[a]Beth Hac′ce·rem;
[b]For disaster appears out of
the north,
And great destruction.
2 I have likened the daughter
of Zion
To a lovely and delicate
woman.
3 The [a]shepherds with their
flocks shall come to her.
They shall pitch *their* tents
against her all around.
Each one shall pasture in
his own place."

4 "Prepare[a] war against her;
Arise, and let us go up [b]at
noon.
Woe to us, for the day goes
away,

For the shadows of the
evening are lengthening.
5 Arise, and let us go by night,
And let us destroy her
palaces."

6 For thus has the LORD of hosts
said:

"Cut down trees,
And build a mound against
Jerusalem.
This *is* the city to be
punished.
She *is* full of oppression in
her midst.
7 [a]As a fountain [1]wells up with
water,
So she wells up with her
wickedness.
[b]Violence and plundering are
heard in her.
Before Me continually *are*
[2]grief and wounds.
8 Be instructed, O Jerusalem,
Lest [a]My soul depart from
you;
Lest I make you desolate,
A land not inhabited."

9 Thus says the LORD of hosts:

"They shall thoroughly glean
as a vine the remnant of
Israel;
As a grape-gatherer, put
your hand back into the
branches."

10 To whom shall I speak and
give warning,
That they may hear?
Indeed their [a]ear *is*
uncircumcised,
And they cannot give heed.
Behold, [b]the word of the LORD
is a reproach to them;
They have no delight in it.

11 Therefore I am full of the
fury of the LORD.
[a]I am weary of holding *it* in.
"I will pour it out [b]on the
children outside,
And on the assembly of
young men together;
For even the husband shall
be taken with the wife,
The aged with *him who is*
full of days.
12 And [a]their houses shall be
turned over to others,
Fields and wives together;
For I will stretch out My hand
Against the inhabitants of
the land," says the LORD.
13 "Because from the least of
them even to the greatest
of them,
Everyone *is* given to
[a]covetousness;
And from the prophet even
to the [b]priest,
Everyone deals falsely.
14 They have also [a]healed
the [1]hurt of My people
[2]slightly,
[b]Saying, 'Peace, peace!'
When *there is* no peace.
15 Were they [a]ashamed when
they had committed
abomination?
No! They were not at all
ashamed;
Nor did they know how to
blush.
Therefore they shall fall
among those who fall;
At the time I punish them,
They shall be cast down,"
says the LORD.

16 Thus says the LORD:

"Stand in the ways and see,
And ask for the [a]old paths,
where the good way *is*,

7 [a]Is. 57:20 [b]Ps. 55:9 [1]*gushes* [2]*sickness*
8 [a]Hos. 9:12
10 [a][Acts 7:51] [b]Jer. 8:9; 20:8
11 [a]Jer. 20:9 [b]Jer. 9:21
12 [a]Deut. 28:30
13 [a]Is. 56:11; Jer. 8:10; 22:17 [b]Jer. 5:31; 23:11
14 [a]Jer. 8:11–15 [b]Jer. 4:10; 23:17 [1]Lit. *crushing* [2]Superficially
15 [a]Jer. 3:3; 8:12
16 [a]Jer. 18:15

And walk in it;
Then you will find [b]rest for your souls.
But they said, 'We will not walk *in it.*'
17 Also, I set [a]watchmen over you, *saying,*
[b]'Listen to the sound of the trumpet!'
But they said, 'We will not listen.'
18 Therefore hear, you nations,
And know, O congregation, what *is* among them.
19 [a]Hear, O earth!
Behold, I will certainly bring [b]calamity on this people—
[c]The fruit of their thoughts,
Because they have not heeded My words
Nor My law, but rejected it.
20 [a]For what purpose to Me
Comes frankincense [b]from Shē'ba,
And [c]sweet cane from a far country?
[d]Your burnt offerings *are* not acceptable,
Nor your sacrifices sweet to Me."

21 Therefore thus says the LORD:

"Behold, I will lay stumbling blocks before this people,
And the fathers and the sons together shall fall on them.
The neighbor and his friend shall perish."

22 Thus says the LORD:

"Behold, a people comes from the [a]north country,
And a great nation will be raised from the farthest parts of the earth.
23 They will lay hold on bow and spear;
They *are* cruel and have no mercy;
Their voice [a]roars like the sea;
And they ride on horses,
As men of war set in array against you, O daughter of Zion."

24 We have heard the report of it;
Our hands grow feeble.
[a]Anguish has taken hold of us,
Pain as of a woman in [1]labor.
25 Do not go out into the field,
Nor walk by the way.
Because of the sword of the enemy,
Fear *is* on every side.
26 O daughter of my people,
[a]Dress in sackcloth
[b]And roll about in ashes!
[c]Make mourning *as for* an only son, most bitter lamentation;
For the plunderer will suddenly come upon us.

27 "I have set you *as* an assayer *and* [a]a fortress among My people,
That you may know and test their way.
28 [a]They *are* all stubborn rebels, [b]walking as slanderers.
They are [c]bronze and iron,
They *are* all corrupters;
29 The bellows blow fiercely,
The lead is consumed by the fire;
The smelter refines in vain,

16 [b]Matt. 11:29
17 [a]Hab. 2:1 [b]Deut. 4:1
19 [a]Is. 1:2 [b]Jer. 19:3, 15 [c]Prov. 1:31
20 [a]Mic. 6:6, 7 [b]Is. 60:6 [c]Is. 43:24 [d]Jer. 7:21–23
22 [a]Jer. 1:15; 10:22; 50:41–43
23 [a]Is. 5:30
24 [a]Jer. 4:31; 13:21; 49:24 [1]*childbirth*
26 [a]Jer. 4:8 [b]Mic. 1:10 [c][Zech. 12:10]
27 [a]Jer. 1:18
28 [a]Jer. 5:23 [b]Jer. 9:4 [c]Ezek. 22:18

For the wicked are not
drawn off.
30 *People* will call them
[a]rejected silver,
Because the LORD has
rejected them."

7

7 The word that came to
Jer·e·mī′ah from the LORD,
saying,
2 [a]"Stand in the gate of the
LORD's house, and proclaim
there this word, and say, 'Hear
the word of the LORD, all *you*
of Judah who enter in at these
gates to worship the LORD!' "
3 Thus says the LORD of hosts,
the God of Israel: [a]"Amend your
ways and your doings, and I will
cause you to dwell in this place.
4 [a]"Do not trust in these lying words, saying, 'The temple
of the LORD, the temple of the
LORD, the temple of the LORD *are*
these.'
5 "For if you thoroughly amend
your ways and your doings, if
you thoroughly [a]execute [1]judg-
ment between a man and his
neighbor,
6 "*if* you do not oppress the
stranger, the fatherless, and the
widow, and do not shed innocent blood in this place, [a]or walk
after other gods to your hurt,
7 [a]"then I will cause you to
dwell in this place, in [b]the land
that I gave to your fathers forever and ever.
8 "Behold, you trust in [a]lying
words that cannot profit.
9 [a]"Will you steal, murder,
commit adultery, swear falsely,
burn incense to Bā′al, and [b]walk
after other gods whom you do
not know,
10 [a]"and *then* come and stand
before Me in this house [b]which
is called by My name, and say,
'We are delivered to do all these
abominations'?
11 "Has [a]this house, which is
called by My name, become a
[b]den of thieves in your eyes? Behold, I, even I, have seen *it*," says
the LORD.
12 "But go now to [a]My place
which *was* in Shī′lōh, [b]where I
set My name at the first, and see
[c]what I did to it because of the
wickedness of My people Israel.
13 "And now, because you have
done all these works," says the
LORD, "and I spoke to you, [a]rising
up early and speaking, but you
did not hear, and I [b]called you,
but you did not answer,
14 "therefore I will do to the
house which is called by My
name, in which you trust, and
to this place which I gave to you
and your fathers, as I have done
to [a]Shī′lōh.
15 "And I will cast you out of
My sight, [a]as I have cast out all
your brethren—[b]the whole posterity of Ē′phra·im.
16 "Therefore [a]do not pray for
this people, nor lift up a cry or
prayer for them, nor make intercession to Me; [b]for I will not
hear you.
17 "Do you not see what they do
in the cities of Judah and in the
streets of Jerusalem?
18 [a]"The children gather wood,
the fathers kindle the fire, and
the women knead dough, to
make cakes for the queen of
heaven; and *they* [b]pour out drink
offerings to other gods, that they
may provoke Me to anger.
19 [a]"Do they provoke Me to anger?" says the LORD. "*Do they*
not *provoke* themselves, to the
shame of their own faces?"

30 [a]Is. 1:22

CHAPTER 7

2 [a]Jer. 17:19; 26:2
3 [a]Jer. 4:1; 18:11; 26:13
4 [a]Mic. 3:11
5 [a]Jer. 21:12; 22:3 [1]*justice*
6 [a]Deut. 6:14, 15
7 [a]Deut. 4:40 [b]Jer. 3:18
8 [a]Jer. 5:31; 14:13, 14
9 [a]1 Kin. 18:21 [b]Ex. 20:3
10 [a]Ezek. 23:39 [b]Jer. 7:11, 14; 32:34; 34:15
11 [a]Is. 56:7 [b]Matt. 21:13
12 [a]Josh. 18:1 [b]Deut. 12:11 [c]1 Sam. 4:10
13 [a]2 Chr. 36:15 [b]Prov. 1:24
14 [a]1 Sam. 4:10, 11
15 [a]2 Kin. 17:23 [b]Ps. 78:67
16 [a]Ex. 32:10; Jer. 11:14 [b]Jer. 15:1
18 [a]Jer. 44:17 [b]Jer. 19:13
19 [a]Deut. 32:16, 21

20 Therefore thus says the Lord GOD: "Behold, My anger and My fury will be poured out on this place—on man and on beast, on the trees of the field and on the fruit of the ground. And it will burn and not be quenched."

21 Thus says the LORD of hosts, the God of Israel: [a]"Add your burnt offerings to your sacrifices and eat meat.

22 [a]"For I did not speak to your fathers, or command them in the day that I brought them out of the land of Egypt, concerning burnt offerings or sacrifices.

23 "But this is what I commanded them, saying, [a]'Obey My voice, and [b]I will be your God, and you shall be My people. And walk in all the ways that I have commanded you, that it may be well with you.'

24 [a]"Yet they did not obey or incline their ear, but [b]followed[1] the counsels *and* the [2]dictates of their evil hearts, and [c]went[3] backward and not forward.

25 "Since the day that your fathers came out of the land of Egypt until this day, I have even [a]sent to you all My servants the prophets, daily rising up early and sending *them.*

26 [a]"Yet they did not obey Me or incline their ear, but [b]stiffened their neck. [c]They did worse than their fathers.

27 "Therefore [a]you shall speak all these words to them, but they will not obey you. You shall also call to them, but they will not answer you.

28 "So you shall say to them, 'This *is* a nation that does not obey the voice of the LORD their God [a]nor receive correction. [b]Truth has perished and has been cut off from their mouth.

29 [a]'Cut off your hair and cast *it* away, and take up a lamentation on the desolate heights; for the LORD has rejected and forsaken the generation of His wrath.'

30 "For the children of Judah have done evil in My sight," says the LORD. [a]"They have set their abominations in the house which is called by My name, to [1]pollute it.

31 "And they have built the [a]high places of Tō'phet, which *is* in the Valley of the Son of Hin'nom, to [b]burn their sons and their daughters in the fire, [c]which I did not command, nor did it come into My heart.

32 "Therefore behold, [a]the days are coming," says the LORD, "when it will no more be called Tō'phet, or the Valley of the Son of Hin'nom, but the Valley of Slaughter; [b]for they will bury in Tō'phet until there is no room.

33 "The [a]corpses of this people will be food for the birds of the heaven and for the beasts of the earth. And no one will frighten *them away.*

34 "Then I will cause to [a]cease from the cities of Judah and from the streets of Jerusalem the voice of mirth and the voice of gladness, the voice of the bridegroom and the voice of the bride. For [b]the land shall be desolate.

8

"At that time," says the LORD, "they shall bring out the bones of the kings of Judah, and the bones of its princes, and the bones of the priests, and the bones of the prophets, and the bones of the inhabitants of Jerusalem, out of their graves.

21 [a]Jer. 6:20
22 [a][Hos. 6:6]
23 [a]Deut. 6:3 [b][Ex. 19:5, 6]
24 [a]Ps. 81:11 [b]Deut. 29:19 [c]Jer. 32:33 [1]*walked in* [2]*stubbornness* or *imagination* [3]Lit. *they were*
25 [a]2 Chr. 36:15
26 [a]Jer. 11:8 [b]Neh. 9:17 [c]Jer. 16:12
27 [a]Ezek. 2:7
28 [a]Jer. 5:3 [b]Jer. 9:3
29 [a]Mic. 1:16
30 [a]Dan. 9:27; 11:31 [1]*defile*
31 [a]2 Kin. 23:10 [b]Ps. 106:38 [c]Deut. 17:3
32 [a]Jer. 19:6 [b]2 Kin. 23:10
33 [a]Jer. 9:22; 19:11
34 [a]Is. 24:7, 8 [b]Lev. 26:33

2 "They shall spread them before the sun and the moon and all the host of heaven, which they have loved and which they have served and after which they have walked, which they have sought and [a]which they have worshiped. They shall not be gathered [b]nor buried; they shall be like refuse on the face of the earth.
3 "Then [a]death shall be chosen rather than life by all the [1]residue of those who remain of this evil family, who remain in all the places where I have driven them," says the LORD of hosts.
4 "Moreover you shall say to them, 'Thus says the LORD:

"Will they fall and not rise?
Will one turn away and not return?
5 Why has this people [a]slidden back,
Jerusalem, in a perpetual backsliding?
[b]They hold fast to deceit,
[c]They refuse to return.
6 [a]I listened and heard,
But they do not speak aright.
[b]No man repented of his wickedness,
Saying, 'What have I done?'
Everyone turned to his own course,
As the horse rushes into the battle.

7 "Even [a]the stork in the heavens
Knows her appointed times;
And the turtledove, the swift, and the swallow
Observe the time of their coming.
But [b]My people do not know the judgment of the LORD.

8 "How can you say, 'We *are* wise,
[a]And the law of the LORD *is* with us'?
Look, the false pen of the scribe certainly works falsehood.
9 [a]The wise men are ashamed,
They are dismayed and taken.
Behold, they have rejected the word of the LORD;
So [b]what wisdom do they have?
10 Therefore [a]I will give their wives to others,
And their fields to those who will inherit *them;*
Because from the least even to the greatest
Everyone is given to [b]covetousness;
From the prophet even to the priest
Everyone deals falsely.
11 For they have [a]healed the hurt of the daughter of My people [1]slightly,
Saying, [b]'Peace, peace!'
When *there is* no peace.
12 Were they [a]ashamed when they had committed abomination?
No! They were not at all ashamed,
Nor did they know how to blush.
Therefore they shall fall among those who fall;
In the time of their punishment
They shall be cast down,"
says the LORD.

CHAPTER 8

2 [a]2 Kin. 23:5 [b]Jer. 22:19
3 [a]Rev. 9:6 [1]*remnant*
5 [a]Jer. 7:24 [b]Jer. 9:6 [c]Jer. 5:3
6 [a]Ps. 14:2 [b]Mic. 7:2
7 [a]Song 2:12 [b]Jer. 5:4; 9:3
8 [a]Rom. 2:17
9 [a]Jer. 6:15 [b]Jer. 4:22
10 [a]Deut. 28:30 [b]Is. 56:11; 57:17
11 [a]Jer. 6:14 [b]Ezek. 13:10 [1]Superficially
12 [a]Jer. 3:3; 6:15

13 "I will surely [1]consume
them," says the LORD.
"No grapes *shall be* [a]on the
vine,
Nor figs on the [b]fig tree,
And the leaf shall fade;
And *the things* I have given
them shall [c]pass away
from them." ' "

14 "Why do we sit still?
[a]Assemble yourselves,
And let us enter the fortified
cities,
And let us be silent there.
For the LORD our God has
put us to silence
And given us [b]water[1] of gall
to drink,
Because we have sinned
against the LORD.

15 "*We* [a]looked for peace, but
no good *came;*
And for a time of health,
and there was trouble!
16 The snorting of His horses
was heard from [a]Dan.
The whole land trembled at
the sound of the neighing
of His [b]strong ones;
For they have come and
devoured the land and
all that is in it,
The city and those who
dwell in it."

17 "For behold, I will send
serpents among you,
Vipers which cannot be
[a]charmed,
And they shall bite you,"
says the LORD.

18 I would comfort myself in
sorrow;
My heart *is* faint in me.
19 Listen! The voice,
The cry of the daughter of
my people
From [a]a far country:
"*Is* not the LORD in Zion?
Is not her King in her?"

"Why have they provoked
Me to anger
With their carved images—
With foreign idols?"

20 "The harvest is past,
The summer is ended,
And we are not saved!"

21 [a]For the hurt of the daughter
of my people I am hurt.
I am [b]mourning;
Astonishment has taken
hold of me.
22 *Is there* no [a]balm in Gil'ē·ad,
Is there no physician there?
Why then is there no
recovery
For the health of the
daughter of my people?

9 Oh, [a]that my head were
waters,
And my eyes a fountain of
tears,
That I might weep day and
night
For the slain of the daughter
of my people!
2 Oh, that I had in the
wilderness
A lodging place for travelers;
That I might leave my
people,
And go from them!
For [a]they *are* all adulterers,
An assembly of treacherous
men.

3 "And *like* their bow [a]they
have bent their tongues
for lies.

13 [a]Joel 1:17 [b]Matt. 21:19 [c]Deut. 28:39, 40 [1]Or *take them away*
14 [a]Jer. 4:5 [b]Jer. 9:15 [1]Bitter or poisonous water
15 [a]Jer. 14:19
16 [a]Jer. 4:15 [b]Jer. 47:3
17 [a]Ps. 58:4, 5
19 [a]Is. 39:3
21 [a]Jer. 9:1 [b]Joel 2:6
22 [a]Jer. 46:11

CHAPTER 9

1 [a]Is. 22:4
2 [a]Jer. 5:7, 8; 23:10
3 [a]Ps. 64:3

They are not valiant for the
truth on the earth.
For they proceed from [b]evil
to evil,
And they [c]do not know Me,"
says the LORD.
4 "Everyone[a] take heed to his
[1]neighbor,
And do not trust any
brother;
For every brother will
utterly supplant,
And every neighbor will
[b]walk with slanderers.
5 Everyone will [a]deceive his
neighbor,
And will not speak the truth;
They have taught their
tongue to speak lies;
They weary themselves to
commit iniquity.
6 Your dwelling place *is* in the
midst of deceit;
Through deceit they refuse
to know Me," says the
LORD.

7 Therefore thus says the LORD
of hosts:

"Behold, [a]I will refine them
and [1]try them;
[b]For how shall I deal with the
daughter of My people?
8 Their tongue *is* an arrow
shot out;
It speaks [a]deceit;
One speaks [b]peaceably to
his neighbor with his
mouth,
But [1]in his heart he [2]lies in
wait.
9 [a]Shall I not punish them for
these *things?*" says the
LORD.
"Shall I not avenge Myself
on such a nation as
this?"

3 [b]Jer. 4:22; 13:23 [c]1 Sam. 2:12
4 [a]Mic. 7:5, 6 [b]Jer. 6:28 [1]*friend*
5 [a]Is. 59:4
7 [a]Is. 1:25 [b]Hos. 11:8 [1]*test*
8 [a]Ps. 12:2 [b]Ps. 55:21 [1]Inwardly he [2]*sets his ambush*
9 [a]Jer. 5:9, 29
10 [a]Hos. 4:3 [b]Jer. 4:25 [1]Or *pastures*
11 [a]Is. 25:2 [b]Is. 13:22; 34:13
12 [a]Hos. 14:9
13 [a]Jer. 3:25; 7:24
14 [a]Jer. 7:24; 11:8 [b]Gal. 1:14 [1]*stubbornness* or *imagination*
15 [a]Ps. 80:5 [b]Lam. 3:15 [1]Bitter or poisonous water
16 [a]Lev. 26:33

10 I will take up a weeping
and wailing for the
mountains,
And [a]for the [1]dwelling
places of the wilderness
a lamentation,
Because they are burned up,
So that no one can pass
through;
Nor can *men* hear the voice
of the cattle.
[b]Both the birds of the
heavens and the beasts
have fled;
They are gone.

11 "I will make Jerusalem [a]a
heap of ruins, [b]a den of
jackals.
I will make the cities of
Judah desolate, without
an inhabitant."

12 [a]Who *is* the wise man who
may understand this? And *who*
is he to whom the mouth of the
LORD has spoken, that he may declare it? Why does the land perish *and* burn up like a wilderness,
so that no one can pass through?
13 And the LORD said, "Because
they have forsaken My law
which I set before them, and
have [a]not obeyed My voice, nor
walked according to it,
14 "but they have [a]walked according to the [1]dictates of their
own hearts and after the Bā'-
als, [b]which their fathers taught
them,"
15 therefore thus says the LORD
of hosts, the God of Israel: "Behold, I will [a]feed them, this people, [b]with wormwood, and give
them [1]water of gall to drink.
16 "I will [a]scatter them also
among the Gentiles, whom neither they nor their fathers have

known. [b]And I will send a sword
after them until I have consumed
them."
17 Thus says the LORD of hosts:

"Consider and call for [a]the
mourning women,
That they may come;
And send for skillful *wailing*
women,
That they may come.
18 Let them make haste
And take up a wailing
for us,
That [a]our eyes may run with
tears,
And our eyelids gush with
water.
19 For a voice of wailing is
heard from Zion:
'How we are plundered!
We are greatly ashamed,
Because we have forsaken
the land,
Because we have been cast
out of [a]our dwellings.' "

20 Yet hear the word of the
LORD, O women,
And let your ear receive the
word of His mouth;
Teach your daughters
wailing,
And everyone her neighbor
a lamentation.
21 For death has come through
our windows,
Has entered our palaces,
To kill off [a]the children—
[1]*no longer to be* outside!
And the young men—[2]*no
longer* on the streets!
22 Speak, "Thus says the LORD:

'Even the carcasses of men
shall fall [a]as refuse on
the open field,

16 [b]Ezek. 5:2
17 [a]2 Chr. 35:25
18 [a]Jer. 9:1; 14:17
19 [a]Lev. 18:28
21 [a]Jer. 6:11; 18:21 [1]Lit. *from outside* [2]Lit. *from the square*
22 [a]Jer. 8:1, 2
23 [a][Eccl. 9:11] [b]Ps. 33:16–18
24 [a]1 Cor. 1:31 [b]Mic. 7:18 [1]*justice*
25 [a][Rom. 2:28, 29]
26 [a]Jer. 25:23 [b][Rom. 2:28]
CHAPTER 10
2 [a][Lev. 18:3; 20:23]

Like cuttings after the
harvester,
And no one shall gather
them.' "

23 Thus says the LORD:

[a]"Let not the wise *man* glory
in his wisdom,
Let not the mighty *man*
glory in his [b]might,
Nor let the rich *man* glory
in his riches;
24 But [a]let him who glories
glory in this,
That he understands and
knows Me,
That I *am* the LORD,
exercising
lovingkindness,
[1]judgment, and
righteousness in the
earth.
[b]For in these I delight," says
the LORD.

25 "Behold, the days are coming," says the LORD, "that [a]I will
punish all *who are* circumcised
with the uncircumcised—
26 "Egypt, Judah, Ē′dom, the
people of Am′mon, Mō′ab, and
all *who are* in the [a]farthest corners, who dwell in the wilderness. For all *these* nations *are*
uncircumcised, and all the house
of Israel *are* [b]uncircumcised in
the heart."

10

Hear the word which
the LORD speaks to you,
O house of Israel.
2 Thus says the LORD:

[a]"Do not learn the way of the
Gentiles;
Do not be dismayed at the
signs of heaven,

For the Gentiles are
dismayed at them.
3 For the customs of the
peoples *are* [1]futile;
For [a]*one* cuts a tree from the
forest,
The work of the hands of
the workman, with the
ax.
4 They decorate it with silver
and gold;
They [a]fasten it with nails
and hammers
So that it will not topple.
5 They *are* upright, like a
palm tree,
And [a]they cannot speak;
They must be [b]carried,
Because they cannot go *by
themselves.*
Do not be afraid of them,
For [c]they cannot do evil,
Nor can they do any good."

6 Inasmuch as *there is* none
[a]like You, O LORD
(You *are* great, and Your
name *is* great in might),
7 [a]Who would not fear You,
O King of the nations?
For this is Your rightful due.
For [b]among all the wise *men*
of the nations,
And in all their kingdoms,
There is none like You.
8 But they are altogether
[a]dull-hearted and foolish;
A wooden idol *is* a
[1]worthless doctrine.
9 Silver is beaten into plates;
It is brought from Tar'shish,
And [a]gold from Ū'phaz,
The work of the craftsman
And of the hands of the
metalsmith;
Blue and purple *are* their
clothing;
They *are* all [b]the work of
skillful *men.*
10 But the LORD *is* the true God;
He *is* [a]the living God and
the [b]everlasting King.
At His wrath the earth will
tremble,
And the nations will not
be able to endure His
indignation.

11 Thus you shall say to them:
[a]"The gods that have not made
the heavens and the earth [b]shall
perish from the earth and from
under these heavens."

12 He [a]has made the earth by
His power,
He has [b]established the
world by His wisdom,
And [c]has stretched out the
heavens at His discretion.
13 [a]When He utters His voice,
There is a [1]multitude of
waters in the heavens:
[b]"And He causes the vapors to
ascend from the ends of
the earth.
He makes lightning for the
rain,
He brings the wind out of
His treasuries."

14 [a]Everyone is [b]dull-hearted,
without knowledge;
[c]Every metalsmith is put to
shame by an image;
[d]For his molded image *is*
falsehood,
And *there is* no breath in
them.
15 They *are* futile, a work of
errors;
In the time of their
punishment they shall
perish.

---

3 [a]Is. 40:19; 45:20 [1]Lit. *vanity*
4 [a]Is. 41:7
5 [a]Ps. 115:5 [b]Ps. 115:7 [c]Is. 41:23, 24
6 [a]Ex. 15:11
7 [a]Rev. 15:4 [b]Ps. 89:6
8 [a]Hab. 2:18 [1]*vain teaching*
9 [a]Dan. 10:5 [b]Ps. 115:4
10 [a]1 Tim. 6:17 [b]Ps. 10:16
11 [a]Ps. 96:5 [b]Zeph. 2:11
12 [a]Jer. 51:15 [b]Ps. 93:1 [c]Job 9:8
13 [a]Job 38:34 [b]Ps. 135:7 [1]Or *noise*
14 [a]Jer. 51:17 [b]Prov. 30:2 [c]Is. 42:17; 44:11 [d]Hab. 2:18

16 [a]The Portion of Jacob *is* not
like them,
For He *is* the Maker of all
things,
And [b]Israel *is* the tribe of
His inheritance;
[c]The LORD of hosts *is* His
name.

17 [a]Gather up your wares from
the land,
O [1]inhabitant of the fortress!

18 For thus says the LORD:

"Behold, I will [a]throw out at
this time
The inhabitants of the land,
And will distress them,
[b]That they may find *it so.*"

19 [a]Woe is me for my hurt!
My wound is severe.
But I say, [b]"Truly this *is* an
infirmity,
And [c]I must bear it."
20 [a]My tent is plundered,
And all my cords are
broken;
My children have gone from
me,
And they *are* [b]no more.
There is no one to pitch my
tent anymore,
Or set up my curtains.

21 For the shepherds have
become dull-hearted,
And have not sought the
LORD;
Therefore they shall not
prosper,
And all their flocks shall be
[a]scattered.
22 Behold, the noise of the
report has come,
And a great commotion out
of the [a]north country,
To make the cities of Judah
desolate, a [b]den of
jackals.

23 O LORD, I know the [a]way of
man *is* not in himself;
It is not in man who walks
to direct his own steps.
24 O LORD, [a]correct me, but
with justice;
Not in Your anger, lest You
bring me to nothing.
25 [a]Pour out Your fury on the
Gentiles, [b]who do not
know You,
And on the families who do
not call on Your name;
For they have eaten up
Jacob,
[c]Devoured him and
consumed him,
And made his dwelling
place desolate.

11

The word that came to
Jer·e·mi′ah from the
LORD, saying,
2 "Hear the words of this covenant, and speak to the men of
Judah and to the inhabitants of
Jerusalem;
3 "and say to them, 'Thus says
the LORD God of Israel: [a]"Cursed
is the man who does not obey
the words of this covenant
4 "which I commanded your
fathers in the day I brought
them out of the land of Egypt,
[a]from the iron furnace, saying,
[b]'Obey My voice, and do according to all that I command you;
so shall you be My people, and I
will be your God,'
5 "that I may establish the
[a]oath which I have sworn to your
fathers, to give them [b]'a land
flowing with milk and honey,' as

---

16 [a]Lam. 3:24 [b]Deut. 32:9 [c]Is. 47:4
17 [a]Jer. 6:1 [1]Or *you who dwell under siege*
18 [a]1 Sam. 25:29 [b]Ezek. 6:10
19 [a]Jer. 8:21 [b]Ps. 77:10 [c]Mic. 7:9
20 [a]Jer. 4:20 [b]Jer. 31:15
21 [a]Jer. 23:2
22 [a]Jer. 5:15 [b]Jer. 9:11
23 [a]Prov. 16:1; 20:24
24 [a]Jer. 30:11
25 [a]Ps. 79:6, 7 [b]Job 18:21 [c]Jer. 8:16

CHAPTER 11

3 [a]Deut. 27:26
4 [a]Deut. 4:20 [b]Lev. 26:3
5 [a]Ps. 105:9 [b]Ex. 3:8

it is this day.’ ’ ” And I answered
and said, [1]“So be it, LORD.”
6 Then the LORD said to me,
“Proclaim all these words in the
cities of Judah and in the streets
of Jerusalem, saying: ‘Hear the
words of this covenant [a]and do
them.
7 ‘For I earnestly exhorted
your fathers in the day I brought
them up out of the land of Egypt,
until this day, [a]rising early and
exhorting, saying, “Obey My
voice.”
8 [a]‘Yet they did not obey or
incline their ear, but [b]everyone
[1]followed the dictates of his
evil heart; therefore I will bring
upon them all the words of this
covenant, which I commanded
them to do, but *which* they have
not done.’ ”
9 And the LORD said to me,
[a]“A conspiracy has been found
among the men of Judah and
among the inhabitants of
Jerusalem.
10 “They have turned back
to [a]the iniquities of their forefathers who refused to hear My
words, and they have gone after
other gods to serve them; the
house of Israel and the house
of Judah have broken My covenant which I made with their
fathers.”
11 Therefore thus says the
LORD: “Behold, I will surely
bring calamity on them which
they will not be able to [1]escape;
and [a]though they cry out to Me,
I will not listen to them.
12 “Then the cities of Judah and
the inhabitants of Jerusalem
will go and [a]cry out to the gods
to whom they offer incense, but
they will not save them at all in
the time of their trouble.
13 “For *according to* the number of your [a]cities were your
gods, O Judah; and *according
to* the number of the streets of
Jerusalem you have set up altars
to *that* shameful thing, altars to
burn incense to Bā′al.
14 “So [a]do not pray for this people, or lift up a cry or prayer for
them; for I will not hear *them* in
the time that they cry out to Me
because of their trouble.

15 “What[a] has My beloved to do
in My house,
Having [b]done lewd deeds
with many?
And [c]the holy flesh has
passed from you.
When you do evil, then you
[d]rejoice.
16 The LORD called your name,
[a]Green Olive Tree, Lovely
and of Good Fruit.
With the noise of a great
tumult
He has kindled fire on it,
And its branches are
broken.

17 “For the LORD of hosts, [a]who
planted you, has pronounced
doom against you for the evil
of the house of Israel and of
the house of Judah, which they
have done against themselves to
provoke Me to anger in offering
incense to Bā′al.”
18 Now the LORD gave me
knowledge *of it*, and I know *it*;
for You showed me their doings.
19 But I *was* like a docile lamb
brought to the slaughter; and I
did not know that they had devised schemes against me, *saying*, “Let us destroy the tree with
its fruit, [a]and let us cut him off
from [b]the land of the living, that

5 [1]Heb. *Amen*
6 [a][Rom. 2:13]
7 [a]Jer. 35:15
8 [a]Jer. 7:26 [b]Jer. 13:10 [1]*walked in the stubbornness* or *imagination*
9 [a]Ezek. 22:25
10 [a]Ezek. 20:18
11 [a]Prov. 1:28 [1]Lit. *go out*
12 [a]Deut. 32:37
13 [a]Jer. 2:28
14 [a]Ex. 32:10
15 [a]Ps. 50:16 [b]Ezek. 16:25 [c][Titus 1:15] [d]Prov. 2:14
16 [a]Ps. 52:8
17 [a]Is. 5:2
19 [a]Ps. 83:4 [b]Ps. 27:13

his name may be remembered
no more."

20 But, O LORD of hosts,
You who judge righteously,
[a]Testing the [1]mind and the heart,
Let me see Your [b]vengeance on them,
For to You I have revealed my cause.

21 "Therefore thus says the
LORD concerning the men of
[a]An'a·thoth who seek your life,
saying, [b]'Do not prophesy in the
name of the LORD, lest you die by
our hand'—
22 "therefore thus says the LORD
of hosts: 'Behold, I will punish them. The young men shall
die by the sword, their sons
and their daughters shall [a]die by
famine;
23 'and there shall be no remnant of them, for I will bring
catastrophe on the men of An'-
a·thoth, *even* [a]the year of their
punishment.' "

CHAPTER 12

12 Righteous [a]*are* You,
O LORD, when I plead with You;
Yet let me talk with You about *Your* judgments.
[b]Why does the way of the wicked prosper?
Why are those happy who deal so treacherously?
2 You have planted them, yes, they have taken root;
They grow, yes, they bear fruit.
[a]You *are* near in their mouth
But far from their [1]mind.
3 But You, O LORD, [a]know me;
You have seen me,
And You have [b]tested my heart toward You.
Pull them out like sheep for the slaughter,
And prepare them for [c]the day of slaughter.
4 How long will [a]the land mourn,
And the herbs of every field wither?
[b]The beasts and birds are consumed,
[c]For the wickedness of those who dwell there,
Because they said, "He will not see our final end."

5 "If you have run with the footmen, and they have wearied you,
Then how can you contend with horses?
And *if* in the land of peace,
In which you trusted, *they* wearied you,
Then how will you do in [a]the [1]floodplain of the Jordan?
6 For even [a]your brothers, the house of your father,
Even they have dealt treacherously with you;
Yes, they have called [1]a multitude after you.
[b]Do not believe them,
Even though they speak [2]smooth words to you.

7 "I have forsaken My house, I have left My heritage;
I have given the dearly beloved of My soul into the hand of her enemies.
8 My heritage is to Me like a lion in the forest;
It cries out against Me;
Therefore I have [a]hated it.

20 [a]Ps. 7:9 [b]Jer. 15:15 [1]Most secret parts, lit. *kidneys*
21 [a]Jer. 1:1; 12:5, 6 [b]Mic. 2:6
22 [a]Jer. 9:21
23 [a]Jer. 23:12

1 [a]Ps. 51:14 [b]Mal. 3:15
2 [a]Matt. 15:8 [1]Most secret parts, lit. *kidneys*
3 [a]Ps. 17:3 [b]Jer. 11:20 [c]James 5:5
4 [a]Hos. 4:3 [b]Jer. 9:10 [c]Ps. 107:34
5 [a]Josh. 3:15 [1]Or *thicket*
6 [a]Jer. 9:4, 5 [b]Prov. 26:25 [1]Or *abundantly* [2]Lit. *good*
8 [a]Hos. 9:15

9 My [1]heritage *is* to Me *like* a
speckled vulture;
The vultures all around *are*
against her.
Come, assemble all the
beasts of the field,
[a]Bring them to devour!

10 "Many [a]rulers[1] have
destroyed [b]My vineyard,
They have [c]trodden My
portion underfoot;
They have made My
[2]pleasant portion a
desolate wilderness.
11 They have made it [a]desolate;
Desolate, it mourns to Me;
The whole land is made
desolate,
Because [b]no one takes *it* to
heart.
12 The plunderers have come
On all the desolate heights
in the wilderness,
For the sword of the LORD
shall devour
From *one* end of the land
to the *other* end of the
land;
No flesh shall have peace.
13 [a]They have sown wheat but
reaped thorns;
They have [1]put themselves
to pain *but* do not profit.
But be ashamed of your
harvest
Because of the fierce anger
of the LORD."

14 Thus says the LORD: "Against
all My evil neighbors who [a]touch
the inheritance which I have
caused My people Israel to inherit—behold, I will [b]pluck them
out of their land and pluck out
the house of Judah from among
them.
15 [a]"Then it shall be, after I have
plucked them out, that I will
return and have compassion on
them [b]and bring them back, everyone to his heritage and everyone to his land.
16 "And it shall be, if they will
learn carefully the ways of My
people, [a]to swear by My name,
'As the LORD lives,' as they taught
My people to swear by Bā'al,
then they shall be [b]established
in the midst of My people.
17 "But if they do not [a]obey, I
will utterly pluck up and destroy
that nation," says the LORD.

13 Thus the LORD said to
me: "Go and get yourself
a linen sash, and put it [1]around
your waist, but do not put it in
water."
2 So I got a [1]sash according to
the word of the LORD, and put *it*
around my waist.
3 And the word of the LORD
came to me the second time,
saying,
4 "Take the [1]sash that you acquired, which *is* [2]around your
waist, and arise, go to the
[3]Eū·phrā'tēs, and hide it there in
a hole in the rock."
5 So I went and hid it by the
Eū·phrā'tēs, as the LORD commanded me.
6 Now it came to pass after
many days that the LORD said to
me, "Arise, go to the Eū·phrā'tēs,
and take from there the sash
which I commanded you to hide
there."
7 Then I went to the Eū·phrā'-
tēs and dug, and I took the
[1]sash from the place where I
had hidden it; and there was the
sash, ruined. It was profitable
for nothing.
8 Then the word of the LORD
came to me, saying,

9 [a]Lev. 26:22 [1]*inheritance*
10 [a]Jer. 6:3; 23:1 [b]Is. 5:1–7 [c]Is. 63:18 [1]Lit. *shepherds* or *pastors* [2]*desired portion* of land
11 [a]Jer. 10:22; 22:6 [b]Is. 42:25
13 [a]Hag. 1:6 [1]Or *strained*
14 [a]Zech. 2:8 [b]Deut. 30:3
15 [a]Ezek. 28:25 [b]Amos 9:14
16 [a][Jer. 4:2] [b][1 Pet. 2:5]
17 [a]Is. 60:12

CHAPTER 13

1 [1]Lit. *upon your loins*
2 [1]*waistband*
4 [1]*waistband* [2]Lit. *upon your loins* [3]Heb. *Perath*
7 [1]*waistband*

9 "Thus says the LORD: 'In this manner [a]I will ruin the pride of Judah and the great [b]pride of Jerusalem.

10 'This evil people, who [a]refuse to hear My words, who [b]follow[1] the dictates of their hearts, and walk after other gods to serve them and worship them, shall be just like this sash which is profitable for nothing.

11 'For as the sash clings to the waist of a man, so I have caused the whole house of Israel and the whole house of Judah to cling to Me,' says the LORD, 'that [a]they may become My people, [b]for renown, for praise, and for [c]glory; but they would [d]not hear.'

12 "Therefore you shall speak to them this word: 'Thus says the LORD God of Israel: "Every bottle shall be filled with wine." ' And they will say to you, 'Do we not certainly know that every bottle will be filled with wine?'

13 "Then you shall say to them, 'Thus says the LORD: "Behold, I will fill all the inhabitants of this land—even the kings who sit on David's throne, the priests, the prophets, and all the inhabitants of Jerusalem—[a]with drunkenness!

14 "And [a]I will dash them [1]one against another, even the fathers and the sons together," says the LORD. "I will not pity nor spare nor have mercy, but will destroy them." ' "

15 Hear and give ear:
Do not be proud,
For the LORD has spoken.
16 [a]Give glory to the LORD your
God
Before He causes [b]darkness,
And before your feet
stumble
On the dark mountains,
And while you are [c]looking
for light,
He turns it into [d]the shadow
of death
And makes *it* dense
darkness.
17 But if you will not hear it,
My soul will [a]weep in secret
for *your* pride;
My eyes will weep bitterly
And run down with tears,
Because the LORD's flock
has been taken captive.

18 Say to [a]the king and to the
queen mother,
"Humble yourselves;
Sit down,
For your rule shall collapse,
the crown of your glory."
19 The cities of the South shall
be shut up,
And no one shall open
them;
Judah shall be carried away
captive, all of it;
It shall be wholly carried
away captive.

20 Lift up your eyes and see
Those who come from the
[a]north.
Where *is* the flock *that* was
given to you,
Your beautiful sheep?
21 What will you say when He
punishes you?
For you have taught them
To be chieftains, to be head
over you.
Will not [a]pangs seize you,
Like a woman in [1]labor?
22 And if you say in your heart,
[a]"Why have these things come
upon me?"

9 [a]Lev. 26:19 [b]Zeph. 3:11
10 [a]Jer. 16:12 [b]Jer. 7:24; 16:12 [1]*walk in the stubbornness* or *imagination*
11 [a][Ex. 19:5, 6] [b]Jer. 33:9 [c]Is. 43:21 [d]Jer. 7:13, 24, 26
13 [a]Is. 51:17; 63:6
14 [a]Jer. 19:9–11 [1]Lit. *a man against his brother*
16 [a]Josh. 7:19 [b]Amos 8:9 [c]Is. 59:9 [d]Ps. 44:19
17 [a]Jer. 9:1; 14:17
18 [a]Jer. 22:26
20 [a]Jer. 10:22; 46:20
21 [a]Jer. 6:24 [1]*childbirth*
22 [a]Jer. 16:10

For the greatness of your iniquity
[b]Your skirts have been uncovered,
Your heels [1]made bare.
23 Can the Ethiopian change his skin or the leopard its spots?
Then may you also do good who are accustomed to do evil.

24 "Therefore I will [a]scatter them [b]like stubble
That passes away by the wind of the wilderness.
25 [a]This is your lot,
The portion of your measures from Me," says the LORD,
"Because you have forgotten Me
And trusted in [b]falsehood.
26 Therefore [a]I will uncover your skirts over your face,
That your shame may appear.
27 I have seen your adulteries
And your *lustful* [a]neighings,
The lewdness of your harlotry,
Your abominations [b]on the hills in the fields.
Woe to you, O Jerusalem!
Will you still not be made clean?"

14

The word of the LORD that came to Jer·e·mī'ah concerning the droughts.

2 "Judah mourns,
And [a]her gates languish;
They [b]mourn for the land,
And [c]the cry of Jerusalem has gone up.
3 Their nobles have sent their lads for water;
They went to the cisterns *and* found no water.
They returned with their vessels empty;
They were [a]ashamed and confounded
[b]And covered their heads.
4 Because the ground is parched,
For there was [a]no rain in the land,
The plowmen were ashamed;
They covered their heads.
5 Yes, the deer also gave birth in the field,
But [1]left because there was no grass.
6 And [a]the wild donkeys stood in the desolate heights;
They sniffed at the wind like jackals;
Their eyes failed because *there was* no grass."

7 O LORD, though our iniquities testify against us,
Do it [a]for Your name's sake;
For our backslidings are many,
We have sinned against You.
8 [a]O the Hope of Israel, his Savior in time of trouble,
Why should You be like a stranger in the land,
And like a traveler *who* turns aside to tarry for a night?
9 Why should You be like a man astonished,
Like a mighty one [a]*who* cannot save?
Yet You, O LORD, [b]*are* in our midst,

22 [b]Is. 47:2 [1]Lit. *suffer violence*
24 [a]Jer. 9:16 [b]Hos. 13:3
25 [a]Job 20:29 [b]Jer. 10:14
26 [a]Lam. 1:8
27 [a]Jer. 5:7, 8 [b]Is. 65:7; Ezek. 6:13

CHAPTER 14

2 [a]Is. 3:26 [b]Jer. 8:21 [c]1 Sam. 5:12
3 [a]Ps. 40:14 [b]2 Sam. 15:30
4 [a]Jer. 3:3
5 [1]*abandoned* her young
6 [a]Jer. 2:24
7 [a]Ps. 25:11
8 [a]Jer. 17:13
9 [a]Is. 59:1 [b]Ex. 29:45

And we are called by Your
name;
Do not leave us!

10 Thus says the LORD to this
people:

[a]"Thus they have loved to
wander;
They have not restrained
their feet.
Therefore the LORD does not
accept them;
[b]He will remember their
iniquity now,
And punish their sins."

11 Then the LORD said to me,
[a]"Do not pray for this people, for
their good.
12 [a]"When they fast, I will not
hear their cry; and [b]when they
offer burnt offering and grain
offering, I will not accept them.
But [c]I will consume them by the
sword, by the famine, and by the
pestilence."
13 [a]Then I said, "Ah, Lord GOD!
Behold, the prophets say to them,
'You shall not see the sword, nor
shall you have famine, but I will
give you [1]assured [b]peace in this
place.' "
14 And the LORD said to me,
[a]"The prophets prophesy lies in
My name. [b]I have not sent them,
commanded them, nor spoken
to them; they prophesy to you
a false vision, [1]divination, a
worthless thing, and the [c]deceit
of their heart.
15 "Therefore thus says the
LORD concerning the prophets who prophesy in My name,
whom I did not send, [a]and who
say, 'Sword and famine shall not
be in this land'—'By sword and
famine those prophets shall be
consumed!
16 'And the people to whom they
prophesy shall be cast out in the
streets of Jerusalem because of
the famine and the sword; [a]they
will have no one to bury them—
them nor their wives, their sons
nor their daughters—for I will
pour their wickedness on them.'
17 "Therefore you shall say this
word to them:

[a]'Let my eyes flow with tears
night and day,
And let them not cease;
[b]For the virgin daughter of
my people
Has been broken with a
mighty stroke, with a
very severe blow.
18 If I go out to [a]the field,
Then behold, those slain
with the sword!
And if I enter the city,
Then behold, those sick
from famine!
Yes, both prophet and
[b]priest go about in a land
they do not know.' "

19 [a]Have You utterly rejected
Judah?
Has Your soul loathed Zion?
Why have You stricken us so
that [b]*there is* no healing
for us?
[c]We looked for peace, but
there was no good;
And for the time of healing,
and there was trouble.
20 We acknowledge, O LORD,
our wickedness
And the iniquity of our
[a]fathers,
For [b]we have sinned against
You.

10 [a]Jer. 2:23–25 [b]Hos. 8:13
11 [a]Ex. 32:10
12 [a]Ezek. 8:18 [b]Jer. 6:20 [c]Jer. 9:16
13 [a]Jer. 4:10 [b]Jer. 8:11; 23:17 [1]*true*
14 [a]Jer. 27:10 [b]Jer. 29:8, 9 [c]Jer. 23:16 [1]Telling the future by signs and omens
15 [a]Ezek. 14:10
16 [a]Ps. 79:2, 3
17 [a]Jer. 9:1; 13:17 [b]Jer. 8:21
18 [a]Ezek. 7:15 [b]Jer. 23:11
19 [a]Lam. 5:22 [b]Jer. 15:18 [c]Jer. 8:15
20 [a]Jer. 3:25 [b]Dan. 9:8

21 Do not abhor *us*, for Your
name's sake;
Do not disgrace the throne
of Your glory.
[a]Remember, do not break
Your covenant with us.
22 [a]Are there any among [b]the
idols of the nations that
can cause [c]rain?
Or can the heavens give
showers?
[d]*Are* You not He, O LORD our
God?
Therefore we will wait for
You,
Since You have made all
these.

15

Then the LORD said to
me, [a]"*Even* if [b]Moses and
[c]Samuel stood before Me, My
[1]mind *would* not *be* favorable
toward this people. Cast *them*
out of My sight, and let them go
forth.
2 "And it shall be, if they say to
you, 'Where should we go?' then
you shall tell them, 'Thus says
the LORD:

[a]"Such as *are* for death, to
death;
And such as *are* for the
sword, to the sword;
And such as *are* for the
famine, to the famine;
And such as *are* for
the [b]captivity, to the
captivity." '

3 "And I will [a]appoint over
them four forms *of destruction*,"
says the LORD: "the sword to
slay, the dogs to drag, [b]the birds
of the heavens and the beasts of
the earth to devour and destroy.
4 "I will hand them over to
[a]trouble, to all kingdoms of the
earth, because of [b]Ma·nas'seh
the son of Hez·e·kī'ah, king
of Judah, for what he did in
Jerusalem.

5 "For who will have pity on
you, O Jerusalem?
Or who will bemoan you?
Or who will turn aside to
ask how you are doing?
6 [a]You have forsaken Me," says
the LORD,
"You have [b]gone backward.
Therefore I will stretch out
My hand against you
and destroy you;
[c]I am [1]weary of relenting!
7 And I will winnow them
with a winnowing fan in
the gates of the land;
I will [a]bereave *them* of
children;
I will destroy My people,
Since they [b]do not return
from their ways.
8 Their widows will be
increased to Me more
than the sand of the
seas;
I will bring against them,
Against the mother of the
young men,
A plunderer at noonday;
I will cause anguish and
terror to fall on them
[a]suddenly.
9 "She[a] languishes who has
borne seven;
She has breathed her last;
[b]Her sun has gone down
While *it was* yet day;
She has been ashamed and
confounded.
And the remnant of them I
will deliver to the sword
Before their enemies," says
the LORD.

21 [a]Ps. 106:45
22 [a]Zech. 10:1 [b]Deut. 32:21 [c]Jer. 5:24 [d]Ps. 135:7

CHAPTER 15

1 [a]Ezek. 14:14 [b]Ex. 32:11–14 [c]1 Sam. 7:9 [1]Lit. *soul was not toward*
2 [a]Zech. 11:9 [b]Jer. 9:16; 16:13
3 [a]Ezek. 14:21 [b]Jer. 7:33
4 [a]Deut. 28:25 [b]2 Kin. 24:3, 4
6 [a]Jer. 2:13 [b]Jer. 7:24 [c]Jer. 20:16 [1]*tired*
7 [a]Jer. 18:21 [b]Is. 9:13
8 [a]Is. 29:5
9 [a]1 Sam. 2:5 [b]Amos 8:9

10 [a]Woe is me, my mother,
That you have borne me,
A man of strife and a man of contention to the whole [1]earth!
I have neither lent for interest,
Nor have men lent to me for interest.
Every one of them curses me.

11 The LORD said:

"Surely it will be well with your remnant;
Surely I will cause [a]the enemy to intercede with you
In the time of adversity and in the time of affliction.
12 Can anyone break iron,
The northern iron and the bronze?
13 Your wealth and your treasures
I will give as [a]plunder without price,
Because of all your sins,
Throughout your territories.
14 And I will [1]make *you* cross over with your enemies
[a]Into a land *which* you do not know;
For a [b]fire is kindled in My anger,
Which shall burn upon you."

15 O LORD, [a]You know;
Remember me and [1]visit me,
And [b]take vengeance for me on my persecutors.
In Your enduring patience, do not take me away.
Know that [c]for Your sake I have suffered rebuke.
16 Your words were found, and I [a]ate them,
And [b]Your word was to me the joy and rejoicing of my heart;
For I am called by Your name,
O LORD God of hosts.
17 [a]I did not sit in the assembly of the mockers,
Nor did I rejoice;
I sat alone because of Your hand,
For You have filled me with indignation.
18 Why is my [a]pain perpetual
And my wound incurable,
Which refuses to be healed?
Will You surely be to me [b]like an unreliable stream,
As waters *that* [1]fail?

19 Therefore thus says the LORD:

[a]"If you return,
Then I will bring you back;
You shall [b]stand before Me;
If you [c]take out the precious from the vile,
You shall be as My mouth.
Let them return to you,
But you must not return to them.
20 And I will make you to this people a fortified bronze [a]wall;
And they will fight against you,
But [b]they shall not prevail against you;
For I *am* with you to save you
And deliver you," says the LORD.
21 "I will deliver you from the hand of the wicked,
And I will redeem you from the grip of the terrible."

10 [a]Job 3:1 [1]Or *land*
11 [a]Jer. 40:4, 5
13 [a]Ps. 44:12
14 [a]Jer. 16:13 [b]Deut. 32:22 [1]So with MT, Vg.; LXX, Syr., Tg. *cause you to serve* (cf. 17:4)
15 [a]Jer. 12:3 [b]Jer. 20:12 [c]Ps. 69:7–9 [1]*attend to*
16 [a]Ezek. 3:1, 3 [b][Job 23:12]
17 [a]Ps. 26:4, 5
18 [a]Jer. 10:19; 30:15 [b]Job 6:15 [1]Or *cannot be trusted*
19 [a]Zech. 3:7 [b]Jer. 15:1 [c]Ezek. 22:26; 44:23
20 [a]Ezek. 3:9 [b]Jer. 1:8, 19; 20:11; 37:21; 38:13; 39:11, 12

16
The word of the LORD also
came to me, saying,
2 "You shall not take a wife,
nor shall you have sons or
daughters in this place."
3 For thus says the LORD concerning the sons and daughters
who are born in this place, and
concerning their mothers who
bore them and their fathers who
begot them in this land:
4 "They shall die [a]gruesome
deaths; they shall not be
[b]lamented nor shall they be
[c]buried, *but* they shall be [d]like
refuse on the face of the earth.
They shall be consumed by
the sword and by famine, and
their [e]corpses shall be meat for
the birds of heaven and for the
beasts of the earth."
5 For thus says the LORD: [a]"Do
not enter the house of mourning, nor go to lament or bemoan
them; for I have taken away My
peace from this people," says
the LORD, "lovingkindness and
mercies.
6 "Both the great and the small
shall die in this land. They shall
not be buried; [a]neither shall men
lament for them, [b]cut themselves,
nor [c]make themselves bald for
them.
7 "Nor shall *men* break *bread*
in mourning for them, to comfort them for the dead; nor shall
men give them the cup of consolation to [a]drink for their father
or their mother.
8 "Also you shall not go into
the house of feasting to sit with
them, to eat and drink."
9 For thus says the LORD of
hosts, the God of Israel: "Behold,
[a]I will cause to cease from this
place, before your eyes and in
your days, the voice of [1]mirth

CHAPTER 16

4 [a]Jer. 15:2
[b]Jer. 22:18; 25:33
[c]Jer. 14:16; 19:11
[d]Ps. 83:10
[e]Ps. 79:2

5 [a]Ezek. 24:17, 22, 23

6 [a]Jer. 22:18
[b]Deut. 14:1
[c]Is. 22:12

7 [a]Prov. 31:6

9 [a]Rev. 18:23
[1]*rejoicing*

10 [a]Deut. 29:24

11 [a]Jer. 22:9

12 [a]Jer. 7:26
[b]Jer. 3:17; 18:12
[1]*walks after the stubbornness* or *imagination*

13 [a]Deut. 4:26; 28:36, 63
[b]Jer. 15:14

14 [a]Jer. 23:7, 8

15 [a]Jer. 3:18
[b]Jer. 24:6; 30:3; 32:37

16 [a]Amos 4:2

and the voice of gladness, the
voice of the bridegroom and the
voice of the bride.
10 "And it shall be, when you
show this people all these words,
and they say to you, [a]'Why has
the LORD pronounced all this
great disaster against us? Or
what *is* our iniquity? Or what *is*
our sin that we have committed
against the LORD our God?'
11 "then you shall say to them,
[a]'Because your fathers have forsaken Me,' says the LORD; 'they
have walked after other gods
and have served them and worshiped them, and have forsaken
Me and not kept My law.
12 'And you have done [a]worse
than your fathers, for behold,
[b]each one [1]follows the dictates
of his own evil heart, so that no
one listens to Me.
13 [a]'Therefore I will cast you
out of this land [b]into a land that
you do not know, neither you
nor your fathers; and there you
shall serve other gods day and
night, where I will not show you
favor.'
14 "Therefore behold, the [a]days
are coming," says the LORD, "that
it shall no more be said, 'The
LORD lives who brought up the
children of Israel from the land
of Egypt,'
15 "but, 'The LORD lives who
brought up the children of Israel
from the land of the [a]north and
from all the lands where He had
driven them.' For [b]I will bring
them back into their land which
I gave to their fathers.
16 "Behold, I will send for many
[a]fishermen," says the LORD, "and
they shall fish them; and afterward I will send for many hunt-
ers, and they shall hunt them

from every mountain and every
hill, and out of the holes of the
rocks.
17 "For My [a]eyes *are* on all their
ways; they are not hidden from
My face, nor is their iniquity
hidden from My eyes.
18 "And first I will repay [a]double
for their iniquity and their sin,
because [b]they have defiled My
land; they have filled My inheritance with the carcasses of
their detestable and abominable
idols."

19 O LORD, [a]my strength and
my fortress,
[b]My refuge in the day of
affliction,
The Gentiles shall come to
You
From the ends of the earth
and say,
"Surely our fathers have
inherited lies,
Worthlessness and
[c]unprofitable *things*."
20 Will a man make gods for
himself,
[a]Which *are* not gods?

21 "Therefore behold, I will
this once cause them to
know,
I will cause them to know
My hand and My might;
And they shall know that
[a]My name *is* the LORD.

17 "The sin of Judah *is*
[a]written with a [b]pen of
iron;
With the point of a diamond
it is [c]engraved
On the tablet of their heart,
And on the horns of your
altars,
2 While their children
remember
Their altars and their
[a]wooden[1] images
By the green trees on the
high hills.
3 O My mountain in the field,
I will give as plunder
your wealth, all your
treasures,
And your high places of sin
within all your borders.
4 And you, even yourself,
Shall let go of your heritage
which I gave you;
And I will cause you to
serve your enemies
In [a]the land which you do
not know;
For [b]you have kindled a fire
in My anger *which* shall
burn forever."

5 Thus says the LORD:

[a]"Cursed *is* the man who
trusts in man
And makes [b]flesh his
[1]strength,
Whose heart departs from
the LORD.
6 For he shall be [a]like a shrub
in the desert,
And [b]shall not see when
good comes,
But shall inhabit the
parched places in the
wilderness,
[c]*In* a salt land *which is* not
inhabited.

7 "Blessed[a] *is* the man who
trusts in the LORD,
And whose hope is the
LORD.
8 For he shall be [a]like a tree
planted by the waters,

17 [a]Heb. 4:13
18 [a]Jer. 17:18 [b][Ezek. 43:7]
19 [a]Ps. 18:1, 2 [b]Jer. 17:17 [c]Is. 44:10
20 [a]Gal. 4:8
21 [a]Amos 5:8

CHAPTER 17

1 [a]Jer. 2:22 [b]Job 19:24 [c]2 Cor. 3:3
2 [a]Judg. 3:7 [1]Heb. *Asherim*, Canaanite deities
4 [a]Jer. 16:13 [b]Jer. 15:14
5 [a]Is. 30:1, 2; 31:1 [b]Is. 31:3 [1]Lit. *arm*
6 [a]Jer. 48:6 [b]Job 20:17 [c]Deut. 29:23
7 [a][Is. 30:18]
8 [a][Ps. 1:3]

Which spreads out its roots
by the river,
And will not [1]fear when
heat comes;
But its leaf will be green,
And will not be anxious in
the year of drought,
Nor will cease from yielding
fruit.

9 "The [a]heart *is* deceitful above
all *things*,
And [1]desperately wicked;
Who can know it?
10 I, the LORD, [a]search the
heart,
I test the [1]mind,
[b]Even to give every man
according to his ways,
According to the fruit of his
doings.

11 "*As* a partridge that [1]broods
but does not hatch,
So is he who gets riches, but
not by right;
It [a]will leave him in the
midst of his days,
And at his end he will be [b]a
fool."

12 A glorious high throne from
the beginning
Is the place of our sanctuary.
13 O LORD, [a]the hope of Israel,
[b]All who forsake You shall be
ashamed.

"Those who depart from Me
Shall be [c]written in the
earth,
Because they have forsaken
the LORD,
The [d]fountain of living
waters."

14 Heal me, O LORD, and I shall
be healed;
Save me, and I shall be
saved,
For [a]You *are* my praise.
15 Indeed they say to me,
[a]"Where *is* the word of the
LORD?
Let it come now!"
16 As for me, [a]I have not
hurried away from *being*
a shepherd *who* follows
You,
Nor have I desired the
woeful day;
You know what came out of
my lips;
It was right there before
You.
17 Do not be a terror to me;
[a]You *are* my hope in the day
of doom.
18 [a]Let them be ashamed who
persecute me,
But [b]do not let me be put to
shame;
Let them be dismayed,
But do not let me be
dismayed.
Bring on them the day of
doom,
And [c]destroy[1] them with
double destruction!

19 Thus the LORD said to me:
"Go and stand in the gate of the
children of the people, by which
the kings of Judah come in and
by which they go out, and in all
the gates of Jerusalem;
20 "and say to them, [a]'Hear the
word of the LORD, you kings of
Judah, and all Judah, and all the
inhabitants of Jerusalem, who
enter by these gates.
21 'Thus says the LORD: [a]"Take
heed to yourselves, and bear no
burden on the Sabbath day, nor
bring *it* in by the gates of Jerusalem;

8 [1]Qr., Tg. *see*
9 [a][Eccl. 9:3] [1]Or *incurably sick*
10 [a]Rev. 2:23 [b]Rom. 2:6 [1]Most secret parts, lit. *kidneys*
11 [a]Ps. 55:23 [b]Luke 12:20 [1]Sits on eggs
13 [a]Jer. 14:8 [b][Is. 1:28] [c]Luke 10:20 [d]Jer. 2:13
14 [a]Deut. 10:21
15 [a]Is. 5:19
16 [a]Jer. 1:4–12
17 [a]Jer. 16:19
18 [a]Ps. 35:4; 70:2 [b]Ps. 25:2 [c]Jer. 11:20 [1]Lit. *crush*
20 [a]Jer. 19:3, 4
21 [a]Neh. 13:19

22 "nor carry a burden out of
your houses on the Sabbath day,
nor do any work, but hallow the
Sabbath day, as I [a]commanded
your fathers.
23 [a]"But they did not obey nor
incline their ear, but [1]made their
neck stiff, that they might not
hear nor receive instruction.
24 "And it shall be, [a]if you heed
Me carefully," says the LORD, "to
bring no burden through the
gates of this city on the [b]Sabbath
day, but hallow the Sabbath day,
to do no work in it,
25 [a]"then shall enter the gates
of this city kings and princes
sitting on the throne of David,
riding in chariots and on horses,
they and their princes, accompanied by the men of Judah
and the inhabitants of Jerusalem; and this city shall remain
forever.
26 "And they shall come from
the cities of Judah and from
[a]the places around Jerusalem,
from the land of Benjamin and
from [b]the [1]lowland, from the
mountains and from [c]the [2]South,
bringing burnt offerings and
sacrifices, grain offerings and
incense, bringing [d]sacrifices of
praise to the house of the LORD.
27 "But if you will not heed Me
to hallow the Sabbath day, such
as not carrying a burden when
entering the gates of Jerusalem
on the Sabbath day, then [a]I will
kindle a fire in its gates, [b]and
it shall devour the palaces of
Jerusalem, and it shall not be
[c]quenched." ' "

18 The word which came
to Jer·e·mi'ah from the
LORD, saying:
2 "Arise and go down to the
potter's house, and there I will
cause you to hear My words."
3 Then I went down to the
potter's house, and there he
was, making something at the
[1]wheel.
4 And the vessel that he [1]made
of clay was [2]marred in the hand
of the potter; so he made it again
into another vessel, as it seemed
good to the potter to make.
5 Then the word of the LORD
came to me, saying:
6 "O house of Israel, [a]can I not
do with you as this potter?" says
the LORD. "Look, [b]as the clay *is*
in the potter's hand, so *are* you
in My hand, O house of Israel!
7 "The instant I speak concerning a nation and concerning
a kingdom, to [a]pluck up, to pull
down, and to destroy *it*,
8 [a]"if that nation against whom
I have spoken turns from its evil,
[b]I will relent of the disaster that I
thought to bring upon it.
9 "And the instant I speak concerning a nation and concerning
a kingdom, to build and to plant
it,
10 "if it does evil in My sight so
that it does not obey My voice,
then I will relent concerning the
good with which I said I would
benefit it.
11 "Now therefore, speak to the
men of Judah and to the inhabitants of Jerusalem, saying, 'Thus
says the LORD: "Behold, I am
fashioning a disaster and devising a plan against you. [a]Return
now every one from his evil way,
and make your ways and your
doings [b]good." ' "
12 And they said, [a]"That is hope-
less! So we will walk according
to our own plans, and we will

22 [a]Ex. 20:8; 31:13
23 [a]Jer. 7:24, 26 [1]Were stubborn
24 [a]Jer. 11:4; 26:3 [b]Ex. 16:23–30; 20:8–10
25 [a]Jer. 22:4
26 [a]Jer. 33:13 [b]Zech. 7:7 [c]Judg. 1:9 [d]Ps. 107:22; 116:17 [1]Heb. *shephelah* [2]Heb. *Negev*
27 [a]Lam. 4:11 [b]2 Kin. 25:9 [c]Jer. 7:20

CHAPTER 18

3 [1]Potter's wheel
4 [1]*was making* [2]*ruined*
6 [a]Rom. 9:20, 21 [b]Is. 64:8
7 [a]Jer. 1:10
8 [a][Ezek. 18:21; 33:11] [b]Jer. 26:3
11 [a]2 Kin. 17:13 [b]Jer. 7:3–7
12 [a]Jer. 2:25

every one [1]obey the [b]dictates[2] of
his evil heart."
13 Therefore thus says the
LORD:

[a]"Ask now among the
Gentiles,
Who has heard such things?
The virgin of Israel has
done [b]a very horrible
thing.
14 Will *a man* [1]leave the snow
water of Lebanon,
Which comes from the rock
of the field?
Will the cold flowing waters
be forsaken for strange
waters?

15 "Because My people have
forgotten [a]Me,
They have burned incense
to worthless idols.
And they have caused
themselves to stumble in
their ways,
From the [b]ancient paths,
To walk in pathways and
not on a highway,
16 To make their land [a]desolate
and a perpetual [b]hissing;
Everyone who passes by it
will be astonished
And shake his head.
17 [a]I will scatter them [b]as with
an east wind before the
enemy;
[c]I will [1]show them the back
and not the face
In the day of their calamity."

18 Then they said, [a]"Come
and let us devise plans against
Jer·e·mī'ah; [b]for the law shall
not perish from the priest, nor
counsel from the wise, nor the
word from the prophet. Come
and let us attack him with the
tongue, and let us not give heed
to any of his words."

19 Give heed to me, O LORD,
And listen to the voice of
those who contend with
me!
20 [a]Shall evil be repaid for
good?
For they have [b]dug a pit for
my life.
Remember that I [c]stood
before You
To speak good [1]for them,
To turn away Your wrath
from them.
21 Therefore [a]deliver up their
children to the famine,
And pour out their *blood*
By the force of the sword;
Let their wives *become*
widows
And [b]bereaved of their
children.
Let their men be put to
death,
Their young men *be* slain
By the sword in battle.
22 Let a cry be heard from
their houses,
When You bring a troop
suddenly upon them;
For they have dug a pit to
take me,
And hidden snares for my
feet.
23 Yet, LORD, You know all their
counsel
Which is against me, to slay
me.
[a]Provide no atonement for
their iniquity,
Nor blot out their sin from
Your sight;
But let them be overthrown
before You.
Deal *thus* with them
In the time of Your [b]anger.

---

12 [b]Jer. 3:17; 23:17 [1]Lit. *do* [2]*stubbornness* or *imagination*
13 [a]Jer. 2:10, 11 [b]Jer. 5:30
14 [1]*forsake*
15 [a]Jer. 2:13, 32 [b]Jer. 6:16
16 [a]Jer. 19:8 [b]1 Kin. 9:8
17 [a]Jer. 13:24 [b]Ps. 48:7 [c]Jer. 2:27 [1]So with LXX, Syr., Tg., Vg.; MT *look them in*
18 [a]Jer. 11:19 [b]Lev. 10:11
20 [a]Ps. 109:4 [b]Jer. 5:26 [c]Jer. 14:7—15:1 [1]*concerning*
21 [a]Ps. 109:9–20 [b]Jer. 15:7, 8
23 [a]Ps. 35:14; 109:14 [b]Jer. 7:20

19 Thus says the LORD: "Go
and get a potter's earthen
flask, and *take* some of the elders of the people and some of
the elders of the priests.
2 "And go out to [a]the Valley of
the Son of Hin′nom, which *is* by
the entry of the Potsherd Gate;
and proclaim there the words
that I will tell you,
3 [a]"and say, 'Hear the word of
the LORD, O kings of Judah and
inhabitants of Jerusalem. Thus
says the LORD of hosts, the God
of Israel: "Behold, I will bring
such a catastrophe on this place,
that whoever hears of it, his ears
will [b]tingle.
4 "Because they [a]have forsaken
Me and made this an alien place,
because they have burned incense in it to other gods whom
neither they, their fathers, nor
the kings of Judah have known,
and have filled this place with
[b]the blood of the innocents
5 [a]"(they have also built the
high places of Bā′al, to burn
their sons with fire *for* burnt offerings to Bā′al, [b]which I did not
command or speak, nor did it
come into My mind),
6 "therefore behold, the days
are coming," says the LORD,
"that this place shall no more
be called Tō′phet or [a]the Valley
of the Son of Hin′nom, but the
Valley of Slaughter.
7 "And I will make void the
counsel of Judah and Jerusalem
in this place, [a]and I will cause
them to fall by the sword before
their enemies and by the hands
of those who seek their lives;
their [b]corpses I will give as meat
for the birds of the heaven and
for the beasts of the earth.
8 "I will make this city [a]deso-
late and a hissing; everyone
who passes by it will be astonished and hiss because of all its
plagues.
9 "And I will cause them to
eat the [a]flesh of their sons and
the flesh of their daughters, and
everyone shall eat the flesh of
his friend in the siege and in
the desperation with which their
enemies and those who seek
their lives shall drive them to
despair." '
10 [a]"Then you shall break the
flask in the sight of the men who
go with you,
11 "and say to them, 'Thus says
the LORD of hosts: [a]"Even so I will
break this people and this city,
as *one* breaks a potter's vessel,
which cannot be [1]made whole
again; and they shall [b]bury *them*
in Tō′phet till *there is* no place
to bury.
12 "Thus I will do to this place,"
says the LORD, "and to its inhabitants, and make this city like
Tō′phet.
13 "And the houses of Jerusalem and the houses of the kings
of Judah shall be defiled [a]like
the place of Tō′phet, because of
all the houses on whose [b]roofs
they have burned incense to all
the host of heaven, and [c]poured
out drink offerings to other
gods." ' "
14 Then Jer·e·mi′ah came from
Tō′phet, where the LORD had sent
him to prophesy; and he stood in
[a]the court of the Lord's house
and said to all the people,
15 "Thus says the LORD of hosts,
the God of Israel: 'Behold, I will
bring on this city and on all her
towns all the doom that I have
pronounced against it, because
[a]they have stiffened their necks

CHAPTER 19
2 [a]Josh. 15:8
3 [a]Jer. 17:20 [b]1 Sam. 3:11
4 [a]Is. 65:11 [b]2 Kin. 21:12
5 [a]Jer. 7:31; 32:35 [b]Lev. 18:21
6 [a]Josh. 15:8
7 [a]Lev. 26:17 [b]Ps. 79:2
8 [a]Jer. 18:16; 49:13; 50:13
9 [a]Lev. 26:29
10 [a]Jer. 51:63, 64
11 [a]Is. 30:14 [b]Jer. 7:32 [1]*restored*
13 [a]2 Kin. 23:10 [b]Zeph. 1:5 [c]Jer. 7:18
14 [a]2 Chr. 20:5
15 [a]Neh. 9:17, 29

that they might not hear My
words.' "

20 Now [a]Pash'hur the son of
[b]Im'mer, the priest who
was also chief governor in the
house of the LORD, heard that
Jer·e·mi'ah prophesied these
things.
2 Then Pash'hur struck Jer·e-
mi'ah the prophet, and put him
in the stocks that *were* in the
high [a]gate of Benjamin, which
was by the house of the LORD.
3 And it happened on the
next day that Pash'hur brought
Jer·e·mi'ah out of the stocks.
Then Jer·e·mi'ah said to him,
"The LORD has not called your
name Pash'hur, but [1]Mā'gor-
Mis·sā'bib.
4 "For thus says the LORD: 'Behold, I will make you a terror to
yourself and to all your friends;
and they shall fall by the sword
of their enemies, and your eyes
shall see *it*. I will [a]give all Judah into the hand of the king
of Babylon, and he shall carry
them captive to Babylon and
slay them with the sword.
5 'Moreover I [a]will deliver all
the wealth of this city, all its produce, and all its precious things;
all the treasures of the kings of
Judah I will give into the hand
of their enemies, who will plunder them, seize them, and [b]carry
them to Babylon.
6 'And you, Pash'hur, and all
who dwell in your house, shall
go into captivity. You shall go to
Babylon, and there you shall die,
and be buried there, you and all
your friends, to whom you have
[a]prophesied lies.' "

7 O LORD, You [1]induced me,
and I was persuaded;
[a]You are stronger than I, and
have prevailed.
[b]I am [2]in derision daily;
Everyone mocks me.
8 For when I spoke, I cried
out;
[a]I shouted, "Violence and
plunder!"
Because the word of the
LORD was made to me
A reproach and a derision
daily.
9 Then I said, "I will not make
mention of Him,
Nor speak anymore in His
name."
But *His word* was in my
heart like a [a]burning fire
Shut up in my bones;
I was weary of holding *it*
back,
And [b]I could not.
10 [a]For I heard many [1]mocking:
"Fear on every side!"
"Report," *they say,* "and we
will report it!"
[b]All my acquaintances
watched for my
stumbling, *saying,*
"Perhaps he can be induced;
Then we will prevail against
him,
And we will take our
revenge on him."

11 But the LORD *is* [a]with me as
a mighty, awesome One.
Therefore my persecutors
will stumble, and will
not [b]prevail.
They will be greatly
ashamed, for they will
not prosper.
Their [c]everlasting confusion
will never be forgotten.
12 But, O LORD of hosts,
You who [a]test the righteous,

CHAPTER 20
1 [a]Ezra 2:37, 38 [b]1 Chr. 24:14
2 [a]Jer. 37:13
3 [1]Lit. *Fear on Every Side*
4 [a]Jer. 21:4–10
5 [a]2 Kin. 20:17 [b]Is. 39:6
6 [a]Jer. 14:13–15
7 [a]Jer. 1:6, 7 [b]Lam. 3:14 [1]*enticed* or *persuaded* [2]Lit. *a laughing-stock all the day*
8 [a]Jer. 6:7
9 [a]Ps. 39:3 [b]Job 32:18
10 [a]Ps. 31:13 [b]Ps. 41:9; 55:13, 14 [1]*slandering*
11 [a]Jer. 1:18, 19 [b]Jer. 15:20; 17:18 [c]Jer. 23:40
12 [a][Jer. 11:20; 17:10]

And see the [1]mind and
heart,
[b]Let me see Your vengeance
on them;
For I have pleaded my cause
before You.

13 Sing to the LORD! Praise the
LORD!
For [a]He has delivered the
life of the poor
From the hand of evildoers.

14 [a]Cursed *be* the day in which
I was born!
Let the day not be blessed
in which my mother
bore me!
15 Let the man *be* cursed
Who brought news to my
father, saying,
"A male child has been born
to you!"
Making him very glad.
16 And let that man be like the
cities
Which the LORD [a]overthrew,
and did not relent;
Let him [b]hear the cry in the
morning
And the shouting at noon,
17 [a]Because he did not kill me
from the womb,
That my mother might have
been my grave,
And her womb always
enlarged *with me.*
18 [a]Why did I come forth from
the womb to [b]see [1]labor
and sorrow,
That my days should be
consumed with shame?

21 The word which came
to Jer·e·mī′ah from the
LORD when [a]King Zed·e·kī′ah
sent to him [b]Pash′hur the son
of Mel·chī′ah, and [c]Zeph·a·nī′ah
the son of Mā·a·sēi′ah, the priest,
saying,
2 [a]"Please inquire of the LORD
for us, for [1]Ne·bū·chad·nez′zar
king of Babylon makes war
against us. Perhaps the LORD
will deal with us according to all
His wonderful works, that *the
king* may go away from us."
3 Then Jer·e·mī′ah said to
them, "Thus you shall say to
Zed·e·kī′ah,
4 'Thus says the LORD God of
Israel: "Behold, I will turn back
the weapons of war that *are*
in your hands, with which you
fight against the king of Babylon and the [1]Chal·dē′ans who
besiege you outside the walls;
and [a]I will assemble them in the
midst of this city.
5 "I [a]Myself will fight against
you with an [b]outstretched hand
and with a strong arm, even in
anger and fury and great wrath.
6 "I will strike the inhabitants of this city, both man and
beast; they shall die of a great
pestilence.
7 "And afterward," says the
LORD, [a]"I will deliver Zed·e·kī′ah
king of Judah, his servants and
the people, and such as are left in
this city from the pestilence and
the sword and the famine, into
the hand of Ne·bū·chad·nez′zar
king of Babylon, into the hand
of their enemies, and into the
hand of those who seek their
life; and he shall strike them
with the edge of the sword. [b]He
shall not spare them, or have
pity or mercy." '
8 "Now you shall say to this
people, 'Thus says the LORD: "Behold, [a]I set before you the way of
life and the way of death.
9 "He who [a]remains in this city

12 [b]Ps. 54:7; 59:10 [1]Most secret parts, lit. *kidneys*
13 [a]Ps. 35:9, 10; 109:30, 31
14 [a]Job 3:3
16 [a]Gen. 19:25 [b]Jer. 18:22
17 [a]Job 3:10, 11
18 [a]Job 3:20 [b]Lam. 3:1 [1]*toil*

CHAPTER 21

1 [a]2 Kin. 24:17, 18 [b]Jer. 38:1 [c]2 Kin. 25:18
2 [a]Jer. 37:3, 7 [1]Heb. *Nebuchadrezzar,* and so elsewhere in the book
4 [a]Is. 13:4 [1]Or *Babylonians,* and so elsewhere in the book
5 [a]Is. 63:10 [b]Ex. 6:6
7 [a]Jer. 37:17; 39:5; 52:9 [b]2 Chr. 36:17
8 [a]Deut. 30:15, 19
9 [a]Jer. 38:2

shall die by the sword, by famine, and by pestilence; but he who goes out and [1]defects to the Chal·dē′ans who besiege you, he shall [b]live, and his life shall be as a prize to him.
10 "For I have [a]set My face against this city for adversity and not for good," says the LORD. [b]"It shall be given into the hand of the king of Babylon, and he shall [c]burn it with fire." '
11 "And concerning the house of the king of Judah, *say*, 'Hear the word of the LORD,
12 'O house of David! Thus says the LORD:

[a]"Execute[1] judgment [b]in the morning;
And deliver *him who is* plundered
Out of the hand of the oppressor,
Lest My fury go forth like fire
And burn so that no one can quench *it*,
Because of the evil of your doings.

13 "Behold, [a]I *am* against you,
O [1]inhabitant of the valley,
And rock of the plain," says the LORD,
"Who say, [b]'Who shall come down against us?
Or who shall enter our dwellings?'
14 But I will punish you according to the [a]fruit of your [1]doings," says the LORD;
"I will kindle a fire in its forest,
And [b]it shall devour all things around it." ' "

9 [b]Jer. 39:18 [1]Lit. *falls away to*
10 [a]Amos 9:4 [b]Jer. 38:3 [c]Jer. 34:2, 22; 37:10
12 [a]Zech. 7:9 [b]Ps. 101:8 [1]*Dispense justice*
13 [a][Ezek. 13:8] [b]Jer. 49:4 [1]*dweller*
14 [a]Is. 3:10, 11 [b]2 Chr. 36:19 [1]*deeds*

CHAPTER 22

2 [a]Jer. 17:20
3 [a]Jer. 21:12 [b]Jer. 7:6 [1]*Dispense justice*
4 [a]Jer. 17:25
5 [a]Matt. 23:38; Heb. 6:13, 17 [1]Obey
6 [a]Song 4:1
7 [a]Is. 37:24 [b]Jer. 21:14
8 [a]Deut. 29:24–26

22 Thus says the LORD: "Go down to the house of the king of Judah, and there speak this word,
2 "and say, [a]'Hear the word of the LORD, O king of Judah, you who sit on the throne of David, you and your servants and your people who enter these gates!
3 'Thus says the LORD: [a]"Execute[1] judgment and righteousness, and deliver the plundered out of the hand of the oppressor. Do no wrong and do no violence to the stranger, the [b]fatherless, or the widow, nor shed innocent blood in this place.
4 "For if you indeed do this thing, [a]then shall enter the gates of this house, riding on horses and in chariots, accompanied by servants and people, kings who sit on the throne of David.
5 "But if you will not [1]hear these words, [a]I swear by Myself," says the LORD, "that this house shall become a desolation." ' "
6 For thus says the LORD to the house of the king of Judah:

"You *are* [a]Gil′ē·ad to Me,
The head of Lebanon;
Yet I surely will make you a wilderness,
Cities *which* are not inhabited.
7 I will prepare destroyers against you,
Everyone with his weapons;
They shall cut down [a]your choice cedars
[b]And cast *them* into the fire.

8 "And many nations will pass by this city; and everyone will say to his neighbor, [a]'Why has the LORD done so to this great city?'

9 "Then they will answer,
[a]'Because they have forsaken
the covenant of the LORD their
God, and worshiped other gods
and served them.' "

10 Weep not for [a]the dead, nor
bemoan him;
Weep bitterly for him [b]who
goes away,
For he shall return no more,
Nor see his native country.

11 For thus says the LORD concerning [a]Shal'lum[1] the son of
Jō·sī'ah, king of Judah, who
reigned instead of Jō·sī'ah his
father, [b]who went from this
place: "He shall not return here
anymore,
12 "but he shall die in the place
where they have led him captive, and shall see this land no
more.

13 "Woe[a] to him who
builds his house by
unrighteousness
And his [1]chambers by
injustice,
[b]*Who* uses his neighbor's
service without wages
And gives him nothing for
his work,
14 Who says, 'I will build
myself a wide house
with spacious [1]chambers,
And cut out windows for it,
Paneling *it* with cedar
And painting *it* with
vermilion.'

15 "Shall you reign because
you enclose *yourself* in
cedar?
Did not your father eat and
drink,
And do justice and
righteousness?
Then [a]*it was* well with him.
16 He [1]judged the cause of the
poor and needy;
Then *it was* well.
Was not this knowing Me?"
says the LORD.
17 "Yet[a] your eyes and your
heart *are* for nothing but
your covetousness,
For shedding innocent
blood,
And practicing oppression
and violence."

18 Therefore thus says the LORD
concerning Je·hoi'a·kim the son
of Jō·sī'ah, king of Judah:

[a]"They shall not lament for
him,
Saying, [b]'Alas, my brother!'
or 'Alas, my sister!'
They shall not lament for
him,
Saying, 'Alas, master!' or
'Alas, his glory!'
19 [a]He shall be buried with the
burial of a donkey,
Dragged and cast out
beyond the gates of
Jerusalem.

20 "Go up to Lebanon, and cry
out,
And lift up your voice in
Bā'shan;
Cry from Ab'a·rim,
For all your lovers are
destroyed.
21 I spoke to you in your
prosperity,
But you said, 'I will not
hear.'
[a]This *has been* your manner
from your youth,

---

9 [a]2 Chr. 34:25
10 [a]2 Kin. 22:20 [b]Jer. 14:17; 22:11
11 [a]1 Chr. 3:15 [b]2 Kin. 23:34 [1]Or *Jehoahaz*
13 [a]2 Kin. 23:35 [b]James 5:4 [1]Lit. *roof chambers, upper chambers*
14 [1]Lit. *roof chambers, upper chambers*
15 [a]Ps. 128:2
16 [1]Defended
17 [a]Ezek. 19:6
18 [a]Jer. 16:4, 6 [b]1 Kin. 13:30
19 [a]Jer. 36:30
21 [a]Jer. 3:24, 25; 32:30

That you did not obey My voice.
22 The wind shall eat up all [a]your [1]rulers,
And your lovers shall go into captivity;
Surely then you will be ashamed and humiliated
For all your wickedness.
23 O inhabitant of Lebanon,
Making your nest in the cedars,
How gracious will you be when pangs come upon you,
Like [a]the pain of a woman in [1]labor?

24 "*As* I live," says the LORD,
[a]"though [1]Cō·nī′ah the son of
Je·hoi′a·kim, king of Judah,
[b]were the [2]signet on My right
hand, yet I would pluck you off;
25 [a]"and I will give you into the
hand of those who seek your
life, and into the hand *of those*
whose face you fear—the hand
of Ne·bū·chad·nez′zar king of
Babylon and the hand of the
[1]Chal·dē′ans.
26 [a]"So I will cast you out, and
your mother who bore you, into
another country where you were
not born; and there you shall
die.
27 "But to the land to which
they desire to return, there they
shall not return.

28 "Is this man [1]Cō·nī′ah a despised, broken idol—
[a]A vessel in which *is* no pleasure?
Why are they cast out, he and his descendants,
And cast into a land which they do not know?

22 [a]Jer. 23:1 [1]Lit. *shepherds*
23 [a]Jer. 6:24 [1]*childbirth*
24 [a]2 Kin. 24:6, 8 [b]Hag. 2:23 [1]Or *Jeconiah* or *Jehoiachin* [2]*signet ring*
25 [a]Jer. 34:20 [1]Or *Babylonians*
26 [a]2 Kin. 24:15
28 [a]Hos. 8:8 [1]See note at v. 24
29 [a]Deut. 32:1
30 [a]Matt. 1:12 [b]Jer. 36:30

CHAPTER 23

1 [a]Jer. 10:21
2 [a]Ex. 32:34
3 [a]Jer. 32:37
4 [a]Jer. 3:15
5 [a]Jer. 33:14; Matt. 1:1, 6; Luke 3:31; [John 1:45; 7:42]; Rev. 22:16 [b]Ps. 72:2 [1]*act wisely* [2]*justice* [3]*land*

29 [a]O earth, earth, earth,
Hear the word of the LORD!
30 Thus says the LORD:
'Write this man down as [a]childless,
A man *who* shall not prosper in his days;
For [b]none of his descendants shall prosper,
Sitting on the throne of David,
And ruling anymore in Judah.' "

23

"Woe [a]to the shepherds
who destroy and scatter
the sheep of My pasture!" says
the LORD.
2 Therefore thus says the LORD
God of Israel against the shepherds who feed My people: "You
have scattered My flock, driven
them away, and not attended to
them. [a]Behold, I will attend to
you for the evil of your doings,"
says the LORD.
3 "But [a]I will gather the remnant of My flock out of all countries where I have driven them,
and bring them back to their
folds; and they shall be fruitful
and increase.
4 "I will set up [a]shepherds over
them who will feed them; and
they shall fear no more, nor
be dismayed, nor shall they be
lacking," says the LORD.

5 "Behold, [a]*the* days are coming," says the LORD, ☆
"That I will raise to David a Branch of righteousness;
A King shall reign and [1]prosper,
[b]And execute [2]judgment and righteousness in the [3]earth.

☆ 6 [a]In His days Judah will be saved,
And Israel [b]will dwell safely;
Now [c]this *is* His name by which He will be called:

[1]THE LORD OUR RIGHTEOUSNESS.

7 "Therefore, behold, [a]*the* days
are coming," says the LORD, "that
they shall no longer say, 'As the
LORD lives who brought up the
children of Israel from the land
of Egypt,'
8 "but, 'As the LORD lives who
brought up and led the descendants of the house of Israel from
the north country [a]and from all
the countries where I had driven
them.' And they shall dwell in
their own [b]land."

9 My heart within me is broken
Because of the prophets;
[a]All my bones shake.
I am like a drunken man,
And like a man whom wine has overcome,
Because of the LORD,
And because of His holy words.
10 For [a]the land is full of adulterers;
For [b]because of a curse the land mourns.
[c]The pleasant places of the wilderness are dried up.
Their course of life is evil,
And their might *is* not right.

11 "For [a]both prophet and priest are profane;
Yes, [b]in My house I have found their wickedness,"
says the LORD.

12 "Therefore[a] their way shall be to them
Like slippery *ways;*
In the darkness they shall be driven on
And fall in them;
For I [b]will bring disaster on them,
The year of their punishment," says the LORD.
13 "And I have seen [1]folly in the prophets of Samaria:
[a]They prophesied by Bā′al
And [b]caused My people Israel to err.
14 Also I have seen a horrible thing in the prophets of Jerusalem:
[a]They commit adultery and walk in lies;
They also [b]strengthen the hands of evildoers,
So that no one turns back from his wickedness.
All of them are like [c]Sod′om to Me,
And her inhabitants like Go·mor′rah.

15 "Therefore thus says the
LORD of hosts concerning the
prophets:

'Behold, I will feed them with [a]wormwood,
And make them drink the water of gall;
For from the prophets of Jerusalem
[1]Profaneness has gone out into all the land.' "

16 Thus says the LORD of hosts:

"Do not listen to the words of the prophets who prophesy to you.

6 [a]Zech. 14:11 [b]Jer. 32:37 [c][Rom. 3:22; 1 Cor. 1:30] [1]Heb. *YHWH Tsidkenu*
7 [a]Jer. 16:14
8 [a]Is. 43:5, 6 [b]Gen. 12:7
9 [a]Hab. 3:16
10 [a]Jer. 9:2 [b]Hos. 4:2 [c]Jer. 9:10
11 [a]Zeph. 3:4 [b]Jer. 7:30; 32:34
12 [a][Prov. 4:19] [b]Jer. 11:23
13 [a]Jer. 2:8 [b]Is. 9:16 [1]Lit. *distastefulness*
14 [a]Jer. 29:23 [b]Ezek. 13:22, 23 [c]Is. 1:9, 10
15 [a]Jer. 9:15 [1]Or *Pollution*

They make you worthless;
[a]They speak a vision of their own heart,
Not from the mouth of the LORD.
17 They continually say to those who despise Me,
'The LORD has said, [a]"You shall have peace" ';
And *to* everyone who [b]walks according to the [1]dictates of his own heart, they say,
[c]'No evil shall come upon you.' "

18 For [a]who has stood in the counsel of the LORD,
And has perceived and heard His word?
Who has marked His word and heard *it?*
19 Behold, a [a]whirlwind of the LORD has gone forth in fury—
A violent whirlwind!
It will fall violently on the head of the wicked.
20 The [a]anger of the LORD will not turn back
Until He has executed and performed the thoughts of His heart.
[b]In the latter days you will understand it perfectly.

21 "I[a] have not sent these prophets, yet they ran.
I have not spoken to them, yet they prophesied.
22 But if they had stood in My counsel,
And had caused My people to hear My words,
Then they would have [a]turned them from their evil way
And from the evil of their doings.

23 "*Am* I a God near at hand," says the LORD,
"And not a God afar off?
24 Can anyone [a]hide himself in secret places,
So I shall not see him?" says the LORD;
[b]"Do I not fill heaven and earth?" says the LORD.

25 "I have heard what the
prophets have said who prophesy lies in My name, saying, 'I
have dreamed, I have dreamed!'
26 "How long will *this* be in
the heart of the prophets who
prophesy lies? Indeed *they are*
prophets of the deceit of their
own heart,
27 "who try to make My people
forget My name by their dreams
which everyone tells his neighbor, [a]as their fathers forgot My
name for Bā'al.

28 "The prophet who has a dream, let him tell a dream;
And he who has My word, let him speak My word faithfully.
What *is* the chaff to the wheat?" says the LORD.
29 "*Is* not My word like a [a]fire?" says the LORD,
"And like a hammer *that* breaks the rock in pieces?

30 "Therefore behold, [a]I *am*
against the prophets," says the
LORD, "who steal My words every one from his neighbor.
31 "Behold, I *am* [a]against the
prophets," says the LORD, "who

16 [a]Jer. 14:14
17 [a]Ezek. 13:10 [b]Deut. 29:19; Jer. 3:17 [c]Mic. 3:11 [1]*stubbornness* or *imagination*
18 [a][1 Cor. 2:16]
19 [a]Amos 1:14
20 [a]Jer. 30:24 [b]Gen. 49:1
21 [a]Jer. 14:14; 23:32; 27:15
22 [a]Jer. 25:5
24 [a][Ps. 139:7] [b][1 Kin. 8:27]
27 [a]Judg. 3:7
29 [a]Jer. 5:14
30 [a]Deut. 18:20
31 [a]Ezek. 13:9

use their tongues and say, 'He
says.'
32 "Behold, I *am* against those
who prophesy false dreams,"
says the LORD, "and tell them,
and cause My people to err by
their [a]lies and by [b]their reckless-
ness. Yet I did not send them or
command them; therefore they
shall not [c]profit this people at
all," says the LORD.
33 "So when these people or the
prophet or the priest ask you,
saying, 'What is [a]the [1]oracle of
the LORD?' you shall then say to
them, [2]'What oracle?' I will even
forsake you," says the LORD.
34 "And *as for* the prophet and
the priest and the people who
say, 'The [1]oracle of the LORD!' I
will even punish that man and
his house.
35 "Thus every one of you shall
say to his neighbor, and every
one to his brother, 'What has the
LORD answered?' and, 'What has
the LORD spoken?'
36 "And the [1]oracle of the LORD
you shall mention no more. For
every man's word will be his
oracle, for you have [a]perverted
the words of the living God, the
LORD of hosts, our God.
37 "Thus you shall say to the
prophet, 'What has the LORD answered you?' and, 'What has the
LORD spoken?'
38 "But since you say, 'The [1]or-
acle of the LORD!' therefore thus
says the LORD: 'Because you say
this word, "The oracle of the
LORD!" and I have sent to you,
saying, "Do not say, 'The oracle
of the LORD!' "
39 'therefore behold, I, even I,
[a]will utterly forget you and forsake you, and the city that I gave
you and your fathers, and *will
cast you* out of My presence.
40 'And I will bring [a]an everlasting reproach upon you, and a
perpetual [b]shame, which shall
not be forgotten.' "

24 The [a]LORD showed me, and
there were two baskets of
figs set before the temple of the
LORD, after Ne·bū·chad·nez′zar
[b]king of Babylon had carried
away captive [c]Jec·o·nī′ah the son
of Je·hoi′a·kim, king of Judah,
and the princes of Judah with
the craftsmen and smiths, from
Jerusalem, and had brought
them to Babylon.
2 One basket *had* very good
figs, like the figs *that are* first
ripe; and the other basket *had*
very bad figs which could not be
eaten, they were so [a]bad.
3 Then the LORD said to me,
"What do you see, Jer·e·mī′ah?"
And I said, "Figs, the good figs,
very good; and the bad, very
bad, which cannot be eaten, they
are so bad."
4 Again the word of the LORD
came to me, saying,
5 "Thus says the LORD, the God
of Israel: 'Like these good figs,
so will I [1]acknowledge those who
are carried away captive from
Judah, whom I have sent out of
this place for *their own* good,
into the land of the Chal·dē′ans.
6 'For I will set My eyes on
them for good, and [a]I will bring
them back to this land; [b]I will
build them and not pull *them*
down, and I will plant them and
not pluck *them* up.
7 'Then I will give them [a]a
heart to know Me, that I *am*
the LORD; and they shall be [b]My
people, and I will be their God,

32 [a]Lam. 2:14; 3:37 [b]Zeph. 3:4 [c]Jer. 7:8
33 [a]Mal. 1:1 [1]*burden, prophecy* [2]LXX, Tg., Vg. *'You are the burden.'*
34 [1]*burden, prophecy*
36 [a]Deut. 4:2 [1]*burden, prophecy*
38 [1]*burden, prophecy*
39 [a]Hos. 4:6
40 [a]Jer. 20:11 [b]Mic. 3:5–7

CHAPTER 24

1 [a]Amos 7:1, 4; 8:1 [b]2 Kin. 24:12–16 [c]Jer. 22:24–28; 29:2
2 [a]Jer. 29:17
5 [1]*regard*
6 [a]Jer. 12:15; 29:10 [b]Jer. 32:41; 33:7; 42:10
7 [a][Deut. 30:6] [b]Jer. 30:22; 31:33; 32:38

for they shall return to Me [c]with
their whole heart.
8 'And as the bad [a]figs which
cannot be eaten, they are so bad'—
surely thus says the LORD—'so
will I give up Zed·e·kī'ah the king
of Judah, his princes, the [b]residue
of Jerusalem who remain in this
land, and [c]those who dwell in the
land of Egypt.
9 'I will deliver them to [a]trouble
into all the kingdoms of the
earth, for *their* harm, [b]*to be* a
reproach and a byword, a taunt
and a curse, in all places where
I shall drive them.
10 'And I will send the sword,
the famine, and the pestilence
among them, till they are [1]con-
sumed from the land that I gave
to them and their fathers.' "

25

The word that came to
Jer·e·mī'ah concerning
all the people of Judah, [a]in the
fourth year of [b]Je·hoi'a·kim the
son of Jō·sī'ah, king of Judah
(which *was* the first year of
Ne·bū·chad·nez'zar king of Babylon),
2 which Jer·e·mī'ah the prophet
spoke to all the people of Judah
and to all the inhabitants of Jerusalem, saying:
3 [a]"From the thirteenth year of
Jō·sī'ah the son of Ā'mon, king
of Judah, even to this day, this *is*
the twenty-third year in which
the word of the LORD has come
to me; and I have spoken to you,
rising early and speaking, [b]but
you have not listened.
4 "And the LORD has sent to
you all His servants the prophets, [a]rising early and sending
them, but you have not listened
nor inclined your ear to hear.
5 "They said, [a]'Repent now everyone of his evil way and his
evil doings, and dwell in the
land that the LORD has given to
you and your fathers forever
and ever.
6 'Do not go after other gods
to serve them and worship them,
and do not provoke Me to anger
with the works of your hands;
and I will not harm you.'
7 "Yet you have not listened
to Me," says the LORD, "that you
might [a]provoke Me to anger with
the works of your hands to your
own hurt.
8 "Therefore thus says the
LORD of hosts: 'Because you have
not heard My words,
9 'behold, I will send and take
[a]all the families of the north,' says
the LORD, 'and Ne·bū·chad·nez'-
zar the king of Babylon, [b]My
servant, and will bring them
against this land, against its inhabitants, and against these nations all around, and will utterly
destroy them, and [c]make them
an astonishment, a hissing, and
perpetual desolations.
10 'Moreover I will [1]take from
them the [a]voice of mirth and the
voice of gladness, the voice of
the bridegroom and the voice of
the bride, [b]the sound of the millstones and the light of the lamp.
11 'And this whole land shall
be a desolation *and* an astonishment, and these nations shall
serve the king of Babylon seventy [a]years.
12 'Then it will come to pass,
[a]when [1]seventy years are completed, *that* I will punish the
king of Babylon and that nation,
the land of the Chal·dē'ans, for
their iniquity,' says the LORD;
[b]'and I will make it a perpetual
desolation.
13 'So I will bring on that land

7 [c]Jer. 29:13
8 [a]Jer. 29:17 [b]Jer. 39:9 [c]Jer. 44:1, 26–30
9 [a]Deut. 28:25, 37 [b]Ps. 44:13, 14
10 [1]*destroyed*

CHAPTER 25

1 [a]Jer. 36:1 [b]2 Kin. 24:1, 2
3 [a]Jer. 1:2 [b]Jer. 7:13; 11:7, 8, 10
4 [a]Jer. 7:13, 25
5 [a]Jer. 18:11
7 [a]Deut. 32:21
9 [a]Jer. 1:15 [b]Is. 45:1 [c]Jer. 18:16
10 [a]Rev. 18:23 [b]Eccl. 12:4 [1]Lit. *cause to perish from them*
11 [a]Jer. 29:10
12 [a]Ezra 1:1 [b]Is. 13:20 [1]Beginning circa 605 B.C. (2 Kin. 24:1) and ending circa 536 B.C. (Ezra 1:1)

all My words which I have pronounced against it, all that is
written in this book, which
Jer·e·mī′ah has prophesied concerning all the nations.
14 [a]‘(For many nations [b]and
great kings shall [c]be served
by them also; [d]and I will repay
them according to their deeds
and according to the works of
their own hands.)’ ”
15 For thus says the LORD God
of Israel to me: “Take this [a]wine
cup of [1]fury from My hand, and
cause all the nations, to whom I
send you, to drink it.
16 “And [a]they will drink and
stagger and go mad because of
the sword that I will send among
them.”
17 Then I took the cup from the
LORD’s hand, and made all the
nations drink, to whom the LORD
had sent me:
18 Jerusalem and the cities of
Judah, its kings and its princes,
to make them [a]a desolation, an
astonishment, a hissing, and [b]a
curse, as *it is* this day;
19 Pharaoh king of Egypt, his
servants, his princes, and all his
people;
20 all the mixed multitude, all
the kings of [a]the land of Uz,
all the kings of the land of the
[b]Phi·lis′tines (namely, Ash′-
ke·lon, Gā′za, Ek′ron, and [c]the
remnant of Ash′dod);
21 [a]Ē′dom, Mō′ab, and the people of Am′mon;
22 all the kings of [a]Tȳre, all the
kings of Sī′don, and the kings of
the coastlands which *are* across
the [b]sea;
23 [a]Dē′dan, Tē′ma, Buz, and all
who are in the farthest corners;
24 all the kings of Arabia and all
the kings of the [a]mixed multitude who dwell in the desert;
25 all the kings of Zim′rī, all
the kings of [a]Ē′lam, and all the
kings of the [b]Mēdes;
26 [a]all the kings of the north,
far and near, one with another;
and all the kingdoms of the
world which *are* on the face of
the earth. Also the king of [1]Shē′-
shach shall drink after them.
27 “Therefore you shall say to
them, ‘Thus says the LORD of
hosts, the God of Israel: [a]“Drink,
[b]be drunk, and vomit! Fall and
rise no more, because of the
sword which I will send among
you.” ’
28 “And it shall be, if they refuse to take the cup from your
hand to drink, then you shall
say to them, ‘Thus says the LORD
of hosts: “You shall certainly
drink!
29 “For behold, [a]I begin to bring
calamity on the city [b]which is
called by My name, and should
you be utterly unpunished? You
shall not be unpunished, for [c]I
will call for a sword on all the
inhabitants of the earth,” says
the LORD of hosts.’
30 “Therefore prophesy against
them all these words, and say to
them:

‘The LORD will [a]roar from on
high,
And utter His voice from
[b]His holy habitation;
He will roar mightily
against [c]His fold.
He will give [d]a shout, as
those who tread *the*
grapes,
Against all the inhabitants
of the earth.

14 [a]Jer. 50:9; 51:27, 28 [b]Jer. 51:27 [c]Jer. 27:7 [d]Jer. 50:29; 51:6, 24
15 [a]Rev. 14:10 [1]*wrath*
16 [a]Nah. 3:11
18 [a]Jer. 25:9, 11 [b]Jer. 24:9
20 [a]Job 1:1 [b]Jer. 47:1–7 [c]Is. 20:1
21 [a]Jer. 49:7
22 [a]Jer. 47:4 [b]Jer. 49:23
23 [a]Jer. 49:7, 8
24 [a]Ezek. 30:5
25 [a]Jer. 49:34 [b]Jer. 51:11, 28
26 [a]Jer. 50:9 [1]A code word for Babylon, Jer. 51:41
27 [a]Hab. 2:16 [b]Is. 63:6
29 [a]Ezek. 9:6 [b]Dan. 9:18 [c]Ezek. 38:21
30 [a]Amos 1:2 [b]Ps. 11:4 [c]1 Kin. 9:3 [d]Is. 16:9

31 A noise will come to the
ends of the earth—
For the LORD has [a]a
controversy with the
nations;
[b]He will plead His case with
all flesh.
He will give those *who are*
wicked to the sword,'
says the LORD."

32 Thus says the LORD of hosts:

"Behold, disaster shall go
forth
From nation to nation,
And [a]a great whirlwind
shall be raised up
From the farthest parts of
the earth.

33 [a]"And at that day the slain of
the LORD shall be from *one* end
of the earth even to the *other*
end of the earth. They shall not
be [b]lamented, [c]or gathered, or
buried; they shall become refuse
on the ground.

34 "Wail,[a] shepherds, and cry!
Roll about *in the ashes,*
You leaders of the flock!
For the days of your
slaughter and your
dispersions are fulfilled;
You shall fall like a precious
vessel.
35 And the shepherds will have
no [1]way to flee,
Nor the leaders of the flock
to escape.
36 A voice of the cry of the
shepherds,
And a wailing of the leaders
to the flock *will be*
heard.
For the LORD has plundered
their pasture,

31 [a]Mic. 6:2 [b]Is. 66:16
32 [a]Jer. 23:19; 30:23
33 [a]Is. 34:2, 3; 66:16 [b]Jer. 16:4, 6 [c]Ps. 79:3
34 [a]Jer. 4:8; 6:26
35 [1]Or *refuge*

CHAPTER 26

2 [a]Jer. 19:14 [b]Matt. 28:20 [c]Acts 20:27
3 [a]Jer. 36:3–7 [b]Jer. 18:8
4 [a]Lev. 26:14, 15
5 [a]Jer. 25:4; 29:19
6 [a]1 Sam. 4:10, 11 [b]Is. 65:15

37 And the peaceful dwellings
are cut down
Because of the fierce anger
of the LORD.
38 He has left His lair like the
lion;
For their land is desolate
Because of the fierceness of
the Oppressor,
And because of His fierce
anger."

26 In the beginning of the
reign of Je·hoi′a·kim the
son of Jō·sī′ah, king of Judah,
this word came from the LORD,
saying,
2 "Thus says the LORD: 'Stand
in [a]the court of the LORD's house,
and speak to all the cities of Judah, which come to worship *in*
the LORD's house, [b]all the words
that I command you to speak to
them. [c]Do not diminish a word.
3 [a]'Perhaps everyone will listen and turn from his evil way,
that I may [b]relent concerning
the calamity which I purpose
to bring on them because of the
evil of their doings.'
4 "And you shall say to them,
'Thus says the LORD: [a]"If you
will not listen to Me, to walk in
My law which I have set before
you,
5 "to heed the words of My
servants the prophets [a]whom I
sent to you, both rising up early
and sending *them* (but you have
not heeded),
6 "then I will make this house
like [a]Shī′lōh, and will make this
city [b]a curse to all the nations of
the earth."'"
7 So the priests and the prophets and all the people heard
Jer·e·mī′ah speaking these
words in the house of the LORD.

8 Now it happened, when
Jer·e·mī′ah had made an end of
speaking all that the LORD had
commanded *him* to speak to all
the people, that the priests and
the prophets and all the people
seized him, saying, "You will
surely die!
9 "Why have you prophesied
in the name of the LORD, saying,
'This house shall be like Shī′lōh,
and this city shall be [a]desolate,
without an inhabitant'?" And
all the people were gathered
against Jer·e·mī′ah in the house
of the LORD.
10 When the princes of Judah
heard these things, they came
up from the king's house to the
house of the LORD and sat down
in the entry of the New Gate of
the LORD's *house.*
11 And the priests and the
prophets spoke to the princes
and all the people, saying, [1]"This
man deserves to [a]die! For he has
prophesied against this city, as
you have heard with your ears."
12 Then Jer·e·mī′ah spoke to all
the princes and all the people,
saying: "The LORD sent me to
prophesy against this house and
against this city with all the
words that you have heard.
13 "Now therefore, [a]amend your
ways and your doings, and obey
the voice of the LORD your God;
then the LORD will relent concerning the doom that He has
pronounced against you.
14 "As for me, here [a]I am, in
your hand; do with me as seems
good and [1]proper to you.
15 "But know for certain that
if you put me to death, you will
surely bring innocent blood on
yourselves, on this city, and on
its inhabitants; for truly the LORD
has sent me to you to speak all
these words in your hearing."
16 So the princes and all the
people said to the priests and
the prophets, "This man does
not deserve to die. For he has
spoken to us in the name of the
LORD our God."
17 [a]Then certain of the elders
of the land rose up and spoke to
all the assembly of the people,
saying:
18 [a]"Mī′cah of Mō′re·sheth
prophesied in the days of
Hez·e·kī′ah king of Judah, and
spoke to all the people of Judah,
saying, 'Thus says the LORD of
hosts:

[b]"Zion shall be plowed *like* a
field,
Jerusalem shall become
[c]heaps of ruins,
And the mountain of the
[1]temple
Like the [2]bare hills of the
forest." '

19 "Did Hez·e·kī′ah king of Judah and all Judah ever put him
to death? [a]Did he not fear the
LORD and [b]seek the LORD's favor?
And the LORD [c]relented concerning the doom which He had
pronounced against them. [d]But
we are doing great evil against
ourselves."
20 Now there was also a man
who prophesied in the name
of the LORD, Ū·rī′jah the son of
She·māi′ah of Kir′jath Jē′a·rim,
who prophesied against this city
and against this land according
to all the words of Jer·e·mī′ah.
21 And when Je·hoi′a·kim the
king, with all his mighty men
and all the princes, heard his
words, the king sought to put

9 [a]Jer. 9:11
11 [a]Jer. 38:4 [1]Lit. *A judgment of death to this man*
13 [a]Jer. 7:3
14 [a]Jer. 38:5 [1]*right*
17 [a]Acts 5:34
18 [a]Mic. 1:1 [b]Mic. 3:12 [c]Jer. 9:11 [1]Lit. *house* [2]Lit. *high places*
19 [a]2 Chr. 32:26 [b]2 Kin. 20:1–19 [c]Ex. 32:14 [d][Acts 5:39]

him to death; but when Ū·rī′jah
heard *it,* he was afraid and fled,
and went to Egypt.
22 Then Je·hoi′a·kim the king
sent men to Egypt: El·nā′than
the son of Ach′bor, and *other*
men *who went* with him to
Egypt.
23 And they brought Ū·rī′jah
from Egypt and brought him to
Je·hoi′a·kim the king, who killed
him with the sword and cast his
dead body into the graves of the
[1]common people.
24 Nevertheless [a]the hand of
A·hī′kam the son of Shā′phan
was with Jer·e·mī′ah, so that
they should not give him into
the hand of the people to put
him to death.

27

In[1] the beginning of the
reign of [2]Je·hoi′a·kim the
son of Jō·sī′ah, [a]king of Judah,
this word came to Jer·e·mī′ah
from the LORD, saying,
2 "Thus says the LORD to me:
'Make for yourselves bonds and
yokes, [a]and put them on your
neck,
3 'and send them to the king
of Ē′dom, the king of Mō′ab,
the king of the Am′mon·ītes, the
king of Tȳre, and the king of
Sī′don, by the hand of the messengers who come to Jerusalem
to Zed·e·kī′ah king of Judah.
4 'And command them to say
to their masters, "Thus says the
LORD of hosts, the God of Israel—thus you shall say to your
masters:
5 [a]'I have made the earth, the
man and the beast that *are* on
the ground, by My great power
and by My outstretched arm,
and [b]have given it to whom it
seemed proper to Me.
6 [a]'And now I have given all
these lands into the hand of
Ne·bū·chad·nez′zar the king of
Babylon, [b]My servant; and [c]the
beasts of the field I have also
given him to serve him.
7 [a]'So all nations shall serve
him and his son and his son's
son, [b]until the time of his land
comes; [c]and then many nations
and great kings shall make him
serve them.
8 'And it shall be, *that* the nation and kingdom which will not
serve Ne·bū·chad·nez′zar the
king of Babylon, and which will
not put its neck under the yoke
of the king of Babylon, that nation I will punish,' says the LORD,
'with the sword, the famine, and
the pestilence, until I have consumed them by his hand.
9 'Therefore do not listen to
your prophets, your diviners,
your [1]dreamers, your soothsayers, or your sorcerers, who
speak to you, saying, "You shall
not serve the king of Babylon."
10 'For they prophesy a [a]lie to
you, to remove you far from
your land; and I will drive you
out, and you will perish.
11 'But the nations that bring
their necks under the yoke of
the king of Babylon and serve
him, I will let them remain in
their own land,' says the LORD,
'and they shall till it and dwell
in it.' " ' "
12 I also spoke to [a]Zed·e·kī′ah
king of Judah according to all
these words, saying, "Bring your
necks under the yoke of the king
of Babylon, and serve him and
his people, and live!
13 [a]"Why will you die, you and
your people, by the sword, by
the famine, and by the pestilence, as the LORD has spoken

23 [1]Lit. *sons of the people*
24 [a]2 Kin. 22:12–14

CHAPTER 27

1 [a]Jer. 27:3, 12, 20; 28:1 [1]LXX omits v. 1. [2]So with MT, Tg., Vg.; some Heb. mss., Arab., Syr. *Zedekiah* (cf. 27:3, 12; 28:1)
2 [a]Jer. 28:10, 12
5 [a]Is. 45:12 [b]Dan. 4:17, 25, 32
6 [a]Jer. 28:14 [b]Jer. 25:9; 43:10 [c]Dan. 2:38
7 [a]2 Chr. 36:20 [b][Dan. 5:26] [c]Jer. 25:14
9 [1]Lit. *dreams*
10 [a]Jer. 23:16, 32; 28:15
12 [a]Jer. 28:1; 38:17
13 [a][Ezek. 18:31]

against the nation that will not
serve the king of Babylon?
14 "Therefore [a]do not listen to
the words of the prophets who
speak to you, saying, 'You shall
not serve the king of Babylon,'
for they prophesy [b]a lie to you;
15 "for I have [a]not sent them,"
says the LORD, "yet they prophesy a lie in My name, that I may
drive you out, and that you may
perish, you and the prophets
who prophesy to you."
16 Also I spoke to the priests
and to all this people, saying,
"Thus says the LORD: 'Do not listen to the words of your prophets who prophesy to you, saying, "Behold, [a]the vessels of the
LORD's house will now shortly
be brought back from Babylon";
for they prophesy a lie to you.
17 'Do not listen to them; serve
the king of Babylon, and live!
Why should this city be laid
waste?
18 'But if they *are* prophets, and
if the word of the LORD is with
them, let them now make intercession to the LORD of hosts, that
the vessels which are left in the
house of the LORD, *in* the house
of the king of Judah, and at Jerusalem, do not go to Babylon.'
19 "For thus says the LORD of
hosts [a]concerning the pillars,
concerning the Sea, concerning
the carts, and concerning the
remainder of the vessels that
remain in this city,
20 "which Ne·bū·chad·nez′-
zar king of Babylon did not
take, when he carried away
[a]captive Jec·o·nī′ah the son of
Je·hoi′a·kim, king of Judah,
from Jerusalem to Babylon,
and all the nobles of Judah and
Jerusalem—

14 [a]Jer. 23:16 [b]Jer. 14:14; 23:21; 29:8, 9
15 [a]Jer. 23:21; 29:9
16 [a]Dan. 1:2
19 [a]2 Kin. 25:13–17
20 [a]Jer. 24:1
21 [a]Jer. 20:5
22 [a]2 Kin. 25:13 [b]2 Chr. 36:21; Jer. 29:10; 32:5 [c]Ezra 1:7; 7:19

CHAPTER 28

1 [a]Jer. 27:1 [b]Jer. 51:59 [c]Ezek. 11:1
2 [a]Jer. 27:12
3 [a]Jer. 27:16 [b]Dan. 1:2
4 [1]*Jehoiachin*, 2 Kin. 24:12
6 [a]1 Kin. 1:36

21 "yes, thus says the LORD of
hosts, the God of Israel, concerning the [a]vessels that remain
in the house of the LORD, and in
the house of the king of Judah
and of Jerusalem:
22 'They shall be [a]carried to
Babylon, and there they shall be
until the day that I [b]visit them,'
says the LORD. 'Then [c]I will bring
them up and restore them to this
place.' "

28 And [a]it happened in the
same year, at the begin-
ning of the reign of Zed·e·kī′ah
king of Judah, in the [b]fourth
year *and* in the fifth month, *that*
Han·a·nī′ah the son of [c]Ā′zur the
prophet, who *was* from Gib′-
ē·on, spoke to me in the house
of the LORD in the presence of
the priests and of all the people,
saying,
2 "Thus speaks the LORD of
hosts, the God of Israel, saying:
'I have broken [a]the yoke of the
king of Babylon.
3 [a]'Within two full years I will
bring back to this place all the
vessels of the LORD's house, that
Ne·bū·chad·nez′zar king of Babylon [b]took away from this place
and carried to Babylon.
4 'And I will bring back to
this place [1]Jec·o·nī′ah the son of
Je·hoi′a·kim, king of Judah, with
all the captives of Judah who
went to Babylon,' says the LORD,
'for I will break the yoke of the
king of Babylon.' "
5 Then the prophet Jer·e·mī′ah
spoke to the prophet Han·a·nī′ah
in the presence of the priests
and in the presence of all the
people who stood in the house
of the LORD,
6 and the prophet Jer·e·mī′ah
said, [a]"Amen! The LORD do so;

the LORD perform your words
which you have prophesied, to
bring back the vessels of the
LORD's house and all who were
carried away captive, from Babylon to this place.
7 "Nevertheless hear now this
word that I speak in your hearing and in the hearing of all the
people:
8 "The prophets who have been
before me and before you of old
prophesied against many countries and great kingdoms—of
war and disaster and pestilence.
9 "As for [a]the prophet who
prophesies of [b]peace, when the
word of the prophet comes to
pass, the prophet will be known
as one whom the LORD has truly
sent."
10 Then Han·a·nī'ah the prophet
took the [a]yoke off the prophet
Jer·e·mī'ah's neck and broke it.
11 And Han·a·nī'ah spoke in
the presence of all the people,
saying, "Thus says the LORD:
'Even so I will break the yoke
of Ne·bū·chad·nez'zar king of
Babylon [a]from the neck of all
nations within the space of two
full years.' " And the prophet
Jer·e·mī'ah went his way.
12 Now the word of the LORD
came to Jer·e·mī'ah, after Han·a-
nī'ah the prophet had broken
the yoke from the neck of the
prophet Jer·e·mī'ah, saying,
13 "Go and tell Han·a·nī'ah, saying, 'Thus says the LORD: "You
have broken the yokes of wood,
but you have made in their place
yokes of iron."
14 'For thus says the LORD of
hosts, the God of Israel: [a]"I have
put a yoke of iron on the neck
of all these nations, that they
may serve Ne·bū·chad·nez'zar
king of Babylon; and they shall
serve him. [b]I have given him the
beasts of the field also." ' "
15 Then the prophet Jer·e·mī'ah
said to Han·a·nī'ah the prophet,
"Hear now, Han·a·nī'ah, the LORD
has not sent you, but [a]you make
this people trust in a [b]lie.
16 "Therefore thus says the
LORD: 'Behold, I will cast you
from the face of the earth. This
year you shall [a]die, because you
have taught [b]rebellion against
the LORD.' "
17 So Han·a·nī'ah the prophet
died the same year in the seventh month.

29 Now these *are* the words
of the letter that Jer·e-
mī'ah the prophet sent from
Jerusalem to the remainder of
the elders who were [a]carried
away captive—to the priests,
the prophets, and all the people
whom Ne·bū·chad·nez'zar had
carried away captive from Jerusalem to Babylon.
2 (This happened after [a]Jec-
o·nī'ah[1] the king, the [b]queen
mother, the [2]eunuchs, the princes
of Judah and Jerusalem, the
craftsmen, and the smiths had
departed from Jerusalem.)
3 *The letter was sent* by the
hand of El·ā'sah the son of [a]Shā'-
phan, and Gem·a·rī'ah the son
of Hil·kī'ah, whom Zed·e·kī'ah
king of Judah sent to Babylon,
to Ne·bū·chad·nez'zar king of
Babylon, saying,

4 Thus says the LORD of
hosts, the God of Israel, to
all who were carried away
captive, whom I have caused
to be carried away from
Jerusalem to Babylon:

9 [a]Deut. 18:22 [b]Jer. 23:17
10 [a]Jer. 27:2
11 [a]Jer. 27:7
14 [a]Deut. 28:48 [b]Jer. 27:6
15 [a]Ezek. 13:22 [b]Jer. 27:10; 29:9
16 [a]Jer. 20:6 [b]Deut. 13:5
CHAPTER 29
1 [a]Jer. 27:20
2 [a]2 Kin. 24:12–16 [b]Jer. 13:18 [1]*Jehoiachin*, 2 Kin. 24:12; 2 Chr. 36:10 [2]Or *officers*
3 [a]2 Chr. 34:8

5 Build houses and dwell *in them;* plant gardens and eat their fruit.
6 Take wives and beget sons and daughters; and take wives for your sons and give your daughters to husbands, so that they may bear sons and daughters—that you may be increased there, and not diminished.
7 And seek the peace of the city where I have caused you to be carried away captive, [a]and pray to the LORD for it; for in its peace you will have peace.
8 For thus says the LORD of hosts, the God of Israel: Do not let your prophets and your diviners who are in your midst [a]deceive you, nor listen to your dreams which you cause to be dreamed.
9 For they prophesy [a]falsely to you in My name; I have not sent them, says the LORD.
10 For thus says the LORD: After [a]seventy years are completed at Babylon, I will visit you and perform My good word toward you, and cause you to [b]return to this place.
11 For I know the thoughts that I think toward you, says the LORD, thoughts of peace and not of evil, to give you a future and a hope.
12 Then you will [a]call upon Me and go and pray to Me, and I will [b]listen to you.
13 And [a]you will seek Me and find *Me,* when you search for Me [b]with all your heart.
14 [a]I will be found by you, says the LORD, and I will bring you back from your captivity; [b]I will gather you from all the nations and from all the places where I have driven you, says the LORD, and I will bring you to the place from which I cause you to be carried away captive.
15 Because you have said, "The LORD has raised up prophets for us in Babylon"—
16 [a]therefore thus says the LORD concerning the king who sits on the throne of David, concerning all the people who dwell in this city, and concerning your brethren who have not gone out with you into captivity—
17 thus says the LORD of hosts: Behold, I will send on them the sword, the famine, and the pestilence, and will make them like [a]rotten figs that cannot be eaten, they are so bad.
18 And I will pursue them with the sword, with famine, and with pestilence; and I [a]will deliver them to trouble among all the kingdoms of the earth—to be [b]a curse, an astonishment, a hissing, and a reproach among all the nations where I have driven them,
19 because they have not heeded My words, says the LORD, which [a]I sent to them by My servants the prophets, rising up early and sending *them;* neither would you heed, says the LORD.
20 Therefore hear the word of the LORD, all you of the captivity, whom I have sent from Jerusalem to Babylon.

7 [a]1 Tim. 2:2
8 [a]Eph. 5:6
9 [a]Jer. 28:15; 37:19
10 [a]Dan. 9:2 [b][Jer. 24:6, 7]
12 [a]Ps. 50:15 [b]Ps. 145:19
13 [a]Deut. 30:1–3 [b]Jer. 24:7
14 [a][Is. 55:6, 7] [b]Jer. 23:8; 32:37
16 [a]Jer. 38:2, 3, 17–23
17 [a]Jer. 24:3, 8–10
18 [a]Deut. 28:25 [b]Jer. 26:6; 42:18
19 [a]Jer. 25:4; 26:5; 35:15

21 Thus says the LORD of
hosts, the God of Israel,
concerning Ā′hab the son
of Kō·laī′ah, and Zed·e·kī′ah
the son of Mā·a·sēi′ah, who
prophesy a [a]lie to you in My
name: Behold, I will deliver
them into the hand of
Ne·bū·chad·nez′zar king of
Babylon, and he shall slay
them before your eyes.
22 [a]And because of them a
curse shall be taken up by
all the captivity of Judah
who *are* in Babylon, saying,
"The LORD make you like
Zed·e·kī′ah and Ā′hab,
[b]whom the king of Babylon
roasted in the fire";
23 because [a]they have done
disgraceful things in Israel,
have committed adultery
with their neighbors' wives,
and have spoken lying
words in My name, which I
have not commanded them.
Indeed I [b]know, and *am* a
witness, says the LORD.

24 You shall also speak
to She·māi′ah the
Ne·hel′a·mīte, saying,
25 Thus speaks the LORD of
hosts, the God of Israel,
saying: You have sent
letters in your name to
all the people who *are* at
Jerusalem, [a]to Zeph·a·nī′ah
the son of Mā·a·sēi′ah the
priest, and to all the priests,
saying,
26 "The LORD has made you
priest instead of Je·hoi′a·da
the priest, so that there
should be [a]officers *in*
the house of the LORD
over every man *who* is
[b]demented and considers
himself a prophet, that you
should [c]put him in prison
and in the stocks.
27 Now therefore, why have
you not rebuked Jer·e·mī′ah
of An′a·thoth who makes
himself a prophet to you?
28 For he has sent to us *in*
Babylon, saying, 'This
captivity is long; build
houses and dwell *in them,*
and plant gardens and eat
their fruit.' "
29 Now Zeph·a·nī′ah the
priest read this letter in the
hearing of Jer·e·mī′ah the
prophet.
30 Then the word of the LORD
came to Jer·e·mī′ah, saying:
31 Send to all those
in captivity, saying,
Thus says the LORD
concerning She·māi′ah
the Ne·hel′a·mīte: Because
She·māi′ah has prophesied
to you, [a]and I have not sent
him, and he has caused you
to trust in a [b]lie—
32 therefore thus says the
LORD: Behold, I will punish
She·māi′ah the Ne·hel′a·mīte
and his [1]family: he shall not
have anyone to dwell among
this people, nor shall he see
the good that I will do for
My people, says the LORD,
[a]because he has taught
rebellion against the LORD.

30 The word that came to
Jer·e·mī′ah from the LORD,
saying,
2 "Thus speaks the LORD God
of Israel, saying: 'Write in a
book for yourself all the words
that I have spoken to you.
3 'For behold, the days are
coming,' says the LORD, 'that [a]I

21 [a]Lam. 2:14
22 [a]Is. 65:15 [b]Dan. 3:6, 21
23 [a]Jer. 23:14 [b][Prov. 5:21]
25 [a]Jer. 21:1
26 [a]Jer. 20:1 [b]John 10:20 [c]Jer. 20:1, 2
31 [a]Jer. 28:15 [b]Ezek. 13:8–16, 22, 23
32 [a]Jer. 28:16 [1]*descendants*, lit. *seed*

CHAPTER 30

3 [a]Ezek. 39:25

will bring back from captivity
My people Israel and Judah,'
says the LORD. [b]'And I will cause
them to return to the land that
I gave to their fathers, and they
shall possess it.' "
4 Now these *are* the words
that the LORD spoke concerning
Israel and Judah.
5 "For thus says the LORD:

'We have heard a voice of
trembling,
Of [1]fear, and not of peace.
6 Ask now, and see,
Whether a [1]man is ever in
[2]labor with child?
So why do I see every man
with his hands on his
loins
[a]Like a woman in labor,
And all faces turned pale?
7 [a]Alas! For that day *is* great,
[b]So that none *is* like it;
And it *is* the time of Jacob's
trouble,
But he shall be saved out
of it.

8 'For it shall come to pass in
that day,'
Says the LORD of hosts,
'*That* I will break his yoke
from your neck,
And will burst your bonds;
Foreigners shall no more
enslave them.
☆9 But they shall serve the
LORD their God,
And [a]David their king,
Whom I will [b]raise up for
them.

10 'Therefore [a]do not fear, O My
servant Jacob,' says the
LORD,
'Nor be dismayed, O Israel;
For behold, I will save you
from afar,
And your seed [b]from the
land of their captivity.
Jacob shall return, have rest
and be quiet,
And no one shall make *him*
afraid.
11 For I *am* with [a]you,' says the
LORD, 'to save you;
[b]Though I make a full end of
all nations where I have
scattered you,
[c]Yet I will not make a
complete end of you.
But I will correct you [d]in
justice,
And will not let you go
altogether unpunished.'

12 "For thus says the LORD:

[a]'Your affliction *is* incurable,
Your wound *is* severe.
13 *There is* no one to plead
your cause,
That you may be bound up;
[a]You have no healing
medicines.
14 [a]All your lovers have
forgotten you;
They do not seek you;
For I have wounded you
with the wound [b]of an
enemy,
With the chastisement [c]of a
cruel one,
For the multitude of your
iniquities,
[d]*Because* your sins have
increased.
15 Why [a]do you cry about your
affliction?
Your sorrow *is* incurable.
Because of the multitude of
your iniquities,
Because your sins have
increased,

3 [b]Jer. 16:15
5 [1]*dread*
6 [a]Jer. 4:31; 6:24 [1]Lit. *male can give birth* [2]*childbirth*
7 [a]Amos 5:18 [b]Dan. 9:12; 12:1
9 [a]Hos. 3:5 [b][Luke 1:69; Acts 2:30; 13:23]
10 [a]Is. 41:13; 43:5; 44:2 [b]Jer. 3:18
11 [a][Is. 43:2–5] [b]Amos 9:8 [c]Jer. 4:27; 46:27, 28 [d]Ps. 6:1
12 [a]Jer. 15:18
13 [a]Jer. 8:22
14 [a]Lam. 1:2 [b]Job 13:24; 16:9; 19:11 [c]Job 30:21 [d]Jer. 5:6
15 [a]Jer. 15:18

I have done these things to
you.

16 'Therefore all those who
devour you [a]shall be
devoured;
And all your adversaries,
every one of them, shall
go into [b]captivity;
Those who plunder you
shall become [c]plunder,
And all who prey upon you
I will make a [d]prey.
17 [a]For I will restore health to
you
And heal you of your
wounds,' says the LORD,
'Because they called you an
outcast *saying*:
"This *is* Zion;
No one seeks her." '

18 "Thus says the LORD:

'Behold, I will bring back the
captivity of Jacob's tents,
And [a]have mercy on his
dwelling places;
The city shall be built upon
its own [1]mound,
And the palace shall remain
according to its own
plan.
19 Then [a]out of them shall
proceed thanksgiving
And the voice of those who
make merry;
[b]I will multiply them, and
they shall not diminish;
I will also glorify them, and
they shall not be small.
20 Their children also shall be
[a]as before,
And their congregation
shall be established
before Me;
And I will punish all who
oppress them.

16 [a]Jer. 10:25 [b]Is. 14:2 [c]Ezek. 39:10 [d]Jer. 2:3
17 [a]Jer. 33:6
18 [a]Ps. 102:13 [1]*ruins*
19 [a]Is. 51:11 [b]Zech. 10:8
20 [a]Is. 1:26
21 [a]Gen. 49:10 [b]Num. 16:5
22 [a]Ezek. 36:28
23 [a]Jer. 23:19, 20; 25:32 [1]Or *sweeping*
24 [a]Gen. 49:1

CHAPTER 31

1 [a]Jer. 30:24 [b]Jer. 30:22
2 [a]Num. 10:33
3 [a]Mal. 1:2 [b]Rom. 11:28 [c]Hos. 11:4 [1]Lit. *from afar*

21 Their nobles shall be from
among them,
[a]And their governor shall
come from their midst;
Then I will [b]cause him to
draw near,
And he shall approach Me;
For who *is* this who pledged
his heart to approach
Me?' says the LORD.
22 'You shall be [a]My people,
And I will be your God.' "

23 Behold, the [a]whirlwind of
the LORD
Goes forth with fury,
A [1]continuing whirlwind;
It will fall violently on the
head of the wicked.
24 The fierce anger of the LORD
will not return until He
has done it,
And until He has performed
the intents of His heart.

[a]In the latter days you will
consider it.

31

"At [a]the same time," says
the LORD, [b]"I will be the
God of all the families of Israel,
and they shall be My people."
2 Thus says the LORD:

"The people who survived
the sword
Found grace in the
wilderness—
Israel, when [a]I went to give
him rest."

3 The LORD has appeared [1]of
old to me, *saying*:
"Yes, [a]I have loved you with
[b]an everlasting love;
Therefore with
lovingkindness I have
[c]drawn you.

4 Again [a]I will build you, and
you shall be rebuilt,
O virgin of Israel!
You shall again be adorned
with your [b]tambourines,
And shall go forth in the
dances of those who
rejoice.
5 [a]You shall yet plant vines
on the mountains of
Samaria;
The planters shall plant and
[1]eat *them* as ordinary
food.
6 For there shall be a day
When the watchmen will cry
on Mount Ē′phra·im,
[a]'Arise, and let us go up *to*
Zion,
To the LORD our God.' "

7 For thus says the LORD:

[a]"Sing with gladness for
Jacob,
And shout among the chief
of the nations;
Proclaim, give praise, and
say,
'O LORD, save Your people,
The remnant of Israel!'
8 Behold, I will bring them
[a]from the north country,
And [b]gather them from the
ends of the earth,
Among them the blind and
the lame,
The woman with child
And the one who labors
with child, together;
A great throng shall return
there.
9 [a]They shall come with
weeping,
And with supplications I
will lead them.
I will cause them to walk
[b]by the rivers of waters,
In a straight way in which
they shall not stumble;
For I am a Father to Israel,
And Ē′phra·im *is* My
[c]firstborn.

10 "Hear the word of the LORD,
O nations,
And declare *it* in the [1]isles
afar off, and say,
'He who scattered Israel [a]will
gather him,
And keep him as a shepherd
does his flock.'
11 For [a]the LORD has redeemed
Jacob,
And ransomed him [b]from
the hand of one stronger
than he.
12 Therefore they shall come
and sing in [a]the height of
Zion,
Streaming to [b]the goodness
of the LORD—
For wheat and new wine
and oil,
For the young of the flock
and the herd;
Their souls shall be like a
[c]well-watered garden,
[d]And they shall sorrow no
more at all.

13 "Then shall the virgin rejoice
in the dance,
And the young men and the
old, together;
For I will turn their
mourning to joy,
Will comfort them,
And make them rejoice
rather than sorrow.
14 I will [1]satiate the soul of the
priests with abundance,
And My people shall
be satisfied with My
goodness, says the
LORD."

---

4 [a]Jer. 33:7 [b]Judg. 11:34
5 [a]Amos 9:14 [1]Lit. *treat them as common*
6 [a][Mic. 4:2]
7 [a]Is. 12:5, 6
8 [a]Jer. 3:12, 18; 23:8 [b]Ezek. 20:34, 41; 34:13
9 [a][Jer. 50:4] [b]Is. 35:8; 43:19; 49:10, 11 [c]Ex. 4:22
10 [a]Is. 40:11 [1]Or *coastlands*
11 [a]Is. 44:23; 48:20 [b]Is. 49:24
12 [a]Ezek. 17:23 [b]Hos. 3:5 [c]Is. 58:11 [d]Is. 35:10; 65:19
14 [1]Fill to the full

☆ **15** Thus says the LORD:

[a]"A voice was heard in
[b]Rā′mah,
Lamentation *and* bitter
[c]weeping,
Rachel weeping for her
children,
Refusing to be comforted
for her children,
Because [d]they *are* no more."

16 Thus says the LORD:

"Refrain your voice from
[a]weeping,
And your eyes from tears;
For your work shall be
rewarded, says the LORD,
And they shall come back
from the land of the
enemy.
17 There is [a]hope in your
future, says the LORD,
That *your* children shall
come back to their own
border.

18 "I have surely heard
Ē′phra·im bemoaning
himself:
'You have [a]chastised me, and
I was chastised,
Like an untrained bull;
[b]Restore me, and I will
return,
For You *are* the LORD my
God.
19 Surely, [a]after my turning, I
repented;
And after I was instructed,
I struck myself on the
thigh;
I was [b]ashamed, yes, even
humiliated,
Because I bore the reproach
of my youth.'

15 [a]Matt. 2:17, 18 [b]Josh. 18:25 [c]Gen. 37:35 [d]Jer. 10:20
16 [a][Is. 25:8; 30:19]
17 [a]Jer. 29:11
18 [a]Ps. 94:12 [b]Lam. 5:21
19 [a]Deut. 30:2 [b]Ezek. 36:31
20 [a]Is. 63:15 [b][Hos. 14:4] [1]Lit. *inward parts*
21 [a]Jer. 50:5 [1]Or *Return*
22 [a]Jer. 2:18, 23, 36 [b]Jer. 3:6, 8, 11, 12, 14, 22
23 [a]Is. 1:26 [b][Zech. 8:3]
24 [a]Jer. 33:12
25 [1]*fully satisfied*
26 [a]Prov. 3:24
27 [a]Ezek. 36:9–11

20 *Is* Ē′phra·im My dear son?
Is he a pleasant child?
For though I spoke against
him,
I earnestly remember him
still;
[a]Therefore My [1]heart yearns
for him;
[b]I will surely have mercy on
him, says the LORD.

21 "Set up signposts,
Make landmarks;
[a]Set your heart toward the
highway,
The way in *which* you went.
[1]Turn back, O virgin of
Israel,
Turn back to these your
cities.
22 How long will you [a]gad
about,
O you [b]backsliding
daughter?
For the LORD has created a
new thing in the earth—
A woman shall encompass
a man."

23 Thus says the LORD of hosts,
the God of Israel: "They shall
again use this speech in the land
of Judah and in its cities, when I
bring back their captivity: [a]'The
LORD bless you, O home of justice, *and* [b]mountain of holiness!'
24 "And there shall dwell in Judah itself, and [a]in all its cities together, farmers and those going
out with flocks.
25 "For I have [1]satiated the
weary soul, and I have replen-
ished every sorrowful soul."
26 After this I awoke and looked
around, and my sleep was [a]sweet
to me.
27 "Behold, the days are coming, says the LORD, that [a]I will

sow the house of Israel and the
house of Judah with the seed of
man and the seed of beast.
28 "And it shall come to pass,
that as I have [a]watched over
them [b]to pluck up, to break
down, to throw down, to destroy,
and to afflict, so I will watch
over them [c]to build and to plant,
says the LORD.
29 [a]"In those days they shall say
no more:

'The fathers have eaten sour
grapes,
And the children's teeth are
set on edge.'

30 [a]"But every one shall die for
his own iniquity; every man who
eats the sour grapes, his teeth
shall be set on edge.
☆ **31** "Behold, the [a]days are coming, says the LORD, when I will
make a new covenant with the
house of Israel and with the
house of Judah—
32 "not according to the covenant that I made with their
fathers in the day *that* [a]I took
them by the hand to lead them
out of the land of Egypt, My covenant which they broke, [1]though
I was a husband to them, says
the LORD.
☆ 33 [a]"But this *is* the covenant
that I will make with the house
of Israel after those days, says
the LORD: [b]I will put My law in
their minds, and write it on their
[1]hearts; [c]and I will be their God,
and they shall be My people.
☆ 34 "No more shall every man
teach his neighbor, and every
man his brother, saying, 'Know
the LORD,' for [a]they all shall know
Me, from the least of them to the
greatest of them, says the LORD.

28 [a]Jer. 44:27 [b]Jer. 1:10; 18:7 [c]Jer. 24:6
29 [a]Ezek. 18:2, 3
30 [a][Gal. 6:5, 7]
31 [a]Luke 22:20; Heb. 8:8–12; 10:16, 17
32 [a]Deut. 1:31 [1]So with MT, Tg., Vg.; LXX, Syr. *and I turned away from them*
33 [a]Jer. 32:40; Heb. 10:16 [b]Ps. 40:8; [2 Cor. 3:3] [c]Jer. 24:7; 30:22; 32:38 [1]Lit. *inward parts*
34 [a][John 6:45] [b][Acts 10:43; 13:39; Rom. 11:27]
35 [a]Gen. 1:14–18 [b]Is. 51:15 [c]Jer. 10:16
36 [a]Ps. 148:6
37 [a]Jer. 33:22 [b][Rom. 11:2–5, 26, 27]
38 [a]Zech. 14:10
39 [a]Zech. 2:1, 2
40 [a]Neh. 3:28

For [b]I will forgive their iniquity,
and their sin I will remember no
more."

35 Thus says the LORD,
[a]Who gives the sun for a
light by day,
The ordinances of the moon
and the stars for a light
by night,
Who disturbs [b]the sea,
And its waves roar
[c](The LORD of hosts *is* His
name):

36 "If [a]those ordinances depart
From before Me, says the
LORD,
Then the seed of Israel shall
also cease
From being a nation before
Me forever."

37 Thus says the LORD:

[a]"If heaven above can be
measured,
And the foundations of
the earth searched out
beneath,
I will also [b]cast off all the
seed of Israel
For all that they have done,
says the LORD.

38 "Behold, the days are coming, says the LORD, that the city
shall be built for the LORD [a]from
the Tower of Ha·nan'el to the
Corner Gate.
39 [a]"The surveyor's line shall
again extend straight forward
over the hill Gā'reb; then it shall
turn toward Gō'ath.
40 "And the whole valley of the
dead bodies and of the ashes,
and all the fields as far as the
Brook Kid'ron, [a]to the corner

of the Horse Gate toward the
east, [b]*shall be* holy to the LORD.
It shall not be plucked up or
thrown down anymore forever."

32 The word that came to
Jer·e·mi′ah from the
LORD [a]in the tenth year of Zed·e-
ki′ah king of Judah, which
was the eighteenth year of
Ne·bu·chad·nez′zar.
2 For then the king of Babylon's army besieged Jerusalem,
and Jer·e·mi′ah the prophet was
shut up [a]in the court of the
prison, which *was in* the king of
Judah's house.
3 For Zed·e·ki′ah king of Judah had shut him up, saying,
"Why do you [a]prophesy and say,
'Thus says the LORD: [b]"Behold, I
will give this city into the hand
of the king of Babylon, and he
shall take it;
4 "and Zed·e·ki′ah king of Judah [a]shall not escape from the
hand of the Chal·de′ans, but
shall surely be delivered into
the hand of the king of Babylon,
and shall speak with him [1]face
to face, and see him [b]eye to eye;
5 "then he shall [a]lead Zed·e-
ki′ah to Babylon, and there he
shall be [b]until I visit him," says
the LORD; [c]"though you fight
with the Chal·de′ans, you shall
not succeed" '?"
6 And Jer·e·mi′ah said, "The
word of the LORD came to me,
saying,
7 'Behold, Han′a·mel the son of
Shal′lum your uncle will come to
you, saying, "Buy my field which
is in An′a·thoth, for the [a]right of
redemption *is* yours to buy *it.*" '
8 "Then Han′a·mel my uncle's
son came to me in the court
of the prison according to the
word of the LORD, and said to
me, 'Please buy my field that
is in An′a·thoth, which *is* in the
country of Benjamin; for the
right of inheritance *is* yours, and
the redemption yours; buy *it* for
yourself.' Then I knew that this
was the word of the LORD.
9 "So I bought the field from
Han′a·mel, the son of my uncle who *was* in An′a·thoth,
and [a]weighed *out to* him the
money—seventeen shekels of
silver.
10 "And I signed the [1]deed
and sealed *it,* took witnesses,
and weighed the money on the
scales.
11 "So I took the purchase deed,
both that which was sealed *according* to the law and custom,
and that which was open;
12 "and I gave the purchase
deed to [a]Bar′uch the son of
Ne·ri′ah, son of Mah′sei·ah, in
the presence of Han′a·mel my
uncle's *son,* and in the presence
of the [b]witnesses who signed
the purchase deed, before all
the Jews who sat in the court
of the prison.
13 "Then I charged [a]Bar′uch before them, saying,
14 'Thus says the LORD of hosts,
the God of Israel: "Take these
deeds, both this purchase deed
which is sealed and this deed
which is open, and put them in
an earthen vessel, that they may
last many days."
15 'For thus says the LORD of
hosts, the God of Israel: "Houses
and fields and vineyards shall be
[a]possessed again in this land." '
16 "Now when I had delivered
the purchase deed to Bar′uch
the son of Ne·ri′ah, I prayed to
the LORD, saying:
17 'Ah, Lord GOD! Behold, [a]You

40 [b][Joel 3:17]
CHAPTER 32
1 [a]Jer. 39:1, 2
2 [a]Jer. 33:1; 37:21; 39:14
3 [a]Jer. 26:8, 9 [b]Jer. 21:3–7; 34:2
4 [a]Jer. 34:3; 38:18, 23; 39:5; 52:9 [b]Jer. 39:5 [1]Lit. *mouth to mouth*
5 [a]Ezek. 12:12, 13 [b]Jer. 27:22 [c]Jer. 21:4; 33:5
7 [a]Ruth 4:4
9 [a]Zech. 11:12
10 [1]Lit. *book*
12 [a]Jer. 36:4 [b]Is. 8:2
13 [a]Jer. 36:4
15 [a][Jer. 31:5, 12, 14]
17 [a]2 Kin. 19:15

have made the heavens and
the earth by Your great power
and outstretched arm. [b]There is
nothing too [1]hard for You.
18 '*You* show [a]lovingkindness
to thousands, and repay the iniquity of the fathers into the
bosom of their children after
them—the Great, [b]the Mighty
God, whose name *is* [c]the LORD of
hosts.
19 '*You are* [a]great in counsel
and mighty in [1]work, for Your
[b]eyes *are* open to all the ways
of the sons of men, [c]to give everyone according to his ways
and according to the fruit of his
doings.
20 'You have set signs and wonders in the land of Egypt, to this
day, and in Israel and among
other men; and You have made
Yourself [a]a name, as it is this
day.
21 'You [a]have brought Your
people Israel out of the land of
Egypt with signs and wonders,
with a strong hand and an outstretched arm, and with great
terror;
22 'You have given them this
land, of which You swore to their
fathers to give them—[a]"a land
flowing with milk and honey."
23 'And they came in and took
possession of it, but [a]they have
not obeyed Your voice or walked
in Your law. They have done
nothing of all that You commanded them to do; therefore
You have caused all this calamity to come upon them.
24 'Look, the siege mounds!
They have come to the city to
take it; and the city has been
given into the hand of the
Chal·dē′ans who fight against
it, because of [a]the sword and

17 [b]Luke 18:27 [1]*difficult*
18 [a]Deut. 5:9, 10 [b][Is. 9:6] [c]Jer. 10:16
19 [a]Is. 28:29 [b]Prov. 5:21 [c]Jer. 17:10 [1]*deed*
20 [a]Is. 63:12
21 [a]Ex. 6:6
22 [a]Ex. 3:8, 17
23 [a][Neh. 9:26]
24 [a]Jer. 14:12
27 [a][Num. 16:22]
29 [a]2 Chr. 36:19 [b]Jer. 19:13
30 [a]Jer. 2:7; 3:25; 7:22–26
31 [a]2 Kin. 23:27; 24:3
32 [a]Dan. 9:8 [b]Jer. 23:14

famine and pestilence. What
You have spoken has happened;
there You see *it!*
25 'And You have said to me,
O Lord GOD, "Buy the field for
money, and take witnesses"!—
yet the city has been given into
the hand of the Chal·dē′ans.' "
26 Then the word of the LORD
came to Jer·e·mī′ah, saying,
27 "Behold, I *am* the LORD, the
[a]God of all flesh. Is there anything too hard for Me?
28 "Therefore thus says
the LORD: 'Behold, I will give
this city into the hand of the
Chal·dē′ans, into the hand of
Ne·bū·chad·nez′zar king of Babylon, and he shall take it.
29 'And the Chal·dē′ans who
fight against this city shall come
and [a]set fire to this city and burn
it, with the houses [b]on whose
roofs they have offered incense
to Bā′al and poured out drink offerings to other gods, to provoke
Me to anger;
30 'because the children of Israel and the children of Judah
[a]have done only evil before Me
from their youth. For the children of Israel have provoked Me
only to anger with the work of
their hands,' says the LORD.
31 'For this city has been to Me
a provocation of My anger and
My fury from the day that they
built it, even to this day; [a]so I
will remove it from before My
face
32 'because of all the evil of the
children of Israel and the children of Judah, which they have
done to provoke Me to anger—
[a]they, their kings, their princes,
their priests, [b]their prophets, the
men of Judah, and the inhabitants of Jerusalem.

33 'And they have turned to
Me the [a]back, and not the face;
though I taught them, [b]rising
up early and teaching *them*, yet
they have not listened to receive
instruction.
34 'But they [a]set their abominations in [1]the house which is
called by My name, to defile it.
35 'And they built the high
places of Bā′al which *are* in the
Valley of the Son of Hin′nom,
to [a]cause their sons and their
daughters to pass through *the
fire* to [b]Mō′lech, [c]which I did not
command them, nor did it come
into My mind that they should
do this abomination, to cause
Judah to sin.'
36 "Now therefore, thus says
the LORD, the God of Israel, concerning this city of which you
say, 'It shall be delivered into the
hand of the king of Babylon by
the sword, by the famine, and by
the pestilence':
37 'Behold, I will [a]gather them
out of all countries where I have
driven them in My anger, in My
fury, and in great wrath; I will
bring them back to this place,
and I will cause them [b]to dwell
safely.
38 'They shall be [a]My people,
and I will be their God;
39 'then I will [a]give them one
heart and one way, that they
may fear Me forever, for the
good of them and their children
after them.
40 'And [a]I will make an everlasting covenant with them, that
I will not turn away from doing
them good; but [b]I will put My
fear in their hearts so that they
will not depart from Me.
41 'Yes, [a]I will rejoice over them
to do them good, and [b]I will
[1]assuredly plant them in this
land, with all My heart and with
all My soul.'
42 "For thus says the LORD:
[a]'Just as I have brought all this
great calamity on this people, so
I will bring on them all the good
that I have promised them.
43 'And fields will be bought in
this land [a]of which you say, "*It is*
desolate, without man or beast;
it has been given into the hand
of the Chal·dē′ans."
44 'Men will buy fields for
money, sign deeds and seal
them, and take witnesses, in
[a]the land of Benjamin, in the
places around Jerusalem, in the
cities of Judah, in the cities of
the mountains, in the cities of
the [1]lowland, and in the cities
of the [2]South; for [b]I will cause
their captives to return,' says the
LORD."

33

Moreover the word of the
LORD came to Jer·e·mī′ah
a second time, while he was
still [a]shut up in the court of the
prison, saying,
2 "Thus says the LORD [a]who
made it, the LORD who formed it
to establish it [b](the[1] LORD *is* His
name):
3 [a]'Call to Me, and I will answer you, and show you great
and [1]mighty things, which you
do not know.'
4 "For thus says the LORD,
the God of Israel, concerning
the houses of this city and the
houses of the kings of Judah,
which have been pulled down *to
fortify* against [a]the siege mounds
and the sword:
5 'They come to fight with the
Chal·dē′ans, but *only* to [a]fill their
places with the dead bodies of
men whom I will slay in My

33 [a]Jer. 2:27; 7:24 [b]Jer. 7:13
34 [a]Jer. 7:10–12, 30; 23:11 [1]The temple
35 [a]Jer. 7:31; 19:5 [b]Lev. 18:21 [c]Jer. 7:31
37 [a]Deut. 30:3 [b]Jer. 33:16
38 [a][Jer. 24:7; 30:22; 31:33]
39 [a][Ezek. 11:19]
40 [a]Is. 55:3 [b][Jer. 31:33]
41 [a]Deut. 30:9 [b]Amos 9:15 [1]*truly*
42 [a]Jer. 31:28
43 [a]Jer. 33:10
44 [a]Jer. 17:26 [b]Jer. 33:7, 11 [1]Heb. *shephelah* [2]Heb. *Negev*

CHAPTER 33

1 [a]Jer. 32:2, 3
2 [a]Is. 37:26 [b]Ex. 15:3 [1]Heb. *YHWH*
3 [a]Jer. 29:12 [1]*inaccessible*
4 [a]Is. 22:10
5 [a]2 Kin. 23:14

anger and My fury, all for whose
wickedness I have hidden My
face from this city.
6 'Behold, [a]I will bring it health
and healing; I will heal them and
reveal to them the abundance of
peace and truth.
7 'And [a]I will cause the captives
of Judah and the captives of
Israel to return, and will rebuild
those places [b]as at the first.
8 'I will [a]cleanse them from
all their iniquity by which they
have sinned against Me, and I
will pardon all their iniquities
by which they have sinned and
by which they have transgressed
against Me.
9 [a]'Then it shall be to Me a
name of joy, a praise, and an
honor before all nations of the
earth, who shall hear all the
good that I do to them; they
shall [b]fear and tremble for all
the goodness and all the prosperity that I provide for it.'
10 "Thus says the LORD: 'Again
there shall be heard in this
place—[a]of which you say, "It
is desolate, without man and
without beast"—in the cities of
Judah, in the streets of Jerusalem that are desolate, without
man and without inhabitant and
without beast,
11 'the [a]voice of joy and the
voice of gladness, the voice of
the bridegroom and the voice of
the bride, the voice of those who
will say:

[b]"Praise the LORD of hosts,
For the LORD *is* good,
For His mercy *endures*
forever"—

and of those *who will* bring [c]the
sacrifice of praise into the house
of the LORD. For I will cause the
captives of the land to return as
at the first,' says the LORD.
12 "Thus says the LORD of hosts:
[a]'In this place which is desolate,
without man and without beast,
and in all its cities, there shall
again be a dwelling place of
shepherds causing *their* flocks
to lie down.
13 [a]'In the cities of the mountains, in the cities of the lowland,
in the cities of the South, in the
land of Benjamin, in the places
around Jerusalem, and in the
cities of Judah, the flocks shall
again [b]pass under the hands of
him who counts *them,*' says the
LORD.
14 [a]'Behold, the days are coming,' says the LORD, 'that [b]I will
perform that good thing which
I have promised to the house
of Israel and to the house of
Judah:

15 'In those days and at that time ☆
I will cause to grow up to David
A [a]Branch of righteousness;
He shall execute judgment and righteousness in the earth.
16 In those days Judah will be saved, ☆
And Jerusalem will dwell safely.
And this *is the name* by which she will be called:

[1]THE LORD OUR
[a]RIGHTEOUSNESS.'

17 "For thus says the LORD: 'David shall never [a]lack a man to
sit on the throne of the house of
Israel;

6 [a]Jer. 30:17
7 [a]Jer. 30:3; 32:44 [b]Is. 1:26
8 [a]Zech. 13:1
9 [a]Is. 62:7 [b]Is. 60:5
10 [a]Jer. 32:43
11 [a]Rev. 18:23 [b]Is. 12:4 [c]Lev. 7:12
12 [a]Is. 65:10
13 [a]Jer. 17:26; 32:44 [b]Lev. 27:32
14 [a]Jer. 23:5; 31:27, 31 [b]Jer. 29:10; 32:42
15 [a]Jer. 23:5; [Matt. 1:1, 6; Luke 3:31; John 1:45; 7:42]; Rev. 22:16
16 [a][Rom. 3:22; 1 Cor. 1:30] [1]Heb. *YHWH Tsidkenu;* cf. Jer. 23:5, 6
17 [a]2 Sam. 7:16

18 'nor shall the [a]priests, the
Lē'vītes, lack a man to [b]offer
burnt offerings before Me, to
[1]kindle grain offerings, and to
sacrifice continually.' "
19 And the word of the LORD
came to Jer·e·mī'ah, saying,
20 "Thus says the LORD: 'If you
can break My covenant with the
day and My covenant with the
night, so that there will not be
day and night in their season,
21 'then [a]My covenant may also
be broken with David My servant, so that he shall not have a
son to reign on his throne, and
with the Lē'vītes, the priests, My
ministers.
22 'As [a]the host of heaven cannot be numbered, nor the sand
of the sea measured, so will I
[b]multiply the descendants of David My servant and the [c]Lē'vītes
who minister to Me.' "
23 Moreover the word of the
LORD came to Jer·e·mī'ah, saying,
24 "Have you not considered
what these people have spoken,
saying, 'The two families which
the LORD has chosen, He has
also cast them off'? Thus they
have [a]despised My people, as if
they should no more be a nation
before them.
25 "Thus says the LORD: 'If
[a]My covenant *is* not with day
and night, *and if* I have not
[b]appointed the ordinances of
heaven and earth,
26 [a]'then I will [b]cast away the
descendants of Jacob and David
My servant, *so* that I will not
take *any* of his descendants *to
be* rulers over the descendants
of Abraham, Isaac, and Jacob.
For I will cause their captives to

18 [a]Ezek. 44:15 [b][1 Pet. 2:5, 9] [1]*burn*
21 [a]2 Sam. 23:5; Ps. 89:34
22 [a]Gen. 15:5; 22:17 [b]Jer. 30:19 [c]Is. 66:21
24 [a]Esth. 3:6–8
25 [a]Gen. 8:22 [b]Ps. 74:16; 104:19
26 [a]Jer. 31:37 [b]Rom. 11:1, 2

CHAPTER 34

1 [a]2 Kin. 25:1 [b]Jer. 1:15; 25:9
2 [a]2 Chr. 36:11, 12 [b]Jer. 21:10; 32:3, 28
3 [a]2 Kin. 25:4, 5 [b]Jer. 32:4; 39:5, 6 [1]Lit. *mouth to mouth*
5 [a]2 Chr. 16:14; 21:19 [b]Dan. 2:46 [c]Jer. 22:18
7 [a]2 Kin. 18:13; 19:8

return, and will have mercy on
them.' "

34

The word which came to
Jer·e·mī'ah from the LORD,
[a]when Ne·bū·chad·nez'zar king
of Babylon and all his army, [b]all
the kingdoms of the earth under
his dominion, and all the people,
fought against Jerusalem and all
its cities, saying,
2 "Thus says the LORD, the
God of Israel: 'Go and [a]speak to
Zed·e·kī'ah king of Judah and
tell him, "Thus says the LORD:
'Behold, [b]I will give this city into
the hand of the king of Babylon,
and he shall burn it with fire.
3 'And [a]you shall not escape
from his hand, but shall surely
be taken and delivered into his
hand; your eyes shall see the
eyes of the king of Babylon, he
shall speak with you [b]face[1] to
face, and you shall go to Babylon.' " '
4 "Yet hear the word of the
LORD, O Zed·e·kī'ah king of Judah! Thus says the LORD concerning you: 'You shall not die
by the sword.
5 'You shall die in peace; as in
[a]the ceremonies of your fathers,
the former kings who were before you, [b]so they shall burn
incense for you and [c]lament for
you, *saying*, "Alas, lord!" For I
have pronounced the word, says
the LORD.' "
6 Then Jer·e·mī'ah the prophet
spoke all these words to Zed·e-
kī'ah king of Judah in Jerusalem,
7 when the king of Babylon's
army fought against Jerusalem
and all the cities of Judah that
were left, against Lā'chish and
A·zē'kah; for *only* [a]these fortified cities remained of the cities
of Judah.

8 *This is* the word that came
to Jer·e·mi'ah from the LORD,
after King Zed·e·ki'ah had made
a covenant with all the people
who *were* at Jerusalem to proclaim [a]liberty to them:
9 [a]that every man should set
free his male and female slave—
a Hebrew man or woman—[b]that
no one should keep a Jewish
brother in bondage.
10 Now when all the princes
and all the people, who had entered into the covenant, heard
that everyone should set free his
male and female slaves, that no
one should keep them in bondage anymore, they obeyed and
let *them* go.
11 But afterward they changed
their minds and made the male
and female slaves return, whom
they had set free, and brought
them into subjection as male
and female slaves.
12 Therefore the word of the
LORD came to Jer·e·mi'ah from
the LORD, saying,
13 "Thus says the LORD, the God
of Israel: 'I made a [a]covenant
with your fathers in the day that
I brought them out of the land of
Egypt, out of the house of bondage, saying,
14 "At the end of [a]seven years
let every man set free his Hebrew brother, who [1]has been
sold to him; and when he has
served you six years, you shall
let him go free from you." But
your fathers did not obey Me
nor incline their ear.
15 'Then you [1]recently turned
and did what was right in My
sight—every man proclaiming
liberty to his neighbor; and you
[a]made a covenant before Me [b]in
the house which is called by My
name.
16 'Then you turned around and
[a]profaned My name, and every
one of you brought back his
male and female slaves, whom
you had set at liberty, at their
pleasure, and brought them
back into subjection, to be your
male and female slaves.'
17 "Therefore thus says the
LORD: 'You have not obeyed Me
in proclaiming liberty, every one
to his brother and every one to
his neighbor. [a]Behold, I proclaim
liberty to you,' says the LORD—
[b]'to the sword, to pestilence, and
to famine! And I will deliver you
to [c]trouble among all the kingdoms of the earth.
18 'And I will give the men who
have transgressed My covenant,
who have not performed the
words of the covenant which
they made before Me, when
[a]they cut the calf in two and
passed between the parts of it—
19 'the princes of Judah, the
princes of Jerusalem, the [1]eu-
nuchs, the priests, and all the
people of the land who passed
between the parts of the calf—
20 'I will [a]give them into the
hand of their enemies and into
the hand of those who seek their
life. Their [b]dead bodies shall
be for meat for the birds of the
heaven and the beasts of the
earth.
21 'And I will give Zed·e·ki'ah
king of Judah and his princes
into the hand of their enemies,
into the hand of those who seek
their life, and into the hand
of the king of Babylon's army
[a]which has gone back from you.
22 [a]'Behold, I will command,'
says the LORD, 'and cause them

8 [a]Ex. 21:2
9 [a]Neh. 5:11 [b]Lev. 25:39–46
13 [a]Ex. 24:3, 7, 8
14 [a]Deut. 15:12 [1]Or *sold himself*
15 [a]Neh. 10:29 [b]Jer. 7:10 [1]Lit. *today*
16 [a]Ex. 20:7
17 [a][Matt. 7:2] [b]Jer. 32:24, 36 [c]Deut. 28:25, 64
18 [a]Gen. 15:10, 17
19 [1]Or *officers*
20 [a]Jer. 22:25 [b]Jer. 7:33; 16:4; 19:7
21 [a]Jer.37:5–11; 39:4–7
22 [a]Jer. 37:8, 10

to return to this city. They will
fight against it [b]and take it and
burn it with fire; and [c]I will
make the cities of Judah a desolation without inhabitant.' "

35
The word which came to
Jer·e·mī′ah from the LORD
in the days of Je·hoi′a·kim the
son of Jō·sī′ah, king of Judah,
saying,
2 "Go to the house of the [a]Rē′-
chab·ītes, speak to them, and
bring them into the house of the
LORD, into one of [b]the chambers,
and give them wine to drink."
3 Then I took Jā·az·a·nī′ah the
son of Jer·e·mī′ah, the son of
Ha·baz·zi·nī′ah, his brothers and
all his sons, and the whole house
of the Rē′chab·ītes,
4 and I brought them into
the house of the LORD, into the
chamber of the sons of Hā′nan
the son of Ig·da·lī′ah, a man of
God, which *was* by the chamber of the princes, above the
chamber of Mā·a·sē′iah the son
of Shal′lum, [a]the keeper of the
[1]door.
5 Then I set before the sons
of the house of the Rē′chab·ītes
bowls full of wine, and cups; and
I said to them, "Drink wine."
6 But they said, "We will drink
no wine, for [a]Jon′a·dab the son
of Rē′chab, our father, commanded us, saying, 'You shall
drink [b]no wine, you nor your
sons, forever.
7 'You shall not build a house,
sow seed, plant a vineyard,
nor have *any of these*; but all
your days you shall dwell in
tents, [a]that you may live many
days in the land where you are
sojourners.'
8 "Thus we have [a]obeyed the
voice of Jon′a·dab the son of
Rē′chab, our father, in all that
he charged us, to drink no wine
all our days, we, our wives, our
sons, or our daughters,
9 "nor to build ourselves
houses to dwell in; nor do we
have vineyard, field, or seed.
10 "But we have dwelt in tents,
and have obeyed and done according to all that Jon′a·dab our
father commanded us.
11 "But it came to pass, when
Ne·bū·chad·nez′zar king of Babylon came up into the land, that
we said, 'Come, let us [a]go to Jerusalem for fear of the army of
the Chal·dē′ans and for fear of
the army of the Syrians.' So we
dwell at Jerusalem."
12 Then came the word of the
LORD to Jer·e·mī′ah, saying,
13 "Thus says the LORD of hosts,
the God of Israel: 'Go and tell
the men of Judah and the inhabitants of Jerusalem, "Will you
not [a]receive instruction to [1]obey
My words?" says the LORD.
14 "The words of Jon′a·dab the
son of Rē′chab, which he commanded his sons, not to drink
wine, are performed; for to this
day they drink none, and obey
their father's commandment.
[a]But although I have spoken to
you, [b]rising early and speaking,
you did not [1]obey Me.
15 "I have also sent to you all
My [a]servants the prophets, rising
up early and sending *them*, saying, [b]'Turn now everyone from
his evil way, amend your doings,
and do not go after other gods to
serve them; then you will [c]dwell
in the land which I have given
you and your fathers.' But you
have not inclined your ear, nor
obeyed Me.
16 "Surely the sons of Jon′a·dab

22 [b]Jer. 38:3; 39:1, 2, 8; 52:7, 13 [c]Jer. 9:11; 44:2, 6

CHAPTER 35

2 [a]1 Chr. 2:55 [b]1 Kin. 6:5, 8

4 [a]1 Chr. 9:18, 19 [1]Lit. *threshold*

6 [a]2 Kin. 10:15, 23 [b]Luke 1:15

7 [a]Ex. 20:12

8 [a][Col. 3:20]

11 [a]Jer. 4:5–7; 8:14

13 [a]Jer. 6:10; 17:23; 32:33 [1]*listen to*

14 [a]2 Chr. 36:15 [b]Jer. 7:13; 25:3 [1]*listen to*

15 [a]Jer. 26:4, 5; 29:19 [b]Jer. 18:11; 25:5, 6 [c]Jer. 7:7; 25:5, 6

the son of Rē′chab have performed the commandment of
their [a]father, which he commanded them, but this people
has not obeyed Me." '
17 "Therefore thus says the
LORD God of hosts, the God of
Israel: 'Behold, I will bring on
Judah and on all the inhabitants
of Jerusalem all the doom that I
have pronounced against them;
[a]because I have spoken to them
but they have not heard, and
I have called to them but they
have not answered.' "
18 And Jer·e·mī′ah said to
the house of the Rē′chab·ītes,
"Thus says the LORD of hosts,
the God of Israel: 'Because you
have obeyed the commandment
of Jon′a·dab your father, and
kept all his precepts and done
according to all that he commanded you,
19 'therefore thus says the LORD
of hosts, the God of Israel: "Jon′-
a·dab the son of Rē′chab shall
not lack a man to [a]stand before
Me forever." ' "

36 Now it came to pass in
the [a]fourth year of Je·hoi′-
a·kim the son of Jō·sī′ah, king
of Judah, *that* this word came
to Jer·e·mī′ah from the LORD,
saying:
2 "Take a [a]scroll of a book and
[b]write on it all the words that I
have spoken to you against Israel, against Judah, and against
[c]all the nations, from the day I
spoke to you, from the days of
[d]Jō·sī′ah even to this day.
3 "It [a]may be that the house of
Judah will hear all the adversities which I purpose to bring
upon them, that everyone may
[b]turn from his evil way, that I

16 [a][Heb. 12:9]
17 [a]Prov. 1:24
19 [a]Jer. 15:19

CHAPTER 36

1 [a]Jer. 25:1, 3; 45:1
2 [a]Zech. 5:1 [b]Jer. 30:2 [c]Jer. 25:15 [d]Jer. 25:3
3 [a]Jer. 26:3 [b]Jon. 3:8
4 [a]Jer. 32:12 [b]Jer. 45:1 [1]Lit. *from Jeremiah's mouth*
6 [a]Acts 27:9 [1]Lit. *from my mouth*

may forgive their iniquity and
their sin."
4 Then Jer·e·mī′ah [a]called
Bar′uch the son of Ne·rī′ah; and
[b]Bar′uch wrote on a scroll of
a book, [1]at the instruction of
Jer·e·mī′ah, all the words of the
LORD which He had spoken to
him.
5 And Jer·e·mī′ah commanded
Bar′uch, saying, "I *am* confined,
I cannot go into the house of the
LORD.
6 "You go, therefore, and read
from the scroll which you have
written [1]at my instruction, the
words of the LORD, in the hearing of the people in the LORD's
house on [a]the day of fasting.
And you shall also read them
in the hearing of all Judah who
come from their cities.
7 "It may be that they will
present their supplication before the LORD, and everyone will
turn from his evil way. For great
is the anger and the fury that the
LORD has pronounced against
this people."
8 And Bar′uch the son of
Ne·rī′ah did according to all that
Jer·e·mī′ah the prophet commanded him, reading from the
book the words of the LORD in
the LORD's house.
9 Now it came to pass in the
fifth year of Je·hoi′a·kim the
son of Jō·sī′ah, king of Judah, in
the ninth month, *that* they proclaimed a fast before the LORD to
all the people in Jerusalem, and
to all the people who came from
the cities of Judah to Jerusalem.
10 Then Bar′uch read from the
book the words of Jer·e·mī′ah
in the house of the LORD, in the
chamber of Gem·a·rī′ah the son
of Shā′phan the scribe, in the

upper court at the [a]entry of the
New Gate of the LORD's house,
in the [1]hearing of all the people.
11 When Mī·chaī′ah the son of
Gem·a·rī′ah, the son of Shā′-
phan, heard all the words of the
LORD from the book,
12 he then went down to the
king's house, into the scribe's
chamber; and there all the
princes were sitting—[a]E·lish′-
a·ma the scribe, De·laī′ah the
son of She·māi′ah, [b]El·nā′than
the son of Ach′bor, Gem·a·rī′ah
the son of Shā′phan, Zed·e-
kī′ah the son of Han·a·nī′ah, and
all the princes.
13 Then Mī·chaī′ah declared
to them all the words that he
had heard when Bar′uch read
the book in the hearing of the
people.
14 Therefore all the princes sent
Je·hū′dī the son of Neth·a·nī′ah,
the son of Shel·e·mī′ah, the son
of Cū′shī, to Bar′uch, saying,
"Take in your hand the scroll
from which you have read in
the hearing of the people, and
come." So Bar′uch the son of
Ne·rī′ah took the scroll in his
hand and came to them.
15 And they said to him, "Sit
down now, and read it in our
hearing." So Bar′uch read *it* in
their hearing.
16 Now it happened, when they
had heard all the words, that
they looked in fear from one
to another, and said to Bar′uch,
"We will surely tell the king of
all these words."
17 And they asked Bar′uch, saying, "Tell us now, how did you
write all these words—[1]at his
instruction?"
18 So Bar′uch answered them,
"He proclaimed with his mouth
all these words to me, and I
wrote *them* with ink in the
book."
19 Then the princes said to
Bar′uch, "Go and hide, you and
Jer·e·mī′ah; and let no one know
where you are."
20 And they went to the king,
into the court; but they stored
the scroll in the chamber of
E·lish′a·ma the scribe, and told
all the words in the hearing of
the king.
21 So the king sent Je·hū′dī to
bring the scroll, and he took
it from E·lish′a·ma the scribe's
chamber. And Je·hū′dī read it
in the hearing of the king and
in the hearing of all the princes
who stood beside the king.
22 Now the king was sitting in
[a]the winter house in the ninth
month, with *a fire* burning on
the hearth before him.
23 And it happened, when
Je·hū′dī had read three or four
columns, *that the king* cut it
with the scribe's knife and cast
it into the fire that *was* on the
hearth, until all the scroll was
consumed in the fire that *was* on
the hearth.
24 Yet they were [a]not afraid, nor
did they [b]tear their garments,
the king nor any of his servants
who heard all these words.
25 Nevertheless El·nā′than,
De·laī′ah, and Gem·a·rī′ah implored the king not to burn the
scroll; but he would not listen to
them.
26 And the king commanded
Je·rah′mē·el [1]the king's son,
Se·rāi′ah the son of Az′ri·el, and
Shel·e·mī′ah the son of Ab·dē′el,
to seize Bar′uch the scribe and
Jer·e·mī′ah the prophet, but the
LORD hid them.

10 [a]Jer. 26:10 [1]Lit. *ears*
12 [a]Jer. 41:1 [b]Jer. 26:22
17 [1]Lit. *with his mouth*
22 [a]Amos 3:15
24 [a][Ps. 36:1] [b]Is. 36:22; 37:1
26 [1]Or *son of Hammelech*

27 Now after the king had
burned the scroll with the words
which Bar′uch had written [1]at
the instruction of Jer·e·mī′ah,
the word of the LORD came to
Jer·e·mī′ah, saying:
28 "Take yet another scroll, and
write on it all the former words
that were in the first scroll which
Je·hoi′a·kim the king of Judah
has burned.
29 "And you shall say to Je·hoi′-
a·kim king of Judah, 'Thus says
the LORD: "You have burned
this scroll, saying, [a]'Why have
you written in it that the king
of Babylon will certainly come
and destroy this land, and cause
man and beast to [b]cease from
here?' "
30 'Therefore thus says the LORD
concerning Je·hoi′a·kim king of
Judah: [a]"He shall have no one to
sit on the throne of David, and
his dead body shall be [b]cast out
to the heat of the day and the
frost of the night.
31 "I will punish him, his [1]fam-
ily, and his servants for their iniquity; and I will bring on them,
on the inhabitants of Jerusalem,
and on the men of Judah all the
doom that I have pronounced
against them; but they did not
heed." ' "
32 Then Jer·e·mī′ah took another scroll and gave it to
Bar′uch the scribe, the son of
Ne·rī′ah, who wrote on it [1]at
the instruction of Jer·e·mī′ah all
the words of the book which
Je·hoi′a·kim king of Judah had
burned in the fire. And besides,
there were added to them many
similar words.

37 Now King [a]Zed·e·kī′ah
the son of Jō·sī′ah reigned
instead of Cō·nī′ah the son of
Je·hoi′a·kim, whom Ne·bū·chad-
nez′zar king of Babylon made
king in the land of Judah.
2 [a]But neither he nor his servants nor the people of the land
gave heed to the words of the
LORD which He spoke by the
prophet Jer·e·mī′ah.
3 And Zed·e·kī′ah the king sent
Je·hū′cal the son of Shel·e·mī′ah,
and [a]Zeph·a·nī′ah the son of
Mā·a·sē′i′ah, the priest, to the
prophet Jer·e·mī′ah, saying,
[b]"Pray now to the LORD our God
for us."
4 Now Jer·e·mī′ah was coming
and going among the people,
for they had not *yet* put him in
prison.
5 Then [a]Pharaoh's army came
up from Egypt; and when the
Chal·dē′ans who were besieging
Jerusalem heard news of them,
they departed from Jerusalem.
6 Then the word of the LORD
came to the prophet Jer·e·mī′ah,
saying,
7 "Thus says the LORD, the God
of Israel, 'Thus you shall say to
the king of Judah, [a]who sent you
to Me to inquire of Me: "Behold,
Pharaoh's army which has come
up to help you will return to
Egypt, to their own land.
8 [a]"And the Chal·dē′ans shall
come back and fight against this
city, and take it and burn it with
fire." '
9 "Thus says the LORD: 'Do
not deceive yourselves, saying,
"The Chal·dē′ans will surely depart from us," for they will not
depart.
10 [a]'For though you had defeated the whole army of the
Chal·dē′ans who fight against
you, and there remained *only*
wounded men among them, they

27 [1]Lit. *from Jeremiah's mouth*
29 [a]Jer. 32:3 [b]Jer. 25:9–11; 26:9
30 [a]Jer. 22:30 [b]Jer. 22:19
31 [1]Lit. *seed*
32 [1]Lit. *from Jeremiah's mouth*

CHAPTER 37

1 [a]2 Kin. 24:17
2 [a]2 Chr. 36:12–16
3 [a]Jer. 21:1, 2; 29:25; 52:24 [b]Jer. 42:2
5 [a]Ezek. 17:15
7 [a]Jer. 21:2
8 [a]Jer. 34:22
10 [a]Jer. 21:4, 5

would rise up, every man in
his tent, and burn the city with
fire.' "
11 And it happened, when the
army of the Chal·dē'ans left *the
siege* of Jerusalem for fear of
Pharaoh's army,
12 that Jer·e·mī'ah went out of
Jerusalem to go into the land of
Benjamin to claim his property
there among the people.
13 And when he was in the Gate
of Benjamin, a captain of the
guard *was* there whose name *was*
I·rī'jah the son of Shel·e·mī'ah,
the son of Han·a·nī'ah; and he
seized Jer·e·mī'ah the prophet,
saying, "You are defecting to the
Chal·dē'ans!"
14 Then Jer·e·mī'ah said,
[1]"False! I am not defecting to
the Chal·dē'ans." But he did not
listen to him. So I·rī'jah seized
Jer·e·mī'ah and brought him to
the princes.
15 Therefore the princes were
angry with Jer·e·mī'ah, and
they struck him [a]and put him in
prison in the [b]house of Jonathan
the scribe. For they had made
that the prison.
16 When Jer·e·mī'ah entered
[a]the dungeon and the cells, and
Jer·e·mī'ah had remained there
many days,
17 then Zed·e·kī'ah the king
sent and took him *out*. The king
asked him secretly in his house,
and said, "Is there *any* word
from the LORD?" And Jer·e·mī'ah
said, "There is." Then he said,
"You shall be [a]delivered into the
hand of the king of Babylon!"
18 Moreover Jer·e·mī'ah said to
King Zed·e·kī'ah, "What offense
have I committed against you,
against your servants, or against
this people, that you have put
me in prison?
19 "Where now *are* your prophets who prophesied to you, saying, 'The king of Babylon will
not come against you or against
this land'?
20 "Therefore please hear now,
O my lord the king. Please, let
my petition be accepted before
you, and do not make me return
to the house of Jonathan the
scribe, lest I die there."
21 Then Zed·e·kī'ah the king
commanded that they should
commit Jer·e·mī'ah [a]to the
court of the prison, and that
they should give him daily a
piece of bread from the bakers'
street, [b]until all the bread in the
city was gone. Thus Jer·e·mī'ah
remained in the court of the
prison.

38

Now Sheph·a·tī'ah the son
of Mat'tan, Ged·a·lī'ah the
son of Pash'hur, [a]Jū'cal[1] the son
of Shel·e·mī'ah, and [b]Pash'hur
the son of Mal·chī'ah [c]heard the
words that Jer·e·mī'ah had spoken to all the people, saying,
2 "Thus says the LORD: [a]'He
who remains in this city shall
die by the sword, by famine, and
by pestilence; but he who goes
over to the Chal·dē'ans shall
live; his life shall be as a prize to
him, and he shall live.'
3 "Thus says the LORD: [a]'This
city shall surely be [b]given into
the hand of the king of Babylon's army, which shall take
it.' "
4 Therefore the princes said
to the king, "Please, [a]let this
man be put to death, for thus he
[1]weakens the hands of the men
of war who remain in this city,
and the hands of all the people,

14 [1]*a lie*
15 [a]Jer. 20:2 [b]Jer. 38:26
16 [a]Jer. 38:6
17 [a]Jer. 21:7
21 [a]Jer. 32:2; 38:13, 28 [b]Jer. 38:9; 52:6

CHAPTER 38

1 [a]Jer. 37:3 [b]Jer. 21:1 [c]Jer. 21:8 [1]*Jehucal,* Jer. 37:3
2 [a]Jer. 21:9
3 [a]Jer. 21:10; 32:3 [b]Jer. 34:2
4 [a]Jer. 26:11 [1]Is discouraging

by speaking such words to them.
For this man does not seek the
[2]welfare of this people, but their
harm."
5 Then Zed·e·kī′ah the king
said, "Look, he *is* in your hand.
For the king can *do* nothing
against you."
6 [a]So they took Jer·e·mī′ah
and cast him into the dungeon
of Mal·chī′ah [1]the king's son,
which *was* in the court of the
prison, and they let Jer·e·mī′ah
down with ropes. And in the
dungeon *there was* no water, but
mire. So Jer·e·mī′ah sank in the
mire.
7 [a]Now Ē′bed-Mē′lech the Ethiopian, one of the [1]eunuchs, who
was in the king's house, heard
that they had put Jer·e·mī′ah in
the dungeon. When the king was
sitting at the Gate of Benjamin,
8 Ē′bed-Mē′lech went out of
the king's house and spoke to
the king, saying:
9 "My lord the king, these
men have done evil in all that
they have done to Jer·e·mī′ah
the prophet, whom they have
cast into the dungeon, and he is
likely to die from hunger in the
place where he is. For *there is*
[a]no more bread in the city."
10 Then the king commanded
Ē′bed-Mē′lech the Ethiopian,
saying, "Take from here thirty
men with you, and lift Jer·e·mī′ah
the prophet out of the dungeon
before he dies."
11 So Ē′bed-Mē′lech took the
men with him and went into
the house of the king under the
treasury, and took from there
old clothes and old rags, and
let them down by ropes into the
dungeon to Jer·e·mī′ah.
12 Then Ē′bed-Mē′lech the
Ethiopian said to Jer·e·mī′ah,
"Please put these old clothes
and rags under your armpits, under the ropes." And Jer·e·mī′ah
did so.
13 So they pulled Jer·e·mī′ah
up with ropes and lifted him out
of the dungeon. And Jer·e·mī′ah
remained [a]in the court of the
prison.
14 Then Zed·e·kī′ah the king
sent and had Jer·e·mī′ah the
prophet brought to him at the
third entrance of the house of
the LORD. And the king said
to Jer·e·mī′ah, "I will [a]ask you
something. Hide nothing from
me."
15 Jer·e·mī′ah said to Zed·e-
kī′ah, "If I declare *it* to you, will
you not surely put me to death?
And if I give you advice, you will
not listen to me."
16 So Zed·e·kī′ah the king swore
secretly to Jer·e·mī′ah, saying,
"*As* the LORD lives, [a]who made
our very souls, I will not put you
to death, nor will I give you into
the hand of these men who seek
your life."
17 Then Jer·e·mī′ah said to
Zed·e·kī′ah, "Thus says the LORD,
the God of hosts, the God of Israel: 'If you surely [a]surrender[1]
[b]to the king of Babylon's princes,
then your soul shall live; this
city shall not be burned with
fire, and you and your house
shall live.
18 'But if you do not [1]surrender
to the king of Babylon's princes,
then this city shall be given
into the hand of the Chal·dē′ans;
they shall burn it with fire, and
[a]you shall not escape from their
hand.' "
19 And Zed·e·kī′ah the king
said to Jer·e·mī′ah, "I am afraid

4 [2]Well-being; lit. *peace*
6 [a]Jer. 37:21 [1]Or *son of Hammelech*
7 [a]Jer. 39:16 [1]Or *officers*
9 [a]Jer. 37:21
13 [a]Jer. 37:21
14 [a]Jer. 21:1, 2; 37:17
16 [a]Is. 57:16
17 [a]2 Kin. 24:12 [b]Jer. 39:3 [1]Lit. *go out*
18 [a]Jer. 32:4; 34:3 [1]Lit. *go out*

of the Jews who have [a]defected
to the Chal·dē′ans, lest they deliver me into their hand, and
they [b]abuse me."
20 But Jer·e·mī′ah said, "They
shall not deliver *you.* Please,
obey the voice of the LORD which
I speak to you. So it shall be
[a]well with you, and your soul
shall live.
21 "But if you refuse to [1]sur-
render, this *is* the word that the
LORD has shown me:
22 'Now behold, all the [a]women
who are left in the king of Judah's house *shall be* surrendered
to the king of Babylon's princes,
and those *women* shall say:

"Your close friends have [1]set
upon you
And prevailed against you;
Your feet have sunk in the
mire,
And they have [2]turned away
again."

23 'So they shall surrender all
your wives and [a]children to the
Chal·dē′ans. [b]You shall not escape from their hand, but shall
be taken by the hand of the
king of Babylon. And you shall
cause this city to be burned with
fire.' "
24 Then Zed·e·kī′ah said to
Jer·e·mī′ah, "Let no one know of
these words, and you shall not
die.
25 "But if the princes hear that
I have talked with you, and they
come to you and say to you, 'Declare to us now what you have
said to the king, and also what
the king said to you; do not hide
it from us, and we will not put
you to death,'
26 "then you shall say to them,
[a]'I presented my request before
the king, that he would not make
me return [b]to Jonathan's house
to die there.' "
27 Then all the princes came to
Jer·e·mī′ah and asked him. And
he told them according to all
these words that the king had
commanded. So they stopped
speaking with him, for the conversation had not been heard.
28 Now [a]Jer·e·mī′ah remained
in the court of the prison until the day that Jerusalem was
taken. And he was *there* when
Jerusalem was taken.

39

In the [a]ninth year of
Zed·e·kī′ah king of Ju-
dah, in the tenth month, Ne·bū-
chad·nez′zar king of Babylon
and all his army came against
Jerusalem, and besieged it.
2 In the [a]eleventh year of
Zed·e·kī′ah, in the fourth month,
on the ninth *day* of the month,
the [1]city was penetrated.
3 [a]Then all the princes of the
king of Babylon came in and
sat in the Middle Gate: Ner′-
gal-Sha·rē′zer, Sam′gar-Nē′bō,
Sar′se·chim, [1]Rab·sar′is, Ner′-
gal-Sa·rē′zer, [2]Rab′mag, with the
rest of the princes of the king of
Babylon.
4 [a]So it was, when Zed·e·kī′ah
the king of Judah and all the
men of war saw them, that they
fled and went out of the city by
night, by way of the king's garden, by the gate between the two
walls. And he went out by way
of the [1]plain.
5 But the Chal·dē′an army
pursued them and [a]overtook
Zed·e·kī′ah in the plains of Jericho. And when they had captured him, they brought him

19 [a]Jer. 39:9 [b]1 Sam. 31:4
20 [a]Jer. 40:9
21 [1]Lit. *go out*
22 [a]Jer. 8:10 [1]Or *misled* [2]Deserted you
23 [a]Jer. 39:6; 41:10 [b]Jer. 39:5
26 [a]Jer. 37:20 [b]Jer. 37:15
28 [a]Jer. 37:21; 39:14

CHAPTER 39

1 [a]2 Kin. 25:1–12
2 [a]Jer. 1:3 [1]*city wall was breached*
3 [a]Jer. 1:15; 38:17 [1]A title, probably *Chief Officer;* also v. 13 [2]A title, probably *Troop Commander;* also v. 13
4 [a]Jer. 52:7 [1]Or *Arabah;* the Jordan Valley
5 [a]Jer. 21:7; 32:4; 38:18, 23

up to Ne·bū·chad·nez′zar king
of Babylon, to [b]Rib′lah in the
land of Hā′math, where he pronounced judgment on him.
6 Then the king of Babylon
killed the sons of Zed·e·kī′ah
before his [a]eyes in Rib′lah; the
king of Babylon also killed all
the [b]nobles of Judah.
7 Moreover [a]he put out Zed·e-
kī′ah's eyes, and bound him with
bronze [1]fetters to carry him off
to Babylon.
8 [a]And the Chal·dē′ans burned
the king's house and the houses
of the people with [b]fire, and broke
down the [c]walls of Jerusalem.
9 [a]Then Ne·bū·za·rad′an the
captain of the guard carried
away captive to Babylon the
remnant of the people who remained in the city and those who
[b]defected to him, with the rest of
the people who remained.
10 But Ne·bū·za·rad′an the captain of the guard left in the
land of Judah the [a]poor people,
who had nothing, and gave them
vineyards and fields [1]at the same
time.
11 Now Ne·bū·chad·nez′zar
king of Babylon gave charge
concerning Jer·e·mī′ah to
Ne·bū·za·rad′an the captain of
the guard, saying,
12 "Take him and look after
him, and do him no [a]harm; but
do to him just as he says to
you."
13 So Ne·bū·za·rad′an the captain of the guard sent Ne·bū-
shas′ban, Rab·sar′is, Ner′gal-
Sha·rē′zer, Rab′mag, and all the
king of Babylon's chief officers;
14 then they sent *someone* [a]to
take Jer·e·mī′ah from the court
of the prison, and committed
him [b]to Ged·a·lī′ah the son of
[c]A·hī′kam, the son of Shā′phan,
that he should take him home.
So he dwelt among the people.
15 Meanwhile the word of the
LORD had come to Jer·e·mī′ah
while he was shut up in the
court of the prison, saying,
16 "Go and speak to [a]Ē′bed-
Mē′lech the Ethiopian, saying,
'Thus says the LORD of hosts, the
God of Israel: "Behold, [b]I will
bring My words upon this city
for adversity and not for good,
and they shall be *performed* in
that day before you.
17 "But I will deliver you in that
day," says the LORD, "and you
shall not be given into the hand
of the men of whom you *are*
afraid.
18 "For I will surely deliver you,
and you shall not fall by the
sword; but [a]your life shall be
as a prize to you, [b]because you
have put your trust in Me," says
the LORD.' "

40 The word that came to
Jer·e·mī′ah from the LORD
[a]after Ne·bū·za·rad′an the captain of the guard had let him go
from Rā′mah, when he had taken
him bound in chains among all
who were carried away captive
from Jerusalem and Judah, who
were carried away captive to
Babylon.
2 And the captain of the guard
took Jer·e·mī′ah and [a]said to
him: "The LORD your God has
pronounced this doom on this
place.
3 "Now the LORD has brought
it, and has done just as He
said. [a]Because you *people* have
sinned against the LORD, and not
obeyed His voice, therefore this
thing has come upon you.

5 [b]2 Kin. 23:33
6 [a]Deut. 28:34 [b]Jer. 34:19–21
7 [a]Ezek. 12:13 [1]*chains*
8 [a]2 Kin. 25:9 [b]Jer. 21:10 [c]Neh. 1:3
9 [a]2 Kin. 25:8, 11, 12, 20 [b]Jer. 38:19
10 [a]Jer. 40:7 [1]Lit. *on that day*
12 [a]Jer. 1:18, 19; 15:20, 21
14 [a]Jer. 38:28 [b]Jer. 40:5 [c]Jer. 26:24
16 [a]Jer. 38:7, 12 [b][Dan. 9:12]
18 [a]Jer. 21:9; 45:5 [b]Ps. 37:40

CHAPTER 40

1 [a]Jer. 39:9, 11
2 [a]Jer. 50:7
3 [a]Dan. 9:11

4 "And now look, I free you this day from the chains that [1]*were* on your hand. [a]If it seems good to you to come with me to Babylon, come, and I will look after you. But if it seems wrong for you to come with me to Babylon, remain here. See, [b]all the land *is* before you; wherever it seems good and convenient for you to go, go there."

5 Now while Jer·e·mī′ah had not yet gone back, *Ne·bū·za-rad′an said,* "Go back to [a]Ged·a·lī′ah the son of A·hī′kam, the son of Shā′phan, [b]whom the king of Babylon has made governor over the cities of Judah, and dwell with him among the people. Or go wherever it seems convenient for you to go." So the captain of the guard gave him rations and a gift and let him go.

6 [a]Then Jer·e·mī′ah went to Ged·a·lī′ah the son of A·hī′kam, to [b]Miz′pah, and dwelt with him among the people who were left in the land.

7 [a]And when all the captains of the armies who *were* in the fields, they and their men, heard that the king of Babylon had made Ged·a·lī′ah the son of A·hī′kam governor in the land, and had committed to him men, women, children, and [b]the poorest of the land who had not been carried away captive to Babylon,

8 then they came to Ged·a·lī′ah at Miz′pah—[a]Ish′ma·el the son of Neth·a·nī′ah, [b]Jō·hā′nan and Jonathan the sons of Ka·rē′ah, Se·rāi′ah the son of Tan′hu·meth, the sons of Ē′phaī the Ne·toph′a·thīte, and [c]Jez·a·nī′ah[1] the son of a [d]Mā′a·cha·thīte, they and their men.

9 And Ged·a·lī′ah the son of A·hī′kam, the son of Shā′phan, took an oath before them and their men, saying, "Do not be afraid to serve the Chal·dē′ans. Dwell in the land and serve the king of Babylon, and it shall be [a]well with you.

10 "As for me, I will indeed dwell at Miz′pah and serve the Chal·dē′ans who come to us. But you, gather wine and summer fruit and oil, put *them* in your vessels, and dwell in your cities that you have taken."

11 Likewise, when all the Jews who *were* in Mō′ab, among the Am′mon·ītes, in Ē′dom, and who *were* in all the countries, heard that the king of Babylon had left a remnant of Judah, and that he had set over them Ged·a·lī′ah the son of A·hī′kam, the son of Shā′phan,

12 then all the Jews [a]returned out of all places where they had been driven, and came to the land of Judah, to Ged·a·lī′ah at Miz′pah, and gathered wine and summer fruit in abundance.

13 Moreover Jō·hā′nan the son of Ka·rē′ah and all the captains of the forces that *were* in the fields came to Ged·a·lī′ah at Miz′pah,

14 and said to him, [1]"Do you certainly know that [a]Bā′a·lis the king of the Am′mon·ītes has sent Ish′ma·el the son of Neth·a·nī′ah to murder you?" But Ged·a·lī′ah the son of A·hī′kam did not believe them.

15 Then Jō·hā′nan the son of Ka·rē′ah spoke secretly to Ged·a·lī′ah in Miz′pah, saying, "Let me go, please, and I will kill Ish′ma·el the son of Neth·a·nī′ah, and no one will know *it*. Why

4 [a]Jer. 39:12 [b]Gen. 20:15 [1]Or *are*
5 [a]Jer. 39:14 [b]Jer. 41:10
6 [a]Jer. 39:14 [b]Judg. 20:1
7 [a]2 Kin. 25:23, 24 [b]Jer. 39:10
8 [a]Jer. 41:1–10 [b]Jer. 41:11; 43:2 [c]Jer. 42:1 [d]Deut. 3:14 [1]*Jaazaniah,* 2 Kin. 25:23
9 [a]Jer. 27:11; 38:17–20
12 [a]Jer. 43:5
14 [a]Jer. 41:10 [1]Or *Certainly you know that*

should he murder you, so that
all the Jews who are gathered to
you would be scattered, and the
[a]remnant in Judah perish?"
16 But Ged·a·lī'ah the son of
A·hī'kam said to Jō·hā'nan the
son of Ka·rē'ah, "You shall not
do this thing, for you speak
falsely concerning Ish'ma·el."

41 Now it came to pass in the
seventh month [a]*that* Ish'-
ma·el the son of Neth·a·nī'ah, the
son of E·lish'a·ma, of the royal
[1]family and of the officers of
the king, came with ten men to
Ged·a·lī'ah the son of A·hī'kam,
at [b]Miz'pah. And there they ate
bread together in Miz'pah.
2 Then Ish'ma·el the son of
Neth·a·nī'ah, and the ten men
who were with him, arose and
[a]struck Ged·a·lī'ah the son of
[b]A·hī'kam, the son of Shā'phan,
with the sword, and killed him
whom the king of Babylon had
made [c]governor over the land.
3 Ish'ma·el also struck down
all the Jews who were with him,
that is, with Ged·a·lī'ah at Miz'-
pah, and the Chal·dē'ans who
were found there, the men of
war.
4 And it happened, on the
second day after he had killed
Ged·a·lī'ah, when as yet no one
knew *it,*
5 that certain men came from
Shē'chem, from Shī'lōh, and
from Samaria, eighty men [a]with
their beards shaved and their
clothes torn, having cut themselves, with offerings and incense in their hand, to bring
them to [b]the house of the LORD.
6 Now Ish'ma·el the son of
Neth·a·nī'ah went out from Miz'-
pah to meet them, weeping as
he went along; and it happened
as he met them that he said to
them, "Come to Ged·a·lī'ah the
son of A·hī'kam!"
7 So it was, when they came
into the midst of the city, that
Ish'ma·el the son of Neth·a·nī'ah
[a]killed them *and cast them* into
the midst of a [1]pit, he and the
men who were with him.
8 But ten men were found
among them who said to Ish'-
ma·el, "Do not kill us, for we
have treasures of wheat, barley,
oil, and honey in the field." So
he desisted and did not kill them
among their brethren.
9 Now the [1]pit into which Ish'-
ma·el had cast all the dead bodies of the men whom he had
slain, because of Ged·a·lī'ah,
was [a]the same one Ā'sa the king
had made for fear of Bā'a·sha
king of Israel. Ish'ma·el the son
of Neth·a·nī'ah filled it with *the*
slain.
10 Then Ish'ma·el carried away
captive all the [a]rest of the people
who *were* in Miz'pah, [b]the king's
daughters and all the people
who remained in Miz'pah,
[c]whom Ne·bū·za·rad'an the captain of the guard had committed
to Ged·a·lī'ah the son of A·hī'-
kam. And Ish'ma·el the son of
Neth·a·nī'ah carried them away
captive and departed to go over
to [d]the Am'mon·ītes.
11 But when [a]Jō·hā'nan the son
of Ka·rē'ah and all the captains
of the forces that *were* with him
heard of all the evil that Ish'-
ma·el the son of Neth·a·nī'ah
had done,
12 they took all the men and
went to fight with Ish'ma·el the
son of Neth·a·nī'ah; and they
found him by [a]the great pool
that *is* in Gib'ē·on.

15 [a]Jer. 42:2

CHAPTER 41

1 [a]2 Kin. 25:25 [b]Jer. 40:6, 10 [1]Lit. *seed*

2 [a]2 Kin. 25:25 [b]Jer. 26:24 [c]Jer. 40:5

5 [a]Deut. 14:1 [b]1 Sam. 1:7

7 [a]Ps. 55:23 [1]Or *cistern*

9 [a]1 Kin. 15:22 [1]Or *cistern*

10 [a]Jer. 40:11, 12 [b]Jer. 43:6 [c]Jer. 40:7 [d]Jer. 40:14

11 [a]Jer. 40:7, 8, 13–16

12 [a]2 Sam. 2:13

13 So it was, when all the people who *were* with Ish′ma·el saw
Jō·hā′nan the son of Ka·rē′ah,
and all the captains of the forces
who *were* with him, that they
were glad.
14 Then all the people whom
Ish′ma·el had carried away captive from Miz′pah turned around
and came back, and went to
Jō·hā′nan the son of Ka·rē′ah.
15 But Ish′ma·el the son of
Neth·a·nī′ah escaped from
Jō·hā′nan with eight men and
went to the Am′mon·ītes.
16 Then Jō·hā′nan the son of
Ka·rē′ah, and all the captains
of the forces that were with
him, took from Miz′pah all the
[a]rest of the people whom he had
recovered from Ish′ma·el the
son of Neth·a·nī′ah after he had
murdered Ged·a·lī′ah the son of
A·hī′kam—the mighty men of
war and the women and the
children and the eunuchs, whom
he had brought back from Gib′-
ē·on.
17 And they departed and dwelt
in the habitation of [a]Chim′ham,
which is near Bethlehem, as they
went on their way to [b]Egypt,
18 because of the Chal·dē′ans;
for they were afraid of them,
because Ish′ma·el the son of
Neth·a·nī′ah had murdered
Ged·a·lī′ah the son of A·hī′kam,
[a]whom the king of Babylon had
made governor in the land.

42 Now all the captains of
the forces, [a]Jō·hā′nan the
son of Ka·rē′ah, Jez·a·nī′ah
the son of Hō·shaī′ah, and all
the people, from the least to the
greatest, came near
2 and said to Jer·e·mī′ah the
prophet, [a]"Please, let our petition be acceptable to you, and
[b]pray for us to the LORD your
God, for all this remnant (since
we are left *but* [c]a few of many,
as you can see),
3 "that the LORD your God may
show us [a]the way in which we
should walk and the thing we
should do."
4 Then Jer·e·mī′ah the prophet
said to them, "I have heard. Indeed, I will pray to the LORD your
God according to your words,
and it shall be, *that* [a]whatever
the LORD answers you, I will declare *it* to you. I will [b]keep nothing back from you."
5 So they said to Jer·e·mī′ah,
[a]"Let the LORD be a true and
faithful witness between us, if
we do not do according to everything which the LORD your God
sends us by you.
6 "Whether *it is* [1]pleasing or
[2]displeasing, we will [a]obey the
voice of the LORD our God to
whom we send you, [b]that it may
be well with us when we obey
the voice of the LORD our God."
7 And it happened after ten
days that the word of the LORD
came to Jer·e·mī′ah.
8 Then he called Jō·hā′nan the
son of Ka·rē′ah, all the captains
of the forces which *were* with
him, and all the people from the
least even to the greatest,
9 and said to them, "Thus says
the LORD, the God of Israel, to
whom you sent me to present
your petition before Him:
10 'If you will still remain in
this land, then [a]I will build you
and not pull *you* down, and I will
plant you and not pluck *you* up.
For I [b]relent concerning the disaster that I have brought upon
you.
11 'Do not be afraid of the king

16 [a]Jer. 40:11, 12; 43:4–7
17 [a]2 Sam. 19:37, 38 [b]Jer. 43:7
18 [a]Jer. 40:5

CHAPTER 42

1 [a]Jer. 40:8, 13; 41:11
2 [a]Jer. 15:11 [b]Is. 37:4 [c]Lev. 26:22
3 [a]Ezra 8:21
4 [a]1 Kin. 22:14 [b]1 Sam. 3:17, 18
5 [a]Gen. 31:50
6 [a]Ex. 24:7 [b]Jer. 7:23 [1]Lit. *good* [2]Lit. *evil*
10 [a]Jer. 24:6; 31:28; 33:7 [b][Jer. 18:8]

of Babylon, of whom you are afraid; do not be afraid of him,' says the LORD, [a]"for I *am* with you, to save you and deliver you from his hand.

12 'And [a]I will show you mercy, that he may have mercy on you and cause you to return to your own land.'

13 "But if [a]you say, 'We will not dwell in this land,' disobeying the voice of the LORD your God,

14 "saying, 'No, but we will go to the land of [a]Egypt where we shall see no war, nor hear the sound of the trumpet, nor be hungry for bread, and there we will dwell'—

15 "Then hear now the word of the LORD, O remnant of Judah! Thus says the LORD of hosts, the God of Israel: 'If you [a]wholly[1] set [b]your faces to enter Egypt, and go to dwell there,

16 'then it shall be *that* the [a]sword which you feared shall overtake you there in the land of Egypt; the famine of which you were afraid shall follow close after you there *in* Egypt; and there you shall die.

17 'So shall it be with all the men who set their faces to go to Egypt to dwell there. They shall die by the sword, by famine, and by pestilence. And [a]none of them shall remain or escape from the disaster that I will bring upon them.'

18 "For thus says the LORD of hosts, the God of Israel: 'As My anger and My fury have been [a]poured out on the inhabitants of Jerusalem, so will My fury be poured out on you when you enter Egypt. And [b]you shall be an oath, an astonishment, a curse, and a reproach; and you shall see this place no more.'

19 "The LORD has said concerning you, O remnant of Judah, [a]'Do not go to Egypt!' Know certainly that I have [1]admonished you this day.

20 "For you [1]were hypocrites in your hearts when you sent me to the LORD your God, saying, 'Pray for us to the LORD our God, and according to all that the LORD your God says, so declare to us and we will do *it*.'

21 "And I have this day declared *it* to you, but you have [a]not obeyed the voice of the LORD your God, or anything which He has sent you by me.

22 "Now therefore, know certainly that you [a]shall die by the sword, by famine, and by pestilence in the place where you desire to go to dwell."

43 Now it happened, when Jer·e·mi′ah had stopped speaking to all the people all the [a]words of the LORD their God, for which the LORD their God had sent him to them, all these words,

2 [a]that Az·a·ri′ah the son of Hō·shai′ah, Jō·hā′nan the son of Ka·rē′ah, and all the proud men spoke, saying to Jer·e·mi′ah, "You speak falsely! The LORD our God has not sent you to say, 'Do not go to Egypt to dwell there.'

3 "But [a]Bar′uch the son of Ne·ri′ah has [1]set you against us, to deliver us into the hand of the Chal·dē′ans, that they may put us to death or carry us away captive to Babylon."

4 So Jō·hā′nan the son of Ka·rē′ah, all the captains of the forces, and all the people would

11 [a]Rom. 8:31
12 [a]Ps. 106:46
13 [a]Jer. 44:16
14 [a]Jer. 41:17; 43:7
15 [a]Deut. 17:16 [b]Luke 9:51 [1]Or *surely*
16 [a]Ezek. 11:8
17 [a]Jer. 44:14, 28
18 [a]Jer. 7:20 [b]Is. 65:15
19 [a]Deut. 17:16 [1]*warned*
20 [1]Lit. *used deceit against your souls*
21 [a]Is. 30:1–7
22 [a]Ezek. 6:11

CHAPTER 43

1 [a]Jer. 42:9–18
2 [a]Jer. 42:1
3 [a]Jer. 36:4; 45:1 [1]Or *incited*

[a]not obey the voice of the LORD,
to remain in the land of Judah.
5 But Jō·hā′nan the son of
Ka·rē′ah and all the captains of
the forces took [a]all the remnant
of Judah who had returned to
dwell in the land of Judah, from
all nations where they had been
driven—
6 men, women, children, [a]the
king's daughters, [b]and every
person whom Ne·bū·za·rad′an
the captain of the guard had
left with Ged·a·lī′ah the son of
A·hī′kam, the son of Shā′phan,
and Jer·e·mī′ah the prophet and
Bar′uch the son of Ne·rī′ah.
7 [a]So they went to the land of
Egypt, for they did not obey the
voice of the LORD. And they went
as far as [b]Tah′pan·hēs.
8 Then the [a]word of the LORD
came to Jer·e·mī′ah in Tah′-
pan·hēs, saying,
9 "Take large stones in your
hand, and hide them in the sight
of the men of Judah, in the [1]clay
in the brick courtyard which
is at the entrance to Pharaoh's
house in Tah′pan·hēs;
10 "and say to them, 'Thus says
the LORD of hosts, the God of
Israel: "Behold, I will send and
bring Ne·bū·chad·nez′zar the
king of Babylon, [a]My servant,
and will set his throne above
these stones that I have hidden.
And he will spread his royal pavilion over them.
11 [a]"When he comes, he shall
strike the land of Egypt *and deliver* to death [b]*those appointed*
for death, and to captivity *those
appointed* for captivity, and to
the sword *those appointed* for
the sword.
12 [1]"I will kindle a fire in the
houses of [a]the gods of Egypt,

4 [a]2 Kin. 25:26
5 [a]Jer. 40:11, 12
6 [a]Jer. 41:10 [b]Jer. 39:10; 40:7
7 [a]Jer. 42:19 [b]Jer. 2:16; 44:1
8 [a]Jer. 44:1–30
9 [1]Or *mortar*
10 [a]Jer. 25:9; 27:6
11 [a]Jer. 25:15–19; 44:13; 46:1, 2, 13–26 [b]Jer. 15:2
12 [a]Jer. 46:25 [1]So with MT, Tg.; LXX, Syr., Vg. *He*
13 [1]Lit. *House of the Sun*, ancient On, later called Heliopolis

CHAPTER 44

1 [a]Jer. 46:14 [b]Jer. 43:7 [c]Is. 19:13 [d]Ezek. 29:14; 30:14 [1]Ancient Memphis
2 [a]Jer. 4:7; 9:11; 34:22
3 [a]Jer. 19:4 [b]Deut. 13:6; 32:17
4 [a]Jer. 7:25; 25:4; 26:5; 29:19
6 [1]Or *became a ruin*

and he shall burn them and
carry them away captive. And he
shall array himself with the land
of Egypt, as a shepherd puts on
his garment, and he shall go out
from there in peace.
13 "He shall also break the *sacred* pillars of [1]Beth Shem′esh
that *are* in the land of Egypt;
and the houses of the gods of
the Egyptians he shall burn with
fire." ' "

44

The word that came to
Jer·e·mī′ah concerning all
the Jews who dwell in the land
of Egypt, who dwell at [a]Mig′-
dōl, at [b]Tah′pan·hēs, at [c]Noph,[1]
and in the country of [d]Path′ros,
saying,
2 "Thus says the LORD of hosts,
the God of Israel: 'You have
seen all the calamity that I have
brought on Jerusalem and on all
the cities of Judah; and behold,
this day they *are* [a]a desolation,
and no one dwells in them,
3 'because of their wickedness
which they have committed to
provoke Me to anger, in that
they went [a]to burn incense *and*
to [b]serve other gods whom they
did not know, they nor you nor
your fathers.
4 'However [a]I have sent to
you all My servants the prophets, rising early and sending
them, saying, "Oh, do not do this
abominable thing that I hate!"
5 'But they did not listen or incline their ear to turn from their
wickedness, to burn no incense
to other gods.
6 'So My fury and My anger
were poured out and kindled
in the cities of Judah and in the
streets of Jerusalem; and they
[1]are wasted *and* desolate, as it is
this day.'

7 “Now therefore, thus says
the LORD, the God of hosts, the
God of Israel: ‘Why do you commit *this* great evil [a]against yourselves, to cut off from you man
and woman, child and infant,
out of Judah, leaving none to
remain,
8 ‘in that you [a]provoke Me to
wrath with the works of your
hands, burning incense to other
gods in the land of Egypt where
you have gone to dwell, that you
may cut yourselves off and be [b]a
curse and a reproach among all
the nations of the earth?
9 ‘Have you forgotten the wickedness of your fathers, the wickedness of the kings of Judah, the
wickedness of their wives, your
own wickedness, and the wickedness of your wives, which they
committed in the land of Judah
and in the streets of Jerusalem?
10 ‘They have not been [a]hum-
bled,[1] to this day, nor have they
[b]feared; they have not walked
in My law or in My statutes
that I set before you and your
fathers.’
11 “Therefore thus says the
LORD of hosts, the God of Israel: ‘Behold, [a]I will set My face
against you for catastrophe and
for [1]cutting off all Judah.
12 ‘And I will take the remnant
of Judah who have set their
faces to go into the land of
Egypt to dwell there, and [a]they
shall all be consumed *and* fall
in the land of Egypt. They shall
be consumed by the sword *and*
by famine. They shall die, from
the least to the greatest, by the
sword and by famine; and [b]they
shall be an oath, an astonishment, a curse and a reproach!
13 [a]‘For I will punish those who
dwell in the land of Egypt, as
I have punished Jerusalem, by
the sword, by famine, and by
pestilence,
14 ‘so that none of the remnant
of Judah who have gone into
the land of Egypt to dwell there
shall escape or survive, lest they
return to the land of Judah, to
which they [a]desire[1] to return
and dwell. For [b]none shall return
except those who escape.’ ”
15 Then all the men who knew
that their wives had burned
incense to other gods, with
all the women who stood by,
a great multitude, and all the
people who dwelt in the land
of Egypt, in Path′ros, answered
Jer·e·mī′ah, saying:
16 “*As for* the word that you
have spoken to us in the name
of the LORD, [a]we will not listen to
you!
17 “But we will certainly do
[a]whatever has gone out of our
own mouth, to burn incense to
the [b]queen of heaven and pour
out drink offerings to her, as we
have done, we and our fathers,
our kings and our princes, in the
cities of Judah and in the streets
of Jerusalem. For *then* we had
plenty of [1]food, were well-off,
and saw no trouble.
18 “But since we stopped burning incense to the queen of
heaven and pouring out drink
offerings to her, we have lacked
everything and have been consumed by the sword and by
famine.”
19 *The women also said,* [a]“And
when we burned incense to the
queen of heaven and poured out
drink offerings to her, did we
make cakes for her, to worship
her, and pour out drink offerings

7 [a]Num. 16:38

8 [a]Jer. 25:6, 7; 44:3 [b]Jer. 42:18

10 [a]Jer. 6:15; 8:12 [b][Prov. 28:14] [1]Lit. *crushed*

11 [a]Amos 9:4 [1]*destroying*

12 [a]Jer. 42:15–17, 22 [b]Is. 65:15

13 [a]Jer. 43:11

14 [a]Jer. 22:26, 27 [b]Jer. 44:28 [1]Lit. *lift up their soul*

16 [a]Jer. 6:16

17 [a]Num. 30:12 [b]Jer. 7:18 [1]Lit. *bread*

19 [a]Jer. 7:18

to her without our husbands' *permission?*"

20 Then Jer·e·mi'ah spoke to all the people—the men, the women, and all the people who had given him *that* answer—saying:

21 "The incense that you burned in the cities of Judah and in the streets of Jerusalem, you and your fathers, your kings and your princes, and the people of the land, did not the LORD remember them, and did it *not* come into His mind?

22 "So the LORD could no longer bear *it*, because of the evil of your doings *and* because of the abominations which you committed. Therefore your land is a desolation, an astonishment, a curse, and without an inhabitant, [a]as *it is* this day.

23 "Because you have burned incense and because you have sinned against the LORD, and have not obeyed the voice of the LORD or walked in His law, in His statutes or in His testimonies, [a]therefore this calamity has happened to you, as *at* this day."

24 Moreover Jer·e·mi'ah said to all the people and to all the women, "Hear the word of the LORD, all Judah who *are* in the land of Egypt!

25 "Thus says the LORD of hosts, the God of Israel, saying: 'You and your wives have spoken with your mouths and fulfilled with your hands, saying, "We will surely keep our vows that we have made, to burn incense to the queen of heaven and pour out drink offerings to her." You will surely keep your vows and perform your vows!'

26 "Therefore hear the word of the LORD, all Judah who dwell in the land of Egypt: 'Behold, [a]I have sworn by My [b]great name,' says the LORD, 'that [c]My name shall no more be named in the mouth of any man of Judah in all the land of Egypt, saying, "The Lord GOD lives."

27 'Behold, I will watch over them for adversity and not for good. And all the men of Judah who *are* in the land of Egypt [a]shall be consumed by the sword and by famine, until there is an end to them.

28 'Yet [a]a small number who escape the sword shall return from the land of Egypt to the land of Judah; and all the remnant of Judah, who have gone to the land of Egypt to dwell there, shall know whose words will stand, Mine or theirs.

29 'And this *shall be* a sign to you,' says the LORD, 'that I will punish you in this place, that you may know that My words will surely [a]stand against you for adversity.'

30 "Thus says the LORD: 'Behold, [a]I will give Pharaoh Hoph'ra king of Egypt into the hand of his enemies and into the hand of those who seek his life, as I gave [b]Zed·e·ki'ah king of Judah into the hand of Ne·bu·chad·nez'zar king of Babylon, his enemy who sought his life.' "

CHAPTER 45

45 The [a]word that Jer·e·mi'ah the prophet spoke to [b]Bar'uch the son of Ne·ri'ah, when he had written these words in a book [1]at the instruction of Jer·e·mi'ah, in the [c]fourth year of Je·hoi'a·kim the son of Jo·si'ah, king of Judah, saying,

2 "Thus says the LORD, the God of Israel, to you, O Bar'uch:

22 [a]Jer. 25:11, 18, 38
23 [a]Dan. 9:11, 12
26 [a]Heb. 6:13 [b]Jer. 10:6 [c]Ezek. 20:39
27 [a]Ezek. 7:6
28 [a]Is. 10:19; 27:12, 13
29 [a][Ps. 33:11]
30 [a]Ezek. 29:3; 30:21 [b]Jer. 39:5
1 [a]Jer. 36:1, 4, 32 [b]Jer. 32:12, 16; 43:3 [c]Jer. 25:1; 36:1; 46:2 [1]Lit. *from Jeremiah's mouth*

3 'You said, "Woe is me now!
For the LORD has added grief to
my sorrow. I [a]fainted in my sighing, and I find no rest." '
4 "Thus you shall say to him,
'Thus says the LORD: "Behold,
[a]what I have built I will break
down, and what I have planted I
will pluck up, that is, this whole
land.
5 "And do you seek great
things for yourself? Do not seek
them; for behold, [a]I will bring
adversity on all flesh," says the
LORD. "But I will give your [b]life
to you as a prize in all places,
wherever you go." ' "

46

46 The word of the LORD
which came to Jer·e-
mī'ah the prophet against [a]the
nations.
2 Against [a]Egypt.
[b]Concerning the army of
Pharaoh Nē'cho, king of Egypt,
which was by the River Eū·phrā'-
tēs in Car'chem·ish, and which
Ne·bū·chad·nez'zar king of Babylon [c]defeated in the [d]fourth
year of Je·hoi'a·kim the son of
Jō·sī'ah, king of Judah:

3 "Order[1] the [2]buckler and
shield,
And draw near to battle!
4 Harness the horses,
And mount up, you
horsemen!
Stand forth with *your*
helmets,
Polish the spears,
[a]Put on the armor!
5 Why have I seen them
dismayed *and* turned
back?
Their mighty ones are
beaten down;
They have speedily fled,
And did not look back,
For [a]fear *was* all around,"
says the LORD.
6 "Do not let the swift flee
away,
Nor the mighty man escape;
They will [a]stumble and fall
Toward the north, by the
River Eū·phrā'tēs.

7 "Who *is* this coming up [a]like
a flood,
Whose waters move like the
rivers?
8 Egypt rises up like a flood,
And *its* waters move like
the rivers;
And he says, 'I will go up
and cover the earth,
I will destroy the city and its
inhabitants.'
9 Come up, O horses, and
rage, O chariots!
And let the mighty men
come forth:
[1]The Ethiopians and [2]the
Lib'yans who handle the
shield,
And the Lyd'i·ans [a]who
handle *and* bend the
bow.
10 For this *is* [a]the day of the
Lord GOD of hosts,
A day of vengeance,
That He may avenge
Himself on His
adversaries.
[b]The sword shall devour;
It shall be [1]satiated and
made drunk with their
blood;
For the Lord GOD of hosts
[c]has a sacrifice
In the north country by the
River Eū·phrā'tēs.

11 "Go[a] up to Gil'ē·ad and take
balm,

3 [a]Ps. 6:6; 69:3
4 [a]Is. 5:5
5 [a]Jer. 25:17–26 [b]Jer. 21:9; 38:2; 39:18
CHAPTER 46
1 [a]Jer. 25:15
2 [a]Jer. 25:17–19 [b]2 Kin. 23:33–35 [c]2 Chr. 35:20 [d]Jer. 45:1
3 [1]*Set in order* [2]A small shield
4 [a]Jer. 51:11, 12
5 [a]Jer. 49:29
6 [a]Dan. 11:19
7 [a]Jer. 47:2
9 [a]Is. 66:19 [1]Heb. *Cush* [2]Heb. *Put*
10 [a]Joel 1:15 [b]Deut. 32:42 [c]Is. 34:6 [1]Filled to the full
11 [a]Jer. 8:22

[b]O virgin, the daughter of
Egypt;
In vain you will use many
medicines;
[c]You shall not be cured.
12 The nations have heard of
your [a]shame,
And your cry has filled the
land;
For the mighty man has
stumbled against the
mighty;
They both have fallen
together."

13 The word that the LORD
spoke to Jer·e·mī'ah the prophet,
how Ne·bū·chad·nez'zar king of
Babylon would come *and* [a]strike
the land of Egypt.

14 "Declare in Egypt, and
proclaim in [a]Mig'dōl;
Proclaim in [1]Noph and in
[b]Tah'pan·hēs;
Say, 'Stand fast and prepare
yourselves,
For the sword devours all
around you.'
15 Why are your valiant *men*
swept away?
They did not stand
Because the LORD drove
them away.
16 He made many fall;
Yes, [a]one fell upon another.
And they said, 'Arise!
[b]Let us go back to our own
people
And to the land of our
nativity
From the oppressing sword.'
17 They cried there,
'Pharaoh, king of Egypt, *is*
but a noise.
He has passed by the
appointed time!'

11 [b]Is. 47:1 [c]Ezek. 30:21
12 [a]Jer. 2:36
13 [a]Is. 19:1
14 [a]Jer. 44:1 [b]Ezek. 30:18 [1]Ancient Memphis
16 [a]Lev. 26:36, 37 [b]Jer. 51:9
18 [a]Jer. 48:15
19 [a]Jer. 48:18 [b]Is. 20:4 [1]Ancient Memphis
20 [a]Hos. 10:11 [b]Jer. 1:14
21 [a][Ps. 37:13] [1]Lit. *calves of the stall*
22 [a][Is. 29:4]
23 [a]Is. 10:34 [b]Judg. 6:5; 7:12

18 "*As* I live," says the King,
[a]Whose name *is* the LORD of
hosts,
"Surely as Tā'bor *is* among
the mountains
And as Car'mel by the sea,
so he shall come.
19 O [a]you daughter dwelling in
Egypt,
Prepare yourself [b]to go into
captivity!
For [1]Noph shall be waste
and desolate, without
inhabitant.

20 "Egypt *is* a very pretty
[a]heifer,
But destruction comes, it
comes [b]from the north.
21 Also her mercenaries are in
her midst like [1]fat bulls,
For they also are turned
back,
They have fled away
together.
They did not stand,
For [a]the day of their
calamity had come upon
them,
The time of their
punishment.
22 [a]Her noise shall go like a
serpent,
For they shall march with
an army
And come against her with
axes,
Like those who chop wood.

23 "They shall [a]cut down her
forest," says the LORD,
"Though it cannot be
searched,
Because they *are*
innumerable,
And more numerous than
[b]grasshoppers.

24 The daughter of Egypt shall
be ashamed;
She shall be delivered into
the hand
Of [a]the people of the north."

25 The LORD of hosts, the God of
Israel, says: "Behold, I will bring
punishment on [1]Ā′mon of [a]No,[2]
and Pharaoh and Egypt, [b]with
their gods and their kings—Pharaoh and those who [c]trust in
him.
26 [a]"And I will deliver them
into the hand of those who
seek their lives, into the hand
of Ne·bū·chad·nez′zar king of
Babylon and the hand of his
servants. [b]Afterward it shall be
inhabited as in the days of old,"
says the LORD.

27 "But[a] do not fear, O My
servant Jacob,
And do not be dismayed,
O Israel!
For behold, I will [b]save you
from afar,
And your offspring from the
land of their captivity;
Jacob shall return, have rest
and be at ease;
No one shall make *him*
afraid.
28 Do not fear, O Jacob My
servant," says the LORD,
"For I *am* with you;
For I will make a complete
end of all the nations
To which I have driven you,
But I will not make [a]a
complete end of you.
I will rightly [b]correct you,
For I will not leave you
wholly unpunished."

47

The word of the LORD
that came to Jer·e·mī′ah
the prophet [a]against the Phi·lis′-
tines, [b]before Pharaoh attacked
Gā′za.

2 Thus says the LORD:

"Behold, [a]waters rise [b]out of
the north,
And shall be an overflowing
flood;
They shall overflow the land
and all that is in it,
The city and those who
dwell within;
Then the men shall cry,
And all the inhabitants of
the land shall wail.
3 At the [a]noise of the
stamping hooves of his
strong horses,
At the rushing of his
chariots,
At the rumbling of his
wheels,
The fathers will not look
back for *their* children,
[1]Lacking courage,
4 Because of the day that
comes to plunder all the
[a]Phi·lis′tines,
To cut off from [b]Tȳre and
Sī′don every helper who
remains;
For the LORD shall plunder
the Phi·lis′tines,
[c]The remnant of the country
of [d]Caph′tor.[1]
5 [a]Baldness has come upon
Gā′za,
[b]Ash′ke·lon is cut off
With the remnant of their
valley.
How long will you cut
yourself?

6 "O you [a]sword of the LORD,
How long until you are
quiet?

24 [a]Jer. 1:15
25 [a]Ezek. 30:14–16 [b]Jer. 43:12, 13 [c]Is. 30:1–5; 31:1–3 [1]A sun god [2]Ancient Thebes
26 [a]Ezek. 32:11 [b]Ezek. 29:8–14
27 [a]Is. 41:13, 14; 43:5; 44:2 [b]Is. 11:11
28 [a]Amos 9:8, 9 [b]Jer. 30:11

CHAPTER 47

1 [a]Zeph. 2:4, 5 [b]Amos 1:6
2 [a]Is. 8:7, 8 [b]Jer. 1:14
3 [a]Jer. 8:16 [1]Lit. *From sinking hands*
4 [a]Is. 14:29–31 [b]Jer. 25:22 [c]Ezek. 25:16 [d]Gen. 10:14 [1]Cappadocia in Asia Minor
5 [a]Mic. 1:16 [b]Jer. 25:20
6 [a]Ezek. 21:3–5

Put yourself up into your
scabbard,
Rest and be still!
7 How can [1]it be quiet,
Seeing the LORD has [a]given
it a charge
Against Ash'ke·lon and
against the seashore?
There He has [b]appointed it."

7 [a]Ezek. 14:17
[b]Mic. 6:9
[1]Lit. *you*

CHAPTER 48

48 Against [a]Mō'ab.
Thus says the LORD of
hosts, the God of Israel:

"Woe to [b]Nē'bō!
For it is plundered,
[c]Kir·jath'a·im is shamed *and*
taken;
[1]The high stronghold is
shamed and dismayed—
2 [a]No more praise of Mō'ab.
In [b]Hesh'bon they have
devised evil against her:
'Come, and let us cut her off
as a nation.'
You also shall be cut down,
O [c]Madmen![1]
The sword shall pursue you;
3 A voice of crying *shall be*
from [a]Hor·ō·nā'īm:
'Plundering and great
destruction!'

4 "Mō'ab is destroyed;
[1]Her little ones have caused
a cry to be heard;
5 [a]For in the Ascent of Lū'hith
they ascend with
continual weeping;
For in the descent of
Hor·ō·nā'īm the enemies
have heard a cry of
destruction.

6 "Flee, save your lives!
And be like [1]the [a]juniper in
the wilderness.

1 [a]Is. 15:1—16:14; 25:10
[b]Is. 15:2
[c]Num. 32:37
[1]Heb. *Misgab*

2 [a]Is. 16:14
[b]Jer. 49:3
[c]Is. 10:31
[1]A city of Moab

3 [a]Is. 15:5

4 [1]So with MT, Tg., Vg.; LXX *Proclaim it in Zoar*

5 [a]Is. 15:5

6 [a]Jer. 17:6
[1]Or *Aroer*, a city of Moab

7 [a]Jer. 9:23
[b]Jer. 48:13
[c]Jer. 49:3

8 [a]Jer. 6:26

9 [a]Ps. 55:6

10 [a]1 Sam. 15:3, 9

11 [a]Zeph. 1:12
[1]Heb. uses masc. and fem. pronouns interchangeably in this chapter.

12 [1]Lit. *tippers* of wine bottles

7 For because you have
trusted in your works
and your [a]treasures,
You also shall be taken.
And [b]Chē'mosh shall go
forth into captivity,
His [c]priests and his princes
together.
8 And [a]the plunderer shall
come against every city;
No one shall escape.
The valley also shall perish,
And the plain shall be
destroyed,
As the LORD has spoken.

9 "Give[a] wings to Mō'ab,
That she may flee and get
away;
For her cities shall be
desolate,
Without any to dwell in
them.
10 [a]Cursed *is* he who does
the work of the LORD
deceitfully,
And cursed *is* he who keeps
back his sword from
blood.

11 "Mō'ab has been at ease
from [1]his youth;
He [a]has settled on his dregs,
And has not been emptied
from vessel to vessel,
Nor has he gone into
captivity.
Therefore his taste
remained in him,
And his scent has not
changed.

12 "Therefore behold, the days
are coming," says the
LORD,
"That I shall send him [1]wine-
workers
Who will tip him over

And empty his vessels
And break the bottles.
13 Mō′ab shall be ashamed of
[a]Chē′mosh,
As the house of Israel [b]was
ashamed of [c]Beth′el,
their confidence.

14 "How can you say, [a]'We *are*
mighty
And strong men for the
war'?
15 Mō′ab is plundered and
gone up *from* her cities;
Her chosen young men
have [a]gone down to the
slaughter," says [b]the
King,
Whose name *is* the LORD of
hosts.

16 "The calamity of Mō′ab *is*
near at hand,
And his affliction comes
quickly.
17 Bemoan him, all you who
are around him;
And all you who know his
name,
Say, [a]'How the strong staff
is broken,
The beautiful rod!'

18 "O [a]daughter inhabiting
[b]Dī′bon,
Come down from *your* glory,
And sit in thirst;
For the plunderer of Mō′ab
has come against you,
He has destroyed your
strongholds.
19 O inhabitant of [a]A·rō′er,
[b]Stand by the way and
watch;
Ask him who flees
And her who escapes;
Say, 'What has happened?'

13 [a]1 Kin. 11:7 [b]Hos. 10:6 [c]1 Kin. 12:29; 13:32–34
14 [a]Is. 16:6
15 [a]Jer. 50:27 [b]Jer. 46:18; 51:57
17 [a]Is. 9:4; 14:4, 5
18 [a]Is. 47:1 [b]Is. 15:2
19 [a]Deut. 2:36 [b]1 Sam. 4:13, 14, 16
20 [a]Is. 16:7 [b]Num. 21:13
24 [a]Amos 2:2
25 [a]Ps. 75:10 [b]Ezek. 30:21 [1]Strength
26 [a]Jer. 25:15
27 [a]Zeph. 2:8 [b]Jer. 2:26 [c]Lam. 2:15
28 [a]Ps. 55:6, 7 [b]Song 2:14
29 [a]Is. 16:6

20 Mō′ab is shamed, for he is
broken down.
[a]Wail and cry!
Tell it in [b]Ar′non, that Mō′ab
is plundered.

21 "And judgment has come on
the plain country:
On Hō′lon and Jah′zah and
Meph′a·ath,
22 On Dī′bon and Nē′bō and
Beth Dib·la·thā′im,
23 On Kir·jath′a·im and Beth
Gā′mūl and Beth Mē′on,
24 On [a]Ker′i·oth and Boz′rah,
On all the cities of the land
of Mō′ab,
Far or near.
25 [a]The [1]horn of Mō′ab is cut
off,
And his [b]arm is broken,"
says the LORD.

26 "Make[a] him drunk,
Because he exalted *himself*
against the LORD.
Mō′ab shall wallow in his
vomit,
And he shall also be in
derision.
27 For [a]was not Israel a
derision to you?
[b]Was he found among
thieves?
For whenever you speak of
him,
You shake *your head in*
[c]*scorn.*
28 You who dwell in Mō′ab,
Leave the cities and [a]dwell
in the rock,
And be like [b]the dove *which*
makes her nest
In the sides of the cave's
mouth.

29 "We have heard the [a]pride of
Mō′ab

(He *is* exceedingly proud),
Of his loftiness and
arrogance and [b]pride,
And of the haughtiness of
his heart."

30 "I know his wrath," says the
LORD,
"But it *is* not right;
[a]His [1]lies have made nothing
right.
31 Therefore [a]I will wail for
Mō′ab,
And I will cry out for all
Mō′ab;
[1]I will mourn for the men of
Kir Hē′res.
32 [a]O vine of Sib′mah! I will
weep for you with the
weeping of [b]Jā′zer.
Your plants have gone over
the sea,
They reach to the sea of
Jā′zer.
The plunderer has fallen on
your summer fruit and
your vintage.
33 [a]Joy and gladness are taken
From the plentiful field
And from the land of Mō′ab;
I have caused wine to [1]fail
from the winepresses;
No one will tread with
joyous shouting—
Not joyous shouting!

34 "From[a] the cry of Hesh′bon to
[b]Ē·le·ā′leh and to Jā′haz
They have uttered their
voice,
[c]From Zō′ar to Hor·ō·nā′im,
Like [1]a three-year-old heifer;
For the waters of Nim′rim
also shall be desolate.

35 "Moreover," says the LORD,
"I will cause to cease in
Mō′ab
[a]The one who offers
sacrifices in the [1]high
places
And burns incense to his
gods.
36 Therefore [a]My heart shall
wail like flutes for Mō′ab,
And like flutes My heart
shall wail
For the men of Kir Hē′res.
Therefore [b]the riches they
have acquired have
perished.

37 "For [a]every head *shall be*
bald, and every beard
clipped;
On all the hands *shall be*
cuts, and [b]on the loins
sackcloth—
38 A general lamentation
On all the [a]housetops of
Mō′ab,
And in its streets;
For I have [b]broken Mō′ab
like a vessel in which *is*
no pleasure," says the
LORD.
39 "They shall wail:
'How she is broken down!
How Mō′ab has turned her
back with shame!'
So Mō′ab shall be a derision
And a dismay to all those
about her."

40 For thus says the LORD:

"Behold, [a]one shall fly like an
eagle,
And [b]spread his wings over
Mō′ab.
41 Ker′i·oth is taken,
And the strongholds are
surprised;
[a]The mighty men's hearts
in Mō′ab on that day
shall be

29 [b]Jer. 49:16
30 [a]Jer. 50:36 [1]*idle talk*
31 [a]Is. 15:5; 16:7, 11 [1]So with DSS, LXX, Vg.; MT *He*
32 [a]Is. 16:8, 9 [b]Num. 21:32
33 [a]Joel 1:12 [1]*cease*
34 [a]Is. 15:4–6 [b]Num. 32:3, 37 [c]Is. 15:5, 6 [1]Or *The Third Eglath,* an unknown city, Is. 15:5
35 [a]Is. 15:2; 16:12 [1]Places for pagan worship
36 [a]Is. 15:5; 16:11 [b]Is. 15:7
37 [a]Is. 15:2, 3 [b]Gen. 37:34
38 [a]Is. 15:3 [b]Jer. 22:28
40 [a]Deut. 28:49 [b]Is. 8:8
41 [a]Is. 13:8; 21:3

Like the heart of a woman
in birth pangs.
42 And Mō′ab shall be
destroyed [a]as a people,
Because he exalted *himself*
against the LORD.
43 [a]Fear and the pit and the
snare *shall be* upon you,
O inhabitant of Mō′ab," says
the LORD.
44 "He who flees from the fear
shall fall into the pit,
And he who gets out of the
pit shall be caught in the
[a]snare.
For upon Mō′ab, upon it [b]I
will bring
The year of their
punishment," says the
LORD.

45 "Those who fled stood under
the shadow of Hesh′bon
Because of exhaustion.
But [a]a fire shall come out of
Hesh′bon,
A flame from the midst of
[b]Sī′hon,
And [c]shall devour the brow
of Mō′ab,
The crown of the head of
the sons of tumult.
46 [a]Woe to you, O Mō′ab!
The people of Chē′mosh
perish;
For your sons have been
taken captive,
And your daughters captive.

47 "Yet I will bring back the
captives of Mō′ab
[a]In the latter days," says the
LORD.

Thus far *is* the judgment of
Mō′ab.

49 Against the [a]Am′mon·ītes.
Thus says the LORD:

"Has Israel no sons?
Has he no heir?
Why *then* does [1]Mil′com
inherit [b]Gad,
And his people dwell in its
cities?
2 [a]Therefore behold, the days
are coming," says the
LORD,
"That I will cause to be heard
an alarm of war
In [b]Rab′bah of the
Am′mon·ītes;
It shall be a desolate mound,
And her [1]villages shall be
burned with fire.
Then Israel shall take
possession of his
inheritance," says the
LORD.

3 "Wail, O [a]Hesh′bon, for Aī is
plundered!
Cry, you daughters of
Rab′bah,
[b]Gird yourselves with
sackcloth!
Lament and run to and fro
by the walls;
For [1]Mil′com shall go into
captivity
With his [c]priests and his
princes together.
4 Why [a]do you boast in the
valleys,
[1]Your flowing valley,
O [b]backsliding daughter?
Who trusted in her
[c]treasures, [d]*saying,*
'Who will come against me?'
5 Behold, I will bring fear
upon you,"
Says the Lord GOD of hosts,
"From all those who are
around you;
You shall be driven out,
everyone headlong,

42 [a]Ps. 83:4
43 [a]Is. 24:17, 18
44 [a]Is. 24:18 [b]Jer. 11:23
45 [a]Num. 21:28, 29 [b]Ps. 135:11 [c]Num. 24:17
46 [a]Num. 21:29
47 [a]Jer. 49:6, 39

CHAPTER 49

1 [a]Ezek. 21:28–32; 25:1–7 [b]Amos 1:13–15 [1]Heb. *Malcam*, lit. *their king;* an Ammonite god, 1 Kin. 11:5; *Molech*, Lev. 18:21
2 [a]Amos 1:13–15 [b]Ezek. 25:5 [1]Lit. *daughters*
3 [a]Jer. 48:2 [b]Is. 32:11 [c]Jer. 48:7 [1]See v. 1
4 [a]Jer. 9:23 [b]Jer. 3:14 [c]Jer. 48:7 [d]Jer. 21:13 [1]Lit. *Your valley is flowing*

And no one will gather
those who wander off.
6 But [a]afterward I will bring
back
The captives of the people
of Am′mon," says the
LORD.

7 [a]Against Ē′dom.
Thus says the LORD of hosts:

[b]"*Is* wisdom no more in
Tē′man?
[c]Has counsel perished from
the prudent?
Has their wisdom
[d]vanished?
8 Flee, turn back, dwell in the
depths, O inhabitants of
[a]Dē′dan!
For I will bring the calamity
of Esau upon him,
The time *that* I will punish
him.
9 [a]If grape-gatherers came to
you,
Would they not leave *some*
gleaning grapes?
If thieves by night,
Would they not destroy until
they have enough?
10 [a]But I have made Esau
bare;
I have uncovered his secret
places,
And he shall not be able to
hide himself.
His descendants are
plundered,
His brethren and his
neighbors,
And [b]he *is* no more.
11 Leave your fatherless
children,
I will preserve *them* alive;
And let your widows trust
in Me."

12 For thus says the LORD: "Behold, [a]those whose judgment
was not to drink of the cup have
assuredly drunk. And *are* you
the one who will altogether go
unpunished? You shall not go
unpunished, but you shall surely
drink *of it.*
13 "For [a]I have sworn by Myself," says the LORD, "that [b]Boz′-
rah shall become a desolation, a
reproach, a [1]waste, and a curse.
And all its cities shall be perpetual [2]wastes."

14 [a]I have heard a message
from the LORD,
And an ambassador has
been sent to the nations:
"Gather together, come
against her,
And rise up to battle!

15 "For indeed, I will make you
small among nations,
Despised among men.
16 Your fierceness has
deceived you,
The [a]pride of your heart,
O you who dwell in the
clefts of the rock,
Who hold the height of the
hill!
[b]Though you make your [c]nest
as high as the eagle,
[d]I will bring you down from
there," says the LORD.

17 "Ē′dom also shall be an
astonishment;
[a]Everyone who goes by it
will be astonished
And will hiss at all its
plagues.
18 [a]As in the overthrow of
Sod′om and Go·mor′rah
And their neighbors," says
the LORD,

6 [a]Jer. 48:47
7 [a]Ezek. 25:12–14; 35:1–15 [b]Gen. 36:11 [c]Is. 19:11 [d]Jer. 8:9
8 [a]Jer. 25:23
9 [a]Obad. 5, 6
10 [a]Mal. 1:3 [b]Is. 17:14
12 [a]Jer. 25:29
13 [a]Amos 6:8 [b]Is. 34:6; 63:1 [1]*ruin* [2]*ruins*
14 [a]Obad. 1–4
16 [a]Jer. 48:29 [b]Obad. 3, 4 [c]Job 39:27 [d]Amos 9:2
17 [a]Jer. 18:16; 49:13; 50:13
18 [a]Deut. 29:23

"No one shall remain there,
Nor shall a son of man
dwell in it.

19 "Behold,[a] he shall come up
like a lion from [b]the
[1]floodplain of the Jordan
Against the dwelling place
of the strong;
But I will suddenly make
him run away from her.
And who *is* a chosen *man*
that I may appoint over
her?
For [c]who *is* like Me?
Who will arraign Me?
And [d]who *is* that shepherd
Who will withstand Me?"

20 [a]Therefore hear the counsel
of the LORD that He has
taken against Ē′dom,
And His purposes that He
has proposed against the
inhabitants of Tē′man:
Surely the least of the flock
shall [1]draw them out;
Surely He shall make their
dwelling places desolate
with them.
21 [a]The earth shakes at the
noise of their fall;
At the cry its noise is heard
at the Red Sea.
22 Behold, [a]He shall come up
and fly like the eagle,
And spread His wings over
Boz′rah;
The heart of the mighty men
of Ē′dom in that day
shall be
Like the heart of a woman
in birth pangs.

23 [a]Against Damascus.

[b]"Hā′math and Ar′pad are
shamed,
For they have heard bad
news.
They are fainthearted;
[c]*There is* [1]trouble on the sea;
It cannot be quiet.
24 Damascus has grown feeble;
She turns to flee,
And fear has seized *her.*
[a]Anguish and sorrows have
taken her like a woman
in [1]labor.
25 Why is [a]the city of praise
not deserted, the city of
My joy?
26 [a]Therefore her young men
shall fall in her streets,
And all the men of war shall
be cut off in that day,"
says the LORD of hosts.
27 "I[a] will kindle a fire in the
wall of Damascus,
And it shall consume the
palaces of Ben-Hā′dad."

28 [a]Against Kē′dar and against
the kingdoms of Hā′zor, which
Ne·bū·chad·nez′zar king of Babylon shall strike.
Thus says the LORD:

"Arise, go up to Kē′dar,
And devastate [b]the men of
the East!
29 Their [a]tents and their flocks
they shall take away.
They shall take for
themselves their
curtains,
All their vessels and their
camels;
And they shall cry out to
them,
[b]'Fear *is* on every side!'

30 "Flee, get far away! Dwell in
the depths,
O inhabitants of Hā′zor!"
says the LORD.

19 [a]Jer. 50:44 [b]Jer. 12:5 [c]Ex. 15:11 [d]Job 41:10 [1]Or *thicket*
20 [a]Jer. 50:45 [1]Or *drag them away*
21 [a]Jer. 50:46
22 [a]Jer. 48:40, 41
23 [a]Amos 1:3, 5 [b]Jer. 39:5 [c][Is. 57:20] [1]*anxiety*
24 [a]Is. 13:8 [1]*childbirth*
25 [a]Jer. 33:9
26 [a]Jer. 50:30
27 [a]Amos 1:4
28 [a]Ezek. 27:21 [b]Judg. 6:3
29 [a]Ps. 120:5 [b]Jer. 46:5

"For Ne·bū·chad·nez′zar king
of Babylon has taken
counsel against you,
And has conceived a plan
against you.
31 "Arise, go up to [a]the wealthy
nation that dwells
securely," says the LORD,
"Which has neither gates nor
bars,
[b]Dwelling alone.
32 Their camels shall be for
booty,
And the multitude of their
cattle for plunder.
I will [a]scatter to all winds
those [1]in the farthest
corners,
And I will bring their
calamity from all its
sides," says the LORD.
33 "Hā′zor [a]shall be a dwelling
for jackals, a desolation
forever;
No one shall reside there,
Nor son of man dwell in it."

34 The word of the LORD that
came to Jer·e·mī′ah the prophet
against [a]Ē′lam, in the [b]beginning
of the reign of Zed·e·kī′ah king
of Judah, saying,
35 "Thus says the LORD of hosts:

'Behold, I will break [a]the
[1]bow of Ē′lam,
The foremost of their might.
36 Against Ē′lam I will bring
the four winds
From the four quarters of
heaven,
And scatter them toward all
those winds;
There shall be no nations
where the outcasts of
Ē′lam will not go.
37 For I will cause Ē′lam to be
dismayed before their
enemies
And before those who seek
their life.
[a]I will bring disaster upon
them,
My fierce anger,' says the
LORD;
'And I will send the sword
after them
Until I have consumed them.
38 I will [a]set My throne in
Ē′lam,
And will destroy from
there the king and the
princes,' says the LORD.

39 'But it shall come to pass [a]in
the latter days:
I will bring back the
captives of Ē′lam,' says
the LORD."

50

The word that the LORD
spoke [a]against Babylon
and against the land of the
Chal·dē′ans by Jer·e·mī′ah the
prophet.

2 "Declare among the nations,
Proclaim, and [1]set up a
standard;
Proclaim—do not conceal
it—
Say, 'Babylon is [a]taken, [b]Bel
is shamed.
[2]Mer′o·dach is broken in
pieces;
[c]Her idols are humiliated,
Her images are broken in
pieces.'
3 [a]For out of the north [b]a
nation comes up against
her,
Which shall make her land
desolate,

31 [a]Ezek. 38:11 [b]Num. 23:9
32 [a]Ezek. 5:10 [1]Lit. *cut off at the corner,* Jer. 9:26; 25:23
33 [a]Mal. 1:3
34 [a]Jer. 25:25 [b]2 Kin. 24:17, 18
35 [a]Is. 22:6 [1]Power
37 [a]Jer. 9:16
38 [a]Jer. 43:10
39 [a]Jer. 48:47

CHAPTER 50

1 [a]Is. 13:1; 47:1
2 [a]Is. 21:9 [b]Is. 46:1 [c]Jer. 43:12, 13 [1]*lift* [2]Or *Marduk;* a Babylonian god
3 [a]Jer. 51:48 [b]Is. 13:17, 18, 20

And no one shall dwell
therein.
They shall [1]move, they shall
depart,
Both man and beast.

4 "In those days and in that
time," says the LORD,
"The children of Israel shall
come,
[a]They and the children of
Judah together;
[b]With continual weeping
they shall come,
[c]And seek the LORD their
God.
5 They shall ask the way to
Zion,
With their faces toward it,
saying,
'Come and let us join
ourselves to the LORD
In [a]a perpetual covenant
That will not be forgotten.'

6 "My people have been [a]lost
sheep.
Their shepherds have led
them [b]astray;
They have turned them
away *on* [c]the mountains.
They have gone from
mountain to hill;
They have forgotten their
resting place.
7 All who found them have
[a]devoured them;
And [b]their adversaries said,
[c]'We have not offended,
Because they have sinned
against the LORD, [d]the
habitation of justice,
The LORD, [e]the hope of their
fathers.'

8 "Move[a] from the midst of
Babylon,
Go out of the land of the
Chal·dē′ans;
And be like the [1]rams before
the flocks.
9 [a]For behold, I will raise and
cause to come up against
Babylon
An assembly of great
nations from the north
country,
And they shall array
themselves against her;
From there she shall be
captured.
Their arrows *shall be* like
those of [1]an expert
warrior;
[b]None shall return in vain.
10 And Chal·dē′a shall become
plunder;
[a]All who plunder her shall be
satisfied," says the LORD.

11 "Because[a] you were glad,
because you rejoiced,
You destroyers of My
heritage,
Because you have grown fat
[b]like a heifer threshing
grain,
And you [1]bellow like bulls,
12 Your mother shall be deeply
ashamed;
She who bore you shall be
ashamed.
Behold, the least of the
nations *shall be* a
[a]wilderness,
A dry land and a desert.
13 Because of the wrath of the
LORD
She shall not be inhabited,
[a]But she shall be wholly
desolate.
[b]Everyone who goes by
Babylon shall be
horrified
And hiss at all her plagues.

---

3 [1]Or *wander*
4 [a]Hos. 1:11 [b]Ezra 3:12, 13 [c]Hos. 3:5
5 [a]Jer. 31:31
6 [a]Is. 53:6 [b]Jer. 23:1 [c][Jer. 2:20; 3:6, 23]
7 [a]Ps. 79:7 [b]Zech. 11:5 [c]Jer. 2:3 [d][Ps. 90:1; 91:1] [e]Ps. 22:4
8 [a]Is. 48:20 [1]*male goats*
9 [a]Jer. 15:14; 51:27 [b]2 Sam. 1:22 [1]So with some Heb. mss., LXX, Syr.; MT, Tg., Vg. *a warrior who makes childless*
10 [a][Rev. 17:16]
11 [a]Is. 47:6 [b]Hos. 10:11 [1]Or *neigh like steeds*
12 [a]Jer. 51:43
13 [a]Jer. 25:12 [b]Jer. 49:17

14 "Put[a] yourselves in array
against Babylon all
around,
All you who bend the bow;
Shoot at her, spare no
arrows,
For she has sinned against
the LORD.
15 Shout against her all
around;
She has [a]given her hand,
Her foundations have fallen,
[b]Her walls are thrown down;
For [c]it *is* the vengeance of
the LORD.
Take vengeance on her.
As she has done, so do to
her.
16 Cut off the sower from
Babylon,
And him who handles the
sickle at harvest time.
For fear of the oppressing
sword
[a]Everyone shall turn to his
own people,
And everyone shall flee to
his own land.

17 "Israel *is* like [a]scattered
sheep;
[b]The lions have driven *him*
away.
First [c]the king of Assyria
devoured him;
Now at last this
[d]Ne·bū·chad·nez'zar king
of Babylon has broken
his bones."

18 Therefore thus says the LORD
of hosts, the God of Israel:

"Behold, I will punish the
king of Babylon and his
land,
As I have punished the king
of [a]Assyria.

19 [a]But I will bring back Israel
to his home,
And he shall feed on
Car'mel and Bā'shan;
His soul shall be satisfied
on Mount Ē'phra·im and
Gil'ē·ad.
20 In those days and in that
time," says the LORD,
[a]"The iniquity of Israel shall
be sought, but *there
shall be* none;
And the sins of Judah, but
they shall not be found;
For I will pardon those
[b]whom I preserve.

21 "Go up against the land of
Mer·a·thā'im, against it,
And against the inhabitants
of [a]Pē'kod.
[1]Waste and utterly destroy
them," says the LORD,
"And do [b]according to all that
I have commanded you.
22 [a]A sound of battle *is* in the
land,
And of great destruction.
23 How [a]the hammer of the
whole earth has been cut
apart and broken!
How Babylon has become
a desolation among the
nations!
24 I have laid a snare for you;
You have indeed been
[a]trapped, O Babylon,
And you were not aware;
You have been found and
also caught,
Because you have
[b]contended against the
LORD.
25 The LORD has opened His
armory,
And has brought out
[a]the weapons of His
indignation;

14 [a]Jer. 51:2
15 [a]Lam. 5:6 [b]Jer. 51:58 [c]Jer. 51:6, 11
16 [a]Is. 13:14
17 [a]2 Kin. 24:10, 14 [b]Jer. 2:15 [c]2 Kin. 15:29; 17:6; 18:9–13 [d]2 Kin. 24:10–14; 25:1–7
18 [a]Ezek. 31:3, 11, 12
19 [a]Is. 65:10
20 [a][Jer. 31:34] [b]Is. 1:9
21 [a]Ezek. 23:23 [b]2 Sam. 16:11 [1]Or *Attack* with the sword
22 [a]Jer. 51:54
23 [a]Jer. 51:20–24
24 [a]Dan. 5:30 [b][Is. 45:9]
25 [a]Is. 13:5

For this *is* the work of the
Lord GOD of hosts
In the land of the
Chal·dē′ans.
26 Come against her from the
farthest border;
Open her storehouses;
Cast her up as heaps of
ruins,
And destroy her utterly;
Let nothing of her be left.
27 Slay all her [a]bulls,
Let them go down to the
slaughter.
Woe to them!
For their day has come, the
time of [b]their punishment.
28 The voice of those who flee
and escape from the
land of Babylon
[a]Declares in Zion the
vengeance of the LORD
our God,
The vengeance of His
temple.

29 "Call together the archers
against Babylon.
All you who bend the bow,
encamp against it all
around;
Let none of them [1]escape.
[a]Repay her according to her
work;
According to all she has
done, do to her;
[b]For she has been proud
against the LORD,
Against the Holy One of
Israel.
30 [a]Therefore her young men
shall fall in the streets,
And all her men of war
shall be cut off in that
day," says the LORD.
31 "Behold, I *am* against you,
O most haughty one!" says
the Lord GOD of hosts;
"For your day has come,
[1]The time *that* I will punish
you.
32 The most [a]proud shall
stumble and fall,
And no one will raise him
up;
[b]I will kindle a fire in his
cities,
And it will devour all
around him."

33 Thus says the LORD of hosts:

"The children of Israel *were*
oppressed,
Along with the children of
Judah;
All who took them captive
have held them fast;
They have refused to let
them go.
34 [a]Their Redeemer *is* strong;
[b]The LORD of hosts *is* His
name.
He will thoroughly plead
their [c]case,
That He may give rest to the
land,
And disquiet the inhabitants
of Babylon.

35 "A sword *is* against the
Chal·dē′ans," says the
LORD,
"Against the inhabitants of
Babylon,
And [a]against her princes
and [b]her wise men.
36 A sword *is* [a]against the
soothsayers, and they
will be fools.
A sword *is* against her
mighty men, and they
will be dismayed.
37 A sword *is* against their
horses,
Against their chariots,

27 [a]Is. 34:7 [b]Jer. 48:44
28 [a]Jer. 51:10
29 [a]Jer. 51:56 [b][Is. 47:10] [1]Qr., some Heb. mss., LXX, Tg. add *to her*
30 [a]Jer. 49:26; 51:4
31 [1]So with MT, Tg.; LXX, Vg. *The time of your punishment*
32 [a]Mal. 4:1 [b]Jer. 21:14
34 [a]Rev. 18:8 [b]Is. 47:4 [c]Jer. 51:36; Mic. 7:9
35 [a]Dan. 5:30 [b]Is. 47:13
36 [a]Is. 44:25

And against all [a]the mixed
peoples who *are* in her
midst;
And [b]they will become like
women.
A sword *is* against her
treasures, and they will
be robbed.
38 [a]A [1]drought *is* against her
waters, and they will be
dried up.
For it *is* the land of carved
images,
And they are insane with
their idols.

39 "Therefore[a] the wild desert
beasts shall dwell *there*
with the jackals,
And the ostriches shall
dwell in it.
[b]It shall be inhabited no
more forever,
Nor shall it be dwelt in
from generation to
generation.
40 [a]As God overthrew Sod′om
and Go·mor′rah
And their neighbors," says
the LORD,
"So no one shall reside
there,
Nor son of man [b]dwell in it.

41 "Behold,[a] a people shall
come from the north,
And a great nation and
many kings
Shall be raised up from the
ends of the earth.
42 [a]They shall hold the bow and
the lance;
[b]They *are* cruel and shall not
show mercy.
[c]Their voice shall roar like
the sea;
They shall ride on horses,
Set in array, like a man for
the battle,
Against you, O daughter of
Babylon.

43 "The king of Babylon has
[a]heard the report about
them,
And his hands grow feeble;
Anguish has taken hold of
him,
Pangs as of a woman in
[b]childbirth.

44 "Behold,[a] he shall come
up like a lion from the
[1]floodplain of the
Jordan
Against the dwelling place
of the strong;
But I will make them
suddenly run away from
her.
And who *is* a chosen *man*
that I may appoint over
her?
For who *is* like Me?
Who will arraign Me?
And [b]who *is* that shepherd
Who will withstand Me?"

45 Therefore hear [a]the counsel
of the LORD that He has
taken against Babylon,
And His [b]purposes that He
has proposed against the
land of the Chal·dē′ans:
[c]Surely the least of the flock
shall draw them out;
Surely He will make their
dwelling place desolate
with them.
46 [a]At the noise of the taking of
Babylon
The earth trembles,
And the cry is heard among
the nations.

37 [a]Jer. 25:20 [b]Jer. 51:30
38 [a]Rev. 16:12 [1]So with MT, Tg., Vg.; Syr. *sword;* LXX omits *A drought is*
39 [a]Rev. 18:2 [b]Is. 13:20
40 [a]Is. 13:19 [b]Is. 13:20
41 [a]Jer. 6:22; 25:14; 51:27
42 [a]Jer. 6:23 [b]Is. 13:18 [c]Is. 5:30
43 [a]Jer. 51:31 [b]Jer. 6:24
44 [a]Jer. 49:19–21 [b]Job 41:10 [1]Or *thicket*
45 [a]Jer. 51:10, 11 [b]Jer. 51:29 [c]Jer. 49:19, 20
46 [a]Rev. 18:9

51

Thus says the LORD:
"Behold, I will raise up
against [a]Babylon,
Against those who dwell in
[1]Leb Kā'maī,
[b]A destroying wind.
2 And I will send [a]winnowers
to Babylon,
Who shall winnow her and
empty her land.
[b]For in the day of doom
They shall be against her all
around.
3 Against *her* [a]let the archer
bend his bow,
And lift himself up against
her in his armor.
Do not spare her young
men;
[b]Utterly destroy all her army.
4 Thus the slain shall fall
in the land of the
Chal·dē'ans,
[a]And *those* thrust through in
her streets.
5 For Israel is [a]not forsaken,
nor Judah,
By his God, the LORD of
hosts,
Though their land was filled
with sin against the Holy
One of Israel."

6 [a]Flee from the midst of
Babylon,
And every one save his life!
Do not be cut off in her
iniquity,
For [b]this *is* the time of the
LORD's vengeance;
[c]He shall recompense her.
7 [a]Babylon *was* a golden cup
in the LORD's hand,
That made all the earth
drunk.
[b]The nations drank her wine;
Therefore the nations [c]are
deranged.
8 Babylon has suddenly
[a]fallen and been
destroyed.
[b]Wail for her!
[c]Take balm for her pain;
Perhaps she may be healed.

9 We would have healed
Babylon,
But she is not healed.
Forsake her, and [a]let us go
everyone to his own
country;
[b]For her judgment reaches to
heaven and is lifted up
to the skies.
10 The LORD has [a]revealed our
righteousness.
Come and let us [b]declare
in Zion the work of the
LORD our God.

11 [a]Make[1] the arrows bright!
Gather the shields!
[b]The LORD has raised up the
spirit of the kings of the
Mēdes.
[c]For His plan *is* against
Babylon to destroy it,
Because it *is* [d]the vengeance
of the LORD,
The vengeance for His
temple.
12 [a]Set up the standard on the
walls of Babylon;
Make the guard strong,
Set up the watchmen,
Prepare the ambushes.
For the LORD has both
devised and done
What He spoke against the
inhabitants of Babylon.
13 [a]O you who dwell by many
waters,
Abundant in treasures,
Your end has come,

CHAPTER 51

1 [a]Is. 47:1 [b]Jer. 4:11 [1]Lit. *The Midst of Those Who Rise Up Against Me;* a code word for Chaldea, Babylonia

2 [a]Jer. 15:7 [b]Jer. 50:14

3 [a]Jer. 50:14, 29 [b]Jer. 50:21

4 [a]Jer. 49:26; 50:30, 37

5 [a][Jer. 33:24–26; 46:28]

6 [a]Rev. 18:4 [b]Jer. 50:15 [c]Jer. 25:14

7 [a]Rev. 17:4 [b]Rev. 14:8 [c]Jer. 25:16

8 [a]Is. 21:9 [b]Rev. 18:9, 11, 19 [c]Jer. 46:11

9 [a]Is. 13:14 [b]Rev. 18:5

10 [a]Ps. 37:6 [b]Jer. 50:28

11 [a]Jer. 46:4, 9 [b]Is. 13:17 [c]Jer. 50:45 [d]Jer. 50:28 [1]*Polish the arrows!*

12 [a]Nah. 2:1; 3:14

13 [a]Rev. 17:1, 15

The measure of your
covetousness.
14 [a]The LORD of hosts has sworn
by Himself:
"Surely I will fill you with
men, [b]as with locusts,
And they shall lift [c]up a
shout against you."

15 [a]He has made the earth by
His power;
He has established the
world by His wisdom,
And [b]stretched out
the heaven by His
understanding.
16 When He utters *His* voice—
There is a multitude of
waters in the heavens:
[a]"He causes the vapors to
ascend from the ends of
the earth;
He makes lightnings for the
rain;
He brings the wind out of
His treasuries."

17 [a]Everyone is dull-hearted,
without knowledge;
Every metalsmith is put to
shame by the carved
image;
[b]For his molded image *is*
falsehood,
And *there is* no breath in
them.
18 They *are* futile, a work of
errors;
In the time of their
punishment they shall
perish.
19 The Portion of Jacob *is* not
like them,
For He *is* the Maker of all
things;
And *Israel is* the tribe of His
inheritance.

14 [a]Jer. 49:13 [b]Nah. 3:15 [c]Jer. 50:15
15 [a]Gen. 1:1, 6 [b]Job 9:8
16 [a]Ps. 135:7
17 [a]Jer. 10:14 [b]Jer. 50:2
20 [a]Is. 10:5, 15
22 [a]2 Chr. 36:17
24 [a]Jer. 50:15, 29
25 [a]Zech. 4:7

The LORD of hosts *is* His
name.

20 "You[a] *are* My battle-ax *and*
weapons of war:
For with you I will break the
nation in pieces;
With you I will destroy
kingdoms;
21 With you I will break in
pieces the horse and its
rider;
With you I will break in
pieces the chariot and its
rider;
22 With you also I will break in
pieces man and woman;
With you I will break in
pieces [a]old and young;
With you I will break in
pieces the young man
and the maiden;
23 With you also I will break in
pieces the shepherd and
his flock;
With you I will break in
pieces the farmer and
his yoke of oxen;
And with you I will break
in pieces governors and
rulers.

24 "And[a] I will repay Babylon
And all the inhabitants of
Chal·dē′a
For all the evil they have
done
In Zion in your sight," says
the LORD.

25 "Behold, I *am* against you,
[a]O destroying mountain,
Who destroys all the earth,"
says the LORD.
"And I will stretch out My
hand against you,
Roll you down from the
rocks,

[b]And make you a burnt
mountain.
26 They shall not take from
you a stone for a corner
Nor a stone for a
foundation,
[a]But you shall be desolate
forever," says the LORD.

27 [a]Set up a banner in the land,
Blow the trumpet among the
nations!
[b]Prepare the nations against
her,
Call [c]the kingdoms together
against her:
Ar′a·rat, Min′nī, and
Ash′ke·naz.
Appoint a general against
her;
Cause the horses to come
up like the bristling
locusts.
28 Prepare against her the
nations,
With the kings of the Mēdes,
Its governors and all its
rulers,
All the land of his dominion.
29 And the land will tremble
and sorrow;
For every [a]purpose of the
LORD shall be performed
against Babylon,
[b]To make the land of
Babylon a desolation
without inhabitant.
30 The mighty men of Babylon
have ceased fighting,
They have remained in their
strongholds;
Their might has failed,
[a]They became *like* women;
They have burned her
dwelling places,
[b]The bars of her *gate* are
broken.

25 [b]Rev. 8:8
26 [a]Jer. 50:26, 40
27 [a]Is. 13:2 [b]Jer. 25:14 [c]Jer. 50:41, 42
29 [a]Jer. 50:45 [b]Jer. 50:13; 51:26, 43
30 [a]Is. 19:16 [b]Lam. 2:9
31 [a]Jer. 50:24
32 [a]Jer. 50:38
33 [a]Is. 21:10 [b]Hab. 3:12 [c]Rev. 14:15
34 [a]Jer. 50:17 [b]Is. 24:1–3
36 [a]Jer. 50:34

31 [a]One runner will run to meet
another,
And one messenger to meet
another,
To show the king of Babylon
that his city is taken on
all sides;
32 [a]The passages are blocked,
The reeds they have burned
with fire,
And the men of war are
terrified.

33 For thus says the LORD of
hosts, the God of Israel:

"The daughter of Babylon *is*
[a]like a threshing floor
When [b]*it is* time to thresh her;
Yet a little while
[c]And the time of her harvest
will come."

34 "Ne·bū·chad·nez′zar the king
of Babylon
Has [a]devoured me, he has
crushed me;
He has made me an [b]empty
vessel,
He has swallowed me up
like a monster;
He has filled his stomach
with my delicacies,
He has spit me out.
35 Let the violence *done* to me
and my flesh *be* upon
Babylon,"
The inhabitant of Zion will
say;
"And my blood be upon the
inhabitants of Chal·dē′a!"
Jerusalem will say.

36 Therefore thus says the LORD:

"Behold, [a]I will plead your
case and take vengeance
for you.

[b]I will dry up her sea and
make her springs dry.
37 [a]Babylon shall become a
heap,
A dwelling place for jackals,
[b]An astonishment and a
hissing,
Without an inhabitant.
38 They shall roar together like
lions,
They shall growl like lions'
whelps.
39 In their excitement I will
prepare their feasts;
[a]I will make them drunk,
That they may rejoice,
And sleep a perpetual sleep
And not awake," says the
LORD.
40 "I will bring them down
Like lambs to the slaughter,
Like rams with male goats.

41 "Oh, how [a]She'shach[1] is
taken!
Oh, how [b]the praise of the
whole earth is seized!
How Babylon has become
desolate among the
nations!
42 [a]The sea has come up over
Babylon;
She is covered with the
multitude of its waves.
43 [a]Her cities are a desolation,
A dry land and a wilderness,
A land where [b]no one
dwells,
Through which no son of
man passes.
44 I will punish [a]Bel[1] in
Babylon,
And I will bring out of his
mouth what he has
swallowed;
And the nations shall not
stream to him anymore.

36 [b]Jer. 50:38
37 [a]Is. 13:22 [b]Jer. 25:9, 11
39 [a]Jer. 51:57
41 [a]Jer. 25:26 [b]Is. 13:19 [1]A code word for Babylon, Jer. 25:26
42 [a]Is. 8:7, 8
43 [a]Jer. 50:39, 40 [b]Is. 13:20
44 [a]Jer. 50:2 [b]Jer. 50:15 [1]A Babylonian god
45 [a][Rev. 18:4] [1]Lit. *his soul*
46 [a]2 Kin. 19:7
48 [a]Is. 44:23; 48:20; 49:13 [b]Jer. 50:3, 41
50 [a]Jer. 44:28 [b][Deut. 4:29–31]

Yes, [b]the wall of Babylon
shall fall.

45 "My[a] people, go out of the
midst of her!
And let everyone deliver
[1]himself from the fierce
anger of the LORD.
46 And lest your heart faint,
And you fear [a]for the rumor
that *will be* heard in the
land
(A rumor will come *one*
year,
And after that, in *another*
year
A rumor *will come,*
And violence in the land,
Ruler against ruler),
47 Therefore behold, the days
are coming
That I will bring judgment
on the carved images of
Babylon;
Her whole land shall be
ashamed,
And all her slain shall fall in
her midst.
48 Then [a]the heavens and the
earth and all that *is* in
them
Shall sing joyously over
Babylon;
[b]For the plunderers shall
come to her from the
north," says the LORD.

49 As Babylon *has caused* the
slain of Israel to fall,
So at Babylon the slain of
all the earth shall fall.
50 [a]You who have escaped the
sword,
Get away! Do not stand still!
[b]Remember the LORD afar off,
And let Jerusalem come to
your mind.

51 [a]We are ashamed because we
have heard reproach.
Shame has covered our
faces,
For strangers [b]have come
into the [1]sanctuaries of
the LORD's house.

52 "Therefore behold, the days
are coming," says the
LORD,
"That I will bring judgment
on her carved images,
And throughout all her land
the wounded shall groan.
53 [a]Though Babylon were to
[1]mount up to heaven,
And though she were to
fortify the height of her
strength,
Yet from Me plunderers
would come to her," says
the LORD.

54 [a]The sound of a cry *comes*
from Babylon,
And great destruction
from the land of the
Chal·dē′ans,
55 Because the LORD is
plundering Babylon
And silencing her loud
voice,
Though her waves roar like
great waters,
And the noise of their voice
is uttered,
56 Because the plunderer
comes against her,
against Babylon,
And her mighty men are
taken.
Every one of their bows is
broken;
[a]For the LORD *is* the God of
recompense,
He will surely repay.

57 "And I will make drunk
Her princes and [a]wise men,
Her governors, her deputies,
and her mighty men.
And they shall sleep a
perpetual sleep
And not awake," says [b]the
King,
Whose name *is* the LORD of
hosts.

58 Thus says the LORD of hosts:

"The broad walls of Babylon
shall be utterly [a]broken,[1]
And her high gates shall be
burned with fire;
[b]The people will labor in
vain,
And the nations, because of
the fire;
And they shall be weary."

59 The word which Jer·e·mī′ah
the prophet commanded
Se·rāi′ah the son of [a]Ne·rī′ah,
the son of Mah′sēi·ah, when he
went with Zed·e·kī′ah the king
of Judah to Babylon in the fourth
year of his reign. And Se·rāi′ah
was the quartermaster.
60 So Jer·e·mī′ah [a]wrote in a
book all the evil that would
come upon Babylon, all these
words that are written against
Babylon.
61 And Jer·e·mī′ah said to Se-
rāi′ah, "When you arrive in Babylon and see it, and read all
these words,
62 "then you shall say, 'O LORD,
You have spoken against this
place to cut it off, so that [a]none
shall remain in it, neither man
nor beast, but it shall be desolate forever.'
63 "Now it shall be, when you
have finished reading this book,

51 [a]Ps. 44:15; 79:4 [b]Lam. 1:10 [1]*holy places*
53 [a]Amos 9:2 [1]*ascend*
54 [a]Jer. 50:22
56 [a]Jer. 50:29
57 [a]Jer. 50:35 [b]Jer. 46:18; 48:15
58 [a]Jer. 50:15 [b]Hab. 2:13 [1]Lit. *laid utterly bare*
59 [a]Jer. 32:12
60 [a]Jer. 36:2
62 [a]Jer. 50:3, 39

[a]*that* you shall tie a stone to it and throw it out into the Eūphrā′tēs.

64 "Then you shall say, 'Thus Babylon shall sink and not rise from the catastrophe that I will bring upon her. And they shall be weary.' " Thus far *are* the words of Jer·e·mī′ah.

52 Zed·e·kī′ah *was* [a]twenty-one years old when he became king, and he reigned eleven years in Jerusalem. His mother's name *was* Ha·mū′tal the daughter of Jer·e·mī′ah of [b]Lib′nah.

2 He also did evil in the sight of the LORD, according to all that Je·hoi′a·kim had done.

3 For because of the anger of the LORD *this* happened in Jerusalem and Judah, till He finally cast them out from His presence. Then Zed·e·kī′ah [a]rebelled against the king of Babylon.

4 Now it came to pass in the [a]ninth year of his reign, in the tenth month, on the tenth *day* of the month, *that* Ne·bū·chad·nez′zar king of Babylon and all his army came against Jerusalem and encamped against it; and *they* built a siege wall against it all around.

5 So the city was besieged until the eleventh year of King Zed·e·kī′ah.

6 By the fourth month, on the ninth day of the month, the famine had become so severe in the city that there was no food for the people of the land.

7 Then the city *wall* was broken through, and all the men of war fled and went out of the city at night by way of the gate between the two walls, which *was* by the king's garden, even though the Chal·dē′ans *were* near the city all around. And they went by way of the [1]plain.

8 But the army of the Chal·dē′ans pursued the king, and they overtook Zed·e·kī′ah in the plains of Jericho. All his army was scattered from him.

9 [a]So they took the king and brought him up to the king of Babylon at Rib′lah in the land of Hā′math, and he pronounced judgment on him.

10 [a]Then the king of Babylon killed the sons of Zed·e·kī′ah before his eyes. And he killed all the princes of Judah in Rib′lah.

11 He also [a]put out the eyes of Zed·e·kī′ah; and the king of Babylon bound him in [1]bronze fetters, took him to Babylon, and put him in prison till the day of his death.

12 [a]Now in the fifth month, on the tenth *day* of the month ([b]which *was* the nineteenth year of King Ne·bū·chad·nez′zar king of Babylon), [c]Ne·bū·za·rad′an, the captain of the guard, *who* served the king of Babylon, came to Jerusalem.

13 He burned the house of the LORD and the king's house; all the houses of Jerusalem, that is, all the houses of the great, he burned with fire.

14 And all the army of the Chal·dē′ans who *were* with the captain of the guard broke down all the walls of Jerusalem all around.

15 [a]Then Ne·bū·za·rad′an the captain of the guard carried away captive *some* of the poor people, the rest of the people who remained in the city, the defectors who had deserted to

63 [a]Rev. 18:21

CHAPTER 52

1 [a]2 Kin. 24:18 [b]Josh. 10:29

3 [a]2 Chr. 36:13

4 [a]Jer. 39:1

7 [1]Or *Arabah;* the Jordan Valley

9 [a]Jer. 32:4; 39:5

10 [a]Ezek. 12:13

11 [a]Ezek. 12:13 [1]*shackles*

12 [a]2 Kin. 25:8–21 [b]Jer. 52:29 [c]Jer. 39:9

15 [a]Jer. 39:9

the king of Babylon, and the rest
of the craftsmen.
16 But Ne·bū·za·rad′an the captain of the guard left *some* of the
poor of the land as vinedressers
and farmers.
17 [a]The [b]bronze pillars that
were in the house of the LORD,
and the carts and the bronze
Sea that *were* in the house of
the LORD, the Chal·dē′ans broke
in pieces, and carried all their
bronze to Babylon.
18 They also took away [a]the
pots, the shovels, the trimmers, the [1]bowls, the spoons,
and all the bronze utensils with
which the *priests* ministered.
19 The basins, the firepans, the
bowls, the pots, the lampstands,
the spoons, and the cups, whatever *was* solid gold and whatever *was* solid silver, the captain
of the guard took away.
20 The two pillars, one Sea, the
twelve bronze bulls which *were*
under *it, and* the carts, which
King Solomon had made for the
house of the LORD—[a]the bronze
of all these articles was beyond
measure.
21 Now *concerning* the [a]pillars:
the height of one pillar *was* eighteen [1]cubits, a measuring line of
twelve cubits could measure its
circumference, and its thickness
was [2]four fingers; *it was* hollow.
22 A capital of bronze *was* on
it; and the height of one capital
was five cubits, with a network
and pomegranates all around
the capital, all of bronze. The
second pillar, with pomegranates was the same.
23 There were ninety-six pomegranates on the sides; [a]all the
pomegranates, all around on the
network, *were* one hundred.

17 [a]Jer. 27:19 [b]1 Kin. 7:15, 23, 27, 50
18 [a]Ex. 27:3 [1]*basins*
20 [a]1 Kin. 7:47
21 [a]2 Kin. 25:17 [1]18 inches each [2]3 inches
23 [a]1 Kin. 7:20
24 [a]2 Kin. 25:18 [b]Jer. 21:1; 29:25
25 [1]Lit. *eunuch*
28 [a]2 Kin. 24:2 [b]2 Kin. 24:12 [c]2 Kin. 24:14
29 [a]Jer. 39:9
31 [a]2 Kin. 25:27–30 [b]Gen. 40:13, 20 [1]Or *Awil-Marduk;* lit. *The Man of Marduk* [2]Showed favor to

24 [a]The captain of the guard
took Se·rāi′ah the chief priest,
[b]Zeph·a·nī′ah the second priest,
and the three doorkeepers.
25 He also took out of the city
an [1]officer who had charge of
the men of war, seven men of
the king's close associates who
were found in the city, the principal scribe of the army who
mustered the people of the land,
and sixty men of the people of
the land who were found in the
midst of the city.
26 And Ne·bū·za·rad′an the
captain of the guard took these
and brought them to the king of
Babylon at Rib′lah.
27 Then the king of Babylon
struck them and put them to
death at Rib′lah in the land of
Hā′math. Thus Judah was carried
away captive from its own land.
28 [a]These *are* the people whom
Ne·bū·chad·nez′zar carried away
captive: [b]in the seventh year,
[c]three thousand and twenty-
three Jews;
29 [a]in the eighteenth year of
Ne·bū·chad·nez′zar he carried
away captive from Jerusalem
eight hundred and thirty-two
persons;
30 in the twenty-third year of
Ne·bū·chad·nez′zar, Ne·bū·za-
rad′an the captain of the guard
carried away captive of the Jews
seven hundred and forty-five
persons. All the persons *were*
four thousand six hundred.
31 [a]Now it came to pass in the
thirty-seventh year of the captivity of Je·hoi′a·chin king of Judah, in the twelfth month, on the
twenty-fifth *day* of the month,
that [1]Ē′vil-Me·rō′dach king of
Babylon, in the *first* year of his
reign, [b]lifted[2] up the head of

Je·hoi′a·chin king of Judah and
brought him out of prison.
32 And he spoke kindly to him
and gave him a more prominent
seat than those of the kings who
were with him in Babylon.
33 So [1]Je·hoi′a·chin changed
from his prison garments, [a]and
he ate bread regularly before
the *king* all the days of his life.
34 And as for his provisions,
there was a regular ration given
him by the king of Babylon, a
portion for each day until the
day of his death, all the days of
his life.

33 [a]2 Sam. 9:7, 13 [1]Lit. *he*

The Book of
LAMENTATIONS

LAMENTATIONS describes the funeral of a city. It is a tearstained portrait of the once proud Jerusalem, now reduced to rubble by the invading Babylonian hordes. In a five-poem dirge, Jeremiah exposes his emotions. A death has occurred; Jerusalem lies barren.

Jeremiah writes his lament in acrostic or alphabetical fashion. Beginning each chapter with the first letter *A* (aleph) he progresses verse by verse through the Hebrew alphabet, literally weeping from *A* to Z. And then, in the midst of this terrible holocaust, Jeremiah triumphantly cries out, "Great *is* Your faithfulness" (3:23). In the face of death and destruction, with life seemingly coming apart, Jeremiah turns tragedy into a triumph of faith. God has never failed him in the past. God has promised to remain faithful in the future. In the light of the God he knows and loves, Jeremiah finds hope and comfort.

The Hebrew title of this book comes from the first word of chapters 1, 2, and 4: *Ekah*, "Ah, how!" Another Hebrew word *Ginoth* ("Elegies" or "Lamentations") has also been used as the title because it better represents the content of the book. The Greek title *Threnoi* means "Dirges" or "Laments," and the Latin title *Threni* ("Tears" or "Lamentations") was derived from this word. The subtitle in Jerome's Vulgate reads: "*Id est lamentationes Jeremiae prophetae*," and this became the basis for the English title "The Lamentations of Jeremiah."

CHAPTER 1

HOW lonely sits the city
That was full of people!
[a]*How* like a widow is she,
Who *was* great among the nations!
The [b]princess among the provinces
Has become a [1]slave!

2 She [a]weeps bitterly in the [b]night,
Her tears *are* on her cheeks;
Among all her lovers
She has none to comfort *her*.
All her friends have dealt treacherously with her;
They have become her enemies.

3 [a]Judah has gone into captivity,
Under affliction and hard servitude;
[b]She dwells among the [1]nations,
She finds no [c]rest;
All her persecutors overtake her in dire straits.

4 The roads to Zion mourn
Because no one comes to the [1]set feasts.
All her gates are [a]desolate;
Her priests sigh,
Her virgins are afflicted,
And she *is* in bitterness.

5 Her adversaries [a]have become [1]the master,
Her enemies prosper;
For the LORD has afflicted her
[b]Because of the multitude of her transgressions.

1 [a]Is. 47:7–9 [b]Ezra 4:20 [1]Lit. *forced laborer*
2 [a]Jer. 13:17 [b]Job 7:3
3 [a]Jer. 52:27 [b]Lam. 2:9 [c]Deut. 28:65 [1]*Gentiles*
4 [a]Is. 27:10 [1]*appointed*
5 [a]Deut. 28:43 [b]Dan. 9:7, 16 [1]Lit. *her head*

Her [c]children have gone
into captivity before the
enemy.

6 And from the daughter of
Zion
All her splendor has
departed.
Her princes have become
like deer
That find no pasture,
That [1]flee without strength
Before the pursuer.

7 In the days of her affliction
and roaming,
Jerusalem [a]remembers all
her pleasant things
That she had in the days of
old.
When her people fell into
the hand of the enemy,
With no one to help her,
The adversaries saw her
And mocked at her
[1]downfall.

8 [a]Jerusalem has sinned
gravely,
Therefore she has become
[1]vile.
All who honored her
despise her
Because [b]they have seen her
nakedness;
Yes, she sighs and turns
away.

9 Her uncleanness *is* in her
skirts;
She [a]did not consider her
destiny;
Therefore her collapse was
awesome;
She had no comforter.
"O LORD, behold my
affliction,
For *the* enemy is exalted!"

10 The adversary has spread
his hand
Over all her [1]pleasant
things;
For she has seen [a]the
nations enter her
[2]sanctuary,
Those whom You
commanded
[b]Not to enter Your assembly.

11 All her people sigh,
[a]They [1]seek bread;
They have given their
[2]valuables for food to
restore life.
"See, O LORD, and consider,
For I am scorned."

12 "*Is it* nothing to you, all you
who [1]pass by?
Behold and see
[a]If there is any sorrow like
my sorrow,
Which has been brought on
me,
Which the LORD has
inflicted
In the day of His fierce
anger.

13 "From above He has sent fire
into my bones,
And it overpowered them;
He has [a]spread a net for my
feet
And turned me back;
He has made me desolate
And faint all the day.

14 "The[a] yoke of my
transgressions was
[1]bound;
They were woven together
by His hands,
And thrust upon my neck.
He made my strength fail;

5 [c]Jer. 52:28
6 [1]Lit. *are gone*
7 [a]Ps. 137:1 [1]Vg. *Sabbaths*
8 [a][1 Kin. 8:46] [b]Ezek. 16:37 [1]LXX, Vg. *moved* or *removed*
9 [a]Is. 47:7
10 [a]Jer. 51:51 [b]Deut. 23:3 [1]*desirable* [2]*holy place,* the temple
11 [a]Jer. 38:9; 52:6 [1]*hunt food* [2]*desirable things*
12 [a]Dan. 9:12 [1]Lit. *pass by this way*
13 [a]Ezek. 12:13; 17:20
14 [a]Deut. 28:48 [1]So with MT, Tg.; LXX, Syr., Vg. *watched over*

The Lord delivered me
into the hands of *those*
whom I am not able to
withstand.

15 "The Lord has trampled
underfoot all my mighty
men in my midst;
He has called an assembly
against me
To crush my young men;
[a]The Lord trampled *as* in a
winepress
The virgin daughter of
Judah.

16 "For these *things* I weep;
My eye, [a]my eye overflows
with water;
Because the comforter, who
should restore my life,
Is far from me.
My children are desolate
Because the enemy
prevailed."

17 [a]Zion [1]spreads out her hands,
But no one comforts her;
The LORD has commanded
concerning Jacob
That those [b]around him
become his adversaries;
Jerusalem has become an
unclean thing among
them.

18 "The LORD is [a]righteous,
For I [b]rebelled against His
[1]commandment.
Hear now, all peoples,
And behold my sorrow;
My virgins and my young
men
Have gone into captivity.

19 "I called for my lovers,
But they deceived me;
My priests and my elders
Breathed their last in the
city,
While they sought food
To restore their life.

20 "See, O LORD, that I *am* in
distress;
My [a]soul[1] is troubled;
My heart is overturned
within me,
For I have been very
rebellious.
[b]Outside the sword bereaves,
At home *it is* like death.

21 "They have heard that I sigh,
But no one comforts me.
All my enemies have heard
of my trouble;
They are [a]glad that You have
done *it*.
Bring on [b]the day You have
[1]announced,
That they may become like
me.

22 "Let[a] all their wickedness
come before You,
And do to them as You have
done to me
For all my transgressions;
For my sighs *are* many,
And my heart *is* faint."

2 How the Lord has covered
the daughter of Zion
With a [a]cloud in His anger!
[b]He cast down from heaven
to the earth
[c]The beauty of Israel,
And did not remember [d]His
footstool
In the day of His anger.

2 The Lord has swallowed up
and has [a]not pitied
All the dwelling places of
Jacob.

15 [a][Rev. 14:19]
16 [a]Eccl. 4:1
17 [a]Jer. 4:31 [b]2 Kin. 24:2–4 [1]Prays
18 [a]Dan. 9:7, 14 [b]1 Sam. 12:14, 15 [1]Lit. *mouth*
20 [a]Is. 16:11 [b]Ezek. 7:15 [1]Lit. *inward parts*
21 [a]Ps. 35:15 [b][Jer. 46] [1]*proclaimed*
22 [a]Ps. 109:15; 137:7, 8

CHAPTER 2

1 [a][Lam. 3:44] [b]Matt. 11:23 [c]2 Sam. 1:19 [d]Ps. 99:5
2 [a]Lam. 3:43

He has thrown down in His wrath
The strongholds of the daughter of Judah;
He has brought *them* down to the ground;
[b]He has profaned the kingdom and its princes.

3 He has cut off in fierce anger
Every [1]horn of Israel;
[a]He has drawn back His right hand
From before the enemy.
[b]He has blazed against Jacob like a flaming fire
Devouring all around.

4 [a]Standing like an enemy, He has bent His bow;
With His right hand, like an adversary,
He has slain [b]all *who were* pleasing to His eye;
On the tent of the daughter of Zion,
He has poured out His fury like fire.

5 [a]The Lord was like an enemy.
He has swallowed up Israel,
He has swallowed up all her palaces;
[b]He has destroyed her strongholds,
And has increased mourning and lamentation
In the daughter of Judah.

6 He has done violence [a]to His [1]tabernacle,
[b]*As if it were* a garden;
He has destroyed His place of assembly;
The LORD has caused
The appointed feasts and Sabbaths to be forgotten in Zion.
In His burning indignation
He has [c]spurned the king and the priest.

7 The Lord has spurned His altar,
He has [a]abandoned His sanctuary;
He has [1]given up the walls of her palaces
Into the hand of the enemy.
[b]They have made a noise in the house of the LORD
As on the day of a set feast.

8 The LORD has [1]purposed to destroy
The [a]wall of the daughter of Zion.
[b]He has stretched out a line;
He has not withdrawn His hand from destroying;
Therefore He has caused the rampart and wall to lament;
They languished together.

9 Her gates have sunk into the ground;
He has destroyed and [a]broken her bars.
[b]Her king and her princes *are* among the [1]nations;
[c]The Law *is* no *more*,
And her [d]prophets find no [2]vision from the LORD.

10 The elders of the daughter of Zion
[a]Sit on the ground *and* keep silence;
[1]They [b]throw dust on their heads
And [c]gird themselves with sackcloth.

2 [b]Ps. 89:39, 40
3 [a]Ps. 74:11 [b]Ps. 89:46 [1]Strength
4 [a]Is. 63:10 [b]Ezek. 24:25
5 [a]Jer. 30:14 [b]Jer. 52:13
6 [a]Ps. 80:12; 89:40 [b]Is. 1:8 [c]Is. 43:28 [1]Lit. *booth*
7 [a]Ezek. 24:21 [b]Ps. 74:3–8 [1]*delivered*
8 [a]Jer. 52:14 [b][Is. 34:11] [1]*determined*
9 [a]Jer. 51:30 [b]Deut. 28:36 [c]2 Chr. 15:3 [d]Ps. 74:9 [1]*Gentiles* [2]Prophetic revelation
10 [a]Is. 3:26 [b]Job 2:12 [c]Is. 15:3 [1]A sign of mourning

The virgins of Jerusalem
Bow their heads to the ground.

11 [a]My eyes fail with tears,
My [1]heart is troubled;
[b]My [2]bile is poured on the ground
Because of the destruction of the daughter of my people,
Because [c]the children and the infants
Faint in the streets of the city.

12 They say to their mothers,
"Where *is* grain and wine?"
As they swoon like the wounded
In the streets of the city,
As their life is poured out
In their mothers' bosom.

13 How shall I [a]console[1] you?
To what shall I liken you,
O daughter of Jerusalem?
What shall I compare with you, that I may comfort you,
O virgin daughter of Zion?
For your ruin *is* spread wide as the sea;
Who can heal you?

14 Your [a]prophets have seen for you
False and deceptive visions;
They have not [b]uncovered your iniquity,
To bring back your captives,
But have envisioned for you false [c]prophecies and delusions.

15 All who [1]pass by [a]clap *their* hands at you;
They hiss [b]and shake their heads
At the daughter of Jerusalem:
"*Is* this the city that is called
[c]'The perfection of beauty,
The joy of the whole earth'?"

16 [a]All your enemies have opened their mouth against you;
They hiss and gnash *their* teeth.
They say, [b]"We have swallowed *her* up!
Surely this *is* the [c]day we have waited for;
We have found *it,* [d]we have seen *it!*"

17 The LORD has done what He [a]purposed;
He has fulfilled His word
Which He commanded in days of old.
He has thrown down and has not pitied,
And He has caused an enemy to [b]rejoice over you;
He has exalted the [1]horn of your adversaries.

18 Their heart cried out to the Lord,
"O wall of the daughter of Zion,
[a]Let tears run down like a river day and night;
Give yourself no relief;
Give [1]your eyes no rest.

19 "Arise, [a]cry out in the night,
At the beginning of the watches;
[b]Pour out your heart like water before the face of the Lord.

11 [a]Lam. 3:48 [b]Job 16:13 [c]Lam. 4:4 [1]Lit. *inward parts* [2]Lit. *liver*

13 [a]Lam. 1:12 [1]Or *bear witness to*

14 [a]Jer. 2:8; 23:25–29; 29:8, 9; 37:19 [b]Is. 58:1 [c]Jer. 23:33–36

15 [a]Ezek. 25:6 [b]Ps. 44:14 [c][Ps. 48:2; 50:2] [1]Lit. *pass by this way*

16 [a]Job 16:9, 10 [b]Ps. 56:2; 124:3 [c]Lam. 1:21 [d]Ps. 35:21

17 [a]Lev. 26:16 [b]Ps. 38:16 [1]Strength

18 [a]Jer. 14:17 [1]Lit. *the daughter of your eye*

19 [a]Ps. 119:147 [b]Ps. 42:4; 62:8

Lift your hands toward Him
For the life of your young
children,
Who faint from hunger [c]at
the head of every street."

20 "See, O LORD, and consider!
To whom have You done
this?
[a]Should the women eat their
offspring,
The children [1]they have
cuddled?
Should the priest and
prophet be slain
In the sanctuary of the
Lord?

21 "Young[a] and old lie
On the ground in the streets;
My virgins and my young
men
Have fallen by the [b]sword;
You have slain *them* in the
day of Your anger,
You have slaughtered *and*
not pitied.

22 "You have invited as to a
feast day
[a]The terrors that surround
me.
In the day of the LORD's
anger
There was no refugee or
survivor.
[b]Those whom I have borne
and brought up
My enemies have
[c]destroyed."

3

I *am* the man *who* has seen
affliction by the rod of
His wrath.
2 He has led me and made *me*
walk
In darkness and not *in* light.
3 Surely He has turned His
hand against me
Time and time again
throughout the day.

4 He has aged [a]my flesh and
my skin,
And [b]broken my bones.
5 He has besieged me
And surrounded *me* with
bitterness and [1]woe.
6 [a]He has set me in dark
places
Like the dead of long ago.

7 [a]He has hedged me in so that
I cannot get out;
He has made my chain
heavy.
8 Even [a]when I cry and shout,
He shuts out my prayer.
9 He has blocked my ways
with hewn stone;
He has made my paths
crooked.

10 [a]He *has been* to me a bear
lying in wait,
Like a lion in [1]ambush.
11 He has turned aside my
ways and [a]torn me in
pieces;
He has made me desolate.
12 He has bent His bow
And [a]set me up as a target
for the arrow.

13 He has caused [a]the [1]arrows
of His quiver
To pierce my [2]loins.
14 I have become the [a]ridicule
of all my people—
[b]Their taunting song all the
day.
15 [a]He has filled me with
bitterness,
He has made me drink
wormwood.

---

19 [c]Is. 51:20
20 [a]Lev. 26:29 [1]Vg. *a span long*
21 [a]2 Chr. 36:17 [b]Jer. 18:21
22 [a]Ps. 31:13 [b]Hos. 9:12 [c]Jer. 16:2–4; 44:7

CHAPTER 3

4 [a]Job 16:8 [b]Ps. 51:8
5 [1]*hardship* or *weariness*
6 [a][Ps. 88:5, 6; 143:3]
7 [a]Hos. 2:6
8 [a]Job 30:20
10 [a]Is. 38:13 [1]Lit. *secret places*
11 [a]Hos. 6:1
12 [a]Job 7:20; 16:12
13 [a]Job 6:4 [1]Lit. *sons of* [2]Lit. *kidneys*
14 [a]Jer. 20:7 [b]Job 30:9
15 [a]Jer. 9:15

16 He has also broken my teeth
[a]with gravel,
And [1]covered me with ashes.
17 You have moved my soul far
from peace;
I have forgotten [1]prosperity.
18 [a]And I said, "My strength
and my hope
Have perished from the
LORD."

19 Remember my affliction and
roaming,
[a]The wormwood and the
[1]gall.
20 My soul still remembers
And [1]sinks within me.
21 This I recall to my mind,
Therefore I have [a]hope.

22 [a]*Through* the LORD's mercies
we are not consumed,
Because His compassions
[b]fail not.
23 *They are* new [a]every
morning;
Great *is* Your faithfulness.
24 "The LORD *is* my [a]portion,"
says my soul,
"Therefore I [b]hope in Him!"

25 The LORD *is* good to those
who [a]wait for Him,
To the soul *who* seeks Him.
26 *It is* good that *one* should
[a]hope [b]and wait quietly
For the salvation of the
LORD.
27 [a]*It is* good for a man to bear
The yoke in his youth.

28 [a]Let him sit alone and keep
silent,
Because *God* has laid *it* on
him;
29 [a]Let him put his mouth in the
dust—
There may yet be hope.
30 [a]Let him give *his* cheek to
the one who strikes him,
And be full of reproach.

31 [a]For the Lord will not cast off
forever.
32 Though He causes grief,
Yet He will show
compassion
According to the multitude
of His mercies.
33 For [a]He does not afflict
[1]willingly,
Nor grieve the children of
men.

34 To crush under one's feet
All the prisoners of the earth,
35 To turn aside the justice *due*
a man
Before the face of the Most
High,
36 Or subvert a man in his
cause—
[a]The Lord does not approve.

37 Who *is* he [a]*who* speaks and
it comes to pass,
When the Lord has not
commanded *it*?
38 *Is it* not from the mouth of
the Most High
That [a]woe and well-being
proceed?
39 [a]Why should a living man
[1]complain,
[b]A man for the punishment
of his sins?

40 Let us search out and
examine our ways,
And turn back to the LORD;
41 [a]Let us lift our hearts and
hands
To God in heaven.
42 [a]We have transgressed and
rebelled;
You have not pardoned.

16 [a][Prov. 20:17] [1]Lit. *bent me down in*
17 [1]Lit. *good*
18 [a]Ps. 31:22
19 [a]Jer. 9:15 [1]*bitterness*
20 [1]Lit. *bowed down*
21 [a]Ps. 130:7
22 [a][Mal. 3:6] [b]Ps. 78:38
23 [a]Is. 33:2
24 [a]Ps. 16:5; 73:26; 119:57 [b]Mic. 7:7
25 [a]Is. 30:18
26 [a][Rom. 4:16–18] [b]Ps. 37:7
27 [a]Ps. 94:12
28 [a]Jer. 15:17
29 [a]Job 42:6
30 [a]Is. 50:6
31 [a]Ps. 77:7; 94:14
33 [a][Ezek. 33:11] [1]Lit. *from His heart*
36 [a][Hab. 1:13]
37 [a][Ps. 33:9–11]
38 [a]Job 2:10
39 [a]Prov. 19:3 [b]Mic. 7:9 [1]Or *murmur*
41 [a]Ps. 86:4
42 [a]Dan. 9:5

43 You have covered *Yourself*
with anger
And pursued us;
You have slain *and* not
pitied.
44 You have covered Yourself
with a cloud,
That prayer should not pass
through.
45 You have made us an
[a]offscouring and refuse
In the midst of the peoples.

46 [a]All our enemies
Have opened their mouths
against us.
47 [a]Fear and a snare have come
upon us,
[b]Desolation and destruction.
48 [a]My eyes overflow with
rivers of water
For the destruction of the
daughter of my people.

49 [a]My eyes flow and do not
cease,
Without interruption,
50 Till the LORD from heaven
[a]Looks down and sees.
51 My eyes bring suffering to
my soul
Because of all the daughters
of my city.

52 My enemies [a]without cause
Hunted me down like a bird.
53 They [1]silenced my life [a]in
the pit
And [b]threw [2]stones at me.
54 [a]The waters flowed over my
head;
[b]I said, "I am cut off!"

55 [a]I called on Your name,
O LORD,
From the lowest [b]pit.
56 [a]You have heard my voice:
"Do not hide Your ear
From my sighing, from my
cry for help."
57 You [a]drew near on the day I
called on You,
And said, [b]"Do not fear!"

58 O Lord, You have [a]pleaded
the case for my soul;
[b]You have redeemed my life.
59 O LORD, You have seen [1]*how*
I am wronged;
[a]Judge my case.
60 You have seen all their
vengeance,
All their [a]schemes against
me.

61 You have heard their
reproach, O LORD,
All their schemes against
me,
62 The lips of my enemies
And their whispering
against me all the day.
63 Look at their [a]sitting down
and their rising up;
I *am* their taunting song.

64 [a]Repay them, O LORD,
According to the work of
their hands.
65 Give them [1]a veiled heart;
Your curse *be* upon them!
66 In Your anger,
Pursue and destroy them
[a]From under the heavens of
the [b]LORD.

4 How the gold has become
dim!
How changed the fine gold!
The stones of the sanctuary
are [1]scattered
At the head of every street.

2 The precious sons of Zion,
[1]Valuable as fine gold,

45 [a]1 Cor. 4:13
46 [a]Lam. 2:16
47 [a]Is. 24:17, 18 [b]Is. 51:19
48 [a]Jer. 4:19; 14:17
49 [a]Jer. 14:17
50 [a]Is. 63:15
52 [a]Ps. 35:7, 19
53 [a]Jer. 37:16 [b]Dan. 6:17 [1]LXX *put to death* [2]Lit. *a stone on*
54 [a]Ps. 69:2 [b]Is. 38:10
55 [a]Ps. 130:1 [b]Jer. 38:6–13
56 [a]Ps. 3:4
57 [a]James 4:8 [b]Is. 41:10, 14
58 [a]Jer. 51:36 [b]Ps. 71:23
59 [a]Ps. 9:4 [1]Lit. *my wrong*
60 [a]Jer. 11:19
63 [a]Ps. 139:2
64 [a]Ps. 28:4
65 [1]A Jewish tradition *sorrow of*
66 [a]Deut. 25:19 [b]Ps. 8:3

CHAPTER 4

1 [1]Lit. *poured out*
2 [1]Lit. *Weighed against*

How they are [2]regarded [a]as
clay pots,
The work of the hands of
the potter!

3 Even the jackals present
their breasts
To nurse their young;
But the daughter of my
people *is* cruel,
[a]Like ostriches in the
wilderness.

4 The tongue of the infant
clings
To the roof of its mouth for
thirst;
[a]The young children ask for
bread,
But no one breaks *it* for
them.

5 Those who ate delicacies
Are desolate in the streets;
Those who were brought up
in scarlet
[a]Embrace ash heaps.

6 The punishment of the
iniquity of the daughter
of my people
Is greater than the
punishment of the [a]sin of
Sod'om,
Which was [b]overthrown in a
moment,
With no hand to help her!

7 Her [1]Naz'ir·ītes were
[2]brighter than snow
And whiter than milk;
They were more ruddy in
body than rubies,
Like sapphire in their
[3]appearance.

8 *Now* their appearance is
blacker than soot;

They go unrecognized in the
streets;
[a]Their skin clings to their
bones,
It has become as dry as
wood.

9 *Those* slain by the sword
are better off
Than *those* who die of
hunger;
For these [a]pine away,
Stricken *for lack* of the
fruits of the [b]field.

10 The hands of the
[a]compassionate women
Have [1]cooked their [b]own
children;
They became [c]food for
them
In the destruction of the
daughter of my people.

11 The LORD has fulfilled His
fury,
[a]He has poured out His fierce
anger.
[b]He kindled a fire in Zion,
And it has devoured its
foundations.

12 The kings of the earth,
And all inhabitants of the
world,
Would not have believed
That the adversary and the
enemy
Could [a]enter the gates of
Jerusalem—

13 [a]Because of the sins of her
prophets
And the iniquities of her
priests,
[b]Who shed in her midst
The blood of the just.

2 [a]Is. 30:14 [2]*reckoned*
3 [a]Job 39:14–17
4 [a]Ps. 22:15
5 [a]Job 24:8
6 [a]Ezek. 16:48 [b]Gen. 19:25
7 [1]Or *nobles* [2]Or *purer* [3]Lit. *polishing*
8 [a]Ps. 102:5
9 [a]Lev. 26:39 [b]Jer. 16:4
10 [a]Lam. 2:20 [b]Is. 49:15 [c]Deut. 28:57 [1]*boiled*
11 [a]Jer. 7:20 [b]Deut. 32:22
12 [a]Jer. 21:13
13 [a]Jer. 5:31 [b]Matt. 23:31

14 They wandered blind in the
streets;
[a]They have defiled
themselves with blood,
[b]So that no one would touch
their garments.

15 They cried out to them,
"Go away, [a]unclean!
Go away, go away,
Do not touch us!"
When they fled and
wandered,
Those among the nations
said,
"They shall no longer dwell
here."

16 The [1]face of the LORD
scattered them;
He no longer regards them.
[a]*The people* do not respect
the priests
Nor show favor to the
elders.

17 Still [a]our eyes failed us,
Watching vainly for our
help;
In our watching we watched
For a nation *that* could not
save *us.*

18 [a]They [1]tracked our steps
So that we could not walk in
our streets.
[b]Our end was near;
Our days were over,
For our end had come.

19 Our pursuers were [a]swifter
Than the eagles of the
heavens.
They pursued us on the
mountains
And lay in wait for us in the
wilderness.

20 The [a]breath of our nostrils,
the anointed of the LORD,
[b]Was caught in their pits,
Of whom we said, "Under
his shadow
We shall live among the
nations."

21 Rejoice and be glad,
O daughter of [a]Ē'dom,
You who dwell in the land
of Uz!
[b]The cup shall also pass over
to you
And you shall become
drunk and make yourself
naked.

22 [a]*The punishment of*
your iniquity [1]is
accomplished,
O daughter of Zion;
He will no longer send you
into captivity.
[b]He will punish your iniquity,
O daughter of Ē'dom;
He will uncover your sins!

5 Remember, [a]O LORD, what
has come upon us;
Look, and behold [b]our
reproach!
2 [a]Our inheritance has been
turned over to aliens,
And our houses to
foreigners.
3 We have become orphans
and waifs,
Our mothers *are* like
[a]widows.

4 We pay for the water we
drink,
And our wood comes at a
price.
5 [a]*They* pursue at our [1]heels;
We labor *and* have no rest.

14 [a]Jer. 2:34 [b]Num. 19:16
15 [a]Lev. 13:45, 46
16 [a]Lam. 5:12 [1]Tg. *anger*
17 [a]2 Kin. 24:7
18 [a]2 Kin. 25:4 [b]Ezek. 7:2, 3, 6 [1]Lit. *hunted*
19 [a]Deut. 28:49
20 [a]Gen. 2:7 [b]Jer. 52:9
21 [a]Ps. 83:3–6 [b]Jer. 25:15
22 [a][Is. 40:2] [b]Ps. 137:7 [1]*has been completed*

CHAPTER 5

1 [a]Ps. 89:50 [b]Lam. 2:15
2 [a]Ps. 79:1
3 [a]Jer. 15:8; 18:21
5 [a]Jer. 28:14 [1]Lit. *necks*

6 [a]We have given our hand [b]*to*
the Egyptians
And the [c]Assyrians, to be
satisfied with bread.

7 [a]Our fathers sinned *and are*
no more,
But we bear their iniquities.
8 Servants rule over us;
There is none to deliver *us*
from their hand.
9 We get our bread *at the risk*
of our lives,
Because of the sword in the
wilderness.

10 Our skin is hot as an
oven,
Because of the fever of
famine.
11 They [a]ravished the women
in Zion,
The maidens in the cities of
Judah.
12 Princes were hung up by
their hands,
And elders were not
respected.
13 Young men [a]ground at the
millstones;
Boys staggered under *loads*
of wood.
14 The elders have ceased
gathering at the gate,
And the young men from
their [a]music.

15 The joy of our heart has
ceased;
Our dance has turned into
[a]mourning.
16 [a]The crown has fallen *from*
our head.
Woe to us, for we have
sinned!
17 Because of this our heart is
faint;
[a]Because of these *things* our
eyes grow dim;
18 Because of Mount Zion
which is [a]desolate,
With foxes walking about
on it.

19 You, O LORD, [a]remain
forever;
[b]Your throne from generation
to generation.
20 [a]Why do You forget us
forever,
And forsake us for so long
a time?
21 [a]Turn us back to You, O LORD,
and we will be [1]restored;
Renew our days as of old,
22 Unless You have utterly
rejected us,
And are very angry with us!

6 [a]Gen. 24:2 [b]Hos. 9:3; 12:1 [c]Hos. 5:13
7 [a]Jer. 31:29
11 [a]Zech. 14:2
13 [a]Judg. 16:21
14 [a]Jer. 7:34
15 [a]Amos 8:10
16 [a]Ps. 89:39
17 [a]Ps. 6:7
18 [a]Is. 27:10
19 [a]Ps. 9:7 [b]Ps. 45:6
20 [a]Ps. 13:1; 44:24
21 [a]Jer. 31:18 [1]*returned*

The Book of
EZEKIEL

EZEKIEL, a priest and a prophet, ministers during the darkest days of Judah's history: the seventy-year period of Babylonian captivity. Carried to Babylon before the final assault on Jerusalem, Ezekiel uses prophecies, parables, signs, and symbols to dramatize God's message to His exiled people. Though they are like dry bones in the sun, God will reassemble them and breathe life into the nation once again. Present judgment will be followed by future glory so that "you shall know that I *am* the LORD" (6:7).

The Hebrew name *Yehezke'l* means "God Strengthens" or "Strengthened by God." Ezekiel is indeed strengthened by God for the prophetic ministry to which he is called (3:8, 9). The name occurs twice in this book and nowhere else in the Old Testament. The Greek form in the Septuagint is *Iezekiel* and the Latin form in the Vulgate is *Ezechiel.*

CHAPTER 1

NOW it came to pass in the
thirtieth year, in the fourth
month, on the fifth *day* of the
month, as I *was* among the captives by [a]the River Chē'bar, *that*
[b]the heavens were opened and I
saw [c]visions[1] of God.
2 On the fifth *day* of the month,
which *was* in the fifth year of
King Je·hoi'a·chin's captivity,
3 the word of the LORD came
expressly to E·zēk'i·el the priest,
the son of Bū'zī, in the land of
the [1]Chal·dē'ans by the River
Chē'bar; and [a]the hand of the
LORD was upon him there.
4 Then I looked, and behold,
[a]a whirlwind was coming [b]out
of the north, a great cloud with
raging fire engulfing itself; and
brightness *was* all around it and
radiating out of its midst like the
color of amber, out of the midst
of the fire.
5 [a]Also from within it *came* the
likeness of four living creatures.
And [b]this *was* their appearance:
they had [c]the likeness of a man.
6 Each one had four faces, and
each one had four wings.
7 Their [1]legs *were* straight,
and the soles of their feet *were*
like the soles of calves' feet.
They sparkled [a]like the color of
burnished bronze.
8 [a]The hands of a man *were*
under their wings on their four
sides; and each of the four had
faces and wings.
9 Their wings touched one another. *The creatures* did not turn
when they went, but each one
went straight [a]forward.
10 As for [a]the likeness of their
faces, *each* [b]had the face of a
man; each of the four had [c]the
face of a lion on the right side,
[d]each of the four had the face of
an ox on the left side, [e]and each
of the four had the face of an
eagle.
11 Thus *were* their faces. Their
wings stretched upward; two
wings of each one touched one
another, and [a]two covered their
bodies.

1 [a]Ezek. 3:15, 23; 10:15 [b]Rev. 4:1; 19:11 [c]Ezek. 8:3 [1]So with MT, LXX, Vg.; Syr., Tg. *a vision*
3 [a]Ezek. 3:14, 22 [1]Or *Babylonians,* and so elsewhere in the book
4 [a]Jer. 23:19; 25:32 [b]Jer. 1:14
5 [a]Rev. 4:6–8 [b]Ezek. 10:8 [c]Ezek. 10:14
7 [a]Dan. 10:6 [1]Lit. *feet*
8 [a]Ezek. 10:8, 21
9 [a]Ezek. 1:12; 10:20–22
10 [a]Rev. 4:7 [b]Num. 2:10 [c]Num. 2:3 [d]Num. 2:18 [e]Num. 2:25
11 [a]Is. 6:2

12 And [a]each one went straight
forward; they went wherever the
spirit wanted to go, and they did
not turn when they went.
13 As for the likeness of the living creatures, their appearance
was like burning coals of fire,
[a]like the appearance of torches
going back and forth among the
living creatures. The fire was
bright, and out of the fire went
lightning.
14 And the living creatures ran
back and forth, [a]in appearance
like a flash of lightning.
15 Now as I looked at the living
creatures, behold, [a]a wheel *was*
on the earth beside each living
creature with its four faces.
16 [a]The appearance of the
wheels and their workings *was*
[b]like the color of beryl, and all
four had the same likeness. The
appearance of their workings
was, as it were, a wheel in the
middle of a wheel.
17 When they moved, they went
toward any one of four directions; they did not turn aside
when they went.
18 As for their rims, they were
so high they were awesome; and
their rims *were* [a]full of eyes, all
around the four of them.
19 [a]When the living creatures
went, the wheels went beside
them; and when the living creatures were lifted up from the
earth, the wheels were lifted up.
20 Wherever the spirit wanted
to go, they went, *because* there
the spirit went; and the wheels
were lifted together with them,
[a]for the spirit of the [1]living creatures *was* in the wheels.
21 When those went, *these* went;
when those stood, *these* stood;
and when those were lifted up
from the earth, the wheels were
lifted up together with them, for
the spirit of the [1]living creatures
was in the wheels.
22 [a]The likeness of the [1]firma-
ment above the heads of the
[2]living creatures *was* like the
color of an awesome [b]crystal,
stretched out [c]over their heads.
23 And under the firmament
their wings *spread out* straight,
one toward another. Each one
had two which covered one side,
and each one had two which
covered the other side of the
body.
24 [a]When they went, I heard
the noise of their wings, [b]like
the noise of many waters, like
[c]the voice of the Almighty, a tumult like the noise of an army;
and when they stood still, they
let down their wings.
25 A voice came from above the
firmament that *was* over their
heads; whenever they stood,
they let down their wings.
26 [a]And above the firmament
over their heads *was* the likeness of a throne, [b]in appearance
like a sapphire stone; on the
likeness of the throne *was* a
likeness with the appearance of
a man high above [c]it.
27 Also from the appearance
of His waist and upward [a]I saw,
as it were, the color of amber
with the appearance of fire all
around within it; and from the
appearance of His waist and
downward I saw, as it were, the
appearance of fire with brightness all around.
28 [a]Like the appearance of a
rainbow in a cloud on a rainy
day, so *was* the appearance of
the brightness all around it.
[b]This *was* the appearance of

12 [a]Ezek. 10:11, 22
13 [a]Rev. 4:5
14 [a][Matt. 24:27]
15 [a]Ezek. 10:9
16 [a]Ezek. 10:9, 10 [b]Dan. 10:6
18 [a]Ezek. 10:12
19 [a]Ezek. 10:16, 17
20 [a]Ezek. 10:17 [1]Lit. *living creature;* LXX, Vg. *spirit of life;* Tg. *creatures*
21 [1]See note at v. 20
22 [a]Ezek. 10:1 [b]Rev. 4:6 [c]Ezek. 10:1 [1]Or *expanse* [2]So with LXX, Tg., Vg.; MT *living creature*
24 [a]Ezek. 3:13; 10:5 [b]Rev. 1:15 [c]Job 37:4, 5
26 [a]Ezek. 10:1 [b]Ex. 24:10, 16 [c]Ezek. 8:2
27 [a]Ezek. 8:2
28 [a]Rev. 4:3; 10:1 [b]Ezek. 3:23; 8:4

the likeness of the glory of the
LORD.
So when I saw *it*, [c]I fell on
my face, and I heard a voice of
One speaking.

2 And He said to me, "Son of
man, [a]stand on your feet,
and I will speak to you."
2 Then [a]the Spirit entered me
when He spoke to me, and set
me on my feet; and I heard Him
who spoke to me.
3 And He said to me: "Son of
man, I am sending you to the
children of Israel, to a rebellious
nation that has [a]rebelled against
Me; [b]they and their fathers have
transgressed against Me to this
very day.
4 [a]"For *they are* [1]impudent and
stubborn children. I am sending
you to them, and you shall say to
them, 'Thus says the Lord GOD.'
5 [a]"As for them, whether they
hear or whether they refuse—for
they *are* a [b]rebellious house—yet
they [c]will know that a prophet
has been among them.
6 "And you, son of man, [a]do not
be afraid of them nor be afraid
of their words, though [b]briers
and thorns *are* with you and you
dwell among scorpions; [c]do not
be afraid of their words or dismayed by their looks, [d]though
they *are* a rebellious house.
7 [a]"You shall speak My words
to them, whether they hear or
whether they refuse, for they *are*
rebellious.
8 "But you, son of man, hear
what I say to you. Do not be
rebellious like that rebellious
house; open your mouth and
[a]eat what I give you."
9 Now when I looked, there
was [a]a hand stretched out to me;
and behold, [b]a scroll of a book
was in it.
10 Then He spread it before me;
and *there was* writing on the
inside and on the outside, and
written on it *were* lamentations
and mourning and woe.

3 Moreover He said to me,
"Son of man, eat what you
find; [a]eat this scroll, and go,
speak to the house of Israel."
2 So I opened my mouth, and
He caused me to eat that scroll.
3 And He said to me, "Son of
man, feed your belly, and fill
your stomach with this scroll
that I give you." So I [a]ate, and it
was in my mouth [b]like honey in
sweetness.
4 Then He said to me: "Son of
man, go to the house of Israel
and speak with My words to
them.
5 "For you *are* not sent to a
people of unfamiliar speech and
of hard language, *but* to the
house of Israel,
6 "not to many people of unfamiliar speech and of hard language, whose words you cannot
understand. Surely, [a]had I sent
you to them, they would have
listened to you.
7 "But the house of Israel will
not listen to you, [a]because they
will not listen to Me; [b]for all the
house of Israel *are* [1]impudent
and hard-hearted.
8 "Behold, I have made your
face strong against their faces,
and your forehead strong against
their foreheads.
9 [a]"Like adamant stone, harder
than flint, I have made your
forehead; [b]do not be afraid of
them, nor be dismayed at their
looks, though they *are* a rebellious house."

---

28 [c]Dan. 8:17

CHAPTER 2

1 [a]Dan. 10:11
2 [a]Ezek. 3:24
3 [a]Ezek. 5:6; 20:8, 13, 18 [b]Jer. 3:25
4 [a]Ezek. 3:7 [1]Lit. *stiff-faced and hard-hearted sons*
5 [a]Ezek. 3:11, 26, 27 [b]Ezek. 3:26 [c]Ezek. 33:33
6 [a]Jer. 1:8, 17 [b]Mic. 7:4 [c][1 Pet. 3:14] [d]Ezek. 3:9, 26, 27
7 [a]Jer. 1:7, 17
8 [a]Rev. 10:9
9 [a][Ezek. 8:3] [b]Ezek. 3:1

CHAPTER 3

1 [a]Ezek. 2:8, 9
3 [a]Rev. 10:9 [b]Ps. 19:10; 119:103
6 [a]Matt. 11:21
7 [a]John 15:20, 21 [b]Ezek. 2:4 [1]Lit. *strong of forehead*
9 [a]Mic. 3:8 [b]Jer. 1:8, 17

10 Moreover He said to me:
"Son of man, receive into your
heart all My words that I speak
to you, and hear with your ears.
11 "And go, get to the captives,
to the children of your people,
and speak to them and tell
them, [a]'Thus says the Lord GOD,'
whether they hear, or whether
they refuse."
12 Then [a]the Spirit lifted me up,
and I heard behind me a great
thunderous voice: "Blessed *is*
the [b]glory of the LORD from His
place!"
13 *I* also *heard* the [a]noise of the
wings of the living creatures
that touched one another, and
the noise of the wheels beside
them, and a great thunderous
noise.
14 So the Spirit lifted me up
and took me away, and I went
in bitterness, in the [1]heat of my
spirit; but [a]the hand of the LORD
was strong upon me.
15 Then I came to the captives
at Tel Ā′bib, who dwelt by the
River Chē′bar; and [a]I sat where
they sat, and remained there
astonished among them seven
days.
16 Now it [a]came to pass at the
end of seven days that the word
of the LORD came to me, saying,
17 [a]"Son of man, I have made
you [b]a watchman for the house
of Israel; therefore hear a word
from My mouth, and give them
[c]warning from Me:
18 "When I say to the wicked,
'You shall surely die,' and you
give him no warning, nor speak
to warn the wicked from his
wicked way, to save his life, that
same wicked *man* [a]shall die in
his iniquity; but his blood I will
require at your hand.

11 [a]Ezek. 2:5, 7
12 [a]Acts 8:39 [b]Ezek. 1:28; 8:4
13 [a]Ezek. 1:24; 10:5
14 [a]2 Kin. 3:15 [1]Or *anger*
15 [a]Job 2:13
16 [a]Jer. 42:7
17 [a]Ezek. 33:7–9 [b]Jer. 6:17 [c][Lev. 19:17]
18 [a][John 8:21, 24]
19 [a]Acts 18:6; 20:26
20 [a]Ezek. 18:24; 33:18
22 [a]Ezek. 1:3 [b]Ezek. 8:4
23 [a]Ezek. 1:28 [b]Ezek. 1:1 [c]Ezek. 1:28
24 [a]Ezek. 2:2
25 [a]Ezek. 4:8
26 [a]Luke 1:20, 22

19 "Yet, if you warn the wicked,
and he does not turn from his
wickedness, nor from his wicked
way, he shall die in his iniquity;
[a]but you have delivered your
soul.
20 "Again, when a [a]righteous
man turns from his righteousness and commits iniquity, and
I lay a stumbling block before
him, he shall die; because you
did not give him warning, he
shall die in his sin, and his righteousness which he has done
shall not be remembered; but
his blood I will require at your
hand.
21 "Nevertheless if you warn
the righteous *man* that the righteous should not sin, and he
does not sin, he shall surely live
because he took warning; also
you will have delivered your
soul."
22 [a]Then the hand of the LORD
was upon me there, and He said
to me, "Arise, go out [b]into the
plain, and there I shall talk with
you."
23 So I arose and went out into
the plain, and behold, [a]the glory
of the LORD stood there, like the
glory which I [b]saw by the River
Chē′bar; [c]and I fell on my face.
24 Then [a]the Spirit entered me
and set me on my feet, and
spoke with me and said to me:
"Go, shut yourself inside your
house.
25 "And you, O son of man,
surely [a]they will put ropes on
you and bind you with them, so
that you cannot go out among
them.
26 [a]"I will make your tongue
cling to the roof of your mouth,
so that you shall be mute and

[b]not be [1]one to rebuke them, [c]for
they *are* a rebellious house.
27 [a]"But when I speak with you,
I will open your mouth, and you
shall say to them, [b]'Thus says
the Lord GOD.' He who hears, let
him hear; and he who refuses,
let him refuse; for they *are* a
rebellious house.

4

"You also, son of man, take a
clay tablet and lay it before
you, and portray on it a city, Jerusalem.
2 [a]"Lay siege against it, build a
[b]siege wall against it, and heap
up a mound against it; set camps
against it also, and place battering rams against it all around.
3 "Moreover take for yourself
an iron plate, and set it *as* an
iron wall between you and the
city. Set your face against it, and
it shall be [a]besieged, and you
shall lay siege against it. [b]This
will be a sign to the house of
Israel.
4 "Lie also on your left side,
and lay the iniquity of the house
of Israel upon it. *According* to
the number of the days that you
lie on it, you shall bear their
iniquity.
5 "For I have laid on you the
years of their iniquity, according
to the number of the days, three
hundred and ninety days; [a]so
you shall bear the iniquity of the
house of Israel.
6 "And when you have com-
pleted them, lie again on your
right side; then you shall bear
the iniquity of the house of Judah forty days. I have laid on
you a day for each year.
7 "Therefore you shall set your
face toward the siege of Jerusalem; your arm *shall be* uncovered, and you shall prophesy
against it.
8 [a]"And surely I will [1]restrain
you so that you cannot turn
from one side to another till you
have ended the days of your
siege.
9 "Also take for yourself wheat,
barley, beans, lentils, millet, and
spelt; put them into one vessel,
and make bread of them for
yourself. *During* the number of
days that you lie on your side,
three hundred and ninety days,
you shall eat it.
10 "And your food which you
eat *shall be* by weight, twenty
shekels a day; from time to time
you shall eat it.
11 "You shall also drink water by measure, one-sixth of a
hin; from time to time you shall
drink.
12 "And you shall eat it *as* barley cakes; and bake it using fuel
of human waste in their sight."
13 Then the LORD said, "So [a]shall
the children of Israel eat their
defiled bread among the Gentiles, where I will drive them."
14 So I said, [a]"Ah, Lord GOD! Indeed I have never defiled myself
from my youth till now; I have
never eaten [b]what died of itself
or was torn by beasts, nor has
[c]abominable[1] flesh ever come
into my mouth."
15 Then He said to me, "See, I
am giving you cow dung instead
of human waste, and you shall
prepare your bread over it."
16 Moreover He said to me,
"Son of man, surely I will cut
off the [a]supply of bread in Jerusalem; they shall [b]eat bread
by weight and with anxiety, and
shall [c]drink water by measure
and with dread,

26 [b]Hos. 4:17 [c]Ezek. 2:5–7 [1]Lit. *one who rebukes*
27 [a]Ezek. 24:27; 33:22 [b]Ezek. 3:11

CHAPTER 4

2 [a]Jer. 6:6 [b]2 Kin. 25:1
3 [a]Jer. 39:1, 2 [b]Ezek. 12:6, 11; 24:24, 27
5 [a]Num. 14:34
8 [a]Ezek. 3:25 [1]Lit. *put ropes on*
13 [a]Hos. 9:3
14 [a]Acts 10:14 [b]Lev. 17:15; 22:8 [c]Deut. 14:3 [1]Ritually unclean flesh, Lev. 7:18
16 [a]Is. 3:1 [b]Ezek. 4:10, 11; 12:19 [c]Ezek. 4:11

17 "that they may lack bread and water, and be dismayed with one another, and [a]waste away because of their iniquity.

5 "And you, son of man, take a sharp sword, take it as a barber's razor, [a]and pass *it* over your head and your beard; then take scales to weigh and divide the *hair*.

2 [a]"You shall burn with fire one-third in the midst of [b]the city, when [c]the days of the siege are finished; then you shall take one-third and strike around *it* with the sword, and one-third you shall scatter in the wind: I will draw out a sword after [d]them.

3 [a]"You shall also take a small number of them and bind them in the edge of your *garment*.

4 "Then take some of them again and [a]throw them into the midst of the fire, and burn them in the fire. From there a fire will go out into all the house of Israel.

5 "Thus says the Lord GOD: 'This *is* Jerusalem; I have set her in the midst of the nations and the countries all around her.

6 'She has rebelled against My judgments by doing wickedness more than the nations, and against My statutes more than the countries that *are* all around her; for they have refused My judgments, and they have not walked in My statutes.'

7 "Therefore thus says the Lord GOD: 'Because you have [1]multiplied *disobedience* more than the nations that *are* all around you, have not walked in My statutes [a]nor kept My judgments, [2]nor even done according to the judgments of the nations that *are* all around you'—

8 "therefore thus says the Lord GOD: 'Indeed I, even I, *am* against you and will execute judgments in your midst in the sight of the nations.

9 [a]'And I will do among you what I have never done, and the like of which I will never do again, because of all your abominations.

10 'Therefore fathers [a]shall eat *their* sons in your midst, and sons shall eat their fathers; and I will execute judgments among you, and all of you who remain I will [b]scatter to all the winds.

11 'Therefore, *as* I live,' says the Lord GOD, 'surely, because you have [a]defiled My sanctuary with all your [b]detestable things and with all your abominations, therefore I will also diminish *you*; [c]My eye will not spare, nor will I have any pity.

12 [a]'One-third of you shall die of the pestilence, and be consumed with famine in your midst; and one-third shall fall by the sword all around you; and [b]I will scatter another third to all the winds, and I will draw out a sword after [c]them.

13 'Thus shall My anger [a]be spent, and I will [b]cause My fury to rest upon them, [c]and I will be avenged; [d]and they shall know that I, the LORD, have spoken *it* in My zeal, when I have spent My fury upon them.

14 'Moreover [a]I will make you a waste and a reproach among the nations that *are* all around you, in the sight of all who pass by.

15 'So [1]it shall be a [a]reproach, a taunt, a [b]lesson, and an astonishment to the nations that *are*

17 [a]Lev. 26:39

CHAPTER 5

1 [a]Is. 7:20

2 [a]Ezek. 5:12 [b]Ezek. 4:1 [c]Ezek. 4:8, 9 [d]Lev. 26:25

3 [a]Jer. 40:6; 52:16

4 [a]Jer. 41:1, 2; 44:14

7 [a]Jer. 2:10, 11 [1]Or *raged* [2]So with MT, LXX, Tg., Vg.; many Heb. mss., Syr. *but have done* (cf. 11:12)

9 [a][Amos 3:2]

10 [a]Jer. 19:9 [b]Zech. 2:6; 7:14

11 [a][Jer. 7:9–11] [b]Ezek. 11:21 [c]Ezek. 7:4, 9; 8:18; 9:10

12 [a]Ezek. 6:12 [b]Jer. 9:16 [c]Jer. 43:10, 11; 44:27

13 [a]Lam. 4:11 [b]Ezek. 21:17 [c]Is. 1:24 [d]Ezek. 36:6; 38:19

14 [a]Lev. 26:31

15 [a]Jer. 24:9 [b][Is. 26:9] [1]LXX, Syr., Tg., Vg. *you*

all around you, when I execute
judgments among you in anger
and in fury and in [c]furious rebukes. I, the LORD, have spoken.
16 'When I [a]send against them
the terrible arrows of famine
which shall be for destruction,
which I will send to destroy you,
I will increase the famine upon
you and cut off your [b]supply of
bread.
17 'So I will send against you
famine and [a]wild beasts, and
they will bereave you. [b]Pestilence
and blood shall pass through
you, and I will bring the sword
against you. I, the LORD, have
spoken.' "

6

Now the word of the LORD
came to me, saying:
2 "Son of man, [a]set your face
toward the [b]mountains of Israel,
and prophesy against them,
3 "and say, 'O mountains of
Israel, hear the word of the Lord
GOD! Thus says the Lord GOD to
the mountains, to the hills, to the
ravines, and to the valleys: "Indeed I, *even* I, will bring a sword
against you, and [a]I will destroy
your [1]high places.
4 "Then your altars shall be
desolate, your incense altars
shall be broken, and [a]I will cast
down your slain *men* before
your idols.
5 "And I will lay the corpses
of the children of Israel before
their idols, and I will scatter your
bones all around your altars.
6 "In all your dwelling places
the cities shall be laid waste,
and the [1]high places shall be
desolate, so that your altars may
be laid waste and made desolate, your idols may be broken
and made to cease, your incense
altars may be cut down, and
your works may be abolished.
7 "The slain shall fall in your
midst, and [a]you shall know that
I *am* the LORD.
8 [a]"Yet I will leave a remnant,
so that you may have *some* who
escape the sword among the nations, when you are [b]scattered
through the countries.
9 "Then those of you who escape will [a]remember Me among
the nations where they are carried captive, because [b]I was
crushed by their adulterous
heart which has departed from
Me, and [c]by their eyes which
play the harlot after their idols;
[d]they will loathe themselves for
the evils which they committed
in all their abominations.
10 "And they shall know that
I *am* the LORD; I have not said
in vain that I would bring this
calamity upon them."
11 'Thus says the Lord GOD:
[a]"Pound[1] your fists and stamp
your feet, and say, 'Alas, for
all the evil abominations of the
house of Israel! [b]For they shall
fall by the sword, by famine, and
by pestilence.
12 'He who is far off shall die
by the pestilence, he who is near
shall fall by the sword, and he
who remains and is besieged
shall die by the famine. [a]Thus
will I spend My fury upon them.
13 'Then you shall know that I
am the LORD, when their slain
are among their idols all around
their altars, [a]on every high hill,
[b]on all the mountaintops, [c]under
every green tree, and under every thick oak, wherever they
offered sweet incense to all their
idols.
14 'So I will [a]stretch out My

15 [c]Ezek. 5:8; 25:17
16 [a]Deut. 32:23 [b]Lev. 26:26
17 [a]Lev. 26:22 [b]Ezek. 38:22

CHAPTER 6

2 [a]Ezek. 20:46; 21:2; 25:2 [b]Ezek. 36:1
3 [a]Lev. 26:30 [1]Places for pagan worship
4 [a]Lev. 26:30
6 [1]Places for pagan worship
7 [a]Ezek. 7:4, 9
8 [a]Jer. 44:28 [b]Ezek. 5:12
9 [a][Deut. 4:29] [b]Ps. 78:40 [c]Ezek. 20:7, 24 [d]Ezek. 20:43; 36:31
11 [a]Ezek. 21:14 [b]Ezek. 5:12 [1]Lit. *Strike your hands*
12 [a]Ezek. 5:13
13 [a]Jer. 2:20; 3:6 [b]Hos. 4:13 [c]Is. 57:5
14 [a]Is. 5:25

hand against them and make the land desolate, yes, more desolate than the wilderness toward [b]Dib′lah, in all their dwelling places. Then they shall know that I *am* the LORD.' " ' "

7 Moreover the word of the LORD came to me, saying,
2 "And you, son of man, thus says the Lord GOD to the land of Israel:

[a]'An end! The end has come
upon the four corners of the land.
3 Now the end *has come* upon you,
And I will send My anger against you;
I will judge you [a]according to your ways,
And I will repay you for all your abominations.
4 [a]My eye will not spare you,
Nor will I have pity;
But I will repay your ways,
And your abominations will be in your midst;
[b]Then you shall know that I *am* the LORD!'

5 "Thus says the Lord GOD:

'A disaster, a singular [a]disaster;
Behold, it has come!
6 An end has come,
The end has come;
It has dawned for you;
Behold, it has come!
7 [a]Doom has come to you, you who dwell in the land;
[b]The time has come,
A day of trouble *is* near,
And not of rejoicing in the mountains.
8 Now upon you I will soon [a]pour out My fury,
And spend My anger upon you;
I will judge you according to your ways;
And I will repay you for all your abominations.
9 'My eye will not spare,
Nor will I have pity;
I will [1]repay you according to your ways,
And your abominations will be in your midst.
Then you shall know that I *am* the LORD who strikes.

10 'Behold, the day!
Behold, it has come!
[a]Doom has gone out;
The rod has blossomed,
Pride has budded.
11 [a]Violence has risen up into a rod of wickedness;
None of them *shall remain,*
None of their multitude,
None of [1]them;
[b]Nor *shall there be* wailing for them.
12 The time has come,
The day draws near.

'Let not the buyer [a]rejoice,
Nor the seller [b]mourn,
For wrath *is* on their whole multitude.
13 For the seller shall not return to what has been sold,
Though he may still be alive;
For the vision concerns the whole multitude,
And it shall not turn back;
No one will strengthen himself
Who lives in iniquity.

14 'They have blown the trumpet and made everyone ready,

14 [b]Num. 33:46

CHAPTER 7

2 [a]Amos 8:2, 10

3 [a][Rom. 2:6]

4 [a]Ezek. 5:11 [b]Ezek. 12:20

5 [a]2 Kin. 21:12, 13

7 [a]Ezek. 7:10 [b]Zeph. 1:14, 15

8 [a]Ezek. 20:8, 21

9 [1]Lit. *give*

10 [a]Ezek. 7:7

11 [a]Jer. 6:7 [b]Jer. 16:5, 6 [1]Or *their wealth*

12 [a]Prov. 20:14 [b]Is. 24:2

But no one goes to battle;
For My wrath *is* on all their multitude.
15 [a]The sword *is* outside,
And the pestilence and famine within.
Whoever *is* in the field
Will die by the sword;
And whoever *is* in the city,
Famine and pestilence will devour him.

16 'Those who [a]survive will escape and be on the mountains
Like doves of the valleys,
All of them mourning,
Each for his iniquity.
17 Every [a]hand will be feeble,
And every knee will be *as* weak *as* water.
18 They will also [a]be girded with sackcloth;
Horror will cover them;
Shame *will be* on every face,
Baldness on all their heads.

19 'They will throw their silver into the streets,
And their gold will be like refuse;
Their [a]silver and their gold will not be able to deliver them
In the day of the wrath of the LORD;
They will not satisfy their souls,
Nor fill their stomachs,
Because it became their stumbling block of iniquity.

20 'As for the beauty of his ornaments,
He set it in majesty;
[a]But they made from it
The images of their abominations—
Their detestable things;
Therefore I have made it
Like refuse to them.
21 I will give it as [a]plunder
Into the hands of strangers,
And to the wicked of the earth as spoil;
And they shall defile it.
22 I will turn My face from them,
And they will defile My secret place;
For robbers shall enter it and defile it.

23 'Make a chain,
For [a]the land is filled with crimes of blood,
And the city is full of violence.
24 Therefore I will bring the [a]worst of the Gentiles,
And they will possess their houses;
I will cause the pomp of the strong to cease,
And their holy places shall be [b]defiled.
25 [1]Destruction comes;
They will seek peace, but *there shall be* none.
26 [a]Disaster will come upon disaster,
And rumor will be upon rumor.
[b]Then they will seek a vision from a prophet;
But the law will perish from the priest,
And counsel from the elders.

27 'The king will mourn,
The prince will be clothed with desolation,

15 [a]Jer. 14:18
16 [a]Ezek. 6:8; 14:22
17 [a]Is. 13:7
18 [a]Amos 8:10
19 [a]Zeph. 1:18
20 [a]Jer. 7:30
21 [a]2 Kin. 24:13
23 [a]2 Kin. 21:16
24 [a]Ezek. 21:31; 28:7 [b]Ezek. 24:21
25 [1]Lit. *Shuddering*
26 [a]Jer. 4:20 [b]Ps. 74:9

And the hands of the
common people will
tremble.
I will do to them according
to their way,
And according to what they
deserve I will judge them;
Then they shall know that I
am the LORD!' "

8 And it came to pass in
the sixth year, in the sixth
month, on the fifth *day* of the
month, as I sat in my house
with [a]the elders of Judah sitting
before me, that [b]the hand of the
Lord GOD fell upon me there.
2 [a]Then I looked, and there was
a likeness, like the appearance
of fire—from the appearance of
His waist and downward, fire;
and from His waist and upward,
like the appearance of brightness, [b]like the color of amber.
3 He [a]stretched out the form of
a hand, and took me by a lock of
my hair; and [b]the Spirit lifted me
up between earth and heaven,
and [c]brought me in visions of
God to Jerusalem, to the door of
the north gate of the inner *court,*
[d]where the seat of the image of
jealousy *was,* which [e]provokes[1]
to jealousy.
4 And behold, the [a]glory of the
God of Israel *was* there, like the
vision that I [b]saw in the plain.
5 Then He said to me, "Son of
man, lift your eyes now toward
the north." So I lifted my eyes toward the north, and there, north
of the altar gate, was this image
of jealousy in the entrance.
6 Furthermore He said to
me, "Son of man, do you see
what they are doing, the great
[a]abominations that the house of
Israel commits here, to make Me
go far away from My sanctuary?
Now turn again, you will see
greater abominations."
7 So He brought me to the
door of the court; and when I
looked, there was a hole in the
wall.
8 Then He said to me, "Son
of man, dig into the wall"; and
when I dug into the wall, there
was a door.
9 And He said to me, "Go
in, and see the wicked abominations which they are doing
there."
10 So I went in and saw, and
there—every [a]sort of [b]creeping
thing, abominable beasts, and
all the idols of the house of Israel, [1]portrayed all around on
the walls.
11 And there stood before them
[a]seventy men of the elders of
the house of Israel, and in their
midst stood Jā·az·a·nī'ah the son
of Shā'phan. Each man had a
censer in his hand, and a thick
cloud of incense went up.
12 Then He said to me, "Son of
man, have you seen what the elders of the house of Israel do in
the dark, every man in the room
of his idols? For they say, [a]'The
LORD does not see us, the LORD
has forsaken the land.' "
13 And He said to me, "Turn
again, *and* you will see greater
abominations that they are
doing."
14 So He brought me to the
door of the north gate of the
LORD's house; and to my dismay,
women were sitting there weeping for [1]Tam'mūz.
15 Then He said to me, "Have
you seen *this,* O son of man?
Turn again, you will see greater
abominations than these."

CHAPTER 8

1 [a]Ezek. 14:1; 20:1; 33:31 [b]Ezek. 1:3; 3:22

2 [a]Ezek. 1:26, 27 [b]Ezek. 1:4, 27

3 [a]Dan. 5:5 [b]Ezek. 3:14 [c]Ezek. 11:1, 24; 40:2 [d]Ezek. 5:11 [e]Deut. 32:16, 21 [1]Arouses the LORD's jealousy

4 [a]Ezek. 3:12; 9:3 [b]Ezek. 1:28; 3:22, 23

6 [a]2 Kin. 23:4, 5

10 [a]Ex. 20:4 [b]Rom. 1:23 [1]Or *carved*

11 [a]Num. 11:16, 25

12 [a]Ezek. 9:9

14 [1]A Sumerian fertility god similar to the Gr. god Adonis

16 So He brought me into the
inner court of the LORD's house;
and there, at the door of the
temple of the LORD, [a]between
the porch and the altar, [b]*were*
about twenty-five men [c]with
their backs toward the temple of
the LORD and their faces toward
the east, and they were worshiping [d]the sun toward the east.
17 And He said to me, "Have
you seen *this,* O son of man? Is
it a trivial thing to the house of
Judah to commit the abominations which they commit here?
For they have [a]filled the land
with violence; then they have returned to provoke Me to anger.
Indeed they put the branch to
their nose.
18 [a]"Therefore I also will act
in fury. My [b]eye will not spare
nor will I have pity; and though
they [c]cry in My ears with a loud
voice, I will not hear them."

9

Then He called out in my
hearing with a loud voice,
saying, "Let those who have
charge over the city draw near,
each *with* a [1]deadly weapon in
his hand."
2 And suddenly six men came
from the direction of the upper gate, which faces north,
each with his [1]battle-ax in his
hand. [a]One man among them
was clothed with linen and had
a writer's inkhorn [2]at his side.
They went in and stood beside
the bronze altar.
3 Now [a]the glory of the God
of Israel had gone up from the
cherub, where it had been, to the
threshold of the [1]temple. And He
called to the man clothed with
linen, who *had* the writer's inkhorn at his side;
4 and the LORD said to him,

16 [a]Joel 2:17 [b]Ezek. 11:1 [c]Jer. 2:27; 32:33 [d]Deut. 4:19

17 [a]Ezek. 9:9

18 [a]Ezek. 5:13; 16:42; 24:13 [b]Ezek. 5:11; 7:4, 9; 9:5, 10 [c]Mic. 3:4

CHAPTER 9

1 [1]Or *destroying*

2 [a]Lev. 16:4 [1]Lit. *shattering weapon* [2]Lit. *upon his loins*

3 [a]Ezek. 3:23; 8:4; 10:4, 18; 11:22, 23 [1]Lit. *house*

4 [a]Rev. 7:2, 3; 9:4; 14:1 [b]Jer. 13:17

5 [a]Ezek. 7:9 [b]Ezek. 5:11 [1]Lit. *ears* [2]Lit. *strike*

6 [a]2 Chr. 36:17 [b]Rev. 9:4 [c]Jer. 25:29 [d]Ezek. 8:11, 12, 16 [1]Lit. *Slay to destruction* [2]Lit. *house*

7 [1]Lit. *house*

8 [a]Josh. 7:6 [b]Ezek. 11:13

9 [a]2 Kin. 21:16 [b]Ezek. 8:12 [c]Is. 29:15

10 [a]Ezek. 5:11; 7:4; 8:18 [b]Ezek. 11:21

"Go through the midst of the
city, through the midst of Jerusalem, and put [a]a mark on the
foreheads of the men [b]who sigh
and cry over all the abominations that are done within it."
5 To the others He said in my
[1]hearing, "Go after him through
the city and [a]kill;[2] [b]do not let
your eye spare, nor have any
pity.
6 [a]"Utterly[1] slay old *and* young
men, maidens and little children and women; but [b]do not
come near anyone on whom
is the mark; and [c]begin at My
sanctuary." [d]So they began with
the elders who *were* before the
[2]temple.
7 Then He said to them, "Defile
the [1]temple, and fill the courts
with the slain. Go out!" And they
went out and killed in the city.
8 So it was, that while they
were killing them, I was left
alone; and I [a]fell on my face and
cried out, and said, [b]"Ah, Lord
GOD! Will You destroy all the
remnant of Israel in pouring out
Your fury on Jerusalem?"
9 Then He said to me, "The iniquity of the house of Israel and
Judah *is* exceedingly great, and
[a]the land is full of bloodshed,
and the city full of perversity;
for they say, [b]'The LORD has forsaken the land, and [c]the LORD
does not see!'
10 "And as for Me also, My [a]eye
will neither spare, nor will I
have pity, *but* [b]I will recompense
their deeds on their own head."
11 Just then, the man clothed
with linen, who *had* the inkhorn
at his side, reported back and
said, "I have done as You commanded me."

10 And I looked, and there in the [a]firmament[1] that was above the head of the cherubim, there appeared something like a sapphire stone, having the appearance of the likeness of a throne.

2 [a]Then He spoke to the man clothed with linen, and said, "Go in among the wheels, under the cherub, fill your hands with [b]coals of fire from among the cherubim, and [c]scatter *them* over the city." And he went in as I watched.

3 Now the cherubim were standing on the [1]south side of the [2]temple when the man went in, and the [a]cloud filled the inner court.

4 [a]Then the glory of the LORD went up from the cherub, *and paused* over the threshold of the [1]temple; and [b]the house was filled with the cloud, and the court was full of the brightness of the LORD's [c]glory.

5 And the [a]sound of the wings of the cherubim was heard *even* in the outer court, like [b]the voice of Almighty God when He speaks.

6 Then it happened, when He commanded the man clothed in linen, saying, "Take fire from among the wheels, from among the cherubim," that he went in and stood beside the wheels.

7 And the cherub stretched out his hand from among the cherubim to the fire that *was* among the cherubim, and took *some of it* and put *it* into the hands of the *man* clothed with linen, who took *it* and went out.

8 [a]The cherubim appeared to have the form of a man's hand under their wings.

9 [a]And when I looked, there were four wheels by the cherubim, one wheel by one cherub and another wheel by each other cherub; the wheels appeared *to have* the color of a [b]beryl stone.

10 *As for* their appearance, all four looked alike—as it were, a wheel in the middle of a wheel.

11 [a]When they went, they went toward *any of* their four directions; they did not turn aside when they went, but followed in the direction the head was facing. They did not turn aside when they went.

12 And their whole body, with their back, their hands, their wings, and the wheels that the four had, *were* [a]full of eyes all around.

13 As for the wheels, they were called in my [1]hearing, "Wheel."

14 [a]Each one had four faces: the first face *was* the face of a cherub, the second face the face of a man, the third the face of a lion, and the fourth the face of an eagle.

15 And the cherubim were lifted up. This *was* [a]the living creature I saw by the River Chē′bar.

16 [a]When the cherubim went, the wheels went beside them; and when the cherubim lifted their wings to mount up from the earth, the same wheels also did not turn from beside them.

17 [a]When [1]*the cherubim* stood still, *the wheels* stood still, and when [2]*one* was lifted up, [3]*the other* lifted itself up, for the spirit of the living creature *was* in them.

18 Then [a]the glory of the LORD [b]departed from the threshold of the [1]temple and stood over the cherubim.

CHAPTER 10

1 [a]Ezek. 1:22, 26 [1]*expanse*

2 [a]Dan. 10:5 [b]Ezek. 1:13 [c]Rev. 8:5

3 [a]1 Kin. 8:10, 11 [1]Lit. *right* [2]Lit. *house*

4 [a]Ezek. 1:28 [b]Ezek. 43:5 [c]Ezek. 11:22, 23 [1]Lit. *house*

5 [a]Ezek. 1:24 [b][Ps. 29:3]

8 [a]Ezek. 1:8; 10:21

9 [a]Ezek. 1:15 [b]Ezek. 1:16

11 [a]Ezek. 1:17

12 [a]Rev. 4:6, 8

13 [1]Lit. *ears*

14 [a]Ezek. 1:6, 10, 11

15 [a]Ezek. 1:3, 5

16 [a]Ezek. 1:19

17 [a]Ezek. 1:12, 20, 21 [1]Lit. *they* [2]Lit. *they were* [3]Lit. *they lifted them*

18 [a]Ezek. 10:4 [b]Hos. 9:12 [1]Lit. *house*

19 And [a]the cherubim lifted their
wings and mounted up from the
earth in my sight. When they
went out, the wheels *were* beside
them; and they stood at the door
of the [b]east gate of the LORD's
house, and the glory of the God
of Israel *was* above them.
20 [a]This *is* the living creature I
saw under the God of Israel [b]by
the River Chē'bar, and I knew
they *were* cherubim.
21 [a]Each one had four faces and
each one four wings, and the
likeness of the hands of a man
was under their wings.
22 And [a]the likeness of their
faces *was* the same *as* the faces
which I had seen by the River
Chē'bar, their appearance and
their persons. [b]They each went
straight forward.

11

Then [a]the Spirit lifted me
up and brought me to
[b]the East Gate of the LORD's
house, which faces eastward;
and there [c]at the door of the gate
were twenty-five men, among
whom I saw Jā·az·a·nī'ah the
son of Az'zur, and Pel·a·tī'ah
the son of Be·nā'i·ah, princes of
the people.
2 And He said to me: "Son of
man, these *are* the men who
devise iniquity and give wicked
[1]counsel in this city,
3 "who say, '*The time is* not
[a]near to build houses; [b]this *city*
is the [1]caldron, and we *are* the
meat.'
4 "Therefore prophesy against
them, prophesy, O son of man!"
5 Then [a]the Spirit of the LORD
fell upon me, and said to me,
"Speak! 'Thus says the LORD:
"Thus you have said, O house
of Israel; for [b]I know the things
that come into your mind.
6 [a]"You have multiplied your
slain in this city, and you have
filled its streets with the slain."
7 'Therefore thus says the
Lord GOD: [a]"Your slain whom
you have laid in its midst, they
are the meat, and this *city is* the
caldron; [b]but I shall bring you
out of the midst of it.
8 "You have [a]feared the sword;
and I will bring a sword upon
you," says the Lord GOD.
9 "And I will bring you out
of its midst, and deliver you
into the hands of strangers, and
[a]execute judgments on you.
10 [a]"You shall fall by the sword.
I will judge you at [b]the border
of Israel. [c]Then you shall know
that I *am* the LORD.
11 [a]"This *city* shall not be your
[1]caldron, nor shall you be the
meat in its midst. I will judge
you at the border of Israel.
12 "And you shall know that I
am the LORD; for you have not
walked in My statutes nor executed My judgments, but [a]have
done according to the customs
of the Gentiles which *are* all
around you." ' "
13 Now it happened, while I was
prophesying, that [a]Pel·a·tī'ah the
son of Be·nā'i·ah died. Then [b]I
fell on my face and cried with a
loud voice, and said, "Ah, Lord
GOD! Will You make a complete
end of the remnant of Israel?"
14 Again the word of the LORD
came to me, saying,
15 "Son of man, your brethren,
your relatives, your countrymen,
and all the house of Israel in its
entirety, *are* those about whom
the inhabitants of Jerusalem
have said, 'Get far away from
the LORD; this land has been
given to us as a possession.'

---

19 [a]Ezek. 11:22 [b]Ezek. 11:1
20 [a]Ezek. 1:22 [b]Ezek. 1:1
21 [a]Ezek. 1:6, 8; 10:14; 41:18, 19
22 [a]Ezek. 1:10 [b]Ezek. 1:9, 12

CHAPTER 11

1 [a]Ezek. 3:12, 14 [b]Ezek. 10:19 [c]Ezek. 8:16
2 [1]Advice
3 [a]2 Pet. 3:4 [b]Jer. 1:13 [1]Pot
5 [a]Ezek. 2:2; 3:24 [b][Jer. 16:17; 17:10]
6 [a]Ezek. 7:23; 22:2–6, 9, 12, 27
7 [a]Mic. 3:2, 3 [b]Ezek. 11:9
8 [a]Jer. 42:16
9 [a]Ezek. 5:8
10 [a]Jer. 39:6; 52:10 [b]2 Kin. 14:25 [c]Ps. 9:16
11 [a]Ezek. 11:3, 7 [1]Pot
12 [a]Deut. 12:30, 31
13 [a]Acts 5:5 [b]Ezek. 9:8

16 "Therefore say, 'Thus says the Lord GOD: "Although I have cast them far off among the Gentiles, and although I have scattered them among the countries, [a]yet I shall be a little [1]sanctuary for them in the countries where they have gone." '

17 "Therefore say, 'Thus says the Lord GOD: [a]"I will gather you from the peoples, assemble you from the countries where you have been scattered, and I will give you the land of Israel." '

18 "And they will go there, and they will take away all its [a]detestable things and all its abominations from there.

19 "Then [a]I will give them one heart, and I will put [b]a new spirit within [1]them, and take [c]the stony heart out of their flesh, and give them a heart of flesh,

20 [a]"that they may walk in My statutes and keep My judgments and do them; [b]and they shall be My people, and I will be their God.

21 "But *as for those* whose hearts follow the desire for their detestable things and their abominations, [a]I will recompense their deeds on their own heads," says the Lord GOD.

22 So the cherubim [a]lifted up their wings, with the wheels beside them, and the glory of the God of Israel *was* high above them.

23 And [a]the glory of the LORD went up from the midst of the city and stood [b]on the mountain, [c]which *is* on the east side of the city.

24 Then [a]the Spirit took me up and brought me in a vision by the Spirit of God into [1]Chal·dē′a, to those in captivity. And the vision that I had seen went up from me.

25 So I spoke to those in captivity of all the things the LORD had shown me.

12

Now the word of the LORD came to me, saying:

2 "Son of man, you dwell in the midst of [a]a rebellious house, which [b]has eyes to see but does not see, and ears to hear but does not hear; [c]for they *are* a rebellious house.

3 "Therefore, son of man, prepare your belongings for captivity, and go into captivity by day in their sight. You shall go from your place into captivity to another place in their sight. It may be that they will consider, though they *are* a rebellious house.

4 "By day you shall bring out your belongings in their sight, as though going into captivity; and at evening you shall go in their sight, like those who go into captivity.

5 "Dig through the wall in their sight, and carry *your belongings* out through it.

6 "In their sight you shall bear *them* on *your* shoulders *and* carry *them* out at twilight; you shall cover your face, so that you cannot see the ground, [a]for I have made you a sign to the house of Israel."

7 So I did as I was commanded. I brought out my belongings by day, as though going into captivity, and at evening I dug through the wall with my hand. I brought *them* out at twilight, *and* I bore *them* on *my* shoulder in their sight.

8 And in the morning the word of the LORD came to me, saying,

16 [a]Is. 8:14 [1]*holy place*
17 [a]Jer. 3:12, 18; 24:5
18 [a]Ezek. 37:23
19 [a]Jer. 32:39 [b]Ezek. 18:31 [c]Zech. 7:12 [1]Lit. *you* (pl.)
20 [a]Ps. 105:45 [b]Jer. 24:7
21 [a]Ezek. 9:10
22 [a]Ezek. 1:19
23 [a]Ezek. 8:4; 9:3 [b]Zech. 14:4 [c]Ezek. 43:2
24 [a]Ezek. 8:3 [1]Or *Babylon*, and so elsewhere in the book

CHAPTER 12

2 [a]Ezek. 2:3, 6–8 [b]Jer. 5:21 [c]Ezek. 2:5
6 [a]Ezek. 4:3; 24:24

9 "Son of man, has not the
house of Israel, [a]the rebellious
house, said to you, [b]'What are
you doing?'
10 "Say to them, 'Thus says the
Lord GOD: "This [a]burden[1] *concerns* the prince in Jerusalem
and all the house of Israel who
are among them." '
11 "Say, [a]'I *am* a sign to you. As
I have done, so shall it be done
to them; [b]they shall be carried
away into captivity.'
12 "And [a]the prince who *is*
among them shall bear *his belongings* on *his* shoulder at twilight and go out. They shall dig
through the wall to carry *them*
out through it. He shall cover his
face, so that he cannot see the
ground with *his* eyes.
13 "I will also spread My [a]net
over him, and he shall be caught
in My snare. [b]I will bring him
to Babylon, *to* the land of the
Chal·dē′ans; yet he shall not see
it, though he shall die there.
14 [a]"I will scatter to every wind
all who *are* around him to help
him, and all his troops; and [b]I
will draw out the sword after
them.
15 [a]"Then they shall know that
I *am* the LORD, when I scatter
them among the nations and
disperse them throughout the
countries.
16 [a]"But I will spare a few of
their men from the sword, from
famine, and from pestilence,
that they may declare all their
abominations among the Gentiles wherever they go. Then
they shall know that I *am* the
LORD."
17 Moreover the word of the
LORD came to me, saying,
18 "Son of man, [a]eat your

9 [a]Ezek. 2:5 [b]Ezek. 17:12; 24:19
10 [a]Mal. 1:1 [1]*oracle, prophecy*
11 [a]Ezek. 12:6 [b]2 Kin. 25:4, 5, 7
12 [a]Jer. 39:4; 52:7
13 [a]Jer. 52:9 [b]Jer. 52:11
14 [a]Ezek. 5:10 [b]Ezek. 5:2, 12
15 [a]Ezek. 6:7, 14; 12:16, 20
16 [a]Ezek. 6:8–10
18 [a]Ezek. 4:16 [1]*shaking*
19 [a]Zech. 7:14 [b]Ps. 107:34
22 [a]Ezek. 11:3; 12:27
23 [a]Zeph. 1:14 [1]Lit. *word*
24 [a]Ezek. 13:6 [b]Lam. 2:14 [1]Lit. *vain*
25 [a][Luke 21:33] [b][Is. 14:24]
27 [a]Ezek. 12:22 [b]Dan. 10:14

bread with [1]quaking, and drink
your water with trembling and
anxiety.
19 "And say to the people of the
land, 'Thus says the Lord GOD to
the inhabitants of Jerusalem *and*
to the land of Israel: "They shall
eat their bread with anxiety, and
drink their water with dread, so
that her land may [a]be emptied of
all who are in it, [b]because of the
violence of all those who dwell
in it.
20 "Then the cities that are inhabited shall be laid waste, and
the land shall become desolate;
and you shall know that I *am* the
LORD." ' "
21 And the word of the LORD
came to me, saying,
22 "Son of man, what *is* this
proverb *that* you *people* have
about the land of Israel, which
says, [a]'The days are prolonged,
and every vision fails'?
23 "Tell them therefore, 'Thus
says the Lord GOD: "I will lay
this proverb to rest, and they
shall no more use it as a proverb
in Israel." ' But say to them, [a]' "The
days are at hand, and the [1]fulfill-
ment of every vision.
24 "For [a]no more shall there be
any [b]false[1] vision or flattering
divination within the house of
Israel.
25 "For I *am* the LORD. I speak,
and [a]the word which I speak will
come to pass; it will no more
be postponed; for in your days,
O rebellious house, I will say the
word and [b]perform it," says the
Lord GOD.' "
26 Again the word of the LORD
came to me, saying,
27 [a]"Son of man, look, the house
of Israel is saying, 'The vision
that he sees *is* [b]for many days

from now, and he prophesies of
times far off.'
28 [a]"Therefore say to them,
'Thus says the Lord GOD: "None
of My words will be postponed
any more, but the word which
I speak [b]will be done," says the
Lord GOD.' "
13 And the word of the LORD
came to me, saying,
2 "Son of man, prophesy
[a]against the prophets of Israel
who prophesy, and say to [b]those
who prophesy out of their own
[c]heart,[1] 'Hear the word of the
LORD!' "
3 Thus says the Lord GOD:
"Woe to the foolish prophets,
who follow their own spirit and
have seen [1]nothing!
4 "O Israel, your prophets are
[a]like foxes in the deserts.
5 "You [a]have not gone up into
the [1]gaps to build a wall for the
house of Israel to stand in battle
on the day of the LORD.
6 [a]"They have envisioned futility and false divination, saying,
'Thus says the LORD!' But the
LORD has [b]not sent them; yet
they hope that the word may [1]be
confirmed.
7 "Have you not seen a futile
vision, and have you not spoken false divination? You say,
'The LORD says,' but I have not
spoken."
8 Therefore thus says the Lord
GOD: "Because you have spoken
nonsense and envisioned lies,
therefore I *am* indeed against
you," says the Lord GOD.
9 "My hand will be [a]against
the prophets who envision futility and who [b]divine lies; they
shall not be in the assembly of
My people, [c]nor be written in
the record of the house of Israel,
[d]nor shall they enter into the
land of Israel. [e]Then you shall
know that I *am* the Lord GOD.
10 "Because, indeed, because
they have seduced My people,
saying, [a]'Peace!' when *there is*
no peace—and one builds a wall,
and they [b]plaster[1] it with untempered *mortar*—
11 "say to those who plaster *it*
with untempered *mortar,* that
it will fall. [a]There will be flooding rain, and you, O great hailstones, shall fall; and a stormy
wind shall tear *it* down.
12 "Surely, when the wall has
fallen, will it not be said to you,
'Where *is* the mortar with which
you plastered *it?*' "
13 Therefore thus says the Lord
GOD: "I will cause a stormy wind
to break forth in My fury; and
there shall be a flooding rain in
My anger, and great hailstones
in fury to consume *it.*
14 "So I will break down the
wall you have plastered with
untempered *mortar,* and bring
it down to the ground, so that its
foundation will be uncovered; it
will fall, and you shall be consumed in the midst of it. [a]Then
you shall know that I *am* the
LORD.
15 "Thus will I accomplish My
wrath on the wall and on those
who have plastered it with untempered *mortar;* and I will say
to you, 'The wall *is* no *more,* nor
those who plastered it,
16 '*that is,* the prophets of Israel who prophesy concerning
Jerusalem, and who [a]see visions
of peace for her when *there is*
no peace,' " says the Lord GOD.
17 "Likewise, son of man, [a]set
your face against the daughters
of your people, [b]who prophesy

28 [a]Ezek. 12:23, 25 [b]Jer. 4:7

CHAPTER 13

2 [a]Ezek. 22:25–28 [b]Ezek. 13:17 [c]Jer. 14:14; 23:16, 26 [1]Inspiration

3 [1]No vision

4 [a]Song 2:15

5 [a]Ps. 106:23 [1]*breaches*

6 [a]Ezek. 22:28 [b]Jer. 27:8–15 [1]Come true

9 [a]Jer. 23:30 [b]Jer. 20:3–6 [c]Ezra 2:59, 62 [d]Jer. 20:3–6 [e]Ezek. 11:10, 12

10 [a]Jer. 6:14; 8:11 [b]Ezek. 22:28 [1]Or *whitewash*

11 [a]Ezek. 38:22

14 [a]Ezek. 13:9, 21, 23; 14:8

16 [a]Jer. 6:14; 8:11; 28:9

17 [a]Ezek. 20:46; 21:2 [b]Ezek. 13:2

out of their own [1]heart; prophesy against them,
18 "and say, 'Thus says the Lord
GOD: "Woe to the *women* who
sew *magic* charms [1]on their
sleeves and make veils for the
heads of people of every height
to hunt souls! Will you [a]hunt the
souls of My people, and keep
yourselves alive?
19 "And will you profane Me
among My people [a]for handfuls
of barley and for pieces of bread,
killing people who should not
die, and keeping people alive
who should not live, by your lying to My people who listen to
lies?"
20 'Therefore thus says the
Lord GOD: "Behold, I *am* against
your *magic* charms by which
you hunt souls there like [1]birds.
I will tear them from your arms,
and let the souls go, the souls
you hunt like birds.
21 "I will also tear off your veils
and deliver My people out of
your hand, and they shall no
longer be as prey in your hand.
[a]Then you shall know that I *am*
the LORD.
22 "Because with [a]lies you have
made the heart of the righteous
sad, whom I have not made sad;
and you have [b]strengthened the
hands of the wicked, so that he
does not turn from his wicked
way to save his life.
23 "Therefore [a]you shall no longer envision futility nor practice
divination; for I will deliver My
people out of your hand, and
you shall know that I *am* the
LORD." ' "

14 Now [a]some of the elders
of Israel came to me and
sat before me.
2 And the word of the LORD
came to me, saying,
3 "Son of man, these men have
set up their idols in their hearts,
and put before them [a]that which
causes them to stumble into iniquity. [b]Should I let Myself be
inquired of at all by them?
4 "Therefore speak to them,
and say to them, 'Thus says
the Lord GOD: "Everyone of the
house of Israel who sets up his
idols in his heart, and puts before him what causes him to
stumble into iniquity, and then
comes to the prophet, I the LORD
will answer him who comes, according to the multitude of his
idols,
5 "that I may seize the house
of Israel by their heart, because
they are all estranged from Me
by their idols." '
6 "Therefore say to the house of
Israel, 'Thus says the Lord GOD:
"Repent, turn away from your
idols, and [a]turn your faces away
from all your abominations.
7 "For anyone of the house of
Israel, or of the strangers who
dwell in Israel, who separates
himself from Me and sets up
his idols in his heart and puts
before him what causes him
to stumble into iniquity, then
comes to a prophet to inquire of
him concerning Me, I the LORD
will answer him by Myself.
8 [a]"I will set My face against
that man and make him a [b]sign
and a proverb, and I will cut him
off from the midst of My people.
[c]Then you shall know that I *am*
the LORD.
9 "And if the prophet is induced to speak anything, I the
LORD [a]have induced that prophet,
and I will stretch out My hand

17 [1]Inspiration
18 [a][2 Pet. 2:14] [1]Lit. *over all the joints of My hands;* Vg. *under every elbow;* LXX, Tg. *on all elbows of the hands*
19 [a]Mic. 3:5
20 [1]Lit. *flying ones*
21 [a]Ezek. 13:9
22 [a]Jer. 28:15 [b]Jer. 23:14
23 [a]Mic. 3:5, 6

CHAPTER 14

1 [a]Ezek. 8:1; 20:1; 33:31
3 [a]Ezek. 7:19 [b]Ezek. 20:3, 31
6 [a]Is. 2:20; 30:22; 55:6, 7
8 [a]Jer. 44:11 [b]Num. 26:10 [c]Ezek. 6:7; 13:14
9 [a]2 Thess. 2:11

against him and destroy him
from among My people Israel.
10 "And they shall bear their
iniquity; the punishment of the
prophet shall be the same as
the punishment of the one who
inquired,
11 "that the house of Israel may
[a]no longer stray from Me, nor
be profaned anymore with all
their transgressions, [b]but that
they may be My people and I
may be their God," says the Lord
GOD.' "
12 The word of the LORD came
again to me, saying:
13 "Son of man, when a land
sins against Me by persistent
unfaithfulness, I will stretch out
My hand against it; I will cut off
its [a]supply of bread, send famine
on it, and cut off man and beast
from it.
14 [a]"Even *if* these three men,
Noah, Daniel, and Job, were in
it, they would deliver *only* themselves [b]by their righteousness,"
says the Lord GOD.
15 "If I cause [a]wild beasts to
pass through the land, and they
[1]empty it, and make it so desolate that no man may pass
through because of the beasts,
16 "*even* [a]*though* these three
men *were* [1]in it, *as* I live," says
the Lord GOD, "they would deliver neither sons nor daughters; only they would be delivered, and the land would be
[b]desolate.
17 "Or *if* [a]I bring a sword on
that land, and say, 'Sword, go
through the land,' and I [b]cut off
man and beast from it,
18 "even [a]*though* these three
men *were* in it, *as* I live," says
the Lord GOD, "they would deliver neither sons nor daughters,
but only they themselves would
be delivered.
19 "Or *if* I send [a]a pestilence
into that land and [b]pour out My
fury on it in blood, and cut off
from it man and beast,
20 "even [a]*though* Noah, Daniel,
and Job *were* in it, *as* I live," says
the Lord GOD, "they would deliver neither son nor daughter;
they would deliver *only* themselves by their righteousness."
21 For thus says the Lord GOD:
"How much more it shall be
when [a]I send My four [1]severe
judgments on Jerusalem—the
sword and famine and wild
beasts and pestilence—to cut off
man and beast from it?
22 [a]"Yet behold, there shall be
left in it a remnant who will
be [b]brought out, *both* sons and
daughters; surely they will come
out to you, and [c]you will see their
ways and their doings. Then you
will be comforted concerning
the disaster that I have brought
upon Jerusalem, all that I have
brought upon it.
23 "And they will comfort you,
when you see their ways and
their doings; and you shall
know that I have done nothing
[a]without cause that I have done
in it," says the Lord GOD.

15

Then the word of the LORD
came to me, saying:
2 "Son of man, how is the wood
of the vine *better* than any other
wood, the vine branch which is
among the trees of the forest?
3 "Is wood taken from it to
make any object? Or can *men*
make a peg from it to hang any
vessel on?
4 "Instead, [a]it is thrown into
the fire for fuel; the fire devours
both ends of it, and its middle

---

11 [a]2 Pet. 2:15 [b]Ezek. 11:20; 37:27
13 [a]Is. 3:1
14 [a]Jer. 15:1 [b][Prov. 11:4]
15 [a]Lev. 26:22 [1]Lit. *bereave it of children*
16 [a]Ezek. 14:14, 18, 20 [b]Ezek. 15:8; 33:28, 29 [1]Lit. *in the midst of it*
17 [a]Lev. 26:25 [b]Zeph. 1:3
18 [a]Ezek. 14:14
19 [a]2 Sam. 24:15 [b]Ezek. 7:8
20 [a]Ezek. 14:14
21 [a]Ezek. 5:17; 33:27 [1]Lit. *evil*
22 [a]Ezek. 12:16; 36:20 [b]Ezek. 6:8 [c]Ezek. 20:43
23 [a]Jer. 22:8, 9

CHAPTER 15

4 [a][John 15:6]

is burned. Is it useful for *any*
work?
5 "Indeed, when it was whole,
no object could be made from it.
How much less will it be useful
for *any* work when the fire has
devoured it, and it is burned?
6 "Therefore thus says the
Lord GOD: 'Like the wood of
the vine among the trees of the
forest, which I have given to the
fire for fuel, so I will give up
the inhabitants of Jerusalem;
7 'and [a]I will set My face
against them. [b]They will go out
from *one* fire, but *another* fire
shall devour them. [c]Then you
shall know that I *am* the LORD,
when I set My face against
them.
8 'Thus I will make the land
desolate, because they have persisted in unfaithfulness,' says
the Lord GOD."

16 Again the word of the
LORD came to me, saying,
2 "Son of man, [a]cause Jerusalem to know her abominations,
3 "and say, 'Thus says the Lord
GOD to Jerusalem: "Your [1]birth
[a]and your nativity *are* from
the land of Cā'naan; [b]your father *was* an Am'o·rīte and your
mother a Hit'tīte.
4 "*As for* your nativity, [a]on the
day you were born your na-
vel cord was not cut, nor were
you washed in water to cleanse
you; you were not rubbed with
salt nor wrapped in swaddling
cloths.
5 "No eye pitied you, to do
any of these things for you, to
have compassion on you; but
you were thrown out into the
open field, when you yourself
were [1]loathed on the day you
were born.
6 "And when I passed by you
and saw you struggling in your
own blood, I said to you in your
blood, 'Live!' Yes, I said to you in
your blood, 'Live!'
7 [a]"I made you [1]thrive like a
plant in the field; and you grew,
matured, and became very beautiful. *Your* breasts were formed,
your hair grew, but you *were*
naked and bare.
8 "When I passed by you again
and looked upon you, indeed
your time *was* the time of love;
[a]so I spread [1]My wing over you
and covered your nakedness.
Yes, I [b]swore an oath to you and
entered into a [c]covenant with
you, and [d]you became Mine,"
says the Lord GOD.
9 "Then I washed you in water;
yes, I thoroughly washed off
your blood, and I anointed you
with oil.
10 "I clothed you in embroidered cloth and gave you sandals of [1]badger skin; I clothed
you with fine linen and covered
you with silk.
11 "I adorned you with ornaments, [a]put bracelets on your
wrists, [b]and a chain on your
neck.
12 "And I put a [1]jewel in your
nose, earrings in your ears, and
a beautiful crown on your head.
13 "Thus you were adorned with
gold and silver, and your clothing *was of* fine linen, silk, and
embroidered cloth. [a]You ate *pastry of* fine flour, honey, and oil.
You were exceedingly [b]beautiful,
and succeeded to royalty.
14 [a]"Your fame went out
among the nations because of
your beauty, for it *was* perfect
through My splendor which I

7 [a]Ezek. 14:8 [b]Is. 24:18 [c]Ezek. 7:4

CHAPTER 16

2 [a]Ezek. 20:4; 22:2

3 [a]Ezek. 21:30 [b]Ezek. 16:45 [1]*origin and your birth*

4 [a]Hos. 2:3

5 [1]*abhorred*

7 [a]Ex. 1:7 [1]Lit. *a myriad*

8 [a]Ruth 3:9 [b]Gen. 22:16–18 [c]Ex. 24:6–8 [d][Ex. 19:5] [1]Or *the corner of My garment*

10 [1]Or *dolphin* or *dugong*

11 [a]Gen. 24:22, 47 [b]Prov. 1:9

12 [1]Lit. *ring*

13 [a]Deut. 32:13, 14 [b]Ps. 48:2

14 [a]Lam. 2:15

had bestowed on you," says the
Lord GOD.
15 [a]"But you trusted in your
own beauty, [b]played the harlot because of your fame, and
poured out your harlotry on everyone passing by who *would*
have it.
16 [a]"You took some of your garments and adorned multicolored
[1]high places for yourself, and
played the harlot on them. *Such*
things should not happen, nor
be.
17 "You have also taken your
beautiful jewelry from My gold
and My silver, which I had given
you, and made for yourself male
images and played the harlot
with them.
18 "You took your embroidered
garments and covered them, and
you set My oil and My incense
before them.
19 "Also [a]My food which I gave
you—the pastry of fine flour, oil,
and honey *which* I fed you—you
set it before them as [1]sweet incense; and *so* it was," says the
Lord GOD.
20 [a]"Moreover you took your
sons and your daughters, whom
you bore to Me, and these you
sacrificed to them to be devoured. *Were* your *acts* of harlotry a small matter,
21 "that you have slain My children and offered them up to
them by causing them to pass
through *the* [a]*fire*?
22 "And in all your abominations and acts of harlotry you
did not remember the days of
your [a]youth, [b]when you were naked and bare, struggling in your
blood.
23 "Then it was so, after all your
wickedness—'Woe, woe to you!'
says the Lord GOD—
24 "*that* [a]you also built for
yourself a shrine, and [b]made a
[1]high place for yourself in every
street.
25 "You built your high places
[a]at the head of every road, and
made your beauty to be abhorred. You offered yourself to
everyone who passed by, and
multiplied your acts of harlotry.
26 "You also committed harlotry
with [a]the Egyptians, your very
fleshly neighbors, and increased
your acts of harlotry to [b]provoke
Me to anger.
27 "Behold, therefore, I stretched
out My hand against you, diminished your [1]allotment, and gave
you up to the will of those who
hate you, [a]the daughters of the
Phi·lis′tines, who were ashamed
of your lewd behavior.
28 "You also played the harlot with the [a]Assyrians, because
you were insatiable; indeed you
played the harlot with them and
still were not satisfied.
29 "Moreover you multiplied
your acts of harlotry as far as
the land of the trader, [a]Chal·dē′a;
and even then you were not
satisfied.
30 "How degenerate is your
heart!" says the Lord GOD, "seeing you do all these *things*, the
deeds of a brazen harlot.
31 [a]"You erected your shrine at
the head of every road, and built
your [1]high place in every street.
Yet you were not like a harlot,
because you scorned [b]payment.
32 "*You are* an adulterous wife,
who takes strangers instead of
her husband.
33 "Men make payment to all
harlots, but [a]you made your

15 [a]Mic. 3:11 [b]Is. 1:21; 57:8
16 [a]Ezek. 7:20 [1]Places for pagan worship
19 [a]Hos. 2:8 [1]Or *a sweet aroma*
20 [a]Jer. 7:31
21 [a]Jer. 19:5
22 [a]Jer. 2:2 [b]Ezek. 16:4–6
24 [a]Jer. 11:13 [b]Jer. 2:20; 3:2 [1]Place for pagan worship
25 [a]Prov. 9:14
26 [a]Ezek. 16:26; 20:7, 8 [b]Deut. 31:20
27 [a]Ezek. 16:57 [1]Allowance of food
28 [a]Jer. 2:18, 36
29 [a]Ezek. 23:14–17
31 [a]Ezek. 16:24, 39 [b]Is. 52:3 [1]Place for pagan worship
33 [a]Hos. 8:9, 10

payments to all your lovers, and
[1]hired them to come to you from
all around for your harlotry.
34 "You are the opposite of
other women in your harlotry,
because no one solicited you
to be a harlot. In that you gave
payment but no payment was
given you, therefore you are the
opposite."
35 'Now then, O harlot, hear the
word of the LORD!
36 'Thus says the Lord GOD:
"Because your filthiness was
poured out and your nakedness
uncovered in your harlotry with
your lovers, and with all your
abominable idols, and because
of [a]the blood of your children
which you gave to them,
37 "surely, therefore, [a]I will
gather all your lovers with
whom you took pleasure, all
those you loved, *and* all those
you hated; I will gather them
from all around against you and
will uncover your nakedness to
them, that they may see all your
nakedness.
38 "And I will judge you as
[a]women who break wedlock or
[b]shed blood are judged; I will
bring blood upon you in fury
and jealousy.
39 "I will also give you into their
hand, and they shall throw down
your shrines and break down
[a]your [1]high places. [b]They shall
also strip you of your clothes,
take your beautiful jewelry, and
leave you naked and bare.
40 [a]"They shall also bring up an
assembly against you, [b]and they
shall stone you with stones and
thrust you through with their
swords.
41 "They shall [a]burn your
houses with fire, and [b]execute
judgments on you in the sight of
many women; and I will make
you [c]cease playing the harlot,
and you shall no longer hire
lovers.
42 "So [a]I will lay to rest My fury
toward you, and My jealousy
shall depart from you. I will be
quiet, and be angry no more.
43 "Because [a]you did not remember the days of your youth,
but [1]agitated Me with all these
things, surely [b]I will also recompense your [2]deeds on *your
own* head," says the Lord GOD.
"And you shall not commit
lewdness in addition to all your
abominations.
44 "Indeed everyone who quotes
proverbs will use *this* proverb
against you: 'Like mother, like
daughter!'
45 "You *are* your mother's
daughter, [1]loathing husband and
children; and you *are* the [a]sister
of your sisters, who loathed their
husbands and children; [b]your
mother *was* a Hit′tīte and your
father an Am′o·rīte.
46 "Your elder sister *is* Samaria,
who dwells with her daughters
to the north of you; and [a]your
younger sister, who dwells to the
south of you, *is* Sod′om and her
daughters.
47 "You did not walk in their
ways nor act according to their
abominations; but, as *if that
were* too little, [a]you became
more corrupt than they in all
your ways.
48 "*As* I live," says the Lord GOD,
"neither [a]your sister Sod′om nor
her daughters have done as you
and your daughters have done.
49 "Look, this was the iniquity
of your sister Sod′om: She and
her daughter had pride, [a]fullness

33 [1]Or *bribed*
36 [a]Jer. 2:34
37 [a]Lam. 1:8
38 [a]Lev. 20:10 [b]Gen. 9:6
39 [a]Ezek. 16:24, 31 [b]Hos. 2:3 [1]Places for pagan worship
40 [a]Ezek. 23:45–47 [b]John 8:5, 7
41 [a]Deut. 13:16 [b]Ezek. 5:8; 23:10, 48 [c]Ezek. 23:27
42 [a]Ezek. 5:13; 21:17
43 [a]Ps. 78:42 [b]Ezek. 9:10; 11:21; 22:31 [1]So with LXX, Syr., Tg., Vg.; MT *were agitated with Me* [2]Lit. *way*
45 [a]Ezek. 23:2–4 [b]Ezek. 16:3 [1]Or *despising*
46 [a]Is. 1:10
47 [a]Ezek. 5:6, 7
48 [a]Matt. 10:15; 11:24
49 [a]Gen. 13:10

of food, and abundance of idleness; neither did she strengthen
the hand of the poor and needy.
50 "And they were haughty and
[a]committed abomination before
Me; therefore [b]I took them away
as [1]I saw *fit.*
51 "Samaria did not commit
[a]half of your sins; but you have
multiplied your abominations
more than they, and [b]have justified your sisters by all the abominations which you have done.
52 "You who judged your sisters, bear your own shame also,
because the sins which you
committed were more abominable than theirs; they are more
righteous than you. Yes, be disgraced also, and bear your own
shame, because you justified
your sisters.
53 [a]"When I bring back their
captives, the captives of Sod'om
and her daughters, and the captives of Samaria and her daughters, then *I will also bring back*
[b]the captives of your captivity
among them,
54 "that you may bear your own
shame and be disgraced by all
that you did when [a]you comforted them.
55 "When your sisters, Sod'om
and her daughters, return to
their former state, and Samaria
and her daughters return to
their former state, then you and
your daughters will return to
your former state.
56 "For your sister Sod'om was
not a byword in your mouth in
the days of your pride,
57 "before your wickedness was
uncovered. It was like the time of
the [a]reproach of the daughters
of [1]Syria and all *those* around
her, and of [b]the daughters of the
Phi·lis'tines, who despise you
everywhere.
58 [a]"You have paid for your
lewdness and your abominations," says the LORD.
59 'For thus says the Lord GOD:
"I will deal with you as you have
done, who [a]despised [b]the oath
by breaking the covenant.
60 "Nevertheless I will [a]remem-
ber My covenant with you in the
days of your youth, and I will establish [b]an everlasting covenant
with you.
61 "Then [a]you will remember
your ways and be ashamed,
when you receive your older and
your younger sisters; for I will
give them to you for [b]daughters,
[c]but not because of My covenant
with you.
62 [a]"And I will establish My
covenant with you. Then you
shall know that I *am* the LORD,
63 "that you may [a]remember
and be ashamed, [b]and never
open your mouth anymore because of your shame, when I
provide you an atonement for all
you have done," says the Lord
GOD.' "

17 And the word of the LORD
came to me, saying,
2 "Son of man, pose a riddle, and speak a [a]parable to the
house of Israel,
3 "and say, 'Thus says the Lord
GOD:

[a]"A great eagle with large
wings and long pinions,
Full of feathers of various
colors,
Came to Lebanon
And [b]took from the cedar
the highest branch.
4 He cropped off its topmost
young twig

50 [a]Gen. 13:13; 18:20; 19:5 [b]Gen. 19:24 [1]Vg. *you saw;* LXX *he saw;* Tg. *as was revealed to Me*
51 [a]Ezek. 23:11 [b]Jer. 3:8–11
53 [a]Is. 1:9 [b]Jer. 20:16
54 [a]Ezek. 14:22
57 [a]2 Kin. 16:5 [b]Ezek. 16:27 [1]Heb. *Aram;* so with MT, LXX, Tg., Vg.; many Heb. mss., Syr. *Edom*
58 [a]Ezek. 23:49
59 [a]Ezek. 17:13 [b]Deut. 29:12
60 [a]Ps. 106:45 [b]Is. 55:3
61 [a]Ezek. 20:43; 36:31 [b][Gal. 4:26] [c]Jer. 31:31
62 [a]Hos. 2:19, 20
63 [a]Ezek. 36:31, 32 [b][Rom. 3:19]

CHAPTER 17

2 [a]Ezek. 20:49; 24:3
3 [a]Ezek. 17:12 [b]2 Kin. 24:12

And carried it to a land of trade;
He set it in a city of merchants.
5 Then he took some of the seed of the land
And planted it in [a]a fertile field;
He placed *it* by abundant waters
And set it [b]like a willow tree.
6 And it grew and became a spreading vine [a]of low stature;
Its branches turned toward him,
But its roots were under it.
So it became a vine,
Brought forth branches,
And put forth shoots.

7 "But there was [1]another great eagle with large wings and many feathers;
And behold, [a]this vine bent its roots toward him,
And stretched its branches toward him,
From the garden terrace where it had been planted,
That he might water it.
8 It was planted in [1]good soil by many waters,
To bring forth branches, bear fruit,
And become a majestic vine." '

9 "Say, 'Thus says the Lord GOD:

"Will it thrive?
[a]Will he not pull up its roots,
Cut off its fruit,
And leave it to wither?
All of its spring leaves will wither,
And no great power or many people
Will be needed to pluck it up by its roots.
10 Behold, *it is* planted,
Will it thrive?
[a]Will it not utterly wither when the east wind touches it?
It will wither in the garden terrace where it grew." ' "

11 Moreover the word of the
LORD came to me, saying,
12 "Say now to [a]the rebellious
house: 'Do you not know what
these *things mean?*' Tell *them,*
'Indeed [b]the king of Babylon
went to Jerusalem and took its
king and princes, and led them
with him to Babylon.
13 [a]'And he took the king's offspring, made a covenant with
him, [b]and put him under oath.
He also took away the mighty of
the land,
14 'that the kingdom might be
[a]brought low and not lift itself
up, *but* that by keeping his covenant it might stand.
15 'But [a]he rebelled against him
by sending his ambassadors
to Egypt, [b]that they might give
him horses and many people.
[c]Will he prosper? Will he who
does such *things* escape? Can
he break a covenant and still be
delivered?
16 '*As* I live,' says the Lord GOD,
'surely [a]in the place *where* the
king *dwells* who made him king,
whose oath he despised and
whose covenant he broke—with
him in the midst of Babylon he
shall die.
17 [a]'Nor will Pharaoh with *his*

5 [a]Deut. 8:7–9 [b]Is. 44:4
6 [a]Ezek. 17:14
7 [a]Ezek. 17:15 [1]So with LXX, Syr., Vg.; MT, Tg. *one*
8 [1]Lit. *a good field*
9 [a]2 Kin. 25:7
10 [a]Hos. 13:15
12 [a]Ezek. 2:3–5; 12:9 [b]2 Kin. 24:11–16
13 [a]2 Kin. 24:17 [b]2 Chr. 36:13
14 [a]Ezek. 29:14
15 [a]2 Kin. 24:20 [b]Deut. 17:16 [c]Ezek. 17:9
16 [a]Ezek. 12:13
17 [a]Jer. 37:7

mighty army and great company
do anything in the war, [b]when
they heap up a siege mound and
build a [1]wall to cut off many
persons.
18 'Since he despised the oath
by breaking the covenant, and
in fact [a]gave[1] his hand and still
did all these *things*, he shall not
escape.' "
19 Therefore thus says the Lord
GOD: "*As* I live, surely My oath
which he despised, and My covenant which he broke, I will
recompense on his own head.
20 "I will [a]spread My net over
him, and he shall be taken in My
snare. I will bring him to Babylon and [b]try him there for the
[1]treason which he committed
against Me.
21 [a]"All his [1]fugitives with all his
troops shall fall by the sword,
and those who remain shall be
[b]scattered to every wind; and
you shall know that I, the LORD,
have spoken."
22 Thus says the Lord GOD: "I
will take also *one* of the highest
[a]branches of the high cedar and
set *it* out. I will crop off from the
topmost of its young twigs [b]a
tender one, and will [c]plant *it* on a
high and prominent mountain.
23 [a]"On the mountain height of
Israel I will plant it; and it will
bring forth boughs, and bear
fruit, and be a majestic cedar.
[b]Under it will dwell birds of
every sort; in the shadow of its
branches they will dwell.
24 "And all the trees of the field
shall know that I, the LORD, [a]have
brought down the high tree and
exalted the low tree, dried up
the green tree and made the dry
tree flourish; [b]I, the LORD, have
spoken and have done *it*."

17 [b]Jer. 52:4
[1]Or *siege wall*

18 [a]1 Chr. 29:24
[1]Took an oath

20 [a]Ezek. 12:13
[b]Ezek. 20:36
[1]Lit. *unfaithful act*

21 [a]Ezek. 12:14
[b]Ezek. 12:15; 22:15
[1]So with MT, Vg.; many Heb. mss., Syr. *choice men;* Tg. *mighty men;* LXX omits *All his fugitives*

22 [a][Zech. 3:8]
[b]Is. 53:2
[c][Ps. 2:6]

23 [a][Is. 2:2, 3]
[b]Dan. 4:12

24 [a]Amos 9:11
[b]Ezek. 22:14

CHAPTER 18

2 [a]Lam. 5:7

4 [a]Num. 16:22; 27:16
[b][Rom. 6:23]

6 [a]Ezek. 22:9
[b]Lev. 18:20; 20:10
[c]Lev. 18:19; 20:18
[1]At the mountain shrines

7 [a]Ex. 22:21
[b]Deut. 24:12
[c]Deut. 15:7, 11
[d]Is. 58:7

8 [a]Ex. 22:25
[1]Lent money at interest

18

The word of the LORD
came to me again, say-
ing,
2 "What do you mean when
you use this proverb concerning
the land of Israel, saying:

'The [a]fathers have eaten sour
grapes,
And the children's teeth are
set on edge'?

3 "*As* I live," says the Lord GOD,
"you shall no longer use this
proverb in Israel.

4 "Behold, all souls are [a]Mine;
The soul of the father
As well as the soul of the
son is Mine;
[b]The soul who sins shall die.
5 But if a man is just
And does what is lawful and
right;
6 [a]If he has not eaten [1]on the
mountains,
Nor lifted up his eyes to
the idols of the house of
Israel,
Nor [b]defiled his neighbor's
wife,
Nor approached [c]a woman
during her impurity;
7 If he has not [a]oppressed
anyone,
But has restored to the
debtor his [b]pledge;
Has robbed no one by
violence,
But has [c]given his bread to
the hungry
And covered the naked with
[d]clothing;
8 If he has not [1]exacted [a]usury
Nor taken any increase,
But has withdrawn his hand
from iniquity

And [b]executed true
[2]judgment between man
and man;
9 *If* he has walked in My
statutes
And kept My judgments
faithfully—
He *is* just;
He shall surely [a]live!"
Says the Lord GOD.

10"If he begets a son *who is* a
robber
Or [a]a shedder of blood,
Who does any of these
things
11 And does none of those
duties,
But has eaten [1]on the
mountains
Or defiled his neighbor's
wife;
12 If he has oppressed the poor
and needy,
Robbed by violence,
Not restored the pledge,
Lifted his eyes to the idols,
Or [a]committed abomination;
13 If he has exacted usury
Or taken increase—
Shall he then live?
He shall not live!
If he has done any of these
abominations,
He shall surely die;
[a]His blood shall be upon him.

14"*If,* however, he begets a son
Who sees all the sins which
his father has done,
And considers but does not
do likewise;
15 [a]*Who* has not eaten [1]on the
mountains,
Nor lifted his eyes to the
idols of the house of
Israel,

8 [b]Zech. 8:16
[2]*justice*
9 [a]Amos 5:4
10 [a]Num. 35:31
11 [1]At the mountain shrines
12 [a]Ezek. 8:6, 17
13 [a]Lev. 20:9, 11–13, 16, 27
15 [a]Ezek. 18:6
[1]At the mountain shrines
17 [1]So with MT, Tg., Vg.; LXX *iniquity* (cf. v. 8)
18 [a]Ezek. 3:18
19 [a]Ex. 20:5
20 [a]Ezek. 18:4
[b]Deut. 24:16
[c]Is. 3:10, 11
[d]Rom. 2:6–9
21 [a]Ezek. 18:27; 33:12, 19

Nor defiled his neighbor's
wife;
16 Has not oppressed anyone,
Nor withheld a pledge,
Nor robbed by violence,
But has given his bread to
the hungry
And covered the naked with
clothing;
17 *Who* has withdrawn his
hand from [1]the poor
And not received usury or
increase,
But has executed My
judgments
And walked in My
statutes—
He shall not die for the
iniquity of his father;
He shall surely live!

18"*As for* his father,
Because he cruelly
oppressed,
Robbed his brother by
violence,
And did what *is* not good
among his people,
Behold, [a]he shall die for his
iniquity.

19 "Yet you say, 'Why [a]should
the son not bear the guilt of the
father?' Because the son has
done what is lawful and right,
and has kept all My statutes and
observed them, he shall surely
live.
20 [a]"The soul who sins shall
die. [b]The son shall not bear the
guilt of the father, nor the father
bear the guilt of the son. [c]The
righteousness of the righteous
shall be upon himself, [d]and the
wickedness of the wicked shall
be upon himself.
21 "But [a]if a wicked man turns
from all his sins which he has

committed, keeps all My statutes, and does what is lawful
and right, he shall surely live; he
shall not die.
22 [a]"None of the transgressions
which he has committed shall
be remembered against him; because of the righteousness which
he has done, he shall [b]live.
23 [a]"Do I have any pleasure at
all that the wicked should die?"
says the Lord GOD, "*and* not that
he should turn from his ways
and live?
24 "But [a]when a righteous man
turns away from his righteousness and commits iniquity, and
does according to all the abominations that the wicked *man*
does, shall he live? [b]All the righteousness which he has done
shall not be remembered; because of the unfaithfulness of
which he is guilty and the sin
which he has committed, because of them he shall die.
25 "Yet you say, [a]'The way of
the Lord is not fair.' Hear now,
O house of Israel, is it not My
way which is fair, and your ways
which are not fair?
26 [a]"When a righteous *man*
turns away from his righteousness, commits iniquity, and dies
in it, it is because of the iniquity
which he has done that he dies.
27 "Again, [a]when a wicked *man*
turns away from the wickedness
which he committed, and does
what is lawful and right, he preserves himself alive.
28 "Because he [a]considers and
turns away from all the transgressions which he committed,
he shall surely live; he shall not
die.
29 [a]"Yet the house of Israel says,
'The way of the Lord is not fair.'

22 [a]Ezek. 18:24; 33:16 [b][Ps. 18:20–24]
23 [a][Ezek. 18:32; 33:11]
24 [a]Ezek. 3:20; 18:26; 33:18 [b][2 Pet. 2:20]
25 [a]Ezek. 18:29; 33:17, 20
26 [a]Ezek. 18:24
27 [a]Ezek. 18:21
28 [a]Ezek. 18:14
29 [a]Ezek. 18:25
30 [a]Ezek. 7:3; 33:20 [b]Matt. 3:2
31 [a]Eph. 4:22, 23 [b]Jer. 32:39
32 [a]Lam. 3:33 [b][Prov. 4:2, 5, 6]

CHAPTER 19

1 [a]Ezek. 26:17; 27:2
3 [a]2 Kin. 23:31, 32
4 [a]2 Kin. 23:33, 34

O house of Israel, is it not My
ways which are fair, and your
ways which are not fair?
30 [a]"Therefore I will judge you,
O house of Israel, every one according to his ways," says the
Lord GOD. [b]"Repent, and turn
from all your transgressions, so
that iniquity will not be your
ruin.
31 [a]"Cast away from you all the
transgressions which you have
committed, and get yourselves a
[b]new heart and a new spirit. For
why should you die, O house of
Israel?
32 "For [a]I have no pleasure in
the death of one who dies," says
the Lord GOD. "Therefore turn
and [b]live!"

19

"Moreover [a]take up a lamentation for the princes
of Israel,
2 "and say:

'What *is* your mother?
A lioness:
She lay down among the
lions;
Among the young lions she
nourished her cubs.
3 She brought up one of her
cubs,
And [a]he became a young
lion;
He learned to catch prey,
And he devoured men.
4 The nations also heard of
him;
He was trapped in their pit,
And they brought him with
chains to the land of
[a]Egypt.

5 'When she saw that she
waited, *that* her hope
was lost,

She took [a]another of her
cubs *and* made him a
young lion.
6 [a]He roved among the lions,
And [b]became a young lion;
He learned to catch prey;
He devoured men.
7 [1]He knew their desolate
places,
And laid waste their cities;
The land with its fullness
was desolated
By the noise of his roaring.
8 [a]Then the nations set against
him from the provinces
on every side,
And spread their net over
him;
[b]He was trapped in their pit.
9 [a]They put him in a cage with
[1]chains,
And brought him to the king
of Babylon;
They brought him in nets,
That his voice should no
longer be heard on [b]the
mountains of Israel.

10 'Your mother *was* [a]like a
vine in your [1]bloodline,
Planted by the waters,
[b]Fruitful and full of branches
Because of many waters.
11 She had strong branches for
scepters of rulers.
[a]She towered in stature above
the thick branches,
And was seen in her height
amid the [1]dense foliage.
12 But she was [a]plucked up in
fury,
She was cast down to the
ground,
And the [b]east wind dried
her fruit.
Her strong branches were
broken and withered;
The fire consumed them.
13 And now she *is* planted in
the wilderness,
In a dry and thirsty land.
14 [a]Fire has come out from a
rod of her branches
And devoured her fruit,
So that she has no strong
branch—a scepter for
ruling.' "

[b]This *is* a lamentation, and
has become a lamentation.

20 It came to pass in the
seventh year, in the fifth
month, on the tenth *day* of the
month, *that* [a]certain of the elders of Israel came to inquire of
the LORD, and sat before me.
2 Then the word of the LORD
came to me, saying,
3 "Son of man, speak to the
elders of Israel, and say to them,
'Thus says the Lord GOD: "Have
you come to inquire of Me? *As* I
live," says the Lord GOD, [a]"I will
not be inquired of by you." '
4 "Will you judge them, son
of man, will you judge *them?*
Then [a]make known to them the
abominations of their fathers.
5 "Say to them, 'Thus says the
Lord GOD: "On the day when [a]I
chose Israel and raised My hand
in an oath to the descendants of
the house of Jacob, and made
Myself [b]known to them in the
land of Egypt, I raised My hand
in an oath to them, saying, [c]'I *am*
the LORD your God.'
6 "On that day I raised My
hand in an oath to them, [a]to
bring them out of the land of
Egypt into a land that I had
searched out for them, [b]'flowing
with milk and honey,' [c]the glory
of all lands.
7 "Then I said to them, 'Each
of you, [a]throw away [b]the

---

5 [a]2 Kin. 23:34
6 [a]2 Kin. 24:8, 9 [b]Ezek. 19:3
7 [1]LXX *He stood in insolence;* Tg. *He destroyed its palaces;* Vg. *He learned to make widows*
8 [a]2 Kin. 24:2, 11 [b]Ezek. 19:4
9 [a]2 Chr. 36:6 [b]Ezek. 6:2 [1]Or *hooks*
10 [a]Ezek. 17:6 [b]Deut. 8:7–9 [1]Lit. *blood,* so with MT, Syr., Vg.; LXX *like a flower on a pomegranate tree;* Tg. *in your likeness*
11 [a]Dan. 4:11 [1]Or *many branches*
12 [a]Jer. 31:27, 28 [b]Hos. 13:5
14 [a]Judg. 9:15 [b]Lam. 2:5

CHAPTER 20

1 [a]Ezek. 8:1, 11, 12; 14:1
3 [a]Ezek. 7:26; 14:3
4 [a]Ezek. 16:2; 22:2
5 [a]Ex. 6:6–8 [b]Deut. 4:34 [c]Ex. 20:2
6 [a]Jer. 32:22 [b]Ex. 3:8 [c]Jer. 11:5; 32:22
7 [a]Ezek. 18:31 [b]2 Chr. 15:8

abominations which are before
his eyes, and do not defile yourselves with [c]the idols of Egypt. I
am the LORD your God.'
8 "But they rebelled against
Me and would not [1]obey Me.
They did not all cast away the
abominations which were before their eyes, nor did they
forsake the idols of Egypt. Then
I said, 'I will [a]pour out My fury
on them and fulfill My anger
against them in the midst of the
land of Egypt.'
9 [a]"But I acted for My name's
sake, that it should not be profaned before the Gentiles among
whom they *were*, in whose sight
I had made Myself [b]known to
them, to bring them out of the
land of Egypt.
10 "Therefore I [a]made them go
out of the land of Egypt and
brought them into the wilderness.
11 [a]"And I gave them My statutes and [1]showed them My judgments, [b]'which, *if* a man does, he
shall live by them.'
12 "Moreover I also gave them
My [a]Sabbaths, to be a sign between them and Me, that they
might know that I *am* the LORD
who sanctifies them.
13 "Yet the house of Israel
[a]rebelled against Me in the wilderness; they did not walk in My
statutes; they [b]despised My judgments, [c]'which, *if* a man does, he
shall live by them'; and they
greatly [d]defiled My Sabbaths.
Then I said I would pour out My
fury on them in the [e]wilderness,
to consume them.
14 [a]"But I acted for My name's
sake, that it should not be profaned before the Gentiles, in
whose sight I had brought them
out.
15 "So [a]I also raised My hand
in an oath to them in the wilderness, that I would not bring them
into the land which I had given
them, [b]'flowing with milk and
honey,' [c]the glory of all lands,
16 [a]'because they despised My
judgments and did not walk in
My statutes, but profaned My
Sabbaths; for [b]their heart went
after their idols.
17 [a]"Nevertheless My eye
spared them from destruction. I
did not make an end of them in
the wilderness.
18 "But I said to their children
in the wilderness, 'Do not walk
in the statutes of your fathers,
nor observe their judgments,
nor defile yourselves with their
idols.
19 'I *am* the LORD your God:
[a]Walk in My statutes, keep My
judgments, and do them;
20 [a]'hallow My Sabbaths, and
they will be a sign between Me
and you, that you may know
that I *am* the LORD your God.'
21 "Notwithstanding, [a]the children rebelled against Me; they
did not walk in My statutes,
and were not careful to observe
My judgments, [b]'which, *if* a man
does, he shall live by them';
but they profaned My Sabbaths.
Then I said I would pour out My
fury on them and fulfill My anger
against them in the wilderness.
22 "Nevertheless I [1]withdrew
My hand and acted for My
name's sake, that it should not
be profaned in the sight of the
Gentiles, in whose sight I had
brought them out.
23 "Also I raised My hand in an
oath to those in the wilderness,

7 [c]Lev. 18:3
8 [a]Ezek. 7:8 [1]Lit. *listen to*
9 [a]Num. 14:13 [b]Josh. 2:10; 9:9, 10
10 [a]Ex. 13:18
11 [a]Neh. 9:13 [b]Lev. 18:5 [1]Lit. *made known to*
12 [a]Deut. 5:12
13 [a]Num. 14:22 [b]Prov. 1:25 [c]Lev. 18:5 [d]Ex. 16:27 [e]Num. 14:29
14 [a]Ezek. 20:9, 20
15 [a]Num. 14:28 [b]Ex. 3:8 [c]Ezek. 20:6
16 [a]Ezek. 20:13, 24 [b]Amos 5:25
17 [a][Ps. 78:38]
19 [a]Deut. 5:32
20 [a]Jer. 17:22
21 [a]Num. 25:1 [b]Lev. 18:5
22 [1]Refrained from judgment

that [a]I would scatter them among
the Gentiles and disperse them
throughout the countries,
24 [a]"because they had not executed My judgments, but had
despised My statutes, profaned
My Sabbaths, and [b]their eyes
were fixed on their fathers'
idols.
25 "Therefore [a]I also gave them
up to statutes *that were* not
good, and judgments by which
they could not live;
26 "and I pronounced them
unclean because of their ritual
gifts, in that they caused all
[1]their firstborn to pass [a]through
the fire, that I might make them
desolate and that they [b]might
know that I am the LORD." '
27 "Therefore, son of man,
speak to the house of Israel, and
say to them, 'Thus says the Lord
GOD: "In this too your fathers
have [a]blasphemed Me, by being
unfaithful to Me.
28 "When I brought them into
the land *concerning* which I had
raised My hand in an oath to give
them, and [a]they saw all the high
hills and all the thick trees, there
they offered their sacrifices and
provoked Me with their offerings. There they also sent up
their [b]sweet aroma and poured
out their drink offerings.
29 "Then I said to them, 'What
is this [1]high place to which you
go?' So its name is called [2]Bā'-
mah to this day." '
30 "Therefore say to the house of
Israel, 'Thus says the Lord GOD:
"Are you defiling yourselves in
the manner of your [a]fathers, and
committing harlotry according
to their [b]abominations?
31 "For when you offer [a]your
gifts and make your sons pass
through the fire, you defile yourselves with all your idols, even
to this day. So shall I be inquired
of by you, O house of Israel? *As*
I live," says the Lord GOD, "I will
[b]not be inquired of by you.
32 [a]"What you have in your
mind shall never be, when you
say, 'We will be like the Gentiles,
like the families in other countries, serving wood and stone.'
33 "*As* I live," says the Lord
GOD, "surely with a mighty hand,
[a]with an outstretched arm, and
with fury poured out, I will rule
over you.
34 "I will bring you out from
the peoples and gather you out
of the countries where you are
scattered, with a mighty hand,
with an outstretched arm, and
with fury poured out.
35 "And I will bring you into the
wilderness of the peoples, and
there [a]I will plead My case with
you face to face.
36 [a]"Just as I pleaded My case
with your fathers in the wilderness of the land of Egypt, so I
will plead My case with you,"
says the Lord GOD.
37 "I will make you [a]pass under
the rod, and I will bring you into
the bond of the [b]covenant;
38 [a]"I will purge the rebels
from among you, and those who
transgress against Me; I will
bring them out of the country
where they dwell, but [b]they shall
not enter the land of Israel. Then
you will know that I *am* the
LORD.
39 "As for you, O house of Israel," thus says the Lord GOD:
[a]"Go, serve every one of you his
idols—and hereafter—if you will
not obey Me; [b]but profane My

23 [a]Lev. 26:33
24 [a]Ezek. 20:13, 16 [b]Ezek. 6:9
25 [a]Rom. 1:24
26 [a]Jer. 32:35 [b]Ezek. 6:7; 20:12, 20 [1]Lit. *that open the womb*
27 [a]Rom. 2:24
28 [a]Ezek. 6:13 [b]Ezek. 16:19
29 [1]Place for pagan worship [2]Lit. *High Place*
30 [a]Judg. 2:19 [b]Jer. 7:26; 16:12
31 [a]Ezek. 16:20; 20:26 [b]Ezek. 20:3
32 [a]Ezek. 11:5
33 [a]Jer. 21:5
35 [a]Jer. 2:9, 35; Ezek. 17:20
36 [a]Num. 14:21–23, 28
37 [a]Lev. 27:32 [b]Ps. 89:30–34
38 [a]Ezek. 34:17 [b]Jer. 44:14
39 [a]Amos 4:4 [b]Is. 1:13–15

holy name no more with your gifts and your idols.

40 "For [a]on My holy mountain, on the mountain height of Israel," says the Lord GOD, "there [b]all the house of Israel, all of them in the land, shall serve Me; there [c]I will accept them, and there I will require your offerings and the firstfruits of your [1]sacrifices, together with all your holy things.

41 "I will accept you as a [a]sweet aroma when I bring you out from the peoples and gather you out of the countries where you have been scattered; and I will be hallowed in you before the Gentiles.

42 [a]"Then you shall know that I *am* the LORD, [b]when I bring you into the land of Israel, into the country *for* which I raised My hand in an oath to give to your fathers.

43 "And [a]there you shall remember your ways and all your doings with which you were defiled; and [b]you shall [1]loathe yourselves in your own sight because of all the evils that you have committed.

44 [a]"Then you shall know that I *am* the LORD, when I have dealt with you [b]for My name's sake, not according to your wicked ways nor according to your corrupt doings, O house of Israel," says the Lord GOD.' "

45 Furthermore the word of the LORD came to me, saying,

46 [a]"Son of man, set your face toward the south; [1]preach against the south and prophesy against the forest land, the [2]South,

47 "and say to the forest of the South, 'Hear the word of the LORD! Thus says the Lord GOD: "Behold, [a]I will kindle a fire in you, and it shall devour [b]every green tree and every dry tree in you; the blazing flame shall not be quenched, and all faces [c]from the south to the north shall be scorched by it.

48 "All flesh shall see that I, the LORD, have kindled it; it shall not be quenched." ' "

49 Then I said, "Ah, Lord GOD! They say of me, 'Does he not speak [a]parables?' "

21 And the word of the LORD came to me, saying,

2 [a]"Son of man, set your face toward Jerusalem, [b]preach[1] against the holy places, and prophesy against the land of Israel;

3 "and say to the land of Israel, 'Thus says the LORD: "Behold, I *am* [a]against you, and I will draw My sword out of its sheath and cut off both [b]righteous and wicked from you.

4 "Because I will cut off both righteous and wicked from you, therefore My sword shall go out of its sheath against all flesh [a]from south *to* north,

5 "that all flesh may know that I, the LORD, have drawn My sword out of its sheath; it [a]shall not return anymore." '

6 [a]"Sigh therefore, son of man, with [1]a breaking heart, and sigh with bitterness before their eyes.

7 "And it shall be when they say to you, 'Why are you sighing?' that you shall answer, 'Because of the news; when it comes, every heart will melt, [a]all hands will be feeble, every spirit will faint, and all knees will be weak *as* water. Behold, it is

40 [a]Is. 2:2, 3 [b]Ezek. 37:22 [c]Zech. 8:20–22 [1]*offerings*
41 [a]Phil. 4:18
42 [a]Ezek. 36:23; 38:23 [b]Ezek. 11:17; 34:13; 36:24
43 [a]Ezek. 16:61 [b]Lev. 26:39 [1]Or *despise*
44 [a]Ezek. 24:24 [b]Ezek. 36:22
46 [a]Ezek. 21:2 [1]*proclaim*, lit. *drop* [2]Heb. *Negev*
47 [a]Jer. 21:14 [b]Luke 23:31 [c]Ezek. 21:4
49 [a]Ezek. 12:9; 17:2

CHAPTER 21

2 [a]Ezek. 20:46 [b]Amos 7:16 [1]*proclaim*, lit. *drop*
3 [a]Ezek. 5:8 [b]Job 9:22
4 [a]Ezek. 20:47
5 [a][Is. 45:23; 55:11]
6 [a]Is. 22:4 [1]Emotional distress, lit. *the breaking of your loins*
7 [a]Ezek. 7:17

coming and shall be brought to pass,' says the Lord GOD."

8 Again the word of the LORD came to me, saying,

9 "Son of man, prophesy and say, 'Thus says the LORD!' Say:

[a]'A sword, a sword is
sharpened
And also polished!
10 Sharpened to make a
dreadful slaughter,
Polished to flash like
lightning!
Should we then make
mirth?
It despises the scepter of My
son,
As it does all wood.
11 And He has given it to be
polished,
That it may be handled;
This sword is sharpened,
and it is polished
To be given into the hand of
[a]the slayer.'

12 "Cry and wail, son of man;
For it will be against My
people,
Against all the princes of
Israel.
Terrors including the sword
will be against My
people;
Therefore [a]strike *your* thigh.

13 "Because *it is* [a]a testing,
And what if *the sword*
despises even the
scepter?
[b]*The scepter* shall be no
more,"

says the Lord GOD.

14 "You therefore, son of man,
prophesy,
And [a]strike *your* hands
together.
The third time let the sword
do double *damage*.
It *is* the sword *that* slays,
The sword that slays the
great *men*,
That enters their [b]private
chambers.
15 I have set the point of the
sword against all their
gates,
That the heart may melt and
many may stumble.
Ah! [a]*It is* made bright;
It is grasped for slaughter:

16 "Swords[a1] at the ready!
Thrust right!
Set your blade!
Thrust left—
Wherever your [2]edge is
ordered!

17 "I also will [a]beat My fists
together,
And [b]I will cause My fury to
rest;
I, the LORD, have spoken."

18 The word of the LORD came
to me again, saying:
19 "And son of man, appoint for
yourself two ways for the sword
of the king of Babylon to go;
both of them shall go from the
same land. Make a sign; put *it* at
the head of the road to the city.
20 "Appoint a road for the
sword to go to [a]Rab′bah of the
Am′mon·ītes, and to Judah, into
fortified Jerusalem.
21 "For the king of Babylon
stands at the parting of the road,
at the fork of the two roads, to
use divination: he shakes the
arrows, he consults the [1]images,
he looks at the liver.

9 [a]Deut. 32:41
11 [a]Ezek. 21:19
12 [a]Jer. 31:19
13 [a]Job 9:23 [b]Ezek. 21:27
14 [a]Num. 24:10 [b]1 Kin. 20:30
15 [a]Ezek. 21:10, 28
16 [a]Ezek. 14:17 [1]Lit. *Sharpen yourself!* or *Unite yourself!* [2]Lit. *face*
17 [a]Ezek. 22:13 [b]Ezek. 5:13; 16:42; 24:13
20 [a]Jer. 49:2
21 [1]Heb. *teraphim*

22 “In his right hand is the
divination for Jerusalem: to set
up battering rams, to call for a
slaughter, to [a]lift the voice with
shouting, [b]to set battering rams
against the gates, to heap up a
siege mound, and to build a wall.
23 “And it will be to them like
a false divination in the eyes of
those who [a]have sworn oaths
with them; but he will bring
their iniquity to remembrance,
that they may be taken.
24 “Therefore thus says the Lord
GOD: ‘Because you have made
your iniquity to be remembered,
in that your transgressions are
uncovered, so that in all your doings your sins appear—because
you have come to remembrance,
you shall be taken in hand.
25 ‘Now to you, O [a]profane,
wicked prince of Israel, [b]whose
day has come, whose iniquity
shall end,
26 ‘thus says the Lord GOD:

“Remove the turban, and
take off the crown;
Nothing *shall remain* the
same.
[a]Exalt the humble, and
humble the exalted.
27 [1]Overthrown, overthrown,
I will make it overthrown!
[a]It shall be no *longer,*
Until He comes whose right
it is,
And I will give it *to* [b]*Him.*” ’

28 “And you, son of man, prophesy and say, ‘Thus says the
Lord GOD [a]concerning the Am′-
mon·ītes and concerning their
reproach,’ and say:

‘A sword, a sword *is* drawn,
Polished for slaughter,
For consuming, for
flashing—
29 While they [a]see false visions
for you,
While they divine a lie to
you,
To bring you on the necks of
the wicked, the slain
[b]Whose day has come,
Whose iniquity *shall* end.

30 ‘Return[a] *it* to its sheath.
[b]I will judge you
In the place where you were
created,
[c]In the land of your [1]nativity.
31 I will [a]pour out My
indignation on you;
I will [b]blow against you with
the fire of My wrath,
And deliver you into the
hands of brutal men *who
are* skillful to [c]destroy.
32 You shall be fuel for the fire;
Your blood shall be in the
midst of the land.
[a]You shall not be remembered,
For I the LORD have
spoken.’ ”

22

Moreover the word of the
LORD came to me, saying,
2 “Now, son of man, [a]will
you judge, will you judge [b]the
bloody city? Yes, show her all
her abominations!
3 “Then say, ‘Thus says the
Lord GOD: “The city sheds
[a]blood in her own midst, that
her time may come; and she
makes idols within herself to
defile herself.
4 “You have become guilty by
the blood which you have [a]shed,
and have defiled yourself with
the idols which you have made.
You have caused your days to
draw near, and have come to

22 [a]Jer. 51:14 [b]Ezek. 4:2
23 [a]Ezek. 17:16, 18
25 [a]Jer. 52:2 [b]Ezek. 21:29
26 [a]Luke 1:52
27 [a][Luke 1:32, 33] [b][Jer. 23:5, 6] [1]Or *Distortion, Ruin*
28 [a]Ezek. 25:1–7
29 [a]Ezek. 12:24; 13:6–9; 22:28 [b]Job 18:20
30 [a]Jer. 47:6, 7 [b]Gen. 15:14 [c]Ezek. 16:3 [1]Or *origin*
31 [a]Ezek. 7:8 [b]Ezek. 22:20, 21 [c]Hab. 1:6–10
32 [a]Ezek. 25:10

CHAPTER 22

2 [a]Ezek. 20:4 [b]Nah. 3:1
3 [a]Ezek. 24:6, 7
4 [a]2 Kin. 21:16

the end of your years; [b]therefore I have made you a reproach to the nations, and a mockery to all countries.

5 "*Those* near and *those* far from you will mock you as [1]infamous *and* full of tumult.

6 "Look, [a]the princes of Israel: each one has used his [1]power to shed blood in you.

7 "In you they have [a]made light of father and mother; in your midst they have [b]oppressed the stranger; in you they have mistreated the [1]fatherless and the widow.

8 "You have despised My holy things and [a]profaned My Sabbaths.

9 "In you are [a]men who slander to cause bloodshed; [b]in you are those who eat on the mountains; in your midst they commit lewdness.

10 "In you men [a]uncover their fathers' nakedness; in you they violate women who are [b]set apart during their impurity.

11 "One commits abomination [a]with his neighbor's wife; [b]another lewdly defiles his daughter-in-law; and another in you violates his sister, his father's [c]daughter.

12 "In you [a]they take bribes to shed blood; [b]you take usury and increase; you have made profit from your neighbors by extortion, and [c]have forgotten Me," says the Lord GOD.

13 "Behold, therefore, I [a]beat My fists at the dishonest profit which you have made, and at the bloodshed which has been in your midst.

14 [a]"Can your heart endure, or can your hands remain strong, in the days when I shall deal with you? [b]I, the LORD, have spoken, and will do *it*.

15 [a]"I will scatter you among the nations, disperse you throughout the countries, and [b]remove your filthiness completely from you.

16 "You shall defile yourself in the sight of the nations; then [a]you shall know that I *am* the LORD." ' "

17 The word of the LORD came to me, saying,

18 "Son of man, [a]the house of Israel has become dross to Me; they *are* all bronze, tin, iron, and lead, in the midst of a [b]furnace; they have become dross from silver.

19 "Therefore thus says the Lord GOD: 'Because you have all become dross, therefore behold, I will gather you into the midst of Jerusalem.

20 '*As men* gather silver, bronze, iron, lead, and tin into the midst of a furnace, to blow fire on it, to [a]melt *it;* so I will gather *you* in My anger and in My fury, and I will leave *you there* and melt you.

21 'Yes, I will gather you and blow on you with the fire of My wrath, and you shall be melted in its midst.

22 'As silver is melted in the midst of a furnace, so shall you be melted in its midst; then you shall know that I, the LORD, have [a]poured out My fury on you.' "

23 And the word of the LORD came to me, saying,

24 "Son of man, say to her: 'You *are* a land that is [a]not [1]cleansed or rained on in the day of indignation.'

25 [a]"The conspiracy of her [1]prophets in her midst is like a

4 [b]Deut. 28:37
5 [1]Lit. *defiled of name*
6 [a]Is. 1:23 [1]Lit. *arm*
7 [a]Lev. 20:9 [b]Ex. 22:22 [1]Lit. *orphan*
8 [a]Lev. 19:30
9 [a]Lev. 19:16 [b]Ezek. 18:6, 11
10 [a]Lev. 18:7, 8 [b]Lev. 18:19; 20:18
11 [a]Ezek. 18:11 [b]Lev. 18:15 [c]Lev. 18:9
12 [a]Ex. 23:8 [b]Ex. 22:25 [c]Ezek. 23:35
13 [a]Ezek. 21:17
14 [a]Ezek. 21:7 [b]Ezek. 17:24
15 [a]Deut. 4:27 [b]Ezek. 23:27, 48
16 [a]Ps. 9:16
18 [a]Is. 1:22 [b]Prov. 17:3
20 [a]Is. 1:25
22 [a]Ezek. 20:8, 33
24 [a]Ezek. 24:13 [1]So with MT, Syr., Vg.; LXX *showered upon*
25 [a]Hos. 6:9 [1]So with MT, Vg.; LXX *princes;* Tg. *scribes*

roaring lion tearing the prey;
they [b]have devoured [2]people;
[c]they have taken treasure and
precious things; they have made
many widows in her midst.
26 [a]"Her priests have [1]vio-
lated My law and [b]profaned
My holy things; they have not
[c]distinguished between the holy
and unholy, nor have they made
known *the difference* between
the unclean and the clean; and
they have hidden their eyes
from My Sabbaths, so that I am
profaned among them.
27 "Her [a]princes in her midst
are like wolves tearing the prey,
to shed blood, to destroy [1]peo-
ple, and to get dishonest gain.
28 [a]"Her prophets plastered
them with untempered *mortar,*
[b]seeing false visions, and divin-
ing [c]lies for them, saying, 'Thus
says the Lord GOD,' when the
LORD had not spoken.
29 "The people of the land have
used oppressions, committed
robbery, and mistreated the poor
and needy; and they wrongfully
[a]oppress the stranger.
30 [a]"So I sought for a man
among them who would [b]make
a wall, and [c]stand in the gap
before Me on behalf of the land,
that I should not destroy it; but I
found no one.
31 "Therefore I have [a]poured
out My indignation on them; I
have consumed them with the
fire of My wrath; and I have recompensed [b]their deeds on their
own heads," says the Lord GOD.

23 The word of the LORD
came again to me,
saying:

2 "Son of man, there were [a]two
women,
The daughters of one
mother.
3 [a]They committed harlotry in
Egypt,
They committed harlotry in
[b]their youth;
Their breasts were there
embraced,
Their virgin bosom was
there pressed.
4 Their names: [1]Ō·hō′lah the
elder and [2]Ō·hol′i·bah
[a]her sister;
[b]They were Mine,
And they bore sons and
daughters.
As for their names,
Samaria *is* Ō·hō′lah, and
Jerusalem *is* Ō·hol′i·bah.

5 "Ō·hō′lah played the harlot
even though she was
Mine;
And she lusted for her
lovers, the neighboring
[a]Assyrians,
6 *Who were* clothed in purple,
Captains and rulers,
All of them desirable young
men,
Horsemen riding on horses.
7 Thus she committed her
harlotry with them,
All of them choice men of
Assyria;
And with all for whom she
lusted,
With all their idols, she
defiled herself.
8 She has never given up her
harlotry *brought* [a]from
Egypt,
For in her youth they had
lain with her,
Pressed her virgin bosom,
And poured out their
immorality upon her.

25 [b]Matt. 23:14 [c]Mic. 3:11 [2]Lit. *souls*
26 [a]Mal. 2:8 [b]1 Sam. 2:29 [c]Lev. 10:10 [1]Lit. *done violence to*
27 [a]Is. 1:23 [1]Lit. *souls*
28 [a]Ezek. 13:10 [b]Ezek. 13:6, 7 [c]Jer. 23:25–32
29 [a]Ex. 23:9
30 [a]Jer. 5:1 [b]Ezek. 13:5 [c]Ps. 106:23
31 [a]Ezek. 22:22 [b]Ezek. 9:10
CHAPTER 23
2 [a]Ezek. 16:44–46
3 [a]Lev. 17:7 [b]Ezek. 16:22
4 [a]Jer. 3:6, 7 [b]Ezek. 16:8, 20 [1]Lit. *Her Own Tabernacle* [2]Lit. *My Tabernacle Is in Her*
5 [a]Hos. 5:13; 8:9, 10
8 [a]Ezek. 23:3, 19

9 "Therefore I have delivered her
Into the hand of her lovers,
Into the hand of the [a]Assyrians,
For whom she lusted.
10 They uncovered her nakedness,
Took away her sons and daughters,
And slew her with the sword;
She became a byword among women,
For they had executed judgment on her.

11 "Now [a]although her sister
Ō·hol′i·bah saw *this,* [b]she became
more corrupt in her lust than she,
and in her harlotry more corrupt
than her sister's harlotry.

12 "She lusted for the neighboring [a]Assyrians,
[b]Captains and rulers,
Clothed most gorgeously,
Horsemen riding on horses,
All of them desirable young men.
13 Then I saw that she was defiled;
Both *took* the same way.
14 But she increased her harlotry;
She looked at men portrayed on the wall,
Images of [a]Chal·dē′ans portrayed in vermilion,
15 Girded with belts around their waists,
Flowing turbans on their heads,
All of them looking like captains,
In the manner of the Babylonians of Chal·dē′a,
The land of their nativity.
16 [a]As soon as her eyes saw them,
She lusted for them
And sent [b]messengers to them in Chal·dē′a.

17 "Then the [1]Babylonians came to her, into the bed of love,
And they defiled her with their immorality;
So she was defiled by them, [a]and alienated herself from them.
18 She revealed her harlotry and uncovered her nakedness.
Then [a]I [b]alienated Myself from her,
As I had alienated Myself from her sister.

19 "Yet she multiplied her harlotry
In calling to remembrance the days of her youth,
[a]When she had played the harlot in the land of Egypt.
20 For she lusted for her [1]paramours,
Whose flesh *is like* the flesh of donkeys,
And whose issue *is like* the issue of horses.
21 Thus you called to remembrance the lewdness of your youth,
When the [a]Egyptians pressed your bosom
Because of your youthful breasts.

22 "Therefore, Ō·hol′i·bah, thus
says the Lord GOD:

[a]'Behold, I will stir up your lovers against you,

9 [a]2 Kin. 17:3
11 [a]Jer. 3:8 [b]Jer. 3:8–11
12 [a]2 Kin. 16:7, 8 [b]Ezek. 23:6, 23
14 [a]Ezek. 8:10; 16:29
16 [a]2 Kin. 24:1 [b]Is. 57:9
17 [a]Ezek. 23:22, 28 [1]Lit. *sons of Babel*
18 [a]Jer. 6:8 [b]Jer. 12:8
19 [a]Ezek. 23:2
20 [1]Illicit lovers
21 [a]Ezek. 16:26
22 [a]Ezek. 16:37–41; 23:28

From whom you have
alienated yourself,
And I will bring them against
you from every side:
23 The Babylonians,
All the Chal·dē′ans,
[a]Pē′kod, Shō′a, Kō′a,
[b]All the Assyrians with them,
All of them desirable young
men,
Governors and rulers,
Captains and men of
renown,
All of them riding on horses.
24 And they shall come against
you
With chariots, wagons, and
war-horses,
With a horde of people.
They shall array against you
Buckler, shield, and helmet
all around.

'I will delegate judgment to
them,
And they shall judge you
according to their
judgments.
25 I will set My [a]jealousy
against you,
And they shall deal
furiously with you;
They shall remove your
nose and your ears,
And your remnant shall fall
by the sword;
They shall take your sons
and your daughters,
And your remnant shall be
devoured by fire.
26 [a]They shall also strip you of
your clothes
And take away your
beautiful jewelry.

27 'Thus [a]I will make you cease
your lewdness and your
[b]harlotry
Brought from the land of
Egypt,
So that you will not lift your
eyes to them,
Nor remember Egypt
anymore.'

28 "For thus says the Lord GOD:
'Surely I will deliver you into the
hand of [a]those you hate, into the
hand *of those* [b]from whom you
alienated yourself.
29 [a]'They will deal hatefully
with you, take away all you have
worked for, and [b]leave you naked and bare. The nakedness
of your harlotry shall be uncovered, both your lewdness and
your harlotry.
30 'I will do these *things* to
you because you have [a]gone as
a harlot after the Gentiles, because you have become defiled
by their idols.
31 'You have walked in the way
of your sister; therefore I will
put her [a]cup in your hand.'
32 "Thus says the Lord GOD:

'You shall drink of your
sister's cup,
The deep and wide one;
[a]You shall be laughed to
scorn
And held in derision;
It contains much.
33 You will be filled with
drunkenness and sorrow,
The cup of horror and
desolation,
The cup of your sister
Samaria.
34 You shall [a]drink and drain it,
You shall break its [1]shards,
And tear at your own
breasts;
For I have spoken,'
Says the Lord GOD.

23 [a]Jer. 50:21 [b]Ezek. 23:12
25 [a]Ex. 34:14
26 [a]Is. 3:18–23
27 [a]Ezek. 16:41; 22:15 [b]Ezek. 23:3, 19
28 [a]Ezek. 16:37–41 [b]Ezek. 23:17
29 [a]Deut. 28:48 [b]Ezek. 16:39
30 [a]Ezek. 6:9
31 [a]Jer. 7:14, 15; 25:15
32 [a]Ezek. 22:4, 5
34 [a]Is. 51:17 [1]Earthenware fragments

35 "Therefore thus says the
Lord GOD:

'Because you [a]have forgotten
Me and [b]cast Me behind
your back,
Therefore you shall bear the
penalty
Of your lewdness and your
harlotry.' "

36 The LORD also said to me:
"Son of man, will you [a]judge
Ō·hō'lah and Ō·hol'i·bah? Then
[b]declare to them their abominations.
37 "For they have commit-
ted adultery, and [a]blood *is* on
their hands. They have committed adultery with their idols,
and even *sacrificed* their sons
[b]whom they bore to Me, passing
them through *the fire,* to devour
them.
38 "Moreover they have done
this to Me: They have [a]defiled
My sanctuary on the same day
and [b]profaned My Sabbaths.
39 "For after they had slain
their children for their idols, on
the same day they came into My
sanctuary to profane it; and indeed [a]thus they have done in the
midst of My house.
40 "Furthermore you sent for
men to come from afar, [a]to whom
a messenger *was* sent; and there
they came. And you [b]washed
yourself for them, [c]painted your
eyes, and adorned yourself with
ornaments.
41 "You sat on a stately [a]couch,
with a table prepared before it,
[b]on which you had set My incense and My oil.
42 "The sound of a carefree
multitude *was* with her, and
[1]Sa·bē'ans *were* brought from
the wilderness with men of the
common sort, who put bracelets
on their [2]wrists and beautiful
crowns on their heads.
43 "Then I said concerning *her*
who had grown old in adulteries,
'Will they commit harlotry with
her now, and she *with them?*'
44 "Yet they went in to her, as
men go in to a woman who plays
the harlot; thus they went in
to Ō·hō'lah and Ō·hol'i·bah, the
lewd women.
45 "But righteous men will
[a]judge them after the manner of
adulteresses, and after the manner of women who shed blood,
because they *are* adulteresses,
and [b]blood *is* on their hands.
46 "For thus says the Lord GOD:
[a]'Bring up an assembly against
them, give them up to trouble
and plunder.
47 [a]'The assembly shall stone
them with stones and [1]execute
them with their swords; [b]they
shall slay their sons and their
daughters, and burn their houses
with fire.
48 'Thus [a]I will cause lewdness
to cease from the land, [b]that all
women may be taught not to
practice your lewdness.
49 'They shall repay you for
your lewdness, and you shall
[a]pay for your idolatrous sins.
[b]Then you shall know that I *am*
the Lord GOD.' "

24 Again, in the ninth year,
in the tenth month, on the
tenth *day* of the month, the word
of the LORD came to me, saying,
2 "Son of man, write down the
name of the day, this very day—
the king of Babylon started his
siege against Jerusalem [a]this
very day.
3 [a]"And utter a parable to the

35 [a]Jer. 3:21 [b]1 Kin. 14:9
36 [a]Ezek. 20:4; 22:2 [b]Is. 58:1
37 [a]Ezek. 16:38 [b]Ezek. 16:20, 21, 36, 45; 20:26, 31
38 [a]2 Kin. 21:4, 7 [b]Ezek. 22:8
39 [a]2 Kin. 21:2–8
40 [a]Is. 57:9 [b]Ruth 3:3 [c]Jer. 4:30
41 [a]Is. 57:7 [b]Prov. 7:17
42 [1]Or *drunkards* [2]Lit. *hands*
45 [a]Ezek. 16:38 [b]Ezek. 23:37
46 [a]Ezek. 16:40
47 [a]Ezek. 16:40 [b]Ezek. 24:21 [1]Lit. *cut down*
48 [a]Ezek. 22:15 [b]Deut. 13:11
49 [a]Ezek. 23:35 [b]Ezek. 20:38, 42, 44; 25:5

CHAPTER 24

2 [a]2 Kin. 25:1
3 [a]Ezek. 17:12

rebellious house, and say to them, 'Thus says the Lord GOD:

[b]"Put on a pot, set *it* on,
And also pour water into it.
4 Gather pieces *of meat* in it,
Every good piece,
The thigh and the shoulder.
Fill *it* with choice [1]cuts;
5 Take the choice of the flock.
Also pile *fuel* bones under it,
Make it boil well,
And let the cuts simmer
in it."

6 'Therefore thus says the Lord GOD:

"Woe to [a]the bloody city,
To the pot whose scum *is*
in it,
And whose scum is not
gone from it!
Bring it out piece by piece,
On which no [b]lot has fallen.
7 For her blood is in her
midst;
She set it on top of a rock;
[a]She did not pour it on the
ground,
To cover it with dust.
8 That it may raise up fury
and take vengeance,
[a]I have set her blood on top
of a rock,
That it may not be covered."

9 'Therefore thus says the Lord GOD:

[a]"Woe to the bloody city!
I too will make the pyre
great.
10 Heap on the wood,
Kindle the fire;
Cook the meat well,
Mix in the spices,
And let the [1]cuts be
burned up.

11 "Then set the pot empty on
the coals,
That it may become hot and
its bronze may burn,
That [a]its filthiness may be
melted in it,
That its scum may be
consumed.
12 She has [1]grown weary with
[2]lies,
And her great scum has not
gone from her.
Let her scum *be* in the fire!
13 In your [a]filthiness *is*
lewdness.
Because I have cleansed
you, and you were not
cleansed,
You will [b]not be cleansed of
your filthiness anymore,
[c]Till I have caused My fury to
rest upon you.
14 [a]I, the LORD, have spoken *it;*
[b]It shall come to pass, and I
will do *it;*
I will not hold back,
[c]Nor will I spare,
Nor will I relent;
According to your ways
And according to your
deeds
[1]They will judge you,"
Says the Lord GOD.' "

15 Also the word of the LORD came to me, saying,
16 "Son of man, behold, I take away from you the desire of your eyes with one stroke; yet you shall [a]neither mourn nor weep, nor shall your tears run down.
17 "Sigh in silence, [a]make no mourning for the dead; [b]bind your turban on your head, and

3 [b]Jer. 1:13
4 [1]Lit. *bones*
6 [a]Ezek. 22:2, 3, 27 [b]Nah. 3:10
7 [a]Lev. 17:13
8 [a][Matt. 7:2]
9 [a]Hab. 2:12
10 [1]Lit. *bones*
11 [a]Ezek. 22:15
12 [1]Or *wearied Me* [2]Or *toil*
13 [a]Ezek. 23:36–48 [b]Jer. 6:28–30 [c]Ezek. 5:13; 8:18; 16:42
14 [a][1 Sam. 15:29] [b]Is. 55:11 [c]Ezek. 5:11 [1]LXX, Syr., Tg., Vg. *I*
16 [a]Jer. 16:5
17 [a]Jer. 16:5 [b]Lev. 10:6; 21:10

[c]put your sandals on your feet;
[d]do not cover *your* [1]lips, and do
not eat man's bread *of sorrow.*"
18 So I spoke to the people in
the morning, and at evening my
wife died; and the next morning
I did as I was commanded.
19 And the people said to me,
[a]"Will you not tell us what these
things signify to us, that you behave so?"
20 Then I answered them, "The
word of the LORD came to me,
saying,
21 'Speak to the house of Israel,
"Thus says the Lord GOD: 'Behold, [a]I will profane My sanctuary, [1]your arrogant boast, the
desire of your eyes, the [2]delight
of your soul; [b]and your sons and
daughters whom you left behind
shall fall by the sword.
22 'And you shall do as I have
done; [a]you shall not cover *your*
[1]lips nor eat man's bread *of
sorrow.*
23 'Your turbans shall be on
your heads and your sandals
on your feet; [a]you shall neither
mourn nor weep, but [b]you shall
pine away in your iniquities and
mourn with one another.
24 'Thus [a]E·zēk′i·el is a sign to
you; according to all that he has
done you shall do; [b]and when
this comes, [c]you shall know that
I *am* the Lord GOD.' "
25 'And you, son of man—*will
it* not *be* in the day when I take
from them [a]their stronghold,
their joy and their glory, the
desire of their eyes, and [1]that on
which they set their minds, their
sons and their daughters:
26 '*that* on that day [a]one who
escapes will come to you to let
you hear *it* with *your* ears?
27 [a]'On that day your mouth
will be opened to him who has
escaped; you shall speak and no
longer be mute. Thus you will
be a sign to them, and they shall
know that I *am* the LORD.' "

25

The word of the LORD
came to me, saying,
2 "Son of man, [a]set your face
[b]against the Am′mon·ītes, and
prophesy against them.
3 "Say to the Am′mon·ītes,
'Hear the word of the Lord
GOD! Thus says the Lord GOD:
[a]"Because you said, 'Aha!' against
My sanctuary when it was profaned, and against the land of
Israel when it was desolate, and
against the house of Judah when
they went into captivity,
4 "indeed, therefore, I will deliver you as a possession to the
[1]men of the East, and they shall
set their encampments among
you and make their dwellings
among you; they shall eat your
fruit, and they shall drink your
milk.
5 "And I will make [a]Rab′bah [b]a
stable for camels and Am′mon
a resting place for flocks. [c]Then
you shall know that I *am* the
LORD."
6 'For thus says the Lord GOD:
"Because you [a]clapped *your*
hands, stamped your feet, and
[b]rejoiced in heart with all your
disdain for the land of Israel,
7 "indeed, therefore, I will
[a]stretch out My hand against
you, and give you as plunder
to the nations; I will cut you
off from the peoples, and I will
cause you to perish from the
countries; I will destroy you, and
you shall know that I *am* the
LORD."
8 'Thus says the Lord GOD:
"Because [a]Mō′ab and [b]Sē′ir say,

---

17 [c]2 Sam. 15:30 [d]Mic. 3:7 [1]Lit. *moustache*
19 [a]Ezek. 12:9; 37:18
21 [a]Jer. 7:14 [b]Ezek. 23:25, 47 [1]Lit. *the pride of your strength* [2]Lit. *compassion*
22 [a]Jer. 16:6, 7 [1]Lit. *moustache*
23 [a]Job 27:15 [b]Lev. 26:39
24 [a]Is. 20:3 [b]Jer. 17:15 [c]Ezek. 6:7; 25:5
25 [a]Ezek. 24:21 [1]Lit. *the lifting up of their soul*
26 [a]Ezek. 33:21
27 [a]Ezek. 3:26; 33:22

CHAPTER 25

2 [a]Ezek. 35:2 [b]Jer. 49:1
3 [a]Ezek. 26:2
4 [1]Lit. *sons*
5 [a]Ezek. 21:20 [b]Is. 17:2 [c]Ezek. 24:24
6 [a]Job 27:23 [b]Ezek. 36:5
7 [a]Ezek. 35:3
8 [a]Amos 2:1, 2 [b]Ezek. 35:2, 5

'Look! The house of Judah *is*
like all the nations,'
9 "therefore, behold, I will
clear the territory of Mō′ab of
cities, of the cities on its frontier,
the glory of the country, Beth
Jesh′i·moth, Bā′al Mē′on, and
[a]Kir·jath′a·im.
10 [a]"To the men of the East I will
give it as a possession, together
with the Am′mon·ītes, that the
Am′mon·ītes [b]may not be remembered among the nations.
11 "And I will execute judgments upon Mō′ab, and they
shall know that I *am* the LORD."
12 'Thus says the Lord GOD:
[a]"Because of what Ē′dom did
against the house of Judah
by taking vengeance, and has
greatly offended by avenging
itself on them,"
13 'therefore thus says the Lord
GOD: "I will also stretch out My
hand against Ē′dom, cut off man
and beast from it, and make it
desolate from Tē′man; [1]Dē′dan
shall fall by the sword.
14 [a]"I will lay My vengeance
on Ē′dom by the hand of My
people Israel, that they may do
in Ē′dom according to My anger
and according to My fury; and
they shall know My vengeance,"
says the Lord GOD.
15 'Thus says the Lord GOD:
[a]"Because [b]the Phi·lis′tines dealt
vengefully and took vengeance
with [1]a spiteful heart, to destroy
because of the [2]old hatred,"
16 'therefore thus says the Lord
GOD: [a]"I will stretch out My hand
against the Phi·lis′tines, and I
will cut off the [b]Cher′e·thītes
[c]and destroy the remnant of the
seacoast.
17 "I will [a]execute great vengeance on them with furious
rebukes; [b]and they shall know
that I *am* the LORD, when I lay
My vengeance upon them." ' "

26 And it came to pass in the
eleventh year, on the first
day of the month, *that* the word
of the LORD came to me, saying,
2 "Son of man, [a]because Tȳre
has said against Jerusalem,
[b]'Aha! She is broken who *was*
the gateway of the peoples; now
she is turned over to me; I shall
be filled; she is laid waste.'
3 "Therefore thus says the Lord
GOD: 'Behold, I *am* against you,
O Tȳre, and will cause many nations to come up against you, as
the sea causes its waves to come
up.
4 'And they shall destroy the
walls of Tȳre and break down
her towers; I will also scrape her
dust from her, and [a]make her
like the top of a rock.
5 'It shall be *a place for* spreading nets [a]in the midst of the sea,
for I have spoken,' says the Lord
GOD; 'it shall become plunder
for the nations.
6 'Also her daughter *villages*
which *are* in the fields shall be
slain by the sword. [a]Then they
shall know that I am the LORD.'
7 "For thus says the Lord GOD:
'Behold, I will bring against Tȳre
from the north [a]Ne·bū·chad·nez′-
zar[1] king of Babylon, [b]king of
kings, with horses, with chariots, and with horsemen, and an
army with many people.
8 'He will slay with the sword
your daughter *villages* in the
fields; he will [a]heap up a siege
mound against you, build a wall
against you, and raise a [1]defense
against you.
9 'He will direct his battering
rams against your walls, and

9 [a]Jer. 48:23
10 [a]Ezek. 25:4 [b]Ezek. 21:32
12 [a]Obad. 10–14
13 [1]Or *even to Dedan they shall fall*
14 [a]Is. 11:14
15 [a]Jer. 25:20 [b]2 Chr. 28:18 [1]Lit. *spite in soul* [2]Or *perpetual*
16 [a]Zeph. 2:4 [b]1 Sam. 30:14 [c]Jer. 47:4
17 [a]Ezek. 5:15 [b]Ps. 9:16

CHAPTER 26

2 [a]Jer. 25:22 [b]Ezek. 25:3
4 [a]Ezek. 26:14
5 [a]Ezek. 27:32
6 [a]Ezek. 25:5
7 [a]Jer. 27:3–6 [b]Dan. 2:37, 47 [1]Heb. *Nebuchadrezzar,* and so elsewhere in the book
8 [a]Ezek. 21:22 [1]Lit. *a large shield*

with his axes he will break down
your towers.
10 'Because of the abundance of
his horses, their dust will cover
you; your walls will shake at the
noise of the horsemen, the wagons, and the chariots, when he
enters your gates, as men enter
a city that has been breached.
11 'With the hooves of his
[a]horses he will trample all your
streets; he will slay your people
by the sword, and your strong
pillars will fall to the ground.
12 'They will plunder your
riches and pillage your merchandise; they will break down
your walls and destroy your
pleasant houses; they will lay
your stones, your timber, and
your soil in the [a]midst of the
water.
13 [a]'I will put an end to the
sound of [b]your songs, and the
sound of your harps shall be
heard no more.
14 [a]'I will make you like the
top of a rock; you shall be *a*
place for spreading nets, and
you shall never be rebuilt, for I
the LORD have spoken,' says the
Lord GOD.
15 "Thus says the Lord GOD to
Tyre: 'Will the coastlands not
[a]shake at the sound of your fall,
when the wounded cry, when
slaughter is made in the midst of
you?
16 'Then all the [a]princes of the
sea will [b]come down from their
thrones, lay aside their robes,
and take off their embroidered
garments; they will clothe themselves with trembling; [c]they will
sit on the ground, [d]tremble *every*
moment, and [e]be astonished at
you.
17 'And they will take up a

11 [a]Hab. 1:8
12 [a]Ezek. 27:27, 32
13 [a]Is. 14:11; 24:8 [b]Rev. 18:22
14 [a]Ezek. 26:4, 5
15 [a]Jer. 49:21
16 [a]Is. 23:8 [b]Jon. 3:6 [c]Job 2:13 [d]Ezek. 32:10 [e]Ezek. 27:35
17 [a]Ezek. 27:2–36 [b]Is. 23:4
18 [a]Ezek. 26:15
20 [a]Ezek. 32:18 [b]Ezek. 32:23
21 [a]Ezek. 27:36; 28:19 [b]Ps. 37:10, 36

CHAPTER 27

2 [a]Ezek. 26:17
3 [a]Ezek. 26:17; 28:2 [b]Is. 23:3 [1]Lit. *sit* or *dwell*

[a]lamentation for you, and say to
you:

"How you have perished,
O one inhabited by
seafaring men,
O renowned city,
Who was [b]strong at sea,
She and her inhabitants,
Who caused their terror *to*
be on all her inhabitants!
18 Now [a]the coastlands
tremble on the day of
your fall;
Yes, the coastlands by the
sea are troubled at your
departure." '

19 "For thus says the Lord GOD:
'When I make you a desolate city,
like cities that are not inhabited,
when I bring the deep upon you,
and great waters cover you,
20 'then I will bring you down
[a]with those who descend into
the Pit, to the people of old,
and I will make you dwell in
the lowest part of the earth, in
places desolate from antiquity,
with those who go down to the
Pit, so that you may never be
inhabited; and I shall establish
glory [b]in the land of the living.
21 [a]'I will make you a terror, and you *shall be* no *more;*
[b]though you are sought for, you
will never be found again,' says
the Lord GOD."

27

The word of the LORD
came again to me, saying,
2 "Now, son of man, [a]take up a
lamentation for Tyre,
3 "and say to Tyre, [a]'You who
[1]are situated at the entrance of
the sea, [b]merchant of the peoples on many coastlands, thus
says the Lord GOD:

"O Tȳre, you have said,
[c]'I *am* perfect in beauty.'
4 Your borders *are* in the midst of the seas.
Your builders have perfected your beauty.
5 They [1]made all *your* planks of fir trees from [a]Sē'nir;
They took a cedar from Lebanon to make you a mast.
6 *Of* [a]oaks from Bā'shan they made your oars;
The company of Ash'ur·ītes have inlaid your planks
With ivory from [b]the coasts of [1]Cyprus.
7 Fine embroidered linen from Egypt was what you spread for your sail;
Blue and purple from the coasts of E·li'shah was what covered you.

8 "Inhabitants of Sī'don and Ar'vad were your oarsmen;
Your wise men, O Tȳre, were in you;
They became your pilots.
9 Elders of [a]Gē'bal and its wise men
Were in you to caulk your seams;
All the ships of the sea
And their oarsmen were in you
To market your merchandise.

10 "Those from Persia, [1]Lyd'i·a, and [2]Lib'ya
Were in your army as men of war;
They hung shield and helmet in you;
They gave splendor to you.

3 [c]Ezek. 28:12
5 [a]Deut. 3:9 [1]*built*
6 [a]Is. 2:12, 13 [b]Jer. 2:10 [1]Heb. *Kittim,* western lands, especially Cyprus
9 [a]1 Kin. 5:18
10 [1]Heb. *Lud* [2]Heb. *Put*
11 [a]Ezek. 27:3
12 [a]Gen. 10:4
13 [a]Gen. 10:2 [b]Rev. 18:13
14 [a]Gen. 10:3
15 [a]Gen. 10:7
17 [a]Judg. 11:33 [b]Jer. 8:22
19 [1]LXX, Syr. *from Uzal*

11 Men of Ar'vad with your army *were* on your walls *all* around,
And the men of Gam'mad were in your towers;
They hung their shields on your walls *all* around;
They made [a]your beauty perfect.

12 [a]"Tar'shish *was* your merchant because of your many
luxury goods. They gave you
silver, iron, tin, and lead for your
goods.
13 [a]"Jā'van, Tū'bal, and Mē'-
shech *were* your traders. They
bartered [b]human lives and vessels of bronze for your merchandise.
14 "Those from the house of
[a]Tō·gar'mah traded for your
wares with horses, steeds, and
mules.
15 "The men of [a]Dē'dan *were*
your traders; many isles *were*
the market of your hand. They
brought you ivory tusks and eb-
ony as payment.
16 "Syria *was* your merchant
because of the abundance of
goods you made. They gave you
for your wares emeralds, purple,
embroidery, fine linen, corals,
and rubies.
17 "Judah and the land of Israel
were your traders. They traded
for your merchandise wheat of
[a]Min'nith, millet, honey, oil, and
[b]balm.
18 "Damascus *was* your merchant because of the abundance
of goods you made, because of
your many luxury items, with
the wine of Hel'bon and with
white wool.
19 "Dan and Jā'van paid for
your wares, [1]traversing back

and forth. Wrought iron, cassia, and cane were among your
merchandise.
20 [a]"Dē′dan *was* your merchant
in saddlecloths for riding.
21 "Arabia and all the princes of
[a]Kē′dar *were* your regular merchants. They traded with you in
lambs, rams, and goats.
22 "The merchants of [a]Shē′ba
and Rā′a·mah *were* your merchants. They traded for your
wares the choicest spices, all
kinds of precious stones, and
gold.
23 [a]"Har′an, Can′neh, Eden, the
merchants of [b]Shē′ba, Assyria,
and Chil′mad *were* your merchants.
24 "These *were* your merchants
in choice items—in purple
clothes, in embroidered garments, in chests of multicolored
apparel, in sturdy woven cords,
which were in your marketplace.

25 "The [a]ships of Tar′shish
were carriers of your
merchandise.
You were filled and very
glorious [b]in the midst of
the seas.
26 Your oarsmen brought you
into many waters,
But [a]the east wind broke
you in the midst of the
seas.

27 "Your [a]riches, wares, and
merchandise,
Your mariners and pilots,
Your caulkers and
merchandisers,
All your men of war who
are in you,
And the entire company
which *is* in your midst,
Will fall into the midst of
the seas on the day of
your ruin.
28 The [a]common-land[1] will
shake at the sound of the
cry of your pilots.

29 "All [a]who handle the oar,
The mariners,
All the pilots of the sea
Will come down from their
ships *and* stand on the
[1]shore.
30 They will make their voice
heard because of you;
They will cry bitterly and
[a]cast dust on their heads;
They [b]will roll about in ashes;
31 They will [a]shave themselves
completely bald because
of you,
Gird themselves with
sackcloth,
And weep for you
With bitterness of heart *and*
bitter wailing.
32 In their wailing for you
They will [a]take up a
lamentation,
And lament for you:
[b]'What *city is* like Tȳre,
Destroyed in the midst of
the sea?

33 'When[a] your wares went out
by sea,
You satisfied many people;
You enriched the kings of
the earth
With your many luxury
goods and your
merchandise.
34 But [a]you are broken by the
seas in the depths of the
waters;
[b]Your merchandise and the
entire company will fall
in your midst.

20 [a]Gen. 25:3
21 [a]Is. 60:7
22 [a]Gen. 10:7
23 [a]2 Kin. 19:12 [b]Gen. 25:3
25 [a]Is. 2:16 [b]Ezek. 27:4
26 [a]Ps. 48:7
27 [a][Prov. 11:4]
28 [a]Ezek. 26:15 [1]*open lands* or *pasturelands*
29 [a]Rev. 18:17 [1]Lit. *land*
30 [a]Rev. 18:19 [b]Jer. 6:26
31 [a]Ezek. 29:18
32 [a]Ezek. 26:17 [b]Rev. 18:18
33 [a]Rev. 18:19
34 [a]Ezek. 26:19 [b]Ezek. 27:27

35 [a]All the inhabitants of the
isles will be astonished
at you;
Their kings will be greatly
afraid,
And *their* countenance will
be troubled.
36 The merchants among the
peoples [a]will hiss at you;
[b]You will become a horror,
and *be* no [c]more
forever.' " ' "

28

The word of the LORD
came to me again, saying,
2 "Son of man, say to the
prince of Tyre, 'Thus says the
Lord GOD:

"Because your heart *is*
[a]lifted[1] up,
And [b]you say, 'I *am* a god,
I sit *in* the seat of gods,
[c]In the midst of the seas,'
[d]Yet you *are* a man, and not
a god,
Though you set your heart
as the heart of a god
3 (Behold, [a]you *are* wiser than
Daniel!
There is no secret that can
be hidden from you!
4 With your wisdom and your
understanding
You have gained [a]riches for
yourself,
And gathered gold
and silver into your
treasuries;
5 [a]By your great wisdom in
trade you have increased
your riches,
And your heart is lifted up
because of your riches),"

6 'Therefore thus says the Lord
GOD:

"Because you have set your
heart as the heart of a
god,
7 Behold, therefore, I will
bring [a]strangers against
you,
[b]The most terrible of the
nations;
And they shall draw their
swords against the
beauty of your wisdom,
And defile your splendor.
8 They shall throw you down
into the [a]Pit,
And you shall die the death
of the slain
In the midst of the seas.

9 "Will you still [a]say before
him who slays you,
'I *am* a god'?
But you *shall be* a man, and
not a god,
In the hand of him who
slays you.
10 You shall die the death of
[a]the uncircumcised
By the hand of aliens;
For I have spoken," says the
Lord GOD.' "

11 Moreover the word of the
LORD came to me, saying,
12 "Son of man, [a]take up a lamentation for the king of Tyre,
and say to him, 'Thus says the
Lord GOD:

[b]"You *were* the seal of
perfection,
Full of wisdom and perfect
in beauty.
13 You were in [a]Eden, the
garden of God;
Every precious stone *was*
your covering:
The sardius, topaz, and
diamond,

35 [a]Ezek. 26:15, 16
36 [a]Jer. 18:16 [b]Ezek. 26:2 [c]Ps. 37:10, 36

CHAPTER 28

2 [a]Jer. 49:16 [b]Ezek. 28:9 [c]Ezek. 27:3, 4 [d]Is. 31:3 [1]Proud
3 [a]Dan. 1:20; 2:20–23, 28; 5:11, 12
4 [a]Zech. 9:1–3
5 [a]Ps. 62:10
7 [a]Ezek. 26:7 [b]Ezek. 7:24; 21:31; 30:11
8 [a]Is. 14:15
9 [a]Ezek. 28:2
10 [a]Ezek. 31:18; 32:19, 21, 25, 27
12 [a]Ezek. 27:2 [b]Ezek. 27:3; 28:3
13 [a]Ezek. 31:8, 9; 36:35

Beryl, onyx, and jasper,
Sapphire, turquoise, and
emerald with gold.
The workmanship of [b]your
timbrels and pipes
Was prepared for you on the
day you were created.

14 "You *were* the anointed
[a]cherub who covers;
I established you;
You were on [b]the holy
mountain of God;
You walked back and forth
in the midst of fiery
stones.
15 You *were* perfect in your
ways from the day you
were created,
Till [a]iniquity was found in
you.

16 "By the abundance of your
trading
You became filled with
violence within,
And you sinned;
Therefore I cast you as a
profane thing
Out of the mountain of God;
And I destroyed you,
[a]O covering cherub,
From the midst of the fiery
stones.

17 "Your [a]heart was [1]lifted up
because of your beauty;
You corrupted your wisdom
for the sake of your
splendor;
I cast you to the ground,
I laid you before kings,
That they might gaze at you.

18 "You defiled your sanctuaries
By the multitude of your
iniquities,
By the iniquity of your
trading;
Therefore I brought fire
from your midst;
It devoured you,
And I turned you to ashes
upon the earth
In the sight of all who saw
you.
19 All who knew you among
the peoples are
astonished at you;
[a]You have become a horror,
And *shall be* no [b]more
forever." ' "

20 Then the word of the LORD
came to me, saying,
21 "Son of man, [a]set your face
[b]toward Sī'don, and prophesy
against her,
22 "and say, 'Thus says the Lord
GOD:

[a]"Behold, I *am* against you,
O Sī'don;
I will be glorified in your
midst;
And [b]they shall know that I
am the LORD,
When I execute judgments
in her and am [c]hallowed
in her.
23 [a]For I will send pestilence
upon her,
And blood in her streets;
The wounded shall be
judged in her midst
By the sword against her on
every side;
Then they shall know that I
am the LORD.

24 "And there shall no longer
be a pricking brier or [a]a painful thorn for the house of Israel
from among all *who are* around
them, who [b]despise them. Then

13 [b]Ezek. 26:13
14 [a]Ex. 25:20 [b]Ezek. 20:40
15 [a][Is. 14:12]
16 [a]Ezek. 28:14
17 [a]Ezek. 28:2, 5 [1]Proud
19 [a]Ezek. 26:21 [b]Ezek. 27:36
21 [a]Ezek. 6:2; 25:2; 29:2 [b]Is. 23:2, 4, 12
22 [a]Ex. 14:4, 17 [b]Ps. 9:16 [c]Ezek. 28:25
23 [a]Ezek. 38:22
24 [a]Josh. 23:13 [b]Ezek. 16:57; 25:6, 7

they shall know that I *am* the
Lord GOD."
25 'Thus says the Lord GOD:
"When I have [a]gathered the
house of Israel from the peoples
among whom they are scattered,
and am [b]hallowed in them in
the sight of the Gentiles, then
they will dwell in their own
land which I gave to My servant
Jacob.
26 "And they will [a]dwell [1]safely
there, [b]build houses, and [c]plant
vineyards; yes, they will dwell
securely, when I execute judgments on all those around them
who despise them. Then they
shall know that I *am* the LORD
their God." ' "

29

In the tenth year, in
the tenth *month,* on the
twelfth *day* of the month, the
word of the LORD came to me,
saying,
2 "Son of man, [a]set your face
against Pharaoh king of Egypt,
and prophesy against him, and
[b]against all Egypt.
3 "Speak, and say, 'Thus says
the Lord GOD:

[a]"Behold, I *am* against you,
O Pharaoh king of Egypt,
O great [b]monster who lies in
the midst of his rivers,
[c]Who has said, 'My [1]River *is*
my own;
I have made *it* for myself.'
4 But [a]I will put hooks in your
jaws,
And cause the fish of your
rivers to stick to your
scales;
I will bring you up out of
the midst of your rivers,
And all the fish in your
rivers will stick to your
scales.

25 [a]Is. 11:12, 13 [b]Ezek. 28:22

26 [a]Jer. 23:6 [b]Amos 9:13, 14 [c]Jer. 31:5 [1]*securely*

CHAPTER 29

2 [a]Ezek. 28:21 [b]Is. 19:1

3 [a]Jer. 44:30 [b]Ps. 74:13, 14 [c]Ezek. 28:2 [1]The Nile

4 [a]Ezek. 38:4

5 [a]Ezek.32:4–6 [b]Jer. 8:2; 16:4; 25:33 [c]Jer. 7:33; 34:20 [1]Lit. *face of the field* [2]So with MT, LXX, Vg.; some Heb. mss., Tg. *buried*

6 [a]Is. 36:6

7 [a]Ezek. 17:17 [1]So with MT, Vg.; LXX, Syr. *hand*

8 [a]Ezek. 14:17; 32:11–13

9 [a]Ezek. 30:7, 8

10 [a]Ezek. 30:12 [b]Ezek. 30:6 [1]Or *the tower*

11 [a]Ezek. 32:13

5 I will leave you in the
wilderness,
You and all the fish of your
rivers;
You shall fall on the [1]open
[a]field;
[b]You shall not be picked up
or [2]gathered.
[c]I have given you as food
To the beasts of the field
And to the birds of the
heavens.

6 "Then all the inhabitants of
Egypt
Shall know that I *am* the
LORD,
Because they have been
a [a]staff of reed to the
house of Israel.
7 [a]When they took hold of you
with the hand,
You broke and tore all their
[1]shoulders;
When they leaned on you,
You broke and made all
their backs quiver."

8 'Therefore thus says the
Lord GOD: "Surely I will bring [a]a
sword upon you and cut off from
you man and beast.
9 "And the land of Egypt shall
become [a]desolate and waste;
then they will know that I *am*
the LORD, because he said, 'The
River *is* mine, and I have made
it.'
10 "Indeed, therefore, I *am*
against you and against your
rivers, [a]and I will make the land
of Egypt utterly waste and desolate, [b]from [1]Mig'dōl *to* Sȳ·ē'nē,
as far as the border of Ethiopia.
11 [a]"Neither foot of man shall
pass through it nor foot of beast
pass through it, and it shall be
uninhabited forty years.

12 [a]"I will make the land of
Egypt desolate in the midst of
the countries *that are* desolate;
and among the cities *that are*
laid waste, her cities shall be
desolate forty years; and I will
[b]scatter the Egyptians among
the nations and disperse them
throughout the countries."
13 'Yet, thus says the Lord GOD:
"At the [a]end of forty years I will
gather the Egyptians from the
peoples among whom they were
scattered.
14 "I will bring back the captives of Egypt and cause them
to return to the land of Path′-
ros, to the land of their origin,
and there they shall be a [a]lowly
kingdom.
15 "It shall be the lowliest of
kingdoms; it shall never again
exalt itself above the nations, for
I will diminish them so that they
will not rule over the nations
anymore.
16 "No longer shall it be [a]the
confidence of the house of Israel,
but will remind them of *their*
iniquity when they turned to follow them. Then they shall know
that I *am* the Lord GOD." ' "
17 And it came to pass in the
twenty-seventh year, in the first
month, on the first *day* of the
month, *that* the word of the
LORD came to me, saying,
18 "Son of man, [a]Ne·bū·chad-
nez′zar king of Babylon caused
his army to labor strenuously
against Tȳre; every head *was*
made [b]bald, and every shoulder
rubbed raw; yet neither he nor
his army received wages from
Tȳre, for the labor which they
expended on it.
19 "Therefore thus says the Lord
GOD: 'Surely I will give the land
of Egypt to [a]Ne·bū·chad·nez′zar
king of Babylon; he shall take
away her wealth, carry off her
spoil, and remove her pillage;
and that will be the wages for
his army.
20 'I have given him the land of
Egypt *for* his labor, because they
[a]worked for Me,' says the Lord
GOD.
21 'In that day [a]I will cause the
[1]horn of the house of Israel to
spring forth, and I will [b]open
your mouth to speak in their
midst. Then they shall know
that I *am* the LORD.' "

30 The word of the LORD
came to me again, saying,
2 "Son of man, prophesy and
say, 'Thus says the Lord GOD:

[a]"Wail, 'Woe to the day!'
3 For [a]the day *is* near,
Even the day of the LORD *is*
near;
It will be a day of clouds,
the time of the Gentiles.
4 The sword shall come upon
Egypt,
And great anguish shall be
in [1]Ethiopia,
When the slain fall in Egypt,
And they [a]take away her
wealth,
And [b]her foundations are
broken down.

5 "Ethiopia, [1]Lib′ya, [2]Lyd′i·a,
[a]all the mingled people, Chub,
and the men of the lands who
are allied, shall fall with them by
the sword."
6 'Thus says the LORD:

"Those who uphold Egypt
shall fall,
And the pride of her power
shall come down.

12 [a]Ezek. 30:7, 26 [b]Ezek. 30:23, 26
13 [a]Jer. 46:26
14 [a]Ezek. 17:6, 14
16 [a]Is. 30:2, 3; 36:4, 6
18 [a]Jer. 25:9; 27:6 [b]Ezek. 27:31
19 [a]Jer. 43:10–13
20 [a]Jer. 25:9
21 [a]Ps. 92:10; 132:17 [b]Ezek. 24:27 [1]Strength

CHAPTER 30

2 [a]Is. 13:6; 15:2
3 [a]Joel 2:1
4 [a]Ezek. 29:19 [b]Jer. 50:15 [1]Heb. *Cush*
5 [a]Jer. 25:20, 24 [1]Heb. *Put* [2]Heb. *Lud*

[a]From [1]Mig′dōl *to* Sȳ·ē′nē
Those within her shall fall
by the sword,"
Says the Lord GOD.

7 "They[a] shall be desolate in
the midst of the desolate
countries,
And her cities shall be in
the midst of the cities
that are laid waste.
8 Then they will know that I
am the LORD,
When I have set a fire in
Egypt
And all her helpers are
destroyed.
9 On that day [a]messengers
shall go forth from Me in
ships
To make the [1]careless
Ethiopians afraid,
And great anguish shall
come upon them,
As on the day of Egypt;
For indeed it is coming!"

10 'Thus says the Lord GOD:

[a]"I will also make a multitude
of Egypt to cease
By the hand of
Ne·bū·chad·nez′zar king
of Babylon.
11 He and his people with him,
[a]the most terrible of the
nations,
Shall be brought to destroy
the land;
They shall draw their
swords against Egypt,
And fill the land with the
slain.
12 [a]I will make the rivers dry,
And [b]sell the land into the
hand of the wicked;
I will make the land waste,
and all that is in it,
By the hand of aliens.
I, the LORD, have spoken."

13 'Thus says the Lord GOD:

"I will also [a]destroy the
idols,
And cause the images to
cease from [1]Noph;
[b]There shall no longer be
princes from the land of
Egypt;
[c]I will put fear in the land of
Egypt.
14 I will make [a]Path′ros
desolate,
Set fire to [b]Zō′an,
[c]And execute judgments in
[1]No.
15 I will pour My fury on [1]Sin,
the strength of Egypt;
[a]I will cut off the multitude
of [2]No,
16 And [a]set a fire in Egypt;
Sin shall have great pain,
No shall be split open,
And Noph *shall be in*
distress daily.
17 The young men of [1]Ā′ven
and Pī Bē′seth shall fall
by the sword,
And these *cities* shall go
into captivity.
18 [a]At [1]Te·haph′ne·hēs the day
shall also be [2]darkened,
When I break the yokes of
Egypt there.
And her arrogant strength
shall cease in her;
As for her, a cloud shall
cover her,
And her daughters shall go
into captivity.
19 Thus I will [a]execute
judgments on Egypt,
Then they shall know that I
am the LORD." ' "

6 [a]Ezek. 29:10 [1]Or *the tower*
7 [a]Ezek. 29:12
9 [a]Is. 18:1, 2 [1]Or *secure*
10 [a]Ezek. 29:19
11 [a]Ezek. 28:7; 31:12
12 [a]Is. 19:5, 6 [b]Is. 19:4
13 [a]Is. 19:1 [b]Zech. 10:11 [c]Is. 19:16 [1]Ancient Memphis
14 [a]Ezek. 29:14 [b]Ps. 78:12, 43 [c]Nah. 3:8–10 [1]Ancient Thebes
15 [a]Jer. 46:25 [1]Ancient Pelusium [2]Ancient Thebes
16 [a]Ezek. 30:8
17 [1]Ancient On, Heliopolis
18 [a]Jer. 2:16 [1]*Tahpanhes*, Jer. 43:7 [2]So with many Heb. mss., Bg., LXX, Syr., Tg., Vg.; MT *refrained*
19 [a][Ps. 9:16]

20 And it came to pass in the
eleventh year, in the first *month,*
on the seventh *day* of the month,
that the word of the LORD came
to me, saying,
21 "Son of man, I have [a]broken
the arm of Pharaoh king of Egypt;
and see, [b]it has not been ban-
daged for healing, nor a [1]splint
put on to bind it, to make it
strong enough to hold a sword.
22 "Therefore thus says the
Lord GOD: 'Surely I *am* [a]against
Pharaoh king of Egypt, and will
[b]break his arms, both the strong
one and the one that was broken; and I will make the sword
fall out of his hand.
23 [a]'I will scatter the Egyptians
among the nations, and disperse
them throughout the countries.
24 'I will strengthen the arms
of the king of Babylon and put
My sword in his hand; but I will
break Pharaoh's arms, and he
will groan before him with the
groanings of a mortally wounded
man.
25 'Thus I will strengthen the
arms of the king of Babylon,
but the arms of Pharaoh shall
fall down; [a]they shall know that
I *am* the LORD, when I put My
sword into the hand of the king
of Babylon and he stretches it
out against the land of Egypt.
26 [a]'I will scatter the Egyptians
among the nations and disperse
them throughout the countries.
Then they shall know that I *am*
the LORD.' "

31

31 Now it came to pass in
the [a]eleventh year, in the
third *month,* on the first *day* of
the month, *that* the word of the
LORD came to me, saying,
2 "Son of man, say to Pharaoh
king of Egypt and to his multitude:

[a]'Whom are you like in your
greatness?
3 [a]Indeed Assyria *was* a cedar
in Lebanon,
With fine branches that
shaded the forest,
And of high stature;
And its top was among the
thick boughs.
4 [a]The waters made it grow;
Underground waters gave it
height,
With their rivers running
around the place where
it was planted,
And sent out [1]rivulets to all
the trees of the field.
5 'Therefore [a]its height was
exalted above all the
trees of the field;
Its boughs were multiplied,
And its branches became
long because of the
abundance of water,
As it sent them out.
6 All the [a]birds of the heavens
made their nests in its
boughs;
Under its branches all
the beasts of the field
brought forth their
young;
And in its shadow all great
nations [1]made their
home.
7 'Thus it was beautiful in
greatness and in the
length of its branches,
Because its roots reached to
abundant waters.
8 The cedars in the [a]garden of
God could not hide it;

21 [a]Jer. 48:25 [b]Jer. 46:11 [1]Lit. *bandage*
22 [a]Jer. 46:25 [b]Ps. 37:17
23 [a]Ezek. 29:12; 30:17, 18, 26
25 [a]Ps. 9:16
26 [a]Ezek. 29:12

CHAPTER 31

1 [a]Ezek. 30:20; 32:1
2 [a]Ezek. 31:18
3 [a]Dan. 4:10, 20–23
4 [a]Jer. 51:36 [1]Or *channels*
5 [a]Dan. 4:11
6 [a]Dan. 4:12, 21 [1]Lit. *dwelled*
8 [a]Gen. 2:8, 9; 13:10

The fir trees were not like
its boughs,
And the [1]chestnut trees were
not like its branches;
No tree in the garden of
God was like it in beauty.
9 I made it beautiful with a
multitude of branches,
So that all the trees of Eden
envied it,
That *were* in the garden of
God.'

10 "Therefore thus says the
Lord GOD: 'Because you have
increased in height, and it set
its top among the thick boughs,
and [a]its heart was [1]lifted up in
its height,
11 'therefore I will deliver it
into the hand of the [a]mighty
one of the nations, and he shall
surely deal with it; I have driven
it out for its wickedness.
12 'And aliens, [a]the most terrible of the nations, have cut it
down and left it; its branches
have fallen [b]on the mountains
and in all the valleys; its boughs
lie [c]broken by all the rivers of
the land; and all the peoples of
the earth have gone from under
its shadow and left it.

13 'On [a]its ruin will remain all
the birds of the heavens,
And all the beasts of the
field will come to its
branches—

14 'So that no trees by the waters
may ever again exalt themselves
for their height, nor set their
tops among the thick boughs,
that no tree which drinks water
may ever be high enough to
reach up to them.

'For [a]they have all been
delivered to death,
[b]To the depths of the earth,
Among the children of men
who go down to the Pit.'

15 "Thus says the Lord GOD:
'In the day when it [a]went down
to [1]hell, I caused mourning. I
covered the deep because of it.
I restrained its rivers, and the
great waters were held back. I
caused Lebanon to [2]mourn for
it, and all the trees of the field
wilted because of it.
16 'I made the nations [a]shake
at the sound of its fall, when I
[b]cast it down to [1]hell together
with those who descend into the
Pit; and [c]all the trees of Eden,
the choice and best of Lebanon, all that drink water, [d]were
comforted in the depths of the
earth.
17 'They also went down to hell
with it, with those slain by the
sword; and *those who were* its
strong arm [a]dwelt in its shadows among the nations.
18 [a]"To which of the trees in
Eden will you then be likened
in glory and greatness? Yet you
shall be brought down with the
trees of Eden to the depths of
the earth; [b]you shall lie in the
midst of the uncircumcised, with
those slain by the sword. This *is*
Pharaoh and all his multitude,'
says the Lord GOD."

32 And it came to pass in
the twelfth year, in the
[a]twelfth *month,* on the first *day*
of the month, *that* the word of
the LORD came to me, saying,
2 "Son of man, [a]take up a lamentation for Pharaoh king of
Egypt, and say to him:

8 [1]Or *plane,* Heb. *armon*
10 [a]Dan. 5:20 [1]Proud
11 [a]Ezek. 30:10
12 [a]Ezek. 28:7; 30:11; 32:12 [b]Ezek. 32:5; 35:8 [c]Ezek. 30:24, 25
13 [a]Is. 18:6
14 [a]Ps. 82:7 [b]Ezek. 32:18
15 [a]Ezek. 32:22, 23 [1]Or *Sheol* [2]Lit. *be darkened*
16 [a]Ezek. 26:15 [b]Is. 14:15 [c]Is. 14:8 [d]Ezek. 32:31 [1]Or *Sheol*
17 [a]Lam. 4:20
18 [a]Ezek. 32:19 [b]Ezek. 28:10; 32:19, 21
CHAPTER 32
1 [a]Ezek. 31:1; 33:21
2 [a]Ezek. 27:2

[b]'You are like a young lion
among the nations,
And [c]you *are* like a monster
in the seas,
[d]Bursting forth in your rivers,
Troubling the waters with
your feet,
And [e]fouling their rivers.

3 'Thus says the Lord GOD:

"I will therefore [a]spread
My net over you with
a company of many
people,
And they will draw you up
in My net.
4 Then [a]I will leave you on the
land;
I will cast you out on the
open fields,
[b]And cause to [1]settle on
you all the birds of the
heavens.
And with you I will fill the
beasts of the whole
earth.
5 I will lay your flesh [a]on the
mountains,
And fill the valleys with
your carcass.

6 "I will also water the land
with the flow of your
blood,
Even to the mountains;
And the riverbeds will be
full of you.
7 When *I* put out your light,
[a]I will cover the heavens, and
make its stars dark;
I will cover the sun with a
cloud,
And the moon shall not give
her light.
8 All the [1]bright lights of the
heavens I will make dark
over you,

2 [b]Ezek. 19:2–6 [c]Ezek. 29:3 [d]Jer. 46:7, 8 [e]Ezek. 34:18
3 [a]Ezek. 12:13; 17:20
4 [a]Ezek. 29:5 [b]Is. 18:6; Ezek. 31:13 [1]Lit. *sit* or *dwell*
5 [a]Ezek. 31:12
7 [a]Rev. 6:12, 13; 8:12
8 [1]Or *shining*
10 [a]Ezek. 26:16
11 [a]Jer. 46:26
12 [a]Ezek. 28:7; 30:11; 31:12 [b]Ezek. 29:19
13 [a]Ezek. 29:11
14 [1]Lit. *sink;* settle, grow clear

And bring darkness upon
your land,"
Says the Lord GOD.

9 'I will also trouble the hearts
of many peoples, when I bring
your destruction among the nations, into the countries which
you have not known.
10 'Yes, I will make many peoples astonished at you, and their
kings shall be horribly afraid of
you when I brandish My sword
before them; and [a]they shall
tremble *every* moment, every
man for his own life, in the day
of your fall.
11 [a]"For thus says the Lord GOD:
"The sword of the king of Babylon shall come upon you.
12 "By the swords of the mighty
warriors, all of them [a]the most
terrible of the nations, I will
cause your multitude to fall.

[b]"They shall plunder the
pomp of Egypt,
And all its multitude shall
be destroyed.
13 Also I will destroy all its
animals
From beside its great
waters;
[a]The foot of man shall
muddy them no more,
Nor shall the hooves of
animals muddy them.
14 Then I will make their
waters [1]clear,
And make their rivers run
like oil,"
Says the Lord GOD.

15 "When I make the land of
Egypt desolate,
And the country is destitute
of all that once filled it,

When I strike all who dwell in it,
[a]Then they shall know that I *am* the LORD.

16 "This *is* the [a]lamentation
With which they shall lament her;
The daughters of the nations shall lament her;
They shall lament for her, for Egypt,
And for all her multitude,"
Says the Lord GOD.' "

17 It came to pass also in the
twelfth year, on the fifteenth *day*
of the month, [a]*that* the word of
the LORD came to me, saying:

18 "Son of man, wail over the multitude of Egypt,
And [a]cast them down to the depths of the earth,
Her and the daughters of the famous nations,
With those who go down to the Pit:
19 'Whom [a]do you surpass in beauty?
[b]Go down, be placed with the uncircumcised.'

20 "They shall fall in the midst of *those* slain by the sword;
She is delivered to the sword,
[a]Drawing her and all her multitudes.
21 [a]The strong among the mighty
Shall speak to him out of the midst of hell
With those who help him:
'They have [b]gone down,
They lie with the uncircumcised, slain by the sword.'

15 [a]Ps. 9:16
16 [a]Ezek. 26:17
17 [a]Ezek. 32:1; 33:21
18 [a]Ezek. 26:20; 31:14
19 [a]Ezek. 31:2, 18 [b]Ezek. 28:10
20 [a]Ps. 28:3
21 [a]Is. 1:31; 14:9, 10 [b]Ezek. 32:19, 25
22 [a]Ezek. 31:3, 16
23 [a]Is. 14:15 [b]Ezek. 32:24–27, 32
24 [a]Jer. 25:25; 49:34–39 [b]Ezek. 32:21 [c]Ezek. 32:23
25 [a]Ps. 139:8
26 [a]Gen. 10:2

22 "Assyria[a] *is* there, and all her company,
With their graves all around her,
All of them slain, fallen by the sword.
23 [a]Her graves are set in the recesses of the Pit,
And her company is all around her grave,
All of them slain, fallen by the sword,
Who [b]caused terror in the land of the living.

24 "There *is* [a]Ē′lam and all her multitude,
All around her grave,
All of them slain, fallen by the sword,
Who have [b]gone down uncircumcised to the lower parts of the earth,
[c]Who caused their terror in the land of the living;
Now they bear their shame with those who go down to the Pit.
25 They have set her [a]bed in the midst of the slain,
With all her multitude,
With her graves all around it,
All of them uncircumcised, slain by the sword;
Though their terror was caused
In the land of the living,
Yet they bear their shame
With those who go down to the Pit;
It was put in the midst of the slain.

26 "There *are* [a]Mē′shech and Tū′bal and all their multitudes,

With all their graves
around it,
All of them [b]uncircumcised,
slain by the sword,
Though they caused their
terror in the land of the
living.
27 [a]They do not lie with the
mighty
Who are fallen of the
uncircumcised,
Who have gone down to hell
with their weapons of
war;
They have laid their swords
under their heads,
But their iniquities will be
on their bones,
Because of the terror of the
mighty in the land of the
living.
28 Yes, you shall be broken
in the midst of the
uncircumcised,
And lie with *those* slain by
the sword.

29 "There *is* [a]Ē'dom,
Her kings and all her
princes,
Who despite their might
Are laid beside *those* slain
by the sword;
They shall lie with the
uncircumcised,
And with those who go
down to the Pit.
30 [a]There *are* the princes of the
north,
All of them, and all the
[b]Sī·dō'ni·ans,
Who have gone down with
the slain
In shame at the terror which
they caused by their
might;
They lie uncircumcised with
those slain by the sword,
And bear their shame with
those who go down to
the Pit.

31 "Pharaoh will see them
And be [a]comforted over all
his multitude,
Pharaoh and all his army,
Slain by the sword,"
Says the Lord GOD.

32 "For I have caused My terror
in the land of the living;
And he shall be placed
in the midst of the
uncircumcised
With *those* slain by the
sword,
Pharaoh and all his
multitude,"
Says the Lord GOD.

33 Again the word of the
LORD came to me, saying,
2 "Son of man, speak to [a]the
children of your people, and
say to them: [b]'When I bring the
sword upon a land, and the people of the land take a man from
their territory and make him
their [c]watchman,
3 'when he sees the sword
coming upon the land, if he
blows the trumpet and warns
the people,
4 'then whoever hears the
sound of the trumpet and does
[a]not take warning, if the sword
comes and takes him away, [b]his
blood shall be on his *own* head.
5 'He heard the sound of the
trumpet, but did not take warning; his blood shall be upon himself. But he who takes warning
will [1]save his life.
6 'But if the watchman sees
the sword coming and does
not blow the trumpet, and the

26 [b]Ezek. 32:19
27 [a]Is. 14:18, 19
29 [a]Ezek. 25:12–14
30 [a]Jer. 1:15; 25:26 [b]Ezek. 28:21–23
31 [a]Ezek. 14:22; 31:16

CHAPTER 33

2 [a]Ezek. 3:11 [b]Ezek. 14:17 [c]2 Sam. 18:24, 25
4 [a]Zech. 1:4 [b][Acts 18:6]
5 [1]Or *deliver his soul*

people are not warned, and the
sword comes and takes *any* person from among them, [a]he is
taken away in his iniquity; but
his blood I will require at the
watchman's hand.'
7 [a]"So you, son of man: I have
made you a watchman for the
house of Israel; therefore you
shall hear a word from My
mouth and warn them for Me.
8 "When I say to the wicked,
'O wicked *man,* you shall surely
die!' and you do not speak to
warn the wicked from his way,
that wicked *man* shall die in his
iniquity; but his blood I will require at your hand.
9 "Nevertheless if you warn
the wicked to turn from his way,
and he does not turn from his
way, he shall die in his iniquity;
but you have [1]delivered your
soul.
10 "Therefore you, O son of
man, say to the house of Israel:
'Thus you say, "If our transgressions and our sins *lie* upon us,
and we [a]pine[1] away in them,
[b]how can we then live?" '
11 "Say to them: '*As* I live,' says
the Lord GOD, [a]"I have no pleasure in the death of the wicked,
but that the wicked [b]turn from
his way and live. Turn, turn from
your evil ways! For [c]why should
you die, O house of Israel?'
12 "Therefore you, O son of
man, say to the children of your
people: 'The [a]righteousness of
the righteous man shall not deliver him in the day of his transgression; as for the wickedness
of the wicked, [b]he shall not fall
because of it in the day that he
turns from his wickedness; nor
shall the righteous be able to
live because of *his righteousness* in the day that he sins.'
13 "When I say to the righteous
that he shall surely live, [a]but
he trusts in his own righteousness and commits iniquity, none
of his righteous works shall be
remembered; but because of the
iniquity that he has committed,
he shall die.
14 "Again, [a]when I say to the
wicked, 'You shall surely die,' if
he turns from his sin and does
[1]what is lawful and [2]right,
15 "*if* the wicked [a]restores the
pledge, [b]gives back what he has
stolen, and walks in [c]the statutes
of life without committing iniquity, he shall surely live; he shall
not die.
16 [a]"None of his sins which he
has committed shall be remembered against him; he has done
what is lawful and right; he shall
surely live.
17 [a]"Yet the children of your
people say, 'The way of the Lord
is not [1]fair.' But it is their way
which is not fair!
18 [a]"When the righteous turns
from his righteousness and
commits iniquity, he shall die
because of it.
19 "But when the wicked turns
from his wickedness and does
what is lawful and right, he shall
live because of it.
20 "Yet you say, [a]'The way of
the Lord is not [1]fair.' O house
of Israel, I will judge every one
of you according to his own
ways."
21 And it came to pass in the
twelfth year [a]of our captivity, in
the tenth *month,* on the fifth *day*
of the month, [b]*that* one who had
escaped from Jerusalem came

6 [a]Ezek. 33:8
7 [a]Is. 62:6
9 [1]Or *saved your life*
10 [a]Ezek. 24:23 [b]Is. 49:14 [1]Or *waste away*
11 [a][2 Sam. 14:14] [b][Acts 3:19] [c]Ezek. 18:30, 31
12 [a]Ezek. 3:20; 18:24, 26 [b][2 Chr. 7:14]
13 [a]Ezek. 3:20; 18:24
14 [a]Ezek. 3:18, 19; 18:27 [1]*justice* [2]*righteousness*
15 [a]Ezek. 18:7 [b]Lev. 6:2, 4, 5 [c]Ezek. 20:11, 13, 21
16 [a][Is. 1:18; 43:25]
17 [a]Ezek. 18:25, 29 [1]Or *equitable*
18 [a]Ezek. 18:26
20 [a]Ezek. 18:25, 29 [1]Or *equitable*
21 [a]Ezek. 1:2 [b]Ezek. 24:26

to me and said, [c]"The city has been [1]captured!"

22 Now [a]the hand of the LORD had been upon me the evening before the man came who had escaped. And He had [b]opened my mouth; so when he came to me in the morning, my mouth was opened, and I was no longer mute.

23 Then the word of the LORD came to me, saying:

24 "Son of man, [a]they who inhabit those [b]ruins in the land of Israel are saying, [c]'Abraham was only one, and he inherited the land. [d]But we *are* many; the land has been given to us as a [e]possession.'

25 "Therefore say to them, 'Thus says the Lord GOD: [a]"You eat *meat* with blood, you [b]lift up your eyes toward your idols, and [c]shed blood. Should you then possess the [d]land?

26 "You rely on your sword, you commit abominations, and you [a]defile one another's wives. Should you then possess the land?" '

27 "Say thus to them, 'Thus says the Lord GOD: "*As* I live, surely [a]those who *are* in the ruins shall fall by the sword, and the one who *is* in the open field [b]I will give to the beasts to be devoured, and those who *are* in the strongholds and [c]caves shall die of the pestilence.

28 [a]"For I will make the land most desolate, [1]her [b]arrogant strength shall cease, and [c]the mountains of Israel shall be so desolate that no one will pass through.

29 "Then they shall know that I *am* the LORD, when I have made the land most desolate because of all their abominations which they have committed." '

30 "As for you, son of man, the children of your people are talking about you beside the walls and in the doors of the houses; and they [a]speak to one another, everyone saying to his brother, 'Please come and hear what the word is that comes from the LORD.'

31 "So [a]they come to you as people do, they [b]sit before you *as* My people, and they [c]hear your words, but they do not do them; [d]for with their mouth they show much love, *but* [e]their hearts pursue their *own* gain.

32 "Indeed you *are* to them as a very lovely song of one who has a pleasant voice and can play well on an instrument; for they hear your words, but they do [a]not do them.

33 [a]"And when this comes to pass—surely it will come—then [b]they will know that a prophet has been among them."

34

And the word of the LORD came to me, saying,

2 "Son of man, prophesy against the shepherds of Israel, prophesy and say to them, 'Thus says the Lord GOD to the shepherds: [a]"Woe to the shepherds of Israel who feed themselves! Should not the shepherds feed the flocks?

3 [a]"You eat the fat and clothe yourselves with the wool; you [b]slaughter the fatlings, *but* you do not feed the flock.

4 [a]"The weak you have not strengthened, nor have you healed those who were sick, nor bound up the broken, nor brought back what was driven away, nor [b]sought what was lost;

21 [c]2 Kin. 25:4 [1]Lit. *struck down*
22 [a]Ezek. 1:3; 8:1; 37:1 [b]Ezek. 24:27
24 [a]Ezek. 34:2 [b]Ezek. 36:4 [c]Is. 51:2 [d][Matt. 3:9] [e]Ezek. 11:15
25 [a]Lev. 3:17; 7:26; 17:10–14; 19:26 [b]Ezek. 18:6 [c]Ezek. 22:6, 9 [d]Deut. 29:28
26 [a]Ezek. 18:6; 22:11
27 [a]Ezek. 33:24 [b]Ezek. 39:4 [c]1 Sam. 13:6
28 [a]Jer. 44:2, 6, 22 [b]Ezek. 7:24; 24:21 [c]Ezek. 6:2, 3, 6 [1]Lit. *pride of her strength*
30 [a]Is. 29:13
31 [a]Ezek. 14:1 [b]Ezek. 8:1 [c]Is. 58:2 [d]Ps. 78:36, 37 [e][Matt. 13:22]
32 [a][Matt. 7:21–28]
33 [a]1 Sam. 3:20 [b]Ezek. 2:5

CHAPTER 34

2 [a]Zech. 11:17
3 [a]Zech. 11:16 [b]Ezek. 33:25, 26
4 [a]Zech. 11:16 [b]Luke 15:4

but with [c]force and [1]cruelty you
have ruled them.
5 [a]"So they were [b]scattered because *there was* no shepherd;
[c]and they became food for all
the beasts of the field when they
were scattered.
6 "My sheep [a]wandered through
all the mountains, and on every
high hill; yes, My flock was scattered over the whole face of the
earth, and no one was seeking or
searching *for them.*"
7 'Therefore, you shepherds,
hear the word of the LORD:
8 "*As* I live," says the Lord
GOD, "surely because My flock
became a prey, and My flock
[a]became food for every beast of
the field, because *there was* no
shepherd, nor did My shepherds
search for My flock, [b]but the
shepherds fed themselves and
did not feed My flock"—
9 'therefore, O shepherds, hear
the word of the LORD!
10 'Thus says the Lord GOD:
"Behold, I *am* [a]against the shepherds, and [b]I will require My
flock at their hand; I will cause
them to cease feeding the sheep,
and the shepherds shall [c]feed
themselves no more; for I will
[d]deliver My flock from their
mouths, that they may no longer
be food for them."
11 'For thus says the Lord GOD:
"Indeed I Myself will search for
My sheep and seek them out.
12 "As a [a]shepherd seeks out his
flock on the day he is among his
scattered sheep, so will I seek
out My sheep and deliver them
from all the places where they
were scattered on [b]a cloudy and
dark day.
13 "And [a]I will bring them out
from the peoples and gather
them from the countries, and
will bring them to their own
land; I will feed them on the
mountains of Israel, [1]in the valleys and in all the inhabited
places of the country.
14 [a]"I will feed them in good
pasture, and their fold shall be
on the high mountains of Israel.
[b]There they shall lie down in a
good fold and feed in rich pasture on the mountains of Israel.
15 "I will feed My flock, and I
will make them lie down," says
the Lord GOD.
16 [a]"I will seek what was lost
and bring back what was driven
away, bind up the broken and
strengthen what was sick;
but I will destroy [b]the fat and
the strong, and feed them [c]in
judgment."
17 'And *as for* you, O My flock,
thus says the Lord GOD: [a]"Behold,
I shall judge between sheep and
sheep, between rams and goats.
18 "*Is it* too little for you to
have eaten up the good pasture,
that you must tread down with
your feet the [1]residue of your
pasture—and to have drunk of
the clear waters, that you must
foul the residue with your feet?
19 "And *as for* My flock, they
eat what you have trampled with
your feet, and they drink what
you have fouled with your feet."
20 'Therefore thus says the Lord
GOD to them: [a]"Behold, I Myself
will judge between the fat and
the lean sheep.
21 "Because you have pushed
with side and shoulder, butted all
the weak ones with your horns,
and scattered them abroad,
22 "therefore I will save My
flock, and they shall no longer

4 [c][1 Pet. 5:3] [1]*harshness* or *rigor*
5 [a]Ezek. 33:21 [b]Matt. 9:36 [c]Is. 56:9
6 [a]1 Pet. 2:25
8 [a]Ezek. 34:5, 6 [b]Ezek. 34:2, 10
10 [a]Jer. 21:13; 52:24–27 [b]Heb. 13:17 [c]Ezek. 34:2, 8 [d]Ezek. 13:23
12 [a]Jer. 31:10 [b]Ezek. 30:3
13 [a]Jer. 23:3 [1]Or *by the streams*
14 [a][John 10:9] [b]Jer. 33:12
16 [a]Mic. 4:6 [b]Is. 10:16 [c]Jer. 10:24
17 [a][Matt. 25:32]
18 [1]*remainder*
20 [a]Ezek. 34:17

be a prey; and I will judge between sheep and sheep.
23 "I will establish one [a]shep-
herd over them, and he shall
feed them—[b]My servant David.
He shall feed them and be their
shepherd.
24 "And [a]I, the LORD, will be
their God, and My servant David [b]a prince among them; I, the
LORD, have spoken.
25 [a]"I will make a covenant of
peace with them, and [b]cause
wild beasts to cease from the
land; and they [c]will dwell safely
in the wilderness and sleep in
the woods.
26 "I will make them and the
places all around [a]My hill [b]a
blessing; and I will [c]cause showers to come down in their season; there shall be [d]showers of
blessing.
27 "Then [a]the trees of the field
shall yield their fruit, and the
earth shall yield her increase.
They shall be safe in their land;
and they shall know that I *am*
the LORD, when I have [b]broken
the bands of their yoke and delivered them from the hand of
those who [c]enslaved them.
28 "And they shall no longer be
a prey for the nations, nor shall
beasts of the land devour them;
but [a]they shall dwell safely, and
no one shall make *them* afraid.
29 "I will raise up for them a
[a]garden[1] of renown, and they
shall [b]no longer be consumed
with hunger in the land, [c]nor
bear the shame of the Gentiles
anymore.
30 "Thus they shall know that
[a]I, the LORD their God, *am* with
them, and they, the house of
Israel, *are* [b]My people," says the
Lord GOD.'
31 "You are My [a]flock, the flock
of My pasture; you *are* men, *and*
I *am* your God," says the Lord
GOD.

35

Moreover the word of the
LORD came to me, saying,
2 "Son of man, set your face
against [a]Mount Sē'ir and [b]proph-
esy against it,
3 "and say to it, 'Thus says the
Lord GOD:

"Behold, O Mount Sē'ir, I *am*
against you;
[a]I will stretch out My hand
against you,
And make you [1]most
desolate;
4 I shall lay your cities waste,
And you shall be desolate.
Then you shall know that I
am the LORD.

5 [a]"Because you have had an
[1]ancient hatred, and have shed
the blood of the children of Israel by the power of the sword at
the time of their calamity, [b]when
their iniquity *came to an* end,
6 "therefore, *as* I live," says
the Lord GOD, "I will prepare
you for [a]blood, and blood shall
pursue you; [b]since you have not
hated [1]blood, therefore blood
shall pursue you.
7 "Thus I will make Mount
Sē'ir [1]most desolate, and cut off
from it the [a]one who leaves and
the one who returns.
8 "And I will fill its mountains
with the slain; on your hills and
in your valleys and in all your
ravines those who are slain by
the sword shall fall.
9 [a]"I will make you [1]perpetu-
ally desolate, and your cities
shall be uninhabited; [b]then you
shall know that I *am* the LORD.

23 [a][Is. 40:11] [b]Jer. 30:9
24 [a]Ex. 29:45 [b]Ezek. 37:24, 25
25 [a]Ezek. 37:26 [b]Is. 11:6–9 [c]Jer. 23:6
26 [a]Is. 56:7 [b]Zech. 8:13 [c]Lev. 26:4 [d]Ps. 68:9
27 [a]Is. 4:2 [b]Jer. 2:20 [c]Jer. 25:14
28 [a]Jer. 30:10
29 [a][Is. 11:1] [b]Ezek. 36:29 [c]Ezek. 36:3, 6, 15 [1]Lit. *planting place*
30 [a]Ezek. 34:24 [b]Ezek. 14:11; 36:28
31 [a]Ps. 100:3

CHAPTER 35

2 [a]Ezek. 25:12–14 [b]Amos 1:11
3 [a]Ezek. 6:14 [1]Lit. *a desolation and a waste*
5 [a]Ezek. 25:12 [b]Ps. 137:7 [1]Or *everlasting*
6 [a]Is. 63:1–6 [b]Ps. 109:17 [1]Or *bloodshed*
7 [a]Judg. 5:6 [1]Lit. *a waste and a desolation*
9 [a]Jer. 49:13 [b]Ezek. 36:11 [1]Lit. *desolated forever*

10 "Because you have said, 'These two nations and these two countries shall be mine, and we will [a]possess them,' although [b]the LORD was there,

11 "therefore, *as* I live," says the Lord GOD, "I will do [a]according to your anger and according to the envy which you showed in your hatred against them; and I will make Myself known among them when I judge you.

12 [a]"Then you shall know that I *am* the LORD. I have [b]heard all your [c]blasphemies which you have spoken against the mountains of Israel, saying, 'They are desolate; they are given to us to consume.'

13 "Thus [a]with your mouth you have [1]boasted against Me and multiplied your [b]words against Me; I have heard *them.*"

14 'Thus says the Lord GOD: [a]"The whole earth will rejoice when I make you desolate.

15 [a]"As you rejoiced because the inheritance of the house of Israel was desolate, [b]so I will do to you; you shall be desolate, O Mount Sē′ir, as well as all of Ē′dom—all of it! Then they shall know that I *am* the LORD." '

36

"And you, son of man, prophesy to the [a]mountains of Israel, and say, 'O mountains of Israel, hear the word of the LORD!

2 'Thus says the Lord GOD: "Because [a]the enemy has said of you, 'Aha! [b]The [1]ancient heights [c]have become our possession,' " '

3 "therefore prophesy, and say, 'Thus says the Lord GOD: "Because they made *you* desolate and swallowed you up on every side, so that you became the possession of the rest of the nations, [a]and you are taken up by the lips of [b]talkers and slandered by the people"—

4 'therefore, O mountains of Israel, hear the word of the Lord GOD! Thus says the Lord GOD to the mountains, the hills, the [1]rivers, the valleys, the desolate wastes, and the cities that have been forsaken, which [a]became plunder and [b]mockery to the rest of the nations all around—

5 'therefore thus says the Lord GOD: [a]"Surely I have spoken in My burning jealousy against the rest of the nations and against all Ē′dom, [b]who gave My land to themselves as a possession, with wholehearted joy *and* [1]spiteful minds, in order to plunder its open country." '

6 "Therefore prophesy concerning the land of Israel, and say to the mountains, the hills, the rivers, and the valleys, 'Thus says the Lord GOD: "Behold, I have spoken in My jealousy and My fury, because you have [a]borne the shame of the nations."

7 'Therefore thus says the Lord GOD: "I have [a]raised My hand in an oath that surely the nations that *are* around you shall [b]bear their own shame.

8 "But you, O mountains of Israel, you shall shoot forth your branches and yield your fruit to My people Israel, for they are about to come.

9 "For indeed I *am* for you, and I will turn to you, and you shall be tilled and sown.

10 "I will multiply men upon you, all the house of Israel, all of it; and the cities shall be inhabited and [a]the ruins rebuilt.

11 [a]"I will multiply upon you man and beast; and they shall

10 [a]Ps. 83:4–12 [b][Ps. 48:1–3; 132:13, 14]
11 [a][James 2:13]
12 [a]Ps. 9:16 [b]Zeph. 2:8 [c]Is. 52:5
13 [a][1 Sam. 2:3] [b]Ezek. 36:3 [1]Lit. *made yourself great*
14 [a]Is. 65:13, 14
15 [a]Obad. 12, 15 [b]Lam. 4:21

CHAPTER 36

1 [a]Ezek. 6:2, 3
2 [a]Ezek. 25:3; 26:2 [b]Deut. 32:13 [c]Ezek. 35:10 [1]Or *everlasting*
3 [a]Deut. 28:37 [b]Ezek. 35:13
4 [a]Ezek. 34:8, 28 [b]Ps. 79:4 [1]Or *ravines*
5 [a]Deut. 4:24 [b]Ezek. 35:10, 12 [1]Lit. *scorning souls*
6 [a]Ps. 74:10; 123:3, 4
7 [a]Ezek. 20:5 [b]Jer. 25:9, 15, 29
10 [a]Amos 9:14
11 [a]Jer. 31:27; 33:12

into them, and they lived, and
stood upon their feet, an exceedingly great army.
11 Then He said to me, "Son of
man, these bones are the [a]whole
house of Israel. They indeed say,
[b]'Our bones are dry, our hope is
lost, and we ourselves are cut
off!'
12 "Therefore prophesy and say
to them, 'Thus says the Lord
GOD: "Behold, [a]O My people,
I will open your graves and
cause you to come up from your
graves, and [b]bring you into the
land of Israel.
13 "Then you shall know that
I *am* the LORD, when I have
opened your graves, O My people, and brought you up from
your graves.
14 "I [a]will put My Spirit in you,
and you shall live, and I will
place you in your own land.
Then you shall know that I, the
LORD, have spoken *it* and performed *it*," says the LORD.' "
15 Again the word of the LORD
came to me, saying,
16 "As for you, son of man,
[a]take a stick for yourself and
write on it: 'For Judah and for
[b]the children of Israel, his companions.' Then take another
stick and write on it, 'For Joseph, the stick of Ē′phra·im, and
for all the house of Israel, his
companions.'
17 "Then [a]join them one to another for yourself into one stick,
and they will become one in
your hand.
18 "And when the children of
your people speak to you, saying, [a]'Will you not show us what
you *mean* by these?'—
19 [a]"say to them, 'Thus says the
Lord GOD: "Surely I will take
[b]the stick of Joseph, which *is* in
the hand of Ē′phra·im, and the
tribes of Israel, his companions;
and I will join them with it, with
the stick of Judah, and make
them one stick, and they will be
one in My hand." '
20 "And the sticks on which
you write will be in your hand
[a]before their eyes.
21 "Then say to them, 'Thus
says the Lord GOD: "Surely [a]I
will take the children of Israel
from among the nations, wherever they have gone, and will
gather them from every side and
bring them into their own land;
22 "and [a]I will make them one
nation in the land, on the mountains of Israel; and [b]one king
shall be king over them all; they
shall no longer be two nations,
nor shall they ever be divided
into two kingdoms again.
23 [a]"They shall not defile themselves anymore with their idols,
nor with their detestable things,
nor with any of their transgressions; but [b]I will deliver them
from all their dwelling places in
which they have sinned, and will
cleanse them. Then they shall
be My people, and I will be their
God.
24 [a]"David My servant *shall be* ☆
king over them, and [b]they shall
all have one shepherd; [c]they
shall also walk in My judgments
and observe My statutes, and do
them.
25 [a]"Then they shall dwell in ☆
the land that I have given to
Jacob My servant, where your
fathers dwelt; and they shall
dwell there, they, their children,
and their children's children,
[b]forever; and [c]My servant David
shall be their prince forever.

11 [a]Ezek. 36:10 [b]Ps. 141:7
12 [a]Is. 26:19; 66:14 [b]Ezek. 36:24
14 [a]Ezek. 36:27
16 [a]Num. 17:2, 3 [b]2 Chr. 11:12, 13, 16; 15:9; 30:11, 18
17 [a]Hos. 1:11
18 [a]Ezek. 12:9; 24:19
19 [a]Zech. 10:6 [b]Ezek. 37:16, 17
20 [a]Ezek. 12:3
21 [a]Ezek. 36:24
22 [a]Jer. 3:18 [b]Ezek. 34:23
23 [a]Ezek. 36:25 [b]Ezek. 36:28, 29
24 [a]Is. 40:11; [Luke 1:32]; 1 Pet. 2:25 [b][John 10:16] [c]Ezek. 36:27
25 [a]Ezek. 36:28; Rev. 21:3; 22:3 [b]Is. 60:21 [c]John 12:34

26 "Moreover I will [1]make [a]a
covenant of peace with them,
and it shall be an everlasting
covenant with them; I will establish them and [b]multiply them,
and I will set My [c]sanctuary in
their midst forevermore.
27 [a]"My tabernacle also shall
be with them; indeed I will be
[b]their God, and they shall be My
people.
28 [a]"The nations also will know
that I, the LORD, [b]sanctify Israel,
when My sanctuary is in their
midst forevermore." ' "

38

Now the word of the LORD
came to me, saying,
2 [a]"Son of man, [b]set your face
against [c]Gog, of the land of [d]Mā'-
gog, [1]the prince of Rosh, [e]Mē'-
shech, and Tū'bal, and prophesy
against him,
3 "and say, 'Thus says the Lord
GOD: "Behold, I *am* against you,
O Gog, the prince of Rosh, Mē'-
shech, and Tū'bal.
4 [a]"I will turn you around, put
hooks into your jaws, and [b]lead
you out, with all your army,
horses, and horsemen, [c]all splen-
didly clothed, a great company
with bucklers and shields, all of
them handling swords.
5 "Persia, [1]Ethiopia, and [2]Lib'ya
are with them, all of them *with*
shield and helmet;
6 [a]"Gō'mer and all its troops;
the house of [b]Tō·gar'mah *from*
the far north and all its troops—
many people *are* with you.
7 [a]"Prepare yourself and be
ready, you and all your companies that are gathered about
you; and be a guard for them.
8 [a]"After many days [b]you will
be visited. In the latter years you
will come into the land of those
brought back from the sword
[c]*and* gathered from many people on [d]the mountains of Israel,
which had long been desolate;
they were brought out of the nations, and now all of them [e]dwell
safely.
9 "You will ascend, coming
[a]like a storm, covering the [b]land
like a cloud, you and all your
troops and many peoples with
you."
10 'Thus says the Lord GOD:
"On that day it shall come to
pass *that* thoughts will arise in
your mind, and you will make
an evil plan:
11 "You will say, 'I will go up
against a land of [a]unwalled villages; I will [b]go to a peaceful
people, [c]who dwell [1]safely, all
of them dwelling without walls,
and having neither bars nor
gates'—
12 "to take plunder and to
take booty, to stretch out your
hand against the waste places
that are again inhabited, [a]and
against a people gathered from
the nations, who have acquired
livestock and goods, who dwell
in the midst of the land.
13 [a]"Shē'ba, [b]Dē'dan, the merchants [c]of Tar'shish, and all
[d]their young lions will say to you,
'Have you come to take plunder?
Have you gathered your army to
take booty, to carry away silver
and gold, to take away livestock and goods, to take great
plunder?' " '
14 "Therefore, son of man,
prophesy and say to Gog, 'Thus
says the Lord GOD: [a]"On that day
when My people Israel [b]dwell
safely, will you not know *it*?
15 [a]"Then you will come from
your place out of the far north,
you and many peoples with you,

26 [a]Is. 55:3 [b]Ezek. 36:10 [c][2 Cor. 6:16] [1]Lit. *cut*
27 [a][John 1:14] [b]Ezek. 11:20
28 [a]Ezek. 36:23 [b]Ezek. 20:12

CHAPTER 38

2 [a]Ezek. 39:1 [b]Ezek. 35:2, 3 [c]Rev. 20:8 [d]Gen. 10:2 [e]Ezek. 32:26 [1]Tg., Vg., Aquila *the chief prince of Meshech,* also v. 3
4 [a]2 Kin. 19:28 [b]Is. 43:17 [c]Ezek. 23:12
5 [1]Heb. *Cush* [2]Heb. *Put*
6 [a]Gen. 10:2 [b]Ezek. 27:14
7 [a]Is. 8:9, 10
8 [a]Is. 24:22 [b]Is. 29:6 [c]Ezek. 34:13 [d]Ezek. 36:1, 4 [e]Ezek. 34:25; 39:26
9 [a]Is. 28:2 [b]Jer. 4:13
11 [a]Zech. 2:4 [b]Jer. 49:31 [c]Ezek. 38:8 [1]*securely*
12 [a]Ezek. 38:8
13 [a]Ezek. 27:22 [b]Ezek. 27:15, 20 [c]Ezek. 27:12 [d]Ezek. 19:3, 5
14 [a]Is. 4:1 [b]Ezek. 38:8, 11
15 [a]Ezek. 39:2

all of them riding on horses, a
great company and a mighty
army.
16 "You will come up against
My people Israel like a cloud, to
cover the land. It will be in the
latter days that I will bring you
against My land, so that the nations may [a]know Me, when I am
[b]hallowed in you, O Gog, before
their eyes."
17 'Thus says the Lord GOD:
"Are *you* he of whom I have spoken in former days by My servants the prophets of Israel, who
prophesied for years in those
days that I would bring you
against them?
18 "And it will come to pass at
the same time, when Gog comes
against the land of Israel," says
the Lord GOD, "*that* My fury will
show in My face.
19 "For [a]in My jealousy [b]*and* in
the fire of My wrath I have spoken: [c]'Surely in that day there
shall be a great [1]earthquake in
the land of Israel,
20 'so that [a]the fish of the sea,
the birds of the heavens, the
beasts of the field, all creeping
things that creep on the earth,
and all men who *are* on the
face of the earth shall shake at
My presence. [b]The mountains
shall be thrown down, the steep
places shall fall, and every wall
shall fall to the ground.'
21 "I will [a]call for [b]a sword
against Gog throughout all My
mountains," says the Lord GOD.
[c]"Every man's sword will be
against his brother.
22 "And I will [a]bring him to
judgment with [b]pestilence and
bloodshed; [c]I will rain down on
him, on his troops, and on the
many peoples who *are* with him,
flooding rain, [d]great hailstones,
fire, and brimstone.
23 "Thus I will magnify Myself
and [a]sanctify Myself, [b]and I will
be known in the eyes of many
nations. Then they shall know
that I *am* the LORD." '

39 "And [a]you, son of man,
prophesy against Gog,
and say, 'Thus says the Lord
GOD: "Behold, I *am* against you,
O Gog, [1]the prince of Rosh, Mē′-
shech, and Tū′bal;
2 "and I will [a]turn you around
and lead you on, [b]bringing you
up from the far north, and bring
you against the mountains of
Israel.
3 "Then I will knock the bow
out of your left hand, and cause
the arrows to fall out of your
right hand.
4 [a]"You shall [1]fall upon the
mountains of Israel, you and all
your troops and the peoples who
are with you; [b]I will give you to
birds of prey of every sort and
to the beasts of the field to be
devoured.
5 "You shall [1]fall on [2]the open
field; for I have spoken," says
the Lord GOD.
6 [a]"And I will send fire on Mā′-
gog and on those who live [1]in
security in [b]the coastlands. Then
they shall know that I *am* the
LORD.
7 [a]"So I will make My holy
name known in the midst of My
people Israel, and I will not *let*
them [b]profane My holy name
anymore. [c]Then the nations
shall know that *I am* the LORD,
the Holy One in Israel.
8 [a]"Surely it is coming, and it
shall be done," says the Lord
GOD. "This *is* the day [b]of which I
have spoken.

16 [a]Ezek. 35:11 [b]Ezek. 28:22
19 [a]Ezek. 36:5, 6 [b]Ps. 89:46 [c]Rev. 16:18 [1]Lit. *shaking*
20 [a]Hos. 4:3 [b]Jer. 4:24
21 [a]Ps. 105:16 [b]Ezek. 14:17 [c]1 Sam. 14:20
22 [a]Is. 66:16 [b]Ezek. 5:17 [c]Ps. 11:6 [d]Rev. 16:21
23 [a]Ezek. 36:23 [b]Ezek. 37:28; 38:16

CHAPTER 39

1 [a]Ezek. 38:2, 3 [1]Tg., Vg., Aquila *the chief prince of Meshech*
2 [a]Ezek. 38:8 [b]Ezek. 38:15
4 [a]Ezek. 38:4, 21 [b]Ezek. 33:27 [1]Be slain
5 [1]Be slain [2]Lit. *the face of the field*
6 [a]Amos 1:4, 7, 10 [b]Ps. 72:10 [1]*securely* or *confidently*
7 [a]Ezek. 39:25 [b]Lev. 18:21 [c]Ezek. 38:16
8 [a]Rev. 16:17; 21:6 [b]Ezek. 38:17

9 "Then those who dwell in the cities of Israel will go out and set on fire and burn the weapons, both the shields and bucklers, the bows and arrows, the [1]javelins and spears; and they will make fires with them for seven years.

10 "They will not take wood from the field nor cut down *any* from the forests, because they will make fires with the weapons; [a]and they will plunder those who plundered them, and pillage those who pillaged them," says the Lord GOD.

11 "It will come to pass in that day *that* I will give Gog a burial place there in Israel, the valley of those who pass by east of the sea; and it will obstruct travelers, because there they will bury Gog and all his multitude. Therefore they will call *it* the Valley of [1]Hā′mon Gog.

12 "For seven months the house of Israel will be burying them, [a]in order to cleanse the land.

13 "Indeed all the people of the land will be burying, and they will gain [a]renown for it on the day that [b]I am glorified," says the Lord GOD.

14 "They will set apart men regularly employed, with the help of [1]a search party, to pass through the land and bury those bodies remaining on the ground, in order [a]to cleanse it. At the end of seven months they will make a search.

15 "The search party will pass through the land; and *when anyone* sees a man's bone, he shall [1]set up a marker by it, till the buriers have buried it in the Valley of Hā′mon Gog.

16 "*The* name of *the* city *will* also *be* [1]Ha·mō′nah. Thus they shall [a]cleanse the land." '

17 "And as for you, son of man, thus says the Lord GOD, [a]'Speak to every sort of bird and to every beast of the field:

[b]"Assemble yourselves and
come;
Gather together from all
sides to My [c]sacrificial
meal
Which I am sacrificing for
you,
A great sacrificial meal [d]on
the mountains of Israel,
That you may eat flesh and
drink blood.
18 [a]You shall eat the flesh of the
mighty,
Drink the blood of the
princes of the earth,
Of rams and lambs,
Of goats and bulls,
All of them [b]fatlings of
Bā′shan.
19 You shall eat fat till you are
full,
And drink blood till you are
drunk,
At My sacrificial meal
Which I am sacrificing for
you.
20 [a]You shall be filled at My
table
With horses and riders,
[b]With mighty men
And with all the men of
war," says the Lord GOD.

21 [a]"I will set My glory among the nations; all the nations shall see My judgment which I have executed, and [b]My hand which I have laid on them.

22 [a]"So the house of Israel shall know that I *am* the LORD their God from that day forward.

9 [1]Lit. *hand staffs*
10 [a]Is. 14:2; 33:1
11 [1]Lit. *The Multitude of Gog*
12 [a]Deut. 21:23
13 [a]Zeph. 3:19, 20 [b]Ezek. 28:22
14 [a]Ezek. 39:12 [1]Lit. *those who pass through*
15 [1]*build*
16 [a]Ezek. 39:12 [1]Lit. *Multitude*
17 [a]Rev. 19:17, 18 [b]Is. 18:6 [c]Zeph. 1:7 [d]Ezek. 39:4
18 [a]Rev. 19:18 [b]Deut. 32:14
20 [a]Ps. 76:5, 6 [b]Rev. 19:18
21 [a]Ezek. 36:23; 38:23 [b]Ex. 7:4
22 [a]Ex. 39:7, 28

23 [a]"The Gentiles shall know
that the house of Israel went
into captivity for their iniquity;
because they were unfaithful to
Me, therefore [b]I hid My face
from them. I [c]gave them into the
hand of their enemies, and they
all fell by the sword.
24 [a]"According to their uncleanness and according to their
transgressions I have dealt with
them, and hidden My face from
them." '
25 "Therefore thus says the
Lord GOD: [a]'Now I will bring
back the captives of Jacob, and
have mercy on the [b]whole house
of Israel; and I will be jealous
for My holy name—
26 [a]'after they have borne their
shame, and all their unfaithfulness in which they were unfaithful to Me, when they [b]dwelt
safely in their *own* land and no
one made *them* afraid.
27 [a]'When I have brought them
back from the peoples and
gathered them out of their enemies' lands, and I [b]am hallowed
in them in the sight of many
nations,
28 [a]'then they shall know that I
am the LORD their God, who sent
them into captivity among the
nations, but also brought them
back to their land, and left none
of them [1]captive any longer.
29 [a]'And I will not hide My face
from them anymore; for I shall
have [b]poured out My Spirit on
the house of Israel,' says the
Lord GOD."

CHAPTER 40

40 In the twenty-fifth year
of our captivity, at the beginning of the year, on the tenth
day of the month, in the fourteenth year after [a]the city was
[1]captured, on the very same day
[b]the hand of the LORD was upon
me; and He took me there.
2 [a]In the visions of God He
took me into the land of Israel
and [b]set me on a very high
mountain; on it toward the south
was something like the structure
of a city.
3 He took me there, and behold, *there was* a man whose
appearance *was* [a]like the appearance of bronze. [b]He had a
line of flax [c]and a measuring rod
in his hand, and he stood in the
gateway.
4 And the man said to me,
[a]"Son of man, look with your
eyes and hear with your ears,
and [1]fix your mind on everything I show you; for you *were*
brought here so that I might
show *them* to you. [b]Declare to
the house of Israel everything
you see."
5 Now there was [a]a wall all
around the outside of the [1]tem-
ple. In the man's hand was a
measuring rod six [2]cubits *long*,
each being a cubit and a handbreadth; and he measured the
width of the wall structure, one
rod; and the height, one rod.
6 Then he went to the gateway
which faced [a]east; and he went
up its stairs and measured the
threshold of the gateway, *which
was* one rod wide, and the other
threshold *was* one rod wide.
7 Each gate chamber *was* one
rod long and one rod wide; between the gate chambers *was
a space of* five cubits; and the
threshold of the gateway by the
vestibule of the inside gate *was*
one rod.
8 He also measured the vestibule of the inside gate, one rod.

23 [a]Ezek. 36:18–20, 23 [b]Is. 1:15; 59:2 [c]Lev. 26:25
24 [a]Ezek. 36:19
25 [a]Ezek. 34:13; 36:24 [b]Hos. 1:11
26 [a]Dan. 9:16 [b]Lev. 26:5, 6
27 [a]Ezek. 28:25, 26 [b]Ezek. 36:23, 24; 38:16
28 [a]Ezek. 34:30 [1]Lit. *there*
29 [a]Is. 54:8, 9 [b][Joel 2:28]

CHAPTER 40

1 [a]Ezek. 33:21 [b]Ezek. 1:3; 3:14, 22; 37:1 [1]Lit. *struck*
2 [a]Ezek. 1:1; 3:14; 8:3; 37:1 [b]Rev. 21:10
3 [a]Dan. 10:6 [b]Ezek. 47:3 [c]Rev. 11:1; 21:15
4 [a]Ezek. 44:5 [b]Ezek. 43:10 [1]Lit. *set your heart*
5 [a]Ezek. 42:20 [1]Lit. *house* [2]A royal cubit of about 21 inches
6 [a]Ezek. 43:1

9 Then he measured the vestibule of the gateway, eight cubits; and the gateposts, two cubits. The vestibule of the gate *was* on the inside.

10 In the eastern gateway *were* three gate chambers on one side and three on the other; the three *were* all the same size; also the gateposts were of the same size on this side and that side.

11 He measured the width of the entrance to the gateway, ten cubits; *and* the length of the gate, thirteen cubits.

12 *There was* a [1]space in front of the gate chambers, one cubit *on this side* and one cubit on that side; the gate chambers *were* six cubits on this side and six cubits on that side.

13 Then he measured the gateway from the roof of *one* gate chamber to the roof of the other; the width *was* twenty-five cubits, as door faces door.

14 He measured the gateposts, sixty cubits high, and the court all around the gateway *extended* to the gatepost.

15 *From* the front of the entrance gate to the front of the vestibule of the inner gate *was* fifty cubits.

16 *There were* [a]beveled window *frames* in the gate chambers and in their intervening archways on the inside of the gateway all around, and likewise in the vestibules. *There were* windows all around on the inside. And on each gatepost *were* [b]palm trees.

17 Then he brought me into [a]the outer court; and *there were* [b]chambers and a pavement made all around the court; [c]thirty chambers faced the pavement.

18 The pavement was by the side of the gateways, corresponding to the length of the gateways; *this was* the lower pavement.

19 Then he measured the width from the front of the lower gateway to the front of the inner court exterior, one hundred cubits toward the east and the north.

20 On the outer court was also a gateway facing north, and he measured its length and its width.

21 Its gate chambers, three on this side and three on that side, its gateposts and its archways, had the same measurements as the first gate; its length *was* fifty cubits and its width twenty-five cubits.

22 Its windows and those of its archways, and also its palm trees, *had* the same measurements as the gateway facing east; it was ascended by seven steps, and its archway *was* in front of it.

23 A gate of the inner court was opposite the northern gateway, just as the eastern *gateway;* and he measured from gateway to gateway, one hundred cubits.

24 After that he brought me toward the south, and there a gateway was facing south; and he measured its gateposts and archways according to these same measurements.

25 *There were* windows in it and in its archways all around like those windows; its length *was* fifty cubits and its width twenty-five cubits.

26 Seven steps led up to it, and its archway *was* in front of them; and it had palm trees on its gate-

12 [1]Lit. *border*

16 [a]1 Kin. 6:4 [b]1 Kin. 6:29, 32, 35

17 [a]Rev. 11:2 [b]1 Kin. 6:5 [c]Ezek. 45:5

posts, one on this side and one
on that side.
27 *There was* also a gateway
on the inner court, facing south;
and he measured from gateway
to gateway toward the south,
one hundred cubits.
28 Then he brought me to the
inner court through the southern gateway; he measured the
southern gateway according to
these same measurements.
29 Also its gate chambers, its
gateposts, and its archways
were according to these same
measurements; *there were* windows in it and in its archways all
around; *it was* fifty cubits long
and twenty-five cubits wide.
30 *There were* archways all
around, [a]twenty-five cubits long
and five cubits wide.
31 Its archways faced the outer
court, palm trees *were* on its
gateposts, and going up to it
were eight steps.
32 And he brought me into the
inner court facing east; he measured the gateway according to
these same measurements.
33 Also its gate chambers, its
gateposts, and its archways
were according to these same
measurements; and *there were*
windows in it and in its archways all around; *it was* fifty cubits long and twenty-five cubits
wide.
34 Its archways faced the outer
court, and palm trees *were* on
its gateposts on this side and on
that side; and going up to it *were*
eight steps.
35 Then he brought me to the
north gateway and measured
it according to these same
measurements—
36 also its gate chambers, its

30 [a]Ezek. 40:21, 25, 33, 36
38 [a]2 Chr. 4:6
39 [a]Lev. 4:2, 3 [b]Lev. 5:6; 6:6; 7:1
44 [a]1 Chr. 6:31, 32; 16:41–43; 25:1–7

gateposts, and its archways.
It had windows all around; its
length *was* fifty cubits and its
width twenty-five cubits.
37 Its gateposts faced the outer
court, palm trees *were* on its
gateposts on this side and on
that side, and going up to it *were*
eight steps.
38 *There was* a chamber and its
entrance by the gateposts of the
gateway, where they [a]washed
the burnt offering.
39 In the vestibule of the gateway *were* two tables on this side
and two tables on that side, on
which to slay the burnt offering,
[a]the sin offering, and [b]the trespass offering.
40 At the outer side of the *vestibule*, as one goes up to the
entrance of the northern gateway, *were* two tables; and on the
other side of the vestibule of the
gateway *were* two tables.
41 Four tables *were* on this side
and four tables on that side, by
the side of the gateway, eight tables on which they slaughtered
the sacrifices.
42 *There were* also four tables
of hewn stone for the burnt offering, one cubit and a half long,
one cubit and a half wide, and
one cubit high; on these they
laid the instruments with which
they slaughtered the burnt offering and the sacrifice.
43 Inside *were* hooks, a handbreadth wide, fastened all
around; and the flesh of the sacrifices *was* on the tables.
44 Outside the inner gate *were*
the chambers for [a]the singers
in the inner court, one facing
south at the side of the northern
gateway, and the other facing

north at the side of the [1]southern
gateway.
45 Then he said to me, "This
chamber which faces south *is*
for [a]the priests who have charge
of the temple.
46 "The chamber which faces
north *is* for the priests [a]who
have charge of the altar; these
are the sons of [b]Zā′dok, from the
sons of Levi, who come near the
LORD to minister to Him."
47 And he measured the court,
one hundred cubits long and
one hundred cubits wide, four-
square. The altar *was* in front of
the temple.
48 Then he brought me to the
[a]vestibule of the temple and
measured the doorposts of the
vestibule, five cubits on this side
and five cubits on that side; and
the width of the gateway was
three cubits on this side and
three cubits on that side.
49 [a]The length of the vestibule
was twenty cubits, and the width
eleven cubits; and by the steps
which led up to it *there were*
[b]pillars by the doorposts, one
on this side and another on that
side.

41 Then he [a]brought me into
the [1]sanctuary and mea-
sured the doorposts, six cubits
wide on one side and six cubits wide on the other side—the
width of the tabernacle.
2 The width of the entryway
was ten cubits, and the side walls
of the entrance *were* five cubits
on this side and five cubits on
the other side; and he measured
its length, forty cubits, and its
width, twenty cubits.
3 Also he went inside and
measured the doorposts, two cubits; and the entrance, six cubits
high; and the width of the entrance, seven cubits.
4 [a]He measured the length,
twenty cubits; and the width,
twenty cubits, beyond the sanctuary; and he said to me, "This *is*
the Most Holy *Place.*"
5 Next, he measured the wall
of the [1]temple, six cubits. The
width of each side chamber all
around the temple *was* four cubits on every side.
6 [a]The side chambers *were*
in three stories, one above the
other, thirty chambers in each
story; they rested on [1]ledges
which *were* for the side chambers all around, that they might
be supported, but [b]not fastened
to the wall of the temple.
7 As one went up from story
to story, the side chambers
[a]became wider all around, because their supporting ledges in
the wall of the temple ascended
like steps; therefore the width of
the structure increased as one
went up *from* the lowest *story* to
the highest by way of the middle
one.
8 I also saw an elevation all
around the temple; it was the
foundation of the side cham-
bers, [a]a full rod, *that is,* six cubits *high.*
9 The thickness of the outer
wall of the side chambers *was*
five cubits, and so also the remaining terrace by the place
of the side chambers of the
[1]temple.
10 And between *it and* the *wall*
chambers was a width of twenty
cubits all around the temple on
every side.
11 The doors of the side chambers opened on the terrace,
one door toward the north and

44 [1]So with LXX; MT, Vg. *eastern*
45 [a]Lev. 8:35
46 [a]Num. 18:5 [b]1 Kin. 2:35
48 [a]1 Kin. 6:3
49 [a]1 Kin. 6:3 [b]1 Kin. 7:15–22

CHAPTER 41

1 [a]Ezek. 40:2, 3, 17 [1]Heb. *heykal;* the main room in the temple, the holy place, Ex. 26:33
4 [a]1 Kin. 6:20
5 [1]Lit. *house*
6 [a]1 Kin. 6:5–10 [b]1 Kin. 6:6, 10 [1]Lit. *the wall*
7 [a]1 Kin. 6:8
8 [a]Ezek. 40:5
9 [1]Lit. *house*

another toward the south; and
the width of the terrace *was* five
cubits all around.
12 The building that faced the
separating courtyard at its western end *was* seventy cubits wide;
the wall of the building *was* five
cubits thick all around, and its
length ninety cubits.
13 So he measured the temple,
one [a]hundred cubits long; and
the separating courtyard with
the building and its walls *was*
one hundred cubits long;
14 also the width of the eastern
face of the temple, including the
separating courtyard, *was* one
hundred cubits.
15 He measured the length of
the building behind it, facing the
separating courtyard, with its
[a]galleries on the one side and on
the other side, one hundred cubits, as well as the inner [1]temple
and the porches of the court,
16 their doorposts and [a]the beveled window frames. And the
galleries all around their three
stories opposite the threshold
were paneled with [b]wood from
the ground to the windows—the
windows were covered—
17 from the space above the
door, even to the inner [1]room,
as well as outside, and on every
wall all around, inside and outside, by measure.
18 And *it was* made [a]with cherubim and [b]palm trees, a palm
tree between cherub and cherub.
Each cherub had two faces,
19 [a]so that the face of a man
was toward a palm tree on one
side, and the face of a young lion
toward a palm tree on the other
side; thus *it was* made throughout the temple all around.
20 From the floor to the space
above the door, and on the wall
of the sanctuary, cherubim and
palm trees *were* carved.
21 The [a]doorposts of the temple
were square, *as was* the front of
the sanctuary; their appearance
was similar.
22 [a]The altar *was* of wood, three
cubits high, and its length two
cubits. Its corners, its length,
and its sides *were* of wood; and
he said to me, "This *is* [b]the table
that *is* [c]before the LORD."
23 [a]The temple and the sanctuary had two doors.
24 The doors had two [a]panels
apiece, two folding panels: two
panels for one door and two
panels for the other *door.*
25 Cherubim and palm trees
were carved on the doors of the
temple just as they *were* carved
on the walls. A wooden canopy
was on the front of the vestibule
outside.
26 *There were* [a]beveled window
frames and palm trees on one
side and on the other, on the
sides of the vestibule—also on
the side chambers of the temple
and on the canopies.

42
Then he [a]brought me out
into the outer court, by
the way toward the [b]north; and
he brought me into [c]the chamber
which *was* opposite the separating courtyard, and which *was*
opposite the building toward the
north.
2 Facing the length, *which was*
one hundred cubits (the width
was fifty cubits), was the north
door.
3 Opposite the inner court of
twenty *cubits,* and opposite the
[a]pavement of the outer court,
was [b]gallery against gallery in
three *stories.*

13 [a]Ezek. 40:47
15 [a]Ezek. 42:3, 5 [1]Or *sanctuary*
16 [a]Ezek. 40:16, 25 [b]1 Kin. 6:15
17 [1]Lit. *house;* the Most Holy Place
18 [a]1 Kin. 6:29 [b]Ezek. 40:16
19 [a]Ezek. 1:10; 10:14
21 [a]1 Kin. 6:33
22 [a]Ex. 30:1–3 [b]Ex. 25:23, 30 [c]Ex. 30:8
23 [a]1 Kin. 6:31–35
24 [a]1 Kin. 6:34
26 [a]Ezek. 40:16

CHAPTER 42

1 [a]Ezek. 41:1 [b]Ezek. 40:20 [c]Ezek. 41:12, 15
3 [a]Ezek. 40:17 [b]Ezek. 41:15, 16; 42:5

4 In front of the chambers,
toward the inside, *was* a walk
ten cubits wide, at a distance of
one cubit; and their doors faced
north.
5 Now the upper chambers
were shorter, because the galleries took away *space* from them
more than from the lower and
middle stories of the building.
6 For they *were* in three *stories*
and did not have pillars like the
pillars of the courts; therefore
the upper level was [1]shortened
more than the lower and middle
levels from the ground up.
7 And a wall which *was* outside ran parallel to the chambers, at the front of the chambers, toward the outer court; its
length *was* fifty cubits.
8 The length of the chambers
toward the outer court *was*
fifty cubits, whereas that facing
the temple *was* one [a]hundred
cubits.
9 At the lower chambers *was*
the entrance on the east side,
as one goes into them from the
outer court.
10 Also *there were* chambers in
the thickness of the wall of the
court toward the east, opposite
the separating courtyard and
opposite the building.
11 [a]*There was* a walk in front
of them also, and their appearance *was* like the chambers
which *were* toward the north;
they *were* as long and as wide
as the others, and all their exits
and entrances *were* according to
plan.
12 And corresponding to the
doors of the chambers that *were*
facing south, as one enters them,
there was a door in front of the
walk, the way directly in front of
the wall toward the east.
13 Then he said to me, "The
north chambers *and* the south
chambers, which *are* opposite
the separating courtyard, *are*
the holy chambers where the
priests who approach the LORD
[a]shall eat the most holy offerings. There they shall lay the
most holy offerings—[b]the grain
offering, the sin offering, and
the trespass offering—for the
place *is* holy.
14 [a]"When the priests enter
them, they shall not go out of
the holy *chamber* into the outer
court; but there they shall leave
their garments in which they
minister, for they *are* holy. They
shall put on other garments;
then they may approach *that*
which *is* for the people."
15 Now when he had finished
measuring the inner [1]temple, he
brought me out through the gateway that faces toward the [a]east,
and measured it all around.
16 He measured the east side
with the [1]measuring rod, five
hundred rods by the measuring
rod all around.
17 He measured the north side,
five hundred rods by the measuring rod all around.
18 He measured the south side,
five hundred rods by the measuring rod.
19 He came around to the west
side *and* measured five hundred
rods by the measuring rod.
20 He measured it on the four
sides; [a]it had a wall all around,
[b]five hundred *cubits* long and
five hundred wide, to separate
the holy areas from the [1]com-
mon.

6 [1]Or *narrowed*
8 [a]Ezek. 41:13, 14
11 [a]Ezek. 42:4
13 [a]Lev. 6:16, 26; 24:9 [b]Lev. 2:3, 10; 6:14, 17, 25
14 [a]Ezek. 44:19
15 [a]Ezek. 40:6; 43:1 [1]Lit. *house*
16 [1]About 10.5 feet, Ezek. 40:5
20 [a]Ezek. 40:5 [b]Ezek. 45:2 [1]Or *profane*

43 Afterward he brought me
to the gate, the gate [a]that
faces toward the east.
2 [a]And behold, the glory of the
God of Israel came from the way
of the east. [b]His voice *was* like
the sound of many waters; [c]and
the earth shone with His glory.
3 *It was* [a]like the appearance
of the vision which I saw—like
the vision which I saw when [1]I
came [b]to destroy the city. The visions *were* like the vision which
I saw [c]by the River Chē′bar; and
I fell on my face.
4 [a]And the glory of the LORD
came into the [1]temple by way of
the gate which faces toward the
east.
5 [a]The Spirit lifted me up and
brought me into the inner court;
and behold, [b]the glory of the
LORD filled the [1]temple.
6 Then I heard *Him* speaking
to me from the temple, while [a]a
man stood beside me.
7 And He said to me, "Son of
man, *this is* [a]the place of My
throne and [b]the place of the
soles of My feet, [c]where I will
dwell in the midst of the children of Israel forever. [d]No more
shall the house of Israel defile
My holy name, they nor their
kings, by their [1]harlotry or with
[e]the carcasses of their kings on
their high places.
8 [a]"When they set their threshold by My threshold, and their
doorpost by My doorpost, with a
wall between them and Me, they
defiled My holy name by the
abominations which they committed; therefore I have consumed them in My anger.
9 "Now let them put their harlotry and the carcasses of their
kings far away from Me, and I
will dwell in their midst forever.
10 "Son of man, [a]describe the
[1]temple to the house of Israel,
that they may be ashamed of
their iniquities; and let them
measure the pattern.
11 "And if they are ashamed of
all that they have done, make
known to them the design of the
[1]temple and its arrangement, its
exits and its entrances, its entire
design and all its [a]ordinances,
all its forms and all its laws.
Write *it* down in their sight, so
that they may keep its whole design and all its ordinances, and
[b]perform them.
12 "This *is* the law of the [1]tem-
ple: The whole area surrounding
[a]the mountaintop *is* most holy.
Behold, this *is* the law of the
temple.
13 "These are the measurements
of the [a]altar in cubits [b](the [1]cubit
is one cubit and a handbreadth):
the base one cubit high and one
cubit wide, with a rim all around
its edge of one span. This *is* the
height of the altar:
14 "from the base on the ground
to the lower ledge, two cubits;
the width of the ledge, one cubit;
from the smaller ledge to the
larger ledge, four cubits; and the
width of the ledge, *one* cubit.
15 "The altar hearth *is* four
cubits high, with four [a]horns
extending upward from the
[1]hearth.
16 "The altar hearth *is* twelve
cubits long, twelve wide, [a]square
at its four corners;
17 "the ledge, fourteen *cubits*
long and fourteen wide on its
four sides, with a rim of half
a cubit around it; its base, one

CHAPTER 43

1 [a]Ezek. 10:19; 46:1

2 [a]Ezek. 11:23 [b]Rev. 1:15; 14:2 [c]Rev. 18:1

3 [a]Ezek. 1:4–28 [b]Jer. 1:10 [c]Ezek. 1:28; 3:23 [1]Some Heb. mss., Vg. *He*

4 [a]Ezek. 10:19; 11:23 [1]Lit. *house*

5 [a]Ezek. 3:12, 14; 8:3 [b]1 Kin. 8:10, 11 [1]Lit. *house*

6 [a]Ezek. 1:26; 40:3

7 [a]Ps. 99:1 [b]1 Chr. 28:2 [c]Joel 3:17 [d]Ezek. 39:7 [e]Lev. 26:30 [1]Unfaithful idolatry

8 [a]Ezek. 8:3; 23:39; 44:7

10 [a]Ezek. 40:4 [1]Lit. *house*

11 [a]Ezek. 44:5 [b]Ezek. 11:20 [1]Lit. *house*

12 [a]Ezek. 40:2 [1]Lit. *house*

13 [a]Ex. 27:1–8 [b]Ezek. 41:8 [1]A royal cubit of about 21 inches

15 [a]Ex. 27:2 [1]Heb. *ariel*

16 [a]Ex. 27:1

cubit all around; and [a]its steps
face toward the east."
18 And He said to me, "Son of
man, thus says the Lord GOD:
'These *are* the ordinances for
the altar on the day when it is
made, for sacrificing [a]burnt offerings on it, and for [b]sprinkling
blood on it.
19 'You shall give [a]a young bull
for a sin offering to [b]the priests,
the Lē'vītes, who are of the seed
of [c]Zā'dok, who approach Me to
minister to Me,' says the Lord
GOD.
20 'You shall take some of its
blood and put *it* on the four
horns of the altar, on the four
corners of the ledge, and on the
rim around it; thus you shall
cleanse it and make atonement
for it.
21 'Then you shall also take the
bull of the sin offering, and [a]burn
it in the appointed place of the
[1]temple, [b]outside the sanctuary.
22 'On the second day you shall
offer a kid of the goats without
blemish for a sin offering; and
they shall cleanse the altar, as
they cleansed *it* with the bull.
23 'When you have finished
cleansing *it*, you shall offer a
young bull without blemish, and
a ram from the flock without
blemish.
24 'When you offer them before
the LORD, [a]the priests shall throw
salt on them, and they will offer
them up *as* a burnt offering to
the LORD.
25 'Every day for [a]seven days
you shall prepare a goat *for* a sin
offering; they shall also prepare
a young bull and a ram from the
flock, both without blemish.
26 'Seven days they shall make
atonement for the altar and purify it, and so [1]consecrate [2]*it*.
27 [a]'When these days are over it
shall be, on the eighth day and
thereafter, that the priests shall
offer your burnt offerings and
your peace offerings on the altar; and I will [b]accept you,' says
the Lord GOD."

44 Then He brought me back
to the outer gate of the
sanctuary [a]which faces toward
the east, but it *was* shut.
2 And the LORD said to me,
"This gate shall be shut; it shall
not be opened, and no man shall
enter by it, [a]because the LORD
God of Israel has entered by it;
therefore it shall be shut.
3 "*As for* the [a]prince, *because*
he *is* the prince, he may sit in it
to [b]eat bread before the LORD; he
shall enter by way of the vestibule of the gateway, and go out
the same way."
4 Also He brought me by way
of the north gate to the front
of the [1]temple; so I looked, and
[a]behold, the glory of the LORD
filled the house of the LORD; [b]and
I fell on my face.
5 And the LORD said to me,
[a]"Son of man, [1]mark well, see
with your eyes and hear with
your ears, all that I say to you
concerning all the [b]ordinances
of the house of the LORD and all
its laws. Mark well who may enter the house and all who go out
from the sanctuary.
6 "Now say to the [a]rebellious,
to the house of Israel, 'Thus says
the Lord GOD: "O house of Israel,
[b]let Us have no more of all your
abominations.
7 [a]"When you brought in [b]for-
eigners, [c]uncircumcised in heart
and uncircumcised in flesh, to

17 [a]Ex. 20:26
18 [a]Ex. 40:29 [b]Lev. 1:5, 11
19 [a]Lev. 8:14 [b]Ezek. 44:15, 16 [c]Ezek. 40:46
21 [a]Ex. 29:14 [b]Heb. 13:11 [1]Lit. *house*
24 [a]Lev. 2:13
25 [a]Ex. 29:35
26 [1]Lit. *fill its hands* [2]LXX, Syr. *themselves*
27 [a]Lev. 9:1–4 [b]Ezek. 20:40, 41

CHAPTER 44

1 [a]Ezek. 43:1
2 [a]Ezek. 43:2–4
3 [a]Gen. 31:54 [b]Ezek. 46:2, 8
4 [a]Ezek. 3:23; 43:5 [b]Ezek. 1:28; 43:3 [1]Lit. *house*
5 [a]Ezek. 40:4 [b]Ezek. 43:10, 11 [1]Lit. *set your heart*
6 [a]Ezek. 2:5 [b]1 Pet. 4:3
7 [a]Acts 21:28 [b]Lev. 22:25 [c]Lev. 26:41

be in My sanctuary to defile
it—My house—and when you
offered [d]My food, [e]the fat and
the blood, then they broke My
covenant because of all your
abominations.
8 “And you have not [a]kept
charge of My holy things, but
you have set *others* to keep
charge of My sanctuary for
you.”
9 ‘Thus says the Lord GOD:
[a]“No foreigner, uncircumcised
in heart or uncircumcised in
flesh, shall enter My sanctuary,
including any foreigner who *is*
among the children of Israel.
10 [a]“And the Lē′vītes who went
far from Me, when Israel went
astray, who strayed away from
Me after their idols, they shall
bear their iniquity.
11 “Yet they shall be ministers
in My sanctuary, [a]*as* gatekeepers of the house and ministers
of the house; [b]they shall slay the
burnt offering and the sacrifice
for the people, and [c]they shall
stand before them to minister to
them.
12 “Because they ministered
to them before their idols and
[a]caused[1] the house of Israel to
fall into iniquity, therefore I
have [b]raised My hand in an oath
against them,” says the Lord
GOD, “that they shall bear their
iniquity.
13 [a]“And they shall not come
near Me to minister to Me as
priest, nor come near any of
My holy things, nor into the
Most Holy *Place;* but they shall
[b]bear their shame and their
abominations which they have
committed.
14 “Nevertheless I will make
them [a]keep charge of the temple,

7 [d]Lev. 21:17 [e]Lev. 3:16
8 [a]Lev. 22:2
9 [a]Ezek. 44:7
10 [a]2 Kin. 23:8
11 [a]1 Chr. 26:1–19 [b]2 Chr. 29:34; 30:17 [c]Num. 16:9
12 [a]Is. 9:16 [b]Ps. 106:26 [1]Lit. *became a stumbling block of iniquity to the house of Israel*
13 [a]2 Kin. 23:9 [b]Ezek. 32:30
14 [a]Num. 18:4
15 [a]Ezek. 40:46 [b][1 Sam. 2:35] [c]Ezek. 44:10 [d]Deut. 10:8 [e]Ezek. 44:7
16 [a]Num. 18:5, 7, 8 [b]Ezek. 41:22
17 [a]Ex. 28:39–43; 39:27–29
18 [a]Ex. 28:40; 39:28
19 [a]Ezek. 42:14 [b]Lev. 6:27
20 [a]Lev. 21:5 [b]Num. 6:5
21 [a]Lev. 10:9
22 [a]Lev. 21:7, 13, 14
23 [a]Mal. 2:6–8

for all its work, and for all that
has to be done in it.
15 [a]“But the priests, the Lē′-
vītes, [b]the sons of Zā′dok, who
kept charge of My sanctuary
[c]when the children of Israel
went astray from Me, they shall
come near Me to minister to Me;
and they [d]shall stand before Me
to offer to Me the [e]fat and the
blood,” says the Lord GOD.
16 “They shall [a]enter My sanctuary, and they shall come near
[b]My table to minister to Me, and
they shall keep My charge.
17 “And it shall be, whenever
they enter the gates of the inner court, that [a]they shall put on
linen garments; no wool shall
come upon them while they
minister within the gates of the
inner court or within the house.
18 [a]“They shall have linen turbans on their heads and linen
trousers on their bodies; they
shall not clothe themselves with
anything that causes sweat.
19 “When they go out to the
outer court, to the outer court
to the people, [a]they shall take
off their garments in which they
have ministered, leave them in
the holy chambers, and put on
other garments; and in their
holy garments they shall [b]not
sanctify the people.
20 [a]“They shall neither shave
their heads nor let their hair
grow [b]long, but they shall keep
their hair well trimmed.
21 [a]“No priest shall drink wine
when he enters the inner court.
22 “They shall not take as wife
a [a]widow or a divorced woman,
but take virgins of the descendants of the house of Israel, or
widows of priests.
23 “And [a]they shall teach My

people *the difference* between
the holy and the unholy, and
cause them to [b]discern between
the unclean and the clean.
24 [a]"In controversy they shall
stand as judges, *and* judge it according to My judgments. They
shall keep My laws and My statutes in all My appointed meet-
ings, [b]and they shall hallow My
Sabbaths.
25 "They shall not defile *themselves* by coming near a dead
person. Only for father or
mother, for son or daughter, for
brother or unmarried sister may
they defile themselves.
26 [a]"After he is cleansed, they
shall count seven days for him.
27 "And on the day that he goes
to the sanctuary to minister in
the sanctuary, [a]he must offer his
sin offering [b]in the inner court,"
says the Lord GOD.
28 "It shall be, in regard to their
inheritance, *that* I [a]*am* their inheritance. You shall give them
no [b]possession in Israel, for I *am*
their possession.
29 [a]"They shall eat the grain offering, the sin offering, and the
trespass offering; [b]every dedicated thing in Israel shall be
theirs.
30 "The [a]best[1] of all firstfruits
of any kind, and every sacrifice
of any kind from all your sacrifices, shall be the priest's; also
you [b]shall give to the priest the
first of your ground meal, [c]to
cause a blessing to rest on your
house.
31 "The priests shall not eat
anything, bird or beast, that
[a]died naturally or was torn *by
wild beasts.*

45 "Moreover, when you [a]di-
vide the land by lot into
inheritance, you shall [b]set apart
a district for the LORD, a holy
section of the land; its length
shall be twenty-five thousand
cubits, and the width ten thousand. It *shall be* holy throughout
its territory all around.
2 "Of this there shall be a
square plot for the sanctuary,
[a]five hundred by five hundred
rods, with fifty cubits around it
for an open space.
3 "So this is the district you
shall measure: twenty-five thousand *cubits* long and ten thousand wide; [a]in it shall be the
sanctuary, the Most Holy *Place.*
4 "It shall be [a]a holy *section* of
the land, belonging to the priests,
the ministers of the sanctuary,
who come near to minister to
the LORD; it shall be a place for
their houses and a holy place for
the sanctuary.
5 [a]"*An area* twenty-five thousand *cubits* long and ten thousand wide shall belong to the
Lē′vītes, the ministers of the
[1]temple; they shall have [b]twenty[2]
chambers as a possession.
6 [a]"You shall appoint as the
property of the city *an area*
five thousand *cubits* wide and
twenty-five thousand long, ad-
jacent to the district of the holy
section; it shall belong to the
whole house of Israel.
7 [a]"The prince shall have *a section* on one side and the other of
the holy district and the city's
property; and bordering on the
holy district and the city's property, extending westward on the
west side and eastward on the
east side, the length *shall be* side
by side with one of the *tribal*
portions, from the west border
to the east border.

23 [b]Lev. 20:25
24 [a]Deut. 17:8, 9 [b]Ezek. 22:26
26 [a]Num. 6:10; 19:11, 13–19
27 [a]Lev. 5:3, 6 [b]Ezek. 44:17
28 [a]Num. 18:20 [b]Ezek. 45:4
29 [a]Lev. 7:6 [b]Lev. 27:21, 28
30 [a]Num. 3:13; 18:12 [b]Neh. 10:37 [c][Mal. 3:10] [1]Lit. *first*
31 [a]Lev. 22:8

CHAPTER 45

1 [a]Ezek. 47:22 [b]Ezek. 48:8, 9
2 [a]Ezek. 42:20
3 [a]Ezek. 48:10
4 [a]Ezek. 48:10, 11
5 [a]Ezek. 48:13 [b]Ezek. 40:17 [1]Lit. *house* [2]So with MT, Tg., Vg.; LXX *a possession, cities of dwelling*
6 [a]Ezek. 48:15
7 [a]Ezek. 48:21

8 “The land shall be his possession in Israel; and [a]My princes
shall no more oppress My people, but they shall give *the rest*
of the land to the house of Israel,
according to their tribes.”
9 ‘Thus says the Lord GOD:
[a]“Enough, O princes of Israel!
[b]Remove violence and plundering, execute justice and righteousness, and stop dispossess-
ing My people,” says the Lord
GOD.
10 “You shall have [a]honest
scales, an honest ephah, and an
honest bath.
11 “The ephah and the bath
shall be of the same measure, so
that the bath contains one-tenth
of a homer, and the ephah one-
tenth of a homer; their measure
shall be according to the homer.
12 “The [a]shekel *shall be* twenty
gerahs; twenty shekels, twenty-
five shekels, *and* fifteen shekels
shall be your mina.
13 “This *is* the offering which
you shall offer: you shall give
one-sixth of an ephah from a
homer of wheat, and one-sixth
of an ephah from a homer of
barley.
14 “The ordinance concerning
oil, the bath of oil, *is* one-tenth
of a bath from a kor. *A kor is* a
homer or ten baths, for ten baths
are a homer.
15 “And one lamb shall be given
from a flock of two hundred,
from the rich pastures of Israel.
These shall be for grain offerings, burnt offerings, and peace
offerings, [a]to make atonement
for them,” says the Lord GOD.
16 “All the people of the land
shall give this offering for the
prince in Israel.
17 “Then it shall be the [a]prince’s
part *to give* burnt offerings,
grain offerings, and drink offerings, at the feasts, the New
Moons, the Sabbaths, and at all
the appointed seasons of the
house of Israel. He shall prepare
the sin offering, the grain offering, the burnt offering, and the
peace offerings to make atonement for the house of Israel.”
18 ‘Thus says the Lord GOD: “In
the first *month,* on the first *day*
of the month, you shall take a
young bull without blemish and
[a]cleanse the sanctuary.
19 [a]“The priest shall take some
of the blood of the sin offering
and put *it* on the doorposts of
the [1]temple, on the four corners
of the ledge of the altar, and on
the gateposts of the gate of the
inner court.
20 “And so you shall do on the
seventh *day* of the month [a]for
everyone who has sinned unintentionally or in ignorance.
Thus you shall make atonement
for the temple.
21 [a]“In the first *month,* on the
fourteenth day of the month,
you shall observe the Passover,
a feast of seven days; unleavened bread shall be eaten.
22 “And on that day the prince
shall prepare for himself and for
all the people of the land [a]a bull
for a sin offering.
23 “On the [a]seven days of the
feast he shall prepare a burnt
offering to the LORD, seven bulls
and seven rams without blemish, daily for seven days, [b]and a
kid of the goats daily *for* a sin
offering.
24 [a]“And he shall prepare a
grain offering of one ephah for
each bull and one ephah for

8 [a]Ezek. 22:27
9 [a]Ezek. 44:6 [b]Jer. 22:3
10 [a]Lev. 19:36
12 [a]Ex. 30:13
15 [a]Lev. 1:4; 6:30
17 [a]Ezek. 46:4–12
18 [a]Lev. 16:16, 33
19 [a]Ezek. 43:20 [1]Lit. *house*
20 [a]Lev. 4:27
21 [a]Ex. 12:18
22 [a]Lev. 4:14
23 [a]Lev. 23:8 [b]Num. 28:15, 22, 30; 29:5, 11, 16, 19
24 [a]Ezek. 46:5, 7

each ram, together with a hin of
oil for each ephah.
25 “In the seventh *month,* on
the fifteenth day of the month,
at the [a]feast, he shall do likewise
for seven days, according to the
sin offering, the burnt offering,
the grain offering, and the oil.”

CHAPTER 46

46 ‘Thus says the Lord GOD:
“The gateway of the inner
court that faces toward the east
shall be shut the six [a]working
days; but on the Sabbath it shall
be opened, and on the day of the
New Moon it shall be opened.
2 [a]“The prince shall enter by
way of the vestibule of the gateway from the outside, and stand
by the gatepost. The priests shall
prepare his burnt offering and
his peace offerings. He shall
worship at the threshold of the
gate. Then he shall go out, but
the gate shall not be shut until
evening.
3 “Likewise the people of the
land shall worship at the entrance to this gateway before
the LORD on the Sabbaths and
the New Moons.
4 “The burnt offering that [a]the
prince offers to the LORD on
the [b]Sabbath day *shall be* six
lambs without blemish, and a
ram without blemish;
5 [a]“and the grain offering *shall
be one* ephah for a ram, and the
grain offering for the lambs, [1]as
much as he wants to give, as
well as a hin of oil with every
ephah.
6 “On the day of the New Moon
it shall be a young bull without
blemish, six lambs, and a ram;
they shall be without blemish.
7 “He shall prepare a grain offering of an ephah for a bull, an
ephah for a ram, [1]as much as he
wants to give for the lambs, and
a hin of oil with every ephah.
8 [a]“When the prince enters, he
shall go in by way of the vestibule of the gateway, and go out
the same way.
9 “But when the people of the
land [a]come before the LORD on
the appointed feast days, whoever enters by way of the north
[b]gate to worship shall go out
by way of the south gate; and
whoever enters by way of the
south gate shall go out by way of
the north gate. He shall not return by way of the gate through
which he came, but shall go out
through the opposite gate.
10 “The prince shall then be in
their midst. When they go in, he
shall go in; and when they go
out, he shall go out.
11 “At the festivals and the appointed feast days [a]the grain
offering shall be an ephah for
a bull, an ephah for a ram, as
much as he wants to give for
the lambs, and a hin of oil with
every ephah.
12 “Now when the prince makes
a voluntary burnt offering or
voluntary peace offering to the
LORD, the gate that faces toward
the east [a]shall then be opened
for him; and he shall prepare his
burnt offering and his peace offerings as he did on the Sabbath
day. Then he shall go out, and
after he goes out the gate shall
be shut.
13 [a]“You shall daily make a
burnt offering to the LORD *of* a
lamb of the first year without
blemish; you shall prepare it
[1]every morning.
14 “And you shall prepare a
grain offering with it every morning, a sixth of an ephah, and a

---

25 [a]Num. 29:12

CHAPTER 46

1 [a]Ex. 20:9

2 [a]Ezek. 44:3

4 [a]Ezek. 45:17 [b]Num. 28:9, 10

5 [a]Ezek. 45:24; 46:7, 11 [1]Lit. *the gift of his hand*

7 [1]Lit. *as much as his hand can reach*

8 [a]Ezek. 44:3; 46:2

9 [a]Ex. 23:14–17; 34:23 [b]Ezek. 48:31, 33

11 [a]Ezek. 46:5, 7

12 [a]Ezek. 44:3; 46:1, 2, 8

13 [a]Num. 28:3–5 [1]Lit. *morning by morning*

third of a hin of oil to moisten
the fine flour. This grain offering
is a perpetual ordinance, to be
made regularly to the LORD.
15 "Thus they shall prepare the
lamb, the grain offering, and the
oil, *as* a [a]regular burnt offering
every morning."
16 'Thus says the Lord GOD:
"If the prince gives a gift *of
some* of his inheritance to any
of his sons, it shall belong to his
sons; it is their possession by
inheritance.
17 "But if he gives a gift of some
of his inheritance to one of his
servants, it shall be his until
[a]the year of liberty, after which
it shall return to the prince. But
his inheritance shall belong to
his sons; it shall become theirs.
18 "Moreover [a]the prince shall
not take any of the people's inheritance by evicting them from
their property; he shall provide
an inheritance for his sons from
his own property, so that none
of My people may be scattered
from his property." ' "
19 Now he brought me through
the entrance, which *was* at the
side of the gate, into the holy
[a]chambers of the priests which
face toward the north; and there
a place *was* situated at their extreme western end.
20 And he said to me, "This *is*
the place where the priests shall
[a]boil the trespass offering and
the sin offering, *and* where they
shall [b]bake the grain offering, so
that they do not bring *them* out
into the outer court [c]to sanctify
the people."
21 Then he brought me out into
the outer court and caused me
to pass by the four corners of
the court; and in fact, in every
corner of the court *there was
another* court.
22 In the four corners of the
court *were* enclosed courts, forty
cubits long and thirty wide;
all four corners *were* the same
size.
23 *There was* a row *of building
stones* all around in them, all
around the four of them; and
[1]cooking hearths were made
under the rows of stones all
around.
24 And he said to me, "These
are the [1]kitchens where the ministers of the [2]temple shall [a]boil
the sacrifices of the people."

47

Then he brought me back
to the door of the [1]temple;
and there was [a]water, flowing
from under the threshold of the
temple toward the east, for the
front of the temple faced east;
the water was flowing from under the right side of the temple,
south of the altar.
2 He brought me out by way
of the north gate, and led me
around on the outside to the
outer gateway that faces [a]east;
and there was water, running
out on the right side.
3 And when [a]the man went out
to the east with the line in his
hand, he measured one thousand cubits, and he brought me
through the waters; the water
came up to my ankles.
4 Again he measured one thousand and brought me through
the waters; the water *came up
to my* knees. Again he measured
one thousand and brought me
through; the water *came up to
my* waist.
5 Again he measured one
thousand, *and it was* a river
that I could not cross; for the

15 [a]Ex. 29:42
17 [a]Lev. 25:10
18 [a]Ezek. 45:8
19 [a]Ezek. 42:13
20 [a]2 Chr. 35:13 [b]Lev. 2:4, 5, 7 [c]Ezek. 44:19
23 [1]Lit. *boiling places*
24 [a]Ezek. 46:20 [1]Lit. *house of those who boil* [2]Lit. *house*

CHAPTER 47

1 [a]Joel 3:18 [1]Lit. *house*
2 [a]Ezek. 44:1, 2
3 [a]Ezek. 40:3

water was too deep, water in
which one must swim, a river
that could not be crossed.
6 He said to me, "Son of man,
have you seen *this?*" Then he
brought me and returned me to
the bank of the river.
7 When I returned, there, along
the bank of the river, *were* very
many [a]trees on one side and the
other.
8 Then he said to me: "This
water flows toward the eastern
region, goes down into the [1]valley, and enters the sea. *When it*
reaches the sea, *its* waters are
healed.
9 "And it shall be *that* every
living thing that moves, wherever [1]the rivers go, will live.
There will be a very great multitude of fish, because these waters go there; for they will be
healed, and everything will live
wherever the river goes.
10 "It shall be *that* fishermen
will stand by it from En Ge'di to
En Eg·lā'im; they will be *places*
for spreading their nets. Their
fish will be of the same kinds
as the fish [a]of the Great Sea, exceedingly many.
11 "But its swamps and marshes
will not be healed; they will be
given over to salt.
12 [a]"Along the bank of the river,
on this side and that, will grow
all *kinds of* trees used for food;
[b]their leaves will not wither, and
their fruit will not fail. They will
bear fruit every month, because
their water flows from the sanctuary. Their fruit will be for food,
and their leaves for [c]medicine."[1]
13 Thus says the Lord GOD:
"These *are* the [a]borders by which
you shall divide the land as an
inheritance among the twelve
tribes of Israel. [b]Joseph *shall
have two* portions.
14 "You shall inherit it equally
with one another; for I [a]raised
My hand in an oath to give it to
your fathers, and this land shall
[b]fall to you as your inheritance.
15 "This *shall be* the border of
the land on the north: from the
Great Sea, *by* [a]the road to Heth'lon, as one goes to [b]Zē'dad,
16 [a]"Hā'math, [b]Be·rō'thah, Sib'rā·im (which *is* between the border of Damascus and the border
of Hā'math), to Hā'zar Hat'ti·con
(which *is* on the border of Hau'ran).
17 "Thus the boundary shall be
from the Sea to [a]Hā'zar Ē'nan,
the border of Damascus; and as
for the north, northward, it is the
border of Hā'math. *This is* the
north side.
18 "On the east side you shall
mark out the border from between Hau'ran and Damascus,
and between Gil'ē·ad and the
land of Israel, along the Jordan,
and along the eastern side of the
sea. *This is* the east side.
19 "The south side, toward the
[1]South, *shall be* from Tā'mar
to [a]the waters of [2]Mer'i·bah by
Kā'desh, along the brook to the
Great Sea. *This is* the south side,
toward the South.
20 "The west side *shall be* the
Great Sea, from the *southern*
boundary until one comes to a
point opposite Hā'math. This *is*
the west side.
21 "Thus you shall [a]divide this
land among yourselves according to the tribes of Israel.
22 "It shall be that you will divide it by [a]lot as an inheritance
for yourselves, [b]and for the
strangers who dwell among you

7 [a][Rev. 22:2]
8 [1]Or *Arabah,* the Jordan Valley
9 [1]Lit. *two rivers*
10 [a]Num. 34:3
12 [a]Ezek. 47:7 [b][Jer. 17:8] [c][Rev. 22:2] [1]Or *healing*
13 [a]Num. 34:1–29 [b]Gen. 48:5
14 [a]Ezek. 20:5, 6, 28, 42 [b]Ezek. 48:29
15 [a]Ezek. 48:1 [b]Num. 34:7, 8
16 [a]Num. 34:8 [b]2 Sam. 8:8
17 [a]Num. 34:9
19 [a]Ps. 81:7 [1]Heb. *Negev* [2]Lit. *Strife*
21 [a]Ezek. 45:1
22 [a]Num. 26:55, 56 [b][Eph. 3:6]

34 "on the west side, four thousand five hundred *cubits* with their three gates: one gate for Gad, one gate for Ash′er, and one gate for Naph′ta·lī.

35 "All the way around *shall be* eighteen thousand *cubits;* [a]and the name of the city from *that* day *shall be:* [b]THE[1] LORD *IS* THERE."

35 [a]Jer. 23:6; 33:16 [b]Joel 3:21 [1]Heb. *YHWH Shammah*

The Book of
DANIEL

DANIEL'S life and ministry bridge the entire seventy-year period of Babylonian captivity. Deported to Babylon at the age of sixteen, and handpicked for government service, Daniel becomes God's prophetic mouthpiece to the gentile and Jewish world declaring God's present and eternal purpose. Nine of the twelve chapters in his book revolve around dreams, including God-given visions involving trees, animals, beasts, and images. In both his personal adventures and prophetic visions, Daniel shows God's guidance, intervention, and power in the affairs of men.

The name *Daniye'l* or *Dani'el* means "God Is My Judge," and the book is, of course, named after the author and principal character. The Greek form *Daniel* in the Septuagint is the basis for the Latin and English titles.

IN the third year of the reign
of [a]Je·hoi'a·kim king of Judah, Ne·bū·chad·nez'zar king of
Babylon came to Jerusalem and
besieged it.
2 And the Lord gave Je·hoi'-
a·kim king of Judah into his
hand, with [a]some of the articles
of [1]the house of God, which he
carried [b]into the land of Shī'nar
to the house of his god; [c]and
he brought the articles into the
treasure house of his god.
3 Then the king instructed
Ash'pe·naz, the master of his
eunuchs, to bring [a]some of the
children of Israel and some
of the king's descendants and
some of the nobles,
4 young men [a]in whom *there*
was no blemish, but good-
looking, gifted in all wisdom,
possessing knowledge and quick
to understand, who *had* ability
to serve in the king's palace,
and [b]whom they might teach the
language and [1]literature of the
Chal·dē'ans.
5 And the king appointed for
them a daily provision of the
king's delicacies and of the wine
which he drank, and three years
of training for them, so that at
the end of *that time* they might
[a]serve before the king.
6 Now from among those of
the sons of Judah were Daniel, Han·a·nī'ah, Mish'a·el, and
Az·a·rī'ah.
7 [a]To them the chief of the
eunuchs gave names: [b]he gave
Daniel *the name* Bel·te·shaz'-
zar; to Han·a·nī'ah, Shad'rach;
to Mish'a·el, Mē'shach; and to
Az·a·rī'ah, A·bed'-Ne·gō'.
8 But Daniel purposed in his
heart that he would not defile
himself [a]with the portion of the
king's delicacies, nor with the
wine which he drank; therefore
he requested of the chief of the
eunuchs that he might not defile
himself.
9 Now [a]God had brought Daniel into the favor and [1]goodwill
of the chief of the eunuchs.
10 And the chief of the eunuchs
said to Daniel, "I fear my lord
the king, who has appointed
your food and drink. For why

CHAPTER 1

1 [a]2 Kin. 24:1, 2
2 [a]Jer. 27:19, 20 [b]Zech. 5:11 [c]2 Chr. 36:7 [1]The temple
3 [a]Is. 39:7
4 [a]Lev. 24:19, 20 [b]Acts 7:22 [1]Lit. *writing* or *book*
5 [a]Dan. 1:19
7 [a]2 Kin. 24:17 [b]Dan. 2:26; 4:8; 5:12
8 [a]Hos. 9:3
9 [a]Gen. 39:21 [1]*kindness*

should he see your faces looking worse than the young men who *are* your age? Then you would endanger my head before the king."

11 So Daniel said to [1]the steward whom the chief of the eunuchs had set over Daniel, Han·a·nī'ah, Mish'a·el, and Az·a·rī'ah,

12 "Please test your servants for ten days, and let them give us vegetables to eat and water to drink.

13 "Then let our appearance be examined before you, and the appearance of the young men who eat the portion of the king's delicacies; and as you see fit, *so* deal with your servants."

14 So he consented with them in this matter, and tested them ten days.

15 And at the end of ten days their features appeared better and fatter in flesh than all the young men who ate the portion of the king's delicacies.

16 Thus [1]the steward took away their portion of delicacies and the wine that they were to drink, and gave them vegetables.

17 As for these four young men, [a]God gave them [b]knowledge and skill in all literature and wisdom; and Daniel had [c]understanding in all visions and dreams.

18 Now at the end of the days, when the king had said that they should be brought in, the chief of the eunuchs brought them in before Ne·bū·chad·nez'zar.

19 Then the king [1]interviewed them, and among them all none was found like Daniel, Han·a·nī'ah, Mish'a·el, and Az·a·rī'ah; therefore [a]they served before the king.

20 [a]And in all matters of wisdom *and* understanding about which the king examined them, he found them ten times better than all the magicians *and* astrologers who *were* in all his realm.

21 [a]Thus Daniel continued until the first year of King Cyrus.

2 Now in the second year of Ne·bū·chad·nez'zar's reign, Ne·bū·chad·nez'zar had dreams; [a]and his spirit was *so* troubled that [b]his sleep left him.

2 [a]Then the king gave the command to call the magicians, the astrologers, the sorcerers, and the Chal·dē'ans to tell the king his dreams. So they came and stood before the king.

3 And the king said to them, "I have had a dream, and my spirit is anxious to [1]know the dream."

4 Then the Chal·dē'ans spoke to the king in Ar·a·mā'ic, [a]"O[1] king, live forever! Tell your servants the dream, and we will give the interpretation."

5 The king answered and said to the Chal·dē'ans, "My [1]decision is firm: if you do not make known the dream to me, and its interpretation, you shall be [a]cut in pieces, and your houses shall be made an ash heap.

6 [a]"However, if you tell the dream and its interpretation, you shall receive from me gifts, rewards, and great honor. Therefore tell me the dream and its interpretation."

7 They answered again and said, "Let the king tell his servants the dream, and we will give its interpretation."

8 The king answered and said, "I know for certain that you would gain time, because you see that my decision is firm:

9 "if you do not make known

11 [1]Or *Melzar*

16 [1]Or *Melzar*

17 [a][James 1:5–7] [b]Acts 7:22 [c]2 Chr. 26:5

19 [a]Gen. 41:46 [1]Lit. *talked with them*

20 [a]1 Kin. 10:1

21 [a]Dan. 6:28; 10:1

CHAPTER 2

1 [a]Gen. 40:5–8; 41:1, 8 [b]Esth. 6:1

2 [a]Ex. 7:11

3 [1]Or *understand*

4 [a]Dan. 3:9; 5:10; 6:6, 21 [1]The original language of Daniel 2:4b through 7:28 is Aramaic.

5 [a]Ezra 6:11 [1]The command

6 [a]Dan. 5:16

the dream to me, *there is only*
one decree for you! For you
have agreed to speak lying and
corrupt words before me till the
[1]time has changed. Therefore
tell me the dream, and I shall
know that you can [2]give me its
interpretation.”
10 The Chal·dē′ans answered
the king, and said, “There is not
a man on earth who can tell the
king's matter; therefore no king,
lord, or ruler has *ever* asked
such things of any magician,
astrologer, or Chal·dē′an.
11 “*It is* a [1]difficult thing that
the king requests, and there is
no other who can tell it to the
king [a]except the gods, whose
dwelling is not with flesh.”
12 For this reason the king was
angry and very furious, and gave
the command to destroy all the
wise *men* of Babylon.
13 So the decree went out, and
they began killing the wise *men*;
and they sought [a]Daniel and his
companions, to kill *them*.
14 Then with counsel and wisdom Daniel answered Ar′i·och,
the captain of the king's guard,
who had gone out to kill the
wise *men* of Babylon;
15 he answered and said to Ar′-
i·och the king's captain, “Why
is the decree from the king so
[1]urgent?” Then Ar′i·och made
the decision known to Daniel.
16 So Daniel went in and
asked the king to give him time,
that he might tell the king the
interpretation.
17 Then Daniel went to his
house, and made the decision
known to Han·a·nī′ah, Mish′a·el,
and Az·a·rī′ah, his companions,
18 [a]that they might seek mercies from the God of heaven
concerning this secret, so that
Daniel and his companions
might not perish with the rest of
the wise *men* of Babylon.
19 Then the secret was revealed
to Daniel [a]in a night vision.
So Daniel blessed the God of
heaven.
20 Daniel answered and said:

[a]“Blessed be the name of God
forever and ever,
[b]For wisdom and might are
His.
21 And He changes [a]the times
and the seasons;
[b]He removes kings and
raises up kings;
[c]He gives wisdom to the wise
And knowledge to those
who have understanding.
22 [a]He reveals deep and secret
things;
[b]He knows what *is* in the
darkness,
And [c]light dwells with Him.

23 “I thank You and praise You,
O God of my fathers;
You have given me wisdom
and might,
And have now made known
to me what we [a]asked of
You,
For You have made
known to us the king's
[1]demand.”

24 Therefore Daniel went to
Ar′i·och, whom the king had appointed to destroy the wise *men*
of Babylon. He went and said
thus to him: “Do not destroy the
wise *men* of Babylon; take me
before the king, and I will tell
the king the interpretation.”
25 Then Ar′i·och quickly
brought Daniel before the king,

9 [1]Situation [2]Or *declare to me*
11 [a]Dan. 5:11 [1]Or *rare*
13 [a]Dan. 1:19, 20
15 [1]Or *harsh*
18 [a][Matt. 18:19]
19 [a]Job 33:15
20 [a]Ps. 113:2 [b][Jer. 32:19]
21 [a]Esth. 1:13 [b][Ps. 75:6, 7] [c][James 1:5]
22 [a]Ps. 25:14 [b][Heb. 4:13] [c]Dan. 5:11, 14
23 [a]Dan. 2:18, 29, 30 [1]Lit. *word*

and said thus to him, "I have
found a man of the [1]captives of
Judah, who will make known to
the king the interpretation."
26 The king answered and
said to Daniel, whose name
was Bel·te·shaz′zar, "Are you
able to make known to me the
dream which I have seen, and its
interpretation?"
27 Daniel answered in the presence of the king, and said, "The
secret which the king has de-
manded, the wise *men*, the astrologers, the magicians, and the
soothsayers cannot declare to
the king.
28 [a]"But there is a God in heaven
who reveals secrets, and He has
made known to King Ne·bū-
chad·nez′zar [b]what will be in the
latter days. Your dream, and the
visions of your head upon your
bed, were these:
29 "As for you, O king, thoughts
came *to* your *mind while* on your
bed, *about* what would come to
pass after this; [a]and He who reveals secrets has made known
to you what will be.
30 [a]"But as for me, this secret
has not been revealed to me because I have more wisdom than
anyone living, but for *our* sakes
who make known the interpretation to the king, [b]and that you
may [1]know the thoughts of your
heart.
31 "You, O king, were watching;
and behold, a great image! This
great image, whose splendor
was excellent, stood before you;
and its form *was* awesome.
32 [a]"This image's head *was* of
fine gold, its chest and arms
of silver, its belly and [1]thighs of
bronze,
33 "its legs of iron, its feet partly
of iron and partly of [1]clay.
34 "You watched while a stone
was cut out [a]without hands,
which struck the image on its
feet of iron and clay, and broke
them in pieces.
35 [a]"Then the iron, the clay, the
bronze, the silver, and the gold
were crushed together, and became [b]like chaff from the summer threshing floors; the wind
carried them away so that [c]no
trace of them was found. And
the stone that struck the image
[d]became a great mountain [e]and
filled the whole earth.
36 "This *is* the dream. Now we
will tell the interpretation of it
before the king.
37 [a]"You, O king, *are* a king of
kings. [b]For the God of heaven
has given you a kingdom, power,
strength, and glory;
38 [a]"and wherever the children
of men dwell, or the beasts of
the field and the birds of the
heaven, He has given *them* into
your hand, and has made you
ruler over them all—[b]you *are*
this head of gold.
39 "But after you shall arise
[a]another kingdom [b]inferior to
yours; then another, a third
kingdom of bronze, which shall
rule over all the earth.
40 "And [a]the fourth kingdom
shall be as strong as iron, inasmuch as iron breaks in pieces
and shatters everything; and like
iron that crushes, *that kingdom*
will break in pieces and crush
all the others.
41 "Whereas you saw the feet
and toes, partly of potter's clay
and partly of iron, the kingdom
shall be divided; yet the strength
of the iron shall be in it, just as

25 [1]Lit. *sons of the captivity*
28 [a]Gen. 40:8 [b]Gen. 49:1
29 [a][Dan. 2:22, 28]
30 [a]Acts 3:12 [b]Dan. 2:47 [1]Understand
32 [a]Dan. 2:38, 45 [1]Or *sides*
33 [1]Or *baked clay,* also vv. 34, 35, 42
34 [a][Zech. 4:6]
35 [a][Rev. 16:14] [b]Hos. 13:3 [c]Ps. 37:10, 36 [d][Is. 2:2, 3] [e]Ps. 80:9
37 [a]Jer. 27:6, 7 [b]Ezra 1:2
38 [a]Dan. 4:21, 22 [b]Dan. 2:32
39 [a]Dan. 5:28, 31 [b]Dan. 2:32
40 [a]Dan. 7:7, 23

you saw the iron mixed with ceramic clay.
42 "And *as* the toes of the feet
were partly of iron and partly
of clay, [a]*so* the kingdom shall
be partly strong and partly
[1]fragile.
43 "As you saw iron mixed with
ceramic clay, they will mingle
with the seed of men; but they
will not adhere to one another,
just as iron does not mix with
clay.
☆ 44 "And in the days of these
kings [a]the God of heaven will set
up a kingdom [b]which shall never
be destroyed; and the kingdom
shall not be left to other people;
[c]it shall [1]break in pieces and
[2]consume all these kingdoms,
and it shall stand forever.
45 [a]"Inasmuch as you saw that
the stone was cut out of the
mountain without hands, and
that it broke in pieces the iron,
the bronze, the clay, the silver,
and the gold—the great God has
made known to the king what
will come to pass after this. The
dream is certain, and its interpretation is sure."
46 [a]Then King Ne·bū·chad·nez′-
zar fell on his face, prostrate
before Daniel, and commanded
that they should present an offering [b]and incense to him.
47 The king answered Daniel,
and said, "Truly [a]your God *is* the
God of [b]gods, the Lord of kings,
and a revealer of secrets, since
you could reveal this secret."
48 [a]Then the king promoted
Daniel [b]and gave him many
great gifts; and he made him
ruler over the whole province of
Babylon, and [c]chief administra-
tor over all the wise *men* of Babylon.

42 [a]Dan. 7:24
[1]Or *brittle*

44 [a]Dan. 2:28, 37
[b][Luke 1:32, 33]
[c]Is. 60:12
[1]Or *crush*
[2]Lit. *put an end to*

45 [a]Dan. 2:35

46 [a]Acts 10:25; 14:13
[b]Ezra 6:10

47 [a]Dan. 3:28, 29; 4:34–37
[b][Deut. 10:17]

48 [a][Prov. 14:35; 21:1]
[b]Dan. 2:6
[c]Dan. 4:9; 5:11

49 [a]Dan. 1:7; 3:12
[b]Esth. 2:19, 21; 3:2
[1]The king's court

CHAPTER 3

1 [1]About 90 feet

4 [a]Dan. 4:1; 6:25
[1]Lit. *with strength*

6 [a]Jer. 29:22

49 Also Daniel petitioned the
king, [a]and he set Shad′rach, Mē′-
shach, and A·bed′-Ne·gō′ over
the affairs of the province of
Babylon; but Daniel [b]*sat* in [1]the
gate of the king.

3 Ne·bū·chad·nez′zar the king
made an image of gold,
whose height *was* [1]sixty cubits
and its width six cubits. He set
it up in the plain of Dū′ra, in the
province of Babylon.
2 And King Ne·bū·chad·nez′-
zar sent *word* to gather together
the satraps, the administrators, the governors, the counselors, the treasurers, the judges,
the magistrates, and all the officials of the provinces, to come to
the dedication of the image
which King Ne·bū·chad·nez′zar
had set up.
3 So the satraps, the administrators, the governors, the
counselors, the treasurers, the
judges, the magistrates, and all
the officials of the provinces
gathered together for the dedication of the image that King
Ne·bū·chad·nez′zar had set up;
and they stood before the image that Ne·bū·chad·nez′zar had
set up.
4 Then a herald cried [1]aloud:
"To you it is commanded, [a]O peoples, nations, and languages,
5 "*that* at the time you hear
the sound of the horn, flute,
harp, lyre, *and* psaltery, in symphony with all kinds of music,
you shall fall down and worship the gold image that King
Ne·bū·chad·nez′zar has set up;
6 "and whoever does not fall
down and worship shall [a]be cast
immediately into the midst of a
burning fiery furnace."
7 So at that time, when all the

people heard the sound of the horn, flute, harp, *and* lyre, in symphony with all kinds of music, all the people, nations, and languages fell down *and* worshiped the gold image which King Ne·bū·chad·nez′zar had set up.

8 Therefore at that time certain Chal·dē′ans [a]came forward and accused the Jews.

9 They spoke and said to King Ne·bū·chad·nez′zar, [a]"O king, live forever!

10 "You, O king, have made a decree that everyone who hears the sound of the horn, flute, harp, lyre, *and* psaltery, in symphony with all kinds of music, shall fall down and worship the gold image;

11 "and whoever does not fall down and worship shall be cast into the midst of a burning fiery furnace.

12 [a]"There are certain Jews whom you have set over the affairs of the province of Babylon: Shad′rach, Mē′shach, and A·bed′-Ne·gō′; these men, O king, have [b]not paid due regard to you. They do not serve your gods or worship the gold image which you have set up."

13 Then Ne·bū·chad·nez′zar, in [a]rage and fury, gave the command to bring Shad′rach, Mē′shach, and A·bed′-Ne·gō′. So they brought these men before the king.

14 Ne·bū·chad·nez′zar spoke, saying to them, "*Is it* true, Shad′rach, Mē′shach, and A·bed′-Ne·gō′, *that* you do not serve my gods or worship the gold image which I have set up?

15 "Now if you are ready at the time you hear the sound of the horn, flute, harp, lyre, *and* psaltery, in symphony with all kinds of music, and you fall down and worship the image which I have made, [a]*good!* But if you do not worship, you shall be cast immediately into the midst of a burning fiery furnace. [b]And who *is* the god who will deliver you from my hands?"

16 Shad′rach, Mē′shach, and A·bed′-Ne·gō′ answered and said to the king, "O Ne·bū·chad·nez′zar, [a]we have no need to answer you in this matter.

17 "If that *is the case,* our [a]God whom we serve is able to [b]deliver us from the burning fiery furnace, and He will deliver *us* from your hand, O king.

18 "But if not, let it be known to you, O king, that we do not serve your gods, nor will we [a]worship the gold image which you have set up."

19 Then Ne·bū·chad·nez′zar was full of fury, and the expression on his face changed toward Shad′rach, Mē′shach, and A·bed′-Ne·gō′. He spoke and commanded that they heat the furnace seven times more than it was usually heated.

20 And he commanded certain mighty men of valor who *were* in his army to bind Shad′rach, Mē′shach, and A·bed′-Ne·gō′, *and* cast *them* into the burning fiery furnace.

21 Then these men were bound in their coats, their trousers, their turbans, and their *other* garments, and were cast into the midst of the burning fiery furnace.

22 Therefore, because the king's command was [1]urgent, and the furnace exceedingly hot, the

8 [a]Dan. 6:12, 13
9 [a]Dan. 2:4; 5:10; 6:6, 21
12 [a]Dan. 2:49 [b]Dan. 1:8; 6:12, 13
13 [a]Dan. 2:12; 3:19
15 [a]Luke 13:9 [b]Ex. 5:2
16 [a][Matt. 10:19]
17 [a][Is. 26:3, 4] [b]1 Sam. 17:37
18 [a]Job 13:15
22 [1]Or *harsh*

flame of the fire killed those
men who took up Shad′rach,
Mē′shach, and A·bed′-Ne·gō′.
23 And these three men, Shad′-
rach, Mē′shach, and A·bed′-
Ne·gō′, fell down bound into
the midst of the burning fiery
furnace.
24 Then King Ne·bū·chad·nez′-
zar was astonished; and he rose
in haste *and* spoke, saying to his
[1]counselors, "Did we not cast
three men bound into the midst
of the fire?" They answered and
said to the king, "True, O king."
25 "Look!" he answered, "I see
four men loose, [a]walking in the
midst of the fire; and they are
not hurt, and the form of the
fourth is like [b]the[1] Son of God."
26 Then Ne·bū·chad·nez′zar
went near the [1]mouth of the
burning fiery furnace *and* spoke,
saying, "Shad′rach, Mē′shach,
and A·bed′-Ne·gō′, servants of
the [a]Most High God, come out,
and come *here*." Then Shad′-
rach, Mē′shach, and A·bed′-
Ne·gō′ came from the midst of
the fire.
27 And the satraps, administrators, governors, and the king's
counselors gathered together,
and they saw these men [a]on
whose bodies the fire had no
power; the hair of their head
was not singed nor were their
garments affected, and the smell
of fire was not on them.
28 Ne·bū·chad·nez′zar spoke,
saying, "Blessed be the God
of Shad′rach, Mē′shach, and
A·bed′-Ne·gō′, who sent His
[a]Angel[1] and delivered His servants who trusted in Him, and
they have frustrated the king's
word, and yielded their bodies,
that they should not serve nor
worship any god except their
own God!
29 [a]"Therefore I make a decree
that any people, nation, or language which speaks anything
amiss against the [b]God of Shad′-
rach, Mē′shach, and A·bed′-
Ne·gō′ shall be [c]cut in pieces,
and their houses shall be made
an ash heap; [d]because there is
no other God who can deliver
like this."
30 Then the king [1]promoted
Shad′rach, Mē′shach, and A·bed′-
Ne·gō′ in the province of Babylon.

4 Ne·bū·chad·nez′zar the king,

[a]To all peoples, nations, and
languages that dwell in all
the earth:

Peace be multiplied to you.

2 I thought it good to declare
the signs and wonders [a]that
the Most High God has
worked for me.

3 [a]How great *are* His signs,
And how mighty His
wonders!
His kingdom *is* [b]an
everlasting kingdom,
And His dominion *is* from
generation to generation.

4 I, Ne·bū·chad·nez′zar, was
at rest in my house, and
flourishing in my palace.
5 I saw a dream which made
me afraid, [a]and the thoughts
on my bed and the visions
of my head [b]troubled me.
6 Therefore I issued a decree
to bring in all the wise *men*
of Babylon before me, that

24 [1]High officials
25 [a]Is. 43:2 [b][Ps. 34:7] [1]Or *a son of the gods*
26 [a][Dan. 4:2, 3, 17, 34, 35] [1]Lit. *door*
27 [a]Heb. 11:34
28 [a][Ps. 34:7, 8] [1]Or *angel*
29 [a]Dan. 6:26 [b]Dan. 2:46, 47; 4:34–37 [c]Dan. 2:5 [d]Dan. 6:27
30 [1]Lit. *caused to prosper*

CHAPTER 4

1 [a]Dan. 3:4; 6:25
2 [a]Dan. 3:26
3 [a]2 Sam. 7:16 [b][Dan. 2:44; 4:34; 6:26]
5 [a]Dan. 2:28, 29 [b]Dan. 2:1

they might make known to
me the interpretation of the
dream.
7 [a]Then the magicians, the
astrologers, the Chal·dē′ans,
and the soothsayers came
in, and I told them the
dream; but they did not
make known to me its
interpretation.
8 But at last Daniel came
before me [a](his name *is*
Bel·te·shaz′zar, according
to the name of my god; [b]in
him *is* the Spirit of the Holy
God), and I told the dream
before him, *saying:*
9 "Bel·te·shaz′zar, [a]chief of the
magicians, because I know
that the Spirit of the Holy
God *is* in you, and no secret
troubles you, explain to me
the visions of my dream
that I have seen, and its
interpretation.
10 "These *were* the visions of
my head *while* on my bed:

I was looking, and behold,
[a]A tree in the midst of the
earth,
And its height was great.
11 The tree grew and became
strong;
Its height reached to the
heavens,
And it could be seen to the
ends of all the earth.
12 Its leaves *were* lovely,
Its fruit abundant,
And in it *was* food for all.
[a]The beasts of the field found
shade under it,
The birds of the heavens
dwelt in its branches,
And all flesh was fed
from it.

13 "I saw in the visions of
my head *while* on my bed,
and there was [a]a watcher,
[b]a holy one, coming down
from heaven.
14 He cried [1]aloud and said
thus:

[a]'Chop down the tree and cut
off its branches,
Strip off its leaves and
scatter its fruit.
[b]Let the beasts get out from
under it,
And the birds from its
branches.
15 Nevertheless leave the
stump and roots in the
earth,
Bound with a band of iron
and bronze,
In the tender grass of the
field.
Let it be wet with the dew of
heaven,
And *let* him graze with the
beasts
On the grass of the earth.
16 Let his heart be changed
from *that of* a man,
Let him be given the heart
of a beast,
And let seven [a]times[1] pass
over him.

17 'This decision *is* by the
decree of the watchers,
And the sentence by the
word of the holy ones,
In order [a]that the living may
know
[b]That the Most High rules in
the kingdom of men,
[c]Gives it to whomever He
will,
And sets over it the [d]lowest
of men.'

7 [a]Dan. 2:2
8 [a]Dan. 1:7 [b]Dan. 2:11; 4:18; 5:11, 14
9 [a]Dan. 2:48; 5:11
10 [a]Ezek. 31:3
12 [a]Lam. 4:20
13 [a][Dan. 4:17, 23] [b]Deut. 33:2
14 [a]Ezek. 31:10–14 [b]Ezek. 31:12, 13 [1]Lit. *with strength*
16 [a]Dan. 11:13; 12:7 [1]Possibly *years*
17 [a]Ps. 9:16; 83:18 [b]Dan. 2:21; 4:25, 32; 5:21 [c]Jer. 27:5–7 [d]1 Sam. 2:8

18 "This dream I, King
Ne·bū·chad·nezʹzar,
have seen. Now you,
Bel·te·shazʹzar, declare its
interpretation, [a]since all the
wise *men* of my kingdom
are not able to make known
to me the interpretation; but
you *are* able, [b]for the Spirit
of the Holy God *is* in you."

19 Then Daniel, [a]whose name
was Bel·te·shazʹzar, was
astonished for a time, and
his thoughts [b]troubled
him. *So* the king spoke,
and said, "Bel·te·shazʹzar,
do not let the dream or its
interpretation trouble you."
Bel·te·shazʹzar answered
and said, "My lord, *may*
[c]the dream [1]concern those
who hate you, and its
interpretation [2]concern your
enemies!
20 [a]The tree that you saw,
which grew and became
strong, whose height
reached to the heavens and
which *could be* seen by all
the earth,
21 whose leaves *were* lovely
and its fruit abundant, in
which *was* food for all,
under which the beasts of
the field dwelt, and in whose
branches the birds of the
heaven had their home—
22 [a]it *is* you, O king, who
have grown and become
strong; for your greatness
has grown and reaches
to the heavens, [b]and your
dominion to the end of the
earth.
23 [a]And inasmuch as the king
saw a watcher, a holy one,
coming down from heaven
and saying, 'Chop down
the tree and destroy it, but
leave its stump and roots
in the earth, *bound* with a
band of iron and bronze in
the tender grass of the field;
let it be wet with the dew of
heaven, [b]and let him graze
with the beasts of the field,
till seven [1]times pass over
him';
24 this is the interpretation,
O king, and this is the
decree of the Most High,
which has come upon my
lord the king:
25 They shall [a]drive you from
men, your dwelling shall
be with the beasts of the
field, and they shall make
you [b]eat grass like oxen.
They shall wet you with the
dew of heaven, and seven
[1]times shall pass over you,
[c]till you know that the Most
High rules in the kingdom
of men, and [d]gives it to
whomever He chooses.
26 And inasmuch as they gave
the command to leave the
stump *and* roots of the
tree, your kingdom shall be
assured to you, after you
come to know that [a]Heaven[1]
rules.
27 Therefore, O king, let my
advice be acceptable to
you; [a]break off your sins by
being righteous, and your
iniquities by showing mercy
to *the* poor. [b]Perhaps there
may be [c]a [1]lengthening of
your prosperity."

28 All *this* came upon King
Ne·bū·chad·nezʹzar.
29 At the end of the twelve
months he was walking

18 [a]Gen. 41:8, 15 [b]Dan. 4:8, 9; 5:11, 14
19 [a]Dan. 4:8 [b]Dan. 7:15, 28; 8:27 [c]2 Sam. 18:32 [1]*be for* [2]*for*
20 [a]Dan. 4:10–12
22 [a]Dan. 2:37, 38 [b]Jer. 27:6–8
23 [a]Dan. 4:13–15 [b]Dan. 5:21 [1]Possibly *years*
25 [a]Dan. 4:32; 5:21 [b]Ps. 106:20 [c]Dan. 4:2, 17, 32 [d]Jer. 27:5 [1]Possibly *years*
26 [a]Matt. 21:25 [1]God
27 [a][1 Pet. 4:8] [b][Ps. 41:1–3] [c]1 Kin. 21:29 [1]*prolonging*

[1]about the royal palace of
Babylon.
30 The king [a]spoke, saying,
"Is not this great Babylon,
that I have built for a royal
dwelling by my mighty
power and for the honor of
my majesty?"
31 [a]While the word *was still* in
the king's mouth, [b]a voice
fell from heaven: "King
Ne·bū·chad·nez′zar, to you it
is spoken: the kingdom has
departed from you!
32 And [a]they shall drive
you from men, and your
dwelling *shall be* with the
beasts of the field. They
shall make you eat grass
like oxen; and seven [1]times
shall pass over you, until
you know that the Most
High rules in the kingdom
of men, and gives it to
whomever He chooses."
33 That very hour the word
was fulfilled concerning
Ne·bū·chad·nez′zar; he was
driven from men and ate
grass like oxen; his body
was wet with the dew of
heaven till his hair had
grown like eagles' *feathers*
and his nails like birds'
claws.

34 And [a]at the end of the [1]time
I, Ne·bū·chad·nez′zar, lifted
my eyes to heaven, and my
understanding returned
to me; and I blessed the
Most High and praised and
honored Him [b]who lives
forever:

For His dominion *is* [c]an
everlasting dominion,
And His kingdom *is* from
generation to generation.
35 [a]All the inhabitants of the
earth *are* reputed as
nothing;
[b]He does according to His
will in the army of
heaven
And *among* the inhabitants
of the earth.
[c]No one can restrain His
hand
Or say to Him, [d]"What have
You done?"

36 At the same time my
reason returned to me,
[a]and for the glory of my
kingdom, my honor and
splendor returned to me.
My counselors and nobles
resorted to me, I was
[b]restored to my kingdom,
and excellent majesty was
[c]added to me.
37 Now I, Ne·bū·chad·nez′zar,
[a]praise and extol and honor
the King of heaven, [b]all of
whose works *are* truth, and
His ways justice. [c]And those
who walk in pride He is
able to put down.

CHAPTER 5

5 Bel·shaz′zar the king [a]made
a great feast for a thousand
of his lords, and drank wine in
the presence of the thousand.
2 While he tasted the wine,
Bel·shaz′zar gave the command to bring the gold and silver vessels [a]which his [1]father
Ne·bū·chad·nez′zar had taken
from the temple which *had been*
in Jerusalem, that the king and
his lords, his wives, and his concubines might drink from them.
3 Then they brought the gold
[a]vessels that had been taken

29 [1]Or *upon*
30 [a]Prov. 16:18
31 [a]Luke 12:20 [b]Dan. 4:24
32 [a][Dan. 4:25] [1]Possibly *years*
34 [a]Dan. 4:26 [b][Rev. 4:10] [c][Luke 1:33] [1]Lit. *days*
35 [a]Is. 40:15, 17 [b]Ps. 115:3; 135:6 [c]Job 34:29 [d]Rom. 9:20
36 [a]Dan. 4:26 [b]2 Chr. 20:20 [c][Prov. 22:4]
37 [a]Dan. 2:46, 47; 3:28, 29 [b][Ps. 33:4] [c]Ex. 18:11
1 [a]Esth. 1:3
2 [a]Dan. 1:2 [1]Or *ancestor*
3 [a]2 Chr. 36:10

from the temple of the house of
God which *had been* in Jerusalem; and the king and his lords,
his wives, and his concubines
drank from them.
4 They drank wine, [a]and
praised the gods of gold and silver, bronze and iron, wood and
stone.
5 [a]In the same hour the fingers
of a man's hand appeared and
wrote opposite the lampstand
on the plaster of the wall of the
king's palace; and the king saw
the part of the hand that wrote.
6 Then the king's countenance
changed, and his thoughts troubled him, so that the joints of
his hips were loosened and his
[a]knees knocked against each
other.
7 [a]The king cried [1]aloud to
bring in [b]the astrologers, the
Chal·dē′ans, and the soothsayers. The king spoke, saying to
the wise *men* of Babylon, "Whoever reads this writing, and tells
me its interpretation, shall be
clothed with purple and *have* a
chain of gold around his neck;
[c]and he shall be the third ruler
in the kingdom."
8 Now all the king's wise *men*
came, [a]but they could not read
the writing, or make known to
the king its interpretation.
9 Then King Bel·shaz′zar was
greatly [a]troubled, his countenance was changed, and his
lords were [1]astonished.
10 The queen, because of the
words of the king and his lords,
came to the banquet hall. The
queen spoke, saying, "O king,
live forever! Do not let your
thoughts trouble you, nor let
your countenance change.
11 [a]"There is a man in your
kingdom in whom *is* the Spirit
of the Holy God. And in the
days of your [1]father, light and
understanding and wisdom, like
the wisdom of the gods, were
found in him; and King Ne·bū-
chad·nez′zar your [1]father—your
father the king—made him chief
of the magicians, astrologers,
Chal·dē′ans, *and* soothsayers.
12 "Inasmuch as an excel-
lent spirit, knowledge, understanding, interpreting dreams,
solving riddles, and [1]explain-
ing enigmas were found in this
Daniel, [a]whom the king named
Bel·te·shaz′zar, now let Daniel
be called, and he will give the
interpretation."
13 Then Daniel was brought in
before the king. The king spoke,
and said to Daniel, "*Are* you
that Daniel [1]who is one of the
captives from Judah, whom my
[2]father the king brought from
Judah?
14 "I have heard of you, that
[a]the [1]Spirit of God *is* in you, and
that light and understanding
and excellent wisdom are found
in you.
15 "Now [a]the wise *men*, the astrologers, have been brought in
before me, that they should read
this writing and make known to
me its interpretation, but they
could not give the interpretation
of the thing.
16 "And I have heard of you,
that you can give interpretations
and [1]explain enigmas. [a]Now if
you can read the writing and
make known to me its interpretation, you shall be clothed with
purple and *have* a chain of gold
around your neck, and shall be
the third ruler in the kingdom."
17 Then Daniel answered, and

4 [a]Rev. 9:20
5 [a]Dan. 4:31
6 [a]Ezek. 7:17; 21:7
7 [a]Dan. 4:6, 7; 5:11, 15 [b]Is. 47:13 [c]Dan. 6:2, 3 [1]Lit. *with strength*
8 [a]Dan. 2:27; 4:7; 5:15
9 [a]Dan. 2:1; 5:6 [1]*perplexed*
11 [a]Dan. 2:48; 4:8, 9, 18 [1]Or *ancestor*
12 [a]Dan. 1:7; 4:8 [1]Lit. *untying knots*
13 [1]Lit. *who is of the sons of the captivity* [2]Or *ancestor*
14 [a]Dan. 4:8, 9, 18; 5:11, 12 [1]Or *spirit of the gods*
15 [a]Dan. 5:7, 8
16 [a]Dan. 5:7, 29 [1]Lit. *untie knots*

said before the king, "Let your
gifts be for yourself, and give
your rewards to another; yet I
will read the writing to the king,
and make known to him the
interpretation.
18 "O king, [a]the Most High God
gave Ne·bū·chad·nez′zar your
[1]father a kingdom and majesty,
glory and honor.
19 "And because of the majesty
that He gave him, [a]all peoples,
nations, and languages trembled
and feared before him. Whomever he wished, he [b]executed;
whomever he wished, he kept
alive; whomever he wished, he
set up; and whomever he wished,
he put down.
20 [a]"But when his heart was
lifted up, and his spirit was hardened in pride, he was deposed
from his kingly throne, and they
took his glory from him.
21 "Then he was [a]driven from
the sons of men, his heart was
made like the beasts, and his
dwelling *was* with the wild donkeys. They fed him with grass
like oxen, and his body was wet
with the dew of heaven, [b]till he
[1]knew that the Most High God
rules in the kingdom of men,
and appoints over it whomever
He chooses.
22 "But you his son, Bel·shaz′-
zar, [a]have not humbled your heart,
although you knew all this.
23 [a]"And you have [1]lifted yourself up against the Lord of
heaven. They have brought the
[b]vessels of [2]His house before
you, and you and your lords,
your wives and your concubines,
have drunk wine from them.
And you have praised the gods
of silver and gold, bronze and
iron, wood and stone, [c]which
do not see or hear or know; and
the God who *holds* your breath
in His hand [d]and owns all your
ways, you have not glorified.
24 "Then the [1]fingers of the
hand were sent from Him, and
this writing was written.
25 "And this is the inscription
that was written:

[1]MENE, MENE, [2]TEKEL,
[3]UPHARSIN.

26 "This *is* the interpretation
of *each* word. MENE: God has
numbered your kingdom, and
finished it;
27 "TEKEL: [a]You have been
weighed in the balances, and
found wanting;
28 "PERES: Your kingdom has
been divided, and given to the
[a]Mēdes and [b]Persians."[1]
29 Then Bel·shaz′zar gave the
command, and they clothed
Daniel with purple and *put* a
chain of gold around his neck,
and made a proclamation concerning him [a]that he should be
the third ruler in the kingdom.
30 [a]That very night Bel·shaz′-
zar, king of the Chal·dē′ans, was
slain.
31 [a]And Da·rī′us the Mēde received the kingdom, *being* about
sixty-two years old.

6

It pleased Da·rī′us to set
over the kingdom one hun-
dred and twenty satraps, to be
over the whole kingdom;
2 and over these, three governors, of whom Daniel *was* one,
that the satraps might give account to them, so that the king
would suffer no loss.
3 Then this Daniel distinguished himself above the governors and satraps, [a]because an

18 [a]Dan. 2:37, 38; 4:17, 22, 25 [1]Or *ancestor*
19 [a]Jer. 27:7 [b]Dan. 2:12, 13; 3:6
20 [a]Dan. 4:30, 37
21 [a]Dan. 4:32, 33 [b]Ezek. 17:24 [1]Recognized
22 [a]2 Chr. 33:23; 36:12
23 [a]Dan. 5:3, 4 [b]Ex. 40:9 [c]Ps. 115:5, 6 [d][Jer. 10:23] [1]Exalted [2]The temple
24 [1]Lit. *palm*
25 [1]Lit. *a mina* (50 shekels) from the verb "to number" [2]Lit. *a shekel* from the verb "to weigh" [3]Lit. *and half-shekels* from the verb "to divide"; pl. of *Peres,* v. 28
27 [a]Ps. 62:9
28 [a]Dan. 5:31; 9:1 [b]Dan. 6:28 [1]Aram. *Paras,* consonant with *Peres*
29 [a]Dan. 5:7, 16
30 [a]Jer. 51:31, 39, 57
31 [a]Dan. 2:39; 9:1

CHAPTER 6

3 [a]Dan. 5:12

excellent spirit *was* in him; and
the king gave thought to setting
him over the whole realm.
4 [a]So the governors and satraps sought to find *some* charge
against Daniel concerning the
kingdom; but they could find no
charge or fault, because he *was*
faithful; nor was there any error
or fault found in him.
5 Then these men said, "We
shall not find any charge against
this Daniel unless we find *it*
against him concerning the law
of his God."
6 So these governors and satraps thronged before the king,
and said thus to him: [a]"King
Da·rī'us, live forever!
7 "All the governors of the
kingdom, the administrators
and satraps, the counselors and
advisors, have [a]consulted together to establish a royal statute and to make a firm decree,
that whoever petitions any god
or man for thirty days, except
you, O king, shall be cast into
the den of lions.
8 "Now, O king, establish the
decree and sign the writing, so
that it cannot be changed, according to the [a]law of the Mēdes
and Persians, which [1]does not
alter."
9 Therefore King Da·rī'us
signed the written decree.
10 Now when Daniel knew that
the writing was signed, he went
home. And in his upper room,
with his windows open [a]toward
Jerusalem, he knelt down on his
knees [b]three times that day, and
prayed and gave thanks before
his God, as was his custom since
early days.
11 Then these men assembled
and found Daniel praying and
making supplication before his
God.
12 [a]And they went before the
king, and spoke concerning
the king's decree: "Have you
not signed a decree that every
man who petitions any god or
man within thirty days, except
you, O king, shall be cast into
the den of lions?" The king answered and said, "The thing *is*
true, [b]according to the law of
the Mēdes and Persians, which
[1]does not alter."
13 So they answered and said
before the king, "That Daniel,
[a]who is [1]one of the captives from
Judah, [b]does not show due regard
for you, O king, or for the decree
that you have signed, but makes
his petition three times a day."
14 And the king, when he heard
these words, [a]was greatly displeased with himself, and set *his*
heart on Daniel to deliver him;
and he [1]labored till the going
down of the sun to deliver him.
15 Then these men [1]approached
the king, and said to the king,
"Know, O king, that *it is* [a]the
law of the Mēdes and Persians
that no decree or statute which
the king establishes may be
changed."
16 So the king gave the command, and they brought Daniel
and cast *him* into the den of
lions. *But* the king spoke, saying to Daniel, "Your God, whom
you serve continually, He will
deliver you."
17 [a]Then a stone was brought
and laid on the mouth of the
den, [b]and the king sealed it with
his own signet ring and with the
signets of his lords, that the purpose concerning Daniel might
not be changed.

4 [a]Eccl. 4:4
6 [a]Neh. 2:3
7 [a]Ps. 59:3; 62:4; 64:2–6
8 [a]Esth. 1:19; 8:8 [1]Lit. *does not pass away*
10 [a]Jon. 2:4 [b]Ps. 55:17
12 [a]Dan. 3:8–12 [b]Dan. 6:8, 15 [1]Lit. *does not pass away*
13 [a]Dan. 1:6; 5:13 [b]Dan. 3:12 [1]Lit. *of the sons of the captivity*
14 [a]Mark 6:26 [1]*strove*
15 [a]Dan. 6:8, 12 [1]Lit. *thronged before*
17 [a]Lam. 3:53 [b]Matt. 27:66

18 Now the king went to his palace and spent the night fasting;
and no [1]musicians were brought
before him. [a]Also his sleep [2]went
from him.
19 Then the [a]king arose very
early in the morning and went
in haste to the den of lions.
20 And when he came to the
den, he cried out with a [1]lament-
ing voice to Daniel. The king
spoke, saying to Daniel, "Daniel,
servant of the living God, [a]has
your God, whom you serve continually, been able to deliver you
from the lions?"
21 Then Daniel said to the king,
[a]"O king, live forever!
22 [a]"My God sent His angel and
[b]shut the lions' mouths, so that
they have not hurt me, because I
was found innocent before Him;
and also, O king, I have done no
wrong before you."
23 Now the king was exceedingly glad for him, and commanded that they should take
Daniel up out of the den. So
Daniel was taken up out of the
den, and no injury whatever was
found on him, [a]because he believed in his God.
24 And the king gave the command, [a]and they brought those
men who had accused Daniel,
and they cast *them* into the den
of lions—them, [b]their children,
and their wives; and the lions
overpowered them, and broke
all their bones in pieces before
they ever came to the bottom of
the den.
25 [a]Then King Da·rī'us wrote:

To all peoples, nations, and
languages that dwell in all
the earth:

Peace be multiplied to you.

26 [a]I make a decree that in
every dominion of my
kingdom *men must* [b]tremble
and fear before the God of
Daniel.

[c]For He *is* the living God,
And steadfast forever;
His kingdom *is the one*
which shall not be
[d]destroyed,
And His dominion *shall*
endure to the end.
27 He delivers and rescues,
[a]And He works signs and
wonders
In heaven and on earth,
Who has delivered Daniel
from the [1]power of the
lions.

28 So this Daniel prospered in
the reign of Da·rī'us [a]and in the
reign of [b]Cyrus the Persian.

7 In the first year of Bel·shaz'-
zar king of Babylon, [a]Daniel
[1]had a dream and [b]visions of his
head *while* on his bed. Then he
wrote down the dream, telling
[2]the main facts.
2 Daniel spoke, saying, "I saw
in my vision by night, and behold, the four winds of heaven
were stirring up the Great Sea.
3 "And four great beasts [a]came
up from the sea, each different
from the other.
4 "The first *was* [a]like a lion, and
had eagle's wings. I watched till
its wings were plucked off; and
it was lifted up from the earth
and made to stand on two feet
like a man, and a [b]man's heart
was given to it.
5 [a]"And suddenly another
beast, a second, like a bear. It

---

18 [a]Dan. 2:1 [1]Exact meaning unknown [2]Or *fled*
19 [a]Dan. 3:24
20 [a]Dan. 3:17 [1]Or *grieved*
21 [a]Dan. 2:4; 6:6
22 [a]Dan. 3:28 [b]Heb. 11:33
23 [a]Heb. 11:33
24 [a]Deut. 19:18, 19 [b]Deut. 24:16
25 [a]Dan. 4:1
26 [a]Dan. 3:29 [b]Ps. 99:1 [c]Dan. 4:34; 6:20 [d]Dan. 2:44; 4:3; 7:14, 27
27 [a]Dan. 4:2, 3 [1]Lit. *hand*
28 [a]Dan. 1:21 [b]Ezra 1:1, 2

CHAPTER 7

1 [a][Amos 3:7] [b][Dan. 2:28] [1]Lit. *saw* [2]Lit. *the head* or *chief of the words*
3 [a]Rev. 13:1; 17:8
4 [a]Deut. 28:49 [b]Dan. 4:16, 34
5 [a]Dan. 2:39

was raised up on one side, and
had three ribs in its mouth between its teeth. And they said
thus to it: 'Arise, devour much
flesh!'
6 "After this I looked, and
there was another, like a leopard, which had on its back four
wings of a bird. The beast also
had [a]four heads, and dominion
was given to it.
7 "After this I saw in the night
visions, and behold, [a]a fourth
beast, dreadful and terrible, exceedingly strong. It had huge
iron teeth; it was devouring,
breaking in pieces, and tram-
pling the residue with its feet. It
was different from all the beasts
that *were* before it, [b]and it had
ten horns.
8 "I was considering the horns,
and [a]there was another horn,
a little one, coming up among
them, before whom three of the
first horns were plucked out
by the roots. And there, in this
horn, *were* eyes like the eyes [b]of
a man, [c]and a mouth speaking
[1]pompous words.

9 "I[a] watched till thrones were
[1]put in place,
And [b]the Ancient of Days
was seated;
[c]His garment *was* white as
snow,
And the hair of His head
was like pure wool.
His throne *was* a fiery
flame,
[d]Its wheels a burning fire;
10 [a]A fiery stream issued
And came forth from before
Him.
[b]A thousand thousands
ministered to Him;
Ten thousand times ten
thousand stood before
Him.
[c]The [1]court was seated,
And the books were opened.

11 "I watched then because of
the sound of the [1]pompous words
which the horn was speaking; [a]I
watched till the beast was slain,
and its body destroyed and given
to the burning flame.
12 "As for the rest of the beasts,
they had their dominion taken
away, yet their lives were prolonged for a season and a time.

13 "I was watching in the night ☆
visions,
And behold, [a]*One* like the
Son of Man,
Coming with the clouds of
heaven!
He came to the Ancient of
Days,
And they brought Him near
before Him.
14 [a]Then to Him was given ☆
dominion and glory and
a kingdom,
That all [b]peoples, nations,
and languages should
serve Him.
His dominion *is* [c]an
everlasting dominion,
Which shall not pass away,
And His kingdom *the one*
Which shall not be
destroyed.

15 "I, Daniel, was grieved in my
spirit [1]within *my* body, and the
visions of my head troubled me.
16 "I came near to one of those
who stood by, and asked him
the truth of all this. So he told
me and made known to me the
interpretation of these things:

6 [a]Dan. 8:8, 22
7 [a]Dan. 2:40 [b]Rev. 12:3; 13:1
8 [a]Dan. 8:9 [b]Rev. 9:7 [c]Rev. 13:5, 6 [1]Lit. *great things*
9 [a][Rev. 20:4] [b]Ps. 90:2 [c]Rev. 1:14 [d]Ezek. 1:15 [1]Or *set up*
10 [a]Is. 30:33; 66:15 [b]Rev. 5:11 [c][Rev. 20:11–15] [1]Or *judgment*
11 [a][Rev. 19:20; 20:10] [1]Lit. *great*
13 [a][Matt. 24:30; 26:64; Mark 13:26; 14:62; Luke 21:27; Rev. 1:7, 13; 14:14]
14 [a][Matt. 28:18; John 3:35, 36; 1 Cor. 15:27; Eph. 1:22; Phil. 2:9–11; Rev. 1:6; 11:15] [b]Dan. 3:4 [c]Mic. 4:7; [Luke 1:33]; John 12:34; Heb. 12:28
15 [1]Lit. *in the midst of its sheath*

17 'Those great beasts, which
are four, *are* four [1]kings *which*
arise out of the earth.
18 'But [a]the saints of the Most
High shall receive the kingdom,
and possess the kingdom forever, even forever and ever.'
19 "Then I wished to know the
truth about the fourth beast,
which was different from all
the others, exceedingly dreadful, *with* its teeth of iron and its
nails of bronze, *which* devoured,
broke in pieces, and trampled
the residue with its feet;
20 "and the ten horns that *were*
on its head, and the other *horn*
which came up, before which
three fell, namely, that horn
which had eyes and a mouth
which spoke [1]pompous words,
whose appearance *was* greater
than his fellows.
21 "I was watching; [a]and the
same horn was making war
against the saints, and prevail-
ing against them,
22 "until the Ancient of Days
came, [a]and a judgment was made
in favor of the saints of the Most
High, and the time came for the
saints to possess the kingdom.
23 "Thus he said:

'The fourth beast shall be
[a]A fourth kingdom on earth,
Which shall be different
from all *other* kingdoms,
And shall devour the whole
earth,
Trample it and break it in
pieces.
24 [a]The ten horns *are* ten kings
Who shall arise from this
kingdom.
And another shall rise after
them;
He shall be different from
the first *ones*,
And shall subdue three
kings.
25 [a]He shall speak *pompous*
words against the Most
High,
Shall [b]persecute[1] the saints
of the Most High,
And shall [c]intend to change
times and law.
Then [d]*the saints* shall be
given into his hand
[e]For a time and times and
half a time.

26 'But[a] the court shall be
seated,
And they shall [b]take away
his dominion,
To consume and destroy *it*
forever.
27 Then the [a]kingdom and
dominion,
And the greatness of the
kingdoms under the
whole heaven,
Shall be given to the people,
the saints of the Most
High.
[b]His kingdom *is* an
everlasting kingdom,
[c]And all dominions shall
serve and obey Him.'

28 "This *is* the end of the [1]ac-
count. As for me, Daniel, [a]my
thoughts greatly troubled me,
and my countenance changed;
but I [b]kept the matter in my
heart."

CHAPTER 8

8 In[1] the third year of the
reign of King Bel·shaz′zar
a vision appeared *to* me—to me,
Daniel—after the one that appeared to me [a]the first time.
2 I saw in the vision, and it so
happened while I was looking,

17 [1]Representing their kingdoms, v. 23
18 [a]Is. 60:12–14
20 [1]Lit. *great things*
21 [a]Rev. 11:7; 13:7; 17:14
22 [a][Rev. 1:6]
23 [a]Dan. 2:40
24 [a]Rev. 13:1; 17:12
25 [a]Rev. 13:1–6 [b]Rev. 17:6 [c]Dan. 2:21 [d]Rev. 13:7; 18:24 [e]Rev. 12:14 [1]Lit. *wear out*
26 [a][Dan. 2:35; 7:10, 22] [b]Rev. 19:20
27 [a]Dan. 7:14, 18, 22 [b][Luke 1:32, 33] [c]Is. 60:12
28 [a]Dan. 8:27 [b]Luke 2:19, 51 [1]Lit. *word*

CHAPTER 8

1 [a]Dan. 7:1 [1]The Hebrew language resumes in Dan. 8:1.

that I *was* in [a]Shū′shan,[1] the
[2]citadel, which *is* in the province
of Ē′lam; and I saw in the vision
that I was by the River Ū′laī.
3 Then I lifted my eyes and
saw, and there, standing beside
the river, was a ram which had
two horns, and the two horns
were high; but one *was* [a]higher
than the other, and the higher
one came up last.
4 I saw the ram pushing westward, northward, and southward, so that no animal could
[1]withstand him; nor *was there*
any that could deliver from his
hand, [a]but he did according to
his will and became great.
5 And as I was considering,
suddenly a male goat came from
the west, across the surface of
the whole earth, without touching the ground; and the goat
had a notable [a]horn between his
eyes.
6 Then he came to the ram that
had two horns, which I had seen
standing beside the river, and
ran at him with furious power.
7 And I saw him confronting
the ram; he was moved with
rage against him, [1]attacked the
ram, and broke his two horns.
There was no power in the ram
to withstand him, but he cast
him down to the ground and
trampled him; and there was no
one that could deliver the ram
from his hand.
8 Therefore the male goat
grew very great; but when he
became strong, the large horn
was broken, and in place of it
[a]four notable ones came up toward the four winds of heaven.
9 [a]And out of one of them came
a little horn which grew exceedingly great toward the south,
[b]toward the east, and toward the
[c]Glorious *Land.*
10 [a]And it grew up to [b]the host
of heaven; and [c]it cast down
some of the host and *some* of
the stars to the ground, and
trampled them.
11 [a]He even exalted *himself* as
high as [b]the Prince of the host;
[c]and by him [d]the daily *sacri-*
fices were taken away, and the
place of [1]His sanctuary was cast
down.
12 Because of transgression,
[a]an army was given over *to the*
horn to oppose the daily *sacri-*
fices; and he cast [b]truth down to
the ground. He [c]did *all this* and
prospered.
13 Then I heard [a]a holy one
speaking; and *another* holy one
said to that certain *one* who was
speaking, "How long *will* the
vision *be, concerning* the daily
sacrifices and the transgression
[1]of desolation, the giving of both
the sanctuary and the host to be
trampled underfoot?"
14 And he said to me, "For two
thousand three hundred [1]days;
then the sanctuary shall be
cleansed."
15 Then it happened, when I,
Daniel, had seen the vision and
[a]was seeking the meaning, that
suddenly there stood before me
[b]one having the appearance of a
man.
16 And I heard a man's voice
[a]between *the banks of* the Ū′laī,
who called, and said, [b]"Gabriel,
make this *man* understand the
vision."
17 So he came near where I
stood, and when he came I was
afraid and [a]fell on my face; but
he said to me, "Understand, son

2 [a]Esth. 1:2; 2:8 [1]Or *Susa* [2]Or *fortified palace*
3 [a]Dan. 7:5
4 [a]Dan. 5:19 [1]Lit. *stand before him*
5 [a]Dan. 8:8, 21; 11:3
7 [1]Lit. *struck*
8 [a]Dan. 7:6; 8:22; 11:4
9 [a]Dan. 11:21 [b]Dan. 11:25 [c]Ps. 48:2
10 [a]Dan. 11:28 [b]Is. 14:13 [c]Rev. 12:4
11 [a]Dan. 8:25; 11:36, 37 [b]Josh. 5:14 [c]Dan. 11:31; 12:11 [d]Ex. 29:38 [1]The temple
12 [a]Dan. 11:31 [b]Is. 59:14 [c]Dan. 8:4; 11:36
13 [a]Dan. 4:13, 23 [1]Or *making desolate*
14 [1]Lit. *evening-mornings*
15 [a]1 Pet. 1:10 [b]Ezek. 1:26
16 [a]Dan. 12:6, 7 [b]Luke 1:19, 26
17 [a]Rev. 1:17

of man, that the vision *refers* to
the time of the end."
18 [a]Now, as he was speaking
with me, I was in a deep sleep
with my face to the ground; [b]but
he touched me, and stood me
upright.
19 And he said, "Look, I am
making known to you what
shall happen in the latter time
of the indignation; [a]for at the appointed time the end *shall be*.
20 "The ram which you saw,
having the two horns—*they are*
the kings of Media and Persia.
21 "And the [1]male goat *is* the
[2]kingdom of Greece. The large
horn that *is* between its eyes [a]*is*
the first king.
22 [a]"As for the broken *horn* and
the four that stood up in its
place, four kingdoms shall arise
out of that nation, but not with
its power.

23 "And in the latter time of
their kingdom,
When the transgressors
have reached their
fullness,
A king shall arise,
[a]Having fierce [1]features,
Who understands sinister
schemes.
24 His power shall be mighty,
[a]but not by his own
power;
He shall destroy [1]fearfully,
[b]And shall prosper and
thrive;
[c]He shall destroy the mighty,
and *also* the holy people.

25 "Through[a] his cunning
He shall cause deceit to
prosper under his [1]rule;
[b]And he shall exalt *himself* in
his heart.

18 [a]Luke 9:32 [b]Ezek. 2:2
19 [a]Hab. 2:3
21 [a]Dan. 11:3 [1]*shaggy male* [2]Lit. *king*, representing his kingdom, Dan. 7:17, 23
22 [a]Dan. 11:4
23 [a]Deut. 28:50 [1]Lit. *countenance*
24 [a]Rev. 17:13 [b]Dan. 11:36 [c]Dan. 7:25 [1]Or *extraordinarily*
25 [a]Dan. 11:21 [b]Dan. 8:11–13; 11:36; 12:7 [c]Rev. 19:19, 20 [d]Job 34:20 [1]Lit. *hand*
26 [a]Ezek. 12:27
27 [a]Dan. 7:28; 8:17 [1]*amazed*

CHAPTER 9

1 [a]Dan. 1:21
2 [a]2 Chr. 36:21
3 [a]Neh. 1:4
4 [a]Ex. 20:6
5 [a]1 Kin. 8:47, 48

He shall destroy many in
their prosperity.
[c]He shall even rise against
the Prince of princes;
But he shall be [d]broken
without *human* [1]means.

26 "And the vision of the
evenings and mornings
Which was told is true;
[a]Therefore seal up the vision,
For *it refers* to many days *in
the future*."

27 [a]And I, Daniel, fainted and
was sick for days; afterward I
arose and went about the king's
business. I was [1]astonished by
the vision, but no one understood it.

9 In the first year [a]of Da·rī'us
the son of A·has·ū·ē'rus, of
the lineage of the Mēdes, who
was made king over the realm of
the Chal·dē'ans—
2 in the first year of his reign I,
Daniel, understood by the books
the number of the years *specified*
by the word of the LORD through
[a]Jer·e·mī'ah the prophet, that He
would accomplish seventy years
in the desolations of Jerusalem.
3 [a]Then I set my face toward
the Lord God to make request by
prayer and supplications, with
fasting, sackcloth, and ashes.
4 And I prayed to the LORD
my God, and made confession,
and said, "O [a]Lord, great and
awesome God, who keeps His
covenant and mercy with those
who love Him, and with those
who keep His commandments,
5 [a]"we have sinned and committed iniquity, we have done
wickedly and rebelled, even by
departing from Your precepts
and Your judgments.

6 [a]"Neither have we heeded Your servants the prophets, who spoke in Your name to our kings and our princes, to our fathers and all the people of the land.
7 "O Lord, [a]righteousness *belongs* to You, but to us shame of face, as *it is* this day—to the men of Judah, to the inhabitants of Jerusalem and all Israel, those near and those far off in all the countries to which You have driven them, because of the unfaithfulness which they have committed against You.
8 "O Lord, to us *belongs* shame of face, to our kings, our princes, and our fathers, because we have sinned against You.
9 [a]"To the Lord our God *belong* mercy and forgiveness, though we have rebelled against Him.
10 "We have not obeyed the voice of the LORD our God, to walk in His laws, which He set before us by His servants the prophets.
11 "Yes, [a]all Israel has transgressed Your law, and has departed so as not to obey Your voice; therefore the curse and the oath written in the [b]Law of Moses the servant of God have been poured out on us, because we have sinned against Him.
12 "And He has [a]confirmed His words, which He spoke against us and against our judges who judged us, by bringing upon us a great disaster; [b]for under the whole heaven such has never been done as what has been done to Jerusalem.
13 [a]"As *it is* written in the Law of Moses, all this disaster has come upon us; [b]yet we have not made our prayer before the LORD our God, that we might turn from our iniquities and understand Your truth.
14 "Therefore the LORD has [a]kept the disaster in mind, and brought it upon us; for [b]the LORD our God *is* righteous in all the works which He does, though we have not obeyed His voice.
15 "And now, O Lord our God, [a]who brought Your people out of the land of Egypt with a mighty hand, and made Yourself [b]a name, as *it is* this day—we have sinned, we have done wickedly!
16 "O Lord, [a]according to all Your righteousness, I pray, let Your anger and Your fury be turned away from Your city Jerusalem, [b]Your holy mountain; because for our sins, [c]and for the iniquities of our fathers, [d]Jerusalem and Your people [e]*are* a reproach to all *those* around us.
17 "Now therefore, our God, hear the prayer of Your servant, and his supplications, [a]and [b]for the Lord's sake [1]cause Your face to shine on [2]Your sanctuary, [c]which is desolate.
18 [a]"O my God, incline Your ear and hear; open Your eyes [b]and see our desolations, and the city [c]which is called by Your name; for we do not present our supplications before You because of our righteous deeds, but because of Your great mercies.
19 "O Lord, hear! O Lord, forgive! O Lord, listen and act! Do not delay for Your own sake, my God, for Your city and Your people are called by Your name."
20 Now while I *was* speaking, praying, and confessing my sin and the sin of my people Israel, and presenting my supplication

6 [a]2 Chr. 36:15
7 [a]Neh. 9:33
9 [a][Ps. 130:4, 7]
11 [a]Is. 1:3–6 [b]Lev. 26:14
12 [a]Zech. 1:6 [b]Lam. 1:12; 2:13
13 [a]Deut. 28:15–68 [b]Is. 9:13
14 [a]Jer. 31:28; 44:27 [b]Neh. 9:33
15 [a]Neh. 1:10 [b]Neh. 9:10
16 [a]1 Sam. 12:7 [b]Zech. 8:3 [c]Ex. 20:5 [d]Lam. 2:16 [e]Ps. 79:4
17 [a]Num. 6:24–26 [b]Lam. 5:18 [c][John 16:24] [1]Be gracious [2]The temple
18 [a]Is. 37:17 [b]Ex. 3:7 [c]Jer. 25:29

before the LORD my God for the
holy mountain of my God,
21 yes, while I *was* speaking in
prayer, the man [a]Gabriel, whom
I had seen in the vision at the
beginning, [1]being caused to fly
swiftly, reached me about the
time of the evening offering.
22 And he informed *me*, and
talked with me, and said, "O
Daniel, I have now come forth to
give you skill to understand.
23 "At the beginning of your
supplications the [1]command
went out, and I have come to tell
you, for you *are* greatly [a]beloved;
therefore [b]consider the matter,
and understand the vision:

24 "Seventy [1]weeks are
determined
For your people and for
your holy city,
To finish the transgression,
[2]To make an end of sins,
[a]To make reconciliation for
iniquity,
[b]To bring in everlasting
righteousness,
To seal up vision and
prophecy,
[c]And to anoint [3]the Most Holy.

☆ 25 "Know therefore and
understand,
That from the going forth of
the command
To restore and build
Jerusalem
Until [a]Messiah [b]the Prince,
There shall be seven weeks
and sixty-two weeks;
The [1]street shall be built
again, and the [2]wall,
Even in troublesome times.

☆ 26 "And after the sixty-two
weeks
[a]Messiah shall [1]be cut off,
[b]but not for Himself;
And [c]the people of the
prince who is to come
[d]Shall destroy the city and
the sanctuary.
The end of it *shall be* with a
flood,
And till the end of the
war desolations are
determined.
27 Then he shall confirm [a]a
[1]covenant with [b]many for
one week;
But in the middle of the week
He shall bring an end to
sacrifice and offering.
And on the wing of
abominations shall be
one who makes desolate,
[c]Even until the
consummation, which is
determined,
Is poured out on the
[2]desolate."

10 In the third year of Cyrus
king of Persia a message
was revealed to Daniel, whose
[a]name was called Bel·te·shaz′-
zar. The message *was* true, [1]but
the appointed time *was* long;
and he understood the message,
and had understanding of the
vision.
2 In those days I, Daniel, was
mourning three full weeks.
3 I ate no [1]pleasant food, no
meat or wine came into my
mouth, nor did I anoint myself at
all, till three whole weeks were
fulfilled.
4 Now on the twenty-fourth
day of the first month, as I was
by the side of the great river,
that *is*, the [1]Ti′gris,
5 I lifted my eyes and looked,
and behold, a certain man clothed

21 [a]Dan. 8:16
[1]Or *being weary with weariness*

23 [a]Dan. 10:11, 19
[b]Matt. 24:15
[1]Lit. *word*

24 [a][Is. 53:10]
[b]Rev. 14:6
[c]Ps. 45:7
[1]Lit. *sevens*, and so throughout the chapter
[2]So with Qr., LXX, Syr., Vg.; Kt., Theodotion *To seal up*
[3]The Most Holy Place

25 [a]John 1:41; 4:25
[b]Is. 55:4
[1]Or *open square*
[2]Or *moat*

26 [a][Is. 53:8]; Matt. 27:50; Mark 9:12; 15:37; [Luke 23:46; 24:26]; John 19:30; Acts 8:32
[b][1 Pet. 2:21]
[c]Matt. 22:7
[d]Matt. 24:2; Mark 13:2; Luke 19:43, 44
[1]Suffer the death penalty

27 [a]Is. 42:6
[b][Matt. 26:28]
[c]Dan. 11:36
[1]Or *treaty*
[2]Or *desolator*

CHAPTER 10

1 [a]Dan. 1:7
[1]Or *and of great conflict;*

3 [1]*desirable*

4 [1]Heb. *Hiddekel*

in [a]linen, whose waist *was* [b]girded with gold of Ū′phaz!

6 His body *was* like beryl, his face like the appearance of lightning, his eyes like torches of fire, his arms and feet like burnished bronze in color, [a]and the sound of his words like the voice of a multitude.

7 And I, Daniel, alone saw the vision, for the men who were with me did not see the vision; but a great terror fell upon them, so that they fled to hide themselves.

8 Therefore I was left alone when I saw this great vision, and no strength remained in me; for my [1]vigor was turned to [2]frailty in me, and I retained no strength.

9 Yet I heard the sound of his words; and while I heard the sound of his words I was in a deep sleep on my face, with my face to the ground.

10 [a]Suddenly, a hand touched me, which made me tremble on my knees and *on* the palms of my hands.

11 And he said to me, "O Daniel, [a]man greatly beloved, understand the words that I speak to you, and stand upright, for I have now been sent to you." While he was speaking this word to me, I stood trembling.

12 Then he said to me, [a]"Do not fear, Daniel, for from the first day that you set your heart to understand, and to humble yourself before your God, [b]your words were heard; and I have come because of your words.

13 [a]"But the prince of the kingdom of Persia withstood me twenty-one days; and behold, [b]Michael, one of the chief princes, came to help me, for I had been left alone there with the kings of Persia.

14 "Now I have come to make you understand what will happen to your people [a]in the latter days, [b]for the vision *refers* to *many* days yet *to come.*"

15 When he had spoken such words to me, [a]I [1]turned my face toward the ground and became speechless.

16 And suddenly, [a]*one* having the likeness of the [1]sons of men [b]touched my lips; then I opened my mouth and spoke, saying to him who stood before me, "My lord, because of the vision [c]my sorrows have [2]overwhelmed me, and I have retained no strength.

17 "For how can this servant of my lord talk with you, my lord? As for me, no strength remains in me now, nor is any breath left in me."

18 Then again, *the one* having the likeness of a man touched me and strengthened me.

19 [a]And he said, "O man greatly beloved, [b]fear not! Peace *be* to you; be strong, yes, be strong!" So when he spoke to me I was strengthened, and said, "Let my lord speak, for you have strengthened me."

20 Then he said, "Do you know why I have come to you? And now I must return to fight [a]with the prince of Persia; and when I have gone forth, indeed the prince of Greece will come.

21 "But I will tell you what is noted in the Scripture of Truth. (No one upholds me against these, [a]except Michael your prince.

5 [a]Ezek. 9:2; 10:2 [b]Rev. 1:13; 15:6
6 [a][Rev. 1:15]
8 [1]Lit. *splendor* [2]Lit. *ruin*
10 [a]Dan. 9:21
11 [a]Dan. 9:23
12 [a]Rev. 1:17 [b]Acts 10:4
13 [a]Dan. 10:20 [b]Dan. 10:21; 12:1
14 [a]Dan. 2:28 [b]Dan. 8:26; 10:1
15 [a]Dan. 8:18; 10:9 [1]Lit. *set*
16 [a]Dan. 8:15 [b]Jer. 1:9 [c]Dan. 10:8, 9 [1]Theodotion, Vg. *the son;* LXX *a hand* [2]Or *turned upon*
19 [a]Dan. 10:11 [b]Judg. 6:23
20 [a]Dan. 10:13
21 [a][Rev. 12:7]

11

“Also [a]in the first year of [b]Da·rī′us the Mēde, I, *even* I, stood up to confirm and strengthen him.)

2 “And now I will tell you the truth: Behold, three more kings will arise in Persia, and the fourth shall be far richer than *them* all; by his strength, through his riches, he shall stir up all against the realm of Greece.

3 “Then [a]a mighty king shall arise, who shall rule with great dominion, and [b]do according to his will.

4 “And when he has arisen, [a]his kingdom shall be broken up and divided toward the four winds of heaven, but not among his posterity [b]nor according to his dominion with which he ruled; for his kingdom shall be uprooted, even for others besides these.

5 “Also the king of the South shall become strong, as well as *one* of his princes; and he shall gain power over him and have dominion. His dominion *shall be* a great dominion.

6 “And at the end of *some* years they shall join forces, for the daughter of the king of the South shall go to the king of the North to make an agreement; but she shall not retain the power of her [1]authority, and neither he nor his [1]authority shall stand; but she shall be given up, with those who brought her, and with him who begot her, and with him who strengthened her in *those* times.

7 “But from a branch of her roots *one* shall arise in his place, who shall come with an army, enter the fortress of the king of the North, and deal with them and prevail.

8 “And he shall also carry their gods captive to Egypt, with their [1]princes *and* their precious articles of silver and gold; and he shall continue *more* years than the king of the North.

9 “Also *the king of the North* shall come to the kingdom of the king of the South, but shall return to his own land.

10 “However his sons shall stir up strife, and assemble a multitude of great forces; and *one* shall certainly come [a]and overwhelm and pass through; then he shall return [b]to his fortress and stir up strife.

11 “And the king of the South shall be [a]moved with rage, and go out and fight with him, with the king of the North, who shall muster a great multitude; but the [b]multitude shall be given into the hand of his *enemy.*

12 “When he has taken away the multitude, his heart will be [1]lifted up; and he will cast down tens of thousands, but he will not prevail.

13 “For the king of the North will return and muster a multitude greater than the former, and shall certainly come at the end of some years with a great army and much equipment.

14 “Now in those times many shall rise up against the king of the South. Also, [1]violent men of your people shall exalt themselves [2]in fulfillment of the vision, but they shall [a]fall.

15 “So the king of the North shall come and [a]build a siege mound, and take a fortified city; and the [1]forces of the South shall not withstand *him.* Even

CHAPTER 11

1 [a]Dan. 9:1 [b]Dan. 5:31

3 [a]Dan. 7:6; 8:5 [b]Dan. 8:4; 11:16, 36

4 [a]Zech. 2:6 [b]Dan. 8:22

6 [1]Lit. *arm*

8 [1]Or *molded images*

10 [a]Is. 8:8 [b]Dan. 11:7

11 [a]Prov. 16:14 [b][Ps. 33:10, 16]

12 [1]Proud

14 [a]Job 9:13 [1]Or *robbers,* lit. *sons of breakage* [2]Lit. *to establish*

15 [a]Ezek. 4:2; 17:17 [1]Lit. *arms*

his choice troops *shall have* no strength to resist.

16 "But he who comes against him [a]shall do according to his own will, and [b]no one shall stand against him. He shall stand in the Glorious Land with destruction in his [1]power.

17 "He shall also [a]set his face to enter with the strength of his whole kingdom, and [1]upright ones with him; thus shall he do. And he shall give him the daughter of women to destroy it; but she shall not stand *with him*, [b]or be for him.

18 "After this he shall turn his face to the coastlands, and shall take many. But a ruler shall bring the reproach against them to an end; and with the reproach removed, he shall turn back on him.

19 "Then he shall turn his face toward the fortress of his own land; but he shall [a]stumble and fall, [b]and not be found.

20 "There shall arise in his place one who imposes taxes *on* the glorious kingdom; but within a few days he shall be destroyed, but not in anger or in battle.

21 "And in his place [a]shall arise a vile person, to whom they will not give the honor of royalty; but he shall come in peaceably, and seize the kingdom by intrigue.

22 "With the [1]force of a [a]flood they shall be swept away from before him and be broken, [b]and also the prince of the covenant.

23 "And after the league *is made* with him [a]he shall act deceitfully, for he shall come up and become strong with a small *number of* people.

24 "He shall enter peaceably, even into the richest places of

16 [a]Dan. 8:4, 7 [b]Josh. 1:5 [1]Lit. *hand*

17 [a]2 Chr. 20:3 [b]Dan. 9:26 [1]Or *bring equitable terms*

19 [a]Jer. 46:6 [b]Ps. 37:36

21 [a]Dan. 7:8

22 [a]Dan. 9:26 [b]Dan. 8:10, 11 [1]Lit. *arms*

23 [a]Dan. 8:25

24 [1]*booty*

26 [1]Or *overflow*

27 [a]Hab. 2:3

30 [a]Jer. 2:10 [1]Heb. *Kittim*, western lands, especially Cyprus

31 [a]Dan. 8:11–13; 12:11 [1]Lit. *arms*

the province; and he shall do *what* his fathers have not done, nor his forefathers: he shall disperse among them the plunder, [1]spoil, and riches; and he shall devise his plans against the strongholds, but *only* for a time.

25 "He shall stir up his power and his courage against the king of the South with a great army. And the king of the South shall be stirred up to battle with a very great and mighty army; but he shall not stand, for they shall devise plans against him.

26 "Yes, those who eat of the portion of his delicacies shall destroy him; his army shall [1]be swept away, and many shall fall down slain.

27 "Both these kings' hearts *shall be* bent on evil, and they shall speak lies at the same table; but it shall not prosper, for the end *will* still *be* at the [a]appointed time.

28 "While returning to his land with great riches, his heart shall be *moved* against the holy covenant; so he shall do *damage* and return to his own land.

29 "At the appointed time he shall return and go toward the south; but it shall not be like the former or the latter.

30 [a]"For ships from [1]Cyprus shall come against him; therefore he shall be grieved, and return in rage against the holy covenant, and do *damage*. So he shall return and show regard for those who forsake the holy covenant.

31 "And [1]forces shall be mustered by him, [a]and they shall defile the sanctuary fortress; then they shall take away the daily

sacrifices, and place *there* the
abomination of desolation.
32 "Those who do wickedly
against the covenant he shall
[1]corrupt with flattery; but the
people who know their God
shall be strong, and carry out
great exploits.
33 "And those of the people who
understand shall instruct many;
yet *for many* days they shall fall
by sword and flame, by captivity
and plundering.
34 "Now when they fall, they
shall be aided with a little help;
but many shall join with them
by [1]intrigue.
35 "And *some* of those of understanding shall fall, [a]to refine
them, purify *them,* and make
them white, *until* the time of the
end; because *it is* still for the appointed time.
36 "Then the king shall do according to his own will: he shall
[a]exalt and magnify himself
above every god, shall speak
blasphemies against the God of
gods, and shall prosper till the
wrath has been accomplished;
for what has been determined
shall be done.
37 "He shall regard neither the
[1]God of his fathers nor the desire of women, [a]nor regard any
god; for he shall exalt himself
above *them* all.
38 "But in their place he shall
honor a god of fortresses; and
a god which his fathers did not
know he shall honor with gold
and silver, with precious stones
and pleasant things.
39 "Thus he shall act against
the strongest fortresses with
a foreign god, which he shall
acknowledge, *and* advance *its*
glory; and he shall cause them
to rule over many, and divide the
land for [1]gain.
40 "At the [a]time of the end
the king of the South shall attack him; and the king of the
North shall come against him
[b]like a whirlwind, with chariots, [c]horsemen, and with many
ships; and he shall enter the
countries, overwhelm *them,* and
pass through.
41 "He shall also enter the Glorious Land, and many *countries*
shall be overthrown; but these
shall escape from his hand:
[a]Ē′dom, Mō′ab, and the [1]promi-
nent people of Am′mon.
42 "He shall stretch out his hand
against the countries, and the
land of [a]Egypt shall not escape.
43 "He shall have power over
the treasures of gold and silver,
and over all the precious things
of Egypt; also the Lib′yans and
Ethiopians *shall follow* [a]at his
heels.
44 "But news from the east and
the north shall trouble him;
therefore he shall go out with
great fury to destroy and annihilate many.
45 "And he shall plant the tents
of his palace between the seas
and [a]the glorious holy mountain; [b]yet he shall come to his
end, and no one will help him.

12

"At that time Michael
shall stand up,
The great prince who stands
watch over the sons of
your people;
[a]And there shall be a time of
trouble,
Such as never was since
there was a nation,
Even to that time.

32 [1]*pollute*
34 [1]Or *slipperiness, flattery*
35 [a]Dan. 12:10
36 [a]Dan. 7:8, 25
37 [a]Is. 14:13 [1]Or *gods*
39 [1]*profit*
40 [a]Dan. 11:27, 35; 12:4, 9 [b]Is. 21:1 [c]Rev. 9:16
41 [a]Is. 11:14 [1]Lit. *chief of the sons of Ammon*
42 [a]Joel 3:19
43 [a]Ex. 11:8
45 [a]Ps. 48:2 [b]Rev. 19:20

CHAPTER 12
1 [a]Jer. 30:7

And at that time your people
[b]shall be delivered,
Every one who is found
[c]written in the book.
2 And many of those who
sleep in the dust of the
earth shall awake,
[a]Some to everlasting life,
Some to shame [b]*and*
everlasting [1]contempt.
3 Those who are wise shall
[a]shine
Like the brightness of the
firmament,
[b]And those who turn many
to righteousness
[c]Like the stars forever and
ever.

4 "But you, Daniel, [a]shut up
the words, and seal the book
until the time of the end; many
shall [b]run to and fro, and knowledge shall increase."
5 Then I, Daniel, looked; and
there stood two others, one on
this riverbank and the other on
that [a]riverbank.
6 And *one* said to the man
clothed in [a]linen, who *was* above
the waters of the river, [b]"How
long shall the fulfillment of these
wonders *be?*"
7 Then I heard the man clothed
in linen, who *was* above the waters of the river, when he [a]held
up his right hand and his left
hand to heaven, and swore by
Him [b]who lives forever, [c]that
it shall be for a time, times,
and half *a time;* [d]and when the
power of [e]the holy people has
been completely shattered, all
these *things* shall be finished.
8 Although I heard, I did not
understand. Then I said, "My
lord, what *shall be* the end of
these *things?*"
9 And he said, "Go *your way,*
Daniel, for the words *are* closed
up and sealed till the time of the
end.
10 [a]"Many shall be purified,
made white, and refined, [b]but
the wicked shall do wickedly;
and none of the wicked shall
understand, but [c]the wise shall
understand.
11 "And from the time *that* the
daily *sacrifice* is taken away,
and the abomination of desolation is set up, *there shall be*
one thousand two hundred and
ninety days.
12 "Blessed *is* he who waits,
and comes to the one thousand
three hundred and thirty-five
days.
13 "But you, go *your way* till the
end; [a]for you shall rest, [b]and will
arise to your inheritance at the
end of the days."

1 [b]Rom. 11:26 [c]Ex. 32:32
2 [a][John 5:28, 29] [b][Is. 66:24] [1]Lit. *abhorrence*
3 [a]Matt. 13:43 [b][James 5:19, 20] [c]1 Cor. 15:41
4 [a]Rev. 22:10 [b]Amos 8:12
5 [a]Dan. 10:4
6 [a]Ezek. 9:2 [b]Dan. 8:13; 12:8
7 [a]Deut. 32:40 [b]Dan. 4:34 [c]Dan. 7:25 [d]Luke 21:24 [e]Dan. 8:24
10 [a]Zech. 13:9 [b]Is. 32:6, 7 [c]John 7:17; 8:47
13 [a]Rev. 14:13 [b]Ps. 1:5

The Book of

HOSEA

HOSEA, whose name means "Salvation," ministers to the northern kingdom of Israel (also called Ephraim, after its largest tribe). Outwardly, the nation is enjoying a time of prosperity and growth; but inwardly, moral corruption and spiritual adultery permeate the people. Hosea, instructed by God to marry a woman named Gomer, finds his domestic life to be an accurate and tragic dramatization of the unfaithfulness of God's people. During his half century of prophetic ministry, Hosea repeatedly echoes his threefold message: God abhors the sins of His people; judgment is certain; but God's loyal love stands firm.

The names Hosea, Joshua, and Jesus are all derived from the same Hebrew root word. The word *hoshea* means "salvation," but "Joshua" and "Jesus" include an additional idea: "Yahweh Is Salvation." As God's messenger, Hosea offers the possibility of salvation if only the nation will turn from idolatry back to God.

Israel's last king, Hoshea, has the same name as the prophet even though the English Bible spells them differently. Hosea in the Greek and Latin is *Osee*.

CHAPTER 1

THE word of the LORD that
came to Hō·sē′a the son
of Be·ē′rī, in the days of [a]Uz-
zī′ah, [b]Jō′tham, [c]Ā′haz, *and*
[d]Hez·e·kī′ah, kings of Judah, and
in the days of [e]Jer·o·bō′am the
son of Jō′ash, king of Israel.
2 When the LORD began to
speak by Hō·sē′a, the LORD said
to Hō·sē′a:

[a]"Go, take yourself a wife of
harlotry
And children of harlotry,
For [b]the land has committed
great [1]harlotry
By departing from the
LORD."

3 So he went and took Gō′mer
the daughter of Dib·lā′im, and
she conceived and bore him a
son.
4 Then the LORD said to him:

"Call his name Jez′rē·el,
For in a little *while*
[a]I will avenge the bloodshed
of Jez′rē·el on the house
of Jē′hū,
[b]And bring an end to the
kingdom of the house of
Israel.
5 [a]It shall come to pass in that
day
That I will break the bow
of Israel in the Valley of
Jez′rē·el."

6 And she conceived again and
bore a daughter. Then *God* said
to him:

"Call her name
[1]Lō-Rū·ha′mah,
[a]For I will no longer have
mercy on the house of
Israel,
[2]But I will utterly take them
away.

1 [a]Amos 1:1 [b]2 Chr. 27 [c]2 Chr. 28 [d]2 Chr. 29:1—32:33 [e]2 Kin. 13:13; 14:23–29

2 [a]Hos. 3:1 [b]Jer. 2:13 [1]Spiritual adultery

4 [a]2 Kin. 10:11 [b]2 Kin. 15:8–10; 17:6, 23; 18:11

5 [a]2 Kin. 15:29

6 [a]2 Kin. 17:6 [1]Lit. *No-Mercy* [2]Or *That I may forgive them at all*

7 [a]Yet I will have mercy on the
house of Judah,
Will save them by the LORD
their God,
And [b]will not save them by
bow,
Nor by sword or battle,
By horses or horsemen."

8 Now when she had weaned
Lō-Rū·ha′mah, she conceived
and bore a son.
9 Then *God* said:

"Call his name [1]Lō-Am′mi,
For you *are* not My people,
And I will not be your *God*.

10 "Yet [a]the number of the
children of Israel
Shall be as the sand of the
sea,
Which cannot be measured
or numbered.
[b]And it shall come to pass
In the place where it was
said to them,
'You *are* [1]not My [c]people,'
There it shall be said to them,
'*You* are [d]sons of the living
God.'
11 [a]Then the children of Judah
and the children of Israel
Shall be gathered together,
And appoint for themselves
one head;
And they shall come up out
of the land,
For great *will be* the day of
Jez′rē·el!

2 Say to your brethren, [1]'My
people,'
And to your sisters, [2]'Mercy
is shown.'

2 "Bring[1] charges against your
mother, [2]bring charges;
For [a]she *is* not My wife, nor
am I her Husband!
Let her put away her
[b]harlotries from her
sight,
And her adulteries from
between her breasts;
3 Lest [a]I strip her naked
And expose her, as in the
day she was [b]born,
And make her like a
wilderness,
And set her like a dry land,
And slay her with [c]thirst.

4 "I will not have mercy on her
children,
For they *are* the [a]children of
harlotry.
5 For their mother has played
the harlot;
She who conceived them
has behaved shamefully.
For she said, 'I will go after
my lovers,
[a]Who give *me* my bread and
my water,
My wool and my linen,
My oil and my drink.'

6 "Therefore, behold,
[a]I will hedge up your way
with thorns,
And [1]wall her in,
So that she cannot find her
paths.
7 She will [1]chase her lovers,
But not overtake them;
Yes, she will seek them, but
not find *them*.
Then she will say,
[a]'I will go and return to my
[b]first husband,
For then *it was* better for
me than now.'
8 For she did not [a]know
That I gave her grain, new
wine, and oil,

---

7 [a]2 Kin. 19:29–35 [b][Zech. 4:6]
9 [1]Lit. *Not-My-People*
10 [a]Gen. 22:17; 32:12 [b]1 Pet. 2:10 [c]Rom. 9:26 [d][John 1:12] [1]Heb. *lo-ammi*, v. 9
11 [a]Is. 11:11–13

CHAPTER 2

1 [1]Heb. *Ammi*, Hos. 1:9, 10 [2]Heb. *Ruhamah*, Hos. 1:6
2 [a]Is. 50:1 [b]Ezek. 16:25 [1]Or *Contend with* [2]Or *contend*
3 [a]Jer. 13:22, 26 [b]Ezek. 16:4–7, 22 [c]Amos 8:11–13
4 [a]John 8:41
5 [a]Hos. 2:8, 12
6 [a]Lam. 3:7, 9 [1]Lit. *wall up her wall*
7 [a]Luke 15:17, 18 [b]Ezek. 16:8; 23:4 [1]Or *pursue*
8 [a]Is. 1:3

And multiplied her silver
and gold—
Which they prepared for
Bā'al.

9 "Therefore I will return and
take away
My grain in its time
And My new wine in its
season,
And will take back My wool
and My linen,
Given to cover her
nakedness.
10 Now [a]I will uncover her
lewdness in the sight of
her lovers,
And no one shall deliver her
from My hand.
11 [a]I will also cause all her
mirth to cease,
Her feast days,
Her New Moons,
Her Sabbaths—
All her appointed feasts.

12 "And I will destroy her vines
and her fig trees,
Of which she has said,
'These *are* my wages that my
lovers have given me.'
So I will make them a
forest,
And the beasts of the field
shall eat them.
13 I will punish her
For the days of the Bā'als
to which she burned
incense.
She decked herself with her
earrings and jewelry,
And went after her lovers;
But Me she forgot," says the
LORD.

14 "Therefore, behold, I will
allure her,

10 [a]Ezek. 16:37
11 [a]Amos 5:21; 8:10
14 [1]Lit. *to her heart*
15 [a]Josh. 7:26 [b]Ezek.16:8–14 [c]Ex. 15:1
16 [1]Heb. *Ishi* [2]Heb. *Baali*
17 [a]Ex. 23:13
18 [a]Job 5:23 [b]Is. 2:4 [c]Lev. 26:5
20 [a][Jer. 31:33, 34]

Will bring her into the
wilderness,
And speak [1]comfort to her.
15 I will give her her vineyards
from there,
And [a]the Valley of Ā'chor as
a door of hope;
She shall sing there,
As in [b]the days of her youth,
[c]As in the day when she
came up from the land
of Egypt.

16 "And it shall be, in that day,"
Says the LORD,
"*That* you will call Me [1]'My
Husband,'
And no longer call Me [2]'My
Master,'
17 For [a]I will take from her
mouth the names of the
Bā'als,
And they shall be
remembered by their
name no more.
18 In that day I will make a
[a]covenant for them
With the beasts of the field,
With the birds of the air,
And *with* the creeping
things of the ground.
Bow and sword of battle
[b]I will shatter from the
earth,
To make them [c]lie down
safely.

19 "I will betroth you to Me
forever;
Yes, I will betroth you to Me
In righteousness and justice,
In lovingkindness and
mercy;
20 I will betroth you to Me in
faithfulness,
And [a]you shall know the
LORD.

21 "It shall come to pass in that day
That [a]I will answer," says the LORD;
"I will answer the heavens,
And they shall answer the earth.
22 The earth shall answer
With grain,
With new wine,
And with oil;
They shall answer [1]Jez′rē·el.
23 Then [a]I will sow her for Myself in the earth,
[b]And I will have mercy on *her who had* [1]not obtained mercy;
Then [c]I will say to *those who were* [2]not My people,
'You *are* [3]My people!'
And they shall say, '*You are* my God!' "

3 Then the LORD said to me,
"Go again, love a woman
who is loved by a [a]lover[1] and is
committing adultery, just like
the love of the LORD for the children of Israel, who look to other
gods and love *the* raisin cakes *of*
the pagans."
2 So I bought her for myself for
fifteen *shekels* of silver, and one
and one-half homers of barley.
3 And I said to her, "You shall
[a]stay with me many days; you
shall not play the harlot, nor
shall you have a man—so, too,
will I *be* toward you."
4 For the children of Israel
shall abide many days [a]without
king or prince, without sacrifice
or *sacred* pillar, without [b]ephod
or [c]teraphim.
5 Afterward the children of Israel shall return and [a]seek the
LORD their God and [b]David their
king. They shall fear the LORD
and His goodness in the [c]latter
days.

4 Hear the word of the LORD,
You children of Israel,
For the LORD *brings* a [a]charge[1] against the inhabitants of the land:

"There is no truth or mercy
Or [b]knowledge of God in the land.
2 *By* swearing and lying,
Killing and stealing and committing adultery,
They break all restraint,
With bloodshed [1]upon bloodshed.
3 Therefore [a]the land will mourn;
And [b]everyone who dwells there will waste away
With the beasts of the field
And the birds of the air;
Even the fish of the sea will be taken away.

4 "Now let no man contend, or rebuke another;
For your people *are* like those [a]who contend with the priest.
5 Therefore you shall stumble [a]in the day;
The prophet also shall stumble with you in the night;
And I will destroy your mother.
6 [a]My people are destroyed for lack of knowledge.
Because you have rejected knowledge,
I also will reject you from being priest for Me;
[b]Because you have forgotten the law of your God,

---

21 [a]Zech. 8:12
22 [1]Lit. *God Will Sow*
23 [a]Jer. 31:27 [b]Hos. 1:6 [c]Hos. 1:10 [1]Heb. *lo-ruhamah* [2]Heb. *lo-ammi* [3]Heb. *ammi*

CHAPTER 3

1 [a]Jer. 3:20 [1]Lit. *friend* or *husband*
3 [a]Deut. 21:13
4 [a]Hos. 10:3 [b]Ex. 28:4–12 [c]Judg. 17:5; 18:14, 17
5 [a]Jer. 50:4 [b]Jer. 30:9 [c][Is. 2:2, 3]

CHAPTER 4

1 [a]Is. 1:18 [b]Jer. 4:22 [1]A legal complaint
2 [1]Lit. *touching*
3 [a]Amos 5:16; 8:8 [b]Zeph. 1:3
4 [a]Deut. 17:12
5 [a]Jer. 15:8
6 [a]Is. 5:13 [b]Ezek. 22:26

I also will forget your
children.

7 "The more they increased,
The more they sinned
against Me;
[a]I[1] will change [2]their glory
into shame.
8 They eat up the sin of My
people;
They set their [1]heart on
their iniquity.
9 And it shall be: [a]like people,
like priest.
So I will punish them for
their ways,
And [1]reward them for their
deeds.
10 For [a]they shall eat, but not
have enough;
They shall commit harlotry,
but not increase;
Because they have ceased
obeying the LORD.

11 "Harlotry, wine, and new
wine [a]enslave the heart.
12 My people ask counsel from
their [a]wooden *idols*,
And their [1]staff informs
them.
For [b]the spirit of harlotry
has caused *them* to
stray,
And they have played the
harlot against their God.
13 [a]They offer sacrifices on the
mountaintops,
And burn incense on the
hills,
Under oaks, poplars, and
terebinths,
Because their shade *is* good.
[b]Therefore your daughters
commit harlotry,
And your brides commit
adultery.
14 "I will not punish your
daughters when they
commit harlotry,
Nor your brides when they
commit adultery;
For *the men* themselves go
apart with harlots,
And offer sacrifices with a
[a]ritual harlot.
Therefore people *who* do
not understand will be
trampled.

15 "Though you, Israel, play the
harlot,
Let not Judah offend.
[a]Do not come up to Gil′gal,
Nor go up to [b]Beth[1] Ā′ven,
[c]Nor swear an oath, *saying*,
'As the LORD lives'—

16 "For Israel [a]is stubborn
Like a stubborn calf;
Now the LORD will let them
forage
Like a lamb in [1]open
country.

17 "Ē′phra·im *is* joined to idols,
[a]Let him alone.
18 Their drink [1]is rebellion,
They commit harlotry
continually.
[a]Her [2]rulers [3]dearly love
dishonor.
19 [a]The wind has wrapped her
up in its wings,
And [b]they shall be ashamed
because of their
sacrifices.

5

"Hear this, O priests!
Take heed, O house of
Israel!
Give ear, O house of the
king!
For [1]yours *is* the judgment,

---

7 [a]1 Sam. 2:30 [1]So with MT, LXX, Vg.; scribal tradition, Syr., Tg. *They will change* [2]So with MT, LXX, Syr., Tg., Vg.; scribal tradition *My glory*

8 [1]Desires

9 [a]Is. 24:2 [1]*repay*

10 [a]Lev. 26:26

11 [a]Is. 5:12; 28:7

12 [a]Jer. 2:27 [b]Is. 44:19, 20 [1]Diviner's rod

13 [a]Is. 1:29; 57:5, 7 [b]Amos 7:17

14 [a]Deut. 23:18

15 [a]Hos. 9:15; 12:11 [b]1 Kin. 12:29 [c]Amos 8:14 [1]Lit. *House of Idolatry* or *Wickedness*

16 [a]Jer. 3:6; 7:24; 8:5 [1]Lit. *a large place*

17 [a]Matt. 15:14

18 [a]Mic. 3:11 [1]Or *has turned aside* [2]Lit. *shields* [3]Heb. difficult; a Jewish tradition *shamefully love, 'Give!'*

19 [a]Jer. 51:1 [b]Is. 1:29

CHAPTER 5

1 [1]Or *to you*

Because [a]you have been a
snare to Miz′pah
And a net spread on
Tā′bor.
2 The revolters are [a]deeply
involved in slaughter,
Though I rebuke them all.
3 [a]I know Ē′phra·im,
And Israel is not hidden
from Me;
For now, O Ē′phra·im, [b]you
commit harlotry;
Israel is defiled.

4 "They[1] do not direct their
deeds
Toward turning to their God,
For [a]the spirit of harlotry is
in their midst,
And they do not know the
LORD.
5 The [a]pride of Israel testifies
to his face;
Therefore Israel and
Ē′phra·im stumble in
their iniquity;
Judah also stumbles with
them.

6 "With their flocks and herds
[a]They shall go to seek the
LORD,
But they will not find *Him*;
He has withdrawn Himself
from them.
7 They have [a]dealt
treacherously with the
LORD,
For they have begotten
[1]pagan children.
Now a New Moon shall
devour them and their
heritage.

8 "Blow[a] the ram's horn in
Gib′ē·ah,
The trumpet in Rā′mah!
[b]Cry aloud *at* [c]Beth Ā′ven,
'*Look* behind you,
O Benjamin!'
9 Ē′phra·im shall be desolate
in the day of rebuke;
Among the tribes of Israel
I make known what is
sure.

10 "The princes of Judah are
like those who [a]remove a
landmark;
I will pour out My wrath on
them like water.
11 Ē′phra·im is [a]oppressed *and*
broken in judgment,
Because he willingly walked
by [b]*human* precept.
12 Therefore I *will be* to
Ē′phra·im like a moth,
And to the house of Judah
[a]like rottenness.

13 "When Ē′phra·im saw his
sickness,
And Judah *saw* his
[a]wound,
Then Ē′phra·im went [b]to
Assyria
And sent to King Jā′reb;
Yet he cannot cure you,
Nor heal you of your wound.
14 For [a]I *will be* like a lion to
Ē′phra·im,
And like a young lion to the
house of Judah.
[b]I, *even* I, will tear *them* and
go away;
I will take *them* away, and
no one shall rescue.
15 I will return again to My
place
Till they [1]acknowledge their
offense.
Then they will seek My
face;
In their affliction they will
earnestly seek Me."

1 [a]Hos. 6:9
2 [a]Is. 29:15
3 [a]Amos 3:2; 5:12 [b]Hos. 4:17
4 [a]Hos. 4:12 [1]Or *Their deeds will not allow them to turn*
5 [a]Hos. 7:10
6 [a]Prov. 1:28
7 [a]Jer. 3:20 [1]Lit. *strange*
8 [a]Joel 2:1 [b]Is. 10:30 [c]Josh. 7:2
10 [a]Deut. 19:14; 27:17
11 [a]Deut. 28:33 [b]Mic. 6:16
12 [a]Prov. 12:4
13 [a]Jer. 30:12–15 [b]2 Kin. 15:19
14 [a]Lam. 3:10 [b]Ps. 50:22
15 [1]Lit. *become guilty or bear punishment*

6

Come,[a] and let us return to
the LORD;
For [b]He has torn, but [c]He
will heal us;
He has stricken, but He will
[1]bind us up.
☆2 [a]After two days He will
revive us;
On the third day He will
raise us up,
That we may live in His
sight.
3 [a]Let us know,
Let us pursue the
knowledge of the LORD.
His going forth is
established [b]as the
morning;
[c]He will come to us [d]like the
rain,
Like the latter *and* former
rain to the earth.

4 "O Ē′phra·im, what shall I do
to you?
O Judah, what shall I do to
you?
For your faithfulness is like
a morning cloud,
And like the early dew it
goes away.
5 Therefore I have hewn *them*
by the prophets,
I have slain them by [a]the
words of My mouth;
And [1]your judgments *are*
like light *that* goes forth.
6 For I desire [a]mercy[1] and [b]not
sacrifice,
And the [c]knowledge of
God more than burnt
offerings.

7 "But like [1]men they
transgressed the
covenant;
There they dealt
treacherously with Me.
8 [a]Gil′ē·ad *is* a city of evildoers
And [1]defiled with blood.
9 As bands of robbers lie in
wait for a man,
So the company of [a]priests
[b]murder on the way to
Shē′chem;
Surely they commit
[c]lewdness.
10 I have seen a horrible thing
in the house of Israel:
There *is* the [1]harlotry of
Ē′phra·im;
Israel is defiled.
11 Also, O Judah, a harvest is
appointed for you,
When I return the captives
of My people.

7

"When I would have healed
Israel,
Then the iniquity of
Ē′phra·im was uncovered,
And the wickedness of
Samaria.
For [a]they have committed
fraud;
A thief comes in;
A band of robbers [1]takes
spoil outside.
2 They [1]do not consider in
their hearts
That [a]I remember all their
wickedness;
Now their own deeds have
surrounded them;
They are before My face.
3 They make a [a]king glad
with their wickedness,
And princes [b]with their lies.

4 "They[a] *are* all adulterers.
Like an oven heated by a
baker—
He ceases stirring *the fire*
after kneading the
dough,
Until it is leavened.

CHAPTER 6

1 [a]Is. 1:18 [b]Deut. 32:39 [c]Jer. 30:17 [1]Bandage

2 [a]Luke 24:46; Acts 10:40; [1 Cor. 15:4]

3 [a]Is. 54:13 [b]2 Sam. 23:4 [c]Ps. 72:6 [d]Job 29:23

5 [a][Jer. 23:29] [1]Or *the judgments on you*

6 [a]Matt. 9:13; 12:7 [b][Mic. 6:6–8] [c][John 17:3] [1]Or *faithfulness* or *loyalty*

7 [1]Or *Adam*

8 [a]Hos. 12:11 [1]Lit. *foot-tracked*

9 [a]Hos. 5:1 [b]Jer. 7:9, 10 [c]Ezek. 22:9; 23:27

10 [1]Spiritual adultery

CHAPTER 7

1 [a]Hos. 5:1 [1]*plunders*

2 [a]Jer. 14:10; 17:1 [1]Lit. *do not say to*

3 [a]Hos. 1:1 [b][Rom. 1:32]

4 [a]Jer. 9:2; 23:10

5 In the day of our king
Princes have made *him* sick,
[1]inflamed with [a]wine;
He stretched out his hand
with scoffers.
6 They prepare their heart
like an oven,
While they lie in wait;
[1]Their baker sleeps all night;
In the morning it burns like
a flaming fire.
7 They are all hot, like an
oven,
And have devoured their
judges;
All their kings have fallen.
[a]None among them calls
upon Me.

8 "E′phra·im [a]has mixed
himself among the
peoples;
E′phra·im is a cake
unturned.
9 [a]Aliens have devoured his
strength,
But he does not know *it*;
Yes, gray hairs are here and
there on him,
Yet he does not know *it*.
10 And the [a]pride of Israel
testifies to his face,
But [b]they do not return to
the LORD their God,
Nor seek Him for all this.

11 "E′phra·im[a] also is like a silly
dove, without [1]sense—
[b]They call to Egypt,
They go to [c]Assyria.
12 Wherever they go, I will
[a]spread My net on them;
I will bring them down like
birds of the air;
I will chastise them
[b]According to what their
congregation has heard.

13 "Woe to them, for they have
fled from Me!
Destruction to them,
Because they have
transgressed against Me!
Though [a]I redeemed them,
Yet they have spoken lies
against Me.
14 [a]They did not cry out to Me
with their heart
When they wailed upon
their beds.

"They [1]assemble together for
grain and new [b]wine,
[2]They rebel against Me;
15 Though I disciplined *and*
strengthened their arms,
Yet they devise evil against
Me;
16 They return, *but* not [1]to the
Most High;
[a]They are like a treacherous
bow.
Their princes shall fall by
the sword
For the [b]cursings of their
tongue.
This *shall be* their derision
[c]in the land of Egypt.

8 "*Set* the [1]trumpet to your
mouth!
He shall come [a]like an eagle
against the house of the
LORD,
Because they have
transgressed My
covenant
And rebelled against My
law.
2 [a]Israel will cry to Me,
'My God, [b]we know You!'
3 Israel has rejected the good;
The enemy will pursue him.

4 "They[a] set up kings, but not
by Me;

---

5 [a]Is. 28:1, 7
[1]Lit. *with the heat of*

6 [1]So with MT, Vg.; Syr., Tg. *Their anger;* LXX *Ephraim*

7 [a]Is. 64:7

8 [a]Ps. 106:35

9 [a]Hos. 8:7

10 [a]Hos. 5:5
[b]Is. 9:13

11 [a]Hos. 11:11
[b]Is. 30:3
[c]Hos. 5:13; 8:9
[1]Lit. *heart*

12 [a]Ezek. 12:13
[b]Lev. 26:14

13 [a]Mic. 6:4

14 [a]Job 35:9, 10
[b]Amos 2:8
[1]So with MT, Tg.; Vg. *thought upon;* LXX *slashed themselves for* (cf. 1 Kin. 18:28)
[2]So with MT, Syr., Tg.; LXX omits *They rebel against Me;* Vg. *They departed from Me*

16 [a]Ps. 78:57
[b]Ps. 73:9
[c]Hos. 8:13; 9:3
[1]Or *upward*

CHAPTER 8

1 [a]Deut. 28:49
[1]*ram's horn,* Heb. *shophar*

2 [a]Ps. 78:34
[b]Titus 1:16

4 [a]2 Kin. 15:23, 25

They made princes, but I did
not acknowledge *them.*
From their silver and gold
They made idols for
themselves—
That they might be cut off.
5 Your [1]calf [2]is rejected,
O Samaria!
My anger is aroused against
them—
[a]How long until they attain
to innocence?
6 For from Israel *is* even this:
A [a]workman made it, and it
is not God;
But the calf of Samaria shall
be broken to pieces.

7 "They[a] sow the wind,
And reap the whirlwind.
The stalk has no bud;
It shall never produce meal.
If it should produce,
[b]Aliens would swallow it up.
8 [a]Israel is swallowed up;
Now they are among the
Gentiles
[b]Like a vessel in which *is* no
pleasure.
9 For they have gone up to
Assyria,
Like [a]a wild donkey alone
by itself;
Ē'phra·im [b]has hired lovers.
10 Yes, though they have hired
among the nations,
Now [a]I will gather them;
And they shall [1]sorrow a
little,
Because of the [2]burden of
[b]the king of princes.

11 "Because Ē'phra·im has
made many altars for
sin,
They have become for him
altars for sinning.
12 I have written for him [a]the
great things of My law,
But they were considered a
strange thing.
13 *For* the sacrifices of My
offerings [a]they sacrifice
flesh and eat *it,*
[b]*But* the LORD does not
accept them.
[c]Now He will remember their
iniquity and punish their
sins.
They shall return to Egypt.

14 "For[a] Israel has forgotten [b]his
Maker,
And has built [1]temples;
Judah also has multiplied
[c]fortified cities;
But [d]I will send fire upon his
cities,
And it shall devour his
[2]palaces."

9

Do[a] not rejoice, O Israel,
with joy like *other*
peoples,
For you have played the
harlot against your God.
You have made love *for*
[b]hire on every threshing
floor.
2 The threshing floor and the
winepress
Shall not feed them,
And the new wine shall fail
in her.

3 They shall not dwell in [a]the
LORD's land,
[b]But Ē'phra·im shall return
to Egypt,
And [c]shall eat unclean
things in Assyria.
4 They shall not offer wine
offerings to the LORD,
Nor [a]shall their [b]sacrifices
be pleasing to Him.

---

5 [a]Jer. 13:27 [1]Golden calf image [2]Or *has rejected you*
6 [a]Is. 40:19
7 [a]Prov. 22:8 [b]Hos. 7:9
8 [a]2 Kin. 17:6 [b]Jer. 22:28; 25:34
9 [a]Jer. 2:24 [b]Ezek. 16:33, 34
10 [a]Ezek. 16:37; 22:20 [b]Is. 10:8 [1]Or *begin to diminish* [2]Or *oracle* or *proclamation*
12 [a][Deut. 4:6–8]
13 [a]Zech. 7:6 [b]Jer. 14:10 [c]Amos 8:7
14 [a]Deut. 32:18 [b]Is. 29:23 [c]Num. 32:17 [d]Jer. 17:27 [1]Or *palaces* [2]Or *citadels*

CHAPTER 9

1 [a]Is. 22:12, 13 [b]Jer. 44:17
3 [a][Lev. 25:23] [b]Hos. 7:16; 8:13 [c]Ezek. 4:13
4 [a]Jer. 6:20 [b]Hos. 8:13

It shall be like bread of
mourners to them;
All who eat it shall be
defiled.
For their bread *shall be* for
their *own* life;
It shall not come into the
house of the LORD.

5 What will you do in the
appointed day,
And in the day of the feast
of the LORD?
6 For indeed they are gone
because of destruction.
Egypt shall gather them up;
Memphis shall bury them.
[a]Nettles shall possess their
valuables of silver;
Thorns *shall be* in their
tents.

7 The [a]days of punishment
have come;
The days of recompense
have come.
Israel knows!
The prophet *is* a [b]fool,
[c]The spiritual man *is* insane,
Because of the greatness of
your iniquity and great
enmity.
8 The [a]watchman of Ē′phra·im
is with my God;
But the prophet *is* a
[1]fowler's snare in all his
ways—
Enmity in the house of his
God.
9 [a]They are deeply corrupted,
As in the days of [b]Gib′ē·ah.
He will remember their
iniquity;
He will punish their sins.

10 "I found Israel
Like grapes in the
[a]wilderness;
I saw your fathers
As the [b]firstfruits on the fig
tree in its first season.
But they went to [c]Bā′al
Pē′or,
And [1]separated themselves
to that shame;
[d]They became an
abomination like the
thing they loved.
11 *As for* Ē′phra·im, their glory
shall fly away like a
bird—
No birth, no pregnancy, and
no conception!
12 Though they bring up their
children,
Yet I will bereave them to
the last man.
Yes, [a]woe to them when I
depart from them!
13 Just [a]as I saw Ē′phra·im
like Tȳre, planted in a
pleasant place,
So Ē′phra·im will bring
out his children to the
murderer."

14 Give them, O LORD—
What will You give?
Give them [a]a miscarrying
womb
And dry breasts!

15 "All their wickedness *is* in
[a]Gil′gal,
For there I hated them.
Because of the evil of their
deeds
I will drive them from My
house;
I will love them no more.
[b]All their princes *are*
rebellious.
16 Ē′phra·im is [a]stricken,
Their root is dried up;
They shall bear no fruit.

6 [a]Is. 5:6; 7:23
7 [a]Is. 10:3 [b]Lam. 2:14 [c]Mic. 2:11
8 [a]Ezek. 3:17; 33:7 [1]One who catches birds in a trap or snare
9 [a]Hos. 10:9 [b]Judg. 19:22
10 [a]Jer. 2:2 [b]Is. 28:4 [c]Num. 25:3 [d]Ps. 81:12 [1]Or *dedicated*
12 [a]Deut. 31:17
13 [a]Ezek. 26—28
14 [a]Luke 23:29
15 [a]Hos. 4:15; 12:11 [b]Is. 1:23
16 [a]Hos. 5:11

Yes, were they to bear
children,
I would kill the darlings of
their womb."

17 My God will [a]cast them
away,
Because they did not obey
Him;
And they shall be
[b]wanderers among the
nations.

10

Israel [a]empties *his* vine;
He brings forth fruit for
himself.
According to the multitude
of his fruit
[b]He has increased the altars;
According to the bounty of
his land
They have embellished *his*
sacred pillars.
2 Their heart is [a]divided;[1]
Now they are held guilty.
He will break down their
altars;
He will ruin their *sacred*
pillars.

3 For now they say,
"We have no king,
Because we did not fear the
LORD.
And as for a king, what
would he do for us?"
4 They have spoken words,
Swearing falsely in making
a covenant.
Thus judgment springs up
[a]like hemlock in the
furrows of the field.

5 The inhabitants of Samaria
fear
Because of the [a]calf[1] of Beth
Ā′ven.
For its people mourn for it,
And [2]its priests shriek for
it—
Because its [b]glory has
departed from it.
6 *The idol* also shall be
carried to Assyria
As a present for King
[a]Jā′reb.
Ē′phra·im shall receive
shame,
And Israel shall be ashamed
of his own counsel.

7 *As for* Samaria, her king is
cut off
Like a twig on the water.
8 Also the [a]high places of
[1]Ā′ven, [b]the sin of Israel,
Shall be destroyed.
The thorn and thistle shall
grow on their altars;
[c]They shall say to the
mountains, "Cover us!"
And to the hills, "Fall on us!"

9 "O Israel, you have sinned
from the days of
[a]Gib′ē·ah;
There they stood.
The [b]battle in Gib′ē·ah
against the children of
[1]iniquity
Did not [2]overtake them.
10 When *it is* My desire, I will
chasten them.
[a]Peoples shall be gathered
against them
When I bind them [1]for their
two transgressions.
11 Ē′phra·im *is* [a]a trained
heifer
That loves to thresh *grain*;
But I harnessed her fair
neck,
I will make Ē′phra·im [1]pull
a plow.
Judah shall plow;
Jacob shall break his clods."

---

17 [a][Zech. 10:6] [b]Lev. 26:33

CHAPTER 10

1 [a]Nah. 2:2 [b]Jer. 2:28

2 [a]1 Kin. 18:21 [1]Divided in loyalty

4 [a]Amos 5:7

5 [a]Hos. 8:5, 6; 13:2 [b]Hos. 9:11 [1]Lit. *calves, images* [2]*idolatrous priests*

6 [a]Hos. 5:13

8 [a]Hos. 4:15 [b]1 Kin. 13:34 [c]Luke 23:30 [1]Lit. *Idolatry* or *Wickedness*

9 [a]Hos. 9:9 [b]Judg. 20 [1]So with many Heb. mss., LXX, Vg.; MT *unruliness* [2]Or *overcome*

10 [a]Jer. 16:16 [1]Or *in their two habitations*

11 [a][Mic. 4:13] [1]Lit. *to ride*

12 Sow for yourselves righteousness;
Reap in mercy;
[a]Break up your fallow ground,
For *it is* time to seek the LORD,
Till He [b]comes and rains righteousness on you.

13 [a]You have plowed wickedness;
You have reaped iniquity.
You have eaten the fruit of lies,
Because you trusted in your own way,
In the multitude of your mighty men.
14 Therefore tumult shall arise among your people,
And all your fortresses shall be plundered
As Shal′man plundered Beth Ar′bel in the day of battle—
A mother dashed in pieces upon *her* children.
15 Thus it shall be done to you, O Beth′el,
Because of your great wickedness.
At dawn the king of Israel
Shall be cut off utterly.

☆ 11 "When Israel *was* a [1]child, I loved him,
And out of Egypt [a]I called My [b]son.
2 [1]*As* they called them,
So they [a]went [2]from them;
They sacrificed to the Bā′als,
And burned incense to carved images.

3 "I[a] taught Ē′phra·im to walk,
Taking them by [1]their arms;
But they did not know that [b]I healed them.
4 I drew them with [1]gentle cords,
With bands of love,
And [a]I was to them as those who take the yoke from their [2]neck.
[b]I stooped *and* fed them.

5 "He shall not return to the land of Egypt;
But the Assyrian shall be his king,
Because they refused to repent.
6 And the sword shall slash in his cities,
Devour his districts,
And consume *them*,
Because of their own counsels.
7 My people are bent on [a]backsliding from Me.
Though [1]they call [2]to the Most High,
None at all exalt *Him*.

8 "How[a] can I give you up, Ē′phra·im?
How can I hand you over, Israel?
How can I make you like [b]Ad′mah?
How can I set you like Ze·boi′im?
My heart [1]churns within Me;
My sympathy is stirred.
9 I will not execute the fierceness of My anger;
I will not again destroy Ē′phra·im.
[a]For I *am* God, and not man,
The Holy One in your midst;
And I will not [1]come with terror.

12 [a]Jer. 4:3 [b]Hos. 6:3

13 [a][Prov. 22:8]

CHAPTER 11

1 [a]Matt. 2:15 [b]Ex. 4:22, 23 [1]Or *youth*

2 [a]2 Kin. 17:13–15 [1]So with MT, Vg.; LXX *Just as I called them;* Tg. interprets as *I sent prophets to a thousand of them.* [2]So with MT, Tg., Vg.; LXX *from My face*

3 [a]Deut. 1:31; 32:10, 11 [b]Ex. 15:26 [1]Some Heb. mss., LXX, Syr., Vg. *My arms*

4 [a]Lev. 26:13 [b]Ps. 78:25 [1]Lit. *cords of a man* [2]Lit. *jaws*

7 [a]Jer. 3:6, 7; 8:5 [1]The prophets [2]Or *upward*

8 [a]Jer. 9:7 [b]Gen. 14:8; 19:24, 25 [1]Lit. *turns over*

9 [a]Num. 23:19 [1]Or *enter a city*

10 "They shall walk after the
LORD.
[a]He will roar like a lion.
When He roars,
Then *His* sons shall come
trembling from the west;
11 They shall come trembling
like a bird from Egypt,
[a]Like a dove from the land of
Assyria.
[b]And I will let them dwell in
their houses,"
Says the LORD.

12 "Ē′phra·im has encircled Me
with lies,
And the house of Israel with
deceit;
But Judah still walks with
God,
Even with the [1]Holy One
who is faithful.

12

"Ē′phra·im [a]feeds on the
wind,
And pursues the east wind;
He daily increases lies and
[1]desolation.
[b]Also they make a [2]covenant
with the Assyrians,
And [c]oil is carried to Egypt.

2 "The[a] LORD also *brings* a
[1]charge against Judah,
And will punish Jacob
according to his ways;
According to his deeds He
will recompense him.
3 He took his brother [a]by the
heel in the womb,
And in his strength he
[b]struggled with God.
4 Yes, he struggled with the
Angel and prevailed;
He wept, and sought favor
from Him.
He found Him *in* [a]Beth′el,
And there He spoke to us—

5 That is, the LORD God of
hosts.
The LORD *is* His [a]memorable
name.
6 [a]So you, by *the help of* your
God, return;
Observe mercy and justice,
And wait on your God
continually.

7 "A cunning [1]Cā′naan·ite!
[a]Deceitful scales *are* in his
hand;
He loves to oppress.
8 And Ē′phra·im said,
[a]'Surely I have become rich,
I have found wealth for
myself;
In all my labors
They shall find in me no
iniquity that *is* sin.'

9 "But I *am* the LORD your God,
Ever since the land of
Egypt;
[a]I will again make you dwell
in tents,
As in the days of the
appointed feast.
10 [a]I have also spoken by the
prophets,
And have multiplied visions;
I have given [1]symbols
[2]through the witness of
the prophets."

11 Though [a]Gil′ē·ad *has* idols—
Surely they are [1]vanity—
Though they sacrifice bulls
in [b]Gil′gal,
Indeed their altars *shall be*
heaps in the furrows of
the field.

12 Jacob [a]fled to the country of
Syria;
[b]Israel served for a spouse,

10 [a][Joel 3:16]
11 [a]Is. 11:11; 60:8 [b]Ezek. 28:25, 26; 34:27, 28
12 [1]Or *holy ones*

CHAPTER 12

1 [a]Job 15:2, 3 [b]2 Kin. 17:4 [c]Is. 30:6 [1]*ruin* [2]Or *treaty*
2 [a]Mic. 6:2 [1]A legal complaint
3 [a]Gen. 25:26 [b]Gen. 32:24–28
4 [a][Gen. 28:12–19; 35:9–15]
5 [a]Ex. 3:15
6 [a]Mic. 6:8
7 [a]Amos 8:5 [1]Or *merchant*
8 [a]Rev. 3:17
9 [a]Lev. 23:42
10 [a]2 Kin. 17:13 [1]Or *parables* [2]Lit. *by the hand*
11 [a]Hos. 6:8 [b]Hos. 9:15 [1]*worthless*
12 [a]Gen. 28:5 [b]Gen. 29:20, 28

And for a wife he tended
sheep.
13 [a]By a prophet the LORD
brought Israel out of
Egypt,
And by a prophet he was
preserved.
14 Ē'phra·im [a]provoked *Him* to
anger most bitterly;
Therefore his Lord will
leave the guilt of his
bloodshed upon him,
[b]And return his reproach
upon him.

13 When Ē'phra·im spoke,
trembling,
He exalted *himself* in Israel;
But when he offended
through Bā'al *worship*,
he died.
2 Now they sin more and
more,
And have made for
themselves molded
images,
Idols of their silver,
according to their skill;
All of it *is* the work of
craftsmen.
They say of them,
"Let [1]the men who sacrifice
[2]kiss the calves!"
3 Therefore they shall be like
the morning cloud
And like the early dew that
passes away,
[a]Like chaff blown off from a
threshing floor
And like smoke from a
chimney.

4 "Yet [a]I *am* the LORD your God
Ever since the land of
Egypt,
And you shall know no God
but Me;
For [b]*there is* no savior
besides Me.
5 [a]I [1]knew you in the
wilderness,
[b]In the land of [2]great
drought.
6 [a]When they had pasture,
they were filled;
They were filled and their
heart was exalted;
Therefore they forgot Me.

7 "So [a]I will be to them like a
lion;
Like [b]a leopard by the road I
will lurk;
8 I will meet them [a]like a bear
deprived *of her cubs;*
I will tear open their rib
cage,
And there I will devour
them like a lion.
The [1]wild beast shall tear
them.

9 "O Israel, [1]you are destroyed,
But [2]your help *is* from Me.
10 [1]I will be your King;
[a]Where *is any other,*
That he may save you in all
your cities?
And your judges to whom
[b]you said,
'Give me a king and
princes'?
11 [a]I gave you a king in My
anger,
And took *him* away in My
wrath.

12 "The[a] iniquity of Ē'phra·im *is*
bound up;
His sin *is* stored up.
13 [a]The sorrows of a woman
in childbirth shall come
upon him.
He *is* an unwise son,

13 [a]Ex. 12:50, 51; 13:3
14 [a]Ezek. 18:10–13 [b]Dan. 11:18

CHAPTER 13

2 [1]Or *those who offer human sacrifice* [2]Worship with kisses
3 [a]Dan. 2:35
4 [a]Is. 43:11 [b]Is. 43:11; 45:21, 22
5 [a]Deut. 2:7; 32:10 [b]Deut. 8:15 [1]Cared for you [2]Lit. *droughts*
6 [a]Deut. 8:12, 14; 32:13–15
7 [a]Lam. 3:10 [b]Jer. 5:6
8 [a]2 Sam. 17:8 [1]Lit. *beast of the field*
9 [1]Lit. *it* or *he destroyed you* [2]Lit. *in your help*
10 [a]Deut. 32:38 [b]1 Sam. 8:5, 6 [1]LXX, Syr., Tg., Vg. *Where is your king?*
11 [a]1 Sam. 8:7; 10:17–24
12 [a]Deut. 32:34, 35
13 [a]Is. 13:8

For he should not stay long
where children are born.

14 "I will ransom them from the
[1]power of [2]the grave;
I will redeem them from
death.
[a]O Death, [3]I will be your
plagues!
O [4]Grave, [5]I will be your
destruction!
[b]Pity is hidden from My
eyes."

15 Though he is fruitful among
his brethren,
[a]An east wind shall come;
The wind of the LORD
shall come up from the
wilderness.
Then his spring shall
become dry,
And his fountain shall be
dried up.
He shall plunder the
treasury of every
desirable prize.
16 Samaria [1]is held guilty,
For she has [a]rebelled against
her God.
They shall fall by the sword,
Their infants shall be
dashed in pieces,
And their women with child
[b]ripped open.

14 O Israel, [a]return to the
LORD your God,
For you have stumbled
because of your iniquity;
2 Take words with you,
And return to the LORD.
Say to Him,
"Take away all iniquity;
Receive *us* graciously,
For we will offer the
[a]sacrifices[1] of our lips.
3 Assyria shall [a]not save us,
[b]We will not ride on horses,
Nor will we say anymore to
the work of our hands,
'*You are* our gods.'
[c]For in You the fatherless
finds mercy."

4 "I will heal their [a]backsliding,
I will [b]love them freely,
For My anger has turned
away from him.
5 I will be like the [a]dew to
Israel;
He shall [1]grow like the lily,
And [2]lengthen his roots like
Lebanon.
6 His branches shall [1]spread;
[a]His beauty shall be like an
olive tree,
And [b]his fragrance like
Lebanon.
7 [a]Those who dwell under his
shadow shall return;
They shall be revived *like*
grain,
And [1]grow like a vine.
Their [2]scent *shall be* like the
wine of Lebanon.

8 "Ē′phra·im *shall say,*
'What have I to do anymore
with idols?'
I have heard and observed
him.
I *am* like a green cypress
tree;
[a]Your fruit is found in Me."

9 Who *is* wise?
Let him understand these
things.
Who is prudent?
Let him know them.
For [a]the ways of the LORD
are right;
The righteous walk in them,
But transgressors stumble
in them.

---

14 [a][1 Cor. 15:54, 55] [b]Jer. 15:6 [1]Lit. *hand* [2]Or *Sheol* [3]LXX *where is your punishment?* [4]Or *Sheol* [5]LXX *where is your sting?*
15 [a]Jer. 4:11, 12
16 [a]2 Kin. 18:12 [b]2 Kin. 15:16 [1]LXX *shall be disfigured*

CHAPTER 14

1 [a][Joel 2:13]
2 [a][Heb. 13:15] [1]Lit. *bull calves;* LXX *fruit*
3 [a]Hos. 7:11; 10:13; 12:1 [b][Ps. 33:17] [c]Ps. 10:14; 68:5
4 [a]Jer. 14:7 [b][Eph. 1:6]
5 [a]Prov. 19:12 [1]Lit. *bud* or *sprout* [2]Lit. *strike*
6 [a]Ps. 52:8; 128:3 [b]Gen. 27:27 [1]Lit. *go*
7 [a]Dan. 4:12 [1]Lit. *bud* or *sprout* [2]Lit. *remembrance*
8 [a][John 15:4]
9 [a][Prov. 10:29]

The Book of JOEL

DISASTER strikes the southern kingdom of Judah without warning. An ominous black cloud descends upon the land—the dreaded locusts. In a matter of hours, every living green thing has been stripped bare. Joel, God's spokesman during the reign of Joash (835–796 B.C.), seizes this occasion to proclaim God's message. Although the locust plague has been a terrible judgment for sin, God's future judgments during the day of the Lord will make that plague pale by comparison. In that day, God will destroy His enemies, but bring unparalleled blessing to those who faithfully obey Him.

The Hebrew name *Yo'el* means "Yahweh Is God." This name is appropriate to the theme of the book, which emphasizes God's sovereign work in history. The courses of nature and nations are in His hand. The Greek equivalent is *Ioel*, and the Latin is *Joel*.

THE word of the LORD that came to [a]Jō'el the son of Pethū'el.

2 Hear this, you elders,
And give ear, all you inhabitants of the land!
[a]Has *anything like* this happened in your days,
Or even in the days of your fathers?
3 [a]Tell your children about it,
Let your children *tell* their children,
And their children another generation.

4 [a]What the chewing [1]locust left, the [b]swarming locust has eaten;
What the swarming locust left, the crawling locust has eaten;
And what the crawling locust left, the consuming locust has eaten.

5 Awake, you [a]drunkards, and weep;
And wail, all you drinkers of wine,
Because of the new wine,
[b]For it has been cut off from your mouth.
6 For [a]a nation has come up against My land,
Strong, and without number;
[b]His teeth *are* the teeth of a lion,
And he has the fangs of a [1]fierce lion.
7 He has [a]laid waste My vine,
And [1]ruined My fig tree;
He has stripped it bare and thrown *it* away;
Its branches are made white.

8 [a]Lament like a virgin girded with sackcloth
For [b]the husband of her youth.
9 [a]The grain offering and the drink offering
Have been cut off from the house of the LORD;

CHAPTER 1

1 [a]Acts 2:16
2 [a]Joel 2:2
3 [a]Ps. 78:4
4 [a]Deut. 28:38 [b]Is. 33:4 [1]Exact identity of these locusts unknown
5 [a]Is. 5:11; 28:1 [b]Is. 32:10
6 [a]Joel 2:2, 11, 25 [b]Rev. 9:8 [1]Or *lioness*
7 [a]Is. 5:6 [1]Or *splintered*
8 [a]Is. 22:12 [b]Jer. 3:4
9 [a]Joel 1:13; 2:14

The priests [b]mourn, who
minister to the LORD.
10 The field is wasted,
[a]The land mourns;
For the grain is ruined,
[b]The new wine is dried up,
The oil fails.

11 [a]Be ashamed, you farmers,
Wail, you vinedressers,
For the wheat and the
barley;
Because the harvest of the
field has perished.
12 [a]The vine has dried up,
And the fig tree has withered;
The pomegranate tree,
The palm tree also,
And the apple tree—
All the trees of the field are
withered;
Surely [b]joy has withered
away from the sons of
men.

13 [a]Gird yourselves and lament,
you priests;
Wail, you who minister
before the altar;
Come, lie all night in
sackcloth,
You who minister to my God;
For the grain offering and
the drink offering
Are withheld from the
house of your God.
14 [a]Consecrate a fast,
Call [b]a sacred assembly;
Gather the elders
And [c]all the inhabitants of
the land
Into the house of the LORD
your God,
And cry out to the LORD.

15 [a]Alas for the day!
For [b]the day of the LORD *is*
at hand;
It shall come as destruction
from the Almighty.
16 Is not the food [a]cut off
before our eyes,
[b]Joy and gladness from the
house of our God?
17 The seed shrivels under the
clods,
Storehouses are in
shambles;
Barns are broken down,
For the grain has withered.
18 How [a]the animals groan!
The herds of cattle are
restless,
Because they have no
pasture;
Even the flocks of sheep
[1]suffer punishment.

19 O LORD, [a]to You I cry out;
For [b]fire has devoured the
[1]open pastures,
And a flame has burned all
the trees of the field.
20 The beasts of the field also
[a]cry out to You,
For [b]the water brooks are
dried up,
And fire has devoured the
[1]open pastures.

2 Blow [a]the [1]trumpet in Zion,
And [b]sound an alarm in My
holy mountain!
Let all the inhabitants of the
land tremble;
For [c]the day of the LORD is
coming,
For it is at hand:
2 [a]A day of darkness and
gloominess,
A day of clouds and thick
darkness,
Like the morning *clouds*
spread over the
mountains.

9 [b]Joel 2:17
10 [a]Jer. 12:11 [b]Is. 24:7
11 [a]Jer. 14:3, 4
12 [a]Joel 1:10 [b]Jer. 48:33
13 [a]Jer. 4:8
14 [a]Joel 2:15, 16 [b]Lev. 23:36 [c]2 Chr. 20:13
15 [a][Jer. 30:7] [b]Is. 13:6
16 [a]Is. 3:1 [b]Deut. 12:7
18 [a]Hos. 4:3 [1]LXX, Vg. *are made desolate*
19 [a][Ps. 50:15] [b]Jer. 9:10 [1]Lit. *pastures of the wilderness*
20 [a]Ps. 104:21; 147:9 [b]1 Kin. 17:7; 18:5 [1]Lit. *pastures of the wilderness*

CHAPTER 2

1 [a]Jer. 4:5 [b]Num. 10:5 [c][Obad. 15] [1]*ram's horn*
2 [a]Amos 5:18

[b]A people *come,* great and strong,
[c]The like of whom has never been;
Nor will there ever be any *such* after them,
Even for many successive generations.

3 A fire devours before them,
And behind them a flame burns;
The land *is* like [a]the Garden of Eden before them,
[b]And behind them a desolate wilderness;
Surely nothing shall escape them.
4 [a]Their appearance is like the appearance of horses;
And like [1]swift steeds, so they run.
5 [a]With a noise like chariots
Over mountaintops they leap,
Like the noise of a flaming fire that devours the stubble,
Like a strong people set in battle array.

6 Before them the people writhe in pain;
[a]All faces [1]are drained of color.
7 They run like mighty men,
They climb the wall like men of war;
Every one marches in formation,
And they do not break [a]ranks.
8 They do not push one another;
Every one marches in his own [1]column.
Though they lunge between the weapons,
They are not [2]cut down.
9 They run to and fro in the city,
They run on the wall;
They climb into the houses,
They [a]enter at the windows [b]like a thief.

10 [a]The earth quakes before them,
The heavens tremble;
[b]The sun and moon grow dark,
And the stars diminish their brightness.
11 [a]The LORD gives voice before His army,
For His camp is very great;
[b]For strong *is the One* who executes His word.
For the [c]day of the LORD *is* great and very terrible;
[d]Who can endure it?

12 "Now, therefore," says the LORD,
[a]"Turn to Me with all your heart,
With fasting, with weeping, and with mourning."
13 So [a]rend your heart, and not [b]your garments;
Return to the LORD your God,
For He *is* [c]gracious and merciful,
Slow to anger, and of great kindness;
And He relents from doing harm.
14 [a]Who knows *if* He will turn and relent,
And leave [b]a blessing behind Him—
[c]A grain offering and a drink offering
For the LORD your God?

2 [b]Joel 1:6; 2:11, 25 [c]Dan. 9:12; 12:1
3 [a]Is. 51:3 [b]Zech. 7:14
4 [a]Rev. 9:7 [1]Or *horsemen*
5 [a]Rev. 9:9
6 [a]Nah. 2:10 [1]LXX, Tg., Vg. *gather blackness*
7 [a]Prov. 30:27
8 [1]Lit. *highway* [2]Halted by losses
9 [a]Jer. 9:21 [b]John 10:1
10 [a]Ps. 18:7 [b]Is. 13:10; 34:4
11 [a]Jer. 25:30 [b]Rev. 18:8 [c]Amos 5:18 [d][Mal. 3:2]
12 [a]Jer. 4:1
13 [a][Ps. 34:18; 51:17] [b]Gen. 37:34 [c][Ex. 34:6]
14 [a]Jer. 26:3 [b]Hag. 2:19 [c]Joel 1:9, 13

15 [a]Blow the [1]trumpet in Zion,
[b]Consecrate a fast,
Call a sacred assembly;
16 Gather the people,
[a]Sanctify the congregation,
Assemble the elders,
Gather the children and
nursing babes;
[b]Let the bridegroom go out
from his chamber,
And the bride from her
dressing room.
17 Let the priests, who minister
to the LORD,
Weep [a]between the porch
and the altar;
Let them say, [b]"Spare Your
people, O LORD,
And do not give Your
heritage to reproach,
That the nations should
[1]rule over them.
[c]Why should they say among
the peoples,
'Where *is* their God?' "

18 Then the LORD will [a]be
zealous for His land,
And pity His people.
19 The LORD will answer and
say to His people,
"Behold, I will send you
[a]grain and new wine and
oil,
And you will be satisfied by
them;
I will no longer make you
a reproach among the
nations.

20 "But [a]I will remove far from
you [b]the northern *army*,
And will drive him away
into a barren and
desolate land,
With his face toward the
eastern sea
And his back [c]toward the
western sea;
His stench will come up,
And his foul odor will rise,
Because he has done
[1]monstrous things."

21 Fear not, O land;
Be glad and rejoice,
For the LORD has done
[1]marvelous things!
22 Do not be afraid, you beasts
of the field;
For [a]the open pastures are
springing up,
And the tree bears its fruit;
The fig tree and the vine
yield their strength.
23 Be glad then, you children
of Zion,
And [a]rejoice in the LORD
your God;
For He has given you the
[1]former rain faithfully,
And He [b]will cause the rain
to come down for you—
The former rain,
And the latter rain in the
first *month*.
24 The threshing floors shall
be full of wheat,
And the vats shall overflow
with new wine and oil.

25 "So I will restore to you the
years [a]that the swarming
[1]locust has eaten,
The crawling locust,
The consuming locust,
And the chewing locust,
My great army which I sent
among you.
26 You shall [a]eat in plenty and
be satisfied,
And praise the name of the
LORD your God,
Who has dealt wondrously
with you;

15 [a]Num. 10:3 [b]Joel 1:14 [1]*ram's horn*
16 [a]Ex. 19:10 [b]Ps. 19:5
17 [a]Matt. 23:35 [b]Ex. 32:11, 12 [c]Ps. 42:10 [1]Or *speak a proverb against them*
18 [a][Is. 60:10; 63:9, 15]
19 [a][Mal. 3:10]
20 [a]Ex. 10:19 [b]Jer. 1:14, 15 [c]Deut. 11:24 [1]Lit. *great*
21 [1]Lit. *great*
22 [a]Joel 1:19
23 [a]Is. 41:16 [b]Lev. 26:4 [1]Or *teacher of righteousness*
25 [a]Joel 1:4–7; 2:2–11 [1]Exact identity of these locusts unknown
26 [a]Lev. 26:5

And My people shall never
be put to [b]shame.
27 Then you shall know that
I *am* [a]in the midst of
Israel:
[b]I *am* the LORD your God
And there is no other.
My people shall never be
put to shame.

28 "And[a] it shall come to pass
afterward
That [b]I will pour out My
Spirit on all flesh;
[c]Your sons and your
[d]daughters shall
prophesy,
Your old men shall dream
dreams,
Your young men shall see
visions.
29 And also on *My*
[a]menservants and on *My*
maidservants
I will pour out My Spirit in
those days.

30 "And [a]I will show wonders in
the heavens and in the
earth:
Blood and fire and pillars of
smoke.
31 [a]The sun shall be turned into
darkness,
And the moon into blood,
[b]Before the coming of the
great and awesome day
of the LORD.
32 And it shall come to pass
That [a]whoever calls on the
name of the LORD
Shall be [1]saved.
For [b]in Mount Zion and in
Jerusalem there shall be
[2]deliverance,
As the LORD has said,
Among [c]the remnant whom
the LORD calls.

26 [b]Is. 45:17
27 [a]Lev. 26:11, 12 [b][Is. 45:5, 6]
28 [a]Ezek. 39:29 [b]Zech. 12:10 [c]Is. 54:13 [d]Acts 21:9
29 [a][Gal. 3:28]
30 [a]Matt. 24:29
31 [a]Is. 13:9, 10; 34:4 [b][Mal. 4:1, 5, 6]
32 [a]Rom. 10:13 [b]Is. 46:13 [c][Mic. 4:7] [1]Or *delivered* [2]Or *salvation*

CHAPTER 3

1 [a]Jer. 30:3
2 [a]Zech. 14:2 [b]Is. 66:16
3 [a]Nah. 3:10
4 [a]Amos 1:6–8 [1]Or *render Me repayment* [2]Or *repay Me* [3]Or *repayment*
5 [1]Lit. *precious good things*

3 "For behold, [a]in those days
and at that time,
When I bring back the
captives of Judah and
Jerusalem,
2 [a]I will also gather all nations,
And bring them down to the
Valley of Je·hosh′a·phat;
And I [b]will enter into
judgment with them
there
On account of My people,
My heritage Israel,
Whom they have scattered
among the nations;
They have also divided up
My land.
3 They have [a]cast lots for My
people,
Have given a boy *as
payment* for a harlot,
And sold a girl for wine,
that they may drink.

4 "Indeed, what have you to do
with Me,
[a]O Tȳre and Sī′don, and all
the coasts of Phi·lis′ti·a?
Will you [1]retaliate against
Me?
But if you [2]retaliate against
Me,
Swiftly and speedily I will
return your [3]retaliation
upon your own head;
5 Because you have taken My
silver and My gold,
And have carried into your
temples My [1]prized
possessions.
6 Also the people of Judah
and the people of
Jerusalem
You have sold to the
Greeks,
That you may remove them
far from their borders.

7 "Behold, [a]I will raise them
Out of the place to which
you have sold them,
And will return your
[1]retaliation upon your
own head.
8 I will sell your sons and
your daughters
Into the hand of the people
of Judah,
And they will sell them to
the [a]Sa·bē′ans,[1]
To a people [b]far off;
For the LORD has spoken."

9 [a]Proclaim this among the
nations:
"Prepare for war!
Wake up the mighty men,
Let all the men of war draw
near,
Let them come up.
10 [a]Beat your plowshares into
swords
And your [1]pruning hooks
into spears;
[b]Let the weak say, 'I *am*
strong.' "
11 Assemble and come, all you
nations,
And gather together all
around.
Cause [a]Your mighty ones to
go down there, O LORD.

12 "Let the nations be wakened,
and come up to the
Valley of Je·hosh′a·phat;
For there I will sit to [a]judge
all the surrounding
nations.
13 [a]Put in the sickle, for [b]the
harvest is ripe.
Come, go down;
For the [c]winepress is full,
The vats overflow—
For their wickedness *is*
great."

7 [a]Jer. 23:8
[1]Or *repayment*

8 [a]Ezek. 23:42
[b]Jer. 6:20
[1]Lit. *Shebaites*, Is. 60:6; Ezek. 27:22

9 [a]Ezek. 38:7

10 [a][Is. 2:4]
[b]Zech. 12:8
[1]*pruning knives*

11 [a]Is. 13:3

12 [a]Is. 2:4

13 [a]Rev. 14:15
[b]Jer. 51:33
[c][Is. 63:3]

14 [a]Joel 2:1

16 [a][Is. 51:5, 6]

17 [a]Zech. 8:3

18 [a]Ezek. 47:1
[1]Heb. *Shittim*

14 Multitudes, multitudes in the
valley of decision!
For [a]the day of the LORD
is near in the valley of
decision.
15 The sun and moon will grow
dark,
And the stars will diminish
their brightness.
16 The LORD also will roar from
Zion,
And utter His voice from
Jerusalem;
The heavens and earth will
shake;
[a]But the LORD will be a
shelter for His people,
And the strength of the
children of Israel.

17 "So you shall know that I *am*
the LORD your God,
Dwelling in Zion My [a]holy
mountain.
Then Jerusalem shall be
holy,
And no aliens shall ever
pass through her again."

18 And it will come to pass in
that day
That the mountains shall
drip with new wine,
The hills shall flow with
milk,
And all the brooks of Judah
shall be flooded with
water;
A [a]fountain shall flow from
the house of the LORD
And water the Valley of
[1]Acacias.

19 "Egypt shall be a desolation,
And Ē′dom a desolate
wilderness,
Because of violence *against*
the people of Judah,

For they have shed innocent
blood in their land.
20 But Judah shall abide
forever,
And Jerusalem from
generation to generation.

21 For I will [a]acquit them of
the guilt of bloodshed,
whom I had not
acquitted;
For the LORD dwells in
Zion."

21 [a]Is. 4:4

The Book of AMOS

AMOS prophesies during a period of national optimism in Israel. Business is booming and boundaries are bulging. But below the surface, greed and injustice are festering. Hypocritical religious motions have replaced true worship, creating a false sense of security and a growing callousness to God's disciplining hand. Famine, drought, plagues, death, destruction—nothing can force the people to their knees.

Amos, the farmer-turned-prophet, lashes out at sin unflinchingly, trying to visualize the nearness of God's judgment and mobilize the nation to repentance. The nation, like a basket of rotting fruit, stands ripe for judgment because of its hypocrisy and spiritual indifference.

The name *Amos* is derived from the Hebrew root *amas*, "to lift a burden, to carry." Thus, his name means "Burden" or "Burden-Bearer." Amos lives up to the meaning of his name by bearing up under his divinely given burden of declaring judgment to rebellious Israel. The Greek and Latin titles are both transliterated in English as *Amos*.

THE words of Ā′mos, who was among the [a]sheepbreeders of [b]Te·kō′a, which he saw concerning Israel in the days of [c]Uz·zī′ah king of Judah, and in the days of [d]Jer·o·bō′am the son of Jō′ash, king of Israel, two years before the [e]earthquake.

2 And he said:

"The LORD [a]roars from Zion,
And utters His voice from Jerusalem;
The pastures of the shepherds mourn,
And the top of [b]Car′mel withers."

3 Thus says the LORD:

"For three transgressions of [a]Damascus, and for four,
I will not turn away its *punishment*,
Because they have [b]threshed Gil′ē·ad with implements of iron.
4 [a]But I will send a fire into the house of Haz′a·el,
Which shall devour the palaces of [b]Ben-Hā′dad.
5 I will also break the *gate* [a]bar of Damascus,
And cut off the inhabitant from the Valley of Ā′ven,
And the one who [1]holds the scepter from [2]Beth Eden.
The people of Syria shall go captive to Kir,"
Says the LORD.

6 Thus says the LORD:

"For three transgressions of [a]Gā′za, and for four,
I will not turn away its *punishment*,
Because they took captive the whole captivity

CHAPTER 1

1 [a]2 Kin. 3:4; Amos 7:14 [b]2 Sam. 14:2 [c]2 Chr. 26:1–23 [d]Amos 7:10 [e]Zech. 14:5

2 [a]Joel 3:16 [b]1 Sam. 25:2

3 [a]Is. 8:4; 17:1–3 [b]2 Kin. 10:32, 33

4 [a]Jer. 49:27; 51:30 [b]2 Kin. 6:24

5 [a]Jer. 51:30 [1]Rules [2]Lit. *House of Eden*

6 [a]Jer. 47:1, 5

To deliver *them* up to
Ē′dom.
7 [a]But I will send a fire upon
the wall of Gā′za,
Which shall devour its
palaces.
8 I will cut off the inhabitant
[a]from Ash′dod,
And the one who holds the
scepter from Ash′ke·lon;
I will [b]turn My hand against
Ek′ron,
And [c]the remnant of the
Phi·lis′tines shall perish,"
Says the Lord GOD.

9 Thus says the LORD:

"For three transgressions of
[a]Tȳre, and for four,
I will not turn away its
punishment,
Because they delivered up
the whole captivity to
Ē′dom,
And did not remember the
covenant of brotherhood.
10 But I will send a fire upon
the wall of Tȳre,
Which shall devour its
palaces."

11 Thus says the LORD:

"For three transgressions of
[a]Ē′dom, and for four,
I will not turn away its
punishment,
Because he pursued his
[b]brother with the sword,
And cast off all pity;
His anger tore perpetually,
And he kept his wrath
forever.
12 But [a]I will send a fire upon
Tē′man,
Which shall devour the
palaces of Boz′rah."

13 Thus says the LORD:

"For three transgressions of
[a]the people of Am′mon,
and for four,
I will not turn away its
punishment,
Because they ripped open
the women with child in
Gil′ē·ad,
That they might enlarge
their territory.
14 But I will kindle a fire in the
wall of [a]Rab′bah,
And it shall devour its
palaces,
[b]Amid shouting in the day of
battle,
And a tempest in the day of
the whirlwind.
15 [a]Their king shall go into
captivity,
He and his princes
together,"
Says the LORD.

2 Thus says the LORD:

[a]"For three transgressions of
Mō′ab, and for four,
I will not turn away its
punishment,
Because he [b]burned the
bones of the king of
Ē′dom to lime.
2 But I will send a fire upon
Mō′ab,
And it shall devour the
palaces of [a]Ker′i·oth;
Mō′ab shall die with tumult,
With shouting *and* trumpet
sound.
3 And I will cut off [a]the judge
from its midst,
And slay all its princes with
him,"
Says the LORD.

7 [a]Jer. 47:1
8 [a]Zeph. 2:4 [b]Ps. 81:14 [c]Ezek. 25:16
9 [a]Is. 23:1–18
11 [a]Is. 21:11 [b]Obad. 10–12
12 [a]Obad. 9, 10
13 [a]Ezek. 25:2
14 [a]Deut. 3:11 [b]Amos 2:2
15 [a]Jer. 49:3

CHAPTER 2

1 [a]Zeph. 2:8–11 [b]2 Kin. 3:26, 27
2 [a]Jer. 48:24, 41
3 [a]Num. 24:17

4 Thus says the LORD:

"For three transgressions of
[a]Judah, and for four,
I will not turn away its
punishment,
[b]Because they have despised
the law of the LORD,
And have not kept His
commandments.
[c]Their lies lead them astray,
Lies [d]which their fathers
followed.
5 [a]But I will send a fire upon
Judah,
And it shall devour the
palaces of Jerusalem."

6 Thus says the LORD:

"For three transgressions of
[a]Israel, and for four,
I will not turn away its
punishment,
Because [b]they sell the
righteous for silver,
And the [c]poor for a pair of
sandals.
7 They [1]pant after the dust of
the earth *which is* on the
head of the poor,
And [a]pervert the way of the
humble.
[b]A man and his father go in
to the *same* girl,
[c]To defile My holy name.
8 They lie down [a]by every
altar on clothes [b]taken in
pledge,
And drink the wine of [1]the
condemned *in* the house
of their god.

9 "Yet *it was* I *who* destroyed
the [a]Am'o·rīte before
them,
Whose height *was* like the
[b]height of the cedars,
And he *was as* strong as the
oaks;
Yet I [c]destroyed his fruit
above
And his roots beneath.
10 Also *it was* [a]I *who* brought
you up from the land of
Egypt,
And [b]led you forty years
through the wilderness,
To possess the land of the
Am'o·rīte.
11 I raised up some of your
sons as [a]prophets,
And some of your young
men as [b]Naz'ir·ītes.
Is it not so, O you children
of Israel?"
Says the LORD.
12 "But you gave the Naz'ir·ītes
wine to drink,
And commanded the
prophets [a]saying,
'Do not prophesy!'

13 "Behold,[a] I am [1]weighed
down by you,
As a cart full of sheaves [2]is
weighed down.
14 [a]Therefore [1]flight shall perish
from the swift,
The strong shall not
strengthen his power,
[b]Nor shall the mighty
[2]deliver himself;
15 He shall not stand who
handles the bow,
The swift of foot shall not
[1]escape,
Nor shall he who rides a
horse deliver himself.
16 The most [1]courageous men
of might
Shall flee naked in that day,"
Says the LORD.

3 Hear this word that the LORD has spoken against you,

---

4 [a]Hos. 12:2 [b]Lev. 26:14 [c]Jer. 16:19 [d]Ezek. 20:13, 16, 18
5 [a]Hos. 8:14
6 [a]2 Kin. 17:7–18; 18:12 [b]Is. 29:21 [c]Amos 4:1; 5:11; 8:6
7 [a]Amos 5:12 [b]Ezek. 22:11 [c]Lev. 20:3 [1]Or *trample on*
8 [a]1 Cor. 8:10 [b]Ex. 22:26 [1]Or *those punished by fines*
9 [a]Num. 21:25 [b]Ezek. 31:3 [c][Mal. 4:1]
10 [a]Ex. 12:51 [b]Deut. 2:7
11 [a]Num. 12:6 [b]Num. 6:2, 3
12 [a]Is. 30:10
13 [a]Is. 1:14 [1]Or *tottering under* [2]Or *totters*
14 [a]Jer. 46:6 [b]Ps. 33:16 [1]Or *the place of refuge* [2]Lit. *save his soul* or *life*
15 [1]Or *save*
16 [1]Lit. *strong of his heart among the mighty*

O children of Israel, against the whole family which I brought up from the land of Egypt, saying:

2 "You[a] only have I known of
all the families of the
earth;
[b]Therefore I will punish you
for all your iniquities."

3 Can two walk together,
unless they are agreed?
4 Will a lion roar in the forest,
when he has no prey?
Will a young lion [1]cry out of
his den, if he has caught
nothing?
5 Will a bird fall into a snare
on the earth, where there
is no [1]trap for it?
Will a snare spring up from
the earth, if it has caught
nothing at all?
6 If a [1]trumpet is blown in a
city, will not the people
be afraid?
[a]If there is calamity in a city,
will not the LORD have
done *it*?

7 Surely the Lord GOD does
nothing,
Unless [a]He reveals His
secret to His servants
the prophets.
8 A lion has roared!
Who will not fear?
The Lord GOD has spoken!
[a]Who can but prophesy?

9 "Proclaim in the palaces at
[1]Ash'dod,
And in the palaces in the
land of Egypt, and say:
'Assemble on the mountains
of Samaria;
See great tumults in her
midst,
And the [2]oppressed within
her.
10 For they [a]do not know to do
right,'
Says the LORD,
'Who store up violence
and [1]robbery in their
palaces.' "

11 Therefore thus says the Lord GOD:

"An adversary *shall be* all
around the land;
He shall sap your strength
from you,
And your palaces shall be
plundered."

12 Thus says the LORD:

"As a shepherd [1]takes from
the mouth of a lion
Two legs or a piece of an
ear,
So shall the children of
Israel be taken out
Who dwell in Samaria—
In the corner of a bed and
[2]on the edge of a couch!
13 Hear and testify against the
house of Jacob,"
Says the Lord GOD, the God
of hosts,
14 "That in the day I punish
Israel for their
transgressions,
I will also visit *destruction*
on the altars of [a]Beth'el;
And the horns of the altar
shall be cut off
And fall to the ground.
15 I will [1]destroy [a]the winter
house along with [b]the
summer house;
The [c]houses of ivory shall
perish,

CHAPTER 3

2 [a][Deut. 7:6] [b][Rom. 2:9]

4 [1]Lit. *give his voice*

5 [1]Or *bait* or *lure*

6 [a]Is. 45:7 [1]*ram's horn*

7 [a][John 15:15]

8 [a]Acts 4:20

9 [1]So with MT; LXX *Assyria* [2]Or *oppression*

10 [a]Jer. 4:22 [1]Or *devastation*

12 [1]Or *snatches* [2]Heb. uncertain, possibly *on the cover*

14 [a]Amos 4:4

15 [a]Jer. 36:22 [b]Judg. 3:20 [c]1 Kin. 22:39 [1]Lit. *strike*

And the great houses shall
have an end,"
Says the LORD.

4

Hear this word, you [a]cows
of Bā'shan, who *are*
on the mountain of
Samaria,
Who oppress the [b]poor,
Who crush the needy,
Who say to [1]your husbands,
"Bring *wine*, let us
[c]drink!"
2 [a]The Lord GOD has sworn by
His holiness:
"Behold, the days shall come
upon you
When He will take you
away [b]with fishhooks,
And your posterity with
fishhooks.
3 [a]You will go out *through*
broken *walls*,
Each one straight ahead of
her,
And you will [1]be cast into
Har'mon,"
Says the LORD.

4 "Come[a] to Beth'el and
transgress,
At [b]Gil'gal multiply
transgression;
[c]Bring your sacrifices every
morning,
[d]Your tithes every three
[1]days.
5 [a]Offer a sacrifice of
thanksgiving with
leaven,
Proclaim *and* announce [b]the
freewill offerings;
For this you love,
You children of Israel!"
Says the Lord GOD.

6 "Also I gave you [1]cleanness
of teeth in all your cities,
And lack of bread in all
your places;
[a]Yet you have not returned
to Me,"
Says the LORD.

7 "I also withheld rain from you,
When *there were* still three
months to the harvest.
I made it rain on one city,
I withheld rain from another
city.
One part was rained upon,
And where it did not rain
the part withered.
8 So two *or* three cities
wandered to another city
to drink water,
But they were not satisfied;
Yet you have not returned
to Me,"
Says the LORD.

9 "I[a] blasted you with blight
and mildew.
When your gardens
increased,
Your vineyards,
Your fig trees,
And your olive trees,
[b]The locust devoured *them*;
Yet you have not returned
to Me,"
Says the LORD.

10 "I sent among you a plague
[a]after the manner of
Egypt;
Your young men I killed
with a sword,
Along with your captive
horses;
I made the stench of your
camps come up into your
nostrils;
Yet you have not returned
to Me,"
Says the LORD.

CHAPTER 4

1 [a]Ps. 22:12 [b]Amos 2:6 [c]Prov. 23:20 [1]Lit. *their masters* or *lords*

2 [a]Ps. 89:35 [b]Jer. 16:16

3 [a]Ezek. 12:5 [1]Or *cast them*

4 [a]Ezek. 20:39 [b]Hos. 4:15 [c]Num. 28:3 [d]Deut. 14:28 [1]Or *years*, Deut. 14:28

5 [a]Lev. 7:13 [b]Lev. 22:18

6 [a]Jer. 5:3 [1]Hunger

9 [a]Hag. 2:17 [b]Joel 1:4, 7

10 [a]Ps. 78:50

11 "I overthrew *some* of you,
As God overthrew [a]Sod′om
and Go·mor′rah,
And you were like a
firebrand plucked from
the burning;
Yet you have not returned
to Me,"
Says the LORD.

12 "Therefore thus will I do to
you, O Israel;
Because I will do this to
you,
[a]Prepare to meet your God,
O Israel!"

13 For behold,
He who forms mountains,
And creates the [1]wind,
[a]Who declares to man what
[2]his thought *is*,
And makes the morning
darkness,
[b]Who treads the high places
of the earth—
[c]The LORD God of hosts *is*
His name.

CHAPTER 5

5 Hear this word which I [a]take
up against you, a lamentation, O house of Israel:

2 The virgin of Israel has
fallen;
She will rise no more.
She lies forsaken on her
land;
There is no one to raise
her up.

3 For thus says the Lord GOD:

"The city that goes out by a
thousand
Shall have a hundred left,
And that which goes out by
a hundred
Shall have ten left to the
house of Israel."

4 For thus says the LORD to the
house of Israel:

[a]"Seek Me [b]and live;
5 But do not seek [a]Beth′el,
Nor enter Gil′gal,
Nor pass over to
[b]Bē·er·shē′ba;
For Gil′gal shall surely go
into captivity,
And [c]Beth′el shall come to
nothing.
6 [a]Seek the LORD and live,
Lest He break out like fire
in the house of Joseph,
And devour *it*,
With no one to quench *it* in
Beth′el—
7 You who [a]turn justice to
wormwood,
And lay righteousness to
rest in the earth!"

8 He made the [a]Plēi′a·dēs and
Ō·rī′on;
He turns the shadow of
death into morning
[b]And makes the day dark as
night;
He [c]calls for the waters of
the sea
And pours them out on the
face of the earth;
[d]The LORD *is* His name.
9 He [1]rains ruin upon the
strong,
So that fury comes upon the
fortress.

10 [a]They hate the one who
rebukes in the gate,
And they [b]abhor the one
who speaks uprightly.
11 [a]Therefore, because you
[1]tread down the poor

4:11 [a]Is. 13:19
12 [a]Jer. 5:22
13 [a]Ps. 139:2 [b]Mic. 1:3 [c]Is. 47:4 [1]Or *spirit* [2]Or *His*

CHAPTER 5

1 [a]Jer. 7:29; 9:10, 17
4 [a][Jer. 29:13] [b][Is. 55:3]
5 [a]Amos 4:4 [b]Amos 8:14 [c]Hos. 4:15
6 [a][Is. 55:3, 6, 7]
7 [a]Amos 6:12
8 [a]Job 9:9; 38:31 [b]Ps. 104:20 [c]Job 38:34 [d][Amos 4:13]
9 [1]Or *flashes forth destruction*
10 [a]Is. 29:21; 66:5 [b]1 Kin. 22:8
11 [a]Amos 2:6 [1]*trample*

And take grain [2]taxes from
him,
Though [b]you have built
houses of hewn stone,
Yet you shall not dwell in
them;
You have planted [3]pleasant
vineyards,
But you shall not drink wine
from them.
12 For I [a]know your manifold
transgressions
And your mighty sins:
[b]Afflicting the just *and*
taking bribes;
[c]Diverting the poor *from*
justice at the gate.
13 Therefore [a]the prudent keep
silent at that time,
For it *is* an evil time.

14 Seek good and not evil,
That you may live;
So the LORD God of hosts
will be with you,
[a]As you have spoken.
15 [a]Hate evil, love good;
Establish justice in the gate.
[b]It may be that the LORD God
of hosts
Will be gracious to the
remnant of Joseph.

16 Therefore the LORD God of
hosts, the Lord, says this:

"*There shall be* wailing in all
streets,
And they shall say in all the
highways,
'Alas! Alas!'
They shall call the farmer to
mourning,
[a]And skillful lamenters to
wailing.
17 In all vineyards *there shall*
be wailing,
For [a]I will pass through
you,"
Says the LORD.

18 [a]Woe to you who desire the
day of the LORD!
For what good *is* [b]the day of
the LORD to you?
It *will be* darkness, and not
light.
19 It *will be* [a]as though a man
fled from a lion,
And a bear met him!
Or *as though* he went into
the house,
Leaned his hand on the
wall,
And a serpent bit him!
20 *Is* not the day of the LORD
darkness, and not light?
Is it not very dark, with no
brightness in it?

21 "I[a] hate, I despise your feast
days,
And [b]I do not savor your
sacred assemblies.
22 [a]Though you offer Me burnt
offerings and your grain
offerings,
I will not accept *them*,
Nor will I regard your
fattened peace offerings.
23 Take away from Me the
noise of your songs,
For I will not hear the
melody of your stringed
instruments.
24 [a]But let justice run down like
water,
And righteousness like a
mighty stream.

25 "Did[a] you offer Me sacrifices
and offerings
In the wilderness forty
years, O house of Israel?

11 [b]Mic. 6:15 [2]Or *tribute* [3]*desirable*
12 [a]Hos. 5:3 [b]Amos 2:6 [c]Is. 29:21
13 [a]Amos 6:10
14 [a]Mic. 3:11
15 [a]Rom. 12:9 [b]Joel 2:14
16 [a]Jer. 9:17
17 [a]Ex. 12:12
18 [a]Is. 5:19 [b]Joel 2:2
19 [a]Jer. 48:44
21 [a]Is. 1:11–16 [b]Lev. 26:31
22 [a]Mic. 6:6, 7
24 [a]Mic. 6:8
25 [a]Deut. 32:17

26 You also carried [1]Sik′kuth[2]
[a]your king
And [2]Chī′un, your idols,
The star of your gods,
Which you made for
yourselves.
27 Therefore I will send you
into captivity [a]beyond
Damascus,"
Says the LORD, [b]whose name
is the God of hosts.

6 Woe [a]to you *who are* at
[b]ease in Zion,
And [c]trust in Mount
Samaria,
Notable persons in the
[d]chief nation,
To whom the house of Israel
comes!
2 [a]Go over to [b]Cal′neh and see;
And from there go to
[c]Hā′math the great;
Then go down to Gath of
the Phi·lis′tines.
[d]*Are you* better than these
kingdoms?
Or is their territory greater
than your territory?
3 *Woe to* you who [a]put far off
the day of [b]doom,
[c]Who cause [d]the seat of
violence to come near;
4 Who lie on beds of ivory,
Stretch out on your couches,
Eat lambs from the flock
And calves from the midst
of the stall;
5 [a]Who sing idly to the sound
of stringed instruments,
And invent for yourselves
[b]musical instruments
[c]like David;
6 Who [a]drink wine from
bowls,
And anoint yourselves with
the best ointments,
[b]But are not grieved for the
affliction of Joseph.
7 Therefore they shall now go
[a]captive as the first of
the captives,
And those who recline
at banquets shall be
removed.

8 [a]The Lord GOD has sworn by
Himself,
The LORD God of hosts says:
"I abhor [b]the pride of Jacob,
And hate his palaces;
Therefore I will deliver up
the city
And all that is in it."

9 Then it shall come to pass,
that if ten men remain in one
house, they shall die.
10 And when [1]a relative *of the*
dead, with one who will burn
the bodies, picks up the [2]bodies
to take them out of the house, he
will say to one inside the house,
"*Are there* any more with you?"
Then someone will say, "None."
And he will say, [a]"Hold your
tongue! [b]For we dare not mention the name of the LORD."

11 For behold, [a]the LORD gives
a command:
[b]He will break the great
house into bits,
And the little house into
pieces.

12 Do horses run on rocks?
Does *one* plow *there* with
oxen?
Yet [a]you have turned justice
into gall,
And the fruit of righteousness
into wormwood,
13 You who rejoice over [1]Lo
Dē′bar,

26 [a]1 Kin. 11:33 [1]LXX, Vg. *tabernacle of Moloch* [2]A pagan deity
27 [a]2 Kin. 17:6 [b]Amos 4:13

CHAPTER 6

1 [a]Luke 6:24 [b]Zeph. 1:12 [c]Is. 31:1 [d]Ex. 19:5
2 [a]Jer. 2:10 [b]Is. 10:9 [c]2 Kin. 18:34 [d]Nah. 3:8
3 [a]Is. 56:12 [b]Amos 5:18 [c]Amos 5:12 [d]Ps. 94:20
5 [a]Is. 5:12; Amos 5:23 [b]1 Chr. 15:16; 16:42 [c]1 Chr. 23:5
6 [a]Amos 2:8; 4:1 [b]Gen. 37:25
7 [a]Amos 5:27
8 [a]Jer. 51:14 [b]Amos 8:7
10 [a]Amos 5:13 [b]Amos 8:3 [1]Lit. *his loved one* or *uncle* [2]Lit. *bones*
11 [a]Is. 55:11 [b]Amos 3:15
12 [a]Hos. 10:4
13 [1]Lit. *Nothing*

Who say, "Have we not
taken [2]Kar·nā'im for
ourselves
By our own strength?"

14 "But, behold, [a]I will raise up
a nation against you,
O house of Israel,"
Says the LORD God of hosts;
"And they will afflict you from
the [b]entrance of Hā'math
To the Valley of the
Ar'a·bah."

7 Thus the Lord GOD showed
me: Behold, He formed locust
swarms at the [1]beginning of the
late crop; indeed *it was* the late
crop after the king's mowings.
2 And so it was, when they had
finished eating the grass of the
land, that I said:

"O Lord GOD, forgive, I pray!
[a]Oh,[1] that Jacob may stand,
For he *is* small!"
3 So [a]the LORD relented
concerning this.
"It shall not be," said the
LORD.

4 Thus the Lord GOD showed
me: Behold, the Lord GOD called
[1]for conflict by fire, and it consumed the great deep and devoured the [2]territory.
5 Then I said:

"O Lord GOD, cease, I pray!
[a]Oh, that Jacob may stand,
For he *is* small!"
6 So the LORD relented
concerning this.
"This also shall not be," said
the Lord GOD.

7 Thus He showed me: Behold,
the Lord stood on a wall *made*
with a plumb line, with a plumb
line in His hand.
8 And the LORD said to me,
"Ā'mos, what do you see?" And
I said, "A plumb line." Then the
Lord said:

"Behold, [a]I am setting a
plumb line
In the midst of My people
Israel;
[b]I will not pass by them
anymore.
9 [a]The [1]high places of Isaac
shall be desolate,
And the [2]sanctuaries of
Israel shall be laid waste.
[b]I will rise with the sword
against the house of
Jer·o·bō'am."

10 Then Am·a·zī'ah the [a]priest of
[b]Beth'el sent to [c]Jer·o·bō'am king
of Israel, saying, "Ā'mos has conspired against you in the midst
of the house of Israel. The land is
not able to [1]bear all his words.
11 "For thus Ā'mos has said:

'Jer·o·bō'am shall die by the
sword,
And Israel shall surely be
led away [a]captive
From their own land.' "

12 Then Am·a·zī'ah said to
Ā'mos:

"Go, you seer!
Flee to the land of Judah.
There eat bread,
And there prophesy.
13 But [a]never again prophesy
at Beth'el,
[b]For it *is* the king's
[1]sanctuary,
And it *is* the royal
[2]residence."

---

13 [2]Lit. *Horns,* a symbol of strength

14 [a]Jer. 5:15 [b]1 Kin. 8:65

CHAPTER 7

1 [1]Lit. *beginning of the sprouting of*

2 [a]Is. 51:19 [1]Or *How shall Jacob stand*

3 [a]Jon. 3:10

4 [1]*to contend* [2]Lit. *portion*

5 [a]Amos 7:2, 3

8 [a]2 Kin. 21:13 [b]Mic. 7:18

9 [a]Gen. 46:1 [b]2 Kin.15:8–10 [1]Places of pagan worship [2]Or *holy places*

10 [a]1 Kin. 12:31, 32; 13:33 [b]Amos 4:4 [c]2 Kin. 14:23 [1]Or *endure*

11 [a]Amos 5:27; 6:7

13 [a]Amos 2:12 [b]1 Kin. 12:29, 32 [1]Or *holy place* [2]Lit. *house*

14 Then Ā′mos answered, and said to Am·a·zī′ah:

"I *was* no prophet,
Nor *was* I [a]a son of a prophet,
But I *was* a [b]sheepbreeder
And a tender of sycamore fruit.
15 Then the LORD took me [1]as I followed the flock,
And the LORD said to me,
'Go, [a]prophesy to My people Israel.'
16 Now therefore, hear the word of the LORD:
You say, 'Do not prophesy against Israel,
And [a]do not [1]spout against the house of Isaac.'

17 "Therefore[a] thus says the LORD:

[b]'Your wife shall be a harlot in the city;
Your sons and daughters shall fall by the sword;
Your land shall be divided by *survey* line;
You shall die in a [c]defiled land;
And Israel shall surely be led away captive
From his own land.'"

8

Thus the Lord GOD showed me: Behold, a basket of summer fruit.
2 And He said, "Ā′mos, what do you see?" So I said, "A basket of summer fruit." Then the LORD said to me:

[a]"The end has come upon My people Israel;
[b]I will not pass by them anymore.

3 And [a]the songs of the temple
Shall be wailing in that day,"
Says the Lord GOD—
"Many dead bodies everywhere,
[b]They shall be thrown out in silence."

4 Hear this, you who [1]swallow up the needy,
And make the poor of the land fail,

5 Saying:

"When will the New Moon be past,
That we may sell grain?
And [a]the Sabbath,
That we may [1]trade wheat?
[b]Making the ephah small and the shekel large,
Falsifying the scales by [c]deceit,
6 That we may buy the poor for [a]silver,
And the needy for a pair of sandals—
Even sell the bad wheat?"

7 The LORD has sworn by [a]the pride of Jacob:
"Surely [b]I will never forget any of their works.
8 [a]Shall the land not tremble for this,
And everyone mourn who dwells in it?
All of it shall swell like [1]the River,
Heave and subside
[b]Like the River of Egypt.

9 "And it shall come to pass in that day," says the Lord GOD,

---

14 [a]1 Kin. 20:35 [b]Zech. 13:5
15 [a]Amos 3:8 [1]Lit. *from behind*
16 [a]Ezek. 21:2 [1]Lit. *drip*
17 [a]Jer. 28:12; 29:21, 32 [b]Zech. 14:2 [c]Hos. 9:3

CHAPTER 8

2 [a]Ezek. 7:2 [b]Amos 7:8
3 [a]Amos 5:23 [b]Amos 6:9, 10
4 [1]Or *trample on*, Amos 2:7
5 [a]Neh. 13:15 [b]Mic. 6:10, 11 [c]Lev. 19:35, 36 [1]Lit. *open*
6 [a]Amos 2:6
7 [a]Amos 6:8 [b]Hos. 7:2; 8:13
8 [a]Hos. 4:3 [b]Amos 9:5 [1]The Nile; some Heb. mss., LXX, Tg., Syr., Vg. *River* (cf. 9:5); MT *the light*

[a]"That I will make the sun go
down at noon,
And I will darken the earth
in [1]broad daylight;
10 I will turn your feasts into
[a]mourning,
[b]And all your songs into
lamentation;
[c]I will bring sackcloth on
every waist,
And baldness on every
head;
I will make it like mourning
for an only *son,*
And its end like a bitter day.

11 "Behold, the days are
coming," says the Lord
GOD,
"That I will send a famine on
the land,
Not a famine of bread,
Nor a thirst for water,
But [a]of hearing the words of
the LORD.
12 They shall wander from sea
to sea,
And from north to east;
They shall run to and fro,
seeking the word of the
LORD,
But shall [a]not find *it.*

13 "In that day the fair virgins
And strong young men
Shall faint from thirst.
14 Those who [a]swear by [b]the
[1]sin of Samaria,
Who say,
'As your god lives, O Dan!'
And, 'As the way of
[c]Bē·er·shē′ba lives!'
They shall fall and never
rise again."

9 I saw the Lord standing by
the altar, and He said:

9 [a]Job 5:14
[1]Lit. *a day of light*

10 [a]Ezek. 7:18
[b]Ezek. 27:31
[c][Zech. 12:10]

11 [a]Ezek. 7:26

12 [a]Hos. 5:6

14 [a]Hos. 4:15
[b]Deut. 9:21
[c]Amos 5:5
[1]Or *Ashima,* a Syrian goddess

CHAPTER 9

1 [a]Hab. 3:13
[b]Amos 2:14
[1]Capitals of the pillars

2 [a]Ps. 139:8
[b]Jer. 51:53
[1]Or *Sheol*

3 [a]Jer. 23:24

4 [a]Lev. 26:33
[b]Jer. 21:10; 39:16; 44:11

5 [a]Mic. 1:4
[b]Amos 8:8
[1]The Nile

"Strike the [1]doorposts, that
the thresholds may
shake,
And [a]break them on the
heads of them all.
I will slay the last of them
with the sword.
[b]He who flees from them
shall not get away,
And he who escapes from
them shall not be
delivered.

2 "Though[a] they dig into [1]hell,
From there My hand shall
take them;
[b]Though they climb up to
heaven,
From there I will bring them
down;
3 And though they [a]hide
themselves on top of
Car′mel,
From there I will search and
take them;
Though they hide from My
sight at the bottom of
the sea,
From there I will command
the serpent, and it shall
bite them;
4 Though they go into
captivity before their
enemies,
From there [a]I will command
the sword,
And it shall slay them.
[b]I will set My eyes on them
for harm and not for
good."

5 The Lord GOD of hosts,
He who touches the earth
and it [a]melts,
[b]And all who dwell there
mourn;
All of it shall swell like [1]the
River,

And subside like the River
of Egypt.
6 He who builds His [a]layers[1]
in the sky,
And has founded His strata
in the earth;
Who [b]calls for the waters of
the sea,
And pours them out on the
face of the earth—
[c]The LORD *is* His name.

7 "*Are* you not like the [1]people
of Ethiopia to Me,
O children of Israel?" says
the LORD.
"Did I not bring up Israel
from the land of Egypt,
The [a]Phi·lis′tines from
[b]Caph′tor,[2]
And the Syrians from [c]Kir?

8 "Behold, [a]the eyes of the
Lord GOD *are* on the
sinful kingdom,
And I [b]will destroy it from
the face of the earth;
Yet I will not utterly destroy
the house of Jacob,"
Says the LORD.

9 "For surely I will command,
And will [1]sift the house of
Israel among all nations,
As *grain* is sifted in a sieve;
[a]Yet not the smallest [2]grain
shall fall to the ground.
10 All the sinners of My people
shall die by the sword,
[a]Who say, 'The calamity
shall not overtake nor
confront us.'

11 "On[a] that day I will raise up ☆
The [1]tabernacle of David,
which has fallen down,
And [2]repair its damages;
I will raise up its ruins,
And rebuild it as in the days
of old;
12 [a]That they may possess the
remnant of [b]Ē′dom,[1]
And all the Gentiles who are
called by My name,"
Says the LORD who does this
thing.

13 "Behold, [a]the days are
coming," says the LORD,
"When the plowman shall
overtake the reaper,
And the treader of grapes
him who sows seed;
[b]The mountains shall drip
with sweet wine,
And all the hills shall flow
with it.
14 [a]I will bring back the
captives of My people
Israel;
[b]They shall build the waste
cities and inhabit *them;*
They shall plant vineyards
and drink wine from
them;
They shall also make
gardens and eat fruit
from them.
15 I will plant them in their
land,
[a]And no longer shall they be
pulled up
From the land I have given
them,"
Says the LORD your God.

---

6 [a]Ps. 104:3, 13 [b]Amos 5:8 [c]Amos 4:13; 5:27 [1]Or *stairs*
7 [a]Jer. 47:4 [b]Deut. 2:23 [c]Amos 1:5 [1]Lit. *sons of the Ethiopians* [2]Crete
8 [a]Amos 9:4 [b]Jer. 5:10; 30:11
9 [a][Is. 65:8–16] [1]*shake* [2]Lit. *pebble*
10 [a]Amos 6:3
11 [a]Acts 15:16–18 [1]Lit. *booth;* a figure of a deposed dynasty [2]Lit. *wall up its breaches*
12 [a]Obad. 19 [b]Num. 24:18 [1]LXX *mankind*
13 [a]Lev. 26:5 [b]Joel 3:18
14 [a]Jer. 30:3, 18 [b]Is. 61:4
15 [a]Ezek. 34:28; 37:25

The Book of OBADIAH

A STRUGGLE that began in the womb between twin brothers, Esau and Jacob, eventuates in a struggle between their respective descendants, the Edomites and the Israelites. For the Edomites' stubborn refusal to aid Israel, first during the time of wilderness wandering (Num. 20:14–21) and later during a time of invasion, they are roundly condemned by Obadiah. This little-known prophet describes their crimes, tries their case, and pronounces their judgment: total destruction.

The Hebrew name *Obadyah* means "Worshiper of Yahweh" or "Servant of Yahweh." The Greek title in the Septuagint is *Obdiou*, and the Latin title in the Vulgate is *Abdias*.

THE vision of Ō·ba·dī′ah.

Thus says the Lord GOD
[a]concerning Ē′dom
[b](We have heard a report
from the LORD,
And a messenger has been
sent among the nations,
saying,
"Arise, and let us rise up
against her for battle"):

2 "Behold, I will make you
small among the nations;
You shall be greatly
despised.
3 The [a]pride of your heart has
deceived you,
You who dwell in the clefts
of the rock,
Whose habitation is high;
[b]*You* who say in your heart,
'Who will bring me down to
the ground?'
4 [a]Though you ascend *as* high
as the eagle,
And though you [b]set your
nest among the stars,
From there I will bring you
down," says the LORD.

5 "If [a]thieves had come to you,
If robbers by night—
Oh, how you will be cut
off!—
Would they not have stolen
till they had enough?
If grape-gatherers had come
to you,
[b]Would they not have left
some gleanings?

6 "Oh, how Esau shall be
searched out!
How his hidden treasures
shall be sought after!
7 All the men in your
confederacy
Shall force you to the
border;
[a]The men at peace with you
Shall deceive you *and*
prevail against you.
Those who eat your bread
shall lay a [1]trap for you.
[b]No[2] one is aware of it.

8 "Will[a] I not in that day," says
the LORD,
"Even destroy the wise *men*
from Ē′dom,

1 [a]Is. 21:11 [b]Jer. 49:14–16
3 [a]Jer. 49:16 [b]Rev. 18:7
4 [a]Job 20:6 [b]Hab. 2:9
5 [a]Jer. 49:9 [b]Deut. 24:21
7 [a]Jer. 38:22 [b]Is. 19:11 [1]Or *wound or plot* [2]Or *There is no understanding in him*
8 [a][Job 5:12–14]

And understanding from the mountains of Esau?
9 Then your [a]mighty men, O [b]Tē′man, shall be dismayed,
To the end that everyone from the mountains of Esau
May be cut off by slaughter.

10 "For [a]violence against your brother Jacob,
Shame shall cover you,
And [b]you shall be cut off forever.
11 In the day that you [a]stood on the other side—
In the day that strangers carried captive his forces,
When foreigners entered his gates
And [b]cast lots for Jerusalem—
Even you *were* as one of them.

12 "But you should not have [a]gazed[1] on the day of your brother
[2]In the day of his captivity;
Nor should you have [b]rejoiced over the children of Judah
In the day of their destruction;
Nor should you have spoken proudly
In the day of distress.
13 You should not have entered the gate of My people
In the day of their calamity.
Indeed, you should not have [1]gazed on their affliction
In the day of their calamity,
Nor laid *hands* on their substance
In the day of their calamity.
14 You should not have stood at the crossroads
To cut off those among them who escaped;
Nor should you have [1]delivered up those among them who remained
In the day of distress.

15 "For[a] the day of the LORD upon all the nations *is* near;
[b]As you have done, it shall be done to you;
Your [1]reprisal shall return upon your own head.
16 [a]For as you drank on My holy mountain,
So shall all the nations drink continually;
Yes, they shall drink, and swallow,
And they shall be as though they had never been.

17 "But on Mount Zion there [a]shall be [1]deliverance,
And there shall be holiness;
The house of Jacob shall possess their possessions.
18 The house of Jacob shall be a fire,
And the house of Joseph [a]a flame;
But the house of Esau *shall be* stubble;
They shall kindle them and devour them,
And no survivor shall *remain* of the house of Esau,"
For the LORD has spoken.

19 The [1]South [a]shall possess the mountains of Esau,

9 [a]Ps. 76:5 [b]Jer. 49:7
10 [a]Gen. 27:41 [b]Ezek. 35:9
11 [a]Ps. 83:5–8 [b]Nah. 3:10
12 [a]Mic. 4:11; 7:10 [b][Prov. 17:5] [1]Gloated over [2]Lit. *On the day he became a foreigner*
13 [1]Gloated over
14 [1]Handed over to the enemy
15 [a]Ezek. 30:3 [b]Hab. 2:8 [1]Or *reward*
16 [a]Joel 3:17
17 [a]Amos 9:8 [1]Or *salvation*
18 [a]Zech. 12:6
19 [a]Is. 11:14 [1]Heb. *Negev*

[b]And the Lowland shall
possess Phi·lis′ti·a.
They shall possess the fields
of Ē′phra·im
And the fields of Samaria.
Benjamin *shall possess*
Gil′ē·ad.
20 And the captives of this host
of the children of Israel
Shall possess the land of the
Cā′naan·ītes
As [a]far as Zar′e·phath.
The captives of Jerusalem
who are in Se·phar′ad
[b]Shall possess the cities of
the [1]South.
21 Then [a]saviors[1] shall come to
Mount Zion
To judge the mountains of
Esau,
And the [b]kingdom shall be
the LORD's.

19 [b]Zeph. 2:7
20 [a]1 Kin. 17:9 [b]Jer. 32:44 [1]Heb. *Negev*
21 [a][James 5:20] [b][Rev. 11:15] [1]*deliverers*

The Book of
JONAH

NINEVEH is northeast; Tarshish is west. When God calls Jonah to preach repentance to the wicked Ninevites, the prophet knows that God's mercy may follow. He turns down the assignment and heads for Tarshish instead. But once God has dampened his spirits (by tossing him out of the boat and into the water) and has demonstrated His protection (by moving him out of the water and into the fish), Jonah realizes God is serious about His command. Nineveh must hear the word of the Lord; therefore Jonah goes. Although the preaching is a success, the preacher comes away angry and discouraged and he must learn firsthand of God's compassion for sinful men.

Yonah is the Hebrew word for "dove." The Septuagint hellenized this word into *Ionas*, and the Latin Vulgate used the title *Jonas*.

NOW the word of the LORD
came to [a]Jonah the son of
A·mit′taī, saying,
2 "Arise, go to [a]Nin′e·veh, that
[b]great city, and cry out against it;
for [c]their wickedness has come
up before Me."
3 But Jonah arose to flee to
Tar′shish from the presence
of the LORD. He went down to
[a]Jop′pa, and found a ship going to Tar′shish; so he paid the
fare, and went down into it, to
go with them to [b]Tar′shish [c]from
the presence of the LORD.
4 But [a]the LORD [1]sent out a
great wind on the sea, and there
was a mighty tempest on the
sea, so that the ship was about
to be broken up.
5 Then the mariners were
afraid; and every man cried out
to his god, and threw the cargo
that *was* in the ship into the sea,
to lighten [1]the load. But Jonah
had gone down [a]into the lowest
parts of the ship, had lain down,
and was fast asleep.
6 So the captain came to him,
and said to him, "What do you
mean, sleeper? Arise, [a]call on
your God; [b]perhaps your God
will consider us, so that we may
not perish."
7 And they said to one another,
"Come, let us [a]cast lots, that we
may know for whose cause this
trouble *has come* upon us." So
they cast lots, and the lot fell on
Jonah.
8 Then they said to him,
[a]"Please tell us! For whose cause
is this trouble upon us? What is
your occupation? And where do
you come from? What is your
country? And of what people are
you?"
9 So he said to them, "I *am* a
Hebrew; and I fear [1]the LORD,
the God of heaven, [a]who made
the sea and the dry *land*."
10 Then the men were exceedingly afraid, and said to him,
"Why have you done this?" For
the men knew that he fled from
the presence of the LORD, because he had told them.
11 Then they said to him, "What
shall we do to you that the sea
may be calm for us?"—for the

CHAPTER 1

1 [a]2 Kin. 14:25
2 [a]Is. 37:37 [b]Gen. 10:11, 12 [c]Gen. 18:20
3 [a]Josh. 19:46 [b]Is. 23:1 [c]Gen. 4:16
4 [a]Ps. 107:25 [1]Lit. *hurled*
5 [a]1 Sam. 24:3 [1]Lit. *from upon them*
6 [a]Ps. 107:28 [b]Joel 2:14
7 [a]Josh. 7:14
8 [a]Josh. 7:19
9 [a][Neh. 9:6] [1]Heb. *YHWH*

sea was growing more tempestuous.
12 And he said to them, [a]"Pick
me up and [1]throw me into the
sea; then the sea will become
calm for you. For I know that
this great tempest *is* because of
me."
13 Nevertheless the men rowed
hard to return to land, [a]but they
could not, for the sea continued to grow more tempestuous
against them.
14 Therefore they cried out to
the LORD and said, "We pray,
O LORD, please do not let us
perish for this man's life, and
[a]do not charge us with innocent
blood; for You, O LORD, [b]have
done as it pleased You."
15 So they picked up Jonah and
threw him into the sea, [a]and the
sea ceased from its raging.
16 Then the men [a]feared the
LORD exceedingly, and offered
a sacrifice to the LORD and took
vows.
17 Now the LORD had prepared
a great fish to swallow Jonah.
And [a]Jonah was in the belly of
the fish three days and three
nights.

2 Then Jonah prayed to the LORD his God from the fish's belly.
2 And he said:

"I [a]cried out to the LORD
because of my affliction,
[b]And He answered me.

"Out of the belly of Shē′ōl I
cried,
And You heard my voice.
3 [a]For You cast me into the
deep,
Into the heart of the seas,
And the floods surrounded
me;
[b]All Your billows and Your
waves passed over me.
4 [a]Then I said, 'I have been
cast out of Your sight;
Yet I will look again [b]toward
Your holy temple.'
5 The [a]waters surrounded me,
even to my soul;
The deep closed around me;
Weeds were wrapped
around my head.
6 I went down to the
[1]moorings of the
mountains;
The earth with its bars
closed behind me
forever;
Yet You have brought up my
[a]life from the pit,
O LORD, my God.

7 "When my soul fainted
within me,
I remembered the LORD;
[a]And my prayer went *up* to
You,
Into Your holy temple.

8 "Those who regard
[a]worthless idols
Forsake their own [1]Mercy.
9 But I will [a]sacrifice to You
With the voice of
thanksgiving;
I will pay what I have
[b]vowed.
[c]Salvation *is* of the [d]LORD."

10 So the LORD spoke to the
fish, and it vomited Jonah onto
dry *land*.

3 Now the word of the LORD
came to Jonah the second
time, saying,
2 "Arise, go to Nin′e·veh, that

12 [a]John 11:50 [1]Lit. *hurl*
13 [a][Prov. 21:30]
14 [a]Deut. 21:8 [b]Ps. 115:3
15 [a][Ps. 89:9; 107:29]
16 [a]Acts 5:11
17 [a][Matt. 12:40]

CHAPTER 2

2 [a]Ps. 120:1 [b]Ps. 65:2
3 [a]Ps. 88:6 [b]Ps. 42:7
4 [a]Ps. 31:22 [b]1 Kin. 8:38
5 [a]Lam. 3:54
6 [a][Ps. 16:10] [1]*foundations* or *bases*
7 [a]Ps. 18:6
8 [a]Jer. 10:8 [1]Or *Loving-kindness*
9 [a]Hos. 14:2 [b][Eccl. 5:4, 5] [c]Ps. 3:8 [d][Jer. 3:23]

great city, and preach to it the
message that I tell you."
3 So Jonah arose and went to
Nin′e·veh, according to the word
of the LORD. Now Nin′e·veh was
an exceedingly great city, [1]a
three-day journey *in extent.*
4 And Jonah began to enter
the city on the first day's walk.
Then [a]he cried out and said, "Yet
forty days, and Nin′e·veh shall
be overthrown!"
5 So the [a]people of Nin′e·veh
believed God, proclaimed a fast,
and put on sackcloth, from the
greatest to the least of them.
6 Then word came to the king
of Nin′e·veh; and he arose from
his throne and laid aside his
robe, covered *himself* with sackcloth [a]and sat in ashes.
7 [a]And he caused *it* to be proclaimed and published throughout Nin′e·veh by the decree of
the king and his [1]nobles, saying,

Let neither man nor beast,
herd nor flock, taste
anything; do not let them
eat, or drink water.
8 But let man and beast be
covered with sackcloth, and
cry mightily to God; yes, [a]let
every one turn from his evil
way and from [b]the violence
that is in his hands.
9 [a]Who can tell *if* God will
turn and relent, and turn
away from His fierce anger,
so that we may not perish?

10 [a]Then God saw their works,
that they turned from their evil
way; and God relented from the
disaster that He had said He
would bring upon them, and He
did not do it.

CHAPTER 3

3 [1]Exact meaning unknown
4 [a][Deut. 18:22]
5 [a][Matt. 12:41]
6 [a]Job 2:8
7 [a]2 Chr. 20:3 [1]Lit. *great ones*
8 [a]Is. 58:6 [b]Is. 59:6
9 [a]Joel 2:14
10 [a]Jer. 18:8

CHAPTER 4

2 [a]Jon. 1:3 [b]Joel 2:13
3 [a]1 Kin. 19:4 [b]Jon. 4:8
6 [1]Heb. *kikayon*, exact identity unknown [2]Lit. *rejoiced with great joy*
8 [a]Jon. 4:3

4 But it displeased Jonah exceedingly, and he became
angry.
2 So he prayed to the LORD,
and said, "Ah, LORD, was not
this what I said when I was
still in my country? Therefore I
[a]fled previously to Tar′shish; for
I know that You *are* a [b]gracious
and merciful God, slow to anger and abundant in lovingkindness, One who relents from doing harm.
3 [a]"Therefore now, O LORD,
please take my life from me, for
[b]*it is* better for me to die than to
live!"
4 Then the LORD said, "*Is it*
right for you to be angry?"
5 So Jonah went out of the
city and sat on the east side of
the city. There he made himself
a shelter and sat under it in the
shade, till he might see what
would become of the city.
6 And the LORD God prepared
a [1]plant and made it come up
over Jonah, that it might be
shade for his head to deliver
him from his misery. So Jonah
[2]was very grateful for the plant.
7 But as morning dawned the
next day God prepared a worm,
and it *so* damaged the plant that
it withered.
8 And it happened, when the
sun arose, that God prepared a
vehement east wind; and the sun
beat on Jonah's head, so that
he grew faint. Then he wished
death for himself, and said, [a]"*It*
is better for me to die than to
live."
9 Then God said to Jonah, "*Is*
it right for you to be angry
about the plant?" And he said,
"*It is* right for me to be angry,
even to death!"

10 But the LORD said, "You have
had pity on the plant for which
you have not labored, nor made
it grow, which [1]came up in a
night and perished in a night.
11 "And should I not pity Nin'-
e·veh, [a]that great city, in which
are more than one hundred and
twenty thousand persons [b]who
cannot discern between their
right hand and their left—and
much livestock?"

10 [1]Lit. *was a son of a night*

11 [a]Jon. 1:2; 3:2, 3 [b]Deut. 1:39

The Book of

MICAH

MICAH, called from his rustic home to be a prophet, leaves his familiar surroundings to deliver a stern message of judgment to the princes and people of Jerusalem. Burdened by the abusive treatment of the poor by the rich and influential, the prophet turns his verbal rebukes upon any who would use their social or political power for personal gain. One-third of Micah's book exposes the sins of his countrymen; another third pictures the punishment God is about to send; and the final third holds out the hope of restoration once that discipline has ended. Through it all, God's righteous demands upon His people are clear: "to do justly, to love mercy, and to walk humbly with your God" (6:8).

The name *Michayahu* ("Who Is Like Yahweh?") is shortened to *Michaia*. In 7:18, Micah hints at his own name with the phrase "Who is a God like You?" The Greek and Latin titles of this book are *Michaias* and *Micha*.

CHAPTER 1

THE word of the LORD that came to [a]Mī′cah of Mō′resheth in the days of [b]Jō′tham, Ā′haz, *and* Hez·e·kī′ah, kings of Judah, which he saw concerning Samaria and Jerusalem.

2 Hear, all you peoples!
Listen, O earth, and all that is in it!
Let the Lord GOD be a witness against you,
The Lord from [a]His holy temple.

3 For behold, the LORD is coming out of His place;
He will come down
And tread on the high places of the earth.
4 [a]The mountains will melt under Him,
And the valleys will split
Like wax before the fire,
Like waters poured down a steep place.
5 All this is for the transgression of Jacob
And for the sins of the house of Israel.
What *is* the transgression of Jacob?
Is it not Samaria?
And what *are* the [a]high places of Judah?
Are they not Jerusalem?

6 "Therefore I will make Samaria [a]a heap of ruins in the field,
Places for planting a vineyard;
I will pour down her stones into the valley,
And I will [b]uncover her foundations.
7 All her carved images shall be beaten to pieces,
And all her [a]pay as a harlot shall be burned with the fire;
All her idols I will lay desolate,
For she gathered *it* from the pay of a harlot,
And they shall return to the [b]pay of a harlot."

1 [a]Jer. 26:18 [b]Is. 1:1
2 [a][Ps. 11:4]
4 [a]Amos 9:5
5 [a]Deut. 32:13; 33:29
6 [a]2 Kin. 19:25 [b]Ezek. 13:14
7 [a]Hos. 2:5 [b]Deut. 23:18

8 Therefore I will wail and
howl,
I will go stripped and naked;
[a]I will make a wailing like
the jackals
And a mourning like the
ostriches,
9 For her wounds *are*
incurable.
For [a]it has come to Judah;
It has come to the gate of
My people—
To Jerusalem.

10 [a]Tell *it* not in Gath,
Weep not at all;
In [1]Beth Aph′rah
Roll yourself in the dust.
11 Pass by in naked shame, you
inhabitant of [1]Shā′phir;
The inhabitant of [2]Zā′a·nan
does not go out.
Beth Ē′zel mourns;
Its place to stand is taken
away from you.

12 For the inhabitant of
[1]Mā′roth [2]pined for good,
But [a]disaster came down
from the LORD
To the gate of Jerusalem.
13 O inhabitant of [a]Lā′chish,
Harness the chariot to the
swift steeds
(She *was* the beginning of
sin to the daughter of
Zion),
For the transgressions of
Israel were [b]found in
you.

14 Therefore you shall [a]give
presents to [1]Mō′re·sheth
Gath;
The houses of [b]Ach′zib[2] *shall*
be a lie to the kings of
Israel.

15 I will yet bring an heir to
you, O inhabitant of
[a]Ma·rē′shah;[1]
The glory of Israel shall
come to [b]A·dul′lam.[2]
16 Make yourself [a]bald and cut
off your hair,
Because of your [b]precious
children;
Enlarge your baldness like
an eagle,
For they shall go from you
into [c]captivity.

2

Woe to those who devise
iniquity,
And [1]work out evil on their
beds!
At [a]morning light they
practice it,
Because it is in the power of
their hand.
2 They [a]covet fields and take
them by violence,
Also houses, and seize *them*.
So they oppress a man and
his house,
A man and his inheritance.

3 Therefore thus says the LORD:

"Behold, against this [a]family I
am devising [b]disaster,
From which you cannot
remove your necks;
Nor shall you walk
haughtily,
For this *is* an evil time.
4 In that day *one* shall take up
a proverb against you,
And [a]lament with a bitter
lamentation, saying:
'We are utterly destroyed!
He has changed the
[1]heritage of my people;
How He has removed *it*
from me!

8 [a]Ps. 102:6
9 [a]2 Kin. 18:13
10 [a]2 Sam. 1:20 [1]Lit. *House of Dust*
11 [1]Lit. *Beautiful* [2]Lit. *Going Out*
12 [a]Is. 59:9–11 [1]Lit. *Bitterness* [2]Lit. *was sick*
13 [a]Is. 36:2 [b]Ezek. 23:11
14 [a]2 Sam. 8:2 [b]Josh. 15:44 [1]Lit. *Possession of Gath* [2]Lit. *Lie*
15 [a]Josh. 15:44 [b]2 Chr. 11:7 [1]Lit. *Inheritance* [2]Lit. *Refuge*
16 [a]Job 1:20 [b]Lam. 4:5 [c]Amos 7:11, 17

CHAPTER 2

1 [a]Hos. 7:6, 7 [1]Plan
2 [a]Is. 5:8
3 [a]Jer. 8:3 [b]Amos 5:13
4 [a]2 Sam. 1:17 [1]Lit. *portion*

To [2]a turncoat He has
divided our fields.' "

5 Therefore you will have
no [1]one to determine
boundaries by lot
In the assembly of the LORD.

6 "Do not prattle," *you say to those* who [1]prophesy.
So they shall not prophesy
[2]to you;
[3]They shall not return insult
for insult.
7 *You who are* named the
house of Jacob:
"Is the Spirit of the LORD
restricted?
Are these His doings?
Do not My words do good
To him who walks
uprightly?

8 "Lately My people have risen
up as an enemy—
You pull off the robe with
the garment
From those who trust *you*,
as they pass by,
Like men returned from war.
9 The women of My people
you cast out
From their pleasant houses;
From their children
You have taken away My
glory forever.

10 "Arise and depart,
For this *is* not *your* [a]rest;
Because it is [b]defiled, it shall
destroy,
Yes, with utter destruction.
11 If a man should walk in a
false spirit
And speak a lie, *saying*,
'I will [1]prophesy to you [2]of
wine and drink,'
Even he would be the
[a]prattler of this people.

12 "I[a] will surely assemble all of
you, O Jacob,
I will surely gather the
remnant of Israel;
I will put them together [b]like
sheep of [1]the fold,
Like a flock in the midst of
their pasture;
[c]They shall make a loud
noise because of *so many* people.
13 The one who breaks open
will come up before them;
They will break out,
Pass through the gate,
And go out by it;
[a]Their king will pass before
them,
[b]With the LORD at their head."

3

And I said:

"Hear now, O heads of Jacob,
And you [a]rulers of the house
of Israel:
[b]*Is it* not for you to know
justice?
2 You who hate good and love
evil;
Who strip the skin from [1]My
people,
And the flesh from their
bones;
3 Who also [a]eat the flesh of
My people,
Flay their skin from them,
Break their bones,
And chop *them* in pieces
Like *meat* for the pot,
[b]Like flesh in the caldron."

4 Then [a]they will cry to the
LORD,
But He will not hear them;

4 [2]Lit. *one turning back*, an apostate

5 [1]Lit. *one casting a surveyor's line*

6 [1]Or *preach*, lit. *drip* words [2]Lit. *to these* [3]Vg. *He shall not take shame*

10 [a]Deut. 12:9 [b]Lev. 18:25

11 [a]Is. 30:10 [1]Or *preach*, lit. *drip* [2]*concerning*

12 [a][Mic. 4:6, 7] [b]Jer. 31:10 [c]Ezek. 33:22; 36:37 [1]Heb. *Bozrah*

13 [a][Hos. 3:5] [b]Is. 52:12

CHAPTER 3

1 [a]Ezek. 22:27 [b]Jer. 5:4, 5

2 [1]Lit. *them*

3 [a]Ps. 14:4; 27:2 [b]Ezek. 11:3, 6, 7

4 [a]Jer. 11:11

He will even hide His face
from them at that time,
Because they have been evil
in their deeds.

5 Thus says the LORD
[a]concerning the prophets
Who make my people stray;
Who chant [1]"Peace"
[2]While they [b]chew with their
teeth,
But who prepare war
against him
[c]Who puts nothing into their
mouths:
6 "Therefore[a] you shall have
night without [1]vision,
And you shall have darkness
without divination;
The sun shall go down on
the prophets,
And the day shall be dark
for [b]them.
7 So the seers shall be
ashamed,
And the diviners abashed;
Indeed they shall all cover
their lips;
[a]For *there is* no answer from
God."

8 But truly I am full of power
by the Spirit of the LORD,
And of justice and might,
[a]To declare to Jacob his
transgression
And to Israel his sin.
9 Now hear this,
You heads of the house of
Jacob
And rulers of the house of
Israel,
Who abhor justice
And [1]pervert all equity,
10 [a]Who build up Zion with
[b]bloodshed
And Jerusalem with iniquity:
11 [a]Her heads judge for a bribe,

5 [a]Ezek. 13:10, 19 [b]Matt. 7:15 [c]Ezek. 13:18 [1]All is well [2]For those who feed them
6 [a]Is. 8:20–22; 29:10–12 [b]Is. 29:10 [1]Prophetic revelation
7 [a]Amos 8:11
8 [a]Is. 58:1
9 [1]Lit. *twist*
10 [a]Jer. 22:13, 17 [b]Hab. 2:12
11 [a]Is. 1:23 [b]Jer. 6:13 [c]Is. 48:2 [1]Lit. *silver*
12 [a]Jer. 26:18 [b]Ps. 79:1 [c]Mic. 4:1, 2 [1]Lit. *house*

CHAPTER 4

1 [a]Is. 2:2–4
3 [a]Is. 2:4 [1]*pruning knives*

[b]Her priests teach for pay,
And her prophets divine for
[1]money.
[c]Yet they lean on the LORD,
and say,
"Is not the LORD among us?
No harm can come upon us."
12 Therefore because of you
Zion shall be [a]plowed *like* a
field,
[b]Jerusalem shall become
heaps of ruins,
And [c]the mountain of the
[1]temple
Like the bare hills of the
forest.

4

Now [a]it shall come to pass
in the latter days
That the mountain of the
LORD's house
Shall be established on the
top of the mountains,
And shall be exalted above
the hills;
And peoples shall flow to it.
2 Many nations shall come
and say,
"Come, and let us go up to
the mountain of the
LORD,
To the house of the God of
Jacob;
He will teach us His ways,
And we shall walk in His
paths."
For out of Zion the law shall
go forth,
And the word of the LORD
from Jerusalem.
3 He shall judge between
many peoples,
And rebuke strong nations
afar off;
They shall beat their swords
into [a]plowshares,
And their spears into
[1]pruning hooks;

Nation shall not lift up
sword against nation,
[b]Neither shall they learn war
anymore.

4 [a]But everyone shall sit under
his vine and under his
fig tree,
And no one shall make
them afraid;
For the mouth of the LORD of
hosts has spoken.
5 For all people walk each in
the name of his god,
But [a]we will walk in the
name of the LORD our
God
Forever and ever.

6 "In that day," says the LORD,
[a]"I will assemble the lame,
[b]I will gather the outcast
And those whom I have
afflicted;
7 I will make the lame [a]a
remnant,
And the outcast a strong
nation;
So the LORD [b]will reign over
them in Mount Zion
From now on, even forever.
8 And you, O tower of the
flock,
The stronghold of the
daughter of Zion,
To you shall it come,
Even the former dominion
shall come,
The kingdom of the
daughter of Jerusalem."

9 Now why do you cry aloud?
[a]*Is there* no king in your
midst?
Has your counselor
perished?
For [b]pangs have seized you
like a woman in [1]labor.
10 Be in pain, and labor to
bring forth,
O daughter of Zion,
Like a woman in birth pangs.
For now you shall go forth
from the city,
You shall dwell in the field,
And to [a]Babylon you
shall go.
There you shall be delivered;
There the [b]LORD will [c]redeem
you
From the hand of your
enemies.

11 [a]Now also many nations have
gathered against you,
Who say, "Let her be defiled,
And let our eye [b]look upon
Zion."
12 But they do not know [a]the
thoughts of the LORD,
Nor do they understand His
counsel;
For He will gather them [b]like
sheaves to the threshing
floor.

13 "Arise[a] and [b]thresh,
O daughter of Zion;
For I will make your horn
iron,
And I will make your hooves
bronze;
You shall [c]beat in pieces
many peoples;
[d]I will consecrate their gain
to the LORD,
And their substance to [e]the
Lord of the whole earth."

5 Now gather yourself in
troops,
O daughter of troops;
He has laid siege against us;
They will [a]strike the judge of
Israel with a rod on the
cheek.

---

3 [b]Ps. 72:7
4 [a]Zech. 3:10
5 [a]Zech. 10:12
6 [a]Ezek. 34:16 [b]Ps. 147:2
7 [a]Mic. 2:12 [b][Is. 9:6; 24:23]
9 [a]Jer. 8:19 [b]Is. 13:8 [1]*childbirth*
10 [a]Amos 5:27 [b][Is. 45:13] [c]Ps. 18:17
11 [a]Lam. 2:16 [b]Obad. 12
12 [a][Is. 55:8, 9] [b]Is. 21:10
13 [a]Jer. 51:33 [b]Is. 41:15 [c]Dan. 2:44 [d]Is. 18:7 [e]Zech. 4:14

CHAPTER 5

1 [a]Lam. 3:30; Matt. 27:30; Mark 15:19

☆ **2** "But you, [a]Bethlehem
[b]Eph′ra·thah,
Though you are little
[c]among the [d]thousands of Judah,
Yet out of you shall come forth to Me
The One to be [e]Ruler in Israel,
[f]Whose goings forth *are* from of old,
From [1]everlasting."

3 Therefore He shall give them up,
Until the time *that* [a]she who is in labor has given birth;
Then [b]the remnant of His brethren
Shall return to the children of Israel.
4 And He shall stand and [a]feed[1] *His flock*
In the strength of the LORD,
In the majesty of the name of the LORD His God;
And they shall abide,
For now He [b]shall be great
To the ends of the earth;
5 And this *One* [a]shall be peace.

When the Assyrian comes into our land,
And when he treads in our palaces,
Then we will raise against him
Seven shepherds and eight princely men.
6 They shall [1]waste with the sword the land of Assyria,
And the land of [a]Nim′rod at its entrances;
Thus He shall [b]deliver *us* from the Assyrian,
When he comes into our land
And when he treads within our borders.

7 Then [a]the remnant of Jacob
Shall be in the midst of many peoples,
[b]Like dew from the LORD,
Like showers on the grass,
That [1]tarry for no man
Nor [2]wait for the sons of men.
8 And the remnant of Jacob
Shall be among the Gentiles,
In the midst of many peoples,
Like a [a]lion among the beasts of the forest,
Like a young lion among flocks of sheep,
Who, if he passes through,
Both treads down and tears in pieces,
And none can deliver.
9 Your hand shall be lifted against your adversaries,
And all your enemies shall be [1]cut off.

10 "And it shall be in that day," says the LORD,
"That I will [a]cut[1] off your [b]horses from your midst
And destroy your [c]chariots.
11 I will cut off the cities of your land
And throw down all your strongholds.
12 I will cut off sorceries from your hand,
And you shall have no [a]soothsayers.
13 [a]Your carved images I will also cut off,
And your *sacred* pillars from your midst;

2 [a]Matt. 2:6; Luke 2:4, 11; John 7:42 [b]Gen. 35:19; 48:7; [c]1 Sam. 23:23 [d]Ex. 18:25 [e][Is. 9:6] [f]Ps. 90:2; [John 1:1] [1]Lit. *the days of eternity*
3 [a]Mic. 4:10 [b]Mic. 4:7; 7:18
4 [a][Is. 40:11; 49:9] [b]Ps. 72:8 [1]*shepherd*
5 [a][Is. 9:6]
6 [a]Gen. 10:8–11 [b]Is. 14:25 [1]*devastate*
7 [a]Mic. 5:3 [b]Deut. 32:2 [1]*wait* [2]*delay*
8 [a]Num. 24:9
9 [1]*destroyed*
10 [a]Zech. 9:10 [b]Deut. 17:16 [c]Is. 2:7; 22:18 [1]*destroy*
12 [a]Is. 2:6
13 [a]Zech. 13:2

You shall [b]no more worship
the work of your hands;
14 I will pluck your [1]wooden
images from your midst;
Thus I will destroy your
cities.
15 And I will [a]execute
vengeance in anger and
fury
On the nations that have not
[1]heard."

CHAPTER 6

6 Hear now what the LORD
says:

"Arise, plead your case before
the mountains,
And let the hills hear your
voice.
2 [a]Hear, O you mountains, [b]the
LORD's complaint,
And you strong foundations
of the earth;
For [c]the LORD has a
complaint against His
people,
And He will [1]contend with
Israel.

3 "O My people, what [a]have I
done to you?
And how have I [b]wearied
you?
Testify against Me.
4 [a]For I brought you up from
the land of Egypt,
I redeemed you from the
house of bondage;
And I sent before you
Moses, Aaron, and
Miriam.
5 O My people, remember
now
What [a]Bā′lak king of Mō′ab
counseled,
And what Bā′laam the son
of Bē′or answered him,
From [1]Acacia Grove to
Gil′gal,
That you may know [b]the
righteousness of the
LORD."

6 With what shall I come
before the LORD,
And bow myself before the
High God?
Shall I come before Him
with burnt offerings,
With calves a year old?
7 [a]Will the LORD be pleased
with thousands of rams,
Ten thousand [b]rivers of oil?
[c]Shall I give my firstborn *for*
my transgression,
[1]The fruit of my body *for* the
sin of my soul?

8 He has [a]shown you, O man,
what *is* good;
And what does the LORD
require of you
But [b]to do justly,
To love [1]mercy,
And to walk humbly with
your God?

9 The LORD's voice cries to the
city—
Wisdom shall see Your
name:

"Hear the rod!
Who has appointed it?
10 Are there yet the treasures
of wickedness
In the house of the wicked,
And the short measure *that*
is an abomination?
11 Shall I count pure *those*
with [a]the wicked scales,
And with the bag of
deceitful weights?
12 For her rich men are full of
[a]violence,

13 [b]Is. 2:8
14 [1]Heb. *Asherim,* Canaanite deities
15 [a][2 Thess. 1:8] [1]*obeyed*
2 [a]Ps. 50:1, 4 [b]Hos. 12:2 [c][Is. 1:18] [1]*bring charges against*
3 [a]Jer. 2:5, 31 [b]Is. 43:22, 23
4 [a][Deut. 4:20]
5 [a]Num. 22:5, 6 [b]Judg. 5:11 [1]Heb. *Shittim,* Num. 25:1; Josh. 2:1; 3:1
7 [a]Is. 1:11 [b]Job 29:6 [c]2 Kin. 16:3 [1]My own child
8 [a][Deut. 10:12] [b]Gen. 18:19 [1]Or *lovingkindness*
11 [a]Hos. 12:7
12 [a]Mic. 2:1, 2

Her inhabitants have spoken
lies,
And [b]their tongue is
deceitful in their mouth.

13 "Therefore I will also [a]make
you sick by striking you,
By making *you* desolate
because of your sins.
14 [a]You shall eat, but not be
satisfied;
[1]Hunger *shall be* in your
midst.
[2]You may carry *some* away,
but shall not save *them;*
And what you do rescue
I will give over to the
sword.

15 "You shall [a]sow, but not reap;
You shall tread the olives,
but not anoint yourselves
with oil;
And *make* sweet wine, but
not drink wine.
16 For the statutes of [a]Om′rī are
[b]kept;
All the works of Ā′hab's
house *are done;*
And you walk in their
counsels,
That I may make you a
[1]desolation,
And your inhabitants a
hissing.
Therefore you shall bear the
[c]reproach of [2]My people."

7

Woe is me!
For I am like those who
gather summer fruits,
Like those who [a]glean
vintage grapes;
There is no cluster to eat
Of the first-ripe fruit *which*
[b]my soul desires.
2 The [a]faithful[1] *man* has
perished from the earth,
And *there is* no one upright
among men.
They all lie in wait for blood;
[b]Every man hunts his brother
with a net.

3 That they may successfully
do evil with both
hands—
The prince asks *for gifts,*
The judge *seeks* a [a]bribe,
And the great *man* utters his
evil desire;
So they scheme together.
4 The best of them *is* [a]like a
brier;
The most upright *is sharper*
than a thorn hedge;
The day of your watchman
and your punishment
comes;
Now shall be their
perplexity.

5 [a]Do not trust in a friend;
Do not put your confidence
in a companion;
Guard the doors of your
mouth
From her who lies in your
[b]bosom.
6 For [a]son dishonors father,
Daughter rises against her
mother,
Daughter-in-law against her
mother-in-law;
A man's enemies *are*
the men of his own
household.
7 Therefore I will look to the
LORD;
I will [a]wait for the God of
my salvation;
My God will hear me.

8 [a]Do not rejoice over me, my
enemy;
[b]When I fall, I will arise;

12 [b]Jer. 9:2–6, 8
13 [a]Lev. 26:16
14 [a]Lev. 26:26 [1]Or *Emptiness* or *Humiliation* [2]Tg., Vg. *You shall take hold*
15 [a]Amos 5:11
16 [a]1 Kin. 16:25, 26 [b]Hos. 5:11 [c]Is. 25:8 [1]Or *object of horror* [2]So with MT, Tg., Vg.; LXX *nations*

CHAPTER 7

1 [a]Is. 17:6 [b]Is. 28:4
2 [a]Is. 57:1 [b]Hab. 1:15 [1]Or *loyal*
3 [a]Mic. 3:11
4 [a]Ezek. 2:6
5 [a]Jer. 9:4 [b]Deut. 28:56
6 [a]Matt. 10:36
7 [a]Is. 25:9
8 [a]Prov. 24:17 [b][Prov. 24:16]

When I sit in darkness,
The LORD *will be* a light to me.
9 [a]I will bear the indignation of the LORD,
Because I have sinned against Him,
Until He pleads my [b]case
And executes justice for me.
He will bring me forth to the light;
I will see His righteousness.
10 Then *she who is* my enemy will see,
And [a]shame will cover her who said to me,
[b]"Where is the LORD your God?"
My eyes will see her;
Now she will be trampled down
Like mud in the streets.

11 *In* the day when your [a]walls are to be built,
In that day [1]the decree shall go far and wide.
12 *In* that day [a]they[1] shall come to you
From Assyria and the [2]fortified cities,
From the [3]fortress to [4]the River,
From sea to sea,
And mountain *to* mountain.
13 Yet the land shall be desolate
Because of those who dwell in it,
And [a]for the fruit of their deeds.

14 Shepherd Your people with Your staff,
The flock of Your heritage,
Who dwell [1]solitarily *in* a [a]woodland,
In the midst of Car′mel;
Let them feed *in* Bā′shan and Gil′ē·ad,
As in days of old.

15 "As[a] in the days when you came out of the land of Egypt,
I will show [1]them [b]wonders."

16 The nations [a]shall see and be ashamed of all their might;
[b]They shall put *their* hand over *their* mouth;
Their ears shall be deaf.
17 They shall lick the [a]dust like a serpent;
[b]They shall crawl from their holes like [1]snakes of the earth.
[c]They shall be afraid of the LORD our God,
And shall fear because of You.
18 [a]Who *is* a God like You,
[b]Pardoning iniquity
And passing over the transgression of [c]the remnant of His heritage?

[d]He does not retain His anger forever,
Because He delights *in* [e]mercy.[1]
19 He will again have compassion on us,
And will subdue our iniquities.

You will cast all [1]our sins
Into the depths of the sea.
20 [a]You will give truth to Jacob ☆
And [1]mercy to Abraham,
[b]Which You have sworn to our fathers
From days of old.

9 [a]Lam. 3:39, 40 [b]Jer. 50:34
10 [a]Ps. 35:26 [b]Ps. 42:3
11 [a][Amos 9:11] [1]Or *the boundary shall be extended*
12 [a][Is. 11:16; 19:23–25] [1]Lit. *he,* collective of the captives [2]Heb. *arey mazor,* possibly *cities of Egypt* [3]Heb. *mazor,* possibly *Egypt* [4]The Euphrates
13 [a]Jer. 21:14
14 [a]Is. 37:24 [1]Alone
15 [a]Ps. 68:22; 78:12 [b]Ex. 34:10 [1]Lit. *him,* collective for the captives
16 [a]Is. 26:11 [b]Job 21:5
17 [a][Is. 49:23] [b]Ps. 18:45 [c]Jer. 33:9 [1]Lit. *crawlers*
18 [a]Ex. 15:11 [b]Ex. 34:6, 7, 9 [c]Mic. 4:7 [d]Ps. 103:8, 9, 13 [e][Ezek. 33:11] [1]Or *lovingkindness*
19 [1]Lit. *their*
20 [a]Luke 1:72, 73 [b]Ps. 105:9 [1]Or *lovingkindness*

The Book of
NAHUM

"FOR everyone to whom much is given, from him much will be required" (Luke 12:48). Nineveh had been given the privilege of knowing the one true God. Under Jonah's preaching this great gentile city had repented, and God had graciously stayed His judgment. However, a hundred years later, Nahum proclaims the downfall of this same city. The Assyrians have forgotten their revival and have returned to their habits of violence, idolatry, and arrogance. As a result, Babylon will so destroy the city that no trace of it will remain—a prophecy fulfilled in painful detail.

The Hebrew word *nahum* ("comfort," "consolation") is a shortened form of Nehemiah ("Comfort of Yahweh"). The destruction of the capital city of Assyria is a message of comfort and consolation to Judah and all who live in fear of the cruelty of the Assyrians. The title of this book in the Greek and Latin Bibles is *Naoum* and *Nahum*.

CHAPTER 1

THE [1]burden [a]against Nin′e-veh. The book of the vision of Nā′hum the El′kosh·īte.

2 God *is* [a]jealous, and the
LORD avenges;
The LORD avenges and *is*
furious.
The LORD will take vengeance
on His adversaries,
And He reserves *wrath* for
His enemies;
3 The LORD *is* [a]slow to anger
and [b]great in power,
And will not at all acquit
the wicked.

[c]The LORD has His way
In the whirlwind and in the
storm,
And the clouds *are* the dust
of His feet.
4 [a]He rebukes the sea and
makes it dry,
And dries up all the rivers.
[b]Bā′shan and Car′mel wither,
And the flower of Lebanon
wilts.

5 The mountains quake before
Him,
The hills melt,
And the earth [1]heaves at His
presence,
Yes, the world and all who
dwell in it.
6 Who can stand before His
indignation?
And [a]who can endure the
fierceness of His anger?
His fury is poured out like
fire,
And the rocks are thrown
down by Him.

7 [a]The LORD *is* good,
A stronghold in the day of
trouble;
And [b]He knows those who
trust in Him.
8 But with an overflowing
flood
He will make an utter end
of its place,
And darkness will pursue
His enemies.

1 [a]Zeph. 2:13 [1]*oracle, prophecy*
2 [a]Ex. 20:5
3 [a]Ex. 34:6, 7 [b][Job 9:4] [c]Ps. 18:17
4 [a]Matt. 8:26 [b]Is. 33:9
5 [1]Tg. *burns*
6 [a][Mal. 3:2]
7 [a][Jer. 33:11] [b]2 Tim. 2:19

9 [a]What do you [1]conspire
against the LORD?
[b]He will make an utter end
of it.
Affliction will not rise up a
second time.
10 For while tangled [a]*like*
thorns,
[b]And while drunken *like*
drunkards,
[c]They shall be devoured like
stubble fully dried.
11 From you comes forth *one*
Who plots evil against the
LORD,
A [1]wicked counselor.

12 Thus says the LORD:

"Though *they are* [1]safe, and
likewise many,
Yet in this manner they will
be [a]cut down
When he passes through.
Though I have afflicted
you,
I will afflict you no more;
13 For now I will break off his
yoke from you,
And burst your bonds
apart."

14 The LORD has given a
command concerning
you:
[1]"Your name shall be
perpetuated no longer.
Out of the house of your
gods
I will cut off the carved
image and the molded
image.
I will dig your [a]grave,
For you are [b]vile."[2]

15 Behold, on the mountains
The [a]feet of him who brings
good tidings,
Who proclaims peace!
O Judah, keep your
appointed feasts,
Perform your vows.
For the [1]wicked one shall no
more pass through you;
He is [b]utterly cut off.

2 He[1] who scatters has come
up before your face.
Man the fort!
Watch the road!
Strengthen *your* flanks!
Fortify *your* power mightily.

2 For the LORD will restore the
excellence of Jacob
Like the excellence of Israel,
For the emptiers have
emptied them out
And ruined their vine
branches.

3 The shields of his mighty
men *are* made red,
The valiant men *are* in
scarlet.
The chariots *come* with
flaming torches
In the day of his
preparation,
And [1]the spears are
brandished.
4 The chariots rage in the
streets,
They jostle one another in
the broad roads;
They seem like torches,
They run like lightning.

5 He remembers his nobles;
They stumble in their walk;
They make haste to her
walls,
And the defense is prepared.
6 The gates of the rivers are
opened,
And the palace is dissolved.

---

9 [a]Ps. 2:1 [b]1 Sam. 3:12 [1]Or *devise*

10 [a]2 Sam. 23:6 [b]Nah. 3:11 [c]Mal. 4:1

11 [1]Lit. *counselor of Belial*

12 [a][Is. 10:16–19, 33, 34] [1]Or *at peace* or *complete*

14 [a]Ezek. 32:22, 23 [b]Nah. 3:6 [1]Lit. *No more of your name shall be fruitful* [2]Or *contemptible*

15 [a]Rom. 10:15 [b]Is. 29:7, 8 [1]Lit. *one of Belial*

CHAPTER 2

1 [1]Vg. *He who destroys*

3 [1]Lit. *the cypresses are shaken;* LXX, Syr. *the horses rush about;* Vg. *the drivers are stupefied*

7 [1]It is decreed:
She shall be led away
captive,
She shall be brought up;
And her maidservants shall
lead *her* as with the
voice of doves,
Beating their breasts.

8 Though Nin′e·veh of old
was like a pool of water,
Now they flee away.
[1]"Halt! Halt!" *they cry;*
But no one turns back.
9 [1]Take spoil of silver!
Take spoil of [a]gold!
There is no end of treasure,
Or wealth of every desirable
prize.
10 She is empty, desolate, and
waste!
The heart melts, and the
knees shake;
Much pain *is* in every side,
And all their faces [1]are
drained of color.

11 Where *is* the dwelling of the
[a]lions,
And the feeding place of the
young lions,
Where the lion walked, the
lioness *and* lion's cub,
And no one made *them*
afraid?
12 The lion tore in pieces
enough for his cubs,
[1]Killed for his lionesses,
[a]Filled his caves with prey,
And his dens with [2]flesh.

13 "Behold, [a]I *am* against you,"
says the LORD of hosts, "I will burn
[1]your chariots in smoke, and the
sword shall devour your young
lions; I will cut off your prey from
the earth, and the voice of your
[b]messengers shall be heard no
more."

3 Woe to the [a]bloody city!
It *is* all full of lies *and*
robbery.
Its [1]victim never departs.
2 The noise of a whip
And the noise of rattling
wheels,
Of galloping horses,
Of [1]clattering chariots!
3 Horsemen charge with
bright sword and
glittering spear.
There is a multitude of slain,
A great number of bodies,
Countless corpses—
They stumble over the
corpses—
4 Because of the multitude
of [1]harlotries of the
[2]seductive harlot,
[a]The mistress of sorceries,
Who sells nations through
her harlotries,
And families through her
sorceries.

5 "Behold, I *am* [a]against you,"
says the LORD of hosts;
[b]"I will lift your skirts over
your face,
I will show the nations your
nakedness,
And the kingdoms your
shame.
6 I will cast abominable filth
upon you,
Make you [a]vile,[1]
And make you [b]a spectacle.
7 It shall come to pass *that* all
who look upon you
[a]Will flee from you, and say,
[b]'Nin′e·veh is laid waste!
[c]Who will bemoan her?'
Where shall I seek
comforters for you?"

7 [1]Heb. *Huzzab*
8 [1]Lit. *Stand*
9 [a]Zeph. 1:18 [1]*Plunder*
10 [1]LXX, Tg., Vg. *gather blackness;* Joel 2:6
11 [a]Job 4:10, 11
12 [a]Jer. 51:34 [1]Lit. *Strangled* [2]Torn flesh
13 [a]Nah. 3:5 [b]2 Kin. 18:17–25; 19:9–13, 23 [1]Lit. *her*

CHAPTER 3

1 [a]Hab. 2:12 [1]Lit. *prey*
2 [1]*bounding* or *jolting*
4 [a]Is. 47:9–12 [1]Spiritual unfaithfulness [2]Lit. *goodly charm,* in a bad sense
5 [a]Nah. 2:13 [b]Is. 47:2, 3
6 [a]Nah. 1:14 [b]Heb. 10:33 [1]*despicable*
7 [a]Rev. 18:10 [b]Jon. 3:3; 4:11 [c]Jer. 15:5

8 [a]Are you better than [b]No[1] Ā′mon
That *was* situated by the [2]River,
That had the waters around her,
Whose rampart *was* the sea,
Whose wall *was* the sea?
9 Ethiopia and Egypt *were* her strength,
And *it was* boundless;
[a]Put and Lū′bim were [1]your helpers.
10 Yet she *was* carried away,
She went into captivity;
[a]Her young children also were dashed to pieces
[b]At the head of every street;
They [c]cast lots for her honorable men,
And all her great men were bound in chains.
11 You also will be [a]drunk;
You will be hidden;
You also will seek refuge from the enemy.

12 All your strongholds *are* [a]fig trees with ripened figs:
If they are shaken,
They fall into the mouth of the eater.
13 Surely, [a]your people in your midst *are* women!
The gates of your land are wide open for your enemies;
Fire shall devour the [b]bars of your *gates.*

14 Draw your water for the siege!
[a]Fortify your strongholds!
Go into the clay and tread the mortar!
Make strong the brick kiln!
15 There the fire will devour you,
The sword will cut you off;
It will eat you up like a [a]locust.

Make yourself many—like the locust!
Make yourself many— like the *swarming* locusts!
16 You have multiplied your [a]merchants more than the stars of heaven.
The locust plunders and flies away.
17 [a]Your commanders *are* like *swarming* locusts,
And your generals like great grasshoppers,
Which camp in the hedges on a cold day;
When the sun rises they flee away,
And the place where they *are* is not known.

18 [a]Your shepherds slumber,
O [b]king of Assyria;
Your nobles rest *in the dust.*
Your people are [c]scattered on the mountains,
And no one gathers them.
19 Your injury *has* no healing,
[a]Your wound is severe.
[b]All who hear news of you
Will clap *their* hands over you,
For upon whom has not your wickedness passed continually?

---

8 [a]Amos 6:2 [b]Jer. 46:25 [1]Ancient Thebes; Tg., Vg. *populous Alexandria* [2]Lit. *rivers,* the Nile and the surrounding canals
9 [a]Ezek. 27:10 [1]LXX *her*
10 [a]Hos. 13:16 [b]Lam. 2:19 [c]Joel 3:3
11 [a]Nah. 1:10
12 [a]Rev. 6:12, 13
13 [a]Is. 19:16 [b]Jer. 51:30
14 [a]Nah. 2:1
15 [a]Joel 1:4
16 [a]Rev. 18:3, 11–19
17 [a]Rev. 9:7
18 [a]Ps. 76:5, 6 [b]Jer. 50:18 [c]1 Kin. 22:17
19 [a]Mic. 1:9 [b]Lam. 2:15

The Book of
HABAKKUK

HABAKKUK ministers during the "death throes" of the nation of Judah. Although repeatedly called to repentance, the nation stubbornly refuses to change her sinful ways. Habakkuk, knowing the hardheartedness of his countrymen, asks God how long this intolerable condition can continue. God replies that the Babylonians will be His chastening rod upon the nation—an announcement that sends the prophet to his knees. He acknowledges that the just in any generation shall live by faith (2:4), not by sight. Habakkuk concludes by praising God's wisdom even though he does not fully understand God's ways.

Habaqquq is an unusual Hebrew name derived from the verb *habaq*, "embrace." Thus his name probably means "One Who Embraces" or "Clings." At the end of his book this name becomes appropriate because Habakkuk chooses to cling firmly to God regardless of what happens to his nation (3:16–19). The Greek title in the Septuagint is *Ambakouk*, and the Latin title in Jerome's Vulgate is *Habacuc*.

THE [1]burden which the prophet
Ha·bak'kuk saw.

2 O LORD, how long shall I cry,
[a]And You will not hear?
Even cry out to You,
[b]"Violence!"
And You will [c]not save.
3 Why do You show me
iniquity,
And cause *me* to see
[1]trouble?
For plundering and violence
are before me;
There is strife, and
contention arises.
4 Therefore the law is
powerless,
And justice never goes
forth.
For the [a]wicked surround
the righteous;
Therefore perverse
judgment proceeds.

5 "Look[a] among the nations
and watch—
Be utterly astounded!
For *I will* work a work in
your days
Which you would not believe,
though it were told *you.*
6 For indeed I am [a]raising up
the Chal·dē'ans,
A bitter and hasty [b]nation
Which marches through the
breadth of the earth,
To possess dwelling places
that are not theirs.
7 They are terrible and
dreadful;
Their judgment and their
dignity proceed from
themselves.
8 Their horses also are
[a]swifter than leopards,
And more fierce than
evening wolves.
Their [1]chargers [2]charge
ahead;
Their cavalry comes from
afar;
They fly as the [b]eagle *that*
hastens to eat.

CHAPTER 1

1 [1]*oracle, prophecy*

2 [a]Lam. 3:8 [b]Mic. 2:1, 2; 3:1–3 [c][Job 21:5–16]

3 [1]Or *toil*

4 [a]Jer. 12:1

5 [a]Is. 29:14

6 [a]2 Kin. 24:2 [b]Ezek. 7:24; 21:31

8 [a]Jer. 4:13 [b]Hos. 8:1 [1]Lit. *horsemen* [2]Lit. *spring about*

9 "They all come for violence;
Their faces are set *like* the
east wind.
They gather captives like
sand.
10 They scoff at kings,
And princes are scorned by
them.
They deride every
stronghold,
For they heap up earthen
mounds and seize it.
11 Then *his* [1]mind changes, and
he transgresses;
He commits offense,
[a]*Ascribing* this power to his
god."

12 Are You not [a]from
everlasting,
O LORD my God, my Holy
One?
We shall not die.
O LORD, [b]You have
appointed them for
judgment;
O Rock, You have marked
them for [c]correction.
13 *You are* of purer eyes than
to behold evil,
And cannot look on
wickedness.
Why do You look on those
who deal treacherously,
And hold Your tongue when
the wicked devours
A *person* more righteous
than he?
14 *Why* do You make men like
fish of the sea,
Like creeping things *that*
have no ruler over them?

15 They take up all of them
with a hook,
They catch them in their net,
And gather them in their
dragnet.
Therefore they rejoice and
are glad.
16 Therefore [a]they sacrifice to
their net,
And burn incense to their
dragnet;
Because by them their share
is [1]sumptuous
And their food plentiful.
17 Shall they therefore empty
their net,
And continue to slay nations
without pity?

2 I will [a]stand my watch
And set myself on the
rampart,
And watch to see what He
will say to me,
And what I will answer
when I am corrected.

2 Then the LORD answered me
and said:

[a]"Write the vision
And make *it* plain on
tablets,
That he may run who reads
it.
3 For [a]the vision *is* yet for an
appointed time;
But at the end it will speak,
and it will [b]not lie.
Though it tarries, [c]wait for
it;
Because it will [d]surely come,
It will not tarry.

4 "Behold the proud,
His soul is not upright in
him;
But the [a]just shall live by his
faith.

5 "Indeed, because he
transgresses by wine,
He is a proud man,

11 [a]Dan. 5:4
[1]Lit. *spirit* or *wind*

12 [a]Ps. 90:2; 93:2
[b]Is. 10:5–7
[c]Jer. 25:9

16 [a]Deut. 8:17
[1]Lit. *fat*

CHAPTER 2

1 [a]Is. 21:8, 11

2 [a]Is. 8:1

3 [a]Dan. 8:17, 19; 10:14
[b]Ezek. 12:24, 25
[c][Heb. 10:37, 38]
[d][2 Pet. 3:9]

4 [a][John 3:36]; Rom. 1:17

And he does not stay at home.
Because he [a]enlarges his desire as [1]hell,
And he *is* like death, and cannot be satisfied,
He gathers to himself all nations
And heaps up for himself all peoples.

6 "Will not all these [a]take up a proverb against him,
And a taunting riddle against him, and say,
'Woe to him who increases
What is not his—how long?
And to him who loads himself with [1]many pledges'?
7 Will not [1]your creditors rise up suddenly?
Will they not awaken who oppress you?
And you will become their booty.
8 [a]Because you have plundered many nations,
All the remnant of the people shall plunder you,
Because of men's [1]blood
And the violence of the land *and* the city,
And of all who dwell in it.

9 "Woe to him who covets evil gain for his house,
That he may [a]set his nest on high,
That he may be delivered from the [1]power of disaster!
10 You give shameful counsel to your house,
Cutting off many peoples,
And sin *against* your soul.
11 For the stone will cry out from the wall,
And the beam from the timbers will answer it.

12 "Woe to him who builds a town with bloodshed,
Who establishes a city by iniquity!
13 Behold, *is it* not of the LORD of hosts
That the peoples labor [1]to feed the fire,
And nations weary themselves in vain?
14 For the earth will be filled
With the knowledge of the glory of the LORD,
As the waters cover the sea.

15 "Woe to him who gives drink to his neighbor,
[1]Pressing *him to* your [a]bottle,
Even to make *him* drunk,
That you may look on [2]his nakedness!
16 You are filled with shame instead of glory.
You also—drink!
And [1]be exposed as uncircumcised!
The cup of the LORD's right hand *will be* turned against you,
And utter shame will be on your glory.
17 For the violence *done to* Lebanon will cover you,
And the plunder of beasts *which* made them afraid,
Because of men's blood
And the violence of the land *and* the city,
And of all who dwell in it.

18 "What profit is the image, that its maker should carve it,
The molded image, a teacher of lies,

5 [a]Is. 5:11–15 [1]Or *Sheol*
6 [a]Mic. 2:4 [1]Syr., Vg. *thick clay*
7 [1]Lit. *those who bite you*
8 [a]Is. 33:1 [1]Or *bloodshed*
9 [a]Obad. 4 [1]Lit. *hand of evil*
13 [1]Lit. *for what satisfies fire,* for what is of no lasting value
15 [a]Hos. 7:5 [1]Lit. *Attaching* or *Joining* [2]Lit. *their*
16 [1]DSS, LXX *reel!*; Syr., Vg. *fall fast asleep!*

That the maker of its mold
should trust in it,
To make mute idols?
19 Woe to him who says to
wood, 'Awake!'
To silent stone, 'Arise! It
shall teach!'
Behold, it is overlaid with
gold and silver,
Yet in it there is no breath
at all.

20 "But[a] the LORD is in His holy
temple.
Let all the earth keep
silence before Him."

3

A prayer of Ha·bak'kuk the
prophet, on [1]Shig·i·ōn'oth.

2 O LORD, I have heard Your
speech *and* was afraid;
O LORD, revive Your work in
the midst of the years!
In the midst of the years
make *it* known;
In wrath remember mercy.

3 God came from Tē'man,
The Holy One from Mount
Par'an. Sē'lah

His glory covered the
heavens,
And the earth was full of
His praise.
4 *His* brightness was like the
light;
He had rays *flashing* from
His hand,
And there His power *was*
hidden.
5 Before Him went pestilence,
And fever followed at His
feet.

6 He stood and measured the
earth;
He looked and startled the
nations.
[a]And the everlasting
mountains were
scattered,
The perpetual hills bowed.
His ways *are* everlasting.
7 I saw the tents of Cūsh'an in
affliction;
The curtains of the land of
Mid'i·an trembled.

8 O LORD, were *You* displeased
with the rivers,
Was Your anger against the
rivers,
Was Your wrath against the
sea,
That You rode on Your
horses,
Your chariots of salvation?
9 Your bow was made quite
ready;
Oaths were sworn over *Your*
[1]arrows. Sē'lah

You divided the earth with
rivers.
10 The mountains saw You *and*
trembled;
The overflowing of the
water passed by.
The deep uttered its voice,
And [a]lifted its hands on
high.
11 The [a]sun and moon stood
still in their habitation;
At the light of Your arrows
they went,
At the shining of Your
glittering spear.

12 You marched through the
land in indignation;
You [1]trampled the nations in
anger.
13 You went forth for the
salvation of Your people,

20 [a]Zeph. 1:7

CHAPTER 3

1 [1]Exact meaning unknown

6 [a]Nah. 1:5

9 [1]Lit. *tribes* or *rods*, cf. v. 14

10 [a]Ex. 14:22

11 [a]Josh. 10:12–14

12 [1]Or *threshed*

For salvation with Your
Anointed.
You struck the head from
the house of the wicked,
By laying bare from
foundation to neck.
Sē′lah

14 You thrust through with his
own arrows
The head of his villages.
They came out like a
whirlwind to scatter me;
Their rejoicing was like
feasting on the poor in
secret.
15 [a]You walked through the sea
with Your horses,
Through the heap of great
waters.

16 When I heard, [a]my body
trembled;
My lips quivered at *the* voice;
Rottenness entered my
bones;
And I trembled in myself,
That I might rest in the day
of trouble.
When he comes up to the
people,
He will invade them with
his troops.

17 Though the fig tree may not
blossom,
Nor fruit be on the vines;
Though the labor of the
olive may fail,
And the fields yield no food;
Though the flock may be cut
off from the fold,
And there be no herd in the
stalls—
18 Yet I will [a]rejoice in the
LORD,
I will joy in the God of my
salvation.

19 [1]The LORD God is my
strength;
He will make my feet like
[a]deer's *feet*,
And He will make me [b]walk
on my high hills.

To the Chief Musician. With
my stringed instruments.

15 [a]Ps. 77:19

16 [a]Ps. 119:120

18 [a]Is. 41:16; 61:10

19 [a]2 Sam. 22:34 [b]Deut. 32:13; 33:29 [1]Heb. *YHWH Adonai*

The Book of

ZEPHANIAH

DURING Judah's hectic political and religious history, reform comes from time to time. Zephaniah's forceful prophecy may be a factor in the reform that occurs during Josiah's reign—a "revival" that produces outward change, but does not fully remove the inward heart of corruption which characterizes the nation. Zephaniah hammers home his message repeatedly that the day of the Lord, Judgment Day, is coming when the malignancy of sin will be dealt with. Israel and her gentile neighbors will soon experience the crushing hand of God's wrath. But after the chastening process is complete, blessing will come in the person of the Messiah, who will be the cause for praise and singing.

Tsephan-yah means "Yahweh Hides" or "Yahweh Has Hidden." Zephaniah was evidently born during the latter part of the reign of King Manasseh. His name may mean that he was "hidden" from Manasseh's atrocities. The Greek and Latin title is *Sophonias*.

CHAPTER 1

THE word of the LORD which came to Zeph·a·nī′ah the son of Cū′shī, the son of Ged·a·lī′ah, the son of Am·a·rī′ah, the son of Hez·e·kī′ah, in the days of [a]Jō·sī′ah the son of Ā′mon, king of Judah.

2 "I will [1]utterly consume everything
From the face of the land,"
Says the LORD;
3 "I[a] will consume man and beast;
I will consume the birds of the heavens,
The fish of the sea,
And the [1]stumbling blocks along with the wicked.
I will cut off man from the face of the [2]land,"
Says the LORD.

4 "I will stretch out My hand against Judah,
And against all the inhabitants of Jerusalem.
[1]I will cut off every trace of Bā′al from this place,
The names of the [a]idolatrous[2] priests with the *pagan* priests—
5 Those [a]who worship the host of heaven on the housetops;
Those who worship and swear *oaths* by the LORD,
But who *also* swear [b]by [1]Mil′com;
6 [a]Those who have turned back from *following* the LORD,
And [b]have not sought the LORD, nor inquired of Him."

7 [a]Be silent in the presence of the Lord GOD;
[b]For the day of the LORD *is* at hand,
For [c]the LORD has prepared a sacrifice;
He has [1]invited His guests.

8 "And it shall be,
In the day of the LORD's sacrifice,

1 [a]2 Kin. 22:1, 2
2 [1]Lit. *make a complete end of,* Jer. 8:13
3 [a]Hos. 4:3 [1]Idols [2]*ground*
4 [a]Hos. 10:5 [1]Fulfilled in 2 Kin. 23:4, 5 [2]Heb. *chemarim*
5 [a]2 Kin. 23:12 [b]Josh. 23:7 [1]Or *Malcam,* an Ammonite god, 1 Kin. 11:5; Jer. 49:1; *Molech,* Lev. 18:21
6 [a]Is. 1:4 [b]Hos. 7:7
7 [a]Zech. 2:13 [b]Is. 13:6 [c]Jer. 46:10 [1]Lit. *set apart, consecrated*

That I will punish [a]the
princes and the king's
children,
And all such as are clothed
with foreign apparel.
9 In the same day I will punish
All those who [a]leap over the
threshold,
Who fill their masters'
houses with violence and
deceit.

10 "And there shall be on that
day," says the LORD,
"The sound of a mournful cry
from [a]the Fish Gate,
A wailing from the Second
Quarter,
And a loud crashing from
the hills.
11 [a]Wail, you inhabitants of
[1]Mak'tesh!
For all the merchant people
are cut down;
All those who handle money
are cut off.

12 "And it shall come to pass at
that time
That I will search Jerusalem
with lamps,
And punish the men
Who are [a]settled[1] in
complacency,
[b]Who say in their heart,
'The LORD will not do good,
Nor will He do evil.'
13 Therefore their goods shall
become booty,
And their houses a
desolation;
They shall build houses, but
not inhabit *them;*
They shall plant vineyards,
but [a]not drink their wine."

14 [a]The great day of the LORD *is*
near;
It is near and hastens
quickly.
The noise of the day of the
LORD is bitter;
There the mighty men shall
cry out.
15 [a]That day *is* a day of wrath,
A day of trouble and
distress,
A day of devastation and
desolation,
A day of darkness and
gloominess,
A day of clouds and thick
darkness,
16 A day of [a]trumpet and alarm
Against the fortified cities
And against the high towers.

17 "I will bring distress upon
men,
And they shall [a]walk like
blind men,
Because they have sinned
against the LORD;
Their blood shall be poured
out like dust,
And their flesh like refuse."

18 [a]Neither their silver nor their
gold
Shall be able to deliver
them
In the day of the LORD's
wrath;
But the whole land shall be
devoured
By the fire of His jealousy,
For He will make speedy
riddance
Of all those who dwell in the
land.

2 Gather[a] yourselves together,
yes, gather together,
O [1]undesirable nation,
2 Before the decree is issued,
Or the day passes like chaff,

8 [a]Jer. 39:6
9 [a]1 Sam. 5:5
10 [a]2 Chr. 33:14
11 [a]James 5:1 [1]A market district of Jerusalem, lit. *Mortar*
12 [a]Jer. 48:11 [b]Ps. 94:7 [1]Lit. *on their lees;* like the dregs of wine
13 [a]Deut. 28:39
14 [a]Joel 2:1, 11
15 [a]Is. 22:5
16 [a]Jer. 4:19
17 [a]Deut. 28:29
18 [a]Ezek. 7:19

CHAPTER 2
1 [a]Joel 1:14; 2:16 [1]Or *shameless*

Before the LORD's fierce
anger comes upon you,
Before the day of the LORD's
anger comes upon you!
3 [a]Seek the LORD, [b]all you
meek of the earth,
Who have upheld His
justice.
Seek righteousness, seek
humility.
[c]It may be that you will be
hidden
In the day of the LORD's
anger.

4 For [a]Gā'za shall be forsaken,
And Ash'ke·lon desolate;
They shall drive out Ash'dod
[b]at noonday,
And Ek'ron shall be
uprooted.
5 Woe to the inhabitants of
[a]the seacoast,
The nation of the
Cher'e·thītes!
The word of the LORD *is*
against you,
O [b]Cā'naan, land of the
Phi·lis'tines:
"I will destroy you;
So there shall be no
inhabitant."

6 The seacoast shall be
pastures,
With [1]shelters for shepherds
[a]and folds for flocks.
7 The coast shall be for [a]the
remnant of the house of
Judah;
They shall feed *their* flocks
there;
In the houses of Ash'ke·lon
they shall lie down at
evening.
For the LORD their God will
[b]intervene[1] for them,
And [c]return their captives.

3 [a]Amos 5:6
[b]Ps. 76:9
[c]Amos 5:14, 15

4 [a]Zech. 9:5
[b]Jer. 6:4

5 [a]Ezek. 25:15–17
[b]Josh. 13:3

6 [a]Is. 17:2
[1]Underground huts or cisterns, lit. *excavations*

7 [a][Mic. 5:7, 8]
[b]Luke 1:68
[c]Jer. 29:14
[1]Lit. *visit them*

8 [a]Jer. 48:27
[b]Ezek. 25:3
[c]Jer. 49:1

9 [a]Is. 15:1–9
[b]Amos 1:13
[c]Deut. 29:23
[1]Lit. *Possessed by nettles*
[2]Or *permanent ruin*

10 [a]Is. 16:6

11 [a]Mal. 1:11
[b]Gen. 10:5

12 [a]Is. 18:1–7
[b]Ps. 17:13

13 [a]Is.10:5–27; 14:24–27

8 "I[a] have heard the reproach of
Mō'ab,
And [b]the insults of the
people of Am'mon,
With which they have
reproached My people,
And [c]made arrogant threats
against their borders.
9 Therefore, as I live,"
Says the LORD of hosts, the
God of Israel,
"Surely [a]Mō'ab shall be like
Sod'om,
And [b]the people of Am'mon
like Go·mor'rah—
[c]Overrun[1] with weeds and
saltpits,
And a [2]perpetual desolation.
The residue of My people
shall plunder them,
And the remnant of My
people shall possess
them."

10 This they shall have [a]for
their pride,
Because they have
reproached and made
arrogant threats
Against the people of the
LORD of hosts.
11 The LORD *will be* awesome to
them,
For He will reduce to
nothing all the gods of
the earth;
[a]*People* shall worship Him,
Each one from his place,
Indeed all [b]the shores of the
nations.

12 "You[a] Ethiopians also,
You shall be slain by [b]My
sword."

13 And He will stretch out His
hand against the north,
[a]Destroy Assyria,

And make Nin′e·veh a
desolation,
As dry as the wilderness.
14 The herds shall lie down in
her midst,
[a]Every beast of the nation.
Both the [b]pelican and the
bittern
Shall lodge on the capitals *of*
her *pillars;*
Their voice shall sing in the
windows;
Desolation *shall be* at the
threshold;
For He will lay bare the
[c]cedar work.
15 This is the rejoicing city
[a]That dwelt securely,
[b]That said in her heart,
"I *am it,* and *there is* none
besides me."
How has she become a
desolation,
A place for beasts to lie
down!
Everyone who passes by her
[c]Shall hiss and [d]shake his fist.

CHAPTER 3

3 Woe to her who is rebellious
and polluted,
To the oppressing city!
2 She has not obeyed *His*
voice,
She has not received
correction;
She has not trusted in the
LORD,
She has not drawn near to
her God.

3 [a]Her princes in her midst *are*
roaring lions;
Her judges *are* [b]evening
wolves
That leave not a bone till
morning.
4 Her [a]prophets are insolent,
treacherous people;
Her priests have [1]polluted
the sanctuary,
They have done [b]violence to
the law.
5 The LORD *is* righteous in her
midst,
He will do no
unrighteousness.
[1]Every morning He brings
His justice to light;
He never fails,
But [a]the unjust knows no
shame.

6 "I have cut off nations,
Their fortresses are
devastated;
I have made their streets
desolate,
With none passing by.
Their cities are destroyed;
There is no one, no
inhabitant.
7 [a]I said, 'Surely you will fear
Me,
You will receive
instruction'—
So that her dwelling would
not be cut off,
Despite everything for which
I punished her.
But [1]they rose early and
[b]corrupted all their deeds.

8 "Therefore [a]wait for Me," says
the LORD,
"Until the day I rise up [1]for
plunder;
My determination *is* to
[b]gather the nations
To My assembly of
kingdoms,
To pour on them My
indignation,
All My fierce anger;
All the earth [c]shall be
devoured
With the fire of My jealousy.

14 [a]Is. 13:21 [b]Is. 14:23; 34:11 [c]Jer. 22:14

15 [a]Is. 47:8 [b]Rev. 18:7 [c]Lam. 2:15 [d]Nah. 3:19

3 [a]Ezek. 22:27 [b]Hab. 1:8

4 [a]Hos. 9:7 [b]Ezek. 22:26 [1]Or *profaned*

5 [a]Jer. 3:3 [1]Lit. *Morning by morning*

7 [a]Jer. 8:6 [b]Gen. 6:12 [1]They were eager

8 [a]Hab. 2:3 [b]Joel 3:2 [c]Zeph. 1:18 [1]LXX, Syr. *for witness;* Tg. *for the day of My revelation for judgment;* Vg. *for the day of My resurrection that is to come*

9 "For then I will restore to
the peoples [a]a pure
[1]language,
That they all may call on the
name of the LORD,
To serve Him with one
accord.
10 [a]From beyond the rivers of
Ethiopia
My worshipers,
The daughter of My
dispersed ones,
Shall bring My offering.
11 In that day you shall not be
shamed for any of your
deeds
In which you transgress
against Me;
For then I will take away
from your midst
Those who [a]rejoice in your
pride,
And you shall no longer be
haughty
In My holy mountain.
12 I will leave in your midst
[a]A meek and humble people,
And they shall trust in the
name of the LORD.
13 [a]The remnant of Israel [b]shall
do no unrighteousness
[c]And speak no lies,
Nor shall a deceitful tongue
be found in their mouth;
For [d]they shall feed *their*
flocks and lie down,
And no one shall make *them*
afraid."

14 [a]Sing, O daughter of Zion!
Shout, O Israel!
Be glad and rejoice with all
your heart,
O daughter of Jerusalem!
15 The LORD has taken away
your judgments,
He has cast out your enemy.
[a]The King of Israel, the LORD,
[b]*is* in your midst;
You shall [1]see disaster no
more.

16 In that day [a]it shall be said to
Jerusalem:
"Do not fear;
Zion, [b]let not your hands be
weak.
17 The LORD your God [a]in your
midst,
The Mighty One, will save;
[b]He will rejoice over you with
gladness,
He will quiet *you* with His
love,
He will rejoice over you with
singing."

18 "I will gather those who
[a]sorrow over the
appointed assembly,
Who are among you,
To whom its reproach *is* a
burden.
19 Behold, at that time
I will deal with all who
afflict you;
I will save the [a]lame,
And gather those who were
driven out;
I will appoint them for praise
and fame
In every land where they
were put to shame.
20 At that time [a]I will bring you
back,
Even at the time I gather
you;
For I will give you [1]fame and
praise
Among all the peoples of the
earth,
When I return your captives
before your eyes,"
Says the LORD.

9 [a]Is. 19:18; 57:19 [1]Lit. *lip*
10 [a]Ps. 68:31
11 [a]Is. 2:12; 5:15
12 [a]Is. 14:32
13 [a][Mic. 4:7] [b]Is. 60:21 [c]Rev. 14:5 [d]Ezek. 34:13–15, 28
14 [a]Is. 12:6
15 [a][John 1:49] [b]Ezek. 48:35 [1]So with Heb. mss., LXX, Bg.; MT, Vg. *fear*
16 [a]Is. 35:3, 4 [b]Heb. 12:12
17 [a]Zeph. 3:5, 15 [b]Is. 62:5; 65:19
18 [a]Lam. 2:6
19 [a][Mic. 4:6, 7]
20 [a]Is. 11:12 [1]Lit. *a name*

The Book of HAGGAI

WITH the Babylonian exile in the past, and a newly returned group of Jews back in the land, the work of rebuilding the temple can begin. However, sixteen years after the process is begun, the people have yet to finish the project, for their personal affairs have interfered with God's business. Haggai preaches a fiery series of sermonettes designed to stir up the nation to finish the temple. He calls the builders to renewed courage in the Lord, renewed holiness of life, and renewed faith in God who controls the future.

The etymology and meaning of *Haggay* is uncertain, but it is probably derived from the Hebrew word *hag*, "festival." It may also be an abbreviated form of *haggiah*, "festival of Yahweh." Thus, Haggai's name means "Festal" or "Festive," possibly because he was born on the day of a major feast, such as Tabernacles (Haggai's second message takes place during that feast, 2:1). The title in the Septuagint is *Aggaios* and in the Vulgate it is *Aggaeus*.

IN [a]the second year of King
Da·rī′us, in the sixth month, on
the first day of the month, the
word of the LORD came by
[b]Hag′gaī the prophet to [c]Ze-
rub′ba·bel the son of She·al′-
ti·el, governor of Judah, and to
[d]Joshua the son of [e]Je·hoz′a·dak,
the high priest, saying,
2 "Thus speaks the LORD of
hosts, saying: 'This people says,
"The time has not come, the time
that the LORD's house should be
built." ' "
3 Then the word of the LORD
[a]came by Hag′gaī the prophet,
saying,
4 "*Is it* [a]time for you yourselves
to dwell in your paneled houses,
and this [1]temple *to lie* in ruins?"
5 Now therefore, thus says the
LORD of hosts: [a]"Consider your
ways!

6 "You have [a]sown much, and
bring in little;
You eat, but do not have
enough;
You drink, but you are not
filled with drink;
You clothe yourselves, but
no one is warm;
And [b]he who earns wages,
Earns wages *to put* into a
bag with holes."

7 Thus says the LORD of hosts:
"Consider your ways!
8 "Go up to the [a]mountains
and bring wood and build the
[1]temple, that I may take pleasure
in it and be glorified," says the
LORD.
9 [a]"*You* looked for much, but
indeed *it came to* little; and when
you brought it home, [b]I blew it
away. Why?" says the LORD of
hosts. "Because of My house that
is in ruins, while every one of you
runs to his own house.
10 "Therefore [a]the heavens
above you withhold the dew, and
the earth withholds its fruit.
11 "For I [a]called for a drought on
the land and the mountains, on
the grain and the new wine and

CHAPTER 1

1 [a]Ezra 4:24 [b]Ezra 5:1; 6:14 [c]Ezra 2:2 [d]Ezra 5:2, 3 [e]1 Chr. 6:15

3 [a]Ezra 5:1

4 [a]2 Sam. 7:2 [1]Lit. *house*

5 [a]Lam. 3:40

6 [a]Deut. 28:38–40 [b]Zech. 8:10

8 [a]Ezra 3:7 [1]Lit. *house*

9 [a]Hag. 2:16 [b]Hag. 2:17

10 [a]Deut. 28:23

11 [a]1 Kin. 17:1

the oil, on whatever the ground
brings forth, on men and livestock, and on [b]all the labor of
your hands."
12 [a]Then Ze·rub′ba·bel the son
of She·al′ti·el, and Joshua the
son of Je·hoz′a·dak, the high
priest, with all the remnant of
the people, obeyed the voice
of the LORD their God, and the
words of Hag′gaī the prophet,
as the LORD their God had sent
him; and the people feared the
presence of the LORD.
13 Then Hag′gaī, the LORD's messenger, spoke the LORD's message
to the people, saying, [a]"I *am* with
you, says the LORD."
14 So [a]the LORD stirred up the
spirit of Ze·rub′ba·bel the son of
She·al′ti·el, [b]governor of Judah,
and the spirit of Joshua the son
of Je·hoz′a·dak, the high priest,
and the spirit of all the remnant
of the people; [c]and they came
and worked on the house of the
LORD of hosts, their God,
15 on the twenty-fourth day of
the sixth month, in the second
year of King Da·rī′us.

2 In the seventh *month,* on the
twenty-first of the month,
the word of the LORD came [1]by
Hag′gaī the prophet, saying:
2 "Speak now to Ze·rub′ba·bel
the son of She·al′ti·el, governor
of Judah, and to Joshua the son
of Je·hoz′a·dak, the high priest,
and to the remnant of the people, saying:
3 [a]'Who is left among you who
saw this [1]temple in its former
glory? And how do you see it
now? In comparison with it, [b]*is
this* not in your eyes as nothing?
4 'Yet now [a]be strong, Ze·rub′-
ba·bel,' says the LORD; 'and be
strong, Joshua, son of Je·hoz′-
a·dak, the high priest; and be
strong, all you people of the
land,' says the LORD, 'and work;
for I *am* with you,' says the LORD
of hosts.
5 [a]'*According to* the word that
I covenanted with you when
you came out of Egypt, so [b]My
Spirit remains among you; do
not fear!'
6 "For thus says the LORD of
hosts: [a]'Once more (it *is* a little
while) [b]I will shake heaven and
earth, the sea and dry land;
7 'and I will shake all nations,
and they shall come to [a]the [1]De-
sire of All Nations, and I will fill
this [2]temple with [b]glory,' says the
LORD of hosts.
8 'The silver *is* Mine, and the
gold *is* Mine,' says the LORD of
hosts.
9 [a]'The glory of this latter
[1]temple shall be greater than the
former,' says the LORD of hosts.
'And in this place I will give
[b]peace,' says the LORD of hosts."
10 On the twenty-fourth *day* of
the ninth *month,* in the second
year of Da·rī′us, the word of
the LORD came by Hag′gaī the
prophet, saying,
11 "Thus says the LORD of hosts:
'Now, [a]ask the priests *concerning the* law, saying,
12 "If one carries holy meat in
the fold of his garment, and
with the edge he touches bread
or stew, wine or oil, or any food,
will it become holy?" '" Then
the priests answered and said,
"No."
13 And Hag′gaī said, "If *one
who is* [a]unclean *because* of a
dead body touches any of these,
will it be unclean?" So the priests
answered and said, "It shall be
unclean."

11 [b]Hag. 2:17
12 [a]Ezra 5:2
13 [a][Matt. 28:20]
14 [a]Ezra 1:1 [b]Hag. 2:21 [c]Ezra 5:2, 8

CHAPTER 2

1 [1]Lit. *by the hand of*
3 [a]Ezra 3:12, 13 [b]Zech. 4:10 [1]Lit. *house*
4 [a]Zech. 8:9
5 [a]Ex. 29:45, 46 [b][Neh. 9:20]
6 [a]Heb. 12:26 [b][Joel 3:16]
7 [a]Gen. 49:10 [b]Is. 60:7 [1]Or *desire of all nations* [2]Lit. *house*
9 [a][John 1:14] [b]Ps. 85:8, 9 [1]Lit. *house*
11 [a]Mal. 2:7
13 [a]Num. 19:11, 22

14 Then Hag′gai answered and
said, [a]" 'So is this people, and so
is this nation before Me,' says
the LORD, 'and so is every work
of their hands; and what they
offer there is unclean.
15 'And now, carefully [a]consider
from this day forward: from before stone was laid upon stone
in the temple of the LORD—
16 'since those *days,* [a]when *one*
came to a heap of twenty ephahs,
there were *but* ten; when *one*
came to the wine vat to draw out
fifty baths from the press, there
were *but* twenty.
17 [a]'I struck you with blight and
mildew and hail [b]in all the labors of your hands; [c]yet you did
not *turn* to Me,' says the LORD.
18 'Consider now from this day
forward, from the twenty-fourth
day of the ninth month, from
[a]the day that the foundation of
the LORD's temple was laid—
consider it:
19 [a]'Is the seed still in the barn?
As yet the vine, the fig tree, the
pomegranate, and the olive tree
have not yielded *fruit. But* from
this day I will [b]bless *you.*' "
20 And again the word of the
LORD came to Hag′gai on the
twenty-fourth day of the month,
saying,
21 "Speak to Ze·rub′ba·bel, [a]gov-
ernor of Judah, saying:

[b]'I will shake heaven and
earth.
22 [a]I will overthrow the throne
of kingdoms;
I will destroy the strength of
the Gentile kingdoms.
[b]I will overthrow the chariots
And those who ride in them;
The horses and their riders
shall come down,
Every one by the sword of
his brother.

23 'In that day,' says the LORD of
hosts, 'I will take you, Ze·rub′-
ba·bel My servant, the son of
She·al′ti·el,' says the LORD, [a]'and
will make you like a signet *ring;*
for [b]I have chosen you,' says the
LORD of hosts."

14 [a][Titus 1:15]
15 [a]Hag. 1:5, 7; 2:18
16 [a]Zech. 8:10
17 [a]Deut. 28:22 [b]Hag. 1:11 [c]Amos 4:6–11
18 [a]Zech. 8:9
19 [a]Zech. 8:12 [b][Mal. 3:10]
21 [a]Zech. 4:6–10 [b]Hag. 2:6, 7
22 [a][Dan. 2:44] [b]Mic. 5:10
23 [a]Song 8:6 [b]Is. 42:1; 43:10

The Book of

ZECHARIAH

FOR a dozen years or more, the task of rebuilding the temple has been half completed. Zechariah is commissioned by God to encourage the people in their unfinished responsibility. Rather than exhorting them to action with strong words of rebuke, Zechariah seeks to encourage them to action by reminding them of the future importance of the temple. The temple must be built, for one day the Messiah's glory will inhabit it. But future blessing is contingent upon present obedience. The people are not merely building a building; they are building the future. With that as their motivation, they can enter into the building project with wholehearted zeal, for their Messiah is coming.

Zekar-yah means "Yahweh Remembers" or "Yahweh Has Remembered." This theme dominates the whole book: Israel will be blessed because Yahweh remembers the covenant He made with the fathers. The Greek and Latin version of his name is *Zacharias*.

CHAPTER 1

IN the eighth month [a]of the second year of Da·rī′us, the word
of the LORD came [b]to Zech·a·rī′ah
the son of Ber·e·chī′ah, the son
of [c]Id′dō the prophet, saying,
2 "The LORD has been very angry with your fathers.
3 "Therefore say to them, 'Thus
says the LORD of hosts: "Return
[a]to Me," says the LORD of hosts,
"and I will return to you," says
the LORD of hosts.
4 "Do not be like your fathers,
[a]to whom the former prophets
preached, saying, 'Thus says the
LORD of hosts: [b]"Turn now from
your evil ways and your evil
deeds." ' But they did not hear
nor heed Me," says the LORD.

5 "Your fathers, where *are*
they?
And the prophets, do they
live forever?
6 Yet surely [a]My words and
My statutes,
Which I commanded My
servants the prophets,
Did they not overtake your
fathers?

"So they returned and said:

[b]'Just as the LORD of hosts
determined to do to us,
According to our ways and
according to our deeds,
So He has dealt with us.' " ' "

7 On the twenty-fourth day of
the eleventh month, which is the
month She·bat′, in the second
year of Da·rī′us, the word of the
LORD came to Zech·a·rī′ah the
son of Ber·e·chī′ah, the son of
Id′dō the prophet:
8 I saw by night, and behold, [a]a
man riding on a red horse, and it
stood among the myrtle trees in
the hollow; and behind him *were*
[b]horses: red, sorrel, and white.
9 Then I said, [a]"My lord, what
are these?" So the angel who
talked with me said to me, "I will
show you what they *are*."
10 And the man who stood

1 [a]Zech. 7:1 [b]Matt. 23:35 [c]Neh. 12:4, 16
3 [a][Mal. 3:7–10]
4 [a]2 Chr. 36:15, 16 [b]Is. 31:6
6 [a][Is. 55:11] [b]Lam. 1:18; 2:17
8 [a][Rev. 6:4] [b][Zech. 6:2–7]
9 [a]Zech. 4:4, 5, 13; 6:4

among the myrtle trees answered and said, [a]"These *are the ones* whom the LORD has sent to walk to and fro throughout the earth."
11 [a]So they answered the Angel of the LORD, who stood among the myrtle trees, and said, "We have walked to and fro throughout the earth, and behold, all the earth is [1]resting quietly."
12 Then the Angel of the LORD answered and said, "O LORD of hosts, [a]how long will You not have mercy on Jerusalem and on the cities of Judah, against which You were angry [b]these seventy years?"
13 And the LORD answered the angel who talked to me, *with* [a]good *and* comforting words.
14 So the angel who spoke with me said to me, [1]"Proclaim, saying, 'Thus says the LORD of hosts:

"I am [a]zealous[2] for Jerusalem
And for Zion with great
[3]zeal.
15 I am exceedingly angry with
the nations at ease;
For [a]I was a little angry,
And they helped—*but* with
evil *intent*."

16 'Therefore thus says the LORD:

[a]"I am returning to Jerusalem
with mercy;
My [b]house [c]shall be built in
it," says the LORD of hosts,
"And [d]a *surveyor's* line shall
be stretched out over
Jerusalem." '

17 "Again proclaim, saying, 'Thus says the LORD of hosts:

"My cities shall again [1]spread
out through prosperity;
[a]The LORD will again comfort
Zion,
And [b]will again choose
Jerusalem." ' "

18 Then I raised my eyes and looked, and there *were* four [a]horns.
19 And I said to the angel who talked with me, "What *are* these?" So he answered me, [a]"These *are* the [1]horns that have scattered Judah, Israel, and Jerusalem."
20 Then the LORD showed me four craftsmen.
21 And I said, "What are these coming to do?" So he said, "These *are* the [a]horns that scattered Judah, so that no one could lift up his head; but [1]the craftsmen are coming to terrify them, to cast out the horns of the nations that [b]lifted up *their* horn against the land of Judah to scatter it."

2 Then I raised my eyes and looked, and behold, [a]a man with a measuring line in his hand.
2 So I said, "Where are you going?" And he said to me, [a]"To measure Jerusalem, to see what *is* its width and what *is* its length."
3 And there *was* the angel who talked with me, going out; and another angel was coming out to meet him,
4 who said to him, "Run, speak to this young man, saying: [a]'Jerusalem shall be inhabited *as* towns without walls, because of the multitude of men and livestock in it.
5 'For I,' says the LORD, 'will be [a]a wall of fire all around her, [b]and I will be the glory in her midst.' "
6 "Up, up! Flee [a]from the land

10 [a][Heb. 1:14]
11 [a][Ps. 103:20, 21] [1]Lit. *sitting and quiet*
12 [a]Ps. 74:10 [b]Jer. 25:11, 12; 29:10
13 [a]Jer. 29:10
14 [a]Zech. 8:2 [1]Lit. *Cry out* [2]Or *jealous* [3]Or *jealousy*
15 [a]Is. 47:6
16 [a][Zech. 2:10; 8:3] [b]Ezra 6:14, 15 [c]Is. 44:28 [d]Zech. 2:1–3
17 [a][Is. 40:1, 2; 51:3] [b]Zech. 2:12 [1]Or *overflow with good*
18 [a][Lam. 2:17]
19 [a]Ezra 4:1, 4, 7 [1]Kingdoms or powers
21 [a][Ps. 75:10] [b]Ps. 75:4, 5 [1]Lit. *these*

CHAPTER 2

1 [a]Jer. 31:39
2 [a]Rev. 11:1
4 [a]Jer. 31:27
5 [a][Is. 26:1] [b][Is. 60:19]
6 [a]Is. 48:20

of the north," says the LORD; "for
I have [b]spread you abroad like
the four winds of heaven," says
the LORD.
7 "Up, Zion! [a]Escape, you who
dwell with the daughter of Babylon."
8 For thus says the LORD of
hosts: "He sent Me after glory, to
the nations which plunder you;
for he who [a]touches you touches
the [1]apple of His eye.
9 "For surely I will [a]shake My
hand against them, and they
shall become [1]spoil for their servants. Then [b]you will know that
the LORD of hosts has sent Me.
10 [a]"Sing and rejoice, O daughter of Zion! For behold, I am
coming and I [b]will dwell in your
midst," says the LORD.
11 [a]"Many nations shall be
joined to the LORD [b]in that day,
and they shall become [c]My people. And I will dwell in your
midst. Then [d]you will know that
the LORD of hosts has sent Me to
you.
12 "And the LORD will [a]take possession of Judah as His inheritance in the Holy Land, and will
again choose Jerusalem.
13 [a]"Be silent, all flesh, before
the LORD, for He is aroused [b]from
His holy habitation!"

3 Then he showed me [a]Joshua
the high priest standing before the Angel of the LORD, and
[b]Satan[1] standing at his right hand
to oppose him.
2 And the LORD said to Satan,
[a]"The LORD rebuke you, Satan!
The LORD who [b]has chosen Jerusalem rebuke you! [c]*Is* this not a
brand plucked from the fire?"
3 Now Joshua was clothed
with [a]filthy garments, and was
standing before the Angel.

6 [b]Deut. 28:64
7 [a]Is. 48:20
8 [a]Deut. 32:10 [1]Lit. *pupil*
9 [a]Is. 19:16 [b]Zech. 4:9 [1]*booty or plunder*
10 [a]Is. 12:6 [b][Lev. 26:12]
11 [a][Is. 2:2, 3] [b]Zech. 3:10 [c]Ex. 12:49 [d]Ezek. 33:33
12 [a][Deut. 32:9]
13 [a]Hab. 2:20 [b]Ps. 68:5

CHAPTER 3

1 [a]Hag. 1:1 [b]Ps. 109:6 [1]Lit. *the Adversary*
2 [a][Jude 9] [b][Rom. 8:33] [c]Amos 4:11
3 [a]Is. 64:6
4 [a]Is. 61:10
5 [a]Ex. 29:6
7 [a]Lev. 8:35 [b]Deut. 17:9, 12 [c]Zech. 3:4
8 [a]Ps. 71:7 [b]Is. 42:1 [c]Is. 11:1; 53:2; Jer. 23:5 [1]Lit. *men of a sign* or *wonder*
9 [a][Zech. 4:10] [b]Ps. 118:22 [c]Jer. 31:34; 50:20

4 Then He answered and spoke
to those who stood before Him,
saying, "Take away the filthy
garments from him." And to him
He said, "See, I have removed
your iniquity from you, [a]and I
will clothe you with rich robes."
5 And I said, "Let them put a
clean [a]turban on his head." So
they put a clean turban on his
head, and they put the clothes
on him. And the Angel of the
LORD stood by.
6 Then the Angel of the LORD
admonished Joshua, saying,
7 "Thus says the LORD of hosts:

'If you will walk in My ways,
And if you will [a]keep My
command,
Then you shall also [b]judge
My house,
And likewise have charge of
My courts;
I will give you places to walk
Among these who [c]stand
here.

8 'Hear, O Joshua, the high
priest,
You and your companions
who sit before you,
For they are [a]a[1] wondrous
sign;
For behold, I am bringing
forth [b]My Servant the
[c]BRANCH.
9 For behold, the stone
That I have laid before
Joshua:
[a]Upon the stone *are* [b]seven
eyes.
Behold, I will engrave its
inscription,'
Says the LORD of hosts,
'And [c]I will remove the
iniquity of that land in
one day.

10 [a]In that day,' says the LORD of
hosts,
'Everyone will invite his
neighbor
[b]Under his vine and under
his fig tree.' "

4 Now [a]the angel who talked
with me came back and
wakened me, [b]as a man who is
wakened out of his sleep.
2 And he said to me, "What do
you see?" So I said, "I am looking, and there *is* [a]a lampstand
of solid gold with a bowl on top
of it, [b]and on the *stand* seven
lamps with seven pipes to the
seven lamps.
3 [a]"Two olive trees *are* by it,
one at the right of the bowl and
the other at its left."
4 So I answered and spoke
to the angel who talked with
me, saying, "What *are* these, my
lord?"
5 Then the angel who talked
with me answered and said to
me, "Do you not know what these
are?" And I said, "No, my lord."
6 So he answered and said to
me:

"This *is* the word of the LORD
to [a]Ze·rub'ba·bel:
[b]'Not by might nor by power,
but by My Spirit,'
Says the LORD of hosts.
7 'Who *are* you, [a]O great
mountain?
Before Ze·rub'ba·bel *you
shall become* a plain!
And he shall bring forth
[b]the capstone
[c]With shouts of "Grace, grace
to it!" ' "

8 Moreover the word of the
LORD came to me, saying:

10 [a]Zech. 2:11 [b]Is. 36:16

CHAPTER 4

1 [a]Zech. 1:9; 2:3 [b]Dan. 8:18

2 [a]Rev. 1:12 [b][Rev. 4:5]

3 [a]Rev. 11:3, 4

6 [a]Hag. 1:1 [b]Hos. 1:7

7 [a]Jer. 51:25 [b]Ps. 118:22 [c]Ezra 3:10, 11, 13

9 [a]Ezra 3:8–10; 5:16 [b]Ezra 6:14, 15 [c]Zech. 2:9, 11; 6:15 [d][Is. 43:16] [1]Lit. *house*

10 [a]Hag. 2:3 [b]2 Chr. 16:9 [1]Lit. *plummet stone*

11 [a]Zech. 4:3

12 [1]Lit. *into the hands of*

14 [a]Rev. 11:4 [b]Zech. 3:1–7 [1]Lit. *sons of fresh oil*

CHAPTER 5

1 [a]Ezek. 2:9

3 [a]Mal. 4:6

9 "The hands of Ze·rub'ba·bel
[a]Have laid the foundation of
this [1]temple;
His hands [b]shall also finish
it.
Then [c]you will know
That the [d]LORD of hosts has
sent Me to you.
10 For who has despised the
day of [a]small things?
For these seven rejoice to
see
The [1]plumb line in the hand
of Ze·rub'ba·bel.
[b]They are the eyes of the
LORD,
Which scan to and fro
throughout the whole
earth."

11 Then I answered and said to
him, "What *are* these [a]two olive
trees—at the right of the lampstand and at its left?"
12 And I further answered and
said to him, "What *are these* two
olive branches that *drip* [1]into
the receptacles of the two gold
pipes from which the golden *oil*
drains?"
13 Then he answered me and
said, "Do you not know what
these *are?*" And I said, "No, my
lord."
14 So he said, [a]"These *are* the
two [1]anointed ones, [b]who stand
beside the Lord of the whole
earth."

5 Then I turned and raised my
eyes, and saw there a flying
[a]scroll.
2 And he said to me, "What do
you see?" So I answered, "I see a
flying scroll. Its length *is* twenty
cubits and its width ten cubits."
3 Then he said to me, "This *is*
the [a]curse that goes out over the
face of the whole earth: 'Every

thief shall be expelled,' according *to* this side of *the scroll;* and, 'Every perjurer shall be expelled,' according *to* that side of it."

4 "I will send out *the curse,*"
says the LORD of hosts;
"It shall enter the house of
the [a]thief
And the house of [b]the one
who swears falsely by
My name.
It shall remain in the midst
of his house
And consume [c]it, with its
timber and stones."

5 Then the angel who talked
with me came out and said to
me, "Lift your eyes now, and see
what this *is* that goes forth."
6 So I asked, "What *is* it?" And
he said, "It *is* a [1]basket that is
going forth." He also said, "This
is their resemblance throughout
the earth:
7 "Here *is* a lead disc lifted
up, and this *is* a woman sitting
inside the basket";
8 then he said, "This *is* Wickedness!"
And he thrust her down
into the basket, and threw the
lead [1]cover over its mouth.
9 Then I raised my eyes and
looked, and there *were* two
women, coming with the wind in
their wings; for they had wings
like the wings of a [a]stork, and
they lifted up the basket between
earth and heaven.
10 So I said to the [a]angel who
talked with me, "Where are they
carrying the basket?"
11 And he said to me, "To [a]build
a house for it in [b]the land of [1]Shi'nar;
when it is ready, *the basket*
will be set there on its base."

4 [a]Ex. 20:15 [b]Lev. 19:12 [c]Lev. 14:34, 35

6 [1]Heb. *ephah,* a measuring container, and so elsewhere

8 [1]Lit. *stone*

9 [a]Lev. 11:13, 19

10 [a]Zech. 5:5

11 [a]Jer. 29:5, 28 [b]Gen. 10:10 [1]Babylon

CHAPTER 6

2 [a]Zech. 1:8 [b]Rev. 6:5

4 [a]Zech. 5:10

5 [a][Heb. 1:7, 14] [b]Dan. 7:10

6 [a]Jer. 1:14 [1]The chariot

7 [a]Zech. 1:10

8 [a]Eccl. 10:4

11 [a]Ex. 29:6 [1]Lit. *crowns*

6

Then I turned and raised
my eyes and looked, and behold,
four chariots *were* coming
from between two mountains,
and the mountains *were* mountains
of bronze.
2 With the first chariot *were*
[a]red horses, with the second
chariot [b]black horses,
3 with the third chariot white
horses, and with the fourth
chariot dappled horses—strong
steeds.
4 Then I answered [a]and said to
the angel who talked with me,
"What *are* these, my lord?"
5 And the angel answered and
said to me, [a]"These *are* four spirits
of heaven, who go out from
their [b]station before the Lord of
all the earth.
6 [1]"The one with the black
horses is going to [a]the north
country, the white are going after
them, and the dappled are going
toward the south country."
7 Then the strong *steeds* went
out, eager to go, that they might
[a]walk to and fro throughout the
earth. And He said, "Go, walk to
and fro throughout the earth." So
they walked to and fro throughout
the earth.
8 And He called to me, and
spoke to me, saying, "See, those
who go toward the north country
have given rest to My [a]Spirit
in the north country."
9 Then the word of the LORD
came to me, saying:
10 "Receive *the gift* from the
captives—from Hel'daī, Tō·bī'jah,
and Je·daī'ah, who have
come from Babylon—and go the
same day and enter the house of
Jō·sī'ah the son of Zeph·a·nī'ah.
11 "Take the silver and gold,
make [a]an[1] elaborate crown, and

set *it* on the head of [b]Joshua the
son of Je·hoz′a·dak, the high
priest.
☆ 12 "Then speak to him, saying,
'Thus says the LORD of hosts,
saying:

"Behold, [a]the Man whose
name *is* the [b]BRANCH!
From His place He shall
[1]branch out,
[c]And He shall build the
temple of the LORD;
☆ 13 Yes, He shall build the
temple of the LORD.
He [a]shall bear the glory,
And shall sit and rule on
His throne;
So [b]He shall be a priest on
His throne,
And the counsel of peace
shall be between [1]them
both." '

14 "Now the [1]elaborate crown
shall be [a]for a memorial in the
temple of the LORD [2]for Hē′lem,
Tō·bī′jah, Je·daī′ah, and Hen the
son of Zeph·a·nī′ah.
15 "Even [a]those from afar shall
come and build the temple of the
LORD. Then you shall know that
the LORD of hosts has sent Me to
you. And *this* shall come to pass
if you diligently obey the voice
of the LORD your God."

7 Now in the fourth year of
King Da·rī′us it came to pass
that the word of the LORD came
to Zech·a·rī′ah, on the fourth *day*
of the ninth month, Chis′lev,
2 when [1]*the people* sent [2]She-
rē′zer, with Reg′em-Mel′ech and
his men, *to* [3]the house of God,
[4]to pray before the LORD,
3 *and* to [a]ask the priests who
were in the house of the LORD of
hosts, and the prophets, saying,
"Should I weep in [b]the fifth
month and [1]fast as I have done
for so many years?"
4 Then the word of the LORD of
hosts came to me, saying,
5 "Say to all the people of the
land, and to the priests: 'When
you [a]fasted and mourned in
the fifth [b]and seventh *months*
[c]during those seventy years, did
you really fast [d]for Me—for Me?
6 [a]'When you eat and when
you drink, do you not eat and
drink *for yourselves*?
7 '*Should you* not *have obeyed*
the words which the LORD proclaimed through the [a]former
prophets when Jerusalem and
the cities around it were inhabited and prosperous, and [b]the
[1]South and the Lowland were
inhabited?' "
8 Then the word of the LORD
came to Zech·a·rī′ah, saying,
9 "Thus says the LORD of hosts:

[a]'Execute true justice,
Show [1]mercy and
compassion
Everyone to his brother.
10 [a]Do not oppress the widow
or the fatherless,
The alien or the poor.
[b]Let none of you plan evil in
his heart
Against his brother.'

11 "But they refused to heed,
[a]shrugged[1] their shoulders, and
[b]stopped[2] their ears so that they
could not hear.
12 "Yes, they made their [a]hearts
like flint, [b]refusing to hear the
law and the words which the
LORD of hosts had sent by His
Spirit through the former prophets. [c]Thus great wrath came from
the LORD of hosts.

---

11 [b]Hag. 1:1
12 [a]John 1:45 [b]Zech. 3:8 [c][Matt. 16:18; Eph. 2:20; Heb. 3:3] [1]Lit. *sprout up*
13 [a]Is. 22:24 [b]Ps. 110:4; [Heb. 3:1] [1]Both offices
14 [a]Ex. 12:14 [1]Lit. *crowns* [2]So with MT, Tg., Vg.; Syr. *for Heldai* (cf. v. 10); LXX *for the patient ones*
15 [a]Is. 57:19

CHAPTER 7

2 [1]Lit. *they*, cf. v. 5 [2]Or *Sar-Ezer* [3]Heb. *Bethel* [4]Or *to entreat the favor of*
3 [a]Mal. 2:7 [b]Zech. 8:19 [1]Lit. *consecrate myself*
5 [a][Is. 58:1–9] [b]Jer. 41:1 [c]Zech. 1:12 [d][Rom. 14:6]
6 [a]1 Chr. 29:22
7 [a]Zech. 1:4 [b]Jer. 17:26 [1]Heb. *Negev*
9 [a]Jer. 7:28 [1]Or *lovingkindness*
10 [a]Ex. 22:22 [b]Mic. 2:1
11 [a]Neh. 9:29 [b]Jer. 17:23 [1]Lit. *gave a stubborn* or *rebellious shoulder* [2]Lit. *made their ears heavy*
12 [a]Ezek. 11:19 [b]Neh. 9:29, 30 [c]Dan. 9:11, 12

13 "Therefore it happened, *that*
just as He proclaimed and they
would not hear, so [a]they called
out and I would not listen," says
the LORD of hosts.
14 "But [a]I scattered them with
a whirlwind among all the nations which they had not known.
Thus the land became desolate after them, so that no one
passed through or returned; for
they made the pleasant land
desolate."

8 Again the word of the LORD
of hosts came, saying,
2 "Thus says the LORD of hosts:

[a]'I am [1]zealous for Zion with
great [2]zeal;
With great [3]fervor I am
zealous for her.'

3 "Thus says the LORD:

[a]'I will return to Zion,
And [b]dwell in the midst of
Jerusalem.
Jerusalem [c]shall be called
the City of Truth,
[d]The Mountain of the LORD of
hosts,
[e]The Holy Mountain.'

4 "Thus says the LORD of hosts:

[a]'Old men and old women
shall again sit
In the streets of Jerusalem,
Each one with his staff in
his hand
Because of [1]great age.
5 The streets of the city
Shall be [a]full of boys and
girls
Playing in its streets.'

6 "Thus says the LORD of hosts:

'If it is [1]marvelous in the
eyes of the remnant of
this people in these days,
[a]Will it also be marvelous in
My eyes?'
Says the LORD of hosts.

7 "Thus says the LORD of hosts:

'Behold, [a]I will save My
people from the land of
the [1]east
And from the land of the
[2]west;
8 I will [a]bring them *back*,
And they shall dwell in the
midst of Jerusalem.
[b]They shall be My people
And I will be their God,
[c]In truth and righteousness.'

9 "Thus says the LORD of hosts:

[a]'Let your hands be strong,
You who have been hearing
in these days
These words by the mouth
of [b]the prophets,
Who *spoke* in [c]the day the
foundation was laid
For the house of the LORD of
hosts,
That the temple might be
built.
10 For before these days
There were no [a]wages for
man nor any hire for
beast;
There was no peace from
the enemy for whoever
went out or came in;
For I set all men, everyone,
against his neighbor.

11 [a]'But now I *will* not *treat* the
remnant of this people as in the
former days,' says the LORD of
hosts.

13 [a]Prov. 1:24–28
14 [a]Deut. 4:27; 28:64

CHAPTER 8

2 [a]Zech. 1:14 [1]Or *jealous* [2]Or *jealousy* [3]Lit. *heat* or *rage*
3 [a]Zech. 1:16 [b]Zech. 2:10, 11 [c]Is. 1:21 [d][Is. 2:2, 3] [e]Jer. 31:23
4 [a]Is. 65:20 [1]Lit. *many days*
5 [a]Jer. 30:19, 20
6 [a][Luke 1:37] [1]Or *wonderful*
7 [a]Is. 11:11 [1]Lit. *rising sun* [2]Lit. *setting sun*
8 [a]Zeph. 3:20 [b][Jer. 30:22; 31:1, 33] [c]Jer. 4:2
9 [a]Hag. 2:4 [b]Ezra 5:1, 2; 6:14 [c]Hag. 2:18
10 [a]Hag. 1:6, 9
11 [a]Hag. 2:15–19

12 'For[a] the [1]seed *shall be* prosperous,
The vine shall give its fruit,
[b]The ground shall give her increase,
And [c]the heavens shall give their dew—
I will cause the remnant of this people
To possess all these.
13 And it shall come to pass
That just as you were [a]a curse among the nations,
O house of Judah and house of Israel,
So I will save you, and [b]you shall be a blessing.
Do not fear,
Let your hands be strong.'

14 "For thus says the LORD of hosts:

[a]'Just as I determined to [1]punish you
When your fathers provoked Me to wrath,'
Says the LORD of hosts,
[b]'And I would not relent,
15 So again in these days
I am determined to do good
To Jerusalem and to the house of Judah.
Do not fear.
16 These *are* the things you shall [a]do:
[b]Speak each man the truth to his neighbor;
Give judgment in your gates for truth, justice, and peace;
17 [a]Let none of you think evil in [1]your heart against your neighbor;
And do not love a false oath.
For all these *are things* that I hate,'
Says the LORD."

12 [a]Joel 2:22 [b]Ps. 67:6 [c]Hag. 1:10 [1]Lit. *seed of peace*
13 [a]Jer. 42:18 [b]Gen. 12:2
14 [a]Jer. 31:28 [b][2 Chr. 36:16] [1]Lit. *bring calamity to you*
16 [a]Zech. 7:9, 10 [b][Eph. 4:25]
17 [a]Prov. 3:29 [1]Lit. *his*
19 [a]Jer. 52:6 [b]Jer. 52:12 [c]2 Kin. 25:25 [d]Jer. 52:4 [e]Esth. 8:17 [f]Zech. 8:16
21 [a][Is. 2:2, 3]
22 [a]Is. 60:3; 66:23
23 [a]Is. 3:6 [b][Is. 45:14] [c]1 Cor. 14:25 [1]Lit. *wing*, corner of a garment

CHAPTER 9

1 [a]Is. 17:1 [b]Amos 1:3–5 [1]*oracle, prophecy*

18 Then the word of the LORD of hosts came to me, saying,
19 "Thus says the LORD of hosts:

[a]'The fast of the fourth *month*,
[b]The fast of the fifth,
[c]The fast of the seventh,
[d]And the fast of the tenth,
Shall be [e]joy and gladness and cheerful feasts
For the house of Judah.
[f]Therefore love truth and peace.'

20 "Thus says the LORD of hosts:

'Peoples shall yet come,
Inhabitants of many cities;
21 The inhabitants of one *city* shall go to another, saying,
[a]"Let us continue to go and pray before the LORD,
And seek the LORD of hosts.
I myself will go also."
22 Yes, [a]many peoples and strong nations
Shall come to seek the LORD of hosts in Jerusalem,
And to pray before the LORD.'

23 "Thus says the LORD of hosts:
'In those days ten men [a]from
every language of the nations
shall [b]grasp the [1]sleeve of a Jewish man, saying, "Let us go with
you, for we have heard [c]*that*
God *is* with you." ' "

9

The [1]burden of the word of the LORD
Against the land of Had'rach,
And [a]Damascus its resting place
(For [b]the eyes of men
And all the tribes of Israel
Are on the LORD);

2 Also *against* [a]Hā′math,
which borders on it,
And *against* [b]Tȳre and
[c]Sī′don, though they are
very [d]wise.

3 For Tȳre built herself a
tower,
Heaped up silver like the
dust,
And gold like the mire of
the streets.
4 Behold, [a]the Lord will cast
her out;
He will destroy [b]her power
in the sea,
And she will be devoured
by fire.

5 Ash′ke·lon shall see *it* and
fear;
Gā′za also shall be very
sorrowful;
And [a]Ek′ron, for He dried
up her expectation.
The king shall perish from
Gā′za,
And Ash′ke·lon shall not be
inhabited.

6 "A[1] mixed race shall settle [a]in
Ash′dod,
And I will cut off the pride
of the [b]Phi·lis′tines.
7 I will take away the blood
from his mouth,
And the abominations from
between his teeth.
But he who remains, even
he *shall be* for our God,
And shall be like a leader in
Judah,
And Ek′ron like a Jeb′ū·sīte.
8 [a]I will camp around My
house
Because of the army,
Because of him who passes
by and him who returns.

No more shall an oppressor
pass through them,
For now I have seen with
My eyes.

9 "Rejoice [a]greatly, O daughter ☆
of Zion!
Shout, O daughter of
Jerusalem!
Behold, [b]your King is
coming to you;
He *is* just and having
salvation,
Lowly and riding on a
donkey,
A colt, the foal of a donkey.
10 I [a]will cut off the chariot
from Ē′phra·im
And the horse from
Jerusalem;
The [b]battle bow shall be cut
off.
He shall speak peace to the
nations;
His dominion *shall be* [c]'from
sea to sea,
And from the River to the
ends of the earth.'
11 "As for you also,
Because of the blood of your
covenant,
I will set your [a]prisoners
free from the waterless
pit.
12 Return to the stronghold,
[a]You prisoners of hope.
Even today I declare
That I will restore [b]double
to you.
13 For I have bent Judah, My
bow,
Fitted the bow with
Ē′phra·im,
And raised up your sons,
O Zion,
Against your sons,
O Greece,

2 [a]Jer. 49:23 [b]Is. 23 [c]1 Kin. 17:9 [d]Ezek. 28:3
4 [a]Is. 23:1 [b]Ezek. 26:17
5 [a]Zeph. 2:4, 5
6 [a]Amos 1:8 [b]Ezek. 25:15–17 [1]Lit. *An illegitimate one*
8 [a][Ps. 34:7]
9 [a]Zech. 2:10 [b][Jer. 23:5, 6]; Matt. 21:5; Mark 11:7, 9; Luke 19:35–38; John 12:15
10 [a]Hos. 1:7 [b]Hos. 2:18 [c]Ps. 72:8
11 [a]Is. 42:7
12 [a]Is. 49:9 [b]Is. 61:7

And made you like the
sword of a mighty man."

14 Then the LORD will be seen
over them,
And [a]His arrow will go forth
like lightning.
The Lord GOD will blow the
trumpet,
And go [b]with whirlwinds
from the south.
15 The LORD of hosts will
[a]defend them;
They shall devour and
subdue with slingstones.
They shall drink *and* roar as
if with wine;
They shall be filled *with
blood* like [1]basins,
Like the corners of the altar.
16 The LORD their God will
[a]save them in that day,
As the flock of His people.
For [b]they *shall be like* the
[1]jewels of a crown,
[c]Lifted like a banner over His
land—
17 For [a]how great is [1]its
goodness
And how great [1]its [b]beauty!
[c]Grain shall make the young
men thrive,
And new wine the young
women.

10

Ask [a]the LORD for [b]rain
In [c]the time of the [1]latter
rain.
The LORD will make
[2]flashing clouds;
He will give them showers
of rain,
Grass in the field for
everyone.

2 For the [a]idols[1] speak
delusion;
The diviners envision [b]lies,
And tell false dreams;
They [c]comfort in vain.
Therefore *the people* wend
their way like [d]sheep;
They are [2]in trouble
[e]because *there is* no
shepherd.

3 "My anger is kindled against
the [a]shepherds,
[b]And I will punish the
[1]goatherds.
For the LORD of hosts [c]will
visit His flock,
The house of Judah,
And [d]will make them as His
royal horse in the battle.
4 From him comes [a]the
cornerstone,
From him [b]the tent peg,
From him the battle bow,
From him every [1]ruler
together.
5 They shall be like mighty
men,
Who [a]tread down *their
enemies*
In the mire of the streets in
the battle.
They shall fight because the
LORD is with them,
And the riders on horses
shall be put to shame.

6 "I will strengthen the house
of Judah,
And I will save the house of
Joseph.
[a]I will bring them back,
Because I [b]have mercy on
them.
They shall be as though I
had not cast them aside;
For I *am* the LORD their God,
And I [c]will hear them.
7 *Those of* Ē′phra·im shall be
like a mighty man,

---

14 [a]Ps. 18:14 [b]Is. 21:1
15 [a]Zech. 12:8 [1]Sacrificial basins
16 [a]Jer. 31:10, 11 [b]Is. 62:3 [c]Is. 11:12 [1]Lit. *stones*
17 [a][Ps. 31:19] [b][Ps. 45:1–16] [c]Joel 3:18 [1]Lit. *His*

CHAPTER 10

1 [a][Jer. 14:22] [b][Deut. 11:13, 14] [c][Joel 2:23] [1]Spring rain [2]Or *lightning flashes*
2 [a]Jer. 10:8 [b]Jer. 27:9 [c]Job 13:4 [d]Jer. 50:6, 17 [e]Ezek. 34:5–8 [1]Heb. *teraphim* [2]*afflicted*
3 [a]Jer. 25:34–36 [b]Ezek. 34:17 [c]Luke 1:68 [d]Song 1:9 [1]Leaders
4 [a]Is. 28:16 [b]Is. 22:23 [1]Or *despot*
5 [a]Ps. 18:42
6 [a]Jer. 3:18 [b]Hos. 1:7 [c]Zech. 13:9

And their [a]heart shall
rejoice as if with wine.
Yes, their children shall see
it and be glad;
Their heart shall rejoice in
the LORD.
8 I will [a]whistle for them and
gather them,
For I will redeem them;
[b]And they shall increase as
they once increased.

9 "I[a] will [1]sow them among the
peoples,
And they shall [b]remember
Me in far countries;
They shall live, together
with their children,
And they shall return.
10 [a]I will also bring them back
from the land of Egypt,
And gather them from
Assyria.
I will bring them into the
land of Gil′ē·ad and
Lebanon,
[b]Until no *more room* is found
for them.
11 [a]He shall pass through the
sea with affliction,
And strike the waves of the
sea:
All the depths of [1]the River
shall dry up.
Then [b]the pride of Assyria
shall be brought down,
And [c]the scepter of Egypt
shall depart.

12 "So I will strengthen them in
the LORD,
And [a]they shall walk up and
down in His name,"
Says the LORD.

11 Open [a]your doors,
O Lebanon,
That fire may devour your
cedars.
2 Wail, O cypress, for the
[a]cedar has fallen,
Because the mighty *trees*
are ruined.
Wail, O oaks of Bā′shan,
[b]For the thick forest has
come down.
3 *There is* the sound of
wailing [a]shepherds!
For their glory is in ruins.
There is the sound of
roaring lions!
For the [1]pride of the Jordan
is in ruins.

4 Thus says the LORD my God,
"Feed the flock for slaughter,
5 "whose owners slaughter
them and [a]feel no guilt; those
who sell them [b]say, 'Blessed be
the LORD, for I am rich'; and their
shepherds do [c]not pity them.
6 "For I will no longer pity the
inhabitants of the land," says the
LORD. "But indeed I will give everyone into his neighbor's hand
and into the hand of his king.
They shall [1]attack the land, and I
will not deliver *them* from their
hand."
7 So I fed the flock for slaughter, [1]in particular [a]the poor of
the flock. I took for myself two
staffs: the one I called [2]Beauty,
and the other I called [3]Bonds;
and I fed the flock.
8 I [1]dismissed the three shepherds [a]in one month. My soul
loathed them, and their soul also
abhorred me.
9 Then I said, "I will not feed
you. [a]Let what is dying die, and
what is perishing perish. Let
those that are left eat each other's flesh."
10 And I took my staff, [1]Beauty,

7 [a]Ps. 104:15
8 [a]Is. 5:26 [b]Ezek. 36:37
9 [a]Hos. 2:23 [b]Deut. 30:1 [1]Or *scatter*
10 [a]Is. 11:11 [b]Is. 49:19, 20
11 [a]Is. 11:15 [b]Zeph. 2:13 [c]Ezek. 30:13 [1]The Nile
12 [a]Mic. 4:5

CHAPTER 11
1 [a]Zech. 10:10
2 [a]Ezek. 31:3 [b]Is. 32:19
3 [a]Jer. 25:34–36 [1]Or *floodplain, thicket*
5 [a][Jer. 2:3]; 50:7 [b]Hos. 12:8 [c]Ezek. 34:2, 3
6 [1]Lit. *strike*
7 [a]Zeph. 3:12 [1]So with MT, Tg., Vg.; LXX *for the Canaanites* [2]Or *Grace* [3]Or *Unity*
8 [a]Hos. 5:7 [1]Or *destroyed*, lit. *cut off*
9 [a]Jer. 15:2
10 [1]Or *Grace*

and cut it in two, that I might
break the covenant which I had
made with all the peoples.
11 So it was broken on that day.
Thus [a]the[1] poor of the flock, who
were watching me, knew that it
was the word of the LORD.
☆ 12 Then I said to them, "If it is
[1]agreeable to you, give *me* my
wages; and if not, refrain." So
they [a]weighed out for my wages
thirty *pieces* of silver.
☆ 13 And the LORD said to me,
"Throw it to the [a]potter"—that
princely price they set on me. So
I took the thirty *pieces* of silver
and threw them into the house
of the LORD for the potter.
14 Then I cut in two my other
staff, [1]Bonds, that I might break
the brotherhood between Judah
and Israel.
15 And the LORD said to me,
[a]"Next, take for yourself the implements of a foolish shepherd.
16 "For indeed I will raise up a
shepherd in the land *who* will
not care for those who are cut
off, nor seek the young, nor heal
those that are broken, nor feed
those that still stand. But he will
eat the flesh of the fat and tear
their hooves in [a]pieces.

17 "Woe[a] to the worthless
    shepherd,
Who leaves the flock!
A sword *shall be* against his
    arm
And against his right eye;
His arm shall completely
    wither,
And his right eye shall be
    totally blinded."

12 The [1]burden of the word
of the LORD against Is-
rael. Thus says the LORD, [a]who
stretches out the heavens, lays
the foundation of the earth, and
[b]forms the spirit of man within
him:
2 "Behold, I will make Jerusalem [a]a cup of [1]drunkenness to all
the surrounding peoples, when
they lay siege against Judah and
Jerusalem.
3 [a]"And it shall happen in that
day that I will make Jerusalem [b]a very heavy stone for all
peoples; all who would heave it
away will surely be cut in pieces,
though all nations of the earth
are gathered against it.
4 "In that day," says the LORD,
[a]"I will strike every horse with
confusion, and its rider with
madness; I will open My eyes
on the house of Judah, and will
strike every horse of the peoples
with blindness.
5 "And the governors of Judah
shall say in their heart, 'The inhabitants of Jerusalem *are* my
strength in the LORD of hosts,
their God.'
6 "In that day I will make the
governors of Judah [a]like a fire-
pan in the woodpile, and like a
fiery torch in the sheaves; they
shall devour all the surrounding
peoples on the right hand and
on the left, but Jerusalem shall
be inhabited again in her own
place—Jerusalem.
7 "The LORD will save the tents
of Judah first, so that the glory
of the house of David and the
glory of the inhabitants of Jerusalem shall not become greater
than that of Judah.
8 "In that day the LORD will
defend the inhabitants of Jerusalem; the one who is feeble
among them in that day shall
be like David, and the house of

11 [a]Zeph. 3:12 [1]So with MT, Tg., Vg.; LXX *the Canaanites*
12 [a]Ex. 21:32; Matt. 26:15; 27:9, 10 [1]*good in your sight*
13 [a]Matt. 27:3–10
14 [1]Or *Unity*
15 [a]Is. 56:11
16 [a]Ezek. 34:1–10
17 [a]Jer. 23:1

CHAPTER 12

1 [a]Is. 42:5; 44:24 [b][Is. 57:16] [1]*oracle, prophecy*
2 [a]Is. 51:17 [1]Lit. *reeling*
3 [a]Zech. 12:4, 6, 8; 13:1 [b]Matt. 21:44
4 [a]Ezek. 38:4
6 [a]Obad. 18

David *shall be* like God, like the
Angel of the LORD before them.
9 "It shall be in that day *that* I
will seek to [a]destroy all the nations that come against Jerusalem.
☆ **10** [a]"And I will pour on the house
of David and on the inhabitants
of Jerusalem the Spirit of grace
and supplication; then they will
[b]look on Me whom they pierced.
Yes, they will mourn for Him [c]as
one mourns for *his* only *son,* and
grieve for Him as one grieves for
a firstborn.
11 "In that day there shall be a
great [a]mourning in Jerusalem,
[b]like the mourning at Hā′dad
Rim′mon in the plain of [1]Me-
gid′dō.
12 [a]"And the land shall mourn,
every family by itself: the family of the house of David by
itself, and their wives by themselves; the family of the house
of [b]Nathan by itself, and their
wives by themselves;
13 "the family of the house of
Levi by itself, and their wives by
themselves; the family of Shim′-
ē·ī by itself, and their wives by
themselves;
14 "all the families that remain,
every family by itself, and their
wives by themselves.

13

"In that [a]day [b]a fountain
shall be opened for the
house of David and for the inhabitants of Jerusalem, for sin
and for [c]uncleanness.
2 "It shall be in that day," says
the LORD of hosts, "*that* I will
[a]cut off the names of the idols
from the land, and they shall
no longer be remembered. I will
also cause [b]the prophets and the
unclean spirit to depart from the
land.
3 "It shall come to pass *that* if
anyone still prophesies, then his
father and mother who begot
him will say to him, 'You shall
[a]not live, because you have spoken lies in the name of the LORD.'
And his father and mother who
begot him [b]shall thrust him
through when he prophesies.
4 "And it shall be in that day
that [a]every prophet will be
ashamed of his vision when he
prophesies; they will not wear [b]a
robe of coarse hair to deceive.
5 [a]"But he will say, 'I *am* no
prophet, I *am* a farmer; for a
man taught me to keep cattle
from my youth.'
6 "And *one* will say to him,
'What are these wounds between your [1]arms?' Then he will
answer, '*Those* with which I was
wounded in the house of my
friends.'

7 "Awake, O sword, against ☆
[a]My Shepherd,
Against the Man [b]who is My
Companion,"
Says the LORD of hosts.
[c]"Strike the Shepherd,
And the sheep will be
scattered;
Then I will turn My hand
against [d]the little ones.
8 And it shall come to pass in
all the land,"
Says the LORD,
"*That* [a]two-thirds in it shall
be cut off *and* die,
[b]But *one*-third shall be left
in it:
9 I will bring the *one*-third
[a]through the fire,
Will [b]refine them as silver is
refined,
And test them as gold is
tested.

9 [a]Hag. 2:22
10 [a][Joel 2:28, 29] [b]John 19:34, 37; 20:27; [Rev. 1:7] [c]Jer. 6:26
11 [a][Rev. 1:7] [b]2 Kin. 23:29 [1]Heb. *Megiddon*
12 [a][Matt. 24:30] [b]Luke 3:31

CHAPTER 13

1 [a][Rev. 21:6, 7] [b][Heb. 9:14] [c]Ezek. 36:25
2 [a]Ex. 23:13 [b]Jer. 23:14, 15
3 [a]Deut. 18:20 [b]Deut. 13:6–11
4 [a][Mic. 3:6, 7] [b]2 Kin. 1:8
5 [a]Amos 7:14
6 [1]Or *hands*
7 [a]Is. 40:11 [b][John 10:30] [c]Matt. 26:31, 56, 67; Mark 14:27; 1 Pet. 5:4; Rev. 7:16, 17 [d]Luke 12:32
8 [a]Ezek. 5:2, 4, 12 [b][Rom. 11:5]
9 [a]Is. 48:10 [b]1 Pet. 1:6, 7

[c]They will call on My name,
And I will answer them.
[d]I will say, 'This *is* My people';
And each one will say, 'The LORD *is* my God.' "

14

Behold, [a]the day of the LORD is coming,
And your [1]spoil will be divided in your midst.
2 For [a]I will gather all the nations to battle against Jerusalem;
The city shall be taken,
The houses [1]rifled,
And the women ravished.
Half of the city shall go into captivity,
But the remnant of the people shall not be cut off from the city.

3 Then the LORD will go forth
And fight against those nations,
As He fights in the day of battle.
4 And in that day His feet will stand [a]on the Mount of Olives,
Which faces Jerusalem on the east.
And the Mount of Olives shall be split in two,
From east to west,
[b]*Making* a very large valley;
Half of the mountain shall move toward the north
And half of it toward the south.

5 Then you shall flee *through* My mountain valley,
For the mountain valley shall reach to Ā'zal.
Yes, you shall flee
As you fled from the [a]earthquake
In the days of Uz·zī'ah king of Judah.

[b]Thus the LORD my God will come,
And [c]all the saints with [1]You.

6 It shall come to pass in that day
That there will be no light;
The [1]lights will diminish.
7 It shall be one day
[a]Which is known to the LORD—
Neither day nor night.
But at [b]evening time it shall happen
That it will be light.

8 And in that day it shall be
That living [a]waters shall flow from Jerusalem,
Half of them toward [1]the eastern sea
And half of them toward [2]the western sea;
In both summer and winter it shall occur.
9 And the LORD shall be [a]King over all the earth.
In that day it shall be—
[b]"The LORD *is* one,"
And His name one.

10 All the land shall be turned
into a plain from Gē'ba to Rim'-
mon south of Jerusalem. [1]*Je-*
rusalem shall be raised up and
[a]inhabited in her place from
Benjamin's Gate to the place of
the First Gate and the Corner
Gate, [b]and *from* the Tower of
Ha·nan'el to the king's winepresses.

---

9 [c]Ps. 50:15 [d]Hos. 2:23

CHAPTER 14

1 [a][Is. 13:6, 9] [1]*plunder* or *booty*

2 [a]Zech. 12:2, 3 [1]Or *plundered*

4 [a]Ezek. 11:23 [b]Joel 3:12

5 [a]Amos 1:1 [b]Matt. 24:30, 31; 25:31 [c]Joel 3:11 [1]Or *you;* LXX, Tg., Vg. *Him*

6 [1]Lit. *glorious ones*

7 [a]Matt. 24:36 [b]Is. 30:26

8 [a]Ezek. 47:1–12 [1]The Dead Sea [2]The Mediterranean Sea

9 [a][Rev. 11:15] [b]Deut. 6:4

10 [a]Zech. 12:6 [b]Jer. 31:38 [1]Lit. *She*

11 *The people* shall dwell
in it;
And [a]no longer shall there
be utter destruction,
[b]But Jerusalem shall be
safely inhabited.

12 And this shall be the plague
with which the LORD will strike
all the people who fought against
Jerusalem:

Their flesh shall [1]dissolve
while they stand on their
feet,
Their eyes shall dissolve in
their sockets,
And their tongues shall
dissolve in their mouths.

13 It shall come to pass in that
day
That [a]a great panic from
the LORD will be among
them.
Everyone will seize the
hand of his neighbor,
And raise [b]his hand against
his neighbor's hand;
14 Judah also will fight at
Jerusalem.
[a]And the wealth of all the
surrounding nations
Shall be gathered together:
Gold, silver, and apparel in
great abundance.

15 [a]Such also shall be the
plague
On the horse *and* the mule,
On the camel and the
donkey,
And on all the cattle that
will be in those camps.
So *shall* this plague *be.*

16 And it shall come to pass
that everyone who is left of all
the nations which came against
Jerusalem shall [a]go up from year
to year to [b]worship the King, the
LORD of hosts, and to keep [c]the
Feast of Tabernacles.
17 [a]And it shall be *that* which-
ever of the families of the earth
do not come up to Jerusalem to
worship the King, the LORD of
hosts, on them there will be no
rain.
18 If the family of [a]Egypt will
not come up and enter in, [b]they
shall have no *rain;* they shall receive the plague with which the
LORD strikes the nations who do
not come up to keep the Feast of
Tabernacles.
19 This shall be the [1]punish-
ment of Egypt and the punishment of all the nations that do
not come up to keep the Feast of
Tabernacles.
20 In that day [a]"HOLINESS TO
THE LORD" shall be *engraved*
on the bells of the horses. The
[b]pots in the LORD's house shall be
like the bowls before the altar.
21 Yes, [1]every pot in Jerusalem
and Judah shall be holiness to
the LORD of hosts. Everyone who
sacrifices shall come and take
them and cook in them. In that
day there shall no longer be a
[a]Cā'naan·īte [b]in the house of the
LORD of hosts.

11 [a]Jer. 31:40 [b]Jer. 23:6
12 [1]Lit. *decay*
13 [a]1 Sam. 14:15, 20 [b]Judg. 7:22
14 [a]Ezek. 39:10, 17
15 [a]Zech. 14:12
16 [a][Is. 2:2, 3; 60:6–9; 66:18–21] [b]Is. 27:13 [c]Lev. 23:34–44
17 [a]Is. 60:12
18 [a]Is. 19:21 [b]Deut. 11:10
19 [1]Lit. *sin*
20 [a]Is. 23:18 [b]Ezek. 46:20
21 [a]Is. 35:8 [b][Eph. 2:19–22] [1]Or *on every pot . . . shall be engraved "HOLINESS TO THE LORD OF HOSTS"*

The Book of

MALACHI

MALACHI, a prophet in the days of Nehemiah, directs his message of judgment to a people plagued with corrupt priests, wicked practices, and a false sense of security in their privileged relationship with God. Using the question-and-answer method, Malachi probes deeply into their problems of hypocrisy, infidelity, mixed marriages, divorce, false worship, and arrogance. So sinful has the nation become that God's words to the people no longer have any impact. For four hundred years after Malachi's ringing condemnations, God remains silent. Only with the coming of John the Baptist (prophesied in 3:1) does God again communicate to His people through a prophet's voice.

The name *Mal'aki* ("My Messenger") is probably a shortened form of *Mal'akya*, "Messenger of Yahweh," and it is appropriate to the book which speaks of the coming of the "messenger of the covenant" ("messenger" is mentioned three times in 2:7; 3:1). The Septuagint used the title *Malachias* even though it also translated it "by the hand of his messenger." The Latin title is *Maleachi*.

THE [1]burden of the word of the LORD to Israel [2]by Mal′a·chī.

2 "I[a] have loved you," says the LORD.
"Yet you say, 'In what way have You loved us?'
Was not Esau Jacob's brother?"
Says the LORD.
"Yet [b]Jacob I have loved;
3 But Esau I have hated,
And [a]laid waste his mountains and his heritage
For the jackals of the wilderness."

4 Even though Ē′dom has said,
"We have been impoverished,
But we will return and build the desolate places,"

Thus says the LORD of hosts:

"They may build, but I will [a]throw down;
They shall be called the Territory of Wickedness,
And the people against whom the LORD will have indignation forever.
5 Your eyes shall see,
And you shall say,
[a]'The LORD is magnified beyond the border of Israel.'

6 "A son [a]honors *his* father,
And a servant *his* master.
[b]If then I am the Father,
Where *is* My honor?
And if I *am* a Master,
Where *is* My reverence?
Says the LORD of hosts
To you priests who despise My name.
[c]Yet you say, 'In what way have we despised Your name?'

7 "You offer [a]defiled food on My altar,

CHAPTER 1

1 [1]*oracle, prophecy* [2]Lit. *by the hand of*

2 [a]Deut. 4:37; 7:8; 23:5 [b]Rom. 9:13

3 [a]Jer. 49:18

4 [a]Jer. 49:16–18

5 [a]Ps. 35:27

6 [a][Ex. 20:12] [b]Luke 6:46 [c]Mal. 2:14

7 [a]Deut. 15:21

But say,
'In what way have we defiled You?'
By saying,
[b]'The table of the LORD is [1]contemptible.'
8 And [a]when you offer the blind as a sacrifice,
Is it not evil?
And when you offer the lame and sick,
Is it not evil?
Offer it then to your governor!
Would he be pleased with you?
Would he [b]accept[1] you favorably?"
Says the LORD of hosts.

9 "But now entreat God's favor,
That He may be gracious to us.
[a]*While* this is being *done* by your hands,
Will He accept you favorably?"
Says the LORD of hosts.
10 "Who *is there* even among you who would shut the doors,
[a]So that you would not kindle fire *on* My altar in vain?
I have no pleasure in you,"
Says the LORD of hosts,
[b]"Nor will I accept an offering from your hands.
11 For [a]from the rising of the sun, even to its going down,
My name *shall be* great [b]among the Gentiles;
[c]In every place [d]incense *shall be* offered to My name,
And a pure offering;
[e]For My name shall be great among the nations,"
Says the LORD of hosts.

12 "But you profane it,
In that you say,
[a]'The table of the [1]LORD is defiled;
And its fruit, its food, *is* contemptible.'
13 You also say,
'Oh, what a [a]weariness!'
And you sneer at it,"
Says the LORD of hosts.
"And you bring the stolen, the lame, and the sick;
Thus you bring an offering!
[b]Should I accept this from your hand?"
Says the LORD.
14 "But cursed *be* [a]the deceiver
Who has in his flock a male,
And takes a vow,
But sacrifices to the Lord [b]what is blemished—
For [c]I *am* a great King,"
Says the LORD of hosts,
"And My name *is to be* feared among the nations.

2 "And now, O [a]priests, this commandment is for you.
2 [a]If you will not hear,
And if you will not take *it* to heart,
To give glory to My name,"
Says the LORD of hosts,
"I will send a curse upon you,
And I will curse your blessings.
Yes, I have cursed them [b]already,
Because you do not take *it* to heart.

3 "Behold, I will rebuke your descendants
And spread [a]refuse on your faces,

7 [b]Ezek. 41:22 [1]Or *to be despised*
8 [a]Lev. 22:22 [b][Job 42:8] [1]Lit. *lift up your face*
9 [a]Hos. 13:9
10 [a]1 Cor. 9:13 [b]Is. 1:11
11 [a]Is. 59:19 [b]Is. 60:3, 5 [c]1 Tim. 2:8 [d]Rev. 8:3 [e]Is. 66:18, 19
12 [a]Mal. 1:7 [1]So with Bg.; MT *Lord*
13 [a]Is. 43:22 [b]Lev. 22:20
14 [a]Mal. 1:8 [b]Lev.22:18–20 [c]Ps. 47:2

CHAPTER 2

1 [a]Mal. 1:6
2 [a][Deut. 28:15] [b]Mal. 3:9
3 [a]Ex. 29:14

The refuse of your solemn
feasts;
And *one* will [b]take you away
[1]with it.
4 Then you shall know
that I have sent this
commandment to you,
That My covenant with Levi
may continue,"
Says the LORD of hosts.
5 "My[a] covenant was with him,
one of life and peace,
And I gave them to him
[b]*that he might* fear *Me;*
So he feared Me
And was reverent before My
name.
6 [a]The[1] law of truth was in his
mouth,
And [2]injustice was not
found on his lips.
He walked with Me in peace
and equity,
And [b]turned many away
from iniquity.

7 "For[a] the lips of a priest
should keep knowledge,
And *people* should seek the
law from his mouth;
[b]For he is the messenger of
the LORD of hosts.
8 But you have departed from
the way;
You [a]have caused many to
stumble at the law.
[b]You have corrupted the
covenant of Levi,"
Says the LORD of hosts.
9 "Therefore [a]I also have made
you contemptible and
base
Before all the people,
Because you have not kept
My ways
But have shown [b]partiality
in the law."

3 [b]1 Kin. 14:10
[1]Lit. *to it*

5 [a]Num. 25:12
[b]Deut. 33:9

6 [a]Deut. 33:10
[b]Jer. 23:22
[1]Or *True instruction*
[2]Or *unrighteousness*

7 [a]Deut. 17:8–11
[b][Gal. 4:14]

8 [a]Jer. 18:15
[b]Neh. 13:29

9 [a]1 Sam. 2:30
[b]Deut. 1:17

10 [a]1 Cor. 8:6
[b]Job 31:15

11 [a]Ezra 9:1, 2

12 [a]Neh. 13:29
[1]Talmud, Vg. *teacher and student*

14 [a]Mal. 3:5
[b]Prov. 2:17

15 [a]Matt. 19:4, 5

10 [a]Have we not all one Father?
[b]Has not one God created us?
Why do we deal
treacherously with one
another
By profaning the covenant
of the fathers?
11 Judah has dealt
treacherously,
And an abomination has
been committed in Israel
and in Jerusalem,
For Judah has [a]profaned
The LORD's holy *institution*
which He loves:
He has married the
daughter of a foreign
god.
12 May the LORD cut off from
the tents of Jacob
The man who does this,
being [1]awake and aware,
Yet [a]who brings an offering
to the LORD of hosts!

13 And this is the second thing
you do:
You cover the altar of the
LORD with tears,
With weeping and crying;
So He does not regard the
offering anymore,
Nor receive *it* with goodwill
from your hands.
14 Yet you say, "For what
reason?"
Because the LORD has been
witness
Between you and [a]the wife
of your youth,
With whom you have dealt
treacherously;
[b]Yet she is your companion
And your wife by covenant.
15 But [a]did He not make *them*
one,
Having a remnant of the
Spirit?

And why one?
He seeks [b]godly offspring.
Therefore take heed to your spirit,
And let none deal treacherously with the wife of his youth.

16 "For [a]the LORD God of Israel says
That He hates divorce,
For it covers one's garment with violence,"
Says the LORD of hosts.
"Therefore take heed to your spirit,
That you do not deal treacherously."

17 [a]You have wearied the LORD with your words;
Yet you say,
"In what way have we wearied *Him?*"
In that you say,
[b]"Everyone who does evil
Is good in the sight of the LORD,
And He delights in them,"
Or, "Where *is* the God of justice?"

☆ 3 "Behold, [a]I send My messenger,
And he will [b]prepare the way before Me.
And the Lord, whom you seek,
Will suddenly come to His temple,
[c]Even the Messenger of the covenant,
In whom you delight.
Behold, [d]He is coming,"
Says the LORD of hosts.

2 "But who can endure [a]the day of His coming?
And [b]who can stand when He appears?
For [c]He *is* like a refiner's fire
And like launderers' soap.
3 [a]He will sit as a refiner and a purifier of silver;
He will purify the sons of Levi,
And [1]purge them as gold and silver,
That they may [b]offer to the LORD
An offering in righteousness.

4 "Then [a]the offering of Judah and Jerusalem
Will be [1]pleasant to the LORD,
As in the days of old,
As in former years.
5 And I will come near you for judgment;
I will be a swift witness
Against sorcerers,
Against adulterers,
[a]Against perjurers,
Against those who [b]exploit wage earners and [c]widows and orphans,
And against those who turn away an alien—
Because they do not fear Me,"
Says the LORD of hosts.

6 "For I *am* the LORD, [a]I do not change;
[b]Therefore you are not consumed, O sons of Jacob.
7 Yet from the days of [a]your fathers
You have gone away from My ordinances
And have not kept *them.*
[b]Return to Me, and I will return to you,"

15 [b][1 Cor. 7:14]
16 [a][Matt. 5:31; 19:6–8]
17 [a]Is. 43:22, 24 [b]Is. 5:20

CHAPTER 3

1 [a]Matt. 11:10; Mark 1:2; Luke 1:76; 7:27; John 1:23; 2:14, 15 [b][Is. 40:3] [c]Is. 63:9 [d]Hag. 2:7
2 [a][Mal. 4:1] [b]Rev. 6:17 [c][Matt. 3:10–12]
3 [a]Is. 1:25 [b][1 Pet. 2:5] [1]Or *refine*
4 [a]Mal. 1:11 [1]*pleasing*
5 [a]Zech. 5:4 [b]James 5:4 [c]Ex. 22:22
6 [a][Rom. 11:29] [b][Lam. 3:22]
7 [a]Acts 7:51 [b]Zech. 1:3

Says the LORD of hosts.
[c]"But you said,
'In what way shall we
return?'

8 "Will a man rob God?
Yet you have robbed Me!
But you say,
'In what way have we robbed
You?'
[a]In tithes and offerings.
9 You are cursed with a curse,
For you have robbed Me,
Even this whole nation.
10 [a]Bring all the tithes into the
[b]storehouse,
That there may be food in
My house,
And try Me now in this,"
Says the LORD of hosts,
"If I will not open for you the
[c]windows of heaven
And [d]pour out for you *such*
blessing
That *there will* not *be room*
enough *to receive it.*

11 "And I will rebuke [a]the
devourer for your sakes,
So that he will not destroy
the fruit of your ground,
Nor shall the vine fail to
bear fruit for you in the
field,"
Says the LORD of hosts;
12 "And all nations will call you
blessed,
For you will be [a]a delightful
land,"
Says the LORD of hosts.

13 "Your[a] words have been
[1]harsh against Me,"
Says the LORD,
"Yet you say,
'What have we spoken
against You?'
14 [a]You have said,
'It is useless to serve God;
What profit *is it* that we
have kept His ordinance,
And that we have walked as
mourners
Before the LORD of hosts?
15 So now [a]we call the proud
blessed,
For those who do
wickedness are [1]raised
up;
They even [b]tempt God and
go free.' "

16 Then those [a]who feared
the LORD [b]spoke to one
another,
And the LORD listened and
heard *them;*
So [c]a book of remembrance
was written before Him
For those who fear the LORD
And who [1]meditate on His
name.

17 "They[a] shall be Mine," says
the LORD of hosts,
"On the day that I make
them My [b]jewels.[1]
And [c]I will spare them
As a man spares his own
son who serves him."
18 [a]Then you shall again
discern
Between the righteous and
the wicked,
Between one who serves
God
And one who does not serve
Him.

4

"For behold, [a]the day is
coming,
Burning like an oven,
And all [b]the proud, yes, all
who do wickedly will be
[c]stubble.

---

7 [c]Mal. 1:6
8 [a]Neh. 13:10–12
10 [a]Prov. 3:9, 10 [b]1 Chr. 26:20 [c]Gen. 7:11 [d]2 Chr. 31:10
11 [a]Amos 4:9
12 [a]Dan. 8:9
13 [a]Mal. 2:17 [1]Lit. *strong*
14 [a]Job 21:14
15 [a]Ps. 73:12 [b]Ps. 95:9 [1]Lit. *built*
16 [a]Ps. 66:16 [b]Heb. 3:13 [c]Ps. 56:8 [1]Or *esteem*
17 [a]Ex. 19:5 [b]Is. 62:3 [c]Ps. 103:13 [1]Lit. *special treasure*
18 [a][Ps. 58:11]

CHAPTER 4

1 [a][2 Pet. 3:7] [b]Mal. 3:18 [c]Obad. 18

And the day which is coming
shall burn them up,"
Says the LORD of hosts,
"That will [d]leave them
neither root nor branch.
2 But to you who [a]fear My
name
The [b]Sun of Righteousness
shall arise
With healing in His wings;
And you shall go out
And grow fat like stall-fed
calves.
3 [a]You shall trample the
wicked,
For they shall be ashes under
the soles of your feet
On the day that I do *this*,"
Says the LORD of hosts.

4 "Remember the [a]Law of
Moses, My servant,
Which I commanded him in
Hō′reb for all Israel,
With [b]*the* statutes and
judgments.
5 Behold, I will send you ☆
[a]E·lī′jah the prophet
[b]Before the coming of the
great and dreadful day
of the LORD.
6 And [a]he will turn ☆
The hearts of the fathers to
the children,
And the hearts of the
children to their
fathers,
Lest I come and [b]strike the
earth with [c]a curse."

1 [d]Amos 2:9
2 [a]Mal. 3:16 [b]Luke 1:78
3 [a]Mic. 7:10
4 [a]Ex. 20:3 [b]Deut. 4:10
5 [a][Matt. 11:14; 17:10–13; Mark 9:11–13; Luke 1:17]; John 1:21 [b]Joel 2:31
6 [a]Luke 1:17 [b]Zech. 14:12 [c]Zech. 5:3

The New Testament

The Words of Christ in Red

The Gospel According to
MATTHEW

MATTHEW is the gospel written by a Jew to Jews about a Jew. Matthew is the writer, his countrymen are the readers, and Jesus Christ is the subject. Matthew's design is to present Jesus as the King of the Jews, the long-awaited Messiah. Through a carefully selected series of Old Testament quotations, Matthew documents Jesus Christ's claim to be the Messiah. His genealogy, baptism, messages, and miracles all point to the same inescapable conclusion: Christ is King. Even in His death, seeming defeat is turned to victory by the Resurrection, and the message again echoes forth: the King of the Jews lives.

At an early date this gospel was given the title *Kata Matthaion*, "According to Matthew." As this title suggests, other gospel accounts were known at that time (the word "Gospel" was added later). Matthew ("Gift of the Lord") was also surnamed Levi (Mark 2:14; Luke 5:27).

★ THE book of the [a]genealogy[1]
of Jesus Christ, [b]the Son of
David, [c]the Son of Abraham:
2 [a]Abraham begot Isaac, [b]Isaac
begot Jacob, and Jacob begot
[c]Judah and his brothers.
3 [a]Judah begot Per′ez and Zē′-
rah by Tā′mar, [b]Per′ez begot Hez′-
ron, and Hez′ron begot Ram.
4 Ram begot Am·min′a·dab,
Am·min′a·dab begot Nah′shon,
and Nah′shon begot Sal′mon.
5 Sal′mon begot [a]Bō′az by Rā′-
hab, Bō′az begot Ō′bed by Ruth,
Ō′bed begot Jesse,
★ 6 and [a]Jesse begot David the
king.
[b]David the king begot Solomon by her [1]*who had been the*
wife of Ū·rī′ah.
7 [a]Solomon begot Rē·ho·bō′am,
Rē·ho·bō′am begot [b]A·bī′jah, and
A·bī′jah begot [1]Ā′sa.
8 Ā′sa begot [a]Je·hosh′a·phat, Je-
hosh′a·phat begot Jō′ram, and Jō′-
ram begot [b]Uz·zī′ah.
9 Uz·zī′ah begot Jō′tham, Jō′-
tham begot [a]Ā′haz, and Ā′haz
begot Hez·e·kī′ah.
10 [a]Hez·e·kī′ah begot Ma·nas′-
seh, Ma·nas′seh begot [1]Ā′mon,
and Ā′mon begot [b]Jō·sī′ah.
11 [a]Jō·sī′ah begot [1]Jec·o·nī′ah and
his brothers about the time they
were [b]carried away to Babylon.
12 And after they were brought
to Babylon, [a]Jec·o·nī′ah begot
She·al′ti·el, and She·al′ti·el begot
[b]Ze·rub′ba·bel.
13 Ze·rub′ba·bel begot A·bī′ud,
A·bī′ud begot E·lī′a·kim, and
E·lī′a·kim begot Ā′zor.
14 Ā′zor begot Zā′dok, Zā′dok
begot Ā′chim, and Ā′chim begot
E·lī′ud.
15 E·lī′ud begot El·ē·ā′zar, El·ē-
ā′zar begot Mat′than, and Mat′-
than begot Jacob.
16 And Jacob begot Joseph the
husband of [a]Mary, of whom was
born Jesus who is called Christ.
17 So all the generations from
Abraham to David *are* fourteen
generations, from David until
the captivity in Babylon *are*
fourteen generations, and from
the captivity in Babylon until the
Christ *are* fourteen generations.

CHAPTER 1

1 [a]Luke 3:23 [b]John 7:42 [c]Gen. 12:3; 22:18 [1]Lit. *generation*
2 [a]Gen. 21:2, 12 [b]Gen. 25:26; 28:14 [c]Gen. 29:35
3 [a]Gen. 38:27; 49:10 [b]Ruth 4:18–22
5 [a]Ruth 2:1; 4:1–13
6 [a]1 Sam. 16:1 [b]2 Sam. 7:12; 12:24 [1]Words in italic type have been added for clarity. They are not found in the original Greek.
7 [a]1 Chr. 3:10 [b]2 Chr. 11:20 [1]NU *Asaph*
8 [a]1 Chr. 3:10 [b]2 Kin. 15:13
9 [a]2 Kin. 15:38
10 [a]2 Kin. 20:21 [b]1 Kin. 13:2 [1]NU *Amos*
11 [a]1 Chr. 3:15, 16 [b]2 Kin. 24:14–16 [1]Or *Coniah* or *Jehoiachin*
12 [a]1 Chr. 3:17 [b]Ezra 3:2
16 [a]Matt. 13:55

★ 18 Now the [a]birth of Jesus
Christ was as follows: After His
mother Mary was betrothed to
Joseph, before they came together, she was found with child
[b]of the Holy Spirit.
19 Then Joseph her husband,
being [1]a just *man,* and not wanting [a]to make her a public example, was minded to put her away
secretly.
20 But while he thought about
these things, behold, an angel
of the Lord appeared to him in
a dream, saying, "Joseph, son of
David, do not be afraid to take
to you Mary your wife, [a]for that
which is [1]conceived in her is of
the Holy Spirit.
21 [a]"And she will bring forth
a Son, and you shall call His
name [1]JESUS, [b]for He will save
His people from their sins."
22 So all this was done that it
might be fulfilled which was
spoken by the Lord through the
prophet, saying:
★ 23 [a]*"Behold,*[1] *the virgin shall*
be with child, and bear a Son,
and they shall call His name
Im·man′ū·el," which is translated, "God with us."
24 Then Joseph, being aroused
from sleep, did as the angel of
the Lord commanded him and
took to him his wife,
25 and [1]did not know her till she
had brought forth [a]her[2] firstborn
Son. And he called His name
JESUS.

★ **2** Now after [a]Jesus was born
in Bethlehem of Judea in the
days of Her′od the king, behold,
[1]wise men [b]from the East came
to Jerusalem,
2 saying, [a]"Where is He who
has been born King of the Jews?
For we have seen [b]His star in the
East and have come to worship
Him."
3 When Her′od the king heard
this, he was troubled, and all
Jerusalem with him.
4 And when he had gathered
all [a]the chief priests and [b]scribes
of the people together, [c]he inquired of them where the Christ
was to be born.
5 So they said to him, "In Bethlehem of Judea, for thus it is
written by the prophet:

6 *'But*[a] *you, Bethlehem, in the* ★
land of Judah,
Are not the least among the
rulers of Judah;
For out of you shall come a
Ruler
[b]*Who will shepherd My*
people Israel.' "

7 Then Her′od, when he had
secretly called the [1]wise men,
determined from them what
time the [a]star appeared.
8 And he sent them to Bethlehem and said, "Go and search
carefully for the young Child,
and when you have found *Him,*
bring back word to me, that
I may come and worship Him
also."
9 When they heard the king,
they departed; and behold, the
star which they had seen in the
East went before them, till it
came and stood over where the
young Child was.
10 When they saw the star, they
rejoiced with exceedingly great
joy.
11 And when they had come
into the house, they saw the
young Child with Mary His
mother, and fell down and worshiped Him. And when they had

18 [a]Luke 1:27 [b]Luke 1:35
19 [a]Deut. 24:1 [1]*an upright*
20 [a]Luke 1:35 [1]Lit. *begotten*
21 [a]Luke 1:31; 2:21 [b]John 1:29 [1]Lit. *Savior*
23 [a]Is. 7:14 [1]Words in oblique type in the New Testament are quoted from the Old Testament.
25 [a]Luke 2:7, 21 [1]Kept her a virgin [2]NU *a Son*

CHAPTER 2

1 [a]Mic. 5:2; Luke 2:4–7 [b]Gen. 25:6 [1]Gr. *magoi*
2 [a]Luke 2:11 [b][Num. 24:17]
4 [a]2 Chr. 36:14 [b]2 Chr. 34:13 [c]Mal. 2:7
6 [a]Mic. 5:2 [b][Rev. 2:27]
7 [a]Num. 24:17 [1]Gr. *magoi*

opened their treasures, [a]they
presented gifts to Him: gold,
frankincense, and myrrh.
12 Then, being divinely warned
[a]in a dream that they should not
return to Her′od, they departed
for their own country another
way.
13 Now when they had departed, behold, an angel of the
Lord appeared to Joseph in a
dream, saying, "Arise, take the
young Child and His mother,
flee to Egypt, and stay there until I bring you word; for Her′od
will seek the young Child to
destroy Him."
14 When he arose, he took the
young Child and His mother by
night and departed for Egypt,
★ 15 and was there until the death
of Her′od, that it might be fulfilled which was spoken by the
Lord through the prophet, saying, [a]*"Out of Egypt I called My*
Son."
16 Then Her′od, when he saw
that he was deceived by the wise
men, was exceedingly angry; and
he sent forth and put to death all
the male children who were in
Bethlehem and in all its districts,
from two years old and under,
according to the time which he
had determined from the wise
men.
17 Then was fulfilled what
was spoken by Jer·e·mī′ah the
prophet, saying:

★ 18 *"A [a]voice was heard in*
Rā′mah,
Lamentation, weeping, and
great mourning,
Rachel weeping for her
children,
Refusing to be comforted,
Because they are no more."

19 Now when Her′od was dead,
behold, an angel of the Lord appeared in a dream to Joseph in
Egypt,
20 [a]saying, "Arise, take the
young Child and His mother,
and go to the land of Israel, for
those who [b]sought the young
Child's life are dead."
21 Then he arose, took the young
Child and His mother, and came
into the land of Israel.
22 But when he heard that Ar-
che·lā′us was reigning over Judea instead of his father Her′od,
he was afraid to go there. And
being warned by God in a
[a]dream, he turned aside [b]into
the region of Galilee.
23 And he came and dwelt in ★
a city called [a]Nazareth, that it
might be fulfilled [b]which was
spoken by the prophets, "He
shall be called a Naz′a·rēne."

3

In those days [a]John the Baptist came preaching [b]in the
wilderness of Judea,
2 and saying, "Repent, for [a]the
kingdom of heaven is at hand!"
3 For this is he who was spo- ★
ken of by the prophet Ī·sāi′ah,
saying:

[a]*"The voice of one crying in*
the wilderness:
[b]*'Prepare the way of the LORD;*
Make His paths straight.'"

4 Now [a]John himself was
clothed in camel's hair, with a
leather belt around his waist;
and his food was [b]locusts and
[c]wild honey.
5 [a]Then Jerusalem, all Judea,
and all the region around the
Jordan went out to him
6 [a]and were baptized by him in
the Jordan, confessing their sins.

11 [a]Is. 60:6
12 [a]Matt. 1:20
15 [a]Hos. 11:1
18 [a]Jer. 31:15
20 [a]Luke 2:39 [b]Matt. 2:16
22 [a]Matt. 2:12, 13, 19 [b]Luke 2:39
23 [a]John 1:45, 46 [b]Judg. 13:5

CHAPTER 3

1 [a]Mark 1:3–8 [b]Josh. 14:10
2 [a]Dan. 2:44
3 [a]Is. 40:3 [b]Luke 1:76
4 [a]Mark 1:6 [b]Lev. 11:22 [c]1 Sam. 14:25, 26
5 [a]Mark 1:5
6 [a]Acts 19:4, 18

7 But when he saw many of the Phar′i·sees and Sad′dū·cees coming to his baptism, he said to them, [a]"Brood of vipers! Who warned you to flee from [b]the wrath to come?

8 "Therefore bear fruits worthy of repentance,

9 "and do not think to say to yourselves, [a]'We have Abraham as *our* father.' For I say to you that God is able to raise up children to Abraham from these stones.

10 "And even now the ax is laid to the root of the trees. [a]Therefore every tree which does not bear good fruit is cut down and thrown into the fire.

☆ 11 [a]"I indeed baptize you with water unto repentance, but He who is coming after me is mightier than I, whose sandals I am not worthy to carry. [b]He will baptize you with the Holy Spirit [1]and fire.

12 [a]"His winnowing fan *is* in His hand, and He will thoroughly clean out His threshing floor, and gather His wheat into the barn; but He will [b]burn up the chaff with unquenchable fire."

13 [a]Then Jesus came [b]from Galilee to John at the Jordan to be baptized by him.

14 And John *tried to* prevent Him, saying, "I need to be baptized by You, and are You coming to me?"

15 But Jesus answered and said to him, "Permit *it to be so* now, for thus it is fitting for us to fulfill all righteousness." Then he allowed Him.

★ 16 [a]When He had been baptized, Jesus came up immediately from the water; and behold, the heavens were opened to Him, and [1]He saw [b]the Spirit of God descending like a dove and alighting upon Him.

17 [a]And suddenly a voice *came* from heaven, saying, [b]"This is My beloved Son, in whom I am well pleased."

4 Then [a]Jesus was led up by [b]the Spirit into the wilderness to be tempted by the devil.

2 And when He had fasted forty days and forty nights, afterward He was hungry.

3 Now when the tempter came to Him, he said, "If You are the Son of God, command that these stones become bread."

4 But He answered and said, "It is written, [a]*'Man shall not live by bread alone, but by every word that proceeds from the mouth of God.'* "

5 Then the devil took Him up [a]into the holy city, set Him on the pinnacle of the temple,

6 and said to Him, "If You are the Son of God, throw Yourself down. For it is written:

[a]'He shall give His angels
charge over you,'

and,

[a]'In their hands they shall
bear you up,
Lest you dash your foot
against a stone.' "

7 Jesus said to him, "It is written again, [a]*'You shall not [1]tempt the* L*ORD your God.'* "

8 Again, the devil took Him up on an exceedingly high mountain, and [a]showed Him all the kingdoms of the world and their glory.

9 And he said to Him, "All

7 [a]Matt. 12:34 [b][1 Thess. 1:10]
9 [a]John 8:33
10 [a]Matt. 7:19
11 [a]Luke 3:16 [b][Acts 2:3, 4] [1]M omits *and fire*
12 [a]Mal. 3:3 [b]Matt. 13:30
13 [a]Mark 1:9–11 [b]Matt. 2:22
16 [a]Mark 1:10 [b][Is. 11:2]; John 1:32 [1]Or *he*
17 [a]John 12:28 [b]Ps. 2:7

CHAPTER 4

1 [a]Mark 1:12 [b]Ezek. 3:14
4 [a]Deut. 8:3
5 [a]Neh. 11:1, 18
6 [a]Ps. 91:11 [b]Ps. 91:12
7 [a]Deut. 6:16 [1]*test*
8 [a][1 John 2:15–17]

these things I will give You if You
will fall down and worship me."
10 Then Jesus said to him,
[1]"Away with you, Satan! For it is
written, [a]*'You shall worship the*
LORD your God, and Him only
you shall serve.'"
11 Then the devil [a]left Him, and
behold, [b]angels came and ministered to Him.
12 [a]Now when Jesus heard that
John had been put in prison, He
departed to Galilee.
13 And leaving Nazareth, He
came and dwelt in Ca·per'na·um,
which is by the sea, in the regions of Zeb'ū·lun and Naph'-
ta·lī,
14 that it might be fulfilled
which was spoken by Ī·sāi'ah
the prophet, saying:

★ 15 *"The[a] land of Zeb'ū·lun and*
the land of Naph'ta·lī,
By the way of the sea,
beyond the Jordan,
Galilee of the Gentiles:
16 [a]*The people who sat in*
darkness have seen a
great light,
And upon those who sat in
the region and shadow
of death
Light has dawned."

17 [a]From that time Jesus began
to preach and to say, [b]"Repent,
for the kingdom of heaven [1]is at
hand."
18 [a]And Jesus, walking by the
Sea of Galilee, saw two brothers, Simon [b]called Peter, and
Andrew his brother, casting a
net into the sea; for they were
fishermen.
19 Then He said to them, "Follow Me, and [a]I will make you
fishers of men."

10 [a]Deut. 6:13; 10:20 [1]M *Get behind Me*
11 [a][James 4:7] [b][Heb. 1:14]
12 [a]John 4:43
15 [a]Is. 9:1, 2
16 [a]Luke 2:32
17 [a]Mark 1:14, 15 [b]Matt. 3:2; 10:7 [1]*has drawn near*
18 [a]Mark 1:16–20 [b]John 1:40–42
19 [a]Luke 5:10
20 [a]Mark 10:28
21 [a]Mark 1:19
23 [a]Matt. 9:35 [b][Matt. 24:14] [c]Mark 1:34
24 [a]Luke 4:40 [1]Lit. *the report of Him*
25 [a]Mark 3:7, 8 [1]Lit. *Ten Cities*

CHAPTER 5

1 [a]Mark 3:13
2 [a][Matt. 7:29]
3 [a]Luke 6:20–23
4 [a]Rev. 21:4
5 [a]Ps. 37:11 [b][Rom. 4:13] [1]Or *land*

20 [a]They immediately left *their*
nets and followed Him.
21 [a]Going on from there, He
saw two other brothers, James
the son of Zeb'e·dee, and John
his brother, in the boat with
Zeb'e·dee their father, mending
their nets. He called them,
22 and immediately they left
the boat and their father, and
followed Him.
23 And Jesus went about all
Galilee, [a]teaching in their synagogues, preaching [b]the gospel
of the kingdom, [c]and healing all
kinds of sickness and all kinds
of disease among the people.
24 Then [1]His fame went throughout all Syria; and they [a]brought
to Him all sick people who were
afflicted with various diseases
and torments, and those who
were demon-possessed, epilep-
tics, and paralytics; and He
healed them.
25 [a]Great multitudes followed
Him—from Galilee, and *from*
[1]De·cap'o·lis, Jerusalem, Judea,
and beyond the Jordan.
5 And seeing the multitudes,
[a]He went up on a mountain,
and when He was seated His
disciples came to Him.
2 Then He opened His mouth
and [a]taught them, saying:

3 "Blessed[a] *are* the poor in
spirit,
For theirs is the kingdom
of heaven.
4 [a]Blessed *are* those who
mourn,
For they shall be
comforted.
5 [a]Blessed *are* the meek,
For [b]they shall inherit the
[1]earth.

6 Blessed *are* those who
[a]hunger and thirst for
righteousness,
[b]For they shall be filled.
7 Blessed *are* the merciful,
[a]For they shall obtain
mercy.
8 [a]Blessed *are* the pure in
heart,
For [b]they shall see God.
9 Blessed *are* the
peacemakers,
For they shall be called
sons of God.
10 [a]Blessed *are* those who
are persecuted for
righteousness' sake,
For theirs is the kingdom
of heaven.

11 [a]"Blessed are you when they
revile and persecute you, and
say all kinds of [b]evil against you
falsely for My sake.
12 [a]"Rejoice and be exceedingly
glad, for great *is* your reward in
heaven, for [b]so they persecuted
the prophets who were before
you.
13 "You are the salt of the earth;
[a]but if the salt loses its flavor,
how shall it be seasoned? It is
then good for nothing but to be
thrown out and trampled underfoot by men.
14 [a]"You are the light of the
world. A city that is set on a hill
cannot be hidden.
15 "Nor do they [a]light a lamp
and put it under a basket, but on
a lampstand, and it gives light to
all *who are* in the house.
16 "Let your light so shine before men, [a]that they may see
your good works and [b]glorify
your Father in heaven.
17 [a]"Do not think that I came to
destroy the Law or the Prophets.
I did not come to destroy but to
fulfill.
18 "For assuredly, I say to you,
[a]till heaven and earth pass away,
one [1]jot or one [2]tittle will by no
means pass from the law till all
is fulfilled.
19 [a]"Whoever therefore breaks
one of the least of these commandments, and teaches men
so, shall be called least in the
kingdom of heaven; but whoever does and teaches *them*, he
shall be called great in the kingdom of heaven.
20 "For I say to you, that unless
your righteousness exceeds [a]*the
righteousness* of the scribes and
Phar'i·sees, you will by no means
enter the kingdom of heaven.
21 "You have heard that it was
said to those [1]of old, [a]*'You shall
not murder,* and whoever murders will be in danger of the
judgment.'
22 "But I say to you that [a]whoever
is angry with his brother [1]with-
out a cause shall be in danger of
the judgment. And whoever says
to his brother, [b]'Ra'ca!'[2] shall be
in danger of the council. But
whoever says, [3]'You fool!' shall
be in danger of [4]hell fire.
23 "Therefore [a]if you bring your
gift to the altar, and there remember that your brother has
something against you,
24 [a]"leave your gift there before
the altar, and go your way. First
be reconciled to your brother, and
then come and offer your gift.
25 [a]"Agree with your adversary
quickly, [b]while you are on the
way with him, lest your adversary deliver you to the judge,
the judge hand you over to the
officer, and you be thrown into
prison.

6 [a]Luke 1:53 [b][Is. 55:1; 65:13]
7 [a]Ps. 41:1
8 [a]Ps. 15:2; 24:4 [b]1 Cor. 13:12
10 [a]1 Pet. 3:14
11 [a]Luke 6:22 [b]1 Pet. 4:14
12 [a]1 Pet. 4:13, 14 [b]Acts 7:52
13 [a]Luke 14:34
14 [a][John 8:12]
15 [a]Luke 8:16
16 [a]1 Pet. 2:12 [b][John 15:8]
17 [a]Rom. 10:4
18 [a]Luke 16:17 [1]Gr. *iota*, Heb. *yod*, the smallest letter [2]The smallest stroke in a Heb. letter
19 [a][James 2:10]
20 [a][Rom. 10:3]
21 [a]Ex. 20:13; Deut. 5:17 [1]*in ancient times*
22 [a][1 John 3:15] [b][James 2:20; 3:6] [1]NU omits *without a cause* [2]Lit., in Aram., *Empty head* [3]Gr. *More* [4]Gr. *Gehenna*
23 [a]Matt. 8:4
24 [a][Job 42:8]
25 [a]Luke 12:58, 59 [b][Is. 55:6]

26 "Assuredly, I say to you, you will by no means get out of there till you have paid the last penny.

27 "You have heard that it was said [1]to those of old, [a]*'You shall not commit adultery.'*

28 "But I say to you that whoever [a]looks at a woman to lust for her has already committed adultery with her in his heart.

29 [a]"If your right eye causes you to [1]sin, [b]pluck it out and cast *it* from you; for it is more profitable for you that one of your members perish, than for your whole body to be cast into hell.

30 "And if your right hand causes you to [1]sin, cut it off and cast *it* from you; for it is more profitable for you that one of your members perish, than for your whole body to be cast into hell.

31 "Furthermore it has been said, [a]'Whoever divorces his wife, let him give her a certificate of divorce.'

32 "But I say to you that [a]whoever divorces his wife for any reason except [1]sexual immorality causes her to commit adultery; and whoever marries a woman who is divorced commits adultery.

33 "Again you have heard that [a]it was said to those of [1]old, [b]'You shall not swear falsely, but [c]shall perform your oaths to the Lord.'

34 "But I say to you, [a]do not swear at all: neither by heaven, for it is [b]God's throne;

35 "nor by the earth, for it is His footstool; nor by Jerusalem, for it is the city of [a]the great King.

36 "Nor shall you swear by your head, because you cannot make one hair white or black.

27 [a]Ex. 20:14; Deut. 5:18 [1]NU, M omit *to those of old*

28 [a]Prov. 6:25

29 [a]Mark 9:43 [b][Col. 3:5] [1]Lit. *stumble* or *offend*

30 [1]Lit. *stumble* or *offend*

31 [a]Deut. 24:1

32 [a][Luke 16:18] [1]Or *fornication*

33 [a]Matt. 23:16 [b]Lev. 19:12 [c]Deut. 23:23 [1]*ancient times*

34 [a]James 5:12 [b]Is. 66:1

35 [a]Ps. 48:2

37 [a][Col. 4:6] [1]Lit. *your word be yes yes*

38 [a]Ex. 21:24; Lev. 24:20; Deut. 19:21

39 [a]Luke 6:29 [b]Is. 50:6

41 [a]Matt. 27:32

42 [a]Luke 6:30–34

43 [a]Lev. 19:18 [b]Deut. 23:3–6

44 [a]Luke 6:27 [b][Rom. 12:20] [c]Acts 7:60 [1]NU *But I say to you, love your enemies and pray for those who persecute you*

45 [a]Job 25:3

46 [a]Luke 6:32

47 [1]M *friends* [2]NU *Gentiles*

48 [a][Col. 1:28; 4:12] [b]Eph. 5:1

37 [a]"But let [1]your 'Yes' be 'Yes,' and your 'No,' 'No.' For whatever is more than these is from the evil one.

38 "You have heard that it was said, [a]*'An eye for an eye and a tooth for a tooth.'*

39 [a]"But I tell you not to resist an evil person. [b]But whoever slaps you on your right cheek, turn the other to him also.

40 "If anyone wants to sue you and take away your tunic, let him have *your* cloak also.

41 "And whoever [a]compels you to go one mile, go with him two.

42 "Give to him who asks you, and [a]from him who wants to borrow from you do not turn away.

43 "You have heard that it was said, [a]*'You shall love your neighbor* [b]and hate your enemy.'

44 [1]"But I say to you, [a]love your enemies, bless those who curse you, [b]do good to those who hate you, and pray [c]for those who spitefully use you and persecute you,

45 "that you may be sons of your Father in heaven; for [a]He makes His sun rise on the evil and on the good, and sends rain on the just and on the unjust.

46 [a]"For if you love those who love you, what reward have you? Do not even the tax collectors do the same?

47 "And if you greet your [1]brethren only, what do you do more *than others?* Do not even the [2]tax collectors do so?

48 [a]"Therefore you shall be perfect, just [b]as your Father in heaven is perfect.

6 "Take heed that you do not do your charitable deeds before men, to be seen by them.

Otherwise you have no reward
from your Father in heaven.
2 "Therefore, [a]when you do a
charitable deed, do not sound
a trumpet before you as the
hypocrites do in the synagogues
and in the streets, that they may
have glory from men. Assuredly,
I say to you, they have their reward.
3 "But when you do a charitable deed, do not let your left
hand know what your right
hand is doing,
4 "that your charitable deed
may be in secret; and your Father
who sees in secret [a]will Himself
reward you [1]openly.
5 "And when you pray, you
shall not be like the [1]hypocrites.
For they love to pray standing in
the synagogues and on the corners of the streets, that they may
be seen by men. Assuredly, I say
to you, they have their reward.
6 "But you, when you pray, [a]go
into your room, and when you
have shut your door, pray to your
Father who *is* in the secret *place*;
and your Father who sees in secret will reward you [1]openly.
7 "And when you pray, [a]do not
use vain repetitions as the heathen *do*. [b]For they think that
they will be heard for their many
words.
8 "Therefore do not be like
them. For your Father [a]knows
the things you have need of before you ask Him.
9 "In this [a]manner, therefore,
pray:

[b]Our Father in heaven,
Hallowed be Your [c]name.
10 Your kingdom come.
[a]Your will be done
On earth [b]as *it is* in heaven.
11 Give us this day our [a]daily
bread.
12 And [a]forgive us our debts,
As we forgive our debtors.
13 [a]And do not lead us into
temptation,
But [b]deliver us from the evil
one.
[1]For Yours is the kingdom
and the power and the
glory forever. Amen.

14 [a]"For if you forgive men their
trespasses, your heavenly Father
will also forgive you.
15 "But [a]if you do not forgive men
their trespasses, neither will your
Father forgive your trespasses.
16 "Moreover, [a]when you fast,
do not be like the [1]hypocrites,
with a sad countenance. For
they disfigure their faces that
they may appear to men to be
fasting. Assuredly, I say to you,
they have their reward.
17 "But you, when you fast,
[a]anoint your head and wash your
face,
18 "so that you do not appear
to men to be fasting, but to your
Father who *is* in the secret *place*;
and your Father who sees in secret will reward you [1]openly.
19 [a]"Do not lay up for yourselves treasures on earth, where
moth and rust destroy and where
thieves break in and steal;
20 [a]"but lay up for yourselves
treasures in heaven, where neither moth nor rust destroys and
where thieves do not break in
and steal.
21 "For where your treasure is,
there your heart will be also.
22 [a]"The lamp of the body is
the eye. If therefore your eye is
[1]good, your whole body will be
full of light.

CHAPTER 6

2 [a]Rom. 12:8

4 [a]Luke 14:12–14
[1]NU omits *openly*

5 [1]*pretenders*

6 [a]2 Kin. 4:33
[1]NU omits *openly*

7 [a]Eccl. 5:2
[b]1 Kin. 18:26

8 [a][Rom. 8:26, 27]

9 [a]Luke 11:2–4
[b][Matt. 5:9, 16]
[c]Mal. 1:11

10 [a]Matt. 26:42
[b]Ps. 103:20

11 [a]Prov. 30:8

12 [a][Matt. 18:21, 22]

13 [a][2 Pet. 2:9]
[b]John 17:15
[1]NU omits the rest of v. 13.

14 [a]Mark 11:25

15 [a]Matt. 18:35

16 [a]Is. 58:3–7
[1]*pretenders*

17 [a]Ruth 3:3

18 [1]NU, M omit *openly*

19 [a]Prov. 23:4

20 [a]Matt. 19:21

22 [a]Luke 11:34, 35
[1]Clear, or healthy

23 "But if your eye is [1]bad, your
whole body will be full of darkness. If therefore the light that is
in you is darkness, how great *is*
that darkness!
24 [a]"No one can serve two masters; for either he will hate the
one and love the other, or else
he will be loyal to the one and
despise the other. [b]You cannot
serve God and [1]mammon.
25 "Therefore I say to you, [a]do
not worry about your life, what
you will eat or what you will
drink; nor about your body, what
you will put on. Is not life more
than food and the body more
than clothing?
26 [a]"Look at the birds of the air,
for they neither sow nor reap
nor gather into barns; yet your
heavenly Father feeds them.
Are you not of more value than
they?
27 "Which of you by worry-
ing can add one [1]cubit to his
[2]stature?
28 "So why do you worry about
clothing? Consider the lilies of
the field, how they grow: they
neither toil nor spin;
29 "and yet I say to you that
even Solomon in all his glory
was not [1]arrayed like one of
these.
30 "Now if God so clothes the
grass of the field, which today
is, and tomorrow is thrown into
the oven, *will He* not much more
clothe you, O you of little faith?
31 "Therefore do not worry,
saying, 'What shall we eat?' or
'What shall we drink?' or 'What
shall we wear?'
32 "For after all these things the
Gentiles seek. For your heavenly
Father knows that you need all
these things.
33 "But [a]seek first the kingdom
of God and His righteousness,
and all these things shall be
added to you.
34 "Therefore do not worry
about tomorrow, for tomorrow
will worry about its own things.
Sufficient for the day *is* its own
trouble.

7 "Judge[1] [a]not, that you be not
judged.
2 "For with what [1]judgment
you judge, you will be judged;
[a]and with the measure you use,
it will be measured back to you.
3 [a]"And why do you look at
the speck in your brother's eye,
but do not consider the plank in
your own eye?
4 "Or how can you say to your
brother, 'Let me remove the
speck from your eye'; and look,
a plank *is* in your own eye?
5 "Hypocrite! First remove
the plank from your own eye,
and then you will see clearly
to remove the speck from your
brother's eye.
6 [a]"Do not give what is holy to
the dogs; nor cast your pearls
before swine, lest they trample
them under their feet, and turn
and tear you in pieces.
7 [a]"Ask, and it will be given
to you; seek, and you will find;
knock, and it will be opened to
you.
8 "For [a]everyone who asks receives, and he who seeks finds,
and to him who knocks it will be
opened.
9 [a]"Or what man is there
among you who, if his son asks
for bread, will give him a stone?
10 "Or if he asks for a fish, will
he give him a serpent?
11 "If you then, [a]being evil, know
how to give good gifts to your

23 [1]Evil, or unhealthy
24 [a]Luke 16:9, 11, 13 [b][Gal. 1:10] [1]Lit., in Aram., *riches*
25 [a]Luke 12:22
26 [a]Luke 12:24
27 [1]About 18 inches [2]*height*
29 [1]*dressed*
33 [a][1 Tim. 4:8]

CHAPTER 7

1 [a]Rom. 14:3 [1]Condemn
2 [a]Luke 6:38 [1]Condemnation
3 [a]Luke 6:41
6 [a]Prov. 9:7, 8
7 [a][Mark 11:24]
8 [a]Prov. 8:17
9 [a]Luke 11:11
11 [a]Gen. 6:5; 8:21

children, how much more will
your Father who is in heaven
give good things to those who
ask Him!
12 "Therefore, [a]whatever you
want men to do to you, do also
to them, for [b]this is the Law and
the Prophets.
13 [a]"Enter by the narrow gate;
for wide *is* the gate and broad
is the way that leads to destruction, and there are many who go
in by it.
14 [1]"Because narrow *is* the gate
and [2]difficult *is* the way which
leads to life, and there are few
who find it.
15 [a]"Beware of false prophets,
[b]who come to you in sheep's
clothing, but inwardly they are
ravenous wolves.
16 [a]"You will know them by
their fruits. [b]Do men gather
grapes from thornbushes or figs
from thistles?
17 "Even so, [a]every good tree
bears good fruit, but a bad tree
bears bad fruit.
18 "A good tree cannot bear bad
fruit, nor *can* a bad tree bear
good fruit.
19 [a]"Every tree that does not
bear good fruit is cut down and
thrown into the fire.
20 "Therefore by their fruits you
will know them.
21 "Not everyone who says to
Me, [a]'Lord, Lord,' shall enter the
kingdom of heaven, but he who
[b]does the will of My Father in
heaven.
22 "Many will say to Me in that
day, 'Lord, Lord, have we [a]not
prophesied in Your name, cast
out demons in Your name, and
done many wonders in Your
name?'
23 "And [a]then I will declare to
them, 'I never knew you; [b]depart
from Me, you who practice
lawlessness!'
24 "Therefore [a]whoever hears
these sayings of Mine, and does
them, I will liken him to a wise
man who built his house on the
rock:
25 "and the rain descended, the
floods came, and the winds blew
and beat on that house; and it
did not fall, for it was founded
on the rock.
26 "But everyone who hears
these sayings of Mine, and does
not do them, will be like a foolish man who built his house on
the sand:
27 "and the rain descended, the
floods came, and the winds blew
and beat on that house; and it
fell. And great was its fall."
28 And so it was, when Jesus
had ended these sayings, that
[a]the people were astonished at
His teaching,
29 [a]for He taught them as one
having authority, and not as the
scribes.

8
When He had come down
from the mountain, great
multitudes followed Him.
2 [a]And behold, a leper came
and [b]worshiped Him, saying,
"Lord, if You are willing, You can
make me clean."
3 Then Jesus put out *His* hand
and touched him, saying, "I am
willing; be cleansed." Immediately his leprosy [a]was cleansed.
4 And Jesus said to him, [a]"See
that you tell no one; but go your
way, show yourself to the priest,
and offer the gift that [b]Moses
[c]commanded, as a testimony to
them."
5 [a]Now when Jesus had entered Ca·per′na·um, a [b]centurion

---

12 [a]Luke 6:31 [b]Gal. 5:14
13 [a]Luke 13:24
14 [1]NU, M *How narrow . . . !* [2]*confined*
15 [a]Jer. 23:16 [b]Mic. 3:5
16 [a]Matt. 7:20; 12:33 [b]Luke 6:43
17 [a]Matt. 12:33
19 [a][John 15:2, 6]
21 [a]Luke 6:46 [b]Rom. 2:13
22 [a]Num. 24:4
23 [a][2 Tim. 2:19] [b]Ps. 5:5; 6:8
24 [a]Luke 6:47–49
28 [a]Matt. 13:54
29 [a][John 7:46]

CHAPTER 8

2 [a]Mark 1:40–45 [b]John 9:38
3 [a]Luke 4:27
4 [a]Mark 5:43 [b]Luke 5:14 [c]Deut. 24:8
5 [a]Luke 7:1–3 [b]Matt. 27:54

came to Him, pleading with Him,

6 saying, "Lord, my servant is lying at home paralyzed, dreadfully tormented."

7 And Jesus said to him, "I will come and heal him."

8 The centurion answered and said, "Lord, [a]I am not worthy that You should come under my roof. But only [b]speak a word, and my servant will be healed.

9 "For I also am a man under authority, having soldiers under me. And I say to this *one,* 'Go,' and he goes; and to another, 'Come,' and he comes; and to my servant, 'Do this,' and he does *it.*"

10 When Jesus heard *it,* He marveled, and said to those who followed, "Assuredly, I say to you, I have not found such great faith, not even in Israel!

☆ 11 "And I say to you that [a]many will come from east and west, and sit down with Abraham, Isaac, and Jacob in the kingdom of heaven.

12 "But [a]the sons of the kingdom [b]will be cast out into outer darkness. There will be weeping and gnashing of teeth."

13 Then Jesus said to the centurion, "Go your way; and as you have believed, *so* let it be done for you." And his servant was healed that same hour.

14 [a]Now when Jesus had come into Peter's house, He saw [b]his wife's mother lying sick with a fever.

15 So He touched her hand, and the fever left her. And she arose and served [1]them.

16 [a]When evening had come, they brought to Him many who were demon-possessed. And He cast out the spirits with a word, and healed all who were sick,

17 that it might be fulfilled ★ which was spoken by Ī·sāi′ah the prophet, saying:

> [a]*"He Himself took our*
> *infirmities*
> *And bore our sicknesses."*

18 And when Jesus saw great multitudes about Him, He gave a command to depart to the other side.

19 [a]Then a certain scribe came and said to Him, "Teacher, I will follow You wherever You go."

20 And Jesus said to him, "Foxes have holes and birds of the air *have* nests, but the Son of Man has nowhere to lay *His* head."

21 [a]Then another of His disciples said to Him, "Lord, [b]let me first go and bury my father."

22 But Jesus said to him, "Follow Me, and let the dead bury their own dead."

23 Now when He got into a boat, His disciples followed Him.

24 [a]And suddenly a great tempest arose on the sea, so that the boat was covered with the waves. But He was asleep.

25 Then His disciples came to *Him* and awoke Him, saying, "Lord, save us! We are perishing!"

26 But He said to them, "Why are you fearful, O you of little faith?" Then [a]He arose and rebuked the winds and the sea, and there was a great calm.

27 So the men marveled, saying, [1]"Who can this be, that even the winds and the sea obey Him?"

28 [a]When He had come to the other side, to the country of the [1]Ger′ge·sēnes, there met Him two

8 [a]Luke 15:19, 21 [b]Ps. 107:20
11 [a]Is. 2:2, 3; Mal. 1:11
12 [a][Matt. 21:43] [b]Luke 13:28
14 [a]Mark 1:29–31 [b]1 Cor. 9:5
15 [1]NU, M *Him*
16 [a]Luke 4:40, 41
17 [a]Is. 53:4
19 [a]Luke 9:57, 58
21 [a]Luke 9:59, 60 [b]1 Kin. 19:20
24 [a]Mark 4:37
26 [a]Ps. 65:7; 89:9; 107:29
27 [1]Lit. *What sort of man is this*
28 [a]Mark 5:1–4 [1]NU *Gadarenes*

demon-possessed *men,* coming out of the tombs, exceedingly fierce, so that no one could pass that way.

29 And suddenly they cried out, saying, "What have we to do with You, Jesus, You Son of God? Have You come here to torment us before the time?"

30 Now a good way off from them there was a herd of many swine feeding.

31 So the demons begged Him, saying, "If You cast us out, [1]permit us to go away into the herd of swine."

32 And He said to them, "Go." So when they had come out, they went into the herd of swine. And suddenly the whole herd of swine ran violently down the steep place into the sea, and perished in the water.

33 Then those who kept *them* fled; and they went away into the city and told everything, including what *had happened* to the demon-possessed *men.*

34 And behold, the whole city came out to meet Jesus. And when they saw Him, [a]they begged *Him* to depart from their region.

CHAPTER 9

9 So He got into a boat, crossed over, [a]and came to His own city.

2 [a]Then behold, they brought to Him a paralytic lying on a bed. [b]When Jesus saw their faith, He said to the paralytic, "Son, be of good cheer; your sins are forgiven you."

3 And at once some of the scribes said within themselves, "This Man blasphemes!"

4 But Jesus, [a]knowing their thoughts, said, "Why do you think evil in your hearts?

5 "For which is easier, to say, '*Your* sins are forgiven you,' or to say, 'Arise and walk'?

6 "But that you may know that the Son of Man has power on earth to forgive sins"—then He said to the paralytic, "Arise, take up your bed, and go to your house."

7 And he arose and departed to his house.

8 Now when the multitudes saw *it,* they [a]marveled[1] and glorified God, who had given such power to men.

9 [a]As Jesus passed on from there, He saw a man named Matthew sitting at the tax office. And He said to him, "Follow Me." So he arose and followed Him.

10 [a]Now it happened, as Jesus sat at the table in the house, *that* behold, many tax collectors and sinners came and sat down with Him and His disciples.

11 And when the Phar'i·sees saw *it,* they said to His disciples, "Why does your Teacher eat with [a]tax collectors and [b]sinners?"

12 When Jesus heard *that,* He said to them, "Those who are well have no need of a physician, but those who are sick.

13 "But go and learn what *this* means: [a]'*I desire mercy and not sacrifice.*' For I did not come to call the righteous, [b]but sinners, [1]to repentance."

14 Then the disciples of John came to Him, saying, [a]"Why do we and the Phar'i·sees fast [1]often, but Your disciples do not fast?"

15 And Jesus said to them, "Can [a]the [1]friends of the bridegroom mourn as long as the bridegroom is with them? But the

8:31 [1]NU *send us into*

34 [a]Luke 5:8; Acts 16:39

9:1 [a]Matt. 4:13; 11:23

2 [a]Luke 5:18–26 [b]Matt. 8:10

4 [a]Matt. 12:25

8 [a]John 7:15 [1]NU *were afraid*

9 [a]Luke 5:27

10 [a]Mark 2:15

11 [a]Matt. 11:19 [b][Gal. 2:15]

13 [a]Hos. 6:6 [b]1 Tim. 1:15 [1]NU omits *to repentance*

14 [a]Luke 5:33–35; 18:12 [1]NU brackets *often* as disputed.

15 [a]John 3:29 [1]Lit. *sons of the bridechamber*

days will come when the bridegroom will be taken away from them, and [b]then they will fast.

16 "No one puts a piece of unshrunk cloth on an old garment; for [1]the patch pulls away from the garment, and the tear is made worse.

17 "Nor do they put new wine into old wineskins, or else the wineskins [1]break, the wine is spilled, and the wineskins are ruined. But they put new wine into new wineskins, and both are preserved."

18 [a]While He spoke these things to them, behold, a ruler came and worshiped Him, saying, "My daughter has just died, but come and lay Your hand on her and she will live."

19 So Jesus arose and followed him, and so *did* His [a]disciples.

20 [a]And suddenly, a woman who had a flow of blood for twelve years came from behind and [b]touched the hem of His garment.

21 For she said to herself, "If only I may touch His garment, I shall be made well."

22 But Jesus turned around, and when He saw her He said, "Be of good cheer, daughter; [a]your faith has made you well." And the woman was made well from that hour.

23 [a]When Jesus came into the ruler's house, and saw [b]the flute players and the noisy crowd wailing,

24 He said to them, [a]"Make room, for the girl is not dead, but sleeping." And they ridiculed Him.

25 But when the crowd was put outside, He went in and [a]took her by the hand, and the girl arose.

26 And the [a]report of this went out into all that land.

27 When Jesus departed from there, [a]two blind men followed Him, crying out and saying, [b]"Son of David, have mercy on us!"

28 And when He had come into the house, the blind men came to Him. And Jesus said to them, "Do you believe that I am able to do this?" They said to Him, "Yes, Lord."

29 Then He touched their eyes, saying, "According to your faith let it be to you."

30 And their eyes were opened. And Jesus sternly warned them, saying, [a]"See *that* no one knows *it.*"

31 [a]But when they had departed, they [1]spread the news about Him in all that [2]country.

32 [a]As they went out, behold, they brought to Him a man, mute and demon-possessed.

33 And when the demon was cast out, the mute spoke. And the multitudes marveled, saying, "It was never seen like this in Israel!"

34 But the Phar'i·sees said, [a]"He casts out demons by the ruler of the demons."

35 Then Jesus went about all the cities and villages, [a]teaching in their synagogues, preaching the gospel of the kingdom, and healing every sickness and every disease [1]among the people.

36 [a]But when He saw the multitudes, He was moved with compassion for them, because they were [1]weary and scattered, [b]like sheep having no shepherd.

37 Then He said to His disciples,

15 [b]Acts 13:2, 3; 14:23
16 [1]Lit. *that which is put on*
17 [1]*burst*
18 [a]Luke 8:41–56
19 [a]Matt. 10:2–4
20 [a]Luke 8:43 [b]Matt. 14:36; 23:5
22 [a]Luke 7:50; 8:48; 17:19; 18:42
23 [a]Mark 5:38 [b]2 Chr. 35:25
24 [a]Acts 20:10
25 [a]Mark 1:31
26 [a]Matt. 4:24
27 [a]Matt. 20:29–34 [b]Luke 18:38, 39
30 [a]Matt. 8:4
31 [a]Mark 7:36 [1]Lit. *made Him known* [2]Lit. *land*
32 [a]Matt. 12:22, 24
34 [a]Luke 11:15
35 [a]Matt. 4:23 [1]NU omits *among the people*
36 [a]Mark 6:34 [b]Num. 27:17 [1]NU, M *harassed*

[a]"The harvest truly *is* plentiful,
but the laborers *are* few.
38 [a]"Therefore pray the Lord of
the harvest to send out laborers
into His harvest."

10 And [a]when He had called
His twelve disciples to
Him, He gave them power *over*
unclean spirits, to cast them out,
and to heal all kinds of sickness
and all kinds of disease.
2 Now the names of the twelve
apostles are these: first, Simon,
[a]who is called Peter, and Andrew
his brother; James the *son* of
Zeb'e·dee, and John his brother;
3 Philip and Bartholomew;
Thomas and Matthew the tax
collector; James the *son* of Al-
phaē'us, and [1]Leb·baē'us, whose
surname was Thad·daē'us;
4 [a]Simon the [1]Can'a·nīte, and
Judas [b]Is·car'i·ot, who also betrayed Him.
5 These twelve Jesus sent out
and commanded them, saying:
[a]"Do not go into the way of the
Gentiles, and do not enter a city
of [b]the Samaritans.
6 [a]"But go rather to the [b]lost
sheep of the house of Israel.
7 [a]"And as you go, preach, saying, [b]'The kingdom of heaven [1]is
at hand.'
8 "Heal the sick, [1]cleanse the
lepers, [2]raise the dead, cast out
demons. [a]Freely you have received, freely give.
9 [a]"Provide neither gold nor
silver nor [b]copper in your money
belts,
10 "nor bag for *your* journey,
nor two tunics, nor sandals, nor
staffs; [a]for a worker is worthy of
his food.
11 [a]"Now whatever city or town
you enter, inquire who in it is
worthy, and stay there till you
go out.
12 "And when you go into a
household, greet it.
13 [a]"If the household is worthy,
let your peace come upon it.
[b]But if it is not worthy, let your
peace return to you.
14 [a]"And whoever will not receive you nor hear your words,
when you depart from that
house or city, [b]shake off the dust
from your feet.
15 "Assuredly, I say to you, [a]it
will be more tolerable for the
land of Sod'om and Go·mor'rah
in the day of judgment than for
that city!
16 [a]"Behold, I send you out as
sheep in the midst of wolves.
[b]Therefore be wise as serpents
and [c]harmless[1] as doves.
17 "But beware of men, for
[a]they will deliver you up to councils and [b]scourge you in their
synagogues.
18 [a]"You will be brought before governors and kings for My
sake, as a testimony to them and
to the Gentiles.
19 [a]"But when they deliver you
up, do not worry about how or
what you should speak. For [b]it
will be given to you in that hour
what you should speak;
20 [a]"for it is not you who speak,
but the Spirit of your Father who
speaks in you.
21 [a]"Now brother will deliver
up brother to death, and a father
his child; and children will rise
up against parents and cause
them to be put to death.
22 "And [a]you will be hated by
all for My name's sake. [b]But he
who endures to the end will be
saved.

37 [a]Luke 10:2
38 [a]2 Thess. 3:1

CHAPTER 10

1 [a]Luke 6:13
2 [a]John 1:42
3 [1]NU omits *Lebbaeus, whose surname was*
4 [a]Acts 1:13 [b]John 13:2, 26 [1]NU *Cananaean*
5 [a]Matt. 4:15 [b]John 4:9
6 [a]Matt. 15:24 [b]Jer. 50:6
7 [a]Luke 9:2 [b]Matt. 3:2 [1]*has drawn near*
8 [a][Acts 8:18] [1]NU *raise the dead, cleanse the lepers* [2]M omits *raise the dead*
9 [a]1 Sam. 9:7 [b]Mark 6:8
10 [a]1 Tim. 5:18
11 [a]Luke 10:8
13 [a]Luke 10:5 [b]Ps. 35:13
14 [a]Mark 6:11 [b]Acts 13:51
15 [a]Matt. 11:22, 24
16 [a]Luke 10:3 [b]Eph. 5:15 [c][Phil. 2:14–16] [1]*innocent*
17 [a]Mark 13:9 [b]Acts 5:40; 22:19; 26:11
18 [a]2 Tim. 4:16
19 [a]Luke 12:11, 12; 21:14, 15 [b]Ex. 4:12
20 [a]2 Sam. 23:2
21 [a]Mic. 7:6
22 [a]Luke 21:17 [b]Mark 13:13

23 [a]"When they persecute you
in this city, flee to another. For
assuredly, I say to you, you will
not have [b]gone through the cities of Israel [c]before the Son of
Man comes.
24 [a]"A disciple is not above *his*
teacher, nor a servant above his
master.
25 "It is enough for a disciple
that he be like his teacher, and a
servant like his master. If [a]they
have called the master of the
house [1]Bē·el′ze·bub, how much
more *will they call* those of his
household!
26 "Therefore do not fear them.
[a]For there is nothing covered
that will not be revealed, and
hidden that will not be known.
27 "Whatever I tell you in the
dark, [a]speak in the light; and
what you hear in the ear, preach
on the housetops.
28 [a]"And do not fear those who
kill the body but cannot kill the
soul. But rather [b]fear Him who
is able to destroy both soul and
body in [1]hell.
29 "Are not two [a]sparrows sold
for a [1]copper coin? And not one
of them falls to the ground apart
from your Father's will.
30 [a]"But the very hairs of your
head are all numbered.
31 "Do not fear therefore; you
are of more value than many
sparrows.
32 [a]"Therefore whoever confesses Me before men, [b]him I
will also confess before My Father who is in heaven.
33 [a]"But whoever denies Me before men, him I will also deny
before My Father who is in
heaven.
34 [a]"Do not think that I came
to bring peace on earth. I did
not come to bring peace but a
sword.
35 "For I have come to [a]*'set*[1] *a* ☆
*man against his father, a daugh-
ter against her mother, and a
daughter-in-law against her
mother-in-law';*
36 "and [a]*'a man's enemies will
be those of his own household.'*
37 [a]"He who loves father or
mother more than Me is not
worthy of Me. And he who loves
son or daughter more than Me is
not worthy of Me.
38 [a]"And he who does not take
his cross and follow after Me is
not worthy of Me.
39 [a]"He who finds his life will
lose it, and he who loses his life
for My sake will find it.
40 [a]"He who receives you receives Me, and he who receives
Me receives Him who sent Me.
41 [a]"He who receives a prophet
in the name of a prophet shall
receive a prophet's reward. And
he who receives a righteous man
in the name of a righteous man
shall receive a righteous man's
reward.
42 [a]"And whoever gives one of
these little ones only a cup of
cold *water* in the name of a
disciple, assuredly, I say to you,
he shall by no means lose his
reward."

11 Now it came to pass, when
Jesus finished command-
ing His twelve disciples, that He
departed from there to [a]teach
and to preach in their cities.
2 [a]And when John had heard
[b]in prison about the works of
Christ, he [1]sent two of his disciples
3 and said to Him, "Are You
[a]the Coming One, or do we look
for another?"

---

23 [a]Acts 8:1 [b][Mark 13:10] [c]Matt. 16:28
24 [a]John 15:20
25 [a]John 8:48, 52 [1]NU, M *Beelzebul*; a Philistine deity, 2 Kin. 1:2, 3
26 [a]Mark 4:22
27 [a]Acts 5:20
28 [a]Luke 12:4 [b]Luke 12:5 [1]Gr. *Gehenna*
29 [a]Luke 12:6, 7 [1]Gr. *assarion*, a coin worth about 1/16 of a denarius
30 [a]Luke 21:18
32 [a]Luke 12:8 [b][Rev. 3:5]
33 [a]2 Tim. 2:12
34 [a][Luke 12:49]
35 [a]Mic. 7:6 [1]*alienate a man from*
36 [a]John 13:18
37 [a]Luke 14:26
38 [a][Mark 8:34]
39 [a]John 12:25
40 [a]Luke 9:48
41 [a]1 Kin. 17:10
42 [a]Mark 9:41

CHAPTER 11

1 [a]Luke 23:5
2 [a]Luke 7:18–35 [b]Matt. 4:12; 14:3 [1]NU *sent by his*
3 [a]John 6:14

4 Jesus answered and said
to them, "Go and tell John the
things which you hear and see:
★ 5 [a]"*The* blind see and *the* lame
walk; *the* lepers are cleansed
and *the* deaf hear; *the* dead are
raised up and [b]*the* poor have the
gospel preached to them.
6 "And blessed is he who is not
[a]offended because of Me."
7 [a]As they departed, Jesus began to say to the multitudes concerning John: "What did you go
out into the wilderness to see?
[b]A reed shaken by the wind?
8 "But what did you go out
to see? A man clothed in soft
garments? Indeed, those who
wear soft *clothing* are in kings'
houses.
9 "But what did you go out to
see? A prophet? Yes, I say to you,
[a]and more than a prophet.
★ 10 "For this is *he* of whom it is
written:

[a]*'Behold, I send My messenger*
before Your face,
Who will prepare Your way
before You.'

11 "Assuredly, I say to you,
among those born of women
there has not risen one greater
than John the Baptist; but he
who is least in the kingdom of
heaven is greater than he.
12 [a]"And from the days of John
the Baptist until now the kingdom of heaven suffers violence,
and the violent take it by force.
★ 13 [a]"For all the prophets and the
law prophesied until John.
14 "And if you are willing to receive *it,* he is [a]E·lī′jah who is to
come.
15 [a]"He who has ears to hear, let
him hear!

5 [a]Is. 29:18; 35:4–6 [b]Ps. 22:26; Is. 61:1
6 [a][Rom. 9:32]
7 [a]Luke 7:24 [b][Eph. 4:14]
9 [a]Luke 1:76; 20:6
10 [a]Mal. 3:1
12 [a]Luke 16:16
13 [a]Mal. 4:4–6
14 [a]Luke 1:17
15 [a]Luke 8:8
16 [a]Luke 7:31
17 [1]Lit. *beat your breast*
19 [a]Matt. 9:10 [b]Luke 7:35 [1]*wine drinker* [2]NU *works*
20 [a]Luke 10:13–15, 18
21 [a]Jon. 3:6–8
22 [a]Matt. 10:15; 11:24
23 [a]Is. 14:13 [1]NU *will you be exalted to heaven? No, you will be*
24 [a]Matt. 10:15
25 [a]Luke 10:21, 22

16 [a]"But to what shall I liken this
generation? It is like children
sitting in the marketplaces and
calling to their companions,
17 "and saying:

'We played the flute for you,
And you did not dance;
We mourned to you,
And you did not [1]lament.'

18 "For John came neither eating nor drinking, and they say,
'He has a demon.'
19 "The Son of Man came eating and drinking, and they say,
'Look, a glutton and a [1]wine-
bibber, [a]a friend of tax collectors
and sinners!' [b]But wisdom is
justified by her [2]children."
20 [a]Then He began to rebuke
the cities in which most of His
mighty works had been done,
because they did not repent:
21 "Woe to you, Chō·rā′zin! Woe
to you, Beth·sā′i·da! For if the
mighty works which were done
in you had been done in Tȳre
and Sī′don, they would have repented long ago [a]in sackcloth
and ashes.
22 "But I say to you, [a]it will be
more tolerable for Tȳre and Sī′-
don in the day of judgment than
for you.
23 "And you, Ca·per′na·um,
[a]who[1] are exalted to heaven, will
be brought down to Hā′dēs; for
if the mighty works which were
done in you had been done in
Sod′om, it would have remained
until this day.
24 "But I say to you [a]that it shall
be more tolerable for the land of
Sod′om in the day of judgment
than for you."
25 [a]At that time Jesus answered
and said, "I thank You, Father,

Lord of heaven and earth, that
[b]You have hidden these things
from *the* wise and prudent [c]and
have revealed them to babes.
26 "Even so, Father, for so it
seemed good in Your sight.
27 [a]"All things have been delivered to Me by My Father, and no
one knows the Son except the
Father. [b]Nor does anyone know
the Father except the Son, and
the one to whom the Son wills
to reveal *Him.*
28 "Come to [a]Me, all *you* who
labor and are heavy laden, and I
will give you rest.
29 "Take My yoke upon you
[a]and learn from Me, for I am
[1]gentle and [b]lowly in heart, [c]and
you will find rest for your souls.
30 [a]"For My yoke *is* easy and
My burden is light."

12 At that time [a]Jesus went
through the grainfields
on the Sabbath. And His disciples were hungry, and began
to [b]pluck heads of grain and to
eat.
2 And when the Phar′i·sees saw
it, they said to Him, "Look, Your
disciples are doing what is not
lawful to do on the Sabbath!"
3 But He said to them, "Have
you not read [a]what David did
when he was hungry, he and
those who were with him:
4 "how he entered the house
of God and ate [a]the showbread
which was not lawful for him to
eat, nor for those who were with
him, [b]but only for the priests?
5 "Or have you not read in the
[a]law that on the Sabbath the
priests in the temple [1]profane
the Sabbath, and are blameless?
6 "Yet I say to you that in this
place there is [a]*One* greater than
the temple.
7 "But if you had known what
this means, [a]*'I desire mercy and*
not sacrifice,' you would not
have condemned the guiltless.
8 "For the Son of Man is Lord
[1]even of the Sabbath."
9 [a]Now when He had departed
from there, He went into their
synagogue.
10 And behold, there was a man
who had a withered hand. And
they asked Him, saying, [a]"Is it
lawful to heal on the Sabbath?"—
that they might accuse Him.
11 Then He said to them, "What
man is there among you who
has one sheep, and if it falls into
a pit on the Sabbath, will not lay
hold of it and lift *it* out?
12 "Of how much more value
then is a man than a sheep?
Therefore it is lawful to do good
on the Sabbath."
13 Then He said to the man,
"Stretch out your hand." And
he stretched *it* out, and it was
restored as whole as the other.
14 Then [a]the Phar′i·sees went
out and plotted against Him,
how they might destroy Him.
15 But when Jesus knew *it,* [a]He
withdrew from there. [b]And great
[1]multitudes followed Him, and
He healed them all.
16 Yet He [a]warned them not to
make Him known,
17 that it might be fulfilled
which was spoken by Ī·sāi′ah
the prophet, saying:

18 *"Behold!*[a] *My Servant whom* ★
I have chosen,
My Beloved [b]*in whom My*
soul is well pleased!
I will put My Spirit upon
Him,
And He will declare justice
to the Gentiles.

25 [b]Ps. 8:2 [c]Matt. 16:17
27 [a]Matt. 28:18 [b]John 1:18; 6:46; 10:15
28 [a][John 6:35–37]
29 [a][Phil. 2:5] [b]Zech. 9:9 [c]Jer. 6:16 [1]*meek*
30 [a][1 John 5:3]

CHAPTER 12

1 [a]Luke 6:1–5 [b]Deut. 23:25
3 [a]1 Sam. 21:6
4 [a]Lev. 24:5 [b]Ex. 29:32
5 [a]Num. 28:9 [1]*desecrate*
6 [a][Is. 66:1, 2]
7 [a][Hos. 6:6]
8 [1]NU, M omit *even*
9 [a]Mark 3:1–6
10 [a]John 9:16
14 [a]Mark 3:6
15 [a]Mark 3:7 [b]Matt. 19:2 [1]NU brackets *multitudes* as disputed.
16 [a]Matt. 8:4; 9:30; 17:9
18 [a]Is. 42:1–4; 49:3 [b]Matt. 3:17; 17:5

19 *He will not quarrel nor cry*
out,
Nor will anyone hear His
voice in the streets.
20 *A bruised reed He will not*
break,
And smoking flax He will
not quench,
Till He sends forth justice to
victory;
21 *And in His name Gentiles*
will trust."

22 [a]Then one was brought to
Him who was demon-possessed,
blind and mute; and He healed
him, so that the [1]blind and mute
man both spoke and saw.
23 And all the multitudes were
amazed and said, "Could this be
the [a]Son of David?"
24 [a]Now when the Phar′i·sees
heard *it* they said, "This *fellow*
does not cast out demons except
by [1]Bē·el′ze·bub, the ruler of the
demons."
25 But Jesus [a]knew their
thoughts, and said to them:
"Every kingdom divided against
itself is brought to desolation,
and every city or house divided
against itself will not stand.
26 "If Satan casts out Satan, he
is divided against himself. How
then will his kingdom stand?
27 "And if I cast out demons by
Bē·el′ze·bub, by whom do your
sons cast *them* out? Therefore
they shall be your judges.
28 "But if I cast out demons by
the Spirit of God, [a]surely the
kingdom of God has come upon
you.
29 [a]"Or how can one enter a
strong man's house and plunder
his goods, unless he first binds
the strong man? And then he
will plunder his house.
30 "He who is not with Me is
against Me, and he who does not
gather with Me scatters abroad.
31 "Therefore I say to you,
[a]every sin and blasphemy will
be forgiven men, [b]but the blasphemy *against* the Spirit will
not be forgiven men.
32 "Anyone who [a]speaks a word
against the Son of Man, [b]it will
be forgiven him; but whoever
speaks against the Holy Spirit,
it will not be forgiven him, either in this age or in the *age* to
come.
33 "Either make the tree good
and [a]its fruit good, or else make
the tree bad and its fruit bad; for
a tree is known by *its* fruit.
34 [a]"Brood[1] of vipers! How
can you, being evil, speak good
things? [b]For out of the abundance of the heart the mouth
speaks.
35 "A good man out of the good
treasure [1]of his heart brings
forth good things, and an evil
man out of the evil treasure
brings forth evil things.
36 "But I say to you that for
every idle word men may speak,
they will give account of it in the
day of judgment.
37 "For by your words you will
be justified, and by your words
you will be condemned."
38 [a]Then some of the scribes
and Phar′i·sees answered, saying, "Teacher, we want to see a
sign from You."
39 But He answered and said to
them, "An evil and [a]adulterous
generation seeks after a sign,
and no sign will be given to it
except the sign of the prophet
Jonah.
40 [a]"For as Jonah was three days
and three nights in the belly of

22 [a]Luke 11:14, 15 [1]NU omits *blind and*
23 [a]Matt. 9:27; 21:9
24 [a]Matt. 9:34 [1]NU, M *Beelzebul,* a Philistine deity
25 [a]Matt. 9:4
28 [a][Dan. 2:44; 7:14]
29 [a]Is. 49:24
31 [a]Mark 3:28–30 [b]Acts 7:51
32 [a]John 7:12, 52 [b]1 Tim. 1:13
33 [a]Matt. 7:16–18
34 [a]Matt. 3:7; 23:33 [b]Luke 6:45 [1]*Offspring*
35 [1]NU, M omit *of his heart*
38 [a]Mark 8:11
39 [a]Matt. 16:4
40 [a]Jon. 1:17

the great fish, so will the Son
of Man be three days and three
nights in the heart of the earth.
41 [a]"The men of Nin′e·veh will
rise up in the judgment with
this generation and [b]condemn
it, [c]because they repented at the
preaching of Jonah; and indeed
a greater than Jonah *is* here.
42 [a]"The queen of the South will
rise up in the judgment with this
generation and condemn it, for
she came from the ends of the
earth to hear the wisdom of Solomon; and indeed a greater than
Solomon *is* here.
43 [a]"When an unclean spirit
goes out of a man, [b]he goes
through dry places, seeking rest,
and finds none.
44 "Then he says, 'I will return
to my house from which I came.'
And when he comes, he finds *it*
empty, swept, and put in order.
45 "Then he goes and takes with
him seven other spirits more
wicked than himself, and they
enter and dwell there; [a]and the
last *state* of that man is worse
than the first. So shall it also be
with this wicked generation."
46 While He was still talking
to the multitudes, [a]behold, His
mother and [b]brothers stood
outside, seeking to speak with
Him.
47 Then one said to Him, "Look,
[a]Your mother and Your brothers
are standing outside, seeking to
speak with You."
48 But He answered and said
to the one who told Him, "Who
is My mother and who are My
brothers?"
49 And He stretched out His
hand toward His disciples and
said, "Here are My mother and
My [a]brothers!
50 "For [a]whoever does the will
of My Father in heaven is My
brother and sister and mother."

13

On the same day Jesus
went out of the house
[a]and sat by the sea.
2 [a]And great multitudes were
gathered together to Him, so
that [b]He got into a boat and sat;
and the whole multitude stood
on the shore.
3 Then He spoke many things
to them in parables, saying:
[a]"Behold, a sower went out to
sow.
4 "And as he sowed, some *seed*
fell by the wayside; and the birds
came and devoured them.
5 "Some fell on stony places,
where they did not have much
earth; and they immediately
sprang up because they had no
depth of earth.
6 "But when the sun was up
they were scorched, and because
they had no root they withered
away.
7 "And some fell among thorns,
and the thorns sprang up and
choked them.
8 "But others fell on good
ground and yielded a crop: some
[a]a hundredfold, some sixty, some
thirty.
9 [a]"He who has ears to hear, let
him hear!"
10 And the disciples came and
said to Him, "Why do You speak
to them in parables?"
11 He answered and said to
them, "Because [a]it has been
given to you to know the [1]mys-
teries of the kingdom of heaven,
but to them it has not been
given.
12 [a]"For whoever has, to him
more will be given, and he will
have abundance; but whoever

41 [a]Luke 11:32 [b]Jer. 3:11 [c]Jon. 3:5
42 [a]1 Kin. 10:1–13
43 [a]Luke 11:24–26 [b][1 Pet. 5:8]
45 [a][2 Pet. 2:20–22]
46 [a]Luke 8:19–21 [b]John 2:12; 7:3, 5
47 [a]Matt. 13:55, 56
49 [a]John 20:17
50 [a]John 15:14

CHAPTER 13

1 [a]Mark 4:1–12
2 [a]Luke 8:4 [b]Luke 5:3
3 [a]Luke 8:5
8 [a]Gen. 26:12
9 [a]Matt. 11:15
11 [a]Mark 4:10, 11 [1]*secret* or *hidden truths*
12 [a]Matt. 25:29

does not have, even what he has
will be taken away from him.
13 "Therefore I speak to them in
parables, because seeing they do
not see, and hearing they do not
hear, nor do they understand.
★ 14 "And in them the prophecy of
Ī·sāi′ah is fulfilled, which says:

[a]*'Hearing you will hear and*
shall not understand,
And seeing you will see and
not [b]*perceive;*
15 *For the hearts of this people*
have grown dull.
Their ears [a]*are hard of*
hearing,
And their eyes they have
[b]*closed,*
Lest they should see with
their eyes and hear with
their ears,
Lest they should understand
with their hearts and
turn,
So that I [1]*should* [c]*heal*
them.'

16 "But [a]blessed *are* your eyes
for they see, and your ears for
they hear;
17 "for assuredly, I say to you
[a]that many prophets and righteous *men* desired to see what
you see, and did not see *it*, and
to hear what you hear, and did
not hear *it*.
18 [a]"Therefore hear the parable
of the sower:
19 "When anyone hears the
word [a]of the kingdom, and does
not understand *it*, then the
wicked *one* comes and snatches
away what was sown in his
heart. This is he who received
seed by the wayside.
20 "But he who received the
seed on stony places, this is he
who hears the word and immediately [a]receives it with joy;
21 "yet he has no root in himself,
but endures only for a while. For
when [a]tribulation or persecution
arises because of the word, immediately [b]he stumbles.
22 "Now [a]he who received seed
[b]among the thorns is he who
hears the word, and the cares of
this world and the deceitfulness
of riches choke the word, and he
becomes unfruitful.
23 "But he who received seed
on the good ground is he who
hears the word and understands
it, who indeed bears [a]fruit and
produces: some a hundredfold,
some sixty, some thirty."
24 Another parable He put forth
to them, saying: "The kingdom
of heaven is like a man who
sowed good seed in his field;
25 "but while men slept, his
enemy came and sowed tares
among the wheat and went his
way.
26 "But when the grain had
sprouted and produced a crop,
then the tares also appeared.
27 "So the servants of the owner
came and said to him, 'Sir, did
you not sow good seed in your
field? How then does it have
tares?'
28 "He said to them, 'An enemy
has done this.' The servants said
to him, 'Do you want us then to
go and gather them up?'
29 "But he said, 'No, lest while
you gather up the tares you also
uproot the wheat with them.
30 'Let both grow together until
the harvest, and at the time of
harvest I will say to the reapers, "First gather together the
tares and bind them in bundles

14 [a]Is. 6:9, 10; Ezek. 12:2 [b][John 3:36]
15 [a]Heb. 5:11 [b]Luke 19:42 [c]Acts 28:26, 27 [1]NU, M *would*
16 [a]Luke 10:23, 24
17 [a]Heb. 11:13
18 [a]Mark 4:13–20
19 [a]Matt. 4:23
20 [a]Is. 58:2
21 [a][Acts 14:22] [b]Matt. 11:6
22 [a]1 Tim. 6:9 [b]Jer. 4:3
23 [a]Col. 1:6

to burn them, but [a]gather the wheat into my barn." ' "

31 Another parable He put forth to them, saying: [a]"The kingdom of heaven is like a mustard seed, which a man took and sowed in his field,

32 "which indeed is the least of all the seeds; but when it is grown it is greater than the herbs and becomes a [a]tree, so that the birds of the air come and nest in its branches."

33 [a]Another parable He spoke to them: "The kingdom of heaven is like leaven, which a woman took and hid in three [1]measures of meal till [b]it was all leavened."

34 [a]All these things Jesus spoke to the multitude in parables; and without a parable He did not speak to them,

35 that it might be fulfilled which was spoken by the prophet, saying:

> [a]*"I will open My mouth in*
> *parables;*
> [b]*I will utter things kept*
> *secret from the*
> *foundation of the world."*

36 Then Jesus sent the multitude away and went into the house. And His disciples came to Him, saying, "Explain to us the parable of the tares of the field."

37 He answered and said to them: "He who sows the good seed is the Son of Man.

38 [a]"The field is the world, the good seeds are the sons of the kingdom, but the tares are [b]the sons of the wicked *one.*

39 "The enemy who sowed them is the devil, [a]the harvest is the end of the age, and the reapers are the angels.

40 "Therefore as the tares are gathered and burned in the fire, so it will be at the end of this age.

41 "The Son of Man will send out His angels, [a]and they will gather out of His kingdom all things that offend, and those who practice lawlessness,

42 [a]"and will cast them into the furnace of fire. [b]There will be wailing and gnashing of teeth.

43 [a]"Then the righteous will shine forth as the sun in the kingdom of their Father. [b]He who has ears to hear, let him hear!

44 "Again, the kingdom of heaven is like treasure hidden in a field, which a man found and hid; and for joy over it he goes and [a]sells all that he has and [b]buys that field.

45 "Again, the kingdom of heaven is like a merchant seeking beautiful pearls,

46 "who, when he had found [a]one pearl of great price, went and sold all that he had and bought it.

47 "Again, the kingdom of heaven is like a dragnet that was cast into the sea and [a]gathered some of every kind,

48 "which, when it was full, they drew to shore; and they sat down and gathered the good into vessels, but threw the bad away.

49 "So it will be at the end of the age. The angels will come forth, [a]separate the wicked from among the just,

50 "and cast them into the furnace of fire. There will be wailing and gnashing of teeth."

30 [a]Matt. 3:12
31 [a]Luke 13:18, 19
32 [a]Ezek. 17:22–24; 31:3–9
33 [a]Luke 13:20, 21 [b][1 Cor. 5:6] [1]Gr. *sata,* same as a Heb. *seah;* approximately 2 pecks in all
34 [a]Ps. 78:2; Mark 4:33, 34
35 [a]Ps. 78:2 [b]Eph. 3:9
38 [a]Rom. 10:18 [b]John 8:44
39 [a]Rev. 14:15
41 [a]Matt. 18:7
42 [a]Rev. 19:20; 20:10 [b]Matt. 8:12; 13:50
43 [a][Dan. 12:3] [b]Matt. 13:9
44 [a]Phil. 3:7, 8 [b][Is. 55:1]
46 [a]Prov. 2:4; 3:14, 15; 8:10, 19
47 [a]Matt. 22:9, 10
49 [a]Matt. 25:32

51 [1]Jesus said to them, "Have
you understood all these things?"
They said to Him, "Yes, [2]Lord."
52 Then He said to them, "Therefore every [1]scribe instructed
[2]concerning the kingdom of
heaven is like a householder
who brings out of his treasure
[a]*things* new and old."
53 Now it came to pass, when
Jesus had finished these parables, that He departed from
there.
54 [a]When He had come to His
own country, He taught them
in their synagogue, so that
they were astonished and said,
"Where did this *Man* get this wisdom and *these* mighty works?
55 [a]"Is this not the carpenter's
son? Is not His mother called
Mary? And [b]His brothers [c]James,
[1]Jō′sēs, Simon, and Judas?
56 "And His sisters, are they not
all with us? Where then did this
Man get all these things?"
57 So they [a]were offended at
Him. But Jesus said to them, [b]"A
prophet is not without honor
except in his own country and in
his own house."
58 Now [a]He did not do many
mighty works there because of
their unbelief.

14 At that time [a]Her′od the
tetrarch heard the report
about Jesus
2 and said to his servants,
"This is John the Baptist; he is
risen from the dead, and therefore these powers are at work in
him."
3 [a]For Her′od had laid hold of
John and bound him, and put
him in prison for the sake of
He·rō′di·as, his brother Philip's
wife.
4 Because John had said to
him, [a]"It is not lawful for you to
have her."
5 And although he wanted to
put him to death, he feared the
multitude, [a]because they counted
him as a prophet.
6 But when Her′od's birthday
was celebrated, the daughter of
He·rō′di·as danced before them
and pleased Her′od.
7 Therefore he promised with
an oath to give her whatever she
might ask.
8 So she, having been prompted
by her mother, said, "Give me
John the Baptist's head here on
a platter."
9 And the king was sorry; nevertheless, because of the oaths
and because of those who sat
with him, he commanded *it* to
be given to *her.*
10 So he sent and had John beheaded in prison.
11 And his head was brought on
a platter and given to the girl, and
she brought *it* to her mother.
12 Then his disciples came and
took away the body and buried
it, and went and told Jesus.
13 [a]When Jesus heard *it,* He
departed from there by boat to
a deserted place by Himself. But
when the multitudes heard it,
they followed Him on foot from
the cities.
14 And when Jesus went out He
saw a great multitude; and He
[a]was moved with compassion
for them, and healed their sick.
15 [a]When it was evening, His
disciples came to Him, saying,
"This is a deserted place, and
the hour is already late. Send
the multitudes away, that they
may go into the villages and buy
themselves food."
16 But Jesus said to them, "They

51 [1]NU omits *Jesus said to them* [2]NU omits *Lord*
52 [a]Song 7:13 [1]A scholar of the Old Testament [2]Or *for*
54 [a]Luke 4:16
55 [a]John 6:42 [b]Matt. 12:46 [c]Mark 15:40 [1]NU *Joseph*
57 [a]Matt. 11:6 [b]Luke 4:24
58 [a]Mark 6:5, 6

CHAPTER 14

1 [a]Mark 6:14–29
3 [a]Luke 3:19, 20
4 [a]Lev. 18:16; 20:21
5 [a]Luke 20:6
13 [a]John 6:1, 2
14 [a]Mark 6:34
15 [a]Luke 9:12

do not need to go away. You give
them something to eat."
17 And they said to Him, "We
have here only five loaves and
two fish."
18 He said, "Bring them here to
Me."
19 Then He commanded the
multitudes to sit down on the
grass. And He took the five loaves
and the two fish, and looking
up to heaven, [a]He blessed and
broke and gave the loaves to the
disciples; and the disciples gave
to the multitudes.
20 So they all ate and were
filled, and they took up twelve
baskets full of the fragments
that remained.
21 Now those who had eaten
were about five thousand men,
besides women and children.
22 Immediately Jesus [1]made
His disciples get into the boat
and go before Him to the other
side, while He sent the multitudes away.
23 [a]And when He had sent the
multitudes away, He went up
on the mountain by Himself to
pray. [b]Now when evening came,
He was alone there.
24 But the boat was now [1]in
the middle of the sea, tossed
by the waves, for the wind was
contrary.
25 Now in the fourth watch of
the night Jesus went to them,
walking on the sea.
26 And when the disciples saw
Him [a]walking on the sea, they
were troubled, saying, "It is a
ghost!" And they cried out for
fear.
27 But immediately Jesus spoke
to them, saying, [1]"Be of good
[a]cheer! [2]It is I; do not be afraid."
28 And Peter answered Him
and said, "Lord, if it is You, command me to come to You on the
water."
29 So He said, "Come." And
when Peter had come down out
of the boat, he walked on the
water to go to Jesus.
30 But when he saw [1]that the
wind *was* boisterous, he was
afraid; and beginning to sink
he cried out, saying, "Lord, save
me!"
31 And immediately Jesus
stretched out *His* hand and
caught him, and said to him, "O
you of [a]little faith, why did you
doubt?"
32 And when they got into the
boat, the wind ceased.
33 Then those who were in the
boat [1]came and worshiped Him,
saying, "Truly [a]You are the Son
of God."
34 [a]When they had crossed
over, they came [1]to the land of
Gen·nes′a·ret.
35 And when the men of that
place recognized Him, they sent
out into all that surrounding
region, brought to Him all who
were sick,
36 and begged Him that they
might only [a]touch the hem of
His garment. And [b]as many as
touched *it* were made perfectly
well.

15 Then [a]the scribes and
Phar′i·sees who were
from Jerusalem came to Jesus,
saying,
2 [a]"Why do Your disciples
transgress the tradition of the elders? For they do not wash their
hands when they eat bread."
3 He answered and said to
them, "Why do you also transgress the commandment of God
because of your tradition?

19 [a]Matt. 15:36; 26:26
22 [1]*invited, strongly urged*
23 [a]Mark 6:46 [b]John 6:16
24 [1]NU *many furlongs away from the land*
26 [a]Job 9:8
27 [a]Acts 23:11; 27:22, 25, 36 [1]*Take courage* [2]Lit. *I am*
30 [1]NU brackets *that* and *boisterous* as disputed.
31 [a]Matt. 6:30; 8:26
33 [a]Ps. 2:7 [1]NU omits *came and*
34 [a]Mark 6:53 [1]NU *to land at*
36 [a][Mark 5:24–34] [b][Luke 6:19]

CHAPTER 15
1 [a]Mark 7:1
2 [a]Mark 7:5

4 "For God commanded, saying, [a]*'Honor your father and your mother'*; and, [b]*'He who curses father or mother, let him be put to death.'*
5 "But you say, 'Whoever says to his father or mother, [a]"Whatever profit you might have received from me *is* a gift *to God*"—
6 'then he need not honor his father [1]or mother.' Thus you have made the [2]commandment of God of no effect by your tradition.
7 [a]"Hypocrites! Well did Ī·sāi′ah prophesy about you, saying:

★ 8 *'These[a] people [1]draw near to*
Me with their mouth,
And honor Me with their
lips,
But their heart is far from
Me.
9 *And in vain they worship*
Me,
[a]*Teaching as doctrines the*
commandments of
men.' "

10 [a]When He had called the
multitude to *Himself*, He said to
them, "Hear and understand:
11 [a]"Not what goes into the
mouth defiles a man; but what
comes out of the mouth, this defiles a man."
12 Then His disciples came and
said to Him, "Do You know that
the Phar′i·sees were offended
when they heard this saying?"
13 But He answered and said,
[a]"Every plant which My heavenly Father has not planted will
be uprooted.
14 "Let them alone. [a]They are
blind leaders of the blind. And
if the blind leads the blind, both
will fall into a ditch."

4 [a][Deut. 5:16] [b]Ex. 21:17
5 [a]Mark 7:11, 12
6 [1]NU omits *or mother* [2]NU *word*
7 [a]Mark 7:6
8 [a]Ps. 78:36; Is. 29:13 [1]NU omits *draw near to Me with their mouth, And*
9 [a][Col. 2:18–22]
10 [a]Mark 7:14
11 [a][Acts 10:15]
13 [a][John 15:2]
14 [a]Luke 6:39
15 [a]Mark 7:17
16 [a]Matt. 16:9
17 [a][1 Cor. 6:13]
18 [a][James 3:6]
19 [a]Prov. 6:14
21 [a]Mark 7:24–30
22 [a]Matt. 1:1; 22:41, 42
24 [a]Matt. 10:5, 6
26 [a]Matt. 7:6

15 [a]Then Peter answered and
said to Him, "Explain this parable to us."
16 So Jesus said, [a]"Are you also
still without understanding?
17 "Do you not yet understand
that [a]whatever enters the mouth
goes into the stomach and is
eliminated?
18 "But [a]those things which
proceed out of the mouth come
from the heart, and they defile a
man.
19 [a]"For out of the heart proceed evil thoughts, murders,
adulteries, fornications, thefts,
false witness, blasphemies.
20 "These are *the things* which
defile a man, but to eat with unwashed hands does not defile a
man."
21 [a]Then Jesus went out from
there and departed to the region
of Tȳre and Sī′don.
22 And behold, a woman of Cā′-
naan came from that region and
cried out to Him, saying, "Have
mercy on me, O Lord, [a]Son of
David! My daughter is severely
demon-possessed."
23 But He answered her not a
word. And His disciples came
and urged Him, saying, "Send
her away, for she cries out after us."
24 But He answered and said,
[a]"I was not sent except to the lost
sheep of the house of Israel."
25 Then she came and wor-
shiped Him, saying, "Lord, help
me!"
26 But He answered and said,
"It is not good to take the children's bread and throw *it* to the
little [a]dogs."
27 And she said, "Yes, Lord,
yet even the little dogs eat the

crumbs which fall from their
masters' table."
28 Then Jesus answered and
said to her, "O woman, [a]great
is your faith! Let it be to you as
you desire." And her daughter
was healed from that very hour.
29 [a]Jesus departed from there,
[b]skirted the Sea of Galilee, and
went up on the mountain and
sat down there.
30 [a]Then great multitudes came
to Him, having with them *the*
lame, blind, mute, [1]maimed, and
many others; and they laid them
down at Jesus' [b]feet, and He
healed them.
31 So the multitude marveled
when they saw *the* mute speaking, *the* [1]maimed made whole,
the lame walking, and *the* blind
seeing; and they [a]glorified the
God of Israel.
32 [a]Now Jesus called His disciples to *Himself* and said, "I have
compassion on the multitude,
because they have now continued with Me three days and
have nothing to eat. And I do not
want to send them away hungry,
lest they faint on the way."
33 [a]Then His disciples said
to Him, "Where could we get
enough bread in the wilderness
to fill such a great multitude?"
34 Jesus said to them, "How
many loaves do you have?" And
they said, "Seven, and a few
little fish."
35 So He commanded the multitude to sit down on the ground.
36 And [a]He took the seven
loaves and the fish and [b]gave
thanks, broke *them* and gave
them to His disciples; and the
disciples *gave* to the multitude.
37 So they all ate and were
filled, and they took up seven
large baskets full of the fragments that were left.
38 Now those who ate were four
thousand men, besides women
and children.
39 [a]And He sent away the multitude, got into the boat, and came
to the region of [1]Mag'da·la.

16 Then the [a]Phar'i·sees and
Sad'dū·cees came, and
testing Him asked that He would
show them a sign from heaven.
2 He answered and said to
them, "When it is evening you
say, '*It will be* fair weather, for
the sky is red';
3 "and in the morning, '*It will
be* foul weather today, for the
sky is red and threatening.'
[1]Hypocrites! You know how to
discern the face of the sky, but
you cannot *discern* the signs of
the times.
4 [a]"A wicked and adulterous
generation seeks after a sign,
and no sign shall be given to it
except the sign of [1]the prophet
Jonah." And He left them and
departed.
5 Now [a]when His disciples had
come to the other side, they had
forgotten to take bread.
6 Then Jesus said to them,
[a]"Take heed and beware of the
[1]leaven of the Phar'i·sees and
the Sad'dū·cees."
7 And they reasoned among
themselves, saying, "*It is* because we have taken no bread."
8 But Jesus, being aware of
it, said to them, "O you of little
faith, why do you reason among
yourselves because you [1]have
brought no bread?
9 [a]"Do you not yet understand,
or remember the five loaves of
the five thousand and how many
baskets you took up?

28 [a]Luke 7:9
29 [a]Mark 7:31–37 [b]Matt. 4:18
30 [a]Is. 35:5, 6 [b]Luke 7:38; 8:41; 10:39 [1]*crippled*
31 [a]Luke 5:25, 26; 19:37, 38 [1]*crippled*
32 [a]Mark 8:1–10
33 [a]2 Kin. 4:43
36 [a]Matt. 14:19; 26:27 [b]Luke 22:19
39 [a]Mark 8:10 [1]NU *Magadan*

CHAPTER 16

1 [a]Mark 8:11
3 [1]NU omits *Hypocrites*
4 [a]Matt. 12:39 [1]NU omits *the prophet*
5 [a]Mark 8:14
6 [a]Luke 12:1 [1]*yeast*
8 [1]NU *have no bread*
9 [a]Matt. 14:15–21

10 [a]"Nor the seven loaves of the
four thousand and how many
large baskets you took up?
11 "How is it you do not understand that I did not speak
to you concerning bread?—*but*
to beware of the [1]leaven of the
Phar′i·sees and Sad′dū·cees."
12 Then they understood that
He did not tell *them* to beware
of the leaven of bread, but of the
[1]doctrine of the Phar′i·sees and
Sad′dū·cees.
13 When Jesus came into the
region of Caes·a·rē′a Phi·lip′pī,
He asked His disciples, saying,
[a]"Who do men say that I, the
Son of Man, am?"
14 So they said, [a]"Some *say*
John the Baptist, some E·lī′jah,
and others Jer·e·mī′ah or [b]one of
the prophets."
15 He said to them, "But who do
[a]you say that I am?"
16 Simon Peter answered and
said, [a]"You are the Christ, the
Son of the living God."
17 Jesus answered and said to
him, "Blessed are you, Simon
Bar-Jō′nah, [a]for flesh and blood
has not revealed *this* to you, but
[b]My Father who is in heaven.
18 "And I also say to you that
[a]you are Peter, and [b]on this rock
I will build My church, and [c]the
gates of Hā′dēs shall not [1]prevail
against it.
19 [a]"And I will give you the keys
of the kingdom of heaven, and
whatever you bind on earth [1]will
be bound in heaven, and whatever you loose on earth will be
loosed in heaven."
20 [a]Then He commanded His
disciples that they should tell
no one that He was Jesus the
Christ.
21 From that time Jesus began
[a]to show to His disciples that He
must go to Jerusalem, and suffer
many things from the elders and
chief priests and scribes, and be
killed, and be raised the third
day.
22 Then Peter took Him aside
and began to rebuke Him, saying, [1]"Far be it from You, Lord;
this shall not happen to You!"
23 But He turned and said to
Peter, "Get behind Me, [a]Satan!
[b]You are [1]an offense to Me, for
you are not mindful of the things
of God, but the things of men."
24 [a]Then Jesus said to His disciples, "If anyone desires to
come after Me, let him deny
himself, and take up his cross,
and [b]follow Me.
25 "For [a]whoever desires to save
his life will lose it, but whoever
loses his life for My sake will
find it.
26 "For what [a]profit is it to a
man if he gains the whole world,
and loses his own soul? Or [b]what
will a man give in exchange for
his soul?
27 "For [a]the Son of Man will ☆
come in the glory of His Father
[b]with His angels, [c]and then He
will reward each according to
his works.
28 "Assuredly, I say to you,
[a]there are some standing here
who shall not taste death till
they see the Son of Man coming
in His kingdom."

17 Now [a]after six days Jesus
took Peter, James, and
John his brother, led them up on
a high mountain by themselves;
2 and He was transfigured before them. His face shone like
the sun, and His clothes became
as white as the light.

10 [a]Matt. 15:32–38
11 [1]*yeast*
12 [1]*teaching*
13 [a]Luke 9:18
14 [a]Matt. 14:2 [b]Matt. 21:11
15 [a]John 6:67
16 [a]Acts 8:37; 9:20
17 [a][Eph. 2:8] [b]Gal. 1:16
18 [a]John 1:42 [b][Eph. 2:20] [c]Is. 38:10 [1]*be victorious*
19 [a]Matt. 18:18 [1]Or *will have been bound . . . will have been loosed*
20 [a]Luke 9:21
21 [a]Luke 9:22; 18:31; 24:46
22 [1]Lit. *Merciful to You,* (May God be merciful)
23 [a]Matt. 4:10 [b][Rom. 8:7] [1]*a stumbling block*
24 [a][2 Tim. 3:12] [b][1 Pet. 2:21]
25 [a]John 12:25
26 [a]Luke 12:20, 21 [b]Ps. 49:7, 8
27 [a]Mark 8:38 [b][Dan. 7:10] [c]Rom. 2:6
28 [a]Luke 9:27

CHAPTER 17

1 [a]Mark 9:2–8

3 And behold, Moses and E·lī′-
jah appeared to them, talking
with Him.
4 Then Peter answered and
said to Jesus, "Lord, it is good
for us to be here; if You wish, [1]let
us make here three tabernacles:
one for You, one for Moses, and
one for E·lī′jah."
★ 5 [a]While he was still speaking, behold, a bright cloud overshadowed them; and suddenly a
voice came out of the cloud, saying, [b]"This is My beloved Son,
[c]in whom I am well pleased.
[d]Hear Him!"
6 [a]And when the disciples
heard *it,* they fell on their faces
and were greatly afraid.
7 But Jesus came and [a]touched
them and said, "Arise, and do
not be afraid."
8 When they had lifted up their
eyes, they saw no one but Jesus
only.
9 Now as they came down
from the mountain, Jesus commanded them, saying, "Tell the
vision to no one until the Son of
Man is risen from the dead."
10 And His disciples asked
Him, saying, [a]"Why then do the
scribes say that E·lī′jah must
come first?"
11 Jesus answered and said to
them, "Indeed, E·lī′jah is coming [1]first and will [a]restore all
things.
12 [a]"But I say to you that E·lī′jah
has come already, and they [b]did
not know him but did to him
whatever they wished. Likewise
[c]the Son of Man is also about to
suffer at their hands."
13 [a]Then the disciples understood that He spoke to them of
John the Baptist.
14 [a]And when they had come
to the multitude, a man came to
Him, kneeling down to Him and
saying,
15 "Lord, have mercy on my
son, for he is [1]an epileptic and
suffers severely; for he often
falls into the fire and often into
the water.
16 "So I brought him to Your
disciples, but they could not cure
him."
17 Then Jesus answered and
said, "O [1]faithless and [a]perverse
generation, how long shall I be
with you? How long shall I bear
with you? Bring him here to
Me."
18 And Jesus [a]rebuked the demon, and it came out of him;
and the child was cured from
that very hour.
19 Then the disciples came to
Jesus privately and said, "Why
could we not cast it out?"
20 So Jesus said to them, "Because of your [1]unbelief; for assuredly, I say to you, [a]if you
have faith as a mustard seed,
you will say to this mountain,
'Move from here to there,' and
it will move; and nothing will be
impossible for you.
21 [1]"However, this kind does
not go out except by prayer and
fasting."
22 [a]Now while they were [1]stay-
ing in Galilee, Jesus said to them,
"The Son of Man is about to be
betrayed into the hands of men,
23 "and they will kill Him, and ☆
the third day He will be raised
up." And they were exceedingly
[a]sorrowful.
24 [a]When they had come to
[1]Ca·per′na·um, those who received the [2]*temple* tax came
to Peter and said, "Does your
Teacher not pay the *temple* tax?"

4 [1]NU *I will make*
5 [a]2 Pet. 1:17 [b]Mark 1:11 [c]Is. 42:1; Matt. 3:17; 12:18 [d][Deut. 18:15, 19]
6 [a]2 Pet. 1:18
7 [a]Dan. 8:18
10 [a]Mal. 4:5
11 [a][Mal. 4:6] [1]NU omits *first*
12 [a]Mark 9:12, 13 [b]Matt. 14:3, 10 [c]Matt. 16:21
13 [a]Matt. 11:14
14 [a]Mark 9:14–28
15 [1]Lit. *moonstruck*
17 [a]Phil. 2:15 [1]*unbelieving*
18 [a]Luke 4:41
20 [a]Luke 17:6 [1]NU *little faith*
21 [1]NU omits v. 21.
22 [a]Mark 8:31 [1]NU *gathering together*
23 [a]John 16:6; 19:30; Acts 10:40
24 [a]Mark 9:33 [1]NU *Capharnaum,* here and elsewhere [2]Lit. *double drachma*

25 He said, "Yes." And when he
had come into the house, Jesus
anticipated him, saying, "What
do you think, Simon? From
whom do the kings of the earth
take customs or taxes, from their
sons or from [a]strangers?"
26 Peter said to Him, "From
strangers." Jesus said to him,
"Then the sons are free.
27 "Nevertheless, lest we offend them, go to the sea, cast
in a hook, and take the fish that
comes up first. And when you
have opened its mouth, you will
find a [1]piece of money; take that
and give it to them for Me and
you."

18 At [a]that time the disciples came to Jesus, say-
ing, "Who then is greatest in the
kingdom of heaven?"
2 Then Jesus called a little
[a]child to Him, set him in the
midst of them,
3 and said, "Assuredly, I say to
you, [a]unless you are converted
and become as little children,
you will by no means enter the
kingdom of heaven.
4 [a]"Therefore whoever humbles himself as this little child is
the greatest in the kingdom of
heaven.
5 [a]"Whoever receives one little
child like this in My name receives Me.
6 [a]"But whoever causes one
of these little ones who believe
in Me to sin, it would be better
for him if a millstone were hung
around his neck, and he were
drowned in the depth of the
sea.
7 "Woe to the world because
of [1]offenses! For [a]offenses must
come, but [b]woe to that man by
whom the offense comes!
8 [a]"If your hand or foot causes
you to sin, cut it off and cast *it*
from you. It is better for you to
enter into life lame or maimed,
rather than having two hands
or two feet, to be cast into the
everlasting fire.
9 "And if your eye causes you
to sin, pluck it out and cast *it*
from you. It is better for you
to enter into life with one eye,
rather than having two eyes, to
be cast into [1]hell fire.
10 "Take heed that you do not
despise one of these little ones,
for I say to you that in heaven
[a]their angels always [b]see the
face of My Father who is in
heaven.
11 [a]"For[1] the Son of Man has
come to save that which was
lost.
12 [a]"What do you think? If a
man has a hundred sheep, and
one of them goes astray, does he
not leave the ninety-nine and go
to the mountains to seek the one
that is straying?
13 "And if he should find it, assuredly, I say to you, he rejoices
more over that *sheep* than over
the ninety-nine that did not go
astray.
14 "Even so it is not the [a]will
of your Father who is in heaven
that one of these little ones
should perish.
15 "Moreover [a]if your brother
sins against you, go and tell him
his fault between you and him
alone. If he hears you, [b]you have
gained your brother.
16 "But if he will not hear, take
with you one or two more, that
[a]*'by the mouth of two or three*
witnesses every word may be
established.'
17 "And if he refuses to hear

25 [a][Is. 60:10–17]
27 [1]Gr. *stater,* the exact temple tax for two

CHAPTER 18
1 [a]Luke 9:46–48; 22:24–27
2 [a]Matt. 19:14
3 [a]Luke 18:16
4 [a][Matt. 20:27; 23:11]
5 [a][Matt. 10:42]
6 [a]Mark 9:42
7 [a][1 Cor. 11:19] [b]Matt. 26:24; 27:4, 5 [1]*enticements to sin*
8 [a]Matt. 5:29, 30
9 [1]Gr. *Gehenna*
10 [a][Heb. 1:14] [b]Luke 1:19
11 [a]Luke 9:56 [1]NU omits v. 11.
12 [a]Luke 15:4–7
14 [a][1 Tim. 2:4]
15 [a]Lev. 19:17 [b][James 5:20]
16 [a]Deut. 17:6; 19:15

them, tell *it* to the church. But
if he refuses even to hear the
church, let him be to you like a
[a]heathen and a tax collector.
18 "Assuredly, I say to you,
[a]whatever you bind on earth
will be bound in heaven, and
whatever you loose on earth will
be loosed in heaven.
19 [a]"Again[1] I say to you that if
two of you agree on earth concerning anything that they ask,
[b]it will be done for them by My
Father in heaven.
20 "For where two or three are
gathered [a]together in My name,
I am there in the midst of them."
21 Then Peter came to Him and
said, "Lord, how often shall my
brother sin against me, and I forgive him? [a]Up to seven times?"
22 Jesus said to him, "I do not
say to you, [a]up to seven times,
but up to seventy times seven.
23 "Therefore the kingdom of
heaven is like a certain king
who wanted to settle accounts
with his servants.
24 "And when he had begun to
settle accounts, one was brought
to him who owed him ten thousand talents.
25 "But as he was not able to
pay, his master commanded
[a]that he be sold, with his wife
and children and all that he had,
and that payment be made.
26 "The servant therefore fell
down before him, saying, 'Master, have patience with me, and I
will pay you all.'
27 "Then the master of that servant was moved with compassion, released him, and forgave
him the debt.
28 "But that servant went out
and found one of his fellow servants who owed him a hundred
denarii; and he laid hands on
him and took *him* by the throat,
saying, 'Pay me what you owe!'
29 "So his fellow servant fell
down [1]at his feet and begged
him, saying, 'Have patience with
me, and I will pay you [2]all.'
30 "And he would not, but went
and threw him into prison till he
should pay the debt.
31 "So when his fellow servants
saw what had been done, they
were very grieved, and came
and told their master all that
had been done.
32 "Then his master, after he
had called him, said to him,
'You wicked servant! I forgave
you [a]all that debt because you
begged me.
33 'Should you not also have
had compassion on your fellow
servant, just as I had pity on
you?'
34 "And his master was angry,
and delivered him to the tortur-
ers until he should pay all that
was due to him.
35 [a]"So My heavenly Father
also will do to you if each of you,
from his heart, does not forgive
his brother [1]his trespasses."

19

Now it came to pass,
[a]when Jesus had finished
these sayings, *that* He departed
from Galilee and came to the
region of Judea beyond the Jordan.
2 [a]And great multitudes followed Him, and He healed them
there.
3 The Phar'i·sees also came
to Him, testing Him, and saying to Him, "Is it lawful for a
man to divorce his wife for *just*
any reason?"
4 And He answered and said
to them, "Have you not read that

17 [a][2 Thess. 3:6, 14]
18 [a][John 20:22, 23]
19 [a][1 Cor. 1:10] [b][1 John 3:22; 5:14] [1]NU, M *Again, assuredly, I say*
20 [a]Acts 20:7
21 [a]Luke 17:4
22 [a]Col. 3:13
25 [a]2 Kin. 4:1
29 [1]NU omits *at his feet* [2]NU, M omit *all*
32 [a]Luke 7:41–43
35 [a]James 2:13 [1]NU omits *his trespasses*

CHAPTER 19

1 [a]Mark 10:1–12
2 [a]Matt. 12:15

He who [1]made *them* at the beginning [a]*'made them male and*
female,'
5 "and said, [a]*'For this reason*
a man shall leave his father
and mother and be joined to his
wife, and [b]*the two shall become*
one flesh'?
6 "So then, they are no longer two but one flesh. Therefore
what God has joined together,
let not man separate."
7 They said to Him, [a]"Why
then did Moses command to
give a certificate of divorce, and
to put her away?"
8 He said to them, "Moses, because of the [a]hardness of your
hearts, permitted you to divorce
your [b]wives, but from the beginning it was not so.
9 [a]"And I say to you, whoever
divorces his wife, except for
[1]sexual immorality, and marries
another, commits adultery; and
whoever marries her who is divorced commits adultery."
10 His disciples said to Him,
[a]"If such is the case of the man
with *his* wife, it is better not to
marry."
11 But He said to them, [a]"All
cannot accept this saying, but
only *those* to whom it has been
given:
12 "For there are [1]eunuchs
who were born thus from *their*
mother's womb, and [a]there are
eunuchs who were made eu-
nuchs by men, and there are
eunuchs who have made themselves eunuchs for the kingdom
of heaven's sake. He who is able
to accept *it*, let him accept *it*."
13 [a]Then little children were
brought to Him that He might
put *His* hands on them and pray,
but the disciples rebuked them.
14 But Jesus said, "Let the little
children come to Me, and do not
forbid them; for [a]of such is the
kingdom of heaven."
15 And He laid *His* hands on
them and departed from there.
16 [a]Now behold, one came and
said to Him, [b]"Good[1] Teacher,
what good thing shall I do that I
may have eternal life?"
17 So He said to him, [1]"Why
do you call Me good? [2]No one
is [a]good but One, *that is*, God.
But if you want to enter into life,
[b]keep the commandments."
18 He said to Him, "Which
ones?" Jesus said, [a]"*'You shall*
not murder,' 'You shall not com-
mit adultery,' 'You shall not
steal,' 'You shall not bear false
witness,'
19 [a]*'Honor your father and your*
mother,' and, [b]*'You shall love*
your neighbor as yourself.'"
20 The young man said to Him,
"All these things I have [a]kept
[1]from my youth. What do I still
lack?"
21 Jesus said to him, "If you
want to be perfect, [a]go, sell what
you have and give to the poor,
and you will have treasure in
heaven; and come, follow Me."
22 But when the young man
heard that saying, he went away
sorrowful, for he had great
possessions.
23 Then Jesus said to His disciples, "Assuredly, I say to you
that [a]it is hard for a rich man to
enter the kingdom of heaven.
24 "And again I say to you, it is
easier for a camel to go through
the eye of a needle than for a
rich man to enter the kingdom
of God."
25 When His disciples heard *it*,
they were greatly astonished,

4 [a]Gen. 1:27; 5:2 [1]NU *created*
5 [a]Gen. 2:24 [b][1 Cor. 6:16; 7:2]
7 [a]Deut. 24:1–4
8 [a]Heb. 3:15 [b]Mal. 2:16
9 [a][Matt. 5:32] [1]Or *fornication*
10 [a][Prov. 21:19]
11 [a][1 Cor. 7:2, 7, 9, 17]
12 [a][1 Cor. 7:32] [1]Emasculated men
13 [a]Luke 18:15
14 [a]Matt. 18:3, 4
16 [a]Mark 10:17–30 [b]Luke 10:25 [1]NU omits *Good*
17 [a]Nah. 1:7 [b]Lev. 18:5 [1]NU *Why do you ask Me about what is good?* [2]NU *There is One who is good. But*
18 [a]Ex. 20:13–16
19 [a]Ex. 20:12–16; Deut. 5:16–20 [b]Lev. 19:18
20 [a][Phil. 3:6, 7] [1]NU omits *from my youth*
21 [a]Acts 2:45; 4:34, 35
23 [a][1 Tim. 6:9]

saying, "Who then can be
saved?"
26 But Jesus looked at *them*
and said to them, "With men this
is impossible, but [a]with God all
things are possible."
27 Then Peter answered and
said to Him, "See, [a]we have left
all and followed You. Therefore
what shall we have?"
28 So Jesus said to them, "Assuredly I say to you, that in
the regeneration, when the Son
of Man sits on the throne of
His glory, [a]you who have followed Me will also sit on twelve
thrones, judging the twelve
tribes of Israel.
29 [a]"And everyone who has left
houses or brothers or sisters or
father or mother [1]or wife or children or [2]lands, for My name's
sake, shall receive a hundredfold, and inherit eternal life.
30 [a]"But many *who are* first will
be last, and the last first.

20

"For the kingdom of
heaven is like a land-
owner who went out early in the
morning to hire laborers for his
vineyard.
2 "Now when he had agreed
with the laborers for a denarius
a day, he sent them into his
vineyard.
3 "And he went out about the
third hour and saw others standing idle in the marketplace,
4 "and said to them, 'You also
go into the vineyard, and whatever is right I will give you.' So
they went.
5 "Again he went out about the
sixth and the ninth hour, and did
likewise.
6 "And about the eleventh hour
he went out and found others
standing [1]idle, and said to them,
'Why have you been standing
here idle all day?'
7 "They said to him, 'Because
no one hired us.' He said to
them, 'You also go into the vineyard, [1]and whatever is right you
will receive.'
8 "So when evening had come,
the owner of the vineyard said
to his steward, 'Call the laborers and give them *their* wages,
beginning with the last to the
first.'
9 "And when those came who
were hired about the eleventh
hour, they each received a denarius.
10 "But when the first came,
they supposed that they would
receive more; and they likewise
received each a denarius.
11 "And when they had received
it, they [1]complained against the
landowner,
12 "saying, 'These last *men*
have worked *only* one hour, and
you made them equal to us who
have borne the burden and the
heat of the day.'
13 "But he answered one of
them and said, 'Friend, I am doing you no wrong. Did you not
agree with me for a denarius?
14 'Take *what is* yours and go
your way. I wish to give to this
last man *the same* as to you.
15 [a]'Is it not lawful for me to do
what I wish with my own things?
Or [b]is your eye evil because I am
good?'
16 [a]"So the last will be first,
and the first last. [b]For[1] many are
called, but few chosen."
17 [a]Now Jesus, going up to Jerusalem, took the twelve disciples aside on the road and said
to them,
18 [a]"Behold, we are going up to

26 [a]Jer. 32:17
27 [a]Deut. 33:9
28 [a]Luke 22:28–30
29 [a]Mark 10:29, 30 [1]NU omits *or wife* [2]Lit. *fields*
30 [a]Luke 13:30

CHAPTER 20

6 [1]NU omits *idle*
7 [1]NU omits the rest of v. 7.
11 [1]*grumbled*
15 [a][Rom. 9:20, 21] [b]Deut. 15:9
16 [a]Matt. 19:30 [b]Matt. 22:14 [1]NU omits the rest of v. 16.
17 [a]Mark 10:32–34
18 [a]Matt. 16:21; 26:47–57

Jerusalem, and the Son of Man will be betrayed to the chief priests and to the scribes; and they will condemn Him to death,

19 [a]"and deliver Him to the Gentiles to [b]mock and to [c]scourge and to [d]crucify. And the third day He will [e]rise again."

20 [a]Then the mother of [b]Zeb′-e·dee's sons came to Him with her sons, kneeling down and asking something from Him.

21 And He said to her, "What do you wish?" She said to Him, "Grant that these two sons of mine [a]may sit, one on Your right hand and the other on the left, in Your kingdom."

22 But Jesus answered and said, "You do not know what you ask. Are you able to drink [a]the cup that I am about to drink, [1]and be baptized with [b]the baptism that I am baptized with?" They said to Him, "We are able."

23 So He said to them, [a]"You will indeed drink My cup, [1]and be baptized with the baptism that I am baptized with; but to sit on My right hand and on My left is not Mine to give, but *it is for those* for whom it is prepared by My Father."

24 [a]And when the ten heard *it*, they were greatly displeased with the two brothers.

25 But Jesus called them to *Himself* and said, "You know that the rulers of the Gentiles lord it over them, and those who are great exercise authority over them.

26 "Yet [a]it shall not be so among you; but [b]whoever desires to become great among you, let him be your servant.

27 [a]"And whoever desires to be first among you, let him be your slave—

28 [a]"just as the [b]Son of Man did not come to be served, [c]but to serve, and [d]to give His life a ransom [e]for many." ★

29 [a]Now as they went out of Jericho, a great multitude followed Him.

30 And behold, [a]two blind men sitting by the road, when they heard that Jesus was passing by, cried out, saying, "Have mercy on us, O Lord, [b]Son of David!"

31 Then the multitude [a]warned them that they should be quiet; but they cried out all the more, saying, "Have mercy on us, O Lord, Son of David!"

32 So Jesus stood still and called them, and said, "What do you want Me to do for you?"

33 They said to Him, "Lord, that our eyes may be opened."

34 So Jesus had [a]compassion and touched their eyes. And immediately their eyes received sight, and they followed Him.

21

Now [a]when they drew near Jerusalem, and came to [1]Beth′pha·gē, at [b]the Mount of Olives, then Jesus sent two disciples,

2 saying to them, "Go into the village opposite you, and immediately you will find a donkey tied, and a colt with her. Loose *them* and bring *them* to Me.

3 "And if anyone says anything to you, you shall say, 'The Lord has need of them,' and immediately he will send them."

4 [1]All this was done that it might be fulfilled which was spoken by the prophet, saying:

5 *"Tell[a] the daughter of Zion,* ★
'Behold, your King is coming
to you,

---

19 [a]Matt. 27:2 [b]Matt. 26:67, 68; 27:29, 41 [c]Matt. 27:26 [d]Acts 3:13–15 [e]Matt. 28:5, 6

20 [a]Mark 10:35–45 [b]Matt. 4:21; 10:2

21 [a][Matt. 19:28]

22 [a]Luke 22:42 [b]Luke 12:50 [1]NU omits *and be baptized with the baptism that I am baptized with*

23 [a][Acts 12:2] [1]NU omits *and be baptized with the baptism that I am baptized with*

24 [a]Mark 10:41

26 [a][1 Pet. 5:3] [b]Matt. 23:11

27 [a][Matt. 18:4]

28 [a]John 13:4 [b][Phil. 2:6, 7] [c]Luke 22:27 [d][Is. 53:10–12; Dan. 9:24, 26] [e][Rom. 5:15, 19]

29 [a]Mark 10:46–52

30 [a]Matt. 9:27 [b][Ezek. 37:21–25]

31 [a]Matt. 19:13

34 [a]Matt. 9:36; 14:14; 15:32; 18:27

CHAPTER 21

1 [a]Luke 19:29–38 [b][Zech. 14:4] [1]M *Bethsphage*

4 [1]NU omits *All*

5 [a]Is. 62:11; Zech. 9:9

Lowly, and sitting on a
donkey,
A colt, the foal of a
donkey.' "

6 [a]So the disciples went and
did as Jesus commanded them.
7 They brought the donkey
and the colt, [a]laid their clothes
on them, [1]and set *Him* on them.
8 And a very great multitude
spread their clothes on the road;
[a]others cut down branches from
the trees and spread *them* on
the road.
★ 9 Then the multitudes who
went before and those who followed cried out, saying:

"Hō·san'na to the Son of
David!
[a]'*Blessed is He who comes in*
the name of the L*ORD*!'
Hō·san'na in the highest!"

10 [a]And when He had come
into Jerusalem, all the city was
moved, saying, "Who is this?"
11 So the multitudes said, "This
is Jesus, [a]the prophet from Nazareth of Galilee."
★ **12** [a]Then Jesus went into the
temple [1]of God and drove out all
those who bought and sold in
the temple, and overturned the
tables of the [b]money changers
and the seats of those who sold
doves.
13 And He said to them, "It
is written, [a]'*My house shall be*
called a house of prayer,' but
you have made it a [b]'*den of*
thieves.' "
14 Then *the* blind and *the* lame
came to Him in the temple, and
He healed them.
★ 15 But when the chief priests
and scribes saw the wonderful
things that He did, and the children crying out in the temple and
saying, "Hō·san'na to the [a]Son of
David!" they were [1]indignant
16 and said to Him, "Do You
hear what these are saying?"
And Jesus said to them, "Yes.
Have you never read,

[a]'*Out of the mouth of babes*
and nursing infants
You have perfected
praise'?"

17 Then He left them and [a]went
out of the city to Beth'a·ny, and
He lodged there.
18 [a]Now in the morning, as He
returned to the city, He was
hungry.
19 [a]And seeing a fig tree by the
road, He came to it and found
nothing on it but leaves, and
said to it, "Let no fruit grow on
you ever again." Immediately
the fig tree withered away.
20 [a]And when the disciples saw
it, they marveled, saying, "How
did the fig tree wither away so
soon?"
21 So Jesus answered and said
to them, "Assuredly, I say to you,
[a]if you have faith and [b]do not
doubt, you will not only do what
was done to the fig tree, [c]but
also if you say to this mountain,
'Be removed and be cast into the
sea,' it will be done.
22 "And [a]whatever things you
ask in prayer, believing, you will
receive."
23 [a]Now when He came into the
temple, the chief priests and the
elders of the people confronted
Him as He was teaching, and
[b]said, "By what authority are
You doing these things? And
who gave You this authority?"

6 [a]Mark 11:4
7 [a]2 Kin. 9:13 [1]NU *and He sat*
8 [a]Lev. 23:40
9 [a]Ps. 118:26; Matt. 23:39
10 [a]John 2:13, 15
11 [a]John 6:14; 7:40; 9:17
12 [a]Ps. 69:9; 119:139; Is. 56:7; Mal. 3:1; Mark 11:15–18 [b]Deut. 14:25 [1]NU omits *of God*
13 [a]Is. 56:7 [b]Jer. 7:11
15 [a]Ps. 118:26; John 7:42 [1]*angry*
16 [a]Ps. 8:2
17 [a]John 11:1, 18; 12:1
18 [a]Mark 11:12–14, 20–24
19 [a]Mark 11:13
20 [a]Mark 11:20
21 [a]Matt. 17:20 [b]James 1:6 [c]1 Cor. 13:2
22 [a]Matt. 7:7–11
23 [a]Luke 20:1–8 [b]Ex. 2:14

24 But Jesus answered and said
to them, "I also will ask you
one thing, which if you tell Me,
I likewise will tell you by what
authority I do these things:
25 "The [a]baptism of [b]John—
where was it from? From heaven
or from men?" And they reasoned among themselves, saying, "If we say, 'From heaven,'
He will say to us, 'Why then did
you not believe him?'
26 "But if we say, 'From men,'
we [a]fear the multitude, [b]for all
count John as a prophet."
27 So they answered Jesus and
said, "We do not know." And He
said to them, "Neither will I tell
you by what authority I do these
things.
28 "But what do you think? A
man had two sons, and he came
to the first and said, 'Son, go,
work today in my [a]vineyard.'
29 "He answered and said, 'I
will not,' but afterward he regretted it and went.
30 "Then he came to the second
and said likewise. And he answered and said, 'I *go*, sir,' but
he did not go.
31 "Which of the two did the will
of *his* father?" They said to Him,
"The first." Jesus said to them,
[a]"Assuredly, I say to you that tax
collectors and harlots enter the
kingdom of God before you.
32 "For [a]John came to you in
the way of righteousness, and
you did not believe him; [b]but tax
collectors and harlots believed
him; and when you saw *it*, you
did not afterward [1]relent and
believe him.
33 "Hear another parable:
There was a certain landowner
[a]who planted a vineyard and set
a hedge around it, dug a winepress in it and built a tower. And
he leased it to vinedressers and
[b]went into a far country.
34 "Now when vintage-time
drew near, he sent his servants
to the vinedressers, that they
might receive its fruit.
35 [a]"And the vinedressers took
his servants, beat one, killed
one, and stoned another.
36 "Again he sent other servants, more than the first, and
they did likewise to them.
37 "Then last of all he sent his
[a]son to them, saying, 'They will
respect my son.'
38 "But when the vinedressers
saw the son, they said among
themselves, [a]'This is the heir.
[b]Come, let us kill him and seize
his inheritance.'
39 [a]"So they took him and cast
him out of the vineyard and
killed *him*.
40 "Therefore, when the owner
of the vineyard comes, what will
he do to those vinedressers?"
41 [a]They said to Him, [b]"He will
destroy those wicked men mis-
erably, [c]and lease *his* vineyard
to other vinedressers who will
[1]render to him the fruits in their
seasons."
42 Jesus said to them, "Have you ☆
never read in the Scriptures:

[a]'The stone which the
builders rejected
Has become the chief
cornerstone.
This was the LORD's doing,
And it is marvelous in our
eyes'?

43 "Therefore I say to you, [a]the
kingdom of God will be taken
from you and given to a nation
bearing the fruits of it.

25 [a][John 1:29–34] [b]John 1:15–28
26 [a]Matt. 14:5; 21:46 [b]Mark 6:20
28 [a]Matt. 20:1; 21:33
31 [a]Luke 7:29, 37–50
32 [a]Luke 3:1–12; 7:29 [b]Luke 3:12, 13 [1]*regret it*
33 [a]Luke 20:9–19 [b]Matt. 25:14
35 [a][1 Thess. 2:15]
37 [a][John 3:16]
38 [a][Heb. 1:2] [b]John 11:53
39 [a][Acts 2:23]
41 [a]Luke 20:16 [b][Luke 21:24] [c][Acts 13:46] [1]*give*
42 [a]Ps. 118:22, 23; Is. 28:16; Acts 4:11; [Rom. 9:33]; Eph. 2:20; [1 Pet. 2:6, 7]
43 [a][Matt. 8:12]

☆ 44 "And [a]whoever falls on this stone will be broken; but on whomever it falls, [b]it will grind him to powder."

45 Now when the chief priests and Phar′i·sees heard His parables, they [1]perceived that He was speaking of them.

46 But when they sought to lay hands on Him, they [a]feared the multitudes, because [b]they took Him for a prophet.

22

And Jesus answered [a]and spoke to them again by parables and said:

2 "The kingdom of heaven is like a certain king who arranged a marriage for his son,

3 "and sent out his servants to call those who were invited to the wedding; and they were not willing to come.

4 "Again, he sent out other servants, saying, 'Tell those who are invited, "See, I have prepared my dinner; [a]my oxen and fatted cattle *are* killed, and all things *are* ready. Come to the wedding." '

5 "But they made light of it and went their ways, one to his own farm, another to his business.

6 "And the rest seized his servants, treated *them* [1]spitefully, and killed *them.*

7 "But when the king heard *about it,* he was furious. And he sent out [a]his armies, destroyed those murderers, and burned up their city.

8 "Then he said to his servants, 'The wedding is ready, but those who were invited were not [a]worthy.

9 'Therefore go into the highways, and as many as you find, invite to the wedding.'

10 "So those servants went out into the highways and [a]gathered together all whom they found, both bad and good. And the wedding *hall* was filled with guests.

11 "But when the king came in to see the guests, he saw a man there [a]who did not have on a wedding garment.

12 "So he said to him, 'Friend, how did you come in here without a wedding garment?' And he was [a]speechless.

13 "Then the king said to the servants, 'Bind him hand and foot, [1]take him away, and cast *him* [a]into outer darkness; there will be weeping and gnashing of teeth.'

14 [a]"For many are called, but few *are* chosen."

15 [a]Then the Phar′i·sees went and plotted how they might entangle Him in *His* talk.

16 And they sent to Him their disciples with the [a]He·rō′di·ans, saying, "Teacher, we know that You are true, and teach the way of God in truth; nor do You care about anyone, for You do not [1]regard the person of men.

17 "Tell us, therefore, what do You think? Is it lawful to pay taxes to Caesar, or not?"

18 But Jesus [1]perceived their wickedness, and said, "Why do you test Me, *you* hypocrites?

19 "Show Me the tax money." So they brought Him a denarius.

20 And He said to them, "Whose image and inscription *is* this?"

21 They said to Him, "Caesar's." And He said to them, [a]"Render[1] therefore to Caesar the things that are [b]Caesar's, and to God the things that are [c]God's."

22 When they had heard *these words,* they marveled, and left Him and went their way.

44 [a]Is. 8:14, 15; [Rom. 9:33]; 1 Pet. 2:6–8 [b]Is. 60:12; [Dan. 2:44]
45 [1]*knew*
46 [a]Matt. 21:26 [b]Matt. 21:11

CHAPTER 22

1 [a][Rev. 19:7–9]
4 [a]Prov. 9:2
6 [1]*insolently*
7 [a][Dan. 9:26]
8 [a]Matt. 10:11
10 [a]Matt. 13:38, 47, 48
11 [a][Col. 3:10, 12]
12 [a][Rom. 3:19]
13 [a]Matt. 8:12; 25:30 [1]NU omits *take him away, and*
14 [a]Matt. 20:16
15 [a]Mark 12:13–17
16 [a]Mark 3:6; 8:15; 12:13 [1]Lit. *look at the face of*
18 [1]*knew*
21 [a]Matt. 17:25 [b][Rom. 13:1–7] [c][1 Cor. 3:23; 6:19, 20; 12:27] [1]*Pay*

23 [a]The same day the Sad′dū·cees, [b]who say there is no resurrection, came to Him and asked Him,

24 saying: "Teacher, [a]Moses said that if a man dies, having no children, his brother shall marry his wife and raise up offspring for his brother.

25 "Now there were with us seven brothers. The first died after he had married, and having no offspring, left his wife to his brother.

26 "Likewise the second also, and the third, even to the seventh.

27 "Last of all the woman died also.

28 "Therefore, in the resurrection, whose wife of the seven will she be? For they all had her."

29 Jesus answered and said to them, "You are [1]mistaken, [a]not knowing the Scriptures nor the power of God.

30 "For in the resurrection they neither marry nor are given in marriage, but [a]are like angels [1]of God in heaven.

31 "But concerning the resurrection of the dead, have you not read what was spoken to you by God, saying,

32 [a]'*I am the God of Abraham, the God of Isaac, and the God of Jacob*'? God is not the God of the dead, but of the living."

33 And when the multitudes heard *this,* [a]they were astonished at His teaching.

34 [a]But when the Phar′i·sees heard that He had silenced the Sad′dū·cees, they gathered together.

35 Then one of them, [a]a lawyer, asked *Him a question,* testing Him, and saying,

36 "Teacher, which *is* the great commandment in the law?"

37 Jesus said to him, [a]" '*You shall love the* LORD *your God with all your heart, with all your soul, and with all your mind.*'

38 "This is *the* first and great commandment.

39 "And *the* second *is* like it: [a]'*You shall love your neighbor as yourself.*'

40 [a]"On these two commandments hang all the Law and the Prophets."

41 [a]While the Phar′i·sees were gathered together, Jesus asked them,

42 saying, "What do you think about the Christ? Whose Son is He?" They said to Him, "*The* [a]*Son* of David."

43 He said to them, "How then does David in the Spirit call Him '*Lord,*' saying:

44 '*The*[a] LORD *said to my Lord,*
"*Sit at My right hand,*
Till I make Your enemies
Your footstool" '? ☆

45 "If David then calls Him '*Lord,*' how is He his Son?"

46 [a]And no one was able to answer Him a word, [b]nor from that day on did anyone dare question Him anymore.

23

Then Jesus spoke to the multitudes and to His disciples,

2 saying: [a]"The scribes and the Phar′i·sees sit in Moses' seat.

3 "Therefore whatever they tell you [1]to observe, *that* observe and do, but do not do according to their works; for [a]they say, and do not do.

4 [a]"For they bind heavy burdens, hard to bear, and lay *them*

23 [a]Luke 20:27–40 [b]Acts 23:8
24 [a]Deut. 25:5
29 [a]John 20:9 [1]*deceived*
30 [a][1 John 3:2] [1]NU omits *of God*
32 [a]Ex. 3:6, 15
33 [a]Matt. 7:28
34 [a]Mark 12:28–31
35 [a]Luke 7:30; 10:25; 11:45, 46, 52; 14:3
37 [a]Deut. 6:5; 10:12; 30:6
39 [a]Lev. 19:18
40 [a][Matt. 7:12]
41 [a]Luke 20:41–44
42 [a]Matt. 1:1; 21:9
44 [a]Ps. 110:1; Acts 2:32–35; Eph. 1:19–23
46 [a]Luke 14:6 [b]Mark 12:34

CHAPTER 23

2 [a]Neh. 8:4, 8
3 [a][Rom. 2:19] [1]NU omits *to observe*
4 [a]Luke 11:46

on men's shoulders; but they *themselves* will not move them with one of their fingers.

5 "But all their works they do to [a]be seen by men. They make their phylacteries broad and enlarge the borders of their garments.

6 [a]"They love the [1]best places at feasts, the best seats in the synagogues,

7 "greetings in the marketplaces, and to be called by men, 'Rabbi, Rabbi.'

8 [a]"But you, do not be called 'Rabbi'; for One is your [1]Teacher, [2]the Christ, and you are all brethren.

9 "Do not call anyone on earth your father; [a]for One is your Father, He who is in heaven.

10 "And do not be called teachers; for One is your Teacher, the Christ.

11 "But [a]he who is greatest among you shall be your servant.

12 [a]"And whoever exalts himself will be [1]humbled, and he who humbles himself will be [2]exalted.

13 "But [a]woe to you, scribes and Phar′i·sees, hypocrites! For you shut up the kingdom of heaven against men; for you neither go in *yourselves*, nor do you allow those who are entering to go in.

14 [1]"Woe to you, scribes and Phar′i·sees, hypocrites! [a]For you devour widows' houses, and for a pretense make long prayers. Therefore you will receive greater condemnation.

15 "Woe to you, scribes and Phar′i·sees, hypocrites! For you travel land and sea to win one proselyte, and when he is won, you make him twice as much a son of [1]hell as yourselves.

16 "Woe to you, [a]blind guides, who say, [b]'Whoever swears by the temple, it is nothing; but whoever swears by the gold of the temple, he is obliged *to perform it.*'

17 "Fools and blind! For which is greater, the gold [a]or the temple that [1]sanctifies the gold?

18 "And, 'Whoever swears by the altar, it is nothing; but whoever swears by the gift that is on it, he is obliged *to perform it.*'

19 "Fools and blind! For which is greater, the gift [a]or the altar that sanctifies the gift?

20 "Therefore he who [1]swears by the altar, swears by it and by all things on it.

21 "He who swears by the temple, swears by it and by [a]Him who [1]dwells in it.

22 "And he who swears by heaven, swears by [a]the throne of God and by Him who sits on it.

23 "Woe to you, scribes and Phar′i·sees, hypocrites! [a]For you pay tithe of mint and anise and cummin, and [b]have neglected the weightier *matters* of the law: justice and mercy and faith. These you ought to have done, without leaving the others undone.

24 "Blind guides, who strain out a gnat and swallow a camel!

25 "Woe to you, scribes and Phar′i·sees, hypocrites! [a]For you cleanse the outside of the cup and dish, but inside they are full of extortion and [1]self-indulgence.

26 "Blind Phar′i·see, first cleanse the inside of the cup and dish, that the outside of them may be clean also.

5 [a][Matt. 6:1–6, 16–18]
6 [a]Luke 11:43; 20:46 [1]Or *place of honor*
8 [a][James 3:1] [1]*Leader* [2]NU omits *the Christ*
9 [a][Mal. 1:6]
11 [a]Matt. 20:26, 27
12 [a]Luke 14:11; 18:14 [1]*put down* [2]*lifted up*
13 [a]Luke 11:52
14 [a]Mark 12:40 [1]NU omits v. 14.
15 [1]Gr. *Gehenna*
16 [a]Matt. 15:14; 23:24 [b][Matt. 5:33, 34]
17 [a]Ex. 30:29 [1]NU *sanctified*
19 [a]Ex. 29:37
20 [1]Swears an oath
21 [a]1 Kin. 8:13 [1]M *dwelt*
22 [a]Matt. 5:34
23 [a]Luke 11:42; 18:12 [b][Hos. 6:6]
25 [a]Luke 11:39 [1]M *unrighteousness*

27 "Woe to you, scribes and
Phar′i·sees, hypocrites! [a]For you
are like whitewashed tombs
which indeed appear beautiful
outwardly, but inside are full
of dead *men's* bones and all
uncleanness.
28 "Even so you also outwardly
appear righteous to men, but
inside you are full of hypocrisy
and lawlessness.
29 [a]"Woe to you, scribes and
Phar′i·sees, hypocrites! Because you build the tombs of the
prophets and [1]adorn the monu-
ments of the righteous,
30 "and say, 'If we had lived
in the days of our fathers, we
would not have been partakers
with them in the blood of the
prophets.'
31 "Therefore you are witnesses
against yourselves that [a]you are
sons of those who murdered the
prophets.
32 [a]"Fill up, then, the measure
of your fathers' *guilt*.
33 "Serpents, [a]brood[1] of vipers!
How can you escape the condemnation of hell?
34 [a]"Therefore, indeed, I send
you prophets, wise men, and
scribes: [b]*some* of them you will
kill and crucify, and [c]*some* of
them you will scourge in your
synagogues and persecute from
city to city,
35 [a]"that on you may come all
the righteous blood shed on
the earth, [b]from the blood of
righteous Abel to [c]the blood of
Zech·a·rī′ah, son of Ber·e·chī′ah,
whom you murdered between
the temple and the altar.
36 "Assuredly, I say to you, all
these things will come upon this
generation.
37 [a]"O Jerusalem, Jerusalem,
the one who kills the prophets
[b]and stones those who are sent
to her! How often [c]I wanted to
gather your children together, as
a hen gathers her chicks [d]under
her wings, but you were not
willing!
38 "See! Your house is left to
you desolate;
39 "for I say to you, you shall
see Me no more till you say,
[a]*'Blessed is He who comes in the
name of the* LORD!*'*"

24

Then [a]Jesus went out and
departed from the tem-
ple, and His disciples came up
to show Him the buildings of the
temple.
2 And Jesus said to them, "Do
you not see all these things? Assuredly, I say to you, [a]not *one*
stone shall be left here upon
another, that shall not be thrown
down."
3 Now as He sat on the Mount
of Olives, [a]the disciples came to
Him privately, saying, [b]"Tell us,
when will these things be? And
what *will be* the sign of Your coming, and of the end of the age?"
4 And Jesus answered and
said to them: [a]"Take heed that
no one deceives you.
5 "For [a]many will come in My
name, saying, 'I am the Christ,'
[b]and will deceive many.
6 "And you will hear of [a]wars
and rumors of wars. See that
you are not troubled; for [1]all
these things must come to pass,
but the end is not yet.
7 "For [a]nation will rise against
nation, and kingdom against
kingdom. And there will be
[b]famines, [1]pestilences, and earthquakes in various places.
8 "All these *are* the beginning
of sorrows.

27 [a]Acts 23:3
29 [a]Luke 11:47, 48 [1]*decorate*
31 [a][Acts 7:51, 52]
32 [a][1 Thess. 2:16]
33 [a]Matt. 3:7; 12:34 [1]*offspring*
34 [a]Luke 11:49 [b]Acts 7:54–60; 22:19 [c]2 Cor. 11:24, 25
35 [a]Rev. 18:24 [b]Gen. 4:8 [c]2 Chr. 24:20, 21
37 [a]Luke 13:34, 35 [b]2 Chr. 24:20, 21; 36:15, 16 [c]Deut. 32:11, 12 [d]Ps. 17:8; 91:4
39 [a]Ps. 118:26

CHAPTER 24

1 [a]Mark 13:1
2 [a]Luke 19:44
3 [a]Mark 13:3 [b][1 Thess. 5:1–3]
4 [a][Col. 2:8, 18]
5 [a]John 5:43 [b]Matt. 24:11
6 [a][Rev. 6:2–4] [1]NU omits *all*
7 [a]Hag. 2:22 [b]Rev. 6:5, 6 [1]NU omits *pestilences*

9 [a]"Then they will deliver you
up to tribulation and kill you,
and you will be hated by all nations for My name's sake.
10 "And then many will be offended, will betray one another,
and will hate one another.
11 "Then [a]many false prophets
will rise up and [b]deceive many.
12 "And because lawlessness
will abound, the love of many
will grow [a]cold.
13 [a]"But he who endures to the
end shall be saved.
14 "And this [a]gospel of the kingdom [b]will be preached in all the
world as a witness to all the
nations, and then the end will
come.
15 [a]"Therefore when you see
the [b]*'abomination of desolation,'* spoken of by Daniel the
prophet, standing in the holy
place" [c](whoever reads, let him
understand),
16 "then let those who are in
Judea flee to the mountains.
17 "Let him who is on the
housetop not go down to take
anything out of his house.
18 "And let him who is in the
field not go back to get his
clothes.
19 "But [a]woe to those who are
pregnant and to those who are
nursing babies in those days!
20 "And pray that your flight
may not be in winter or on the
Sabbath.
21 "For [a]then there will be great
tribulation, such as has not been
since the beginning of the world
until this time, no, nor ever shall
be.
22 "And unless those days were
shortened, no flesh would be
saved; [a]but for the [1]elect's sake
those days will be shortened.

9 [a]Matt. 10:17
11 [a]2 Pet. 2:1 [b][1 Tim. 4:1]
12 [a][2 Thess. 2:3]
13 [a]Matt. 10:22
14 [a]Matt. 4:23 [b]Rom. 10:18
15 [a]Mark 13:14 [b]Dan. 9:27; 11:31; 12:11 [c]Dan. 9:23
19 [a]Luke 23:29
21 [a]Dan. 9:26
22 [a]Is. 65:8, 9 [1]*chosen ones'*
23 [a]Luke 17:23
24 [a][2 Thess. 2:9] [b][2 Tim. 2:19]
27 [a]Luke 17:24
28 [a]Luke 17:37
29 [a][Dan. 7:11] [b]Ezek. 32:7
30 [a][Dan. 7:13, 14] [b]Zech. 12:12; Rev. 1:7; 14:14
31 [a][1 Cor. 15:52] [1]*chosen ones*
32 [a]Luke 21:29
33 [a][James 5:9] [1]Or *He*

23 [a]"Then if anyone says to you,
'Look, here *is* the Christ!' or
'There!' do not believe *it.*
24 "For [a]false christs and false
prophets will rise and show great
signs and wonders to deceive, [b]if
possible, even the elect.
25 "See, I have told you beforehand.
26 "Therefore if they say to you,
'Look, He is in the desert!' do
not go out; *or* 'Look, *He is* in the
inner rooms!' do not believe *it.*
27 [a]"For as the lightning comes
from the east and flashes to the
west, so also will the coming of
the Son of Man be.
28 [a]"For wherever the carcass
is, there the eagles will be gathered together.
29 [a]"Immediately after the tribulation of those days [b]the sun
will be darkened, and the moon
will not give its light; the
stars will fall from heaven, and
the powers of the heavens will
be shaken.
30 [a]"Then the sign of the Son ☆
of Man will appear in heaven,
[b]and then all the tribes of the
earth will mourn, and they will
see the Son of Man coming on
the clouds of heaven with power
and great glory.
31 [a]"And He will send His angels with a great sound of a
trumpet, and they will gather
together His [1]elect from the four
winds, from one end of heaven
to the other.
32 "Now learn [a]this parable from
the fig tree: When its branch has
already become tender and puts
forth leaves, you know that summer *is* near.
33 "So you also, when you see
all these things, know [a]that [1]it is
near—at the doors!

34 "Assuredly, I say to you, [a]this generation will by no means pass away till all these things take place.

35 [a]"Heaven and earth will pass away, but My words will by no means pass away.

36 [a]"But of that day and hour no one knows, not even the angels of [1]heaven, [b]but My Father only.

37 "But as the days of Noah *were,* so also will the coming of the Son of Man be.

38 [a]"For as in the days before the flood, they were eating and drinking, marrying and giving in marriage, until the day that Noah entered the ark,

39 "and did not know until the flood came and took them all away, so also will the coming of the Son of Man be.

40 [a]"Then two *men* will be in the field: one will be taken and the other left.

41 "Two *women will be* grinding at the mill: one will be taken and the other left.

42 [a]"Watch therefore, for you do not know what [1]hour your Lord is coming.

43 [a]"But know this, that if the master of the house had known what [1]hour the thief would come, he would have watched and not allowed his house to be broken into.

44 [a]"Therefore you also be ready, for the Son of Man is coming at an hour you do not expect.

45 [a]"Who then is a faithful and wise servant, whom his master made ruler over his household, to give them food [1]in due season?

46 [a]"Blessed *is* that servant whom his master, when he comes, will find so doing.

47 "Assuredly, I say to you that [a]he will make him ruler over all his goods.

48 "But if that evil servant says in his heart, 'My master [a]is delaying [1]his coming,'

49 "and begins to beat *his* fellow servants, and to eat and drink with the drunkards,

50 "the master of that servant will come on a day when he is not looking for *him* and at an hour that he is [a]not aware of,

51 "and will cut him in two and appoint *him* his portion with the hypocrites. [a]There shall be weeping and gnashing of teeth.

25 "Then the kingdom of heaven shall be likened to ten virgins who took their lamps and went out to meet [a]the bridegroom.

2 [a]"Now five of them were wise, and five *were* foolish.

3 "Those who *were* foolish took their lamps and took no oil with them,

4 "but the wise took oil in their vessels with their lamps.

5 "But while the bridegroom was delayed, [a]they all slumbered and slept.

6 "And at midnight [a]a cry was *heard:* 'Behold, the bridegroom [1]is coming; go out to meet him!'

7 "Then all those virgins arose and [a]trimmed their lamps.

8 "And the foolish said to the wise, 'Give us *some* of your oil, for our lamps are going out.'

9 "But the wise answered, saying, '*No,* lest there should not be enough for us and you; but go rather to those who sell, and buy for yourselves.'

10 "And while they went to buy, the bridegroom came, and those who were ready went in with

34 [a][Matt. 10:23; 16:28; 23:36]
35 [a]Luke 21:33
36 [a]Acts 1:7 [b]Zech. 14:7 [1]NU adds *nor the Son*
38 [a][Gen. 6:3–5]
40 [a]Luke 17:34
42 [a]Matt. 25:13 [1]NU *day*
43 [a]Luke 12:39 [1]Lit. *watch of the night*
44 [a][1 Thess. 5:6]
45 [a]Luke 12:42–46 [1]*at the right time*
46 [a]Rev. 16:15
47 [a]Matt. 25:21, 23
48 [a][2 Pet. 3:4–9] [1]NU omits *his coming*
50 [a]Mark 13:32
51 [a]Matt. 8:12; 25:30

CHAPTER 25

1 [a][Eph. 5:29, 30]
2 [a]Matt. 13:47; 22:10
5 [a]1 Thess. 5:6
6 [a][1 Thess. 4:16] [1]NU omits *is coming*
7 [a]Luke 12:35

him to the wedding; and [a]the
door was shut.
11 "Afterward the other virgins
came also, saying, [a]'Lord, Lord,
open to us!'
12 "But he answered and said,
'Assuredly, I say to you, [a]I do not
know you.'
13 [a]"Watch therefore, for you
[b]know neither the day nor the
hour [1]in which the Son of Man
is coming.
14 [a]"For *the kingdom of heaven*
is [b]like a man traveling to a far
country, *who* called his own servants and delivered his goods to
them.
15 "And to one he gave five
talents, to another two, and to
another one, [a]to each according
to his own ability; and immediately he went on a journey.
16 "Then he who had received
the five talents went and traded
with them, and made another
five talents.
17 "And likewise he who *had*
received two gained two more
also.
18 "But he who had received
one went and dug in the ground,
and hid his lord's money.
19 "After a long time the lord of
those servants came and settled
accounts with them.
20 "So he who had received
five talents came and brought
five other talents, saying, 'Lord,
you delivered to me five talents;
look, I have gained five more
talents besides them.'
21 "His lord said to him, 'Well
done, good and faithful servant;
you were [a]faithful over a few
things, [b]I will make you ruler
over many things. Enter into
[c]the joy of your lord.'
22 "He also who had received

10 [a]Luke 13:25
11 [a][Matt. 7:21–23]
12 [a][Hab. 1:13]
13 [a]Mark 13:35 [b]Matt. 24:36, 42 [1]NU omits the rest of v. 13.
14 [a]Luke 19:12–27 [b]Matt. 21:33
15 [a][Rom. 12:6]
21 [a][1 Cor. 4:2] [b][Luke 12:44; 22:29, 30] [c][Heb. 12:2]
23 [a]Matt. 24:45, 47; 25:21 [b][Ps. 16:11]
26 [a]Matt. 18:32
29 [a]Matt. 13:12
30 [a]Matt. 8:12; 22:13 [b]Matt. 7:23; 8:12; 24:51 [c]Ps. 112:10
31 [a][1 Thess. 4:16] [1]NU omits *holy*

two talents came and said, 'Lord,
you delivered to me two talents;
look, I have gained two more
talents besides them.'
23 "His lord said to him, [a]'Well
done, good and faithful servant;
you have been faithful over a
few things, I will make you ruler
over many things. Enter into
[b]the joy of your lord.'
24 "Then he who had received
the one talent came and said,
'Lord, I knew you to be a hard
man, reaping where you have
not sown, and gathering where
you have not scattered seed.
25 'And I was afraid, and went
and hid your talent in the
ground. Look, *there* you have
what is yours.'
26 "But his lord answered and
said to him, 'You [a]wicked and
lazy servant, you knew that I
reap where I have not sown, and
gather where I have not scattered seed.
27 'So you ought to have depos-
ited my money with the bank-
ers, and at my coming I would
have received back my own with
interest.
28 'Therefore take the talent
from him, and give *it* to him who
has ten talents.
29 [a]'For to everyone who has,
more will be given, and he will
have abundance; but from him
who does not have, even what
he has will be taken away.
30 'And cast the unprofitable
servant [a]into the outer darkness. [b]There will be weeping and
[c]gnashing of teeth.'
31 [a]"When the Son of Man
comes in His glory, and all the
[1]holy angels with Him, then He
will sit on the throne of His
glory.

32 [a]"All the nations will be gathered before Him, and [b]He will
separate them one from another,
as a shepherd divides *his* sheep
from the goats.
33 "And He will set the [a]sheep
on His right hand, but the goats
on the left.
34 "Then the King will say to
those on His right hand, 'Come,
you blessed of My Father, [a]in-
herit the kingdom [b]prepared for
you from the foundation of the
world:
35 [a]'for I was hungry and you
gave Me food; I was thirsty and
you gave Me drink; [b]I was a
stranger and you took Me in;
36 'I *was* [a]naked and you
clothed Me; I was sick and you
visited Me; [b]I was in prison and
you came to Me.'
37 "Then the righteous will answer Him, saying, 'Lord, when
did we see You hungry and feed
You, or thirsty and give *You*
drink?
38 'When did we see You a
stranger and take *You* in, or naked and clothe *You?*
39 'Or when did we see You sick,
or in prison, and come to You?'
40 "And the King will answer
and say to them, 'Assuredly, I
say to you, [a]inasmuch as you did
it to one of the least of these My
brethren, you did *it* to Me.'
41 "Then He will also say to
those on the left hand, [a]'Depart
from Me, you cursed, [b]into the
everlasting fire prepared for [c]the
devil and his angels:
42 'for I was hungry and you
gave Me no food; I was thirsty
and you gave Me no drink;
43 'I was a stranger and you
did not take Me in, naked and
you did not clothe Me, sick and
in prison and you did not visit
Me.'
44 "Then they also will answer
[1]Him, saying, 'Lord, when did
we see You hungry or thirsty or
a stranger or naked or sick or in
prison, and did not minister to
You?'
45 "Then He will answer them,
saying, 'Assuredly, I say to you,
[a]inasmuch as you did not do *it* to
one of the least of these, you did
not do *it* to Me.'
46 "And [a]these will go away into
everlasting punishment, but the
righteous into eternal life."

26

Now it came to pass,
when Jesus had finished
all these sayings, *that* He said to
His disciples,
2 [a]"You know that after two
days is the Passover, and the
Son of Man will be delivered up
to be crucified."
3 [a]Then the chief priests, [1]the
scribes, and the elders of the
people assembled at the palace of the high priest, who was
called Cā′i·a·phas,
4 and [a]plotted to take Jesus by
[1]trickery and kill *Him.*
5 But they said, "Not during
the feast, lest there be an uproar
among the [a]people."
6 And when Jesus was in
[a]Beth′a·ny at the house of Simon
the leper,
7 a woman came to Him having an alabaster flask of very
costly fragrant oil, and she
poured *it* on His head as He sat
at the table.
8 [a]But when His disciples saw
it, they were indignant, saying,
"Why this waste?
9 "For this fragrant oil might
have been sold for much and
given to *the* poor."

32 [a][2 Cor. 5:10] [b]Ezek. 20:38
33 [a][John 10:11, 27, 28]
34 [a][Rom. 8:17] [b]Mark 10:40
35 [a]Is. 58:7 [b][Heb. 13:2]
36 [a][James 2:15, 16] [b]2 Tim. 1:16
40 [a]Mark 9:41
41 [a]Matt. 7:23 [b]Matt. 13:40, 42 [c][2 Pet. 2:4]
44 [1]NU, M omit *Him*
45 [a]Prov. 14:31
46 [a][Dan. 12:2]

CHAPTER 26

2 [a]Luke 22:1, 2
3 [a]John 11:47 [1]NU omits *the scribes*
4 [a]Acts 4:25–28 [1]*deception*
5 [a]Matt. 21:26
6 [a]Mark 14:3–9
8 [a]John 12:4

10 But when Jesus was aware of *it*, He said to them, "Why do you trouble the woman? For she has done a good work for Me.

11 [a]"For you have the poor with you always, but [b]Me you do not have always.

12 "For in pouring this fragrant oil on My body, she did *it* for My [a]burial.

13 "Assuredly, I say to you, wherever this gospel is preached in the whole world, what this woman has done will also be told as a memorial to her."

★ 14 [a]Then one of the twelve, called [b]Judas Is·car'i·ot, went to the chief priests

15 and said, [a]"What are you willing to give me if I deliver Him to you?" And they counted out to him thirty pieces of silver.

16 So from that time he sought opportunity to betray Him.

17 [a]Now on the first *day of the Feast* of Unleavened Bread the disciples came to Jesus, saying to Him, "Where do You want us to prepare for You to eat the Passover?"

18 And He said, "Go into the city to a certain man, and say to him, 'The Teacher says, [a]"My time is at hand; I will keep the Passover at your house with My disciples." ' "

19 So the disciples did as Jesus had directed them; and they prepared the Passover.

20 [a]When evening had come, He sat down with the twelve.

21 Now as they were eating, He said, "Assuredly, I say to you, one of you will [a]betray Me."

22 And they were exceedingly sorrowful, and each of them began to say to Him, "Lord, is it I?"

23 He answered and said, [a]"He who dipped *his* hand with Me in the dish will betray Me.

24 "The Son of Man indeed goes just [a]as it is written of Him, but [b]woe to that man by whom the Son of Man is betrayed! [c]It would have been good for that man if he had not been born."

25 Then Judas, who was betraying Him, answered and said, "Rabbi, is it I?" He said to him, "You have said it."

26 [a]And as they were eating, [b]Jesus took bread, [1]blessed and broke *it*, and gave *it* to the disciples and said, "Take, eat; [c]this is My body."

27 Then He took the cup, and gave thanks, and gave *it* to them, saying, [a]"Drink from it, all of you.

28 "For [a]this is My blood [b]of the [1]new covenant, which is shed [c]for many for the [2]remission of sins.

29 "But [a]I say to you, I will not drink of this fruit of the vine from now on [b]until that day when I drink it new with you in My Father's kingdom."

30 [a]And when they had sung a hymn, they went out to the Mount of Olives.

31 Then Jesus said to them, [a]"All ☆
of you will [b]be [1]made to stumble because of Me this night, for it is written:

> [c]*'I will strike the Shepherd,*
> *And the sheep of the flock*
> *will be scattered.'*

32 "But after I have been raised, [a]I will go before you to Galilee."

33 Peter answered and said to Him, "Even if all are [1]made to

---

11 [a][Deut. 15:11] [b][John 13:33; 14:19; 16:5, 28; 17:11]

12 [a]John 19:38–42

14 [a]Ps. 41:9; Mark 14:10, 11; Luke 22:3–6 [b]Matt. 10:4

15 [a]Zech. 11:12

17 [a]Ex. 12:6, 18–20

18 [a]Luke 9:51

20 [a]Mark 14:17–21

21 [a]John 6:70, 71; 13:21

23 [a]Ps. 41:9

24 [a]1 Cor. 15:3 [b]Luke 17:1 [c]John 17:12

26 [a]Mark 14:22–25 [b]1 Cor. 11:23–25 [c][1 Pet. 2:24] [1]M *gave thanks for*

27 [a]Mark 14:23

28 [a][Ex. 24:8] [b]Jer. 31:31 [c]Matt. 20:28 [1]NU omits *new* [2]*forgiveness*

29 [a]Mark 14:25 [b]Acts 10:41

30 [a]Mark 14:26–31

31 [a]Matt. 26:56; Mark 14:50; John 16:32 [b][Matt. 11:6] [c]Zech. 13:7 [1]*caused to take offense at Me*

32 [a]Matt. 28:7, 10, 16

33 [1]*caused to take offense at You*

stumble because of You, I will
never be made to stumble."
34 Jesus said to him, [a]"Assuredly,
I say to you that this night, before the rooster crows, you will
deny Me three times."
35 Peter said to Him, "Even if I
have to die with You, I will not
deny You!" And so said all the
disciples.
36 [a]Then Jesus came with them
to a place called Geth·sem′a·nē,
and said to the disciples, "Sit
here while I go and pray over
there."
37 And He took with Him Peter
and [a]the two sons of Zeb′e·dee,
and He began to be sorrowful and deeply distressed.
38 Then He said to them, [a]"My
soul is exceedingly sorrowful,
even to death. Stay here and
watch with Me."
39 He went a little farther and
fell on His face, and [a]prayed,
saying, [b]"O My Father, if it is
possible, [c]let this cup pass from
Me; nevertheless, [d]not as I will,
but as You *will*."
40 Then He came to the disciples and found them sleeping, and said to Peter, "What?
Could you not watch with Me
one hour?
41 [a]"Watch and pray, lest you
enter into temptation. [b]The spirit
indeed *is* willing, but the flesh *is*
weak."
42 Again, a second time, He
went away and prayed, saying,
"O My Father, [1]if this cup cannot pass away from Me unless I
drink it, Your will be done."
43 And He came and found
them asleep again, for their eyes
were heavy.
44 So He left them, went away

34 [a]John 13:38

36 [a]Mark 14:32–35

37 [a]Matt. 4:21; 17:1

38 [a]John 12:27

39 [a][Heb. 5:7–9] [b]John 12:27 [c]Matt. 20:22 [d]John 5:30; 6:38

41 [a]Luke 22:40, 46 [b][Gal. 5:17]

42 [1]NU *if this may not pass away unless*

45 [a]Matt. 17:22, 23; 20:18, 19 [1]*has drawn near*

47 [a]Acts 1:16

49 [a]2 Sam. 20:9

50 [a]Ps. 41:9; 55:13

51 [a]John 18:10

52 [a]Rev. 13:10 [1]M *die*

53 [a]Dan. 7:10

54 [a]Is. 50:6; 53:2–11

again, and prayed the third time,
saying the same words.
45 Then He came to His disciples and said to them, "Are
you still sleeping and resting?
Behold, the hour [1]is at hand,
and the Son of Man is being
[a]betrayed into the hands of sinners.
46 "Rise, let us be going. See,
My betrayer is at hand."
47 And [a]while He was still
speaking, behold, Judas, one of
the twelve, with a great multitude with swords and clubs,
came from the chief priests and
elders of the people.
48 Now His betrayer had given
them a sign, saying, "Whomever I kiss, He is the One; seize
Him."
49 Immediately he went up
to Jesus and said, "Greetings,
Rabbi!" [a]and kissed Him.
50 But Jesus said to him,
[a]"Friend, why have you come?"
Then they came and laid hands
on Jesus and took Him.
51 And suddenly, [a]one of those
who were with Jesus stretched
out *his* hand and drew his sword,
struck the servant of the high
priest, and cut off his ear.
52 But Jesus said to him, "Put
your sword in its place, [a]for all
who take the sword will [1]perish
by the sword.
53 "Or do you think that I cannot now pray to My Father, and
He will provide Me with [a]more
than twelve legions of angels?
54 "How then could the Scriptures be fulfilled, [a]that it must
happen thus?"
55 In that hour Jesus said to the
multitudes, "Have you come out,
as against a robber, with swords
and clubs to take Me? I sat daily

with you, teaching in the temple,
and you did not seize Me.
56 "But all this was done that
the [a]Scriptures of the prophets
might be fulfilled." Then [b]all the
disciples forsook Him and fled.
57 [a]And those who had laid hold
of Jesus led *Him* away to Cā′-
i·a·phas the high priest, where
the scribes and the elders were
assembled.
58 But [a]Peter followed Him at
a distance to the high priest's
courtyard. And he went in and
sat with the servants to see the
end.
59 Now the chief priests, [1]the elders, and all the council sought
[a]false testimony against Jesus to
put Him to death,
60 [1]but found none. Even though
[a]many false witnesses came forward, they found none. But at
last [b]two [2]false witnesses came
forward
61 and said, "This *fellow* said,
[a]'I am able to destroy the temple
of God and to build it in three
days.'"
62 [a]And the high priest arose
and said to Him, "Do You answer
nothing? What *is it* these men
testify against You?"
63 But [a]Jesus kept silent. And
the high priest answered and
said to Him, [b]"I put You under
oath by the living God: Tell us
if You are the Christ, the Son of
God!"
64 Jesus said to him, "*It is as*
you said. Nevertheless, I say to
you, [a]hereafter you will see the
Son of Man [b]sitting at the right
hand of the Power, and coming
on the clouds of heaven."
65 [a]Then the high priest tore
his clothes, saying, "He has spoken blasphemy! What further
need do we have of witnesses?
Look, now you have heard His
[b]blasphemy!
66 "What do you think?" They
answered and said, [a]"He is deserving of death."
67 [a]Then they spat in His face ★
and beat Him; and [b]others struck
Him with [1]the palms of their
hands,
68 saying, [a]"Prophesy to us,
Christ! Who is the one who
struck You?"
69 [a]Now Peter sat outside in the
courtyard. And a servant girl
came to him, saying, "You also
were with Jesus of Galilee."
70 But he denied it before *them*
all, saying, "I do not know what
you are saying."
71 And when he had gone out
to the gateway, another *girl* saw
him and said to those *who were*
there, "This *fellow* also was with
Jesus of Nazareth."
72 But again he denied with an
oath, "I do not know the Man!"
73 And a little later those who
stood by came up and said to Peter, "Surely you also are *one* of
them, for your [a]speech betrays
you."
74 Then [a]he began to [1]curse and
[2]swear, *saying*, "I do not know
the Man!" Immediately a rooster
crowed.
75 And Peter remembered the
word of Jesus who had said to
him, [a]"Before the rooster crows,
you will deny Me three times." So
he went out and wept bitterly.

27

When morning came, [a]all
the chief priests and el-
ders of the people plotted against
Jesus to put Him to death.
2 And when they had bound
Him, they led Him away and

56 [a]Lam. 4:20 [b]John 18:15
57 [a]John 18:12, 19–24
58 [a]John 18:15, 16
59 [a]Ps. 35:11 [1]NU omits *the elders*
60 [a]Mark 14:55 [b]Deut. 19:15 [1]NU *but found none, even though many false witnesses came forward.* [2]NU omits *false witnesses*
61 [a]John 2:19
62 [a]Mark 14:60
63 [a]Is. 53:7 [b]Lev. 5:1
64 [a]Dan. 7:13 [b][Acts 7:55]
65 [a]2 Kin. 18:37 [b]John 10:30–36
66 [a]Lev. 24:16
67 [a]Is. 50:6; 53:3 [b]Luke 22:63–65 [1]Or *rods,*
68 [a]Mark 14:65
69 [a]John 18:16–18, 25–27
73 [a]Luke 22:59
74 [a]Mark 14:71 [1]*call down curses* [2]Swear oaths
75 [a]Matt. 26:34

CHAPTER 27

1 [a]John 18:28

[a]delivered Him to [1]Pon′ti·us Pilate the governor.

3 [a]Then Judas, His betrayer, seeing that He had been condemned, was remorseful and brought back the thirty [b]pieces of silver to the chief priests and elders,

4 saying, "I have sinned by betraying innocent blood." And they said, "What *is that* to us? You see *to it!*"

5 Then he threw down the pieces of silver in the temple and [a]departed, and went and hanged himself.

6 But the chief priests took the silver pieces and said, "It is not lawful to put them into the treasury, because they are the price of blood."

7 And they consulted together and bought with them the potter's field, to bury strangers in.

8 Therefore that field has been called [a]the Field of Blood to this day.

★ 9 Then was fulfilled what was spoken by Jer·e·mi′ah the prophet, saying, [a]*"And they took the thirty pieces of silver, the value of Him who was priced,* whom they of the children of Israel priced,

★ 10 *"and [a]gave them for the potter's field, as the* Lord *directed me."*

11 Now Jesus stood before the governor. [a]And the governor asked Him, saying, "Are You the King of the Jews?" Jesus said to him, [b]"*It is as* you say."

12 And while He was being accused by the chief priests and elders, [a]He answered nothing.

13 Then Pilate said to Him, [a]"Do You not hear how many things they testify against You?"

2 [a]Acts 3:13 [1]NU omits *Pontius*
3 [a]Matt. 26:14 [b]Matt. 26:15
5 [a]Acts 1:18
8 [a]Acts 1:19
9 [a]Zech. 11:12
10 [a]Jer. 32:6–9; Zech. 11:12, 13
11 [a]Mark 15:2–5 [b]John 18:37
12 [a]John 19:9
13 [a]Matt. 26:62
14 [a]Is. 53:7
15 [a]Luke 23:17–25
16 [1]NU *Jesus Barabbas*
18 [a]Matt. 21:38
20 [a]Acts 3:14
21 [a]Acts 3:14
23 [a]Acts 3:13
24 [a]Deut. 21:6–8 [1]*an uproar* [2]NU omits *just*

14 [a]But He answered him not one word, so that the governor marveled greatly. ★

15 [a]Now at the feast the governor was accustomed to releasing to the multitude one prisoner whom they wished.

16 And at that time they had a notorious prisoner called [1]Ba·rab′bas.

17 Therefore, when they had gathered together, Pilate said to them, "Whom do you want me to release to you? Ba·rab′bas, or Jesus who is called Christ?"

18 For he knew that they had handed Him over because of [a]envy.

19 While he was sitting on the judgment seat, his wife sent to him, saying, "Have nothing to do with that just Man, for I have suffered many things today in a dream because of Him."

20 [a]But the chief priests and elders persuaded the multitudes that they should ask for Ba·rab′bas and destroy Jesus.

21 The governor answered and said to them, "Which of the two do you want me to release to you?" They said, [a]"Ba·rab′bas!"

22 Pilate said to them, "What then shall I do with Jesus who is called Christ?" *They* all said to him, "Let Him be crucified!"

23 Then the governor said, [a]"Why, what evil has He done?" But they cried out all the more, saying, "Let Him be crucified!"

24 When Pilate saw that he could not prevail at all, but rather *that* a [1]tumult was rising, he [a]took water and washed *his* hands before the multitude, saying, "I am innocent of the blood of this [2]just Person. You see *to it.*"

25 And all the people answered
and said, [a]"His blood *be* on us
and on our children."
★ 26 Then he released Ba·rab′-
bas to them; and when [a]he had
[1]scourged Jesus, he delivered
Him to be crucified.
27 [a]Then the soldiers of the governor took Jesus into the [1]Prae-
tō′ri·um and gathered the whole
[2]garrison around Him.
28 And they [a]stripped Him and
[b]put a scarlet robe on Him.
29 [a]When they had [1]twisted a
crown of thorns, they put *it* on
His head, and a reed in His
right hand. And they bowed the
knee before Him and mocked
Him, saying, "Hail, King of the
Jews!"
★ 30 Then [a]they spat on Him, and
took the reed and struck Him on
the head.
31 And when they had mocked
Him, they took the robe off Him,
put His *own* clothes on Him, [a]and
led Him away to be crucified.
32 [a]Now as they came out, [b]they
found a man of Cȳ·rē′nē, Simon
by name. Him they compelled to
bear His cross.
33 [a]And when they had come to
a place called Gol′go·tha, that is
to say, Place of a Skull,
★ 34 [a]they gave Him [1]sour wine
mingled with gall to drink. But
when He had tasted *it*, He would
not drink.
★ 35 [a]Then they crucified Him,
and divided His garments, casting lots, [1]that it might be fulfilled which was spoken by the
prophet:

[b]*"They divided My garments*
among them,
And for My clothing they
cast lots."

36 [a]Sitting down, they kept ★
watch over Him there.
37 And they [a]put up over His
head the accusation written
against Him:

THIS IS JESUS THE KING
OF THE JEWS.

38 [a]Then two robbers were crucified with Him, one on the right
and another on the left.
39 And [a]those who passed by ★
blasphemed Him, wagging their
heads
40 and saying, [a]"You who destroy the temple and build *it* in
three days, save Yourself! [b]If You
are the Son of God, come down
from the cross."
41 Likewise the chief priests
also, mocking with the [1]scribes
and elders, said,
42 "He [a]saved others; Himself
He cannot save. [1]If He is the
King of Israel, let Him now
come down from the cross, and
we will believe [2]Him.
43 [a]"He trusted in God; let Him ★
deliver Him now if He will have
Him; for He said, 'I am the Son
of God.' "
44 [a]Even the robbers who were
crucified with Him reviled Him
with the same thing.
45 [a]Now from the sixth hour
until the ninth hour there was
darkness over all the land.
46 And about the ninth hour ★
[a]Jesus cried out with a loud
voice, saying, "Ē′lī, Ē′lī, la·ma′
sa·bach′tha·nī?" that is, [b]*"My
God, My God, why have You
forsaken Me?"*
47 Some of those who stood
there, when they heard *that*,
said, "This Man is calling for
E·lī′jah!"

25 [a]Josh. 2:19
26 [a][Is. 50:6; 53:5] [1]*flogged* with a Roman scourge
27 [a]Mark 15:16–20 [1]The governor's headquarters [2]*cohort*
28 [a]John 19:2 [b]Luke 23:11
29 [a]Is. 53:3 [1]Lit. *woven*
30 [a]Is. 50:6; 53:5; Matt. 26:67
31 [a]Is. 53:7
32 [a]Heb. 13:12 [b]Mark 15:21
33 [a]John 19:17
34 [a]Ps. 69:21 [1]NU omits *sour*
35 [a]Luke 23:34 [b]Ps. 22:18 [1]NU, M omit the rest of v. 35.
36 [a]Ps. 22:17; Matt. 27:54
37 [a]John 19:19
38 [a]Is. 53:9, 12
39 [a]Ps. 22:7, 8; Mark 15:29
40 [a]John 2:19 [b]Matt. 26:63
41 [1]M *scribes, the Pharisees, and the elders*
42 [a][John 3:14, 15] [1]NU omits *If* [2]NU, M *in Him*
43 [a]Ps. 22:8
44 [a]Luke 23:39–43
45 [a]Mark 15:33–41
46 [a][Heb. 5:7] [b]Ps. 22:1

48 Immediately one of them ran
and took a sponge, [a]filled *it* with
sour wine and put *it* on a reed,
and offered it to Him to drink.
49 The rest said, "Let Him alone;
let us see if E·lī′jah will come to
save Him."
50 And Jesus [a]cried out again
with a loud voice, and [b]yielded
up His spirit.
51 Then, behold, [a]the veil of the
temple was torn in two from top
to bottom; and the earth quaked,
and the rocks were split,
52 and the graves were opened;
and many bodies of the saints
who had fallen asleep were
raised;
53 and coming out of the graves
after His resurrection, they went
into the holy city and appeared
to many.
54 [a]So when the centurion
and those with him, who were
guarding Jesus, saw the earthquake and the things that had
happened, they feared greatly,
saying, [b]"Truly this was the Son
of God!"
55 And many women [a]who followed Jesus from Galilee, ministering to Him, were there looking on from afar,
56 [a]among whom were Mary
Mag′da·lēne, Mary the mother
of James and [1]Jō′sēs, and the
mother of Zeb′e·dee's sons.
★ **57** Now [a]when evening had
come, there came a rich man
from Ar·i·ma·thē′a, named Joseph, who himself had also become a disciple of Jesus.
58 This man went to Pilate and
asked for the body of Jesus.
Then Pilate commanded the
body to be given to him.
59 When Joseph had taken the
body, he wrapped it in a clean
linen cloth,
60 and [a]laid it in his new tomb ★
which he had hewn out of the
rock; and he rolled a large stone
against the door of the tomb,
and departed.
61 And Mary Mag′da·lēne was
there, and the other Mary, sitting [1]opposite the tomb.
62 On the next day, which followed the Day of Preparation,
the chief priests and Phar′i·sees
gathered together to Pilate,
63 saying, "Sir, we remember,
while He was still alive, how
that deceiver said, [a]'After three
days I will rise.'
64 "Therefore command that
the tomb be made secure until
the third day, lest His disciples
come [1]by night and steal Him
away, and say to the people,
'He has risen from the dead.' So
the last deception will be worse
than the first."
65 Pilate said to them, "You
have a guard; go your way, make
it as secure as you know how."
66 So they went and made the
tomb secure, [a]sealing the stone
and setting the guard.

28

Now [a]after the Sabbath,
as the first *day* of the
week began to dawn, Mary
Mag′da·lēne [b]and the other Mary
came to see the tomb.
2 And behold, there was a
great earthquake; for [a]an angel of the Lord descended from
heaven, and came and rolled
back the stone [1]from the door,
and sat on it.
3 [a]His countenance was like
lightning, and his clothing as
white as snow.
4 And the guards shook for

48 [a]Ps. 69:21
50 [a]Luke 23:46 [b][John 19:30]
51 [a]Ex. 26:31
54 [a]Mark 15:39 [b]Matt. 14:33
55 [a]Luke 8:2, 3
56 [a]Mark 15:40, 47; 16:9 [1]NU *Joseph*
57 [a]Is. 53:9; John 19:38–42
60 [a]Is. 53:9
61 [1]*in front of*
63 [a]Mark 8:31; 10:34
64 [1]NU omits *by night*
66 [a]Dan. 6:17

CHAPTER 28

1 [a]Luke 24:1–10 [b]Matt. 27:56, 61
2 [a]Mark 16:5 [1]NU omits *from the door*
3 [a]Dan. 7:9; 10:6

fear of him, and became like
[a]dead *men.*
5 But the angel answered and
said to the women, "Do not be
afraid, for I know that you seek
Jesus who was crucified.
6 "He is not here; for He is
risen, [a]as He said. Come, see the
place where the Lord lay.
7 "And go quickly and tell His
disciples that He is risen from
the dead, and indeed [a]He is going before you into Galilee; there
you will see Him. Behold, I have
told you."
8 So they went out quickly
from the tomb with fear and
great joy, and ran to bring His
disciples word.
9 And [1]as they went to tell
His disciples, behold, [a]Jesus met
them, saying, "Rejoice!" So they
came and held Him by the feet
and worshiped Him.
10 Then Jesus said to them, "Do
not be afraid. Go *and* tell [a]My
brethren to go to Galilee, and
there they will see Me."
11 Now while they were going,
behold, some of the guard came
into the city and reported to the
chief priests all the things that
had happened.
12 When they had assembled
with the elders and consulted
together, they gave a large sum
of money to the soldiers,
13 saying, "Tell them, 'His disciples came at night and stole
Him *away* while we slept.'
14 "And if this comes to the
governor's ears, we will appease
him and make you secure."
15 So they took the money and
did as they were instructed; and
this saying is commonly reported
among the Jews until this day.
16 Then the eleven disciples
went away into Galilee, to the
mountain [a]which Jesus had appointed for them.
17 When they saw Him, they
worshiped Him; but some
[a]doubted.
18 And Jesus came and spoke
to them, saying, [a]"All authority
has been given to Me in heaven
and on earth.
19 [a]"Go [1]therefore and [b]make
disciples of all the nations, baptizing them in the name of the
Father and of the Son and of the
Holy Spirit,
20 [a]"teaching them to observe
all things that I have commanded you; and lo, I am [b]with
you always, *even* to the end of
the age." [1]Amen.

4 [a]Rev. 1:17
6 [a]Matt. 12:40; 16:21; 17:23; 20:19
7 [a]Mark 16:7
9 [a]John 20:14 [1]NU omits *as they went to tell His disciples*
10 [a]John 20:17
16 [a]Matt. 26:32; 28:7, 10
17 [a]John 20:24–29
18 [a][Dan. 7:13, 14]
19 [a]Mark 16:15 [b]Luke 24:47 [1]M omits *therefore*
20 [a][Acts 2:42] [b][Acts 4:31; 18:10; 23:11] [1]NU omits *Amen.*

The Gospel According to
MARK

THE message of Mark's gospel is captured in a single verse: "For even the Son of Man did not come to be served, but to serve, and to give His life a ransom for many" (10:45). Chapter by chapter, the book unfolds the dual focus of Christ's life: service and sacrifice.

Mark portrays Jesus as a Servant on the move, instantly responsive to the will of the Father. By preaching, teaching, and healing, He ministers to the needs of others even to the point of death. After the Resurrection, He commissions His followers to continue His work in His power—servants following in the steps of the perfect Servant.

The ancient title for this gospel was *Kata Markon*, "According to Mark." The author is best known by his Latin name *Marcus*, but in Jewish circles he was called by his Hebrew name *John*. Acts 12:12, 25 refer to him as "John whose surname was Mark."

THE [a]beginning of the gospel
of Jesus Christ, [b]the Son of
God.
★ 2 As it is written in [1]the Prophets:

[a]*"Behold, I send My messenger*
before Your face,
Who will prepare Your way
before You."
★ 3 *"The[a] voice of one crying in*
the wilderness:
'Prepare the way of the Lord;
Make His paths straight.'"

★ 4 [a]John came baptizing in the
wilderness and preaching a baptism of repentance [1]for the remission of sins.
5 [a]Then all the land of Judea,
and those from Jerusalem, went
out to him and were all baptized
by him in the Jordan River, confessing their sins.
6 Now John was [a]clothed with
camel's hair and with a leather
belt around his waist, and he ate
locusts and wild honey.
7 And he preached, saying,
[a]"There comes One after me
who is mightier than I, whose
sandal strap I am not worthy to
stoop down and loose.
8 [a]"I indeed baptized you with
water, but He will baptize you
[b]with the Holy Spirit."
9 [a]It came to pass in those days
that Jesus came from Nazareth
of Galilee, and was baptized by
John in the Jordan.
10 [a]And immediately, coming
up [1]from the water, He saw the
heavens [2]parting and the Spirit
[b]descending upon Him like a
dove.
11 Then a voice came from
heaven, [a]"You are My beloved
Son, in whom I am well pleased."
12 [a]Immediately the Spirit
[1]drove Him into the wilderness.
13 And He was there in the
wilderness forty days, tempted
by Satan, and was with the wild
beasts; [a]and the angels ministered to Him.
14 [a]Now after John was put in

CHAPTER 1

1 [a]Luke 3:22 [b]Matt. 14:33
2 [a]Mal. 3:1 [1]NU *Isaiah the prophet*
3 [a]Is. 40:3
4 [a]Mal. 4:5, 6; Matt. 3:1 [1]Or *because of forgiveness*
5 [a]Matt. 3:5
6 [a]Matt. 3:4
7 [a]John 1:27
8 [a]Acts 1:5; 11:16 [b]Is. 44:3
9 [a]Matt. 3:13–17
10 [a]Matt. 3:16 [b]Acts 10:38 [1]NU *out of* [2]*torn open*
11 [a]Matt. 3:17; 12:18
12 [a]Matt. 4:1–11 [1]*sent Him out*
13 [a]Matt. 4:10, 11
14 [a]Matt. 4:12

prison, Jesus came to Galilee,
[b]preaching the gospel [1]of the
kingdom of God,
15 and saying, [a]"The time is fulfilled, and [b]the kingdom of God
[1]is at hand. Repent, and believe
in the gospel."
16 [a]And as He walked by the
Sea of Galilee, He saw Simon
and Andrew his brother casting
a net into the sea; for they were
fishermen.
17 Then Jesus said to them,
"Follow Me, and I will make you
become [a]fishers of men."
18 [a]They immediately left their
nets and followed Him.
19 When He had gone a little farther from there, He saw
James the *son* of Zeb′e·dee, and
John his brother, who also *were*
in the boat mending their nets.
20 And immediately He called
them, and they left their father
Zeb′e·dee in the boat with the
hired servants, and went after
Him.
21 [a]Then they went into Ca·per′-
na·um, and immediately on the
Sabbath He entered the [b]syn-
agogue and taught.
22 [a]And they were astonished
at His teaching, for He taught
them as one having authority,
and not as the scribes.
23 Now there was a man in their
synagogue with an [a]unclean
spirit. And he cried out,
24 saying, "Let *us* alone! [a]What
have we to do with You, Jesus
of Nazareth? Did You come to
destroy us? I [b]know who You
are—the [c]Holy One of God!"
25 But Jesus [a]rebuked him, saying, [1]"Be quiet, and come out of
him!"
26 And when the unclean spirit
[a]had convulsed him and cried

14 [b]Matt. 4:23
[1]NU omits *of the kingdom*
15 [a][Gal. 4:4]
[b]Matt. 3:2; 4:17
[1]*has drawn near*
16 [a]Luke 5:2–11
17 [a]Matt. 13:47, 48
18 [a][Luke 14:26]
21 [a]Luke 4:31–37
[b]Matt. 4:23
22 [a]Matt. 7:28, 29; 13:54
23 [a][Matt. 12:43]
24 [a]Matt. 8:28, 29
[b]James 2:19
[c]Ps. 16:10
25 [a][Luke 4:39]
[1]Lit. *Be muzzled*
26 [a]Mark 9:20
27 [1]NU *What is this? A new doctrine with authority! He*
[2]*teaching*
28 [a]Matt. 4:24; 9:31
29 [a]Luke 4:38, 39
32 [a]Matt. 8:16, 17
34 [a]Luke 13:32
[b]Acts 16:17, 18
35 [a]Luke 4:42, 43
[b]Luke 5:16; 6:12; 9:28, 29
[1]*deserted*
37 [a]John 3:26; 12:19
[b][Heb. 11:6]
38 [a]Luke 4:43

out with a loud voice, he came
out of him.
27 Then they were all amazed,
so that they questioned among
themselves, saying, [1]"What is
this? What new [2]doctrine *is* this?
For with authority He commands even the unclean spirits,
and they obey Him."
28 And immediately His [a]fame
spread throughout all the region
around Galilee.
29 [a]Now as soon as they had
come out of the synagogue, they
entered the house of Simon and
Andrew, with James and John.
30 But Simon's wife's mother
lay sick with a fever, and they
told Him about her at once.
31 So He came and took her by
the hand and lifted her up, and
immediately the fever left her.
And she served them.
32 [a]At evening, when the sun
had set, they brought to Him all
who were sick and those who
were demon-possessed.
33 And the whole city was gathered together at the door.
34 Then He healed many who
were sick with various diseases,
and [a]cast out many demons; and
He [b]did not allow the demons to
speak, because they knew Him.
35 Now [a]in the morning, having
risen a long while before daylight, He went out and departed
to a [1]solitary place; and there He
[b]prayed.
36 And Simon and those *who
were* with Him searched for
Him.
37 When they found Him, they
said to Him, [a]"Everyone [b]is looking for You."
38 But He said to them, [a]"Let
us go into the next towns, that I
may preach there also, because

[b]for this purpose I have come
forth."
39 [a]And He was preaching in
their synagogues throughout
all Galilee, and [b]casting out demons.
40 [a]Now a leper came to Him,
imploring Him, kneeling down
to Him and saying to Him, "If
You are willing, You can make
me clean."
41 Then Jesus, moved with
[a]compassion, stretched out *His*
hand and touched him, and
said to him, "I am willing; be
cleansed."
42 As soon as He had spoken,
[a]immediately the leprosy left
him, and he was cleansed.
43 And He strictly warned him
and sent him away at once,
44 and said to him, "See that
you say nothing to anyone; but
go your way, show yourself to
the priest, and offer for your
cleansing those things [a]which
Moses commanded, as a testimony to them."
45 [a]However, he went out and
began to proclaim *it* freely, and
to spread the matter, so that
Jesus could no longer openly
enter the city, but was outside in
deserted places; [b]and they came
to Him from every direction.
2 And again [a]He entered Ca-
per′na·um after *some* days,
and it was heard that He was in
the house.
2 [1]Immediately many gathered
together, so that there was no
longer room to receive *them*,
not even near the door. And He
preached the word to them.
3 Then they came to Him,
bringing a [a]paralytic who was
carried by four *men*.
4 And when they could not
come near Him because of the
crowd, they uncovered the roof
where He was. So when they
had broken through, they let
down the bed on which the paralytic was lying.
5 When Jesus saw their faith,
He said to the paralytic, "Son,
your sins are forgiven you."
6 And some of the scribes were
sitting there and reasoning in
their hearts,
7 "Why does this *Man* speak
blasphemies like this? [a]Who can
forgive sins but God alone?"
8 But immediately, when Jesus perceived in His spirit that
they reasoned thus within themselves, He said to them, "Why do
you reason about these things in
your hearts?
9 [a]"Which is easier, to say to
the paralytic, '*Your* sins are forgiven you,' or to say, 'Arise, take
up your bed and walk'?
10 "But that you may know that
the Son of Man has [1]power on
earth to forgive sins"—He said
to the paralytic,
11 "I say to you, arise, take up
your bed, and go to your house."
12 Immediately he arose, took
up the bed, and went out in the
presence of them all, so that all
were amazed and [a]glorified God,
saying, "We never saw *anything*
like this!"
13 [a]Then He went out again by
the sea; and all the multitude
came to Him, and He taught
them.
14 [a]As He passed by, He saw
Levi the *son* of Al·phae̅′us sitting
at the tax office. And He said to
him, [b]"Follow Me." So he arose
and [c]followed Him.
15 [a]Now it happened, as He was
dining in *Levi's* house, that many

38 [b][Is. 61:1, 2]
39 [a]Matt. 4:23; 9:35 [b]Mark 5:8, 13; 7:29, 30
40 [a]Luke 5:12–14
41 [a]Luke 7:13
42 [a]Matt. 15:28
44 [a]Lev. 14:1–32
45 [a]Luke 5:15 [b]Mark 2:2, 13; 3:7

CHAPTER 2

1 [a]Matt. 9:1
2 [1]NU omits *Immediately*
3 [a]Matt. 4:24; 8:6
7 [a]Is. 43:25
9 [a]Matt. 9:5
10 [1]*authority*
12 [a][Phil. 2:11]
13 [a]Matt. 9:9
14 [a]Luke 5:27–32 [b]John 1:43; 12:26; 21:22 [c]Luke 18:28
15 [a]Matt. 9:10

tax collectors and sinners also
sat together with Jesus and His
disciples; for there were many,
and they followed Him.
16 And when the scribes [1]and
Phar'i·sees saw Him eating with
the tax collectors and sinners,
they said to His disciples, "How
is it that He eats and drinks with
tax collectors and sinners?"
17 When Jesus heard *it*, He said
to them, [a]"Those who are well
have no need of a physician,
but those who are sick. I did not
come to call *the* righteous, but
sinners, [1]to repentance."
18 [a]The disciples of John and
of the Phar'i·sees were fasting.
Then they came and said to
Him, "Why do the disciples of
John and of the Phar'i·sees fast,
but Your disciples do not fast?"
19 And Jesus said to them, "Can
the [1]friends of the bridegroom
fast while the bridegroom is
with them? As long as they have
the bridegroom with them they
cannot fast.
20 "But the days will come when
the bridegroom will be [a]taken
away from them, and then they
will fast in those days.
21 "No one sews a piece of unshrunk cloth on an old garment;
or else the new piece pulls away
from the old, and the tear is
made worse.
22 "And no one puts new wine
into old wineskins; or else the
new wine bursts the wineskins,
the wine is spilled, and the wineskins are ruined. But new wine
must be put into new wineskins."
23 [a]Now it happened that He
went through the grainfields on
the Sabbath; and as they went
His disciples began [b]to pluck the
heads of grain.
24 And the Phar'i·sees said to
Him, "Look, why do they do
what is [a]not lawful on the Sabbath?"
25 But He said to them, "Have
you never read [a]what David did
when he was in need and hungry, he and those with him:
26 "how he went into the house
of God *in the days* of A·bi'a·thar
the high priest, and ate the showbread, [a]which is not lawful to eat
except for the priests, and also
gave some to those who were
with him?"
27 And He said to them, "The
Sabbath was made for man, and
not man for the [a]Sabbath.
28 "Therefore [a]the Son of Man
is also Lord of the Sabbath."

3

And [a]He entered the synagogue again, and a man was
there who had a withered hand.
2 So they [a]watched Him closely,
whether He would [b]heal him on
the Sabbath, so that they might
[1]accuse Him.
3 And He said to the man who
had the withered hand, [1]"Step
forward."
4 Then He said to them, "Is
it lawful on the Sabbath to do
good or to do evil, to save life or
to kill?" But they kept silent.
5 And when He had looked
around at them with anger, being grieved by the [a]hardness of
their hearts, He said to the man,
"Stretch out your hand." And he
stretched *it* out, and his hand
was restored [1]as whole as the
other.
6 [a]Then the Phar'i·sees went ★
out and immediately plotted with
[b]the He·rō'di·ans against Him,
how they might destroy Him.
7 But Jesus withdrew with His
disciples to the sea. And a great

16 [1]NU *of the*
17 [a]Matt. 9:12, 13; 18:11 [1]NU omits *to repentance*
18 [a]Luke 5:33–38
19 [1]Lit. *sons of the bridechamber*
20 [a]Acts 1:9; 13:2, 3; 14:23
23 [a]Luke 6:1–5 [b]Deut. 23:25
24 [a]Ex. 20:10; 31:15
25 [a]1 Sam. 21:1–6
26 [a]Lev. 24:5–9
27 [a]Deut. 5:14
28 [a]Matt. 12:8

CHAPTER 3

1 [a]Luke 6:6–11
2 [a]Luke 14:1; 20:20 [b]Luke 13:14 [1]*bring charges against*
3 [1]Lit. *Arise into the midst*
5 [a]Zech. 7:12 [1]NU omits *as whole as the other*
6 [a]Ps. 2:2; Mark 12:13 [b]Matt. 22:16

multitude from Galilee followed
Him, [a]and from Judea
8 and Jerusalem and Id·ū·mē′a
and beyond the Jordan; and
those from Tȳre and Sī′don,
a great multitude, when they
heard how [a]many things He was
doing, came to Him.
9 So He told His disciples that
a small boat should be kept
ready for Him because of the
multitude, lest they should crush
Him.
10 For He healed [a]many, so
that as many as had afflictions
pressed about Him to [b]touch
Him.
11 [a]And the unclean spirits,
whenever they saw Him, fell
down before Him and cried out,
saying, [b]"You are the Son of
God."
12 But [a]He sternly warned them
that they should not make Him
known.
13 [a]And He went up on the
mountain and called to *Him*
those He Himself wanted. And
they came to Him.
14 Then He appointed twelve,
[1]that they might be with Him
and that He might send them
out to preach,
15 and to have [1]power [2]to heal
sicknesses and to cast out demons:
16 [1]Simon, [a]to whom He gave
the name Peter;
17 James the *son* of Zeb′e·dee
and John the brother of James,
to whom He gave the name
Bō·a·ner′gēs, that is, "Sons of
Thunder";
18 Andrew, Philip, Bartholomew, Matthew, Thomas, James
the *son* of Al·phaē′us, Thad-
daē′us, Simon the Can′a·nīte;
19 and Judas Is·car′i·ot, who
also betrayed Him. And they
went into a house.
20 Then the multitude came together again, [a]so that they could
not so much as eat bread.
21 But when His [a]own people
heard *about this*, they went out
to lay hold of Him, [b]for they
said, "He is out of His mind."
22 And the scribes who came
down from Jerusalem said, [a]"He
has Bē·el′ze·bub," and, "By the
[b]ruler of the demons He casts
out demons."
23 [a]So He called them to *Him-*
self and said to them in parables:
"How can Satan cast out Satan?
24 "If a kingdom is divided
against itself, that kingdom cannot stand.
25 "And if a house is divided
against itself, that house cannot
stand.
26 "And if Satan has risen up
against himself, and is divided,
he cannot stand, but has an
end.
27 [a]"No one can enter a strong
man's house and plunder his
goods, unless he first binds the
strong man. And then he will
plunder his house.
28 [a]"Assuredly, I say to you, all
sins will be forgiven the sons of
men, and whatever blasphemies
they may utter;
29 "but he who blasphemes
against the Holy Spirit never
has forgiveness, but is subject to
eternal condemnation"—
30 because they [a]said, "He has
an unclean spirit."
31 [a]Then His brothers and His
mother came, and standing outside they sent to Him, calling
Him.
32 And a multitude was sitting
around Him; and they said to

7 [a]Luke 6:17
8 [a]Mark 5:19
10 [a]Luke 7:21 [b]Matt. 9:21; 14:36
11 [a]Luke 4:41 [b]Matt. 8:29; 14:33
12 [a]Mark 1:25, 34
13 [a]Luke 9:1
14 [1]NU adds *whom He also named apostles*
15 [1]*authority* [2]NU omits *to heal sicknesses and*
16 [a]John 1:42 [1]NU *and He appointed the twelve: Simon . . .*
20 [a]Mark 6:31
21 [a]Mark 6:3 [b]John 7:5; 10:20
22 [a]Matt. 9:34; 10:25 [b][John 12:31; 14:30; 16:11]
23 [a]Matt. 12:25–29
27 [a][Is. 49:24, 25]
28 [a]Luke 12:10
30 [a]Matt. 9:34
31 [a]Matt. 12:46–50

Him, "Look, Your mother and Your brothers [1]are outside seeking You."

33 But He answered them, saying, "Who is My mother, or My brothers?"

34 And He looked around in a circle at those who sat about Him, and said, "Here are My mother and My brothers!

35 "For whoever does the [a]will of God is My brother and My sister and mother."

4 And [a]again He began to teach by the sea. And a great multitude was gathered to Him, so that He got into a boat and sat *in it* on the sea; and the whole multitude was on the land facing the sea.

2 Then He taught them many things by parables, [a]and said to them in His teaching:

3 "Listen! Behold, a sower went out to sow.

4 "And it happened, as he sowed, *that* some *seed* fell by the wayside; and the birds [1]of the air came and devoured it.

5 "Some fell on stony ground, where it did not have much earth; and immediately it sprang up because it had no depth of earth.

6 "But when the sun was up it was scorched, and because it had no root it withered away.

7 "And some *seed* fell among thorns; and the thorns grew up and choked it, and it yielded no [1]crop.

8 "But other *seed* fell on good ground and yielded a crop that sprang up, increased and produced: some thirtyfold, some sixty, and some a hundred."

9 And He said [1]to them, "He who has ears to hear, let him hear!"

10 [a]But when He was alone, those around Him with the twelve asked Him about the parable.

11 And He said to them, "To you it has been given to [a]know the [1]mystery of the kingdom of God; but to [b]those who are outside, all things come in parables,

12 "so that ★

[a]'Seeing they may see and
not perceive,
And hearing they may hear
and not understand;
Lest they should turn,
And their sins be forgiven
them.'"

13 And He said to them, "Do you not understand this parable? How then will you understand all the parables?

14 [a]"The sower sows the word.

15 "And these are the ones by the wayside where the word is sown. When they hear, Satan comes immediately and takes away the word that was sown in their hearts.

16 "These likewise are the ones sown on stony ground who, when they hear the word, immediately receive it with gladness;

17 "and they have no root in themselves, and so endure only for a time. Afterward, when tribulation or persecution arises for the word's sake, immediately they stumble.

18 "Now these are the ones sown among thorns; *they are* the ones who hear the word,

19 "and the [a]cares of this world, [b]the deceitfulness of riches, and the desires for other things

32 [1]NU, M add *and Your sisters*
35 [a]Eph. 6:6

CHAPTER 4

1 [a]Luke 8:4–10
2 [a]Mark 12:38
4 [1]NU, M omit *of the air*
7 [1]Lit. *fruit*
9 [1]NU, M omit *to them*
10 [a]Luke 8:9
11 [a][1 Cor. 2:10–16] [b][Col. 4:5] [1]*secret* or *hidden truths*
12 [a]Is. 6:9, 10; 43:8
14 [a]Matt. 13:18–23
19 [a]Luke 21:34 [b]1 Tim. 6:9, 10, 17

entering in choke the word, and
it becomes unfruitful.
20 "But these are the ones sown
on good ground, those who hear
the word, [1]accept *it*, and bear
[a]fruit: some thirtyfold, some
sixty, and some a hundred."
21 [a]Also He said to them, "Is a
lamp brought to be put under a
basket or under a bed? Is it not
to be set on a lampstand?
22 [a]"For there is nothing hidden
which will not be revealed, nor
has anything been kept secret
but that it should come to light.
23 [a]"If anyone has ears to hear,
let him hear."
24 Then He said to them, "Take
heed what you hear. [a]With the
same measure you use, it will
be measured to you; and to you
who hear, more will be given.
25 [a]"For whoever has, to him
more will be given; but whoever
does not have, even what he has
will be taken away from him."
26 And He said, [a]"The kingdom
of God is as if a man should
[1]scatter seed on the ground,
27 "and should sleep by night
and rise by day, and the seed
should sprout and [a]grow, he
himself does not know how.
28 "For the earth [a]yields crops
by itself: first the blade, then the
head, after that the full grain in
the head.
29 "But when the grain ripens,
immediately [a]he puts in the
sickle, because the harvest has
come."
30 Then He said, [a]"To what shall
we liken the kingdom of God?
Or with what parable shall we
picture it?
31 "*It is* like a mustard seed
which, when it is sown on the
ground, is smaller than all the
seeds on earth;
32 "but when it is sown, it grows
up and becomes greater than
all herbs, and shoots out large
branches, so that the birds of the
air may nest under its shade."
33 [a]And with many such parables He spoke the word to them
as they were able to hear *it*.
34 But without a parable He did
not speak to them. And when
they were alone, [a]He explained
all things to His disciples.
35 [a]On the same day, when evening had come, He said to them,
"Let us cross over to the other
side."
36 Now when they had left the
multitude, they took Him along
in the boat as He was. And other
little boats were also with Him.
37 And a great windstorm arose,
and the waves beat into the boat,
so that it was already filling.
38 But He was in the stern,
asleep on a pillow. And they
awoke Him and said to Him,
[a]"Teacher, [b]do You not care that
we are perishing?"
39 Then He arose and [a]rebuked
the wind, and said to the sea,
[b]"Peace,[1] be still!" And the wind
ceased and there was a great
calm.
40 But He said to them, "Why
are you so fearful? [a]How[1] *is it*
that you have no faith?"
41 And they feared exceedingly,
and said to one another, "Who
can this be, that even the wind
and the sea obey Him!"

5

Then [a]they came to the other
side of the sea, to the country of the [1]Gad′a·rēnes.
2 And when He had come out
of the boat, immediately there

20 [a][Rom. 7:4] [1]*receive*
21 [a]Matt. 5:15
22 [a]Matt. 10:26, 27
23 [a]Matt. 11:15; 13:9, 43
24 [a]Matt. 7:2
25 [a]Luke 8:18; 19:26
26 [a][Matt. 13:24–30, 36–43] [1]*sow*
27 [a][2 Pet. 3:18]
28 [a][John 12:24]
29 [a]Rev. 14:15
30 [a]Matt. 13:31, 32
33 [a]Matt. 13:34, 35
34 [a]Luke 24:27, 45
35 [a]Luke 8:22, 25
38 [a][Matt. 23:8–10] [b]Ps. 44:23
39 [a]Luke 4:39 [b]Ps. 65:7; 89:9; 93:4; 104:6, 7 [1]Lit. *Be quiet*
40 [a]Matt. 14:31, 32 [1]NU *Have you still no faith?*

CHAPTER 5

1 [a]Matt. 8:28–34 [1]NU *Gerasenes*

met Him out of the tombs a man
with an [a]unclean spirit,
3 who had *his* dwelling among
the tombs; and no one could
bind [1]him, not even with chains,
4 because he had often been
bound with shackles and chains.
And the chains had been pulled
apart by him, and the shackles
broken in pieces; neither could
anyone tame him.
5 And always, night and day,
he was in the mountains and in
the tombs, crying out and cutting himself with stones.
6 When he saw Jesus from afar,
he ran and worshiped Him.
7 And he cried out with a loud
voice and said, "What have I to
do with You, Jesus, Son of the
Most High God? I [a]implore[1] You
by God that You do not torment
me."
8 For He said to him, [a]"Come
out of the man, unclean spirit!"
9 Then He asked him, "What *is*
your name?" And he answered,
saying, "My name *is* Legion; for
we are many."
10 Also he begged Him earnestly that He would not send
them out of the country.
11 Now a large herd of [a]swine
was feeding there near the
mountains.
12 So all the demons begged
Him, saying, "Send us to the
swine, that we may enter them."
13 And [1]at once Jesus gave them
permission. Then the unclean
spirits went out and entered the
swine (there were about two
thousand); and the herd ran violently down the steep place into
the sea, and drowned in the sea.
14 So those who fed the swine
fled, and they told *it* in the city
and in the country. And they
went out to see what it was that
had happened.
15 Then they came to Jesus,
and saw the one *who had been*
[a]demon-possessed and had the
legion, [b]sitting and [c]clothed and
in his right mind. And they were
afraid.
16 And those who saw it told
them how it happened to him
who had been demon-possessed,
and about the swine.
17 Then [a]they began to plead
with Him to depart from their
region.
18 And when He got into the
boat, [a]he who had been demon-
possessed begged Him that he
might be with Him.
19 However, Jesus did not permit him, but said to him, "Go
home to your friends, and tell
them what great things the Lord
has done for you, and how He
has had compassion on you."
20 And he departed and began
to [a]proclaim in [1]De·cap'o·lis all
that Jesus had done for him; and
all [b]marveled.
21 [a]Now when Jesus had crossed
over again by boat to the other
side, a great multitude gathered
to Him; and He was by the sea.
22 [a]And behold, one of the rulers of the synagogue came, Jā·ī'-
rus by name. And when he saw
Him, he fell at His feet
23 and begged Him earnestly,
saying, "My little daughter lies
at the point of death. Come and
[a]lay Your hands on her, that she
may be healed, and she will
live."
24 So *Jesus* went with him, and
a great multitude followed Him
and thronged Him.
25 Now a certain woman [a]had a
flow of blood for twelve years,

2 [a]Mark 1:23; 7:25
3 [1]NU adds *anymore*
7 [a]Acts 19:13 [1]*adjure*
8 [a]Mark 1:25; 9:25
11 [a]Deut. 14:8
13 [1]NU *He gave*
15 [a]Matt. 4:24; 8:16 [b]Luke 10:39 [c][Is. 61:10]
17 [a]Acts 16:39
18 [a]Luke 8:38, 39
20 [a]Ps. 66:16 [b]Matt. 9:8, 33 [1]Lit. *Ten Cities*
21 [a]Luke 8:40
22 [a]Matt. 9:18–26
23 [a]Acts 9:17; 28:8
25 [a]Lev. 15:19, 25

26 and had suffered many
things from many physicians.
She had spent all that she had
and was no better, but rather
grew worse.
27 When she heard about Jesus,
she came behind *Him* in the
crowd and [a]touched His garment.
28 For she said, "If only I may
touch His clothes, I shall be
made well."
29 Immediately the fountain of
her blood was dried up, and she
felt in *her* body that she was
healed of the [1]affliction.
30 And Jesus, immediately
knowing in Himself that [a]power
had gone out of Him, turned
around in the crowd and said,
"Who touched My clothes?"
31 But His disciples said to Him,
"You see the multitude thronging
You, and You say, 'Who touched
Me?' "
32 And He looked around to see
her who had done this thing.
33 But the woman, [a]fearing and
trembling, knowing what had
happened to her, came and fell
down before Him and told Him
the whole truth.
34 And He said to her, "Daughter, [a]your faith has made you
well. [b]Go in peace, and be healed
of your affliction."
35 [a]While He was still speaking, *some* came from the ruler
of the synagogue's *house* who
said, "Your daughter is dead. Why
trouble the Teacher any further?"
36 As soon as Jesus heard the
word that was spoken, He said to
the ruler of the synagogue, "Do
not be afraid; only [a]believe."
37 And He permitted no one to
follow Him except Peter, James,
and John the brother of James.
38 Then He came to the house
of the ruler of the synagogue,
and saw [1]a tumult and those
who [a]wept and wailed loudly.
39 When He came in, He said to
them, "Why make this commotion and weep? The child is not
dead, but [a]sleeping."
40 And they ridiculed Him. [a]But
when He had put them all outside, He took the father and the
mother of the child, and those
who were with Him, and entered
where the child was lying.
41 Then He took the child by
the hand, and said to her, "Tal′-
i·tha, cū′mi," which is translated,
"Little girl, I say to you, arise."
42 Immediately the girl arose
and walked, for she was twelve
years *of age*. And they were
[a]overcome with great amazement.
43 But [a]He commanded them
strictly that no one should know
it, and said that *something*
should be given her to eat.

6 Then [a]He went out from
there and came to His own
country, and His disciples followed Him.
2 And when the Sabbath had
come, He began to teach in the
synagogue. And many hearing
Him were [a]astonished, saying,
[b]"Where *did* this Man *get* these
things? And what wisdom *is* this
which is given to Him, that such
mighty works are performed by
His hands!
3 "Is this not the carpenter,
the Son of Mary, and [a]brother of
James, Jō′sēs, Judas, and Simon?
And are not His sisters here with
us?" So they [b]were offended at
Him.
4 But Jesus said to them, [a]"A
prophet is not without honor

27 [a]Matt. 14:35, 36
29 [1]*suffering*
30 [a]Luke 6:19; 8:46
33 [a][Ps. 89:7]
34 [a]Matt. 9:22 [b]Luke 7:50; 8:48
35 [a]Luke 8:49
36 [a][John 11:40]
38 [a]Acts 9:39 [1]*an uproar*
39 [a]John 11:4, 11
40 [a]Acts 9:40
42 [a]Mark 1:27; 7:37
43 [a][Matt. 8:4; 12:16–19; 17:9]

CHAPTER 6

1 [a]Matt. 13:54
2 [a]Matt. 7:28 [b]John 6:42
3 [a]Matt. 12:46 [b][Matt. 11:6]
4 [a]John 4:44

except in his own country,
among his own relatives, and in
his own house."
5 [a]Now He could do no mighty
work there, except that He laid
His hands on a few sick people
and healed *them.*
6 And [a]He marveled because
of their unbelief. [b]Then He went
about the villages in a circuit,
teaching.
7 [a]And He called the twelve to
Himself, and began to send them
out [b]two *by* two, and gave them
power over unclean spirits.
8 He commanded them to take
nothing for the journey except a
staff—no bag, no bread, no copper in *their* money belts—
9 but [a]to wear sandals, and not
to put on two tunics.
10 [a]Also He said to them, "In
whatever place you enter a
house, stay there till you depart
from that place.
11 [a]"And [1]whoever will not receive you nor hear you, when
you depart from there, [b]shake
off the dust under your feet as
a testimony against them. [2]As-
suredly, I say to you, it will be
more tolerable for Sod′om and
Go·mor′rah in the day of judgment than for that city!"
12 So they went out and
preached that *people* should repent.
13 And they cast out many demons, [a]and anointed with oil
many who were sick, and healed
them.
14 [a]Now King Her′od heard *of
Him,* for His name had become
well known. And he said, "John
the Baptist is risen from the
dead, and therefore [b]these powers are at work in him."
15 [a]Others said, "It is E·lī′jah."

5 [a]Gen. 19:22; 32:25
6 [a]Is. 59:16 [b]Matt. 9:35
7 [a]Mark 3:13, 14 [b][Eccl. 4:9, 10]
9 [a][Eph. 6:15]
10 [a]Matt. 10:11
11 [a]Matt. 10:14 [b]Acts 13:51; 18:6 [1]NU *whatever place* [2]NU omits the rest of v. 11.
13 [a][James 5:14]
14 [a]Luke 9:7–9 [b]Luke 19:37
15 [a]Mark 8:28 [b]Matt. 21:11 [1]NU, M *a prophet, like one*
16 [a]Luke 3:19
18 [a]Lev. 18:16; 20:21
19 [1]*held a grudge*
20 [a]Matt. 14:5; 21:26 [1]NU *was very perplexed, yet*
21 [a]Matt. 14:6 [b]Gen. 40:20
23 [a]Esth. 5:3, 6; 7:2

And others said, "It is [1]the
Prophet, [b]or like one of the
prophets."
16 [a]But when Her′od heard, he
said, "This is John, whom I beheaded; he has been raised from
the dead!"
17 For Her′od himself had sent
and laid hold of John, and bound
him in prison for the sake of
He·rō′di·as, his brother Philip's
wife; for he had married her.
18 Because John had said to
Her′od, [a]"It is not lawful for you
to have your brother's wife."
19 Therefore He·rō′di·as [1]held it
against him and wanted to kill
him, but she could not;
20 for Her′od [a]feared John,
knowing that he *was* a just and
holy man, and he protected him.
And when he heard him, he
[1]did many things, and heard him
gladly.
21 [a]Then an opportune day
came when Her′od [b]on his birthday gave a feast for his nobles,
the high officers, and the chief
men of Galilee.
22 And when He·rō′di·as'
daughter herself came in and
danced, and pleased Her′od and
those who sat with him, the king
said to the girl, "Ask me whatever you want, and I will give *it*
to you."
23 He also swore to her,
[a]"Whatever you ask me, I will
give you, up to half my kingdom."
24 So she went out and said to
her mother, "What shall I ask?"
And she said, "The head of John
the Baptist!"
25 Immediately she came in
with haste to the king and asked,
saying, "I want you to give me

at once the head of John the
Baptist on a platter."
26 [a]And the king was exceedingly sorry; *yet*, because of the
oaths and because of those who
sat with him, he did not want to
refuse her.
27 Immediately the king sent an
executioner and commanded his
head to be brought. And he went
and beheaded him in prison,
28 brought his head on a platter, and gave it to the girl; and
the girl gave it to her mother.
29 When his disciples heard *of*
it, they came and [a]took away his
corpse and laid it in a tomb.
30 [a]Then the apostles gathered
to Jesus and told Him all things,
both what they had done and
what they had taught.
31 [a]And He said to them, "Come
aside by yourselves to a deserted place and rest a while."
For [b]there were many coming
and going, and they did not even
have time to eat.
32 [a]So they departed to a deserted place in the boat by themselves.
33 But [1]the multitudes saw them
departing, and many [a]knew Him
and ran there on foot from all the
cities. They arrived before them
and came together to Him.
34 [a]And Jesus, when He came
out, saw a great multitude and
was moved with compassion for
them, because they were like
[b]sheep not having a shepherd.
So [c]He began to teach them
many things.
35 [a]When the day was now far
spent, His disciples came to Him
and said, "This is a deserted
place, and already the hour *is*
late.
36 "Send them away, that they
may go into the surrounding
country and villages and buy
themselves [1]bread; for they have
nothing to eat."
37 But He answered and said to
them, "You give them something
to eat." And they said to Him,
[a]"Shall we go and buy two hundred denarii worth of bread and
give them *something* to eat?"
38 But He said to them, "How
many loaves do you have? Go
and see." And when they found
out they said, [a]"Five, and two
fish."
39 Then He [a]commanded them
to make them all sit down in
groups on the green grass.
40 So they sat down in ranks, in
hundreds and in fifties.
41 And when He had taken the
five loaves and the two fish, He
[a]looked up to heaven, [b]blessed
and broke the loaves, and gave
them to His disciples to set before them; and the two fish He
divided among *them* all.
42 So they all ate and were
filled.
43 And they took up twelve baskets full of fragments and of the
fish.
44 Now those who had eaten
the loaves were [1]about five thousand men.
45 [a]Immediately He [1]made His
disciples get into the boat and
go before Him to the other side,
to Beth·sā′i·da, while He sent the
multitude away.
46 And when He had sent them
away, He [a]departed to the mountain to pray.
47 Now when evening came,
the boat was in the middle of
the sea; and He *was* alone on the
land.
48 Then He saw them straining

26 [a]Matt. 14:9
29 [a]1 Kin. 13:29, 30
30 [a]Luke 9:10
31 [a]Matt. 14:13 [b]Mark 3:20
32 [a]Matt. 14:13–21
33 [a][Col. 1:6] [1]NU, M *they*
34 [a]Matt. 9:36; 14:14 [b]Num. 27:17 [c]Luke 9:11
35 [a]Matt. 14:15
36 [1]NU *something to eat* and omits the rest of v. 36.
37 [a]2 Kin. 4:43
38 [a]John 6:9
39 [a]Matt. 15:35
41 [a]John 11:41, 42 [b]Matt. 15:36; 26:26
44 [1]NU, M omit *about*
45 [a]John 6:15–21 [1]*invited, strongly urged*
46 [a]Luke 5:16

at rowing, for the wind was
against them. Now about the
fourth watch of the night He
came to them, walking on the
sea, and [a]would have passed
them by.
49 And when they saw Him
walking on the sea, they supposed it was a [a]ghost, and cried
out;
50 for they all saw Him and
were troubled. But immediately
He talked with them and said to
them, [a]"Be[1] of good cheer! It is I;
do not be [b]afraid."
51 Then He went up into the
boat to them, and the wind
[a]ceased. And they were greatly
[b]amazed in themselves beyond
measure, and marveled.
52 For [a]they had not understood
about the loaves, because their
[b]heart was hardened.
53 [a]When they had crossed
over, they came to the land of
Gen·nes′a·ret and anchored
there.
54 And when they came out
of the boat, immediately [1]the
people recognized Him,
55 ran through that whole surrounding region, and began
to carry about on beds those
who were sick to wherever they
heard He was.
56 Wherever He entered, into
villages, cities, or the country,
they laid the sick in the marketplaces, and begged Him that
[a]they might just touch the [b]hem
of His garment. And as many as
touched Him were made well.

7 Then [a]the Phar′i·sees and
some of the scribes came
together to Him, having come
from Jerusalem.
2 Now [1]when they saw some
of His disciples eat bread with
defiled, that is, with [a]unwashed
hands, [2]they found fault.
3 For the Phar′i·sees and all
the Jews do not eat unless they
wash *their* hands [1]in a special
way, holding the [a]tradition of the
elders.
4 *When they come* from the
marketplace, they do not eat
unless they wash. And there are
many other things which they
have received and hold, *like* the
washing of cups, pitchers, copper vessels, and couches.
5 [a]Then the Phar′i·sees and
scribes asked Him, "Why do
Your disciples not walk according to the tradition of the elders,
but eat bread with unwashed
hands?"
6 He answered and said to ★
them, "Well did Ī·sāi′ah prophesy of you [a]hypocrites, as it is
written:

[b]*'This people honors Me with*
their lips,
But their heart is far from Me.
7 *And in vain they worship Me,*
Teaching as doctrines the
commandments of men.'

8 "For laying aside the commandment of God, you hold the
tradition of men—[1]the washing
of pitchers and cups, and many
other such things you do."
9 He said to them, "*All too* well
[a]you [1]reject the commandment
of God, that you may keep your
tradition.
10 "For Moses said, [a]*'Honor*
your father and your mother';
and, [b]*'He who curses father or*
mother, let him be put to death.'
11 "But you say, 'If a man says to
his father or mother, [a]"Whatever
profit you might have received

48 [a]Luke 24:28
49 [a]Matt. 14:26
50 [a]Matt. 9:2 [b]Is. 41:10 [1]*Take courage*
51 [a]Ps. 107:29 [b]Mark 1:27; 2:12; 5:42; 7:37
52 [a]Mark 8:17, 18 [b]Mark 3:5; 16:14
53 [a]Matt. 14:34–36
54 [1]Lit. *they*
56 [a]Matt. 9:20 [b]Num. 15:38, 39

CHAPTER 7

1 [a]Matt. 15:1–20
2 [a]Matt. 15:20 [1]NU omits *when* [2]NU omits *they found fault*
3 [a]Gal. 1:14 [1]Lit. *with the fist*
5 [a]Matt. 15:2
6 [a]Matt. 23:13–29 [b]Is. 29:13
8 [1]NU omits the rest of v. 8.
9 [a]Prov. 1:25 [1]*set aside*
10 [a]Ex. 20:12; Deut. 5:16 [b]Ex. 21:17
11 [a]Matt. 15:5; 23:18

from me *is* Cor′ban"—' (that is, a gift *to God*),

12 "then you no longer let him do anything for his father or his mother,

13 "making the word of God of no effect through your tradition which you have handed down. And many such things you do."

14 [a]When He had called all the multitude to *Himself*, He said to them, "Hear Me, everyone, and [b]understand:

15 "There is nothing that enters a man from outside which can defile him; but the things which come out of him, those are the things that [a]defile a man.

16 [a]"If[1] anyone has ears to hear, let him hear!"

17 [a]When He had entered a house away from the crowd, His disciples asked Him concerning the parable.

18 So He said to them, [a]"Are you thus without understanding also? Do you not perceive that whatever enters a man from outside cannot defile him,

19 "because it does not enter his heart but his stomach, and is eliminated, [1]*thus* purifying all foods?"

20 And He said, [a]"What comes out of a man, that defiles a man.

21 [a]"For from within, out of the heart of men, [b]proceed evil thoughts, [c]adulteries, [d]fornications, murders,

22 "thefts, [a]covetousness, wickedness, [b]deceit, [c]lewdness, an evil eye, [d]blasphemy, [e]pride, foolishness.

23 "All these evil things come from within and defile a man."

24 [a]From there He arose and went to the region of Tȳre [1]and Sī′don. And He entered a house and wanted no one to know *it*, but He could not be [b]hidden.

25 For a woman whose young daughter had an unclean spirit heard about Him, and she came and [a]fell at His feet.

26 The woman was a [1]Greek, a [2]Sȳ′rō-Phoe·ni′cian by birth, and she kept [3]asking Him to cast the demon out of her daughter.

27 But Jesus said to her, "Let the children be filled first, for it is not good to take the children's bread and throw *it* to the little dogs."

28 And she answered and said to Him, "Yes, Lord, yet even the little dogs under the table eat from the children's crumbs."

29 Then He said to her, "For this saying go your way; the demon has gone out of your daughter."

30 And when she had come to her house, she found the demon gone out, and her daughter lying on the bed.

31 [a]Again, departing from the region of Tȳre and Sī′don, He came through the midst of the region of De·cap′o·lis to the Sea of Galilee.

32 Then [a]they brought to Him one who was deaf and had an impediment in his speech, and they begged Him to put His hand on him.

33 And He took him aside from the multitude, and put His fingers in his ears, and [a]He spat and touched his tongue.

34 Then, [a]looking up to heaven, [b]He sighed, and said to him, "Eph′pha·tha," that is, "Be opened."

35 [a]Immediately his ears were opened, and the [1]impediment of his tongue was loosed, and he spoke plainly.

36 Then [a]He commanded them

14 [a]Matt. 15:10 [b]Matt. 16:9, 11, 12
15 [a]Is. 59:3
16 [a]Matt. 11:15 [1]NU omits v. 16.
17 [a]Matt. 15:15
18 [a][Heb. 5:11–14]
19 [1]NU sets off the final phrase as Mark's comment that Jesus has declared all foods clean.
20 [a]Ps. 39:1
21 [a]Gen. 6:5; 8:21 [b][Gal. 5:19–21] [c]2 Pet. 2:14 [d]1 Thess. 4:3
22 [a]Luke 12:15 [b]Rom. 1:28, 29 [c]1 Pet. 4:3 [d]Rev. 2:9 [e]1 John 2:16
24 [a]Matt. 15:21 [b]Mark 2:1, 2 [1]NU omits *and Sidon*
25 [a]John 11:32
26 [1]*Gentile* [2]A Syrian of Phoenicia [3]*begging*
31 [a]Matt. 15:29
32 [a]Luke 11:14
33 [a]Mark 8:23
34 [a]Mark 6:41 [b]John 11:33, 38
35 [a]Is. 35:5, 6 [1]Lit. *bond*
36 [a]Mark 5:43

that they should tell no one;
but the more He commanded
them, the more widely they proclaimed *it.*
37 And they were [a]astonished
beyond measure, saying, "He
has done all things well. He
[b]makes both the deaf to hear
and the mute to speak."

8

8 In those days, [a]the multitude
being very great and hav-
ing nothing to eat, Jesus called
His disciples *to Him* and said
to them,
2 "I have [a]compassion on the
multitude, because they have
now continued with Me three
days and have nothing to eat.
3 "And if I send them away
hungry to their own houses,
they will faint on the way; for
some of them have come from
afar."
4 Then His disciples answered
Him, "How can one satisfy these
people with bread here in the
wilderness?"
5 [a]He asked them, "How many
loaves do you have?" And they
said, "Seven."
6 So He commanded the multitude to sit down on the ground.
And He took the seven loaves
and gave thanks, broke *them*
and gave *them* to His disciples
to set before *them;* and they set
them before the multitude.
7 They also had a few small
fish; and [a]having blessed them,
He said to set them also before
them.
8 So they ate and were filled,
and they took up seven large
baskets of leftover fragments.
9 Now those who had eaten
were about four thousand. And
He sent them away,
10 [a]immediately got into the boat
with His disciples, and came to
the region of Dal·ma·nū′tha.
11 [a]Then the Phar′i·sees came
out and began to dispute with
Him, seeking from Him a sign
from heaven, testing Him.
12 But He [a]sighed deeply in
His spirit, and said, "Why does
this generation seek a sign? Assuredly, I say to you, [b]no sign shall
be given to this generation."
13 And He left them, and getting
into the boat again, departed to
the other side.
14 [a]Now [1]the disciples had forgotten to take bread, and they
did not have more than one loaf
with them in the boat.
15 [a]Then He charged them, saying, "Take heed, beware of the
[1]leaven of the Phar′i·sees and
the leaven of Her′od."
16 And they reasoned among
themselves, saying, "*It is* because we have no bread."
17 But Jesus, being aware of *it,*
said to them, "Why do you reason because you have no bread?
[a]Do you not yet perceive nor
understand? Is your heart [1]still
hardened?
18 "Having eyes, do you not
see? And having ears, do you not
hear? And do you not remember?
19 [a]"When I broke the five
loaves for the five thousand,
how many baskets full of fragments did you take up?" They
said to Him, "Twelve."
20 "Also, [a]when I broke the
seven for the four thousand,
how many large baskets full
of fragments did you take up?"
And they said, "Seven."
21 So He said to them, "How *is*
it [a]you do not understand?"

37 [a]Mark 6:51; 10:26 [b]Matt. 12:22

CHAPTER 8

1 [a]Matt. 15:32–39
2 [a]Mark 1:41; 6:34
5 [a]Mark 6:38
7 [a]Matt. 14:19
10 [a]Matt. 15:39
11 [a]Matt. 12:38; 16:1
12 [a]Mark 7:34 [b]Matt. 12:39
14 [a]Matt. 16:5 [1]NU, M *they*
15 [a]Luke 12:1 [1]*yeast*
17 [a]Mark 6:52; 16:14 [1]NU omits *still*
19 [a]Matt. 14:20
20 [a]Matt. 15:37
21 [a][Mark 6:52]

22 Then He came to Beth·sā′-
i·da; and they brought a [a]blind
man to Him, and begged Him to
[b]touch him.
23 So He took the blind man by
the hand and led him out of the
town. And when [a]He had spit
on his eyes and put His hands
on him, He asked him if he saw
anything.
24 And he looked up and said,
"I see men like trees, walking."
25 Then He put *His* hands on
his eyes again and made him
look up. And he was restored
and saw everyone clearly.
26 Then He sent him away to
his house, saying, [1]"Neither go
into the town, [a]nor tell anyone in
the town."
27 [a]Now Jesus and His disciples went out to the towns of
Caes·a·rē′a Phi·lip′pī; and on the
road He asked His disciples,
saying to them, "Who do men
say that I am?"
28 So they answered, [a]"John the
Baptist; but some *say,* [b]E·lī′jah;
and others, one of the prophets."
29 He said to them, "But who
do you say that I am?" Peter answered and said to Him, [a]"You
are the Christ."
30 [a]Then He strictly warned
them that they should tell no
one about Him.
31 And [a]He began to teach them
that the Son of Man must suffer
many things, and be [b]rejected by
the elders and chief priests and
scribes, and be [c]killed, and after
three days rise again.
32 He spoke this word openly.
Then Peter took Him aside and
began to rebuke Him.
33 But when He had turned
around and looked at His disciples, He [a]rebuked Peter, saying,

22 [a]John 9:1 [b]Luke 18:15
23 [a]Mark 7:33
26 [a]Mark 5:43; 7:36 [1]NU *"Do not even go into the town."*
27 [a]Luke 9:18–20
28 [a]Matt. 14:2 [b]Luke 9:7, 8
29 [a]John 1:41; 4:42; 6:69; 11:27
30 [a]Matt. 8:4; 16:20
31 [a]Matt. 16:21; 20:19 [b]Mark 10:33 [c]Mark 9:31; 10:34
33 [a][Rev. 3:19] [1]*setting your mind on*
34 [a]Luke 14:27
35 [a]John 12:25
38 [a]Matt. 10:33 [b]2 Tim. 1:8, 9; 2:12

CHAPTER 9

1 [a]Luke 9:27 [b][Matt. 24:30] [1]*having come*
2 [a]Matt. 17:1–8
3 [a]Dan. 7:9

"Get behind Me, Satan! For you
are not [1]mindful of the things of
God, but the things of men."
34 When He had called the people to *Himself,* with His disciples
also, He said to them, [a]"Whoever
desires to come after Me, let him
deny himself, and take up his
cross, and follow Me.
35 "For [a]whoever desires to save
his life will lose it, but whoever
loses his life for My sake and the
gospel's will save it.
36 "For what will it profit a man
if he gains the whole world, and
loses his own soul?
37 "Or what will a man give in
exchange for his soul?
38 [a]"For whoever [b]is ashamed
of Me and My words in this
adulterous and sinful generation, of him the Son of Man also
will be ashamed when He comes
in the glory of His Father with
the holy angels."
9 And He said to them, [a]"Assuredly, I say to you that
there are some standing here
who will not taste death till they
see [b]the kingdom of God [1]pres-
ent with power."
2 [a]Now after six days Jesus
took Peter, James, and John, and
led them up on a high mountain
apart by themselves; and He
was transfigured before them.
3 His clothes became shining,
exceedingly [a]white, like snow,
such as no launderer on earth
can whiten them.
4 And E·lī′jah appeared to
them with Moses, and they were
talking with Jesus.
5 Then Peter answered and said
to Jesus, "Rabbi, it is good for us
to be here; and let us make three
tabernacles: one for You, one for
Moses, and one for E·lī′jah"—

6 because he did not know
what to say, for they were greatly
afraid.
★ 7 And a [a]cloud came and overshadowed them; and a voice
came out of the cloud, saying,
"This is [b]My beloved Son. [c]Hear
Him!"
8 Suddenly, when they had
looked around, they saw no one
anymore, but only Jesus with
themselves.
9 [a]Now as they came down
from the mountain, He commanded them that they should
tell no one the things they had
seen, till the Son of Man had
risen from the dead.
10 So they kept this word to
themselves, questioning [a]what
the rising from the dead meant.
11 And they asked Him, saying,
"Why do the scribes say [a]that
E·lī′jah must come first?"
☆ 12 Then He answered and told
them, "Indeed, E·lī′jah is coming
first and restores all things. And
[a]how is it written concerning the
Son of Man, that He must suffer many things and [b]be treated
with contempt?
13 "But I say to you that [a]E·lī′jah
has also come, and they did to
him whatever they wished, as it
is written of him."
14 [a]And when He came to the
disciples, He saw a great multitude around them, and scribes
disputing with them.
15 Immediately, when they saw
Him, all the people were greatly
amazed, and running to *Him*,
greeted Him.
16 And He asked the scribes,
"What are you discussing with
them?"
17 Then [a]one of the crowd answered and said, "Teacher, I
brought You my son, who has a
mute spirit.
18 "And wherever it seizes him,
it throws him down; he foams
at the mouth, gnashes his teeth,
and becomes rigid. So I spoke to
Your disciples, that they should
cast it out, but they could not."
19 He answered him and said,
"O [a]faithless[1] generation, how
long shall I be with you? How
long shall I [2]bear with you?
Bring him to Me."
20 Then they brought him to
Him. And [a]when he saw Him,
immediately the spirit convulsed
him, and he fell on the ground
and wallowed, foaming at the
mouth.
21 So He asked his father, "How
long has this been happening to
him?" And he said, "From childhood.
22 "And often he has thrown
him both into the fire and into
the water to destroy him. But if
You can do anything, have compassion on us and help us."
23 Jesus said to him, [a]"If[1] you
can believe, all things *are* possible to him who believes."
24 Immediately the father of the
child cried out and said with
tears, "Lord, I believe; [a]help my
unbelief!"
25 When Jesus saw that the
people came running together,
He [a]rebuked the unclean spirit,
saying to it: "Deaf and dumb
spirit, I command you, come out
of him and enter him no more!"
26 Then *the spirit* cried out,
convulsed him greatly, and came
out of him. And he became as
one dead, so that many said, "He
is dead."
27 But Jesus took him by the

7 [a]Ex. 40:34 [b]Ps. 2:7; [Is. 42:1]; Mark 1:11 [c]Acts 3:22
9 [a]Matt. 17:9–13
10 [a]John 2:19–22
11 [a]Mal. 4:5
12 [a]Ps. 22:6; Is. 53:3; Dan. 9:26; Mal. 4:5, 6 [b]Luke 23:11; Phil. 2:7
13 [a]Luke 1:17
14 [a]Matt. 17:14–19
17 [a]Luke 9:38
19 [a]John 4:48 [1]*unbelieving* [2]*put up with*
20 [a]Mark 1:26
23 [a]John 11:40 [1]NU " *'If You can!' All things*
24 [a]Luke 17:5
25 [a]Mark 1:25

hand and lifted him up, and he
arose.
28 [a]And when He had come into
the house, His disciples asked
Him privately, "Why could we
not cast it out?"
29 So He said to them, "This
kind can come out by nothing
but [a]prayer [1]and fasting."
30 Then they departed from
there and passed through Galilee, and He did not want anyone
to know *it*.
31 [a]For He taught His disciples
and said to them, "The Son of
Man is being betrayed into the
hands of men, and they will [b]kill
Him. And after He is killed, He
will [c]rise the third day."
32 But they [a]did not understand
this saying, and were afraid to
ask Him.
33 [a]Then He came to Ca·per′-
na·um. And when He was in the
house He asked them, "What
was it you [1]disputed among
yourselves on the road?"
34 But they kept silent, for on
the road they had [a]disputed
among themselves who *would
be the* [b]greatest.
35 And He sat down, called the
twelve, and said to them, [a]"If
anyone desires to be first, he
shall be last of all and servant of
all."
36 Then [a]He took a little child
and set him in the midst of them.
And when He had taken him in
His arms, He said to them,
37 "Whoever receives one of
these little children in My name
receives Me; and [a]whoever receives Me, receives not Me but
Him who sent Me."
38 [a]Now John answered Him,
saying, "Teacher, we saw someone who does not follow us
casting out demons in Your
name, and we forbade him because he does not follow us."
39 But Jesus said, "Do not forbid him, [a]for no one who works
a miracle in My name can soon
afterward speak evil of Me.
40 "For [a]he who is not against
[1]us is on [2]our side.
41 [a]"For whoever gives you a
cup of water to drink in My
name, because you belong to
Christ, assuredly, I say to you,
he will by no means lose his reward.
42 [a]"But whoever causes one of
these little ones who believe in
Me [1]to stumble, it would be better for him if a millstone were
hung around his neck, and he
were thrown into the sea.
43 [a]"If your hand causes you to
sin, cut it off. It is better for you
to enter into life [1]maimed, rather
than having two hands, to go
to [2]hell, into the fire that shall
never be quenched—
44 [1]"where

[a]*'Their worm does not die*
And the fire is not
quenched.'

45 "And if your foot causes you
to sin, cut it off. It is better for
you to enter life lame, rather
than having two feet, to be cast
into [1]hell, [2]into the fire that shall
never be quenched—
46 "where

[a]*'Their worm does not die*
And the fire is not
quenched.'

47 "And if your eye causes you
to sin, pluck it out. It is better
for you to enter the kingdom of

28 [a]Matt. 17:19
29 [a][James 5:16] [1]NU omits *and fasting*
31 [a]Luke 9:44 [b]Matt. 16:21; 27:50 [c]1 Cor. 15:4
32 [a]Luke 2:50; 18:34
33 [a]Matt. 18:1–5 [1]*discussed*
34 [a][Prov. 13:10] [b]Luke 22:24; 23:46; 24:46
35 [a]Luke 22:26, 27
36 [a]Mark 10:13–16
37 [a]Matt. 10:40
38 [a]Num. 11:27–29
39 [a]1 Cor. 12:3
40 [a][Matt. 12:30] [1]M *you* [2]M *your*
41 [a]Matt. 10:42
42 [a]Luke 17:1, 2 [1]To fall into sin
43 [a]Matt. 5:29, 30; 18:8, 9 [1]*crippled* [2]Gr. *Gehenna*
44 [a]Is. 66:24 [1]NU omits v. 44.
45 [1]Gr. *Gehenna* [2]NU omits the rest of v. 45 and all of v. 46.
46 [a]Is. 66:24

God with one eye, rather than
having two eyes, to be cast into
[1]hell fire—
48 "where

[a]*'Their worm does not die*
And the [b]*fire is not*
quenched.'

49 "For everyone will be
[a]seasoned with fire, [b]and[1] every
sacrifice will be seasoned with
salt.
50 [a]"Salt *is* good, but if the salt
loses its flavor, how will you
season it? [b]Have salt in yourselves, and [c]have peace with one
another."

10 Then [a]He arose from
there and came to the
region of Judea by the other side
of the Jordan. And multitudes
gathered to Him again, and as
He was accustomed, He taught
them again.
2 [a]The Phar'i·sees came and
asked Him, "Is it lawful for a
man to divorce *his* wife?" testing
Him.
3 And He answered and said
to them, "What did Moses command you?"
4 They said, [a]"Moses permitted *a man* to write a certificate
of divorce, and to dismiss *her*."
5 And Jesus answered and
said to them, "Because of the
hardness of your heart he wrote
you this [1]precept.
6 "But from the beginning of
the creation, God [a]*'made them*
male and female.'
7 [a]*'For this reason a man shall*
leave his father and mother and
be joined to his wife,
8 *'and the two shall become*
one flesh'; so then they are no
longer two, but one flesh.

9 "Therefore what God has
joined together, let not man separate."
10 In the house His disciples
also asked Him again about the
same *matter*.
11 So He said to them, [a]"Whoever divorces his wife and marries another commits adultery
against her.
12 "And if a woman divorces
her husband and marries another, she commits adultery."
13 [a]Then they brought little
children to Him, that He might
touch them; but the disciples rebuked those who brought *them*.
14 But when Jesus saw *it*, He
was greatly displeased and said
to them, "Let the little children
come to Me, and do not forbid
them; for [a]of such is the kingdom of God.
15 "Assuredly, I say to you,
[a]whoever does not receive the
kingdom of God as a little child
will [b]by no means enter it."
16 And He took them up in His
arms, laid *His* hands on them,
and blessed them.
17 [a]Now as He was going out
on the road, one came running,
knelt before Him, and asked
Him, "Good Teacher, what shall
I [b]do that I may inherit eternal
life?"
18 So Jesus said to him, "Why
do you call Me good? No one *is*
good but One, *that is*, [a]God.
19 "You know the command-
ments: [a]*'Do not commit adul-*
tery,' 'Do not murder,' 'Do not
steal,' 'Do not bear false wit-
ness,' 'Do not defraud,' *'Honor*
your father and your mother.'"
20 And he answered and said to
Him, "Teacher, all these things I
have [a]kept from my youth."

47 [1]Gr. *Gehenna*
48 [a]Is. 66:24 [b]Jer. 7:20
49 [a][Matt. 3:11] [b]Lev. 2:13 [1]NU omits the rest of v. 49.
50 [a]Matt. 5:13 [b]Col. 4:6 [c]Rom. 12:18; 14:19

CHAPTER 10

1 [a]Matt. 19:1–9
2 [a]Matt. 19:3
4 [a]Deut. 24:1–4
5 [1]*command*
6 [a]Gen. 1:27; 5:2
7 [a]Gen. 2:24
11 [a][Matt. 5:32; 19:9]
13 [a]Luke 18:15–17
14 [a][1 Pet. 2:2]
15 [a]Matt. 18:3, 4; 19:14 [b]Luke 13:28
17 [a]Matt. 19:16–30 [b]John 6:28
18 [a]1 Sam. 2:2
19 [a]Ex. 20:12–16; Deut. 5:16–20
20 [a]Phil. 3:6

21 Then Jesus, looking at him,
loved him, and said to him, "One
thing you lack: Go your way,
[a]sell whatever you have and give
to the poor, and you will have
[b]treasure in heaven; and come,
[c]take up the cross, and follow
Me."
22 But he was sad at this word,
and went away sorrowful, for he
had great possessions.
23 [a]Then Jesus looked around
and said to His disciples, "How
hard it is for those who have
riches to enter the kingdom of
God!"
24 And the disciples were astonished at His words. But Jesus answered again and said to
them, "Children, how hard it is
[1]for those [a]who trust in riches to
enter the kingdom of God!
25 "It is easier for a camel to
go through the eye of a needle
than for a [a]rich man to enter the
kingdom of God."
26 And they were greatly astonished, saying among themselves,
"Who then can be saved?"
27 But Jesus looked at them
and said, "With men *it is* impossible, but not [a]with God; for with
God all things are possible."
28 [a]Then Peter began to say to
Him, "See, we have left all and
followed You."
29 So Jesus answered and said,
"Assuredly, I say to you, there is
no one who has left house or
brothers or sisters or father or
mother [1]or wife or children
or [2]lands, for My sake and the
gospel's,
30 [a]"who shall not receive a
hundredfold now in this time—
houses and brothers and sisters
and mothers and children and
lands, with [b]persecutions—and
in the age to come, eternal life.
31 [a]"But many *who are* first will
be last, and the last first."
32 [a]Now they were on the road,
going up to Jerusalem, and Jesus was going before them; and
they were amazed. And as they
followed they were afraid. [b]Then
He took the twelve aside again
and began to tell them the things
that would happen to Him:
33 "Behold, we are going up to
Jerusalem, and the Son of Man
will be betrayed to the chief
priests and to the scribes; and
they will condemn Him to death
and deliver Him to the Gentiles;
34 "and they will mock Him,
and [1]scourge Him, and spit on
Him, and kill Him. And the third
day He will rise again."
35 [a]Then James and John, the
sons of Zeb'e·dee, came to Him,
saying, "Teacher, we want You to
do for us whatever we ask."
36 And He said to them, "What
do you want Me to do for you?"
37 They said to Him, "Grant
us that we may sit, one on Your
right hand and the other on Your
left, in Your glory."
38 But Jesus said to them, "You
do not know what you ask. Are
you able to drink the [a]cup that
I drink, and be baptized with
the [b]baptism that I am baptized
with?"
39 They said to Him, "We are
able." So Jesus said to them,
[a]"You will indeed drink the cup
that I drink, and with the baptism I am baptized with you will
be baptized;
40 "but to sit on My right hand
and on My left is not Mine to
give, but *it is for those* [a]for
whom it is prepared."

21 [a][Luke 12:33; 16:9] [b]Matt. 6:19, 20; 19:21 [c][Mark 8:34]
23 [a]Matt. 19:23
24 [a][1 Tim. 6:17] [1]NU omits *for those who trust in riches*
25 [a][Matt. 13:22; 19:24]
27 [a]Jer. 32:17
28 [a]Luke 18:28
29 [1]NU omits *or wife* [2]Lit. *fields*
30 [a]Luke 18:29, 30 [b][1 Pet. 4:12, 13]
31 [a]Luke 13:30
32 [a]Matt. 20:17–19 [b]Mark 8:31; 9:31
34 [1]*flog Him* with a Roman scourge
35 [a][James 4:3]
38 [a]John 18:11 [b]Luke 12:50
39 [a]Acts 12:2
40 [a][Heb. 11:16]

41 [a]And when the ten heard *it,*
they began to be greatly displeased with James and John.
42 But Jesus called them to
Himself and said to them, [a]"You
know that those who are considered rulers over the Gentiles lord
it over them, and their great ones
exercise authority over them.
43 [a]"Yet it shall not be so among
you; but whoever desires to become great among you shall be
your servant.
44 "And whoever of you desires
to be first shall be slave of all.
☆ 45 "For even [a]the Son of Man
did not come to be served, but
to serve, and [b]to give His life a
ransom for many."
46 [a]Now they came to Jericho.
As He went out of Jericho with
His disciples and a great multitude, blind Bar·ti·maē′us, the
son of Ti·maē′us, sat by the road
begging.
47 And when he heard that it
was Jesus of Nazareth, he began
to cry out and say, "Jesus, [a]Son
of David, [b]have mercy on me!"
48 Then many warned him to
be quiet; but he cried out all
the more, "Son of David, have
mercy on me!"
49 So Jesus stood still and commanded him to be called. Then
they called the blind man, saying to him, "Be of good cheer.
Rise, He is calling you."
50 And throwing aside his
garment, he rose and came to
Jesus.
51 So Jesus answered and said
to him, "What do you want Me
to do for you?" The blind man
said to Him, [1]"Rab·bō′nī, that I
may receive my sight."
52 Then Jesus said to him, "Go
your way; [a]your faith has [1]made

41 [a]Matt. 20:24
42 [a]Luke 22:25
43 [a]Mark 9:35
45 [a]Luke 22:27; John 13:14; [Phil. 2:7, 8] [b][2 Cor. 5:21; 1 Tim. 2:5, 6; Titus 2:14]
46 [a]Luke 18:35–43
47 [a]Rev. 22:16 [b]Matt. 15:22
51 [1]Lit. *My Great One*
52 [a]Matt. 9:22 [1]Lit. *saved you*

CHAPTER 11

1 [a]Matt. 21:1–9 [1]M *Bethsphage*
4 [1]NU, M *a*
7 [a]Zech. 9:9
8 [a]Matt. 21:8
9 [a]Ps. 118:25, 26
10 [a]Ps. 148:1 [1]NU omits *in the name of the Lord*

you well." And immediately he
received his sight and followed
Jesus on the road.

11 Now [a]when they drew
near Jerusalem, to [1]Beth′-
pha·gē and Beth′a·ny, at the
Mount of Olives, He sent two of
His disciples;
2 and He said to them, "Go
into the village opposite you;
and as soon as you have entered
it you will find a colt tied, on
which no one has sat. Loose it
and bring *it.*
3 "And if anyone says to you,
'Why are you doing this?' say,
'The Lord has need of it,' and immediately he will send it here."
4 So they went their way, and
found [1]the colt tied by the door
outside on the street, and they
loosed it.
5 But some of those who stood
there said to them, "What are
you doing, loosing the colt?"
6 And they spoke to them just
as Jesus had commanded. So
they let them go.
7 [a]Then they brought the colt ★
to Jesus and threw their clothes
on it, and He sat on it.
8 [a]And many spread their
clothes on the road, and others
cut down leafy branches from
the trees and spread *them* on
the road.
9 Then those who went before ★
and those who followed cried
out, saying:

"Hō·san′na!
[a]*'Blessed is He who comes in*
the name of the LORD!'
10 Blessed *is* the kingdom of
our father David
That comes [1]in the name of
the Lord!
[a]Hō·san′na in the highest!"

11 [a]And Jesus went into Jerusalem and into the temple. So
when He had looked around at
all things, as the hour was already late, He went out to Beth'-
a·ny with the twelve.
12 [a]Now the next day, when
they had come out from Beth'-
a·ny, He was hungry.
13 [a]And seeing from afar a fig
tree having leaves, He went to
see if perhaps He would find
something on it. When He came
to it, He found nothing but
leaves, for it was not the season
for figs.
14 In response Jesus said to it,
"Let no one eat fruit from you
ever again." And His disciples
heard *it.*
15 [a]So they came to Jerusalem.
Then Jesus went into the temple
and began to drive out those
who bought and sold in the temple, and overturned the tables
of the money changers and the
seats of those who sold [b]doves.
16 And He would not allow anyone to carry wares through the
temple.
17 Then He taught, saying to
them, "Is it not written, [a]*'My
house shall be called a house
of prayer for all nations'*? But
you have made it a [b]*'den of
thieves.'* "
18 And [a]the scribes and chief
priests heard it and sought how
they might destroy Him; for they
feared Him, because [b]all the
people were astonished at His
teaching.
19 When evening had come, He
went out of the city.
20 [a]Now in the morning, as they
passed by, they saw the fig tree
dried up from the roots.
21 And Peter, remembering,
said to Him, "Rabbi, look! The
fig tree which You cursed has
withered away."
22 So Jesus answered and said
to them, "Have faith in God.
23 "For [a]assuredly, I say to you,
whoever says to this mountain,
'Be removed and be cast into
the sea,' and does not doubt in
his heart, but believes that those
things he says will be done, he
will have whatever he says.
24 "Therefore I say to you,
[a]whatever things you ask when
you pray, believe that you receive *them,* and you will have
them.
25 "And whenever you stand
praying, [a]if you have anything
against anyone, forgive him, that
your Father in heaven may also
forgive you your trespasses.
26 [1]"But [a]if you do not forgive, neither will your Father in
heaven forgive your trespasses."
27 Then they came again to Jerusalem. [a]And as He was walking
in the temple, the chief priests,
the scribes, and the elders came
to Him.
28 And they said to Him, "By
what [a]authority are You doing
these things? And who gave
You this authority to do these
things?"
29 But Jesus answered and said
to them, "I also will ask you one
question; then answer Me, and I
will tell you by what authority I
do these things:
30 "The [a]baptism of John—was
it from heaven or from men?
Answer Me."
31 And they reasoned among
themselves, saying, "If we say,
'From heaven,' He will say, 'Why
then did you not believe him?'
32 "But if we say, 'From men' "

11 [a]Matt. 21:12
12 [a]Matt. 21:18–22
13 [a]Matt. 21:19
15 [a]John 2:13–16 [b]Lev. 14:22
17 [a]Is. 56:7 [b]Jer. 7:11
18 [a]Matt. 21:45, 46 [b]Matt. 7:28
20 [a]Matt. 21:19–22
23 [a]Matt. 17:20; 21:21
24 [a]Matt. 7:7
25 [a][Col. 3:13]
26 [a]Matt. 6:15; 18:35 [1]NU omits v. 26.
27 [a]Luke 20:1–8
28 [a]John 5:27
30 [a]Luke 7:29, 30

—they feared the people, for [a]all
counted John to have been a
prophet indeed.
33 So they answered and said to
Jesus, "We do not know." And Jesus answered and said to them,
"Neither will I tell you by what
authority I do these things."

12 Then [a]He began to speak
to them in parables: "A
man planted a vineyard and set a
hedge around *it*, dug *a place for*
the wine vat and built a tower.
And he leased it to [1]vinedressers
and went into a far country.
2 "Now at vintage-time he sent
a servant to the vinedressers,
that he might receive some of
the fruit of the vineyard from
the vinedressers.
3 "And they took *him* and beat
him and sent *him* away empty-
handed.
4 "Again he sent them another
servant, [1]and at him they threw
stones, wounded *him* in the
head, and sent *him* away shamefully treated.
5 "And again he sent another,
and him they killed; and many
others, [a]beating some and killing some.
6 "Therefore still having one
son, his beloved, he also sent
him to them last, saying, 'They
will respect my son.'
7 "But those [1]vinedressers said
among themselves, 'This is the
heir. Come, let us kill him, and
the inheritance will be ours.'
8 "So they took him and [a]killed
him and cast *him* out of the vineyard.
9 "Therefore what will the
owner of the vineyard do? He
will come and destroy the vinedressers, and give the vineyard
to others.

32 [a]Matt. 3:5; 14:5

CHAPTER 12

1 [a]Luke 20:9–19 [1]*tenant farmers*

4 [1]NU omits *and at him they threw stones*

5 [a]2 Chr. 36:16

7 [1]*tenant farmers*

8 [a][Acts 2:23]

10 [a]Ps. 118:22, 23; Is. 28:16; Acts 4:11; [Rom. 9:33]; Eph. 2:20; [1 Pet. 2:6, 7]

12 [a]John 7:25, 30, 44

13 [a]Luke 20:20–26

14 [a]Acts 18:26 [1]Court no man's favor [2]Lit. *look at the face of men*

15 [a]Luke 12:1

17 [a][Eccl. 5:4, 5] [1]*Pay*

18 [a]Luke 20:27–38 [b]Acts 23:8

19 [a]Deut. 25:5

10 "Have you not even read this ☆
Scripture:

[a]'The stone which the
builders rejected
Has become the chief
cornerstone.
11 *This was the LORD's doing,*
And it is marvelous in our
eyes'?"

12 [a]And they sought to lay
hands on Him, but feared the
multitude, for they knew He
had spoken the parable against
them. So they left Him and went
away.
13 [a]Then they sent to Him
some of the Phar′i·sees and the
He·rō′di·ans, to catch Him in *His*
words.
14 When they had come, they
said to Him, "Teacher, we know
that You are true, and [1]care about
no one; for You do not [2]regard
the person of men, but teach the
[a]way of God in truth. Is it lawful
to pay taxes to Caesar, or not?
15 "Shall we pay, or shall we
not pay?" But He, knowing their
[a]hypocrisy, said to them, "Why
do you test Me? Bring Me a denarius that I may see *it*."
16 So they brought *it*. And He
said to them, "Whose image and
inscription *is* this?" They said to
Him, "Caesar's."
17 And Jesus answered and said
to them, [1]"Render to Caesar the
things that are Caesar's, and to
[a]God the things that are God's."
And they marveled at Him.
18 [a]Then *some* Sad′dū·cees,
[b]who say there is no resurrection, came to Him; and they
asked Him, saying:
19 "Teacher, [a]Moses wrote to
us that if a man's brother dies,

and leaves *his* wife behind, and
leaves no children, his brother
should take his wife and raise
up offspring for his brother.
20 "Now there were seven
brothers. The first took a wife;
and dying, he left no offspring.
21 "And the second took her,
and he died; nor did he leave
any offspring. And the third
likewise.
22 "So the seven had her and
left no offspring. Last of all the
woman died also.
23 "Therefore, in the resurrection, when they rise, whose wife
will she be? For all seven had
her as wife."
24 Jesus answered and said to
them, "Are you not therefore
[1]mistaken, because you do not
know the Scriptures nor the
power of God?
25 "For when they rise from the
dead, they neither marry nor are
given in marriage, but [a]are like
angels in heaven.
26 "But concerning the dead,
that they [a]rise, have you not
read in the book of Moses, in
the *burning* bush *passage,* how
God spoke to him, saying, [b]*'I am
the God of Abraham, the God of
Isaac, and the God of Jacob'* ?
27 "He is not the God of the
dead, but the God of the living.
You are therefore greatly [1]mis-
taken."
28 [a]Then one of the scribes
came, and having heard them
reasoning together, [1]perceiv-
ing that He had answered them
well, asked Him, "Which is the
[2]first commandment of all?"
29 Jesus answered him, "The
[1]first of all the commandments
is: [a]*'Hear, O Israel, the LORD our
God, the LORD is one.*
30 *'And you shall* [a]*love the
LORD your God with all your
heart, with all your soul, with
all your mind, and with all your
strength.'* [1]This *is* the first commandment.
31 "And the second, like *it,* is
this: [a]*'You shall love your neighbor as yourself.'* There is no
other commandment greater
than [b]these."
32 So the scribe said to Him,
"Well *said,* Teacher. You have
spoken the truth, for there is one
God, [a]and there is no other but
He.
33 "And to love Him with all
the heart, with all the understanding, [1]with all the soul, and
with all the strength, and to love
one's neighbor as oneself, [a]is
more than all the whole burnt
offerings and sacrifices."
34 Now when Jesus saw that
he answered wisely, He said to
him, "You are not far from the
kingdom of God." [a]But after that
no one dared question Him.
35 [a]Then Jesus answered and
said, while He taught in the temple, "How *is it* that the scribes
say that the Christ is the Son of
David?
36 "For David himself said [a]by ☆
the Holy Spirit:

> [b]*'The LORD said to my Lord,*
> *"Sit at My right hand,*
> *Till I make Your enemies*
> *Your footstool."'*

37 "Therefore David himself
calls Him *'Lord'*; how is He *then*
his [a]Son?" And the common
people heard Him gladly.
38 Then [a]He said to them in
His teaching, [b]"Beware of the
scribes, who desire to go around

24 [1]Or *deceived*
25 [a][1 Cor. 15:42, 49, 52]
26 [a][Rev. 20:12, 13] [b]Ex. 3:6, 15
27 [1]Or *deceived*
28 [a]Matt. 22:34–40 [1]NU *seeing* [2]*foremost*
29 [a]Deut. 6:4, 5 [1]*foremost*
30 [a][Deut. 10:12; 30:6] [1]NU omits the rest of v. 30.
31 [a]Lev. 19:18 [b][Rom. 13:9]
32 [a]Deut. 4:39
33 [a][Hos. 6:6] [1]NU omits *with all the soul*
34 [a]Matt. 22:46
35 [a]Luke 20:41–44
36 [a]2 Sam. 23:2 [b]Ps. 110:1; Eph. 1:19–23; Col. 3:1; Heb. 1:13
37 [a][Acts 2:29–31]
38 [a]Mark 4:2 [b]Matt. 23:1–7

in long robes, [c]*love* greetings in
the marketplaces,
39 "the [a]best seats in the synagogues, and the best places at
feasts,
40 [a]"who devour widows' houses,
and [1]for a pretense make long
prayers. These will receive
greater condemnation."
41 [a]Now Jesus sat opposite the
treasury and saw how the people put money [b]into the treasury.
And many *who were* rich put in
much.
42 Then one poor widow came
and threw in two [1]mites, which
make a [2]quadrans.
43 So He called His disciples to
Himself and said to them, "Assuredly, I say to you that [a]this
poor widow has put in more
than all those who have given to
the treasury;
44 "for they all put in out of
their abundance, but she out of
her poverty put in all that she
had, [a]her whole livelihood."

13

Then [a]as He went out of
the temple, one of His
disciples said to Him, "Teacher,
see what manner of stones and
what buildings *are here!*"
2 And Jesus answered and
said to him, "Do you see these
great buildings? [a]Not *one* stone
shall be left upon another, that
shall not be thrown down."
3 Now as He sat on the Mount
of Olives opposite the tem-
ple, [a]Peter, [b]James, [c]John, and
[d]Andrew asked Him privately,
4 [a]"Tell us, when will these
things be? And what *will be* the
sign when all these things will
be fulfilled?"
5 And Jesus, answering them,
began to say: [a]"Take heed that
no one deceives you.

38 [c]Matt. 23:7
39 [a]Luke 14:7
40 [a]Matt. 23:14 [1]*for appearance' sake*
41 [a]Luke 21:1–4 [b]2 Kin. 12:9
42 [1]Gr. *lepta*, very small copper coins [2]A Roman coin
43 [a][2 Cor. 8:12]
44 [a]Deut. 24:6

CHAPTER 13

1 [a]Luke 21:5–36
2 [a]Luke 19:44
3 [a]Matt. 16:18 [b]Mark 1:19 [c]Mark 1:19 [d]John 1:40
4 [a]Matt. 24:3
5 [a]Eph. 5:6
8 [a]Hag. 2:22 [b]Matt. 24:8 [1]NU omits *and troubles* [2]Lit. *birth pangs*
9 [a]Matt. 10:17, 18; 24:9 [1]NU, M *stand*
10 [a]Matt. 24:14
11 [a]Luke 12:11; 21:12–17 [b]Acts 2:4; 4:8, 31 [1]NU omits *or premeditate*
12 [a]Mic. 7:6
13 [a]Luke 21:17 [b]Matt. 10:22; 24:13 [1]*bears patiently*
14 [a]Matt. 24:15 [b]Dan. 9:27; 11:31; 12:11 [c]Luke 21:21 [1]NU omits *spoken of by Daniel the prophet*

6 "For many will come in My
name, saying, 'I am *He*,' and will
deceive many.
7 "But when you hear of wars
and rumors of wars, do not be
troubled; for *such things* must
happen, but the end *is* not yet.
8 "For nation will rise against
nation, and [a]kingdom against
kingdom. And there will be
earthquakes in various places,
and there will be famines [1]and
troubles. [b]These *are* the beginnings of [2]sorrows.
9 "But [a]watch out for yourselves, for they will deliver you
up to councils, and you will be
beaten in the synagogues. You
will [1]be brought before rulers
and kings for My sake, for a testimony to them.
10 "And [a]the gospel must first
be preached to all the nations.
11 [a]"But when they arrest *you*
and deliver you up, do not worry
beforehand, [1]or premeditate
what you will speak. But whatever is given you in that hour,
speak that; for it is not you who
speak, [b]but the Holy Spirit.
12 "Now [a]brother will betray
brother to death, and a father
his child; and children will rise
up against parents and cause
them to be put to death.
13 [a]"And you will be hated by
all for My name's sake. But [b]he
who [1]endures to the end shall be
saved.
14 [a]"So when you see the [b]*'abomination of desolation,'* [1]spoken of
by Daniel the prophet, standing
where it ought not" (let the reader
understand), "then [c]let those who
are in Judea flee to the mountains.
15 "Let him who is on the housetop not go down into the house,

nor enter to take anything out of
his house.
16 "And let him who is in the
field not go back to get his
clothes.
17 [a]"But woe to those who are
pregnant and to those who are
nursing babies in those days!
18 "And pray that your flight
may not be in winter.
19 [a]"For *in* those days there will
be tribulation, such as has not
been since the beginning of the
creation which God created until this time, nor ever shall be.
20 "And unless the Lord had
shortened those days, no flesh
would be saved; but for the
elect's sake, whom He chose, He
shortened the days.
21 [a]"Then if anyone says to you,
'Look, here *is* the Christ!' or,
'Look, *He is* there!' do not believe it.
22 "For false christs and false
prophets will rise and show
signs and [a]wonders to deceive,
if possible, even the [1]elect.
23 "But [a]take heed; see, I have
told you all things beforehand.
24 [a]"But in those days, after that
tribulation, the sun will be darkened, and the moon will not give
its light;
25 "the stars of heaven will fall,
and the powers in the heavens
will be [a]shaken.
26 [a]"Then they will see the Son
of Man coming in the clouds
with great power and glory.
27 "And then He will send His
angels, and gather together His
[1]elect from the four winds, from
the farthest part of earth to the
farthest part of heaven.
28 [a]"Now learn this parable from
the fig tree: When its branch has
already become tender, and puts
forth leaves, you know that summer is near.
29 "So you also, when you see
these things happening, know
that [1]it is near—at the doors!
30 "Assuredly, I say to you, this
generation will by no means
pass away till all these things
take place.
31 "Heaven and earth will pass
away, but [a]My words will by no
means pass away.
32 "But of that day and hour [a]no
one knows, not even the angels
in heaven, nor the Son, but only
the [b]Father.
33 [a]"Take heed, watch and pray;
for you do not know when the
time is.
34 [a]"*It is* like a man going to a
far country, who left his house
and gave [b]authority to his servants, and to each his work, and
commanded the doorkeeper to
watch.
35 [a]"Watch therefore, for you
do not know when the mas-
ter of the house is coming—in
the evening, at midnight, at the
crowing of the rooster, or in the
morning—
36 "lest, coming suddenly, he
find you sleeping.
37 "And what I say to you, I say
to all: Watch!"

14 After [a]two days it was
the Passover and [b]*the
Feast* of Unleavened Bread. And
the chief priests and the scribes
sought how they might take
Him by [1]trickery and put *Him*
to death.
2 But they said, "Not during
the feast, lest there be an uproar
of the people."
3 [a]And being in Beth'a·ny at
the house of Simon the leper,
as He sat at the table, a woman

17 [a]Luke 21:23
19 [a]Dan. 9:26; 12:1
21 [a]Luke 17:23; 21:8
22 [a]Rev. 13:13, 14 [1]*chosen ones*
23 [a][2 Pet. 3:17]
24 [a]Zeph. 1:15
25 [a]Is. 13:10; 34:4
26 [a][Dan. 7:13, 14]
27 [1]*chosen ones*
28 [a]Luke 21:29
29 [1]Or *He*
31 [a]Is. 40:8
32 [a]Matt. 25:13 [b]Acts 1:7
33 [a]1 Thess. 5:6
34 [a]Matt. 24:45; 25:14 [b][Matt. 16:19]
35 [a]Matt. 24:42, 44

CHAPTER 14

1 [a]Luke 22:1, 2 [b]Ex. 12:1–27 [1]*deception*
3 [a]Luke 7:37

came having an alabaster flask
of very costly [1]oil of spikenard.
Then she broke the flask and
poured *it* on His head.
4 But there were some who
were indignant among themselves, and said, "Why was this
fragrant oil wasted?
5 "For it might have been
sold for more than three hundred [a]denarii and given to the
poor." And they [b]criticized[1] her
sharply.
6 But Jesus said, "Let her alone.
Why do you trouble her? She
has done a good work for Me.
7 [a]"For you have the poor with
you always, and whenever you
wish you may do them good;
[b]but Me you do not have always.
8 "She has done what she
could. She has come beforehand
to anoint My body for burial.
9 "Assuredly, I say to you, wherever this gospel is [a]preached
in the whole world, what this
woman has done will also be
told as a memorial to her."
10 [a]Then Judas Is·car'i·ot, one
of the twelve, went to the chief
priests to betray Him to them.
11 And when they heard *it*, they
were glad, and promised to give
him money. So he sought how
he might conveniently betray
Him.
12 [a]Now on the first day of
Unleavened Bread, when they
[1]killed the Passover *lamb*, His
disciples said to Him, "Where do
You want us to go and prepare,
that You may eat the Passover?"
13 And He sent out two of His
disciples and said to them, "Go
into the city, and a man will
meet you carrying a pitcher of
water; follow him.
14 "Wherever he goes in, say
to the master of the house,
'The Teacher says, "Where is
the guest room in which I may
eat the Passover with My disciples?" '
15 "Then he will show you a
large upper room, furnished *and*
prepared; there make ready for
us."
16 So His disciples went out, and
came into the city, and found it
just as He had said to them; and
they prepared the Passover.
17 [a]In the evening He came with
the twelve.
18 Now as they sat and ate,
Jesus said, "Assuredly, I say to
you, [a]one of you who eats with
Me will betray Me."
19 And they began to be sorrowful, and to say to Him one by
one, "*Is* it I?" [1]And another *said*,
"*Is* it I?"
20 He answered and said to
them, "*It is* one of the twelve,
who dips with Me in the dish.
21 [a]"The Son of Man indeed
goes just as it is written of Him,
but woe to that man by whom
the Son of Man is betrayed! It
would have been good for that
man if he had never been born."
22 [a]And as they were eating,
Jesus took bread, blessed and
broke *it*, and gave *it* to them
and said, "Take, [1]eat; this is My
[b]body."
23 Then He took the cup, and
when He had given thanks He
gave *it* to them, and they all
drank from it.
24 And He said to them, "This is
My blood of the [1]new covenant,
which is shed for many.
25 "Assuredly, I say to you, I
will no longer drink of the fruit
of the vine until that day when I

3 [1]Perfume of pure nard
5 [a]Matt. 18:28 [b]John 6:61 [1]*scolded*
7 [a]Deut. 15:11 [b][John 7:33; 8:21; 14:2, 12; 16:10, 17, 28]
9 [a]Luke 24:47
10 [a]Matt. 10:2–4
12 [a]Matt. 26:17–19 [1]*sacrificed*
17 [a]Matt. 26:20–24
18 [a]John 6:70, 71; 13:18
19 [1]NU omits the rest of v. 19.
21 [a]Luke 22:22
22 [a]1 Cor. 11:23–25 [b][1 Pet. 2:24] [1]NU omits *eat*
24 [1]NU omits *new*

drink it new in the kingdom of
God."
26 [a]And when they had sung
[1]a hymn, they went out to the
Mount of Olives.
☆ **27** [a]Then Jesus said to them,
"All of you will be made to stumble [1]because of Me this night, for
it is written:

[b]*'I will strike the Shepherd,*
And the sheep will be
scattered.'

28 "But [a]after I have been raised,
I will go before you to Galilee."
29 [a]Peter said to Him, "Even if
all are made to [1]stumble, yet I
will not *be.*"
30 Jesus said to him, "Assuredly, I say to you that today, *even*
this night, before the rooster
crows twice, you will deny Me
three times."
31 But he spoke more vehemently, "If I have to die with You,
I will not deny You!" And they all
said likewise.
32 [a]Then they came to a place
which was named Geth·sem'-
a·nē; and He said to His disciples, "Sit here while I pray."
33 And He [a]took Peter, James,
and John with Him, and He began to be troubled and deeply
distressed.
34 Then He said to them, [a]"My
soul is exceedingly sorrowful,
even to death. Stay here and
watch."
35 He went a little farther, and
fell on the ground, and prayed
that if it were possible, the hour
might pass from Him.
★ 36 And He said, [a]"Abba, Father,
[b]all things *are* possible for You.
Take this cup away from Me;
[c]nevertheless, not what I will,
but what You *will.*"
37 Then He came and found
them sleeping, and said to Peter,
"Simon, are you sleeping? Could
you not watch one hour?
38 [a]"Watch and pray, lest you
enter into temptation. [b]The spirit
indeed *is* willing, but the flesh *is*
weak."
39 Again He went away and
prayed, and spoke the same
words.
40 And when He returned, He
found them asleep again, for
their eyes were heavy; and they
did not know what to answer
Him.
41 Then He came the third
time and said to them, "Are you
still sleeping and resting? It is
enough! [a]The hour has come;
behold, the Son of Man is being
betrayed into the hands of sinners.
42 [a]"Rise, let us be going. See,
My betrayer is at hand."
43 [a]And immediately, while He
was still speaking, Judas, one
of the twelve, with a great multitude with swords and clubs,
came from the chief priests and
the scribes and the elders.
44 Now His betrayer had given
them a signal, saying, "Whomever I [a]kiss, He is the One; seize
Him and lead *Him* away safely."
45 As soon as he had come,
immediately he went up to Him
and said to Him, "Rabbi, Rabbi!"
and kissed Him.
46 Then they laid their hands
on Him and took Him.
47 And one of those who stood
by drew his sword and struck
the servant of the high priest,
and cut off his ear.
48 [a]Then Jesus answered and

26 [a]Matt. 26:30 [1]Or *hymns*
27 [a]Matt. 26:31–35 [b]Zech. 13:7; Matt. 26:56 [1]NU omits *because of Me this night*
28 [a]Mark 16:7
29 [a]John 13:37, 38 [1]*fall away*
32 [a]Luke 22:40–46
33 [a]Mark 5:37; 9:2; 13:3
34 [a]John 12:27
36 [a]Gal. 4:6 [b][Heb. 5:7] [c]Is. 50:5; John 5:30; 6:38
38 [a]Luke 21:36 [b][Rom. 7:18, 21–24]
41 [a]John 13:1; 17:1
42 [a]John 13:21; 18:1, 2
43 [a]Luke 22:47–53
44 [a][Prov. 27:6]
48 [a]Matt. 26:55

said to them, "Have you come
out, as against a robber, with
swords and clubs to take Me?
49 "I was daily with you in the
temple [a]teaching, and you did
not seize Me. But [b]the Scriptures
must be fulfilled."
50 [a]Then they all forsook Him
and fled.
51 Now a certain young man
followed Him, having a linen
cloth thrown around *his* naked
body. And the young men laid
hold of him,
52 and he left the linen cloth
and fled from them naked.
53 [a]And they led Jesus away to
the high priest; and with him
were [b]assembled all the [c]chief
priests, the elders, and the
scribes.
54 But [a]Peter followed Him at
a distance, right into the courtyard of the high priest. And
he sat with the servants and
warmed himself at the fire.
55 [a]Now the chief priests and
all the council sought testimony
against Jesus to put Him to
death, but found none.
56 For many bore [a]false witness
against Him, but their testimonies [1]did not agree.
★ 57 [a]Then some rose up and bore
false witness against Him, saying,
58 "We heard Him say, [a]'I will
destroy this temple made with
hands, and within three days I
will build another made without
hands.' "
59 But not even then did their
testimony agree.
60 [a]And the high priest stood
up in the midst and asked Jesus,
saying, "Do You answer nothing? What *is it* these men testify
against You?"

61 But [a]He kept silent and answered nothing. [b]Again the high
priest asked Him, saying to Him,
"Are You the Christ, the Son of
the Blessed?"
62 Jesus said, "I am. [a]And you
will see the Son of Man sitting
at the right hand of the Power,
and coming with the clouds of
heaven."
63 Then the high priest tore his
clothes and said, "What further
need do we have of witnesses?
64 "You have heard the [a]blas-
phemy! What do you think?"
And they all condemned Him to
be deserving of [b]death.
65 Then some began to [a]spit ★
on Him, and to blindfold Him,
and to beat Him, and to say to
Him, "Prophesy!" And the officers [1]struck Him with the palms
of their hands.
66 [a]Now as Peter was below in
the courtyard, one of the servant
girls of the high priest came.
67 And when she saw Peter
warming himself, she looked at
him and said, "You also were
with [a]Jesus of Nazareth."
68 But he denied it, saying, "I
neither know nor understand
what you are saying." And he
went out on the porch, and a
rooster crowed.
69 [a]And the servant girl saw
him again, and began to say to
those who stood by, "This is *one*
of them."
70 But he denied it again. [a]And
a little later those who stood by
said to Peter again, "Surely you
are *one* of them; [b]for you are
a Galilean, [1]and your [2]speech
shows *it.*"
71 Then he began to curse and
swear, "I do not know this Man
of whom you speak!"

49 [a]Matt. 21:23 [b]Is. 53:7
50 [a]Ps. 88:8
53 [a]Matt. 26:57–68 [b]Mark 15:1 [c]John 7:32; 18:3; 19:6
54 [a]John 18:15
55 [a]Matt. 26:59
56 [a]Ex. 20:16 [1]*were not consistent*
57 [a]Ps. 35:11
58 [a]John 2:19
60 [a]Matt. 26:62
61 [a]Is. 53:7 [b]Luke 22:67–71
62 [a]Luke 22:69
64 [a]John 10:33, 36 [b]John 19:7
65 [a]Is. 50:6; 52:14; Lam. 3:30 [1]NU *received Him with slaps*
66 [a]John 18:16–18, 25–27
67 [a]John 1:45
69 [a]Matt. 26:71
70 [a]Luke 22:59 [b]Acts 2:7 [1]NU omits the rest of v. 70. [2]*accent*

72 [a]A second time *the* rooster
crowed. Then Peter called to
mind the word that Jesus had
said to him, "Before the rooster
crows twice, you will deny Me
three times." And when he
thought about it, he wept.

★ **15** Immediately, [a]in the morning, the chief priests held
a consultation with the elders
and scribes and the whole council; and they bound Jesus, led
Him away, and [b]delivered *Him* to
Pilate.
2 [a]Then Pilate asked Him, "Are
You the King of the Jews?" He
answered and said to him, "*It is*
as you say."
★ 3 And the chief priests accused Him of many things, but
He [a]answered nothing.
4 [a]Then Pilate asked Him
again, saying, "Do You answer
nothing? See how many things
[1]they testify against You!"
5 [a]But Jesus still answered
nothing, so that Pilate marveled.
6 Now [a]at the feast he was accustomed to releasing one prisoner to them, whomever they
requested.
7 And there was one named
Ba·rab′bas, *who was* chained
with his fellow rebels; they had
committed murder in the rebellion.
8 Then the multitude, [1]crying
aloud, began to ask *him to do*
just as he had always done for
them.
9 But Pilate answered them,
saying, "Do you want me to
release to you the King of the
Jews?"
10 For he knew that the chief
priests had handed Him over
because of envy.
11 But [a]the chief priests stirred
up the crowd, so that he should
rather release Ba·rab′bas to
them.
12 Pilate answered and said to
them again, "What then do you
want me to do *with Him* whom
you call the [a]King of the Jews?"
13 So they cried out again,
"Crucify Him!"
14 Then Pilate said to them,
"Why, [a]what evil has He done?"
But they cried out all the more,
"Crucify Him!"
15 [a]So Pilate, wanting to gratify
the crowd, released Ba·rab′bas
to them; and he delivered Jesus,
after he had scourged *Him*, to be
[b]crucified.
16 [a]Then the soldiers led
Him away into the hall called
[1]Prae·tō′ri·um, and they called
together the whole garrison.
17 And they clothed Him with
purple; and they twisted a crown
of thorns, put it on His *head*,
18 and began to salute Him,
"Hail, King of the Jews!"
19 Then they [a]struck Him on ★
the head with a reed and spat on
Him; and bowing the knee, they
worshiped Him.
20 And when they had [a]mocked
Him, they took the purple off
Him, put His own clothes on Him,
and led Him out to crucify Him.
21 [a]Then they compelled a certain man, Simon a Cȳ·rē′ni·an,
the father of Alexander and Rū′-
fus, as he was coming out of the
country and passing by, to bear
His cross.
22 [a]And they brought Him to
the place Gol′go·tha, which is
translated, Place of a Skull.
23 [a]Then they gave Him wine
mingled with myrrh to drink,
but He did not take *it*.

72 [a]Matt. 26:75

CHAPTER 15

1 [a]Ps. 2:2 [b]Acts 3:13
2 [a]Matt. 27:11–14
3 [a]Is. 53:7; John 19:9
4 [a]Matt. 27:13 [1]NU *of which they accuse You*
5 [a]Is. 53:7
6 [a]Matt. 27:15–26
8 [1]NU *going up*
11 [a]Acts 3:14
12 [a]Mic. 5:2
14 [a]1 Pet. 2:21–23
15 [a]Matt. 27:26 [b][Is. 53:8]
16 [a]Matt. 27:27–31 [1]The governor's headquarters
19 [a][Is. 50:6; 52:14; 53:5]; Mic. 5:1
20 [a]Luke 22:63; 23:11
21 [a]Matt. 27:32
22 [a]John 19:17–24
23 [a]Matt. 27:34

24 And when they crucified Him,
[a]they divided His garments, casting lots for them *to determine*
what every man should take.
25 Now [a]it was the third hour,
and they crucified Him.
26 And [a]the inscription of His
[1]accusation was written above:

THE KING OF THE JEWS.

★ 27 [a]With Him they also crucified
two robbers, one on His right
and the other on His left.
★ 28 [1]So the Scripture was fulfilled
which says, [a]*"And He was numbered with the transgressors."*
★ 29 And [a]those who passed by
blasphemed Him, [b]wagging their
heads and saying, "Aha! [c]*You*
who destroy the temple and build
it in three days,
30 "save Yourself, and come
down from the cross!"
★ 31 Likewise the chief priests
also, [a]mocking among themselves with the scribes, said, "He
saved [b]others; Himself He cannot
save.
32 "Let the Christ, the King of Israel, descend now from the cross,
that we may see and [1]believe."
Even [a]those who were crucified
with Him reviled Him.
33 Now [a]when the sixth hour
had come, there was darkness
over the whole land until the
ninth hour.
★ 34 And at the ninth hour Jesus cried out with a loud voice,
saying, "Ē′lō·ī, Ē′lō·ī, la·ma′ sa-
bach′tha·nī?" which is translated,
[a]*"My God, My God, why have
You forsaken Me?"*
35 Some of those who stood
by, when they heard *that,* said,
"Look, He is calling for E·lī′jah!"
★ 36 Then [a]someone ran and filled

24 [a]Ps. 22:18
25 [a]John 19:14
26 [a]Matt. 27:37 [1]*crime*
27 [a]Is. 53:9, 12; Luke 22:37
28 [a]Is. 53:12 [1]NU omits v. 28.
29 [a]Ps. 22:6, 7; 69:7 [b]Ps. 109:25 [c]John 2:19–21
31 [a]Ps. 22:8; Luke 18:32 [b]John 11:43, 44
32 [a]Matt. 27:44 [1]M *believe Him*
33 [a]Luke 23:44–49
34 [a]Ps. 22:1
36 [a]John 19:29 [b]Ps. 69:21
37 [a]Matt. 27:50
38 [a]Ex. 26:31–33
39 [a]Luke 23:47 [1]NU *He thus breathed His last*
40 [a]Matt. 27:55 [b]Ps. 38:11
41 [a]Luke 8:2, 3
42 [a]John 19:38–42
43 [a]Luke 2:25, 38; 23:51
45 [a]Is. 53:9, 12
46 [a]Matt. 27:59, 60

a sponge full of sour wine, put *it*
on a reed, and [b]offered *it* to Him
to drink, saying, "Let Him alone;
let us see if E·lī′jah will come to
take Him down."
37 [a]And Jesus cried out with
a loud voice, and breathed His
last.
38 Then [a]the veil of the temple
was torn in two from top to bottom.
39 So [a]when the centurion, who
stood opposite Him, saw that [1]He
cried out like this and breathed
His last, he said, "Truly this Man
was the Son of God!"
40 [a]There were also women
looking on [b]from afar, among
whom were Mary Mag′da·lēne,
Mary the mother of James the
Less and of Jō′sēs, and Sa·lō′mē,
41 who also [a]followed Him and
ministered to Him when He
was in Galilee, and many other
women who came up with Him
to Jerusalem.
42 [a]Now when evening had
come, because it was the Preparation Day, that is, the day before
the Sabbath,
43 Joseph of Ar·i·ma·thē′a, a
prominent council member, who
[a]was himself waiting for the
kingdom of God, coming and
taking courage, went in to Pilate
and asked for the body of Jesus.
44 Pilate marveled that He was
already dead; and summoning
the centurion, he asked him if He
had been dead for some time.
45 So when he found out from ★
the centurion, [a]he granted the
body to Joseph.
46 [a]Then he bought fine linen,
took Him down, and wrapped
Him in the linen. And he laid
Him in a tomb which had been
hewn out of the rock, and rolled

a stone against the door of the
tomb.
47 And Mary Mag'da·lēne and
Mary *the mother* of Jō'sēs observed where He was laid.

16 Now [a]when the Sabbath
was past, Mary Mag'-
da·lēne, Mary *the mother* of
James, and Sa·lō'mē [b]bought
spices, that they might come and
anoint Him.
2 [a]Very early in the morning,
on the first *day* of the week, they
came to the tomb when the sun
had risen.
3 And they said among themselves, "Who will roll away the
stone from the door of the tomb
for us?"
4 But when they looked up,
they saw that the stone had been
rolled away—for it was very
large.
5 [a]And entering the tomb,
they saw a young man clothed
in a long white robe sitting on
the right side; and they were
alarmed.
6 [a]But he said to them, "Do not
be alarmed. You seek Jesus of
Nazareth, who was crucified. He
is risen! He is not here. See the
place where they laid Him.
7 "But go, tell His disciples—
and Peter—that He is going
[1]before you into Galilee; there
you will see Him, [a]as He said to
you."
8 So they went out [1]quickly
and fled from the tomb, for they
trembled and were amazed. [a]And
they said nothing to anyone, for
they were afraid.
9 [1]Now when *He* rose early on
the first *day* of the week, He appeared first to Mary Mag'da·lēne,
[a]out of whom He had cast seven
demons.
10 [a]She went and told those
who had been with Him, as they
mourned and wept.
11 [a]And when they heard that
He was alive and had been seen
by her, they did not believe.
12 After that, He appeared in
another form [a]to two of them as
they walked and went into the
country.
13 And they went and told *it* to
the rest, *but* they did not believe
them either.
14 [a]Later He appeared to the
eleven as they sat at the table;
and He rebuked their unbelief
and hardness of heart, because
they did not believe those who
had seen Him after He had
risen.
15 [a]And He said to them, "Go
into all the world [b]and preach the
gospel to every creature.
16 [a]"He who believes and is baptized will be saved; [b]but he who
does not believe will be condemned.
17 "And these [a]signs will follow
those who [1]believe: [b]In My name
they will cast out demons; [c]they
will speak with new tongues;
18 [a]"they[1] will take up serpents;
and if they drink anything deadly,
it will by no means hurt them;
[b]they will lay hands on the sick,
and they will recover."
19 So then, [a]after the Lord had ★
spoken to them, He was [b]received
up into heaven, and [c]sat down at
the right hand of God.
20 And they went out and
preached everywhere, the Lord
working with *them* [a]and con-
firming the word through the
accompanying signs. Amen.

CHAPTER 16

1 [a]John 20:1–8 [b]Luke 23:56
2 [a]Luke 24:1
5 [a]John 20:11, 12
6 [a]Matt. 28:6
7 [a]Matt. 26:32; 28:16, 17 [1]*ahead of*
8 [a]Matt. 28:8 [1]NU, M omit *quickly*
9 [a]Luke 8:2 [1]Vv. 9–20 are bracketed in NU as not in the original text. They are lacking in Codex Sinaiticus and Codex Vaticanus, although nearly all other mss. of Mark contain them.
10 [a]Luke 24:10
11 [a]Luke 24:11, 41
12 [a]Luke 24:13–35
14 [a]1 Cor. 15:5
15 [a]Matt. 28:19 [b][Col. 1:23]
16 [a][John 3:18, 36] [b][John 12:48]
17 [a]Acts 5:12 [b]Luke 10:17 [c][Acts 2:4] [1]*have believed*
18 [a]Acts 28:3–6 [b]James 5:14 [1]NU *and in their hands they will*
19 [a]Acts 1:2, 3 [b]Luke 9:51; 24:51 [c][Ps. 110:1]
20 [a][Heb. 2:4]

The Gospel According to

LUKE

LUKE, a physician, writes with the compassion and warmth of a family doctor as he carefully documents the perfect humanity of the Son of Man, Jesus Christ. Luke emphasizes Jesus' ancestry, birth, and early life before moving carefully and chronologically through His earthly ministry. Growing belief and growing opposition develop side by side. Those who believe are challenged to count the cost of discipleship. Those who oppose will not be satisfied until the Son of Man hangs lifeless on a cross. But the Resurrection insures that His purpose will be fulfilled: "to seek and to save that which was lost" (19:10).

Kata Loukan, "According to Luke," is the ancient title that was added to this gospel at a very early date. The Greek name *Luke* appears only three times in the New Testament (Col. 4:14; 2 Tim. 4:11; Philem. 24).

INASMUCH as many have taken in hand to set in order a narrative of those [a]things which [1]have been fulfilled among us,
2 just as those who [a]from the beginning were [b]eyewitnesses and ministers of the word [c]delivered them to us,
3 it seemed good to me also, having [1]had perfect understanding of all things from the very first, to write to you an orderly account, [a]most excellent Thē-oph′i·lus,
4 [a]that you may know the certainty of those things in which you were instructed.
5 There was [a]in the days of Her′od, the king of Judea, a certain priest named Zach·a·rī′as, [b]of the division of [c]A·bī′jah. His [d]wife *was* of the daughters of Aaron, and her name *was* Elizabeth.
6 And they were both righteous before God, walking in all the commandments and ordinances of the Lord blameless.
7 But they had no child, because Elizabeth was barren, and they were both well advanced in years.
8 So it was, that while he was serving as priest before God in the order of his division,
9 according to the custom of the priesthood, [1]his lot fell [a]to burn incense when he went into the temple of the Lord.
10 [a]And the whole multitude of the people was praying outside at the hour of incense.
11 Then an angel of the Lord appeared to him, standing on the right side of [a]the altar of incense.
12 And when Zach·a·rī′as saw *him*, [a]he was troubled, and fear fell upon him.
13 But the angel said to him, "Do not be afraid, Zach·a·rī′as, for your prayer is heard; and your wife Elizabeth will bear you a son, and [a]you shall call his name John.
14 "And you will have joy and gladness, and [a]many will rejoice at his birth.
15 "For he will be [a]great in the sight of the Lord, and [b]shall

CHAPTER 1

1 [a]John 20:31 [1]Or *are most surely believed*
2 [a]Acts 1:21, 22 [b]Acts 1:2 [c]Heb. 2:3
3 [a]Acts 1:1 [1]Lit. *accurately followed*
4 [a][John 20:31]
5 [a]Matt. 2:1 [b]1 Chr. 24:1, 10 [c]Neh. 12:4 [d]Lev. 21:13, 14
9 [a]Ex. 30:7, 8 [1]*he was chosen by lot*
10 [a]Lev. 16:17
11 [a]Ex. 30:1
12 [a]Luke 2:9
13 [a]Luke 1:57, 60, 63
14 [a]Luke 1:58
15 [a][Luke 7:24–28] [b]Num. 6:3

drink neither wine nor strong
drink. He will also be filled with
the Holy Spirit, [c]even from his
mother's womb.
16 "And he will turn many of
the children of Israel to the Lord
their God.
☆ 17 [a]"He will also go before Him
in the spirit and power of E·lī′-
jah, *'to turn the hearts of the*
fathers to the children,' and the
disobedient to the wisdom of
the just, to make ready a people
prepared for the Lord."
18 And Zach·a·rī′as said to the
angel, [a]"How shall I know this?
For I am an old man, and my
wife is well advanced in years."
19 And the angel answered and
said to him, "I am [a]Gabriel, who
stands in the presence of God,
and was sent to speak to you and
bring you [1]these glad [b]tidings.
20 "But behold, [a]you will be
mute and not able to speak until
the day these things take place,
because you did not believe my
words which will be fulfilled in
their own time."
21 And the people waited for
Zach·a·rī′as, and marveled that
he lingered so long in the temple.
22 But when he came out, he
could not speak to them; and
they perceived that he had seen
a vision in the temple, for he
beckoned to them and remained
speechless.
23 So it was, as soon as [a]the
days of his service were completed, that he departed to his
own house.
24 Now after those days his
wife Elizabeth conceived; and
she hid herself five months, saying,
25 "Thus the Lord has dealt
with me, in the days when He
looked on *me,* to [a]take away my
reproach among people."
26 Now in the sixth month the
angel Gabriel was sent by God
to a city of Galilee named Nazareth,
27 to a virgin [a]betrothed to a ★
man whose name was Joseph, of
the house of David. The virgin's
name *was* Mary.
28 And having come in, the angel said to her, [a]"Rejoice, highly
favored *one,* [b]the Lord *is* with
you; [1]blessed *are* you among
women!"
29 But [1]when she saw *him,* [a]she
was troubled at his saying, and
considered what manner of
greeting this was.
30 Then the angel said to her,
"Do not be afraid, Mary, for you
have found [a]favor with God.
31 [a]"And behold, you will con- ★
ceive in your womb and bring
forth a Son, and [b]shall call His
name JESUS.
32 "He will be great, [a]and will
be called the Son of the Highest;
and [b]the Lord God will give Him
the [c]throne of His [d]father David.
33 [a]"And He will reign over the ☆
house of Jacob forever, and of
His kingdom there will be no
end."
34 Then Mary said to the angel,
"How can this be, since I [1]do not
know a man?"
35 And the angel answered and
said to her, [a]"*The* Holy Spirit
will come upon you, and the
power of the Highest will overshadow you; therefore, also, that
Holy One who is to be born will
be called [b]the Son of God.
36 "Now indeed, Elizabeth your
relative has also conceived a son
in her old age; and this is now

15 [c]Jer. 1:5
17 [a]Mal. 4:5, 6; Matt. 3:1–3; 11:14
18 [a]Gen. 17:17
19 [a]Dan. 8:16 [b]Luke 2:10 [1]*this good news*
20 [a]Ezek. 3:26; 24:27
23 [a]2 Kin. 11:5
25 [a]Gen. 30:23
27 [a]Is. 7:14; Matt. 1:18
28 [a]Dan. 9:23 [b]Judg. 6:12 [1]NU omits *blessed are you among women*
29 [a]Luke 1:12 [1]NU omits *when she saw him*
30 [a]Luke 2:52
31 [a]Is. 7:14; Matt. 1:21, 25 [b]Luke 2:21
32 [a]Mark 5:7 [b]2 Sam. 7:12, 13, 16 [c]2 Sam. 7:14–17 [d]Matt. 1:1
33 [a][Dan. 2:44]; Obad. 21; Mic. 4:7; Heb. 1:8]; 2 Pet. 1:11
34 [1]Am a virgin
35 [a]Matt. 1:20 [b][Heb. 1:2, 8]

the sixth month for her who was called barren.
37 "For [a]with God nothing will be impossible."
38 Then Mary said, "Behold the maidservant of the Lord! Let it be to me according to your word." And the angel departed from her.
39 Now Mary arose in those days and went into the hill country with haste, [a]to a city of Judah,
40 and entered the house of Zach·a·rī′as and greeted Elizabeth.
41 And it happened, when Elizabeth heard the greeting of Mary, that the babe leaped in her womb; and Elizabeth was [a]filled with the Holy Spirit.
42 Then she spoke out with a loud voice and said, [a]"Blessed *are* you among women, and blessed *is* the fruit of your womb!
43 "But why *is* this *granted* to me, that the mother of my Lord should come to me?
44 "For indeed, as soon as the voice of your greeting sounded in my ears, the babe leaped in my womb for joy.
45 [a]"Blessed *is* she who [1]believed, for there will be a fulfillment of those things which were told her from the Lord."
46 And Mary said:

[a]"My soul [1]magnifies the
Lord,
47 And my spirit has [a]rejoiced
in [b]God my Savior.
48 For [a]He has regarded
the lowly state of His
maidservant;
For behold, henceforth [b]all
generations will call me
blessed.
49 For He who is mighty [a]has
done great things for me,
And [b]holy *is* His name.
50 And [a]His mercy *is* on those
who fear Him
From generation to
generation.
51 [a]He has shown strength with
His arm;
[b]He has scattered *the* proud
in the imagination of
their hearts.
52 [a]He has put down the mighty
from *their* thrones,
And exalted *the* lowly.
53 He has [a]filled *the* hungry
with good things,
And *the* rich He has sent
away empty.
54 He has helped His [a]servant
Israel,
[b]In remembrance of *His*
mercy,
55 [a]As He spoke to our [b]fathers,
To Abraham and to his [c]seed
forever."

56 And Mary remained with her about three months, and returned to her house.
57 Now Elizabeth's full time came for her to be delivered, and she brought forth a son.
58 When her neighbors and relatives heard how the Lord had shown great mercy to her, they [a]rejoiced with her.
59 So it was, [a]on the eighth day, that they came to circumcise the child; and they would have called him by the name of his father, Zach·a·rī′as.
60 His mother answered and said, [a]"No; he shall be called John."
61 But they said to her, "There is no one among your relatives who is called by this name."

37 [a]Jer. 32:17
39 [a]Josh. 21:9
41 [a]Acts 6:3
42 [a]Judg. 5:24
45 [a]John 20:29 [1]Or *believed that there*
46 [a]1 Sam. 2:1–10 [1]Declares the greatness of
47 [a]Hab. 3:18 [b]1 Tim. 1:1; 2:3
48 [a]Ps. 138:6 [b]Luke 11:27
49 [a]Ps. 71:19; 126:2, 3 [b]Ps. 111:9
50 [a]Ps. 103:17
51 [a]Ps. 98:1; 118:15 [b][1 Pet. 5:5]
52 [a]1 Sam. 2:7, 8
53 [a][Matt. 5:6]
54 [a]Is. 41:8 [b][Jer. 31:3]
55 [a]Gen. 17:19 [b][Rom. 11:28] [c]Gen. 17:7
58 [a][Rom. 12:15]
59 [a]Gen. 17:12
60 [a]Luke 1:13, 63

62 So they made signs to his
father—what he would have him
called.
63 And he asked for a writing
tablet, and wrote, saying, "His
name is John." So they all marveled.
64 Immediately his mouth was
opened and his tongue *loosed,*
and he spoke, praising God.
65 Then fear came on all who
dwelt around them; and all these
sayings were discussed throughout all the hill country of Judea.
66 And all those who heard
them [a]kept *them* in their hearts,
saying, "What kind of child will
this be?" And [b]the hand of the
Lord was with him.
67 Now his father Zach·a·rī′as
[a]was filled with the Holy Spirit,
and prophesied, saying:

68 "Blessed[a] *is* the Lord God of
Israel,
For [b]He has visited and
redeemed His people,
69 [a]And has raised up a horn of
salvation for us
In the house of His servant
David,
70 [a]As He spoke by the mouth
of His holy prophets,
Who *have been* [b]since the
world began,
71 That we should be saved
from our enemies
And from the hand of all
who hate us,
72 [a]To perform the mercy
promised to our fathers
And to remember His holy
covenant,
73 [a]The oath which He swore to
our father Abraham:
74 To grant us that we,
Being delivered from the
hand of our enemies,
Might [a]serve Him without
fear,
75 [a]In holiness and righteousness
before Him all the days
of our life.

76 "And you, child, will be
called the [a]prophet of the
Highest;
For [b]you will go before
the face of the Lord to
prepare His ways,
77 To give [a]knowledge of
salvation to His people
By the remission of their
sins,
78 Through the tender mercy
of our God,
With which the [1]Dayspring
from on high [2]has visited
us;
79 [a]To give light to those who ☆
sit in darkness and the
shadow of death,
To [b]guide our feet into the
way of peace."

80 So [a]the child grew and became strong in spirit, and [b]was
in the deserts till the day of his
manifestation to Israel.

2 And it came to pass in those
days *that* a decree went out
from Caesar Au·gus′tus that all
the world should be registered.
2 [a]This census first took place
while Quī·rin′i·us was governing
Syria.
3 So all went to be registered,
everyone to his own city.
4 Joseph also went up from ★
Galilee, out of the city of Nazareth, into Judea, to [a]the city of
David, which is called Bethlehem, [b]because he was of the
house and lineage of David,
5 to be registered with Mary,

66 [a]Luke 2:19 [b]Acts 11:21
67 [a]Joel 2:28
68 [a]1 Kin. 1:48 [b]Ex. 3:16
69 [a]Ps. 132:17
70 [a]Rom. 1:2 [b]Acts 3:21
72 [a]Lev. 26:42
73 [a]Gen. 12:3; 22:16–18
74 [a][Heb. 9:14]
75 [a][Eph. 4:24]
76 [a]Matt. 3:3; 11:9 [b]Is. 40:3
77 [a][Mark 1:4]
78 [1]Lit. *Dawn;* the Messiah [2]NU *shall visit*
79 [a]Is. 9:2; 2 Cor. 4:6; Eph. 5:8 [b][John 10:4; 14:27; 16:33]
80 [a]Luke 2:40 [b]Matt. 3:1

CHAPTER 2

2 [a]Acts 5:37
4 [a]1 Sam. 16:1; Mic. 5:2 [b]Matt. 1:16

[a]his betrothed [1]wife, who was
with child.
6 So it was, that while they
were there, the days were completed for her to be delivered.
7 And [a]she brought forth her
firstborn Son, and wrapped Him
in swaddling cloths, and laid
Him in a [1]manger, because there
was no room for them in the
inn.
8 Now there were in the same
country shepherds living out in
the fields, keeping watch over
their flock by night.
9 And [1]behold, an angel of the
Lord stood before them, and the
glory of the Lord shone around
them, [a]and they were greatly
afraid.
10 Then the angel said to them,
[a]"Do not be afraid, for behold, I
bring you good tidings of great
joy [b]which will be to all people.
★ 11 [a]"For there is born to you this
day in the city of David [b]a Savior, [c]who is Christ the Lord.
12 "And this *will be* the sign
to you: You will find a Babe
wrapped in swaddling cloths,
lying in a [1]manger."
13 [a]And suddenly there was
with the angel a multitude of
the heavenly host praising God
and saying:

14 "Glory[a] to God in the highest,
And on earth [b]peace,
[c]goodwill[1] toward men!"

15 So it was, when the angels
had gone away from them into
heaven, that the shepherds said
to one another, "Let us now go
to Bethlehem and see this thing
that has come to pass, which the
Lord has made known to us."
16 And they came with haste
and found Mary and Joseph,
and the Babe lying in a manger.
17 Now when they had seen
Him, they made [1]widely known
the saying which was told them
concerning this Child.
18 And all those who heard *it*
marveled at those things which
were told them by the shepherds.
19 [a]But Mary kept all these
things and pondered *them* in her
heart.
20 Then the shepherds returned,
glorifying and [a]praising God for
all the things that they had heard
and seen, as it was told them.
21 [a]And when eight days were
completed [1]for the circumcision of the Child, His name was
called [b]JESUS, the name given by
the angel [c]before He was conceived in the womb.
22 Now when [a]the days of her
purification according to the law
of Moses were completed, they
brought Him to Jerusalem to
present *Him* to the Lord
23 [a](as it is written in the law
of the Lord, [b]*"Every male who*
opens the womb shall be called
holy to the LORD"),
24 and to offer a sacrifice according to what is said in the
law of the Lord, [a]*"A pair of tur-*
tledoves or two young pigeons."
25 And behold, there was a
man in Jerusalem whose name
was Sim'ē·on, and this man *was*
just and devout, [a]waiting for the
Consolation of Israel, and the
Holy Spirit was upon him.
26 And it had been revealed to
him by the Holy Spirit that he
would not [a]see death before he
had seen the Lord's Christ.
27 So he came [a]by the Spirit
into the temple. And when the
parents brought in the Child

5 [a][Matt. 1:18] [1]NU omits *wife*
7 [a]Matt. 1:25 [1]*feed trough*
9 [a]Luke 1:12 [1]NU omits *behold*
10 [a]Luke 1:13, 30 [b]Gen. 12:3
11 [a]Is. 9:6; Mic. 5:2 [b]Matt. 1:21 [c]Acts 2:36
12 [1]*feed trough*
13 [a]Dan. 7:10
14 [a]Luke 19:38 [b]Is. 57:19 [c][Eph. 2:4, 7] [1]NU *toward men of goodwill*
17 [1]NU omits *widely*
19 [a]Gen. 37:11
20 [a]Luke 19:37
21 [a]Lev. 12:3 [b][Matt. 1:21] [c]Luke 1:31 [1]NU *for His circumcision*
22 [a]Lev. 12:2–8
23 [a]Deut. 18:4 [b]Ex. 13:2, 12, 15
24 [a]Lev. 12:2, 8
25 [a]Mark 15:43
26 [a][Heb. 11:5]
27 [a]Matt. 4:1

Jesus, to do for Him according
to the custom of the law,
28 he took Him up in his arms
and blessed God and said:

29 "Lord, [a]now You are letting
Your servant depart in
peace,
According to Your word;
30 For my eyes [a]have seen Your
salvation
31 Which You have prepared
before the face of all
peoples,
★ 32 [a]A light to *bring* revelation to
the Gentiles,
And the glory of Your people
Israel."

33 [1]And Joseph and His mother
marveled at those things which
were spoken of Him.
☆ 34 Then Sim′ē·on blessed them,
and said to Mary His mother,
"Behold, this *Child* is destined
for the [a]fall and rising of many
in Israel, and for [b]a sign which
will be spoken against
35 "(yes, [a]a sword will pierce
through your own soul also),
that the thoughts of many hearts
may be revealed."
36 Now there was one, Anna,
a prophetess, the daughter of
Phan′ū·el, of the tribe of [a]Ash′er.
She was of a great age, and
had lived with a husband seven
years from her virginity;
37 and this woman *was* a widow
[1]of about eighty-four years, who
did not depart from the temple,
but served *God* with fastings
and prayers [a]night and day.
38 And coming in that instant
she gave thanks to [1]the Lord,
and spoke of Him to all those
who [a]looked for redemption in
Jerusalem.

39 So when they had performed
all things according to the law of
the Lord, they returned to Galilee, to their *own* city, Nazareth.
40 [a]And the Child grew and became strong [1]in spirit, filled with
wisdom; and the grace of God
was upon Him.
41 His parents went to [a]Jerusa-
lem [b]every year at the Feast of
the Passover.
42 And when He was twelve
years old, they went up to Jerusalem according to the [a]custom
of the feast.
43 When they had finished the
[a]days, as they returned, the Boy
Jesus lingered behind in Jerusalem. And [1]Joseph and His
mother did not know *it;*
44 but supposing Him to have
been in the company, they went
a day's journey, and sought Him
among *their* relatives and acquaintances.
45 So when they did not find
Him, they returned to Jerusalem, seeking Him.
46 Now so it was *that* after
three days they found Him in
the temple, sitting in the midst
of the teachers, both listening
to them and asking them questions.
47 And [a]all who heard Him were
astonished at His understanding
and answers.
48 So when they saw Him, they
were amazed; and His mother
said to Him, "Son, why have
You done this to us? Look, Your
father and I have sought You
anxiously."
49 And He said to them, "Why
did you seek Me? Did you not
know that I must be [a]about [b]My
Father's business?"
50 But [a]they did not understand

29 [a]Gen. 46:30
30 [a][Is. 52:10]
32 [a]Is. 9:2; 42:6; Acts 10:45; 13:47; 28:28
33 [1]NU *And His father and mother*
34 [a][1 Pet. 2:7, 8] [b]Acts 4:1–3; 17:32; 28:22
35 [a]Ps. 42:10
36 [a]Josh. 19:24
37 [a]1 Tim. 5:5 [1]NU *until she was eighty-four*
38 [a]Mark 15:43 [1]NU *God*
40 [a]Luke 1:80; 2:52 [1]NU omits *in spirit*
41 [a]John 4:20 [b]Deut. 16:1, 16
42 [a]Ex. 23:14, 15
43 [a]Ex. 12:15 [1]NU *His parents*
47 [a]Matt. 7:28; 13:54; 22:33
49 [a]John 9:4 [b][Luke 4:22, 32]
50 [a]John 7:15, 46

the statement which He spoke to
them.
51 Then He went down with
them and came to Nazareth, and
was [1]subject to them, but His
mother [a]kept all these things in
her heart.
52 And Jesus [a]increased in wisdom and stature, [b]and in favor
with God and men.

3

3 Now in the fifteenth year
of the reign of Tī·bē′ri·us
Caesar, [a]Pon′ti·us Pilate being
governor of Judea, Her′od being
tetrarch of Galilee, his brother
Philip tetrarch of Ī·tu·rē′a and the
region of Trach·o·nī′tis, and Lȳ-
sā′ni·as tetrarch of Ab·i·lē′nē,
2 [1]while [a]An′nas and Cā′i·a-
phas were high priests, the word
of God came to [b]John the son of
Zach·a·rī′as in the wilderness.
3 [a]And he went into all the region around the Jordan, preaching a baptism of repentance [b]for
the remission of sins,
★ 4 as it is written in the book of
the words of Ī·sāi′ah the prophet,
saying:

[a]*"The voice of one crying in*
the wilderness:
'Prepare the way of the LORD*;*
Make His paths straight.
5 *Every valley shall be filled*
And every mountain and
hill brought low;
The crooked places shall be
made straight
And the rough ways
smooth;
6 *And* [a]*all flesh shall see the*
salvation of God.'"

7 Then he said to the multitudes that came out to be baptized by him, [a]"Brood[1] of vipers!
Who warned you to flee from
the wrath to come?
8 "Therefore bear fruits [a]wor-
thy of repentance, and do not
begin to say to yourselves, 'We
have Abraham as *our* father.'
For I say to you that God is able
to raise up children to Abraham
from these stones.
9 "And even now the ax is laid
to the root of the trees. Therefore [a]every tree which does not
bear good fruit is cut down and
thrown into the fire."
10 So the people asked him, saying, [a]"What shall we do then?"
11 He answered and said to
them, [a]"He who has two tunics,
let him give to him who has
none; and he who has food, [b]let
him do likewise."
12 Then [a]tax collectors also came
to be baptized, and said to him,
"Teacher, what shall we do?"
13 And he said to them, [a]"Collect
no more than what is appointed
for you."
14 Likewise the soldiers asked
him, saying, "And what shall we
do?" So he said to them, "Do not
[1]intimidate anyone [a]or accuse
falsely, and be content with your
wages."
15 Now as the people were in
expectation, and all reasoned in
their hearts about John, whether
he was the Christ *or* not,
16 John answered, saying to all,
[a]"I indeed baptize you with water; but One mightier than I is
coming, whose sandal strap I
am not worthy to loose. He will
[b]baptize you with the Holy Spirit
and fire.
17 "His winnowing fan *is* in His
hand, and He will thoroughly
clean out His threshing floor,
and [a]gather the wheat into His

51 [a]Dan. 7:28 [1]*obedient*
52 [a][Col. 2:2, 3] [b]1 Sam. 2:26

CHAPTER 3

1 [a]Matt. 27:2
2 [a]Acts 4:6 [b]Luke 1:13 [1]NU, M *in the high priesthood of Annas and Caiaphas*
3 [a]Mark 1:4 [b]Luke 1:77
4 [a]Is. 40:3–5
6 [a]Is. 52:10
7 [a]Matt. 3:7; 12:34; 23:33 [1]*Offspring*
8 [a][2 Cor. 7:9–11]
9 [a]Matt. 7:19
10 [a][Acts 2:37, 38; 16:30, 31]
11 [a]2 Cor. 8:14 [b]Is. 58:7
12 [a]Luke 7:29
13 [a]Luke 19:8
14 [a]Ex. 20:16; 23:1 [1]Lit. *shake down* for money
16 [a]Matt. 3:11, 12 [b]John 7:39; 20:22
17 [a]Matt. 13:24–30

barn; but the chaff He will burn
with unquenchable fire."
18 And with many other ex-
hortations he preached to the
people.
19 [a]But Her′od the tetrarch, being rebuked by him concerning
He·rō′di·as, his [1]brother Philip's
wife, and for all the evils which
Her′od had done,
20 also added this, above all,
that he shut John up in prison.
21 When all the people were
baptized, [a]it came to pass that
Jesus also was baptized; and
while He prayed, the heaven
was opened.
22 And the Holy Spirit descended in bodily form like a
dove upon Him, and a voice
came from heaven which said,
"You are My beloved Son; in You
I am [a]well pleased."
23 Now Jesus Himself began
His ministry at [a]about thirty
years of age, being (as was supposed) [b]*the* son of Joseph, *the*
son of Hē′lī,
24 *the son* of Mat′that, *the son*
of Levi, *the son* of Mel′chī, *the*
son of Jan′na, *the son* of Joseph,
25 *the son* of Mat·ta·thī′ah, *the*
son of Ā′mos, *the son* of Nā′-
hum, *the son* of Es′lī, *the son* of
Nag′ga·ī,
26 *the son* of Mā′ath, *the son* of
Mat·ta·thī′ah, *the son* of Sem′e·ī,
the son of Joseph, *the son* of
Judah,
27 *the son* of Jō·an′nas, *the son*
of Rhē′sa, *the son* of [a]Ze·rub′-
ba·bel, *the son* of She·al′ti·el, *the*
son of Nē′rī,
28 *the son* of Mel′chī, *the son*
of Ad′dī, *the son* of Cō′sam, *the*
son of El·mō′dam, *the son* of Er,
29 *the son* of Jō′sē, *the son* of
El·i·ē′zer, *the son* of Jō′rim, *the*
son of Mat′that, *the son* of Levi,
30 *the son* of Sim′ē·on, *the son*
of Judah, *the son* of Joseph, *the*
son of Jō′nan, *the son* of E·lī′-
a·kim,
31 *the son* of Mē′le·a, *the son* of ★
Mē′nan, *the son* of Mat′ta·thah,
the son of [a]Nathan, [b]*the son* of
David,
32 [a]*the son* of Jesse, *the son*
of Ō′bed, *the son* of Bō′az, *the*
son of Sal′mon, *the son* of Nah′-
shon,
33 *the son* of Am·min′a·dab, *the*
son of Ram, *the son* of Hez′ron,
the son of Per′ez, *the son* of Judah,
34 *the son* of Jacob, *the son* of
Isaac, *the son* of Abraham, [a]*the*
son of Tē′rah, *the son* of Nā′hor,
35 *the son* of Sē′rug, *the son* of
Rē′ū, *the son* of Pē′leg, *the son*
of Ē′ber, *the son* of Shē′lah,
36 [a]*the son* of Cā·ī′nan, *the*
son of [b]Ar·phā′xad, [c]*the son* of
Shem, *the son* of Noah, *the son*
of Lā′mech,
37 *the son* of Me·thū′se·lah, *the*
son of Ē′noch, *the son* of Jar′ed,
the son of Ma·hal′a·lel, *the son*
of Cā·ī′nan,
38 *the son* of Ē′nosh, *the son* of
Seth, *the son* of Adam, [a]*the son*
of God.

CHAPTER 4

4 Then [a]Jesus, being filled with
the Holy Spirit, returned
from the Jordan and [b]was led by
the Spirit [1]into the wilderness,
2 being [1]tempted for forty days
by the devil. And [a]in those days
He ate nothing, and afterward,
when they had ended, He was
hungry.
3 And the devil said to Him,
"If You are [a]the Son of God,
command this stone to become
bread."

19 [a]Mark 6:17 [1]NU *brother's wife*
21 [a]Matt. 3:13–17
22 [a]2 Pet. 1:17
23 [a][Num. 4:3, 35, 39, 43, 47] [b]John 6:42
27 [a]Ezra 2:2; 3:8
31 [a]Zech. 12:12 [b]2 Sam. 5:14; 7:12; Is. 9:7; Jer. 23:5
32 [a]Ruth 4:18–22
34 [a]Gen. 11:24, 26–30; 12:3
36 [a]Gen. 11:12 [b]Gen. 10:22, 24; 11:10–13 [c]Gen. 5:6–32; 9:27; 11:10
38 [a]Gen. 5:1, 2

CHAPTER 4

1 [a]Matt. 4:1–11 [b]Luke 2:27 [1]NU *in*
2 [a]Ex. 34:28 [1]*tested*
3 [a]John 20:31

4 But Jesus answered him,
saying, "It is written, [a]*'Man shall*
not live by bread alone, [1]*but by*
every word of God.'"
5 [1]Then the devil, taking Him
up on a high mountain, showed
Him all the kingdoms of the
world in a moment of time.
6 And the devil said to Him,
"All this authority I will give You,
and their glory; for [a]*this* has
been delivered to me, and I give
it to whomever I wish.
7 "Therefore, if You will worship before me, all will be
Yours."
8 And Jesus answered and said
to him, [1]"Get behind Me, Satan!
[2]For it is written, [a]*'You shall*
worship the LORD *your God, and*
Him only you shall serve.'"
9 [a]Then he brought Him to
Jerusalem, set Him on the pinnacle of the temple, and said to
Him, "If You are the Son of God,
throw Yourself down from here.
10 "For it is written:

[a]*'He shall give His angels*
charge over you,
To keep you,'

11 "and,

[a]*'In their hands they shall*
bear you up,
Lest you dash your foot
against a stone.'"

12 And Jesus answered and
said to him, "It has been said,
[a]*'You shall not* [1]*tempt the* LORD
your God.'"
13 Now when the devil had
ended every [1]temptation, he departed from Him [a]until an opportune time.
14 [a]Then Jesus returned [b]in the
power of the Spirit to [c]Galilee,
and [d]news of Him went out
through all the surrounding region.
15 And He [a]taught in their synagogues, [b]being glorified by all.
16 So He came to [a]Nazareth,
where He had been brought up.
And as His custom was, [b]He
went into the synagogue on the
Sabbath day, and stood up to
read.
17 And He was handed the
book of the prophet Ī·sāi′ah.
And when He had opened the
book, He found the place where
it was written:

18 *"The*[a] *Spirit of the* LORD *is* ★
upon Me,
Because He has anointed Me
To preach the gospel to the
poor;
He has sent Me [1]*to heal the*
brokenhearted,
To proclaim liberty to the
captives
And recovery of sight to the
blind,
To [b]*set at liberty those who*
are [2]*oppressed;*
19 *To proclaim the acceptable*
year of the LORD."

20 Then He closed the book,
and gave *it* back to the atten-
dant and sat down. And the eyes
of all who were in the synagogue were fixed on Him.
21 And He began to say to them,
"Today this Scripture is [a]fulfilled
in your hearing."
22 So all bore witness to Him,
and [a]marveled at the gracious
words which proceeded out of
His mouth. And they said, [b]"Is
this not Joseph's son?"
23 He said to them, "You will

4 [a]Deut. 8:3 [1]NU omits *but by every word of God*
5 [1]NU *And taking Him up, he showed Him*
6 [a][Rev. 13:2, 7]
8 [a]Deut. 6:13; 10:20 [1]NU omits *Get behind Me, Satan* [2]NU, M omit *For*
9 [a]Matt. 4:5–7
10 [a]Ps. 91:11
11 [a]Ps. 91:12
12 [a]Deut. 6:16 [1]*test*
13 [a][Heb. 4:15] [1]*testing*
14 [a]Matt. 4:12 [b]John 4:43 [c]Acts 10:37 [d]Matt. 4:24
15 [a]Matt. 4:23 [b]Is. 52:13
16 [a]Mark 6:1 [b]Acts 13:14–16; 17:2
18 [a]Is. 49:8, 9; 61:1, 2 [b][Dan. 9:24] [1]NU omits *to heal the brokenhearted* [2]*downtrodden*
21 [a]Acts 13:29
22 [a][Ps. 45:2] [b]John 6:42

surely say this proverb to Me,
'Physician, heal yourself! Whatever we have heard done in
[a]Ca·per'na·um,[1] do also here in
[b]Your country.' "
24 Then He said, "Assuredly, I
say to you, no [a]prophet is accepted in his own country.
25 "But I tell you truly, [a]many
widows were in Israel in the
days of E·lī'jah, when the heaven
was shut up three years and six
months, and there was a great
famine throughout all the land;
26 "but to none of them was
E·lī'jah sent except to [1]Zar'-
e·phath, *in the region* of Sī'don,
to a woman *who was* a widow.
27 [a]"And many lepers were in
Israel in the time of E·lī'sha the
prophet, and none of them was
cleansed except Nā'a·man the
Syrian."
28 So all those in the synagogue, when they heard these
things, were [a]filled with [1]wrath,
29 [a]and rose up and thrust Him
out of the city; and they led Him
to the brow of the hill on which
their city was built, that they
might throw Him down over the
cliff.
30 Then [a]passing through the
midst of them, He went His way.
31 Then [a]He went down to
Ca·per'na·um, a city of Galilee,
and was teaching them on the
Sabbaths.
32 And they were [a]astonished
at His teaching, [b]for His word
was with authority.
33 [a]Now in the synagogue there
was a man who had a spirit of
an unclean demon. And he cried
out with a loud voice,
34 saying, "Let *us* alone! What
have we to do with You, Jesus
of Nazareth? Did You come to
destroy us? [a]I know who You
are—[b]the Holy One of God!"
35 But Jesus rebuked him, saying, [1]"Be quiet, and come out
of him!" And when the demon
had thrown him in *their* midst,
it came out of him and did not
hurt him.
36 Then they were all amazed
and spoke among themselves,
saying, "What a word this *is!* For
with authority and power He
commands the unclean spirits,
and they come out."
37 And the report about Him
went out into every place in the
surrounding region.
38 [a]Now He arose from the
synagogue and entered Si-
mon's house. But Simon's wife's
mother was [1]sick with a high
fever, and they [b]made request of
Him concerning her.
39 So He stood over her and
[a]rebuked the fever, and it left
her. And immediately she arose
and served them.
40 [a]When the sun was setting,
all those who had any that
were sick with various diseases
brought them to Him; and He
laid His hands on every one of
them and healed them.
41 [a]And demons also came out
of many, crying out and saying,
[b]"You are [1]the Christ, the Son of
God!" And He, [c]rebuking *them,*
did not allow them to [2]speak,
for they knew that He was the
Christ.
42 [a]Now when it was day, He departed and went into a deserted
place. And the crowd sought
Him and came to Him, and tried
to keep Him from leaving them;
43 but He said to them, "I must
[a]preach the kingdom of God to

23 [a]Matt. 4:13; 11:23 [b]Matt. 13:54 [1]NU *Capharnaum,* here and elsewhere
24 [a]John 4:44
25 [a]1 Kin. 17:9
26 [1]Gr. *Sarepta*
27 [a]2 Kin. 5:1–14
28 [a]Luke 6:11 [1]*rage*
29 [a]John 8:37; 10:31
30 [a]John 8:59; 10:39
31 [a]Matt. 4:13
32 [a]Matt. 7:28, 29 [b][John 6:63; 7:46; 8:26, 28, 38, 47; 12:49, 50]
33 [a]Mark 1:23
34 [a]Luke 4:41 [b]Ps. 16:10
35 [1]Lit. *Be muzzled*
38 [a]Mark 1:29–31 [b]Mark 5:23 [1]*afflicted with*
39 [a]Luke 8:24
40 [a]Matt. 8:16, 17
41 [a]Mark 1:34; 3:11 [b]Mark 8:29 [c]Mark 1:25, 34; 3:11 [1]NU omits *the Christ* [2]Or *say that they knew*
42 [a]Mark 1:35–38
43 [a][John 9:4]

the other cities also, because for
this purpose I have been sent."
44 [a]And He was preaching in
the synagogues of [1]Galilee.

5

So [a]it was, as the multitude
pressed about Him to [b]hear
the word of God, that He stood
by the Lake of Gen·nes′a·ret,
2 and saw two boats standing
by the lake; but the fishermen
had gone from them and were
washing *their* nets.
3 Then He got into one of the
boats, which was Simon's, and
asked him to put out a little from
the land. And He [a]sat down and
taught the multitudes from the
boat.
4 When He had stopped speaking, He said to Simon, [a]"Launch
out into the deep and let down
your nets for a catch."
5 But Simon answered and said
to Him, "Master, we have toiled
all night and caught [a]nothing;
nevertheless [b]at Your word I will
let down the net."
6 And when they had done
this, they caught a great number
of fish, and their net was breaking.
7 So they signaled to *their*
partners in the other boat to
come and help them. And they
came and filled both the boats,
so that they began to sink.
8 When Simon Peter saw *it*, he
fell down at Jesus' knees, saying, [a]"Depart from me, for I am
a sinful man, O Lord!"
9 For he and all who were
with him were [a]astonished at
the catch of fish which they had
taken;
10 and so also *were* James and
John, the sons of Zeb′e·dee, who
were partners with Simon. And
Jesus said to Simon, "Do not be

44 [a]Matt. 4:23; 9:35 [1]NU *Judea*

CHAPTER 5

1 [a]Mark 1:16–20 [b]Acts 13:44

3 [a]John 8:2

4 [a]John 21:6

5 [a]John 21:3 [b]Ps. 33:9

8 [a]1 Kin. 17:18

9 [a]Mark 5:42; 10:24, 26

10 [a]Matt. 4:19

11 [a]Matt. 4:20; 19:27 [1]*left behind*

12 [a]Mark 1:40–44 [b]Lev. 13:14 [1]*begged*

13 [a]John 5:9

14 [a]Matt. 8:4 [b]Lev. 13:1–3; 14:2–32

15 [a]Mark 1:45 [b]John 6:2

16 [a]Luke 9:10 [b]Matt. 14:23

17 [1]NU *with Him to heal*

18 [a]Mark 2:3–12

afraid. [a]From now on you will
catch men."
11 So when they had brought
their boats to land, [a]they [1]for-
sook all and followed Him.
12 [a]And it happened when He
was in a certain city, that behold,
a man who was full of [b]leprosy
saw Jesus; and he fell on *his*
face and [1]implored Him, saying,
"Lord, if You are willing, You can
make me clean."
13 Then He put out *His* hand and
touched him, saying, "I am willing; be cleansed." [a]Immediately
the leprosy left him.
14 [a]And He charged him to tell
no one, "But go and show yourself to the priest, and make an
offering for your cleansing, as a
testimony to them, [b]just as Moses commanded."
15 However, [a]the report went
around concerning Him all the
more; and [b]great multitudes
came together to hear, and to be
healed by Him of their infirmities.
16 [a]So He Himself *often* withdrew into the wilderness and
[b]prayed.
17 Now it happened on a certain day, as He was teaching,
that there were Phar′i·sees and
teachers of the law sitting by,
who had come out of every town
of Galilee, Judea, and Jerusalem. And the power of the Lord
was *present* [1]to heal them.
18 [a]Then behold, men brought
on a bed a man who was paralyzed, whom they sought to
bring in and lay before Him.
19 And when they could not
find how they might bring him
in, because of the crowd, they
went up on the housetop and let
him down with *his* bed through

the tiling into the midst [a]before
Jesus.
20 When He saw their faith, He
said to him, "Man, your sins are
forgiven you."
21 [a]And the scribes and the
Phar'i·sees began to reason, saying, "Who is this who speaks
blasphemies? [b]Who can forgive
sins but God alone?"
22 But when Jesus [a]perceived
their thoughts, He answered and
said to them, "Why are you reasoning in your hearts?
23 "Which is easier, to say, 'Your
sins are forgiven you,' or to say,
'Rise up and walk'?
24 "But that you may know that
the Son of Man has power on
earth to forgive sins"—He said
to the man who was paralyzed,
[a]"I say to you, arise, take up your
bed, and go to your house."
25 Immediately he rose up before them, took up what he had
been lying on, and departed to
his own house, [a]glorifying God.
26 And they were all amazed,
and they [a]glorified God and were
filled with fear, saying, "We have
seen strange things today!"
27 [a]After these things He went
out and saw a tax collector
named Levi, sitting at the tax
office. And He said to him, [b]"Follow Me."
28 So he left all, rose up, and
[a]followed Him.
29 [a]Then Levi gave Him a great
feast in his own house. And
[b]there were a great number of
tax collectors and others who
sat down with them.
30 [1]And their scribes and the
Phar'i·sees [2]complained against
His disciples, saying, [a]"Why do
You eat and drink with tax collectors and sinners?"
31 Jesus answered and said to
them, "Those who are well have
no need of a physician, but those
who are sick.
32 [a]"I have not come to call *the*
righteous, but sinners, to repentance."
33 Then they said to Him,
[a]"Why[1] do the disciples of John
fast often and make prayers,
and likewise those of the Phar'-
i·sees, but Yours eat and drink?"
34 And He said to them, "Can
you make the friends of the
bridegroom fast while the
[a]bridegroom is with them?
35 "But the days will come when
the bridegroom will be taken
away from them; then they will
fast in those days."
36 [a]Then He spoke a parable
to them: "No one [1]puts a piece
from a new garment on an old
one; otherwise the new makes a
tear, and also the piece that was
taken out of the new does not
match the old.
37 "And no one puts new wine
into old wineskins; or else the
new wine will burst the wineskins and be spilled, and the
wineskins will be ruined.
38 "But new wine must be put
into new wineskins, [1]and both
are preserved.
39 "And no one, having drunk
old *wine*, [1]immediately desires
new; for he says, 'The old is [2]bet-
ter.' "

6 Now [a]it happened [1]on the
second Sabbath after the
first that He went through
the grainfields. And His disciples plucked the heads of grain
and ate *them*, rubbing *them* in
their hands.
2 And some of the Phar'i·sees
said to them, "Why are you

19 [a]Matt. 15:30
21 [a]Mark 2:6, 7 [b]Is. 43:25
22 [a]John 2:25
24 [a]Luke 7:14
25 [a]Acts 3:8
26 [a]Luke 1:65; 7:16
27 [a]Matt. 9:9–17 [b]John 12:26; 21:19, 22
28 [a]Mark 10:28
29 [a]Matt. 9:9, 10 [b]Luke 15:1
30 [a]Luke 15:2 [1]NU *But the Pharisees and their scribes* [2]*grumbled*
32 [a]1 Tim. 1:15
33 [a]Matt. 9:14 [1]NU omits *Why do*, making the verse a statement
34 [a]John 3:29
36 [a]Mark 2:21, 22 [1]NU *tears a piece from a new garment and puts it on an old one*
38 [1]NU omits *and both are preserved*
39 [1]NU omits *immediately* [2]NU *good*

CHAPTER 6

1 [a]Matt. 12:1–8 [1]NU *on a Sabbath that He went*

doing [a]what is not lawful to do
on the Sabbath?"
3 But Jesus answering them
said, "Have you not even read
this, [a]what David did when he
was hungry, he and those who
were with him:
4 "how he went into the house
of God, took and ate the showbread, and also gave some to
those with him, [a]which is not
lawful for any but the priests to
eat?"
5 And He said to them, "The
Son of Man is also Lord of the
Sabbath."
6 [a]Now it happened on another
Sabbath, also, that He entered
the synagogue and taught. And
a man was there whose right
hand was withered.
7 So the scribes and Phar'-
i·sees watched Him closely,
whether He would [a]heal on the
Sabbath, that they might find an
[b]accusation against Him.
8 But He [a]knew their thoughts,
and said to the man who had the
withered hand, "Arise and stand
here." And he arose and stood.
9 Then Jesus said to them, "I
will ask you one thing: [a]Is it lawful on the Sabbath to do good
or to do evil, to save life or [1]to
destroy?"
10 And when He had looked
around at them all, He said to
[1]the man, "Stretch out your
hand." And he did so, and his
hand was restored [2]as whole as
the other.
11 But they were filled with
rage, and discussed with one
another what they might do to
Jesus.
12 Now it came to pass in those
days that He went out to the
mountain to pray, and continued
all night in [a]prayer to God.
13 And when it was day, He
called His disciples to *Himself;*
[a]and from them He chose [b]twelve
whom He also named apostles:
14 Simon, [a]whom He also
named Peter, and Andrew his
brother; James and John; Philip
and Bartholomew;
15 Matthew and Thomas; James
the *son* of Al·phae̅'us, and Simon
called the Zealot;
16 Judas [a]*the son* of James, and
[b]Judas Is·car'i·ot who also became a traitor.
17 And He came down with
them and stood on a level place
with a crowd of His disciples
[a]and a great multitude of people
from all Judea and Jerusalem,
and from the seacoast of Ty̅re
and Si̅'don, who came to hear
Him and be healed of their diseases,
18 as well as those who were
tormented with unclean spirits.
And they were healed.
19 And the whole multitude
[a]sought to [b]touch Him, for
[c]power went out from Him and
healed *them* all.
20 Then He lifted up His eyes
toward His disciples, and said:

[a]"Blessed *are you* poor,
For yours is the kingdom
of God.
21 [a]Blessed *are you* who hunger
now,
For you shall be [b]filled.[1]
[c]Blessed *are you* who weep
now,
For you shall [d]laugh.
22 [a]Blessed are you when men
hate you,
And when they [b]exclude
you,

2 [a]Ex. 20:10
3 [a]1 Sam. 21:6
4 [a]Lev. 24:9
6 [a]Mark 3:1–6
7 [a]Luke 13:14; 14:1–6 [b]Luke 20:20
8 [a]Matt. 9:4
9 [a]John 7:23 [1]M *to kill*
10 [1]NU, M *him* [2]NU omits *as whole as the other*
12 [a]Mark 1:35
13 [a]John 6:70 [b]Matt. 10:1
14 [a]John 1:42
16 [a]Jude 1 [b]Luke 22:3–6
17 [a]Mark 3:7, 8
19 [a]Matt. 9:21; 14:36 [b]Mark 5:27, 28 [c]Luke 8:46
20 [a]Matt. 5:3–12; [11:5]
21 [a]Is. 55:1; 65:13 [b][Rev. 7:16] [c][Is. 61:3] [d]Ps. 126:5 [1]*satisfied*
22 [a]1 Pet. 2:19; 3:14; 4:14 [b][John 16:2]

And revile *you,* and cast
out your name as evil,
For the Son of Man's sake.
23 [a]Rejoice in that day and leap
for joy!
For indeed your reward *is*
great in heaven,
For [b]in like manner
their fathers did to the
prophets.

24 "But[a] woe to you [b]who are
rich,
For [c]you have received
your consolation.
25 [a]Woe to you who are full,
For you shall hunger.
[b]Woe to you who laugh now,
For you shall mourn and
[c]weep.
26 [a]Woe [1]to you when [2]all men
speak well of you,
For so did their fathers to
the false prophets.

27 [a]"But I say to you who hear:
Love your enemies, do good to
those who hate you,
28 [a]"bless those who curse you,
and [b]pray for those who spitefully use you.
29 [a]"To him who strikes you on
the *one* cheek, offer the other
also. [b]And from him who takes
away your cloak, do not withhold *your* tunic either.
30 [a]"Give to everyone who asks
of you. And from him who takes
away your goods do not ask
them back.
31 [a]"And just as you want men
to do to you, you also do to them
likewise.
32 [a]"But if you love those who
love you, what credit is that to
you? For even sinners love those
who love them.
33 "And if you do good to those
who do good to you, what credit
is that to you? For even sinners
do the same.
34 [a]"And if you lend *to those*
from whom you hope to receive
back, what credit is that to you?
For even sinners lend to sinners
to receive as much back.
35 "But [a]love your enemies,
[b]do good, and [c]lend, [1]hoping for
nothing in return; and your reward will be great, and [d]you will
be sons of the Most High. For
He is kind to the unthankful and
evil.
36 [a]"Therefore be merciful, just
as your Father also is merciful.
37 [a]"Judge not, and you shall
not be judged. Condemn not,
and you shall not be condemned.
[b]Forgive, and you will be forgiven.
38 [a]"Give, and it will be given
to you: good measure, pressed
down, shaken together, and running over will be put into your
[b]bosom. For [c]with the same measure that you use, it will be measured back to you."
39 And He spoke a parable to
them: [a]"Can the blind lead the
blind? Will they not both fall
into the ditch?
40 [a]"A disciple is not above his
teacher, but everyone who is
perfectly trained will be like his
teacher.
41 [a]"And why do you look at
the speck in your brother's eye,
but do not perceive the plank in
your own eye?
42 "Or how can you say to your
brother, 'Brother, let me remove
the speck that *is* in your eye,'
when you yourself do not see
the plank that *is* in your own
eye? Hypocrite! First remove the
plank from your own eye, and

23 [a]James 1:2 [b]Acts 7:51
24 [a]James 5:1–6 [b]Luke 12:21 [c]Luke 16:25
25 [a][Is. 65:13] [b][Prov. 14:13] [c]James 4:9
26 [a][John 15:19] [1]NU, M omit *to you* [2]M omits *all*
27 [a]Rom. 12:20
28 [a]Rom. 12:14 [b]Acts 7:60
29 [a]Matt. 5:39–42 [b][1 Cor. 6:7]
30 [a]Deut. 15:7, 8
31 [a]Matt. 7:12
32 [a]Matt. 5:46
34 [a]Matt. 5:42
35 [a][Rom. 13:10] [b]Heb. 13:16 [c]Ps. 37:26 [d]Matt. 5:46 [1]*expecting*
36 [a]Matt. 5:48
37 [a]Matt. 7:1–5 [b]Matt. 18:21–35
38 [a][Prov. 19:17; 28:27] [b]Ps. 79:12 [c]James 2:13
39 [a]Matt. 15:14; 23:16
40 [a][John 13:16; 15:20]
41 [a]Matt. 7:3

then you will see clearly to remove the speck that is in your
brother's eye.
43 [a]"For a good tree does not
bear bad fruit, nor does a bad
tree bear good fruit.
44 "For [a]every tree is known
by its own fruit. For *men* do
not gather figs from thorns, nor
do they gather grapes from a
bramble bush.
45 [a]"A good man out of the good
treasure of his heart brings forth
good; and an evil man out of the
evil [1]treasure of his heart brings
forth evil. For out [b]of the abundance of the heart his mouth
speaks.
46 [a]"But why do you call Me
'Lord, Lord,' and not do the
things which I say?
47 [a]"Whoever comes to Me,
and hears My sayings and does
them, I will show you whom he
is like:
48 "He is like a man building a
house, who dug deep and laid
the foundation on the rock. And
when the flood arose, the stream
beat vehemently against that
house, and could not shake it,
for it was [1]founded on the rock.
49 "But he who heard and did
nothing is like a man who built
a house on the earth without a
foundation, against which the
stream beat vehemently; and
immediately it [1]fell. And the ruin
of that house was great."

7 Now when He concluded all
His sayings in the hearing of
the people, He [a]entered Ca·per'-
na·um.
2 And a certain centurion's
servant, who was dear to him,
was sick and ready to die.
3 So when he heard about Jesus, he sent elders of the Jews to
Him, pleading with Him to come
and heal his servant.
4 And when they came to Jesus, they begged Him earnestly,
saying that the one for whom He
should do this was deserving,
5 "for he loves our nation, and
has built us a synagogue."
6 Then Jesus went with them.
And when He was already not
far from the house, the centurion sent friends to Him, saying
to Him, "Lord, do not trouble
Yourself, for I am not worthy
that You should enter under my
roof.
7 "Therefore I did not even
think myself worthy to come to
You. But [a]say the word, and my
servant will be healed.
8 "For I also am a man placed
under [a]authority, having soldiers
under me. And I say to one, 'Go,'
and he goes; and to another,
'Come,' and he comes; and to
my servant, 'Do this,' and he
does *it*."
9 When Jesus heard these
things, He marveled at him, and
turned around and said to the
crowd that followed Him, "I say
to you, I have not found such
great faith, not even in Israel!"
10 And those who were sent,
returning to the house, found
the servant well [1]who had been
sick.
11 Now it happened, the day
after, *that* He went into a city
called Nā'in; and many of His
disciples went with Him, and a
large crowd.
12 And when He came near the
gate of the city, behold, a dead
man was being carried out, the
only son of his mother; and she
was a widow. And a large crowd
from the city was with her.

43 [a]Matt. 7:16–18, 20
44 [a]Matt. 12:33
45 [a]Matt. 12:35 [b]Matt. 12:34 [1]NU omits *treasure of his heart*
46 [a]Mal. 1:6
47 [a]James 1:22–25
48 [1]NU *well built*
49 [1]NU *collapsed*

CHAPTER 7

1 [a]Matt. 8:5–13
7 [a]Ps. 33:9; 107:20
8 [a][Mark 13:34]
10 [1]NU omits *who had been sick*

13 When the Lord saw her, He
had [a]compassion on her and
said to her, [b]"Do not weep."
14 Then He came and touched
the open coffin, and those who
carried *him* stood still. And He
said, "Young man, I say to you,
[a]arise."
15 So he who was dead [a]sat up
and began to speak. And He
[b]presented him to his mother.
16 [a]Then fear [1]came upon all,
and they [b]glorified God, saying,
[c]"A great prophet has risen up
among us"; and, [d]"God has visited His people."
17 And this report about Him
went throughout all Judea and
all the surrounding region.
18 [a]Then the disciples of John
reported to him concerning all
these things.
19 And John, calling two of
his disciples to *him*, sent *them*
to [1]Jesus, saying, "Are You [a]the
Coming One, or [2]do we look for
another?"
20 When the men had come to
Him, they said, "John the Baptist
has sent us to You, saying, 'Are
You the Coming One, or do we
look for another?' "
21 And that very hour He cured
many of [1]infirmities, afflictions,
and evil spirits; and to many
blind He gave sight.
★ 22 [a]Jesus answered and said
to them, "Go and tell John the
things you have seen and heard:
[b]that *the* blind [c]see, *the* lame
[d]walk, *the* lepers are [e]cleansed,
the deaf [f]hear, *the* dead are
raised, [g]*the* poor have the gospel
preached to them.
23 "And blessed is *he* who is not
[1]offended because of Me."
24 [a]When the messengers of
John had departed, He began
to speak to the multitudes concerning John: "What did you go
out into the wilderness to see? A
reed shaken by the wind?
25 "But what did you go out to
see? A man clothed in soft garments? Indeed those who are
gorgeously appareled and live
in luxury are in kings' courts.
26 "But what did you go out to
see? A prophet? Yes, I say to you,
and more than a prophet.
27 "This is *he* of whom it is written: ★

> [a]*'Behold, I send My*
> *messenger before Your*
> *face,*
> *Who will prepare Your way*
> *before You.'*

28 "For I say to you, among
those born of women there is
[1]not a [a]greater prophet than
John the Baptist; but he who is
least in the kingdom of God is
greater than he."
29 And when all the people
heard *Him*, even the tax collectors [1]justified God, [a]having been
baptized with the baptism of
John.
30 But the Phar'i·sees and [1]lawyers rejected [a]the will of God
for themselves, not having been
baptized by him.
31 [1]And the Lord said, [a]"To what
then shall I liken the men of this
generation, and what are they
like?
32 "They are like children sitting in the marketplace and calling to one another, saying:

> 'We played the flute for you,
> And you did not dance;
> We mourned to you,
> And you did not weep.'

13 [a]John 11:35 [b]Luke 8:52
14 [a]Acts 9:40
15 [a]John 11:44 [b]2 Kin. 4:36
16 [a]Luke 1:65 [b]Luke 5:26 [c]Luke 24:19 [d]Luke 1:68 [1]*seized them all*
18 [a]Matt. 11:2–19
19 [a][Zech. 9:9] [1]NU *the Lord* [2]*should we expect*
21 [1]*illnesses*
22 [a]Matt. 11:4 [b]Is. 35:5, 6 [c]John 9:7 [d]Matt. 15:31 [e]Luke 17:12–14 [f]Mark 7:37 [g][Is. 61:1–3]
23 [1]*caused to stumble*
24 [a]Matt. 11:7
27 [a]Is. 40:3; Mal. 3:1
28 [a][Luke 1:15] [1]NU *none greater than John;*
29 [a]Luke 3:12 [1]*declared the righteousness of*
30 [a]Acts 20:27 [1]*the experts in the law*
31 [a]Matt. 11:16 [1]NU, M omit *And the Lord said*

33 "For [a]John the Baptist came
[b]neither eating bread nor drinking wine, and you say, 'He has a
demon.'
34 "The Son of Man has come
[a]eating and drinking, and you
say, 'Look, a glutton and a [1]wine-
bibber, a friend of tax collectors
and sinners!'
35 [a]"But wisdom is justified by
all her children."
36 [a]Then one of the Phar′i·sees
asked Him to eat with him.
And He went to the Phar′i·see's
house, and sat down to eat.
37 And behold, a woman in the
city who was a sinner, when
she knew that *Jesus* sat at the
table in the Phar′i·see's house,
brought an alabaster flask of
fragrant oil,
38 and stood at His feet behind
Him weeping; and she began
to wash His feet with her tears,
and wiped *them* with the hair
of her head; and she kissed His
feet and anointed *them* with the
fragrant oil.
39 Now when the Phar′i·see who
had invited Him saw *this*, he
spoke to himself, saying, [a]"This
Man, if He were a prophet, would
know who and what manner of
woman *this is* who is touching
Him, for she is a sinner."
40 And Jesus answered and said
to him, "Simon, I have something to say to you." So he said,
"Teacher, say it."
41 "There was a certain creditor
who had two debtors. One owed
five hundred [a]denarii, and the
other fifty.
42 "And when they had nothing
with which to repay, he freely
forgave them both. Tell Me,
therefore, which of them will
love him more?"

33 [a]Matt. 3:1 [b]Luke 1:15
34 [a]Luke 15:2 [1]An excessive drinker
35 [a]Matt. 11:19
36 [a]John 11:2
39 [a]Luke 15:2
41 [a]Matt. 18:28
44 [a]Gen. 18:4; 19:2; 43:24
45 [a]Rom. 16:16
46 [a]Ps. 23:5
47 [a][1 Tim. 1:14]
48 [a]Matt. 9:2
49 [a]Luke 5:21
50 [a]Matt. 9:22
CHAPTER 8
1 [1]*proclaiming the good news*
2 [a]Matt. 27:55 [b]Mark 16:9 [1]*sicknesses*

43 Simon answered and said, "I
suppose the *one* whom he forgave more." And He said to him,
"You have rightly judged."
44 Then He turned to the
woman and said to Simon, "Do
you see this woman? I entered
your house; you gave Me no
[a]water for My feet, but she has
washed My feet with her tears
and wiped *them* with the hair of
her head.
45 "You gave Me no [a]kiss, but
this woman has not ceased to
kiss My feet since the time I
came in.
46 [a]"You did not anoint My head
with oil, but this woman has
anointed My feet with fragrant
oil.
47 [a]"Therefore I say to you, her
sins, which *are* many, are forgiven, for she loved much. But
to whom little is forgiven, *the
same* loves little."
48 Then He said to her, [a]"Your
sins are forgiven."
49 And those who sat at the
table with Him began to say to
themselves, [a]"Who is this who
even forgives sins?"
50 Then He said to the woman,
[a]"Your faith has saved you. Go in
peace."
8 Now it came to pass, afterward, that He went through
every city and village, preaching
and [1]bringing the glad tidings
of the kingdom of God. And the
twelve *were* with Him,
2 and [a]certain women who had
been healed of evil spirits and
[1]infirmities—Mary called Mag′-
da·lēne, [b]out of whom had come
seven demons,
3 and Jō·an′na the wife of
Chū′za, Her′od's steward, and
Susanna, and many others who

provided for [1]Him from their
[2]substance.
4 [a]And when a great multitude had gathered, and they had
come to Him from every city, He
spoke by a parable:
5 "A sower went out to sow his
seed. And as he sowed, some
fell by the wayside; and it was
trampled down, and the birds of
the air devoured it.
6 "Some fell on rock; and as
soon as it sprang up, it withered
away because it lacked moisture.
7 "And some fell among thorns,
and the thorns sprang up with it
and choked it.
8 "But others fell on good
ground, sprang up, and yielded
[1]a crop a hundredfold." When
He had said these things He
cried, [a]"He who has ears to hear,
let him hear!"
9 [a]Then His disciples asked
Him, saying, "What does this
parable mean?"
★ 10 And He said, "To you it has
been given to know the [1]myster-
ies of the kingdom of God, but
to the rest *it is given* in parables,
that

[a]*'Seeing they may not see,*
And hearing they may not
understand.'

11 [a]"Now the parable is this:
The seed is the [b]word of God.
12 "Those by the wayside are
the ones who hear; then the
devil comes and takes away the
word out of their hearts, lest they
should believe and be saved.
13 "But the ones on the rock
are those who, when they hear,
receive the word with joy; and
these have no root, who believe
for a while and in time of [1]temp-
tation fall away.
14 "Now the ones *that* fell
among thorns are those who,
when they have heard, go out
and are choked with cares,
[a]riches, and pleasures of life,
and bring no fruit to maturity.
15 "But the ones *that* fell on
the good ground are those who,
having heard the word with a
noble and good heart, keep *it*
and bear fruit with [a]patience.[1]
16 [a]"No one, when he has lit a
lamp, covers it with a vessel or
puts *it* under a bed, but sets *it*
on a lampstand, that those who
enter may see the [b]light.
17 [a]"For nothing is secret that
will not be [b]revealed, nor *any-*
thing hidden that will not be
known and come to light.
18 "Therefore take heed how
you hear. [a]For whoever has, to
him *more* will be given; and
whoever does not have, even
what he [1]seems to [b]have will be
taken from him."
19 [a]Then His mother and brothers came to Him, and could not
approach Him because of the
crowd.
20 And it was told Him *by some,*
who said, "Your mother and Your
brothers are standing outside,
desiring to see You."
21 But He answered and said
to them, "My mother and My
brothers are these who hear the
word of God and do it."
22 [a]Now it happened, on a certain day, that He got into a boat
with His disciples. And He said
to them, "Let us cross over to the
other side of the lake." And they
launched out.
23 But as they sailed He fell
asleep. And a windstorm came

3 [1]NU, M *them* [2]*possessions*
4 [a]Mark 4:1–9
8 [a]Luke 14:35 [1]Lit. *fruit*
9 [a]Matt. 13:10–23
10 [a]Is. 6:9 [1]*secret* or *hidden truths*
11 [a][1 Pet. 1:23] [b]Luke 5:1; 11:28
13 [1]*testing*
14 [a]1 Tim. 6:9, 10
15 [a][Heb. 10:36–39] [1]*endurance*
16 [a]Luke 11:33 [b]Matt. 5:14
17 [a]Luke 12:2 [b][2 Cor. 5:10]
18 [a]Matt. 25:29 [b]Matt. 13:12 [1]*thinks that he has*
19 [a]Mark 3:31–35
22 [a]Matt. 8:23–27

down on the lake, and they were filling *with water,* and were in [1]jeopardy.

24 And they came to Him and awoke Him, saying, "Master, Master, we are perishing!" Then He arose and rebuked the wind and the raging of the water. And they ceased, and there was a calm.

25 But He said to them, [a]"Where is your faith?" And they were afraid, and marveled, saying to one another, [b]"Who can this be? For He commands even the winds and water, and they obey Him!"

26 [a]Then they sailed to the country of the [1]Gad′a·rēnes, which is opposite Galilee.

27 And when He stepped out on the land, there met Him a certain man from the city who had demons [1]for a long time. And he wore no clothes, nor did he live in a house but in the tombs.

28 When he saw Jesus, he [a]cried out, fell down before Him, and with a loud voice said, [b]"What have I to do with [c]You, Jesus, Son of the Most High God? I beg You, do not torment me!"

29 For He had commanded the unclean spirit to come out of the man. For it had often seized him, and he was kept under guard, bound with chains and shackles; and he broke the bonds and was driven by the demon into the wilderness.

30 Jesus asked him, saying, "What is your name?" And he said, "Legion," because many demons had entered him.

31 And they begged Him that He would not command them to go out [a]into the abyss.

32 Now a herd of many [a]swine was feeding there on the mountain. So they begged Him that He would permit them to enter them. And He permitted them.

33 Then the demons went out of the man and entered the swine, and the herd ran violently down the steep place into the lake and drowned.

34 When those who fed *them* saw what had happened, they fled and told *it* in the city and in the country.

35 Then they went out to see what had happened, and came to Jesus, and found the man from whom the demons had departed, [a]sitting at the [b]feet of Jesus, clothed and in his [c]right mind. And they were afraid.

36 They also who had seen *it* told them by what means he who had been demon-possessed was [1]healed.

37 [a]Then the whole multitude of the surrounding region of the [1]Gad′a·rēnes [b]asked Him to [c]depart from them, for they were seized with great [d]fear. And He got into the boat and returned.

38 Now [a]the man from whom the demons had departed begged Him that he might be with Him. But Jesus sent him away, saying,

39 "Return to your own house, and tell what great things God has done for you." And he went his way and proclaimed throughout the whole city what great things Jesus had done for him.

40 So it was, when Jesus returned, that the multitude welcomed Him, for they were all waiting for Him.

41 [a]And behold, there came a man named Jā·ī′rus, and he was a ruler of the synagogue.

23 [1]*danger*
25 [a]Luke 9:41 [b]Luke 4:36; 5:26
26 [a]Mark 5:1–17 [1]NU *Gerasenes*
27 [1]NU *and for a long time wore no clothes*
28 [a]Mark 1:26; 9:26 [b]Mark 1:23, 24 [c]Luke 4:41
31 [a][Rev. 20:1, 3]
32 [a]Lev. 11:7
35 [a][Matt. 11:28] [b]Luke 10:39; 17:16 [c][2 Tim. 1:7]
36 [1]*delivered*
37 [a]Matt. 8:34 [b]Luke 4:34 [c]Acts 16:39 [d]Luke 5:26 [1]NU *Gerasenes*
38 [a]Mark 5:18–20
41 [a]Mark 5:22–43

And he fell down at Jesus' feet
and begged Him to come to his
house,
42 for he had an only daughter
about twelve years of age, and
she [a]was dying. But as He went,
the multitudes thronged Him.
43 [a]Now a woman, having a
[b]flow of blood for twelve years,
who had spent all her livelihood
on physicians and could not be
healed by any,
44 came from behind and
[a]touched the border of His garment. And immediately her flow
of blood stopped.
45 And Jesus said, "Who
touched Me?" When all denied
it, Peter [1]and those with him
said, "Master, the multitudes
throng and press You, [2]and You
say, 'Who touched Me?' "
46 But Jesus said, "Somebody
touched Me, for I perceived
[a]power going out from Me."
47 Now when the woman saw
that she was not hidden, she
came trembling; and falling
down before Him, she declared
to Him in the presence of all
the people the reason she had
touched Him and how she was
healed immediately.
48 And He said to her, "Daughter, [1]be of good cheer; [a]your
faith has made you well. [b]Go in
peace."
49 [a]While He was still speaking,
someone came from the ruler of
the synagogue's *house*, saying
to him, "Your daughter is dead.
Do not trouble the [1]Teacher."
50 But when Jesus heard *it*, He
answered him, saying, "Do not
be afraid; [a]only believe, and she
will be made well."
51 When He came into the
house, He permitted no one to
go [1]in except [2]Peter, James, and
John, and the father and mother
of the girl.
52 Now all wept and mourned
for her; but He said, [a]"Do not
weep; she is not dead, [b]but sleeping."
53 And they ridiculed Him,
knowing that she was dead.
54 But He [1]put them all outside,
took her by the hand and called,
saying, "Little girl, [a]arise."
55 Then her spirit returned, and
she arose immediately. And He
commanded that she be given
something to eat.
56 And her parents were astonished, but [a]He charged them to
tell no one what had happened.

9 Then [a]He called His twelve
disciples together and [b]gave
them power and authority over
all demons, and to cure diseases.
2 [a]He sent them to preach the
kingdom of God and to heal the
sick.
3 [a]And He said to them, "Take
nothing for the journey, neither
staffs nor bag nor bread nor
money; and do not have two tunics apiece.
4 [a]"Whatever house you enter,
stay there, and from there depart.
5 [a]"And whoever will not receive you, when you go out of
that city, [b]shake off the very dust
from your feet as a testimony
against them."
6 [a]So they departed and went
through the towns, preaching
the gospel and healing everywhere.
7 [a]Now Her'od the tetrarch
heard of all that was done by
Him; and he was perplexed,

42 [a]Luke 7:2
43 [a]Matt. 9:20 [b]Luke 15:19–22
44 [a]Mark 6:56
45 [1]NU omits *and those with him* [2]NU omits the rest of v. 45.
46 [a]Mark 5:30
48 [a]Luke 7:50 [b]John 8:11 [1]NU omits *be of good cheer*
49 [a]Mark 5:35 [1]NU adds *anymore*
50 [a][Mark 11:22–24]
51 [1]NU adds *with Him* [2]NU, M *Peter, John, and James*
52 [a]Luke 7:13 [b][John 11:11, 13]
54 [a]John 11:43 [1]NU omits *put them all outside*
56 [a]Matt. 8:4; 9:30

CHAPTER 9

1 [a]Matt. 10:1, 2 [b][John 14:12]
2 [a]Matt. 10:7, 8
3 [a]Luke 10:4–12; 22:35
4 [a]Mark 6:10
5 [a]Matt. 10:14 [b]Acts 13:51
6 [a]Mark 6:12
7 [a]Matt. 14:1, 2

because it was said by some that
John had risen from the dead,
8 and by some that E·lī′jah
had appeared, and by others
that one of the old prophets had
risen again.
9 Her′od said, "John I have
beheaded, but who is this of
whom I hear such things?" [a]So
he sought to see Him.
10 [a]And the apostles, when they
had returned, told Him all that
they had done. [b]Then He took
them and went aside privately
into a deserted place belonging
to the city called Beth·sā′i·da.
11 But when the multitudes
knew *it*, they followed Him; and
He received them and spoke to
them about the kingdom of God,
and healed those who had need
of healing.
12 [a]When the day began to
wear away, the twelve came and
said to Him, "Send the multitude
away, that they may go into the
surrounding towns and country,
and lodge and get provisions;
for we are in a deserted place
here."
13 But He said to them, "You
give them something to eat."
And they said, "We have no
more than five loaves and two
fish, unless we go and buy food
for all these people."
14 For there were about five
thousand men. Then He said to
His disciples, "Make them sit
down in groups of fifty."
15 And they did so, and made
them all sit down.
16 Then He took the five loaves
and the two fish, and looking
up to heaven, He [a]blessed and
broke them, and gave *them* to
the disciples to set before the
multitude.
17 So they all ate and were
[1]filled, and twelve baskets of the
leftover fragments were taken
up by them.
18 [a]And it happened, as He was
alone praying, *that* His disciples
joined Him, and He asked them,
saying, "Who do the crowds say
that I am?"
19 So they answered and said,
[a]"John the Baptist, but some *say*
E·lī′jah; and others *say* that one
of the old prophets has risen
again."
20 He said to them, "But who
do you say that I am?" [a]Peter
answered and said, "The Christ
of God."
21 [a]And He strictly warned and
commanded them to tell this to
no one,
22 saying, [a]"The Son of Man
must suffer many things, and
be rejected by the elders and
chief priests and scribes, and be
killed, and be raised the third
day."
23 [a]Then He said to *them* all,
"If anyone desires to come after
Me, let him deny himself, and
take up his cross [1]daily, and follow Me.
24 [a]"For whoever desires to save
his life will lose it, but whoever
loses his life for My sake will
save it.
25 [a]"For what profit is it to a man
if he gains the whole world, and
is himself destroyed or lost?
26 [a]"For whoever is ashamed of
Me and My words, of him the
Son of Man will be [b]ashamed
when He comes in His *own*
glory, and *in His* Father's, and of
the holy angels.
27 [a]"But I tell you truly, there
are some standing here who

9 [a]Luke 23:8
10 [a]Mark 6:30 [b]Matt. 14:13
12 [a]John 6:1, 5
16 [a]Luke 22:19; 24:30
17 [1]*satisfied*
18 [a]Matt. 16:13–16
19 [a]Matt. 14:2
20 [a]John 6:68, 69
21 [a]Matt. 8:4; 16:20
22 [a]Matt. 16:21; 17:22
23 [a]Matt. 10:38; 16:24 [1]M omits *daily*
24 [a][John 12:25]
25 [a]Mark 8:36
26 [a][Rom. 1:16] [b]Matt. 10:33
27 [a]Matt. 16:28

shall not taste death till they see
the kingdom of God."
28 [a]Now it came to pass, about
eight days after these sayings,
that He took Peter, John, and
James and went up on the mountain to pray.
29 As He prayed, the appearance of His face was altered,
and His robe *became* white *and*
glistening.
30 And behold, two men talked
with Him, who were [a]Moses and
[b]E·lī'jah,
31 who appeared in glory and
spoke of His [1]decease which He
was about to accomplish at Jerusalem.
32 But Peter and those with
him [a]were heavy with sleep; and
when they were fully awake,
they saw His glory and the two
men who stood with Him.
33 Then it happened, as they
were parting from Him, *that*
Peter said to Jesus, "Master, it is
good for us to be here; and let us
make three [1]tabernacles: one for
You, one for Moses, and one for
E·lī'jah"—not knowing what he
said.
34 While he was saying this, a
cloud came and overshadowed
them; and they were fearful as
they entered the [a]cloud.
35 And a voice came out of the
cloud, saying, [a]"This is [1]My beloved Son. [b]Hear Him!"
36 When the voice had ceased,
Jesus was found alone. [a]But they
kept quiet, and told no one in
those days any of the things
they had seen.
37 [a]Now it happened on the
next day, when they had come
down from the mountain, that a
great multitude met Him.
38 Suddenly a man from the
multitude cried out, saying,
"Teacher, I implore You, look on
my son, for he is my only child.
39 "And behold, a spirit seizes
him, and he suddenly cries out;
it convulses him so that he foams
at the mouth; and it departs
from him with great difficulty,
bruising him.
40 "So I implored Your disciples
to cast it out, but they could
not."
41 Then Jesus answered and
said, "O [1]faithless and perverse
generation, how long shall I be
with you and [2]bear with you?
Bring your son here."
42 And as he was still coming,
the demon threw him down and
convulsed *him.* Then Jesus rebuked the unclean spirit, healed
the child, and gave him back to
his father.
43 And they were all amazed at
the majesty of God. But while
everyone marveled at all the
things which Jesus did, He said
to His disciples,
44 [a]"Let these words sink down
into your ears, for the Son of
Man is about to be betrayed into
the hands of men."
45 [a]But they did not understand
this saying, and it was hidden
from them so that they did not
perceive it; and they were afraid
to ask Him about this saying.
46 [a]Then a dispute arose among
them as to which of them would
be greatest.
47 And Jesus, [a]perceiving the
thought of their heart, took a
[b]little child and set him by Him,
48 and said to them, [a]"Whoever
receives this little child in My
name receives Me; and [b]whoever
receives Me [c]receives Him who

28 [a]Mark 9:2–8
30 [a]Heb. 11:23–29 [b]2 Kin. 2:1–11
31 [1]Death, lit. *departure*
32 [a]Dan. 8:18; 10:9
33 [1]*tents*
34 [a]Ex. 13:21
35 [a][Matt. 3:17; 12:18] [b]Acts 3:22 [1]NU *My Son, the Chosen One*
36 [a]Matt. 17:9
37 [a]Mark 9:14–27
41 [1]*unbelieving* [2]*put up with*
44 [a]Matt. 17:22
45 [a]Mark 9:32
46 [a]Matt. 18:1–5
47 [a]Matt. 9:4 [b]Luke 18:17
48 [a]Matt. 18:5 [b]John 12:44 [c]John 13:20

sent Me. [d]For he who is least
among you all will be great."
49 [a]Now John answered and
said, "Master, we saw someone casting out demons in Your
name, and we forbade him because he does not follow with
us."
50 But Jesus said to him, "Do
not forbid *him,* for [a]he who is
not against [1]us is on [2]our side."
51 Now it came to pass, when
the time had come for [a]Him to
be received up, that He steadfastly set His face to go to Jerusalem,
52 and sent messengers before
His face. And as they went, they
entered a village of the Samaritans, to prepare for Him.
53 But [a]they did not receive
Him, because His face was *set*
for the journey to Jerusalem.
54 And when His disciples
[a]James and John saw *this,* they
said, "Lord, do You want us to
command fire to come down
from heaven and consume them,
[1]just as [b]E·lí'jah did?"
55 But He turned and rebuked
them, [1]and said, "You do not
know what manner of [a]spirit
you are of.
56 [1]"For [a]the Son of Man did not
come to destroy men's lives but
to save *them.*" And they went to
another village.
57 [a]Now it happened as they
journeyed on the road, *that*
someone said to Him, "Lord,
I will follow You wherever You
go."
58 And Jesus said to him, "Foxes
have holes and birds of the air
have nests, but the Son of Man
[a]has nowhere to lay *His* head."
59 [a]Then He said to another,
"Follow Me." But he said, "Lord,
let me first go and bury my father."
60 Jesus said to him, "Let the
dead bury their own dead, but
you go and preach the kingdom
of God."
61 And another also said, "Lord,
[a]I will follow You, but let me first
go *and* bid them farewell who
are at my house."
62 But Jesus said to him, "No
one, having put his hand to the
plow, and looking back, is [a]fit
for the kingdom of God."

10 After these things the
Lord appointed [1]seventy
others also, and [a]sent them two
by two before His face into every
city and place where He Himself
was about to go.
2 Then He said to them, [a]"The
harvest truly *is* great, but the
laborers *are* few; therefore [b]pray
the Lord of the harvest to send
out laborers into His harvest.
3 "Go your way; [a]behold, I
send you out as lambs among
wolves.
4 [a]"Carry neither money bag,
knapsack, nor sandals; and
[b]greet no one along the road.
5 [a]"But whatever house you
enter, first say, 'Peace to this
house.'
6 "And if a son of peace is
there, your peace will rest on it;
if not, it will return to you.
7 [a]"And remain in the same
house, [b]eating and drinking
such things as they give, for [c]the
laborer is worthy of his wages.
Do not go from house to house.
8 "Whatever city you enter,
and they receive you, eat such
things as are set before you.
9 [a]"And heal the sick there,
and say to them, [b]'The kingdom
of God has come near to you.'

48 [d]Eph. 3:8
49 [a]Mark 9:38–40
50 [a]Luke 11:23 [1]NU *you* [2]NU *your*
51 [a]Mark 16:19
53 [a]John 4:4, 9
54 [a]Mark 3:17 [b]2 Kin. 1:10, 12 [1]NU omits *just as Elijah did*
55 [a][2 Tim. 1:7] [1]NU omits the rest of v. 55.
56 [a]John 3:17; 12:47 [1]NU omits *For the Son of Man did not come to destroy men's lives but to save them.*
57 [a]Matt. 8:19–22
58 [a]Luke 2:7; 8:23
59 [a]Matt. 8:21, 22
61 [a]1 Kin. 19:20
62 [a]2 Tim. 4:10

CHAPTER 10

1 [a]Mark 6:7 [1]NU *seventy-two others*
2 [a]John 4:35 [b]2 Thess. 3:1
3 [a]Matt. 10:16
4 [a]Luke 9:3–5 [b]2 Kin. 4:29
5 [a]Matt. 10:12
7 [a]Matt. 10:11 [b]1 Cor. 10:27 [c]1 Tim. 5:18
9 [a]Mark 3:15 [b]Matt. 3:2; 10:7

10 "But whatever city you enter, and they do not receive you, go out into its streets and say,
11 [a]'The very dust of your city which clings to [1]us we wipe off against you. Nevertheless know this, that the kingdom of God has come near you.'
12 [1]"But I say to you that [a]it will be more tolerable in that Day for Sod′om than for that city.
13 [a]"Woe to you, Chō·rā′zin! Woe to you, Beth·sā′i·da! [b]For if the mighty works which were done in you had been done in Tȳre and Sī′don, they would have repented long ago, sitting in sackcloth and ashes.
14 "But it will be more tolerable for Tȳre and Sī′don at the judgment than for you.
15 [a]"And you, Ca·per′na·um, [1]who are [b]exalted to heaven, [c]will be brought down to Hā′dēs.
16 [a]"He who hears you hears Me, [b]he who rejects you rejects Me, and [c]he who rejects Me rejects Him who sent Me."
17 Then [a]the [1]seventy returned with joy, saying, "Lord, even the demons are subject to us in Your name."
18 And He said to them, [a]"I saw Satan fall like lightning from heaven.
19 "Behold, [a]I give you the authority to trample on serpents and scorpions, and over all the power of the enemy, and nothing shall by any means hurt you.
20 "Nevertheless do not rejoice in this, that the spirits are subject to you, but [1]rather rejoice because [a]your names are written in heaven."
21 [a]In that hour Jesus rejoiced in the Spirit and said, "I thank You, Father, Lord of heaven and earth, that You have hidden these things from *the* wise and prudent and revealed them to babes. Even so, Father, for so it seemed good in Your sight.
22 [a]"All[1] things have been delivered to Me by My Father, and [b]no one knows who the Son is except the Father, and who the Father is except the Son, and *the one* to whom the Son wills to reveal *Him.*"
23 Then He turned to *His* disciples and said privately, [a]"Blessed *are* the eyes which see the things you see;
24 "for I tell you [a]that many prophets and kings have desired to see what you see, and have not seen *it,* and to hear what you hear, and have not heard *it.*"
25 And behold, a certain [1]lawyer stood up and tested Him, saying, [a]"Teacher, what shall I do to inherit eternal life?"
26 He said to him, "What is written in the law? What is your reading *of it?*"
27 So he answered and said, [a]"*'You shall love the* LORD *your God with all your heart, with all your soul, with all your strength, and with all your mind,'* and [b]*'your neighbor as yourself.'* "
28 And He said to him, "You have answered rightly; do this and [a]you will live."
29 But he, wanting to [a]justify himself, said to Jesus, "And who is my neighbor?"
30 Then Jesus answered and said: "A certain *man* went down from Jerusalem to Jericho, and fell among [1]thieves, who stripped him of his clothing, wounded

11 [a]Acts 13:51 [1]NU *our feet*
12 [a]Matt. 10:15; 11:24 [1]NU, M omit *But*
13 [a]Matt. 11:21–23 [b]Ezek. 3:6
15 [a]Matt. 11:23 [b]Is. 14:13–15 [c]Ezek. 26:20 [1]NU *will you be exalted to heaven? You will be thrust down to Hades!*
16 [a]John 13:20 [b]1 Thess. 4:8 [c]John 5:23
17 [a]Luke 10:1 [1]NU *seventy-two*
18 [a]John 12:31
19 [a]Mark 16:18
20 [a]Is. 4:3 [1]NU, M omit *rather*
21 [a]Matt. 11:25–27
22 [a]John 3:35; 5:27; 17:2 [b][John 1:18; 6:44, 46] [1]M *And turning to the disciples He said, "All*
23 [a]Matt. 13:16, 17
24 [a]1 Pet. 1:10, 11
25 [a]Matt. 19:16–19; 22:35 [1]*expert in the law*
27 [a]Deut. 6:5 [b]Lev. 19:18
28 [a]Ezek. 20:11, 13, 21
29 [a]Luke 16:15
30 [1]*robbers*

him, and departed, leaving *him*
half dead.
31 "Now by chance a certain
priest came down that road. And
when he saw him, [a]he passed by
on the other side.
32 "Likewise a Lē′vīte, when he
arrived at the place, came and
looked, and passed by on the
other side.
33 "But a certain [a]Samaritan,
as he journeyed, came where he
was. And when he saw him, he
had [b]compassion.
34 "So he went to *him* and ban-
daged his wounds, pouring on
oil and wine; and he set him on
his own animal, brought him to
an inn, and took care of him.
35 "On the next day, [1]when
he departed, he took out two
[a]denarii, gave *them* to the inn-
keeper, and said to him, 'Take
care of him; and whatever more
you spend, when I come again, I
will repay you.'
36 "So which of these three do
you think was neighbor to him
who fell among the thieves?"
37 And he said, "He who showed
mercy on him." Then Jesus said
to him, [a]"Go and do likewise."
38 Now it happened as they
went that He entered a certain
village; and a certain woman
named [a]Martha welcomed Him
into her house.
39 And she had a sister called
Mary, [a]who also [b]sat at [1]Jesus'
feet and heard His word.
40 But Martha was distracted
with much serving, and she approached Him and said, "Lord,
do You not care that my sister has left me to serve alone?
Therefore tell her to help me."
41 And [1]Jesus answered and
said to her, "Martha, Martha,
you are worried and troubled
about many things.
42 "But [a]one thing is needed,
and Mary has chosen that good
part, which will not be taken
away from her."

11 Now it came to pass, as
He was praying in a cer-
tain place, when He ceased, *that*
one of His disciples said to Him,
"Lord, teach us to pray, as John
also taught his disciples."
2 So He said to them, "When
you pray, say:

[a]Our[1] Father [2]in heaven,
Hallowed be Your name.
Your kingdom come.
[3]Your will be done
On earth as *it is* in heaven.
3 Give us day by day our daily
bread.
4 And [a]forgive us our sins,
For we also forgive everyone
who is indebted to us.
And do not lead us into
temptation,
[1]But deliver us from the evil
one."

5 And He said to them, "Which
of you shall have a friend, and
go to him at midnight and say
to him, 'Friend, lend me three
loaves;
6 'for a friend of mine has
come to me on his journey, and I
have nothing to set before him';
7 "and he will answer from
within and say, 'Do not trouble
me; the door is now shut, and
my children are with me in bed;
I cannot rise and give to you'?
8 "I say to you, [a]though he will
not rise and give to him because
he is his friend, yet because of
his persistence he will rise and
give him as many as he needs.

31 [a]Ps. 38:11
33 [a]John 4:9 [b]Luke 15:20
35 [a]Matt. 20:2 [1]NU omits *when he departed*
37 [a]Prov. 14:21
38 [a]John 11:1; 12:2, 3
39 [a][1 Cor. 7:32–40] [b]Acts 22:3 [1]NU *the Lord's*
41 [1]NU *the Lord*
42 [a][Ps. 27:4]

CHAPTER 11

2 [a]Matt. 6:9–13 [1]NU omits *Our* [2]NU omits *in heaven* [3]NU omits the rest of v. 2.
4 [a][Eph. 4:32] [1]NU omits *But deliver us from the evil one*
8 [a][Luke 18:1–5]

9 [a]"So I say to you, ask, and it
will be given to you; [b]seek, and
you will find; knock, and it will
be opened to you.
10 "For everyone who asks receives, and he who seeks finds,
and to him who knocks it will be
opened.
11 [a]"If a son asks for [1]bread
from any father among you, will
he give him a stone? Or if *he*
asks for a fish, will he give him
a serpent instead of a fish?
12 "Or if he asks for an egg, will
he offer him a scorpion?
13 "If you then, being evil, know
how to give [a]good gifts to your
children, how much more will
your heavenly Father give the
Holy Spirit to those who ask
Him!"
14 [a]And He was casting out a
demon, and it was mute. So it
was, when the demon had gone
out, that the mute spoke; and the
multitudes marveled.
15 But some of them said, [a]"He
casts out demons by [1]Bē·el′-
ze·bub, the ruler of the demons."
16 Others, testing *Him,* [a]sought
from Him a sign from heaven.
17 [a]But [b]He, knowing their
thoughts, said to them: "Every
kingdom divided against itself
is brought to desolation, and a
house *divided* against a house
falls.
18 "If Satan also is divided
against himself, how will his
kingdom stand? Because you
say I cast out demons by Bē·el′-
ze·bub.
19 "And if I cast out demons by
Bē·el′ze·bub, by whom do your
sons cast *them* out? Therefore
they will be your judges.
20 "But if I cast out demons
[a]with the finger of God, surely
the kingdom of God has come
upon you.
21 [a]"When a strong man, fully
armed, guards his own palace,
his goods are in peace.
22 "But [a]when a stronger than
he comes upon him and overcomes him, he takes from him
all his armor in which he trusted,
and divides his [1]spoils.
23 [a]"He who is not with Me is
against Me, and he who does not
gather with Me scatters.
24 [a]"When an unclean spirit
goes out of a man, he goes
through dry places, seeking rest;
and finding none, he says, 'I will
return to my house from which I
came.'
25 "And when he comes, he
finds *it* swept and put in order.
26 "Then he goes and takes with
him seven other spirits more
wicked than himself, and they
enter and dwell there; and [a]the
last *state* of that man is worse
than the first."
27 And it happened, as He
spoke these things, that a certain woman from the crowd
raised her voice and said to
Him, [a]"Blessed *is* the womb that
bore You, and *the* breasts which
nursed You!"
28 But He said, [a]"More than
that, blessed *are* those who hear
the word of God and keep it!"
29 [a]And while the crowds were
thickly gathered together, He
began to say, "This is an evil
generation. It seeks a [b]sign, and
no sign will be given to it except
the sign of Jonah [1]the prophet.
30 "For as [a]Jonah became a sign
to the Nin′e·vītes, so also the
Son of Man will be to this generation.
31 [a]"The queen of the South will

9 [a][John 15:7] [b]Is. 55:6
11 [a]Matt. 7:9 [1]NU omits *bread from any father among you, will he give him a stone? Or if he asks for*
13 [a]James 1:17
14 [a]Matt. 9:32–34; 12:22, 24
15 [a]Matt. 9:34; 12:24 [1]NU, M *Beelzebul*
16 [a]Matt. 12:38; 16:1
17 [a]Matt. 12:25–29 [b]John 2:25
20 [a]Ex. 8:19
21 [a]Mark 3:27
22 [a][Is. 53:12] [1]*plunder*
23 [a]Matt. 12:30
24 [a]Matt. 12:43–45
26 [a][2 Pet. 2:20]
27 [a]Luke 1:28, 48
28 [a][Luke 8:21]
29 [a]Matt. 12:38–42 [b]1 Cor. 1:22 [1]NU omits *the prophet*
30 [a]Jon. 1:17; 2:10; 3:3–10
31 [a]1 Kin. 10:1–9

rise up in the judgment with the
men of this generation and condemn them, for she came from
the ends of the earth to hear
the wisdom of Solomon; and
indeed a [b]greater than Solomon
is here.
32 "The men of Nin′e·veh will
rise up in the judgment with this
generation and condemn it, for
[a]they repented at the preaching
of Jonah; and indeed a greater
than Jonah *is* here.
33 [a]"No one, when he has lit a
lamp, puts *it* in a secret place or
under a [b]basket, but on a lampstand, that those who come in
may see the light.
34 [a]"The lamp of the body is the
eye. Therefore, when your eye is
[1]good, your whole body also is
full of light. But when *your eye*
is [2]bad, your body also *is* full of
darkness.
35 "Therefore take heed that
the light which is in you is not
darkness.
36 "If then your whole body *is*
full of light, having no part dark,
the whole *body* will be full of
light, as when the bright shining
of a lamp gives you light."
37 And as He spoke, a certain
Phar′i·see asked Him to dine
with him. So He went in and sat
down to eat.
38 [a]When the Phar′i·see saw *it*,
he marveled that He had not
first washed before dinner.
39 [a]Then the Lord said to him,
"Now you Phar′i·sees make
the outside of the cup and dish
clean, but [b]your inward part is
full of [1]greed and wickedness.
40 "Foolish ones! Did not [a]He
who made the outside make the
inside also?
41 [a]"But rather give alms of
[1]such things as you have; then
indeed all things are clean to
you.
42 [a]"But woe to you Phar′i·sees!
For you tithe mint and rue and
all manner of herbs, and [b]pass
by justice and the [c]love of God.
These you ought to have done,
without leaving the others undone.
43 [a]"Woe to you Phar′i·sees! For
you love the [1]best seats in the
synagogues and greetings in the
marketplaces.
44 [a]"Woe to you, [1]scribes and
Phar′i·sees, hypocrites! [b]For you
are like graves which are not
seen, and the men who walk over
them are not aware *of them*."
45 Then one of the lawyers
answered and said to Him,
"Teacher, by saying these things
You reproach us also."
46 And He said, "Woe to you
also, lawyers! [a]For you load men
with burdens hard to bear, and
you yourselves do not touch the
burdens with one of your fingers.
47 [a]"Woe to you! For you build
the tombs of the prophets, and
your fathers killed them.
48 "In fact, you bear witness
that you approve the deeds of
your fathers; for they indeed
killed them, and you build their
tombs.
49 "Therefore the wisdom of
God also said, [a]'I will send them
prophets and apostles, and *some*
of them they will kill and persecute,'
50 "that the blood of all the
prophets which was shed from
the foundation of the world may
be required of this generation,
51 [a]"from the blood of Abel to
[b]the blood of Zech·a·rī′ah who

31 [b][Rom. 9:5]
32 [a]Jon. 3:5
33 [a]Mark 4:21 [b]Matt. 5:15
34 [a]Matt. 6:22, 23 [1]Clear, or healthy [2]Evil, or unhealthy
38 [a]Mark 7:2, 3
39 [a]Matt. 23:25 [b]Titus 1:15 [1]Lit. *eager grasping or robbery*
40 [a]Gen. 1:26, 27
41 [a][Luke 12:33; 16:9] [1]Or *what is inside*
42 [a]Matt. 23:23 [b][Mic. 6:7, 8] [c]John 5:42
43 [a]Mark 12:38, 39 [1]Or *places of honor*
44 [a]Matt. 23:27 [b]Ps. 5:9 [1]NU omits *scribes and Pharisees, hypocrites*
46 [a]Matt. 23:4
47 [a]Matt. 23:29
49 [a]Matt. 23:34
51 [a]Gen. 4:8 [b]2 Chr. 24:20, 21

perished between the altar and
the temple. Yes, I say to you, it
shall be required of this generation.
52 [a]"Woe to you lawyers! For
you have taken away the key of
knowledge. You did not enter in
yourselves, and those who were
entering in you hindered."
53 [1]And as He said these things
to them, the scribes and the
Phar'i·sees began to assail *Him*
vehemently, and to cross-examine Him about many things,
54 lying in wait for Him, [1]and
[a]seeking to catch Him in something He might say, [2]that they
might accuse Him.

12 In [a]the meantime, when
an innumerable multitude of people had gathered together, so that they trampled one
another, He began to say to His
disciples first *of all,* [b]"Beware
of the [1]leaven of the Phar'i·sees,
which is hypocrisy.
2 [a]"For there is nothing covered
that will not be revealed, nor
hidden that will not be known.
3 "Therefore whatever you
have spoken in the dark will be
heard in the light, and what you
have spoken in the ear in inner
rooms will be proclaimed on the
housetops.
4 [a]"And I say to you, [b]My
friends, do not be afraid of those
who kill the body, and after that
have no more that they can do.
5 "But I will show you whom
you should fear: Fear Him who,
after He has killed, has power to
cast into hell; yes, I say to you,
[a]fear Him!
6 "Are not five sparrows sold
for two [1]copper coins? And [a]not
one of them is forgotten before
God.
7 "But the very hairs of your
head are all numbered. Do not
fear therefore; you are of more
value than many sparrows.
8 [a]"Also I say to you, whoever
confesses Me [b]before men, him
the Son of Man also will confess
before the angels of God.
9 "But he who [a]denies Me before men will be denied before
the angels of God.
10 "And [a]anyone who speaks a
word against the Son of Man,
it will be forgiven him; but to
him who blasphemes against
the Holy Spirit, it will not be
forgiven.
11 [a]"Now when they bring you
to the synagogues and magistrates and authorities, do not
worry about how or what you
should answer, or what you
should say.
12 "For the Holy Spirit will
[a]teach you in that very hour
what you ought to say."
13 Then one from the crowd
said to Him, "Teacher, tell my
brother to divide the inheritance
with me."
14 But He said to him, [a]"Man,
who made Me a judge or an arbitrator over you?"
15 And He said to them, [a]"Take
heed and beware of [1]covetousness, for one's life does not consist in the abundance of the
things he possesses."
16 Then He spoke a parable to
them, saying: "The ground of a
certain rich man yielded plentifully.
17 "And he thought within himself, saying, 'What shall I do,
since I have no room to store my
crops?'
18 "So he said, 'I will do this:
I will pull down my barns and

52 [a]Matt. 23:13
53 [1]NU *And when He left there*
54 [a]Mark 12:13 [1]NU omits *and seeking* [2]NU omits *that they might accuse Him*

CHAPTER 12

1 [a]Mark 8:15 [b]Matt. 16:12 [1]*yeast*
2 [a]Matt. 10:26; [1 Cor. 4:5]
4 [a]Is. 51:7, 8, 12, 13 [b][John 15:13–15]
5 [a]Ps. 119:120
6 [a]Matt. 6:26 [1]Gr. *assarion,* a coin worth about 1/16 of a denarius
8 [a]Matt. 10:32 [b]Ps. 119:46
9 [a]Matt. 10:33
10 [a][Matt. 12:31, 32]
11 [a]Mark 13:11
12 [a][John 14:26]
14 [a][John 18:36]
15 [a][1 Tim. 6:6–10] [1]NU *all covetousness*

build greater, and there I will
store all my crops and my
goods.
19 ‘And I will say to my soul,
[a]“Soul, you have many goods
laid up for many years; take
your ease; [b]eat, drink, *and* be
merry.” ’
20 “But God said to him, ‘Fool!
This night [a]your soul will be required of you; [b]then whose will
those things be which you have
provided?’
21 “So *is* he who lays up treasure for himself, [a]and is not rich
toward God.”
22 Then He said to His disciples, “Therefore I say to you, [a]do
not worry about your life, what
you will eat; nor about the body,
what you will put on.
23 “Life is more than food, and
the body *is more* than clothing.
24 “Consider the ravens, for
they neither sow nor reap,
which have neither storehouse
nor barn; and [a]God feeds them.
Of how much more value are
you than the birds?
25 “And which of you by wor-
rying can add one cubit to his
stature?
26 “If you then are not able to
do *the* least, why [1]are you anxious for the rest?
27 “Consider the lilies, how they
grow: they neither toil nor spin;
and yet I say to you, even [a]Sol-
omon in all his glory was not
[1]arrayed like one of these.
28 “If then God so clothes the
grass, which today is in the field
and tomorrow is thrown into
the oven, how much more *will
He clothe* you, O *you* of [a]little
faith?
29 “And do not seek what you
should eat or what you should
drink, nor have an anxious
mind.
30 “For all these things the nations of the world seek after,
and your Father [a]knows that you
need these things.
31 [a]“But seek [1]the kingdom of
God, and all these things shall
be added to you.
32 “Do not fear, little flock, for
[a]it is your Father’s good pleasure
to give you the kingdom.
33 [a]“Sell what you have and
give [b]alms; [c]provide yourselves
money bags which do not grow
old, a treasure in the heavens
that does not fail, where no thief
approaches nor moth destroys.
34 “For where your treasure is,
there your heart will be also.
35 [a]“Let your waist be girded
and [b]*your* lamps burning;
36 “and you yourselves be like
men who wait for their master,
when he will return from the
wedding, that when he comes
and knocks they may open to
him immediately.
37 [a]“Blessed *are* those servants
whom the master, when he
comes, will find watching. Assuredly, I say to you that he will
gird himself and have them sit
down *to eat*, and will come and
serve them.
38 “And if he should come in
the second watch, or come in the
third watch, and find *them* so,
blessed are those servants.
39 [a]“But know this, that if the
master of the house had known
what hour the thief would come,
he would [1]have watched and not
allowed his house to be broken
into.
40 [a]“Therefore you also be
ready, for the Son of Man is

19 [a]Eccl. 11:9 [b][Eccl. 2:24; 3:13; 5:18; 8:15]
20 [a]Ps. 52:7 [b]Ps. 39:6
21 [a][James 2:5; 5:1–5]
22 [a]Matt. 6:25–33
24 [a]Job 38:41
26 [1]*do you worry*
27 [a]1 Kin. 10:4–7 [1]*clothed*
28 [a]Matt. 6:30; 8:26; 14:31; 16:8
30 [a]Matt. 6:31, 32
31 [a]Matt. 6:33 [1]NU *His kingdom, and these things*
32 [a][Matt. 11:25, 26]
33 [a]Matt. 19:21 [b]Luke 11:41 [c]Matt. 6:20
35 [a][1 Pet. 1:13] [b][Matt. 25:1–13]
37 [a]Matt. 24:46
39 [a]Rev. 3:3; 16:15 [1]NU *not have allowed*
40 [a]Mark 13:33

coming at an hour you do not
expect."
41 Then Peter said to Him,
"Lord, do You speak this parable
only to us, or to all *people?*"
42 And the Lord said, [a]"Who
then is that faithful and wise
steward, whom *his* master will
make ruler over his household,
to give *them their* portion of
food [1]in due season?
43 "Blessed *is* that servant
whom his master will find so
doing when he comes.
44 [a]"Truly, I say to you that he
will make him ruler over all that
he has.
45 [a]"But if that servant says in
his heart, 'My master is delaying
his coming,' and begins to beat
the male and female servants,
and to eat and drink and be
drunk,
46 "the master of that servant
will come on a [a]day when he is
not looking for *him,* and at an
hour when he is not aware, and
will cut him in two and appoint
him his portion with the unbelievers.
47 "And [a]that servant who [b]knew
his master's will, and did not
prepare *himself* or do according
to his will, shall be beaten with
many *stripes.*
48 [a]"But he who did not know,
yet committed things deserving of stripes, shall be beaten
with few. For everyone to whom
much is given, from him much
will be required; and to whom
much has been committed, of
him they will ask the more.
49 [a]"I came to send fire on the
earth, and how I wish it were
already kindled!
50 "But [a]I have a baptism to be
baptized with, and how distressed
I am till it is [b]accomplished!
51 [a]"Do *you* suppose that I came
to give peace on earth? I tell you,
not at all, [b]but rather division.
52 [a]"For from now on five in
one house will be divided: three
against two, and two against
three.
53 [a]"Father will be divided
against son and son against father, mother against daughter and
daughter against mother, mother-
in-law against her daughter-in-
law and daughter-in-law against
her mother-in-law."
54 Then He also said to the
multitudes, [a]"Whenever you see
a cloud rising out of the west,
immediately you say, 'A shower
is coming'; and so it is.
55 "And when *you see* the [a]south
wind blow, you say, 'There will
be hot weather'; and there is.
56 "Hypocrites! You can discern
the face of the sky and of the
earth, but how *is it* you do not
discern [a]this time?
57 "Yes, and why, even of yourselves, do you not judge what is
right?
58 [a]"When you go with your adversary to the magistrate, make
every effort [b]along the way to
settle with him, lest he drag you
to the judge, the judge deliver
you to the officer, and the officer
throw you into prison.
59 "I tell you, you shall not depart from there till you have
paid the very last mite."

13

There were present at
that season some who
told Him about the Galileans
whose blood Pilate had [1]mingled
with their sacrifices.
2 And Jesus answered and
said to them, "Do you suppose

42 [a]Matt. 24:45, 46; 25:21 [1]*at the right time*
44 [a]Matt. 24:47; 25:21
45 [a]2 Pet. 3:3, 4
46 [a]1 Thess. 5:3
47 [a]Deut. 25:2 [b][James 4:17]
48 [a][Lev. 5:17]
49 [a]Luke 12:51
50 [a]Mark 10:38 [b]John 12:27; 19:30
51 [a]Matt. 10:34–36 [b]John 7:43; 9:16; 10:19
52 [a]Mark 13:12
53 [a]Matt. 10:21, 36
54 [a]Matt. 16:2, 3
55 [a]Job 37:17
56 [a]Luke 19:41–44
58 [a]Prov. 25:8 [b][Is. 55:6]

CHAPTER 13

1 [1]*mixed*

that these Galileans were worse
sinners than all *other* Galileans, because they suffered such
things?
3 "I tell you, no; but unless you
repent you will all likewise perish.
4 "Or those eighteen on whom
the tower in Sī·lō′am fell and
killed them, do you think that
they were worse sinners than all
other men who dwelt in Jerusalem?
5 "I tell you, no; but unless you
repent you will all likewise perish."
6 He also spoke this parable:
[a]"A certain *man* had a fig tree
planted in his vineyard, and he
came seeking fruit on it and
found none.
7 "Then he said to the keeper
of his vineyard, 'Look, for three
years I have come seeking fruit
on this fig tree and find none.
Cut it down; why does it [1]use up
the ground?'
8 "But he answered and said
to him, 'Sir, let it alone this year
also, until I dig around it and
fertilize *it*.
9 [1]'And if it bears fruit, *well*.
But if not, after that you can [a]cut
it down.' "
10 Now He was teaching in one
of the synagogues on the Sabbath.
11 And behold, there was a
woman who had a spirit of infirmity eighteen years, and was
bent over and could in no way
[1]raise *herself* up.
12 But when Jesus saw her, He
called *her* to *Him* and said to
her, "Woman, you are loosed
from your [a]infirmity."
13 [a]And He laid *His* hands on
her, and immediately she was
made straight, and glorified God.
14 But the ruler of the synagogue answered with indignation, because Jesus had [a]healed
on the Sabbath; and he said to
the crowd, [b]"There are six days
on which men ought to work;
therefore come and be healed
on them, and [c]not on the Sabbath day."
15 The Lord then answered him
and said, [1]"Hypocrite! [a]Does not
each one of you on the Sabbath
loose his ox or donkey from the
stall, and lead *it* away to water
it?
16 "So ought not this woman,
[a]being a daughter of Abraham,
whom Satan has bound—think
of it—for eighteen years, be
loosed from this bond on the
Sabbath?"
17 And when He said these
things, all His adversaries were
put to shame; and all the multitude rejoiced for all the glorious
things that were [a]done by Him.
18 [a]Then He said, "What is the
kingdom of God like? And to
what shall I compare it?
19 "It is like a mustard seed,
which a man took and put in his
garden; and it grew and became
a [1]large tree, and the birds of the
air nested in its branches."
20 And again He said, "To what
shall I liken the kingdom of
God?
21 "It is like [1]leaven, which a
woman took and hid in three
[a]measures[2] of meal till it was all
leavened."
22 [a]And He went through the
cities and villages, teaching, and
journeying toward Jerusalem.
23 Then one said to Him, "Lord,

6 [a]Matt. 21:19
7 [1]*waste*
9 [a][John 15:2] [1]NU *And if it bears fruit after that, well. But if not, you can*
11 [1]*straighten up*
12 [a]Luke 7:21; 8:2
13 [a]Acts 9:17
14 [a][Luke 6:6–11; 14:1–6] [b]Ex. 20:9; 23:12 [c]Mark 3:2
15 [a]Luke 14:5 [1]NU, M *Hypocrites*
16 [a]Luke 19:9
17 [a]Mark 5:19, 20
18 [a]Mark 4:30–32
19 [1]NU omits *large*
21 [a]Matt. 13:33 [1]*yeast* [2]Gr. *sata,* same as Heb. *seah;* approximately 2 pecks in all
22 [a]Mark 6:6

are there [a]few who are saved?"
And He said to them,
24 [a]"Strive to enter through the
narrow gate, for [b]many, I say to
you, will seek to enter and will
not be able.
25 [a]"When once the Master of
the house has risen up and [b]shut
the door, and you begin to stand
outside and knock at the door,
saying, [c]'Lord, Lord, open for
us,' and He will answer and
say to you, [d]'I do not know you,
where you are from,'
26 "then you will begin to say,
'We ate and drank in Your presence, and You taught in our
streets.'
27 [a]"But He will say, 'I tell you I
do not know you, where you are
from. [b]Depart from Me, all you
workers of iniquity.'
28 [a]"There will be weeping and
gnashing of teeth, [b]when you
see Abraham and Isaac and Jacob and all the prophets in the
kingdom of God, and yourselves
thrust out.
29 "They will come from the
east and the west, from the north
and the south, and sit down in
the kingdom of God.
30 [a]"And indeed there are last
who will be first, and there are
first who will be last."
31 [1]On that very day some
Phar′i·sees came, saying to Him,
"Get out and depart from here,
for Her′od wants to kill You."
32 And He said to them, "Go,
tell that fox, 'Behold, I cast out
demons and perform cures today and tomorrow, and the third
day [a]I shall be [1]perfected.'
33 "Nevertheless I must journey
today, tomorrow, and the *day*
following; for it cannot be that a
prophet should perish outside of
Jerusalem.
34 [a]"O Jerusalem, Jerusalem,
the one who kills the prophets
and stones those who are sent
to her! How often I wanted to
gather your children together, as
a hen *gathers* her brood under
her wings, but you were not willing!
35 "See! [a]Your house is left to ☆
you desolate; and [1]assuredly, I
say to you, you shall not see Me
until *the time* comes when you
say, [b]*'Blessed is He who comes*
in the name of the LORD!' "

14 Now it happened, as He
went into the house of
one of the rulers of the Phar′-
i·sees to eat bread on the Sabbath, that they watched Him
closely.
2 And behold, there was a certain man before Him who had
dropsy.
3 And Jesus, answering, spoke
to the lawyers and Phar′i·sees,
saying, [a]"Is it lawful to heal on
the [1]Sabbath?"
4 But they kept silent. And He
took *him* and healed him, and
let him go.
5 Then He answered them,
saying, [a]"Which of you, having a
[1]donkey or an ox that has fallen
into a pit, will not immediately
pull him out on the Sabbath
day?"
6 And they could not answer
Him regarding these things.
7 So He told a parable to those
who were invited, when He
noted how they chose the best
places, saying to them:
8 "When you are invited by
anyone to a wedding feast, do
not sit down in the best place,

23 [a][Matt. 7:14; 20:16]
24 [a][Matt. 7:13] [b][John 7:34; 8:21; 13:33]
25 [a]Is. 55:6 [b]Matt. 25:10 [c]Luke 6:46 [d]Matt. 7:23; 25:12
27 [a][Matt. 7:23; 25:41] [b]Ps. 6:8
28 [a]Matt. 8:12; 13:42; 24:51 [b]Matt. 8:11
30 [a][Matt. 19:30; 20:16]
31 [1]NU *In that very hour*
32 [a][Heb. 2:10; 5:9; 7:28] [1]Resurrected
34 [a]Matt. 23:37–39
35 [a]Lev. 26:31, 32; Ps. 69:25; Is. 1:7; Jer. 22:5; Dan. 9:27 [b]Ps. 118:26; Matt. 21:9 [1]NU, M omit *assuredly*

CHAPTER 14

3 [a]Matt. 12:10 [1]NU adds *or not*
5 [a][Ex. 23:5] [1]NU, M *son*

lest one more honorable than you be invited by him;

9 "and he who invited you and him come and say to you, 'Give place to this man,' and then you begin with shame to take the lowest place.

10 [a]"But when you are invited, go and sit down in the lowest place, so that when he who invited you comes he may say to you, 'Friend, go up higher.' Then you will have glory in the presence of those who sit at the table with you.

11 [a]"For whoever exalts himself will be [1]humbled, and he who humbles himself will be exalted."

12 Then He also said to him who invited Him, "When you give a dinner or a supper, do not ask your friends, your brothers, your relatives, nor rich neighbors, lest they also invite you back, and you be repaid.

13 "But when you give a feast, invite [a]*the* poor, *the* [1]maimed, *the* lame, *the* blind.

14 "And you will be [a]blessed, because they cannot repay you; for you shall be repaid at the resurrection of the just."

15 Now when one of those who sat at the table with Him heard these things, he said to Him, [a]"Blessed *is* he who shall eat [1]bread in the kingdom of God!"

16 [a]Then He said to him, "A certain man gave a great supper and invited many,

17 "and [a]sent his servant at supper time to say to those who were invited, 'Come, for all things are now ready.'

18 "But they all with one *accord* began to make excuses. The first said to him, 'I have bought a piece of ground, and I must go and see it. I ask you to have me excused.'

19 "And another said, 'I have bought five yoke of oxen, and I am going to test them. I ask you to have me excused.'

20 "Still another said, 'I have married a wife, and therefore I cannot come.'

21 "So that servant came and reported these things to his master. Then the master of the house, being angry, said to his servant, 'Go out quickly into the streets and lanes of the city, and bring in here *the* poor and *the* [1]maimed and *the* lame and *the* blind.'

22 "And the servant said, 'Master, it is done as you commanded, and still there is room.'

23 "Then the master said to the servant, 'Go out into the highways and hedges, and compel *them* to come in, that my house may be filled.

24 'For I say to you [a]that none of those men who were invited shall taste my supper.' "

25 Now great multitudes went with Him. And He turned and said to them,

26 [a]"If anyone comes to Me [b]and does not hate his father and mother, wife and children, brothers and sisters, [c]yes, and his own life also, he cannot be My disciple.

27 "And [a]whoever does not bear his cross and come after Me cannot be My disciple.

28 "For [a]which of you, intending to build a tower, does not sit down first and count the cost, whether he has *enough* to finish *it*—

29 "lest, after he has laid the

10 [a]Prov. 25:6, 7
11 [a]Matt. 23:12 [1]*put down*
13 [a]Neh. 8:10, 12 [1]*crippled*
14 [a][Matt. 25:34–40]
15 [a]Rev. 19:9 [1]M *dinner*
16 [a]Matt. 22:2–14
17 [a]Prov. 9:2, 5
21 [1]*crippled*
24 [a][Acts 13:46]
26 [a]Deut. 13:6; 33:9 [b]Rom. 9:13 [c]Rev. 12:11
27 [a]Luke 9:23
28 [a]Prov. 24:27

foundation, and is not able to
finish, all who see *it* begin to
mock him,
30 "saying, 'This man began to
build and was not able to finish'?
31 "Or what king, going to
make war against another king,
does not sit down first and consider whether he is able with
ten thousand to meet him who
comes against him with twenty
thousand?
32 "Or else, while the other is
still a great way off, he sends a
delegation and asks conditions
of peace.
33 "So likewise, whoever of you
[a]does not forsake all that he has
cannot be My disciple.
34 [a]"Salt *is* good; but if the salt
has lost its flavor, how shall it be
seasoned?
35 "It is neither fit for the land
nor for the [1]dunghill, *but* men
throw it out. He who has ears to
hear, let him hear!"

15 Then [a]all the tax collectors and the sinners drew
near to Him to hear Him.
2 And the Phar′i·sees and
scribes complained, saying,
"This Man [1]receives sinners [a]and
eats with them."
3 So He spoke this parable to
them, saying:
4 [a]"What man of you, having a
hundred sheep, if he loses one of
them, does not leave the ninety-
nine in the wilderness, and go
after the one which is lost until
he finds it?
5 "And when he has found *it*,
he lays *it* on his shoulders, rejoicing.
6 "And when he comes home,
he calls together *his* friends
and neighbors, saying to them,
[a]'Rejoice with me, for I have
found my sheep [b]which was
lost!'
7 "I say to you that likewise
there will be more joy in heaven
over one sinner who repents
[a]than over ninety-nine [1]just persons who [b]need no repentance.
8 "Or what woman, having
ten silver [1]coins, if she loses
one coin, does not light a lamp,
sweep the house, and search
carefully until she finds *it*?
9 "And when she has found *it*,
she calls *her* friends and neighbors together, saying, 'Rejoice
with me, for I have found the
piece which I lost!'
10 "Likewise, I say to you, there
is joy in the presence of the angels of God over one sinner who
repents."
11 Then He said: "A certain man
had two sons.
12 "And the younger of them
said to *his* father, 'Father, give
me the portion of goods that
falls *to me.*' So he divided to
them [a]*his* livelihood.
13 "And not many days after,
the younger son gathered all together, journeyed to a far country, and there wasted his possessions with [1]prodigal living.
14 "But when he had spent all,
there arose a severe famine in
that land, and he began to be in
want.
15 "Then he went and joined
himself to a citizen of that country, and he sent him into his
fields to feed swine.
16 "And he would gladly have
filled his stomach with the [1]pods
that the swine ate, and no one
gave him *anything*.
17 "But when he came to himself, he said, 'How many of my

33 [a]Matt. 19:27
34 [a][Mark 9:50]
35 [1]*rubbish heap*

CHAPTER 15

1 [a][Matt. 9:10–13]
2 [a]Gal. 2:12 [1]*welcomes*
4 [a]Matt. 18:12–14
6 [a][Rom. 12:15] [b][1 Pet. 2:10, 25]
7 [a][Luke 5:32] [b][Mark 2:17] [1]*upright*
8 [1]Gr. *drachma,* a valuable coin often worn in a ten-piece garland by married women
12 [a]Mark 12:44
13 [1]*wasteful*
16 [1]*carob pods*

father's hired servants have
bread enough and to spare, and
I perish with hunger!
18 'I will arise and go to my father, and will say to him, "Father,
[a]I have sinned against heaven
and before you,
19 "and I am no longer worthy
to be called your son. Make
me like one of your hired servants." '
20 "And he arose and came to
his father. But [a]when he was
still a great way off, his father
saw him and had compassion,
and ran and fell on his neck and
kissed him.
21 "And the son said to him,
'Father, I have sinned against
heaven [a]and in your sight, and
am no longer worthy to be called
your son.'
22 "But the father said to his
servants, [1]'Bring out the best
robe and put *it* on him, and put
a ring on his hand and sandals
on *his* feet.
23 'And bring the fatted calf
here and kill *it*, and let us eat
and be merry;
24 [a]'for this my son was dead
and is alive again; he was lost
and is found.' And they began to
be merry.
25 "Now his older son was in
the field. And as he came and
drew near to the house, he heard
music and dancing.
26 "So he called one of the
servants and asked what these
things meant.
27 "And he said to him, 'Your
brother has come, and because
he has received him safe and
sound, your father has killed the
fatted calf.'
28 "But he was angry and would
not go in. Therefore his father
came out and pleaded with him.
29 "So he answered and said
to *his* father, 'Lo, these many
years I have been serving you;
I never transgressed your commandment at any time; and yet
you never gave me a young goat,
that I might make merry with
my friends.
30 'But as soon as this son of
yours came, who has devoured
your livelihood with harlots, you
killed the fatted calf for him.'
31 "And he said to him, 'Son,
you are always with me, and all
that I have is yours.
32 'It was right that we should
make merry and be glad, [a]for
your brother was dead and is
alive again, and was lost and is
found.' "

16 He also said to His disciples: "There was a certain
rich man who had a steward,
and an accusation was brought
to him that this man was [1]wast-
ing his goods.
2 "So he called him and said to
him, 'What is this I hear about
you? Give an [a]account of your
stewardship, for you can no longer be steward.'
3 "Then the steward said
within himself, 'What shall I
do? For my master is taking
the stewardship away from me.
I cannot dig; I am ashamed to
beg.
4 'I have resolved what to do,
that when I am put out of the
stewardship, they may receive
me into their houses.'
5 "So he called every one of
his master's debtors to *him*, and
said to the first, 'How much do
you owe my master?'
6 "And he said, 'A hundred

18 [a]2 Sam. 12:13; 24:10, 17
20 [a][Eph. 2:13, 17]
21 [a]Ps. 51:4
22 [1]NU *Quickly bring*
24 [a]Luke 9:60; 15:32
32 [a]Luke 15:24

CHAPTER 16

1 [1]*squandering*
2 [a][Rom. 14:12]

[1]measures of oil.' So he said
to him, 'Take your bill, and sit
down quickly and write fifty.'
7 "Then he said to another,
'And how much do you owe?' So
he said, 'A hundred [1]measures of
wheat.' And he said to him, 'Take
your bill, and write eighty.'
8 "So the master commended
the unjust steward because he
had dealt shrewdly. For the sons
of this world are more shrewd in
their generation than [a]the sons
of light.
9 "And I say to you, [a]make
friends for yourselves by unrighteous [1]mammon, that when
[2]you fail, they may receive you
into an everlasting home.
10 [a]"He who *is* faithful in *what*
is least is faithful also in much;
and he who is unjust in *what is*
least is unjust also in much.
11 "Therefore if you have not
been faithful in the unrighteous
mammon, who will commit to
your trust the true *riches*?
12 "And if you have not been
faithful in what is another man's,
who will give you what is your
[a]own?
13 [a]"No servant can serve two
masters; for either he will hate
the one and love the other, or
else he will be loyal to the one
and despise the other. You cannot serve God and mammon."
14 Now the Phar′i·sees, [a]who
were lovers of money, also heard
all these things, and they [1]de-
rided Him.
15 And He said to them, "You
are those who [a]justify yourselves [b]before men, but [c]God
knows your hearts. For [d]what is
highly esteemed among men is
an abomination in the sight of
God.
16 [a]"The law and the prophets
were until John. Since that time
the kingdom of God has been
preached, and everyone is pressing into it.
17 [a]"And it is easier for heaven
and earth to pass away than for
one [1]tittle of the law to fail.
18 [a]"Whoever divorces his wife
and marries another commits
adultery; and whoever marries
her who is divorced from *her*
husband commits adultery.
19 "There was a certain rich
man who was clothed in purple
and fine linen and [1]fared sumptuously every day.
20 "But there was a certain
beggar named Laz′a·rus, full of
sores, who was laid at his gate,
21 "desiring to be fed with [1]the
crumbs which fell from the rich
man's table. Moreover the dogs
came and licked his sores.
22 "So it was that the beggar
died, and was carried by the
angels to [a]Abraham's bosom.
The rich man also died and was
buried.
23 "And being in torments in
Hā′dēs, he lifted up his eyes and
saw Abraham afar off, and Laz′-
a·rus in his bosom.
24 "Then he cried and said, 'Father Abraham, have mercy on
me, and send Laz′a·rus that he
may dip the tip of his finger in
water and [a]cool my tongue; for I
[b]am tormented in this flame.'
25 "But Abraham said, 'Son,
[a]remember that in your lifetime
you received your good things,
and likewise Laz′a·rus evil
things; but now he is comforted
and you are tormented.
26 'And besides all this, between
us and you there is a great gulf
fixed, so that those who want to

6 [1]Gr. *batos*, same as Heb. *bath;* 8 or 9 gallons each

7 [1]Gr. *koros*, same as Heb. *kor;* 10 or 12 bushels each

8 [a][Eph. 5:8]

9 [a]Dan. 4:27 [1]Lit., in Aram., *wealth* [2]NU *it fails*

10 [a]Matt. 25:21

12 [a][1 Pet. 1:3, 4]

13 [a]Matt. 6:24

14 [a]Matt. 23:14 [1]Lit. *turned up their nose at*

15 [a]Luke 10:29 [b][Matt. 6:2, 5, 16] [c]Ps. 7:9 [d]1 Sam. 16:7

16 [a]Matt. 3:1–12; 4:17; 11:12, 13

17 [a]Is. 40:8; 51:6 [1]The smallest stroke in a Heb. letter

18 [a]1 Cor. 7:10, 11

19 [1]*lived in luxury*

21 [1]NU *what fell*

22 [a]Matt. 8:11

24 [a]Zech. 14:12 [b][Mark 9:42–48]

25 [a]Luke 6:24

pass from here to you cannot,
nor can those from there pass
to us.'
27 "Then he said, 'I beg you
therefore, father, that you would
send him to my father's house,
28 'for I have five brothers, that
he may testify to them, lest they
also come to this place of torment.'
29 "Abraham said to him, [a]'They
have Moses and the prophets;
let them hear them.'
30 "And he said, 'No, father
Abraham; but if one goes to
them from the dead, they will
repent.'
31 "But he said to him, [a]'If they
do not hear Moses and the
prophets, [b]neither will they be
persuaded though one rise from
the dead.' "

17 Then He said to the disciples, [a]"It is impossible
that no [1]offenses should come,
but [b]woe *to him* through whom
they do come!
2 "It would be better for him
if a millstone were hung around
his neck, and he were thrown
into the sea, than that he should
[1]offend one of these little ones.
3 "Take heed to yourselves. [a]If
your brother sins [1]against you,
[b]rebuke him; and if he repents,
forgive him.
4 "And if he sins against you
seven times in a day, and seven
times in a day returns [1]to you,
saying, 'I repent,' you shall forgive him."
5 And the apostles said to the
Lord, "Increase our faith."
6 [a]So the Lord said, "If you
have faith as a mustard seed,
you can say to this mulberry
tree, 'Be pulled up by the roots

29 [a]Acts 15:21; 17:11
31 [a][John 5:46] [b]John 12:10, 11

CHAPTER 17

1 [a][1 Cor. 11:19] [b][2 Thess. 1:6] [1]*stumbling blocks*
2 [1]*cause one of these little ones to stumble*
3 [a][Matt. 18:15, 21] [b][Prov. 17:10] [1]NU omits *against you*
4 [1]M omits *to you*
6 [a][Mark 9:23; 11:23]
8 [a][Luke 12:37]
9 [1]NU omits the rest of v. 9; M omits *him*
10 [a]Rom. 3:12; 11:35
11 [a]Luke 9:51, 52
12 [a]Lev. 13:46
14 [a]Matt. 8:4
15 [a]Luke 5:25; 18:43
16 [a]2 Kin. 17:24

and be planted in the sea,' and it
would obey you.
7 "And which of you, having
a servant plowing or tending
sheep, will say to him when
he has come in from the field,
'Come at once and sit down to
eat'?
8 "But will he not rather say to
him, 'Prepare something for my
supper, and gird yourself [a]and
serve me till I have eaten and
drunk, and afterward you will
eat and drink'?
9 "Does he thank that servant
because he did the things that
were commanded [1]him? I think
not.
10 "So likewise you, when you
have done all those things which
you are commanded, say, 'We
are [a]unprofitable servants. We
have done what was our duty
to do.' "
11 Now it happened [a]as He went
to Jerusalem that He passed
through the midst of Samaria
and Galilee.
12 Then as He entered a certain
village, there met Him ten men
who were lepers, [a]who stood
afar off.
13 And they lifted up *their*
voices and said, "Jesus, Master,
have mercy on us!"
14 So when He saw *them,* He
said to them, [a]"Go, show yourselves to the priests." And so it
was that as they went, they were
cleansed.
15 And one of them, when he
saw that he was healed, returned, and with a loud voice
[a]glorified God,
16 and fell down on *his* face at
His feet, giving Him thanks. And
he was a [a]Samaritan.
17 So Jesus answered and said,

"Were there not ten cleansed?
But where *are* the nine?
18 "Were there not any found
who returned to give glory to
God except this foreigner?"
19 [a]And He said to him, "Arise,
go your way. Your faith has made
you well."
20 Now when He was asked by
the Phar′i·sees when the kingdom of God would come, He
answered them and said, "The
kingdom of God does not come
with observation;
21 [a]"nor will they say, [1]'See
here!' or 'See there!' For indeed,
[b]the kingdom of God is [2]within
you."
22 Then He said to the disciples,
[a]"The days will come when you
will desire to see one of the days
of the Son of Man, and you will
not see *it*.
23 [a]"And they will say to you,
[1]'Look here!' or 'Look there!'
Do not go after *them* or follow
them.
24 [a]"For as the lightning that
flashes out of one *part* under
heaven shines to the other *part*
under heaven, so also the Son of
Man will be in His day.
25 [a]"But first He must suffer
many things and be [b]rejected by
this generation.
26 [a]"And as it [b]was in the [c]days
of [d]Noah, so it will be also in the
days of the Son of Man:
27 "They ate, they drank, they
married wives, they were given
in marriage, until the [a]day that
Noah entered the ark, and the
flood came and [b]destroyed them
all.
28 [a]"Likewise as it was also in
the days of Lot: They ate, they
drank, they bought, they sold,
they planted, they built;
29 "but on [a]the day that Lot
went out of Sod′om it rained fire
and brimstone from heaven and
destroyed *them* all.
30 "Even so will it be in the
day when the Son of Man [a]is
revealed.
31 "In that day, he [a]who is on
the housetop, and his [1]goods *are*
in the house, let him not come
down to take them away. And
likewise the one who is in the
field, let him not turn back.
32 [a]"Remember Lot's wife.
33 [a]"Whoever seeks to save his
life will lose it, and whoever
loses his life will preserve it.
34 [a]"I tell you, in that night there
will be two [1]*men* in one bed: the
one will be taken and the other
will be left.
35 [a]"Two *women* will be grinding together: the one will be
taken and the other left.
36 [1]"Two *men* will be in the
field: the one will be taken and
the other left."
37 And they answered and said
to Him, [a]"Where, Lord?" So He
said to them, "Wherever the
body is, there the eagles will be
gathered together."

18 Then He spoke a parable to them, that men
[a]always ought to pray and not
lose heart,
2 saying: "There was in a certain city a judge who did not
fear God nor [1]regard man.
3 "Now there was a widow in
that city; and she came to him,
saying, [1]'Get justice for me from
my adversary.'
4 "And he would not for a
while; but afterward he said
within himself, 'Though I do not
fear God nor regard man,
5 [a]'yet because this widow

19 [a]Matt. 9:22
21 [a]Luke 17:23 [b][Rom. 14:17] [1]NU reverses *here* and *there* [2]*in your midst*
22 [a]Matt. 9:15
23 [a]Matt. 24:23 [1]NU reverses *here* and *there*
24 [a]Matt. 24:27
25 [a]Mark 8:31; 9:31; 10:33 [b]Luke 9:22
26 [a]Matt. 24:37–39 [b][Gen. 6:5–7] [c][Gen. 6:8–13] [d]1 Pet. 3:20
27 [a]Gen. 7:1–16 [b]Gen. 7:19–23
28 [a]Gen. 19
29 [a]Gen. 19:16, 24, 29
30 [a][2 Thess. 1:7]
31 [a]Mark 13:15 [1]*possessions*
32 [a]Gen. 19:26
33 [a]Matt. 10:39; 16:25
34 [a][1 Thess. 4:17] [1]Or *people*
35 [a]Matt. 24:40, 41
36 [1]NU, M omit v. 36.
37 [a]Matt. 24:28

CHAPTER 18

1 [a]Luke 11:5–10
2 [1]*respect*
3 [1]*Avenge me on*
5 [a]Luke 11:8

troubles me I will [1]avenge her,
lest by her continual coming she
weary me.' "
6 Then the Lord said, "Hear
what the unjust judge said.
7 "And [a]shall God not avenge
His own elect who cry out day
and night to Him, though He
bears long with them?
8 "I tell you [a]that He will
avenge them speedily. Nevertheless, when the Son of Man
comes, will He really find faith
on the earth?"
9 Also He spoke this parable
to some [a]who trusted in themselves that they were righteous,
and despised others:
10 "Two men went up to the
temple to pray, one a Phar'i·see
and the other a tax collector.
11 "The Phar'i·see [a]stood and
prayed thus with himself, [b]'God,
I thank You that I am not like
other men—extortioners, unjust,
adulterers, or even as this tax
collector.
12 'I fast twice a week; I give
tithes of all that I possess.'
13 "And the tax collector, standing afar off, would not so much
as raise *his* eyes to heaven, but
beat his breast, saying, 'God, be
merciful to me a sinner!'
14 "I tell you, this man went
down to his house justified
rather than the other; [a]for everyone who exalts himself will be
[1]humbled, and he who humbles
himself will be exalted."
15 [a]Then they also brought infants to Him that He might touch
them; but when the disciples
saw *it*, they rebuked them.
16 But Jesus called them to *Him*
and said, "Let the little children come to Me, and do not
forbid them; for [a]of such is the
kingdom of God.
17 [a]"Assuredly, I say to you,
whoever does not receive the
kingdom of God as a little child
will by no means enter it."
18 [a]Now a certain ruler asked
Him, saying, "Good Teacher,
what shall I do to inherit eternal
life?"
19 So Jesus said to him, "Why
do you call Me good? No one *is*
good but [a]One, *that is*, God.
20 "You know the command-
ments: [a]*'Do not commit adultery,' 'Do not murder,' 'Do not
steal,' 'Do not bear false witness,'* [b]*'Honor your father and
your mother.'* "
21 And he said, "All [a]these things
I have kept from my youth."
22 So when Jesus heard these
things, He said to him, "You still
lack one thing. [a]Sell all that you
have and distribute to the poor,
and you will have treasure in
heaven; and come, follow Me."
23 But when he heard this, he
became very sorrowful, for he
was very rich.
24 And when Jesus saw that he
became very sorrowful, He said,
[a]"How hard it is for those who
have riches to enter the kingdom of God!
25 "For it is easier for a camel
to go through the eye of a needle
than for a rich man to enter the
kingdom of God."
26 And those who heard it said,
"Who then can be saved?"
27 But He said, [a]"The things
which are impossible with men
are possible with God."
28 [a]Then Peter said, "See, we
have left [1]all and followed You."
29 So He said to them, "Assuredly, I say to you, [a]there is no one

5 [1]*vindicate*
7 [a]Rev. 6:10
8 [a]Heb. 10:37
9 [a]Luke 10:29; 16:15
11 [a]Ps. 135:2 [b]Is. 1:15; 58:2
14 [a]Luke 14:11 [1]*put down*
15 [a]Mark 10:13–16
16 [a]1 Pet. 2:2
17 [a]Mark 10:15
18 [a]Matt. 19:16–29
19 [a]Ps. 86:5; 119:68
20 [a]Ex. 20:12–16; Deut. 5:16–20 [b]Eph. 6:2; Col. 3:20
21 [a]Phil. 3:6
22 [a]Matt. 6:19, 20; 19:21
24 [a]Mark 10:23
27 [a]Jer. 32:17
28 [a]Matt. 19:27 [1]NU *our own*
29 [a]Deut. 33:9

who has left house or parents or
brothers or wife or children, for
the sake of the kingdom of God,
30 [a]"who shall not receive many
times more in this present time,
and in the age to come eternal
life."
31 [a]Then He took the twelve
aside and said to them, "Behold,
we are going up to Jerusalem,
and all things [b]that are written
by the prophets concerning the
Son of Man will be [1]accom-
plished.
32 "For [a]He will be delivered to
the Gentiles and will be mocked
and insulted and spit upon.
33 "They will scourge *Him* and
kill Him. And the third day He
will rise again."
34 [a]But they understood none
of these things; this saying was
hidden from them, and they did
not know the things which were
spoken.
35 [a]Then it happened, as He
was coming near Jericho, that
a certain blind man sat by the
road begging.
36 And hearing a multitude
passing by, he asked what it
meant.
37 So they told him that Jesus
of Nazareth was passing by.
38 And he cried out, saying, "Jesus, [a]Son of David, have mercy
on me!"
39 Then those who went before warned him that he should
be quiet; but he cried out all
the more, "Son of David, have
mercy on me!"
40 So Jesus stood still and commanded him to be brought to
Him. And when he had come
near, He asked him,
41 saying, "What do you want
Me to do for you?" He said,
"Lord, that I may receive my
sight."
42 Then Jesus said to him, "Receive your sight; [a]your faith has
made you well."
43 And immediately he re-
ceived his sight, and followed
Him, [a]glorifying God. And all
the people, when they saw *it*,
gave praise to God.

19

Then *Jesus* entered and
passed through [a]Jericho.
2 Now behold, *there was* a
man named Zac·chaē′us who
was a chief tax collector, and he
was rich.
3 And he sought to [a]see who
Jesus was, but could not because of the crowd, for he was
of short stature.
4 So he ran ahead and climbed
up into a sycamore tree to see
Him, for He was going to pass
that *way*.
5 And when Jesus came to
the place, He looked up [1]and
saw him, and said to him,
"Zac·chaē′us, [2]make haste and
come down, for today I must
stay at your house."
6 So he [1]made haste and came
down, and received Him joyfully.
7 But when they saw *it*, they
all [1]complained, saying, [a]"He
has gone to be a guest with a
man who is a sinner."
8 Then Zac·chaē′us stood and
said to the Lord, "Look, Lord,
I give half of my goods to the
[a]poor; and if I have taken anything from anyone by [b]false accusation, [c]I restore fourfold."
9 And Jesus said to him, "Today salvation has come to this
house, because [a]he also is [b]a son
of Abraham;
10 [a]"for the Son of Man has

30 [a]Job 42:10
31 [a]Matt. 16:21; 17:22; 20:17 [b]Ps. 22 [1]*fulfilled*
32 [a]Acts 3:13
34 [a]Luke 2:50; 9:45
35 [a]Matt. 20:29–34
38 [a]Matt. 9:27
42 [a]Luke 17:19
43 [a]Luke 5:26

CHAPTER 19

1 [a]Josh. 6:26
3 [a]John 12:21
5 [1]NU omits *and saw him* [2]*hurry*
6 [1]*hurried*
7 [a]Luke 5:30; 15:2 [1]*grumbled*
8 [a][Ps. 41:1] [b]Luke 3:14 [c]Ex. 22:1
9 [a][Gal. 3:7] [b][Luke 13:16]
10 [a]Matt. 18:11

come to seek and to save that
which was lost."
11 Now as they heard these
things, He spoke another parable, because He was near Jerusalem and because [a]they thought
the kingdom of God would appear immediately.
12 [a]Therefore He said: "A certain nobleman went into a far
country to receive for himself a
kingdom and to return.
13 "So he called ten of his servants, delivered to them ten [1]mi-
nas, and said to them, 'Do business till I come.'
14 [a]"But his citizens hated him,
and sent a delegation after him,
saying, 'We will not have this
man to reign over us.'
15 "And so it was that when he
returned, having received the
kingdom, he then commanded
these servants, to whom he had
given the money, to be called to
him, that he might know how
much every man had gained by
trading.
16 "Then came the first, saying,
'Master, your mina has earned
ten minas.'
17 "And he said to him, [a]'Well
done, good servant; because you
were [b]faithful in a very little,
have authority over ten cities.'
18 "And the second came, saying, 'Master, your mina has
earned five minas.'
19 "Likewise he said to him,
'You also be over five cities.'
20 "Then another came, saying, 'Master, here is your mina,
which I have kept put away in a
handkerchief.
21 [a]'For I feared you, because
you are [1]an austere man. You
collect what you did not deposit,
and reap what you did not sow.'
22 "And he said to him, [a]'Out
of your own mouth I will judge
you, *you* wicked servant. [b]You
knew that I was an austere man,
collecting what I did not deposit
and reaping what I did not sow.
23 'Why then did you not put
my money in the bank, that at
my coming I might have collected it with interest?'
24 "And he said to those who
stood by, 'Take the mina from
him, and give *it* to him who has
ten minas.'
25 ("But they said to him, 'Master, he has ten minas.')
26 'For I say to you, [a]that to
everyone who has will be given;
and from him who does not
have, even what he has will be
taken away from him.
27 'But bring here those enemies of mine, who did not want
me to reign over them, and slay
them before me.' "
28 When He had said this, [a]He
went on ahead, going up to Jerusalem.
29 [a]And it came to pass, when
He drew near to [1]Beth′pha·gē
and [b]Beth′a·ny, at the mountain
called [c]Ol′i·vet, *that* He sent two
of His disciples,
30 saying, "Go into the village
opposite *you*, where as you enter you will find a colt tied,
on which no one has ever sat.
Loose it and bring *it here*.
31 "And if anyone asks you,
'Why are you loosing *it*?' thus
you shall say to him, 'Because
the Lord has need of it.' "
32 So those who were sent went
their way and found *it* just [a]as
He had said to them.
33 But as they were loosing the
colt, the owners of it said to

11 [a]Acts 1:6
12 [a]Matt. 25:14–30
13 [1]Gr. *mna*, same as Heb. *minah*, each worth about three months' salary
14 [a][John 1:11]
17 [a]Matt. 25:21, 23 [b]Luke 16:10
21 [a]Matt. 25:24 [1]*a severe*
22 [a]Job 15:6 [b]Matt. 25:26
26 [a]Luke 8:18
28 [a]Mark 10:32
29 [a]Matt. 21:1 [b]John 12:1 [c]Acts 1:12 [1]M *Bethsphage*
32 [a]Luke 22:13

them, "Why are you loosing the colt?"

34 And they said, "The Lord has need of him."

35 Then they brought him to Jesus. [a]And they threw their own clothes on the colt, and they set Jesus on him.

36 And as He went, *many* spread their clothes on the road.

37 Then, as He was now drawing near the descent of the Mount of Olives, the whole multitude of the disciples began to [a]rejoice and praise God with a loud voice for all the mighty works they had seen,

★ 38 saying:

> [a]" *'Blessed is the King who*
> *comes in the name of the*
> *LORD!'*
> [b]Peace in heaven and glory
> in the highest!"

39 And some of the Phar′i·sees called to Him from the crowd, "Teacher, rebuke Your disciples."

40 But He answered and said to them, "I tell you that if these should keep silent, [a]the stones would immediately cry out."

41 Now as He drew near, He saw the city and [a]wept over it,

42 saying, "If you had known, even you, especially in this [a]your day, the things *that* [b]*make* for your [c]peace! But now they are hidden from your eyes.

43 "For days will come upon you when your enemies will [a]build an embankment around you, surround you and close you in on every side,

44 [a]"and level you, and your children within you, to the ground; and [b]they will not leave in you one stone upon another, [c]because you did not know the time of your visitation."

45 [a]Then He went into the temple and began to drive out those who [1]bought and sold in it,

46 saying to them, "It is written, [a]*'My house* [1]*is a house of prayer,'* but you have made it a [b]*'den of thieves.'* "

47 And He [a]was teaching daily in the temple. But [b]the chief priests, the scribes, and the leaders of the people sought to destroy Him,

48 and were unable to do anything; for all the people were very attentive to [a]hear Him.

20 Now [a]it happened on one of those days, as He taught the people in the temple and preached the gospel, *that* the chief priests and the scribes, together with the elders, confronted *Him*

2 and spoke to Him, saying, "Tell us, [a]by what authority are You doing these things? Or who is he who gave You this authority?"

3 But He answered and said to them, "I also will ask you one thing, and answer Me:

4 "The [a]baptism of John—was it from heaven or from men?"

5 And they reasoned among themselves, saying, "If we say, 'From heaven,' He will say, 'Why [1]then did you not believe him?'

6 "But if we say, 'From men,' all the people will stone us, [a]for they are persuaded that John was a prophet."

7 So they answered that they did not know where *it was* from.

8 And Jesus said to them, "Neither will I tell you by what authority I do these things."

35 [a]2 Kin. 9:13
37 [a]Luke 13:17; 18:43
38 [a]Ps. 118:26 [b][Eph. 2:14]
40 [a]Hab. 2:11
41 [a]John 11:35
42 [a]Heb. 3:13 [b][Acts 10:36] [c][Rom. 5:1]
43 [a]Jer. 6:3, 6
44 [a]1 Kin. 9:7, 8 [b]Matt. 24:2 [c][1 Pet. 2:12]
45 [a]Mark 11:11, 15–17 [1]NU *were selling, saying*
46 [a]Is. 56:7 [b]Jer. 7:11 [1]NU *shall be*
47 [a]Luke 21:37; 22:53 [b]John 7:19; 8:37
48 [a]Luke 21:38

CHAPTER 20

1 [a]Matt. 21:23–27
2 [a]Acts 4:7; 7:27
4 [a]John 1:26, 31
5 [1]NU, M omit *then*
6 [a]Luke 7:24–30

9 Then He began to tell the
people this parable: [a]"A certain
man planted a vineyard, leased
it to [1]vinedressers, and went into
a far country for a long time.
10 "Now at [1]vintage-time he [a]sent
a servant to the vinedressers, that
they might give him some of the
fruit of the vineyard. But the vinedressers beat him and sent *him*
away empty-handed.
11 "Again he sent another servant; and they beat him also,
treated *him* shamefully, and sent
him away empty-handed.
12 "And again he sent a third;
and they wounded him also and
cast *him* out.
13 "Then the owner of the vineyard said, 'What shall I do? I will
send my beloved son. Probably
they will respect *him* when they
see him.'
14 "But when the vinedressers
saw him, they reasoned among
themselves, saying, 'This is the
[a]heir. Come, [b]let us kill him, that
the inheritance may be [c]ours.'
15 "So they cast him out of the
vineyard and [a]killed *him*. Therefore what will the owner of the
vineyard do to them?
16 "He will come and destroy
those vinedressers and give the
vineyard to [a]others." And when
they heard *it* they said, "Certainly not!"
☆17 Then He looked at them and
said, "What then is this that is
written:

[a]'The stone which the
builders rejected
Has become the chief
cornerstone'?

☆18 "Whoever falls on that stone
will be [a]broken; but [b]on whomever it falls, it will grind him to
powder."
19 And the chief priests and the
scribes that very hour sought
to lay hands on Him, but they
[1]feared the people—for they
knew He had spoken this parable against them.
20 [a]So they watched *Him*, and
sent spies who pretended to be
righteous, that they might seize
on His words, in order to deliver
Him to the power and the authority of the governor.
21 Then they asked Him, saying,
[a]"Teacher, we know that You say
and teach rightly, and You do not
show personal favoritism, but
teach the way of God in truth:
22 "Is it lawful for us to pay
taxes to Caesar or not?"
23 But He perceived their craftiness, and said to them, [1]"Why do
you test Me?
24 "Show Me a denarius. Whose
image and inscription does it
have?" They answered and said,
"Caesar's."
25 And He said to them,
[a]"Render[1] therefore to Caesar
the things that are Caesar's,
and to God the things that are
God's."
26 But they could not catch Him
in His words in the presence of
the people. And they marveled
at His answer and kept silent.
27 [a]Then some of the Sad′-
dū·cees, [b]who deny that there is
a resurrection, came to *Him* and
asked Him,
28 saying: "Teacher, Moses wrote
to us *that* if a man's brother dies,
having a wife, and he dies without
children, his brother should take
his wife and raise up offspring for
his brother.

9 [a]Mark 12:1–12 [1]*tenant farmers*
10 [a][1 Thess. 2:15] [1]Lit. *the season*
14 [a][Heb. 1:1–3] [b]Matt. 27:21–23 [c]John 11:47, 48
15 [a]Luke 23:33
16 [a]Rom. 11:1, 11
17 [a]Ps. 118:22; Acts 4:10, 11; Eph. 2:20
18 [a]Is. 8:14, 15; 1 Pet. 2:7, 8 [b][Dan. 2:34, 35, 44, 45]
19 [1]M *were afraid—for*
20 [a]Matt. 22:15
21 [a]Mark 12:14
23 [1]NU omits *Why do you test Me?*
25 [a][1 Pet. 2:13–17] [1]*Pay*
27 [a]Mark 12:18–27 [b]Acts 23:6, 8

29 "Now there were seven
brothers. And the first took a
wife, and died without children.
30 "And the second [1]took her as
wife, and he died childless.
31 "Then the third took her, and
in like manner the seven [1]also;
and they left no children, and
died.
32 "Last of all the woman died
also.
33 "Therefore, in the resurrection, whose wife does she become? For all seven had her as
wife."
34 Jesus answered and said
to them, "The sons of this age
marry and are given in marriage.
35 "But those who are [a]counted
worthy to attain that age, and
the resurrection from the dead,
neither marry nor are given in
marriage;
36 "nor can they die anymore,
for [a]they are equal to the angels
and are sons of God, [b]being sons
of the resurrection.
37 "But even Moses showed in
the *burning* bush *passage* that
the dead are raised, when he
called the Lord [a]*'the God of
Abraham, the God of Isaac, and
the God of Jacob.'*
38 "For He is not the God of the
dead but of the living, for [a]all
live to Him."
39 Then some of the scribes answered and said, "Teacher, You
have spoken well."
40 But after that they dared not
question Him anymore.
41 And He said to them, [a]"How
can they say that the Christ is
the Son of David?
☆ 42 "Now David himself said in
the Book of Psalms:

[a]*'The LORD said to my Lord,
"Sit at My right hand,*
43 *Till I make Your enemies
Your footstool."'*

44 "Therefore David calls Him
'Lord'; [a]how is He then his
Son?"
45 [a]Then, in the hearing of all
the people, He said to His disciples,
46 [a]"Beware of the scribes,
who desire to go around in long
robes, [b]love greetings in the
marketplaces, the best seats in
the synagogues, and the best
places at feasts,
47 [a]"who devour widows'
houses, and for a [b]pretense make
long prayers. These will receive
greater condemnation."

21
And He looked up [a]and
saw the rich putting their
gifts into the treasury,
2 and He saw also a certain
[a]poor widow putting in two
[b]mites.[1]
3 So He said, "Truly I say to
you [a]that this poor widow has
put in more than all;
4 "for all these out of their
abundance have put in offerings [1]for God, but she out of her
poverty put in [a]all the livelihood
that she had."
5 [a]Then, as some spoke of the
temple, how it was [1]adorned
with beautiful stones and dona-
tions, He said,
6 "These things which you
see—the days will come in which
[a]not *one* stone shall be left upon
another that shall not be thrown
down."
7 So they asked Him, saying,
"Teacher, but when will these
things be? And what sign *will*

30 [1]NU omits the rest of v. 30.
31 [1]NU, M *also left no children*
35 [a]Phil. 3:11
36 [a][1 John 3:2] [b]Rom. 8:23
37 [a]Ex. 3:1–6, 15
38 [a][Rom. 6:10, 11; 14:8, 9]
41 [a]Matt. 22:41–46
42 [a]Ps. 110:1; Eph. 1:19–23
44 [a]Rom. 1:3; 9:4, 5
45 [a]Matt. 23:1–7
46 [a]Matt. 23:5 [b]Luke 11:43; 14:7
47 [a]Matt. 23:14 [b][Matt. 6:5, 6]

CHAPTER 21

1 [a]Mark 12:41–44
2 [a][2 Cor. 6:10] [b]Mark 12:42 [1]Gr. *lepta*, very small copper coins
3 [a][2 Cor. 8:12]
4 [a][2 Cor. 8:12] [1]NU omits *for God*
5 [a]Mark 13:1 [1]*decorated*
6 [a]Luke 19:41–44

there be when these things are about to take place?"

8 And He said: [a]"Take heed that you not be deceived. For many will come in My name, saying, 'I am *He*,' and, 'The time has drawn near.' [1]Therefore do not [2]go after them.

9 "But when you hear of [a]wars and commotions, do not be terrified; for these things must come to pass first, but the end *will* not *come* immediately."

10 [a]Then He said to them, "Nation will rise against nation, and kingdom against kingdom.

11 "And there will be great [a]earthquakes in various places, and famines and pestilences; and there will be fearful sights and great signs from heaven.

12 [a]"But before all these things, they will lay their hands on you and persecute *you*, delivering *you* up to the synagogues and [b]prisons. [c]You will be brought before kings and rulers [d]for My name's sake.

13 "But [a]it will turn out for you as an occasion for testimony.

14 [a]"Therefore settle *it* in your hearts not to meditate beforehand on what you will [1]answer;

15 "for I will give you a mouth and wisdom [a]which all your adversaries will not be able to contradict or [1]resist.

16 [a]"You will be betrayed even by parents and brothers, relatives and friends; and they will put [b]*some* of you to death.

17 "And [a]you will be hated by all for My name's sake.

18 [a]"But not a hair of your head shall be lost.

19 "By your patience possess your souls.

20 [a]"But when you see Jerusalem surrounded by armies, then know that its desolation is near.

21 "Then let those who are in Judea flee to the mountains, let those who are in the midst of her depart, and let not those who are in the country enter her.

22 "For these are the days of vengeance, that [a]all things which are written may be fulfilled.

23 [a]"But woe to those who are pregnant and to those who are nursing babies in those days! For there will be great distress in the land and wrath upon this people.

24 "And they will fall by the edge of the sword, and be led away captive into all nations. And Jerusalem will be trampled by Gentiles [a]until the times of the Gentiles are fulfilled.

25 [a]"And there will be signs in the sun, in the moon, and in the stars; and on the earth distress of nations, with perplexity, the sea and the waves roaring;

26 "men's hearts failing them from fear and the expectation of those things which are coming on the earth, [a]for the powers of the heavens will be shaken.

27 "Then they will see the Son of Man [a]coming in a cloud with power and great glory. ☆

28 "Now when these things begin to happen, look up and lift up your heads, because [a]your redemption draws near."

29 [a]Then He spoke to them a parable: "Look at the fig tree, and all the trees.

30 "When they are already budding, you see and know for yourselves that summer is now near.

31 "So you also, when you see these things happening, know

8 [a]Eph. 5:6 [1]NU omits *Therefore* [2]*follow*
9 [a]Rev. 6:4
10 [a]Matt. 24:7
11 [a]Rev. 6:12
12 [a][Rev. 2:10] [b]Acts 4:3; 5:18; 12:4; 16:24 [c]Acts 25:23 [d]1 Pet. 2:13
13 [a][Phil. 1:12–14, 28]
14 [a]Luke 12:11 [1]*say in defense*
15 [a]Acts 6:10 [1]*withstand*
16 [a]Mic. 7:6 [b]Acts 7:59; 12:2
17 [a]Matt. 10:22
18 [a]Matt. 10:30
20 [a]Mark 13:14
22 [a][Dan. 9:24–27]
23 [a]Matt. 24:19
24 [a][Dan. 9:27; 12:7]
25 [a][2 Pet. 3:10–12]
26 [a]Matt. 24:29
27 [a]Dan. 7:13; Rev. 1:7; 14:14
28 [a][Rom. 8:19, 23]
29 [a]Mark 13:28

that the kingdom of God is
near.
32 "Assuredly, I say to you, this
generation will by no means
pass away till all things take
place.
33 [a]"Heaven and earth will pass
away, but My [b]words will by no
means pass away.
34 "But [a]take heed to yourselves,
lest your hearts be weighed
down with [1]carousing, drunkenness, and [b]cares of this life, and
that Day come on you unexpectedly.
35 "For [a]it will come as a snare
on all those who dwell on the
face of the whole earth.
36 [a]"Watch therefore, and [b]pray
always that you may [1]be counted
[c]worthy to escape all these things
that will come to pass, and [d]to
stand before the Son of Man."
37 [a]And in the daytime He was
teaching in the temple, but [b]at
night He went out and stayed on
the mountain called Ol'i·vet.
38 Then early in the morning
all the people came to Him in
the temple to hear Him.

22

Now [a]the Feast of Unleavened Bread drew near,
which is called Passover.
2 And [a]the chief priests and
the scribes sought how they
might kill Him, for they feared
the people.
3 [a]Then Satan entered Judas,
surnamed Is·car'i·ot, who was
numbered among the [b]twelve.
4 So he went his way and conferred with the chief priests and
captains, how he might betray
Him to them.
5 And they were glad, and
[a]agreed to give him money.
6 So he promised and sought
opportunity to [a]betray Him to
them in the absence of the multitude.
7 [a]Then came the Day of Unleavened Bread, when the Passover must be [1]killed.
8 And He sent Peter and John,
saying, "Go and prepare the
Passover for us, that we may
eat."
9 So they said to Him, "Where
do You want us to prepare?"
10 And He said to them, "Behold, when you have entered
the city, a man will meet you
carrying a pitcher of water; follow him into the house which he
enters.
11 "Then you shall say to the
master of the house, 'The Teacher
says to you, "Where is the guest
room where I may eat the Passover with My disciples?" '
12 "Then he will show you a
large, furnished upper room;
there make ready."
13 So they went and [a]found it
just as He had said to them, and
they prepared the Passover.
14 [a]When the hour had come,
He sat down, and the [1]twelve
apostles with Him.
15 Then He said to them, "With
fervent desire I have desired to
eat this Passover with you before I suffer;
16 "for I say to you, I will no
longer eat of it [a]until it is fulfilled in the kingdom of God."
17 Then He took the cup, and
gave thanks, and said, "Take this
and divide *it* among yourselves;
18 "for [a]I say to you, [1]I will not
drink of the fruit of the vine until the kingdom of God comes."
19 [a]And He took bread, gave
thanks and broke *it*, and gave
it to them, saying, "This is My

33 [a]Matt. 24:35 [b]Is. 40:8
34 [a]1 Thess. 5:6 [b]Luke 8:14 [1]*dissipation*
35 [a]Rev. 3:3; 16:15
36 [a]Matt. 24:42; 25:13 [b]Luke 18:1 [c]Luke 20:35 [d][Eph. 6:13] [1]NU *have strength to*
37 [a]John 8:1, 2 [b]Luke 22:39

CHAPTER 22

1 [a]Matt. 26:2–5
2 [a]John 11:47
3 [a]Mark 14:10, 11 [b]Matt. 10:2–4
5 [a]Zech. 11:12
6 [a]Ps. 41:9
7 [a]Matt. 26:17–19 [1]Sacrificed
13 [a]Luke 19:32
14 [a]Mark 14:17 [1]NU omits *twelve*
16 [a][Rev. 19:9]
18 [a]Mark 14:25 [1]NU adds *from now on*
19 [a]Matt. 26:26

[b]body which is given for you; [c]do
this in remembrance of Me."
20 Likewise He also *took* the
cup after supper, saying, [a]"This
cup *is* the new covenant in My
blood, which is shed for you.
21 [a]"But behold, the hand of
My betrayer *is* with Me on the
table.
22 [a]"And truly the Son of Man
goes [b]as it has been determined,
but woe to that man by whom
He is betrayed!"
23 [a]Then they began to question among themselves, which
of them it was who would do
this thing.
24 [a]Now there was also a dispute among them, as to which of
them should be considered the
greatest.
25 [a]And He said to them, "The
kings of the Gentiles exercise
lordship over them, and those
who exercise authority over
them are called 'benefactors.'
26 [a]"But not so *among* you; on
the contrary, [b]he who is greatest among you, let him be as the
younger, and he who governs as
he who serves.
27 [a]"For who *is* greater, he
who sits at the table, or he who
serves? *Is* it not he who sits at
the table? Yet [b]I am among you
as the One who serves.
28 "But you are those who have
continued with Me in [a]My trials.
29 "And [a]I bestow upon you a
kingdom, just as My Father bestowed *one* upon Me,
30 "that [a]you may eat and drink
at My table in My kingdom, [b]and
sit on thrones judging the twelve
tribes of Israel."
31 [1]And the Lord said, "Simon,
Simon! Indeed, [a]Satan has asked

19 [b][1 Pet. 2:24] [c]1 Cor. 11:23–26
20 [a]1 Cor. 10:16
21 [a]John 13:21, 26, 27
22 [a]Matt. 26:24 [b]Acts 2:23
23 [a]John 13:22, 25
24 [a]Mark 9:34
25 [a]Mark 10:42–45
26 [a][1 Pet. 5:3] [b]Luke 9:48
27 [a][Luke 12:37] [b]Phil. 2:7
28 [a][Heb. 2:18; 4:15]
29 [a]Matt. 24:47
30 [a][Matt. 8:11] [b][Rev. 3:21]
31 [a]1 Pet. 5:8 [b]Amos 9:9 [1]NU omits *And the Lord said*
32 [a][John 17:9, 11, 15] [b]John 21:15–17
34 [a]John 13:37, 38
35 [a]Matt. 10:9
37 [a]Is. 53:12; Matt. 27:38; Mark 15:28 [1]*fulfilled*
39 [a]John 18:1 [b]Luke 21:37
40 [a]Mark 14:32–42
41 [a]Matt. 26:39
42 [a]Is. 50:5; John 4:34; 5:30; 6:38; 8:29
43 [a]Matt. 4:11 [1]NU brackets vv. 43 and 44 as not in the original text.

for you, that he may [b]sift *you* as
wheat.
32 "But [a]I have prayed for you,
that your faith should not fail;
and when you have returned to
Me, [b]strengthen your brethren."
33 But he said to Him, "Lord, I
am ready to go with You, both to
prison and to death."
34 [a]Then He said, "I tell you,
Peter, the rooster shall not crow
this day before you will deny
three times that you know Me."
35 [a]And He said to them, "When
I sent you without money bag,
knapsack, and sandals, did you
lack anything?" So they said,
"Nothing."
36 Then He said to them, "But
now, he who has a money bag,
let him take *it*, and likewise a
knapsack; and he who has no
sword, let him sell his garment
and buy one.
37 "For I say to you that this ☆
which is written must still be
[1]accomplished in Me: [a]*'And He
was numbered with the transgressors.'* For the things concerning Me have an end."
38 So they said, "Lord, look,
here *are* two swords." And He
said to them, "It is enough."
39 [a]Coming out, [b]He went to the
Mount of Olives, as He was accustomed, and His disciples also
followed Him.
40 [a]When He came to the place,
He said to them, "Pray that you
may not enter into temptation."
41 [a]And He was withdrawn from
them about a stone's throw, and
He knelt down and prayed,
42 saying, "Father, if it is Your ★
will, take this cup away from
Me; nevertheless [a]not My will,
but Yours, be done."
43 [1]Then [a]an angel appeared to

Him from heaven, strengthening
Him.
44 [a]And being in agony, He
prayed more earnestly. Then His
sweat became like great drops
of blood falling down to the
ground.
45 When He rose up from
prayer, and had come to His disciples, He found them sleeping
from sorrow.
46 Then He said to them, "Why
[a]do you sleep? Rise and [b]pray,
lest you enter into temptation."
★ **47** And while He was still speaking, [a]behold, a multitude; and he
who was called [b]Judas, one of
the twelve, went before them
and drew near to Jesus to kiss
Him.
48 But Jesus said to him, "Judas, are you betraying the Son
of Man with a [a]kiss?"
49 When those around Him saw
what was going to happen, they
said to Him, "Lord, shall we
strike with the sword?"
50 And [a]one of them struck the
servant of the high priest and
cut off his right ear.
51 But Jesus answered and
said, "Permit even this." And He
touched his ear and healed him.
52 [a]Then Jesus said to the chief
priests, captains of the temple,
and the elders who had come
to Him, "Have you come out, as
against a [b]robber, with swords
and clubs?
53 "When I was with you daily
in the [a]temple, you did not try to
seize Me. But this is your [b]hour,
and the power of darkness."
54 [a]Having arrested Him, they
led *Him* and brought Him into
the high priest's house. [b]But Peter followed at a distance.
55 [a]Now when they had kindled
a fire in the midst of the courtyard and sat down together, Peter sat among them.
56 And a certain servant girl,
seeing him as he sat by the fire,
looked intently at him and said,
"This man was also with Him."
57 But he denied [1]Him, saying,
"Woman, I do not know Him."
58 [a]And after a little while another saw him and said, "You
also are of them." But Peter said,
"Man, I am not!"
59 [a]Then after about an hour
had passed, another confidently
affirmed, saying, "Surely this
fellow also was with Him, for he
is a [b]Galilean."
60 But Peter said, "Man, I do
not know what you are saying!"
Immediately, while he was still
speaking, [1]the rooster crowed.
61 And the Lord turned and
looked at Peter. Then [a]Peter remembered the word of the Lord,
how He had said to him, [b]"Before
the rooster [1]crows, you will deny
Me three times."
62 So Peter went out and wept
bitterly.
63 [a]Now the men who held Jesus mocked Him and [b]beat Him.
64 [1]And having blindfolded
Him, they [a]struck Him on the
face and asked Him, saying,
"Prophesy! Who is the one who
struck You?"
65 And many other things they
blasphemously spoke against
Him.
66 [a]As soon as it was day, [b]the
elders of the people, both chief
priests and scribes, came together and led Him into their
council, saying,
67 [a]"If You are the Christ, tell
us." But He said to them, "If I

44 [a][Heb. 5:7]
46 [a]Luke 9:32 [b]Luke 22:40
47 [a]John 18:3–11 [b]Ps. 41:9; Acts 1:16, 17
48 [a][Prov. 27:6]
50 [a]Matt. 26:51
52 [a]Matt. 26:55 [b]Luke 23:32
53 [a]Luke 19:47, 48 [b][John 12:27]
54 [a]Matt. 26:57 [b]John 18:15
55 [a]Mark 14:66–72
57 [1]NU *it*
58 [a]John 18:25
59 [a]Mark 14:70 [b]Acts 1:11; 2:7
60 [1]NU, M *a rooster*
61 [a]Matt. 26:75 [b]John 13:38 [1]NU adds *today*
63 [a]Ps. 69:1, 4, 7–9 [b]Is. 50:6
64 [a]Zech. 13:7 [1]NU *And having blindfolded Him, they asked Him*
66 [a]Matt. 27:1 [b]Acts 4:26
67 [a]Matt. 26:63–66

tell you, you will [b]by no means
believe.
68 "And if I [1]also ask *you,* you
will by no means answer [2]Me or
let *Me* go.
69 [a]"Hereafter the Son of Man
will sit on the right hand of the
power of God."
70 Then they all said, "Are You
then the Son of God?" So He
said to them, [a]"You *rightly* say
that I am."
71 [a]And they said, "What further testimony do we need? For
we have heard it ourselves from
His own mouth."
23 Then [a]the whole multitude of them arose and
led Him to [b]Pilate.
2 And they began to [a]accuse
Him, saying, "We found this *fel-*
low [b]perverting [1]the nation, and
[c]forbidding to pay taxes to Caesar, saying [d]that He Himself is
Christ, a King."
3 [a]Then Pilate asked Him, saying, "Are You the King of the
Jews?" He answered him and
said, "*It is as* you say."
4 So Pilate said to the chief
priests and the crowd, [a]"I find no
fault in this Man."
5 But they were the more
fierce, saying, "He stirs up the
people, teaching throughout all
Judea, beginning from [a]Galilee
to this place."
6 When Pilate heard [1]of Galilee, he asked if the Man were a
Galilean.
7 And as soon as he knew that
He belonged to [a]Her′od's juris-
diction, he sent Him to Her′od,
who was also in Jerusalem at
that time.
8 Now when Her′od saw Jesus,
[a]he was exceedingly glad; for he
had desired for a long *time* to
see Him, because [b]he had heard
many things about Him, and he
hoped to see some miracle done
by Him.
9 Then he questioned Him ★
with many words, but He answered him [a]nothing.
10 And the chief priests and
scribes stood and vehemently
accused Him.
11 [a]Then Her′od, with his [1]men
of war, treated Him with contempt and mocked *Him,* arrayed
Him in a gorgeous robe, and
sent Him back to Pilate.
12 That very day [a]Pilate and
Her′od became friends with
each other, for previously they
had been at enmity with each
other.
13 [a]Then Pilate, when he had
called together the chief priests,
the rulers, and the people,
14 said to them, [a]"You have
brought this Man to me, as one
who misleads the people. And
indeed, [b]having examined *Him*
in your presence, I have found
no fault in this Man concerning
those things of which you accuse Him;
15 "no, neither did Her′od, for
[1]I sent you back to him; and indeed nothing deserving of death
has been done by Him.
16 [a]"I will therefore chastise
Him and release *Him*"
17 [a](for[1] it was necessary for
him to release one to them at the
feast).
18 And [a]they all cried out at
once, saying, "Away with this
Man, and release to us Ba·rab′-
bas"—
19 who had been thrown into
prison for a certain rebellion
made in the city, and for murder.

67 [b]Luke 20:5–7
68 [1]NU omits *also* [2]NU omits the rest of v. 68.
69 [a]Heb. 1:3; 8:1
70 [a]Matt. 26:64; 27:11
71 [a]Mark 14:63

CHAPTER 23

1 [a]John 18:28 [b]Luke 3:1; 13:1
2 [a]Acts 24:2 [b]Acts 17:7 [c]Matt. 17:27 [d]John 19:12 [1]NU *our*
3 [a]1 Tim. 6:13
4 [a][1 Pet. 2:22]
5 [a]John 7:41
6 [1]NU omits *of Galilee*
7 [a]Luke 3:1; 9:7; 13:31
8 [a]Luke 9:9 [b]Matt. 14:1
9 [a]Is. 53:7; John 19:9
11 [a]Is. 53:3 [1]*troops*
12 [a]Acts 4:26, 27
13 [a]Mark 15:14
14 [a]Luke 23:1, 2 [b]Luke 23:4
15 [1]NU *he sent Him back to us*
16 [a]John 19:1
17 [a]John 18:39 [1]NU omits v. 17.
18 [a]Acts 3:13–15

20 Pilate, therefore, wishing to
release Jesus, again called out to
them.
21 But they shouted, saying,
"Crucify *Him*, crucify Him!"
22 Then he said to them the
third time, "Why, what evil has
He done? I have found no reason
for death in Him. I will therefore
chastise Him and let *Him* go."
23 But they were insistent, de-
manding with loud voices that
He be crucified. And the voices
of these men [1]and of the chief
priests prevailed.
24 So [a]Pilate gave sentence that
it should be as they requested.
25 [a]And he released [1]to them
the one they requested, who for
rebellion and murder had been
thrown into prison; but he delivered Jesus to their will.
26 [a]Now as they led Him away,
they laid hold of a certain man,
Simon a Cȳ·rē′ni·an, who was
coming from the country, and on
him they laid the cross that he
might bear *it* after Jesus.
27 And a great multitude of
the people followed Him, and
women who also mourned and
lamented Him.
28 But Jesus, turning to them,
said, "Daughters of Jerusalem,
do not weep for Me, but weep for
yourselves and for your children.
29 [a]"For indeed the days are
coming in which they will say,
'Blessed *are* the barren, wombs
that never bore, and breasts
which never nursed!'
30 "Then they will begin [a]*'to say
to the mountains, "Fall on us!"
and to the hills, "Cover us!"'*
31 [a]"For if they do these things
in the green wood, what will be
done in the dry?"
★ 32 [a]There were also two others,
criminals, led with Him to be put
to death.
33 And [a]when they had come to
the place called Calvary, there
they crucified Him, and the
criminals, one on the right hand
and the other on the left.
34 [1]Then Jesus said, "Father,
[a]forgive them, for [b]they do not
know what they do." And [c]they
divided His garments and cast
lots.
35 And [a]the people stood look- ★
ing on. But even the [b]rulers with
them sneered, saying, "He saved
others; let Him save Himself if
He is the Christ, the chosen of
God."
36 The soldiers also mocked ★
Him, coming and offering Him
[a]sour wine,
37 and saying, "If You are the
King of the Jews, save Yourself."
38 [a]And an inscription also was
[1]written over Him in letters of
Greek, Latin, and Hebrew:

THIS IS THE KING
OF THE JEWS.

39 [a]Then one of the criminals
who were hanged blasphemed
Him, saying, [1]"If You are the
Christ, save Yourself and us."
40 But the other, answering, rebuked him, saying, "Do you not
even fear God, seeing you are
under the same condemnation?
41 "And we indeed justly, for we
receive the due reward of our
deeds; but this Man has done
[a]nothing wrong."
42 Then he said [1]to Jesus, "Lord,
remember me when You come
into Your kingdom."
43 And Jesus said to him, "Assuredly, I say to you, today you
will be with Me in [a]Paradise."

23 [1]NU omits *and of the chief priests*
24 [a]Mark 15:15
25 [a]Is. 53:8 [1]NU, M omit *to them*
26 [a]Matt. 27:32
29 [a]Matt. 24:19
30 [a]Hos. 10:8; Rev. 6:16, 17; 9:6
31 [a][Jer. 25:29]
32 [a]Is. 53:9, 12
33 [a]John 19:17–24
34 [a]1 Cor. 4:12 [b]Acts 3:17 [c]Matt. 27:35 [1]NU brackets the first sentence as a later addition.
35 [a]Ps. 22:17; [Zech. 12:10] [b]Ps. 22:7, 8; Matt. 27:39
36 [a]Ps. 69:21
38 [a]John 19:19 [1]NU omits *written* and *in letters of Greek, Latin, and Hebrew*
39 [a]Mark 15:32 [1]NU *Are You not the Christ? Save*
41 [a][Heb. 7:26]
42 [1]NU *"Jesus, remember me*
43 [a][Rev. 2:7]

44 [a]Now it [1]was about the sixth
hour, and there was darkness
over all the earth until the ninth
hour.
45 Then the sun was [1]darkened,
and [a]the veil of the temple was
torn in [2]two.
46 And when Jesus had cried
out with a loud voice, He said,
"Father, [a]'*into Your hands I com-*
mit My spirit.'" [b]Having said
this, He breathed His last.
47 [a]So when the centurion saw
what had happened, he glorified
God, saying, "Certainly this was
a righteous Man!"
48 And the whole crowd who
came together to that sight, seeing what had been done, beat
their breasts and returned.
49 [a]But all His acquaintances,
and the women who followed
Him from Galilee, stood at a distance, watching these things.
50 [a]Now behold, *there was* a
man named Joseph, a council
member, a good and just man.
51 He had not consented to their
decision and deed. *He was* from
Ar·i·ma·thē′a, a city of the Jews,
[a]who[1] himself was also waiting
for the kingdom of God.
52 This man went to Pilate and
asked for the body of Jesus.
53 [a]Then he took it down,
wrapped it in linen, and laid it
in a tomb *that was* hewn out of
the rock, where no one had ever
lain before.
54 That day was [a]the Preparation, and the Sabbath drew near.
55 And the women [a]who had
come with Him from Galilee followed after, and [b]they observed
the tomb and how His body was
laid.
56 Then they returned and
[a]prepared spices and fragrant

44 [a]Matt. 27:45–56
[1]NU adds *already*

45 [a]Matt. 27:51
[1]NU *obscured*
[2]*the middle*

46 [a]Ps. 31:5
[b]John 19:30

47 [a]Mark 15:39

49 [a]Ps. 38:11

50 [a]Matt. 27:57–61

51 [a]Luke 2:25, 38
[1]NU *who was waiting*

53 [a]Mark 15:46

54 [a]Matt. 27:62

55 [a]Luke 8:2
[b]Mark 15:47

56 [a]Mark 16:1
[b]Ex. 20:10

CHAPTER 24

1 [a]John 20:1–8
[b]Luke 23:56
[1]NU omits *and certain other women with them*

2 [a]Mark 16:4

3 [a]Mark 16:5

4 [a]John 20:12
[1]NU omits *greatly*

6 [a]Luke 9:22

7 [a]Luke 9:44; 11:29, 30; 18:31–33

8 [a]John 2:19–22

9 [a]Mark 16:10

10 [a]Luke 8:3

11 [a]Luke 24:25
[1]*nonsense*

12 [a]John 20:3–6
[1]NU omits *lying*

oils. And they rested on the
Sabbath [b]according to the commandment.
24 Now [a]on the first *day* of
the week, very early in
the morning, they, [1]and certain
other women with them, came
to the tomb [b]bringing the spices
which they had prepared.
2 [a]But they found the stone
rolled away from the tomb.
3 [a]Then they went in and did
not find the body of the Lord
Jesus.
4 And it happened, as they
were [1]greatly perplexed about
this, that [a]behold, two men stood
by them in shining garments.
5 Then, as they were afraid
and bowed *their* faces to the
earth, they said to them, "Why
do you seek the living among
the dead?
6 "He is not here, but is risen!
[a]Remember how He spoke to
you when He was still in Galilee,
7 "saying, 'The Son of Man
must be [a]delivered into the hands
of sinful men, and be crucified,
and the third day rise again.'"
8 And [a]they remembered His
words.
9 [a]Then they returned from the
tomb and told all these things to
the eleven and to all the rest.
10 It was Mary Mag′da·lēne,
[a]Jō·an′na, Mary *the mother* of
James, and the other *women*
with them, who told these things
to the apostles.
11 [a]And their words seemed to
them like [1]idle tales, and they
did not believe them.
12 [a]But Peter arose and ran to
the tomb; and stooping down,
he saw the linen cloths [1]lying
by themselves; and he departed,

marveling to himself at what
had happened.
13 [a]Now behold, two of them
were traveling that same day to
a village called Em·mā′us, which
was [1]seven miles from Jerusalem.
14 And they talked together of
all these things which had happened.
15 So it was, while they conversed and reasoned, that [a]Jesus
Himself drew near and went
with them.
16 But [a]their eyes were restrained, so that they did not
know Him.
17 And He said to them, "What
kind of conversation *is* this that
you have with one another as
you [1]walk and are sad?"
18 Then the one [a]whose name
was Clē′o·pas answered and
said to Him, "Are You the only
stranger in Jerusalem, and have
You not known the things which
happened there in these days?"
19 And He said to them, "What
things?" So they said to Him,
"The things concerning Jesus of
Nazareth, [a]who was a Prophet
[b]mighty in deed and word before
God and all the people,
20 [a]"and how the chief priests
and our rulers delivered Him
to be condemned to death, and
crucified Him.
21 "But we were hoping [a]that
it was He who was going to redeem Israel. Indeed, besides all
this, today is the third day since
these things happened.
22 "Yes, and [a]certain women of
our company, who arrived at the
tomb early, astonished us.
23 "When they did not find His
body, they came saying that they
had also seen a vision of angels
who said He was alive.
24 "And [a]certain of those *who*
were with us went to the tomb
and found *it* just as the women
had said; but Him they did not
see."
25 Then He said to them, "O
foolish ones, and slow of heart
to believe in all that the prophets have spoken!
26 [a]"Ought not the Christ to
have suffered these things and
to enter into His [b]glory?"
27 And beginning at [a]Moses and
[b]all the Prophets, He [1]expounded
to them in all the Scriptures the
things concerning Himself.
28 Then they drew near to the
village where they were going, and [a]He [1]indicated that He
would have gone farther.
29 But [a]they constrained Him,
saying, [b]"Abide with us, for it
is toward evening, and the day
is far spent." And He went in to
stay with them.
30 Now it came to pass, as [a]He
sat at the table with them, that
He took bread, blessed and
broke *it*, and gave it to them.
31 Then their eyes were opened
and they knew Him; and He
vanished from their sight.
32 And they said to one another, "Did not our heart burn
within us while He talked with
us on the road, and while He
opened the Scriptures to us?"
33 So they rose up that very
hour and returned to Jerusalem,
and found the eleven and those
who were with them gathered
together,
34 saying, "The Lord is risen
indeed, and [a]has appeared to
Simon!"

13 [a]Mark 16:12 [1]Lit. *60 stadia*
15 [a][Matt. 18:20]
16 [a]John 20:14; 21:4
17 [1]NU *walk? And they stood still, looking sad.*
18 [a]John 19:25
19 [a]Matt. 21:11 [b]Acts 7:22
20 [a]Acts 13:27, 28
21 [a]Luke 1:68; 2:38
22 [a]Mark 16:10
24 [a]Luke 24:12
26 [a]Acts 17:2, 3 [b][1 Pet. 1:10–12]
27 [a][Deut. 18:15] [b][Is. 7:14; 9:6] [1]*explained*
28 [a]Mark 6:48 [1]*acted as if*
29 [a]Gen. 19:2, 3 [b][John 14:23]
30 [a]Matt. 14:19
34 [a]1 Cor. 15:5

35 And they told about the
things *that had happened* on the
road, and how He was [1]known to
them in the breaking of bread.
36 [a]Now as they said these
things, Jesus Himself stood in
the midst of them, and said to
them, "Peace to you."
37 But they were terrified and
frightened, and supposed they
had seen [a]a spirit.
38 And He said to them, "Why
are you troubled? And why do
doubts arise in your hearts?
39 "Behold My hands and My
feet, that it is I Myself. [a]Handle
Me and see, for a [b]spirit does not
have flesh and bones as you see
I have."
40 [1]When He had said this, He
showed them His hands and His
feet.
41 But while they still did not
believe [a]for joy, and marveled,
He said to them, [b]"Have you any
food here?"
42 So they gave Him a piece of
a broiled fish [1]and some honeycomb.
43 [a]And He took *it* and ate in
their presence.
44 Then He said to them, [a]"These
are the words which I spoke to
you while I was still with you,
that all things must be fulfilled
which were written in the Law
of Moses and *the* Prophets and
the Psalms concerning Me."
45 And [a]He opened their understanding, that they might comprehend the Scriptures.
46 Then He said to them, [a]"Thus
it is written, [1]and thus it was
necessary for the Christ to suffer and to rise from the dead the
third day,
47 "and that repentance and
[a]remission of sins should be
preached in His name [b]to all nations, beginning at Jerusalem.
48 "And [a]you are witnesses of
these things.
49 [a]"Behold, I send the Promise
of My Father upon you; but tarry
in the city [1]of Jerusalem until
you are endued with power from
on high."
50 And He led them out [a]as far
as Beth′a·ny, and He lifted up
His hands and blessed them.
51 [a]Now it came to pass, while ★
He blessed them, that He was
parted from them and carried
up into heaven.
52 [a]And they worshiped Him,
and returned to Jerusalem with
great joy,
53 and were continually [a]in the
temple [1]praising and blessing
God. [2]Amen.

35 [1]*recognized*
36 [a]Mark 16:14
37 [a]Mark 6:49
39 [a]John 20:20, 27 [b][1 Cor. 15:50]
40 [1]Some printed New Testaments omit v. 40. It is found in nearly all Gr. mss.
41 [a]Gen. 45:26 [b]John 21:5
42 [1]NU omits *and some honeycomb*
43 [a]Acts 10:39–41
44 [a]Matt. 16:21; 17:22; 20:18
45 [a]Acts 16:14
46 [a]Acts 17:3 [1]NU *that the Christ should suffer and rise*
47 [a]Acts 5:31; 10:43; 13:38; 26:18 [b][Jer. 31:34]
48 [a][Acts 1:8]
49 [a]Joel 2:28 [1]NU omits *of Jerusalem*
50 [a]Acts 1:12
51 [a]Ps. 68:18; Mark 16:19
52 [a]Matt. 28:9
53 [a]Acts 2:46 [1]NU omits *praising and* [2]NU omits *Amen.*

The Gospel According to
JOHN

JUST as a coin has two sides, both valid, so Jesus Christ has two natures, both valid. Luke presents Christ in His humanity as the Son of Man; John portrays Him in His deity as the Son of God. John's purpose is crystal clear: to set forth Christ in His deity in order to spark believing faith in his readers. John's gospel is topical, not primarily chronological, and it revolves around seven miracles and seven "I am" statements of Christ.

Following an extended eyewitness description of the Upper Room meal and discourse, John records events leading up to the Resurrection, the final climactic proof that Jesus is who He claims to be—the Son of God.

The title of the Fourth Gospel follows the same format as the titles of the synoptic Gospels: *Kata Ioannen*, "According to John." As with the others, the word "Gospel" was added later. *Ioannes* is derived from the Hebrew name *Johanan*, "Yahweh Has Been Gracious."

IN the beginning [a]was the Word,
and the [b]Word was [c]with God,
and the Word was [d]God.
2 [a]He was in the beginning
with God.
3 [a]All things were made through
Him, and without Him nothing
was made that was made.
4 [a]In Him was life, and [b]the life
was the light of men.
5 And [a]the light shines in the
darkness, and the darkness did
not [1]comprehend it.
6 There was a [a]man sent from
God, whose name *was* John.
7 This man came for a [a]witness,
to bear witness of the Light, that
all through him might [b]believe.
8 He was not that Light, but
was sent to bear witness of that
[a]Light.
9 [a]That[1] was the true Light
which gives light to every man
coming into the world.
10 He was in the world, and the
world was made through Him,
and [a]the world did not know
Him.
11 [a]He came to His [1]own, and ★
His [2]own did not receive Him.
12 But [a]as many as received
Him, to them He gave the [1]right
to become children of God,
to those who believe in His
name:
13 [a]who were born, not of blood,
nor of the will of the flesh, nor
of the will of man, but of God.
14 [a]And the Word [b]became
[c]flesh and dwelt among us, and
[d]we beheld His glory, the glory
as of the only begotten of the
Father, [e]full of grace and truth.
15 [a]John bore witness of Him
and cried out, saying, "This was
He of whom I said, [b]'He who
comes after me [1]is preferred
before me, [c]for He was before
me.' "
16 [1]And of His [a]fullness we
have all received, and grace for
grace.
17 For [a]the law was given
through Moses, *but* [b]grace
and [c]truth came through Jesus
Christ.

CHAPTER 1

1 [a]1 John 1:1
[b]Rev. 19:13
[c][John 17:5]
[d][1 John 5:20]
2 [a]Gen. 1:1
3 [a][Col. 1:16, 17]
4 [a][1 John 5:11]
[b]John 8:12; 9:5; 12:46
5 [a][John 3:19]
[1]Or *overcome*
6 [a]Matt. 3:1–17
7 [a]John 3:25–36; 5:33–35
[b][John 3:16]
8 [a]Is. 9:2; 49:6
9 [a]Is. 49:6
[1]Or *That was the true Light which, coming into the world, gives light to every man.*
10 [a]Heb. 1:2
11 [a]Is. 53:3; [Luke 19:14]
[1]His own things or domain
[2]His own people
12 [a]Gal. 3:26
[1]*authority*
13 [a][1 Pet. 1:23]
14 [a]Rev. 19:13
[b]Gal. 4:4
[c]Heb. 2:11
[d]Is. 40:5
[e][John 8:32; 14:6; 18:37]
15 [a]John 3:32
[b][Matt. 3:11]
[c][Col. 1:17]
[1]*ranks higher than I*
16 [a][Col. 1:19; 2:9]
[1]NU *For*
17 [a][Ex. 20:1]
[b][Rom. 5:21; 6:14]
[c][John 8:32; 14:6; 18:37]

18 [a]No one has seen God at any time. [b]The only begotten [1]Son, who is in the bosom of the Father, He has declared *Him.*

19 Now this is [a]the testimony of John, when the Jews sent priests and Lē′vītes from Jerusalem to ask him, "Who are you?"

20 [a]He confessed, and did not deny, but confessed, "I am not the Christ."

21 And they asked him, "What then? Are you E·lī′jah?" He said, "I am not." "Are you [a]the Prophet?" And he answered, "No."

22 Then they said to him, "Who are you, that we may give an answer to those who sent us? What do you say about yourself?"

★ 23 He said: [a]"I *am*

> [b]*'The voice of one crying in*
> *the wilderness:*
> *"Make straight the way of*
> *the* LORD,"'

as the prophet Ī·sāi′ah said."

24 Now those who were sent were from the Phar′i·sees.

25 And they asked him, saying, "Why then do you baptize if you are not the Christ, nor E·lī′jah, nor the Prophet?"

26 John answered them, saying, [a]"I baptize with water, [b]but there stands One among you whom you do not know.

27 [a]"It is He who, coming after me, [1]is preferred before me, whose sandal strap I am not worthy to loose."

28 These things were done [a]in [1]Beth·ab′a·ra beyond the Jordan, where John was baptizing.

29 The next day John saw Jesus coming toward him, and said, "Behold! [a]The Lamb of God [b]who takes away the sin of the world!

30 "This is He of whom I said, 'After me comes a Man who [1]is preferred before me, for He was before me.'

31 "I did not know Him; but that He should be revealed to Israel, [a]therefore I came baptizing with water."

32 [a]And John bore witness, saying, "I saw the Spirit descending from heaven like a dove, and He remained upon Him.

33 "I did not know Him, but ★
He who sent me to baptize with water said to me, 'Upon whom you see the Spirit descending, and remaining on Him, [a]this is He who baptizes with the Holy Spirit.'

34 "And I have seen and testified that this is the [a]Son of God."

35 Again, the next day, John stood with two of his disciples.

36 And looking at Jesus as He walked, he said, [a]"Behold the Lamb of God!"

37 The two disciples heard him speak, and they [a]followed Jesus.

38 Then Jesus turned, and seeing them following, said to them, "What do you seek?" They said to Him, "Rabbi" (which is to say, when translated, Teacher), "where are You staying?"

39 He said to them, "Come and see." They came and saw where He was staying, and remained with Him that day (now it was about the tenth hour).

40 One of the two who heard John *speak,* and followed Him, was [a]Andrew, Simon Peter's brother.

41 He first found his own brother Simon, and said to him,

18 [a]Ex. 33:20 [b]John 14:9 [1]NU *God*
19 [a]John 5:33
20 [a]Luke 3:15
21 [a]Deut. 18:15, 18
23 [a]Matt. 3:3 [b]Is. 40:3
26 [a]Matt. 3:11 [b]Mal. 3:1
27 [a]Acts 19:4 [1]*ranks higher than I*
28 [a]Judg. 7:24 [1]NU, M *Bethany*
29 [a]Rev. 5:6–14 [b][1 Pet. 2:24]
30 [1]*ranks higher than I*
31 [a]Matt. 3:6
32 [a]Mark 1:10
33 [a]Is. 42:1; 61:1; Matt. 3:11
34 [a]John 11:27
36 [a]John 1:29
37 [a]Matt. 4:20, 22
40 [a]Matt. 4:18

"We have found the [1]Messiah"
(which is translated, the Christ).
42 And he brought him to Jesus.
Now when Jesus looked at him,
He said, "You are Simon the son
of [1]Jonah. [a]You shall be called
Cē′phas" (which is translated, [2]A
Stone).
43 The following day Jesus
wanted to go to Galilee, and He
found [a]Philip and said to him,
"Follow Me."
44 Now [a]Philip was from
Beth·sā′i·da, the city of Andrew
and Peter.
45 Philip found [a]Na·than′a·el
and said to him, "We have found
Him of whom [b]Moses in the law,
and also the [c]prophets, wrote—
Jesus [d]of Nazareth, the [e]son of
Joseph."
46 And Na·than′a·el said to him,
[a]"Can anything good come out
of Nazareth?" Philip said to him,
"Come and see."
47 Jesus saw Na·than′a·el coming toward Him, and said of him,
"Behold, [a]an Israelite indeed, in
whom is no deceit!"
48 Na·than′a·el said to Him,
"How do You know me?" Jesus
answered and said to him, "Before Philip called you, when you
were under the fig tree, I saw
you."
49 Na·than′a·el answered and
said to Him, "Rabbi, [a]You are the
Son of God! You are [b]the King of
Israel!"
50 Jesus answered and said to
him, "Because I said to you, 'I
saw you under the fig tree,' do
you believe? You will see greater
things than these."
51 And He said to him, "Most assuredly, I say to you, [a]hereafter[1]
you shall see heaven open, and
the angels of God ascending
and descending upon the Son of
Man."

2 On the third day there was a
[a]wedding in [b]Cā′na of Galilee, and the [c]mother of Jesus
was there.
2 Now both Jesus and His disciples were invited to the wedding.
3 And when they ran out of
wine, the mother of Jesus said to
Him, "They have no wine."
4 Jesus said to her, [a]"Woman,
[b]what does your concern have
to do with Me? [c]My hour has not
yet come."
5 His mother said to the servants, "Whatever He says to you,
do *it.*"
6 Now there were set there six
waterpots of stone, [a]according
to the manner of purification of
the Jews, containing twenty or
thirty gallons apiece.
7 Jesus said to them, "Fill the
waterpots with water." And they
filled them up to the brim.
8 And He said to them, "Draw
some out now, and take *it* to the
master of the feast." And they
took *it.*
9 When the master of the feast
had tasted [a]the water that was
made wine, and did not know
where it came from (but the servants who had drawn the water
knew), the master of the feast
called the bridegroom.
10 And he said to him, "Every
man at the beginning sets out
the good wine, and when the
guests have well drunk, then the
inferior. You have kept the good
wine until now!"
11 This [a]beginning of signs Jesus did in Cā′na of Galilee, [b]and
[1]manifested His glory; and His
disciples believed in Him.

41 [1]Lit. *Anointed One*
42 [a]Matt. 16:18 [1]NU *John* [2]Gr. *Petros,* usually translated *Peter*
43 [a]John 6:5; 12:21, 22; 14:8, 9
44 [a]John 12:21
45 [a]John 21:2 [b]Luke 24:27 [c][Zech. 6:12] [d][Matt. 2:23] [e]Luke 3:23
46 [a]John 7:41, 42, 52
47 [a]Ps. 32:2; 73:1
49 [a]Matt. 14:33 [b]Matt. 21:5
51 [a]Gen. 28:12 [1]NU omits *hereafter*

CHAPTER 2

1 [a][Heb. 13:4] [b]John 4:46 [c]John 19:25
4 [a]John 19:26 [b]2 Sam. 16:10 [c]John 7:6, 8, 30; 8:20
6 [a][Mark 7:3]
9 [a]John 4:46
11 [a]John 4:54 [b][John 1:14] [1]*revealed*

12 After this He went down to
[a]Ca·per′na·um, He, His mother,
[b]His brothers, and His disciples;
and they did not stay there many
days.
13 [a]Now the Passover of the
Jews was at hand, and Jesus
went up to Jerusalem.
★ 14 [a]And He found in the temple those who sold oxen and
sheep and doves, and the money
changers [1]doing business.
15 When He had made a whip
of cords, He drove them all out
of the temple, with the sheep
and the oxen, and poured out
the changers' money and overturned the tables.
16 And He said to those who
sold doves, "Take these things
away! Do not make [a]My Father's
house a house of merchandise!"
★ 17 Then His disciples remembered that it was written, [a]*"Zeal
for Your house [1]has eaten Me
up."*
18 So the Jews answered and
said to Him, [a]"What sign do You
show to us, since You do these
things?"
19 Jesus answered and said to
them, [a]"Destroy this temple, and
in three days I will raise it up."
20 Then the Jews said, "It has
taken forty-six years to build
this temple, and will You raise it
up in three days?"
21 But He was speaking [a]of the
temple of His body.
22 Therefore, when He had risen
from the dead, [a]His disciples remembered that He had said this
[1]to them; and they believed the
Scripture and the word which
Jesus had said.
23 Now when He was in Jerusalem at the Passover, during
the feast, many believed in His
name when they saw the [a]signs
which He did.
24 But Jesus did not commit
Himself to them, because He
[a]knew all *men*,
25 and had no need that anyone
should testify of man, for [a]He
knew what was in man.

3 There was a man of the
Phar′i·sees named Nic·o·dē′-
mus, a ruler of the Jews.
2 [a]This man came to Jesus by
night and said to Him, "Rabbi,
we know that You are a teacher
come from God; for [b]no one can
do these signs that You do unless
[c]God is with him."
3 Jesus answered and said to
him, "Most assuredly, I say to
you, [a]unless one is born [1]again,
he cannot see the kingdom of
God."
4 Nic·o·dē′mus said to Him,
"How can a man be born when
he is old? Can he enter a second
time into his mother's womb
and be born?"
5 Jesus answered, "Most assuredly, I say to you, [a]unless one
is born of water and the Spirit,
he cannot enter the kingdom of
God.
6 "That which is born of the
flesh is [a]flesh, and that which is
born of the Spirit is spirit.
7 "Do not marvel that I said to
you, 'You must be born again.'
8 [a]"The wind blows where it
wishes, and you hear the sound
of it, but cannot tell where it
comes from and where it goes.
So is everyone who is born of
the Spirit."
9 Nic·o·dē′mus answered and
said to Him, [a]"How can these
things be?"
10 Jesus answered and said to
him, "Are you the teacher of

12 [a]Matt. 4:13 [b]Matt. 12:46; 13:55
13 [a]Deut. 16:1–6
14 [a]Mal. 3:1; Mark 11:15, 17 [1]Lit. *sitting*
16 [a]Luke 2:49
17 [a]Ps. 69:9 [1]NU, M *will eat*
18 [a]Matt. 12:38
19 [a]Matt. 26:61; 27:40
21 [a][1 Cor. 3:16; 6:19]
22 [a]Luke 24:8 [1]NU, M omit *to them*
23 [a][Acts 2:22]
24 [a]Rev. 2:23
25 [a]Matt. 9:4

CHAPTER 3

2 [a]John 7:50; 19:39 [b]John 9:16, 33 [c][Acts 10:38]
3 [a][1 Pet. 1:23] [1]Or *from above*
5 [a][Acts 2:38]
6 [a]1 Cor. 15:50
8 [a]Eccl. 11:5
9 [a]John 6:52, 60

Israel, and do not know these
things?
11 [a]"Most assuredly, I say to
you, We speak what We know
and testify what We have seen,
and [b]you do not receive Our witness.
12 "If I have told you earthly
things and you do not believe,
how will you believe if I tell you
heavenly things?
13 [a]"No one has ascended to
heaven but He who came down
from heaven, *that is,* the Son of
Man [1]who is in heaven.
14 [a]"And as Moses lifted up the
serpent in the wilderness, even
so [b]must the Son of Man be
lifted up,
15 "that whoever [a]believes in
Him should [1]not perish but [b]have
eternal life.
16 [a]"For God so loved the world
that He gave His only begotten
[b]Son, that whoever believes in
Him should not perish but have
everlasting life.
17 [a]"For God did not send His
Son into the world to condemn
the world, but that the world
through Him might be saved.
18 [a]"He who believes in Him
is not condemned; but he who
does not believe is condemned
already, because he has not believed in the name of the only
begotten Son of God.
19 "And this is the condemnation, [a]that the light has come
into the world, and men loved
darkness rather than light, because their deeds were evil.
20 "For [a]everyone practicing
evil hates the light and does not
come to the light, lest his deeds
should be exposed.
21 "But he who does the truth
comes to the light, that his deeds
may be clearly seen, that they
have been [a]done in God."
22 After these things Jesus and
His disciples came into the land
of Judea, and there He remained
with them [a]and baptized.
23 Now John also was baptizing in Aē′non near [a]Sā′lim, because there was much water
there. [b]And they came and were
baptized.
24 For [a]John had not yet been
thrown into prison.
25 Then there arose a dispute
between *some* of John's disciples and the Jews about purification.
26 And they came to John and
said to him, "Rabbi, He who was
with you beyond the Jordan,
[a]to whom you have testified—
behold, He is baptizing, and all
[b]are coming to Him!"
27 John answered and said, [a]"A
man can receive nothing unless
it has been given to him from
heaven.
28 "You yourselves bear me witness, that I said, [a]'I am not the
Christ,' but, [b]'I have been sent
before Him.'
29 [a]"He who has the bride is the
bridegroom; but [b]the friend of
the bridegroom, who stands and
hears him, rejoices greatly because of the bridegroom's voice.
Therefore this joy of mine is
fulfilled.
30 [a]"He must increase, but I
must decrease.
31 [a]"He who comes from above
[b]is above all; [c]he who is of the
earth is earthly and speaks of
the earth. [d]He who comes from
heaven is above all.
32 "And [a]what He has seen and
heard, that He testifies; and no
one receives His testimony.

11 [a][Matt. 11:27] [b]John 3:32; 8:14
13 [a]Eph. 4:9 [1]NU omits *who is in heaven*
14 [a]Num. 21:9 [b]John 8:28; 12:34; 19:18
15 [a]John 6:47 [b]John 3:36 [1]NU omits *not perish but*
16 [a]Rom. 5:8 [b][Is. 9:6]
17 [a]Luke 9:56
18 [a]John 5:24; 6:40, 47; 20:31
19 [a][John 1:4, 9–11]
20 [a]Eph. 5:11, 13
21 [a]1 Cor. 15:10
22 [a]John 4:1, 2
23 [a]1 Sam. 9:4 [b]Matt. 3:5, 6
24 [a]Matt. 4:12; 14:3
26 [a]John 1:7, 15, 27, 34 [b]Mark 2:2; 3:10; 5:24
27 [a]1 Cor. 3:5, 6; 4:7
28 [a]John 1:19–27 [b]Mal. 3:1
29 [a][2 Cor. 11:2] [b]Song 5:1
30 [a][Is. 9:7]
31 [a]John 3:13; 8:23 [b]Matt. 28:18 [c]1 Cor. 15:47 [d]John 6:33
32 [a]John 3:11; 15:15

33 "He who has received His testimony [a]has certified that God is true.

★ 34 [a]"For He whom God has sent speaks the words of God, for God does not give the Spirit [b]by measure.

35 [a]"The Father loves the Son, and has given all things into His hand.

36 [a]"He who believes in the Son has everlasting life; and he who does not believe the Son shall not see life, but the [b]wrath of God abides on him."

4

Therefore, when the Lord knew that the Phar′i·sees had heard that Jesus made and [a]baptized more disciples than John

2 (though Jesus Himself did not baptize, but His disciples),

3 He left Judea and departed again to Galilee.

4 But He needed to go through Samaria.

5 So He came to a city of Samaria which is called Sȳ′char, near the plot of ground that [a]Jacob [b]gave to his son Joseph.

6 Now Jacob's well was there. Jesus therefore, being wearied from *His* journey, sat thus by the well. It was about the sixth hour.

7 A woman of Samaria came to draw water. Jesus said to her, "Give Me a drink."

8 For His disciples had gone away into the city to buy food.

9 Then the woman of Samaria said to Him, "How is it that You, being a Jew, ask a drink from me, a Samaritan woman?" For [a]Jews have no dealings with [b]Samaritans.

10 Jesus answered and said to her, "If you knew the [a]gift of God, and who it is who says to you, 'Give Me a drink,' you would have asked Him, and He would have given you [b]living water."

11 The woman said to Him, "Sir, You have nothing to draw with, and the well is deep. Where then do You get that living water?

12 "Are You greater than our father Jacob, who gave us the well, and drank from it himself, as well as his sons and his livestock?"

13 Jesus answered and said to her, "Whoever drinks of this water will thirst again,

14 "but [a]whoever drinks of the water that I shall give him will never thirst. But the water that I shall give him [b]will become in him a fountain of water springing up into everlasting life."

15 [a]The woman said to Him, "Sir, give me this water, that I may not thirst, nor come here to draw."

16 Jesus said to her, "Go, call your husband, and come here."

17 The woman answered and said, "I have no husband." Jesus said to her, "You have well said, 'I have no husband,'

18 "for you have had five husbands, and the one whom you now have is not your husband; in that you spoke truly."

19 The woman said to Him, "Sir, [a]I perceive that You are a prophet.

20 "Our fathers worshiped on [a]this mountain, and you *Jews* say that in [b]Jerusalem is the place where one ought to worship."

21 Jesus said to her, "Woman, believe Me, the hour is coming [a]when you will neither on

33 [a]1 John 5:10
34 [a]Deut. 18:18; John 7:16 [b]John 1:16
35 [a][Heb. 2:8]
36 [a]John 3:16, 17; 6:47 [b]Rom. 1:18
CHAPTER 4
1 [a]John 3:22, 26
5 [a]Gen. 33:19 [b]Gen. 48:22
9 [a]Acts 10:28 [b]2 Kin. 17:24
10 [a][Rom. 5:15] [b]Is. 12:3; 44:3
14 [a][John 6:35, 58] [b]John 7:37, 38
15 [a]John 6:34, 35; 17:2, 3
19 [a]Luke 7:16, 39; 24:19
20 [a]Judg. 9:7 [b]Deut. 12:5, 11
21 [a]1 Tim. 2:8

this mountain, nor in Jerusalem,
worship the Father.
22 "You worship [a]what you do
not know; we know what we
worship, for [b]salvation is of the
Jews.
23 "But the hour is coming, and
now is, when the true worshipers will [a]worship the Father in
[b]spirit [c]and truth; for the Father
is seeking such to worship Him.
24 [a]"God *is* Spirit, and those
who worship Him must worship
in spirit and truth."
25 The woman said to Him, "I
know that Messiah [a]is coming"
(who is called Christ). "When
He comes, [b]He will tell us all
things."
26 Jesus said to her, [a]"I who
speak to you am *He.*"
27 And at this *point* His disciples came, and they marveled
that He talked with a woman;
yet no one said, "What do You
seek?" or, "Why are You talking
with her?"
28 The woman then left her wa-
terpot, went her way into the
city, and said to the men,
29 "Come, see a Man [a]who told
me all things that I ever did.
Could this be the Christ?"
30 Then they went out of the
city and came to Him.
31 In the meantime His disciples urged Him, saying, "Rabbi,
eat."
32 But He said to them, "I have
food to eat of which you do not
know."
33 Therefore the disciples said
to one another, "Has anyone
brought Him *anything* to eat?"
34 Jesus said to them, [a]"My food
is to do the will of Him who sent
Me, and to [b]finish His work.
35 "Do you not say, 'There are
still four months and *then* comes
[a]the harvest'? Behold, I say to
you, lift up your eyes and look at
the fields, [b]for they are already
white for harvest!
36 [a]"And he who reaps receives
wages, and gathers fruit for eternal life, that [b]both he who sows
and he who reaps may rejoice
together.
37 "For in this the saying is true:
[a]'One sows and another reaps.'
38 "I sent you to reap that for
which you have not labored;
[a]others have labored, and you
have entered into their labors."
39 And many of the Samaritans of that city believed in Him
[a]because of the word of the
woman who testified, "He told
me all that I *ever* did."
40 So when the Samaritans had
come to Him, they urged Him to
stay with them; and He stayed
there two days.
41 And many more believed because of His own [a]word.
42 Then they said to the woman,
"Now we believe, not because of
what you said, for [a]we ourselves
have heard *Him* and we know
that this is indeed [1]the Christ,
the Savior of the world."
43 Now after the two days He
departed from there and went to
Galilee.
44 For [a]Jesus Himself testified
that a prophet has no honor in
his own country.
45 So when He came to Galilee, the Galileans received Him,
[a]having seen all the things He
did in Jerusalem at the feast;
[b]for they also had gone to the
feast.
46 So Jesus came again to Cā́na
of Galilee [a]where He had made
the water wine. And there was

22 [a][2 Kin. 17:28–41] [b][Rom. 3:1; 9:4, 5]
23 [a][Heb. 13:10–14] [b]Phil. 3:3 [c][John 1:17]
24 [a]2 Cor. 3:17
25 [a]Deut. 18:15 [b]John 4:29, 39
26 [a]Matt. 26:63, 64
29 [a]John 4:25
34 [a]Ps. 40:7, 8 [b][John 6:38; 17:4; 19:30]
35 [a]Gen. 8:22 [b]Matt. 9:37
36 [a]Dan. 12:3 [b]1 Thess. 2:19
37 [a]1 Cor. 3:5–9
38 [a][1 Pet. 1:12]
39 [a]John 4:29
41 [a]Luke 4:32
42 [a]1 John 4:14 [1]NU omits *the Christ*
44 [a]Matt. 13:57
45 [a]John 2:13, 23; 3:2 [b]Deut. 16:16
46 [a]John 2:1, 11

a certain [1]nobleman whose son
was sick at Ca·per′na·um.
47 When he heard that Jesus
had come out of Judea into Galilee, he went to Him and implored Him to come down and
heal his son, for he was at the
point of death.
48 Then Jesus said to him,
[a]"Unless you *people* see signs
and wonders, you will by no
means believe."
49 The nobleman said to Him,
"Sir, come down before my child
dies!"
50 Jesus said to him, "Go your
way; your son lives." So the man
believed the word that Jesus
spoke to him, and he went his
way.
51 And as he was now going
down, his servants met him
and told *him*, saying, "Your son
lives!"
52 Then he inquired of them the
hour when he got better. And
they said to him, "Yesterday at
the seventh hour the fever left
him."
53 So the father knew that *it*
was at the same hour in which
Jesus said to him, "Your son
lives." And he himself believed,
and his whole household.
54 This again *is* the second sign
Jesus did when He had come out
of Judea into Galilee.

5 After [a]this there was a feast
of the Jews, and Jesus [b]went
up to Jerusalem.
2 Now there is in Jerusalem
[a]by the Sheep *Gate* a pool, which
is called in Hebrew, [1]Be·thes′da,
having five porches.
3 In these lay a great multitude
of sick people, blind, lame, [1]par-
alyzed, [2]waiting for the moving
of the water.
4 For an angel went down at
a certain time into the pool and
stirred up the water; then whoever stepped in first, after the
stirring of the water, was made
well of whatever disease he had.
5 Now a certain man was there
who had an infirmity thirty-eight
years.
6 When Jesus saw him lying
there, and knew that he already
had been *in that condition* a
long time, He said to him, "Do
you want to be made well?"
7 The sick man answered Him,
"Sir, I have no man to put me
into the pool when the water is
stirred up; but while I am coming, another steps down before
me."
8 Jesus said to him, [a]"Rise,
take up your bed and walk."
9 And immediately the man
was made well, took up his bed,
and walked. And [a]that day was
the Sabbath.
10 The Jews therefore said to
him who was cured, "It is the
Sabbath; [a]it is not lawful for you
to carry your bed."
11 He answered them, "He who
made me well said to me, 'Take
up your bed and walk.' "
12 Then they asked him, "Who
is the Man who said to you,
'Take up your bed and walk'?"
13 But the one who was [a]healed
did not know who it was, for Jesus had withdrawn, a multitude
being in *that* place.
14 Afterward Jesus found him
in the temple, and said to him,
"See, you have been made well.
[a]Sin no more, lest a worse thing
come upon you."
15 The man departed and told
the Jews that it was Jesus who
had made him well.

46 [1]*royal official*
48 [a]1 Cor. 1:22

CHAPTER 5

1 [a]Deut. 16:16
[b]John 2:13
2 [a]Neh. 3:1, 32; 12:39
[1]NU *Bethzatha*
3 [1]*withered*
[2]NU omits the rest of v. 3 and all of v. 4.
8 [a]Luke 5:24
9 [a]John 9:14
10 [a]Jer. 17:21, 22
13 [a]Luke 13:14; 22:51
14 [a]John 8:11

16 For this reason the Jews
[a]persecuted Jesus, [1]and sought
to kill Him, because He had done
these things on the Sabbath.
17 But Jesus answered them,
[a]"My Father has been working
until now, and I have been working."
18 Therefore the Jews [a]sought
all the more to kill Him, because
He not only broke the Sabbath,
but also said that God was His
Father, [b]making Himself equal
with God.
19 Then Jesus answered and
said to them, "Most assuredly, I
say to you, [a]the Son can do nothing of Himself, but what He sees
the Father do; for whatever He
does, the Son also does in like
manner.
20 "For [a]the Father loves the
Son, and [b]shows Him all things
that He Himself does; and He
will show Him greater works
than these, that you may marvel.
21 "For as the Father raises the
dead and gives life to *them,*
[a]even so the Son gives life to
whom He will.
22 "For the Father judges no
one, but [a]has committed all judgment to the Son,
23 "that all should honor the
Son just as they honor the Father. [a]He who does not honor the
Son does not honor the Father
who sent Him.
24 "Most assuredly, I say to you,
[a]he who hears My word and believes in Him who sent Me has
everlasting life, and shall not
come into judgment, [b]but has
passed from death into life.
25 "Most assuredly, I say to you,
the hour is coming, and now is,
when [a]the dead will hear the
voice of the Son of God; and
those who hear will live.
26 "For [a]as the Father has life in
Himself, so He has granted the
Son to have [b]life in Himself,
27 "and [a]has given Him authority to execute judgment also,
[b]because He is the Son of Man.
28 "Do not marvel at this; for
the hour is coming in which all
who are in the graves will [a]hear
His voice
29 [a]"and come forth—[b]those
who have done good, to the resurrection of life, and those who
have done evil, to the resurrection of condemnation.
30 [a]"I can of Myself do nothing.
As I hear, I judge; and My judgment is righteous, because [b]I do
not seek My own will but the
will of the Father who sent Me.
31 [a]"If I bear witness of Myself,
My witness is not [1]true.
32 [a]"There is another who bears
witness of Me, and I know that
the witness which He witnesses
of Me is true.
33 "You have sent to John, [a]and
he has borne witness to the
truth.
34 "Yet I do not receive testimony from man, but I say these
things that you may be saved.
35 "He was the burning and
[a]shining lamp, and [b]you were
willing for a time to rejoice in
his light.
36 "But [a]I have a greater witness than John's; for [b]the works
which the Father has given Me
to finish—the very [c]works that I
do—bear witness of Me, that the
Father has sent Me.
37 "And the Father Himself, who
sent Me, [a]has testified of Me. You
have neither heard His voice at
any time, [b]nor seen His form.

16 [a]John 8:37; 10:39 [1]NU omits *and sought to kill Him*
17 [a][John 9:4; 17:4]
18 [a]John 7:1, 19 [b]John 10:30
19 [a]John 5:30; 6:38; 8:28; 12:49; 14:10
20 [a]Matt. 3:17 [b][Matt. 11:27]
21 [a][John 11:25]
22 [a][Acts 17:31]
23 [a]1 John 2:23
24 [a]John 3:16, 18; 6:47 [b][1 John 3:14]
25 [a][Col. 2:13]
26 [a]Ps. 36:9 [b]1 Cor. 15:45
27 [a][Acts 10:42; 17:31] [b]Dan. 7:13
28 [a][1 Thess. 4:15–17]
29 [a]Is. 26:19 [b]Dan. 12:2
30 [a]John 5:19 [b]Matt. 26:39
31 [a]John 8:14 [1]*valid* as testimony
32 [a][Matt. 3:17]
33 [a][John 1:15, 19, 27, 32]
35 [a]2 Pet. 1:19 [b]Mark 6:20
36 [a]1 John 5:9 [b]John 3:2; 10:25; 17:4 [c]John 9:16; 10:38
37 [a]Matt. 3:17 [b]1 John 4:12

38 "But you do not have His word abiding in you, because whom He sent, Him you do not believe.

39 [a]"You search the Scriptures, for in them you think you have eternal life; and [b]these are they which testify of Me.

40 [a]"But you are not willing to come to Me that you may have life.

41 [a]"I do not receive honor from men.

42 "But I know you, that you do not have the love of God in you.

43 "I have come in My Father's name, and you do not receive Me; if another comes in his own name, him you will receive.

44 [a]"How can you believe, who receive honor from one another, and do not seek [b]the honor that *comes* from the only God?

45 "Do not think that I shall accuse you to the Father; [a]there is *one* who accuses you—Moses, in whom you trust.

46 "For if you believed Moses, you would believe Me; [a]for he wrote about Me.

47 "But if you [a]do not believe his writings, how will you believe My words?"

6 After [a]these things Jesus went over the Sea of Galilee, which is *the Sea* of [b]Tī·bē'ri·as.

2 Then a great multitude followed Him, because they saw His signs which He performed on those who were [a]diseased.[1]

3 And Jesus went up on the mountain, and there He sat with His disciples.

4 [a]Now the Passover, a feast of the Jews, was near.

5 [a]Then Jesus lifted up *His* eyes, and seeing a great multitude coming toward Him, He said to [b]Philip, "Where shall we buy bread, that these may eat?"

6 But this He said to test him, for He Himself knew what He would do.

7 Philip answered Him, [a]"Two hundred denarii worth of bread is not sufficient for them, that every one of them may have a little."

8 One of His disciples, [a]Andrew, Simon Peter's brother, said to Him,

9 "There is a lad here who has five barley loaves and two small fish, [a]but what are they among so many?"

10 Then Jesus said, "Make the people sit down." Now there was much grass in the place. So the men sat down, in number about five thousand.

11 And Jesus took the loaves, and when He had given thanks He distributed *them* [1]to the disciples, and the disciples to those sitting down; and likewise of the fish, as much as they wanted.

12 So when they were filled, He said to His disciples, "Gather up the fragments that remain, so that nothing is lost."

13 Therefore they gathered *them* up, and filled twelve baskets with the fragments of the five barley loaves which were left over by those who had eaten.

14 Then those men, when they had seen the sign that Jesus did, said, "This is truly [a]the Prophet who is to come into the world."

15 Therefore when Jesus perceived that they were about to come and take Him by force to make Him [a]king, He departed again to the mountain by Himself alone.

39 [a]Is. 8:20; 34:16 [b]Luke 24:27
40 [a][John 1:11; 3:19]
41 [a]1 Thess. 2:6
44 [a]John 12:43 [b][Rom. 2:29]
45 [a]Rom. 2:12
46 [a]Deut. 18:15, 18
47 [a]Luke 16:29, 31

CHAPTER 6

1 [a]Mark 6:32 [b]John 6:23; 21:1
2 [a]Matt. 4:23; 8:16; 9:35; 14:36; 15:30; 19:2 [1]*sick*
4 [a]Deut. 16:1
5 [a]Matt. 14:14 [b]John 1:43
7 [a]Num. 11:21, 22
8 [a]John 1:40
9 [a]2 Kin. 4:43
11 [1]NU omits *to the disciples, and the disciples*
14 [a]Gen. 49:10
15 [a][John 18:36]

16 [a]Now when evening came,
His disciples went down to the
sea,
17 got into the boat, and went
over the sea toward Ca·per′-
na·um. And it was already dark,
and Jesus had not come to
them.
18 Then the sea arose because a
great wind was blowing.
19 So when they had rowed
about [1]three or four miles, they
saw Jesus walking on the sea
and drawing near the boat; and
they were [a]afraid.
20 But He said to them, [a]"It is I;
do not be afraid."
21 Then they willingly received
Him into the boat, and immediately the boat was at the land
where they were going.
22 On the following day, when
the people who were standing
on the other side of the sea saw
that there was no other boat
there, except [1]that one [2]which
His disciples had entered, and
that Jesus had not entered the
boat with His disciples, but
His disciples had gone away
alone—
23 however, other boats came
from Tī·bē′ri·as, near the place
where they ate bread after the
Lord had given thanks—
24 when the people therefore
saw that Jesus was not there,
nor His disciples, they also got
into boats and came to Ca·per′-
na·um, [a]seeking Jesus.
25 And when they found Him
on the other side of the sea, they
said to Him, "Rabbi, when did
You come here?"
26 Jesus answered them and
said, "Most assuredly, I say to
you, you seek Me, not because
you saw the signs, but because
you ate of the loaves and were
filled.
27 [a]"Do not labor for the food
which perishes, but [b]for the food
which endures to everlasting
life, which the Son of Man will
give you, [c]because God the Father has set His seal on Him."
28 Then they said to Him, "What
shall we do, that we may work
the works of God?"
29 Jesus answered and said to
them, [a]"This is the work of God,
that you believe in Him whom
He sent."
30 Therefore they said to Him,
[a]"What sign will You perform
then, that we may see it and
believe You? What work will
You do?
31 [a]"Our fathers ate the manna
in the desert; as it is written, [b]*'He
gave them bread from heaven to
eat.'* "
32 Then Jesus said to them,
"Most assuredly, I say to you,
Moses did not give you the bread
from heaven, but [a]My Father
gives you the true bread from
heaven.
33 "For the bread of God is He
who comes down from heaven
and gives life to the world."
34 [a]Then they said to Him,
"Lord, give us this bread always."
35 And Jesus said to them, [a]"I
am the bread of life. [b]He who
comes to Me shall never hunger,
and he who believes in Me shall
never [c]thirst.
36 [a]"But I said to you that you
have seen Me and yet [b]do not
believe.
37 [a]"All that the Father gives Me
will come to Me, and [b]the one
who comes to Me I will [1]by no
means cast out.

16 [a]Matt. 14:23
19 [a]Matt. 17:6 [1]Lit. *25 or 30 stadia*
20 [a]Is. 43:1, 2
22 [1]NU omits *that* [2]NU omits *which His disciples had entered*
24 [a]Luke 4:42
27 [a]Matt. 6:19 [b]John 4:14 [c]Acts 2:22
29 [a][1 John 3:23]
30 [a]Matt. 12:38; 16:1
31 [a]Ex. 16:15 [b]Ex. 16:4, 15; Neh. 9:15; Ps. 78:24
32 [a]John 3:13, 16
34 [a]John 4:15
35 [a]John 6:48, 58 [b]John 4:14; 7:37 [c]Is. 55:1, 2
36 [a]John 6:26, 64; 15:24 [b]John 10:26
37 [a]John 6:45 [b]2 Tim. 2:19 [1]*certainly not*

38 "For I have come down from heaven, [a]not to do My own will, [b]but the will of Him who sent Me.

39 "This is the will of the Father who sent Me, [a]that of all He has given Me I should lose nothing, but should raise it up at the last day.

40 "And this is the will of Him who sent Me, [a]that everyone who sees the Son and believes in Him may have everlasting life; and I will raise him up at the last day."

41 The Jews then [1]complained about Him, because He said, "I am the bread which came down from heaven."

42 And they said, [a]"Is not this Jesus, the son of Joseph, whose father and mother we know? How is it then that He says, 'I have come down from heaven'?"

43 Jesus therefore answered and said to them, [1]"Do not murmur among yourselves.

44 [a]"No one can come to Me unless the Father who sent Me [b]draws him; and I will raise him up at the last day.

45 "It is written in the prophets, [a]*'And they shall all be taught by God.'* [b]Therefore everyone who [1]has heard and learned from the Father comes to Me.

46 [a]"Not that anyone has seen the Father, [b]except He who is from God; He has seen the Father.

47 "Most assuredly, I say to you, [a]he who believes [1]in Me has everlasting life.

48 [a]"I am the bread of life.

49 [a]"Your fathers ate the manna in the wilderness, and are dead.

50 [a]"This is the bread which comes down from heaven, that one may eat of it and not die.

51 "I am the living bread [a]which came down from heaven. If anyone eats of this bread, he will live forever; and [b]the bread that I shall give is My flesh, which I shall give for the life of the world."

52 The Jews therefore [a]quarreled among themselves, saying, "How can this Man give us *His* flesh to eat?"

53 Then Jesus said to them, "Most assuredly, I say to you, unless [a]you eat the flesh of the Son of Man and drink His blood, you have no life in you.

54 [a]"Whoever eats My flesh and drinks My blood has eternal life, and I will raise him up at the last day.

55 "For My flesh is [1]food indeed, and My blood is [2]drink indeed.

56 "He who eats My flesh and drinks My blood [a]abides in Me, and I in him.

57 "As the living Father sent Me, and I live because of the Father, so he who feeds on Me will live because of Me.

58 [a]"This is the bread which came down from heaven—not [b]as your fathers ate the manna, and are dead. He who eats this bread will live forever."

59 These things He said in the synagogue as He taught in Ca·per'na·um.

60 [a]Therefore many of His disciples, when they heard *this,* said, "This is a [1]hard saying; who can understand it?"

61 When Jesus knew in Himself that His disciples [1]complained about this, He said to them, "Does this [2]offend you?

62 [a]"*What* then if you should

38 [a]Matt. 26:39 [b]John 4:34
39 [a]John 10:28; 17:12; 18:9
40 [a]John 3:15, 16; 4:14; 6:27, 47, 54
41 [1]*grumbled*
42 [a]Matt. 13:55
43 [1]*Stop grumbling*
44 [a]Song 1:4 [b][Phil. 1:29; 2:12, 13]
45 [a]Is. 54:13 [b]John 6:37 [1]M *hears and has learned*
46 [a]John 1:18 [b]Matt. 11:27
47 [a][John 3:16, 18] [1]NU omits *in Me*
48 [a]John 6:33, 35
49 [a]John 6:31, 58
50 [a]John 6:51, 58
51 [a]John 3:13 [b]Heb. 10:5
52 [a]John 7:43; 9:16; 10:19
53 [a]Matt. 26:26
54 [a]John 4:14; 6:27, 40
55 [1]NU *true food* [2]NU *true drink*
56 [a][1 John 3:24; 4:15, 16]
58 [a]John 6:49–51 [b]Ex. 16:14–35
60 [a]John 6:66 [1]*difficult*
61 [1]*grumbled* [2]*make you stumble*
62 [a]Acts 1:9; 2:32, 33

see the Son of Man ascend
where He was before?
63 [a]"It is the Spirit who gives
life; the [b]flesh profits nothing.
The [c]words that I speak to you
are spirit, and *they* are life.
64 "But [a]there are some of you
who do not believe." For [b]Jesus
knew from the beginning who
they were who did not believe,
and who would betray Him.
65 And He said, "Therefore [a]I
have said to you that no one can
come to Me unless it has been
granted to him by My Father."
66 [a]From that *time* many of His
disciples went [1]back and walked
with Him no more.
67 Then Jesus said to the twelve,
"Do you also want to go away?"
68 But Simon Peter answered
Him, "Lord, to whom shall we
go? You have [a]the words of eternal life.
69 [a]"Also we have come to believe and know that You are the
[1]Christ, the Son of the living
God."
70 Jesus answered them, [a]"Did I
not choose you, the twelve, [b]and
one of you is a devil?"
71 He spoke of [a]Judas Is·car'-
i·ot, *the son* of Simon, for it was
he who would [b]betray Him, being one of the twelve.

7 After these things Jesus
walked in Galilee; for He
did not want to walk in Judea,
[a]because the [1]Jews sought to kill
Him.
2 [a]Now the Jews' Feast of Tabernacles was at hand.
3 [a]His brothers therefore said
to Him, "Depart from here and
go into Judea, that Your disciples
also may see the works that You
are doing.
4 "For no one does anything
in secret while he himself seeks
to be known openly. If You do
these things, show Yourself to
the world."
5 For [a]even His [b]brothers did ★
not believe in Him.
6 Then Jesus said to them,
[a]"My time has not yet come, but
your time is always ready.
7 [a]"The world cannot hate you,
but it hates Me [b]because I testify
of it that its works are evil.
8 "You go up to this feast. I am
not [1]yet going up to this feast,
[a]for My time has not yet fully
come."
9 When He had said these
things to them, He remained in
Galilee.
10 But when His brothers had
gone up, then He also went up
to the feast, not openly, but as it
were in secret.
11 Then [a]the Jews sought Him
at the feast, and said, "Where is
He?"
12 And [a]there was much complaining among the people concerning Him. [b]Some said, "He
is good"; others said, "No, on
the contrary, He deceives the
people."
13 However, no one spoke
openly of Him [a]for fear of the
Jews.
14 Now about the middle of ★
the feast Jesus went up into the
temple and [a]taught.
15 [a]And the Jews marveled, saying, "How does this Man know
letters, having never studied?"
16 [1]Jesus answered them and
said, [a]"My doctrine is not Mine,
but His who sent Me.
17 [a]"If anyone wills to do His
will, he shall know concerning
the doctrine, whether it is from

63 [a]2 Cor. 3:6 [b]John 3:6 [c][John 6:68; 14:24]
64 [a]John 6:36 [b]John 2:24, 25; 13:11
65 [a]John 6:37, 44, 45
66 [a]Luke 9:62 [1]Or *away;* lit. *to the back*
68 [a]Acts 5:20
69 [a]Luke 9:20 [1]NU *Holy One of God.*
70 [a]Luke 6:13 [b][John 13:27]
71 [a]John 12:4; 13:2, 26 [b]Matt. 26:14–16

CHAPTER 7

1 [a]John 5:18; 7:19, 25; 8:37, 40 [1]The ruling authorities
2 [a]Lev. 23:34
3 [a]Matt. 12:46
5 [a]Ps. 69:8; Mic. 7:6 [b]Mark 3:21
6 [a]John 2:4; 8:20
7 [a][John 15:19] [b]John 3:19
8 [a]John 8:20 [1]NU omits *yet*
11 [a]John 11:56
12 [a]John 9:16; 10:19 [b]Luke 7:16
13 [a][John 9:22; 12:42; 19:38]
14 [a]Ps. 22:22; Mark 6:34
15 [a]Matt. 13:54
16 [a]John 3:11 [1]NU, M *So Jesus*
17 [a]John 3:21; 8:43

God or *whether* I speak on My
own *authority.*
18 [a]"He who speaks from himself seeks his own glory; but He
who [b]seeks the glory of the One
who sent Him is true, and [c]no
unrighteousness is in Him.
19 [a]"Did not Moses give you the
law, yet none of you keeps the
law? [b]Why do you seek to kill
Me?"
20 The people answered and
said, [a]"You have a demon. Who
is seeking to kill You?"
21 Jesus answered and said to
them, "I did one work, and you
all marvel.
22 [a]"Moses therefore gave you
circumcision (not that it is from
Moses, [b]but from the fathers),
and you circumcise a man on
the Sabbath.
23 "If a man receives circumcision on the Sabbath, so that the
law of Moses should not be broken, are you angry with Me because [a]I made a man completely
well on the Sabbath?
24 [a]"Do not judge according to
appearance, but judge with righteous judgment."
25 Now some of them from Jerusalem said, "Is this not He
whom they seek to [a]kill?
26 "But look! He speaks boldly,
and they say nothing to Him.
[a]Do the rulers know indeed that
this is [1]truly the Christ?
27 [a]"However, we know where
this Man is from; but when the
Christ comes, no one knows
where He is from."
28 Then Jesus cried out, as He
taught in the temple, saying,
[a]"You both know Me, and you
know where I am from; and [b]I
have not come of Myself, but He
who sent Me [c]is true, [d]whom you
do not know.
29 [1]"But [a]I know Him, for I am
from Him, and He sent Me."
30 Therefore [a]they sought to
take Him; but [b]no one laid a
hand on Him, because His hour
had not yet come.
31 And [a]many of the people believed in Him, and said, "When
the Christ comes, will He do
more signs than these which
this *Man* has done?"
32 The Phar′i·sees heard the
crowd murmuring these things
concerning Him, and the Phar′-
i·sees and the chief priests sent
officers to take Him.
33 Then Jesus said [1]to them, [a]"I
shall be with you a little while
longer, and *then* I [b]go to Him
who sent Me.
34 "You [a]will seek Me and not
find *Me,* and where I am you
[b]cannot come."
35 Then the Jews said among
themselves, "Where does He intend to go that we shall not
find Him? Does He intend to go
to [a]the Dispersion among the
Greeks and teach the Greeks?
36 "What is this thing that He
said, 'You will seek Me and not
find Me, and where I am you
cannot come'?"
37 [a]On the last day, that great
day of the feast, Jesus stood and
cried out, saying, [b]"If anyone
thirsts, let him come to Me and
drink.
38 [a]"He who believes in Me, as
the Scripture has said, [b]out of
his heart will flow rivers of living water."
39 [a]But this He spoke concerning the Spirit, whom those [1]be-
lieving in Him would receive;
for the [2]Holy Spirit was not yet

18 [a]John 5:41 [b]John 8:50 [c][2 Cor. 5:21]
19 [a]Deut. 33:4 [b]Matt. 12:14
20 [a]John 8:48, 52
22 [a]Lev. 12:3 [b]Gen. 17:9–14
23 [a]John 5:8, 9, 16
24 [a]Prov. 24:23
25 [a]Matt. 21:38; 26:4
26 [a]John 7:48 [1]NU omits *truly*
27 [a]Luke 4:22
28 [a]John 8:14 [b]John 5:43 [c]Rom. 3:4 [d]John 1:18; 8:55
29 [a]Matt. 11:27 [1]NU, M omit *But*
30 [a]Mark 11:18 [b]John 7:32, 44; 8:20; 10:39
31 [a]Matt. 12:23
33 [a]John 13:33 [b][1 Pet. 3:22] [1]NU, M omit *to them*
34 [a]Hos. 5:6 [b][Matt. 5:20]
35 [a]James 1:1
37 [a]Lev. 23:36 [b][Is. 55:1]
38 [a]Deut. 18:15 [b]Is. 12:3; 43:20; 44:3; 55:1
39 [a]Is. 44:3 [1]NU *who believed* [2]NU omits *Holy*

given, because Jesus was not yet
[b]glorified.
40 Therefore [1]many from the
crowd, when they heard this
saying, said, "Truly this is [a]the
Prophet."
41 Others said, "This is [a]the
Christ." But some said, "Will the
Christ come out of Galilee?
42 [a]"Has not the Scripture said
that the Christ comes from the
seed of David and from the town
of Bethlehem, [b]where David
was?"
43 So [a]there was a division
among the people because of
Him.
44 Now [a]some of them wanted
to take Him, but no one laid
hands on Him.
45 Then the officers came to
the chief priests and Phar′i·sees,
who said to them, "Why have
you not brought Him?"
46 The officers answered, [a]"No
man ever spoke like this Man!"
47 Then the Phar′i·sees answered them, "Are you also deceived?
48 "Have any of the rulers or
the Phar′i·sees believed in Him?
49 "But this crowd that does not
know the law is accursed."
50 Nic·o·dē′mus [a](he who came
to [1]Jesus [2]by night, being one of
them) said to them,
51 [a]"Does our law judge a man
before it hears him and knows
what he is doing?"
52 They answered and said to
him, "Are you also from Galilee?
Search and look, for [a]no prophet
[1]has arisen out of Galilee."
53 [1]And everyone went to his
own house.

8

But Jesus went to the Mount
of Olives.
2 Now [1]early in the morning
He came again into the temple,
and all the people came to Him;
and He sat down and [a]taught
them.
3 Then the scribes and Phar′i·sees brought to Him a woman
caught in adultery. And when
they had set her in the midst,
4 they said to Him, "Teacher,
[1]this woman was caught in
[a]adultery, in the very act.
5 [a]"Now [1]Moses, in the law,
commanded us [2]that such
should be stoned. But what do
You [3]say?"
6 This they said, testing Him,
that they [a]might have *something*
of which to accuse Him. But Jesus stooped down and wrote on
the ground with *His* finger, [1]as
though He did not hear.
7 So when they continued asking Him, He [1]raised Himself up
and said to them, [a]"He who is
without sin among you, let him
throw a stone at her first."
8 And again He stooped down
and wrote on the ground.
9 Then those who heard *it,*
[a]being[1] convicted by *their* conscience, went out one by one,
beginning with the oldest *even*
to the last. And Jesus was left
alone, and the woman standing
in the midst.
10 When Jesus had raised Himself up [1]and saw no one but the
woman, He said to her, "Woman,
where are those accusers [2]of
yours? Has no one condemned
you?"
11 She said, "No one, Lord."
And Jesus said to her, [a]"Neither
do I condemn you; go [1]and [b]sin
no more."
12 Then Jesus spoke to them
again, saying, [a]"I am the light of
the world. He who [b]follows Me

---

39 [b]John 12:16; 13:31; 17:5
40 [a]Deut. 18:15, 18 [1]NU *some*
41 [a]John 4:42; 6:69
42 [a]Mic. 5:2 [b]1 Sam. 16:1, 4
43 [a]John 7:12
44 [a]John 7:30
46 [a]Luke 4:22
50 [a]John 3:1, 2; 19:39 [1]Lit. *Him* [2]NU *before*
51 [a]Deut. 1:16, 17; 19:15
52 [a][Is. 9:1, 2] [1]NU *is to rise*
53 [1]NU brackets 7:53 through 8:11 as not in the original text. They are present in over 900 mss. of John.

CHAPTER 8

2 [a]John 8:20; 18:20 [1]M *very early*
4 [a]Ex. 20:14 [1]M *we found this woman*
5 [a]Lev. 20:10 [1]M *in our law Moses commanded* [2]NU, M *to stone such* [3]M adds *about her*
6 [a]Matt. 22:15 [1]NU, M omit *as though He did not hear*
7 [a]Deut. 17:7 [1]M *He looked up*
9 [a]Rom. 2:22 [1]NU, M omit *being convicted by their conscience*
10 [1]NU omits *and saw no one but the woman;* M *He saw her and said,* [2]NU, M omit *of yours*
11 [a][John 3:17] [b][John 5:14] [1]NU, M add *from now on*
12 [a]John 1:4; 9:5; 12:35 [b]1 Thess. 5:5

shall not walk in darkness, but have the light of life."

13 The Phar′i·sees therefore said to Him, [a]"You bear witness of Yourself; Your witness is not [1]true."

14 Jesus answered and said to them, "Even if I bear witness of Myself, My witness is true, for I know where I came from and where I am going; but [a]you do not know where I come from and where I am going.

15 [a]"You judge according to the flesh; [b]I judge no one.

16 "And yet if I do judge, My judgment is true; for [a]I am not alone, but I *am* with the Father who sent Me.

17 [a]"It is also written in your law that the testimony of two men is true.

18 "I am One who bears witness of Myself, and [a]the Father who sent Me bears witness of Me."

19 Then they said to Him, "Where is Your Father?" Jesus answered, [a]"You know neither Me nor My Father. [b]If you had known Me, you would have known My Father also."

20 These words Jesus spoke in [a]the treasury, as He taught in the temple; and [b]no one laid hands on Him, for [c]His hour had not yet come.

21 Then Jesus said to them again, "I am going away, and [a]you will seek Me, and [b]will die in your sin. Where I go you cannot come."

22 So the Jews said, "Will He kill Himself, because He says, 'Where I go you cannot come'?"

23 And He said to them, [a]"You are from beneath; I am from above. [b]You are of this world; I am not of this world.

24 [a]"Therefore I said to you that you will die in your sins; [b]for if you do not believe that I am *He*, you will die in your sins."

25 Then they said to Him, "Who are You?" And Jesus said to them, "Just what I [a]have been saying to you from the beginning.

26 "I have many things to say and to judge concerning you, but [a]He who sent Me is true; and [b]I speak to the world those things which I heard from Him."

27 They did not understand that He spoke to them of the Father.

28 Then Jesus said to them, "When you [a]lift[1] up the Son of Man, [b]then you will know that I am *He,* and [c]*that* I do nothing of Myself; but [d]as My Father taught Me, I speak these things.

29 "And [a]He who sent Me is with Me. [b]The Father has not left Me alone, [c]for I always do those things that please Him."

30 As He spoke these words, [a]many believed in Him.

31 Then Jesus said to those Jews who believed Him, "If you [a]abide in My word, you are My disciples indeed.

32 "And you shall know the [a]truth, and [b]the truth shall make you free."

33 They answered Him, [a]"We are Abraham's descendants, and have never been in bondage to anyone. How *can* You say, 'You will be made free'?"

34 Jesus answered them, "Most assuredly, I say to you, [a]whoever commits sin is a slave of sin.

35 "And [a]a slave does not abide in the house forever, *but* a son abides forever.

36 [a]"Therefore if the Son makes you free, you shall be free indeed.

13 [a]John 5:31 [1]*valid* as testimony
14 [a]John 7:28; 9:29
15 [a]John 7:24 [b][John 3:17; 12:47; 18:36]
16 [a]John 16:32
17 [a]Deut. 17:6; 19:15
18 [a]John 5:37
19 [a]John 16:3 [b]John 14:7
20 [a]Mark 12:41, 43 [b]John 2:4; 7:30 [c]John 7:8
21 [a]John 7:34; 13:33 [b]John 8:24
23 [a]John 3:31 [b]1 John 4:5
24 [a]John 8:21 [b][Mark 16:16]
25 [a]John 4:26
26 [a]John 7:28 [b]John 3:32; 15:15
28 [a]John 3:14; 12:32; 19:18 [b][Rom. 1:4] [c]John 5:19, 30 [d]John 3:11 [1]Crucify
29 [a]John 14:10 [b]John 8:16; 16:32 [c]John 4:34; 5:30; 6:38
30 [a]John 7:31; 10:42; 11:45
31 [a][John 14:15, 23]
32 [a][John 1:14, 17; 14:6] [b][Rom. 6:14, 18, 22]
33 [a][Matt. 3:9]
34 [a]2 Pet. 2:19
35 [a]Gal. 4:30
36 [a]Gal. 5:1

37 "I know that you are Abraham's descendants, but [a]you
seek to kill Me, because My
word has no place in you.
38 [a]"I speak what I have seen
with My Father, and you do
what you have [1]seen with your
father."
39 They answered and said to
Him, [a]"Abraham is our father."
Jesus said to them, [b]"If you were
Abraham's children, you would
do the works of Abraham.
40 [a]"But now you seek to kill
Me, a Man who has told you the
truth [b]which I heard from God.
Abraham did not do this.
41 "You do the deeds of your
father." Then they said to Him,
"We were not born of fornication; [a]we have one Father—
God."
42 Jesus said to them, [a]"If God
were your Father, you would
love Me, for [b]I proceeded forth
and came from God; [c]nor have I
come of Myself, but He sent Me.
43 [a]"Why do you not understand
My speech? Because you are not
able to listen to My word.
44 [a]"You are of *your* father the
devil, and the [b]desires of your
father you want to [c]do. He was
a murderer from the beginning,
and [d]does not stand in the truth,
because there is no truth in him.
When he speaks a lie, he speaks
from his own *resources,* for he is
a liar and the father of it.
45 "But because I tell the truth,
you do not believe Me.
46 "Which of you convicts Me
of sin? And if I tell the truth, why
do you not believe Me?
47 [a]"He who is of God hears
God's words; therefore you do
not hear, because you are not of
God."
48 Then the Jews answered and
said to Him, "Do we not say
rightly that You are a Samaritan
and [a]have a demon?"
49 Jesus answered, "I do not
have a demon; but I honor My
Father, and [a]you dishonor Me.
50 "And [a]I do not seek My *own*
glory; there is One who seeks
and judges.
51 "Most assuredly, I say to you,
[a]if anyone keeps My word he
shall never see death."
52 Then the Jews said to Him,
"Now we know that You [a]have a
demon! [b]Abraham is dead, and
the prophets; and You say, 'If
anyone keeps My word he shall
never taste death.'
53 "Are You greater than our father Abraham, who is dead? And
the prophets are dead. [a]Who do
You make Yourself out to be?"
54 Jesus answered, [a]"If I honor
Myself, My honor is nothing. [b]It
is My Father who honors Me, of
whom you say that He is [1]your
God.
55 "Yet [a]you have not known
Him, but I know Him. And if I
say, 'I do not know Him,' I shall
be a liar like you; but I do know
Him and [b]keep His word.
56 "Your father Abraham [a]re-
joiced to see My day, [b]and he
saw *it* and was glad."
57 Then the Jews said to Him,
"You are not yet fifty years old,
and have You seen Abraham?"
58 Jesus said to them, "Most
assuredly, I say to you, [a]before
Abraham was, [b]I AM."
59 Then [a]they took up stones
to throw at Him; but Jesus hid
Himself and went out of the temple, [b]going[1] through the midst of
them, and so passed by.

37 [a]John 7:19
38 [a][John 3:32; 5:19, 30; 14:10, 24] [1]NU *heard from*
39 [a]Matt. 3:9 [b][Rom. 2:28]
40 [a]John 8:37 [b]John 8:26
41 [a]Is. 63:16
42 [a]1 John 5:1 [b]John 16:27; 17:8, 25 [c]Gal. 4:4
43 [a][John 7:17]
44 [a]Matt. 13:38 [b]1 John 2:16, 17 [c][1 John 3:8–10, 15] [d][Jude 6]
47 [a]1 John 4:6
48 [a]John 7:20; 10:20
49 [a]John 5:41
50 [a]John 5:41; 7:18
51 [a]John 5:24; 11:26
52 [a]John 7:20; 10:20 [b]Zech. 1:5
53 [a]John 10:33; 19:7
54 [a]John 5:31, 32 [b]Acts 3:13 [1]NU, M *our*
55 [a]John 7:28, 29 [b][John 15:10]
56 [a]Luke 10:24 [b]Heb. 11:13
58 [a]Mic. 5:2 [b]Rev. 1:8
59 [a]John 10:31; 11:8 [b]Luke 4:30 [1]NU omits the rest of v. 59.

9 Now as *Jesus* passed by, He
saw a man who was blind
from birth.
2 And His disciples asked Him,
saying, "Rabbi, [a]who sinned, this
man or his parents, that he was
born blind?"
3 Jesus answered, "Neither this
man nor his parents sinned, [a]but
that the works of God should be
revealed in him.
4 [a]"I[1] must work the works
of Him who sent Me while it is
[b]day; *the* night is coming when
no one can work.
5 "As long as I am in the world,
[a]I am the light of the world."
6 When He had said these
things, [a]He spat on the ground
and made clay with the saliva;
and He anointed the eyes of the
blind man with the clay.
7 And He said to him, "Go,
wash [a]in the pool of Sī·lō′am"
(which is translated, Sent). So
[b]he went and washed, and came
back seeing.
8 Therefore the neighbors and
those who previously had seen
that he was [1]blind said, "Is not
this he who sat and begged?"
9 Some said, "This is he." Others *said,* [1]"He is like him." He
said, "I am *he.*"
10 Therefore they said to him,
"How were your eyes opened?"
11 He answered and said, [a]"A
Man called Jesus made clay and
anointed my eyes and said to me,
'Go to [1]the pool of Sī·lō′am and
wash.' So I went and washed,
and I received sight."
12 Then they said to him,
"Where is He?" He said, "I do
not know."
13 They brought him who formerly was blind to the Phar′-
i·sees.
14 Now it was a Sabbath when
Jesus made the clay and opened
his eyes.
15 Then the Phar′i·sees also
asked him again how he had received his sight. He said to them,
"He put clay on my eyes, and I
washed, and I see."
16 Therefore some of the Phar′-
i·sees said, "This Man is not
from God, because He does not
[1]keep the Sabbath." Others said,
[a]"How can a man who is a sinner do such signs?" And [b]there
was a division among them.
17 They said to the blind
man again, "What do you say
about Him because He opened
your eyes?" He said, [a]"He is a
prophet."
18 But the Jews did not believe concerning him, that he
had been blind and received his
sight, until they called the parents of him who had received
his sight.
19 And they asked them, saying, "Is this your son, who you
say was born blind? How then
does he now see?"
20 His parents answered them
and said, "We know that this is
our son, and that he was born
blind;
21 "but by what means he now
sees we do not know, or who
opened his eyes we do not know.
He is of age; ask him. He will
speak for himself."
22 His parents said these *things*
because [a]they feared the Jews,
for the Jews had agreed already
that if anyone confessed *that* He
was Christ, he [b]would be put out
of the synagogue.
23 Therefore his parents said,
"He is of age; ask him."
24 So they again called the man

CHAPTER 9

2 [a]John 9:34

3 [a]John 11:4

4 [a][John 4:34; 5:19, 36; 17:4] [b]John 11:9, 10; 12:35 [1]NU *We*

5 [a][John 1:5, 9; 3:19; 8:12; 12:35, 46]

6 [a]Mark 7:33; 8:23

7 [a]Neh. 3:15 [b]2 Kin. 5:14

8 [1]NU *a beggar*

9 [1]NU *"No, but he is like him."*

11 [a]John 9:6, 7 [1]NU omits *the pool of*

16 [a]John 3:2; 9:33 [b]John 7:12, 43; 10:19 [1]*observe*

17 [a][John 4:19; 6:14]

22 [a]Acts 5:13 [b]John 16:2

who was blind, and said to him,
[a]"Give God the glory! [b]We know
that this Man is a sinner."
25 He answered and said,
"Whether He is a sinner *or not* I
do not know. One thing I know:
that though I was blind, now I
see."
26 Then they said to him again,
"What did He do to you? How
did He open your eyes?"
27 He answered them, "I told
you already, and you did not
listen. Why do you want to hear
it again? Do you also want to
become His disciples?"
28 Then they reviled him and
said, "You are His disciple, but
we are Moses' disciples.
29 "We know that God [a]spoke to
[b]Moses; *as for* this *fellow,* [c]we do
not know where He is from."
30 The man answered and said
to them, [a]"Why, this is a marvelous thing, that you do not know
where He is from; yet He has
opened my eyes!
31 "Now we know that [a]God
does not hear sinners; but if anyone is a worshiper of God and
does His will, He hears him.
32 "Since the world began it
has been unheard of that anyone opened the eyes of one who
was born blind.
33 [a]"If this Man were not from
God, He could do nothing."
34 They answered and said
to him, [a]"You were completely
born in sins, and are you teaching us?" And they [1]cast him out.
35 Jesus heard that they had cast
him out; and when He had [a]found
him, He said to him, "Do you
[b]believe in [c]the Son of [1]God?"
36 He answered and said, "Who
is He, Lord, that I may believe in
Him?"
37 And Jesus said to him, "You
have both seen Him and [a]it is He
who is talking with you."
38 Then he said, "Lord, I believe!" And he [a]worshiped Him.
39 And Jesus said, [a]"For judgment I have come into this world,
[b]that those who do not see may
see, and that those who see may
be made blind."
40 Then *some* of the Phar'i·sees
who were with Him heard these
words, [a]and said to Him, "Are we
blind also?"
41 Jesus said to them, [a]"If you
were blind, you would have no
sin; but now you say, 'We see.'
Therefore your sin remains.

10

"Most assuredly, I say to
you, he who does not en-
ter the sheepfold by the door,
but climbs up some other way,
the same is a thief and a robber.
2 "But he who enters by the
door is the shepherd of the sheep.
3 "To him the doorkeeper
opens, and the sheep hear his
voice; and he calls his own sheep
by [a]name and leads them out.
4 "And when he brings out his
own sheep, he goes before them;
and the sheep follow him, for
they know his voice.
5 "Yet they will by no means
follow a [a]stranger, but will flee
from him, for they do not know
the voice of strangers."
6 Jesus used this illustration,
but they did not understand the
things which He spoke to them.
7 Then Jesus said to them
again, "Most assuredly, I say to
you, I am the door of the sheep.
8 "All who *ever* came [1]before
Me are thieves and robbers, but
the sheep did not hear them.
9 [a]"I am the door. If anyone
enters by Me, he will be saved,

24 [a]Josh. 7:19 [b]John 9:16
29 [a]Num. 12:6–8 [b][John 5:45–47] [c]John 7:27, 28; 8:14
30 [a]John 3:10
31 [a]Zech. 7:13
33 [a]John 3:2; 9:16
34 [a]John 9:2 [1]Excommunicated him
35 [a]John 5:14 [b]John 1:7; 16:31 [c]Matt. 14:33; 16:16 [1]NU *Man*
37 [a]John 4:26
38 [a]Matt. 8:2
39 [a][John 3:17; 5:22, 27; 12:47] [b]Matt. 13:13; 15:14
40 [a][Rom. 2:19]
41 [a]John 15:22, 24

CHAPTER 10

3 [a]John 20:16
5 [a][2 Cor. 11:13–15]
8 [1]M omits *before Me*
9 [a][Eph. 2:18]

and will go in and out and find
pasture.
10 "The thief does not come
except to steal, and to kill, and
to destroy. I have come that they
may have life, and that they may
have *it* more abundantly.
11 [a]"I am the good shepherd.
The good shepherd gives His life
for the sheep.
12 "But a [1]hireling, *he who is*
not the shepherd, one who does
not own the sheep, sees the wolf
coming and [a]leaves the sheep
and flees; and the wolf catches
the sheep and scatters them.
13 "The hireling flees because
he is a hireling and does not
care about the sheep.
14 "I am the good shepherd;
and [a]I know My *sheep,* and [b]am
known by My own.
15 [a]"As the Father knows Me,
even so I know the Father; [b]and I
lay down My life for the sheep.
16 "And [a]other sheep I have
which are not of this fold; them
also I must bring, and they will
hear My voice; [b]and there will
be one flock *and* one shepherd.
17 "Therefore My Father [a]loves
Me, [b]because I lay down My life
that I may take it again.
18 "No one takes it from Me,
but I lay it down of Myself. I
[a]have power to lay it down, and
I have power to take it again.
[b]This command I have received
from My Father."
19 Therefore [a]there was a division again among the Jews because of these sayings.
20 And many of them said, [a]"He
has a demon and is [1]mad. Why
do you listen to Him?"
21 Others said, "These are not
the words of one who has a demon. [a]Can a demon [b]open the
eyes of the blind?"
22 Now it was the Feast of Dedication in Jerusalem, and it was
winter.
23 And Jesus walked in the
temple, [a]in Solomon's porch.
24 Then the Jews surrounded
Him and said to Him, "How long
do You keep us in [1]doubt? If You
are the Christ, tell us plainly."
25 Jesus answered them, "I told
you, and you do not believe. [a]The
works that I do in My Father's
name, they [b]bear witness of Me.
26 "But [a]you do not believe, because you are not of My sheep,
[1]as I said to you.
27 [a]"My sheep hear My voice,
and I know them, and they follow Me.
28 "And I give them eternal life,
and they shall never perish; neither shall anyone snatch them
out of My hand.
29 [a]"My Father, [b]who has given
them to Me, is greater than all;
and no one is able to snatch
them out of My Father's hand.
30 [a]"I and *My* Father are one."
31 Then [a]the Jews took up
stones again to stone Him.
32 Jesus answered them, "Many
good works I have shown you
from My Father. For which of
those works do you stone Me?"
33 The Jews answered Him, saying, "For a good work we do not
stone You, but for [a]blasphemy,
and because You, being a Man,
[b]make Yourself God."
34 Jesus answered them, "Is it
not written in your law, [a]*'I said,
"You are gods"'*?
35 "If He called them gods, [a]to
whom the word of God came
(and the Scripture [b]cannot be
broken),

11 [a]Is. 40:11
12 [a]Zech. 11:16, 17 [1]*hired man*
14 [a]2 Tim. 2:19 [b]2 Tim. 1:12
15 [a]Matt. 11:27 [b][John 15:13; 19:30]
16 [a]Is. 42:6; 56:8 [b]Eph. 2:13–18
17 [a]John 5:20 [b][Heb. 2:9]
18 [a][John 2:19; 5:26] [b][John 6:38; 14:31; 17:4; Acts 2:24, 32]
19 [a]John 7:43; 9:16
20 [a]John 7:20 [1]*insane*
21 [a][Ex. 4:11] [b]John 9:6, 7, 32, 33
23 [a]Acts 3:11; 5:12
24 [1]Suspense
25 [a]John 5:36; 10:38 [b]Matt. 11:4
26 [a][John 8:47] [1]NU omits *as I said to you*
27 [a]John 10:4, 14
29 [a]John 14:28 [b][John 17:2, 6, 12, 24]
30 [a]John 17:11, 21–24
31 [a]John 8:59
33 [a]Matt. 9:3 [b]John 5:18
34 [a]Ps. 82:6
35 [a]Matt. 5:17, 18 [b]1 Pet. 1:25

36 "do you say of Him [a]whom
the Father sanctified and [b]sent
into the world, 'You are blaspheming,' [c]because I said, 'I am
[d]the Son of God'?
37 [a]"If I do not do the works of
My Father, do not believe Me;
38 "but if I do, though you do
not believe Me, [a]believe the
works, that you may know and
[1]believe [b]that the Father *is* in Me,
and I in Him."
39 [a]Therefore they sought again
to seize Him, but He escaped out
of their hand.
40 And He went away again
beyond the Jordan to the place
[a]where John was baptizing at
first, and there He stayed.
41 Then many came to Him and
said, "John performed no sign,
[a]but all the things that John spoke
about this Man were true."
42 And many believed in Him
there.

11 Now a certain *man* was
sick, Laz'a·rus of Beth'-
a·ny, the town of [a]Mary and her
sister Martha.
2 [a]It was *that* Mary who
anointed the Lord with fragrant
oil and wiped His feet with her
hair, whose brother Laz'a·rus
was sick.
3 Therefore the sisters sent to
Him, saying, "Lord, behold, he
whom You love is sick."
4 When Jesus heard *that*, He
said, "This sickness is not unto
death, but for the glory of God,
that the Son of God may be glorified through it."
5 Now Jesus loved Martha and
her sister and Laz'a·rus.
6 So, when He heard that he
was sick, [a]He stayed two more
days in the place where He was.
7 Then after this He said to *the*
disciples, "Let us go to Judea
again."
8 *The* disciples said to Him,
"Rabbi, lately the Jews sought
to [a]stone You, and are You going
there again?"
9 Jesus answered, "Are there
not twelve hours in the day? [a]If
anyone walks in the day, he does
not stumble, because he sees the
[b]light of this world.
10 "But [a]if one walks in the
night, he stumbles, because the
light is not in him."
11 These things He said, and
after that He said to them, "Our
friend Laz'a·rus [a]sleeps, but I go
that I may wake him up."
12 Then His disciples said,
"Lord, if he sleeps he will get
well."
13 However, Jesus spoke of his
death, but they thought that He
was speaking about taking rest
in sleep.
14 Then Jesus said to them
plainly, "Laz'a·rus is dead.
15 "And I am glad for your
sakes that I was not there, that
you may believe. Nevertheless
let us go to him."
16 Then [a]Thomas, who is called
the Twin, said to his fellow disciples, "Let us also go, that we
may die with Him."
17 So when Jesus came, He
found that he had already been
in the tomb four days.
18 Now Beth'a·ny was near Jerusalem, about [1]two miles away.
19 And many of the Jews had
joined the women around Martha and Mary, to comfort them
concerning their brother.
20 Then Martha, as soon as she
heard that Jesus was coming,
went and met Him, but Mary
was sitting in the house.

36 [a]John 6:27 [b]John 3:17 [c]John 5:17, 18 [d]Luke 1:35
37 [a]John 10:25; 15:24
38 [a]John 5:36 [b]John 14:10, 11 [1]NU *understand*
39 [a]John 7:30, 44
40 [a]John 1:28
41 [a][John 1:29, 36; 3:28–36; 5:33]

CHAPTER 11

1 [a]Luke 10:38, 39
2 [a]Matt. 26:7
6 [a]John 10:40
8 [a]John 8:59; 10:31
9 [a]John 9:4; 12:35 [b]Is. 9:2
10 [a]John 12:35
11 [a]Matt. 9:24
16 [a]John 14:5; 20:26–28
18 [1]Lit. *15 stadia*

21 Now Martha said to Jesus,
"Lord, if You had been here, my
brother would not have died.
22 "But even now I know that
[a]whatever You ask of God, God
will give You."
23 Jesus said to her, "Your
brother will rise again."
24 Martha said to Him, [a]"I know
that he will rise again in the resurrection at the last day."
25 Jesus said to her, "I am [a]the
resurrection and the life. [b]He
who believes in Me, though he
may [c]die, he shall live.
26 "And whoever lives and believes in Me shall never die. Do
you believe this?"
27 She said to Him, "Yes, Lord,
[a]I believe that You are the Christ,
the Son of God, who is to come
into the world."
28 And when she had said these
things, she went her way and
secretly called Mary her sister,
saying, "The Teacher has come
and is calling for you."
29 As soon as she heard *that,*
she arose quickly and came to
Him.
30 Now Jesus had not yet come
into the town, but [1]was in the
place where Martha met Him.
31 [a]Then the Jews who were
with her in the house, and comforting her, when they saw that
Mary rose up quickly and went
out, followed her, [1]saying, "She
is going to the tomb to weep
there."
32 Then, when Mary came
where Jesus was, and saw Him,
she [a]fell down at His feet, saying
to Him, [b]"Lord, if You had been
here, my brother would not have
died."
33 Therefore, when Jesus saw
her weeping, and the Jews who
came with her weeping, He
groaned in the spirit and was
troubled.
34 And He said, "Where have
you laid him?" They said to Him,
"Lord, come and see."
35 [a]Jesus wept.
36 Then the Jews said, "See how
He loved him!"
37 And some of them said,
"Could not this Man, [a]who
opened the eyes of the blind,
also have kept this man from
dying?"
38 Then Jesus, again groaning
in Himself, came to the tomb.
It was a cave, and a [a]stone lay
against it.
39 Jesus said, "Take away the
stone." Martha, the sister of
him who was dead, said to Him,
"Lord, by this time there is a
stench, for he has been *dead*
four days."
40 Jesus said to her, "Did I not
say to you that if you would believe you would [a]see the glory of
God?"
41 Then they took away the
stone [1]*from the place* where the
dead man was lying. And Jesus
lifted up *His* eyes and said, "Father, I thank You that You have
heard Me.
42 "And I know that You always
hear Me, but [a]because of the
people who are standing by I
said *this,* that they may believe
that You sent Me."
43 Now when He had said these
things, He cried with a loud
voice, "Laz'a·rus, come forth!"
44 And he who had died came
out bound hand and foot with
[a]graveclothes, and [b]his face was
wrapped with a cloth. Jesus said
to them, "Loose him, and let
him go."

22 [a][John 9:31; 11:41]
24 [a][John 5:29]
25 [a]John 5:21; 6:39, 40, 44 [b]1 John 5:10 [c]1 Cor. 15:22
27 [a]Matt. 16:16
30 [1]NU *was still*
31 [a]John 11:19, 33 [1]NU *supposing that she was going*
32 [a]Rev. 1:17 [b]John 11:21
35 [a]Luke 19:41
37 [a]John 9:6, 7
38 [a]Matt. 27:60, 66
40 [a][John 11:4, 23]
41 [1]NU omits *from the place where the dead man was lying*
42 [a]John 12:30; 17:21
44 [a]John 19:40 [b]John 20:7

45 Then many of the Jews who had come to Mary, [a]and had seen the things Jesus did, believed in Him.

46 But some of them went away to the Phar′i·sees and [a]told them the things Jesus did.

47 [a]Then the chief priests and the Phar′i·sees gathered a council and said, [b]"What shall we do? For this Man works many signs.

48 "If we let Him alone like this, everyone will believe in Him, and the Romans will come and take away both our place and nation."

49 And one of them, [a]Cā′i·a·phas, being high priest that year, said to them, "You know nothing at all,

50 [a]"nor do you consider that it is expedient for [1]us that one man should die for the people, and not that the whole nation should perish."

51 Now this he did not say on his own *authority;* but being high priest that year he prophesied that Jesus would die for the nation,

52 and [a]not for that nation only, but [b]also that He would gather together in one the children of God who were scattered abroad.

53 Then, from that day on, they plotted to [a]put Him to death.

54 [a]Therefore Jesus no longer walked openly among the Jews, but went from there into the country near the wilderness, to a city called [b]Ē′phra·im, and there remained with His disciples.

55 [a]And the Passover of the Jews was near, and many went from the country up to Jerusalem before the Passover, to [b]purify themselves.

56 [a]Then they sought Jesus, and spoke among themselves as they stood in the temple, "What do you think—that He will not come to the feast?"

57 Now both the chief priests and the Phar′i·sees had given a command, that if anyone knew where He was, he should report *it,* that they might [a]seize Him.

12

Then, six days before the Passover, Jesus came to Beth′a·ny, [a]where Laz′a·rus was [1]who had been dead, whom He had raised from the dead.

2 [a]There they made Him a supper; and Martha served, but Laz′a·rus was one of those who sat at the table with Him.

3 Then [a]Mary took a pound of very costly oil of [b]spikenard, anointed the feet of Jesus, and wiped His feet with her hair. And the house was filled with the fragrance of the oil.

4 But one of His disciples, [a]Judas Is·car′i·ot, Simon's *son,* who would betray Him, said,

5 "Why was this fragrant oil not sold for [1]three hundred denarii and given to the poor?"

6 This he said, not that he cared for the poor, but because he was a thief, and [a]had the money box; and he used to take what was put in it.

7 But Jesus said, "Let her alone; [1]she has kept this for the day of My burial.

8 "For [a]the poor you have with you always, but Me you do not have always."

9 Now a great many of the Jews knew that He was there; and they came, not for Jesus' sake only, but that they might also see Laz′a·rus, [a]whom He had raised from the dead.

---

45 [a]John 2:23; 10:42; 12:11, 18

46 [a]John 5:15

47 [a]Ps. 2:2 [b]Acts 4:16

49 [a]Luke 3:2

50 [a]John 18:14 [1]NU *you*

52 [a]Is. 49:6 [b][Eph. 2:14–17]

53 [a]Matt. 26:4

54 [a]John 4:1, 3; 7:1 [b]2 Chr. 13:19

55 [a]John 2:13; 5:1; 6:4 [b]Num. 9:10, 13; 31:19, 20

56 [a]John 7:11

57 [a]Matt. 26:14–16

CHAPTER 12

1 [a]John 11:1, 43 [1]NU omits *who had been dead*

2 [a]Mark 14:3; Luke 10:38–41

3 [a]John 11:2 [b]Song 1:12

4 [a]John 13:26

5 [1]About one year's wages for a worker

6 [a]John 13:29

7 [1]NU *that she may keep*

8 [a]Mark 14:7

9 [a]John 11:43, 44

10 [a]But the chief priests plotted
to put Laz′a·rus to death also,
11 [a]because on account of him
many of the Jews went away
and believed in Jesus.
12 [a]The next day a great multitude that had come to the feast,
when they heard that Jesus was
coming to Jerusalem,
★ 13 took branches of palm trees
and went out to meet Him, and
cried out:

"Hō·san′na!
[a]'*Blessed is He who comes in*
the name of the L*ORD*!'
The King of Israel!"

14 [a]Then Jesus, when He had
found a young donkey, sat on it;
as it is written:

★ 15 "*Fear*[a] *not, daughter of Zion;*
Behold, your King is
coming,
Sitting on a donkey's colt."

16 [a]His disciples did not understand these things at first; [b]but
when Jesus was glorified, [c]then
they remembered that these
things were written about Him
and *that* they had done these
things to Him.
17 Therefore the people, who
were with Him when He called
Laz′a·rus out of his tomb and
raised him from the dead, bore
witness.
18 [a]For this reason the people
also met Him, because they
heard that He had done this
sign.
19 The Phar′i·sees therefore
said among themselves, [a]"You
see that you are accomplishing
nothing. Look, the world has
gone after Him!"

20 Now there [a]were certain
Greeks among those [b]who came
up to worship at the feast.
21 Then they came to Philip,
[a]who was from Beth·sā′i·da of
Galilee, and asked him, saying,
"Sir, we wish to see Jesus."
22 Philip came and told Andrew, and in turn Andrew and
Philip told Jesus.
23 But Jesus answered them,
saying, [a]"The hour has come
that the Son of Man should be
glorified.
24 "Most assuredly, I say to you,
[a]unless a grain of wheat falls
into the ground and dies, it remains alone; but if it dies, it produces much [1]grain.
25 [a]"He who loves his life will
lose it, and he who hates his
life in this world will keep it for
eternal life.
26 "If anyone serves Me, let him
[a]follow Me; and [b]where I am,
there My servant will be also.
If anyone serves Me, him *My*
Father will honor.
27 [a]"Now My soul is troubled,
and what shall I say? 'Father,
save Me from this hour'? [b]But
for this purpose I came to this
hour.
28 "Father, glorify Your name."
[a]Then a voice came from heaven,
saying, "I have both glorified *it*
and will glorify *it* again."
29 Therefore the people who
stood by and heard *it* said that it
had thundered. Others said, "An
angel has spoken to Him."
30 Jesus answered and said,
[a]"This voice did not come because of Me, but for your sake.
31 "Now is the judgment of this
world; now [a]the ruler of this
world will be cast out.
32 "And I, [a]if I am [1]lifted up from

10 [a]Luke 16:31
11 [a]John 11:45; 12:18
12 [a]Matt. 21:4–9
13 [a]Ps. 118:25, 26
14 [a]Matt. 21:7
15 [a]Is. 40:9; Zech. 9:9
16 [a]Luke 18:34 [b]John 7:39; 12:23 [c][John 14:26]
18 [a]John 12:11
19 [a]John 11:47, 48
20 [a]Acts 17:4 [b]1 Kin. 8:41, 42
21 [a]John 1:43, 44; 14:8–11
23 [a]John 13:32
24 [a]1 Cor. 15:36 [1]Lit. *fruit*
25 [a]Mark 8:35
26 [a][Matt. 16:24] [b]John 14:3; 17:24
27 [a][Matt. 26:38, 39] [b]Luke 22:53
28 [a]Matt. 3:17; 17:5
30 [a]John 11:42
31 [a][2 Cor. 4:4]
32 [a]John 3:14; 8:28 [1]Crucified

the earth, will draw [b]all *peoples* to Myself."

33 [a]This He said, signifying by what death He would die.

34 The people answered Him, [a]"We have heard from the law that the Christ remains forever; and how *can* You say, 'The Son of Man must be lifted up'? Who is this Son of Man?"

35 Then Jesus said to them, "A little while longer [a]the light is with you. [b]Walk while you have the light, lest darkness overtake you; [c]he who walks in darkness does not know where he is going.

36 "While you have the light, believe in the light, that you may become [a]sons of light." These things Jesus spoke, and departed, and [b]was hidden from them.

37 But although He had done so many [a]signs before them, they did not believe in Him,

38 that the word of Ī·sāi′ah the prophet might be fulfilled, which he spoke:

> [a]*"Lord, who has believed our*
> *report?*
> *And to whom has the arm of*
> *the* L*ORD* *been revealed?"*

39 Therefore they could not believe, because Ī·sāi′ah said again:

> ★ 40 *"He*[a] *has blinded their eyes*
> *and hardened their*
> *hearts,*
> [b]*Lest they should see with*
> *their eyes,*
> *Lest they should understand*
> *with their hearts and*
> *turn,*
> *So that I should heal them."*

41 [a]These things Ī·sāi′ah said [1]when he saw His glory and spoke of Him.

42 Nevertheless even among the rulers many believed in Him, but [a]because of the Phar′i·sees they did not confess *Him,* lest they should be put out of the synagogue;

43 [a]for they loved the praise of men more than the praise of God.

44 Then Jesus cried out and said, [a]"He who believes in Me, [b]believes not in Me [c]but in Him who sent Me.

45 "And [a]he who sees Me sees Him who sent Me.

46 [a]"I have come *as* a light into the world, that whoever believes in Me should not abide in darkness.

47 "And if anyone hears My words and does not [1]believe, [a]I do not judge him; for [b]I did not come to judge the world but to save the world.

48 [a]"He who rejects Me, and does not receive My words, has that which judges him—[b]the word that I have spoken will judge him in the last day.

49 "For [a]I have not spoken on My own *authority;* but the Father who sent Me gave Me a command, [b]what I should say and what I should speak.

50 "And I know that His command is everlasting life. Therefore, whatever I speak, just as the Father has told Me, so I [a]speak."

13

Now [a]before the Feast of the Passover, when Jesus knew that [b]His hour had come that He should depart from this world to the Father, having loved His own who were in the world, He [c]loved them to the end.

32 [b][Rom. 5:18]
33 [a]John 18:32; 21:19
34 [a]Mic. 4:7
35 [a][John 1:9; 7:33; 8:12] [b]Eph. 5:8 [c][1 John 2:9–11]
36 [a]Luke 16:8 [b]John 8:59
37 [a]John 11:47
38 [a]Is. 53:1
40 [a]Is. 6:9, 10 [b]Matt. 13:14
41 [a]Is. 6:1 [1]NU *because*
42 [a]John 7:13; 9:22
43 [a]John 5:41, 44
44 [a]Mark 9:37 [b][John 3:16, 18, 36; 11:25, 26] [c][John 5:24]
45 [a][John 14:9]
46 [a]John 1:4, 5; 8:12; 12:35, 36
47 [a]John 5:45 [b]John 3:17 [1]NU *keep them*
48 [a][Luke 10:16] [b]Deut. 18:18, 19
49 [a]John 8:38 [b]Deut. 18:18
50 [a]John 5:19; 8:28

CHAPTER 13

1 [a]Matt. 26:2 [b]John 12:23; 17:1 [c]John 15:9

2 And [1]supper being ended,
[a]the devil having already put it
into the heart of Judas Is·car′i·ot,
Simon's *son,* to betray Him,
3 Jesus, knowing [a]that the Father had given all things into His
hands, and that He [b]had come
from God and [c]was going to
God,
4 [a]rose from supper and laid
aside His garments, took a towel
and girded Himself.
5 After that, He poured water
into a basin and began to wash
the disciples' feet, and to wipe
them with the towel with which
He was girded.
6 Then He came to Simon
Peter. And *Peter* said to Him,
[a]"Lord, are You washing my
feet?"
7 Jesus answered and said to
him, "What I am doing you [a]do
not understand now, [b]but you
will know after this."
8 Peter said to Him, "You shall
never wash my feet!" Jesus answered him, [a]"If I do not wash
you, you have no part with Me."
9 Simon Peter said to Him,
"Lord, not my feet only, but also
my hands and *my* head!"
10 Jesus said to him, "He who
is bathed needs only to wash
his feet, but is completely clean;
and [a]you are clean, but not all of
you."
11 For [a]He knew who would
betray Him; therefore He said,
"You are not all clean."
12 So when He had washed
their feet, taken His garments,
and sat down again, He said
to them, "Do you [1]know what I
have done to you?
13 [a]"You call Me Teacher and
Lord, and you say well, for *so* I
am.
14 [a]"If I then, *your* Lord and
Teacher, have washed your feet,
[b]you also ought to wash one another's feet.
15 "For [a]I have given you an
example, that you should do as I
have done to you.
16 [a]"Most assuredly, I say to
you, a servant is not greater
than his master; nor is he who
is sent greater than he who sent
him.
17 [a]"If you know these things,
blessed are you if you do them.
18 "I do not speak concerning ★
all of you. I know whom I have
chosen; but that the [a]Scripture
may be fulfilled, [b]*'He who eats*
[1]*bread with Me has lifted up his*
heel against Me.'
19 [a]"Now I tell you before it
comes, that when it does come
to pass, you may believe that I
am *He.*
20 [a]"Most assuredly, I say to
you, he who receives whomever
I send receives Me; and he who
receives Me receives Him who
sent Me."
21 [a]When Jesus had said these
things, [b]He was troubled in spirit,
and testified and said, "Most assuredly, I say to you, [c]one of you
will betray Me."
22 Then the disciples looked at
one another, perplexed about
whom He spoke.
23 Now [a]there was [1]leaning on
Jesus' bosom one of His disciples, whom Jesus loved.
24 Simon Peter therefore mo-
tioned to him to ask who it was
of whom He spoke.
25 Then, leaning [1]back on Jesus'
breast, he said to Him, "Lord,
who is it?"
26 Jesus answered, "It is he to
whom I shall give a piece of

2 [a]Luke 22:3 [1]NU *during supper*
3 [a]Acts 2:36 [b]John 8:42; 16:28 [c]John 17:11; 20:17
4 [a][Luke 22:27]
6 [a]Matt. 3:14
7 [a]John 12:16; 16:12 [b]John 13:19
8 [a][1 Cor. 6:11]
10 [a][John 15:3]
11 [a]John 6:64; 18:4
12 [1]*understand*
13 [a]Matt. 23:8, 10
14 [a]Luke 22:27 [b][Rom. 12:10]
15 [a][1 Pet. 2:21–24]
16 [a]Matt. 10:24
17 [a][James 1:25]
18 [a]John 15:25; 17:12 [b]Ps. 41:9 [1]NU *My bread has*
19 [a]John 14:29; 16:4
20 [a]Matt. 10:40
21 [a]Luke 22:21 [b]John 12:27 [c]1 John 2:19
23 [a]John 19:26; 20:2; 21:7, 20 [1]*reclining*
25 [1]NU, M add *thus*

bread when I have dipped *it.*"
And having dipped the bread,
He gave *it* to [a]Judas Is·car′i·ot,
the son of Simon.
27 [a]Now after the piece of bread,
Satan entered him. Then Jesus
said to him, "What you do, do
quickly."
28 But no one at the table knew
for what reason He said this to
him.
29 For some thought, because
[a]Judas had the money box, that
Jesus had said to him, "Buy
those things we need for the
feast," or that he should give
something to the poor.
30 Having received the piece of
bread, he then went out immediately. And it was night.
31 So, when he had gone out,
Jesus said, [a]"Now the Son of
Man is glorified, and [b]God is
glorified in Him.
32 "If God is glorified in Him,
God will also glorify Him in
Himself, and [a]glorify Him immediately.
33 "Little children, I shall be
with you a [a]little while longer.
You will seek Me; [b]and as I said
to the Jews, 'Where I am going,
you cannot come,' so now I say
to you.
34 [a]"A new commandment I
give to you, that you love one
another; as I have loved you,
that you also love one another.
35 [a]"By this all will know that
you are My disciples, if you have
love for one another."
36 Simon Peter said to Him,
"Lord, where are You going?"
Jesus answered him, "Where I
[a]am going you cannot follow Me
now, but [b]you shall follow Me
afterward."
37 Peter said to Him, "Lord,

26 [a]John 6:70, 71; 12:4
27 [a]Luke 22:3
29 [a]John 12:6
31 [a]John 12:23 [b][1 Pet. 4:11]
32 [a]John 12:23
33 [a]John 12:35; 14:19; 16:16–19 [b][John 7:34; 8:21]
34 [a]1 Thess. 4:9
35 [a]1 John 2:5
36 [a]John 13:33; 14:2; 16:5 [b]2 Pet. 1:14
37 [a]Mark 14:29–31
38 [a]John 18:25–27

CHAPTER 14

1 [a][John 14:27; 16:22, 24]
2 [a]John 13:33, 36 [1]Lit. *dwellings* [2]NU *would I have told you that I go* or *I would have told you; for I go*
3 [a][Acts 1:11] [b][John 12:26]
5 [a]Matt. 10:3
6 [a][Heb. 9:8; 10:19, 20] [b][John 1:14, 17; 8:32; 18:37] [c][John 11:25] [d]1 Tim. 2:5 [e][John 10:7–9]
7 [a]John 8:19
9 [a]Col. 1:15
10 [a]John 10:38; 14:11, 20 [b]John 5:19; 14:24

why can I not follow You now?
I will [a]lay down my life for Your
sake."
38 Jesus answered him, "Will
you lay down your life for My
sake? Most assuredly, I say to
you, the rooster shall not [a]crow
till you have denied Me three
times.

14 "Let [a]not your heart be
troubled; you believe in
God, believe also in Me.
2 "In My Father's house are
many [1]mansions; if *it were* not
so, [2]I would have told you. [a]I go
to prepare a place for you.
3 "And if I go and prepare a
place for you, [a]I will come again
and receive you to Myself; that
[b]where I am, *there* you may be
also.
4 "And where I go you know,
and the way you know."
5 [a]Thomas said to Him, "Lord,
we do not know where You are
going, and how can we know
the way?"
6 Jesus said to him, "I am [a]the
way, [b]the truth, and [c]the life. [d]No
one comes to the Father [e]except
through Me.
7 [a]"If you had known Me, you
would have known My Father
also; and from now on you know
Him and have seen Him."
8 Philip said to Him, "Lord,
show us the Father, and it is sufficient for us."
9 Jesus said to him, "Have I
been with you so long, and yet
you have not known Me, Philip?
[a]He who has seen Me has seen
the Father; so how can you say,
'Show us the Father'?
10 "Do you not believe that [a]I
am in the Father, and the Father
in Me? The words that I speak to
you [b]I do not speak on My own

authority; but the Father who
dwells in Me does the works.
11 "Believe Me that I *am* in the
Father and the Father in Me, [a]or
else believe Me for the sake of
the works themselves.
12 [a]"Most assuredly, I say to
you, he who believes in Me, the
works that I do he will do also;
and greater *works* than these
he will do, because I go to My
Father.
13 [a]"And whatever you ask in
My name, that I will do, that the
Father may be [b]glorified in the
Son.
14 "If you [1]ask anything in My
name, I will do *it.*
15 [a]"If you love Me, [1]keep My
commandments.
16 "And I will pray the Father,
and [a]He will give you another
[1]Helper, that He may abide with
you forever—
17 [a]"the Spirit of truth, [b]whom
the world cannot receive, because it neither sees Him nor
knows Him; but you know Him,
for He dwells with you [c]and will
be in you.
18 [a]"I will not leave you orphans; [b]I will come to you.
19 "A little while longer and the
world will see Me no more, but
[a]you will see Me. [b]Because I live,
you will live also.
20 "At that day you will know
that [a]I *am* in My Father, and you
in Me, and I in you.
21 [a]"He who has My commandments and keeps them, it is he
who loves Me. And he who loves
Me will be loved by My Father,
and I will love him and [1]mani-
fest Myself to him."
22 [a]Judas (not Is·car'i·ot) said
to Him, "Lord, how is it that You
will manifest Yourself to us, and
not to the world?"
23 Jesus answered and said to
him, "If anyone loves Me, he will
keep My word; and My Father
will love him, [a]and We will come
to him and make Our home with
him.
24 "He who does not love Me
does not keep My words; and
[a]the word which you hear is not
Mine but the Father's who sent
Me.
25 "These things I have spoken
to you while being present with
you.
26 "But [a]the [1]Helper, the Holy
Spirit, whom the Father will
[b]send in My name, [c]He will teach
you all things, and bring to your
[d]remembrance all things that I
said to you.
27 [a]"Peace I leave with you, My
peace I give to you; not as the
world gives do I give to you. Let
not your heart be troubled, neither let it be afraid.
28 "You have heard Me [a]say to
you, 'I am going away and coming *back* to you.' If you loved
Me, you would rejoice because [1]I
said, [b]'I am going to the Father,'
for [c]My Father is greater than I.
29 "And [a]now I have told you before it comes, that when it does
come to pass, you may believe.
30 "I will no longer talk much
with you, [a]for the ruler of this
world is coming, and he has
[b]nothing in Me.
31 "But that the world may
know that I love the Father, and
[a]as the Father gave Me commandment, so I do. Arise, let us
go from here.

15
"I am the true vine, and
My Father is the vine-
dresser.

11 [a]John 5:36; 10:38
12 [a]Luke 10:17
13 [a]Matt. 7:7 [b]John 13:31
14 [1]NU *ask Me*
15 [a]1 John 5:3 [1]NU *you will keep*
16 [a]Rom. 8:15 [1]*Comforter,* Gr. *Parakletos*
17 [a][1 John 4:6; 5:7] [b][1 Cor. 2:14] [c][1 John 2:27]
18 [a][Matt. 28:20] [b][John 14:3, 28]
19 [a]John 16:16, 22 [b][1 Cor. 15:20]
20 [a]John 10:38; 14:11
21 [a]1 John 2:5 [1]*reveal*
22 [a]Luke 6:16
23 [a]Rev. 3:20; 21:3
24 [a]John 5:19
26 [a]Luke 24:49 [b]John 15:26 [c]1 Cor. 2:13 [d]John 2:22; 12:16 [1]*Comforter,* Gr. *Parakletos*
27 [a][Phil. 4:7]
28 [a]John 14:3, 18 [b]John 16:16 [c][Phil. 2:6] [1]NU omits *I said*
29 [a]John 13:19
30 [a][John 12:31] [b][Heb. 4:15]
31 [a]Is. 50:5; John 10:18

2 [a]"Every branch in Me that does not bear fruit He [1]takes away; and every *branch* that bears fruit He prunes, that it may bear [b]more fruit.
3 [a]"You are already clean because of the word which I have spoken to you.
4 [a]"Abide in Me, and I in you. As the branch cannot bear fruit of itself, unless it abides in the vine, neither can you, unless you abide in Me.
5 "I am the vine, you *are* the branches. He who abides in Me, and I in him, bears much [a]fruit; for without Me you can do [b]nothing.
6 "If anyone does not abide in Me, [a]he is cast out as a branch and is withered; and they gather them and throw *them* into the fire, and they are burned.
7 "If you abide in Me, and My words [a]abide in you, [b]you[1] will ask what you desire, and it shall be done for you.
8 [a]"By this My Father is glorified, that you bear much fruit; [b]so you will be My disciples.
9 "As the Father [a]loved Me, I also have loved you; abide in My love.
10 [a]"If you keep My commandments, you will abide in My love, just as I have kept My Father's commandments and abide in His love.
11 "These things I have spoken to you, that My joy may remain in you, and [a]*that* your joy may be full.
12 [a]"This is My [b]commandment, that you love one another as I have loved you.
13 [a]"Greater love has no one than this, than to lay down one's life for his friends.
14 [a]"You are My friends if you do whatever I command you.
15 "No longer do I call you servants, for a servant does not know what his master is doing; but I have called you friends, [a]for all things that I heard from My Father I have made known to you.
16 [a]"You did not choose Me, but I chose you and [b]appointed you that you should go and bear fruit, and *that* your fruit should remain, that whatever you ask the Father [c]in My name He may give you.
17 "These things I command you, that you love one another.
18 [a]"If the world hates you, you know that it hated Me before *it hated* you.
19 [a]"If you were of the world, the world would love its own. Yet [b]because you are not of the world, but I chose you out of the world, therefore the world hates you.
20 "Remember the word that I said to you, [a]'A servant is not greater than his master.' If they persecuted Me, they will also persecute you. [b]If they kept My word, they will keep yours also.
21 "But [a]all these things they will do to you for My name's sake, because they do not know Him who sent Me.
22 [a]"If I had not come and spoken to them, they would have no sin, [b]but now they have no excuse for their sin.
23 [a]"He who hates Me hates My Father also.
24 "If I had not done among them [a]the works which no one else did, they would have no sin; but now they have [b]seen and also hated both Me and My Father.

CHAPTER 15

2 [a]Matt. 15:13 [b][Matt. 13:12] [1]Or *lifts up*
3 [a][John 13:10; 17:17]
4 [a][Col. 1:23]
5 [a]Hos. 14:8 [b]2 Cor. 3:5
6 [a]Matt. 3:10
7 [a]1 John 2:14 [b]John 14:13; 16:23 [1]NU omits *you will*
8 [a][Matt. 5:16] [b]John 8:31
9 [a]John 5:20; 17:26
10 [a]John 14:15
11 [a]1 John 1:4
12 [a]1 John 3:11 [b]Rom. 12:9
13 [a]1 John 3:16
14 [a][Matt. 12:50; 28:20]
15 [a]Gen. 18:17
16 [a]John 6:70; 13:18; 15:19 [b][Col. 1:6] [c]John 14:13; 16:23, 24
18 [a]1 John 3:13
19 [a]1 John 4:5 [b]John 17:14
20 [a]John 13:16 [b]Ezek. 3:7
21 [a]Matt. 10:22; 24:9
22 [a]John 9:41; 15:24 [b][James 4:17]
23 [a]1 John 2:23
24 [a]John 3:2 [b]John 14:9

25 "But *this happened* that the
word might be fulfilled which is
written in their law, [a]*'They hated
Me without a cause.'*
26 [a]"But when the [1]Helper
comes, whom I shall send to
you from the Father, the Spirit
of truth who proceeds from the
Father, [b]He will testify of Me.
27 "And [a]you also will bear witness, because [b]you have been
with Me from the beginning.

16 "These things I have
spoken to you, that you
[a]should not be made to stumble.
2 [a]"They will put you out of
the synagogues; yes, the time is
coming [b]that whoever kills you
will think that he offers God
service.
3 "And [a]these things they will
do [1]to you because they have not
known the Father nor Me.
4 "But these things I have told
you, that when [1]the time comes,
you may remember that I told
you of them. And these things I
did not say to you at the beginning, because I was with you.
5 "But now I [a]go away to Him
who sent Me, and none of you
asks Me, 'Where are You going?'
6 "But because I have said
these things to you, [a]sorrow has
filled your heart.
7 "Nevertheless I tell you the
truth. It is to your advantage
that I go away; for if I do not go
away, the Helper will not come
to you; but [a]if I depart, I will
send Him to you.
8 "And when He has [a]come, He
will convict the world of sin, and
of righteousness, and of judgment:
9 [a]"of sin, because they do not
believe in Me;
10 [a]"of righteousness, [b]because
I go to My Father and you see
Me no more;
11 [a]"of judgment, because [b]the
ruler of this world is judged.
12 "I still have many things to
say to you, [a]but you cannot bear
them now.
13 "However, when He, [a]the
Spirit of truth, has come, [b]He
will guide you into all truth;
for He will not speak on His
own *authority,* but whatever He
hears He will speak; and He will
tell you things to come.
14 [a]"He will glorify Me, for He
will take of what is Mine and
declare *it* to you.
15 [a]"All things that the Father
has are Mine. Therefore I said
that He [1]will take of Mine and
declare *it* to you.
16 "A [a]little while, and you will
not see Me; and again a little while, and you will see Me,
[b]because I go to the Father."
17 Then *some* of His disciples
said among themselves, "What
is this that He says to us, 'A little
while, and you will not see Me;
and again a little while, and you
will see Me'; and, 'because I go
to the Father'?"
18 They said therefore, "What is
this that He says, 'A little while'?
We do not [1]know what He is saying."
19 Now Jesus knew that they
desired to ask Him, and He said
to them, "Are you inquiring
among yourselves about what I
said, 'A little while, and you will
not see Me; and again a little
while, and you will see Me'?
20 "Most assuredly, I say to you
that you will weep and [a]lament,
but the world will rejoice; and
you will be sorrowful, but your
sorrow will be turned into [b]joy.

---

25 [a]Ps. 35:19; 69:4; 109:3–5
26 [a]Luke 24:49 [b]1 John 5:6 [1]*Comforter,* Gr. *Parakletos*
27 [a]Luke 24:48 [b]Luke 1:2

CHAPTER 16

1 [a]Matt. 11:6
2 [a]John 9:22 [b]Acts 8:1
3 [a]John 8:19; 15:21 [1]NU, M omit *to you*
4 [1]NU *their*
5 [a]John 7:33; 13:33; 14:28; 17:11
6 [a][John 16:20, 22]
7 [a]Acts 2:33
8 [a]Acts 1:8; 2:1–4, 37
9 [a]Acts 2:22
10 [a]Acts 2:32 [b]John 5:32
11 [a]Acts 26:18 [b][Luke 10:18]
12 [a]Mark 4:33
13 [a][John 14:17] [b]John 14:26
14 [a]John 15:26
15 [a]Matt. 11:27 [1]NU, M *takes of Mine and will declare*
16 [a]John 7:33; 12:35; 13:33; 14:19; 19:40–42; 20:19 [b]John 13:3
18 [1]*understand*
20 [a]Mark 16:10 [b]Luke 24:32, 41

21 [a]"A woman, when she is in labor, has sorrow because her hour has come; but as soon as she has given birth to the child, she no longer remembers the anguish, for joy that a human being has been born into the world.

22 "Therefore you now have sorrow; but I will see you again and [a]your heart will rejoice, and your joy no one will take from you.

23 "And in that day you will ask Me nothing. [a]Most assuredly, I say to you, whatever you ask the Father in My name He will give you.

24 "Until now you have asked nothing in My name. Ask, and you will receive, [a]that your joy may be [b]full.

25 "These things I have spoken to you in figurative language; but the time is coming when I will no longer speak to you in figurative language, but I will tell you [a]plainly about the Father.

26 "In that day you will ask in My name, and I do not say to you that I shall pray the Father for you;

27 [a]"for the Father Himself loves you, because you have loved Me, and [b]have believed that I came forth from God.

28 [a]"I came forth from the Father and have come into the world. Again, I leave the world and go to the Father."

29 His disciples said to Him, "See, now You are speaking plainly, and using no figure of speech!

30 "Now we are sure that [a]You know all things, and have no need that anyone should question You. By this [b]we believe that You came forth from God."

31 Jesus answered them, "Do you now believe?

32 [a]"Indeed the hour is coming, yes, has now come, that you will be scattered, [b]each to his [1]own, and will leave Me alone. And [c]yet I am not alone, because the Father is with Me.

33 "These things I have spoken to you, that [a]in Me you may have peace. [b]In the world you [1]will have tribulation; but be of good cheer, [c]I have overcome the world."

17

Jesus spoke these words, lifted up His eyes to heaven, and said: "Father, [a]the hour has come. Glorify Your Son, that Your Son also may glorify You,

2 [a]"as You have given Him authority over all flesh, that He [1]should give eternal life to as many [b]as You have given Him.

3 "And [a]this is eternal life, that they may know You, [b]the only true God, and Jesus Christ [c]whom You have sent.

4 [a]"I have glorified You on the earth. [b]I have finished the work [c]which You have given Me to do.

5 "And now, O Father, glorify Me together [1]with Yourself, with the glory [a]which I had with You before the world was.

6 [a]"I have [1]manifested Your name to the men [b]whom You have given Me out of the world. [c]They were Yours, You gave them to Me, and they have kept Your word.

7 "Now they have known that all things which You have given Me are from You.

8 "For I have given to them the ★
words [a]which You have given Me;

21 [a]Is. 13:8; 26:17; 42:14
22 [a]1 Pet. 1:8
23 [a]Matt. 7:7
24 [a]John 17:13 [b]John 15:11
25 [a]John 7:13
27 [a][John 14:21, 23] [b]John 3:13
28 [a]John 13:1, 3; 16:5, 10, 17
30 [a]John 21:17 [b]John 17:8
32 [a]Matt. 26:31, 56 [b]John 20:10 [c]John 8:29 [1]*own things* or *place*
33 [a][Eph. 2:14] [b]2 Tim. 3:12 [c]Rom. 8:37 [1]NU, M omit *will*

CHAPTER 17

1 [a]John 12:23
2 [a]John 3:35 [b]John 6:37, 39; 17:6, 9, 24 [1]M *shall*
3 [a]Jer. 9:23, 24 [b]1 Cor. 8:4 [c]John 3:34
4 [a]John 13:31 [b]John 4:34; 19:30 [c]John 14:31
5 [a]Phil. 2:6 [1]Lit. *alongside*
6 [a]Ps. 22:22 [b]John 6:37 [c]Ezek. 18:4 [1]*revealed*
8 [a]John 8:28

and they have received *them*,
[b]and have known surely that I
came forth from You; and they
have believed that [c]You sent Me.
9 "I pray for them. [a]I do not
pray for the world but for those
whom You have given Me, for
they are Yours.
10 "And all Mine are Yours, and
[a]Yours are Mine, and I am glorified in them.
11 [a]"Now I am no longer in the
world, but these are in the world,
and I come to You. Holy Father,
[b]keep[1] through Your name those
whom You have given Me, that
they may be one [c]as We *are*.
12 "While I was with them [1]in
the world, [a]I kept them in [2]Your
name. Those whom You gave Me
I have kept; and [b]none of them
is [3]lost [c]except the son of [4]perdi-
tion, [d]that the Scripture might be
fulfilled.
13 "But now I come to You,
and these things I speak in the
world, that they may have My
joy fulfilled in themselves.
14 "I have given them Your
word; [a]and the world has hated
them because they are not of the
world, [b]just as I am not of the
world.
15 "I do not pray that You should
take them out of the world, but
[a]that You should keep them from
the evil one.
16 "They are not of the world,
just as I am not of the world.
17 [a]"Sanctify[1] them by Your
truth. [b]Your word is truth.
18 [a]"As You sent Me into the
world, I also have sent them into
the world.
19 "And [a]for their sakes I sanctify Myself, that they also may
be sanctified by the truth.
20 "I do not pray for these alone,
but also for those who [1]will believe in Me through their word;
21 [a]"that they all may be one,
as [b]You, Father, *are* in Me, and
I in You; that they also may be
one in Us, that the world may
believe that You sent Me.
22 "And the [a]glory which You
gave Me I have given them, [b]that
they may be one just as We are
one:
23 "I in them, and You in Me;
[a]that they may be made perfect
in one, and that the world may
know that You have sent Me, and
have loved them as You have
loved Me.
24 [a]"Father, I desire that they
also whom You gave Me may be
with Me where I am, that they
may behold My glory which You
have given Me; [b]for You loved
Me before the foundation of the
world.
25 "O righteous Father! [a]The
world has not known You, but
[b]I have known You; and [c]these
have known that You sent Me.
26 [a]"And I have declared to them
Your name, and will declare *it*,
that the love [b]with which You
loved Me may be in them, and I
in them."

18 When Jesus had spoken
these words, [a]He went
out with His disciples over [b]the
Brook Kid′ron, where there was
a garden, which He and His disciples entered.
2 And Judas, who betrayed
Him, also knew the place; [a]for
Jesus often met there with His
disciples.
3 [a]Then Judas, having received
a detachment *of troops*, and officers from the chief priests and
Phar′i·sees, came there with lan-
terns, torches, and weapons.

8 [b]John 8:42; 16:27, 30 [c]Deut. 18:15, 18
9 [a][1 John 5:19]
10 [a]John 16:15
11 [a]John 13:1 [b][1 Pet. 1:5] [c]John 10:30 [1]NU, M *keep them through Your name which You have given Me*
12 [a]Heb. 2:13 [b]1 John 2:19 [c]John 6:70 [d]Ps. 41:9; 109:8 [1]NU omits *in the world* [2]NU *Your name which You gave Me. And I guarded them;* (or *it;*) [3]*destroyed* [4]*destruction*
14 [a]John 15:19 [b]John 8:23
15 [a]1 John 5:18
17 [a][Eph. 5:26] [b]Ps. 119:9, 142, 151 [1]*Set them apart*
18 [a]John 4:38; 20:21
19 [a][Heb. 10:10]
20 [1]NU, M omit *will*
21 [a][Gal. 3:28] [b]John 10:38; 17:11, 23
22 [a]1 John 1:3 [b][2 Cor. 3:18]
23 [a][Col. 3:14]
24 [a][1 Thess. 4:17] [b]John 17:5
25 [a]John 15:21 [b]John 7:29; 8:55; 10:15 [c]John 3:17; 17:3, 8, 18, 21, 23
26 [a]John 17:6 [b]John 15:9

CHAPTER 18

1 [a]Mark 14:26, 32 [b]2 Sam. 15:23
2 [a]Luke 21:37; 22:39
3 [a]Luke 22:47–53

4 Jesus therefore, [a]knowing all
things that would come upon
Him, went forward and said to
them, "Whom are you seeking?"
5 They answered Him, [a]"Jesus
[1]of Nazareth." Jesus said to
them, "I am *He.*" And Judas,
who [b]betrayed Him, also stood
with them.
6 Now when He said to them,
"I am *He,*" they drew back and
fell to the ground.
7 Then He asked them again,
"Whom are you seeking?" And
they said, "Jesus of Nazareth."
8 Jesus answered, "I have told
you that I am *He.* Therefore, if
you seek Me, let these go their
way,"
9 that the saying might be
fulfilled which He spoke, [a]"Of
those whom You gave Me I have
lost none."
10 [a]Then Simon Peter, having
a sword, drew it and struck the
high priest's servant, and cut off
his right ear. The servant's name
was Mal'chus.
11 So Jesus said to Peter, "Put
your sword into the sheath.
Shall I not drink [a]the cup which
My Father has given Me?"
12 Then the detachment *of
troops* and the captain and the
officers of the Jews arrested Jesus and bound Him.
13 And [a]they led Him away to
[b]An'nas first, for he was the
father-in-law of [c]Cā'i·a·phas who
was high priest that year.
14 [a]Now it was Cā'i·a·phas who
advised the Jews that it was [1]ex-
pedient that one man should die
for the people.
15 [a]And Simon Peter followed
Jesus, and so *did* [b]another[1] disciple. Now that disciple was
known to the high priest, and
went with Jesus into the courtyard of the high priest.
16 [a]But Peter stood at the door
outside. Then the other disciple,
who was known to the high
priest, went out and spoke to her
who kept the door, and brought
Peter in.
17 Then the servant girl who
kept the door said to Peter, "You
are not also *one* of this Man's
disciples, are you?" He said, "I
am [a]not."
18 Now the servants and officers who had made a fire of
coals stood there, for it was cold,
and they warmed themselves.
And Peter stood with them and
warmed himself.
19 The high priest then asked
Jesus about His disciples and
His doctrine.
20 Jesus answered him, [a]"I
spoke openly to the world. I
always taught [b]in synagogues
and [c]in the temple, where [1]the
Jews always meet, and in secret
I have said nothing.
21 "Why do you ask Me? Ask
[a]those who have heard Me what
I said to them. Indeed they know
what I said."
22 And when He had said these
things, one of the officers who
stood by [a]struck[1] Jesus with the
palm of his hand, saying, "Do
You answer the high priest like
that?"
23 Jesus answered him, "If I
have spoken evil, bear witness
of the evil; but if well, why do
you strike Me?"
24 [a]Then An'nas sent Him
bound to [b]Cā'i·a·phas the high
priest.
25 Now Simon Peter stood and
warmed himself. [a]Therefore
they said to him, "You are not

4 [a]John 6:64; 13:1, 3; 19:28
5 [a]Matt. 21:11 [b]Ps. 41:9 [1]Lit. *the Nazarene*
9 [a][John 6:39; 17:12]
10 [a]Matt. 26:51
11 [a]Matt. 20:22; 26:39
13 [a]Matt. 26:57 [b]Luke 3:2 [c]Matt. 26:3
14 [a]John 11:50 [1]*advantageous*
15 [a]Mark 14:54 [b]John 20:2–5 [1]M *the other*
16 [a]Matt. 26:69
17 [a]Matt. 26:34
20 [a]Luke 4:15 [b]John 6:59 [c]Mark 14:49 [1]NU *all the Jews meet*
21 [a]Mark 12:37
22 [a]Jer. 20:2 [1]Lit. *gave Jesus a slap,*
24 [a]Matt. 26:57 [b]John 11:49
25 [a]Luke 22:58–62

also *one* of His disciples, are
you?" He denied *it* and said, "I
am not!"
26 One of the servants of the
high priest, a relative *of him*
whose ear Peter cut off, said,
"Did I not see you in the garden
with Him?"
27 Peter then denied again; and
[a]immediately a rooster crowed.
28 [a]Then they led Jesus from
Cā′i·a·phas to the Prae·tō′ri·um,
and it was early morning. [b]But
they themselves did not go
into the [1]Prae·tō′ri·um, lest they
should be defiled, but that they
might eat the Passover.
29 [a]Pilate then went out to them
and said, "What accusation do
you bring against this Man?"
30 They answered and said to
him, "If He were not [1]an evildoer, we would not have delivered Him up to you."
31 Then Pilate said to them,
"You take Him and judge Him
according to your law." Therefore the Jews said to him, "It is
not lawful for us to put anyone
to death,"
32 [a]that the saying of Jesus
might be fulfilled which He
spoke, [b]signifying by what death
He would die.
33 [a]Then Pilate entered the
[1]Prae·tō′ri·um again, called Jesus, and said to Him, "Are You
the King of the Jews?"
34 Jesus answered him, "Are
you speaking for yourself about
this, or did others tell you this
concerning Me?"
35 Pilate answered, "Am I a
Jew? Your own nation and the
chief priests have delivered You
to me. What have You done?"
36 [a]Jesus answered, [b]"My kingdom is not of this world. If My

27 [a]John 13:38
28 [a]Mark 15:1 [b]Acts 10:28; 11:3 [1]The governor's headquarters
29 [a]Matt. 27:11–14
30 [1]*a criminal*
32 [a]Matt. 20:17–19; 26:2 [b]John 3:14; 8:28; 12:32, 33
33 [a]Matt. 27:11 [1]The governor's headquarters
36 [a]1 Tim. 6:13 [b][Dan. 2:44; 7:14]
37 [a][Matt. 5:17; 20:28] [b]Is. 55:4 [c][John 14:6] [d]John 8:47; 10:27
38 [a]John 19:4, 6
39 [a]Luke 23:17–25
40 [a]Is. 53:3; Acts 3:14 [b]Luke 23:19

CHAPTER 19

1 [a]Matt. 20:19; 27:26
3 [a]Is. 50:6 [1]NU *And they came up to Him and said*
4 [a]John 18:33, 38
6 [a]Acts 3:13

kingdom were of this world, My
servants would fight, so that I
should not be delivered to the
Jews; but now My kingdom is
not from here."
37 Pilate therefore said to Him,
"Are You a king then?" Jesus
answered, "You say *rightly* that
I am a king. For this cause I
was born, and for this cause I
have come into the world, [a]that
I should bear [b]witness to the
truth. Everyone who [c]is of the
truth [d]hears My voice."
38 Pilate said to Him, "What is
truth?" And when he had said
this, he went out again to the
Jews, and said to them, [a]"I find
no fault in Him at all.
39 [a]"But you have a custom that
I should release someone to you
at the Passover. Do you therefore want me to release to you
the King of the Jews?"
40 [a]Then they all cried again, ★
saying, "Not this Man, but
Ba·rab′bas!" [b]Now Ba·rab′bas
was a robber.

19

So then [a]Pilate took Jesus
and scourged *Him*.
2 And the soldiers twisted a
crown of thorns and put *it* on
His head, and they put on Him a
purple robe.
3 [1]Then they said, "Hail, King
of the Jews!" And they [a]struck
Him with their hands.
4 Pilate then went out again,
and said to them, "Behold, I am
bringing Him out to you, [a]that
you may know that I find no
fault in Him."
5 Then Jesus came out, wearing the crown of thorns and the
purple robe. And *Pilate* said to
them, "Behold the Man!"
6 [a]Therefore, when the chief
priests and officers saw Him,

they cried out, saying, "Crucify
Him, crucify *Him!*" Pilate said to
them, "You take Him and crucify
Him, for I find no fault in Him."
7 The Jews answered him, [a]"We
have a law, and according to [1]our
law He ought to die, because [b]He
made Himself the Son of God."
8 Therefore, when Pilate heard
that saying, he was the more
afraid,
★ 9 and went again into the
Prae·tō′ri·um, and said to Jesus,
"Where are You from?" [a]But Jesus gave him no answer.
10 Then Pilate said to Him, "Are
You not speaking to me? Do You
not know that I have [1]power to
crucify You, and [1]power to release You?"
11 Jesus answered, [a]"You could
have no power at all against Me
unless it had been given you
from above. Therefore [b]the one
who delivered Me to you has the
greater sin."
12 From then on Pilate sought
to release Him, but the Jews
cried out, saying, "If you let this
Man go, you are not Caesar's
friend. [a]Whoever makes himself
a king speaks against Caesar."
13 [a]When Pilate therefore heard
that saying, he brought Jesus out
and sat down in the judgment
seat in a place that is called *The*
Pavement, but in Hebrew, Gab′-
ba·tha.
14 Now [a]it was the Preparation
Day of the Passover, and about
the sixth hour. And he said to
the Jews, "Behold your King!"
15 But they cried out, "Away
with *Him,* away with *Him!* Crucify Him!" Pilate said to them,
"Shall I crucify your King?" The
chief priests answered, [a]"We
have no king but Caesar!"
16 [a]Then he delivered Him to
them to be crucified. So they
took Jesus [1]and led *Him* away.
17 [a]And He, bearing His cross,
[b]went out to a place called *the*
Place of a Skull, which is called
in Hebrew, Gol′go·tha,
18 where they crucified Him, ★
and [a]two others with Him, one
on either side, and Jesus in the
center.
19 [a]Now Pilate wrote a title and
put *it* on the cross. And the writing was:

JESUS OF NAZARETH, THE
KING OF THE JEWS.

20 Then many of the Jews read
this title, for the place where
Jesus was crucified was near
the city; and it was written in
Hebrew, Greek, *and* Latin.
21 Therefore the chief priests of
the Jews said to Pilate, "Do not
write, 'The King of the Jews,'
but, 'He said, "I am the King of
the Jews." ' "
22 Pilate answered, "What I
have written, I have written."
23 [a]Then the soldiers, when
they had crucified Jesus, took
His garments and made four
parts, to each soldier a part, and
also the tunic. Now the tunic
was without seam, woven from
the top in one piece.
24 They said therefore among ★
themselves, "Let us not tear it,
but cast lots for it, whose it shall
be," that the Scripture might be
fulfilled which says:

[a]*"They divided My garments*
among them,
And for My clothing they
cast lots."

7 [a]Lev. 24:16 [b]Matt. 26:63–66 [1]NU *the law*
9 [a]Is. 53:7
10 [1]*authority*
11 [a][Luke 22:53] [b]Rom. 13:1
12 [a]Luke 23:2
13 [a]1 Sam. 15:24
14 [a]Matt. 27:62
15 [a][Gen. 49:10]
16 [a]Luke 23:24 [1]NU omits *and led Him away*
17 [a]Mark 15:21, 22 [b]Num. 15:36
18 [a]Is. 53:12
19 [a]Matt. 27:37
23 [a]Luke 23:34
24 [a]Ps. 22:18

Therefore the soldiers did these
things.
25 [a]Now there stood by the
cross of Jesus His mother, and
His mother's sister, Mary the
wife of [b]Clō′pas, and Mary Mag′-
da·lēne.
26 When Jesus therefore saw
His mother, and [a]the disciple
whom He loved standing by, He
said to His mother, [b]"Woman,
behold your son!"
27 Then He said to the disciple, "Behold your mother!" And
from that hour that disciple took
her [a]to his own *home*.
28 After this, Jesus, [1]knowing
that all things were now accomplished, [a]that the Scripture might
be fulfilled, said, "I thirst!"
★ 29 Now a vessel full of sour
wine was sitting there; and [a]they
filled a sponge with sour wine,
put *it* on hyssop, and put *it* to
His mouth.
30 So when Jesus had received
the sour wine, He said, [a]"It is
finished!" And bowing His head,
He gave up His spirit.
31 [a]Therefore, because it was
the Preparation *Day*, [b]that the
bodies should not remain on the
cross on the Sabbath (for that
Sabbath was a [c]high day), the
Jews asked Pilate that their legs
might be broken, and *that* they
might be taken away.
32 Then the soldiers came and
broke the legs of the first and
of the other who was crucified
with Him.
★ 33 But when they came to Jesus
and saw that He was already
dead, [a]they did not break His
legs.
34 But one of the soldiers
pierced His side with a spear,
and immediately [a]blood and water came out.
35 And he who has seen has
testified, and his testimony is
[a]true; and he knows that he is
telling the truth, so that you may
[b]believe.
36 For these things were done ★
that the Scripture should be fulfilled, [a]*"Not one of His bones
shall be broken."*
37 And again another Scripture ★
says, [a]*"They shall look on Him
whom they pierced."*
38 [a]After this, Joseph of Ar·i-
ma·thē′a, being a disciple of Jesus, but secretly, [b]for fear of the
Jews, asked Pilate that he might
take away the body of Jesus;
and Pilate gave *him* permission.
So he came and took the body
of Jesus.
39 And [a]Nic·o·dē′mus, who at
first came to Jesus by night,
also came, bringing a mixture of
[b]myrrh and aloes, about a hundred pounds.
40 Then they took the body of
Jesus, and [a]bound it in strips of
linen with the spices, as the custom of the Jews is to bury.
41 Now in the place where He
was crucified there was a garden, and in the garden a new
tomb in which no one had yet
been laid.
42 So [a]there they laid Jesus,
[b]because of the Jews' Preparation *Day*, for the tomb was
nearby.

20
Now on the [a]first *day* of
the week Mary Mag′-
da·lēne went to the tomb early,
while it was still dark, and saw
that the [b]stone had been taken
away from the tomb.
2 Then she ran and came to
Simon Peter, and to the [a]other

25 [a]Mark 15:40 [b]Luke 24:18
26 [a]John 13:23; 20:2; 21:7, 20, 24 [b]John 2:4
27 [a]John 1:11; 16:32
28 [a]Ps. 22:15 [1]M *seeing*
29 [a]Ps. 69:21; Matt. 27:48, 50
30 [a]John 17:4
31 [a]Mark 15:42 [b]Deut. 21:23 [c]Ex. 12:16
33 [a][Ex. 12:46; Num. 9:12]; Ps. 34:20
34 [a][1 John 5:6, 8]
35 [a]John 21:24 [b][John 20:31]
36 [a][Ex. 12:46; Num. 9:12]; Ps. 34:20
37 [a]Ps. 22:16, 17; Zech. 12:10; 13:6
38 [a]Luke 23:50–56 [b][John 7:13; 9:22; 12:42]
39 [a]John 3:1, 2; 7:50 [b]Matt. 2:11
40 [a]John 20:5, 7
42 [a]Is. 53:9 [b]John 19:14, 31

CHAPTER 20

1 [a]Matt. 28:1–8 [b]Matt. 27:60, 66; 28:2
2 [a]John 21:23, 24

disciple, [b]whom Jesus loved, and
said to them, "They have taken
away the Lord out of the tomb,
and we do not know where they
have laid Him."
3 [a]Peter therefore went out,
and the other disciple, and were
going to the tomb.
4 So they both ran together,
and the other disciple outran Peter and came to the tomb first.
5 And he, stooping down and
looking in, saw [a]the linen cloths
lying *there;* yet he did not go in.
6 Then Simon Peter came,
following him, and went into
the tomb; and he saw the linen
cloths lying *there,*
7 and [a]the [1]handkerchief that
had been around His head, not
lying with the linen cloths, but
folded together in a place by
itself.
8 Then the [a]other disciple, who
came to the tomb first, went in
also; and he saw and believed.
9 For as yet they did not [1]know
the [a]Scripture, that He must rise
again from the dead.
10 Then the disciples went away
again to their own homes.
11 [a]But Mary stood outside by
the tomb weeping, and as she
wept she stooped down *and
looked* into the tomb.
12 And she saw two angels in
white sitting, one at the head
and the other at the feet, where
the body of Jesus had lain.
13 Then they said to her,
"Woman, why are you weep-
ing?" She said to them, "Because
they have taken away my Lord,
and I do not know where they
have laid Him."
14 [a]Now when she had said
this, she turned around and saw
Jesus standing *there,* and [b]did
not know that it was Jesus.
15 Jesus said to her, "Woman,
why are you weeping? Whom
are you seeking?" She, supposing Him to be the gardener, said
to Him, "Sir, if You have carried
Him away, tell me where You
have laid Him, and I will take
Him away."
16 Jesus said to her, [a]"Mary!"
She turned and said to [1]Him,
"Rab·bō′nī!" (which is to say,
Teacher).
17 Jesus said to her, "Do not
cling to Me, for I have not yet
[a]ascended to My Father; but go
to [b]My brethren and say to them,
[c]'I am ascending to My Father
and your Father, and *to* [d]My God
and your God.' "
18 [a]Mary Mag′da·lēne came and
told the [1]disciples that she had
seen the Lord, and *that* He had
spoken these things to her.
19 [a]Then, the same day at evening, being the first *day* of the
week, when the doors were shut
where the disciples were [1]as-
sembled, for [b]fear of the Jews,
Jesus came and stood in the
midst, and said to them, [c]"Peace
be with you."
20 When He had said this, He
[a]showed them *His* hands and
His side. [b]Then the disciples
were glad when they saw the
Lord.
21 So Jesus said to them again,
"Peace to you! [a]As the Father
has sent Me, I also send you."
22 And when He had said this,
He breathed on *them,* and said
to them, "Receive the Holy
Spirit.
23 [a]"If you forgive the sins of
any, they are forgiven them; if

2 [b]John 13:23; 19:26; 21:7, 20, 24
3 [a]Luke 24:12
5 [a]John 19:40
7 [a]John 11:44 [1]*face cloth*
8 [a]John 21:23, 24
9 [a]Ps. 16:10 [1]*understand*
11 [a]Mark 16:5
14 [a]Matt. 28:9 [b]John 21:4
16 [a]John 10:3 [1]NU adds *in Hebrew*
17 [a]Heb. 4:14 [b]Heb. 2:11 [c]John 16:28; 17:11 [d]Eph. 1:17
18 [a]Luke 24:10, 23 [1]NU *disciples, "I have seen the Lord,"*
19 [a]Luke 24:36 [b]John 9:22; 19:38 [c]John 14:27; 16:33 [1]NU omits *assembled*
20 [a]Acts 1:3 [b]John 16:20, 22
21 [a]John 17:18, 19
23 [a]Matt. 16:19; 18:18

you retain the *sins* of any, they
are retained."
24 Now Thomas, [a]called the
Twin, one of the twelve, was not
with them when Jesus came.
25 The other disciples therefore
said to him, "We have seen the
Lord." So he said to them, "Unless I see in His hands the print
of the nails, and put my finger
into the print of the nails, and
put my hand into His side, I will
not believe."
26 And after eight days His disciples were again inside, and
Thomas with them. Jesus came,
the doors being shut, and stood
in the midst, and said, "Peace to
you!"
★27 Then He said to Thomas,
"Reach your finger here, and
look at My hands; and [a]reach
your hand *here*, and put *it* into
My side. Do not be [b]unbelieving,
but believing."
28 And Thomas answered and
said to Him, "My Lord and my
God!"
29 Jesus said to him, [1]"Thomas,
because you have seen Me, you
have believed. [a]Blessed *are* those
who have not seen and *yet* have
believed."
30 And [a]truly Jesus did many
other signs in the presence of
His disciples, which are not written in this book;
31 [a]but these are written that
[b]you may believe that Jesus [c]is
the Christ, the Son of God, [d]and
that believing you may have life
in His name.

21
After these things Jesus
showed Himself again
to the disciples at the [a]Sea of
Tī·bē′ri·as, and in this way He
showed *Himself:*
2 Simon Peter, [a]Thomas called
the Twin, [b]Na·than′a·el of [c]Cā′na
in Galilee, [d]the *sons* of Zeb′-
e·dee, and two others of His
disciples were together.
3 Simon Peter said to them,
"I am going fishing." They said
to him, "We are going with you
also." They went out and [1]im-
mediately got into the boat, and
that night they caught nothing.
4 But when the morning had
now come, Jesus stood on the
shore; yet the disciples [a]did not
know that it was Jesus.
5 Then [a]Jesus said to them,
"Children, have you any food?"
They answered Him, "No."
6 And He said to them, [a]"Cast
the net on the right side of the
boat, and you will find *some*."
So they cast, and now they were
not able to draw it in because of
the multitude of fish.
7 Therefore [a]that disciple
whom Jesus loved said to Peter, "It is the Lord!" Now when
Simon Peter heard that it was
the Lord, he put on *his* outer
garment (for he had removed it),
and plunged into the sea.
8 But the other disciples came
in the little boat (for they were
not far from land, but about two
hundred cubits), dragging the
net with fish.
9 Then, as soon as they had
come to land, they saw a fire of
coals there, and fish laid on it,
and bread.
10 Jesus said to them, "Bring
some of the fish which you have
just caught."
11 Simon Peter went up and
dragged the net to land, full
of large fish, one hundred and
fifty-three; and although there
were so many, the net was not
broken.

24 [a]John 11:16
27 [a]Ps. 22:16; Zech. 12:10; 13:6; 1 John 1:1 [b]Mark 16:14
29 [a]1 Pet. 1:8 [1]NU, M omit *Thomas*
30 [a]John 21:25
31 [a]Luke 1:4 [b]1 John 5:13 [c]Luke 2:11 [d]John 3:15, 16; 5:24

CHAPTER 21

1 [a]John 6:1
2 [a]John 20:24 [b]John 1:45–51 [c]John 2:1 [d]Matt. 4:21
3 [1]NU omits *immediately*
4 [a]John 20:14
5 [a]Luke 24:41
6 [a]Luke 5:4, 6, 7
7 [a]John 13:23; 20:2

12 Jesus said to them, [a]"Come
and eat breakfast." Yet none of
the disciples dared ask Him,
"Who are You?"—knowing that
it was the Lord.
13 Jesus then came and took
the bread and gave it to them,
and likewise the fish.
14 This *is* now [a]the third time
Jesus showed Himself to His
disciples after He was raised
from the dead.
15 So when they had eaten
breakfast, Jesus said to Simon
Peter, "Simon, *son* of [1]Jonah, do
you love Me more than these?"
He said to Him, "Yes, Lord; You
know that I [2]love You." He said
to him, [a]"Feed My lambs."
16 He said to him again a second time, "Simon, *son* of [1]Jonah,
do you love Me?" He said to
Him, "Yes, Lord; You know that
I [2]love You." [a]He said to him,
"Tend My [b]sheep."
17 He said to him the third time,
"Simon, *son* of [1]Jonah, do you
[2]love Me?" Peter was grieved
because He said to him the third
time, "Do you [2]love Me?" And he
said to Him, "Lord, [a]You know
all things; You know that I [2]love
You." Jesus said to him, "Feed
My sheep.
18 [a]"Most assuredly, I say to
you, when you were younger,
you girded yourself and walked
where you wished; but when
you are old, you will stretch out
your hands, and another will
gird you and carry *you* where
you do not wish."
19 This He spoke, signifying
[a]by what death he would glorify
God. And when He had spoken
this, He said to him, [b]"Follow
Me."
20 Then Peter, turning around,
saw the disciple [a]whom Jesus
loved following, [b]who also had
leaned on His breast at the supper, and said, "Lord, who is the
one who betrays You?"
21 Peter, seeing him, said to Jesus, "But Lord, what *about* this
man?"
22 Jesus said to him, "If I [1]will
that he remain [a]till I come, what
is that to you? You follow Me."
23 Then this saying went out
among the brethren that this disciple would not die. Yet Jesus did
not say to him that he would not
die, but, "If I will that he remain
till I come, what *is that* to you?"
24 This is the disciple who
[a]testifies of these things, and
wrote these things; and we know
that his testimony is true.
25 [a]And there are also many
other things that Jesus did,
which if they were written one
by one, [b]I suppose that even the
world itself could not contain
the books that would be written.
Amen.

12 [a]Acts 10:41
14 [a]John 20:19, 26
15 [a]Acts 20:28 [1]NU *John* [2]*have affection for*
16 [a]Heb. 13:20 [b]Ps. 79:13 [1]NU *John* [2]*have affection for*
17 [a]John 2:24, 25; 16:30 [1]NU *John* [2]*have affection for*
18 [a]Acts 12:3, 4
19 [a]2 Pet. 1:13, 14 [b][Matt. 4:19; 16:24]
20 [a]John 13:23; 20:2 [b]John 13:25
22 [a][Rev. 2:25; 3:11; 22:7, 20] [1]*desire*
24 [a]John 19:35
25 [a]John 20:30 [b]Amos 7:10

THE ACTS

of the Apostles

JESUS' last recorded words have come to be known as the Great Commission: "You shall be witnesses to Me in Jerusalem, and in all Judea and Samaria, and to the end of the earth" (1:8). The Book of Acts, written by Luke, is the story of the men and women who took that commission seriously and began to spread the news of a risen Savior to the most remote corners of the known world.

Each section of the book (1—7; 8—12; 13—28) focuses on a particular audience, a key personality, and a significant phase in the expansion of the gospel message.

As the second volume in a two-part work by Luke, this book probably had no separate title. But all available Greek manuscripts designate it by the title *Praxeis*, "Acts," or by an expanded title like "The Acts of the Apostles." *Praxeis* was commonly used in Greek literature to summarize the accomplishments of outstanding men. While the apostles are mentioned collectively at several points, this book really records the acts of Peter (1—12) and of Paul (13—28).

THE former account I made,
O [a]Thē·oph′i·lus, of all that
Jesus began both to do and
teach,
2 [a]until the day in which [1]He
was taken up, after He through
the Holy Spirit [b]had given commandments to the apostles
whom He had chosen,
3 [a]to whom He also presented
Himself alive after His suffering
by many [1]infallible proofs, being
seen by them during forty days
and speaking of the things pertaining to the kingdom of God.
4 [a]And being assembled together with *them,* He commanded them not to depart from
Jerusalem, but to wait for the
Promise of the Father, "which,"
He said, "you have [b]heard from
Me;
5 [a]"for John truly baptized
with water, [b]but you shall be
baptized with the Holy Spirit
not many days from now."
6 Therefore, when they had
come together, they asked Him,
saying, "Lord, will You at this
time restore the kingdom to Israel?"
7 And He said to them, [a]"It is
not for you to [b]know times or
seasons which the Father has
put in His own authority.
8 [a]"But you shall receive power
[b]when the Holy Spirit has come
upon you; and [c]you shall be [1]wit-
nesses to Me in Jerusalem, and
in all Judea and [d]Samaria, and
to the [e]end of the earth."
9 [a]Now when He had spoken
these things, while they watched,
[b]He was taken up, and a cloud
received Him out of their sight.
10 And while they looked steadfastly toward heaven as He went
up, behold, two men stood by
them [a]in white apparel,
11 who also said, "Men of Gali- ☆
lee, why do you stand gazing up
into heaven? This *same* Jesus,

CHAPTER 1

1 [a]Luke 1:3

2 [a]Mark 16:19 [b]Matt. 28:19 [1]He ascended into heaven.

3 [a]Mark 16:12, 14 [1]*unmistakable*

4 [a]Luke 24:49 [b][John 14:16, 17, 26; 15:26]

5 [a]Matt. 3:11 [b][Joel 2:28]

7 [a]1 Thess. 5:1 [b]Matt. 24:36

8 [a][Acts 2:1, 4] [b]Luke 24:49 [c]Luke 24:48 [d]Acts 8:1, 5, 14 [e]Col. 1:23 [1]NU *My witnesses*

9 [a]Luke 24:50, 51 [b]Acts 1:2

10 [a]John 20:12

who was taken up from you into
heaven, [a]will so come in like
manner as you saw Him go into
heaven."
12 [a]Then they returned to Jerusalem from the mount called
Ol′i·vet, which is near Jerusalem, a Sabbath day's journey.
13 And when they had entered,
they went up [a]into the upper
room where they were staying: [b]Peter, James, John, and
Andrew; Philip and Thomas;
Bartholomew and Matthew;
James *the son* of Al·phae̅′us and
[c]Simon the Zealot; and [d]Judas
the son of James.
14 [a]These all continued with
one [1]accord in prayer [2]and supplication, with [b]the women and
Mary the mother of Jesus, and
with [c]His brothers.
15 And in those days Peter
stood up in the midst of the [1]dis-
ciples (altogether the number
[a]of names was about a hundred
and twenty), and said,
★ 16 "Men *and* brethren, this Scripture had to be fulfilled, [a]which
the Holy Spirit spoke before by
the mouth of David concerning
Judas, [b]who became a guide to
those who arrested Jesus;
17 "for [a]he was numbered with
us and obtained a part in [b]this
ministry."
18 [a](Now this man purchased
a field with [b]the [1]wages of iniquity; and falling headlong, he
burst open in the middle and all
his [2]entrails gushed out.
19 And it became known to all
those dwelling in Jerusalem; so
that field is called in their own
language, Akel Da′ma, that is,
Field of Blood.)
★ 20 "For it is written in the Book
of Psalms:

[a]'Let his dwelling place be
[1]desolate,
And let no one live in it';

and,

[b]'Let another take his [2]office.'

21 "Therefore, of these men
who have accompanied us all
the time that the Lord Jesus
went in and out among us,
22 "beginning from the baptism
of John to that day when [a]He
was taken up from us, one of
these must [b]become a witness
with us of His resurrection."
23 And they proposed two: Joseph called [a]Bar′sa·bas, who
was surnamed Jus′tus, and
Mat·thi̅′as.
24 And they prayed and said,
"You, O Lord, [a]who know the
hearts of all, show which of
these two You have chosen
25 [a]"to take part in this ministry
and apostleship from which Judas by transgression fell, that he
might go to his own place."
26 And they cast their lots, and
the lot fell on Mat·thi̅′as. And he
was numbered with the eleven
apostles.

2 When [a]the Day of Pentecost
had fully come, [b]they were all
[1]with one accord in one place.
2 And suddenly there came
a sound from heaven, as of a
rushing mighty wind, and [a]it
filled the whole house where
they were sitting.
3 Then there appeared to them
[1]divided tongues, as of fire, and
one sat upon each of them.
4 And [a]they were all filled with
the Holy Spirit and began [b]to
speak with other tongues, as the
Spirit gave them utterance.

11 [a]Dan. 7:13; [Matt. 24:30; 26:64; Mark 14:62; Luke 21:27; Rev. 1:7; 14:14]
12 [a]Luke 24:52
13 [a]Acts 9:37, 39; 20:8 [b]Matt. 10:2–4 [c]Luke 6:15 [d]Jude 1
14 [a]Acts 2:1, 46 [b]Luke 23:49, 55 [c]Matt. 13:55 [1]*purpose* or *mind* [2]NU omits *and supplication*
15 [a]Rev. 3:4 [1]NU *brethren*
16 [a]Ps. 41:9; 55:12–14, 20; Matt. 26:14–16, 21–25, 47–50 [b]Luke 22:47
17 [a]Matt. 10:4 [b]Acts 1:25
18 [a]Matt. 27:3–10 [b]Mark 14:21 [1]*reward of unrighteousness* [2]*intestines*
20 [a]Ps. 69:25 [b]Ps. 109:8; John 17:12 [1]*deserted* [2]Gr. *episkopen*, position of overseer
22 [a]Acts 1:9 [b]Acts 1:8; 2:32
23 [a]Acts 15:22
24 [a]1 Sam. 16:7
25 [a]Acts 1:17

CHAPTER 2

1 [a]Lev. 23:15 [b]Acts 1:14 [1]NU *together*
2 [a]Acts 4:31
3 [1]Or *tongues as of fire, distributed and resting on each*
4 [a]Acts 1:5 [b]Mark 16:17

5 And there were dwelling
in Jerusalem Jews, [a]devout
men, from every nation under
heaven.
6 And when this sound oc-
curred, the [a]multitude came
together, and were confused,
because everyone heard them
speak in his own language.
7 Then they were all amazed
and marveled, saying to one another, "Look, are not all these
who speak [a]Galileans?
8 "And how *is it that* we hear,
each in our own [1]language in
which we were born?
9 "Par′thi·ans and Mēdes
and Ē′lam·ītes, those dwelling
in Mes·o·po·tā′mi·a, Judea and
[a]Cap·pa·dō′ci·a, Pon′tus and
Asia,
10 "Phryg′i·a and Pam·phyl′i·a,
Egypt and the parts of Lib′ya
adjoining Cȳ·rē′nē, visitors from
Rome, both Jews and proselytes,
11 "Crē′tans and [1]Arabs—we
hear them speaking in our own
tongues the wonderful works of
God."
12 So they were all amazed
and perplexed, saying to one
another, "Whatever could this
mean?"
13 Others mocking said, "They
are full of new wine."
14 But Peter, standing up with
the eleven, raised his voice and
said to them, "Men of Judea and
all who dwell in Jerusalem, let
this be known to you, and heed
my words.
15 "For these are not drunk, as
you suppose, [a]since it is *only* [1]the
third hour of the day.
16 "But this is what was spoken
by the prophet Jō′el:

17 *'And[a] it shall come to pass in*
the last days, says God,
[b]That I will pour out of My
Spirit on all flesh;
Your sons and [c]your
daughters shall
prophesy,
Your young men shall see
visions,
Your old men shall dream
dreams.
18 *And on My menservants*
and on My maidservants
I will pour out My Spirit in
those days;
[a]And they shall prophesy.
19 *[a]I will show wonders in*
heaven above
And signs in the earth
beneath:
Blood and fire and vapor of
smoke.
20 *[a]The sun shall be turned into*
darkness,
And the moon into blood,
Before the coming of the
great and awesome day
of the LORD*.*
21 *And it shall come to pass*
That [a]whoever calls on the
name of the LORD
Shall be saved.'

22 "Men of Israel, hear these
words: Jesus of Nazareth, a Man
attested by God to you [a]by miracles, wonders, and signs which
God did through Him in your
midst, as you yourselves also
know—
23 "Him, [a]being delivered by the
determined purpose and fore-
knowledge of God, [b]you [1]have
taken by lawless hands, have
crucified, and put to death;
24 [a]"whom God raised up, having [1]loosed the [2]pains of death,

5 [a]Acts 8:2
6 [a]Acts 4:32
7 [a]Acts 1:11
8 [1]*dialect*
9 [a]1 Pet. 1:1
11 [1]*Arabians*
15 [a]1 Thess. 5:7 [1]9 A.M.
17 [a]Joel 2:28–32 [b]Acts 10:45 [c]Acts 21:9
18 [a]1 Cor. 12:10
19 [a]Joel 2:30
20 [a]Matt. 24:29
21 [a]Rom. 10:13
22 [a]John 3:2; 5:6
23 [a]Luke 22:22 [b]Acts 5:30 [1]NU omits *have taken*
24 [a][Rom. 8:11] [1]*destroyed* or *abolished* [2]Lit. *birth pangs*

because it was not possible that
He should be held by it.
★ 25 "For David says concerning
Him:

[a]*'I foresaw the* LORD *always*
before my face,
For He is at my right
hand, that I may not be
shaken.
26 *Therefore my heart rejoiced,*
and my tongue was glad;
Moreover my flesh also will
rest in hope.
27 *For You will not leave my*
soul in [a]*Hā'dēs,*
Nor will You allow Your Holy
One to see [b]*corruption.*
28 *You have made known to*
me the ways of life;
You will make me full of joy
in Your presence.'

29 "Men *and* brethren, let *me*
speak freely to you [a]of the patri-
arch David, that he is both dead
and buried, and his tomb is with
us to this day.
★ 30 "Therefore, being a prophet,
[a]and knowing that God had
sworn with an oath to him that
of the fruit of his body, [1]ac-
cording to the flesh, He would
raise up the Christ to sit on his
throne,
★ 31 "he, foreseeing this, spoke
concerning the resurrection of
the Christ, [a]that His soul was not
left in Hā'dēs, nor did His flesh
see corruption.
32 [a]"This Jesus God has raised
up, [b]of which we are all witnesses.
★ 33 "Therefore [a]being exalted
[1]to [b]the right hand of God, and
[c]having received from the Father
the promise of the Holy Spirit,
He [d]poured out this which you
now see and hear.
34 "For David did not ascend ★
into the heavens, but he says
himself:

[a]*'The* LORD *said to my Lord,*
"Sit at My right hand,
35 *Till I make Your enemies*
Your footstool."'

36 "Therefore let all the house
of Israel know assuredly that
God has made this Jesus, whom
you crucified, both Lord and
Christ."
37 Now when they heard *this,*
[a]they were cut to the heart, and
said to Peter and the rest of
the apostles, "Men *and* brethren,
what shall we do?"
38 Then Peter said to them,
[a]"Repent, and let every one of
you be baptized in the name of
Jesus Christ for the [1]remission
of sins; and you shall receive the
gift of the Holy Spirit.
39 "For the promise is to you
and [a]to your children, and [b]to all
who are afar off, as many as the
Lord our God will call."
40 And with many other words
he testified and exhorted them,
saying, "Be saved from this [1]per-
verse generation."
41 Then those who [1]gladly received his word were baptized;
and that day about three thousand souls were added *to them.*
42 [a]And they continued steadfastly in the apostles' [1]doctrine
and fellowship, in the breaking
of bread, and in prayers.
43 Then fear came upon every
soul, and [a]many wonders and
signs were done through the
apostles.
44 Now all who believed were

25 [a]Ps. 16:8–11
27 [a]Acts 2:31, 32; Heb. 13:20 [b]Acts 13:30–37
29 [a]Acts 13:36
30 [a]Ps. 132:11 [1]NU *He would seat one on his throne,*
31 [a]Ps. 16:10; Is. 53:10
32 [a]Acts 2:24 [b]Acts 1:8; 3:15
33 [a]Ps. 110:1; [Acts 5:31] [b][Heb. 10:12] [c][John 14:26] [d]Matt. 3:11; Acts 2:1–11, 17; 10:45 [1]Possibly *by*
34 [a]Ps. 68:18; 110:1; John 20:17; 1 Cor. 15:25; Eph. 1:20; Heb. 1:13
37 [a]Luke 3:10, 12, 14
38 [a]Luke 24:47 [1]*forgiveness*
39 [a]Joel 2:28, 32 [b]Eph. 2:13
40 [1]*crooked*
41 [1]NU omits *gladly*
42 [a]Acts 1:14 [1]*teaching*
43 [a]Acts 2:22

together, and [a]had all things in common,
45 and [1]sold their possessions and goods, and [a]divided[2] them among all, as anyone had need.
46 [a]So continuing daily with one accord [b]in the temple, and [c]breaking bread from house to house, they ate their food with gladness and simplicity of heart,
47 praising God and having favor with all the people. And [a]the Lord added [1]to the church daily those who were being saved.

3 Now Peter and John went up together [a]to the temple at the hour of prayer, [b]the ninth *hour.*
2 And [a]a certain man lame from his mother's womb was carried, whom they laid daily at the gate of the temple which is called Beautiful, [b]to [1]ask alms from those who entered the temple;
3 who, seeing Peter and John about to go into the temple, asked for alms.
4 And fixing his eyes on him, with John, Peter said, "Look at us."
5 So he gave them his attention, expecting to receive something from them.
6 Then Peter said, "Silver and gold I do not have, but what I do have I give you: [a]In the name of Jesus Christ of Nazareth, rise up and walk."
7 And he took him by the right hand and lifted *him* up, and immediately his feet and ankle bones received strength.
8 So he, [a]leaping up, stood and walked and entered the temple with them—walking, leaping, and praising God.
9 [a]And all the people saw him walking and praising God.
10 Then they knew that it was he who [a]sat begging alms at the Beautiful Gate of the temple; and they were filled with wonder and amazement at what had happened to him.
11 Now as the lame man who was healed held on to Peter and John, all the people ran together to them in the porch [a]which is called Solomon's, greatly amazed.
12 So when Peter saw *it,* he responded to the people: "Men of Israel, why do you marvel at this? Or why look so intently at us, as though by our own power or godliness we had made this man walk?
13 [a]"The God of Abraham, Isaac, and Jacob, the God of our fathers, [b]glorified His Servant Jesus, whom you [c]delivered up and [d]denied in the presence of Pilate, when he was determined to let *Him* go.
14 "But you denied [a]the Holy One [b]and the Just, and [c]asked for a murderer to be granted to you,
15 "and killed the [1]Prince of life, [a]whom God raised from the dead, [b]of which we are witnesses.
16 [a]"And His name, through faith in His name, has made this man strong, whom you see and know. Yes, the faith which *comes* through Him has given him this perfect soundness in the presence of you all.
17 "Yet now, brethren, I know that [a]you did *it* in ignorance, as *did* also your rulers.
18 "But [a]those things which God ★
foretold [b]by the mouth of all His

44 [a]Acts 4:32, 34, 37; 5:2
45 [a]Is. 58:7 [1]*would sell* [2]*distributed*
46 [a]Acts 1:14 [b]Luke 24:53 [c]Acts 2:42; 20:7
47 [a]Acts 5:14 [1]NU omits *to the church*

CHAPTER 3

1 [a]Acts 2:46 [b]Ps. 55:17
2 [a]Acts 14:8 [b]John 9:8 [1]Beg
6 [a]Acts 4:10
8 [a]Is. 35:6
9 [a]Acts 4:16, 21
10 [a]John 9:8
11 [a]John 10:23
13 [a]John 5:30 [b]John 7:39; 12:23; 13:31 [c]Matt. 27:2 [d]Matt. 27:20
14 [a]Mark 1:24 [b]Acts 7:52 [c]John 18:40
15 [a]Acts 2:24 [b]Acts 2:32 [1]Or *Originator*
16 [a]Matt. 9:22
17 [a]Luke 23:34
18 [a]Acts 26:22 [b]Ps. 22; Is. 53; 1 Pet. 1:10

prophets, that the Christ would
suffer, He has thus fulfilled.
19 [a]"Repent therefore and be
converted, that your sins may
be blotted out, so that times of
refreshing may come from the
presence of the Lord,
20 "and that He may send [1]Je-
sus Christ, who was [2]preached
to you before,
21 [a]"whom heaven must receive
until the times of [b]restoration of
all things, [c]which God has spoken by the mouth of all His holy
prophets since [1]the world began.
★ 22 "For Moses truly said to the
fathers, [a]*'The Lord your God*
will raise up for you a Prophet
like me from your brethren.
Him you shall hear in all things,
whatever He says to you.
23 *'And it shall be that every soul*
who will not hear that Prophet
shall be utterly destroyed from
among the people.'
24 "Yes, and [a]all the prophets,
from Samuel and those who follow, as many as have spoken,
have also [1]foretold these days.
★ 25 [a]"You are sons of the prophets, and of the covenant which
God made with our fathers, saying to Abraham, [b]*'And in your*
seed all the families of the earth
shall be blessed.'
26 "To you [a]first, God, having
raised up His Servant Jesus,
sent Him to bless you, [b]in turning away every one of *you* from
your iniquities."

4 Now as they spoke to the
people, the priests, the captain of the temple, and the [a]Sad′-
dū·cees came upon them,
2 being greatly disturbed that
they taught the people and
preached in Jesus the resurrection from the dead.
3 And they laid hands on them,
and put *them* in custody until
the next day, for it was already
evening.
4 However, many of those who
heard the word believed; and the
number of the men came to be
about five thousand.
5 And it came to pass, on the
next day, that their rulers, elders, and scribes,
6 as well as [a]An′nas the high
priest, Cā′i·a·phas, John, and Alexander, and as many as were
of the family of the high priest,
were gathered together at Jerusalem.
7 And when they had set them
in the midst, they asked, [a]"By
what power or by what name
have you done this?"
8 [a]Then Peter, filled with the
Holy Spirit, said to them, "Rulers of the people and elders of
Israel:
9 "If we this day are judged
for a good deed *done* to a helpless man, by what means he has
been made well,
10 "let it be known to you all,
and to all the people of Israel,
[a]that by the name of Jesus Christ
of Nazareth, whom you crucified, [b]whom God raised from the
dead, by Him this man stands
here before you whole.
11 "This is the [a]*'stone which* ★
was rejected by you builders,
which has become the chief cor-
nerstone.'
12 [a]"Nor is there salvation in any
other, for there is no other name
under heaven given among men
by which we must be saved."
13 Now when they saw the
boldness of Peter and John, [a]and
perceived that they were unedu-
cated and untrained men, they

19 [a][Acts 2:38; 26:20]
20 [1]NU, M *Christ Jesus* [2]NU, M *ordained for you before*
21 [a]Acts 1:11 [b]Matt. 17:11 [c]Luke 1:70 [1]Or *time*
22 [a]Deut. 18:15, 18, 19
24 [a]Luke 24:25 [1]NU, M *proclaimed*
25 [a][Rom. 9:4, 8] [b]Gen. 12:3; 18:18; 22:18; 26:4; 28:14
26 [a][Rom. 1:16; 2:9] [b]Matt. 1:21

CHAPTER 4

1 [a]Matt. 22:23
6 [a]Luke 3:2
7 [a]Matt. 21:23
8 [a]Luke 12:11, 12
10 [a]Acts 2:22; 3:6, 16 [b]Acts 2:24
11 [a]Ps. 118:22; Is. 28:16; 1 Pet. 2:4–8
12 [a][1 Tim. 2:5, 6]
13 [a][1 Cor. 1:27]

marveled. And they realized that
they had been with Jesus.
14 And seeing the man who
had been healed [a]standing with
them, they could say nothing
against it.
15 But when they had com-
manded them to go aside out
of the council, they conferred
among themselves,
16 saying, [a]"What shall we do
to these men? For, indeed, that a
[1]notable miracle has been done
through them *is* [b]evident[2] to all
who dwell in Jerusalem, and we
cannot deny *it*.
17 "But so that it spreads no
further among the people, let
us severely threaten them, that
from now on they speak to no
man in this name."
18 [a]So they called them and
commanded them not to speak
at all nor teach in the name of
Jesus.
19 But Peter and John answered
and said to them, [a]"Whether it is
right in the sight of God to listen
to you more than to God, you
judge.
20 [a]"For we cannot but speak
the things which [b]we have seen
and heard."
21 So when they had further
threatened them, they let them
go, finding no way of punishing
them, [a]because of the people,
since they all [b]glorified God for
[c]what had been done.
22 For the man was over forty
years old on whom this miracle
of healing had been performed.
23 And being let go, [a]they went
to their own *companions* and
reported all that the chief priests
and elders had said to them.
24 So when they heard that,
they raised their voice to God
with one accord and said: "Lord,
[a]You *are* God, who made heaven
and earth and the sea, and all
that is in them,
25 "who [1]by the mouth of Your ★
servant David have said:

[a]'Why did the nations rage,
And the people plot vain
things?
26 *The kings of the earth took*
their stand,
And the rulers were
gathered together
Against the L*ORD and*
against His Christ.'

27 "For [a]truly against [b]Your
holy Servant Jesus, [c]whom You
anointed, both Her′od and Pon′-
ti·us Pilate, with the Gentiles
and the people of Israel, were
gathered together
28 [a]"to do whatever Your hand
and Your purpose determined
before to be done.
29 "Now, Lord, look on their
threats, and grant to Your servants [a]that with all boldness
they may speak Your word,
30 "by stretching out Your hand
to heal, [a]and that signs and wonders may be done [b]through the
name of [c]Your holy Servant Jesus."
31 And when they had prayed,
[a]the place where they were assembled together was shaken;
and they were all filled with the
Holy Spirit, [b]and they spoke the
word of God with boldness.
32 Now the multitude of those
who believed [a]were of one heart
and one soul; [b]neither did anyone say that any of the things he
possessed was his own, but they
had all things in common.
33 And with [a]great power the

14 [a]Acts 3:11
16 [a]John 11:47 [b]Acts 3:7–10 [1]*remarkable sign* [2]*well known*
18 [a]Acts 5:28, 40
19 [a]Acts 5:29
20 [a]Acts 1:8; 2:32 [b][1 John 1:1, 3]
21 [a]Acts 5:26 [b]Matt. 15:31 [c]Acts 3:7, 8
23 [a]Acts 2:44–46; 12:12
24 [a]Ex. 20:11
25 [a]Ps. 2:1, 2 [1]NU *through the Holy Spirit, by the mouth of our father, Your servant David,*
27 [a]Luke 22:2; 23:1, 8 [b][Luke 1:35] [c]John 10:36
28 [a]Acts 2:23; 3:18
29 [a]Acts 4:13, 31; 9:27; 13:46; 14:3; 19:8; 26:26
30 [a]Acts 2:43; 5:12 [b]Acts 3:6, 16 [c]Acts 4:27
31 [a]Acts 2:2, 4; 16:26 [b]Acts 4:29
32 [a]Rom. 15:5, 6 [b]Acts 2:44
33 [a][Acts 1:8]

apostles gave [b]witness to the
resurrection of the Lord Jesus.
And [c]great grace was upon them
all.
34 Nor was there anyone among
them who lacked; [a]for all who
were possessors of lands or
houses sold them, and brought
the proceeds of the things that
were sold,
35 [a]and laid *them* at the apostles' feet; [b]and they distributed
to each as anyone had need.
36 And [1]Jō′sēs, who was also
named Bar′na·bas by the apostles (which is translated Son of
[2]Encouragement), a Lē′vīte of
the country of Cyprus,
37 [a]having land, sold *it*, and
brought the money and laid *it* at
the apostles' feet.

5 But a certain man named
An·a·nī′as, with Sap·phī′ra
his wife, sold a possession.
2 And he kept back *part* of
the proceeds, his wife also being aware *of it*, and brought a
certain part and laid *it* at the
apostles' feet.
3 [a]But Peter said, "An·a·nī′as,
why has [b]Satan filled your heart
to lie to the Holy Spirit and keep
back *part* of the price of the
land for yourself?
4 "While it remained, was it not
your own? And after it was sold,
was it not in your own control?
Why have you conceived this
thing in your heart? You have not
lied to men but to God."
5 Then An·a·nī′as, hearing
these words, [a]fell down and
breathed his last. So great fear
came upon all those who heard
these things.
6 And the young men arose
and [a]wrapped him up, carried
him out, and buried *him*.
7 Now it was about three hours
later when his wife came in, not
knowing what had happened.
8 And Peter answered her,
"Tell me whether you sold the
land for so much?" She said,
"Yes, for so much."
9 Then Peter said to her, "How
is it that you have agreed together [a]to test the Spirit of the
Lord? Look, the feet of those
who have buried your husband
are at the door, and they will
carry you out."
10 [a]Then immediately she fell
down at his feet and breathed
her last. And the young men
came in and found her dead, and
carrying *her* out, buried *her* by
her husband.
11 [a]So great fear came upon all
the church and upon all who
heard these things.
12 And [a]through the hands of
the apostles many signs and
wonders were done among the
people. [b]And they were all with
one accord in Solomon's Porch.
13 Yet [a]none of the rest dared
join them, [b]but the people esteemed them highly.
14 And believers were increasingly added to the Lord, multitudes of both men and women,
15 so that they brought the sick
out into the streets and laid
them on beds and couches, [a]that
at least the shadow of Peter
passing by might fall on some of
them.
16 Also a multitude gathered
from the surrounding cities to
Jerusalem, bringing [a]sick people
and those who were tormented
by unclean spirits, and they
were all healed.
17 [a]Then the high priest rose up,
and all those who *were* with him

33 [b]Acts 1:22 [c]Rom. 6:15
34 [a]Acts 2:45
35 [a]Acts 4:37; 5:2 [b]Acts 2:45; 6:1
36 [1]NU *Joseph* [2]Or *Consolation*
37 [a]Acts 4:34, 35; 5:1, 2

CHAPTER 5

3 [a]Deut. 23:21 [b]Luke 22:3
5 [a]Acts 5:10, 11
6 [a]John 19:40
9 [a]Acts 5:3, 4
10 [a]Acts 5:5
11 [a]Acts 2:43; 5:5; 19:17
12 [a]Acts 2:43; 4:30; 6:8; 14:3; 15:12 [b]Acts 3:11; 4:32
13 [a]John 9:22 [b]Acts 2:47; 4:21
15 [a]Acts 19:12
16 [a]Mark 16:17, 18
17 [a]Acts 4:1, 2, 6

(which is the sect of the Sad′-
dū·cees), and they were filled
with [1]indignation,
18 [a]and laid their hands on the
apostles and put them in the
common prison.
19 But at night [a]an angel of the
Lord opened the prison doors
and brought them out, and said,
20 "Go, stand in the temple
and speak to the people [a]all the
words of this life."
21 And when they heard *that*,
they entered the temple early in
the morning and taught. [a]But the
high priest and those with him
came and called the [1]council together, with all the [2]elders of the
children of Israel, and sent to the
prison to have them brought.
22 But when the officers came
and did not find them in the
prison, they returned and reported,
23 saying, "Indeed we found the
prison shut securely, and the
guards standing [1]outside before
the doors; but when we opened
them, we found no one inside!"
24 Now when [1]the high priest,
[a]the captain of the temple, and
the chief priests heard these
things, they wondered what the
outcome would be.
25 So one came and told them,
[1]saying, "Look, the men whom
you put in prison are standing
in the temple and teaching the
people!"
26 Then the captain went with
the officers and brought them
without violence, [a]for they feared
the people, lest they should be
stoned.
27 And when they had brought
them, they set *them* before the
council. And the high priest
asked them,
28 saying, [a]"Did we not strictly
command you not to teach in
this name? And look, you have
filled Jerusalem with your doctrine, [b]and intend to bring this
Man's [c]blood on us!"
29 But Peter and the *other* apostles answered and said: [a]"We
ought to obey God rather than
men.
30 [a]"The God of our fathers
raised up Jesus whom you murdered by [b]hanging on a tree.
31 [a]"Him God has exalted to
His right hand *to be* [b]Prince and
[c]Savior, [d]to give repentance to
Israel and forgiveness of sins.
32 "And [a]we are His witnesses
to these things, and *so* also *is*
the Holy Spirit [b]whom God has
given to those who obey Him."
33 When they heard *this*, they
were [a]furious[1] and plotted to kill
them.
34 Then one in the council
stood up, a Phar′i·see named
[a]Ga·mā′li·el, a teacher of the law
held in respect by all the people,
and commanded them to put
the apostles outside for a little
while.
35 And he said to them: "Men of
Israel, [1]take heed to yourselves
what you intend to do regarding
these men.
36 "For some time ago Theū′das
rose up, claiming to be somebody. A number of men, about
four hundred, [1]joined him. He
was slain, and all who obeyed
him were scattered and came to
nothing.
37 "After this man, Judas of
Galilee rose up in the days of the
census, and drew away many
people after him. He also perished, and all who obeyed him
were dispersed.

17 [1]*jealousy*
18 [a]Luke 21:12
19 [a]Acts 12:7; 16:26
20 [a][John 6:63, 68; 17:3]
21 [a]Acts 4:5, 6 [1]Sanhedrin [2]*council of elders* or *senate*
23 [1]NU, M omit *outside*
24 [a]Acts 4:1; 5:26 [1]NU omits *the high priest*
25 [1]NU, M omit *saying*
26 [a]Matt. 21:26
28 [a]Acts 4:17, 18 [b]Acts 2:23, 36 [c]Matt. 23:35
29 [a]Acts 4:19
30 [a]Acts 3:13, 15 [b][1 Pet. 2:24]
31 [a][Acts 2:33, 36] [b]Acts 3:15 [c]Matt. 1:21 [d]Luke 24:47
32 [a]John 15:26, 27 [b]Acts 2:4; 10:44
33 [a]Acts 2:37; 7:54 [1]*cut to the quick*
34 [a]Acts 22:3
35 [1]*be careful*
36 [1]*followed*

38 "And now I say to you, keep away from these men and let them alone; for if this plan or this work is of men, it will come to nothing;

39 [a]"but if it is of God, you cannot overthrow it—lest you even be found [b]to fight against God."

40 And they agreed with him, and when they had [a]called for the apostles [b]and beaten *them,* they commanded that they should not speak in the name of Jesus, and let them go.

41 So they departed from the presence of the council, [a]rejoicing that they were counted worthy to suffer shame for [1]His name.

42 And daily [a]in the temple, and in every house, [b]they did not cease teaching and preaching Jesus *as* the Christ.

CHAPTER 6

6 Now in those days, [a]when *the number of* the disciples was multiplying, there arose a complaint against the Hebrews by the [b]Hel′len·ists,[1] because their widows were neglected [c]in the daily distribution.

2 Then the twelve summoned the multitude of the disciples and said, [a]"It is not desirable that we should leave the word of God and serve tables.

3 "Therefore, brethren, [a]seek out from among you seven men of *good* reputation, full of the Holy Spirit and wisdom, whom we may appoint over this [b]business;

4 "but we [a]will give ourselves continually to prayer and to the ministry of the word."

5 And the saying pleased the whole multitude. And they chose Stephen, [a]a man full of faith and the Holy Spirit, and [b]Philip, Proch′o·rus, Nī·cā′nor, Tī′mon, Par′me·nas, and [c]Nic′o·las, a proselyte from An′ti·och,

6 whom they set before the apostles; and [a]when they had prayed, [b]they laid hands on them.

7 Then [a]the word of God spread, and the number of the disciples multiplied greatly in Jerusalem, and a great many [b]of the priests were obedient to the faith.

8 And Stephen, full of [1]faith and power, did great [a]wonders and signs among the people.

9 Then there arose some from what is called the Synagogue of the Freedmen (Cȳ·rē′ni·ans, Alexandrians, and those from Ci·li′ci·a and Asia), disputing with Stephen.

10 And [a]they were not able to resist the wisdom and the Spirit by which he spoke.

11 [a]Then they secretly induced men to say, "We have heard him speak blasphemous words against Moses and God."

12 And they stirred up the people, the elders, and the scribes; and they came upon *him,* seized him, and brought *him* to the council.

13 They also set up false witnesses who said, "This man does not cease to speak [1]blasphemous words against this holy place and the law;

14 [a]"for we have heard him say that this Jesus of Nazareth will destroy this place and change the customs which Moses delivered to us."

15 And all who sat in the council, looking steadfastly at him, saw his face as the face of an angel.

39 [a]1 Cor. 1:25 [b]Acts 7:51; 9:5
40 [a]Acts 4:18 [b]Matt. 10:17
41 [a][1 Pet. 4:13–16] [1]NU *the name;* M *the name of Jesus*
42 [a]Acts 2:46 [b]Acts 4:20, 29

CHAPTER 6

1 [a]Acts 2:41; 4:4 [b]Acts 9:29; 11:20 [c]Acts 4:35; 11:29 [1]Greek-speaking Jews
2 [a]Ex. 18:17
3 [a]1 Tim. 3:7 [b]1 Tim. 3:8–13
4 [a]Acts 2:42
5 [a]Acts 6:3; 11:24 [b]Acts 8:5, 26; 21:8 [c]Rev. 2:6, 15
6 [a]Acts 1:24 [b][2 Tim. 1:6]
7 [a]Acts 12:24 [b]John 12:42
8 [a]Acts 2:43; 5:12; 8:15; 14:3 [1]NU *grace*
10 [a]Luke 21:15
11 [a]1 Kin. 21:10, 13
13 [1]NU omits *blasphemous*
14 [a]Acts 10:38; 25:8

7 Then the high priest said,
"Are these things so?"
2 And he said, [a]"Brethren and
fathers, listen: The [b]God of glory
appeared to our father Abraham
when he was in Mes·o·po·tā′-
mi·a, before he dwelt in [c]Har′an,
3 "and said to him, [a]*'Get out
of your country and from your
relatives, and come to a land
that I will show you.'*
4 "Then [a]he came out of the
land of the Chal·dē′ans and
dwelt in Har′an. And from there,
when his father was [b]dead, He
moved him to this land in which
you now dwell.
5 "And *God* gave him no inheritance in it, not even *enough*
to set his foot on. But even when
Abraham had no child, [a]He
promised to give it to him for a
possession, and to his descendants after him.
6 "But God spoke in this way:
[a]that his descendants would
dwell in a foreign land, and
that they would bring them into
[b]bondage and oppress *them* four
hundred years.
7 [a]*'And the nation to whom
they will be in bondage I will
[b]judge,'* said God, [c]*'and after that
they shall come out and serve
Me in this place.'*
8 [a]"Then He gave him the
covenant of circumcision; [b]and
so *Abraham* begot Isaac and
circumcised him on the eighth
day; [c]and Isaac *begot* Jacob, and
[d]Jacob *begot* the twelve patriarchs.
9 [a]"And the patriarchs, becoming envious, [b]sold Joseph into
Egypt. [c]But God was with him
10 "and delivered him out of all
his troubles, [a]and gave him favor
and wisdom in the presence of
Pharaoh, king of Egypt; and he
made him governor over Egypt
and all his house.
11 [a]"Now a famine and great
[1]trouble came over all the land
of Egypt and Cā′naan, and our
fathers found no sustenance.
12 [a]"But when Jacob heard that
there was grain in Egypt, he sent
out our fathers first.
13 "And the [a]second *time* Joseph was made known to his
brothers, and Joseph's family
became known to the Pharaoh.
14 [a]"Then Joseph sent and
called his father Jacob and [b]all
his relatives to *him,* [1]seventy-
five people.
15 [a]"So Jacob went down to
Egypt; [b]and he died, he and our
fathers.
16 "And [a]they were carried back
to Shē′chem and laid in [b]the
tomb that Abraham bought for a
sum of money from the sons of
Hā′mor, *the father* of Shē′chem.
17 "But when [a]the time of the
promise drew near which God
had sworn to Abraham, [b]the
people grew and multiplied in
Egypt
18 "till another king [a]arose who
did not know Joseph.
19 "This man dealt treacherously with our people, and oppressed our forefathers, [a]making
them expose their babies, so
that they might not live.
20 [a]"At this time Moses was
born, and [b]was well pleasing
to God; and he was brought up
in his father's house for three
months.
21 "But [a]when he was set out,
[b]Pharaoh's daughter took him
away and brought him up as her
own son.
22 "And Moses was learned in

CHAPTER 7

2 [a]Acts 22:1 [b]Ps. 29:3 [c]Gen. 11:31, 32
3 [a]Gen. 12:1
4 [a]Gen. 11:31; 15:7 [b]Gen. 11:32
5 [a]Gen. 12:7; 13:15; 15:3, 18; 17:8; 26:3
6 [a]Gen. 15:13, 14, 16; 47:11, 12 [b]Ex. 1:8–14; 12:40, 41
7 [a]Gen. 15:14 [b]Ex. 14:13–31 [c]Ex. 3:12
8 [a]Gen. 17:9–14 [b]Gen. 21:1–5 [c]Gen. 25:21–26 [d]Gen. 29:31—30:24; 35:18, 22–26
9 [a]Gen. 37:4, 11, 28 [b]Gen. 37:28 [c]Gen. 39:2, 21, 23
10 [a]Gen. 41:38–44
11 [a]Gen. 41:54; 42:5 [1]*affliction*
12 [a]Gen. 42:1, 2
13 [a]Gen. 45:4, 16
14 [a]Gen. 45:9, 27 [b]Deut. 10:22 [1]Or *seventy,* Ex. 1:5
15 [a]Gen. 46:1–7 [b]Gen. 49:33
16 [a]Josh. 24:32 [b]Gen. 23:16
17 [a]Gen. 15:13 [b]Ex. 1:7–9
18 [a]Ex. 1:8
19 [a]Ex. 1:22
20 [a]Ex. 2:1, 2 [b]Heb. 11:23
21 [a]Ex. 2:3, 4 [b]Ex. 2:5–10

all the wisdom of the Egyptians,
and was [a]mighty in words and
deeds.
23 [a]"Now when he was forty
years old, it came into his heart
to visit his brethren, the children
of Israel.
24 "And seeing one of *them*
suffer wrong, he defended
and avenged him who was oppressed, and struck down the
Egyptian.
25 "For he supposed that his
brethren would have understood
that God would deliver them by
his hand, but they did not understand.
26 "And the next day he appeared to *two of* them as they
were fighting, and *tried to* reconcile them, saying, 'Men, you
are brethren; why do you wrong
one another?'
27 "But he who did his neighbor
wrong pushed him away, saying,
[a]*'Who made you a ruler and a*
judge over us?
28 *'Do you want to kill me as*
you did the Egyptian yester-
day?'
29 [a]"Then, at this saying, Moses
fled and became a dweller in the
land of Mid'i·an, where he [b]had
two sons.
30 [a]"And when forty years had
passed, an Angel [1]of the Lord
appeared to him in a flame of
fire in a bush, in the wilderness
of Mount Sinai.
31 "When Moses saw *it,* he
marveled at the sight; and as he
drew near to observe, the voice
of the Lord came to him,
32 "*saying,* [a]*'I am the God of*
your fathers—the God of Abra-
ham, the God of Isaac, and the
God of Jacob.' And Moses trembled and dared not look.
33 [a]*'Then the* LORD *said to him,*
"Take your sandals off your feet,
for the place where you stand is
holy ground.
34 *"I have surely* [a]*seen the op-*
pression of My people who are
in Egypt; I have heard their
groaning and have come down
to deliver them. And now come,
I will [b]*send you to Egypt."'*
35 "This Moses whom they rejected, saying, [a]*'Who made you*
a ruler and a judge?' is the one
God sent *to be* a ruler and a
deliverer [b]by the hand of the
Angel who appeared to him in
the bush.
36 [a]"He brought them out, after he had [b]shown wonders and
signs in the land of Egypt, [c]and
in the Red Sea, [d]and in the wilderness forty years.
37 "This is that Moses who said ★
to the children of Israel, [a]*'The*
LORD your God will raise up for
you a Prophet like me from your
brethren. [b]*Him*[1] *you shall hear.'*
38 [a]"This is he who was in the
[1]congregation in the wilderness
with [b]the Angel who spoke to
him on Mount Sinai, and *with*
our fathers, [c]the one who received the living [d]oracles[2] to give
to us,
39 "whom our fathers [a]would
not obey, but rejected. And in
their hearts they turned back to
Egypt,
40 [a]"saying to Aaron, *'Make us*
gods to go before us; as for this
Moses who brought us out of the
land of Egypt, we do not know
what has become of him.'
41 [a]"And they made a calf in
those days, offered sacrifices to
the idol, and [b]rejoiced in the
works of their own hands.
42 "Then [a]God turned and gave

22 [a]Luke 24:19
23 [a]Ex. 2:11, 12
27 [a]Ex. 2:14
29 [a]Heb. 11:27 [b]Ex. 2:15, 21, 22; 4:20; 18:3
30 [a]Ex. 3:1–10 [1]NU omits *of the Lord*
32 [a]Ex. 3:6, 15
33 [a]Ex. 3:5, 7, 8, 10
34 [a]Ex. 2:24, 25 [b]Ps. 105:26
35 [a]Ex. 2:14 [b]Ex. 14:21
36 [a]Ex. 12:41; 33:1 [b]Ps. 105:27 [c]Ex. 14:21 [d]Ex. 16:1, 35
37 [a]Deut. 18:15, 18, 19 [b]Matt. 17:5 [1]NU, M omit *Him you shall hear*
38 [a]Ex. 19:3 [b]Gal. 3:19 [c]Deut. 5:27 [d]Heb. 5:12 [1]Gr. *ekklesia, assembly* or *church* [2]*sayings*
39 [a]Ps. 95:8–11
40 [a]Ex. 32:1, 23
41 [a]Deut. 9:16 [b]Ex. 32:6, 18, 19
42 [a][2 Thess. 2:11]

them up to worship [b]the host of
heaven, as it is written in the
book of the Prophets:

[c]*'Did you offer Me*
slaughtered animals and
sacrifices during forty
years in the wilderness,
O house of Israel?
43 *You also took up the*
tabernacle of Mō'loch,
And the star of your god
Rem'phan,
Images which you made to
worship;
And [a]I will carry you away
beyond Babylon.'

44 "Our fathers had the tabernacle of witness in the wilderness, as He appointed, instruct-
ing Moses [a]to make it according
to the pattern that he had seen,
45 [a]"which our fathers, having
received it in turn, also brought
with Joshua into the land possessed by the Gentiles, [b]whom
God drove out before the face
of our fathers until the [c]days of
David,
46 [a]"who found favor before
God and [b]asked to find a dwelling for the God of Jacob.
47 [a]"But Solomon built Him a
house.
48 "However, [a]the Most High
does not dwell in temples made
with hands, as the prophet says:

49 *'Heaven[a] is My throne,*
And earth is My footstool.
What house will you build
for Me? says the LORD,
Or what is the place of My
rest?
50 *Has My hand not [a]made all*
these things?'

51 "*You* [a]stiff-necked[1] and [b]un-
circumcised in heart and ears!
You always resist the Holy Spirit;
as your fathers *did,* so *do* you.
52 [a]"Which of the prophets did
your fathers not persecute? And
they killed those who foretold
the coming of [b]the Just One, of
whom you now have become the
betrayers and murderers,
53 [a]"who have received the law
by the direction of angels and
have not kept *it.*"
54 [a]When they heard these
things they were [1]cut to the
heart, and they gnashed at him
with *their* teeth.
55 But he, [a]being full of the
Holy Spirit, gazed into heaven
and saw the [b]glory of God, and
Jesus standing at the right hand
of God,
56 and said, "Look! [a]I see the
heavens opened and the [b]Son of
Man standing at the right hand
of God!"
57 Then they cried out with a
loud voice, stopped their ears,
and ran at him with one accord;
58 and they cast *him* out of
the city and stoned *him.* And
[a]the witnesses laid down their
clothes at the feet of a young
man named Saul.
59 And they stoned Stephen as
he was calling on *God* and saying, "Lord Jesus, [a]receive my
spirit."
60 Then he knelt down and cried
out with a loud voice, [a]"Lord, do
not charge them with this sin."
And when he had said this, he
fell asleep.

8 Now Saul was consenting
to his death. At that time a
great persecution arose against
the church which was at Jerusalem; and [a]they were all scattered

42 [b]2 Kin. 21:3 [c]Amos 5:25–27
43 [a]Jer. 25:9–12
44 [a][Heb. 8:5]
45 [a]Josh. 3:14; 18:1; 23:9 [b]Ps. 44:2 [c]2 Sam. 6:2–15
46 [a]2 Sam. 7:1–13 [b]1 Chr. 22:7
47 [a]1 Kin. 6:1–38; 8:20, 21
48 [a]1 Kin. 8:27
49 [a]Is. 66:1, 2
50 [a]Ps. 102:25
51 [a]Ex. 32:9 [b]Lev. 26:41 [1]*stubborn*
52 [a]2 Chr. 36:16 [b]Acts 3:14; 22:14
53 [a]Ex. 20:1
54 [a]Acts 5:33 [1]*furious*
55 [a]Acts 6:5 [b][Ex. 24:17]
56 [a]Matt. 3:16 [b]Dan. 7:13
58 [a]Acts 22:20
59 [a]Ps. 31:5
60 [a]Matt. 5:44

CHAPTER 8

1 [a]Acts 8:4; 11:19

throughout the regions of Judea
and Samaria, except the apostles.
2 And devout men carried Stephen *to his burial,* and [a]made
great lamentation over him.
3 As for Saul, [a]he made havoc
of the church, entering every
house, and dragging off men
and women, committing *them* to
prison.
4 Therefore [a]those who were
scattered went everywhere
preaching the word.
5 Then [a]Philip went down
to [1]the city of Samaria and
preached Christ to them.
6 And the multitudes with one
accord heeded the things spoken by Philip, hearing and seeing the miracles which he did.
7 For [a]unclean spirits, crying
with a loud voice, came out of
many who were possessed; and
many who were paralyzed and
lame were healed.
8 And there was great joy in
that city.
9 But there was a certain man
called Simon, who previously
[a]practiced [1]sorcery in the city
and [b]astonished the [2]people of
Samaria, claiming that he was
someone great,
10 to whom they all gave heed,
from the least to the greatest,
saying, "This man is the great
power of God."
11 And they heeded him because he had astonished them
with his [1]sorceries for a long
time.
12 But when they believed
Philip as he preached the things
[a]concerning the kingdom of God
and the name of Jesus Christ,
both men and women were baptized.
13 Then Simon himself also believed; and when he was baptized he continued with Philip,
and was amazed, seeing the
miracles and signs which were
done.
14 Now when the [a]apostles who
were at Jerusalem heard that
Samaria had received the word
of God, they sent Peter and John
to them,
15 who, when they had come
down, prayed for them [a]that they
might receive the Holy Spirit.
16 For [a]as yet He had fallen
upon none of them. [b]They had
only been baptized in [c]the name
of the Lord Jesus.
17 Then [a]they laid hands on
them, and they received the
Holy Spirit.
18 And when Simon saw that
through the laying on of the
apostles' hands the Holy Spirit
was given, he offered them
money,
19 saying, "Give me this power
also, that anyone on whom I
lay hands may receive the Holy
Spirit."
20 But Peter said to him, "Your
money perish with you, because
[a]you thought that [b]the gift of
God could be purchased with
money!
21 "You have neither part nor
portion in this matter, for your
[a]heart is not right in the sight of
God.
22 "Repent therefore of this
your wickedness, and pray God
[a]if perhaps the thought of your
heart may be forgiven you.
23 "For I see that you are
[a]poisoned by bitterness and
bound by iniquity."
24 Then Simon answered and
said, [a]"Pray to the Lord for me,

2 [a]Gen. 23:2
3 [a]Phil. 3:6
4 [a]Matt. 10:23
5 [a]Acts 6:5; 8:26, 30 [1]Or *a*
7 [a]Mark 16:17
9 [a]Acts 8:11; 13:6 [b]Acts 5:36 [1]*magic* [2]Or *nation*
11 [1]*magic arts*
12 [a]Acts 1:3; 8:4
14 [a]Acts 5:12, 29, 40
15 [a]Acts 2:38; 19:2
16 [a]Acts 19:2 [b]Matt. 28:19 [c]Acts 10:48; 19:5
17 [a]Acts 6:6; 19:6
20 [a][Matt. 10:8] [b][Acts 2:38; 10:45; 11:17]
21 [a]Jer. 17:9
22 [a]2 Tim. 2:25
23 [a]Heb. 12:15
24 [a]James 5:16

that none of the things which you have spoken may come upon me."

25 So when they had testified and preached the word of the Lord, they returned to Jerusalem, preaching the gospel in many villages of the Samaritans.

26 Now an angel of the Lord spoke to [a]Philip, saying, "Arise and go toward the south along the road which goes down from Jerusalem to Gā´za." This is [1]desert.

27 So he arose and went. And behold, [a]a man of Ethiopia, a eunuch of great authority under Can·dā´cē the queen of the Ethiopians, who had charge of all her treasury, and [b]had come to Jerusalem to worship,

28 was returning. And sitting in his chariot, he was reading Ī·sāi´ah the prophet.

29 Then the Spirit said to Philip, "Go near and overtake this chariot."

30 So Philip ran to him, and heard him reading the prophet Ī·sāi´ah, and said, "Do you understand what you are reading?"

31 And he said, "How can I, unless someone guides me?" And he asked Philip to come up and sit with him.

★ 32 The place in the Scripture which he read was this:

[a]*"He was led as a sheep to the*
slaughter;
And as a lamb before its
shearer is silent,
[b]*So He opened not His*
mouth.

33 *In His humiliation His*
[a]*justice was taken away,*
And who will declare His
generation?
For His life is [b]*taken from*
the earth."

34 So the eunuch answered Philip and said, "I ask you, of whom does the prophet say this, of himself or of some other man?"

35 Then Philip opened his mouth, [a]and beginning at this Scripture, preached Jesus to him.

36 Now as they went down the road, they came to some water. And the eunuch said, "See, *here is* water. [a]What hinders me from being baptized?"

37 [1]Then Philip said, [a]"If you believe with all your heart, you may." And he answered and said, [b]"I believe that Jesus Christ is the Son of God."

38 So he commanded the chariot to stand still. And both Philip and the eunuch went down into the water, and he baptized him.

39 Now when they came up out of the water, [a]the Spirit of the Lord caught Philip away, so that the eunuch saw him no more; and he went on his way rejoicing.

40 But Philip was found at [1]A·zō´tus. And passing through, he preached in all the cities till he came to [a]Caes·a·rē´a.

9 Then [a]Saul, still breathing threats and murder against the disciples of the Lord, went to the high priest

2 and asked [a]letters from him to the synagogues of Damascus, so that if he found any who were of the Way, whether men or women, he might bring them bound to Jerusalem.

26 [a]Acts 6:5 [1]Or *a deserted place*
27 [a]Ps. 68:31; 87:4 [b]John 12:20
32 [a]Is. 53:7, 8 [b]Matt. 27:12–14; John 19:9
33 [a]Luke 23:1–25 [b]Luke 23:33–46
35 [a]Luke 24:27
36 [a]Acts 10:47; 16:33
37 [a][Mark 16:16] [b]Matt. 16:16 [1]NU, M omit v. 37. It is found in Western texts, including the Latin tradition.
39 [a]Ezek. 3:12, 14
40 [a]Acts 21:8 [1]Same as Heb. *Ashdod*

CHAPTER 9

1 [a]Acts 7:57; 8:1, 3; 26:10, 11
2 [a]Acts 22:5

3 [a]As he journeyed he came near Damascus, and suddenly a light shone around him from heaven.

4 Then he fell to the ground, and heard a voice saying to him, "Saul, Saul, [a]why are you persecuting Me?"

5 And he said, "Who are You, Lord?" Then the Lord said, "I am Jesus, whom you are persecuting. [1]It *is* hard for you to kick against the goads."

6 So he, trembling and astonished, said, "Lord, what do You want me to do?" Then the Lord *said* to him, "Arise and go into the city, and you will be told what you must do."

7 And [a]the men who journeyed with him stood speechless, hearing a voice but seeing no one.

8 Then Saul arose from the ground, and when his eyes were opened he saw no one. But they led him by the hand and brought *him* into Damascus.

9 And he was three days without sight, and neither ate nor drank.

10 Now there was a certain disciple at Damascus [a]named An·a·nī′as; and to him the Lord said in a vision, "An·a·nī′as." And he said, "Here I am, Lord."

11 So the Lord *said* to him, "Arise and go to the street called Straight, and inquire at the house of Judas for *one* called Saul [a]of Tar′sus, for behold, he is praying.

12 "And in a vision he has seen a man named An·a·nī′as coming in and putting *his* hand on him, so that he might receive his sight."

13 Then An·a·nī′as answered, "Lord, I have heard from many about this man, [a]how much [1]harm he has done to Your saints in Jerusalem.

14 "And here he has authority from the chief priests to bind all [a]who call on Your name."

15 But the Lord said to him, "Go, for [a]he is a chosen vessel of Mine to bear My name before [b]Gentiles, [c]kings, and the [d]children[1] of Israel.

16 "For [a]I will show him how many things he must suffer for My [b]name's sake."

17 [a]And An·a·nī′as went his way and entered the house; and [b]laying his hands on him he said, "Brother Saul, the Lord [1]Jesus, who appeared to you on the road as you came, has sent me that you may receive your sight and [c]be filled with the Holy Spirit."

18 Immediately there fell from his eyes *something* like scales, and he received his sight at once; and he arose and was baptized.

19 So when he had received food, he was strengthened. [a]Then Saul spent some days with the disciples at Damascus.

20 Immediately he preached [1]the Christ in the synagogues, that He is the Son of God.

21 Then all who heard were amazed, and said, [a]"Is this not he who destroyed those who called on this name in Jerusalem, and has come here for that purpose, so that he might bring them bound to the chief priests?"

22 But Saul increased all the more in strength, [a]and confounded the Jews who dwelt in Damascus, proving that this *Jesus* is the Christ.

23 Now after many days were past, [a]the Jews plotted to kill him.

3 [a]1 Cor. 15:8
4 [a][Matt. 25:40]
5 [1]NU, M omit the rest of v. 5 and begin v. 6 with *But arise and go*
7 [a][Acts 22:9; 26:13]
10 [a]Acts 22:12
11 [a]Acts 21:39; 22:3
13 [a]Acts 9:1 [1]*bad things*
14 [a]Acts 7:59; 9:2, 21
15 [a]Eph. 3:7, 8 [b]Rom. 1:5; 11:13 [c]Acts 25:22, 23; 26:1 [d]Rom. 1:16; 9:1–5 [1]Lit. *sons*
16 [a]Acts 20:23 [b]2 Cor. 4:11
17 [a]Acts 22:12, 13 [b]Acts 8:17 [c]Acts 2:4; 4:31; 8:17; 13:52 [1]M omits *Jesus*
19 [a]Acts 26:20
20 [1]NU *Jesus*
21 [a]Gal. 1:13, 23
22 [a]Acts 18:28
23 [a]2 Cor. 11:26

24 [a]But their plot became known
to Saul. And they watched the
gates day and night, to kill him.
25 Then the disciples took him
by night and [a]let *him* down
through the wall in a large basket.
26 And [a]when Saul had come
to Jerusalem, he tried to join
the disciples; but they were all
afraid of him, and did not believe that he was a disciple.
27 [a]But Bar′na·bas took him and
brought *him* to the apostles. And
he declared to them how he had
seen the Lord on the road, and
that He had spoken to him, [b]and
how he had preached boldly at
Damascus in the name of Jesus.
28 So [a]he was with them at Jerusalem, coming in and going out.
29 And he spoke boldly in the
name of the Lord Jesus and disputed against the [a]Hel′len·ists,[1]
[b]but they attempted to kill him.
30 When the brethren found
out, they brought him down to
Caes·a·rē′a and sent him out to
Tar′sus.
31 [a]Then the [1]churches throughout all Judea, Galilee, and Samaria had peace and were [b]edi-
fied.[2] And walking in the [c]fear
of the Lord and in the [d]comfort
of the Holy Spirit, they were
[e]multiplied.
32 Now it came to pass, as Peter went [a]through all *parts of
the country,* that he also came
down to the saints who dwelt in
Lyd′da.
33 There he found a certain
man named Aē·nē′as, who had
been bedridden eight years and
was paralyzed.
34 And Peter said to him,
"Aē·nē′as, [a]Jesus the Christ heals
you. Arise and make your bed."
Then he arose immediately.
35 So all who dwelt at Lyd′da
and [a]Sharon saw him and
[b]turned to the Lord.
36 At Jop′pa there was a certain disciple named [1]Tab′i·tha,
which is translated [2]Dor′cas. This
woman was full [a]of good works
and charitable deeds which she
did.
37 But it happened in those days
that she became sick and died.
When they had washed her, they
laid *her* in [a]an upper room.
38 And since Lyd′da was near
Jop′pa, and the disciples had
heard that Peter was there, they
sent two men to him, imploring
him not to delay in coming to
them.
39 Then Peter arose and went
with them. When he had come,
they brought *him* to the upper room. And all the widows
stood by him weeping, showing
the tunics and garments which
Dor′cas had made while she was
with them.
40 But Peter [a]put them all out,
and [b]knelt down and prayed.
And turning to the body he
[c]said, "Tab′i·tha, arise." And she
opened her eyes, and when she
saw Peter she sat up.
41 Then he gave her *his* hand
and lifted her up; and when he
had called the saints and widows, he presented her alive.
42 And it became known
throughout all Jop′pa, [a]and
many believed on the Lord.
43 So it was that he stayed many
days in Jop′pa with [a]Simon, a
tanner.

10 There was a certain man
in [a]Caes·a·rē′a called
Cornelius, a centurion of what

24 [a]2 Cor. 11:32
25 [a]Josh. 2:15
26 [a]Acts 22:17–20; 26:20
27 [a]Acts 4:36; 13:2 [b]Acts 9:20, 22
28 [a]Gal. 1:18
29 [a]Acts 6:1; 11:20 [b]2 Cor. 11:26 [1]Greek-speaking Jews
31 [a]Acts 5:11; 8:1; 16:5 [b][Eph. 4:16, 29] [c]Ps. 34:9 [d]John 14:16 [e]Acts 16:5 [1]NU *church . . . was* [2]*built up*
32 [a]Acts 8:14
34 [a][Acts 3:6, 16; 4:10]
35 [a]1 Chr. 5:16; 27:29 [b]Acts 11:21; 15:19
36 [a]1 Tim. 2:10 [1]Lit., in Aram., *Gazelle* [2]Lit., in Gr., *Gazelle*
37 [a]Acts 1:13; 9:39
40 [a]Matt. 9:25 [b]Acts 7:60 [c]Mark 5:41, 42
42 [a]John 11:45
43 [a]Acts 10:6

CHAPTER 10

1 [a]Acts 8:40; 23:23

was called the Italian [1]Regiment,
2 [a]a devout *man* and one who
[b]feared God with all his household, who gave [1]alms generously to the people, and prayed to God always.
3 About [1]the ninth hour of the day [a]he saw clearly in a vision an angel of God coming in and saying to him, "Cornelius!"
4 And when he observed him, he was afraid, and said, "What is it, lord?" So he said to him, "Your prayers and your alms have come up for a memorial before God.
5 "Now [a]send men to Jop′pa, and send for Simon whose surname is Peter.
6 "He is lodging with [a]Simon, a tanner, whose house is by the sea. [b]He[1] will tell you what you must do."
7 And when the angel who spoke to him had departed, Cornelius called two of his household servants and a devout soldier from among those who waited on him continually.
8 So when he had explained all *these* things to them, he sent them to Jop′pa.
9 The next day, as they went on their journey and drew near the city, [a]Peter went up on the housetop to pray, about [1]the sixth hour.
10 Then he became very hungry and wanted to eat; but while they made ready, he fell into a trance
11 and [a]saw heaven opened and an object like a great sheet bound at the four corners, descending to him and let down to the earth.
12 In it were all kinds of four-

1 [1]*Cohort*

2 [a]Acts 8:2; 9:22; 22:12
[b][Acts 10:22, 35; 13:16, 26]
[1]*charitable gifts*

3 [a]Acts 10:30; 11:13
[1]3 P.M.

5 [a]Acts 11:13, 14

6 [a]Acts 9:43
[b]Acts 11:14
[1]NU, M omit the rest of v. 6.

9 [a]Acts 10:9–32; 11:5–14
[1]Noon

11 [a]Acts 7:56

14 [a]Deut. 14:3, 7

15 [a][Rom. 14:14]
[1]Declared clean

17 [1]*was perplexed*

19 [a]Acts 11:12

20 [a]Acts 15:7–9

21 [1]NU, M omit *who had been sent to him from Cornelius*

22 [a]Acts 22:12

23 [a]Acts 10:45; 11:12

footed animals of the earth, wild beasts, creeping things, and birds of the air.
13 And a voice came to him, "Rise, Peter; kill and eat."
14 But Peter said, "Not so, Lord! [a]For I have never eaten anything common or unclean."
15 And a voice *spoke* to him again the second time, [a]"What God has [1]cleansed you must not call common."
16 This was done three times. And the object was taken up into heaven again.
17 Now while Peter [1]wondered within himself what this vision which he had seen meant, behold, the men who had been sent from Cornelius had made inquiry for Simon's house, and stood before the gate.
18 And they called and asked whether Simon, whose surname was Peter, was lodging there.
19 While Peter thought about the vision, [a]the Spirit said to him, "Behold, three men are seeking you.
20 [a]"Arise therefore, go down and go with them, doubting nothing; for I have sent them."
21 Then Peter went down to the men [1]who had been sent to him from Cornelius, and said, "Yes, I am he whom you seek. For what reason have you come?"
22 And they said, "Cornelius *the* centurion, a just man, one who fears God and [a]has a good reputation among all the nation of the Jews, was divinely instructed by a holy angel to summon you to his house, and to hear words from you."
23 Then he invited them in and lodged *them.* On the next day Peter went away with them, [a]and

some brethren from Jop′pa accompanied him.
24 And the following day they
entered Caes·a·rē′a. Now Cornelius was waiting for them, and
had called together his relatives
and close friends.
25 As Peter was coming in, Cornelius met him and fell down at
his feet and worshiped *him.*
26 But Peter lifted him up, saying, [a]"Stand up; I myself am also
a man."
27 And as he talked with him,
he went in and found many who
had come together.
28 Then he said to them, "You
know how [a]unlawful it is for a
Jewish man to keep company
with or go to one of another
nation. But [b]God has shown me
that I should not call any man
common or unclean.
29 "Therefore I came without
objection as soon as I was sent
for. I ask, then, for what reason
have you sent for me?"
30 So Cornelius said, [1]"Four
days ago I was fasting until
this hour; and at the ninth hour
I prayed in my house, and behold, [a]a man stood before me [b]in
bright clothing,
31 "and said, 'Cornelius, [a]your
prayer has been heard, and
[b]your [1]alms are remembered in
the sight of God.
32 'Send therefore to Jop′pa
and call Simon here, whose surname is Peter. He is lodging in
the house of Simon, a tanner, by
the sea. [1]When he comes, he will
speak to you.'
33 "So I sent to you immediately,
and you have done well to come.
Now therefore, we are all present
before God, to hear all the things
commanded you by God."

34 Then Peter opened *his* mouth
and said: [a]"In truth I perceive
that God shows no partiality.
35 "But [a]in every nation whoever fears Him and works righteousness is [b]accepted by Him.
36 "The word which *God* sent to
the [1]children of Israel, [a]preaching
peace through Jesus Christ—[b]He
is Lord of all—
37 "that word you know, which
was proclaimed throughout all
Judea, and [a]began from Galilee
after the baptism which John
preached:
38 "how [a]God anointed Jesus of
Nazareth with the Holy Spirit
and with power, who [b]went about
doing good and healing all who
were oppressed by the devil, [c]for
God was with Him.
39 "And we are [a]witnesses of
all things which He did both in
the land of the Jews and in Jerusalem, whom [1]they [b]killed by
hanging on a tree.
40 "Him [a]God raised up on ★
the third day, and showed Him
openly,
41 [a]"not to all the people, but to
witnesses chosen before by God,
even to us [b]who ate and drank
with Him after He arose from
the dead.
42 "And [a]He commanded us to
preach to the people, and to
testify [b]that it is He who was
ordained by God *to be* Judge [c]of
the living and the dead.
43 [a]"To Him all the prophets
witness that, through His name,
[b]whoever believes in Him will
receive [c]remission[1] of sins."
44 While Peter was still speaking these words, [a]the Holy Spirit
fell upon all those who heard the
word.

26 [a]Acts 14:14, 15
28 [a]John 4:9; 18:28 [b][Acts 10:14, 35; 15:8, 9]
30 [a]Acts 1:10 [b]Matt. 28:3 [1]NU *Four days ago to this hour, at the ninth hour*
31 [a]Dan. 10:12 [b]Heb. 6:10 [1]*charitable gifts*
32 [1]NU omits the rest of v. 32.
34 [a]Deut. 10:17
35 [a][Eph. 2:13] [b]Ps. 15:1, 2
36 [a]Is. 57:19 [b]Rom. 10:12 [1]Lit. *sons*
37 [a]Luke 4:14
38 [a]Luke 4:18 [b]Matt. 4:23 [c]John 3:2; 8:29
39 [a]Acts 1:8 [b]Acts 2:23 [1]NU, M *they also*
40 [a]Hos. 6:2; Acts 2:24; 1 Cor. 15:4
41 [a][John 14:17, 19, 22; 15:27] [b]Luke 24:30, 41–43
42 [a]Matt. 28:19 [b]John 5:22, 27 [c]1 Pet. 4:5
43 [a]Zech. 13:1 [b]Gal. 3:22 [c]Acts 13:38, 39 [1]*forgiveness*
44 [a]Acts 4:31

45 [a]And [1]those of the circumcision who believed were astonished, as many as came with
Peter, [b]because the gift of the
Holy Spirit had been poured out
on the Gentiles also.
46 For they heard them speak
with tongues and magnify God.
Then Peter answered,
47 "Can anyone forbid water,
that these should not be baptized who have received the
Holy Spirit [a]just as we *have*?"
48 [a]And he commanded them to
be baptized [b]in the name of the
Lord. Then they asked him to
stay a few days.

11 Now the apostles and
brethren who were in
Judea heard that the Gentiles
had also received the word of
God.
2 And when Peter came up to
Jerusalem, [a]those of the circumcision contended with him,
3 saying, [a]"You went in to uncircumcised men [b]and ate with
them!"
4 But Peter explained *it* to
them [a]in order from the beginning, saying:
5 [a]"I was in the city of Jop′pa
praying; and in a trance I saw
a vision, an object descending
like a great sheet, let down from
heaven by four corners; and it
came to me.
6 "When I observed it intently
and considered, I saw four-footed
animals of the earth, wild beasts,
creeping things, and birds of the
air.
7 "And I heard a voice saying
to me, 'Rise, Peter; kill and eat.'
8 "But I said, 'Not so, Lord! For
nothing common or unclean has
at any time entered my mouth.'
9 "But the voice answered me
again from heaven, 'What God
has cleansed you must not call
common.'
10 "Now this was done three
times, and all were drawn up
again into heaven.
11 "At that very moment, three
men stood before the house
where I was, having been sent
to me from Caes·a·rē′a.
12 "Then [a]the Spirit told me to
go with them, doubting nothing.
Moreover [b]these six brethren accompanied me, and we entered
the man's house.
13 [a]"And he told us how he had
seen an angel standing in his
house, who said to him, 'Send
men to Jop′pa, and call for Simon whose surname is Peter,
14 'who will tell you words by
which you and all your household will be saved.'
15 "And as I began to speak, the
Holy Spirit fell upon them, [a]as
upon us at the beginning.
16 "Then I remembered the
word of the Lord, how He said,
[a]'John indeed baptized with water, but [b]you shall be baptized
with the Holy Spirit.'
17 [a]"If therefore God gave them
the same gift as *He gave* us
when we believed on the Lord
Jesus Christ, [b]who was I that I
could withstand God?"
18 When they heard these things
they became silent; and they glorified God, saying, [a]"Then God
has also granted to the Gentiles
repentance to life."
19 [a]Now those who were scattered after the persecution that
arose over Stephen traveled as
far as Phoe·ni′ci·a, Cyprus, and
An′ti·och, preaching the word to
no one but the Jews only.
20 But some of them were men

45 [a]Acts 10:23 [b]Acts 11:18 [1]The Jews
47 [a]Acts 2:4; 10:44; 11:17; 15:8
48 [a]1 Cor. 1:14–17 [b]Acts 2:38; 8:16; 19:5

CHAPTER 11

2 [a]Acts 10:45
3 [a]Acts 10:28 [b]Gal. 2:12
4 [a]Luke 1:3
5 [a]Acts 10:9
12 [a][John 16:13] [b]Acts 10:23
13 [a]Acts 10:30
15 [a]Acts 2:1–4; 15:7–9
16 [a]John 1:26, 33 [b]Is. 44:3
17 [a][Acts 15:8, 9] [b]Acts 10:47
18 [a]Rom. 10:12, 13; 15:9, 16
19 [a]Acts 8:1, 4

from Cyprus and Cȳ·rē′nē, who, when they had come to An′ti·och, spoke to [a]the Hel′len·ists, preaching the Lord Jesus.
21 And [a]the hand of the Lord was with them, and a great number believed and [b]turned to the Lord.
22 Then news of these things came to the ears of the church in Jerusalem, and they sent out [a]Bar′na·bas to go as far as An′ti·och.
23 When he came and had seen the grace of God, he was glad, and [a]encouraged them all that with purpose of heart they should continue with the Lord.
24 For he was a good man, [a]full of the Holy Spirit and of faith. [b]And a great many people were added to the Lord.
25 Then Bar′na·bas departed for [a]Tar′sus to seek Saul.
26 And when he had found him, he brought him to An′ti·och. So it was that for a whole year they assembled with the church and taught a great many people. And the disciples were first called Christians in An′ti·och.
27 And in these days [a]prophets came from Jerusalem to An′ti·och.
28 Then one of them, named [a]Ag′a·bus, stood up and showed by the Spirit that there was going to be a great famine throughout all the world, which also happened in the days of [b]Clau′di·us Caesar.
29 Then the disciples, each according to his ability, determined to send [a]relief to the brethren dwelling in Judea.
30 [a]This they also did, and sent it to the elders by the hands of Bar′na·bas and Saul.

12 Now about that time Her′od the king stretched out *his* hand to harass some from the church.
2 Then he killed James [a]the brother of John with the sword.
3 And because he saw that it pleased the Jews, he proceeded further to seize Peter also. Now it was *during* [a]the Days of Unleavened Bread.
4 So [a]when he had arrested him, he put *him* in prison, and delivered *him* to four [1]squads of soldiers to keep him, intending to bring him before the people after Passover.
5 Peter was therefore kept in prison, but [1]constant prayer was offered to God for him by the church.
6 And when Her′od was about to bring him out, that night Peter was sleeping, bound with two chains between two soldiers; and the guards before the door were [1]keeping the prison.
7 Now behold, [a]an angel of the Lord stood by *him,* and a light shone in the prison; and he struck Peter on the side and raised him up, saying, "Arise quickly!" And his chains fell off *his* hands.
8 Then the angel said to him, "Gird yourself and tie on your sandals"; and so he did. And he said to him, "Put on your garment and follow me."
9 So he went out and followed him, and [a]did not know that what was done by the angel was real, but thought [b]he was seeing a vision.
10 When they were past the first and the second guard posts, they came to the iron gate that leads to the city, [a]which opened

20 [a]Acts 6:1; 9:29
21 [a]Luke 1:66 [b]Acts 9:35; 14:1
22 [a]Acts 4:36; 9:27
23 [a]Acts 13:43; 14:22
24 [a]Acts 6:5 [b]Acts 5:14; 11:21
25 [a]Acts 9:11, 30
27 [a]1 Cor. 12:28
28 [a]Acts 21:10 [b]Acts 18:2
29 [a]1 Cor. 16:1
30 [a]Acts 12:25

CHAPTER 12

2 [a]Matt. 4:21; 20:23
3 [a]Ex. 12:15; 23:15
4 [a]John 21:18 [1]Gr. *tetrads,* squads of four
5 [1]NU *constantly* or *earnestly*
6 [1]*guarding*
7 [a]Acts 5:19
9 [a]Ps. 126:1 [b]Acts 10:3, 17; 11:5
10 [a]Acts 5:19; 16:26

to them of its own accord; and
they went out and went down
one street, and immediately the
angel departed from him.
11 And when Peter had come to
himself, he said, "Now I know
for certain that [a]the Lord has
sent His angel, and [b]has delivered me from the hand of Her′od
and *from* all the expectation of
the Jewish people."
12 So, when he had considered
this, [a]he came to the house of
Mary, the mother of [b]John whose
surname was Mark, where many
were gathered together [c]praying.
13 And as Peter knocked at the
door of the gate, a girl named
Rhō′da came to answer.
14 When she recognized Peter's
voice, because of *her* gladness
she did not open the gate, but
ran in and announced that Peter
stood before the gate.
15 But they said to her, "You are
beside yourself!" Yet she kept
insisting that it was so. So they
said, [a]"It is his angel."
16 Now Peter continued knock-
ing; and when they opened *the
door* and saw him, they were
astonished.
17 But [a]motioning to them with
his hand to keep silent, he declared to them how the Lord
had brought him out of the
prison. And he said, "Go, tell
these things to James and to the
brethren." And he departed and
went to another place.
18 Then, as soon as it was day,
there was no small [1]stir among
the soldiers about what had become of Peter.
19 But when Her′od had
searched for him and not found
him, he examined the guards and
commanded that *they* should be
put to death. And he went down
from Judea to Caes·a·rē′a, and
stayed *there.*
20 Now Her′od had been very
angry with the people of [a]Tȳre
and Sī′don; but they came to
him with one accord, and having made Blas′tus [1]the king's
personal aide their friend, they
asked for peace, because [b]their
country was [2]supplied with food
by the king's *country.*
21 So on a set day Her′od, arrayed in royal apparel, sat on
his throne and gave an oration
to them.
22 And the people kept shouting, "The voice of a god and not
of a man!"
23 Then immediately an angel
of the Lord [a]struck him, because
[b]he did not give glory to God.
And he was eaten by worms and
[1]died.
24 But [a]the word of God grew
and multiplied.
25 And [a]Bar′na·bas and Saul
returned [1]from Jerusalem when
they had [b]fulfilled *their* ministry, and they also [c]took with
them [d]John whose surname was
Mark.

13 Now [a]in the church that
was at An′ti·och there
were certain prophets and
teachers: [b]Bar′na·bas, Sim′ē·on
who was called Nī′ger, [c]Lū′cius
of Cȳ·rē′nē, Man′a·en who had
been brought up with Her′od the
tetrarch, and Saul.
2 As they ministered to the
Lord and fasted, the Holy Spirit
said, [a]"Now separate to Me Bar′-
na·bas and Saul for the work [b]to
which I have called them."
3 Then, [a]having fasted and
prayed, and laid hands on them,
they sent *them* away.

11 [a][Ps. 34:7] [b]Job 5:19
12 [a]Acts 4:23 [b]Acts 13:5, 13; 15:37 [c]Acts 12:5
15 [a][Matt. 18:10]
17 [a]Acts 13:16; 19:33; 21:40
18 [1]*disturbance*
20 [a]Matt. 11:21 [b]Ezek. 27:17 [1]*who was in charge of the king's bedchamber* [2]Lit. *nourished*
23 [a]2 Sam. 24:16, 17 [b]Ps. 115:1 [1]*breathed his last*
24 [a]Acts 6:7; 19:20
25 [a]Acts 11:30 [b]Acts 11:30 [c]Acts 13:5, 13 [d]Acts 12:12; 15:37 [1]NU, M *to*

CHAPTER 13

1 [a]Acts 14:26 [b]Acts 11:22 [c]Rom. 16:21
2 [a]Gal. 1:15; 2:9 [b]Heb. 5:4
3 [a]Acts 6:6

★ **4** So, being sent out by the
Holy Spirit, they went down to
Se·leū′ci·a, and from there they
sailed to [a]Cyprus.
5 And when they arrived in
Sal′a·mis, [a]they preached the
word of God in the synagogues
of the Jews. They also had [b]John
as *their* assistant.
6 Now when they had gone
through [1]the island to Pā′phos,
they found [a]a certain sorcerer,
a false prophet, a Jew whose
name *was* Bar-Jē′sus,
7 who was with the proconsul,
Ser′gi·us Paul′us, an intelligent
man. This man called for Bar′-
na·bas and Saul and sought to
hear the word of God.
8 But [a]El′y·mas the sorcerer (for
so his name is translated) [1]with-
stood them, seeking to turn the
proconsul away from the faith.
9 Then Saul, who also *is called*
Paul, [a]filled with the Holy Spirit,
looked intently at him
10 and said, "O full of all deceit
and all fraud, [a]*you* son of the
devil, *you* enemy of all righteousness, will you not cease
perverting the straight ways of
the Lord?
11 "And now, indeed, [a]the hand
of the Lord *is* upon you, and you
shall be blind, not seeing the sun
for a time." And immediately a
dark mist fell on him, and he
went around seeking someone
to lead him by the hand.
12 Then the proconsul believed,
when he saw what had been
done, being astonished at the
teaching of the Lord.
13 Now when Paul and his
party set sail from Pā′phos, they
came to Per′ga in Pam·phyl′i·a;
and [a]John, departing from them,
returned to Jerusalem.
14 But when they departed from
Per′ga, they came to An′ti·och
in Pi·sid′i·a, and [a]went into the
synagogue on the Sabbath day
and sat down.
15 And [a]after the reading of the
Law and the Prophets, the rulers
of the synagogue sent to them,
saying, "Men *and* brethren, if
you have [b]any word of [1]exhorta-
tion for the people, say on."
16 Then Paul stood up, and mo-
tioning with *his* hand said, "Men
of Israel, and [a]you who fear God,
listen:
17 "The God of this people
[1]Israel [a]chose our fathers, and
exalted the people [b]when they
dwelt as strangers in the land of
Egypt, and with [2]an uplifted arm
He [c]brought them out of it.
18 "Now [a]for a time of about
forty years He put up with their
ways in the wilderness.
19 "And when He had destroyed
[a]seven nations in the land of Cā′-
naan, [b]He distributed their land
to them by allotment.
20 "After that [a]He gave *them*
judges for about four hundred
and fifty years, [b]until Samuel
the prophet.
21 [a]"And afterward they asked
for a king; so God gave them
[b]Saul the son of Kish, a man of
the tribe of Benjamin, for forty
years.
22 "And [a]when He had removed
him, [b]He raised up for them
David as king, to whom also He
gave testimony and said, [c]'*I have
found David* the *son* of Jesse, [d]*a
man after My own heart,* who
will do all My will.'
23 [a]"From this man's seed, ac- ★
cording [b]to *the* promise, God
raised up for Israel [c]a[1] Savior—
Jesus—

4 [a]Acts 4:36
5 [a][Acts 13:46] [b]Acts 12:25; 15:37
6 [a]Acts 8:9 [1]NU *the whole island*
8 [a]Ex. 7:11 [1]*opposed*
9 [a]Acts 2:4; 4:8
10 [a]Matt. 13:38
11 [a]1 Sam. 5:6
13 [a]Acts 15:38
14 [a]Acts 16:13
15 [a]Luke 4:16 [b]Heb. 13:22 [1]*encouragement*
16 [a]Acts 10:35
17 [a]Deut. 7:6–8 [b]Acts 7:17 [c]Ex. 14:8 [1]M omits *Israel* [2]Mighty power
18 [a]Num. 14:34
19 [a]Deut. 7:1 [b]Josh. 14:1, 2; 19:51
20 [a]Judg. 2:16 [b]1 Sam. 3:20
21 [a]1 Sam. 8:5 [b]1 Sam. 10:20–24
22 [a]1 Sam. 15:23, 26, 28 [b]1 Sam. 16:1, 12, 13 [c]Ps. 89:20 [d]1 Sam. 13:14
23 [a]Is. 11:1 [b]Ps. 132:11 [c][Matt. 1:21] [1]M *salvation, after*

24 [a]"after John had first
preached, before His coming,
the baptism of repentance to all
the people of Israel.
25 "And as John was finishing
his course, he said, [a]'Who do
you think I am? I am not *He*. But
behold, [b]there comes One after
me, the sandals of whose feet I
am not worthy to loose.'
26 "Men *and* brethren, sons of
the [1]family of Abraham, and
[a]those among you who fear God,
[b]to you the [2]word of this salvation has been sent.
27 "For those who dwell in Jerusalem, and their rulers, [a]because
they did not know Him, nor even
the voices of the Prophets which
are read every Sabbath, have
fulfilled *them* in condemning
Him.
28 [a]"And though they found no
cause for death *in Him*, they
asked Pilate that He should be
put to death.
29 [a]"Now when they had fulfilled all that was written concerning Him, [b]they took *Him*
down from the tree and laid *Him*
in a tomb.
30 [a]"But God raised Him from
the dead.
31 [a]"He was seen for many days
by those who came up with Him
from Galilee to Jerusalem, who
are His witnesses to the people.
32 "And we declare to you glad
tidings—[a]that promise which
was made to the fathers.
★ 33 "God has fulfilled this for
us their children, in that He has
raised up Jesus. As it is also
written in the second Psalm:

> [a]*'You are My Son,*
> *Today I have begotten You.'*

34 "And that He raised Him ★
from the dead, no more to return
to [1]corruption, He has spoken
thus:

> [a]*'I will give you the sure*
> [2]*mercies of David.'*

35 "Therefore He also says in ★
another *Psalm:*

> [a]*'You will not allow Your Holy*
> *One to see corruption.'*

36 "For David, after he had
served [1]his own generation by
the will of God, [a]fell asleep, was
buried with his fathers, and [2]saw
corruption;
37 "but He whom God raised up
[1]saw no corruption.
38 "Therefore let it be known
to you, brethren, that [a]through
this Man is preached to you the
forgiveness of sins;
39 "and [a]by Him everyone who
believes is justified from all
things from which you could
not be justified by the law of
Moses.
40 "Beware therefore, lest what
has been spoken in the prophets
come upon you:

> 41 *'Behold,*[a] *you despisers,*
> *Marvel and perish!*
> *For I work a work in your*
> *days,*
> *A work which you will by*
> *no means believe,*
> *Though one were to declare*
> *it to you.'"*

42 [1]So when the Jews went out
of the synagogue, the Gentiles
begged that these words might
be preached to them the next
Sabbath.

---

24 [a][Luke 3:3]
25 [a]Mark 1:7 [b]John 1:20, 27
26 [a]Ps. 66:16 [b]Matt. 10:6 [1]*stock* [2]*message*
27 [a]Luke 23:34
28 [a]Matt. 27:22, 23
29 [a]Luke 18:31 [b]Matt. 27:57–61
30 [a]Matt. 12:39, 40; 28:6
31 [a]Acts 1:3, 11
32 [a][Gen. 3:15]
33 [a]Ps. 2:7; [Heb. 1:5; 5:5]
34 [a]Ps. 89:28; Is. 55:3 [1]*the state of decay* [2]*blessings*
35 [a]Ps. 16:10
36 [a]Acts 2:29 [1]*in his* [2]*underwent decay*
37 [1]*underwent no decay*
38 [a]Jer. 31:34
39 [a][Is. 53:11]
41 [a]Hab. 1:5
42 [1]Or *And when they went out of the synagogue of the Jews;* NU *And when they went out, they begged*

43 Now when the congregation
had broken up, many of the
Jews and devout proselytes followed Paul and Bar′na·bas, who,
speaking to them, [a]persuaded
them to continue in [b]the grace of
God.
44 On the next Sabbath almost
the whole city came together to
hear the word of God.
45 But when the Jews saw the
multitudes, they were filled with
envy; and contradicting and
blaspheming, they [a]opposed the
things spoken by Paul.
46 Then Paul and Bar′na·bas
grew bold and said, [a]"It was
necessary that the word of God
should be spoken to you first;
but [b]since you reject it, and
judge yourselves unworthy of
everlasting life, behold, [c]we turn
to the Gentiles.
★ 47 "For so the Lord has commanded us:

[a]*'I have set you as a light to*
the Gentiles,
That you should be for
salvation to the ends of
the earth.' "

48 Now when the Gentiles
heard this, they were glad and
glorified the word of the Lord.
[a]And as many as had been appointed to eternal life believed.
49 And the word of the Lord
was being spread throughout all
the region.
50 But the Jews stirred up the
devout and prominent women
and the chief men of the city,
[a]raised up persecution against
Paul and Bar′na·bas, and expelled them from their region.
51 [a]But they shook off the dust
from their feet against them,
and came to Ī·cō′ni·um.
52 And the disciples [a]were filled
with joy and [b]with the Holy
Spirit.

14

Now it happened in Ī·cō′-
ni·um that they went to-
gether to the synagogue of the
Jews, and so spoke that a great
multitude both of the Jews and
of the [a]Greeks believed.
2 But the unbelieving Jews
stirred up the Gentiles and [1]poi-
soned their [2]minds against the
brethren.
3 Therefore they stayed there
a long time, speaking boldly in
the Lord, [a]who was bearing witness to the word of His grace,
granting signs and [b]wonders to
be done by their hands.
4 But the multitude of the city
was [a]divided: part sided with
the Jews, and part with the
[b]apostles.
5 And when a violent attempt
was made by both the Gentiles
and Jews, with their rulers, [a]to
abuse and stone them,
6 they became aware of it and
[a]fled to Lys′tra and Der′bē, cities
of Lyc·ā·ō′ni·a, and to the surrounding region.
7 And they were preaching the
gospel there.
8 [a]And in Lys′tra a certain
man without strength in his feet
was sitting, a cripple from his
mother's womb, who had never
walked.
9 *This* man heard Paul speaking. [1]Paul, observing him intently and seeing that he had
faith to be healed,
10 said with a loud voice, [a]"Stand
up straight on your feet!" And
he leaped and walked.
11 Now when the people saw

43 [a]Acts 11:23 [b]Titus 2:11
45 [a]1 Pet. 4:4
46 [a]Rom. 1:16 [b]Ex. 32:10 [c]Acts 18:6
47 [a]Is. 42:6; 49:6
48 [a][Acts 2:47]
50 [a]2 Tim. 3:11
51 [a]Matt. 10:14
52 [a]John 16:22 [b]Acts 2:4; 4:8, 31; 13:9

CHAPTER 14

1 [a]Acts 18:4
2 [1]*embittered* [2]Lit. *souls*
3 [a]Heb. 2:4 [b]Acts 5:12
4 [a]Luke 12:51 [b]Acts 13:2, 3
5 [a]2 Tim. 3:11
6 [a]Matt. 10:23
8 [a]Acts 3:2
9 [1]Lit. *Who*
10 [a][Is. 35:6]

what Paul had done, they raised their voices, saying in the Lyc·ā·ō′ni·an *language,* [a]"The gods have come down to us in the likeness of men!"

12 And Bar′na·bas they called [1]Zeūs, and Paul, [2]Her′mēs, because he was the chief speaker.

13 Then the priest of Zeūs, whose temple was in front of their city, brought oxen and garlands to the gates, [a]intending to sacrifice with the multitudes.

14 But when the apostles Bar′na·bas and Paul heard this, [a]they tore their clothes and ran in among the multitude, crying out

15 and saying, "Men, [a]why are you doing these things? [b]We also are men with the same nature as you, and preach to you that you should turn from [c]these useless things [d]to the living God, [e]who made the heaven, the earth, the sea, and all things that are in them,

16 [a]"who in bygone generations allowed all nations to walk in their own ways.

17 [a]"Nevertheless He did not leave Himself without witness, in that He did good, [b]gave us rain from heaven and fruitful seasons, filling our hearts with [c]food and gladness."

18 And with these sayings they could scarcely restrain the multitudes from sacrificing to them.

19 [a]Then Jews from An′ti·och and Ī·cō′ni·um came there; and having persuaded the multitudes, [b]they stoned Paul *and* dragged *him* out of the city, supposing him to be [c]dead.

20 However, when the disciples gathered around him, he rose up and went into the city. And the next day he departed with Bar′na·bas to Der′bē.

21 And when they had preached the gospel to that city [a]and made many disciples, they returned to Lys′tra, Ī·cō′ni·um, and An′ti·och,

22 strengthening the souls of the disciples, [a]exhorting *them* to continue in the faith, and *saying,* [b]"We must through many tribulations enter the kingdom of God."

23 So when they had [a]appointed elders in every church, and prayed with fasting, they commended them to the Lord in whom they had believed.

24 And after they had passed through Pi·sid′i·a, they came to Pam·phyl′i·a.

25 Now when they had preached the word in Per′ga, they went down to At·ta·lī′a.

26 From there they sailed to An′ti·och, where they had been commended to the grace of God for the work which they had completed.

27 Now when they had come and gathered the church together, [a]they reported all that God had done with them, and that He had [b]opened the door of faith to the Gentiles.

28 So they stayed there a long time with the disciples.

15 And [a]certain *men* came down from Judea and taught the brethren, [b]"Unless you are circumcised according to the custom of Moses, you cannot be saved."

2 Therefore, when Paul and Bar′na·bas had no small dissension and dispute with them, they determined that [a]Paul and

11 [a]Acts 8:10; 28:6
12 [1]*Jupiter* [2]*Mercury*
13 [a]Dan. 2:46
14 [a]Matt. 26:65
15 [a]Acts 10:26 [b]James 5:17 [c]1 Cor. 8:4 [d]1 Thess. 1:9 [e]Rev. 14:7
16 [a]Ps. 81:12
17 [a]Rom. 1:19, 20 [b]Deut. 11:14 [c]Ps. 145:16
19 [a]Acts 13:45, 50; 14:2–5 [b]2 Cor. 11:25 [c][2 Cor. 12:1–4]
21 [a]Matt. 28:19
22 [a]Acts 11:23 [b][2 Tim. 2:12; 3:12]
23 [a]Titus 1:5
27 [a]Acts 15:4, 12 [b]2 Cor. 2:12

CHAPTER 15

1 [a]Gal. 2:12 [b]Phil. 3:2
2 [a]Gal. 2:1

Bar′na·bas and certain others of
them should go up to Jerusalem,
to the apostles and elders, about
this question.
3 So, [a]being sent on their
way by the church, they passed
through Phoe·ni′ci·a and Samaria, [b]describing the conver-
sion of the Gentiles; and they
caused great joy to all the brethren.
4 And when they had come to
Jerusalem, they were received
by the church and the apostles
and the elders; and they reported all things that God had
done with them.
5 But some of the sect of the
Phar′i·sees who believed rose
up, saying, "It is necessary to circumcise them, and to command
them to keep the law of Moses."
6 Now the apostles and elders
came together to consider this
matter.
7 And when there had been
much dispute, Peter rose up *and*
said to them: [a]"Men *and* brethren, you know that a good while
ago God chose among us, that by
my mouth the Gentiles should
hear the word of the gospel and
believe.
8 "So God, [a]who knows the
heart, [1]acknowledged them by
[b]giving them the Holy Spirit,
just as *He did* to us,
9 [a]"and made no distinction
between us and them, [b]purifying
their hearts by faith.
10 "Now therefore, why do you
test God [a]by putting a yoke on
the neck of the disciples which
neither our fathers nor we were
able to bear?
11 "But [a]we believe that through
the grace of the Lord Jesus
[1]Christ we shall be saved in the
same manner as they."

12 Then all the multitude kept
silent and listened to Bar′na·bas
and Paul declaring how many
miracles and wonders God had
[a]worked through them among
the Gentiles.
13 And after they had [1]become
silent, [a]James answered, saying, "Men *and* brethren, listen to
me:
14 [a]"Simon has declared how
God at the first visited the Gentiles to take out of them a people
for His name.
15 "And with this the words of
the prophets agree, just as it is
written:

16 *'After[a] this I will return*
And will rebuild the
tabernacle of David,
which has fallen down;
I will rebuild its ruins,
And I will set it up;
17 *So that the rest of mankind*
may seek the L*ORD*,
Even all the Gentiles who
are called by My name,
Says the [1]L*ORD who does all*
these things.'

18 [1]"Known to God from eternity are all His works.
19 "Therefore [a]I judge that we
should not trouble those from
among the Gentiles who [b]are
turning to God,
20 "but that we [a]write to them to
abstain [b]from things polluted by
idols, [c]*from* [1]sexual immorality,
[d]*from* things strangled, and *from*
blood.
21 "For Moses has had throughout many generations those who
preach him in every city, [a]being
read in the synagogues every
Sabbath."
22 Then it pleased the apostles

3 [a]Rom. 15:24 [b]Acts 14:27; 15:4, 12
7 [a]Acts 10:20
8 [a]Acts 1:24 [b]Acts 2:4; 10:44, 47 [1]*bore witness to*
9 [a]Rom. 10:12 [b]Acts 10:15, 28
10 [a]Matt. 23:4
11 [a]Rom. 3:4; 5:15 [1]NU, M omit *Christ*
12 [a]Acts 14:27; 15:3, 4
13 [a]Acts 12:17 [1]*stopped speaking*
14 [a]Acts 15:7
16 [a]Amos 9:11, 12
17 [1]NU L*ORD*, who makes these things
18 [1]NU (continuing v. 17) *known from eternity (of old).'*
19 [a]Acts 15:28; 21:25 [b]1 Thess. 1:9
20 [a]Acts 21:25 [b][1 Cor. 8:1; 10:20, 28] [c][1 Cor. 6:9] [d]Lev. 3:17 [1]Or *fornication*
21 [a]Acts 13:15, 27

and elders, with the whole church, to send chosen men of their own company to An′ti·och with Paul and Bar′na·bas, *namely,* Judas who was also named [a]Bar′sa·bas,[1] and Silas, leading men among the brethren.
23 They wrote this *letter* by them:

The apostles, the elders, and the brethren,

To the brethren who are of the Gentiles in An′ti·och, Syria, and Ci·li′ci·a:

Greetings.

24 Since we have heard that [a]some who went out from us have troubled you with words, [b]unsettling your souls, [1]saying, "*You must* be circumcised and keep the law"—to whom we gave no *such* commandment—
25 it seemed good to us, being assembled with one [1]accord, to send chosen men to you with our beloved Bar′na·bas and Paul,
26 [a]men who have risked their lives for the name of our Lord Jesus Christ.
27 We have therefore sent Judas and Silas, who will also report the same things by word of mouth.
28 For it seemed good to the Holy Spirit, and to us, to lay upon you no greater burden than these necessary things:
29 [a]that you abstain from things offered to idols, [b]from blood, from things strangled, and from [c]sexual[1] immorality. If you keep yourselves from these, you will do well.

Farewell.

30 So when they were sent off, they came to An′ti·och; and when they had gathered the multitude together, they delivered the letter.
31 When they had read it, they rejoiced over its encouragement.
32 Now Judas and Silas, themselves being [a]prophets also, [b]exhorted and strengthened the brethren with many words.
33 And after they had stayed *there* for a time, they were [a]sent back with greetings from the brethren to [1]the apostles.
34 [1]However, it seemed good to Silas to remain there.
35 [a]Paul and Bar′na·bas also remained in An′ti·och, teaching and preaching the word of the Lord, with many others also.
36 Then after some days Paul said to Bar′na·bas, "Let us now go back and visit our brethren in every city where we have preached the word of the Lord, *and see* how they are doing."
37 Now Bar′na·bas [1]was determined to take with them [a]John called Mark.
38 But Paul insisted that they should not take with them [a]the one who had departed from them in Pam·phyl′i·a, and had not gone with them to the work.
39 Then the contention became so sharp that they parted from one another. And so Bar′na·bas took Mark and sailed to [a]Cyprus;
40 but Paul chose Silas and

22 [a]Acts 1:23 [1]NU, M *Barsabbas*
24 [a]Titus 1:10, 11 [b]Gal. 1:7; 5:10 [1]NU omits *saying, "You must be circumcised and keep the law"*
25 [1]*purpose* or *mind*
26 [a]Acts 13:50; 14:19
29 [a]Acts 15:20; 21:25 [b]Lev. 17:14 [c]Col. 3:5 [1]Or *fornication*
32 [a]Eph. 4:11 [b]Acts 14:22; 18:23
33 [a]Heb. 11:31 [1]NU *those who had sent them*
34 [1]NU, M omit v. 34.
35 [a]Acts 13:1
37 [a]Acts 12:12, 25 [1]*resolved*
38 [a]Acts 13:13
39 [a]Acts 4:36; 13:4

departed, [a]being [1]commended
by the brethren to the grace of
God.
41 And he went through Syria
and Ci·li′ci·a, [a]strengthening the
churches.

16
Then he came to [a]Der′bē
and Lys′tra. And behold,
a certain disciple was there,
[b]named Timothy, [c]*the* son of
a certain Jewish woman who
believed, but his father *was*
Greek.
2 He was well spoken of by
the brethren who were at Lys′tra
and Ī·cō′ni·um.
3 Paul wanted to have him go
on with him. And he [a]took *him*
and circumcised him because
of the Jews who were in that
region, for they all knew that his
father was Greek.
4 And as they went through
the cities, they delivered to them
the [a]decrees to keep, [b]which
were determined by the apostles
and elders at Jerusalem.
5 [a]So the churches were
strengthened in the faith, and
increased in number daily.
6 Now when they had gone
through Phryg′i·a and the region
of [a]Galatia, they were forbidden
by the Holy Spirit to preach the
word in [1]Asia.
7 After they had come to Mys′-
i·a, they tried to go into Bi·thyn′-
i·a, but the [1]Spirit did not permit
them.
8 So passing by Mys′i·a, they
[a]came down to Trō′as.
9 And a vision appeared to
Paul in the night. A [a]man of
Mac·e·dō′ni·a stood and pleaded
with him, saying, "Come over to
Mac·e·dō′ni·a and help us."
10 Now after he had seen the
vision, immediately we sought
to go [a]to Mac·e·dō′ni·a, concluding that the Lord had called us
to preach the gospel to them.
11 Therefore, sailing from
Trō′as, we ran a straight course
to Sam′o·thrāce, and the next
day came to Nē·ap′o·lis,
12 and from there to [a]Phi·lip′pī,
which is the [1]foremost city of
that part of Mac·e·dō′ni·a, a col-
ony. And we were staying in that
city for some days.
13 And on the Sabbath day we
went out of the city to the riverside, where prayer was custom-
arily made; and we sat down
and spoke to the women who
met *there*.
14 Now a certain woman named
Lyd′i·a heard *us*. She was a
seller of purple from the city of
[a]Thȳ·a·tī′ra, who worshiped God.
[b]The Lord opened her heart to
heed the things spoken by Paul.
15 And when she and her household were baptized, she begged
us, saying, "If you have judged
me to be faithful to the Lord,
come to my house and stay." So
[a]she persuaded us.
16 Now it happened, as we went
to prayer, that a certain slave
girl [a]possessed with a spirit of
divination met us, who brought
her masters [b]much profit by fortune-telling.
17 This girl followed Paul and
us, and cried out, saying, "These
men are the servants of the Most
High God, who proclaim to us
the way of salvation."
18 And this she did for many
days. But Paul, [a]greatly [1]an-
noyed, turned and said to the
spirit, "I command you in the
name of Jesus Christ to come
out of her." [b]And he came out
that very hour.

40 [a]Acts 11:23; 14:26 [1]*committed*
41 [a]Acts 16:5

CHAPTER 16

1 [a]Acts 14:6 [b]Rom. 16:21 [c]2 Tim. 1:5; 3:15
3 [a][Gal. 2:3; 5:2]
4 [a]Acts 15:19–21 [b]Acts 15:28, 29
5 [a]Acts 2:47; 15:41
6 [a]Gal. 1:1, 2 [1]The Roman province of Asia
7 [1]NU adds *of Jesus*
8 [a]2 Cor. 2:12
9 [a]Acts 10:30
10 [a]2 Cor. 2:13
12 [a]Phil. 1:1 [1]Lit. *first*
14 [a]Rev. 1:11; 2:18, 24 [b]Luke 24:45
15 [a]Judg. 19:21
16 [a]1 Sam. 28:3, 7 [b]Acts 19:24
18 [a]Mark 1:25, 34 [b]Mark 16:17 [1]*distressed*

19 But [a]when her masters saw
that their hope of profit was
gone, they seized Paul and Silas
and [b]dragged *them* into the marketplace to the authorities.
20 And they brought them to
the magistrates, and said, "These
men, being Jews, [a]exceedingly
trouble our city;
21 "and they teach customs
which are not lawful for us,
being Romans, to receive or observe."
22 Then the multitude rose up
together against them; and the
magistrates tore off their clothes
[a]and commanded *them* to be
beaten with rods.
23 And when they had laid many
stripes on them, they threw *them*
into prison, commanding the
jailer to keep them securely.
24 Having received such a
charge, he put them into the
inner prison and fastened their
feet in the stocks.
25 But at midnight Paul and
Silas were praying and singing
hymns to God, and the prisoners
were listening to them.
26 [a]Suddenly there was a great
earthquake, so that the foundations of the prison were shaken;
and immediately [b]all the doors
were opened and everyone's
chains were loosed.
27 And the keeper of the prison,
awaking from sleep and seeing
the prison doors open, supposing the prisoners had fled, drew
his sword and was about to kill
himself.
28 But Paul called with a loud
voice, saying, "Do yourself no
harm, for we are all here."
29 Then he called for a light,
ran in, and fell down trembling
before Paul and Silas.
30 And he brought them out
and said, [a]"Sirs, what must I do
to be saved?"
31 So they said, [a]"Believe on the
Lord Jesus Christ, and you will
be saved, you and your household."
32 Then they spoke the word of
the Lord to him and to all who
were in his house.
33 And he took them the same
hour of the night and washed
their stripes. And immediately
he and all his *family* were baptized.
34 Now when he had brought
them into his house, [a]he set food
before them; and he rejoiced,
having believed in God with all
his household.
35 And when it was day, the
magistrates sent the [1]officers,
saying, "Let those men go."
36 So the keeper of the prison
reported these words to Paul,
saying, "The magistrates have
sent to let you go. Now therefore
depart, and go in peace."
37 But Paul said to them, "They
have beaten us openly, uncondemned [a]Romans, *and* have
thrown *us* into prison. And now
do they put us out secretly? No
indeed! Let them come themselves and get us out."
38 And the officers told these
words to the magistrates, and
they were afraid when they
heard that they were Romans.
39 Then they came and pleaded
with them and brought *them*
out, and [a]asked *them* to depart
from the city.
40 So they went out of the
prison [a]and entered *the house of*
Lyd'i·a; and when they had seen
the brethren, they encouraged
them and departed.

19 [a]Acts 16:16; 19:25, 26 [b]Matt. 10:18
20 [a]Acts 17:8
22 [a]1 Thess. 2:2
26 [a]Acts 4:31 [b]Acts 5:19; 12:7, 10
30 [a]Acts 2:37; 9:6; 22:10
31 [a][John 3:16, 36; 6:47]
34 [a]Luke 5:29; 19:6
35 [1]*lictors,* lit. *rod bearers*
37 [a]Acts 22:25–29
39 [a]Matt. 8:34
40 [a]Acts 16:14

17 Now when they had
passed through Am·phip′-
o·lis and Ap·ol·lō′ni·a, they came
to [a]Thes·sa·lo·nī′ca, where there
was a synagogue of the Jews.
2 Then Paul, as his custom
was, [a]went in to them, and for
three Sabbaths [b]reasoned with
them from the Scriptures,
3 explaining and demonstrat-
ing [a]that the Christ had to suffer
and rise again from the dead,
and *saying*, "This Jesus whom I
preach to you is the Christ."
4 [a]And some of them were persuaded; and a great multitude
of the devout Greeks, and not
a few of the leading women,
joined Paul and [b]Silas.
5 But the Jews [1]who were not
persuaded, [2]becoming [a]envious,
took some of the evil men from
the marketplace, and gathering
a mob, set all the city in an
uproar and attacked the house
of [b]Jason, and sought to bring
them out to the people.
6 But when they did not find
them, they dragged Jason and
some brethren to the rulers of
the city, crying out, [a]"These who
have turned the world upside
down have come here too.
7 "Jason has [1]harbored them,
and these are all acting contrary
to the decrees of Caesar, [a]saying
there is another king—Jesus."
8 And they troubled the crowd
and the rulers of the city when
they heard these things.
9 So when they had taken security from Jason and the rest,
they let them go.
10 Then [a]the brethren immediately sent Paul and Silas away
by night to Be·rē′a. When they
arrived, they went into the synagogue of the Jews.

CHAPTER 17
1 [a]1 Thess. 1:1
2 [a]Luke 4:16 [b]1 Thess. 2:1–16
3 [a]Acts 18:5, 28
4 [a]Acts 28:24 [b]Acts 15:22, 27, 32, 40
5 [a]Acts 13:45 [b]Rom. 16:21 [1]NU omits *who were not persuaded* [2]M omits *becoming envious*
6 [a][Acts 16:20]
7 [a]1 Pet. 2:13 [1]*welcomed*
10 [a]Acts 9:25; 17:14
11 [a]John 5:39 [1]Lit. *noble*
14 [a]Matt. 10:23
15 [a]Acts 18:5
16 [a]2 Pet. 2:8 [1]*full of idols*
18 [a]1 Cor. 15:12 [1]NU, M add *also* [2]Lit. *seed picker,* an idler who makes a living picking up scraps
19 [1]Lit. *Hill of Ares,* or *Mars' Hill*

11 These were more [1]fair-minded
than those in Thes·sa·lo·nī′ca, in
that they received the word with
all readiness, and [a]searched
the Scriptures daily *to find out*
whether these things were so.
12 Therefore many of them believed, and also not a few of the
Greeks, prominent women as
well as men.
13 But when the Jews from
Thes·sa·lo·nī′ca learned that the
word of God was preached by
Paul at Be·rē′a, they came there
also and stirred up the crowds.
14 [a]Then immediately the brethren sent Paul away, to go to the
sea; but both Silas and Timothy
remained there.
15 So those who conducted
Paul brought him to Athens; and
[a]receiving a command for Silas
and Timothy to come to him
with all speed, they departed.
16 Now while Paul waited for
them at Athens, [a]his spirit was
provoked within him when he
saw that the city was [1]given over
to idols.
17 Therefore he reasoned in the
synagogue with the Jews and
with the *Gentile* worshipers,
and in the marketplace daily
with those who happened to be
there.
18 [1]Then certain Ep·i·cū·rē′an
and Stoic philosophers encoun-
tered him. And some said, "What
does this [2]babbler want to say?"
Others said, "He seems to be
a proclaimer of foreign gods,"
because he preached to them
[a]Jesus and the resurrection.
19 And they took him and
brought him to the [1]Ar·e·op′-
a·gus, saying, "May we know
what this new doctrine *is* of
which you speak?

20 "For you are bringing some
strange things to our ears. Therefore we want to know what these
things mean."
21 For all the A·thē′ni·ans and
the foreigners who were there
spent their time in nothing else
but either to tell or to hear some
new thing.
22 Then Paul stood in the midst
of the [1]Ar·e·op′a·gus and said,
"Men of Athens, I perceive that
in all things you are very religious;
23 "for as I was passing through
and considering the objects of
your worship, I even found an
altar with this inscription:

TO THE UNKNOWN GOD.

Therefore, the One whom you
worship without knowing, Him
I proclaim to you:
24 [a]"God, who made the world
and everything in it, since He is
[b]Lord of heaven and earth, [c]does
not dwell in temples made with
hands.
25 "Nor is He worshiped with
men's hands, as though He
needed anything, since He [a]gives
to all life, breath, and all things.
26 "And He has made from one
[1]blood every nation of men to
dwell on all the face of the earth,
and has determined their preap-
pointed times and [a]the boundaries of their dwellings,
27 [a]"so that they should seek
the Lord, in the hope that they
might grope for Him and find
Him, [b]though He is not far from
each one of us;
28 "for [a]in Him we live and move
and have our being, [b]as also some
of your own poets have said, 'For
we are also His offspring.'

22 [1]Lit. *Hill of Ares*, or *Mars' Hill*
24 [a]Acts 14:15 [b]Matt. 11:25 [c]Acts 7:48–50
25 [a]Is. 42:5
26 [a]Deut. 32:8 [1]NU omits *blood*
27 [a][Rom. 1:20] [b]Jer. 23:23, 24
28 [a][Heb. 1:3] [b]Titus 1:12
29 [a]Is. 40:18, 19
30 [a][Rom. 3:25] [b][Titus 2:11, 12]
31 [a]Acts 10:42 [b]Acts 2:24

CHAPTER 18

2 [a]1 Cor. 16:19
3 [a]Acts 20:34
4 [a]Acts 17:2
5 [a]Acts 17:14, 15

29 "Therefore, since we are the
offspring of God, [a]we ought not
to think that the Divine Nature
is like gold or silver or stone,
something shaped by art and
man's devising.
30 "Truly, [a]these times of ignorance God overlooked, but [b]now
commands all men everywhere
to repent,
31 "because He has appointed a
day on which [a]He will judge the
world in righteousness by the
Man whom He has ordained. He
has given assurance of this to all
by [b]raising Him from the dead."
32 And when they heard of the
resurrection of the dead, some
mocked, while others said, "We
will hear you again on this *matter.*"
33 So Paul departed from
among them.
34 However, some men joined
him and believed, among them
Dī·o·nys′i·us the Ar·e·op′a·gīte,
a woman named Dam′a·ris, and
others with them.

18

After these things Paul
departed from Athens
and went to Corinth.
2 And he found a certain Jew
named [a]A·qui′la, born in Pon′-
tus, who had recently come from
Italy with his wife Pri·scil′la
(because Clau′di·us had commanded all the Jews to depart
from Rome); and he came to
them.
3 So, because he was of the
same trade, he stayed with them
[a]and worked; for by occupation
they were tentmakers.
4 [a]And he reasoned in the synagogue every Sabbath, and persuaded both Jews and Greeks.
5 [a]When Silas and Timothy
had come from Mac·e·dō′ni·a,

Paul was [b]compelled [1]by the
Spirit, and testified to the Jews
that Jesus *is* the Christ.
6 But [a]when they opposed
him and blasphemed, [b]he shook
his garments and said to them,
[c]"Your blood *be* upon your *own*
heads; [d]I *am* clean. [e]From now
on I will go to the Gentiles."
7 And he departed from there
and entered the house of a certain *man* named [1]Jus′tus, *one*
who worshiped God, whose
house was next door to the synagogue.
8 [a]Then Cris′pus, the ruler of
the synagogue, believed on the
Lord with all his household. And
many of the Corinthians, hearing, believed and were baptized.
9 Now [a]the Lord spoke to Paul
in the night by a vision, "Do not
be afraid, but speak, and do not
keep silent;
10 [a]"for I am with you, and no
one will attack you to hurt you;
for I have many people in this
city."
11 And he continued *there* a
year and six months, teaching
the word of God among them.
12 When Gal′li·ō was proconsul
of A·chā′i·a, the Jews with one
accord rose up against Paul and
brought him to the [1]judgment
seat,
13 saying, "This *fellow* per-
suades men to worship God contrary to the law."
14 And when Paul was about to
open *his* mouth, Gal′li·ō said to
the Jews, "If it were a matter of
wrongdoing or wicked crimes,
O Jews, there would be reason
why I should bear with you.
15 "But if it is a [a]question of
words and names and your own
law, look *to it* yourselves; for

5 [b]Acts 18:28 [1]Or *in his spirit* or *in the Spirit*
6 [a]Acts 13:45 [b]Neh. 5:13 [c]2 Sam. 1:16 [d][Ezek. 3:18, 19] [e]Acts 13:46–48; 28:28
7 [1]NU *Titius Justus*
8 [a]1 Cor. 1:14
9 [a]Acts 23:11
10 [a]Jer. 1:18, 19
12 [1]Gr. *bema*
15 [a]Acts 23:29; 25:19
17 [a]1 Cor. 1:1 [1]NU *they all*
18 [a]Acts 21:24 [b]Rom. 16:1 [1]Lit. *many days*
21 [a]Acts 19:21; 20:16 [b]1 Cor. 4:19 [1]NU omits *I must by all means keep this coming feast in Jerusalem*
22 [a]Acts 8:40 [1]To Jerusalem
23 [a]Gal. 1:2 [b]Acts 14:22; 15:32, 41 [1]*successively*
24 [a]Titus 3:13
25 [a]Rom. 12:11 [b]Acts 19:3

I do not want to be a judge of
such *matters*."
16 And he drove them from the
judgment seat.
17 Then [1]all the Greeks took
[a]Sos′the·nēs, the ruler of the
synagogue, and beat *him* before
the judgment seat. But Gal′li·ō
took no notice of these things.
18 So Paul still remained [1]a
good while. Then he took leave
of the brethren and sailed for
Syria, and Pri·scil′la and A·qui′la
were with him. [a]He had *his* hair
cut off at [b]Cen′chrē·a, for he had
taken a vow.
19 And he came to Eph′e·sus,
and left them there; but he himself entered the synagogue and
reasoned with the Jews.
20 When they asked *him* to stay
a longer time with them, he did
not consent,
21 but took leave of them, saying, [a]"I[1] must by all means keep
this coming feast in Jerusalem;
but I will return again to you,
[b]God willing." And he sailed
from Eph′e·sus.
22 And when he had landed
at [a]Caes·a·rē′a, and [1]gone up
and greeted the church, he went
down to An′ti·och.
23 After he had spent some time
there, he departed and went
over the region of [a]Galatia and
Phryg′i·a [1]in order, [b]strength-
ening all the disciples.
24 [a]Now a certain Jew named
A·pol′los, born at Alexandria, an
eloquent man *and* mighty in the
Scriptures, came to Eph′e·sus.
25 This man had been instructed
in the way of the Lord; and being [a]fervent in spirit, he spoke
and taught accurately the things
of the Lord, [b]though he knew
only the baptism of John.

26 So he began to speak boldly
in the synagogue. When A·qui′la
and Pri·scil′la heard him, they
took him aside and explained to
him the way of God more accurately.
27 And when he desired to cross
to A·chā′i·a, the brethren wrote,
exhorting the disciples to receive him; and when he arrived,
[a]he greatly helped those who
had believed through grace;
28 for he vigorously refuted the
Jews publicly, [a]showing from
the Scriptures that Jesus is the
Christ.

19 And it happened, while
[a]A·pol′los was at Corinth,
that Paul, having passed through
[b]the upper regions, came to
Eph′e·sus. And finding some
disciples
2 he said to them, "Did you receive the Holy Spirit when you
believed?" So they said to him,
[a]"We have not so much as heard
whether there is a Holy Spirit."
3 And he said to them, "Into
what then were you baptized?"
So they said, [a]"Into John's baptism."
4 Then Paul said, [a]"John indeed baptized with a baptism of
repentance, saying to the people
that they should believe on Him
who would come after him, that
is, on Christ Jesus."
5 When they heard *this,* they
were baptized [a]in the name of
the Lord Jesus.
6 And when Paul had [a]laid
hands on them, the Holy Spirit
came upon them, and [b]they spoke
with tongues and prophesied.
7 Now the men were about
twelve in all.
8 [a]And he went into the synagogue and spoke boldly for three
months, reasoning and persuad-
ing [b]concerning the things of the
kingdom of God.
9 But [a]when some were hardened and did not believe, but
spoke evil [b]of the Way before
the multitude, he departed from
them and withdrew the disciples,
reasoning daily in the school of
Tȳ·ran′nus.
10 And [a]this continued for two
years, so that all who dwelt in
Asia heard the word of the Lord
Jesus, both Jews and Greeks.
11 Now [a]God worked unusual
miracles by the hands of Paul,
12 [a]so that even handkerchiefs
or aprons were brought from
his body to the sick, and the
diseases left them and the evil
spirits went out of them.
13 [a]Then some of the itinerant
Jewish exorcists [b]took it upon
themselves to call the name of
the Lord Jesus over those who
had evil spirits, saying, [1]"We [2]ex-
orcise you by the Jesus whom
Paul [c]preaches."
14 Also there were seven sons
of Scē′va, a Jewish chief priest,
who did so.
15 And the evil spirit answered
and said, "Jesus I know, and
Paul I know; but who are you?"
16 Then the man in whom the
evil spirit was leaped on them,
[1]overpowered them, and prevailed against [2]them, so that they
fled out of that house naked and
wounded.
17 This became known both to
all Jews and Greeks dwelling in
Eph′e·sus; and [a]fear fell on them
all, and the name of the Lord
Jesus was magnified.
18 And many who had believed
came [a]confessing and telling
their deeds.

18:27 [a]1 Cor. 3:6
28 [a]Acts 9:22; 17:3; 18:5

CHAPTER 19

1 [a]1 Cor. 1:12; 3:5, 6 [b]Acts 18:23
2 [a]1 Sam. 3:7
3 [a]Acts 18:25
4 [a]Matt. 3:11
5 [a]Acts 8:12, 16; 10:48
6 [a]Acts 6:6; 8:17 [b]Acts 2:4; 10:46
8 [a]Acts 17:2; 18:4 [b]Acts 1:3; 28:23
9 [a]2 Tim. 1:15 [b]Acts 9:2; 19:23; 22:4; 24:14
10 [a]Acts 19:8; 20:31
11 [a]Mark 16:20
12 [a]Acts 5:15
13 [a]Matt. 12:27 [b]Mark 9:38 [c]1 Cor. 1:23; 2:2 [1]NU *I* [2]*adjure,* solemnly command
16 [1]M *and they overpowered them* [2]NU *both of them*
17 [a]Luke 1:65; 7:16
18 [a]Matt. 3:6

19 Also, many of those who
had practiced magic brought
their books together and burned
them in the sight of all. And
they counted up the value of
them, and *it* totaled fifty thousand *pieces* of silver.
20 [a]So the word of the Lord
grew mightily and prevailed.
21 [a]When these things were accomplished, Paul [b]purposed in
the Spirit, when he had passed
through [c]Mac·e·dō′ni·a and
A·chā′i·a, to go to Jerusalem,
saying, "After I have been there,
[d]I must also see Rome."
22 So he sent into Mac·e·dō′ni·a
two of those who ministered to
him, [a]Timothy and [b]Ē·ras′tus, but
he himself stayed in Asia for a
time.
23 And [a]about that time there
arose a great commotion about
[b]the Way.
24 For a certain man named
De·mē′tri·us, a silversmith, who
made silver shrines of [1]Diana,
brought [a]no small profit to the
craftsmen.
25 He called them together with
the workers of similar occupation, and said: "Men, you know
that we have our prosperity by
this trade.
26 "Moreover you see and hear
that not only at Eph′e·sus, but
throughout almost all Asia, this
Paul has persuaded and turned
away many people, saying that
[a]they are not gods which are
made with hands.
27 "So not only is this trade of
ours in danger of falling into
disrepute, but also the temple of
the great goddess Diana may be
despised and [1]her magnificence
destroyed, whom all Asia and
the world worship."
28 Now when they heard *this,*
they were full of wrath and cried
out, saying, "Great *is* Diana of
the E·phē′si·ans!"
29 So the whole city was filled
with confusion, and rushed
into the theater with one accord, having seized [a]Gā′i·us and
[b]Ar·is·tar′chus, Mac·e·dō′ni·ans,
Paul's travel companions.
30 And when Paul wanted to
go in to the people, the disciples
would not allow him.
31 Then some of the [1]officials of
Asia, who were his friends, sent
to him pleading that he would
not venture into the theater.
32 Some therefore cried one
thing and some another, for the
assembly was confused, and
most of them did not know why
they had come together.
33 And they drew Alexan-
der out of the multitude, the
Jews putting him forward. And
[a]Alexander [b]motioned with his
hand, and wanted to make his
defense to the people.
34 But when they found out that
he was a Jew, all with one voice
cried out for about two hours,
"Great *is* Diana of the E·phē′-
si·ans!"
35 And when the city clerk had
quieted the crowd, he said: "Men
of Eph′e·sus, what man is there
who does not know that the
city of the E·phē′si·ans is temple
guardian of the great goddess
[1]Diana, and of the *image* which
fell down from [2]Zeūs?
36 "Therefore, since these things
cannot be denied, you ought to
be quiet and do nothing rashly.
37 "For you have brought these
men here who are neither robbers of temples nor blasphemers of [1]your goddess.

20 [a]Acts 6:7; 12:24
21 [a]Rom. 15:25 [b]Acts 20:22 [c]Acts 20:1 [d]Rom. 1:13; 15:22–29
22 [a]1 Tim. 1:2 [b]Rom. 16:23
23 [a]2 Cor. 1:8 [b]Acts 9:2
24 [a]Acts 16:16, 19 [1]Gr. *Artemis*
26 [a]Is. 44:10–20
27 [1]NU *she be deposed from her magnificence*
29 [a]Rom. 16:23 [b]Col. 4:10
31 [1]*Asiarchs, rulers of Asia,* the province
33 [a]2 Tim. 4:14 [b]Acts 12:17
35 [1]Gr. *Artemis* [2]*heaven*
37 [1]NU *our*

38 "Therefore, if De·mē′tri·us and his fellow craftsmen have a [1]case against anyone, the courts are open and there are proconsuls. Let them bring charges against one another.
39 "But if you have any other inquiry to make, it shall be determined in the lawful assembly.
40 "For we are in danger of being [1]called in question for today's uproar, there being no reason which we may give to account for this disorderly gathering."
41 And when he had said these things, he dismissed the assembly.

20 After the uproar had ceased, Paul called the disciples to *himself*, embraced *them*, and [a]departed to go to Mac·e·dō′ni·a.
2 Now when he had gone over that region and encouraged them with many words, he came to [a]Greece
3 and stayed three months. And [a]when the Jews plotted against him as he was about to sail to Syria, he decided to return through Mac·e·dō′ni·a.
4 And Sop′a·ter of Be·rē′a accompanied him to Asia—also [a]Ar·is·tar′chus and Secundus of the Thes·sa·lō′ni·ans, and [b]Gā′i·us of Der′bē, and [c]Timothy, and [d]Tych′i·cus and [e]Troph′i·mus of Asia.
5 These men, going ahead, waited for us at [a]Trō′as.
6 But we sailed away from Phil·ip′pī after [a]the Days of Unleavened Bread, and in five days joined them [b]at Trō′as, where we stayed seven days.
7 Now on [a]the first *day* of the week, when the disciples came together [b]to break bread, Paul, ready to depart the next day, spoke to them and continued his message until midnight.
8 There were many lamps [a]in the upper room where [1]they were gathered together.
9 And in a window sat a certain young man named Eū′ty·chus, who was sinking into a deep sleep. He was overcome by sleep; and as Paul continued speaking, he fell down from the third story and was taken up dead.
10 But Paul went down, [a]fell on him, and embracing *him* said, [b]"Do not trouble yourselves, for his life is in him."
11 Now when he had come up, had broken bread and eaten, and talked a long while, even till daybreak, he departed.
12 And they brought the young man in alive, and they were not a little comforted.
13 Then we went ahead to the ship and sailed to As′sos, there intending to take Paul on board; for so he had [1]given orders, intending himself to go on foot.
14 And when he met us at As′sos, we took him on board and came to Mit·y·lē′nē.
15 We sailed from there, and the next *day* came opposite Chī′os. The following *day* we arrived at Sā′mos and stayed at Trō·gyl′li·um. The next *day* we came to Mī·lē′tus.
16 For Paul had decided to sail past Eph′e·sus, so that he would not have to spend time in Asia; for [a]he was hurrying [b]to be at Jerusalem, if possible, on [c]the Day of Pentecost.
17 From Mī·lē′tus he sent to

38 [1]Lit. *matter*
40 [1]Or *charged with rebellion concerning today*

CHAPTER 20

1 [a]1 Tim. 1:3
2 [a]Acts 17:15; 18:1
3 [a]2 Cor. 11:26
4 [a]Col. 4:10 [b]Acts 19:29 [c]Acts 16:1 [d]Eph. 6:21 [e]2 Tim. 4:20
5 [a]2 Tim. 4:13
6 [a]Ex. 12:14, 15 [b]2 Tim. 4:13
7 [a]1 Cor. 16:2 [b]Acts 2:42, 46; 20:11
8 [a]Acts 1:13 [1]NU, M *we*
10 [a]1 Kin. 17:21 [b]Matt. 9:23, 24
13 [1]*arranged it*
16 [a]Acts 18:21; 19:21; 21:4 [b]Acts 24:17 [c]Acts 2:1

Eph'e·sus and called for the elders of the church.
18 And when they had come to him, he said to them: "You know, [a]from the first day that I came to Asia, in what manner I always lived among you,
19 "serving the Lord with all humility, with many tears and trials which happened to me [a]by the plotting of the Jews;
20 "how [a]I kept back nothing that was helpful, but proclaimed it to you, and taught you publicly and from house to house,
21 [a]"testifying to Jews, and also to Greeks, [b]repentance toward God and faith toward our Lord Jesus Christ.
22 "And see, now [a]I go bound in the spirit to Jerusalem, not knowing the things that will happen to me there,
23 "except that [a]the Holy Spirit testifies in every city, saying that chains and tribulations await me.
24 [1]"But [a]none of these things move me; nor do I count my life dear to myself, [b]so that I may finish my [2]race with joy, [c]and the ministry [d]which I received from the Lord Jesus, to testify to the gospel of the grace of God.
25 "And indeed, now I know that you all, among whom I have gone preaching the kingdom of God, will see my face no more.
26 "Therefore I testify to you this day that I *am* [a]innocent[1] of the blood of all *men*.
27 "For I have not [1]shunned to declare to you [a]the whole counsel of God.
28 [a]"Therefore take heed to yourselves and to all the flock, among which the Holy Spirit [b]has made you overseers, to shepherd the church [1]of God [c]which He purchased [d]with His own blood.
29 "For I know this, that after my departure [a]savage wolves will come in among you, not sparing the flock.
30 "Also [a]from among yourselves men will rise up, speaking [1]perverse things, to draw away the disciples after themselves.
31 "Therefore watch, and remember that [a]for three years I did not cease to warn everyone night and day with tears.
32 "So now, brethren, I commend you to God and [a]to the word of His grace, which is able [b]to build you up and give you [c]an inheritance among all those who are sanctified.
33 "I have coveted no one's silver or gold or apparel.
34 [1]"Yes, you yourselves know [a]that these hands have provided for my necessities, and for those who were with me.
35 "I have shown you in every way, [a]by laboring like this, that you must support the weak. And remember the words of the Lord Jesus, that He said, 'It is more blessed to give than to receive.' "
36 And when he had said these things, he knelt down and prayed with them all.
37 Then they all [a]wept [1]freely, and [b]fell on Paul's neck and kissed him,
38 sorrowing most of all for the words which he spoke, that they would see his face no more. And they accompanied him to the ship.

21 Now it came to pass, that when we had departed from them and set sail, running a

18 [a]Acts 18:19; 19:1, 10; 20:4, 16
19 [a]Acts 20:3
20 [a]Acts 20:27
21 [a]Acts 18:5; 19:10 [b]Mark 1:15
22 [a]Acts 19:21
23 [a]Acts 21:4, 11
24 [a]Acts 21:13 [b]2 Tim. 4:7 [c]Acts 1:17 [d]Gal. 1:1 [1]NU *But I do not count my life of any value or dear to myself* [2]*course*
26 [a]Acts 18:6 [1]Lit. *clean*
27 [a]Luke 7:30 [1]*avoided declaring*
28 [a]1 Pet. 5:2 [b]1 Cor. 12:28 [c]Eph. 1:7, 14 [d]Heb. 9:14 [1]M *of the Lord and God*
29 [a]Matt. 7:15
30 [a]1 Tim. 1:20 [1]*misleading*
31 [a]Acts 19:8, 10; 24:17
32 [a]Heb. 13:9 [b]Acts 9:31 [c][Heb. 9:15]
34 [a]Acts 18:3 [1]NU, M omit *Yes*
35 [a]Rom. 15:1
37 [a]Acts 21:13 [b]Gen. 45:14 [1]Lit. *much*

straight course we came to Cōs,
the following *day* to Rhōdes,
and from there to Pat′a·ra.
2 And finding a ship sailing
over to Phoe·ni′ci·a, we went
aboard and set sail.
3 When we had sighted Cy-
prus, we passed it on the left,
sailed to Syria, and landed at
Tȳre; for there the ship was to
unload her cargo.
4 And finding [1]disciples, we
stayed there seven days. [a]They
told Paul through the Spirit not
to go up to Jerusalem.
5 When we had come to the
end of those days, we departed
and went on our way; and they
all accompanied us, with wives
and children, till *we were* out of
the city. And [a]we knelt down on
the shore and prayed.
6 When we had taken our leave
of one another, we boarded the
ship, and they returned [a]home.
7 And when we had finished
our voyage from Tȳre, we came
to Ptol·e·mā′is, greeted the brethren, and stayed with them one
day.
8 On the next *day* we [1]who
were Paul's companions departed and came to [a]Caes·a·rē′a,
and entered the house of Philip
[b]the evangelist, [c]who was *one* of
the seven, and stayed with him.
9 Now this man had four virgin daughters [a]who prophesied.
10 And as we stayed many days,
a certain prophet named [a]Ag′-
a·bus came down from Judea.
11 When he had come to us, he
took Paul's belt, bound his *own*
hands and feet, and said, "Thus
says the Holy Spirit, [a]'So shall
the Jews at Jerusalem bind the
man who owns this belt, and
deliver *him* into the hands of the
Gentiles.' "
12 Now when we heard these
things, both we and those from
that place pleaded with him not
to go up to Jerusalem.
13 Then Paul answered, [a]"What
do you mean by weeping and
breaking my heart? For I am
ready not only to be bound, but
also to die at Jerusalem for the
name of the Lord Jesus."
14 So when he would not be
persuaded, we ceased, saying,
[a]"The will of the Lord be done."
15 And after those days we
[1]packed and went up to Jerusalem.
16 Also some of the disciples
from Caes·a·rē′a went with us
and brought with them a certain
Mnā′son of Cyprus, an early
disciple, with whom we were to
lodge.
17 [a]And when we had come
to Jerusalem, the brethren received us gladly.
18 On the following *day* Paul
went in with us to [a]James, and
all the elders were present.
19 When he had greeted them,
[a]he told in detail those things
which God had done among the
Gentiles [b]through his ministry.
20 And when they heard *it*, they
glorified the Lord. And they said
to him, "You see, brother, how
many myriads of Jews there are
who have believed, and they are
all [a]zealous for the law;
21 "but they have been informed
about you that you teach all the
Jews who are among the Gentiles to forsake Moses, saying
that they ought not to circumcise *their* children nor to walk
according to the customs.
22 [1]"What then? The assembly

CHAPTER 21

4 [a][Acts 20:23; 21:12] [1]NU *the disciples*

5 [a]Acts 9:40; 20:36

6 [a]John 1:11

8 [a]Acts 8:40; 21:16 [b]Eph. 4:11 [c]Acts 6:5 [1]NU omits *who were Paul's companions*

9 [a]Joel 2:28

10 [a]Acts 11:28

11 [a]Acts 20:23; 21:33; 22:25

13 [a]Acts 20:24, 37

14 [a]Luke 11:2; 22:42

15 [1]*made preparations*

17 [a]Acts 15:4

18 [a]Gal. 1:19; 2:9

19 [a]Rom. 15:18, 19 [b]Acts 1:17; 20:24

20 [a]Acts 15:1; 22:3

22 [1]NU *What then is to be done? They will certainly hear*

must certainly meet, for they
will hear that you have come.
23 "Therefore do what we tell
you: We have four men who
have taken a vow.
24 "Take them and be purified
with them, and pay their ex-
penses so that they may [a]shave
their heads, and that all may
know that those things of which
they were informed concerning
you are nothing, but *that* you
yourself also walk orderly and
keep the law.
25 "But concerning the Gentiles
who believe, we have written
and decided [1]that they should
observe no such thing, except[a]
that they should keep themselves from *things* offered to
idols, from blood, from things
strangled, and from [2]sexual immorality."
26 Then Paul took the men, and
the next day, having been purified with them, [a]entered the
temple [b]to announce the [1]expira-
tion of the days of purification,
at which time an offering should
be made for each one of them.
27 Now when the seven days
were almost ended, [a]the Jews
from Asia, seeing him in the
temple, stirred up the whole
crowd and [b]laid hands on him,
28 crying out, "Men of Israel,
help! This is the man [a]who
teaches all *men* everywhere
against the people, the law, and
this place; and furthermore he
also brought Greeks into the
temple and has defiled this holy
place."
29 (For they had [1]previously
seen [a]Troph′i·mus the E·phē′-
si·an with him in the city, whom
they supposed that Paul had
brought into the temple.)
30 And [a]all the city was disturbed; and the people ran together, seized Paul, and dragged
him out of the temple; and immediately the doors were shut.
31 Now as they were [a]seeking
to kill him, news came to the
commander of the [1]garrison that
all Jerusalem was in an uproar.
32 [a]He immediately took soldiers and centurions, and ran
down to them. And when they
saw the commander and the soldiers, they stopped beating Paul.
33 Then the [a]commander came
near and took him, and [b]com-
manded *him* to be bound with
two chains; and he asked who
he was and what he had done.
34 And some among the multitude cried one thing and some
another. So when he could not
ascertain the truth because of
the tumult, he commanded him
to be taken into the barracks.
35 When he reached the stairs,
he had to be carried by the soldiers because of the violence of
the mob.
36 For the multitude of the people followed after, crying out,
[a]"Away with him!"
37 Then as Paul was about to
be led into the barracks, he said
to the commander, "May I speak
to you?" He replied, "Can you
speak Greek?
38 [a]"Are you not the Egyptian
who some time ago stirred up a
rebellion and led the four thousand assassins out into the wilderness?"
39 But Paul said, [a]"I am a Jew
from Tar′sus, in Ci·li′ci·a, a citizen of no [1]mean city; and I implore you, permit me to speak to
the people."
40 So when he had given him

24 [a]Acts 18:18
25 [a]Acts 15:19, 20, 29 [1]NU omits *that they should observe no such thing, except* [2]*fornication*
26 [a]Acts 21:24; 24:18 [b]Num. 6:13 [1]*completion*
27 [a]Acts 20:19; 24:18 [b]Acts 26:21
28 [a]Acts 6:13; 24:6
29 [a]Acts 20:4 [1]M omits *previously*
30 [a]Acts 16:19; 26:21
31 [a]2 Cor. 11:23 [1]*cohort*
32 [a]Acts 23:27; 24:7
33 [a]Acts 24:7 [b]Acts 20:23; 21:11
36 [a]John 19:15
38 [a]Acts 5:36
39 [a]Acts 9:11; 22:3 [1]*insignificant*

permission, Paul stood on the
stairs and [a]motioned with his
hand to the people. And when
there was a great silence, he
spoke to *them* in the [b]Hebrew
language, saying,

22 "Brethren[a] and fathers,
hear my defense before
you now."
2 And when they heard that he
spoke to them in the [a]Hebrew
language, they kept all the more
silent. Then he said:
3 [a]"I am indeed a Jew, born in
Tar'sus of Ci·li'ci·a, but brought
up in this city [b]at the feet of
[c]Ga·mā'li·el, taught [d]according
to the strictness of our fathers'
law, and [e]was zealous toward
God [f]as you all are today.
4 [a]"I persecuted this Way to
the death, binding and delivering into prisons both men and
women,
5 "as also the high priest bears
me witness, and [a]all the council
of the elders, [b]from whom I also
received letters to the brethren,
and went to Damascus [c]to bring
in chains even those who were
there to Jerusalem to be punished.
6 "Now [a]it happened, as I journeyed and came near Damascus
at about noon, suddenly a great
light from heaven shone around
me.
7 "And I fell to the ground
and heard a voice saying to me,
'Saul, Saul, why are you persecuting Me?'
8 "So I answered, 'Who are
You, Lord?' And He said to me,
'I am Jesus of Nazareth, whom
you are persecuting.'
9 "And [a]those who were with
me indeed saw the light [1]and
were afraid, but they did not
hear the voice of Him who spoke
to me.
10 "So I said, 'What shall I do,
Lord?' And the Lord said to me,
'Arise and go into Damascus,
and there you will be told all
things which are appointed for
you to do.'
11 "And since I could not see for
the glory of that light, being led
by the hand of those who were
with me, I came into Damascus.
12 "Then [a]a certain An·a·nī'as,
a devout man according to the
law, [b]having a good testimony
with all the [c]Jews who dwelt
there,
13 "came to me; and he stood
and said to me, 'Brother Saul,
receive your sight.' And at that
same hour I looked up at him.
14 "Then he said, [a]'The God of
our fathers [b]has chosen you that
you should [c]know His will, and
[d]see the Just One, [e]and hear the
voice of His mouth.
15 [a]'For you will be His witness
to all men of [b]what you have
seen and heard.
16 'And now why are you waiting? Arise and be baptized, [a]and
wash away your sins, [b]calling on
the name of the Lord.'
17 "Now [a]it happened, when I
returned to Jerusalem and was
praying in the temple, that I was
in a trance
18 "and [a]saw Him saying to me,
[b]'Make haste and get out of Jerusalem quickly, for they will
not receive your testimony concerning Me.'
19 "So I said, 'Lord, [a]they know
that in every synagogue I imprisoned and [b]beat those who
believe on You.
20 [a]'And when the blood of Your
martyr Stephen was shed, I also

40 [a]Acts 12:17 [b]Acts 22:2

CHAPTER 22

1 [a]Acts 7:2

2 [a]Acts 21:40

3 [a]2 Cor. 11:22 [b]Deut. 33:3 [c]Acts 5:34 [d]Acts 23:6; 26:5 [e]Gal. 1:14 [f][Rom. 10:2]

4 [a]1 Tim. 1:13

5 [a]Acts 23:14; 24:1; 25:15 [b]Luke 22:66 [c]Acts 9:2

6 [a]Acts 9:3; 26:12, 13

9 [a]Acts 9:7 [1]NU omits *and were afraid*

12 [a]Acts 9:17 [b]Acts 10:22 [c]1 Tim. 3:7

14 [a]Acts 3:13; 5:30 [b]Acts 9:15; 26:16 [c]Acts 3:14; 7:52 [d]1 Cor. 9:1; 15:8 [e]Gal. 1:12

15 [a]Acts 23:11 [b]Acts 4:20; 26:16

16 [a]Heb. 10:22 [b]Rom. 10:13

17 [a]Acts 9:26; 26:20

18 [a]Acts 22:14 [b]Matt. 10:14

19 [a]Acts 8:3; 22:4 [b]Matt. 10:17

20 [a]Acts 7:54—8:1

was standing by [b]consenting
[1]to his death, and guarding the
clothes of those who were killing him.'
21 "Then He said to me, 'Depart, [a]for I will send you far from
here to the Gentiles.' "
22 And they listened to him
until this word, and *then* they
raised their voices and said,
[a]"Away with such a *fellow* from
the earth, for [b]he is not fit to
live!"
23 Then, as they cried out and
[1]tore off *their* clothes and threw
dust into the air,
24 the commander ordered him
to be brought into the barracks,
and said that he should be examined under scourging, so that he
might know why they shouted
so against him.
25 And as they bound him with
thongs, Paul said to the centurion who stood by, [a]"Is it lawful
for you to scourge a man who is
a Roman, and uncondemned?"
26 When the centurion heard
that, he went and told the commander, saying, "Take care what
you do, for this man is a Roman."
27 Then the commander came
and said to him, "Tell me, are
you a Roman?" He said, "Yes."
28 The commander answered,
"With a large sum I obtained
this citizenship." And Paul said,
"But I was born *a citizen.*"
29 Then immediately those who
were about to examine him withdrew from him; and the commander was also afraid after he
found out that he was a Roman,
and because he had bound him.
30 The next day, because he
wanted to know for certain why
he was accused by the Jews, he
released him from *his* bonds,
and commanded the chief
priests and all their council to
appear, and brought Paul down
and set him before them.

23

Then Paul, looking ear-
nestly at the council, said,
"Men *and* brethren, [a]I have lived
in all good conscience before
God until this day."
2 And the high priest An·a·nī′as
commanded those who stood
by him [a]to strike him on the
mouth.
3 Then Paul said to him, "God
will strike you, *you* whitewashed
wall! For you sit to judge me according to the law, and [a]do you
command me to be struck contrary to the law?"
4 And those who stood by
said, "Do you revile God's high
priest?"
5 Then Paul said, [a]"I did not
know, brethren, that he was the
high priest; for it is written,
[b]*'You shall not speak evil of a
ruler of your people.'* "
6 But when Paul perceived that
one part were Sad′dū·cees and
the other Phar′i·sees, he cried
out in the council, "Men *and*
brethren, [a]I am a Phar′i·see, the
son of a Phar′i·see; [b]concerning
the hope and resurrection of the
dead I am being judged!"
7 And when he had said this,
a dissension arose between the
Phar′i·sees and the Sad′dū·cees;
and the assembly was divided.
8 [a]For Sad′dū·cees say that
there is no resurrection—and
no angel or spirit; but the Phar′-
i·sees confess both.
9 Then there arose a loud outcry. And the scribes of the Phar′-
i·sees' party arose and protested,
saying, [a]"We find no evil in this
man; [1]but [b]if a spirit or an angel

20 [b]Luke 11:48 [1]NU omits *to his death*
21 [a]Acts 9:15
22 [a]Acts 21:36 [b]Acts 25:24
23 [1]Lit. *threw*
25 [a]Acts 16:37

CHAPTER 23

1 [a]2 Tim. 1:3
2 [a]John 18:22
3 [a]Deut. 25:1, 2
5 [a]Lev. 5:17, 18 [b]Ex. 22:28
6 [a]Phil. 3:5 [b]Acts 24:15, 21; 26:6; 28:20
8 [a]Matt. 22:23
9 [a]Acts 25:25; 26:31 [b]Acts 22:6, 7, 17, 18 [1]NU *what if a spirit or an angel has spoken to him?* omitting the last clause

has spoken to him, [c]let us not
fight against God."
10 Now when there arose a
great dissension, the commander, fearing lest Paul might
be pulled to pieces by them,
commanded the soldiers to go
down and take him by force
from among them, and bring
him into the barracks.
11 But [a]the following night the
Lord stood by him and said,
[1]"Be of good cheer, Paul; for
as you have testified for Me in
[b]Jerusalem, so you must also
bear witness at [c]Rome."
12 And when it was day, [a]some
of the Jews banded together
and bound themselves under an
oath, saying that they would neither eat nor drink till they had
[b]killed Paul.
13 Now there were more than
forty who had formed this conspiracy.
14 They came to the chief priests
and [a]elders, and said, "We have
bound ourselves under a great
oath that we will eat nothing
until we have killed Paul.
15 "Now you, therefore, together with the council, suggest
to the commander that he be
brought down to you [1]tomorrow,
as though you were going to
make further inquiries concerning him; but we are ready to kill
him before he comes near."
16 So when Paul's sister's son
heard of their ambush, he went
and entered the barracks and
told Paul.
17 Then Paul called one of the
centurions to *him* and said, "Take
this young man to the commander, for he has something to
tell him."
18 So he took him and brought
him to the commander and said,
"Paul the prisoner called me to
him and asked *me* to bring this
young man to you. He has something to say to you."
19 Then the commander took
him by the hand, went aside,
and asked privately, "What is it
that you have to tell me?"
20 And he said, [a]"The Jews have
agreed to ask that you bring
Paul down to the council tomorrow, as though they were going
to inquire more fully about him.
21 "But do not yield to them,
for more than forty of them lie
in wait for him, men who have
bound themselves by an oath
that they will neither eat nor
drink till they have killed him;
and now they are ready, waiting
for the promise from you."
22 So the commander let the
young man depart, and commanded *him*, "Tell no one that
you have revealed these things
to me."
23 And he called for two centurions, saying, "Prepare two hundred soldiers, seventy horsemen,
and two hundred spearmen to
go to [a]Caes·a·rē′a at the third
hour of the night;
24 "and provide mounts to set
Paul on, and bring *him* safely to
Felix the governor."
25 He wrote a letter in the following manner:

26 Clau′di·us Lys′i·as,

To the most excellent
governor Felix:

Greetings.

27 [a]This man was seized by the
Jews and was about to be

9 [c]Acts 5:39
11 [a]Acts 18:9; 27:23, 24 [b]Acts 21:18, 19; 22:1–21 [c]Acts 28:16, 17, 23 [1]*Take courage*
12 [a]Acts 23:21, 30; 25:3 [b]Acts 9:23, 24; 25:3; 26:21; 27:42
14 [a]Acts 4:5, 23; 6:12; 22:5; 24:1; 25:15
15 [1]NU omits *tomorrow*
20 [a]Acts 23:12
23 [a]Acts 8:40; 23:33
27 [a]Acts 21:30, 33; 24:7

killed by them. Coming with
the troops I rescued him,
having learned that he was
a Roman.
28 [a]And when I wanted to
know the reason they
accused him, I brought him
before their council.
29 I found out that he was
accused [a]concerning
questions of their law, [b]but
had nothing charged against
him deserving of death or
chains.
30 And [a]when it was told
me that [1]the Jews lay in
wait for the man, I sent
him immediately to you,
and [b]also commanded his
accusers to state before you
the charges against him.

Farewell.

31 Then the soldiers, as they
were commanded, took Paul and
brought *him* by night to An·tip′-
a·tris.
32 The next day they left the
horsemen to go on with him,
and returned to the barracks.
33 When they came to [a]Caes·a-
rē′a and had delivered the [b]letter
to the governor, they also presented Paul to him.
34 And when the governor had
read *it,* he asked what province he was from. And when he
understood that *he was* from
[a]Ci·li′ci·a,
35 he said, [a]"I will hear you
when your accusers also have
come." And he commanded him
to be kept in [b]Her′od's [1]Prae·tō′-
ri·um.

24

Now after [a]five days
[b]An·a·nī′as the high priest
came down with the elders and
a certain orator *named* Ter·tul′-
lus. These gave evidence to the
governor against Paul.
2 And when he was called
upon, Ter·tul′lus began his accusation, saying: "Seeing that
through you we enjoy great
peace, and [1]prosperity is being
brought to this nation by your
foresight,
3 "we accept *it* always and in
all places, most noble Felix, with
all thankfulness.
4 "Nevertheless, not to be tedious to you any further, I beg
you to hear, by your [1]courtesy, a
few words from us.
5 [a]"For we have found this man
a plague, a creator of dissension
among all the Jews throughout
the world, and a ringleader of
the sect of the Naz′a·rēnes.
6 [a]"He even tried to profane
the temple, and we seized him,
[1]and wanted [b]to judge him according to our law.
7 [a]"But the commander Lys′i·as
came by and with great violence
took *him* out of our hands,
8 [a]"commanding his accusers
to come to you. By examining
him yourself you may ascertain
all these things of which we accuse him."
9 And the Jews also [1]assented,
maintaining that these things
were so.
10 Then Paul, after the governor had nodded to him to speak,
answered: "Inasmuch as I know
that you have been for many
years a judge of this nation, I do
the more cheerfully answer for
myself,
11 "because you may ascertain
that it is no more than twelve
days since I went up to Jerusalem [a]to worship.

---

28 [a]Acts 22:30
29 [a]Acts 18:15; 25:19 [b]Acts 25:25; 26:31
30 [a]Acts 23:20 [b]Acts 24:8; 25:6 [1]NU *there would be a plot against the man*
33 [a]Acts 8:40 [b]Acts 23:26–30
34 [a]Acts 6:9; 21:39
35 [a]Acts 24:1, 10; 25:16 [b]Matt. 27:27 [1]Headquarters

CHAPTER 24

1 [a]Acts 21:27 [b]Acts 23:2, 30, 35; 25:2
2 [1]Or *reforms are*
4 [1]*graciousness*
5 [a]1 Pet. 2:12, 15
6 [a]Acts 21:28 [b]John 18:31 [1]NU ends the sentence here and omits the rest of v. 6, all of v. 7, and the first clause of v. 8.
7 [a]Acts 21:33; 23:10
8 [a]Acts 23:30
9 [1]NU, M *joined the attack*
11 [a]Acts 21:15, 18, 26, 27; 24:17

12 [a]"And they neither found me in the temple disputing with anyone nor inciting the crowd, either in the synagogues or in the city.

13 "Nor can they prove the things of which they now accuse me.

14 "But this I confess to you, that according to [a]the Way which they call a sect, so I worship the [b]God of my fathers, believing all things which are written in [c]the Law and in the Prophets.

15 [a]"I have hope in God, which they themselves also accept, [b]that there will be a resurrection [1]of *the* dead, both of *the* just and *the* unjust.

16 [a]"This *being* so, I myself always strive to have a conscience without offense toward God and men.

17 "Now after many years [a]I came to bring alms and offerings to my nation,

18 [a]"in the midst of which some Jews from Asia found me [b]purified in the temple, neither with a mob nor with tumult.

19 [a]"They ought to have been here before you to object if they had anything against me.

20 "Or else let those who are *here* themselves say [1]if they found any wrongdoing in me while I stood before the council,

21 "unless *it is* for this one statement which I cried out, standing among them, [a]'Concerning the resurrection of the dead I am being judged by you this day.' "

22 But when Felix heard these things, having more accurate knowledge of *the* [a]Way, he adjourned the proceedings and said, "When [b]Lys'i·as the commander comes down, I will make a decision on your case."

23 So he commanded the centurion to keep Paul and to let *him* have liberty, and [a]told him not to forbid any of his friends to provide for or visit him.

24 And after some days, when Felix came with his wife Drū·sil'la, who was Jewish, he sent for Paul and heard him concerning the [a]faith in Christ.

25 Now as he reasoned about righteousness, self-control, and the judgment to come, Felix was afraid and answered, "Go away for now; when I have a convenient time I will call for you."

26 Meanwhile he also hoped that [a]money would be given him by Paul, [1]that he might release him. Therefore he sent for him more often and conversed with him.

27 But after two years Por'ci·us Fes'tus succeeded Felix; and Felix, [a]wanting to do the Jews a favor, left Paul bound.

25 Now when Fes'tus had come to the province, after three days he went up from [a]Caes·a·rē'a to Jerusalem.

2 [a]Then the [1]high priest and the chief men of the Jews informed him against Paul; and they petitioned him,

3 asking a favor against him, that he would summon him to Jerusalem—[a]while *they* lay in ambush along the road to kill him.

4 But Fes'tus answered that Paul should be kept at Caes·a·rē'a, and that he himself was going *there* shortly.

5 "Therefore," he said, "let those who have authority among you go down with *me* and accuse

12 [a]Acts 25:8; 28:17
14 [a]Acts 9:2; 24:22 [b]2 Tim. 1:3 [c]Acts 26:22; 28:23
15 [a]Acts 23:6; 26:6, 7; 28:20 [b][Dan. 12:2] [1]NU omits *of the dead*
16 [a]Acts 23:1
17 [a]Rom. 15:25–28
18 [a]Acts 21:27; 26:21 [b]Acts 21:26
19 [a][Acts 23:30; 25:16]
20 [1]NU, M *what wrongdoing they found*
21 [a][Acts 23:6; 24:15; 28:20]
22 [a]Acts 9:2; 18:26; 19:9, 23; 22:4 [b]Acts 23:26; 24:7
23 [a]Acts 23:16; 27:3; 28:16
24 [a][Rom. 10:9]
26 [a]Ex. 23:8 [1]NU omits *that he might release him*
27 [a]Acts 12:3; 23:35; 25:9, 14

CHAPTER 25

1 [a]Acts 8:40; 25:4, 6, 13
2 [a]Acts 24:1; 25:15 [1]NU *chief priests*
3 [a]Acts 23:12, 15

this man, to see [a]if there is any
fault in him."
6 And when he had remained
among them more than ten days,
he went down to Caes·a·rē'a.
And the next day, sitting on the
judgment seat, he commanded
Paul to be brought.
7 When he had come, the
Jews who had come down from
Jerusalem stood about [a]and
laid many serious complaints
against Paul, which they could
not prove,
8 while he answered for himself, [a]"Neither against the law of
the Jews, nor against the temple,
nor against Caesar have I offended in anything at all."
9 But Fes'tus, [a]wanting to do
the Jews a favor, answered Paul
and said, [b]"Are you willing to go
up to Jerusalem and there be
judged before me concerning
these things?"
10 So Paul said, "I stand at Caesar's judgment seat, where I
ought to be judged. To the Jews
I have done no wrong, as you
very well know.
11 [a]"For if I am an offender, or
have committed anything deserving of death, I do not object
to dying; but if there is nothing
in these things of which these
men accuse me, no one can deliver me to them. [b]I appeal to
Caesar."
12 Then Fes'tus, when he had
conferred with the council, answered, "You have appealed to
Caesar? To Caesar you shall
go!"
13 And after some days King
A·grip'pa and Ber·nī'cē came to
Caes·a·rē'a to greet Fes'tus.
14 When they had been there
many days, Fes'tus laid Paul's
case before the king, saying:
[a]"There is a certain man left a
prisoner by Felix,
15 [a]"about whom the chief
priests and the elders of the
Jews informed *me*, when I was
in Jerusalem, asking for a judgment against him.
16 [a]"To them I answered, 'It is
not the custom of the Romans to
deliver any man [1]to destruction
before the accused meets the accusers face to face, and has opportunity to answer for himself
concerning the charge against
him.'
17 "Therefore when they had
come together, [a]without any delay, the next day I sat on the
judgment seat and commanded
the man to be brought in.
18 "When the accusers stood
up, they brought no accusation
against him of such things as I
[1]supposed,
19 [a]"but had some questions
against him about their own
religion and about a certain Jesus, who had died, whom Paul
affirmed to be alive.
20 "And because I was uncertain of such questions, I asked
whether he was willing to go to
Jerusalem and there be judged
concerning these matters.
21 "But when Paul [a]appealed to
be reserved for the decision of
Au·gus'tus, I commanded him to
be kept till I could send him to
Caesar."
22 Then [a]A·grip'pa said to Fes'-
tus, "I also would like to hear
the man myself." "Tomorrow,"
he said, "you shall hear him."
23 So the next day, when
A·grip'pa and Ber·nī'cē had
come with great [1]pomp, and had
entered the auditorium with the

5 [a]Acts 18:14; 25:18
7 [a]Acts 24:5, 13
8 [a]Acts 6:13; 24:12; 28:17
9 [a]Acts 12:2; 24:27 [b]Acts 25:20
11 [a]Acts 18:14; 23:29; 25:25; 26:31 [b]Acts 26:32; 28:19
14 [a]Acts 24:27
15 [a]Acts 24:1; 25:2, 3
16 [a]Acts 25:4, 5 [1]NU omits *to destruction,* although it is implied
17 [a]Acts 25:6, 10
18 [1]*suspected*
19 [a]Acts 18:14, 15; 23:29
21 [a]Acts 25:11, 12
22 [a]Acts 9:15
23 [1]*pageantry*

commanders and the prominent
men of the city, at Fes′tus' command [a]Paul was brought in.
24 And Fes′tus said: "King
A·grip′pa and all the men who
are here present with us, you see
this man about whom [a]the whole
assembly of the Jews petitioned
me, both at Jerusalem and here,
crying out that he was [b]not fit to
live any longer.
25 "But when I found that [a]he
had committed nothing deserving of death, [b]and that he himself had appealed to Au·gus′tus,
I decided to send him.
26 "I have nothing certain to
write to my lord concerning him.
Therefore I have brought him
out before you, and especially
before you, King A·grip′pa, so
that after the examination has
taken place I may have something to write.
27 "For it seems to me unreasonable to send a prisoner and not
to specify the charges against
him."

26

Then A·grip′pa said to
Paul, "You are permitted
to speak for yourself." So Paul
stretched out his hand and answered for himself:
2 "I think myself [a]happy,
King A·grip′pa, because today I
shall answer [b]for myself before
you concerning all the things
of which I am [c]accused by the
Jews,
3 "especially because you are
expert in all customs and questions which have to do with the
Jews. Therefore I beg you to
hear me patiently.
4 "My manner of life from my
youth, which was spent from
the beginning among my own
nation at Jerusalem, all the Jews
know.
5 "They knew me from the
first, if they were willing to testify, that according to [a]the strictest sect of our religion I lived a
Phar′i·see.
6 [a]"And now I stand and am
judged for the hope of [b]the promise made by God to our fathers.
7 "To this *promise* [a]our twelve
tribes, earnestly serving *God*
[b]night and day, [c]hope to attain. For this hope's sake, King
A·grip′pa, I am accused by the
Jews.
8 "Why should it be thought in-
credible by you that God raises
the dead?
9 [a]"Indeed, I myself thought I
must do many things [1]contrary
to the name of [b]Jesus of Nazareth.
10 [a]"This I also did in Jerusalem, and many of the saints I
shut up in prison, having received authority [b]from the chief
priests; and when they were put
to death, I cast my vote against
them.
11 [a]"And I punished them often in every synagogue and
compelled *them* to blaspheme;
and being exceedingly enraged
against them, I persecuted *them*
even to foreign cities.
12 [a]"While thus occupied, as I
journeyed to Damascus with authority and commission from
the chief priests,
13 "at midday, O king, along the
road I saw a light from heaven,
brighter than the sun, shining
around me and those who journeyed with me.
14 "And when we all had fallen
to the ground, I heard a voice
speaking to me and saying in

23 [a]Acts 9:15
24 [a]Acts 25:2, 3, 7 [b]Acts 21:36; 22:22
25 [a]Acts 23:9, 29; 26:31 [b]Acts 25:11, 12

CHAPTER 26

2 [a][1 Pet. 3:14; 4:14] [b][1 Pet. 3:15, 16] [c]Acts 21:28; 24:5, 6
5 [a]Phil. 3:5
6 [a]Acts 23:6 [b]Acts 13:32
7 [a]James 1:1 [b]1 Thess. 3:10 [c]Phil. 3:11
9 [a]1 Tim. 1:12, 13 [b]Acts 2:22; 10:38 [1]*against*
10 [a]Acts 8:1–3; 9:13 [b]Acts 9:14
11 [a]Acts 22:19
12 [a]Acts 9:3–8; 22:6–11; 26:12–18

the Hebrew language, 'Saul,
Saul, why are you persecuting
Me? *It is* hard for you to kick
against the goads.'
15 "So I said, 'Who are You,
Lord?' And He said, 'I am Jesus,
whom you are persecuting.
16 'But rise and stand on your
feet; for I have appeared to you
for this purpose, [a]to make you a
minister and a witness both of
the things which you have seen
and of the things which I will yet
reveal to you.
17 'I will [1]deliver you from the
Jewish people, as well as *from*
the Gentiles, [a]to whom I [2]now
send you,
18 [a]'to open their eyes, *in order*
[b]to turn *them* from darkness
to light, and *from* the power of
Satan to God, [c]that they may receive forgiveness of sins and [d]an
inheritance among those who
are [e]sanctified[1] by faith in Me.'
19 "Therefore, King A·grip'pa, I
was not disobedient to the heavenly vision,
20 "but [a]declared first to those
in Damascus and in Jerusalem,
and throughout all the region of
Judea, and *then* to the Gentiles,
that they should repent, turn to
God, and do [b]works befitting
repentance.
21 "For these reasons the Jews
seized me in the temple and
tried to kill *me*.
22 "Therefore, having obtained
help from God, to this day I
stand, witnessing both to small
and great, saying no other things
than those [a]which the prophets
and [b]Moses said would come—
23 [a]'that the Christ would suffer, [b]that He would be the first to
rise from the dead, and [c]would
proclaim light to the *Jewish* people and to the Gentiles."
24 Now as he thus made his
defense, Fes'tus said with a loud
voice, "Paul, [a]you are beside
yourself! Much learning is driving you mad!"
25 But he said, "I am not [1]mad,
most noble Fes'tus, but speak
the words of truth and reason.
26 "For the king, before whom I
also speak freely, [a]knows these
things; for I am convinced that
none of these things escapes his
attention, since this thing was
not done in a corner.
27 "King A·grip'pa, do you believe the prophets? I know that
you do believe."
28 Then A·grip'pa said to Paul,
"You almost persuade me to become a Christian."
29 And Paul said, [a]"I would to
God that not only you, but also
all who hear me today, might
become both almost and altogether such as I am, except for
these chains."
30 When he had said these
things, the king stood up, as well
as the governor and Ber·nī'cē
and those who sat with them;
31 and when they had gone
aside, they talked among themselves, saying, [a]"This man is doing nothing deserving of death
or chains."
32 Then A·grip'pa said to Fes'-
tus, "This man might have been
set [a]free [b]if he had not appealed
to Caesar."

27
And when [a]it was de-
cided that we should sail
to Italy, they delivered Paul and
some other prisoners to *one*
named Julius, a centurion of the
Au·gus'tan Regiment.

16 [a]Acts 22:15
17 [a]Acts 22:21 [1]*rescue* [2]NU, M omit *now*
18 [a]Is. 35:5; 42:7, 16 [b]1 Pet. 2:9 [c]Luke 1:77 [d]Col. 1:12 [e]Acts 20:32 [1]*set apart*
20 [a]Acts 9:19, 20, 22; 11:26 [b]Matt. 3:8
22 [a]Rom. 3:21 [b]John 5:46
23 [a]Luke 24:26 [b]1 Cor. 15:20, 23 [c]Luke 2:32
24 [a][1 Cor. 1:23; 2:13, 14; 4:10]
25 [1]*out of my mind*
26 [a]Acts 26:3
29 [a]1 Cor. 7:7
31 [a]Acts 23:9, 29; 25:25
32 [a]Acts 28:18 [b]Acts 25:11

CHAPTER 27
1 [a]Acts 25:12, 25

2 So, entering a ship of Ad·ra·myt′ti·um, we put to sea, meaning to sail along the coasts of Asia. [a]Ar·is·tar′chus, a Mac·e·dō′ni·an of Thes·sa·lo·nī′ca, was with us.

3 And the next *day* we landed at Sī′don. And Julius [a]treated Paul kindly and gave *him* liberty to go to his friends and receive care.

4 When we had put to sea from there, we sailed under *the shelter of* Cyprus, because the winds were contrary.

5 And when we had sailed over the sea which is off Ci·li′ci·a and Pam·phyl′i·a, we came to Mȳ′ra, *a city* of Ly′ci·a.

6 There the centurion found [a]an Alexandrian ship sailing to Italy, and he put us on board.

7 When we had sailed slowly many days, and arrived with difficulty off Cnī′dus, the wind not permitting us to proceed, we sailed under *the shelter of* [a]Crēte off Sal·mō′nē.

8 Passing it with difficulty, we came to a place called Fair Havens, near the city *of* La·sē′a.

9 Now when much time had been spent, and sailing was now dangerous [a]because [1]the Fast was already over, Paul advised them,

10 saying, "Men, I perceive that this voyage will end with disaster and much loss, not only of the cargo and ship, but also our lives."

11 Nevertheless the centurion was more persuaded by the helmsman and the owner of the ship than by the things spoken by Paul.

12 And because the harbor was not suitable to winter in, the majority advised to set sail from there also, if by any means they could reach Phoenix, a harbor of Crēte opening toward the southwest and northwest, *and* winter *there.*

13 When the south wind blew softly, supposing that they had obtained *their* desire, putting out to sea, they sailed close by Crēte.

14 But not long after, a tempestuous head wind arose, called [1]Eū·roc′ly·don.

15 So when the ship was caught, and could not head into the wind, we let *her* [1]drive.

16 And running under *the shelter of* an island called [1]Clau′da, we secured the skiff with difficulty.

17 When they had taken it on board, they used cables to undergird the ship; and fearing lest they should run aground on the [1]Syr′tis *Sands,* they struck sail and so were driven.

18 And because we were exceedingly tempest-tossed, the next *day* they lightened the ship.

19 On the third *day* [a]we threw the ship's tackle overboard with our own hands.

20 Now when neither sun nor stars appeared for many days, and no small tempest beat on *us,* all hope that we would be saved was finally given up.

21 But after long abstinence from food, then Paul stood in the midst of them and said, "Men, you should have listened to me, and not have sailed from Crēte and incurred this disaster and loss.

22 "And now I urge you to take [1]heart, for there will be no loss

2 [a]Acts 19:29
3 [a]Acts 24:23; 28:16
6 [a]Acts 28:11
7 [a]Titus 1:5, 12
9 [a]Lev. 16:29–31; 23:27–29 [1]The Day of Atonement, late September or early October
14 [1]A southeast wind that stirs up broad waves; NU *Euraquilon,* a northeaster
15 [1]*be driven*
16 [1]NU *Cauda*
17 [1]M *Syrtes*
19 [a]Jon. 1:5
22 [1]*courage*

of life among you, but only of the ship.

23 [a]"For there stood by me this night an angel of the God to whom I belong and [b]whom I serve,

24 "saying, 'Do not be afraid, Paul; you must be brought before Caesar; and indeed God has granted you all those who sail with you.'

25 "Therefore take heart, men, [a]for I believe God that it will be just as it was told me.

26 "However, [a]we must run aground on a certain island."

27 Now when the fourteenth night had come, as we were driven up and down in the Ā·dri·at′ic *Sea*, about midnight the sailors sensed that they were drawing near some land.

28 And they took soundings and found *it* to be twenty fathoms; and when they had gone a little farther, they took soundings again and found *it* to be fifteen fathoms.

29 Then, fearing lest we should run aground on the rocks, they dropped four anchors from the stern, and [1]prayed for day to come.

30 And as the sailors were seeking to escape from the ship, when they had let down the skiff into the sea, under pretense of putting out anchors from the prow,

31 Paul said to the centurion and the soldiers, "Unless these men stay in the ship, you cannot be saved."

32 Then the soldiers cut away the ropes of the skiff and let it fall off.

33 And as day was about to dawn, Paul implored *them* all to take food, saying, "Today is the fourteenth day you have waited and continued without food, and eaten nothing.

34 "Therefore I urge you to take nourishment, for this is for your survival, [a]since not a hair will fall from the head of any of you."

35 And when he had said these things, he took bread and [a]gave thanks to God in the presence of them all; and when he had broken *it* he began to eat.

36 Then they were all encouraged, and also took food themselves.

37 And in all we were two hundred and seventy-six [a]persons on the ship.

38 So when they had eaten enough, they lightened the ship and threw out the wheat into the sea.

39 When it was day, they did not recognize the land; but they observed a bay with a beach, onto which they planned to run the ship if possible.

40 And they [1]let go the anchors and left *them* in the sea, meanwhile loosing the rudder ropes; and they hoisted the mainsail to the wind and made for shore.

41 But striking [1]a place where two seas met, [a]they ran the ship aground; and the prow stuck fast and remained immovable, but the stern was being broken up by the violence of the waves.

42 And the soldiers' plan was to kill the prisoners, lest any of them should swim away and escape.

43 But the centurion, wanting to save Paul, kept them from *their* purpose, and commanded that those who could swim should

23 [a]Acts 18:9; 23:11 [b]Dan. 6:16
25 [a]Rom. 4:20, 21
26 [a]Acts 28:1
29 [1]Or *wished*
34 [a][Matt. 10:30]
35 [a][1 Tim. 4:3, 4]
37 [a]Acts 2:41; 7:14
40 [1]*cast off*
41 [a]2 Cor. 11:25 [1]A reef

jump *overboard* first and get to land,
44 and the rest, some on boards and some on *parts* of the ship. And so it was [a]that they all escaped safely to land.

28 Now when they had escaped, they then found out that [a]the island was called Malta.
2 And the [a]natives[1] showed us unusual kindness; for they kindled a fire and made us all welcome, because of the rain that was falling and because of the cold.
3 But when Paul had gathered a bundle of sticks and laid *them* on the fire, a viper came out because of the heat, and fastened on his hand.
4 So when the natives saw the creature hanging from his hand, they said to one another, "No doubt this man is a murderer, whom, though he has escaped the sea, yet justice does not allow to live."
5 But he shook off the creature into the fire and [a]suffered no harm.
6 However, they were expecting that he would swell up or suddenly fall down dead. But after they had looked for a long time and saw no harm come to him, they changed their minds and [a]said that he was a god.
7 In that region there was an estate of the [1]leading citizen of the island, whose name was Pub′li·us, who received us and entertained us courteously for three days.
8 And it happened that the father of Pub′li·us lay sick of a fever and dysentery. Paul went in to him and [a]prayed, and [b]he laid his hands on him and healed him.
9 So when this was done, the rest of those on the island who had diseases also came and were healed.
10 They also honored us in many [a]ways; and when we departed, they provided such things as were [b]necessary.
11 After three months we sailed in [a]an Alexandrian ship whose figurehead was the [1]Twin Brothers, which had wintered at the island.
12 And landing at Syracuse, we stayed three days.
13 From there we circled round and reached Rhē′gi·um. And after one day the south wind blew; and the next day we came to Pū·tē′o·lī,
14 where we found [a]brethren, and were invited to stay with them seven days. And so we went toward Rome.
15 And from there, when the brethren heard about us, they came to meet us as far as Ap′pi·ī Forum and Three Inns. When Paul saw them, he thanked God and took courage.
16 Now when we came to Rome, the centurion delivered the prisoners to the captain of the guard; but [a]Paul was permitted to dwell by himself with the soldier who guarded him.
17 And it came to pass after three days that Paul called the leaders of the Jews together. So when they had come together, he said to them: "Men *and* brethren, [a]though I have done nothing against our people or the customs of our fathers, yet [b]I was delivered as a prisoner from

44 [a]Acts 27:22, 31

CHAPTER 28

1 [a]Acts 27:26
2 [a]Col. 3:11 [1]Lit. *barbarians*
5 [a]Mark 16:18
6 [a]Acts 12:22; 14:11
7 [1]Magistrate
8 [a][James 5:14, 15] [b]Mark 5:23; 6:5; 7:32; 16:18
10 [a]Matt. 15:6 [b][Phil. 4:19]
11 [a]Acts 27:6 [1]Gr. *Dioskouroi,* Zeus's sons Castor and Pollux
14 [a]Rom. 1:8
16 [a]Acts 23:11; 24:25; 27:3
17 [a]Acts 23:29; 24:12, 13; 26:31 [b]Acts 21:33

Jerusalem into the hands of the
Romans,
18 "who, [a]when they had examined me, wanted to let *me* go,
because there was no cause for
putting me to death.
19 "But when the [1]Jews spoke
against *it,* [a]I was compelled to
appeal to Caesar, not that I had
anything of which to accuse my
nation.
20 "For this reason therefore I
have called for you, to see *you*
and speak with *you,* because
[a]for the hope of Israel I am
bound with [b]this chain."
21 Then they said to him, "We
neither received letters from
Judea concerning you, nor have
any of the brethren who came
reported or spoken any evil of
you.
22 "But we desire to hear from
you what you think; for concerning this sect, we know that [a]it is
spoken against everywhere."
23 So when they had appointed
him a day, many came to him
at *his* lodging, [a]to whom he explained and solemnly testified
of the kingdom of God, per-
suading them concerning Jesus
[b]from both the Law of Moses
and the Prophets, from morning
till evening.
24 And [a]some were persuaded
by the things which were spoken, and some disbelieved.
25 So when they did not agree
among themselves, they departed after Paul had said one
word: "The Holy Spirit spoke
rightly through Ī·sāi′ah the
prophet to [1]our fathers,
26 "saying, ★

[a]*'Go to this people and say:*
"Hearing you will hear, and
shall not understand;
And seeing you will see, and
not perceive;
27 *For the hearts of this people*
have grown dull.
Their ears are hard of
hearing,
And their eyes they have
closed,
Lest they should see with
their eyes and hear with
their ears,
Lest they should understand
with their hearts and
turn,
So that I should heal them."'

28 "Therefore let it be known ★
to you that the salvation of God
has been sent [a]to the Gentiles,
and they will hear it!"
29 [1]And when he had said these
words, the Jews departed and
had a great dispute among themselves.
30 Then Paul dwelt two whole
years in his own rented house,
and received all who came to
him,
31 [a]preaching the kingdom of
God and teaching the things
which concern the Lord Jesus
Christ with all confidence, no
one forbidding him.

18 [a]Acts 22:24; 24:10; 25:8; 26:32
19 [a]Acts 25:11, 21, 25 [1]The ruling authorities
20 [a]Acts 26:6, 7 [b]Eph. 3:1; 4:1; 6:20
22 [a][1 Pet. 2:12; 3:16; 4:14, 16]
23 [a]Luke 24:27 [b]Acts 26:6, 22
24 [a]Acts 14:4; 19:9
25 [1]NU *your*
26 [a]Is. 6:9, 10; Matt. 13:14, 15; Luke 8:10; Rom. 11:8
28 [a]Is. 42:6; 49:6; Rom. 11:11
29 [1]NU omits v. 29.
31 [a]Eph. 6:19

The Epistle of Paul the Apostle to the ROMANS

ROMANS, Paul's greatest work, is placed first among his thirteen epistles in the New Testament. While the four Gospels present the words and works of Jesus Christ, Romans explores the significance of His sacrificial death. Using a question-and-answer format, Paul records the most systematic presentation of doctrine in the Bible. Romans is more than a book of theology; it is also a book of practical exhortation. The good news of Jesus Christ is more than facts to be believed; it is also a life to be lived—a life of righteousness befitting the person, "justified freely by [God's] grace through the redemption that is in Christ Jesus" (3:24).

Although some manuscripts omit "in Rome" in 1:7, 15, the title *Pros Romaious,* "To the Romans," has been associated with the epistle almost from the beginning.

PAUL, a bondservant of Jesus Christ, [a]called *to be* an
apostle, [b]separated to the gospel
of God
2 [a]which He promised before
[b]through His prophets in the
Holy Scriptures,
★ 3 concerning His Son Jesus
Christ our Lord, who [1]was [a]born
of the seed of David according
to the flesh,
★ 4 *and* [a]declared *to be* the Son
of God with power according
[b]to the Spirit of holiness, by the
resurrection from the dead.
5 Through Him [a]we have received grace and apostleship for
[b]obedience to the faith among
all nations [c]for His name,
6 among whom you also are
the called of Jesus Christ;

7 To all who are in Rome,
beloved of God, [a]called *to be*
saints:

[b]Grace to you and peace from
God our Father and the Lord
Jesus Christ.

CHAPTER 1

1 [a]1 Tim. 1:11 [b]Acts 9:15; 13:2
2 [a]Acts 26:6 [b]Gal. 3:8
3 [a]Ps. 89:3, 4; 132:11; Is. 11:1; Gal. 4:4 [1]*came*
4 [a]Ps. 2:7; Acts 9:20; 13:33 [b]Ps. 16:10, 11; [Heb. 9:14]
5 [a]Eph. 3:8 [b]Acts 6:7 [c]Acts 9:15
7 [a]1 Cor. 1:2, 24 [b]1 Cor. 1:3
8 [a]1 Cor. 1:4 [b]Rom. 16:19
9 [a]Rom. 9:1 [b]Acts 27:23 [c]1 Thess. 3:10 [1]Or *in*
11 [a]Rom. 15:29
12 [a]Titus 1:4
13 [a][1 Thess. 2:18] [b]Phil. 4:17

8 First, [a]I thank my God
through Jesus Christ for you
all, that [b]your faith is spoken of
throughout the whole world.
9 For [a]God is my witness,
[b]whom I serve [1]with my spirit
in the gospel of His Son, that
[c]without ceasing I make mention
of you always in my prayers,
10 making request if, by some
means, now at last I may find a
way in the will of God to come
to you.
11 For I long to see you, that [a]I
may impart to you some spiritual gift, so that you may be
established—
12 that is, that I may be encouraged together with you by [a]the
mutual faith both of you and
me.
13 Now I do not want you to be
unaware, brethren, that I often
planned to come to you (but
[a]was hindered until now), that
I might have some [b]fruit among
you also, just as among the other
Gentiles.
14 I am a debtor both to Greeks

and to barbarians, both to wise
and to unwise.
15 So, as much as is in me, *I am*
ready to preach the gospel to
you who are in Rome also.
16 For [a]I am not ashamed of the
gospel [1]of Christ, for [b]it is the
power of God to salvation for
everyone who believes, [c]for the
Jew first and also for the Greek.
17 For [a]in it the righteousness
of God is revealed from faith to
faith; as it is written, [b]*"The just*
shall live by faith."
18 [a]For the wrath of God is revealed from heaven against all
ungodliness and [b]unrighteous-
ness of men, who [1]suppress the
truth in unrighteousness,
19 because [a]what may be known
of God is [1]manifest [2]in them, for
[b]God has shown *it* to them.
20 For since the creation of the
world [a]His invisible *attributes*
are clearly seen, being understood by the things that are
made, *even* His eternal power
and [1]Godhead, so that they are
without excuse,
21 because, although they knew
God, they did not glorify *Him*
as God, nor were thankful, but
[a]became futile in their thoughts,
and their foolish hearts were
darkened.
22 [a]Professing to be wise, they
became fools,
23 and changed the glory of
the [a]incorruptible [b]God into an
image made like [1]corruptible
man—and birds and four-footed
animals and creeping things.
24 [a]Therefore God also gave
them up to uncleanness, in the
lusts of their hearts, [b]to dishonor
their bodies [c]among themselves,
25 who exchanged [a]the truth of
God [b]for the lie, and worshiped

16 [a]Ps. 40:9, 10 [b]1 Cor. 1:18, 24 [c]Acts 3:26 [1]NU omits *of Christ*

17 [a]Rom. 3:21; 9:30 [b]Hab. 2:4

18 [a][Acts 17:30] [b]2 Thess. 2:10 [1]*hold down*

19 [a][Acts 14:17; 17:24] [b][John 1:9] [1]*evident* [2]*among*

20 [a]Ps. 19:1–6 [1]*divine nature, deity*

21 [a]Jer. 2:5

22 [a]Jer. 10:14

23 [a]1 Tim. 1:17; 6:15, 16 [b]Deut. 4:16–18 [1]*perishable*

24 [a]Eph. 4:18, 19 [b]1 Cor. 6:18 [c]Lev. 18:22

25 [a]1 Thess. 1:9 [b]Is. 44:20

26 [a]Lev. 18:22 [1]Lit. *females*

27 [1]Lit. *males* [2]Lit. *female*

28 [a]Eph. 5:4

29 [1]NU omits *sexual immorality* [2]*greed* [3]*malice*

31 [1]*without understanding* [2]NU omits *unforgiving*

32 [a][Rom. 2:2] [b][Rom. 6:21] [c]Hos. 7:3

CHAPTER 2

1 [a][Rom. 1:20] [b][Matt. 7:1–5]

and served the creature rather
than the Creator, who is blessed
forever. Amen.
26 For this reason God gave
them up to [a]vile passions. For
even their [1]women exchanged
the natural use for what is
against nature.
27 Likewise also the [1]men,
leaving the natural use of the
[2]woman, burned in their lust for
one another, [1]men with [1]men
committing what is shameful,
and receiving in themselves the
penalty of their error which was
due.
28 And even as they did not like
to retain God in *their* knowledge, God gave them over to
a debased mind, to do those
things [a]which are not fitting;
29 being filled with all unrighteousness, [1]sexual immorality,
wickedness, [2]covetousness, [3]ma-
liciousness; full of envy, murder,
strife, deceit, evil-mindedness;
they are whisperers,
30 backbiters, haters of God,
violent, proud, boasters, inven-
tors of evil things, disobedient to
parents,
31 [1]undiscerning, untrustworthy,
unloving, [2]unforgiving, unmerci-
ful;
32 who, [a]knowing the righteous
judgment of God, that those who
practice such things [b]are deserving of death, not only do the
same but also [c]approve of those
who practice them.

2

Therefore you are [a]inexcus-
able, O man, whoever you
are who judge, [b]for in whatever
you judge another you condemn
yourself; for you who judge
practice the same things.
2 But we know that the judgment of God is according to

truth against those who practice such things.
3 And do you think this, O man, you who judge those practicing such things, and doing the same, that you will escape the judgment of God?
4 Or do you despise [a]the riches of His goodness, [b]forbearance, and [c]longsuffering, [d]not knowing that the goodness of God leads you to repentance?
5 But in accordance with your hardness and your [1]impenitent heart [a]you are [2]treasuring up for yourself wrath in the day of wrath and revelation of the righteous judgment of God,
6 who [a]*"will render to each one according to his deeds"*:
7 eternal life to those who by patient continuance in doing good seek for glory, honor, and immortality;
8 but to those who are self-seeking and [a]do not obey the truth, but obey unrighteousness—indignation and wrath,
9 tribulation and anguish, on every soul of man who does evil, of the Jew [a]first and also of the [1]Greek;
10 [a]but glory, honor, and peace to everyone who works what is good, to the Jew first and also to the Greek.
11 For [a]there is no partiality with God.
12 For as many as have sinned without law will also perish without law, and as many as have sinned in the law will be judged by the law
13 (for [a]not the hearers of the law *are* just in the sight of God, but the doers of the law will be justified;
14 for when Gentiles, who do not have the law, by nature do the things in the law, these, although not having the law, are a law to themselves,
15 who show the [a]work of the law written in their hearts, their [b]conscience also bearing witness, and between themselves *their* thoughts accusing or else excusing *them*)
16 [a]in the day when God will judge the secrets of men [b]by Jesus Christ, [c]according to my gospel.

17 [1]Indeed [a]you are called a Jew, and [b]rest[2] on the law, [c]and make your boast in God,
18 and [a]know *His* will, and [b]approve the things that are excellent, being instructed out of the law,
19 and [a]are confident that you yourself are a guide to the blind, a light to those who are in darkness,
20 an instructor of the foolish, a teacher of babes, [a]having the form of knowledge and truth in the law.
21 [a]You, therefore, who teach another, do you not teach yourself? You who preach that a man should not steal, do you steal?
22 You who say, "Do not commit adultery," do you commit adultery? You who abhor idols, [a]do you rob temples?
23 You who [a]make your boast in the law, do you dishonor God through breaking the law?
24 For [a]*"the name of God is* [b]*blasphemed among the Gentiles because of you,"* as it is written.

25 [a]For circumcision is indeed profitable if you keep the law; but if you are a breaker of the

4 [a][Eph. 1:7, 18; 2:7] [b][Rom. 3:25] [c]Ex. 34:6 [d]Is. 30:18
5 [a][Deut. 32:34] [1]*unrepentant* [2]*storing*
6 [a]Ps. 62:12; Prov. 24:12
8 [a][2 Thess. 1:8]
9 [a]1 Pet. 4:17 [1]Gentile
10 [a][1 Pet. 1:7]
11 [a]Deut. 10:17
13 [a][James 1:22, 25]
15 [a]1 Cor. 5:1 [b]Acts 24:25
16 [a][Matt. 25:31] [b]Acts 10:42; 17:31 [c]1 Tim. 1:11
17 [a]John 8:33 [b]Mic. 3:11 [c]Is. 48:1, 2 [1]NU *But if* [2]*rely*
18 [a]Deut. 4:8 [b]Phil. 1:10
19 [a]Matt. 15:14
20 [a][2 Tim. 3:5]
21 [a]Matt. 23:3
22 [a]Mal. 3:8
23 [a]Rom. 2:17; 9:4
24 [a]Ezek. 16:27 [b]Is. 52:5; Ezek. 36:22
25 [a][Gal. 5:3]

law, your circumcision has become uncircumcision.
26 Therefore, [a]if an uncircumcised man keeps the righteous
requirements of the law, will not
his uncircumcision be counted
as circumcision?
27 And will not the physically
uncircumcised, if he fulfills the
law, [a]judge you who, *even* with
your [1]written *code* and circumcision, *are* a transgressor of the
law?
28 For [a]he is not a Jew who *is*
one outwardly, nor *is* circumcision that which *is* outward in the
flesh;
29 but *he is* a Jew [a]who *is one*
inwardly; and [b]circumcision *is*
that of the heart, [c]in the Spirit,
not in the letter; [d]whose [1]praise
is not from men but from God.

3

What advantage then has
the Jew, or what *is* the profit
of circumcision?
2 Much in every way! Chiefly
because [a]to them were committed the [1]oracles of God.
3 For what if [a]some did not believe? [b]Will their unbelief make
the faithfulness of God without
effect?
4 [a]Certainly not! Indeed, let
[b]God be [1]true but [c]every man a
liar. As it is written:

[d]*"That You may be justified in*
Your words,
And may overcome when
You are judged."

5 But if our unrighteousness
demonstrates the righteousness
of God, what shall we say? *Is*
God unjust who inflicts wrath?
[a](I speak as a man.)
6 Certainly not! For then [a]how
will God judge the world?
7 For if the truth of God has
increased through my lie to His
glory, why am I also still judged
as a sinner?
8 And *why* not *say,* [a]"Let us do
evil that good may come"?—as
we are slanderously reported
and as some affirm that we say.
Their [1]condemnation is just.
9 What then? Are we better
than they? Not at all. For we
have previously charged both
Jews and Greeks that [a]they are
all under sin.
10 As it is written:

[a]*"There is none righteous, no,*
not one;
11 *There is none who*
understands;
There is none who seeks
after God.
12 *They have all turned aside;*
They have together become
unprofitable;
There is none who does
good, no, not one."
13 *"Their*[a] *throat is an open*
[1]*tomb;*
With their tongues they
have practiced deceit";
[b]*"The poison of asps is under*
their lips";
14 *"Whose*[a] *mouth is full of*
cursing and bitterness."
15 *"Their*[a] *feet are swift to shed*
blood;
16 *Destruction and misery are*
in their ways;
17 *And the way of peace they*
have not known."
18 *"There*[a] *is no fear of God*
before their eyes."

19 Now we know that whatever
[a]the law says, it says to those
who are under the law, that
[b]every mouth may be stopped,

26 [a][Acts 10:34]
27 [a]Matt. 12:41 [1]Lit. *letter*
28 [a][Gal. 6:15]
29 [a][1 Pet. 3:4] [b]Phil. 3:3 [c]Deut. 30:6 [d][1 Cor. 4:5] [1]A play on words—*Jew* is literally *praise.*

CHAPTER 3

2 [a]Deut. 4:5–8 [1]*sayings,* Scriptures
3 [a]Heb. 4:2 [b][2 Tim. 2:13]
4 [a]Job 40:8 [b][John 3:33] [c]Ps. 62:9 [d]Ps. 51:4 [1]Found true
5 [a]Gal. 3:15
6 [a][Gen. 18:25]
8 [a]Rom. 5:20 [1]Lit. *judgment*
9 [a]Gal. 3:22
10 [a]Ps. 14:1–3; 53:1–3; Eccl. 7:20
13 [a]Ps. 5:9 [b]Ps. 140:3 [1]*grave*
14 [a]Ps. 10:7
15 [a]Prov. 1:16; Is. 59:7, 8
18 [a]Ps. 36:1
19 [a]John 10:34 [b]Job 5:16

and all the world may become [1]guilty before God.

20 Therefore [a]by the deeds of the law no flesh will be justified in His sight, for by the law *is* the knowledge of sin.

21 But now [a]the righteousness of God apart from the law is revealed, [b]being witnessed by the Law [c]and the Prophets,

22 even the righteousness of God, through faith in Jesus Christ, to all [1]and on all who believe. For [a]there is no difference;

23 for [a]all have sinned and fall short of the glory of God,

24 being justified [1]freely [a]by His grace [b]through the redemption that is in Christ Jesus,

25 whom God set forth [a]*as* a [1]propitiation [b]by His blood, through faith, to demonstrate His righteousness, because in His forbearance God had passed over [c]the sins that were previously committed,

26 to demonstrate at the present time His righteousness, that He might be just and the justifier of the one who has faith in Jesus.

27 [a]Where *is* boasting then? It is excluded. By what law? Of works? No, but by the law of faith.

28 Therefore we conclude [a]that a man is [1]justified by faith apart from the deeds of the law.

29 Or *is He* the God of the Jews only? *Is He* not also the God of the Gentiles? Yes, of the Gentiles also,

30 since [a]*there is* one God who will justify the circumcised by faith and the uncircumcised through faith.

31 Do we then make void the law through faith? Certainly not! On the contrary, we establish the law.

4 What then shall we say that [a]Abraham our [b]father[1] has found according to the flesh?

2 For if Abraham was [a]justified by works, he has *something* to boast about, but not before God.

3 For what does the Scripture say? [a]*"Abraham believed God, and it was* [1]*accounted to him for righteousness."*

4 Now [a]to him who works, the wages are not counted [1]as grace but [1]as debt.

5 But to him who [a]does not work but believes on Him who justifies [b]the ungodly, his faith is accounted for righteousness,

6 just as David also [a]describes the blessedness of the man to whom God imputes righteousness apart from works:

7 *"Blessed[a] are those whose*
lawless deeds are
forgiven,
And whose sins are covered;
8 *Blessed is the man to whom*
the LORD *shall not*
impute sin."

9 *Does* this blessedness then *come* upon the circumcised *only,* or upon the uncircumcised also? For we say that faith was accounted to Abraham for righteousness.

10 How then was it accounted? While he was circumcised, or uncircumcised? Not while circumcised, but while uncircumcised.

11 And [a]he received the sign of circumcision, a seal of the righteousness of the faith which *he*

19 [1]*accountable*
20 [a][Gal. 2:16]
21 [a]Acts 15:11 [b]John 5:46 [c]1 Pet. 1:10
22 [a][Col. 3:11] [1]NU omits *and on all*
23 [a]Gal. 3:22
24 [a][Eph. 2:8] [b][Heb. 9:12, 15] [1]*without any cost*
25 [a]Lev. 16:15 [b]Col. 1:20 [c]Acts 14:16; 17:30 [1]*mercy seat*
27 [a][1 Cor. 1:29]
28 [a]Gal. 2:16 [1]*declared righteous*
30 [a][Gal. 3:8, 20]

CHAPTER 4

1 [a]Is. 51:2 [b]James 2:21 [1]Or *(fore)father according to the flesh has found?*
2 [a]Rom. 3:20, 27
3 [a]Gen. 15:6 [1]*imputed, credited, reckoned, counted*
4 [a]Rom. 11:6 [1]*according to*
5 [a][Eph. 2:8, 9] [b]Josh. 24:2
6 [a]Ps. 32:1, 2
7 [a]Ps. 32:1, 2
11 [a]Gen. 17:10

had while still uncircumcised, that [b]he might be the father of all those who believe, though they are uncircumcised, that righteousness might be imputed to them also,

12 and the father of circumcision to those who not only *are* of the circumcision, but who also walk in the steps of the faith which our father [a]Abraham *had while still* uncircumcised.

13 For the promise that he would be the [a]heir of the world *was* not to Abraham or to his seed through the law, but through the righteousness of faith.

14 For [a]if those who are of the law *are* heirs, faith is made void and the promise made of no effect,

15 because [a]the law brings about wrath; for where there is no law *there is* no transgression.

16 Therefore *it is* of faith that *it might be* [a]according to grace, [b]so that the promise might be [1]sure to all the seed, not only to those who are of the law, but also to those who are of the faith of Abraham, [c]who is the father of us all

17 (as it is written, [a]*"I have made you a father of many nations"*) in the presence of Him whom he believed—God, [b]who gives life to the dead and calls those [c]things which do not exist as though they did;

18 who, contrary to hope, in hope believed, so that he became the father of many nations, according to what was spoken, [a]*"So shall your descendants be."*

19 And not being weak in faith, [a]he did not consider his own body, already dead (since he was about a hundred years old), [b]and the deadness of Sarah's womb.

20 He did not waver at the promise of God through unbelief, but was strengthened in faith, giving glory to God,

21 and being fully convinced that what He had promised [a]He was also able to perform.

22 And therefore [a]*"it was accounted to him for righteousness."*

23 Now [a]it was not written for his sake alone that it was imputed to him,

24 but also for us. It shall be imputed to us who believe [a]in Him who raised up Jesus our Lord from the dead,

25 [a]who was delivered up because of our offenses, and [b]was raised because of our justification.

5

Therefore, [a]having been justified by faith, [1]we have [b]peace with God through our Lord Jesus Christ,

2 [a]through whom also we have access by faith into this grace [b]in which we stand, and [c]rejoice in hope of the glory of God.

3 And not only *that,* but [a]we also glory in tribulations, [b]knowing that tribulation produces [1]perseverance;

4 [a]and perseverance, [1]character; and character, hope.

5 [a]Now hope does not disappoint, [b]because the love of God has been poured out in our hearts by the Holy Spirit who was given to us.

6 For when we were still without strength, [1]in due time [a]Christ died for the ungodly.

7 For scarcely for a righteous man will one die; yet perhaps

11 [b]Luke 19:9
12 [a]Rom. 4:18–22
13 [a]Gen. 17:4–6; 22:17
14 [a]Gal. 3:18
15 [a]Rom. 3:20
16 [a][Rom. 3:24] [b][Gal. 3:22] [c]Is. 51:2 [1]*certain*
17 [a]Gen. 17:5 [b][Rom. 8:11] [c]Rom. 9:26
18 [a]Gen. 15:5
19 [a]Gen. 17:17 [b]Heb. 11:11
21 [a][Heb. 11:19]
22 [a]Gen. 15:6
23 [a]Rom. 15:4
24 [a]Acts 2:24
25 [a]Is. 53:4, 5 [b][1 Cor. 15:17]

CHAPTER 5

1 [a]Is. 32:17 [b][Eph. 2:14] [1]Some ancient mss. *let us have*
2 [a][Eph. 2:18; 3:12] [b]1 Cor. 15:1 [c]Heb. 3:6
3 [a]Matt. 5:11, 12 [b]James 1:3 [1]*endurance*
4 [a][James 1:12] [1]*approved character*
5 [a]Phil. 1:20 [b]2 Cor. 1:22
6 [a][Rom. 4:25; 5:8; 8:32] [1]*at the right time*

for a good man someone would even dare to die.

★ 8 But [a]God demonstrates His own love toward us, in that while we were still sinners, Christ died for us.

9 Much more then, having now been justified [a]by His blood, we shall be saved [b]from wrath through Him.

10 For [a]if when we were enemies [b]we were reconciled to God through the death of His Son, much more, having been reconciled, we shall be saved [c]by His life.

11 And not only *that*, but we also [a]rejoice in God through our Lord Jesus Christ, through whom we have now received the reconciliation.

12 Therefore, just as [a]through one man sin entered the world, and [b]death through sin, and thus death spread to all men, because all sinned—

13 (For until the law sin was in the world, but [a]sin is not imputed when there is no law.

14 Nevertheless death reigned from Adam to Moses, even over those who had not sinned according to the likeness of the transgression of Adam, [a]who is a type of Him who was to come.

15 But the free gift *is* not like the [1]offense. For if by the one man's offense many died, much more the grace of God and the gift by the grace of the one Man, Jesus Christ, abounded [a]to many.

16 And the gift *is* not like *that which came* through the one who sinned. For the judgment *which came* from one *offense resulted* in condemnation, but the free gift *which came* from many [1]offenses *resulted* in justification.

17 For if by the one man's [1]offense death reigned through the one, much more those who receive abundance of grace and of the gift of righteousness will reign in life through the One, Jesus Christ.)

18 Therefore, as through [1]one man's offense *judgment came* to all men, resulting in condemnation, even so through [a]one[2] Man's righteous act *the free gift came* [b]to all men, resulting in justification of life. ★

19 For as by one man's disobedience many were made sinners, so also by [a]one Man's obedience many will be made righteous.

20 Moreover [a]the law entered that the offense might abound. But where sin abounded, grace [b]abounded much more,

21 so that as sin reigned in death, even so grace might reign through righteousness to eternal life through Jesus Christ our Lord.

6 What shall we say then? [a]Shall we continue in sin that grace may abound?

2 Certainly not! How shall we who [a]died to sin live any longer in it?

3 Or do you not know that [a]as many of us as were baptized into Christ Jesus [b]were baptized into His death?

4 Therefore we were [a]buried with Him through baptism into death, that [b]just as Christ was raised from the dead by [c]the glory of the Father, [d]even so we also should walk in newness of life.

5 [a]For if we have been united together in the likeness of His death, certainly we also shall be *in the likeness* of *His* resurrection,

8 [a]Is. 53:5; [John 3:16; 15:13]
9 [a]Eph. 2:13 [b]1 Thess. 1:10
10 [a][Rom. 8:32] [b]2 Cor. 5:18 [c]John 14:19
11 [a][Gal. 4:9]
12 [a][1 Cor. 15:21] [b]Gen. 2:17
13 [a]1 John 3:4
14 [a][1 Cor. 15:21, 22]
15 [a][Is. 53:11] [1]*trespass* or *false step*
16 [1]*trespasses*
17 [1]*trespass*
18 [a]Is. 53:11, 12; [1 Cor. 15:21, 45] [b][John 12:32] [1]Or *one trespass* [2]Or *one righteous act*
19 [a][Phil. 2:8]
20 [a]John 15:22 [b]1 Tim. 1:14

CHAPTER 6

1 [a]Rom. 3:8; 6:15
2 [a][Gal. 2:19]
3 [a][Gal. 3:27] [b][1 Cor. 15:29]
4 [a]Col. 2:12 [b]1 Cor. 6:14 [c]John 2:11 [d][Gal. 6:15]
5 [a]Phil. 3:10

6 knowing this, that [a]our old man was crucified with *Him,* that [b]the body of sin might be [1]done away with, that we should no longer be slaves of sin.

7 For [a]he who has died has been [1]freed from sin.

8 Now [a]if we died with Christ, we believe that we shall also live with Him,

9 knowing that [a]Christ, having been raised from the dead, dies no more. Death no longer has dominion over Him.

10 For *the death* that He died, [a]He died to sin once for all; but *the life* that He lives, [b]He lives to God.

11 Likewise you also, [1]reckon yourselves to be [a]dead indeed to sin, but [b]alive to God in Christ Jesus our Lord.

12 [a]Therefore do not let sin reign in your mortal body, that you should obey it in its lusts.

13 And do not present your [a]members *as* [1]instruments of unrighteousness to sin, but [b]present yourselves to God as being alive from the dead, and your members *as* [1]instruments of righteousness to God.

14 For [a]sin shall not have dominion over you, for you are not under law but under grace.

15 What then? Shall we sin [a]because we are not under law but under grace? Certainly not!

16 Do you not know that [a]to whom you present yourselves slaves to obey, you are that one's slaves whom you obey, whether of sin *leading* to death, or of obedience *leading* to righteousness?

17 But God be thanked that *though* you were slaves of sin, yet you obeyed from the heart [a]that form of doctrine to which you were [1]delivered.

18 And [a]having been set free from sin, you became slaves of righteousness.

19 I speak in human *terms* because of the weakness of your flesh. For just as you presented your members *as* slaves of uncleanness, and of lawlessness *leading* to *more* lawlessness, so now present your members *as* slaves of righteousness [1]for holiness.

20 For when you were [a]slaves of sin, you were free in regard to righteousness.

21 [a]What fruit did you have then in the things of which you are now ashamed? For [b]the end of those things *is* death.

22 But now [a]having been set free from sin, and having become slaves of God, you have your fruit [1]to holiness, and the end, everlasting life.

23 For [a]the wages of sin *is* death, but [b]the [1]gift of God *is* eternal life in Christ Jesus our Lord.

7 Or do you not know, brethren (for I speak to those who know the law), that the law [1]has dominion over a man as long as he lives?

2 For [a]the woman who has a husband is bound by the law to *her* husband as long as he lives. But if the husband dies, she is released from the law of *her* husband.

3 So then [a]if, while *her* husband lives, she marries another man, she will be called an adulteress; but if her husband dies, she is free from that law, so that she is no adulteress, though she has married another man.

4 Therefore, my brethren, you

6 [a]Gal. 2:20; 5:24; 6:14 [b]Col. 2:11 [1]*rendered inoperative*
7 [a]1 Pet. 4:1 [1]*cleared*
8 [a]2 Tim. 2:11
9 [a]Rev. 1:18
10 [a]Heb. 9:27 [b]Luke 20:38
11 [a][Rom. 6:2; 7:4, 6] [b][Gal. 2:19] [1]*consider*
12 [a]Ps. 19:13
13 [a]Col. 3:5 [b]1 Pet. 2:24; 4:2 [1]Or *weapons*
14 [a][Gal. 5:18]
15 [a]1 Cor. 9:21
16 [a]2 Pet. 2:19
17 [a]2 Tim. 1:13 [1]*entrusted*
18 [a]John 8:32
19 [1]*unto sanctification*
20 [a]John 8:34
21 [a]Rom. 7:5 [b]Rom. 1:32
22 [a]Rom. 6:18; 8:2 [1]*unto sanctification*
23 [a]Gen. 2:17 [b]1 Pet. 1:4 [1]*free gift*

CHAPTER 7

1 [1]*rules*
2 [a]1 Cor. 7:39
3 [a][Matt. 5:32]

also have become [a]dead to the
law through the body of Christ,
that you may be married to another—to Him who was raised
from the dead, that we should
[b]bear fruit to God.
5 For when we were in the
flesh, the sinful passions which
were aroused by the law [a]were
at work in our members [b]to bear
fruit to death.
6 But now we have been delivered from the law, having died
to what we were held by, so that
we should serve [a]in the newness
of the Spirit and not *in* the old-
ness of the letter.
7 What shall we say then? *Is*
the law sin? Certainly not! On
the contrary, [a]I would not have
known sin except through the
law. For I would not have known
covetousness unless the law had
said, [b]*"You shall not covet."*
8 But [a]sin, taking opportunity
by the commandment, produced
in me all *manner of evil* desire.
For [b]apart from the law sin *was*
dead.
9 I was alive once without the
law, but when the commandment came, sin revived and I
died.
10 And the commandment,
[a]which *was* to *bring* life, I found
to *bring* death.
11 For sin, taking occasion by
the commandment, deceived
me, and by it killed *me*.
12 Therefore [a]the law *is* holy,
and the commandment holy and
just and good.
13 Has then what is good become death to me? Certainly
not! But sin, that it might appear
sin, was producing death in me
through what is good, so that
sin through the commandment
might become exceedingly sinful.
14 For we know that the law is
spiritual, but I am carnal, [a]sold
under sin.
15 For what I am doing, I do
not understand. [a]For what I will
to do, that I do not practice; but
what I hate, that I do.
16 If, then, I do what I will not to
do, I agree with the law that *it is*
good.
17 But now, *it is* no longer I who
do it, but sin that dwells in me.
18 For I know that [a]in me (that
is, in my flesh) nothing good
dwells; for to will is present with
me, but *how* to perform what is
good I do not find.
19 For the good that I will *to do*,
I do not do; but the evil I will not
to do, that I practice.
20 Now if I do what I will not *to*
do, it is no longer I who do it, but
sin that dwells in me.
21 I find then a law, that evil is
present with me, the one who
wills to do good.
22 For I [a]delight in the law of
God according to [b]the inward
man.
23 But [a]I see another law in [b]my
members, warring against the
law of my mind, and bringing
me into captivity to the law of
sin which is in my members.
24 O wretched man that I am!
Who will deliver me [a]from this
body of death?
25 [a]I thank God—through Jesus
Christ our Lord! So then, with
the mind I myself serve the law
of God, but with the flesh the
law of sin.

8

There is therefore now no
condemnation to those who
are in Christ Jesus, [a]who[1] do not

4 [a]Gal. 2:19; 5:18 [b]Gal. 5:22
5 [a]Rom. 6:13 [b]James 1:15
6 [a]Rom. 2:29
7 [a]Rom. 3:20 [b]Ex. 20:17; Deut. 5:21; Acts 20:33
8 [a]Rom. 4:15 [b]1 Cor. 15:56
10 [a]Lev. 18:5
12 [a]Ps. 19:8
14 [a]2 Kin. 17:17
15 [a][Gal. 5:17]
18 [a][Gen. 6:5; 8:21]
22 [a]Ps. 1:2 [b][2 Cor. 4:16]
23 [a][Gal. 5:17] [b]Rom. 6:13, 19
24 [a][1 Cor. 15:51, 52]
25 [a]1 Cor. 15:57

CHAPTER 8

1 [a]Gal. 5:16 [1]NU omits the rest of v. 1.

walk according to the flesh, but
according to the Spirit.
2 For [a]the law of [b]the Spirit of
life in Christ Jesus has made
me free from [c]the law of sin and
death.
3 For [a]what the law could not
do in that it was weak through
the flesh, [b]God *did* by sending
His own Son in the likeness of
sinful flesh, on account of sin:
He condemned sin in the flesh,
4 that the righteous requirement of the law might be fulfilled in us who [a]do not walk
according to the flesh but according to the Spirit.
5 For [a]those who live according to the flesh set their minds
on the things of the flesh, but
those *who live* according to the
Spirit, [b]the things of the Spirit.
6 For [a]to be [1]carnally minded
is death, but to be spiritually
minded *is* life and peace.
7 Because [a]the [1]carnal mind *is*
enmity against God; for it is not
subject to the law of God, [b]nor
indeed can be.
8 So then, those who are in the
flesh cannot please God.
9 But you are not in the flesh
but in the Spirit, if indeed the
Spirit of God dwells in you. Now
if anyone does not have the
Spirit of Christ, he is not His.
10 And if Christ *is* in you, the
body *is* dead because of sin, but
the Spirit *is* life because of righteousness.
11 But if the Spirit of [a]Him
who raised Jesus from the dead
dwells in you, [b]He who raised
Christ from the dead will also
give life to your mortal bodies
[1]through His Spirit who dwells
in you.
12 [a]Therefore, brethren, we are
debtors—not to the flesh, to live
according to the flesh.
13 For [a]if you live according to
the flesh you will die; but if by
the Spirit you [b]put to death the
deeds of the body, you will live.
14 For [a]as many as are led by
the Spirit of God, these are sons
of God.
15 For [a]you did not receive the
spirit of bondage again [b]to fear,
but you received the [c]Spirit of
adoption by whom we cry out,
[d]"Abba,[1] Father."
16 [a]The Spirit Himself bears
witness with our spirit that we
are children of God,
17 and if children, then [a]heirs—
heirs of God and joint heirs with
Christ, [b]if indeed we suffer with
Him, that we may also be glorified together.
18 For I consider that [a]the sufferings of this present time are
not worthy *to be compared* with
the glory which shall be revealed
in us.
19 For [a]the earnest expectation
of the creation eagerly waits
for the revealing of the sons of
God.
20 For [a]the creation was sub-
jected to futility, not willingly,
but because of Him who sub-
jected *it* in hope;
21 because the creation itself
also will be delivered from the
bondage of [1]corruption into the
glorious [a]liberty of the children
of God.
22 For we know that the whole
creation [a]groans and labors with
birth pangs together until now.
23 Not only *that,* but we also
who have [a]the firstfruits of
the Spirit, [b]even we ourselves
groan [c]within ourselves, eagerly

2 [a]Rom. 6:18, 22 [b][1 Cor. 15:45] [c]Rom. 7:24, 25
3 [a]Acts 13:39 [b][2 Cor. 5:21]
4 [a]Gal. 5:16, 25
5 [a]John 3:6 [b][Gal. 5:22–25]
6 [a]Gal. 6:8 [1]*fleshly*
7 [a]James 4:4 [b]1 Cor. 2:14 [1]*fleshly*
11 [a]Acts 2:24 [b]1 Cor. 6:14 [1]Or *because of*
12 [a][Rom. 6:7, 14]
13 [a]Gal. 6:8 [b]Eph. 4:22
14 [a][Gal. 5:18]
15 [a]Heb. 2:15 [b]2 Tim. 1:7 [c][Is. 56:5] [d]Mark 14:36 [1]Lit., in Aram., *Father*
16 [a]Eph. 1:13
17 [a]Acts 26:18 [b]Phil. 1:29
18 [a]2 Cor. 4:17
19 [a][2 Pet. 3:13]
20 [a]Gen. 3:17–19
21 [a][2 Cor. 3:17] [1]*decay*
22 [a]Jer. 12:4, 11
23 [a]2 Cor. 5:5 [b]2 Cor. 5:2, 4 [c][Luke 20:36]

waiting for the adoption, the [d]redemption of our body.

24 For we were saved in this hope, but [a]hope that is seen is not hope; for why does one still hope for what he sees?

25 But if we hope for what we do not see, we eagerly wait for *it* with perseverance.

26 Likewise the Spirit also helps in our weaknesses. For [a]we do not know what we should pray for as we ought, but [b]the Spirit Himself makes intercession [1]for us with groanings which cannot be uttered.

27 Now [a]He who searches the hearts knows what the mind of the Spirit *is,* because He makes intercession for the saints [b]according to *the will of* God.

28 And we know that all things work together for good to those who love God, to those [a]who are the called according to *His* purpose.

29 For whom [a]He foreknew, [b]He also predestined [c]*to be* conformed to the image of His Son, [d]that He might be the firstborn among many brethren.

30 Moreover whom He predestined, these He also [a]called; whom He called, these He also [b]justified; and whom He justified, these He also [c]glorified.

31 What then shall we say to these things? [a]If God *is* for us, who *can be* against us?

32 [a]He who did not spare His own Son, but [b]delivered Him up for us all, how shall He not with Him also freely give us all things?

33 Who shall bring a charge against God's elect? [a]*It is* God who justifies.

34 [a]Who *is* he who condemns? *It is* Christ who died, and furthermore is also risen, [b]who is even at the right hand of God, [c]who also makes intercession for us.

35 Who shall separate us from the love of Christ? *Shall* tribulation, or distress, or persecution, or famine, or nakedness, or peril, or sword?

36 As it is written:

> [a]*"For Your sake we are killed*
> *all day long;*
> *We are accounted as sheep*
> *for the slaughter."*

37 [a]Yet in all these things we are more than conquerors through Him who loved us.

38 For I am persuaded that neither death nor life, nor angels nor [a]principalities nor powers, nor things present nor things to come,

39 nor height nor depth, nor any other created thing, shall be able to separate us from the love of God which is in Christ Jesus our Lord.

9 I [a]tell the truth in Christ, I am not lying, my conscience also bearing me witness in the Holy Spirit,

2 [a]that I have great sorrow and continual grief in my heart.

3 For [a]I could wish that I myself were accursed from Christ for my brethren, my [1]countrymen according to the flesh,

4 who are Israelites, [a]to whom *pertain* the adoption, [b]the glory, [c]the covenants, [d]the giving of the law, [e]the service *of God,* and [f]the promises;

5 [a]of whom *are* the fathers and from [b]whom, according to the flesh, Christ *came,* [c]who is over

23 [d]Eph. 1:14; 4:30
24 [a]Heb. 11:1
26 [a]Matt. 20:22 [b]Eph. 6:18 [1]NU omits *for us*
27 [a]1 Chr. 28:9 [b]1 John 5:14
28 [a]2 Tim. 1:9
29 [a]2 Tim. 2:19 [b]Eph. 1:5, 11 [c][2 Cor. 3:18] [d]Heb. 1:6
30 [a][1 Pet. 2:9; 3:9] [b][Gal. 2:16] [c]John 17:22
31 [a]Num. 14:9
32 [a]Rom. 5:6, 10 [b][Rom. 4:25]
33 [a]Is. 50:8, 9
34 [a]John 3:18 [b]Mark 16:19 [c]Heb. 7:25; 9:24
36 [a]Ps. 44:22
37 [a]1 Cor. 15:57
38 [a][Eph. 1:21]

CHAPTER 9

1 [a]2 Cor. 1:23
2 [a]Rom. 10:1
3 [a]Ex. 32:32 [1]Or *relatives*
4 [a]Ex. 4:22 [b]1 Sam. 4:21 [c]Acts 3:25 [d]Ps. 147:19 [e]Heb. 9:1, 6 [f][Acts 2:39; 13:32]
5 [a]Deut. 10:15 [b][Luke 1:34, 35; 3:23] [c]Jer. 23:6

all, *the* eternally blessed God.
Amen.
6 [a]But it is not that the word
of God has taken no effect. For
[b]they *are* not all Israel who *are*
of Israel,
7 [a]nor *are they* all children
because they are the seed of
Abraham; but, [b]*"In Isaac your
seed shall be called."*
8 That is, those who *are* the
children of the flesh, these *are*
not the children of God; but
[a]the children of the promise are
counted as the seed.
9 For this *is* the word of promise: [a]*"At this time I will come
and Sarah shall have a son."*
10 And not only *this,* but when
[a]Rebecca also had conceived by
one man, *even* by our father
Isaac
11 (for *the children* not yet being born, nor having done any
good or evil, that the purpose of
God according to election might
stand, not of works but of [a]Him
who calls),
12 it was said to her, [a]*"The older
shall serve the younger."*
13 As it is written, [a]*"Jacob I have
loved, but Esau I have hated."*
14 What shall we say then?
[a]*Is there* unrighteousness with
God? Certainly not!
15 For He says to Moses, [a]*"I
will have mercy on whomever I
will have mercy, and I will have
compassion on whomever I will
have compassion."*
16 So then *it is* not of him who
wills, nor of him who runs, but
of God who shows mercy.
17 For [a]the Scripture says to the
Pharaoh, [b]*"For this very purpose
I have raised you up, that I may
show My power in you, and that*

6 [a]Num. 23:19 [b][Gal. 6:16]
7 [a][Gal. 4:23] [b]Gen. 21:12
8 [a]Gal. 4:28
9 [a]Gen. 18:10, 14
10 [a]Gen. 25:21
11 [a][Rom. 4:17; 8:28]
12 [a]Gen. 25:23
13 [a]Mal. 1:2, 3
14 [a]Deut. 32:4
15 [a]Ex. 33:19
17 [a]Gal. 3:8 [b]Ex. 9:16
18 [a]Ex. 4:21
19 [a]2 Chr. 20:6
20 [a]Is. 29:16
21 [a]Prov. 16:4 [b]2 Tim. 2:20
22 [a][1 Thess. 5:9] [b][1 Pet. 2:8]
23 [a][Col. 1:27] [b][Rom. 8:28–30]
24 [a][Rom. 8:28] [b]Rom. 3:29
25 [a]Hos. 2:23
26 [a]Hos. 1:10

*My name may be declared in all
the earth."*
18 Therefore He has mercy on
whom He wills, and whom He
wills He [a]hardens.
19 You will say to me then,
"Why does He still find fault?
For [a]who has resisted His will?"
20 But indeed, O man, who are
you to reply against God? [a]Will
the thing formed say to him who
formed *it,* "Why have you made
me like this?"
21 Does not the [a]potter have
power over the clay, from the
same lump to make [b]one vessel
for honor and another for dishonor?
22 *What* if God, wanting to
show *His* wrath and to make
His power known, endured with
much longsuffering [a]the vessels
of wrath [b]prepared for destruction,
23 and that He might make
known [a]the riches of His glory
on the vessels of mercy, which
He had [b]prepared beforehand
for glory,
24 even us whom He [a]called,
[b]not of the Jews only, but also of
the Gentiles?
25 As He says also in Hō·sē'a:

[a]*"I will call them My people,*
who were not My people,
And her beloved, who was
not beloved."
26 *"And[a] it shall come to pass*
in the place where it was
said to them,
'You are not My people,'
There they shall be called
sons of the living God."

27 Ī·sāi'ah also cries out concerning Israel:

[a]"Though the number of the
children of Israel be as
the sand of the sea,
[b]The remnant will be saved.
28 *For [1]He will finish the*
work and cut it short in
righteousness,
[a]Because the LORD *will make*
a short work upon the
earth."

29 And as Ī·sāi′ah said before:

[a]"Unless the LORD *of*
[1]Sab′a·ōth had left us a
seed,
[b]We would have become like
Sod′om,
And we would have been
made like Go·mor′rah."

30 What shall we say then?
[a]That Gentiles, who did not pursue righteousness, have attained
to righteousness, [b]even the righteousness of faith;
31 but Israel, [a]pursuing the law
of righteousness, [b]has not attained to the law [1]of righteousness.
★ 32 Why? Because *they did* not
seek it by faith, but as it were,
[1]by the works of the law. For
[a]they stumbled at that stumbling
stone.
★ 33 As it is written:

[a]"Behold, I lay in Zion a
stumbling stone and
rock of offense,
And [b]whoever believes on
Him will not be put to
shame."

10 Brethren, my heart's desire and prayer to God
for [1]Israel is that they may be
saved.
2 For I bear them witness [a]that
they have a zeal for God, but not
according to knowledge.
3 For they being ignorant
of [a]God's righteousness, and
seeking to establish their own
[b]righteousness, have not submit-
ted to the righteousness of God.
4 For [a]Christ *is* the end of the
law for righteousness to everyone who believes.
5 For Moses writes about the
righteousness which is of the
law, *[a]"The man who does those*
things shall live by them."
6 But the righteousness of faith
speaks in this way, *[a]"Do not say*
in your heart, 'Who will ascend
into heaven?'" (that is, to bring
Christ down *from above*)
7 or, *[a]"'Who will descend into*
the abyss?'" (that is, to bring
Christ up from the dead).
8 But what does it say? *[a]"The*
word is near you, in your mouth
and in your heart" (that is, the
word of faith which we preach):
9 that [a]if you confess with your
mouth the Lord Jesus and believe in your heart that God has
raised Him from the dead, you
will be saved.
10 For with the heart one believes unto righteousness, and
with the mouth confession is
made unto salvation.
11 For the Scripture says, ★
[a]"Whoever believes on Him will
not be put to shame."
12 For [a]there is no distinction
between Jew and Greek, for [b]the
same Lord over all [c]is rich to all
who call upon Him.
13 For *[a]"whoever calls [b]on the*
name of the LORD *shall be saved."*
14 How then shall they call on
Him in whom they have not
believed? And how shall they

27 [a]Is. 10:22, 23 [b]Rom. 11:5
28 [a]Is. 10:23; 28:22 [1]NU *the* LORD *will finish the work and cut it short upon the earth*
29 [a]Is. 1:9 [b]Is. 13:19 [1]Lit., in Heb., *Hosts*
30 [a]Rom. 4:11 [b]Rom. 1:17; 3:21; 10:6
31 [a][Rom. 10:2–4] [b][Gal. 5:4] [1]NU omits *of righteousness*
32 [a]Is. 8:14, 15; [1 Cor. 1:23] [1]NU *by works*, omitting *of the law*
33 [a]Is. 8:14; 28:16 [b]Rom. 5:5; 10:11

CHAPTER 10

1 [1]NU *them*
2 [a]Acts 21:20
3 [a][Rom. 1:17] [b][Phil. 3:9]
4 [a][Gal. 3:24; 4:5]
5 [a]Lev. 18:5
6 [a]Deut. 30:12–14
7 [a]Deut. 30:13
8 [a]Deut. 30:14
9 [a]Luke 12:8
11 [a]Is. 28:16
12 [a]Rom. 3:22, 29 [b]Acts 10:36 [c]Eph. 1:7
13 [a]Joel 2:32 [b]Acts 9:14

believe in Him of whom they
have not heard? And how shall
they hear [a]without a preacher?
15 And how shall they preach
unless they are sent? As it is
written:

> [a]*"How beautiful are the feet*
> *of those who* [1]*preach the*
> *gospel of peace,*
> *Who bring glad tidings of*
> *good things!"*

★ 16 But they have not all obeyed
the gospel. For Ī·sāi′ah says,
[a]*"*LORD, *who has believed our*
report?"
17 So then faith *comes* by hearing, and hearing by the word of
God.
18 But I say, have they not
heard? Yes indeed:

> [a]*"Their sound has gone out to*
> *all the earth,*
> [b]*And their words to the ends*
> *of the world."*

19 But I say, did Israel not
know? First Moses says:

> [a]*"I will provoke you to*
> *jealousy by those who*
> *are not a nation,*
> *I will move you to anger by*
> *a* [b]*foolish nation."*

20 But Ī·sāi′ah is very bold and
says:

> [a]*"I was found by those who*
> *did not seek Me;*
> *I was made manifest to*
> *those who did not ask*
> *for Me."*

21 But to Israel he says:

> [a]*"All day long I have stretched*
> *out My hands*
> *To a disobedient and*
> *contrary people."*

11 I say then, [a]has God
cast away His people?
[b]Certainly not! For [c]I also am
an Israelite, of the seed of Abraham, *of* the tribe of Benjamin.
2 God has not cast away His
people whom [a]He foreknew. Or
do you not know what the Scripture says of E·lī′jah, how he
pleads with God against Israel,
saying,
3 [a]*"*LORD, *they have killed Your*
prophets and torn down Your
altars, and I alone am left, and
they seek my life"?
4 But what does the divine
response say to him? [a]*"I have*
reserved for Myself seven thou-
sand men who have not bowed
the knee to Bā′al."
5 [a]Even so then, at this present
time there is a remnant according to the election of grace.
6 And [a]if by grace, then *it is*
no longer of works; otherwise
grace is no longer grace. [1]But
if *it is* of works, it is no longer
grace; otherwise work is no longer work.
7 What then? [a]Israel has not
obtained what it seeks; but the
elect have obtained it, and the
rest were [b]blinded.
8 Just as it is written:

> [a]*"God has given them a spirit*
> *of stupor,*
> [b]*Eyes that they should not*
> *see*
> *And ears that they should*
> *not hear,*
> *To this very day."*

---

14 [a]Titus 1:3
15 [a]Is. 52:7; Nah. 1:15 [1]NU omits *preach the gospel of peace, Who*
16 [a]Is. 53:1
18 [a]Ps. 19:4 [b]1 Kin. 18:10
19 [a]Deut. 32:21 [b]Titus 3:3
20 [a]Is. 65:1
21 [a]Is. 65:2

CHAPTER 11

1 [a]Jer. 46:28 [b]1 Sam. 12:22 [c]2 Cor. 11:22
2 [a][Rom. 8:29]
3 [a]1 Kin. 19:10, 14
4 [a]1 Kin. 19:18
5 [a]Rom. 9:27
6 [a]Rom. 4:4 [1]NU omits the rest of v. 6.
7 [a]Rom. 9:31 [b]2 Cor. 3:14
8 [a]Is. 29:10, 13 [b]Deut. 29:3, 4

★ 9 And David says:

[a]"Let their table become a
snare and a trap,
A stumbling block and a
recompense to them.
10 *Let their eyes be darkened,*
so that they do not see,
And bow down their back
always."

11 I say then, have they stumbled
that they should fall? Certainly
not! But [a]through their [1]fall, to
provoke them to [b]jealousy, salvation *has come* to the Gentiles.
12 Now if their [1]fall *is* riches
for the world, and their failure riches for the Gentiles, how
much more their fullness!
13 For I speak to you Gentiles;
inasmuch as [a]I am an apostle to
the Gentiles, I magnify my ministry,
14 if by any means I may provoke to jealousy *those who*
are my flesh and [a]save some of
them.
15 For if their being cast away
is the reconciling of the world,
what *will* their acceptance *be*
[a]but life from the dead?
16 For if [a]the firstfruit *is* holy, the
lump *is* also *holy;* and if the root
is holy, so *are* the branches.
17 And if [a]some of the branches
were broken off, [b]and you, being
a wild olive tree, were grafted in
among them, and with them became a partaker of the root and
[1]fatness of the olive tree,
18 [a]do not boast against the
branches. But if you do boast,
remember that you do not support the root, but the root *sup-*
ports you.
19 You will say then, "Branches
were broken off that I might be
grafted in."
20 Well *said.* Because of [a]un-
belief they were broken off, and
you stand by faith. Do not be
haughty, but fear.
21 For if God did not spare the
natural branches, He may not
spare you either.
22 Therefore consider the goodness and severity of God: on
those who fell, severity; but
toward you, [1]goodness, [a]if you
continue in *His* goodness. Otherwise [b]you also will be cut off.
23 And they also, [a]if they do
not continue in unbelief, will
be grafted in, for God is able to
graft them in again.
24 For if you were cut out of
the olive tree which is wild by
nature, and were grafted contrary to nature into a cultivated
olive tree, how much more will
these, who *are* natural *branches,*
be grafted into their own olive
tree?
25 For I do not desire, brethren,
that you should be ignorant of
this mystery, lest you should be
[a]wise in your own [1]opinion, that
[b]blindness in part has happened
to Israel [c]until the fullness of the
Gentiles has come in.
26 And so all Israel will be ☆
[1]saved, as it is written:

[a]"The Deliverer will come out
of Zion,
And He will turn away
ungodliness from Jacob;
27 *For [a]this is My covenant*
with them,
When I take away their sins."

28 Concerning the gospel *they*
are enemies for your sake, but
concerning the election *they are*

9 [a]Ps. 69:22, 23
11 [a]Is. 42:6, 7 [b]Rom. 10:19 [1]*trespass*
12 [1]*trespass*
13 [a]Acts 9:15; 22:21
14 [a]1 Cor. 9:22
15 [a][Is. 26:16–19]
16 [a]Lev. 23:10
17 [a]Jer. 11:16 [b][Eph. 2:12] [1]*richness*
18 [a][1 Cor. 10:12]
20 [a]Heb. 3:19
22 [a]1 Cor. 15:2 [b][John 15:2] [1]NU adds *of God*
23 [a][2 Cor. 3:16]
25 [a]Rom. 12:16 [b]2 Cor. 3:14 [c]Luke 21:24 [1]*estimation*
26 [a]Is. 59:20, 21 [1]Or *delivered*
27 [a]Is. 27:9

[a]beloved for the sake of the fathers.
29 For the gifts and the calling
of God *are* [a]irrevocable.
30 For as you [a]were once disobedient to God, yet have now
obtained mercy through their
disobedience,
31 even so these also have now
been disobedient, that through
the mercy shown you they also
may obtain mercy.
32 For God has [1]committed
them [a]all to disobedience, that
He might have mercy on all.
33 Oh, the depth of the riches
both of the wisdom and knowledge of God! How unsearchable
are His judgments and His ways
past finding out!

34 *"For who has known the*
[a]mind of the LORD?
Or [b]who has become His
counselor?"
35 *"Or[a] who has first given to*
Him
And it shall be repaid to
him?"

36 For [a]of Him and through Him
and to Him *are* all things, [b]to
whom *be* glory forever. Amen.

12

I [a]beseech[1] you therefore,
brethren, by the mercies
of God, that you present your
bodies [b]a living sacrifice, holy,
acceptable to God, *which is* your
[2]reasonable service.
2 And [a]do not be conformed to
this world, but [b]be transformed
by the renewing of your mind,
that you may [c]prove what *is* that
good and acceptable and perfect
will of God.
3 For I say, [a]through the grace
given to me, to everyone who
is among you, [b]not to think of
himself more highly than he
ought to think, but to think soberly, as God has dealt [c]to each
one a measure of faith.
4 For [a]as we have many members in one body, but all the
members do not have the same
function,
5 so [a]we, *being* many, are one
body in Christ, and individually
members of one another.
6 Having then gifts differing
according to the grace that is
[a]given to us, *let us use them:* if
prophecy, *let us [b]prophesy* in
proportion to our faith;
7 or ministry, *let us use it* in *our*
ministering; [a]he who teaches, in
teaching;
8 [a]he who exhorts, in exhortation; [b]he who gives, with liberality; [c]he who leads, with diligence; he who shows mercy,
[d]with cheerfulness.
9 [a]*Let* love *be* without hypocrisy. [b]Abhor what is evil. Cling
to what is good.
10 [a]*Be* kindly affectionate to
one another with brotherly love,
[b]in honor giving preference to
one another;
11 not lagging in diligence, fervent in spirit, serving the Lord;
12 [a]rejoicing in hope, [b]patient[1]
in tribulation, [c]continuing steadfastly in prayer;
13 [a]distributing to the needs of
the saints, [b]given[1] to hospitality.
14 [a]Bless those who persecute
you; bless and do not curse.
15 [a]Rejoice with those who rejoice, and weep with those who
weep.
16 [a]Be of the same mind toward
one another. [b]Do not set your
mind on high things, but associate with the humble. Do not be
wise in your own opinion.

---

28 [a]Deut. 7:8; 10:15
29 [a]Num. 23:19
30 [a][Eph. 2:2]
32 [a][Gal. 3:22] [1]*shut them all up in*
34 [a]Is. 40:13; Jer. 23:18 [b]Job 36:22
35 [a]Job 41:11
36 [a]Heb. 2:10 [b]Heb. 13:21

CHAPTER 12

1 [a]2 Cor. 10:1–4 [b]Heb. 10:18, 20 [1]*urge* [2]*rational*
2 [a]1 John 2:15 [b]Eph. 4:23 [c][1 Thess. 4:3]
3 [a]Gal. 2:9 [b]Prov. 25:27 [c][Eph. 4:7]
4 [a]1 Cor. 12:12–14
5 [a][1 Cor. 10:17]
6 [a][John 3:27] [b]Acts 11:27
7 [a]Eph. 4:11
8 [a]Acts 15:32 [b][Matt. 6:1–3] [c][Acts 20:28] [d]2 Cor. 9:7
9 [a]1 Tim. 1:5 [b]Ps. 34:14
10 [a]Heb. 13:1 [b]Phil. 2:3
12 [a]Luke 10:20 [b]Luke 21:19 [c]Luke 18:1 [1]*persevering*
13 [a]1 Cor. 16:1 [b]1 Tim. 3:2 [1]Lit. *pursuing*
14 [a][Matt. 5:44]
15 [a][1 Cor. 12:26]
16 [a][Phil. 2:2; 4:2] [b]Jer. 45:5

17 [a]Repay no one evil for evil.
[b]Have[1] regard for good things in
the sight of all men.
18 If it is possible, as much as
depends on you, [a]live peaceably
with all men.
19 Beloved, [a]do not avenge
yourselves, but *rather* give
place to wrath; for it is written,
[b]*"Vengeance is Mine, I will repay,"* says the Lord.
20 Therefore

[a]*"If your enemy is hungry,*
feed him;
If he is thirsty, give him a
drink;
For in so doing you will
heap coals of fire on his
head."

21 Do not be overcome by evil,
but [a]overcome evil with good.

13 Let every soul be [a]subject
to the governing authorities.
For there is no authority
except from God, and the authorities
that exist are appointed
by God.
2 Therefore whoever resists
[a]the authority resists the ordinance
of God, and those who
resist will [1]bring judgment on
themselves.
3 For rulers are not a terror
to good works, but to evil. Do
you want to be unafraid of the
authority? [a]Do what is good, and
you will have praise from the
same.
4 For he is God's minister to
you for good. But if you do evil,
be afraid; for he does not bear
the sword in vain; for he is God's
minister, an avenger to *execute*
wrath on him who practices evil.
5 Therefore [a]*you* must be
subject, not only because of
wrath [b]but also for conscience'
sake.
6 For because of this you also
pay taxes, for they are God's
ministers attending continually
to this very thing.
7 [a]Render therefore to all their
due: taxes to whom taxes *are*
due, customs to whom customs,
fear to whom fear, honor to
whom honor.
8 Owe no one anything except
to love one another, for [a]he who
loves another has fulfilled the
law.
9 For the commandments,
[a]*"You shall not commit adultery," "You shall not murder,"*
"You shall not steal," [1]*"You shall*
not bear false witness," "You
shall not covet," and if *there is*
any other commandment, are
all summed up in this saying,
namely, [b]*"You shall love your*
neighbor as yourself."
10 Love does no harm to a
neighbor; therefore [a]love *is* the
fulfillment of the law.
11 And *do* this, knowing the
time, that now *it is* high time [a]to
awake out of sleep; for now our
salvation *is* nearer than when
we *first* believed.
12 The night is far spent, the
day is at hand. [a]Therefore let us
cast off the works of darkness,
and [b]let us put on the armor of
light.
13 [a]Let us walk [1]properly, as
in the day, [b]not in revelry and
drunkenness, [c]not in lewdness
and lust, [d]not in strife and envy.
14 But [a]put on the Lord Jesus
Christ, and [b]make no provision
for the flesh, to *fulfill its* lusts.

14 Receive[a] one who is weak
in the faith, *but* not to
disputes over doubtful things.

17 [a][Matt. 5:39] [b]2 Cor. 8:21 [1]Or *Provide good*
18 [a]Heb. 12:14
19 [a]Lev. 19:18 [b]Deut. 32:35
20 [a]Prov. 25:21, 22
21 [a][Rom. 12:1, 2]

CHAPTER 13

1 [a]1 Pet. 2:13
2 [a][Titus 3:1] [1]Lit. *receive*
3 [a]1 Pet. 2:14
5 [a]Eccl. 8:2 [b][1 Pet. 2:13, 19]
7 [a]Matt. 22:21
8 [a][Gal. 5:13, 14]
9 [a]Ex. 20:13–17; Deut. 5:17–21 [b]Lev. 19:18 [1]NU omits *"You shall not bear false witness,"*
10 [a][Matt. 7:12; 22:39, 40]
11 [a][1 Cor. 15:34]
12 [a]Eph. 5:11 [b][Eph. 6:11, 13]
13 [a]Phil. 4:8 [b]Prov. 23:20 [c][1 Cor. 6:9] [d]James 3:14 [1]*decently*
14 [a]Gal. 3:27 [b][Gal. 5:16]

CHAPTER 14

1 [a][1 Cor. 8:9; 9:22]

2 For one believes he [a]may eat
all things, but he who is weak
eats *only* vegetables.
3 Let not him who eats despise
him who does not eat, and [a]let
not him who does not eat judge
him who eats; for God has received him.
4 [a]Who are you to judge another's servant? To his own master he stands or falls. Indeed, he
will be made to stand, for God is
able to make him stand.
5 [a]One person esteems *one* day
above another; another esteems
every day *alike*. Let each be fully
convinced in his own mind.
6 He who [a]observes the day,
observes *it* to the Lord; [1]and he
who does not observe the day,
to the Lord he does not observe
it. He who eats, eats to the Lord,
for [b]he gives God thanks; and
he who does not eat, to the Lord
he does not eat, and gives God
thanks.
7 For [a]none of us lives to himself, and no one dies to himself.
8 For if we [a]live, we live to the
Lord; and if we die, we die to
the Lord. Therefore, whether we
live or die, we are the Lord's.
9 For [a]to this end Christ died
[1]and rose and lived again, that
He might be [b]Lord of both the
dead and the living.
10 But why do you judge your
brother? Or why do you show
contempt for your brother? For
[a]we shall all stand before the
judgment seat of [1]Christ.
☆ 11 For it is written:

[a]"As I live, says the LORD,
Every knee shall bow to Me,
And every tongue shall
confess to God."

12 So then [a]each of us shall give
account of himself to God.
13 Therefore let us not judge
one another [1]anymore, but
rather resolve this, [a]not to put
a stumbling block or a cause to
fall in *our* brother's way.
14 I know and am convinced ☆
by the Lord Jesus [a]that *there is*
nothing unclean of itself; but to
him who considers anything to
be unclean, to him *it is* unclean.
15 Yet if your brother is grieved
because of *your* food, you are no
longer walking in love. [a]Do not
destroy with your food the one
for whom Christ died.
16 [a]Therefore do not let your
good be spoken of as evil;
17 [a]for the kingdom of God is
not eating and drinking, but
righteousness and [b]peace and
joy in the Holy Spirit.
18 For he who serves Christ in
[1]these things [a]*is* acceptable to
God and approved by men.
19 [a]Therefore let us pursue the
things *which make* for peace
and the things by which [b]one
may [1]edify another.
20 [a]Do not destroy the work of
God for the sake of food. [b]All
things indeed *are* pure, [c]but *it is*
evil for the man who eats with
[1]offense.
21 *It is* good neither to eat [a]meat
nor drink wine nor *do anything*
by which your brother stumbles
[1]or is offended or is made weak.
22 [1]Do you have faith? Have *it*
to yourself before God. [a]Happy
is he who does not condemn
himself in what he approves.
23 But he who doubts is condemned if he eats, because *he*
does not *eat* from faith; for
[a]whatever *is* not from faith is
[1]sin.

2 [a][Titus 1:15]
3 [a][Col. 2:16]
4 [a]James 4:11, 12
5 [a]Gal. 4:10
6 [a]Gal. 4:10 [b][1 Tim. 4:3] [1]NU omits the rest of this sentence.
7 [a][Gal. 2:20]
8 [a]2 Cor. 5:14, 15
9 [a]2 Cor. 5:15 [b]Acts 10:36 [1]NU omits *and rose*
10 [a]2 Cor. 5:10 [1]NU *God*
11 [a]Is. 45:23; Phil. 2:9–11
12 [a]1 Pet. 4:5
13 [a]1 Cor. 8:9 [1]*any longer*
14 [a]1 Cor. 10:25
15 [a]1 Cor. 8:11
16 [a][Rom. 12:17]
17 [a]1 Cor. 8:8 [b][Rom. 8:6]
18 [a]2 Cor. 8:21 [1]NU *this thing*
19 [a]Rom. 12:18 [b]1 Cor. 14:12 [1]*build up*
20 [a]Rom. 14:15 [b]Acts 10:15 [c]1 Cor. 8:9–12 [1]A feeling of giving offense
21 [a]1 Cor. 8:13 [1]NU omits the rest of v. 21.
22 [a][1 John 3:21] [1]NU *The faith which you have—have*
23 [a]Titus 1:15 [1]M puts Rom. 16:25–27 here.

15 We [a]then who are strong
ought to bear with the
[1]scruples of the weak, and not to
please ourselves.
2 [a]Let each of us please *his*
neighbor for *his* good, leading to
[1]edification.
★ 3 [a]For even Christ did not
please Himself; but as it is written, [b]*"The reproaches of those
who reproached You fell on
Me."*
4 For [a]whatever things were
written before were written for
our learning, that we through
the [1]patience and comfort of the
Scriptures might have hope.
5 [a]Now may the God of patience and comfort grant you to
be like-minded toward one another, according to Christ Jesus,
6 that you may [a]with one mind
and one mouth glorify the God
and Father of our Lord Jesus
Christ.
7 Therefore [a]receive one another, just [b]as Christ also received [1]us, to the glory of God.
8 Now I say that [a]Jesus Christ
has become a [1]servant to the circumcision for the truth of God,
[b]to confirm the promises *made*
to the fathers,
9 and [a]that the Gentiles might
glorify God for *His* mercy, as it
is written:

[b]*"For this reason I will confess
to You among the
Gentiles,
And sing to Your name."*

10 And again he says:

[a]*"Rejoice, O Gentiles, with His
people!"*

11 And again:

[a]*"Praise the LORD, all you
Gentiles!
Laud Him, all you peoples!"*

12 And again, Ī·sāi'ah says: ★

[a]*"There shall be a root of
Jesse;
And He who shall rise to
reign over the Gentiles,
In Him the Gentiles shall
hope."*

13 Now may the God of hope
fill you with all [a]joy and peace in
believing, that you may abound
in hope by the power of the Holy
Spirit.
14 Now [a]I myself am confident
concerning you, my brethren,
that you also are full of goodness, [b]filled with all knowledge,
able also to admonish [1]one another.
15 Nevertheless, brethren, I
have written more boldly to you
on *some* points, as reminding
you, [a]because of the grace given
to me by God,
16 that [a]I might be a minister
of Jesus Christ to the Gentiles,
ministering the gospel of God,
that the [b]offering [1]of the Gentiles might be acceptable, sanctified by the Holy Spirit.
17 Therefore I have reason to
glory in Christ Jesus [a]in the
things *which pertain* to God.
18 For I will not dare to speak
of any of those things [a]which
Christ has not accomplished
through me, in word and deed,
[b]to make the Gentiles obedient—
19 [a]in mighty signs and wonders, by the power of the Spirit
of God, so that from Jerusalem
and round about to Il·lyr'i·cum

CHAPTER 15
1 [a][Gal. 6:1, 2] [1]*weaknesses*
2 [a]1 Cor. 9:22; 10:24, 33 [1]*building up*
3 [a]Matt. 26:39 [b]Ps. 69:9
4 [a]1 Cor. 10:11 [1]*perseverance*
5 [a]1 Cor. 1:10
6 [a]Acts 4:24
7 [a]Rom. 14:1, 3 [b]Rom. 5:2 [1]NU, M *you*
8 [a]Matt. 15:24 [b]2 Cor. 1:20 [1]*minister*
9 [a]John 10:16 [b]2 Sam. 22:50; Ps. 18:49
10 [a]Deut. 32:43
11 [a]Ps. 117:1
12 [a]Is. 11:1, 10
13 [a]Rom. 12:12; 14:17
14 [a]2 Pet. 1:12 [b]1 Cor. 1:5; 8:1, 7, 10 [1]M *others*
15 [a]Rom. 1:5; 12:3
16 [a]Rom. 11:13 [b][Is. 66:20] [1]Consisting of
17 [a]Heb. 2:17; 5:1
18 [a]Acts 15:12; 21:19 [b]Rom. 1:5
19 [a]Acts 19:11

I have fully preached the gospel
of Christ.
20 And so I have made it my
aim to preach the gospel, not
where Christ was named, [a]lest I
should build on another man's
foundation,
☆ 21 but as it is written:

> [a]*"To whom He was not*
> *announced, they shall*
> *see;*
> *And those who have not*
> *heard shall understand."*

22 For this reason [a]I also have
been much hindered from coming to you.
23 But now no longer having a
place in these parts, and [a]having
a great desire these many years
to come to you,
24 whenever I journey to Spain,
[1]I shall come to you. For I hope
to see you on my journey, [a]and
to be helped on my way there
by you, if first I may [b]enjoy your
company for a while.
25 But now [a]I am going to Jerusalem to [1]minister to the saints.
26 For [a]it pleased those from
Mac·e·dō'ni·a and A·chā'i·a to
make a certain contribution for
the poor among the saints who
are in Jerusalem.
27 It pleased them indeed, and
they are their debtors. For [a]if the
Gentiles have been partakers of
their spiritual things, [b]their duty
is also to minister to them in
material things.
28 Therefore, when I have performed this and have sealed to
them [a]this fruit, I shall go by
way of you to Spain.
29 [a]But I know that when I
come to you, I shall come in the
fullness of the blessing [1]of the
gospel of Christ.
30 Now I beg you, brethren,
through the Lord Jesus Christ,
and [a]through the love of the
Spirit, [b]that you strive together
with me in prayers to God for
me,
31 [a]that I may be delivered from
those in Judea who [1]do not believe, and that [b]my service for
Jerusalem may be acceptable to
the saints,
32 [a]that I may come to you with
joy [b]by the will of God, and may
[c]be refreshed together with you.
33 Now [a]the God of peace *be*
with you all. Amen.

16 I commend to you
Phoē'bē our sister, who is
a servant of the church in [a]Cen'-
chrē·a,
2 [a]that you may receive her in
the Lord [b]in a manner worthy
of the saints, and assist her in
whatever business she has need
of you; for indeed she has been
a helper of many and of myself
also.
3 Greet [a]Pri·scil'la and A·qui'la,
my fellow workers in Christ Jesus,
4 who risked their own necks
for my life, to whom not only
I give thanks, but also all the
churches of the Gentiles.
5 Likewise *greet* [a]the church
that is in their house. Greet my
beloved E·paē'ne·tus, who is [b]the
firstfruits of [1]A·chā'i·a to Christ.
6 Greet Mary, who labored
much for us.
7 Greet An·dron'i·cus and Jū'-
ni·a, my countrymen and my fellow prisoners, who are of note
among the [a]apostles, who also
[b]were in Christ before me.

20 [a][2 Cor. 10:13, 15, 16]
21 [a]Is. 52:15
22 [a]Rom. 1:13
23 [a]Acts 19:21; 23:11
24 [a]Acts 15:3 [b]Rom. 1:12 [1]NU omits *I shall come to you* and joins *Spain* with the next sentence.
25 [a]Acts 19:21 [1]*serve*
26 [a]1 Cor. 16:1
27 [a]Rom. 11:17 [b]1 Cor. 9:11
28 [a]Phil. 4:17
29 [a][Rom. 1:11] [1]NU omits *of the gospel*
30 [a]Phil. 2:1 [b]2 Cor. 1:11
31 [a]2 Tim. 3:11; 4:17 [b]2 Cor. 8:4 [1]*are disobedient*
32 [a]Rom. 1:10 [b]Acts 18:21 [c]1 Cor. 16:18
33 [a]1 Cor. 14:33

CHAPTER 16

1 [a]Acts 18:18
2 [a]Phil. 2:29 [b]Phil. 1:27
3 [a]Acts 18:2, 18, 26
5 [a]1 Cor. 16:19 [b]1 Cor. 16:15 [1]NU *Asia*
7 [a]Acts 1:13, 26 [b]Gal. 1:22

8 Greet Am′pli·as, my beloved
in the Lord.
9 Greet Ur·bā′nus, our fellow
worker in Christ, and Stā′chys,
my beloved.
10 Greet A·pel′lēs, approved in
Christ. Greet those who are of
the *household* of Ar·is·tob′ū·lus.
11 Greet He·rō′di·on, my [1]coun-
tryman. Greet those who are
of the *household* of Nar·cis′sus
who are in the Lord.
12 Greet Trȳ·phē′na and Trȳ-
phō′sa, who have labored in the
Lord. Greet the beloved Per′sis,
who labored much in the Lord.
13 Greet Rū′fus, [a]chosen in the
Lord, and his mother and mine.
14 Greet A·syn′cri·tus, Phlē′gon,
Her′mas, Pat′ro·bas, Her′mēs,
and the brethren who are with
them.
15 Greet Phi·lol′o·gus and Ju-
lia, Ne′re·us and his sister, and
Ō·lym′pas, and all the saints
who are with them.
16 [a]Greet one another with
a holy kiss. [1]The churches of
Christ greet you.
17 Now I urge you, brethren,
note those [a]who cause divisions
and offenses, contrary to the
doctrine which you learned, and
[b]avoid them.
18 For those who are such do not
serve our Lord [1]Jesus Christ, but
[a]their own belly, and [b]by smooth
words and flattering speech deceive the hearts of the simple.
19 For [a]your obedience has become known to all. Therefore
I am glad on your behalf; but I
want you to be [b]wise in what is
good, and [1]simple concerning
evil.
20 And [a]the God of peace
[b]will crush Satan under your
feet shortly. [c]The grace of our
Lord Jesus Christ *be* with you.
Amen.
21 [a]Timothy, my fellow worker,
and [b]Lū′cius, [c]Jason, and [d]Sō-
sip′a·ter, my countrymen, greet
you.
22 I, Ter′ti·us, who wrote *this*
epistle, greet you in the Lord.
23 [a]Gā′i·us, my host and *the*
host of the whole church, greets
you. [b]Ē·ras′tus, the treasurer of
the city, greets you, and Quar′-
tus, a brother.
24 [a]The[1] grace of our Lord Jesus
Christ *be* with you all. Amen.
25 [1]Now [a]to Him who is able
to establish you [b]according to
my gospel and the preaching of
Jesus Christ, [c]according to the
revelation of the mystery [d]kept
secret since the world began
26 but [a]now made manifest, and
by the prophetic Scriptures made
known to all nations, according
to the commandment of the everlasting God, for [b]obedience to
the faith—
27 to [a]God, alone wise, *be* glory
through Jesus Christ forever.
Amen.

11 [1]Or *relative*
13 [a]2 John 1
16 [a]1 Cor. 16:20 [1]NU *All the churches*
17 [a][Acts 15:1] [b][1 Cor. 5:9]
18 [a]Phil. 3:19 [b]Col. 2:4 [1]NU, M omit *Jesus*
19 [a]Rom. 1:8 [b]Matt. 10:16 [1]*innocent*
20 [a]Rom. 15:33 [b]Gen. 3:15 [c]1 Cor. 16:23
21 [a]Acts 16:1 [b]Acts 13:1 [c]Acts 17:5 [d]Acts 20:4
23 [a]1 Cor. 1:14 [b]Acts 19:22
24 [a]1 Thess. 5:28 [1]NU omits v. 24.
25 [a][Eph. 3:20] [b]Rom. 2:16 [c]Eph. 1:9 [d]Col. 1:26; 2:2; 4:3 [1]M puts Rom. 16:25–27 after Rom. 14:23.
26 [a]Eph. 1:9 [b]Rom. 1:5
27 [a]Jude 25

The First Epistle of Paul the Apostle to the

CORINTHIANS

CORINTH, the most important city in Greece during Paul's day, was a bustling hub of worldwide commerce, degraded culture, and idolatrous religion. There Paul founded a church (Acts 18:1–17), and two of his letters are addressed "To the church of God which is at Corinth" (1:2; 2 Cor. 1:1).

First Corinthians reveals the problems, pressures, and struggles of a church called out of a pagan society. Paul addresses a variety of problems in the lifestyle of the Corinthian church: factions, lawsuits, immorality, questionable practices, abuse of the Lord's Supper, and spiritual gifts. In addition to words of discipline, Paul shares words of counsel in answer to questions raised by the Corinthian believers.

The oldest recorded title of this epistle is *Pros Korinthious A*, in effect, the "First to the Corinthians." The *A* was no doubt a later addition to distinguish this book from Second Corinthians.

CHAPTER 1

PAUL, [a]called *to be* an apostle
of Jesus Christ [b]through the
will of God, and [c]Sos′the·nēs *our*
brother,

2 To the church of God which
is at Corinth, to those who
[a]are [1]sanctified in Christ Jesus,
[b]called *to be* saints, with all who
in every place call on the name
of Jesus Christ [c]our Lord, [d]both
theirs and ours:

3 [a]Grace to you and peace from
God our Father and the Lord Jesus Christ.
4 [a]I thank my God always concerning
you for the grace of
God which was given to you by
Christ Jesus,
5 that you were enriched in
everything by Him [a]in all [1]utterance
and all knowledge,
6 even as [a]the testimony of
Christ was confirmed [1]in you,
7 so that you come short in
no gift, eagerly [a]waiting for the
revelation of our Lord Jesus
Christ,
8 [a]who will also confirm you
to the end, [b]*that you may be*
blameless in the day of our Lord
Jesus Christ.
9 [a]God *is* faithful, by whom
you were called into [b]the fellowship
of His Son, Jesus Christ our
Lord.
10 Now I plead with you, brethren,
by the name of our Lord
Jesus Christ, [a]that you all [1]speak
the same thing, and *that* there
be no [2]divisions among you, but
that you be perfectly joined together
in the same mind and in
the same judgment.
11 For it has been declared to
me concerning you, my brethren,
by those of Chlō′ē's *household,*
that there are [1]contentions
among you.
12 Now I say this, that [a]each of
you says, "I am of Paul," or "I am
of [b]A·pol′los," or "I am of [c]Cē′phas,"
or "I am of Christ."
13 [a]Is Christ divided? Was Paul

1 [a]Rom. 1:1 [b]2 Cor. 1:1 [c]Acts 18:17
2 [a][Acts 15:9] [b]Rom. 1:7 [c][1 Cor. 8:6] [d][Rom. 3:22] [1]*set apart*
3 [a]Rom. 1:7
4 [a]Rom. 1:8
5 [a][1 Cor. 12:8] [1]*speech*
6 [a]2 Tim. 1:8 [1]Or *among*
7 [a]Phil. 3:20
8 [a]1 Thess. 3:13; 5:23 [b]Col. 1:22; 2:7
9 [a]Is. 49:7 [b][John 15:4]
10 [a]2 Cor. 13:11 [1]Have a uniform testimony [2]*schisms* or *dissensions*
11 [1]*quarrels*
12 [a]1 Cor. 3:4 [b]Acts 18:24 [c]John 1:42
13 [a]2 Cor. 11:4

crucified for you? Or were you
baptized in the name of Paul?
14 I thank God that I baptized
[a]none of you except [b]Cris′pus
and [c]Gā′i·us,
15 lest anyone should say that I
had baptized in my own name.
16 Yes, I also baptized the household of [a]Steph′a·nas. Besides, I do
not know whether I baptized any
other.
17 For Christ did not send me to
baptize, but to preach the gospel, [a]not with wisdom of words,
lest the cross of Christ should be
made of no effect.
18 For the [1]message of the cross
is [a]foolishness to [b]those who are
perishing, but to us [c]who are
being saved it is the [d]power of
God.
19 For it is written:

[a]*"I will destroy the wisdom of*
the wise,
And bring to nothing the
understanding of the
prudent."

20 [a]Where *is* the wise? Where
is the scribe? Where *is* the [1]dis-
puter of this age? [b]Has not God
made foolish the wisdom of this
world?
21 For since, in the [a]wisdom of
God, the world through wisdom
did not know God, it pleased
God through the foolishness of
the message preached to save
those who believe.
22 For [a]Jews request a sign, and
Greeks seek after wisdom;
23 but we preach Christ crucified, [a]to the Jews a [1]stumbling
block and to the [2]Greeks [b]fool-
ishness,
24 but to those who are called,
both Jews and Greeks, Christ

14 [a]John 4:2 [b]Acts 18:8 [c]Rom. 16:23
16 [a]1 Cor. 16:15, 17
17 [a][1 Cor. 2:1, 4, 13]
18 [a]1 Cor. 2:14 [b]2 Cor. 2:15 [c][1 Cor. 15:2] [d]Rom. 1:16 [1]Lit. *word*
19 [a]Is. 29:14
20 [a]Is. 19:12; 33:18 [b]Job 12:17 [1]*debater*
21 [a]Dan. 2:20
22 [a]Matt. 12:38
23 [a]Luke 2:34 [b][1 Cor. 2:14] [1]Gr. *skandalon, offense* [2]NU *Gentiles*
24 [a][Rom. 1:4] [b]Col. 2:3
26 [a]John 7:48 [1]*consider* [2]*well-born*
27 [a]Matt. 11:25
28 [1]*insignificant* or *lowly*
30 [a][2 Cor. 5:21]
31 [a]Jer. 9:23, 24

CHAPTER 2

1 [1]NU *mystery*
2 [a]Gal. 6:14
3 [a]Acts 18:1 [b][2 Cor. 4:7]
4 [a]2 Pet. 1:16 [b]Rom. 15:19 [1]NU omits *human*

[a]the power of God and [b]the wisdom of God.
25 Because the foolishness of
God is wiser than men, and the
weakness of God is stronger
than men.
26 For [1]you see your calling,
brethren, [a]that not many wise
according to the flesh, not many
mighty, not many [2]noble, *are*
called.
27 But [a]God has chosen the
foolish things of the world to put
to shame the wise, and God has
chosen the weak things of the
world to put to shame the things
which are mighty;
28 and the [1]base things of the
world and the things which are
despised God has chosen, and
the things which are not, to
bring to nothing the things that
are,
29 that no flesh should glory in
His presence.
30 But of Him you are in Christ
Jesus, who became for us wisdom
from God—and [a]righteousness
and sanctification and redemption—
31 that, as it is written, [a]*"He*
who glories, let him glory in the
LORD."

2 And I, brethren, when I
came to you, did not come
with excellence of speech or of
wisdom declaring to you the
[1]testimony of God.
2 For I determined not to know
anything among you [a]except Jesus Christ and Him crucified.
3 [a]I was with you [b]in weakness,
in fear, and in much trembling.
4 And my speech and my
preaching [a]*were* not with per-
suasive words of [1]human wisdom, [b]but in demonstration of
the Spirit and of power,

5 that your faith should not be
in the wisdom of men but in the
[a]power of God.
6 However, we speak wisdom
among those who are mature,
yet not the wisdom of this age,
nor of the rulers of this age, who
are coming to nothing.
7 But we speak the wisdom
of God in a mystery, the hidden
wisdom which God [1]ordained
before the ages for our glory,
8 which none of the rulers of
this age knew; for [a]had they
known, they would not have
[b]crucified the Lord of glory.
9 But as it is written:

[a]*"Eye has not seen, nor ear*
heard,
Nor have entered into the
heart of man
The things which God has
prepared for those who
love Him."

10 But [a]God has revealed *them*
to us through His Spirit. For the
Spirit searches all things, yes,
the deep things of God.
11 For what man knows the
things of a man except the
[a]spirit of the man which is in
him? [b]Even so no one knows the
things of God except the Spirit
of God.
12 Now we have received, not
the spirit of the world, but [a]the
Spirit who is from God, that we
might know the things that have
been freely given to us by God.
13 These things we also speak,
not in words which man's wisdom teaches but which the
[1]Holy Spirit teaches, comparing
spiritual things with spiritual.
14 [a]But the natural man does
not receive the things of the
Spirit of God, for they are foolishness to him; nor can he know
them, because they are spiritually discerned.
15 But he who is spiritual
judges all things, yet he himself
is *rightly* judged by no one.
16 For [a]*"who has known the*
mind of the LORD *that he may*
instruct Him?" [b]But we have the
mind of Christ.

3 And I, brethren, could not
speak to you as to spiritual
people but as to carnal, as to
[a]babes in Christ.
2 I fed you with [a]milk and not
with solid food; [b]for until now
you were not able *to receive it*,
and even now you are still not
able;
3 for you are still carnal. For
where *there are* envy, strife, and
divisions among you, are you
not carnal and [1]behaving like
mere men?
4 For when one says, "I am
of Paul," and another, "I *am* of
A·pol′los," are you not carnal?
5 Who then is Paul, and who *is*
A·pol′los, but [a]ministers through
whom you believed, as the Lord
gave to each one?
6 [a]I planted, [b]A·pol′los watered,
[c]but God gave the increase.
7 So then [a]neither he who
plants is anything, nor he who
waters, but God who gives the
increase.
8 Now he who plants and he
who waters are one, [a]and each
one will receive his own reward
according to his own labor.
9 For [a]we are God's fellow
workers; you are God's field,
you are [b]God's building.
10 [a]According to the grace of
God which was given to me, as
a wise master builder I have

5 [a]1 Thess. 1:5
7 [1]*predetermined*
8 [a]Luke 23:34 [b]Matt. 27:33–50
9 [a][Is. 64:4; 65:17]
10 [a]Matt. 11:25; 13:11; 16:17
11 [a][James 2:26] [b]Rom. 11:33
12 [a][Rom. 8:15]
13 [1]NU omits *Holy*
14 [a]Matt. 16:23
16 [a]Is. 40:13 [b][John 15:15]

CHAPTER 3

1 [a]Heb. 5:13
2 [a]1 Pet. 2:2 [b]John 16:12
3 [1]Lit. *walking according to man*
5 [a]2 Cor. 3:3, 6; 4:1; 5:18; 6:4
6 [a]Acts 18:4 [b]Acts 18:24–27 [c][2 Cor. 3:5]
7 [a][Gal. 6:3]
8 [a]Ps. 62:12
9 [a]2 Cor. 6:1 [b][Eph. 2:20–22]
10 [a]Rom. 1:5

laid [b]the foundation, and another builds on it. But let each
one take heed how he builds on
it.
11 For no other foundation can
anyone lay than [a]that which is
laid, [b]which is Jesus Christ.
12 Now if anyone builds on this
foundation *with* gold, silver, precious stones, wood, hay, straw,
13 each one's work will become
clear; for the Day [a]will declare
it, because [b]it will be revealed
by fire; and the fire will test each
one's work, of what sort it is.
14 If anyone's work which he
has built on *it* endures, he will
receive a reward.
15 If anyone's work is burned,
he will suffer loss; but he himself will be saved, yet so as
through fire.
16 [a]Do you not know that you
are the temple of God and *that*
the Spirit of God dwells in you?
17 If anyone [1]defiles the temple
of God, God will destroy him.
For the temple of God is holy,
which *temple* you are.
18 [a]Let no one deceive himself.
If anyone among you seems to
be wise in this age, let him become a fool that he may become
wise.
19 For the wisdom of this world
is foolishness with God. For it is
written, [a]*"He catches the wise in
their own craftiness"*;
20 and again, [a]*"The* LORD *knows
the thoughts of the wise, that
they are futile."*
21 Therefore let no one boast in
men. For [a]all things are yours:
22 whether Paul or A·pol′los or
Cē′phas, or the world or life
or death, or things present or
things to come—all are yours.

10 [b]1 Cor. 4:15
11 [a]Is. 28:16 [b]Eph. 2:20
13 [a]1 Pet. 1:7 [b]Luke 2:35
16 [a]2 Cor. 6:16
17 [1]*destroys*
18 [a]Prov. 3:7
19 [a]Job 5:13
20 [a]Ps. 94:11
21 [a][2 Cor. 4:5]
23 [a]2 Cor. 10:7

CHAPTER 4

1 [a]Col. 1:25 [b]Titus 1:7
3 [1]Lit. *day*
5 [a]Matt. 7:1 [b]Matt. 10:26 [c]1 Cor. 3:13 [d]Rom. 2:29 [1]*motives*
6 [1]*arrogant*
7 [a]John 3:27 [1]*distinguishes you*
8 [a]Rev. 3:17
9 [a]Heb. 10:33

23 And [a]you *are* Christ's, and
Christ *is* God's.

4 Let a man so consider us,
as [a]servants of Christ [b]and
stewards of the mysteries of
God.
2 Moreover it is required in
stewards that one be found faithful.
3 But with me it is a very small
thing that I should be judged by
you or by a human [1]court. In
fact, I do not even judge myself.
4 For I know of nothing against
myself, yet I am not justified by
this; but He who judges me is
the Lord.
5 [a]Therefore judge nothing before the time, until the Lord
comes, who will both bring to
[b]light the hidden things of darkness and [c]reveal the [1]counsels
of the hearts. [d]Then each one's
praise will come from God.
6 Now these things, brethren,
I have figuratively transferred
to myself and A·pol′los for your
sakes, that you may learn in
us not to think beyond what is
written, that none of you may
be [1]puffed up on behalf of one
against the other.
7 For who [1]makes you differ
from another? And [a]what do you
have that you did not receive?
Now if you did indeed receive *it*,
why do you boast as if you had
not received *it*?
8 You are already full! [a]You are
already rich! You have reigned
as kings without us—and indeed
I could wish you did reign, that
we also might reign with you!
9 For I think that God has displayed us, the apostles, last, as
men condemned to death; for
we have been made a [a]spectacle

[1]to the world, both to angels and
to men.
10 We *are* [a]fools for Christ's
sake, but you *are* wise in Christ!
[b]We *are* weak, but you *are*
strong! You *are* distinguished,
but we *are* dishonored!
11 To the present hour we both
hunger and thirst, and we are
poorly clothed, and beaten, and
homeless.
12 [a]And we labor, working with
our own hands. [b]Being reviled,
we bless; being persecuted, we
endure;
13 being defamed, we [1]entreat.
[a]We have been made as the filth
of the world, the offscouring of
all things until now.
14 I do not write these things to
shame you, but [a]as my beloved
children I warn *you.*
15 For though you might have
ten thousand instructors in
Christ, yet *you do* not *have* many
fathers; for [a]in Christ Jesus I
have begotten you through the
gospel.
16 Therefore I urge you, [a]imitate
me.
17 For this reason I have sent
[a]Timothy to you, [b]who is my
beloved and faithful son in the
Lord, who will [c]remind you of
my ways in Christ, as I [d]teach
everywhere [e]in every church.
18 [a]Now some are [1]puffed up,
as though I were not coming to
you.
19 [a]But I will come to you shortly,
[b]if the Lord wills, and I will know,
not the word of those who are
puffed up, but the power.
20 For [a]the kingdom of God *is*
not in word but in [b]power.
21 What do you want? [a]Shall
I come to you with a rod, or in
love and a spirit of gentleness?

5 It is actually reported *that
there is* sexual immorality
among you, and such sexual immorality as is not even [1]named
among the Gentiles—that a man
has his father's [a]wife!
2 [a]And you are [1]puffed up, and
have not rather [b]mourned, that
he who has done this deed might
be taken away from among you.
3 [a]For I indeed, as absent in
body but present in spirit, have
already judged (as though I
were present) him who has so
done this deed.
4 In the [a]name of our Lord
Jesus Christ, when you are gathered together, along with my
spirit, [b]with the power of our
Lord Jesus Christ,
5 [a]deliver such a one to [b]Satan
for the destruction of the flesh,
that his spirit may be saved in
the day of the Lord [1]Jesus.
6 [a]Your glorying *is* not good.
Do you not know that [b]a little
leaven leavens the whole lump?
7 Therefore [1]purge out the old
leaven, that you may be a new
lump, since you truly are unleavened. For indeed [a]Christ, our
[b]Passover, was sacrificed [2]for us.
8 Therefore [a]let us keep the
feast, [b]not with old leaven, nor
[c]with the leaven of malice and
wickedness, but with the unleavened *bread* of sincerity and
truth.
9 I wrote to you in my epistle
[a]not to [1]keep company with sexually immoral people.
10 Yet *I* certainly *did* not *mean*
with the sexually immoral people of this world, or with the
covetous, or extortioners, or
idolaters, since then you would
need to go [a]out of the world.
11 But now I have written to

---

9 [1]Lit. *theater*
10 [a]Acts 17:18; 26:24 [b]2 Cor. 13:9
12 [a]Acts 18:3; 20:34 [b]Matt. 5:44
13 [a]Lam. 3:45 [1]*exhort, encourage*
14 [a]1 Thess. 2:11
15 [a]Gal. 4:19
16 [a][1 Cor. 11:1]
17 [a]Acts 19:22 [b]1 Tim. 1:2, 18 [c]1 Cor. 11:2 [d]1 Cor. 7:17 [e]1 Cor. 14:33
18 [a]1 Cor. 5:2 [1]*arrogant*
19 [a]Acts 19:21; 20:2 [b]Acts 18:21
20 [a]1 Thess. 1:5 [b]1 Cor. 2:4
21 [a]2 Cor. 10:2

CHAPTER 5

1 [a]Lev. 18:6–8 [1]NU omits *named*
2 [a]1 Cor. 4:18 [b]2 Cor. 7:7–10 [1]*arrogant*
3 [a]Col. 2:5
4 [a][Matt. 18:20] [b][John 20:23]
5 [a]1 Tim. 1:20 [b][Acts 26:18] [1]NU omits *Jesus*
6 [a]1 Cor. 3:21 [b]Gal. 5:9
7 [a]Is. 53:7 [b]John 19:14 [1]*clean out* [2]NU omits *for us*
8 [a]Ex. 12:15 [b]Deut. 16:3 [c]Matt. 16:6
9 [a]2 Cor. 6:14 [1]*associate*
10 [a]John 17:15

you not to keep company [a]with
anyone named a brother, who is
sexually immoral, or covetous,
or an idolater, or a reviler, or a
drunkard, or an extortioner—
[b]not even to eat with such a person.
12 For what *have* I *to do* with
judging those also who are outside? Do you not judge those
who are inside?
13 But those who are outside
God judges. Therefore [a]*"put
away from yourselves the evil
person."*

6

Dare any of you, having a
matter against another, go
to law before the unrighteous,
and not before the [a]saints?
2 Do you not know that [a]the
saints will judge the world? And
if the world will be judged by
you, are you unworthy to judge
the smallest matters?
3 Do you not know that we
shall [a]judge angels? How much
more, things that pertain to this
life?
4 If then you have [1]judgments
concerning things pertaining to
this life, do you appoint those
who are least esteemed by the
church to judge?
5 I say this to your shame. Is it
so, that there is not a wise man
among you, not even one, who
will be able to judge between his
brethren?
6 But brother goes to law
against brother, and that before
unbelievers!
7 Now therefore, it is already
an utter failure for you that you
go to law against one another.
[a]Why do you not rather accept
wrong? Why do you not rather
let yourselves be cheated?
8 No, you yourselves do wrong
and cheat, and *you do* these
things *to your* brethren!
9 Do you not know that the
unrighteous will not inherit the
kingdom of God? Do not be
deceived. [a]Neither fornicators,
nor idolaters, nor adulterers, nor
[1]homosexuals, nor [2]sodomites,
10 nor thieves, nor covetous,
nor drunkards, nor revilers,
nor extortioners will inherit the
kingdom of God.
11 And such were [a]some of you.
[b]But you were washed, but you
were [1]sanctified, but you were
justified in the name of the Lord
Jesus and by the Spirit of our
God.
12 [a]All things are lawful for me,
but all things are not [1]helpful.
All things are lawful for me, but
I will not be brought under the
power of [2]any.
13 [a]Foods for the stomach and
the stomach for foods, but God
will destroy both it and them.
Now the body *is* not for [b]sexual
immorality but [c]for the Lord,
[d]and the Lord for the body.
14 And [a]God both raised up the
Lord and will also raise us up
[b]by His power.
15 Do you not know that [a]your
bodies are members of Christ?
Shall I then take the members of
Christ and make *them* members
of a harlot? Certainly not!
16 Or do you not know that he
who is joined to a harlot is one
body *with her*? For [a]*"the two,"* He
says, *"shall become one flesh."*
17 [a]But he who is joined to the
Lord is one spirit *with Him.*
18 [a]Flee sexual immorality.
Every sin that a man does is
outside the body, but he who
commits sexual immorality sins
[b]against his own body.

11 [a]Matt. 18:17 [b]Gal. 2:12
13 [a]Deut. 13:5; 17:7, 12; 19:19; 21:21; 22:21, 24; 24:7

CHAPTER 6

1 [a]Dan. 7:22
2 [a]Ps. 49:14
3 [a]2 Pet. 2:4
4 [1]*courts*
7 [a][Prov. 20:22]
9 [a]Gal. 5:21 [1]*catamites,* those submitting to homosexuals [2]*male homosexuals*
11 [a][1 Cor. 12:2] [b]Heb. 10:22 [1]*set apart*
12 [a]1 Cor. 10:23 [1]*profitable* [2]Or *anything*
13 [a]Matt. 15:17 [b]Gal. 5:19 [c]1 Thess. 4:3 [d][Eph. 5:23]
14 [a]2 Cor. 4:14 [b]Eph. 1:19
15 [a]Rom. 12:5
16 [a]Gen. 2:24
17 [a][John 17:21–23]
18 [a]Heb. 13:4 [b]Rom. 1:24

19 Or [a]do you not know that
your body is the temple of the
Holy Spirit *who is* in you, whom
you have from God, [b]and you are
not your own?
20 For [a]you were bought at a
price; therefore glorify God in
your body [1]and in your spirit,
which are God's.

7 Now concerning the things
of which you wrote to me:
[a]*It is* good for a man not to touch
a woman.
2 Nevertheless, because of
sexual immorality, let each man
have his own wife, and let each
woman have her own husband.
3 [a]Let the husband render to
his wife the affection due her,
and likewise also the wife to her
husband.
4 The wife does not have authority over her own body, but
the husband *does.* And likewise
the husband does not have authority over his own body, but
the wife *does.*
5 [a]Do not deprive one another
except with consent for a time,
that you may give yourselves to
fasting and prayer; and come together again so that [b]Satan does
not tempt you because of your
lack of self-control.
6 But I say this as a conces-
sion, [a]not as a commandment.
7 For [a]I wish that all men were
even as I myself. But each one
has his own gift from God, one
in this manner and another in
that.
8 But I say to the unmarried
and to the widows: [a]It is good
for them if they remain even as
I am;
9 but [a]if they cannot exercise
self-control, let them marry. For
it is better to marry than to burn
with passion.
10 Now to the married I command, *yet* not I but the [a]Lord:
[b]A wife is not to depart from *her*
husband.
11 But even if she does depart,
let her remain unmarried or be
reconciled to *her* husband. And
a husband is not to divorce *his*
wife.
12 But to the rest I, not the Lord,
say: If any brother has a wife
who does not believe, and she is
willing to live with him, let him
not divorce her.
13 And a woman who has a
husband who does not believe, if
he is willing to live with her, let
her not divorce him.
14 For the unbelieving husband
is sanctified by the wife, and the
unbelieving wife is sanctified by
the husband; otherwise [a]your
children would be unclean, but
now they are holy.
15 But if the unbeliever departs,
let him depart; a brother or a sister is not under bondage in such
cases. But God has called us [a]to
peace.
16 For how do you know, O wife,
whether you will [a]save *your* husband? Or how do you know,
O husband, whether you will
save *your* wife?
17 But as God has distributed to
each one, as the Lord has called
each one, so let him walk. And
[a]so I [1]ordain in all the churches.
18 Was anyone called while
circumcised? Let him not become uncircumcised. Was anyone called while uncircumcised?
[a]Let him not be circumcised.
19 [a]Circumcision is nothing and
uncircumcision is nothing, but

19 [a]2 Cor. 6:16 [b]Rom. 14:7
20 [a]2 Pet. 2:1 [1]NU omits the rest of v. 20.

CHAPTER 7

1 [a]1 Cor. 7:8, 26
3 [a]Ex. 21:10
5 [a]Joel 2:16 [b]1 Thess. 3:5
6 [a]2 Cor. 8:8
7 [a]Acts 26:29
8 [a]1 Cor. 7:1, 26
9 [a]1 Tim. 5:14
10 [a]Mark 10:6–10 [b][Matt. 5:32]
14 [a]Mal. 2:15
15 [a]Rom. 12:18
16 [a]1 Pet. 3:1
17 [a]1 Cor. 4:17 [1]*direct*
18 [a]Acts 15:1
19 [a][Gal. 3:28; 5:6; 6:15]

[b]keeping the commandments of
God *is what matters.*
20 Let each one remain in the
same calling in which he was
called.
21 Were you called *while* a slave?
Do not be concerned about it; but
if you can be made free, rather
use *it.*
22 For he who is called in the
Lord *while* a slave is [a]the Lord's
freedman. Likewise he who is
called *while* free is [b]Christ's
slave.
23 [a]You were bought at a price;
do not become slaves of men.
24 Brethren, let each one remain with [a]God in that *state* in
which he was called.
25 Now concerning virgins: [a]I
have no commandment from the
Lord; yet I give judgment as one
[b]whom the Lord in His mercy
has made [c]trustworthy.
26 I suppose therefore that this
is good because of the present
distress—[a]that *it is* good for a
man to remain as he is:
27 Are you bound to a wife? Do
not seek to be loosed. Are you
loosed from a wife? Do not seek
a wife.
28 But even if you do marry,
you have not sinned; and if a virgin marries, she has not sinned.
Nevertheless such will have
trouble in the flesh, but I would
spare you.
29 But [a]this I say, brethren, the
time *is* short, so that from now
on even those who have wives
should be as though they had
none,
30 those who weep as though
they did not weep, those who rejoice as though they did not rejoice, those who buy as though
they did not possess,
31 and those who use this world
as not [a]misusing *it.* For [b]the form
of this world is passing away.
32 But I want you to be without [1]care. [a]He who is unmarried [2]cares for the things of the
Lord—how he may please the
Lord.
33 But he who is married cares
about the things of the world—
how he may please *his* wife.
34 There is a difference between a wife and a virgin. The
unmarried woman [a]cares about
the things of the Lord, that she
may be holy both in body and
in spirit. But she who is married
cares about the things of the
world—how she may please *her*
husband.
35 And this I say for your own
profit, not that I may put a leash
on you, but for what is proper,
and that you may serve the Lord
without distraction.
36 But if any man thinks he is
behaving improperly toward his
[1]virgin, if she is past the flower
of youth, and thus it must be, let
him do what he wishes. He does
not sin; let them marry.
37 Nevertheless he who stands
steadfast in his heart, having no
necessity, but has power over
his own will, and has so determined in his heart that he will
keep his [1]virgin, does well.
38 [a]So then he who gives [1]*her* in
marriage does well, but he who
does not give *her* in marriage
does better.
39 [a]A wife is bound by law as
long as her husband lives; but if
her husband dies, she is at liberty to be married to whom she
wishes, [b]only in the Lord.
40 But she is happier if she remains as she is, [a]according to

19 [b][John 15:14]
22 [a][John 8:36] [b]1 Pet. 2:16
23 [a]1 Pet. 1:18, 19
24 [a][Col. 3:22–24]
25 [a]2 Cor. 8:8 [b]1 Tim. 1:13, 16 [c]1 Tim. 1:12
26 [a]1 Cor. 7:1, 8
29 [a]1 Pet. 4:7
31 [a]1 Cor. 9:18 [b][1 John 2:17]
32 [a]1 Tim. 5:5 [1]*concern* [2]*is concerned about*
34 [a]Luke 10:40
36 [1]Or *virgin daughter*
37 [1]Or *virgin daughter*
38 [a]Heb. 13:4 [1]NU *his own virgin*
39 [a]Rom. 7:2 [b]2 Cor. 6:14
40 [a]1 Cor. 7:6, 25

my judgment—and [b]I think I also
have the Spirit of God.

8 Now [a]concerning things
offered to idols: We know
that we all have [b]knowledge.
[c]Knowledge [1]puffs up, but love
[2]edifies.
2 And [a]if anyone thinks that he
knows anything, he knows nothing yet as he ought to know.
3 But if anyone loves God, this
one is known by Him.
4 Therefore concerning the
eating of things offered to idols,
we know that [a]an idol *is* nothing
in the world, [b]and that *there is*
no other God but one.
5 For even if there are [a]so-
called gods, whether in heaven
or on earth (as there are many
gods and many lords),
6 yet [a]for us *there is* one God,
the Father, [b]of whom *are* all
things, and we for Him; and
[c]one Lord Jesus Christ, [d]through
whom *are* all things, and
[e]through whom we *live.*
7 However, *there is* not in
everyone that knowledge; for
some, [a]with consciousness of
the idol, until now eat *it* as a
thing offered to an idol; and
their conscience, being weak, is
[b]defiled.
8 But [a]food does not commend
us to God; for neither if we eat
are we the better, nor if we do
not eat are we the worse.
9 But [a]beware lest somehow
this liberty of yours become [b]a
[1]stumbling block to those who
are weak.
10 For if anyone sees you who
have knowledge eating in an
idol's temple, will not [a]the conscience of him who is weak be
emboldened to eat those things
offered to idols?

40 [b]1 Thess. 4:8

CHAPTER 8

1 [a]Acts 15:20 [b]Rom. 14:14 [c]Rom. 14:3 [1]*makes arrogant* [2]*builds up*

2 [a][1 Cor. 13:8–12]

4 [a]Is. 41:24 [b]Deut. 4:35, 39; 6:4

5 [a][John 10:34]

6 [a]Mal. 2:10 [b]Acts 17:28 [c]John 13:13 [d]John 1:3 [e]Rom. 5:11

7 [a][1 Cor. 10:28] [b]Rom. 14:14, 22

8 [a][Rom. 14:17]

9 [a]Gal. 5:13 [b]Rom. 14:13, 21 [1]*cause of offense*

10 [a]1 Cor. 10:28

11 [a]Rom. 14:15, 20

12 [a]Matt. 25:40

13 [a]Rom. 14:21

CHAPTER 9

1 [a]Acts 9:15 [b]1 Cor. 15:8 [c]1 Cor. 3:6; 4:15

2 [a]2 Cor. 12:12 [1]*certification*

4 [a][1 Thess. 2:6, 9] [1]*authority*

5 [a]Matt. 13:55 [b]Matt. 8:14 [1]Lit. *a sister*, a wife

6 [a]Acts 4:36

7 [a]2 Cor. 10:4 [b]Deut. 20:6 [c]John 21:15

9 [a]Deut. 25:4

10 [a]2 Tim. 2:6

11 And [a]because of your knowledge shall the weak brother perish, for whom Christ died?
12 But [a]when you thus sin
against the brethren, and wound
their weak conscience, you sin
against Christ.
13 Therefore, [a]if food makes my
brother stumble, I will never
again eat meat, lest I make my
brother stumble.

9 Am [a]I not an apostle? Am I
not free? [b]Have I not seen
Jesus Christ our Lord? [c]Are you
not my work in the Lord?
2 If I am not an apostle to others, yet doubtless I am to you.
For you are [a]the [1]seal of my
apostleship in the Lord.
3 My defense to those who examine me is this:
4 [a]Do we have no [1]right to eat
and drink?
5 Do we have no right to take
along [1]a believing wife, as *do*
also the other apostles, [a]the
brothers of the Lord, and [b]Cē′-
phas?
6 Or *is it* only Bar′na·bas and
I [a]*who* have no right to refrain
from working?
7 Who ever [a]goes to war at his
own expense? Who [b]plants a
vineyard and does not eat of its
fruit? Or who [c]tends a flock and
does not drink of the milk of the
flock?
8 Do I say these things as a
mere man? Or does not the law
say the same also?
9 For it is written in the law of
Moses, [a]*"You shall not muzzle
an ox while it treads out the
grain."* Is it oxen God is concerned about?
10 Or does He say *it* altogether
for our sakes? For our sakes, no
doubt, *this* is written, that [a]he

who plows should plow in hope,
and he who threshes in hope
should be partaker of his hope.
11 [a]If we have sown spiritual
things for you, *is it* a great thing
if we reap your material things?
12 If others are partakers of
this right over you, *are* we not
even more? [a]Nevertheless we
have not used this right, but
endure all things [b]lest we hinder
the gospel of Christ.
13 [a]Do you not know that those
who minister the holy things
eat *of the things* of the [b]temple,
and those who serve at the altar
partake of *the offerings of* the
altar?
14 Even so [a]the Lord has commanded [b]that those who preach
the gospel should live from the
gospel.
15 But [a]I have used none of
these things, nor have I written
these things that it should be
done so to me; for [b]it *would be*
better for me to die than that
anyone should make my boasting void.
16 For if I preach the gospel,
I have nothing to boast of, for
[a]necessity is laid upon me; yes,
woe is me if I do not preach the
gospel!
17 For if I do this willingly, [a]I
have a reward; but if against my
will, [b]I have been entrusted with
a stewardship.
18 What is my reward then?
That [a]when I preach the gospel,
I may present the gospel [1]of
Christ without charge, that I
[b]may not abuse my authority in
the gospel.
19 For though I am [a]free from
all *men*, [b]I have made myself a
servant to all, [c]that I might win
the more;
20 and [a]to the Jews I became as
a Jew, that I might win Jews; to
those *who are* under the law, as
under the [1]law, that I might win
those *who are* under the law;
21 [a]to [b]those *who are* without
law, as without law [c](not being
without [1]law toward God, but
under [2]law toward Christ), that
I might win those *who are* without law;
22 [a]to the weak I became [1]as
weak, that I might win the weak.
[b]I have become all things to all
men, [c]that I might by all means
save some.
23 Now this I do for the gospel's
sake, that I may be partaker of it
with *you*.
24 Do you not know that those
who run in a race all run, but
one receives the prize? [a]Run in
such a way that you may [1]obtain
it.
25 And everyone who competes
for the prize [1]is temperate in all
things. Now they *do it* to obtain
a perishable crown, but we *for*
[a]an imperishable *crown*.
26 Therefore I run thus: [a]not
with uncertainty. Thus I fight:
not as *one who* beats the air.
27 [a]But I discipline my body
and [b]bring *it* into subjection,
lest, when I have preached to
others, I myself should become
[c]disqualified.

10

Moreover, brethren, I do
not want you to be un-
aware that all our fathers were
under [a]the cloud, all passed
through [b]the sea,
2 all were baptized into Moses
in the cloud and in the sea,
3 all ate the same [a]spiritual
food,
4 and all drank the same [a]spir-
itual drink. For they drank of

11 [a]Rom. 15:27

12 [a][Acts 18:3; 20:33] [b]2 Cor. 11:12

13 [a]Lev. 6:16, 26; 7:6, 31 [b]Num. 18:8–31

14 [a]Matt. 10:10 [b]Rom. 10:15

15 [a]Acts 18:3; 20:33 [b]2 Cor. 11:10

16 [a][Rom. 1:14]

17 [a]1 Cor. 3:8, 14; 9:18 [b]Gal. 2:7

18 [a]1 Cor. 10:33 [b]1 Cor. 7:31; 9:12 [1]NU omits *of Christ*

19 [a]1 Cor. 9:1 [b]Gal. 5:13 [c]Matt. 18:15

20 [a]Acts 16:3; 21:23–26 [1]NU adds *though not being myself under the law*

21 [a][Gal. 2:3; 3:2] [b][Rom. 2:12, 14] [c][1 Cor. 7:22] [1]NU *God's law* [2]NU *Christ's law*

22 [a]Rom. 14:1; 15:1 [b]1 Cor. 10:33 [c]Rom. 11:14 [1]NU omits *as*

24 [a]Gal. 2:2 [1]*win*

25 [a]James 1:12 [1]*exercises self-control*

26 [a]2 Tim. 2:5

27 [a][Rom. 8:13] [b][Rom. 6:18] [c]Jer. 6:30

CHAPTER 10

1 [a]Ex. 13:21, 22 [b]Ex. 14:21, 22, 29

3 [a]Ex. 16:4, 15, 35

4 [a]Ex. 17:5–7

that spiritual Rock that followed
them, and that Rock was Christ.
5 But with most of them God
was not well pleased, for *their*
bodies [a]were scattered in the
wilderness.
6 Now these things became
our examples, to the intent that
we should not lust after evil
things as [a]they also lusted.
7 [a]And do not become idolaters as *were* some of them. As
it is written, [b]*"The people sat*
down to eat and drink, and rose
up to play."
8 [a]Nor let us commit sexual
immorality, as [b]some of them
did, and [c]in one day twenty-
three thousand fell;
9 nor let us [1]tempt Christ, as
[a]some of them also tempted, and
[b]were destroyed by serpents;
10 nor complain, as [a]some of
them also complained, and [b]were
destroyed by [c]the destroyer.
11 Now [1]all these things happened to them as examples, and
[a]they were written for our [2]ad-
monition, [b]upon whom the ends
of the ages have come.
12 Therefore [a]let him who
thinks he stands take heed lest
he fall.
13 No temptation has overtaken
you except such as is common to
man; but [a]God *is* faithful, [b]who
will not allow you to be tempted
beyond what you are able, but
with the temptation will also
make the way of escape, that
you may be able to [1]bear *it*.
14 Therefore, my beloved, [a]flee
from idolatry.
15 I speak as to [a]wise men;
judge for yourselves what I say.
16 [a]The cup of blessing which
we bless, is it not the [1]commu-
nion of the blood of Christ? [b]The
bread which we break, is it not
the communion of the body of
Christ?
17 For [a]we, *though* many, are
one bread *and* one body; for we
all partake of that one bread.
18 Observe [a]Israel [b]after the
flesh: [c]Are not those who eat of
the sacrifices [1]partakers of the
altar?
19 What am I saying then? [a]That
an idol is anything, or what is offered to idols is anything?
20 Rather, that the things which
the Gentiles [a]sacrifice [b]they sacrifice to demons and not to God,
and I do not want you to have
fellowship with demons.
21 [a]You cannot drink the cup
of the Lord and [b]the cup of demons; you cannot partake of the
[c]Lord's table and of the table of
demons.
22 Or do we [a]provoke the Lord
to jealousy? [b]Are we stronger
than He?
23 All things are lawful [1]for me,
but not all things are [a]helpful;
all things are lawful [1]for me, but
not all things [2]edify.
24 Let no one seek his own,
but each one [a]the other's *well-*
being.
25 [a]Eat whatever is sold in the
meat market, asking no questions for conscience' sake;
26 for [a]*"the earth is the* L*ORD's*,
and all its fullness."
27 If any of those who do not
believe invites you *to dinner*,
and you desire to go, [a]eat whatever is set before you, asking no
question for conscience' sake.
28 But if anyone says to you,
"This was offered to idols," do
not eat it [a]for the sake of the one
who told you, and for conscience'

5 [a]Num. 14:29, 37; 26:65
6 [a]Num. 11:4, 34
7 [a]1 Cor. 5:11; 10:14 [b]Ex. 32:6
8 [a]Rev. 2:14 [b]Num. 25:1–9 [c]Ps. 106:29
9 [a]Ex. 17:2, 7 [b]Num. 21:6–9 [1]*test*
10 [a]Ex. 16:2 [b]Num. 14:37 [c]Ex. 12:23
11 [a]Rom. 15:4 [b]Phil. 4:5 [1]NU omits *all* [2]*instruction*
12 [a]Rom. 11:20
13 [a]1 Cor. 1:9 [b]Ps. 125:3 [1]*endure*
14 [a]2 Cor. 6:17
15 [a]1 Cor. 8:1
16 [a]Matt. 26:26–28 [b]Acts 2:42 [1]*fellowship* or *sharing*
17 [a]1 Cor. 12:12, 27
18 [a]Rom. 4:12 [b]Rom. 4:1 [c]Lev. 3:3; 7:6, 14 [1]*fellowshippers* or *sharers*
19 [a]1 Cor. 8:4
20 [a]Lev. 17:7 [b]Deut. 32:17
21 [a]2 Cor. 6:15, 16 [b]Deut. 32:38 [c][1 Cor. 11:23–29]
22 [a]Deut. 32:21 [b]Ezek. 22:14
23 [a]1 Cor. 6:12 [1]NU omits *for me* [2]*build up*
24 [a]Phil. 2:4
25 [a][1 Tim. 4:4]
26 [a]Ps. 24:1
27 [a]Luke 10:7, 8
28 [a][1 Cor. 8:7, 10, 12]

sake; [1]for [b]*"the earth is the LORD's,*
and all its fullness."
29 "Conscience," I say, not your
own, but that of the other. For
[a]why is my liberty judged by
another *man's* conscience?
30 But if I partake with thanks,
why am I evil spoken of for *the*
food [a]over which I give thanks?
31 [a]Therefore, whether you eat
or drink, or whatever you do, do
all to the glory of God.
32 [a]Give no offense, either to
the Jews or to the Greeks or to
the church of God,
33 just [a]as I also please all *men*
in all *things*, not seeking my
own profit, but the *profit* of
many, that they may be saved.

11 Imitate[a] me, just as I also
imitate Christ.
2 Now I praise you, brethren,
that you remember me in all
things and keep the traditions
just as I delivered *them* to you.
3 But I want you to know
that [a]the head of every man is
Christ, [b]the head of woman *is*
man, and [c]the head of Christ
is God.
4 Every man praying or [a]proph-
esying, having *his* head covered,
dishonors his head.
5 But every woman who prays
or prophesies with *her* head uncovered dishonors her head, for
that is one and the same as if her
head were [a]shaved.
6 For if a woman is not covered,
let her also be shorn. But if it
is [a]shameful for a woman to be
shorn or shaved, let her be covered.
7 For a man indeed ought not
to cover *his* head, since [a]he is
the image and glory of God; but
woman is the glory of man.
8 For man is not from woman,
but woman [a]from man.
9 Nor was man created for
the woman, but woman [a]for the
man.
10 For this reason the woman
ought to have *a symbol of* authority on *her* head, because of
the angels.
11 Nevertheless, [a]neither *is* man
independent of woman, nor
woman independent of man, in
the Lord.
12 For as woman *came* from
man, even so man also *comes*
through woman; but all things
are from God.
13 Judge among yourselves. Is
it proper for a woman to pray to
God with her head uncovered?
14 Does not even nature itself
teach you that if a man has long
hair, it is a dishonor to him?
15 But if a woman has long hair,
it is a glory to her; for *her* hair is
given [1]to her for a covering.
16 But [a]if anyone seems to be
contentious, we have no such
custom, [b]nor *do* the churches of
God.
17 Now in giving these instructions I do not praise *you,* since
you come together not for the
better but for the worse.
18 For first of all, when you
come together as a church, [a]I
hear that there are divisions
among you, and in part I believe it.
19 For [a]there must also be factions among you, [b]that those
who are approved may be [1]rec-
ognized among you.
20 Therefore when you come
together in one place, it is not to
eat the Lord's Supper.
21 For in eating, each one takes
his own supper ahead of *others;*

---

28 [b]Ps. 24:1 [1]NU omits the rest of v. 28.
29 [a]Rom. 14:16
30 [a]Rom. 14:6
31 [a]Col. 3:17
32 [a]Rom. 14:13
33 [a]Rom. 15:2

CHAPTER 11

1 [a]Eph. 5:1
3 [a]Eph. 1:22; 4:15; 5:23 [b]Gen. 3:16 [c]John 14:28
4 [a]1 Cor. 12:10
5 [a]Deut. 21:12
6 [a]Num. 5:18
7 [a]Gen. 1:26, 27; 5:1; 9:6
8 [a]Gen. 2:21–23
9 [a]Gen. 2:18
11 [a][Gal. 3:28]
15 [1]M omits *to her*
16 [a]1 Tim. 6:4 [b]1 Cor. 7:17
18 [a]1 Cor. 1:10–12; 3:3
19 [a]1 Tim. 4:1 [b][Deut. 13:3] [1]Lit. *manifest, evident*

and one is hungry and [a]another
is drunk.
22 What! Do you not have
houses to eat and drink in? Or
do you despise [a]the church of
God and [b]shame [1]those who
have nothing? What shall I say
to you? Shall I praise you in
this? I do not praise *you.*
23 For [a]I received from the Lord
that which I also delivered to
you: [b]that the Lord Jesus on the
same night in which He was betrayed took bread;
24 and when He had given
thanks, He broke *it* and said,
[1]"Take, eat; this is My body
which is [2]broken for you; do this
in remembrance of Me."
25 In the same manner *He* also
took the cup after supper, saying, "This cup is the new covenant in My blood. This do, as
often as you drink *it,* in remembrance of Me."
26 For as often as you eat this
bread and drink this cup, you
proclaim the Lord's death [a]till
He comes.
27 Therefore whoever eats [a]this
bread or drinks *this* cup of the
Lord in an unworthy manner
will be guilty of the body and
[1]blood of the Lord.
28 But [a]let a man examine himself, and so let him eat of the
bread and drink of the cup.
29 For he who eats and drinks
[1]in an unworthy manner eats
and drinks judgment to himself,
not discerning the [2]Lord's body.
30 For this reason many *are*
weak and sick among you, and
many [1]sleep.
31 For [a]if we would judge ourselves, we would not be judged.
32 But when we are judged, [a]we
are chastened by the Lord, that
we may not be condemned with
the world.
33 Therefore, my brethren,
when you [a]come together to eat,
wait for one another.
34 But if anyone is hungry, let
him eat at home, lest you come
together for judgment. And the
rest I will set in order when I
come.

12

Now [a]concerning spiri-
tual *gifts,* brethren, I do
not want you to be ignorant:
2 You know [a]that[1] you were
Gentiles, carried away to these
[b]dumb[2] idols, however you were
led.
3 Therefore I make known
to you that no one speaking by
the Spirit of God calls Jesus [1]ac-
cursed, and [a]no one can say that
Jesus is Lord except by the Holy
Spirit.
4 [a]There are [1]diversities of
gifts, but [b]the same Spirit.
5 [a]There are differences of
ministries, but the same Lord.
6 And there are diversities of
activities, but it is the same God
[a]who works [1]all in all.
7 But the manifestation of the
Spirit is given to each one for
the profit *of all:*
8 for to one is given [a]the word
of wisdom through the Spirit, to
another [b]the word of knowledge
through the same Spirit,
9 [a]to another faith by the same
Spirit, to another [b]gifts of healings by [1]the same Spirit,
10 [a]to another the working of
miracles, to another [b]prophecy,
to another [c]discerning of spirits,
to another [d]*different* kinds of
tongues, to another the interpretation of tongues.
11 But one and the same Spirit
works all these things, [a]distributing

21 [a]Jude 12
22 [a]1 Cor. 10:32 [b]James 2:6 [1]The poor
23 [a]1 Cor. 15:3 [b]Matt. 26:26–28
24 [1]NU omits *Take, eat* [2]NU omits *broken*
26 [a]John 14:3
27 [a][John 6:51] [1]NU, M *the blood*
28 [a]2 Cor. 13:5
29 [1]NU omits *in an unworthy manner* [2]NU omits *Lord's*
30 [1]Are dead
31 [a][1 John 1:9]
32 [a]Ps. 94:12
33 [a]1 Cor. 14:26

CHAPTER 12

1 [a]1 Cor. 12:4; 14:1, 37
2 [a]Eph. 2:11 [b]Ps. 115:5 [1]NU, M *that when* [2]*mute, silent*
3 [a]Matt. 16:17 [1]Gr. *anathema*
4 [a]Rom. 12:3–8 [b]Eph. 4:4 [1]*allotments* or *various kinds*
5 [a]Rom. 12:6
6 [a]1 Cor. 15:28 [1]*all things in*
8 [a]1 Cor. 2:6, 7 [b]Rom. 15:14
9 [a]2 Cor. 4:13 [b]Mark 3:15; 16:18 [1]NU *one*
10 [a]Mark 16:17 [b]Rom. 12:6 [c]1 John 4:1 [d]Acts 2:4–11
11 [a]Rom. 12:6

to each one individually [b]as He wills.

12 For [a]as the body is one and has many members, but all the members of that one body, being many, are one body, [b]so also *is* Christ.

13 For [a]by one Spirit we were all baptized into one body—[b]whether Jews or Greeks, whether slaves or free—and [c]have all been made to drink [1]into one Spirit.

14 For in fact the body is not one member but many.

15 If the foot should say, "Because I am not a hand, I am not of the body," is it therefore not of the body?

16 And if the ear should say, "Because I am not an eye, I am not of the body," is it therefore not of the body?

17 If the whole body *were* an eye, where *would be* the hearing? If the whole *were* hearing, where *would be* the smelling?

18 But now [a]God has set the members, each one of them, in the body [b]just as He pleased.

19 And if they were all one member, where *would* the body *be?*

20 But now indeed *there are* many members, yet one body.

21 And the eye cannot say to the hand, "I have no need of you"; nor again the head to the feet, "I have no need of you."

22 No, much rather, those members of the body which seem to be weaker are necessary.

23 And those *members* of the body which we think to be less honorable, on these we bestow greater honor; and our unpresentable *parts* have greater modesty,

24 but our presentable *parts* have no need. But God composed the body, having given greater honor to that *part* which lacks it,

25 that there should be no [1]schism in the body, but *that* the members should have the same care for one another.

26 And if one member suffers, all the members suffer with *it;* or if one member is honored, all the members rejoice with *it.*

27 Now [a]you are the body of Christ, and [b]members individually.

28 And [a]God has appointed these in the church: first [b]apostles, second [c]prophets, third teachers, after that [d]miracles, then [e]gifts of healings, [f]helps, [g]administrations, varieties of tongues.

29 *Are* all apostles? *Are* all prophets? *Are* all teachers? *Are* all workers of miracles?

30 Do all have gifts of healings? Do all speak with tongues? Do all interpret?

31 But [a]earnestly desire the [1]best gifts. And yet I show you a more excellent way.

13

Though I speak with the tongues of men and of angels, but have not love, I have become sounding brass or a clanging cymbal.

2 And though I have *the gift of* [a]prophecy, and understand all mysteries and all knowledge, and though I have all faith, [b]so that I could remove mountains, but have not love, I am nothing.

3 And [a]though I bestow all my goods to feed *the poor,* and though I give my body [1]to be burned, but have not love, it profits me nothing.

4 [a]Love suffers long *and* is [b]kind; love [c]does not envy; love

---

11 [b][John 3:8]

12 [a]Rom. 12:4, 5 [b][Gal. 3:16]

13 [a][Rom. 6:5] [b]Col. 3:11 [c][John 7:37–39] [1]NU omits *into*

18 [a]1 Cor. 12:28 [b]Rom. 12:3

25 [1]*division*

27 [a]Rom. 12:5 [b]Eph. 5:30

28 [a]Eph. 4:11 [b][Eph. 2:20; 3:5] [c]Acts 13:1 [d]1 Cor. 12:10, 29 [e]1 Cor. 12:9, 30 [f]Num. 11:17 [g]Rom. 12:8

31 [a]1 Cor. 14:1, 39 [1]NU *greater*

CHAPTER 13

2 [a]1 Cor. 12:8–10, 28; 14:1 [b]Matt. 17:20; 21:21

3 [a]Matt. 6:1, 2 [1]NU *so I may boast*

4 [a]Prov. 10:12; 17:9 [b]Eph. 4:32 [c]Gal. 5:26

does not parade itself, is not
[1]puffed up;
5 does not behave rudely,
[a]does not seek its own, is not
provoked, [1]thinks no evil;
6 [a]does not rejoice in iniquity,
but [b]rejoices in the truth;
7 [a]bears all things, believes all
things, hopes all things, endures
all things.
8 Love never fails. But whether
there are prophecies, they will
fail; whether *there are* tongues,
they will cease; whether *there is*
knowledge, it will vanish away.
9 [a]For we know in part and we
prophesy in part.
10 But when that which is [1]per-
fect has come, then that which is
in part will be done away.
11 When I was a child, I spoke
as a child, I understood as a
child, I thought as a child; but
when I became a man, I put
away childish things.
12 For [a]now we see in a mirror,
dimly, but then [b]face to face. Now
I know in part, but then I shall
know just as I also am known.
13 And now abide faith, hope,
love, these three; but the greatest of these *is* love.

14

Pursue love, and [a]desire
spiritual *gifts*, [b]but especially that you may prophesy.
2 For he who [a]speaks in a
tongue does not speak to men
but to God, for no one understands *him*; however, in the spirit
he speaks mysteries.
3 But he who prophesies
speaks [a]edification and [b]exhorta-
tion and comfort to men.
4 He who speaks in a tongue
edifies himself, but he who
prophesies edifies the church.
5 I wish you all spoke with
tongues, but even more that you

4 [1]*arrogant*
5 [a]1 Cor. 10:24 [1]*keeps no accounts of evil*
6 [a]Rom. 1:32 [b]2 John 4
7 [a]Gal. 6:2
9 [a]1 Cor. 8:2; 13:12
10 [1]*complete*
12 [a]Phil. 3:12 [b][1 John 3:2]

CHAPTER 14

1 [a]1 Cor. 12:31; 14:39 [b]Num. 11:25, 29
2 [a]Acts 2:4; 10:46
3 [a]Rom. 14:19; 15:2 [b]1 Tim. 4:13
5 [1]NU *and*
6 [a]1 Cor. 14:26
10 [1]*meaning*
11 [1]Lit. *barbarian*
12 [1]*eager* [2]*building up*
13 [a]1 Cor. 12:10
15 [a]Col. 3:16

prophesied; [1]for he who prophesies *is* greater than he who
speaks with tongues, unless
indeed he interprets, that the
church may receive edification.
6 But now, brethren, if I come
to you speaking with tongues,
what shall I profit you unless I speak to you either by
[a]revelation, by knowledge, by
prophesying, or by teaching?
7 Even things without life,
whether flute or harp, when they
make a sound, unless they make
a distinction in the sounds, how
will it be known what is piped or
played?
8 For if the trumpet makes an
uncertain sound, who will prepare for battle?
9 So likewise you, unless you
utter by the tongue words easy
to understand, how will it be
known what is spoken? For you
will be speaking into the air.
10 There are, it may be, so many
kinds of languages in the world,
and none of them *is* without
[1]significance.
11 Therefore, if I do not know
the meaning of the language, I
shall be a [1]foreigner to him who
speaks, and he who speaks *will
be* a foreigner to me.
12 Even so you, since you are
[1]zealous for spiritual *gifts*, *let
it be* for the [2]edification of the
church *that* you seek to excel.
13 Therefore let him who speaks
in a tongue pray that he may
[a]interpret.
14 For if I pray in a tongue, my
spirit prays, but my understanding is unfruitful.
15 What is *the conclusion* then?
I will pray with the spirit, and
I will also pray with the understanding. [a]I will sing with the

spirit, and I will also sing [b]with
the understanding.
16 Otherwise, if you bless with
the spirit, how will he who occu-
pies the place of the uninformed
say "Amen" [a]at your giving of
thanks, since he does not understand what you say?
17 For you indeed give thanks
well, but the other is not edi-
fied.
18 I thank my God I speak with
tongues more than you all;
19 yet in the church I would
rather speak five words with my
understanding, that I may teach
others also, than ten thousand
words in a tongue.
20 Brethren, [a]do not be children
in understanding; however, in
malice [b]be babes, but in understanding be mature.
21 [a]In the law it is written:

[b]*"With men of other tongues*
and other lips
I will speak to this people;
And yet, for all that, they
will not hear Me,"

says the Lord.
22 Therefore tongues are for a
[a]sign, not to those who believe
but to unbelievers; but prophesying is not for unbelievers but
for those who believe.
23 Therefore if the whole church
comes together in one place,
and all speak with tongues, and
there come in *those who are*
uninformed or unbelievers, [a]will
they not say that you are [1]out of
your mind?
24 But if all prophesy, and an
unbeliever or an uninformed
person comes in, he is convinced
by all, he is convicted by all.
25 [1]And thus the secrets of his
heart are revealed; and so, falling down on *his* face, he will
worship God and report [a]that
God is truly among you.
26 How is it then, brethren?
Whenever you come together,
each of you has a psalm, [a]has
a teaching, has a tongue, has
a revelation, has an interpretation. [b]Let all things be done for
[1]edification.
27 If anyone speaks in a tongue,
let there be two or at the most
three, *each* in turn, and let one
interpret.
28 But if there is no interpreter,
let him keep silent in church,
and let him speak to himself and
to God.
29 Let two or three prophets
speak, and [a]let the others judge.
30 But if *anything* is revealed to
another who sits by, [a]let the first
keep silent.
31 For you can all prophesy one
by one, that all may learn and all
may be encouraged.
32 And [a]the spirits of the prophets are subject to the prophets.
33 For God is not *the author* of
[1]confusion but of peace, [a]as in
all the churches of the saints.
34 [a]Let [1]your women keep silent
in the churches, for they are not
permitted to speak; but *they are*
to be submissive, as the [b]law
also says.
35 And if they want to learn
something, let them ask their
own husbands at home; for it is
shameful for women to speak in
church.
36 Or did the word of God come
originally from you? Or *was it*
you only that it reached?
37 [a]If anyone thinks himself to
be a prophet or spiritual, let him
acknowledge that the things

15 [b]Ps. 47:7
16 [a]1 Cor. 11:24
20 [a]Ps. 131:2 [b][1 Pet. 2:2]
21 [a]John 10:34 [b]Is. 28:11, 12
22 [a]Mark 16:17
23 [a]Acts 2:13 [1]*insane*
25 [a]Is. 45:14 [1]NU omits *And thus*
26 [a]1 Cor. 12:8–10; 14:6 [b][2 Cor. 12:19] [1]*building up*
29 [a]1 Cor. 12:10
30 [a][1 Thess. 5:19, 20]
32 [a]1 John 4:1
33 [a]1 Cor. 11:16 [1]*disorder*
34 [a]1 Tim. 2:11 [b]Gen. 3:16 [1]NU omits *your*
37 [a]2 Cor. 10:7

which I write to you are the
commandments of the Lord.
38 But [1]if anyone is ignorant, let
him be ignorant.
39 Therefore, brethren, [a]desire
earnestly to prophesy, and do not
forbid to speak with tongues.
40 [a]Let all things be done decently and in order.

15 Moreover, brethren, I declare to you the gospel
[a]which I preached to you, which
also you received and [b]in which
you stand,
2 [a]by which also you are saved,
if you hold fast that word which
I preached to you—unless [b]you
believed in vain.
★3 For [a]I delivered to you first
of all that [b]which I also received:
that Christ died for our sins
[c]according to the Scriptures,
★4 and that He was buried, and
that He rose again the third day
[a]according to the Scriptures,
5 [a]and that He was seen by
[1]Cē′phas, then [b]by the twelve.
6 After that He was seen by
over five hundred brethren at
once, of whom the greater part
remain to the present, but some
have [1]fallen asleep.
7 After that He was seen by
James, then [a]by all the apostles.
8 [a]Then last of all He was seen
by me also, as by one born out of
due time.
9 For I am [a]the least of the apostles, who am not worthy to be
called an apostle, because [b]I persecuted the church of God.
10 But [a]by the grace of God I am
what I am, and His grace toward
me was not in vain; but I labored
more abundantly than they all,
[b]yet not I, but the grace of God
which was with me.
11 Therefore, whether *it was* I

38 [1]NU *if anyone does not recognize this, he is not recognized.*

39 [a]1 Cor. 12:31

40 [a]1 Cor. 14:33

CHAPTER 15

1 [a][Gal. 1:11] [b][Rom. 5:2; 11:20]

2 [a]Rom. 1:16 [b]Gal. 3:4

3 [a]1 Cor. 11:2, 23 [b][Gal. 1:12] [c]Ps. 22:15; Is. 53:5–12

4 [a]Gen. 1:9–13; Ps. 16:9–11; 68:18; 110:1; Is. 53:10; Hos. 6:2; Jon. 1:17; 2:10

5 [a]Luke 24:34 [b]Matt. 28:17 [1]Peter

6 [1]Died

7 [a]Acts 1:3, 4

8 [a][Acts 9:3–8; 22:6–11; 26:12–18]

9 [a]Eph. 3:8 [b]Acts 8:3

10 [a]Eph. 3:7, 8 [b]Phil. 2:13

13 [a][1 Thess. 4:14]

15 [a]Acts 2:24

17 [a][Rom. 4:25]

18 [a]Job 14:12 [1]Died

19 [a]2 Tim. 3:12

20 [a]1 Pet. 1:3 [b]Acts 26:23 [1]Died

21 [a]Rom. 5:12; 6:23 [b]John 11:25

22 [a][John 5:28, 29]

23 [a][1 Thess. 4:15–17]

24 [a][Dan. 2:44; 7:14, 27; 2 Pet. 1:11]

or they, so we preach and so you
believed.
12 Now if Christ is preached
that He has been raised from the ☆
dead, how do some among you
say that there is no resurrection
of the dead?
13 But if there is no resurrection of the dead, [a]then Christ is
not risen.
14 And if Christ is not risen,
then our preaching *is* empty and
your faith *is* also empty.
15 Yes, and we are found false
witnesses of God, because [a]we
have testified of God that He
raised up Christ, whom He did
not raise up—if in fact the dead
do not rise.
16 For if *the* dead do not rise,
then Christ is not risen.
17 And if Christ is not risen,
your faith *is* futile; [a]you are still
in your sins!
18 Then also those who have
[1]fallen [a]asleep in Christ have perished.
19 [a]If in this life only we have
hope in Christ, we are of all men
the most pitiable.
20 But now [a]Christ is risen from
the dead, *and* has become [b]the
firstfruits of those who have
[1]fallen asleep.
21 For [a]since by man *came*
death, [b]by Man also *came* the
resurrection of the dead.
22 For as in Adam all die, even so
in Christ all shall [a]be made alive.
23 But [a]each one in his own
order: Christ the firstfruits, afterward those *who are* Christ's
at His coming.
24 Then *comes* the end, when ☆
He delivers [a]the kingdom to God
the Father, when He puts an end
to all rule and all authority and
power.

☆ 25 For He must reign [a]till He
has put all enemies under His
feet.
☆ 26 [a]The last enemy *that* will be
destroyed *is* death.
☆ 27 For [a]*"He has put all things*
under His feet." But when He
says "all things are put under
Him," it is evident that He who
put all things under Him is ex-
cepted.
☆ 28 [a]Now when all things are
made subject to Him, then [b]the
Son Himself will also be subject
to Him who put all things under
Him, that God may be all in all.
29 Otherwise, what will they do
who are baptized for the dead, if
the dead do not rise at all? Why
then are they baptized for the
dead?
30 And [a]why do we stand in
[1]jeopardy every hour?
31 I affirm, by [a]the boasting in
you which I have in Christ Jesus
our Lord, [b]I die daily.
32 If, in the manner of men, [a]I
have fought with beasts at Eph′-
e·sus, what advantage *is it* to
me? If *the* dead do not rise, [b]*"Let*
us eat and drink, for tomorrow
we die!"
33 Do not be deceived: [a]"Evil
company corrupts good habits."
34 [a]Awake to righteousness,
and do not sin; [b]for some do not
have the knowledge of God. [c]I
speak *this* to your shame.
35 But someone will say, [a]"How
are the dead raised up? And
with what body do they come?"
36 Foolish one, [a]what you sow is
not made alive unless it dies.
37 And what you sow, you do
not sow that body that shall be,
but mere grain—perhaps wheat
or some other *grain.*
38 But God gives it a body as
He pleases, and to each seed its
own body.
39 All flesh *is* not the same
flesh, but *there is* one *kind* [1]of
flesh of men, another flesh of
animals, another of fish, *and*
another of birds.
40 *There are* also [1]celestial bodies and [2]terrestrial bodies; but
the glory of the celestial *is* one,
and the *glory* of the terrestrial *is*
another.
41 *There is* one glory of the sun,
another glory of the moon, and
another glory of the stars; for
one star differs from *another*
star in glory.
42 [a]So also *is* the resurrection
of the dead. *The body* is sown in
corruption, it is raised in incorruption.
43 [a]It is sown in dishonor, it
is raised in glory. It is sown in
weakness, it is raised in power.
44 It is sown a natural body, it
is raised a spiritual body. There
is a natural body, and there is a
spiritual body.
45 And so it is written, [a]*"The*
first man Adam became a living
being." [b]The last Adam *became*
[c]a life-giving spirit.
46 However, the spiritual is not
first, but the natural, and afterward the spiritual.
47 [a]The first man *was* of the
earth, [b]*made*[1] of dust; the second
Man *is* [2]the Lord [c]from heaven.
48 As *was* the [1]*man* of dust, so
also *are* those *who are* [1]*made*
of dust; [a]and as *is* the heavenly
Man, so also *are* those *who are*
heavenly.
49 And [a]as we have borne the
image of the *man* of dust, [b]we[1]
shall also bear the image of the
heavenly *Man.*
50 Now this I say, brethren, that

25 [a]Ps. 110:1; Matt. 22:44
26 [a][2 Tim. 1:10; Rev. 20:14; 21:4]
27 [a]Ps. 8:6; 110:1
28 [a][Phil. 3:21] [b]1 Cor. 3:23; 11:3; 12:6
30 [a]2 Cor. 11:26 [1]*danger*
31 [a]1 Thess. 2:19 [b]Rom. 8:36
32 [a]2 Cor. 1:8 [b]Is. 22:13; 56:12
33 [a][1 Cor. 5:6]
34 [a]Rom. 13:11 [b][1 Thess. 4:5] [c]1 Cor. 6:5
35 [a]Ezek. 37:3
36 [a]John 12:24
39 [1]NU, M omit *of flesh*
40 [1]*heavenly* [2]*earthly*
42 [a][Dan. 12:3]
43 [a][Phil. 3:21]
45 [a]Gen. 2:7 [b][Rom. 5:14] [c]John 5:21; 6:57
47 [a]John 3:31 [b]Gen. 2:7; 3:19 [c]John 3:13 [1]*earthy* [2]NU omits *the Lord*
48 [a]Phil. 3:20 [1]*earthy*
49 [a]Gen. 5:3 [b]Rom. 8:29 [1]M *let us also bear*

[a]flesh and blood cannot inherit
the kingdom of God; nor does
corruption inherit incorruption.
51 Behold, I tell you a [1]mystery:
[a]We shall not all sleep, [b]but we
shall all be changed—
52 in a moment, in the twin-
kling of an eye, at the last trumpet. [a]For the trumpet will sound,
and the dead will be raised
incorruptible, and we shall be
changed.
53 For this corruptible must put
on incorruption, and [a]this mortal *must* put on immortality.
54 So when this corruptible has
put on incorruption, and this
mortal has put on immortality,
then shall be brought to pass the
saying that is written: [a]*"Death is*
swallowed up in victory."

55 *"O*[a1] *Death, where is your*
sting?
O Hā'dēs, where is your
victory?"

56 The sting of death *is* sin, and
[a]the strength of sin *is* the law.
57 [a]But thanks *be* to God, who
gives us [b]the victory through our
Lord Jesus Christ.
58 [a]Therefore, my beloved brethren, be steadfast, immovable, always abounding in the work of
the Lord, knowing [b]that your labor is not in vain in the Lord.

16 Now concerning [a]the
collection for the saints,
as I have given orders to the
churches of Galatia, so you must
do also:
2 [a]On the first *day* of the week
let each one of you lay something aside, storing up as he
may prosper, that there be no
collections when I come.
3 And when I come, [a]whomever
you approve by *your* letters I
will send to bear your gift to
Jerusalem.
4 [a]But if it is fitting that I go
also, they will go with me.
5 Now I will come to you [a]when
I pass through Mac·e·dō'ni·a (for
I am passing through Mac·e·dō'-
ni·a).
6 And it may be that I will remain, or even spend the winter
with you, that you may [a]send me
on my journey, wherever I go.
7 For I do not wish to see you
now on the way; but I hope to
stay a while with you, [a]if the
Lord permits.
8 But I will tarry in Eph'e·sus
until [a]Pentecost.
9 For [a]a great and effective
door has opened to me, and
[b]*there are* many adversaries.
10 And [a]if Timothy comes, see
that he may be with you without
fear; for [b]he does the work of the
Lord, as I also *do*.
11 [a]Therefore let no one despise
him. But send him on his journey [b]in peace, that he may come
to me; for I am waiting for him
with the brethren.
12 Now concerning *our* brother
[a]A·pol'los, I strongly urged him
to come to you with the brethren, but he was quite unwilling
to come at this time; however, he
will come when he has a convenient time.
13 [a]Watch, [b]stand fast in the
faith, be brave, [c]be strong.
14 [a]Let all *that* you *do* be done
with love.
15 I urge you, brethren—you
know [a]the household of Steph'-
a·nas, that it is [b]the firstfruits
of A·chā'i·a, and *that* they have
devoted themselves to [c]the ministry of the saints—

50 [a][John 3:3, 5]
51 [a][1 Thess. 4:15] [b][Phil. 3:21] [1]*hidden truth*
52 [a]Matt. 24:31
53 [a]2 Cor. 5:4
54 [a]Is. 25:8
55 [a]Hos. 13:14 [1]NU *O Death, where is your victory? O Death, where is your sting?*
56 [a][Rom. 3:20; 4:15; 7:8]
57 [a][Rom. 7:25] [b][1 John 5:4]
58 [a]2 Pet. 3:14 [b][1 Cor. 3:8]

CHAPTER 16

1 [a]Gal. 2:10
2 [a]Acts 20:7
3 [a]2 Cor. 3:1; 8:18
4 [a]2 Cor. 8:4, 19
5 [a]2 Cor. 1:15, 16
6 [a]Acts 15:3
7 [a]James 4:15
8 [a]Lev. 23:15–22
9 [a]Acts 14:27 [b]Acts 19:9
10 [a]Acts 19:22 [b]Phil. 2:20
11 [a]1 Tim. 4:12 [b]Acts 15:33
12 [a]1 Cor. 1:12; 3:5
13 [a]Matt. 24:42 [b]Phil. 1:27; 4:1 [c][Eph. 3:16; 6:10]
14 [a][1 Pet. 4:8]
15 [a]1 Cor. 1:16 [b]Rom. 16:5 [c]2 Cor. 8:4

16 [a]that you also submit to such,
and to everyone who works and
[b]labors with *us.*
17 I am glad about the coming of Steph'a·nas, For·tu·nā'tus,
and A·chā'i·cus, [a]for what was
lacking on your part they supplied.
18 [a]For they refreshed my spirit
and yours. Therefore [b]acknowl-
edge such men.
19 The churches of Asia greet
you. A·qui'la and Pri·scil'la
greet you heartily in the Lord,
[a]with the church that is in their
house.
20 All the brethren greet you.
[a]Greet one another with a holy
kiss.
21 [a]The salutation with my own
hand—Paul's.
22 If anyone [a]does not love the
Lord Jesus Christ, [b]let him be
[1]accursed. [c]O[2] Lord, come!
23 [a]The grace of our Lord Jesus
Christ *be* with you.
24 My love *be* with you all in
Christ Jesus. Amen.

16 [a]Heb. 13:17 [b][Heb. 6:10]
17 [a]2 Cor. 11:9
18 [a]Col. 4:8 [b]Phil. 2:29
19 [a]Rom. 16:5
20 [a]Rom. 16:16
21 [a]Col. 4:18
22 [a]Eph. 6:24 [b]Gal. 1:8, 9 [c]Jude 14, 15 [1]Gr. *anathema* [2]Aram. *Marana tha;* possibly *Maran atha, Our Lord has come*
23 [a]Rom. 16:20

The Second Epistle of Paul the Apostle to the

CORINTHIANS

SINCE Paul's first letter, the Corinthian church had been swayed by false teachers who stirred the people against Paul. They claimed he was fickle, proud, unimpressive in appearance and speech, dishonest, and unqualified as an apostle of Jesus Christ. Paul sent Titus to Corinth to deal with these difficulties, and upon his return, rejoiced to hear of the Corinthians' change of heart. Paul wrote this letter to express his thanksgiving for the repentant majority and to appeal to the rebellious minority to accept his authority. Throughout the book he defends his conduct, character, and calling as an apostle of Jesus Christ.

To distinguish this epistle from First Corinthians, it was given the title *Pros Korinthious B,* the "Second to the Corinthians." The *A* and *B* were probably later additions to *Pros Korinthious.*

PAUL, [a]an apostle of Jesus Christ by the will of God, and [b]Timothy *our* brother,

To the church of God which is at Corinth, [c]with all the saints who are in all A·chā'i·a:

2 [a]Grace to you and peace from God our Father and the Lord Jesus Christ.

3 [a]Blessed *be* the God and Father of our Lord Jesus Christ, the Father of mercies and God of all comfort,
4 who [a]comforts us in all our tribulation, that we may be able to comfort those who are in any [1]trouble, with the comfort with which we ourselves are comforted by God.
5 For as [a]the sufferings of Christ abound in us, so our [1]consolation also abounds through Christ.
6 Now if we are afflicted, [a]*it is* for your consolation and salvation, which is effective for enduring the same sufferings which we also suffer. Or if we are comforted, *it is* for your consolation and salvation.
7 And our hope for you *is* steadfast, because we know that [a]as you are partakers of the sufferings, so also *you will partake* of the consolation.
8 For we do not want you to be ignorant, brethren, of [a]our [1]trouble which came to us in Asia: that we were burdened beyond measure, above strength, so that we despaired even of life.
9 Yes, we had the sentence of death in ourselves, that we should [a]not trust in ourselves but in God who raises the dead,
10 [a]who delivered us from so great a death, and [1]does deliver us; in whom we trust that He will still deliver *us,*
11 you also [a]helping together in prayer for us, that thanks may be given by many persons on [1]our behalf [b]for the gift *granted* to us through many.
12 For our boasting is this: the

CHAPTER 1

1 [a]2 Tim. 1:1
[b]1 Cor. 16:10
[c]Col. 1:2

2 [a]Rom. 1:7

3 [a]1 Pet. 1:3

4 [a]Is. 51:12; 66:13
[1]*tribulation*

5 [a]2 Cor. 4:10
[1]*comfort*

6 [a]2 Cor. 4:15; 12:15

7 [a][Rom. 8:17]

8 [a]Acts 19:23
[1]*tribulation*

9 [a]Jer. 17:5, 7

10 [a][2 Pet. 2:9]
[1]NU *shall*

11 [a]Rom. 15:30
[b]2 Cor. 4:15; 9:11
[1]M *your behalf*

testimony of our conscience that
we conducted ourselves in the
world in [1]simplicity and [a]godly
sincerity, [b]not with fleshly wisdom but by the grace of God,
and more abundantly toward
you.
13 For we are not writing any
other things to you than what
you read or understand. Now I
trust you will understand, even
to the end
14 (as also you have understood
us in part), [a]that we are your
boast as [b]you also *are* ours, in
the day of the Lord Jesus.
15 And in this confidence [a]I intended to come to you before,
that you might have [b]a second
benefit—
16 to pass by way of you to
Mac·e·dō′ni·a, [a]to come again
from Mac·e·dō′ni·a to you, and
be helped by you on my way to
Judea.
17 Therefore, when I was plan-
ning this, did I do it lightly? Or
the things I plan, do I plan [a]ac-
cording to the flesh, that with
me there should be Yes, Yes, and
No, No?
18 But *as* God *is* [a]faithful, our
[1]word to you was not Yes and
No.
19 For [a]the Son of God, Jesus
Christ, who was preached among
you by us—by me, [b]Sil·vā′nus,
and [c]Timothy—was not Yes and
No, [d]but in Him was Yes.
20 [a]For all the promises of God
in Him *are* Yes, and in Him Amen,
to the glory of God through us.
21 Now He who establishes
us with you in Christ and [a]has
anointed us *is* God,
22 who [a]also has sealed us and
[b]given us the Spirit in our hearts
as a guarantee.

12 [a]2 Cor. 2:17 [b][1 Cor. 2:4] [1]The opposite of duplicity
14 [a]2 Cor. 5:12 [b]Phil. 2:16
15 [a]1 Cor. 4:19 [b]Rom. 1:11; 15:29
16 [a]1 Cor. 16:3–6
17 [a]2 Cor. 10:2; 11:18
18 [a]1 John 5:20 [1]*message*
19 [a]Mark 1:1 [b]1 Pet. 5:12 [c]2 Cor. 1:1 [d][Heb. 13:8]
20 [a][Rom. 15:8, 9]
21 [a][1 John 2:20, 27]
22 [a][Eph. 4:30] [b][Eph. 1:14]
23 [a]Gal. 1:20 [b]1 Cor. 4:21
24 [a][1 Pet. 5:3] [b]Rom. 11:20 [1]*rule*

CHAPTER 2

1 [a]2 Cor. 1:23
2 [a]2 Cor. 7:8
3 [a]2 Cor. 12:21 [b]Gal. 5:10
4 [a][2 Cor. 2:9; 7:8, 12] [1]*tribulation*
5 [a][1 Cor. 5:1] [b]Gal. 4:12
6 [a]1 Cor. 5:4, 5
7 [a]Gal. 6:1
9 [a]2 Cor. 7:15; 10:6
10 [1]NU *indeed, what I have forgiven, if I have forgiven anything, I did it for your sakes*

23 Moreover [a]I call God as witness against my soul, [b]that to
spare you I came no more to
Corinth.
24 Not [a]that we [1]have dominion
over your faith, but are fellow
workers for your joy; for [b]by
faith you stand.
2 But I determined this within
myself, [a]that I would not
come again to you in sorrow.
2 For if I make you [a]sorrowful,
then who is he who makes me
glad but the one who is made
sorrowful by me?
3 And I wrote this very thing
to you, lest, when I came, [a]I
should have sorrow over those
from whom I ought to have joy,
[b]having confidence in you all
that my joy is *the joy* of you all.
4 For out of much [1]affliction
and anguish of heart I wrote to
you, with many tears, [a]not that
you should be grieved, but that
you might know the love which
I have so abundantly for you.
5 But [a]if anyone has caused
grief, he has not [b]grieved me, but
all of you to some extent—not to
be too severe.
6 This punishment which *was*
inflicted [a]by the majority *is* sufficient for such a man,
7 [a]so that, on the contrary, you
ought rather to forgive and comfort *him,* lest perhaps such a one
be swallowed up with too much
sorrow.
8 Therefore I urge you to reaf-
firm *your* love to him.
9 For to this end I also wrote,
that I might put you to the test,
whether you are [a]obedient in all
things.
10 Now whom you forgive anything, I also *forgive.* For [1]if indeed I have forgiven anything, I

have forgiven that one for your
sakes in the presence of Christ,
11 lest Satan should take advantage of us; for we are not
ignorant of his devices.
12 Furthermore, [a]when I came
to Trō'as to *preach* Christ's gospel, and [b]a [1]door was opened to
me by the Lord,
13 [a]I had no rest in my spirit,
because I did not find Titus my
brother; but taking my leave of
them, I departed for Mac·e·dō'-
ni·a.
14 Now thanks *be* to God who
always leads us in triumph in
Christ, and through us [1]diffuses
the fragrance of His knowledge
in every place.
15 For we are to God the fragrance of Christ [a]among those
who are being saved and [b]among
those who are perishing.
16 [a]To the one *we are* the aroma
of death *leading* to death, and to
the other the aroma of life *leading* to life. And [b]who *is* sufficient
for these things?
17 For we are not, as [1]so many,
[a]peddling[2] the word of God; but
as [b]of sincerity, but as from God,
we speak in the sight of God in
Christ.

3 Do [a]we begin again to commend ourselves? Or do we
need, as some *others,* [b]epistles of
commendation to you or *letters*
of commendation from you?
2 [a]You are our epistle written
in our hearts, known and read
by all men;
3 clearly you are an epistle of
Christ, [a]ministered by us, written not with ink but by the Spirit
of the living God, not [b]on tablets
of stone but [c]on tablets of flesh,
that is, of the heart.

12 [a]Acts 16:8 [b]1 Cor. 16:9 [1]Opportunity
13 [a]2 Cor. 7:6, 13; 8:6
14 [1]*manifests*
15 [a][1 Cor. 1:18] [b][2 Cor. 4:3]
16 [a]Luke 2:34 [b][1 Cor. 15:10]
17 [a]2 Pet. 2:3 [b]2 Cor. 1:12 [1]M *the rest* [2]*adulterating for gain*

CHAPTER 3

1 [a]2 Cor. 5:12; 10:12, 18; 12:11 [b]Acts 18:27
2 [a]1 Cor. 9:2
3 [a]1 Cor. 3:5 [b]Ex. 24:12; 31:18; 32:15 [c]Ps. 40:8
5 [a][John 15:5] [b]1 Cor. 15:10
6 [a]1 Cor. 3:5 [b]Jer. 31:31 [c]Rom. 2:27 [d]Gal. 3:10 [e]John 6:63 [1]Or *spirit*
7 [a]Rom. 7:10 [b]Ex. 34:1 [c]Ex. 34:29
8 [a][Gal. 3:5]
9 [a][Rom. 1:17; 3:21]
12 [a]Eph. 6:19
13 [a]Ex. 34:33–35 [b][Gal. 3:23]
14 [a]Is. 6:9, 10; Acts 28:26

4 And we have such trust
through Christ toward God.
5 [a]Not that we are sufficient of
ourselves to think of anything as
being from ourselves, but [b]our
sufficiency *is* from God,
6 who also made us sufficient
as [a]ministers of [b]the new covenant, not [c]of the letter but of
the [1]Spirit; for [d]the letter kills,
[e]but the Spirit gives life.
7 But if [a]the ministry of death,
[b]written *and* engraved on stones,
was glorious, [c]so that the children of Israel could not look
steadily at the face of Moses because of the glory of his countenance, which *glory* was passing
away,
8 how will [a]the ministry of the
Spirit not be more glorious?
9 For if the ministry of condemnation *had* glory, the ministry [a]of righteousness exceeds
much more in glory.
10 For even what was made glorious had no glory in this respect, because of the glory that
excels.
11 For if what is passing away
was glorious, what remains *is*
much more glorious.
12 Therefore, since we have
such hope, [a]we use great boldness of speech—
13 unlike Moses, [a]*who* put a veil
over his face so that the children
of Israel could not look steadily
at [b]the end of what was passing
away.
14 But [a]their minds were blinded. ★
For until this day the same veil
remains unlifted in the reading
of the Old Testament, because the
veil is taken away in Christ.
15 But even to this day, when
Moses is read, a veil lies on their
heart.

16 Nevertheless [a]when one turns to the Lord, [b]the veil is taken away.

17 Now [a]the Lord is the Spirit; and where the Spirit of the Lord *is*, there *is* [b]liberty.

18 But we all, with unveiled face, beholding [a]as in a mirror [b]the glory of the Lord, [c]are being transformed into the same image from glory to glory, just as [1]by the Spirit of the Lord.

4 Therefore, since we have this ministry, [a]as we have received mercy, we [b]do not lose heart.

2 But we have renounced the hidden things of shame, not walking in craftiness nor [1]handling the word of God deceitfully, but by manifestation of the truth [a]commending ourselves to every man's conscience in the sight of God.

3 But even if our gospel is veiled, [a]it is veiled to those who are perishing,

4 whose minds [a]the god of this age [b]has blinded, who do not believe, lest [c]the light of the gospel of the glory of Christ, [d]who is the image of God, should shine on them.

5 [a]For we do not preach ourselves, but Christ Jesus the Lord, and [b]ourselves your bondservants for Jesus' sake.

6 For it is the God [a]who commanded light to shine out of darkness, who has [b]shone in our hearts to *give* the light of the knowledge of the glory of God in the face of Jesus Christ.

7 But we have this treasure in earthen vessels, [a]that the excellence of the power may be of God and not of us.

8 *We are* [a]hard-pressed on every side, yet not crushed; *we are* perplexed, but not in despair;

9 persecuted, but not [a]forsaken; [b]struck down, but not destroyed—

10 [a]always carrying about in the body the dying of the Lord Jesus, [b]that the life of Jesus also may be manifested in our body.

11 For we who live [a]are always delivered to death for Jesus' sake, that the life of Jesus also may be manifested in our mortal flesh.

12 So then death is working in us, but life in you.

13 And since we have [a]the same spirit of faith, according to what is written, [b]*"I believed and therefore I spoke,"* we also believe and therefore speak,

14 knowing that [a]He who raised up the Lord Jesus will also raise us up with Jesus, and will present *us* with you.

15 For [a]all things *are* for your sakes, that [b]grace, having spread through the many, may cause thanksgiving to abound to the glory of God.

16 Therefore we [a]do not lose heart. Even though our outward man is perishing, yet the inward *man* is [b]being renewed day by day.

17 For [a]our light affliction, which is but for a moment, is working for us a far more exceeding *and* eternal weight of glory,

18 [a]while we do not look at the things which are seen, but at the things which are not seen. For the things which are seen *are* temporary, but the things which are not seen *are* eternal.

5 For we know that if [a]our earthly [1]house, *this* tent, is destroyed, we have a building from

16 [a]Rom. 11:23 [b]Is. 25:7
17 [a][1 Cor. 15:45] [b]Gal. 5:1, 13
18 [a]1 Cor. 13:12 [b][2 Cor. 4:4, 6] [c][Rom. 8:29, 30] [1]Or *from the Lord, the Spirit*

CHAPTER 4

1 [a]1 Cor. 7:25 [b]2 Cor. 4:16
2 [a]2 Cor. 5:11 [1]*adulterating the word of God*
3 [a][1 Cor. 1:18]
4 [a]John 12:31 [b]John 12:40 [c][2 Cor. 3:8, 9] [d][John 1:18]
5 [a]1 Cor. 1:13 [b]1 Cor. 9:19
6 [a]Gen. 1:3 [b]2 Pet. 1:19
7 [a]1 Cor. 2:5
8 [a]2 Cor. 1:8; 7:5
9 [a][Heb. 13:5] [b]Ps. 37:24
10 [a]Phil. 3:10 [b]Rom. 8:17
11 [a]Rom. 8:36
13 [a]2 Pet. 1:1 [b]Ps. 116:10
14 [a][Rom. 8:11]
15 [a]Col. 1:24 [b]2 Cor. 1:11
16 [a]2 Cor. 4:1 [b][Is. 40:29, 31]
17 [a]Rom. 8:18
18 [a][Heb. 11:1, 13]

CHAPTER 5

1 [a]Job 4:19 [1]Physical body

God, a house [b]not made with
hands, eternal in the heavens.
2 For in this [a]we groan, earnestly desiring to be clothed with
our [1]habitation which is from
heaven,
3 if indeed, [a]having been
clothed, we shall not be found
naked.
4 For we who are in *this* tent
groan, being burdened, not because we want to be unclothed,
[a]but further clothed, that mortality may be swallowed up by life.
5 Now He who has prepared
us for this very thing *is* God,
who also [a]has given us the Spirit
as [1]a guarantee.
6 So *we are* always confident,
knowing that while we are at
home in the body we are absent
from the Lord.
7 For [a]we walk by faith, not by
sight.
8 We are confident, yes, [a]well
pleased rather to be absent from
the body and to be present with
the Lord.
9 Therefore we make it our
aim, whether present or absent,
to be well pleasing to Him.
☆ 10 [a]For we must all appear before the judgment seat of Christ,
[b]that each one may receive the
things *done* in the body, according to what he has done,
whether good or bad.
11 Knowing, therefore, [a]the terror of the Lord, we persuade
men; but we are well known to
God, and I also trust are well
known in your consciences.
12 For [a]we do not commend
ourselves again to you, but give
you opportunity [b]to boast on our
behalf, that you may have *an
answer* for those who boast in
appearance and not in heart.

1 [b]Mark 14:58
2 [a]Rom. 8:23 [1]*dwelling*
3 [a]Rev. 3:18
4 [a]1 Cor. 15:53
5 [a]Rom. 8:23 [1]*down payment, earnest*
7 [a]Heb. 11:1
8 [a]Phil. 1:23
10 [a]Matt. 16:27; Acts 10:42; Rom. 2:16; 14:10, 12 [b]Gal. 6:7; Eph. 6:8
11 [a][Heb. 10:31; 12:29]
12 [a]2 Cor. 3:1 [b]2 Cor. 1:14
13 [a]2 Cor. 11:1, 16; 12:11
14 [a][Rom. 5:15; 6:6]
15 [a][Rom. 6:11]
16 [a]2 Cor. 10:3 [b][Matt. 12:50]
17 [a][John 6:63] [b][Rom. 8:9] [c]Is. 43:18; 65:17 [d][Rom. 6:3–10]
18 [a]Rom. 5:10
19 [a][Rom. 3:24] [1]*reckoning*
20 [a]Eph. 6:20
21 [a]Is. 53:6, 9 [b][Rom. 1:17; 3:21]; 1 Cor. 1:30

CHAPTER 6

1 [a]1 Cor. 3:9 [b]2 Cor. 5:20

13 For [a]if we are beside ourselves, *it is* for God; or if we are
of sound mind, *it is* for you.
14 For the love of Christ compels us, because we judge thus:
that [a]if One died for all, then all
died;
15 and He died for all, [a]that
those who live should live no
longer for themselves, but for
Him who died for them and rose
again.
16 [a]Therefore, from now on,
we regard no one according to
the flesh. Even though we have
known Christ according to the
flesh, [b]yet now we know *Him
thus* no longer.
17 Therefore, if anyone [a]*is* in
Christ, *he is* [b]a new creation;
[c]old things have passed away;
behold, all things have become
[d]new.
18 Now all things *are* of God,
[a]who has reconciled us to Himself through Jesus Christ, and
has given us the ministry of reconciliation,
19 that is, that [a]God was in Christ
reconciling the world to Himself,
not [1]imputing their trespasses to
them, and has committed to us
the word of reconciliation.
20 Now then, we are [a]ambassa-
dors for Christ, as though God
were pleading through us: we
implore *you* on Christ's behalf,
be reconciled to God.
21 For [a]He made Him who knew ★
no sin *to be* sin for us, that we
might become [b]the righteousness of God in Him.

6

We then, *as* [a]workers together *with Him* also [b]plead
with *you* not to receive the grace
of God in vain.
2 For He says: ★

[a]*"In an acceptable time I have*
heard you,
And in the day of salvation I
have helped you."
Behold, now *is* the accepted
time; behold, now *is* the day of
salvation.
3 [a]We give no offense in anything, that our ministry may not
be blamed.
4 But in all *things* we commend ourselves [a]as ministers of
God: in much [1]patience, in tribulations, in needs, in distresses,
5 [a]in stripes, in imprisonments,
in tumults, in labors, in sleeplessness, in fastings;
6 by purity, by knowledge, by
longsuffering, by kindness, by
the Holy Spirit, by [1]sincere love,
7 [a]by the word of truth, by [b]the
power of God, by [c]the armor of
righteousness on the right hand
and on the left,
8 by honor and dishonor, by
evil report and good report; as
deceivers, and *yet* true;
9 as unknown, and [a]*yet* well
known; [b]as dying, and behold
we live; [c]as chastened, and *yet*
not killed;
10 as sorrowful, yet always
rejoicing; as poor, yet making
many [a]rich; as having nothing,
and *yet* possessing all things.
11 O Corinthians! [1]We have spoken openly to you, [a]our heart is
wide open.
12 You are not restricted by us,
but [a]you are restricted by your
own affections.
13 Now in return for the same
[a](I speak as to children), you
also be open.
14 [a]Do not be unequally yoked
together with unbelievers. For
[b]what [1]fellowship has righteousness with lawlessness? And what
[2]communion has light with darkness?
15 And what accord has Christ
with Bē′li·al? Or what part has a
believer with an unbeliever?
16 And what agreement has the
temple of God with idols? For
[a]you[1] are the temple of the living
God. As God has said:

[b]*"I will dwell in them*
And walk among them.
I will be their God,
And they shall be My
people."

17 Therefore

[a]*"Come out from among them*
And be separate, says the
Lord.
Do not touch what is
unclean,
And I will receive you."
18 *"I* [a]*will be a Father to you,*
And you shall be My [b]*sons*
and daughters,
Says the LORD *Almighty."*

7

Therefore,[a] having these
promises, beloved, let us
cleanse ourselves from all filthiness of the flesh and spirit, per-
fecting holiness in the fear of
God.
2 Open *your hearts* to us. We
have wronged no one, we have
corrupted no one, [a]we have
cheated no one.
3 I do not say *this* to condemn;
for [a]I have said before that you
are in our hearts, to die together
and to live together.
4 [a]Great *is* my boldness of
speech toward you, [b]great *is*
my boasting on your behalf. [c]I
am filled with comfort. I am

2 [a]Is. 49:8
3 [a]Rom. 14:13
4 [a]1 Cor. 4:1 [1]*endurance*
5 [a]2 Cor. 11:23
6 [1]Lit. *unhypocritical*
7 [a]2 Cor. 7:14 [b]1 Cor. 2:4 [c]2 Cor. 10:4
9 [a]2 Cor. 4:2; 5:11 [b]1 Cor. 4:9, 11 [c]Ps. 118:18
10 [a][2 Cor. 8:9]
11 [a]2 Cor. 7:3 [1]Lit. *Our mouth is open*
12 [a]2 Cor. 12:15
13 [a]1 Cor. 4:14
14 [a]1 Cor. 5:9 [b]Eph. 5:6, 7, 11 [1]*in common* [2]*fellowship*
16 [a][1 Cor. 3:16, 17; 6:19] [b]Ezek. 37:26, 27 [1]NU *we*
17 [a]Is. 52:11
18 [a]2 Sam. 7:14 [b][Rom. 8:14]

CHAPTER 7

1 [a][1 John 3:3]
2 [a]Acts 20:33
3 [a]2 Cor. 6:11, 12
4 [a]2 Cor. 3:12 [b]1 Cor. 1:4 [c]Phil. 2:17

exceedingly joyful in all our
tribulation.
5 For indeed, [a]when we came
to Mac·e·dō′ni·a, our bodies had
no rest, but [b]we were troubled
on every side. [c]Outside *were*
conflicts, inside *were* fears.
6 Nevertheless [a]God, who comforts the downcast, comforted
us by [b]the coming of Titus,
7 and not only by his coming,
but also by the [1]consolation with
which he was comforted in you,
when he told us of your earnest
desire, your mourning, your zeal
for me, so that I rejoiced even
more.
8 For even if I made you [a]sorry
with my letter, I do not regret
it; [b]though I did regret it. For I
perceive that the same epistle
made you sorry, though only for
a while.
9 Now I rejoice, not that you
were made sorry, but that your
sorrow led to repentance. For
you were made sorry in a godly
manner, that you might suffer
loss from us in nothing.
10 For [a]godly sorrow produces
repentance *leading* to salvation,
not to be regretted; [b]but the
sorrow of the world produces
death.
11 For observe this very thing,
that you sorrowed in a godly
manner: What diligence it produced in you, *what* [a]clearing
of yourselves, *what* indignation,
what fear, *what* vehement desire, *what* zeal, *what* vindication! In all *things* you proved
yourselves to be [b]clear in this
matter.
12 Therefore, although I wrote
to you, *I did* not *do it* for the
sake of him who had done the
wrong, nor for the sake of him
who suffered wrong, [a]but that
our care for you in the sight of
God might appear to you.
13 Therefore we have been
comforted in your comfort. And
we rejoiced exceedingly more
for the joy of Titus, because his
spirit [a]has been refreshed by
you all.
14 For if in anything I have
boasted to him about you, I am
not ashamed. But as we spoke
all things to you in truth, even so
our boasting to Titus was found
true.
15 And his affections are greater
for you as he remembers [a]the
obedience of you all, how with
fear and trembling you received
him.
16 Therefore I rejoice that [a]I
have confidence in you in everything.

8 Moreover, brethren, we
make known to you the
grace of God bestowed on the
churches of Mac·e·dō′ni·a:
2 that in a great trial of affliction the abundance of their
joy and [a]their deep poverty
abounded in the riches of their
liberality.
3 For I bear witness that according to *their* ability, yes, and
beyond *their* ability, *they were*
freely willing,
4 imploring us with much urgency [1]that we would receive the
gift and [a]the fellowship of the
ministering to the saints.
5 And not *only* as we had
hoped, but they first [a]gave themselves to the Lord, and *then* to
us by the [b]will of God.
6 So [a]we urged Titus, that as
he had begun, so he would also
complete this grace in you as
well.

5 [a]2 Cor. 2:13 [b]2 Cor. 4:8 [c]Deut. 32:25
6 [a]2 Cor. 1:3, 4 [b]2 Cor. 2:13; 7:13
7 [1]*comfort*
8 [a]2 Cor. 2:2 [b]2 Cor. 2:4
10 [a]Matt. 26:75 [b]Prov. 17:22
11 [a]Eph. 5:11 [b]2 Cor. 2:5–11
12 [a]2 Cor. 2:4
13 [a]Rom. 15:32
15 [a]2 Cor. 2:9
16 [a]2 Thess. 3:4

CHAPTER 8

2 [a]Mark 12:44
4 [a]Rom. 15:25, 26 [1]NU, M omit *that we would receive,* thus changing text to *urgency for the favor and fellowship*
5 [a][Rom. 12:1, 2] [b][Eph. 6:6]
6 [a]2 Cor. 8:17; 12:18

7 But as [a]you abound in everything—in faith, in speech, in
knowledge, in all diligence, and
in your love for us—*see* [b]that
you abound in this grace also.
8 [a]I speak not by commandment, but I am testing the sincerity of your love by the diligence of others.
9 For you know the grace of
our Lord Jesus Christ, [a]that
though He was rich, yet for your
sakes He became poor, that you
through His poverty might become [b]rich.
10 And in this [a]I give advice: [b]It
is to your advantage not only to
be doing what you began and
[c]were desiring to do a year ago;
11 but now you also must complete the doing *of it;* that as
there was a readiness to desire
it, so *there* also *may be* a completion out of what *you* have.
12 For [a]if there is first a willing
mind, *it is* accepted according to
what one has, *and* not according
to what he does not have.
13 For *I do* not *mean* that others
should be eased and you burdened;
14 but by an equality, *that* now
at this time your abundance
may supply their lack, that their
abundance also may *supply* your
lack—that there may be equality.
15 As it is written, [a]*"He who*
gathered much had nothing left
over, and he who gathered little
had no lack."
16 But thanks *be* to God who
[1]puts the same earnest care for
you into the heart of Titus.
17 For he not only accepted the
exhortation, but being more diligent, he went to you of his own
accord.

7 [a][1 Cor. 1:5; 12:13] [b]2 Cor. 9:8
8 [a]1 Cor. 7:6
9 [a]Phil. 2:6, 7 [b]Rom. 9:23
10 [a]1 Cor. 7:25, 40 [b][Heb. 13:16] [c]2 Cor. 9:2
12 [a]Mark 12:43, 44
15 [a]Ex. 16:18
16 [1]NU *has put*
18 [a]2 Cor. 12:18
19 [a]1 Cor. 16:3, 4 [b]2 Cor. 4:15
21 [a]Rom. 12:17
23 [a]2 Cor. 7:13, 14 [b]Phil. 2:25 [1]Lit. *apostles,* "sent ones"
24 [a]2 Cor. 7:4, 14; 9:2 [1]NU, M omit *and*

CHAPTER 9

1 [a]Gal. 2:10
2 [a]2 Cor. 8:10
3 [a]2 Cor. 8:6, 17

18 And we have sent with him
[a]the brother whose praise *is* in
the gospel throughout all the
churches,
19 and not only *that,* but who
was also [a]chosen by the churches
to travel with us with this gift,
which is administered by us [b]to
the glory of the Lord Himself
and *to show* your ready mind,
20 avoiding this: that anyone
should blame us in this lavish
gift which is administered by
us—
21 [a]providing honorable things,
not only in the sight of the Lord,
but also in the sight of men.
22 And we have sent with them
our brother whom we have often
proved diligent in many things,
but now much more diligent,
because of the great confidence
which *we have* in you.
23 If *anyone inquires* about
[a]Titus, *he is* my partner and fellow worker concerning you. Or if
our brethren *are inquired about,*
they are [b]messengers[1] of the
churches, the glory of Christ.
24 Therefore show to them, [1]and
before the churches, the proof of
your love and of our [a]boasting
on your behalf.

9 Now concerning [a]the ministering to the saints, it is
superfluous for me to write to
you;
2 for I know your willingness,
about which I boast of you to the
Mac·e·dō′ni·ans, that A·chā′i·a
was ready a [a]year ago; and your
zeal has stirred up the majority.
3 [a]Yet I have sent the brethren,
lest our boasting of you should
be in vain in this respect, that, as
I said, you may be ready;
4 lest if *some* Mac·e·dō′ni·ans
come with me and find you

unprepared, we (not to mention
you!) should be ashamed of this
[1]confident boasting.
5 Therefore I thought it necessary to [1]exhort the brethren to
go to you ahead of time, and prepare your generous gift beforehand, which *you had* previously
promised, that it may be ready
as *a matter of* generosity and
not as a [2]grudging obligation.
6 [a]But this *I say:* He who sows
sparingly will also reap sparingly, and he who sows [1]bounti-
fully will also reap [1]bountifully.
7 *So let* each one *give* as
he purposes in his heart, [a]not
grudgingly or of [1]necessity; for
[b]God loves a cheerful giver.
8 [a]And God *is* able to make
all grace abound toward you,
that you, always having all sufficiency in all *things,* may have
an abundance for every good
work.
9 As it is written:

[a]*"He has dispersed abroad,*
He has given to the poor;
His righteousness endures
forever."

10 Now [1]may He who [a]supplies
seed to the sower, and bread
for food, [2]supply and multiply the seed you have *sown*
and increase the fruits of your
[b]righteousness,
11 while *you are* enriched in everything for all liberality, [a]which
causes thanksgiving through us
to God.
12 For the administration of this
service not only [a]supplies the
needs of the saints, but also
is abounding through many
thanksgivings to God,
13 while, through the proof of
this ministry, they [a]glorify God
for the obedience of your confession to the gospel of Christ,
and for *your* liberal [b]sharing
with them and all *men,*
14 and by their prayer for you,
who long for you because of the
exceeding [a]grace of God in you.
15 Thanks *be* to God [a]for His
indescribable gift!

10

Now [a]I, Paul, myself am
pleading with you by the
meekness and gentleness of
Christ—[b]who in presence *am*
lowly among you, but being absent am bold toward you.
2 But I beg *you* [a]that when I
am present I may not be bold
with that confidence by which I
intend to be bold against some,
who think of us as if we walked
according to the flesh.
3 For though we walk in the
flesh, we do not war according
to the flesh.
4 [a]For the weapons [b]of our warfare *are* not [1]carnal but [c]mighty
in God [d]for pulling down strongholds,
5 [a]casting down arguments
and every high thing that exalts itself against the knowledge
of God, bringing every thought
into captivity to the obedience
of Christ,
6 [a]and being ready to punish
all disobedience when [b]your
obedience is fulfilled.
7 [a]Do you look at things according to the outward appearance? [b]If anyone is convinced
in himself that he is Christ's, let
him again consider this in himself, that just as he *is* Christ's,
even [1]so [c]we *are* Christ's.
8 For even if I should boast
somewhat more [a]about our authority, which the Lord gave

4 [1]NU *confidence.*
5 [1]*encourage* [2]Lit. *covetousness*
6 [a]Prov. 11:24; 22:9 [1]*with blessings*
7 [a]Deut. 15:7 [b]Rom. 12:8 [1]*compulsion*
8 [a][Prov. 11:24]
9 [a]Ps. 112:9
10 [a]Is. 55:10 [b]Hos. 10:12 [1]NU omits *may* [2]NU *will supply*
11 [a]2 Cor. 1:11
12 [a]2 Cor. 8:14
13 [a][Matt. 5:16] [b][Heb. 13:16]
14 [a]2 Cor. 8:1
15 [a][James 1:17]

CHAPTER 10

1 [a]Rom. 12:1 [b]1 Thess. 2:7
2 [a]1 Cor. 4:21
4 [a]Eph. 6:13 [b]1 Tim. 1:18 [c]Acts 7:22 [d]Jer. 1:10 [1]*of the flesh*
5 [a]1 Cor. 1:19
6 [a]2 Cor. 13:2, 10 [b]2 Cor. 7:15
7 [a][John 7:24] [b]1 Cor. 1:12; 14:37 [c]1 Cor. 3:23 [1]NU *as we are.*
8 [a]2 Cor. 13:10

[1]us for [2]edification and not for
your destruction, [b]I shall not be
ashamed—
9 lest I seem to terrify you by
letters.
10 "For *his* letters," they say,
"*are* weighty and powerful, but
[a]*his* bodily presence *is* weak,
and *his* [b]speech contemptible."
11 Let such a person consider
this, that what we are in word by
letters when we are absent, such
we will also *be* in deed when we
are present.
12 [a]For we dare not class ourselves or compare ourselves
with those who commend themselves. But they, measuring
themselves by themselves, and
comparing themselves among
themselves, are not wise.
13 [a]We, however, will not boast
beyond measure, but within the
limits of the sphere which God
appointed us—a sphere which
especially includes you.
14 For we are not overextend-
ing ourselves (as though *our
authority* did not extend to you),
[a]for it was to you that we came
with the gospel of Christ;
15 not boasting of things beyond measure, *that is*, [a]in other
men's labors, but having hope,
that as your faith is increased,
we shall be greatly enlarged by
you in our sphere,
16 to preach the gospel in the
regions beyond you, *and* not to
boast in another man's sphere
of accomplishment.
17 But [a]*"he who glories, let him
glory in the* LORD."
18 For [a]not he who commends
himself is approved, but [b]whom
the Lord commends.

11

Oh, that you would
bear with me in a little

8 [b]2 Cor. 7:14 [1]NU omits *us* [2]*building up*
10 [a]Gal. 4:13 [b]2 Cor. 11:6
12 [a]2 Cor. 5:12
13 [a]2 Cor. 10:15
14 [a]1 Cor. 3:5, 6
15 [a]Rom. 15:20
17 [a]Jer. 9:24
18 [a]Prov. 27:2 [b]Rom. 2:29

CHAPTER 11

1 [a]2 Cor. 11:4, 16, 19
2 [a]Gal. 4:17 [b]Hos. 2:19 [c]Col. 1:28 [d]Lev. 21:13
3 [a]Gen. 3:4, 13 [b]Eph. 6:24 [1]NU adds *and purity*
4 [a]Gal. 1:6–8
5 [a]2 Cor. 12:11
6 [a][1 Cor. 1:17] [b][Eph. 3:4] [c][2 Cor. 12:12] [1]NU omits *been*
7 [a]1 Cor. 9:18 [1]*putting myself down*
9 [a]Acts 20:33 [b]Phil. 4:10
10 [a]Rom. 1:9; 9:1 [b]1 Cor. 9:15

[a]folly—and indeed you do bear
with me.
2 For I am [a]jealous for you
with godly jealousy. For [b]I have
betrothed you to one husband,
[c]that I may present *you* [d]*as* a
chaste virgin to Christ.
3 But I fear, lest somehow, as
[a]the serpent deceived Eve by his
craftiness, so your minds [b]may
be corrupted from the [1]simplic-
ity that is in Christ.
4 For if he who comes preaches
another Jesus whom we have not
preached, or *if* you receive a different spirit which you have not
received, or a [a]different gospel
which you have not accepted—
you may well put up with it!
5 For I consider that [a]I am not
at all inferior to the most eminent apostles.
6 Even though [a]*I am* untrained
in speech, yet *I am* not [b]in
knowledge. But [c]we have [1]been
thoroughly manifested among
you in all things.
7 Did I commit sin in [1]hum-
bling myself that you might be
exalted, because I preached the
gospel of God to you [a]free of
charge?
8 I robbed other churches, taking wages *from them* to minister
to you.
9 And when I was present with
you, and in need, [a]I was a burden to no one, for what I lacked
[b]the brethren who came from
Mac·e·dō′ni·a supplied. And in
everything I kept myself from
being burdensome to you, and
so I will keep *myself*.
10 [a]As the truth of Christ is in
me, [b]no one shall stop me from
this boasting in the regions of
A·chā′i·a.

11 Why? [a]Because I do not love
you? God knows!
12 But what I do, I will also
continue to do, [a]that I may cut
off the opportunity from those
who desire an opportunity to be
regarded just as we are in the
things of which they boast.
13 For such [a]*are* false apostles,
[b]deceitful workers, transform-
ing themselves into apostles of
Christ.
14 And no wonder! For Satan
himself transforms himself into
[a]an angel of light.
15 Therefore *it is* no great thing
if his ministers also transform
themselves into ministers of
righteousness, [a]whose end will
be according to their works.
16 I say again, let no one think
me a fool. If otherwise, at least
receive me as a fool, that I also
may boast a little.
17 What I speak, [a]I speak not
according to the Lord, but as
it were, foolishly, in this confidence of boasting.
18 Seeing that many boast according to the flesh, I also will
boast.
19 For you put up with fools
gladly, [a]since you *yourselves* are
wise!
20 For you put up with it [a]if one
brings you into bondage, if one
devours *you,* if one takes *from
you,* if one exalts himself, if one
strikes you on the face.
21 To *our* shame [a]I say that
we were too weak for that! But
[b]in whatever anyone is bold—I
speak foolishly—I am bold also.
22 Are they [a]Hebrews? So *am* I.
Are they Israelites? So *am* I. Are
they the seed of Abraham? So
am I.
23 Are they ministers of Christ?—
I speak as a fool—I *am* more:
[a]in labors more abundant, [b]in
stripes above measure, in prisons more frequently, [c]in deaths
often.
24 From the Jews five times I
received [a]forty [b]*stripes* minus
one.
25 Three times I was [a]beaten
with rods; [b]once I was stoned;
three times I [c]was shipwrecked;
a night and a day I have been in
the deep;
26 *in* journeys often, *in* perils
of waters, *in* perils of robbers,
[a]*in* perils of *my own* countrymen, [b]*in* perils of the Gentiles, *in*
perils in the city, *in* perils in the
wilderness, *in* perils in the sea,
in perils among false brethren;
27 in weariness and toil, [a]in
sleeplessness often, [b]in hunger
and thirst, in [c]fastings often, in
cold and nakedness—
28 besides the other things, what
comes upon me daily: [a]my deep
concern for all the churches.
29 [a]Who is weak, and I am not
weak? Who is made to stumble,
and I do not burn *with indignation?*
30 If I must boast, [a]I will boast
in the things which concern my
[1]infirmity.
31 [a]The God and Father of
our Lord Jesus Christ, [b]who is
blessed forever, knows that I am
not lying.
32 [a]In Damascus the governor,
under Ar′e·tas the king, was
guarding the city of the Dam′-
a·scēnes with a garrison, desiring to arrest me;
33 but I was let down in a basket
through a window in the wall,
and escaped from his hands.

11 [a]2 Cor. 6:11; 12:15
12 [a]1 Cor. 9:12
13 [a]Phil. 1:15 [b]Phil. 3:2
14 [a]Gal. 1:8
15 [a][Phil. 3:19]
17 [a]1 Cor. 7:6
19 [a]1 Cor. 4:10
20 [a][Gal. 2:4; 4:3, 9; 5:1]
21 [a]2 Cor. 10:10 [b]Phil. 3:4
22 [a]Phil. 3:4–6
23 [a]1 Cor. 15:10 [b]Acts 9:16 [c]1 Cor. 15:30
24 [a]Deut. 25:3 [b]2 Cor. 6:5
25 [a]Acts 16:22, 23; 21:32 [b]Acts 14:5, 19 [c]Acts 27:1–44
26 [a]Acts 9:23, 24; 13:45, 50; 17:5, 13 [b]Acts 14:5, 19; 19:23; 27:42
27 [a]Acts 20:31 [b]1 Cor. 4:11 [c]Acts 9:9; 13:2, 3; 14:23
28 [a]Acts 20:18
29 [a][1 Cor. 8:9, 13; 9:22]
30 [a][2 Cor. 12:5, 9, 10] [1]*weakness*
31 [a]1 Thess. 2:5 [b]Rom. 9:5
32 [a]Acts 9:19–25

12 It is [1]doubtless not profitable for me to boast. I will
come to [a]visions and [b]revelations
of the Lord:
2 I know a man [a]in Christ who
fourteen years ago—whether
in the body I do not know, or
whether out of the body I do
not know, God knows—such a
one [b]was caught up to the third
heaven.
3 And I know such a man—
whether in the body or out of
the body I do not know, God
knows—
4 how he was caught up into
[a]Paradise and heard inexpressible words, which it is not lawful
for a man to utter.
5 Of such a one I will boast;
yet of myself I will not [a]boast,
except in my infirmities.
6 For though I might desire to
boast, I will not be a fool; for
I will speak the truth. But I refrain, lest anyone should think
of me above what he sees me *to
be* or hears from me.
7 And lest I should be exalted
above measure by the abundance
of the revelations, a [a]thorn in the
flesh was given to me, [b]a messenger of Satan to [1]buffet me,
lest I be exalted above measure.
8 [a]Concerning this thing I
pleaded with the Lord three
times that it might depart from
me.
9 And He said to me, "My
grace is sufficient for you, for
My strength is made perfect
in weakness." Therefore most
gladly [a]I will rather boast in my
infirmities, [b]that the power of
Christ may rest upon me.
10 Therefore [a]I take pleasure
in infirmities, in reproaches, in
needs, in persecutions, in distresses, for Christ's sake. [b]For
when I am weak, then I am
strong.
11 I have become [a]a fool [1]in
boasting; you have compelled
me. For I ought to have been
commended by you; for [b]in
nothing was I behind the most
eminent apostles, though [c]I am
nothing.
12 [a]Truly the signs of an apostle were accomplished among
you with all perseverance, in
signs and [b]wonders and mighty
[c]deeds.
13 For what is it in which you
were inferior to other churches,
except that I myself was not
burdensome to you? Forgive me
this wrong!
14 [a]Now *for* the third time I am
ready to come to you. And I will
not be burdensome to you; for [b]I
do not seek yours, but you. [c]For
the children ought not to lay up
for the parents, but the parents
for the children.
15 And I will very gladly spend
and be spent [a]for your souls;
though [b]the more abundantly I
love you, the less I am loved.
16 But be that *as it may,* [a]I did
not burden you. Nevertheless,
being crafty, I caught you by
cunning!
17 Did I take advantage of you
by any of those whom I sent to
you?
18 I urged Titus, and sent our
[a]brother with *him.* Did Titus
take advantage of you? Did we
not walk in the same spirit? Did
we not *walk* in the same steps?
19 [a]Again,[1] do you think that
we excuse ourselves to you? [b]We
speak before God in Christ. [c]But
we do all things, beloved, for
your edification.

CHAPTER 12

1 [a]Acts 16:9; 18:9; 22:17, 18; 23:11; 26:13–15; 27:23 [b][Gal. 1:12; 2:2] [1]NU *necessary, though not profitable, to boast*
2 [a]Rom. 16:7 [b]Acts 22:17
4 [a]Luke 23:43
5 [a]2 Cor. 11:30
7 [a]Ezek. 28:24 [b]Job 2:7 [1]*beat*
8 [a]Matt. 26:44
9 [a]2 Cor. 11:30 [b][1 Pet. 4:14]
10 [a][Rom. 5:3; 8:35] [b]2 Cor. 13:4
11 [a]2 Cor. 5:13; 11:1, 16; 12:6 [b]2 Cor. 11:5 [c]1 Cor. 3:7; 13:2; 15:9 [1]NU omits *in boasting*
12 [a]Rom. 15:18 [b]Acts 15:12 [c]Acts 14:8–10; 16:16–18; 19:11, 12; 20:6–12; 28:1–10
14 [a]2 Cor. 1:15; 13:1, 2 [b][1 Cor. 10:24–33] [c]1 Cor. 4:14
15 [a][2 Tim. 2:10] [b]2 Cor. 6:12, 13
16 [a]2 Cor. 11:9
18 [a]2 Cor. 8:18
19 [a]2 Cor. 5:12 [b][Rom. 9:1, 2] [c]1 Cor. 10:33 [1]NU *You have been thinking for a long time that we*

20 For I fear lest, when I come, I
shall not find you such as I wish,
and *that* [a]I shall be found by you
such as you do not wish; lest
there be contentions, jealousies,
outbursts of wrath, selfish ambitions, backbitings, whisperings,
conceits, tumults;
21 lest, when I come again, my
God [a]will humble me among you,
and I shall mourn for many [b]who
have sinned before and have
not repented of the uncleanness,
[c]fornication, and lewdness which
they have practiced.

CHAPTER 13

13 This *will be* [a]the third
time I am coming to you.
[b]*"By the mouth of two or three
witnesses every word shall be
established."*
2 [a]I have told you before, and
foretell as if I were present the
second time, and now being absent [1]I write to those [b]who have
sinned before, and to all the rest,
that if I come again [c]I will not
spare—
3 since you seek a proof of
Christ [a]speaking in me, who is
not weak toward you, but mighty
[b]in you.
4 [a]For though He was crucified
in weakness, yet [b]He lives by the
power of God. For [c]we also are
weak in Him, but we shall live
with Him by the power of God
toward you.
5 Examine yourselves *as to*
whether you are in the faith. Test
yourselves. Do you not know
yourselves, [a]that Jesus Christ is
in you?—unless indeed you [1]are
[b]disqualified.
6 But I trust that you will know
that we are not disqualified.
7 Now [1]I pray to God that you
do no evil, not that we should
appear approved, but that you
should do what is honorable,
though [a]we may seem disqualified.
8 For we can do nothing against
the truth, but for the truth.
9 For we are glad [a]when we
are weak and you are strong.
And this also we pray, [b]that you
may be made complete.
10 [a]Therefore I write these
things being absent, lest being present I should use sharp-
ness, according to the [b]authority
which the Lord has given me for
edification and not for destruction.
11 Finally, brethren, farewell.
Become complete. [a]Be of good
comfort, be of one mind, live in
peace; and the God of love [b]and
peace will be with you.
12 [a]Greet one another with a
holy kiss.
13 All the saints greet you.
14 [a]The grace of the Lord Jesus
Christ, and the love of God, and
[b]the [1]communion of the Holy
Spirit *be* with you all. Amen.

---

20 [a]1 Cor. 4:21
21 [a]2 Cor. 2:1, 4 [b]2 Cor. 13:2 [c]1 Cor. 5:1

CHAPTER 13

1 [a]2 Cor. 12:14 [b]Deut. 17:6; 19:15
2 [a]2 Cor. 10:2 [b]2 Cor. 12:21 [c]2 Cor. 1:23; 10:11 [1]NU omits *I write*
3 [a]Matt. 10:20 [b][1 Cor. 9:2]
4 [a][1 Pet. 3:18] [b][Rom. 1:4; 6:4] [c][2 Cor. 10:3, 4]
5 [a][Gal. 4:19] [b]1 Cor. 9:27 [1]*do not stand the test*
7 [a]2 Cor. 6:9 [1]NU *we*
9 [a]1 Cor. 4:10 [b][1 Thess. 3:10]
10 [a]1 Cor. 4:21 [b]2 Cor. 10:8
11 [a]Rom. 12:16, 18 [b]Rom. 15:33
12 [a]Rom. 16:16
14 [a]Rom. 16:24 [b]Phil. 2:1 [1]*fellowship*

The Epistle of Paul the Apostle to the

GALATIANS

THE Galatians, having launched their Christian experience by faith, seem content to leave their voyage of faith and chart a new course based on works—a course Paul finds disturbing. His letter to the Galatians is a vigorous attack against the gospel of works and defense of the gospel of faith.

Paul begins by setting forth his credentials as an apostle with a message from God: blessing comes from God on the basis of faith, not law. The law declares men guilty and imprisons them; faith sets men free to enjoy liberty in Christ. But liberty is not license. Freedom in Christ means freedom to produce the fruits of righteousness through a Spirit-led lifestyle.

The book is called *Pros Galatas,* "To the Galatians," and it is the only letter of Paul that is specifically addressed to a number of churches ("To the churches of Galatia," 1:2). The name *Galatians* was given to this Celtic people because they originally lived in Gaul before their migration to Asia Minor.

CHAPTER 1

PAUL, an apostle (not from men nor through man, but [a]through Jesus Christ and God the Father [b]who raised Him from the dead),

2 and all the brethren who are with me,

To the churches of Galatia:

3 Grace to you and peace from God the Father and our Lord Jesus Christ,

4 [a]who gave Himself for our sins, that He might deliver us [b]from this present evil age, according to the will of our God and Father,

5 to whom *be* glory forever and ever. Amen.

6 I marvel that you are turning away so soon [a]from Him who called you in the grace of Christ, to a different gospel,

7 [a]which is not another; but there are some [b]who trouble you and want to [c]pervert[1] the gospel of Christ.

8 But even if [a]we, or an angel from heaven, preach any other gospel to you than what we have preached to you, let him be [1]accursed.

9 As we have said before, so now I say again, if anyone preaches any other gospel to you [a]than what you have received, let him be accursed.

10 For [a]do I now [b]persuade men, or God? Or [c]do I seek to please men? For if I still pleased men, I would not be a bondservant of Christ.

11 [a]But I make known to you, brethren, that the gospel which was preached by me is not according to man.

12 For [a]I neither received it from man, nor was I taught *it,* but *it came* [b]through the revelation of Jesus Christ.

13 For you have heard of my former conduct in Judaism, how [a]I persecuted the church of God beyond measure and [b]*tried to* destroy it.

1 [a]Acts 9:6 [b]Acts 2:24
4 [a][Matt. 20:28] [b]Heb. 2:5
6 [a]Gal. 1:15; 5:8
7 [a]2 Cor. 11:4 [b]Gal. 5:10, 12 [c]2 Cor. 2:17 [1]*distort*
8 [a]1 Cor. 16:22 [1]Gr. *anathema*
9 [a]Deut. 4:2
10 [a]1 Thess. 2:4 [b]1 Sam. 24:7 [c]1 Thess. 2:4
11 [a]1 Cor. 15:1
12 [a]1 Cor. 15:1 [b][Eph. 3:3–5]
13 [a]Acts 9:1 [b]Acts 8:3; 22:4, 5

14 And I advanced in Judaism beyond many of my contemporaries in my own nation, [a]being more exceedingly zealous [b]for the traditions of my fathers.

15 But when it pleased God, [a]who separated me from my mother's womb and called *me* through His grace,

16 [a]to reveal His Son in me, that [b]I might preach Him among the Gentiles, I did not immediately confer with [c]flesh and blood,

17 nor did I go up to Jerusalem to those *who were* apostles before me; but I went to Arabia, and returned again to Damascus.

18 Then after three years [a]I went up to Jerusalem to see [1]Peter, and remained with him fifteen days.

19 But [a]I saw none of the other apostles except [b]James, the Lord's brother.

20 (Now *concerning* the things which I write to you, indeed, before God, I do not lie.)

21 [a]Afterward I went into the regions of Syria and Ci·li′ci·a.

22 And I was unknown by face to the churches of Judea which [a]*were* in Christ.

23 But they were [a]hearing only, "He who formerly [b]persecuted us now preaches the faith which he once *tried to* destroy."

24 And they [a]glorified God in me.

2 Then after fourteen years [a]I went up again to Jerusalem with Bar′na·bas, and also took Titus with *me.*

2 And I went up [1]by revelation, and communicated to them that gospel which I preach among the Gentiles, but [a]privately to those who were of reputation, lest by any means [b]I might run, or had run, in vain.

3 Yet not even Titus who *was* with me, being a Greek, was compelled to be circumcised.

4 And *this occurred* because of [a]false brethren secretly brought in (who came in by stealth to spy out our [b]liberty which we have in Christ Jesus, [c]that they might bring us into bondage),

5 to whom we did not yield submission even for an hour, that [a]the truth of the gospel might continue with you.

6 But from those [a]who seemed to be something—whatever they were, it makes no difference to me; [b]God [1]shows personal favoritism to no man—for those who seemed *to be something* [c]added nothing to me.

7 But on the contrary, [a]when they saw that the gospel for the uncircumcised [b]had been committed to me, as *the gospel* for the circumcised *was* to Peter

8 (for He who worked effectively in Peter for the apostleship to the [a]circumcised [b]also [c]worked effectively in me toward the Gentiles),

9 and when James, [1]Cē′phas, and John, who seemed to be [a]pillars, perceived [b]the grace that had been given to me, they gave me and Bar′na·bas the right hand of fellowship, [c]that we *should go* to the Gentiles and they to the circumcised.

10 *They desired* only that we should remember the poor, [a]the very thing which I also was eager to do.

11 [a]Now when [1]Peter had come to An′ti·och, I [2]withstood him to his face, because he was to be blamed;

14 [a]Acts 26:9 [b]Jer. 9:14
15 [a]Is. 49:1, 5
16 [a][2 Cor. 4:5–7] [b]Acts 9:15 [c]Matt. 16:17
18 [a]Acts 9:26 [1]NU *Cephas*
19 [a]1 Cor. 9:5 [b]Matt. 13:55
21 [a]Acts 9:30
22 [a]Rom. 16:7
23 [a]Acts 9:20, 21 [b]Acts 8:3
24 [a]Acts 11:18

CHAPTER 2

1 [a]Acts 15:2
2 [a]Acts 15:1–4 [b]Phil. 2:16 [1]*because of*
4 [a]Acts 15:1, 24 [b]Gal. 3:25; 5:1, 13 [c]Gal. 4:3, 9
5 [a][Gal. 1:6; 2:14; 3:1]
6 [a]Gal. 2:9; 6:3 [b]Acts 10:34 [c]2 Cor. 11:5; 12:11 [1]Lit. *does not receive the face of a man*
7 [a]Acts 9:15; 13:46; 22:21 [b]1 Thess. 2:4
8 [a]1 Pet. 1:1 [b]Acts 9:15 [c][Gal. 3:5]
9 [a]Matt. 16:18 [b]Rom. 1:5 [c]Acts 13:3 [1]Peter
10 [a]Acts 11:30
11 [a]Acts 15:35 [1]NU *Cephas* [2]*opposed*

12 for before certain men came
from James, [a]he would eat with
the Gentiles; but when they
came, he withdrew and separated himself, fearing [1]those
who were of the circumcision.
13 And the rest of the Jews also
played the hypocrite with him,
so that even Bar′na·bas was carried away with their hypocrisy.
14 But when I saw that they
were not straightforward about
[a]the truth of the gospel, I said to
Peter [b]before *them* all, [c]"If you,
being a Jew, live in the manner
of Gentiles and not as the Jews,
[1]why do you compel Gentiles to
live as [2]Jews?
15 [a]"We *who are* Jews by nature,
and not [b]sinners of the Gentiles,
16 [a]"knowing that a man is not
[1]justified by the works of the
law but [b]by faith in Jesus Christ,
even we have believed in Christ
Jesus, that we might be justified
by faith in Christ and not [c]by
the works of the law; for by the
works of the law no flesh shall
be justified.
17 "But if, while we seek to be
justified by Christ, we ourselves
also are found [a]sinners, *is* Christ
therefore a minister of sin? Certainly not!
18 "For if I build again those
things which I destroyed, I make
myself a transgressor.
19 "For I [a]through the law [b]died
to the law that I might [c]live to
God.
★ 20 "I have been [a]crucified with
Christ; it is no longer I who live,
but Christ lives in me; and the
life which I now live in the flesh
[b]I live by faith in the Son of God,
[c]who loved me and gave Himself
for me.
21 "I do not set aside the grace
of God; for [a]if righteousness
comes through the law, then
Christ died [1]in vain."

3 O foolish Galatians! Who
has bewitched you [1]that you
should not obey the truth, before
whose eyes Jesus Christ was
clearly portrayed [2]among you as
crucified?
2 This only I want to learn
from you: Did you receive the
Spirit by the works of the law,
[a]or by the hearing of faith?
3 Are you so foolish? [a]Having
begun in the Spirit, are you
now being made perfect by [b]the
flesh?
4 [a]Have you suffered so [1]many
things in vain—if indeed *it was*
in vain?
5 Therefore He who supplies
the Spirit to you and works miracles among you, *does He do it*
by the works of the law, or by
the hearing of faith?—
6 just as Abraham [a]*"believed
God, and it was accounted to
him for righteousness."*
7 Therefore know that *only*
[a]those who are of faith are sons
of Abraham.
8 And [a]the Scripture, foresee- ★
ing that God would justify the
Gentiles by faith, preached the
gospel to Abraham beforehand,
saying, [b]*"In you all the nations
shall be blessed."*
9 So then those who *are* of
faith are blessed with believing
Abraham.
10 For as many as are of the
works of the law are under the
curse; for it is written, [a]*"Cursed
is everyone who does not continue in all things which are
written in the book of the law, to
do them."*
11 But that no one is [1]justified

12 [a][Acts 10:28; 11:2, 3] [1]Jewish Christians
14 [a]Gal. 1:6; 2:5 [b]1 Tim. 5:20 [c][Acts 10:28] [1]NU *how can you* [2]Some interpreters stop the quotation here.
15 [a][Acts 15:10] [b]Matt. 9:11
16 [a]Acts 13:38, 39 [b]Rom. 1:17 [c]Ps. 143:2 [1]*declared righteous*
17 [a][1 John 3:8]
19 [a]Rom. 8:2 [b][Rom. 6:2, 14; 7:4] [c][Rom. 6:11]
20 [a][Rom. 6:6] [b]2 Cor. 5:15 [c]Is. 53:12; Eph. 5:2
21 [a]Heb. 7:11 [1]*for nothing*

CHAPTER 3

1 [1]NU omits *that you should not obey the truth* [2]NU omits *among you*
2 [a]Rom. 10:16, 17
3 [a][Gal. 4:9] [b]Heb. 7:16
4 [a]Heb. 10:35 [1]Or *great*
6 [a]Gen. 15:6
7 [a]John 8:39
8 [a]Rom. 9:17 [b]Gen. 12:3; 18:18; 22:18; 26:4; 28:14
10 [a]Deut. 27:26
11 [1]*declared righteous*

by the law in the sight of God *is*
evident, for [a]*"the just shall live*
by faith."
12 Yet [a]the law is not of faith,
but [b]*"the man who does them*
shall live by them."
13 [a]Christ has redeemed us
from the curse of the law, having become a curse for us (for it
is written, [b]*"Cursed is everyone*
who hangs on a tree"),
★ 14 [a]that the blessing of Abraham
might come upon the [b]Gentiles
in Christ Jesus, that we might
receive [c]the promise of the Spirit
through faith.
15 Brethren, I speak in the manner of men: [a]Though *it is* only a
man's covenant, yet *if it is* confirmed, no one annuls or adds
to it.
★ 16 Now to Abraham and his
Seed were the promises made.
He does not say, "And to seeds,"
as of many, but as of [a]one, [b]*"And*
to your Seed," who is [c]Christ.
17 And this I say, *that* the law,
[a]which was four hundred and
thirty years later, cannot annul
the covenant that was confirmed
before by God [1]in Christ, [b]that it
should make the promise of no
effect.
18 For if [a]the inheritance *is* of
the law, [b]*it is* no longer of promise; but God gave *it* to Abraham
by promise.
19 What purpose then *does* the
law *serve?* [a]It was added because of transgressions, till the
[b]Seed should come to whom the
promise was made; *and it was*
[c]appointed through angels by
the hand [d]of a mediator.
20 Now a mediator does not
mediate for one *only,* [a]but God
is one.
21 *Is* the law then against the

11 [a]Hab. 2:4
12 [a]Rom. 4:4, 5 [b]Lev. 18:5
13 [a][Rom. 8:3] [b]Deut. 21:23
14 [a]Gen. 12:3; 22:18; [Rom. 4:1–5, 9, 16] [b]Is. 49:6; Rom. 3:29, 30 [c]Is. 32:15
15 [a]Heb. 9:17
16 [a]Gen. 22:18 [b]Gen. 12:3, 7; 13:15; 24:7 [c][1 Cor. 12:12]
17 [a]Ex. 12:40 [b][Rom. 4:13] [1]NU omits *in Christ*
18 [a][Rom. 8:17] [b]Rom. 4:14
19 [a]John 15:22 [b]Gal. 4:4 [c]Acts 7:53 [d]Ex. 20:19
20 [a][Rom. 3:29]
22 [a]Rom. 11:32 [b]Rom. 4:11
23 [1]Lit. *confined*
24 [a]Rom. 10:4 [b]Acts 13:39 [1]In a household, the guardian responsible for the care and discipline of the children
26 [a]John 1:12
27 [a][Rom. 6:3] [b]Rom. 10:12; 13:14
28 [a]Col. 3:11 [b][1 Cor. 12:13] [c][Eph. 2:15, 16]
29 [a]Gen. 21:10; Heb. 11:18 [b]Rom. 4:11; Gal. 3:7 [c]Gen. 12:3; 18:18; Rom. 8:17

CHAPTER 4

3 [a]Col. 2:8, 20
4 [a][Gen. 49:10] [b][John 1:14] [c]Gen. 3:15; Is. 7:14; Matt. 1:25] [d][Matt. 5:17]; Luke 2:21, 27 [1]Or *made*
5 [a][Matt. 20:28]

promises of God? Certainly not!
For if there had been a law
given which could have given
life, truly righteousness would
have been by the law.
22 But the Scripture has confined [a]all under sin, [b]that the
promise by faith in Jesus Christ
might be given to those who believe.
23 But before faith came, we
were kept under guard by the
law, [1]kept for the faith which
would afterward be revealed.
24 Therefore [a]the law was our
[1]tutor *to bring us* to Christ, [b]that
we might be justified by faith.
25 But after faith has come, we
are no longer under a tutor.
26 For you [a]are all sons of God
through faith in Christ Jesus.
27 For [a]as many of you as were
baptized into Christ [b]have put
on Christ.
28 [a]There is neither Jew nor
Greek, [b]there is neither slave
nor free, there is neither male
nor female; for you are all [c]one
in Christ Jesus.
29 And [a]if you *are* Christ's, then ★
you are Abraham's [b]seed, and
[c]heirs according to the promise.

4

Now I say *that* the heir, as
long as he is a child, does not
differ at all from a slave, though
he is master of all,
2 but is under guardians and
stewards until the time appointed by the father.
3 Even so we, when we were
children, [a]were in bondage under the elements of the world.
4 But [a]when the fullness of the ★
time had come, God sent forth
His Son, [b]born[1] [c]of a woman,
[d]born under the law,
5 [a]to redeem those who were

under the law, [b]that we might
receive the adoption as sons.
6 And because you are sons,
God has sent forth [a]the Spirit of
His Son into your hearts, crying
out, [1]"Abba, Father!"
7 Therefore you are no longer
a slave but a son, [a]and if a son,
then an heir [1]of God [2]through
Christ.
8 But then, indeed, [a]when you
did not know God, [b]you served
those which by nature are not
gods.
9 But now [a]after you have
known God, or rather are known
by God, [b]how *is it that* you turn
again to [c]the weak and beggarly
elements, to which you desire
again to be in bondage?
10 [a]You observe days and
months and seasons and years.
11 I am afraid for you, [a]lest I
have labored for you in vain.
12 Brethren, I urge you to become like me, for I *became* like
you. [a]You have not injured me at
all.
13 You know that [a]because of
physical infirmity I preached
the gospel to you at the first.
14 And my trial which was in
my flesh you did not despise or
reject, but you received me [a]as
an [1]angel of God, [b]*even* as Christ
Jesus.
15 [1]What then was the blessing
you *enjoyed*? For I bear you witness that, if possible, you would
have plucked out your own eyes
and given them to me.
16 Have I therefore become your
enemy because I tell you the
truth?
17 They [a]zealously court you,
but for no good; yes, they want
to exclude you, that you may be
zealous for them.
18 But it is good to be zealous
in a good thing always, and not
only when I am present with
you.
19 [a]My little children, for whom
I labor in birth again until Christ
is formed in you,
20 I would like to be present
with you now and to change my
tone; for I have doubts about
you.
21 Tell me, you who desire to be
under the law, do you not hear
the law?
22 For it is written that Abraham had two sons: [a]the one by
a bondwoman, [b]the other by a
freewoman.
23 But he *who was* of the bondwoman [a]was born according to
the flesh, [b]and he of the freewoman through promise,
24 which things are symbolic.
For these are [1]the two covenants:
the one from Mount [a]Sinai which
gives birth to bondage, which is
Hā′gar—
25 for this Hā′gar is Mount Sinai in Arabia, and corresponds
to Jerusalem which now is, and
is in bondage with her children—
26 but the [a]Jerusalem above is
free, which is the mother of us
all.
27 For it is written:

[a]*"Rejoice, O barren,*
You who do not bear!
Break forth and shout,
You who are not in labor!
For the desolate has many
more children
Than she who has a
husband."

28 Now [a]we, brethren, as Isaac
was, are [b]children of promise.

5 [b][John 1:12]
6 [a][Rom. 5:5; 8:9, 15, 16] [1]Lit., in Aram., *Father*
7 [a][Rom. 8:16, 17] [1]NU *through God* [2]NU omits *through Christ*
8 [a]Eph. 2:12 [b]Rom. 1:25
9 [a][1 Cor. 8:3] [b]Col. 2:20 [c]Heb. 7:18
10 [a]Rom. 14:5
11 [a]1 Thess. 3:5
12 [a]2 Cor. 2:5
13 [a]1 Cor. 2:3
14 [a]Mal. 2:7 [b][Luke 10:16] [1]Or *messenger*
15 [1]NU *Where*
17 [a]Rom. 10:2
19 [a]1 Cor. 4:15
22 [a]Gen. 16:15 [b]Gen. 21:2
23 [a]Rom. 9:7, 8 [b]Heb. 11:11
24 [a]Deut. 33:2 [1]NU, M omit *the*
26 [a][Is. 2:2]
27 [a]Is. 54:1
28 [a]Gal. 3:29 [b]Acts 3:25

29 But, as [a]he who was born
according to the flesh then persecuted him *who was born* according to the Spirit, [b]even so *it*
is now.
30 Nevertheless what does [a]the
Scripture say? [b]*"Cast out the*
bondwoman and her son, for
[c]*the son of the bondwoman shall*
not be heir with the son of the
freewoman."
31 So then, brethren, we are not
children of the bondwoman but
of the free.

5 [a]Stand[1] fast therefore in the
liberty by which Christ has
made us free, and do not be
entangled again with a [b]yoke of
bondage.
2 Indeed I, Paul, say to you
that [a]if you become circumcised,
Christ will profit you nothing.
3 And I testify again to every
man who becomes circumcised
[a]that he is [1]a debtor to keep the
whole law.
4 [a]You have become estranged
from Christ, you who *attempt*
to be justified by law; [b]you have
fallen from grace.
5 For we through the Spirit eagerly [a]wait for the hope of righteousness by faith.
6 For [a]in Christ Jesus neither
circumcision nor uncircumcision avails anything, but [b]faith
working through love.
7 You [a]ran well. Who hindered
you from obeying the truth?
8 This persuasion does not
come from Him who calls you.
9 [a]A little leaven leavens the
whole lump.
10 I have confidence in you, in
the Lord, that you will have no
other mind; but he who troubles
you shall bear his judgment,
whoever he is.
11 And I, brethren, if I still
preach circumcision, [a]why do I
still suffer persecution? Then [b]the
offense of the cross has ceased.
12 [a]I could wish that those [b]who
trouble you would even [1]cut
themselves off!
13 For you, brethren, have been
called to liberty; only [a]do not
use liberty as an [b]opportunity
for the flesh, but [c]through love
serve one another.
14 For [a]all the law is fulfilled
in one word, *even* in this: [b]*"You*
shall love your neighbor as your-
self."
15 But if you bite and devour
one another, beware lest you be
consumed by one another!
16 I say then: [a]Walk in the Spirit,
and you shall not fulfill the lust
of the flesh.
17 For [a]the flesh lusts against
the Spirit, and the Spirit against
the flesh; and these are contrary
to one another, [b]so that you do
not do the things that you wish.
18 But [a]if you are led by the
Spirit, you are not under the law.
19 Now [a]the works of the flesh
are evident, which are: [1]adultery,
[2]fornication, uncleanness, lewdness,
20 idolatry, sorcery, hatred, contentions, jealousies, outbursts of
wrath, selfish ambitions, dissensions, heresies,
21 envy, [1]murders, drunkenness,
revelries, and the like; of which
I tell you beforehand, just as I
also told *you* in time past, that
[a]those who practice such things
will not inherit the kingdom of
God.
22 But [a]the fruit of the Spirit is
[b]love, joy, peace, longsuffering,
kindness, [c]goodness, [d]faithful-
ness,

29 [a]Gen. 21:9 [b]Gal. 5:11
30 [a][Gal. 3:8, 22] [b]Gen. 21:10, 12 [c][John 8:35]

CHAPTER 5

1 [a]Phil. 4:1 [b]Acts 15:10 [1]NU *For freedom Christ has made us free; stand fast therefore, and*
2 [a]Acts 15:1
3 [a][Rom. 2:25] [1]*obligated*
4 [a][Rom. 9:31] [b]Heb. 12:15
5 [a]Rom. 8:24
6 [a][Gal. 6:15] [b]1 Thess. 1:3
7 [a]1 Cor. 9:24
9 [a]1 Cor. 5:6
11 [a]1 Cor. 15:30 [b][1 Cor. 1:23]
12 [a]Josh. 7:25 [b]Acts 15:1, 2 [1]*mutilate themselves*
13 [a]1 Cor. 8:9 [b]1 Pet. 2:16 [c]1 Cor. 9:19
14 [a]Matt. 7:12; 22:40 [b]Lev. 19:18
16 [a]Rom. 6:12
17 [a]Rom. 7:18, 22, 23; 8:5 [b]Rom. 7:15
18 [a][Rom. 6:14; 7:4; 8:14]
19 [a]Eph. 5:3, 11 [1]NU omits *adultery* [2]*sexual immorality*
21 [a]1 Cor. 6:9, 10 [1]NU omits *murders*
22 [a][John 15:2] [b][Col. 3:12–15] [c]Rom. 15:14 [d]1 Cor. 13:7

23 [1]gentleness, self-control. [a]Against such there is no law.

24 And those *who are* Christ's [a]have crucified the flesh with its passions and desires.

25 [a]If we live in the Spirit, let us also walk in the Spirit.

26 [a]Let us not become conceited, provoking one another, envying one another.

6 Brethren, if a man is [1]overtaken in any trespass, you who *are* spiritual restore such a one in a spirit of [a]gentleness, considering yourself lest you also be tempted.

2 [a]Bear one another's burdens, and so fulfill [b]the law of Christ.

3 For [a]if anyone thinks himself to be something, when [b]he is nothing, he deceives himself.

4 But [a]let each one examine his own work, and then he will have rejoicing in himself alone, and [b]not in another.

5 For [a]each one shall bear his own load.

6 [a]Let him who is taught the word share in all good things with him who teaches.

7 Do not be deceived, God is not mocked; for [a]whatever a man sows, that he will also reap.

8 For he who sows to his flesh will of the flesh reap corruption, but he who sows to the Spirit will of the Spirit reap [a]everlasting life.

9 And [a]let us not grow weary while doing good, for in due season we shall reap [b]if we do not lose heart.

10 [a]Therefore, as we have opportunity, [b]let us do good to all, [c]especially to those who are of the household of faith.

11 See with what large letters I have written to you with my own hand!

12 As many as desire to make a good showing in the flesh, these *would* compel you to be circumcised, [a]only that they may not suffer persecution for the cross of Christ.

13 For not even those who are circumcised keep the law, but they desire to have you circumcised that they may boast in your flesh.

14 But God forbid that I should boast except in the [a]cross of our Lord Jesus Christ, by [1]whom the world has been crucified to me, and [b]I to the world.

15 For [a]in Christ Jesus neither circumcision nor uncircumcision avails anything, but a new creation.

16 And as many as walk according to this rule, peace and mercy *be* upon them, and upon the Israel of God.

17 From now on let no one trouble me, for I bear in my body the marks of the Lord Jesus.

18 Brethren, the grace of our Lord Jesus Christ *be* with your spirit. Amen.

23 [a]1 Tim. 1:9 [1]*meekness*
24 [a]Rom. 6:6
25 [a][Rom. 8:4, 5]
26 [a]Phil. 2:3

CHAPTER 6

1 [a]Eph. 4:2 [1]*caught*
2 [a]Rom. 15:1 [b][James 2:8]
3 [a]Rom. 12:3 [b][2 Cor. 3:5]
4 [a]1 Cor. 11:28 [b]Luke 18:11
5 [a][Rom. 2:6]
6 [a]1 Cor. 9:11, 14
7 [a][Rom. 2:6]
8 [a][Rom. 6:8]
9 [a]1 Cor. 15:58 [b][James 5:7, 8]
10 [a]Prov. 3:27 [b]Titus 3:8 [c]Rom. 12:13
12 [a]Gal. 5:11
14 [a][1 Cor. 1:18] [b]Col. 2:20 [1]Or *which,* the cross
15 [a]1 Cor. 7:19

The Epistle of Paul the Apostle to the
EPHESIANS

EPHESIANS is addressed to a group of believers who are rich beyond measure in Jesus Christ, yet living as beggars, and only because they are ignorant of their wealth. Paul begins by describing in chapters 1—3 the contents of the Christian's heavenly "bank account": adoption, acceptance, redemption, forgiveness, wisdom, inheritance, the seal of the Holy Spirit, life, grace, citizenship—in short, every spiritual blessing. In chapters 4—6 the Christian learns a spiritual walk rooted in his spiritual wealth. "For we are His workmanship, created in Christ Jesus [1—3] for good works, . . . that we should walk in them [4—6]" (2:10).

The traditional title of this epistle is *Pros Ephesious*, "To the Ephesians." Many ancient manuscripts, however, omit *en Epheso*, "in Ephesus," in 1:1. This has led a number of scholars to challenge the traditional view that this message was directed specifically to the Ephesians. The encyclical theory proposes that it was a circular letter sent by Paul to the churches of Asia. It is argued that Ephesians is really a Christian treatise designed for general use: it involves no controversy and deals with no specific problems in any particular church. Some scholars accept an ancient tradition that Ephesians is Paul's letter to the Laodiceans (Col. 4:16), but there is no way to be sure. If Ephesians began as a circular letter, it eventually became associated with Ephesus, the foremost of the Asian churches. Another plausible option is that this epistle was directly addressed to the Ephesians, but written in such a way as to make it helpful for all the churches in Asia.

PAUL, an apostle of Jesus Christ by the will of God,

To the saints who are in Eph′e·sus, and faithful in Christ Jesus:

2 Grace to you and peace from God our Father and the Lord Jesus Christ.

3 [a]Blessed *be* the God and Father of our Lord Jesus Christ, who has blessed us with every spiritual blessing in the heavenly *places* in Christ,
4 just as [a]He chose us in Him
[b]before the foundation of the world, that we should [c]be holy and without blame before Him in love,
5 [a]having predestined us to
[b]adoption as sons by Jesus Christ to Himself, [c]according to the good pleasure of His will,
6 to the praise of the glory of His grace, [a]by which He [1]made us accepted in [b]the Beloved.
7 [a]In Him we have redemption through His blood, the forgiveness of sins, according to [b]the riches of His grace
8 which He made to abound toward us in all wisdom and [1]prudence,
9 [a]having made known to us the mystery of His will, according

CHAPTER 1

3 [a]2 Cor. 1:3

4 [a]Rom. 8:28 [b]1 Pet. 1:2 [c]Luke 1:75

5 [a][Rom. 8:29] [b]John 1:12 [c][1 Cor. 1:21]

6 [a][Rom. 3:24] [b]Matt. 3:17 [1]Lit. *bestowed grace (favor) upon us*

7 [a][Heb. 9:12] [b][Rom. 3:24, 25]

8 [1]*understanding*

9 [a][Rom. 16:25]

to His good pleasure [b]which He
purposed in Himself,
10 that in the dispensation of
[a]the fullness of the times [b]He
might gather together in one
[c]all things in Christ, [1]both which
are in heaven and which are on
earth—in Him.
11 [a]In Him also we have obtained an inheritance, being
predestined according to [b]the
purpose of Him who works all
things according to the counsel
of His will,
12 [a]that we [b]who first trusted in
Christ should be to the praise of
His glory.
13 In Him you also *trusted,* after you heard [a]the word of truth,
the gospel of your salvation;
in whom also, having believed,
[b]you were sealed with the Holy
Spirit of promise,
14 [a]who[1] is the [2]guarantee of
our inheritance [b]until the redemption of [c]the purchased possession, [d]to the praise of His
glory.
15 Therefore I also, [a]after I
heard of your faith in the Lord
Jesus and your love for all the
saints,
16 [a]do not cease to give thanks
for you, making mention of you
in my prayers:
17 that [a]the God of our Lord
Jesus Christ, the Father of glory,
[b]may give to you the spirit of
wisdom and revelation in the
knowledge of Him,
18 [a]the eyes of your [1]under-
standing being enlightened;
that you may know what is [b]the
hope of His calling, what are the
riches of the glory of His inheritance in the saints,
19 and what *is* the exceeding
greatness of His power toward
us who believe, [a]according to the
working of His mighty power
20 which He worked in Christ
when [a]He raised Him from
the dead and [b]seated *Him* at
His right hand in the heavenly
places,
21 [a]far above all [b]principality[1]
and [2]power and [3]might and dominion, and every name that is
named, not only in this age but
also in that which is to come.
22 And [a]He put all *things* un- ☆
der His feet, and gave Him [b]*to
be* head over all *things* to the
church,
23 [a]which is His body, [b]the fullness of Him [c]who fills all in all.

2 And [a]you *He made alive,*
[b]who were dead in tres-
passes and sins,
2 [a]in which you once walked
according to the [1]course of this
world, according to [b]the prince
of the power of the air, the spirit
who now works in [c]the sons of
disobedience,
3 [a]among whom also we all
once conducted ourselves in
[b]the lusts of our flesh, fulfilling
the desires of the flesh and of
the mind, and [c]were by nature
children of wrath, just as the
others.
4 But God, [a]who is rich in
mercy, because of His [b]great
love with which He loved us,
5 [a]even when we were dead
in trespasses, [b]made us alive together with Christ (by grace you
have been saved),
6 and raised *us* up together,
and made *us* sit together [a]in the
heavenly *places* in Christ Jesus,
7 that in the ages to come He
might show the exceeding riches
of His grace in [a]*His* kindness toward us in Christ Jesus.

9 [b][2 Tim. 1:9]
10 [a]Gal. 4:4 [b]1 Cor. 3:22 [c][Col. 1:16, 20] [1]NU, M omit *both*
11 [a]Rom. 8:17 [b]Is. 46:10
12 [a]2 Thess. 2:13 [b]James 1:18
13 [a]John 1:17 [b][2 Cor. 1:22]
14 [a]2 Cor. 5:5 [b]Rom. 8:23 [c][Acts 20:28] [d]1 Pet. 2:9 [1]NU *which* [2]*down payment, earnest*
15 [a]Col. 1:4
16 [a]Rom. 1:9
17 [a]John 20:17 [b]Col. 1:9
18 [a]Acts 26:18 [b]Eph. 2:12 [1]NU, M *hearts*
19 [a]Col. 2:12
20 [a]Acts 2:24 [b]Ps. 110:1
21 [a]Phil. 2:9, 10 [b][Rom. 8:38, 39] [1]*rule* [2]*authority* [3]*power*
22 [a]Ps. 8:6; 110:1; Matt. 28:18; 1 Cor. 15:27 [b]Heb. 2:7, 8
23 [a]Rom. 12:5 [b]Col. 2:9 [c][1 Cor. 12:6]

CHAPTER 2

1 [a]Col. 2:13 [b]Eph. 4:18
2 [a]Col. 1:21 [b]Eph. 6:12 [c]Col. 3:6 [1]Gr. *aion,* aeon
3 [a]1 Pet. 4:3 [b]Gal. 5:16 [c][Ps. 51:5]
4 [a]Rom. 10:12 [b]John 3:16
5 [a]Rom. 5:6, 8 [b][Rom. 6:4, 5]
6 [a]Eph. 1:20
7 [a]Titus 3:4

8 [a]For by grace you have been saved [b]through faith, and that not of yourselves; [c]*it is* the gift of God,

9 not of [a]works, lest anyone should [b]boast.

10 For we are [a]His workmanship, created in Christ Jesus for good works, which God prepared beforehand that we should walk in them.

11 Therefore remember that you, once Gentiles in the flesh—who are called Uncircumcision by what is called [a]the Circumcision made in the flesh by hands—

12 that at that time you were without Christ, being aliens from the commonwealth of Israel and strangers from the covenants of promise, having no hope and without God in the world.

13 But now in Christ Jesus you who once were far off have been brought near by the blood of Christ.

14 For He Himself is our peace, who has made both one, and has broken down the middle wall of separation,

15 having abolished in His flesh the enmity, *that is,* the law of commandments *contained* in ordinances, so as to create in Himself one [a]new man *from* the two, *thus* making peace,

16 and that He might [a]reconcile them both to God in one body through the cross, thereby [b]putting to death the enmity.

17 And He came and preached peace to you who were afar off and to those who were near.

18 For [a]through Him we both have access [b]by one Spirit to the Father.

19 Now, therefore, you are no longer strangers and foreigners, but fellow citizens with the saints and members of the household of God,

20 having been [a]built [b]on the ★ foundation of the [c]apostles and prophets, Jesus Christ Himself being [d]the chief corner*stone,*

21 in whom the whole building, being fitted together, grows into [a]a holy temple in the Lord,

22 [a]in whom you also are being built together for a [b]dwelling place of God in the Spirit.

3 For this reason I, Paul, the prisoner of Christ Jesus for you Gentiles—

2 if indeed you have heard of the [1]dispensation of the grace of God [a]which was given to me for you,

3 [a]how that by revelation [b]He made known to me the mystery (as I have briefly written already,

4 by which, when you read, you may understand my knowledge in the mystery of Christ),

5 which in other ages was not made known to the sons of men, as it has now been revealed by the Spirit to His holy apostles and prophets:

6 that the Gentiles [a]should be fellow heirs, of the same body, and partakers of His promise in Christ through the gospel,

7 [a]of which I became a minister [b]according to the gift of the grace of God given to me by [c]the effective working of His power.

8 To me, [a]who am less than the least of all the saints, this grace was given, that I should preach among the Gentiles [b]the unsearchable riches of Christ,

8 [a][2 Tim. 1:9] [b]Rom. 4:16 [c][John 1:12, 13]
9 [a]Rom. 4:4, 5; 11:6 [b]Rom. 3:27
10 [a]Is. 19:25
11 [a][Col. 2:11]
15 [a]Gal. 6:15
16 [a][Col. 1:20–22] [b][Rom. 6:6]
18 [a]John 10:9 [b]1 Cor. 12:13
20 [a]1 Pet. 2:4 [b]Matt. 16:18 [c]1 Cor. 12:28 [d]Ps. 118:22; Luke 20:17
21 [a]1 Cor. 3:16, 17
22 [a]1 Pet. 2:5 [b]John 17:23

CHAPTER 3

2 [a]Acts 9:15 [1]*stewardship*
3 [a]Acts 22:17, 21; 26:16 [b][Rom. 11:25; 16:25]
6 [a]Gal. 3:28, 29
7 [a]Rom. 15:16 [b]Rom. 1:5 [c]Rom. 15:18
8 [a][1 Cor. 15:9] [b][Col. 1:27; 2:2, 3]

9 and to make all see what *is* the [1]fellowship of the mystery, which from the beginning of the ages has been hidden in God who [a]created all things [2]through Jesus Christ;

10 [a]to the intent that now [b]the [1]manifold wisdom of God might be made known by the church [c]to the [2]principalities and powers in the heavenly *places,*

11 [a]according to the eternal purpose which He accomplished in Christ Jesus our Lord,

12 in whom we have boldness and access [a]with confidence through faith in Him.

13 [a]Therefore I ask that you do not lose heart at my tribulations for you, [b]which is your glory.

14 For this reason I bow my knees to the [a]Father [1]of our Lord Jesus Christ,

15 from whom the whole family in heaven and earth is named,

16 that He would grant you, [a]according to the riches of His glory, [b]to be strengthened with might through His Spirit in [c]the inner man,

17 [a]that Christ may dwell in your hearts through faith; that you, [b]being rooted and grounded in love,

18 [a]may be able to comprehend with all the saints [b]what *is* the width and length and depth and height—

19 to know the love of Christ which passes knowledge; that you may be filled [a]with all the fullness of God.

20 Now [a]to Him who is able to do exceedingly abundantly [b]above all that we ask or think, [c]according to the power that works in us,

21 [a]to Him *be* glory in the church by Christ Jesus to all generations, forever and ever. Amen.

4

I, therefore, the prisoner [1]of the Lord, [2]beseech you to [a]walk worthy of the calling with which you were called,

2 with all lowliness and gentleness, with longsuffering, bearing with one another in love,

3 endeavoring to keep the unity of the Spirit [a]in the bond of peace.

4 [a]*There is* one body and one Spirit, just as you were called in one hope of your calling;

5 [a]one Lord, [b]one faith, [c]one baptism;

6 [a]one God and Father of all, who *is* above all, and [b]through all, and in [1]you all.

7 But [a]to each one of us grace was given according to the measure of Christ's gift.

8 Therefore He says: ★

> [a]*"When He ascended on high,*
> *He led captivity captive,*
> *And gave gifts to men."*

9 [a](Now this, *"He ascended"*—what does it mean but that He also [1]first descended into the lower parts of the earth?

10 He who descended is also the ★
One [a]who ascended far above all the heavens, [b]that He might fill all things.)

11 And He Himself gave some *to be* apostles, some prophets, some evangelists, and some pastors and teachers,

12 for the equipping of the saints for the work of ministry, [a]for the [1]edifying of [b]the body of Christ,

13 till we all come to the unity of

---

9 [a]Heb. 1:2 [1]NU, M *stewardship* (dispensation) [2]NU omits *through Jesus Christ*
10 [a]1 Pet. 1:12 [b][1 Tim. 3:16] [c]Col. 1:16; 2:10, 15 [1]*variegated* or *many-sided* [2]*rulers*
11 [a][Eph. 1:4, 11]
12 [a]Heb. 4:16; 10:19, 35
13 [a]Phil. 1:14 [b]2 Cor. 1:6
14 [a]Eph. 1:3 [1]NU omits *of our Lord Jesus Christ*
16 [a][Phil. 4:19] [b]Col. 1:11 [c]Rom. 7:22
17 [a]John 14:23 [b]Col. 1:23
18 [a]Eph. 1:18 [b]Rom. 8:39
19 [a]Eph. 1:23
20 [a]Rom. 16:25 [b]1 Cor. 2:9 [c]Col. 1:29
21 [a]Rom. 11:36

CHAPTER 4

1 [a]1 Thess. 2:12 [1]Lit. *in* [2]*exhort, encourage*
3 [a]Col. 3:14
4 [a]Rom. 12:5
5 [a]1 Cor. 1:13 [b]Jude 3 [c][Heb. 6:6]
6 [a]Mal. 2:10 [b]Rom. 11:36 [1]NU omits *you;* M *us*
7 [a][1 Cor. 12:7, 11]
8 [a]Ps. 68:18; Mark 16:19; Acts 1:9; [1 Cor. 12:4–11]
9 [a]John 3:13; 20:17 [1]NU omits *first*
10 [a]Ps. 68:18; Acts 1:9 [b][Acts 2:33; Eph. 1:23]
12 [a]1 Cor. 14:26 [b]Col. 1:24 [1]*building up*

the faith [a]and of the knowledge
of the Son of God, to [b]a perfect
man, to the measure of the stature of the fullness of Christ;
14 that we should no longer be
[a]children, tossed to and fro and
carried about with every wind
of doctrine, by the trickery of
men, in the cunning craftiness
of [b]deceitful plotting,
15 but, speaking the truth in love,
may grow up in all things into
Him who is the [a]head—Christ—
16 [a]from whom the whole body,
joined and knit together by what
every joint supplies, according to
the effective working by which
every part does its share, causes
growth of the body for the edify-
ing of itself in love.
17 This I say, therefore, and testify in the Lord, that you should
[a]no longer walk as [1]the rest of
the Gentiles walk, in the futility
of their mind,
18 having their understanding
darkened, being alienated from
the life of God, because of the ignorance that is in them, because
of the [a]blindness of their heart;
19 [a]who, being past feeling,
[b]have given themselves over to
lewdness, to work all uncleanness with greediness.
20 But you have not so learned
Christ,
21 if indeed you have heard Him
and have been taught by Him, as
the truth is in Jesus:
22 that you [a]put off, concerning
your former conduct, the old
man which grows corrupt according to the deceitful lusts,
23 and [a]be renewed in the spirit
of your mind,
24 and that you [a]put on the new
man which was created accord-

13 [a]Col. 2:2 [b]1 Cor. 14:20
14 [a]1 Cor. 14:20 [b]Rom. 16:18
15 [a]Eph. 1:22
16 [a]Col. 2:19
17 [a]Eph. 2:2; 4:22 [1]NU omits *the rest of*
18 [a]Rom. 1:21
19 [a]1 Tim. 4:2 [b]1 Pet. 4:3
22 [a]Col. 3:8
23 [a][Rom. 12:2]
24 [a][Rom. 6:4; 7:6; 12:2]
25 [a]Zech. 8:16 [b]Rom. 12:5
26 [a]Ps. 4:4; 37:8
27 [a][Rom. 12:19] [1]*an opportunity*
28 [a]Acts 20:35 [b]Luke 3:11
29 [a]Col. 3:8 [b]1 Thess. 5:11 [c]Col. 3:16 [1]*building up*
30 [a]Is. 7:13
31 [a]Col. 3:8, 19 [b]James 4:11 [c]Titus 3:3 [1]*loud quarreling*
32 [a]2 Cor. 6:10 [b][Mark 11:25]

CHAPTER 5

1 [a]Luke 6:36 [b]1 Pet. 1:14–16
2 [a]1 Thess. 4:9 [b]Gal. 1:4 [c]2 Cor. 2:14, 15
3 [a]Col. 3:5–7 [b][Luke 12:15]
4 [a]Matt. 12:34, 35 [b]Titus 3:9

ing to God, in true righteousness
and holiness.
25 Therefore, putting away lying, [a]*"Let each one of you speak
truth with his neighbor,"* for [b]we
are members of one another.
26 [a]*"Be angry, and do not sin"*:
do not let the sun go down on
your wrath,
27 [a]nor give [1]place to the devil.
28 Let him who stole steal no
longer, but rather [a]let him labor, working with *his* hands
what is good, that he may have
something [b]to give him who has
need.
29 [a]Let no corrupt word proceed
out of your mouth, but [b]what is
good for necessary [1]edification,
[c]that it may impart grace to the
hearers.
30 And [a]do not grieve the Holy
Spirit of God, by whom you
were sealed for the day of redemption.
31 [a]Let all bitterness, wrath, anger, [1]clamor, and [b]evil speaking
be put away from you, [c]with all
malice.
32 And [a]be kind to one another,
tenderhearted, [b]forgiving one
another, even as God in Christ
forgave you.

5 Therefore[a] be imitators of
God as dear [b]children.
2 And [a]walk in love, [b]as Christ
also has loved us and given
Himself for us, an offering and
a sacrifice to God [c]for a sweet-
smelling aroma.
3 But fornication and all [a]un-
cleanness or [b]covetousness, let it
not even be named among you,
as is fitting for saints;
4 [a]neither filthiness, nor [b]fool-
ish talking, nor coarse jesting,

[c]which are not fitting, but rather
[d]giving of thanks.
5 For [1]this you know, that no
fornicator, unclean person, nor
covetous man, who is an idolater, has any [a]inheritance in the
kingdom of Christ and God.
6 Let no one deceive you with
empty words, for because of
these things the wrath of God
comes upon the sons of disobedience.
7 Therefore do not be [a]partak-
ers with them.
8 For you were once darkness,
but now *you are* [a]light in the
Lord. Walk as children of light
9 (for [a]the fruit of the [1]Spirit *is*
in all goodness, righteousness,
and truth),
10 [a]finding out what is acceptable to the Lord.
11 And have [a]no fellowship with
the unfruitful works of darkness, but rather [1]expose *them.*
12 [a]For it is shameful even to
speak of those things which are
done by them in secret.
13 But [a]all things that are [1]ex-
posed are made manifest by the
light, for whatever makes manifest is light.
★ 14 Therefore He says:

[a]"Awake, you who sleep,
Arise from the dead,
And Christ will give you
light."

15 [a]See then that you walk [1]cir-
cumspectly, not as fools but as
wise,
16 [a]redeeming the time, [b]be-
cause the days are evil.
17 [a]Therefore do not be unwise,
but [b]understand [c]what the will
of the Lord *is.*

4 [c]Rom. 1:28 [d]Phil. 4:6
5 [a]1 Cor. 6:9, 10 [1]NU *know this*
7 [a]1 Tim. 5:22
8 [a]1 Thess. 5:5
9 [a]Gal. 5:22 [1]NU *light*
10 [a][Rom. 12:1, 2]
11 [a]2 Cor. 6:14 [1]*reprove*
12 [a]Rom. 1:24
13 [a][John 3:20, 21] [1]*reproved*
14 [a][Is. 26:19; 60:1]
15 [a]Col. 4:5 [1]*carefully*
16 [a]Col. 4:5 [b]Eccl. 11:2
17 [a]Col. 4:5 [b][Rom. 12:2] [c]1 Thess. 4:3
18 [a]Prov. 20:1; 23:31
19 [a]Acts 16:25 [b]James 5:13
20 [a]Ps. 34:1 [b][1 Pet. 2:5]
21 [a][Phil. 2:3] [1]NU *Christ*
22 [a]Col. 3:18—4:1
23 [a][1 Cor. 11:3] [b]Col. 1:18
24 [a]Titus 2:4, 5
25 [a]Col. 3:19 [b]Acts 20:28
26 [a]John 3:5 [b][John 15:3; 17:17] [1]*set it apart*
27 [a]Col. 1:22 [b]Song 4:7
30 [a]Gen. 2:23 [1]NU omits the rest of v. 30.

18 And [a]do not be drunk with
wine, in which is dissipation; but
be filled with the Spirit,
19 speaking to one another [a]in
psalms and hymns and spiritual songs, singing and making
[b]melody in your heart to the
Lord,
20 [a]giving thanks always for all
things to God the Father [b]in the
name of our Lord Jesus Christ,
21 [a]submitting to one another in
the fear of [1]God.
22 Wives, [a]submit to your own
husbands, as to the Lord.
23 For [a]the husband is head of
the wife, as also [b]Christ is head
of the church; and He is the Savior of the body.
24 Therefore, just as the church
is subject to Christ, so *let* the
wives *be* to their own husbands
[a]in everything.
25 [a]Husbands, love your wives,
just as Christ also loved the
church and [b]gave Himself for
her,
26 that He might [1]sanctify and
cleanse her [a]with the washing of
water [b]by the word,
27 [a]that He might present her
to Himself a glorious church,
[b]not having spot or wrinkle or
any such thing, but that she
should be holy and without
blemish.
28 So husbands ought to love
their own wives as their own
bodies; he who loves his wife
loves himself.
29 For no one ever hated his
own flesh, but nourishes and
cherishes it, just as the Lord
does the church.
30 For [a]we are members of His
body, [1]of His flesh and of His
bones.

31 [a]*"For this reason a man shall*
leave his father and mother and
be joined to his wife, and the
[b]*two shall become one flesh."*
32 This is a great mystery, but I
speak concerning Christ and the
church.
33 Nevertheless [a]let each one
of you in particular so love his
own wife as himself, and let the
wife *see* that she [b]respects *her*
husband.

CHAPTER 6

6 Children, [a]obey your parents in the Lord, for this is
right.
2 [a]*"Honor your father and*
mother," which is the first commandment with promise:
3 *"that it may be well with you*
and you may live long on the
earth."
4 And [a]you, fathers, do not
provoke your children to wrath,
but [b]bring them up in the training and admonition of the Lord.
5 [a]Bondservants, be obedient
to those who are your masters
according to the flesh, [b]with fear
and trembling, [c]in sincerity of
heart, as to Christ;
6 [a]not with eyeservice, as menpleasers, but as bondservants
of Christ, doing the will of God
from the heart,
7 with goodwill doing service,
as to the Lord, and not to men,
8 [a]knowing that whatever good
anyone does, he will receive the
same from the Lord, whether *he*
is a slave or free.
9 And you, masters, do the
same things to them, giving up
threatening, knowing that [1]your
own [a]Master also is in heaven,
and [b]there is no partiality with
Him.

10 Finally, my brethren, be strong
in the Lord and in the power of
His might.
11 [a]Put on the whole armor of
God, that you may be able to
stand against the [1]wiles of the
devil.
12 For we do not wrestle against
flesh and blood, but against
[a]principalities, against powers,
against [b]the rulers of [1]the darkness of this age, against spiritual
hosts of wickedness in the heavenly *places.*
13 [a]Therefore take up the whole
armor of God, that you may be
able to withstand [b]in the evil day,
and having done all, to stand.
14 Stand therefore, [a]having
girded your waist with truth,
[b]having put on the breastplate of
righteousness,
15 [a]and having shod your feet
with the preparation of the gospel of peace;
16 above all, taking [a]the shield
of faith with which you will be
able to quench all the fiery darts
of the wicked one.
17 And [a]take the helmet of salvation, and [b]the sword of the
Spirit, which is the word of God;
18 [a]praying always with all
prayer and supplication in the
Spirit, [b]being watchful to this
end with all perseverance and
[c]supplication for all the saints—
19 and for me, that utterance
may be given to me, [a]that I may
open my mouth boldly to make
known the mystery of the gospel,
20 for which [a]I am an ambassador in chains; that in it I
may speak boldly, as I ought to
speak.

31 [a]Gen. 2:24 [b][1 Cor. 6:16]
33 [a]Col. 3:19 [b]1 Pet. 3:1, 6
1 [a]Col. 3:20
2 [a]Deut. 5:16
4 [a]Col. 3:21 [b]Gen. 18:19
5 [a][1 Tim. 6:1] [b]2 Cor. 7:15 [c]1 Chr. 29:17
6 [a]Col. 3:22
8 [a]Rom. 2:6
9 [a]Col. 4:1 [b]Rom. 2:11 [1]NU *He who is both their Master and yours is*
11 [a][2 Cor. 6:7] [1]*schemings*
12 [a]Rom. 8:38 [b]Luke 22:53 [1]NU *this darkness,*
13 [a][2 Cor. 10:4] [b]Eph. 5:16
14 [a]Is. 11:5 [b]Is. 59:17
15 [a]Is. 52:7
16 [a]1 John 5:4
17 [a]1 Thess. 5:8 [b][Heb. 4:12]
18 [a]Luke 18:1 [b][Matt. 26:41] [c]Phil. 1:4
19 [a]Col. 4:3
20 [a]2 Cor. 5:20

21 But that you also may know
my affairs *and* how I am doing,
[a]Tych′i·cus, a beloved brother
and [b]faithful minister in the
Lord, will make all things known
to you;
22 [a]whom I have sent to you for
this very purpose, that you may
know our affairs, and *that* he
may [b]comfort your hearts.
23 Peace to the brethren, and
love with faith, from God the Father and the Lord Jesus Christ.
24 Grace *be* with all those who
love our Lord Jesus Christ in
sincerity. Amen.

21 [a]Acts 20:4 [b]1 Cor. 4:1, 2
22 [a]Col. 4:8 [b]2 Cor. 1:6

The Epistle of Paul the Apostle to the
PHILIPPIANS

PAUL writes a thank-you note to the believers at Philippi for their help in his hour of need, and he uses the occasion to send along some instruction on Christian unity. His central thought is simple: Only in Christ are real unity and joy possible. With Christ as your model of humility and service, you can enjoy a oneness of purpose, attitude, goal, and labor—a truth Paul illustrates from his own life, and one the Philippians desperately need to hear. Within their own ranks, fellow workers in the Philippian church are at odds, hindering the work in proclaiming new life in Christ. Because of this, Paul exhorts the church to "stand fast . . . be of the same mind . . . rejoice in the Lord always . . . but in everything by prayer and supplication, with thanksgiving, let your requests be made known . . . and the peace of God, which surpasses all understanding, will guard your hearts and minds through Christ Jesus" (4:1, 2, 4, 6, 7).

This epistle is called *Pros Philippesious*, "To the Philippians." The church at Philippi was the first church Paul founded in Macedonia.

PAUL and Timothy, bondservants of Jesus Christ,

To all the saints in Christ Jesus who are in Phi·lip′pī, with the [1]bishops and [a]deacons:

2 Grace to you and peace from God our Father and the Lord Jesus Christ.

3 [a]I thank my God upon every remembrance of you,
4 always in [a]every prayer of mine making request for you all with joy,
5 [a]for your fellowship in the gospel from the first day until now,
6 being confident of this very thing, that He who has begun [a]a good work in you will complete *it* until the day of Jesus Christ;
7 just as it is right for me to think this of you all, because I have you in my heart, inasmuch as both in my chains and in the defense and confirmation of the gospel, you all are partakers with me of grace.
8 For God is my witness, how greatly I long for you all with the affection of Jesus Christ.
9 And this I pray, that your love may abound still more and more in knowledge and all discernment,
10 that you may approve the things that are excellent, that you may be sincere and without offense till the day of Christ,
11 being filled with the fruits of righteousness [a]which *are* by Jesus Christ, [b]to the glory and praise of God.
12 But I want you to know, brethren, that the things *which happened* to me have actually turned out for the furtherance of the gospel,
13 so that it has become evident [a]to the whole [1]palace guard, and to all the rest, that my chains are in Christ;

CHAPTER 1

1 [a][1 Tim. 3:8–13] [1]Lit. *overseers*
3 [a]1 Cor. 1:4
4 [a]Eph. 1:16
5 [a][Rom. 12:13]
6 [a][John 6:29]
11 [a]Col. 1:6 [b]John 15:8
13 [a]Phil. 4:22 [1]Or *Praetorium*

14 and most of the brethren in
the Lord, having become confident by my chains, are much
more bold to speak the word
without fear.
15 Some indeed preach Christ
even from envy and strife, and
some also from goodwill:
16 [1]The former preach Christ
from selfish ambition, not sincerely, supposing to add affliction to my chains;
17 but the latter out of love,
knowing that I am appointed for
the defense of the gospel.
18 What then? Only *that* in every way, whether in pretense or
in truth, Christ is preached; and
in this I rejoice, yes, and will rejoice.
19 For I know that [a]this will turn
out for my deliverance through
your prayer and the supply of
the Spirit of Jesus Christ,
20 according to my earnest expectation and hope that in nothing I shall be ashamed, but [a]with
all boldness, as always, so now
also Christ will be magnified in
my body, whether by life [b]or by
death.
21 For to me, to live *is* Christ,
and to die *is* gain.
22 But if *I* live on in the flesh,
this *will mean* fruit from *my*
labor; yet what I shall choose I
[1]cannot tell.
23 [1]For I am hard-pressed between the two, having a [a]desire
to depart and be with Christ,
which is [b]far better.
24 Nevertheless to remain in the
flesh *is* more needful for you.
25 And being confident of this,
I know that I shall remain and
continue with you all for your
progress and joy of faith,
26 that [a]your rejoicing for me
may be more abundant in Jesus
Christ by my coming to you
again.
27 Only [a]let your conduct be
worthy of the gospel of Christ,
so that whether I come and see
you or am absent, I may hear of
your affairs, that you stand fast
in one spirit, [b]with one mind
[c]striving together for the faith of
the gospel,
28 and not in any way terrified
by your adversaries, which is to
them a proof of perdition, but [1]to
you of salvation, and that from
God.
29 For to you [a]it has been
granted on behalf of Christ, [b]not
only to believe in Him, but also
to [c]suffer for His sake,
30 [a]having the same conflict
[b]which you saw in me and now
hear *is* in me.

2 Therefore if *there is* any
[1]consolation in Christ, if any
comfort of love, if any fellowship
of the Spirit, if any [a]affection
and mercy,
2 [a]fulfill my joy [b]by being like-
minded, having the same love,
being of [c]one accord, of one
mind.
3 [a]*Let* nothing *be done* through
selfish ambition or conceit, but
[b]in lowliness of mind let each esteem others better than himself.
4 [a]Let each of you look out not
only for his own interests, but
also for the interests of [b]others.
5 [a]Let this mind be in you
which was also in Christ Jesus,
6 who, [a]being in the form of
God, did not consider it [1]robbery
to be equal with God,
7 [a]but [1]made Himself of no
reputation, taking the form [b]of a
bondservant, *and* [c]coming in the
likeness of men.

16 [1]NU reverses vv. 16 and 17.
19 [a]Job 13:16, LXX
20 [a]Eph. 6:19, 20 [b][Rom. 14:8]
22 [1]*do not know*
23 [a][2 Cor. 5:2, 8] [b][Ps. 16:11] [1]NU, M *But*
26 [a]2 Cor. 1:14
27 [a]Eph. 4:1 [b]Eph. 4:3 [c]Jude 3
28 [1]NU *of your salvation*
29 [a][Matt. 5:11, 12] [b]Eph. 2:8 [c][2 Tim. 3:12]
30 [a]Col. 1:29; 2:1 [b]Acts 16:19–40

CHAPTER 2

1 [a]Col. 3:12 [1]Or *encouragement*
2 [a]John 3:29 [b]Rom. 12:16 [c]Phil. 4:2
3 [a]Gal. 5:26 [b]Rom. 12:10
4 [a]1 Cor. 13:5 [b]Rom. 15:1, 2
5 [a][Matt. 11:29]
6 [a]2 Cor. 4:4 [1]Or *something to be held onto to be equal*
7 [a]Ps. 22:6 [b]Is. 42:1 [c][John 1:14] [1]*emptied Himself of His privileges*

8 And being found in appearance as a man, He humbled Himself and [a]became [b]obedient to *the point of* death, even the death of the cross.

★ 9 [a]Therefore God also [b]has highly exalted Him and [c]given Him the name which is above every name,

10 [a]that at the name of Jesus every knee should bow, of those in heaven, and of those on earth, and of those under the earth,

☆ 11 and [a]*that* every tongue should confess that Jesus Christ *is* Lord, to the glory of God the Father.

12 Therefore, my beloved, [a]as you have always obeyed, not as in my presence only, but now much more in my absence, [b]work out your own salvation with [c]fear and trembling;

13 for [a]it is God who works in you both to will and to do [b]for *His* good pleasure.

14 Do all things [a]without [1]complaining and [b]disputing,[2]

15 that you may become blameless and [1]harmless, children of God without fault in the midst of a crooked and perverse generation, among whom you shine as [a]lights in the world,

16 holding fast the word of life, so that [a]I may rejoice in the day of Christ that [b]I have not run in vain or labored in [c]vain.

17 Yes, and if [a]I am being poured out *as a drink offering* on the sacrifice [b]and service of your faith, [c]I am glad and rejoice with you all.

18 For the same reason you also be glad and rejoice with me.

19 But I trust in the Lord Jesus to send [a]Timothy to you shortly, that I also may be encouraged when I know your [1]state.

20 For I have no one [a]likeminded, who will sincerely care for your state.

21 For all seek their own, not the things which are of Christ Jesus.

22 But you know his proven character, [a]that as a son with *his* father he served with me in the gospel.

23 Therefore I hope to send him at once, as soon as I see how it goes with me.

24 But I trust in the Lord that I myself shall also come shortly.

25 Yet I considered it necessary to send to you [a]E·paph·ro·dī′tus, my brother, fellow worker, and [b]fellow soldier, [c]but your messenger and [d]the one who ministered to my need;

26 [a]since he was longing for you all, and was distressed because you had heard that he was sick.

27 For indeed he was sick almost unto death; but God had mercy on him, and not only on him but on me also, lest I should have sorrow upon sorrow.

28 Therefore I sent him the more eagerly, that when you see him again you may rejoice, and I may be less sorrowful.

29 Receive him therefore in the Lord with all gladness, and hold such men in esteem;

30 because for the work of Christ he came close to death, [1]not regarding his life, [a]to supply what was lacking in your service toward me.

3 Finally, my brethren, [a]rejoice in the Lord. For me to write the same things to you *is* not tedious, but for you *it is* safe.

---

8 [a]Matt. 26:39 [b]Heb. 5:8

9 [a]Heb. 2:9 [b]Ps. 68:18; 110:1; Is. 52:13; Acts 2:33 [c]Is. 9:6; Luke 1:32; Eph. 1:21

10 [a]Is. 45:23

11 [a]John 13:13; [Rom. 10:9; 14:9]

12 [a]Phil. 1:5, 6; 4:15 [b]John 6:27, 29 [c]Eph. 6:5

13 [a]Heb. 13:20, 21 [b]Eph. 1:5

14 [a]1 Pet. 4:9 [b]Rom. 14:1 [1]*grumbling* [2]*arguing*

15 [a]Matt. 5:15, 16 [1]*innocent*

16 [a]2 Cor. 1:14 [b]Gal. 2:2 [c]1 Thess. 3:5

17 [a]2 Tim. 4:6 [b]Rom. 15:16 [c]2 Cor. 7:4

19 [a]Rom. 16:21 [1]*condition*

20 [a]2 Tim. 3:10

22 [a]1 Cor. 4:17

25 [a]Phil. 4:18 [b]Philem. 2 [c]2 Cor. 8:23 [d]2 Cor. 11:9

26 [a]Phil. 1:8

30 [a]1 Cor. 16:17 [1]*risking*

CHAPTER 3

1 [a]1 Thess. 5:16

2 [a]Beware of dogs, beware of
[b]evil workers, [c]beware of the
mutilation!
3 For we are [a]the circumcision,
[b]who worship [1]God in the Spirit,
rejoice in Christ Jesus, and have
no confidence in the flesh,
4 though [a]I also might have
confidence in the flesh. If anyone else thinks he may have
confidence in the flesh, I [b]more
so:
5 circumcised the eighth day,
of the stock of Israel, [a]*of* the
tribe of Benjamin, [b]a Hebrew
of the Hebrews; concerning the
law, [c]a Phar'i·see;
6 concerning zeal, [a]persecuting
the church; concerning the righteousness which is in the law,
blameless.
7 But [a]what things were gain
to me, these I have counted loss
for Christ.
8 Yet indeed I also count all
things loss [a]for the excellence of
the knowledge of Christ Jesus
my Lord, for whom I have suffered the loss of all things, and
count them as rubbish, that I
may gain Christ
9 and be found in Him, not
having [a]my own righteousness,
which *is* from the law, but [b]that
which *is* through faith in Christ,
the righteousness which is from
God by faith;
10 that I may know Him and the
[a]power of His resurrection, and
[b]the fellowship of His sufferings,
being conformed to His death,
11 if, by any means, I may [a]at-
tain[1] to the resurrection from
the dead.
12 Not that I have already [a]at-
tained,[1] or am already [b]perfected;
but I press on, that I may lay
hold of that for which Christ Jesus has also laid hold of me.
13 Brethren, I do not count
myself to have [1]apprehended;
but one thing *I do*, [a]forgetting
those things which are behind
and [b]reaching forward to those
things which are ahead,
14 [a]I press toward the goal for
the prize of [b]the upward call of
God in Christ Jesus.
15 Therefore let us, as many as
are [a]mature, [b]have this mind;
and if in anything you think
otherwise, [c]God will reveal even
this to you.
16 Nevertheless, to *the degree*
that we have already [1]attained,
[a]let us walk [b]by the same [2]rule,
let us be of the same mind.
17 Brethren, [a]join in following
my example, and note those
who so walk, as [b]you have us for
a pattern.
18 For many walk, of whom I
have told you often, and now
tell you even weeping, *that they
are* [a]the enemies of the cross of
Christ:
19 [a]whose end *is* destruction,
[b]whose god *is their* belly, and
[c]*whose* glory *is* in their shame—
[d]who set their mind on earthly
things.
20 For [a]our citizenship is in
heaven, [b]from which we also
[c]eagerly wait for the Savior, the
Lord Jesus Christ,
21 [a]who will transform our lowly
body that it may be [b]conformed
to His glorious body, [c]according
to the working by which He is
able even to [d]subdue all things
to Himself.

4
Therefore, my beloved and
[a]longed-for brethren, [b]my
joy and crown, so [c]stand fast in
the Lord, beloved.

2 [a]Gal. 5:15 [b]Ps. 119:115 [c]Rom. 2:28
3 [a]Deut. 30:6 [b]Rom. 7:6 [1]NU, M *in the Spirit of God*
4 [a]2 Cor. 5:16; 11:18 [b]2 Cor. 11:22, 23
5 [a]Rom. 11:1 [b]2 Cor. 11:22 [c]Acts 23:6
6 [a]Acts 8:3; 22:4, 5; 26:9–11
7 [a]Matt. 13:44
8 [a]Jer. 9:23
9 [a]Rom. 10:3 [b]Rom. 1:17
10 [a]Eph. 1:19, 20 [b][Rom. 6:3–5]
11 [a]Acts 26:6–8 [1]Lit. *arrive at*
12 [a][1 Tim. 6:12, 19] [b]Heb. 12:23 [1]*obtained it*
13 [a]Luke 9:62 [b]Heb. 6:1 [1]*laid hold of it*
14 [a]2 Tim. 4:7 [b]Heb. 3:1
15 [a]1 Cor. 2:6 [b]Gal. 5:10 [c]Hos. 6:3
16 [a]Gal. 6:16 [b]Rom. 12:16; 15:5 [1]*arrived* [2]NU omits *rule* and the rest of v. 16.
17 [a][1 Cor. 4:16; 11:1] [b]Titus 2:7, 8
18 [a]Gal. 1:7
19 [a]2 Cor. 11:15 [b]1 Tim. 6:5 [c]Hos. 4:7 [d]Rom. 8:5
20 [a]Eph. 2:6, 19 [b]Acts 1:11 [c]1 Cor. 1:7
21 [a][1 Cor. 15:43–53] [b]1 John 3:2 [c]Eph. 1:19 [d][1 Cor. 15:28]

CHAPTER 4

1 [a]Phil. 1:8 [b]2 Cor. 1:14 [c]Phil. 1:27

2 I implore Eū·ō′di·a and I implore Syn′ty·chē [a]to be of the same mind in the Lord.

3 [1]And I urge you also, true companion, help these women who [a]labored with me in the gospel, with Clem′ent also, and the rest of my fellow workers, whose names *are* in [b]the Book of Life.

4 [a]Rejoice in the Lord always. Again I will say, rejoice!

5 Let your [1]gentleness be known to all men. [a]The Lord *is* at hand.

6 [a]Be anxious for nothing, but in everything by prayer and supplication, with [b]thanksgiving, let your requests be made known to God;

7 and [a]the peace of God, which surpasses all understanding, will guard your hearts and minds through Christ Jesus.

8 Finally, brethren, whatever things are [a]true, whatever things *are* [b]noble, whatever things *are* [c]just, [d]whatever things *are* pure, whatever things *are* [e]lovely, whatever things *are* of good report, if *there is* any virtue and if *there is* anything praiseworthy—meditate on these things.

9 The things which you learned and received and heard and saw in me, these do, and [a]the God of peace will be with you.

10 But I rejoiced in the Lord greatly that now at last [a]your[1] care for me has flourished again; though you surely did care, but you lacked opportunity.

11 Not that I speak in regard to need, for I have learned in whatever state I am, [a]to be content:

12 [a]I know how to [1]be abased, and I know how to [2]abound. Everywhere and in all things I have learned both to be full and to be hungry, both to abound and to suffer need.

13 I can do all things [a]through [1]Christ who strengthens me.

14 Nevertheless you have done well that [a]you shared in my distress.

15 Now you Phi·lip′pi·ans know also that in the beginning of the gospel, when I departed from Mac·e·dō′ni·a, [a]no church shared with me concerning giving and receiving but you only.

16 For even in Thes·sa·lo·nī′ca you sent *aid* once and again for my necessities.

17 Not that I seek the gift, but I seek [a]the fruit that abounds to your account.

18 Indeed I [1]have all and abound. I am full, having received from [a]E·paph·ro·dī′tus the things *sent* from you, [b]a sweet-smelling aroma, [c]an acceptable sacrifice, well pleasing to God.

19 And my God [a]shall supply all your need according to His riches in glory by Christ Jesus.

20 [a]Now to our God and Father *be* glory forever and ever. Amen.

21 Greet every saint in Christ Jesus. The brethren [a]who are with me greet you.

22 All the saints greet you, but especially those who are of Caesar's household.

23 The grace of our Lord Jesus Christ be with [1]you all. Amen.

2 [a]Phil. 2:2; 3:16
3 [a]Rom. 16:3 [b]Luke 10:20 [1]NU, M *Yes*
4 [a]Rom. 12:12
5 [a][James 5:7–9] [1]*graciousness* or *forbearance*
6 [a]Matt. 6:25 [b][1 Thess. 5:17, 18]
7 [a][John 14:27]
8 [a]Eph. 4:25 [b]2 Cor. 8:21 [c]Deut. 16:20 [d]1 Thess. 5:22 [e]1 Cor. 13:4–7
9 [a]Rom. 15:33
10 [a]2 Cor. 11:9 [1]*you have revived your care*
11 [a]1 Tim. 6:6, 8
12 [a]1 Cor. 4:11 [1]*live humbly* [2]*live in prosperity*
13 [a]John 15:5 [1]NU *Him who*
14 [a]Phil. 1:7
15 [a]2 Cor. 11:8, 9
17 [a]Titus 3:14
18 [a]Phil. 2:25 [b]Heb. 13:16 [c]2 Cor. 9:12 [1]Or *have received all*
19 [a]Ps. 23:1
20 [a]Rom. 16:27
21 [a]Gal. 1:2
23 [1]NU *your spirit*

The Epistle of Paul the Apostle to the

COLOSSIANS

IF Ephesians can be labeled the epistle portraying the "church of Christ," then Colossians must surely be the "Christ of the church." Ephesians focuses on the body; Colossians focuses on the Head. Like Ephesians, the little Book of Colossians divides neatly in half with the first portion doctrinal (1 and 2) and the second practical (3 and 4). Paul's purpose is to show that Christ is preeminent—first and foremost in everything—and the Christian's life should reflect that priority. Because believers are rooted in Him, alive in Him, hidden in Him, and complete in Him, it is utterly inconsistent for them to live life without Him. Clothed in His love, with His peace ruling in their hearts, they are equipped to make Christ first in every area of life.

This epistle became known as *Pros Kolossaeis*, "To the Colossians," because of 1:2. Paul also wanted it to be read in the neighboring church at Laodicea (4:16).

PAUL, [a]an apostle of Jesus
Christ by the will of God, and
Timothy our brother,

2 To the saints [a]and faithful
brethren in Christ *who are* in
Co·los′sē:

[b]Grace to you and peace from
God our Father [1]and the Lord
Jesus Christ.

3 [a]We give thanks to the God
and Father of our Lord Jesus
Christ, praying always for you,
4 [a]since we heard of your faith
in Christ Jesus and of [b]your love
for all the saints;
5 because of the hope [a]which
is laid up for you in heaven, of
which you heard before in the
word of the truth of the gospel,
6 which has come to you, [a]as
it has also in all the world, and
[b]is bringing forth [1]fruit, as *it is*
also among you since the day
you heard and knew [c]the grace
of God in truth;
7 as you also learned from
[a]Ep′a·phras, our dear fellow servant,
who is [b]a faithful minister
of Christ on your behalf,
8 who also declared to us your
[a]love in the Spirit.
9 [a]For this reason we also,
since the day we heard it, do
not cease to pray for you, and to
ask [b]that you may be filled with
[c]the knowledge of His will [d]in
all wisdom and spiritual understanding;
10 [a]that you may walk worthy
of the Lord, [b]fully pleasing
Him, [c]being fruitful in every
good work and increasing in the
[d]knowledge of God;
11 [a]strengthened with all might,
according to His glorious power,
[b]for all patience and longsuffering
[c]with joy;
12 [a]giving thanks to the Father
who has qualified us to be partakers
of [b]the inheritance of the
saints in the light.
13 He has delivered us from
[a]the power of darkness [b]and

CHAPTER 1

1 [a]Eph. 1:1
2 [a]1 Cor. 4:17 [b]Gal. 1:3 [1]NU omits *and the Lord Jesus Christ*
3 [a]Phil. 1:3
4 [a]Eph. 1:15 [b][Heb. 6:10]
5 [a][1 Pet. 1:4]
6 [a]Matt. 24:14 [b]John 15:16 [c]Eph. 3:2 [1]NU, M add *and growing*
7 [a]Philem. 23 [b]2 Cor. 11:23
8 [a]Rom. 15:30
9 [a]Eph. 1:15–17 [b]1 Cor. 1:5 [c][Rom. 12:2] [d]Eph. 1:8
10 [a]Eph. 4:1 [b]1 Thess. 4:1 [c]Heb. 13:21 [d]2 Pet. 3:18
11 [a][Eph. 3:16; 6:10] [b]Eph. 4:2 [c][Acts 5:41]
12 [a][Eph. 5:20] [b]Eph. 1:11
13 [a]Eph. 6:12 [b]2 Pet. 1:11

[1]conveyed *us* into the kingdom
of the Son of His love,
14 [a]in whom we have redemption [1]through His blood, the forgiveness of sins.
15 He is [a]the image of the invisible God, [b]the firstborn over all
creation.
16 For [a]by Him all things were
created that are in heaven and
that are on earth, visible and
invisible, whether thrones or
[b]dominions or [1]principalities or
[2]powers. All things were created
[c]through Him and for Him.
17 [a]And He is before all things,
and in Him [b]all things consist.
18 And [a]He is the head of the
body, the church, who is the beginning, [b]the firstborn from the
dead, that in all things He may
have the preeminence.
19 For it pleased *the Father that*
[a]in Him all the fullness should
dwell,
20 and [a]by Him to reconcile
[b]all things to Himself, by Him,
whether things on earth or
things in heaven, [c]having made
peace through the blood of His
cross.
21 And you, [a]who once were
alienated and enemies in your
mind [b]by wicked works, yet now
He has [c]reconciled
22 [a]in the body of His flesh
through death, [b]to present you
holy, and blameless, and above
reproach in His sight—
23 if indeed you continue [a]in the
faith, grounded and steadfast,
and are [b]not moved away from
the hope of the gospel which
you heard, [c]which was preached
to every creature under heaven,
[d]of which I, Paul, became a minister.
24 [a]I now rejoice in my sufferings
[b]for you, and fill up in my flesh
[c]what is lacking in the afflictions
of Christ, for [d]the sake of His
body, which is the church,
25 of which I became a minister
according to [a]the [1]stewardship
from God which was given to
me for you, to fulfill the word of
God,
26 [a]the [1]mystery which has been
hidden from ages and from generations, [b]but now has been revealed to His saints.
27 [a]To them God willed to make
known what are [b]the riches of
the glory of this mystery among
the Gentiles: [1]which is [c]Christ in
you, [d]the hope of glory.
28 Him we preach, [a]warning
every man and teaching every
man in all wisdom, [b]that we may
present every man perfect in
Christ Jesus.
29 To this *end* I also labor, striving according to His working
which works in me [a]mightily.

2

For I want you to know what
a great [a]conflict[1] I have for
you and those in Lā·o·di·cē′a,
and *for* as many as have not
seen my face in the flesh,
2 that their hearts may be encouraged, being knit together in
love, and *attaining* to all riches
of the full assurance of understanding, to the knowledge of
the mystery of God, [1]both of the
Father and of Christ,
3 [a]in whom are hidden all the
treasures of wisdom and knowledge.
4 Now this I say [a]lest anyone
should deceive you with persua-
sive words.
5 For [a]though I am absent in
the flesh, yet I am with you in
spirit, rejoicing [1]to see [b]your *good*

---

13 [1]*transferred*
14 [a]Eph. 1:7 [1]NU, M omit *through His blood*
15 [a]2 Cor. 4:4 [b]Rev. 3:14
16 [a]Heb. 1:2, 3 [b][Eph. 1:20, 21] [c]Heb. 2:10 [1]*rulers* [2]*authorities*
17 [a][John 17:5] [b]Heb. 1:3
18 [a]Eph. 1:22 [b]Rev. 1:5
19 [a]John 1:16
20 [a]Eph. 2:14 [b]2 Cor. 5:18 [c]Eph. 1:10
21 [a][Eph. 2:1] [b]Titus 1:15 [c]2 Cor. 5:18, 19
22 [a]2 Cor. 5:18 [b][Eph. 5:27]
23 [a]Eph. 3:17 [b][John 15:6] [c]Col. 1:6 [d]Col. 1:25
24 [a]2 Cor. 7:4 [b]Eph. 3:1, 13 [c][2 Cor. 1:5; 12:15] [d]Eph. 1:23
25 [a]Gal. 2:7 [1]*dispensation* or *administration*
26 [a][1 Cor. 2:7] [b][2 Tim. 1:10] [1]*secret* or *hidden truth*
27 [a]2 Cor. 2:14 [b]Rom. 9:23 [c][Rom. 8:10, 11] [d]1 Tim. 1:1 [1]M *who*
28 [a]Acts 20:20 [b]Eph. 5:27
29 [a]Eph. 3:7

CHAPTER 2

1 [a]Phil. 1:30 [1]*struggle*
2 [1]NU omits *both of the Father and*
3 [a]1 Cor. 1:24, 30
4 [a]Rom. 16:18
5 [a]1 Thess. 2:17 [b]1 Cor. 14:40 [1]Lit. *and seeing*

order and the [c]steadfastness of
your faith in Christ.
6 [a]As you therefore have received Christ Jesus the Lord, so
walk in Him,
7 [a]rooted and built up in Him
and established in the faith, as
you have been taught, abounding [1]in it with thanksgiving.
8 Beware lest anyone [1]cheat
you through philosophy and
empty deceit, according to [a]the
tradition of men, according to
the [b]basic principles of the world,
and not according to Christ.
9 For [a]in Him dwells all the
fullness of the Godhead [1]bodily;
10 and you are complete in Him,
who is the [a]head of all [1]principality and power.
11 In Him you were also [a]circumcised with the circumcision
made without hands, by [b]putting
off the body [1]of the sins of the
flesh, by the circumcision of
Christ,
12 [a]buried with Him in baptism,
in which you also were raised
with *Him* through [b]faith in the
working of God, [c]who raised
Him from the dead.
13 And you, being dead in your
trespasses and the uncircumcision of your flesh, He has made
alive together with Him, having
forgiven you all trespasses,
14 [a]having wiped out the [1]handwriting of requirements that was
against us, which was contrary
to us. And He has taken it out of
the way, having nailed it to the
cross.
15 [a]Having disarmed [b]principalities and powers, He made
a public spectacle of them, triumphing over them in it.
16 So let no one [a]judge you in
food or in drink, or regarding a

5 [c]1 Pet. 5:9
6 [a]1 Thess. 4:1
7 [a]Eph. 2:21 [1]NU omits *in it*
8 [a]Gal. 1:14 [b]Gal. 4:3, 9, 10 [1]Lit. *plunder you or take you captive*
9 [a][John 1:14] [1]*in bodily form*
10 [a][Eph. 1:20, 21] [1]*rule and authority*
11 [a]Deut. 10:16 [b]Rom. 6:6; 7:24 [1]NU omits *of the sins*
12 [a]Rom. 6:4 [b]Eph. 1:19, 20 [c]Acts 2:24
14 [a][Eph. 2:15, 16] [1]*certificate of debt with its*
15 [a][Is. 53:12] [b]Eph. 6:12
16 [a]Rom. 14:3 [1]*feast day*
17 [a]Heb. 8:5; 10:1 [1]Lit. *body*
18 [1]NU omits *not*
19 [a]Eph. 4:15 [b]Eph. 1:23; 4:16
20 [a]Rom. 6:2–5 [b]Gal. 4:3, 9 [1]NU, M omit *Therefore*
21 [a]1 Tim. 4:3
22 [a]Titus 1:14
23 [a]1 Tim. 4:8 [1]*severe treatment, asceticism*

CHAPTER 3

1 [a]Col. 2:12 [b]Ps. 68:18; 110:1; Eph. 1:20
2 [a][Matt. 6:19–21]
3 [a][Rom. 6:2] [b][2 Cor. 5:7]
4 [a][1 John 3:2] [b]John 14:6 [c]1 Cor. 15:43
5 [a][Rom. 8:13] [b][Rom. 6:13]

[1]festival or a new moon or sabbaths,
17 [a]which are a shadow of
things to come, but the [1]substance is of Christ.
18 Let no one cheat you of your
reward, taking delight in *false*
humility and worship of angels, intruding into those things
which he has [1]not seen, vainly
puffed up by his fleshly mind,
19 and not holding fast to [a]the
Head, from whom all the body,
nourished and knit together by
joints and ligaments, [b]grows
with the increase *that is* from
God.
20 [1]Therefore, if you [a]died with
Christ from the basic principles
of the world, [b]why, as *though* living in the world, do you subject
yourselves to regulations—
21 [a]"Do not touch, do not taste,
do not handle,"
22 which all concern things
which perish with the using—
[a]according to the commandments and doctrines of men?
23 [a]These things indeed have an
appearance of wisdom in self-imposed religion, *false* humility,
and [1]neglect of the body, *but are*
of no value against the indulgence of the flesh.

3 If then you were [a]raised with ★
Christ, seek those things
which are above, [b]where Christ
is, sitting at the right hand of
God.
2 Set your mind on things
above, not on things on the
[a]earth.
3 [a]For you died, [b]and your life
is hidden with Christ in God.
4 [a]When Christ *who is* [b]our life
appears, then you also will appear with Him in [c]glory.
5 [a]Therefore put to death [b]your

members which are on the earth:
[c]fornication, uncleanness, passion, evil desire, and covetousness, [d]which is idolatry.
6 [a]Because of these things the
wrath of God is coming upon
[b]the sons of disobedience,
7 [a]in which you yourselves
once walked when you lived in
them.
8 [a]But now you yourselves are
to put off all these: anger, wrath,
malice, blasphemy, filthy language out of your mouth.
9 Do not lie to one another,
since you have put off the old
man with his deeds,
10 and have put on the new
man who [a]is renewed in knowledge [b]according to the image of
Him who [c]created him,
11 where there is neither [a]Greek
nor Jew, circumcised nor uncircumcised, barbarian, Scyth'i·an,
slave *nor* free, [b]but Christ *is* all
and in all.
12 Therefore, [a]as *the* elect of
God, holy and beloved, [b]put on
tender mercies, kindness, humility, meekness, longsuffering;
13 [a]bearing with one another,
and forgiving one another, if
anyone has a complaint against
another; even as Christ forgave
you, so you also *must do.*
14 [a]But above all these things
[b]put on love, which is the [c]bond
of perfection.
15 And let [a]the peace of God
rule in your hearts, [b]to which
also you were called [c]in one
body; and [d]be thankful.
16 Let the word of Christ dwell
in you richly in all wisdom,
teaching and admonishing one
another [a]in psalms and hymns
and spiritual songs, singing with
grace in your hearts to the Lord.
17 And [a]whatever you do in
word or deed, *do* all in the name
of the Lord Jesus, giving thanks
to God the Father through Him.
18 [a]Wives, submit to your own
husbands, [b]as is fitting in the
Lord.
19 [a]Husbands, love your wives
and do not be [b]bitter toward
them.
20 [a]Children, obey your parents
[b]in all things, for this is well
pleasing to the Lord.
21 [a]Fathers, do not provoke
your children, lest they become
discouraged.
22 [a]Bondservants, obey in all
things your masters according
to the flesh, not with eyeservice,
as men-pleasers, but in sincerity
of heart, fearing God.
23 [a]And whatever you do, do it
heartily, as to the Lord and not
to men,
24 [a]knowing that from the Lord
you will receive the reward of
the inheritance; [b]for[1] you serve
the Lord Christ.
25 But he who does wrong will
be repaid for what he has done,
and [a]there is no partiality.
4 Masters,[a] give your bondservants what is just and
fair, knowing that you also have
a Master in heaven.
2 [a]Continue earnestly in prayer,
being vigilant in it [b]with thanksgiving;
3 [a]meanwhile praying also for
us, that God would [b]open to us a
door for the word, to speak [c]the
[1]mystery of Christ, [d]for which I
am also in chains,
4 that I may make it manifest,
as I ought to speak.
5 [a]Walk in [b]wisdom toward
those *who are* outside, [c]redeem-
ing the time.

5 [c]Eph. 5:3
[d]Eph. 4:19; 5:3, 5
6 [a]Rom. 1:18
[b][Eph. 2:2]
7 [a]1 Cor. 6:11
8 [a]Eph. 4:22
10 [a]Rom. 12:2
[b][Rom. 8:29]
[c][Eph. 2:10]
11 [a]Gal. 3:27, 28
[b]Eph. 1:23
12 [a][1 Pet. 1:2]
[b]1 John 3:17
13 [a][Mark 11:25]
14 [a]1 Pet. 4:8
[b][1 Cor. 13]
[c]Eph. 4:3
15 [a][John 14:27]
[b]1 Cor. 7:15
[c]Eph. 4:4
[d][1 Thess. 5:18]
16 [a]Eph. 5:19
17 [a]1 Cor. 10:31
18 [a]1 Pet. 3:1
[b][Eph. 5:22—6:9]
19 [a][Eph. 5:25]
[b]Eph. 4:31
20 [a]Eph. 6:1
[b]Eph. 5:24
21 [a]Eph. 6:4
22 [a]Eph. 6:5
23 [a][Eccl. 9:10]
24 [a]Eph. 6:8
[b]1 Cor. 7:22
[1]NU omits *for*
25 [a]Rom. 2:11

CHAPTER 4

1 [a]Eph. 6:9
2 [a]Luke 18:1
[b]Col. 2:7
3 [a]Eph. 6:19
[b]1 Cor. 16:9
[c]Eph. 3:3, 4; 6:19
[d]Eph. 6:20
[1]*hidden truth*
5 [a]Eph. 5:15
[b][Matt. 10:16]
[c]Eph. 5:16

6 *Let* your speech always *be*
[a]with grace, [b]seasoned with salt,
[c]that you may know how you
ought to answer each one.
7 [a]Tych'i·cus, a beloved brother,
faithful minister, and fellow servant in the Lord, will tell you all
the news about me.
8 [a]I am sending him to you for
this very purpose, that [1]he may
know your circumstances and
comfort your hearts,
9 with [a]Ō·nes'i·mus, a faithful
and beloved brother, who is *one*
of you. They will make known
to you all things which *are hap-*
pening here.
10 [a]Ar·is·tar'chus my fellow
prisoner greets you, with [b]Mark
the cousin of Bar'na·bas (about
whom you received instructions:
if he comes to you, welcome
him),
11 and Jesus who is called Jus'-
tus. These *are my* only fellow
workers for the kingdom of God
who are of the circumcision;
they have proved to be a comfort to me.
12 [a]Ep'a·phras, who is *one* of
you, a bondservant of Christ,
greets you, always [b]laboring fervently for you in prayers, that
you may stand [c]perfect and
[1]complete in all the will of God.
13 For I bear him witness that
he has a great [1]zeal for you, and
those who are in Lā·o·di·cē'a,
and those in Hī·er·ap'o·lis.
14 [a]Luke the beloved physician
and [b]Dē'mas greet you.
15 Greet the brethren who are
in Lā·o·di·cē'a, and [1]Nym'phas
and [a]the church that *is* in [2]his
house.
16 Now when [a]this epistle is
read among you, see that it is
read also in the church of the
Lā·o·di·cē'ans, and that you
likewise read the *epistle* from
Lā·o·di·cē'a.
17 And say to [a]Ar·chip'pus, "Take
heed to [b]the ministry which you
have received in the Lord, that
you may fulfill it."
18 [a]This salutation by my own
hand—Paul. [b]Remember my
chains. Grace *be* with you. Amen.

6 [a]Eccl. 10:12 [b]Mark 9:50 [c]1 Pet. 3:15
7 [a]2 Tim. 4:12
8 [a]Eph. 6:22 [1]NU *you may know our circumstances and he may comfort*
9 [a]Philem. 10
10 [a]Acts 19:29; 20:4; 27:2 [b]2 Tim. 4:11
12 [a]Philem. 23 [b]Rom. 15:30 [c]Matt. 5:48 [1]NU *fully assured*
13 [1]NU *concern*
14 [a]2 Tim. 4:11 [b]2 Tim. 4:10
15 [a]Rom. 16:5 [1]NU *Nympha* [2]NU *her*
16 [a]1 Thess. 5:27
17 [a]Philem. 2 [b]2 Tim. 4:5
18 [a]1 Cor. 16:21 [b]Heb. 13:3

The First Epistle of Paul the Apostle to the

THESSALONIANS

PAUL has many pleasant memories of the days he spent with the infant Thessalonian church. Their faith, hope, love, and perseverance in the face of persecution are exemplary. Paul's labors as a spiritual parent to the fledgling church have been richly rewarded, and his affection is visible in every line of his letter.

Paul encourages them to excel in their newfound faith, to increase in their love for one another, and to rejoice, pray, and give thanks always. He closes his letter with instruction regarding the return of the Lord, whose advent signifies hope and comfort for believers both living and dead.

Because this is the first of Paul's two canonical letters to the church at Thessalonica, it received the title *Pros Thessalonikeis A*, the "First to the Thessalonians."

PAUL, [a]Sil·vā′nus, and Timothy,

To the church of the [b]Thessa·lō′ni·ans in God the Father and the Lord Jesus Christ:

Grace to you and peace [1]from God our Father and the Lord Jesus Christ.

2 [a]We give thanks to God always for you all, making mention of you in our prayers,

3 remembering without ceasing [a]your work of faith, [b]labor of love, and patience of hope in our Lord Jesus Christ in the sight of our God and Father,

4 knowing, beloved brethren, [a]your election by God.

5 For [a]our gospel did not come to you in word only, but also in power, [b]and in the Holy Spirit [c]and in much assurance, as you know what kind of men we were among you for your sake.

6 And [a]you became followers of us and of the Lord, having received the word in much affliction, [b]with joy of the Holy Spirit,

7 so that you became examples to all in Mac·e·dō′ni·a and A·chā′i·a who believe.

8 For from you the word of the Lord [a]has sounded forth, not only in Mac·e·dō′ni·a and A·chā′i·a, but also [b]in every place. Your faith toward God has gone out, so that we do not need to say anything.

9 For they themselves declare concerning us [a]what manner of entry we had to you, [b]and how you turned to God from idols to serve the living and true God,

10 and [a]to wait for His Son from heaven, whom He raised from the dead, *even* Jesus who delivers us [b]from the wrath to come.

2 For you yourselves know, brethren, that our coming to you was not in vain.

2 But [1]even after we had suffered before and were spitefully treated at [a]Phi·lip′pī, as you know, we were [b]bold in our God

CHAPTER 1

1 [a]1 Pet. 5:12 [b]Acts 17:1–9 [1]NU omits *from God our Father and the Lord Jesus Christ*

2 [a]Rom. 1:8

3 [a]John 6:29 [b]Rom. 16:6

4 [a]Col. 3:12

5 [a]Mark 16:20 [b]2 Cor. 6:6 [c]Heb. 2:3

6 [a]1 Cor. 4:16; 11:1 [b]Acts 5:41; 13:52

8 [a]Rom. 10:18 [b]Rom. 1:8; 16:19

9 [a]1 Thess. 2:1 [b]1 Cor. 12:2

10 [a][Rom. 2:7] [b]Rom. 5:9

CHAPTER 2

2 [a]Acts 14:5; 16:19–24 [b]Acts 17:1–9 [1]NU, M omit *even*

to speak to you the gospel of
God in much conflict.
3 [a]For our exhortation *did* not
come from error or uncleanness,
nor *was it* in deceit.
4 But as [a]we have been approved by God [b]to be entrusted
with the gospel, even so we
speak, [c]not as pleasing men, but
God [d]who tests our hearts.
5 For [a]neither at any time did
we use flattering words, as you
know, nor a [1]cloak for covetousness—[b]God *is* witness.
6 [a]Nor did we seek glory from
men, either from you or from
others, when [b]we might have
[c]made demands [d]as apostles of
Christ.
7 But [a]we were gentle among
you, just as a nursing *mother*
cherishes her own children.
8 So, affectionately longing for
you, we were well pleased [a]to
impart to you not only the gospel of God, but also [b]our own
lives, because you had become
dear to us.
9 For you remember, brethren,
our [a]labor and toil; for laboring
night and day, [b]that we might
not be a burden to any of you,
we preached to you the gospel
of God.
10 [a]You *are* witnesses, and God
also, [b]how devoutly and justly
and blamelessly we behaved
ourselves among you who believe;
11 as you know how we ex-
horted, and comforted, and
[1]charged every one of you, as a
father *does* his own children,
12 [a]that you would walk worthy
of God [b]who calls you into His
own kingdom and glory.
13 For this reason we also thank
God [a]without ceasing, because

3 [a]2 Cor. 7:2
4 [a]1 Cor. 7:25 [b]Titus 1:3 [c]Gal. 1:10 [d]Prov. 17:3
5 [a]2 Cor. 2:17 [b]Rom. 1:9 [1]*pretext for greed*
6 [a]1 Tim. 5:17 [b]1 Cor. 9:4 [c]2 Cor. 11:9 [d]1 Cor. 9:1
7 [a]1 Cor. 2:3
8 [a]Rom. 1:11 [b]2 Cor. 12:15
9 [a]Acts 18:3; 20:34, 35 [b]2 Cor. 12:13
10 [a]1 Thess. 1:5 [b]2 Cor. 7:2
11 [1]NU, M *implored*
12 [a]Eph. 4:1 [b]1 Cor. 1:9
13 [a]1 Thess. 1:2, 3 [b]Mark 4:20 [c][Gal. 4:14] [d][1 Pet. 1:23]
14 [a]Gal. 1:22 [b]Acts 17:5
15 [a]Acts 2:23 [b]Matt. 5:12; 23:34, 35 [c]Esth. 3:8 [1]*hostile*
16 [a]Luke 11:52 [b]Gen. 15:16 [c]Matt. 24:6
17 [a]1 Cor. 5:3
18 [a]Rom. 1:13; 15:22
19 [a]2 Cor. 1:14 [b]Prov. 16:31 [c]Jude 24 [d]1 Cor. 15:23

CHAPTER 3

2 [a]Rom. 16:21

when you [b]received the word
of God which you heard from
us, you welcomed *it* [c]not *as* the
word of men, but as it is in truth,
the word of God, which also
effectively [d]works in you who
believe.
14 For you, brethren, became
imitators [a]of the churches of
God which are in Judea in
Christ Jesus. For [b]you also suffered the same things from your
own countrymen, just as they
did from the Judeans,
15 [a]who killed both the Lord
Jesus and [b]their own prophets,
and have persecuted us; and
they do not please God [c]and are
[1]contrary to all men,
16 [a]forbidding us to speak to
the Gentiles that they may be
saved, so as always [b]to fill up *the*
measure of their sins; [c]but wrath
has come upon them to the uttermost.
17 But we, brethren, having
been taken away from you for
a short time [a]in presence, not in
heart, endeavored more eagerly
to see your face with great desire.
18 Therefore we wanted to
come to you—even I, Paul, time
and again—but [a]Satan hindered
us.
19 For [a]what *is* our hope, or joy,
or [b]crown of rejoicing? *Is it* not
even you in the [c]presence of our
Lord Jesus Christ [d]at His coming?
20 For you are our glory and
joy.

3 Therefore, when we could
no longer endure it, we
thought it good to be left in Athens alone,
2 and sent [a]Timothy, our
brother and minister of God, and

our fellow laborer in the gospel
of Christ, to establish you and
encourage you concerning your
faith,
3 [a]that no one should be shaken
by these afflictions; for you
yourselves know that [b]we are
appointed to this.
4 [a]For, in fact, we told you before when we were with you that
we would suffer tribulation, just
as it happened, and you know.
5 For this reason, when I could
no longer endure it, I sent to
know your faith, [a]lest by some
means the tempter had tempted
you, and [b]our labor might be in
vain.
6 [a]But now that Timothy has
come to us from you, and brought
us good news of your faith and
love, and that you always have
good remembrance of us, greatly
desiring to see us, [b]as we also *to
see* you—
7 therefore, brethren, in all our
affliction and distress [a]we were
comforted concerning you by
your faith.
8 For now we live, if you [a]stand
fast in the Lord.
9 For what thanks can we render to God for you, for all the joy
with which we rejoice for your
sake before our God,
10 night and day praying exceedingly that we may see your
face [a]and perfect what is lacking
in your faith?
11 Now may our God and Father Himself, and our Lord Jesus
Christ, [a]direct our way to you.
12 And may the Lord make you
increase and [a]abound in love to
one another and to all, just as
we *do* to you,
13 so that He may estab-
lish [a]your hearts blameless in
holiness before our God and
Father at the coming of our Lord
Jesus Christ with all His saints.

4 Finally then, brethren, we
urge and exhort in the Lord
Jesus [a]that you should abound
more and more, [b]just as you received from us how you ought to
walk and to please God;
2 for you know what com-
mandments we gave you through
the Lord Jesus.
3 For this is [a]the will of God,
[b]your sanctification: [c]that you
should abstain from sexual immorality;
4 [a]that each of you should know
how to possess his own vessel in
sanctification and honor,
5 [a]not in passion of lust, [b]like
the Gentiles [c]who do not know
God;
6 that no one should take
advantage of and defraud his
brother in this matter, because
the Lord [a]*is* the avenger of all
such, as we also forewarned you
and testified.
7 For God did not call us to
uncleanness, [a]but in holiness.
8 [a]Therefore he who rejects
this does not reject man, but
God, [b]who[1] has also given us His
Holy Spirit.
9 But concerning brotherly
love you have no need that I
should write to you, for [a]you
yourselves are taught by God [b]to
love one another;
10 and indeed you do so toward all the brethren who are
in all Mac·e·dō′ni·a. But we urge
you, brethren, [a]that you increase
more and more;
11 that you also aspire to lead
a quiet life, [a]to mind your own
business, and [b]to work with your

3 [a]Eph. 3:13 [b]Acts 9:16; 14:22
4 [a]Acts 20:24
5 [a]1 Cor. 7:5 [b]Gal. 2:2
6 [a]Acts 18:5 [b]Phil. 1:8
7 [a]2 Cor. 1:4
8 [a]Phil. 4:1
10 [a]2 Cor. 13:9
11 [a]Mark 1:3
12 [a]Phil. 1:9
13 [a]2 Thess. 2:17

CHAPTER 4

1 [a]1 Cor. 15:58 [b]Phil. 1:27
3 [a][Rom. 12:2] [b]Eph. 5:27 [c][1 Cor. 6:15–20]
4 [a]Rom. 6:19
5 [a]Col. 3:5 [b]Eph. 4:17, 18 [c]1 Cor. 15:34
6 [a]2 Thess. 1:8
7 [a]Lev. 11:44
8 [a]Luke 10:16 [b]1 Cor. 2:10 [1]NU *who also gives*
9 [a][Jer. 31:33, 34] [b]Matt. 22:39
10 [a]1 Thess. 3:12
11 [a]2 Thess. 3:11 [b]Acts 20:35

own hands, as we commanded
you,
12 [a]that you may walk properly
toward those who are outside,
and *that* you may lack nothing.
13 But I do not want you to be
ignorant, brethren, concerning
those who have [1]fallen asleep,
lest you sorrow [a]as others [b]who
have no hope.
14 For [a]if we believe that Jesus
died and rose again, even so
God will bring with Him [b]those
who [1]sleep in Jesus.
15 For this we say to you [a]by the
word of the Lord, that [b]we who
are alive *and* remain until the
coming of the Lord will by no
means precede those who are
[1]asleep.
16 For [a]the Lord Himself will descend from heaven with a shout,
with the voice of an archangel,
and with [b]the trumpet of God.
[c]And the dead in Christ will rise
first.
17 [a]Then we who are alive *and*
remain shall be caught up together with them [b]in the clouds
to meet the Lord in the air. And
thus [c]we shall always be with
the Lord.
18 [a]Therefore comfort one another with these words.

5

But concerning [a]the times
and the seasons, brethren,
you have no need that I should
write to you.
2 For you yourselves know
perfectly that [a]the day of the
Lord so comes as a thief in the
night.
3 For when they say, "Peace and
safety!" then [a]sudden destruction comes upon them, [b]as labor
pains upon a pregnant woman.
And they shall not escape.
4 [a]But you, brethren, are not
in darkness, so that this Day
should overtake you as a thief.
5 You are all [a]sons of light and
sons of the day. We are not of the
night nor of darkness.
6 [a]Therefore let us not sleep,
as others *do*, but [b]let us watch
and be [1]sober.
7 For [a]those who sleep, sleep at
night, and those who get drunk
[b]are drunk at night.
8 But let us who are of the day
be sober, [a]putting on the breastplate of faith and love, and *as* a
helmet the hope of salvation.
9 For [a]God did not appoint us
to wrath, [b]but to obtain salvation
through our Lord Jesus Christ,
10 [a]who died for us, that whether
we wake or sleep, we should live
together with Him.
11 Therefore [1]comfort each
other and [2]edify one another,
just as you also are doing.
12 And we urge you, brethren,
[a]to recognize those who labor
among you, and are over you in
the Lord and [1]admonish you,
13 and to esteem them very
highly in love for their work's
sake. [a]Be at peace among yourselves.
14 Now we [1]exhort you, brethren, [a]warn those who are [2]un-
ruly, [b]comfort the fainthearted,
[c]uphold the weak, [d]be patient
with all.
15 [a]See that no one renders evil
for evil to anyone, but always
[b]pursue what is good both for
yourselves and for all.
16 [a]Rejoice always,
17 [a]pray without ceasing,
18 in everything give thanks;
for this is the will of God in
Christ Jesus for you.
19 [a]Do not quench the Spirit.
20 [a]Do not despise prophecies.

12 [a]Rom. 13:13
13 [a]Lev. 19:28 [b][Eph. 2:12] [1]Died
14 [a]1 Cor. 15:13 [b]1 Cor. 15:20, 23 [1]Or *through Jesus sleep*
15 [a]1 Kin. 13:17; 20:35 [b]1 Cor. 15:51, 52 [1]Dead
16 [a][Matt. 24:30, 31] [b][1 Cor. 15:52] [c][1 Cor. 15:23]
17 [a][1 Cor. 15:51–53] [b]Acts 1:9 [c]John 14:3; 17:24
18 [a]1 Thess. 5:11

CHAPTER 5

1 [a]Matt. 24:3
2 [a][2 Pet. 3:10]
3 [a]Is. 13:6–9 [b]Hos. 13:13
4 [a]1 John 2:8
5 [a]Eph. 5:8
6 [a]Matt. 25:5 [b][1 Pet. 5:8] [1]*self-controlled*
7 [a][Luke 21:34] [b]Acts 2:15
8 [a]Eph. 6:14
9 [a]Rom. 9:22 [b][2 Thess. 2:13]
10 [a]2 Cor. 5:15
11 [1]Or *encourage* [2]*build one another up*
12 [a]1 Cor. 16:18 [1]*instruct* or *warn*
13 [a]Mark 9:50
14 [a]2 Thess. 3:6, 7, 11 [b]Heb. 12:12 [c]Rom. 14:1; 15:1 [d]Gal. 5:22 [1]*encourage* [2]*insubordinate* or *idle*
15 [a]Lev. 19:18 [b]Gal. 6:10
16 [a][2 Cor. 6:10]
17 [a]Eph. 6:18
19 [a]Eph. 4:30
20 [a]1 Cor. 14:1, 31

21 [a]Test all things; [b]hold fast
what is good.
22 Abstain from every form of
evil.
23 Now may [a]the God of peace
Himself [b]sanctify[1] you completely; and may your whole
spirit, soul, and body [c]be preserved blameless at the coming
of our Lord Jesus Christ.

21 [a]1 John 4:1 [b]Phil. 4:8
23 [a]Phil. 4:9 [b]1 Thess. 3:13 [c]1 Cor. 1:8, 9 [1]*set you apart*
24 [a][1 Cor. 10:13] [b]Phil. 1:6
27 [1]*letter* [2]NU omits *holy*

24 He who calls you *is* [a]faithful,
who also will [b]do *it*.
25 Brethren, pray for us.
26 Greet all the brethren with a
holy kiss.
27 I charge you by the Lord that
this [1]epistle be read to all the
[2]holy brethren.
28 The grace of our Lord Jesus
Christ *be* with you. Amen.

The Second Epistle of Paul the Apostle to the

THESSALONIANS

SINCE Paul's first letter, the seeds of false doctrine have been sown among the Thessalonians, causing them to waver in their faith. Paul removes these destructive seeds and again plants the seeds of truth. He begins by commending the believers on their faithfulness in the midst of persecution and encouraging them that present suffering will be repaid with future glory. Therefore, in the midst of persecution, expectation can be high.

Paul then deals with the central matter of his letter: a misunderstanding spawned by false teachers regarding the coming day of the Lord. Despite reports to the contrary, that Day has not yet come, and Paul recounts the events that must first take place. Laboring for the gospel, rather than lazy resignation, is the proper response.

As the second letter in Paul's Thessalonian correspondence, this was entitled *Pros Thessalonikeis B*, the "Second to the Thessalonians."

PAUL, Sil·vā'nus, and Timothy,

To the church of the Thes·sa-
lō'ni·ans in God our Father and
the Lord Jesus Christ:

2 [a]Grace to you and peace from
God our Father and the Lord Jesus Christ.

3 We are bound to thank God
always for you, brethren, as it is
fitting, because your faith grows
exceedingly, and the love of every one of you all abounds toward each other,
4 so that [a]we ourselves boast
of you among the churches of
God [b]for your patience and faith
[c]in all your persecutions and
[1]tribulations that you endure,
5 *which is* [a]manifest[1] evidence
of the righteous judgment of
God, that you may be counted
worthy of the kingdom of God,
[b]for which you also suffer;
6 [a]since *it is* a righteous thing
with God to repay with [1]tribula-
tion those who trouble you,
7 and to *give* you who are
troubled [a]rest with us when [b]the
Lord Jesus is revealed from
heaven with His mighty angels,
8 in flaming fire taking vengeance on those who do not
know God, and on those who do
not obey the gospel of our Lord
Jesus Christ.
9 [a]These shall be punished with
everlasting destruction from the
presence of the Lord and [b]from
the glory of His power,
10 when He comes, in that Day,
[a]to be [b]glorified in His saints and
to be admired among all those
who [1]believe, because our testimony among you was believed.
11 Therefore we also pray
always for you that our God
would [a]count you worthy of *this*
calling, and fulfill all the good
pleasure of *His* goodness and
[b]the work of faith with power,
12 [a]that the name of our Lord
Jesus Christ may be glorified in

CHAPTER 1

2 [a]1 Cor. 1:3

4 [a]2 Cor. 7:4 [b]1 Thess. 1:3 [c]1 Thess. 2:14 [1]*afflictions*

5 [a]Phil. 1:28 [b]1 Thess. 2:14 [1]*plain*

6 [a]Rev. 6:10 [1]*affliction*

7 [a]Rev. 14:13 [b]Jude 14

9 [a]Phil. 3:19 [b]Deut. 33:2

10 [a]Matt. 25:31 [b]John 17:10 [1]NU, M *have believed*

11 [a]Col. 1:12 [b]1 Thess. 1:3

12 [a][Col. 3:17]

you, and you in Him, according
to the grace of our God and the
Lord Jesus Christ.

2

Now, brethren, [a]concerning
the coming of our Lord Jesus Christ [b]and our gathering
together to Him, we ask you,
2 [a]not to be soon shaken in
mind or troubled, either by spirit
or by word or by letter, as if from
us, as though the day of [1]Christ
had come.
3 Let no one deceive you by
any means; for *that Day will not*
come [a]unless the falling away
comes first, and [b]the man of [1]sin
is revealed, [c]the son of perdition,
4 who opposes and [a]exalts
himself [b]above all that is called
God or that is worshiped, so that
he sits [1]as God in the temple of
God, showing himself that he is
God.
5 Do you not remember that
when I was still with you I told
you these things?
6 And now you know what is
restraining, that he may be revealed in his own time.
7 For [a]the [1]mystery of lawlessness is already at work; only [2]He
who now restrains *will do so* until [2]He is taken out of the way.
8 And then the lawless one
will be revealed, [a]whom the Lord
will consume [b]with the breath of
His mouth and destroy [c]with the
brightness of His coming.
9 The coming of the *lawless*
one is [a]according to the working
of Satan, with all power, [b]signs,
and lying wonders,
10 and with all unrighteous deception among [a]those who perish, because they did not receive
[b]the love of the truth, that they
might be saved.

CHAPTER 2

1 [a][1 Thess. 4:15–17] [b]Matt. 24:31
2 [a]Matt. 24:4 [1]NU *the Lord*
3 [a]1 Tim. 4:1 [b]Dan. 7:25; 8:25; 11:36 [c]John 17:12 [1]NU *lawlessness*
4 [a]Is. 14:13, 14 [b]1 Cor. 8:5 [1]NU omits *as God*
7 [a]1 John 2:18 [1]*hidden truth* [2]Or *he*
8 [a]Dan. 7:10 [b]Is. 11:4 [c]Heb. 10:27
9 [a]John 8:41 [b]Deut. 13:1
10 [a]2 Cor. 2:15 [b]1 Cor. 16:22
11 [a]Rom. 1:28 [b]1 Tim. 4:1
12 [a]Rom. 1:32
13 [a]Eph. 1:4 [b]1 Thess. 1:4 [c][1 Pet. 1:2] [1]*under obligation* [2]*being set apart by*
14 [a]1 Pet. 5:10
15 [a]1 Cor. 16:13 [b]1 Cor. 11:2 [1]*letter*
16 [a][Rev. 1:5] [b]1 Pet. 1:3
17 [a]1 Cor. 1:8 [1]*strengthen*

CHAPTER 3

1 [a]Eph. 6:19
2 [a]Rom. 15:31 [b]Acts 28:24
3 [a]1 Cor. 1:9 [b]John 17:15
4 [a]2 Cor. 7:16
5 [a]1 Chr. 29:18

11 And [a]for this reason God will
send them strong delusion, [b]that
they should believe the lie,
12 that they all may be condemned who did not believe the
truth but [a]had pleasure in unrighteousness.
13 But we are [1]bound to give
thanks to God always for you,
brethren beloved by the Lord,
because God [a]from the beginning [b]chose you for salvation
[c]through [2]sanctification by the
Spirit and belief in the truth,
14 to which He called you by
our gospel, for [a]the obtaining
of the glory of our Lord Jesus
Christ.
15 Therefore, brethren, [a]stand
fast and hold [b]the traditions
which you were taught, whether
by word or our [1]epistle.
16 Now may our Lord Jesus
Christ Himself, and our God and
Father, [a]who has loved us and
given *us* everlasting consolation
and [b]good hope by grace,
17 comfort your hearts [a]and [1]es-
tablish you in every good word
and work.

3

Finally, brethren, [a]pray for
us, that the word of the Lord
may run *swiftly* and be glorified,
just as *it is* with you,
2 and [a]that we may be delivered from unreasonable and
wicked men; [b]for not all have
faith.
3 But [a]the Lord is faithful, who
will establish you and [b]guard
you from the evil one.
4 And [a]we have confidence in
the Lord concerning you, both
that you do and will do the
things we command you.
5 Now may [a]the Lord direct
your hearts into the love of God
and into the patience of Christ.

6 But we command you, brethren, in the name of our Lord
Jesus Christ, [a]that you withdraw
[b]from every brother who walks
[c]disorderly and not according to
the tradition which [1]he received
from us.
7 For you yourselves know
how you ought to follow us, for
we were not disorderly among
you;
8 nor did we eat anyone's bread
[1]free of charge, but worked with
[a]labor and toil night and day,
that we might not be a burden to
any of you,
9 not because we do not have
[a]authority, but to make ourselves
an example of how you should
follow us.
10 For even when we were with
you, we commanded you this: If
anyone will not work, neither
shall he eat.
11 For we hear that there are
some who walk among you in a
disorderly manner, not working
at all, but are [a]busybodies.
12 Now those who are such we
command and [1]exhort through
our Lord Jesus Christ [a]that they
work in quietness and eat their
own bread.
13 But *as for* you, brethren, [a]do
not grow weary *in* doing good.
14 And if anyone does not obey
our word in this [1]epistle, note
that person and [a]do not keep
company with him, that he may
be ashamed.
15 [a]Yet do not count *him* as an
enemy, [b]but [1]admonish *him* as a
brother.
16 Now may [a]the Lord of peace
Himself give you peace always
in every way. The Lord *be* with
you all.
17 [a]The salutation of Paul with
my own hand, which is a sign in
every [1]epistle; so I write.
18 [a]The grace of our Lord Jesus
Christ *be* with you all. Amen.

6 [a]Rom. 16:17 [b]1 Cor. 5:1 [c]1 Thess. 4:11 [1]NU, M *they*
8 [a]1 Thess. 2:9 [1]Lit. *for nothing*
9 [a]1 Cor. 9:4, 6–14
11 [a]1 Pet. 4:15
12 [a]Eph. 4:28 [1]*encourage*
13 [a]Gal. 6:9
14 [a]Matt. 18:17 [1]*letter*
15 [a]Lev. 19:17 [b]Titus 3:10 [1]*warn*
16 [a]Rom. 15:33
17 [a]1 Cor. 16:21 [1]*letter*
18 [a]Rom. 16:20, 24

The First Epistle of Paul the Apostle to

TIMOTHY

PAUL, the aged and experienced apostle, writes to the young pastor Timothy who is facing a heavy burden of responsibility in the church at Ephesus. The task is challenging: false doctrine must be erased, public worship safeguarded, and mature leadership developed. In addition to the conduct of the church, Paul talks pointedly about the conduct of the minister. Timothy must be on his guard lest his youthfulness become a liability, rather than an asset, to the gospel. He must be careful to avoid false teachers and greedy motives, pursuing instead righteousness, godliness, faith, love, perseverance, and the gentleness that befits a man of God.

The Greek title for this letter is *Pros Timotheon A*, the "First to Timothy." *Timothy* means "honoring God" or "honored by God," and probably was given to him by his mother Eunice.

PAUL, an apostle of Jesus
Christ, by the commandment
of God our Savior and the Lord
Jesus Christ, our hope,

2 To Timothy, a [a]true son in the
faith:

[b]Grace, mercy, *and* peace
from God our Father and Jesus
Christ our Lord.

3 As I urged you [a]when I went
into Mac·e·dō′ni·a—remain in
Eph′e·sus that you may [1]charge
some [b]that they teach no other
doctrine,
4 [a]nor give heed to fables
and endless genealogies, which
cause disputes rather than godly
edification which is in faith.
5 Now [a]the purpose of the commandment is love [b]from a pure
heart, *from* a good conscience,
and *from* [1]sincere faith,
6 from which some, having
strayed, have turned aside to
[a]idle talk,
7 desiring to be teachers of the

CHAPTER 1

2 [a]Titus 1:4
[b]Gal. 1:3

3 [a]Acts 20:1, 3
[b]Gal. 1:6, 7
[1]*command*

4 [a]Titus 1:14

5 [a]Rom. 13:8–10
[b]Eph. 6:24
[1]Lit. *unhypocritical*

6 [a]1 Tim. 6:4, 20

8 [a]Rom. 7:12, 16

10 [1]*opposed*

11 [a]1 Tim. 6:15
[b]1 Cor. 9:17

12 [a]1 Cor. 15:10
[b]1 Cor. 7:25
[c]Col. 1:25

13 [a]Acts 8:3
[1]*violently arrogant*

law, understanding neither what
they say nor the things which
they affirm.
8 But we know that the law *is*
[a]good if one uses it lawfully,
9 knowing this: that the law is
not made for a righteous person,
but for *the* lawless and insubordinate, for *the* ungodly and for
sinners, for *the* unholy and profane, for murderers of fathers
and murderers of mothers, for
manslayers,
10 for fornicators, for sodomites, for kidnappers, for liars,
for perjurers, and if there is any
other thing that is [1]contrary to
sound doctrine,
11 according to the glorious
gospel of the [a]blessed God which
was [b]committed to my trust.
12 And I thank Christ Jesus
our Lord who has [a]enabled me,
[b]because He counted me faithful,
[c]putting *me* into the ministry,
13 although [a]I was formerly a
blasphemer, a persecutor, and
an [1]insolent man; but I obtained

mercy because [b]I did *it* ignorantly
in unbelief.
14 [a]And the grace of our Lord
was exceedingly abundant,
[b]with faith and love which are
in Christ Jesus.
★15 [a]This *is* a faithful saying
and worthy of all acceptance,
that [b]Christ Jesus came into the
world to save sinners, of whom I
am chief.
16 However, for this reason
I obtained mercy, that in me
first Jesus Christ might show
all longsuffering, as a pattern to
those who are going to believe
on Him for everlasting life.
17 Now to [a]the King eternal,
[b]immortal, [c]invisible, to [1]God
[d]who alone is wise, [e]*be* honor
and glory forever and ever.
Amen.
18 This [1]charge I commit to
you, son Timothy, according to
the prophecies previously made
concerning you, that by them
you may wage the good warfare,
19 having faith and a good conscience, which some having rejected, concerning the faith have
suffered shipwreck,
20 of whom are [a]Hy̆·me·naē′us
and [b]Alexander, whom I delivered to Satan that they may
learn not to [c]blaspheme.

2 Therefore I [1]exhort first
of all that supplications,
prayers, intercessions, *and* giving of thanks be made for all
men,
2 [a]for kings and [b]all who are
in [1]authority, that we may lead
a quiet and peaceable life in all
godliness and [2]reverence.
3 For this *is* [a]good and acceptable in the sight [b]of God our
Savior,
4 [a]who desires all men to be
saved [b]and to come to the knowledge of the truth.
5 [a]For *there is* one God and
[b]one Mediator between God and
men, *the* Man Christ Jesus,
6 [a]who gave Himself a ransom
for all, to be testified in due
time,
7 [a]for which I was appointed
a preacher and an apostle—I
am speaking the truth [1]in Christ
and not lying—[b]a teacher of the
Gentiles in faith and truth.
8 I desire therefore that the
men pray [a]everywhere, [b]lifting
up holy hands, without wrath
and doubting;
9 in like manner also, that
the [a]women adorn themselves
in modest apparel, with propri-
ety and [1]moderation, not with
braided hair or gold or pearls or
costly clothing,
10 [a]but, which is proper for
women professing godliness,
with good works.
11 Let a woman learn in silence
with all submission.
12 And [a]I do not permit a woman
to teach or to have authority
over a man, but to be in silence.
13 For Adam was formed first,
then Eve.
14 And Adam was not deceived,
but the woman being deceived,
fell into transgression.
15 Nevertheless she will be
saved in childbearing if they
continue in faith, love, and holiness, with self-control.

3 This *is* a faithful saying: If
a man desires the position
of a [1]bishop, he desires a good
work.
2 A bishop then must be
blameless, the husband of one
wife, temperate, sober-minded,

13 [b]John 4:21
14 [a]Rom. 5:20 [b]2 Tim. 1:13; 2:22
15 [a]2 Tim. 2:11 [b]Is. 53:5; 61:1; Hos. 6:1–3; Matt. 1:21; 9:13
17 [a]Ps. 10:16 [b]Rom. 1:23 [c]Heb. 11:27 [d]Rom. 16:27 [e]1 Chr. 29:11 [1]NU *the only God,*
18 [1]*command*
20 [a]2 Tim. 2:17, 18 [b]2 Tim. 4:14 [c]Acts 13:45

CHAPTER 2
1 [1]*encourage*
2 [a]Ezra 6:10 [b][Rom. 13:1] [1]*a prominent place* [2]*dignity*
3 [a]Rom. 12:2 [b]2 Tim. 1:9
4 [a]Ezek. 18:23, 32 [b][John 17:3]
5 [a]Gal. 3:20 [b][Heb. 9:15]
6 [a]Mark 10:45
7 [a]Eph. 3:7, 8 [b][Gal. 1:15, 16] [1]NU omits *in Christ*
8 [a]Luke 23:34 [b]Ps. 134:2
9 [a]1 Pet. 3:3 [1]*discretion*
10 [a]1 Pet. 3:4
12 [a]1 Cor. 14:34

CHAPTER 3
1 [1]Lit. *overseer*

of good behavior, hospitable,
able to teach;
3 not [1]given to wine, not violent, [2]not greedy for money,
but gentle, not quarrelsome, not
[3]covetous;
4 one who rules his own house
well, having *his* children in submission with all reverence
5 (for if a man does not know
how to rule his own house, how
will he take care of the church
of God?);
6 not a [1]novice, lest being
puffed up with pride he fall into
the *same* condemnation as the
devil.
7 Moreover he must have a
good testimony among those
who are outside, lest he fall into
reproach and the [a]snare of the
devil.
8 Likewise deacons *must be*
reverent, not double-tongued,
[a]not given to much wine, not
greedy for money,
9 holding the [1]mystery of the
faith with a pure conscience.
10 But let these also first be
tested; then let them serve as
deacons, being *found* blameless.
11 Likewise, *their* wives *must
be* reverent, not [1]slanderers,
temperate, faithful in all things.
12 Let deacons be the husbands
of one wife, ruling *their* children
and their own houses well.
13 For those who have served
well as deacons [a]obtain for themselves a good standing and great
boldness in the faith which is in
Christ Jesus.
14 These things I write to you,
though I hope to come to you
shortly;
15 but if I am delayed, *I write*
so that you may know how you
ought to conduct yourself in
the house of God, which is the
church of the living God, the pillar and [1]ground of the truth.
16 And without controversy
great is the [1]mystery of godliness:

[a]God[2] was manifested in the
flesh,
[b]Justified in the Spirit,
[c]Seen by angels,
[d]Preached among the
Gentiles,
[e]Believed on in the world,
[f]Received up in glory.

4 Now the Spirit [1]expressly
says that in latter times
some will depart from the faith,
giving heed [a]to deceiving spirits
and doctrines of demons,
2 [a]speaking lies in hypocrisy,
having their own conscience
[b]seared with a hot iron,
3 forbidding to marry, *and
commanding* to abstain from
foods which God created to be
received with thanksgiving by
those who believe and know the
truth.
4 For every creature of God
is good, and nothing is to be
refused if it is received with
thanksgiving;
5 for it is [1]sanctified by the
word of God and prayer.
6 If you instruct the brethren
in these things, you will be a
good minister of Jesus Christ,
[a]nourished in the words of faith
and of the good doctrine which
you have carefully followed.
7 But [a]reject profane and old
wives' fables, and [b]exercise
yourself toward godliness.
8 For [a]bodily exercise profits a
little, but godliness is profitable
for all things, [b]having promise of

3 [1]*addicted* [2]NU omits *not greedy for money* [3]*loving money*
6 [1]*new convert*
7 [a]2 Tim. 2:26
8 [a]Ezek. 44:21
9 [1]*hidden truth*
11 [1]*malicious gossips*
13 [a]Matt. 25:21
15 [1]*foundation, mainstay*
16 [a][John 1:14] [b][Matt. 3:16] [c]Matt. 28:2 [d]Rom. 10:18 [e]Col. 1:6, 23 [f]Luke 24:51 [1]*hidden truth* [2]NU *Who*

CHAPTER 4

1 [a]Rev. 16:14 [1]*explicitly*
2 [a]Matt. 7:15 [b]Eph. 4:19
5 [1]*set apart*
6 [a]2 Tim. 3:14
7 [a]2 Tim. 2:16 [b]Heb. 5:14
8 [a]1 Cor. 8:8 [b]Ps. 37:9

the life that now is and of that
which is to come.
9 This *is* a faithful saying and
worthy of all acceptance.
10 For to this *end* [1]we both labor
and suffer reproach, because we
trust in the living God, [a]who is
the Savior of all men, especially
of those who believe.
11 These things command and
teach.
12 Let no one [1]despise your
youth, but be an [a]example to the
believers in word, in conduct, in
love, [2]in spirit, in faith, in purity.
13 Till I come, give attention to
reading, to exhortation, to [1]doc-
trine.
14 [a]Do not neglect the gift that
is in you, which was given to
you by prophecy [b]with the laying on of the hands of the elder-
ship.
15 Meditate on these things;
give yourself entirely to them,
that your progress may be evident to all.
16 Take heed to yourself and to
the doctrine. Continue in them,
for in doing this you will save
both yourself and those who
hear you.

5 Do not rebuke an older man,
but exhort *him* as a father,
younger men as brothers,
2 older women as mothers,
younger women as sisters, with
all purity.
3 Honor widows who are really widows.
4 But if any widow has children or grandchildren, let them
first learn to show piety at home
and [a]to repay their parents; for
this is [1]good and acceptable before God.
5 Now she who is really a
widow, and left alone, trusts in
God and continues in supplications and prayers [a]night and
day.
6 But she who lives in [1]plea-
sure is dead while she lives.
7 And these things command,
that they may be blameless.
8 But if anyone does not provide for his own, [a]and especially for those of his household,
[b]he has denied the faith [c]and is
worse than an unbeliever.
9 Do not let a widow under
sixty years old be taken into the
number, *and not unless* she has
been the wife of one man,
10 well reported for good works:
if she has brought up children, if
she has lodged strangers, if she
has washed the saints' feet, if
she has relieved the afflicted, if
she has diligently followed every good work.
11 But [1]refuse *the* younger widows; for when they have begun
to grow wanton against Christ,
they desire to marry,
12 having condemnation because they have cast off their
first [1]faith.
13 And besides they learn *to
be* idle, wandering about from
house to house, and not only
idle but also gossips and busybodies, saying things which they
ought not.
14 Therefore I desire that *the*
younger *widows* marry, bear
children, manage the house, give
no opportunity to the adversary
to speak reproachfully.
15 For some have already turned
aside after Satan.
16 If any believing [1]man or
woman has widows, let them
[2]relieve them, and do not let
the church be burdened, that it

10 [a]Ps. 36:6 [1]NU *we labor and strive,*
12 [a]1 Pet. 5:3 [1]*look down on your youthfulness* [2]NU omits *in spirit*
13 [1]teaching
14 [a]2 Tim. 1:6 [b]Acts 6:6

CHAPTER 5

4 [a]Gen. 45:10 [1]NU, M omit *good and*
5 [a]Acts 26:7
6 [1]*indulgence*
8 [a]Is. 58:7 [b]2 Tim. 3:5 [c]Matt. 18:17
11 [1]Refuse to enroll
12 [1]Or *solemn promise*
16 [1]NU omits *man or* [2]*give aid to*

may relieve those who are really widows.

17 Let the elders who rule well be counted worthy of double honor, especially those who labor in the word and doctrine.

18 For the Scripture says, [a]*"You shall not muzzle an ox while it treads out the grain,"* and, [b]"The laborer *is* worthy of his wages."

19 Do not receive an accusation against an elder except [a]from two or three witnesses.

20 Those who are sinning rebuke in the presence of all, that the rest also may fear.

21 I charge *you* before God and the Lord Jesus Christ and the [1]elect angels that you observe these things without [a]prejudice, doing nothing with partiality.

22 Do not lay hands on anyone hastily, nor [a]share in other people's sins; keep yourself pure.

23 No longer drink only water, but use a little wine for your stomach's sake and your frequent [1]infirmities.

24 Some men's sins are [a]clearly evident, preceding *them* to judgment, but those of some *men* follow later.

25 Likewise, the good works *of some* are clearly evident, and those that are otherwise cannot be hidden.

6 Let as many [a]bondservants as are under the yoke count their own masters worthy of all honor, so that the name of God and *His* doctrine may not be blasphemed.

2 And those who have believing masters, let them not despise *them* because they are brethren, but rather serve *them* because those who are benefited are believers and beloved. Teach and exhort these things.

3 If anyone teaches otherwise and does not consent to [a]wholesome words, *even* the words of our Lord Jesus Christ, [b]and to the [1]doctrine which accords with godliness,

4 he is proud, knowing nothing, but is obsessed with disputes and arguments over words, from which come envy, strife, reviling, evil suspicions,

5 [1]useless wranglings of men of corrupt minds and destitute of the truth, who suppose that godliness is a *means of* gain. [2]From [a]such withdraw yourself.

6 Now godliness with [a]contentment is great gain.

7 For we brought nothing into *this* world, [1]*and it is* [a]certain we can carry nothing out.

8 And having food and clothing, with these we shall be [a]content.

9 But those who desire to be rich fall into temptation and a snare, and *into* many foolish and harmful lusts which drown men in destruction and perdition.

10 For the love of money is a root of all *kinds of* evil, for which some have strayed from the faith in their greediness, and pierced themselves through with many sorrows.

11 But you, O man of God, flee these things and pursue righteousness, godliness, faith, love, patience, gentleness.

12 Fight the good fight of faith, lay hold on eternal life, to which you were also called and have confessed the good confession in the presence of many witnesses.

18 [a]Deut. 25:4 [b]Luke 10:7
19 [a]Deut. 17:6; 19:15
21 [a]Deut. 1:17 [1]*chosen*
22 [a]Eph. 5:6, 7
23 [1]*illnesses*
24 [a]Gal. 5:19–21

CHAPTER 6

1 [a]Eph. 6:5
3 [a]2 Tim. 1:13 [b]Titus 1:1 [1]*teaching*
5 [a]2 Tim. 3:5 [1]NU, M *constant friction* [2]NU omits the rest of v. 5.
6 [a]Heb. 13:5
7 [a]Job 1:21 [1]NU omits *and it is certain*
8 [a]Prov. 30:8, 9

13 I urge you in the sight of
God who gives life to all things,
and *before* Christ Jesus [a]who
witnessed the good confession
before Pon′ti·us Pilate,
14 that you keep *this* commandment without spot, blameless
until our Lord Jesus Christ's appearing,
15 which He will manifest in
His own time, *He who is* the
blessed and only [1]Potentate, the
King of kings and Lord of lords,
16 who alone has immortality,
dwelling in [a]unapproachable
light, [b]whom no man has seen
or can see, to whom *be* honor
and everlasting power. Amen.
17 Command those who are
rich in this present age not to
be haughty, nor to trust in uncertain [a]riches but in the living
God, who gives us richly all
things [b]to enjoy.
18 *Let them* do good, that they
be rich in good works, ready to
give, willing to share,
19 [a]storing up for themselves a
good foundation for the time to
come, that they may lay hold on
eternal life.
20 O Timothy! [a]Guard what
was committed to your trust,
[b]avoiding the profane *and* [1]idle
babblings and contradictions of
what is falsely called knowledge—
21 by professing it some have
strayed concerning the faith.
Grace *be* with you. Amen.

13 [a]John 18:36, 37
15 [1]*Sovereign*
16 [a]Dan. 2:22 [b]John 6:46
17 [a]Jer. 9:23; 48:7 [b]Eccl. 5:18, 19
19 [a][Matt. 6:20, 21; 19:21]
20 [a][2 Tim. 1:12, 14] [b]Titus 1:14 [1]*empty chatter*

The Second Epistle of Paul the Apostle to

TIMOTHY

PRISON is the last place from which to expect a letter of encouragement, but that is where Paul's second letter to Timothy originates. He begins by assuring Timothy of his continuing love and prayers, and reminds him of his spiritual heritage and responsibilities. Only the one who perseveres, whether as a soldier, athlete, farmer, or minister of Jesus Christ, will reap the reward. Paul warns Timothy that his teaching will come under attack as men desert the truth for ear-itching words (4:3). But Timothy has Paul's example to guide him and God's Word to fortify him as he faces growing opposition and glowing opportunities in the last days.

Paul's last epistle received the title *Pros Timotheon B*, the "Second to Timothy." When Paul's epistles were collected together, the *B* was probably added to distinguish this letter from the first letter he wrote to Timothy.

PAUL, an apostle of [1]Jesus
Christ by the will of God,
according to the [a]promise of life
which is in Christ Jesus,

2 To Timothy, a [a]beloved son:

Grace, mercy, *and* peace
from God the Father and Christ
Jesus our Lord.

3 I thank God, whom I serve
with a pure conscience, as *my*
[a]forefathers *did,* as without ceasing I remember you in my prayers
night and day,
4 greatly desiring to see you,
being mindful of your tears, that
I may be filled with joy,
5 when I call to remembrance
[a]the [1]genuine faith that is in you,
which dwelt first in your grandmother Lō′is and [b]your mother
Eū′nice, and I am persuaded is
in you also.
6 Therefore I remind you [a]to
stir up the gift of God which is
in you through the laying on of
my hands.

CHAPTER 1

1 [a]Titus 1:2 [1]NU, M *Christ Jesus*

2 [a]1 Tim. 1:2

3 [a]Acts 24:14

5 [a]1 Tim. 1:5; 4:6 [b]Acts 16:1 [1]Lit. *unhypocritical*

6 [a]1 Tim. 4:14

7 [a]Rom. 8:15 [b][Acts 1:8]

8 [a][Rom. 1:16] [b]1 Tim. 2:6 [c]Eph. 3:1

9 [a][Rom. 3:20] [b]Rom. 8:28 [c]Rom. 16:25

10 [a]Eph. 1:9

11 [a]Acts 9:15 [1]NU omits *of the Gentiles*

12 [a]1 Pet. 4:19

7 For [a]God has not given us a
spirit of fear, [b]but of power and
of love and of a sound mind.
8 [a]Therefore do not be ashamed
of [b]the testimony of our Lord,
nor of me [c]His prisoner, but
share with me in the sufferings
for the gospel according to the
power of God,
9 who has saved us and called
us with a holy calling, [a]not according to our works, but [b]according
to His own purpose and grace
which was given to us in Christ
Jesus [c]before time began,
10 but [a]has now been revealed
by the appearing of our Savior
Jesus Christ, *who* has abolished
death and brought life and immortality to light through the
gospel,
11 [a]to which I was appointed
a preacher, an apostle, and a
teacher [1]of the Gentiles.
12 For this reason I also suffer
these things; nevertheless I am
not ashamed, [a]for I know whom
I have believed and am persuaded that He is able to keep

what I have committed to Him
until that Day.
13 [a]Hold fast [b]the pattern of
[c]sound words which you have
heard from me, in faith and love
which are in Christ Jesus.
14 That good thing which was
committed to you, keep by the
Holy Spirit who dwells in us.
15 This you know, that all those
in Asia have turned away from
me, among whom are Phy̆′-
gel·lus and Her·mog′e·nēs.
16 The Lord grant mercy to the
[a]household of On·e·siph′o·rus,
for he often refreshed me, and
was not ashamed of my chain;
17 but when he arrived in Rome,
he sought me out very zealously
and found *me.*
18 The Lord [a]grant to him that
he may find mercy from the
Lord [b]in that Day—and you
know very well how many ways
he [c]ministered [1]*to me* at Eph′-
e·sus.

2

You therefore, [a]my son, [b]be
strong in the grace that is in
Christ Jesus.
2 And the things that you have
heard from me among many witnesses, commit these to faithful
men who will be able to teach
others also.
3 You therefore must [a]endure[1]
hardship [b]as a good soldier of
Jesus Christ.
4 [a]No one engaged in warfare
entangles himself with the affairs of *this* life, that he may
please him who enlisted him as
a soldier.
5 And also [a]if anyone competes
in athletics, he is not crowned
unless he competes according to
the rules.
6 The hardworking farmer must
be first to partake of the crops.

13 [a]Titus 1:9 [b]Rom. 2:20; 6:17 [c]1 Tim. 6:3

16 [a]2 Tim. 4:19

18 [a]Mark 9:41 [b]2 Thess. 1:10 [c]Heb. 6:10 [1]*to me* from Vg., a few Gr. mss.

CHAPTER 2

1 [a]1 Tim. 1:2 [b]Eph. 6:10

3 [a]2 Tim. 4:5 [b]1 Tim. 1:18 [1]NU *You must share*

4 [a][2 Pet. 2:20]

5 [a][1 Cor. 9:25]

7 [a]Prov. 2:6 [1]NU *the Lord will give you*

8 [a]Rom. 1:3, 4 [b]1 Cor. 15:4 [c]Rom. 2:16

9 [a]Acts 9:16 [b]Eph. 3:1 [c]Acts 28:31

10 [a]Eph. 3:13 [b]2 Cor. 1:6 [1]*chosen ones*

11 [a]Rom. 6:5, 8

12 [a][Rom. 5:17; 8:17] [b]Matt. 10:33

13 [a]Num. 23:19

14 [a]Titus 3:9 [1]*battle*

15 [a]2 Pet. 1:10

16 [1]*empty chatter* [2]*lead*

17 [a]1 Tim. 1:20

18 [a]1 Cor. 15:12

7 Consider what I say, and
[1]may the Lord [a]give you understanding in all things.
8 Remember that Jesus Christ,
[a]of the seed of David, [b]was raised
from the dead [c]according to my
gospel,
9 [a]for which I suffer trouble as
an evildoer, [b]*even* to the point of
chains; [c]but the word of God is
not chained.
10 Therefore [a]I endure all things
for the sake of the [1]elect, [b]that
they also may obtain the salvation which is in Christ Jesus
with eternal glory.
11 *This is* a faithful saying:

For [a]if we died with *Him,*
We shall also live with *Him.*
12 [a]If we endure,
We shall also reign with
Him.
[b]If we deny *Him,*
He also will deny us.
13 If we are faithless,
He remains faithful;
He [a]cannot deny Himself.

14 Remind *them* of these things,
[a]charging *them* before the Lord
not to [1]strive about words to no
profit, to the ruin of the hearers.
15 [a]Be diligent to present yourself approved to God, a worker
who does not need to be ashamed,
rightly dividing the word of
truth.
16 But shun profane *and* [1]idle
babblings, for they will [2]increase
to more ungodliness.
17 And their message will spread
like cancer. [a]Hy̆·me·naē′us and
Phi·lē′tus are of this sort,
18 who have strayed concerning
the truth, [a]saying that the resurrection is already past; and they
overthrow the faith of some.

19 Nevertheless [a]the solid foundation of God stands, having this
seal: "The Lord [b]knows those
who are His," and, "Let everyone
who names the name of [1]Christ
depart from iniquity."
20 But in a great house there
are not only [a]vessels of gold and
silver, but also of wood and clay,
some for honor and some for
dishonor.
21 Therefore if anyone cleanses
himself from the latter, he will
be a vessel for honor, [1]sancti-
fied and useful for the Master,
[a]prepared for every good work.
22 [a]Flee also youthful lusts; but
pursue righteousness, faith, love,
peace with those who call on the
Lord out of a pure heart.
23 But avoid foolish and ignorant disputes, knowing that they
generate strife.
24 And [a]a servant of the Lord
must not quarrel but be gentle
to all, [b]able to teach, [c]patient,
25 [a]in humility correcting those
who are in opposition, [b]if God
perhaps will grant them repentance, [c]so that they may know
the truth,
26 and *that* they may come to
their senses *and* [a]*escape* the
snare of the devil, having been
taken captive by him to *do* his
will.

3

3 But know this, that [a]in the
last days [1]perilous times will
come:
2 For men will be lovers of
themselves, lovers of money,
boasters, proud, blasphemers,
disobedient to parents, unthankful, unholy,
3 unloving, [1]unforgiving, slanderers, without self-control, brutal, despisers of good,
4 [a]traitors, headstrong, haughty,
lovers of pleasure rather than lovers of God,
5 [a]having a form of godliness
but [b]denying its power. And
[c]from such people turn away!
6 For [a]of this sort are those
who creep into households and
make captives of gullible women
loaded down with sins, led away
by various lusts,
7 always learning and never
able [a]to come to the knowledge
of the truth.
8 [a]Now as Jan′nēs and Jam′-
brēs resisted Moses, so do these
also resist the truth: [b]men of corrupt minds, [c]disapproved concerning the faith;
9 but they will progress no further, for their folly will be manifest to all, [a]as theirs also was.
10 [a]But you have carefully followed my doctrine, manner of
life, purpose, faith, longsuffering, love, perseverance,
11 persecutions, afflictions,
which happened to me [a]at An′-
ti·och, [b]at Ī·cō′ni·um, [c]at Lys′-
tra—what persecutions I endured. And [d]out of *them* all the
Lord delivered me.
12 Yes, and [a]all who desire to
live godly in Christ Jesus will
suffer persecution.
13 [a]But evil men and impostors
will grow worse and worse, deceiving and being deceived.
14 But you must [a]continue in the
things which you have learned
and been assured of, knowing
from whom you have learned
them,
15 and that from childhood you
have known [a]the Holy Scriptures, which are able to make
you wise for salvation through
faith which is in Christ Jesus.
16 [a]All Scripture *is* given by

19 [a][1 Cor. 3:11] [b][Nah. 1:7] [1]NU, M *the Lord*
20 [a]Rom. 9:21
21 [a]2 Tim. 3:17 [1]*set apart*
22 [a]1 Tim. 6:11
24 [a]Titus 3:2 [b]Titus 1:9 [c]1 Tim. 3:3
25 [a]Gal. 6:1 [b]Acts 8:22 [c]1 Tim. 2:4
26 [a]1 Tim. 3:7

CHAPTER 3

1 [a]1 Tim. 4:1 [1]*times of stress*
3 [1]*irreconcilable*
4 [a]2 Pet. 2:10
5 [a]Titus 1:16 [b]1 Tim. 5:8 [c]2 Thess. 3:6
6 [a]Matt. 23:14
7 [a]1 Tim. 2:4
8 [a]Ex. 7:11, 12, 22; 8:7; 9:11 [b]1 Tim. 6:5 [c]Rom. 1:28
9 [a]Ex. 7:11, 12; 8:18; 9:11
10 [a]1 Tim. 4:6
11 [a]Acts 13:44–52 [b]Acts 14:1–6, 19 [c]Acts 14:8–20 [d]Ps. 34:19
12 [a][Ps. 34:19]
13 [a]2 Thess. 2:11
14 [a]2 Tim. 1:13
15 [a]John 5:39
16 [a][2 Pet. 1:20]

inspiration of God, [b]and *is* profitable for doctrine, for reproof,
for correction, for [1]instruction in
righteousness,
17 [a]that the man of God may be
complete, [b]thoroughly equipped
for every good work.

4 I [a]charge *you* [1]therefore before God and the Lord Jesus
Christ, [b]who will judge the living
and the dead [2]at His appearing
and His kingdom:
2 Preach the word! Be ready
in season *and* out of season.
[a]Convince, [b]rebuke, [c]exhort, with
all longsuffering and teaching.
3 [a]For the time will come when
they will not endure [b]sound doctrine, [c]but according to their
own desires, *because* they have
itching ears, they will heap up
for themselves teachers;
4 and they will turn *their* ears
away from the truth, and [a]be
turned aside to fables.
5 But you be watchful in all
things, [a]endure afflictions, do
the work of [b]an evangelist, fulfill
your ministry.
6 For [a]I am already being
poured out as a drink offering,
and the time of [b]my departure is
at hand.
7 [a]I have fought the good fight,
I have finished the race, I have
kept the faith.
8 Finally, there is laid up for
me [a]the crown of righteousness,
which the Lord, the righteous
[b]Judge, will give to me [c]on that
Day, and not to me only but also
to all who have loved His appearing.
9 Be diligent to come to me
quickly;
10 for [a]Dē′mas has forsaken
me, [b]having loved this present
world, and has departed for
Thes·sa·lo·nī′ca—Crescens for
Galatia, Titus for Dal·mā′tia.
11 Only Luke is with me. Get
[a]Mark and bring him with you,
for he is useful to me for ministry.
12 And [a]Tych′i·cus I have sent to
Eph′e·sus.
13 Bring the cloak that I left
with Car′pus at Trō′as when you
come—and the books, especially
the parchments.
14 [a]Alexander the coppersmith
did me much harm. May the
Lord repay him according to his
works.
15 You also must beware of
him, for he has greatly resisted
our words.
16 At my first defense no one
stood with me, but all forsook
me. [a]May it not be charged
against them.
17 [a]But the Lord stood with me
and strengthened me, [b]so that
the message might be preached
fully through me, and *that* all
the Gentiles might hear. Also I
was delivered [c]out of the mouth
of the lion.
18 [a]And the Lord will deliver
me from every evil work and
preserve *me* for His heavenly
kingdom. [b]To Him *be* glory forever and ever. Amen!
19 Greet [a]Pris′ca and A·qui′la,
and the household of [b]On·e·siph′-
o·rus.
20 [a]Ē·ras′tus stayed in Corinth,
but [b]Troph′i·mus I have left in
Mī·lē′tus sick.
21 Do your utmost to come
before winter. Eū·bū′lus greets
you, as well as Pū′dens, Lī′nus,
Clau′di·a, and all the brethren.
22 The Lord [1]Jesus Christ be
with your spirit. Grace be with
you. Amen.

16 [b]Rom. 4:23; 15:4 [1]*training, discipline*
17 [a]1 Tim. 6:11 [b]2 Tim. 2:21

CHAPTER 4

1 [a]1 Tim. 5:21 [b]Acts 10:42 [1]NU omits *therefore* [2]NU *and by*
2 [a]Titus 2:15 [b]1 Tim. 5:20 [c]1 Tim. 4:13
3 [a]2 Tim. 3:1 [b]1 Tim. 1:10 [c]2 Tim. 3:6
4 [a]1 Tim. 1:4
5 [a]2 Tim. 1:8 [b]Acts 21:8
6 [a]Phil. 2:17 [b][Phil. 1:23]
7 [a]1 Cor. 9:24–27
8 [a]James 1:12 [b]John 5:22 [c]2 Tim. 1:12
10 [a]Col. 4:14 [b]1 John 2:15
11 [a]Acts 12:12, 25; 15:37–39
12 [a]Acts 20:4
14 [a]1 Tim. 1:20
16 [a]Acts 7:60
17 [a]Acts 23:11 [b]Acts 9:15 [c]1 Sam. 17:37
18 [a]Ps. 121:7 [b]Rom. 11:36
19 [a]Acts 18:2 [b]2 Tim. 1:16
20 [a]Rom. 16:23 [b]Acts 20:4; 21:29
22 [1]NU omits *Jesus Christ*

The Epistle of Paul the Apostle to

TITUS

TITUS, a young pastor, faces the unenviable assignment of setting in order the church at Crete. Paul writes advising him to appoint elders, men of proven spiritual character in their homes and businesses, to oversee the work of the church. But elders are not the only individuals in the church who are required to excel spiritually. Men and women, young and old, each have their vital functions to fulfill in the church if they are to be living examples of the doctrine they profess. Throughout his letter to Titus, Paul stresses the necessary, practical working out of salvation in the daily lives of both the elders and the congregation. Good works are desirable and profitable for all believers.

This third Pastoral Epistle is simply titled *Pros Titon*, "To Titus." Ironically, this was also the name of the Roman general who destroyed Jerusalem in A.D. 70 and succeeded his father Vespasian as emperor.

CHAPTER 1

PAUL, a bondservant of God and an apostle of Jesus Christ, according to the faith of God's elect and [a]the acknowledgment of the truth [b]which accords with godliness,
2 in hope of eternal life which God, who [a]cannot lie, promised before time began,
3 but has in due time manifested His word through preaching, which was committed to me according to the commandment of God our Savior;

4 To [a]Titus, a true son in *our* common faith:

Grace, mercy, *and* peace from God the Father and [1]the Lord Jesus Christ our Savior.

5 For this reason I left you in Crēte, that you should [a]set in order the things that are lacking, and appoint elders in every city as I commanded you—
6 if a man is blameless, the husband of one wife, [a]having faithful children not accused of [1]dissipation or insubordination.
7 For a [1]bishop must be blameless, as a steward of God, not self-willed, not quick-tempered, [a]not given to wine, not violent, not greedy for money,
8 but hospitable, a lover of what is good, sober-minded, just, holy, self-controlled,
9 holding fast the faithful word as he has been taught, that he may be able, by sound doctrine, both to exhort and convict those who contradict.
10 For there are many insubordinate, both idle [a]talkers and deceivers, especially those of the circumcision,
11 whose mouths must be stopped, who subvert whole households, teaching things which they ought not, [a]for the sake of dishonest gain.
12 [a]One of them, a prophet of their own, said, "Crē′tans *are* always liars, evil beasts, lazy gluttons."

1 [a]2 Tim. 2:25 [b][1 Tim. 3:16]
2 [a]Num. 23:19
4 [a]2 Cor. 2:13; 8:23 [1]NU *Christ Jesus*
5 [a]1 Cor. 11:34
6 [a]1 Tim. 3:2–4 [1]*debauchery*, lit. *incorrigibility*
7 [a]Lev. 10:9 [1]Lit. *overseer*
10 [a]James 1:26
11 [a]1 Tim. 6:5
12 [a]Acts 17:28

13 This testimony is true. [a]Therefore rebuke them sharply, that they may be sound in the faith,
14 not giving heed to Jewish fables and [a]commandments of men who turn from the truth.
15 [a]To the pure all things are pure, but to those who are defiled and unbelieving nothing is pure; but even their mind and conscience are defiled.
16 They profess to [a]know God, but [b]in works they deny *Him*, being [1]abominable, disobedient, [c]and disqualified for every good work.

2 But as for you, speak the things which are proper for sound doctrine:
2 that the older men be sober, reverent, temperate, sound in faith, in love, in patience;
3 the older women likewise, that they be reverent in behavior, not slanderers, not given to much wine, teachers of good things—
4 that they admonish the young women to love their husbands, to love their children,
5 *to be* discreet, chaste, [a]homemakers, good, [b]obedient to their own husbands, [c]that the word of God may not be blasphemed.
6 Likewise, exhort the young men to be sober-minded,
7 in all things showing yourself *to be* [a]a pattern of good works; in doctrine *showing* integrity, reverence, [b]incorruptibility,[1]
8 sound speech that cannot be condemned, that one who is an opponent may be ashamed, having nothing evil to say of [1]you.
9 *Exhort* [a]bondservants to be obedient to their own masters, to be well pleasing in all *things*, not answering back,

13 [a]2 Cor. 13:10
14 [a]Is. 29:13
15 [a]1 Cor. 6:12
16 [a]Matt. 7:20–23; 25:12 [b][2 Tim. 3:5, 7] [c]Rom. 1:28 [1]*detestable*

CHAPTER 2

5 [a]1 Tim. 5:14 [b]1 Cor. 14:34 [c]Rom. 2:24
7 [a]1 Tim. 4:12 [b]Eph. 6:24 [1]NU omits *incorruptibility*
8 [1]NU, M *us*
9 [a]1 Tim. 6:1
10 [1]*thieving* [2]*honesty*
11 [a][Rom. 5:15]
13 [a]1 Cor. 1:7 [b][Col. 3:4]
14 [a]Is. 53:10–12; Gal. 1:4 [b]Ezek. 37:23; [Heb. 1:3; 9:14] [c]Ex. 15:16
15 [a]2 Tim. 4:2

CHAPTER 3

1 [a]1 Pet. 2:13 [b]Col. 1:10
3 [a]1 Cor. 6:11
4 [a]Titus 2:11 [b]1 Tim. 2:3
5 [a][Rom. 3:20] [b]John 3:3
6 [a]Ezek. 36:26

10 not [1]pilfering, but showing all good [2]fidelity, that they may adorn the doctrine of God our Savior in all things.
11 For [a]the grace of God that brings salvation has appeared to all men,
12 teaching us that, denying ungodliness and worldly lusts, we should live soberly, righteously, and godly in the present age,
13 [a]looking for the blessed [b]hope and glorious appearing of our great God and Savior Jesus Christ,
14 [a]who gave Himself for us, ★
that He might redeem us from every lawless deed [b]and purify for Himself [c]*His* own special people, zealous for good works.
15 Speak these things, [a]exhort, and rebuke with all authority. Let no one despise you.

3 Remind them [a]to be subject to rulers and authorities, to obey, [b]to be ready for every good work,
2 to speak evil of no one, to be peaceable, gentle, showing all humility to all men.
3 For [a]we ourselves were also once foolish, disobedient, deceived, serving various lusts and pleasures, living in malice and envy, hateful and hating one another.
4 But when [a]the kindness and the love of [b]God our Savior toward man appeared,
5 [a]not by works of righteousness which we have done, but according to His mercy He saved us, through [b]the washing of regeneration and renewing of the Holy Spirit,
6 [a]whom He poured out on us abundantly through Jesus Christ our Savior,

7 that having been justified by
His grace [a]we should become
heirs according to the hope of
eternal life.
8 [a]This is a faithful saying, and
these things I want you to affirm constantly, that those who
have believed in God should be
careful to maintain good works.
These things are good and profitable to men.
9 But [a]avoid foolish disputes,
genealogies, contentions, and
strivings about the law; for they
are unprofitable and useless.
10 [a]Reject a divisive man after
the first and second [1]admoni-
tion,
11 knowing that such a person

7 [a][Rom. 8:17, 23, 24]

8 [a]1 Tim. 1:15

9 [a]2 Tim. 2:23

10 [a]Matt. 18:17 [1]*warning*

12 [a]Acts 20:4

13 [a]Acts 18:24

is warped and sinning, being
self-condemned.
12 When I send Ar′te·mas to
you, or [a]Tych′i·cus, be diligent to
come to me at Ni·cop′o·lis, for I
have decided to spend the winter there.
13 Send Zē′nas the lawyer and
[a]A·pol′los on their journey with
haste, that they may lack nothing.
14 And let our *people* also learn
to maintain good works, to *meet*
urgent needs, that they may not
be unfruitful.
15 All who *are* with me greet
you. Greet those who love us in
the faith. Grace *be* with you all.
Amen.

The Epistle of Paul the Apostle to

PHILEMON

DOES Christian brotherly love really work, even in situations of extraordinary tension and difficulty? Will it work, for example, between a prominent slave owner and one of his runaway slaves? Paul has no doubt! He writes a "postcard" to Philemon, his beloved brother and fellow worker, on behalf of Onesimus—a deserter, thief, and formerly worthless slave, but now Philemon's brother in Christ. With much tact and tenderness, Paul asks Philemon to receive Onesimus back with the same gentleness with which he would receive Paul himself. Any debt Onesimus owes, Paul promises to make good. Knowing Philemon, Paul is confident that brotherly love and forgiveness will carry the day.

Since this letter is addressed to Philemon in verse 1, it becomes known as *Pros Philemona,* "To Philemon." Like First and Second Timothy and Titus, it is addressed to an individual, but unlike the Pastoral Epistles, Philemon is also addressed to a family and a church (v. 2).

PAUL, a [a]prisoner of Christ Jesus, and Timothy *our* brother,

To Phī·lē′mon our beloved *friend* and fellow laborer,
2 to [1]the beloved Ap′phi·a, [a]Ar·chip′pus our fellow soldier, and to the church in your house:

3 Grace to you and peace from God our Father and the Lord Jesus Christ.

4 [a]I thank my God, making mention of you always in my prayers,
5 [a]hearing of your love and faith which you have toward the Lord Jesus and toward all the saints,
6 that the sharing of your faith may become effective [a]by the acknowledgment of [b]every good thing which is in [1]you in Christ Jesus.
7 For we [1]have great [2]joy and [3]consolation in your love, because the [4]hearts of the saints have been refreshed by you, brother.
8 Therefore, though I might be very bold in Christ to command you what is fitting,
9 *yet* for love's sake I rather appeal *to you*—being such a one as Paul, the aged, and now also a prisoner of Jesus Christ—
10 I appeal to you for my son [a]Ō·nes′i·mus, whom I have begotten *while* in my chains,
11 who once was unprofitable to you, but now is profitable to you and to me.
12 I am sending him [1]back. You therefore receive him, that is, my own [2]heart,
13 whom I wished to keep with me, that on your behalf he might minister to me in my chains for the gospel.
14 But without your consent I wanted to do nothing, [a]that your good deed might not be by

1 [a]Eph. 3:1
2 [a]Col. 4:17 [1]NU *our sister Apphia*
4 [a]2 Thess. 1:3
5 [a]Col. 1:4
6 [a]Phil. 1:9 [b][1 Thess. 5:18] [1]NU, M *us*
7 [1]NU *had* [2]M *thanksgiving* [3]*comfort* [4]Lit. *inward parts,* heart, liver, and lungs
10 [a]Col. 4:9
12 [1]NU *back to you in person, that is, my own heart,* [2]See v. 7.
14 [a]2 Cor. 9:7

compulsion, as it were, but voluntary.
15 For perhaps he departed for
a while for this *purpose*, that
you might receive him forever,
16 no longer as a slave but more
than a slave—a beloved brother,
especially to me but how much
more to you, both in the [a]flesh
and in the Lord.
17 If then you count me as a partner, receive him as *you would* me.
18 But if he has wronged you or
owes anything, put that on my
account.
19 I, Paul, am writing with my
own [a]hand. I will repay—not to
mention to you that you owe me
even your own self besides.
20 Yes, brother, let me have joy
from you in the Lord; refresh my
heart in the Lord.
21 [a]Having confidence in your
obedience, I write to you, knowing that you will do even more
than I say.
22 But, meanwhile, also prepare a guest room for me, for [a]I
trust that [b]through your prayers
I shall be granted to you.
23 [a]Ep'a·phras, my fellow prisoner in Christ Jesus, greets you,
24 *as do* [a]Mark, [b]Ar·is·tar'chus,
[c]Dē'mas, [d]Luke, my fellow laborers.
25 [a]The grace of our Lord Jesus Christ *be* with your spirit.
Amen.

16 [a]Col. 3:22
19 [a]1 Cor. 16:21
21 [a]2 Cor. 7:16
22 [a]Phil. 1:25; 2:24 [b]2 Cor. 1:11
23 [a]Col. 1:7; 4:12
24 [a]Acts 12:12, 25; 15:37–39 [b]Acts 19:29; 27:2 [c]Col. 4:14 [d]2 Tim. 4:11
25 [a]2 Tim. 4:22

The Epistle to the
HEBREWS

MANY Jewish believers, having stepped out of Judaism into Christianity, want to reverse their course in order to escape persecution by their countrymen. The writer of Hebrews exhorts them to "go on to perfection" (6:1). His appeal is based on the superiority of Christ over the Judaic system. Christ is better than the angels, for they worship Him. He is better than Moses, for He created him. He is better than the Aaronic priesthood, for His sacrifice was once for all time. He is better than the law, for He mediates a better covenant. In short, there is more to be gained in Christ than to be lost in Judaism. Pressing on in Christ produces tested faith, self-discipline, and a visible love seen in good works.

Although the King James Version uses the title "The Epistle of Paul the Apostle to the Hebrews," there is no early manuscript evidence to support it. The oldest and most reliable title is simply *Pros Ebraious*, "To Hebrews."

GOD, who [1]at various times
and [a]in various ways spoke
in time past to the fathers by the
prophets,
2 has in these last days spoken to us by *His* Son, whom He
has appointed heir of all things,
through whom also He made the
[1]worlds;
★ 3 [a]who being the brightness of
His glory and the express [b]image
of His person, and [c]upholding
all things by the word of His
power, [d]when He had [1]by Himself [2]purged [3]our sins, [e]sat down
at the right hand of the Majesty
on high,
4 having become so much better than the angels, as [a]He has
by inheritance obtained a more
excellent name than they.
★ 5 For to which of the angels
did He ever say:

[a]"You are My Son,
Today I have begotten You"?

And again:

[b]"I will be to Him a Father,
And He shall be to Me a Son"?

6 But when He again brings ★
[a]the firstborn into the world, He
says:

[b]"Let all the angels of God worship Him."

7 And of the angels He says:

[a]"Who makes His angels spirits
And His ministers a flame of fire."

8 But to the Son *He says:* ★

[a]"Your throne, O God, is forever and ever;
A [1]scepter of righteousness is the scepter of Your kingdom.
9 *You have loved righteousness and hated lawlessness;* ★

CHAPTER 1

1 [a]Num. 12:6, 8 [1]Or *in many portions*

2 [1]Or *ages*, Gr. *aiones*, aeons

3 [a]John 1:14 [b]2 Cor. 4:4 [c]Col. 1:17 [d][Heb. 7:27] [e]Ps. 110:1 [1]NU omits *by Himself* [2]*cleansed* [3]NU omits *our*

4 [a][Phil. 2:9, 10]

5 [a]Ps. 2:7 [b]2 Sam. 7:14

6 [a]Ps. 89:27; [Rom. 8:29] [b]Deut. 32:43, LXX, DSS; Ps. 97:7; 1 Pet. 3:22; Rev. 5:11–13

7 [a]Ps. 104:4

8 [a]Ps. 45:6, 7 [1]A ruler's staff

Therefore God, Your God,
[a]has anointed You
With the oil of gladness
more than Your
companions."

10 And:

[a]"You, LORD, in the beginning
laid the foundation of
the earth,
And the heavens are the
work of Your hands.
11 *[a]They will perish, but You*
remain;
And [b]they will all grow old
like a garment;
12 *Like a cloak You will fold*
them up,
And they will be changed.
But You are the [a]same,
And Your years will not fail."

★ 13 But to which of the angels
has He ever said:

[a]"Sit at My right hand,
Till I make Your enemies
Your footstool"?

14 [a]Are they not all ministering
spirits sent forth to minister for
those who will [b]inherit salvation?

2 Therefore we must give [1]the
more earnest heed to the
things we have heard, lest we
drift away.
2 For if the word [a]spoken
through angels proved steadfast, and [b]every transgression
and disobedience received a just
[1]reward,
3 [a]how shall we escape if we
neglect so great a salvation,
[b]which at the first began to be
spoken by the Lord, and was
[c]confirmed to us by those who
heard *Him,*
4 [a]God also bearing witness
[b]both with signs and wonders,
with various miracles, and [c]gifts[1]
of the Holy Spirit, [d]according to
His own will?
5 For He has not put [a]the world
to come, of which we speak, in
subjection to angels.
6 But one testified in a certain
place, saying:

[a]"What is man that You are
mindful of him,
Or the son of man that You
take care of him?
7 *You have made him [1]a little*
lower than the angels;
You have crowned him with
glory and honor,
[2]And set him over the works
of Your hands.
8 *[a]You have put all things in*
subjection under his
feet."

For in that He put all in subjection under him, He left nothing
that is not put under him. But
now [b]we do not yet see all things
put under him.
9 But we see Jesus, [a]who was
made [1]a little lower than the
angels, for the suffering of death
[b]crowned with glory and honor,
that He, by the grace of God,
might taste death [c]for everyone.
10 For it was fitting for Him,
[a]for whom *are* all things and by
whom *are* all things, in bringing many sons to glory, to make
the captain of their salvation
[b]perfect through sufferings.
11 For [a]both He who [1]sanctifies
and those who are being sanctified [b]*are* all of one, for which
reason [c]He is not ashamed to
call them brethren,
12 saying:

9 [a]Ps. 45:6, 7; Is. 61:1, 3
10 [a]Ps. 102:25–27
11 [a][Is. 34:4] [b]Is. 50:9; 51:6
12 [a]Heb. 13:8
13 [a]Ps. 110:1
14 [a]Ps. 103:20 [b]Rom. 8:17

CHAPTER 2

1 [1]*all the more careful attention*
2 [a]Acts 7:53 [b]Num. 15:30 [1]*retribution* or *penalty*
3 [a]Heb. 10:28 [b]Matt. 4:17 [c]Luke 1:2
4 [a]Mark 16:20 [b]Acts 2:22, 43 [c]1 Cor. 12:4, 7, 11 [d]Eph. 1:5, 9 [1]*distributions*
5 [a][2 Pet. 3:13]
6 [a]Ps. 8:4–6
7 [1]Or *for a little while* [2]NU, M omit the rest of v. 7.
8 [a]Matt. 28:18 [b]1 Cor. 15:25, 27
9 [a]Phil. 2:7–9 [b]Acts 2:33; 3:13 [c][John 3:16] [1]Or *for a little while*
10 [a]Col. 1:16 [b]Heb. 5:8, 9; 7:28
11 [a]Heb. 10:10 [b]Acts 17:26 [c]Matt. 28:10 [1]*sets apart*

★ [a]*"I will declare Your name to*
My brethren;
In the midst of the assembly
I will sing praise to You."

★ 13 And again:

[a]*"I will put My trust in Him."*

And again:

[b]*"Here am I and the children*
whom God has given
Me."

14 Inasmuch then as the children have partaken of flesh
and blood, He [a]Himself likewise
shared in the same, [b]that through
death He might destroy him who
had the power of [c]death, that is,
the devil,
15 and release those who
[a]through fear of death were all
their lifetime subject to bondage.
16 For indeed He does not [1]give
aid to angels, but He does [2]give
aid to the seed of Abraham.
17 Therefore, in all things He
had [a]to be made like *His* brethren, that He might be [b]a merciful and faithful High Priest
in things *pertaining* to God, to
make propitiation for the sins of
the people.
18 [a]For in that He Himself has
suffered, being [1]tempted, He
is able to aid those who are
tempted.

3

3 Therefore, holy brethren,
partakers of the heavenly
calling, consider the Apostle
and High Priest of our confession, Christ Jesus,
2 who was faithful to Him who
appointed Him, as [a]Moses also
was faithful in all His house.

12 [a]Ps. 22:22
13 [a]2 Sam. 22:3; Is. 8:17 [b]Is. 8:18
14 [a]John 1:14 [b]Col. 2:15 [c]2 Tim. 1:10
15 [a][Luke 1:74]
16 [1]Or *take on* the nature of [2]Or *take on*
17 [a]Phil. 2:7 [b][Heb. 4:15; 5:1–10]
18 [a][Heb. 4:15, 16] [1]*tested*

CHAPTER 3

2 [a]Num. 12:7
3 [a]Zech. 6:12, 13
4 [a][Eph. 2:10]
5 [a]Heb. 3:2 [b]Ex. 14:31 [c]Deut. 18:15, 18, 19
6 [a]Heb. 1:2 [b][1 Cor. 3:16] [c][Matt. 10:22] [1]NU omits *firm to the end*
7 [a]Acts 1:16 [b]Ps. 95:7–11
13 [1]*encourage*

3 For this One has been
counted worthy of more glory
than Moses, inasmuch as [a]He
who built the house has more
honor than the house.
4 For every house is built by
someone, but [a]He who built all
things *is* God.
5 [a]And Moses indeed *was* faithful in all His house as [b]a servant,
[c]for a testimony of those things
which would be spoken *after-*
ward,
6 but Christ as [a]a Son over His
own house, [b]whose house we are
[c]if we hold fast the confidence
and the rejoicing of the hope
[1]firm to the end.
7 Therefore, as [a]the Holy Spirit
says:

[b]*"Today, if you will hear His*
voice,
8 *Do not harden your hearts*
as in the rebellion,
In the day of trial in the
wilderness,
9 *Where your fathers tested*
Me, tried Me,
And saw My works forty
years.
10 *Therefore I was angry with*
that generation,
And said, 'They always go
astray in their heart,
And they have not known
My ways.'
11 *So I swore in My wrath,*
'They shall not enter My
rest.'"

12 Beware, brethren, lest there
be in any of you an evil heart of
unbelief in departing from the
living God;
13 but [1]exhort one another daily,
while it is called *"Today,"* lest any

of you be hardened through the deceitfulness of sin.

14 For we have become partakers of Christ if we hold the beginning of our confidence steadfast to the end,

15 while it is said:

> [a]*"Today, if you will hear His voice,*
> *Do not harden your hearts as in the rebellion."*

16 [a]For who, having heard, rebelled? Indeed, *was it* not all who came out of Egypt, *led* by Moses?

17 Now with whom was He angry forty years? *Was it* not with those who sinned, [a]whose corpses fell in the wilderness?

18 And [a]to whom did He swear that they would not enter His rest, but to those who did not obey?

19 So we see that they could not enter in because of [a]unbelief.

4 Therefore, since a promise remains of entering His rest, [a]let us fear lest any of you seem to have come short of it.

2 For indeed the gospel was preached to us as well as to them; but the word which they heard did not profit them, [1]not being mixed with faith in those who heard *it.*

3 For we who have believed do enter that rest, as He has said:

> [a]*"So I swore in My wrath,*
> *'They shall not enter My rest,' "*

although the works were finished from the foundation of the world.

4 For He has spoken in a certain place of the seventh *day* in this way: [a]*"And God rested on the seventh day from all His works"*;

5 and again in this *place:* [a]*"They shall not enter My rest."*

6 Since therefore it remains that some *must* enter it, and those to whom it was first preached did not enter because of disobedience,

7 again He designates a certain day, saying in David, *"Today,"* after such a long time, as it has been said:

> [a]*"Today, if you will hear His voice,*
> *Do not harden your hearts."*

8 For if [1]Joshua had [a]given them rest, then He would not afterward have spoken of another day.

9 There remains therefore a rest for the people of God.

10 For he who has entered His rest has himself also ceased from his works as God *did* from His.

11 [a]Let us therefore be diligent to enter that rest, lest anyone fall according to the same example of disobedience.

12 For the word of God *is* [a]living and powerful, and [b]sharper than any [c]two-edged sword, piercing even to the division of soul and spirit, and of joints and marrow, and is [d]a discerner of the thoughts and intents of the heart.

13 [a]And there is no creature hidden from His sight, but all things *are* [b]naked and open to the eyes of Him to whom we *must give* account.

---

15 [a]Ps. 95:7, 8
16 [a]Num. 14:2, 11, 30
17 [a]Num. 14:22, 23
18 [a]Num. 14:30
19 [a]1 Cor. 10:11, 12

CHAPTER 4

1 [a]Heb. 12:15
2 [1]NU, M *since they were not united by faith with those who heeded it*
3 [a]Ps. 95:11
4 [a]Gen. 2:2
5 [a]Ps. 95:11
7 [a]Ps. 95:7, 8
8 [a]Josh. 22:4 [1]Gr. *Jesus,* same as Heb. *Joshua*
11 [a]2 Pet. 1:10
12 [a]Ps. 147:15 [b]Is. 49:2 [c]Eph. 6:17 [d]1 Cor. 14:24, 25
13 [a]Ps. 33:13–15; 90:8 [b]Job 26:6

14 Seeing then that we have
a great [a]High Priest who has
passed through the heavens, Jesus the Son of God, [b]let us hold
fast *our* confession.
15 For [a]we do not have a High
Priest who cannot sympathize
with our weaknesses, but [b]was
in all *points* tempted as *we are,*
[c]*yet* without sin.
16 [a]Let us therefore come boldly
to the throne of grace, that we
may obtain mercy and find grace
to help in time of need.
5 For every high priest taken
from among men [a]is ap-
pointed for men in things *per-*
taining to God, that he may offer
both gifts and sacrifices for sins.
2 He can [1]have compassion on
those who are ignorant and going astray, since he himself is
also subject to [a]weakness.
3 Because of this he is required
as for the people, so also for
[a]himself, to offer *sacrifices* for
sins.
4 And no man takes this honor
to himself, but he who is called
by God, just as [a]Aaron *was.*
★5 [a]So also Christ did not glorify Himself to become High
Priest, but *it was* He who said to
Him:

[b]*"You are My Son,*
Today I have begotten You."

★6 As *He* also says in another
place:

[a]*"You are a priest forever*
According to the order of
Mel·chiz'e·dek";

7 who, in the days of His
flesh, when He had [a]offered up
prayers and supplications, [b]with
vehement cries and tears to Him
[c]who was able to save Him from
death, and was heard [d]because
of His godly fear,
8 though He was a Son, *yet* He
learned [a]obedience by the things
which He suffered.
9 And [a]having been perfected,
He became the author of eternal
salvation to all who obey Him,
10 called by God as High Priest
[a]*"according to the order of*
Mel·chiz'e·dek,"
11 of whom [a]we have much to
say, and hard to explain, since
you have become [b]dull of hearing.
12 For though by this time you
ought to be teachers, you need
someone to teach you again the
first principles of the [1]oracles of
God; and you have come to need
[a]milk and not solid food.
13 For everyone who partakes
only of milk *is* unskilled in the
word of righteousness, for he is
[a]a babe.
14 But solid food belongs to
those who are [1]of full age, *that*
is, those who by reason of [2]use
have their senses exercised [a]to
discern both good and evil.
6 Therefore, [a]leaving the dis-
cussion of the elementary
principles of Christ, let us go on
to [1]perfection, not laying again
the foundation of repentance
from [b]dead works and of faith
toward God,
2 [a]of the doctrine of baptisms,
[b]of laying on of hands, [c]of resurrection of the dead, [d]and of eternal judgment.
3 And this [1]we will do if God
permits.
4 For *it is* impossible for those
who were once enlightened, and
have tasted [a]the heavenly gift,

14 [a]Heb. 2:17; 7:26 [b]Heb. 10:23
15 [a]Is. 53:3–5 [b]Luke 22:28 [c]2 Cor. 5:21
16 [a][Eph. 2:18]

CHAPTER 5

1 [a]Heb. 2:17; 8:3
2 [a]Heb. 7:28 [1]*deal gently with*
3 [a]Lev. 9:7; 16:6
4 [a]Ex. 28:1
5 [a]John 8:54 [b]Ps. 2:7
6 [a]Ps. 110:4
7 [a]Matt. 26:39, 42, 44 [b]Ps. 22:1 [c]Matt. 26:53 [d]Matt. 26:39
8 [a]Phil. 2:8
9 [a]Heb. 2:10
10 [a]Ps. 110:4
11 [a][John 16:12] [b][Matt. 13:15]
12 [a]1 Cor. 3:1–3 [1]*sayings,* Scriptures
13 [a]Eph. 4:14
14 [a]Is. 7:15 [1]*mature* [2]*practice*

CHAPTER 6

1 [a]Heb. 5:12 [b][Heb. 9:14] [1]*maturity*
2 [a]Acts 19:3–5 [b][Acts 8:17] [c]Acts 17:31 [d]Acts 24:25
3 [1]M *let us do*
4 [a][John 4:10]

and [b]have become partakers of
the Holy Spirit,
5 and have tasted the good
word of God and the powers of
the age to come,
6 [1]if they fall away, to renew
them again to repentance, [a]since
they crucify again for themselves the Son of God, and put
Him to an open shame.
7 For the earth which drinks in
the rain that often comes upon
it, and bears herbs useful for
those by whom it is cultivated,
[a]receives blessing from God;
8 [a]but if it bears thorns and
briers, *it is* rejected and near to
being cursed, whose end *is* to be
burned.
9 But, beloved, we are confident of better things concerning
you, yes, things that accompany
salvation, though we speak in
this manner.
10 For [a]God *is* not unjust to
forget [b]your work and [1]labor of
love which you have shown toward His name, *in that* you have
[c]ministered to the saints, and do
minister.
11 And we desire that each one
of you show the same diligence
[a]to the full assurance of hope
until the end,
12 that you do not become
[1]sluggish, but imitate those who
through faith and patience [a]in-
herit the promises.
13 For when God made a promise to Abraham, because He
could swear by no one greater,
[a]He swore by Himself,
14 saying, [a]*"Surely blessing I
will bless you, and multiplying I
will multiply you."*
15 And so, after he had patiently endured, he obtained the
[a]promise.
16 For men indeed swear by the
greater, and [a]an oath for confirmation *is* for them an end of all
dispute.
17 Thus God, determining to
show more abundantly to [a]the
heirs of promise [b]the [1]immuta-
bility of His counsel, [2]confirmed
it by an oath,
18 that by two [1]immutable
things, in which it *is* impossible
for God to [a]lie, we [2]might have
strong consolation, who have
fled for refuge to lay hold of the
hope [b]set before *us*.
19 This *hope* we have as an an-
chor of the soul, both sure and
steadfast, [a]and which enters the
Presence behind the veil,
20 [a]where the forerunner has
entered for us, *even* Jesus,
[b]having become High Priest forever according to the order of
Mel·chiz′e·dek.

7

For this [a]Mel·chiz′e·dek, king
of Sā′lem, priest of the Most
High God, who met Abraham
returning from the slaughter of
the kings and blessed him,
2 to whom also Abraham gave
a tenth part of all, first being
translated "king of righteousness," and then also king of Sā′-
lem, meaning "king of peace,"
3 without father, without
mother, without genealogy, having neither beginning of days
nor end of life, but made like
the Son of God, remains a priest
continually.
4 Now consider how great this
man *was*, to whom even the pa-
triarch Abraham gave a tenth of
the [1]spoils.
5 And indeed [a]those who are of
the sons of Levi, who receive the
priesthood, have a commandment to receive tithes from the

4 [b][Gal. 3:2, 5]
6 [a]Heb. 10:29 [1]Or *and have fallen away*
7 [a]Ps. 65:10
8 [a]Is. 5:6
10 [a]Rom. 3:4 [b]1 Thess. 1:3 [c]Rom. 15:25 [1]NU omits *labor of*
11 [a]Col. 2:2
12 [a]Heb. 10:36 [1]*lazy*
13 [a]Gen. 22:16, 17
14 [a]Gen. 22:16, 17
15 [a]Gen. 12:4; 21:5
16 [a]Ex. 22:11
17 [a]Heb. 11:9 [b]Rom. 11:29 [1]*unchangeableness of His purpose* [2]*guaranteed*
18 [a]Num. 23:19 [b][Col. 1:5] [1]*unchangeable* [2]M omits *might*
19 [a]Lev. 16:2, 15
20 [a][Heb. 4:14] [b]Heb. 3:1; 5:10, 11

CHAPTER 7
1 [a]Gen. 14:18–20
4 [1]*plunder*
5 [a]Num. 18:21–26

people according to the law, that
is, from their brethren, though
they have come from the loins of
Abraham;
6 but he whose genealogy is not
derived from them received tithes
from Abraham [a]and blessed [b]him
who had the promises.
7 Now beyond all contradic-
tion the lesser is blessed by the
better.
8 Here mortal men receive
tithes, but there he *receives them*,
[a]of whom it is witnessed that he
lives.
9 Even Levi, who receives
tithes, paid tithes through Abraham, so to speak,
10 for he was still in the loins of
his father when Mel·chiz′e·dek
met him.
11 [a]Therefore, if perfection were
through the Le·vit′i·cal priesthood (for under it the people
received the law), what further
need *was there* that another
priest should rise according to
the order of Mel·chiz′e·dek, and
not be called according to the
order of Aaron?
12 For the priesthood being
changed, of necessity there is
also a change of the law.
13 For He of whom these things
are spoken belongs to another
tribe, from which no man has
[1]officiated at the altar.
★ 14 For *it is* evident that [a]our
Lord arose from [b]Judah, of
which tribe Moses spoke nothing concerning [1]priesthood.
15 And it is yet far more evident
if, in the likeness of Mel·chiz′-
e·dek, there arises another priest
16 who has come, not according to the law of a fleshly commandment, but according to the
power of an endless life.

6 [a]Gen. 14:19, 20 [b][Rom. 4:13]
8 [a]Heb. 5:6; 6:20
11 [a]Heb. 7:18; 8:7
13 [1]*served*
14 [a]Gen. 49:8–10; Is. 1:1; 11:1; Mic. 5:2 [b]Matt. 1:2 [1]NU *priests*
17 [a]Ps. 110:4 [1]NU *it is testified*
18 [a][Rom. 8:3]
19 [a][Acts 13:39] [b]Heb. 6:18, 19 [c]Rom. 5:2 [1]*complete*
21 [a]Ps. 110:4 [1]NU ends the quotation after *forever.*
22 [a]Heb. 8:6 [1]*guarantee*
25 [a]Jude 24 [b]Rom. 8:34 [1]*completely* or *forever*
26 [a]Heb. 4:15 [b]Eph. 1:20 [1]*innocent*

17 For [1]He testifies: ★

[a]*“You are a priest forever*
According to the order of
Mel·chiz′e·dek.”

18 For on the one hand there is
an annulling of the former commandment because of [a]its weakness and unprofitableness,
19 for [a]the law made nothing
[1]perfect; on the other hand, *there*
is the bringing in of [b]a better
hope, through which [c]we draw
near to God.
20 And inasmuch as *He was* not
made priest without an oath
21 (for they have become priests ★
without an oath, but He with an
oath by Him who said to Him:

[a]*“The* L*ORD has sworn*
And will not relent,
‘You are a priest [1]*forever*
According to the order of
Mel·chiz′e·dek’”),

22 by so much more Jesus has
become a [1]surety of a [a]better
covenant.
23 Also there were many priests,
because they were prevented by
death from continuing.
24 But He, because He continues forever, has an unchangeable priesthood.
25 Therefore He is also [a]able to
save [1]to the uttermost those who
come to God through Him, since
He always lives [b]to make intercession for them.
26 For such a High Priest was
fitting for us, [a]*who is* holy, [1]harm-
less, undefiled, separate from
sinners, [b]and has become higher
than the heavens;
27 who does not need daily, as
those high priests, to offer up

sacrifices, first for His [a]own sins and then for the people's, for this He did once for all when He offered up Himself.

28 For the law appoints as high priests men who have weakness, but the word of the oath, which came after the law, *appoints* the Son who has been perfected forever.

8 Now *this is* the main point of the things we are saying: We have such a High Priest, [a]who is seated at the right hand of the throne of the Majesty in the heavens,

2 a Minister of [a]the [1]sanctuary and of [b]the true tabernacle which the Lord erected, and not man.

3 For [a]every high priest is appointed to offer both gifts and sacrifices. Therefore [b]*it is* necessary that this One also have something to offer.

4 For if He were on earth, He would not be a priest, since there are priests who offer the gifts according to the law;

5 who serve [a]the copy and [b]shadow of the heavenly things, as Moses was divinely instructed when he was about to make the tabernacle. For He said, [c]*"See that you make all things according to the pattern shown you on the mountain."*

6 But now [a]He has obtained a more excellent ministry, inasmuch as He is also Mediator of a [b]better covenant, which was established on better promises.

7 For if that [a]first *covenant* had been faultless, then no place would have been sought for a second.

★ 8 Because finding fault with them, He says: [a]*"Behold, the days are coming, says the LORD, when I will make a new covenant with the house of Israel and with the house of Judah—*

9 *"not according to the covenant that I made with their fathers in the day when I took them by the hand to lead them out of the land of Egypt; because they did not continue in My covenant, and I disregarded them, says the LORD.*

10 *"For this is the covenant that I will make with the house of Israel after those days, says the [a]LORD: I will put My laws in their mind and write them on their hearts; and [b]I will be their God, and they shall be My people.*

11 [a]*"None of them shall teach his neighbor, and none his brother, saying, 'Know the [b]LORD,' for all shall know Me, from the least of them to the greatest of them.*

12 *"For I will be merciful to their unrighteousness, [a]and their sins [1]and their lawless deeds I will remember no more."*

13 [a]In that He says, *"A new covenant,"* He has made the first obsolete. Now what is becoming obsolete and growing old is ready to vanish away.

9 Then indeed, even the first *covenant* had ordinances of divine service and [a]the earthly sanctuary.

2 For a tabernacle was prepared: the first *part,* in which *was* the lampstand, the table, and the showbread, which is called the [1]sanctuary;

3 [a]and behind the second veil, the part of the tabernacle which is called the Holiest of All,

4 which had the [a]golden censer and [b]the ark of the covenant overlaid on all sides with gold,

---

27 [a]Lev. 9:7; 16:6

CHAPTER 8

1 [a]Col. 3:1

2 [a]Heb. 9:8, 12 [b]Heb. 9:11, 24 [1]Lit. *holies*

3 [a]Heb. 5:1; 8:4 [b][Eph. 5:2]

5 [a]Heb. 9:23, 24 [b]Col. 2:17 [c]Ex. 25:40

6 [a][2 Cor. 3:6–8] [b]Heb. 7:22

7 [a]Ex. 3:8; 19:5

8 [a]Jer. 31:31–34; Matt. 26:26–28; 1 Cor. 11:25

10 [a]Jer. 31:33 [b]Zech. 8:8

11 [a]Is. 54:13 [b]Jer. 31:34

12 [a]Rom. 11:27 [1]NU omits *and their lawless deeds*

13 [a][2 Cor. 5:17]

CHAPTER 9

1 [a]Ex. 25:8

2 [1]*holy place,* lit. *holies*

3 [a]Ex. 26:31–35; 40:3

4 [a]Lev. 16:12 [b]Ex. 25:10

in which *were* [c]the golden pot
that had the manna, [d]Aaron's
rod that budded, and [e]the tablets
of the covenant;
5 and [a]above it were the cherubim of glory overshadowing the
mercy seat. Of these things we
cannot now speak in detail.
6 Now when these things had
been thus prepared, [a]the priests
always went into the first part of
the tabernacle, performing the
services.
7 But into the second part the
high priest *went* alone [a]once a
year, not without blood, which
he offered for [b]himself and *for*
the people's sins *committed* in
ignorance;
8 the Holy Spirit indicating
this, that [a]the way into the Holiest of All was not yet made
manifest while the first tabernacle was still standing.
9 It *was* symbolic for the present time in which both gifts and
sacrifices are offered [a]which cannot make him who performed
the service perfect in regard to
the conscience—
10 *concerned* only with [a]foods
and drinks, [b]various [1]washings,
[c]and fleshly ordinances imposed
until the time of reformation.
11 But Christ came *as* High
Priest of [a]the good things [1]to
come, with the greater and more
perfect tabernacle not made
with hands, that is, not of this
creation.
12 Not [a]with the blood of goats
and calves, but [b]with His own
blood He entered the Most Holy
Place [c]once for all, [d]having obtained eternal redemption.
13 For if [a]the blood of bulls
and goats and [b]the ashes of a
heifer, sprinkling the unclean,
[1]sanctifies for the [2]purifying of
the flesh,
14 how much more shall the
blood of Christ, who through the
eternal Spirit offered Himself
without [1]spot to God, [a]cleanse
your conscience from [b]dead
works [c]to serve the living God?
15 And for this reason [a]He is
the Mediator of the new covenant, by means of death, for
the redemption of the transgressions under the first covenant,
that [b]those who are called may
receive the promise of the eternal inheritance.
16 For where there *is* a testament, there must also of necessity be the death of the testator.
17 For [a]a testament *is* in force
after men are dead, since it has
no power at all while the testator lives.
18 [a]Therefore not even the first
covenant was dedicated without
blood.
19 For when Moses had spoken
every [1]precept to all the people
according to the law, [a]he took
the blood of calves and goats,
[b]with water, scarlet wool, and
hyssop, and sprinkled both the
book itself and all the people,
20 saying, [a]*"This is the* [b]*blood
of the covenant which God has
commanded you."*
21 Then likewise [a]he sprinkled
with blood both the tabernacle
and all the vessels of the ministry.
22 And according to the law almost all things are [1]purified with
blood, and [a]without shedding of
blood there is no [2]remission.
23 Therefore *it was* necessary
that [a]the copies of the things
in the heavens should be [1]puri-
fied with these, but the heavenly

4 [c]Ex. 16:33 [d]Num. 17:1–10 [e]Ex. 25:16; 34:29
5 [a]Lev. 16:2
6 [a]Num. 18:2–6; 28:3
7 [a]Ex. 30:10 [b]Heb. 5:3
8 [a][John 14:6]
9 [a]Heb. 7:19
10 [a]Col. 2:16 [b]Num. 19:7 [c]Eph. 2:15 [1]Lit. *baptisms*
11 [a]Heb. 10:1 [1]NU *that have come*
12 [a]Heb. 10:4 [b]Eph. 1:7 [c]Zech. 3:9 [d][Dan. 9:24]
13 [a]Lev. 16:14, 15 [b]Num. 19:2 [1]*sets apart* [2]*cleansing*
14 [a]1 John 1:7 [b]Heb. 6:1 [c]Luke 1:74 [1]*blemish*
15 [a]Rom. 3:25 [b]Heb. 3:1
17 [a]Gal. 3:15
18 [a]Ex. 24:6
19 [a]Ex. 24:5, 6 [b]Lev. 14:4, 7 [1]*command*
20 [a][Matt. 26:28] [b]Ex. 24:3–8
21 [a]Ex. 29:12, 36
22 [a]Lev. 17:11 [1]*cleansed* [2]*forgiveness*
23 [a]Heb. 8:5 [1]*cleansed*

things themselves with better
sacrifices than these.
24 For [a]Christ has not entered
the holy places made with hands,
which are [1]copies of [b]the true, but
into heaven itself, now [c]to appear
in the presence of God for us;
25 not that He should offer Himself often, as [a]the high priest enters the Most Holy Place every
year with blood of another—
26 He then would have had to
suffer often since the foundation of the world; but now, once
at the end of the ages, He has
appeared to put away sin by the
sacrifice of Himself.
27 [a]And as it is appointed for
men to die once, [b]but after this
the judgment,
★ 28 so [a]Christ was [b]offered once
to bear the sins [c]of many. To
those who [d]eagerly wait for Him
He will appear a second time,
apart from sin, for salvation.

10 For the law, having a
[a]shadow of the good
things to come, *and* not the very
image of the things, [b]can never
with these same sacrifices,
which they offer continually
year by year, make those who
approach perfect.
2 For then would they not
have ceased to be offered? For
the worshipers, once [1]purified,
would have had no more consciousness of sins.
3 But in those *sacrifices there
is* a reminder of sins every year.
4 For [a]*it is* not possible that the
blood of bulls and goats could
take away sins.
★ 5 Therefore, when He came
into the world, He said:

[a]"Sacrifice and offering You
did not desire,
But a body You have
prepared for Me.
6 *In burnt offerings and*
sacrifices for sin
You had no pleasure.
7 *Then I said, 'Behold, I have*
come—
In the volume of the book it
is written of Me—
To do Your will, O God.'"

8 Previously saying, *"Sacrifice
and offering, burnt offerings,
and offerings for sin You did not
desire, nor had pleasure in them"*
(which are offered according to
the law),
9 then He said, *"Behold, I have
come to do Your will, [1]O God."*
He takes away the first that He
may establish the second.
10 [a]By that will we have been
[1]sanctified [b]through the offering
of the body of Jesus Christ once
for all.
11 And every priest stands
[a]ministering daily and offering
repeatedly the same sacrifices,
which can never take away
sins.
12 [a]But this Man, after He had ★
offered one sacrifice for sins forever, sat down [b]at the right hand
of God,
13 from that time waiting [a]till ★
His enemies are made His footstool.
14 For by one offering He has
perfected forever those who are
being [1]sanctified.
15 But the Holy Spirit also witnesses to us; for after He had
said before,
16 [a]*"This is the covenant that I* ★
*will make with them after those
days, says the* L**ORD**: *I will put
My laws into their hearts, and in
their minds I will write them,"*

24 [a]Heb. 6:20 [b]Heb. 8:2 [c]Rom. 8:34 [1]*representations*
25 [a]Heb. 9:7
27 [a]Gen. 3:19 [b][2 Cor. 5:10]
28 [a]Rom. 6:10 [b]Is. 53:10–12; 1 Pet. 2:24 [c]Matt. 26:28 [d]Titus 2:13

CHAPTER 10

1 [a]Heb. 8:5 [b]Heb. 7:19; 9:9
2 [1]*cleansed*
4 [a]Mic. 6:6, 7
5 [a]Ps. 40:6–8
9 [1]NU, M omit *O God*
10 [a]John 17:19 [b][Heb. 9:12] [1]*set apart*
11 [a]Num. 28:3
12 [a]Col. 3:1 [b]Ps. 110:1
13 [a]Ps. 110:1
14 [1]*set apart*
16 [a]Jer. 31:33, 34

17 *then He adds,* [a]*"Their sins and their lawless deeds I will remember no more."*

18 Now where there is [1]remission of these, *there is* no longer an offering for sin.

19 Therefore, brethren, having [a]boldness[1] to enter [b]the Holiest by the blood of Jesus,

20 by a new and [a]living way which He consecrated for us, through the veil, that is, His flesh,

21 and *having* a High Priest over the house of God,

22 let us [a]draw near with a true heart [b]in full assurance of faith, having our hearts sprinkled from an evil conscience and our bodies washed with pure water.

23 Let us hold fast the confession of *our* hope without wavering, for [a]He who promised *is* faithful.

24 And let us consider one another in order to stir up love and good works,

25 [a]not forsaking the assembling of ourselves together, as *is* the manner of some, but exhorting *one another,* and [b]so much the more as you see [c]the Day approaching.

26 For [a]if we sin willfully [b]after we have received the knowledge of the truth, there [c]no longer remains a sacrifice for sins,

27 but a certain fearful expectation of judgment, and [a]fiery indignation which will devour the adversaries.

28 Anyone who has rejected Moses' law dies without mercy on *the testimony of* two or three [a]witnesses.

29 [a]Of how much worse punishment, do you suppose, will he be thought worthy who has trampled the Son of God underfoot, [b]counted the blood of the covenant by which he was sanctified a common thing, [c]and insulted the Spirit of grace?

30 For we know Him who said, [a]*"Vengeance is Mine, I will repay,"* [1]says the Lord. And again, [b]*"The* LORD *will judge His people."*

31 [a]It is a fearful thing to fall into the hands of the living God.

32 But [a]recall the former days in which, after you were [1]illuminated, you endured a great struggle with sufferings:

33 partly while you were made [a]a spectacle both by reproaches and tribulations, and partly while [b]you became companions of those who were so treated;

34 for you had compassion on [1]me [a]in my chains, and [b]joyfully accepted the plundering of your [2]goods, knowing that [c]you have a better and an enduring possession for yourselves [3]in heaven.

35 Therefore do not cast away your confidence, [a]which has great reward.

36 [a]For you have need of endurance, so that after you have done the will of God, [b]you may receive the promise:

37 *"For* [a]*yet a little while,*
And [b]*He*[1] *who is coming will come and will not* [2]*tarry.*

38 *Now* [a]*the*[1] *just shall live by faith;*
But if anyone draws back,
My soul has no pleasure in him."

39 But we are not of those [a]who draw back to [1]perdition, but of

17 [a]Jer. 31:34
18 [1]*forgiveness*
19 [a][Eph. 2:18] [b]Heb. 9:8, 12 [1]*confidence*
20 [a]John 14:6
22 [a]Heb. 7:19; 10:1 [b]Eph. 3:12
23 [a]1 Cor. 1:9; 10:13
25 [a]Acts 2:42 [b]Rom. 13:11 [c]Phil. 4:5
26 [a]Num. 15:30 [b]2 Pet. 2:20 [c]Heb. 6:6
27 [a]Zeph. 1:18
28 [a]Deut. 17:2–6; 19:15
29 [a][Heb. 2:3] [b]1 Cor. 11:29 [c][Matt. 12:31]
30 [a]Deut. 32:35 [b]Deut. 32:36 [1]NU omits *says the Lord*
31 [a][Luke 12:5]
32 [a]Gal. 3:4 [1]*enlightened*
33 [a]1 Cor. 4:9 [b]Phil. 1:7
34 [a]2 Tim. 1:16 [b]Matt. 5:12 [c]Matt. 6:20 [1]NU *the prisoners* instead of *me in my chains* [2]*possessions* [3]NU omits *in heaven*
35 [a]Matt. 5:12
36 [a]Luke 21:19 [b][Col. 3:24]
37 [a]Luke 18:8 [b]Hab. 2:3, 4 [1]Or *that which* [2]*delay*
38 [a]Rom. 1:17 [1]NU *My just one*
39 [a]2 Pet. 2:20 [1]*destruction*

those who [b]believe to the saving
of the soul.

11

Now faith is the [1]sub-
stance of things hoped
for, the [2]evidence [a]of things not
seen.
2 For by it the elders obtained
a *good* testimony.
3 By faith we understand that
[a]the [1]worlds were framed by the
word of God, so that the things
which are seen were not made
of things which are visible.
4 By faith [a]Abel offered to God
a more excellent sacrifice than
Cain, through which he obtained
witness that he was righteous,
God testifying of his gifts; and
through it he being dead still
[b]speaks.
5 By faith Ē'noch was taken
away so that he did not see
death, [a]*"and was not found, be-*
cause God had taken him"; for
before he was taken he had this
testimony, that he pleased God.
6 But without faith *it is* impossible to please *Him,* for he who
comes to God must believe that
He is, and *that* He is a rewarder
of those who diligently seek
Him.
7 By faith [a]Noah, being divinely warned of things not yet
seen, moved with godly fear,
[b]prepared an ark for the saving
of his household, by which he
condemned the world and became heir of [c]the righteousness
which is according to faith.
8 By faith [a]Abraham obeyed
when he was called to go out
to the place which he would receive as an inheritance. And he
went out, not knowing where he
was going.
9 By faith he dwelt in the
land of promise as *in* a foreign
country, [a]dwelling in tents with
Isaac and Jacob, [b]the heirs with
him of the same promise;
10 for he waited for [a]the city
which has foundations, [b]whose
builder and maker *is* God.
11 By faith [a]Sarah herself also
received strength to conceive
seed, and [b]she[1] bore a child
when she was past the age, because she judged Him [c]faithful
who had promised.
12 Therefore from one man,
and him as good as [a]dead, were
born *as many* as the [b]stars of the
sky in multitude—innumerable
as the sand which is by the seashore.
13 These all died in faith, [a]not
having received the [b]promises,
but [c]having seen them afar off
[1]were assured of them, embraced
them and [d]confessed that they
were strangers and pilgrims on
the earth.
14 For those who say such
things [a]declare plainly that they
seek a homeland.
15 And truly if they had called
to mind [a]that *country* from
which they had come out, they
would have had opportunity to
return.
16 But now they desire a better, that is, a heavenly *country.*
Therefore God is not ashamed
[a]to be called their God, for He
has [b]prepared a city for them.
17 By faith Abraham, [a]when he
was tested, offered up Isaac, and
he who had received the promises offered up his only begotten
son,
18 [1]of whom it was said, [a]*"In*
Isaac your seed shall be called,"
19 concluding that God [a]*was*
able to raise *him* up, even from
the dead, from which he also

39 [b]Acts 16:31

CHAPTER 11

1 [a]Rom. 8:24 [1]*realization* [2]Or *confidence*

3 [a]Ps. 33:6 [1]Or *ages,* Gr. *aiones,* aeons

4 [a]Gen. 4:3–5 [b]Heb. 12:24

5 [a]Gen. 5:21–24

7 [a]Gen. 6:13–22 [b]1 Pet. 3:20 [c]Rom. 3:22

8 [a]Gen. 12:1–4

9 [a]Gen. 12:8; 13:3, 18; 18:1, 9 [b]Heb. 6:17

10 [a][Heb. 12:22; 13:14] [b][Rev. 21:10]

11 [a]Gen. 17:19; 18:11–14; 21:1, 2 [b]Luke 1:36 [c]Heb. 10:23 [1]NU omits *she bore a child*

12 [a]Rom. 4:19 [b]Gen. 15:5; 22:17; 32:12

13 [a]Heb. 11:39 [b]Gen. 12:7 [c]John 8:56 [d]Ps. 39:12 [1]NU, M omit *were assured of them*

14 [a]Heb. 13:14

15 [a]Gen. 11:31

16 [a]Ex. 3:6, 15; 4:5 [b][Rev. 21:2]

17 [a]James 2:21

18 [a]Gen. 21:12 [1]*to*

19 [a]Rom. 4:17

received him in a figurative
sense.
20 By faith [a]Isaac blessed Jacob
and Esau concerning things to
come.
21 By faith Jacob, when he was
dying, [a]blessed each of the sons
of Joseph, and worshiped, *lean-*
ing on the top of his staff.
22 By faith [a]Joseph, when he
was dying, made mention of the
departure of the children of Israel, and gave instructions concerning his bones.
23 By faith [a]Moses, when he
was born, was hidden three
months by his parents, because
they saw *he was* a beautiful
child; and they were not afraid
of the king's [b]command.
24 By faith [a]Moses, when he became of age, refused to be called
the son of Pharaoh's daughter,
25 choosing rather to suffer affliction with the people of God
than to enjoy the [1]passing pleasures of sin,
26 esteeming [a]the [1]reproach of
Christ greater riches than the
treasures [2]in Egypt; for he looked
to the [b]reward.
27 By faith [a]he forsook Egypt,
not fearing the wrath of the
king; for he endured as seeing
Him who is invisible.
28 By faith [a]he kept the Passover and the sprinkling of blood,
lest he who destroyed the firstborn should touch them.
29 By faith [a]they passed through
the Red Sea as by dry *land,*
whereas the Egyptians, attempt-
ing to do so, were drowned.
30 By faith [a]the walls of Jericho
fell down after they were encircled for seven days.
31 By faith [a]the harlot Rā'hab
did not perish with those who
[1]did not believe, when [b]she had
received the spies with peace.
32 And what more shall I say?
For the time would fail me to
tell of [a]Gideon and [b]Bar'ak and
[c]Samson and [d]Jeph'thah, also
of [e]David and [f]Samuel and the
prophets:
33 who through faith sub-
dued kingdoms, worked righteousness, obtained promises,
[a]stopped the mouths of lions,
34 [a]quenched the violence of
fire, escaped the edge of the
sword, out of weakness were
made strong, became valiant
in battle, turned to flight the
armies of the aliens.
35 [a]Women received their dead
raised to life again. Others were
[b]tortured, not accepting deliverance, that they might obtain a
better resurrection.
36 Still others had trial of mock-
ings and scourgings, yes, and [a]of
chains and imprisonment.
37 [a]They were stoned, they were
sawn in two, [1]were tempted,
were slain with the sword. [b]They
wandered about [c]in sheepskins
and goatskins, being destitute,
afflicted, tormented—
38 of whom the world was not
worthy. They wandered in deserts and mountains, [a]*in* dens and
caves of the earth.
39 And all these, [a]having obtained a good testimony through
faith, did not receive the promise,
40 God having provided something better for us, that they
should not be [a]made perfect
apart from us.

12
Therefore we also, since
we are surrounded by so
great a cloud of witnesses, [a]let us
lay aside every weight, and the

20 [a]Gen. 27:26–40
21 [a]Gen. 48:1, 5, 16, 20
22 [a]Gen. 50:24, 25
23 [a]Ex. 2:1–3 [b]Ex. 1:16, 22
24 [a]Ex. 2:11–15
25 [1]*temporary*
26 [a]Heb. 13:13 [b]Rom. 8:18 [1]*reviling because of* [2]NU, M *of*
27 [a]Ex. 10:28
28 [a]Ex. 12:21
29 [a]Ex. 14:22–29
30 [a]Josh. 6:20
31 [a]Josh. 2:9; 6:23 [b]Josh. 2:1 [1]*were disobedient*
32 [a]Judg. 6:11; 7:1–25 [b]Judg. 4:6–24 [c]Judg. 13:24—16:31 [d]Judg. 11:1–29; 12:1–7 [e]1 Sam. 16; 17 [f]1 Sam. 7:9–14
33 [a]Dan. 6:22
34 [a]Dan. 3:23–28
35 [a]1 Kin. 17:22 [b]Acts 22:25
36 [a]Gen. 39:20
37 [a]1 Kin. 21:13 [b]2 Kin. 1:8 [c]Zech. 13:4 [1]NU omits *were tempted*
38 [a]1 Kin. 18:4, 13; 19:9
39 [a]Heb. 11:2, 13
40 [a]Heb. 5:9

CHAPTER 12

1 [a]Col. 3:8

sin which so easily ensnares *us,*
and [b]let us run [c]with endurance
the race that is set before us,
★ 2 looking unto Jesus, the [1]au-
thor and [2]finisher of *our* faith,
[a]who for the joy that was set
before Him [b]endured the cross,
despising the shame, and [c]has
sat down at the right hand of the
throne of God.
3 [a]For consider Him who endured such hostility from sinners against Himself, [b]lest you
become weary and discouraged
in your souls.
4 [a]You have not yet resisted to
bloodshed, striving against sin.
5 And you have forgotten the
exhortation which speaks to you
as to sons:

[a]"My son, do not despise the
[1]chastening of the LORD,
Nor be discouraged when
you are rebuked by Him;
6 *For [a]whom the LORD loves*
He chastens,
And scourges every son
whom He receives."

7 [a]If[1] you endure chastening,
God deals with you as with sons;
for what [b]son is there whom a
father does not chasten?
8 But if you are without chastening, [a]of which all have become partakers, then you are
illegitimate and not sons.
9 Furthermore, we have had
human fathers who corrected
us, and we paid *them* respect.
Shall we not much more readily
be in subjection to [a]the Father of
spirits and live?
10 For they indeed for a few days
chastened *us* as seemed *best*
to them, but He for *our* profit,
[a]that *we* may be partakers of His
holiness.
11 Now no [1]chastening seems
to be joyful for the present, but
painful; nevertheless, afterward
it yields [a]the peaceable fruit of
righteousness to those who have
been trained by it.
12 Therefore [a]strengthen the
hands which hang down, and
the feeble knees,
13 and make straight paths for
your feet, so that what is lame
may not be dislocated, but rather
be healed.
14 [a]Pursue peace with all *peo-*
ple, and holiness, [b]without which
no one will see the Lord:
15 looking carefully lest anyone [a]fall short of the grace of
God; lest any [b]root of bitterness
springing up cause trouble, and
by this many become defiled;
16 lest there *be* any [a]fornicator
or [1]profane person like Esau,
[b]who for one morsel of food sold
his birthright.
17 For you know that afterward,
when he wanted to inherit the
blessing, he was [a]rejected, for he
found no place for repentance,
though he sought it diligently
with tears.
18 For you have not come [1]to
[a]the mountain that may be
touched and that burned with
fire, and to blackness and [2]dark-
ness and tempest,
19 and the sound of a trumpet
and the voice of words, so that
those who heard *it* [a]begged that
the word should not be spoken
to them anymore.
20 (For they could not endure
what was commanded: [a]*"And if*
so much as a beast touches the
mountain, it shall be stoned [1]or
shot with an arrow."

1 [b]1 Cor. 9:24 [c]Rom. 12:12
2 [a]Luke 24:26 [b]Ps. 69:7, 19; Phil. 2:8 [c]Ps. 110:1 [1]*originator* [2]*perfecter*
3 [a]Matt. 10:24 [b]Gal. 6:9
4 [a][1 Cor. 10:13]
5 [a]Prov. 3:11, 12 [1]*discipline*
6 [a]Rev. 3:19
7 [a]Deut. 8:5 [b]Prov. 13:24; 19:18; 23:13 [1]NU, M *It is for discipline that you endure; God*
8 [a]1 Pet. 5:9
9 [a][Job 12:10]
10 [a]Lev. 11:44
11 [a]James 3:17, 18 [1]*discipline*
12 [a]Is. 35:3
14 [a]Ps. 34:14 [b]Matt. 5:8
15 [a]Heb. 4:1 [b]Deut. 29:18
16 [a][1 Cor. 6:13–18] [b]Gen. 25:33 [1]*godless*
17 [a]Gen. 27:30–40
18 [a]Deut. 4:11; 5:22 [1]NU *to that which* [2]NU *gloom*
19 [a]Ex. 20:18–26
20 [a]Ex. 19:12, 13 [1]NU, M omit the rest of v. 20.

21 And so terrifying was the
sight *that* Moses said, [a]*"I am exceedingly afraid* and trembling.")
22 But you have come to Mount
Zion and to the city of the living
God, the heavenly Jerusalem,
to an innumerable company of
angels,
23 to the [1]general assembly and
church of [a]the firstborn [b]*who are*
registered in heaven, to God [c]the
Judge of all, to the spirits of just
men [d]made perfect,
24 to Jesus [a]the Mediator of the
new covenant, and to [b]the blood
of sprinkling that speaks better
things [c]than *that of* Abel.
25 See that you do not refuse
Him who speaks. For [a]if they
did not escape who refused Him
who spoke on earth, much more
shall we not escape if we turn
away from Him who *speaks*
from heaven,
26 whose voice then shook the
earth; but now He has promised, saying, [a]*"Yet once more I*
[1]*shake not only the earth, but
also heaven."*
27 Now this, *"Yet once more,"*
indicates the [a]removal of those
things that are being shaken, as
of things that are made, that the
things which cannot be shaken
may remain.
28 Therefore, since we are receiving a kingdom which cannot be shaken, let us have grace,
by which we [1]may [a]serve God
acceptably with reverence and
godly fear.
29 For [a]our God *is* a consuming
fire.

13

Let [a]brotherly love continue.
2 [a]Do not forget to entertain
strangers, for by so *doing* [b]some
have unwittingly entertained
angels.
3 [a]Remember the prisoners
as if chained with them—those
who are mistreated—since you
yourselves are in the body also.
4 [a]Marriage *is* honorable among
all, and the bed undefiled; [b]but
fornicators and adulterers God
will judge.
5 *Let your* conduct *be* without
covetousness; *be* content with
such things as you have. For He
Himself has said, [a]*"I will never
leave you nor forsake you."*
6 So we may boldly say:

> [a]*"The LORD is my helper;*
> *I will not fear.*
> *What can man do to me?"*

7 Remember those who [1]rule
over you, who have spoken the
word of God to you, whose faith
follow, considering the outcome
of *their* conduct.
8 Jesus Christ *is* [a]the same yesterday, today, and forever.
9 Do not be carried [1]about with
various and strange doctrines.
For *it is* good that the heart be
established by grace, not with
foods which have not profited
those who have been occupied
with them.
10 We have an altar from which
those who serve the tabernacle
have no right to eat.
11 For the bodies of those animals, whose blood is brought
into the sanctuary by the high
priest for sin, are burned outside
the camp.
12 Therefore Jesus also, that He
might [1]sanctify the people with
His own blood, suffered outside
the gate.

---

21 [a]Deut. 9:19
23 [a][James 1:18] [b]Luke 10:20 [c]Ps. 50:6; 94:2 [d][Phil. 3:12] [1]*festal gathering*
24 [a]Heb. 8:6; 9:15 [b]Ex. 24:8 [c]Gen. 4:10
25 [a]Heb. 2:2, 3
26 [a]Hag. 2:6 [1]NU *will shake*
27 [a][Is. 34:4; 54:10; 65:17]
28 [a]Heb. 13:15, 21 [1]M omits *may*
29 [a]Ex. 24:17

CHAPTER 13

1 [a]Rom. 12:10
2 [a]Matt. 25:35 [b]Gen. 18:1–22; 19:1
3 [a]Matt. 25:36
4 [a]Prov. 5:18, 19 [b]1 Cor. 6:9
5 [a]Deut. 31:6, 8; Josh. 1:5
6 [a]Ps. 27:1; 118:6
7 [1]*lead*
8 [a]Heb. 1:12
9 [1]NU, M *away*
12 [1]*set apart*

13 Therefore let us go forth to
Him, outside the camp, bearing
[a]His reproach.
14 For here we have no continuing city, but we seek the one to
come.
15 [a]Therefore by Him let us
continually offer [b]the sacrifice
of praise to God, that is, [c]the
fruit of *our* lips, [1]giving thanks
to His name.
16 [a]But do not forget to do good
and to share, for [b]with such sacrifices God is well pleased.
17 [a]Obey those who [1]rule over
you, and be submissive, for
[b]they watch out for your souls,
as those who must give account.
Let them do so with joy and not
with grief, for that would be unprofitable for you.
18 [a]Pray for us; for we are confident that we have [b]a good conscience, in all things desiring to
live honorably.
19 But I especially urge *you* to
do this, that I may be restored to
you the sooner.
20 Now may [a]the God of peace ★
[b]who brought up our Lord Jesus from the dead, [c]that great
Shepherd of the sheep, [d]through
the blood of the everlasting covenant,
21 make you [1]complete in every good work to do His will,
[a]working in [2]you what is well
pleasing in His sight, through
Jesus Christ, to whom *be* glory
forever and ever. Amen.
22 And I appeal to you, brethren, bear with the word of exhortation, for I have written to
you in few words.
23 Know that *our* brother Timothy has been set free, with
whom I shall see you if he comes
shortly.
24 Greet all those who [1]rule over
you, and all the saints. Those
from Italy greet you.
25 Grace *be* with you all. Amen.

13 [a]1 Pet. 4:14
15 [a]Eph. 5:20 [b]Lev. 7:12 [c]Hos. 14:2 [1]Lit. *confessing*
16 [a]Rom. 12:13 [b]Phil. 4:18
17 [a]Phil. 2:29 [b]Ezek. 3:17 [1]*lead*
18 [a]Eph. 6:19 [b]Acts 23:1
20 [a]Rom. 5:1, 2, 10; 15:33 [b]Ps. 16:10, 11; Hos. 6:2; Rom. 4:24 [c]Ps. 23:1; Is. 40:11; 63:11; 1 Pet. 2:25; 5:4 [d]Zech. 9:11
21 [a]Phil. 2:13 [1]*perfect* [2]NU, M *us*
24 [1]*lead*

The Epistle of JAMES

FAITH without works cannot be called faith. "Faith without works is dead" (2:26), and a dead faith is worse than no faith at all. Faith must work, it must produce, it must be visible. Verbal faith is not enough; mental faith is insufficient. Faith must be there, but it must be more. It must inspire action. Throughout his epistle to Jewish believers, James integrates true faith and everyday practical experience by stressing that true faith must manifest itself in works of faith.

Faith endures trials. Trials come and go, but a strong faith will face them head-on and develop endurance. Faith understands temptations. It will not allow us to consent to our lust and slide into sin. Faith obeys the Word. It will not merely hear and not do. Faith produces doers. Faith harbors no prejudice. For James, faith and favoritism cannot coexist. Faith displays itself in works. Faith is more than mere words; it is more than knowledge; it is demonstrated by obedience; and it overtly responds to the promises of God. Faith controls the tongue. This small but immensely powerful part of the body must be held in check. Faith can do it. Faith acts wisely. It gives us the ability to choose wisdom that is heavenly and to shun wisdom that is earthly. Faith produces separation from the world and submission to God. It provides us with the ability to resist the Devil and humbly draw near to God. Finally, faith waits patiently for the coming of the Lord. Through trouble and trial it stifles complaining.

The name *Iakobos* (James) in 1:1 is the basis for the early title *Iakobou Epistole,* "Epistle of James." *Iakobos* is the Greek form of the Hebrew name Jacob, a Jewish name common in the first century.

JAMES, [a]a bondservant of God and of the Lord Jesus Christ,

To the twelve tribes which are scattered abroad:

Greetings.

2 My brethren, [a]count it all joy [b]when you fall into various trials,
3 [a]knowing that the testing of your faith produces [1]patience.
4 But let patience have *its* perfect work, that you may be [1]perfect and complete, lacking nothing.
5 [a]If any of you lacks wisdom, [b]let him ask of God, who gives to all liberally and without reproach, and [c]it will be given to him.
6 [a]But let him ask in faith, with no doubting, for he who doubts is like a wave of the sea driven and tossed by the wind.
7 For let not that man suppose that he will receive anything from the Lord;
8 *he is* [a]a double-minded man, unstable in all his ways.
9 Let the lowly brother glory in his exaltation,
10 but the rich in his humiliation,

CHAPTER 1

1 [a]Acts 12:17

2 [a]Acts 5:41
[b]1 Pet. 1:6

3 [a]Rom. 5:3–5
[1]*endurance* or *perseverance*

4 [1]*mature*

5 [a]1 Kin. 3:9
[b]Matt. 7:7
[c]Jer. 29:12

6 [a][Mark 11:23, 24]

8 [a]James 4:8

because [a]as a flower of the field
he will pass away.
11 For no sooner has the sun
risen with a burning heat than
it withers the grass; its flower
falls, and its beautiful appearance perishes. So the rich man
also will fade away in his pur-
suits.
12 [a]Blessed *is* the man who endures temptation; for when he
has been approved, he will receive [b]the crown of life [c]which
the Lord has promised to those
who love Him.
13 Let no one say when he is
tempted, "I am tempted by God";
for God cannot be tempted by
evil, nor does He Himself tempt
anyone.
14 But each one is tempted
when he is drawn away by his
own desires and enticed.
15 Then, [a]when desire has conceived, it gives birth to sin; and
sin, when it is full-grown, [b]brings
forth death.
16 Do not be deceived, my beloved brethren.
17 [a]Every good gift and every
perfect gift is from above, and
comes down from the Father of
lights, [b]with whom there is no
variation or shadow of turning.
18 [a]Of His own will He brought
us forth by the [b]word of truth,
[c]that we might be a kind of firstfruits of His creatures.
19 [1]So then, my beloved brethren, let every man be swift to
hear, [a]slow to speak, [b]slow to
wrath;
20 for the wrath of man does
not produce the righteousness
of God.
21 Therefore [a]lay aside all filthiness and [1]overflow of wickedness, and receive with meekness
the implanted word, [b]which is
able to save your souls.
22 But [a]be doers of the word,
and not hearers only, deceiving
yourselves.
23 For [a]if anyone is a hearer of
the word and not a doer, he is
like a man observing his natural
face in a mirror;
24 for he observes himself, goes
away, and immediately forgets
what kind of man he was.
25 But [a]he who looks into the
perfect law of liberty and continues *in it*, and is not a forgetful
hearer but a doer of the work,
[b]this one will be blessed in what
he does.
26 If anyone [1]among you thinks
he is religious, and [a]does not
bridle his tongue but deceives
his own heart, this one's religion
is useless.
27 [a]Pure and undefiled religion
before God and the Father is
this: [b]to visit orphans and widows in their trouble, [c]*and* to
keep oneself unspotted from the
world.

2

My brethren, do not hold
the faith of our Lord Jesus
Christ, [a]*the Lord* of glory, with
[b]partiality.
2 For if there should come into
your assembly a man with gold
rings, in [1]fine apparel, and there
should also come in a poor man
in [2]filthy clothes,
3 and you [1]pay attention to the
one wearing the fine clothes and
say to him, "You sit here in a
good place," and say to the poor
man, "You stand there," or, "Sit
here at my footstool,"
4 have you not [1]shown partiality among yourselves, and become judges with evil thoughts?
5 Listen, my beloved brethren:

10 [a]Job 14:2

12 [a]James 5:11 [b][1 Cor. 9:25] [c]Matt. 10:22

15 [a]Job 15:35 [b][Rom. 5:12; 6:23]

17 [a]John 3:27 [b]Num. 23:19

18 [a]John 1:13 [b][1 Pet. 1:3, 23] [c][Eph. 1:12, 13]

19 [a]Prov. 10:19; 17:27 [b]Prov. 14:17; 16:32 [1]NU *Know this* or *This you know*

21 [a]Col. 3:8 [b]Acts 13:26 [1]*abundance*

22 [a]Matt. 7:21–28

23 [a]Luke 6:47

25 [a]James 2:12 [b]John 13:17

26 [a]Ps. 34:13 [1]NU omits *among you*

27 [a]Matt. 25:34–36 [b]Is. 1:17 [c][Rom. 12:2]

CHAPTER 2

1 [a]1 Cor. 2:8 [b]Lev. 19:15

2 [1]*bright* [2]*vile*

3 [1]Lit. *look upon*

4 [1]*differentiated*

[a]Has God not chosen the poor
of this world *to be* [b]rich in faith
and heirs of the kingdom [c]which
He promised to those who love
Him?
6 But [a]you have dishonored
the poor man. Do not the rich
oppress you [b]and drag you into
the courts?
7 Do they not blaspheme that
noble name by which you are
[a]called?
8 If you really fulfill *the* royal
law according to the Scripture,
[a]*"You shall love your neighbor
as yourself,"* you do well;
9 but if you [1]show partiality, you
commit sin, and are convicted
by the law as [a]transgressors.
10 For whoever shall keep the
whole law, and yet [a]stumble in
one *point*, [b]he is guilty of all.
11 For He who said, [a]*"Do not
commit adultery,"* also said,
[b]*"Do not murder."* Now if you
do not commit adultery, but you
do murder, you have become a
transgressor of the law.
12 So speak and so do as those
who will be judged by [a]the law
of liberty.
13 For [a]judgment is without
mercy to the one who has shown
[b]no [c]mercy. [d]Mercy triumphs
over judgment.
14 [a]What *does it* profit, my
brethren, if someone says he has
faith but does not have works?
Can faith save him?
15 [a]If a brother or sister is naked and destitute of daily food,
16 and [a]one of you says to them,
"Depart in peace, be warmed and
filled," but you do not give them
the things which are needed for
the body, what *does it* profit?
17 Thus also faith by itself, if it
does not have works, is dead.
18 But someone will say, "You
have faith, and I have works."
[a]Show me your faith without
[1]your works, [b]and I will show
you my faith by [2]my works.
19 You believe that there is one
God. You do well. Even the demons believe—and tremble!
20 But do you want to know,
O foolish man, that faith without
works is [1]dead?
21 Was not Abraham our father
justified by works [a]when he offered Isaac his son on the altar?
22 Do you see [a]that faith was
working together with his
works, and by [b]works faith was
made [1]perfect?
23 And the Scripture was fulfilled which says, [a]*"Abraham believed God, and it was* [1]*accounted
to him for righteousness."* And
he was called [b]the friend of God.
24 You see then that a man is
justified by works, and not by
faith only.
25 Likewise, [a]was not Rā′hab
the harlot also justified by works
when she received the messengers and sent *them* out another
way?
26 For as the body without the
spirit is dead, so faith without
works is dead also.

3

My brethren, [a]let not many
of you become teachers,
[b]knowing that we shall receive a
stricter judgment.
2 For [a]we all stumble in many
things. [b]If anyone does not stumble in word, [c]he *is* a [1]perfect man,
able also to bridle the whole
body.
3 [1]Indeed, [a]we put bits in
horses' mouths that they may
obey us, and we turn their whole
body.
4 Look also at ships: although

5 [a]1 Cor. 1:27 [b]Luke 12:21 [c]Ex. 20:6
6 [a]1 Cor. 11:22 [b]Acts 13:50
7 [a]1 Pet. 4:16
8 [a]Lev. 19:18
9 [a]Deut. 1:17 [1]Lit. *receive the face*
10 [a]Gal. 3:10 [b]Deut. 27:26
11 [a]Ex. 20:14; Deut. 5:18 [b]Ex. 20:13; Deut. 5:17
12 [a]James 1:25
13 [a]Job 22:6 [b]Prov. 21:13 [c]Mic. 7:18 [d]Rom. 12:8
14 [a]Matt. 7:21–23, 26; 21:28–32
15 [a]Luke 3:11
16 [a][1 John 3:17, 18]
18 [a]Heb. 6:10 [b]James 3:13 [1]NU omits *your* [2]NU omits *my*
20 [1]NU *useless*
21 [a]Gen. 22:9, 10, 12, 16–18
22 [a]Heb. 11:17 [b]John 8:39 [1]*complete*
23 [a]Gen. 15:6 [b]2 Chr. 20:7 [1]*credited*
25 [a]Heb. 11:31

CHAPTER 3

1 [a][Matt. 23:8] [b]Luke 6:37
2 [a]1 Kin. 8:46 [b]Ps. 34:13 [c][Matt. 12:34–37] [1]*mature*
3 [a]Ps. 32:9 [1]NU *Now if*

they are so large and are driven
by fierce winds, they are turned
by a very small rudder wherever
the pilot desires.
5 Even so [a]the tongue is a little member and [b]boasts great
things. See how great a forest a
little fire kindles!
6 And [a]the tongue *is* a fire, a
world of [1]iniquity. The tongue is
so set among our members that
it [b]defiles the whole body, and
sets on fire the course of [2]nature;
and it is set on fire by [3]hell.
7 For every kind of beast and
bird, of reptile and creature of
the sea, is tamed and has been
tamed by mankind.
8 But no man can tame the
tongue. *It is* an unruly evil, [a]full
of deadly poison.
9 With it we bless our God
and Father, and with it we curse
men, who have been made [a]in
the [1]similitude of God.
10 Out of the same mouth proceed blessing and cursing. My
brethren, these things ought not
to be so.
11 Does a spring send forth
fresh *water* and bitter from the
same opening?
12 Can a [a]fig tree, my brethren,
bear olives, or a grapevine bear
figs? [1]Thus no spring yields both
salt water and fresh.
13 [a]Who *is* wise and understanding among you? Let him
show by good conduct *that* his
works *are done* in the meekness
of wisdom.
14 But if you have [a]bitter envy
and [1]self-seeking in your hearts,
[b]do not boast and lie against the
truth.
15 [a]This wisdom does not descend from above, but *is* earthly,
sensual, demonic.
16 For [a]where envy and self-
seeking *exist,* confusion and every evil thing *are* there.
17 But [a]the wisdom that is from
above is first pure, then peaceable, gentle, willing to yield,
full of mercy and good fruits,
[b]without partiality [c]and without
hypocrisy.
18 [a]Now the fruit of righteousness is sown in peace by those
who make peace.

4

Where do [1]wars and fights
come from among you? Do
they not *come* from your *desires
for* pleasure [a]that war in your
members?
2 You lust and do not have. You
murder and covet and cannot
obtain. You fight and [1]war. [2]Yet
you do not have because you do
not ask.
3 [a]You ask and do not receive,
[b]because you ask amiss, that you
may spend *it* on your pleasures.
4 [1]Adulterers and adulteresses! Do you not know that
[a]friendship with the world is enmity with God? [b]Whoever therefore wants to be a friend of the
world makes himself an enemy
of God.
5 Or do you think that the
Scripture says in vain, [a]"The
Spirit who dwells in us yearns
jealously"?
6 But He gives more grace.
Therefore He says:

> [a]*"God resists the proud,*
> *But gives grace to the*
> *humble."*

7 Therefore submit to God.
[a]Resist the devil and he will flee
from you.
8 [a]Draw near to God and He
will draw near to you. [b]Cleanse

---

5 [a]Prov. 12:18; 15:2 [b]Ps. 12:3; 73:8
6 [a]Prov. 16:27 [b][Matt. 12:36; 15:11, 18] [1]*unrighteousness* [2]*existence* [3]Gr. *Gehenna*
8 [a]Ps. 140:3
9 [a]Gen. 1:26; 5:1; 9:6 [1]*likeness*
12 [a]Matt. 7:16–20 [1]NU *Neither can a salty spring produce fresh water.*
13 [a]Gal. 6:4
14 [a]Rom. 13:13 [b]Rom. 2:17 [1]*selfish ambition*
15 [a]Phil. 3:19
16 [a]1 Cor. 3:3
17 [a]1 Cor. 2:6, 7 [b]James 2:1 [c]Rom. 12:9
18 [a]Prov. 11:18

CHAPTER 4

1 [a]Rom. 7:23 [1]*battles*
2 [1]*battle* [2]NU, M omit *Yet*
3 [a]Job 27:8, 9 [b][Ps. 66:18]
4 [a]1 John 2:15 [b]Gal. 1:4 [1]NU omits *Adulterers and*
5 [a]Gen. 6:5
6 [a]Prov. 3:34
7 [a][Eph. 4:27; 6:11]
8 [a]2 Chr. 15:2 [b]Is. 1:16

your hands, *you* sinners; and [c]purify *your* hearts, *you* double-minded.

9 [a]Lament and mourn and weep! Let your laughter be turned to mourning and *your* joy to gloom.

10 [a]Humble yourselves in the sight of the Lord, and He will lift you up.

11 [a]Do not speak evil of one another, brethren. He who speaks evil of a brother [b]and judges his brother, speaks evil of the law and judges the law. But if you judge the law, you are not a doer of the law but a judge.

12 There is one [1]Lawgiver, [a]who is able to save and to destroy. [b]Who[2] are you to judge [3]another?

13 Come now, you who say, "Today or tomorrow [1]we will go to such and such a city, spend a year there, buy and sell, and make a profit";

14 whereas you do not know what *will happen* tomorrow. For what *is* your life? [a]It is even a vapor that appears for a little time and then vanishes away.

15 Instead you *ought* to say, [a]"If the Lord wills, we shall live and do this or that."

16 But now you boast in your arrogance. [a]All such boasting is evil.

17 Therefore, [a]to him who knows to do good and does not do *it,* to him it is sin.

5 Come now, *you* [a]rich, weep and howl for your miseries that are coming upon *you!*

2 Your [a]riches [1]are corrupted, and [b]your garments are moth-eaten.

3 Your gold and silver are corroded, and their corrosion will be a witness against you and will eat your flesh like fire. [a]You have heaped up treasure in the last days.

4 Indeed [a]the wages of the laborers who mowed your fields, which you kept back by fraud, cry out; and [b]the cries of the reapers have reached the ears of the Lord of [1]Sab′a·ōth.

5 You have lived on the earth in pleasure and [1]luxury; you have [2]fattened your hearts [3]as in a day of slaughter.

6 You have condemned, you have murdered the just; he does not resist you.

7 Therefore be patient, brethren, until the coming of the Lord. See *how* the farmer waits for the precious fruit of the earth, waiting patiently for it until it receives the early and latter rain.

8 You also be patient. Establish your hearts, for the coming of the Lord [1]is at hand.

9 Do not [1]grumble against one another, brethren, lest you be [2]condemned. Behold, the Judge is standing at the door!

10 [a]My brethren, take the prophets, who spoke in the name of the Lord, as an example of suffering and [b]patience.

11 Indeed [a]we count them blessed who [b]endure. You have heard of [c]the perseverance of Job and seen [d]the end *intended by* the Lord—that [e]the Lord is very compassionate and merciful.

12 But above all, my brethren, [a]do not swear, either by heaven or by earth or with any other oath. But let your "Yes" be "Yes," and *your* "No," "No," lest you fall into [1]judgment.

8 [c]1 Pet. 1:22
9 [a]Matt. 5:4
10 [a]Job 22:29
11 [a]1 Pet. 2:1–3 [b][Matt. 7:1–5]
12 [a][Matt. 10:28] [b]Rom. 14:4 [1]NU adds *and Judge* [2]NU, M *But who* [3]NU *a neighbor*
13 [1]M *let us*
14 [a]Job 7:7
15 [a]Acts 18:21
16 [a]1 Cor. 5:6
17 [a][Luke 12:47]

CHAPTER 5

1 [a][Luke 6:24]
2 [a]Matt. 6:19 [b]Job 13:28 [1]*have rotted*
3 [a]Rom. 2:5
4 [a]Lev. 19:13 [b]Deut. 24:15 [1]Lit., in Heb., *Hosts*
5 [1]*indulgence* [2]Lit. *nourished* [3]NU omits *as*
8 [1]*has drawn near*
9 [1]Lit. *groan* [2]NU, M *judged*
10 [a]Matt. 5:12 [b]Heb. 10:36
11 [a][Ps. 94:12] [b][James 1:12] [c]Job 1:21, 22; 2:10 [d]Job 42:10 [e]Num. 14:18
12 [a]Matt. 5:34–37 [1]M *hypocrisy*

13 Is anyone among you suffering? Let him [a]pray. Is anyone cheerful? [b]Let him sing
psalms.
14 Is anyone among you sick?
Let him call for the elders of the
church, and let them pray over
him, [a]anointing him with oil in
the name of the Lord.
15 And the prayer of faith will
save the sick, and the Lord will
raise him up. [a]And if he has
committed sins, he will be forgiven.
16 [1]Confess *your* trespasses
to one another, and pray for
one another, that you may be
healed. [a]The effective, [2]fervent
prayer of a righteous man avails
much.
17 E·lī′jah was a man [a]with a
nature like ours, and [b]he prayed
earnestly that it would not rain;
and it did not rain on the land
for three years and six months.
18 And he prayed [a]again, and
the heaven gave rain, and the
earth produced its fruit.
19 Brethren, if anyone among
you wanders from the truth, and
someone [a]turns him back,
20 let him know that he who
turns a sinner from the error of
his way [a]will save [1]a soul from
death and [b]cover a multitude of
sins.

13 [a]Ps. 50:14, 15 [b]Eph. 5:19
14 [a]Mark 6:13; 16:18
15 [a]Is. 33:24
16 [a]Num. 11:2 [1]NU *Therefore confess your sins* [2]*supplication*
17 [a]Acts 14:15 [b]1 Kin. 17:1; 18:1
18 [a]1 Kin. 18:1, 42
19 [a]Gal. 6:1
20 [a]Rom. 11:14 [b][1 Pet. 4:8] [1]NU *his soul*

The First Epistle of

PETER

PERSECUTION can cause either growth or bitterness in the Christian life. Response determines the result. In writing to Jewish believers struggling in the midst of persecution, Peter encourages them to conduct themselves courageously for the Person and program of Christ. Both their character and conduct must be above reproach. Having been born again to a living hope, they are to imitate the Holy One, who has called them. The fruit of that character will be conduct rooted in submission: citizens to government, servants to masters, wives to husbands, husbands to wives, and Christians to one another. Only after submission is fully understood does Peter deal with the difficult area of suffering. The Christians are not to “think it strange concerning the fiery trial which is to try you, as though some strange thing happened to you” (4:12), but are to rejoice as partakers of the suffering of Christ. That response to life is truly the climax of one’s submission to the good hand of God.

This epistle begins with the phrase *Petros apostolos Iesou Christou,* “Peter, an apostle of Jesus Christ.” This is the basis of the early title *Petrou A,* the “First of Peter.”

PETER, an apostle of Jesus
Christ,

To the [1]pilgrims [a]of the Dispersion in Pon′tus, Galatia,
Cap·pa·dō′ci·a, Asia, and Bi-
thyn′i·a,
2 [a]elect [b]according to the fore-
knowledge of God the Father, [c]in
sanctification of the Spirit, for
[d]obedience and [e]sprinkling of
the blood of Jesus Christ:

[f]Grace to you and peace be
multiplied.

3 [a]Blessed *be* the God and Father of our Lord Jesus Christ,
who [b]according to His abundant
mercy [c]has begotten us again to
a living hope [d]through the resurrection of Jesus Christ from the
dead,
4 to an inheritance [1]incorrup-
tible and undefiled and that

CHAPTER 1

1 [a]James 1:1
[1]*sojourners,* temporary residents

2 [a]Eph. 1:4
[b][Rom. 8:29]
[c]2 Thess. 2:13
[d]Rom. 1:5
[e]Heb. 10:22; 12:24
[f]Rom. 1:7

3 [a]Eph. 1:3
[b]Gal. 6:16
[c][John 3:3, 5]
[d]1 Cor. 15:20

4 [a]Col. 1:5
[1]*imperishable*

5 [a]John 10:28

6 [a]Matt. 5:12
[b]2 Cor. 4:17
[c]James 1:2
[1]*distressed*

7 [a]James 1:3
[b]Job 23:10
[c][Rom. 2:7]

8 [a]1 John 4:20
[b]John 20:29
[1]M *known*

does not fade away, [a]reserved in
heaven for you,
5 [a]who are kept by the power
of God through faith for salvation ready to be revealed in the
last time.
6 [a]In this you greatly rejoice,
though now [b]for a little while, if
need be, [c]you have been [1]grieved
by various trials,
7 that [a]the genuineness of your
faith, *being* much more precious
than gold that perishes, though
[b]it is tested by fire, [c]may be
found to praise, honor, and glory
at the revelation of Jesus Christ,
8 [a]whom having not [1]seen you
love. [b]Though now you do not
see *Him,* yet believing, you rejoice with joy inexpressible and
full of glory,
9 receiving the end of your
faith—the salvation of *your* souls.
10 Of this salvation the prophets have inquired and searched

carefully, who prophesied of the
grace *that would come* to you,
11 searching what, or what manner of time, [a]the Spirit of Christ
who was in them was indicating
when He testified beforehand
the sufferings of Christ and the
glories that would follow.
12 To them it was revealed that,
not to themselves, but to [1]us
they were ministering the things
which now have been reported
to you through those who have
preached the gospel to you
by the Holy Spirit sent from
heaven—things which [a]angels
desire to look into.
13 Therefore gird up the loins
of your mind, be sober, and rest
your hope fully upon the grace
that is to be brought to you at
the revelation of Jesus Christ;
14 as obedient children, not
[a]conforming yourselves to the
former lusts, *as* in your ignorance;
15 [a]but as He who called you *is*
holy, you also be holy in all *your*
conduct,
16 because it is written, [a]*"Be
holy, for I am holy."*
17 And if you call on the Father,
who [a]without partiality judges
according to each one's work,
conduct yourselves throughout
the time of your [1]stay *here* in
fear;
18 knowing that you were not redeemed with [1]corruptible things,
like silver or gold, from your aim-
less conduct *received* by tradition
from your fathers,
★ 19 but [a]with the precious blood
of Christ, [b]as of a lamb without
blemish and without spot.
20 [a]He indeed was foreordained
before the foundation of the
world, but was [1]manifest [b]in
these last times for you
21 who through Him believe in
God, [a]who raised Him from the
dead and [b]gave Him glory, so
that your faith and hope are in
God.
22 Since you [a]have purified
your souls in obeying the truth
[1]through the Spirit in [2]sincere
[b]love of the brethren, love one
another fervently with a pure
heart,
23 [a]having been born again, not
of [1]corruptible seed but [2]incor-
ruptible, [b]through the word of
God which lives and abides [3]for-
ever,
24 because

[a]*"All flesh is as grass,*
And all [1]the glory of man as
the flower of the grass.
The grass withers,
And its flower falls away,
25 [a]*But the [1]word of the* LORD
endures forever."

[b]Now this is the word which by
the gospel was preached to you.

2

Therefore, [a]laying aside all
malice, all deceit, hypocrisy,
envy, and all evil speaking,
2 [a]as newborn babes, desire
the pure [b]milk of the word, that
you may grow [1]thereby,
3 if indeed you have [a]tasted
that the Lord *is* gracious.
4 Coming to Him *as to* a living
stone, [a]rejected indeed by men,
but chosen by God *and* precious,
5 you also, as living stones, are
being built up a spiritual house,
a holy priesthood, to offer up
spiritual sacrifices acceptable to
God through Jesus Christ.

11 [a]2 Pet. 1:21
12 [a]Eph. 3:10 [1]NU, M *you*
14 [a][Rom. 12:2]
15 [a][2 Cor. 7:1]
16 [a]Lev. 11:44, 45; 19:2; 20:7
17 [a]Acts 10:34 [1]*sojourning, dwelling* as resident aliens
18 [1]*perishable*
19 [a]Acts 20:28 [b]Ex. 12:5; Is. 53:7
20 [a]Rom. 3:25 [b]Gal. 4:4 [1]*revealed*
21 [a]Acts 2:24 [b]Acts 2:33
22 [a]Acts 15:9 [b]Heb. 13:1 [1]NU omits *through the Spirit* [2]Lit. *unhypocritical*
23 [a]John 1:13 [b]James 1:18 [1]*perishable* [2]*imperishable* [3]NU omits *forever*
24 [a]Is. 40:6–8 [1]NU *its glory as*
25 [a]Is. 40:8 [b][John 1:1] [1]*spoken word*

CHAPTER 2

1 [a]Heb. 12:1
2 [a][Matt. 18:3; 19:14] [b]1 Cor. 3:2 [1]NU adds *up to salvation*
3 [a]Heb. 6:5
4 [a]Ps. 118:22

★ 6 Therefore it is also contained
in the Scripture,

[a]*"Behold, I lay in Zion*
A chief cornerstone, elect,
precious,
And he who believes on
Him will by no means be
put to shame."

★ 7 Therefore, to you who believe, *He is* precious; but to those
who [1]are disobedient,

[a]*"The stone which the*
builders rejected
Has become the chief
cornerstone,"

8 and

★ [a]*"A stone of stumbling*
And a rock of offense."

[b]They stumble, being disobedient to the word, [c]to which they
also were appointed.
9 But you *are* a chosen generation, a royal priesthood, a
holy nation, His own special
people, that you may proclaim
the praises of Him who called
you out of [a]darkness into His
marvelous light;
10 [a]who once *were* not a people
but *are* now the people of God,
who had not obtained mercy but
now have obtained mercy.
11 Beloved, I beg *you* as sojourners and pilgrims, abstain
from fleshly lusts [a]which war
against the soul,
12 [a]having your conduct honorable among the Gentiles, that
when they speak against you as
evildoers, [b]they may, by *your* good
works which they observe, glorify God in the day of visitation.

6 [a]Is. 28:16
7 [a]Ps. 118:22 [1]NU *disbelieve*
8 [a]Is. 8:14 [b]1 Cor. 1:23 [c]Rom. 9:22
9 [a][Acts 26:18]
10 [a]Hos. 1:9, 10; 2:23
11 [a]James 4:1
12 [a]Phil. 2:15 [b]Matt. 5:16; 9:8
13 [a]Matt. 22:21 [1]*institution*
16 [a]Rom. 6:14, 20, 22 [b]Gal. 5:13 [1]*wickedness*
17 [a]Prov. 24:21
18 [a]Eph. 6:5–8
19 [a]Matt. 5:10
20 [a]Luke 6:32–34
21 [a]Matt. 16:24 [b][1 John 2:6] [1]NU *you* [2]NU, M *you*
22 [a]Is. 53:9
23 [a]Is. 53:7 [b]Luke 23:46
24 [a][Heb. 9:28]

13 [a]Therefore submit yourselves
to every [1]ordinance of man for
the Lord's sake, whether to the
king as supreme,
14 or to governors, as to those
who are sent by him for the punishment of evildoers and *for the*
praise of those who do good.
15 For this is the will of God,
that by doing good you may put
to silence the ignorance of foolish men—
16 [a]as free, yet not [b]using liberty as a cloak for [1]vice, but as
bondservants of God.
17 Honor all *people.* Love the
brotherhood. Fear [a]God. Honor
the king.
18 [a]Servants, *be* submissive to
your masters with all fear, not
only to the good and gentle, but
also to the harsh.
19 For this *is* [a]commendable, if
because of conscience toward
God one endures grief, suffering
wrongfully.
20 For [a]what credit *is it* if, when
you are beaten for your faults,
you take it patiently? But when
you do good and suffer, if you
take it patiently, this *is* com-
mendable before God.
21 For [a]to this you were called,
because Christ also suffered for
[1]us, [b]leaving [2]us an example, that
you should follow His steps:

22 *"Who*[a] *committed no sin,* ★
Nor was deceit found in His
mouth";

23 [a]who, when He was reviled, ★
did not revile in return; when
He suffered, He did not threaten,
but [b]committed *Himself* to Him
who judges righteously;
24 [a]who Himself bore our sins ★
in His own body on the tree,

[b]that we, having died to sins, might live for righteousness—[c]by whose [1]stripes you were healed.

★ 25 For [a]you were like sheep going astray, but have now returned [b]to the Shepherd and [1]Overseer of your souls.

3 Wives, likewise, *be* [a]submissive to your own husbands, that even if some do not obey the word, [b]they, without a word, may [c]be won by the conduct of their wives,

2 [a]when they observe your chaste conduct *accompanied* by fear.

3 [a]Do not let your adornment be *merely* outward—arranging the hair, wearing gold, or putting on *fine* apparel—

4 rather *let it be* [a]the hidden person of the heart, with the [1]incorruptible *beauty* of a gentle and quiet spirit, which is very precious in the sight of God.

5 For in this manner, in former times, the holy women who trusted in God also adorned themselves, being submissive to their own husbands,

6 as Sarah obeyed Abraham, [a]calling him lord, whose daughters you are if you do good and are not afraid with any terror.

7 [a]Husbands, likewise, dwell with *them* with understanding, giving honor to the wife, [b]as to the weaker vessel, and as *being* heirs together of the grace of life, [c]that your prayers may not be hindered.

8 Finally, all *of you be* of one mind, having compassion for one another; love as brothers, *be* tenderhearted, *be* [1]courteous;

9 [a]not returning evil for evil or reviling for reviling, but on the contrary [b]blessing, knowing that you were called to this, [c]that you may inherit a blessing.

10 For

[a]"He who would love life
And see good days,
[b]Let him [1]refrain his tongue
from evil,
And his lips from speaking
deceit.
11 *Let him [a]turn away from*
evil and do good;
[b]Let him seek peace and
pursue it.
12 *For the eyes of the* LORD *are*
on the righteous,
[a]And His ears are open to
their prayers;
But the face of the LORD *is*
against those who do
evil."

13 [a]And who *is* he who will harm you if you become followers of what is good?

14 [a]But even if you should suffer for righteousness' sake, *you are* blessed. [b]*"And do not be afraid of their threats, nor be troubled."*

15 But [1]sanctify [2]the Lord God in your hearts, and always [a]*be* ready to *give* a defense to everyone who asks you a reason for the [b]hope that is in you, with meekness and fear;

16 [a]having a good conscience, that when they defame you as evildoers, those who revile your good conduct in Christ may be ashamed.

17 For *it is* better, if it is the will of God, to suffer for doing good than for doing evil.

18 For Christ also suffered once for sins, the just for the unjust, that He might bring [1]us to God,

24 [b]Rom. 7:6 [c]Is. 53:5 [1]*wounds*
25 [a]Is. 53:5, 6 [b]Is. 40:11; [Ezek. 34:23]; Zech. 13:7 [1]Gr. *Episkopos*

CHAPTER 3

1 [a]Eph. 5:22 [b]1 Cor. 7:16 [c]Matt. 18:15
2 [a]1 Pet. 2:12; 3:6
3 [a]1 Tim. 2:9
4 [a]Rom. 2:29 [1]*imperishable*
6 [a]Gen. 18:12
7 [a][Eph. 5:25] [b]1 Cor. 12:23 [c]Job 42:8
8 [1]NU *humble*
9 [a][Prov. 17:13] [b]Matt. 5:44 [c]Matt. 25:34
10 [a]Ps. 34:12–16 [b]James 1:26 [1]*restrain*
11 [a]Ps. 37:27 [b]Rom. 12:18
12 [a]John 9:31
13 [a]Prov. 16:7
14 [a]James 1:12 [b]Is. 8:12
15 [a]Ps. 119:46 [b][Titus 3:7] [1]*set apart* [2]NU *Christ as Lord*
16 [a]Heb. 13:18
18 [1]NU, M *you*

being put to death in the flesh
but made alive by the Spirit,
19 by whom also He went and
preached to the spirits in prison,
20 who formerly were disobedient, [1]when once the Divine longsuffering waited in the days of
Noah, while *the* ark was being
prepared, in which a few, that is,
eight souls, were saved through
water.
21 [a]There is also an antitype
which now saves us—baptism
[b](not the removal of the filth of
the flesh, [c]but the answer of a
good conscience toward God),
through the resurrection of Jesus Christ,
22 who has gone into heaven
and [a]is at the right hand of God,
[b]angels and authorities and powers having been made subject to
Him.

4 Therefore, since Christ suffered [1]for us in the flesh,
arm yourselves also with the
same mind, for he who has suffered in the flesh has ceased
from sin,
2 that he no longer should live
the rest of *his* time in the flesh
for the lusts of men, [a]but for the
will of God.
3 For we *have spent* enough
of our past [1]lifetime in doing
the will of the Gentiles—when
we walked in lewdness, lusts,
drunkenness, revelries, drinking
parties, and abominable idola-
tries.
4 In regard to these, they think
it strange that you do not run
with *them* in the same flood of
dissipation, speaking evil of *you*.
5 They will give an account to
Him who is ready [a]to judge the
living and the dead.
6 For this reason [a]the gospel
was preached also to those who
are dead, that they might be
judged according to men in the
flesh, but [b]live according to God
in the spirit.
7 But [a]the end of all things is at
hand; therefore be serious and
watchful in your prayers.
8 And above all things have
fervent love for one another, for
[a]*"love will cover a multitude of*
sins."
9 [a]*Be* hospitable to one another [b]without grumbling.
10 [a]As each one has received a
gift, minister it to one another,
[b]as good stewards of [c]the manifold grace of God.
11 [a]If anyone speaks, *let him*
speak as the [1]oracles of God. If
anyone ministers, *let him do it*
as with the ability which God
supplies, that [b]in all things God
may be glorified through Jesus Christ, to whom belong the
glory and the [2]dominion forever
and ever. Amen.
12 Beloved, do not think it
strange concerning the fiery
trial which is to try you, as
though some strange thing happened to you;
13 but rejoice [a]to the extent that
you partake of Christ's sufferings, that [b]when His glory is
revealed, you may also be glad
with exceeding joy.
14 If you are [1]reproached for
the name of Christ, [a]blessed *are*
you, for the Spirit of glory and
of God rests upon you. [2]On their
part He is blasphemed, [b]but on
your part He is glorified.
15 But let none of you suffer
as a murderer, a thief, an evildoer, or as a [1]busybody in other
people's matters.
16 Yet if *anyone suffers* as a

20 [1]NU, M *when the longsuffering of God waited patiently*
21 [a]Eph. 5:26 [b][Titus 3:5] [c][Rom. 10:10]
22 [a]Ps. 110:1 [b]Rom. 8:38

CHAPTER 4

1 [1]NU omits *for us*
2 [a]John 1:13
3 [1]NU *time*
5 [a]Acts 10:42
6 [a]1 Pet. 1:12; 3:19 [b][Rom. 8:9, 13]
7 [a]Rom. 13:11
8 [a][Prov. 10:12]
9 [a]Heb. 13:2 [b]2 Cor. 9:7
10 [a]Rom. 12:6–8 [b]1 Cor. 4:1, 2 [c][1 Cor. 12:4]
11 [a]Eph. 4:29 [b][1 Cor. 10:31] [1]*utterances* [2]*sovereignty*
13 [a]James 1:2 [b]2 Tim. 2:12
14 [a]Matt. 5:11 [b]Matt. 5:16 [1]*insulted or reviled* [2]NU omits the rest of v. 14.
15 [1]*meddler*

Christian, let him not be ashamed,
but let him glorify God in this
[1]matter.
17 For the time *has come* [a]for
judgment to begin at the house
of God; and if *it begins* with us
first, [b]what will *be* the end of
those who do not obey the gospel of God?
18 Now

[a]"If the righteous one is
scarcely saved,
Where will the ungodly and
the sinner appear?"

19 Therefore let those who suffer according to the will of God
[a]commit their souls *to Him* in
doing good, as to a faithful Creator.

5 The elders who are among
you I exhort, I who am a fellow elder and a [a]witness of the
sufferings of Christ, and also a
partaker of the [b]glory that will
be revealed:
2 [a]Shepherd the flock of God
which is among you, serving as
overseers, [b]not by compulsion
but [1]willingly, [c]not for dishonest
gain but eagerly;
3 nor as [a]being [1]lords over
[b]those entrusted to you, but [c]be-
ing examples to the flock;
4 and when [a]the Chief Shepherd appears, you will receive
[b]the crown of glory that does not
fade away.
5 Likewise you younger people,
submit yourselves to *your* elders.
Yes, [a]all of *you* be submissive to
one another, and be clothed with
humility, for

[b]"God resists the proud,
But [c]gives grace to the
humble."

6 Therefore humble yourselves
under the mighty hand of God,
that He may exalt you in due
time,
7 casting all your care upon
Him, for He cares for you.
8 Be [1]sober, be [2]vigilant; [3]be-
cause your adversary the devil
walks about like a roaring lion,
seeking whom he may devour.
9 Resist him, steadfast in the
faith, knowing that the same
sufferings are experienced by
your brotherhood in the world.
10 But [1]may the God of all grace,
[a]who called [2]us to His eternal
glory by Christ Jesus, after you
have suffered a while, [3]perfect,
establish, strengthen, and settle
you.
11 [a]To Him *be* the glory and
the dominion forever and ever.
Amen.
12 By [a]Sil·vā′nus, our faithful
brother as I consider him, I have
written to you briefly, exhorting
and testifying [b]that this is the
true grace of God in which you
stand.
13 She who is in Babylon, elect
together with *you,* greets you;
and *so does* [a]Mark my son.
14 Greet one another with a
kiss of love. Peace to you all who
are in Christ Jesus. Amen.

---

16 [1]NU *name*
17 [a]Is. 10:12 [b]Luke 10:12
18 [a]Prov. 11:31
19 [a]2 Tim. 1:12

CHAPTER 5

1 [a]Matt. 26:37 [b]Rom. 8:17, 18
2 [a]Acts 20:28 [b]1 Cor. 9:17 [c]1 Tim. 3:3 [1]NU adds *according to God*
3 [a]Ezek. 34:4 [b]Ps. 33:12 [c]Phil. 3:17 [1]*masters*
4 [a]Heb. 13:20 [b]2 Tim. 4:8
5 [a]Eph. 5:21 [b]Prov. 3:34 [c]Is. 57:15
8 [1]*self-controlled* [2]*watchful* [3]NU, M omit *because*
10 [a]1 Cor. 1:9 [1]NU *the God of all grace,* [2]NU, M *you* [3]NU *will perfect*
11 [a]Rev. 1:6
12 [a]2 Cor. 1:19 [b]Acts 20:24
13 [a]Acts 12:12, 25; 15:37, 39

The Second Epistle of
PETER

FIRST Peter deals with problems from the outside; Second Peter deals with problems from the inside. Peter writes to warn the believers about the false teachers who are peddling damaging doctrine. He begins by urging them to keep close watch on their personal lives. The Christian life demands diligence in pursuing moral excellence, knowledge, self-control, perseverance, godliness, brotherly kindness, and selfless love. By contrast, the false teachers are sensual, arrogant, greedy, and covetous. They scoff at the thought of future judgment and live their lives as if the present would be the pattern for the future. Peter reminds them that although God may be longsuffering in sending judgment, ultimately it will come. In view of that fact, believers should live lives of godliness, blamelessness, and steadfastness.

The statement of authorship in 1:1 is very clear: "Simon Peter, a bondservant and apostle of Jesus Christ." To distinguish this epistle from the first by Peter it was given the Greek title *Petrou B*, the "Second of Peter."

SIMON Peter, a bondservant
and [a]apostle of Jesus Christ,

To those who have [1]obtained
[b]like[2] precious faith with us by
the righteousness of our God
and Savior Jesus Christ:

2 [a]Grace and peace be multiplied to you in the knowledge of
God and of Jesus our Lord,
3 as His [a]divine power has
given to us all things that *pertain*
to life and godliness, through the
knowledge of Him [b]who called
us by glory and virtue,
4 [a]by which have been given
to us exceedingly great and precious promises, that through
these you may be [b]partakers of
the divine nature, having escaped the [1]corruption *that is* in
the world through lust.
5 But also for this very reason,
[a]giving all diligence, add to your
faith virtue, to virtue [b]knowl-
edge,
6 to knowledge self-control,
to self-control [1]perseverance, to
perseverance godliness,
7 to godliness brotherly kindness, and [a]to brotherly kindness
love.
8 For if these things are yours
and abound, *you* will be neither
[1]barren [a]nor unfruitful in the
knowledge of our Lord Jesus
Christ.
9 For he who lacks these things
is [a]shortsighted, even to blindness, and has forgotten that he
was cleansed from his old sins.
10 Therefore, brethren, be even
more diligent [a]to make your call
and election sure, for if you
do these things you will never
stumble;
11 for so an entrance will be
supplied to you abundantly into
the everlasting kingdom of our
Lord and Savior Jesus Christ.
12 For this reason [a]I will not
be negligent to remind you always of these things, [b]though

CHAPTER 1

1 [a]Gal. 2:8 [b]Eph. 4:5 [1]*received* [2]*faith of the same value*
2 [a]Dan. 4:1
3 [a]1 Pet. 1:5 [b]1 Thess. 2:12
4 [a]2 Cor. 1:20; 7:1 [b][2 Cor. 3:18] [1]*depravity*
5 [a]2 Pet. 3:18 [b]2 Pet. 1:2
6 [1]*patience*
7 [a]Gal. 6:10
8 [a][John 15:2] [1]*useless*
9 [a]1 John 2:9–11
10 [a]1 John 3:19
12 [a]Phil. 3:1 [b]1 Pet. 5:12

you know and are established in
the present truth.
13 Yes, I think it is right, [a]as
long as I am in this [1]tent, [b]to stir
you up by reminding *you,*
14 [a]knowing that shortly I *must*
[1]put off my tent, just as [b]our
Lord Jesus Christ showed me.
15 Moreover I will be careful
to ensure that you always have
a reminder of these things after
my [1]decease.
16 For we did not follow [a]cun-
ningly devised fables when we
made known to you the [b]power
and [c]coming of our Lord Jesus
Christ, but were [d]eyewitnesses
of His majesty.
17 For He received from God
the Father honor and glory when
such a voice came to Him from
the Excellent Glory: [a]"This is My
beloved Son, in whom I am well
pleased."
18 And we heard this voice
which came from heaven when
we were with Him on [a]the holy
mountain.
19 [1]And so we have the prophetic word confirmed, which
you do well to heed as a [a]light
that shines in a dark place, [b]until
[c]the day dawns and the morning
star rises in your [d]hearts;
20 knowing this first, that [a]no
prophecy of Scripture is of any
private [1]interpretation,
21 for [a]prophecy never came
by the will of man, [b]but [1]holy
men of God spoke *as they were*
moved by the Holy Spirit.

2

2 But there were also false
prophets among the peo-
ple, even as there will be [a]false
teachers among you, who will
secretly bring in destructive heresies, even denying the Lord
who bought them, *and* bring on
themselves swift destruction.
2 And many will follow their
destructive ways, because of
whom the way of truth will be
blasphemed.
3 By covetousness they will ex-
ploit you with deceptive words;
for a long time their judgment
has not been idle, and their destruction [1]does not slumber.
4 For if God did not spare the
angels who sinned, but cast
them down to [1]hell and delivered
them into chains of darkness, to
be reserved for judgment;
5 and did not spare the ancient
world, but saved Noah, *one of*
eight *people,* a preacher of righteousness, bringing in the flood
on the world of the ungodly;
6 and turning the cities of
[a]Sod'om and Go·mor'rah into
ashes, condemned *them* to destruction, making *them* an example to those who afterward
would live ungodly;
7 and [a]delivered righteous Lot,
who was oppressed by the filthy
conduct of the wicked
8 (for that righteous man, dwelling among them, [a]tormented *his*
righteous soul from day to day by
seeing and hearing *their* lawless
deeds)—
9 *then* [a]the Lord knows how to
deliver the godly out of temptations and to reserve the unjust
under punishment for the day of
judgment,
10 and especially [a]those who
walk according to the flesh in
the lust of uncleanness and despise authority. [b]*They are* pre-
sumptuous, self-willed. They are
not afraid to speak evil of [1]digni-
taries,

---

13 [a][2 Cor. 5:1, 4] [b]2 Pet. 3:1 [1]Body
14 [a][2 Tim. 4:6] [b]John 13:36; 21:18, 19 [1]Die and leave this body
15 [1]Lit. *exodus, departure*
16 [a]1 Cor. 1:17 [b][Eph. 1:19–22] [c][1 Pet. 5:4] [d]Matt. 17:1–5
17 [a]Matt. 17:5
18 [a]Matt. 17:1
19 [a][John 1:4, 5, 9] [b]Prov. 4:18 [c]Rev. 2:28; 22:16 [d][2 Cor. 4:5–7] [1]Or *We also have the more sure prophetic word*
20 [a][Rom. 12:6] [1]Or *origin*
21 [a][2 Tim. 3:16] [b]2 Sam. 23:2 [1]NU *men spoke from God*

CHAPTER 2

1 [a]1 Tim. 4:1, 2
3 [1]M *will not*
4 [1]Lit. *Tartarus*
6 [a]Gen. 19:1–26
7 [a]Gen. 19:16, 29
8 [a]Ps. 119:139
9 [a]Ps. 34:15–19
10 [a]Jude 4, 7, 8 [b]Jude 8 [1]*glorious ones,* lit. *glories*

11 whereas [a]angels, who are
greater in power and might, do
not bring a reviling accusation
against them before the Lord.
12 But these, [a]like natural brute
beasts made to be caught and
destroyed, speak evil of the
things they do not understand,
and will utterly perish in their
own corruption,
13 [a]*and* will receive the wages
of unrighteousness, *as* those
who count it pleasure [b]to [1]ca-
rouse in the daytime. [c]*They are*
spots and blemishes, [2]carousing
in their own deceptions while
[d]they feast with you,
14 having eyes full of [1]adultery
and that cannot cease from sin,
enticing unstable souls. [a]They
have a heart trained in covetous
practices, *and are* accursed children.
15 They have forsaken the right
way and gone astray, following
the way of [a]Bā′laam the *son* of
Bē′or, who loved the wages of
unrighteousness;
16 but he was rebuked for his
iniquity: a dumb donkey speaking with a man's voice restrained
the madness of the prophet.
17 [a]These are wells without water, [1]clouds carried by a tempest,
for whom is reserved the blackness of darkness [2]forever.
18 For when they speak great
swelling *words* of emptiness,
they allure through the lusts of
the flesh, through lewdness, the
ones who [1]have actually escaped
from those who live in error.
19 While they promise them liberty, they themselves are slaves
of [1]corruption; [a]for by whom a
person is overcome, by him also
he is brought into [2]bondage.
20 For if, after they [a]have escaped
the pollutions of the world through
the knowledge of the Lord and
Savior Jesus Christ, they are
[b]again entangled in them and
overcome, the latter end is worse
for them than the beginning.
21 For [a]it would have been better for them not to have known
the way of righteousness, than
having known *it*, to turn from
the holy commandment delivered to them.
22 But it has happened to them
according to the true proverb: [a]*"A
dog returns to his own vomit,"*
and, "a sow, having washed, to
her wallowing in the mire."

3 Beloved, I now write to you
this second epistle (in *both*
of which [a]I stir up your pure
minds by way of reminder),
2 that you may be mindful of
the words [a]which were spoken
before by the holy prophets,
[b]and of the commandment of
[1]us, the apostles of the Lord and
Savior,
3 knowing this first: that scoffers will come in the last days,
[a]walking according to their own
lusts,
4 and saying, "Where is the
promise of His coming? For since
the fathers fell asleep, all things
continue as *they were* from the
beginning of [a]creation."
5 For this they willfully forget:
that [a]by the word of God the
heavens were of old, and the
earth [b]standing out of water and
in the water,
6 [a]by which the world *that*
then existed perished, being
flooded with water.
7 But [a]the heavens and the
earth *which* are now preserved
by the same word, are reserved

11 [a]Jude 9
12 [a]Jude 10
13 [a]Phil. 3:19 [b]Rom. 13:13 [c]Jude 12 [d]1 Cor. 11:20, 21 [1]*revel* [2]*reveling*
14 [a]Jude 11 [1]Lit. *an adulteress*
15 [a]Num. 22:5, 7
17 [a]Jude 12, 13 [1]NU *and mists* [2]NU omits *forever*
18 [1]NU *are barely escaping*
19 [a]John 8:34 [1]*depravity* [2]*slavery*
20 [a]Matt. 12:45 [b][Heb. 6:4–6]
21 [a]Luke 12:47
22 [a]Prov. 26:11

CHAPTER 3

1 [a]2 Pet. 1:13
2 [a]2 Pet. 1:21 [b]Jude 17 [1]NU, M *the apostles of your Lord and Savior* or *your apostles of the Lord and Savior*
3 [a]2 Pet. 2:10
4 [a]Gen. 6:1–7
5 [a]Gen. 1:6, 9 [b]Ps. 24:2; 136:6
6 [a]Gen. 7:11, 12, 21–23
7 [a]2 Pet. 3:10, 12

for [b]fire until the day of judgment and [1]perdition of ungodly
men.
8 But, beloved, do not forget
this one thing, that with the
Lord one day *is* as a thousand
years, and [a]a thousand years as
one day.
9 [a]The Lord is not slack concerning *His* promise, as some
count slackness, but [b]is longsuffering toward [1]us, [c]not willing
that any should perish but [d]that
all should come to repentance.
☆ **10** But [a]the day of the Lord will
come as a thief in the night, in
which [b]the heavens will pass
away with a great noise, and
the elements will melt with fervent heat; both the earth and
the works that are in it will be
[1]burned up.
11 Therefore, since all these
things will be dissolved, what
manner *of persons* ought you to
be [a]in holy conduct and godliness,
12 [a]looking for and hastening
the coming of the day of God,
because of which the heavens
will [b]be dissolved, being on fire,
and the elements will [c]melt with
fervent heat?

7 [b][2 Thess. 1:8] [1]*destruction*
8 [a]Ps. 90:4
9 [a]Hab. 2:3 [b]Is. 30:18 [c]Ezek. 33:11 [d][Rom. 2:4] [1]NU *you*
10 [a]Matt. 24:42, 43; Luke 12:39; 1 Thess. 5:2; Rev. 3:3; 16:15 [b]Ps. 102:25, 26 [1]NU *laid bare*, lit. *found*
11 [a]1 Pet. 1:15
12 [a]1 Cor. 1:7, 8 [b]Ps. 50:3 [c]Mic. 1:4
13 [a]Is. 65:17; 66:22 [b]Rev. 21:1
14 [a]1 Cor. 1:8; 15:58
15 [a]Rom. 2:4
16 [a]1 Cor. 15:24 [b]2 Tim. 3:16
17 [a]Mark 13:23 [b]Eph. 4:14
18 [a]Eph. 4:15 [b]2 Tim. 4:18

13 Nevertheless we, according
to His promise, look for [a]new
heavens and a [b]new earth in
which righteousness dwells.
14 Therefore, beloved, looking forward to these things, be
diligent [a]to be found by Him in
peace, without spot and blameless;
15 and consider *that* [a]the longsuffering of our Lord *is* salvation—as also our beloved
brother Paul, according to the
wisdom given to him, has written to you,
16 as also in all his [a]epistles,
speaking in them of these things,
in which are some things hard to
understand, which untaught and
unstable *people* twist to their
own destruction, as *they do* also
the [b]rest of the Scriptures.
17 You therefore, beloved, [a]since
you know *this* beforehand, [b]be-
ware lest you also fall from your
own steadfastness, being led away
with the error of the wicked;
18 [a]but grow in the grace and
knowledge of our Lord and Savior Jesus Christ. [b]To Him *be*
the glory both now and forever.
Amen.

The First Epistle of

JOHN

GOD is light; God is love; and God is life. John is enjoying a delightful fellowship with that God of light, love, and life, and he desperately desires that his spiritual children enjoy the same fellowship.

God is light. Therefore, to engage in fellowship with Him we must walk in light and not in darkness. As we walk in the light, we will regularly confess our sins, allowing the blood of Christ to continually cleanse us. Two major roadblocks to hinder this walk will be falling in love with the world and falling for the alluring lies of false teachers.

God is love. Since we are His children, we must walk in love. In fact, John says that if we do not love, we do not know God. Love is more than just words; it is actions. Love is giving, not getting. Biblical love is unconditional in its nature. Christ's love fulfilled those qualities, and when that brand of love characterizes us, we will be free of self-condemnation and experience confidence before God.

God is life. Those who fellowship with Him must possess His quality of life. Spiritual life begins with spiritual birth, which occurs through faith in Jesus Christ. Faith in Jesus Christ infuses us with God's life—eternal life.

Although the apostle John's name is not found in this book, it was given the title *Ioannou A*, the "First of John."

THAT [a]which was from the
beginning, which we have
heard, which we have [b]seen with
our eyes, [c]which we have looked
upon, and [d]our hands have handled, concerning the [e]Word of
life—
2 [a]the life [b]was manifested, and
we have seen, [c]and bear witness,
and declare to you that eternal
life which was [d]with the Father
and was manifested to us—
3 that which we have seen and
heard we declare to you, that
you also may have fellowship
with us; and truly our fellowship
is [a]with the Father and with His
Son Jesus Christ.
4 And these things we write to
you [a]that [1]your joy may be full.
5 [a]This is the message which
we have heard from Him and
declare to you, that [b]God is light
and in Him is no darkness at
all.
6 [a]If we say that we have fellowship with Him, and walk
in darkness, we lie and do not
practice the truth.
7 But if we [a]walk in the light
as He is in the light, we have fellowship with one another, and
[b]the blood of Jesus Christ His
Son cleanses us from all sin.
8 If we say that we have no sin,
we deceive ourselves, and the
truth is not in us.
9 If we [a]confess our sins, He is
[b]faithful and just to forgive us
our sins and to [c]cleanse us from
all unrighteousness.
10 If we say that we have not
sinned, we [a]make Him a liar, and
His word is not in us.

CHAPTER 1

1 [a][John 1:1] [b]John 1:14 [c]2 Pet. 1:16 [d]Luke 24:39 [e][John 1:1, 4, 14]

2 [a]John 1:4 [b]Rom. 16:26 [c]John 21:24 [d][John 1:1, 18; 16:28]

3 [a]1 Cor. 1:9

4 [a]John 15:11; 16:24 [1]NU, M *our*

5 [a]1 John 3:11 [b][1 Tim. 6:16]

6 [a][1 John 2:9–11]

7 [a]Is. 2:5 [b][1 Cor. 6:11]

9 [a]Prov. 28:13 [b][Rom. 3:24–26] [c]Ps. 51:2

10 [a]1 John 5:10

2

My little children, these things I write to you, so that you may not sin. And if anyone sins, [a]we have an Advocate with the Father, Jesus Christ the righteous.

2 And [a]He Himself is the propitiation for our sins, and not for ours only but [b]also for the whole world.

3 Now by this we know that we know Him, if we keep His commandments.

4 He who says, "I know Him," and does not keep His commandments, is a [a]liar, and the truth is not in him.

5 But [a]whoever keeps His word, truly the love of God [1]is perfected [b]in him. By this we know that we are in Him.

6 [a]He who says he abides in Him [b]ought himself also to walk just as He walked.

7 [1]Brethren, I write no new commandment to you, but an old commandment which you have had [a]from the beginning. The old commandment is the word which you heard [2]from the beginning.

8 Again, [a]a new commandment I write to you, which thing is true in Him and in you, [b]because the darkness is passing away, and [c]the true light is already shining.

9 [a]He who says he is in the light, and hates his brother, is in darkness until now.

10 [a]He who loves his brother abides in the light, and [b]there is no cause for stumbling in him.

11 But he who [a]hates his brother is in darkness and [b]walks in darkness, and does not know where he is going, because the darkness has blinded his eyes.

12 I write to you, little children,
Because [a]your sins are forgiven you for His name's sake.
13 I write to you, fathers,
Because you have known Him *who is* [a]from the beginning.
I write to you, young men,
Because you have overcome the wicked one.
I write to you, little children,
Because you have [b]known the Father.
14 I have written to you, fathers,
Because you have known Him *who is* from the beginning.
I have written to you, young men,
Because [a]you are strong, and the word of God abides in you,
And you have overcome the wicked one.

15 [a]Do not love the world or the things in the world. [b]If anyone loves the world, the love of the Father is not in him.

16 For all that *is* in the world—the lust of the flesh, [a]the lust of the eyes, and the pride of life—is not of the Father but is of the world.

17 And [a]the world is passing away, and the lust of it; but he who does the will of God abides forever.

18 [a]Little children, [b]it is the last hour; and as you have heard that [c]the[1] Antichrist is coming, [d]even now many antichrists have come, by which we know [e]that it is the last hour.

19 [a]They went out from us, but

CHAPTER 2

1 [a]Heb. 7:25; 9:24

2 [a][Rom. 3:25] [b]John 1:29

4 [a]Rom. 3:4

5 [a]John 14:21, 23 [b][1 John 4:12] [1]*has been completed*

6 [a]John 15:4 [b]1 Pet. 2:21

7 [a]1 John 3:11, 23; 4:21 [1]NU *Beloved* [2]NU omits *from the beginning*

8 [a]John 13:34; 15:12 [b]Rom. 13:12 [c][John 1:9; 8:12; 12:35]

9 [a][1 Cor. 13:2]

10 [a][1 John 3:14] [b]2 Pet. 1:10

11 [a][1 John 2:9; 3:15; 4:20] [b]John 12:35

12 [a][1 Cor. 6:11]

13 [a]John 1:1 [b][Rom. 8:15–17]

14 [a]Eph. 6:10

15 [a][Rom. 12:2] [b]James 4:4

16 [a][Eccl. 5:10, 11]

17 [a]1 Cor. 7:31

18 [a]John 21:5 [b]1 Pet. 4:7 [c]2 Thess. 2:3 [d]2 John 7 [e]1 Tim. 4:1 [1]NU omits *the*

19 [a]Deut. 13:13

they were not of us; for [b]if they
had been of us, they would have
continued with us; but *they went*
out [c]that they might be made
manifest, that none of them were
of us.
20 But [a]you have an anointing
[b]from the Holy One, and [c]you[1]
know all things.
21 I have not written to you because you do not know the truth,
but because you know it, and
that no lie is of the truth.
22 [a]Who is a liar but he who
denies that [b]Jesus is the Christ?
He is antichrist who denies the
Father and the Son.
23 [a]Whoever denies the Son
does not have the [b]Father either;
[c]he who acknowledges the Son
has the Father also.
24 Therefore let that abide in
you [a]which you heard from the
beginning. If what you heard
from the beginning abides in
you, [b]you also will abide in the
Son and in the Father.
25 [a]And this is the promise that
He has promised us—eternal life.
26 These things I have written
to you concerning those who *try*
to [1]deceive you.
27 But the [a]anointing which you
have received from Him abides
in you, and [b]you do not need
that anyone teach you; but as
the same anointing [c]teaches you
concerning all things, and is
true, and is not a lie, and just as
it has taught you, you [1]will abide
in Him.
28 And now, little children,
abide in Him, that [1]when He appears, we may have [a]confidence
and not be ashamed before Him
at His coming.
29 [a]If you know that He is righteous, you know that [b]everyone

19 [b]Matt. 24:24 [c]1 Cor. 11:19
20 [a]2 Cor. 1:21 [b]Acts 3:14 [c][John 16:13] [1]NU *you all know.*
22 [a]2 John 7 [b]1 John 4:3
23 [a]John 15:23 [b]John 5:23 [c]1 John 4:15; 5:1
24 [a]2 John 5, 6 [b]John 14:23
25 [a]John 3:14–16; 6:40; 17:2, 3
26 [1]*lead you astray*
27 [a][John 14:16; 16:13] [b][Jer. 31:33] [c][John 14:16] [1]NU omits *will*
28 [a]1 John 3:21; 4:17; 5:14 [1]NU *if*
29 [a]Acts 22:14 [b]1 John 3:7, 10

CHAPTER 3

1 [a][1 John 4:10] [b][John 1:12] [c]John 15:18, 21; 16:3 [1]NU adds *And we are.* [2]M *you*
2 [a][Rom. 8:15, 16] [b][Rom. 8:18, 19, 23] [c]Rom. 8:29 [d][Ps. 16:11]
3 [a]1 John 4:17
4 [a]Rom. 4:15
5 [a]1 John 1:2; 3:8 [b]John 1:29 [c][2 Cor. 5:21]
8 [a]Matt. 13:38 [b]Luke 10:18
9 [a]John 1:3; 3:3 [b]1 Pet. 1:23

who practices righteousness is
born of Him.
3 Behold [a]what manner of love
the Father has bestowed on
us, that [b]we should be called
children of [1]God! Therefore the
world does not know [2]us, [c]be-
cause it did not know Him.
2 Beloved, [a]now we are children of God; and [b]it has not yet
been revealed what we shall be,
but we know that when He is
revealed, [c]we shall be like Him,
for [d]we shall see Him as He is.
3 [a]And everyone who has this
hope in Him purifies himself,
just as He is pure.
4 Whoever commits sin also
commits lawlessness, and [a]sin is
lawlessness.
5 And you know [a]that He was
manifested [b]to take away our
sins, and [c]in Him there is no
sin.
6 Whoever abides in Him does
not sin. Whoever sins has neither seen Him nor known Him.
7 Little children, let no one
deceive you. He who practices
righteousness is righteous, just
as He is righteous.
8 [a]He who sins is of the devil,
for the devil has sinned from
the beginning. For this purpose
the Son of God was manifested,
[b]that He might destroy the works
of the devil.
9 Whoever has been [a]born of
God does not sin, for [b]His seed
remains in him; and he cannot
sin, because he has been born of
God.
10 In this the children of God
and the children of the devil
are manifest: Whoever does not
practice righteousness is not of
God, nor *is* he who does not love
his brother.

11 For this is the message that
you heard from the beginning,
[a]that we should love one another,
12 not as [a]Cain *who* was of the
wicked one and murdered his
brother. And why did he murder
him? Because his works were
evil and his brother's righteous.
13 Do not marvel, my brethren,
if [a]the world hates you.
14 We know that we have passed
from death to life, because we
love the brethren. He who does
not love [1]*his* brother abides in
death.
15 [a]Whoever hates his brother
is a murderer, and you know
that [b]no murderer has eternal
life abiding in him.
16 [a]By this we know love, [b]because He laid down His life for
us. And we also ought to lay
down *our* lives for the brethren.
17 But [a]whoever has this world's
goods, and sees his brother in
need, and shuts up his heart
from him, how does the love of
God abide in him?
18 My little children, [a]let us not
love in word or in tongue, but in
deed and in truth.
19 And by this we [1]know [a]that
we are of the truth, and shall
[2]assure our hearts before Him.
20 [a]For if our heart condemns
us, God is greater than our heart,
and knows all things.
21 Beloved, if our heart does
not condemn us, [a]we have confidence toward God.
22 And [a]whatever we ask we
receive from Him, because we
keep His commandments [b]and
do those things that are pleasing
in His sight.
23 And this is His commandment: that we should believe on
the name of His Son Jesus Christ
[a]and love one another, as He
gave [1]us commandment.
24 Now [a]he who keeps His commandments [b]abides in Him, and
He in him. And [c]by this we know
that He abides in us, by the
Spirit whom He has given us.

4 Beloved, do not believe every spirit, but [a]test the spirits, whether they are of God; because [b]many false prophets have
gone out into the world.
2 By this you know the Spirit
of God: [a]Every spirit that confesses that Jesus Christ has
come in the flesh is of God,
3 and every spirit that does not
confess [1]that Jesus [2]Christ has
come in the flesh is not of God.
And this is the *spirit* of the Antichrist, which you have heard
was coming, and is now already
in the world.
4 You are of God, little children, and have overcome them,
because He who is in you is
greater than [a]he who is in the
world.
5 [a]They are of the world. Therefore they speak *as* of the world,
and [b]the world hears them.
6 We are of God. He who knows
God hears us; he who is not of
God does not hear us. [a]By this we
know the spirit of truth and the
spirit of error.
7 [a]Beloved, let us love one another, for love is of God; and
everyone who [b]loves is born of
God and knows God.
8 He who does not love does
not know God, for God is love.
9 [a]In this the love of God was
manifested toward us, that God
has sent His only begotten [b]Son
into the world, that we might
live through Him.

11 [a][John 13:34; 15:12]
12 [a]Gen. 4:4, 8
13 [a][John 15:18; 17:14]
14 [1]NU omits *his brother*
15 [a]Matt. 5:21 [b][Gal. 5:20, 21]
16 [a][John 3:16] [b]John 10:11; 15:13
17 [a]Deut. 15:7
18 [a]Ezek. 33:31
19 [a]John 18:37 [1]NU *shall know* [2]*persuade, set at rest*
20 [a][1 Cor. 4:4, 5]
21 [a][1 John 2:28; 5:14]
22 [a]Ps. 34:15 [b]John 8:29
23 [a]Matt. 22:39 [1]M omits *us*
24 [a]John 14:23 [b]John 14:21; 17:21 [c]Rom. 8:9, 14, 16

CHAPTER 4

1 [a]1 Cor. 14:29 [b]Matt. 24:5
2 [a]1 Cor. 12:3
3 [1]NU omits *that* [2]NU omits *Christ has come in the flesh*
4 [a]John 14:30; 16:11
5 [a]John 3:31 [b]John 15:19; 17:14
6 [a][1 Cor. 2:12–16]
7 [a]1 John 3:10, 11, 23 [b]1 Thess. 4:9
9 [a]Rom. 5:8 [b]John 3:16

10 In this is love, [a]not that we
loved God, but that He loved us
and sent His Son [b]*to be* the propitiation for our sins.
11 Beloved, [a]if God so loved us,
we also ought to love one another.
12 [a]No one has seen God at any
time. If we love one another,
God abides in us, and His love
has been perfected in us.
13 [a]By this we know that we
abide in Him, and He in us,
because He has given us of His
Spirit.
14 And [a]we have seen and testify that [b]the Father has sent the
Son *as* Savior of the world.
15 [a]Whoever confesses that
Jesus is the Son of God, God
abides in him, and he in God.
16 And we have known and
believed the love that God has
for us. God is love, and [a]he who
abides in love abides in God,
and God [b]in him.
17 Love has been perfected
among us in this: that [a]we may
have boldness in the day of
judgment; because as He is, so
are we in this world.
18 There is no fear in love; but
perfect love casts out fear, because fear involves torment. But
he who fears has not been made
perfect in love.
19 [a]We love [1]Him because He
first loved us.
20 [a]If someone says, "I love
God," and hates his brother, he
is a liar; for he who does not love
his brother whom he has seen,
[1]how can he love God [b]whom he
has not seen?
21 And [a]this commandment we
have from Him: that he who
loves God *must* love his brother
also.

10 [a]Titus 3:5 [b]1 John 2:2

11 [a]Matt. 18:33

12 [a]John 1:18

13 [a]John 14:20

14 [a]John 1:14 [b]John 3:17; 4:42

15 [a][Rom. 10:9]

16 [a][1 John 3:24] [b][John 14:23]

17 [a]1 John 2:28

19 [a]1 John 4:10 [1]NU omits *Him*

20 [a][1 John 2:4] [b]1 John 4:12 [1]NU *he cannot*

21 [a][Matt. 5:43, 44; 22:39]

CHAPTER 5

1 [a]1 John 2:22; 4:2, 15 [b]John 1:13

2 [a]John 15:10

3 [a]John 14:15 [b]Matt. 11:30; 23:4

4 [a]John 16:33 [b]1 John 2:13; 4:4 [1]M *your*

5 [a]1 Cor. 15:57

6 [a]John 1:31–34 [b][John 14:17]

7 [a][John 1:1] [b]John 10:30 [1]NU, M omit the words from *in heaven* (v. 7) through *on earth* (v. 8). Only 4 or 5 very late mss. contain these words in Greek.

8 [a]John 15:26

9 [a]John 5:34, 37; 8:17, 18 [b][Matt. 3:16, 17] [1]NU *God, that*

10 [a][Rom. 8:16] [b]John 3:18, 33

5

Whoever believes that [a]Jesus
is the Christ is [b]born of God,
and everyone who loves Him
who begot also loves him who is
begotten of Him.
2 By this we know that we
love the children of God, when
we love God and [a]keep His commandments.
3 [a]For this is the love of God,
that we keep His command-
ments. And [b]His commandments
are not burdensome.
4 For [a]whatever is born of God
overcomes the world. And this
is the victory that [b]has overcome
the world—[1]our faith.
5 Who is he who overcomes
the world, but [a]he who believes
that Jesus is the Son of God?
6 This is He who came [a]by
water and blood—Jesus Christ;
not only by water, but by water
and blood. [b]And it is the Spirit
who bears witness, because the
Spirit is truth.
7 For there are three that bear
witness [1]in heaven: the Father,
[a]the Word, and the Holy Spirit;
[b]and these three are one.
8 And there are three that bear
witness on earth: [a]the Spirit, the
water, and the blood; and these
three agree as one.
9 If we receive [a]the witness
of men, the witness of God is
greater; [b]for this is the witness
of [1]God which He has testified
of His Son.
10 He who believes in the Son
of God [a]has the witness in himself; he who does not believe
God [b]has made Him a liar, because he has not believed the
testimony that God has given of
His Son.
11 And this is the testimony:

that God has given us eternal
life, and this life is in His Son.
12 [a]He who has the Son has
[1]life; he who does not have the
Son of God does not have [1]life.
13 These things I have written
to you who believe in the name
of the Son of God, that you may
know that you have eternal life,
[1]and that you may *continue to*
believe in the name of the Son
of God.
14 Now this is the confidence
that we have in Him, that [a]if we
ask anything according to His
will, He hears us.
15 And if we know that He
hears us, whatever we ask, we
know that we have the petitions
that we have asked of Him.
16 If anyone sees his brother
sinning a sin *which does* not *lead*
to death, he will ask, and [a]He
will give him life for those who
commit sin not *leading* to death.
[b]There is sin *leading* to death. [c]I
do not say that he should pray
about that.
17 [a]All unrighteousness is sin,
and there is sin not *leading* to
death.
18 We know that [a]whoever is
born of God does not sin; but
he who has been born of God
[b]keeps[1] [2]himself, and the wicked
one does not touch him.
19 We know that we are of God,
and [a]the whole world lies *under
the sway of* the wicked one.
20 And we know that the [a]Son
of God has come and [b]has given
us an understanding, [c]that we
may know Him who is true; and
we are in Him who is true, in
His Son Jesus Christ. [d]This is the
true God [e]and eternal life.
21 Little children, keep yourselves from idols. Amen.

12 [a][John 3:15, 36; 6:47; 17:2, 3] [1]Or *the life*

13 [1]NU omits the rest of v. 13.

14 [a][1 John 2:28; 3:21, 22]

16 [a]Job 42:8 [b][Matt. 12:31] [c]Jer. 7:16; 14:11

17 [a]1 John 3:4

18 [a][1 Pet. 1:23] [b]James 1:27 [1]*guards* [2]NU *him*

19 [a]Gal. 1:4

20 [a]1 John 4:2 [b]Luke 24:45 [c]John 17:3 [d]Is. 9:6 [e]1 John 5:11, 12

The Second Epistle of

JOHN

"LET him who thinks he stands take heed lest he fall" (1 Cor. 10:12). These words of the apostle Paul could well stand as a subtitle for John's little epistle. The recipients, a chosen lady and her children, were obviously standing. They were walking in truth, remaining faithful to the commandments they had received from the Father. John is deeply pleased to be able to commend them. But he takes nothing for granted. Realizing that standing is just one step removed from falling, he hesitates not at all to issue a reminder: "love one another" (v. 5). The apostle admits that this is not new revelation, but he views it sufficiently important to repeat. Loving one another, he stresses, is equivalent to walking according to God's commandments.

John indicates, however, that this love must be discerning. It is not a naive, unthinking, open-to-anything-and-anyone kind of love. Biblical love is a matter of choice; it is dangerous and foolish to float through life with undiscerning love. False teachers abound who do not acknowledge Christ as having come in the flesh. It is false charity to open the door to false teaching. We must have fellowship with God. We must have fellowship with Christians. But we must not have fellowship with false teachers.

The "elder" of verse 1 has been traditionally identified with the apostle John, resulting in the Greek title *Ioannou B*, the "Second of John."

THE Elder,

To the [1]elect lady and her
children, whom I love in truth,
and not only I, but also all those
who have known [a]the truth,
2 because of the truth which
abides in us and will be with us
forever:

3 [a]Grace, mercy, *and* peace
will be with [1]you from God the
Father and from the Lord Jesus
Christ, the Son of the Father, in
truth and love.

4 I [a]rejoiced greatly that I have
found *some* of your children
walking in truth, as we received
commandment from the Father.
5 And now I plead with you,
lady, not as though I wrote a
new commandment to you, but
that which we have had from
the beginning: [a]that we love one
another.
6 [a]This is love, that we walk according to His commandments.
This is the commandment, that
[b]as you have heard from the beginning, you should walk in it.
7 For [a]many deceivers have
gone out into the world [b]who
do not confess Jesus Christ *as*
coming in the flesh. [c]This is a
deceiver and an antichrist.
8 [a]Look to yourselves, [b]that
[1]we do not lose those things we
worked for, but *that* [1]we may
receive a full reward.
9 [a]Whoever [1]transgresses and
does not abide in the doctrine
of Christ does not have God. He
who abides in the doctrine of

1 [a]Col. 1:5 [1]*chosen*
3 [a]1 Tim. 1:2 [1]NU, M *us*
4 [a]3 John 3, 4
5 [a][John 13:34, 35; 15:12, 17]
6 [a]1 John 2:5; 5:3 [b]1 John 2:24
7 [a]1 John 2:19; 4:1 [b]1 John 4:2 [c]1 John 2:22
8 [a]Mark 13:9 [b]Gal. 3:4 [1]NU *you*
9 [a]John 7:16; 8:31 [1]NU *goes ahead*

Christ has both the Father and
the Son.
10 If anyone comes to you and
[a]does not bring this doctrine, do
not receive him into your house
nor greet him;
11 for he who greets him shares
in his evil deeds.

10 [a]Rom. 16:17

12 [a]3 John 13, 14
[b]John 17:13

13 [a]1 Pet. 5:13

12 [a]Having many things to
write to you, I did not wish *to
do so* with paper and ink; but I
hope to come to you and speak
face to face, [b]that our joy may
be full.
13 [a]The children of your elect
sister greet you. Amen.

The Third Epistle of

JOHN

IN Third John the apostle encourages fellowship with Christian brothers. Following his expression of love for Gaius, John assures him of his prayers for his health and voices his joy over Gaius's persistent walk in truth and for the manner in which he shows hospitality and support for missionaries who have come to his church.

But not everyone in the church feels the same way. Diotrephes' heart is one hundred and eighty degrees removed from Gaius's heart. He is no longer living in love. Pride has taken precedence in his life. He has refused a letter John has written for the church, fearing that his authority might be superseded by that of the apostle. He also has accused John of evil words and refused to accept missionaries. He forbids others to do so and even expels them from the church if they disobey him. John uses this negative example as an opportunity to encourage Gaius to continue his hospitality. Demetrius has a good testimony and may even be one of those turned away by Diotrephes. He is widely known for his good character and his loyalty to the truth. Here he is well commended by John and stands as a positive example for Gaius.

The Greek titles of First, Second, and Third John are *Ioannou A, B,* and *G.* The *G* is gamma, the third letter of the Greek alphabet; *Ioannou G* means the "Third of John."

THE Elder,

To the beloved Gā'i·us, [a]whom
I love in truth:

2 Beloved, I pray that you may
prosper in all things and be in
health, just as your soul prospers.
3 For I [a]rejoiced greatly when
brethren came and testified of
the truth *that is* in you, just as
you walk in the truth.
4 I have no greater [a]joy than to
hear that [b]my children walk in
[1]truth.
5 Beloved, you do faithfully
whatever you do for the brethren [1]and for strangers,
6 who have borne witness of
your love before the church. *If*
you send them forward on their
journey in a manner worthy of
God, you will do well,
7 because they went forth for
His name's sake, [a]taking nothing from the Gentiles.
8 We therefore ought to [a]re-
ceive[1] such, that we may become
fellow workers for the truth.
9 I wrote to the church, but
Dī·ot're·phēs, who loves to have
the preeminence among them,
does not receive us.
10 Therefore, if I come, I will
call to mind his deeds which he
does, [a]prating[1] against us with
malicious words. And not content with that, he himself does
not receive the brethren, and
forbids those who wish to, putting *them* out of the church.
11 Beloved, [a]do not imitate what
is evil, but what is good. [b]He who

1 [a]2 John 1
3 [a]2 John 4
4 [a]1 Thess. 2:19, 20 [b][1 Cor. 4:15] [1]NU *the truth*
5 [1]NU *and especially for*
7 [a]1 Cor. 9:12, 15
8 [a]Matt. 10:40 [1]NU *support*
10 [a]Prov. 10:8, 10 [1]*talking nonsense*
11 [a]Ps. 34:14; 37:27 [b][1 John 2:29; 3:10]

does good is of God, [1]but he who
does evil has not seen [c]God.
12 De·mē′tri·us [a]has a *good* testimony from all, and from the
truth itself. And we also [1]bear
witness, [b]and you know that our
testimony is true.

11 [c][1 John 3:10]
[1]NU, M omit *but*

12 [a]1 Tim. 3:7
[b]John 19:35; 21:24
[1]*testify*

13 [a]2 John 12

13 [a]I had many things to write,
but I do not wish to write to you
with pen and ink;
14 but I hope to see you shortly,
and we shall speak face to face.
Peace to you. Our friends greet
you. Greet the friends by name.

The Epistle of

JUDE

FIGHT! Contend! Do battle! When apostasy arises, when false teachers emerge, when the truth of God is attacked, it is time to fight for the faith. Only believers who are spiritually "in shape" can answer the summons. At the beginning of his letter Jude focuses on the believers' common salvation but then feels compelled to challenge them to contend for the faith. The danger is real. False teachers have crept into the church, turning God's grace into unbounded license to do as they please. Jude reminds such men of God's past dealings with unbelieving Israel, disobedient angels, and wicked Sodom and Gomorrah. In the face of such danger Christians should not be caught off guard. The challenge is great, but so is the God who is able to keep them from stumbling.

The Greek title *Iouda,* "Of Jude," comes from the name *Ioudas* that appears in verse 1. This name, which can be translated Jude or Judas, was popular in the first century because of Judas Maccabaeus (died 160 B.C.), a leader of the Jewish resistance against Syria during the Maccabean revolt.

JUDE, a bondservant of Jesus
Christ, and [a]brother of James,

To those who are [b]called,
[1]sanctified by God the Father,
and [c]preserved in Jesus Christ:

2 Mercy, [a]peace, and love be
multiplied to you.

3 Beloved, while I was very diligent to write to you [a]concerning
our common salvation, I found it
necessary to write to you exhorting [b]you to contend earnestly for
the faith which was once for all
delivered to the saints.
4 For certain men have crept
in unnoticed, who long ago were
marked out for this condemnation, ungodly men, who turn the
grace of our God into lewdness
and deny the only Lord [1]God
and our Lord Jesus Christ.
5 But I want to remind you,
though you once knew this, that
[a]the Lord, having saved the people out of the land of Egypt,
afterward destroyed those who
did not believe.
6 And the angels who did not
keep their [1]proper domain, but
left their own abode, He has reserved in everlasting chains under darkness for the judgment
of the great day;
7 as [a]Sod′om and Go·mor′rah,
and the cities around them in a
similar manner to these, having
given themselves over to sexual immorality and gone after
strange flesh, are set forth as
an example, suffering the [1]ven-
geance of eternal fire.
8 [a]Likewise also these dream-
ers defile the flesh, reject authority, and [b]speak evil of [1]digni-
taries.
9 Yet Michael the archangel, in
[1]contending with the devil, when
he disputed about the body of
Moses, dared not bring against

1 [a]Acts 1:13 [b]Rom. 1:7 [c]John 17:11, 12 [1]NU *beloved*
2 [a]1 Pet. 1:2
3 [a]Titus 1:4 [b]Phil. 1:27
4 [1]NU omits *God*
5 [a]1 Cor. 10:5–10
6 [1]*own*
7 [a]Gen. 19:24 [1]*punishment*
8 [a]2 Pet. 2:10 [b]Ex. 22:28 [1]*glorious ones,* lit. *glories*
9 [1]*arguing*

him a reviling accusation, but
said, [a]"The Lord rebuke you!"
10 [a]But these speak evil of
whatever they do not know; and
whatever they know naturally,
like brute beasts, in these things
they corrupt themselves.
11 Woe to them! For they have
gone in the way [a]of Cain, [b]have
run greedily in the error of Bā′-
laam for profit, and perished [c]in
the rebellion of Kō′rah.
12 These are [1]spots in your love
feasts, while they feast with you
without fear, serving *only* themselves. *They are* clouds without water, carried [2]about by the
winds; late autumn trees without fruit, twice dead, pulled up
by the roots;
13 [a]raging waves of the sea,
[b]foaming up their own shame;
wandering stars [c]for whom is
reserved the blackness of darkness forever.
☆ 14 Now Ē′noch, the seventh
from Adam, prophesied about
these men also, saying, [a]"Behold,
the Lord comes with ten thousands of His saints,
15 "to execute judgment on all,
to convict all who are ungodly
among them of all their ungodly
deeds which they have committed in an ungodly way, and
of all the [a]harsh things which
ungodly sinners have spoken
against Him."
16 These are grumblers, com-
plainers, walking according to
their own lusts; and they [a]mouth
great swelling *words,* [b]flattering
people to gain advantage.
17 [a]But you, beloved, remember
the words which were spoken
before by the apostles of our
Lord Jesus Christ:
18 how they told you that [a]there
would be mockers in the last
time who would walk according
to their own ungodly lusts.
19 These are [1]sensual persons,
who cause divisions, not having
the Spirit.
20 But you, beloved, [a]building
yourselves up on your most
holy faith, [b]praying in the Holy
Spirit,
21 keep yourselves in the love
of God, [a]looking for the mercy
of our Lord Jesus Christ unto
eternal life.
22 And on some have compassion, [1]making a distinction;
23 but [a]others save [1]with fear,
[b]pulling *them* out of the [2]fire,
hating even [c]the garment defiled
by the flesh.

24 [a]Now to Him who is able
to keep [1]you from
stumbling,
And [b]to present *you*
faultless
Before the presence of His
glory with exceeding joy,
25 To [1]God our Savior,
[2]Who alone is wise,
Be glory and majesty,
Dominion and [3]power,
Both now and forever.
Amen.

9 [a]Zech. 3:2
10 [a]2 Pet. 2:12
11 [a]Gen. 4:3–8 [b]2 Pet. 2:15 [c]Num. 16:1–3, 31–35
12 [1]*stains, or hidden reefs* [2]NU, M *along*
13 [a]Is. 57:20 [b][Phil. 3:19] [c]2 Pet. 2:17
14 [a]Matt. 16:27; 25:31
15 [a]1 Sam. 2:3
16 [a]2 Pet. 2:18 [b]Prov. 28:21
17 [a]2 Pet. 3:2
18 [a][1 Tim. 4:1]
19 [1]*soulish or worldly*
20 [a]Col. 2:7 [b][Rom. 8:26]
21 [a]Titus 2:13
22 [1]NU *who are doubting* (or *making distinctions*)
23 [a]Rom. 11:14 [b]Amos 4:11 [c][Zech. 3:4, 5] [1]NU omits *with fear* [2]NU adds *and on some have mercy with fear*
24 [a][Eph. 3:20] [b]Col. 1:22 [1]M *them*
25 [1]NU *the only God our* [2]NU *Through Jesus Christ our Lord, Be glory* [3]NU adds *Before all time,*

THE REVELATION

of Jesus Christ

JUST as Genesis is the book of beginnings, Revelation is the book of consummation. In it, the divine program of redemption is brought to fruition, and the holy name of God is vindicated before all creation. Although there are numerous prophecies in the Gospels and Epistles, Revelation is the only New Testament book that focuses primarily on prophetic events. Its title means "unveiling" or "disclosure." Thus, the book is an unveiling of the character and program of God. Penned by John during his exile on the island of Patmos, Revelation centers around visions and symbols of the resurrected Christ, who alone has authority to judge the earth, to remake it, and to rule it in righteousness.

The title of this book in the Greek text is *Apokalypsis Ioannou,* "Revelation of John." It is also known as the Apocalypse, a transliteration of the word *apokalypsis,* meaning "unveiling," "disclosure," or "revelation." Thus, the book is an unveiling of that which otherwise could not be known. A better title comes from the first verse: *Apokalypsis Iesou Christou,* "Revelation of Jesus Christ." This could be taken as a revelation which came from Christ or as a revelation which is about Christ—both are appropriate. Because of the unified contents of this book, it should not be called Revelations.

CHAPTER 1

THE Revelation of Jesus Christ,
[a]which God gave Him to show
His servants—things which must
[1]shortly take place. And [b]He sent
and signified *it* by His angel to
His servant John,
2 [a]who bore witness to the word
of God, and to the testimony of
Jesus Christ, to all things [b]that he
saw.
3 [a]Blessed *is* he who reads and
those who hear the words of this
prophecy, and keep those things
which are written in it; for [b]the
time *is* near.

4 John, to the seven churches
which are in Asia:

Grace to you and peace from
Him [a]who is and [b]who was and
who is to come, [c]and from the
seven Spirits who are before His
throne,
5 and from Jesus Christ, [a]the ★
faithful [b]witness, the [c]firstborn
from the dead, and [d]the ruler
over the kings of the earth. To
Him [e]who [1]loved us [f]and washed
us from our sins in His own
blood,
6 and has [a]made us [1]kings and
priests to His God and Father,
[b]to Him *be* glory and dominion
forever and ever. Amen.
7 Behold, He is coming with
[a]clouds, and every eye will see
Him, even [b]they who pierced
Him. And all the tribes of the
earth will mourn because of
Him. Even so, Amen.
8 [a]"I am the Alpha and the
Omega, [1]*the* Beginning and *the*
End," says the [2]Lord, [b]"who is

1 [a]John 3:32 [b]Rev. 22:6 [1]*quickly* or *swiftly*
2 [a]1 Cor. 1:6 [b]1 John 1:1
3 [a]Luke 11:28 [b]James 5:8
4 [a]Ex. 3:14 [b]John 1:1 [c][Is. 11:2]
5 [a]John 8:14 [b]Is. 55:4 [c]Ps. 89:27; [Col. 1:18] [d]Rev. 17:14 [e]John 13:34 [f]Heb. 9:14 [1]NU *loves us and freed;* M *loves us and washed*
6 [a]1 Pet. 2:5, 9 [b]1 Tim. 6:16 [1]NU, M *a kingdom*
7 [a]Matt. 24:30 [b]Zech. 12:10–14
8 [a]Is. 41:4 [b]Rev. 4:8; 11:17 [1]NU, M omit *the Beginning and the End* [2]NU, M *Lord God*

and who was and who is to
come, the [c]Almighty."
9 I, John, [1]both your brother
and [a]companion in the tribulation and [b]kingdom and patience
of Jesus Christ, was on the island that is called Pat′mos for
the word of God and for the
testimony of Jesus Christ.
10 [a]I was in the Spirit on [b]the
Lord's Day, and I heard behind
me [c]a loud voice, as of a trumpet,
11 saying, [1]"I am the Alpha and
the Omega, the First and the
Last," and, "What you see, write
in a book and send *it* to the
seven churches [2]which are in
Asia: to Eph′e·sus, to Smyrna,
to Per′ga·mos, to Thȳ·a·tī′ra, to
Sar′dis, to Philadelphia, and to
Lā·o·di·cē′a."
12 Then I turned to see the voice
that spoke with me. And having turned [a]I saw seven golden
lampstands,
13 [a]and in the midst of the seven
lampstands [b]*One* like the Son of
Man, [c]clothed with a garment
down to the feet and [d]girded
about the chest with a golden
band.
14 His head and [a]hair *were*
white like wool, as white as
snow, and [b]His eyes like a flame
of fire;
15 [a]His feet *were* like fine brass,
as if refined in a furnace, and
[b]His voice as the sound of many
waters;
16 [a]He had in His right hand
seven stars, [b]out of His mouth
went a sharp two-edged sword,
[c]and His countenance *was* like
the sun shining in its strength.
17 And [a]when I saw Him, I fell
at His feet as dead. But [b]He laid
His right hand on me, saying [1]to
me, "Do not be afraid; [c]I am the
First and the Last.
18 [a]"I *am* He who lives, and
was dead, and behold, [b]I am
alive forevermore. Amen. And [c]I
have the keys of [1]Hā′dēs and of
Death.
19 [1]"Write the things which
you have [a]seen, [b]and the things
which are, [c]and the things which
will take place after this.
20 "The [1]mystery of the seven
stars which you saw in My right
hand, and the seven golden
lampstands: The seven stars
are [a]the [2]angels of the seven
churches, and [b]the seven lampstands [3]which you saw are the
seven churches.

2

"To the [1]angel of the church
of Eph′e·sus write,
'These things says [a]He who
holds the seven stars in His right
hand, [b]who walks in the midst of
the seven golden lampstands:
2 [a]"I know your works, your
labor, your [1]patience, and that
you cannot [2]bear those who are
evil. And [b]you have tested those
[c]who say they are apostles and
are not, and have found them
liars;
3 "and you have persevered
and have patience, and have
labored for My name's sake and
have [a]not become weary.
4 "Nevertheless I have *this*
against you, that you have left
your first love.
5 "Remember therefore from
where you have fallen; repent
and do the first works, [a]or else
I will come to you quickly and
remove your lampstand from its
place—unless you repent.
6 "But this you have, that you
hate the deeds of the Nic·ō·lā′-
i·tans, which I also hate.

8 [c]Is. 9:6

9 [a]Phil. 1:7 [b][2 Tim. 2:12] [1]NU, M omit *both*

10 [a]Acts 10:10 [b]Acts 20:7 [c]Rev. 4:1

11 [1]NU, M omit *"I am the Alpha and the Omega, the First and the Last," and,* [2]NU, M omit *which are in Asia*

12 [a]Ex. 25:37

13 [a]Rev. 2:1 [b]Ezek. 1:26 [c]Dan. 10:5 [d]Rev. 15:6

14 [a]Dan. 7:9 [b]Dan. 10:6

15 [a]Ezek. 1:7 [b]Ezek. 1:24; 43:2

16 [a]Rev. 1:20; 2:1; 3:1 [b]Is. 49:2 [c]Matt. 17:2

17 [a]Ezek. 1:28 [b]Dan. 8:18; 10:10, 12 [c]Is. 41:4; 44:6; 48:12 [1]NU, M omit *to me*

18 [a]Rom. 6:9 [b]Rev. 4:9 [c]Ps. 68:20 [1]Lit. *Unseen;* the unseen realm

19 [a]Rev. 1:9–18 [b]Rev. 2:1 [c]Rev. 4:1 [1]NU, M *Therefore, write*

20 [a]Rev. 2:1 [b]Zech. 4:2 [1]*hidden truth* [2]Or *messengers* [3]NU, M omit *which you saw*

CHAPTER 2

1 [a]Rev. 1:16 [b]Rev. 1:13 [1]Or *messenger*

2 [a]Ps. 1:6 [b]1 John 4:1 [c]2 Cor. 11:13 [1]*perseverance* [2]*endure*

3 [a]Gal. 6:9

5 [a]Matt. 21:41

7 [a]"He who has an ear, let him
hear what the Spirit says to
the churches. To him who overcomes I will give [b]to eat from
[c]the tree of life, which is in the
midst of the Paradise of God." '
8 "And to the [1]angel of the
church in Smyrna write,
'These things says [a]the First
and the Last, who was dead, and
came to life:
9 "I know your works, tribulation, and poverty (but you
are [a]rich); and *I know* the blasphemy of [b]those who say they
are Jews and are not, [c]but *are* a
[1]synagogue of Satan.
10 [a]"Do not fear any of those
things which you are about to
suffer. Indeed, the devil is about
to throw *some* of you into prison,
that you may be tested, and you
will have tribulation ten days.
[b]Be faithful until death, and I
will give you [c]the crown of life.
11 [a]"He who has an ear, let him
hear what the Spirit says to the
churches. He who overcomes
shall not be hurt by [b]the second
death." '
12 "And to the [1]angel of the
church in Per'ga·mos write,
'These things says [a]He who
has the sharp two-edged sword:
13 "I know your works, and
where you dwell, where Satan's
throne *is.* And you hold fast to
My name, and did not deny My
faith even in the days in which
An'ti·pas *was* My faithful martyr, who was killed among you,
where Satan dwells.
14 "But I have a few things
against you, because you have
there those who hold the doctrine of [a]Bā'laam, who taught
Bā'lak to put a stumbling block
before the children of Israel, [b]to
eat things sacrificed to idols,
[c]and to commit sexual immorality.
15 "Thus you also have those
who hold the doctrine of the
Nic·ō·lā'i·tans, [1]which thing I
hate.
16 "Repent, or else I will come
to you quickly and [a]will fight
against them with the sword of
My mouth.
17 "He who has an ear, let him
hear what the Spirit says to
the churches. To him who overcomes I will give some of the
hidden [a]manna to eat. And I will
give him a white stone, and on
the stone [b]a new name written
which no one knows except him
who receives *it.*" '
18 "And to the [1]angel of the
church in Thy̅·a·tī'ra write,
'These things says the Son of
God, [a]who has eyes like a flame
of fire, and His feet like fine
brass:
19 [a]"I know your works, love,
[1]service, faith, and your [2]pa-
tience; and *as* for your works,
the last *are* more than the first.
20 "Nevertheless I have [1]a few
things against you, because you
allow [2]that woman [a]Jez'e·bel,
who calls herself a prophetess,
[3]to teach and seduce My servants [b]to commit sexual immorality and eat things sacrificed
to idols.
21 "And I gave her time [a]to [1]re-
pent of her sexual immorality,
and she did not repent.
22 "Indeed I will cast her into
a sickbed, and those who commit adultery with her into great
tribulation, unless they repent of
[1]their deeds.
23 "I will kill her children with
death, and all the churches shall

7 [a]Matt. 11:15 [b][Rev. 22:2, 14] [c][Gen. 2:9; 3:22]
8 [a]Rev. 1:8, 17, 18 [1]Or *messenger*
9 [a]Luke 12:21 [b]Rom. 2:17 [c]Rev. 3:9 [1]*congregation*
10 [a]Matt. 10:22 [b]Matt. 24:13 [c]James 1:12
11 [a]Rev. 13:9 [b][Rev. 20:6, 14; 21:8]
12 [a]Rev. 1:16; 2:16 [1]Or *messenger*
14 [a]Num. 31:16 [b]Acts 15:29 [c]1 Cor. 6:13
15 [1]NU, M *likewise.*
16 [a]2 Thess. 2:8
17 [a]Ex. 16:33, 34 [b]Rev. 3:12
18 [a]Rev. 1:14, 15 [1]Or *messenger*
19 [a]Rev. 2:2 [1]NU, M *faith, service* [2]*perseverance*
20 [a]1 Kin. 16:31; 21:25 [b]Ex. 34:15 [1]NU, M *against you that you tolerate* [2]M *your wife Jezebel* [3]NU, M *and teaches and seduces*
21 [a]Rev. 9:20; 16:9, 11 [1]NU, M *repent, and she does not want to repent of her sexual immorality.*
22 [1]NU, M *her*

know that I am He who [a]searches[1]
the minds and hearts. And I will
give to each one of you according to your works.
24 "Now to you I say, [1]and to the
rest in Thy̆·a·tī′ra, as many as do
not have this doctrine, who have
not known the [a]depths of Satan,
as they say, [b]I [2]will put on you no
other burden.
25 "But hold fast [a]what you have
till I come.
26 "And he who overcomes, and
keeps [a]My works until the end,
[b]to him I will give power over
the nations—

☆27 *'He[a] shall rule them with a*
rod of iron;
They shall be dashed to
pieces like the potter's
vessels'—

as I also have received from My
Father;
28 "and I will give him [a]the
morning star.
29 "He who has an ear, let him
hear what the Spirit says to the
churches." '

3

"And to the [1]angel of the
church in Sar′dis write,
'These things says He who
[a]has the seven Spirits of God
and the seven stars: "I know
your works, that you have a
name that you are alive, but you
are dead.
2 "Be watchful, and strengthen
the things which remain, that
are ready to die, for I have not
found your works perfect before
[1]God.
3 [a]"Remember therefore how
you have received and heard;
hold fast and [b]repent. [c]Therefore
if you will not watch, I will come
upon you [d]as a thief, and you
will not know what hour I will
come upon you.
4 [1]"You have [a]a few names
[2]even in Sar′dis who have not
[b]defiled their garments; and they
shall walk with Me [c]in white, for
they are worthy.
5 "He who overcomes [a]shall be
clothed in white garments, and I
will not [b]blot out his name from
the [c]Book of Life; but [d]I will confess his name before My Father
and before His angels.
6 [a]"He who has an ear, let him
hear what the Spirit says to the
churches." '
7 "And to the [1]angel of the ★
church in Philadelphia write,
'These things says [a]He who
is holy, [b]He who is true, [c]*"He*
who has the key of David, [d]*He*
who opens and no one shuts,
and [e]*shuts and no one opens"*:
8 [a]"I know your works. See,
I have set before you [b]an open
door, [1]and no one can shut it; for
you have a little strength, have
kept My word, and have not denied My name.
9 "Indeed I will make [a]*those* of
the synagogue of Satan, who say
they are Jews and are not, but
lie—indeed [b]I will make them
come and worship before your
feet, and to know that I have
loved you.
10 "Because you have kept [1]My
command to persevere, [a]I also
will keep you from the hour of
trial which shall come upon [b]the
whole world, to test those who
dwell [c]on the earth.
11 [1]"Behold, [a]I am coming
quickly! [b]Hold fast what you
have, that no one may take [c]your
crown.
12 "He who overcomes, I will
make him [a]a pillar in the temple

---

23 [a]Jer. 11:20; 17:10 [1]*examines*
24 [a]2 Tim. 3:1–9 [b]Acts 15:28 [1]NU, M omit *and* [2]NU, M omit *will*
25 [a]Rev. 3:11
26 [a][John 6:29] [b][Matt. 19:28]
27 [a]Ps. 2:8, 9; Rev. 12:5; 19:15
28 [a]2 Pet. 1:19

CHAPTER 3

1 [a]Rev. 1:4, 16 [1]Or *messenger*
2 [1]NU, M *My God*
3 [a]1 Tim. 6:20 [b]Rev. 3:19 [c]Matt. 24:42, 43 [d][Rev. 16:15]
4 [a]Acts 1:15 [b][Jude 23] [c]Rev. 4:4; 6:11 [1]NU, M *Nevertheless you* [2]NU, M omit *even*
5 [a][Rev. 19:8] [b]Ex. 32:32 [c]Phil. 4:3 [d]Luke 12:8
6 [a]Rev. 2:7
7 [a]Acts 3:14 [b]1 John 5:20 [c]Is. 9:7; 22:22 [d][Matt. 16:19] [e]Job 12:14 [1]Or *messenger*
8 [a]Rev. 3:1 [b]1 Cor. 16:9 [1]NU, M *which no one can shut*
9 [a]Rev. 2:9 [b]Is. 45:14; 49:23; 60:14
10 [a]2 Pet. 2:9 [b]Luke 2:1 [c]Is. 24:17 [1]Lit. *the word of My patience*
11 [a]Phil. 4:5 [b]Rev. 2:25 [c][Rev. 2:10] [1]NU, M omit *Behold*
12 [a]1 Kin. 7:21

of My God, and he shall [b]go out
no more. [c]I will write on him the
name of My God and the name
of the city of My God, the [d]New
Jerusalem, which [e]comes down
out of heaven from My God.
[f]And *I will write on him* My new
name.
13 [a]"He who has an ear, let him
hear what the Spirit says to the
churches." '
14 "And to the [1]angel of the
church [2]of the Lā·o·di·cē'ans
write,
[a]'These things says the Amen,
[b]the Faithful and True Witness,
[c]the Beginning of the creation of
God:
15 [a]"I know your works, that you
are neither cold nor hot. I could
wish you were cold or hot.
16 "So then, because you are
lukewarm, and neither [1]cold nor
hot, I will vomit you out of My
mouth.
17 "Because you say, [a]'I am rich,
have become wealthy, and have
need of nothing'—and do not
know that you are wretched,
miserable, poor, blind, and naked—
18 "I counsel you [a]to buy from
Me gold refined in the fire, that
you may be rich; and [b]white garments, that you may be clothed,
that the shame of your nakedness may not be revealed; and
anoint your eyes with eye salve,
that you may see.
19 [a]"As many as I love, I rebuke and [b]chasten.[1] Therefore
be [2]zealous and repent.
20 "Behold, [a]I stand at the door
and knock. [b]If anyone hears My
voice and opens the door, [c]I will
come in to him and dine with
him, and he with Me.
21 "To him who overcomes [a]I
will grant to sit with Me on My
throne, as I also overcame and
sat down with My Father on His
throne.
22 [a]"He who has an ear, let him
hear what the Spirit says to the
churches." ' "

4 After these things I looked,
and behold, a door *standing*
[a]open in heaven. And the first
voice which I heard *was* like a
[b]trumpet speaking with me, saying, "Come up here, and I will
show you things which must
take place after this."
2 Immediately [a]I was in the
Spirit; and behold, [b]a throne set
in heaven, and *One* sat on the
throne.
3 [1]And He who sat there was
[a]like a jasper and a sardius stone
in appearance; [b]and *there was* a
rainbow around the throne, in
appearance like an emerald.
4 [a]Around the throne *were*
twenty-four thrones, and on the
thrones I saw twenty-four elders
sitting, [b]clothed in white [1]robes;
and they had crowns of gold on
their heads.
5 And from the throne proceeded [a]lightnings, [1]thunderings,
and voices. [b]Seven lamps of fire
were burning before the throne,
which are [c]the[2] seven Spirits of
God.
6 Before the throne *there* [1]*was*
[a]a sea of glass, like crystal. [b]And
in the midst of the throne, and
around the throne, *were* four living creatures full of eyes in front
and in back.
7 [a]The first living creature *was*
like a lion, the second living
creature like a calf, the third
living creature had a face like a
man, and the fourth living creature *was* like a flying eagle.

12 [b]Ps. 23:6 [c][Rev. 14:1; 22:4] [d][Heb. 12:22] [e]Rev. 21:2 [f][Rev. 2:17; 22:4]

13 [a]Rev. 2:7

14 [a]2 Cor. 1:20 [b]Rev. 1:5; 3:7; 19:11 [c][Col. 1:15] [1]Or *messenger* [2]NU, M *in Laodicea*

15 [a]Rev. 3:1

16 [1]NU, M *hot nor cold*

17 [a]Hos. 12:8

18 [a]Is. 55:1 [b]2 Cor. 5:3

19 [a]Job 5:17 [b]Heb. 12:6 [1]*discipline* [2]*eager*

20 [a]Song 5:2 [b]Luke 12:36, 37 [c][John 14:23]

21 [a]Matt. 19:28

22 [a]Rev. 2:7

CHAPTER 4

1 [a]Ezek. 1:1 [b]Rev. 1:10

2 [a]Rev. 1:10 [b]Is. 6:1

3 [a]Rev. 21:11 [b]Ezek. 1:28 [1]M omits *And He who sat there was*, making the following a description of the throne.

4 [a]Rev. 11:16 [b]Rev. 3:4, 5 [1]NU, M *robes, with crowns*

5 [a]Rev. 8:5; 11:19; 16:18 [b]Ex. 37:23 [c][Rev. 1:4] [1]NU, M *voices, and thunderings.* [2]M omits *the*

6 [a]Rev. 15:2 [b]Ezek. 1:5 [1]NU, M add *something like*

7 [a]Ezek. 1:10; 10:14

8 *The* four living creatures,
each having [a]six wings, were full
of eyes around and within. And
they do not rest day or night,
saying:

[b]"Holy,[1] holy, holy,
[c]Lord God Almighty,
[d]Who was and is and is to
come!"

9 Whenever the living creatures give glory and honor and
thanks to Him who sits on the
throne, [a]who lives forever and
ever,
10 [a]the twenty-four elders fall
down before Him who sits on
the throne and worship Him
who lives forever and ever, and
cast their crowns before the
throne, saying:

11 "You[a] are worthy, [1]O Lord,
To receive glory and honor
and power;
[b]For You created all things,
And by [c]Your will they [2]exist
and were created."

5

5 And I saw in the right *hand*
of Him who sat on the
throne [a]a scroll written inside
and on the back, [b]sealed with
seven seals.
2 Then I saw a strong angel
proclaiming with a loud voice,
[a]"Who is worthy to open the
scroll and to loose its seals?"
3 And no one in heaven or on
the earth or under the earth was
able to open the scroll, or to look
at it.
4 So I wept much, because no
one was found worthy to open
[1]and read the scroll, or to look
at it.
5 But one of the elders said to

8 [a]Is. 6:2
[b]Is. 6:3
[c]Rev. 1:8
[d]Rev. 1:4
[1]M has *holy* nine times.

9 [a]Rev. 1:18

10 [a]Rev. 5:8, 14; 7:11; 11:16; 19:4

11 [a]Rev. 1:6; 5:12
[b]Gen. 1:1
[c]Col. 1:16
[1]NU, M *our Lord and God*
[2]NU, M *existed*

CHAPTER 5

1 [a]Ezek. 2:9, 10
[b]Is. 29:11

2 [a]Rev. 4:11; 5:9

4 [1]NU, M omit *and read*

5 [a]Gen. 49:9
[b]Heb. 7:14
[c]Is. 11:1, 10
[d]Rev. 3:21
[e]Rev. 6:1
[1]NU, M omit *to loose*

6 [a][John 1:29]
[b]Zech. 3:9; 4:10
[c]Rev. 1:4; 3:1; 4:5
[1]NU, M *I saw in the midst . . . a Lamb standing*

7 [a]Rev. 4:2

8 [a]Rev. 4:8–10; 19:4
[b]Rev. 8:3

9 [a]Rev. 14:3
[b]Rev. 4:11
[c]John 1:29
[d][Heb. 9:12]

10 [a]Ex. 19:6
[b]Is. 61:6
[1]NU, M *them*
[2]NU *a kingdom*
[3]NU, M *they*

me, "Do not weep. Behold, [a]the
Lion of the tribe of [b]Judah, [c]the
Root of David, has [d]prevailed to
open the scroll [e]and [1]to loose its
seven seals."
6 And I looked, [1]and behold,
in the midst of the throne and
of the four living creatures, and
in the midst of the elders, stood
[a]a Lamb as though it had been
slain, having seven horns and
[b]seven eyes, which are [c]the seven
Spirits of God sent out into all
the earth.
7 Then He came and took the
scroll out of the right hand [a]of
Him who sat on the throne.
8 Now when He had taken the
scroll, [a]the four living creatures
and the twenty-four elders fell
down before the Lamb, each
having a harp, and golden bowls
full of incense, which are the
[b]prayers of the saints.
9 And [a]they sang a new song,
saying:

[b]"You are worthy to take the
scroll,
And to open its seals;
For You were slain,
And [c]have redeemed us to
God [d]by Your blood
Out of every tribe and
tongue and people and
nation,
10 And have made [1]us [a]kings[2]
and [b]priests to our God;
And [3]we shall reign on the
earth."

11 Then I looked, and I heard
the voice of many angels around
the throne, the living creatures,
and the elders; and the number
of them was ten thousand times
ten thousand, and thousands of
thousands,

★ 12 saying with a loud voice:

"Worthy is the [a]Lamb who
was slain
To receive power and riches
and wisdom,
And strength and honor and
glory and blessing!"

13 And [a]every creature which is in heaven and on the earth and under the earth and such as are in the sea, and all that are in them, I heard saying:

[b]"Blessing and honor and
glory and power
Be to Him [c]who sits on the
throne,
And to the Lamb, forever
and [1]ever!"

14 Then the four living creatures said, "Amen!" And the [1]twenty-four elders fell down and worshiped [2]Him who lives forever and ever.

6

Now [a]I saw when the Lamb opened one of the [1]seals; and I heard [b]one of the four living creatures saying with a voice like thunder, "Come and see."

2 And I looked, and behold, [a]a white horse. [b]He who sat on it had a bow; [c]and a crown was given to him, and he went out [d]conquering and to conquer.

3 When He opened the second seal, [a]I heard the second living creature saying, "Come [1]and see."

4 [a]Another horse, fiery red, went out. And it was granted to the one who sat on it to [b]take peace from the earth, and that *people* should kill one another; and there was given to him a great sword.

5 When He opened the third seal, [a]I heard the third living creature say, "Come and see." So I looked, and behold, [b]a black horse, and he who sat on it had a pair of [c]scales[1] in his hand.

6 And I heard a voice in the midst of the four living creatures saying, "A [1]quart of wheat for a [2]denarius, and three quarts of barley for a denarius; and [a]do not harm the oil and the wine."

7 When He opened the fourth seal, [a]I heard the voice of the fourth living creature saying, "Come and see."

8 [a]So I looked, and behold, a pale horse. And the name of him who sat on it was Death, and Hā′dēs followed with him. And [1]power was given to them over a fourth of the earth, [b]to kill with sword, with hunger, with death, [c]and by the beasts of the earth.

9 When He opened the fifth seal, I saw under [a]the altar [b]the souls of those who had been slain [c]for the word of God and for [d]the testimony which they held.

10 And they cried with a loud voice, saying, [a]"How long, O Lord, [b]holy and true, [c]until You judge and avenge our blood on those who dwell on the earth?"

11 Then a [a]white robe was given to each of them; and it was said to them [b]that they should rest a little while longer, until both *the number of* their fellow servants and their brethren, who would be killed as they *were*, was completed.

12 I looked when He opened the sixth seal, [a]and [1]behold, there was a great earthquake; and [b]the sun became black as sackcloth

---

12 [a]Is. 53:7

13 [a]Phil. 2:10 [b]1 Chr. 29:11 [c]Rev. 4:2, 3; 6:16; 20:11 [1]M adds *Amen*

14 [1]NU, M omit *twenty-four* [2]NU, M omit *Him who lives forever and ever*

CHAPTER 6

1 [a][Rev. 5:5–7, 12; 13:8] [b]Rev. 4:7 [1]NU, M *seven seals*

2 [a]Zech. 1:8; 6:3 [b]Ps. 45:4, 5, LXX [c]Zech. 6:11 [d]Matt. 24:5

3 [a]Rev. 4:7 [1]NU, M omit *and see*

4 [a]Zech. 1:8; 6:2 [b]Matt. 24:6, 7

5 [a]Rev. 4:7 [b]Zech. 6:2, 6 [c]Matt. 24:7 [1]*balances*

6 [a]Rev. 7:3; 9:4 [1]Gr. *choinix,* about 1 quart [2]About 1 day's wage for a worker

7 [a]Rev. 4:7

8 [a]Zech. 6:3 [b]Ezek. 5:12, 17; 14:21; 29:5 [c]Lev. 26:22 [1]*authority*

9 [a]Rev. 8:3 [b][Rev. 20:4] [c]Rev. 1:2, 9 [d]2 Tim. 1:8

10 [a]Zech. 1:12 [b]Rev. 3:7 [c]Rev. 11:18

11 [a]Rev. 3:4, 5; 7:9 [b]Heb. 11:40

12 [a]Matt. 24:7 [b]Joel 2:10, 31; 3:15 [1]NU, M omit *behold*

of hair, and the [2]moon became
like blood.
13 [a]And the stars of heaven fell
to the earth, as a fig tree drops
its late figs when it is shaken by
a mighty wind.
14 [a]Then the sky [1]receded as a
scroll when it is rolled up, and
[b]every mountain and island was
moved out of its place.
15 And the [a]kings of the earth,
the great men, [1]the rich men, the
commanders, the mighty men,
every slave and every free man,
[b]hid themselves in the caves and
in the rocks of the mountains,
16 [a]and said to the mountains
and rocks, "Fall on us and hide
us from the face of Him who
[b]sits on the throne and from the
wrath of the Lamb!
17 "For the great day of His
wrath has come, [a]and who is
able to stand?"

7 After these things I saw four
angels standing at the four
corners of the earth, [a]holding
the four winds of the earth, [b]that
the wind should not blow on
the earth, on the sea, or on any
tree.
2 Then I saw another angel
ascending from the east, having
the seal of the living God. And
he cried with a loud voice to
the four angels to whom it was
granted to harm the earth and
the sea,
3 saying, [a]"Do not harm the
earth, the sea, or the trees till we
have sealed the servants of our
God [b]on their foreheads."
4 [a]And I heard the number of
those who were sealed. [b]One
hundred *and* forty-four thousand [c]of all the tribes of the children of Israel *were* sealed:

12 [2]NU, M *whole moon*

13 [a]Rev. 8:10; 9:1

14 [a]Is. 34:4
[b]Rev. 16:20
[1]Or *split apart*

15 [a]Ps. 2:2–4
[b]Is. 2:10, 19, 21; 24:21
[1]NU, M *the commanders, the rich men,*

16 [a]Luke 23:29, 30
[b]Rev. 20:11

17 [a]Zeph. 1:14

CHAPTER 7

1 [a]Dan. 7:2
[b]Rev. 7:3; 8:7; 9:4

3 [a]Rev. 6:6
[b]Rev. 22:4

4 [a]Rev. 9:16
[b]Rev. 14:1, 3
[c]Gen. 49:1–27

5 [1]NU, M omit *sealed* in vv. 5b–8b.

9 [a]Rom. 11:25
[b]Rev. 5:9
[c]Rev. 3:5, 18; 4:4; 6:11

10 [a]Ps. 3:8

5 of the tribe of Judah
twelve thousand *were*
sealed;
of the tribe of Reuben
twelve thousand *were*
[1]sealed;
of the tribe of Gad
twelve thousand *were*
sealed;
6 of the tribe of Ash′er
twelve thousand *were*
sealed;
of the tribe of Naph′ta·lī
twelve thousand *were*
sealed;
of the tribe of Ma·nas′seh
twelve thousand *were*
sealed;
7 of the tribe of Sim′ē·on
twelve thousand *were*
sealed;
of the tribe of Levi
twelve thousand *were*
sealed;
of the tribe of Is′sa·char
twelve thousand *were*
sealed;
8 of the tribe of Zeb′ū·lun
twelve thousand *were*
sealed;
of the tribe of Joseph
twelve thousand *were*
sealed;
of the tribe of Benjamin
twelve thousand *were*
sealed.

9 After these things I looked,
and behold, [a]a great multitude
which no one could number,
[b]of all nations, tribes, peoples,
and tongues, standing before
the throne and before the Lamb,
[c]clothed with white robes, with
palm branches in their hands,
10 and crying out with a loud
voice, saying, [a]"Salvation *belongs*

to our God [b]who sits on the throne,
and to the Lamb!"
11 [a]All the angels stood around
the throne and the elders and
the four living creatures, and fell
on their faces before the throne
and [b]worshiped God,
12 [a]saying:

"Amen! Blessing and glory
and wisdom,
Thanksgiving and honor
and power and might,
Be to our God forever and
ever.
Amen."

13 Then one of the elders answered, saying to me, "Who
are these arrayed in [a]white
robes, and where did they come
from?"
14 And I said to him, [1]"Sir,
you know." So he said to me,
[a]"These are the ones who come
out of the great tribulation, and
[b]washed their robes and made
them white in the blood of the
Lamb.
15 "Therefore they are before
the throne of God, and serve
Him day and night in His temple. And He who sits on the
throne will [a]dwell among them.
16 [a]"They shall neither hunger
anymore nor thirst anymore;
[b]the sun shall not strike them,
nor any heat;
☆ 17 "for the Lamb who is in the
midst of the throne [a]will shepherd them and lead them to
[1]living fountains of waters. [b]And
God will wipe away every tear
from their eyes."

8 When[a] He opened the seventh seal, there was silence
in heaven for about half an
hour.
2 [a]And I saw the seven angels
who stand before God, [b]and to
them were given seven trumpets.
3 Then another angel, having
a golden censer, came and stood
at the altar. He was given much
incense, that he should offer
it with [a]the prayers of all the
saints upon [b]the golden altar
which was before the throne.
4 And [a]the smoke of the incense, with the prayers of the
saints, ascended before God
from the angel's hand.
5 Then the angel took the censer, filled it with fire from the
altar, and threw *it* to the earth.
And [a]there were noises, thunderings, [b]lightnings, [c]and an
earthquake.
6 So the seven angels who had
the seven trumpets prepared
themselves to sound.
7 The first angel sounded:
[a]And hail and fire followed,
mingled with blood, and they
were thrown [b]to the [1]earth. And
a third [c]of the trees were burned
up, and all green grass was
burned up.
8 Then the second angel
sounded: [a]And *something* like
a great mountain burning with
fire was thrown into the sea,
[b]and a third of the sea [c]became
blood.
9 [a]And a third of the living
creatures in the sea died, and
a third of the ships were destroyed.
10 Then the third angel sounded: [a]And a great star fell from
heaven, burning like a torch,
[b]and it fell on a third of the rivers and on the springs of water.
11 [a]The name of the star is
Wormwood. [b]A third of the waters

10 [b]Rev. 5:13
11 [a]Rev. 4:6 [b]Rev. 4:11; 5:9, 12, 14; 11:16
12 [a]Rev. 5:13, 14
13 [a]Rev. 7:9
14 [a]Rev. 6:9 [b][Heb. 9:14] [1]NU, M *My lord*
15 [a]Is. 4:5, 6
16 [a]Is. 49:10 [b]Ps. 121:6
17 [a]Ps. 23:1 [b]Is. 25:8; Rev. 21:4 [1]NU, M *fountains of the waters of life*

CHAPTER 8

1 [a]Rev. 6:1
2 [a][Matt. 18:10] [b]2 Chr. 29:25–28
3 [a]Rev. 5:8 [b]Ex. 30:1
4 [a]Ps. 141:2
5 [a]Rev. 11:19; 16:18 [b]Rev. 4:5 [c]2 Sam. 22:8
7 [a]Ezek. 38:22 [b]Rev. 16:2 [c]Rev. 9:4, 15–18 [1]NU, M add *and a third of the earth was burned up*
8 [a]Jer. 51:25 [b]Ex. 7:17 [c]Ezek. 14:19
9 [a]Rev. 16:3
10 [a]Is. 14:12 [b]Rev. 14:7; 16:4
11 [a]Ruth 1:20 [b]Ex. 15:23

became wormwood, and many
men died from the water, because
it was made bitter.
12 [a]Then the fourth angel
sounded: And a third of the sun
was struck, a third of the moon,
and a third of the stars, so that a
third of them were darkened. A
third of the day [1]did not shine,
and likewise the night.
13 And I looked, [a]and I heard an
[1]angel flying through the midst
of heaven, saying with a loud
voice, [b]"Woe, woe, woe to the
inhabitants of the earth, because
of the remaining blasts of the
trumpet of the three angels who
are about to sound!"
9 Then the fifth angel sounded:
[a]And I saw a star fallen from
heaven to the earth. To him was
given the key to [b]the [1]bottom-
less pit.
2 And he opened the bottomless pit, and smoke arose out of
the pit like the smoke of a great
furnace. So the [a]sun and the air
were darkened because of the
smoke of the pit.
3 Then out of the smoke locusts came upon the earth. And
to them was given power, [a]as
the scorpions of the earth have
power.
4 They were commanded [a]not
to harm [b]the grass of the earth,
or any green thing, or any tree,
but only those men who do not
have [c]the seal of God on their
foreheads.
5 And [1]they were not given *authority* to kill them, [a]but to torment them *for* five months. Their
torment *was* like the torment of
a scorpion when it strikes a
man.
6 In those days [a]men will seek
death and will not find it; they
will desire to die, and death will
flee from them.
7 [a]The shape of the locusts
was like horses prepared for
battle. [b]On their heads were
crowns of something like gold,
[c]and their faces *were* like the
faces of men.
8 They had hair like women's
hair, and [a]their teeth were like
lions' *teeth.*
9 And they had breastplates
like breastplates of iron, and the
sound of their wings *was* [a]like
the sound of chariots with many
horses running into battle.
10 They had tails like scorpions, and there were stings in
their tails. Their power *was* to
hurt men five months.
11 And they had as king over
them [a]the angel of the bottomless pit, whose name in Hebrew
is [1]A·bad′don, but in Greek he
has the name [2]A·pol′lyon.
12 [a]One woe is past. Behold,
still two more woes are coming
after these things.
13 Then the sixth angel sounded:
And I heard a voice from the
four horns of the [a]golden altar
which is before God,
14 saying to the sixth angel
who had the trumpet, "Release
the four angels who are bound
[a]at the great river Eū·phrā′tēs."
15 So the four angels, who had
been prepared for the hour and
day and month and year, were
released to kill a [a]third of mankind.
16 Now [a]the number of the
army [b]of the horsemen *was* two
hundred million; [c]I heard the
number of them.
17 And thus I saw the horses
in the vision: those who sat on
them had breastplates of fiery

12 [a]Is. 13:10 [1]*had no light*
13 [a]Rev. 14:6; 19:17 [b]Rev. 9:12; 11:14; 12:12 [1]NU, M *eagle*

CHAPTER 9

1 [a]Rev. 8:10 [b]Luke 8:31 [1]Lit. *shaft of the abyss*
2 [a]Joel 2:2, 10
3 [a]Judg. 7:12
4 [a]Rev. 6:6 [b]Rev. 8:7 [c]Rev. 7:2, 3
5 [a][Rev. 9:10; 11:7] [1]The locusts
6 [a]Jer. 8:3
7 [a]Joel 2:4 [b]Nah. 3:17 [c]Dan. 7:8
8 [a]Joel 1:6
9 [a]Joel 2:5–7
11 [a]Eph. 2:2 [1]Lit. *Destruction* [2]Lit. *Destroyer*
12 [a]Rev. 8:13; 11:14
13 [a]Rev. 8:3
14 [a]Rev. 16:12
15 [a]Rev. 8:7–9; 9:18
16 [a]Dan. 7:10 [b]Ezek. 38:4 [c]Rev. 7:4

red, hyacinth blue, and sulfur
yellow; [a]and the heads of the
horses *were* like the heads of
lions; and out of their mouths
came fire, smoke, and brimstone.
18 By these three *plagues* a
third of mankind was killed—by
the fire and the smoke and the
brimstone which came out of
their mouths.
19 For [1]their power is in their
mouth and in their tails; [a]for
their tails *are* like serpents, having heads; and with them they
do harm.
20 But the rest of mankind, who
were not killed by these plagues,
[a]did not repent of the works of
their hands, that they should
not worship [b]demons, [c]and idols
of gold, silver, brass, stone, and
wood, which can neither see nor
hear nor walk.
21 And they did not repent of
their murders [a]or their [1]sorcer-
ies or their sexual immorality or
their thefts.

10

I saw still another mighty
angel coming down from
heaven, clothed with a cloud.
[a]And a rainbow *was* on [b]his
head, his face *was* like the sun,
and [c]his feet like pillars of fire.
2 He had a little book open in
his hand. [a]And he set his right
foot on the sea and *his* left *foot*
on the land,
3 and cried with a loud voice,
as *when* a lion roars. When he
cried out, [a]seven thunders uttered their voices.
4 Now when the seven thunders [1]uttered their voices, I was
about to write; but I heard a
voice from heaven saying [2]to
me, [a]"Seal up the things which
the seven thunders uttered, and
do not write them."
5 The angel whom I saw standing on the sea and on the land
[a]raised up his [1]hand to heaven
6 and swore by Him who lives
forever and ever, [a]who created
heaven and the things that are
in it, the earth and the things
that are in it, and the sea and the
things that are in it, [b]that there
should be delay no longer,
7 but [a]in the days of the sounding of the seventh angel, when
he is about to sound, the mystery of God would be finished,
as He declared to His servants
the prophets.
8 Then the voice which I heard
from heaven spoke to me again
and said, "Go, take the little
book which is open in the hand
of the angel who stands on the
sea and on the earth."
9 So I went to the angel and
said to him, "Give me the little
book." And he said to me, [a]"Take
and eat it; and it will make your
stomach bitter, but it will be as
sweet as honey in your mouth."
10 Then I took the little book
out of the angel's hand and ate
it, [a]and it was as sweet as honey
in my mouth. But when I had
eaten it, [b]my stomach became
bitter.
11 And [1]he said to me, "You
must prophesy again about
many peoples, nations, tongues,
and kings."

11

Then I was given [a]a reed
like a measuring rod.
[1]And the angel stood, saying,
[b]"Rise and measure the temple
of God, the altar, and those who
worship there.
2 "But leave out [a]the court
which is outside the temple, and

17 [a]Is. 5:28, 29
19 [a]Is. 9:15 [1]NU, M *the power of the horses*
20 [a]Deut. 31:29 [b]1 Cor. 10:20 [c]Dan. 5:23
21 [a]Rev. 21:8; 22:15 [1]NU, M *drugs*

CHAPTER 10

1 [a]Rev. 4:3 [b]Rev. 1:16 [c]Rev. 1:15
2 [a]Matt. 28:18
3 [a]Ps. 29:3–9
4 [a]Dan. 8:26; 12:4, 9 [1]NU, M *sounded,* [2]NU, M omit *to me*
5 [a]Dan. 12:7 [1]NU, M *right hand*
6 [a]Rev. 4:11 [b]Rev. 16:17
7 [a]Rev. 11:15
9 [a]Jer. 15:16
10 [a]Ezek. 3:3 [b]Ezek. 2:10
11 [1]NU, M *they*

CHAPTER 11

1 [a]Ezek. 40:3—42:20 [b]Num. 23:18 [1]NU, M omit *And the angel stood*
2 [a]Ezek. 40:17, 20

do not measure it, [b]for it has been given to the Gentiles. And they will [c]tread the holy city underfoot *for* [d]forty-two months.

3 "And I will give *power* to my two [a]witnesses, [b]and they will prophesy [c]one thousand two hundred and sixty days, clothed in sackcloth."

4 These are the [a]two olive trees and the two lampstands standing before the [1]God of the earth.

5 And if anyone wants to harm them, [a]fire proceeds from their mouth and devours their enemies. [b]And if anyone wants to harm them, he must be killed in this manner.

6 These [a]have power to shut heaven, so that no rain falls in the days of their prophecy; and they have power over waters to turn them to blood, and to strike the earth with all plagues, as often as they desire.

7 When they [a]finish their testimony, [b]the beast that ascends [c]out of the bottomless pit [d]will make war against them, overcome them, and kill them.

8 And their dead bodies *will lie* in the street of [a]the great city which spiritually is called Sod'om and Egypt, [b]where also [1]our Lord was crucified.

9 [a]Then *those* from the peoples, tribes, tongues, and nations [1]will see their dead bodies three-and-a-half days, [b]and not allow their dead bodies to be put into graves.

10 [a]And those who dwell on the earth will rejoice over them, make merry, [b]and send gifts to one another, [c]because these two prophets tormented those who dwell on the earth.

11 [a]Now after the three-and-a-half days [b]the breath of life from God entered them, and they stood on their feet, and great fear fell on those who saw them.

12 And [1]they heard a loud voice from heaven saying to them, "Come up here." [a]And they ascended to heaven [b]in a cloud, [c]and their enemies saw them.

13 In the same hour [a]there was a great earthquake, [b]and a tenth of the city fell. In the earthquake seven thousand people were killed, and the rest were afraid [c]and gave glory to the God of heaven.

14 [a]The second woe is past. Behold, the third woe is coming quickly.

15 Then [a]the seventh angel ☆ sounded: [b]And there were loud voices in heaven, saying, [c]"The [1]kingdoms of this world have become *the kingdoms* of our Lord and of His Christ, [d]and He shall reign forever and ever!"

16 And [a]the twenty-four elders who sat before God on their thrones fell on their faces and [b]worshiped God,

17 saying:

"We give You thanks, O Lord
God Almighty,
The One [a]who is and who
was [1]and who is to come,
Because You have taken
Your great power [b]and
reigned.

18 The nations were [a]angry,
and Your [1]wrath has
come,
And the time of the [b]dead,
that they should be
judged,

2 [b]Ps. 79:1 [c]Dan. 8:10 [d]Rev. 12:6; 13:5
3 [a]Rev. 20:4 [b]Rev. 19:10 [c]Rev. 12:6
4 [a]Zech. 4:2, 3, 11, 14 [1]NU, M *Lord*
5 [a]2 Kin. 1:10–12 [b]Num. 16:29
6 [a]1 Kin. 17:1
7 [a]Luke 13:32 [b]Rev. 13:1, 11; 17:8 [c]Rev. 9:1, 2 [d]Dan. 7:21
8 [a]Rev. 14:8 [b]Heb. 13:12 [1]NU, M *their*
9 [a]Rev. 17:15 [b]Ps. 79:2, 3 [1]NU, M *see . . . and will not allow*
10 [a]Rev. 12:12 [b]Esth. 9:19, 22 [c]Rev. 16:10
11 [a]Rev. 11:9 [b]Ezek. 37:5, 9, 10
12 [a]Is. 14:13 [b]Acts 1:9 [c]2 Kin. 2:11, 12 [1]M *I*
13 [a]Rev. 6:12; 8:5; 11:19; 16:18 [b]Rev. 16:19 [c]Rev. 14:7; 16:9; 19:7
14 [a]Rev. 8:13; 9:12
15 [a]Rev. 8:2; 10:7 [b]Is. 27:13 [c]Rev. 12:10 [d]Ex. 15:18 [1]NU, M *kingdom . . . has become the kingdom*
16 [a]Rev. 4:4 [b]Rev. 4:11; 5:9, 12, 14; 7:11
17 [a]Rev. 16:5 [b]Rev. 19:6 [1]NU, M omit *and who is to come*
18 [a]Ps. 2:1 [b]Dan. 7:10 [1]*anger*

And that You should reward
Your servants the
prophets and the saints,
And those who fear Your
name, small and great,
And should destroy those
who destroy the earth."

19 Then [a]the temple of God was
opened in heaven, and the ark
of [1]His covenant was seen in His
temple. And [b]there were lightnings, noises, thunderings, an
earthquake, [c]and great hail.

12

12 Now a great sign ap-
peared in heaven: a
woman clothed with the sun,
with the moon under her feet,
and on her head a garland of
twelve stars.
2 Then being with child, she
cried out [a]in labor and in pain to
give birth.
3 And another sign appeared
in heaven: behold, [a]a great, fiery
red dragon having seven heads
and ten horns, and seven dia-
dems on his heads.
4 [a]His tail drew a third [b]of the
stars of heaven [c]and threw them
to the earth. And the dragon
stood [d]before the woman who
was ready to give birth, [e]to devour her Child as soon as it was
born.
☆ 5 She bore a male Child [a]who
was to rule all nations with
a rod of iron. And her Child
was [b]caught up to God and His
throne.
6 Then [a]the woman fled into
the wilderness, where she has
a place prepared by God, that
they should feed her there [b]one
thousand two hundred and sixty
days.
7 And war broke out in heaven:
[a]Michael and his angels fought
[b]with the dragon; and the dragon
and his angels fought,
8 but they [1]did not prevail, nor
was a place found for [2]them in
heaven any longer.
9 So [a]the great dragon was
cast out, [b]that serpent of old,
called the Devil and Satan, [c]who
deceives the whole world; [d]he
was cast to the earth, and his
angels were cast out with him.
10 Then I heard a loud voice
saying in heaven, [a]"Now salvation, and strength, and the kingdom of our God, and the power
of His Christ have come, for the
accuser of our brethren, [b]who
accused them before our God
day and night, has been cast
down.
11 "And [a]they overcame him by
the blood of the Lamb and by
the word of their testimony, [b]and
they did not love their lives to
the death.
12 "Therefore [a]rejoice, O heavens, and you who dwell in them!
[b]Woe to the inhabitants of the
earth and the sea! For the devil
has come down to you, having
great wrath, [c]because he knows
that he has a short time."
13 Now when the dragon saw
that he had been cast to the
earth, he persecuted [a]the woman
who gave birth to the male
Child.
14 [a]But the woman was given
two wings of a great eagle, [b]that
she might fly [c]into the wilderness to her place, where she is
nourished [d]for a time and times
and half a time, from the presence of the serpent.
15 So the serpent [a]spewed water out of his mouth like a flood
after the woman, that he might

19 [a]Rev. 4:1; 15:5, 8 [b]Rev. 8:5 [c]Rev. 16:21 [1]M *the covenant of the Lord*

CHAPTER 12

2 [a]Is. 26:17; 66:6–9

3 [a]Rev. 13:1; 17:3, 7, 9

4 [a]Rev. 9:10, 19 [b]Rev. 8:7, 12 [c]Dan. 8:10 [d]Rev. 12:2 [e]Matt. 2:16

5 [a]Ps. 2:9; Is. 7:14; 9:6; Rev. 2:27; 19:15 [b]Luke 24:51; Acts 1:9–11

6 [a]Rev. 12:4, 14 [b]Rev. 11:3; 13:5

7 [a]Dan. 10:13, 21; 12:1 [b]Rev. 20:2

8 [1]*were not strong enough* [2]M *him*

9 [a]John 12:31 [b]Gen. 3:1, 4 [c]Rev. 20:3 [d]Rev. 9:1

10 [a]Rev. 11:15 [b]Zech. 3:1

11 [a]Rom. 16:20 [b]Luke 14:26

12 [a]Ps. 96:11 [b]Rev. 8:13 [c]Rev. 10:6

13 [a]Rev. 12:5

14 [a]Ex. 19:4 [b]Rev. 12:6 [c]Rev. 17:3 [d]Dan. 7:25; 12:7

15 [a]Is. 59:19

cause her to be carried away by
the flood.
16 But the earth helped the
woman, and the earth opened
its mouth and swallowed up
the flood which the dragon had
spewed out of his mouth.
17 And the dragon was enraged
with the woman, and he went to
make war with the rest of her
offspring, who keep the commandments of God and have the
testimony of Jesus [1]Christ.

13 Then [1]I stood on the sand
of the sea. And I saw
[a]a beast rising up out of the
sea, [b]having [2]seven heads and
ten horns, and on his horns
ten crowns, and on his heads a
[c]blasphemous name.
2 Now the beast which I saw
was like a leopard, his feet were
like *the feet of* a bear, and his
mouth like the mouth of a lion.
The [a]dragon gave him his power,
his throne, and great authority.
3 And I saw one of his heads
[a]as if it had been mortally
wounded, and his deadly wound
was healed. And [b]all the world
marveled and followed the
beast.
4 So they worshiped the dragon
who gave authority to the beast;
and they worshiped the beast,
saying, [a]"Who *is* like the beast?
Who is able to make war with
him?"
5 And he was given [a]a mouth
speaking great things and blasphemies, and he was given authority to [1]continue for [b]forty-two months.
6 Then he opened his mouth
in blasphemy against God, to
blaspheme His name, [a]His tabernacle, and those who dwell in
heaven.

17 [1]NU, M omit *Christ*

CHAPTER 13

1 [a]Dan. 7:2, 7 [b]Rev. 12:3 [c]Rev. 17:3 [1]NU *he* [2]NU, M *ten horns and seven heads*

2 [a]Rev. 12:3, 9; 13:4, 12

3 [a]Rev. 13:12, 14 [b]Rev. 17:8

4 [a]Rev. 18:18

5 [a]Dan. 7:8, 11, 20, 25; 11:36 [b]Rev. 11:2 [1]M *make war*

6 [a][Col. 2:9]

7 [a]Dan. 7:21 [b]Rev. 11:18 [1]NU, M add *and people*

8 [a]Ex. 32:32 [b]Rev. 17:8

9 [a]Rev. 2:7

10 [a]Is. 33:1 [b]Gen. 9:6 [c]Rev. 14:12 [1]*perseverance*

11 [a]Rev. 11:7

12 [a]Rev. 13:3, 4

13 [a]Matt. 24:24 [b]1 Kin. 18:38

14 [a]Rev. 12:9 [b]2 Thess. 2:9 [c]2 Kin. 20:7 [1]M *my own people*

15 [a]Rev. 16:2

7 It was granted to him [a]to
make war with the saints and to
overcome them. And [b]authority
was given him over every [1]tribe,
tongue, and nation.
8 All who dwell on the earth
will worship him, [a]whose names
have not been written in the
Book of Life of the Lamb slain
[b]from the foundation of the
world.
9 [a]If anyone has an ear, let him
hear.
10 [a]He who leads into captivity
shall go into captivity; [b]he who
kills with the sword must be
killed with the sword. [c]Here is
the [1]patience and the faith of the
saints.
11 Then I saw another beast
[a]coming up out of the earth, and
he had two horns like a lamb
and spoke like a dragon.
12 And he exercises all the authority of the first beast in his
presence, and causes the earth
and those who dwell in it to
worship the first beast, [a]whose
deadly wound was healed.
13 [a]He performs great signs, [b]so
that he even makes fire come
down from heaven on the earth
in the sight of men.
14 [a]And he deceives [1]those who
dwell on the earth [b]by those
signs which he was granted to
do in the sight of the beast, telling those who dwell on the earth
to make an image to the beast
who was wounded by the sword
[c]and lived.
15 He was granted *power* to
give breath to the image of the
beast, that the image of the beast
should both speak [a]and cause as
many as would not worship the
image of the beast to be killed.
16 He causes all, both small

and great, rich and poor, free
and slave, [a]to receive a mark on
their right hand or on their foreheads,
17 and that no one may buy
or sell except one who has [1]the
mark or [a]the name of the beast,
[b]or the number of his name.
18 [a]Here is wisdom. Let him
who has [b]understanding calcu-
late [c]the number of the beast,
[d]for it is the number of a man:
His number *is* 666.

14

14 Then I looked, and be-
hold, [1]a [a]Lamb standing
on Mount Zion, and with Him
[b]one hundred *and* forty-four
thousand, [2]having His Father's
name [c]written on their foreheads.
2 And I heard a voice from
heaven, [a]like the voice of many
waters, and like the voice of
loud thunder. And I heard the
sound of [b]harpists playing their
harps.
3 They sang as it were a new
song before the throne, before
the four living creatures, and the
elders; and no one could learn
that song [a]except the hundred
and forty-four thousand who
were redeemed from the earth.
4 These are the ones who were
not defiled with women, [a]for they
are virgins. These are the ones
[b]who follow the Lamb wherever
He goes. These [c]were [1]redeemed
from *among* men, [d]*being* firstfruits to God and to the Lamb.
5 And [a]in their mouth was
found no [1]deceit, for [b]they are
without fault [2]before the throne
of God.
6 Then I saw another angel
[a]flying in the midst of heaven,
[b]having the everlasting gospel
to preach to those who dwell
on the earth—[c]to every nation,
tribe, tongue, and people—
7 saying with a loud voice,
[a]"Fear God and give glory to
Him, for the hour of His judgment has come; [b]and worship
Him who made heaven and
earth, the sea and springs of
water."
8 And another angel followed,
saying, [a]"Babylon[1] is fallen, is
fallen, that great city, because
[b]she has made all nations drink
of the wine of the wrath of her
fornication."
9 Then a third angel followed
them, saying with a loud voice,
[a]"If anyone worships the beast
and his image, and receives *his*
[b]mark on his forehead or on his
hand,
10 "he himself [a]shall also drink
of the wine of the wrath of God,
which is [b]poured out full strength
into [c]the cup of His indignation.
[d]He shall be tormented with [e]fire
and brimstone in the presence
of the holy angels and in the
presence of the Lamb.
11 "And [a]the smoke of their torment ascends forever and ever;
and they have no rest day or
night, who worship the beast
and his image, and whoever receives the mark of his name."
12 [a]Here is the [1]patience of the
saints; [b]here[2] *are* those who keep
the commandments of God and
the faith of Jesus.
13 Then I heard a voice from
heaven saying [1]to me, "Write:
[a]'Blessed *are* the dead [b]who
die in the Lord from now on.' "
"Yes," says the Spirit, [c]"that they
may rest from their labors, and
their works follow [d]them."
14 Then I looked, and behold, a
white cloud, and on the cloud sat

16 [a]Rev. 7:3; 14:9; 20:4
17 [a]Rev. 14:9–11 [b]Rev. 15:2 [1]NU, M *the mark, the name*
18 [a]Rev. 17:9 [b][1 Cor. 2:14] [c]Rev. 15:2 [d]Rev. 21:17

CHAPTER 14

1 [a]Rev. 5:6 [b]Rev. 7:4; 14:3 [c]Rev. 7:3; 22:4 [1]NU, M *the* [2]NU, M add *His name and*
2 [a]Rev. 1:15; 19:6 [b]Rev. 5:8
3 [a]Rev. 5:9
4 [a][2 Cor. 11:2] [b]Rev. 3:4; 7:17 [c]Rev. 5:9 [d]James 1:18 [1]M adds *by Jesus*
5 [a]Ps. 32:2 [b]Eph. 5:27 [1]NU, M *falsehood* [2]NU, M omit the rest of v. 5.
6 [a]Rev. 8:13 [b]Eph. 3:9 [c]Rev. 13:7
7 [a]Rev. 11:18 [b]Neh. 9:6
8 [a]Is. 21:9 [b]Jer. 51:7 [1]NU *Babylon the great is fallen, is fallen, which has made;* M *Babylon the great is fallen. She has made*
9 [a]Rev. 13:14, 15; 14:11 [b]Rev. 13:16
10 [a]Ps. 75:8 [b]Rev. 18:6 [c]Rev. 16:19 [d]Rev. 20:10 [e]2 Thess. 1:7
11 [a]Is. 34:8–10
12 [a]Rev. 13:10 [b]Rev. 12:17 [1]*steadfastness, perseverance* [2]NU, M omit *here are those*
13 [a]Eccl. 4:1, 2 [b]1 Cor. 15:18 [c]Heb. 4:9, 10 [d][1 Cor. 3:11–15; 15:58] [1]NU, M omit *to me*

One like the Son of Man, having
on His head a golden crown, and
in His hand a sharp sickle.
15 And another angel [a]came out
of the temple, crying with a loud
voice to Him who sat on the
cloud, [b]"Thrust in Your sickle
and reap, for the time has come
[1]for You to reap, for the harvest
[c]of the earth is ripe."
16 So He who sat on the cloud
thrust in His sickle on the earth,
and the earth was reaped.
17 Then another angel came out
of the temple which is in heaven,
he also having a sharp sickle.
18 And another angel came out
from the altar, [a]who had power
over fire, and he cried with a
loud cry to him who had the
sharp sickle, saying, [b]"Thrust in
your sharp sickle and gather the
clusters of the vine of the earth,
for her grapes are fully ripe."
19 So the angel thrust his sickle
into the earth and gathered the
vine of the earth, and threw *it*
into [a]the great winepress of the
wrath of God.
20 And [a]the winepress was
trampled [b]outside the city, and
blood came out of the winepress, [c]up to the horses' bridles,
for one thousand six hundred
[1]furlongs.

15

15 Then [a]I saw another sign
in heaven, great and mar-
velous: [b]seven angels having the
seven last plagues, [c]for in them
the wrath of God is complete.
2 And I saw *something* like [a]a
sea of glass [b]mingled with fire,
and those who have the victory
over the beast, [c]over his image
and [1]over his mark *and* over
the [d]number of his name, standing on the sea of glass, [e]having
harps of God.

15 [a]Rev. 16:17
[b]Joel 3:13
[c]Jer. 51:33
[1]NU, M omit *for You*

18 [a]Rev. 16:8
[b]Joel 3:13

19 [a]Rev. 19:15

20 [a]Is. 63:3
[b]Heb. 13:12
[c]Is. 34:3
[1]Lit. *stadia,* about 184 miles in all

CHAPTER 15

1 [a]Rev. 12:1, 3
[b]Rev. 21:9
[c]Rev. 14:10

2 [a]Rev. 4:6
[b][Matt. 3:11]
[c]Rev. 13:14, 15
[d]Rev. 13:17
[e]Rev. 5:8
[1]NU, M omit *over his mark*

3 [a]Ex. 15:1–21
[b]Rev. 15:3
[c]Deut. 32:3, 4
[d]Ps. 145:17
[1]NU, M *nations*

4 [a]Ex. 15:14
[b]Lev. 11:44
[c]Is. 66:23

5 [a]Num. 1:50
[1]NU, M omit *behold*
[2]*sanctuary,* the inner shrine

6 [a]Ex. 28:6
[1]*sanctuary,* the inner shrine

7 [a]Rev. 4:6
[b]1 Thess. 1:9

8 [a]Ex. 19:18; 40:34
[b]2 Thess. 1:9

CHAPTER 16

1 [a]Rev. 15:1
[b]Rev. 14:10
[1]NU, M *seven bowls*

2 [a]Rev. 8:7
[b]Ex. 9:9–11
[c]Rev. 13:15–17; 14:9
[1]*severe and malignant,* lit. *bad and evil*

3 They sing [a]the song of Moses, the servant of God, and the
song of the [b]Lamb, saying:

[c]"Great and marvelous *are*
Your works,
Lord God Almighty!
[d]Just and true *are* Your ways,
O King of the [1]saints!
4 [a]Who shall not fear You,
O Lord, and glorify Your
name?
For *You* alone *are* [b]holy.
For [c]all nations shall come
and worship before You,
For Your judgments have
been manifested."

5 After these things I looked,
and [1]behold, [a]the [2]temple of the
tabernacle of the testimony in
heaven was opened.
6 And out of the [1]temple
came the seven angels having
the seven plagues, [a]clothed in
pure bright linen, and having
their chests girded with golden
bands.
7 [a]Then one of the four living creatures gave to the seven
angels seven golden bowls full
of the wrath of God [b]who lives
forever and ever.
8 [a]The temple was filled with
smoke [b]from the glory of God
and from His power, and no one
was able to enter the temple till
the seven plagues of the seven
angels were completed.

16

16 Then I heard a loud voice
from the temple saying
[a]to the seven angels, "Go and
pour out the [1]bowls [b]of the wrath
of God on the earth."
2 So the first went and poured
out his bowl [a]upon the earth,
and a [1]foul and [b]loathsome sore
came upon the men [c]who had

the mark of the beast and those
[d]who worshiped his image.
3 Then the second angel
poured out his bowl [a]on the
sea, and [b]it became blood as of
a dead *man;* [c]and every living
creature in the sea died.
4 Then the third angel poured
out his bowl [a]on the rivers and
springs of water, [b]and they became blood.
5 And I heard the angel of the
waters saying:

[a]"You are righteous, [1]O Lord,
The One [b]who is and who
[2]was and who is to be,
Because You have judged
these things.
6 For [a]they have shed the
blood [b]of saints and
prophets,
[c]And You have given them
blood to drink.
[1]For it is their just due."

7 And I heard [1]another from
the altar saying, "Even so, [a]Lord
God Almighty, [b]true and righteous *are* Your judgments."
8 Then the fourth angel
poured out his bowl [a]on the sun,
[b]and power was given to him to
scorch men with fire.
9 And men were scorched with
great heat, and they [a]blasphemed
the name of God who has power
over these plagues; [b]and they
did not repent [c]and give Him
glory.
10 Then the fifth angel poured
out his bowl [a]on the throne of
the beast, [b]and his kingdom became full of darkness; [c]and they
gnawed their tongues because
of the pain.
11 They blasphemed the God of
heaven because of their pains
and their sores, and did not repent of their deeds.
12 Then the sixth angel poured
out his bowl [a]on the great river
Eū·phrā′tēs, [b]and its water was
dried up, [c]so that the way of the
kings from the east might be
prepared.
13 And I saw three unclean
[a]spirits like frogs *coming* out of
the mouth of [b]the dragon, out
of the mouth of the beast, and
out of the mouth of [c]the false
prophet.
14 For they are spirits of demons, [a]performing signs, *which*
go out to the kings [1]of the earth
and of [b]the whole world, to
gather them to [c]the battle of that
great day of God Almighty.
15 [a]"Behold, I am coming as a ☆
thief. Blessed *is* he who watches,
and keeps his garments, [b]lest
he walk naked and they see his
shame."
16 [a]And they gathered them together to the place called in Hebrew, [1]Ar·ma·ged′don.
17 Then the seventh angel
poured out his bowl into the air,
and a loud voice came out of
the temple of heaven, from the
throne, saying, [a]"It is done!"
18 And [a]there were noises and
thunderings and lightnings;
[b]and there was a great earthquake, such a mighty and great
earthquake [c]as had not occurred
since men were on the earth.
19 Now [a]the great city was divided into three parts, and the
cities of the nations fell. And
[b]great Babylon [c]was remembered before God, [d]to give her
the cup of the wine of the fierceness of His wrath.
20 Then [a]every island fled away,

2 [d]Rev. 13:14
3 [a]Rev. 8:8; 11:6 [b]Ex. 7:17–21 [c]Rev. 8:9
4 [a]Rev. 8:10 [b]Ex. 7:17–20
5 [a]Rev. 15:3, 4 [b]Rev. 1:4, 8 [1]NU, M omit *O Lord* [2]NU, M *was, the Holy One*
6 [a]Matt. 23:34 [b]Rev. 11:18 [c]Is. 49:26 [1]NU, M omit *For*
7 [a]Rev. 15:3 [b]Rev. 13:10; 19:2 [1]NU, M omit *another from*
8 [a]Rev. 8:12 [b]Rev. 9:17, 18
9 [a]Rev. 16:11 [b]Dan. 5:22 [c]Rev. 11:13
10 [a]Rev. 13:2 [b]Rev. 8:12; 9:2 [c]Rev. 11:10
12 [a]Rev. 9:14 [b]Jer. 50:38 [c]Is. 41:2, 25; 46:11
13 [a]1 John 4:1 [b]Rev. 12:3, 9 [c]Rev. 13:11, 14; 19:20; 20:10
14 [a]2 Thess. 2:9 [b]Luke 2:1 [c]Rev. 17:14; 19:19; 20:8 [1]NU, M omit *of the earth and*
15 [a]Matt. 24:43; Luke 12:39; Rev. 3:3, 11 [b]2 Cor. 5:3
16 [a]Rev. 19:19 [1]Lit. *Mount Megiddo;* M *Megiddo*
17 [a]Rev. 10:6; 21:6
18 [a]Rev. 4:5 [b]Rev. 11:13 [c]Dan. 12:1
19 [a]Rev. 14:8 [b]Rev. 17:5, 18 [c]Rev. 14:8; 18:5 [d]Is. 51:17
20 [a]Rev. 6:14; 20:11

and the mountains were not
found.
21 And great hail from heaven
fell upon men, *each hailstone*
about the weight of a talent.
Men blasphemed God because
of the plague of the hail, since
that plague was exceedingly
great.

17

17 Then [a]one of the seven
angels who had the seven
bowls came and talked with me,
saying [1]to me, "Come, [b]I will
show you the judgment of [c]the
great harlot [d]who sits on many
waters,
2 [a]"with whom the kings of
the earth committed fornication,
and [b]the inhabitants of the earth
were made drunk with the wine
of her fornication."
3 So he carried me away in
the Spirit [a]into the wilderness.
And I saw a woman sitting [b]on
a scarlet beast *which was* full
of [c]names of blasphemy, having
seven heads and ten horns.
4 The woman [a]was arrayed in
purple and scarlet, [b]and adorned
with gold and precious stones
and pearls, [c]having in her hand
a golden cup [d]full of abominations and the filthiness of [1]her
fornication.
5 And on her forehead a name
was written:

[a]MYSTERY, BABYLON THE
GREAT, THE MOTHER OF
HARLOTS AND OF THE
ABOMINATIONS OF THE
EARTH.

6 I saw [a]the woman, drunk
[b]with the blood of the saints and
with the blood of [c]the martyrs
of Jesus. And when I saw her,
I marveled with great amazement.
7 But the angel said to me,
"Why did you marvel? I will tell
you the [1]mystery of the woman
and of the beast that carries her,
which has the seven heads and
the ten horns.
8 "The beast that you saw was,
and is not, and [a]will ascend out
of the bottomless pit and [b]go
to [1]perdition. And those who
[c]dwell on the earth [d]will marvel,
[e]whose names are not written in
the Book of Life from the foundation of the world, when they
see the beast that was, and is
not, and [2]yet is.
9 [a]"Here *is* the mind which has
wisdom: [b]The seven heads are
seven mountains on which the
woman sits.
10 "There are also seven kings.
Five have fallen, one is, *and*
the other has not yet come.
And when he comes, he must
[a]continue a short time.
11 "The [a]beast that was, and is
not, is himself also the eighth,
and is of the seven, and is going
to [1]perdition.
12 [a]"The ten horns which you
saw are ten kings who have
received no kingdom as yet, but
they receive authority for one
hour as kings with the beast.
13 "These are of one mind, and
they will give their power and
authority to the beast.
14 [a]"These will make war with
the Lamb, and the Lamb will
[b]overcome them, [c]for He is Lord
of lords and King of kings; [d]and
those *who are* with Him *are*
called, chosen, and faithful."
15 Then he said to me, [a]"The
waters which you saw, where

CHAPTER 17

1 [a]Rev. 1:1; 21:9 [b]Rev. 16:19 [c]Nah. 3:4 [d]Jer. 51:13 [1]NU, M omit *to me*

2 [a]Rev. 2:22; 18:3, 9 [b]Jer. 51:7

3 [a]Rev. 12:6, 14; 21:10 [b]Rev. 12:3 [c]Rev. 13:1

4 [a]Rev. 18:12, 16 [b]Dan. 11:38 [c]Jer. 51:7 [d]Rev. 14:8 [1]M *the fornication of the earth*

5 [a]2 Thess. 2:7

6 [a]Rev. 18:24 [b]Rev. 13:15 [c]Rev. 6:9, 10

7 [1]*hidden truth*

8 [a]Rev. 11:7 [b]Rev. 13:10; 17:11 [c]Rev. 3:10 [d]Rev. 13:3 [e]Rev. 13:8 [1]*destruction* [2]NU, M *shall be present*

9 [a]Rev. 13:18 [b]Rev. 13:1

10 [a]Rev. 13:5

11 [a]Rev. 13:3, 12, 14; 17:8 [1]*destruction*

12 [a]Dan. 7:20

14 [a]Rev. 16:14; 19:19 [b]Rev. 19:20 [c]1 Tim. 6:15 [d]Jer. 50:44

15 [a]Is. 8:7

the harlot sits, [b]are peoples, multitudes, nations, and tongues.
16 "And the ten horns which
you [1]saw on the beast, [a]these
will hate the harlot, make her
[b]desolate [c]and naked, eat her
flesh and [d]burn her with fire.
17 [a]"For God has put it into their
hearts to fulfill His purpose, to
be of one mind, and to give their
kingdom to the beast, [b]until the
words of God are fulfilled.
18 "And the woman whom you
saw [a]is that great city [b]which
reigns over the kings of the
earth."

18 After[a] these things I saw
another angel coming
down from heaven, having great
authority, [b]and the earth was il-
luminated with his glory.
2 And he cried [1]mightily with
a loud voice, saying, [a]"Babylon
the great is fallen, is fallen, and
[b]has become a dwelling place of
demons, a prison for every foul
spirit, and [c]a cage for every unclean and hated bird!
3 "For all the nations [a]have
drunk of the wine of the wrath
of her fornication, the kings of
the earth have committed fornication with her, [b]and the merchants of the earth have become
rich through the [1]abundance of
her luxury."
4 And I heard another voice
from heaven saying, [a]"Come out
of her, my people, lest you share
in her sins, and lest you receive
of her plagues.
5 [a]"For her sins [1]have reached
to heaven, and [b]God has remembered her iniquities.
6 [a]"Render to her just as she
rendered [1]to you, and repay her
double according to her works;

15 [b]Rev. 13:7

16 [a]Jer. 50:41 [b]Rev. 18:17, 19 [c]Ezek. 16:37, 39 [d]Rev. 18:8 [1]NU, M *saw, and the beast*

17 [a]2 Thess. 2:11 [b]Rev. 10:7

18 [a]Rev. 11:8; 16:19 [b]Rev. 12:4

CHAPTER 18

1 [a]Rev. 17:1, 7 [b]Ezek. 43:2

2 [a]Is. 13:19; 21:9 [b]Is. 13:21; 34:11, 13–15 [c]Is. 14:23 [1]NU, M omit *mightily*

3 [a]Rev. 14:8 [b]Is. 47:15 [1]Lit. *strengths*

4 [a]Is. 48:20

5 [a]Gen. 18:20 [b]Rev. 16:19 [1]NU, M *have been heaped up*

6 [a]Ps. 137:8 [b]Rev. 14:10 [c]Rev. 16:19 [1]NU, M omit *to you*

7 [a]Ezek. 28:2–8 [b]Is. 47:7, 8 [1]*sensually*

8 [a]Rev. 18:10 [b]Rev. 17:16 [c]Jer. 50:34 [1]NU, M *has judged*

9 [a]Ezek. 26:16; 27:35 [b]Jer. 50:46 [c]Rev. 19:3

10 [a]Is. 21:9 [b]Rev. 18:17, 19

11 [a]Ezek. 27:27–34

12 [a]Rev. 17:4

13 [a]Ezek. 27:13

14 [1]NU, M *been lost to you*

[b]in the cup which she has mixed,
[c]mix double for her.
7 [a]"In the measure that she
glorified herself and lived [1]luxu-
riously, in the same measure
give her torment and sorrow;
for she says in her heart, 'I sit *as*
[b]queen, and am no widow, and
will not see sorrow.'
8 "Therefore her plagues will
come [a]in one day—death and
mourning and famine. And [b]she
will be utterly burned with fire,
[c]for strong *is* the Lord God who
[1]judges her.
9 [a]"The kings of the earth who
committed fornication and lived
luxuriously with her [b]will weep
and lament for her, [c]when they
see the smoke of her burning,
10 "standing at a distance for
fear of her torment, saying,
[a]'Alas, alas, that great city Babylon, that mighty city! [b]For in
one hour your judgment has
come.'
11 "And [a]the merchants of the
earth will weep and mourn over
her, for no one buys their merchandise anymore:
12 [a]"merchandise of gold and
silver, precious stones and
pearls, fine linen and purple,
silk and scarlet, every kind of
citron wood, every kind of object of ivory, every kind of object
of most precious wood, bronze,
iron, and marble;
13 "and cinnamon and incense,
fragrant oil and frankincense,
wine and oil, fine flour and
wheat, cattle and sheep, horses
and chariots, and bodies and
[a]souls of men.
14 "The fruit that your soul
longed for has gone from you,
and all the things which are rich
and splendid have [1]gone from

you, and you shall find them no
more at all.
15 "The merchants of these
things, who became rich by her,
will stand at a distance for fear
of her torment, weeping and
wailing,
16 "and saying, 'Alas, alas, [a]that
great city [b]that was clothed in
fine linen, purple, and scarlet,
and adorned with gold and precious stones and pearls!
17 [a]'For in one hour such great
riches [1]came to nothing.' [b]Every
shipmaster, all who travel by
ship, sailors, and as many as
trade on the sea, stood at a distance
18 [a]"and cried out when they
saw the smoke of her burning,
saying, [b]'What *is* like this great
city?'
19 [a]"They threw dust on their
heads and cried out, weeping
and wailing, and saying, 'Alas,
alas, that great city, in which all
who had ships on the sea became rich by her wealth! [b]For in
one hour she [1]is made desolate.'
20 [a]"Rejoice over her, O heaven,
and *you* [1]holy apostles and
prophets, for [b]God has avenged
you on her!"
21 Then a mighty angel took
up a stone like a great millstone
and threw *it* into the sea, saying,
[a]"Thus with violence the great
city Babylon shall be thrown
down, and [b]shall not be found
anymore.
22 [a]"The sound of harpists, mu-
sicians, flutists, and trumpeters
shall not be heard in you anymore. No craftsman of any craft
shall be found in you anymore,
and the sound of a millstone
shall not be heard in you anymore.
23 [a]"The light of a lamp shall
not shine in you anymore, [b]and
the voice of bridegroom and
bride shall not be heard in you
anymore. For [c]your merchants
were the great men of the earth,
[d]for by your sorcery all the nations were deceived.
24 "And [a]in her was found the
blood of prophets and saints,
and of all who [b]were slain on the
earth."

19 After these things [a]I
[1]heard a loud voice of a
great multitude in heaven, saying, "Alleluia! [b]Salvation and
glory and honor and power *belong* to [2]the Lord our God!
2 "For [a]true and righteous *are*
His judgments, because He has
judged the great harlot who corrupted the earth with her fornication; and He [b]has avenged on
her the blood of His servants
shed by her."
3 Again they said, "Alleluia!
[a]Her smoke rises up forever and
ever!"
4 And [a]the twenty-four elders
and the four living creatures
fell down and worshiped God
who sat on the throne, saying,
[b]"Amen! Alleluia!"
5 Then a voice came from the
throne, saying, [a]"Praise our God,
all you His servants and those
who fear Him, [b]both[1] small and
great!"
6 [a]And I heard, as it were, the
voice of a great multitude, as
the sound of many waters and
as the sound of mighty thunderings, saying, "Alleluia! For [b]the[1]
Lord God Omnipotent reigns!
7 "Let us be glad and rejoice
and give Him glory, for [a]the
marriage of the Lamb has come,

16 [a]Rev. 17:18 [b]Rev. 17:4
17 [a]Rev. 18:10 [b]Is. 23:14 [1]*have been laid waste*
18 [a]Ezek. 27:30 [b]Rev. 13:4
19 [a]Josh. 7:6 [b]Rev. 18:8 [1]*have been laid waste*
20 [a]Jer. 51:48 [b]Luke 11:49 [1]NU, M *saints and apostles*
21 [a]Jer. 51:63, 64 [b]Rev. 12:8; 16:20
22 [a]Jer. 7:34; 16:9; 25:10
23 [a]Jer. 25:10 [b]Jer. 7:34; 16:9 [c]Is. 23:8 [d]2 Kin. 9:22
24 [a]Rev. 16:6; 17:6 [b]Jer. 51:49

CHAPTER 19

1 [a]Rev. 11:15; 19:6 [b]Rev. 4:11 [1]NU, M add *something like* [2]NU, M omit *the Lord*
2 [a]Rev. 15:3; 16:7 [b]Deut. 32:43
3 [a]Is. 34:10
4 [a]Rev. 4:4, 6, 10 [b]1 Chr. 16:36
5 [a]Ps. 134:1 [b]Rev. 11:18 [1]NU, M omit *both*
6 [a]Ezek. 1:24 [b]Rev. 11:15 [1]NU, M *our*
7 [a][Matt. 22:2; 25:10]

and His wife has made herself
ready."
8 And [a]to her it was granted
to be arrayed in fine linen, clean
and bright, [b]for the fine linen is
the righteous acts of the saints.
9 Then he said to me, "Write:
[a]'Blessed *are* those who are
called to the marriage supper of
the Lamb!' " And he said to me,
[b]"These are the true sayings of
God."
10 And [a]I fell at his feet to worship him. But he said to me,
[b]"See *that you do* not *do that!* I
am your [c]fellow servant, and of
your brethren [d]who have the testimony of Jesus. Worship God!
For the [e]testimony of Jesus is the
spirit of prophecy."
11 [a]Now I saw heaven opened,
and behold, [b]a white horse. And
He who sat on him *was* called
[c]Faithful and True, and [d]in righteousness He judges and makes
war.
12 [a]His eyes *were* like a flame
of fire, and on His head *were*
many crowns. [b]He [1]had a name
written that no one knew except
Himself.
★ 13 [a]He *was* clothed with a robe
dipped in blood, and His name is
called [b]The Word of God.
14 [a]And the armies in heaven,
[b]clothed in [1]fine linen, white and
clean, followed Him on white
horses.
15 Now [a]out of His mouth goes
a [1]sharp sword, that with it He
should strike the nations. And
[b]He Himself will rule them with
a rod of iron. [c]He Himself treads
the winepress of the fierceness
and wrath of Almighty God.
16 And [a]He has on *His* robe and
on His thigh a name written:

[b]KING OF KINGS
AND LORD OF LORDS.

17 Then I saw an angel standing in the sun; and he cried
with a loud voice, saying to all
the birds that fly in the midst
of heaven, [a]"Come and gather
together for the [1]supper of the
great God,
18 [a]"that you may eat the flesh
of kings, the flesh of captains,
the flesh of mighty men, the
flesh of horses and of those who
sit on them, and the flesh of
all *people,* [1]free and slave, both
small and great."
19 [a]And I saw the beast, the ☆
kings of the earth, and their
armies, gathered together to
make war against Him who sat
on the horse and against His
army.
20 [a]Then the beast was captured, and with him the false
prophet who worked signs in his
presence, by which he deceived
those who received the mark of
the beast and [b]those who worshiped his image. [c]These two
were cast alive into the lake of
fire [d]burning with brimstone.
21 And the rest [a]were killed
with the sword which proceeded
from the mouth of Him who sat
on the horse. [b]And all the birds
[c]were filled with their flesh.

20 Then I saw an angel coming down from heaven,
[a]having the key to the bottomless pit and a great chain in his
hand.
2 He laid hold of [a]the dragon,
that serpent of old, who is *the*
Devil and Satan, and bound him
for a thousand years;
3 and he cast him into the bottomless pit, and shut him up,

8 [a]Ezek. 16:10 [b]Ps. 132:9
9 [a]Luke 14:15 [b]Rev. 22:6
10 [a]Rev. 22:8 [b]Acts 10:26 [c][Heb. 1:14] [d]1 John 5:10 [e]Luke 24:27
11 [a]Rev. 15:5 [b]Rev. 6:2; 19:19, 21 [c]Rev. 3:7, 14 [d]Is. 11:4
12 [a]Rev. 1:14 [b]Rev. 2:17; 19:16 [1]M adds *names written, and*
13 [a]Is. 63:2, 3 [b][John 1:1, 14]
14 [a]Rev. 14:20 [b]Matt. 28:3 [1]NU, M *pure white linen*
15 [a]Is. 11:4 [b]Ps. 2:8, 9 [c]Is. 63:3–6 [1]M *sharp two-edged*
16 [a]Rev. 2:17; 19:12 [b]Dan. 2:47
17 [a]Ezek. 39:17 [1]NU, M *great supper of God*
18 [a]Ezek. 39:18–20 [1]NU, M *both free*
19 [a]Rev. 16:13–16
20 [a]Rev. 16:13 [b]Rev. 13:8, 12, 13 [c]Dan. 7:11 [d]Rev. 14:10
21 [a]Rev. 19:15 [b]Rev. 19:17, 18 [c]Rev. 17:16

CHAPTER 20

1 [a]Rev. 1:18; 9:1
2 [a]2 Pet. 2:4

and [a]set a seal on him, [b]so that
he should deceive the nations
no more till the thousand years
were finished. But after these
things he must be released for a
little while.
4 And I saw [a]thrones, and they
sat on them, and [b]judgment was
committed to them. Then *I saw*
[c]the souls of those who had been
beheaded for their witness to
Jesus and for the word of God,
[d]who had not worshiped the
beast [e]or his image, and had not
received *his* mark on their foreheads or on their hands. And
they [f]lived and [g]reigned with
Christ for [1]a thousand years.
5 But the rest of the dead did
not live again until the thousand
years were finished. This *is* the
first resurrection.
6 Blessed and holy *is* he who
has part in the first resurrection.
Over such [a]the second death
has no power, but they shall be
[b]priests of God and of Christ,
[c]and shall reign with Him a
thousand years.
7 Now when the thousand
years have expired, Satan will
be released from his prison
8 and will go out [a]to deceive
the nations which are in the
four corners of the earth, [b]Gog
and Mā′gog, [c]to gather them together to battle, whose number
is as the sand of the sea.
9 [a]They went up on the breadth
of the earth and surrounded the
camp of the saints and the beloved city. And fire came down
from God out of heaven and
devoured them.
10 The devil, who deceived
them, was cast into the lake of
fire and brimstone [a]where[1] the
beast and the false prophet *are*.

3 [a]Dan. 6:17 [b]Rev. 12:9; 20:8, 10
4 [a]Dan. 7:9 [b][1 Cor. 6:2, 3] [c]Rev. 6:9 [d]Rev. 13:12 [e]Rev. 13:15 [f]John 14:19 [g]Rom. 8:17 [1]M *the*
6 [a][Rev. 2:11; 20:14] [b]Is. 61:6 [c]Rev. 20:4
8 [a]Rev. 12:9; 20:3, 10 [b]Ezek. 38:2; 39:1, 6 [c]Rev. 16:14
9 [a]Ezek. 38:9, 16
10 [a]Rev. 19:20; 20:14, 15 [b]Rev. 14:10 [1]NU, M *where also*
11 [a]2 Pet. 3:7 [b]Dan. 2:35
12 [a]Rev. 19:5 [b]Dan. 7:10 [c]Ps. 69:28 [d]Matt. 16:27 [1]NU, M *the throne*
13 [a]Rev. 1:18; 6:8; 21:4 [b]Rev. 2:23; 20:12
14 [a]1 Cor. 15:26 [b]Rev. 21:8 [1]NU, M *death, the lake of fire.*
15 [a]Rev. 19:20

CHAPTER 21

1 [a][2 Pet. 3:13] [b]Rev. 20:11
2 [a]Is. 52:1 [b]2 Cor. 11:2 [1]NU, M omit *John*
3 [a]Lev. 26:11
4 [a]Is. 25:8 [b]1 Cor. 15:26 [c]Is. 35:10; 51:11; 65:19

And they [b]will be tormented day
and night forever and ever.
11 Then I saw a great white
throne and Him who sat on it,
from whose face [a]the earth and
the heaven fled away. [b]And there
was found no place for them.
12 And I saw the dead, [a]small
and great, standing before [1]God,
[b]and books were opened. And another [c]book was opened, which
is *the Book* of Life. And the dead
were judged [d]according to their
works, by the things which were
written in the books.
13 The sea gave up the dead
who were in it, [a]and Death and
Hā′dēs delivered up the dead
who were in them. [b]And they
were judged, each one according to his works.
14 Then [a]Death and Hā′dēs
were cast into the lake of fire.
[b]This is the second [1]death.
15 And anyone not found written in the Book of Life [a]was cast
into the lake of fire.

21
Now [a]I saw a new heaven
and a new earth, [b]for the
first heaven and the first earth
had passed away. Also there was
no more sea.
2 Then I, [1]John, saw [a]the holy
city, New Jerusalem, coming
down out of heaven from God,
prepared [b]as a bride adorned for
her husband.
3 And I heard a loud voice
from heaven saying, "Behold,
[a]the tabernacle of God *is* with
men, and He will dwell with
them, and they shall be His people. God Himself will be with
them *and be* their God.
4 [a]"And God will wipe away
every tear from their eyes; [b]there
shall be no more death, [c]nor sorrow, nor crying. There shall be

no more pain, for the former
things have passed away."
5 Then [a]He who sat on the
throne said, [b]"Behold, I make all
things new." And He said [1]to me,
"Write, for [c]these words are true
and faithful."
6 And He said to me, [a]"It[1] is
done! [b]I am the Alpha and the
Omega, the Beginning and the
End. [c]I will give of the fountain
of the water of life freely to him
who thirsts.
7 "He who overcomes [1]shall
inherit all things, and [a]I will be
his God and he shall be My son.
8 [a]"But the cowardly, [1]unbe-
lieving, abominable, murderers,
sexually immoral, sorcerers,
idolaters, and all liars shall have
their part in [b]the lake which
burns with fire and brimstone,
which is the second death."
9 Then one of [a]the seven angels who had the seven bowls
filled with the seven last plagues
came [1]to me and talked with me,
saying, "Come, I will show you
[b]the [2]bride, the Lamb's wife."
10 And he carried me away [a]in
the Spirit to a great and high
mountain, and showed me [b]the
[1]great city, the [2]holy Jerusalem,
descending out of heaven from
God,
11 [a]having the glory of God. Her
light *was* like a most precious
stone, like a jasper stone, clear
as crystal.
12 Also she had a great and
high wall with [a]twelve gates, and
twelve angels at the gates, and
names written on them, which
are *the names* of the twelve
tribes of the children of Israel:
13 [a]three gates on the east, three
gates on the north, three gates
on the south, and three gates on
the west.
14 Now the wall of the city had
twelve foundations, and [a]on
them were the [1]names of the
twelve apostles of the Lamb.
15 And he who talked with me
[a]had a gold reed to measure the
city, its gates, and its wall.
16 The city is laid out as a
square; its length is as great as
its breadth. And he measured
the city with the reed: twelve
thousand [1]furlongs. Its length,
breadth, and height are equal.
17 Then he measured its wall:
one hundred *and* forty-four cubits, *according* to the measure of
a man, that is, of an angel.
18 The construction of its wall
was *of* jasper; and the city *was*
pure gold, like clear glass.
19 [a]The foundations of the wall
of the city *were* adorned with
all kinds of precious stones: the
first foundation *was* jasper, the
second sapphire, the third chal-
cedony, the fourth emerald,
20 the fifth sardonyx, the sixth
sardius, the seventh chrysolite,
the eighth beryl, the ninth topaz, the tenth chrysoprase, the
eleventh jacinth, and the twelfth
amethyst.
21 The twelve gates *were* twelve
[a]pearls: each individual gate
was of one pearl. [b]And the street
of the city *was* pure gold, like
transparent glass.
22 [a]But I saw no temple in it, for ☆
the Lord God Almighty and the
Lamb are its temple.
23 [a]The city had no need of the ☆
sun or of the moon to shine [1]in
it, for the [2]glory of God illumi-
nated it. The Lamb *is* its light.
24 [a]And the nations [1]of those
who are saved shall walk in its

5 [a]Rev. 4:2, 9; 20:11 [b]Is. 43:19 [c]Rev. 19:9; 22:6 [1]NU, M omit *to me*
6 [a]Rev. 10:6; 16:17 [b]Rev. 1:8; 22:13 [c]John 4:10 [1]M omits *It is done*
7 [a]Zech. 8:8 [1]M *I shall give him these things*
8 [a]1 Cor. 6:9 [b]Rev. 20:14 [1]M adds *and sinners,*
9 [a]Rev. 15:1 [b]Rev. 19:7; 21:2 [1]NU, M omit *to me* [2]M *woman, the Lamb's bride*
10 [a]Rev. 1:10 [b]Ezek. 48 [1]NU, M omit *great* [2]NU, M *holy city, Jerusalem*
11 [a]Rev. 15:8; 21:23; 22:5
12 [a]Ezek. 48:31–34
13 [a]Ezek. 48:31–34
14 [a]Eph. 2:20 [1]NU, M *twelve names*
15 [a]Ezek. 40:3
16 [1]Lit. *stadia,* about 1,380 miles in all
19 [a]Is. 54:11
21 [a]Matt. 13:45, 46 [b]Rev. 22:2
22 [a]John 4:21, 23
23 [a]Is. 24:23; 60:19, 20 [1]NU, M omit *in it* [2]M *very glory*
24 [a]Is. 60:3, 5; 66:12 [1]NU, M omit *of those who are saved*

light, and the kings of the earth
bring their glory and honor
[2]into it.
25 [a]Its gates shall not be shut
at all by day [b](there shall be no
night there).
26 [a]And they shall bring the
glory and the honor of the nations into [1]it.
27 But [a]there shall by no means
enter it anything [1]that defiles, or
causes an abomination or a lie,
but only those who are written
in the Lamb's [b]Book of Life.

22

And he showed me [a]a
[1]pure river of water of
life, clear as crystal, proceeding
from the throne of God and of
the Lamb.
2 [a]In the middle of its street,
and on either side of the river,
was [b]the tree of life, which bore
twelve fruits, each *tree* yielding
its fruit every month. The leaves
of the tree *were* [c]for the healing
of the nations.
☆ 3 And [a]there shall be no more
curse, [b]but the throne of God
and of the Lamb shall be in it,
and His [c]servants shall serve
Him.
4 [a]They shall see His face, and
[b]His name *shall be* on their foreheads.
5 [a]There shall be no night
there: They need no lamp nor
[b]light of the sun, for [c]the Lord
God gives them light. [d]And they
shall reign forever and ever.
6 Then he said to me, [a]"These
words *are* faithful and true."
And the Lord God of the [1]holy
prophets [b]sent His angel to show
His servants the things which
must [c]shortly take place.
7 [a]"Behold, I am coming
quickly! [b]Blessed *is* he who
keeps the words of the prophecy
of this book."
8 Now I, John, [1]saw and heard
these things. And when I heard
and saw, [a]I fell down to worship
before the feet of the angel who
showed me these things.
9 Then he said to me, [a]"See
that you do not *do that.* [1]For I
am your fellow servant, and of
your brethren the prophets, and
of those who keep the words of
this book. Worship God."
10 [a]And he said to me, "Do not
seal the words of the prophecy
of this book, [b]for the time is at
hand.
11 "He who is unjust, let him
be unjust still; he who is filthy,
let him be filthy still; he who is
righteous, let him [1]be righteous
still; he who is holy, let him be
holy still."
12 "And behold, I am coming ☆
quickly, and [a]My reward *is* with
Me, [b]to give to every one according to his work.
13 [a]"I am the Alpha and the
Omega, *the* [1]Beginning and *the*
End, the First and the Last."
14 [a]Blessed *are* those who [1]do
His commandments, that they
may have the right [b]to the tree of
life, [c]and may enter through the
gates into the city.
15 [1]But [a]outside *are* [b]dogs and
sorcerers and sexually immoral
and murderers and idolaters,
and whoever loves and practices
a lie.
16 [a]"I, Jesus, have sent My angel to testify to you these things
in the churches. [b]I am the Root
and the Offspring of David, [c]the
Bright and Morning Star."
17 And the Spirit and [a]the bride
say, "Come!" And let him who
hears say, "Come!" [b]And let him

24 [2]M *of the nations to Him*
25 [a]Is. 60:11 [b]Is. 60:20
26 [a]Rev. 21:24 [1]M adds *that they may enter in.*
27 [a]Joel 3:17 [b]Phil. 4:3 [1]NU, M *profane, nor one who causes*

CHAPTER 22

1 [a]Ezek. 47:1 [1]NU, M omit *pure*
2 [a]Ezek. 47:12 [b]Gen. 2:9 [c]Rev. 21:24
3 [a]Zech. 14:11 [b]Ezek. 48:35 [c]Rev. 7:15
4 [a][Matt. 5:8] [b]Rev. 14:1
5 [a]Rev. 21:23 [b]Rev. 7:15 [c]Ps. 36:9 [d]Dan. 7:18, 27
6 [a]Rev. 19:9 [b]Rev. 1:1 [c]Heb. 10:37 [1]NU, M *spirits of the prophets*
7 [a][Rev. 3:11] [b]Rev. 1:3
8 [a]Rev. 19:10 [1]NU, M *am the one who heard and saw*
9 [a]Rev. 19:10 [1]NU, M omit *For*
10 [a]Dan. 8:26 [b]Rev. 1:3
11 [1]NU, M *do right*
12 [a]Is. 40:10; 62:11 [b]Rev. 20:12
13 [a]Is. 41:4 [1]NU, M *First and the Last, the Beginning and the End.*
14 [a]Dan. 12:12 [b][Prov. 11:30] [c]Rev. 21:27 [1]NU *wash their robes,*
15 [a]1 Cor. 6:9 [b]Phil. 3:2 [1]NU, M omit *But*
16 [a]Rev. 1:1 [b]Rev. 5:5 [c]Num. 24:17
17 [a][Rev. 21:2, 9] [b]Is. 55:1

who thirsts come. Whoever desires, let him take the water of
life freely.
18 [1]For I testify to everyone who
hears the words of the prophecy
of this book: [a]If anyone adds to
these things, [2]God will add to
him the plagues that are written
in this book;
19 and if anyone takes away
from the words of the book of
this prophecy, [a]God[1] shall take
away his part from the [2]Book
of Life, from the holy city, and
from the things which are written in this book.
20 He who testifies to these
things says, "Surely I am coming quickly." Amen. Even so,
come, Lord Jesus!
21 The grace of our Lord Jesus
Christ *be* [1]with you all. Amen.

18 [a]Deut. 4:2; 12:32 [1]NU, M omit *For* [2]M *may God add*

19 [a]Ex. 32:33 [1]M *may God take away* [2]NU, M *tree of life*

21 [1]NU *with all;* M *with all the saints*

Concordance

CONCORDANCE

A

ABBA
And He said, "*A* . . . . Mark 14:36
whom we cry out, "*A* . . . . Rom 8:15
crying out, "*A* . . . . Gal 4:6

ABIDE
LORD, who may *a* . . . . Ps 15:1
the Most High shall *a* . . . . Ps 91:1
Helper, that He may *a* . . . . John 14:16
"If you *a* in Me . . . . John 15:7
does the love of God *a* . . . . 1 John 3:17

ABIDES
He who *a* in Me . . . . John 15:5

ABOMINATION
the *a* of desolation . . . . Dan 12:11
the '*a of desolation*' . . . . Matt 24:15

ABUNDANTLY
may have it more *a* . . . . John 10:10

ACCEPTABLE
a time I have heard . . . . Is 49:8
Proclaim the a year . . . . Luke 4:19

ACCESS
whom also we have *a*. . . . . Rom 5:2

ACCORD
daily with one *a* . . . . Acts 2:46

ACCURSED
he who is hanged is *a* . . . . Deut 21:23
not know the law is *a*. . . . . John 7:49
that I myself were *a* . . . . Rom 9:3
of God calls Jesus *a* . . . . 1 Cor 12:3

ACCUSATION
over His head the *a* . . . . Matt 27:37
they might find an *a*. . . . . Luke 6:7
Do not receive an *a* . . . . 1 Tim 5:19

ACCUSER
the *a* of our brethren . . . . Rev 12:10

ACKNOWLEDGE
in all your ways *a*. . . . . Prov 3:6

ACQUAINTED
are *a* with all my ways. . . . . Ps 139:3
a Man of sorrows and *a*. . . . . Is 53:3

ADOPTION
received the Spirit of *a* . . . . Rom 8:15
we might receive the *a*. . . . . Gal 4:5

ADULTERERS
nor idolaters, nor *a* . . . . 1 Cor 6:9
a God will judge . . . . Heb 13:4

ADULTERY
You shall not commit *a* . . . . Ex 20:14
already committed *a* . . . . Matt 5:28
a woman caught in *a* . . . . John 8:3

ADVANTAGE
Satan should take *a*. . . . . 2 Cor 2:11
no one should take *a* . . . . 1 Thess 4:6

ADVERSARY
your *a* the devil walks . . . . 1 Pet 5:8

ADVOCATE
sins, we have an *A* . . . . 1 John 2:1

AFFECTION
to his wife the *a* . . . . 1 Cor 7:3

AFFLICTION
is my comfort in my *a* . . . . Ps 119:50
For our light *a*. . . . . 2 Cor 4:17

AFRAID
garden, and I was *a* . . . . Gen 3:10
I will not be *a* of ten. . . . . Ps 3:6

AGE
and in the *a* to come . . . . Mark 10:30
the powers of the *a* . . . . Heb 6:5

AGES
ordained before the *a* . . . . 1 Cor 2:7
a was not made known . . . . Eph 3:5
at the end of the *a* . . . . Heb 9:26

AGREE
that if two of you *a*. . . . . Matt 18:19
and these three *a* . . . . 1 John 5:8

AIR
of the power of the *a* . . . . Eph 2:2

ALIVE
I kill and I make *a* . . . . Deut 32:39
go down *a* into hell . . . . Ps 55:15
presented Himself *a*. . . . . Acts 1:3
all shall be made *a* . . . . 1 Cor 15:22

trespasses, made us *a* . . . . Eph 2:5
flesh, He has made *a* . . . . Col 2:13
that we who are *a*. . . . . 1 Thess 4:15
the flesh but made *a* . . . . 1 Pet 3:18
and behold, I am *a*. . . . . Rev 1:18
These two were cast *a* . . . . Rev 19:20

ALPHA
"I am the *A* and the . . . . Rev 1:8
"I am the *A* and the . . . . Rev 22:13

ALTAR
Then Noah built an *a*. . . . . Gen 8:20
your gift to the *a*. . . . . Matt 5:23
Isaac his son on the *a* . . . . James 2:21

ALWAYS
lo, I am with you *a* . . . . Matt 28:20
thus we shall *a* . . . . 1 Thess 4:17

AM
to Moses, "I *A* WHO I *A*. . . . . Ex 3:14
Abraham was, I *A* . . . . John 8:58

ANGEL
Now the *A* of the LORD. . . . . Gen 16:7
"Behold, I send an *A* . . . . Ex 23:20
And behold, an *a* . . . . Luke 2:9
For an *a* went down at . . . . John 5:4
A who appeared to him. . . . . . . Acts 7:35

ANGELS
give His a charge . . . . Matt 4:6
but are like *a*. . . . . Matt 22:30
twelve legions of *a*. . . . . Matt 26:53

ANGER
For His *a* is but for a . . . . Ps 30:5
harsh word stirs up *a*. . . . . Prov 15:1
fierceness of His *a* . . . . .Nah 1:6

ANOINT
you shall *a* for Me the . . . . 1 Sam 16:3
a my head with oil . . . . Ps 23:5

ANOINTING
them pray over him, *a* . . . . James 5:14
But you have an *a*. . . . . 1 John 2:20

ANT
Go to the *a* . . . . Prov 6:6

ANTICHRIST
have heard that the *A* . . . . 1 John 2:18
is a deceiver and an *a* . . . . 2 John 7

ANXIOUS
Be *a* for nothing . . . . Phil 4:6

APOSTLE
called to be an *a* . . . . Rom 1:1
the signs of an *a* were . . . . 2 Cor 12:12
a preacher and an *a*. . . . . 1 Tim 2:7
consider the *A* . . . . Heb 3:1

APOSTLES
of the twelve *a* . . . . Matt 10:2
am the least of the *a*. . . . . 1 Cor 15:9
gave some to be *a*. . . . . Eph 4:11

APPEARING
Lord Jesus Christ's *a*. . . . . 1 Tim 6:14
who have loved His *a*. . . . . 2 Tim 4:8

APPOINTED
You have *a* his limits . . . . Job 14:5
And as it is *a* for men . . . . Heb 9:27

APPROVE
do the same but also *a*. . . . . . . Rom 1:32
a the things that are. . . . . Phil 1:10

ARCHANGEL
with the voice of an *a* . . . . 1 Thess 4:16
Yet Michael the *a* . . . . Jude 9

ARISE
A, shine . . . . Is 60:1

ARK
"Make yourself an *a*. . . . . Gen 6:14
Let us bring the *a*. . . . . 1 Sam 4:3

ARM
with an outstretched *a*. . . . . Ex 6:6
You have a mighty *a* . . . . Ps 89:13
therefore His own *a*. . . . . Is 59:16

ARMIES
"I defy the *a* . . . . 1 Sam 17:10
any number to His *a* . . . . Job 25:3
And the *a* in heaven. . . . . Rev 19:14

ARMOR
let us put on the *a*. . . . . Rom 13:12
Put on the whole *a*. . . . . Eph 6:11

AROMA
smelled a soothing *a* . . . . Gen 8:21
a sweet-smelling *a* . . . . Phil 4:18

B

BASKETS
they took up twelve *b* .... Matt 14:20

BATTLE
b is the LORD's............. 1 Sam 17:47
the *b* to the strong .... Eccl 9:11

BEAR
they shall *b* you up............. Ps 91:12
B one another's .... Gal 6:2

BEAST
the mark of the *b* .... Rev 19:20

BEAT
spat in His face and *b* .... Matt 26:67

BEAUTIFUL
has made everything *b* .... Eccl 3:11
my love, you are as *b*.......... Song 6:4
How *b* upon the .... Is 52:7

BED
If I make my *b* in hell........... Ps 139:8
Arise, take up your *b* .... Matt 9:6

BEGINNING
In the *b* God created .... Gen 1:1
In the *b* was the Word .... John 1:1
and the Omega, the *B* .... Rev 21:6

BEGOTTEN
glory as of the only *b*........... John 1:14

BEHOLD
B the Lamb of God............ John 1:36
B what manner of love .... 1 John 3:1

BELIEVE
B in the LORD your God ...... 2 Chr 20:20
because they did not *b*........ Mark 16:14
even to those who *b*........... John 1:12
the Lord Jesus and *b* .... Rom 10:9
comes to God must *b*.......... Heb 11:6
Even the demons *b*........... James 2:19

BELIEVED
Abraham b God .... Rom 4:3
I know whom I have *b*........ 2 Tim 1:12

BELIEVES
that whoever *b* in Him......... John 3:16
with the heart one *b*.......... Rom 10:10

BELIEVING
you ask in prayer, *b* .... Matt 21:22

BELLY
And Jonah was in the *b*......... Jon 1:17

BELOVED
My *b* is mine .... Song 2:16
a song of my *B* .... Is 5:1
for you are greatly *b* .... Dan 9:23

BESTOWED
love the Father has *b* .... 1 John 3:1

BETRAY
you, one of you will *b* .... Matt 26:21

BETRAYED
Man is about to be *b* .... Matt 17:22

BETROTHED
to a virgin *b* to a man .... Luke 1:27

BETTER
b than sacrifice............. 1 Sam 15:22
For it is *b* to marry .... 1 Cor 7:9
Christ, which is far *b*.......... Phil 1:23
b things concerning............ Heb 6:9
b things than that............ Heb 12:24

BEWARE
"*B* of false prophets .... Matt 7:15

BEWITCHED
b you that you should .... Gal 3:1

BIRTH
Now the *b* of Jesus........... Matt 1:18
conceived, it gives *b*......... James 1:15

BIRTHRIGHT
of food sold his *b* .... Heb 12:16

BISHOP
the position of a *b* .... 1 Tim 3:1
b must be blameless........... Titus 1:7

BITTERNESS
root of *b* springing up .... Heb 12:15

BLAMELESS
you holy, and *b*............... Col 1:22
without spot and *b*........... 2 Pet 3:14

BLASPHEME
may learn not to *b* .... 1 Tim 1:20
God, to *b* His name .... Rev 13:6

BLASPHEMED
the name of God is b .... Rom 2:24

BRETHREN
least of these My *b*. . . . . Matt 25:40
firstborn among many *b* . . . . . . Rom 8:29
over five hundred *b* . . . . 1 Cor 15:6

BRIDE
the Spirit and the *b* . . . . Rev 22:17

BRIDEGROOM
b fast while the. . . . . Mark 2:19

BRIGHTNESS
and kings to the *b* . . . . Is 60:3
who being the *b* . . . . Heb 1:3

BRIMSTONE
the lake of fire and *b* . . . . Rev 20:10

BROKEN
is My body which is *b* . . . . 1 Cor 11:24

BROKENHEARTED
He heals the *b* and. . . . . Ps 147:3

BROTHER
Where is Abel your *b*. . . . . Gen 4:9
and a *b* is born for . . . . Prov 17:17
how often shall my *b*. . . . . Matt 18:21

BROTHER'S
Am I my *b* keeper. . . . . Gen 4:9

BROTHERS
b did not believe. . . . . John 7:5

BRUISE
He shall *b* your head . . . . Gen 3:15
the LORD to *b* Him. . . . . Is 53:10

BRUISED
He was *b* for our. . . . . Is 53:5

BUILDER
me, as a wise master *b*. . . . . 1 Cor 3:10
foundations, whose *b*. . . . . Heb 11:10

BUILDING
field, you are God's *b*. . . . . 1 Cor 3:9

BURDEN
Cast your *b* on the . . . . Ps 55:22
easy and My *b* is light . . . . Matt 11:30

BURDENS
Bear one another's *b* . . . . Gal 6:2

BURIAL
she did it for My *b* . . . . Matt 26:12

BURIED
b with Him in baptism. . . . . Col 2:12

BUSYBODIES
but also gossips and *b* . . . . 1 Tim 5:13

C

CALF
and made a molded *c*. . . . . Ex 32:4
And bring the fatted *c* . . . . Luke 15:23

CALL
c upon Him while He. . . . . Is 55:6
'C to Me. . . . . Jer 33:3
They will *c* on My name . . . . . . Zech 13:9
c His name JESUS. . . . . Matt 1:21
How then shall they *c* . . . . Rom 10:14

CALLED
to those who are the *c* . . . . Rom 8:28
But God has *c* us to . . . . 1 Cor 7:15

CALLING
the gifts and the *c*. . . . . Rom 11:29
to walk worthy of the *c* . . . . Eph 4:1

CAMEL
it is easier for a *c* . . . . Matt 19:24
and swallow a *c* . . . . Matt 23:24

CAPTIVITY
every thought into *c*. . . . . 2 Cor 10:5

CARE
casting all your *c* . . . . 1 Pet 5:7

CARNAL
c mind is enmity. . . . . Rom 8:7
for you are still c . . . . 1 Cor 3:3

CARNALLY
c minded is death. . . . . Rom 8:6

CAST
Why are you *c* down . . . . Ps 42:5
c all our sins into . . . . Mic 7:19
In My name they will *c* . . . . . . Mark 16:17
c away your confidence. . . . . . . Heb 10:35

CATCH
down your nets for a *c*. . . . . Luke 5:4

CHARIOT
and overtake this *c*. . . . . Acts 8:29

CHASTEN
C your son while there . . . . . . Prov 19:18
a father does not c . . . . Heb 12:7

CHASTENING
do not despise the c . . . . Job 5:17

CHASTENS
the LORD loves He c . . . . Heb 12:6

CHASTISEMENT
the c for our peace . . . . Is 53:5

CHEERFUL
God loves a c giver . . . . 2 Cor 9:7

CHERUBIM
dwell between the c . . . . Ps 80:1

CHILD
c is known by his . . . . Prov 20:11
Train up a c in the . . . . Prov 22:6
For unto us a C . . . . Is 9:6
c shall lead them . . . . Is 11:6
He took a little c . . . . Mark 9:36

CHILDBEARING
she will be saved in c . . . . 1 Tim 2:15

CHILDREN
c are a heritage . . . . Ps 127:3
and become as little c . . . . Matt 18:3
the right to become c . . . . John 1:12

CHOSE
just as He c us in Him . . . . Eph 1:4
from the beginning c . . . . 2 Thess 2:13

CHOSEN
But you are a c . . . . 1 Pet 2:9

CHRIST
"You are the C . . . . Matt 16:16
It is C who died . . . . Rom 8:34
to be justified by C . . . . Gal 2:17
been crucified with C . . . . Gal 2:20
to me, to live is C . . . . Phil 1:21
confess that Jesus C . . . . Phil 2:11
Jesus C is the same . . . . Heb 13:8
that Jesus is the C . . . . 1 John 5:1

CHRISTIAN
anyone suffers as a C . . . . 1 Pet 4:16

CHRISTIANS
were first called C . . . . Acts 11:26

CHURCH
rock I will build My c . . . . Matt 16:18
body, which is the c . . . . Col 1:24

CHURCHES
strengthening the c . . . . Acts 15:41

CIRCUMCISE
c the foreskin of your . . . . Deut 10:16
is necessary to c them . . . . Acts 15:5

CIRCUMCISION
c is that of the heart . . . . Rom 2:29
C is nothing and . . . . 1 Cor 7:19

CITY
How lonely sits the c . . . . Lam 1:1
c that is set on a . . . . Matt 5:14

CLAY
Shall the c say to him . . . . Is 45:9

CLEAN
He who has c hands and . . . . Ps 24:4

CLEANSE
C me from secret . . . . Ps 19:12
And c me from my sin . . . . Ps 51:2
How can a young man c . . . . Ps 119:9
c the lepers, raise . . . . Matt 10:8

CLOTHED
all her household is c . . . . Prov 31:21
I was naked and you c . . . . Matt 25:36
that you may be c . . . . Rev 3:18

CLOTHING
to you in sheep's c . . . . Matt 7:15

CLOUD
c received Him out of . . . . Acts 1:9
great a c of witnesses . . . . Heb 12:1

CLOUDS
of Man coming on the c . . . . . . Matt 24:30

COLD
of many will grow c . . . . Matt 24:12
that you are neither c . . . . Rev 3:15

COME
who have no money, c . . . . Is 55:1
C to Me, all you who . . . . Matt 11:28
the bride say, "C . . . . Rev 22:17

COMFORT
and Your staff, they c . . . . Ps 23:4
yes, c My people . . . . Is 40:1

CRUCIFY
out again, "C Him. . . . . .Mark 15:13

CRY
and their *c* came up to. . . . . .Ex 2:23
heart and my flesh *c* . . . . Ps 84:2
I *c* out with my whole . . . . Ps 119:145
Does not wisdom *c*. . . . . Prov 8:1
"What shall I *c* . . . . .Is 40:6
His own elect who *c*. . . . . Luke 18:7

CRYING
"The voice of one c . . . . Matt 3:3
nor sorrow, nor *c* . . . . Rev 21:4

CRYSTAL
a sea of glass, like *c*. . . . . Rev 4:6

CUP
My *c* runs over . . . . Ps 23:5
Then He took the *c*. . . . . Matt 26:27
c is the new covenant . . . . . . .1 Cor 11:25

CURSE
c the ground for man's . . . . .Gen 8:21
c a ruler of your . . . . .Ex 22:28
shall not *c* the deaf. . . . . Lev 19:14
C God and die. . . . . Job 2:9
Do not *c* the king . . . . .Eccl 10:20
are cursed with a *c*. . . . . .Mal 3:9
law are under the *c* . . . . Gal 3:10

CURSES
I will curse him who *c*. . . . . .Gen 12:3
c his father or his . . . . Prov 20:20

CYMBAL
or a clanging *c* . . . . .1 Cor 13:1

D

DAILY
Give us this day our *d* . . . . Matt 6:11
I sat *d* with you. . . . . Matt 26:55
take up his cross *d*. . . . . Luke 9:23
the Scriptures *d* . . . . Acts 17:11
our Lord, I die *d* . . . . .1 Cor 15:31

DANCE
mourn, and a time to *d* . . . . .Eccl 3:4
And you did not *d* . . . . Matt 11:17

DANCED
Then David *d* before . . . . .2 Sam 6:14
daughter of Herodias *d* . . . . Matt 14:6

DANCING
saw the calf and the *d* . . . . .Ex 32:19
me my mourning into *d*. . . . . Ps 30:11

DARKNESS
d He called Night . . . . .Gen 1:5
d have seen a great . . . . .Is 9:2
cast out into outer *d*. . . . . Matt 8:12
For you were once *d*. . . . . .Eph 5:8
us from the power of *d* . . . . Col 1:13
called you out of *d* . . . . 1 Pet 2:9
and in Him is no *d* . . . . .1 John 1:5

DARTS
quench all the fiery *d*. . . . . .Eph 6:16

DAUGHTER
Rejoice greatly, O *d* . . . . Zech 9:9
"Fear not, d of Zion . . . . John 12:15
the son of Pharaoh's *d*. . . . . . . .Heb 11:24

DAUGHTERS
d shall prophesy. . . . . Acts 2:17

DAY
God called the light *D* . . . . .Gen 1:5
Remember the Sabbath *d* . . . . .Ex 20:8
d the LORD has made . . . . Ps 118:24
For the *d* of the LORD. . . . . .Joel 2:11
again the third *d*. . . . . .1 Cor 15:4

DEACONS
d be the husbands . . . . 1 Tim 3:12

DEAD
d are raised up and . . . . .Matt 11:5
for this my son was *d*. . . . . Luke 15:24
resurrection of the *d* . . . . .1 Cor 15:12
made alive, who were *d*. . . . . .Eph 2:1
And the *d* in Christ . . . . 1 Thess 4:16

DEADLY
they drink anything *d*. . . . . .Mark 16:18
d wound was healed . . . . Rev 13:3

DEAF
d shall hear the words . . . . .Is 29:18
are cleansed and the *d*. . . . . Matt 11:5

DEATH
Let me die the *d* . . . . Num 23:10
d parts you and me . . . . Ruth 1:17
For in *d* there is no. . . . . Ps 6:5
D and life are in the. . . . . Prov 18:21
the wages of sin is *d*. . . . . Rom 6:23

DIED
in due time Christ *d* . . . . Rom 5:6
Christ *d* for us. . . . . Rom 5:8

DILIGENT
d shall be made rich. . . . . Prov 13:4
Let us therefore be *d* . . . . .Heb 4:11

DIM
His eyes were not *d* . . . . Deut 34:7

DISCERNED
they are spiritually *d* . . . . .1 Cor 2:14

DISCIPLE
d is not above his . . . . Matt 10:24
he cannot be My *d* . . . . Luke 14:26

DISCIPLES
My word, you are My *d* . . . . John 8:31
so you will be My *d* . . . . John 15:8

DISCRETION
woman who lacks *d* . . . . Prov 11:22

DISOBEDIENT
out My hands to a d . . . . Rom 10:21

DISPUTES
foolish and ignorant *d* . . . . 2 Tim 2:23
But avoid foolish *d*. . . . . Titus 3:9

DISQUALIFIED
myself should become *d* . . . . . .1 Cor 9:27

DIVIDED
"Every kingdom *d* . . . . Matt 12:25
and a house *d* against . . . . Luke 11:17

DIVIDING
rightly *d* the word of . . . . 2 Tim 2:15

DIVINATION
shall you practice *d* . . . . Lev 19:26
a spirit of *d* met us . . . . Acts 16:16

DIVINE
d power has given . . . . 2 Pet 1:3

DIVISIONS
note those who cause *d* . . . . . . Rom 16:17

DIVISIVE
Reject a *d* man after. . . . . Titus 3:10

DIVORCE
her a certificate of *d*. . . . . Deut 24:1
a certificate of *d* . . . . .Mark 10:4

DO
men to *d* to you, *d*. . . . . Matt 7:12
without Me you can *d* . . . . John 15:5
good that I will to *d* . . . . Rom 7:19
or whatever you *d*, *d* . . . . .1 Cor 10:31
d all things through . . . . .Phil 4:13

DOCTRINE
with every wind of *d* . . . . Eph 4:14
is contrary to sound *d* . . . . 1 Tim 1:10
is profitable for *d* . . . . 2 Tim 3:16

DOERS
But be *d* of the word . . . . James 1:22

DOG
d returns to his own. . . . . 2 Pet 2:22

DOGS
what is holy to the *d* . . . . Matt 7:6
d eat the crumbs which . . . . . . Matt 15:27

DOMINION
let them have *d*. . . . . .Gen 1:26
made him to have *d* . . . . Ps 8:6

DONKEY
colt, the foal of a d. . . . . Matt 21:5

DOOR
sin lies at the *d* . . . . .Gen 4:7
to you, I am the *d* . . . . John 10:7
I stand at the *d* . . . . Rev 3:20

DOORKEEPER
I would rather be a *d* . . . . Ps 84:10

DOUBLE
worthy of *d* honor . . . . 1 Tim 5:17

DOUBLE-MINDED
he is a *d* man. . . . . James 1:8

DOUBTS
doubting, for he who *d* . . . . . . James 1:6

DOVE
d found no resting . . . . .Gen 8:9
I had wings like a *d* . . . . Ps 55:6
descending like a *d* . . . . Matt 3:16

DRAGON
a great, fiery red *d* . . . . Rev 12:3
they worshiped the *d*. . . . . Rev 13:4

DRAW
You have nothing to *d* . . . . John 4:11
D near to God and He . . . . James 4:8

GIFT
but the *g* of God is . . . . .Rom. 6:23
it is the *g* of God. . . . . .Eph 2:8
Do not neglect the *g*. . . . . 1 Tim 4:14
you to stir up the *g*. . . . . 2 Tim 1:6

GIFTS
and desire spiritual *g*. . . . . .1 Cor 14:1
captive, and gave g . . . . .Eph 4:8

GIVE
G us this day our . . . . Matt 6:11
but what I do have I *g* . . . . Acts 3:6

GLAD
I was *g* when they said . . . . Ps 122:1

GLADNESS
receive it with *g* . . . . .Mark 4:16

GLORIFY
"Father, *g* Your name . . . . .John 12:28

GLORY
"*G* to God in the . . . . Luke 2:14
and we beheld His *g* . . . . John 1:14

GO
'Let My people *g*. . . . . .Ex 5:1
Where can I *g* from . . . . Ps 139:7
I *g* to prepare a place. . . . . .John 14:2

GOAL
I press toward the *g*. . . . . .Phil 3:14

GOD
the *G* of Abraham . . . . Ex 3:6
G is a consuming fire. . . . . Deut 4:24
my people, and your *G* . . . . Ruth 1:16
G is our refuge . . . . Ps 46:1
Counselor, Mighty *G* . . . . .Is 9:6
and I will be their *G*. . . . . .Jer 31:33
in *G* my Savior . . . . .Luke 1:47
"For *G* so loved the. . . . . John 3:16
Christ is the Son of *G* . . . . Acts 8:37
Indeed, let *G* be true . . . . Rom 3:4
G shall supply all . . . . Phil 4:19
for *G* is love. . . . . .1 John 4:8

GODHEAD
the fullness of the *G*. . . . . Col 2:9

GODLINESS
having a form of *g* . . . . 2 Tim 3:5
pertain to life and *g* . . . . 2 Pet 1:3

GOLD
is like apples of *g* . . . . Prov 25:11
more precious than *g*. . . . . 1 Pet 1:7
of the city was pure *g* . . . . .Rev 21:21

GOOD
who went about doing *g* . . . . . Acts 10:38
g man someone would. . . . . Rom 5:7
overcome evil with *g* . . . . Rom 12:21

GOODNESS
Surely *g* and mercy . . . . Ps 23:6

GOODS
and plunder his *g*. . . . . Matt 12:29
Soul, you have many *g* . . . . . . Luke 12:19
has this world's *g*. . . . . .1 John 3:17

GOSPEL
and believe in the *g* . . . . .Mark 1:15
not ashamed of the *g*. . . . . Rom 1:16

GOVERNMENT
and the *g* will be upon. . . . . .Is 9:6

GRACE
But Noah found *g*. . . . . .Gen 6:8
G to you and peace . . . . Rom 1:7
My *g* is sufficient . . . . .2 Cor 12:9
g you have been saved. . . . . .Eph 2:8
But He gives more *g*. . . . . .James 4:6

GRAIN
unless a *g* of wheat . . . . John 12:24

GRAPES
brought forth wild *g*. . . . . .Is 5:2
have eaten sour *g*. . . . . Ezek 18:2

GRASS
The *g* withers . . . . .Is 40:7
"*All flesh is as g* . . . . 1 Pet 1:24

GREAT
and make your name *g* . . . . .Gen 12:2
g is Your faithfulness . . . . Lam 3:23
one pearl of *g* price . . . . Matt 13:46
Then I saw a *g* white . . . . Rev 20:11

GREATER
g things than these. . . . . John 1:50
G love has no one. . . . . .John 15:13

GREATEST
little child is the *g*. . . . . Matt 18:4
be considered the *g* . . . . Luke 22:24

HEARING
or by the *h* of faith . . . . Gal 3:2

HEART
LORD looks at the *h*. . . . . 1 Sam 16:7
My *h* and my flesh cry . . . . Ps 84:2
as he thinks in his *h*. . . . . Prov 23:7
h is deceitful above . . . . Jer 17:9
and take the stony *h* . . . . Ezek 11:19
are the pure in *h*. . . . . Matt 5:8
h will flow rivers . . . . John 7:38
"Let not your *h* . . . . John 14:1

HEARTS
And he will turn the *h* . . . . Mal 4:6
h failing them from . . . . Luke 21:26
will guard your *h* . . . . Phil 4:7
of God rule in your *h* . . . . Col 3:15

HEAVEN
on earth as it is in *h*. . . . . Matt 6:10
"*H* and earth will . . . . Matt 24:35
laid up for you in *h*. . . . . Col 1:5

HEAVENLY
your *h* Father will. . . . . Matt 6:14
h host praising God . . . . Luke 2:13

HEAVENS
h declare the glory . . . . Ps 19:1
For as the *h* are high . . . . Ps 103:11
h are the work of Your . . . . Heb 1:10

HEEL
you shall bruise His *h* . . . . Gen 3:15

HEIGHT
nor *h* nor depth. . . . . Rom 8:39
length and depth and *h* . . . . Eph 3:18

HEIRS
of God and joint *h* . . . . Rom 8:17
should be fellow *h* . . . . Eph 3:6

HELL
go down alive into *h* . . . . Ps 55:15
his soul from *h* . . . . Prov 23:14
"*H* from beneath is. . . . . Is 14:9
to be cast into *h* . . . . Matt 18:9
power to cast into *h* . . . . Luke 12:5
it is set on fire by *h*. . . . . James 3:6

HELMET
And take the *h* of . . . . Eph 6:17

HELP
A very present *h*. . . . . Ps 46:1

HELPER
I will make him a *h* . . . . Gen 2:18
"But when the *H*. . . . . John 15:26

HELPS
the Spirit also *h* . . . . Rom 8:26

HERESIES
in destructive *h*. . . . . 2 Pet 2:1

HIDDEN
Your word I have *h*. . . . . Ps 119:11
h that will not . . . . Matt 10:26

HIGH
know that the Most *H* . . . . Dan 4:17
h thing that exalts . . . . 2 Cor 10:5
and faithful *H* Priest . . . . Heb 2:17

HOLY
where you stand is *h* . . . . Ex 3:5
priests and a *h* nation . . . . Ex 19:6
the LORD your God am *h* . . . . Lev 19:2
God, in His *h* mountain . . . . Ps 48:1
"*H, h, h* is the LORD . . . . Is 6:3
baptize you with the *H* . . . . Mark 1:8
all filled with the *H* . . . . Acts 2:4
receive the *H* Spirit . . . . Acts 19:2
it is written, "*Be h* . . . . 1 Pet 1:16

HOME
to him and make Our *h* . . . . . . John 14:23
to show piety at *h*. . . . . 1 Tim 5:4

HONOR
H your father and your . . . . Matt 15:4
worthy of double *h*. . . . . 1 Tim 5:17

HONORABLE
Marriage is *h* among . . . . Heb 13:4

HOPE
For You are my *h*. . . . . Ps 71:5
O the *H* of Israel. . . . . Jer 14:8
good that one should *h* . . . . Lam 3:26
h does not disappoint . . . . Rom 5:5
And now abide faith, *h* . . . . . . 1 Cor 13:13
were called in one *h*. . . . . Eph 4:4
h which is laid . . . . Col 1:5
Christ in you, the *h*. . . . . Col 1:27
Jesus Christ, our *h* . . . . 1 Tim 1:1
to lay hold of the *h*. . . . . Heb 6:18
us again to a living *h* . . . . 1 Pet 1:3

HORN
h will be exalted. . . . . Ps 112:9

HORSE
The *h* and its rider He . . . . Ex 15:1
h is a vain hope . . . . Ps 33:17

HOSPITABLE
Be *h* to one another . . . . 1 Pet 4:9

HOSTS
LORD of *h* is His name . . . . Is 47:4
against spiritual *h* . . . . Eph 6:12

HOUR
day and *h* no one knows . . . . . Matt 24:36

HOUSE
But as for me and my *h* . . . . . . Josh 24:15
'Set your *h* in order . . . . .Is 38:1
h divided against . . . . Matt 12:25
h are many mansions . . . . John 14:2

HOUSEHOLD
saved, you and your *h* . . . . Acts 16:31

HUMBLE
man Moses was very *h* . . . . Num 12:3
h shall hear of it and . . . . Ps 34:2
associate with the *h* . . . . Rom 12:16
h yourselves under the . . . . 1 Pet 5:6

HUNGER
are those who *h* . . . . Matt 5:6

HUNGRY
gives food to the *h* . . . . Ps 146:7
your soul to the *h* . . . . .Is 58:10
'for I was *h* and you . . . . Matt 25:35

HUSBAND
She also gave to her *h* . . . . .Gen 3:6
h safely trusts her . . . . Prov 31:11
For the unbelieving *h* . . . . .1 Cor 7:14
For the *h* is head of . . . . .Eph 5:23
the *h* of one wife . . . . 1 Tim 3:2

HUSBANDS
H, love your wives . . . . .Eph 5:25

HYPOCRISY
Pharisees, which is *h* . . . . Luke 12:1
Let love be without *h* . . . . Rom 12:9

HYSSOP
Purge me with *h* . . . . Ps 51:7

I

IDLE
i word men may speak . . . . Matt 12:36
they learn to be *i* . . . . 1 Tim 5:13

IDOLS
stolen the household *i* . . . . .Gen 31:19
This was offered to *i* . . . . .1 Cor 10:28
keep yourselves from *i* . . . . . .1 John 5:21

IMITATE
I urge you, *i* me . . . . .1 Cor 4:16
i those who through . . . . .Heb 6:12

IMMORALITY
except sexual *i* . . . . Matt 5:32
abstain from sexual *i* . . . . 1 Thess 4:3

IMMORTALITY
mortal must put on *i* . . . . .1 Cor 15:53

IMPOSSIBLE
and nothing will be *i* . . . . Matt 17:20
God nothing will be *i* . . . . Luke 1:37
without faith it is *i* . . . . .Heb 11:6

INCORRUPTIBLE
dead will be raised *i* . . . . .1 Cor 15:52
corruptible seed but *i* . . . . 1 Pet 1:23

INFIRMITIES
He Himself took our i . . . . Matt 8:17
boast, except in my *i* . . . . .2 Cor 12:5

INHERITANCE
we have obtained an *i* . . . . .Eph 1:11
i incorruptible . . . . 1 Pet 1:4

INIQUITIES
forgives all your *i* . . . . Ps 103:3
was bruised for our *i* . . . . .Is 53:5
i have separated you . . . . .Is 59:2

INIQUITY
If I regard *i* in my . . . . Ps 66:18
has laid on Him the *i* . . . . .Is 53:6

INTEGRITY
In the *i* of my heart . . . . .Gen 20:5
he holds fast to his *i* . . . . Job 2:3
I have walked in my *i* . . . . Ps 26:1
The *i* of the upright . . . . Prov 11:3

INTERCESSION
of many, and made *i* . . . . Is 53:12
Spirit Himself makes *i* . . . . Rom 8:26
always lives to make *i* . . . . Heb 7:25

INTERPRET
pray that he may *i* . . . . .1 Cor 14:13

KNEW
Adam *k* Eve his wife . . . . Gen 4:1
in the womb I *k*. . . . . Jer 1:5
to them, 'I never *k* . . . . Matt 7:23
k what was in man. . . . . John 2:25

KNOCK
k, and it will be. . . . . Matt 7:7
at the door and *k* . . . . Rev 3:20

KNOW
k that my Redeemer. . . . . Job 19:25
k that I am God. . . . . Ps 46:10
We speak what We *k* . . . . John 3:11
k what we worship. . . . . John 4:22

KNOWLEDGE
and the tree of the *k*. . . . . Gen 2:9
k is too wonderful . . . . Ps 139:6
Wise people store up *k* . . . . . . Prov 10:14
k shall increase. . . . . Dan 12:4
you have rejected *k* . . . . Hos 4:6
K puffs up . . . . 1 Cor 8:1

KNOWS
searches the hearts *k*. . . . . Rom 8:27
k the things of God . . . . 1 Cor 2:11
k those who are His . . . . 2 Tim 2:19

L

LABOR
Six days you shall *l* . . . . Ex 20:9
to Me, all you who *l* . . . . Matt 11:28
but rather let him *l*. . . . . Eph 4:28

LABORERS
but the *l* are few . . . . Matt 9:37

LACK
"One thing you *l* . . . . Mark 10:21

LAMB
but where is the *l* . . . . Gen 22:7
took the poor man's *l*. . . . . 2 Sam 12:4
He was led as a *l*. . . . . Is 53:7
The *L* of God who takes . . . . . . John 1:29
of Christ, as of a *l*. . . . . 1 Pet 1:19
by the blood of the *L* . . . . Rev 12:11
supper of the *L*. . . . . Rev 19:9

LAME
blind see and the *l* . . . . Matt 11:5
And a certain man *l* . . . . Acts 3:2

LAMP
Your word is a *l* . . . . Ps 119:105
Nor do they light a *l*. . . . . Matt 5:15
"The *l* of the body. . . . . Matt 6:22

LAND
l that I will show you . . . . Gen 12:1
l flowing with milk. . . . . Ex 3:8

LANGUAGE
whole earth had one *l* . . . . Gen 11:1
speak in his own *l* . . . . Acts 2:6

LAUGH
Why did Sarah *l* . . . . Gen 18:13

LAW
Oh, how I love Your *l* . . . . Ps 119:97
for this is the *L* . . . . Matt 7:12
you are not under *l*. . . . . Rom 6:14
l is fulfilled in one . . . . Gal 5:14
into the perfect *l*. . . . . James 1:25

LEAD
And do not *l* us into . . . . Matt 6:13

LEAVE
a man shall *l* his . . . . Gen 2:24
"I will never l . . . . Heb 13:5

LEAVEN
of heaven is like *l*. . . . . Matt 13:33
and beware of the *l* . . . . Matt 16:6
know that a little *l* . . . . 1 Cor 5:6

LED
For as many as are *l*. . . . . Rom 8:14
l captivity captive. . . . . Eph 4:8

LENDS
has pity on the poor *l*. . . . . Prov 19:17

LENGTH
is your life and the *l*. . . . . Deut 30:20
L of days is in her. . . . . Prov 3:16

LETTER
for the *l* kills . . . . 2 Cor 3:6
or by word or by *l*. . . . . 2 Thess 2:2

LEVIATHAN
"Can you draw out *L* . . . . Job 41:1

LEVITE
"Is not Aaron the *L*. . . . . Ex 4:14

LIAR
for he is a *l* and the .... John 8:44
but every man a *l* .... Rom 3:4
God has made Him a *l* .... 1 John 5:10

LIBERTY
year, and proclaim *l* .... Lev 25:10
to proclaim *l* to the .... Is 61:1
Lord is, there is *l* .... 2 Cor 3:17
the perfect law of *l* .... James 1:25
yet not using *l* .... 1 Pet 2:16

LIE
man, that He should *l* .... Num 23:19
Do not *l* to one .... Col 3:9

LIFE
the breath of *l* .... Gen 2:7
'For the *l* of the .... Lev 17:11
before you today *l* .... Deut 30:15
word has given me *l* .... Ps 119:50
She is a tree of *l* .... Prov 3:18
is that wisdom gives *l* .... Eccl 7:12
not worry about your *l* .... Matt 6:25
l does not consist .... Luke 12:15
so the Son gives *l* .... John 5:21
resurrection and the *l* .... John 11:25
l which I now live .... Gal 2:20
l is hidden with .... Col 3:3
that pertain to *l* .... 2 Pet 1:3
who has the Son has *l* .... 1 John 5:12
the Lamb's Book of *L* .... Rev 21:27
the water of *l* freely .... Rev 22:17

LIFT
I will *l* up my eyes to .... Ps 121:1

LIGHT
"Let there be *l* .... Gen 1:3
The LORD is my *l* .... Ps 27:1
"You are the *l* .... Matt 5:14
"Let your *l* so shine .... Matt 5:16
and the life was the *l* .... John 1:4
Walk as children of *l* .... Eph 5:8
into His marvelous *l* .... 1 Pet 2:9
to you, that God is *l* .... 1 John 1:5
The Lamb is its *l* .... Rev 21:23

LIGHTNING
saw Satan fall like *l* .... Luke 10:18

LIKENESS
according to Our *l* .... Gen 1:26
carved image—any *l* .... Ex 20:4
when I awake in Your *l* .... Ps 17:15

LILY
the *l* of the valleys .... Song 2:1
shall grow like the *l* .... Hos 14:5

LINE
upon precept, *l* upon *l* .... Is 28:10
I am setting a plumb *l* .... Amos 7:8

LIVE
but the just shall *l* .... Hab 2:4
'Man shall not l .... Matt 4:4
to me, to *l* is Christ .... Phil 1:21

LOAVES
have here only five *l* .... Matt 14:17

LONGSUFFERING
is love, joy, peace, *l* .... Gal 5:22

LOOK
"*L* to Me, and be saved .... Is 45:22

LOOKING
l unto Jesus .... Heb 12:2

LOOSE
and whatever you *l* .... Matt 16:19

LORD
L is a man of war .... Ex 15:3
L our God, the *L* .... Deut 6:4
L is near to all who .... Ps 145:18
L is a God of justice .... Is 30:18
L Our Righteousness .... Jer 23:6
L God is my strength .... Hab 3:19
shall worship the L .... Matt 4:10
why do you call Me '*L* .... Luke 6:46
'Who are You, *L* .... Acts 26:15
that Jesus Christ is *L* .... Phil 2:11
L God Omnipotent .... Rev 19:6

LOTS
garments, casting *l* .... Mark 15:24

LOVE
l your neighbor as .... Lev 19:18
l the LORD your God .... Deut 6:5
l covers all sins .... Prov 10:12
a time to *l* .... Eccl 3:8
banner over me was *l* .... Song 2:4
to you, *l* your enemies .... Matt 5:44
"If you *l* Me .... John 14:15
l one another as I .... John 15:12

Let *l* be without .... Rom 12:9
up, but *l* edifies ....1 Cor 8:1
L never fails ....1 Cor 13:8
greatest of these is *l*..........1 Cor 13:13
For the *l* of Christ.............2 Cor 5:14
fruit of the Spirit is *l* .... Gal 5:22
Husbands, *l* your wives ....Eph 5:25
l their husbands .... Titus 2:4
for "*l will cover a* ....1 Pet 4:8
we *l* the brethren ....1 John 3:14
know God, for God is *l*.........1 John 4:8
have left your first *l* ....Rev 2:4

LOVINGKINDNESS
l is better than life ....Ps 63:3

LUKEWARM
because you are *l*...................Rev 3:16

LYING
I hate and abhor *l*............ Ps 119:163
righteous man hates *l* .... Prov 13:5
signs, and *l* wonders ....2 Thess 2:9

M

MAGNIFIED
For You have *m* Your .... Ps 138:2

MAJESTY
splendor of Your *m*................Ps 145:5
eyewitnesses of His *m* .... 2 Pet 1:16
wise, be glory and *m* ....Jude 25

MAKE
Let Us *m* man in Our............Gen 1:26
m Our home with him.........John 14:23

MALICE
laying aside all *m*................ 1 Pet 2:1

MAN
"Let Us make *m* ....Gen 1:26
"You are the *m* ....2 Sam 12:7
"Behold the *M*...................John 19:5
since by *m* came death ......1 Cor 15:21
in Himself one new *m*............Eph 2:15

MANGER
and laid Him in a *m*.............Luke 2:7

MANIFESTED
"I have *m* Your name ....John 17:6
God was *m* in the flesh ....1 Tim 3:16
the love of God was *m*...........1 John 4:9

MANNA
of Israel ate *m*.......................Ex 16:35
Our fathers ate the *m*..........John 6:31
of the hidden *m* ....Rev 2:17

MANNER
in an unworthy *m*...............1 Cor 11:27
as is the *m* of some.............Heb 10:25

MANSIONS
house are many *m* .... John 14:2

MARK
And the LORD set a *m*..........Gen 4:15
M the blameless man............ Ps 37:37
whoever receives the *m*........Rev 14:11

MARRED
so His visage was *m*..............Is 52:14

MARRIAGE
nor are given in *m* .... Matt 22:30
her in *m* does well ....1 Cor 7:38
M is honorable among..........Heb 13:4
the *m* of the Lamb has...........Rev 19:7

MARRY
it is better not to *m*........... Matt 19:10
they neither *m* nor are........ Matt 22:30
let them *m*.........................1 Cor 7:9
forbidding to *m*................... 1 Tim 4:3
the younger widows *m* ...... 1 Tim 5:14

MARVELED
Jesus heard it, He *m*............Matt 8:10
And the multitudes *m* ....Matt 9:33

MARVELOUS
m are Your works .... Ps 139:14
of darkness into His *m* .... 1 Pet 2:9

MASTER
not greater than his *m*........ John 15:20
m builder I have laid ....1 Cor 3:10

MASTERS
can serve two *m*.................Luke 16:13

MEASURE
to each one a *m* .... Rom 12:3

MEDIATOR
is one God and one *M* .... 1 Tim 2:5
as He is also *M*......................Heb 8:6
to Jesus the *M* of the ....Heb 12:24

MEEK
Blessed are the *m*. . . . . Matt 5:5

MEMBERS
that your bodies are *m*. . . . . .1 Cor 6:15

MENSERVANTS
And on My m and on My . . . . . Acts 2:18

MERCIFUL
Blessed are the *m*. . . . . Matt 5:7
saying, 'God be *m*. . . . . Luke 18:13

MERCY
but showing *m* to . . . . Ex 20:6
and abundant in *m*. . . . . Num 14:18
m endures forever . . . . .1 Chr 16:34
do justly, to love *m* . . . . Mic 6:8
that we may obtain *m* . . . . .Heb 4:16

MERRY
m heart makes a. . . . . Prov 15:13
eat, drink, and be *m*. . . . . .Eccl 8:15

MESSIAH
until *M* the Prince . . . . .Dan 9:25
"We have found the *M*. . . . . John 1:41

MIDST
I am there in the *m*. . . . . Matt 18:20

MIGHT
'Not by *m* nor by . . . . Zech 4:6

MIGHTY
How the *m* have fallen. . . . . . . 2 Sam 1:19
The LORD *m* in battle . . . . Ps 24:8
their Redeemer is *m*. . . . . Prov 23:11
Woe to men *m* at . . . . .Is 5:22

MIND
perfect peace, whose *m*. . . . . .Is 26:3
Be of the same *m* . . . . Rom 12:16

MINISTERS
angels spirits, His *m* . . . . Ps 104:4
commend ourselves as *m* . . . . . .2 Cor 6:4

MIRACLES
God worked unusual *m*. . . . . . Acts 19:11
the working of *m* . . . . .1 Cor 12:10

MITES
widow putting in two *m* . . . . . .Luke 21:2

MOCKED
knee before Him and *m*. . . . . . Matt 27:29
deceived, God is not *m* . . . . Gal 6:7

MONEY
tables of the *m* changers . . . . . Matt 21:12
and hid his lord's *m* . . . . Matt 25:18
not greedy for *m*. . . . . 1 Tim 3:3

MORNING
Lucifer, son of the *m* . . . . .Is 14:12
the Bright and *M* Star . . . . Rev 22:16

MOTHER
because she was the *m* . . . . Gen 3:20
leave his father and m. . . . . Matt 19:5
"Behold your *m*!" . . . . John 19:27

MOUNTAIN
you will say to this *m*. . . . . Matt 17:20
with Him on the holy *m*. . . . . . . 2 Pet 1:18

MOUNTAINS
in Judea flee to the *m*. . . . . Matt 24:16

MOURN
a time to *m* .Eccl 3:4
are those who *m*. . . . . Matt 5:4
of the earth will *m* . . . . Rev 1:7

MOURNING
I will turn their *m*. . . . . .Jer 31:13

MULTIPLY
"Be fruitful and *m* . . . . Gen 1:22
m your descendants. . . . . Gen 16:10

MULTITUDE
compassion on the *m*. . . . . Matt 15:32

MURDER
'You shall not m. . . . . Matt 5:21
threats and *m* against . . . . Acts 9:1

MUZZLE
"You shall not m . . . . 1 Tim 5:18

MYSTERIES
the spirit he speaks *m* . . . . .1 Cor 14:2

MYSTERY
Behold, I tell you a *m*. . . . . . . .1 Cor 15:51
made known to us the *m*. . . . . .Eph 1:9

N

NAKED
And they were both *n* . . . . Gen 2:25
N I came from my . . . . Job 1:21
'I was *n* and you . . . . Matt 25:36

in Him should not *p* .... John 3:16
that any should *p* .... 2 Pet 3:9

PERSECUTE
p me wrongfully .... Ps 119:86
when they revile and *p* .... Matt 5:11
Bless those who *p* .... Rom 12:14

PERSEVERANCE
tribulation produces *p* .... Rom 5:3
to this end with all *p* .... Eph 6:18

PERSON
express image of His *p* .... Heb 1:3
let it be the hidden *p* .... 1 Pet 3:4

PERSUADE
"You almost *p* me .... Acts 26:28
the Lord, we *p* men .... 2 Cor 5:11
For do I now *p* men .... Gal 1:10

PERSUADED
p that He is able .... 2 Tim 1:12

PERVERSE
p lips far from you .... Prov 4:24
from this *p* generation .... Acts 2:40

PHYSICIAN
Gilead, is there no *p* .... Jer 8:22
have no need of a *p* .... Matt 9:12
Luke the beloved *p* .... Col 4:14

PIERCED
p My hands and My feet .... Ps 22:16
Me whom they have *p* .... Zech 12:10
of the soldiers *p* .... John 19:34
and they also who *p* .... Rev 1:7

PILLAR
and she became a *p* .... Gen 19:26
and by night in a *p* .... Ex 13:21

PIT
cast him into some *p* .... Gen 37:20
who go down to the *p* .... Ps 28:1
a harlot is a deep *p* .... Prov 23:27
up my life from the *p* .... Jon 2:6
if it falls into a *p* .... Matt 12:11
into the bottomless *p* .... Rev 20:3

PITY
"Have *p* on me .... Job 19:21
for someone to take *p* .... Ps 69:20
And should I not *p* .... Jon 4:11

PLACE
Come, see the *p* .... Matt 28:6
I go to prepare a *p* .... John 14:2
might go to his own *p* .... Acts 1:25

PLAGUES
I will send all My *p* .... Ex 9:14
p that are written .... Rev 22:18

PLANT
a time to *p* .... Eccl 3:2
Him as a tender *p* .... Is 53:2
p which My heavenly .... Matt 15:13

PLANTED
I *p*, Apollos watered .... 1 Cor 3:6

PLAY
p skillfully with a .... Ps 33:3
nursing child shall *p* .... Is 11:8

PLEASANT
how good and how *p* .... Ps 133:1
P words are like a .... Prov 16:24

PLEASE
in the flesh cannot *p* .... Rom 8:8
is impossible to *p* Him .... Heb 11:6

PLEASURE
not a God who takes *p* .... Ps 5:4
for He has no *p* .... Eccl 5:4
shall perform all My *p* .... Is 44:28
your Father's good *p* .... Luke 12:32

PLEASURES
Your right hand are *p* .... Ps 16:11
to enjoy the passing *p* .... Heb 11:25

PLOW
put his hand to the *p* .... Luke 9:62

PLUMB
a *p* line, with a *p* .... Amos 7:7

POISON
"The p of asps is .... Rom 3:13
evil, full of deadly *p* .... James 3:8

POOR
p will never cease .... Deut 15:11
soul grieved for the *p* .... Job 30:25
p man cried out .... Ps 34:6
a slack hand becomes *p* ...... Prov 10:4
the alien or the *p* .... Zech 7:10
p have the gospel .... Matt 11:5

your sakes He became *p* . . . . . . .2 Cor 8:9
should remember the *p* . . . . Gal 2:10
wretched, miserable, *p* . . . . Rev 3:17

PORTION
I will divide Him a *p* . . . . .Is 53:12
"The LORD is my *p* . . . . Lam 3:24
and appoint him his *p* . . . . Matt 24:51
Father, give me the *p* . . . . Luke 15:12

POSSIBLE
God all things are *p* . . . . Matt 19:26
p that the blood . . . . .Heb 10:4

POUR
p My Spirit on your . . . . .Is 44:3
that I will *p* out My . . . . .Joel 2:28

POURED
I am *p* out like water . . . . Ps 22:14
I am already being *p* . . . . 2 Tim 4:6

POVERTY
but it leads to *p*. . . . . Prov 11:24
p might become rich . . . . .2 Cor 8:9

POWER
that I may show My *p* . . . . Ex 9:16
Not by might nor by *p* . . . . Zech 4:6
you are endued with *p*. . . . . Luke 24:49
you shall receive *p* . . . . Acts 1:8
for it is the *p* . . . . Rom 1:16
greatness of His *p* . . . . Eph 1:19
by the word of His *p*. . . . . .Heb 1:3

PRAISE
that has breath *p* . . . . Ps 150:6
Let another man *p* . . . . Prov 27:2
for You are my *p* . . . . .Jer 17:14
You have perfected p. . . . . Matt 21:16
should be to the *p*. . . . . Eph 1:12
the sacrifice of *p*. . . . . .Heb 13:15
saying, "*P* our God . . . . Rev 19:5

PRAISES
enthroned in the *p* . . . . Ps 22:3
it is good to sing *p* . . . . Ps 147:1

PRAY
LORD in ceasing to *p*. . . . . 1 Sam 12:23
"But you, when you *p*. . . . . Matt 6:6
to the mountain to *p* . . . . .Mark 6:46
"Lord, teach us to *p* . . . . Luke 11:1
men always ought to *p* . . . . Luke 18:1
I do not *p* for the. . . . . John 17:9
know what we should *p*. . . . . . . Rom 8:26
p without ceasing . . . . .1 Thess 5:17
Let him *p*. . . . . James 5:13

PRAYER
continually to *p* . . . . Acts 6:4
steadfastly in *p*. . . . . .Rom 12:12
to fasting and *p*. . . . . .1 Cor 7:5
but in everything by *p* . . . . Phil 4:6
And the *p* of faith. . . . . James 5:15

PREACH
that great city, and *p* . . . . Jon 3:2
time Jesus began to *p* . . . . Matt 4:17
p the gospel to the . . . . Luke 4:18
And how shall they *p*. . . . . Rom 10:15
p Christ crucified . . . . .1 Cor 1:23
For we do not *p*. . . . . .2 Cor 4:5
p Christ even from . . . . Phil 1:15
P the word. . . . . 2 Tim 4:2

PREDESTINED
He foreknew, He also *p* . . . . Rom 8:29
having *p* us to . . . . Eph 1:5
inheritance, being *p*. . . . . Eph 1:11

PRESENCE
themselves from the *p* . . . . Gen 3:8
p is fullness of joy . . . . Ps 16:11
Be silent in the *p*. . . . . Zeph 1:7

PRESENT
p your bodies a living . . . . Rom 12:1
absent in body but *p* . . . . .1 Cor 5:3
p you faultless . . . . Jude 24

PREVAIL
our tongue we will *p* . . . . Ps 12:4
of Hades shall not *p*. . . . . Matt 16:18

PRIDE
P goes before . . . . Prov 16:18

PRIEST
so He shall be a *p*. . . . . Zech 6:13
and faithful High *P* . . . . Heb 2:17
we have a great High *P*. . . . . Heb 4:14
p forever according . . . . Heb 5:6

PRIESTHOOD
has an unchangeable *p* . . . . Heb 7:24
house, a holy *p* . . . . 1 Pet 2:5
generation, a royal *p* . . . . 1 Pet 2:9

PRIESTS
to Me a kingdom of *p*. . . . . Ex 19:6
made us kings and *p* . . . . Rev 1:6
but they shall be *p* . . . . Rev 20:6

PRINCE
"Who made you a *p* . . . . Ex 2:14
everlasting Father, *P* . . . . Is 9:6
according to the *p* . . . . Eph 2:2

PRISON
and put him into the *p*. . . . . Gen 39:20
to the spirits in *p* . . . . 1 Pet 3:19

PRIZE
the goal for the *p* . . . . Phil 3:14

PROCLAIM
began to *p* it freely. . . . . .Mark 1:45
knowing, Him I *p* . . . . Acts 17:23
drink this cup, you *p* . . . . 1 Cor 11:26

PRODIGAL
with *p* living . . . . Luke 15:13

PROMISE
but to wait for the *P*. . . . . Acts 1:4
is made void and the *p*. . . . . Rom 4:14
it is no longer of *p* . . . . Gal 3:18
Therefore, since a *p* . . . . .Heb 4:1

PROMISES
For all the *p* of God . . . . .2 Cor 1:20
patience inherit the *p*. . . . . .Heb 6:12

PROPHECY
miracles, to another *p* . . . . . . .1 Cor 12:10
for *p* never came by the. . . . . . 2 Pet 1:21

PROPHESIED
Lord, have we not *p* . . . . Matt 7:22
virgin daughters who *p* . . . . Acts 21:9

PROPHESY
prophets, "Do not *p* . . . . .Is 30:10
the prophets *p* falsely . . . . .Jer 5:31
saying, "*P* to us. . . . . Matt 26:68
your daughters shall p. . . . . Acts 2:17
if prophecy, let us *p* . . . . Rom 12:6
know in part and we *p*. . . . . . . .1 Cor 13:9
desire earnestly to *p* . . . . .1 Cor 14:39

PROPHET
raise up for you a *P* . . . . Deut 18:15
send you Elijah the *p*. . . . . Mal 4:5
p shall receive a . . . . Matt 10:41
with him the false *p* . . . . Rev 19:20

PROPHETS
to be apostles, some *p* . . . . .Eph 4:11
blood of saints and *p* . . . . Rev 16:6

PROPITIATION
set forth to be a *p*. . . . . Rom 3:25
to God, to make *p*. . . . . .Heb 2:17
His Son to be the *p*. . . . . .1 John 4:10

PROSPER
I pray that you may *p*. . . . . 3 John 2

PROUD
He has scattered the *p*. . . . . Luke 1:51
"God resists the p. . . . . 1 Pet 5:5

PROVIDE
"My son, God will *p* . . . . .Gen 22:8
if anyone does not *p*. . . . . 1 Tim 5:8

PROVOKE
you, fathers, do not *p* . . . . .Eph 6:4

PSALMS
to one another in *p*. . . . . .Eph 5:19
Let him sing *p*. . . . . James 5:13

PUNISH
p your iniquity . . . . Lam 4:22
So I will *p* them for . . . . .Hos 4:9

PURE
a mercy seat of *p* gold . . . . Ex 25:17
To such as are *p* . . . . Ps 73:1
whatever things are *p* . . . . Phil 4:8
keep yourself *p*. . . . . 1 Tim 5:22
p all things are *p* . . . . Titus 1:15
babes, desire the *p* . . . . 1 Pet 2:2
just as He is *p* . . . . 1 John 3:3

PURGE
P me with hyssop . . . . Ps 51:7

PURIFY
p the sons of Levi. . . . . .Mal 3:3
and *p* your hearts. . . . . James 4:8

PURPLE
they put on Him a *p*. . . . . John 19:2
She was a seller of *p* . . . . Acts 16:14

PURPOSE
a time for every *p*. . . . . .Eccl 3:1
But for this *p* I came . . . . John 12:27

Q

QUARREL
any fool can start a *q* . . . . Prov 20:3
of the Lord must not *q* . . . . 2 Tim 2:24

QUEEN
Q Vashti also made a . . . . Esth 1:9
"The *q* of the South . . . . Matt 12:42

QUENCH
Do not *q* the Spirit . . . . 1 Thess 5:19

QUIETNESS
in *q* and confidence . . . . Is 30:15

QUIVER
the man who has his *q* . . . . Ps 127:5

R

RACE
I have finished the *r* . . . . 2 Tim 4:7
with endurance the *r* . . . . Heb 12:1

RAIN
given you the former *r* . . . . Joel 2:23
the good, and sends *r* . . . . Matt 5:45
that it would not *r* . . . . James 5:17

RAINBOW
"I set My *r* in the . . . . Gen 9:13
and there was a *r* . . . . Rev 4:3

RAISE
third day He will *r* . . . . Hos 6:2

RAISED
Spirit of Him who *r* . . . . Rom 8:11
"How are the dead *r* . . . . 1 Cor 15:35
and the dead will be *r* . . . . 1 Cor 15:52

RANSOM
"I will *r* them from . . . . Hos 13:14
to give His life a *r* . . . . Mark 10:45
who gave Himself a *r* . . . . 1 Tim 2:6

REAP
r the whirlwind . . . . Hos 8:7
they neither sow nor *r* . . . . Matt 6:26
due season we shall *r* . . . . Gal 6:9

REASON
Come now, and let us *r* . . . . Is 1:18

REBELLION
r is as the sin . . . . 1 Sam 15:23

REBUKE
Do not *r* an older man . . . . 1 Tim 5:1
The Lord *r* you . . . . Jude 9

RECEIVE
believing, you will *r* . . . . Matt 21:22
Ask, and you will *r* . . . . John 16:24
r the Holy Spirit . . . . Acts 19:2
r the Spirit by the . . . . Gal 3:2
suppose that he will *r* . . . . James 1:7
whatever we ask we *r* . . . . 1 John 3:22

RECONCILE
and that He might *r* . . . . Eph 2:16
r all things to . . . . Col 1:20

RECONCILED
were enemies we were *r* . . . . . . Rom 5:10

RED
though they are *r* . . . . Is 1:18
for the sky is *r* . . . . Matt 16:2

REDEEM
r their life from . . . . Ps 72:14
And He shall *r* Israel . . . . Ps 130:8
us, that He might *r* . . . . Titus 2:14

REDEEMED
Christ has *r* us from . . . . Gal 3:13

REDEEMER
For I know that my *R* . . . . Job 19:25
for their *R* is mighty . . . . Prov 23:11
Their *R* is strong . . . . Jer 50:34

REDEMPTION
heads, because your *r* . . . . Luke 21:28
sanctification and *r* . . . . 1 Cor 1:30
In Him we have *r* . . . . Eph 1:7

REFUGE
six cities of *r* . . . . Num 35:6
eternal God is your *r* . . . . Deut 33:27
God is our *r* and . . . . Ps 46:1
who have fled for *r* . . . . Heb 6:18

REGENERATION
the washing of *r* . . . . Titus 3:5

REIGN
righteousness will *r* . . . . Rom 5:17
do not let sin *r* . . . . Rom 6:12

REJECTED
He is despised and *r* . . . . Is 53:3

RIVERS
his heart will flow *r* . . . . John 7:38

ROB
"Will a man *r* God . . . . Mal 3:8

ROCK
you shall strike the *r* . . . . Ex 17:6
R who begot you . . . . Deut 32:18
"The LORD is my *r*. . . . . 2 Sam 22:2
For You are my *r*. . . . . Ps 31:3
been mindful of the *R* . . . . Is 17:10
his house on the *r*. . . . . Matt 7:24
"Some fell on *r* . . . . Luke 8:6

ROD
And Moses took the *r* . . . . Ex 4:20
Your *r* and Your staff . . . . Ps 23:4
The *r* and rebuke give . . . . Prov 29:15
shall come forth a *R*. . . . . Is 11:1
rule them with a r. . . . . Rev 2:27

ROOTED
that you, being *r*. . . . . Eph 3:17
r and built up in Him . . . . Col 2:7

ROSE
I am the *r* of Sharon. . . . . Song 2:1
and blossom as the *r* . . . . Is 35:1
buried, and that He *r* . . . . 1 Cor 15:4

RUBIES
of wisdom is above *r* . . . . Job 28:18
worth is far above *r* . . . . Prov 31:10

RULE
and he shall *r* . . . . Gen 3:16
let the peace of God *r*. . . . . Col 3:15
Let the elders who *r*. . . . . 1 Tim 5:17
Remember those who *r* . . . . Heb 13:7

RUN
r and not be weary. . . . . Is 40:31
that I have not *r* . . . . Phil 2:16

S

SABBATH
"Remember the *S*. . . . . Ex 20:8
S was made for man . . . . Mark 2:27

SACRIFICE
desire mercy and not s . . . . Matt 9:13
God a more excellent *s* . . . . Heb 11:4
offer the *s* of praise . . . . Heb 13:15

SACRIFICES
The *s* of God are a . . . . Ps 51:17
burnt offerings and *s*. . . . . Mark 12:33
s God is well pleased . . . . Heb 13:16

SAINTS
is the death of His *s* . . . . Ps 116:15
war against the *s* . . . . Dan 7:21
the least of all the *s* . . . . Eph 3:8
shed the blood of *s*. . . . . Rev 16:6

SALT
"You are the *s* . . . . Matt 5:13
s loses its flavor . . . . Mark 9:50

SALVATION
the good news of His *s*. . . . . . . 1 Chr 16:23
And He has become my *s* . . . . . Ps 118:14
joy in the God of my *s* . . . . Hab 3:18
"Nor is there *s*. . . . . Acts 4:12
the power of God to *s* . . . . Rom 1:16
work out your own *s* . . . . Phil 2:12
neglect so great a *s* . . . . Heb 2:3

SAMARITAN
But a certain *S* . . . . Luke 10:33
a drink from me, a *S* . . . . John 4:9

SANCTIFICATION
righteousness and *s*. . . . . 1 Cor 1:30
will of God, your *s* . . . . 1 Thess 4:3

SANCTIFIED
husband is *s* by the . . . . 1 Cor 7:14
those who are being *s* . . . . Heb 2:11
who are called, *s* . . . . Jude 1

SANCTUARY
let them make Me a *s*. . . . . Ex 25:8
and the earthly *s* . . . . Heb 9:1

SATAN
S stood up against . . . . 1 Chr 21:1
before the LORD, and *S*. . . . . Job 1:6
"Away with you, *S* . . . . Matt 4:10
"How can *S* cast out. . . . . Mark 3:23
S has asked for you . . . . Luke 22:31

SATISFIES
s your mouth with good . . . . Ps 103:5
s the longing soul. . . . . Ps 107:9

SATISFY
s us early with Your . . . . Ps 90:14
long life I will *s*. . . . . Ps 91:16

SAVE
mighty to *s* . . . . Is 63:1
Jesus, for He will *s* . . . . Matt 1:21
the world to *s* sinners . . . . 1 Tim 1:15

SAVED
through Him might be *s* . . . . . . John 3:17
what must I do to be *s* . . . . Acts 16:30
is that they may be *s* . . . . Rom 10:1
grace you have been *s* . . . . Eph 2:8

SAVIOR
of Israel, your *S* . . . . Is 43:3
the city of David a *S* . . . . Luke 2:11
the Christ, the *S* . . . . John 4:42
to be Prince and *S* . . . . Acts 5:31
and He is the *S* . . . . Eph 5:23
God, who is the *S* . . . . 1 Tim 4:10
of our *S* Jesus Christ . . . . 2 Tim 1:10
God and *S* Jesus Christ . . . . Titus 2:13

SCEPTER
s shall not depart . . . . Gen 49:10
S shall rise out of . . . . Num 24:17

SCORPIONS
on serpents and *s* . . . . Luke 10:19

SCRIPTURE
"Today this *S* . . . . Luke 4:21
S has confined all . . . . Gal 3:22
All *S* is given by . . . . 2 Tim 3:16
that no prophecy of *S* . . . . 2 Pet 1:20

SEA
drowned in the Red *S* . . . . Ex 15:4
the waters cover the *s* . . . . Hab 2:14

SEAT
shall make a mercy *s* . . . . Ex 25:17
before the judgment *s* . . . . 2 Cor 5:10
the mercy *s* . . . . Heb 9:5

SEED
He shall see His *s* . . . . Is 53:10
s is the word of God . . . . Luke 8:11
had left us a s . . . . Rom 9:29
you are Abraham's *s* . . . . Gal 3:29
of corruptible *s* . . . . 1 Pet 1:23

SEEK
will find Him if you *s* . . . . Deut 4:29
early will I *s* You . . . . Ps 63:1
"*S* Me and live . . . . Amos 5:4
of Man has come to *s* . . . . Luke 19:10

SEEN
s Me has *s* the . . . . John 14:9
things which are not *s* . . . . 2 Cor 4:18
heard, which we have *s* . . . . 1 John 1:1

SELF-CONTROL
they cannot exercise *s* . . . . 1 Cor 7:9
gentleness, *s* . . . . Gal 5:23
slanderers, without *s* . . . . 2 Tim 3:3

SELL
s whatever you have . . . . Mark 10:21
no one may buy or *s* . . . . Rev 13:17

SEND
"Whom shall I *s* . . . . Is 6:8
s them a Savior . . . . Is 19:20
"Behold, I *s* you out . . . . Matt 10:16
whom the Father will *s* . . . . . . John 14:26

SEPARATE
let not man *s* . . . . Matt 19:6
Who shall *s* us from . . . . Rom 8:35

SERPENT
s was more cunning . . . . Gen 3:1
"Make a fiery *s* . . . . Num 21:8
will he give him a *s* . . . . Matt 7:10
Moses lifted up the *s* . . . . John 3:14
was cast out, that *s* . . . . Rev 12:9

SERVANT
good and faithful *s* . . . . Matt 25:21

SERVE
Lord your God and *s* . . . . Deut 6:13
You cannot *s* God and . . . . Matt 6:24
but through love *s* . . . . Gal 5:13

SEVENTY
S weeks are . . . . Dan 9:24
up to *s* times seven . . . . Matt 18:22
Then the *s* returned . . . . Luke 10:17

SHADOW
in the *s* of His hand . . . . Is 49:2
which are a *s* of . . . . Col 2:17
the law, having a *s* . . . . Heb 10:1
is no variation or *s* . . . . James 1:17

SHAKE
s the earth . . . . Is 2:19
I will *s* all nations . . . . Hag 2:7
s not only the earth . . . . Heb 12:26

SHAME
hate Zion be put to *s* .... Ps 129:5
is a son who causes *s*.......... Prov 10:5
hide My face from *s*.............Is 50:6
their glory into *s*................Hos 4:7
worthy to suffer *s*. .... Acts 5:41
will not be put to s........... Rom 9:33

SHARE
is taught the word *s* .... Gal 6:6
to do good and to *s*.............Heb 13:16

SHED
which is *s* for many .... Matt 26:28

SHEDDING
blood, and without *s* ....Heb 9:22

SHEEP
slaughter, and as a *s*.............Is 53:7
s will be scattered .... Zech 13:7
having a hundred *s* ....Luke 15:4
and I know My *s*.......... John 10:14
"He was led as a s .... Acts 8:32
like *s* going astray .... 1 Pet 2:25

SHEOL
down to the gates of *S*........ Job 17:16
not leave my soul in *S* .... Ps 16:10
the belly of *S* I cried............ Jon 2:2

SHEPHERD
s My people Israel .... 2 Sam 5:2
The LORD is my *s* .... Ps 23:1
His flock like a *s*..............Is 40:11
'I will strike the S........... Matt 26:31
"I am the good *s*............. John 10:11
S the flock of God .... 1 Pet 5:2
of the throne will *s*........... Rev 7:17

SHIELD
He is a *s* to all who..........2 Sam 22:31
God is a sun and *s* .... Ps 84:11
all, taking the *s*...............Eph 6:16

SHINE
cause His face to *s* .... Ps 67:1
who are wise shall *s*.............Dan 12:3
the righteous will *s*.......... Matt 13:43
among whom you *s* ....Phil 2:15

SHIPWRECK
faith have suffered *s* .... 1 Tim 1:19

SHOUT
S joyfully to the LORD........... Ps 98:4
from heaven with a *s*.......1 Thess 4:16

SHOWBREAD
s which had been taken...... 1 Sam 21:6
s which was not lawful .... Matt 12:4

SICK
I was *s* and you............. Matt 25:36
many are weak and *s*........1 Cor 11:30
faith will save the *s* .... James 5:15

SICKLE
Put in the *s* ....Joel 3:13
"Thrust in Your *s*............. Rev 14:15

SIGHT
by faith, not by *s*..............2 Cor 5:7

SIGN
will give you a *s* ....Is 7:14
we want to see a *s* .... Matt 12:38
For Jews request a *s*..........1 Cor 1:22
Now a great *s* appeared .... Rev 12:1

SILVER
have refined us as *s* .... Ps 66:10
chosen rather than *s* .... Prov 16:16
s has become dross ....Is 1:22
may buy the poor for *s* .... Amos 8:6
him thirty pieces of *s*........ Matt 26:15

SIMPLE
making wise the *s* .... Ps 19:7
LORD preserves the *s* .... Ps 116:6

SIN
and be sure your *s* .... Num 32:23
in *s* my mother .... Ps 51:5
"He who is without *s* .... John 8:7
died to *s* once for all .... Rom 6:10
Him who knew no *s*..........2 Cor 5:21
appeared to put away *s* ....Heb 9:26
"Who committed no s .... 1 Pet 2:22
say that we have no *s*.........1 John 1:8

SING
"*S* to the LORD................ Ex 15:21
I will *s* of mercy and .... Ps 101:1
S us one of the songs.......... Ps 137:3
Let him *s* psalms .... James 5:13

SINNED
You only, have I *s* . . . . Ps 51:4
for all have *s* and . . . . Rom 3:23
say that we have not *s* . . . . 1 John 1:10

SINNER
s who repents than. . . . . Luke 15:7

SINNERS
the righteous, but *s* . . . . Matt 9:13
tax collectors and *s* . . . . Matt 11:19
the world to save *s*. . . . . 1 Tim 1:15

SINS
s have hidden His face. . . . . Is 59:2
the soul who *s* shall . . . . Ezek 18:4
If we confess our *s*. . . . . .1 John 1:9

SIT
but to *s* on My right . . . . Matt 20:23
"S at My right hand . . . . .Heb 1:13
I will grant to *s* . . . . Rev 3:21

SLAIN
s his thousands. . . . . .1 Sam 18:7
Those *s* by the sword . . . . Lam 4:9
the prophets, I have *s*. . . . . .Hos 6:5
is the Lamb who was *s* . . . . Rev 5:12

SLAUGHTER
led as a lamb to the *s*. . . . . .Is 53:7
but the Valley of *S*. . . . . .Jer 7:32

SLAVE
commits sin is a *s*. . . . . John 8:34
you are no longer a *s* . . . . Gal 4:7

SLEEP
He gives His beloved *s*. . . . . Ps 127:2
s will be sweet . . . . Prov 3:24
We shall not all *s* . . . . .1 Cor 15:51
"Awake, you who *s*. . . . . .Eph 5:14

SMITTEN
Him stricken, *s* . . . . .Is 53:4

SMOOTH
and the rough places *s*. . . . . Is 40:4

SNOW
shall be whiter than *s* . . . . Ps 51:7
She is not afraid of *s* . . . . Prov 31:21
shall be as white as *s*. . . . . .Is 1:18

SODOMITES
nor homosexuals, nor *s* . . . . 1 Cor 6:9
for fornicators, for *s*. . . . . 1 Tim 1:10

SOLD
s his birthright . . . . .Gen 25:33
s all that he had . . . . Matt 13:46
s their possessions . . . . Acts 2:45

SOLDIER
hardship as a good *s* . . . . 2 Tim 2:3

SON
s makes a glad father. . . . . Prov 10:1
is born, unto us a *S* . . . . .Is 9:6
fourth is like the *S* . . . . .Dan 3:25
This is My beloved *S* . . . . Matt 3:17
The only begotten *S*. . . . . John 1:18
S can do nothing . . . . John 5:19
Jesus Christ is the *S*. . . . . Acts 8:37
declared to be the *S*. . . . . Rom 1:4
by sending His own *S* . . . . Rom 8:3
not spare His own *S*. . . . . Rom 8:32
God sent forth His *S* . . . . Gal 4:4
the knowledge of the *S* . . . . Eph 4:13
but Christ as a *S*. . . . . .Heb 3:6
though He was a *S*. . . . . .Heb 5:8
This is My beloved *S* . . . . 2 Pet 1:17
Whoever denies the *S*. . . . . .1 John 2:23
God has given of His *S* . . . . . .1 John 5:10
One like the *S* of Man . . . . Rev 1:13

SONG
is my strength and *s*. . . . . Ex 15:2
Sing to Him a new *s*. . . . . Ps 33:3
He has put a new *s*. . . . . Ps 40:3
in the night His *s* . . . . Ps 42:8
to my Well-beloved a *s*. . . . . Is 5:1
as a very lovely *s* . . . . Ezek 33:32
And they sang a new *s* . . . . Rev 5:9

SONS
who are of faith are *s*. . . . . Gal 3:7
the adoption as *s* . . . . Gal 4:5

SORCERER
omens, or a *s*. . . . . Deut 18:10

SORCERERS
outside are dogs and *s*. . . . . Rev 22:15

SORCERESS
shall not permit a *s* . . . . Ex 22:18

SORROW
and He adds no *s* . . . . Prov 10:22
them sleeping from *s*. . . . . Luke 22:45
s produces repentance. . . . . . . .2 Cor 7:10
s as others who have . . . . 1 Thess 4:13
no more death, nor *s* . . . . Rev 21:4

SUPPER
to eat the Lord's *S* ... 1 Cor 11:20
took the cup after *s* ... 1 Cor 11:25
together for the *s* ... Rev 19:17

SUPPLICATION
with all prayer and *s* ... Eph 6:18
by prayer and *s* ... Phil 4:6

SUPPLY
And my God shall *s* ... Phil 4:19

SWORD
to bring peace but a *s* ... Matt 10:34
the *s* of the Spirit ... Eph 6:17
than any two-edged *s* ... Heb 4:12
mouth goes a sharp *s* ... Rev 19:15

SWORDS
shall beat their *s* ... Is 2:4
look, here are two *s* ... Luke 22:38

SWORE
So I s in My wrath ... Heb 3:11
and *s* by Him who lives ... Rev 10:6

SYNAGOGUE
He went into the *s* ... Luke 4:16
but are a *s* of Satan ... Rev 2:9

T

TABERNACLE
you shall make the *t* ... Ex 26:1
How lovely is Your *t* ... Ps 84:1
and will rebuild the t ... Acts 15:16
and more perfect *t* ... Heb 9:11

TABLES
and overturned the *t* ... Matt 21:12
of God and serve *t* ... Acts 6:2

TAKE
T your sandal off your ... Josh 5:15
T My yoke upon you ... Matt 11:29
and *t* up his cross ... Mark 8:34
I urge you to *t* heart ... Acts 27:22

TALENT
went and hid your *t* ... Matt 25:25

TASTE
Oh, *t* and see that the ... Ps 34:8

TAXES
Is it lawful to pay *t* ... Matt 22:17
t to whom *t* ... Rom 13:7

TEACH
t them diligently ... Deut 6:7
T me Your paths ... Ps 25:4

TEARS
GOD will wipe away *t* ... Is 25:8
His feet with her *t* ... Luke 7:38

TEMPLE
So Solomon built the *t* ... 1 Kin 6:14
to inquire in His *t* ... Ps 27:4
"Destroy this *t* ... John 2:19
your body is the *t* ... 1 Cor 6:19
grows into a holy *t* ... Eph 2:21
Then the *t* of God was ... Rev 11:19

TEMPT
Why do you *t* the LORD ... Ex 17:2
t the LORD your God ... Matt 4:7
nor does He Himself *t* ... James 1:13

TEMPTATION
do not lead us into *t* ... Matt 6:13
lest you enter into *t* ... Matt 26:41
t has overtaken you ... 1 Cor 10:13
the man who endures *t* ... James 1:12

TEST
said, "Why do you *t* ... Matt 22:18
T all things ... 1 Thess 5:21
but *t* the spirits ... 1 John 4:1

TESTIFY
t what We have ... John 3:11
t that the Father ... 1 John 4:14

TESTS
gold, but the LORD *t* ... Prov 17:3

THANK
"I *t* You and praise ... Dan 2:23
"I *t* You, Father ... Matt 11:25
t You that I am not ... Luke 18:11

THANKFUL
Be *t* to Him ... Ps 100:4
Him as God, nor were *t* ... Rom 1:21

THANKSGIVING
His presence with *t* ... Ps 95:2
into His gates with *t* ... Ps 100:4
supplication, with *t* ... Phil 4:6

THIEF
known what hour the *t* ... Matt 24:43
upon you as a *t* ... Rev 3:3

THINKS
for as he *t* in his . . . . Prov 23:7
t he stands take heed. . . . . .1 Cor 10:12
t he is religious. . . . . .James 1:26

THIRST
those who hunger and *t* . . . . Matt 5:6
in Me shall never *t*. . . . . John 6:35
anymore nor *t* anymore . . . . Rev 7:16

THORN
a *t* in the flesh was. . . . . .2 Cor 12:7

THOUGHTS
For My *t* are not your . . . . .Is 55:8

THRONE
“Heaven is My *t* . . . . .Is 66:1
come boldly to the *t*. . . . . .Heb 4:16
I saw a great white *t* . . . . Rev 20:11

TIDINGS
I bring you good *t* . . . . Luke 2:10
who bring glad t. . . . . Rom 10:15

TIME
pray to You in a *t* . . . . Ps 32:6
A *t* to be born. . . . . .Eccl 3:2
but *t* and chance. . . . . .Eccl 9:11
t has not yet come . . . . John 7:6

TITHE
For you pay *t* of mint . . . . Matt 23:23

TITHES
to receive *t* from the . . . . .Heb 7:5

TOMORROW
do not worry about *t* . . . . Matt 6:34
drink, for t we die . . . . .1 Cor 15:32

TONGUE
t should confess that . . . . .Phil 2:11
And the *t* is a fire . . . . .James 3:6
every nation, tribe, *t* . . . . .Rev 14:6

TONGUES
will speak with new *t* . . . . . . .Mark 16:17
and they spoke with *t* . . . . Acts 19:6
t are for a sign . . . . .1 Cor 14:22

TRAIN
T up a child in the . . . . Prov 22:6
t of His robe filled . . . . .Is 6:1

TRANSFIGURED
and was *t* before them. . . . . Matt 17:2

TRANSGRESSION
He who covers a *t* . . . . Prov 17:9

TRANSGRESSIONS
was wounded for our *t* . . . . .Is 53:5

TRANSGRESSORS
Then I will teach *t* . . . . Ps 51:13
numbered with the t . . . . .Mark 15:28

TREASURE
one who finds great *t*. . . . . Ps 119:162
“For where your *t*. . . . . Matt 6:21
So is he who lays up *t* . . . . Luke 12:21

TREE
“but of the *t*. . . . . .Gen 2:17
t planted by the . . . . Ps 1:3
t bears good fruit . . . . Matt 7:17
His own body on the *t*. . . . . 1 Pet 2:24
give to eat from the *t* . . . . Rev 2:7

TRESPASSES
forgive men their *t*. . . . . Matt 6:14
not imputing their *t* . . . . .2 Cor 5:19
who were dead in *t* . . . . Eph 2:1

TRIAL
in the day of t. . . . . .Heb 3:8
concerning the fiery *t* . . . . 1 Pet 4:12
t which shall come. . . . . Rev 3:10

TRIBE
the Lion of the *t* . . . . Rev 5:5
blood out of every *t* . . . . Rev 5:9

TRIBULATION
out of the great *t* . . . . Rev 7:14

TRIBULATIONS
t enter the kingdom . . . . Acts 14:22
but we also glory in *t*. . . . . Rom 5:3
not lose heart at my *t*. . . . . .Eph 3:13

TRIUMPH
Let not my enemies *t*. . . . . Ps 25:2
always leads us in *t* . . . . .2 Cor 2:14

TRUE
and Your words are *t* . . . . .2 Sam 7:28
we know that You are *t* . . . . . . Matt 22:16
Indeed, let God be *t* . . . . Rom 3:4
whatever things are *t*. . . . . Phil 4:8

TRUMPET
For the *t* will sound . . . . .1 Cor 15:52
loud voice, as of a *t* . . . . Rev 1:10

TRUST
T in the LORD.................. Ps 37:3
T in the LORD with all........... Prov 3:5
Do not *t* in a friend .... Mic 7:5

TRUTH
Behold, You desire *t*............. Ps 51:6
"I am the way, the *t* .... John 14:6

TURN
yes, let every one *t*............... Jon 3:8
T now from your evil.......... Zech 1:4
on your right cheek, *t* .... Matt 5:39
t the hearts of the............ Luke 1:17
t them from darkness .... Acts 26:18

U

UNBELIEF
because of their *u*.......... Matt 13:58
help my *u* ....Mark 9:24
and He rebuked their *u*......Mark 16:14
you an evil heart of *u*.......... Heb 3:12
enter in because of *u*..........Heb 3:19

UNCLEAN
I am a man of *u* lips...............Is 6:5
any man common or *u*....... Acts 10:28

UNDERSTANDS
is easy to him who *u* .... Prov 14:6
there is none who u.......... Rom 3:11

UNGODLY
Christ died for the *u*........... Rom 5:6

UNHOLY
between the holy and *u*...... Ezek 22:26

UNITY
to dwell together in *u*.......... Ps 133:1
we all come to the *u*...........Eph 4:13

UNJUST
For God is not *u* ....Heb 6:10
the just for the *u*............. 1 Pet 3:18

UNRIGHTEOUS
u man his thoughts ....Is 55:7
u will not inherit the ....1 Cor 6:9

UPHOLDING
u all things by the...............Heb 1:3

UPRIGHT
righteous and *u* is He......... Deut 32:4
Good and *u* is the LORD .... Ps 25:8

UTTERANCE
the Spirit gave them *u*......... Acts 2:4
u may be given to me...........Eph 6:19

V

VALLEY
I walk through the *v*............ Ps 23:4
v shall be exalted ....Is 40:4

VANISH
For the heavens will *v* ....Is 51:6
knowledge, it will *v* ....1 Cor 13:8

VANITY
of vanities, all is *v*...............Eccl 1:2

VEIL
he put a *v* on his face...........Ex 34:33
v of the temple was .... Matt 27:51

VENGEANCE
'You shall not take *v* .... Lev 19:18
written, "*V is Mine*.......... Rom 12:19

VESSEL
to possess his own *v* ....1 Thess 4:4
to the weaker *v*............... 1 Pet 3:7

VICTORY
who gives us the *v* ....1 Cor 15:57
v that has overcome..........1 John 5:4

VIGILANT
Be sober, be *v* .... 1 Pet 5:8

VILE
"Behold, I am *v*................ Job 40:4
them up to *v* passions .... Rom 1:26

VINE
planted you a noble *v* ....Jer 2:21
"I am the true *v*............... John 15:1

VIOLENCE
of heaven suffers *v*.......... Matt 11:12

VIRGIN
"*Behold, the v shall* .... Matt 1:23

VIRGINS
v who took their lamps .... Matt 25:1

VIRTUE
if there is any *v*.................Phil 4:8
us by glory and *v* .... 2 Pet 1:3

without God in the *w*. . . . . .Eph 2:12
Do not love the *w*. . . . . .1 John 2:15

WORM
But I am a *w* . . . . Ps 22:6
w does not die and the. . . . . . . .Mark 9:44

WORMWOOD
end she is bitter as *w*. . . . . Prov 5:4
of the star is *W*. . . . . Rev 8:11

WORSHIP
Oh come, let us *w*. . . . . Ps 95:6
w what you do not know. . . . . . John 4:22

WORTHY
"I am not *w* of the. . . . . Gen 32:10
sandals I am not *w*. . . . . Matt 3:11
and I am no longer *w*. . . . . Luke 15:19
the world was not *w*. . . . . .Heb 11:38
W is the Lamb who . . . . Rev 5:12

WOUND
I *w* and I heal . . . . Deut 32:39
My *w* is incurable. . . . . Job 34:6
and my *w* incurable . . . . .Jer 15:18

WRATH
in My *w* I struck you . . . . .Is 60:10
I will pour out my *w*. . . . . Hos 5:10
For the *w* of God is. . . . . Rom 1:18
nature children of *w* . . . . .Eph 2:3
holy hands, without *w*. . . . . 1 Tim 2:8
for the *w* of man does . . . . James 1:20
of the wine of the *w*. . . . . Rev 14:8

WRESTLE
For we do not *w* . . . . .Eph 6:12

WRITE
w them on the tablet . . . . Prov 7:3
w them on their hearts . . . . .Heb 8:10

Y

YEAR
'In the *Y* of Jubilee . . . . Lev 27:24
the acceptable *y* . . . . .Is 61:2
to Jerusalem every *y* . . . . Luke 2:41
of sins every *y*. . . . . .Heb 10:3

YES
"But let your '*Y*' . . . . Matt 5:37

YOKE
and He will put a *y*. . . . . Deut 28:48
You have broken the *y*. . . . . .Is 9:4
"Take My *y* upon you. . . . . Matt 11:29

YOKED
Do not be unequally *y* . . . . .2 Cor 6:14

YOUNG
y man followed Him . . . . .Mark 14:51
they admonish the *y* . . . . Titus 2:4
I write to you, *y* . . . . .1 John 2:13

YOURS
Y is the kingdom . . . . Matt 6:13
y is the kingdom. . . . . Luke 6:20

YOUTH
speak, for I am a *y* . . . . .Jer 1:6
I have kept from my *y* . . . . Matt 19:20
no one despise your *y* . . . . 1 Tim 4:12

YOUTHFUL
Flee also *y* lusts . . . . 2 Tim 2:22

Z

ZEAL
z has consumed me . . . . Ps 119:139
He shall stir up His *z* . . . . .Is 42:13
have spoken it in My *z* . . . . Ezek 5:13
for Zion with great *z* . . . . Zech 8:2
"Z for Your house has . . . . John 2:17